INDEX OF ECONOMIC ARTICLES
In Journals and Collective Volumes

Index of
Economic Articles

IN JOURNALS AND COLLECTIVE VOLUMES

Volume XV · 1973

Prepared under the auspices of

THE JOURNAL OF ECONOMIC LITERATURE

of the

AMERICAN ECONOMIC ASSOCIATION

MARK PERLMAN, *Managing Editor*
NAOMI PERLMAN, *Associate Editor*
DRUCILLA EKWURZEL, *Assistant Editor*

Assisted by
ASATOSHI MAESHIRO, *classification consultant*
AND STUDENTS FROM THE DEPARTMENT OF ECONOMICS, UNIVERSITY OF PITTSBURGH

Distributed by
RICHARD D. IRWIN, INC.
1818 RIDGE ROAD
HOMEWOOD, ILLINOIS 60430
1977

Library of Congress Catalog Card Number: 61–8020
International Standard Book Number: 0–917290–04–6
Printed in the United States of America

TABLE OF CONTENTS

INTRODUCTORY DISCUSSION

Volume XV continues the new series of the *Index of Economic Articles*, which began with Volume XI (1969). It is linked to the earlier volumes, I–X, in scope and content. The actual classification system in volumes XI–XV differs and is coordinated with the system developed by the American Economic Association Classification Committee in 1967 and used in the sections in the *Journal of Economic Literature* relating to articles and books and in the field of specialization classifications in the *American Economic Association Directory*.

Scope

This volume of the *Index* lists, both by subject category and by author, articles in major economic journals and in collective volumes published during the year 1973. The articles listed include all articles published in English or with English summaries in the journals and books listed below (p. xi).

Relationship to JEL

This *Index* is prepared largely as an adjunct to the bibliographic activities of the *Journal of Economic Literature (JEL)*. Economies of joint production are pursued throughout the production process. Journals included are those indexed in the *JEL* quarterly; collective volumes are selected from the annotated 1973 books; the classification system is a more detailed version of the *JEL* system.

The joint production process involves computerization of the article citations, for use both in *JEL* and in the *Index*. The data-base article citations are then run through various programs. The resultant gains from a reduction in production costs involve some small losses in flexibility in arrangement and data inclusion as well as some relatively small losses with regard to proofreading and classification.

Journals Included

The 206 journals listed are drawn from 219 journals representing, in general, those journals that we believe will be most helpful to research workers and teachers of economics. These journals are listed below on p. xi.

Generally, articles, notes, communications, comments, replies, rejoinders, as well as papers and formal discussions in proceedings and review articles in the included journals have been indexed. There are some exceptions; only articles in English or with English summaries are included—this practice results in a slightly reduced coverage compared with the *JEL* quarterly. For example, articles in foreign languages are indexed in the quarterly from any journal where we regularly print English abstracts; also in some years, available foreign language skills permitted classification of such articles. Articles lacking author identification are omitted, as are articles without economic content. Identical articles appearing in two different journals in 1973 are listed from both sources. The journal issues included are those for 1973, usually falling within a single volume. When a volume of a journal overlaps two calendar years, for example, Fall 1972 to Summer 1973, we include the issues from the two volumes relating to 1973 as best we can determine. As will be noted in the journal listings, there are a few instances where issues of journals are not included because they had not been received at the *JEL* office despite repeated requests.

Collective Volumes

The collective volumes consist of the following:
1. *Festschriften*
2. Conference publications with individual papers
3. Collected essays, original, by one or more authors
4. Collected essays, reprinted, by one or more authors
5. Proceedings volumes with individual papers not included among the journal listings
6. Books of readings

All original articles in English are indexed with the exception of unsigned articles or articles without economic content. Reprinted articles are included if they have not been indexed in the volumes of the *Index of Economic Journals* or the *Index of Economic Articles* covering the period from 1955 on, that is in Volumes V to XIV.

The rule of thumb followed for the inclusion of excerpts from printed articles or books is that the excerpt should represent a substantial portion of the article or of a chapter of a book. The same article or excerpt appearing for the first time in different collective volumes in the same year is cited from both publications.

In the article citation, reference to the book in which the article appeared is by author or editor of the volume. If the same person or persons wrote or edited more than one book included in the 1973 *Index*, it is indicated by a I or II appearing immediately after the name in both the source given in the article citation and the bibliographic reference in the book listing. If the same person wrote one book and edited another in 1973, the inclusion of editor in the reference indicates which book is being cited.

The collective volumes are listed alphabetically by author or editor on pp. xvi with a full bibliographic reference. If there is more than one edition, the publisher cited is the one on the copy the *JEL* received, usually from the American publisher. These books are 1973 publications; two 1972 publications omitted from the 1972 volume are included.

Arrangement

The Index consists of two parts:
1. A Subject Index in which the articles are arranged by subject according to the detailed classification system developed by the *JEL* staff from the American Economic Association Classification Committee systems.
2. An Author Index.

Subject Index

All articles are listed alphabetically under each 4-digit category. The entries are arranged alphabetically, first by author and then under particular authors by title. Since the sort is by computer and the number of programs was constrained by cost compared to frequency of usage, Part II of a two-part article may appear before Part I, or a reply to a comment before the article in question. If an article is written by more than one author, up to three authors are listed; beyond that, only the first author and the term, *et al.*

There is one exception to the alphabetical author arrangement. In the 0322 category, a subdivision of **History of Thought** entitled **Individuals**, the arrangement is first alphabetical by the individual discussed in the article and then alphabetically by the article's author.

Articles with empirical content or discussing a particular geographic area carry a geographic descriptor (see discussion below). Articles listed under subject categories 1210, 1211, 1220, 1221, and 1230, involving generalized comparative economics studies, may involve several countries. Since the number of geographic descriptors in the program is limited to five, these subject categories often serve as substitutes for selecting individual countries, and these articles may carry no geographic descriptors. All articles under this category involve some empirical content.

Author Index

The Author Index is arranged alphabetically. Wherever possible the full first names and middle initial or middle name(s) are used. Wherever it could be definitely ascertained, articles by the same person were grouped together with only one listing of the name and/or initial. Authors' first names and intials are listed differently in various journals and books; for example, an individual may be identified as John L. Smith, J. L. Smith, or John Smith. Thus, despite our best efforts, we were left in doubt in several instances. Joint authors are listed up to three; beyond that, only the first author is listed, followed by *et al.* Articles by joint authors appear more than once, listed under the name of each of its authors, unless it is an *et al.* grouping. Under each author, articles are listed alphabetically. Prefix names are alphabetized according to the first *capitalized* letter. Thus, van Arkadie appears under A and D'Alabro under D.

Geographic Descriptors

Geographic descriptors appear in brackets at the end of any article entry where the article cites data from a particular country or area or refers to a specific geographic area. Research workers interested in these countries thus are made aware of the empirical content in the article. The descriptors used are countries or broader areas, such as southeast Asia (S.E. Asia); articles referring to cities or regions within a country are classified under the country. In general, the country name is written out in full with some adaptations and abbreviations, *e.g.*, U.S. is used for United States, U.K. for United Kingdom, and U.S.S.R. for Union of Soviet Socialist Republics. Abbreviations include: W. for West, E. for East, S. for South, N. for North. A shortened name such as W. Germany is used rather than the correct, but longer, Federal Republic of Germany. When broader regions are used as descriptors, the article may or may not refer to the full unit. For example, O.E.C.D. has been used at times when most, but not all, of the O.E.C.D. member countries are referred to. E.E.C. has been used at times to refer to the six and at times to the nine constituent countries.

The fact that an article carries a geographic descriptor does not necessarily preclude its being primarily theoretical in nature. Any theoretical article drawing on empirical data to demonstrate its findings will carry a geographic descriptor.

Classification System

The classification system is an expansion of the 3-digit classification system with approximately 100 subcategories used in the *Journal of Economic Literature* to a 4-digit system with approximately 300 subcategories. The classification system, itself, is shown on p. xxiv. In most cases the classification heading is self-explanatory; however, in some cases notes have been added to explain where related topics are classified. The basic approach in classification is from the point of view of the researcher rather than from the teacher. Course content does not necessarily coincide with subfields of our classification system. In all cases where there are two or more 4-digit classifications under a 3-digit category, there is a zero classification; in most instances this is labeled "General." The zero or general category has been used both as an inclusive and a residual category; thus, when the subject matter of an article covers all or most of the subcategories, that article appears in the zero or general category. For example, an article discussing *all* aspects of international trade theory appears in the general category. There are also some articles that do not fall in any of the individual subcategories, and these, too, are classified in the general or zero category.

The criterion used in the classifying process is whether a person interested in this topic would wish to have the article drawn to their attention. Slightly over half of the articles are classified in more than one subcategory. From time to time, we find it desirable to add additional subject classifications as particular topics become prominent. For example, in the 1973 *Index* we have added a separate category covering all energy topics, 7230. Previously these articles appeared under 6322, 6323, 6352, 7210, or 7220 depending on the subject matter.

Topical Guide to the Classification System

At the back of this book there is an alphabetical listing of standard economic terms and concepts. References are to the appropriate 4-digit classification numbers, not to page numbers.

LIST OF JOURNALS INDEXED 1973

Accounting Review, Vol. 48.

Acta Oeconomica, Vol. 10; Vol. 11.

Agricultural Economics Research, Vol. 25.

Agricultural Finance Review, Vol. 34.

American Economic Review, Vol. 63.
Includes American Economic Association
Papers and Proceedings of the annual meet-
ing in *63*(2).

American Economist, Vol. 17.

American Historical Review, Vol. 78.

American Journal of Agricultural Economics,
Vol. 55.
Title changed from **Journal of Farm Eco-
nomics** in 1968.

American Journal of Economics and Sociology, Vol. 32.

American Political Science Review, Vol. 67.

American Real Estate and Urban Economics
Association Journal, Vol. 1.

Annales de Sciences Économiques Ap-
pliquées, Issue no. 1, 1973/74.

Annals of the American Academy of Political
and Social Science, Vols. 405–410.

Annals of Economic and Social Measurement, Vol. 2.

Antitrust Bulletin, Vol. 18.

Applied Economics, Vol. 5.

Artha-Vikas, Vol. 9.

Aussenwirtschaft, Vol. 28.

Australian Economic History Review, Vol.
13.
Title changed from **Business Archives and
History** in 1967; prior to 1962 entitled **Bulletin of the Business Archives Council of Australia.**

Australian Economic Papers, Vol. 12.

Australian Economic Review, 1st–4th Quar-
ters, 1973.

Australian Journal of Agricultural Economics, Vol. 17.

Banca Nazionale del Lavoro-Quarterly Review, Issue nos. 104–107.

Bancaria, Vol. 29.

Bangladesh Economic Review, Vol. 1.

Bell Journal of Economics and Management
Science, Vol. 4.

Brookings Papers on Economic Activity, Issue nos. 1–3, 1973.

Bulletin of Economic Research, Vol. 25.
Title changed from **Yorkshire Bulletin of
Economic and Social Research** in 1971.

Bulletin of Indonesian Economic Studies,
Vol. 9.

Bulletin for International Fiscal Documenta-
tion, Vol. 27.

Bulletin Oxford University Institute of Economics and Statistics: see **Oxford Bulletin of
Economics and Statistics.**

Business History Review, Vol. 47.
Title changed from **Bulletin of the Business
Historical Society** in 1954.

Cahiers Économiques de Bruxelles, Issue
nos. 57–60.

California Management Review, Vol. 15, Issue nos. 3–4; Vol. 16, Issue nos. 1–2.

Canadian Journal of Agricultural Economics,
Vol. 21.

Canadian Journal of Economics, Vol. 6.

Chinese Economic Studies, Vol. 6, Issue nos.
3–4; Vol. 7, Issue nos. 1–2.

Hitotsubashi Journal of Economics, Vol. 13, Issue no. 2; Vol. 14, Issue no. 1.

Ifo-Studien, Vol. 19.

Illinois Agricultural Economics, Vol. 13.

L'Impresa, Vol. 15.

Indian Economic Journal, Vol. 20, Issue nos. 3–5; Vol. 21, Issue nos. 1–2.

Indian Economic Review, Vol. 8.

Indiana Business Review, Vol. 48.

L'Industria, Issue no. 1–2, 1973.

Industrial and Labor Relations Review, Vol. 26, Issue nos. 2–4; Vol. 27, Issue no. 1.

Industrial Relations, Vol. 12.

Intermountain Economic Review, Vol. 4.

International Economic Review, Vol. 14.

International Labour Review, Vol. 107; Vol. 108.

International Monetary Fund, Staff Papers, Vol. 20.

International Social Science Journal, Vol. 25.

Irish Banking Review, Issue nos. 3–12, 1973.

Jahrbücher für Nationalökonomie und Statistik, Vol. 187, Issue nos. 2–6; Vol. 188, Issue no. 1.

Journal of Accounting Research, Vol. 11.

Journal of the American Statistical Association, Vol. 68.

Journal of Asian Studies, Vol. 32, Issue nos. 3–4.

Journal of Bank Research, Vol. 3, Issue no. 4; Vol. 4, Issue nos. 1–3.

Journal of Business, Vol. 46.

Journal of Business Research, Vol. 1.

Journal of Common Market Studies, Vol. 11, Issue nos. 3–4; Vol. 12, Issue nos. 1–2.

Journal of Developing Areas, Vol. 7, Issue nos. 2–4; Vol. 8, Issue no. 1.

Journal of Development Studies, Vol. 9, Issue nos. 2–4; Vol. 10, Issue no. 1.

Journal of Econometrics, Vol. 1.

Journal of Economic Education, Vol. 4, Issue no. 2; Vol. 5, Issue no. 1.

Journal of Economic History, Vol. 33.

Journal of Economic Issues, Vol. 7.

Journal of Economic Literature, Vol. 11.

Journal of Economic Theory, Vol. 6.

Journal of Economics and Business, Vol. 25, Issue nos. 2–3; Vol. 26, Issue no. 1.
  Title changed from **Economics and Business Bulletin** in 1972–73.

Journal of Finance, Vol. 28.

Journal of Financial and Quantitative Analysis, Vol. 8.

Journal of Human Resources, Vol. 8; Supplement.

Journal of Industrial Economics, Vol. 21, Issue nos. 2–3; Vol. 22, Issue nos. 1–2.

Journal of International Economics, Vol. 3.

Journal of Law and Economics, Vol. 16.

Journal of Marketing Research, Vol. 10.

Journal of Money, Credit and Banking, Vol. 5.

Journal of Peace Science, Vol. 1, Issue no. 1.

Journal of Political Economy, Vol. 81.

Journal of Public Economics, Vol. 2.

Journal of Regional Science, Vol. 13.

Journal of Risk and Insurance, Vol. 40.

Journal of the Royal Statistical Society, Series A, Vol. 136.

Journal of Transport Economics and Policy, Vol. 7.

Public Finance Quarterly, Vol. 1.

Public Policy, Vol. 21.

Quarterly Journal of Economics, Vol. 87.

Quarterly Review of Agricultural Economics, Vol. 26.

Quarterly Review of Economics and Business, Vol. 13.

Recherches Économiques de Louvain, Vol. 39.

Review of the Economic Conditions in Italy, Vol. 27.

Review of Economic Studies, Vol. 40.

Review of Economics and Statistics, Vol. 55.
  Title changed from The Review of Economic Statistics in 1948.

Review of Income and Wealth, Vol. 19.

Review of Marketing and Agricultural Economics, Vol. 41.

Review of Radical Political Economics, Vol. 5.

Review of Social Economy, Vol. 31.

Revue Économique, Vol. 24.

Revue Roumaine des Sciences Sociales; Série Sciences Économiques, Vol. 17, Issue no. 1.

Rivista Internazionale di Scienze Economiche e Commerciali, Vol. 20.

Schweizerische Zeitschrift für Volkswirtschaft und Statistik, Vol. 109.

Science and Society, Vol. 37.

Scottish Journal of Political Economy, Vol. 20.

Social and Economic Studies, Vol. 22.

Social Research, Vol. 40.

Social Science Quarterly, Vol. 53, Issue no. 4; Vol. 54, Issue nos. 1–3.

Social Security Bulletin, Vol. 36.

South African Journal of Economics, Vol. 41.

Southern Economic Journal, Vol. 39, Issue nos. 3–4; Vol. 40, Issue nos. 1–2.

Southern Quarterly, Vol. 11, Issue nos. 2–4; Vol. 12, Issue no. 1.

Statistica, Vol. 33.

Studii și Cercetări Economicè, Issue nos. 1–4, 1973.

Survey of Current Business, Vol. 53, Issue nos. 1–8, 10–12.

Swedish Journal of Economics, Vol. 75.
  Title changed from Ekonomisk Tidskrift in 1965.

Tahqiqāt-eqtesādi (Quarterly Journal of Economic Research), Vol. 10, Issue no. 31–32.

Tijdschrift Voor Economie, Vol. 18.

Urban Studies, Vol. 10.

Water Resources Research, Vol. 9.

Weltwirtschaftliches Archiv, Vol. 109.

Western Economic Journal, Vol. 11.

World Development, Vol. 1, Issue nos. 1–5, 9.

Yale Law Journal, Vol. 82, Issue nos. 3–8; Vol. 83, Issue nos. 1–2.

Zeitschrift für die gesamte Staatswissenschaft, Vol. 129.

Zeitschrift für Nationalökonomie, Vol. 33.

Zeitschrift für Wirtschaft-und Sozialwissenschaften, Vol. 93.
  Title changed from Schmollers Jahrbuch für Wirtschafts und Sozialwissenschaften in 1972.

LIST OF COLLECTIVE VOLUMES INDEXED 1973

AHAMAD, BASHIR AND BLAUG, MARK, eds. *The Practice of Manpower Forecasting: A Collection of Case Studies.* The Jossey-Bass/Elsevier International Series. Amsterdam: Elsevier Scientific; San Francisco: Jossey-Bass, 1973.

AISLABIE, COLIN, ed. *Proceedings of the Urban Water Economics Symposium.* New South Wales, Australia: University of Newcastle, 1973.

ALBERICI, ADALBERTO AND BARAVELLI, MAURIZIO, eds. *Savings Banks and Savings Facilities in African Countries.* The Credit Markets of Africa, Monograph No. 7. Milan: Cassa di Risparmio Delle Provincie Lombarde, 1973.

ALCHIAN, ARMEN A., ET AL. *The Economics of Charity: Essays on the Comparative Economics and Ethics of Giving and Selling, with Applications to Blood.* London: Institute of Economic Affairs, 1973.

ALDEN, DAURIL, ed. *Colonial Roots of Modern Brazil: Papers of the Newberry Library Conference.* Berkeley and London: University of California Press, 1973.

ALEXANDRIDES, C. G., ed. *International Business Systems Perspectives.* Atlanta: Georgia State University, School of Business Administration, 1973.

ALLEN, G. C., ET AL. *Mergers, Take-Overs and the Structure of Industry.* Foreword by ARTHUR SELDON. London: Institute of Economic Affairs, 1973.

ANDREANO, RALPH L., ed. *Superconcentration/Supercorporation: A Collage of Opinion on the Concentration of Economic Power.* New York: MSS Information, 1973.

ARONSON, ROBERT L., ed. *The Localization of Federal Manpower Planning.* Ithaca: Cornell University, New York State School of Industrial and Labor Relations, 1973.

ARRIGHI, GIOVANNI AND SAUL, JOHN S. *Essays on the Political Economy of Africa.* New York and London: Monthly Review Press, 1973.

AYAL, ELIEZER B., ed. *Micro Aspects of Development.* Praeger Special Studies in International Economics and Development. New York and London: Praeger, 1973.

BAKER, ALAN R. H. AND BUTLIN, ROBIN A., eds. *Studies of Field Systems in the British Isles.* New York and London: Cambridge University Press, 1973.

BALL, R. J., ed. *The International Linkage of National Economic Models.* Contributions to Economic Analysis series, no. 78. Amsterdam and London: North-Holland; New York: American Elsevier, 1973.

BANDERA, V. N. AND MELNYK, Z. L., eds. *The Soviet Economy in Regional Perspective.* Praeger Special Studies in International Economics and Development. New York and London: Praeger, 1973.

BARKIN, DAVID P. AND MANITZAS, NITA R., eds. *Cuba: The Logic of the Revolution.* New York: MSS Information, 1973.

BERG, ALAN; SCRIMSHAW, NEVIN S. AND CALL, DAVID L., eds. *Nutrition, National Development, and Planning: Proceedings of an International Conference Held at Cambridge, Massachusetts, October 19–21, 1971.* Cambridge, Mass., and London: MIT Press, 1973.

BERG, ROBERT L., ed. *Health Status Indexes: Proceedings of a Conference Conducted by Health Services Research, Tucson, Arizona, October 1–4, 1972.* Chicago: Hospital Research and Educational Trust, 1973.

BERGSTEN, C. FRED, ed. *The Future of the International Economic Order: An Agenda for Research.* Lexington, Mass.; Toronto and London: Heath, 1973.

BLAQUIÈRE, AUSTIN, ed. *Topics in Differential Games.* New York: American Elsevier; Amsterdam and London: North-Holland, 1973.

BLOHM, HANS AND STEINBUCH, KARL, eds. *Technological Forecasting in Practice.* Translated from the German edition by FREDERICK AND CHRISTINE CROWLEY. Westmead, England: Saxon House; New York: Lexington Books, [1972] 1973.

BODDEWYN, J. J. AND HOLLANDER, STANLEY C., eds. *Public Policy toward Retailing: An International Symposium.* Lexington, Mass.; Toronto and London: Heath, 1973.

BONILLA, FRANK AND GIRLING, ROBERT, eds. *Structures of Dependency*. Palo Alto, Calif.: Nairobi Bookstore, 1973.

BORNSTEIN, MORRIS, ed. *Plan and Market: Economic Reform in Eastern Europe*. Yale Russian and East European Studies, No. 12. New Haven and London: Yale University Press, 1973.

BOULDING, KENNETH E. *Collected Papers*. Vol. 3. *Political Economy*. Edited by LARRY D. SINGELL. Boulder: Colorado Associated University Press, 1973.

BOULDING, KENNETH E.; PFAFF, MARTIN AND PFAFF, ANITA, eds., *Transfers in an Urbanized Economy: Theories and Effects of the Grants Economy*. Belmont, Calif.: Wadsworth, 1973.

BRITT, STEUART HENDERSON AND BOYD, HARPER W., JR., eds. *Marketing Management and Administrative Action*. Third edition. New York; London; Johannesburg and New Delhi: McGraw-Hill, [1963] 1973.

BUCHANAN, J. M. AND THIRLBY, G. F., eds. *L.S.E. Essays on Cost*. New York: Humanities Press; London: Weidenfeld and Nicolson for the London School of Economics, 1973.

CAGAN, PHILLIP, ET AL. *A New Look at Inflation: Economic Policy in the Early 1970s*. Washington, D.C.: American Enterprise Institute for Public Policy Research, 1973.

CANADIAN AGRICULTURAL ECONOMICS SOCIETY. *Canadian Trade and the Pacific Rim: Marketing and Production Implications*. Ottawa: Author, 1973.

CHAMBERLAIN, NEIL W., ed. *Contemporary Economic Issues*. Revised edition. Irwin Series in Economics. Homewood, Ill.: Irwin; Georgetown, Ont.: Irwin-Dorsey, [1969] 1973.

CLAWSON, MARION, ed. *Modernizing Urban Land Policy*. London and Baltimore: Johns Hopkins University Press for Resources for the Future, Inc., 1973.

COCHRANE, JAMES L. AND ZELENY, MILAN, eds. *Multiple Criteria Decision Making*. Columbia: University of South Carolina Press, 1973.

COLE, H. S. D., ET AL., eds. *Models of Doom: A Critique of the Limits to Growth; With a Reply by the Authors of "The Limits to Growth."* New York: Universe Books, 1973.

THE CONFERENCE BOARD. *Challenge to Leadership: Managing in a Changing World*. New York: Free Press; London: Collier-Macmillan, 1973.

DALY, HERMAN E., ed. *Toward a Steady-State Economy*. San Francisco: Freeman, 1973.

DAMACHI, UKANDI G. AND SEIBEL, HANS DIETER, eds. *Social Change and Economic Development in Nigeria*. Praeger Special Studies in International Economics and Development. New York and London: Praeger, 1973.

DEANE, R. S., ed. *A New Zealand Model: Structure, Policy Uses & Some Simulation Results*. Research Paper No. 8. Wellington: Reserve Bank of New Zealand, 1972.

DESPRES, EMILE. *International Economic Reform: Collected Papers of Emile Despres*. Edited by GERALD M. MEIER. New York; London and Toronto: Oxford University Press, 1973.

DIEBOLD GROUP, INC. *Rethinking the Practice of Management: The Impact of Data Processing, Management Information Systems, and Communications*. Praeger Special Studies in U.S. Economic, Social, and Political Issues. New York and London: Praeger, 1973.

DIERKES, MEINOLF AND BAUER, RAYMOND A., eds. *Corporate Social Accounting*. Praeger Special Studies in U.S. Economic, Social, and Political Issues. New York and London: Praeger, 1973.

DINWIDDY, BRUCE, ed. *Aid Performance and Development Policies of Western Countries: Studies in U.S., U.K., E.E.C., and Dutch Programs*. New York and London: Praeger in association with the Overseas Development Institute, 1973.

ECKAUS, R. S. AND ROSENSTEIN-RODAN, P. N., eds. *Analysis of Development Problems: Studies of the Chilean Economy*. Contributions to Economic Analysis series, no. 83. New York: American Elsevier; Amsterdam and London: North-Holland, 1973.

EDGE, D. O. AND WOLFE, J. N., eds. *Meaning and Control: Essays in Social Aspects of Science and Technology*. Social Issues in the Seventies. New York: Barnes & Noble; London: Tavistock, 1973.

ENTHOVEN, ALAIN C. AND FREEMAN, A. MYRICK, III, eds. *Pollution, Resources, and the Environment*. Problems of the Modern Economy Series. New York: Norton, 1973.

EPSTEIN, T. SCARLETT AND PENNY, DAVID H., eds. *Opportunity and Response: Case Studies in*

Economic Development. Sydney: Angus and Robertson; distributed in the United States by Humanities Press, 1973.

EVERITT, ALAN, ed. *Perspectives in English Urban History.* New York: Barnes & Noble, 1973.

FALK, RICHARD A. AND MENDLOVITZ, SAUL H., eds. *Regional Politics and World Order.* San Francisco: Freeman, 1973.

FARRELL, M. J., ed. *Readings in Welfare Economics: A Selection of Papers from the Review of Economic Studies.* London; Melbourne; Johannesburg and Madras: Macmillan; New York: St. Martin's Press, 1973.

FAYERWEATHER, JOHN, ed. *International Business-Government Affairs: Toward an Era of Accommodation.* Cambridge, Mass.: Ballinger, 1973.

FEDERAL RESERVE BANK OF BOSTON. *Policies for a More Competitive Financial System: A Review of the Report of The President's Commission on Financial Structure and Regulation; Proceedings of a Conference Held at Nantucket, Massachusetts, June, 1972.* Conference Series, No. 8. Boston: Author, 1972.

FLOOK, E. EVELYN AND SANAZARO, PAUL J., eds. *Health Services Research and R&D in Perspective.* Ann Arbor, Mich.: Health Administration Press, 1973.

FÖLDI, TAMÁS, ed. *Economic Development and Planning: Selected Studies.* Budapest: Akadémiai Kiadó, 1973.

FRIEDMANN, JOHN. *Urbanization, Planning, and National Development.* Beverly Hills, Calif., and London: Sage, 1973.

GABRIEL, RICHARD A. AND COHEN, SYLVAN H., eds. *The Environment: Critical Factors in Strategy Development.* New York: MSS Information, 1973.

GHAI, DHARAM, ed. *Economic Independence in Africa.* Nairobi: East African Literature Bureau, 1973.

GIERSCH, HERBERT, ed. *Fiscal Policy and Demand Management: Symposium 1972.* Tübingen: J. C. B. Mohr (Paul Siebeck), 1973.

GINZBERG, ELI AND YOHALEM, ALICE M., eds. *Corporate Lib: Women's Challenge to Management.* Policy Studies in Employment and Welfare, No. 17. Baltimore and London: Johns Hopkins University Press, 1973.

GOLDBERGER, ARTHUR S. AND DUNCAN, OTIS DUDLEY, eds. *Structural Equation Models in the Social Sciences.* Quantitative Studies in Social Relations. New York and London: Seminar Press, 1973.

GOLDSMITH, RAYMOND W., ed. *Institutional Investors and Corporate Stock: A Background Study.* New York and London: National Bureau of Economic Research, 1973.

GOREUX, LOUIS M. AND MANNE, ALAN S., eds. *Multi-Level Planning: Case Studies in Mexico.* Foreword by HOLLIS B. CHENERY. Amsterdam and London: North-Holland; New York: American Elsevier, 1973.

GOUGH, KATHLEEN AND SHARMA, HARI P., eds. *Imperialism and Revolution in South Asia.* New York and London: Monthly Review Press, 1973.

GRIESON, RONALD E., ed. *Urban Economics: Readings and Analysis.* Boston: Little, Brown, 1973.

GRUBEL, HERBERT G. AND MORGAN, THEODORE, eds. *Exchange Rate Policy in Southeast Asia.* Lexington, Mass.; Toronto and London: Heath, 1973.

[HALM, GEORGE N.] *Leading Issues in International Economic Policy: Essays in Honor of George N. Halm.* Edited by C. FRED BERGSTEN AND WILLIAM G. TYLER. Lexington, Mass.: Heath, Lexington Books, 1973.

HARBERGER, ARNOLD C. *Project Evaluation: Collected Papers.* Markham Economics Series. Chicago: Markham, 1973.

HARRISS, C. LOWELL, ed. *Government Spending & Land Values: Public Money & Private Gain.* Committee on Taxation, Resources and Economic Development, No. 6. Madison: University of Wisconsin Press for the Committee on Taxation, Resources and Economic Development, 1973.

HAVEMAN, ROBERT H. AND HAMRIN, ROBERT D., eds. *The Political Economy of Federal Policy.* New York and London: Harper & Row, 1973.

HAWKES, NIGEL, ed. *International Seminar on Trends in Mathematical Modelling, Venice, 13–18*

December 1971. Lecture Notes in Economics and Mathematical Systems, Vol. 80. Berlin and New York: Springer-Verlag, 1973.

HAYNES, W. WARREN; COYNE, THOMAS JOSEPH AND OSBORNE, DALE K., eds. *Readings in Managerial Economics.* Dallas: Business Publications; Georgetown, Ont.: Irwin-Dorsey, 1973.

HEIMANN, FRITZ F., ed. *The Future of Foundations.* Englewood Cliffs, N.J.: Prentice-Hall for the American Assembly, Columbia University, 1973.

HENLEY, DONALD S., ed. *International Business—1973: A Selection of Current Readings.* Assisted by K. ANDERSON, *et al.* MSU International Business and Economic Studies. East Lansing: Michigan State University, Graduate School of Business Administration, Division of Research, 1973.

HICKS, J. R. AND WEBER, W., eds. *Carl Menger and the Austrian School of Economics.* New York and London: Oxford University Press, 1973.

[HICKS, URSULA] *Public Finance, Planning and Economic Development: Essays in Honour of Ursula Hicks.* Edited by WILFRED L. DAVID. New York: St. Martin's Press; London: Macmillan, 1973.

HOLBIK, KAREL, ed. *Monetary Policy in Twelve Industrial Countries.* Boston: Federal Reserve Bank of Boston, 1973.

HUGHES, HELEN, ed. *Prospects for Partnership: Industrialization and Trade Policies in the 1970s.* Baltimore and London: Johns Hopkins University Press for the International Bank for Reconstruction and Development, 1973.

INSTITUTE FOR DEVELOPMENT RESEARCH. *Dualism and Rural Development in East Africa.* Copenhagen: Author, 1973.

IOWA STATE UNIVERSITY CENTER FOR AGRICULTURAL AND RURAL DEVELOPMENT. *U.S. Trade Policy and Agricultural Exports.* Ames: Iowa State University Press, 1973.

JACOBY, HENRY D., ET AL. *Clearing the Air: Federal Policy on Automotive Emissions Control.* Cambridge, Mass.: Ballinger, 1973.

JOHNSON, HARRY G. *Further Essays in Monetary Economics.* American edition. Cambridge, Mass.: Harvard University Press, [1972] 1973.

JOHNSON, HARRY G. AND SWOBODA, ALEXANDER K., eds. *The Economics of Common Currencies: Proceedings of the Madrid Conference on Optimum Currency Areas.* Cambridge, Mass.: Harvard University Press, 1973.

JOHNSON, HARRY G. AND WEISBROD, BURTON A., eds. *The Daily Economist: A Chronicle of Contemporary Subjects Showing the Scope and Originality of Economic Research and Its Application to Real-World Issues.* Englewood Cliffs, N.J.; London; Tokyo and New Delhi: Prentice-Hall, 1973.

JUDGE, GEORGE G. AND TAKAYAMA, TAKASHI, eds. *Studies in Economic Planning over Space and Time.* Contributions to Economic Analysis series, no. 82. Amsterdam and London: North-Holland; New York: American Elsevier, 1973.

KAYE, SEYMOUR P. AND MARSH, ARTHUR, eds. *International Manual on Collective Bargaining for Public Employees.* Foreword by THEODORE W. KHEEL. Praeger Special Studies in International Politics and Government. New York and London: Praeger, 1973.

KISS, T., ed. *The Market of Socialist Economic Integration: Selected Conference Papers.* In Collaboration with T. FÖLDI AND I. SCHWEITZER. Translated by P. AUSTIN. Budapest: Akadémiai Kiadó, 1973.

KLEIN, WALTER H. AND MURPHY, DAVID C., eds. *Policy: Concepts in Organizational Guidance: A Book of Readings.* Boston: Little, Brown, 1973.

KRAUSE, LAWRENCE B. AND SALANT, WALTER S., eds. *European Monetary Unification and Its Meaning for the United States.* Washington, D.C.: Brookings Institution, 1973.

KRAUSS, MELVYN B., ed. *The Economics of Integration: A Book of Readings.* London: Allen & Unwin, 1973.

KUJAWA, DUANE, ed. *American Labor and the Multinational Corporation.* Foreword by ROBERT G. HAWKINS. Praeger Special Studies in International Economics and Development. New York and London: Praeger, 1973.

KUZNETS, SIMON. *Population, Capital, and Growth: Selected Essays.* New York: Norton, 1973.

LEVIN, SAMUEL M. *Essays on American Industrialism: Selected Papers of Samuel M. Levin.* Detroit: Wayne State University College of Liberal Arts, 1973.

LEVITAN, SAR A., ed. *The Federal Social Dollar in Its Own Back Yard.* Washington, D.C.: The Bureau of National Affairs, 1973.

LEVY, MICHAEL E., ed. *Major Economic Issues of the 1970's.* A Report from The Conference Board. New York: The Conference Board, 1973.

LEWIS, JOHN P. AND KAPUR, ISHAN, eds. *The World Bank Group, Multilateral Aid, and the 1970s.* Lexington, Mass.; Toronto and London: Heath, 1973.

LISTER, R. J., ed. *Studies in Optimal Financing.* New York and London: Macmillan, 1973.

LIVINGSTONE, I., ET AL., eds. *The Teaching of Economics in Africa: Report of a Conference Held in April 1969 in Dar es Salaam, United Republic of Tanzania.* London: Chatto and Windus for Sussex University Press; Toronto: Clarke, Irwin, 1973.

MAGNIFICO, GIOVANNI. *European Monetary Unification.* New York and Toronto: Wiley, 1973.

MANDELL, LEWIS, ET AL., eds. *Surveys of Consumers, 1971–72: Contributions to Behavioral Economics.* Ann Arbor: University of Michigan, Institute for Social Research, 1973.

MANGUM, GARTH L. AND ROBSON, R. THAYNE, eds. *Metropolitan Impact of Manpower Programs: A Four-City Comparison.* Salt Lake City: Olympus, 1973.

MASOTTI, L. H. AND HADDEN, J. K., eds. *The Urbanization of the Suburbs.* Urban Affairs Annual Reviews, Vol. 7. Beverly Hills, Calif., and London: Sage, 1973.

MATTILA, JOHN M. AND THOMPSON, WILBUR R., eds. *Proceedings of the Conference on Urban Economics.* Detroit: Wayne State University, Department of Economics, 1973.

MCCLURE, LARRY AND BUAN, CAROLYN, eds. *Essays on Career Education.* Foreword by SIDNEY P. MARLAND, JR. Portland, Ore.: Northwest Regional Educational Laboratory under contract with the U.S. Office of Education/National Institute of Education, 1973.

MESKILL, JOHN, ed. *An Introduction to Chinese Civilization.* New York and London: Columbia University Press, 1973.

METZLER, LLOYD A. *Collected Papers.* Cambridge, Mass.: Harvard University Press, 1973.

MICKIEWICZ, ELLEN, ed. *Handbook of Soviet Social Science Data.* Foreword by KARL W. DEUTSCH. New York: Free Press; London: Collier-Macmillan, 1973.

MIRRLEES, JAMES A. AND STERN, N. H., eds. *Models of Economic Growth: Proceedings of a Conference Held by the International Economic Association at Jerusalem.* New York and Toronto: Wiley, 1973.

MORISHIMA, M., ET AL. *Theory of Demand: Real and Monetary.* London and New York: Oxford University Press, 1973.

MOSKOFF, WILLIAM, ed. *Comparative National Economic Policies: A Reader for Introductory Economics.* Lexington, Mass.; Toronto and London: Heath, 1973.

MOSS, MILTON, ed. *The Measurement of Economic and Social Performance.* Conference on Research in Income and Wealth, Studies in Income and Wealth, vol. 38, New York and London: Columbia University Press for the National Bureau of Economic Research, 1973.

MURRAY, BARBARA B., ed. *Consumerism: The Eternal Triangle: Business, Government, and Consumers.* Pacific Palisades, Calif.: Goodyear, 1973.

MUSGRAVE, RICHARD A., ed. *Broad-Based Taxes: New Options and Sources.* A Supplementary Paper of the Committee for Economic Development. Baltimore and London: Johns Hopkins University Press, 1973.

MYRDAL, GUNNAR. *Against the Stream: Critical Essays on Economics.* New York: Pantheon Books, [1972] 1973.

NISKANEN, WILLIAM A., ET AL., eds. *Benefit-Cost and Policy Analysis 1972: An Aldine Annual on Forecasting, Decision-Making, and Evaluation.* Chicago: Aldine, 1973.

NOVICK, DAVID, ed. *Current Practice in Program Budgeting (PPBS): Analysis and Case Studies Covering Government and Business.* A Rand Corporation Research Study. New York: Crane, Russak, for the Rand Corporation, 1973.

OFORI, I. M., ed. *Factors of Agricultural Growth in West Africa: Proceedings of an International*

Conference Held at Legon, April 1971. Legon, Africa: University of Ghana, Institute of Statistical, Social and Economic Research, 1973.

OKSENBERG, MICHEL, ed. *China's Developmental Experience.* New York: Academy of Political Science, Columbia University, 1973.

OLSON, MANCUR AND LANDSBERG, HANS H., eds. *The No-Growth Society.* New York: Norton, 1973.

OSTROM, VINCENT. *The Intellectual Crisis in American Public Administration.* University, Ala.: University of Alabama Press, 1973.

OTT, DAVID J., ET AL. *Public Claims on U.S. Output: Federal Budget Options in the Last Half of the Seventies.* AEI Domestic Affairs Study, No. 8. Washington, D.C.: American Enterprise Institute for Public Policy Research, 1973.

OWEN, HENRY, ed. *The Next Phase in Foreign Policy.* Washington, D.C.: Brookings Institution, 1973.

PALDA, KRISTIAN S., ed. *Readings in Managerial Economics.* Englewood Cliffs, N.J.: Prentice-Hall, 1973.

PARK, ROLLA EDWARD, ed. *The Role of Analysis in Regulatory Decisionmaking: The Case of Cable Television.* Lexington, Mass.; Toronto and London: Heath, 1973.

PARKIN, MICHAEL, ed. *Essays in Modern Economics: The Proceedings of the Association of University Teachers of Economics: Aberystwyth 1972.* New York: Harper & Row, Barnes & Noble, 1973.

PERKINS, J. O. N., ed. *Macro-Economic Policy: A Comparative Study: Australia, Canada, New Zealand, South Africa.* Toronto and Buffalo: University of Toronto Press, 1973.

PERRY, P. J., ed. *British Agriculture, 1875–1914.* Debates in Economic History. London: Methuen; distributed by Harper & Row, Barnes & Noble, New York, 1973.

POLLOCK, DAVID H. AND RITTER, ARCH R. M., eds. *Latin American Prospects for the 1970s: What Kinds of Revolutions?* Praeger Special Studies in International Politics and Government. New York and London: Praeger, 1973.

POSTAN, M. M. *Essays on Medieval Agriculture and General Problems of the Medieval Economy.* New York and London: Cambridge University Press, 1973. (I)

POSTAN, M. M. *Medieval Trade and Finance.* New York and London: Cambridge University Press, 1973. (II)

POWELL, ALAN A. AND WILLIAMS, ROSS A., eds. *Econometric Studies of Macro and Monetary Relations: Papers Presented at the Second Australasian Conference of Econometricians, Monash University, 9–13 August 1971.* Amsterdam and London: North-Holland; New York: American Elsevier, 1973.

PYNOOS, JON; SCHAFER, ROBERT AND HARTMAN, CHESTER W., eds. *Housing Urban America.* Social Research and Public Policy series. Chicago: Aldine, 1973.

RASMUSSEN, DAVID W. AND HAWORTH, CHARLES T., eds. *The Modern City: Readings in Urban Economics.* New York and London: Harper & Row, 1973.

RECKTENWALD, HORST CLAUS, ed. *Political Economy: A Historical Perspective.* London: Collier-Macmillan, 1973.

REYNOLDS, LLOYD G.; GREEN, GEORGE D. AND LEWIS, DARRELL R., eds. *Current Issues of Economic Policy.* Georgetown, Ont.: Irwin-Dorsey; Homewood, Ill.: Irwin, 1973.

RICHARDS, AUDREY I.; STURROCK, FORD AND FORTT, JEAN M., eds. *Subsistence to Commercial Farming in Present-Day Buganda: An Economic and Anthropological Survey.* African Studies Series, No. 8. New York and London: Cambridge University Press, 1973.

RICKS, R. BRUCE, ed. *National Housing Models: Application of Econometric Techniques to Problems of Housing Research: Proceedings of a Conference Sponsored by the Federal Home Loan Bank System.* Studies in Business, Technology, and Economics. Lexington, Mass.; Toronto and London: Heath, Lexington Books, 1973.

ROBINSON, DEREK. *Incomes Policy and Capital Sharing in Europe.* New York: Harper & Row, Barnes & Noble, 1973.

ROBINSON, JOAN, ed. *After Keynes: Papers Presented to Section F (Economics) at the 1972 Annual*

Meeting of the British Association for the Advancement of Science. British Association series. Oxford: Basil Blackwell, 1973.

[ROSENSTEIN-RODAN, PAUL] *Development and Planning: Essays in Honour of Paul Rosenstein-Rodan*. Edited by JAGDISH N. BHAGWATI AND RICHARD S. ECKAUS. Cambridge, Mass.: MIT Press, 1973.

ROSS, MICEAL, ed. *Operational Research '72: Proceedings of the Sixth IFORS International Conference on Operational Research, Dublin, Ireland, August 21–25, 1972*. New York: American Elsevier; Amsterdam and London: North-Holland, 1973.

ROTTENBERG, SIMON, ed. *The Economics of Crime and Punishment: A Conference Sponsored by American Enterprise Institute for Public Policy Research*. Washington, D.C.: American Enterprise Institute for Public Policy Research, 1973.

RUSSELL, MILTON, ed. *Perspectives in Public Regulation: Essays on Political Economy; Southern Illinois University Conference on Current Issues in Public Utility Regulation and Management, Carbondale, 1972*. Carbondale: Southern Illinois University Press; London and Amsterdam: Feffer and Simons, 1973.

RYBCZYNSKI, T. M., ed. *A New Era in Competition: Papers Read at the Society of Business Economists' Conference at Churchill College, Cambridge, April, 1972*. New York: Harper & Row, Barnes & Noble, 1973.

SCAPERLANDA, ANTHONY E., ed. *Prospects for Eliminating Non-Tariff Distortions*. Foreword by FRANS A. M. ALTING VON GEUSAU. John F. Kennedy Institute Center for International Studies Publication. Groningen, the Netherlands: Academic Book Services Holland for Sijthoff, 1973.

SCOTT, ROBERT E., ed. *Latin American Modernization Problems: Case Studies in the Crises of Change*. Urbana and London: University of Illinois Press, 1973.

SHELDON, ELEANOR BERNERT, ed. *Family Economic Behavior: Problems and Prospects; From a Conference on Social Structure, Family Life Styles, and Economic Behavior, Sponsored by the Institute of Life Insurance at Williamsburg, Virginia, January 1972*. Philadelphia and Toronto: Lippincott, 1973.

SIMHA, S. L. N., ed. *Reform of the Indian Banking System: Proceedings of a Seminar Organized in Madras on December 1 and 2, 1972*. Madras: Orient Longman for the Institute for Financial Management and Research, 1973.

SOKOLOSKI, ADAM A., ed. *Ocean Fishery Management: Discussions and Research*. NOAA Technical Report NMFS CIRC-371. Seattle: U.S. Dept of Commerce, National Oceanic and Atmospheric Administration, 1973.

SOMERS, GERALD G., ed. *The Next Twenty-Five Years of Industrial Relations*. Twenty-Fifth Anniversary Volume. Industrial Relations Research Association Series. Madison, Wisc.: Industrial Relations Research Association, 1973.

STEIN, BRUNO AND MILLER, S. M., eds. *Incentives and Planning in Social Policy*. Chicago: Aldine, 1973.

STEPAN, ALFRED, ed. *Authoritarian Brazil: Origins, Policies, and Future*. New Haven and London: Yale University Press, [1973] 1976.

STREETEN, PAUL, ed. *Trade Strategies for Development: Papers of the Ninth Cambridge Conference on Development Problems, September 1972*. Cambridge University Overseas Studies Committee. New York and Toronto: Wiley, 1973.

STURMTHAL, ADOLF AND SCOVILLE, JAMES G., eds. *The International Labor Movement in Transition: Essays on Africa, Asia, Europe, and South America*. Urbana and London: University of Illinois Press, 1973.

TAX FOUNDATION, INC. *The Challenge of Tax Reform: Proceedings of Tax Foundation's 24th National Conference*. New York: Author, 1973.

TEMIN, PETER, ed. *New Economic History: Selected Readings*. Penguin Modern Economics Readings. Harmondsworth, England; Baltimore and Victoria, Australia: Penguin Books, 1973.

THOMAS, WILLIAM E., JR., ed. *Readings in Cost Accounting, Budgeting, and Control*. Fourth edition. Cincinnati and Brighton, England: South-Western, [1955] 1973.

THORELLI, H. B., ed. *International Marketing Strategy: Selected Readings*. Penguin Modern Management Readings. Harmondsworth, England; Baltimore and Victoria, Australia: Penguin Books, 1973.

THURBER, CLARENCE E. AND GRAHAM, LAWRENCE S., eds. *Development Administration in Latin America.* Comparative Administration Group Series. Durham, N.C.: Duke University Press for Comparative Administration Group of the American Society for Public Administration, 1973.

[TINBERGEN, JAN] *Economic Structure and Development: Essays in Honour of Jan Tinbergen.* Edited by H. C. BOS; H. LINNEMANN AND P. DE WOLFF. Amsterdam and London: North-Holland; New York: American Elsevier, 1973.

TIVEY, LEONARD, ed. *The Nationalized Industries since 1960: A Book of Readings.* Buffalo and Toronto: University of Toronto Press for the Royal Institute of Public Administration, 1973.

TRANTER, N. L., ed. *Population and Industrialization.* Documents in Economic History. New York: Crane, Russak, 1973.

UDIS, BERNARD, ed. *The Economic Consequences of Reduced Military Spending.* Studies in International Development and Economics. Lexington, Mass.; Toronto and London: Heath, Lexington Books, 1973.

ULMAN, LLOYD, ed. *Manpower Programs in the Policy Mix.* Baltimore and London: Johns Hopkins University Press, 1973.

URQUIDI, VICTOR L. AND THORP, ROSEMARY, eds. *Latin America in the International Economy: Proceedings of a Conference Held by the International Economic Association in Mexico City, Mexico.* New York and Toronto: Wiley, Halsted Press, 1973.

WADHVA, CHARAN D., ed. *Some Problems of India's Economic Policy: Selected Readings on Planning, Agriculture and Foreign Trade.* Bombay: Tata McGraw-Hill, 1973.

WADSWORTH, J. E., ed. *The Banks and the Monetary System in the UK, 1959–1971.* London: Methuen; distributed by Harper & Row, Barnes & Noble, New York, 1973.

WEINTRAUB, ANDREW; SCHWARTZ, ELI AND ARONSON, J. RICHARD, eds. *The Economic Growth Controversy.* New York: International Arts and Sciences Press, 1973.

WEINTRAUB, SIDNEY, ET AL. *Keynes and the Monetarists and Other Essays.* New Brunswick, N.J.: Rutgers University Press, 1973.

WESTON, J. FRED AND ORNSTEIN, STANLEY I., eds. *The Impact of Large Firms on the U.S. Economy.* Studies in Business, Technology and Economics. Toronto; London and Lexington, Mass.: Heath, Lexington Books, 1973.

WHITAKER, BEN, ed. *The Fourth World: Victims of Group Oppression; Eight Reports from the Field Work of the Minority Rights Group.* New York: Schocken, 1973.

WIEGAND, G. C., ed. *Toward a New World Monetary System: Proceedings of the First International Monetary Seminar Sponsored by the Committee for Monetary Research and Education, Inc. (CMRE)—1973.* New York: McGraw-Hill, *Engineering and Mining Journal,* 1973.

WILBER, CHARLES K., ed. *The Political Economy of Development and Underdevelopment.* New York: Random House, 1973.

WILLIAMS, B. R., ed. *Science and Technology in Economic Growth: Proceedings of a Conference Held by the International Economic Association at St. Anton, Austria.* New York and Toronto: Wiley, Halsted Press; London: Macmillan Press, 1973.

[WILLIAMSON, HAROLD F.] *Business Enterprise and Economic Change: Essays in Honor of Harold F. Williamson.* Edited by LOUIS P. CAIN AND PAUL J. USELDING. Kent, Ohio: Kent State University Press, 1973.

WOLFE, J. N., ed. *Cost Benefit and Cost Effectiveness: Studies and Analysis.* London: George Allen & Unwin, 1973.

YOUNG, DENNIS R. AND NELSON, RICHARD R., eds. *Public Policy for Day Care of Young Children: Organization, Finance, and Planning.* Lexington, Mass.; Toronto and London: Heath, Lexington Books, in Cooperation with the Urban Institute, Washington, D.C., 1973.

YOUNGSON, A. J., ed. *Economic Development in the Long Run.* New York: St. Martin's Press, 1973.

ZAMMIT, J. ANN, ed. *The Chilean Road to Socialism: Proceedings of an ODEPLAN-IDS Round Table, March 1972.* Austin: University of Texas Press; Sussex, England: University of Sussex, Institute of Development Studies, 1973.

CLASSIFICATION SYSTEM

N.B. Editor's note. Reading this description seems to be unavoidable for anyone seeking to use this classification system.

Subject Index of Articles in Current Periodicals, Collective Volumes, and Government Documents

Abbreviated titles for journals are the same as those used in the *Journal of Economic Literature*. Full titles of journals may be found on pages xi–xv.

Books have been identified by author or editor (noted *ed.*). In rare cases where two books by the same author appear, volumes are distinguished by I or II after the name. In some cases there appear two books by the same person, once as author, once as editor. These may be distinguished by *ed.* noted for the edited volume. Full titles and bibliographic references for books may be found on pages xvi–xxiii.

Geographic Descriptors when appropriate appear in brackets at the end of the article citation.

000 General Economics; Theory; History; Systems

010 GENERAL ECONOMICS

011 General Economics

0110 General

Agnati, Achille. Dal calcolo dell'opinione nei preclassici all'analisi economica dell'esogeneità. (From the Calculus of Consent in the Preclassics to the Economic Analysis of Exogeneity. With English summary.) *Rivista Int. Sci. Econ. Com.*, February 1973, *20*(2), pp. 153–78.

Allen, R. G. D. The Statistician and the British Library of Political and Economic Science. *J. Roy. Statist. Soc.*, Part 2, 1973, *136*, pp. 255–57. [G: U.K.]

Balogh, T. and Balacs, P. Fact and Fancy in International Economic Relations. *World Devel.*, February 1973, *1*(1-2), pp. 76–92.

Bawden, D. Lee. The Neglected Human Factor. *Amer. J. Agr. Econ.*, December 1973, *55*(5), pp. 879–87.

Boulding, Kenneth E. Economics as a Social Science. In *Boulding, K. E.*, 1973, pp. 25–40.

Boulding, Kenneth E. Man as a Commodity. In *Boulding, K. E.*, 1973, pp. 587–603.

Boulding, Kenneth E. Religious Foundations of Economic Progress. In *Boulding, K. E.*, 1973, pp. 41–51.

Boulding, Kenneth E. The Misallocation of Intellectual Resources in Economics. In *Boulding, K. E.*, 1973, pp. 533–52. [G: U.S.]

Bouvier, Leon F. A Survey of Population Textbooks. *Demography*, November 1973, *10*(4), pp. 685–92.

Brown, Lowell S., et al. Are There Real Limits to Growth?—A Reply to Beckerman. *Oxford Econ. Pap.*, November 1973, *25*(3), pp. 455–60.

Burns, E. O. Random Thoughts on Some Problems of Professional Communication. *Australian J. Agr. Econ.*, August 1973, *17*(2), pp. 93–103.

Costin, Frank; Greenough, William T. and Menges, Robert J. Student Ratings of College Teaching: Reliability, Validity, and Usefulness. *J. Econ. Educ.*, Fall 1973, *5*(1), pp. 51–53.

Day, Lincoln H. A Survey of Population Textbooks. *Demography*, November 1973, *10*(4), pp. 693–96.

Francis, Gary. On the Obligation to Publish and the Nature of URPE Literature. *Rev. Radical Polit. Econ.*, Summer 1973, *5*(2), pp. 93–94.

Frankena, Mark and Bhatia, Kul B. Canadian Contributions to Economics Journals, 1968-1972. *Can. J. Econ.*, February 1973, *6*(1), pp. 121–24.

Frazer, William J., Jr. An Assessment of the Impact of the Computer. *Schweiz. Z. Volkswirtsch. Statist.*, December 1973, *109*(4), pp. 579–95.

Gray, Roger W. The Rebirth of Agricultural Economics? *Food Res. Inst. Stud.*, 1973, *12*(3), pp. 253–58.

Grundmann, Helge E. Towards a More Applicable Economic Theory. In *Livingstone, I., et al., eds.*, 1973, pp. 59–65.

Guarnieri, Raymond L. A Suggestion for Rigorizing the Theory of Prediction. *Western Econ. J.*, June 1973, *11*(2), pp. 147–49.

Hogan, Timothy D. Rankings of Ph.D. Programs in Economics and the Relative Publishing Performance of their Ph.D.'s: The Experience of the 1960's. *Western Econ. J.*, December 1973, *11*(4), pp. 429–50. [G: U.S.]

Knapp, John. Economics or Political Economy? *Lloyds Bank Rev.*, January 1973, (107), pp. 19–43.

Leijonhufvud, Axel. Life Among the Econ. *Western Econ. J.*, September 1973, *11*(3), pp. 327–37.

Lovell, Michael C. The Production of Economic Literature: An Interpretation. *J. Econ. Lit.*, March 1973, *11*(1), pp. 27–55.

Lumsden, Keith G. Summary of an Analysis of Student Evaluations of Faculty and Courses. *J. Econ. Educ.*, Fall 1973, *5*(1), pp. 54–56.

Madarász, A. Is Political Economy Timely? *Acta Oecon.*, 1973, *10*(2), pp. 177–200.

Malenbaum, Wilfred. World Resources for the Year 2000. *Ann. Amer. Acad. Polit. Soc. Sci.*, July 1973, *408*, pp. 30–46.

Mighell, Ronald L. and Lane, Elizabeth. Writing and the Economic Researcher. *Agr. Econ. Res.*, January 1973, *25*(1), pp. 15–20.

Mirus, Rolf. Some Implications of Student Evaluation of Teachers. *J. Econ. Educ.*, Fall 1973, *5*(1), pp. 35–46.

Myrdal, Gunnar. How Scientific Are the Social Sciences? In *Myrdal, G.*, 1973, pp. 133–57.

Norton, Hugh S. Reviewing Economics Textbooks: Some Comments on the Process. *J. Econ. Lit.*, September 1973, *11*(3), pp. 889–97.

Perlman, Mark. On the Classification of Economics Material. *J. Econ. Lit.,* September 1973, *11*(3), pp. 898–99.

Perlman, Mark. The Editor's Comment. *J. Econ. Lit.,* March 1973, *11*(1), pp. 56–58.

Raj, K. N. Presidential Address. *Indian Econ. J.,* January-March 1973, *20*(3), pp. 355–62.

Siegfried, John J. and White, Kenneth J. Financial Rewards to Research and Teaching: A Case Study of Academic Economists. *Amer. Econ. Rev.,* May 1973, *63*(2), pp. 309–15. [G: U.S.]

Soper, John C. Soft Research on a Hard Subject: Student Evaluations Reconsidered. *J. Econ. Educ.,* Fall 1973, *5*(1), pp. 22–26.

Stever, Guyford. Impact of Space on World Development. *World Devel.,* February 1973, *1*(1-2), pp. 116–21.

Taeuber, Richard C. Problems of Access: Some Comments. *Ann. Econ. Soc. Measure,* April 1973, *2*(2), pp. 215–20. [G: U.S.]

Tribe, M. Economics Textbooks for Africa. In *Livingstone, I., et al., eds.,* 1973, pp. 181–89. [G: Africa]

Tullock, Gordon. Universities Should Discriminate Against Assistant Professors. *J. Polit. Econ.,* September-October 1973, *81*(5), pp. 1256–57.

Vandermeulen, Alice. Economics Journals: Policies, Trends, and a Warning: Comment. *Southern Econ. J.,* July 1973, *40*(1), pp. 146–48.

Villard, Henry H. Some Reflections on Student Evaluation of Teaching. *J. Econ. Educ.,* Fall 1973, *5*(1), pp. 47–50.

Wall, David. Fashionable Economics? Review Article. *Econ. Develop. Cult. Change,* April 1973, *21*(3), pp. 534–40.

Weber, John A. A Note on Keeping Abreast of Developments in the Field of Finance. *J. Finance,* March 1973, *28*(1), pp. 161–65. [G: U.S.]

Weber, John A. Economics Journals: Policies, Trends, and a Warning: Reply. *Southern Econ. J.,* July 1973, *40*(1), pp. 148–49.

Wiener, Anthony J. The Future of Economic Activity. *Ann. Amer. Acad. Polit. Soc. Sci.,* July 1973, *408*, pp. 47–61.

0111 Teaching of Economics

Amin, Samir. The Place of Economic History in the Teaching of Economics in Africa. In *Livingstone, I., et al., eds.,* 1973, pp. 101–03. [G: Africa]

Bach, G. L. An Agenda for Improving the Teaching of Economics. *Amer. Econ. Rev.,* May 1973, *63*(2), pp. 303–08.

Battalio, Raymond C.; Hulett, Joe R. and Kagel, John H. A Comment on J. J. Siegfried's "The Publishing of Economic Papers and Its Impact on Graduate Faculty Ratings, 1960-1969." *J. Econ. Lit.,* March 1973, *11*(1), pp. 68–70. [G: U.S.; U.K.]

Belshaw, D. G. R. The Role of Agricultural Economics in University Economics Teaching in Africa. In *Livingstone, I., et al., eds.,* 1973, pp. 119–29. [G: Africa]

Bevin, J. H. and Livingstone, I. Economic History and Economics Teaching. In *Livingstone, I., et al., eds.,* 1973, pp. 95–100.

Botha, D. J. J. A School of Economic Studies. *S. Afr. J. Econ.,* September 1973, *41*(3), pp. 281–90.

Bulgaru, Mircea. Unele probleme ale integrării învățămîntului cu cercetarea și producția. (Problems of the Integration of Economic Education into Scientific Research and Production. With English summary.) *Stud. Cercet. Econ.,* 1973, (2), pp. 33–46. [G: Rumania]

Connor, Larry J. Michigan State's Curricula in Agricultural Economics. *Amer. J. Agr. Econ.,* Part II, November 1973, *55*(4), pp. 752–54. [G: U.S.]

Davis, Carlton G. Traditional Graduate Admission Standards as Constraints to Increasing the Supply of Black Professional Agriculturalists: The Florida Experience. *Amer. J. Agr. Econ.,* December 1973, *55*(5), pp. 952–66. [G: U.S.]

Decker, Robert L. Success and Attrition Characteristics in Graduate Studies. *J. Econ. Educ.,* Spring 1973, *4*(2), pp. 130–37. [G: U.S.]

Evans, Dennis A. The Influence of Computers on the Teaching of Statistics. *J. Roy. Statist. Soc.,* Part 2, 1973, *136*, pp. 153–90.

de Gaay Fortman, B. The Teaching of Microeconomics. In *Livingstone, I., et al., eds.,* 1973, pp. 73–77.

Grady, Jesse C. Texas A&M's Curriculum. *Amer. J. Agr. Econ.,* Part II, November 1973, *55*(4), pp. 755–56. [G: U.S.]

Green, R. H. University Economics in Anglophonic Africa: A Modest Critique from a Consumer Viewpoint. In *Livingstone, I., et al., eds.,* 1973, pp. 137–46. [G: Africa]

Hansen, W. Lee. Readings on Effective Teaching. *J. Econ. Educ.,* Fall 1973, *5*(1), pp. 63–67.

Harvey, Charles. Mathematics and the Teaching of Economics. In *Livingstone, I., et al., eds.,* 1973, pp. 131–36.

Hess, Carroll V. Workshop Summary and Evaluation. *Amer. J. Agr. Econ.,* Part II, November 1973, *55*(4), pp. 767–69.

Kelley, Allen C. Individualizing Education through the Use of Technology in Higher Education. *J. Econ. Educ.,* Spring 1973, *4*(2), pp. 77–89.

Kendrick, James G. Techniques for Motivating Students. *Amer. J. Agr. Econ.,* Part II, November 1973, *55*(4), pp. 762–66.

Lewis, Darrell R.; Wentworth, Donald R. and Orvis, Charles C. Economics in the Junior Colleges: Terminal or Transfer? *J. Econ. Educ.,* Spring 1973, *4*(2), pp. 100–10. [G: U.S.]

Lindström, Caj-Gunnar. Företagsekonomin som vetenskapsgren och undervisnings disciplin. (Business Economics as a Branch of Science and Educational Discipline. With English summary.) *Ekon. Samfundets Tidskr.,* 1973, *26*(3), pp. 201–10.

Livingstone, I., et al. A Review of the Debate. In *Livingstone, I., et al., eds.,* 1973, pp. 17–39. [G: Africa]

Makower, H. The Pure Theory of International Trade: The Teaching of It. *Indian Econ. J.,* July-September 1973, *21*(1), pp. 1–18.

Manderscheid, Lester V. Guidelines for Curriculum Changes in Agricultural Economics. *Amer. J. Agr. Econ.,* Part II, November 1973, *55*(4), pp. 740–47.

Mead, R. and Stern, R. D. The Use of a Computer

in the Teaching of Statistics. *J. Roy. Statist. Soc.*, Part 2, 1973, *136*, pp. 191–205.

Mestre, Eloy R. and Lubell, Alfred M. Teaching Undergraduate Economics: An Experimental Program. *J. Econ. Educ.*, Spring 1973, *4*(2), pp. 138–40.

Mochalov, B. On the Training of Economists. *Prob. Econ.*, July 1973, *16*(3), pp. 87–101. [G: U.S.S.R.]

Moore, William J. The Relative Quality of Graduate Programs in Economics, 1958-1972: Who Published and Who Perished. *Western Econ. J.*, March 1973, *11*(1), pp. 1–23. [G: U.S.]

Mosher, A. T. Higher Education in the Rural Social Sciences. *Amer. J. Agr. Econ.*, Part II, November 1973, *55*(4), pp. 711–19.

Mwanza, J. The Adaptation of Economics Teaching to the Needs of African Economic Development. In *Livingstone, I., et al., eds.*, 1973, pp. 41–45. [G: Africa]

Nanus, Burt and Coffey, Robert E. Future-Oriented Business Education. *Calif. Manage. Rev.*, Summer 1973, *15*(4), pp. 28–34.

Ord, H. W. The Employment of Economists in Africa. In *Livingstone, I., et al., eds.*, 1973, pp. 147–51. [G: Africa]

Parker, Edith H. New Directions in Agricultural Economics Curricula, University of California, Davis. *Amer. J. Agr. Econ.*, Part II, November 1973, *55*(4), pp. 748–49. [G: U.S.]

Patinkin, Don. Frank Knight as Teacher. *Amer. Econ. Rev.*, December 1973, *63*(5), pp. 787–810.

Ramsett, David E.; Johnson, Jerry D. and Adams, Curtis. Some Evidence on the Value of Instructors in Teaching Economic Principles. *J. Econ. Educ.*, Fall 1973, *5*(1), pp. 57–62.

Roop, Joseph M. Contingency Management in the Teaching of Economics: Some Results from an Intermediate Microeconomics Course. *Intermountain Econ. Rev.*, Spring 1973, *4*(1), pp. 53–71.

Rothman, Mitchell P. and Scott, James H., Jr. Political Opinions and the TUCE. *J. Econ. Educ.*, Spring 1973, *4*(2), pp. 116–24. [G: U.S.]

Scott, James H., Jr. The Test of Understanding in College Economics and Its Construct Validity: Comment. *J. Econ. Educ.*, Spring 1973, *4*(2), pp. 141–42.

Seers, Dudley. The Debate on the Teaching of Economics in Africa: Foreword. In *Livingstone, I., et al., eds.*, 1973, pp. 9–15. [G: Africa]

Siegfried, John J. A Reply to the Comment of Professors Battalio, Hulett, and Kagel on "The Publishing of Economic Papers and Its Impact on Graduate Faculty Ratings, 1960-1969." *J. Econ. Lit.*, March 1973, *11*(1), pp. 71–73.

Siegfried, John J. and White, Kenneth J. Teaching and Publishing as Determinants of Academic Salaries. *J. Econ. Educ.*, Spring 1973, *4*(2), pp. 90–99. [G: U.S.]

Sjo, John; Orazem, Frank and Biere, Arlo. Undergraduate Program Revision at Kansas State University. *Amer. J. Agr. Econ.*, Part I, November 1973, *55*(4), pp. 604–10. [G: U.S.]

Soper, John C. Programmed Instruction in Large-Lecture Courses. *J. Econ. Educ.*, Spring 1973, *4*(2), pp. 125–29. [G: U.S.]

Stigler, George J. A Sketch of the History of Truth in Teaching. *J. Polit. Econ.*, Part I, March-April 1973, *81*(2), pp. 491–95.

Storey, David A. and Christensen, Robert L. Graduate Programs in Agricultural Economics: Results of a Survey. *Amer. J. Agr. Econ.*, February 1973, *55*(1), pp. 61–64. [G: U.S.; Canada]

Streeten, Paul. Some Comments on the Teaching of Economics. In *Livingstone, I., et al., eds.*, 1973, pp. 46–50.

Thompson, Fred A. The Interaction of Cognition and Affect: The Issue of Free Trade. *J. Econ. Educ.*, Spring 1973, *4*(2), pp. 111–15. [G: U.S.]

Treml, Vladimir G. and Gallik, Dimitri, M. Teaching the History of Economic Thought in the USSR. *Hist. Polit. Econ.*, Spring 1973, *5*(1), pp. 215–42. [G: U.S.S.R.]

Wills, Walter J. SIU's Curriculum in Agricultural Economics. *Amer. J. Agr. Econ.*, Part II, November 1973, *55*(4), pp. 750–51. [G: U.S.]

Woods, Roger. Interdisciplinary Courses and Professional Training in East African Universities. In *Livingstone, I., et al., eds.*, 1973, pp. 105–17. [G: E. Africa]

0112 Role of Economics; Role of Economists

Ady, P. On Economic Advice to Developing Countries. *World Devel.*, February 1973, *1*(1-2), pp. 64–75.

Boulding, Kenneth E. The Role of Economics in the Establishment of Stable Peace. In *Boulding, K. E.*, 1973, pp. 407–11.

Bronfenbrenner, Martin. What the Radical Economists Are Saying. *Harvard Bus. Rev.*, September-October 1973, *51*(5), pp. 26–38, 166–68.

Coddington, Alan. Economists and Policy. *Nat. Westminster Bank Quart. Rev.*, February 1973, pp. 59–68.

Gliazer, L. The Economics of Science and the Science of Economics. *Prob. Econ.*, December 1973, *16*(8), pp. 22–43.

Heilbroner, Robert L. Economics as a "Value-Free" Science. *Soc. Res.*, Spring 1973, *40*(1), pp. 129–43.

Küng, Emil. Economics on the Way into the 21st Century. *Nebr. J. Econ. Bus.*, Summer 1973, *12*(3), pp. 53–63.

Lakhtin, G. The Subject of the Economics of Science. *Prob. Econ.*, December 1973, *16*(8), pp. 3–21.

Mattfeldt, Harald. Zum Problem der wissenschaftlichen Politikberatung am Beispiel des Gesamtindikators des Sachverständigenrats. (With English summary.) *Z. ges. Staatswiss.*, October 1973, *129*(4), pp. 634–42. [G: W. Germany]

Mochalov, B. On the Training of Economists. *Prob. Econ.*, July 1973, *16*(3), pp. 87–101. [G: U.S.S.R.]

Reich, Utz-Peter. Die theoretischen Grundlagen des SPD-Langzeitprogramms. (Theoretical Framework of the SPD-Long-Term-Program. With English summary.) *Z. Wirtschaft. Sozialwissen.*, 1973, *93*(5), pp. 513–35. [G: W. Germany]

Riddell, Tom. A Note on Radical Economics and the

New Economists. *Rev. Radical Polit. Econ.*, Fall 1973, *5*(3), pp. 67–72.

Rotwein, Eugene. The Ideology of Wealth and the Liberal Economic Heritage: The Neglected View. *Soc. Res.*, Summer 1973, *40*(2), pp. 269–92.

Schachter, Gustav. Some Developments in Economic Science Since 1965: Methods, Ideas, Approaches. *Amer. J. Econ. Soc.*, July 1973, *32*(3), pp. 331–35.

Svendsen, K. E. Economic Theory and Public Policy. In *Livingstone, I., et al., eds.*, 1973, pp. 66–72.
[G: Africa]

0113 Relation of Economics to Other Disciplines

Baker, Robert P. Labor History, Social Science, and the Concept of the Working Class. *Labor Hist.*, Winter 1973, *14*(1), pp. 98–105.

Bennett, James T. and Barth, James R. Astronomics: A New Approach to Economics? *J. Polit. Econ.*, November-December 1973, *81*(6), pp. 1473–75.

Boulding, Kenneth E. Economics and the Behavioral Sciences: A Desert Frontier? In *Boulding, K. E.*, 1973, pp. 105–20.

Burns, E. O. Random Thoughts on Some Problems of Professional Communication. *Australian J. Agr. Econ.*, August 1973, *17*(2), pp. 93–103.

Gruchy, Allan G. Law, Politics, and Institutional Economics. *J. Econ. Issues*, December 1973, *7*(4), pp. 623–43. [G: U.S.]

Harvey, Charles. Mathematics and the Teaching of Economics. In *Livingstone, I., et al., eds.*, 1973, pp. 131–36.

Hill, Reuben and Klein, David M. Understanding Family Consumption: Common Ground for Integrating Uncommon Disciplinary Perspectives. In *Sheldon, E. B., ed.*, 1973, pp. 1–22. [G: U.S.]

Hunt, Verl F. The Glass Bead Game of Orthodox Economics: Reply. *Intermountain Econ. Rev.*, Spring 1973, *4*(1), pp. 74–76.

Johnson, Harry G. The Glass Bead Game of Orthodox Economics: Comment. *Intermountain Econ. Rev.*, Spring 1973, *4*(1), pp. 72–73.

Lee, Norman. Interactions between Economic and Eco-systems. In *Robinson, J., ed.*, 1973, pp. 125–33.

Lowry, S. Todd. Lord Mansfield and the Law Merchant: Law and Economics in the Eighteenth Century. *J. Econ. Issues*, December 1973, *7*(4), pp. 605–22. [G: U.K.]

Mestmäcker, Ernst-Joachim. Power, Law and Economic Constitution. *Ger. Econ. Rev.*, 1973, *11*(3), pp. 177–92.

Myrdal, Gunnar. The Need for a Sociology and Psychology of Social Science and Scientists. *World Devel.*, May 1973, *1*(5), pp. 41–46.

Rohrlich, George F. The Potential of *Social* Ecology for Economic Science. *Rev. Soc. Econ.*, April 1973, *31*(1), pp. 31–39.

Samuels, Warren J. Law and Economics: Introduction. *J. Econ. Issues*, December 1973, *7*(4), pp. 535–41.

Seidman, Robert B. Contract Law, the Free Market, and State Intervention: A Jurisprudential Perspective. *J. Econ. Issues*, December 1973, *7*(4), pp. 553–75. [G: Kenya; Ghana]

Woods, Roger. Interdisciplinary Courses and Professional Training in East African Universities. In *Livingstone, I., et al., eds.*, 1973, pp. 105–17.
[G: E. Africa]

0114 Relation of Economics to Social Values

Boulding, Kenneth E. Economic Progress as a Goal in Economic Life. In *Boulding, K. E.*, 1973, pp. 53–86.

Boulding, Kenneth E. Some Questions on the Measurement and Evaluation of Organization. In *Boulding, K. E.*, 1973, pp. 147–59.

Boulding, Kenneth E. The Formation of Values as a Process in Human Learning. In *Boulding, K. E.*, 1973, pp. 457–66.

Boulding, Kenneth E. The Ethnics of Rational Decision. In *Haynes, W. W.; Coyne, T. J. and Osborne, D. K., eds.*, 1973, pp. 8–17.

Bronfenbrenner, Martin. Equality and Equity. *Ann. Amer. Acad. Polit. Soc. Sci.*, September 1973, *409*, pp. 9–23.

Ciucur, Dumitru and Gavrilă, Ilie. Competenţa economică a muncitorului modern din ţara noastră. (The Economic Competence of the Modern Worker in Our Country. With English summary.) *Stud. Cercet. Econ.*, 1973, (4), pp. 15–23.
[G: Rumania]

Dunlap, Riley E.; Gale, Richard P. and Rutherford, Brent M. Concern for Environmental Rights Among College Students. *Amer. J. Econ. Soc.*, January 1973, *32*(1), pp. 45–60. [G: U.S.]

Fernandez, Raul A. The Problem of Heroin Addiction and Radical Political Economy. *Amer. Econ. Rev.*, May 1973, *63*(2), pp. 257–62.

Fusfeld, Daniel R. Types of Radicalism in American Economics. *Amer. Econ. Rev.*, May 1973, *63*(2), pp. 145–51.

Ginger, Ray. American Workers: Views From the Left. *Labor Hist.*, Summer 1973, *14*(3), pp. 425–28. [G: U.S.]

Gramm, Warren S. Natural Selection in Economic Thought: Ideology, Power, and the Keynesian Counterrevolution. *J. Econ. Issues*, March 1973, *7*(1), pp. 1–27.

Gruchy, Allan G. Law, Politics, and Institutional Economics. *J. Econ. Issues*, December 1973, *7*(4), pp. 623–43. [G: U.S.]

Hardesty, John; Clement, Norris C. and Jencks, Clinton E. Ecological Conflicts: A Reply. *Rev. Radical Polit. Econ.*, Summer 1973, *5*(2), pp. 95–102.

Heilbroner, Robert L. Economics as a "Value-Free" Science. *Soc. Res.*, Spring 1973, *40*(1), pp. 129–43.

Henderson, Hazel. Ecologists versus Economists. *Harvard Bus. Rev.*, July-August 1973, *51*(4), pp. 28–36, 152–57.

Küng, Emil. Economics on the Way into the 21st Century. *Nebr. J. Econ. Bus.*, Summer 1973, *12*(3), pp. 53–63.

MacRae, Duncan, Jr. Normative Assumptions in the Study of Public Choice. *Public Choice*, Fall 1973, *16*, pp. 27–41.

Martin, David A. Beyond Positive Economics: Toward Moral Philosophy. *Amer. Econ.*, Spring 1973, *17*(1), pp. 60–69.

Myrdal, Gunnar. Rôle des valeurs et politique sociale. (The Place of Values in Social Policy. With English summary.) *Consommation,* January-March 1973, *20*(1), pp. 5–16.

Myrdal, Gunnar. The Place of Values in Social Policy. In *Myrdal, G.,* 1973, pp. 33–51.

Myrdal, Gunnar. The Need for a Sociology and Psychology of Social Science and Scientists. *World Devel.,* May 1973, *1*(5), pp. 41–46.

Oliver, Henry. Study of Relationships Between Economic and Political Systems. *J. Econ. Issues,* December 1973, *7*(4), pp. 543–51.

Stein, Bruno. Incentives and Planning as Social Policy Tools. In *Stein, B. and Miller, S. M., eds.,* 1973, pp. 3–10.

Weisskopf, Walter A. The Image of Man in Economics. *Soc. Res.,* Autumn 1973, *40*(3), pp. 547–63.

Weisskopf, Walter A. Economic Growth versus Existential Balance. In *Daly, H. E., ed.,* 1973, pp. 240–51.

Weisskopf, Walter A. The Dialetics of Equality. *Ann. Amer. Acad. Polit. Soc. Sci.,* September 1973, *409,* pp. 163–73.

Wingo, Lowdon. The Quality of Life: Toward a Microeconomic Definition. *Urban Stud.,* February 1973, *10*(1), pp. 3–18.

Worland, Stephen T. The Economic Significance of John Rawls' A Theory of Justice. *Nebr. J. Econ. Bus.,* Autumn 1973, *12*(4), pp. 119–26.

Yunker, James A. An Appraisal of Langian Socialism. *Indian Econ. J.,* January-March 1973, *20*(3), pp. 382–413.

0115 Methods Used by Economists

Bisogno, Paolo and Forti, Augusto. International Seminar on Trends in Mathematical Modelling: Introduction. In *Hawkes, N., ed.,* 1973, pp. 1–7.

Boulding, Kenneth E. The Skills of the Economist. In *Rectenwald, H. C., ed.,* 1973, pp. 415–24.

Enzer, Selwyn. Applications of Futures Research to Society's Problems. In *Hawkes, N., ed.,* 1973, pp. 243–87.

Georgescu-Roegen, Nicholas. The Entropy Law and the Economic Problem. In *Daly, H. E., ed.,* 1973, pp. 37–49.

Helmer, Olaf. The Role of Futures Research in Societal Modelling. In *Hawkes, N., ed.,* 1973, pp. 9–13.

Mirrlees, James A. Models of Economic Growth: Introduction. In *Mirrlees, J. A. and Stern, N. H., eds.,* 1973, pp. xi–xxii.

Moiseev, Nikita N. The Present State of Futures Research in the Soviet Union. In *Hawkes, N., ed.,* 1973, pp. 14–19. [G: U.S.S.R.]

Routh, Guy. Methodology. In *Livingstone, I., et al., eds.,* 1973, pp. 51–58.

Shell, Richard L. and Stelzer, David F. Systems Analysis: Aid to Decision Making. In *Klein, W. H. and Murphy, D. C., eds.,* 1973, pp. 34–39.

Shubik, Martin. Some Aspects of Socio-Economic Modelling. In *Hawkes, N., ed.,* 1973, pp. 155–63.

Svendsen, K. E. Economic Theory and Public Policy. In *Livingstone, I., et al., eds.,* 1973, pp. 66–72. [G: Africa]

Tribe, Laurence H. Policy Science: Analysis or Ideology? In *Niskanen, W. A., et al., eds.,* 1973, pp. 3–47.

020 GENERAL ECONOMIC THEORY

0200 General Economic Theory

Allingham, M. G. and Morishima, M. Qualitative Economics and Comparative Statics. In *Morishima, M., et al.,* 1973, pp. 3–69.

Boulding, Kenneth E. The Skills of the Economist. In *Rectenwald, H. C., ed.,* 1973, pp. 415–24.

Boulding, Kenneth E. Economics as a Social Science. In *Boulding, K. E.,* 1973, pp. 25–40.

Bronfenbrenner, Martin. A Skeptical View of Radical Economics. *Amer. Econ.,* Fall 1973, *17*(2), pp. 4–8.

Gintzburger, Alphonse A. Psychoanalysis of a Case of Stagnation. *Econ. Develop. Cult. Change,* January 1973, *21*(2), pp. 227–46.

Gottinger, Hans-Werner. Toward a Fuzzy Reasoning in the Behavioral Sciences. *Ekon.-Mat. Obzor,* 1973, *9*(4), pp. 404–22.

Grundmann, Helge E. Towards a More Applicable Economic Theory. In *Livingstone, I., et al., eds.,* 1973, pp. 59–65.

von Hayek, F. A. Economics and Knowledge. In *Buchanan, J. M. and Thirlby, G. F., eds.,* 1973, pp. 43–68.

Hurwicz, Leonid. The Design of Mechanisms for Resource Allocation. *Amer. Econ. Rev.,* May 1973, *63* (2), pp. 1–30.

Kornai, János and Martos, Béla. Autonomous Control of the Economic System. *Econometrica,* May 1973, *41*(3), pp. 509–28.

Lebowitz, Michael A. The Current Crisis of Economic Theory. *Sci. Soc.,* Winter 1973–1974, *37*(4), pp. 385–403.

Madarász, A. Is Political Economy Timely? *Acta Oecon.,* 1973, *10*(2), pp. 177–200.

Oniki, Hajime. Comparative Dynamics (Sensitivity Analysis) in Optimal Control Theory. *J. Econ. Theory,* June 1973, *6*(3), pp. 265–83.

Rowthorn, Bob. Neoclassical Economics and its Critics: A Marxist View. *Pakistan Econ. Soc. Rev.,* Autumn 1973, *11*(3), pp. 316–48.

Svendsen, K. E. Economic Theory and Public Policy. In *Livingstone, I., et al., eds.,* 1973, pp. 66–72. [G: Africa]

Yunker, James A. An Appraisal of Langian Socialism. *Indian Econ. J.,* January-March 1973, *20*(3), pp. 382–413.

021 General Equilibrium Theory

0210 General

Baudier, Edmond. Competitive Equilibrium in a Game. *Econometrica,* November 1973, *41*(6), pp. 1049–68.

Berndt, Ernst R. and Christensen, Laurits R. The Internal Structure of Functional Relationships: Separability, Substitution and Aggregation. *Rev. Econ. Stud.,* July 1973, *40*(3), pp. 403–10.

Bewley, Truman F. The Equality of the Core and the Set of Equilibria in Economies with Infinitely Many Commodities and a Continuum of Agents. *Int. Econ. Rev.,* June 1973, *14*(2), pp. 383–94.

Bhattacharya, Rabindra Nath and Majumdar,

Mukul. Random Exchange Economies. *J. Econ. Theory,* February 1973, *6*(1), pp. 37–67.

Blaquière, Austin; Juricek, Libuska and Wiese, Karl E. Geometry of Pareto Equilibria in N-Person Differential Games. In *Blaquière, A., ed.,* 1973, pp. 271–310.

Boehm, Volker. Firms and Market Equilibria in a Private Ownership Economy. *Z. Nationalökon.,* 1973, *33*(1–2), pp. 87–102.

Boehm, Volker. On Cores and Equilibria of Productive Economies with a Measure Space of Consumers: An Example. *J. Econ. Theory,* August 1973, *6*(4), pp. 409–12.

Braverman, E. M. A Production Model with Disequilibrium Prices. *Matekon,* Fall 1973, *10*(1), pp. 40–64.

Case, James. Differential Trading Games. In *Blaquière, A., ed.,* 1973, pp. 377–400.

Diéguez, Héctor L. and Porto, Alberto. Un modelo simple de equilibrio general: cambio tecnológico. (A Simple Model of General Equilibrium Technological Change. With English summary.) *Económica,* January-April 1973, *19*(1), pp. 45–69.

Gale, David. Pure Exchange Equilibrium of Dynamic Economic Models. *J. Econ. Theory,* February 1973, *6*(1), pp. 12–36.

Ghafari, R. An Analysis of von Newmann "General Equilibrium." *Tahq. Eq.,* Summer & Autumn 1973, *10*(31&32), pp. 84–103.

Goetz, Charles J. and Buchanan, James M. External Diseconomies in Competitive Supply: Reply. *Amer. Econ. Rev.,* September 1973, *63*(4), pp. 745–48.

Gordon, Peter and Lande, Paul S. The Pricing of Goods and Agricultural Land in Multiregional General Equilibrium: Comment. *Southern Econ. J.,* July 1973, *40*(1), pp. 143–44.

Grandmont, Jean-Michel and Laroque, Guy. Money in the Pure Consumption Loan Model. *J. Econ. Theory,* August 1973, *6*(4), pp. 382–95.

Green, Jerry R. Temporary General Equilibrium in a Sequential Trading Model with Spot and Futures Transactions. *Econometrica,* November 1973, *41*(6), pp. 1103–23.

Habibagahi, Hamid and Quirk, James. Hicksian Stability and Walras' Law. *Rev. Econ. Stud.,* April 1973, *40*(2), pp. 249–58.

Hartwick, John M. The Pricing of Goods and Agricultural Land in Multiregional General Equilibrium: Reply. *Southern Econ. J.,* July 1973, *40* (1), pp. 144–45.

Hay, George A. and McGowan, John J. External Diseconomies in Competitive Supply: Comment. *Amer. Econ. Rev.,* September 1973, *63*(4), pp. 738–40.

Hildenbrand, Werner; Schmeidler, David and Zamir, Shmuel. Existence of Approximate Equilibria and Cores. *Econometrica,* November 1973, *41*(6), pp. 1159–66.

Hillinger, Claude. Sales Maximization as an Explanation of Near Pareto Optimality of the U.S. Economy. *Jahr. Nationalökon. Statist.,* May 1973, *187* (4), pp. 364–67. [G: U.S.]

Juricek, Libuska. Games with Coalitions. In *Blaquière, A., ed.,* 1973, pp. 311–44.

Keiding, Hans. Equilibrium in Economies with Non-

Marketed Goods. *Swedish J. Econ.,* December 1973, *75*(4), pp. 349–61.

Malinvaud, E. Markets for an Exchange Economy with Individual Risks. *Econometrica,* May 1973, *41*(3), pp. 383–410.

Metzler, Lloyd A. Stability of Multiple Markets: The Hicks Conditions. In *Metzler, L. A.,* 1973, pp. 499–515.

Metzler, Lloyd A. Taxes and Subsidies in Leontief's Input-Output Model. In *Metzler, L. A.,* 1973, pp. 568–74.

de Montbrial, Thierry. Intertemporal General Equilibrium and Interest Rates Theory. *Écon. Appl.,* 1973, *26*(2–3–4), pp. 877–917.

Mukherji, Anjan. On the Sensitivity of Stability Results to the Choice of the Numeraire. *Rev. Econ. Stud.,* July 1973, *40*(3), pp. 427–33.

Nichols, Alan. External Diseconomies in Competitive Supply: Comment. *Amer. Econ. Rev.,* September 1973, *63*(4), pp. 741–42.

Nishimura, Osamu. Transaction Activity and Optimal Taxation. *Econ. Stud. Quart.,* August 1973, *24* (2), pp. 16–25.

Osana, Hiroaki. On the Boundedness of an Economy with Externalities. *Rev. Econ. Stud.,* July 1973, *40* (3), pp. 321–31.

Ostroy, Joseph M. The Informational Efficiency of Monetary Exchange. *Amer. Econ. Rev.,* September 1973, *63*(4), pp. 597–610.

Pearce, I. F. and Wise, J. On the Uniqueness of Competitive Equilibrium: Part I, Unbounded Demand. *Econometrica,* September 1973, *41*(5), pp. 817–28.

Perroux, François. The Economic Agent, Equilibrium, and the Choice of Formalisation. *Écon. Appl.,* 1973, *26*(2–3–4), pp. 250–85.

Pryor, Frederic L. Simulation of the Impact of Social and Economic Institutions on the Size Distribution of Income and Wealth. *Amer. Econ. Rev.,* March 1973, *63*(1), pp. 50–72.

Robinson, Stephen M. Irreducibility in the von Neumann Model. *Econometrica,* May 1973, *41*(3), pp. 569–73.

Sandberg, I. W. A Nonlinear Input-Output Model of a Multisectored Economy. *Econometrica,* November 1973, *41*(6), pp. 1167–82.

Schotter, Andrew. Core Allocations and Competitive Equilibrium—A Survey. *Z. Nationalökon.,* 1973, *33*(3–4), pp. 281–313.

Schuster, Helmut. Keynes' Disequilibrium Analysis. *Kyklos,* 1973, *26*(3), pp. 512–44.

Shapley, Lloyd S. Let's Block "Block." *Econometrica,* November 1973, *41*(6), pp. 1201–02.

Shepherd, A. Ross. External Diseconomies in Competitive Supply: Comment. *Amer. Econ. Rev.,* September 1973, *63*(4), pp. 743–44.

Shoven, John B. and Whalley, John. General Equilibrium with Taxes: A Computational Procedure and an Existence Proof. *Rev. Econ. Stud.,* October 1973, *40*(4), pp. 475–89.

Shubik, Martin. Commodity Money, Oligopoly, Credit and Bankruptcy in a General Equilibrium Model. *Western Econ. J.,* March 1973, *11*(1), pp. 24–38.

Shubik, Martin and Whitt, Ward. Fiat Money in an Economy with One Nondurable Good and No

Credit (A Noncooperative Sequential Game). In *Blaquière, A., ed.*, 1973, pp. 401–48.

Sonnenschein, Hugo. Do Walras' Identity and Continuity Characterize the Class of Community Excess Demand Functions? *J. Econ. Theory*, August 1973, *6*(4), pp. 345–54.

Stalford, Harold and Leitmann, George. Sufficiency Conditions for Nash Equilibria in N-Person Differential Games. In *Blaquière, A., ed.*, 1973, pp. 345–76.

Starrett, David A. A Note on Externalities and the Core. *Econometrica*, January 1973, *41*(1), pp. 179–83.

Starr, Ross M. Optimal Production and Allocation under Uncertainty. *Quart. J. Econ.*, February 1973, *87*(1), pp. 81–95.

Stigum, Bernt P. Competitive Equilibria with Infinitely Many Commodities (II) *J. Econ. Theory*, October 1973, *6*(5), pp. 415–45.

Suzumura, Kotaro. Professor Uzawa's Equivalence Theorem: A Note. *Econ. Stud. Quart.*, August 1973, *24*(2), pp. 67–70.

Suzumura, Kotaro. Boundedness of the Closed Economy with Samuelson-Leontief Technology. *Hitotsubashi J. Econ.*, February 1973, *13*(2), pp. 43–46.

Suzumura, Kotaro. The Economic Theory of Organization and Planning: A Review Article. *Econ. Stud. Quart.*, April 1973, *24*(1), pp. 33–51.

Tokita, Tadahiko. Determination of Income and Prices in the Short Run. (In Japanese. With English summary.) *Econ. Stud. Quart.*, December 1973, *24*(3), pp. 31–42.

Womer, Norman K. Lancaster's Version of the Walras-Wald Model. *J. Econ. Theory*, October 1973, *6*(5), pp. 515–19.

022 Microeconomic Theory

0220 General

Arrow, Kenneth J. and Starrett, David A. Cost- and Demand-theoretical Approaches to the Theory of Price Determination. In *Hicks, J. R. and Weber, W., eds.*, 1973, pp. 129–48.

Arrow, Kenneth J. Rawls's Principle of Just Saving. *Swedish J. Econ.*, December 1973, *75*(4), pp. 323–35.

Axelsson, Runo. The Economic Postulate of Rationality—Some Methodological Views. *Swedish J. Econ.*, September 1973, *75*(3), pp. 289–95.

Boadway, Robin W. Similarities and Differences between Public Goods and Public Factors. *Public Finance*, 1973, *28*(3–4), pp. 245–58.

Borglin, Anders. Price Characterization of Stable Allocations in Exchange Economies with Externalities. *J. Econ. Theory*, October 1973, *6*(5), pp. 483–94.

Cazenave, Philippe and Morrisson, Christian. Fonctions d'utilité interdépendantes et théorie de la redistribution en économie de production. (Interdependent Utility Functions and Redistribution Theory in a Production Economy. With English summary.) *Revue Écon.*, September 1973, *24*(5), pp. 725–60.

Coddington, Alan. Bargaining as a Decision Process.

Swedish J. Econ., December 1973, *75*(4), pp. 397–405.

Cross, John G. A Stochastic Learning Model of Economic Behavior. *Quart. J. Econ.*, May 1973, *87*(2), pp. 239–66.

Evans, Alan W. On the Theory of the Valuation and Allocation of Time: Reply. *Scot. J. Polit. Econ.*, February 1973, *20*(1), pp. 73–74.

Flemming, J. S. On the Theory of the Valuation and Allocation of Time: Some Comments. *Scot. J. Polit. Econ.*, February 1973, *20*(1), pp. 65–71.

Frankel, Marvin. Pricing Decisions Under Unknown Demand. *Kyklos*, 1973, *26*(1), pp. 1–24.

von Furstenberg, George M. and Spulber, Nicolas. Is There an Economic System Based on Sovereignty of Each Consumer? *Z. Nationalökon.*, 1973, *33* (3–4), pp. 361–74.

Geary, P. T. and Morishima, M. Demand and Supply under Separability. In *Morishima, M., et al.*, 1973, pp. 87–147.

Goetz, Charles J. and Buchanan, James M. External Diseconomies in Competitive Supply: Reply. *Amer. Econ. Rev.*, September 1973, *63*(4), pp. 745–48.

Hay, George A. and McGowan, John J. External Diseconomies in Competitive Supply: Comment. *Amer. Econ. Rev.*, September 1973, *63*(4), pp. 738–40.

Hebert, Robert F. Wage Cobwebs and Cobweb-Type Phenomena: An Early French Formulation. *Western Econ. J.*, December 1973, *11*(4), pp. 394–403.

Hirshleifer, Jack. Exchange Theory: The Missing Chapter. *Western Econ. J.*, June 1973, *11*(2), pp. 129–46.

Hirshleifer, Jack. Where Are We in the Theory of Information? *Amer. Econ. Rev.*, May 1973, *63*(2), pp. 31–39.

Hull, J.; Moore, P. G. and Thomas, H. Utility and its Measurement. *J. Roy. Statist. Soc.*, Part 2, 1973, *136*, pp. 226–47.

Hurwicz, Leonid and Reiter, Stanley. On the Boundedness of the Feasible Set Without Convexity Assumptions. *Int. Econ. Rev.*, October 1973, *14*(3), pp. 580–86.

Kalman, Peter J. and Intriligator, Michael D. Generalized Comparative Statics with Applications to Consumer Theory and Producer Theory. *Int. Econ. Rev.*, June 1973, *14*(2), pp. 473–86.

Karni, Edi. Transactions Costs and the Demand for Media of Exchange. *Western Econ. J.*, March 1973, *11*(1), pp. 71–80.

Lachmann, L. M. Sir John Hicks as a Neo-Austrian. *S. Afr. J. Econ.*, September 1973, *41*(3), pp. 195–207.

Laibman, David. Values and Prices of Production: The Political Economy of the Transformation Problem. *Sci. Soc.*, Winter 1973–1974, *37*(4), pp. 404–36.

Laing, N. F. Technological Uncertainty and the Pure *Ex Ante* Theory of the Allocation of Resources. *Australian Econ. Pap.*, December 1973, *12*(21), pp. 221–38.

Läufer, Nikolaus K. A. Marktungleichgewichte und die Nichtoptimalität neutralen Revisionsverhaltens. (Market Disequilibria and the Nonoptimality of Neutral Revision Behaviour. With English summary.) *Jahr. Nationalökon. Statist.*, May 1973, *187* (4), pp. 301–29.

Malinvaud, E. Markets for an Exchange Economy with Individual Risks. *Econometrica,* May 1973, *41*(3), pp. 383–410.

Nelson, Phillip. Economics of Information: Discussion. *Amer. Econ. Rev.,* May 1973, *63*(2), pp. 50–51.

Nichols, Alan. External Diseconomies in Competitive Supply: Comment. *Amer. Econ. Rev.,* September 1973, *63*(4), pp. 741–42.

Perroux, François. The Economic Agent, Equilibrium, and the Choice of Formalisation. *Écon. Appl.,* 1973, *26*(2–3–4), pp. 250–85.

Rao, Potluri. On Estimation of Demand and Supply Equations of a Commodity. *Indian Econ. Rev.,* April 1973, *8*(1), pp. 61–68.

Ross, Stephen A. The Economic Theory of Agency: The Principal's Problem. *Amer. Econ. Rev.,* May 1973, *63*(2), pp. 134–39.

Sato, Ryuzo. On the Stability Properties of Dynamic Economic Systems. *Int. Econ. Rev.,* October 1973, *14*(3), pp. 753–64.

Schotter, Andrew. Core Allocations and Competitive Equilibrium—A Survey. *Z. Nationalökon.,* 1973, *33*(3–4), pp. 281–313.

Shepherd, A. Ross. External Diseconomies in Competitive Supply: Comment. *Amer. Econ. Rev.,* September 1973, *63*(4), pp. 743–44.

Suzumura, Kotaro. The Economic Theory of Organization and Planning: A Review Article. *Econ. Stud. Quart.,* April 1973, *24*(1), pp. 33–51.

Telser, L. G. Searching for the Lowest Price. *Amer. Econ. Rev.,* May 1973, *63*(2), pp. 40–49.

Tomasini, Luigi M. Una nota sull'incertezza e la convenienza economica della lite giudiziaria. (A Note on Uncertainty and Economic Profitability of Legal Controversy. With English summary.) *L'Industria,* January-June 1973, (1–2), pp. 125–31.

Vertinsky, Ilan and Uyeno, Dean. Demand for Health Services and the Theory of Time Allocation. *Appl. Econ.,* December 1973, *5*(4), pp. 249–60.

Williamson, Oliver E. Markets and Hierarchies: Some Elementary Considerations. *Amer. Econ. Rev.,* May 1973, *63*(2), pp. 316–25.

0222 Theory of the Household (consumer demand)

Afriat, S. N. On a System of Inequalities in Demand Analysis: An Extension of the Classical Method. *Int. Econ. Rev.,* June 1973, *14*(2), pp. 460–72.

Allingham, M. G. and Morishima, M. Veblen Effects and Portfolio Selection. In *Morishima, M., et al.,* 1973, pp. 242–70.

Anderson, Jock R. Risk Aversion and Polynomial Preference. *Australian Econ. Pap.,* December 1973, *12*(21), pp. 261–62.

Ara, Kenjiro. Some Notes on Utility Function. *Hitotsubashi J. Econ.,* February 1973, *13*(2), pp. 37–42.

Barnett, William A. The Effects of Consumer Bliss on Welfare Economics. *J. Econ. Issues,* March 1973, *7*(1), pp. 29–45.

Batra, Harish. Dynamic Interdependence in Demand for Savings Deposits. *J. Finance,* May 1973, *28*(2), pp. 507–14. [G: U.S.]

Battalio, Raymond C., et al. A Test of Consumer Demand Theory Using Observations of Individual Consumer Purchases. *Western Econ. J.,* December 1973, *11*(4), pp. 411–28.

Becker, Gary S. A Theory of Marriage: Part I. *J. Polit. Econ.,* July-August 1973, *81*(4), pp. 813–46.

Berg, Sanford V. Interdependent Tastes and Fashion Behavior. *Quart. Rev. Econ. Bus.,* Summer 1973, *13*(2), pp. 49–58.

Berhold, Marvin. Multiple Criteria Decision Making in Consumer Behavior. In *Cochrane, J. L. and Zeleny, M., eds.,* 1973, pp. 570–76.

Bernholz, Peter and Faber, Malte. A Note on Stackelberg's Hypothesis Concerning a Relationship between the Price of Land, the Real Rate of Interest and Impatience to Consume. *Z. Nationalökon.,* 1973, *33*(3–4), pp. 375–88.

Betancourt, Roger R. Increasing Risk and Nonseparable Utility Functions. *J. Econ. Theory,* December 1973, *6*(6), pp. 575–81.

Bewley, Truman F. Edgeworth's Conjecture. *Econometrica,* May 1973, *41*(3), pp. 425–54.

Birdsall, William C. and Goldstein, Jon H. The Effect of Interest-Rate Changes on Consumption Allocation Over Time. *Int. Econ. Rev.,* June 1973, *14*(2), pp. 487–92.

Blackorby, Charles, et al. Consistent Intertemporal Decision Making. *Rev. Econ. Stud.,* April 1973, *40* (2), pp. 239–48.

Borch, Karl. Uncertainty and Indifference Curves —A Correction. *Rev. Econ. Stud.,* January 1973, *40*(1), pp. 141.

Bronsard, Camille and Lacroix, Robert. L'équilbre du consommateur en économie monétaire. (Consumer Equilibrium in a Monetary Economy. With English summary.) *Can. J. Econ.,* August 1973, *6* (3), pp. 332–43.

Burness, H. Stuart. Impatience and the Preference for Advancement in the Timing of Satisfactions. *J. Econ. Theory,* October 1973, *6*(5), pp. 495–507.

Burns, Michael E. A Note on the Concept and Measure of Consumer's Surplus. *Amer. Econ. Rev.,* June 1973, *63*(3), pp. 335–44.

Cerny, Martin. Preference Relations and Order-Preserving Functons. *Ekon.-Mat. Obzor,* 1973, *9* (3), pp. 275–91.

Cichetti, Charles J. and Smith, V. Kerry. Interdependent Consumer Decisions: A Production Function Approach. *Australian Econ. Pap.,* December 1973, *12*(21), pp. 239–52.

Crawford, Robert G. Implications of Learning for Economic Models of Uncertainty. *Int. Econ. Rev.,* October 1973, *14*(3), pp. 587–600.

Daems, H. Consumption and Savings Decisions Under Uncertainty: A Numerical Example. *Tijdschr. Econ.,* 1973, *18*(3), pp. 429–40.

D'Albergo, Ernesto. "Relativizzazione" di un teorema. (On the Relativity of a Theorem. With English summary.) *Econ. Int.,* February 1973, *26* (1), pp. 35–45.

Day, Richard H. and Robinson, Stephen M. Economic Decisions with L** Utility. In *Cochrane, J. L. and Zeleny, M., eds.,* 1973, pp. 84–92.

Deschamps, Robert. Risk Aversion and Demand Functions. *Econometrica*, May 1973, *41*(3), pp. 455–65.

Diewert, W. E. Afriat and Revealed Preference Theory. *Rev. Econ. Stud.*, July 1973, *40*(3), pp. 419–25.

Feldman, Allan M. Bilateral Trading, Processes, Pairwise Optimality, and Pareto Optimality. *Rev. Econ. Stud.*, October 1973, *40*(4), pp. 463–73.

Ferber, Robert. Consumer Economics, A Survey. *J. Econ. Lit.*, December 1973, *11*(4), pp. 1303–42.

Fischer, Stanley. A Life Cycle Model of Life Insurance Purchases. *Int. Econ. Rev.*, February 1973, *14*(1), pp. 132–52.

Fishburn, Peter C. A Mixture-Set Axiomatization of Conditional Subjective Expected Utility. *Econometrica*, January 1973, *41*(1), pp. 1–25.

Fishburn, Peter C. Bernoullian Utilities for Multiple-Factor Situations. In *Cochrane, J. L. and Zeleny, M., eds.*, 1973, pp. 47–61.

Frey, Bruno S. Interactions Between Preferences and Consumption in Economic Development. *Scot. J. Polit. Econ.*, February 1973, *20*(1), pp. 53–64.

Galatin, Malcolm. A True Price Index When the Consumer Saves. *Amer. Econ. Rev.*, March 1973, *63*(1), pp. 185–94.

Gamaletsos, Theodore. Further Analysis of Cross-Country Comparison of Consumer Expenditure Patterns. *Europ. Econ. Rev.*, April 1973, *4*(1), pp. 1–20. [G: O.E.C.D.]

Goddard, Frederick O. Consumer Welfare and Product Differentiation: Reply. *Quart. Rev. Econ. Bus.*, Summer 1973, *13*(2), pp. 92–94.

Gørtz, Erik and Vibe-Pedersen, J. Livsindkomstberegninger og deres betydning. (Calculation and Significance of Lifetime Incomes. With English summary.) *Nationalokon. Tidsskr.*, 1973, *111*(1), pp. 25–59. [G: Denmark]

Gottinger, Hans-Werner. Conditional Utility. *Z. Nationalökon.*, 1973, *33*(3–4), pp. 315–24.

Grandmont, Jean-Michel and Laroque, Guy. Money in the Pure Consumption Loan Model. *J. Econ. Theory*, August 1973, *6*(4), pp. 382–95.

Green, Richard; Hassan, Zuhair and Johnson, Stanley R. Price and Income Flexibilities and the Double Logarithmic Demand System: Comment. *Amer. J. Agr. Econ.*, Part I, November 1973, *55*(4), pp. 678–79.

Hatta, Tatsuo. A Note on a Theorem in "Value and Capital." *Western Econ. J.*, June 1973, *11*(2), pp. 164–66.

Herzberger, Hans G. Ordinal Preference and Rational Choice. *Econometrica*, March 1973, *41*(2), pp. 187–237.

Hirschman, Albert O. An Alternative Explanation of Contemporary Harriedness. *Quart. J. Econ.*, November 1973, *87*(4), pp. 634–37.

Houck, James P. Price and Income Flexibilities and the Double Logarithmic Demand System: Reply. *Amer. J. Agr. Econ.*, Part I, November 1973, *55*(4), pp. 679–80.

Jamison, Dean T. and Lau, Lawrence J. Semiorders and the Theory of Choice. *Econometrica*, September 1973, *41*(5), pp. 901–12.

Keeney, Ralph L. Risk Independence and Multiattributed Utility Functions. *Econometrica*, January 1973, *41*(1), pp. 27–34.

Keeney, Ralph L. Concepts of Independence in Multiattribute Utility Theory. In *Cochrane, J. L. and Zeleny, M., eds.*, 1973, pp. 62–71.

Kim, Young Chin. Choice in the Lottery-Insurance Situation Augmented-Income Approach. *Quart. J. Econ.*, February 1973, *87*(1), pp. 148–56.

Klein, Philip A. Demand Theory and the Economist's Propensity to Assume. *J. Econ. Issues*, June 1973, *7*(2), pp. 209–39.

Krelle, Wilhelm. Dynamics of the Utility Function. In *Hicks, J. R. and Weber, W., eds.*, 1973, pp. 92–128.

LaValle, Irving H. On Admissibility and Bayesness When Risk Attitude but Not the Preference Ranking Is Permitted to Vary. In *Cochrane, J. L. and Zeleny, M., eds.*, 1973, pp. 72–83.

Lekachman, Robert. Demand Theory and the Economist's Propensity to Assume: Comment. *J. Econ. Issues*, June 1973, *7*(2), pp. 241–43.

Lluch, Constantino. The Extended Linear Expenditure System. *Europ. Econ. Rev.*, April 1973, *4*(1), pp. 21–32.

Lluch, Constantino and Morishima, M. Demand for Commodities under Uncertain Expectation. In *Morishima, M., et al.*, 1973, pp. 169–83.

Martin, M. J. Durable Goods as a Generalizer of Demand Theory. In *Morishima, M., et al.*, 1973, pp. 184–209.

McCain, Roger A. Consumer Welfare and Product Differentiation: An Agnostic Comment. *Quart. Rev. Econ. Bus.*, Summer 1973, *13*(2), pp. 90–92.

McKean, J. R. and Peterson, R. D. Demand Elasticity, Product Differentiation, and Market Structure. *J. Econ. Theory*, April 1973, *6*(2), pp. 205–09.

McKean, Roland N. Spillovers from the Rising Value of Time. *Quart. J. Econ.*, November 1973, *87*(4), pp. 638–40.

Metcalf, Charles E. Making Inferences from Controlled Income Maintenance Experiments. *Amer. Econ. Rev.*, June 1973, *63*(3), pp. 478–83.

Metwally, Mohktar M. and Timmaiah, G. A Note on the Classical Utility Function for Purpose of the Theory of Taxation. *Finanzarchiv*, 1973, *31*(3), pp. 441–45.

Michael, Robert T. and Becker, Gary S. On the New Theory of Consumer Behavior. *Swedish J. Econ.*, December 1973, *75*(4), pp. 378–96.

Morgenstern, Oskar. Ingolf Stahl: Bargaining Theory. *Swedish J. Econ.*, December 1973, *75*(4), pp. 410–13.

Morishima, M. Separability and Intrinsic Complementarity. In *Morishima, M., et al.*, 1973, pp. 148–65.

Morishima, M. Consumer Behaviour and Liquidity Preference. In *Morishima, M., et al.*, 1973, pp. 215–41.

Morishima, M. Demand for Durable Goods: A Note. In *Morishima, M., et al.*, 1973, pp. 210–11.

Morrison, Clarence C. and Higgins, Richard S. A Note on Comparative Statics Analysis in Equality Constrained Models. *Southern Econ. J.*, April 1973, *39*(4), pp. 638–41.

Nakao, Takeo. An Examination of Duesenberry's Hypothesis on the Growth of Demand for the New

Product. (In Japanese.) *Econ. Stud. Quart.*, April 1973, *24*(1), pp. 18–32.

Näslund, Bertil. Pollution and the Value of Time. *Europ. Econ. Rev.*, June 1973, *4*(2), pp. 181–96.

Nasse, Ph. Un système complet de fonctions de demande: Les équations de Fourgeaud et Nataf. *Econometrica*, November 1973, *41*(6), pp. 1137–58. [G: France]

Ng, Yew-Kwang. The Economic Theory of Clubs: Pareto Optimality Conditions. *Economica, N.S.*, August 1973, *40*(159), pp. 291–98.

Nicosia, Francesco M. Consumer Behavior: Can Economics and Behavioral Science Converge? *Calif. Manage. Rev.*, Winter 1973, *16*(2), pp. 71–78.

Nussbaumer, Adolf. On the Compatibility of Subjective and Objective Theories of Economic Value. In *Hicks, J. R. and Weber, W., eds.,* 1973, pp. 75–91.

Olsen, E. Odgers, Jr. Utility and Profit Maximization by an Owner-Manager. *Southern Econ. J.*, January 1973, *39*(3), pp. 389–95.

Onigkeit, Dietmar. Zur Berechnung von Einkommenselastizitäten für Prognosen. (The Computation of Income Elasticities for Forecasts. With English summary.) *Schweiz. Z. Volkswirtsch. Statist.*, December 1973, *109*(4), pp. 597–602.

Paroush, Jacob. Efficient Purchasing Behavior and Order Relations in Consumption. *Kyklos*, 1973, *26*(1), pp. 91–112.

Peleg, Bezalel and Yaari, Menahem E. On the Existence of a Consistent Course of Action when Tastes are Changing. *Rev. Econ. Stud.*, July 1973, *40*(3), pp. 391–401.

Pham, Chung. On Some Aspects of the Theory of Grants Economics. *Soc. Sci. Quart.*, December 1973, *54*(3), pp. 632–38.

Phelps, Edmund S. The Harried Leisure Class: A Demurrer. *Quart. J. Econ.*, November 1973, *87*(4), pp. 641–45.

Pickering, J. F., et al. Are Goods Goods? Some Empirical Evidence. *Appl. Econ.*, March 1973, *5*(1), pp. 1–18.

Pollak, Robert A. The Risk Independence Axiom. *Econometrica*, January 1973, *41*(1), pp. 35–39.

van Praag, Bernard M. S. and Kapteyn, Arie. Further Evidence on the Individual Welfare Function of Income: An Empirical Investigation in The Netherlands. *Europ. Econ. Rev.*, April 1973, *4*(1), pp. 33–62. [G: Netherlands]

Prochaska, Fred J. and Schrimper, R. A. Opportunity Cost of Time and Other Socioeconomic Effects on Away-From-Home Food Consumption. *Amer. J. Agr. Econ.*, Part I, November 1973, *55*(4), pp. 595–603. [G: U.S.]

Rader, J. Trout. Nice Demand Functions. *Econometrica*, September 1973, *41*(5), pp. 913–35.

Reaume, David M. Cost-Benefit Techniques and Consumer Surplus: A Clarificatory Analysis. *Public Finance*, 1973, *28*(2), pp. 196–211.

Reinhardt, Paul G. A Theory of Household Grocery Inventory Holdings. *Kyklos*, 1973, *26*(3), pp. 497–511.

Roberts, Blaine. Individual Decisions and Standardized Choice. *Z. Nationalökon.*, 1973, *33*(3–4), pp. 353–60.

Roberts, Marc J. On Time. *Quart. J. Econ.*, November 1973, *87*(4), pp. 646–50.

Rubin, Paul H. A Paradox Regarding the Use of Time. *Indian Econ. J.*, January-March 1973, *20*(3), pp. 469–71.

Rubinstein, Mark E. The Fundamental Theorem of Parameter-Preference Security Valuation. *J. Financial Quant. Anal.*, January 1973, *8*(1), pp. 61–69.

Rugg, Donald. The Choice of Journey Destination: A Theoretical and Empirical Analysis. *Rev. Econ. Statist.*, February 1973, *55*(1), pp. 64–72. [G: U.S.]

Sandmo, Agnar. Public Goods and the Technology of Consumption. *Rev. Econ. Stud.*, October 1973, *40*(4), pp. 517–28.

Sankar, U. A Utility Function for Wealth for a Risk-Averter. *J. Econ. Theory*, December 1973, *6*(6), pp. 614–17.

Scitovsky, Tibor. Notes on the Producer Society. *De Economist*, May-June 1973, *121*(3), pp. 225–50.

Scitovsky, Tibor. The Place of Economic Welfare in Human Welfare. *Quart. Rev. Econ. Bus.*, Autumn 1973, *13*(3), pp. 7–19.

Scitovsky, Tibor. A New Approach to the Theory of Consumer Behavior. *Amer. Econ.*, Fall 1973, *17*(2), pp. 29–32.

Sen, Amartya K. Behaviour and the Concept of Preference. *Economica, N.S.*, August 1973, *40*(159), pp. 241–59.

Singh, Balvir and Nagar, A. L. Determination of Consumer Unit Scales. *Econometrica*, March 1973, *41*(2), pp. 347–55.

Smith, Victor E. and Koo, Anthony Y. C. A General Consumption Technology in New Demand Theory. *Western Econ. J.*, September 1973, *11*(3), pp. 243–59.

Sonnenschein, Hugo. The Utility Hypothesis and Market Demand Theory. *Western Econ. J.*, December 1973, *11*(4), pp. 404–10.

Sonnenschein, Hugo. Do Walras' Identity and Continuity Characterize the Class of Community Excess Demand Functions? *J. Econ. Theory*, August 1973, *6*(4), pp. 345–54.

Spence, A. Michael. Time and Communication in Economic and Social Interaction. *Quart. J. Econ.*, November 1973, *87*(4), pp. 651–60.

Stahl, Ingolf. Bargaining as a Decision Process: Comment. *Swedish J. Econ.*, December 1973, *75*(4), pp. 406–09.

Stigum, Bernt P. Revealed Preference—A Proof of Houthakker's Theorem. *Econometrica*, May 1973, *41*(3), pp. 411–23.

Suranyi-Unger, Theodore, Jr. Consumer Behavior and the Hypothesis of Standardized Choice. *Z. Nationalökon.*, 1973, *33*(3–4), pp. 325–51.

Theil, Henri. Some Recent Developments in Consumer Demand Analysis. In *[Tinbergen, J.]*, 1973, pp. 41–73. [G: Netherlands; U.K.]

Tsiang, S. C. Interest Rate and Consumption: Comment. *Int. Econ. Rev.*, June 1973, *14*(2), pp. 493–96.

Vedder, James N. Multiattribute Decision Making under Uncertainty Using Bounded Intervals. In *Cochrane, J. L. and Zeleny, M., eds.,* 1973, pp. 93–107.

Vitaliano, Donald F. A Reconsideration of Some Aspects of the Utility Sacrifice Rules of Taxation. *Public Finance Quart.*, January 1973, *1*(1), pp. 59–65.

Wolf, Charles, Jr. Heresies About Time: Wasted Time, Double-Duty Time, and Past Time. *Quart. J. Econ.*, November 1973, *87*(4), pp. 661–67.

Working, E. J. What Do Statistical "Demand Curves" Show? In *Haynes, W. W.; Coyne, T. J. and Osborne, D. K., eds.*, 1973, pp. 61–73.

Young, Warren L. Compulsory Loans and Consumption-Savings Behaviour: Some Micro- and Macro-Economic Aspects. *Public Finance*, 1973, *28*(3–4), pp. 333–53. [G: Israel]

Zabel, Edward. Consumer Choice, Portfolio Decisions, and Transaction Costs. *Econometrica*, March 1973, *41*(2), pp. 321–35.

Zeckhauser, Richard J. Time as the Ultimate Source of Utility. *Quart. J. Econ.*, November 1973, *87*(4), pp. 668–75.

0223 Theory of Production

Ahmad, Meekal A.; Flesher, John and Over, Mead. An Econometric Test of a Zero Elasticity of Substitution Production Function for Pakistan. *Pakistan Econ. Soc. Rev.*, Winter 1973, *11*(4), pp. 443–53. [G: Pakistan]

Ahmad, Meekal A. The Cobb-Douglas Production Function: A Comment. *Pakistan Econ. Soc. Rev.*, Summer 1973, *11*(2), pp. 219–26.

Atkinson, A. B. Worker Management and the Modern Industrial Enterprise. *Quart. J. Econ.*, August 1973, *87*(3), pp. 375–92.

Bardhan, Pranab K. More on Putty-Clay. *Int. Econ. Rev.*, February 1973, *14*(1), pp. 211–22.

Baumol, William J., et al. Efficiency of Corporate Investment: A Reply. *Rev. Econ. Statist.*, February 1973, *55*(1), pp. 128–31.

Baumol, William J. Income and Substitution Effects in the Linder Theorem. *Quart. J. Econ.*, November 1973, *87*(4), pp. 629–33.

Berndt, Ernst R. and Christensen, Laurits R. The Translog Function and the Substitution of Equipment, Structures, and Labor in U.S. Manufacturing 1929–68. *J. Econometrics*, March 1973, *1*(1), pp. 81–113. [G: U.S.]

Bodenhöfer, Hans-Joachim. X-Effizienz, Innovations-Effizienz und wirtschaftliches Wachstum. (X-Efficiency, Innovation Efficiency, and Economic Growth. With English summary.) *Z. Wirtschaft. Sozialwissen.*, 1973, *93*(6), pp. 671–86.

Bohman, J. and Bohman, M. K. The Neoclassical Theory of Technical Progress: Note. *Amer. Econ. Rev.*, June 1973, *63*(3), pp. 490–93.

Boudreaux, Kenneth J. 'Managerialism' and Risk-Return Performance. *Southern Econ. J.*, January 1973, *39*(3), pp. 366–72. [G: U.S.]

Bowden, Roger J. Some Implications of the Permanent-Income Hypothesis. *Rev. Econ. Stud.*, January 1973, *40*(1), pp. 33–37.

Brechling, Frank. Announcement Effects of Profits Taxation: Discussion. In *Parkin, M., ed.*, 1973, pp. 33–34.

Brite, Robert L. Scale and the Elasticity of Substitution in Cross-Section Production Functions. *J.*

Econ. Bus., Winter 1973, *25*(2), pp. 101–06. [G: U.S.]

Brown, Murray. Toward an Econometric Accommodation of the Capital-Intensity-Perversity Phenomenon. *Econometrica*, September 1973, *41*(5), pp. 937–54.

Burley, H. T. Production Functions for Australian Manufacturing Industries. *Rev. Econ. Statist.*, February 1973, *55*(1), pp. 118–22. [G: Australia]

Carlson, John A. The Production Lag. *Amer. Econ. Rev.*, March 1973, *63*(1), pp. 73–86. [G: U.S.]

Christensen, Laurits R.; Jorgenson, Dale W. and Lau, Lawrence J. Transcendental Logarithmic Production Frontiers. *Rev. Econ. Statist.*, February 1973, *55*(1), pp. 28–45.

Colberg, Marshall R. and King, James P. Theory of Production Abandonment. *Rivista Int. Sci. Econ. Com.*, October 1973, *20*(10), pp. 961–72.

Cornwall, Richard R. A Note on Using Profit Functions to Aggregate Production Functions. *Int. Econ. Rev.*, June 1973, *14*(2), pp. 511–19.

Dietz, James L. Paradise Reswitched. *Rev. Radical Polit. Econ.*, Summer 1973, *5*(2), pp. 1–17.

Diewert, W. E. Functional Forms for Profit and Transformation Functions. *J. Econ. Theory*, June 1973, *6*(3), pp. 284–316.

Donna, Giorgio. Modelli di sviluppo per una teoria dinamica dell'impresa. (Models of Development for a Dynamic Theory of the Firm. With English summary.) *L'Impresa*, 1973, *15*(3–4), pp. 253–64.

Douglas, Aaron J. Stochastic Returns and the Theory of the Firm. *Amer. Econ. Rev.*, May 1973, *63*(2), pp. 129–33.

Emerson, David L. Optimum Firm Location and the Theory of Production. *J. Reg. Sci.*, December 1973, *13*(3), pp. 335–47.

Ethridge, Don. The Inclusion of Wastes in the Theory of the Firm. *J. Polit. Econ.*, November-December 1973, *81*(6), pp. 1430–41.

Ferrer-Pacces, F. M. La rivincita dei gamma. (Gamma's Revenge. With English summary.) *L'Impresa*, 1973, *15*(5–6), pp. 305–08.

Ferrer-Pacces, F. M. Teoria senza ricerca. (Theory Without Research. With English summary.) *L'Impresa*, 1973, *15*(3–4), pp. 187–89.

Fleck, F. H., et al. The Cost-function of a CES-Production Function. *Rivista Int. Sci. Econ. Com.*, January 1973, *20*(1), pp. 18–32.

Fløystad, Gunnar. A Note on Estimating the Elasticity of Substitution Between Labour and Capital from Norwegian Time Series Data. *Swedish J. Econ.*, March 1973, *75*(1), pp. 100–04. [G: Norway]

Friedman, James W. Concavity of Production Functions and Non-Increasing Returns to Scale. *Econometrica*, September 1973, *41*(5), pp. 981–84.

Friend, Irwin and Husic, Frank. Efficiency of Corporate Investment. *Rev. Econ. Statist.*, February 1973, *55*(1), pp. 122–27.

Fuchs, Tomáš and Prič, Jozef. Meranie intenzity ekonomického rastu metódou úplne dynamizovanej substitučnej produkčnej funkcie Cobb-Douglasovho typu. (Measuring the Intensity of Economic Growth by the Method of Totally Dynamised Cobb-Douglas Type Production

Function. With English summary.) *Ekon.-Mat. Obzor,* 1973, *9*(4), pp. 381–92.

Gapinski, James H. Putty-Clay Capital and Small-Sample Properties of Neoclassical Estimators. *J. Polit. Econ.,* January-February 1973, *81*(1), pp. 145–57.

Gapinski, James H. Growth Parameters and Neoclassical Estimates: Effect of an Adaptive Wage-Expectation Scheme. *Southern Econ. J.,* January 1973, *39*(3), pp. 431–33.

Gros-Pietro, Gian M. Produzione industriale e teoria economica. (Industrial Production and Economic Theory. With English summary.) *L'Impresa,* 1973, *15*(3–4), pp. 209–21.

Hall, Robert E. The Specification of Technology with Several Kinds of Output. *J. Polit. Econ.,* July-August 1973, *81*(4), pp. 878–92.

Hamermesh, Daniel S. Price and Quantity Adjustment in Factor Markets. *Western Econ. J.,* March 1973, *11*(1), pp. 118–25.

Hanieski, John F. Technological Change as the Optimization of a Multidimensional Product. In *Cochrane, J. L. and Zeleny, M., eds.,* 1973, pp. 550–69.

Hartman, Richard. Adjustment Costs, Price and Wage Uncertainty, and Investment. *Rev. Econ. Stud.,* April 1973, *40*(2), pp. 259–67.

Hayami, Yujiro and Ruttan, Vernon W. Professor Rosenberg and the Direction of Technological Change: Comment. *Econ. Develop. Cult. Change,* January 1973, *21*(2), pp. 352–55.

Hemmings, Dan B. Leverage, Dividend Policy and the Cost of Capital: Comment. *J. Finance,* December 1973, *28*(5), pp. 1366–70.

Herberg, Horst. On the Convexity of the Production Possibility Set under General Production Conditions. *Z. ges. Staatswiss.,* May 1973, *129*(2), pp. 205–14.

Hicks, John R. [Sir]. The Mainspring of Economic Growth. *Swedish J. Econ.,* December 1973, *75*(4), pp. 336–48.

Hicks, John R. [Sir]. The Austrian Theory of Capital and Its Rebirth in Modern Economics. In *Hicks, J. R. and Weber, W., eds.,* 1973, pp. 190–206.

Hjalmarsson, Lennart. Optimal Structural Change and Related Concepts. *Swedish J. Econ.,* June 1973, *75*(2), pp. 176–92.

Hochman, Eitan; Hochman, Oded and Razin, Assaf. Demand for Investment in Productive and Financial Capital. *Europ. Econ. Rev.,* April 1973, *4*(1), pp. 67–83.

Hu, Sheng Cheng. Capital Mobility and the Effects of Unionization. *Southern Econ. J.,* April 1973, *39*(4), pp. 526–34.

Inselbag, Isik. Financing Decisions and the Theory of the Firm. *J. Financial Quant. Anal.,* December 1973, *8*(5), pp. 763–76.

Jhabvala, Firdaus. The Optimal Allocation of Resources in a Decentralized Model. *Eng. Econ.,* April-May 1973, *18*(3), pp. 169–89.

Jorgenson, Dale W. Technology and Decision Rules in the Theory of Investment Behavior. *Quart. J. Econ.,* November 1973, *87*(4), pp. 523–43.

Kazmi, Aqdas Ali. Cobb-Douglas Production Function: A Reply. *Pakistan Econ. Soc. Rev.,* Summer 1973, *11*(2), pp. 227–29.

Kemp, Murray C. Heterogeneous Capital Goods and Long-Run Stolper-Samuelson Theorems. *Australian Econ. Pap.,* December 1973, *12*(21), pp. 253–60.

Khang, Chulsoon and Uekawa, Yasuo. The Production Possibility Set in a Model Allowing Interindustry Flows: The Necessary and Sufficient Conditions for its Strict Convexity. *J. Int. Econ.,* August 1973, *3*(3), pp. 283–90.

Krauss, Melvyn B.; Johnson, Harry G. and Skouras, Thanos. On the Shape and Location of the Production Possibility Curve. *Economica, N.S.,* August 1973, *40*(159), pp. 305–10.

Krouse, Clement G. On the Theory of Optimal Investment, Dividends, and Growth in the Firm. *Amer. Econ. Rev.,* June 1973, *63*(3), pp. 269–79.

Kuga, Kiyoshi. More about Joint Production. *Int. Econ. Rev.,* February 1973, *14*(1), pp. 196–210.

Kuipers, S. K. The Positive Relation Between Average Labour Productivity and Labour Intensity. *Z. Nationalökon.,* 1973, *33*(1–2), pp. 115–26.

Lacaze, Dominique. Prix duaux et prix du marché. Une théorie du producteur. (Dual Prices and Market Prices: A Theory of the Producer. With English summary.) *Revue Écon.,* March 1973, *24*(2), pp. 273–305.

Lapan, Harvey and Bardhan, Pranab K. Localized Technical Progress and Transfer of Technology and Economic Development. *J. Econ. Theory,* December 1973, *6*(6), pp. 585–95.

Largay, James A., III. Microeconomic Foundations of Variable Costing. *Accounting Rev.,* January 1973, *48*(1), pp. 115–19.

Latham, R. W. and Peel, David A. A Comment on Adjustments Costs and the Flexible Accelerator. *Rech. Écon. Louvain,* September 1973, *39*(3), pp. 371–76.

Leibenstein, Harvey. Notes on X-Efficiency and Technical Progress. In *Ayal, E. B., ed.,* 1973, pp. 18–38.

Litzenberger, Robert H. and Joy, O. Maurice. Inter-Industry Profitability Under Uncertainty. *Western Econ. J.,* September 1973, *11*(3), pp. 338–49. [G: U.S.]

Lofthouse, Stephen. On Paradigms, Methodology and the Theory of the Firm. Part 1. *Rivista Int. Sci. Econ. Com.,* May 1973, *20*(5), pp. 406–48.

Lofthouse, Stephen. On Paradigms, Methodology and the Theory of the Firm. Part 2. *Rivista Int. Sci. Econ. Com.,* June 1973, *20*(6), pp. 566–607.

Lovell, C. A. Knox. Homotheticity and the Average Cost Function. *Western Econ. J.,* December 1973, *11*(4), pp. 506–13. [G: U.S.]

Lovell, C. A. Knox. Technology and Specification Error. *Southern Econ. J.,* July 1973, *40*(1), pp. 110–16. [G: U.S.]

Lovell, C. A. Knox. Estimation and Prediction with CES and VES Production Functions. *Int. Econ. Rev.,* October 1973, *14*(3), pp. 676–92. [G: U.S.]

Lovell, C. A. Knox and Moroney, J. R. Estimating the Elasticity of Substitution: A Correction and Some Further Results. *Southern Econ. J.,* January 1973, *39*(3), pp. 437–41.

Magee, Stephen P. Factor Market Distortions, Production, and Trade: A Survey. *Oxford Econ. Pap.*, March 1973, *25*(1), pp. 1–43.

Mayer, Wolfgang. A General Class of Production Functions with Nonlinear Isoclines. *Southern Econ. J.*, July 1973, *40*(1), pp. 1–8.

McCain, Roger A. The Cost of Supervision and the Quality of Labor: A Determinant of X-Inefficiency. *Miss. Val. J. Bus. Econ.*, Spring 1973, *8*(3), pp. 1–16.

McNicol, David L. The Comparative Statics Properties of the Theory of the Regulated Firm. *Bell J. Econ. Manage. Sci.*, Autumn 1973, *4*(2), pp. 428–53.

Mortensen, Dale T. Generalized Costs of Adjustment and Dynamic Factor Demand Theory. *Econometrica*, July 1973, *41*(4), pp. 657–65.

Mundlak, Yair and Volcani, Zvi. The Correspondence of Efficiency Frontier as a Generalization of the Cost Function. *Int. Econ. Rev.*, February 1973, *14*(1), pp. 223–33.

Nelson, Phillip. The Elasticity of Labor Supply to the Individual Firm. *Econometrica*, September 1973, *41*(5), pp. 853–66.

Nelson, Richard R. and Winter, Sidney G. Toward an Evolutionary Theory of Economic Capabilities. *Amer. Econ. Rev.*, May 1973, *63*(2), pp. 440–49.

Nordhaus, William D. Some Skeptical Thoughts on the Theory of Induced Innovation. *Quart. J. Econ.*, May 1973, *87*(2), pp. 208–19.

Nuti, Domenico M. On the Truncation of Production Flows. *Kyklos*, 1973, *26*(3), pp. 485–96.

Olivera, Julio H. G. On Bernoullian Production Sets. *Quart. J. Econ.*, February 1973, *87*(1), pp. 112–20.

Olsen, E. Odgers, Jr. Utility and Profit Maximization by an Owner-Manager. *Southern Econ. J.*, January 1973, *39*(3), pp. 389–95.

Orosel, Gerhard O. A Note on the Factor–Price Frontier. *Z. Nationalökon.*, 1973, *33*(1–2), pp. 103–14.

Otani, Yoshihiko. Neo-Classical Technology Sets and Properties of Production Possibility Sets. *Econometrica*, July 1973, *41*(4), pp. 667–82.

Palda, Kristian S. Production Functions and Performance Evaluation. In *Palda, K. S., ed.*, 1973, pp. 34–42.

Palmerio, Giovanni. Contributo alla teoria dello sviluppo dell'impresa. (A Contribution to the Theory of the Growth of the Firm. With English summary.) *L'Industria*, January-June 1973, (1–2), pp. 59–88.

Peel, David A. Some Implications of Utility Maximizing Firms: A Note. *Bull. Econ. Res.*, November 1973, *25*(2), pp. 148–51.

Peel, David A. The Non-uniqueness of the Dorfman-Steiner Condition: A Note. *Economica, N.S.*, May 1973, *40*(158), pp. 208–09.

Pfouts, Ralph W. Some Cost and Profit Relationships in the Multi-Product Firm. *Southern Econ. J.*, January 1973, *39*(3), pp. 361–65.

Pol, Jorge E. F. A Note on the Generalized Production Function. *Rev. Econ. Stud.*, January 1973, *40*(1), pp. 139–40.

Powers, John A. Symmetry of Production Stages and Uneconomic Production: Comment. *Southern Econ. J.*, October 1973, *40*(2), pp. 333–34.

Racette, George A. Earnings Retention, New Capital and the Growth of the Firm: A Comment. *Rev. Econ. Statist.*, February 1973, *55*(1), pp. 127–28.

Renas, Steve. Work Effort and the Progressive Income Tax: A Note. *Tijdschr. Econ.*, 1973, *18*(3), pp. 441–43.

Renas, Steve. Short Run Marginal Cost and Marginal Productivity: A Note. *Pakistan Econ. Soc. Rev.*, Summer 1973, *11*(2), pp. 215–18.

Robbins, Lionel [Lord]. Remarks upon Certain Aspects of the Theory of Costs. In *Buchanan, J. M. and Thirlby, G. F., eds.*, 1973, pp. 19–41.

Rosenberg, Nathan. The Direction of Technological Change: Reply. *Econ. Develop. Cult. Change*, January 1973, *21*(2), pp. 356–57.

Roth, Timothy P. Classical vs. Process Analysis and the Form of the Production Function. *Eng. Econ.*, October-November 1973, *19*(1), pp. 47–54.

Rubin, Paul H. The Expansion of Firms. *J. Polit. Econ.*, July-August 1973, *81*(4), pp. 936–49.

Ryan, Terence M. C.E.S. Production Functions in British Manufacturing Industry: A Cross-section Study. *Oxford Econ. Pap.*, July 1973, *25*(2), pp. 241–50. [G: U.K.]

Sakai, Yasuhiro. An Axiomatic Approach to Input Demand Theory. *Int. Econ. Rev.*, October 1973, *14*(3), pp. 735–52.

Salkin, Jay S. The Optimal Level of Production in Generalized Production Functions an Application to South Vietnamese Rice Production. *Malayan Econ. Rev.*, October 1973, *18*(2), pp. 60–67. [G: S. Vietnam]

Samuelson, Paul A. Relative Shares and Elasticities Simplified: Comment. *Amer. Econ. Rev.*, September 1973, *63*(4), pp. 770–71.

Samuelson, Paul A. A Quantum-Theory Model of Economics: Is the Co-ordinating Entrepreneur Just Worth His Profit? In *[Rosenstein-Rodan, P.]*, 1973, pp. 329–35.

Sato, Ryuzo and Koizumi, Tetsunori. The Production Function and the Theory of Distributive Shares. *Amer. Econ. Rev.*, June 1973, *63*(3), pp. 484–89.

Sato, Ryuzo and Koizumi, Tetsunori. Relative Shares and Elasticities Simplified: Reply. *Amer. Econ. Rev.*, September 1973, *63*(4), pp. 772.

Sato, Ryuzo and Koizumi, Tetsunori. On the Elasticities of Substitution and Complementarity. *Oxford Econ. Pap.*, March 1973, *25*(1), pp. 44–56.

Sawhney, Pawan K. and Sawhney, Bansi L. Capacity-Utilization, Concentration, and Price-Cost Margins: Results on Indian Industries. *J. Ind. Econ.*, April 1973, *21*(2), pp. 145–53. [G: India]

Scarth, William M. and Warne, Robert D. The Elasticity of Substitution and the Shape of the Transformation Curve. *Economica, N.S.*, August 1973, *40*(159), pp. 299–304.

Scheffman, D. T. Some Remarks on the Net Production Possibilities Set in Models with Intermediate Goods. *J. Int. Econ.*, August 1973, *3*(3), pp. 291–95.

Scully, Gerald W. Technical Progress, Factor Market Distortions, and the Pattern of Trade. *Econ. Int.*, February 1973, *26*(1), pp. 3–16.

Sieper, E. and Swan, P. L. Monopoly and Competition in the Market for Durable Goods. *Rev. Econ. Stud.*, July 1973, *40*(3), pp. 333–51.

Sjaastad, Larry A. Notes on X-Efficiency and Technical Progress: Comment. In *Ayal, E. B., ed.*, 1973, pp. 38–40.

Stephens, J. Kirker. Returns to Scale and the Average Cost Curve: Comment. *Swedish J. Econ.*, March 1973, *75*(1), pp. 110–11.

Stigler, George J. The Economies of Scale. In *Haynes, W. W.; Coyne, T. J. and Osborne, D. K., eds.*, 1973, pp. 232–49. [G: U.S.]

Stigum, Bernt P. Competitive Equilibria with Infinitely Many Commodities (II) *J. Econ. Theory*, October 1973, *6*(5), pp. 415–45.

Sudit, Ephraim F. Additive Nonhomogeneous Production Functions in Telecommunications. *Bell J. Econ. Manage. Sci.*, Autumn 1973, *4*(2), pp. 499–514.

Sumner, M. T. Announcement Effects of Profits Taxation. In *Parkin, M., ed.*, 1973, pp. 17–32.

Sutton, C. J. Management Behaviour and a Theory of Diversification. *Scot. J. Polit. Econ.*, February 1973, *20*(1), pp. 27–42.

Syrquin, Moshe. Efficient Input Frontiers for the Manufacturing Sector in Mexico 1965–1980. *Int. Econ. Rev.*, October 1973, *14*(3), pp. 657–75. [G: Mexico]

Szabó, K. A Few Thoughts on the Evolution of a Uniform Marxist Theory of the Firm. *Acta Oecon.*, 1973, *11*(4), pp. 325–45.

Talonen, Pentti. Näkökohtia yrityksen kasvusta ja kannattavuudesta. Osa II. (Growth and Profitability of the Firm. Part II. With English summary.) *Liiketaloudellinen Aikak.*, 1973, *22*(4), pp. 248–62.

Tapiero, Charles S. and Leinekugel-Le-Cocq, Armand R. Investissements, utilisation de capacité productive et amortissement: politiques optimales. (Investments, Capacity Utilization and Depreciation: Optimal Policies. With English summary.) *Revue Écon.*, May 1973, *24*(3), pp. 442–59.

Thirlby, G. F. The Economist's Description of Business Behaviour. In *Buchanan, J. M. and Thirlby, G. F., eds.*, 1973, pp. 201–24.

Thompson, Russell G., et al. A Stochastic Investment Model for a Survival Conscious Firm Applied to Shrimp Fishing. *Appl. Econ.*, June 1973, *5*(2), pp. 75–87.

Tisdell, Clement A. Certainty Equivalence and Bias in the Management of Production. *Rev. Marketing Agr. Econ.*, December 1973, *41*(4), pp. 166–78.

Trapeznikov, V. Scientific-Technical Progress and the Effectiveness of Science. *Prob. Econ.*, August 1973, *16*(4), pp. 23–46. [G: U.S.S.R.]

Truett, Dale and Roberts, Blaine. Classical Production Functions, Technical Optimality, and Scale Adjustments of the Firms. *Amer. Econ. Rev.*, December 1973, *63*(5), pp. 975–82.

Tsang, Herbert H. Economic Hypotheses and the Derivation of Production Functions. *Econ. Rec.*, September 1973, *49*(127), pp. 456–63.

Turnovsky, Stephen J. Production Flexibility, Price Uncertainty and the Behavior of the Competitive Firm. *Int. Econ. Rev.*, June 1973, *14*(2), pp. 395–413.

Vaughn, Karen I. Symmetry of Production Stages and Uneconomic Production: Reply. *Southern Econ. J.*, October 1973, *40*(2), pp. 334–35.

Vázquez, Andrés and Puu, Tönu. Factor Demand Functions in the Long-Run Equilibrium. *Rivista Int. Sci. Econ. Com.*, December 1973, *20*(12), pp. 1209–29.

Verstraete, J. Effect of a Change in Scale in One of the Variables on the Coefficients in a Cobb-Douglas Production Function. A Note. *Tijdschr. Econ.*, 1973, *18*(1), pp. 87–91.

Weber, Jean E. and Hawkins, Clark A. The Estimation of Constant Elasticities: Reply. *Southern Econ. J.*, January 1973, *39*(3), pp. 445–47.

Wells, Louis T., Jr. Economic Man and Engineering Man: Choice in a Low-Wage Country. *Public Policy*, Summer 1973, *21*(3), pp. 319–42. [G: Indonesia]

Wolkowitz, Benjamin. Estimation of a Set of Homothetic Production Functions: A Time Series Analysis of American Postwar Manufacturing. *Southern Econ. J.*, April 1973, *39*(4), pp. 626–37. [G: U.S.]

Womer, Norman K. Lancaster's Version of the Walras-Wald Model. *J. Econ. Theory*, October 1973, *6*(5), pp. 515–19.

Woodward, Robert S. The Iso-Outlay Function and Variable Transport Costs. *J. Reg. Sci.*, December 1973, *13*(3), pp. 349–55.

Yarrow, G. K. Managerial Utility Maximization under Uncertainty. *Economica, N.S.*, May 1973, *40*(158), pp. 155–73.

Yunker, James A. A Dynamic Optimization Model of the Soviet Enterprise. *Econ. Planning*, 1973, *13*(1–2), pp. 33–51.

Zabel, Edward. The Competitive Firm, Uncertainty, and Capital Accumulation. *Int. Econ. Rev.*, October 1973, *14*(3), pp. 765–79.

Zanetti, Giovanni. Elementi per un'analisi economica dell'impresa. (Elements for an Economic Analysis of the Firm. With English summary.) *L'Impresa*, 1973, *15*(3–4), pp. 191–207.

Zellner, Arnold and Richard, Jean F. Use of Prior Information in the Analysis and Estimation of Cobb-Douglas Production Function Models. *Int. Econ. Rev.*, February 1973, *14*(1), pp. 107–19.

0224 Theory of Distribution (factor) and Distributive Shares

Bernholz, Peter and Faber, Malte. A Note on Stackelberg's Hypothesis Concerning a Relationship between the Price of Land, the Real Rate of Interest and Impatience to Consume. *Z. Nationalökon.*, 1973, *33*(3–4), pp. 375–88.

Blinder, Alan S. A Model of Inherited Wealth. *Quart. J. Econ.*, November 1973, *87*(4), pp. 608–26. [G: U.S.]

Bruyn-Hundt, M. Naar de meetbaarheid van een rechtvaardige verdeling van de helft voor de helft. (An Approach to the Measurement of Just Distribution of One Half for One Half. With English summary.) *De Economist*, November-December 1973, *121*(6), pp. 626–28, 29. [G: Netherlands]

Chiang, Alpha C. A Simple Generalization of the Kaldor-Pasinetti Theory of Profit Rate and Income Distribution. *Economica, N.S.,* August 1973, *40*(159), pp. 311–13.

Craine, Roger. On the Service Flow from Labour. *Rev. Econ. Stud.,* January 1973, *40*(1), pp. 39–46.

Dasgupta, Partha; Sen, Amartya K. and Starrett, David. Notes on the Measurement of Inequality. *J. Econ. Theory,* April 1973, *6*(2), pp. 180–87.

Dietz, James L. Paradise Reswitched. *Rev. Radical Polit. Econ.,* Summer 1973, *5*(2), pp. 1–17.

Formby, John P. A Clarification of Rent Theory: Reply. *Southern Econ. J.,* July 1973, *40*(1), pp. 131–34.

Harcourt, G. C. The Rate of Profits in Equilibrium Growth Models: A Review Article. *J. Polit. Econ.,* September-October 1973, *81*(5), pp. 1261–77.

Johnson, Harry G. Some Micro-Economic Reflections on Income and Wealth Inequalities. *Ann. Amer. Acad. Polit. Soc. Sci.,* September 1973, *409,* pp. 53–60.

Kamerschen, David R. A Reaffirmation of Marginal Productivity Theory. *Rivista Int. Sci. Econ. Com.,* March 1973, *20*(3), pp. 286–90.

Keiding, Hans. Equilibrium in Economies with Non-Marketed Goods. *Swedish J. Econ.,* December 1973, *75*(4), pp. 349–61.

Khachaturov, T. Improving the Methods of Determining the Effectiveness of Capital Investments. *Prob. Econ.,* September 1973, *16*(5), pp. 3–30. [G: U.S.S.R.]

Mabry, Bevars D. The Economics of Fringe Benefits. *Ind. Relat.,* February 1973, *12*(1), pp. 95–106.

Metzler, Lloyd A. The Rate of Interest and the Marginal Product of Capital. In *Metzler, L. A.,* 1973, pp. 363–89.

Minoguchi, Takeo. Reconsideration of the Theory of Rent. *Hitotsubashi J. Econ.,* February 1973, *13*(2), pp. 29–36.

Nell, Edward J. The Fall of the House of Efficiency. *Ann. Amer. Acad. Polit. Soc. Sci.,* September 1973, *409,* pp. 102–11.

Ophek, Eli. On Samuelson's Analysis of Land Rent. *Amer. J. Econ. Soc.,* July 1973, *32*(3), pp. 306–10.

Peabody, Gerald E. A Primer on the Critique of Marginal Distribution Theory. *Amer. Econ.,* Fall 1973, *17*(2), pp. 23–27.

Rothschild, Michael and Stiglitz, Joseph E. Some Further Results on the Measurement of Inequality. *J. Econ. Theory,* April 1973, *6*(2), pp. 188–204.

Samuelson, Paul A. Relative Shares and Elasticities Simplified: Comment. *Amer. Econ. Rev.,* September 1973, *63*(4), pp. 770–71.

Sato, Ryuzo and Koizumi, Tetsunori. The Production Function and the Theory of Distributive Shares. *Amer. Econ. Rev.,* June 1973, *63*(3), pp. 484–89.

Sato, Ryuzo and Koizumi, Tetsunori. Relative Shares and Elasticities Simplified: Reply. *Amer. Econ. Rev.,* September 1973, *63*(4), pp. 772.

Sato, Ryuzo and Koizumi, Tetsunori. On the Elasticities of Substitution and Complementarity. *Oxford Econ. Pap.,* March 1973, *25*(1), pp. 44–56.

Schuster, Helmut. On the Additivity of Consumers' Rents and the Assessment of External Rent Effects. *Ger. Econ. Rev.,* 1973, *11*(1), pp. 14–20.

Shepherd, A. Ross. A Clarification of Rent Theory: Comment. *Southern Econ. J.,* July 1973, *40*(1), pp. 124–31.

Spandau, Arnt. The Post-Keynesian Model of Income Distribution. *S. Afr. J. Econ.,* March 1973, *41*(1), pp. 1–16.

Tinbergen, J. Naar de meetbaarheid van een rechtvaardige verdeling. (An Approach to the Measurement of a Just Distribution of Income. With English summary.) *De Economist,* March-April 1973, *121*(2), pp. 106–21. [G: Netherlands]

Tinbergen, J. Naar de meetbaarheid van een rechtvaardige verdeling van de helft voor de helft. Naschrift. (An Approach to the Measurement of Just Distribution of One Half for One Half: Reply. With English summary.) *De Economist,* November-December 1973, *121*(6), pp. 628–29. [G: Netherlands]

0225 Price and Market Theory of Firm and Industry in Competition; Single Market Equilibrium

Bronfenbrenner, Martin. Samuelson, Marx, and Their Latest Critics. *J. Econ. Lit.,* March 1973, *11*(1), pp. 58–63.

Davies, J. R. On the Sales Maximization Hypothesis: A Comment. *J. Ind. Econ.,* April 1973, *21*(2), pp. 200–02.

Guarnieri, Raymond L. Short-Run Supply. *Southern Econ. J.,* July 1973, *40*(1), pp. 9–11.

Hamermesh, Daniel S. Price and Quantity Adjustment in Factor Markets. *Western Econ. J.,* March 1973, *11*(1), pp. 118–25.

Herdzina, Klaus. Markstruktur und Wettbewerb. (Market Structure and Competition. On Definition Patterns of Workable Competition. With English summary.) *Z. Wirtschaft. Sozialwissen.,* 1973, *93*(3), pp. 267–84.

Köhler, Walter. Konkurrenzgleichgewicht und Zollwirkung am Brotmarkt. (Equilibrium under Conditions of Competition and Effects of Duties in the Baker's Market. With English summary.) *Jahr. Nationalökon. Statist.,* March 1973, *187*(3), pp. 218–36.

Lacaze, Dominique. Prix duaux et prix du marché. Une théorie du producteur. (Dual Prices and Market Prices: A Theory of the Producer. With English summary.) *Revue Écon.,* March 1973, *24*(2), pp. 273–305.

Merton, Robert C. An Intertemporal Capital Asset Pricing Model. *Econometrica,* September 1973, *41*(5), pp. 867–87.

Metzler, Lloyd A. The Assumptions Implied in Least-Squares Demand Techniques. In *Metzler, L. A.,* 1973, pp. 575–98.

Rothschild, Michael. Models of Market Organization with Imperfect Information: A Survey. *J. Polit. Econ.,* November-December 1973, *81*(6), pp. 1283–1308.

Samuelson, Paul A. Samuelson's "Reply on Marxian Matters." *J. Econ. Lit.,* March 1973, *11*(1), pp. 64–68.

Schimmler, Jörg. Speculation, Profitability, and Price Stability—A Formal Approach. *Rev. Econ. Statist.,* February 1973, *55*(1), pp. 110–14.

Turnovsky, Stephen J. Optimal Stabilization Policies in a Market with Lagged Adjustment in Supply. *Econ. Rec.,* March 1973, *49*(125), pp. 31–49.

Vázquez, Andrés and Puu, Tönu. Factor Demand Functions in the Long-Run Equilibrium. *Rivista Int. Sci. Econ. Com.*, December 1973, *20*(12), pp. 1209–29.

Veendorp, E. C. H. Pure Competition in Disequilibrium Situations. *Weltwirtsch. Arch.*, 1973, *109*(3), pp. 476–94.

Williams, Fred E. The Effect of Market Organization on Competitive Equilibrium: The Multi-Unit Case. *Rev. Econ. Stud.*, January 1973, *40*(1), pp. 97–113.

0226 Price and Market Theory of Firm and Industry in Noncompetitive Relations

Aberle, Gerd. Reaktionshypothesen in Oligopolmodellen und oligopolistisches Marktverhalten. (Reaction Hypotheses in Oligopoly Models and Oligopolistic Market Behavior. With English summary.) *Z. ges. Staatswiss.*, August 1973, *129*(3), pp. 454–77.

Andersen, Per. Økonomisk overlevelse i et stokastisk marked. (The Behaviour of a Monopolist Who Seeks Economic Survival in a Stochastic Market. With English summary.) *Nationalokon. Tidsskr.*, 1973, *111*(2), pp. 266–76.

Aumann, Robert J. Disadvantageous Monopolies. *J. Econ. Theory*, February 1973, *6*(1), pp. 1–11.

Baron, David P. Limit Pricing, Potential Entry, and Barriers to Entry. *Amer. Econ. Rev.*, September 1973, *63*(4), pp. 666–74.

Bergson, Abram. On Monopoly Welfare Losses. *Amer. Econ. Rev.*, December 1973, *63*(5), pp. 853–70.

Cyert, Richard M. and DeGroot, Morris H. An Analysis of Cooperation and Learning in a Duopoly Context. *Amer. Econ. Rev.*, March 1973, *63*(1), pp. 24–37.

Dewey, Donald. Imperfect Competition: Dewey and Heuss: Reply. *Weltwirtsch. Arch.*, 1973, *109* (3), pp. 517–18.

Douglas, Evan J. Price Strategy Duopoly with Product Variation: Comment. *Kyklos*, 1973, *26*(3), pp. 608–11.

Douglas, Evan J. Price Variation Duopoly with Differentiated Products: A Note. *J. Econ. Theory*, December 1973, *6*(6), pp. 618–20.

Eaton, B. Curtis. Comment on "Duopoly and Space." *Can. J. Econ.*, February 1973, *6*(1), pp. 124–27.

Eeckhoudt, Louis R. The "Dorfman-Steiner" Rule: The Intertemporal Case: A Reply. *Z. Nationalökon.*, 1973, *33*(3–4), pp. 431–34.

Eichner, Alfred S. A Theory of the Determination of the Mark-up Under Oligopoly. *Econ. J.*, December 1973, *83*(332), pp. 1184–1200.

Fisher, Franklin M. Stability and Competitive Equilibrium in Two Models of Search and Individual Price Adjustment. *J. Econ. Theory*, October 1973, *6*(5), pp. 446–70.

Formby, John P. On Revenue Maximizing Duopoly. *J. Ind. Econ.*, July 1973, *21*(3), pp. 272–92.

Franke, Jürgen F. A. W. Advertising and Collusion in Oligopoly. *Jahr. Nationalökon. Statist.*, December 1973, *188*(1), pp. 33–50.

Friedman, James W. On Reaction Function Equilibria. *Int. Econ. Rev.*, October 1973, *14*(3), pp. 721–34.

Friedman, James W. A Non-cooperative Equilibrium for Supergames: A Correction. *Rev. Econ. Stud.*, July 1973, *40*(3), pp. 435.

Gandenberger, Otto. Konkurrenzinformation und Wettbewerb. (Information Among Competitors in Respect to Competition. With English summary.) *Jahr. Nationalökon. Statist.*, December 1973, *188*(1), pp. 10–32.

Gannon, Colin A. Central Concentration in Simple Spatial Duopoly: Some Behavioral and Functional Conditions. *J. Reg. Sci.*, December 1973, *13*(3), pp. 357–75.

Gannon, Colin A. Optimization of Market Share in Spatial Competition. *Southern Econ. J.*, July 1973, *40*(1), pp. 66–79.

Goldberg, Victor and Moirao, Sharon. Limit Pricing and Potential Competition. *J. Polit. Econ.*, November-December 1973, *81*(6), pp. 1460–66.

Graeser, Paul. Imperfect Competition: Dewey and Heuss: Comment. *Weltwirtsch. Arch.*, 1973, *109* (3), pp. 514–16.

Greene, Robert L. Peak Load Pricing: An Application. *Quart. Rev. Econ. Bus.*, Autumn 1973, *13*(3), pp. 105–14.

Greenhut, M. L. and Ohta, H. Spatial Configurations and Competitive Equilibrium. *Weltwirtsch. Arch.*, 1973, *109*(1), pp. 87–104.

Gutowski, Armin. Theoretical Approaches to a Concept of Supplier's Power. *Ger. Econ. Rev.*, 1973, *11*(3), pp. 193–215.

Harnett, Donald L. and Hamner, W. Clay. The Value of Information in Bargaining. *Western Econ. J.*, March 1973, *11*(1), pp. 81–88.

Hartwick, John M. and Hartwick, Philip G. Reply to Comment by B. C. Eaton. *Can. J. Econ.*, February 1973, *6*(1), pp. 127–28.

Hauptmann, Harry and Seifert, Hans G. Ein Oligopolspiel mit wirksamen Kapazitätsschranken. (An Oligopoly Game with Effective Capacity Bounds. With English summary.) *Jahr. Nationalökon. Statist.*, December 1973, *188*(1), pp. 51–64.

Helmer, Jean-Yves. Essai sur la croissance de l'entreprise. (Essay on Firm Growth. With English summary.) *Revue Écon.*, March 1973, *24*(2), pp. 235–72.

Hibdon, James E., et al. Market Areas in Spatial Duopoly. *Rivista Int. Sci. Econ. Com.*, March 1973, *20*(3), pp. 267–77.

Hillinger, Claude. Sales Maximization as an Explanation of Near Pareto Optimality of the U.S. Economy. *Jahr. Nationalökon. Statist.*, May 1973, *187* (4), pp. 364–67. [G: U.S.]

Hughes, G. David; Juhasz, Joseph B. and Contini, Bruno. The Influence of Personality on the Bargaining Process. *J. Bus.*, October 1973, *46*(4), pp. 593–604.

Ireland, Norman J. The "Dorfman-Steiner" Rule and Bandwagon Effects. *Z. Nationalökon.*, 1973, *33*(3–4), pp. 427–30.

Maurice, S. Charles and Ferguson, C. E. Factor Demand Elasticity under Monopoly and Monopsony. *Economica, N.S.*, May 1973, *40*(158), pp. 180–86.

McKean, J. R. and Peterson, R. D. Demand Elasticity, Product Differentiation, and Market Structure. *J. Econ. Theory*, April 1973, *6*(2), pp. 205–09.

Müller, Udo and Rumm, Ulrich. Zur Gleichgewichtsproblematik im unvollkommenen Polypol. (The Problem of Equilibrium in the Polypol. With English summary.) *Z. ges. Staatswiss.*, May 1973, *129*(2), pp. 189–204.

Okuguchi, Koji. Quasi-Competitiveness and Cournot Oligopoly. *Rev. Econ. Stud.*, January 1973, *40*(1), pp. 145–48.

Osborne, D. K. On the Rationality of Limit Pricing. *J. Ind. Econ.*, September 1973, *22*(1), pp. 71–80.

Prescott, Edward C. Market Structure and Monopoly Profits: A Dynamic Theory. *J. Econ. Theory*, December 1973, *6*(6), pp. 546–57.

Pursell, G. and Snape, R. H. Economies of Scale, Price Discrimination and Exporting. *J. Int. Econ.*, February 1973, *3*(1), pp. 85–91.

Ribich, Thomas I. Soft Sell for Soft Drinks: An Excise Tax Problem. *Nat. Tax J.*, March 1973, *26*(1), pp. 115–17.

Rousseau, Henri-Paul. Bargaining As Behavior Towards Risk. *Amer. Econ.*, Spring 1973, *17*(1), pp. 4–12.

Sabel, Hermann. On Pricing New Products. *Ger. Econ. Rev.*, 1973, *11*(4), pp. 292–311.

Salop, S. C. Wage Differentials in a Dynamic Theory of the Firm. *J. Econ. Theory*, August 1973, *6*(4), pp. 321–44.

Scheidell, John M. The Price Reducing Potential of Advertising. *Southern Econ. J.*, April 1973, *39*(4), pp. 535–43.

Sellekaerts, Willy and Lesage, Richard. A Reformulation and Empirical Verification of the Administered Prices Inflation Hypothesis: The Canadian Case. *Southern Econ. J.*, January 1973, *39*(3), pp. 345–60.   **[G: Canada]**

Shitovitz, Benyamin. Oligopoly in Markets with a Continuum of Traders. *Econometrica*, May 1973, *41*(3), pp. 467–501.

Shubik, Martin. Price Strategy Duopoly with Product Variation: Reply. *Kyklos*, 1973, *26*(3), pp. 612.

Shubik, Martin. Information, Duopoly and Competitive Markets: A Sensitivity Analysis. *Kyklos*, 1973, *26*(4), pp. 736–61.

Sieper, E. and Swan, P. L. Monopoly and Competition in the Market for Durable Goods. *Rev. Econ. Stud.*, July 1973, *40*(3), pp. 333–51.

Simon, Julian L.; Puig, Carlos M. and Aschoff, John. A Duopoly Simulation and Richer Theory: An End to Cournot. *Rev. Econ. Stud.*, July 1973, *40*(3), pp. 353–66.

Steinmann, Gunter. Informationsgewinnung und Preisentwicklung: Ein mikroökonomischer Erklärungsversuch für die verzögerte Preisanpassung im Konjunkturaufschwung mit Hilfe des Mills-Modells. (Information Problem and Price Development: A Mills-Model-Explanation for Lagged Adjustment of Prices in the Beginning Upswing. With English summary.) *Z. Wirtschaft. Sozialwissen.*, 1973, *93*(4), pp. 411–21.

Stigler, George J. The Kinky Oligopoly Demand Curve and Rigid Prices. In *Haynes, W. W.; Coyne, T. J. and Osborne, D. K., eds.*, 1973, pp. 281–99.   **[G: U.S.]**

Tokita, Tadahiko. Behavior of Oligopolistic Firm and Market Adjustment—A Short Run Macroeconomic Approach. (In Japanese.) *Econ. Stud. Quart.*, April 1973, *24*(1), pp. 9–17.

White, Daniel L. and Walker, Michael C. First Degree Price Discrimination and Profit Maximization. *Southern Econ. J.*, October 1973, *40*(2), pp. 313–18.

Worcester, Dean A., Jr. New Estimates of the Welfare Loss to Monopoly, United States: 1956–1969. *Southern Econ. J.*, October 1973, *40*(2), pp. 234–45.   **[G: U.S.]**

023 Macroeconomic Theory

0230 General

Adie, Douglas K. An International Comparison of the Quantity and Income-Expenditure Theories. *J. Amer. Statist. Assoc.*, March 1973, *68*(341), pp. 63–65.

Akerlof, George A. The Demand for Money: A General-Equilibrium Inventory-Theoretic Approach. *Rev. Econ. Stud.*, January 1973, *40*(1), pp. 115–30.

Allsbrook, Ogden O., Jr. and DeLorme, Charles D., Jr. Monetary Policy, Price Expectations, and the Case of a Positively-Sloped *IS* Curve. *Rivista Int. Sci. Econ. Com.*, March 1973, *20*(3), pp. 278–85.

Andersen, Leonall C. A Note on the Effects of Government Finance on Aggregate Demand for Goods and Services—A Reply. *Public Finance*, 1973, *28*(3–4), pp. 397–406.

Andersen, Leonall C. The State of the Monetarist Debate. *Fed. Res. Bank St. Louis Rev.*, September 1973, *55*(9), pp. 2–8.   **[G: U.S.]**

Andersen, Palle Schelde. Automatic Stabilization in Static and Dynamic Models. *Nationalokon. Tidsskr.*, 1973, *111*(1), pp. 60–85.

Arak, Marcelle and Spiro, Alan. A Theoretical Explanation of the Interest Inelasticity of Money Demand. *Rev. Econ. Statist.*, November 1973, *55*(4), pp. 520–23.   **[G: U.S.]**

Balles, John J. Evaluating Money Market Conditions. *Fed. Res. Bank San Francisco Rev.*, September-October 1973, pp. 3–11.   **[G: U.S.]**

Baltensperger, Ernst. Zur Rolle des Bankensystems in makroökonomischen Modellen. (The Role of the Banking System in Macroeconomic Models. With English summary.) *Kyklos*, 1973, *26*(4), pp. 787–803.

Benavie, Arthur. Imports in Macroeconomic Models. *Int. Econ. Rev.*, June 1973, *14*(2), pp. 530–32.

Bhattacharya, Sourin. Separate Treatment of Demand and Supply Lags and Stability of Multiplier Processes. *Indian Econ. J.*, April-June 1973, *20*(4–5), pp. 570–80.

Blinder, Alan S. and Solow, Robert M. Does Fiscal Policy Matter? *J. Public Econ.*, November 1973, *2*(4), pp. 319–37.

Brunner, Karl and Meltzer, Allan H. Mr. Hicks and the "Monetarists." *Economica*, N.S., February 1973, *40*(157), pp. 44–59.

Brunner, Karl. The State of the Monetarist Debate: A Comment. *Fed. Res. Bank St. Louis Rev.*, September 1973, *55*(9), pp. 9, 12–14.

Cebula, Richard J. Expected Interest Rate Changes

and Monetary Policy: A Brief Note. *Miss. Val. J. Bus. Econ.*, Spring 1973, *8*(3), pp. 71–76.

Cebula, Richard J. Deficit Spending, Expectations, and Fiscal Policy Effectiveness. *Public Finance*, 1973, *28*(3–4), pp. 362–70.

Chand, Sheetal. Period Analysis and Continuous Analysis in Patinkin's Macroeconomic Model—A Critical Note. *J. Econ. Theory*, October 1973, *6*(5), pp. 520–24.

Chen, Chau-Nan. The Monetary Effect of Devaluation: An Alternative Interpretation of the Cooper Paradox. *Western Econ. J.*, December 1973, *11*(4), pp. 475–80.

Chen, Chau-Nan. A Graphical Note on the Aggregative Effect of Payments of Interest on Deposits: Comment. *J. Money, Credit, Banking*, November 1973, *5*(4), pp. 985–87.

Cheng, Juei Ming. On the Stability of Equilibrium of the Manufacturing Market Structure. *Rivista Int. Sci. Econ. Com.*, February 1973, *20*(2), pp. 184–89.

Chick, Victoria. Financial Counterparts of Saving and Investment and Inconsistency in Some Simple Macro Models. *Weltwirtsch. Arch.*, 1973, *109* (4), pp. 621–43.

Chipman, John S. and Moore, James C. Aggregate Demand, Real National Income, and the Compensation Principle. *Int. Econ. Rev.*, February 1973, *14*(1), pp. 153–81.

Christ, Carl F. Monetary and Fiscal Influences on U.S. Money Income, 1891–1970. *J. Money, Credit, Banking*, Part II, February 1973, *5*(1), pp. 279–300.   [G: U.S.]

Chung, Pham. Some Notes on the Assignment Problem. *Public Finance*, 1973, *28*(1), pp. 20–29.

Claassen, Emil-Maria. Alternative Policies to Achieve Internal and External Equilibrium: A Graphical Overview. *Z. Nationalökon.*, 1973, *33* (1–2), pp. 127–31.

Clark, Carolyn. The Demand for Money and the Choice of a Permanent Income Estimate: Some Canadian Evidence, 1926-65. *J. Money, Credit, Banking*, August 1973, *5*(3), pp. 773–93.
                                              [G: Canada]

Clower, Robert W. and Leijonhufvud, Axel. Say's Principle, What it Means and Doesn't Mean: Part I. *Intermountain Econ. Rev.*, Fall 1973, *4*(2), pp. 1–16.

Courbis, Raymond. La théorie des "économies concurrencées" fondement du modèle FIFI. (The Theory of "Competitioned Economies" as a Basis of the Fifi Model. With English summary.) *Revue Écon.*, November 1973, *24*(6), pp. 905–22.

Davidson, Paul and Weintraub, Sidney. Money as Cause and Effect. *Econ. J.*, December 1973, *83* (332), pp. 1117–32.

Dean, James W. and Tower, Edward. Internal and External Balance in an "Almost Classical" World: Rejoinder. *Western Econ. J.*, June 1973, *11*(2), pp. 240.

Dean, James W. and Tower, Edward. More on Internal and External Balance in an "Almost Classical" World. *Western Econ. J.*, June 1973, *11*(2), pp. 232–37.

Desai, Meghnad. Growth Cycles and Inflation in a Model of the Class Struggle. *J. Econ. Theory*, December 1973, *6*(6), pp. 527–45.

Feldstein, Martin S. Tax Incentives, Corporate Saving, and Capital Accumulation in the United States. *J. Public Econ.*, April 1973, *2*(2), pp. 159–71.   [G: U.S.]

Fink, William H. Dollar Surplus and Devaluation. *Rivista Int. Sci. Econ. Com.*, July 1973, *20*(7), pp. 625–39.

Fried, Joel. Money, Exchange and Growth. *Western Econ. J.*, September 1973, *11*(3), pp. 285–301.

Gebauer, Wolfgang. The Theory of Monetarism. *Z. ges. Staatswiss.*, February 1973, *129*(1), pp. 23–45.

Geisel, Martin S. Bayesian Comparisons of Simple Macroeconomic Models. *J. Money, Credit, Banking*, August 1973, *5*(3), pp. 751–72.   [G: U.S.]

Gibson, William E. Interest Rates and Prices in the Long Run: A Study of the Gibson Paradox: Comment. *J. Money, Credit, Banking*, Part II, February 1973, *5*(1), pp. 450–53.   [G: U.S.]

Gordon, Robert J. Interest Rates and Prices in the Long Run: A Study of the Gibson Paradox: Comment. *J. Money, Credit, Banking*, Part II, February 1973, *5*(1), pp. 460–63.   [G: U.S.]

Hahn, Frank H. On Transaction Costs, Inessential Sequence Economies and Money. *Rev. Econ. Stud.*, October 1973, *40*(4), pp. 449–61.

Harvey, C. E. On the Cost-Inflationary Impact of High Interest Rates: Reply. *J. Econ. Issues*, September 1973, *7*(3), pp. 514.

Hebert, Robert F. and Byrns, Ralph T. On the Cost-Inflationary Impact of High Interest Rates: Comment. *J. Econ. Issues*, September 1973, *7*(3), pp. 511–14.

Hendershott, Patric H. Interest Rates and Prices in the Long Run: A Study of the Gibson Paradox: Comment. *J. Money, Credit, Banking*, Part II, February 1973, *5*(1), pp. 454–59.   [G: U.S.]

Hendershott, Patric H. Monetary and Fiscal Influences on U.S. Money Income, 1891–1970: Comment. *J. Money, Credit, Banking*, Part II, February 1973, *5*(1), pp. 311–12.   [G: U.S.]

Henderson, Dale W. and Sargent, Thomas J. Monetary and Fiscal Policy in a Two-Sector Aggregative Model. *Amer. Econ. Rev.*, June 1973, *63*(3), pp. 345–65.

Holub, H. W. and Kuhbier, P. Ein ungleichgewichtiges Modell des Wachstums und der Einkommensverteilung mit endogenen Strukturänderungen. (A Disequilibrated Model of Growth and Income Distribution with Endogenous Structural Change. With English summary.) *Jahr. Nationalökon. Statist.*, May 1973, *187*(4), pp. 289–300.

Horvat, Branko. Labour-Time Prices of Production and the Transformation Problem in a Socialist Economy. *Kyklos*, 1973, *26*(4), pp. 762–86.

Humphrey, Thomas M. Empirical Tests of the Quantity Theory of Money in the United States, 1900–1930. *Hist. Polit. Econ.*, Fall 1973, *5*(2), pp. 285–316.   [G: U.S.]

Johnson, Stanley R. and Smith, Paul E. The Phillips Curve, Expectations, and Stability. *Quart. Rev. Econ. Bus.*, Autumn 1973, *13*(3), pp. 85–91.

Kane, Edward J. Monetary and Fiscal Influence on

U.S. Money Income, 1891–1970: Comment. *J. Money, Credit, Banking*, Part II, February 1973, *5*(1), pp. 301–03. [G: U.S.]

Klein, Lawrence R. The State of the Monetarist Debate: A Comment. *Fed. Res. Bank St. Louis Rev.*, September 1973, *55*(9), pp. 9–12.

Knapp, John. Economics or Political Economy? *Lloyds Bank Rev.*, January 1973, (107), pp. 19–43.

Kumar, Rishi. Demand Policies and Internal-External Balance Under Fixed Exchange Rates—The Mundellian Assignment: A Reformulation and Some Extensions. *Weltwirtsch. Arch.*, 1973, *109* (2), pp. 253–73.

Kymn, Kern O. A Note on Logical Inconsistencies of the Kennedy Wage-Price Guidelines. *Southern Econ. J.*, January 1973, *39*(3), pp. 434–36.

Lachmann, L. M. Sir John Hicks as a Neo-Austrian. *S. Afr. J. Econ.*, September 1973, *41*(3), pp. 195–207.

Laibman, David. Values and Prices of Production: The Political Economy of the Transformation Problem. *Sci. Soc.*, Winter 1973–1974, *37*(4), pp. 404–36.

Laidler, David. Expectations, Adjustment, and the Dynamic Response of Income to Policy Changes. *J. Money, Credit, Banking*, Part I, February 1973, *5*(1), pp. 157–72.

Laidler, David. Monetarist Policy Prescriptions and Their Background. *Manchester Sch. Econ. Soc. Stud.*, March 1973, *41*(1), pp. 59–71. [G: U.K.]

Lebowitz, Michael A. The Current Crisis of Economic Theory. *Sci. Soc.*, Winter 1973–1974, *37*(4), pp. 385–403.

Leijonhufvud, Axel. Effective Demand Failures. *Swedish J. Econ.*, March 1973, *75*(1), pp. 27–48.

Levin, Fred J. Examination of the Money-Stock Control Approach of Burger, Kalish, and Babb. *J. Money, Credit, Banking*, November 1973, *5*(4), pp. 924–38. [G: U.S.]

McCallum, B. T. Friedman's Missing Equation: Another Approach. *Manchester Sch. Econ. Soc. Stud.*, September 1973, *41*(3), pp. 311–28. [G: U.S.]

McGregor, L. and Walters, A. A. Real Balances and Output: A Productivity Model of a Monetary Economy. In *Powell, A. A. and Williams, R. A.*, eds., 1973, pp. 233–59.

Metzler, Lloyd A. Business Cycles and the Theory of Employment. In *Metzler, L. A.*, 1973, pp. 482–96.

Metzler, Lloyd A. The Structure of Taxes, Open-Market Operations, and the Rate of Interest. In *Metzler, L. A.*, 1973, pp. 345–62. [G: U.S.]

Metzler, Lloyd A. Three Lags in the Circular Flow of Income. In *Metzler, L. A.*, 1973, pp. 465–81. [G: U.S.]

Metzler, Lloyd A. Wealth, Saving, and the Rate of Interest. In *Metzler, L. A.*, 1973, pp. 311–44.

Miconi, Gastone. New Aspects of an Old Problem? Inflation. *Rev. Econ. Cond. Italy*, January-March 1973, *27*(1–2), pp. 53–64.

Modigliani, Franco and Shiller, Robert J. Inflation, Rational Expectations and the Term Structure of Interest Rates. *Economica*, *N.S.*, February 1973, *40*(157), pp. 12–43.

Monissen, Hans G. Preise, Löhne und Beschäftigung in dynamischer Betrachtung: Eine einfache Exposition. (Prices, Wages and Employment in Dynamic Perspective: A Simple Exposition. With English summary.) *Kyklos*, 1973, *26*(3), pp. 545–58.

Montazer-Zohour, M. Generalization of Multiplier Theory. *Tahq. Eq.*, Winter & Spring 1973, *10*(29 & 30), pp. 106–45.

Moore, Basil J. Some Macroeconomic Consequences of Corporate Equities. *Can. J. Econ.*, November 1973, *6*(4), pp. 529–44.

Morley, Samuel A. The Relationship Between Money, Income and Prices in the Short and Long Run. *J. Finance*, December 1973, *28*(5), pp. 1119–30.

Needham, Douglas. Monetary and Fiscal Policy under Fixed Exchange Rates: Comment. *Swedish J. Econ.*, March 1973, *75*(1), pp. 112–18.

Ohtsuki, Yoshitaka. Public Investment and Economic Growth—Fiscal Policy and Resource Allocation. (In Japanese. With English summary.) *Econ. Stud. Quart.*, December 1973, *24*(3), pp. 16–30.

Parguez, Alain. Sismondi et la théorie du déséquilibre macro-économique. (Sismondi and Macro-Disequilibrium Theory. With English summary.) *Revue Écon.*, September 1973, *24*(5), pp. 837–66.

Park, Yung C. The Transmission Process and the Relative Effectiveness of Monetary and Fiscal Policy in a Two-Sector Neoclassical Model. *J. Money, Credit, Banking*, May 1973, *5*(2), pp. 595–622.

Patrick, John D. Establishing Convergent Decentralized Policy Assignment. *J. Int. Econ.*, February 1973, *3*(1), pp. 37–51.

Peston, Maurice. A Note on Tax Changes and Fluctuations in National Income. *J. Polit. Econ.*, November-December 1973, *81*(6), pp. 1467–70. [G: U.S.]

Phan, Duc-Loï. Le modèle FIFI et la politique économique à moyen terme. (The Physico-Financial Model and the Medium Term Policy. With English summary.) *Revue Écon.*, November 1973, *24*(6), pp. 923–50. [G: France]

Poole, William and Kornblith, Elinda B. F. The Friedman-Meiselman CMC Paper: New Evidence on an Old Controversy. *Amer. Econ. Rev.*, December 1973, *63*(5), pp. 908–17.

Prachowny, Martin F. J. The Effectiveness of Stabilization Policy in a Small Open Economy. *Weltwirtsch. Arch.*, 1973, *109*(2), pp. 214–31.

Puckett, Richard H. Monetary Policy Effectiveness: The Case of a Positively Sloped I-S Curve: Comment. *J. Finance*, December 1973, *28*(5), pp. 1362–64.

Purvis, Douglas D. Short-Run Dynamics in Models of Money and Growth. *Amer. Econ. Rev.*, March 1973, *63*(1), pp. 12–23.

Rao, B. Bhaskara. Price Behaviour in India: A Note on Professor Raj's Model. *Indian Econ. Rev.*, October 1973, *8*(2), pp. 186–92. [G: India]

Rasche, Robert H. A Comparative Static Analysis of Some Monetarist Propositions. *Fed. Res. Bank St. Louis Rev.*, December 1973, *55*(12), pp. 15–23.

Rea, John D. Trends and Cycles in Money and Bank Credit. *Fed. Res. Bank Kansas City Rev.*, March

1973, pp. 3–9.   [G: U.S.]

Richter, Rudolf. Full Employment and Stable Prices—Compatibility of Targets and Rules. *Ger. Econ. Rev.*, 1973, *11*(2), pp. 108–20.

Roll, Richard. Assets, Money, and Commodity Price Inflation Under Uncertainty: Demand Theory. *J. Money, Credit, Banking*, November 1973, *5*(4), pp. 903–23.

Rose, Hugh. Effective Demand in the Long Run. In *Mirrlees, J. A. and Stern, N. H., eds.*, 1973, pp. 25–47.

Ross, Stephen A. and Wachter, Michael L. Wage Determination, Inflation, and the Industrial Structure. *Amer. Econ. Rev.*, September 1973, *63* (4), pp. 675–92.

Sargent, Thomas J. What Do Regressions of Interest on Inflation Show? *Ann. Econ. Soc. Measure*, July 1973, *2*(3), pp. 289–301.

Sargent, Thomas J. Interest Rates and Prices in the Long Run: A Study of the Gibson Paradox. *J. Money, Credit, Banking*, Part II, February 1973, *5*(1), pp. 385–449.   [G: U.S.]

Sargent, Thomas J. "Rational Expectations": A Correction. *Brookings Pap. Econ. Act.*, 1973, (3), pp. 799–800.

Sargent, Thomas J. Rational Expectations, the Real Rate of Interest, and the Natural Rate of Unemployment. *Brookings Pap. Econ. Act.*, 1973, (2), pp. 429–72.

Scarfe, B. L. A Model of the Inflation Cycle in a Small Open Economy. *Oxford Econ. Pap.*, July 1973, *25* (2), pp. 192–203.

Schmidt, Ádám. Equilibrium of the Budget and of the National Economy. In *Földi, T., ed.*, 1973, pp. 89–115.

Sdralevich, Alberto and Monti, Mario. I modelli macroeconomici per la politica monetaria in Italia: aggregazione e realismo. (Macroeconomic Models for Monetary Policy in Italy: Aggregation and Realism. With English summary.) *L'Industria*, January-June 1973, (1–2), pp. 36–58. [G: Italy]

Sekine, Thomas T. Classical Monetary Theory and the Non-Optimality Theorem. *Z. Nationalökon.*, 1973, *33*(1–2), pp. 1–24.

Shapiro, Harold T. Monetary and Fiscal Influences on U.S. Money Income, 1891–1970: Comment. *J. Money, Credit, Banking*, Part II, February 1973, *5*(1), pp. 304–10.   [G: U.S.]

Silber, William L. Monetary Policy Effectiveness: The Case of a Positively Sloped I-S Curve: Reply. *J. Finance*, December 1973, *28*(5), pp. 1365.

Starrett, David A. Inefficiency and the Demand for "Money" in a Sequence Economy. *Rev. Econ. Stud.*, October 1973, *40*(4), pp. 437–48.

Steindl, Frank G. Price Expectations and Interest Rates. *J. Money, Credit, Banking*, November 1973, *5*(4), pp. 939–49.

Steinmann, Gunter. Lohnentwicklung und Beschäftigungsgrad: Die Neuauflage der Kontroverse zwischen der Keynesschen und der neoklassischen Theorie bei der Diskussion um die Phillips-Kurve. (Wages and the Rate of Employment. With English summary.) *Weltwirtsch. Arch.*, 1973, *109*(1), pp. 105–20.

Tokita, Tadahiko. Determination of Income and Prices in the Short Run. (In Japanese. With Eng-

lish summary.) *Econ. Stud. Quart.*, December 1973, *24*(3), pp. 31–42.

Tokita, Tadahiko. Behavior of Oligopolistic Firm and Market Adjustment—A Short Run Macroeconomic Approach. (In Japanese.) *Econ. Stud. Quart.*, April 1973, *24*(1), pp. 9–17.

Turnovsky, Stephen J. Optimal Stabilization Policies for Deterministic and Stochastic Linear Economic Systems. *Rev. Econ. Stud.*, January 1973, *40*(1), pp. 79–95.

Uzawa, Hirofumi. Towards a Keynesian Model of Monetary Growth. In *Mirrlees, J. A. and Stern, N. H., eds.*, 1973, pp. 53–70.

Verbaan, W. C. and de Ridder, P. B. Uniforme modelstructuur voor meerdere landen. (A Uniform Model Structure for Several Countries. With English summary.) *De Economist*, September-October 1973, *121*(5), pp. 481–520.

Vousden, Neil. Basic Theoretical Issues of Resource Depletion. *J. Econ. Theory*, April 1973, *6*(2), pp. 126–43.

Waud, Roger N. Index Bonds and Economic Stability. *Public Finance*, 1973, *28*(1), pp. 52–68.

Weintraub, Sidney. Keynes and the Theory of Derived Demand. In *Weintraub, S., et al.*, 1973, pp. 51–70.

Wiles, Peter. Cost Inflation and the State of Economic Theory. *Econ. J.*, June 1973, *83*(330), pp. 377–98.

Williams, Raburn and Miller, Roger LeRoy. A Note on the Effects of Government Finance on Aggregate Demand for Goods and Services. *Public Finance*, 1973, *28*(3–4), pp. 393–96.

Zelder, Raymond E.; Ross, Myron H. and Collery, Arnold. Internal and External Balance in an "Almost Classical" World: Reply. *Western Econ. J.*, June 1973, *11*(2), pp. 238–40.

0231 Developments in General Macroeconomic Theory 1930–45

Allsbrook, Ogden O., Jr. Keynes's Involuntary Unemployment Equilibrium: An Alternative View. *S. Afr. J. Econ.*, March 1973, *41*(1), pp. 60–66.

Asimakopulos, A. Keynes, Patinkin, Historical Time, and Equilibrium Analysis. *Can. J. Econ.*, May 1973, *6*(2), pp. 179–88.

Burress, Glenn E. Who First Proposed the Habit Persistence Hypothesis: Keynes or Duesenberry and Modigliani. *Indian Econ. J.*, January-March 1973, *20*(3), pp. 472–78.

Johnson, Harry G. Keynes and the Keynesians. In *Johnson, H. G.*, 1973, pp. 70–76.

Kliman, M. L. and Oksanen, Ernest H. The Keynesian Demand-for-Money Function: Comment. *J. Money, Credit, Banking*, Part I, February 1973, *5*(1), pp. 215–20.

Moggridge, D. E. From the *Treatise* to *The General Theory*: An Exercise in Chronology. *Hist. Polit. Econ.*, Spring 1973, *5*(1), pp. 72–88.

Roe, Alan R. The Case for Flow of Funds and National Balance Sheet Accounts. *Econ. J.*, June 1973, *83*(330), pp. 399–420.   [G: U.K.]

Schuster, Helmut. Keynes' Disequilibrium Analysis. *Kyklos*, 1973, *26*(3), pp. 512–44.

Titmuss, R. and Titmuss, K. Parents' Revolt, 1942. In *Tranter, N. L., ed.,* 1973, pp. 155–62. [G: U.K.]

Uhr, Carl G. The Emergence of the "New Economics" in Sweden: A Review of a Study by Otto Steiger. *Hist. Polit. Econ.,* Spring 1973, *5*(1), pp. 243–60. [G: Sweden]

Weintraub, Sidney. Keynes and the Theory of Derived Demand. In *Weintraub, S., et al.,* 1973, pp. 51–70.

Wells, Paul. Keynes's Dynamic Disequilibrium Theory of Employment. *Quart. Rev. Econ. Bus.,* Winter 1973, *13*(4), pp. 89–93.

Yeager, Leland B. The Keynesian Diversion. *Western Econ. J.,* June 1973, *11*(2), pp. 150–63.

0232 Theory of Aggregate Demand: Consumption

Anthony, William P. and Nosari, Eldon J. A Test of the Permanent Income Hypothesis. *J. Bus. Res.,* Summer 1973, *1*(1), pp. 43–48. [G: U.S.]

Bell, D. J.; Brenneman, Ronald and Steedman, Ian. A Control Theory Analysis of a Finite Optimum Savings Program in a Two-Sector Model. *Int. Econ. Rev.,* June 1973, *14*(2), pp. 520–24.

Bowden, Roger J. Some Implications of the Permanent-Income Hypothesis. *Rev. Econ. Stud.,* January 1973, *40*(1), pp. 33–37.

Burress, Glenn E. Who First Proposed the Habit Persistence Hypothesis: Keynes or Duesenberry and Modigliani. *Indian Econ. J.,* January-March 1973, *20*(3), pp. 472–78.

Burress, Glenn E. A More General Theory of the Short-Run Consumption Function and Recent Data. *Nebr. J. Econ. Bus.,* Autumn 1973, *12*(4), pp. 7–22. [G: U.S.]

Chaudry, M. Anwar. An Econometric Approach to Saving Analysis. *Pakistan Develop. Rev.,* Autumn 1973, *12*(3), pp. 200–31.

Feldstein, Martin S. and Fane, George. Taxes, Corporate Dividend Policy and Personal Savings: The British Postwar Experience. *Rev. Econ. Statist.,* November 1973, *55*(4), pp. 399–411. [G: U.K.]

Ferber, Robert. Consumer Economics, A Survey. *J. Econ. Lit.,* December 1973, *11*(4), pp. 1303–42.

Flemming, J. S. The Consumption Function when Capital Markets are Imperfect: The Permanent Income Hypothesis Reconsidered. *Oxford Econ. Pap.,* July 1973, *25*(2), pp. 160–72.

Glahe, Fred R. A Permanent Restatement of the IS-LM Model. *Amer. Econ.,* Spring 1973, *17*(1), pp. 158–67.

Hansen, Gerd and Staudte, Axel. Eine empirische Überprüfung der Permanent-Income-Hypothese: Eine Erwiderung auf H. Drost. (An Empirical Reexamination of the Permanent Income Hypothesis: A Comment. With English summary.) *Jahr. Nationalökon. Statist.,* March 1973, *187*(3), pp. 269–81.

Hempenius, A. L. On the Specification of Risk Aversion in an Expenditure Equation. *De Economist,* July-August 1973, *121*(4), pp. 375–86.

Hoch, Róbert and Kovács, Ilona. Changes in Income and Consumer Prices Affecting Demand. In *Földi, T., ed.,* 1973, pp. 65–88. [G: Europe; U.S.; Canada]

Janáček, K. Estimating the Aggregate Macroeconomic Consumption Function in Czechoslovakia. *Eastern Europ. Econ.,* Spring 1973, *11*(3), pp. 74–107. [G: Czechoslovakia]

Landsberger, Michael. Children's Age as a Factor Affecting the Simultaneous Determination of Consumption and Labor Supply. *Southern Econ. J.,* October 1973, *40*(2), pp. 279–88. [G: U.S.; Israel]

Leijonhufvud, Axel. Effective Demand Failures. *Swedish J. Econ.,* March 1973, *75*(1), pp. 27–48.

Lluch, Constantino. The Extended Linear Expenditure System. *Europ. Econ. Rev.,* April 1973, *4*(1), pp. 21–32.

Mikesell, Raymond F. and Zinser, James E. The Nature of the Savings Function in Developing Countries: A Survey of the Theoretical and Empirical Literature. *J. Econ. Lit.,* March 1973, *11*(1), pp. 1–26.

Moore, Robert L. Further Test of the Permanent Income Hypothesis Using Postwar Time-Series Data. *Southern Econ. J.,* October 1973, *40*(2), pp. 319–22. [G: U.S.]

Nakao, Takeo. An Examination of Duesenberry's Hypothesis on the Growth of Demand for the New Product. (In Japanese.) *Econ. Stud. Quart.,* April 1973, *24*(1), pp. 18–32.

Nemmers, Erwin E. Real as Opposed to Monetary Underconsumption or Hobson Revisited. *Nebr. J. Econ. Bus.,* Autumn 1973, *12*(4), pp. 69–76.

Okuno, Nobuhiro. Consumption Externalities and Total Demand Curves. *Econ. Stud. Quart.,* August 1973, *24*(2), pp. 61–66.

Parks, Richard W. and Barten, Anton P. A Cross-Country Comparison of the Effects of Prices, Income and Population Composition on Consumption Patterns. *Econ. J.,* September 1973, *83*(331), pp. 834–52.

Pesaran, M. Hashem. An Alternative Econometric Approach to the Permanent Income Hypothesis: An International Comparison: A Comment. *Rev. Econ. Statist.,* May 1973, *55*(2), pp. 259–61.

Powell, A. A. An ELES Consumption Function for the United States. *Econ. Rec.,* September 1973, *49*(127), pp. 337–57. [G: U.S.]

Rao, B. Bhaskara. An Alternative Econometric Approach to the Permanent Income Hypothesis: An International Comparison: A Comment. *Rev. Econ. Statist.,* May 1973, *55*(2), pp. 261.

Vakil, Firouz. Indian Saving Behavior: A Reconciliation of Time Series and Cross Section Evidence. *Rev. Income Wealth,* September 1973, *19*(3), pp. 307–23. [G: India]

Young, Warren L. Compulsory Loans and Consumption-Savings Behaviour: Some Micro- and Macro-Economic Aspects. *Public Finance,* 1973, *28*(3–4), pp. 333–53. [G: Israel]

0233 Theory of Aggregate Demand: Investment

Cass, David. On the Wicksellian Point-Input, Point-Output Model of Capital Accumulation: A Modern View (or, Neoclassicism Slightly Vindicated). *J. Polit. Econ.,* January-February 1973, *81*(1), pp. 71–97.

Chang, John C. and Holt, Charles C. Optimal Investment Orders Under Uncertainty and Dynamic Costs: Theory and Estimates. *Southern Econ. J.*, April 1973, *39*(4), pp. 508–25. [G: U.S.]

Elliott, J. W. Theories of Corporate Investment Behavior Revisited. *Amer. Econ. Rev.*, March 1973, *63*(1), pp. 195–207. [G: U.S.]

Erdös, T. Investments and Economic Growth. *Acta Oecon.*, 1973, *11*(4), pp. 281–303.

Feldstein, Martin S. Tax Incentives, Corporate Saving, and Capital Accumulation in the United States. *J. Public Econ.*, April 1973, *2*(2), pp. 159–71. [G: U.S.]

Gould, John P. and Waud, Roger N. The Neoclassical Model of Investment Behavior: Another View. *Int. Econ. Rev.*, February 1973, *14*(1), pp. 33–48.

Grossman, Steven D. A Test of Speed of Adjustment in Manufacturing Inventory Investment. *Quart. Rev. Econ. Bus.*, Autumn 1973, *13*(3), pp. 21–32. [G: U.S.]

Heubes, Jürgen. Investitionsverhalten in der Industrie der Bundesrepublik Deutschland 1950–1970. (Investment Behavior in the West-German Industry 1950–1970. With English summary.) *Z. ges. Staatswiss.*, October 1973, *129*(4), pp. 685–701. [G: W. Germany]

Horvat, Branko. Real Fixed Capital Costs Under Steady Growth. *Europ. Econ. Rev.*, April 1973, *4*(1), pp. 85–103.

Joyce, Jon M. Cost of Capital and Inventory Investment: Further Evidence. *Southern Econ. J.*, October 1973, *40*(2), pp. 323–29. [G: U.S.]

Laing, N. F. A Theory of Employment Fluctuations in the Full Employment Zone. *Econ. Rec.*, December 1973, *49*(128), pp. 546–59.

Maccini, Louis J. On Optimal Delivery Lags. *J. Econ. Theory*, April 1973, *6*(2), pp. 107–25.

Vartikar, V. S. On Optimizing the Rate of Investment. *Econ. Int.*, February 1973, *26*(1), pp. 17–31. [G: India]

Venieris, Yiannis P. Sales Expectations, Inventory Fluctuations, and Price Behavior. *Southern Econ. J.*, October 1973, *40*(2), pp. 246–61. [G: U.S.]

0234 Theory of Aggregate Supply

Brown, Murray. Toward an Econometric Accommodation of the Capital-Intensity-Perversity Phenomenon. *Econometrica*, September 1973, *41*(5), pp. 937–54.

Cornwall, Richard R. A Note on Using Profit Functions to Aggregate Production Functions. *Int. Econ. Rev.*, June 1973, *14*(2), pp. 511–19.

Fløystad, Gunnar. A Note on Estimating the Elasticity of Substitution Between Labour and Capital from Norwegian Time Series Data. *Swedish J. Econ.*, March 1973, *75*(1), pp. 100–04. [G: Norway]

Goldberger, Arthur S. Dependency Rates and Savings Rates: Further Comment. *Amer. Econ. Rev.*, March 1973, *63*(1), pp. 232–33.

Harris, Donald J. Capital, Distribution, and the Aggregate Production Function. *Amer. Econ. Rev.*, March 1973, *63*(1), pp. 100–13.

Helliwell, John F.; Sparks, Gordon and Frisch, Jack.

The Supply Price of Capital in Macroeconomic Models. In *Powell, A. A. and Williams, R. A., eds.*, 1973, pp. 261–83. [G: Canada; Australia]

Hicks, John R. [Sir]. Recollections and Documents. *Economica, N.S.*, February 1973, *40*(157), pp. 2–11.

Horvat, Branko. Real Fixed Capital Costs Under Steady Growth. *Europ. Econ. Rev.*, April 1973, *4*(1), pp. 85–103.

Ireland, Norman J.; Briscoe, G. and Smyth, David J. Specification Bias and Short-run Returns to Labour: Some Evidence for the United Kingdom. *Rev. Econ. Statist.*, February 1973, *55*(1), pp. 23–27. [G: U.K.]

Kennedy, Charles. The Death-rate of 'Tractors' and the Rate of Depreciation. *Oxford Econ. Pap.*, March 1973, *25*(1), pp. 57–59.

Krivenkov, Iu. P. A Production Model with Circulating Capital. *Matekon*, Summer 1973, *9*(4), pp. 67–79.

Leff, Nathaniel H. Dependency Rates and Savings Rates: Reply. *Amer. Econ. Rev.*, March 1973, *63*(1), pp. 234.

Lovell, C. A. Knox. A Note on Aggregation Bias and Loss. *J. Econometrics*, October 1973, *1*(3), pp. 301–11. [G: U.S.]

Lovell, C. A. Knox. CES and VES Production Functions in a Cross-Section Context. *J. Polit. Econ.*, May-June 1973, *81*(3), pp. 705–20. [G: U.S.]

Sandee, J. A Linear Macro Production Function for Long-Term Use. In *[Tinbergen, J.]*, 1973, pp. 99–110. [G: U.K.; Netherlands]

Stiglitz, Joseph E. Recurrence of Techniques in a Dynamic Economy. In *Mirrlees, J. A. and Stern, N. H., eds.*, 1973, pp. 138–61.

Stiglitz, Joseph E. The Badly Behaved Economy with the Well-Behaved Production Function. In *Mirrlees, J. A. and Stern, N. H., eds.*, 1973, pp. 117–37.

Zellner, Arnold and Richard, Jean F. Use of Prior Information in the Analysis and Estimation of Cobb-Douglas Production Function Models. *Int. Econ. Rev.*, February 1973, *14*(1), pp. 107–19.

0235 Theory of Aggregate Distribution

Adler, John H. Development and Income Distribution. *Finance Develop.*, September 1973, *10*(3), pp. 2–5.

Bernholz, Peter and Faber, Malte. Technical Productivity of Roundabout Processes and Positive Rate of Interest. A Capital Model with Depreciation and n-Period Horizon. *Z. ges. Staatswiss.*, February 1973, *129*(1), pp. 46–61.

Bharadwaj, V. P. and Dave, P. K. An Empirical Test of Kaldor's Macro Model of Income Distribution for Indian Economy. *Indian Econ. J.*, January-March 1973, *20*(3), pp. 515–20. [G: India]

Davidson, Paul. Inequality and the Double Bluff. *Ann. Amer. Acad. Polit. Soc. Sci.*, September 1973, *409*, pp. 24–33.

Dietz, James L. Paradise Reswitched. *Rev. Radical Polit. Econ.*, Summer 1973, *5*(2), pp. 1–17.

Drost, Helmar. Equilibrium Growth and the Relative Income Shares in a Two-sector Growth Model with Fixed Technical Coefficients: A Note.

Jahr. Nationalökon. Statist., May 1973, *187*(4), pp. 368–73.

Fishman, L. The Rate of Interest in a State of Economic Flux: Discussion. In *Parkin, M., ed.*, 1973, pp. 343–44.

Grossman, Herschel I. Aggregate Demand, Job Search, and Employment. *J. Polit. Econ.*, November-December 1973, *81*(6), pp. 1353–69.

Harris, Donald J. Capital, Distribution, and the Aggregate Production Function. *Amer. Econ. Rev.*, March 1973, *63*(1), pp. 100–13.

Helmstädter, Ernst. The Long-Run Movement of the Capital-Output Ratio and of Labour's Share. In *Mirrlees, J. A. and Stern, N. H., eds.*, 1973, pp. 3–17. **[G: U.K.; Germany; U.S.]**

Jaeger, Klaus. Sparverhalten und Vermögenspolitik in neoklassischen und generelleren Modellen. (Savings Behaviour and Distribution of Wealth in Neoclassical and More General Models. With English summary.) *Jahr. Nationalökon. Statist.*, March 1973, *187*(3), pp. 193–208.

Jaeger, Klaus. Income Distribution, Value of Capital, and Two Notions of the Wage-Profit Trade-Off: Comment. *Oxford Econ. Pap.*, July 1973, *25*(2), pp. 286–88.

Kennedy, Charles and Thirlwall, A. P. Technological Change and the Distribution of Income: A Belated Comment. *Int. Econ. Rev.*, October 1973, *14*(3), pp. 780–84.

Mathur, P. N. The Rate of Interest in a State of Economic Flux. In *Parkin, M., ed.*, 1973, pp. 330–42.

Metzler, Lloyd A. The Rate of Interest and the Marginal Product of Capital. In *Metzler, L. A.*, 1973, pp. 363–89.

Minsky, Hyman P. The Strategy of Economic Policy and Income Distribution. *Ann. Amer. Acad. Polit. Soc. Sci.*, September 1973, *409*, pp. 92–101.

Näslund, Bertil. Labor Power and Income Distribution. *Swedish J. Econ.*, June 1973, *75*(2), pp. 128–42.

Spandau, Arnt. Cross-Section Production Functions and Income-Shares in South African Industry. *S. Afr. J. Econ.*, September 1973, *41*(3), pp. 208–33. **[G: S. Africa]**

Stiglitz, Joseph E. Recurrence of Techniques in a Dynamic Economy. In *Mirrlees, J. A. and Stern, N. H., eds.*, 1973, pp. 138–61.

Stiglitz, Joseph E. The Badly Behaved Economy with the Well-Behaved Production Function. In *Mirrlees, J. A. and Stern, N. H., eds.*, 1973, pp. 117–37.

Tarascio, Vincent J. The Pareto Law of Income Distribution. *Soc. Sci. Quart.*, December 1973, *54*(3), pp. 525–33.

Tinbergen, Jan. Labour with Different Types of Skills and Jobs as Production Factors. *De Economist*, May-June 1973, *121*(3), pp. 213–24.

Tyler, William G. A Model of Income Distribution and Economic Development. *Weltwirtsch. Arch.*, 1973, *109*(2), pp. 321–36.

von Weizsäcker, Carl Christian. Modern Capital Theory and the Concept of Exploitation. *Kyklos*, 1973, *26*(2), pp. 245–81.

Woodfield, Alan. Biased Efficiency Growth and the Declining Relative Share of Labor in New Zealand Manufacturing. *Southern Econ. J.*, January 1973, *39*(3), pp. 373–80. **[G: New Zealand]**

024 Welfare Theory

0240 General

Akin, John S.; Fields, Gary S. and Neenan, William B. A Socioeconomic Explanation of Demand for Public Goods. *Public Finance Quart.*, April 1973, *1*(2), pp. 169–89. **[G: U.S.]**

Alchian, Armen A. and Demsetz, Harold. The Property Rights Paradigm. *J. Econ. Hist.*, March 1973, *33*(1), pp. 16–27.

d'Arge, Ralph C. Coase Theorem Symposium. *Natural Res. J.*, October 1973, *13*(4), pp. 557–60.

Arrow, Kenneth J. Rawls's Principle of Just Saving. *Swedish J. Econ.*, December 1973, *75*(4), pp. 323–35.

Asher, Ephraim. Consumers Time-Preferences and Welfare Economics under Socialism. *Scot. J. Polit. Econ.*, November 1973, *20*(3), pp. 283–90.

Atkinson, A. B. How Progressive Should Income Tax Be? In *Parkin, M., ed.*, 1973, pp. 90–109.

Auster, Richard and Silver, Morris. Collective Goods and Collective Decision Mechanisms. *Public Choice*, Spring 1973, *14*, pp. 1–17.

Barnett, William A. The Effects of Consumer Bliss on Welfare Economics. *J. Econ. Issues*, March 1973, *7*(1), pp. 29–45.

Bergstrom, Theodore C. and Goodman, Robert P. Private Demands for Public Goods. *Amer. Econ. Rev.*, June 1973, *63*(3), pp. 280–96.

Birmingham, Robert L. The Consumer as King: The Economics of Precarious Sovereignty. In *Murray, B. B., ed.*, 1973, pp. 212–24. **[G: U.S.]**

Bish, Robert L. and O'Donoghue, Patrick D. Public Goods, Increasing Cost, and Monopsony: Reply. *J. Polit. Econ.*, January-February 1973, *81*(1), pp. 231–36.

Boadway, Robin W.; Maital, Shlomo and Prachowny, Martin F. J. Optimal Tariffs, Optimal Taxes and Public Goods. *J. Public Econ.*, November 1973, *2*(4), pp. 391–403.

Boadway, Robin W. Similarities and Differences between Public Goods and Public Factors. *Public Finance*, 1973, *28*(3–4), pp. 245–58.

Boulding, Kenneth E. Economic Progress as a Goal in Economic Life. In *Boulding, K. E.*, 1973, pp. 53–86.

Brown, Kenneth M. Welfare Implications of Congestion in Public Goods. *Rev. Soc. Econ.*, April 1973, *31*(1), pp. 89–92.

Burns, Michael E. A Note on the Concept and Measure of Consumer's Surplus. *Amer. Econ. Rev.*, June 1973, *63*(3), pp. 335–44.

Chipman, John S. and Moore, James C. Aggregate Demand, Real National Income, and the Compensation Principle. *Int. Econ. Rev.*, February 1973, *14*(1), pp. 153–81.

Clark, Colin. The Marginal Utility of Income. *Oxford Econ. Pap.*, July 1973, *25*(2), pp. 145–59.

D'Albergo, Ernesto. "Relativizzazione" di un teorema. (On the Relativity of a Theorem. With English summary.) *Econ. Int.*, February 1973, *26*(1), pp. 35–45.

Dasgupta, Partha; Sen, Amartya K. and Starrett, David. Notes on the Measurement of Inequality. *J. Econ. Theory,* April 1973, *6*(2), pp. 180–87.

Davis, Otto A. and Whinston, Andrew B. The Economics of Urban Renewal. In *Grieson, R. E., ed.,* 1973, pp. 163–77.

Demsetz, Harold. Joint Supply and Price Discrimination. *J. Law Econ.,* October 1973, *16*(2), pp. 389–405.

Demsetz, Harold. The Private Production of Public Goods: Reply. *J. Law Econ.,* October 1973, *16*(2), pp. 413–15.

Diamond, Peter A. Taxation and Public Production in a Growth Setting. In *Mirrlees, J. A. and Stern, N. H., eds.,* 1973, pp. 215–35.

Ekelund, Robert B., Jr. and Hulett, Joe R. Joint Supply, the Taussig-Pigou Controversy, and the Competitive Provision of Public Goods. *J. Law Econ.,* October 1973, *16*(2), pp. 369–87.

Ellickson, Bryan. A Generalization of the Pure Theory of Public Goods. *Amer. Econ. Rev.,* June 1973, *63*(3), pp. 417–32.

Feldstein, Martin S. On the Optimal Progressivity of the Income Tax. *J. Public Econ.,* November 1973, *2*(4), pp. 357–76.

Ferejohn, John and Page, Talbot. A Note on "Voting or a Price System in a Competitive Market Structure." *Amer. Polit. Sci. Rev.,* March 1973, *67*(1), pp. 157–60.

Fisher, Anthony C. A Paradox in the Theory of Public Investment. *J. Public Econ.,* November 1973, *2*(4), pp. 405–07.

Friedlaender, Ann F. Macro Policy Goals in the Postwar Period: A Study in Revealed Preference. *Quart. J. Econ.,* February 1973, *87*(1), pp. 25–43. [G: U.S.]

von Furstenberg, George M. and Spulber, Nicolas. Is There an Economic System Based on Sovereignty of Each Consumer? *Z. Nationalökon.,* 1973, *33* (3–4), pp. 361–74.

von Furstenberg, George M. Welfare Maximization: Samuelson's Analysis with Public and Private Goods. *Public Finance Quart.,* October 1973, *1* (4), pp. 426–36.

Galbraith, John Kenneth. The Theory of Social Balance. In *Reynolds, L. G.; Green, G. D. and Lewis, D. R., eds.,* 1973, pp. 304–14. [G: U.S.]

Gale, David. Pure Exchange Equilibrium of Dynamic Economic Models. *J. Econ. Theory,* February 1973, *6*(1), pp. 12–36.

Greene, Kenneth V. Attitudes Toward Risk and the Relative Size of the Public Sector. *Public Finance Quart.,* April 1973, *1*(2), pp. 205–18.

Greene, Kenneth V. and Newlon, Daniel H. The Pareto Optimality of Eliminating a Lottery Draft. *Quart. Rev. Econ. Bus.,* Winter 1973, *13*(4), pp. 61–70.

Greene, Kenneth V. Inheritance Unjustified? *J. Law Econ.,* October 1973, *16*(2), pp. 417–19.

Gupta, Rajendra K. Social Welfare Functions. *Indian Econ. J.,* January-March 1973, *20*(3), pp. 414–30.

Güth, Werner. Zur wohlfahrtsökonomischen Bedeutung marktwirtschaftlicher Verhandlungsgleichgewichte. (Welfare Economic Meaning of Market Economies' Competitive Equilibria. With English summary.) *Z. ges. Staatswiss.,* August 1973, *129* (3), pp. 445–53.

Hahn, Frank H. On Optimum Taxation. *J. Econ. Theory,* February 1973, *6*(1), pp. 96–106.

Hayami, Yujiro and Peterson, Willis. Social Return to Public Information Services: Statistical Reporting of U.S. Farm Commodities: Reply. *Amer. Econ. Rev.,* December 1973, *63*(5), pp. 1020–21. [G: U.S.]

Head, John G. Public Goods and Multi-Level Government. In *[Hicks, U.],* 1973, pp. 20–43.

Hildenbrand, Werner and Kirman, Alan P. Size Removes Inequity. *Rev. Econ. Stud.,* July 1973, *40* (3), pp. 305–19.

Homma, Masaaki. A Dynamic Pigovian Policy Under Production Externalities. *Econ. Stud. Quart.,* August 1973, *24*(2), pp. 26–30.

Ireland, Thomas R. Inheritance Justified: Comment. *J. Law Econ.,* October 1973, *16*(2), pp. 421–22.

Isard, Walter and Liossatos, Panagis. Social Injustice and Optimal Space-Time Development. *J. Peace Sci.,* Autumn 1973, *1*(1), pp. 69–93.

Johnson, Harry G. Notes on the Welfare Effects of a Reversed Transfer. *Osaka Econ. Pap.,* March 1973, *21*(38), pp. 45–52.

Koller, Roland H., II. Inheritance Justified: Comment. *J. Law Econ.,* October 1973, *16*(2), pp. 423–24.

Kramer, Gerald H. On a Class of Equilibrium Conditions for Majority Rule. *Econometrica,* March 1973, *41*(2), pp. 285–97.

Loehman, Edna and Whinston, A. Reply to Forster and Logan. *Appl. Econ.,* March 1973, *5*(1), pp. 69–73.

MacRae, Duncan, Jr. Normative Assumptions in the Study of Public Choice. *Public Choice,* Fall 1973, *16,* pp. 27–41.

Maekawa, Koichi. A Note on the Estimation of the Pareto Distribution. *Econ. Stud. Quart.,* December 1973, *24*(3), pp. 63–66.

Maital, Shlomo. Public Goods and Income Distribution: Some Further Results. *Econometrica,* May 1973, *41*(3), pp. 561–68.

Marchand, James R. and Russell, Keith P. Externalities, Liability, Separability, and Resource Allocation. *Amer. Econ. Rev.,* September 1973, *63*(4), pp. 611–20.

Marty, Alvin L. Growth, Satiety, and the Tax Revenue from Money Creation. *J. Polit. Econ.,* September-October 1973, *81*(5), pp. 1136–52.

Minnehan, Robert F. Multiple Objectives and Multigroup Decision Making in Physical Design Situations. In *Cochrane, J. L. and Zeleny, M., eds.,* 1973, pp. 506–16. [G: U.S.]

Mirrlees, James A. National Income and Social Values: Rejoinder. *Bangladesh Econ. Rev.,* January 1973, *1*(1), pp. 101–02.

Mishan, Ezra J. Welfare Criteria: Resolution of a Paradox. *Econ. J.,* September 1973, *83*(331), pp. 747–67.

Mohring, Herbert and Maslove, Allan. The Optimal Provision of Public Goods: Yet Another Comment. *J. Polit. Econ.,* May-June 1973, *81*(3), pp. 778–85.

Ng, Yew-Kwang. The Economic Theory of Clubs:

Pareto Optimality Conditions. *Economica, N.S.,* August 1973, *40*(159), pp. 291–98.

Oi, Walter Y. The Economics of Product Safety. *Bell J. Econ. Manage. Sci.,* Spring 1973, *4*(1), pp. 3–28.

Osana, Hiroaki. On the Boundedness of an Economy with Externalities. *Rev. Econ. Stud.,* July 1973, *40* (3), pp. 321–31.

Ostrom, Vincent. The Work of the Contemporary Political Economists. In *Ostrom, V.,* 1973, pp. 48–73.

Pejovich, Svetozar. Good Old Economic History: Discussion. *J. Econ. Hist.,* March 1973, *33*(1), pp. 41–42.

Peterson, George E. Welfare, Workfare, and Pareto Optimality. *Public Finance Quart.,* July 1973, *1* (3), pp. 323–38.

Pham, Chung. On Some Aspects of the Theory of Grants Economics. *Soc. Sci. Quart.,* December 1973, *54*(3), pp. 632–38.

Phelps, Edmund S. Taxation of Wage Income for Economic Justice. *Quart. J. Econ.,* August 1973, *87*(3), pp. 331–54.

van Praag, Bernard M. S. and Kapteyn, Arie. Further Evidence on the Individual Welfare Function of Income: An Empirical Investigation in The Netherlands. *Europ. Econ. Rev.,* April 1973, *4*(1), pp. 33–62. [G: Netherlands]

Rahman, Md. Anisur. National Income and Social Values. *Bangladesh Econ. Rev.,* January 1973, *1* (1), pp. 95–101.

Ray, Paramesh. Independence of Irrelevant Alternatives. *Econometrica,* September 1973, *41*(5), pp. 987–91.

Reaume, David M. Cost-Benefit Techniques and Consumer Surplus: A Clarificatory Analysis. *Public Finance,* 1973, *28*(2), pp. 196–211.

Roskamp, Karl W. Pareto Optimal Redistribution, Utility Interdependence and Social Optimum. *Weltwirtsch. Arch.,* 1973, *109*(2), pp. 337–44.

Rothschild, Michael and Stiglitz, Joseph E. Some Further Results on the Measurement of Inequality. *J. Econ. Theory,* April 1973, *6*(2), pp. 188–204.

Scitovsky, Tibor. The Place of Economic Welfare in Human Welfare. *Quart. Rev. Econ. Bus.,* Autumn 1973, *13*(3), pp. 7–19.

Sen, Amartya K. On Ignorance and Equal Distribution. *Amer. Econ. Rev.,* December 1973, *63*(5), pp. 1022–24.

Sen, Amartya K. Behaviour and the Concept of Preference. *Economica, N.S.,* August 1973, *40*(159), pp. 241–59.

Shell, Karl. Inventive Activity, Industrial Organisation and Economic Growth. In *Mirrlees, J. A. and Stern, N. H., eds.,* 1973, pp. 77–96.

Shibata, Hirofumi. Public Goods, Increasing Cost, and Monopsony: Comment. *J. Polit. Econ.,* January-February 1973, *81*(1), pp. 223–30.

Simon, Julian L. Does Economic Growth Imply a Growth in Welfare? *J. Econ. Issues,* March 1973, *7*(1), pp. 130–36.

Smith, Lawrence N. and Scherr, Bruce A. Social Return to Public Information Services: Statistical Reporting of U.S. Farm Commodities: Comment. *Amer. Econ. Rev.,* December 1973, *63*(5), pp. 1017–19. [G: U.S.]

Starr, Ross M. Optimal Production and Allocation under Uncertainty. *Quart. J. Econ.,* February 1973, *87*(1), pp. 81–95.

Taylor, Lance. Two Generalizations of Discounting. In *Eckaus, R. S. and Rosenstein-Rodan, P. N., eds.,* 1973, pp. 31–45.

Thompson, Earl A. The Private Production of Public Goods: Comment. *J. Law Econ.,* October 1973, *16* (2), pp. 407–12.

Thompson, Wilbur R. The City as a Distorted Price System. In *Grieson, R. E., ed.,* 1973, pp. 4–14.

Topham, Neville. Micro-Economic Risk and the Social Rate of Discount. In *Parkin, M., ed.,* 1973, pp. 139–55.

Trezza, Bruno. La teoria del second best: una critica. (On the Theory of Second Best: a Critique. With English summary.) *L'Industria,* January-June 1973, (1–2), pp. 18–35.

Tribe, Laurence H. Policy Science: Analysis or Ideology? In *Niskanen, W. A., et al., eds.,* 1973, pp. 3–47.

Tullock, Gordon. Inheritance Rejustified. *J. Law Econ.,* October 1973, *16*(2), pp. 425–28.

Wallich, Henry C. Could Galbraith be Wrong? In *Reynolds, L. G.; Green, G. D. and Lewis, D. R., eds.,* 1973, pp. 315–22. [G: U.S.]

West, E. G. The Bilateral Monopoly Theory of Public Goods: A Critique. *J. Polit. Econ.,* September-October 1973, *81*(5), pp. 1226–35.

Winch, David M. The Pure Theory of Non-Pure Goods. *Can. J. Econ.,* May 1973, *6*(2), pp. 149–63.

Wolfe, J. N. Cost Benefit and Cost Effectiveness: Studies and Analysis: Introduction. In *Wolfe, J. N., ed.,* 1973, pp. 9–14.

Worland, Stephen T. The Economic Significance of John Rawls' A Theory of Justice. *Nebr. J. Econ. Bus.,* Autumn 1973, *12*(4), pp. 119–26.

Zeckhauser, Richard J. Determining the Qualities of a Public Good—A Paradigm on Town Park Location. *Western Econ. J.,* March 1973, *11*(1), pp. 39–60.

0242 Allocative Efficiency Including Theory of Cost/Benefit

Beenhakker, Henri L. Discounting Indices Proposed for Capital Investment Evaluation: A Further Examination. *Eng. Econ.,* April-May 1973, *18*(3), pp. 149–68.

Bernhard, Richard H. Consumer Surplus as an Index of User Benefit from Public Expenditure. *Eng. Econ.,* October-November 1973, *19*(1), pp. 1–33.

Bhagwati, Jagdish N. and Srinivasan, T. N. Smuggling and Trade Policy. *J. Public Econ.,* November 1973, *2*(4), pp. 377–89.

Bhagwati, Jagdish N. and Srinivasan, T. N. The General Equilibrium Theory of Effective Protection and Resource Allocation. *J. Int. Econ.,* August 1973, *3*(3), pp. 259–81.

Brada, Josef C. The Allocative Efficiency of Centrally Planned Foreign Trade: A Programming Approach to the Czech Case. *Europ. Econ. Rev.,* December 1973, *4*(4), pp. 329–46. [G: Czechoslovakia]

Bronsard, Camille. The Computational Economics of Jacques Lesourne. *J. Public Econ.,* July 1973, *2*(3), pp. 271–80.

Brown, Gardner, Jr. and Johnson, M. Bruce. Welfare-Maximizing Price and Output with Stochastic Demand: Reply. *Amer. Econ. Rev.*, March 1973, *63* (1), pp. 230–31.

Bruno, M. Protection and Tariff Change under General Equilibrium. *J. Int. Econ.*, August 1973, *3*(3), pp. 205–25.

Corti, G. Risk, Uncertainty and Cost Benefit: Some Notes on Practical Difficulties for Project Appraisals. In *Wolfe, J. N., ed.*, 1973, pp. 75–87.

Crocker, Thomas D. Contractual Choice. *Natural Res. J.*, October 1973, *13*(4), pp. 561–77.

Culyer, Anthony J. Pareto, Peacock and Rowley, and Policy Towards Natural Monopoly: Comment. *J. Public Econ.*, February 1973, *2*(1), pp. 89–95.

Dougherty, Christopher and Selowsky, Marcelo. Measuring the Effects of the Misallocation of Labour. *Rev. Econ. Statist.*, August 1973, *55*(3), pp. 386–90.   [G: Colombia]

Feldman, Allan M. Bilateral Trading, Processes, Pairwise Optimality, and Pareto Optimality. *Rev. Econ. Stud.*, October 1973, *40*(4), pp. 463–73.

Feldstein, Martin S. The Welfare Loss of Excess Health Insurance. *J. Polit. Econ.*, Part I, March-April 1973, *81*(2), pp. 251–80.   [G: U.S.]

Feldstein, Martin S. Cost-Benefit Analysis in Developing Countries: The Evaluation of Projects Financed by Aid and External Loans. In *[Hicks, U.]*, 1973, pp. 3–19.

Fischer, Dietrich. Kosten-Nutzen-Analysen. (Cost-Benefit-Analyses. With English summary.) *Z. ges. Staatswiss.*, May 1973, *129*(2), pp. 230–45.

Foster, C. D. A Note on the Treatment of Taxation in Cost-benefit Analysis. In *Wolfe, J. N., ed.*, 1973, pp. 63–74.   [G: U.K.]

Green, H. A. John. Public Sector Resource Allocation under Conditions of Risk: Discussion. In *Parkin, M., ed.*, 1973, pp. 137–38.

Guadagni, Alieto A. La evaluación social de los proyectos industriales según "Guidelines for Project Evaluation" de Unido. (Social Evaluation of Industrial Projects According Unidó's "Guidelines for Project Evaluation." With English summary.) *Económica*, May-August 1973, *19*(2), pp. 165–83.

Harberger, Arnold C. On Measuring the Social Opportunity Cost of Public Funds. In *Harberger, A. C.*, 1973, pp. 94–122.

Harberger, Arnold C. Survey of Literature on Cost-Benefit Analysis for Industrial Project Evaluation. In *Harberger, A. C.*, 1973, pp. 23–69.

Hillinger, Claude. Sales Maximization as an Explanation of Near Pareto Optimality of the U.S. Economy. *Jahr. Nationalökon. Statist.*, May 1973, *187* (4), pp. 364–67.   [G: U.S.]

Hirshleifer, Jack. Where Are We in the Theory of Information? *Amer. Econ. Rev.*, May 1973, *63*(2), pp. 31–39.

Hurwicz, Leonid. The Design of Mechanisms for Resource Allocation. *Amer. Econ. Rev.*, May 1973, *63* (2), pp. 1–30.

Laing, N. F. Technological Uncertainty and the Pure *Ex Ante* Theory of the Allocation of Resources. *Australian Econ. Pap.*, December 1973, *12*(21), pp. 221–38.

Lind, Robert C. Spatial Equilibrium, the Theory of Rents, and the Measurement of Benefits from Public Programs. *Quart. J. Econ.*, May 1973, *87* (2), pp. 188–207.

Lloyd, P. J. Optimal Intervention in a Distortion-Ridden Open Economy. *Econ. Rec.*, September 1973, *49*(127), pp. 377–93.

Merewitz, Leonard. Cost Overruns in Public Works. In *Niskanen, W. A., et al., eds.*, 1973, pp. 277–95.   [G: U.S.]

Mirrlees, James A. The Integration of Project and Sector Analysis: Discussion. In *Parkin, M., ed.*, 1973, pp. 167–69.

Naouri, Jean-Charles. Le financement des investissements publics. Les deux taux d'actualisation et la charge morte du transfert fiscal. (Financing Public Expenditure and the Deadweight Loss of Fiscal Transfers. With English summary.) *Revue Écon.*, July 1973, *24*(4), pp. 588–618.

Negishi, Takashi. The Excess of Public Expenditures on Industries. *J. Public Econ.*, July 1973, *2*(3), pp. 231–40.

Nelson, Phillip. Economics of Information: Discussion. *Amer. Econ. Rev.*, May 1973, *63*(2), pp. 50–51.

Nwaneri, V. C. Income Distribution and Project Selection. *Finance Develop.*, September 1973, *10* (3), pp. 27–29, 33.

Peacock, Alan. Cost-benefit Analysis and the Political Control of Public Investment. In *Wolfe, J. N., ed.*, 1973, pp. 17–29.   [G: U.S.; U.K.]

Peacock, Alan T. and Rowley, Charles K. Welfare Economics and the Public Regulation of Natural Monopoly: Reply. *J. Public Econ.*, February 1973, *2*(1), pp. 97–100.

Ray, Alok. Non-Traded Inputs and Effective Protection: A General Equilibrium Analysis. *J. Int. Econ.*, August 1973, *3*(3), pp. 245–57.

Rees, R. Public Sector Resource Allocation under Conditions of Risk. In *Parkin, M., ed.*, 1973, pp. 110–36.

Roberts, Blaine. An Extension of Optimality Criteria: An Axiomatic Approach to Institutional Choice. *J. Polit. Econ.*, Part I, March-April 1973, *81*(2), pp. 386–400.

Roberts, Donald John. Existence of Lindahl Equilibrium with a Measure Space of Consumers. *J. Econ. Theory*, August 1973, *6*(4), pp. 355–81.

Sadler, P. G. The Integration of Project and Sector Analysis. In *Parkin, M., ed.*, 1973, pp. 156–66.

Sadowski, Dieter. Zur Berücksichtigung des Verteilungsaspektes in der Cost-Benefit-Analyse. (The Aspect of Distribution in Cost-Benefit-Analysis. With English summary.) *Z. ges. Staatswiss.*, May 1973, *129*(2), pp. 215–29.

Stern, Nicholas. Homogeneous Utility Functions and Equality in "The Optimum Town." A Note. *Swedish J. Econ.*, June 1973, *75*(2), pp. 204–07.

Taylor, Lance. Investment Project Analysis in Terms of a Model of Optical Growth: The Case of Chile. In *Eckaus, R. S. and Rosenstein-Rodan, P. N., eds.*, 1973, pp. 167–98.   [G: Chile]

Terre, Norbert C.; Warnke, Dale W. and Ameiss, Albert P. Cost/Benefit Analysis of Public Projects. *Manage. Account.*, January 1973, *54*(7), pp. 34–37.

Thomas, H. The Assessment of Project Worth with Applications to Research and Development. In *Wolfe, J. N., ed.,* 1973, pp. 88–114.

Thygesen, Inge. Ranking of Interdependent Investment Projects. In *Ross, M., ed.,* 1973, pp. 531–40.

Visscher, Michael L. Welfare-Maximizing Price and Output with Stochastic Demand: Comment. *Amer. Econ. Rev.,* March 1973, *63*(1), pp. 224–29.

Weinstein, Milton C. and Zeckhauser, Richard J. Critical Ratios and Efficient Allocation. *J. Public Econ.,* April 1973, *2*(2), pp. 147–57.

Weld, John. Coase, Social Cost and Stability: An Integrative Essay. *Natural Res. J.,* October 1973, *13* (4), pp. 595–613.

Williams, Alan. Cost-benefit Analysis: Bastard Science? And/Or Insidious Poison in the Body Politick? In *Wolfe, J. N., ed.,* 1973, pp. 30–60.

Williams, Alan. Cost-Benefit Analysis: Bastard Science? And/Or Insidious Poison in the Body Politick? In *Niskanen, W. A., et al., eds.,* 1973, pp. 48–74.

Wolfe, J. N. Cost Benefit and Cost Effectiveness: Studies and Analysis: Introduction. In *Wolfe, J. N., ed.,* 1973, pp. 9–14.

0243 Redistributive Aspects

Alchian, Armen A. and Allen, William R. The Pure Economics of Giving. In *Alchian, A. A., et al.,* 1973, pp. 3–13.

Behrens, Jean and Smolensky, Eugene. Alternative Definitions of Income Redistribution. *Public Finance,* 1973, *28*(3–4), pp. 315–32.

Bittker, Boris I. Should Foundations Be Third-Class Charities? In *Heimann, F. F., ed.,* 1973, pp. 132–62. [G: U.S.]

Boulding, Kenneth E. Equality and Conflict. *Ann. Amer. Acad. Polit. Soc. Sci.,* September 1973, *409*, pp. 1–8.

Brennan, Geoffrey and Walsh, Cliff. Pareto-Optimal Redistribution Reconsidered. *Public Finance Quart.,* April 1973, *1*(2), pp. 147–68.

Brennan, Geoffrey. Pareto Desirable Redistribution: The Non-Altruistic Dimension. *Public Choice,* Spring 1973, *14*, pp. 43–67.

Brennan, Geoffrey. Pareto Desirable Redistribution: The Case of Malice and Envy. *J. Public Econ.,* April 1973, *2*(2), pp. 173–83.

Brim, Orville G., Jr. Do We Know What We Are Doing? In *Heimann, F. F., ed.,* 1973, pp. 216–58. [G: U.S.]

Bronfenbrenner, Martin. Equality and Equity. *Ann. Amer. Acad. Polit. Soc. Sci.,* September 1973, *409*, pp. 9–23.

Brown, Charles; Fane, George and Medoff, James. The Income Distribution as a Pure Public Good: Comment. *Quart. J. Econ.,* May 1973, *87*(2), pp. 296–303.

Brownlee, Oswald. The Effects of Inflation on the Distribution of Economic Welfare: Comment. *J. Money, Credit, Banking,* Part II, February 1973, *5*(1), pp. 505–06. [G: U.S.]

Buttler, Friedrich. Explikative und normative Theorie der meritorishen Güter—eine Problemanalyse. (A Theory of Merit Goods. With English summary.) *Z. Wirtschaft. Sozialwissen.,* 1973, *93*(2), pp. 129–46.

Canterbery, E. R. and Tuckman, Howard P. The Income Distribution as a Pure Public Good: Comment. *Quart. J. Econ.,* May 1973, *87*(2), pp. 304–10.

Cazenave, Philippe and Morrisson, Christian. Fonctions d'utilité interdépendantes et théorie de la redistribution en économie de production. (Interdependent Utility Functions and Redistribution Theory in a Production Economy. With English summary.) *Revue Écon.,* September 1973, *24*(5), pp. 725–60.

Cooper, Michael H. and Culyer, Anthony J. The Economics of Giving and Selling Blood. In *Alchian, A. A., et al.,* 1973, pp. 109–43.

Culyer, Anthony J. Quids without Quos—A Praxeological Approach. In *Alchian, A. A., et al.,* 1973, pp. 33–61.

Dean, James M. Redistribution and Tax Concessions for Charitable Contributions. *Public Finance,* 1973, *28*(3–4), pp. 371–76.

Faber, Malte. Einstimmigkeitsregel und Einkommensumverteilung. (Rule of Unanimity and Income Redistribution. With English summary.) *Kyklos,* 1973, *26*(1), pp. 36–57.

Friedman, Richard E. Private Foundation-Government Relationships. In *Heimann, F. F., ed.,* 1973, pp. 163–91. [G: U.S.]

Garfinkel, Irwin. Is In-Kind Redistribution Efficient? *Quart. J. Econ.,* May 1973, *87*(2), pp. 320–30.

Hamada, Koichi. A Simple Majority Rule on the Distribution of Income. *J. Econ. Theory,* June 1973, *6*(3), pp. 243–64.

Hart, Jeffrey. Foundations and Social Activism: A Critical View. In *Heimann, F. F., ed.,* 1973, pp. 43–57. [G: U.S.]

Hochman, Harold M. and Rodgers, James D. Utility Interdependence and Income Transfers through Charity. In *Boulding, K. E.; Pfaff, M. and Pfaff, A., eds.,* 1973, pp. 63–77. [G: U.S.]

Hochman, Harold M. and Rodgers, James D. Brennan and Walsh Reconsidered. (Mutt and Jeff Ride Again.) *Public Finance Quart.,* October 1973, *1* (4), pp. 359–71.

Hochman, Harold M.; Rodgers, James D. and Tullock, Gordon. The Income Distribution as a Pure Public Good: Comment. *Quart. J. Econ.,* May 1973, *87*(2), pp. 311–15.

Ireland, Thomas R. and Koch, James V. Blood and American Social Attitudes. In *Alchian, A. A., et al.,* 1973, pp. 145–55. [G: U.S.]

Ireland, Thomas R. The Calculus of Philanthropy. In *Alchian, A. A., et al.,* 1973, pp. 63–78.

James, H. Thomas. Perspectives on Internal Functioning of Foundations. In *Heimann, F. F., ed.,* 1973, pp. 192–215. [G: U.S.]

Jhunjhunwala, Bharat. Hypothetical Compensation: Is it Relevant? *Indian Econ. J.,* January-March 1973, *20*(3), pp. 445–51.

Johnson, David B. The Charity Market: Theory and Practice. In *Alchian, A. A., et al.,* 1973, pp. 79–106. [G: U.S.]

Kessel, Reuben A. The Effects of Inflation on the Distribution of Economic Welfare: Comment. *J. Money, Credit, Banking,* Part II, February 1973,

5(1), pp. 507–08. [G: U.S.]

Labovitz, John R. 1969 Tax Reforms Reconsidered. In *Heimann, F. F., ed.*, 1973, pp. 101–31.
[G: U.S.]

Lancaster, Kelvin. Politically Feasible Income Redistribution in a Democracy. *Amer. Econ.*, Fall 1973, *17*(2), pp. 79–84.

Minsky, Hyman P. The Strategy of Economic Policy and Income Distribution. *Ann. Amer. Acad. Polit. Soc. Sci.*, September 1973, *409*, pp. 92–101.

Molitor, Bruno. Öffentliche Leistungen in verteilungspolitischer Sicht. (Social Goods and Income Redistribution. With English summary.) *Z. Wirtschaft. Sozialwissen.*, 1973, *93*(2), pp. 147–58.

Morrison, Clarence C. and Higgins, Richard S. A Further Note on Distributional Equality. *Southern Econ. J.*, January 1973, *39*(3), pp. 442–43.

Ng, Yew-Kwang. Income Distribution as a Peculiar Public Good: The Paradox of Redistribution and the Paradox of Universal Externality. *Public Finance*, 1973, *28*(1), pp. 1–10.

Nordhaus, William D. The Effects of Inflation on the Distribution of Economic Welfare. *J. Money, Credit, Banking*, Part II, February 1973, *5*(1), pp. 465–504. [G: U.S.]

Parrish, Thomas. The Foundation: "A Special American Institution." In *Heimann, F. F., ed.*, 1973, pp. 7–42. [G: U.S.]

Pauly, Mark V. Income Redistribution as a Local Public Good. *J. Public Econ.*, February 1973, *2*(1), pp. 35–58.

Polinsky, A. Mitchell. A Note on the Measurement of Incidence. *Public Finance Quart.*, April 1973, *1*(2), pp. 219–30.

Rodgers, James D. Distributional Externalities and the Optimal Form of Income Transfers. *Public Finance Quart.*, July 1973, *1*(3), pp. 266–99.

Sadowski, Dieter. Zur Berücksichtigung des Verteilungsaspektes in der Cost-Benefit-Analyse. (The Aspect of Distribution in Cost-Benefit-Analysis. With English summary.) *Z. ges. Staatswiss.*, May 1973, *129*(2), pp. 215–29.

Simon, John G. Foundations and Public Controversy: An Affirmative View. In *Heimann, F. F., ed.*, 1973, pp. 58–100. [G: U.S.]

Szeplaki, Leslie. A Note on the Redistributive Effects of Socialist Wage and Price Policies. *Rivista Int. Sci. Econ. Com.*, November 1973, *20*(11), pp. 1109–15.

Thurow, Lester C. The Income Distribution as a Pure Public Good: Response. *Quart. J. Econ.*, May 1973, *87*(2), pp. 316–19.

Tinbergen, Jan. Actual, Feasible and Optimal Income Inequality in a Three-Level Education Model. *Ann. Amer. Acad. Polit. Soc. Sci.*, September 1973, *409*, pp. 156–62. [G: Netherlands]

Tullock, Gordon. The Charity of the Uncharitable. In *Alchian, A. A., et al.*, 1973, pp. 15–32.

0244 Externalities

Alessio, Frank J. A Neo-Classical Land Use Model: The Influence of Externalities. *Swedish J. Econ.*, December 1973, *75*(4), pp. 414–19.

Artle, Roland and Averous, Christian P. The Telephone System as a Public Good: Static and Dynamic Aspects. *Bell J. Econ. Manage. Sci.*, Spring 1973, *4*(1), pp. 89–100.

Barnett, Andy H. and Yandle, Bruce, Jr. Allocating Environmental Resources. *Public Finance*, 1973, *28*(1), pp. 11–19.

Bergstrom, Theodore C. The Use of Markets to Control Pollution. *Rech. Écon. Louvain*, December 1973, *39*(4), pp. 403–18.

Blair, Roger D. Problems of Pollution Standards: The Clean Air Act of 1970. *Land Econ.*, August 1973, *49*(3), pp. 260–68. [G: U.S.]

Borglin, Anders. Price Characterization of Stable Allocations in Exchange Economies with Externalities. *J. Econ. Theory*, October 1973, *6*(5), pp. 483–94.

Buchanan, James M. The Institutional Structure of Externality. *Public Choice*, Spring 1973, *14*, pp. 69–82.

Buchanan, James M. The Coase Theorem and the Theory of the State. *Natural Res. J.*, October 1973, *13*(4), pp. 579–94.

Byrne, Robert F. and Spiro, Michael H. On Taxation as a Pollution Control Policy. *Swedish J. Econ.*, March 1973, *75*(1), pp. 105–09.

Cheung, Steven N. S. The Fable of the Bees: An Economic Investigation. *J. Law Econ.*, April 1973, *16*(1), pp. 11–33. [G: U.S.]

Chung, Pham. A Note on a Standard Theorem of Welfare Economics. *Indian Econ. J.*, January-March 1973, *20*(3), pp. 440–44.

Common, Michael S. and Pearce, David W. Adaptive Mechanisms, Growth, and the Environment: The Case of Natural Resources. *Can. J. Econ.*, August 1973, *6*(3), pp. 289–300.

Daly, George A. and Giertz, Fred J. Pollution Abatement, Pareto Optimality, and the Market Mechanism. In *Boulding, K. E.; Pfaff, M. and Pfaff, A., eds.*, 1973, pp. 350–58.

Diamond, Peter A. Consumption Externalities and Imperfect Corrective Pricing. *Bell J. Econ. Manage. Sci.*, Autumn 1973, *4*(2), pp. 526–38.

Diamond, Peter A. and Mirrlees, James A. Aggregate Production with Consumption Externalities. *Quart. J. Econ.*, February 1973, *87*(1), pp. 1–24.

Ethridge, Don. The Inclusion of Wastes in the Theory of the Firm. *J. Polit. Econ.*, November-December 1973, *81*(6), pp. 1430–41.

Fisher, Anthony C. Environmental Externalities and the Arrow-Lind Public Investment Theorem. *Amer. Econ. Rev.*, September 1973, *63*(4), pp. 722–25.

Forster, Bruce A. Optimal Consumption Planning in a Polluted Environment. *Econ. Rec.*, December 1973, *49*(128), pp. 534–45.

Frech, H. E., III. Pricing of Pollution: The Coase Theorem in the Long Run. *Bell J. Econ. Manage. Sci.*, Spring 1973, *4*(1), pp. 316–19.

Ghali, Moheb A. On Measuring "Third Party" Effects of a Strike. *Western Econ. J.*, June 1973, *11*(2), pp. 214–27. [G: U.S.]

Gifford, Adam, Jr. and Stone, Courtenay C. Externalities, Liability and the Coase Theorem: A Mathematical Analysis. *Western Econ. J.*, September 1973, *11*(3), pp. 260–69.

Gould, J. R. Meade on External Economies: Should

the Beneficiaries Be Taxed? *J. Law Econ.*, April 1973, *16*(1), pp. 53–66.

Haveman, Robert H. Common Property, Congestion, and Environmental Pollution. *Quart. J. Econ.*, May 1973, *87*(2), pp. 278–87.

Haworth, Joan G. Externalities and the City. In *Rasmussen, D. W. and Haworth, C. T., eds.*, 1973, pp. 28–30. [G: U.S.]

Homma, Masaaki. A Dynamic Pigovian Policy Under Production Externalities. *Econ. Stud. Quart.*, August 1973, *24*(2), pp. 26–30.

Hufbauer, G. C. Environmental Quality, Income Distribution, and Factor Mobility: The Consequences of Local Action. *J. Econ. Issues*, June 1973, *7*(2), pp. 323–35.

Hunt, E. K. and d'Arge, Ralph C. On Lemmings and Other Acquisitive Animals: Propositions on Consumption. *J. Econ. Issues*, June 1973, *7*(2), pp. 337–53.

Inada, Ken-Ichi and Kuga, Kiyoshi. Limitations of the "Coase Theorem" on Liability Rules. *J. Econ. Theory*, December 1973, *6*(6), pp. 606–13.

Johnson, David B. Meade, Bees and Externalities. *J. Law Econ.*, April 1973, *16*(1), pp. 35–52.

Kamien, Morton I.; Schwartz, Nancy L. and Roberts, Donald John. Exclusion, Externalities, and Public Goods. *J. Public Econ.*, July 1973, *2*(3), pp. 217–30.

Kneese, Allen V. and Mäler, Karl-Göran. Bribes and Charges in Pollution Control: An Aspect of the Coase Controversy. *Natural Res. J.*, October 1973, *13*(4), pp. 705–16.

Kolm, Serge-Christophe. Les pollués doivent-ils payer? (With English summary.) *Kyklos,* 1973, *26*(2), pp. 322–36.

Krier, James E. and Montgomery, W. David. Resource Allocation, Information Cost and the Form of Government Intervention. *Natural Res. J.*, January 1973, *13*(1), pp. 89–105.

Kuipers, S. K. and Nentjes, A. Pollution in a Neo-Classical World: The Classics Rehabilitated? *De Economist,* January-February 1973, *121*(1), pp. 52–67.

Lanzillotti, Robert F. and Blair, Roger D. Automobile Pollution, Externalities and Public Policy. *Antitrust Bull.*, Fall, 1973, *18*(3), pp. 431–47. [G: U.S.]

Liebhafsky, H. H. "The Problem of Social Cost" —An Alternative Approach. *Natural Res. J.,* October 1973, *13*(4), pp. 615–76.

McGuire, Thomas. A Note on Lindahl's Voluntary Exchange Theory. *Public Finance*, 1973, *28*(1), pp. 94–97.

Mishan, Ezra J. The Nature of External Diseconomies. In *Grieson, R. E., ed.*, 1973, pp. 234–44.

Näslund, Bertil. Pollution and the Value of Time. *Europ. Econ. Rev.*, June 1973, *4*(2), pp. 181–96.

Ng, Yew-Kwang. Income Distribution as a Peculiar Public Good: The Paradox of Redistribution and the Paradox of Universal Externality. *Public Finance*, 1973, *28*(1), pp. 1–10.

Okuno, Nobuhiro. Consumption Externalities and Total Demand Curves. *Econ. Stud. Quart.*, August 1973, *24*(2), pp. 61–66.

Osana, Hiroaki. On the Boundedness of an Economy with Externalities. *Rev. Econ. Stud.*, July 1973, *40*(3), pp. 321–31.

Osana, Hiroaki. Externalities and the Basic Theorems of Welfare Economics: A Supplementary Note. *J. Econ. Theory*, February 1973, *6*(1), pp. 91–93.

Page, Talbot. Failure of Bribes and Standards for Pollution Abatement. *Natural Res. J.*, October 1973, *13*(4), pp. 677–704.

Richelson, Jeffrey. A Note on Collective Goods and the Theory of Political Entrepreneurship. *Public Choice*, Fall 1973, *16*, pp. 73–75.

Rich, Jack. Natural Resources and External Economies: Regulation of the Pacific Halibut Fishery. In *Sokoloski, A. A., ed.*, 1973, pp. 65–71. [G: U.S.]

Roberts, Donald John. Existence of Lindahl Equilibrium with a Measure Space of Consumers. *J. Econ. Theory*, August 1973, *6*(4), pp. 355–81.

Rose-Ackerman, Susan. Effluent Charges: A Critique. *Can. J. Econ.*, November 1973, *6*(4), pp. 512–28.

Rosenthal, Robert W. Taxation vs. Prohibition of an External Diseconomy by Direct Vote: A Game Theoretic Approach. *Int. Econ. Rev.*, June 1973, *14*(2), pp. 414–20.

Rueter, Frederick H. Externalities in Urban Property Markets: An Empirical Test of the Zoning Ordinance of Pittsburgh. *J. Law Econ.*, October 1973, *16*(2), pp. 313–49. [G: U.S.]

Ruff, Larry E. The Economic Common Sense of Pollution. In *Enthoven, A. C. and Freeman, A. M., III, eds.*, 1973, pp. 37–53. [G: U.S.]

Schatz, Sayre P. Externalities, Divergences, and the Profitability Criterion. *Quart. Rev. Econ. Bus.*, Winter 1973, *13*(4), pp. 19–26.

Seskin, Eugene P. Residential Choice and Air Pollution: A General Equilibrium Model. *Amer. Econ. Rev.*, December 1973, *63*(5), pp. 960–67.

Siebert, Horst. Environment and Regional Growth. *Z. Nationalökon.*, 1973, *33*(1–2), pp. 79–85.

Starrett, David A. A Note on Externalities and the Core. *Econometrica*, January 1973, *41*(1), pp. 179–83.

Strotz, Robert H. and Wright, Colin. Externalities, Welfare Economics, and Environmental Problems. In *Boulding, K. E.; Pfaff, M. and Pfaff, A., eds.*, 1973, pp. 359–73.

Stroup, Richard and Baden, John. Externality, Property Rights, and the Management of our National Forests. *J. Law Econ.*, October 1973, *16*(2), pp. 303–12. [G: U.S.]

Tietenberg, Thomas H. Controlling Pollution by Price and Standard Systems: A General Equilibrium Analysis. *Swedish J. Econ.*, June 1973, *75*(2), pp. 193–203.

Tietenberg, Thomas H. Specific Taxes and the Control of Pollution: A General Equilibrium Analysis. *Quart. J. Econ.*, November 1973, *87*(4), pp. 503–22.

Tybout, Richard A. Pricing of Pollution: The Coase Theorem in the Long Run: Reply. *Bell J. Econ. Manage. Sci.*, Spring 1973, *4*(1), pp. 320–21.

Walsh, Cliff and Tisdell, Clem. Non-marginal Externalities: As Relevant and As Not. *Econ. Rec.*, September 1973, *49*(127), pp. 447–55.

Wedin, Dick. Externalities and Open Field Burning:

A Case Study. *Amer. J. Agr. Econ.*, December 1973, *55*(5), pp. 1026–29. [G: U.S.]

Weissler, Mark L. Snowmobiles and the Environment. *Yale Law J.*, March 1973, *82*(4), pp. 772–86. [G: U.S.]

Weld, John. Coase, Social Cost and Stability: An Integrative Essay. *Natural Res. J.*, October 1973, *13*(4), pp. 595–613.

Wenders, John T. Corrective Taxes and Pollution Abatement. *J. Law Econ.*, October 1973, *16*(2), pp. 365–68.

025 Social Choice

0250 Social Choice

Ames, Edward. The Emerging Theory of Comparative Economic Systems. *Amer. Econ.*, Spring 1973, *17*(1), pp. 22–28.

Auster, Richard and Silver, Morris. Collective Goods and Collective Decision Mechanisms. *Public Choice*, Spring 1973, *14*, pp. 1–17.

Barro, Robert J. The Control of Politicians: An Economic Model. *Public Choice*, Spring 1973, *14*, pp. 19–42.

Barton, David M. Constitutional Choice and Simple Majority Rule: Comment. *J. Polit. Econ.*, Part I, March-April 1973, *81*(2), pp. 471–79.

Barzel, Yoram and Silberberg, Eugene. Is the Act of Voting Rational? *Public Choice*, Fall 1973, *16*, pp. 51–58. [G: U.S.]

Baudier, Edmond. Competitive Equilibrium in a Game. *Econometrica*, November 1973, *41*(6), pp. 1049–68.

Bernholz, Peter. Logrolling, Arrow Paradox and Cyclical Majorities. *Public Choice*, Summer 1973, *15*, pp. 87–95.

Blin, Jean-Marie. Intransitive Social Orderings and the Probability of the Condorcet Effect. *Kyklos*, 1973, *26*(1), pp. 25–35.

Brody, Richard A. and Page, Benjamin I. Indifference, Alienation and Rational Decisions: The Effects of Candidate Evaluations on Turnout and the Vote. *Public Choice*, Summer 1973, *15*, pp. 1–17. [G: U.S.]

Brown, Kenneth M. and Zech, Charles E. Welfare Effects of Announcing Election Forecasts. *Public Choice*, Spring 1973, *14*, pp. 117–23.

Buchanan, James M. The Institutional Structure of Externality. *Public Choice*, Spring 1973, *14*, pp. 69–82.

Buchanan, James M. The Coase Theorem and the Theory of the State. *Natural Res. J.*, October 1973, *13*(4), pp. 579–94.

Campbell, Donald E. Social Choice and Intensity of Preference. *J. Polit. Econ.*, January-February 1973, *81*(1), pp. 211–18.

Conway, William J. Economic Dominants and Community Power: A Reputational and Decisional Analysis. *Amer. J. Econ. Soc.*, July 1973, *32*(3), pp. 269–82.

Faber, Malte. Einstimmigkeitsregel und Einkommensumverteilung. (Rule of Unanimity and Income Redistribution. With English summary.) *Kyklos*, 1973, *26*(1), pp. 36–57.

Fach, Wolfgang. Über einige Schwierigkeiten der Neuen Politischen Ökonomie: Das Beispiel der Koalitionstheorie. (Some Difficulties of the New Political Economy: The Example of the Coalition Theory. With English summary.) *Z. ges. Staatswiss.*, May 1973, *129*(2), pp. 347–74.

Ferejohn, John and Page, Talbot. A Note on "Voting or a Price System in a Competitive Market Structure." *Amer. Polit. Sci. Rev.*, March 1973, *67*(1), pp. 157–60.

Fine, Kit. Conditions for the Existence of Cycles Under Majority and Non-Minority Rules. *Econometrica*, September 1973, *41*(5), pp. 889–99.

Fishburn, Peter C. Transitive Binary Social Choices and Intraprofile Conditions. *Econometrica*, July 1973, *41*(4), pp. 603–15.

Fishburn, Peter C. Summation Social Choice Functions. *Econometrica*, November 1973, *41*(6), pp. 1183–96.

Frech, H. E., III. The Public Choice Theory of Murray N. Rothbard, A Modern Anarchist. *Public Choice*, Spring 1973, *14*, pp. 143–54.

Frey, Bruno S. and Frey, Rene L. The Economic Theory of Politics: A Survey of German Contributions. *Public Choice*, Fall 1973, *16*, pp. 81–89. [G: Germany]

Garrabe, Michel. Échange, transferts et préférences éthiques. (Exchange, Transfers and Ethical Preferences. With English summary.) *Public Finance*, 1973, *28*(3–4), pp. 280–90. [G: France]

Gibbard, Allan. Manipulation of Voting Schemes: A General Result. *Econometrica*, July 1973, *41*(4), pp. 587–601.

Greene, Kenneth V. Attitudes Toward Risk and the Relative Size of the Public Sector. *Public Finance Quart.*, April 1973, *1*(2), pp. 205–18.

Güth, Werner. Zur wohlfahrtsökonomischen Bedeutung marktwirtschaftlicher Verhandlungsgleichgewichte. (Welfare Economic Meaning of Market Economies' Competitive Equilibria. With English summary.) *Z. ges. Staatswiss.*, August 1973, *129*(3), pp. 445–53.

Gwartney, James and Silberman, Jonathan. Distribution of Costs and Benefits and the Significance of Collective Decision Rules. *Soc. Sci. Quart.*, December 1973, *54*(3), pp. 568–78.

Hamada, Koichi. A Simple Majority Rule on the Distribution of Income. *J. Econ. Theory*, June 1973, *6*(3), pp. 243–64.

Hansen, Thomas J. and Prince, Barry L. The Paradox of Voting: An Elementary Solution for the Case of Three Alternatives. *Public Choice*, Summer 1973, *15*, pp. 103–17.

Harlow, Robert L. On the Decline and Possible Fall of PPBS. *Public Finance Quart.*, January 1973, *1*(1), pp. 85–105.

Harnett, Donald L. and Hamner, W. Clay. The Value of Information in Bargaining. *Western Econ. J.*, March 1973, *11*(1), pp. 81–88.

Helman, Amir and Shechter, Mordechai. Collective Decision-Making in a Kibbutz: A Case Study. *Public Finance*, 1973, *28*(2), pp. 139–50. [G: Israel]

Inagaki, M. Intertemporal National Optimality and Temporal Social Preferences. In *Mirrlees,*

J. A. and Stern, N. H., eds., 1973, pp. 241–54.

Intriligator, Michael D. A Probabilistic Model of Social Choice. *Rev. Econ. Stud.,* October 1973, *40* (4), pp. 553–60.

Ireland, Thomas R. Micropolitics and Macroeconomics: Discussion. *Amer. Econ. Rev.,* May 1973, *63*(2), pp. 179–80. [G: U.S.]

Kazmann, Raphael G. Democratic Organization: A Preliminary Mathematical Model. *Public Choice,* Fall 1973, *16,* pp. 17–26.

Klevorick, Alvin K. and Kramer, Gerald H. Social Choice on Pollution Management: The Genossenschaften. *J. Public Econ.,* April 1973, *2*(2), pp. 101–46. [G: W. Germany]

Kramer, Gerald H. On a Class of Equilibrium Conditions for Majority Rule. *Econometrica,* March 1973, *41*(2), pp. 285–97.

Kushner, Harvey W. and Urken, Arnold B. Measuring Power in Voting Bodies. *Public Choice,* Summer 1973, *15,* pp. 77–85.

Lucier, Richard I. The Prediction of Public Choice Behavior in the Washington Tax Substitution Referendum. *Nat. Tax J.,* December 1973, *26*(4), pp. 625–30. [G: U.S.]

MacRae, Duncan, Jr. Normative Assumptions in the Study of Public Choice. *Public Choice,* Fall 1973, *16,* pp. 27–41.

Marz, Roger H.; Casstevens, Thomas W. and Casstevens, Harold T., II. The Hunting of the Paradox. *Public Choice,* Summer 1973, *15,* pp. 97–102.

McCracken, Paul W. The Practice of Political Economy. *Amer. Econ. Rev.,* May 1973, *63*(2), pp. 168–71. [G: U.S.]

Medler, Jerry F. and Tull, Donald S. Poll Positions and Win Probabilities: A Stochastic Model of the Electoral Process. *Public Choice,* Spring 1973, *14,* pp. 125–32.

Mueller, Dennis C. Constitutional Democracy and Social Welfare. *Quart. J. Econ.,* February 1973, *87* (1), pp. 60–80.

Murray, Barbara B. A Pure Theory of Local Expenditures Revisited. In *Mattila, J. M. and Thompson, W. R., eds.,* 1973, pp. 129–39.

Okun, Arthur M. General Economic Conditions and National Elections: Comment. *Amer. Econ. Rev.,* May 1973, *63*(2), pp. 172–77. [G: U.S.]

Ostrom, Vincent. The Work of the Contemporary Political Economists. In *Ostrom, V.,* 1973, pp. 48–73.

Pattanaik, Prasanta K. On the Stability of Sincere Voting Situations. *J. Econ. Theory,* December 1973, *6*(6), pp. 558–74.

Plott, Charles R. Path Independence, Rationality, and Social Choice. *Econometrica,* November 1973, *41*(6), pp. 1075–91.

Rader, J. Trout. An Economic Approach to Social Choice. *Public Choice,* Summer 1973, *15,* pp. 49–75.

Ray, Paramesh. Independence of Irrelevant Alternatives. *Econometrica,* September 1973, *41*(5), pp. 987–91.

Riker, William H. Micropolitics and Macroeconomics: Discussion. *Amer. Econ. Rev.,* May 1973, *63* (2), pp. 178–80. [G: U.S.]

Roberts, Blaine. An Extension of Optimality Criteria:

An Axiomatic Approach to Institutional Choice. *J. Polit. Econ.,* Part I, March-April 1973, *81*(2), pp. 386–400.

Rosenthal, Robert W. Taxation vs. Prohibition of an External Diseconomy by Direct Vote: A Game Theoretic Approach. *Int. Econ. Rev.,* June 1973, *14*(2), pp. 414–20.

Rürup, Bert. Handlungsverzögerungen diskretionärer Fiskalpolitik: Konstruktionsfehler oder Element rationaler Politik? (Decision Lags of Discretionary Fiscal Policy: Defects of Construction or Element of a Rational Policy. With English summary.) *Z. Wirtschaft. Sozialwissen.,* 1973, *93* (1), pp. 35–50.

Shapley, Lloyd S. Let's Block "Block." *Econometrica,* November 1973, *41*(6), pp. 1201–02.

Sloss, Judith. Stable Outcomes in Majority Rule Voting Games. *Public Choice,* Summer 1973, *15,* pp. 19–48.

Smith, John H. Aggregation of Preferences with Variable Electorate. *Econometrica,* November 1973, *41*(6), pp. 1027–41.

Stigler, George J. General Economic Conditions and National Elections. *Amer. Econ. Rev.,* May 1973, *63*(2), pp. 160–67. [G: U.S.]

Tollison, Robert D. and Willet, Thomas D. Some Simple Economics of Voting and Not Voting. *Public Choice,* Fall 1973, *16,* pp. 59–71.

Tribe, Laurence H. Policy Science: Analysis or Ideology? In *Niskanen, W. A., et al., eds.,* 1973, pp. 3–47.

Tullock, Gordon. Constitutional Choice and Simple Majority Rule: Reply. *J. Polit. Econ.,* Part I, March-April 1973, *81*(2), pp. 480–84.

Whitmore, G. A. Health State Preferences and the Social Choice. In *Berg, R. L., ed.,* 1973, pp. 135–45.

Wilson, Ewen M. The Rhodesian Constitution and Predictions for Political Stability. *Public Choice,* Fall 1973, *16,* pp. 77–80. [G: Rhodesia]

Wittman, Donald A. Parties as Utility Maximizers. *Amer. Polit. Sci. Rev.,* June 1973, *67*(2), pp. 490–98.

Zeckhauser, Richard J. Voting Systems, Honest Preferences and Pareto Optimality. *Amer. Polit. Sci. Rev.,* September 1973, *67*(3), pp. 934–46.

030 HISTORY OF THOUGHT; METHODOLOGY

031 History of Economic Thought

0310 General

Agnati, Achille. Dal calcolo dell'opinione nei preclassici all'analisi economica dell'esogeneità. (From the Calculus of Consent in the Preclassics to the Economic Analysis of Exogeneity. With English summary.) *Rivista Int. Sci. Econ. Com.,* February 1973, *20*(2), pp. 153–78.

Arndt, H. W. Development Economics Before 1945. In *[Rosenstein-Rodan, P.],* 1973, pp. 13–29.

Bronfenbrenner, Martin. Samuelson, Marx, and

Their Latest Critics. *J. Econ. Lit.*, March 1973, *11* (1), pp. 58–63.

Carpenter, Kenneth E. and Redlich, Fritz. Research Possibilities in the History of Political Economy Through a Bibliography of Translations. *Hist. Polit. Econ.*, Spring 1973, *5*(1), pp. 268–83.

Ekelund, Robert B., Jr. and Hebert, Robert F. Public Economics at the Ecole des Ponts et Chaussées: 1830–1850. *J. Public Econ.*, July 1973, *2*(3), pp. 241–56.

Groenewegen, P. D. A Note on the Origin of the Phrase, "Supply and Demand" *Econ. J.*, June 1973, *83*(330), pp. 505–09.

Karsten, Siegfried G. Dialetics and the Evolution of Economic Thought. *Hist. Polit. Econ.*, Fall 1973, *5*(2), pp. 399–419.

Kiker, B. F. and Cochrane, James L. War and Human Capital in Western Economic Analysis. *Hist. Polit. Econ.*, Fall 1973, *5*(2), pp. 375–98.

Kleiman, Ephraim. An Early Modern Hebrew Textbook of Economics. *Hist. Polit. Econ.*, Fall 1973, *5*(2), pp. 339–58.

Matsuura, Tamotsu. L'evoluzione del pensiero economico moderno in Giappone. (The Evolution of Modern Economic Thought in Japan. With English summary.) *Rivista Int. Sci. Econ. Com.*, August-September 1973, *20*(8–9), pp. 839–52.
[G: Japan]

Patinkin, Don. In Search of the "Wheel of Wealth": On the Origins of Frank Knight's Circular-Flow Diagram. *Amer. Econ. Rev.*, December 1973, *63* (5), pp. 1037–46.

Pavitt, K. L. R. Malthus and Other Economists: Some Doomsdays Revisited. In *Cole, H. S. D., et al., eds.*, 1973, pp. 137–58.

Rotwein, Eugene. The Ideology of Wealth and the Liberal Economic Heritage: The Neglected View. *Soc. Res.*, Summer 1973, *40*(2), pp. 269–92.

Samuelson, Paul A. Samuelson's "Reply on Marxian Matters." *J. Econ. Lit.*, March 1973, *11*(1), pp. 64–68.

Treml, Vladimir G. and Gallik, Dimitri, M. Teaching the History of Economic Thought in the USSR. *Hist. Polit. Econ.*, Spring 1973, *5*(1), pp. 215–42.
[G: U.S.S.R.]

Van Rompuy, H. Het stagnatieprobleem. Verleden en heden. (The Stagnation-Thesis. With English summary.) *Tijdschr. Econ.*, 1973, *18*(1), pp. 65–86.

Velupillai, K. A Note on the Origin of the 'Correspondence Principle'. *Swedish J. Econ.*, September 1973, *75*(3), pp. 302–04.

Weintraub, Sidney. Keynes and the Theory of Derived Demand. In *Weintraub, S., et al.*, 1973, pp. 51–70.

Weisskopf, Walter A. The Image of Man in Economics. *Soc. Res.*, Autumn 1973, *40*(3), pp. 547–63.

Weisskopf, Walter A. Economic Growth versus Existential Balance. In *Daly, H. E., ed.*, 1973, pp. 240–51.

0311 Ancient, Medieval

Postan, M. M. Why Was Science Backward in the Middle Ages? In *Postan, M. M. (I)*, 1973, pp. 81–86.
[G: W. Europe]

0312 Pre-Classical Except Mercantilist

Rasmussen, Jørgen. Dual Theories and the Classics. In *Institute for Development Research*, 1973, pp. 61–74.

Sekine, Thomas T. The Discovery of International Monetary Equilibrium by Vanderlint, Cantillon, Gervaise and Hume. *Econ. Int.*, May 1973, *26*(2), pp. 262–82.

0313 Mercantilist

Allen, William R. The Interpretation of Mercantilist Economics: Some Historiographical Problems: Rearguard Response. *Hist. Polit. Econ.*, Fall 1973, *5*(2), pp. 496–98.

Coats, A. W. The Interpretation of Mercantilist Economics: Some Historiographical Problems. *Hist. Polit. Econ.*, Fall 1973, *5*(2), pp. 485–95.

Overbeek, Johannes. Mercantilism, Physiocracy and Population Theory. *S. Afr. J. Econ.*, June 1973, *41* (2), pp. 167–74.

0314 Classical

Akhtar, M. A. The Stationary State of Ricardo and Malthus: Comment. *Intermountain Econ. Rev.*, Spring 1973, *4*(1), pp. 77–79.

Black, R. D. Collison. Libero scambio e imperialismo nel pensiero e nella politica economica dei classici inglesi. (Free Trade and Imperialism in English Classical Economic Thought and Policy. With English summary.) *Rivista Int. Sci. Econ. Com.*, July 1973, *20*(7), pp. 640–49. [G: U.S.]

Clower, Robert W. and Leijonhufvud, Axel. Say's Principle, What it Means and Doesn't Mean: Part I. *Intermountain Econ. Rev.*, Fall 1973, *4*(2), pp. 1–16.

Cochrane, James L. Ricardo on the Rate of Profit and Distributive Shares: Comment. *Indian Econ. J.*, January-March 1973, *20*(3), pp. 521–22.

Ekelund, Robert B., Jr. and Olsen, Emilie S. Comte, Mill, and Cairnes: The Positivist-Empiricist Interlude in Late Classical Economics. *J. Econ. Issues*, September 1973, *7*(3), pp. 383–416.

Ferguson, C. E. The Specialization Gap: Barton, Ricardo, and Hollander. *Hist. Polit. Econ.*, Spring 1973, *5*(1), pp. 1–13.

Gootzeit, Michael J. The Corn Laws and Wage Adjustment in a Short-Run Ricardian Model. *Hist. Polit. Econ.*, Spring 1973, *5*(1), pp. 50–71.

Gordon, Scott. The Wage-Fund Controversy: The Second Round. *Hist. Polit. Econ.*, Spring 1973, *5* (1), pp. 14–35.

Grampp, William D. Classical Economics and Its Moral Critics. *Hist. Polit. Econ.*, Fall 1973, *5*(2), pp. 359–74.

Hollander, Samuel. Ricardo's Analysis of the Profit Rate, 1813–15. *Economica, N.S.*, August 1973, *40* (159), pp. 260–82.

Kaushil, S. The Case of Adam Smith's Value Analysis. *Oxford Econ. Pap.*, March 1973, *25*(1), pp. 60–71.

Kittrell, Edward R. Wakefield's Scheme of Systematic Colonization and Classical Economics.

Amer. J. Econ. Soc., January 1973, *32*(1), pp. 87–111.

Kolb, Fredric R. The Stationary State of Ricardo and Malthus: Reply. *Intermountain Econ. Rev.,* Spring 1973, *4*(1), pp. 80.

Lamb, Robert. Adam Smith's Concept of Alienation. *Oxford Econ. Pap.,* July 1973, *25*(2), pp. 275–85.

de Marchi, N. B. and Sturges, R. P. Malthus and Ricardo's Inductivist Critics: Four Letters to William Whewell. *Economica, N.S.,* November 1973, *40*(160), pp. 379–93.

Meek, Ronald L. and Skinner, Andrew S. The Development of Adam Smith's Ideas on the Division of Labour. *Econ. J.,* December 1973, *83*(332), pp. 1094–1116.

Nord, Walter. Adam Smith and Contemporary Social Exchange Theory. *Amer. J. Econ. Soc.,* October 1973, *32*(4), pp. 421–36.

Okishio, Nobuo. On the Convergence of Marx's 'Transformation' Procedure. (In Japanese. With English summary.) *Econ. Stud. Quart.,* August 1973, *24*(2), pp. 40–45.

Prasad, K. N. The Value Approach in the Classical Theory of Distribution-II. *Econ. Aff.,* September-October 1973, *18*(9–10), pp. 475–76.

Prasad, K. N. The Value Approach in the Classical Theory of Distribution. *Econ. Aff.,* August 1973, *18*(8), pp. 372–80.

Prasad, K. N. The Value Approach in the Classical Theory of Distribution—III. *Econ. Aff.,* November-December 1973, *18*(11–12), pp. 503–10.

Samuels, Warren J. Adam Smith and the Economy as a System of Power. *Rev. Soc. Econ.,* October 1973, *31*(2), pp. 123–37.

Staley, Charles E. A Note on Adam Smith's Version of the Vent for Surplus Model. *Hist. Polit. Econ.,* Fall 1973, *5*(2), pp. 438–48.

0315 Austrian, Marshallian, Neoclassical

Borch, Karl. The Place of Uncertainty in the Theories of the Austrian School. In *Hicks, J. R. and Weber, W., eds.,* 1973, pp. 61–74.

Collard, David. Léon Walras and the Cambridge Caricature. *Econ. J.,* June 1973, *83*(330), pp. 465–76.

Gordon, Scott. The Wage-Fund Controversy: The Second Round. *Hist. Polit. Econ.,* Spring 1973, *5*(1), pp. 14–35.

Hicks, John R. [Sir]. The Austrian Theory of Capital and Its Rebirth in Modern Economics. In *Hicks, J. R. and Weber, W., eds.,* 1973, pp. 190–206.

Humphrey, Thomas M. On the Monetary Economics of Chicagoans and Non-Chicagoans: Reply. *Southern Econ. J.,* January 1973, *39*(3), pp. 460–63.

Hunt, E. K. and d'Arge, Ralph C. On Lemmings and Other Acquisitive Animals: Propositions on Consumption. *J. Econ. Issues,* June 1973, *7*(2), pp. 337–53.

Menger, Karl. Austrian Marginalism and Mathematical Economics. In *Hicks, J. R. and Weber, W., eds.,* 1973, pp. 38–60.

Moss, Laurence S. Isaac Butt and the Early Development of the Marginal Utility Theory of Imputa-

tion. *Hist. Polit. Econ.,* Fall 1973, *5*(2), pp. 317–38.

Nussbaumer, Adolf. On the Compatibility of Subjective and Objective Theories of Economic Value. In *Hicks, J. R. and Weber, W., eds.,* 1973, pp. 75–91.

Patinkin, Don. On the Monetary Economics of Chicagoans and Non-Chicagoans: Comment. *Southern Econ. J.,* January 1973, *39*(3), pp. 454–59.

Rothschild, Kurt W. Distributive Aspects of the Austrian Theory. In *Hicks, J. R. and Weber, W., eds.,* 1973, pp. 207–25.

Rowthorn, Bob. Neoclassical Economics and its Critics: A Marxist View. *Pakistan Econ. Soc. Rev.,* Autumn 1973, *11*(3), pp. 316–48.

Streissler, Erich W. and Weber, Wilhelm. The Menger Tradition. In *Hicks, J. R. and Weber, W., eds.,* 1973, pp. 226–32.

Tarascio, Vincent J. Vilfredo Pareto: On the Occasion of the Translation of His Manuel. *Can. J. Econ.,* August 1973, *6*(3), pp. 394–408.

0316 General Equilibrium until 1945

Hicks, John R. [Sir]. Recollections and Documents. *Economica, N.S.,* February 1973, *40*(157), pp. 2–11.

Schuster, Helmut. Keynes' Disequilibrium Analysis. *Kyklos,* 1973, *26*(3), pp. 512–44.

Uhr, Carl G. The Emergence of the "New Economics" in Sweden: A Review of a Study by Otto Steiger. *Hist. Polit. Econ.,* Spring 1973, *5*(1), pp. 243–60. **[G: Sweden]**

Walker, Donald A. Edgeworth's Theory of Recontract. *Econ. J.,* March 1973, *83*(329), pp. 138–49.

0317 Socialist until 1945

Baker, Robert P. Labor History, Social Science, and the Concept of the Working Class. *Labor Hist.,* Winter 1973, *14*(1), pp. 98–105.

Becker, James F. Class Structure and Conflict in the Managerial Phase: I. *Sci. Soc.,* Fall 1973, *37*(3), pp. 259–77.

Bronfenbrenner, Martin. "Samuelson and Marx": Reply. *J. Econ. Lit.,* December 1973, *11*(4), pp. 1367.

Constantinescu, N. N. Cadrul economic, social şi politic în care a apărut Manifestul Partidului Comunist. (The Economic, Social and Political Background Against which the Manifesto of the Communist Party was Published. With English summary.) *Stud. Cercet. Econ.,* 1973, (2), pp. 25–32.

Fusfeld, Daniel R. Types of Radicalism in American Economics. *Amer. Econ. Rev.,* May 1973, *63*(2), pp. 145–51.

Kresl, Peter Karl. Nikolai Bukharin on Economic Imperalism. *Rev. Radical Polit. Econ.,* Spring 1973, *5*(1), pp. 3–12.

Laibman, David. Values and Prices of Production: The Political Economy of the Transformation Problem. *Sci. Soc.,* Winter 1973–1974, *37*(4), pp. 404–36.

Morris, Jacob and Lewin, Haskell. The Skilled Labor

Reduction Problem. *Sci. Soc.*, Winter 1973–1974, *37*(4), pp. 454–72.

Robinson, Joan. "Samuelson and Marx." *J. Econ. Lit.*, December 1973, *11*(4), pp. 1367.

Samuelson, Paul A. "Samuelson and Marx": Reply. *J. Econ. Lit.*, December 1973, *11*(4), pp. 1367.

Smolinski, Leon. Karl Marx and Mathematical Economics. *J. Polit. Econ.*, September-October 1973, *81*(5), pp. 1189–1204.

Szeplaki, Leslie. Some Reflections on Marxian Equilibria and Socialist Economic Policy. *Indian Econ. J.*, January-March 1973, *20*(3), pp. 431–39.

von Weizsäcker, Carl Christian. Morishima on Marx. *Econ. J.*, December 1973, *83*(332), pp. 1245–54.

Wolfstetter, E. Surplus Labour, Synchronised Labor Costs and Marx's Labour Theory of Value. *Econ. J.*, September 1973, *83*(331), pp. 787–809.

0318 Historical and Institutional

Aufhauser, R. Keith. Slavery and Scientific Management. *J. Econ. Hist.*, December 1973, *33*(4), pp. 811–24. [G: U.S.]

Breit, William. The Development of Clarence Ayres's Theoretical Institutionalism. *Soc. Sci. Quart.*, September 1973, *54*(2), pp. 244–57.

Gruchy, Allan G. Law, Politics, and Institutional Economics. *J. Econ. Issues,* December 1973, *7*(4), pp. 623–43. [G: U.S.]

Johnpoll, Bernard K. Manuscript Sources in American Radicalism. *Labor Hist.*, Winter 1973, *14*(1), pp. 92–97. [G: U.S.]

Leathers, Charles G. and Evans, John S. Thorstein Veblen and the New Industrial State. *Hist. Polit. Econ.*, Fall 1973, *5*(2), pp. 420–37.

McNulty, Paul J. Hoxie's Economics in Retrospect: The Making and Unmaking of a Veblenian. *Hist. Polit. Econ.*, Fall 1973, *5*(2), pp. 449–84.

Tilman, Rick. Thorstein Veblen: Incrementalist and Utopian. *Amer. J. Econ. Soc.*, April 1973, *32*(2), pp. 155–69.

032 History of Economic Thought
(continued)

0321 Other Schools Since 1800

Buchanan, James M. Introduction: L.S.E. Cost Theory in Retrospect. In *Buchanan, J. M. and Thirlby, G. F., eds.*, 1973, pp. 1–16.

Ekelund, Robert B., Jr. and Hooks, Donald L. Ellet, Dupuit, and Lardner: On Nineteenth Century Engineers and Economic Analysis. *Nebr. J. Econ. Bus.*, Summer 1973, *12*(3), pp. 43–52.

Humphrey, Thomas M. Empirical Tests of the Quantity Theory of Money in the United States, 1900–1930. *Hist. Polit. Econ.*, Fall 1973, *5*(2), pp. 285–316. [G: U.S.]

Uhr, Carl G. The Emergence of the "New Economics" in Sweden: A Review of a Study by Otto Steiger. *Hist. Polit. Econ.*, Spring 1973, *5*(1), pp. 243–60. [G: Sweden]

0322 Individuals

Ayres, Clarence. E.

Ayers, C. E. and Burger, David H. In Memo-

riam. *Amer. J. Econ. Soc.*, July 1973, *32*(3), pp. 335–36.

Breit, William. The Development of Clarence Ayres's Theoretical Institutionalism. *Soc. Sci. Quart.*, September 1973, *54*(2), pp. 244–57.

Bukharin, Nikolai

Kresl, Peter Karl. Nikolai Bukharin on Economic Imperialism. *Rev. Radical Polit. Econ.*, Spring 1973, *5*(1), pp. 3–12.

Butt, Isaac

Moss, Laurence S. Isaac Butt and the Early Development of the Marginal Utility Theory of Imputation. *Hist. Polit. Econ.*, Fall 1973, *5*(2), pp. 317–38.

Cantillon, Richard

Sekine, Thomas T. The Discovery of International Monetary Equilibrium by Vanderlint, Cantillon, Gervaise and Hume. *Econ. Int.*, May 1973, *26*(2), pp. 262–82.

de Chardin, Pierre Teilhard

Laudadio, Leonard. Teilhard de Chardin on Technological Progress. *Rev. Soc. Econ.*, October 1973, *31*(2), pp. 167–78.

Cheysson, Jean-Jacques Emile

Hebert, Robert F. Wage Cobwebs and Cobweb-Type Phenomena: An Early French Formulation. *Western Econ. J.*, December 1973, *11*(4), pp. 394–403.

Copernicus, Nicolaus

Bieda, K. Copernicus as an Economist. *Econ. Rec.*, March 1973, *49*(125), pp. 89–103.

Cournot, Antoine Augustin

Roy, René. Cournot and Mathematical Economics. In *Rectenwald, H. C., ed.*, 1973, pp. 180–88.

Dewey, John

Levin, Samuel M. John Dewey's Evaluation of Technology. In *Levin, S. M.*, 1973, pp. 157–74.

Edgeworth, Francis Y.

Walker, Donald A. Edgeworth's Theory of Recontract. *Econ. J.*, March 1973, *83*(329), pp. 138–49.

Frisch, Ragnar

Danø, Sven and Rasmussen, Nørregaard. Ragnar Frisch. *Nationalokon. Tidsskr.*, 1973, *111*(1), pp. 5–8.

Lotti, Eraldo. Nuove tecniche di organizzazione della produzione. Estensione di alcuni concetti di Ragnar Frisch. (New Techniques of Industrial Organization. An Extension of Some Ideas of Ragnar Frisch. With English summary.) *L'Impresa*, 1973, *15*(11–12), pp. 701–08.

Medow, Paul. Towards a Reexamination of Ragnar Frisch's Proposal for a Multilateral Trade Clearing Agency in the Light of International Program Budgeting. *Amer. Econ.*, Fall 1973, *17*(2), pp. 51–55.

Furtado, Celso

Furtado, Celso. Adventures of a Brazilian Economist. *Int. Soc. Sci. J.*, 1973, *25*(1–2), pp. 28–38.

Gandhi, Mohandas K.

Koshal, Rajindar K. and Koshal, Manjulika. Gandhian Economic Philosophy. *Amer. J. Econ. Soc.*, April 1973, *32*(2), pp. 191–209.

George, Henry
Frye, Jerry K. Rhetorical Strategies Employed by Henry George and His Followers. *Amer. J. Econ. Soc.*, October 1973, *32*(4), pp. 405–20.

Graham, Frank D.
Metzler, Lloyd A. Graham's Theory of International Values. In *Metzler, L. A.*, 1973, pp. 234–57.

von Hayek, Friedrich A.
Ferguson, C. E. The Specialization Gap: Barton, Ricardo, and Hollander. *Hist. Polit. Econ.*, Spring 1973, *5*(1), pp. 1–13.

Hicks, John R. [Sir]
Hicks, John R. [Sir]. Recollections and Documents. *Economica, N.S.*, February 1973, *40*(157), pp. 2–11.
Lachmann, L. M. Sir John Hicks as a Neo-Austrian. *S. Afr. J. Econ.*, September 1973, *41*(3), pp. 195–207.

Hobbes, Thomas
Ophuls, William. Leviathan or Oblivion? In *Daly, H. E., ed.*, 1973, pp. 215–30.

Hoxie, Robert Franklin
McNulty, Paul J. Hoxie's Economics in Retrospect: The Making and Unmaking of a Veblenian. *Hist. Polit. Econ.*, Fall 1973, *5*(2), pp. 449–84.

Hume, David
Rotwein, Eugène. David Hume as an Economist. In *Rectenwald, H. C., ed.*, 1973, pp. 30–36.
Sekine, Thomas T. The Discovery of International Monetary Equilibrium by Vanderlint, Cantillon, Gervaise and Hume. *Econ. Int.*, May 1973, *26*(2), pp. 262–82.

Jevons, W. Stanley
de Marchi, N. B. The Noxious Influence of Authority: A Correction of Jevons' Charge. *J. Law Econ.*, April 1973, *16*(1), pp. 179–89.   [G: U.K.]

Keynes, John Maynard
Asimakopulos, A. Keynes, Patinkin, Historical Time, and Equilibrium Analysis. *Can. J. Econ.*, May 1973, *6*(2), pp. 179–88.
Howson, Susan. "A Dear Money Man"?: Keynes on Monetary Policy, 1920. *Econ. J.*, June 1973, *83*(330), pp. 456–64.
Hutchison, T. W. *The Collected Writings of John Maynard Keynes*, Volumes I–VI and XV–XVI. *Econ. Hist. Rev., 2nd Ser.*, February 1973, pp. 141–52.
Johnson, Elizabeth S. John Maynard Keynes: Scientist or Politician? In *Robinson, J., ed.*, 1973, pp. 12–25.
Johnson, Elizabeth S. The Collected Writings of John Maynard Keynes: Some Visceral Reactions. In *Parkin, M., ed.*, 1973, pp. 216–27.
Johnson, Harry G. Keynes and the Keynesians. In *Johnson, H. G.*, 1973, pp. 70–76.
Moggridge, D. E. From the *Treatise* to *The General Theory*: An Exercise in Chronology. *Hist. Polit. Econ.*, Spring 1973, *5*(1), pp. 72–88.
Posner, M. V. Making Economic Policy. *Econ. J.*, March 1973, *83*(329), pp. 111–19.
Robinson, Austin. John Maynard Keynes. In *Rectenwald, H. C., ed.*, 1973, pp. 395–405.

Robinson, Joan. What Has Become of the Keynesian Revolution? In *Robinson, J., ed.*, 1973, pp. 1–11.
Samuelson, Paul A. Lord Keynes and the General Theory. In *Rectenwald, H. C., ed.*, 1973, pp. 407–13.
Shackle, G. L. S. Keynes and Today's Establishment in Economic Theory: A View. *J. Econ. Lit.*, June 1973, *11*(2), pp. 516–19.
Wells, Paul. Keynes's Dynamic Disequilibrium Theory of Employment. *Quart. Rev. Econ. Bus.*, Winter 1973, *13*(4), pp. 89–93.
Yeager, Leland B. The Keynesian Diversion. *Western Econ. J.*, June 1973, *11*(2), pp. 150–63.

Knight, Frank
Patinkin, Don. Frank Knight as Teacher. *Amer. Econ. Rev.*, December 1973, *63*(5), pp. 787–810.
Patinkin, Don. In Search of the "Wheel of Wealth": On the Origins of Frank Knight's Circular-Flow Diagram. *Amer. Econ. Rev.*, December 1973, *63*(5), pp. 1037–46.

Lange, Oskar
Neuberger, Egon. The Plan and the Market: The Models of Oskar Lange. *Amer. Econ.*, Fall 1973, *17*(2), pp. 148–53.
Yunker, James A. An Appraisal of Langian Socialism. *Indian Econ. J.*, January-March 1973, *20*(3), pp. 382–413.

Leontief, Wassily
Dorfman, Robert. Wassily Leontief's Contribution to Economics. *Swedish J. Econ.*, December 1973, *75*(4), pp. 430–49.

List, Friedrich
Heuss, Theodor. Friedrich List. In *Rectenwald, H. C., ed.*, 1973, pp. 157–65.

Lösch, August
Parr, John B. Structure and Size in the Urban System of Lösch. *Econ. Geogr.*, July 1973, *49*(3), pp. 185–212.

Malthus, Thomas Robert
Akhtar, M. A. The Stationary State of Ricardo and Malthus: Comment. *Intermountain Econ. Rev.*, Spring 1973, *4*(1), pp. 77–79.
Bonar, James. Malthus and His Work. In *Rectenwald, H. C., ed.*, 1973, pp. 83–89.
Kolb, Fredric R. The Stationary State of Ricardo and Malthus: Reply. *Intermountain Econ. Rev.*, Spring 1973, *4*(1), p. 80.
de Marchi, N. B. and Sturges, R. P. Malthus and Ricardo's Inductivist Critics: Four Letters to William Whewell. *Economica, N.S.*, November 1973, *40*(160), pp. 379–93.
Peacock, Alan T. Malthus in the Twentieth Century. In *Rectenwald, H. C., ed.*, 1973, pp. 91–98.

Marshall, Alfred
Keynes, John Maynard. Alfred Marshall. In *Rectenwald, H. C., ed.*, 1973, pp. 280–93.
Petridis, Anastasios. Alfred Marshall's Attitudes to the Economic Analysis of Trade Unions: A Case of Anomalies in a Competitive System. *Hist. Polit. Econ.*, Spring 1973, *5*(1), pp. 165–98.
Weisskopf, Walter A. Economic Growth versus

Existential Balance. In *Daly, H. E., ed.*, 1973, pp. 240–51.

Marx, Karl

Banke, Niels. Kommentarer til Karl Marx's mindesten. (On Marxian Economics. With English summary.) *Nationalokon. Tidsskr.*, 1973, *111*(1), pp. 112–43.

Baumol, William J. Values vs. Prices: What Marx "Really" Meant. *Amer. Econ.*, Fall 1973, *17*(2), pp. 63–71.

Becker, James F. Class Structure and Conflict in the Managerial Phase: I. *Sci. Soc.*, Fall 1973, *37*(3), pp. 259–77.

Berlin, Isaiah. Karl Marx: His Life and Environment. In *Rectenwald, H. C., ed.*, 1973, pp. 223–38.

Bronfenbrenner, Martin. "Samuelson and Marx": Reply. *J. Econ. Lit.*, December 1973, *11*(4), pp. 1367.

Bronfenbrenner, Martin. Samuelson, Marx, and Their Latest Critics. *J. Econ. Lit.*, March 1973, *11*(1), pp. 58–63.

Fetscher, Iring. Karl Marx on Human Nature. *Soc. Res.*, Autumn 1973, *40*(3), pp. 443–67.

Laibman, David. Values and Prices of Production: The Political Economy of the Transformation Problem. *Sci. Soc.*, Winter 1973–1974, *37*(4), pp. 404–36.

Morris, Jacob and Lewin, Haskell. The Skilled Labor Reduction Problem. *Sci. Soc.*, Winter 1973–1974, *37*(4), pp. 454–72.

Myrdal, Gunnar. A Brief Note on Marx and "Marxism." In *Myrdal, G.*, 1973, pp. 308–16.

Nell, Edward J. Cyclical Accumulation: A Marxian Model of Development. *Amer. Econ. Rev.*, May 1973, *63*(2), pp. 152–59.

Okishio, Nobuo. On the Convergence of Marx's 'Transformation' Procedure. (In Japanese. With English summary.) *Econ. Stud. Quart.*, August 1973, *24*(2), pp. 40–45.

Robinson, Joan. "Samuelson and Marx." *J. Econ. Lit.*, December 1973, *11*(4), pp. 1367.

Samuelson, Paul A. "Samuelson and Marx": Reply. *J. Econ. Lit.*, December 1973, *11*(4), pp. 1367.

Samuelson, Paul A. Samuelson's "Reply on Marxian Matters." *J. Econ. Lit.*, March 1973, *11*(1), pp. 64–68.

Schumpeter, Joseph Alois. Capitalism, Socialism and Democracy: Marx the Economist. In *Rectenwald, H. C., ed.*, 1973, pp. 238–50.

Smolinski, Leon. Karl Marx and Mathematical Economics. *J. Polit. Econ.*, September-October 1973, *81*(5), pp. 1189–1204.

Ullmo, Jean. Sur quelques concepts marxistes. (About Some Marxist Concepts. With English summary.) *Revue Écon.*, January 1973, *24*(1), pp. 109–38.

von Weizsäcker, Carl Christian. Morishima on Marx. *Econ. J.*, December 1973, *83*(332), pp. 1245–54.

Wolfstetter, E. Surplus Labour, Synchronised Labor Costs and Marx's Labour Theory of Value. *Econ. J.*, September 1973, *83*(331), pp. 787–809.

Mattioli, Raffaele

Stammati, Gaetano. Raffaele Mattioli. (Raffaele Mattioli. With English summary.) *Bancaria*, November 1973, *29*(11), pp. 1323–28.

Menger, Karl

Hayek, F. A. The Place of Menger's Grundsatze in the History of Economic Thought. In *Hicks, J. R. and Weber, W., eds.*, 1973, pp. 1–14.

Hutchison, T. W. Some Themes from Investigations into Method. In *Hicks, J. R. and Weber, W., eds.*, 1973, pp. 15–37.

Streissler, Erich W. Menger's Theories of Money and Uncertainty—A Modern Interpretation. In *Hicks, J. R. and Weber, W., eds.*, 1973, pp. 164–89.

Mill, John Stuart

Bush, Winston C. Population and Mill's Peasant-Proprietor Economy. *Hist. Polit. Econ.*, Spring 1973, *5*(1), pp. 110–20.

de Marchi, N. B. The Noxious Influence of Authority: A Correction of Jevons' Charge. *J. Law Econ.*, April 1973, *16*(1), pp. 179–89. [G: U.K.]

Rasmussen, Jørgen. Dual Theories and the Classics. In *Institute for Development Research*, 1973, pp. 61–74.

Stigler, George J. John Stuart Mill: The Nature and Role of Originality in Scientific Progress. In *Rectenwald, H. C., ed.*, 1973, pp. 207–10.

Tatalovich, Anne. John Stuart Mill: The Subjection of Women: An Analysis. *Southern Quart.*, October 1973, *12*(1), pp. 87–105.

Wollheim, Richard. John Stuart Mill and the Limits of State Action. *Soc. Res.*, Spring 1973, *40*(1), pp. 1–30.

Minard, Joseph

Ekelund, Robert B., Jr. and Hebert, Robert F. Public Economics at the Ecole des Ponts et Chaussées: 1830–1850. *J. Public Econ.*, July 1973, *2*(3), pp. 241–56.

von Mises, Ludwig Edler

Gonce, R. A. Natural Law and Ludwig von Mises' Praxeology and Economic Science. *Southern Econ. J.*, April 1973, *39*(4), pp. 490–507.

Navier, Henri

Ekelund, Robert B., Jr. and Hebert, Robert F. Public Economics at the Ecole des Ponts et Chaussées: 1830–1850. *J. Public Econ.*, July 1973, *2*(3), pp. 241–56.

Pareto, Vilfredo

Amoroso, Luigi. The Work of Vilfredo Pareto. In *Rectenwald, H. C., ed.*, 1973, pp. 307–10.

Bousquet, Georges-Henri. Vilfredo Pareto. In *Rectenwald, H. C., ed.*, 1973, pp. 297–306.

Levy, Marion J., Jr. A Sociologist Who Knew Science. *Soc. Sci. Quart.*, December 1973, *54*(3), pp. 469–79.

Lopreato, Joseph. Notes on the Work of Vilfredo Pareto. *Soc. Sci. Quart.*, December 1973, *54*(3), pp. 451–68.

Pizzorno, Alessandro. Vilfredo Pareto and the Crisis of Nineteenth Century Science. *Soc. Sci. Quart.*, December 1973, *54*(3), pp. 480–90.

Tarascio, Vincent J. Vilfredo Pareto: On the Occasion of the Translation of His Manuel. *Can. J. Econ.*, August 1973, *6*(3), pp. 394–408.

Tarascio, Vincent J. The Pareto Law of Income Distribution. *Soc. Sci. Quart.*, December 1973, *54*(3), pp. 525–33.

Tommissen, Piet. La notion d'idéologie dans la pensée de Pareto. (The Meaning of Ideology in Pareto's Sociological Work. With English summary.) *Rivista Int. Sci. Econ. Com.*, March 1973, *20*(3), pp. 219–41.

Perroux, François

Bouckaert, L. François Perroux en de verruiming van het economisch denken. (The Economic Thought of F. Perroux. With English summary.) *Tijdschr. Econ.*, 1973, *18*(1), pp. 9–37.

Pigou, Arthur Cecil

Brahmananda, Palahalli Ramaiya. A. C. Pigou. In *Rectenwald, H. C., ed.*, 1973, pp. 358–67.

Quesnay, François

Foley, V. An Origin of the *Tableau Économique*. *Hist. Polit. Econ.*, Spring 1973, *5*(1), pp. 121–50.

Hecht, Jacqueline. The Life of François Quesnay. In *Rectenwald, H. C., ed.*, 1973, pp. 1–11.

Phillips, Almarin. François Quesnay: The Tableau Économique as a Simple Leontief Model. In *Rectenwald, H. C., ed.*, 1973, pp. 16–21.

Spengler, Joseph John. Quesnay: Philosopher, Empiricist, Economist. In *Rectenwald, H. C., ed.*, 1973, pp. 11–16.

Ricardo, David

Akhtar, M. A. The Stationary State of Ricardo and Malthus: Comment. *Intermountain Econ. Rev.*, Spring 1973, *4*(1), pp. 77–79.

Cochrane, James L. Ricardo on the Rate of Profit and Distributive Shares: Comment. *Indian Econ. J.*, January-March 1973, *20*(3), pp. 521–22.

Ferguson, C. E. The Specialization Gap: Barton, Ricardo, and Hollander. *Hist. Polit. Econ.*, Spring 1973, *5*(1), pp. 1–13.

Gootzeit, Michael J. The Corn Laws and Wage Adjustment in a Short-Run Ricardian Model. *Hist. Polit. Econ.*, Spring 1973, *5*(1), pp. 50–71.

Hollander, Samuel. Ricardo's Analysis of the Profit Rate, 1813–15. *Economica, N.S.*, August 1973, *40*(159), pp. 260–82.

Kolb, Fredric R. The Stationary State of Ricardo and Malthus: Reply. *Intermountain Econ. Rev.*, Spring 1973, *4*(1), pp. 80.

Stigler, George J. The Ricardian Theory of Value and Distribution. In *Rectenwald, H. C., ed.*, 1973, pp. 131–34.

Say, John-Baptiste

Clower, Robert W. and Leijonhufvud, Axel. Say's Principle, What it Means and Doesn't Mean: Part I. *Intermountain Econ. Rev.*, Fall 1973, *4*(2), pp. 1–16.

Reynaud, Pierre-Louis. The Work of Jean-Baptiste Say. In *Rectenwald, H. C., ed.*, 1973, pp. 110–18.

von Schmoller, Gustav

von Beckerath, Erwin. The Work of Gustav von Schmoller. In *Rectenwald, H. C., ed.*, 1973, pp. 275–78.

Schumpeter, Joseph Alois

Haberler, Gottfried. Joseph Alois Schumpeter. In *Rectenwald, H. C., ed.*, 1973, pp. 370–93.

O'Donnell, L. A. Rationalism, Capitalism and the Entrepreneur: The Views of Veblen and Schumpeter. *Hist. Polit. Econ.*, Spring 1973, *5*(1), pp. 199–214.

Simonde de Sismondi, J.C.L.

Parguez, Alain. Sismondi et la théorie du déséquilibre macro-économique. (Sismondi and Macro-Disequilibrium Theory. With English summary.) *Revue Écon.*, September 1973, *24*(5), pp. 837–66.

Smith, Adam

De Gregori, Thomas R. Prodigality or Parsimony: The False Dilemma in Economic Development Theory. *J. Econ. Issues*, June 1973, *7*(2), pp. 259–66.

Kaushil, S. The Case of Adam Smith's Value Analysis. *Oxford Econ. Pap.*, March 1973, *25*(1), pp. 60–71.

Lamb, Robert. Adam Smith's Concept of Alienation. *Oxford Econ. Pap.*, July 1973, *25*(2), pp. 275–85.

Meek, Ronald L. and Skinner, Andrew S. The Development of Adam Smith's Ideas on the Division of Labour. *Econ. J.*, December 1973, *83*(332), pp. 1094–1116.

Nord, Walter. Adam Smith and Contemporary Social Exchange Theory. *Amer. J. Econ. Soc.*, October 1973, *32*(4), pp. 421–36.

Rasmussen, Jørgen. Dual Theories and the Classics. In *Institute for Development Research*, 1973, pp. 61–74.

Samuels, Warren J. Adam Smith and the Economy as a System of Power. *Rev. Soc. Econ.*, October 1973, *31*(2), pp. 123–37.

Samuels, Warren J. Adam Smith and the Economy as a System of Power. *Indian Econ. J.*, January-March 1973, *20*(3), pp. 363–81.

Staley, Charles E. A Note on Adam Smith's Version of the Vent for Surplus Model. *Hist. Polit. Econ.*, Fall 1973, *5*(2), pp. 438–48.

Viner, Jacob. Adam Smith and Laissez-Faire. In *Rectenwald, H. C., ed.*, 1973, pp. 54–62.

Sumner, William Graham

Bannister, Robert C., Jr. William Graham Sumner's Social Darwinism: A Recommendation. *Hist. Polit. Econ.*, Spring 1973, *5*(1), pp. 89–109.

Takada, Yasuma

Hayasaka, Tadashi. Dr. Yasuma Takada in the History of Economics in Japan. (In Japanese. With English summary.) *Econ. Stud. Quart.*, August 1973, *24*(2), pp. 46–60.

von Thünen, Johann Heinrich

Leigh, Arthur Hertel. von Thünen's Theory of Distribution and the Advent of Marginal Analysis. In *Rectenwald, H. C., ed.*, 1973, pp. 146–54.

Salin, Edgar. Johann Heinrich von Thünen in His Age. In *Rectenwald, H. C., ed.*, 1973, pp. 135–45.

Tugan-Baranovsky, M. I.

Kowal, Lubomyr M. The Market and Business Cycle Theories of M. I. Tugan-Baranovsky.

Rivista Int. Sci. Econ. Com., April 1973, *20*(4), pp. 305–34.

Tusi, Khajeh Nasir ed-Din

Sabā, Mohsen. The Economic Ideas of Khajeh Nasir ed-Din Tusi as Stated in the Nasirian Ethics. *Tahq. Eq.,* Summer & Autumn 1973, *10*(31&32), pp. 5–21.

Vaizey, John

Vaizey, John. Emergence of a British Economist. *Int. Soc. Sci. J.,* 1973, *25*(1–2), pp. 154–68.

Veblen, Thorstein

Dorfman, Joseph. Source and Impact of Veblen. In *Rectenwald, H. C., ed.,* 1973, pp. 333–38.

Leathers, Charles G. and Evans, John S. Thorstein Veblen and the New Industrial State. *Hist. Polit. Econ.,* Fall 1973, *5*(2), pp. 420–37.

O'Donnell, L. A. Rationalism, Capitalism and the Entrepreneur: The Views of Veblen and Schumpeter. *Hist. Polit. Econ.,* Spring 1973, *5* (1), pp. 199–214.

Tilman, Rick. Thorstein Veblen: Incrementalist and Utopian. *Amer. J. Econ. Soc.,* April 1973, *32*(2), pp. 155–69.

Wakefield, Edward Gibbon

Kittrell, Edward R. Wakefield's Scheme of Systematic Colonization and Classical Economics. *Amer. J. Econ. Soc.,* January 1973, *32*(1), pp. 87–111.

Walras, Léon

Collard, David. Léon Walras and the Cambridge Caricature. *Econ. J.,* June 1973, *83*(330), pp. 465–76.

Hicks, John R. [Sir] and Recktenwald, Horst Claus. Walras's Economic System. In *Rectenwald, H. C., ed.,* 1973, pp. 261–65.

Howitt, P. W. Walras and Monetary Theory. *Western Econ. J.,* December 1973, *11*(4), pp. 487–99.

Jaffé, William. Léon Walras. In *Rectenwald, H. C., ed.,* 1973, pp. 253–61.

Weber, Max

Bendix, Reinhard. Max Weber: Career and Personal Orientation. In *Rectenwald, H. C., ed.,* 1973, pp. 341–47.

Seligman, Ben Baruch. Max Weber and the Capitalist Spirit. In *Rectenwald, H. C., ed.,* 1973, pp. 348–56.

Whewell, William

Henderson, James P. William Whewell's Mathematical Statements of Price Flexibility, Demand Elasticity and the Giffen Paradox. *Manchester Sch. Econ. Soc. Stud.,* September 1973, *41*(3), pp. 329–42.

Wicksell, Knut

Overbeek, Johannes. Wicksell on Population. *Econ. Develop. Cult. Change,* January 1973, *21*(2), pp. 205–11.

0329 Other Special Topics

Guggenheim, Thomas. Some Early Views on Monetary Integration. In *Johnson, H. G. and Swoboda, A. K., eds.,* 1973, pp. 93–98.

Hamilton, David. What Has Evolutionary Economics to Contribute to Consumption Theory? *J. Econ. Issues,* June 1973, *7*(2), pp. 197–207.

Hochwald, Werner. *The Idea of Progress:* A Review Article. *J. Econ. Issues,* March 1973, *7*(1), pp. 47–59.

Ophuls, William. Leviathan or Oblivion? In *Daly, H. E., ed.,* 1973, pp. 215–30.

Trantner, N. L. Population and Industrialization: Introduction. In *Tranter, N. L., ed.,* 1973, pp. 9–32.

Wang, Tong-eng. Quantitative Analysis of the Progress of the Econometric Movement: An Exploration. *Hist. Polit. Econ.,* Spring 1973, *5*(1), pp. 151–64.   [G: U.S.]

036 Economic Methodology

0360 Economic Methodology

Agnati, Achille. Dal calcolo dell'opinione nei preclassici all'analisi economica dell'esogeneità. (From the Calculus of Consent in the Preclassics to the Economic Analysis of Exogeneity. With English summary.) *Rivista Int. Sci. Econ. Com.,* February 1973, *20*(2), pp. 153–78.

Axelsson, Runo. The Economic Postulate of Rationality—Some Methodological Views. *Swedish J. Econ.,* September 1973, *75*(3), pp. 289–95.

Daly, Herman E. Toward a Steady-State Economy: Introduction. In *Daly, H. E., ed.,* 1973, pp. 1–29.

Ekelund, Robert B., Jr. and Olsen, Emilie S. Comte, Mill, and Cairnes: The Positivist-Empiricist Interlude in Late Classical Economics. *J. Econ. Issues,* September 1973, *7*(3), pp. 383–416.

Fach, Wolfgang. Über einige Schwierigkeiten der Neuen Politischen Ökonomie: Das Beispiel der Koalitionstheorie. (Some Difficulties of the New Political Economy: The Example of the Coalition Theory. With English summary.) *Z. ges. Staatswiss.,* May 1973, *129*(2), pp. 347–74.

Ferrer-Pacces, F. M. Teoria senza ricerca. (Theory Without Research. With English summary.) *L'Impresa,* 1973, *15*(3–4), pp. 187–89.

Gramm, Warren S. Natural Selection in Economic Thought: Ideology, Power, and the Keynesian Counterrevolution. *J. Econ. Issues,* March 1973, *7*(1), pp. 1–27.

Hahn, Frank H. The Winter of our Discontent. *Economica, N.S.,* August 1973, *40*(159), pp. 322–30.

Holmlund, Bertil. Om postulatens status i ekonomisk teori. (The Status of Postulates in Economic Theory. With English summary.) *Ekon. Samfundets Tidskr.,* 1973, *26*(4), pp. 255–69.

Hunt, Verl F. The Glass Bead Game of Orthodox Economics: Reply. *Intermountain Econ. Rev.,* Spring 1973, *4*(1), pp. 74–76.

Johnson, Harry G. The Glass Bead Game of Orthodox Economics: Comment. *Intermountain Econ. Rev.,* Spring 1973, *4*(1), pp. 72–73.

Karsten, Siegfried G. Dialetics and the Evolution of Economic Thought. *Hist. Polit. Econ.,* Fall 1973, *5*(2), pp. 399–419.

Lofthouse, Stephen. On Paradigms, Methodology and the Theory of the Firm. Part 1. *Rivista Int. Sci. Econ. Com.,* May 1973, *20*(5), pp. 406–48.

Lofthouse, Stephen. On Paradigms, Methodology and the Theory of the Firm. Part 2. *Rivista Int. Sci. Econ. Com.,* June 1973, *20*(6), pp. 566–607.

Rothbard, Murray N. Value Implications of Economic Theory. *Amer. Econ.*, Spring 1973, *17*(1), pp. 35–39.

Rotwein, Eugene. Empiricism and Economic Method: Several Views Considered. *J. Econ. Issues*, September 1973, *7*(3), pp. 361–82.

Rousseas, Stephen. Paradigm Polishing versus Critical Thought in Economics. *Amer. Econ.*, Fall 1973, *17*(2), pp. 72–78.

Routh, Guy. Methodology. In *Livingstone, I., et al., eds.*, 1973, pp. 51–58.

Schachter, Gustav. Some Developments in Economic Science Since 1965: Methods, Ideas, Approaches. *Amer. J. Econ. Soc.*, July 1973, *32*(3), pp. 331–35.

Schumacher, E. F. Does Economics Help? An Exploration of Meta-economics. In *Robinson, J., ed.*, 1973, pp. 26–36.

Shaffer, James D. On the Concept of Subsector Studies. *Amer. J. Agr. Econ.*, May 1973, *55*(2), pp. 333–35.

Shapiro, Harold T. Is Verification Possible? The Evaluation of Large Econometric Models. *Amer. J. Agr. Econ.*, May 1973, *55*(2), pp. 250–58.

Velupillai, K. A Note on the Origin of the 'Correspondence Principle'. *Swedish J. Econ.*, September 1973, *75*(3), pp. 302–04.

Wang, Tong-eng. Quantitative Analysis of the Progress of the Econometric Movement: An Exploration. *Hist. Polit. Econ.*, Spring 1973, *5*(1), pp. 151–64. [G: U.S.]

Wong, Stanley. The "F-Twist" and the Methodology of Paul Samuelson. *Amer. Econ. Rev.*, June 1973, *63*(3), pp. 312–25.

040 ECONOMIC HISTORY

041 Economic History: General

0410 General

Amin, Samir. The Place of Economic History in the Teaching of Economics in Africa. In *Livingstone, I., et al., eds.*, 1973, pp. 101–03. [G: Africa]

Bevin, J. H. and Livingstone, I. Economic History and Economics Teaching. In *Livingstone, I., et al., eds.*, 1973, pp. 95–100.

Bolton, G. C. Louis Hartz. *Australian Econ. Hist. Rev.*, September 1973, *13*(2), pp. 168–76.

Chandler, Alfred D., Jr. Decision Making and Modern Institutional Change. *J. Econ. Hist.*, March 1973, *33*(1), pp. 1–15. [G: U.S.]

Constantinescu, N. N. Cadrul economic, social și politic în care a apărut Manifestul Partidului Comunist. (The Economic, Social and Political Background Against which the Manifesto of the Communist Party was Published. With English summary.) *Stud. Cercet. Econ.*, 1973, (2), pp. 25–32.

Derber, Milton. Some Further Thoughts on the Historical Study of Industrial Democracy. *Labor Hist.*, Fall 1973, *14*(4), pp. 599–611.

Hadari, Yitzhak. The Structure of the Private Multinational Enterprise. *Mich. Law Rev.*, March 1973, *71*(4), pp. 729–806.

Pope, David. Economic History and Scientific Inference. *Australian Econ. Hist. Rev.*, March 1973, *13*(1), pp. 1–15.

Supple, Barry. Thinking About Economic Development. In *Youngson, A. J., ed.*, 1973, pp. 19–35.

Trantner, N. L. Population and Industrialization: Introduction. In *Tranter, N. L., ed.*, 1973, pp. 9–32.

0411 Development of the Discipline

Baker, Robert P. Labor History, Social Science, and the Concept of the Working Class. *Labor Hist.*, Winter 1973, *14*(1), pp. 98–105.

Clower, Robert W. Snarks, Quarks, and Other Fictions. In *[Williamson, H. F.]*, 1973, pp. 3–14.

Hartwell, R. M. Good Old Economic History. *J. Econ. Hist.*, March 1973, *33*(1), pp. 28–40.

Hughes, Jonathan R. T. Business Enterprise and Economic Change: Comment. In *[Williamson, H. F.]*, 1973, pp. 304–20.

Parker, William N. Through Growth and Beyond: Three Decades in Economic and Business History. In *[Williamson, H. F.]*, 1973, pp. 15–47. [G: U.S.]

0412 Comparative Intercountry or Intertemporal Economic History

Adams, N. A. Trade as a Handmaiden of Growth: Comment. *Econ. J.*, March 1973, *83*(329), pp. 210–12.

Alchian, Armen A. and Demsetz, Harold. The Property Rights Paradigm. *J. Econ. Hist.*, March 1973, *33*(1), pp. 16–27.

Baker, A. R. H. and Butlin, R. A. Studies of Field Systems in the British Isles: Introduction: Materials and Methods. In *Baker, A. R. H. and Butlin, R. A., eds.*, 1973, pp. 1–40. [G: U.K.]

Baker, Mary Roys. Anglo-Massachusetts Trade Union Roots, 1130–1790. *Labor Hist.*, Summer 1973, *14*(3), pp. 352–96. [G: U.S.; U.K.]

Barsby, Steven L. Great Spurts and the Experience of Non-European Countries. *J. Econ. Issues*, September 1973, *7*(3), pp. 459–74.

Birnberg, Thomas and Resnick, Stephen A. A Model of the Trade and Government Sectors in Colonial Economies. *Amer. Econ. Rev.*, September 1973, *63*(4), pp. 572–87.

Crafts, N. F. R. Trade as a Handmaiden of Growth: An Alternative View. *Econ. J.*, September 1973, *83*(331), pp. 875–84.

Csernok, Attila; Ehrlich, Eva and Szilágyi, Gyorgy. Numerical Results of an International Comparison of Infrastructure Development Over the Last 100 Years. *Europ. Econ. Rev.*, April 1973, *4*(1), pp. 63–65.

Davis, Lance E. Secular Price Change in Historical Perspective: Comment. *J. Money, Credit, Banking*, Part II, February 1973, *5*(1), pp. 270–73.

Dillard, Dudley. Capitalism. In *Wilber, C. K., ed.*, 1973, pp. 60–67. [G: Europe]

Fishlow, Albert. Comparative Consumption Patterns, the Extent of the Market, and Alternative Development Strategies. In *Ayal, E. B., ed.*, 1973, pp. 41–80. [G: U.S.; U.K.; France]

Gitelman, H. M. Perspectives on American Industrial Violence. *Bus. Hist. Rev.*, Spring 1973, *47*(1), pp. 1–23. [G: U.S.]

Griffin, Keith. Underdevelopment in History. In *Wilber, C. K., ed.*, 1973, pp. 68–81.

Habakkuk, H. J. American and British Technology in the Nineteenth Century, 1962. In *Tranter, N. L., ed.*, 1973, pp. 136–40. [G: U.S.; U.K.]

Helmstädter, Ernst. The Long-Run Movement of the Capital-Output Ratio and of Labour's Share. In *Mirrlees, J. A. and Stern, N. H., eds.*, 1973, pp. 3–17. [G: U.K.; Germany; U.S.]

Kemmerer, Donald L. The Role of Gold in the Past Century. In *Wiegand, G. C., ed.*, 1973, pp. 3–13.

Kravis, Irving B. Trade as a Handmaiden of Growth: Reply. *Econ. J.*, March 1973, *83*(329), pp. 212–17.

Kravis, Irving B. Trade as a Handmaiden of Growth: A Reply. *Econ. J.*, September 1973, *83*(331), pp. 885–89.

Nugent, Jeffrey B. Exchange-Rate Movements and Economic Development in the Late Nineteenth Century. *J. Polit. Econ.*, September-October 1973, *81*(5), pp. 1110–35.

Saul, S. B. The Nature and Diffusion of Technology. In *Youngson, A. J., ed.*, 1973, pp. 36–61. [G: U.S.; Europe]

Schwartz, Anna J. Secular Price Change in Historical Perspective. *J. Money, Credit, Banking*, Part II, February 1973, *5*(1), pp. 243–69.

Scoville, James G. Some Determinants of the Structure of Labor Movements. In *Sturmthal, A. and Scoville, J. G., eds.*, 1973, pp. 58–78. [G: U.S.; U.K.]

Sturmthal, Adolf. Industrial Relations Strategies. In *Sturmthal, A. and Scoville, J. G., eds.*, 1973, pp. 1–33. [G: U.S.; U.K.]

Trescott, Paul B. Secular Price Change in Historical Perspective: Comment. *J. Money, Credit, Banking*, Part II, February 1973, *5*(1), pp. 274–78.

Wilber, Charles K. The Human Costs of Economic Development: The West, the Soviet Union, and Underdeveloped Countries Today. In *Wilber, C. K., ed.*, 1973, pp. 324–41. [G: U.S.S.R.; U.S.; U.K.; Japan; Mexico]

Williamson, Jeffrey G. Comparative Consumption Patterns, the Extent of the Market, and Alternative Development Strategies: Comment. In *Ayal, E. B., ed.*, 1973, pp. 80–83. [G: U.S.; U.K.; France]

Youngson, A. J. Economic Development in the Long Run: Introduction. In *Youngson, A. J., ed.*, 1973, pp. 9–17.

042 Economic History: North America (excluding Mexico)

0420 General

Abrahams, Paul P. Brandeis and Lamont on Finance Capitalism. *Bus. Hist. Rev.*, Spring 1973, *47*(1), pp. 72–94. [G: U.S.]

Acheson, T. W. Changing Social Origins of the Canadian Industrial Elite, 1880–1910. *Bus. Hist. Rev.*, Summer 1973, *47*(2), pp. 189–217. [G: Canada]

Aldrich, Mark. Flexible Exchange Rates, Northern Expansion, and the Market for Southern Cotton:

1866–1879. *J. Econ. Hist.*, June 1973, *33*(2), pp. 399–416. [G: U.S.]

Andreano, Ralph. A Note on the Horatio Alger Legend: Statistical Studies of the Nineteenth–Century American Business Elite. In *[Williamson, H. F.]*, 1973, pp. 227–46. [G: U.S.]

Baack, Bennett D. and Ray, Edward J. Tariff Policy and Comparative Advantage in the Iron and Steel Industry: 1870–1929. *Exploration Econ. Hist.*, Fall 1973, *11*(1), pp. 3–23. [G: U.S.]

Becker, William H. American Manufacturers and Foreign Markets, 1870–1900: Business Historians and the "New Economic Determinists." *Bus. Hist. Rev.*, Winter 1973, *47*(4), pp. 466–81. [G: U.S.]

Bertram, Gordon W. The Relevance of the Wheat Boom in Canadian Economic Growth. *Can. J. Econ.*, November 1973, *6*(4), pp. 545–66. [G: Canada]

Booms, Bernard H. Impact of Urban Market Structure on the Level of Inventive Activity in Cities in the Early Nineteen Hundreds. *Land Econ.*, August 1973, *49*(3), pp. 318–25. [G: U.S.]

Broeze, Frank J. A. The New Economic History, the Navigation Acts, and the Continental Tobacco Market, 1770–90. *Econ. Hist. Rev., 2nd Ser.*, November 1973, *26*(4), pp. 668–78. [G: U.K.; U.S.]

Brown, William W. and Reynolds, Morgan O. Debt Peonage Re-examined. *J. Econ. Hist.*, December 1973, *33*(4), pp. 862–71. [G: U.S.]

Chandler, Alfred D., Jr. Decision Making and Modern Institutional Change. *J. Econ. Hist.*, March 1973, *33*(1), pp. 1–15. [G: U.S.]

Cockerell, Hugh. The History of British and American Fire Marks: Comment. *J. Risk Ins.*, December 1973, *40*(4), pp. 639–41. [G: U.S.; U.K.]

Feller, Irwin. Determinants of the Composition of Urban Inventions. *Econ. Geogr.*, January 1973, *49*(1), pp. 47–58. [G: U.S.]

Fogarty, Robert S. Oneida: A Utopian Search for Religious Security. *Labor Hist.*, Spring 1973, *14*(2), pp. 202–27. [G: U.S.]

Fowler, Loretta. The Arapahoe Ranch: An Experiment in Cultural Change and Economic Development. *Econ. Develop. Cult. Change*, April 1973, *21*(3), pp. 446–64. [G: U.S.]

Giddens, Paul H. Historical Origins of the Adoption of the Exxon Name and Trademark. *Bus. Hist. Rev.*, Autumn 1973, *47*(3), pp. 353–66. [G: U.S.]

Gitelman, H. M. Perspectives on American Industrial Violence. *Bus. Hist. Rev.*, Spring 1973, *47*(1), pp. 1–23. [G: U.S.]

Gray, Jean M. New Evidence on the Term Structure of Interest Rates: 1884–1900. *J. Finance*, June 1973, *28*(3), pp. 635–46. [G: U.S.]

Habakkuk, H. J. American and British Technology in the Nineteenth Century, 1962. In *Tranter, N. L., ed.*, 1973, pp. 136–40. [G: U.S.; U.K.]

Haites, Erik F. and Mak, James. The Decline of Steamboating on the Ante-bellum Western Rivers: Some New Evidence and An Alternative Hypothesis. *Exploration Econ. Hist.*, Fall 1973, *11*(1), pp. 25–36. [G: U.S.]

Higgs, Robert. Mortality in Rural America, 1870–

1920: Estimates and Conjectures. *Exploration Econ. Hist.*, Winter 1973, *10*(2), pp. 177–95. [G: U.S.]

Hinderliter, Roger H. and Rockoff, Hugh. The Management of Reserves by Ante-bellum Banks in Eastern Financial Centers. *Exploration Econ. Hist.*, Fall 1973, *11*(1), pp. 37–53. [G: U.S.]

Ishikawa, Tsuneo. Conceptualization of Learning by Doing: A Note on Paul David's "Learning by Doing and . . . the Ante-bellum United States Cotton Textile Industry." *J. Econ. Hist.*, December 1973, *33*(4), pp. 851–61. [G: U.S.]

Jeremy, David J. British Textile Technology Transmission to the United States: The Philadelphia Region Experience, 1770-1820. *Bus. Hist. Rev.*, Spring 1973, *47*(1), pp. 24–52. [G: U.S.]

Johnpoll, Bernard K. Manuscript Sources in American Radicalism. *Labor Hist.*, Winter 1973, *14*(1), pp. 92–97. [G: U.S.]

Johnson, Harry M. The History of British and American Fire Marks: Reply. *J. Risk Ins.*, December 1973, *40*(4), pp. 641–42. [G: U.S.; U.K.]

Keller, Robert R. Estimates of National Income and Product, 1919–1941: The Best of All Possible Worlds. *Exploration Econ. Hist.*, Fall 1973, *11*(1), pp. 87–88. [G: U.S.]

Lefever, Harry G. The Involvement of the Men and Religion Forward Movement in the Cause of Labor Justice, Atlanta, Georgia, 1912–1916. *Labor Hist.*, Fall 1973, *14*(4), pp. 521–35. [G: U.S.]

Levin, Samuel M. Ford Profit Sharing, 1914–1920. In *Levin, S. M.*, 1973, pp. 33–50. [G: U.S.]

Levin, Samuel M. The End of Ford Profit Sharing. In *Levin, S. M.*, 1973, pp. 51–64. [G: U.S.]

Levin, Samuel M. The Ford Unemployment Policy. In *Levin, S. M.*, 1973, pp. 79–88. [G: U.S.]

Loschky, David J. Studies of the Navigation Acts: New Economic Non-History? *Econ. Hist. Rev.*, 2nd Ser., November 1973, *26*(4), pp. 689–91.

McClelland, Peter D. The New Economic History and the Burdens of the Navigation Acts: Comment. *Econ. Hist. Rev.*, 2nd Ser., November 1973, *26*(4), pp. 679–86.

Morris, Stuart. Stalled Professionalism: The Recruitment of Railway Officials in the United States, 1885–1940. *Bus. Hist. Rev.*, Autumn 1973, *47*(3), pp. 317–34. [G: U.S.]

Parker, William N. Through Growth and Beyond: Three Decades in Economic and Business History. In *[Williamson, H. F.]*, 1973, pp. 15–47. [G: U.S.]

Persky, Joseph. The Dominance of the Rural-Industrial South, 1900–1930. *J. Reg. Sci.*, December 1973, *13*(3), pp. 409–19. [G: U.S.]

Porter, Glenn. Recent Trends in Canadian Business and Economic History. *Bus. Hist. Rev.*, Summer 1973, *47*(2), pp. 141–57. [G: Canada]

Poulson, Barry W. and Dowling, J. Malcolm, Jr. The Climacteric in U.S. Economic Growth. *Oxford Econ. Pap.*, November 1973, *25*(3), pp. 420–34. [G: U.S.]

Redlich, Fritz. American Banking and Growth in the Nineteenth Century: Epistemological Reflections. *Exploration Econ. Hist.*, Spring 1973, *10*(3), pp. 305–14. [G: U.S.]

Roy, Patricia E. Direct Management from Abroad: The Formative Years of the British Columbia Electric Railway. *Bus. Hist. Rev.*, Summer 1973, *47*(2), pp. 239–59. [G: Canada]

Shetler, Douglas. Monetary Aggregates Prior to the Civil War: A Closer Look: Comment. *J. Money, Credit, Banking*, November 1973, *5*(4), pp. 1000–06. [G: U.S.]

Singleton, Gregory H. The Genesis of Suburbia: A Complex of Historical Trends. In *Masotti, L. H. and Hadden, J. K., eds.*, 1973, pp. 29–50. [G: U.S.]

Swanson, Dorothy. Annual Bibliography of Periodical Articles on American Labor History, 1972. *Labor Hist.*, Fall 1973, *14*(4), pp. 580–98. [G: U.S.]

Sylla, Richard. Economic History "Von Unten Nach Oben" and "Von Oben Nach Unten": A Reply to Fritz Redlich. *Exploration Econ. Hist.*, Spring 1973, *10*(3), pp. 315–18. [G: U.S.]

Thomas, Robert Paul and Anderson, Terry L. White Population, Labor Force and Extensive Growth of the New England Economy in the Seventeenth Century. *J. Econ. Hist.*, September 1973, *33*(3), pp. 634–67. [G: U.S.]

Walton, Gary M. The Burdens of the Navigation Acts: Reply. *Econ. Hist. Rev.*, 2nd Ser., November 1973, *26*(4), pp. 687–88.

Wilson, Alan. Maritime Business History: A Reconnaissance of Records, Sources, and Prospects. *Bus. Hist. Rev.*, Summer 1973, *47*(2), pp. 260–76. [G: Canada]

Wright, Gavin. New and Old Views on the Economics of Slavery. *J. Econ. Hist.*, June 1973, *33*(2), pp. 452–66. [G: U.S.]

0421 History of Product Prices and Markets

Aduddell, Robert and Cain, Louis. Location and Collusion in the Meat Packing Industry. In *[Williamson, H. F.]*, 1973, pp. 85–117. [G: U.S.]

Blicksilver, Jack. The Life Insurance Company of Georgia: The Formative Years, 1891–1918. In *[Williamson, H. F.]*, 1973, pp. 248–79. [G: U.S.]

Bloch, Ben W. and Pilgrim, John D. A Reappraisal of Some Factors Associated with Fluctuations in the United States in the Interwar Period. *Southern Econ. J.*, January 1973, *39*(3), pp. 327–44. [G: U. S.]

Christensen, Raymond P. and Goolsby, O. Halbert. U.S. Agricultural Trade and Balance of Payments. In *Iowa State University Center for Agricultural and Rural Development*, 1973, pp. 122–40. [G: U.S.]

Decanio, Stephen. Cotton "Overproduction" in Late Nineteenth-Century Southern Agriculture. *J. Econ. Hist.*, September 1973, *33*(3), pp. 608–33.

George, P. J. and Oksanen, Ernest H. Saturation in the Automobile Market in the Late Twenties: Some Further Results. *Exploration Econ. Hist.*, Fall 1973, *11*(1), pp. 73–85. [G: U.S.]

Greer, Douglas F. Some Case History Evidence on the Advertising-Concentration Relationship. *Antitrust Bull.*, Summer 1973, *18*(2), pp. 307–32. [G: U.S.]

Joskow, Paul L. and McKelvey, Edward F. The Fogel-Engerman Iron Model: A Clarifying Note. *J.*

Polit. Econ., September-October 1973, *81*(5), pp. 1236–40.

Levin, Samuel M. The Impact of War on Industrial Technology. In *Levin, S. M.*, 1973, pp. 99–114.
[G: U.S.]

McDougall, Duncan M. The Domestic Availability of Manufactured Commodity Output, Canada, 1870–1915. *Can. J. Econ.*, May 1973, *6*(2), pp. 189–206.
[G: Canada]

Mercer, Lloyd J. and Morgan, W. Douglas. Housing Surplus in the 1920s? Another Evaluation. *Exploration Econ. Hist.*, Spring 1973, *10*(3), pp. 295–303.
[G: U.S.]

Puth, Robert C. From Enforced Segregation to Integration: Market Factors in the Development of a Negro Life Insurance. In *[Williamson, H. F.]*, 1973, pp. 280–301.
[G: U.S.]

Thomas, Robert Paul. Style Change and the Automobile Industry During the Roaring Twenties. In *[Williamson, H. F.]*, 1973, pp. 118–38. [G: U.S.]

Uselding, Paul. An Early Chapter in the Evolution of American Industrial Management. In *[Williamson, H. F.]*, 1973, pp. 51–84. [G: U.S.]

Williamson, Jeffrey G. Late Nineteenth-Century American Retardation: A Neoclassical Analysis. *J. Econ. Hist.*, September 1973, *33*(3), pp. 581–607.
[G: U.S.]

0422 History of Factor Prices and Markets

Abramovitz, Moses and David, Paul A. Economic Growth in America: Historical Parables and Realities. *De Economist*, May-June 1973, *121*(3), pp. 251–72. [G: U.S.]

Adams, Donald R., Jr. Wage Rates in the Iron Industry: Comment. *Exploration Econ. Hist.*, Fall 1973, *11*(1), pp. 89–94. [G: U.S.]

Aufhauser, R. Keith. Slavery and Scientific Management. *J. Econ. Hist.*, December 1973, *33*(4), pp. 811–24. [G: U.S.]

Brito, Dagobert L. and Williamson, Jeffrey G. Skilled Labor and Nineteenth Century Anglo-American Managerial Behavior. *Exploration Econ. Hist.*, Spring 1973, *10*(3), pp. 235–51. [G: U.S.; U.K.]

Coen, Robert M. Labor Force and Unemployment in the 1920's and 1930's: A Re-examination Based on Postwar Experience. *Rev. Econ. Statist.*, February 1973, *55*(1), pp. 46–55. [G: U.S.]

Coen, Robert M. Labor Force and Unemployment in the 1920's and 1930's: Reply. *Rev. Econ. Statist.*, November 1973, *55*(4), pp. 527–28. [G: U.S.]

Conrad, A. H. and Meyer, John R. The Economics of Slavery in the Antebellum South. In *Temin, P., ed.*, 1973, pp. 339–97. [G: U.S.]

David, Paul A. The 'Horndal Effect' in Lowell, 1834-1856: A Short-run Learning Curve for Integrated Cotton Textile Mills. *Exploration Econ. Hist.*, Winter 1973, *10*(2), pp. 131–50. [G: U.S.]

Engerman, Stanley. Some Considerations Relating to Property Rights in Man. *J. Econ. Hist.*, March 1973, *33*(1), pp. 43–65. [G: U.S.]

Foner, Philip S. An Early Trades Union and Its Fate. *Labor Hist.*, Summer 1973, *14*(3), pp. 423–24.
[G: U.S.]

Gitelman, H. M. No Irish Need Apply: Patterns of and Responses to Ethnic Discrimination in the Labor Market. *Labor Hist.*, Winter 1973, *14*(1), pp. 56–68. [G: U.S.]

Goldsmith, Raymond W. The Historical Background: Financial Institutions as Investors in Corporate Stock Before 1952. In *Goldsmith, R. W., ed.*, 1973, pp. 34–90. [G: U.S.]

Gunderson, Gerald. Southern Ante-bellum Income Reconsidered. *Exploration Econ. Hist.*, Winter 1973, *10*(2), pp. 151–76. [G: U.S.]

Gutman, Herbert G. Work, Culture, and Society in Industrializing America, 1815–1919. *Amer. Hist. Rev.*, June 1973, *78*(3), pp. 531–88. [G: U.S.]

Harley, C. K. On the Persistence of Old Techniques: The Case of North American Wooden Shipbuilding. *J. Econ. Hist.*, June 1973, *33*(2), pp. 372–98.
[G: U.S.]

Higgs, Robert. Race, Tenure, and Resource Allocation in Southern Agriculture, 1910. *J. Econ. Hist.*, March 1973, *33*(1), pp. 149–69. [G: U.S.]

Keller, Robert R. Factor Income Distribution in the United States during the 1920's: A Reexamination of Fact and Theory. *J. Econ. Hist.*, March 1973, *33*(1), pp. 252–73. [G: U.S.]

Kenneally, James J. Women and Trade Unions, 1870-1920: The Quandary of the Reformer. *Labor Hist.*, Winter 1973, *14*(1), pp. 42–55.
[G: U.S.]

Kritzberg, Barry. An Unfinished Chapter in White-Collar Unionism: The Formative Years of the Chicago Newspaper Guild. *Labor Hist.*, Summer 1973, *14*(3), pp. 397–413. [G: U.S.]

Lebergott, Stanley. A New Technique for Time Series? Comment. *Rev. Econ. Statist.*, November 1973, *55*(4), pp. 525–27.

LeWarne, Charles P. On the Wobbly Train to Fresno. *Labor Hist.*, Spring 1973, *14*(2), pp. 264–89.
[G: U.S.]

Mak, James and Walton, Gary M. The Persistence of Old Technologies: The Case of Flatboats. *J. Econ. Hist.*, June 1973, *33*(2), pp. 444–51.
[G: U.S.]

Marcus, Irwin M. Labor Discontent in Tioga County, Pennsylvania, 1865–1905. *Labor Hist.*, Summer 1973, *14*(3), pp. 414–22. [G: U.S.]

Marks, George P., III. The New Orleans Screwmen's Benevolent Association, 1850-1861. *Labor Hist.*, Spring 1973, *14*(2), pp. 259–63. [G: U.S.]

McLaughlin, Doris B. The Second Battle of Battle Creek—The Open Shop Movement in the Early Twentieth Century. *Labor Hist.*, Summer 1973, *14*(3), pp. 323–39. [G: U.S.]

Mercer, Lloyd J. Corporate Farming in the United States: Discussion. *J. Econ. Hist.*, March 1973, *33*(1), pp. 291–95.

Passell, Peter. Corporate Farming in the United States: Discussion. *J. Econ. Hist.*, March 1973, *33*(1), pp. 296–98.

Reed, Merl E. The Augusta Textile Mills and the Strike of 1886. *Labor Hist.*, Spring 1973, *14*(2), pp. 228–46. [G: U.S.]

Reid, Joseph D. Sharecropping as an Understandable Market Response—The Post-Bellum South. *J. Econ. Hist.*, March 1973, *33*(1), pp. 106–30.
[G: U.S.]

Reisler, Mark. Mexican Unionization in California

Agriculture, 1927–1936. *Labor Hist.*, Fall 1973, *14*(4), pp. 562–79. [G: U.S.]

Scharnau, Ralph. Elizabeth Morgan, Crusader for Labor Reform. *Labor Hist.*, Summer 1973, *14*(3), pp. 340–51. [G: U.S.]

Shaw, John A. Railroads, Irrigation, and Economic Growth: The San Joaquin Valley of California. *Exploration Econ. Hist.*, Winter 1973, *10*(2), pp. 211–27. [G: U.S.]

Sutch, Richard and Ransom, Roger. The Ex-Slave in the Post-Bellum South: A Study of the Economic Impact of Racism in a Market Environment. *J. Econ. Hist.*, March 1973, *33*(1), pp. 131–48. [G: U.S.]

Temin, Peter. Labor Scarcity in America. In *Temin, P., ed.*, 1973, pp. 165–80. [G: U.S.]

Uselding, Paul and Juba, Bruce. Biased Technical Progress in American Manufacturing, 1839–1899. *Exploration Econ. Hist.*, Fall 1973, *11*(1), pp. 55–72. [G: U.S.]

Walker, Joseph. Labor-Management Relations at Hopewell Village. *Labor Hist.*, Winter 1973, *14* (1), pp. 3–18. [G: U.S.]

Weinstein, James. Labor and Socialism in America. *Labor Hist.*, Summer 1973, *14*(3), pp. 429–34. [G: U.S.]

Wright, Gavin. Race, Tenure, and Resource Allocation in Southern Agriculture, 1910: Discussion. *J. Econ. Hist.*, March 1973, *33*(1), pp. 170–76. [G: U.S.]

Zabler, Jeffrey F. More on Wage Rates in the Iron Industry: Reply. *Exploration Econ. Hist.*, Fall 1973, *11*(1), pp. 95–99. [G: U.S.]

0423 History of Public Economic Policy (all levels)

Armstrong, Christopher and Nelles, H. V. Private Property in Peril: Ontario Businessmen and the Federal System, 1898–1911. *Bus. Hist. Rev.*, Summer 1973, *47*(2), pp. 158–76. [G: Canada]

Asher, Robert. Radicalism and Reform: State Insurance of Workmen's Compensation in Minnesota, 1910-1933. *Labor Hist.*, Winter 1973, *14*(1), pp. 19–41. [G: U.S.]

Blackford, Mansel G. Banking and Bank Legislation in California, 1890–1915. *Bus. Hist. Rev.*, Winter 1973, *47*(4), pp. 482–507. [G: U.S.]

Bliss, Michael. Another Anti-Trust Tradition: Canadian Anti-Combines Policy, 1889–1910. *Bus. Hist. Rev.*, Summer 1973, *47*(2), pp. 177–88. [G: Canada]

Bromley, David G. and Smith, Joel. The Historical Significance of Annexation as a Social Process. *Land Econ.*, August 1973, *49*(3), pp. 294–309. [G: U.S.]

Bucksar, Richard G. The White Pass and Yukon Railway: Past, Present and Future. *Mich. Academician*, Winter 1973, *5*(3), pp. 315–23. [G: Canada]

Carosso, Vincent P. The Wall Street Money Trust from Pujo through Medina. *Bus. Hist. Rev.*, Winter 1973, *47*(4), pp. 421–37. [G: U.S.]

Clark, Duncan W. Politics and Health Services Research: A Cameo Study of Policy in the Health Services in the 1930's. In *Flook, E. E. and*

Sanazaro, P. J., eds., 1973, pp. 109–25. [G: U.S.]

Dyson, Lowell K. The Southern Tenant Farmers Union and Depression Politics. *Polit. Sci. Quart.*, June 1973, *88*(2), pp. 230–52. [G: U.S.]

Friedman, M. and Schwartz, Anna J. The Panic of 1907 and Banking Reform in Its Wake. In *Temin, P., ed.*, 1973, pp. 315–35. [G: U.S.]

Garraty, John A. The New Deal, National Socialism and the Great Depression. *Amer. Hist. Rev.*, October 1973, *78*(4), pp. 907–44. [G: U.S.; Germany]

Glynn, Sean and Lougheed, Alan L. A Comment on United States Economic Policy and the "Dollar Gap" of the 1920's. *Econ. Hist. Rev., 2nd Ser.*, November 1973, *26*(4), pp. 692–94.

Goldin, Claudia Dale. The Economics of Emancipation. *J. Econ. Hist.*, March 1973, *33*(1), pp. 66–85. [G: U.S.]

Graebner, William. The Coal-Mine Operator and Safety: A Study of Business Reform in the Progressive Period. *Labor Hist.*, Fall 1973, *14*(4), pp. 483–505. [G: U.S.]

Graham, Edward D. Special Interests and the Early China Trade. *Mich. Academician*, Fall 1973, *6*(2), pp. 233–42. [G: U.S.]

Gramm, Warren S. Industrial Capitalism and the Breakdown of the Liberal Rule of Law. *J. Econ. Issues*, December 1973, *7*(4), pp. 577–603. [G: U.S.]

Grossman, Jonathan. Wage and Price Controls During the American Revolution. *Mon. Lab. Rev.*, September 1973, *96*(9), pp. 3–10. [G: U.S.]

Grossman, Jonathan. The Origin of the U.S. Department of Labor. *Mon. Lab. Rev.*, March 1973, *96* (3), pp. 3–7. [G: U.S.]

Grossman, Jonathan. Who is the Father of Labor Day? *Labor Hist.*, Fall 1973, *14*(4), pp. 612–23. [G: U.S.]

Gruchy, Allan G. Law, Politics, and Institutional Economics. *J. Econ. Issues*, December 1973, *7*(4), pp. 623–43. [G: U.S.]

Herbst, Anthony F. and Wu, Joseph S. K. Some Evidence of Subsidization: The U.S. Trucking Industry, 1900–1920. *J. Econ. Hist.*, June 1973, *33* (2), pp. 417–33. [G: U.S.]

Hines, Lawrence G. Precursors to Benefit-Cost Analysis in Early United States Public Investment Projects. *Land Econ.*, August 1973, *49*(3), pp. 310–17. [G: U.S.]

Lapping, Mark B. The Emergence of Federal Public Housing: Atlanta's Techwood Project. *Amer. J. Econ. Soc.*, October 1973, *32*(4), pp. 379–86. [G: U.S.]

Levin, Samuel M. Organized Labor and the Equality of Sacrifice Program. In *Levin, S. M.*, 1973, pp. 127–42. [G: U.S.]

Levin, Samuel M. The Economic Background of the National Labor Relations Act. In *Levin, S. M.*, 1973, pp. 89–98. [G: U.S.]

Levin, Samuel M. The Second Industrial Conference and Adjustment of Disputes. In *Levin, S. M.*, 1973, pp. 15–32. [G: U.S.]

Martin, David A. 1853: The End of Bimetallism in the United States. *J. Econ. Hist.*, December 1973, *33*(4), pp. 825–44. [G: U.S.]

Mercer, Lloyd J. Corporate Farming in the United

States: Discussion. *J. Econ. Hist.*, March 1973, *33* (1), pp. 291–95.

Nordhauser, Norman. Origins of Federal Oil Regulation in the 1920's. *Bus. Hist. Rev.*, Spring 1973, *47* (1), pp. 53–71.   [G: U.S.]

Passell, Peter. Corporate Farming in the United States: Discussion. *J. Econ. Hist.*, March 1973, *33* (1), pp. 296–98.

Peppers, Larry C. Full-Employment Surplus Analysis and Structural Change: The 1930s. *Exploration Econ. Hist.*, Winter 1973, *10*(2), pp. 197–210.   [G: U.S.]

Reading, Don C. New Deal Activity and the States, 1933 to 1939. *J. Econ. Hist.*, December 1973, *33* (4), pp. 792–810.   [G: U.S.]

Reps, John W. Public Land, Urban Development Policy, and the American Planning Tradition. In *Clawson, M., ed.*, 1973, pp. 15–48.   [G: U.S.]

Riesenfeld, Stefan A. Enforcement of Money Judgments in Early American History. *Mich. Law Rev.*, March 1973, *71*(4), pp. 691–728. [G: U.S.]

Rolph, Earl R. The Economics of the Nullification Movement. *Western Econ. J.*, December 1973, *11* (4), pp. 381–93.   [G: U.S.]

Scheiber, Harry N. Property Law, Expropriation, and Resource Allocation by Government: The United States, 1789–1910. *J. Econ. Hist.*, March 1973, *33*(1), pp. 232–51.   [G: U.S.]

Scheinberg, Stephen. Invitation to Empire: Tariffs and American Economic Expansion in Canada. *Bus. Hist. Rev.*, Summer 1973, *47*(2), pp. 218–38.   [G: Canada]

Tontz, Robert L. U.S. Trade Policy: Background and Historical Trends. In *Iowa State University Center for Agricultural and Rural Development*, 1973, pp. 17–48.   [G: U.S.]

Weintraub, Andrew. The Economics of Lincoln's Proposal for Compensated Emancipation. *Amer. J. Econ. Soc.*, April 1973, *32*(2), pp. 171–77.   [G: U.S.]

043 Economic History: Ancient and Medieval (until 1453)

0430 General

Baker, A. R. H. and Butlin, R. A. Studies of Field Systems in the British Isles: Conclusion: Problems and Perspectives. In *Baker, A. R. H. and Butlin, R. A., eds.*, 1973, pp. 619–56.   [G: U.K.]

Baker, A. R. H. Field Systems of Southeast England. In *Baker, A. R. H. and Butlin, R. A., eds.*, 1973, pp. 377–429.   [G: U.K.]

Bridbury, A. R. The Black Death. *Econ. Hist. Rev.*, *2nd Ser.*, November 1973, *26*(4), pp. 577–92.   [G: Europe]

Buchanan, R. H. Field Systems of Ireland. In *Baker, A. R. H. and Butlin, R. A., eds.*, 1973, pp. 580–618.   [G: Ireland]

Davies, M. Field Systems of South Wales. In *Baker, A. R. H. and Butlin, R. A., eds.*, 1973, pp. 480–529.   [G: U.K.]

Dobson, R. B. Admissions to the Freedom of the City of York in the Later Middle Ages. *Econ. Hist. Rev.*, *2nd Ser.*, February 1973, *26*(1), pp. 1–22.   [G: U.K.]

Jones, G. R. J. Field Systems of North Wales. In *Baker, A. R. H. and Butlin, R. A., eds.*, 1973, pp. 430–79.   [G: U.K.]

Miller, Edward. Farming of Manors and Direct Management: Rejoinder. *Econ. Hist. Rev.*, *2nd Ser.*, February 1973, *26*(1), pp. 138–40.   [G: U.K.]

Postan, M. M. Economic Relations between Eastern and Western Europe. In *Postan, M. M. (II)*, 1973, pp. 305–34.   [G: Europe]

Postan, M. M. Italians and the Economic Development of England in the Middle Ages. In *Postan, M. M. (II)*, 1973, pp. 335–41.   [G: Italy; U.K.]

Postan, M. M. Private Financial Instruments in Medieval England. In *Postan, M. M. (II)*, 1973, pp. 28–64.   [G: U.K.]

Postan, M. M. The Economic and Political Relations of England and the Hanse from 1400 to 1475. In *Postan, M. M. (II)*, 1973, pp. 232–304.   [G: N. Europe]

Postan, M. M. Glastonbury Estates in the Twelfth Century. In *Postan, M. M. (I)*, 1973, pp. 249–77.   [G: U.K.]

Postan, M. M. Legal Status and Economic Condition in Medieval Villages. In *Postan, M. M. (I)*, 1973, pp. 278–89.   [G: U.K.]

Postan, M. M. Some Social Consequences of the Hundred Years War. In *Postan, M. M. (I)*, 1973, pp. 49–62.   [G: U.K.; France]

Postan, M. M. The Charters of the Villeins. In *Postan, M. M. (I)*, 1973, pp. 107–49.   [G: U.K.]

Postan, M. M. The Costs of the Hundred Years War. In *Postan, M. M. (I)*, 1973, pp. 63–80. [G: U.K.; France]

Postan, M. M. The Economic Foundations of Medieval Economy. In *Postan, M. M. (I)*, 1973, pp. 3–27.   [G: W. Europe]

Postan, M. M. The Fifteenth Century. In *Postan, M. M. (I)*, 1973, pp. 41–48.   [G: U.K.]

Postan, M. M. The Rise of a Money Economy. In *Postan, M. M. (I)*, 1973, pp. 28–40.   [G: W. Europe]

Postan, M. M. Why Was Science Backward in the Middle Ages? In *Postan, M. M. (I)*, 1973, pp. 81–86.   [G: W. Europe]

Postgate, M. R. Field Systems of East Anglia. In *Baker, A. R. H. and Butlin, R. A., eds.*, 1973, pp. 281–324.   [G: U.K.]

Reed, Clyde G. and Anderson, Terry L. An Economic Explanation of English Agricultural Organization in the Twelfth and Thirteenth Centuries: Comment. *Econ. Hist. Rev.*, *2nd Ser.*, February 1973, *26*(1), pp. 134–37.   [G: U.K.]

Roden, D. Field Systems of the Chiltern Hills and Their Environs. In *Baker, A. R. H. and Butlin, R. A., eds.*, 1973, pp. 325–76.   [G: U.K.]

Rosenthal, Joel T. Medieval Longevity: And the Secular Peerage, 1350–1500. *Population Stud.*, July 1973, *27*(2), pp. 287–93.

Sheppard, J. A. Field Systems of Yorkshire. In *Baker, A. R. H. and Butlin, R. A., eds.*, 1973, pp. 145–87.   [G: U.K.]

Thirsk, J. Field Systems of the East Midlands. In *Baker, A. R. H. and Butlin, R. A., eds.*, 1973, pp. 232–80.   [G: U.K.]

Whittington, G. Field Systems of Scotland. In *Baker,*

A. R. H. and Butlin, R. A., eds., 1973, pp. 530–79.
[G: U.K.]

0431 History of Product Prices and Markets

von Loewe, Karl. Commerce and Agriculture in Lithuania, 1400-1600. *Econ. Hist. Rev., 2nd Ser.,* February 1973, *26*(1), pp. 23–37. [G: Lithuania]

Postan, M. M. Credit in Medieval Trade. In *Postan, M. M. (II),* 1973, pp. 1–27. [G: U.K.]

Postan, M. M. Partnership in English Medieval Commerce. In *Postan, M. M. (II),* 1973, pp. 65–91. [G: U.K.]

Postan, M. M. The Medieval Wool Trade. In *Postan, M. M. (II),* 1973, pp. 342–52. [G: U.K.]

Postan, M. M. The Trade of Medieval Europe: The North. In *Postan, M. M. (II),* 1973, pp. 92–231. [G: N. Europe]

0432 History of Factor Prices and Markets

Mate, Mavis. The Indebtedness of Canterbury Cathedral Priory, 1215–95. *Econ. Hist. Rev., 2nd Ser.,* May 1973, *26*(2), pp. 183–97. [G: U.K.]

Postan, M. M. Some Agrarian Evidence of Declining Population in the Later Middle Ages. In *Postan, M. M. (I),* 1973, pp. 186–213. [G: U.K.]

Postan, M. M. The Chronology of Labour Services. In *Postan, M. M. (I),* 1973, pp. 89–106. [G: U.K.]

0433 History of Public Economic Policy (all levels)

Bean, Richard. War and the Birth of the Nation State. *J. Econ. Hist.,* March 1973, *33*(1), pp. 203–21.

May, Alfred N. An Index of Thirteenth-Century Peasant Impoverishment? Manor Court Fines. *Econ. Hist. Rev., 2nd Ser.,* August 1973, *26*(3), pp. 389–402. [G: U.K.]

Postan, M. M. English Studies of the Customs Accounts. In *Postan, M. M. (II),* 1973, pp. 353–60. [G: U.K.]

Ringrose, David R. War and the Birth of the Nation State: Discussion. *J. Econ. Hist.,* March 1973, *33* (1), pp. 222–27.

Roehl, Richard. War and the Birth of the Nation State: Discussion. *J. Econ. Hist.,* March 1973, *33* (1), pp. 228–31.

044 Economic History: Europe

0440 General

Anderson, Otto. Dødelighedsforholdene i Danmark 1735–1839. (Mortality Conditions in Denmark 1735–1839. With English summary.) *Nationalokon. Tidsskr.,* 1973, *111*(2), pp. 277–305. [G: Denmark]

Appleby, Andrew B. Disease or Famine? Mortality in Cumberland and Westmorland, 1580–1640. *Econ. Hist. Rev., 2nd Ser.,* August 1973, *26*(3), pp. 403–32. [G: U.K.]

Baker, A. R. H. and Butlin, R. A. Studies of Field Systems in the British Isles: Conclusion: Problems and Perspectives. In *Baker, A. R. H. and Butlin, R. A., eds.,* 1973, pp. 619–56. [G: U.K.]

Baker, A. R. H. and Butlin, R. A. Studies of Field Systems in the British Isles: Introduction: Materials and Methods. In *Baker, A. R. H. and Butlin, R. A., eds.,* 1973, pp. 1–40. [G: U.K.]

Baker, A. R. H. Field Systems of Southeast England. In *Baker, A. R. H. and Butlin, R. A., eds.,* 1973, pp. 377–429. [G: U.K.]

Barnsby, G. J. The Standard of Living in the Black Country in the Nineteenth Century: A Rejoinder. *Econ. Hist. Rev., 2nd Ser.,* August 1973, *26*(3), pp. 514–16. [G: U.K.]

Black, R. D. Collinson. The Irish Experience in Relation to the Theory and Policy of Economic Development. In *Youngson, A. J., ed.,* 1973, pp. 192–210. [G: Ireland]

Bouwsma, William J. Lawyers in Early Modern Culture. *Amer. Hist. Rev.,* April 1973, *78*(2), pp. 303–27. [G: Europe]

Buchanan, R. H. Field Systems of Ireland. In *Baker, A. R. H. and Butlin, R. A., eds.,* 1973, pp. 580–618. [G: Ireland]

Butlin, R. A. Field Systems of Northumberland and Durham. In *Baker, A. R. H. and Butlin, R. A., eds.,* 1973, pp. 93–144. [G: U.K.]

Chambers, J. D. The Vale of Trent, 1957. In *Tranter, N. L., ed.,* 1973, pp. 122–26. [G: U.K.]

Cockerell, Hugh. The History of British and American Fire Marks: Comment. *J. Risk Ins.,* December 1973, *40*(4), pp. 639–41. [G: U.S.; U.K.]

Coelho, Philip R. P. The Profitability of Imperialism: The British Experience in the West Indies 1768-1772. *Exploration Econ. Hist.,* Spring 1973, *10*(3), pp. 253–80. [G: U.K.]

Coleman, D. C. Gentlemen and Players. *Econ. Hist. Rev., 2nd Ser.,* February 1973, *26*(1), pp. 92–116. [G: U.K.]

Cole, W. A. Eighteenth-Century Economic Growth Revisited. *Exploration Econ. Hist.,* Summer 1973, *10*(4), pp. 327–48. [G: U.K.]

Crouzet, F. Western Europe and Great Britain: 'Catching Up' in the First Half of the Nineteenth Century. In *Youngson, A. J., ed.,* 1973, pp. 98–125. [G: U.K.; W. Europe]

Daff, Trevor. The Establishment of Ironmaking at Scunthorpe 1858-77. *Bull. Econ. Res.,* November 1973, *25*(2), pp. 104–21. [G: U.K.]

Davies, M. Field Systems of South Wales. In *Baker, A. R. H. and Butlin, R. A., eds.,* 1973, pp. 480–529. [G: U.K.]

Deane, Phyllis. The Role of Capital in the Industrial Revolution. *Exploration Econ. Hist.,* Summer 1973, *10*(4), pp. 349–64. [G: U.K.]

Deane, Phyllis and Cole, W. A. British Economic Growth, 1967. In *Tranter, N. L., ed.,* 1973, pp. 127–35. [G: U.K.]

Elliott, G. Field Systems of Northwest England. In *Baker, A. R. H. and Butlin, R. A., eds.,* 1973, pp. 42–92. [G: U.K.]

Espenshade, Thomas J. A Note on the Population of Seventeenth Century London: Comment. *Demography,* November 1973, *10*(4), pp. 659–60. [G: U.K.]

Everitt, Alan. Town and Country in Victorian Leicestershire: The Role of the Village Carrier. In *Eve-*

ritt, A., ed., 1973, pp. 213–40. [G: U.K.]

Everitt, Alan. Perspectives in English Urban History: Introduction. In Everitt, A., ed., 1973, pp. 1–15. [G: U.K.]

Friedlander, Dov. Demographic Patterns and Socioeconomic Characteristics of the Coal-mining Population in England and Wales in the Nineteenth Century. Econ. Develop. Cult. Change, October 1973, 22(1), pp. 39–51. [G: U.K.]

Good, David F. Backwardness and the Role of Banking in Nineteenth-Century European Industrialization. J. Econ. Hist., December 1973, 33(4), pp. 845–50. [G: Europe]

Gourvish, Terence R. A British Business Elite: The Chief Executive Managers of the Railway Industry, 1850–1922. Bus. Hist. Rev., Autumn 1973, 47(3), pp. 289–316. [G: U.K.]

Griffin, Colin P. The Standard of Living in the Black Country in the Nineteenth Century: A Comment. Econ. Hist. Rev., 2nd Ser., August 1973, 26(3), pp. 510–13. [G: U.K.]

Griffith, G. Talbot. Population Problems in the Age of Malthus, 1967. In Tranter, N. L., ed., 1973, pp. 208–10. [G: U.K.]

Griffiths, Brian. The Development of Restrictive Practices in the U.K. Monetary System. Manchester Sch. Econ. Soc. Stud., March 1973, 41(1), pp. 3–18. [G: U.K.]

Groza, Maria and Iovanelli, Marcela. Activizarea și conducerea politică a maselor țărănești de către Partidul Comunist Român în procesul înfăptuirii sarcinilor desăvîrșirii revoluției burghezo-democratice. (The Activation and the Political Leadership of the Peasant Masses by the Romanian Communist Party in the Fulfilment of the Targets of the Completion of the Bourgeois-Democratic Revolution. With English summary.) Stud. Cercet. Econ., 1973, (3), pp. 19–28. [G: Rumania]

Habakkuk, H. J. American and British Technology in the Nineteenth Century, 1962. In Tranter, N. L., ed., 1973, pp. 136–40. [G: U.S.; U.K.]

Hueckel, Glenn. War and the British Economy, 1793–1815: A General Equilibrium Analysis. Exploration Econ. Hist., Summer 1973, 10(4), pp. 365–96. [G: U.K.]

Hyde, Charles K. The Adoption of the Hot Blast by the British Iron Industry: A Reinterpretation. Exploration Econ. Hist., Spring 1973, 10(3), pp. 281–93. [G: U.K.]

Johnson, Harry M. The History of British and American Fire Marks: Reply. J. Risk Ins., December 1973, 40(4), pp. 641–42. [G: U.S.; U.K.]

Jones, G. R. J. Field Systems of North Wales. In Baker, A. R. H. and Butlin, R. A., eds., 1973, pp. 430–79. [G: U.K.]

Lee, Ronald. Population in Preindustrial England: An Econometric Analysis. Quart. J. Econ., November 1973, 87(4), pp. 581–607. [G: U.K.]

Lefgren, John. Famine in Finland: 1867–1868. Intermountain Econ. Rev., Fall 1973, 4(2), pp. 17–31. [G: Finland]

Mantoux, P. The Industrial Revolution in the Eighteenth Century, 1966. In Tranter, N. L., ed., 1973, pp. 211–17. [G: U.K.]

Maragi, Mario. La problematica del prestito su pegno. (Pledge Loan Problems. With English summary.) Bancaria, July 1973, 29(7), pp. 813–19.

Newell, William H. The Agricultural Revolution in Nineteenth-Century France. J. Econ. Hist., December 1973, 33(4), pp. 697–731. [G: France]

North, Douglass C. and Thomas, Robert Paul. European Economic Growth: Comments on the North-Thomas Theory: Reply. Econ. Hist. Rev., 2nd Ser., May 1973, 26(2), pp. 293–94.

Nove, Alec. Russia as an Emergent Country. In Youngson, A. J., ed., 1973, pp. 79–97. [G: U.S.S.R.]

Palliser, David M. York under the Tudors: The Trading Life of the Northern Capital. In Everitt, A., ed., 1973, pp. 39–59. [G: U.K.]

Parker, William N. Technology, Resources, and Economic Change in the West. In Youngson, A. J., ed., 1973, pp. 62–78. [G: W. Europe]

Pollard, Sidney. Industrialization and the European Economy. Econ. Hist. Rev., 2nd Ser., November 1973, 26(4), pp. 636–48. [G: Europe]

Postgate, M. R. Field Systems of East Anglia. In Baker, A. R. H. and Butlin, R. A., eds., 1973, pp. 281–324. [G: U.K.]

Reed, Clyde G. Transactions Costs and Differential Growth in Seventeenth Century Western Europe. J. Econ. Hist., March 1973, 33(1), pp. 177–90. [G: U.K.; Holland; France; Spain]

Richards, E. S. Structural Change in a Regional Economy: Sutherland and the Industrial Revolution, 1780–1830. Econ. Hist. Rev., 2nd Ser., February 1973, 26(1), pp. 63–76. [G: U.K.]

Ringrose, David R. European Economic Growth: Comments on the North-Thomas Theory. Econ. Hist. Rev., 2nd Ser., May 1973, 26(2), pp. 285–92.

Ringrose, David R. The Impact of a New Capital City: Madrid, Toledo, and New Castile, 1560–1660. J. Econ. Hist., December 1973, 33(4), pp. 761–91. [G: Spain]

Roberts, B. K. Field Systems of the West Midlands. In Baker, A. R. H. and Butlin, R. A., eds., 1973, pp. 188–231. [G: U.K.]

Roden, D. Field Systems of the Chiltern Hills and Their Environs. In Baker, A. R. H. and Butlin, R. A., eds., 1973, pp. 325–76. [G: U.K.]

Rostow, W. W. The Beginnings of Modern Growth in Europe: An Essay in Synthesis. J. Econ. Hist., September 1973, 33(3), pp. 547–80.

Schofield, Roger. Dimensions of Illiteracy, 1750–1850. Exploration Econ. Hist., Summer 1973, 10(4), pp. 437–54. [G: U.K.]

Sheppard, J. A. Field Systems of Yorkshire. In Baker, A. R. H. and Butlin, R. A., eds., 1973, pp. 145–87. [G: U.K.]

Shorter, Edward. Female Emancipation, Birth Control, and Fertility in European History. Amer. Hist. Rev., June 1973, 78(3), pp. 605–40. [G: Europe]

Thirsk, J. Field Systems of the East Midlands. In Baker, A. R. H. and Butlin, R. A., eds., 1973, pp. 232–80. [G: U.K.]

Vasile, Radu. Premisele economice ale revoluției române de la 1848. (The Economic Conditions of the 1848 Romanian Revolution. With English summary.) Stud. Cercet. Econ., 1973, (2), pp. 5–24. [G: Rumania]

de Vries, Jan. On the Modernity of the Dutch Republic. *J. Econ. Hist.*, March 1973, *33*(1), pp. 191–202. [G: Holland]

Whittington, G. Field Systems of Scotland. In *Baker, A. R. H. and Butlin, R. A., eds.*, 1973, pp. 530–79. [G: U.K.]

Whyman, John. A Hanoverian Watering-Place: Margate before the Railway. In *Everitt, A., ed.*, 1973, pp. 138–60. [G: U.K.]

Zito, George V. A Note on the Population of Seventeenth Century London: Reply. *Demography*, November 1973, *10*(4), pp. 661–62. [G: U.K.]

0441 History of Product Prices and Markets

Bogucka, Maria. Amsterdam and the Baltic in the First Half of the Seventeenth Century. *Econ. Hist. Rev.*, 2nd Ser., August 1973, *26*(3), pp. 433–47. [G: Netherlands]

Broeze, Frank J. A. The New Economic History, the Navigation Acts, and the Continental Tobacco Market, 1770–90. *Econ. Hist. Rev.*, 2nd Ser., November 1973, *26*(4), pp. 668–78. [G: U.K.; U.S.]

Conacher, H. M. Causes of the Fall of Agricultural Prices between 1875 and 1895. In *Perry, P. J., ed.*, 1973, pp. 18–29. [G: U.K.]

Coppock, J. T. Agricultural Changes in the Chilterns, 1875–1900. In *Perry, P. J., ed.*, 1973, pp. 56–76. [G: U.K.]

Ernle, [Lord]. The Great Depression and Recovery, 1874–1914. In *Perry, P. J., ed.*, 1973, pp. 1–17. [G: U.K.]

Everitt, Alan. The English Urban Inn, 1560–1760. In *Everitt, A., ed.*, 1973, pp. 91–137. [G: U.K.]

Ferrier, R. W. The Armenians and the East India Company in Persia in the Seventeenth and Early Eighteenth Centuries. *Econ. Hist. Rev.*, 2nd Ser., February 1973, *26*(1), pp. 38–62. [G: Persia]

Fletcher, T. W. Lancashire Livestock Farming during the Great Depression. In *Perry, P. J., ed.*, 1973, pp. 77–108. [G: U.K.]

Hammersley, G. The Charcoal Iron Industry and its Fuel, 1540–1750. *Econ. Hist. Rev.*, 2nd Ser., November 1973, *26*(4), pp. 593–613. [G: U.K.]

Jones, Eric L. The Fashion Manipulators: Consumer Tastes and British Industries, 1660–1800. In *[Williamson, H. F.]*, 1973, pp. 198–226. [G: U.K.]

Jones, S. R. H. Price Associations and Competition in the British Pin Industry, 1814–40. *Econ. Hist. Rev.*, 2nd Ser., May 1973, *26*(2), pp. 237–53. [G: U.K.]

Mathias, Peter. Debates in Economic History: Introduction. In *Perry, P. J., ed.*, 1973, pp. xi–xliv. [G: U.K.]

Perren, R. The Landlord and Agricultural Transformation, 1870–1900. In *Perry, P. J., ed.*, 1973, pp. 109–28. [G: U.K.]

Perry, P. J. Where was the 'Great Agricultural Depression'? A Geography of Agricultural Bankruptcy in Late Victorian England and Wales. In *Perry, P. J., ed.*, 1973, pp. 129–48. [G: U.K.]

Trebilcock, Clive. British Armaments and European Industrialization, 1890–1914. *Econ. Hist. Rev.*,

2nd Ser., May 1973, *26*(2), pp. 254–72. [G: U.K.]

0442 History of Factor Prices and Markets

Brito, Dagobert L. and Williamson, Jeffrey G. Skilled Labor and Nineteenth Century Anglo-American Managerial Behavior. *Exploration Econ. Hist.*, Spring 1973, *10*(3), pp. 235–51. [G: U.S.; U.K.]

Hyde, Charles K. The Adoption of Coke-Smelting by the British Iron Industry, 1709–1790. *Exploration Econ. Hist.*, Summer 1973, *10*(4), pp. 397–418. [G: U.K.]

Kahan, Arcadius. Notes on Serfdom in Western and Eastern Europe. *J. Econ. Hist.*, March 1973, *33*(1), pp. 86–99.

Lösche, Peter. Stages in the Evolution of the German Labor Movement. In *Sturmthal, A. and Scoville, J. G., eds.*, 1973, pp. 101–22. [G: Germany]

Merrett, A. J. and Sykes, Allen. Return on Equities and Fixed Interest Securities: 1919–66. In *Lister, R. J., ed.*, 1973, pp. 28–38. [G: U.K.]

Meyer, John R. Notes on Serfdom in Western and Eastern Europe: Discussion. *J. Econ. Hist.*, March 1973, *33*(1), pp. 100–105.

Riley, J. C. Dutch Investment in France, 1781–1787. *J. Econ. Hist.*, December 1973, *33*(4), pp. 732–60. [G: Netherlands; France]

Sellier, François. The French Workers' Movement and Political Unionism. In *Sturmthal, A. and Scoville, J. G., eds.*, 1973, pp. 79–100. [G: France]

Soly, H. Grondspeculatie en kapitalisme te Antwerpen in de 16e eeuw. (Real Estate Speculation and Capitalism in Antwerp in the 16th Century. With English summary.) *Econ. Soc. Tijdschr.*, June 1973, *27*(3), pp. 291–302. [G: Belgium]

Tilly, Richard H. Zeitreihen zum Geldumlauf in Deutschland, 1870–1913. (Time Series Concerning the Aggregate Money Supply in Germany, 1870–1913. With English summary.) *Jahr. Nationalökon. Statist.*, May 1973, *187*(4), pp. 330–63. [G: Germany]

0443 History of Public Economic Policy (all levels)

Barkai, Haim. The Macro-Economics of Tsarist Russia in the Industrialization Era: Monetary Developments, the Balance of Payments and the Gold Standard. *J. Econ. Hist.*, June 1973, *33*(2), pp. 339–71. [G: U.S.S.R.]

Broeze, Frank J. A. The New Economic History, the Navigation Acts, and the Continental Tobacco Market, 1770–90. *Econ. Hist. Rev.*, 2nd Ser., November 1973, *26*(4), pp. 668–78. [G: U.K.; U.S.]

Cox, R. C. W. The Old Centre of Croydon: Victorian Decay and Redevelopment. In *Everitt, A., ed.*, 1973, pp. 184–212. [G: U.K.]

Despres, Emile. Germany's Exchange Control Mechanism. In *Despres, E.*, 1973, pp. 13–27.

Farrar, Marjorie M. Preclusive Purchases: Politics and Economic Warfare in France during the First World War. *Econ. Hist. Rev.*, 2nd Ser., February 1973, *26*(1), pp. 117–33. [G: France]

Gentles, Ian. The Sales of Crown Lands During the

English Revolution. *Econ. Hist. Rev., 2nd Ser.,* November 1973, *26*(4), pp. 614–35.   [G: U.K.]

Gould, J. The Great Debasement and the Supply of Money. *Australian Econ. Hist. Rev.,* September 1973, *13*(2), pp. 177–89.   [G: U.K.]

Heal, Felicity. The Tudors and Church Lands: Economic Problems of the Bishopric of Ely during the Sixteenth Century. *Econ. Hist. Rev., 2nd Ser.,* May 1973, *26*(2), pp. 198–217.   [G: U.K.]

Jago, Charles. The Influence of Debt on the Relations between Crown and Aristocracy in Seventeenth-Century Castile. *Econ. Hist. Rev., 2nd Ser.,* May 1973, *26*(2), pp. 218–36.   [G: U.K.]

Kirby, M. W. The Control of Competition in the British Coal Mining Industry in the Thirties. *Econ. Hist. Rev., 2nd Ser.,* May 1973, *26*(2), pp. 273–84.   [G: U.K.]

Loschky, David J. Studies of the Navigation Acts: New Economic Non-History? *Econ. Hist. Rev., 2nd Ser.,* November 1973, *26*(4), pp. 689–91.

Lowry, S. Todd. Lord Mansfield and the Law Merchant: Law and Economics in the Eighteenth Century. *J. Econ. Issues,* December 1973, *7*(4), pp. 605–22.   [G: U.K.]

Mafeje, Archie. Agrarian Revolution and the Land Question in Buganda. In *Institute for Development Research,* 1973, pp. 127–54.   [G: Uganda; U.K.]

McClelland, Peter D. The New Economic History and the Burdens of the Navigation Acts: Comment. *Econ. Hist. Rev., 2nd Ser.,* November 1973, *26*(4), pp. 679–86.

McCloskey, Donald N. New Perspectives on the Old Poor Law. *Exploration Econ. Hist.,* Summer 1973, *10*(4), pp. 419–36.   [G: U.K.]

McLean, David. Commerce, Finance, and British Diplomatic Support in China, 1885–86. *Econ. Hist. Rev., 2nd Ser.,* August 1973, *26*(3), pp. 464–76.   [G: U.K.; China]

Platt, D. C. M. Further Objections to an "Imperialism of Free Trade," 1830–60. *Econ. Hist. Rev., 2nd Ser.,* February 1973, *26*(1), pp. 77–91.   [G: U.K.]

Walton, Gary M. The Burdens of the Navigation Acts: Reply. *Econ. Hist. Rev., 2nd Ser.,* November 1973, *26*(4), pp. 687–88.

045 Economic History: Asia

0450 General

Bagchi, Amiya Kumar. Foreign Capital and Economic Development in India: A Schematic View. In *Gough, K. and Sharma, H. P., eds.,* 1973, pp. 43–76.   [G: India]

Chen, Nai-Ruenn. Economic Structure of Traditional China. In *Meskill, J., ed.,* 1973, pp. 463–81.   [G: China]

Goldstein, Melvyn C. The Circulation of Estates in Tibet: Reincarnation, Land and Politics. *J. Asian Stud.,* May 1973, *32*(3), pp. 445–55.   [G: Tibet]

Hou, Chi-Ming. Economic Trends in Modern China. In *Meskill, J., ed.,* 1973, pp. 483–513.   [G: China]

Hufbauer, G. C. Occupational Trends and Social Mobility in the West Punjab. *Pakistan Econ. Soc.*

Rev., Spring 1973, *11*(1), pp. 83–103.   [G: India]

Klein, Ira. Death in India, 1871–1921. *J. Asian Stud.,* August 1973, *32*(4), pp. 639–59.   [G: India]

Macpherson, W. J. Economic Development in India under the British Crown, 1858–1947. In *Youngson, A. J., ed.,* 1973, pp. 126–91.   [G: India]

Malaker, C. R. Construction of Nuptiality Tables for the Single Population in India: 1901–1931. *Demography,* November 1973, *10*(4), pp. 525–35.   [G: India]

McCord, William. The Japanese Model. In *Wilber, C. K., ed.,* 1973, pp. 278–83.   [G: Japan]

McLean, David. Commerce, Finance, and British Diplomatic Support in China, 1885–86. *Econ. Hist. Rev., 2nd Ser.,* August 1973, *26*(3), pp. 464–76.   [G: U.K.; China]

Nakamura, Satoru. The Historical Preconditions of the Formations of Capitalism in Japan. *Kyoto Univ. Econ. Rev.,* April–October 1973, *43*(1–2), pp. 30–44.   [G: Japan]

Penny, David H. and Singarimbun, Masri. Economic Activity among the Karo Batak of Indonesia: A Case Study in Economic Change. In *Epstein, T. S. and Penny, D. H., eds.,* 1973, pp. 86–113.   [G: Indonesia]

Rosovsky, H. What are the 'Lessons' of Japanese Economic History. In *Youngson, A. J., ed.,* 1973, pp. 229–53.   [G: Japan]

Yamamura, Kozo. Economic Responsiveness in Japanese Industrialization. In *[Williamson, H. F.],* 1973, pp. 173–97.   [G: Japan]

Yamamura, Kozo. Toward a Reexamination of the Economic History of Tokugawa Japan, 1600–1867. *J. Econ. Hist.,* September 1973, *33*(3), pp. 509–46.   [G: Japan]

Yamamura, Kozo. The Development of Za in Medieval Japan. *Bus. Hist. Rev.,* Winter 1973, *47*(4), pp. 438–65.   [G: Japan]

Zahn, Frank. A Test of the Escape from the Persistence of Backwardness. *J. Devel. Stud.,* April 1973, *9*(3), pp. 403–11.   [G: Japan]

0452 History of Factor Prices and Markets

Mazumdar, D. Labour Supply in Early Industrialization: the Case of the Bombay Textile Industry. *Econ. Hist. Rev., 2nd Ser.,* August 1973, *26*(3), pp. 477–96.   [G: India]

Taira, Koji. Labor Markets, Unions, and Employers in Inter-war Japan. In *Sturmthal, A. and Scoville, J. G., eds.,* 1973, pp. 149–77.   [G: Japan]

0453 History of Public Economic Policy (all levels)

Chung, N. H. Paul and Chong, Fei Wan. The Currency Reform of the Straits Settlements and Malay States: Misunderstood Intention. *Malayan Econ. Rev.,* April 1973, *18*(1), pp. 48–54.   [G: Malaya]

Hsü, King-yi. Agrarian Policies of the Chinese Communists: Extraction of Rural Resources During the Kiangsi Period. *Mich. Academician,* Spring 1973, *5*(4), pp. 515–28.   [G: China]

046 Economic History: Africa

0460 General

Amin, Samir. Underdevelopment and Dependence in Black Africa—Their Historical Origins and Contemporary Forms. *Soc. Econ. Stud.,* March 1973, *22*(1), pp. 177–96. [G: Africa]

Arrighi, Giovanni. The Political Economy of Rhodesia. In *Arrighi, G. and Saul, J. S.,* 1973, pp. 336–77. [G: Rhodesia]

Mafeje, Archie. Agrarian Revolution and the Land Question in Buganda. In *Institute for Development Research,* 1973, pp. 127–54. [G: Uganda; U.K.]

0461 History of Product Prices and Markets

Fortt, J. M. and Hougham, D. A. Environment, Population and Economic History. In *Richards, A. I.; Sturrock, F. and Fortt, J. M., eds.,* 1973, pp. 17–46. [G: Uganda]

0463 History of Public Economic Policy (all levels)

Botha, D. J. J. On Tariff Policy: The Formative Years. *S. Afr. J. Econ.,* December 1973, *41*(4), pp. 321–55. [G: S.Africa]

Ehrlich, Cyril. Building and Caretaking: Economic Policy in British Tropical Africa, 1890–1960. *Econ. Hist. Rev., 2nd Ser.,* November 1973, *26*(4), pp. 649–67. [G: Africa]

Fortt, J. M. Land Tenure and the Emergence of Large Scale Farming. In *Richards, A. I.; Sturrock, F. and Fortt, J. M., eds.,* 1973, pp. 66–84. [G: Uganda]

Seidman, Robert B. Contract Law, the Free Market, and State Intervention: A Jurisprudential Perspective. *J. Econ. Issues,* December 1973, *7*(4), pp. 553–75. [G: Kenya; Ghana]

047 Economic History: Latin America and Caribbean

0470 General

Baer, Werner and Villela, Annibal V. Industrial Growth and Industrialization: Revisions in the Stages of Brazil's Economic Development. *J. Devel. Areas,* January 1973, *7*(2), pp. 217–34. [G: Brazil]

Coelho, Philip R. P. The Profitability of Imperialism: The British Experience in the West Indies 1768-1772. *Exploration Econ. Hist.,* Spring 1973, *10*(3), pp. 253–80. [G: U.K.]

French, Christopher J. Eighteenth-Century Shipping Tonnage Measurements. *J. Econ. Hist.,* June 1973, *33*(2), pp. 434–43. [G: British West Indies]

Gedicks, Al. The Nationalization of Copper in Chile: Antecedents and Consequences. *Rev. Radical Polit. Econ.,* Fall 1973, *5*(3), pp. 1–25. [G: Chile]

Green, W. A. The Planter Class and the British West Indian Sugar Production, before and after Eman-

cipation. *Econ. Hist. Rev., 2nd Ser.,* August 1973, *26*(3), pp. 448–63. [G: Caribbean]

Higman, B. W. Household Structure and Fertility on Jamaican Slave Plantations: A Nineteenth-Century Example. *Population Stud.,* November 1973, *27*(3), pp. 527–50. [G: Jamaica]

Johnson, Harold B., Jr. A Preliminary Inquiry into Money, Prices, and Wages in Rio de Janeiro, 1763–1823. In *Alden, D., ed.,* 1973, pp. 231–83. [G: Brazil]

Kane, N. Stephen. Bankers and Diplomats: The Diplomacy of the Dollar in Mexico, 1921–1924. *Bus. Hist. Rev.,* Autumn 1973, *47*(3), pp. 335–52. [G: Mexico]

Lagos, Ricardo. The Historical Background to the Present Economic Situation in Chile. In *Zammit, J. A., ed.,* 1973, pp. 41–45. [G: Chile]

Leff, Nathaniel H. Tropical Trade and Development in the Nineteenth Century: The Brazilian Experience. *J. Polit. Econ.,* May-June 1973, *81*(3), pp. 678–96. [G: Brazil]

Taylor, Frank F. The Tourist Industry in Jamaica, 1919–1939. *Soc. Econ. Stud.,* June 1973, *22*(2), pp. 205–28. [G: Jamaica]

0472 History of Factor Prices and Markets

MacLachlan, Colin M. The Indian Labor Structure in the Portuguese Amazon, 1700–1800. In *Alden, D., ed.,* 1973, pp. 199–230. [G: Brazil]

Schwartz, Stuart B. Free Labor in a Slave Economy: The *Lavrodores de Cana* of Colonial Bahia. In *Alden, D., ed.,* 1973, pp. 147–97. [G: Brazil]

0473 History of Public Economic Policy (all levels)

Love, Joseph. External Financing and Domestic Politics: The Case of São Paulo, Brazil, 1889–1937. In *Scott, R. E., ed.,* 1973, pp. 236–59. [G: Brazil]

048 Economic History: Oceania

0480 General

Barwick, Diane. Coranderrk and Cumeroogunga: Pioneers and Policy. In *Epstein, T. S. and Penny, D. H., eds.,* 1973, pp. 11–68. [G: Australia]

Martin, A. W. Australia and the Hartz 'Fragment' Thesis. *Australian Econ. Hist. Rev.,* September 1973, *13*(2), pp. 131–47. [G: Australia]

McCarty, J. W. Australia as a Region of Recent Settlement in the Nineteenth Century. *Australian Econ. Hist. Rev.,* September 1973, *13*(2), pp. 148–67. [G: Australia]

McLean, I. W. The Adoption of Harvest Machinery in Victoria in the Late Nineteenth Century. *Australian Econ. Hist. Rev.,* March 1973, *13*(1), pp. 41–56. [G: Australia]

Pool, D. I. Estimates of New Zealand Maori Vital Rates from the Mid-Nineteenth Century to World War I. *Population Stud.,* March 1973, *27*(1), pp. 117–25. [G: New Zealand]

Schedvin, C. B. A Century of Money in Australia. *Econ. Rec.,* December 1973, *49*(128), pp. 588–605. [G: Australia]

Snooks, G. D. Innovation and the Growth of the Firm: Hume Enterprises 1910–40. *Australian Econ. Hist. Rev.*, March 1973, *13*(1), pp. 16–40. [G: Australia]

Snooks, G. D. Depression and Recovery in Western Australia, 1928–29 to 1938–39: A Deviation from the Norm. *Econ. Rec.*, September 1973, *49*(127), pp. 420–39. [G: Australia]

Snooks, G. D. The Growth Process of the Firm: A Case Study. *Australian Econ. Pap.*, December 1973, *12*(21), pp. 162–74. [G: Australia]

0481 History of Product Prices and Markets

Bambrick, Susan. Australian Price Levels, 1890–1970. *Australian Econ. Hist. Rev.*, March 1973, *13*(1), pp. 57–71. [G: Australia]

McLean, I. W. Growth and Technological Change in Agriculture: Victoria 1870–1910. *Econ. Rec.*, December 1973, *49*(128), pp. 560–74. [G: Australia]

0483 History of Public Economic Policy (all levels)

Boehm, E. A. Australia's Economic Depression of the 1930s. *Econ. Rec.*, December 1973, *49*(128), pp. 606–23. [G: Australia]

Cain, Neville. Political Economy and the Tariff: Australia in the 1920s. *Australian Econ. Pap.*, June 1973, *12*(20), pp. 1–20. [G: Australia]

Hawke, G. R. The Government and the Depression of the 1930s in New Zealand: An Essay Towards a Revision. *Australian Econ. Hist. Rev.*, March 1973, *13*(1), pp. 72–95. [G: New Zealand]

050 ECONOMIC SYSTEMS

051 Capitalist Economic Systems

0510 Market Economies

Ackerman, Robert W. How Companies Respond to Social Demands. *Harvard Bus. Rev.*, July-August 1973, *51*(4), pp. 88–98.

Alchian, Armen A. and Demsetz, Harold. The Property Rights Paradigm. *J. Econ. Hist.*, March 1973, *33*(1), pp. 16–27.

Anderson, W. T., Jr. and Sharpe, L. K. The New American Marketplace: Life-Style in Revolution. In *Thorelli, H. B., ed.,* 1973, pp. 146–53. [G: U.S.]

Andrews, Kenneth R. Can the Best Corporations be Made Moral? *Harvard Bus. Rev.*, May-June 1973, *51*(3), pp. 57–64.

Banke, Niels. Kommentarer til Karl Marx's mindesten. (On Marxian Economics. With English summary.) *Nationalokon. Tidsskr.*, 1973, *111*(1), pp. 112–43.

Becker, James F. Class Structure and Conflict in the Managerial Phase: II. *Sci. Soc.*, Winter 1973–1974, *37*(4), pp. 437–53.

Becsky, Gy. An Analysis of the Economic Growth in Developed Capitalist Countries: Comment and Criticism. *Acta Oecon.*, 1973, *11*(2–3), pp. 247–62.

Bichi, C. Inflaţia în ţările capitaliste şi apologia ei. (Inflation in the Capitalist Countries and its Apology. With English summary.) *Stud. Cercet. Econ.*, 1973, (1), pp. 163–79.

Boulding, Kenneth E. Economic Progress as a Goal in Economic Life. In *Boulding, K. E.,* 1973, pp. 53–86.

Boulding, Kenneth E. Is Scarcity Dead? In *Boulding, K. E.,* 1973, pp. 311–21. [G: U.S.]

Boulding, Kenneth E. Religious Foundations of Economic Progress. In *Boulding, K. E.,* 1973, pp. 41–51.

Boulding, Kenneth E. The Changing Framework of American Capitalism. In *Boulding, K. E.,* 1973, pp. 251–56. [G: U.S.]

Boulding, Kenneth E. The Future Corporation and Public Attitudes. In *Boulding, K. E.,* 1973, pp. 175–93. [G: U.S.]

Boulding, Kenneth E. The Public Image of American Economic Institutions. In *Boulding, K. E.,* 1973, pp. 127–45. [G: U.S.]

Boulding, Kenneth E. The Scientific-Military-Industrial Complex. In *Boulding, K. E.,* 1973, pp. 351–60. [G: U.S.]

Bradshaw, T. F. Corporate Social Reform: An Executive's Viewpoint. *Calif. Manage. Rev.*, Summer 1973, *15*(4), pp. 85–89.

Brummet, R. Lee. Total Performance Measurement. *Manage. Account.*, November 1973, *55*(5), pp. 11–15.

Cardoso, Fernando Henrique. Imperialism and Dependency in Latin America. In *Bonilla, F. and Girling, R., eds.,* 1973, pp. 7–16.

Carnoy, Martin. Financial Institutions and Dependency. In *Bonilla, F. and Girling, R., eds.,* 1973, pp. 34–45. [G: U.S.]

Cherry, Robert. Class Struggle and the Nature of the Working Class. *Rev. Radical Polit. Econ.*, Summer 1973, *5*(2), pp. 47–86. [G: U.S.]

England, Richard and Bluestone, Barry. Ecology and Social Conflict. In *Daly, H. E., ed.,* 1973, pp. 190–214. [G: U.S.]

Epstein, Edwin M. Dimensions of Corporate Power, Pt. 1. *Calif. Manage. Rev.*, Winter 1973, *16*(2), pp. 9–23. [G: U.S.]

Flores, Guillermo V. and Bailey, Ronald. Internal Colonialism and Racial Minorities in the U.S.: An Overview. In *Bonilla, F. and Girling, R., eds.,* 1973, pp. 149–60. [G: U.S.]

Galbraith, John Kenneth. Power and the Useful Economist. *Amer. Econ. Rev.*, March 1973, *63*(1), pp. 1–11. [G: U.S.]

Galbraith, John Kenneth. The Theory of Social Balance. In *Reynolds, L. G.; Green, G. D. and Lewis, D. R., eds.,* 1973, pp. 304–14. [G: U.S.]

Gramm, Warren S. Industrial Capitalism and the Breakdown of the Liberal Rule of Law. *J. Econ. Issues,* December 1973, *7*(4), pp. 577–603. [G: U.S.]

Gray, Daniel H. Methodology: One Approach to the Corporate Social Audit. *Calif. Manage. Rev.*, Summer 1973, *15*(4), pp. 106–09.

Grayson, C. Jackson, Jr. Let's Get Back to the Competitive Market System. *Harvard Bus. Rev.*, November-December 1973, *51*(6), pp. 103–12. [G: U.S.]

Habermas, Jürgen. What Does a Crisis Mean Today? Legitimation Problems in Late Capitalism. *Soc. Res.*, Winter 1973, *40*(4), pp. 643–67.

Hardesty, John; Clement, Norris C. and Jencks, Clinton E. Ecological Conflicts: A Reply. *Rev. Radical Polit. Econ.*, Summer 1973, *5*(2), pp. 95–102.

Havrilesky, Thomas M. Legitimating the Corporate State. *Amer. Econ.*, Spring 1973, *17*(1), pp. 169–73.

Henderson, Hazel. Ecologists versus Economists. *Harvard Bus. Rev.*, July-August 1973, *51*(4), pp. 28–36, 152–57.

Jaeger, Klaus. Zur Problematik der Gewinnbeteiligung der Arbeitnehmer als Mittel der Vermögenspolitik. (Profit-Sharing as an Instrument of Ownership Policy. With English summary.) *Z. Wirtschaft. Sozialwissen.*, 1973, *93*(6), pp. 687–707. [G: W. Germany]

Katona, George; Strumpel, Burkhard and Zahn, E. The Sociocultural Environment. In *Thorelli, H. B., ed.*, 1973, pp. 135–45. [G: U.S.; W. Germany; U.K.; Italy]

Krusius-Ahrenberg, Lolo. Kring företagsdemokratin i tyska förbundsrepubliken. (On Industrial Democracy in the Federal Republic of Germany. With English summary.) *Ekon. Samfundets Tidskr.*, 1973, *26*(4), pp. 270–99. [G: W. Germany]

Lancaster, Kelvin. The Dynamic Inefficiency of Capitalism. *J. Polit. Econ.*, September-October 1973, *81*(5), pp. 1092–1109.

Leathers, Charles G. and Evans, John S. Thorstein Veblen and the New Industrial State. *Hist. Polit. Econ.*, Fall 1973, *5*(2), pp. 420–37.

Levin, Samuel M. Technology and Liberty. In *Levin, S. M.*, 1973, pp. 115–26. [G: U.S.]

Levin, Samuel M. Thoughts on Industrial Democracy. In *Levin, S. M.*, 1973, pp. 143–56. [G: U.S.]

Luoma, Väinö. Yritys ja yhteiskunta. (The Enterprise and Society: The Social Responsibility of Management in Outline. With English summary.) *Liiketaloudellinen Aikak.*, 1973, *22*(1), pp. 18–28.

McCall, David B. Profit: Spur for Solving Social Ills. *Harvard Bus. Rev.*, May-June 1973, *51*(3), pp. 46–54, 180–82. [G: U.S.]

Mestmäcker, Ernst-Joachim. Wettbewerbspolitik in der Industriegesellschaft. (Policy of Competition in the Industrial Society. With English summary.) *Z. ges. Staatswiss.*, February 1973, *129*(1), pp. 89–101. [G: W. Germany]

Moore, Philip W. Corporate Social Reform: An Activist's Viewpoint. *Calif. Manage. Rev.*, Summer 1973, *15*(4), pp. 90–96.

Myrdal, Gunnar. The Place of Values in Social Policy. In *Myrdal, G.*, 1973, pp. 33–51.

Nader, Ralph. A Citizen's Guide to the American Economy. In *Haveman, R. H. and Hamrin, R. D., eds.*, 1973, pp. 33–42. [G: U.S.]

O'Donnell, L. A. Rationalism, Capitalism and the Entrepreneur: The Views of Veblen and Schumpeter. *Hist. Polit. Econ.*, Spring 1973, *5*(1), pp. 199–214.

Pásara, Luís and Santistevan, Jorge. "Industrial Communities" and Trade Unions in Peru: A Preliminary Analysis. *Int. Lab. Rev.*, August-September 1973, *108*(2–3), pp. 127–42. [G: Peru]

Pejovich, Svetozar. Good Old Economic History: Discussion. *J. Econ. Hist.*, March 1973, *33*(1), pp. 41–42.

Pochkin, P. The Effectiveness of Production in Bourgeois Literature. *Prob. Econ.*, June 1973, *16*(2), pp. 84–102.

Richman, Barry. New Paths to Corporate Social Responsibility. *Calif. Manage. Rev.*, Spring 1973, *15*(3), pp. 20–36.

Robinson, Derek. Capital-Sharing Schemes. In *Robinson, D.*, 1973, pp. 137–57.

Robinson, Derek. Trade Union Views on Workers' Negotiated Savings Plans for Capital Formation. In *Robinson, D.*, 1973, pp. 76–104. [G: W. Europe]

Robinson, Derek. Workers' Savings Plans for Capital Formation in Germany. In *Robinson, D.*, 1973, pp. 105–36. [G: W. Germany]

Salgo, Harvey. The Obsolescence of Growth: Capitalism and the Environmental Crisis. *Rev. Radical Polit. Econ.*, Fall 1973, *5*(3), pp. 26–45.

Schmidt, Benicio Viero. Dependency and the Multinational Corporation. In *Bonilla, F. and Girling, R., eds.*, 1973, pp. 17–33. [G: U.S.; Latin America]

Shocker, Allan D. and Sethi, S. Prakash. An Approach to Incorporating Societal Preferences in Developing Corporate Action Strategies. *Calif. Manage. Rev.*, Summer 1973, *15*(4), pp. 97–105.

Sunkel, Osvaldo. Transnational Capitalism and National Disintegration in Latin America. *Soc. Econ. Stud.*, March 1973, *22*(1), pp. 132–76. [G: Latin America]

Votaw, Dow. Genius Becomes Rare: A Comment on the Doctrine of Social Responsibility Pt. II. *Calif. Manage. Rev.*, Spring 1973, *15*(3), pp. 5–19.

Wachtel, Howard M. Theses on Poverty and Inequality. *Amer. Econ.*, Fall 1973, *17*(2), pp. 17–22.

Weaver, James H. Economic Growth, Inequality, Hierarchy, Alienation: The Impact of Socialization Processes in Capitalist Society. *Amer. Econ.*, Fall 1973, *17*(2), pp. 9–16. [G: U.S.]

Weisskopf, Thomas E. Capitalism and Underdevelopment in the Modern World. In *Reynolds, L. G.; Green, G. D. and Lewis, D. R., eds.*, 1973, pp. 518–29.

Williams, B. R. The Basis of Science Policy in Market Economies. In *Williams, B. R., ed.*, 1973, pp. 416–31.

Winter, Ralph K., Jr. Economic Regulation vs. Competition: Ralph Nader and Creeping Capitalism. *Yale Law J.*, April 1973, *82*(5), pp. 890–902. [G: U.S.]

Wolfe, Alan. Waiting for Righty: A Critique of the "Fascism" Hypothesis. *Rev. Radical Polit. Econ.*, Fall 1973, *5*(3), pp. 46–66.

052 Socialist and Communist Economic Systems

0520 Socialist and Communist Economic Systems

Alekseev, V. Protection of the Natural Environment (Economic Aspect) *Prob. Econ.*, November 1973, *16*(7), pp. 24–35.

Allende, Salvador. The Chilean Road to Socialism. In *Zammit, J. A., ed.*, 1973, pp. 17–25. [G: Chile]

Arrighi, Giovanni and Saul, John S. Socialism and Economic Development in Tropical Africa. In *Arrighi, G. and Saul, J. S.*, 1973, pp. 11–43. [G: Tanzania]

Asher, Ephraim. Consumers Time-Preferences and Welfare Economics under Socialism. *Scot. J. Polit. Econ.*, November 1973, *20*(3), pp. 283–90.

Atlas, Z. Profits and Profitability as Criteria of the Effectiveness of Production. *Prob. Econ.*, December 1973, *16*(8), pp. 56–80.

Bácskai, T. The Experience of Savings-Banks in Socialist Economies and its Applicability to Developing Countries. *Acta Oecon.*, 1973, *10*(2), pp. 201–16.

Balassa, Bela. The Firm in the New Economic Mechanism in Hungary. In *Bornstein, M., ed.*, 1973, pp. 347–72. [G: Hungary]

Balázsy, S. Financial Regulating System and Technical Development. *Acta Oecon.*, 1973, *10*(3–4), pp. 315–38. [G: Hungary]

Belen'kii, V. Z.; Volkonskii, V. A. and Pavlov, N. V. Dynamic Input-Output Models in Planning and Price Calculations and Economic Analysis. *Matekon*, Winter 1973-74, *10*(2), pp. 74–101. [G: U.S.S.R.]

Bornstein, Morris. Plan and Market: Economic Reform in Eastern Europe: Introduction. In *Bornstein, M., ed.*, 1973, pp. 1–22. [G: E. Europe]

Brada, Josef C. The Allocative Efficiency of Centrally Planned Foreign Trade: A Programming Approach to the Czech Case. *Europ. Econ. Rev.*, December 1973, *4*(4), pp. 329–46. [G: Czechoslovakia]

Bryson, Phillip J. Dynamic Price Planning in Command Systems: A Partial Equilibrium Approach. *Weltwirtsch. Arch.*, 1973, *109*(3), pp. 495–513.

Bulgaru, Mircea. Modificări în structura social-profesională a populației României în anii Republicii. (Changes in the Social-Professional Structure of Romania's Population in the Years of the Republic. With English summary.) *Stud. Cercet. Econ.*, 1973, (1), pp. 5–11. [G: Rumania]

Burks, R. V. The Political Implications of Economic Reform. In *Bornstein, M., ed.*, 1973, pp. 373–402. [G: E. Europe]

Bzhilianskii, Iu. Political and Economic Problems of Population Under Socialism. *Prob. Econ.*, April 1973, *15*(12), pp. 52–72. [G: U.S.S.R.]

Călin, Oprea and Ciucur, Elena. Rolul prețului de cost în cadrul sistemului informațional economic al întreprinderii. (The Role of the Cost Price in the Economic Informational System of the Enterprise. With English summary.) *Stud. Cercet. Econ.*, 1973, (4), pp. 111–26.

Cameron, Norman. Incentives and Labour Supply in Co-operative Enterprises. *Can. J. Econ.*, February 1973, *6*(1), pp. 16–22. [G: U.S.S.R.]

Chalupski, Z. Characteristics of the Socialist International Market. In *Kiss, T., ed.*, 1973, pp. 57–62.

Ciucur, Dumitru and Gavrilă, Ilie. Competența economică a muncitorului modern din țara noastră. (The Economic Competence of the Modern Worker in Our Country. With English summary.) *Stud. Cercet. Econ.*, 1973, (4), pp. 15–23. [G: Rumania]

Costache, Sandu and Popescu, Constantin. Coordonate ale echilibrului dezvoltării economico-sociale în profil de ramură și teritorial. (Coordinates of the Equilibrium of Economic-Social Development as Regards Branch and Territory. With English summary.) *Stud. Cercet. Econ.*, 1973, (4), pp. 25–38. [G: Rumania]

Crook, Frederick W. Collective Farms in Communist China. *Mon. Lab. Rev.*, March 1973, *96*(3), pp. 45–50. [G: China]

Dobrotă, Niță. Principalele caracteristici ale unei țări în curs de dezvoltare. (The Main Characteristics of a Developing Country. With English summary.) *Stud. Cercet. Econ.*, 1973, (1), pp. 13–26. [G: Rumania]

Drecin, J. and Hetényi, I. Some Thoughts Concerning the Future of our Planning. (In Russian. With English summary.) *Acta Oecon.*, 1973, *11*(2–3), pp. 129–48. [G: E. Europe]

Dumitru, Georgeta and Purcărea, M. Eficiența economică a diversificării producției industriale. (The Economic Efficiency of the Diversification of Industrial Production. With English summary.) *Stud. Cercet. Econ.*, 1973, (2), pp. 63–71.

Ellman, Michael. Bonus Formulae and Soviet Managerial Performance: A Further Comment. *Southern Econ. J.*, April 1973, *39*(4), pp. 652–53. [G: U.S.S.R.]

Enache, Constantin. Unele probleme ale reproducției forței de muncă în socialism. (Some Problems of the Reproduction of Labour in Socialism. With English summary.) *Stud. Cercet. Econ.*, 1973, (4), pp. 5–13.

Feiwel, George R. The Dynamics of Perpetuation: Some Observations on the Efficacy of Soviet Economic Reforms. *Econ. Int.*, May 1973, *26*(2), pp. 233–61. [G: U.S.S.R.]

Fekete, F. The Major Social and Economic Features of Co-operative Farming in Hungary. *Acta Oecon.*, 1973, *11*(1), pp. 19–32. [G: Hungary]

Figueroa, Luis. Participation under the Popular Unity Government. In *Zammit, J. A., ed.*, 1973, pp. 187–91. [G: Chile]

Flakierski, H. The Polish Economic Reform of 1970. *Can. J. Econ.*, February 1973, *6*(1), pp. 1–15. [G: Poland]

Friss, István. Objective Conditions of the Economy and the Extent of Centralization and Decentralization. *Acta Oecon.*, 1973, *10*(3–4), pp. 303–14. [G: Hungary]

Friss, István. Practical Experiences of the Economic Reform in Hungary. *Eastern Europ. Econ.*, Spring 1973, *11*(3), pp. 3–26. [G: Hungary]

Friss, István. On Long–Term National Economic Planning. In *Földi, T., ed.*, 1973, pp. 9–36. [G: E. Europe]

Furubotn, Eirik G. and Pejovich, Svetozar. Property Rights, Economic Decentralization, and the Evolution of the Yugoslav Firm, 1965–1972. *J. Law Econ.*, October 1973, *16*(2), pp. 275–302.
[G: Yugoslavia]

Gadó, O. Plan and Regulators in the Hungarian Economic Management. In *Kiss, T., ed.*, 1973, pp. 79–98. [G: Hungary]

Garcés, Joán E. The Popular Unity Government's Workers' Participation Model: Some Conditioning Factors. In *Zammit, J. A., ed.*, 1973, pp. 181–86. [G: Chile]

Garreton, Oscar. Some Preliminary Facts about the Management and Organization of the Industrial Sector. In *Zammit, J. A., ed.*, 1973, pp. 63–68. [G: Chile]

Gavrilă, Tatiana. Organizarea ştiinţifică a producţiei şi a muncii—factor dinamizator al productivităţii muncii. (The Scientific Organization of Production and Labour—A Stimulating Factor of Labour Productivity. With English summary.) *Stud. Cercet. Econ.*, 1973, (3), pp. 29–39.

Glueck, William F. and Kavran, Dragoljub. The Yugoslav Management System. In *Henley, D. S., ed.*, 1973, pp. 375–89. [G: Yugoslavia]

Goldman, Marshall I. Public Policy Toward Retailing: USSR. In *Boddewyn, J. J. and Hollander, S. C., eds.*, 1972, pp. 337–49. [G: U.S.S.R.]

Granick, David. A Management Model of East European, Centrally-Planned Economies. *Europ. Econ. Rev.*, June 1973, *4*(2), pp. 135–61.

Groza, Maria and Iovanelli, Marcela. Activizarea şi conducerea politică a maselor ţărăneşti de către Partidul Comunist Român în procesul înfăptuirii sarcinilor desăvîrşirii revoluţiei burghezo-democratice. (The Activation and the Political Leadership of the Peasant Masses by the Romanian Communist Party in the Fulfilment of the Targets of the Completion of the Bourgeois-Democratic Revolution. With English summary.) *Stud. Cercet. Econ.*, 1973, (3), pp. 19–28. [G: Rumania]

Hamouz, Frantisek. Implementation of the Comprehensive Program of Socialist Economic Integration. *Czech. Econ. Digest.*, December 1973, (8), pp. 3–46.

Hoffmann, Pavel. Methodological Aspects of Prognoses in the Regional Development of the National Economy. *Czech. Econ. Digest.*, November 1973, (7), pp. 56–73. [G: Czechoslovakia]

Holbik, Karel. The Tasks and Problems of Marxism in Chile's Economy. *Z. ges. Staatswiss.*, May 1973, *129*(2), pp. 333–46. [G: Chile]

Horvat, Branko. Labour-Time Prices of Production and the Transformation Problem in a Socialist Economy. *Kyklos*, 1973, *26*(4), pp. 762–86.

Horwitz, Bertrand and Whitehouse, F. Douglas. Soviet Land Value and Enterprise Location. *Land Econ.*, May 1973, *49*(2), pp. 233–37.
[G: U.S.S.R.]

Hsia, Tao-tai and Haun, Kathryn A. Laws of the People's Republic of China on Industrial and Intellectual Property. *Law Contemp. Probl.*, Summer-Autumn 1973, *38*(2), pp. 274–91. [G: China]

Huszár, J. and Mandel, M. The Investment Decision-Making System in Hungary. *Eastern Europ.*

Econ., Spring 1973, *11*(3), pp. 27–49. [G: Hungary]

Ionescu, Eugen. Procesul economisirii la C.E.C. Tendinţe şi structuri. (The Process of Economizing with the Savings Bank—Trends and Structures. With English summary.) *Stud. Cercet. Econ.*, 1973, (4), pp. 65–71. [G: Rumania]

Jarkovsky, Vladimír. The Dynamic Determination of Economically Efficient Capital Investment and New Technology. *Eastern Europ. Econ.*, Summer 1973, *11*(4), pp. 86–112. [G: Czechoslovakia]

Joxe, Alain. Is the 'Chilean Road to Socialism' Blocked? In *Zammit, J. A., ed.*, 1973, pp. 223–36. [G: Chile]

Kassirov, L. Rent Relationships in the Economic Mechanism of Social Production. *Prob. Econ.*, November 1973, *16*(7), pp. 36–58.

Katsenelinboigen, A. I. On the Various Methods of Describing the Socialist Economy. *Matekon*, Winter 1973-74, *10*(2), pp. 3–25.

Keren, Michael. Concentration Amid Devolution in East Germany's Reforms. In *Bornstein, M., ed.*, 1973, pp. 123–51. [G: E. Germany]

Khromov, P. Labor Productivity and Accumulation. *Prob. Econ.*, February 1973, *15*(10), pp. 30–45. [G: U.S.S.R.]

Komin, A. Problems in the Methodology and Practice of Planned Price Formation. *Prob. Econ.*, May 1973, *16*(1), pp. 35–49. [G: U.S.S.R.]

Koriagin, A. Problems of the Theory of Socialist Reproduction. *Prob. Econ.*, January 1973, *15*(9), pp. 28–46. [G: U.S.S.R.]

Koropeckyj, I. S. Regional Resource Allocation, Growth, and Income Inequality under Socialism. In *Bandera, V. N. and Melnyk, Z. L., eds.*, 1973, pp. 45–62. [G: E. Europe]

Kotov, V. Prices: The Instrument of National Economic Planning and the Basis of the Value Indices of the Plan. *Prob. Econ.*, May 1973, *16*(1), pp. 50–69. [G: U.S.S.R.]

Kovyzhenko, V. Problems in Reducing Complex Labor to Simple Labor in Marxist Political Economy. *Prob. Econ.*, August 1973, *16*(4), pp. 3–22.

Lange, O. Mr. Lerner's "Note on Socialist Economics." In *Farrell, M. J., ed.*, 1973, pp. 44–45.

Lăudatu, Alexandra. Determinarea capacităţii efective optime de producţie în unităţile de construcţii-montaj. (Determining the Best Effective Production Capacity in the Building-Assemblage Units. With English summary.) *Stud. Cercet. Econ.*, 1973, (2), pp. 89–98.

Lerner, Abba P. A Note on Socialist Economics. In *Farrell, M. J., ed.*, 1973, pp. 39–43.

Levin, A. Problems in the Control of Consumer Demand. *Prob. Econ.*, December 1973, *16*(8), pp. 81–104. [G: U.S.S.R.]

Lisandru, N. Necesitatea verigii comerciale cu ridicata în organizarea circulaţiei mărfurilor. (The Necessity of a Wholesale Trade Link in Organizing the Circulation of Goods. With English summary.) *Stud. Cercet. Econ.*, 1973, (1), pp. 133–39.

Mach, Milos. Planning Under Socialism. *Czech. Econ. Digest.*, August 1973, (5), pp. 64–88.

Mach, Milos and Reizer, Jozef. The Place of Commodity-Money Relations in the Socialist System and a Critical Review of the Theory of the So-Called Market Socialism. *Czech. Econ. Digest.*, December 1973, (8), pp. 71–101.

Manove, Michael. Non-Price Rationing of Intermediate Goods in Centrally Planned Economies. *Econometrica*, September 1973, *41*(5), pp. 829–52. [G: U.S.S.R.]

Marschak, Thomas A. Decentralizing the Command Economy: The Study of a Pragmatic Strategy for Reformers. In *Bornstein, M., ed.*, 1973, pp. 23–63.

Matiukha, I. The Rise in Living Standards of Working People in the USSR. *Prob. Econ.*, September 1973, *16*(5), pp. 60–71. [G: U.S.S.R.]

McCain, Roger A. Critical Note on Illyrian Economics. *Kyklos*, 1973, *26*(2), pp. 380–86.

McFarlane, Bruce. Price Rigidity and Excess Capacity in Socialist Economies. *Australian Econ. Pap.*, June 1973, *12*(20), pp. 36–41.

Megyeri, E. Optimal Utilization of Enterprise Funds and Some Problems of Measuring Effectiveness. *Acta Oecon.*, 1973, *11*(4), pp. 347–67. [G: Hungary]

Mesa-Lago, Carmelo. A Continuum Model to Compare Socialist Systems Globally. *Econ. Develop. Cult. Change*, Part I, July 1973, *21*(4), pp. 573–90.

Minc, Bronislaw. Il meccanismo di funzionamento dell'economia socialista. (The Functioning Mechanism of Socialist Economy. With English summary.) *Mondo Aperto*, October 1973, *27*(5), pp. 314–20.

Moldovan, Roman and Botez, Mihai C. Correlation Between Forecasting and Action—An Essential Feature in Planning. *Revue Roumaine Sci. Soc. Serie Sci. Econ.*, 1973, *17*(1), pp. 41–52.

Montias, John Michael. A Framework for Theoretical Analysis of Economic Reforms in Soviet-type Economies. In *Bornstein, M., ed.*, 1973, pp. 65–122.

Nasta, Eliza and Vasilescu, Floarea. Considerații asupra metodologiei de calcul a coeficientului elasticității. (Considerations of the Methodology of Calculating the Elasticity Coefficient. With English summary.) *Stud. Cercet. Econ.*, 1973, (1), pp. 99–109.

Nasta, Eliza and Horja, Gavril. Conținutul și funcțiile contractelor economice în etapa actuală. (The Content and Functions of the Economic Contracts in the Present Stage. With English summary.) *Stud. Cercet. Econ.*, 1973, (4), pp. 47–53. [G: Rumania]

Neuberger, Egon and James, Estelle. The Yugoslav Self-Managed Enterprise: A Systemic Approach. In *Bornstein, M., ed.*, 1973, pp. 245–84. [G: Yugoslavia]

Neuberger, Egon. The Plan and the Market: The Models of Oskar Lange. *Amer. Econ.*, Fall 1973, *17*(2), pp. 148–53.

Notkin, A. The Production Accumulation Norm. *Prob. Econ.*, February 1973, *15*(10), pp. 3–29. [G: U.S.S.R.]

Orleans, Leo A. and Suttmeier, Richard P. The Mao Ethic and Environmental Quality. In *Wilber, C. K., ed.*, 1973, pp. 258–65. [G: China]

Oțoiu, Alexandrina. Cu privire la metodele de evidență a cheltuielilor de producție și de calculație a prețului de cost. (On the Concept and Classifica-

tion of the Accounts Keeping Methods of Production Expenses and of Cost Price Calculation. With English summary.) *Stud. Cercet. Econ.*, 1973, (1), pp. 141–49.

Pajestka, Józef. General Development Relationships and Social Factors for Progress. *Eastern Europ. Econ.*, Fall 1973, *12*(1), pp. 45–81. [G: Poland]

Penkava, Jaromír. Improvements of the Finance and Credit System in Czechoslovakia. *Czech. Econ. Digest.*, August 1973, (5), pp. 3–24. [G: Czechoslovakia]

Pintilie, C. Concepte de bază ale științei conducerii societății socialiste, a ramurilor și unităților lor componente. (Basic Concepts of the Science of Management of the Socialist Society, of their Component Branches and Units. With English summary.) *Stud. Cercet. Econ.*, 1973, (2), pp. 73–87.

Popovici, Otilia. Perfecționarea remunerării muncii. (Improving the Pay for Work. With English summary.) *Stud. Cercet. Econ.*, 1973, (2), pp. 117–26. [G: Rumania]

Portes, Richard. Hungary: The Experience of Market Socialism. In *Zammit, J. A., ed.*, 1973, pp. 367–89. [G: Hungary]

Pozdniakova, N. On the Distribution of Incomes on Collective Farms. *Prob. Econ.*, January 1973, *15*(9), pp. 90–100. [G: U.S.S.R.]

Pricop, Mihai. Asigurarea ritmicității activității de servire a producției de bază. (Ensuring the Rhythmicity of the Activity of Serving Basic Production. With English summary.) *Stud. Cercet. Econ.*, 1973, (4), pp. 55–64.

Prybyla, Jan S. Soviet Economic Reforms in Agriculture. *Weltwirtsch. Arch.*, 1973, *109*(4), pp. 644–87. [G: U.S.S.R.]

Răducanu, Constantin. Determinarea proporției dintre sectorul I și sectorul II necesare realizării echilibrului la nivel intersectorial între cerere și ofertă. (Determining the Proportion Between Sector I and Sector II Necessary for Obtaining an Intersectorial Balance Between Supply and Demand. With English summary.) *Stud. Cercet. Econ.*, 1973, (1), pp. 43–52.

Reese, K. The Soviet Ruble and Comecon Countries. *S. Afr. J. Econ.*, June 1973, *41*(2), pp. 134–45. [G: U.S.S.R.]

Richter, H. V. The Impact of Socialism on Economic Activity in Burma. In *Epstein, T. S. and Penny, D. H., eds.*, 1973, pp. 216–39. [G: Burma]

Ristea, Mihai. Conceptul de operativitate în sistemul informațional contabil. (The Concept of Efficiency in the Book-keeping Information System. With English summary.) *Stud. Cercet. Econ.*, 1973, (4), pp. 99–109.

Robinson, Joan. Chinese Agricultural Communes. In *Wilber, C. K., ed.*, 1973, pp. 209–15. [G: China]

Roșu, V. Armonizarea intereselor în procesul de făurire a societății socialiste multilateral dezvoltate. (Harmonizing the Interests in Building the Many-sidedly Developed Socialist Society. With English summary.) *Stud. Cercet. Econ.*, 1973, (4), pp. 39–46.

Rubinshtein, M. Scientific and Technical Progress and Planned Price Formation. *Prob. Econ.*, July 1973, *16*(3), pp. 22–36. [G: U.S.S.R.]

Rychlewski, Eugeniusz. The Investment System of a Socialist Economy. *Eastern Europ. Econ.,* Fall 1973, *12*(1), pp. 3–44. [G: Poland]

Rzhanitsina, L. Public Consumption Funds in the USSR. *Int. Lab. Rev.,* December 1973, *108*(6), pp. 516–35. [G: U.S.S.R.]

Sandu, C. and Popescu, C. Corelaţia între creşterea productivităţii muncii şi salariul mediu şi influenţa ei asupra mărimii preţului de cost şi a rentabilităţii. (The Correlation Between the Increase of Labour Productivity and the Average Wage and Its Influence on the Proportion of the Cost Price and of Profitableness. With English summary.) *Stud. Cercet. Econ.,* 1973, (1), pp. 35–42.

Saul, John S. African Socialism in One Country: Tanzania. In *Arrighi, G. and Saul, J. S.,* 1973, pp. 237–335. [G: Tanzania]

Sellekaerts, Willy. The Soviet Managerial Evolution. *Marquette Bus. Rev.,* Summer 1973, *17*(2), pp. 84–97. [G: U.S.S.R.]

Sergent, Raisa and Lefter, Viorel. Utilizarea extensivă a capacităţilor de producţie şi influenţa ei asupra preţului de cost. (The Extensive Use of Production Capacities and its Influence on the Cost Price. With English summary.) *Stud. Cercet. Econ.,* 1973, (1), pp. 65–76.

Shtern, Iu. Production Functions and the Possibility of Using Them in Economic Calculations. *Prob. Econ.,* November 1973, *16*(7), pp. 59–83. [G: U.S.S.R.]

Silverman, Bertram. Economic Organization and Social Conscience: Some Dilemmas of Cuban Socialism. In *Barkin, D. P. and Manitzas, N. R., eds.,* 1973, pp. R262–28. [G: Cuba]

Silverman, Bertram. Economic Organization and Social Conscience: Some Dilemmas of Cuban Socialism. In *Zammit, J. A., ed.,* 1973, pp. 391–418. [G: Cuba]

Skarzhinskii, M. A Systems-Structural Approach to the Study of the Basic Economic Law of Socialism. *Prob. Econ.,* April 1973, *15*(12), pp. 3–15. [G: U.S.S.R.]

Solar, Donald. Chile's Dilemma: An Interpretive Analysis. *Amer. Econ.,* Spring 1973, *17*(1), pp. 40–50. [G: Chile]

Şovei, George. Sistem informaţional bancar modern. (A Modern Banking Informational System. With English summary.) *Stud. Cercet. Econ.,* 1973, (4), pp. 127–40.

Starostin, S. and Emdin, G. The Five-Year Plan and the Soviet Way of Life. *Prob. Econ.,* February 1973, *15*(10), pp. 81–103. [G: U.S.S.R.]

Stelu, Şerban. Circuitul economic al ambalajelor. (The Economic Circuit of Packings. With English summary.) *Stud. Cercet. Econ.,* 1973, (2), pp. 157–69.

Stelu, Şerban. Perfectarea contractelor economice. (The Conclusion of Economic Contracts. With English summary.) *Stud. Cercet. Econ.,* 1973, (3), pp. 141–52. [G: Rumania]

Sycheva, L. Economic Foundations of an Optimal Combination of Accumulation and Consumption on Collective Farms. *Prob. Econ.,* February 1973, *15*(10), pp. 46–61. [G: U.S.S.R.]

Szakolczai, G. Capital Taxes, Self-Financing and Capital Transfer. *Acta Oecon.,* 1973, *10*(3–4), pp. 361–76. [G: Hungary]

Szeplaki, Leslie. A Note on the Redistributive Effects of Socialist Wage and Price Policies. *Rivista Int. Sci. Econ. Com.,* November 1973, *20*(11), pp. 1109–15.

Szeplaki, Leslie. Some Reflections on Marxian Equilibria and Socialist Economic Policy. *Indian Econ. J.,* January-March 1973, *20*(3), pp. 431–39.

Tahir, Pervez. Soviet Economic Reform: Progress and Problems. *Pakistan Develop. Rev.,* Spring 1973, *12*(1), pp. 62–67. [G: U.S.S.R.]

Tardos, M. Necessity of Direct Connections between Productive Enterprises and Difficulties of Their Development in the Foreign Trade between CMEA Countries. (In Russian. With English summary.) *Acta Oecon.,* 1973, *11*(4), pp. 369–80.

Timár, M. Results of the New System of Economic Control and Management and its Further Development. *Acta Oecon.,* 1973, *10*(3–4), pp. 277–301. [G: Hungary]

Tinbergen, Jan. Some Thoughts on Mature Socialism. In *Judge, G. G. and Takayama, T., eds.,* 1973, pp. 9–25. [G: E. Europe; India]

Tomic, Radomiro. One View of Chile's Present Political and Economic Situation. In *Zammit, J. A., ed.,* 1973, pp. 31–40. [G: Chile]

Trofimenko, Martha B. Legal Aspects of Economic Centralization. In *Bandera, V. N. and Melnyk, Z. L., eds.,* 1973, pp. 328–45. [G: U.S.S.R.]

Vági, F. The Basis and Main Features of the System of Wage-Mass Regulation. (In Russian.) *Acta Oecon.,* 1973, *11*(1), pp. 65–80.

Van Arkadie, Brian. Problems of Socialism in Tanzania. In *Zammit, J. A., ed.,* 1973, pp. 421–39. [G: Tanzania]

Vanek, Jaroslav. The Yugoslav Economy Viewed through the Theory of Labor Management. *World Devel.,* September 1973, *1*(9), pp. 39–56. [G: Yugoslavia]

Vanek, Jaroslav. Some Fundamental Considerations on Financing and Form of Ownership under Labor Management. In *[Tinbergen, J.],* 1973, pp. 139–52. [G: Yugoslavia]

Vişinoiu, N. Analiza factorială a unor indicatori sintetici ai economiei naţionale. (The Factorial Analysis of Some of the Synthetic Indicators of the National Economy. With English summary.) *Stud. Cercet. Econ.,* 1973, (2), pp. 127–38.

Vişinoiu, N. Utilizarea teoriei grafurilor în studiul relaţiilor dintre mărimile relative ale dinamicii produsului social. (The Utilization of the Theory of Graphs in Studying the Relations Between the Relative Sizes of the Dynamics of the Social Product. With English summary.) *Stud. Cercet. Econ.,* 1973, (3), pp. 85–98.

Vuskovic, Pedro. The Economic Policy of the Popular Unity Government. In *Zammit, J. A., ed.,* 1973, pp. 49–56. [G: Chile]

Ward, Benjamin. Appraising Yugoslav Socialism. In *Zammit, J. A., ed.,* 1973, pp. 441–55. [G: Yugoslavia]

Weinstein, James. Labor and Socialism in America. *Labor Hist.,* Summer 1973, *14*(3), pp. 429–34. [G: U.S.]

Wemelsfelder, J. Kapitaalvoorzieningsproblemen in een op arbeiderszelfbestuur gebaseerde industrie. Het voorbeeld van Joegoslavië. (Problems of Financing Labor-Managed Firms: The Case of Yugo-Slavia. With English summary.) *De Economist*, March-April 1973, *121*(2), pp. 122–56. [G: Yugoslavia]

Weralski, Marian. Problems of Budgetary Policy in Socialist Planned Economies. In *[Hicks, U.]*, 1973, pp. 260–69.

Wilber, Charles K. Economic Development, Central Planning and Allocative Efficiency. In *Wilber, C. K., ed.*, 1973, pp. 221–39. [G: U.S.S.R.]

Winter, E. Radical Egalitarianism: The Chinese Experience. *Amer. Econ.*, Spring 1973, *17*(1), pp. 174–77. [G: China]

Wiseman, Jack. Uncertainty, Costs, and Collectivist Economic Planning. In *Buchanan, J. M. and Thirlby, G. F., eds.*, 1973, pp. 227–43.

Wong, John. Agricultural Production and Socialist Transformation in China: Two Decades After. *Malayan Econ. Rev.*, October 1973, *18*(2), pp. 1–15. [G: China]

Yunker, James A. An Appraisal of Langian Socialism. *Indian Econ. J.*, January-March 1973, *20*(3), pp. 382–413.

Yunker, James A. A Dynamic Optimization Model of the Soviet Enterprise. *Econ. Planning*, 1973, *13*(1–2), pp. 33–51.

Zammit, J. Ann. Introduction: The Context of the Round Table and Subsequent Events. In *Zammit, J. A., ed.*, 1973, pp. 5–13. [G: Chile]

Zinam, Oleg. Impact of Modernization on USSR: Two Revolutions in Conflict. *Econ. Int.*, May 1973, *26*(2), pp. 283–302. [G: U.S.S.R.]

Zinam, Oleg. The Dilemma of Specialization versus Autarky in the USSR: Issues and Solutions. In *Bandera, V. N. and Melnyk, Z. L., eds.*, 1973, pp. 196–213. [G: U.S.S.R.]

Zinam, Oleg. Soviet Dilemma: Modernization Versus Non-Marxist Convergence. *Rivista Int. Sci. Econ. Com.*, June 1973, *20*(6), pp. 526–41. [G: U.S.S.R.]

Zlocha, Nikolaj. Further Progress in the Work Connected with the System of Plan-Based Management. *Czech. Econ. Digest.*, December 1973, (8), pp. 47–70. [G: Czechoslovakia]

053 Comparative Economic Systems

0530 Comparative Economic Systems

Ames, Edward. The Emerging Theory of Comparative Economic Systems. *Amer. Econ.*, Spring 1973, *17*(1), pp. 22–28.

Atkinson, A. B. Worker Management and the Modern Industrial Enterprise. *Quart. J. Econ.*, August 1973, *87*(3), pp. 375–92.

Bandera, V. N. and Melnyk, Z. Lew. The Soviet Economy in Regional Perspective: Introduction. In *Bandera, V. N. and Melnyk, Z. L., eds.*, 1973, pp. xvii–xxi. [G: U.S.S.R.]

Boulding, Kenneth E. Business and Economic Systems. In *Boulding, K. E.*, 1973, pp. 429–47.

Boulding, Kenneth E. Some Questions on the Measurement and Evaluation of Organization. In *Boulding, K. E.*, 1973, pp. 147–59.

Breimyer, Harold F. Man, Physical Resources, and Economic Organization. *Amer. J. Agr. Econ.*, February 1973, *55*(1), pp. 1–9.

Bronfenbrenner, Martin. Samuelson, Marx, and Their Latest Critics. *J. Econ. Lit.*, March 1973, *11*(1), pp. 58–63.

Ciucur, Dumitru and Gavrilă, I. Aspecte ale gîndirii economice burgheze contemporane privind munca productivă. (Aspects of the Contemporary Bourgeois Economic Thinking on Productive Labor. With English summary.) *Stud. Cercet. Econ.*, 1973, (1), pp. 151–61.

Day, Lincoln H. Social Consequences of Zero Economic Growth. In *Weintraub, A.; Schwartz, E. and Aronson, J. R., eds.*, 1973, pp. 116–40.

Feiwel, George R. Growth, Planning, Price Mechanism and Consumer Sovereignty. *Rivista Int. Sci. Econ. Com.*, November 1973, *20*(11), pp. 1041–70.

Ferejohn, John and Page, Talbot. A Note on "Voting or a Price System in a Competitive Market Structure." *Amer. Polit. Sci. Rev.*, March 1973, *67*(1), pp. 157–60.

Goldman, Marshall I. Growth and Environmental Problems of Noncapitalist Nations. In *Weintraub, A.; Schwartz, E. and Aronson, J. R., eds.*, 1973, pp. 98–115.

Green, H. A. John. Public Sector Resource Allocation under Conditions of Risk: Discussion. In *Parkin, M., ed.*, 1973, pp. 137–38.

Herzog, Philippe. À propos de la notion d'économie publique. (Reflexions on Public Economy Notion. With English summary.) *Revue Écon.*, January 1973, *24*(1), pp. 139–62.

Israel, Joachim. Om marknadsekonomins förträfflighet: en sociologisk analys. (The functioning of the market economy: A Critical Analysis from a Sociological Point of View. With English summary.) *Nationalokon. Tidsskr.*, 1973, *111*(2), pp. 221–41.

Jabbar, M. A. Agriculture in Economic Development: The Competitive Approach Versus Soviet Control. *Can. J. Agr. Econ.*, February 1973, *21*(1), pp. 63–64. [G: Canada; U.S.S.R.]

Kuznets, Simon. Notes on Stage of Economic Growth as a System Determinant. In *Kuznets, S.*, 1973, pp. 212–42.

Lindblom, Charles E. The Rediscovery of the Market. In *Reynolds, L. G.; Green, G. D. and Lewis, D. R., eds.*, 1973, pp. 532–43.

Madarász, A. Is Political Economy Timely? *Acta Oecon.*, 1973, *10*(2), pp. 177–200.

McFarlane, Bruce. Price Rigidity and Excess Capacity in Socialist Economies. *Australian Econ. Pap.*, June 1973, *12*(20), pp. 36–41.

Melman, Seymour. Industrial Efficiency under Managerial vs. Cooperative Decision-Making: A Comparative Study of Manufacturing Enterprises in Israel. In *Wilber, C. K., ed.*, 1973, pp. 240–57. [G: Israel]

Oliver, Henry. Study of Relationships Between Economic and Political Systems. *J. Econ. Issues*, December 1973, *7*(4), pp. 543–51.

Peters, Hans-Rudolf. Hauptsächliche Determinanten von Wirtschaftsordnungen. (Main Determining Factors of Economic Orders. With

English summary.) *Z. Wirtschaft. Sozialwissen.*, 1973, *93*(4), pp. 385–409.

Popescu, Maria D. Prospective Considerations on the Modernization of National Economic Structures. *Revue Roumaine Sci. Soc. Serie Sci. Econ.*, 1973, *17*(1), pp. 91–102. [G: Rumania]

Rees, R. Public Sector Resource Allocation under Conditions of Risk. In *Parkin, M., ed.*, 1973, pp. 110–36.

Samuelson, Paul A. Samuelson's "Reply on Marxian Matters." *J. Econ. Lit.*, March 1973, *11*(1), pp. 64–68.

Schumacher, E. F. Buddhist Economics. In *Daly, H. E., ed.*, 1973, pp. 231–39. [G: E. Asia]

Szabó, K. A Few Thoughts on the Evolution of a Uniform Marxist Theory of the Firm. *Acta Oecon.*, 1973, *11*(4), pp. 325–45.

Timberg, Thomas A. Revolution and Growth: Two Case Studies from India. *Polit. Sci. Quart.*, March 1973, *88*(1), pp. 86–93. [G: India]

Varga, Gy. On the System of Preferences. *Acta Oecon.*, 1973, *10*(1), pp. 52–66. [G: Hungary]

Watrin, Christian. On the Question of Measuring the Efficiency of Economic Systems. *Ger. Econ. Rev.*, 1973, *11*(2), pp. 89–107.

Weaver, James H. Growth and Welfare. In *Wilber, C. K., ed.*, 1973, pp. 342–53.

von Weizsäcker, Carl Christian. Modern Capital Theory and the Concept of Exploitation. *Kyklos*, 1973, *26*(2), pp. 245–81.

100 Economic Growth; Development; Planning; Fluctuations

110 ECONOMIC GROWTH; DEVELOPMENT; AND PLANNING THEORY AND POLICY

111 Economic Growth Theory and Models

1110 Growth Theories

Abramovitz, Moses and David, Paul A. Reinterpreting Economic Growth: Parables and Realities. *Amer. Econ. Rev.*, May 1973, *63*(2), pp. 428–39. [G: U.S.]

d'Arge, R. C. and Kogiku, K. C. Economic Growth and the Environment. *Rev. Econ. Stud.*, January 1973, *40*(1), pp. 61–77.

Ayres, Robert U. and Kneese, Allen V. Economic and Ecological Effects of a Stationary Economy. In *Enthoven, A. C. and Freeman, A. M., III, eds.*, 1973, pp. 235–52.

Barsby, Steven L. Great Spurts and the Experience of Non-European Countries. *J. Econ. Issues*, September 1973, *7*(3), pp. 459–74.

Bertram, Gordon W. The Relevance of the Wheat Boom in Canadian Economic Growth. *Can. J. Econ.*, November 1973, *6*(4), pp. 545–66. [G: Canada]

Bhagwati, Jagdish N. and Hansen, Bent. Should Growth Rates Be Evaluated at International Prices? In *[Rosenstein-Rodan, P.]*, 1973, pp. 53–68.

Bodenhöfer, Hans-Joachim. X-Effizienz, Innova-

tions-Effizienz und wirtschaftliches Wachstum. (X-Efficiency, Innovation Efficiency, and Economic Growth. With English summary.) *Z. Wirtschaft. Sozialwissen.*, 1973, *93*(6), pp. 671–86.

Boulding, Kenneth E. The Shadow of the Stationary State. In *Olson, M. and Landsberg, H. H., eds.*, 1973, pp. 89–101.

Bradley, Paul G. Increasing Scarcity: The Case of Energy Resources. *Amer. Econ. Rev.*, May 1973, *63*(2), pp. 119–25.

Britto, Ronald. Some Recent Developments in the Theory of Economic Growth: An Interpretation. *J. Econ. Lit.*, December 1973, *11*(4), pp. 1343–66.

Brooks, Harvey. The Technology of Zero Growth. In *Olson, M. and Landsberg, H. H., eds.*, 1973, pp. 139–52.

Cole, H. S. D. and Curnow, R. C. An Evaluation of the World Models. In *Cole, H. S. D., et al., eds.*, 1973, pp. 108–34.

Cole, H. S. D. The Structure of the World Models. In *Cole, H. S. D., et al., eds.*, 1973, pp. 14–32.

Cole, W. A. Eighteenth-Century Economic Growth Revisited. *Exploration Econ. Hist.*, Summer 1973, *10*(4), pp. 327–48. [G: U.K.]

Cooper, Charles. Choice of Techniques and Technological Change as Problems in Political Economy. *Int. Soc. Sci. J.*, 1973, *25*(3), pp. 293–304.

Daly, Herman E. Toward a Steady-State Economy: Introduction. In *Daly, H. E., ed.*, 1973, pp. 1–29.

Daly, Herman E. The Steady-State Economy: Toward a Political Economy of Biophysical Equilibrium and Moral Growth. In *Daly, H. E., ed.*, 1973, pp. 149–74.

Daly, Herman E. Electric Power, Employment, and Economic Growth: A Case Study in Growth-mania. In *Daly, H. E., ed.*, 1973, pp. 252–77. [G: U.S.]

Day, Lincoln H. Social Consequences of Zero Economic Growth. In *Weintraub, A.; Schwartz, E. and Aronson, J. R., eds.*, 1973, pp. 116–40.

Deane, Phyllis. The Role of Capital in the Industrial Revolution. *Exploration Econ. Hist.*, Summer 1973, *10*(4), pp. 349–64. [G: U.K.]

Dvořák, Jiří and Jezek, Tomás. Some Problems of Strain in the Manpower Balances. *Eastern Europ. Econ.*, Summer 1973, *11*(4), pp. 60–85. [G: Czechoslovakia]

Feiwel, George R. Growth, Planning, Price Mechanism and Consumer Sovereignty. *Rivista Int. Sci. Econ. Com.*, November 1973, *20*(11), pp. 1041–70.

Felderer, Bernhard. Der Zusammenhang zwischen Allokation von Produktionsfaktoren und wirtschaftlichem Wachstum. (The Relation of Factor Allocation and Economic Growth. With English summary.) *Z. ges. Staatswiss.*, October 1973, *129*(4), pp. 589–600. [G: France; W. Germany]

Fishlow, Albert. Comparative Consumption Patterns, the Extent of the Market, and Alternative Development Strategies. In *Ayal, E. B., ed.*, 1973, pp. 41–80. [G: U.S.; U.K.; France]

Fishman, L. The Rate of Interest in a State of Economic Flux: Discussion. In *Parkin, M., ed.*, 1973, pp. 343–44.

Freeman, Christopher. Malthus with a Computer. In *Cole, H. S. D., et al., eds.*, 1973, pp. 5–13.

Frigero, Piercarlo. I modelli macroeconomici di sviluppo come strumento operativo per l'impresa. (Models of Economic Growth as an Operative Instrument of the Firm. With English summary.) *L'Impresa*, 1973, *15*(3–4), pp. 233–39.

Fuchs, Tomáš and Prič, Jozef. Meranie intenzity ekonomického rastu metódou úplne dynamizovanej substitučnej produkčnej funkcie Cobb-Douglasovho typu. (Measuring the Intensity of Economic Growth by the Method of Totally Dynamised Cobb-Douglas Type Production Function. With English summary.) *Ekon.-Mat. Obzor*, 1973, *9*(4), pp. 381–92.

Gale, David. Pure Exchange Equilibrium of Dynamic Economic Models. *J. Econ. Theory*, February 1973, *6*(1), pp. 12–36.

Gerber, Abraham. Energy Supply as a Factor in Economic Growth. In *Weintraub, A.; Schwartz, E. and Aronson, J. R., eds.*, 1973, pp. 82–97.
[G: U.S.]

Goldman, Marshall I. Growth and Environmental Problems of Noncapitalist Nations. In *Weintraub, A.; Schwartz, E. and Aronson, J. R., eds.*, 1973, pp. 98–115.

Goodeve, Charles [Sir]. The Critical Path to Growth. In *Ross, M., ed.*, 1973, pp. 21–27.

Gordon, Scott. Today's Apocalypses and Yesterday's. *Amer. Econ. Rev.*, May 1973, *63*(2), pp. 106–10.

Harcourt, G. C. The Rate of Profits in Equilibrium Growth Models: A Review Article. *J. Polit. Econ.*, September-October 1973, *81*(5), pp. 1261–77.

Heubes, Jürgen. Zyklisches Wachstum. (Cyclical Growth. With English summary.) *Z. ges. Staatswiss.*, February 1973, *129*(1), pp. 62–88.

Hicks, John R. [Sir]. The Mainspring of Economic Growth. *Swedish J. Econ.*, December 1973, *75*(4), pp. 336–48.

Hieser, R. O. The Economic Consequences of Zero Population Growth. *Econ. Rec.*, June 1973, *49* (126), pp. 241–62.

Infante, Ettore F. and Stein, Jerome L. Optimal Growth with Robust Feedback Control. *Rev. Econ. Stud.*, January 1973, *40*(1), pp. 47–60.

Jahoda, Marie. A Postscript on Social Change. In *Cole, H. S. D., et al., eds.*, 1973, pp. 209–15.

Jensen, Rodney C. Aspects of The Spatial Dimension in Economics. *Econ. Anal. Pol.*, March 1973, *4*(1), pp. 1–16.

Johnson, Willard R. Should the Poor Buy No Growth? In *Olson, M. and Landsberg, H. H., eds.*, 1973, pp. 165–89.
[G: U.S.]

Julien, P.-A. and Freeman, Christopher. The Capital and Industrial Output Sub-system. In *Cole, H. S. D., et al., eds.*, 1973, pp. 66–79.

Kelley, Allen C. and Williamson, Jeffrey G. Sources of Growth Methodology in Low-Income Countries: A Critique. *Quart. J. Econ.*, February 1973, *87*(1), pp. 138–47.

Kranzberg, Melvin. Can Technological Progress Continue to Provide for the Future? In *Weintraub, A.; Schwartz, E. and Aronson, J. R., eds.*, 1973, pp. 62–81.

Kuznets, Simon. Modern Economic Growth: Findings and Reflections. *Amer. Econ. Rev.*, June 1973, *63*(3), pp. 247–58.

Kuznets, Simon. Modern Economic Growth: Findings and Reflections. In *Kuznets, S.*, 1973, pp. 165–84.

Kuznets, Simon. Notes on Stage of Economic Growth as a System Determinant. In *Kuznets, S.*, 1973, pp. 212–42.

Kuznets, Simon. Population and Economic Growth. In *Kuznets, S.*, 1973, pp. 1–48.

Kuznets, Simon. Problems in Comparing Recent Growth Rates for Developed and Less-Developed Countries. In *Kuznets, S.*, 1973, pp. 311–42.

Leibenstein, Harvey. Notes on X-Efficiency and Technical Progress. In *Ayal, E. B., ed.*, 1973, pp. 18–38.

Lewis, William Cris. Public Investment Impacts and Regional Economic Growth. *Water Resources Res.*, August 1973, *9*(4), pp. 851–60.

Mackay, Robert J. Stein and Nagatani on Stabilization Policies in a Growing Economy. *Rev. Econ. Stud.*, October 1973, *40*(4), pp. 571–78.

Marstrand, Pauline K. and Pavitt, K. L. R. The Agricultural Sub-system. In *Cole, H. S. D., et al., eds.*, 1973, pp. 56–65.

Marstrand, Pauline K. and Sinclair, T. C. The Pollution Sub-system. In *Cole, H. S. D., et al., eds.*, 1973, pp. 80–89.

Mathur, P. N. The Rate of Interest in a State of Economic Flux. In *Parkin, M., ed.*, 1973, pp. 330–42.

Matthews, R. C. O. Foreign Trade and British Economic Growth. *Scot. J. Polit. Econ.*, November 1973, *20*(3), pp. 195–209.
[G: U.K.]

McKean, Roland N. Growth vs. No Growth: An Evaluation. In *Olson, M. and Landsberg, H. H., eds.*, 1973, pp. 207–27.

Meadows, Dennis L. The Dynamics of Global Equilibrium. In *Hawkes, N., ed.*, 1973, pp. 78–95.

Meadows, Donella H., et al. The Limits to Growth. In *Enthoven, A. C. and Freeman, A. M., III, eds.*, 1973, pp. 212–29.

Meadows, Donella H., et al. A Response to Sussex. In *Cole, H. S. D., et al., eds.*, 1973, pp. 216–40.

Mellor, John W. Accelerated Growth in Agricultural Production and the Intersectoral Transfer of Resources. *Econ. Develop. Cult. Change*, October 1973, *22*(1), pp. 1–16.
[G: Taiwan; India]

Mirrlees, James A. Models of Economic Growth: Introduction. In *Mirrlees, J. A. and Stern, N. H., eds.*, 1973, pp. xi–xxii.

Mishan, Ezra J. Ills, Bads, and Disamenities: The Wages of Growth. In *Olson, M. and Landsberg, H. H., eds.*, 1973, pp. 63–87.

Mishan, Ezra J. Growth and Antigrowth: What Are the Issues? In *Weintraub, A.; Schwartz, E. and Aronson, J. R., eds.*, 1973, pp. 3–38.

Morse, Chandler. Natural Resources as a Constraint on Economic Growth: Discussion. *Amer. Econ. Rev.*, May 1973, *63*(2), pp. 126–28.

Nguyen, D. T. Unwanted Amortisation Funds: A Comment. *Econ. J.*, March 1973, *83*(329), pp. 234–35.

Nordhaus, William D. World Dynamics: Measurement Without Data. *Econ. J.*, December 1973, *83* (332), pp. 1156–83.

North, Douglass C. and Thomas, Robert Paul. European Economic Growth: Comments on the

North-Thomas Theory: Reply. *Econ. Hist. Rev.,* 2nd Ser., May 1973, *26*(2), pp. 293–94.

Olson, Mancur. The No-Growth Society: Introduction. In *Olson, M. and Landsberg, H. H., eds.,* 1973, pp. 1–13.

Olson, Mancur; Landsberg, Hans H. and Fisher, Joseph L. The No-Growth Society: Epilogue. In *Olson, M. and Landsberg, H. H., eds.,* 1973, pp. 229–41.

Ophuls, William. Leviathan or Oblivion? In *Daly, H. E., ed.,* 1973, pp. 215–30.

Page, William. The Non-renewable Resources Subsystem. In *Cole, H. S. D., et al., eds.,* 1973, pp. 33–42.

Page, William. The Population Sub-system. In *Cole, H. S. D., et al., eds.,* 1973, pp. 43–55.

Pasour, E. C., Jr. Economic Growth and Agriculture: An Evaluation of the Compensation Principle. *Amer. J. Agr. Econ.,* Part I, November 1973, *55*(4), pp. 611–16.

Passell, Peter; Roberts, Marc J. and Ross, Leonard. The Limits to Growth: A Review. In *Enthoven, A. C. and Freeman, A. M., III, eds.,* 1973, pp. 230–34.

Pavitt, K. L. R. Malthus and Other Economists: Some Doomsdays Revisited. In *Cole, H. S. D., et al., eds.,* 1973, pp. 137–58.

Poulson, Barry W. and Dowling, J. Malcolm, Jr. The Climacteric in U.S. Economic Growth. *Oxford Econ. Pap.,* November 1973, *25*(3), pp. 420–34.   [G: U.S.]

Randers, Jørgen and Meadows, Donella H. The Carrying Capacity of Our Global Environment: A Look at the Ethical Alternatives. In *Daly, H. E., ed.,* 1973, pp. 283–306.

Ringrose, David R. European Economic Growth: Comments on the North-Thomas Theory. *Econ. Hist. Rev.,* 2nd Ser., May 1973, *26*(2), pp. 285–92.

Roberts, Marc J. On Reforming Economic Growth. In *Olson, M. and Landsberg, H. H., eds.,* 1973, pp. 119–37.

Rosenberg, Nathan. Innovative Responses to Materials Shortages. *Amer. Econ. Rev.,* May 1973, *63*(2), pp. 111–18.

Rostow, W. W. The Beginnings of Modern Growth in Europe: An Essay in Synthesis. *J. Econ. Hist.,* September 1973, *33*(3), pp. 547–80.

Rothschild, Kurt W. Military Expenditure, Exports and Growth. *Kyklos,* 1973, *26*(4), pp. 804–14.   [G: O.E.C.D.]

Sandler, Todd M. and Hogan, Timothy D. The Optimum Population and Growth: A Further Look. *J. Econ. Theory,* December 1973, *6*(6), pp. 582–84.

Schiesser, W. E. The Club of Rome Model. In *Weintraub, A.; Schwartz, E. and Aronson, J. R., eds.,* 1973, pp. 219–29.

Schlüter, Karl-Peter. Eignet sich die Wachstumstheorie zur wirtschaftspolitischen Anwendung? (With English summary.) *Z. ges. Staatswiss.,* October 1973, *129*(4), pp. 613–33.

Scoville, Orlin J. The Agribusiness Sector—An Important Link in Economic Growth Models. *Amer. J. Agr. Econ.,* August 1973, *55*(3), pp. 520–23.

Simmons, Harvey. System Dynamics and Technocracy. In *Cole, H. S. D., et al., eds.,* 1973, pp. 192–208.

Sjaastad, Larry A. Notes on X-Efficiency and Technical Progress: Comment. In *Ayal, E. B., ed.,* 1973, pp. 38–40.

Solow, Robert M. Is the End of the World at Hand? In *Weintraub, A.; Schwartz, E. and Aronson, J. R., eds.,* 1973, pp. 39–61.

Thurow, Lester C. Zero Economic Growth and the Distribution of Income. In *Weintraub, A.; Schwartz, E. and Aronson, J. R., eds.,* 1973, pp. 141–53.

Toms, Miroslav. The Labor Force and Relations Within the Production Process. *Eastern Europ. Econ.,* Summer 1973, *11*(4), pp. 3–59.   [G: Czechoslovakia]

Van Geel, M. Alternatief-Economisch/2 Zero economische groei: betekenis en consequenties. (Zero Economic Growth: Significance and Consequences. With English summary.) *Econ. Soc. Tijdschr.,* August 1973, *27*(4), pp. 347–70.

Van Rompuy, H. Het stagnatieprobleem. Verleden en heden. (The Stagnation-Thesis. With English summary.) *Tijdschr. Econ.,* 1973, *18*(1), pp. 65–86.

Weaver, James H. Economic Growth, Inequality, Hierarchy, Alienation: The Impact of Socialization Processes in Capitalist Society. *Amer. Econ.,* Fall 1973, *17*(2), pp. 9–16.   [G: U.S.]

von Weizsäcker, C. C. Notes on Endogenous Growth of Productivity. In *Mirrlees, J. A. and Stern, N. H., eds.,* 1973, pp. 101–10.

Williamson, Jeffrey G. Comparative Consumption Patterns, the Extent of the Market, and Alternative Development Strategies: Comment. In *Ayal, E. B., ed.,* 1973, pp. 80–83.   [G: U.S.; U.K.; France]

Zeckhauser, Richard J. The Risks of Growth. In *Olson, M. and Landsberg, H. H., eds.,* 1973, pp. 103–18.

1112 One and Two Sector Growth Models and Related Topics

Bade, Robin. Optimal Foreign Investment and International Trade. *Econ. Rec.,* March 1973, *49*(125), pp. 62–75.

Bardhan, Pranab K. More on Putty-Clay. *Int. Econ. Rev.,* February 1973, *14*(1), pp. 211–22.

Bell, D. J.; Brenneman, Ronald and Steedman, Ian. A Control Theory Analysis of a Finite Optimum Savings Program in a Two-Sector Model. *Int. Econ. Rev.,* June 1973, *14*(2), pp. 520–24.

Bertrand, Trent J. Trade and Growth: A Comment. *J. Int. Econ.,* May 1973, *3*(2), pp. 193–95.

Brems, Hans. Nature and Neoclassical Growth. *Ekon. Samfundets Tidskr.,* January 1973, *26*(1), pp. 16–20.

Burmeister, Edwin, et al. The "Saddlepoint Property" and the Structure of Dynamic Heterogeneous Capital Good Models. *Econometrica,* January 1973, *41*(1), pp. 79–95.

Cass, David. On the Wicksellian Point-Input, Point-Output Model of Capital Accumulation: A Modern View (or, Neoclassicism Slightly Vindicated).

J. Polit. Econ., January-February 1973, *81*(1), pp. 71–97.

Christensen, Laurits R.; Jorgenson, Dale W. and Lau, Lawrence J. Transcendental Logarithmic Production Frontiers. *Rev. Econ. Statist.*, February 1973, *55*(1), pp. 28–45.

Craven, John. Stability in a Two-Sector Model with Induced Bias. *Econ. J.*, September 1973, *83*(331), pp. 858–62.

Crouch, Robert L. Economic Development, Foreign Aid and Neoclassical Growth. *J. Devel. Stud.*, April 1973, *9*(3), pp. 353–64.

Davidson, Paul. Inequality and the Double Bluff. *Ann. Amer. Acad. Polit. Soc. Sci.*, September 1973, *409*, pp. 24–33.

Deardorff, Alan V. The Gains from Trade in and out of Steady-state Growth. *Oxford Econ. Pap.*, July 1973, *25*(2), pp. 173–91.

Demery, David and Demery, Lionel. Cross-Section Evidence for Balanced and Unbalanced Growth. *Rev. Econ. Statist.*, November 1973, *55*(4), pp. 459–64.

Denton, Frank T. and Spencer, Byron G. A Simulation Analysis of the Effects of Population Change on a Neoclassical Economy. *J. Polit. Econ.*, Part I, March-April 1973, *81*(2), pp. 356–75. [G: Canada]

Desai, Meghnad. Growth Cycles and Inflation in a Model of the Class Struggle. *J. Econ. Theory*, December 1973, *6*(6), pp. 527–45.

Diamond, Peter A. Taxation and Public Production in a Growth Setting. In *Mirrlees, J. A. and Stern, N. H., eds.*, 1973, pp. 215–35.

Diéguez, Héctor L. and Porto, Alberto. Un modelo simple de equilibrio general: cambio tecnológico. (A Simple Model of General Equilibrium Technological Change. With English summary.) *Económica*, January-April 1973, *19*(1), pp. 45–69.

Dixit, Avinash K. Comparative Dynamics from the Point of View of the Dual. In *Parkin, M., ed.*, 1973, pp. 35–46.

Drost, Helmar. Equilibrium Growth and the Relative Income Shares in a Two-sector Growth Model with Fixed Technical Coefficients: A Note. *Jahr. Nationalökon. Statist.*, May 1973, *187*(4), pp. 368–73.

Forster, Bruce A. Optimal Capital Accumulation in a Polluted Environment. *Southern Econ. J.*, April 1973, *39*(4), pp. 544–47.

Fujita, Masahisa. Optimum Growth in Two-Region, Two-Good Space Systems: The Final State Problem. *J. Reg. Sci.*, December 1973, *13*(3), pp. 385–407.

Gabisch, Günter. Optimal Growth in the Two-Sector Neoclassical Growth Model. *Z. Nationalökon.*, 1973, *33*(3–4), pp. 419–26.

Gapinski, James H. Growth Parameters and Neoclassical Estimates: Effect of an Adaptive Wage-Expectation Scheme. *Southern Econ. J.*, January 1973, *39*(3), pp. 431–33.

Gifford, Adam, Jr. Pollution, Technology, and Economic Growth. *Southern Econ. J.*, October 1973, *40*(2), pp. 210–15.

Glycopantis, D. On the Relative Stability and Optimality of Consumption in Aggregative Growth Models: A Critical Analysis. *Economica, N.S.*, August 1973, *40*(159), pp. 283–90.

Gordon, Nancy M. Ex Ante and Ex Post Substitutability in Economic Growth. *Int. Econ. Rev.*, June 1973, *14*(2), pp. 497–510.

Grossman, Michael and Fuchs, Victor R. Intersectoral Shifts and Aggregate Productivity Change. *Ann. Econ. Soc. Measure*, July 1973, *2*(3), pp. 227–43. [G: U.S.]

Hahn, Frank H. On Some Equilibrium Paths. In *Mirrlees, J. A. and Stern, N. H., eds.*, 1973, pp. 193–206.

Hammond, Peter J. and Mirrlees, James A. Agreeable Plans. In *Mirrlees, J. A. and Stern, N. H., eds.*, 1973, pp. 283–99.

Hammond, P. J. Comparative Dynamics from the Point of View of the Dual: Discussion. In *Parkin, M., ed.*, 1973, pp. 47–49.

Heinemann, Hans-Joachim. Leistungsbilanzsalden, Wirtschaftswachstum und Konsummöglichkeiten. (Current Account, Economic Growth, and Consumption. With English summary.) *Ifo-Studien*, January 1973, *19*(1/2), pp. 1–16.

Helmstädter, Ernst. The Long-Run Movement of the Capital-Output Ratio and of Labour's Share. In *Mirrlees, J. A. and Stern, N. H., eds.*, 1973, pp. 3–17. [G: U.K.; Germany; U.S.]

Henderson, John. A Putty-Clay Growth Model with Induced Technical Change. *Amer. Econ.*, Spring 1973, *17*(1), pp. 13–20.

Holub, H. W. and Kuhbier, P. Ein ungleichgewichtiges Modell des Wachstums und der Einkommensverteilung mit endogenen Strukturänderungen. (A Disequiliberated Model of Growth and Income Distribution with Endogenous Structural Change. With English summary.) *Jahr. Nationalökon. Statist.*, May 1973, *187*(4), pp. 289–300.

Horvat, Branko. Real Fixed Capital Costs Under Steady Growth. *Europ. Econ. Rev.*, April 1973, *4*(1), pp. 85–103.

Horvat, Branko. Fixed Capital Cost, Depreciation Multiplier and the Rate of Interest. *Europ. Econ. Rev.*, June 1973, *4*(2), pp. 163–79.

Inagaki, M. Intertemporal National Optimality and Temporal Social Preferences. In *Mirrlees, J. A. and Stern, N. H., eds.*, 1973, pp. 241–54.

Jaeger, Klaus. Sparverhalten und Vermögenspolitik in neoklassischen und generelleren Modellen. (Savings Behaviour and Distribution of Wealth in Neoclassical and More General Models. With English summary.) *Jahr. Nationalökon. Statist.*, March 1973, *187*(3), pp. 193–208.

Jhabvala, Firdaus. The Optimal Allocation of Resources in a Decentralized Model. *Eng. Econ.*, April-May 1973, *18*(3), pp. 169–89.

Kaiyama, Michihiro. On the Growth Model of a Dual Economy. (In Japanese. With English summary.) *Econ. Stud. Quart.*, December 1973, *24*(3), pp. 1–15.

Kennedy, Charles. A Generalisation of the Theory of Induced Bias in Technical Progress. *Econ. J.*, March 1973, *83*(329), pp. 48–57.

Koopmans, Tjalling C. Some Observations on 'Optimal' Economic Growth and Exhaustible Resources. In *[Tinbergen, J.]*, 1973, pp. 239–55.

Krzyzaniak, Marian. Benefit-Cost and Incidence Study of Transfers, Financed by Taxes on Profits, in a Growing Neoclassical Economy with Two Labor Inputs. *Public Finance,* 1973, *28*(2), pp. 151–77.

Kuipers, S. K. A Demand and Supply Model of Economic Growth. *De Economist,* November-December 1973, *121*(6), pp. 553–608.

Labia, N. A Neo-Classical Growth Model. *S. Afr. J. Econ.,* June 1973, *41*(2), pp. 164–66.

Laing, N. F. A Theory of Employment Fluctuations in the Full Employment Zone. *Econ. Rec.,* December 1973, *49*(128), pp. 546–59.

Layard, Richard. Denison and the Contribution of Education to National Income Growth: A Comment. *J. Polit. Econ.,* July-August 1973, *81*(4), pp. 1013–16.

Mas-Colell, Andreu and Razin, Assaf. A Model of Intersectoral Migration and Growth. *Oxford Econ. Pap.,* March 1973, *25*(1), pp. 72–79.

Mathur, Ashok. Consumption Lag, Harrod's Warranted Growth Path and Its Stability. *Indian Econ. Rev.,* October 1973, *8*(2), pp. 148–71.

Mirman, Leonard J. The Steady State Behavior of a Class of One Sector Growth Models with Uncertain Technology. *J. Econ. Theory,* June 1973, *6*(3), pp. 219–42.

Nordhaus, William D. Some Skeptical Thoughts on the Theory of Induced Innovation. *Quart. J. Econ.,* May 1973, *87*(2), pp. 208–19.

Ohtsuki, Yoshitaka. Public Investment and Economic Growth—Fiscal Policy and Resource Allocation. (In Japanese. With English summary.) *Econ. Stud. Quart.,* December 1973, *24*(3), pp. 16–30.

Orosel, Gerhard O. A Linear Growth Model Including Education. *Z. Nationalökon.,* 1973, *33*(3–4), pp. 251–79.

Parrinello, Sergio. Distribuzione, sviluppo e commercio internazionale. (Distribution, Growth and International Trade. With English summary.) *Econ. Int.,* May 1973, *26*(2), pp. 197–229.

Peleg, Bezalel and Yaari, Menahem E. Price Properties of Optimal Consumption Programmes. In *Mirrlees, J. A. and Stern, N. H., eds.,* 1973, pp. 306–17.

Peterson, David W. The Economic Significance of Auxiliary Functions in Optimal Control. *Int. Econ. Rev.,* February 1973, *14*(1), pp. 234–52.

Pitchford, J. D. The Optimum Population and Growth: A Closer Look. *J. Econ. Theory,* February 1973, *6*(1), pp. 94–95.

Radner, Roy. Optimal Stationary Consumption with Stochastic Production and Resources. *J. Econ. Theory,* February 1973, *6*(1), pp. 68–90.

Ramanathan, R. Adjustment Time in the Two-Sector Growth Model with Fixed Coefficients. *Econ. J.,* December 1973, *83*(332), pp. 1236–44.

Ryder, Harl E., Jr. and Heal, Geoffrey M. Optimum Growth with Intertemporally Dependent Preferences. *Rev. Econ. Stud.,* January 1973, *40*(1), pp. 1–33.

Sengupta, J. K. Adaptive Control in Models of Optimum Economic Growth. *Z. ges. Staatswiss.,* October 1973, *129*(4), pp. 601–12.

Smith, M. A. M. A Note on Fixed Factor Proportions and Net Saving Rates. *Rev. Econ. Stud.,* April 1973, *40*(2), pp. 297–98.

Spaventa, Luigi. Notes on Problems of Transition between Techniques. In *Mirrlees, J. A. and Stern, N. H., eds.,* 1973, pp. 168–87.

Stephens, J. Kirker. Input Quality, Obsolescence, and Unemployment. *Kyklos,* 1973, *26*(2), pp. 282–87.

Stiglitz, Joseph E. Recurrence of Techniques in a Dynamic Economy. In *Mirrlees, J. A. and Stern, N. H., eds.,* 1973, pp. 138–61.

Stiglitz, Joseph E. The Badly Behaved Economy with the Well-Behaved Production Function. In *Mirrlees, J. A. and Stern, N. H., eds.,* 1973, pp. 117–37.

Strassl, Arthur. Equilibrium Growth of Capital and Labor. *Amer. Econ.,* Fall 1973, *17*(2), pp. 33–45.

Strøm, Steinar. Economic Growth and Biological Equilibrium. *Swedish J. Econ.,* June 1973, *75*(2), pp. 164–75.

1113 Multisector Growth Models and Related Topics

Banks, F. E. Growth and Pollution. *Ekon. Samfundets Tidskr.,* 1973, *26*(2), pp. 67–74.

Banks, F. E. On Optimal Transformation Frontier. *Tahq. Eq.,* Summer & Autumn 1973, *10*(31&32), pp. 80–83.

Brock, William A. and Mirman, Leonard J. Optimal Economic Growth and Uncertainty: The No Discounting Case. *Int. Econ. Rev.,* October 1973, *14*(3), pp. 560–73.

Brock, William A. Some Results on the Uniqueness of Steady States in Multisector Models of Optimum Growth when Future Utilities are Discounted. *Int. Econ. Rev.,* October 1973, *14*(3), pp. 535–59.

Chang, Winston W. Intermediate Products, Aggregation, and Economic Growth. *Southern Econ. J.,* July 1973, *40*(1), pp. 56–65.

Eckaus, Richard S. Absorptive Capacity as a Constraint Due to Maturation Processes. In *[Rosenstein-Rodan, P.],* 1973, pp. 79–108.

Gelting, Jørgen H. Boligbyggeri kontra anden investering. (Residential Construction and other Investment. With English summary.) *Nationalokon. Tidsskr.,* 1973, *111*(1), pp. 86–91.

Ghafari, R. An Analysis of von Newmann "General Equilibrium." *Tahq. Eq.,* Summer & Autumn 1973, *10*(31&32), pp. 84–103.

Hagen, Everett E. Economic Growth with Unlimited Foreign Exchange and No Technical Progress. In *[Rosenstein-Rodan, P.],* 1973, pp. 69–78.

Ivanov, N. How Many Specialists are Needed? *Prob. Econ.,* August 1973, *16*(4), pp. 63–81.

McFadden, Daniel. On the Existence of Optimal Development Programmes in Infinite-Horizon Economies. In *Mirrlees, J. A. and Stern, N. H., eds.,* 1973, pp. 260–82.

Peleg, Bezalel. A Weakly Maximal Golden-Rule Program for a Multi-Sector Economy. *Int. Econ. Rev.,* October 1973, *14*(3), pp. 574–79.

Shell, Karl. Inventive Activity, Industrial Organisation and Economic Growth. In *Mirrlees, J. A. and Stern, N. H., eds.,* 1973, pp. 77–96.

1114 Monetary Growth Models

Bolle, Michael. Geld, Wachstum und Beschäftigung. (Money, Growth and Employment. With English summary.) *Z. ges. Staatswiss.*, February 1973, *129* (1), pp. 1–22.

Crouch, Robert L. A New Approach to the Monetisation of Neoclassical Growth Models. In *Powell, A. A. and Williams, R. A.*, eds., 1973, pp. 285–99.

Dornbusch, Rudiger and Frenkel, Jacob A. Inflation and Growth: Alternative Approaches. *J. Money, Credit, Banking*, Part I, February 1973, *5*(1), pp. 141–56.

Fischer, Stanley. A Neoclassical Monetary Growth Model: Comment. *J. Money, Credit, Banking*, May 1973, *5*(2), pp. 704–06.

Fried, Joel. Money, Exchange and Growth. *Western Econ. J.*, September 1973, *11*(3), pp. 285–301.

Holzheu, Franz. Das Geld- und Kreditsystem als Variable im Wachstumsprozess. (The Monetary System as a Variable in the Process of Growth. With English summary.) *Jahr. Nationalökon. Statist.*, January 1973, *187*(2), pp. 97–107.

Jaeger, Klaus. Ein einfaches monetäres Wachstumsmodell mit Produkt- und Prozessinnovationen. (A Simple Monetary Growth Model with Product and Process Innovations. With English summary.) *Z. ges. Staatswiss.*, August 1973, *129*(3), pp. 409–44.

Laumas, Prem S. and Mohabhat, Khan A. Money and Economic Development. *Indian Econ. J.*, April-June 1973, *20*(4–5), pp. 619–29. [G: India]

Marty, Alvin L. Growth, Satiety, and the Tax Revenue from Money Creation. *J. Polit. Econ.*, September-October 1973, *81*(5), pp. 1136–52.

Purvis, Douglas D. Short-Run Dynamics in Models of Money and Growth. *Amer. Econ. Rev.*, March 1973, *63*(1), pp. 12–23.

Richter, Rudolf. Full Employment and Stable Prices—Compatibility of Targets and Rules. *Ger. Econ. Rev.*, 1973, *11*(2), pp. 108–20.

Rose, Hugh. Effective Demand in the Long Run. In *Mirrlees, J. A. and Stern, N. H.*, eds., 1973, pp. 25–47.

Sargent, Thomas J. and Wallace, Neil. The Stability of Models of Money and Growth with Perfect Foresight. *Econometrica*, November 1973, *41*(6), pp. 1043–48.

Uzawa, Hirofumi. Towards a Keynesian Model of Monetary Growth. In *Mirrlees, J. A. and Stern, N. H.*, eds., 1973, pp. 53–70.

Villanueva, Delano P. A Neoclassical Monetary Growth Model: Reply. *J. Money, Credit, Banking*, May 1973, *5*(2), pp. 707–12.

112 Economic Development Models and Theories

1120 Economic Development Models and Theories

Adelman, Irma. Social and Economic Development at the Micro Level—A Tentative Hypothesis. In *Ayal, E. B.*, ed., 1973, pp. 3–13.

Adelman, Irma. Planning for Social Equity. In *[Tinbergen, J.]*, 1973, pp. 181–200.

Adhvaryu, J. H. Area Development and the Theory of Multiplier. *Artha-Vikas*, January-July 1973, *9* (1–2), pp. 55–63.

Adler, John H. The World Bank's Concept of Development—An In-House Dogmengeschichte. In *[Rosenstein-Rodan, P.]*, 1973, pp. 30–50.

Ady, P. On Economic Advice to Developing Countries. *World Devel.*, February 1973, *1*(1-2), pp. 64–75.

Ahluwalia, Montek S. Taxes, Subsidies, and Employment. *Quart. J. Econ.*, August 1973, *87*(3), pp. 393–409.

Ahmad, Meekal A.; Flesher, John and Over, Mead. An Econometric Test of a Zero Elasticity of Substitution Production Function for Pakistan. *Pakistan Econ. Soc. Rev.*, Winter 1973, *11*(4), pp. 443–53. [G: Pakistan]

Ahmad, Rafiq. South Asian Developmental Crisis. *Pakistan Develop. Rev.*, Summer 1973, *12*(2), pp. 181–88. [G: Asia]

Arrighi, Giovanni and Saul, John S. Socialism and Economic Development in Tropical Africa. In *Arrighi, G. and Saul, J. S.*, 1973, pp. 11–43. [G: Tanzania]

Ault, David E. On the Importance of Lags in Technology: An Empirical Test. *Rivista Int. Sci. Econ. Com.*, October 1973, *20*(10), pp. 945–60.

Ayal, Eliezer B. Micro Aspects of Development: Introduction. In *Ayal, E. B.*, ed., 1973, pp. xix–xxxi.

Azhar, B. A. An Econometric Analysis of Price Behaviour in Pakistan. *Pakistan Develop. Rev.*, Winter 1973, *12*(4), pp. 375–92. [G: Pakistan]

Bertolino, Alberto. Un problema fondamentale per lo sviluppo economico: la formazione dei quadri tecnico-economici. (A Basic Problem for Economic Development: The Formation of Technico-economic Personnel. With English summary.) *Rivista Int. Sci. Econ. Com.*, February 1973, *20*(2), pp. 130–38.

Bhagwati, Jagdish N. and Dellalfar, William. The Brain Drain and Income Taxation. *World Devel.*, February 1973, *1*(1-2), pp. 94–101.

Bhalla, A. S. A Disaggregative Approach to Employment in LDCs. *J. Devel. Stud.*, October 1973, *10* (1), pp. 50–65.

Bhattacharya, Debesh. Foreign Aid and Economic Development. *Econ. Aff.*, January–February 1973, *18*(1-2), pp. 41–53.

Blandy, Richard and Wery, René. Population and Employment Growth: Bachue-1. *Int. Lab. Rev.*, May 1973, *107*(5), pp. 441–49.

Boulding, Kenneth E. Human Resource Development as a Learning Process. In *Boulding, K. E.*, 1973, pp. 339–49.

Cebula, Richard J. and Kohn, Robert M. Foreign Capital and Steady-State Growth in Developing Economies. *Pakistan Econ. Soc. Rev.*, Winter 1973, *11*(4), pp. 378–82.

Chakravarty, Sukhamoy. Theory of Development Planning: An Appraisal. In *[Tinbergen, J.]*, 1973, pp. 163–79.

Costa, E. Maximising Employment in Labour-intensive Development Programmes. *Int. Lab. Rev.*, November 1973, *108*(5), pp. 371–94.

Cukor, György. Industrial Development Strategy in

Developing Countries. In *Földi, T., ed.*, 1973, pp. 37–63.

Currie, Lauchlin. The Exchange Constraint on Development—A Partial Solution to the Problem: A Reply. *Econ. J.*, March 1973, *83*(329), pp. 207–10.

Dagnino Pastore, José M. and de Pablo, Juan C. Sobre la restricción de ahorro-inversión en los modelos de dos brechas. (On the Savings Constraint in Two Gap Models. With English summary.) *Económica*, May-August 1973, *19*(2), pp. 157–64.

Day, Richard H. and Nelson, Jon P. A Class of Dynamic Models for Describing and Projecting Industrial Development. *J. Econometrics*, June 1973, *1*(2), pp. 155–90. [G: U.S.; Japan]

Decker, Robert L. The Saving Gap and Foreign Aid. *Intermountain Econ. Rev.*, Fall 1973, *4*(2), pp. 45–54.

De Gregori, Thomas R. Prodigality or Parsimony: The False Dilemma in Economic Development Theory. *J. Econ. Issues*, June 1973, *7*(2), pp. 259–66.

Desai, Padma. Third World Social Scientists in Santiago. *World Devel.*, September 1973, *1*(9), pp. 57–65. [G: LDC's]

Despres, Emile. Determining the Size of a Development Plan: Pakistan. In *Despres, E.*, 1973, pp. 99–132. [G: Pakistan]

Despres, Emile. The Welfare State and Development Expenditure: Pakistan. In *Despres, E.*, 1973, pp. 146–53. [G: Pakistan]

Dixit, Avinash K. Models of Dual Economies. In *Mirrlees, J. A. and Stern, N. H., eds.*, 1973, pp. 325–52.

Dobrotă, Niță. Principalele caracteristici ale unei țări în curs de dezvoltare. (The Main Characteristics of a Developing Country. With English summary.) *Stud. Cercet. Econ.*, 1973, (1), pp. 13–26. [G: Rumania]

Enke, Stephen. Economic Consequences of Rapid Population Growth: A Reply. *Econ. J.*, March 1973, *83*(329), pp. 219–21.

Erdös, T. Investments and Economic Growth. *Acta Oecon.*, 1973, *11*(4), pp. 281–303.

Fedorenko, Nicolai P. Methodological Aspects of Forecasting Long-Term Socio-Economic Development. *Amer. Econ.*, Fall 1973, *17*(2), pp. 46–48.

Freire, Paulo. Pedagogy of the Oppressed. In *Wilber, C. K., ed.*, 1973, pp. 410–26.

Frey, Bruno S. Interactions Between Preferences and Consumption in Economic Development. *Scot. J. Polit. Econ.*, February 1973, *20*(1), pp. 53–64.

Friedman, Irving S. Dilemmas of the Developing Countries—The Sword of Damocles. *Finance Develop.*, March 1973, *10*(1), pp. 12–15, 37.

Friss, István. On Long–Term National Economic Planning. In *Földi, T., ed.*, 1973, pp. 9–36. [G: E. Europe]

Fuchs, Claudio J. and Landsberger, Henry A. "Revolution of Rising Expectations" or "Traditional Life Ways"? A Study of Income Aspirations in a Developing Country. *Econ. Develop. Cult. Change*, January 1973, *21*(2), pp. 212–26. [G: Chile]

Furtado, Celso. The Concept of External Dependence in the Study of Underdevelopment. In *Wilber, C. K., ed.*, 1973, pp. 118–23.

Genovese, Nicola M. and Sobbrio, Giuseppe. Regional Inequality and the Market Mechanism: Comment. *Kyklos*, 1973, *26*(3), pp. 621–23. [G: Italy]

Georgescu-Roegen, Nicholas. The Entropy Law and the Economic Problem. In *Daly, H. E., ed.*, 1973, pp. 37–49.

Ghai, Dharam P. The Concept and Strategies of Economic Independence. In *Ghai, D., ed.*, 1973, pp. 9–34. [G: Africa]

Gintzburger, Alphonse A. Psychoanalysis of a Case of Stagnation. *Econ. Develop. Cult. Change*, January 1973, *21*(2), pp. 227–46.

Girling, Robert. Dependency, Technology and Development. In *Bonilla, F. and Girling, R., eds.*, 1973, pp. 46–62.

Gordon, Wendell. Institutionalized Consumption Patterns in Underdeveloped Countries. *J. Econ. Issues*, June 1973, *7*(2), pp. 267–87.

Goulet, Denis. "Development" . . . or Liberation? In *Wilber, C. K., ed.*, 1973, pp. 354–61. [G: Latin America]

Green, R. H. Economic Independence and Economic Co-operation. In *Ghai, D., ed.*, 1973, pp. 45–87. [G: Africa]

Griffin, Keith. Underdevelopment in Theory. In *Wilber, C. K., ed.*, 1973, pp. 15–25.

Griffin, Keith. Policy Options for Rural Development. *Oxford Bull. Econ. Statist.*, November 1973, *35*(4), pp. 239–74.

Hanson, John R., III. Economic Consequences of Rapid Population Growth: A Comment. *Econ. J.*, March 1973, *83*(329), pp. 217–19.

Harbison, Frederick H. Human Resources and the Development of Modernizing Nations. In *Somers, G. G., ed.*, 1973, pp. 177–86.

Harris, John R. Entrepreneurship and Economic Development. In *[Williamson, H. F.]*, 1973, pp. 141–72. [G: Nigeria]

Hendershot, Gerry E. Population Size, Military Power, and Antinatal Policy. *Demography*, November 1973, *10*(4), pp. 517–24.

Higgins, Benjamin. The Employment Problem in Development. In *Ayal, E. B., ed.*, 1973, pp. 241–75.

Hirschman, Albert O. and Rothschild, Michael. The Changing Tolerance for Income Inequality in the Course of Economic Development; with a Mathematical Appendix. *Quart. J. Econ.*, November 1973, *87*(4), pp. 544–66.

Hoselitz, Bert F. The Development of a Labor Market in the Process of Economic Growth. In *Sturmthal, A. and Scoville, J. G., eds.*, 1973, pp. 34–57.

Ikonicoff, Moïses. Technologie et modèle de consommation dans le Tiers-Monde. (Technology and Consumption Patterns in Under-Developed Countries. With English summary.) *Revue Écon.*, July 1973, *24*(4), pp. 619–40.

Isard, Walter and Liossatos, Panagis. Social Injustice and Optimal Space-Time Development. *J. Peace Sci.*, Autumn 1973, *1*(1), pp. 69–93.

Jackson, Dudley and Turner, H. A. How to Provide

More Employment in a Labour-Surplus Economy. *Int. Lab. Rev.*, April 1973, *107*(4), pp. 315–38.   [G: Morocco]

Jaguaribe, Helio. Foreign Technical Assistance and National Development. In *Thurber, C. E. and Graham, L. S., eds.*, 1973, pp. 109–29.

Jha, L. K. Leaning Against Open Doors? Comment. In *Lewis, J. P. and Kapur, I., eds.*, 1973, pp. 97–101.

Joshi, V. H. The Concept of Regional Analysis: Its Application to the Study of the Development of Backward Regions. *Artha-Vikas*, January-July 1973, *9*(1–2), pp. 64–68.

Kádár, B. Small-Sized Developing Countries in the Regional Arrangements. *Acta Oecon.*, 1973, *10*(2), pp. 217–31.

Kasnacich, Johannes. Le più importanti prospettive macro-economiche del mondo attuale. (The Main Macro-Economic Perspectives of World Development. With English summary.) *Mondo Aperto*, February 1973, *27*(1), pp. 1–8.

Katouzian, M. A. A Two-Sector Model of Population, Growth and Economic Development (1). *Tahq. Eq.*, Summer & Autumn 1973, *10*(31&32), pp. 60–79.

Kelley, Allen C. and Williamson, Jeffrey G. Sources of Growth Methodology in Low-Income Countries: A Critique. *Quart. J. Econ.*, February 1973, *87*(1), pp. 138–47.

Kelley, Allen C. and Williamson, Jeffrey G. Modeling Economic Development and General Equilibrium Histories. *Amer. Econ. Rev.*, May 1973, *63*(2), pp. 450–58.   [G: Japan]

Komló, L. The Industrialization and Integration of Agriculture in a Socialist Country. *Acta Oecon.*, 1973, *10*(1), pp. 67–79.

Krutilla, John V. Some Environmental Effects of Economic Development. In *Enthoven, A. C. and Freeman, A. M., III, eds.*, 1973, pp. 253–62.

Lal, Deepak. Disutility of Effort, Migration, and the Shadow Wage-rate. *Oxford Econ. Pap.*, March 1973, *25*(1), pp. 112–26.

Lapan, Harvey and Bardhan, Pranab K. Localized Technical Progress and Transfer of Technology and Economic Development. *J. Econ. Theory*, December 1973, *6*(6), pp. 585–95.

Leff, Nathaniel H. The Employment Problem in Development: Comment. In *Ayal, E. B., ed.*, 1973, pp. 275–77.

Lell, Hans-Joachim. Integrated Regional Development. *Finance Develop.*, June 1973, *10*(2), pp. 23–25, 38.

Letwin, William. Four Fallacies about Economic Development. In *Reynolds, L. G.; Green, G. D. and Lewis, D. R., eds.*, 1973, pp. 502–17.

Lewis, John P. Wanted in India: A Relevant Radicalism. In *Wadhva, C. D., ed.*, 1973, pp. 216–32.   [G: India]

Lewis, Stephen R., Jr. Agricultural Taxation and Intersectoral Resource Transfers. *Food Res. Inst. Stud.*, 1973, *12*(2), pp. 93–114.

Lissner, Will. Developing Agriculture in Low Income Countries. *Amer. J. Econ. Soc.*, October 1973, *32*(4), pp. 436–38.

Mafeje, Archie. The Fallacy of Dual Economies Revisited. In *Institute for Development Research*, 1973, pp. 25–52.   [G: Africa]

Mas-Colell, Andreu and Razin, Assaf. A Model of Intersectoral Migration and Growth. *Oxford Econ. Pap.*, March 1973, *25*(1), pp. 72–79.

McKee, David L. Regional Inequality and the Market Mechanism: Comment. *Kyklos*, 1973, *26*(3), pp. 624–26.   [G: Italy]

Mellor, John W. Accelerated Growth in Agricultural Production and the Intersectoral Transfer of Resources. *Econ. Develop. Cult. Change*, October 1973, *22*(1), pp. 1–16.   [G: Taiwan; India]

Müller, Jens. Appropriate Technology and Technological Dualism. In *Institute for Development Research*, 1973, pp. 161–76.

Myers, Myron G.; Rogstad, Barry K. and Wehner, Harrison G. A Theoretical Evaluation of Alternative Subsidy Schemes for Regional Development. *Amer. J. Agr. Econ.*, May 1973, *55*(2), pp. 304–12.

Myrdal, Gunnar. Growth and Social Justice. *World Devel.*, March-April 1973, *1*(3–4), pp. 119–20.

Myrdal, Gunnar. "Growth" and "Development." In *Myrdal, G.*, 1973, pp. 182–96.

Myrdal, Gunnar. The Need for Radical Domestic Reforms. In *Myrdal, G.*, 1973, pp. 101–32.

Myrdal, Gunnar. The World Poverty Problem. In *Myrdal, G.*, 1973, pp. 65–100.

Myrdal, Gunnar. Causes and Nature of Development. *Tahq. Eq.*, Winter & Spring 1973, *10*(29 & 30), pp. 3–16.

Naqvi, Syed Nawab Haider. The Balance-of-Payments Problems in Developing Countries. *Pakistan Develop. Rev.*, Autumn 1973, *12*(3), pp. 259–72.

Nell, Edward J. Cyclical Accumulation: A Marxian Model of Development. *Amer. Econ. Rev.*, May 1973, *63*(2), pp. 152–59.

Nelson, Richard R. Microeconomic Theory and Economic Development: Reflections on the Conference. In *Ayal, E. B., ed.*, 1973, pp. 278–85.

Owen, Carol and Witton, Ronald A. A Note on Conditions Supporting the Covariation of External and Internal Conflict. *Econ. Develop. Cult. Change*, October 1973, *22*(1), pp. 114–23.

Pajestka, Jøzef. Need for Greater World-Wide Rationality. In *[Tinbergen, J.]*, 1973, pp. 273–83.

Pajestka, Jøzef. General Development Relationships and Social Factors for Progress. *Eastern Europ. Econ.*, Fall 1973, *12*(1), pp. 45–81.   [G: Poland]

Paldam, Martin. An Empirical Analysis of the Relationship between Inflation and Economic Growth in 12 Countries, 1950 to 1969. *Swedish J. Econ.*, December 1973, *75*(4), pp. 420–27.   [G: W. Europe; U.K.; U.S.]

Papanek, Gustav F. Aid, Foreign Private Investment, Savings, and Growth in Less Developed Countries. *J. Polit. Econ.*, January-February 1973, *81*(1), pp. 120–30.

Pathak, H. N. Developing Entrepreneurship in Backward Regions. *Artha-Vikas*, January-July 1973, *9*(1–2), pp. 47–54.   [G: India]

Pathak, Mahesh T. Development of Backward Areas: Problems and Prospects. *Artha-Vikas*, January-July 1973, *9*(1–2), pp. 25–46. [G: India]

Penrose, Edith. International Patenting and the Less-Developed Countries. *Econ. J.*, September 1973, *83*(331), pp. 768–86.

Perroux, François. Multinational Investments and the Analysis of Development and Integration Poles. *Écon. Soc.*, May-June 1973, *7*(5–6), pp. 831–68.

Popescu, Maria D. Prospective Considerations on the Modernization of National Economic Structures. *Revue Roumaine Sci. Soc. Serie Sci. Econ.*, 1973, *17*(1), pp. 91–102. [G: Rumania]

Pournarakis, E. Capital Accumulation and Industrialization in the Open Dual Economy—A Two Sector Model. *Econ. Int.*, August-November 1973, *26*(3–4), pp. 502–15.

Rahim, Sikander. Economic Development and Unequal Exchange. *Pakistan Econ. Soc. Rev.*, Winter 1973, *11*(4), pp. 463–72.

Randers, Jørgen and Meadows, Donella H. The Carrying Capacity of Our Global Environment: A Look at the Ethical Alternatives. In *Daly, H. E., ed.*, 1973, pp. 283–306.

Ranis, Gustav. Industrial Sector Labor Absorption. *Econ. Develop. Cult. Change*, April 1973, *21*(3), pp. 387–408. [G: Korea; Taiwan]

Ranis, Gustav. The Exchange Constraint on Development—A Partial Solution to the Problem: A Comment. *Econ. J.*, March 1973, *83*(329), pp. 203–07.

Rasmussen, Jørgen. Dual Theories and the Classics. In *Institute for Development Research*, 1973, pp. 61–74.

Roy, René. Demography and Economic Growth: Income Distribution and Way of Life. In *[Tinbergen, J.]*, 1973, pp. 257–71.

Rweyemamu, J. F. A Note on the Theories of Underdevelopment. In *Livingstone, I., et al., eds.*, 1973, pp. 79–81.

Saini, Krishan G. and Neece, Roger N. Poverty versus Pollution: Is There a Choice? *Indian Econ. J.*, January-March 1973, *20*(3), pp. 452–68.

Salvatore, Dominick. Regional Inequality and the Market Mechanism: Reply. *Kyklos*, 1973, *26*(3), pp. 627–33. [G: Italy]

Sankaran, Sundaram. Population and the World Bank. *Finance Develop.*, December 1973, *10*(4), pp. 18–21, 41.

Saul, John S. The Political Aspects of Economic Independence. In *Ghai, D., ed.*, 1973, pp. 123–50.

Schuster, Helmut. Direktinvestitionen und Zahlungsbilanz in Entwicklungsländern. (Direct Investment and the Balance of Payments in Developing Countries. With English summary.) *Z. Wirtschaft. Sozialwissen.*, 1973, *93*(2), pp. 190–96.

Schwartz, Sandra L. Second-hand Machinery in Development, or How to Recognize a Bargain. *J. Devel. Stud.*, July 1973, *9*(4), pp. 544–55.

de Schweinitz, Karl, Jr. The Ethics of Economic Development. *Econ. Develop. Cult. Change*, Part I, July 1973, *21*(4), pp. 717–21.

Scott, Robert E. Latin America and Modernization. In *Scott, R. E., ed.*, 1973, pp. 1–21. [G: Latin America]

Shah, Anil C. and Patel, V. G. An Integrated Strategy for Backward Districts Industrial Development. *Artha-Vikas*, January-July 1973, *9*(1–2), pp. 203–13. [G: India]

Sharif, M. Raihan. Development Planning with Social Justice: Some Clarifications of Concepts and Applications. *Bangladesh Econ. Rev.*, July 1973, *1*(3), pp. 227–42.

Sicherl, Pavle. Time-Distance as a Dynamic Measure of Disparities in Social and Economic Development. *Kyklos*, 1973, *26*(3), pp. 559–75.

Simon, Julian L. Does Economic Growth Imply a Growth in Welfare? *J. Econ. Issues*, March 1973, *7*(1), pp. 130–36.

Singh, Anoop. An Enquiry into the Nature and Implications of a Foreign Exchange Constraint on Development. *Indian Econ. J.*, October–December 1973, *21*(2), pp. 147–57.

Sofranko, Andrew J. and Bealer, Robert C. Modernization Balance, Imbalance, and Domestic Instability. *Econ. Develop. Cult. Change*, October 1973, *22*(1), pp. 52–72.

Steel, William F. Complementarities and Conflicts Between Employment and Output Growth in Low-Income Countries. *Econ. Bull. Ghana, Sec. Ser.*, 1973, *3*(1), pp. 50–66. [G: Ghana]

Stewart, Frances and Streeten, Paul. Conflicts Between Output and Employment Objectives in Developing Countries. *Bangladesh Econ. Rev.*, January 1973, *1*(1), pp. 1–24.

Streeten, Paul. An Institutional Critique of Development Concepts. In *Livingstone, I., et al., eds.*, 1973, pp. 82–94.

Supple, Barry. Thinking About Economic Development. In *Youngson, A. J., ed.*, 1973, pp. 19–35.

Svendsen, K. E. Economic Theory and Public Policy. In *Livingstone, I., et al., eds.*, 1973, pp. 66–72. [G: Africa]

Teubal, Morris. Heavy and Light Industry in Economic Development. *Amer. Econ. Rev.*, September 1973, *63*(4), pp. 588–96.

Thorbecke, Erik. Sector Analysis and Models of Agriculture in Developing Countries. *Food Res. Inst. Stud.*, 1973, *12*(1), pp. 73–89.

Thurber, Clarence E. Islands of Development: A Political and Social Approach to Development Administration in Latin America. In *Thurber, C. E. and Graham, L. S., eds.*, 1973, pp. 15–46. [G: Latin America]

Tinbergen, Jan. Exhaustion and Technological Development: A Macro-Dynamic Policy Model. *Z. Nationalökon.*, 1973, *33*(3–4), pp. 213–34.

Tricković, Vidosav. Science Policy and Development Strategy in Developing Countries. In *Williams, B. R., ed.*, 1973, pp. 287–99.

Tyler, William G. A Model of Income Distribution and Economic Development. *Weltwirtsch. Arch.*, 1973, *109*(2), pp. 321–36.

Vachha, Homiar S. and Iyengar, Sampath S. Financial Institutions and Backward Regions: A Case Study of Gujarat. *Artha-Vikas*, January-July 1973, *9*(1–2), pp. 185–202. [G: India]

Vanek, Jaroslav. A Contribution to the Problem of Economic Development of Bangladesh. *Bangladesh Econ. Rev.*, July 1973, *1*(3), pp. 324–27. [G: Bangladesh]

Vartikar, V. S. On Optimizing the Rate of Investment. *Econ. Int.*, February 1973, *26*(1), pp. 17–31. [G: India]

Watanabe, Tsunehiko. The Process of Industrialization: A Dynamic Simulation. *Osaka Econ. Pap.,* March 1973, *21*(38), pp. 1–43.

Weisskopf, Thomas E. Capitalism and Underdevelopment in the Modern World. In *Reynolds, L. G.; Green, G. D. and Lewis, D. R., eds.,* 1973, pp. 518–29.

West, Robert LeRoy. Economic Dependence and Policy in Developing Countries. In *[Halm, G. N.],* 1973, pp. 157–83.

Whitney, J. B. R. Ecology and Environmental Control. In *Oksenberg, M., ed.,* 1973, pp. 95–109. [G: China]

Wilber, Charles K. Economic Development, Central Planning and Allocative Efficiency. In *Wilber, C. K., ed.,* 1973, pp. 221–39. [G: U.S.S.R.]

Williams, B. R. Science and Technology in Economic Growth: Introduction. In *Williams, B. R., ed.,* 1973, pp. xi–xvii.

Winston, Gordon C. A Note on the Political Economy of Development Theory. *Bangladesh Econ. Rev.,* January 1973, *1*(1), pp. 115–17.

Ylä-Anttila, Pekka. Infrastruktuuri ja teollisuuden kehitys. (Overhead Capital and Industrial Development. With English summary.) *Liiketaloudellinen Aikak.,* 1973, *22*(4), pp. 278–87.

Yotopoulos, Pan A. and Nugent, Jeffrey B. A Balanced-Growth Version of the Linkage Hypothesis: A Test. *Quart. J. Econ.,* May 1973, *87*(2), pp. 157–71.

Youngson, A. J. Economic Development in the Long Run: Introduction. In *Youngson, A. J., ed.,* 1973, pp. 9–17.

113 Economic Planning Theory and Policy

1130 Economic Planning Theory and Policy

Abkin, M. H., et al. System Simulation of Agricultural Development: Some Nigerian Policy Comparisons. *Amer. J. Agr. Econ.,* August 1973, *55*(3), pp. 404–19. [G: Nigeria]

Banerjee, B. P. A Working Plan for Programming and Sustaining the Growth of Small Scale Industries around Calcutta, India. In *Ross, M., ed.,* 1973, pp. 483–89. [G: India]

Banks, F. E. A Note on Stochastic Programming in a Development Plan. *Kyklos,* 1973, *26*(2), pp. 395–98. [G: Egypt]

Beck, Jiř and Nachtigal, Vladimír. K problematice systému makroekonomických modelů v podmínkách ČSSR. (Problems of a System of Macroeconomic Models in the Conditions of Czechoslovakia. With English summary.) *Ekon.-Mat. Obzor,* 1973, *9*(1), pp. 13–29. [G: Czechoslovakia]

Belen'kii, V. Z.; Volkonskii, V. A. and Pavlov, N. V. Dynamic Input-Output Models in Planning and Price Calculations and Economic Analysis. *Matekon,* Winter 1973-74, *10*(2), pp. 74–101. [G: U.S.S.R.]

Bergendorff, Hans G.; Clark, Peter B. and Taylor, Lance. Welfare Gains from Optimization in Dynamic Planning Models. *Econ. Planning,* 1973, *13* (1–2), pp. 75–90. [G: Chile]

Bonnaud, Jean-Jacques and Pagé, Jean-Pierre. L'utilisation d'un modèle de simulation économique dans la procédure de préparation du VIᵉ Plan (1970–1975). (The Utilisation of a Mathematical Economic Model in the Process of Elaboration of the French VIth Plan (1970–1975). With English summary.) *Revue Écon.,* November 1973, *24*(6), pp. 988–1025. [G: France]

Borovskikh, B. Urgent Problems in Planning the Reproduction of Natural Resources. *Prob. Econ.,* November 1973, *16*(7), pp. 3–23.

Brada, Josef C. The Allocative Efficiency of Centrally Planned Foreign Trade: A Programming Approach to the Czech Case. *Europ. Econ. Rev.,* December 1973, *4*(4), pp. 329–46. [G: Czechoslovakia]

Brand, S. S. Economic Development as a Policy Objective. *Finance Trade Rev.,* December 1973, *10* (4), pp. 168–75. [G: S. Africa]

Bryson, Phillip J. Dynamic Price Planning in Command Systems: A Partial Equilibrium Approach. *Weltwirtsch. Arch.,* 1973, *109*(3), pp. 495–513.

Bubnov, Iu. T. Modeling the Distribution and Adjustment to the Annual Production Program. *Matekon,* Fall 1973, *10*(1), pp. 83–92.

Burks, R. V. The Political Implications of Economic Reform. In *Bornstein, M., ed.,* 1973, pp. 373–402. [G: E. Europe]

Clark, Peter B. and Foxley, Alejandro. Target Shooting with a Multisectoral Model. In *Eckaus, R. S. and Rosenstein-Rodan, P. N., eds.,* 1973, pp. 341–66. [G: Chile]

Cohon, Jared L. and Marks, David H. Multiobjective Screening Models and Water Resource Investment. *Water Resources Res.,* August 1973, *9*(4), pp. 826–36.

Costache, Sandu and Popescu, Constantin. Coordonate ale echilibrului dezvoltării economicosociale în profil de ramură şi teritorial. (Coordinates of the Equilibrium of Economic-Social Development as Regards Branch and Territory. With English summary.) *Stud. Cercet. Econ.,* 1973, (4), pp. 25–38. [G: Rumania]

Darvas, Gy. Major Implications of Long-Term Planning on the Fifth Five-Year Plan. *Acta Oecon.,* 1973, *11*(2–3), pp. 149–63. [G: Hungary]

Despres, Emile. Determining the Size of a Development Plan: Pakistan. In *Despres, E.,* 1973, pp. 99–132. [G: Pakistan]

Diwan, Romesh K. Are We Saving Enough for Our Plans? In *Wadhva, C. D., ed.,* 1973, pp. 163–78. [G: India]

Dumitru, Georgeta and Fundătură, D. Îmbunătăţirea utilizării extensive a fondurilor fixe. (Improving the Extensive Use of Productive Fixed Assets. With English summary.) *Stud. Cercet. Econ.,* 1973, (1), pp. 53–64.

Dvorák, Jirí and Jezek, Tomás. Some Problems of Strain in the Manpower Balances. *Eastern Europ. Econ.,* Summer 1973, *11*(4), pp. 60–85. [G: Czechoslovakia]

Fedorenko, N. P. The Present Stage and Future Prospects for the Creation of Automatic Control Systems for Industrial Enterprise. *Matekon,* Fall 1973, *10*(1), pp. 24–39. [G: U.S.S.R.]

Feiwel, George R. Growth, Planning, Price Mechanism and Consumer Sovereignty. *Rivista Int. Sci. Econ. Com.,* November 1973, *20*(11), pp. 1041–70.

Friss, István. On Long–Term National Economic Planning. In *Földi, T., ed.*, 1973, pp. 9–36. [G: E. Europe]

Gács, János and Lackó, Mária. A Study of Planning Behaviour on the National-Economic Level: An Attempt at Analysing a Few Correlations Based on Hungarian Data. *Econ. Planning*, 1973, *13* (1–2), pp. 91–119. [G: Hungary]

Gadgil, D. R. Planning without a Policy Frame. In *Wadhva, C. D., ed.*, 1973, pp. 94–107. [G: India]

Gadó, O. Plan and Regulators in the Hungarian Economic Management. In *Kiss, T., ed.*, 1973, pp. 79–98. [G: Hungary]

Garreton, Oscar. Some Preliminary Facts about the Management and Organization of the Industrial Sector. In *Zammit, J. A., ed.*, 1973, pp. 63–68. [G: Chile]

Ghosh, Ranen. The Public Sector and Economic Development in India–I. *Econ. Aff.*, January–February 1973, *18*(1-2), pp. 9–16, 89–94. [G: India]

Gilbert, Gary G. Investment Planning for Latin American Economic Integration. *J. Common Market Stud.*, June 1973, *11*(4), pp. 314–25. [G: Latin America]

Greenstreet, D. K. Public Administration: A Comparative Analysis of the 1950 Colonial Ten-Year Development Plan and the 1951 'Nkrumah' Development Plan of the Gold Coast (Ghana) *Econ. Bull. Ghana, Sec. Ser.*, 1973, *3*(4), pp. 31–55. [G: Ghana]

Herman, Bohuslav. On the Choice of the Optimal Industry—A Check of a Controversy. *Weltwirtsch. Arch.*, 1973, *109*(1), pp. 70–86.

Higgins, Benjamin. Profits and Planning in Developing Countries. *Écon. Appl.*, 1973, *26*(1), pp. 5–32.

Holešovský, Václav. Planning and the Market in the Czechoslovak Reform. In *Bornstein, M., ed.*, 1973, pp. 313–45. [G: Czechoslovakia]

Husain, Ishrat. Mechanics of Development Planning in Pakistan: A Suggested Framework. *Pakistan Econ. Soc. Rev.*, Winter 1973, *11*(4), pp. 454–62. [G: Pakistan]

Ianovskii, V. S. The Problem of Economic Integration of Enterprises in Industry Production Associations and the Optimization of Current Planning. *Matekon*, Fall 1973, *10*(1), pp. 65–82.

Jarkovsky, Vladimír. The Dynamic Determination of Economically Efficient Capital Investment and New Technology. *Eastern Europ. Econ.*, Summer 1973, *11*(4), pp. 86–112. [G: Czechoslovakia]

Keren, Michael. Concentration Amid Devolution in East Germany's Reforms. In *Bornstein, M., ed.*, 1973, pp. 123–51. [G: E. Germany]

Khachaturov, T. S. Development of Science and Technology in the U.S.S.R. In *Williams, B. R., ed.*, 1973, pp. 147–68. [G: U.S.S.R.]

Komin, A. Problems in the Methodology and Practice of Planned Price Formation. *Prob. Econ.*, May 1973, *16*(1), pp. 35–49. [G: U.S.S.R.]

Kossov, V. V. Relationships in the Development of Industries. *Matekon*, Spring 1973, *9*(3), pp. 89–108.

Kotov, V. Prices: The Instrument of National Economic Planning and the Basis of the Value Indices of the Plan. *Prob. Econ.*, May 1973, *16*(1), pp. 50–69. [G: U.S.S.R.]

Kriesel, Herbert C. and Hedley, Douglas D. Planners as Factors in Agricultural Growth. In *Ofori, I. M., ed.*, 1973, pp. 33–41.

Lăudatu, Alexandra. Determinarea capacității efective optime de producție în unitățile de construcții-montaj. (Determining the Best Effective Production Capacity in the Building-Assemblage Units. With English summary.) *Stud. Cercet. Econ.*, 1973, (2), pp. 89–98.

Lebédel, Claude. Public Policy Toward Retailing: East Germany. In *Boddewyn, J. J. and Hollander, S. C., eds.*, 1972, pp. 101–15. [G: E. Germany]

Levy, Fred D., Jr. Economic Planning in Venezuela. In *Thurber, C. E. and Graham, L. S., eds.*, 1973, pp. 81–108. [G: Venezuela]

Little, I. M. D. and Mirrlees, James A. Further Reflections on the OECD Manual of Project Analysis in Developing Countries. In *[Rosenstein-Rodan, P.]*, 1973, pp. 257–80.

Mach, Milos. Planning Under Socialism. *Czech. Econ. Digest.*, August 1973, (5), pp. 64–88.

Manne, Alan S. Economic Alternatives for Mexico: A Quantitative Analysis. In *Goreux, L. M. and Manne, A. S., eds.*, 1973, pp. 151–72. [G: Mexico]

Manove, Michael. Non-Price Rationing of Intermediate Goods in Centrally Planned Economies. *Econometrica*, September 1973, *41*(5), pp. 829–52. [G: U.S.S.R.]

Martner, Gonzalo. The Popular Unity Government's Efforts in Planning. In *Zammit, J. A., ed.*, 1973, pp. 69–75. [G: Chile]

Miller, S. F. and Halter, A. N. Systems-Simulation in a Practical Policy-Making Setting: The Venezuelan Cattle Industry. *Amer. J. Agr. Econ.*, August 1973, *55*(3), pp. 420–32. [G: Venezuela]

Moldovan, Roman and Botez, Mihai C. Correlation Between Forecasting and Action—An Essential Feature in Planning. *Revue Roumaine Sci. Soc. Serie Sci. Econ.*, 1973, *17*(1), pp. 41–52.

Mosin, V. On the Creation of an Automated System of Planning. *Prob. Econ.*, April 1973, *15*(12), pp. 16–36. [G: U.S.S.R.]

Naqvi, Syed Nawab Haider. Pakistan's Export Possibilities. *Pakistan Develop. Rev.*, Spring 1973, *12* (1), pp. 1–30. [G: Pakistan]

Nasta, Eliza and Vasilescu, Floarea. Considerații asupra metodologiei de calcul a coeficientului elasticității. (Considerations of the Methodology of Calculating the Elasticity Coefficient. With English summary.) *Stud. Cercet. Econ.*, 1973, (1), pp. 99–109.

Nasta, Eliza and Horja, Gavril. Conținutul și funcțiile contractelor economice în etapa actuală. (The Content and Functions of the Economic Contracts in the Present Stage. With English summary.) *Stud. Cercet. Econ.*, 1973, (4), pp. 47–53. [G: Rumania]

Notkin, A. The Production Accumulation Norm. *Prob. Econ.*, February 1973, *15*(10), pp. 3–29. [G: U.S.S.R.]

Pajestka, Jøzef. General Development Relationships and Social Factors for Progress. *Eastern Europ. Econ.*, Fall 1973, *12*(1), pp. 45–81. [G: Poland]

Parrish, Charles J. Bureaucracy, Democracy, and Development: Some Considerations Based on the Chilean Case. In *Thurber, C. E. and Graham, L. S., eds.*, 1973, pp. 229–59. [G: Chile]

Patel, I. G. The Strategy of Indian Planning. In *Wadhva, C. D., ed.*, 1973, pp. 108–15. [G: India]

Pricop, Mihai. Asigurarea ritmicității activității de servire a producției de bază. (Ensuring the Rhythmicity of the Activity of Serving Basic Production. With English summary.) *Stud. Cercet. Econ.*, 1973, (4), pp. 55–64.

Psacharopoulos, George. Substitution Assumptions versus Empirical Evidence in Manpower Planning. *De Economist*, November-December 1973, *121*(6), pp. 609–25. [G: Greece]

Ristea, Mihai. Conceptul de operativitate în sistemul informațional contabil. (The Concept of Efficiency in the Book-keeping Information System. With English summary.) *Stud. Cercet. Econ.*, 1973, (4), pp. 99–109.

Rosenstein-Rodan, Paul N. Planning for Full Employment in Latin America. In *Pollock, D. H. and Ritter, A. R. M., eds.*, 1973, pp. 86–96. [G: Latin America]

Schwartz, Sandra L. Second-hand Machinery in Development, or How to Recognize a Bargain. *J. Devel. Stud.*, July 1973, *9*(4), pp. 544–55.

Sergent, Raisa and Lefter, Viorel. Utilizarea extensivă a capacităților de producție și influența ei asupra prețului de cost. (The Extensive Use of Production Capacities and its Influence on the Cost Price. With English summary.) *Stud. Cercet. Econ.*, 1973, (1), pp. 65–76.

Sharif, M. Raihan. Development Planning with Social Justice: Some Clarifications of Concepts and Applications. *Bangladesh Econ. Rev.*, July 1973, *1*(3), pp. 227–42.

Shtern, Iu. Production Functions and the Possibility of Using Them in Economic Calculations. *Prob. Econ.*, November 1973, *16*(7), pp. 59–83. [G: U.S.S.R.]

Siegel, Gilbert B. Brazil: Diffusion and Centralization of Power. In *Thurber, C. E. and Graham, L. S., eds.*, 1973, pp. 362–81. [G: Brazil]

Sigurdson, Jon. Rural Economic Planning. In *Oksenberg, M., ed.*, 1973, pp. 68–79. [G: China]

Silverman, Bertram. Economic Organization and Social Conscience: Some Dilemmas of Cuban Socialism. In *Barkin, D. P. and Manitzas, N. R., eds.*, 1973, pp. R262–28. [G: Cuba]

Sinha, R. K. Report of the Committee on Taxation of Agricultural Wealth and Income—An Appraisal. *Econ. Aff.*, January–February 1973, *18*(1-2), pp. 17–28. [G: India]

Starostin, S. and Emdin, G. The Five-Year Plan and the Soviet Way of Life. *Prob. Econ.*, February 1973, *15*(10), pp. 81–103. [G: U.S.S.R.]

Szeplaki, Leslie. Pricing and Taxation in a Marxian Two-Sector Model: A Brief Reflection. *J. Econ. Theory*, August 1973, *6*(4), pp. 404–08.

Thurber, Clarence E. Islands of Development: A Political and Social Approach to Development Administration in Latin America. In *Thurber, C. E. and Graham, L. S., eds.*, 1973, pp. 15–46. [G: Latin America]

Tintner, Gerhard and Ferghali, Salwa Ali S. A Note on Stochastic Programming in a Development Plan: Reply. *Kyklos*, 1973, *26*(2), pp. 399–401. [G: Egypt]

Toms, Miroslav. The Labor Force and Relations Within the Production Process. *Eastern Europ. Econ.*, Summer 1973, *11*(4), pp. 3–59. [G: Czechoslovakia]

Ullmo, Bernard. Trois problèmes posés par le modèle physico-financier. (Three Problems Set by the Physico-Financial Model. With English summary.) *Revue Écon.*, November 1973, *24*(6), pp. 1026–71. [G: France]

Usatov, I. The Elaboration of Plans and the System of Prices. *Prob. Econ.*, March 1973, *15*(11), pp. 44–62. [G: U.S.S.R.]

Van Arkadie, Brian. Development of the State Sector and Economic Independence. In *Ghai, D., ed.*, 1973, pp. 88–122. [G: Tanzania]

Vanek, Jaroslav. The Yugoslav Economy Viewed through the Theory of Labor Management. *World Devel.*, September 1973, *1*(9), pp. 39–56. [G: Yugoslavia]

Veverka, Ján. Strukturní model pro vypocty zmen velkoobchodních cen. (Structure Models for Calculating Wholesale Prices Changes. With English summary.) *Ekon.-Mat. Obzor*, 1973, *9*(3), pp. 260–74.

Walters, J., Jr. Public Policy Toward Retailing: Poland. In *Boddewyn, J. J. and Hollander, S. C., eds.*, 1972, pp. 271–82. [G: Poland]

Weiller, Augusto. Arbitrato e programmazione. (Arbitration and Planning. With English summary.) *Bancaria*, December 1973, *29*(12), pp. 1474–80.

Zlocha, Nikolaj. The Role of Economic Production Units /VHJs/ and Enterprises. *Czech. Econ. Digest.*, May 1973, (3), pp. 52–77. [G: Czechoslovakia]

Zucker, Jiří. Uzití metody Monte Carlo k určení charakteristik souboru investic. (The Use of Monte Carlo Method for Determining the Characteristics of a Collection of Investment Assets. With English summary.) *Ekon.-Mat. Obzor*, 1973, *9*(2), pp. 134–49.

1132 Economic Planning Theory

Adelman, Irma. Planning for Social Equity. In *[Tinbergen, J.]*, 1973, pp. 181–200.

Aganbegian, A. G. and Bagrinovsky, K. A. Problem-Complexes in Optimal Planning. *Acta Oecon.*, 1973, *10*(1), pp. 21–27.

Aoki, Masanao. Approximation Scheme for Evaluating Some Terminal Capital Stock. *J. Econ. Theory*, June 1973, *6*(3), pp. 317–19.

Bagrinovsky, K. A. A System of Models for Central Planning. In *Hawkes, N., ed.*, 1973, pp. 21–30. [G: U.S.S.R.]

Baher, G. H. A Planning Model for the Educational Requirements of Economic Development: The Case of Iran. *Tahq. Eq.*, Winter & Spring 1973, *10* (29 & 30), pp. 170–205. [G: Iran]

Berg, Alan and Muscat, Robert. Nutrition Program Planning: An Approach. In *Berg, A.; Scrimshaw, N. S. and Call, D. L., eds.*, 1973, pp. 247–74.

Braverman, E. M. A Production Model with Disequilibrium Prices. *Matekon,* Fall 1973, *10*(1), pp. 40–64.

Bzhilianskii, Iu. Political and Economic Problems of Population Under Socialism. *Prob. Econ.,* April 1973, *15*(12), pp. 52–72. [G: U.S.S.R.]

Chakravarty, Sukhamoy and Lefeber, Louis. An Optimising Planning Model. In *Wadhva, C. D., ed.,* 1973, pp. 51–77. [G: India]

Chakravarty, Sukhamoy. Theory of Development Planning: An Appraisal. In *[Tinbergen, J.],* 1973, pp. 163–79.

Chung, Pham. A Note on the Optimal Product Mix in a Centrally Planned Economy. *J. Polit. Econ.,* Part I, March-April 1973, *81*(2), pp. 427–34.

Clark, Peter B.; Foxley, Alejandro and Jul, Anna Maria. Project Evaluation within a Macroeconomic Framework. In *Eckaus, R. S. and Rosenstein-Rodan, P. N., eds.,* 1973, pp. 199–226. [G: Chile]

Courbis, Raymond. La théorie des "économies concurrencées" fondement du modèle FIFI. (The Theory of "Competitioned Economies" as a Basis of the Fifi Model. With English summary.) *Revue Écon.,* November 1973, *24*(6), pp. 905–22.

Courbis, Raymond and Pagé, Jean-Pierre. Techniques de projection macro-économique et choix du Plan français. (Macro-Economic Forecasting Techniques and Decision Making in the French Planning System. With English summary.) *Revue Écon.,* November 1973, *24*(6), pp. 951–87. [G: France]

Deleau, Michel; Guesnerie, Roger and Malgrange, Pierre. Planification, incertitude et politique économique. II—L'opération Optimix: Résultats numériques. (Planning, Uncertainty and Economic Policy. II—Optimix Operation: Numerical Results. With English summary.) *Revue Écon.,* November 1973, *24*(6), pp. 1072–1103.

Despres, Emile. Price Distortions and Development Planning: Pakistan. In *Despres, E.,* 1973, pp. 133–45. [G: Pakistan]

Drecin, J. and Hetényi, I. Some Thoughts Concerning the Future of our Planning. (In Russian. With English summary.) *Acta Oecon.,* 1973, *11*(2–3), pp. 129–48. [G: E. Europe]

Duloy, John H. and Norton, Roger D. CHAC Results: Economic Alternatives for Mexican Agriculture. In *Goreux, L. M. and Manne, A. S., eds.,* 1973, pp. 373–99. [G: Mexico]

Duloy, John H. and Norton, Roger D. Linking the Agricultural Model and the Economy-Wide Model. In *Goreux, L. M. and Manne, A. S., eds.,* 1973, pp. 435–61. [G: Mexico]

Duloy, John H. and Norton, Roger D. CHAC, A Programming Model of Mexican Agriculture. In *Goreux, L. M. and Manne, A. S., eds.,* 1973, pp. 291–337. [G: Mexico]

Fedorenko, N. and Gofman, K. G. Problems of Optimization in the Planning and Control of the Environment. *Prob. Econ.,* April 1973, *15*(12), pp. 37–51. [G: U.S.S.R.]

Fedorenko, N. On the Elaboration of a System of Optimal Functioning of the Socialist Economy. *Prob. Econ.,* January 1973, *15*(9), pp. 3–27. [G: U.S.S.R.]

Fernández de la Garza, Guillermo and Manne, Alan

S. ENERGETICOS, A Process Analysis of the Energy Sectors. In *Goreux, L. M. and Manne, A. S., eds.,* 1973, pp. 233–75. [G: Mexico]

Fernández de la Garza, Guillermo; Manne, Alan S. and Valencia, José Alberto. Multi-Level Planning for Electric Power Projects. In *Goreux, L. M. and Manne, A. S., eds.,* 1973, pp. 197–231. [G: Mexico]

Franchet, Yves; Inman, Richard A. and Manne, Alan S. Numerical Data for Multi-Sector Planning. In *Goreux, L. M. and Manne, A. S., eds.,* 1973, pp. 85–106. [G: Mexico]

Ginor, Fanny. Importance of the Nutrition Component in Economic Planning. In *Berg, A.; Scrimshaw, N. S. and Call, D. L., eds.,* 1973, pp. 275–81.

Goreux, Louis M. and Manne, Alan S. Multi-Level Planning: Case Studies in Mexico: Introduction. In *Goreux, L. M. and Manne, A. S., eds.,* 1973, pp. 1–14. [G: Mexico]

Granick, David. A Management Model of East European, Centrally-Planned Economies. *Europ. Econ. Rev.,* June 1973, *4*(2), pp. 135–61.

Groves, Theodore. Incentives in Teams. *Econometrica,* July 1973, *41*(4), pp. 617–31.

Halabuk, L. Estimation and Structure of the Second Econometric Model of Hungary. *Matekon,* Summer 1973, *9*(4), pp. 43–66. [G: Hungary]

Hamilton, F. E. Ian. Spatial Dimensions of Soviet Economic Decision Making. In *Bandera, V. N. and Melnyk, Z. L., eds.,* 1973, pp. 235–60. [G: U.S.S.R.]

Hammond, Peter J. and Mirrlees, James A. Agreeable Plans. In *Mirrlees, J. A. and Stern, N. H., eds.,* 1973, pp. 283–99.

Hertz, David B. Planning under Uncertainty. In *Ross, M., ed.,* 1973, pp. 103–22.

Jhabvala, Firdaus. A Model of Motivation in State Enterprises in Underdeveloped Economies. *Indian Econ. Rev.,* October 1973, *8*(2), pp. 172–85.

Khachaturov, T. Improving the Methods of Determining the Effectiveness of Capital Investments. *Prob. Econ.,* September 1973, *16*(5), pp. 3–30. [G: U.S.S.R.]

Komiya, Ryutaro. A Note on Professor Mahalanobis' Model of Indian Economic Planning. In *Wadhva, C. D., ed.,* 1973, pp. 32–41. [G: India]

Kornai, János. Thoughts on Multi-Level Planning Systems. In *Goreux, L. M. and Manne, A. S., eds.,* 1973, pp. 521–51. [G: Mexico]

Kornai, János and Martos, Béla. Autonomous Control of the Economic System. *Econometrica,* May 1973, *41*(3), pp. 509–28.

Kornai, János. Some Intersectoral and Intemporal Choice Problems: Hungarian Experiences in Long-Term Planning. In *[Tinbergen, J.],* 1973, pp. 201–13. [G: Hungary]

Kovács, J. Simplified Model for Level-of-Planning-Consistency Control. *Acta Oecon.,* 1973, *11*(2–3), pp. 177–90.

Lombardini, Siro. Piano e mercato oggi in Italia. (Plan and Market in Italy Today. With English summary.) *L'industria, N. S.,* 1973, (1), pp. 27–34. [G: Italy]

Maki, Wilbur R. and Angus, James E. Development Planning. In *Judge, G. G. and Takayama, T., eds.,* 1973, pp. 43–64.

Manne, Alan S. On Linking ENERGETICOS to DINAMICO. In *Goreux, L. M. and Manne, A. S., eds.*, 1973, pp. 277–89. [G: Mexico]

Marschak, Thomas A. Decentralizing the Command Economy: The Study of a Pragmatic Strategy for Reformers. In *Bornstein, M., ed.*, 1973, pp. 23–63.

McFadden, Daniel. On the Existence of Optimal Development Programmes in Infinite-Horizon Economies. In *Mirrlees, J. A. and Stern, N. H., eds.*, 1973, pp. 260–82.

Megyeri, E. Optimal Utilization of Enterprise Funds and Some Problems of Measuring Effectiveness. *Acta Oecon.*, 1973, *11*(4), pp. 347–67. [G: Hungary]

Mirrlees, James A. The Integration of Project and Sector Analysis: Discussion. In *Parkin, M., ed.*, 1973, pp. 167–69.

Moiseev, Nikita N. Principles of Simulation: Hierarchial Control Systems. In *Hawkes, N., ed.*, 1973, pp. 205–26.

Montias, John Michael. A Framework for Theoretical Analysis of Economic Reforms in Soviet-type Economies. In *Bornstein, M., ed.*, 1973, pp. 65–122.

Nagy, A. Industrial Projection Methods in Hungary. *Acta Oecon.*, 1973, *11*(4), pp. 381–402. [G: Hungary]

Naseem, S. M. Import Substitution: A Survey of Concepts, Measures and Models. *Pakistan Develop. Rev.*, Spring 1973, *12*(1), pp. 31–47.

Nathan, Robert R. Focusing Attention on Nutrition in Development Planning. In *Berg, A.; Scrimshaw, N. S. and Call, D. L., eds.*, 1973, pp. 282–84.

Pajestka, Jøzef. The Socio-Economic Factors of Progress. *Acta Oecon.*, 1973, *10*(1), pp. 3–20.

Pant, S. P. and Takayama, T. An Investigation of Agricultural Planning Models: A Case Study of the Indian's Food Economy. In *Judge, G. G. and Takayama, T., eds.*, 1973, pp. 597–623. [G: India]

Patrick, John D. Establishing Convergent Decentralized Policy Assignment. *J. Int. Econ.*, February 1973, *3*(1), pp. 37–51.

Phan, Duc-Loï. Le modèle FIFI et la politique économique à moyen terme. (The Physico-Financial Model and the Medium Term Policy. With English summary.) *Revue Écon.*, November 1973, *24*(6), pp. 923–50. [G: France]

Prodromidis, Kypriqnos P. Applied Economic Policy with a Quadratic Criterion Function: A Reply. *Appl. Econ.*, September 1973, *5*(3), pp. 229–31.

Qayum, Abdul. Professor Tinbergen's Approach to Economic Planning. *Econ. Int.*, February 1973, *26*(1), pp. 95–115.

Reese, K. The Soviet Ruble and Comecon Countries. *S. Afr. J. Econ.*, June 1973, *41*(2), pp. 134–45. [G: U.S.S.R.]

Roberts, Paul Craig. The Theory of Socialist Planning: Reply. *J. Polit. Econ.*, Part I, March-April 1973, *81*(2), pp. 465–70.

Robinson, J. N. Applied Economic Policy with a Quadratic Criterion Function: A Comment. *Appl. Econ.*, September 1973, *5*(3), pp. 227–28.

Rueda-Williamson, Roberto. Top Priority Programs in National Development Plans. In *Berg, A.; Scrimshaw, N. S. and Call, D. L., eds.*, 1973, pp. 285–89.

Rutgaizer, V. A Comprehensive Plan for the Development of the Service Sector. *Prob. Econ.*, September 1973, *16*(5), pp. 41–59. [G: U.S.S.R.]

Ryvkin, A. A Conference on Problems of Long-Range Planning and Forecasting. *Prob. Econ.*, September 1973, *16*(5), pp. 31–40.

Sadler, P. G. The Integration of Project and Sector Analysis. In *Parkin, M., ed.*, 1973, pp. 156–66.

Scotto di Carlo, Giovampietro. Effetto reddito ed effetto finanziario per la programmazione della politica di bilancio. (Income Effect and Financial Effect in the Planning of the Budget Policy. With English summary.) *L'Industria*, January-June 1973, (1–2), pp. 109–24.

Sebestyén, Joseph. On Models of Planning Regional Development in Hungary. In *Judge, G. G. and Takayama, T., eds.*, 1973, pp. 26–42. [G: Hungary]

Sherman, Howard J. The Theory of Socialist Planning: Comment. *J. Polit. Econ.*, Part I, March-April 1973, *81*(2), pp. 450–58.

Srinivasan, T. N. A Critique of the Optimising Planning Model. In *Wadhva, C. D., ed.*, 1973, pp. 78–93. [G: India]

Suzumura, Kotaro. The Economic Theory of Organization and Planning: A Review Article. *Econ. Stud. Quart.*, April 1973, *24*(1), pp. 33–51.

Taylor, Lance. Investment Project Analysis in Terms of a Model of Optical Growth: The Case of Chile. In *Eckaus, R. S. and Rosenstein-Rodan, P. N., eds.*, 1973, pp. 167–98. [G: Chile]

Uitermark, P. J. The Theory of Socialist Planning: Comment. *J. Polit. Econ.*, Part I, March-April 1973, *81*(2), pp. 459–64.

Wilber, Charles K. Economic Development, Central Planning and Allocative Efficiency. In *Wilber, C. K., ed.*, 1973, pp. 221–39. [G: U.S.S.R.]

Wiseman, Jack. Uncertainty, Costs, and Collectivist Economic Planning. In *Buchanan, J. M. and Thirlby, G. F., eds.*, 1973, pp. 227–43.

Woroniak, Alexander. Regional Aspects of Soviet Planning and Industrial Organization. In *Bandera, V. N. and Melnyk, Z. L., eds.*, 1973, pp. 261–304. [G: U.S.S.R.]

1136 Economic Planning Policy

Allegri, Vincenzo. La politica industriale delle Regioni. (The Industrial Policy of the Italian Regions. With English summary.) *L'industria, N. S.*, 1973, (1), pp. 15–24. [G: Italy]

Balassa, Á. Economic Growth, Equilibrium and Efficiency in the Present Stage of Development. *Acta Oecon.*, 1973, *10*(3–4), pp. 339–60. [G: Hungary]

Balassa, Bela. Planning and Programming in the European Common Market. *Europ. Econ. Rev.*, October 1973, *4*(3), pp. 217–33. [G: E.E.C.]

Bhattacharya, Debesh. A Critical Survey of Indian Planning and its Achievements. *Econ. Aff.*, March 1973, *18*(3), pp. 105–23. [G: India]

Billon, S. A. Centralization of Authority and Regional Management. In *Bandera, V. N. and Melnyk, Z. L., eds.*, 1973, pp. 214–34. [G: U.S.S.R.]

Bravo, Jacques. L'expérience française des budgets de programmes. (The French Experiment in Program Budgeting. With English summary.) *Revue Écon.,* January 1973, *24*(1), pp. 1–65.   [G: France]

Brown, Alan A. and Marer, Paul. Foreign Trade in the East European Reforms. In *Bornstein, M., ed.,* 1973, pp. 153–205.   [G: E. Europe]

Cargill, I. P. M. Efforts to Influence Recipient Performance: Case Study of India. In *Lewis, J. P. and Kapur, I., eds.,* 1973, pp. 89–95.   [G: India]

Carlson, Keith M. The 1973 National Economic Plan: Slowing the Boom. *Fed. Res. Bank St. Louis Rev.,* March 1973, *55*(3), pp. 2–9.   [G: U.S.]

Catanese, Anthony James. Planning in a State of Siege: The Colombia Experience. *Land Econ.,* February 1973, *49*(1), pp. 35–43. [G: Colombia]

Chen, Lihsin. Population Planning in China. *Pakistan Econ. Soc. Rev.,* Autumn 1973, *11*(3), pp. 231–38.   [G: China]

Conroy, Michael E. Rejection of Growth Center Strategy in Latin American Regional Development Planning. *Land Econ.,* November 1973, *49* (4), pp. 371–80.   [G: Latin America]

Corea, Gamani. Economic Planning, the Green Revolution and the 'Food Drive' in Ceylon. In *[Hicks, U.],* 1973, pp. 273–303.   [G: Ceylon]

Courbis, Raymond. Les méthodes de planification française: évolution et perspectives. (The Methods of French Planification: Evolution and Perspectives. With English summary.) *Schweiz. Z. Volkswirtsch. Statist.,* September 1973, *109*(3), pp. 317–40.   [G: France]

Dahyabhai, Indulal. Industrial Development of Backward Areas in Gujarat. *Artha-Vikas,* January-July 1973, *9*(1–2), pp. 240–44.   [G: India]

Deleau, Michel; Guesnerie, Roger and Malgrange, Pierre. Planification, incertitude et politique économique. L'operation Optimix. Une procédure formalisée d'adaptation du Plan à l'aléa. (Planning Uncertainty and Economic Policy. A Formalized Procedure: "Optimix." With English summary.) *Revue Écon.,* September 1973, *24*(5), pp. 801–36.   [G: France]

Eckaus, Richard S. The Chinese Economy at the Present Juncture: Discussion. *Amer. Econ. Rev.,* May 1973, *63*(2), pp. 233–34.   [G: China]

Eidel'man, M. The New Ex Post Interbranch Balance of Production and Distribution of Output in the National Economy of the USSR. *Prob. Econ.,* May 1973, *16*(1), pp. 3–34.   [G: U.S.S.R.]

Elovikov, L. A. Ways of Creating Social and Economic Conditions for the Reproduction of Labor Power in the New Regions of the West Siberian Plains. *Prob. Econ.,* June 1973, *16*(2), pp. 42–54.   [G: U.S.S.R.]

Flakierski, H. The Polish Economic Reform of 1970. *Can. J. Econ.,* February 1973, *6*(1), pp. 1–15.   [G: Poland]

Fremr, Jirí. Wage Developments in the Czechoslovak National Economy Since 1945, and Wage Trends in the 5th Five-Year Plan. *Czech. Econ. Digest.,* September 1973, (6), pp. 105–19.   [G: Czechoslovakia]

Friss, István. Objective Conditions of the Economy and the Extent of Centralization and Decentralization. *Acta Oecon.,* 1973, *10*(3–4), pp. 303–14.   [G: Hungary]

Friss, István. Practical Experiences of the Economic Reform in Hungary. *Eastern Europ. Econ.,* Spring 1973, *11*(3), pp. 3–26.   [G: Hungary]

Furtado, Celso. The Brazilian 'Model' *Soc. Econ. Stud.,* March 1973, *22*(1), pp. 122–31.   [G: Brazil]

Ghuge, V. B. Critique of Development Planning in India. *Econ. Aff.,* August 1973, *18*(8), pp. 357–71.   [G: India]

Gohil, B. K. Provision of Infrastructure in Gujarat. *Artha-Vikas,* January-July 1973, *9*(1–2), pp. 69–99.   [G: India]

Gupta, S. The Role of the Public Sector in Reducing Regional Income Disparity in Indian Plans. *J. Devel. Stud.,* January 1973, *9*(2), pp. 243–60.   [G: India]

Hoffmann, Pavel. Methodological Aspects of Prognoses in the Regional Development of the National Economy. *Czech. Econ. Digest.,* November 1973, (7), pp. 56–73.   [G: Czechoslovakia]

Hroneš, Václav. State Budgets for 1973. *Czech. Econ. Digest.,* May 1973, (3), pp. 25–51.   [G: Czechoslovakia]

Hsiao-wen, Kung. We Must Keep Count: In Refutation of "Statistics Is Useless." *Chinese Econ. Stud.,* Spring 1973, *6*(3), pp. 32–38.   [G: China]

Husák, Gustáv. From the Report of the Central Committee Presidium of the Communist Party of Czechoslovakia on the Implementation of the Decisions of the 14th Congress of the Communist Party of Czechoslovakia. *Czech. Econ. Digest.,* May 1973, (3), pp. 3–24. [G: Czechoslovakia]

Huszár, J. and Mandel, M. The Investment Decision-Making System in Hungary. *Eastern Europ. Econ.,* Spring 1973, *11*(3), pp. 27–49.   [G: Hungary]

Inozemtsev, N. Main Tasks in the Coordination of the National Economic Plans of COMECON Countries. *Prob. Econ.,* October 1973, *16*(6), pp. 20–35.   [G: E. Europe]

Iudina, E. and Oleinik, I. Structural Changes in the Economies of Socialist Countries. *Prob. Econ.,* March 1973, *15*(11), pp. 21–43. [G: U.S.S.R.]

Jensen, Robert G. Regional Pricing and the Economic Evaluation of Land in Soviet Agriculture. In *Bandera, V. N. and Melnyk, Z. L., eds.,* 1973, pp. 305–27.   [G: U.S.S.R.]

Joshi, N. D. Review of the Policy for the Development of Backward Regions in India. *Artha-Vikas,* January-July 1973, *9*(1–2), pp. 11–24. [G: India]

Joshi, V. H. The Concept of Regional Analysis: Its Application to the Study of the Development of Backward Regions. *Artha-Vikas,* January-July 1973, *9*(1–2), pp. 64–68.

Kale, J. D. Attracting Industries to Backward Areas. *Artha-Vikas,* January-July 1973, *9*(1–2), pp. 245–48.   [G: India]

Karcz, Jerzy F. Agricultural Reform in Eastern Europe. In *Bornstein, M., ed.,* 1973, pp. 207–43.   [G: E. Europe]

Kazakevich, L. and Shishankov, V. Economic Collaboration Between the USSR and the Socialist Countries. *Prob. Econ.,* October 1973, *16*(6), pp. 72–92.   [G: E. Europe; U.S.S.R.]

Kormnov, Iu. International Economic Organizations and Their Role in the Collaboration of COMECON Countries. *Prob. Econ.*, October 1973, *16* (6), pp. 36–54. [G: E. Europe]

Kotzenberg, H. R. P. A. The Policy and Programme for the Decentralisation of Industry in South Africa. *Finance Trade Rev.*, December 1973, *10* (4), pp. 137–67. [G: S. Africa]

Laevaert, W. Het Plan 1971–1975 Procedure, doelstellingen en draagwijdte. (The 1971–1975 Plan: Procedures, Aims and Significance. With English summary.) *Econ. Soc. Tijdschr.*, April 1973, *27*(2), pp. 157–71. [G: Belgium]

Levin, A. Problems in the Control of Consumer Demand. *Prob. Econ.*, December 1973, *16*(8), pp. 81–104. [G: U.S.S.R.]

Lynch, Edward. Propositions for Planning New Towns in Venezuela. *J. Devel. Areas,* July 1973, *7*(4), pp. 549–70. [G: Venezuela]

Mănescu, Manea. The Planned Economic-Social Development of Romania. *Revue Roumaine Sci. Soc. Serie Sci. Econ.*, 1973, *17*(1), pp. 13–33. [G: Rumania]

Mishra, G. P. Planning and Land Reform Policy in India. *Econ. Aff.*, May 1973, *18*(5), pp. 217–33. [G: India]

Nuttall, T. The Industry Act and Regional Policy. *Nat. Westminster Bank Quart. Rev.*, November 1973, pp. 55–68. [G: U.K.]

Onoe, Hisao. Problems of Japanese Economic Policy at the Turning-Point in Planning. *Rivista Int. Sci. Econ. Com.*, August-September 1973, *20*(8–9), pp. 794–803. [G: Japan]

Oza, Ghanshyambhai. Inaugural Speech. *Artha-Vikas,* January-July 1973, *9*(1–2), pp. 5–10. [G: India]

Patankar, H. R. Some Observations about Efficacy of Financial Incentives on Industrial Development in Backward Districts. *Artha-Vikas,* January-July 1973, *9*(1–2), pp. 220–29. [G: India]

Patel, V. G. Promotion of Entrepreneurship and Regional Development. *Artha-Vikas,* January-July 1973, *9*(1–2), pp. 214–19. [G: India]

Pathak, H. N. Developing Entrepreneurship in Backward Regions. *Artha-Vikas,* January-July 1973, *9*(1–2), pp. 47–54. [G: India]

Pathak, Mahesh T.; Desai, Mahendra D. and Charan, A. S. Development of Agriculture in Backward Regions of Gujarat: Facts and Issues. *Artha-Vikas,* January-July 1973, *9*(1–2), pp. 100–38. [G: India]

Pathak, Mahesh T. Development of Backward Areas: Problems and Prospects. *Artha-Vikas,* January-July 1973, *9*(1–2), pp. 25–46. [G: India]

Pavliuchenko, V. Some Problems in the Long-Term Planning of Purchases of Licenses. *Prob. Econ.*, March 1973, *15*(11), pp. 92–98. [G: U.S.S.R.]

Penkava, Jaromír. Improvements of the Finance and Credit System in Czechoslovakia. *Czech. Econ. Digest.*, August 1973, (5), pp. 3–24. [G: Czechoslovakia]

Perkins, Dwight H. Plans and Their Implementation in the People's Republic of China. *Amer. Econ. Rev.*, May 1973, *63*(2), pp. 224–31. [G: China]

Pessel', M. Credit and Its Development Under Current Conditions. *Prob. Econ.*, April 1973, *15*(12), pp. 86–99. [G: U.S.S.R.]

Portes, Richard. Hungary: The Experience of Market Socialism. In *Zammit, J. A., ed.,* 1973, pp. 367–89. [G: Hungary]

Potác, Svatopluk. The Role of Credit in the Plan-Based Management of the Czechoslovak Economy. *Czech. Econ. Digest.*, September 1973, (6), pp. 63–104. [G: Czechoslovakia]

Rao, M. R. S. N. Proposed Role of GIIC in Industrialisation of Backward Districts. *Artha-Vikas,* January-July 1973, *9*(1–2), pp. 230–39. [G: India]

Rawski, Thomas G. The Chinese Economy at the Present Juncture: Discussion. *Amer. Econ. Rev.*, May 1973, *63*(2), pp. 234–35. [G: China]

Ritter, Arch R. M. Institutional Strategy and Economic Performance in Revolutionary Cuba. In *Pollock, D. H. and Ritter, A. R. M., eds.,* 1973, pp. 203–59. [G: Cuba]

Robinson, Albert J. A Planned New Town: The Canberra Experiment. *Land Econ.*, August 1973, *49* (3), pp. 362–65. [G: Australia]

Rohlíček, Rudolf. The Role of Finance in Plan-Based Management of the Development of the Czechoslovak Economy. *Czech. Econ. Digest.*, September 1973, (6), pp. 3–62. [G: Czechoslovakia]

Ross, Miceal. Procedures for Integrated Regional Planning. I: The Background to Decentralisation. *Econ. Soc. Rev.*, July 1973, *4*(4), pp. 523–42. [G: Ireland]

Rubinshtein, M. Scientific and Technical Progress and Planned Price Formation. *Prob. Econ.*, July 1973, *16*(3), pp. 22–36. [G: U.S.S.R.]

Rudamoorthy, B. Financing Agriculture in Backward Regions. *Artha-Vikas,* January-July 1973, *9* (1–2), pp. 139–42. [G: India]

Rybakov, O. Some Organizational and Methodological Problems Relating to the Elaboration of Long-Range Plans for Collaboration Between the USSR and Socialist Countries. *Prob. Econ.*, October 1973, *16*(6), pp. 3–19. [G: E. Europe; U.S.S.R.]

Rybakov, O. Improvements in Planning Methods of Collaboration Among COMECON Countries. *Prob. Econ.*, March 1973, *15*(11), pp. 3–20. [G: COMECON]

Rychlewski, Eugeniusz. The Investment System of a Socialist Economy. *Eastern Europ. Econ.*, Fall 1973, *12*(1), pp. 3–44. [G: Poland]

Saxena, P. S. and Dubey, R. M. Rural Unemployment: A Direct Approach. *Econ. Aff.*, June 1973, *18*(6), pp. 265–74, 304. [G: India]

Schlichthaber, Roland. Verkehrsplanung in der Agglomeration aus der Sicht eines Ökonomen. (Traffic Planning in Agglomerations from the Economist's Point of View. With English summary.) *Schweiz. Z. Volkswirtsch. Statist.*, September 1973, *109*(3), pp. 375–84.

Scotto di Carlo, Giovampietro. Programmi quinquennali di spesa pubblica. Il sistema inglese e quello italiano. (Five-Year Public Expenditure Programmes. The British and Italian Systems. With English summary.) *Bancaria,* July 1973, *29* (7), pp. 832–38. [G: Italy]

Shah, Anil C. and Patel, V. G. An Integrated Strategy for Backward Districts Industrial Development. *Artha-Vikas,* January-July 1973, *9*(1–2), pp. 203–13. [G: India]

Shiriaev, Iu. Developing Scientific Foundations for Joint Planning Activity of COMECON Countries.

Prob. Econ., October 1973, *16*(6), pp. 55–71.
[G: E. Europe]

Singer, Hans and Jolly, Richard. Unemployment in an African Setting: Lessons of the Employment Strategy Mission to Kenya. *Int. Lab. Rev.*, February 1973, *107*(2), pp. 103–15. [G: Kenya]

Stelu, Şerban. Perfectarea contractelor economice. (The Conclusion of Economic Contracts. With English summary.) *Stud. Cercet. Econ.*, 1973, (3), pp. 141–52. [G: Rumania]

Timár, M. Results of the New System of Economic Control and Management and its Further Development. *Acta Oecon.*, 1973, *10*(3–4), pp. 277–301. [G: Hungary]

Tweeten, Luther G. Emerging Issues for Sparsely Populated Areas and Regions Under a National Growth Policy. *Amer. J. Agr. Econ.*, December 1973, *55*(5), pp. 840–50. [G: U.S.]

Ujázy, Karol. An Analysis of the Situation in Capital Construction. *Czech. Econ. Digest.*, November 1973, (7), pp. 3–55. [G: Czechoslovakia]

Vachel, Jan and Nentvichová, Božena. 25 Years of Building Czechoslovakia's Socialist Economy. *Czech. Econ. Digest.*, February 1973, (1), pp. 3–93. [G: Czechoslovakia]

Vianelli, Silvio. Problemi economici e programmazione ecologica per la difesa dell'uomo e del suo ambiente. (Economic Problems and Environmental Planning for the Defense of Mankind and its Habitat. With English summary.) *Mondo Aperto*, June-August 1973, *27*(3–4), pp. 185–223.

Waris, Klaus. Styrningen av kreditströmmarna. (Directing the Credit Flows. With English summary.) *Ekon. Samfundets Tidskr.*, 1973, *26*(2), pp. 87–94. [G: Finland]

Zhamin, V. Forecasting the Level of Education. *Prob. Econ.*, March 1973, *15*(11), pp. 73–91. [G: U.S.S.R.]

Zlocha, Nikolaj. Further Progress in the Work Connected with the System of Plan-Based Management. *Czech. Econ. Digest.*, December 1973, (8), pp. 47–70. [G: Czechoslovakia]

114 Economics of War, Defense, and Disarmament

1140 Economics of War and Defense

Allison, Graham T. Organizational and Administrative Factors Affecting Shifts in Defense Expenditures. In *Udis, B., ed.*, 1973, pp. 289–35. [G: U.S.]

Arnell, J. C. Development of Program Budgeting in the Canadian Department of National Defense. In *Novick, D., ed.*, 1973, pp. 79–88. [G: Canada]

Bean, Richard. War and the Birth of the Nation State. *J. Econ. Hist.*, March 1973, *33*(1), pp. 203–21.

Benoit, Emile. Balance of Payments Impact of a Vietnam Disengagement. In *Udis, B., ed.*, 1973, pp. 211–23. [G: U.S.]

Benoit, Emile. Cutting Back Military Spending: The Vietnam Withdrawal and the Recession. *Ann. Amer. Acad. Polit. Soc. Sci.*, March 1973, *406*, pp. 73–79. [G: U.S.]

Biderman, Albert D. Where Do They Go from Here?—Retired Military in America. *Ann. Amer. Acad. Polit. Soc. Sci.*, March 1973, *406*, pp. 146–61. [G: U.S.]

Bobrow, Davis B. Military Research and Development: Implications for the Civil Sector. *Ann. Amer. Acad. Polit. Soc. Sci.*, March 1973, *406*, pp. 117–28. [G: U.S.]

Bohi, Douglas R. Profit Performance in the Defense Industry. *J. Polit. Econ.*, May-June 1973, *81*(3), pp. 721–28. [G: U.S.]

Boulding, Kenneth E. The Scientific-Military-Industrial Complex. In *Boulding, K. E.*, 1973, pp. 351–60. [G: U.S.]

Boulding, Kenneth E. War Industry and the American Economy. In *Boulding, K. E.*, 1973, pp. 483–501. [G: U.S.]

Boulding, Kenneth E. The Impact of the Defense Industry on the Structure of the American Economy. In *Udis, B., ed.*, 1973, pp. 225–52. [G: U.S.]

Clayton, James L. The Ultimate Cost of the Vietnam Conflict. In *Haveman, R. H. and Hamrin, R. D., eds.*, 1973, pp. 107–11. [G: U.S.]

Cumberland, John H. Dimensions of the Impact of Reduced Military Expenditures on Industries, Regions, and Communities. In *Udis, B., ed.*, 1973, pp. 79–147. [G: U.S.]

Daicoff, Darwin W. The Adjustment of DOD Civilian and Military Personnel. In *Udis, B., ed.*, 1973, pp. 167–77. [G: U.S.]

Daicoff, Darwin W. The Community Impact of Military Installations. In *Udis, B., ed.*, 1973, pp. 149–66. [G: U.S.]

Deagle, Edwin A., Jr. Contemporary Professionalism and Future Military Leadership. *Ann. Amer. Acad. Polit. Soc. Sci.*, March 1973, *406*, pp. 162–70. [G: U.S.]

Eaton, B. Curtis. The Individual and the Defense Mass-Layoff. In *Udis, B., ed.*, 1973, pp. 179–209. [G: U.S.]

Eden, Philip. Estimating U.S. Human Capital Loss in Southeast Asia: Reply. *J. Human Res.*, Fall 1973, *8*(4), pp. 526–27. [G: U.S.]

Epps, Thomas W. An Econometric Analysis of the Effectiveness of the U.S. Army's 1971 Paid Advertising Campaign. *Appl. Econ.*, December 1973, *5*(4), pp. 261–69. [G: U.S.]

Etzioni, Amitai. Societal Turnability: A Theoretical Treatment. In *Udis, B., ed.*, 1973, pp. 337–80. [G: U.S.]

Fink, William H. Dollar Surplus and Devaluation. *Rivista Int. Sci. Econ. Com.*, July 1973, *20*(7), pp. 625–39.

Fitzgerald, A. Ernest. Golden Fleece. In *Haveman, R. H. and Hamrin, R. D., eds.*, 1973, pp. 166–74. [G: U.S.]

Fried, Edward R. The Military and the Balance of Payments. *Ann. Amer. Acad. Polit. Soc. Sci.*, March 1973, *406*, pp. 80–85. [G: U.S.]

Galbraith, John Kenneth. Military Power and the Military Budget. In *Haveman, R. H. and Hamrin, R. D., eds.*, 1973, pp. 112–16.

Greene, Kenneth V. and Newlon, Daniel H. Economic Factors Affecting the Likelihood of a Switch to a Volunteer Army. *Public Finance Quart.*, October 1973, *1*(4), pp. 388–98. [G: U.S.]

Greene, Kenneth V. and Newlon, Daniel H. The Pareto Optimality of Eliminating a Lottery Draft.

Quart. Rev. Econ. Bus., Winter 1973, *13*(4), pp. 61–70.

Hanushek, Eric A. The High Cost of Graduate Education in the Military. *Public Policy*, Fall 1973, *21*(4), pp. 525–52. [G: U.S.]

Hause, John C. Enlistment Rates for Military Service and Unemployment. *J. Human Res.*, Winter 1973, *8*(1), pp. 98–109. [G: U.S.]

Hendershot, Gerry E. Population Size, Military Power, and Antinatal Policy. *Demography*, November 1973, *10*(4), pp. 517–24.

Hueckel, Glenn. War and the British Economy, 1793–1815: A General Equilibrium Analysis. *Exploration Econ. Hist.*, Summer 1973, *10*(4), pp. 365–96. [G: U.K.]

Janowitz, Morris. The Social Demography of the All-Volunteer Armed Force. *Ann. Amer. Acad. Polit. Soc. Sci.*, March 1973, *406*, pp. 86–93. [G: U.S.]

Jastrow, Robert. The Purpose of the Lunar Landing. In *The Diebold Group, Inc.*, 1973, pp. 143–52. [G: U.S.]

Kaufman, Richard F. A Profile of the Military-Industrial Complex. In *Haveman, R. H. and Hamrin, R. D., eds.*, 1973, pp. 135–44. [G: U.S.]

Kiker, B. F. and Cochrane, James L. War and Human Capital in Western Economic Analysis. *Hist. Polit. Econ.*, Fall 1973, *5*(2), pp. 375–98.

Klein, Lawrence R. and Mori, Kei. The Impact of Disarmament on Aggregate Economic Activity: An Econometric Analysis. In *Udis, B., ed.*, 1973, pp. 59–77. [G: U.S.]

Knapp, Charles B. A Human Capital Approach to the Burden of the Military Draft. *J. Human Res.*, Fall 1973, *8*(4), pp. 485–96. [G: U.S.]

Koenig, Gilbert. Affectation des ressources et système de conscription en France. (Allocation of Resources and Draft System in France. With English summary.) *Revue Écon.*, January 1973, *24*(1), pp. 66–108. [G: France]

Korb, Lawrence J. National Defense. In *Ott, D. J., et al.*, 1973, pp. 29–52. [G: U.S.]

Lambelet, John C. Towards a Dynamic Two-Theater Model of the East-West Arms Race. *J. Peace Sci.*, Autumn 1973, *1*(1), pp. 1–38. [G: U.S.; U.S.S.R.]

Lazarcik, Gregor. Defense, Education and Health Expenditures and Their Relation to GNP in Eastern Europe, 1960-1970. *Amer. Econ.*, Spring 1973, *17*(1), pp. 29–34. [G: E. Europe]

Lee, Jong Ryool and Milstein, Jeffrey S. A Political Economy of the Vietnam War, 1965–1972. *Peace Sci. Soc.*, 1973, *21*, pp. 41–63. [G: U.S.; Vietnam]

Leitenberg, Milton. The Dynamics of Military Technology Today. *Int. Soc. Sci. J.*, 1973, *25*(3), pp. 336–57.

Levin, Samuel M. Organized Labor and the Equality of Sacrifice Program. In *Levin, S. M.*, 1973, pp. 127–42. [G: U.S.]

Levin, Samuel M. The Impact of War on Industrial Technology. In *Levin, S. M.*, 1973, pp. 99–114. [G: U.S.]

Melman, Seymour. The Pervasive Economic Impact of the Military. In *Haveman, R. H. and Hamrin, R. D., eds.*, 1973, pp. 127–34. [G: U.S.]

Metcalf, Lee. The Vested Oracles: How Industry

Regulates Government. In *Haveman, R. H. and Hamrin, R. D., eds.*, 1973, pp. 52–59. [G: U.S.]

Petrini, Bart F. and Grub, Phillip D. Product Management in High Technology Defense Industry Marketing. *Calif. Manage. Rev.*, Spring 1973, *15*(3), pp. 138–46.

Reich, Michael and Finkelhor, David. The Military-Industrial Complex. In *Reynolds, L. G.; Green, G. D. and Lewis, D. R., eds.*, 1973, pp. 334–46. [G: U.S.]

Ringrose, David. War and the Birth of the Nation State: Discussion. *J. Econ. Hist.*, March 1973, *33*(1), pp. 222–27.

Roehl, Richard. War and the Birth of the Nation State: Discussion. *J. Econ. Hist.*, March 1973, *33*(1), pp. 228–31.

Rothschild, Kurt W. Military Expenditure, Exports and Growth. *Kyklos*, 1973, *26*(4), pp. 804–14. [G: O.E.C.D.]

Scherer, Frederic M. The Problem of Cost Overruns. In *Haveman, R. H. and Hamrin, R. D., eds.*, 1973, pp. 159–65. [G: U.S.]

Schloenbach, Knut. Studies on the Structure of the Armed Forces with the Aid of Simulation. On the Quantitative Methods of Analysis Employed by the Force Structure Commission. *Ger. Econ. Rev.*, 1973, *11*(4), pp. 361–68. [G: W. Germany]

Schultze, Charles L. The Economic Content of National Security Policy. *Foreign Aff.*, April 1973, *51*(3), pp. 522–40. [G: U.S.]

Schultze, Charles L. The Factors Behind Rising Military Expenditures. In *Haveman, R. H. and Hamrin, R. D., eds.*, 1973, pp. 117–26. [G: U.S.]

Udis, Bernard. The Economic Consequences of Reduced Military Spending: Overview and Summary. In *Udis, B., ed.*, 1973, pp. 1–15. [G: U.S.]

Udis, Bernard and Weidenbaum, Murray L. The Many Dimensions of the Military Effort. In *Udis, B., ed.*, 1973, pp. 17–57. [G: U.S.]

Udis, Bernard. The End of Overrun: Prospects for the High Technology Defense Industry and Related Issues. *Ann. Amer. Acad. Polit. Soc. Sci.*, March 1973, *406*, pp. 59–72. [G: U.S.]

Weidenbaum, Murray L. Industrial Adjustments to Military Expenditure Shifts and Cutbacks. In *Udis, B., ed.*, 1973, pp. 253–87. [G: U.S.]

Wever, F. Long-term Scientific Studies in NATO. In *Blohm, H. and Steinbuch, K., eds.*, 1973, pp. 79–81.

Wolf, Charles, Jr. Military-Industrial Complexities. In *Andreano, R. L., ed.*, 1973, pp. R339–04. [G: U.S.]

Ziderman, Adrian. Estimating U.S. Human Capital Loss in Southeast Asia: Comment. *J. Human Res.*, Fall 1973, *8*(4), pp. 524–26. [G: U.S.]

120 ECONOMIC DEVELOPMENT STUDIES

121 Economic Studies of Less Industrialized Countries

1210 General

Adler, John H. Development and Income Distribution. *Finance Develop.*, September 1973, *10*(3), pp. 2–5.

Andic, Suphan. Tax Problems of Developing Countries. *Finanzarchiv,* 1973, *32*(1), pp. 155–59.

Anker, Desmond L. W. Rural Development Problems and Strategies. *Int. Lab. Rev.,* December 1973, *108*(6), pp. 461–84.

Areskoug, Kaj. Foreign-Capital Utilization and Economic Policies in Developing Countries. *Rev. Econ. Statist.,* May 1973, *55*(2), pp. 182–89.

Barg, Benjamin. Nutrition and National Development. In *Berg, A.; Scrimshaw, N. S. and Call, D. L., eds.,* 1973, pp. 49–69.

Bartsch, William H. Notes on Developing Countries and their Statistics: Comment. *Rev. Income Wealth,* June 1973, *19*(2), pp. 211–12.

Bhagwat, Avinash. Main Features of the Employment Problem in Developing Countries. *Int. Monet. Fund Staff Pap.,* March 1973, *20*(1), pp. 78–99.

Bhalla, A. S. A Disaggregative Approach to Employment in LDCs. *J. Devel. Stud.,* October 1973, *10*(1), pp. 50–65.

Blandy, Richard and Wery, René. Population and Employment Growth: Bachue-1. *Int. Lab. Rev.,* May 1973, *107*(5), pp. 441–49.

Brewster, Havelock. Economic Dependence: A Quantitative Interpretation. *Soc. Econ. Stud.,* March 1973, *22*(1), pp. 90–95. [G: Caribbean]

Chandavarkar, Anand G. How Relevant is Finance for Development? *Finance Develop.,* September 1973, *10*(3), pp. 14–16.

Chenery, Hollis B. and Hughes, Helen. Industrialization and Trade Trends: Some Issues for the 1970s. In *Hughes, H., ed.,* 1973, pp. 3–31.

Christian, James W. and Pagoulatos, Emilio. Domestic Financial Markets in Developing Economies: An Econometric Analysis. *Kyklos,* 1973, *26*(1), pp. 75–90.

Costa, E. Maximising Employment in Labour-intensive Development Programmes. *Int. Lab. Rev.,* November 1973, *108*(5), pp. 371–94.

Demery, David and Demery, Lionel. Cross-Section Evidence for Balanced and Unbalanced Growth. *Rev. Econ. Statist.,* November 1973, *55*(4), pp. 459–64.

Edwards, Edgar O. and Todaro, Michael P. Educational Demand and Supply in the Context of Growing Unemployment in Less Developed Countries. *World Devel.,* March-April 1973, *1*(3–4), pp. 107–117.

Eichberg, Henning. "Entwicklungshilfe" Verhaltensumformung nach europäischem Modell? ("Assistance" for Underdeveloped Countries—Transformation of Behaviour According to Western Patterns? With English summary.) *Z. Wirtschaft. Sozialwissen.,* 1973, *93*(6), pp. 641–70.

Elkan, Walter. On the Apparent Benefits of Higher Productivity: An Arithmetical Illustration: Reply. *J. Devel. Stud.,* April 1973, *9*(3), pp. 452–53.

Freivalds, John. Bringing Space Down to Earth: Space Age Technology Transfer and the Developing Countries. *J. Devel. Areas,* October 1973, *8*(1), pp. 83–92.

Glezakos, Constantine. Export Instability and Economic Growth: A Statistical Verification. *Econ. Develop. Cult. Change,* Part I, July 1973, *21*(4), pp. 670–78.

Griffin, Keith. The Effect of Aid and Other Resource Transfers on Savings and Growth in Less-Developed Countries: A Comment. *Econ. J.,* September 1973, *83*(331), pp. 863–66.

Haq, Mahbub. Employment in the 1970's: A New Perspective. In *Wilber, C. K., ed.,* 1973, pp. 266–72.

Haq, Mahbub. The Crisis in Development Strategies. In *Wilber, C. K., ed.,* 1973, pp. 367–72.

Helfgott, Roy B. Multinational Corporations and Manpower Utilization in Developing Nations. *J. Devel. Areas,* January 1973, *7*(2), pp. 235–46. [G: U.S.; Latin America]

Higgins, Benjamin. Profits and Planning in Developing Countries. *Écon. Appl.,* 1973, *26*(1), pp. 5–32.

Howe, James W. The Developing Countries in a Changing International Economic Order: A Survey of Research Needs. In *Bergsten, C. F., ed.,* 1973, pp. 197–264.

Hunter, Guy. Agricultural Administration and Institutions. *Food Res. Inst. Stud.,* 1973, *12*(3), pp. 233–51.

Hunter, Guy. Development—The Search for a New Strategy. In *Dinwiddy, B., ed.,* 1973, pp. 112–34.

Ikonicoff, Moïses. Technologie et modèle de consommation dans le Tiers-Monde. (Technology and Consumption Patterns in Under-Developed Countries. With English summary.) *Revue Écon.,* July 1973, *24*(4), pp. 619–40.

Illich, Ivan. Outwitting the "Developed" Countries. In *Wilber, C. K., ed.,* 1973, pp. 401–09. [G: Latin America]

Jaffe, A. J. Notes on Developing Countries and their Statistics: Reply. *Rev. Income Wealth,* June 1973, *19*(2), pp. 213–14.

Kádár, B. Small-Sized Developing Countries in the Regional Arrangements. *Acta Oecon.,* 1973, *10*(2), pp. 217–31.

Kafka, Alexandre. Adjustment Under the Bretton Woods Code with Special Reference to the Less Developed Countries. In *[Rosenstein-Rodan, P.],* 1973, pp. 210–38.

Kamarck, Andrew M. Climate and Economic Development. *Finance Develop.,* June 1973, *10*(2), pp. 2–8.

Korka, Mihai. Evoluția comerțului invizibil al țărilor în curs de dezvoltare. (The Evolution of the Invisible Trade of the Developing Countries. With English summary.) *Stud. Cercet. Econ.,* 1973, (4), pp. 177–92.

Lent, George E. Taxation of Agricultural Income in Developing Countries. *Bull. Int. Fiscal Doc.,* August 1973, *27*(8), pp. 324–42.

Lewis, Stephen R., Jr. Agricultural Taxation and Intersectoral Resource Transfers. *Food Res. Inst. Stud.,* 1973, *12*(2), pp. 93–114.

Little, I. M. D. and Mirrlees, James A. Further Reflections on the OECD Manual of Project Analysis in Developing Countries. In *[Rosenstein-Rodan, P.],* 1973, pp. 257–80.

Louis, R. Co-operative Development Centres. *Int. Lab. Rev.,* June 1973, *107*(6), pp. 539–51.

Martinoli, Gino. Formazione dei quadri e "stages" all'estero. (Cadres Training and "Stages" abroad. With English summary.) *L'Impresa,* 1973, *15*(2), pp. 147–56.

Mellor, John W. Nutrition and Economic Growth. In *Berg, A.; Scrimshaw, N. S. and Call, D. L., eds.,* 1973, pp. 70–73.

Morrock, Richard. Heritage of Strife: The Effects of Colonialist "Divide and Rule" Strategy Upon the Colonized Peoples. *Sci. Soc.,* Summer 1973, *37*(2), pp. 129–51.

Myrdal, Gunnar. Rôle des valeurs et politique sociale. (The Place of Values in Social Policy. With English summary.) *Consommation,* January–March 1973, *20*(1), pp. 5–16.

Myrdal, Gunnar. The Need for Radical Domestic Reforms. In *Myrdal, G.,* 1973, pp. 101–32.

Naseem, S. M. Import Substitution: A Survey of Concepts, Measures and Models. *Pakistan Develop. Rev.,* Spring 1973, *12*(1), pp. 31–47.

Newlyn, Walter T. The Effect of Aid and Other Resource Transfers on Savings and Growth in Less-Developed Countries: A Comment. *Econ. J.,* September 1973, *83*(331), pp. 867–69.

Novak, George J. Priorities for Statistical Development. *Finance Develop.,* September 1973, *10*(3), pp. 9–13.

Nwaneri, V. C. Income Distribution Criteria for the Analysis of Development Projects. *Finance Develop.,* March 1973, *10*(1), pp. 16–19, 37.

Ohlin, Göran. Industrialization and Trade Trends: Some Issues for the 1970s: Comment. In *Hughes, H., ed.,* 1973, pp. 32–34.

Packard, Philip C. On the Apparent Benefits of Higher Productivity: An Arithmetical Illustration: A Comment. *J. Devel. Stud.,* April 1973, *9*(3), pp. 451–52.

Papanek, Gustav F. The Effect of Aid and Other Resource Transfers on Savings and Growth in Less-Developed Countries: A Reply. *Econ. J.,* September 1973, *83*(331), pp. 870–74.

Penny, David H. Development Studies: Some Reflections. In *Epstein, T. S. and Penny, D. H., eds.,* 1973, pp. 1–10.

Ranis, Gustav. Industrial Sector Labor Absorption. *Econ. Develop. Cult. Change,* April 1973, *21*(3), pp. 387–408. [G: Korea; Taiwan]

Rice, E. B. and Dalrymple, Dana G. Review of Small Farmer Credit in Developing Nations. *Agr. Finance Rev.,* July 1973, *34,* pp. 35–37.

Rogers, Christopher D. Gli accordi internazionali per le materie prime. (The International Agreements on Raw Materials. With English summary.) *Mondo Aperto,* December 1973, *27*(6), pp. 415–28.

Sen, Amartya K. Brain Drain: Causes and Effects. In *Williams, B. R., ed.,* 1973, pp. 385–404. [G: U.S.]

Sharif, M. Raihan. Development Planning with Social Justice: Some Clarifications of Concepts and Applications. *Bangladesh Econ. Rev.,* July 1973, *1*(3), pp. 227–42.

Sharpston, C. H. Competition and the Developing Countries. In *Rybczynski, T. M., ed.,* 1973, pp. 46–54.

Stewart, Frances and Streeten, Paul. Conflicts Between Output and Employment Objectives in Developing Countries. *Bangladesh Econ. Rev.,* January 1973, *1*(1), pp. 1–24.

Stoner, James A. F. and Aram, John D. Effectiveness of Two Technical Assistance Efforts in Differing Environments. *J. Devel. Stud.,* July 1973, *9*(4), pp. 508–17.

Stoutjesdijk, A. LDC Regional Markets: Do They Work? In *Thorelli, H. B., ed.,* 1973, pp. 47–57.

Streeten, Paul. Industrialization and Trade Trends: Some Issues for the 1970s: Comment. In *Hughes, H., ed.,* 1973, pp. 35–39.

Vaitsos, Constantine V. Strategic Choices in the Commercialization of Technology: The Point of View of Developing Countries. *Int. Soc. Sci. J.,* 1973, *25*(3), pp. 370–86.

Ward, Richard J. The Widening Gaps: Are There Tolerance Levels? *Rev. Soc. Econ.,* April 1973, *31* (1), pp. 40–53.

Watanabe, Tsunehiko. The Process of Industrialization: A Dynamic Simulation. *Osaka Econ. Pap.,* March 1973, *21*(38), pp. 1–43.

1211 Comparative Country Studies

Agarwala, R. An Econometric Test of Alternative Constraints on the Growth of Underdeveloped Countries: A Comment. *Rev. Econ. Statist.,* February 1973, *55*(1), pp. 132–33.

Birnberg, Thomas and Resnick, Stephen A. A Model of the Trade and Government Sectors in Colonial Economies. *Amer. Econ. Rev.,* September 1973, *63*(4), pp. 572–87.

Chenery, Hollis B. and Carter, Nicholas G. Foreign Assistance and Development Performance, 1960–1970. *Amer. Econ. Rev.,* May 1973, *63*(2), pp. 459–68.

Despres, Emile. Dimensions and Dilemmas of Economic Development. In *Despres, E.,* 1973, pp. 89–98.

Enweze, Cyril. Structure of Public Expenditures in Selected Developing Countries: A Time Series Study. *Manchester Sch. Econ. Soc. Stud.,* December 1973, *41*(4), pp. 430–63.

Epstein, T. Scarlett. Economic Development and Social Change in South India and New Guinea. In *Epstein, T. S. and Penny, D. H., eds.,* 1973, pp. 131–55. [G: India; New Guinea]

Girgis, Maurice. Development and Trade Patterns in the Arab World. *Weltwirtsch. Arch.,* 1973, *109*(1), pp. 121–68.

Iyoha, Milton Ame. Inflation and "Openness" in Less Developed Economies: A Cross-Country Analysis. *Econ. Develop. Cult. Change,* October 1973, *22*(1), pp. 31–38.

Kingston, Jerry L. Export Instability in Latin America: The Postwar Statistical Record. *J. Devel. Areas,* April 1973, *7*(3), pp. 381–95. [G: Latin America]

O'Loughlin, Carleen. What Is Agricultural Growth? In *Ofori, I. M., ed.,* 1973, pp. 7–13. [G: Central America; W. Africa]

Papanek, Gustav F. Aid, Foreign Private Investment, Savings, and Growth in Less Developed Countries. *J. Polit. Econ.,* January–February 1973, *81*(1), pp. 120–30.

Park, Yung C. The Role of Money in Stabilization Policy in Developing Countries. *Int. Monet. Fund Staff Pap.,* July 1973, *20*(2), pp. 379–418.

Thorbecke, Erik. The Employment Problem: A Critical Evaluation of Four ILO Comprehensive Country Reports. *Int. Lab. Rev.*, May 1973, *107* (5), pp. 393–423. **[G: Colombia; Sri Lanka; Kenya; Iran]**

Torres, James F. Concentration of Political Power and Levels of Economic Development in Latin American Countries. *J. Devel. Areas*, April 1973, *7*(3), pp. 397–409. **[G: Latin America]**

Voivodas, Constantin S. Exports, Foreign Capital Inflow and Economic Growth. *J. Int. Econ.*, November 1973, *3*(4), pp. 337–49.

de Vries, Barend A. The Plight of Small Countries. *Finance Develop.*, September 1973, *10*(3), pp. 6–8, 34.

Wai, U Tun and Patrick, Hugh T. Stock and Bond Issues and Capital Markets in Less Developed Countries. *Int. Monet. Fund Staff Pap.*, July 1973, *20*(2), pp. 253–317.

Weisskopf, Thomas E. An Econometric Test of Alternative Constraints on the Growth of Underdeveloped Countries: A Reply. *Rev. Econ. Statist.*, February 1973, *55*(1), pp. 133–34.

1213 European Countries

Balassa, Á. Economic Growth, Equilibrium and Efficiency in the Present Stage of Development. *Acta Oecon.*, 1973, *10*(3–4), pp. 339–60. **[G: Hungary]**

Brada, Josef C. The Microallocative Impact of the Hungarian Economic Reform of 1968: Some Evidence from the Export Sector. *Econ. Planning*, 1973, *13*(1–2), pp. 1–14. **[G: Hungary]**

Brown, Alan A.; Licari, J. A. and Neuberger, Egon. A Dynamic CES Production Function Interpretation of Hungarian Growth. *Acta Oecon.*, 1973, *11* (4), pp. 305–24. **[G: Hungary]**

Csendes, Béla. Development Trends of Hungarian Agriculture. In *Földi, T., ed.*, 1973, pp. 117–34. **[G: Hungary]**

Dobrescu, Em. Models of Proportions Between the Investment Fund and the Consumption Fund for Forecasting the Development of the Rumanian Economy. *Eastern Europ. Econ.*, Spring 1973, *11* (3), pp. 50–73. **[G: Rumania]**

Dobrotă, Niță. Principalele caracteristici ale unei țări în curs de dezvoltare. (The Main Characteristics of a Developing Country. With English summary.) *Stud. Cercet. Econ.*, 1973, (1), pp. 13–26. **[G: Rumania]**

Donges, Juergen B. Shaping Spain's Export Industry. *World Devel.*, September 1973, *1*(9), pp. 19–37. **[G: Spain]**

Gábor, Ottó and Gede, Miklós. Role of the Engineering Industries in the Development of the Hungarian Economy and in the Transformation of the Economic Structure. *Eastern Europ. Econ.*, Fall 1973, *12*(1), pp. 82–104. **[G: Hungary]**

Gács, János and Lackó, Mária. A Study of Planning Behaviour on the National-Economic Level: An Attempt at Analysing a Few Correlations Based on Hungarian Data. *Econ. Planning*, 1973, *13* (1–2), pp. 91–119. **[G: Hungary]**

Horvat, Branko. The Postwar Evolution of Yugoslav Agricultural Organization: Interaction of Ideology, Practice, and Results. *Eastern Europ. Econ.*,

Winter 1973-74, *12*(2), pp. 3–106. **[G: Yugoslavia]**

Křikava, L.; Mašek, J. and Malek, P. The Czech Experience in Nutrition Improvement. In *Berg, A.; Scrimshaw, N. S. and Call, D. L., eds.*, 1973, pp. 329–34. **[G: Czechoslovakia]**

Mănescu, Manea. The Planned Economic-Social Development of Romania. *Revue Roumaine Sci. Soc. Serie Sci. Econ.*, 1973, *17*(1), pp. 13–33. **[G: Rumania]**

Militaru, St. Analiza statistică a corelației dintre acumulare și consum în R.S. România. (Statistical Analysis of the Correlation Between Accumulation and Consumption in the Socialist Republic of Romania. With English summary.) *Stud. Cercet. Econ.*, 1973, (3), pp. 105–20. **[G: Rumania]**

Újhelyi, T. Foreign Trade in Agricultural and Food Products—The Hungarian National Economy and the World Market. *Acta Oecon.*, 1973, *11*(1), pp. 3–18. **[G: Hungary]**

Varga, Gy. On the System of Preferences. *Acta Oecon.*, 1973, *10*(1), pp. 52–66. **[G: Hungary]**

1214 Asian Countries

Abdullah, Abu A. The Success Story That Wasn't— "Development Policy II: The Pakistan Experience." *Bangladesh Econ. Rev.*, July 1973, *1*(3), pp. 309–16. **[G: Pakistan]**

Aggarwal, R. C. Socio-Economic Objectives of Fifth Plan—A Critique. *Econ. Aff.*, April 1973, *18*(4), pp. 153–63. **[G: India]**

Ahmad, Qazi Kholiquzzaman. A Note on Capacity Utilization in the Jute Manufacturing Industry of Bangladesh. *Bangladesh Econ. Rev.*, January 1973, *1*(1), pp. 103–14. **[G: Bangladesh]**

Ahmad, Qazi Kholiquzzaman and Anwaruzzaman, Chowdhury. Productivity Trends in the Manufacturing Sector of Bangladesh: A Case Study of Selected Industries. *Bangladesh Econ. Rev.*, April 1973, *1*(2), pp. 119–48. **[G: Bangladesh]**

Ahmad, Rafiq. Incentive Taxation for Economic and Social Development. *Pakistan Econ. Soc. Rev.*, Summer 1973, *11*(2), pp. 154–66. **[G: Pakistan]**

Ahmad, Rafiq. South Asian Developmental Crisis. *Pakistan Develop. Rev.*, Summer 1973, *12*(2), pp. 181–88. **[G: Asia]**

Ahmed, Feroz. The Structural Matrix of the Struggle in Bangladesh. In *Gough, K. and Sharma, H. P., eds.*, 1973, pp. 419–48. **[G: Bangladesh]**

Alagh, Yoginder K. and Pathak, Pravin G. Industrial Development in Gujarat: Regional Structure and Policies. *Artha-Vikas*, January-July 1973, *9*(1–2), pp. 143–84. **[G: India]**

Alamgir, Mohiuddin and Berlage, Lodewijk J. J. B. Foodgrain (Rice and Wheat) Demand, Import and Price Policy for Bangladesh. *Bangladesh Econ. Rev.*, January 1973, *1*(1), pp. 25–58. **[G: Bangladesh]**

Arndt, H. W. and Sundrum, R. M. Foreign Capital and Indonesian Economic Growth: A Comment. *Bull. Indonesian Econ. Stud.*, July 1973, *9*(2), pp. 90–95. **[G: Indonesia]**

Arndt, H. W. Survey of Recent Developments. *Bull. Indonesian Econ. Stud.*, July 1973, *9*(2), pp. 1–27. **[G: Indonesia]**

Baher, G. H. A Planning Model for the Educational Requirements of Economic Development: The Case of Iran. *Tahq. Eq.*, Winter & Spring 1973, *10* (29 & 30), pp. 170–205. [G: Iran]

Barlow, Colin. The Socio-Economic Response to Different Institutional Structure. In *Epstein, T. S. and Penny, D. H., eds.*, 1973, pp. 193–202. [G: S.E. Asia]

Bautista, Romeo M. Devaluation and Employment in a Labor-Surplus Economy: The Philippines. *Econ. Int.*, August-November 1973, *26*(3–4), pp. 543–59. [G: Philippines]

Bechtold, Peter K. New Attempts at Arab Cooperation: The Federation of Arab Republics, 1971–? *Middle East J.*, Spring 1973, *27*(2), pp. 152–72.

Belfiglio, Valentine J. India's Economic Relations with Nepal 1947–1967. *Econ. Int.*, August-November 1973, *26*(3–4), pp. 560–78. [G: India; Nepal]

Bhaduri, Amit. A Study in Agricultural Backwardness under Semi-Feudalism. *Econ. J.*, March 1973, *83*(329), pp. 120–37. [G: India]

Bhattacharya, Debesh. A Critical Survey of Indian Planning and its Achievements. *Econ. Aff.*, March 1973, *18*(3), pp. 105–23. [G: India]

Burki, Shahid J. Rapid Population Growth and Urbanization: The Case of Pakistan. *Pakistan Econ. Soc. Rev.*, Autumn 1973, *11*(3), pp. 239–76. [G: Pakistan]

Chattopadhyay, Paresh. Some Trends in India's Economic Development. In *Gough, K. and Sharma, H. P., eds.*, 1973, pp. 103–29. [G: India]

Chaudhry, M. Ghaffar. Rural Income Distribution in Pakistan in the Green Revolution Perspective. *Pakistan Develop. Rev.*, Autumn 1973, *12*(3), pp. 247–58. [G: Pakistan]

Cohen, Benjamin I. Comparative Behavior of Foreign and Domestic Export Firms in a Developing Economy. *Rev. Econ. Statist.*, May 1973, *55*(2), pp. 190–97. [G: S. Korea]

Collier, William L. and Soentoro, Gunawan Wiradi. Recent Changes in Rice Harvesting Methods: Some Serious Social Implications. *Bull. Indonesian Econ. Stud.*, July 1973, *9*(2), pp. 36–45. [G: Indonesia]

Corea, Gamani. Economic Planning, the Green Revolution and the 'Food Drive' in Ceylon. In *[Hicks, U.]*, 1973, pp. 273–303. [G: Ceylon]

Dahyabhai, Indulal. Industrial Development of Backward Areas in Gujarat. *Artha-Vikas*, January-July 1973, *9*(1–2), pp. 240–44. [G: India]

Daroesman, Ruth. An Economic Survey of Bali. *Bull. Indonesian Econ. Stud.*, November 1973, *9*(3), pp. 28–61. [G: Indonesia]

Despres, Emile. Financing of Development: Malaysia. In *Despres, E.*, 1973, pp. 154–83. [G: Malaysia]

Dutta, Amita. Migration in a Trading Economy. *J. Devel. Stud.*, October 1973, *10*(1), pp. 79–91. [G: Ceylon]

Fan, Liang-Shing. The Economy and Foreign Trade of China. *Law Contemp. Probl.*, Summer-Autumn 1973, *38*(2), pp. 249–59. [G: China]

Farooq, Ghazi M. Economic Growth and Changes in the Industrial Structure of Income and Labor Force in Pakistan. *Econ. Develop. Cult. Change*, January 1973, *21*(2), pp. 293–308. [G: Pakistan]

Frankena, Mark. Marketing Characteristics and Prices of Exports of Engineering Goods from India. *Oxford Econ. Pap.*, March 1973, *25*(1), pp. 127–32. [G: India]

Gangulee, Srilata. Rising Real Wages and the Growth of Industrial Output in India, 1946-61. *Amer. Econ.*, Spring 1973, *17*(1), pp. 154–57. [G: India]

Gardezi, Hassan N. Neocolonial Alliances and the Crisis of Pakistan. In *Gough, K. and Sharma, H. P., eds.*, 1973, pp. 130–44. [G: Pakistan]

Garnaut, Ross and Manning, Chris M. An Economic Survey of West Irian, Part II. *Bull. Indonesian Econ. Stud.*, March 1973, *9*(1), pp. 30–64. [G: Indonesia]

Ghafari, R. Saving and Investment and the Effects of Financial Intermediaries on the Rate of Change of G.N.P. in Iran 1936–71. *Tahq. Eq.*, Winter & Spring 1973, *10*(29 & 30), pp. 50–79. [G: Iran]

Ghosh, Arabinda. Size-Structure, Productivity and Growth: A Case Study of West Bengal Agriculture. *Bangladesh Econ. Rev.*, January 1973, *1*(1), pp. 59–70. [G: India]

Ghosh, Ranen. The Public Sector and Economic Development in India–I. *Econ. Aff.*, January–February 1973, *18*(1-2), pp. 9–16, 89–94. [G: India]

Ghuge, V. B. Critique of Development Planning in India. *Econ. Aff.*, August 1973, *18*(8), pp. 357–71. [G: India]

Glassburner, Bruce and Riedel, James. Economic Development Lessons from Hong Kong: A Reply. *Econ. Rec.*, December 1973, *49*(128), pp. 637–43. [G: Hong Kong]

Gotsch, Carl H. Tractor Mechanisation and Rural Development in Pakistan. *Int. Lab. Rev.*, February 1973, *107*(2), pp. 133–66. [G: Pakistan]

Gough, Kathleen. Imperialism and Revolutionary Potential in South Asia. In *Gough, K. and Sharma, H. P., eds.*, 1973, pp. 3–42. [G: S. Asia]

Grenville, Stephen. Survey of Recent Developments. *Bull. Indonesian Econ. Stud.*, March 1973, *9*(1), pp. 1–29. [G: Indonesia]

Gurley, John W. Maoist Economic Development: The New Man in the New China. In *Wilber, C. K., ed.*, 1973, pp. 307–19. [G: China]

Halder, A. and Richards, J. H. Structural Characteristics of India's Foreign Trade and its Effect on the Instability of Export Receipts. *Indian Econ. J.*, October–December 1973, *21*(2), pp. 132–46. [G: India]

Hallwood, C. P. The Impact of Foreign Aid Upon India's International Trade 1951-65. *Bull. Econ. Res.*, November 1973, *25*(2), pp. 129–45. [G: India]

Hansen, Bent. Simulation of Fiscal, Monetary and Exchange Policy in a Primitive Economy: Afghanistan. In *[Tinbergen, J.]*, 1973, pp. 215–37. [G: Afghanistan]

Healey, Derek T. Foreign Capital and Exports in Economic Development: The Experience of Eight Asian Countries. *Econ. Rec.*, September 1973, *49*(127), pp. 394–419.

Hoerr, O. D. Education, Income and Equity in Malaysia. *Econ. Develop. Cult. Change*, January

1973, *21*(2), pp. 247–73. [G: Malaysia]

Hoffmann, Lutz. Import Substitution—Export Expansion and Growth in an Open Developing Economy: The Case of West Malaysia. *Weltwirtsch. Arch.*, 1973, *109*(3), pp. 452–75. [G: W. Malaysia]

Hou, Chi-Ming. Economic Trends in Modern China. In *Meskill, J., ed.*, 1973, pp. 483–513. [G: China]

Hsia, Ronald. Technological Change in the Industrial Growth of Hong Kong. In *Williams, B. R., ed.*, 1973, pp. 335–53. [G: Hong Kong]

Johns, B. L. Import Substitution and Export Potential—The Case of Manufacturing Industry in West Malaysia. *Australian Econ. Pap.*, December 1973, *12*(21), pp. 175–95. [G: Malaysia]

Joshi, N. D. Review of the Policy for the Development of Backward Regions in India. *Artha-Vikas*, January-July 1973, *9*(1–2), pp. 11–24. [G: India]

Joshi, V. H. The Concept of Regional Analysis: Its Application to the Study of the Development of Backward Regions. *Artha-Vikas*, January-July 1973, *9*(1–2), pp. 64–68.

Kale, J. D. Attracting Industries to Backward Areas. *Artha-Vikas*, January-July 1973, *9*(1–2), pp. 245–48. [G: India]

Kehal, H. S. Role of Land Reforms in Punjab's Agricultural Development. *Econ. Aff.*, September-October 1973, *18*(9–10), pp. 434–38, 454. [G: India]

Khan, Mahmood H. "Green Revolution" or "Technocratic Euphoria." Some Problems of Rapid Agricultural Change in Asia. *Econ. Int.*, February 1973, *26*(1), pp. 119–34. [G: Asia]

Khin, Maung Kyi, et al. Process of Communication in Modernisation of Rural Society: A Survey Report on Two Burmese Villages. *Malayan Econ. Rev.*, April 1973, *18*(1), pp. 55–73. [G: Burma]

Koshal, Manjulika and Koshal, Rajindar K. Gandhi's Influence on Indian Economic Planning: A Critical Analysis. *Amer. J. Econ. Soc.*, July 1973, *32*(3), pp. 311–30. [G: India]

Laumas, Prem S. and Mohabhat, Khan A. Money and Economic Development. *Indian Econ. J.*, April-June 1973, *20*(4–5), pp. 619–29. [G: India]

Lee, S. Y. Some Basic Problems of Industrialization in Singapore. *J. Devel. Areas*, January 1973, *7*(2), pp. 185–216. [G: Singapore]

Lockwood, Brian and Moulik, T. K. Seeds of Development in a Delhi Village. In *Epstein, T. S. and Penny, D. H., eds.*, 1973, pp. 157–72. [G: India]

Mangkusuwondo, Suhadi. Dilemmas in Indonesian Economic Development. *Bull. Indonesian Econ. Stud.*, July 1973, *9*(2), pp. 28–35. [G: Indonesia]

Mellor, John W. Accelerated Growth in Agricultural Production and the Intersectoral Transfer of Resources. *Econ. Develop. Cult. Change*, October 1973, *22*(1), pp. 1–16. [G: Taiwan; India]

Mishra, G. P. Planning and Land Reform Policy in India. *Econ. Aff.*, May 1973, *18*(5), pp. 217–33. [G: India]

Mujahid, G. B. S. "Disguised" Unemployment Once Again: East Pakistan, 1951–1961: Comment. *Amer. J. Agr. Econ.*, February 1973, *55*(1), pp. 118–19. [G: Pakistan]

Mujahid, G. B. S. The Measurement of Disguised Unemployment: A Comment. *Can. J. Econ.*, February 1973, *6*(1), pp. 128–29. [G: India]

Mukherjee, Ramkrishna. The Social Background of Bangladesh. In *Gough, K. and Sharma, H. P., eds.*, 1973, pp. 399–418. [G: Bangladesh]

Naqvi, Syed Nawab Haider. Pakistan's Export Possibilities. *Pakistan Develop. Rev.*, Spring 1973, *12* (1), pp. 1–30. [G: Pakistan]

Naseem, S. M. Mass Poverty in Pakistan: Some Preliminary Findings. *Pakistan Develop. Rev.*, Winter 1973, *12*(4), pp. 317–60. [G: Pakistan]

Nayyar, Deepak. An Analysis of the Stagnation in India's Cotton Textile Exports During the Sixties. *Oxford Bull. Econ. Statist.*, February 1973, *35*(1), pp. 1–19. [G: India]

Oldham, C. H. G. Science and Technology Policies. In *Oksenberg, M., ed.*, 1973, pp. 80–94. [G: China]

Patankar, H. R. Some Observations about Efficacy of Financial Incentives on Industrial Development in Backward Districts. *Artha-Vikas*, January-July 1973, *9*(1–2), pp. 220–29. [G: India]

Pathak, H. N. Developing Entrepreneurship in Backward Regions. *Artha-Vikas*, January-July 1973, *9*(1–2), pp. 47–54. [G: India]

Pathak, Mahesh T.; Desai, Mahendra D. and Charan, A. S. Development of Agriculture in Backward Regions of Gujarat: Facts and Issues. *Artha-Vikas*, January-July 1973, *9*(1–2), pp. 100–38. [G: India]

Pathak, Mahesh T. Development of Backward Areas: Problems and Prospects. *Artha-Vikas*, January-July 1973, *9*(1–2), pp. 25–46. [G: India]

Peacock, Alan T. and Shaw, G. K. Fiscal Measures to Create Employment: The Indonesian Case. *Bull. Int. Fiscal Doc.*, November 1973, *27*(11), pp. 443–54. [G: Indonesia]

Penny, David H. and Singarimbun, Masri. Economic Activity among the Karo Batak of Indonesia: A Case Study in Economic Change. In *Epstein, T. S. and Penny, D. H., eds.*, 1973, pp. 86–113. [G: Indonesia]

Ramana, D. V. Towards an Appraisal and a Strategy of Development for the ECAFE Region Countries. *Malayan Econ. Rev.*, October 1973, *18*(2), pp. 16–36. [G: Asia]

Rao, M. R. S. N. Proposed Role of GIIC in Industrialisation of Backward Districts. *Artha-Vikas*, January-July 1973, *9*(1–2), pp. 230–39. [G: India]

Rawski, Thomas G. The Chinese Economy at the Present Juncture: Discussion. *Amer. Econ. Rev.*, May 1973, *63*(2), pp. 234–35. [G: China]

Rawski, Thomas G. Chinese Industrial Production, 1952-1971. *Rev. Econ. Statist.*, May 1973, *55*(2), pp. 169–81. [G: China]

Renaud, Bertrand M. Conflicts Between National Growth and Regional Income Equality in a Rapidly Growing Economy: The Case of Korea. *Econ. Develop. Cult. Change*, April 1973, *21*(3), pp. 429–45. [G: S. Korea]

Richards, P. J. Job Mobility and Unemployment in the Ceylon Urban Labour Market. *Oxford Bull. Econ. Statist.*, February 1973, *35*(1), pp. 49–59. [G: Ceylon]

Rifkin, Susan B. and Kaplinsky, Raphael. Health

Strategy and Development Planning: Lessons from the People's Republic of China. *J. Devel. Stud.*, January 1973, *9*(2), pp. 213–32. [G: China]

Robinson, Warren C. "Disguised" Unemployment Once Again: East Pakistan, 1951–1961: Reply. *Amer. J. Agr. Econ.*, February 1973, *55*(1), pp. 120. [G: Pakistan]

Rosenberg, W. Economic Development Lessons from Hong Kong: A Rejoinder. *Econ. Rec.*, December 1973, *49*(128), pp. 644–45. [G: Hong Kong]

Rosenberg, W. Hong Kong Model for Development? *Econ. Rec.*, December 1973, *49*(128), pp. 629–36. [G: Hong Kong]

Schwartz, Benjamin. China's Developmental Experience, 1949–72. In *Oksenberg, M., ed.*, 1973, pp. 17–26. [G: China]

Shah, Anil C. and Patel, V. G. An Integrated Strategy for Backward Districts Industrial Development. *Artha-Vikas,* January-July 1973, *9*(1–2), pp. 203–13. [G: India]

Sharma, Hari P. The Green Revolution in India: Prelude to a Red One? In *Gough, K. and Sharma, H. P., eds.*, 1973, pp. 77–102. [G: India]

Short, Brock K. The Velocity of Money and *Per Capita* Income in Developing Economies: West Malaysia and Singapore. *J. Devel. Stud.*, January 1973, *9*(2), pp. 291–300. [G: Malaysia; Singapore]

Shourie, Arun. Growth, Poverty and Inequalities. *Foreign Aff.*, January 1973, *51*(2), pp. 340–52. [G: India]

Silcock, T. H. Rationality, Fluency and Impersonality in Rural Thailand. In *Epstein, T. S. and Penny, D. H., eds.*, 1973, pp. 203–15. [G: Thailand]

Singh, Balwinder; Rangi, P. S. and Sankhayan, P. L. Relative Contributions of Area and Productivity in Increasing Production of Major Foodgrain Crops in Panjab (1960–61 to 1969–70) *Econ. Aff.*, March 1973, *18*(3), pp. 124–30. [G: India]

Singh, H. P. Export of Spices. *Econ. Aff.*, March 1973, *18*(3), pp. 131–42. [G: India]

Singh, Tarlok. Enlarging the Economic Base for Domestic Savings. In *[Hicks, U.],* 1973, pp. 181–88. [G: India]

Sinha, J. N. Agrarian Reforms and Employment in Densely Populated Agrarian Economies: A Dissenting View. *Int. Lab. Rev.,* November 1973, *108* (5), pp. 395–421. [G: Japan; India]

Squire, Lyn. Optimal Feeder Roads in Developing Countries: The Case of Thailand. *J. Devel. Stud.,* January 1973, *9*(2), pp. 279–90. [G: Thailand]

Strout, Alan M. Foreign Capital and Indonesian Economic Growth. *Bull. Indonesian Econ. Stud.,* July 1973, *9*(2), pp. 77–90. [G: Indonesia]

Strout, Alan M. Foreign Capital and Indonesian Economic Growth: A Reply. *Bull. Indonesian Econ. Stud.,* July 1973, *9*(2), pp. 96–99. [G: Indonesia]

Subramaniam, V. Has the Indian Economy "Taken-Off". *Econ. Aff.,* August 1973, *18*(8), pp. 381–88. [G: India]

Sussman, Zvi. The Determination of Wages for Unskilled Labor in the Advanced Sector of the Dual Economy of Mandatory Palestine. *Econ. Develop.*

Cult. Change, October 1973, *22*(1), pp. 95–113. [G: Israel]

Swamy, Subramanian. Economic Growth in China and India, 1952–1970: A Comparative Appraisal. *Econ. Develop. Cult. Change,* Part II, July 1973, *21*(4), pp. 1–84. [G: China; India]

Thoburn, J. T. Exports and the Malaysian Engineering Industry: A Case Study of Backward Linkage. *Oxford Bull. Econ. Statist.,* May 1973, *35*(2), pp. 91–117. [G: Malaya]

Thoburn, J. T. Exports and Economic Growth in West Malaysia. *Oxford Econ. Pap.,* March 1973, *25*(1), pp. 88–111. [G: Malaysia]

Timberg, Thomas A. Revolution and Growth: Two Case Studies from India. *Polit. Sci. Quart.,* March 1973, *88*(1), pp. 86–93. [G: India]

Timmer, C. Peter. Choice of Technique in Rice Milling in Java. *Bull. Indonesian Econ. Stud.,* July 1973, *9*(2), pp. 57–76. [G: Indonesia]

Utami, Widya and Ihalauw, John. Some Consequences of Small Farm Size. *Bull. Indonesian Econ. Stud.,* July 1973, *9*(2), pp. 46–56. [G: Indonesia]

Vachha, Homiar S. and Iyengar, Sampath S. Financial Institutions and Backward Regions: A Case Study of Gujarat. *Artha-Vikas,* January-July 1973, *9*(1–2), pp. 185–202. [G: India]

Vanek, Jaroslav. A Contribution to the Problem of Economic Development of Bangladesh. *Bangladesh Econ. Rev.,* July 1973, *1*(3), pp. 324–27. [G: Bangladesh]

Vartikar, V. S. On Optimizing the Rate of Investment. *Econ. Int.,* February 1973, *26*(1), pp. 17–31. [G: India]

Verma, Pramod. Regional Wages and Economic Development: A Case Study of Manufacturing Wages in India, 1950–1960. *J. Devel. Stud.,* October 1973, *10*(1), pp. 16–32. [G: India]

Weisskopf, Thomas E. Dependence and Imperialism in India. *Rev. Radical Polit. Econ.,* Spring 1973, *5*(1), pp. 53–96. [G: India]

Welch, Wilford. The Business Outlook for Southeast Asia. *Harvard Bus. Rev.,* May-June 1973, *51*(3), pp. 72–84. [G: S.E. Asia]

Williams, Maurice J. A Bilateral Viewpoint: Comment. In *Lewis, J. P. and Kapur, I., eds.*, 1973, pp. 103–08. [G: India]

de Wit, Y. B. The *Kabupaten* Program. *Bull. Indonesian Econ. Stud.,* March 1973, *9*(1), pp. 65–85. [G: Indonesia]

Wong, John. Agricultural Production and Socialist Transformation in China: Two Decades After. *Malayan Econ. Rev.,* October 1973, *18*(2), pp. 1–15. [G: China]

1215 African Countries

Abdalla, Ismail-Sabry. Economic Independence Through Socialism: The Egyptian Approach. In *Ghai, D., ed.*, 1973, pp. 190–204. [G: Egypt]

Abkin, M. H., et al. System Simulation of Agricultural Development: Some Nigerian Policy Comparisons. *Amer. J. Agr. Econ.,* August 1973, *55*(3), pp. 404–19. [G: Nigeria]

Addo, John Sackah. Savings Banks and Savings Facilities in African Countries: Ghana. In *Al-*

berici, A. and Baravelli, M., eds., 1973, pp. 37–39. [G: Ghana]

Aguda, Oluwadare. The State and the Economy in the Sudan: From a Political Scientist's Point of View. *J. Devel. Areas,* April 1973, *7*(3), pp. 431–48. [G: Sudan]

Amin, Samir. Underdevelopment and Dependence in Black Africa—Their Historical Origins and Contemporary Forms. *Soc. Econ. Stud.,* March 1973, *22*(1), pp. 177–96. [G: Africa]

Anyanwu, Enoch A. The Contribution of Finance to Industrial Development: The Nigerian Experience. In *[Hicks, U.],* 1973, pp. 59–94. [G: Nigeria]

Arcucci, Francesco and Frediani, Lorenzo. Savings Banks and Savings Facilities in African Countries: Malawi. In *Alberici, A. and Baravelli, M., eds.,* 1973, pp. 55–59. [G: Malawi]

Arrighi, Giovanni. The Political Economy of Rhodesia. In *Arrighi, G. and Saul, J. S.,* 1973, pp. 336–77. [G: Rhodesia]

Awad, M. Dilemmas in Economic Independence: Lessons from Sudan. In *Ghai, D., ed.,* 1973, pp. 205–31. [G: Sudan]

Babingui, Denis. Savings Banks and Savings Facilities in African Countries: Congo Brazzaville. In *Alberici, A. and Baravelli, M., eds.,* 1973, pp. 19–21. [G: Congo Brazzaville]

Belkhodja, Hassen. Savings Banks and Savings Facilities in African Countries: Tunisia. In *Alberici, A. and Baravelli, M., eds.,* 1973, pp. 115–20. [G: Tunisia]

Birara, Jean. Savings Banks and Savings Facilities in African Countries: Rwanda. In *Alberici, A. and Baravelli, M., eds.,* 1973, pp. 81. [G: Rwanda]

Boubacar, Mamadou N'Diaye. Savings Banks and Savings Facilities in African Countries: Dahomey. In *Alberici, A. and Baravelli, M., eds.,* 1973, pp. 23–27. [G: Dahomey]

Braemer, Pierre. Savings Banks and Savings Facilities in African Countries: Mauritania. In *Alberici, A. and Baravelli, M., eds.,* 1973, pp. 63–64. [G: Mauritania]

Chapman, Duane. Economic Aspects of a Nuclear Desalination Agro-Industrial Project in the United Arab Republic. *Amer. J. Agr. Econ.,* August 1973, *55*(3), pp. 433–40. [G: United Arab Republic]

Congo, M. Savings Banks and Savings Facilities in African Countries: Upper Volta. In *Alberici, A. and Baravelli, M., eds.,* 1973, pp. 125–28. [G: Upper Volta]

Davies, David G. A Critical Discussion of I.L.O. Report on Employment in Kenya. *Pakistan Develop. Rev.,* Autumn 1973, *12*(3), pp. 283–92. [G: Kenya]

Dematté, Claudio. Savings Banks and Savings Facilities in African Countries: Mali. In *Alberici, A. and Baravelli, M., eds.,* 1973, pp. 61–62. [G: Mali]

Due, Jean M. Development without Growth—The Case of Ghana in the 1960s? *Econ. Bull. Ghana, Sec. Ser.,* 1973, *3*(1), pp. 3–15. [G: Ghana]

Fortt, J. M. and Hougham, D. A. Environment, Population and Economic History. In *Richards, A. I.; Sturrock, F. and Fortt, J. M., eds.,* 1973, pp. 17–46. [G: Uganda]

Frankel, S. Herbert. Economic Change in Africa in Historical Perspective. In *Youngson, A. J., ed.,* 1973, pp. 211–28. [G: Africa]

Gado, Abdou. Savings Banks and Savings Facilities in African Countries: Niger. In *Alberici, A. and Baravelli, M., eds.,* 1973, pp. 77–79. [G: Niger]

Ghai, Dharam P. The Concept and Strategies of Economic Independence. In *Ghai, D., ed.,* 1973, pp. 9–34. [G: Africa]

Grayson, Leslie E. The Role of Suppliers' Credits in the Industrialization of Ghana. *Econ. Develop. Cult. Change,* April 1973, *21*(3), pp. 477–99. [G: Ghana]

Green, R. H. Economic Independence and Economic Co-operation. In *Ghai, D., ed.,* 1973, pp. 45–87. [G: Africa]

Greenstreet, D. K. Public Administration: A Comparative Analysis of the 1950 Colonial Ten-Year Development Plan and the 1951 'Nkrumah' Development Plan of the Gold Coast (Ghana) *Econ. Bull. Ghana, Sec. Ser.,* 1973, *3*(4), pp. 31–55. [G: Ghana]

el-Hag Musa, Omar. Reconciliation, Rehabilitation and Development Efforts in Southern Sudan. *Middle East J.,* Winter 1973, *27*(1), pp. 1–6. [G: Sudan]

Harris, John R. Entrepreneurship and Economic Development. In *[Williamson, H. F.],* 1973, pp. 141–72. [G: Nigeria]

Harvey, Charles. International Corporations and Economic Independence: A View from Zambia. In *Ghai, D., ed.,* 1973, pp. 176–89. [G: Zambia]

Herzi, Abdurahman Nur. Savings Banks and Savings Facilities in African Countries: Somalia. In *Alberici, A. and Baravelli, M., eds.,* 1973, pp. 93–96. [G: Somalia]

Horton, Alexander Romeo. Savings Banks and Savings Facilities in African Countries: Liberia. In *Alberici, A. and Baravelli, M., eds.,* 1973, pp. 47–48. [G: Liberia]

Idachaba, F. S. Marketing Boards as Potential Stabilizers of Government Revenues in Developing Countries: The Nigerian Experience. *Econ. Bull. Ghana, Sec. Ser.,* 1973, *3*(4), pp. 23–30. [G: Nigeria]

Ikinda, Antoine. Savings Banks and Savings Facilities in African Countries: Gabon. In *Alberici, A. and Baravelli, M., eds.,* 1973, pp. 33–34. [G: Gabon]

Ingham, Barbara M. Ghana Cocoa Farmers—Income, Expenditure Relationships. *J. Devel. Stud.,* April 1973, *9*(3), pp. 365–72. [G: Ghana]

Johnson, A. S. C. Savings Banks and Savings Facilities in African Countries: Sierra Leone. In *Alberici, A. and Baravelli, M., eds.,* 1973, pp. 87–92. [G: Sierra Leone]

Kamau, C. M. Localising Capitalism: The Kenya Experience. In *Ghai, D., ed.,* 1973, pp. 153–75. [G: Kenya]

Kamulegeya, Edric Spencer. Savings Banks and Savings Facilities in African Countries: Uganda. In *Alberici, A. and Baravelli, M., eds.,* 1973, pp. 121–24. [G: Uganda]

Karani, Hiram. Savings Banks and Savings Facilities in African Countries: Kenya. In *Alberici, A. and Baravelli, M., eds.,* 1973, pp. 41–43. [G: Kenya]

Kibaki, M. Economic Independence: A Survey of Issues. In *Ghai, D., ed.,* 1973, pp. 3–8.

Kientz, Jean. Savings Banks and Savings Facilities in African Countries: Madagascar. In *Alberici, A. and Baravelli, M., eds.,* 1973, pp. 49–53.
[G: Madagascar]

Kongbo, Basile. Savings Banks and Savings Facilities in African Countries: Central African Republic. In *Alberici, A. and Baravelli, M., eds.,* 1973, pp. 7–10. [G: Central African Rep.]

Laokole, Jean-Baptiste. Savings Banks and Savings Facilities in African Countries: Chad. In *Alberici, A. and Baravelli, M., eds.,* 1973, pp. 11–17.
[G: Chad]

Mabogunje, Akin L. Manufacturing and the Geography of Development in Tropical Africa. *Econ. Geogr.,* January 1973, *49*(1), pp. 1–20. [G: Africa]

Mankoubi, Bawa Sandani. Savings Banks and Savings Facilities in African Countries: Togo. In *Alberici, A. and Baravelli, M., eds.,* 1973, pp. 111–13.
[G: Togo]

M'Baye, M. Savings Banks and Savings Facilities in African Countries: Senegal. In *Alberici, A. and Baravelli, M., eds.,* 1973, pp. 83–86. [G: Senegal]

Mondanga, Emony. Savings Banks and Savings Facilities in African Countries: Zaire. In *Alberici, A. and Baravelli, M., eds.,* 1973, pp. 129–31.
[G: Zaire]

Nesci, Vincenzo. Savings Banks and Savings Facilities in African Countries: Morocco. In *Alberici, A. and Baravelli, M., eds.,* 1973, pp. 69–76. [G: Morocco]

Nlend, Emmanuel. Savings Banks and Savings Facilities in African Countries: Cameroon. In *Alberici, A. and Baravelli, M., eds.,* 1973, pp. 1–5.
[G: Cameroon]

Onado, Marco and Porteri, Antonio. Savings Banks and Savings Facilities in African Countries: Lesotho. In *Alberici, A. and Baravelli, M., eds.,* 1973, pp. 45–46. [G: Lesotho]

Onitiri, H. M. A. The International Aspects of Economic Independence. In *Ghai, D., ed.,* 1973, pp. 35–44. [G: Africa]

Oyejide, T. Ademola. Tariff Protection and Industrialization via Import Substitution: An Empirical Analysis of the Nigerian Experience. *Econ. Bull. Ghana, Sec. Ser.,* 1973, *3*(3), pp. 20–27. [G: Nigeria]

Oyejide, T. Ademola. Tariff Protection and Industrialization via Import Substitution: An Empirical Analysis of the Nigerian Experience. *Bangladesh Econ. Rev.,* October 1973, *1*(4), pp. 331–40. [G: Nigeria]

Portugués, Juan Marrero. Savings Banks and Savings Facilities in African Countries: Equatorial Guinea. In *Alberici, A. and Baravelli, M., eds.,* 1973, pp. 29–32. [G: Equatorial Guinea]

Rahman El Sheikh, Ahmed Abdel. Savings Banks and Savings Facilities in African Countries: Sudan. In *Alberici, A. and Baravelli, M., eds.,* 1973, pp. 97–101. [G: Sudan]

Richards, A. I. Subsistence to Commercial Farming in Present-Day Buganda: An Economic and Anthropological Survey: Introduction. In *Richards, A. I.; Sturrock, F. and Fortt, J. M., eds.,* 1973, pp. 1–13. [G: Uganda]

Ruozi, Roberto. Savings Banks and Savings Facilities in African Countries: Introduction. In *Alberici, A. and Baravelli, M., eds.,* 1973, pp. ix–xxiii.
[G: Africa]

Rutman, Gilbert L. and Werner, David J. A Test of the 'Uneconomic Culture' Thesis: An Economic Rationale for the 'Sacred Cow.' *J. Devel. Stud.,* July 1973, *9*(4), pp. 566–80. [G: Africa]

Saul, John S. The Political Aspects of Economic Independence. In *Ghai, D., ed.,* 1973, pp. 123–50.

Senghore, Alhagi A. J. Savings Banks and Savings Facilities in African Countries: Gambia. In *Alberici, A. and Baravelli, M., eds.,* 1973, pp. 35–36.
[G: Gambia]

Sidambaram, Mootoosamy. Savings Banks and Savings Facilities in African Countries: Mauritius. In *Alberici, A. and Baravelli, M., eds.,* 1973, pp. 65–67. [G: Mauritius]

Singer, Hans and Jolly, Richard. Unemployment in an African Setting: Lessons of the Employment Strategy Mission to Kenya. *Int. Lab. Rev.,* February 1973, *107*(2), pp. 103–15. [G: Kenya]

Steel, William F. Complementarities and Conflicts Between Employment and Output Growth in Low-Income Countries. *Econ. Bull. Ghana, Sec. Ser.,* 1973, *3*(1), pp. 50–66. [G: Ghana]

Van Arkadie, Brian. Development of the State Sector and Economic Independence. In *Ghai, D., ed.,* 1973, pp. 88–122. [G: Tanzania]

Weinand, Herbert C. Some Spatial Aspects of Economic Development in Nigeria. *J. Devel. Areas,* January 1973, *7*(2), pp. 247–63. [G: Nigeria]

Werlin, Herbert H. The Consequences of Corruption: The Ghanaian Experience. *Polit. Sci. Quart.,* March 1973, *88*(1), pp. 71–85. [G: Ghana]

Yona, Daniel A. N. Savings Banks and Savings Facilities in African Countries: Tanzania. In *Alberici, A. and Baravelli, M., eds.,* 1973, pp. 103–09.
[G: Tanzania]

1216 Latin American and Caribbean Countries

Astiz, Carlos A. The Military Establishment as a Political Elite: The Peruvian Case. In *Pollock, D. H. and Ritter, A. R. M., eds.,* 1973, pp. 203–29.
[G: Peru]

Baer, Donald E. Income and Export Taxation of Agriculture in Costa Rica and Honduras. *J. Devel. Areas,* October 1973, *8*(1), pp. 39–53. [G: Costa Rica; Honduras]

Baer, Werner and Villela, Annibal V. Industrial Growth and Industrialization: Revisions in the Stages of Brazil's Economic Development. *J. Devel. Areas,* January 1973, *7*(2), pp. 217–34.
[G: Brazil]

Barkin, David P. Cuban Agriculture: A Strategy of Economic Development. In *Barkin, D. P. and Manitzas, N. R., eds.,* 1973, pp. R261–21.
[G: Cuba]

Barraclough, Solon and Schatan, Jacobo. Technological Policy and Agricultural Development. *Land Econ.,* May 1973, *49*(2), pp. 175–94. [G: Latin America]

Behrman, Jere R. Aggregative Market Responses in Developing Agriculture: The Postwar Chilean Experience. In *Eckaus, R. S. and Rosenstein-*

Rodan, P. N., eds., 1973, pp. 229–50. [G: Chile]

Behrman, Jere R. Cyclical Sectoral Capacity Utilization in a Developing Economy. In Eckaus, R. S. and Rosenstein-Rodan, P. N., eds., 1973, pp. 251–66. [G: Chile]

Bergendorff, Hans G.; Clark, Peter B. and Taylor, Lance. Welfare Gains from Optimization in Dynamic Planning Models. Econ. Planning, 1973, 13 (1–2), pp. 75–90. [G: Chile]

Bianchi, Andrés. Notes on the Theory of Latin American Economic Development. Soc. Econ. Stud., March 1973, 22(1), pp. 96–121. [G: Latin America]

Bitar, Sergio and Trivelli, Hugo. The Cost of Capital in the Chilean Economy. In Eckaus, R. S. and Rosenstein-Rodan, P. N., eds., 1973, pp. 147–65. [G: Chile]

Blankstein, Charles S. and Zuvekas, Clarence, Jr. Agrarian Reform in Ecuador: An Evaluation of Past Efforts and the Development of a New Approach. Econ. Develop. Cult. Change, October 1973, 22(1), pp. 73–94. [G: Ecuador]

Brown, Lawrence A. and Lentnek, Barry. Innovation Diffusion in a Developing Economy: A Mesoscale View. Econ. Develop. Cult. Change, January 1973, 21(2), pp. 274–92. [G: Mexico]

Cardoso, Fernando Henrique. Imperialism and Dependency in Latin America. In Bonilla, F. and Girling, R., eds., 1973, pp. 7–16.

Catanese, Anthony James. Planning in a State of Siege: The Colombia Experience. Land Econ., February 1973, 49(1), pp. 35–43. [G: Colombia]

Cauas, Jorge. Short-Term Economic Policy. In [Rosenstein-Rodan, P.], 1973, pp. 118–30. [G: Chile]

Cebula, Richard J. The City as a Source of Regional Economic Disparity in Latin America: Comment. Rev. Soc. Econ., April 1973, 31(1), pp. 85–88. [G: Latin America]

Clark, Peter B. and Foxley, Alejandro. Target Shooting with a Multisectoral Model. In Eckaus, R. S. and Rosenstein-Rodan, P. N., eds., 1973, pp. 341–66. [G: Chile]

Despres, Emile. Inflation and Development: Brazil. In Despres, E., 1973, pp. 184–206. [G: Brazil]

Donnelly, John T. External Financing and Short-Term Consequences of External Debt Servicing for Brazilian Economic Development, 1947-1968. J. Devel. Areas, April 1973, 7(3), pp. 411–29. [G: Brazil]

Escobedo, Gilberto. The Response of the Mexican Economy to Policy Actions. Fed. Res. Bank St. Louis Rev., June 1973, 55(6), pp. 15–23. [G: Mexico]

Fernandez, Raul A. The Border Industrial Program on the United States-Mexico Border. Rev. Radical Polit. Econ., Spring 1973, 5(1), pp. 37–52. [G: U.S.; Mexico]

Friedmann, John. Hyperurbanization and National Development in Chile. In Friedmann, J., 1973, pp. 91–114. [G: Chile]

Friedmann, John. Problems of Spatial Development in the Capital Region of Chile. In Friedmann, J., 1973, pp. 187–226. [G: Chile]

Fuchs, Claudio J. and Landsberger, Henry A. "Revolution of Rising Expectations" or "Traditional Life Ways"? A Study of Income Aspirations in a Developing Country. Econ. Develop. Cult. Change, January 1973, 21(2), pp. 212–26. [G: Chile]

Furtado, Celso. The Brazilian "Model" of Development. In Wilber, C. K., ed., 1973, pp. 297–306. [G: Brazil]

Furtado, Celso. The Brazilian 'Model'. Soc. Econ. Stud., March 1973, 22(1), pp. 122–31. [G: Brazil]

Girvan, Norman. The Development of Dependency Economics in the Caribbean and Latin America: Review and Comparison. Soc. Econ. Stud., March 1973, 22(1), pp. 1–33. [G: Caribbean; Latin America]

Grant, C. H. Political Sequel to Alcan Nationalization in Guyana: The International Aspects. Soc. Econ. Stud., June 1973, 22(2), pp. 249–71. [G: Guyana]

Hanson, James S. and Vogel, Robert C. Inflation and Monetary Velocity in Latin America. Rev. Econ. Statist., August 1973, 55(3), pp. 365–70. [G: Latin America]

van Houten, Jan F. Assembly Industries in the Caribbean. Finance Develop., June 1973, 10(2), pp. 19–22, 37. [G: Caribbean]

Ibarra, Jose. Some Aspects of the Popular Unity's Development Model. In Zammit, J. A., ed., 1973, pp. 57–62. [G: Chile]

Kingston, Jerry L. Export Instability in Latin America: The Postwar Statistical Record. J. Devel. Areas, April 1973, 7(3), pp. 381–95. [G: Latin America]

Levy, Fred D., Jr. Economic Planning in Venezuela. In Thurber, C. E. and Graham, L. S., eds., 1973, pp. 81–108. [G: Venezuela]

Manitzas, Nita R. The Setting of the Cuban Revolution. In Barkin, D. P. and Manitzas, N. R., eds., 1973, pp. M260–18. [G: Cuba]

McLeod, Donald. Determinants of Jamaican Government Revenue Shares. J. Devel. Stud., April 1973, 9(3), pp. 427–37. [G: Jamaica]

Mikesell, Raymond F. and Zinser, James E. The Nature of the Savings Function in Developing Countries: A Survey of the Theoretical and Empirical Literature. J. Econ. Lit., March 1973, 11 (1), pp. 1–26.

Müller, Ronald. The Multinational Corporation and the Underdevelopment of the Third World. In Wilber, C. K., ed., 1973, pp. 124–51. [G: S. America]

Pérez, Louis A., Jr. Aspects of Underdevelopment: Tourism in the West Indies. Sci. Soc., Winter 1973–1974, 37(4), pp. 473–80. [G: W. Indies]

Petras, James F. Cuba: Fourteen Years of Revolutionary Government. In Thurber, C. E. and Graham, L. S., eds., 1973, pp. 281–93. [G: Cuba]

Pindling, Lynden O. Focus on the Bahamas: The Way to Independence. World Devel., May 1973, 1(5), pp. 47–48. [G: W. Indies]

Pollock, David H. Ideologies of Latin American Modernization. In Pollock, D. H. and Ritter, A. R. M., eds., 1973, pp. 30–44. [G: Latin America]

Pollock, David H. The Pearson and Prebisch Reports: The Crucial Issue of Unemployment. In Pollock, D. H. and Ritter, A. R. M., eds., 1973, pp. 70–85. [G: Latin America]

Pompermayer, Malori J. Dependency and Unemployment: Some Issues. In *Bonilla, F. and Girling, R., eds.,* 1973, pp. 63–82.

Pone, Maris. Recent Developments in Brazil: A Perspective. In *Pollock, D. H. and Ritter, A. R. M., eds.,* 1973, pp. 185–202. **[G: Brazil]**

Porter, Richard C. The Birth of a Bill Market. *J. Devel. Stud.,* April 1973, *9*(3), pp. 439–50.
[G: Colombia]

Randall, Laura. Inflation and Economic Development in Latin America: Some New Evidence. *J. Devel. Stud.,* January 1973, *9*(2), pp. 317–22.
[G: Argentina; Brazil]

Remes Lenicov, Jorge L. Algunos resultados de la política desarrollista (1958–64): el caso de la industria automotriz. (Some Results of the Development Policy 1958–64; the Case of the Automobile Industry. With English summary.) *Económica,* September-December 1973, *19*(3), pp. 293–329.
[G: Argentina]

Richards, Vincent A. E. Development Prospects in the Commonwealth Caribbean in the 1970s. In *Pollock, D. H. and Ritter, A. R. M., eds.,* 1973, pp. 269–86. **[G: Caribbean]**

Ritter, Arch R. M. Institutional Strategy and Economic Performance in Revolutionary Cuba. In *Pollock, D. H. and Ritter, A. R. M., eds.,* 1973, pp. 203–59. **[G: Cuba]**

Ritter, Arch R. M. and Pollock, David H. Revolution in Latin America: An Overview. In *Pollock, D. H. and Ritter, A. R. M., eds.,* 1973, pp. 3–29.
[G: Latin America]

Rosenstein-Rodan, Paul N. Planning for Full Employment in Latin America. In *Pollock, D. H. and Ritter, A. R. M., eds.,* 1973, pp. 86–96. **[G: Latin America]**

Schmitter, Philippe C. The "Portugalization" of Brazil? In *Stepan, A., ed.,* 1973, pp. 179–232.
[G: Brazil]

Scott, Robert E. Latin America and Modernization. In *Scott, R. E., ed.,* 1973, pp. 1–21. **[G: Latin America]**

Seligson, Mitchell A. Transactions and Community Formation: Fifteen Years of Growth and Stagnation in Central America. *J. Common Market Stud.,* March 1973, *11*(3), pp. 173–90. **[G: Central America]**

Seton, Francis. Shadow Wages in Chile. In *Eckaus, R. S. and Rosenstein-Rodan, P. N., eds.,* 1973, pp. 49–119. **[G: Chile]**

Skidmore, Thomas E. Politics and Economic Policy Making in Authoritarian Brazil, 1937–71. In *Stepan, A., ed.,* 1973, pp. 3–46. **[G: Brazil]**

Smith, Gordon W. Marketing and Economic Development: A Brazilian Case Study, 1930–70. *Food Res. Inst. Stud.,* 1973, *12*(3), pp. 179–98.
[G: Brazil]

Solar, Donald. Chile's Dilemma: An Interpretive Analysis. *Amer. Econ.,* Spring 1973, *17*(1), pp. 40–50. **[G: Chile]**

Syrquin, Moshe. Efficient Input Frontiers for the Manufacturing Sector in Mexico 1965–1980. *Int. Econ. Rev.,* October 1973, *14*(3), pp. 657–75.
[G: Mexico]

Torres, James F. Concentration of Political Power and Levels of Economic Development in Latin American Countries. *J. Devel. Areas,* April 1973, *7*(3), pp. 397–409. **[G: Latin America]**

Tyler, William G. Manufactured Export Promotion in a Semi-Industrialized Economy: The Brazilian Case. *J. Devel. Stud.,* October 1973, *10*(1), pp. 3–15. **[G: Brazil]**

Vandendries, René. An Appraisal of the Reformist Development Strategy of Peru. In *Scott, R. E., ed.,* 1973, pp. 260–84. **[G: Peru]**

Vilas, Carlos M. Aspectos del desarrollo de las corporaciones multinacionales en Argentina. (Aspects of Multinational Corporations Development in Argentina. With English summary.) *Económica,* September-December 1973, *19*(3), pp. 331–68. **[G: Argentina]**

Walter, John P. The City as a Source of Regional Economic Disparity in Latin America. *Rev. Soc. Econ.,* April 1973, *31*(1), pp. 66–84. **[G: Latin America]**

Wesche, Rolf J. Montana Settlement as a Partial Solution to Peru's Economic and Demographic Problems. In *Pollock, D. H. and Ritter, A. R. M., eds.,* 1973, pp. 260–68. **[G: Peru]**

Wilford, W. T. The Central American Common Market: Trade Patterns After a Decade of Union. *Nebr. J. Econ. Bus.,* Summer 1973, *12*(3), pp. 3–22. **[G: Central America]**

Witte, Ann Dryden. Employment in the Manufacturing Sector of Developing Economies: A Study of Mexico and Peru. *J. Devel. Stud.,* October 1973, *10*(1), pp. 33–49. **[G: Mexico; Peru]**

Wood, Harold A. Obstacles to Development in Latin America: An Evaluation of the Planning Process. In *Pollock, D. H. and Ritter, A. R. M., eds.,* 1973, pp. 47–57. **[G: Latin America]**

Worrell, DeLisle. Comment on Three Econometric Models of the Jamaican Economy. *Soc. Econ. Stud.,* June 1973, *22*(2), pp. 272–86. **[G: Jamaica]**

1217 Oceanic Countries

Conroy, J. D. Urbanization in Papua New Guinea: A Development Constraint. *Econ. Rec.,* March 1973, *49*(125), pp. 76–88. **[G: New Guinea]**

Finney, B. R. Big-men, Half-men and Trader-chiefs: Entrepreneurial Styles in Australian New Guinea and French Polynesia. In *Epstein, T. S. and Penny, D. H., eds.,* 1973, pp. 114–30. **[G: New Guinea; Tahiti]**

Fisk, E. K. and Honeybone, D. Belshaw's 'Emergent Fijian Enterprise' after Ten Years. In *Epstein, T. S. and Penny, D. H., eds.,* 1973, pp. 173–92.
[G: Fiji]

Shand, R. T. The Spectrum of Cash Crop Participation in New Guinea Villages. In *Epstein, T. S. and Penny, D. H., eds.,* 1973, pp. 69–85. **[G: New Guinea]**

122 Economic Studies of More Industrialized Countries

1220 General

Baldwin, George B. "Population Policy in Developed Countries" *Finance Develop.,* December 1973, *10*(4), pp. 3–7.

Ball, R. J. The Economic Models of Project LINK. In *Ball, R. J., ed.,* 1973, pp. 65–107. **[G: W. Europe; N. America; Japan]**

Barsby, Steven L. Great Spurts and the Experience of Non-European Countries. *J. Econ. Issues*, September 1973, *7*(3), pp. 459–74.

Lubitz, Raymond. Export-Led Growth in Industrial Economies. *Kyklos*, 1973, *26*(2), pp. 307–21.

Porta, Pier Luigi. Patterns of Association of Output and Employment in the Industrially Advanced Countries. *Rivista Int. Sci. Econ. Com.*, May 1973, *20*(5), pp. 449–69.

Ripley, Duncan M. Systematic Elements in the Linkage of National Stock Market Indices. *Rev. Econ. Statist.*, August 1973, *55*(3), pp. 356–61.

1221 Comparative Country Studies

Blumenfeld, Hans. Growth Rate Comparisons: Soviet Union and German Democratic Republic. *Land Econ.*, May 1973, *49*(2), pp. 122–32.
[G: U.S.S.R.; E. Germany]

Capdevielle, Patricia and Neef, Arthur. Productivity and Unit Labor Costs in 12 Industrial Countries. *Mon. Lab. Rev.*, November 1973, *96*(11), pp. 14–21.

George, Kenneth D. The Changing Structure of Industry in the United Kingdom. In *Rybczynski, T. M., ed.*, 1973, pp. 55–67. [G: U.K.]

Kaye, Seymour P. Summary of Comparative Public Policies and Procedures. In *Kaye, S. P. and Marsh, A., eds.*, 1973, pp. 300–321. [G: U.S.; W. Europe]

Matthews, R. C. O. The Contribution of Science and Technology to Economic Development. In *Williams, B. R., ed.*, 1973, pp. 1–31. [G: U.S.; Canada; Europe; Japan]

Oshima, Keichi. Research and Development and Economic Growth in Japan. In *Williams, B. R., ed.*, 1973, pp. 310–23. [G: Japan]

Paldam, Martin. An Empirical Analysis of the Relationship between Inflation and Economic Growth in 12 Countries, 1950 to 1969. *Swedish J. Econ.*, December 1973, *75*(4), pp. 420–27. [G: W. Europe; U.K.; U.S.]

Perkins, J. O. N. Macro-Economic Policy: Introduction. In *Perkins, J. O. N., ed.*, 1973, pp. 11–16. [G: Australia; Canada; S. Africa; New Zealand]

Perkins, J. O. N. and Nieuwenhuysen, J. P. Macro-Economic Policies in the Four Countries. In *Perkins, J. O. N., ed.*, 1973, pp. 177–208. [G: Australia; New Zealand; Canada; S. Africa]

Phelps Brown, E. H. Levels and Movements of Industrial Productivity and Real Wages Internationally Compared, 1860-1970. *Econ. J.*, March 1973, *83*(329), pp. 58–71. [G: Germany; Sweden; U.K.; U.S.; France]

Szepesi, Gy. and Székely, B. Some Features of the Economic Structure: An International Comparison. *Acta Oecon.*, 1973, *10*(2), pp. 129–46.

Verbaan, W. C. and de Ridder, P. B. Uniforme modelstructuur voor meerdere landen. (A Uniform Model Structure for Several Countries. With English summary.) *De Economist*, September-October 1973, *121*(5), pp. 481–520.

1223 European Countries

Bauch, Vlastislav. The Effect of the Economic Policy of the Communist Party of Czechoslovakia on the Material Situation of the Population of Slovakia.

Czech. Econ. Digest., June 1973, (4), pp. 34–56. [G: Czechoslovakia]

Betz, Horst. The Pattern of Economic Reform in East Germany: Return to Increased Centralization? *Econ. Int.*, May 1973, *26*(2), pp. 318–28. [G: E. Germany]

Brehmer, Ekhard and Bradford, Maxwell R. Incomes and Labor Market Policies in Sweden. *Finance Develop.*, September 1973, *10*(3), pp. 21–23, 35. [G: Sweden]

Čáp, Václav. The Development of Effectiveness of the Czechoslovak Economy. *Czech. Econ. Digest.*, June 1973, (4), pp. 3–33. [G: Czechoslovakia]

Farley, Noel J. J. Outward-looking Policies and Industrialization in a Small Economy: Some Notes on the Irish Case. *Econ. Develop. Cult. Change*, Part I, July 1973, *21*(4), pp. 610–28. [G: Ireland]

Feiwel, George R. The Dynamics of Perpetuation: Some Observations on the Efficacy of Soviet Economic Reforms. *Econ. Int.*, May 1973, *26*(2), pp. 233–61. [G: U.S.S.R.]

Foulon, Alain. Consommation des ménages et consommation publique "divisible": Structure, évolution et financement 1959–1969. (Private Consumption and Public "Divisible" Consumption: Structure, Evolution and Financement. 1959–1969. With English summary.) *Consommation*, April-June 1973, *20*(2), pp. 5–94. [G: France]

Gibson, Norman. Economic Conditions and Policy in Northern Ireland. *Econ. Soc. Rev.*, April 1973, *4*(3), pp. 349–64. [G: U.K.]

Holešovský, Václav. Planning and the Market in the Czechoslovak Reform. In *Bornstein, M., ed.*, 1973, pp. 313–45. [G: Czechoslovakia]

Husák, Gustáv. From the Report of the Central Committee Presidium of the Communist Party of Czechoslovakia on the Implementation of the Decisions of the 14th Congress of the Communist Party of Czechoslovakia. *Czech. Econ. Digest.*, May 1973, (3), pp. 3–24. [G: Czechoslovakia]

Iudina, E. and Oleinik, I. Structural Changes in the Economies of Socialist Countries. *Prob. Econ.*, March 1973, *15*(11), pp. 21–43. [G: U.S.S.R.]

Kux, Jaroslav. Comparative Study of Labour Productivity in Industry Between Czechoslovakia, Hungary, France and Austria. *Czech. Econ. Digest.*, November 1973, (7), pp. 74–95. [G: Czechoslavakia; Hungary; France; Austria]

Lieberman, Sima. Economic Achievement in the German Democratic Republic 1949–1969. *Schweiz. Z. Volkswirtsch. Statist.*, December 1973, *109*(4), pp. 554–78. [G: E. Germany]

Matthews, R. C. O. Foreign Trade and British Economic Growth. *Scot. J. Polit. Econ.*, November 1973, *20*(3), pp. 195–209. [G: U.K.]

Melnyk, Z. Lew. Regional Contribution to Capital Formation in the USSR: The Case of the Ukrainian Republic. In *Bandera, V. N. and Melnyk, Z. L., eds.*, 1973, pp. 104–31. [G: U.S.S.R.]

Modigliani, Franco and Tarantelli, Ezio. A Generalization of the Phillips Curve for a Developing Country. *Rev. Econ. Stud.*, April 1973, *40*(2), pp. 203–23. [G: Italy]

Perroux, François. The Growth of the French Economy 1946–1970 a First Assessment. *Écon. Appl.*, 1973, *26*(2–3–4), pp. 641–46. [G: France]

Rohlícek, Rudolf. The Role of Finance in Plan-Based Management of the Development of the Czechoslovak Economy. *Czech. Econ. Digest.*, September 1973, (6), pp. 3–62. [G: Czechoslovakia]

Tagliacarne, Guglielmo. The Regions Twenty Years Later: Socio-Economic Dynamics of the Regions Between 1951 and 1971. *Rev. Econ. Cond. Italy,* May 1973, *27*(3), pp. 127–61. [G: Italy]

Tilly, Richard H. Zeitreihen zum Geldumlauf in Deutschland, 1870–1913. (Time Series Concerning the Aggregate Money Supply in Germany, 1870–1913. With English summary.) *Jahr. Nationalökon. Statist.,* May 1973, *187*(4), pp. 330–63. [G: Germany]

Tyler, Geoffrey and Neiss, Hubert. Problems and Prospects in East-West Trade. *Finance Develop.,* September 1973, *10*(3), pp. 24–26.

Ujázy, Karol. An Analysis of the Situation in Capital Construction. *Czech. Econ. Digest.,* November 1973, (7), pp. 3–55. [G: Czechoslovakia]

Vachel, Jan and Nentvichová, Božena. 25 Years of Building Czechoslovakia's Socialist Economy. *Czech. Econ. Digest.,* February 1973, (1), pp. 3–93. [G: Czechoslovakia]

Ventriglia, Ferdinando. Results and Prospects of the Policy for Southern Italy. *Rev. Econ. Cond. Italy,* January-March 1973, *27*(1–2), pp. 5–28. [G: Italy]

1224 Asian Countries

Aliber, Robert Z. Japanese Growth and the Equilibrium Foreign Exchange Value of the Yen. *Southern Econ. J.,* January 1973, *39*(3), pp. 406–18. [G: Japan]

Dore, Ronald P. L'effetto di sviluppo ritardato e il Giappone. (Late Development Effect and Japan. With English summary.) *Rivista Int. Sci. Econ. Com.,* August-September 1973, *20*(8–9), pp. 738–57. [G: Japan]

Eckaus, Richard S. The Chinese Economy at the Present Juncture: Discussion. *Amer. Econ. Rev.,* May 1973, *63*(2), pp. 233–34. [G: China]

Ike, Nobutaka. Economic Growth and Intergenerational Change in Japan. *Amer. Polit. Sci. Rev.,* December 1973, *67*(4), pp. 1194–1203. [G: Japan]

Ishi, Hiromitsu. Cyclical Behavior of Government Receipts and Expenditures—A Case Study of Postwar Japan. *Hitotsubashi J. Econ.,* June 1973, *14*(1), pp. 56–83. [G: Japan]

Ivanova, R. Concerning the Development of the Eastern Regions and Their Manpower Supply. *Prob. Econ.,* June 1973, *16*(2), pp. 26–41. [G: U.S.S.R.]

Kelley, Allen C. and Williamson, Jeffrey G. Modeling Economic Development and General Equilibrium Histories. *Amer. Econ. Rev.,* May 1973, *63*(2), pp. 450–58. [G: Japan]

Miyazaki, Yoshikazu. Rapid Economic Growth in Postwar Japan. In *Moskoff, W., ed.,* 1973, pp. 117–39. [G: Japan]

Monroe, Wilbur F. The Contribution of Japanese Exports to Growth in Output. *Nebr. J. Econ. Bus.,* Winter 1973, *12*(1), pp. 11–21. [G: Japan]

Nosse, Tetsuya. Patterns of Government Capital Formation in the Economic Development of Japan,

1878–1967. In *[Hicks, U.],* 1973, pp. 140–80. [G: Japan]

Zahn, Frank. A Test of the Escape from the Persistence of Backwardness. *J. Devel. Stud.,* April 1973, *9*(3), pp. 403–11. [G: Japan]

1225 African Countries

Brand, S. S. Economic Development as a Policy Objective. *Finance Trade Rev.,* December 1973, *10*(4), pp. 168–75. [G: S. Africa]

Brits, R. N. Inflation and Capital Growth in South Africa, 1963–1972. *S. Afr. J. Econ.,* September 1973, *41*(3), pp. 291–97. [G: S. Africa]

Nieuwenhuysen, J. P. Macro-Economic Policy: South Africa. In *Perkins, J. O. N., ed.,* 1973, pp. 130–76. [G: S. Africa]

Steenkamp, W. F. J. Labour and Management in Manufacturing Development. *S. Afr. J. Econ.,* December 1973, *41*(4), pp. 438–51. [G: S. Africa]

1227 Oceanic Countries

Perkins, J. O. N. and Nieuwenhuysen, J. P. Macro-Economic Policy: Australia. In *Perkins, J. O. N., ed.,* 1973, pp. 17–56. [G: Australia]

Rowe, J. W. Macro-Economic Policy: New Zealand. In *Perkins, J. O. N., ed.,* 1973, pp. 94–129. [G: New Zealand]

Whitlam, E. G. Focus on Australia: Change Will Mean Opportunity. *World Devel.,* May 1973, *1*(5), pp. 65. [G: Australia]

1228 North American Countries

Abramovitz, Moses and David, Paul A. Reinterpreting Economic Growth: Parables and Realities. *Amer. Econ. Rev.,* May 1973, *63*(2), pp. 428–39. [G: U.S.]

Abramovitz, Moses and David, Paul A. Economic Growth in America: Historical Parables and Realities. *De Economist,* May-June 1973, *121*(3), pp. 251–72. [G: U.S.]

English, M. D. Macro-Economic Policy: Canada. In *Perkins, J. O. N., ed.,* 1973, pp. 57–93. [G: Canada]

Hale, Carl W. United States' Economic Development, the Business Cycle, and Industrial Complementarity. *Miss. Val. J. Bus. Econ.,* Spring 1973, *8*(3), pp. 47–58. [G: U.S.]

La Tourette, John E. Capital and Output in Postwar Canada. *Amer. Econ.,* Spring 1973, *17*(1), pp. 70–80. [G: Canada]

123 Comparative Economic Studies Involving Both More and Less Industrialized Countries; International Statistical Comparisons

1230 Comparative Economic Studies Involving More and Less Industrialized Countries; International Statistical Comparisons

Adams, N. A. Trade as a Handmaiden of Growth: Comment. *Econ. J.,* March 1973, *83*(329), pp. 210–12.

Allais, Maurice. Inequality and Civilizations. *Soc. Sci. Quart.*, December 1973, *54*(3), pp. 508–24.

Asher, Ephraim and Kumar, T. Krishna. Capital-Labor Substitution and Technical Progress in Planned and Market Oriented Economies: A Comparative Study. *Southern Econ. J.*, July 1973, *40*(1), pp. 103–09. [G: U.S.S.R.; Yugoslavia; Hungary; N. America; Israel]

Ault, David E. On the Importance of Lags in Technology: An Empirical Test. *Rivista Int. Sci. Econ. Com.*, October 1973, *20*(10), pp. 945–60.

Balassa, Bela. Just How Misleading are Official Exchange Rate Conversions?: Comment. *Econ. J.*, December 1973, *83*(332), pp. 1258–67.

Chaudry, M. Anwar. An Econometric Approach to Saving Analysis. *Pakistan Develop. Rev.*, Autumn 1973, *12*(3), pp. 200–31.

Coen, Edward. Relative Growth Rates: The Experience of the Advanced Economies. *Banca Naz. Lavoro Quart. Rev.*, June 1973, *105*, pp. 158–76.

Crafts, N. F. R. Trade as a Handmaiden of Growth: An Alternative View. *Econ. J.*, September 1973, *83*(331), pp. 875–84.

Csernok, Attila; Ehrlich, Eva and Szilágyi, Gyorgy. Numerical Results of an International Comparison of Infrastructure Development Over the Last 100 Years. *Europ. Econ. Rev.*, April 1973, *4*(1), pp. 63–65.

David, Paul A. Just How Misleading are Official Exchange Rate Conversions?: Reply. *Econ. J.*, December 1973, *83*(332), pp. 1267–76.

Decker, Robert L. The Saving Gap and Foreign Aid. *Intermountain Econ. Rev.*, Fall 1973, *4*(2), pp. 45–54.

Diaz-Alejandro, Carlos. Labour Productivity and Other Characteristics of Cement Plants—An International Comparison. In *[Rosenstein-Rodan, P.]*, 1973, pp. 283–315. [G: Latin America]

Drechsler, László. Weighting of Index Numbers in Multilateral International Comparisons. *Rev. Income Wealth*, March 1973, *19*(1), pp. 17–34.

Drtina, František. International Position of Czechoslovak Agriculture. *Czech. Econ. Digest.*, June 1973, (4), pp. 57–76. [G: Czechoslovakia]

Flanagan, Robert J. The U.S. Phillips Curve and International Unemployment Rate Differentials. *Amer. Econ. Rev.*, March 1973, *63*(1), pp. 114–31. [G: U.S.]

Glezakos, Constantine. Export Instability and Economic Growth: A Statistical Verification. *Econ. Develop. Cult. Change*, Part I, July 1973, *21*(4), pp. 670–78.

Goldberger, Arthur S. Dependency Rates and Savings Rates: Further Comment. *Amer. Econ. Rev.*, March 1973, *63*(1), pp. 232–33.

Gregory, Paul; Campbell, John and Cheng, Benjamin. Differences in Fertility Determinants: Developed and Developing Countries. *J. Devel. Stud.*, January 1973, *9*(2), pp. 233–41.

Griffin, Keith. The Effect of Aid and Other Resource Transfers on Savings and Growth in Less-Developed Countries: A Comment. *Econ. J.*, September 1973, *83*(331), pp. 863–66.

Helleiner, Gerald K. Manufactured Exports from Less-Developed Countries and Multinational Firms. *Econ. J.*, March 1973, *83*(329), pp. 21–47.

Herman, Bohuslav. Unemployment and the International Division of Labour. In *Judge, G. G. and Takayama, T.*, eds., 1973, pp. 89–115.

Heston, Alan. A Comparison of Some Short-Cut Methods of Estimating Real Product Per Capita. *Rev. Income Wealth*, March 1973, *19*(1), pp. 79–104.

Hickman, Bert G. and Lau, Lawrence J. Elasticities of Substitution and Export Demands in a World Trade Model. *Europ. Econ. Rev.*, December 1973, *4*(4), pp. 347–80.

Hirsch, Seev and Lev, Baruch. Trade and Per Capita Income Differentials: A Test of the Burenstam-Linder Hypothesis. *World Devel.*, September 1973, *1*(9), pp. 11–17.

Hoselitz, Bert F. The Development of a Labor Market in the Process of Economic Growth. In *Sturmthal, A. and Scoville, J. G.*, eds., 1973, pp. 34–57.

Hsieh, C. Measuring the Effects of Trade Expansion on Employment: A Review of Some Research. *Int. Lab. Rev.*, January 1973, *107*(1), pp. 1–29.

Hsieh, C. Measuring the Effects of Trade Expansion on Employment: A Review of Some Research. *Int. Lab. Rev.*, January 1973, *107*(1), pp. 1–29.

Ihrig, Károly. Agriculture's Contribution to the Growth of Capitalist Economies. In *Földi, T., ed.*, 1973, pp. 135–60.

Jabbar, M. A. Agriculture in Economic Development: The Competitive Approach Versus Soviet Control. *Can. J. Agr. Econ.*, February 1973, *21*(1), pp. 63–64. [G: Canada; U.S.S.R.]

Jansen, M. A. Problems of International Comparisons of National Accounting Aggregates Between Countries with Different Economic Systems. *Rev. Income Wealth*, March 1973, *19*(1), pp. 69–77.

Joshi, Nandini U. Validity of International Comparisons of Relationship between Economic Development and Human Resource Development. *Indian Econ. Rev.*, April 1973, *8*(1), pp. 90–92.

Kossov, V. V. Relationships in the Development of Industries. *Matekon*, Spring 1973, *9*(3), pp. 89–108.

Kravis, Irving B. Trade as a Handmaiden of Growth: Reply. *Econ. J.*, March 1973, *83*(329), pp. 212–17.

Kravis, Irving B. Trade as a Handmaiden of Growth: A Reply. *Econ. J.*, September 1973, *83*(331), pp. 885–89.

Kravis, Irving B. and Kenessey, Zoltan. Output and Prices in the International Comparison Project. *Rev. Income Wealth*, March 1973, *19*(1), pp. 49–67.

Kravis, Irving B. A World of Unequal Incomes. *Ann. Amer. Acad. Polit. Soc. Sci.*, September 1973, *409*, pp. 61–80.

Kuznets, Simon. Modern Economic Growth: Findings and Reflections. *Amer. Econ. Rev.*, June 1973, *63*(3), pp. 247–58.

Kuznets, Simon. Economic Capacity and Population Growth. In *Kuznets, S.*, 1973, pp. 49–93.

Kuznets, Simon. Modern Economic Growth: Findings and Reflections. In *Kuznets, S.*, 1973, pp. 165–84.

Kuznets, Simon. Population and Economic Growth. In *Kuznets, S.*, 1973, pp. 1–48.

Kuznets, Simon. Problems in Comparing Recent Growth Rates for Developed and Less-Developed Countries. In *Kuznets, S.*, 1973, pp. 311–42.

Leff, Nathaniel H. Dependency Rates and Savings Rates: Reply. *Amer. Econ. Rev.*, March 1973, *63* (1), pp. 234.

Liu, Ta-Chung and Yeh, Kung-Chia. Chinese and Other Asian Economies: A Quantitative Evaluation. *Amer. Econ. Rev.*, May 1973, *63*(2), pp. 215–23. [G: China]

Lucas, Robert E., Jr. Some International Evidence on Output-Inflation Tradeoffs. *Amer. Econ. Rev.*, June 1973, *63*(3), pp. 326–34.

MacDonald, A. S. Exchange Rates for National Expenditure on Research and Development. *Econ. J.*, June 1973, *83*(330), pp. 477–94.

Mafeje, Archie. The Fallacy of Dual Economies Revisited. In *Institute for Development Research*, 1973, pp. 25–52. [G: Africa]

Manca, G. Developments in the International Competitive Climate during the 1970s. In *Rybczynski, T. M., ed.*, 1973, pp. 18–36.

Mangahas, Mahar. A Note on "Income Inequality and Economic Growth: The Postwar Experience of Asian Countries." *Malayan Econ. Rev.*, April 1973, *18*(1), pp. 11–14. [G: Asia]

Mason, R. Hal. The Multinational Firm and the Cost of Technology to Developing Countries. *Calif. Manage. Rev.*, Summer 1973, *15*(4), pp. 5–13. [G: Latin America; Europe; Canada]

Moyer, R. International Market Analysis. In *Thorelli, H. B., ed.*, 1973, pp. 162–79.

Naya, Seiji. Fluctuations in Export Earnings and Economic Patterns of Asian Countries. *Econ. Develop. Cult. Change*, Part I, July 1973, *21*(4), pp. 629–41. [G: Asia]

Newlyn, Walter T. The Effect of Aid and Other Resource Transfers on Savings and Growth in Less-Developed Countries: A Comment. *Econ. J.*, September 1973, *83*(331), pp. 867–69.

Oohashi, Ryuken. Working Class in the Present World—Statistics and Their Meaning. *Kyoto Univ. Econ. Rev.*, April–October 1973, *43*(1–2), pp. 1–29.

Owen, Carol and Witton, Ronald A. A Note on Conditions Supporting the Covariation of External and Internal Conflict. *Econ. Develop. Cult. Change*, October 1973, *22*(1), pp. 114–23.

Papanek, Gustav F. The Effect of Aid and Other Resource Transfers on Savings and Growth in Less-Developed Countries: A Reply. *Econ. J.*, September 1973, *83*(331), pp. 870–74.

Paukert, Felix. Income Distribution at Different Levels of Development: A Survey of Evidence. *Int. Lab. Rev.*, August-September 1973, *108*(2–3), pp. 97–125.

Pinto, Aníbal and Kñakal, Jan. The Centre-Periphery System Twenty Years Later. *Soc. Econ. Stud.*, March 1973, *22*(1), pp. 34–89.

Rothschild, Kurt W. Military Expenditure, Exports and Growth. *Kyklos*, 1973, *26*(4), pp. 804–14. [G: O.E.C.D.]

Salazar-Carrillo, Jorge. Price, Purchasing Power and Real Product Comparisons in Latin America. *Rev. Income Wealth*, March 1973, *19*(1), pp. 117–32. [G: Latin America]

Sellekaerts, Willy and Sellekaerts, Brigette. Balance of Payments Deficits, the Adjustment Cost and the Optimum Level of International Reserves. *Weltwirtsch. Arch.*, 1973, *109*(1), pp. 1–18.

Sofranko, Andrew J. and Bealer, Robert C. Modernization Balance, Imbalance, and Domestic Instability. *Econ. Develop. Cult. Change*, October 1973, *22*(1), pp. 52–72.

Stewart, Frances. Trade and Technology. In *Streeten, P., ed.*, 1973, pp. 231–63.

Strober, Myra H. Economic Development and the Hierachy of Earnings. *Ind. Relat.*, February 1973, *12*(1), pp. 65–76.

Studenmund, A. H. A Cross-Sectional Analysis of the Law of Declining International Trade. *Western Econ. J.*, December 1973, *11*(4), pp. 481–86.

Summers, Robert. International Price Comparisons Based Upon Incomplete Data. *Rev. Income Wealth*, March 1973, *19*(1), pp. 1–16.

Sunkel, Osvaldo. Transnational Capitalism and National Disintegration in Latin America. *Soc. Econ. Stud.*, March 1973, *22*(1), pp. 132–76. [G: Latin America]

Taplin, G. B. A Model of World Trade. In *Ball, R. J., ed.*, 1973, pp. 177–223.

Warriner, Doreen. Results of Land Reform in Asian and Latin American Countries. *Food Res. Inst. Stud.*, 1973, *12*(2), pp. 115–31. [G: Asia; Latin America]

Wilber, Charles K. The Human Costs of Economic Development: The West, the Soviet Union, and Underdeveloped Countries Today. In *Wilber, C. K., ed.*, 1973, pp. 324–41. [G: U.S.S.R.; U.S.; U.K.; Japan; Mexico]

Wilford, W. T. Nutrition Levels and Economic Growth: Some Empirical Measures. *J. Econ. Issues*, September 1973, *7*(3), pp. 437–58.

Yotopoulos, Pan A. and Nugent, Jeffrey B. A Balanced-Growth Version of the Linkage Hypothesis: A Test. *Quart. J. Econ.*, May 1973, *87*(2), pp. 157–71.

130 ECONOMIC FLUCTUATIONS; FORECASTING; STABILIZATION; AND INFLATION

131 Economic Fluctuations

1310 General

Aliber, Robert Z. Speculation in the Flexible Exchange Re-Revisited: Reply. *Kyklos*, 1973, *26* (3), pp. 619–20. [G: France]

Bhattacharya, Sourin. Separate Treatment of Demand and Supply Lags and Stability of Multiplier Processes. *Indian Econ. J.*, April-June 1973, *20* (4–5), pp. 570–80.

Biehl, Dieter, et al. Measuring the Demand Effects of Fiscal Policy. In *Giersch, H., ed.*, 1973, pp. 223–41. [G: W. Germany]

Burger, Hendrik. Possible Concepts for Better Planning and Evaluating Fiscal Policy—Experiences in the Netherlands. In *Giersch, H., ed.*, 1973, pp. 210–22. [G: Netherlands]

Giersch, Herbert. On the Desirable Degree of Flexibility of Exchange Rates. *Weltwirtsch. Arch.*, 1973, *109*(2), pp. 191–213.

Heubes, Jürgen. Zyklisches Wachstum. (Cyclical

Growth. With English summary.) *Z. ges. Staatswiss.*, February 1973, *129*(1), pp. 62–88.

Hymans, Saul H. On the Use of Leading Indicators to Predict Cyclical Turning Points. *Brookings Pap. Econ. Act.*, 1973, (2), pp. 339–75. **[G: U.S.]**

Kowal, Lubomyr M. The Market and Business Cycle Theories of M. I. Tugan-Baranovsky. *Rivista Int. Sci. Econ. Com.*, April 1973, *20*(4), pp. 305–34.

Laidler, David. Simultaneous Fluctuations in Prices and Output—A Business Cycle Approach. *Economica, N.S.*, February 1973, *40*(157), pp. 60–72.

Mackay, Robert J. Stein and Nagatani on Stabilization Policies in a Growing Economy. *Rev. Econ. Stud.*, October 1973, *40*(4), pp. 571–78.

Merriam, John H. Forecasting Business Cycle Downturns. *Quart. Rev. Econ. Bus.*, Winter 1973, *13*(4), pp. 71–78. **[G: U.S.]**

Metzler, Lloyd A. Business Cycles and the Theory of Employment. In *Metzler, L. A.*, 1973, pp. 482–96.

Metzler, Lloyd A. Factors Governing the Length of Inventory Cycles. In *Metzler, L. A.*, 1973, pp. 440–64.

Metzler, Lloyd A. Partial Adjustment and the Stability of Inventory Cycles. In *Metzler, L. A.*, 1973, pp. 428–39.

Metzler, Lloyd A. The Nature and Stability of Inventory Cycles. In *Metzler, L. A.*, 1973, pp. 393–427.

Metzler, Lloyd A. Three Lags in the Circular Flow of Income. In *Metzler, L. A.*, 1973, pp. 465–81. **[G: U.S.]**

Neild, R. R. The Effect of Demand on Prices in British Manufacturing Industry: Comment. *Rev. Econ. Stud.*, January 1973, *40*(1), pp. 143–44.

Nell, Edward J. Cyclical Accumulation: A Marxian Model of Development. *Amer. Econ. Rev.*, May 1973, *63*(2), pp. 152–59.

Odewahn, Charles A. and Krislov, Joseph. The Relationship Between Union Contract Rejections and the Business Cycle—A Theoretical Approach. *Nebr. J. Econ. Bus.*, Summer 1973, *12*(3), pp. 23–36.

Pippenger, John E. Speculation in the Flexible Exchange Re-Revisited. *Kyklos*, 1973, *26*(3), pp. 613–18. **[G: France]**

Shiskin, Julius. Measuring Current Economic Fluctuations. *Ann. Econ. Soc. Measure*, January 1973, *2*(1), pp. 1–15. **[G: U.S.]**

Young, Richard M. Inflation and the Distribution of Income and Wealth: Are the Poor Really Hurt? *Fed. Res. Bank Bus. Rev. Phila.*, September 1973, pp. 16–25. **[G: U.S.]**

1313 Fluctuation: Studies

Biehl, Dieter, et al. On the Cyclical Effects of Budgetary Policy from 1960 to 1970 in the Federal Republic of Germany. *Ger. Econ. Rev.*, 1973, *11*(4), pp. 273–91. **[G: W. Germany]**

Blankart, Beat. Arbeitskräftenachfrage im Konjunkturablauf—das Problem des temporären Hortens von Arbeitskräften. (The Demand for Labour During Business Cycles—the Problem of Short-Term Labour Hoarding. With English summary.)

Schweiz. Z. Volkswirtsch. Statist., June 1973, *109*(2), pp. 171–85.

Bloch, Ben W. and Pilgrim, John D. A Reappraisal of Some Factors Associated with Fluctuations in the United States in the Interwar Period. *Southern Econ. J.*, January 1973, *39*(3), pp. 327–44. **[G: U. S.]**

Bretzfelder, Robert B. Sensitivity of State and Regional Income to National Business Cycles. *Surv. Curr. Bus.*, April 1973, *53*(4), pp. 22–33. **[G: U.S.]**

Brown, Alan A.; Licari, J. A. and Neuberger, Egon. A Dynamic CES Production Function Interpretation of Hungarian Growth. *Acta Oecon.*, 1973, *11*(4), pp. 305–24. **[G: Hungary]**

Burger, Albert E. Relative Movements in Wages and Profits. *Fed. Res. Bank St. Louis Rev.*, February 1973, *55*(2), pp. 8–16. **[G: U.S.]**

Cagan, Phillip. Controls and Monetary Policy, 1969–1973. In *Cagan, P., et al.*, 1973, pp. 1–34. **[G: U.S.]**

Carson, Carol S. Inventory-Sales Ratios in Manufacturing and Trade, 1961–72. *Surv. Curr. Bus.*, February 1973, *53*(2), pp. 41–48. **[G: U.S.]**

Dahlstedt, Roy. Cycles in the Finnish Trade with the Soviet Union. *Liiketaloudellinen Aikak.*, 1973, *22*(1), pp. 63–66. **[G: Finland]**

Eckstein, Otto. Instability in the Private and Public Sectors. *Swedish J. Econ.*, March 1973, *75*(1), pp. 19–26. **[G: U.S.]**

Francis, Jack Clark. Has the Inventory Cycle Lost Its Oomph? *Fed. Res. Bank Bus. Rev. Phila.*, February 1973, pp. 19–27. **[G: U.S.]**

Gordon, Robert J. The Welfare Cost of Higher Unemployment. *Brookings Pap. Econ. Act.*, 1973, (1), pp. 133–95. **[G: U.S.]**

Gregory, R. G. and Sheehan, P. J. The Cyclical Sensitivity of Labour Force Participation Rates. *Australian Econ. Rev.*, 2nd Quarter 1973, pp. 9–20. **[G: Australia]**

Hale, Carl W. United States' Economic Development, the Business Cycle, and Industrial Complementarity. *Miss. Val. J. Bus. Econ.*, Spring 1973, *8*(3), pp. 47–58. **[G: U.S.]**

Harshbarger, C. Edward and Doll, Raymond J. Farm Prices and Food Prices: The Relevant Issues. *Fed. Res. Bank Kansas City Rev.*, May 1973, pp. 3–10. **[G: U.S.]**

Haywood, E. The Deviation Cycle: A New Index of the Australian Business Cycle 1950-1973. *Australian Econ. Rev.*, 4th Quarter 1973, pp. 31–39. **[G: Australia]**

Klotz, Benjamin P. Oscillatory Growth in Three Nations. *J. Amer. Statist. Assoc.*, September 1973, *68*(343), pp. 562–67. **[G: U.S.; U.K.; Sweden]**

Klotz, Benjamin P. and Neal, Larry. Spectral and Cross-Spectral Analysis of the Long-Swing Hypothesis. *Rev. Econ. Statist.*, August 1973, *55*(3), pp. 291–98. **[G: U.S.; U.K.; Sweden]**

Lenti, Libero. Business Cycles and Price Trend in Italy. *Rev. Econ. Cond. Italy*, May 1973, *27*(3), pp. 113–26. **[G: Italy]**

Mirer, Thad W. The Distributional Impact of the 1970 Recession. *Rev. Econ. Statist.*, May 1973, *55*(2), pp. 214–24. **[G: U.S.]**

Mirer, Thad W. The Effects of Macroeconomic Fluctuations on the Distribution of Income. *Rev. Income Wealth,* December 1973, *19*(4), pp. 385–406. [G: U.S.]

Okun, Arthur M. Upward Mobility in a High-pressure Economy. *Brookings Pap. Econ. Act.,* 1973, (1), pp. 207–52. [G: U.S.]

Ruggeri, Giuseppe C. Automatic Stabilizers, Business Cycles, and Economic Growth. *Kyklos,* 1973, *26*(2), pp. 288–306. [G: U.S.]

Schiltknecht, Kurt and Zweifel, Peter. Voraussagen der Kommission für Konjunkturfragen und Modellprognosen 1967–1970. (Forecasts of the Federal Commission on Business Cycles and Model's Predictions 1967-1970. With English summary.) *Schweiz. Z. Volkswirtsch. Statist.,* December 1973, *109*(4), pp. 535–53. [G: Switzerland]

Schüler, Manfred. Fiscal Policy in Recession: The German Experience. In *Giersch, H., ed.,* 1973, pp. 195–202. [G: W. Germany]

Snooks, G. D. Depression and Recovery in Western Australia, 1928–29 to 1938–39: A Deviation from the Norm. *Econ. Rec.,* September 1973, *49*(127), pp. 420–39. [G: Australia]

Spitäller, Erich. Incomes Policy in Austria. *Int. Monet. Fund Staff Pap.,* March 1973, *20*(1), pp. 170–202. [G: Austria]

Van Rompuy, E. De stop-go cyclus en de Europese monetaire integratie. (The Stop-go Cycle and the European Monetary Integration. With English summary.) *Tijdschr. Econ.,* 1973, *18*(3), pp. 457–79. [G: U.K.; Europe]

Venieris, Yiannis P. Sales Expectations, Inventory Fluctuations, and Price Behavior. *Southern Econ. J.,* October 1973, *40*(2), pp. 246–61. [G: U.S.]

Wagner, Antonin. Die Auswirkung der öffentlichen Haushalte auf den Konjunkturverlauf in der Schweiz, 1955–1970. (The Effects of Public Finance on Trade Cycles in Switzerland, 1955–1970. With English summary.) *Schweiz. Z. Volkswirtsch. Statist.,* March 1973, *109*(1), pp. 17–57. [G: Switzerland]

132 Economic Forecasting and Forecasting Models

1320 General

Adams, F. Gerard; Clavijo, Fernando and Orsi, Renzo. A Macroeconomic Model of Belgium: Anelise. *Rech. Écon. Louvain,* September 1973, *39*(3), pp. 303–26. [G: Belgium]

Aujac, H. A New Approach to Technological Forecasting in French National Planning. In *Williams, B. R., ed.,* 1973, pp. 96–115. [G: France]

Bain, A. D. and Evans, J. D. Price Formation and Profits: Explanatory and Forecasting Models of Manufacturing Industry Profits in the U.K. *Oxford Bull. Econ. Statist.,* November 1973, *35*(4), pp. 295–308. [G: U.K.]

Blandy, Richard and Wery, René. Population and Employment Growth: Bachue-1. *Int. Lab. Rev.,* May 1973, *107*(5), pp. 441–49.

Bodkin, Ronald G. Econometric Models: Discussion. *Amer. Econ. Rev.,* May 1973, *63*(2), pp. 410–11.

Bonnaud, Jean-Jacques and Pagé, Jean-Pierre. L'utilisation d'un modèle de simulation éco-

nomique dans la procédure de préparation du VIe Plan (1970–1975). (The Utilisation of a Mathematical Economic Model in the Process of Elaboration of the French VIth Plan (1970–1975). With English summary.) *Revue Écon.,* November 1973, *24*(6), pp. 988–1025. [G: France]

Brown, H. James. Shift and Share Projections Revisited: Reply. *J. Reg. Sci.,* April 1973, *13*(1), pp. 121. [G: U.S.]

Chow, Gregory C. and Fair, Ray C. Maximum Likelihood Estimation of Linear Equation Systems with Auto-Regressive Residuals. *Ann. Econ. Soc. Measure,* January 1973, *2*(1), pp. 17–28. [G: U.S.]

Cole, H. S. D. and Curnow, R. C. An Evaluation of the World Models. In *Cole, H. S. D., et al., eds.,* 1973, pp. 108–34.

Cole, H. S. D. The Structure of the World Models. In *Cole, H. S. D., et al., eds.,* 1973, pp. 14–32.

Courbis, Raymond. Les méthodes de planification française: évolution et perspectives. (The Methods of French Planification: Evolution and Perspectives. With English summary.) *Schweiz. Z. Volkswirtsch. Statist.,* September 1973, *109*(3), pp. 317–40. [G: France]

Courbis, Raymond and Pagé, Jean-Pierre. Techniques de projection macro-économique et choix du Plan français. (Macro-Economic Forecasting Techniques and Decision Making in the French Planning System. With English summary.) *Revue Écon.,* November 1973, *24*(6), pp. 951–87. [G: France]

Dagenais, Marcel G. Un modèle annuel de prévision pour l'économie du Québec. (An Annual Forecasting Model of the Quebec Economy. With English summary.) *Can. J. Econ.,* February 1973, *6*(1), pp. 62–78. [G: Canada]

Deane, R. S.; Lumsden, M. A. and Sturm, A. B. Some Simulation Experiments with a New Zealand Model. In *Deane, R. S., ed.,* 1972, pp. 15–64. [G: New Zealand]

Denton, Frank T. and Oksanen, Ernest H. Data Revisions and Forecasting Accuracy: An Econometric Analysis Based on Preliminary and Revised National Accounting Estimates. *Rev. Income Wealth,* December 1973, *19*(4), pp. 437–52.

Dresch, Stephen P. and Goldberg, Robert D. IDIOM: An Inter-Industry, National-Regional Policy Evaluation Model. *Ann. Econ. Soc. Measure,* July 1973, *2*(3), pp. 323–56. [G: U.S.]

Duloy, John H. and Norton, Roger D. Linking the Agricultural Model and the Economy-Wide Model. In *Goreux, L. M. and Manne, A. S., eds.,* 1973, pp. 435–61. [G: Mexico]

Floyd, Charles F. and Sirmans, C. F. Shift and Share Projections Revisited. *J. Reg. Sci.,* April 1973, *13*(1), pp. 115–20. [G: U.S.]

Freeman, Christopher. Malthus with a Computer. In *Cole, H. S. D., et al., eds.,* 1973, pp. 5–13.

Fromm, Gary and Klein, Lawrence R. A Comparison of Eleven Econometric Models of the United States. *Amer. Econ. Rev.,* May 1973, *63*(2), pp. 385–93. [G: U.S.]

Gardini, Attilio and Pezzoli, Ettore. Soluzione e qualche simulazione di un semplice modello statistico aggregato dell'economia italiana (1952–1970). (Solution and Some Simulations of a Simple Aggregate Model of the Italian Economy (1952–1970). With English summary.) *Statistica*, July-September 1973, *33*(3), pp. 429–36.   [G: Italy]

Geisel, Martin S.   Bayesian Comparisons of Simple Macroeconomic Models. *J. Money, Credit, Banking*, August 1973, *5*(3), pp. 751–72.   [G: U.S.]

Goreux, Louis M.   Comparative Analysis of the Programming Models. In *Goreux, L. M. and Manne, A. S., eds.*, 1973, pp. 15–33.   [G: Mexico]

Goreux, Louis M. and Manne, Alan S.   Multi-Level Planning: Case Studies in Mexico: Introduction. In *Goreux, L. M. and Manne, A. S., eds.*, 1973, pp. 1–14.   [G: Mexico]

Granger, C. W. J. and Newbold, P.   Some Comments on the Evaluation of Economic Forecasts. *Appl. Econ.*, March 1973, *5*(1), pp. 35–47.

Granger, C. W. J.   On the Properties of Forecasts Used in Optimal Economic Policy Decisions. *J. Public Econ.*, November 1973, *2*(4), pp. 347–56.

Helliwell, John F., et al.   Some Features and Uses of the Canadian Quarterly Model RDX2. In *Powell, A. A. and Williams, R. A., eds.*, 1973, pp. 27–47.   [G: Canada]

Helliwell, John F., et al.   Comprehensive Linkage of Large Models: Canada and the United States. In *Ball, R. J., ed.*, 1973, pp. 395–426.   [G: Canada; U.S.]

Higgins, C. I. and FitzGerald, V. W.   An Econometric Model of the Australian Economy. *J. Econometrics*, October 1973, *1*(3), pp. 229–65.   [G: Australia]

Hymans, Saul H.   On the Use of Leading Indicators to Predict Cyclical Turning Points. *Brookings Pap. Econ. Act.*, 1973, (2), pp. 339–75.   [G: U.S.]

Julien, P.-A. and Freeman, Christopher.   The Capital and Industrial Output Sub-system. In *Cole, H. S. D., et al., eds.*, 1973, pp. 66–79.

Klacek, Jan and Toms, Miroslav.   Prognostický model pro krátké obdobi. (A Short-Run Forecasting Model. With English summary.) *Ekon.-Mat. Obzor*, 1973, *9*(1), pp. 68–83.   [G: Czechoslovakia]

Lybeck, Johan A.   The Monetary Sector of RDX2: A Note on Some Puzzling Features. *Can. J. Econ.*, November 1973, *6*(4), pp. 595–98.

Manca, G.   Developments in the International Competitive Climate during the 1970s. In *Rybczynski, T. M., ed.*, 1973, pp. 18–36.

Manne, Alan S.   DINAMICO, A Dynamic Multi-Sector, Multi-Skill Model. In *Goreux, L. M. and Manne, A. S., eds.*, 1973, pp. 107–50.   [G: Mexico]

Manne, Alan S.   Economic Alternatives for Mexico: A Quantitative Analysis. In *Goreux, L. M. and Manne, A. S., eds.*, 1973, pp. 151–72.   [G: Mexico]

Marstrand, Pauline K. and Pavitt, K. L. R.   The Agricultural Sub-system. In *Cole, H. S. D., et al., eds.*, 1973, pp. 56–65.

Marstrand, Pauline K. and Sinclair, T. C.   The Pollution Sub-system. In *Cole, H. S. D., et al., eds.*, 1973, pp. 80–89.

McNees, Stephen K.   A Comparison of the GNP Forecasting Accuracy of the Fair and St. Louis Econometric Models. *New Eng. Econ. Rev.*, September-October 1973, pp. 29–34.

McNees, Stephen K.   The Predictive Accuracy of Econometric Forecasts. *New Eng. Econ. Rev.*, September-October 1973, pp. 3–27.

Meadows, Donella H., et al.   A Response to Sussex. In *Cole, H. S. D., et al., eds.*, 1973, pp. 216–40.

Merriam, John H.   Forecasting Business Cycle Downturns. *Quart. Rev. Econ. Bus.*, Winter 1973, *13*(4), pp. 71–78.   [G: U.S.]

Moriguchi, C. and Tatemoto, M.   An Econometric Analysis of a Bilateral Model of International Economic Activity: Japan and U.S.A. In *Ball, R. J., ed.*, 1973, pp. 367–93.   [G: Japan; U.S.]

Nagy, A.   Industrial Projection Methods in Hungary. *Acta Oecon.*, 1973, *11*(4), pp. 381–402.   [G: Hungary]

Nordhaus, William D.   World Dynamics: Measurement Without Data. *Econ. J.*, December 1973, *83* (332), pp. 1156–83.

Page, William.   Population Forecasting. In *Cole, H. S. D., et al., eds.*, 1973, pp. 159–74.

Page, William.   The Non-renewable Resources Subsystem. In *Cole, H. S. D., et al., eds.*, 1973, pp. 33–42.

Page, William.   The Population Sub-system. In *Cole, H. S. D., et al., eds.*, 1973, pp. 43–55.

Prell, Michael J.   How Well Do the Experts Forecast Interest Rates? *Fed. Res. Bank Kansas City Rev.*, September-October 1973, pp. 3–13.   [G: U.S.]

Stekler, H. O. and Schepsman, Martin.   Forecasting with an Index of Leading Series. *J. Amer. Statist. Assoc.*, June 1973, *68*(342), pp. 291–96.

Surrey, A. J. and Bromley, A. J.   Energy Resources. In *Cole, H. S. D., et al., eds.*, 1973, pp. 90–107.

Taplin, G. B.   A Model of World Trade. In *Ball, R. J., ed.*, 1973, pp. 177–223.

Trejo Reyes, Saúl.   Comments on DINAMICO. In *Goreux, L. M. and Manne, A. S., eds.*, 1973, pp. 173–77.   [G: Mexico]

Trejo Reyes, Saúl.   EXPORTA, A Multi-Sector Model for Optimal Growth and Export Policies. In *Goreux, L. M. and Manne, A. S., eds.*, 1973, pp. 179–95.   [G: Mexico]

Tsurumi, Hiroki.   A Comparison of Econometric Macro Models in Three Countries. *Amer. Econ. Rev.*, May 1973, *63*(2), pp. 394–401.   [G: U.S.; Canada; Japan]

Tsurumi, Hiroki.   A Survey of Recent Canadian Macro-Econometric Models. *Can. J. Econ.*, August 1973, *6*(3), pp. 409–28.

Ullmo, Bernard.   Trois problèmes posés par le modèle physico-financier. (Three Problems Set by the Physico-Financial Model. With English summary.) *Revue Écon.*, November 1973, *24*(6), pp. 1026–71.   [G: France]

Verbaan, W. C. and de Ridder, P. B.   Uniforme modelstructuur voor meerdere landen. (A Uniform Model Structure for Several Countries. With English summary.) *De Economist*, September-October 1973, *121*(5), pp. 481–520.

1322 General Forecasts for a Country

Alterman, Jack.   An Overview of BLS Projections. *Mon. Lab. Rev.*, December 1973, *96*(12), pp. 3–7.   [G: U.S.]

Amano, A.   International Capital Movements: Theory and Estimation. In *Ball, R. J., ed.*, 1973, pp. 283–327. [G: Japan]

Andersen, Leonall C. A Comparison of Stabilization Policies: 1966–67 and 1969–70. *J. Money, Credit, Banking*, Part I, February 1973, *5*(1), pp. 26–38. [G: U.S.]

Bloch, Ben W. and Pilgrim, John D. A Reappraisal of Some Factors Associated with Fluctuations in the United States in the Interwar Period. *Southern Econ. J.*, January 1973, *39*(3), pp. 327–44. [G: U. S.]

Deane, R. S. Macroeconometric Relationships within New Zealand: A Preliminary Examination. In *Powell, A. A. and Williams, R. A., eds.*, 1973, pp. 85–114. [G: New Zealand]

Dutta, M. and Sharma, P. L. Alternative Estimators and Predictive Power of Alternative Estimators: An Econometric Model of Puerto Rico. *Rev. Econ. Statist.*, August 1973, *55*(3), pp. 381–85. [G: Puerto Rico]

FitzGerald, V. W. Dynamic Properties of a Non-Linear Econometric Model. In *Powell, A. A. and Williams, R. A., eds.*, 1973, pp. 169–93. [G: Australia]

Franchet, Yves; Inman, Richard A. and Manne, Alan S. Numerical Data for Multi-Sector Planning. In *Goreux, L. M. and Manne, A. S., eds.*, 1973, pp. 85–106. [G: Mexico]

Gardini, Attilio and Pezzoli, Ettore. Relazioni statistiche di un semplice modello aggregativo dell'economia italiana (1951–1970). (Some Statistical Relationships in a Simple Aggregate Model of the Italian Economy (1951–1970). With English summary.) *Statistica*, April-June 1973, *33*(2), pp. 241–73. [G: Italy]

Hansen, Bent. Simulation of Fiscal, Monetary and Exchange Policy in a Primitive Economy: Afghanistan. In *[Tinbergen, J.]*, 1973, pp. 215–37. [G: Afghanistan]

Johnston, Denis F. Population and Labor Force Projections. *Mon. Lab. Rev.*, December 1973, *96*(12), pp. 8–17. [G: U.S.]

Johnston, Denis F. The U.S. Labor Force: Projections to 1990. *Mon. Lab. Rev.*, July 1973, *96*(7), pp. 3–13. [G: U.S.]

Kane, Edward J. Simulations of Stabilization Policies for 1966–1970 *and* A Comparison of Stabilization Policies: 1966–67 and 1969–70: Comment. *J. Money, Credit, Banking*, Part I, February 1973, *5*(1), pp. 39–42. [G: U.S.]

Klein, Lawrence R. and Mori, Kei. The Impact of Disarmament on Aggregate Economic Activity: An Econometric Analysis. In *Udis, B., ed.*, 1973, pp. 59–77. [G: U.S.]

Kutscher, Ronald E. Projections of GNP, Income, Output, and Employment. *Mon. Lab. Rev.*, December 1973, *96*(12), pp. 27–42. [G: U.S.]

Meiselman, David I. Simulations of Stabilization Policies for 1966–1970 *and* A Comparison of Stabilization Policies: 1966–67 and 1969–70: Comment. *J. Money, Credit, Banking*, Part I, February 1973, *5*(1), pp. 43–46. [G: U.S.]

Naqvi, Syed Nawab Haider. Pakistan's Export Possibilities. *Pakistan Develop. Rev.*, Spring 1973, *12* (1), pp. 1–30. [G: Pakistan]

Norton, W. E. and Henderson, J. F. The Structure of a Model of the Australian Economy. In *Powell, A. A. and Williams, R. A., eds.*, 1973, pp. 49–83. [G: Australia]

Ramanujam, M. S. Requirements of Technical Manpower in India: 1965–66 to 1980–81. *Indian Econ. Rev.*, October 1973, *8*(2), pp. 101–24. [G: India]

Rasche, Robert H. Simulations of Stabilization Policies for 1966–1970. *J. Money, Credit, Banking*, Part I, February 1973, *5*(1), pp. 1–25. [G: U.S.]

Ritter, Lawrence S. Reordering National Priorities: A Day of Reckoning. In *Reynolds, L. G.; Green, G. D. and Lewis, D. R., eds.*, 1973, pp. 323–31. [G: U.S.]

Robertson, Ross M., et al. The Uncertain Outlook for 1974. *Indiana Bus. Rev.*, November-December 1973, *48*, pp. 3–15. [G: U.S.]

Rosenblum, Marc. The Great Labor Force Projection Debate: Implications for 1980. *Amer. Econ.*, Fall 1973, *17*(2), pp. 122–29. [G: U.S.]

Rosenthal, Neal H. Projected Changes in Occupations. *Mon. Lab. Rev.*, December 1973, *96*(12), pp. 18–26. [G: U.S.]

Scheper, W. and Reichenbach, H. Die Entwicklung der Anteile der Wirtschaftsbereiche am Bruttoinlandsprodukt—Eine Strukturprognose. (The Development of the Sectoral Shares of Production in Gross National Product. A Forecast of the Production Structure. With English summary) *Weltwirtsch. Arch.*, 1973, *109*(2), pp. 291–320. [G: W. Germany]

Schiltknecht, Kurt and Zweifel, Peter. Voraussagen der Kommission für Konjunkturfragen und Modellprognosen 1967–1970. (Forecasts of the Federal Commission on Business Cycles and Model's Predictions 1967-1970. With English summary.) *Schweiz. Z. Volkswirtsch. Statist.*, December 1973, *109*(4), pp. 535–53. [G: Switzerland]

Šujan, Ivan and Tkáč, Miloslav. The Econometric Forecasting Model of Czechoslovakia. *Econ. Planning*, 1973, *13*(1–2), pp. 15–31. [G: Czechoslovakia]

Teeters, Nancy H. The Payroll Tax and Social-Security Finance. In *Musgrave, R. A., ed.*, 1973, pp. 87–112. [G: U.S.]

Vaciago, Giacomo. Monetary Analysis and Policy: An Aggregated Model for the Italian Economy. *Banca Naz. Lavoro Quart. Rev.*, June 1973, (105), pp. 84–108. [G: Italy]

Vişinoiu, N. Analiza factorială a unor indicatori sintetici ai economiei naţionale. (The Factorial Analysis of Some of the Synthetic Indicators of the National Economy. With English summary.) *Stud. Cercet. Econ.*, 1973, (2), pp. 127–38.

van der Werf, D. Ein Beitrag zur Problematik der Konsumfunktion in der Bundesrepublik Deutschland. (A Contribution to the Problem of Consumption Function in the German Federal Republic. With English summary.) *Weltwirtsch. Arch.*, 1973, *109*(2), pp. 274–90. [G: W. Germany]

Zellner, Arnold and Peck, Stephen C. Simulation Experiments with a Quarterly Macroeconometric

Model of the U.S. Economy. In *Powell, A. A. and Williams, R. A., eds.*, 1973, pp. 149–68. [G: U.S.]

1323 Specific Forecasts for a Sector

Abe, Masatoshi A. Dynamic Micro-economic Models of Production, Investment and Technological Change of the U.S. and Japanese Iron and Steel Industries. In *Judge, G. G. and Takayama, T., eds.*, 1973, pp. 345–67. [G: U.S.; Japan]

Anderson, Kent P. Residential Demand for Electricity: Econometric Estimates for California and the United States. *J. Bus.*, October 1973, *46*(4), pp. 526–53. [G: U.S.]

Baxter, Gary L. Indiana Housing Cycle: 1973 Forecast. *Indiana Bus. Rev.*, May-June 1973, *48*, pp. 10–12. [G: U.S.]

Brown, George H. Census Projections: 1970 to 1985. *Manage. Account.*, January 1973, *54*(7), pp. 11–14. [G: U.S.]

Cummins, J. David. An Econometric Model of the Life Insurance Sector of the U. S. Economy. *J. Risk Ins.*, December 1973, *40*(4), pp. 533–54. [G: U.S.]

Davies, S. W. and Scott, T. W. K. Forecasting Industrial Production. *Nat. Inst. Econ. Rev.*, November 1973, (66), pp. 54–68. [G: U.K.]

Davison, Cecil W. and Martin, Neil R., Jr. Sensitivity of Beef Quantity and Prices—1980 Preview. *Ill. Agr. Econ.*, July 1973, *13*(2), pp. 33–37. [G: U.S.]

Dietrich, J. Kimball and Gutierrez, Alfredo D. An Evaluation of Short-Term Forecasts of Coffee and Cocoa. *Amer. J. Agr. Econ.*, February 1973, *55*(1), pp. 93–99.

Diwan, Romesh K. Are We Saving Enough for Our Plans? In *Wadhva, C. D., ed.*, 1973, pp. 163–78. [G: India]

Duloy, John H.; Kutcher, Gary P. and Norton, Roger D. Investment and Employment Alternatives in the Agricultural District Model. In *Goreux, L. M. and Manne, A. S., eds.*, 1973, pp. 417–33. [G: Mexico]

Duloy, John H. and Norton, Roger D. CHAC, A Programming Model of Mexican Agriculture. In *Goreux, L. M. and Manne, A. S., eds.*, 1973, pp. 291–337. [G: Mexico]

Ferguson, Ian S. Forecasting the Future for Timber. *Australian J. Agr. Econ.*, December 1973, *17*(3), pp. 159–69. [G: Australia]

Fernández de la Garza, Guillermo and Manne, Alan S. ENERGETICOS, A Process Analysis of the Energy Sectors. In *Goreux, L. M. and Manne, A. S., eds.*, 1973, pp. 233–75. [G: Mexico]

Fernández de la Garza, Guillermo; Manne, Alan S. and Valencia, José Alberto. Multi-Level Planning for Electric Power Projects. In *Goreux, L. M. and Manne, A. S., eds.*, 1973, pp. 197–231. [G: Mexico]

Gibson, William E. Interest Rates and Prices in the Long Run: A Study of the Gibson Paradox: Comment. *J. Money, Credit, Banking*, Part II, February 1973, *5*(1), pp. 450–53. [G: U.S.]

Gordon, Robert J. Interest Rates and Prices in the Long Run: A Study of the Gibson Paradox: Comment. *J. Money, Credit, Banking*, Part II, February 1973, *5*(1), pp. 460–63. [G: U.S.]

Graf, Hans G. Zukünftige Verkehrsentwicklung in der Schweiz. (Future Development of Traffic in Switzerland. With English summary.) *Schweiz. Z. Volkswirtsch. Statist.*, September 1973, *109*(3), pp. 341–55. [G: Switzerland]

Hendershott, Patric H. Interest Rates and Prices in the Long Run: A Study of the Gibson Paradox: Comment. *J. Money, Credit, Banking*, Part II, February 1973, *5*(1), pp. 454–59. [G: U.S.]

Higgins, C. I. A Wage-Price Sector for a Quarterly Australian Model. In *Powell, A. A. and Williams, R. A., eds.*, 1973, pp. 115–47. [G: Australia]

Hodgins, Cyril D. and Tanner, J. Ernest. Forecasting Non-residential Building Construction. *Can. J. Econ.*, February 1973, *6*(1), pp. 79–89. [G: Canada]

Kähr, Walter. Die Entwicklung des Energieverbrauchs der Schweiz im Zeitraum 1950 bis 1970 und Vorschau auf das Jahr 2000. (The Development of the Energy Consumption in the Period 1950–1970, with a Forecast for the Year 2000. With English summary.) *Schweiz. Z. Volkswirtsch. Statist.*, September 1973, *109*(3), pp. 385–410. [G: Switzerland]

Keesing, Donald B. and Manne, Alan S. Manpower Projections. In *Goreux, L. M. and Manne, A. S., eds.*, 1973, pp. 55–83. [G: Mexico]

Koshal, Rajindar K. The Future of Higher Education in the State of Ohio: An Econometric Approach. *Ohio State U. Bull. Bus. Res.*, November 1973, *48*(11), pp. 1–3, 5. [G: U.S.]

Krishna, Raj. Government Operations in Foodgrains. In *Wadhva, C. D., ed.*, 1973, pp. 323–39. [G: India]

Mammen, Thampy. Indian Money Market: An Econometric Study. *Int. Econ. Rev.*, February 1973, *14*(1), pp. 49–68. [G: India]

Mann, Jitendar S. A Dynamic Model of the U.S. Tobacco Economy. *Agr. Econ. Res.*, July 1973, *25*(3), pp. 81–92. [G: U.S.]

Price, R. W. R. Some Aspects of the Progressive Income Tax Structure in the UK. *Nat. Inst. Econ. Rev.*, August 1973, (65), pp. 52–63. [G: U.K.]

Sargent, Thomas J. Interest Rates and Prices in the Long Run: A Study of the Gibson Paradox. *J. Money, Credit, Banking*, Part II, February 1973, *5*(1), pp. 385–449. [G: U.S.]

Smith, R. J. Medium-Term Forecasts Reassessed: IV. Domestic Appliances. *Nat. Inst. Econ. Rev.*, May 1973, (64), pp. 68–83. [G: U.K.]

Steindl, Frank G. A Structural Model of the Canadian Monetary Sector: Comment. *Southern Econ. J.*, April 1973, *39*(4), pp. 642. [G: Canada]

Strumpel, Burkhard; Schmiedeskamp, Jay and Schwartz, M. Susan. The Function of Consumer Attitude Data Beyond Econometric Forecasts. In *Mandell, L., et al., eds.*, 1973, pp. 263–88. [G: U.S.]

Vedovato, Giuseppe. Situation and Prospects of the Italian Extractive Industry. *Rev. Econ. Cond. Italy*, July 1973, *27*(4), pp. 225–35. [G: Italy]

1324 Forecasting Models; Theory and Methodology

Ball, R. J. The Economic Models of Project LINK. In *Ball, R. J., ed.*, 1973, pp. 65–107.   [G: W. Europe; N. America; Japan]

Basevi, G. Commodity Trade Equations in Project LINK. In *Ball, R. J., ed.*, 1973, pp. 227–81.   [G: W. Europe; Japan; N. America]

Bombach, Gottfried. Problemstellungen, Methoden und Grenzen mittelfristiger Wirtschafts- und Finanzplanung. (Problems, Methods and Limits of Medium-Termed Economic and Financial Planning. With English summary.) *Schweiz. Z. Volkswirtsch. Statist.*, September 1973, *109*(3), pp. 293–316.

Box, G. E. P. and Jenkins, G. M. Some Comments on a Paper by Chatfield and Prothero and on a Review by Kendall. *J. Roy. Statist. Soc.*, Part 3 1973, *136*, pp. 337–52.

Brewer, Garry D. and Hall, Owen P., Jr. Policy Analysis by Computer Simulation: The Need for Appraisal. *Public Policy*, Summer 1973, *21*(3), pp. 343–65.

Büti, G. Technological Pre-assessment as the Partner of Macroeconomic Forecasting. In *Blohm, H. and Steinbuch, K., eds.*, 1973, pp. 133–38.

Chatfield, C. and Prothero, D. L. Box-Jenkins Seasonal Forecasting: Problems in a Case-study. *J. Roy. Statist. Soc.*, Part 3 1973, *136*, pp. 295–315.

Chow, Gregory C. Multiperiod Predictions from Stochastic Difference Equations by Bayesian Methods. *Econometrica*, January 1973, *41*(1), pp. 109–18.

Cooley, Thomas F. and Prescott, Edward C. Tests of an Adaptive Regression Model. *Rev. Econ. Statist.*, May 1973, *55*(2), pp. 248–56.   [G: U.S.]

Cooper, Ronald L. An Econometric Forecasting Model of the Financial Sector of U.S. Households. *Appl. Econ.*, June 1973, *5*(2), pp. 101–17.   [G: U.S.]

Crotty, James R. Specification Error in Macro-Econometric Models: The Influence of Policy Goals. *Amer. Econ. Rev.*, December 1973, *63*(5), pp. 1025–30.

Crvcanin, Milan. Application de modèles intégrés à la planification des systèmes de transports de la région lausannoise. (Integrated Models Used in Lausanne Area Transportation Study. With English summary.) *Schweiz. Z. Volkswirtsch. Statist.*, September 1973, *109*(3), pp. 357–73.   [G: Switzerland]

Dadayan, V. S. Economic Forecasting and Scientific and Technical Progress. *Amer. Econ.*, Fall 1973, *17*(2), pp. 49–50.

Daub, Mervin. On the Accuracy of Canadian Short-term Economic Forecasts. *Can. J. Econ.*, February 1973, *6*(1), pp. 90–107.   [G: Canada]

Deane, R. S. Macroeconometric Model Simulation: Contexts and Uses. In *Deane, R. S., ed.*, 1972, pp. 7–12.

Dobrescu, Em. Models of Proportions Between the Investment Fund and the Consumption Fund for Forecasting the Development of the Rumanian Economy. *Eastern Europ. Econ.*, Spring 1973, *11*(3), pp. 50–73.   [G: Rumania]

Drettakis, E. G. Missing Data in Econometric Estimation. *Rev. Econ. Stud.*, October 1973, *40*(4), pp. 537–52.   [G: U.K.]

Duloy, John H. and Norton, Roger D. CHAC, A Programming Model of Mexican Agriculture. In *Goreux, L. M. and Manne, A. S., eds.*, 1973, pp. 291–337.   [G: Mexico]

Elliott, J. W. A Direct Comparison of Short-Run GNP Forecasting Models. *J. Bus.*, January 1973, *46*(1), pp. 33–60.   [G: U.S.]

Fedorenko, Nicolai P. Methodological Aspects of Forecasting Long-Term Socio-Economic Development. *Amer. Econ.*, Fall 1973, *17*(2), pp. 46–48.

Francis, Darryl R. The Usefulness of Applied Econometrics to the Policymaker: An Address. *Fed. Res. Bank St. Louis Rev.*, May 1973, *55*(5), pp. 7–10.

Friend, Irwin. Mythology in Finance. *J. Finance*, May 1973, *28*(2), pp. 257–72.

Fromm, Gary and Schink, George R. Aggregation and Econometric Models. *Int. Econ. Rev.*, February 1973, *14*(1), pp. 1–32.

Giles, D. E. A. A Note on Some Recent Developments in Large–Model Estimation. In *Deane, R. S., ed.*, 1972, pp. 89–92.

Giles, D. E. A. The Structural Stability of the Reserve Bank Model. In *Deane, R. S., ed.*, 1972, pp. 75–86.   [G: New Zealand]

Goreux, Louis M. The Problem of Interdependence. In *Goreux, L. M. and Manne, A. S., eds.*, 1973, pp. 35–54.   [G: Mexico]

Halabuk, L. Estimation and Structure of the Second Econometric Model of Hungary. *Matekon*, Summer 1973, *9*(4), pp. 43–66.   [G: Hungary]

Hickman, Bert G. A General Linear Model of World Trade. In *Ball, R. J., ed.*, 1973, pp. 21–43.

Hirsch, Albert A. The BEA Quarterly Model as a Forecasting Instrument. *Surv. Curr. Bus.*, August 1973, *53*(8), pp. 24–38, 52.   [G: U.S.]

Holden, Daina. The Institute's Short Term Forecasting Procedures. *Australian Econ. Rev.*, 2nd Quarter 1973, pp. 45–56.   [G: Australia]

Klein, Lawrence R. and Van Peeterssen, A. Forecasting World Trade within Project LINK. In *Ball, R. J., ed.*, 1973, pp. 429–63. [G: Japan; N. America; W. Europe]

Kornai, János. Thoughts on Multi-Level Planning Systems. In *Goreux, L. M. and Manne, A. S., eds.*, 1973, pp. 521–51.   [G: Mexico]

Kutcher, Gary P. On Decomposing Price-Endogenous Models. In *Goreux, L. M. and Manne, A. S., eds.*, 1973, pp. 499–519.   [G: Mexico]

Lerviks, Alf-Erik. Synpunkter på ekonomiskt modellbyggande. (On Model Construction in Economic Sciences. With English summary.) *Ekon. Samfundets Tidskr.*, 1973, *26*(4), pp. 301–04.

Lybeck, Johan A. The Monetary Sector of the Bank of Finland's Quarterly Model: A Critical Comment. *Ekon. Samfundets Tidskr.*, 1973, *26*(2), pp. 117–21.   [G: Finland]

Manne, Alan S. A Mixed Integer Algorithm for Project Evaluation. In *Goreux, L. M. and Manne, A. S., eds.*, 1973, pp. 477–97.   [G: Mexico]

Manne, Alan S. On Linking ENERGETICOS to DINAMICO. In *Goreux, L. M. and Manne, A. S., eds.*, 1973, pp. 277–89.   [G: Mexico]

Massetti, C. Les incertitudes quantitatives et qualitatives des prévisions du bilan et de l'approvisionnement énergétique européen: ses implications pour l'industrie pétrolière. (The Quantitative and Qualitative Uncertainties of Forecasting the European Energy Balance and Supply: Its Implications for the Mineral Oil Industry. With English summary.) *Schweiz. Z. Volkswirtsch. Statist.*, September 1973, *109*(3), pp. 411–20. [G: Europe]

McNees, Stephen K. The Predictive Accuracy of Econometric Forecasts. *New Eng. Econ. Rev.*, September-October 1973, pp. 3–27.

Meadows, Dennis L. Dynamic Systems Modelling. In *Hawkes, N., ed.*, 1973, pp. 60–77.

Meadows, Dennis L. The Dynamics of Global Equilibrium. In *Hawkes, N., ed.*, 1973, pp. 78–95.

Miller, Thomas A. Economic Adjustment Research for Policy Guidance: An Example from Agriculture. In *Judge, G. G. and Takayama, T., eds.*, 1973, pp. 65–88. [G: U.S.]

Montazer-Zohour, M. Generalization of Multiplier Theory. *Tahq. Eq.*, Winter & Spring 1973, *10*(29 & 30), pp. 106–45.

Moriguchi, C. Forecasting and Simulation Analysis of the World Economy. *Amer. Econ. Rev.*, May 1973, *63*(2), pp. 402–09.

Nordberg, Leif. Om möjligheterna att utnyttja data fran flera länder vid konstruktionen av ekonometriska modeller. (The Possibilities of Using Data from Several Countries in the Construction of Econometric Models. With English summary.) *Ekon. Samfundets Tidskr.*, 1973, *26*(2), pp. 105–16.

Pasternak, Hanoch and Passy, Ury. Bicriterion Functions in Annual Activity Planning. In *Ross, M., ed.*, 1973, pp. 325–41. [G: Israel]

Rhomberg, Rudolf R. Towards a General Trade Model. In *Ball, R. J., ed.*, 1973, pp. 9–20.

Ryvkin, A. A Conference on Problems of Long-Range Planning and Forecasting. *Prob. Econ.*, September 1973, *16*(5), pp. 31–40.

Schiesser, W. E. The Club of Rome Model. In *Weintraub, A.; Schwartz, E. and Aronson, J. R., eds.*, 1973, pp. 219–29.

Schloctern, F. J. M. Meyer Zu and Yajima, Akira. The OECD Trade Model 1970 Version. In *Alexandrides, C. G., ed.*, 1973, pp. 57–78.

Schwarze, Jochen. Probleme der Fehlermessung bei quantitativen ökonomischen Prognosen. (Problems of Measuring of Errors in Quantitative Economic Forecasting. With English summary.) *Z. ges. Staatswiss.*, August 1973, *129*(3), pp. 535–58.

Shapiro, Harold T. Is Verification Possible? The Evaluation of Large Econometric Models. *Amer. J. Agr. Econ.*, May 1973, *55*(2), pp. 250–58.

Sowey, Eric R. Stochastic Stimulation of Macroeconomic Models: Methodology and Interpretation. In *Powell, A. A. and Williams, R. A., eds.*, 1973, pp. 195–230. [G: U.S.]

Sprenger, Rolf-Ulrich. Zur Problematik der Treffsicherheit von langfristigen Verkehrsvorausschätzungen—Methodische Ansätze ter Treffsicherheitsanalyse und ihr Aussagewert für die prognostische Praxis. (Notes on Testing the Accuracy of Long-Term Traffic Forecasts. With English summary.) *Ifo-Studien*, January 1973, *19*(1/2), pp.

17–57. [G: W. Germany]

Šujan, Ivan and Tkáč, Miloslav. The Econometric Forecasting Model of Czechoslovakia. *Econ. Planning*, 1973, *13*(1–2), pp. 15–31. [G: Czechoslovakia]

Thompson, Russell G. and Young, H. Peyton. Forecasting Water Use for Policy Making: A Review. *Water Resources Res.*, August 1973, *9*(4), pp. 792–99.

Waelbroeck, J. The Methodology of Linkage. In *Ball, R. J., ed.*, 1973, pp. 45–61.

Young, H. Peyton and Thompson, Russell G. Forecasting Water Use for Electric Power Generation. *Water Resources Res.*, August 1973, *9*(4), pp. 800–07.

133 General Outlook and Stabilization Theories and Policies

1330 General Outlook

Arndt, H. W. Inflation: New Policy Prescriptions. *Australian Econ. Rev.*, 3rd Quarter 1973, pp. 41–48.

Arndt, H. W. Survey of Recent Developments. *Bull. Indonesian Econ. Stud.*, July 1973, *9*(2), pp. 1–27. [G: Indonesia]

Barber, Clarence L. Presidential Address: A Sense of Proportion. *Can. J. Econ.*, November 1973, *6*(4), pp. 467–82.

Boulding, Kenneth E. America's Economy: The Qualified Uproarious Success. In *Boulding, K. E.*, 1973, pp. 361–81. [G: U.S.]

Bowsher, Norman N. 1973—A Year of Inflation. *Fed. Res. Bank St. Louis Rev.*, December 1973, *55*(12), pp. 2–11. [G: U.S.]

Brady, Eugene A., et al. The Outlook: A Reevaluation of the Forecast for 1973. *Indiana Bus. Rev.*, May-June 1973, *48*, pp. 1–9. [G: U.S.]

Burns, Arthur F. Statement to Congress. *Fed. Res. Bull.*, March 1973, *59*(3), pp. 164–68.

Burns, Arthur F. Statement to Congress. *Fed. Res. Bull.*, August 1973, *59*(8), pp. 567–73. [G: U.S.]

Cacy, J. A. and Miller, Glenn H., Jr. Business and Financial Outlook—A Promising 1973. *Fed. Res. Bank Kansas City Rev.*, January 1973, pp. 11–20. [G: U.S.]

Cacy, J. A. and Stahl, Sheldon W. For 1974—An Uncertain Outlook. *Fed. Res. Bank Kansas City Rev.*, December 1973, pp. 3–11. [G: U.S.]

Cagan, Phillip. Controls and Monetary Policy, 1969–1973. In *Cagan, P., et al.*, 1973, pp. 1–34. [G: U.S.]

Carli, Guido. Crisi monetaria internazionale e politica di ripresa economica-I. (Policies Designed to Overcome the International Monetary Crisis and to Support the Economic Recovery in Italy-I. With English summary.) *Bancaria*, May 1973, *29*(5), pp. 543–62. [G: Italy]

Christ, Carl F. The 1973 Report of the President's Council of Economic Advisers: A Review. *Amer. Econ. Rev.*, September 1973, *63*(4), pp. 515–26. [G: U.S.]

Danciu, Constantin and Mănescu, Gheorghe. Istoria contemporană a României şi reprezentarea viitorului. (The Contemporary History of Romania and the Representation of the Future. With English summary.) *Stud. Cercet. Econ.,* 1973, (3), pp. 5–18. [G: Rumania]

Darnell, Jerome C. Relaxed Controls: A Bigger Year for Corporate Treasurers in '73? *Fed. Res. Bank Bus. Rev. Phila.,* February 1973, pp. 3–11. [G: U.S.]

English, M. D. Macro-Economic Policy: Canada. In *Perkins, J. O. N., ed.,* 1973, pp. 57–93. [G: Canada]

Escobedo, Gilberto. The Response of the Mexican Economy to Policy Actions. *Fed. Res. Bank St. Louis Rev.,* June 1973, *55*(6), pp. 15–23. [G: Mexico]

Fellner, William J. Employment Goals and Monetary-Fiscal Overexpansion. In *Cagan, P., et al.,* 1973, pp. 135–72. [G: U.S.]

Francis, Darryl R. The Problem of Re-Entry to a High-Employment Economy: An Address. *Fed. Res. Bank St. Louis Rev.,* June 1973, *55*(6), pp. 11–14. [G: U.S.]

Francis, Darryl R. Economic Issues in 1974. *Fed. Res. Bank St. Louis Rev.,* October 1973, *55*(10), pp. 14–19. [G: U.S.]

Freeman, S. David. Is There an Energy Crisis? An Overview. *Ann. Amer. Acad. Polit. Soc. Sci.,* November 1973, *410*, pp. 1–10. [G: U.S.]

Gasparini, Innocenzo. Prospettive e problemi dell-'economia giapponese. (Prospects and Problems of Japanese Economy. With English summary.) *Rivista Int. Sci. Econ. Com.,* August-September 1973, *20*(8–9), pp. 730–37. [G: Japan]

Gibson, Norman. Economic Conditions and Policy in Northern Ireland. *Econ. Soc. Rev.,* April 1973, *4* (3), pp. 349–64. [G: U.K.]

Greenwald, Carol S. A New Deflated Composite Index of Leading Indicators. *New Eng. Econ. Rev.,* July-August 1973, pp. 3–18. [G: U.S.]

Gregory, Gene. Japan Enters the Technetronic Age. *Econ. Rec.,* March 1973, *49*(125), pp. 1–14. [G: Japan]

Grenville, Stephen. Survey of Recent Developments. *Bull. Indonesian Econ. Stud.,* March 1973, *9*(1), pp. 1–29. [G: Indonesia]

Hadjimichalakis, Michael G. On the Effectiveness of Monetary Policy as a Stabilization Device. *Rev. Econ. Stud.,* October 1973, *40*(4), pp. 561–70.

Harshbarger, C. Edward. A Look at 1973: Agriculture Has a Tough Act to Follow. *Fed. Res. Bank Kansas City Rev.,* January 1973, pp. 3–10. [G: U.S.]

Henning, John A. and Sufrin, Sidney C. Japan: Steady State or Explosion. *Rivista Int. Sci. Econ. Com.,* August-September 1973, *20*(8–9), pp. 786–93. [G: Japan]

Holbik, Karel. The Tasks and Problems of Marxism in Chile's Economy. *Z. ges. Staatswiss.,* May 1973, *129*(2), pp. 333–46. [G: Chile]

Johnston, Verle; Levy, Yvonne and Chen, Dean. Boom in the West. *Fed. Res. Bank San Francisco Rev.,* May-June 1973, pp. 3–8. [G: U.S.]

Katona, George. Cognitive Processes in Learning: Reactions to Inflation and Change in Taxes. In *Mandell, L., et al., eds.,* 1973, pp. 183–203. [G: U.S.]

Lachmann, L. M. The Budget and Inflation. *S. Afr.*

J. Econ., June 1973, *41*(2), pp. 146–49. [G: S. Africa]

Levy, Michael E. Major Economic Issues of the 1970's. In *Levy, M. E., ed.,* 1973, pp. 1–5. [G: U.S.]

Lewis, John P. Wanted in India: A Relevant Radicalism. In *Wadhva, C. D., ed.,* 1973, pp. 216–32. [G: India]

Liu, Ta-Chung and Yeh, Kung-Chia. Chinese and Other Asian Economies: A Quantitative Evaluation. *Amer. Econ. Rev.,* May 1973, *63*(2), pp. 215–23. [G: China]

McCawley, Peter. Survey of Recent Developments. *Bull. Indonesian Econ. Stud.,* November 1973, *9* (3), pp. 1–27. [G: Indonesia]

McLure, Charles E., Jr. Gradualism and the New Economic Policy: Fiscal Economics in Transition. In *Cagan, P., et al.,* 1973, pp. 35–77. [G: U.S.]

Meiselman, David I. The 1973 Report of the President's Council of Economic Advisers: Whistling in the Dark. *Amer. Econ. Rev.,* September 1973, *63*(4), pp. 527–34. [G: U.S.]

Myrdal, Gunnar. The Future of India. In *Myrdal, G.,* 1973, pp. 245–65. [G: India]

Nieuwenhuysen, J. P. Macro-Economic Policy: South Africa. In *Perkins, J. O. N., ed.,* 1973, pp. 130–76. [G: S. Africa]

Niskanen, William and Berry, Robert. The 1973 Economic Report of the President. *J. Money, Credit, Banking,* May 1973, *5*(2), pp. 693–703. [G: U.S.]

Owen, John E. The US Economy—Prosperity and Problems. *Rivista Int. Sci. Econ. Com.,* October 1973, *20*(10), pp. 973–84. [G: U.S.]

Paish, F. W. The Prospects for Increasing Output. *Lloyds Bank Rev.,* January 1973, (107), pp. 1–18. [G: U.K.]

Parkin, Michael. The 1973 Report of the President's Council of Economic Advisers: A Critique. *Amer. Econ. Rev.,* September 1973, *63*(4), pp. 535–45. [G: U.S.]

Perkins, J. O. N. and Nieuwenhuysen, J. P. Macro-Economic Policy: Australia. In *Perkins, J. O. N., ed.,* 1973, pp. 17–56. [G: Australia]

Perkins, J. O. N. and Nieuwenhuysen, J. P. Macro-Economic Policies in the Four Countries. In *Perkins, J. O. N., ed.,* 1973, pp. 177–208. [G: Australia; New Zealand; Canada; S. Africa]

Ratajczak, Donald and Williams, Robert M. Forecast. Another Year of Prosperity for 1973. *Calif. Manage. Rev.,* Spring 1973, *15*(3), pp. i–v. [G: U.S.]

Richards, Vincent A. E. Development Prospects in the Commonwealth Caribbean in the 1970s. In *Pollock, D. H. and Ritter, A. R. M., eds.,* 1973, pp. 269–86. [G: Caribbean]

Robertson, Ross M., et al. The Uncertain Outlook for 1974. *Indiana Bus. Rev.,* November-December 1973, *48*, pp. 3–15. [G: U.S.]

Rowe, J. W. Macro-Economic Policy: New Zealand. In *Perkins, J. O. N., ed.,* 1973, pp. 94–129. [G: New Zealand]

Saulnier, Raymond J. Is a Tax Increase Inevitable? In *Tax Foundation, Inc.,* 1973, pp. 6–9. [G: U.S.]

Schnittker, John A. The 1972–73 Food Price Spiral.

Brookings Pap. Econ. Act., 1973, (2), pp. 498–507. [G: U.S.]

Schweiger, Irving. 1973 Forecast of Gross National Product, Consumer Spending, Saving, and Housing. *J. Bus.,* January 1973, *46*(1), pp. 6–10. [G: U.S.]

Smith, Curtis R. Despite Damage by Agnes...District Economy Forges Ahead in '72. *Fed. Res. Bank Bus. Rev. Phila.,* February 1973, pp. 12–18. [G: U.S.]

Soloveytchik, George. Nordic Uncertainties and Realities. *Nat. Westminster Bank Quart. Rev.,* May 1973, pp. 31–45. [G: Norway; Sweden; Iceland; Denmark; Finland]

Spencer, Roger W. Strong Credit Demands, But No "Crunch" in Early 1973. *Fed. Res. Bank St. Louis Rev.,* June 1973, *55*(6), pp. 2–10. [G: U.S.]

Spencer, Roger W. Business Recovery Continues. *Fed. Res. Bank St. Louis Rev.,* February 1973, *55* (2), pp. 2–7. [G: U.S.]

Sprinkel, Beryl W. Continued Expansion in 1973 amid Growing Prosperity. *J. Bus.,* January 1973, *46*(1), pp. 1–5. [G: U.S.]

Timár, M. Results of the New System of Economic Control and Management and its Further Development. *Acta Oecon.,* 1973, *10*(3–4), pp. 277–301. [G: Hungary]

Ulmer, Melville J. The Non-Answer to Nixonomics. In *Reynolds, L. G.; Green, G. D. and Lewis, D. R., eds.,* 1973, pp. 81–86. [G: U.S.]

Voet, James R. Current Economic Developments in New Mexico: Business Conditions Monthly Summary and Economic Indicators. *N. Mex. Bus.,* June 1973, *26*(6), pp. 17, 26–27. [G: U.S.]

Vuskovic, Pedro. The Economic Policy of the Popular Unity Government. In *Zammit, J. A., ed.,* 1973, pp. 49–56. [G: Chile]

Weintraub, Sidney. Introduction: Perspectives on Money Wages. In *Weintraub, S., et al.,* 1973, pp. 3–16. [G: U.S.]

Welch, Wilford. The Business Outlook for Southeast Asia. *Harvard Bus. Rev.,* May-June 1973, *51*(3), pp. 72–84. [G: S.E. Asia]

Woodward, John T. Capital Spending Expected to Rise Through First Half of 1974. *Surv. Curr. Bus.,* December 1973, *53*(12), pp. 9–13. [G: U.S.]

1331 Stabilization Theories and Policies

Andersen, Leonall C. A Comparison of Stabilization Policies: 1966–67 and 1969–70. *J. Money, Credit, Banking,* Part I, February 1973, *5*(1), pp. 26–38. [G: U.S.]

Andersen, Leonall C. The State of the Monetarist Debate. *Fed. Res. Bank St. Louis Rev.,* September 1973, *55*(9), pp. 2–8. [G: U.S.]

Andersen, Palle Schelde. Automatic Stabilization in Static and Dynamic Models. *Nationalokon. Tidsskr.,* 1973, *111*(1), pp. 60–85.

Aoki, Masanao. On Sufficient Conditions for Optimal Stabilization Policies. *Rev. Econ. Stud.,* January 1973, *40*(1), pp. 131–38.

Arndt, H. W. Inflation: New Policy Prescriptions. *Australian Econ. Rev.,* 3rd Quarter 1973, pp. 41–48.

Arndt, Sven W. Policy Choices in an Open Economy: Some Dynamic Considerations. *J. Polit. Econ.,* July-August 1973, *81*(4), pp. 916–35.

Balles, John J. Evaluating Money Market Conditions. *Fed. Res. Bank San Francisco Rev.,* September-October 1973, pp. 3–11. [G: U.S.]

Biehl, Dieter, et al. Measuring the Demand Effects of Fiscal Policy. In *Giersch, H., ed.,* 1973, pp. 223–41. [G: W. Germany]

Biehl, Dieter, et al. On the Cyclical Effects of Budgetary Policy from 1960 to 1970 in the Federal Republic of Germany. *Ger. Econ. Rev.,* 1973, *11* (4), pp. 273–91. [G: W. Germany]

Blackaby, F. T. Incomes and Inflation. In *Robinson, J., ed.,* 1973, pp. 55–70.

Blinder, Alan S. and Solow, Robert M. Does Fiscal Policy Matter? *J. Public Econ.,* November 1973, *2*(4), pp. 319–37.

Bosworth, Barry. The Current Inflation: Malign Neglect? *Brookings Pap. Econ. Act.,* 1973, (1), pp. 263–83. [G: U.S.]

Boulding, Kenneth E. Can We Control Inflation in a Garrison State? In *Boulding, K. E.,* 1973, pp. 1–24.

Brandow, G. E. A Discussion of the 1973 Economic Report of the President: The Food Price Problem. *Amer. J. Agr. Econ.,* August 1973, *55*(3), pp. 385–90. [G: U.S.]

Branson, William H. The Use of Variable Tax Rates for Stabilization Purposes. In *Musgrave, R. A., ed.,* 1973, pp. 267–85. [G: U.S.]

Brehmer, Ekhard and Bradford, Maxwell R. Incomes and Labor Market Policies in Sweden. *Finance Develop.,* September 1973, *10*(3), pp. 21–23, 35. [G: Sweden]

Brito, Dagobert L. Estimation, Prediction and Economic Control. *Int. Econ. Rev.,* October 1973, *14* (3), pp. 646–52.

Britto, Ronald and Heller, H. Robert. International Adjustment and Optimal Reserves. *Int. Econ. Rev.,* February 1973, *14*(1), pp. 182–95.

Brunner, Karl. The State of the Monetarist Debate: A Comment. *Fed. Res. Bank St. Louis Rev.,* September 1973, *55*(9), pp. 9, 12–14.

Burchardt, Michael. Die Koordination von Geld- und Fiskalpolitik bei festen Wechselkursen. (The Coordination of Monetary and Fiscal Policies under Fixed Exchange Rates. With English summary.) *Z. Wirtschaft. Sozialwissen.,* 1973, *93*(4), pp. 423–43.

Burke, William. Higher Payout? *Fed. Res. Bank San Francisco Rev.,* July-August 1973, pp. 3–7. [G: U.S.]

Burns, Arthur F. Statement to Congress. *Fed. Res. Bull.,* February 1973, *59*(2), pp. 81–85. [G: U.S.]

Burns, Arthur F. Statements to Congress. *Fed. Res. Bull.,* April 1973, *59*(4), pp. 280–85. [G: U.S.]

Carlson, Keith M. The 1973 National Economic Plan: Slowing the Boom. *Fed. Res. Bank St. Louis Rev.,* March 1973, *55*(3), pp. 2–9. [G: U.S.]

Cauas, Jorge. Short-Term Economic Policy. In *[Rosenstein-Rodan, P.],* 1973, pp. 118–30. [G: Chile]

Chiancone, Aldo. Il sistema svedese dei fondi di riserva per gli investimenti come strumento di stabilizzazione economica. (The Swedish System of Investment Funds as an Instrument of Stabilization Policy. With English summary.) *Rivista Int. Sci. Econ. Com.*, March 1973, *20*(3), pp. 242–66. [G: Sweden]

Chow, Gregory C. Effect of Uncertainty on Optimal Control Policies. *Int. Econ. Rev.*, October 1973, *14*(3), pp. 632–45.

Chow, Gregory C. Problems of Economic Policy from the Viewpoint of Optimal Control. *Amer. Econ. Rev.*, December 1973, *63*(5), pp. 825–37.

Davidson, Paul and Weintraub, Sidney. Money as Cause and Effect. *Econ. J.*, December 1973, *83* (332), pp. 1117–32.

Dieterlen, Pierre and Durand, Huguette. Monetary Policy in France. In *Holbik, K., ed.,* 1973, pp. 117–60. [G: France]

Duggar, Jan W. and Beard, Thomas R. The Concept and Measurement of Defensive Open Market Operations. *Miss. Val. J. Bus. Econ.*, Spring 1973, *8*(3), pp. 29–38. [G: U.S.]

den Dunnen, Emile. Monetary Policy in the Netherlands. In *Holbik, K., ed.,* 1973, pp. 282–328. [G: Netherlands]

Eastburn, David P. Monetary Policy In a "New" Economy. *Fed. Res. Bank Bus. Rev. Phila.*, October 1973, pp. 3–6. [G: U.S.]

Eckel, Dieter. Probleme der Erfolgsmessung der Wirtschaftspolitik. (Problems of Evaluation of Macro-Economic-Policy. With English summary.) *Z. ges. Staatswiss.*, May 1973, *129*(2), pp. 375–84.

Eckstein, Otto. Instability in the Private and Public Sectors. *Swedish J. Econ.*, March 1973, *75*(1), pp. 19–26. [G: U.S.]

Escobedo, Gilberto. The Response of the Mexican Economy to Policy Actions. *Fed. Res. Bank St. Louis Rev.*, June 1973, *55*(6), pp. 15–23. [G: Mexico]

Fabricant, Solomon. The Perennial Problem of Economic Stability. *Amer. Econ.*, Fall 1973, *17*(2), pp. 85–89. [G: U.S.]

Ferrari, Alberto. Monetary Policy in Italy. In *Holbik, K., ed.,* 1973, pp. 214–45. [G: Italy]

Fischer, Stanley and Cooper, J. Phillip. Stabilization Policy and Lags. *J. Polit. Econ.*, July-August 1973, *81*(4), pp. 847–77.

Fishlow, Albert. Some Reflections on Post-1964 Brazilian Economic Policy. In *Stepan, A., ed.,* 1973, pp. 69–118. [G: Brazil]

Francis, Darryl R. The Usefulness of Applied Econometrics to the Policymaker: An Address. *Fed. Res. Bank St. Louis Rev.*, May 1973, *55*(5), pp. 7–10.

Francis, Darryl R. The Problem of Re-Entry to a High-Employment Economy: An Address. *Fed. Res. Bank St. Louis Rev.*, June 1973, *55*(6), pp. 11–14. [G: U.S.]

Friedlaender, Ann F. Macro Policy Goals in the Postwar Period: A Study in Revealed Preference. *Quart. J. Econ.*, February 1973, *87*(1), pp. 25–43. [G: U.S.]

von Furstenberg, George M. and Boughton, James M. Stabilization Goals and the Appropriateness of Fiscal Policy during the Eisenhower and Kennedy-Johnson Administrations. *Public Finance Quart.*, January 1973, *1*(1), pp. 5–28. [G: U.S.]

Galbraith, John Kenneth. Controls or Competition—

What's at Issue? Comment. *Rev. Econ. Statist.*, November 1973, *55*(4), pp. 524.

Galper, Harvey and Wendel, Helmut F. Time Lags in the Federal Expenditure Process and their Stabilization Implications. *Public Finance Quart.*, April 1973, *1*(2), pp. 123–46. [G: U.S.]

Giersch, Herbert. Some Neglected Aspects of Inflation in the World Economy. *Public Finance*, 1973, *28*(2), pp. 105–24.

Giersch, Herbert. On the Desirable Degree of Flexibility of Exchange Rates. *Weltwirtsch. Arch.*, 1973, *109*(2), pp. 191–213.

Gilbert, Ronald D. Okun's Law: Some Additional Evidence. *Nebr. J. Econ. Bus.*, Winter 1973, *12*(1), pp. 51–60. [G: U.S.]

Gordon, Robert J. The Welfare Cost of Higher Unemployment. *Brookings Pap. Econ. Act.*, 1973, (1), pp. 133–95. [G: U.S.]

Granger, C. W. J. On the Properties of Forecasts Used in Optimal Economic Policy Decisions. *J. Public Econ.*, November 1973, *2*(4), pp. 347–56.

Grünärml, Frohmund. Demand Management—Illusion oder Realität? (Demand Management—Illusion or Reality? With English summary.) *Z. Wirtschaft. Sozialwissen.*, 1973, *93*(5), pp. 537–66.

Hagger, A. J. and Rayner, P. J. The Excess Demand for Commodities in Australia, 1950–51 to 1968–69. *Econ. Rec.*, June 1973, *49*(126), pp. 161–93. [G: Australia]

Hansen, Bent. On the Effects of Fiscal and Monetary Policy: A Taxonomic Discussion. *Amer. Econ. Rev.*, September 1973, *63*(4), pp. 546–71. [G: U.S.]

Harshbarger, C. Edward and Doll, Raymond J. Farm Prices and Food Prices: The Relevant Issues. *Fed. Res. Bank Kansas City Rev.*, May 1973, pp. 3–10. [G: U.S.]

Havrilesky, Thomas M. Alternative Monetary Control Responses in a Stochastic Macro Model. *Quart. Rev. Econ. Bus.*, Spring 1973, *13*(1), pp. 37–48.

Haythorne, George V. Prices and Incomes Policy: The Canadian Experience, 1969–1972. *Int. Lab. Rev.*, December 1973, *108*(6), pp. 485–503. [G: Canada]

Hicks, John R. [Sir] and Hicks, Ursula K. [Lady]. British Fiscal Policy. In *Giersch, H., ed.,* 1973, pp. 142–54. [G: U.K.]

Houck, James P. Some Aspects of Income Stabilization for Primary Producers. *Australian J. Agr. Econ.*, December 1973, *17*(3), pp. 200–15. [G: Australia]

Isaac, J. E. Incomes Policy: Unnecessary? Undesirable? Impracticable? *Australian Econ. Rev.*, 1st Quarter 1973, pp. 41–50. [G: Australia]

Isard, Peter. The Effectiveness of Using the Tax System to Curb Inflationary Collective Bargains: An Analysis of the Wallich-Weintraub Plan. *J. Polit. Econ.*, May-June 1973, *81*(3), pp. 729–40. [G: U.S.]

Johnson, Stanley R. and Smith, Paul E. The Phillips Curve, Expectations, and Stability. *Quart. Rev. Econ. Bus.*, Autumn 1973, *13*(3), pp. 85–91.

Kaliski, S. F. and Smith, D. C. Inflation, Unemployment and Incomes Policy. *Can. J. Econ.*, November 1973, *6*(4), pp. 574–91. [G: Canada]

Kane, Edward J. Simulations of Stabilization Policies for 1966–1970 *and* A Comparison of Stabilization Policies: 1966–67 and 1969–70: Comment. *J. Money, Credit, Banking*, Part I, February 1973, *5*(1), pp. 39–42. [G: U.S.]

Kennedy, M. C. Employment Policy: What Went Wrong? In *Robinson, J., ed.*, 1973, pp. 71–87. [G: U.K.]

Kirschen, Etienne S. BENELUX Experience with Public Finance Instruments for Achieving the Objectives of Full Employment and Expansion. In *Giersch, H., ed.*, 1973, pp. 155–69. [G: Belgium; Netherlands]

Klein, Lawrence R. The State of the Monetarist Debate: A Comment. *Fed. Res. Bank St. Louis Rev.*, September 1973, *55*(9), pp. 9–12.

Kmenta, J. and Smith, Paul E. Autonomous Expenditures Versus Money Supply: An Application of Dynamic Multipliers. *Rev. Econ. Statist.*, August 1973, *55*(3), pp. 299–307. [G: U.S.]

Krainer, Robert E. Economic Structure and the Assignment Problem: A Contribution to the Theory of Macro-Economic Policy for Net Creditor Countries. *Can. J. Econ.*, May 1973, *6*(2), pp. 239–47.

Laidler, David. Monetarist Policy Prescriptions and Their Background. *Manchester Sch. Econ. Soc. Stud.*, March 1973, *41*(1), pp. 59–71. [G: U.K.]

La Malfa, Ugo. Contenimento della spesa pubblica e lotta all'inflazione per una solida linea di stabilità. (Containment of Public Expenditure and Fight Against Inflation for Stability. With Engish summary.) *Bancaria*, November 1973, *29* (11), pp. 1342–45. [G: Italy]

Lerner, Abba P. The Challenge of Full Employment with Price Stability: "Incomes Policies." In *Levy, M. E., ed.*, 1973, pp. 14–22. [G: U.S.]

Lewis, Wilfred, Jr. Economic Policy and Inflation in the 1960's—a Review Essay. *Mon. Lab. Rev.*, November 1973, *96*(11), pp. 49–52. [G: U.S.]

Lindauer, John. Stabilization Inflation and the Inflation-Unemployment Trade-off. *Indian Econ. J.*, April-June 1973, *20*(4–5), pp. 541–47.

Madden, Carl H. Controls or Competition—What's at Issue? Reply. *Rev. Econ. Statist.*, November 1973, *55*(4), pp. 524–25.

Maital, Shlomo. Targets, Tradeoffs, and Economic Policy: A Generalized Phillips Curve. *Public Finance Quart.*, January 1973, *1*(1), pp. 67–83.

Matthiessen, Lars. Recent Experience with Fiscal Policy in Sweden. In *Giersch, H., ed.*, 1973, pp. 170–87. [G: Sweden]

McCracken, Paul W. Domestic Economic Policy and Convertibility. *Amer. Econ. Rev.*, May 1973, *63* (2), pp. 199–205.

McCracken, Paul W. The Practice of Political Economy. *Amer. Econ. Rev.*, May 1973, *63*(2), pp. 168–71. [G: U.S.]

Meidner, Rudolf and Andersson, Rolf. The Overall Impact of an Active Labor Market Policy in Sweden. In *Ulman, L., ed.*, 1973, pp. 117–58. [G: Sweden]

Meiselman, David I. Simulations of Stabilization Policies for 1966–1970 *and* A Comparison of Stabilization Policies: 1966–67 and 1969–70: Com-

ment. *J. Money, Credit, Banking*, Part I, February 1973, *5*(1), pp. 43–46. [G: U.S.]

Miller, Ervin. The Pains of Monetary Restraint. *Lloyds Bank Rev.*, July 1973, (109), pp. 36–51. [G: U.S.; U.K.]

Monissen, Hans G. Preise, Löhne und Beschäftigung in dynamischer Betrachtung: Eine einfache Exposition. (Prices, Wages and Employment in Dynamic Perspective: A Simple Exposition. With English summary.) *Kyklos*, 1973, *26*(3), pp. 545–58.

Motley, Brian. Sales versus Income Taxes: A Pedagogic Note. *Oxford Econ. Pap.*, July 1973, *25*(2), pp. 204–12.

Neumann, Manfred J. M. The 1972 Report of the German Council of Economic Experts: Inflation and Stabilization: Review Essay. *J. Money, Credit, Banking*, November 1973, *5*(4), pp. 950–59. [G: W. Germany]

Okun, Arthur M. General Economic Conditions and National Elections: Comment. *Amer. Econ. Rev.*, May 1973, *63*(2), pp. 172–77. [G: U.S.]

Okun, Arthur M. Rules and Roles for Fiscal and Monetary Policy. In *Reynolds, L. G.; Green, G. D. and Lewis, D. R., eds.*, 1973, pp. 62–80. [G: U.S.]

Okun, Arthur M. Upward Mobility in a High-pressure Economy. *Brookings Pap. Econ. Act.*, 1973, (1), pp. 207–52. [G: U.S.]

Park, Yung C. The Role of Money in Stabilization Policy in Developing Countries. *Int. Monet. Fund Staff Pap.*, July 1973, *20*(2), pp. 379–418.

Park, Yung C. The Transmission Process and the Relative Effectiveness of Monetary and Fiscal Policy in a Two-Sector Neoclassical Model. *J. Money, Credit, Banking*, May 1973, *5*(2), pp. 595–622.

Pedersen, Peder J. Har finanspolitikken mistet sin effektivitet? (With English summary.) *Nationaløkon. Tidsskr.*, 1973, *111*(3), pp. 327–41. [G: Denmark]

Pettersen, Oystein. Stochastic Properties of Cumulative Feedback in a Simple Model. *Swedish J. Econ.*, September 1973, *75*(3), pp. 296–301.

Phelps Brown, E. H. How Phase II Worked in the United States. *Lloyds Bank Rev.*, July 1973, (109), pp. 1–16. [G: U.S.]

Phelps, Edmund S. Optimal Stabilization Paths: Comment. *J. Money, Credit, Banking*, Part II, February 1973, *5*(1), pp. 563–65.

Pindyck, Robert S. Optimal Policies for Economic Stabilization. *Econometrica*, May 1973, *41*(3), pp. 529–60.

Popkin, Joel. Prices in 1972: An Analysis of Changes During Phase 2. *Mon. Lab. Rev.*, February 1973, *96*(2), pp. 16–23. [G: U.S.]

Prachowny, Martin F. J. The Effectiveness of Stabilization Policy in a Small Open Economy. *Weltwirtsch. Arch.*, 1973, *109*(2), pp. 214–31.

Rasche, Robert H. Simulations of Stabilization Policies for 1966–1970. *J. Money, Credit, Banking*, Part I, February 1973, *5*(1), pp. 1–25. [G: U.S.]

Rasminsky, Louis. Canadian Monetary Policy and the Problem of Inflation. In *Moskoff, W., ed.*, 1973, pp. 56–62. [G: Canada]

Richter, Rudolf. Full Employment and Stable

Prices—Compatibility of Targets and Rules. *Ger. Econ. Rev.*, 1973, *11*(2), pp. 108–20.

Rose, Hugh. Optimal Stabilization Paths: Comment. *J. Money, Credit, Banking*, Part II, February 1973, *5*(1), pp. 566–67.

Ruggeri, Giuseppe C. Automatic Stabilizers, Business Cycles, and Economic Growth. *Kyklos*, 1973, *26*(2), pp. 288–306. [G: U.S.]

Rürup, Bert. Handlungsverzögerungen diskretionärer Fiskalpolitik: Konstruktionsfehler oder Element rationaler Politik? (Decision Lags of Discretionary Fiscal Policy: Defects of Construction or Element of a Rational Policy. With English summary.) *Z. Wirtschaft. Sozialwissen.*, 1973, *93* (1), pp. 35–50.

Salant, Walter S. Some Intellectual Contributions of the Truman Council of Economic Advisers to Policy-Making. *Hist. Polit. Econ.*, Spring 1973, *5* (1), pp. 36–49.

Scarth, William M. The Effects on Stabilization Policy of Several Monetary Reform Proposals. *J. Econ. Bus.*, Spring-Summer 1973, *25*(3), pp. 154–58.

Scarth, William M. The Financing of Stabilization Policies: Evidence for the Canadian Economy. *Can. J. Econ.*, August 1973, *6*(3), pp. 301–18. [G: Canada]

Schiff, Frank W. Alternative Tax and Spending Policies, 1971–1976. In *Giersch, H., ed.*, 1973, pp. 188–94. [G: U.S.]

Schlesinger, Helmut and Bockelmann, Horst. Monetary Policy in the Federal Republic of Germany. In *Holbik, K., ed.*, 1973, pp. 161–213. [G: W. Germany]

Schüler, Manfred. Fiscal Policy in Recession: The German Experience. In *Giersch, H., ed.*, 1973, pp. 195–202. [G: W. Germany]

Selowsky, Marcelo. Cost of Price Stabilization in a Strongly Inflationary Economy. *Quart. J. Econ.*, February 1973, *87*(1), pp. 44–59. [G: Chile]

Snowbarger, Marvin and Kirk, John. A Cross-Sectional Model of Built-In Flexibility, 1954–1969. *Nat. Tax J.*, June 1973, *26*(2), pp. 241–49. [G: U.S.]

Snyder, Wayne W. Are the Budgets of State and Local Governments Destabilizing? A Six Country Comparison. *Europ. Econ. Rev.*, June 1973, *4*(2), pp. 197–213.

Solow, Robert M. What Happened to Full Employment? *Quart. Rev. Econ. Bus.*, Summer 1973, *13* (2), pp. 7–20. [G: U.S.]

Spencer, Roger W. The National Plans to Curb Unemployment and Inflation. *Fed. Res. Bank St. Louis Rev.*, April 1973, *55*(4), pp. 2–13. [G: U.S.]

Spitäller, Erich. Incomes Policy in Austria. *Int. Monet. Fund Staff Pap.*, March 1973, *20*(1), pp. 170–202. [G: Austria]

Stammati, Gaetano. Italian Experience with Fiscal Policy. In *Giersch, H., ed.*, 1973, pp. 203–09. [G: Italy]

Stein, Jerome L. and Infante, Ettore F. Optimal Stabilization Paths. *J. Money, Credit, Banking*, Part II, February 1973, *5*(1), pp. 525–62.

Stigler, George J. General Economic Conditions and National Elections. *Amer. Econ. Rev.*, May 1973,

63(2), pp. 160–67. [G: U.S.]

Sumner, M. T. Investment and Corporate Taxation. *J. Polit. Econ.*, July-August 1973, *81*(4), pp. 982–93. [G: U.K.]

Turnovsky, Stephen J. Optimal Stabilization Policies for Deterministic and Stochastic Linear Economic Systems. *Rev. Econ. Stud.*, January 1973, *40*(1), pp. 79–95.

Ulman, Lloyd. Introduction: The Problems in Policy Context. In *Ulman, L., ed.*, 1973, pp. 1–13. [G: U.S.; Sweden]

Van Lam, Ngo. The Pursuit of Growth and Stability Through Taxation of Agricultural Exports: Thailand's Experience: A Comment. *Public Finance*, 1973, *28*(2), pp. 227–32. [G: Thailand]

Van Roy, Edward. Ngo Van Lam on the Rice Premium: A Rejoinder. *Public Finance*, 1973, *28* (2), pp. 233–36.

Wagner, Antonin. Die Auswirkung der öffentlichen Haushalte auf den Konjunkturverlauf in der Schweiz, 1955–1970. (The Effects of Public Finance on Trade Cycles in Switzerland, 1955–1970. With English summary.) *Schweiz. Z. Volkswirtsch. Statist.*, March 1973, *109*(1), pp. 17–57. [G: Switzerland]

Waud, Roger N. Index Bonds and Economic Stability. *Public Finance*, 1973, *28*(1), pp. 52–68.

Williams, William V., et al. The Stability, Growth and Stabilizing Influence of State Taxes. *Nat. Tax J.*, June 1973, *26*(2), pp. 267–74. [G: U.S.]

1332 Wage and Price Controls

Bourgoignie, Th. Overheid en bedrijfsleven/3 La réglementation des prix en Belgique. (Price Regulation in Belgium. With English summary.) *Econ. Soc. Tijdschr.*, August 1973, *27*(4), pp. 387–400. [G: Belgium]

Estey, Marten. Wage Stabilization Policy and the Nixon Administration. In *Cagan, P., et al.*, 1973, pp. 107–33. [G: U.S.]

Gordon, Robert J. The Response of Wages and Prices to the First Two Years of Controls. *Brookings Pap. Econ. Act.*, 1973, (3), pp. 765–78. [G: U.S.]

Grayson, C. Jackson, Jr. Let's Get Back to the Competitive Market System. *Harvard Bus. Rev.*, November-December 1973, *51*(6), pp. 103–12. [G: U.S.]

Grossman, Jonathan. Wage and Price Controls During the American Revolution. *Mon. Lab. Rev.*, September 1973, *96*(9), pp. 3–10. [G: U.S.]

Hempel, George H. Wage and Price Controls for State and Local Governments: Their Effectiveness and the Potential Effects of Phase III. *Public Policy*, Summer 1973, *21*(3), pp. 425–36. [G: U.S.]

Kymn, Kern O. A Note on Logical Inconsistencies of the Kennedy Wage-Price Guidelines. *Southern Econ. J.*, January 1973, *39*(3), pp. 434–36.

Mitchell, D. J. B. and Azevedo, R. A Pay Board Assessment of Wage Controls. *Mon. Lab. Rev.*, April 1973, *96*(4), pp. 21–23. [G: U.S.]

Mouly, Jean. Prices, Wages, Unemployment: Inflation in Contemporary Economic Theory. *Int. Lab. Rev.*, October 1973, *108*(4), pp. 329–43.

Nakayama, Toshiko. Second Quarter Price Pressures

Bring Freeze, Phase 4. *Mon. Lab. Rev.*, September 1973, *96*(9), pp. 69–73. [G: U.S.]

Pen, Jan. Trade Union Attitudes Toward Central Wage Policy: Remarks on the Dutch Experience. In *Sturmthal, A. and Scoville, J. G., eds.*, 1973, pp. 259–82. [G: Netherlands]

Poole, William. Wage-Price Controls: Where Do We Go from Here? *Brookings Pap. Econ. Act.*, 1973, (1), pp. 285–99. [G: U.S.]

Robinson, Derek. Industrial Relations Aspects of Incomes Policies. In *Robinson, D.*, 1973, pp. 42–75.

Robinson, Derek. Prices and Incomes Policies—Recent Developments in Some European Countries. In *Robinson, D.*, 1973, pp. 11–41. [G: Austria; Finland; Ireland; Netherlands]

Sheehan, P. J. The Real Income Guarantee: A Fiscal Policy to Control Inflation. *Australian Econ. Rev.*, 4th Quarter 1973, pp. 9–14. [G: Australia]

Shuptrine, F. Kelly. Upper-Middle Class and Working Class Opinions of the Wage/Price Freeze. *Marquette Bus. Rev.*, Winter 1973, *17*(4), pp. 182–87. [G: U.S.]

Sonne, A. Monopol-og priskontrol under en stabiliseringspolitik. (Monopoly and Price Control in a Stabilization Policy. With English summary.) *Nationalokon. Tidsskr.*, 1973, *111*(1), pp. 154–64. [G: Denmark]

Tantazzi, Angelo. Il controllo dei prezzi industriali. (The Control of Industrial Prices. With English summary.) *L'industria, N. S.*, 1973, (1), pp. 39–56. [G: Italy]

Taymans, A. L. The Use of Productivity Gains in the Price Control Program of the United States. *Econ. Soc. Tijdschr.*, April 1973, *27*(2), pp. 181–90. [G: U.S.]

Tullock, Gordon. Inflation and Unemployment: The Discussion Continued: Comment. *J. Money, Credit, Banking*, August 1973, *5*(3), pp. 826–35.

Väyrynen, Olavi. Priskontrollen i samhällspolitiken. (Price Control in Public Policy. With English summary.) *Ekon. Samfundets Tidskr.*, 1973, *26*(2), pp. 75–86.

134 Inflation and Deflation

1340 General

Alchian, Armen A. and Klein, Benjamin. On a Correct Measure of Inflation. *J. Money, Credit, Banking*, Part I, February 1973, *5*(1), pp. 173–91.

Balogh, T. and Balacs, P. Fact and Fancy in International Economic Relations. *World Devel.*, March-April 1973, *1*(3–4), pp. 71–105.

Boulding, Kenneth E. Can We Control Inflation in a Garrison State? In *Boulding, K. E.*, 1973, pp. 1–24.

Brinner, Roger. Inflation, Deferral and the Neutral Taxation of Capital Gains. *Nat. Tax J.*, December 1973, *26*(4), pp. 565–73. [G: U.S.]

Cagan, Phillip. Controls and Monetary Policy, 1969–1973. In *Cagan, P., et al.*, 1973, pp. 1–34. [G: U.S.]

Davis, Lance E. Secular Price Change in Historical Perspective: Comment. *J. Money, Credit, Banking*, Part II, February 1973, *5*(1), pp. 270–73.

Dell'Amore, Giordano. Attualità del risparmio e in-

segnamenti della storia della Cassa di Risparmio delle Provincie Lombarde. (The Present Need for Saving and the Lessons from the History of the Cassa di Risparmio delle Provincie Lombarde. With English summary.) *Bancaria*, November 1973, *29*(11), pp. 1329–37. [G: Italy]

Eichner, Alfred S. A Theory of the Determination of the Mark-up Under Oligopoly. *Econ. J.*, December 1973, *83*(332), pp. 1184–1200.

Gibson, William E. Interest Rates and Prices in the Long Run: A Study of the Gibson Paradox: Comment. *J. Money, Credit, Banking*, Part II, February 1973, *5*(1), pp. 450–53. [G: U.S.]

Gillion, C. Econometric Models and Current Economic Issues. In *Deane, R. S., ed.*, 1972, pp. 67–73. [G: New Zealand]

Gordon, Robert J. Interest Rates and Prices in the Long Run: A Study of the Gibson Paradox: Comment. *J. Money, Credit, Banking*, Part II, February 1973, *5*(1), pp. 460–63. [G: U.S.]

Haberler, Gottfried. International Aspects of U.S. Inflation. In *Cagan, P., et al.*, 1973, pp. 79–105. [G: U.S.]

Hamdani, Daood H. Fiscal Measures Against Inflation and Unemployment in Canada: 1973 Budget and Other Developments. *Bull. Int. Fiscal Doc.*, June 1973, *27*(6), pp. 223–40. [G: Canada]

Haythorne, George V. Prices and Incomes Policy: The Canadian Experience, 1969–1972. *Int. Lab. Rev.*, December 1973, *108*(6), pp. 485–503. [G: Canada]

Hendershott, Patric H. and Van Horne, James C. Expected Inflation Implied by Capital Market Rates. *J. Finance*, May 1973, *28*(2), pp. 301–14. [G: U.S.]

Hendershott, Patric H. Interest Rates and Prices in the Long Run: A Study of the Gibson Paradox: Comment. *J. Money, Credit, Banking*, Part II, February 1973, *5*(1), pp. 454–59. [G: U.S.]

Holt, Charles C., et al. Manpower Policies to Reduce Inflation and Unemployment. In *Ulman, L., ed.*, 1973, pp. 51–82. [G: U.S.]

Johnson, Harry G. Secular Inflation and the International Monetary System. *J. Money, Credit, Banking*, Part II, February 1973, *5*(1), pp. 509–19.

Lindauer, John. Stabilization Inflation and the Inflation-Unemployment Trade-off. *Indian Econ. J.*, April-June 1973, *20*(4–5), pp. 541–47.

Miller, Ervin. The Pains of Monetary Restraint. *Lloyds Bank Rev.*, July 1973, (109), pp. 36–51. [G: U.S.; U.K.]

Mouly, Jean. Prices, Wages, Unemployment: Inflation in Contemporary Economic Theory. *Int. Lab. Rev.*, October 1973, *108*(4), pp. 329–43.

Myrdal, Gunnar. "Stagflation." In *Myrdal, G.*, 1973, pp. 17–32.

Phelps Brown, E. H. How Phase II Worked in the United States. *Lloyds Bank Rev.*, July 1973, (109), pp. 1–16. [G: U.S.]

Sargent, Thomas J. Interest Rates and Prices in the Long Run: A Study of the Gibson Paradox. *J. Money, Credit, Banking*, Part II, February 1973, *5*(1), pp. 385–449. [G: U.S.]

Schwartz, Anna J. Secular Price Change in Historical Perspective. *J. Money, Credit, Banking*, Part II, February 1973, *5*(1), pp. 243–69.

Shapiro, A. A. Inflation, Lags, and the Demand for Money. *Int. Econ. Rev.*, February 1973, *14*(1), pp. 81–96. [G: U.S.]

Shinkai, Yoichi. A Model of Imported Inflation. *J. Polit. Econ.*, July-August 1973, *81*(4), pp. 962–71.

Sreenivas, M. A. Prices, Money Wages and Real Output: A Case Study of Indian Manufacturing Sector. *Indian Econ. J.*, April-June 1973, *20*(4–5), pp. 604–18. [G: India]

Stott, Alexander L. Capital Recovery in a World of Inflation. In *Tax Foundation, Inc.*, 1973, pp. 35–42. [G: U.S.]

Stroobants-Vanden Bossche, G. Inflatie: een actueel probleem voor het bedrijfsleven? (Inflation: A Topical Business Problem? With English summary.) *Econ. Soc. Tijdschr.*, April 1973, *27*(2), pp. 115–28.

Tobin, James. More on Inflation: Reply. *J. Money, Credit, Banking*, November 1973, *5*(4), pp. 982–84.

Trescott, Paul B. Secular Price Change in Historical Perspective: Comment. *J. Money, Credit, Banking*, Part II, February 1973, *5*(1), pp. 274–78.

Willett, Thomas D. Secular Inflation and the International Monetary System: Comment. *J. Money, Credit, Banking*, Part II, February 1973, *5*(1), pp. 520–23.

Young, Richard M. Inflation and the Distribution of Income and Wealth: Are the Poor Really Hurt? *Fed. Res. Bank Bus. Rev. Phila.*, September 1973, pp. 16–25. [G: U.S.]

1342 Inflation Theories; Studies Illustrating Inflation Theories

Arndt, H. W. Inflation: New Policy Prescriptions. *Australian Econ. Rev.*, 3rd Quarter 1973, pp. 41–48.

Arndt, H. W. Survey of Recent Developments. *Bull. Indonesian Econ. Stud.*, July 1973, *9*(2), pp. 1–27. [G: Indonesia]

Azhar, B. A. An Econometric Analysis of Price Behaviour in Pakistan. *Pakistan Develop. Rev.*, Winter 1973, *12*(4), pp. 375–92. [G: Pakistan]

Baxter, J. L. Inflation in the Context of Relative Deprivation and Social Justice. *Scot. J. Polit. Econ.*, November 1973, *20*(3), pp. 263–82. [G: U.K.]

Beare, John B. Wage and Price Change Relationships in Post-War Canada. *Can. J. Econ.*, May 1973, *6*(2), pp. 260–65. [G: Canada]

Bechter, Dan M. Money and Inflation. *Fed. Res. Bank Kansas City Rev.*, July-August 1973, pp. 3–6. [G: U.S.]

Behrman, Jere R. and Mujica, Jorge G. A Study of Quarterly Nominal Wage Change Determination in an Inflationary Developing Economy. In *Eckaus, R. S. and Rosenstein-Rodan, P. N., eds.*, 1973, pp. 399–416. [G: Chile]

Behrman, Jere R. Price Determination in an Inflationary Economy: The Dynamics of Chilean Inflation Revisited. In *Eckaus, R. S. and Rosenstein-Rodan, P. N., eds.*, 1973, pp. 369–97. [G: Chile]

Bichi, C. Inflația în țările capitaliste și apologia ei. (Inflation in the Capitalist Countries and its Apology. With English summary.) *Stud. Cercet. Econ.*, 1973, (1), pp. 163–79.

Blackaby, F. T. Incomes and Inflation. In *Robinson, J., ed.*, 1973, pp. 55–70.

Blinder, Alan S. Note: Can Income Tax Increases Be Inflationary? *Nat. Tax J.*, June 1973, *26*(2), pp. 295–301.

Boelaert, Remi. Unemployment-Inflation Trade-Offs in EEC-Countries. *Weltwirtsch. Arch.*, 1973, *109*(3), pp. 418–51. [G: E.E.C.]

Bose, Swadesh R. The Price Situation in Bangladesh—A Preliminary Analysis. *Bangladesh Econ. Rev.*, July 1973, *1*(3), pp. 243–68. [G: Bangladesh]

Bosworth, Barry. The Current Inflation: Malign Neglect? *Brookings Pap. Econ. Act.*, 1973, (1), pp. 263–83. [G: U.S.]

Bourgoignie, Th. Overheid en bedrijfsleven/3 La réglementation des prix en Belgique. (Price Regulation in Belgium. With English summary.) *Econ. Soc. Tijdschr.*, August 1973, *27*(4), pp. 387–400. [G: Belgium]

Bowen, John and Hinshaw, Elton. Inflation and Stagnation in Brazil: Comment. *Econ. Develop. Cult. Change*, April 1973, *21*(3), pp. 522–25. [G: Brazil]

Bowsher, Norman N. 1973—A Year of Inflation. *Fed. Res. Bank St. Louis Rev.*, December 1973, *55*(12), pp. 2–11. [G: U.S.]

Brandow, G. E. A Discussion of the 1973 Economic Report of the President: The Food Price Problem. *Amer. J. Agr. Econ.*, August 1973, *55*(3), pp. 385–90. [G: U.S.]

Brechling, Frank. Wage Inflation and the Structure of Regional Unemployment. *J. Money, Credit, Banking*, Part II, February 1973, *5*(1), pp. 355–79.

Brits, R. N. Inflation and Capital Growth in South Africa, 1963–1972. *S. Afr. J. Econ.*, September 1973, *41*(3), pp. 291–97. [G: S. Africa]

Bronfenbrenner, Martin. On "Let-'er-Rip" Inflation Policy. *Southern Econ. J.*, January 1973, *39*(3), pp. 424–26.

Brownlee, Oswald. The Effects of Inflation on the Distribution of Economic Welfare: Comment. *J. Money, Credit, Banking*, Part II, February 1973, *5*(1), pp. 505–06. [G: U.S.]

Brunner, Karl, et al. Fiscal and Monetary Policies in Moderate Inflation: Case Studies of Three Countries. *J. Money, Credit, Banking*, Part II, February 1973, *5*(1), pp. 313–53. [G: U.S.; Germany; Italy]

Congdon, Timothy G. Why Has Inflation Accelerated? *Nat. Westminster Bank Quart. Rev.*, February 1973, pp. 6–19. [G: U.K.]

Coste, Roger. Inflation et processus de décision. (Inflation and Decision Making Process. With English summary.) *Consommation*, April-June 1973, *20*(2), pp. 95–116.

Dahmén, Erik. Inflation: Economics or Politics? *Nat. Westminster Bank Quart. Rev.*, November 1973, pp. 16–26.

Dalton, James A. Administered Inflation and Business Pricing: Another Look. *Rev. Econ. Statist.*, November 1973, *55*(4), pp. 516–19. [G: U.S.]

Dasmahapatra, Rajkrishna. Recent Rise in Bank Rate

in India and its Probable Consequences. *Econ. Aff.*, June 1973, *18*(6), pp. 299–304. [G: India]

Desai, Meghnad. Growth Cycles and Inflation in a Model of the Class Struggle. *J. Econ. Theory*, December 1973, *6*(6), pp. 527–45.

Despres, Emile. Inflation and Development: Brazil. In *Despres, E.*, 1973, pp. 184–206. [G: Brazil]

Diz, Adolfo. L'inflazione e il sistema monetario internazionale: Intervento. (Inflation and the International Monetary System: Discussion. With English summary.) *Bancaria*, October 1973, *29*(10), pp. 1220–24.

Donner, Arthur W. and Lazar, Fred. Some Comments on the Canadian Phillips Curve. *Economica, N.S.*, May 1973, *40*(158), pp. 195–207. [G: Canada]

Dornbusch, Rudiger and Frenkel, Jacob A. Inflation and Growth: Alternative Approaches. *J. Money, Credit, Banking*, Part I, February 1973, *5*(1), pp. 141–56.

Eastburn, David P. Monetary Policy In a "New" Economy. *Fed. Res. Bank Bus. Rev. Phila.*, October 1973, pp. 3–6. [G: U.S.]

Emminger, Otmar. L'inflazione e il sistema monetario internazionale. (Inflation and the International Monetary System. With English summary.) *Bancaria*, October 1973, *29*(10), pp. 1206–19.

Fekete, Janos. L'inflazione e il sistema monetario internazionale: Intervento. (Inflation and the International Monetary System: Discussion. With English summary.) *Bancaria*, October 1973, *29*(10), pp. 1225–28.

Fellner, William J. Employment Goals and Monetary-Fiscal Overexpansion. In *Cagan, P., et al.*, 1973, pp. 135–72. [G: U.S.]

Franco, G. Robert. A Model of French Post-War Inflation. *Econ. Int.*, May 1973, *26*(2), pp. 329–48. [G: France]

Franke, Jürgen F. A. W. Marktmacht und Inflation. (Market Power and Inflation. With English summary.) *Z. Wirtschaft. Sozialwissen.*, 1973, *93*(3), pp. 285–305.

Fried, Joel. Inflation-unemployment Trade-offs under Fixed and Floating Exchange Rates. *Can. J. Econ.*, February 1973, *6*(1), pp. 43–52.

Gardini, Attilio and Pezzoli, Ettore. Relazioni statistiche di un semplice modello aggregativo dell-'economia italiana (1951–1970). (Some Statistical Relationships in a Simple Aggregate Model of the Italian Economy (1951–1970). With English summary.) *Statistica*, April-June 1973, *33*(2), pp. 241–73. [G: Italy]

Gardini, Attilio and Pezzoli, Ettore. Soluzione e qualche simulazione di un semplice modello statistico aggregato dell'economia italiana (1952–1970). (Solution and Some Simulations of a Simple Aggregate Model of the Italian Economy (1952–1970). With English summary.) *Statistica*, July-September 1973, *33*(3), pp. 429–36. [G: Italy]

Giersch, Herbert. Some Neglected Aspects of Inflation in the World Economy. *Public Finance*, 1973, *28*(2), pp. 105–24.

Godfrey, Leslie G. and Taylor, Jim. Earnings Changes in the United Kingdom, 1954–70: Excess Labour Supply, Expected Inflation and Union In-

fluence. *Oxford Bull. Econ. Statist.*, August 1973, *35*(3), pp. 197–216. [G: U.K.]

Hagger, A. J. and Rayner, P. J. The Excess Demand for Commodities in Australia, 1950–51 to 1968–69. *Econ. Rec.*, June 1973, *49*(126), pp. 161–93. [G: Australia]

Hanson, James S. and Vogel, Robert C. Inflation and Monetary Velocity in Latin America. *Rev. Econ. Statist.*, August 1973, *55*(3), pp. 365–70. [G: Latin America]

Harvey, C. E. On the Cost-Inflationary Impact of High Interest Rates: Reply. *J. Econ. Issues*, September 1973, *7*(3), pp. 514.

Hasson, Joseph. The Impact of Dollar Devaluation on Domestic Prices. *J. Econ. Bus.*, Fall 1973, *26*(1), pp. 25–40. [G: U.S.]

Hebert, Robert F. and Byrns, Ralph T. On the Cost-Inflationary Impact of High Interest Rates: Comment. *J. Econ. Issues*, September 1973, *7*(3), pp. 511–14.

Hempel, George H. Wage and Price Controls for State and Local Governments: Their Effectiveness and the Potential Effects of Phase III. *Public Policy*, Summer 1973, *21*(3), pp. 425–36. [G: U.S.]

Holt, Charles C. Wage Inflation and the Structure of Regional Unemployment: Comment. *J. Money, Credit, Banking*, Part II, February 1973, *5*(1), pp. 380–81.

Isaac, J. E. Incomes Policy: Unnecessary? Undesirable? Impracticable? *Australian Econ. Rev.*, 1st Quarter 1973, pp. 41–50. [G: Australia]

Iyoha, Milton Ame. Inflation and "Openness" in Less Developed Economies: A Cross-Country Analysis. *Econ. Develop. Cult. Change*, October 1973, *22*(1), pp. 31–38.

Johnson, Harry G. Inflation: A 'Monetarist' View. In *Johnson, H. G.*, 1973, pp. 325–37.

Jonson, P. D. and Mahoney, D. M. Price Expectations in Australia. *Econ. Rec.*, March 1973, *49* (125), pp. 50–61. [G: Australia]

Jonson, P. D. Our Current Inflationary Experience. *Australian Econ. Rev.*, 2nd Quarter 1973, pp. 21–26. [G: Australia]

Kaliski, S. F. and Smith, D. C. Inflation, Unemployment and Incomes Policy. *Can. J. Econ.*, November 1973, *6*(4), pp. 574–91. [G: Canada]

Kessel, Reuben A. The Effects of Inflation on the Distribution of Economic Welfare: Comment. *J. Money, Credit, Banking*, Part II, February 1973, *5*(1), pp. 507–08. [G: U.S.]

Klijn, Nico. The Effects of a 9.42 Per Cent Price Increase for Iron and Steel on Other Prices. *Australian Econ. Rev.*, 4th Quarter 1973, pp. 27–30. [G: Australia]

Knight, J. B. and Mabro, Robert. On the Determination of the General Wage Level: A Rejoinder. *Econ. J.*, June 1973, *83*(330), pp. 520–22.

Koot, Ronald S. Price Expectations and Monetary Adjustments in Latin America. *Schweiz. Z. Volkswirtsch. Statist.*, June 1973, *109*(2), pp. 223–32. [G: Latin America]

Laidler, David. The Influence of Money on Real Income and Inflation:—A Simple Model with some Empirical Tests for the United States 1953–72. *Manchester Sch. Econ. Soc. Stud.*, December

1973, *41*(4), pp. 367–95. [G: U.S.]

Laidler, David. Simultaneous Fluctuations in Prices and Output—A Business Cycle Approach. *Economica, N.S.,* February 1973, *40*(157), pp. 60–72.

Laidler, David. The Current Inflation—The Problem of Explanation and the Problem of Policy. In *Robinson, J., ed.,* 1973, pp. 37–54. [G: U.K.]

Lécaillon, Jacques and Botalla-Gambetta, Brigitte. Inflation, répartition et chômage dans la France contemporaine. (Inflation, Distribution and Unemployment in Today's France. With English summary.) *Revue Écon.,* May 1973, *24*(3), pp. 373–400. [G: France]

Lenti, Libero. Business Cycles and Price Trend in Italy. *Rev. Econ. Cond. Italy,* May 1973, *27*(3), pp. 113–26. [G: Italy]

LeRoy, Stephen F. Interest Rates and the Inflation Premium. *Fed. Res. Bank Kansas City Rev.,* May 1973, pp. 11–18.

Lucas, Robert E., Jr. Some International Evidence on Output-Inflation Tradeoffs. *Amer. Econ. Rev.,* June 1973, *63*(3), pp. 326–34.

Lucas, Robert E., Jr. Wage Inflation and the Structure of Regional Unemployment: Comment. *J. Money, Credit, Banking,* Part II, February 1973, *5*(1), pp. 382–84.

Magnifico, Giovanni. The Theory of Optimum Currency Areas and European Monetary Unification. In *Magnifico, G.,* 1973, pp. 43–84. [G: E.E.C.]

McCormick, B. J. Trade Unions and Wage Inflation in the UK: A Reappraisal: Discussion. In *Parkin, M., ed.,* 1973, pp. 328–29. [G: U.K.]

Miconi, Gastone. New Aspects of an Old Problem? Inflation. *Rev. Econ. Cond. Italy,* January-March 1973, *27*(1–2), pp. 53–64.

Modigliani, Franco and Shiller, Robert J. Inflation, Rational Expectations and the Term Structure of Interest Rates. *Economica, N.S.,* February 1973, *40*(157), pp. 12–43.

Morley, Samuel A. Inflation and Stagnation in Brazil: Reply. *Econ. Develop. Cult. Change,* April 1973, *21*(3), pp. 530–33. [G: Brazil]

Mulvey, C. and Trevithick, J. A. Trade Unions and Wage Inflation. *Econ. Soc. Rev.,* January 1973, *4* (2), pp. 209–29.

Neild, R. R. The Effect of Demand on Prices in British Manufacturing Industry: Comment. *Rev. Econ. Stud.,* January 1973, *40*(1), pp. 143–44.

Neumann, Manfred J. M. The 1972 Report of the German Council of Economic Experts: Inflation and Stabilization: Review Essay. *J. Money, Credit, Banking,* November 1973, *5*(4), pp. 950–59. [G: W. Germany]

Neumann, Manfred J. M. Special Drawing Rights and Inflation. *Weltwirtsch. Arch.,* 1973, *109*(2), pp. 232–52.

Nordhaus, William D. The Effects of Inflation on the Distribution of Economic Welfare. *J. Money, Credit, Banking,* Part II, February 1973, *5*(1), pp. 465–504. [G: U.S.]

O'Brien, James M. Inflation and Unemployment: The Great Debate. *Fed. Res. Bank Bus. Rev. Phila.,* January 1973, pp. 13–18. [G: U.S.]

Olienyk, John and Fan, Liang-Shing. Inflation in a Growing Economy: A Monetaristic Elucidation.

Intermountain Econ. Rev., Fall 1973, *4*(2), pp. 75–76.

Oudet, Bruno A. The Variation of the Return of Stocks in Periods of Inflation. *J. Financial Quant. Anal.,* March 1973, *8*(2), pp. 247–58. [G: U.S.]

Packer, Arnold H. and Park, Seong H. Distortions in Relative Wages and Shifts in the Phillips Curve. *Rev. Econ. Statist.,* February 1973, *55*(1), pp. 16–22. [G: U.S.]

Paldam, Martin. An Empirical Analysis of the Relationship between Inflation and Economic Growth in 12 Countries, 1950 to 1969. *Swedish J. Econ.,* December 1973, *75*(4), pp. 420–27. [G: W. Europe; U.K.; U.S.]

Parkin, Michael. The Short-Run and Long-Run Trade-Offs Between Inflation and Unemployment in Australia. *Australian Econ. Pap.,* December 1973, *12*(21), pp. 127–44. [G: Australia]

Parkin, Michael. The 1973 Report of the President's Council of Economic Advisers: A Critique. *Amer. Econ. Rev.,* September 1973, *63*(4), pp. 535–45. [G: U.S.]

Perry, George L. The Success of Anti-Inflation Policies in the United States. *J. Money, Credit, Banking,* Part II, February 1973, *5*(1), pp. 569–93. [G: U.S.]

Perry, George L. Capacity in Manufacturing. *Brookings Pap. Econ. Act.,* 1973, (3), pp. 701–42. [G: U.S.]

Phelps, Edmund S. Inflation in the Theory of Public Finance. *Swedish J. Econ.,* March 1973, *75*(1), pp. 67–82.

Phlips, Louis. Illusions in Testing for Administered Prices: A Reply. *J. Ind. Econ.,* April 1973, *21*(2), pp. 196–99.

Purdy, D. L. and Zis, G. Trade Unions and Wage Inflation in the UK: A Reappraisal. In *Parkin, M., ed.,* 1973, pp. 294–327. [G: U.K.]

Randall, Laura. Inflation and Economic Development in Latin America: Some New Evidence. *J. Devel. Stud.,* January 1973, *9*(2), pp. 317–22. [G: Argentina; Brazil]

Ratchford, B. U. Interest Rates and Inflation. *Nebr. J. Econ. Bus.,* Spring 1973, *12*(2), pp. 45–54.

Ripley, Frank C. and Segal, Lydia. Price Determination in 395 Manufacturing Industries. *Rev. Econ. Statist.,* August 1973, *55*(3), pp. 263–71. [G: U.S.]

Roll, Richard. Assets, Money, and Commodity Price Inflation Under Uncertainty: Demand Theory. *J. Money, Credit, Banking,* November 1973, *5*(4), pp. 903–23.

Rose, Klaus and Bender, Dieter. Flexible Wechselkurse und Inflationsimport. (Flexible Exchange Rates and Import of Inflation. With English summary.) *Jahr. Nationalökon. Statist.,* August 1973, *187*(6), pp. 481–506.

Rose, Peter S. The Impact of Policy Variables on Price-Level Movements. *Miss. Val. J. Bus. Econ.,* Fall 1973, *9*(1), pp. 1–11. [G: U.S.]

Ross, Howard N. Illusions in Testing for Administered Prices. *J. Ind. Econ.,* April 1973, *21*(2), pp. 187–95.

Ross, Stephen A. and Wachter, Michael L. Wage Determination, Inflation, and the Industrial

Structure. *Amer. Econ. Rev.*, September 1973, *63* (4), pp. 675–92.

Sargent, Thomas J. and Wallace, Neil. Rational Expectations and the Dynamics of Hyperinflation. *Int. Econ. Rev.*, June 1973, *14*(2), pp. 328–50.

Sargent, Thomas J. What Do Regressions of Interest on Inflation Show? *Ann. Econ. Soc. Measure,* July 1973, *2*(3), pp. 289–301.

Sargent, Thomas J. and Wallace, Neil. The Stability of Models of Money and Growth with Perfect Foresight. *Econometrica,* November 1973, *41*(6), pp. 1043–48.

Scarfe, B. L. A Model of the Inflation Cycle in a Small Open Economy. *Oxford Econ. Pap.,* July 1973, *25* (2), pp. 192–203.

Sellekaerts, Willy and Lesage, Richard. A Reformulation and Empirical Verification of the Administered Prices Inflation Hypothesis: The Canadian Case. *Southern Econ. J.,* January 1973, *39*(3), pp. 345–60. [G: Canada]

Selowsky, Marcelo. Cost of Price Stabilization in a Strongly Inflationary Economy. *Quart. J. Econ.,* February 1973, *87*(1), pp. 44–59. [G: Chile]

Severn, Alan K. Further Evidence on the Formation of Price Expectations. *Quart. Rev. Econ. Bus.,* Winter 1973, *13*(4), pp. 27–35. [G: U.S.]

Sharot, T. Unemployment Dispersion as a Determinant of Wage Inflation in the U.K. 1925–66—A Note. *Manchester Sch. Econ. Soc. Stud.,* June 1973, *41*(2), pp. 225–28. [G: U.K.]

Sheehan, P. J. The Real Income Guarantee: A Fiscal Policy to Control Inflation. *Australian Econ. Rev.,* 4th Quarter 1973, pp. 9–14. [G: Australia]

Shin, Kilman. The Rate of Interest and Inflation: An International Comparison. *Econ. Int.,* August-November 1973, *26*(3–4), pp. 603–22.

Silveira, Antonio M. Interest Rate and Rapid Inflation: The Evidence from the Brazilian Economy. *J. Money, Credit, Banking,* August 1973, *5*(3), pp. 794–805. [G: Brazil]

Sonne, A. Monopol-og priskontrol under en stabiliseringspolitik. (Monopoly and Price Control in a Stabilization Policy. With English summary.) *Nationalokon. Tidsskr.,* 1973, *111*(1), pp. 154–64. [G: Denmark]

Struyk, Raymond J. Price Determinants in the Republic of Vietnam, 1966–1970. *Malayan Econ. Rev.,* April 1973, *18*(1), pp. 74–80. [G: S. Vietnam]

Sundrum, R. M. Money Supply and Prices: A Reinterpretation. *Bull. Indonesian Econ. Stud.,* November 1973, *9*(3), pp. 73–86. [G: Indonesia]

Thomas, R. L. Unemployment Dispersion as a Determinant of Wage Inflation in the U.K. 1925–66—A Rejoinder. *Manchester Sch. Econ. Soc. Stud.,* June 1973, *41*(2), pp. 229–33. [G: U.K.]

Tobin, James. More on Inflation: Reply. *J. Money, Credit, Banking,* November 1973, *5*(4), pp. 982–84.

Tokita, Tadahiko. Behavior of Oligopolistic Firm and Market Adjustment—A Short Run Macroeconomic Approach. (In Japanese.) *Econ. Stud. Quart.,* April 1973, *24*(1), pp. 9–17.

Tuckwell, R. H. The Wage-Price Link. *Econ. Anal. Pol.,* September 1973, *4*(2), pp. 76–87. [G: Australia]

Tullock, Gordon. Inflation and Unemployment: The Discussion Continued: Comment. *J. Money, Credit, Banking,* August 1973, *5*(3), pp. 826–35.

Turner, H. A. and Jackson, D. A. S. A Riposte to Knight and Mabro. *Econ. J.,* June 1973, *83*(330), pp. 523–25.

Verdoorn, P. J. Some Long-Run Dynamic Elements of Factor Price Inflation. In *[Tinbergen, J.],* 1973, pp. 111–37.

Verma, Krishnanand. Price Rise in India (1949–72). *Econ. Aff.,* June 1973, *18*(6), pp. 281–90. [G: India]

Vuchelen, Jozef. Gezinsbesparingen en inflatie: een mogelijke benadering voor de Belgische ervaring. (With English summary.) *Cah. Écon. Bruxelles,* 3rd Trimestre 1973, (59), pp. 413–42. [G: Belgium]

Whitehead, C. M. E. Inflation and the New Housing Market. *Oxford Bull. Econ. Statist.,* November 1973, *35*(4), pp. 275–93. [G: U.K.]

Wicke, Lutz. Zinserhöhungen bei festverzinslichen Wertpapieren während einer schleichdenden Inflation. (Are Increases in the Interest Rates of Fixed-Interest-Bearing Securities During a Creeping Inflation a Compensation for Losses of Real Value? With English summary.) *Z. Wirtschaft. Sozialwissen.,* 1973, *93*(5), pp. 567–85.

Wiles, Peter. Cost Inflation and the State of Economic Theory. *Econ. J.,* June 1973, *83*(330), pp. 377–98.

Wilson, Thomas. Pensions, Inflation and Growth. In *Robinson, J., ed.,* 1973, pp. 88–114. [G: W. Europe]

Wittenberg, J. I. The Effective Rate of Inflation. *Rev. Marketing Agr. Econ.,* June and September 1973, *41*(2–3), pp. 93–94. [G: U.K.]

Wogart, Jan P. Inflation and Stagnation in Brazil: Comment. *Econ. Develop. Cult. Change,* April 1973, *21*(3), pp. 526–29. [G: Brazil]

200 Quantitative Economic Methods and Data

210 ECONOMETRIC, STATISTICAL, AND MATHEMATICAL METHODS, AND MODELS

211 Econometric and Statistical Methods and Models

2110 General

Băjan, Ana. Verificarea existenţei legăturilor statistice prin metoda distribuţiilor condiţionate şi prin analiza dispersională. (Verifying the Existence of Statistical Connections Through the Method of Conditioned Distributions and Through the Dispersional Analysis. With English summary.) *Stud. Cercet. Econ.,* 1973, (1), pp. 77–97.

Baron, David P. Point Estimation and Risk Preferences. *J. Amer. Statist. Assoc.,* December 1973, *68* (344), pp. 944–50.

Belsley, David A. and Kuh, Edwin. Time-Varying Parameter Structures: An Overview. *Ann. Econ. Soc. Measure,* October 1973, *2*(4), pp. 375–79.

Berger, Agnes and Gold, Ruth Z. Note on Cochran's Q-Test for the Comparison of Correlated Proportions. *J. Amer. Statist. Assoc.*, December 1973, *68* (344), pp. 989–93.

Bliemel, Friedhelm. Theil's Forecast Accuracy Coefficient: A Clarification. *J. Marketing Res.*, November 1973, *10*(4), pp. 444–46.

Bradley, Edwin L. The Equivalence of Maximum Likelihood and Weighted Least Squares Estimates in the Exponential Family. *J. Amer. Statist. Assoc.*, March 1973, *68*(341), pp. 199–200.

Brito, Dagobert L. Estimation, Prediction and Economic Control. *Int. Econ. Rev.*, October 1973, *14* (3), pp. 646–52.

Burstein, Herman. Close Approximations of Percentage Points of the Chi-Square Distribution and Poisson Confidence Limits. *J. Amer. Statist. Assoc.*, September 1973, *68*(343), pp. 581–84.

Clark, Peter K. A Subordinated Stochastic Process Model with Finite Variance for Speculative Prices. *Econometrica*, January 1973, *41*(1), pp. 135–55. [G: U.S.]

Drettakis, E. G. Missing Data in Econometric Estimation. *Rev. Econ. Stud.*, October 1973, *40*(4), pp. 537–52. [G: U.K.]

DuMouchel, William H. Stable Distributions in Statistical Inference: 1. Symmetric Stable Distributions Compared to Other Symmetric Long-Tailed Distributions. *J. Amer. Statist. Assoc.*, June 1973, *68*(342), pp. 469–77.

Dyer, Alan R. Discrimination Procedures for Separate Families of Hypotheses. *J. Amer. Statist. Assoc.*, December 1973, *68*(344), pp. 970–74.

Ebbeler, Donald H. Measuring the Permanent Component of a Series for Serially Correlated Observations. *J. Amer. Statist. Assoc.*, September 1973, *68*(343), pp. 579–80.

Evans, Dennis A. The Influence of Computers on the Teaching of Statistics. *J. Roy. Statist. Soc.*, Part 2, 1973, *136*, pp. 153–90.

Frosini, Benito Vittorio. Su alcune diseguaglianze concernenti lo scarto medio assoluto. (On Some Inequalities Concerning Mean Deviation. With English summary.) *Statistica*, January-March 1973, *33*(1), pp. 41–61.

Goldberger, Arthur S. Correlations Between Binary Outcomes and Probabilistic Predictions. *J. Amer. Statist. Assoc.*, March 1973, *68*(341), pp. 84.

Han, Chien-Pai. Double Sampling with Partial Information on Auxiliary Variables. *J. Amer. Statist. Assoc.*, December 1973, *68*(344), pp. 914–18.

Hardaker, J. B. and Tanago, A. G. Assessment of the Output of a Stochastic Decision Model. *Australian J. Agr. Econ.*, December 1973, *17*(3), pp. 170–78.

Johnson, K. H. and Lyon, H. L. Experimental Evidence on Combining Cross-Section and Time Series Information. *Rev. Econ. Statist.*, November 1973, *55*(4), pp. 465–74.

Judge, G. G.; Yancey, T. A. and Bock, M. E. Properties of Estimators After Preliminary Tests of Significance When Stochastic Restrictions Are Used in Regression. *J. Econometrics*, March 1973, *1*(1), pp. 29–47.

Kraemer, Helena C. Improved Approximation to the Non-Null Distribution of the Correlation Co-

efficient. *J. Amer. Statist. Assoc.*, December 1973, *68*(344), pp. 1004–08.

Kulldorff, Gunnar and Vännman, Kerstin. Estimation of the Location and Scale Parameters of a Pareto Distribution by Linear Functions of Order Statistics. *J. Amer. Statist. Assoc.*, March 1973, *68* (341), pp. 218–27.

Land, Charles E. Standard Confidence Limits for Linear Functions of the Normal Mean and Variance. *J. Amer. Statist. Assoc.*, December 1973, *68* (344), pp. 960–63.

Ling, Robert F. A Probability Theory of Cluster Analysis. *J. Amer. Statist. Assoc.*, March 1973, *68* (341), pp. 159–64.

Little, Charles H. and Doeksen, Gerald A. Measurement of Leakage by the Use of an Input-Output Model: Reply. *Amer. J. Agr. Econ.*, Part I, November 1973, *55*(4), pp. 682.

Luscia, Fausta. Un risultato sull'indipendenza. (A Result on Independence. With English summary.) *Rivista Int. Sci. Econ. Com.*, October 1973, *20* (10), pp. 1025–28.

Malkovich, J. F. and Afifi, A. A. On Tests for Multivariate Normality. *J. Amer. Statist. Assoc.*, March 1973, *68*(341), pp. 176–79.

Mandelbrot, Benoit B. A Subordinated Stochastic Process Model with Finite Variance for Speculative Prices: Comment. *Econometrica*, January 1973, *41*(1), pp. 157–59.

Mayer, Lawrence S. Estimating a Correlation Coefficient When One Variable Is Not Directly Observed. *J. Amer. Statist. Assoc.*, June 1973, *68* (342), pp. 420–21.

Mead, R. and Stern, R. D. The Use of a Computer in the Teaching of Statistics. *J. Roy. Statist. Soc.*, Part 2, 1973, *136*, pp. 191–205.

Metzler, Lloyd A. The Assumptions Implied in Least-Squares Demand Techniques. In *Metzler, L. A.*, 1973, pp. 575–98.

Mondani, Aristide. Alcune semplici rappresentazioni integrali di funzioni a gradino. (A Few Simple Integral Representations of Step Functions. With English summary.) *Rivista Int. Sci. Econ. Com.*, November 1973, *20*(11), pp. 1127–34.

Montgomery, David B. and Morrison, Donald G. A Note on Adjusting R^2. *J. Finance*, September 1973, *28*(4), pp. 1009–13.

Mustafa, Gholam. Measurement of Leakage by the Use of an Input-Output Model: Comment. *Amer. J. Agr. Econ.*, Part I, November 1973, *55*(4), pp. 680–82.

Nicholson, R. J. Econometrics: Measurement in Economics. *Bull. Econ. Res.*, May 1973, *25*(1), pp. 3–21.

Olivieri, Dario. Tavole della dimensione minima di un campione necessaria per la stima di una probabilità. (Tables of a Sample Minimum Size Necessary for the Estimate of a Probability. With English summary.) *Rivista Int. Sci. Econ. Com.*, April 1973, *20*(4), pp. 371–98.

Quintano, Claudio. Regressione e correlazione lineare di variabili multidimensionali. (Linear Regression and Linear Correlation of Multidimensional Variables. With English summary.) *Rivista Int. Sci. Econ. Com.*, January 1973, *20*(1), pp. 48–62.

Sands, Saul. Estimating Data Withheld in Grouped Size Distributions. *J. Amer. Statist. Assoc.,* June 1973, *68*(342), pp. 306–11.

Schlossmacher, E. J. An Iterative Technique for Absolute Deviations Curve Fitting. *J. Amer. Statist. Assoc.,* December 1973, *68*(344), pp. 857–59.

Schönfeld, Peter. A Note on the Measurability of the Pseudo-Inverse. *J. Econometrics,* October 1973, *1* (3), pp. 313–14.

Schuessler, Karl. Ratio Variables and Path Models. In *Goldberger, A. S. and Duncan, O. D., eds.,* 1973, pp. 201–28.

Shaw, William H. Paradoxes, Problems and Progress. *J. Amer. Statist. Assoc.,* March 1973, *68*(341), pp. 7–10.

Sowey, Eric R. A Classified Bibliography of Monte Carlo Studies in Econometrics. *J. Econometrics,* December 1973, *1*(4), pp. 377–95.

Tate, Merle W. and Hyer, Leon A. Inaccuracy of the X^2 Test of Goodness of Fit when Expected Frequencies Are Small. *J. Amer. Statist. Assoc.,* December 1973, *68*(344), pp. 836–41.

Wang, Tong-eng. Quantitative Analysis of the Progress of the Econometric Movement: An Exploration. *Hist. Polit. Econ.,* Spring 1973, *5*(1), pp. 151–64.   [G: U.S.]

Weinstein, Milton C. and Zeckhauser, Richard J. Critical Ratios and Efficient Allocation. *J. Public Econ.,* April 1973, *2*(2), pp. 147–57.

Zanella, Angelo. Sulle procedure di classificazione simultanea. (Some Aspects of Simultaneous Test Procedures. With English summary.) *Statistica,* January-March 1973, *33*(1), pp. 63–120.

2112 Inferential Problems in Simultaneous Equation Systems

Ågren, Anders. Extensions of the Fix-Point Method I. The GEID Estimator and the Fractional Fix-Point Method. *Écon. Appl.,* 1973, *26*(2–3–4), pp. 561–82.

Anderson, T. W. and Sawa, Takamitsu. Distributions of Estimates of Coefficients of a Single Equation in a Simultaneous System and Their Asymptotic Expansions. *Econometrica,* July 1973, *41*(4), pp. 683–714.

Basmann, R. L. and Richardson, D. H. The Exact Finite Sample Distribution of a Non-Consistent Structural Variance Estimator. *Econometrica,* January 1973, *41*(1), pp. 41–58.

Belsley, David A. A Test for Systematic Variation in Regression Coefficients. *Ann. Econ. Soc. Measure,* October 1973, *2*(4), pp. 495–99.

Bergström, Reinhold. Investigations of the Fix-Point and Iterative Instrumental Variables Methods. Convergence Properties, Comparative Studies and Applications. *Écon. Appl.,* 1973, *26*(2–3–4), pp. 505–35.

Berndt, Ernst R. and Christensen, Laurits R. The Translog Function and the Substitution of Equipment, Structures, and Labor in U.S. Manufacturing 1929–68. *J. Econometrics,* March 1973, *1*(1), pp. 81–113.   [G: U.S.]

Bodin, Lennart. Extensions of the Fix-Point Method II: The Recursive Fix-Point Method. *Écon. Appl.,* 1973, *26*(2–3–4), pp. 583–607.

Bowden, Roger J. Note on Coefficient Restrictions in Estimating Sets of Demand Relations. *Econometrica,* May 1973, *41*(3), pp. 575–79.

Bowden, Roger J. The Theory of Parametric Identification. *Econometrica,* November 1973, *41*(6), pp. 1069–74.

Carter, R. A. L. Least Squares as an Exploratory Estimator. *Can. J. Econ.,* February 1973, *6*(1), pp. 108–14.

Chow, Gregory C. and Fair, Ray C. Maximum Likelihood Estimation of Linear Equation Systems with Auto-Regressive Residuals. *Ann. Econ. Soc. Measure,* January 1973, *2*(1), pp. 17–28.   [G: U.S.]

Chow, Gregory C. On the Computation of Full-Information Maximum Likelihood Estimates for Nonlinear Equation Systems. *Rev. Econ. Statist.,* February 1973, *55*(1), pp. 104–09.

Christensen, Laurits R. Simultaneous Statistical Inference in the Normal Multiple Linear Regression Model. *J. Amer. Statist. Assoc.,* June 1973, *68* (342), pp. 457–61.

Cooper, J. Phillip and Fischer, Stanley. The Use of the Secant Method in Econometric Models. *J. Bus.,* April 1973, *46*(2), pp. 274–77.

Court, R. H. Efficient Estimation of the Reduced Form from Incomplete Econometric Models. *Rev. Econ. Stud.,* July 1973, *40*(3), pp. 411–17.

Dhrymes, Phoebus J. Small Sample and Asymptotic Relations Between Maximum Likelihood and Three Stage Least Squares Estimators. *Econometrica,* March 1973, *41*(2), pp. 357–64.

Dhrymes, Phoebus J. A Simple Proof of the Asymptotic Efficiency of 3SLS Relative to 2SLS Estimators. *Western Econ. J.,* June 1973, *11*(2), pp. 187–90.

Dhrymes, Phoebus J. Restricted and Unrestricted Reduced Forms: Asymptotic Distribution and Relative Efficiency. *Econometrica,* January 1973, *41*(1), pp. 119–34.

Drettakis, E. G. An Expository Note on the Derivation of the Two Stage and Three Stage Least Squares Estimators. *Bull. Econ. Res.,* November 1973, *25*(2), pp. 146–47.

Dutta, M. and Sharma, P. L. Alternative Estimators and Predictive Power of Alternative Estimators: An Econometric Model of Puerto Rico. *Rev. Econ. Statist.,* August 1973, *55*(3), pp. 381–85.   [G: Puerto Rico]

Ebbeler, Donald H. and McDonald, James B. An Analysis of the Properties of the Exact Finite Sample Distribution of a Nonconsistent GCL Structural Variance Estimator. *Econometrica,* January 1973, *41*(1), pp. 59–65.

Edgerton, David L. The Combined Use of Predictors and Taylor Series in Nonlinear Interdependent Systems. *Écon. Appl.,* 1973, *26*(2–3–4), pp. 537–59.

Fair, Ray C. A Comparison of Alternative Estimators of Macroeconomic Models. *Int. Econ. Rev.,* June 1973, *14*(2), pp. 261–77.

Faliva, Mario. Stimatori lineari ottimali dei parametri in un modello di regressione lineare con vincoli di diseguaglianza sui parametri. (An Optimal Linear Estimator of Parameters in the Linear Regression Model with Inequality Constraints.

With English summary.) *Statistica,* July-September 1973, *33*(3), pp. 363–94.

Froehlich, B. R. Some Estimators for a Random Coefficient Regression Model. *J. Amer. Statist. Assoc.,* June 1973, *68*(342), pp. 329–35.

Froehlich, B. R. A Note on Some Monte Carlo Results on Non-Negative Variance Estimators for a Random Coefficient Regression Model. *Amer. J. Agr. Econ.,* May 1973, *55*(2), pp. 231–34.

Geary, R. C. A Method of Estimating the Elements of an Interindustry Matrix Knowing the Row and Column Totals. *Econ. Soc. Rev.,* July 1973, *4*(4), pp. 477–85.

Goldberger, Arthur S. Efficient Estimation in Overidentified Models: A Interpretive Analysis. In *Goldberger, A. S. and Duncan, O. D., eds.,* 1973, pp. 131–52.

Goldberger, Arthur S. Structural Equation Models: An Overview. In *Goldberger, A. S. and Duncan, O. D., eds.,* 1973, pp. 1–18.

Guilkey, David K. and Schmidt, Peter. Estimation of Seemingly Unrelated Regressions with Vector Autoregressive Errors. *J. Amer. Statist. Assoc.,* September 1973, *68*(343), pp. 642–47.

Hambor, John C.; Phillips, Llad and Votey, Harold L., Jr. Optimal Community Educational Attainment: A Simultaneous Equation Approach. *Rev. Econ. Statist.,* February 1973, *55*(1), pp. 98–103. [G: U.S.]

Hannan, E. J. and Terrell, R. D. Multiple Equation Systems with Stationary Errors. *Econometrica,* March 1973, *41*(2), pp. 299–320.

Hatanaka, Michio. On the Existence and the Approximation Formulae for the Moments of the *k*-Class Estimators. *Econ. Stud. Quart.,* August 1973, *24*(2), pp. 1–15.

Hendry, D. F. On Asymptotic Theory and Finite Sample Experiments. *Economica, N.S.,* May 1973, *40*(158), pp. 210–17.

Henry, E. W. A Note on the Logarithmic Transformation of the RAS. *Econ. Soc. Rev.,* July 1973, *4*(4), pp. 487–92.

Jöreskog, Karl G. A General Method for Estimating a Linear Structural Equation System. In *Goldberger, A. S. and Duncan, O. D., eds.,* 1973, pp. 85–112.

Klein, Lawrence R. The Treatment of Undersized Samples in Econometrics. In *Powell, A. A. and Williams, R. A., eds.,* 1973, pp. 3–26.

Klein, Roger W. K-Class Estimators: The Optimum Normalization for Finite Samples. *J. Amer. Statist. Assoc.,* June 1973, *68*(342), pp. 445–51.

Land, Kenneth C. Identification, Parameter Estimation, and Hypothesis Testing in Recursive Sociological Models. In *Goldberger, A. S. and Duncan, O. D., eds.,* 1973, pp. 19–49.

Leamer, Edward E. Multicollinearity: A Bayesian Interpretation. *Rev. Econ. Statist.,* August 1973, *55*(3), pp. 371–80.

Lyttkens, Ejnar. The Fix-point Method for Estimating Interdependent Systems with the Underlying Model Specification. *J. Roy. Statist. Soc.,* Part 3 1973, *136*, pp. 353–75.

Maddala, G. S. and Mount, T. D. A Comparative Study of Alternative Estimators for Variance Components Models Used in Econometric Ap-

plications. *J. Amer. Statist. Assoc.,* June 1973, *68*(342), pp. 324–28.

Mariano, Roberto S. Approximations to the Distribution Functions of the Ordinary Least-Squares and Two-Stage Least-Squares Estimators in the Case of Two Included Endogenous Variables. *Econometrica,* January 1973, *41*(1), pp. 67–77.

Mariano, Roberto S. Approximations to the Distribution Functions of Theil's *K*-Class Estimators. *Econometrica,* July 1973, *41*(4), pp. 715–21.

Mullet, Gary M. and Murray, Tracy. More on the Game of Maximizing R^2 *Australian Econ. Pap.,* December 1973, *12*(21), pp. 263–66.

Nagar, A. L. and Ullah, Aman. Note on Approximate Skewness and Kurtosis of the Two-Stage Least-Square Estimator. *Indian Econ. Rev.,* April 1973, *8*(1), pp. 69–80.

Neary, Peter. Relative Efficiency of Regression Using Original Data or First Differences: The Case of Autocorrelated Disturbances. *Econ. Soc. Rev.,* October 1973, *5*(1), pp. 47–58.

Nicholson, R. J. and Topham, N. Step-wise Regression and Principal Components Analysis in Estimating a Relationship in an Econometric Model. *Manchester Sch. Econ. Soc. Stud.,* June 1973, *41*(2), pp. 187–205.

Oberhofer, W. and Kmenta, J. Estimation of Standard Errors of the Characteristic Roots of a Dynamic Econometric Model. *Econometrica,* January 1973, *41*(1), pp. 171–77.

Pagan, Adrian. Efficient Estimation of Models with Composite Disturbance Terms. *J. Econometrics,* December 1973, *1*(4), pp. 329–40.

Paraskevopoulos, Christos C. The Impact of Regional Wage Differentials. *Growth Change,* April 1973, *4*(2), pp. 40–42. [G: U.S.]

Phillips, P. C. B. The Problem of Identification in Finite Parameter Continuous Time Models. *J. Econometrics,* December 1973, *1*(4), pp. 351–62.

Rao, Potluri. On Estimation of Demand and Supply Equations of a Commodity. *Indian Econ. Rev.,* April 1973, *8*(1), pp. 61–68.

Revankar, Nagesh S. and Hartley, Michael J. An Independence Test and Conditional Unbiased Predictions in the Context of Simultaneous Equation Systems. *Int. Econ. Rev.,* October 1973, *14*(3), pp. 625–31.

Savin, N. E. Systems *k*-Class Estimators. *Econometrica,* November 1973, *41*(6), pp. 1125–36.

Sawa, Takamitsu. Almost Unbiased Estimator in Simultaneous Equations Systems. *Int. Econ. Rev.,* February 1973, *14*(1), pp. 97–106.

Sawa, Takamitsu. The Mean Square Error of a Combined Estimator and Numerical Comparison with the TSLS Estimator. *J. Econometrics,* June 1973, *1*(2), pp. 115–32.

Schmidt, Peter. The Asymptotic Distribution of Dynamic Multipliers. *Econometrica,* January 1973, *41*(1), pp. 161–64.

Srivastava, V. K. The Efficiency of an Improved Method of Estimating Seemingly Unrelated Regression Equations. *J. Econometrics,* December 1973, *1*(4), pp. 341–50.

Theil, Henri. A Simple Modification of the Two-Stage Least-Squares Procedure for Undersized Samples. In *Goldberger, A. S. and Duncan, O. D., eds.*, 1973, pp. 113–29.

Tomek, William G. R^2 in TSLS and GLS Estimation. *Amer. J. Agr. Econ.*, Part I, November 1973, *55*(4), pp. 670.

Wiley, David E. The Identification Problem for Structural Equation Models with Unmeasured Variables. In *Goldberger, A. S. and Duncan, O. D., eds.*, 1973, pp. 69–83.

Wu, Roland Y. On Some Aspects of Linearly Aggregated Macro Models. *Int. Econ. Rev.*, October 1973, *14*(3), pp. 785–88.

Zvára, Karel. Odvození trístupnové metody nejmensích ctvercu prímym vyuzitím identifikacních omezení. (Derivation of the Three-Stage Least-Squares Method by Means of Direct Use of Identification Restrictions. With English summary.) *Ekon.-Mat. Obzor,* 1973, *9*(3), pp. 292–304.

2113 Distributed Lags and Serially Correlated Disturbance Terms; Miscellaneous Single Equation Inferential Problems

Aigner, Dennis J. Regression With a Binary Independent Variable Subject to Errors of Observation. *J. Econometrics,* March 1973, *1*(1), pp. 49–59.

Aigner, Dennis J. An Errors-In-Variables Model in Which Least Squares Is Consistent. *Int. Econ. Rev.*, February 1973, *14*(1), pp. 256–57.

Amemiya, Takeshi. Regression Analysis When the Variance of the Dependent Variable Is Proportional to the Square of Its Expectation. *J. Amer. Statist. Assoc.,* December 1973, *68*(344), pp. 928–34.

Amemiya, Takeshi. Generalized Least Squares with an Estimated Autocovariance Matrix. *Econometrica,* July 1973, *41*(4), pp. 723–32.

Amemiya, Takeshi. Regression Analysis when the Dependent Variable is Truncated Normal. *Econometrica,* November 1973, *41*(6), pp. 997–1016.

Arora, Swarnjit S. Error Components Regression Models and Their Applications. *Ann. Econ. Soc. Measure,* October 1973, *2*(4), pp. 451–61.

Balestra, Pietro. Best Quadratic Unbiased Estimators of the Variance-Covariance Matrix in Normal Regression. *J. Econometrics,* March 1973, *1*(1), pp. 17–28.

Basmann, R. L.; Battalio, Raymond C. and Kagel, John H. Comment on R. P. Byron's "The Restricted Aitken Estimation of Sets of Demand Relations." *Econometrica,* March 1973, *41*(2), pp. 365–70.

Belsley, David A. On the Determination of Systematic Parameter Variation in the Linear Regression Model. *Ann. Econ. Soc. Measure,* October 1973, *2*(4), pp. 487–94.

Belsley, David A. The Applicability of the Kalman Filter in the Determination of Systematic Parameter Variation. *Ann. Econ. Soc. Measure,* October 1973, *2*(4), pp. 531–33.

Belsley, David A. The Relative Power of the τ-Test: A Furthering Comment. *Rev. Econ. Statist.,* February 1973, *55*(1), pp. 132.

Bergmann, Barbara R. Combining Microsimulation and Regression: A "Prepared" Regression of Poverty Incidence on Unemployment and Growth. *Econometrica,* September 1973, *41*(5), pp. 955–63.

Bhansali, R. J. A Monte Carlo Comparison of the Regression Method and the Spectral Methods of Prediction. *J. Amer. Statist. Assoc.,* September 1973, *68*(343), pp. 621–25.

Blattberg, Robert C. Evaluation of the Power of the Durbin-Watson Statistic for Non-First Order Serial Correlation Alternatives. *Rev. Econ. Statist.,* November 1973, *55*(4), pp. 508–15.

Blomqvist, A. G. Hypothesis Tests and Confidence Intervals for Steady-State Coefficients in Models with Lagged Dependent Variables: Some Notes in Fieller's Method. *Oxford Bull. Econ. Statist.,* February 1973, *35*(1), pp. 69–74.

Bock, M. E.; Judge, G. G. and Yancey, T. A. Some Comments on Estimation in Regression After Preliminary Tests of Significance. *J. Econometrics,* June 1973, *1*(2), pp. 191–200.

Bock, M. E.; Yancey, T. A. and Judge, G. G. The Statistical Consequences of Preliminary Test Estimators in Regression. *J. Amer. Statist. Assoc.,* March 1973, *68*(341), pp. 109–16.

Bodkin, Ronald G. and Murthy, K. S. R. The Orders-Shipments Mechanism in Canadian Producer Goods Industries. *J. Amer. Statist. Assoc.,* June 1973, *68*(342), pp. 297–305.   [G: Canada]

Brewer, K. R. W. Some Consequences of Temporal Aggregation and Systematic Sampling for ARMA and ARMAX Models. *J. Econometrics,* June 1973, *1*(2), pp. 133–54.

Brook, Richard and Wallace, T. D. A Note on Extraneous Information in Regression. *J. Econometrics,* October 1973, *1*(3), pp. 315–16.

Byron, R. P. The Restricted Aitken Estimation of Sets of Demand Relations: Reply. *Econometrica,* March 1973, *41*(2), pp. 371–74.

Casson, M. C. Linear Regression with Error in the Deflating Variable. *Econometrica,* July 1973, *41*(4), pp. 751–59.

Cleur, Eugene M. A Simulation Study on the Powers of Three Tests for Serial Correlation in the Errors from Least Squares Analysis. *Statistica,* April-June 1973, *33*(2), pp. 285–300.

Cohen, Malcolm; Gillingham, Robert and Heien, Dale. A Monte Carlo Study of Complex Finite Distributed Lag Structures. *Ann. Econ. Soc. Measure,* January 1973, *2*(1), pp. 53–63.

Conlisk, John. Choice of Response Functional Form in Designing Subsidy Experiments. *Econometrica,* July 1973, *41*(4), pp. 643–56.

Cooley, Thomas F. and Prescott, Edward C. Systematic (Non-Random) Variation Models Varying Parameter Regression: A Theory and Some Applications. *Ann. Econ. Soc. Measure,* October 1973, *2*(4), pp. 463–73.

Cooley, Thomas F. and Prescott, Edward C. Tests of an Adaptive Regression Model. *Rev. Econ. Statist.,* May 1973, *55*(2), pp. 248–56.   [G: U.S.]

Cooley, Thomas F. and Prescott, Edward C. An Adaptive Regression Model. *Int. Econ. Rev.,* June 1973, *14*(2), pp. 364–71.

Cooper, J. Phillip. Time-Varying Regression Coefficients: A Mixed Estimation Approach and Operational Limitations of the General Markov Structure. *Ann. Econ. Soc. Measure*, October 1973, *2* (4), pp. 525–30.

Cote, R.; Manson, A. R. and Hader, R. J. Minimum Bias Approximation of a General Regression Model. *J. Amer. Statist. Assoc.*, September 1973, *68*(343), pp. 633–38.

Creedy, John. A Problem in the Estimation of Double-Log Engel Curves. *Oxford Bull. Econ. Statist.*, August 1973, *35*(3), pp. 217–22. [G: U.K.]

Dagenais, Marcel G. The Use of Incomplete Observations in Multiple Regression Analysis: A Generalized Least Squares Approach. *J. Econometrics*, December 1973, *1*(4), pp. 317–28.

Ebbeler, Donald H. A Note on Large-Sample Approximations in Lognormal Linear Models. *J. Amer. Statist. Assoc.*, March 1973, *68*(341), pp. 231.

Ebbeler, Donald H. On the Measurement of the Permanent Component of a Series. *J. Amer. Statist. Assoc.*, June 1973, *68*(342), pp. 343–47.

Ellenberg, Jonas H. The Joint Distribution of the Standardized Least Squares Residuals from a General Linear Regression. *J. Amer. Statist. Assoc.*, December 1973, *68*(344), pp. 941–43.

Fabrycy, Mark Z. Economic Theory and Multicollinearity. *Amer. Econ.*, Spring 1973, *17*(1), pp. 81–84.

Feldstein, Martin S. Multicollinearity and the Mean Square Error of Alternative Estimators. *Econometrica*, March 1973, *41*(2), pp. 337–46.

Fitts, John. Testing for Autocorrelation in the Autoregressive Moving Average Error Model. *J. Econometrics*, December 1973, *1*(4), pp. 363–76.

Forsythe, Alan B., et al. A Stopping Rule for Variable Selection in Multiple Regression. *J. Amer. Statist. Assoc.*, March 1973, *68*(341), pp. 75–77.

Friedman, Philip. Suggestions for the Analysis of Qualitative Dependent Variables. *Public Finance Quart.*, July 1973, *1*(3), pp. 345–55.

Frome, Edward L.; Kutner, Michael H. and Beauchamp, John J. Regression Analysis of Poisson-Distributed Data. *J. Amer. Statist. Assoc.*, December 1973, *68*(344), pp. 935–40.

Fuller, Wayne A. and Battese, George E. Transformations for Estimation of Linear Models with Nested-Error Structure. *J. Amer. Statist. Assoc.*, September 1973, *68*(343), pp. 626–32.

Gallant, A. R. and Fuller, Wayne A. Fitting Segmented Polynomial Regression Models Whose Join Points Have to Be Estimated. *J. Amer. Statist. Assoc.*, March 1973, *68*(341), pp. 144–47.

Gapinski, James H. Putty-Clay Capital and Small-Sample Properties of Neoclassical Estimators. *J. Polit. Econ.*, January-February 1973, *81*(1), pp. 145–57.

Geary, R. C. Identification of Cause and Effect in Simple Least Squares Regression. *Econ. Soc. Rev.*, October 1973, *5*(1), pp. 1–6.

Gehan, Edmund A. and Siddiqui, M. M. Simple Regression Methods for Survival Time Studies. *J. Amer. Statist. Assoc.*, December 1973, *68*(344), pp. 848–56.

Godfrey, Leslie G. A Note on the Treatment of Serial Correlation. *Can. J. Econ.*, November 1973, *6*(4), pp. 567–73.

Goldberger, Arthur S. Structural Equation Models: An Overview. In *Goldberger, A. S. and Duncan, O. D., eds.*, 1973, pp. 1–18.

Goldfeld, Stephen M. and Quandt, Richard E. The Estimation of Structural Shifts by Switching Regressions. *Ann. Econ. Soc. Measure*, October 1973, *2*(4), pp. 475–85.

Grassini, Maurizio. The Transformation Matrix in the Linear Statistical Model with Serially Correlated Errors Generated by Autoregressive Schemes. *Statistica*, July-September 1973, *33*(3), pp. 395–407.

Grether, D. M. and Maddala, G. S. Errors in Variables and Serially Correlated Disturbances in Distributed Lag Models. *Econometrica*, March 1973, *41*(2), pp. 255–62.

Hartley, H. O. and Jayatillake, K. S. E. Estimation for Linear Models with Unequal Variances. *J. Amer. Statist. Assoc.*, March 1973, *68*(341), pp. 189–92.

Henry, Neil W. Measurement Models for Continuous and Discrete Variables. In *Goldberger, A. S. and Duncan, O. D., eds.*, 1973, pp. 51–67.

Huang, Cliff J. Normality of Disturbance Terms and Specification of the Production Functional Forms. *Southern Econ. J.*, July 1973, *40*(1), pp. 12–18.

Hulett, Joe R. On the Use of Regression Analysis with a Qualitative Dependent Variable. *Public Finance Quart.*, July 1973, *1*(3), pp. 339–44.

Johansson, Johny K. A Generalized Logistic Function with an Application to the Effect of Advertising. *J. Amer. Statist. Assoc.*, December 1973, *68* (344), pp. 824–27.

Larnac, Pierre-Marie. Retards moyens et multiplicateurs dynamiques. (Mean Lags and Dynamic Multipliers. With English summary.) *Revue Écon.*, July 1973, *24*(4), pp. 646–64.

Leone, Fred C. and Moussa-Hamouda, Effat. Relative Efficiencies of 'O-BLUE' Estimators in Simple Linear Regression. *J. Amer. Statist. Assoc.*, December 1973, *68*(344), pp. 953–59.

Levenbach, Hans. The Estimation of Heteroscedasticity from a Marginal Likelihood Function. *J. Amer. Statist. Assoc.*, June 1973, *68*(342), pp. 436–39.

Levi, Maurice D. Errors in the Variables Bias in the Presence of Correctly Measured Variables. *Econometrica*, September 1973, *41*(5), pp. 985–86.

Lyttkens, Ejnar. Investigation of the Fix-Point (FP) and Iterative Instrumental Variables (IIV) and Related Estimation Methods: Various Theoretical Aspects. *Écon. Appl.*, 1973, *26*(2–3–4), pp. 423–70.

Maddala, G. S. and Rao, A. S. Tests for Serial Correlation in Regression Models with Lagged Dependent Variables and Serially Correlated Errors. *Econometrica*, July 1973, *41*(4), pp. 761–74.

Martin, Warren S. The Effects of Scaling on the Correlation Coefficient: A Test of Validity. *J. Marketing Res.*, August 1973, *10*(3), pp. 316–18.

McCallum, B. T. A Note Concerning Asymptotic Covariance Expressions. *Econometrica*, May 1973, *41*(3), pp. 581–83.

Mehran, Farhad. Variance of the MVUE for the Lognormal Mean. *J. Amer. Statist. Assoc.*, September 1973, *68*(343), pp. 726–27.

Merriwether, Jacob D. Small Sample Properties of Distributed Lag Estimators with Misspecified Lag Structures. *J. Amer. Statist. Assoc.*, September 1973, *68*(343), pp. 568–74.

Miron, John R. On the Estimation of a Partial Adjustment Model with Autocorrelated Errors. *Int. Econ. Rev.*, October 1973, *14*(3), pp. 653–56.

Nicholson, R. J. and Topham, N. Step-wise Regression and Principal Components Analysis in Estimating a Relationship in an Econometric Model. *Manchester Sch. Econ. Soc. Stud.*, June 1973, *41*(2), pp. 187–205.

Olshen, Richard A. The Conditional Level of the F-Test. *J. Amer. Statist. Assoc.*, September 1973, *68*(343), pp. 692–98.

Pesaran, M. Hashem. Exact Maximum Likelihood Estimation of a Regression Equation with a First-Order Moving-Average Error. *Rev. Econ. Stud.*, October 1973, *40*(4), pp. 529–35.

Pesaran, M. Hashem. The Small Sample Problem of Truncation Remainders in the Estimation of Distributed Lag Models with Autocorrelated Errors. *Int. Econ. Rev.*, February 1973, *14*(1), pp. 120–31.

Poirier, Dale J. Piecewise Regression Using Cubic Splines. *J. Amer. Statist. Assoc.*, September 1973, *68*(343), pp. 515–24.

Quandt, Richard E. The Estimation of Constant Elasticities: Comment. *Southern Econ. J.*, January 1973, *39*(3), pp. 444–45.

Rizvi, M. Haseeb and Solomon, Herbert. Selection of Largest Multiple Correlation Coefficients: Asymptotic Case. *J. Amer. Statist. Assoc.*, March 1973, *68*(341), pp. 184–88.

Rosenberg, Barr. A Survey of Stochastic Parameter Regression. *Ann. Econ. Soc. Measure*, October 1973, *2*(4), pp. 381–97.

Rosenberg, Barr. The Analysis of a Cross Section of Time Series by Stochastically Convergent Parameter Regression. *Ann. Econ. Soc. Measure*, October 1973, *2*(4), pp. 399–428.

Sawa, Takamitsu and Hiromatsu, Takeshi. Minimax Regret Significance Points for a Preliminary Test in Regression Analysis. *Econometrica*, November 1973, *41*(6), pp. 1093–1101.

Scadding, John L. The Sampling Distribution of the Liviatan Estimator of the Geometric Distributed Lag Parameter. *Econometrica*, May 1973, *41*(3), pp. 503–08.

Schmidt, Peter. Calculating the Power of the Minimum Standard Error Choice Criterion. *Int. Econ. Rev.*, February 1973, *14*(1), pp. 253–55.

Schmidt, Peter. On the Difference Between Conditional and Unconditional Asymptotic Distributions of Estimates in Distributed Lag Models with Integer-Valued Parameters. *Econometrica*, January 1973, *41*(1), pp. 165–69.

Schmidt, Peter and Waud, Roger N. The Almon Lag Technique and the Monetary Versus Fiscal Policy Debate. *J. Amer. Statist. Assoc.*, March 1973, *68*(341), pp. 11–19.

Shiller, Robert J. A Distributed Lag Estimator Derived from Smoothness Priors. *Econometrica*, July 1973, *41*(4), pp. 775–88.

Sielken, R. L., Jr. and Hartley, H. O. Two Linear

Programming Algorithms for Unbiased Estimation of Linear Models. *J. Amer. Statist. Assoc.*, September 1973, *68*(343), pp. 639–41.

Smith, V. Kerry. Least Squares Regression with Cauchy Errors. *Oxford Bull. Econ. Statist.*, August 1973, *35*(3), pp. 223–31.

Stefansky, Wilhelmine and Kaiser, Henry F. Note on Discrete Approximations. *J. Amer. Statist. Assoc.*, March 1973, *68*(341), pp. 232–34.

Swamy, P. A. V. B. Criteria, Constraints and Multicollinearity in Random Coefficient Regression Models. *Ann. Econ. Soc. Measure*, October 1973, *2*(4), pp. 429–50.

Tillman, J. A. The Efficiency of Taking First Differences in Regression Analysis: A Note. *Econ. Soc. Rev.*, July 1973, *4*(4), pp. 543–49.

Willassen, Yngve. Three Econometric Applications of Split-variable and NIPALS Modelling. *Écon. Appl.*, 1973, *26*(2–3–4), pp. 471–504.

Wu, De-Min. Alternative Tests of Independence Between Stochastic Regressors and Disturbances. *Econometrica*, July 1973, *41*(4), pp. 733–50.

Yancey, T. A.; Judge, G. G. and Bock, M. E. Wallace's Weak Mean Square Error Criterion for Testing Linear Restrictions in Regression: A Tighter Bound. *Econometrica*, November 1973, *41*(6), pp. 1203–06.

2114 Multivariate Analysis, Information Theory, and Other Special Inferential Problems; Queuing Theory; Markov Chain

Aigner, Dennis J. An Errors-In-Variables Model in Which Least Squares Is Consistent. *Int. Econ. Rev.*, February 1973, *14*(1), pp. 256–57.

Brumelle, Shelby L. and Schwab, Bernhard. Capital Budgeting with Uncertain Future Opportunities: A Markovian Approach. *J. Financial Quant. Anal.*, January 1973, *8*(1), pp. 111–22.

Cooper, J. Phillip. Time-Varying Regression Coefficients: A Mixed Estimation Approach and Operational Limitations of the General Markov Structure. *Ann. Econ. Soc. Measure*, October 1973, *2*(4), pp. 525–30.

Devore, Jay L. Reconstructing a Noisy Markov Chain. *J. Amer. Statist. Assoc.*, June 1973, *68*(342), pp. 394–98.

Devore, Jay L. Reconstructing a Noisy Markov Chain Using Near-Neighbor Rules. *J. Amer. Statist. Assoc.*, September 1973, *68*(343), pp. 599–602.

Fisher, Lloyd and Van Ness, John W. Admissible Discriminant Analysis. *J. Amer. Statist. Assoc.*, September 1973, *68*(343), pp. 603–07.

Goldfeld, Stephen M. and Quandt, Richard E. The Estimation of Structural Shifts by Switching Regressions. *Ann. Econ. Soc. Measure*, October 1973, *2*(4), pp. 475–85.

Goldfeld, Stephen M. and Quandt, Richard E. A Markov Model for Switching Regressions. *J. Econometrics*, March 1973, *1*(1), pp. 3–15.

Hirshleifer, Jack. Where Are We in the Theory of Information? *Amer. Econ. Rev.*, May 1973, *63*(2), pp. 31–39.

Kenny, David A. Cross-lagged and Synchronous Common Factors in Panel Data. In *Goldberger,*

A. S. and Duncan, O. D., eds., 1973, pp. 153–65.

Moore, Dan H., II. Evaluation of Five Discrimination Procedures for Binary Variables. *J. Amer. Statist. Assoc.*, June 1973, *68*(342), pp. 399–404.

Nath, G. Baikunth. Correlation in a Truncated Bivariate Normal Distribution. *Statistica*, October-December 1973, *33*(4), pp. 563–87.

Nicholson, R. J. and Topham, N. Step-wise Regression and Principal Components Analysis in Estimating a Relationship in an Econometric Model. *Manchester Sch. Econ. Soc. Stud.*, June 1973, *41* (2), pp. 187–205.

Sarris, Alexander H. A Bayesian Approach to Estimation of Time-Varying Regression Coefficients. *Ann. Econ. Soc. Measure,* October 1973, *2*(4), pp. 501–23.

Wiley, David E.; Schmidt, William H. and Bramble, William J. Studies of a Class of Covariance Structure Models. *J. Amer. Statist. Assoc.*, June 1973, *68*(342), pp. 317–23.

2115 Bayesian Statistics and Statistical Decision Theory

Adamec, Štefan. Problémy ekonometrie a rozhodovania. (Problems of Econometrics and Decision. With English summary.) *Ekon.-Mat. Obzor,* 1973, *9*(1), pp. 84–91.

Anderson, Robert J., Jr. A Nesting Theorem on Efficiency of Bayesian or Mixed Regression Model Estimators. *Int. Econ. Rev.*, October 1973, *14*(3), pp. 789–90.

Baron, David P. Point Estimation and Risk Preferences. *J. Amer. Statist. Assoc.*, December 1973, *68* (344), pp. 944–50.

Bassin, William M. A Bayesian Optimal Overhaul Interval Model for the Weibull Restoration Process Case. *J. Amer. Statist. Assoc.*, September 1973, *68*(343), pp. 575–78.

Chow, Gregory C. Multiperiod Predictions from Stochastic Difference Equations by Bayesian Methods. *Econometrica*, January 1973, *41*(1), pp. 109–18.

Cooley, Thomas F. and Prescott, Edward C. Tests of an Adaptive Regression Model. *Rev. Econ. Statist.*, May 1973, *55*(2), pp. 248–56. [G: U.S.]

de Cristofaro, Rodolfo. Probabilità delle ipotesi e loro accettazione. (Probability of Hypotheses and their Acceptance. With English summary.) *Statistica,* January-March 1973, *33*(1), pp. 13–40.

de Cristofaro, Rodolfo. Il confronto tra varianze nell-'inferenza bayesiana. (A Bayesian Approach to the Comparison of Variances. With English summary.) *Statistica,* October-December 1973, *33*(4), pp. 547–59.

Dalrymple, Brent B. Risk Analysis Applied to Commodity Speculation. *J. Econ. Bus.*, Winter 1973, *25*(2), pp. 127–30.

Dayananda, R. A. and Evans, I. G. Bayesian Acceptance-Sampling Schemes for Two-Sided Tests of the Mean of a Normal Distribution of Known Variance. *J. Amer. Statist. Assoc.*, March 1973, *68* (341), pp. 131–36.

DeGroot, Morris H. Doing What Comes Naturally: Interpreting a Tail Area as a Posterior Probability or as a Likelihood Ratio. *J. Amer. Statist. Assoc.,* December 1973, *68*(344), pp. 966–69.

Efron, Bradley and Morris, Carl. Stein's Estimation Rule and Its Competitors—An Empirical Bayes Approach. *J. Amer. Statist. Assoc.,* March 1973, *68* (341), pp. 117–30.

Fishburn, Peter C. A Mixture-Set Axiomatization of Conditional Subjective Expected Utility. *Econometrica,* January 1973, *41*(1), pp. 1–25.

Geisel, Martin S. Bayesian Comparisons of Simple Macroeconomic Models. *J. Money, Credit, Banking,* August 1973, *5*(3), pp. 751–72. [G: U.S.]

Halpern, Elkan F. Polynomial Regression from a Bayesian Approach. *J. Amer. Statist. Assoc.,* March 1973, *68*(341), pp. 137–43.

Hampton, J. M.; Moore, P. G. and Thomas, H. Subjective Probability and Its Measurement. *J. Roy. Statist. Soc.,* Part 1, 1973, *136*, pp. 21–42.

Hull, J.; Moore, P. G. and Thomas, H. Utility and its Measurement. *J. Roy. Statist. Soc.,* Part 2, 1973, *136*, pp. 226–47.

Kelejian, Harry H. Information Lost in Aggregation: A Bayesian Approach—A Further Note. *Econometrica,* March 1973, *41*(2), pp. 375.

Leamer, Edward E. Multicollinearity: A Bayesian Interpretation. *Rev. Econ. Statist.*, August 1973, *55*(3), pp. 371–80.

Mehta, J. S. and Swamy, P. A. V. B. Bayesian Analysis of a Bivariate Normal Distribution with Incomplete Observations. *J. Amer. Statist. Assoc.,* December 1973, *68*(344), pp. 922–27.

Sarris, Alexander H. A Bayesian Approach to Estimation of Time-Varying Regression Coefficients. *Ann. Econ. Soc. Measure,* October 1973, *2*(4), pp. 501–23.

Shiller, Robert J. A Distributed Lag Estimator Derived from Smoothness Priors. *Econometrica,* July 1973, *41*(4), pp. 775–88.

Swamy, P. A. V. B. and Mehta, J. S. Bayesian Analysis of Error Components Regression Models. *J. Amer. Statist. Assoc.,* September 1973, *68*(343), pp. 648–58.

Zellner, Arnold and Richard, Jean F. Use of Prior Information in the Analysis and Estimation of Cobb-Douglas Production Function Models. *Int. Econ. Rev.,* February 1973, *14*(1), pp. 107–19.

Zellner, Arnold and Williams, Anne D. Bayesian Analysis of the Federal Reserve–MIT–Penn Model's Almon Lag Consumption Function. *J. Econometrics,* October 1973, *1*(3), pp. 267–99. [G: U.S.]

2116 Time Series and Spectral Analysis

Bhansali, R. J. A Monte Carlo Comparison of the Regression Method and the Spectral Methods of Prediction. *J. Amer. Statist. Assoc.,* September 1973, *68*(343), pp. 621–25.

Box, G. E. P. and Jenkins, G. M. Some Comments on a Paper by Chatfield and Prothero and on a Review by Kendall. *J. Roy. Statist. Soc.,* Part 3 1973, *136*, pp. 337–52.

Brewer, K. R. W. Some Consequences of Temporal Aggregation and Systematic Sampling for ARMA and ARMAX Models. *J. Econometrics,* June 1973, *1*(2), pp. 133–54.

Chatfield, C. and Prothero, D. L. Box-Jenkins Seasonal Forecasting: Problems in a Case-study. *J. Roy. Statist. Soc.*, Part 3 1973, *136*, pp. 295–315.

Cogger, Kenneth O. Specification Analysis. *J. Amer. Statist. Assoc.*, December 1973, *68*(344), pp. 899–905.

Ebbeler, Donald H. On the Measurement of the Permanent Component of a Series. *J. Amer. Statist. Assoc.*, June 1973, *68*(342), pp. 343–47.

Fase, M. M. G.; Koning, J. and Volgenant, A. F. An Experimental Look at Seasonal Adjustment. *De Economist*, September-October 1973, *121*(5), pp. 441–80.

Johnson, Dudley D. Properties of Alternative Seasonal Adjustment Techniques: A Comment on the OMB Model. *J. Bus.*, April 1973, *46*(2), pp. 284–303.

Mentasti, Flaminio. Osservazioni cicliche attorno alla circolazione monetaria: filtrazione mediante processo di convoluzione. (Convolution Approach in Digital Filtering of Currency Circulation Time Series. With English summary.) *L'Industria,* January-June 1973, (1–2), pp. 176–87.

Phillips, P. C. B. The Problem of Identification in Finite Parameter Continuous Time Models. *J. Econometrics,* December 1973, *1*(4), pp. 351–62.

Schips, B. and Stier, W. Einige Bemerkungen über die Rolle der Spektralanalyse in der empirischen Wirtschaftsforschung. (Some Remarks on the Role of Spectral Analysis for Empirical Economic Research. With English summary.) *Schweiz. Z. Volkswirtsch. Statist.,* June 1973, *109*(2), pp. 233–43.

Shapiro, S. H. On Computing Bayes Risks. *J. Amer. Statist. Assoc.*, June 1973, *68*(342), pp. 485–86.

Shiskin, Julius. Measuring Current Economic Fluctuations. *Ann. Econ. Soc. Measure,* January 1973, *2*(1), pp. 1–15. [G: U.S.]

2117 Survey Methods; Sampling Methods

Berg, Sanford V. The CPS Viewed from the Outside. *Ann. Econ. Soc. Measure,* April 1973, *2*(2), pp. 99–104. [G: U.S.]

Borus, Michael E. and Nestel, Gilbert. Response Bias in Reports of Father's Education and Socioeconomic Status. *J. Amer. Statist. Assoc.*, December 1973, *68*(344), pp. 816–20. [G: U.S.]

Buse, R. C. Increasing Response Rates in Mailed Questionnaires? *Amer. J. Agr. Econ.*, August 1973, *55*(3), pp. 503–08.

Conlisk, John. Choice of Response Functional Form in Designing Subsidy Experiments. *Econometrica,* July 1973, *41*(4), pp. 643–56.

Folsom, Ralph E., et al. The Two Alternate Questions Randomized Response Model for Human Surveys. *J. Amer. Statist. Assoc.*, September 1973, *68*(343), pp. 525–30.

Jarvis, Lovell S. Un ejemplo del uso de modelos económicos para la construcción de datos no disponibles: la estimación de la existencia de vacunos desagregado en Argentina 1937–1967. (An Example of the Use of Economics Models for the Construction of Unavailable Data. The Appreciation of the Existence of Disaggregated Cattle in Argentina—1937–1967. With English summary.) *Económica,* January-April 1973, *19*(1), pp. 71–117. [G: Argentina]

Jennergren, L. Peter. An Optimal Sampling Policy for a Matched Sampling Problem. *J. Amer. Statist. Assoc.*, March 1973, *68*(341), pp. 148–50.

Jones, H. J. M.; Lawson, H. B. and Newman, D. Population Census: Some Recent British Developments in Methodology. *J. Roy. Statist. Soc.*, Part 4, 1973, *136*, pp. 505–20. [G: U.K.]

Kaufman, G. M. and King, Benjamin. A Bayesian Analysis of Nonresponse in Dichotomous Processes. *J. Amer. Statist. Assoc.*, September 1973, *68* (343), pp. 670–78.

Koch, Gary G. An Alternative Approach to Multivariate Response Error Models for Sample Survey Data with Applications to Estimators Involving Subclass Means. *J. Amer. Statist. Assoc.*, December 1973, *68*(344), pp. 906–13.

Lee, Kok-Huat. Variance Estimation in Stratified Sampling. *J. Amer. Statist. Assoc.*, June 1973, *68* (342), pp. 336–42.

Lee, Kok-Huat. Using Partially Balanced Designs for the Half Sample Replication Method of Variance Estimation. *J. Amer. Statist. Assoc.*, September 1973, *68*(343), pp. 612–14.

Martin, Warren S. The Effects of Scaling on the Correlation Coefficient: A Test of Validity. *J. Marketing Res.*, August 1973, *10*(3), pp. 316–18.

Olson, Edwin G. Determining Sample Size for State Tax Impact Studies. *Nat. Tax J.,* March 1973, *26* (1), pp. 99–102. [G: U.S.]

Porter, Richard D. On the Use of Survey Sample Weights in the Linear Model. *Ann. Econ. Soc. Measure,* April 1973, *2*(2), pp. 141–58.

Regan, Opal G. Statistical Reforms Accelerated by Sixth Census Errors. *J. Amer. Statist. Assoc.*, September 1973, *68*(343), pp. 540–46. [G: U.S.]

Smith, James D. New Perspectives in Government Data Distribution: The Current Population Survey. *Ann. Econ. Soc. Measure,* April 1973, *2*(2), pp. 131–39. [G: U.S.]

Sudman, Seymour and Bradburn, Norman M. Effects of Time and Memory Factors on Response in Surveys. *J. Amer. Statist. Assoc.*, December 1973, *68*(344), pp. 805–15.

Thompson, Marvin M. and Shapiro, Gary. The Current Population Survey: An Overview. *Ann. Econ. Soc. Measure,* April 1973, *2*(2), pp. 105–29. [G: U.S.]

2118 Theory of Index Numbers and Aggregation

Alchian, Armen A. and Klein, Benjamin. On a Correct Measure of Inflation. *J. Money, Credit, Banking,* Part I, February 1973, *5*(1), pp. 173–91.

Blin, Jean-Marie. The General Concept of Multidimensional Consistency: Some Algebraic Aspects of the Aggregation Problem. In *Cochrane, J. L. and Zeleny, M., eds.,* 1973, pp. 164–78.

Drechsler, László. Weighting of Index Numbers in Multilateral International Comparisons. *Rev. Income Wealth,* March 1973, *19*(1), pp. 17–34.

Galatin, Malcolm. A True Price Index When the Consumer Saves. *Amer. Econ. Rev.*, March 1973, *63*(1), pp. 185–94.

Hulten, Charles R. Divisia Index Numbers. *Econometrica,* November 1973, *41*(6), pp. 1017–25.

Leamer, Edward E. Empirically Weighted Indexes for Import Demand Functions. *Rev. Econ. Statist.,* November 1973, *55*(4), pp. 441–50.

Lovell, C. A. Knox. A Note on Aggregation Bias and Loss. *J. Econometrics,* October 1973, *1*(3), pp. 301–11. **[G: U.S.]**

Mirrlees, James A. National Income and Social Values: Rejoinder. *Bangladesh Econ. Rev.,* January 1973, *1*(1), pp. 101–02.

Mukherjee, M. and Rao, D. S. Prasada. On Consistent Intergroup Comparisons of Purchasing Power of Money. *Rev. Income Wealth,* March 1973, *19*(1), pp. 35–47.

Rahman, Md. Anisur. National Income and Social Values. *Bangladesh Econ. Rev.,* January 1973, *1* (1), pp. 95–101.

Scheel, William C. A Critique of the Interest-Adjusted Net Cost Index. *J. Risk Ins.,* June 1973, *40*(2), pp. 245–61.

Sondermann, Dieter. Optimale Aggregation von grossen linearen Gleichungssystemen. (Optimal Aggregation of Great Systems of Linear Equations.) *Z. Nationalökon.,* 1973, *33*(3–4), pp. 235–50.

Theil, Henri. Measuring the Quality of the Consumer's Basket. *De Economist,* July-August 1973, *121*(4), pp. 333–46. **[G: Netherlands]**

Theil, Henri. A New Index Number Formula. *Rev. Econ. Statist.,* November 1973, *55*(4), pp. 498–502.

Vişinoiu, N. Aspecte privind teoria tabelelor de indici. (Aspects on the Theory of Index Tables. With English summary.) *Stud. Cercet. Econ.,* 1973, (1), pp. 111–21.

212 Construction, Analysis, and Use of Econometric Models

2120 Construction, Analysis, and Use of Econometric Models

Aigner, Dennis J. and Goldfeld, Stephen M. Simulation and Aggregation: A Reconsideration. *Rev. Econ. Statist.,* February 1973, *55*(1), pp. 114–18.

Burns, M. E. A Note on the Choice of Data in Econometric Studies. *Econ. Rec.,* March 1973, *49* (125), pp. 24–30.

Burrows, Paul and Godfrey, Leslie G. Identifying and Estimating the Parameters of a Symmetrical Model of Inventory Investment. *Appl. Econ.,* September 1973, *5*(3), pp. 193–97.

Choucri, Nazil. Applications of Econometric Analysis to Forecasting in International Relations. *Peace Sci. Soc.,* 1973, *21,* pp. 15–39. **[G: U.K.]**

Chow, Gregory C. Multiperiod Predictions from Stochastic Difference Equations by Bayesian Methods. *Econometrica,* January 1973, *41*(1), pp. 109–18.

Courbis, Raymond and Pagé, Jean-Pierre. Techniques de projection macro-économique et choix du Plan français. (Macro-Economic Forecasting Techniques and Decision Making in the French Planning System. With English summary.) *Revue Écon.,* November 1973, *24*(6), pp. 951–87. **[G: France]**

Crotty, James R. Specification Error in Macro-Econometric Models: The Influence of Policy Goals. *Amer. Econ. Rev.,* December 1973, *63*(5), pp. 1025–30.

Deleau, Michel; Guesnerie, Roger and Malgrange, Pierre. Planification, incertitude et politique économique. II—L'opération Optimix: Résultats numériques. (Planning, Uncertainty and Economic Policy. II—Optimix Operation: Numerical Results. With English summary.) *Revue Écon.,* November 1973, *24*(6), pp. 1072–1103.

Edgerton, David L. The Combined Use of Predictors and Taylor Series in Nonlinear Interdependent Systems. *Écon. Appl.,* 1973, *26*(2–3–4), pp. 537–59.

Fromm, Gary and Klein, Lawrence R. A Comparison of Eleven Econometric Models of the United States. *Amer. Econ. Rev.,* May 1973, *63*(2), pp. 385–93. **[G: U.S.]**

Fromm, Gary and Schink, George R. Aggregation and Econometric Models. *Int. Econ. Rev.,* February 1973, *14*(1), pp. 1–32.

Granger, C. W. J. and Newbold, P. Some Comments on the Evaluation of Economic Forecasts. *Appl. Econ.,* March 1973, *5*(1), pp. 35–47.

Hall, Robert E. The Specification of Technology with Several Kinds of Output. *J. Polit. Econ.,* July-August 1973, *81*(4), pp. 878–92.

Heien, Dale; Matthews, Jim and Womack, Abner. A Methods Note on the Gauss-Seidel Algorithm for Solving Econometric Models. *Agr. Econ. Res.,* July 1973, *25*(3), pp. 71–80.

Hickman, Bert G.; Klein, Lawrence R. and Rhomberg, Rudolf R. Background, Organization and Preliminary Results of Project LINK. In *Alexandrides, C. G., ed.,* 1973, pp. 19–56.

Johansen, Leif. Targets and Instruments under Uncertainty. In *[Tinbergen, J.],* 1973, pp. 3–20.

Kaplan, G. A. Some Problems of Control by Minimum Mean-Square Deviation from Goals. *Matekon,* Summer 1973, *9*(4), pp. 3–9.

Lerviks, Alf-Erik. Synpunkter på ekonomiskt modellbyggande. (On Model Construction in Economic Sciences. With English summary.) *Ekon. Samfundets Tidskr.,* 1973, *26*(4), pp. 301–04.

Lybeck, Johan A. The Monetary Sector of the Bank of Finland's Quarterly Model: A Critical Comment. *Ekon. Samfundets Tidskr.,* 1973, *26*(2), pp. 117–21. **[G: Finland]**

McLaren, J. Alec. An Income Tax Simulation Model for the State of Minnesota. *Nat. Tax J.,* March 1973, *26*(1), pp. 71–77. **[G: U.S.]**

McNees, Stephen K. The Predictive Accuracy of Econometric Forecasts. *New Eng. Econ. Rev.,* September-October 1973, pp. 3–27.

Meissner, Werner. Econometric Models: Cognitive Aims and Aspiration Levels. *Écon. Appl.,* 1973, *26* (2–3–4), pp. 367–84.

Nordberg, Leif. Om möjligheterna att utnyttja data från flera länder vid konstruktionen av ekonometriska modeller. (The Possibilities of Using Data from Several Countries in the Construction of Econometric Models. With English summary.)

Ekon. Samfundets Tidskr., 1973, *26*(2), pp. 105–16.

Schwarze, Jochen. Probleme der Fehlermessung bei quantitativen ökonomischen Prognosen. (Problems of Measuring of Errors in Quantitative Economic Forecasting. With English summary.) *Z. ges. Staatswiss.*, August 1973, *129*(3), pp. 535–58.

Scioli, Frank P., Jr. and Cook, Thomas J. Experimental Design in Policy Impact Analysis. *Soc. Sci. Quart.*, September 1973, *54*(2), pp. 271–80.

Shapiro, Harold T. Is Verification Possible? The Evaluation of Large Econometric Models. *Amer. J. Agr. Econ.*, May 1973, *55*(2), pp. 250–58.

Smith, V. Kerry and Loeb, Peter D. Misspecification and the Small Sample Properties of Econometric Estimators. *Appl. Econ.*, September 1973, *5*(3), pp. 167–79. [G: U.S.]

Trivedi, P. K. Retail Inventory Investment Behaviour. *J. Econometrics*, March 1973, *1*(1), pp. 61–80. [G: U.K.]

Zeleny, Milan and Cochrane, James L. A Priori and A Posteriori Goals in Macroeconomic Policy Making. In *Cochrane, J. L. and Zeleny, M., eds.*, 1973, pp. 373–91.

213 Mathematical Methods and Models

2130 General

Afriat, S. N. A Theorem on Shadow Prices. *Econometrica*, November 1973, *41*(6), pp. 1197–99.

Aganbegian, A. G. and Bagrinovsky, K. A. Problem-Complexes in Optimal Planning. *Acta Oecon.*, 1973, *10*(1), pp. 21–27.

Berndt, Ernst R. and Christensen, Laurits R. The Internal Structure of Functional Relationships: Separability, Substitution and Aggregation. *Rev. Econ. Stud.*, July 1973, *40*(3), pp. 403–10.

Bhattacharya, Rabindra Nath and Majumdar, Mukul. Random Exchange Economies. *J. Econ. Theory*, February 1973, *6*(1), pp. 37–67.

Burns, Tom and Meeker, L. D. A Mathematical Model of Multi-Dimensional Evaluation, Decision-Making, and Social Interaction. In *Cochrane, J. L. and Zeleny, M., eds.*, 1973, pp. 141–63.

Cox, James C. A Theorem on Additively-Separable, Quasi-Concave Functions. *J. Econ. Theory*, April 1973, *6*(2), pp. 210–12.

Cuénod, Michel. Identification Procedures for Dynamic Systems. In *Ross, M., ed.*, 1973, pp. 75–100.

Fromm, Gary. Implications to and from Economic Theory in Models of Complex Systems. *Amer. J. Agr. Econ.*, May 1973, *55*(2), pp. 259–71.

Ginsberg, William. Concavity and Quasiconcavity in Economics. *J. Econ. Theory*, December 1973, *6*(6), pp. 596–605.

Gottinger, Hans-Werner. Toward a Fuzzy Reasoning in the Behavioral Sciences. *Ekon.-Mat. Obzor*, 1973, *9*(4), pp. 404–22.

Hurwicz, Leonid and Reiter, Stanley. On the Boundedness of the Feasible Set Without Convexity Assumptions. *Int. Econ. Rev.*, October 1973, *14*(3), pp. 580–86.

Kane, Julius; Vertinsky, Ilan and Thomson, William. KSIM: A Methodology for Interactive Resource Policy Simulation. *Water Resources Res.*, February 1973, *9*(1), pp. 65–79.

Kendall, M. G. A Computer Method of Analysing the Structure of Behavioural Models. In *Hawkes, N., ed.*, 1973, pp. 170–77.

Moiseev, Nikita N. Operations Research in the U.S.S.R.—Development and Perspectives. In *Ross, M., ed.*, 1973, pp. 41–55. [G: U.S.S.R.]

Teodorescu, N. Mathematical Modelling of Cybernetic Systems. In *Hawkes, N., ed.*, 1973, pp. 182–94.

Uekawa, Yasuo; Kemp, Murray C. and Wegge, Leon L. P- and PN-Matrices, Minkowski- and Metzler-Matrices, and Generalizations of the Stolper-Samuelson and Samuelson-Rybczynski Theorems. *J. Int. Econ.*, February 1973, *3*(1), pp. 53–76.

Vişinoiu, N. Utilizarea teoriei grafurilor în studiul relaţiilor dintre mărimile relative ale dinamicii produsului social. (The Utilization of the Theory of Graphs in Studying the Relations Between the Relative Sizes of the Dynamics of the Social Product. With English summary.) *Stud. Cercet. Econ.*, 1973, (3), pp. 85–98.

Zhuravlev, Y. I. Algorithms for Assessing the Quality of Expert Data. In *Hawkes, N., ed.*, 1973, pp. 238–42.

Zoutendijk, G. Nonlinear Programming. In *Ross, M., ed.*, 1973, pp. 555–57.

2132 Optimization Techniques

Ang, James S. Reliability of Using the Mean Absolute Deviation to Derive Efficient E, V Farm Plans: Comment. *Amer. J. Agr. Econ.*, Part I, November 1973, *55*(4), pp. 675–77.

Balquière, Austin and Caussin, Pierre. Differential Games with Time Lag. In *Blaquière, A., ed.*, 1973, pp. 151–78.

Barták, Rudolf and Hynar, Ladislav. Optimální cesty. (Optimal Routes. With English summary.) *Ekon.-Mat. Obzor*, 1973, *9*(2), pp. 167–83.

Blaquière, Austin and Caussin, Pierre. Further Geometric Aspects of Differential Games. In *Blaquière, A., ed.*, 1973, pp. 101–49.

Blaquière, Austin; Juricek, Libuska and Wiese, Karl E. Geometry of Pareto Equilibria in N-Person Differential Games. In *Blaquière, A., ed.*, 1973, pp. 271–310.

Boehlje, Michael. Optimization and Decision Models: The Use of Statistical Search Procedures. *Can. J. Agr. Econ.*, July 1973, *21*(2), pp. 43–53.

Chow, Gregory C. Effect of Uncertainty on Optimal Control Policies. *Int. Econ. Rev.*, October 1973, *14*(3), pp. 632–45.

Chow, Gregory C. Problems of Economic Policy from the Viewpoint of Optimal Control. *Amer. Econ. Rev.*, December 1973, *63*(5), pp. 825–37.

Ciletti, Michael D. Differential Games with Information Time Lag. In *Blaquière, A., ed.*, 1973, pp. 179–268.

Cox, James C. Properties of Functions which are Solutions to Maximization Problems. *J. Econ. Theory*, August 1973, *6*(4), pp. 396–98.

Fazel, Hassan. Optimization and Decision Models. *Can. J. Agr. Econ.*, July 1973, *21*(2), pp. 54–58.

Infante, Ettore F. and Stein, Jerome L. Optimal

Growth with Robust Feedback Control. *Rev. Econ. Stud.*, January 1973, *40*(1), pp. 47–60.

Isaacs, Rufus. Some Fundamentals of Differential Games. In *Blaquière, A., ed.*, 1973, pp. 1–42.

Kazakova, M. F. A "Branches-Bounds" Type Method for the Generalized Knapsack Problem. *Matekon*, Spring 1973, *9*(3), pp. 47–54.

Morrison, Clarence C. and Higgins, Richard S. A Note on Comparative Statics Analysis in Equality Constrained Models. *Southern Econ. J.*, April 1973, *39*(4), pp. 638–41.

Oniki, Hajime. Comparative Dynamics (Sensitivity Analysis) in Optimal Control Theory. *J. Econ. Theory*, June 1973, *6*(3), pp. 265–83.

Pchenitchny, Boris N. ε-Strategies in Differential Games. In *Blaquière, A., ed.*, 1973, pp. 45–99.

Peterson, David W. The Economic Significance of Auxiliary Functions in Optimal Control. *Int. Econ. Rev.*, February 1973, *14*(1), pp. 234–52.

Stalford, Harold and Leitmann, George. Sufficiency Conditions for Nash Equilibria in N-Person Differential Games. In *Blaquière, A., ed.*, 1973, pp. 345–76.

Stern, Ronald J. and Ben-Israel, Adi. On Linear Optimal Control Problems with Multiple Quadratic Criteria. In *Cochrane, J. L. and Zeleny, M., eds.*, 1973, pp. 366–72.

Švábová, Milada and Marunová, Eva. Zobecnění MODI-metody pro žiskání optimálního řešení jednoho typu trojrozměrného dopravního problému. (Generalization of Modi-Method for Getting the Optimal Solution of One Type of Three-Dimensional Transportation Problem. With English summary.) *Ekon.-Mat. Obzor*, 1973, *9*(2), pp. 201–11.

Thomson, K. J. and Hazell, P. B. R. Reliability of Using the Mean Absolute Deviation to Derive Efficient *E*, *V* Farm Plans: Reply. *Amer. J. Agr. Econ.*, Part I, November 1973, *55*(4), pp. 677–78.

Turnovsky, Stephen J. Optimal Stabilization Policies for Deterministic and Stochastic Linear Economic Systems. *Rev. Econ. Stud.*, January 1973, *40*(1), pp. 79–95.

Yu, P. L. Introduction to Domination Structures in Multicriteria Decision Problems. In *Cochrane, J. L. and Zeleny, M., eds.*, 1973, pp. 249–61.

Zimmermann, Karel. Solution of Some Optimization Problems in Extremal Vector Space. (In Russian. With English summary.) *Ekon.-Mat. Obzor*, 1973, *9*(3), pp. 336–50.

2133 Existence and Stability Conditions of Equilibrium

Allingham, M. G. and Morishima, M. Qualitative Economics and Comparative Statics. In *Morishima, M., et al.*, 1973, pp. 3–69.

Conlisk, John. Quick Stability Checks and Matrix Norms. *Economica, N.S.*, November 1973, *40*(160), pp. 402–09.

Hahn, Frank H. On Some Equilibrium Paths. In *Mirrlees, J. A. and Stern, N. H., eds.*, 1973, pp. 193–206.

Metzler, Lloyd A. Stability of Multiple Markets: The Hicks Conditions. In *Metzler, L. A.*, 1973, pp. 499–515.

Mukherji, Anjan. On the Sensitivity of Stability Results to the Choice of the Numeraire. *Rev. Econ. Stud.*, July 1973, *40*(3), pp. 427–33.

Sato, Ryuzo. On the Stability Properties of Dynamic Economic Systems. *Int. Econ. Rev.*, October 1973, *14*(3), pp. 753–64.

2134 Computational Techniques

Candler, Wilfred V.; Cartwright, R. Wayne and Penn, J. B. The Substitution of Analytic for Simulation Algorithms: Comment. *Amer. J. Agr. Econ.*, May 1973, *55*(2), pp. 235–39.

Dellepiane, Nicola. Localizzazione delle attività interne: metodi quantitativi di ottimizzazione. (Locating facilities: Optimizing Techniques. With English summary.) *L'Impresa*, 1973, *15*(2), pp. 157–63.

Farebrother, R. W. Simplified Samuelson Conditions for Cubic and Quartic Equations. *Manchester Sch. Econ. Soc. Stud.*, December 1973, *41*(4), pp. 396–400.

Glückaufová, Dagmar and Turková, Dana. Některá rozšíření metody zobecněných horních mezí. (Some Extensions of Generalized Upper Bounding Technique. With English summary.) *Ekon.-Mat. Obzor*, 1973, *9*(4), pp. 423–49.

Jennergren, L. Peter. A Price Schedules Decomposition Algorithm for Linear Programming Problems. *Econometrica*, September 1973, *41*(5), pp. 965–80.

Klema, Virginia. A Note on Matrix Factorization. *Ann. Econ. Soc. Measure*, July 1973, *2*(3), pp. 317–22.

Moeller, John F. Development of a Microsimulation Model for Evaluating Economic Implications of Income Transfer and Tax Policies. *Ann. Econ. Soc. Measure*, April 1973, *2*(2), pp. 183–87.

Sielken, R. L., Jr. and Hartley, H. O. Two Linear Programming Algorithms for Unbiased Estimation of Linear Models. *J. Amer. Statist. Assoc.*, September 1973, *68*(343), pp. 639–41.

Sirenko, E. I. Methods for Solving Linear Programming Problems on Analogue Computers. *Matekon*, Winter 1973-74, *10*(2), pp. 56–63.

Thompson, S. C. The Substitution of Analytic for Simulation Algorithms: Response. *Amer. J. Agr. Econ.*, May 1973, *55*(2), pp. 240–41.

2135 Construction, Analysis, and Use of Mathematical Programming Models

Alemany, Ricardo; Fernandez, Pedro and Pousa, Aurora G. Algorithm for Solving a Class of Linear Programing Problems Related to Reservoir Management and Design. *Water Resources Res.*, October 1973, *9*(5), pp. 1227–34.

Baron, David P. Stochastic Programming and Risk Aversion. In *Cochrane, J. L. and Zeleny, M., eds.*, 1973, pp. 124–38.

Chernov, Iu. P. Problems of Fractional Programming with Linear, Separable, and Quadratic Functions. *Matekon*, Spring 1973, *9*(3), pp. 22–40.

Chervak, Iu. Iu. On the Problem of Constructing Supplementary Constraints in Gomory's Integer

Linear Programming Method. *Matekon*, Winter 1973-74, *10*(2), pp. 52–55.

Chobot, Michal. Stochasticky prístup k ciel'ovému programovaniu. (Stochastic Approaches to Goal Programming. With English summary.) *Ekon.-Mat. Obzor*, 1973, *9*(3), pp. 305–19.

Day, Richard H. and Nelson, Jon P. A Class of Dynamic Models for Describing and Projecting Industrial Development. *J. Econometrics*, June 1973, *1*(2), pp. 155–90. **[G: U.S.; Japan]**

Dinkelbach, Werner and Isermann, Heinz. On Decision Making under Multiple Criteria and under Incomplete Information. In *Cochrane, J. L. and Zeleny, M., eds.*, 1973, pp. 302–12.

Dyer, James S. An Empirical Investigation of a Man-Machine Interactive Approach to the Solution of the Multiple Criteria Problem. In *Cochrane, J. L. and Zeleny, M., eds.*, 1973, pp. 202–16.

Eastman, John and ReVelle, Charles. Linear Decision Rule in Reservoir Management and Design: 3. Direct Capacity Determination and Intraseasonal Constraints. *Water Resources Res.*, February 1973, *9*(1), pp. 29–42.

Evans, John P. and Steuer, Ralph E. Generating Efficient Extreme Points in Linear Multiple Objective Programming: Two Algorithms and Computing Experience. In *Cochrane, J. L. and Zeleny, M., eds.*, 1973, pp. 349–65.

Hammer, Peter L. Some Developments in 0–1 Programming. In *Ross, M., ed.*, 1973, pp. 551–54.

Jennergren, L. Peter. A Price Schedules Decomposition Algorithm for Linear Programming Problems. *Econometrica*, September 1973, *41*(5), pp. 965–80.

Malinnikov, V. V. The Decompostiion Method in the Solution of Large-Scale Linear Programming Problems with Block Structure. *Matekon*, Spring 1973, *9*(3), pp. 41–46.

Moiseev, Nikita N. Principles of Simulation: Hierarchial Control Systems. In *Hawkes, N., ed.*, 1973, pp. 205–26.

Morin, Thomas L. Pathology of a Dynamic Programming Sequencing Algorithm. *Water Resources Res.*, October 1973, *9*(5), pp. 1178–85.

Paris, Quirino and Rausser, Gordon C. Sufficient Conditions for Aggregation of Linear Programming Models. *Amer. J. Agr. Econ.*, Part I, November 1973, *55*(4), pp. 659–66.

Pasternak, Hanoch and Passy, Ury. Bicriterion Mathematical Programs with Boolean Variables. In *Cochrane, J. L. and Zeleny, M., eds.*, 1973, pp. 327–48.

Polterovich, V. M. On the Formulation of Integer Linear Programming Problems. *Matekon*, Winter 1973-74, *10*(2), pp. 36–51.

Sengupta, S. Sankar; Podrebarac, Michael L. and Fernando, T. D. H. Probabilities of Optima in Multi-Objective Linear Programmes. In *Cochrane, J. L. and Zeleny, M., eds.*, 1973, pp. 217–35. **[G: Canada]**

Votiakov, A. A. Integer Programming: A Comparison of Cutoffs. *Matekon*, Summer 1973, *9*(4), pp. 80–94.

Windsor, James S. Optimization Model for the Operation of Flood Control Systems. *Water Resources Res.*, October 1973, *9*(5), pp. 1219–26.

Young, H. Peyton and Thompson, Russell G. Least-Cost Allocation and Valuation Model for Water Resources. *Water Resources Res.*, October 1973, *9*(5), pp. 1186–95.

Zeleny, Milan. Compromise Programming. In *Cochrane, J. L. and Zeleny, M., eds.*, 1973, pp. 262–301.

Zukhovitskii, S. T.; Poliak, R. A. and Primak, M. E. Concave Multiperson Games: Numerical Methods. *Matekon*, Summer 1973, *9*(4), pp. 10–30.

214 Computer Programs

2140 Computer Programs

Almon, Clopper. Programs and Methods for Input-Output Analysis—A Preview. *Ann. Econ. Soc. Measure*, July 1973, *2*(3), pp. 307–08.

Dagli, Ates, et al. Microdata Processing Package. *Ann. Econ. Soc. Measure*, July 1973, *2*(3), pp. 303–05.

Dathe, H. M. Cybernetic Models as Aids in Normative Forecasting. In *Blohm, H. and Steinbuch, K., eds.*, 1973, pp. 39–53.

Dyer, James S. An Empirical Investigation of a Man-Machine Interactive Approach to the Solution of the Multiple Criteria Problem. In *Cochrane, J. L. and Zeleny, M., eds.*, 1973, pp. 202–16.

Eisner, Mark and Pindyck, Robert S. A Generalized Approach to Estimation as Implemented in the TROLL/1 System. *Ann. Econ. Soc. Measure*, January 1973, *2*(1), pp. 29–51.

Francis, Ivor. A Comparison of Several Analysis of Variance Programs. *J. Amer. Statist. Assoc.*, December 1973, *68*(344), pp. 860–65.

Freiden, Alan. A Program for the Estimation of Dymanic Economic Relations from a Time Series of Cross Sections. *Ann. Econ. Soc. Measure*, January 1973, *2*(1), pp. 89–91.

Holland, Paul W. Computer Research Center for Economics and Management Science: The Data-Analysis Project (March 1973) *Ann. Econ. Soc. Measure*, April 1973, *2*(2), pp. 221–24.

Jones, Lonnie L. and Mustafa, Gholam. RIMLOC: A Computer Algorithm for Regional Input-Output Analyses. *Ann. Econ. Soc. Measure*, July 1973, *2*(3), pp. 313–16.

Kendall, M. G. A Computer Method of Analysing the Structure of Behavioural Models. In *Hawkes, N., ed.*, 1973, pp. 170–77.

Liew, C. K. A Computer Program for Dynamic Multipliers. *Econometrica*, November 1973, *41*(6), pp. 1207.

Robinson, Randall S. BANKMOD: An Interactive Simulation Aid for Bank Financial Planning. *J. Bank Res.*, Autumn 1973, *4*(3), pp. 212–24.

Shapiro, Jeremy F. Computer Research Center for Economics and Management Science: The Mathematical Programming Project (March 1973) *Ann. Econ. Soc. Measure*, April 1973, *2*(2), pp. 224–25.

Sirenko, E. I. Methods for Solving Linear Programming Problems on Analogue Computers. *Matekon*, Winter 1973-74, *10*(2), pp. 56–63.

Wolff, Edward. IOPE: Input/Output Program for Economists. *Ann. Econ. Soc. Measure*, July 1973, *2*(3), pp. 309–12.

Zelinka, Jan and Pražák, Ivo. Systém programů pro ekonomicko-matematické úlohy. (System of Computer Programs for Economic-Mathematical Calculations. With English summary.) *Ekon.-Mat. Obzor,* 1973, *9*(4), pp. 393–403.

220 ECONOMIC AND SOCIAL STATISTICS

2200 General

Allen, Jodie T. A Guide to the 1960–1971 Current Population Survey Files. *Ann. Econ. Soc. Measure,* April 1973, *2*(2), pp. 189–99. [G: U.S.]

Berg, Sanford V. The CPS Viewed from the Outside. *Ann. Econ. Soc. Measure,* April 1973, *2*(2), pp. 99–104. [G: U.S.]

Clague, Ewan. Developments in Labor Statistics. In *Somers, G. G., ed.,* 1973, pp. 37–46. [G: U.S.]

Hsaio-wen, Kung. We Must Keep Count: In Refutation of "Statistics Is Useless." *Chinese Econ. Stud.,* Spring 1973, *6*(3), pp. 32–38. [G: China]

Kraseman, Thomas W. Statistics and Analysis. *Mon. Lab. Rev.,* January 1973, *96*(1), pp. 58–59. [G: U.S.]

Kuznets, Simon. Data for Quantitative Economic Analysis: Problems of Demand and Supply. In *Kuznets, S.,* 1973, pp. 243–62.

Kuznets, Simon. The Measurement of Economic and Social Performance: Concluding Remarks. In *Moss, M., ed.,* 1973, pp. 579–92. [G: U.S.]

Wilson, J. Harold. Statistics and Decision-making in Government— Bradshaw Revisited: The Address of the President (with Proceedings). *J. Roy. Statist. Soc.,* Part 1, 1973, *136,* pp. 1–20. [G: U.K.]

221 National Income Accounting

2210 National Income Accounting Theory and Procedures

Aidenoff, Abraham. A Proposal for a System of Economic and Social Accounts: Comment. In *Moss, M., ed.,* 1973, pp. 153–59. [G: U.S.]

Bain, A. D. Flow of Funds Analysis: Survey. *Econ. J.,* December 1973, *83*(332), pp. 1055–93.

Blohm, Margareta and Ohlsson, Ingvar. Experience in Measurement of Welfare Components and their Regional Implications. *Rev. Income Wealth,* June 1973, *19*(2), pp. 167–88. [G: Sweden]

Boulding, Kenneth E. Fun and Games with the Gross National Product—The Role of Misleading Indicators in Social Policy. In *Reynolds, L. G.; Green, G. D. and Lewis, D. R., eds.,* 1973, pp. 112–22.

Boulding, Kenneth E. Fun and Games with the Gross National Product: The Role of Misleading Indicators in Social Policy. In *Boulding, K. E.,* 1973, pp. 467–82.

Boulding, Kenneth E. The Need for Reform of National Income Statistics. In *Boulding, K. E.,* 1973, pp. 581–86. [G: U.S.]

Carlin, Thomas A. and Smith, Allen G. A New Approach in Accounting for Our Nation's Farm Income. *Agr. Finance Rev.,* July 1973, *34,* pp. 1–6. [G: U.S.]

Christensen, Laurits R. and Jorgenson, Dale W. Measuring Economic Performance in the Private Sector. In *Moss, M., ed.,* 1973, pp. 233–338. [G: U.S.]

Christensen, Laurits R. and Jorgenson, Dale W. Measuring Economic Performance in the Private Sector: Reply to Kendrick. In *Moss, M., ed.,* 1973, pp. 350–51. [G: U.S.]

Christensen, Laurits R. and Jorgenson, Dale W. Measuring Economic Performance in the Private Sector: Reply to Eisner. In *Moss, M., ed.,* 1973, pp. 349–50. [G: U.S.]

Denison, Edward F. A Proposal for a System of Economic and Social Accounts: Comment. In *Moss, M., ed.,* 1973, pp. 159–60. [G: U.S.]

Denton, Frank T. and Oksanen, Ernest H. Data Revisions and Forecasting Accuracy: An Econometric Analysis Based on Preliminary and Revised National Accounting Estimates. *Rev. Income Wealth,* December 1973, *19*(4), pp. 437–52.

Edde, Richard. Production, Income and Expenditure. *S. Afr. J. Econ.,* September 1973, *41*(3), pp. 268–80.

Eisner, Robert. A Framework for the Measurement of Economic and Social Performance: Comment. In *Moss, M., ed.,* 1973, pp. 99–102. [G: U.S.]

Eisner, Robert. Measuring Economic Performance in the Private Sector: Comment. In *Moss, M., ed.,* 1973, pp. 343–49. [G: U.S.]

Enthoven, Adolf J. H. Standardized Accountancy and Economic Development. *Finance Develop.,* March 1973, *10*(1), pp. 28–31.

Foulon, Alain. Consommation des ménages et consommation publique "divisible": Structure, évolution et financement 1959–1969. (Private Consumption and Public "Divisible" Consumption: Structure, Evolution and Financement. 1959–1969. With English summary.) *Consommation,* April-June 1973, *20*(2), pp. 5–94. [G: France]

Frey, Helmuth E. The Treatment of Import Duties in National Accounts, A Comment on A. L. Gaathon: Exchange Rate Problems in National Accounting of Developing Countries. *Rev. Income Wealth,* June 1973, *19*(2), pp. 203–05.

Gaathon, A. L. Exchange Rate Problems in National Accounting of Developing Countries: Reply. *Rev. Income Wealth,* June 1973, *19*(2), pp. 207–09.

Geary, R. C. Reflections on National Accounting. *Rev. Income Wealth,* September 1973, *19*(3), pp. 221–51.

Haig, Bryan D. The Treatment of Banks in the Social Accounts. *Econ. Rec.,* December 1973, *49*(128), pp. 624–28. [G: Australia]

Haig, Bryan D. The Treatment of Stock Appreciation in the Measurement of National Income. *Rev. Income Wealth,* December 1973, *19*(4), pp. 429–36.

Hartle, Douglas G. A Proposal for a System of Economic and Social Accounts: Comment. In *Moss, M., ed.,* 1973, pp. 146–53. [G: U.S.]

Heston, Alan. A Comparison of Some Short-Cut Methods of Estimating Real Product Per Capita. *Rev. Income Wealth,* March 1973, *19*(1), pp. 79–104.

Jansen, M. A. Problems of International Comparisons of National Accounting Aggregates Between

Countries with Different Economic Systems. *Rev. Income Wealth*, March 1973, *19*(1), pp. 69–77.

Jaszi, George. A Framework for the Measurement of Economic and Social Performance: Comment. In *Moss, M., ed.*, 1973, pp. 84–99. **[G: U.S.]**

Juster, F. Thomas. A Framework for the Measurement of Economic and Social Performance. In *Moss, M., ed.*, 1973, pp. 25–84. **[G: U.S.]**

Juster, F. Thomas. A Framework for the Measurement of Economic and Social Performance: Reply. In *Moss, M., ed.*, 1973, pp. 105–09. **[G: U.S.]**

Kendrick, John W. Measuring Economic Performance in the Private Sector: Comment. In *Moss, M., ed.*, 1973, pp. 338–43. **[G: U.S.]**

Kovács, J. Simplified Model for Level-of-Planning-Consistency Control. *Acta Oecon.*, 1973, *11*(2–3), pp. 177–90.

Kravis, Irving B. and Kenessey, Zoltan. Output and Prices in the International Comparison Project. *Rev. Income Wealth*, March 1973, *19*(1), pp. 49–67.

Kreps, Clifton H., Jr. Statistics for Public Policy Formation: New Needs. *Nebr. J. Econ. Bus.*, Winter 1973, *12*(1), pp. 61–63.

Kurabayashi, Yoshimasa. Use of National Accounts as a Basis of Economic Data System. *Hitotsubashi J. Econ.*, June 1973, *14*(1), pp. 22–43. **[G: Japan]**

Mirrlees, James A. National Income and Social Values: Rejoinder. *Bangladesh Econ. Rev.*, January 1973, *1*(1), pp. 101–02.

Moser, Claus A. and Beesley, I. B. United Kingdom Official Statistics and the European Communities. *J. Roy. Statist. Soc.*, Part 4, 1973, *136*, pp. 539–72. **[G: U.K.; E.E.C.]**

Myrdal, Gunnar. Causes and Nature of Development. *Tahq. Eq.*, Winter & Spring 1973, *10*(29 & 30), pp. 3–16.

Novak, George J. Priorities for Statistical Development. *Finance Develop.*, September 1973, *10*(3), pp. 9–13.

Rahman, Md. Anisur. National Income and Social Values. *Bangladesh Econ. Rev.*, January 1973, *1*(1), pp. 95–101.

Rawski, Thomas G. Chinese Industrial Production, 1952-1971. *Rev. Econ. Statist.*, May 1973, *55*(2), pp. 169–81. **[G: China]**

Ruggles, Nancy and Ruggles, Richard. A Proposal for a System of Economic and Social Accounts. In *Moss, M., ed.*, 1973, pp. 111–46. **[G: U.S.]**

Salazar-Carrillo, Jorge. Price, Purchasing Power and Real Product Comparisons in Latin America. *Rev. Income Wealth*, March 1973, *19*(1), pp. 117–32. **[G: Latin America]**

Schimmler, Harry. On National Accounts at Constant Prices. *Rev. Income Wealth*, December 1973, *19*(4), pp. 457–61.

Scitovsky, Tibor. The Place of Economic Welfare in Human Welfare. *Quart. Rev. Econ. Bus.*, Autumn 1973, *13*(3), pp. 7–19.

Sevaldson, Per. Price Differentiation and Computation of National Accounts Figures at Constant Prices. *Rev. Income Wealth*, December 1973, *19*(4), pp. 453–56.

Solow, Robert M. A Framework for the Measurement of Economic and Social Performance: Com-

ment. In *Moss, M., ed.*, 1973, pp. 102–05. **[G: U.S.]**

Weinrobe, Maurice D. Accounting for Pollution: Pollution Abatement and the National Product. *Land Econ.*, May 1973, *49*(2), pp. 115–21.

Wood, G. Donald, Jr. Problems of Comparisons in Africa with Special Regard to Kenya. *Rev. Income Wealth*, March 1973, *19*(1), pp. 105–16. **[G: Africa; Kenya]**

2212 National Income Accounts

Arndt, H. W. Regional Income Estimates. *Bull. Indonesian Econ. Stud.*, November 1973, *9*(3), pp. 87–102. **[G: Indonesia]**

Behrman, Jere R. Cyclical Sectoral Capacity Utilization in a Developing Economy. In *Eckaus, R. S. and Rosenstein-Rodan, P. N., eds.*, 1973, pp. 251–66. **[G: Chile]**

Boulding, Kenneth E. The Impact of the Defense Industry on the Structure of the American Economy. In *Udis, B., ed.*, 1973, pp. 225–52. **[G: U.S.]**

Carlin, Thomas A. and Reinsel, Edward I. Combining Income and Wealth: An Analysis of Farm Family "Well-Being." *Amer. J. Agr. Econ.*, February 1973, *55*(1), pp. 38–44. **[G: U.S.]**

Carson, Carol S. Inventory-Sales Ratios in Manufacturing and Trade, 1961–72. *Surv. Curr. Bus.*, February 1973, *53*(2), pp. 41–48. **[G: U.S.]**

Christensen, Laurits R. and Jorgenson, Dale W. U.S. Income, Saving, and Wealth, 1929–1969. *Rev. Income Wealth*, December 1973, *19*(4), pp. 329–62. **[G: U.S.]**

Desai, Padma. Soviet Industrial Production: Estimates of Gross Outputs by Branches and Groups. *Oxford Bull. Econ. Statist.*, May 1973, *35*(2), pp. 153–71. **[G: U.S.S.R.]**

Elliott, J. W. A Direct Comparison of Short-Run GNP Forecasting Models. *J. Bus.*, January 1973, *46*(1), pp. 33–60. **[G: U.S.]**

Gottsegen, Jack J. GNP by Major Industry, 1972. *Surv. Curr. Bus.*, April 1973, *53*(4), pp. 19–21. **[G: U.S.]**

Harberger, Arnold C. On Estimating the Rate of Return to Capital in Colombia. In *Harberger, A. C.*, 1973, pp. 132–56. **[G: Columbia]**

Helmstädter, Ernst. The Long-Run Movement of the Capital-Output Ratio and of Labour's Share. In *Mirrlees, J. A. and Stern, N. H., eds.*, 1973, pp. 3–17. **[G: U.K.; Germany; U.S.]**

Janowitz, Barbara S. The Effects of Demographic Factors on Age Composition and the Implications for Per Capita Income. *Demography*, November 1973, *10*(4), pp. 507–15. **[G: U.S.]**

Keller, Robert R. Estimates of National Income and Product, 1919–1941: The Best of All Possible Worlds. *Exploration Econ. Hist.*, Fall 1973, *11*(1), pp. 87–88. **[G: U.S.]**

La Tourette, John E. Public and Private Capital and the Capital Coefficient in Canada: Reply. *Quart. Rev. Econ. Bus.*, Spring 1973, *13*(1), pp. 100–04. **[G: Canada]**

La Tourette, John E. Capital and Output in Postwar Canada. *Amer. Econ.*, Spring 1973, *17*(1), pp. 70–80. **[G: Canada]**

Odling-Smee, J. C. Personal Saving Revisited: More Statistics, Fewer Facts. *Oxford Bull. Econ. Statist.,* February 1973, *35*(1), pp. 21–29. [G: U.K.]

Palmer, John P. Public and Private Capital and the Capital Coefficient in Canada: Comment. *Quart. Rev. Econ. Bus.,* Spring 1973, *13*(1), pp. 97–100. [G: Canada]

Sharples, Jerry and Prindle, Allen. Income Characteristics of Farm Families in the Corn Belt. *Agr. Finance Rev.,* July 1973, *34,* pp. 12–17. [G: U.S.]

Stone, Richard. Economic and Demographic Accounts and the Distribution of Income. *Acta Oecon.,* 1973, *11*(2–3), pp. 165–76.

Vachel, Jan and Nentvichová, Božena. 25 Years of Building Czechoslovakia's Socialist Economy. *Czech. Econ. Digest.,* February 1973, (1), pp. 3–93. [G: Czechoslovakia]

Vakil, Firouz. Indian Saving Behavior: A Reconciliation of Time Series and Cross Section Evidence. *Rev. Income Wealth,* September 1973, *19*(3), pp. 307–23. [G: India]

Wisman, Jon D. and Sawers, Larry. Wealth Taxation for the United States. *J. Econ. Issues,* September 1973, *7*(3), pp. 417–36. [G: U.S.]

Young, Warren L. Compulsory Loans, Disposable Income, and Quarterly Consumption Behaviour in Israel: 1964–1969. *Finanzarchiv,* 1973, *32*(1), pp. 98–115. [G: Israel]

2213 Income Distribution

Allais, Maurice. Inequality and Civilizations. *Soc. Sci. Quart.,* December 1973, *54*(3), pp. 508–24.

Azfar, Javaid. The Distribution of Income in Pakistan—1966–67. *Pakistan Econ. Soc. Rev.,* Spring 1973, *11*(1), pp. 40–66. [G: Pakistan]

Baerwaldt, Nancy A. and Morgan, James N. Trends in Inter-Family Transfers. In *Mandell, L., et al., eds.,* 1973, pp. 205–32. [G: U.S.]

Balintfy, Joseph L. and Goodman, Seymour S. Socio-Economic Factors in Income Inequality: A Log-Normal Hypothesis. *Z. Nationalökon.,* 1973, *33* (3–4), pp. 389–402. [G: U.S.]

Bates, Timothy. The Economic Origins of Political Power in America. In *Haveman, R. H. and Hamrin, R. D., eds.,* 1973, pp. 26–32. [G: U.S.]

Berry, R. Albert. Land Distribution, Income Distribution, and the Productive Efficiency of Colombian Agriculture. *Food Res. Inst. Stud.,* 1973, *12* (3), pp. 199–232. [G: Colombia]

Bhagwati, Jagdish N. Education, Class Structure and Income Equality. *World Devel.,* May 1973, *1*(5), pp. 21–36. [G: India]

Bird, Richard M. and De Wulf, Luc H. Taxation and Income Distribution in Latin America: A Critical Review of Empirical Studies. *Int. Monet. Fund Staff Pap.,* November 1973, *20*(3), pp. 639–82. [G: Latin America]

Blinder, Alan S. A Model of Inherited Wealth. *Quart. J. Econ.,* November 1973, *87*(4), pp. 608–26. [G: U.S.]

Bressler, Barry. Family Size and Income Inequality. *Amer. Econ.,* Fall 1973, *17*(2), pp. 113–21. [G: U.S.]

Bretzfelder, Robert B. State and Regional Personal Income, 1959–1972. *Surv. Curr. Bus.,* August 1973, *53*(8), pp. 39–49. [G: U.S.]

Brittain, John A. Research on the Transmission of Material Wealth. *Amer. Econ. Rev.,* May 1973, *63* (2), pp. 335–45.

Browning, Thomas L. and Reinsel, Edward I. Distribution of Farm Program Payments by Income of Sole Proprietors. *Agr. Econ. Res.,* April 1973, *25* (2), pp. 41–44. [G: U.S.]

Brownlee, Oswald. The Effects of Inflation on the Distribution of Economic Welfare: Comment. *J. Money, Credit, Banking,* Part II, February 1973, *5*(1), pp. 505–06. [G: U.S.]

Bruyn-Hundt, M. Naar de meetbaarheid van een rechtvaardige verdeling van de helft voor de helft. (An Approach to the Measurement of Just Distribution of One Half for One Half. With English summary.) *De Economist,* November-December 1973, *121*(6), pp. 626–28, 29. [G: Netherlands]

Carlin, Thomas A. Economic Position of Farm Families When Money Income and Net Worth are Combined. *Agr. Econ. Res.,* July 1973, *25*(3), pp. 61–70. [G: U.S.]

Chaudhry, M. Ghaffar. Rural Income Distribution in Pakistan in the Green Revolution Perspective. *Pakistan Develop. Rev.,* Autumn 1973, *12*(3), pp. 247–58. [G: Pakistan]

Cherry, Robert. Class Struggle and the Nature of the Working Class. *Rev. Radical Polit. Econ.,* Summer 1973, *5*(2), pp. 47–86. [G: U.S.]

Dovring, Folke. Distribution of Farm Size and Income: Analysis by Exponential Functions. *Land Econ.,* May 1973, *49*(2), pp. 133–47. [G: U.S.]

Eapen, A. T. and Eapen, Ana N. Income Redistributive Effects of State and Local Fiscs: Connecticut, A Case Study. *Public Finance Quart.,* October 1973, *1*(4), pp. 372–87. [G: U.S.]

Ewusi, Kodwo. Changes in Distribution of Earnings of Africans in Recorded Employment in Uganda. *Econ. Bull. Ghana, Sec. Ser.,* 1973, *3*(1), pp. 39–49. [G: Uganda]

Farbman, Michael. Income Concentration in the Southern United States. *Rev. Econ. Statist.,* August 1973, *55*(3), pp. 333–40. [G: U.S.]

Foulon, Alain; Hatchuel, Georges and Kende, Pierre. Un premier bilan de la redistribution des revenus en France; Les impôts et cotisations sociales à la charge des ménages en 1965. (Balance of the Redistribution of Incomes in France: Personal Taxes and Social Security Contributions in 1965. With English summary.) *Consommation,* October-December 1973, *20*(4), pp. 5–133. [G: France]

Frankena, Mark. Income Distributional Effects of Urban Transit Subsidies. *J. Transp. Econ. Policy,* September 1973, *7*(3), pp. 215–30. [G: Canada]

Freeman, A. Myrick, III. Income Distribution and Environmental Quality. In *Enthoven, A. C. and Freeman, A. M., III, eds.,* 1973, pp. 100–06. [G: U.S.]

Girling, Robert. Dependency and Persistent Income Inequality. In *Bonilla, F. and Girling, R., eds.,* 1973, pp. 83–101. [G: Latin America]

Gørtz, Erik and Vibe-Pedersen, J. Livsindkomstberegninger og deres betydning. (Calculation and

Significance of Lifetime Incomes. With English summary.) *Nationalokon. Tidsskr.*, 1973, *111*(1), pp. 25–59. [G: Denmark]

Gupta, S. The Role of the Public Sector in Reducing Regional Income Disparity in Indian Plans. *J. Devel. Stud.*, January 1973, *9*(2), pp. 243–60. [G: India]

Hamblin, Mary and Prell, Michael J. Income of Men and Women: Why Do They Differ? *Fed. Res. Bank Kansas City Rev.*, April 1973, pp. 3–11. [G: U.S.]

Hanlon, Richard A. Differences in Reporting Family Income. *Mon. Lab. Rev.*, April 1973, *96*(4), pp. 46–48. [G: U.S.]

Hight, Joseph E. and Pollock, Richard. Income Distribution Effects of Higher Education Expenditures in California, Florida and Hawaii. *J. Human Res.*, Summer 1973, *8*(3), pp. 318–30. [G: U.S.]

Isbister, John. Birth Control, Income Redistribution, and the Rate of Saving: The Case of Mexico. *Demography*, February 1973, *10*(1), pp. 85–98. [G: Mexico]

Jonish, James E. and Kau, James B. State Differentials in Income Inequality. *Rev. Soc. Econ.*, October 1973, *31*(2), pp. 179–90. [G: U.S.]

Kakwani, N. C. and Podder, N. On the Estimation of Lorenz Curves from Grouped Observations. *Int. Econ. Rev.*, June 1973, *14*(2), pp. 278–92. [G: Australia]

Karageorgas, Dionysios. The Distribution of Tax Burden by Income Groups in Greece. *Econ. J.*, June 1973, *83*(330), pp. 436–48. [G: Greece]

Kessel, Reuben A. The Effects of Inflation on the Distribution of Economic Welfare: Comment. *J. Money, Credit, Banking*, Part II, February 1973, *5*(1), pp. 507–08. [G: U.S.]

Khandker, R. H. Distribution of Income and Wealth in Pakistan. *Pakistan Econ. Soc. Rev.*, Spring 1973, *11*(1), pp. 1–39. [G: Pakistan]

Kravis, Irving B. A World of Unequal Incomes. *Ann. Amer. Acad. Polit. Soc. Sci.*, September 1973, *409*, pp. 61–80.

Krelle, Wilhelm and Siebke, Jürgen. Vermögensverteilung und Vermögenspolitik in der Bundesrepublik Deutschland. Ein Überblick. (Distribution of Wealth and Policy of Wealth Distribution in the Federal Republic of Germany. A Survey. With English summary.) *Z. ges. Staatswiss.*, August 1973, *129*(3), pp. 478–503. [G: Germany]

Krzyzaniak, Marian and Özmucur, Süleyman. The Distribution of Income and the Short-run Burden of Taxes in Turkey, 1968. *Finanzarchiv*, 1973, *32* (1), pp. 69–97. [G: Turkey]

Lampman, Robert J. Measured Inequality of Income: What Does It Mean and What Can It Tell Us? *Ann. Amer. Acad. Polit. Soc. Sci.*, September 1973, *409*, pp. 81–91. [G: U.S.]

Michal, Jan M. Size-Distribution of Earnings and Household Incomes in Small Socialist Countries. *Rev. Income Wealth*, December 1973, *19*(4), pp. 407–28. [G: Czechoslovakia; Yugoslavia; Hungary]

Mirer, Thad W. The Distributional Impact of the 1970 Recession. *Rev. Econ. Statist.*, May 1973, *55* (2), pp. 214–24. [G: U.S.]

Mirer, Thad W. The Effects of Macroeconomic Fluctuations on the Distribution of Income. *Rev. Income Wealth*, December 1973, *19*(4), pp. 385–406. [G: U.S.]

Morley, Samuel A. and Smith, Gordon W. The Effect of Changes in the Distribution of Income on Labor, Foreign Investment, and Growth in Brazil. In *Stepan, A., ed.*, 1973, pp. 119–41. [G: Brazil]

Naseem, S. M. Mass Poverty in Pakistan: Some Preliminary Findings. *Pakistan Develop. Rev.*, Winter 1973, *12*(4), pp. 317–60. [G: Pakistan]

Nordhaus, William D. The Effects of Inflation on the Distribution of Economic Welfare. *J. Money, Credit, Banking*, Part II, February 1973, *5*(1), pp. 465–504. [G: U.S.]

Nwaneri, V. C. Income Distribution Criteria for the Analysis of Development Projects. *Finance Develop.*, March 1973, *10*(1), pp. 16–19, 37.

Paukert, Felix. Income Distribution at Different Levels of Development: A Survey of Evidence. *Int. Lab. Rev.*, August-September 1973, *108*(2–3), pp. 97–125.

Pechman, Joseph A. The Rich, the Poor, and the Taxes They Pay. In *Reynolds, L. G.; Green, G. D. and Lewis, D. R., eds.*, 1973, pp. 260–82. [G: U.S.]

Pryor, Frederic L. Simulation of the Impact of Social and Economic Institutions on the Size Distribution of Income and Wealth. *Amer. Econ. Rev.*, March 1973, *63*(1), pp. 50–72.

Sakashita, Noboru and Kamoike, Osamu. National Growth and Regional Income Inequality: A Consistent Model. *Int. Econ. Rev.*, June 1973, *14*(2), pp. 372–82.

Scitovsky, Tibor. Inequalities: Open and Hidden, Measured and Immeasurable. *Ann. Amer. Acad. Polit. Soc. Sci.*, September 1973, *409*, pp. 112–19.

Šefer, Berislav. Income Distribution in Yugoslavia. In *Moskoff, W., ed.*, 1973, pp. 201–16. [G: Yugoslavia]

Singer, Dan and Walzer, Norman. The Distribution of Income in Large Urban Areas. *Nebr. J. Econ. Bus.*, Autumn 1973, *12*(4), pp. 91–101. [G: U.S.]

Theil, Henri and Friedman, Yoram. Regional Per Capita Incomes and Income Inequalities: Point Estimates and Their Standard Errors. *J. Amer. Statist. Assoc.*, September 1973, *68*(343), pp. 531–39.

Thurow, Lester C. Zero Economic Growth and the Distribution of Income. In *Weintraub, A.; Schwartz, E. and Aronson, J. R., eds.*, 1973, pp. 141–53.

Tinbergen, J. Naar de meetbaarheid van een rechtvaardige verdeling. (An Approach to the Measurement of a Just Distribution of Income. With English summary.) *De Economist*, March-April 1973, *121*(2), pp. 106–21. [G: Netherlands]

Tinbergen, J. Naar de meetbaarheid van een rechtvaardige verdeling van de helft voor de helft. Naschrift. (An Approach to the Measurement of Just Distribution of One Half for One Half: Reply. With English summary.) *De Economist*, November-December 1973, *121*(6), pp. 628–29. [G: Netherlands]

Tinbergen, Jan. Tendencies and Determinants of Income Distribution in Western Countries—A

Note. In *[Rosenstein-Rodan, P.]*, 1973, pp. 178–84.   [G: U.K.; U.S.]

van de Woestijne, W. J. Toepassing van de Wet van Pareto op de lage inkomens. (Application of Pareto's Law to Low Incomes. With English summary.) *De Economist*, January-February 1973, *121*(1), pp. 29–51.

Young, Richard M. Inflation and the Distribution of Income and Wealth: Are the Poor Really Hurt? *Fed. Res. Bank Bus. Rev. Phila.*, September 1973, pp. 16–25.   [G: U.S.]

222 Input-Output

2220 Input-Output

Ahmed, Iftikhar. Sectoral Employment Response in an Input-Output Framework: The Case of Bangladesh. *Bangladesh Econ. Rev.*, July 1973, *1*(3), pp. 317–23.   [G: Bangladesh]

Bartsch, William H. Notes on Developing Countries and their Statistics: Comment. *Rev. Income Wealth*, June 1973, *19*(2), pp. 211–12.

Belen'kii, V. Z.; Volkonskii, V. A. and Pavlov, N. V. Dynamic Input-Output Models in Planning and Price Calculations and Economic Analysis. *Matekon*, Winter 1973-74, *10*(2), pp. 74–101.   [G: U.S.S.R.]

Bezdek, Roger H. Interindustry Manpower Analysis: Theoretical Potential and Empirical Problems. *Amer. Econ.*, Spring 1973, *17*(1), pp. 147–53.

Blin, Jean-Marie. A Further Procedure for Ordering an Input-output Matrix: Some Empirical Evidence. *Econ. Planning*, 1973, *13*(1–2), pp. 121–29.   [G: U.S.; Norway; Japan; Italy; India]

Czamanski, Stan. Linkages between Industries in Urban-Regional Complexes. In *Judge, G. G. and Takayama, T., eds.*, 1973, pp. 180–204. [G: U.S.]

Dorfman, Robert. Wassily Leontief's Contribution to Economics. *Swedish J. Econ.*, December 1973, *75*(4), pp. 430–49.

Eidel'man, M. The New Ex Post Interbranch Balance of Production and Distribution of Output in the National Economy of the USSR. *Prob. Econ.*, May 1973, *16*(1), pp. 3–34.   [G: U.S.S.R.]

Geary, R. C. A Method of Estimating the Elements of an Interindustry Matrix Knowing the Row and Column Totals. *Econ. Soc. Rev.*, July 1973, *4*(4), pp. 477–85.

Henry, E. W. Relative Efficiency of RAS Versus Least Squares Methods of Updating Input-Output Structures, as Adjudged by Application to Irish Data. *Econ. Soc. Rev.*, October 1973, *5*(1), pp. 7–29.   [G: Ireland]

Herfindahl, Orris C. and Kneese, Allen V. Measuring Social and Economic Change: Benefits and Costs of Environmental Pollution. In *Moss, M., ed.*, 1973, pp. 441–503.   [G: U.S.]

Jaffe, A. J. Notes on Developing Countries and their Statistics: Reply. *Rev. Income Wealth*, June 1973, *19*(2), pp. 213–14.

Konius, A. A. Commensuration of Labor by Means of an Input-Output Table. *Matekon*, Summer 1973, *9*(4), pp. 31–42.

Merz, C. M.; Gibson, T. A. and Seitz, C. Ward. Impact of the Space Shuttle Program on the National Economy. *Eng. Econ.*, January-February 1973, *18*(2), pp. 115–33.   [G: U.S.]

Morley, Samuel A. and Smith, Gordon W. The Effect of Changes in the Distribution of Income on Labor, Foreign Investment, and Growth in Brazil. In *Stepan, A., ed.*, 1973, pp. 119–41. [G: Brazil]

Park, Se-Hark. On Input-Output Multipliers with Errors in Input-Output Coefficients. *J. Econ. Theory*, August 1973, *6*(4), pp. 399–403.

Ramanujam, M. S. Requirements of Technical Manpower in India: 1965–66 to 1980–81. *Indian Econ. Rev.*, October 1973, *8*(2), pp. 101–24. [G: India]

Ritz, Philip M. and Roberts, Eugene P. Industry Inventory Requirements: An Input-Output Analysis. *Surv. Curr. Bus.*, November 1973, *53*(11), pp. 15–22.   [G: U.S.]

Robinson, Sherman and Markandya, Anil. Complexity and Adjustment in Input-Output Systems. *Oxford Bull. Econ. Statist.*, May 1973, *35*(2), pp. 119–34.

Sandberg, I. W. A Nonlinear Input-Output Model of a Multisectored Economy. *Econometrica*, November 1973, *41*(6), pp. 1167–82.

Seton, Francis. Shadow Wages in Chile. In *Eckaus, R. S. and Rosenstein-Rodan, P. N., eds.*, 1973, pp. 49–119.   [G: Chile]

Stone, Richard. Process, Capacity and Control in an Input-Output System. *L'Industria*, January-June 1973, (1–2), pp. 3–17.

Thage, Bent. Udenrigshandelen i input-output analysen. (With English summary.) *Nationalokon. Tidsskr.*, 1973, *111*(3), pp. 361–81.   [G: Denmark]

Vickrey, William. Measuring Social and Economic Change: Benefits and Costs of Environmental Pollution: Comment. In *Moss, M., ed.*, 1973, pp. 503–08.   [G: U.S.]

Volkov, A. M. and Senchagov, V. K. Problems of Depreciation and Its Reflection in the Input-Output Balance. *Matekon*, Spring 1973, *9*(3), pp. 55–66.

Walderhaug, Albert J. The Composition of Value Added in the 1963 Input-Output Study. *Surv. Curr. Bus.*, April 1973, *53*(4), pp. 34–44.   [G: U.S.]

Walter, Ingo. The Pollution Content of American Trade. *Western Econ. J.*, March 1973, *11*(1), pp. 61–70.   [G: U.S.]

Yotopoulos, Pan A. and Nugent, Jeffrey B. A Balanced-Growth Version of the Linkage Hypothesis: A Test. *Quart. J. Econ.*, May 1973, *87*(2), pp. 157–71.

223 Financial Accounts

2230 Financial Accounts; Financial Statistics

Bain, A. D. Flow of Funds Analysis: Survey. *Econ. J.*, December 1973, *83*(332), pp. 1055–93.

Cohen, Jacob and Miller, Richard K. A Flow-of-Funds Model of the Stock Market. *J. Econ. Bus.*, Winter 1973, *25*(2), pp. 71–82.   [G: U.S.]

Goldsmith, Raymond W. Basic Considerations. In *Goldsmith, R. W., ed.*, 1973, pp. 1–33. [G: U.S.]

Goldsmith, Raymond W. The Position of Institutional Investors and of Corporate Stock in the

National Balance Sheets and the Flow of Funds Accounts of the United States of America, 1952–68. In *Goldsmith, R. W., ed.*, 1973, pp. 91–164. [G: U.S.]

L'Esperance, Wilford L. Estimating Corporate Net Income in Ohio. *Ohio State U. Bull. Bus. Res.*, October 1973, *48*(10), pp. 4–5. [G: U.S.]

Mallinson, Eugenie and Pickering, Margaret H. New Series for Large Manufacturing Corporations. *Fed. Res. Bull.*, October 1973, *59*(10), pp. 731–33. [G: U.S.]

Nissen, Anton. Revision of the Money Stock Measures and Member Bank Reserves and Deposits. *Fed. Res. Bull.*, February 1973, *59*(2), pp. 61–79. [G: U.S.]

Odling-Smee, J. C. Personal Saving Revisited: More Statistics, Fewer Facts. *Oxford Bull. Econ. Statist.*, February 1973, *35*(1), pp. 21–29. [G: U.K.]

Petersen, Russell J. Price-Level Changes and Company Wealth. *Manage. Account.*, February 1973, *54*(8), pp. 17–20.

Roe, Alan R. The Case for Flow of Funds and National Balance Sheet Accounts. *Econ. J.*, June 1973, *83*(330), pp. 399–420. [G: U.K.]

Schedvin, C. B. A Century of Money in Australia. *Econ. Rec.*, December 1973, *49*(128), pp. 588–605. [G: Australia]

Smith, James D. New Perspectives in Government Data Distribution: The Current Population Survey. *Ann. Econ. Soc. Measure*, April 1973, *2*(2), pp. 131–39. [G: U.S.]

224 National Wealth and Balance Sheets

2240 National Wealth and Balance Sheets

Bossons, John. The Distribution of Assets Among Individuals of Different Age and Wealth. In *Goldsmith, R. W., ed.*, 1973, pp. 394–428. [G: U.S.]

Christensen, Laurits R. and Jorgenson, Dale W. Measuring Economic Performance in the Private Sector: Reply to Kendrick. In *Moss, M., ed.*, 1973, pp. 350–51. [G: U.S.]

Christensen, Laurits R. and Jorgenson, Dale W. Measuring Economic Performance in the Private Sector. In *Moss, M., ed.*, 1973, pp. 233–338. [G: U.S.]

Christensen, Laurits R. and Jorgenson, Dale W. Measuring Economic Performance in the Private Sector: Reply to Eisner. In *Moss, M., ed.*, 1973, pp. 349–50. [G: U.S.]

Eisner, Robert. A Framework for the Measurement of Economic and Social Performance: Comment. In *Moss, M., ed.*, 1973, pp. 99–102. [G: U.S.]

Eisner, Robert. Measuring Economic Performance in the Private Sector: Comment. In *Moss, M., ed.*, 1973, pp. 343–49. [G: U.S.]

Goldsmith, Raymond W. The Position of Institutional Investors and of Corporate Stock in the National Balance Sheets and the Flow of Funds Accounts of the United States of America, 1952–68. In *Goldsmith, R. W., ed.*, 1973, pp. 91–164. [G: U.S.]

Gupta, Suraj B. Financial Progress, Banking Expansion, and Saving. *Indian Econ. J.*, April-June 1973, *20*(4–5), pp. 548–69.

Harberger, Arnold C. On Estimating the Rate of Return to Capital in Colombia. In *Harberger, A. C.*, 1973, pp. 132–56. [G: Columbia]

Harbury, C. D. and McMahon, P. C. Inheritance and the Characteristics of Top Wealth Leavers in Britain. *Econ. J.*, September 1973, *83*(331), pp. 810–33. [G: U.K.]

Jaszi, George. A Framework for the Measurement of Economic and Social Performance: Comment. In *Moss, M., ed.*, 1973, pp. 84–99. [G: U.S.]

Jenkins, Glenn P. The Measurement of Rates of Return and Taxation from Private Capital in Canada. In *Niskanen, W. A., et al., eds.*, 1973, pp. 211–45. [G: Canada]

Juster, F. Thomas. A Framework for the Measurement of Economic and Social Performance: Reply. In *Moss, M., ed.*, 1973, pp. 105–09. [G: U.S.]

Juster, F. Thomas. A Framework for the Measurement of Economic and Social Performance. In *Moss, M., ed.*, 1973, pp. 25–84. [G: U.S.]

Kendrick, John W. Measuring Economic Performance in the Private Sector: Comment. In *Moss, M., ed.*, 1973, pp. 338–43. [G: U.S.]

McClung, Nelson. Editing Census Microdata Files for Income and Wealth. *Ann. Econ. Soc. Measure*, April 1973, *2*(2), pp. 201–08. [G: U.S.]

Milgram, Grace. Estimates of the Value of Land in the United States Held by Various Sectors of the Economy, Annually, 1952 to 1968. In *Goldsmith, R. W., ed.*, 1973, pp. 343–77. [G: U.S.]

Nelson, Ralph L. Estimates of Balance Sheets and Income Statements of Foundations and Colleges and Universities. In *Goldsmith, R. W., ed.*, 1973, pp. 378–91. [G: U.S.]

Smith, James D. New Perspectives in Government Data Distribution: The Current Population Survey. *Ann. Econ. Soc. Measure*, April 1973, *2*(2), pp. 131–39. [G: U.S.]

Solow, Robert M. A Framework for the Measurement of Economic and Social Performance: Comment. In *Moss, M., ed.*, 1973, pp. 102–05. [G: U.S.]

Tice, Helen Stone and Duff, Virginia A. Basic Statistical Data. In *Goldsmith, R. W., ed.*, 1973, pp. 269–342. [G: U.S.]

Vuchelen, J. Het gezinsvermogen 1952–1971. (With English summary.) *Cah. Écon. Bruxelles*, 4th Quarter 1973, (60), pp. 573–605. [G: Belgium]

225 Social Indicators and Social Accounts

2250 Social Indicators and Social Accounts

Aidenoff, Abraham. A Proposal for a System of Economic and Social Accounts: Comment. In *Moss, M., ed.*, 1973, pp. 153–59. [G: U.S.]

Andrews, Frank M. Social Indicators and Socioeconomic Development. *J. Devel. Areas*, October 1973, *8*(1), pp. 3–12.

Aukrust, Odd and Nordbotten, Svein. Files of Individual Data and their Potentials for Social Research. *Rev. Income Wealth*, June 1973, *19*(2), pp. 189–201. [G: Norway]

Bauer, Raymond A. The Future of Corporate Social

Accounting. In *Dierkes, M. and Bauer, R. A., eds.,* 1973, pp. 389–405. [G: U.S.]

Bauer, Raymond A. The State of the Art of Social Auditing. In *Dierkes, M. and Bauer, R. A., eds.,* 1973, pp. 3–40.

Bernolak, Imre. Is Growth Obsolete? Comment. In *Moss, M., ed.,* 1973, pp. 536–40. [G: U.S.]

Bitar, Sergio and Trivelli, Hugo. The Cost of Capital in the Chilean Economy. In *Eckaus, R. S. and Rosenstein-Rodan, P. N., eds.,* 1973, pp. 147–65. [G: Chile]

Brummet, R. Lee. Nonfinancial Measures in Social Accounts. In *Dierkes, M. and Bauer, R. A., eds.,* 1973, pp. 345–50.

Burnham, John B. Societal Values in Power Generation. In *Dierkes, M. and Bauer, R. A., eds.,* 1973, pp. 260–70. [G: U.S.]

Butcher, Bernard L. The Program Management Approach. In *Dierkes, M. and Bauer, R. A., eds.,* 1973, pp. 276–84. [G: U.S.]

Chen, Martin K. The G Index for Program Priority. In *Berg, R. L., ed.,* 1973, pp. 28–34. [G: U.S.]

Colantoni, C. S.; Cooper, W. W. and Dietzer, H. J. Budgetary Disclosure and Social Accounting. In *Dierkes, M. and Bauer, R. A., eds.,* 1973, pp. 365–86.

Corbin, Donald A. Guidelines for Reporting Corporate Environmental Impact. In *Dierkes, M. and Bauer, R. A., eds.,* 1973, pp. 321–26.

Curtin, Richard T. Index Construction: An Appraisal of the Index of Consumer Sentiment. In *Mandell, L., et al., eds.,* 1973, pp. 253–61. [G: U.S.]

Day, George S. The Role of the Consumer in the Corporate Social Audit. In *Dierkes, M. and Bauer, R. A., eds.,* 1973, pp. 117–29.

Denison, Edward F. A Proposal for a System of Economic and Social Accounts: Comment. In *Moss, M., ed.,* 1973, pp. 159–60. [G: U.S.]

Denison, Edward F. Is Growth Obsolete? Comment. In *Moss, M., ed.,* 1973, pp. 546–48. [G: U.S.]

Drobny, Neil L. Social Accounting in Environmental Planning. In *Dierkes, M. and Bauer, R. A., eds.,* 1973, pp. 248–59. [G: U.S.]

Eason, Warren W. Handbook of Soviet Social Science Data: Demography. In *Mickiewicz, E., ed.,* 1973, pp. 49–63. [G: U.S.S.R.]

Eisner, Robert. A Framework for the Measurement of Economic and Social Performance: Comment. In *Moss, M., ed.,* 1973, pp. 99–102. [G: U.S.]

Elliott-Jones, M. F. Matrix Methods in Corporate Social Accounting. In *Dierkes, M. and Bauer, R. A., eds.,* 1973, pp. 351–64.

Field, Mark G. Handbook of Soviet Social Science Data: Health. In *Mickiewicz, E., ed.,* 1973, pp. 101–18. [G: U.S.S.R.]

Finkelstein, Larry. Concepts for Reporting on Corporations' Community Involvement. In *Dierkes, M. and Bauer, R. A., eds.,* 1973, pp. 219–24. [G: U.S.]

Flamholtz, Eric. The Role of Human Resource Accounting in Social Accounting. In *Dierkes, M. and Bauer, R. A., eds.,* 1973, pp. 166–82.

Flanagan, John C. Inputs to Social Accounts Gained from Studies of Individuals' Quality of Life. In *Dierkes, M. and Bauer, R. A., eds.,* 1973, pp. 50–56.

Fox, Karl A. and van Moeseke, Paul. Derivation and Implications of a Scalar Measure of Social Income. In *[Tinbergen, J.],* 1973, pp. 21–40.

Francis, M. E. Accounting and the Evaluation of Social Programs: A Critical Comment. *Accounting Rev.,* April 1973, *48*(2), pp. 245–57.

Gastil, Raymond D. Social Accounting versus Social Responsibility. In *Dierkes, M. and Bauer, R. A., eds.,* 1973, pp. 93–106.

Ghez, Gilbert R. The Measurement of Output of the Nonmarket Sector: The Evaluation of Housewives' Time: Comment. In *Moss, M., ed.,* 1973, pp. 190–92. [G: U.S.; Israel]

Gordon, Robert A. An Explicit Estimation of the Prevalence of Commitment to a Training School, to Age 18, by Race and by Sex. *J. Amer. Statist. Assoc.,* September 1973, *68*(343), pp. 547–53. [G: U.S.]

Gray, Daniel H. One Way to Go about Inventing Social Accounting. In *Dierkes, M. and Bauer, R. A., eds.,* 1973, pp. 315–20.

Griliches, Zvi. Measuring Performance in Education: Comment. In *Moss, M., ed.,* 1973, pp. 433–35. [G: U.S.]

Gronau, Reuben. The Measurement of Output of the Nonmarket Sector: The Evaluation of Housewives' Time. In *Moss, M., ed.,* 1973, pp. 163–90. [G: U.S.; Israel]

Grove, Ernest W. Evaluating Performance in the Public Sector: Comment. In *Moss, M., ed.,* 1973, pp. 394–97. [G: U.S.]

Hartle, Douglas G. A Proposal for a System of Economic and Social Accounts: Comment. In *Moss, M., ed.,* 1973, pp. 146–53. [G: U.S.]

Herfindahl, Orris C. and Kneese, Allen V. Measuring Social and Economic Change: Benefits and Costs of Environmental Pollution. In *Moss, M., ed.,* 1973, pp. 441–503. [G: U.S.]

Hollander, Gayle D. Handbook of Soviet Social Science Data: Communications. In *Mickiewicz, E., ed.,* 1973, pp. 175–96. [G: U.S.S.R.]

Jaszi, George. A Framework for the Measurement of Economic and Social Performance: Comment. In *Moss, M., ed.,* 1973, pp. 84–99. [G: U.S.]

Juster, F. Thomas. A Framework for the Measurement of Economic and Social Performance: Reply. In *Moss, M., ed.,* 1973, pp. 105–09. [G: U.S.]

Juster, F. Thomas. A Framework for the Measurement of Economic and Social Performance. In *Moss, M., ed.,* 1973, pp. 25–84. [G: U.S.]

Katz, Sidney, et al. Measuring the Health Status of Populations. In *Berg, R. L., ed.,* 1973, pp. 39–51. [G: U.S.]

Lal, Deepak. Employment, Income Distribution and a Poverty Redressal Index. *World Devel.,* March–April 1973, *1*(3–4), pp. 121–25.

Lamson, Robert W. Corporate Accounting for Environmental Effects. In *Dierkes, M. and Bauer, R. A., eds.,* 1973, pp. 230–47.

Lawler, Edward E., III. Quality of Working Life and Social Accounts. In *Dierkes, M. and Bauer, R. A., eds.,* 1973, pp. 154–65. [G: U.S.]

Leontief, Wassily W. National Income, Economic Structure, and Environmental Externalities. In *Moss, M., ed.,* 1973, pp. 565–76. [G: U.S.]

Leveson, Irving. Strategies against Urban Poverty. In *Boulding, K. E.; Pfaff, M. and Pfaff, A., eds.,* 1973, pp. 130–59. [G: U.S.]

Levine, Daniel S. and Yett, Donald E. A Method for Constructing Proxy Measures of Health Status. In *Berg, R. L., ed.,* 1973, pp. 12–22. [G: U.S.]

Levy, Girard W. Urban Social Indicators and Corporate Social Accounts. In *Dierkes, M. and Bauer, R. A., eds.,* 1973, pp. 212–18.

Marcus, Sumner. The Basic Issues: Societal Demands and the Viability of Social Accounting: Introduction. In *Dierkes, M. and Bauer, R. A., eds.,* 1973, pp. 43–49. [G: U.S.]

Mathias, Robert A. An Approach Toward Corporate Social Measures. In *Dierkes, M. and Bauer, R. A., eds.,* 1973, pp. 285–91.

McElyea, Steward D. Auditing Corporate Social Impact in a Period of Rising Social Concern. In *Dierkes, M. and Bauer, R. A., eds.,* 1973, pp. 308–14.

Meyer, John R. Is Growth Obsolete? Comment. In *Moss, M., ed.,* 1973, pp. 548–54. [G: U.S.]

Monsen, R. Joseph. Is Social Accounting a Mirage? In *Dierkes, M. and Bauer, R. A., eds.,* 1973, pp. 107–10.

Morton, Henry W. Handbook of Soviet Social Science Data: Housing. In *Mickiewicz, E., ed.,* 1973, pp. 119–35. [G: U.S.S.R.]

Moser, Claus A. Social Indicators—Systems, Methods and Problems. *Rev. Income Wealth,* June 1973, *19*(2), pp. 133–41.

Myers, John G. Measuring and Monitoring the Impact of Advertising. In *Dierkes, M. and Bauer, R. A., eds.,* 1973, pp. 130–41.

Nolan, Joseph T. The Social Audit: One Corporation's Experience. In *Dierkes, M. and Bauer, R. A., eds.,* 1973, pp. 292–96. [G: U.S.]

Nordhaus, William D. and Tobin, James. Is Growth Obsolete? In *Moss, M., ed.,* 1973, pp. 509–32. [G: U.S.]

Nordhaus, William D. and Tobin, James. Is Growth Obsolete? Reply to Meyer. In *Moss, M., ed.,* 1973, pp. 563–64. [G: U.S.]

Nordhaus, William D. and Tobin, James. Is Growth Obsolete? Reply to Denison and Usher. In *Moss, M., ed.,* 1973, pp. 554–63. [G: U.S.]

Olson, Mancur. Evaluating Performance in the Public Sector: Reply. In *Moss, M., ed.,* 1973, pp. 397–409. [G: U.S.]

Olson, Mancur. Evaluating Performance in the Public Sector. In *Moss, M., ed.,* 1973, pp. 355–84. [G: U.S.]

Pfaff, Martin. Economic Life-Styles, Values, and Subjective Welfare—An Empirical Approach: Response. In *Sheldon, E. B., ed.,* 1973, pp. 126–38. [G: U.S.]

Pool, A. Jonathan, et al. Handbook of Soviet Social Science Data: Education. In *Mickiewicz, E., ed.,* 1973, pp. 137–58. [G: U.S.S.R.]

Regan, Opal G. Statistical Reforms Accelerated by Sixth Census Errors. *J. Amer. Statist. Assoc.,* September 1973, *68*(343), pp. 540–46. [G: U.S.]

Ritter, Lawrence S. Reordering National Priorities: A Day of Reckoning. In *Reynolds, L. G.; Green, G. D. and Lewis, D. R., eds.,* 1973, pp. 323–31. [G: U.S.]

Rivlin, Alice M. Measuring Performance in Education. In *Moss, M., ed.,* 1973, pp. 411–28. [G: U.S.]

Ruggles, Nancy and Ruggles, Richard. A Proposal for a System of Economic and Social Accounts. In *Moss, M., ed.,* 1973, pp. 111–46. [G: U.S.]

Schultze, Charles L. Evaluating Performance in the Public Sector: Comment. In *Moss, M., ed.,* 1973, pp. 384–94. [G: U.S.]

Singer, S. Fred. Is There an Optimum Level of Population? In *Weintraub, A.; Schwartz, E. and Aronson, J. R., eds.,* 1973, pp. 154–64. [G: U.S.]

Singer, S. Fred. Is Growth Obsolete? Comment. In *Moss, M., ed.,* 1973, pp. 532–36. [G: U.S.]

Solow, Robert M. A Framework for the Measurement of Economic and Social Performance: Comment. In *Moss, M., ed.,* 1973, pp. 102–05. [G: U.S.]

Stone, Richard. Economic and Demographic Accounts and the Distribution of Income. *Acta Oecon.,* 1973, *11*(2–3), pp. 165–76.

Stone, Richard. A System of Social Matrices. *Rev. Income Wealth,* June 1973, *19*(2), pp. 143–66. [G: U.K.]

Strumpel, Burkhard. Economic Life-Styles, Values, and Subjective Welfare—An Empirical Approach. In *Sheldon, E. B., ed.,* 1973, pp. 69–125. [G: U.S.]

Terleckyj, Nestor E. Measuring Performance in Education: Comment. In *Moss, M., ed.,* 1973, pp. 435–37. [G: U.S.]

Toan, Arthur B., Jr. Publicly Reporting on Corporate Social Impact. In *Dierkes, M. and Bauer, R. A., eds.,* 1973, pp. 327–44. [G: U.S.]

Usher, Dan. Is Growth Obsolete? Comment. In *Moss, M., ed.,* 1973, pp. 540–45. [G: U.S.]

Vickrey, William. Measuring Social and Economic Change: Benefits and Costs of Environmental Pollution: Comment. In *Moss, M., ed.,* 1973, pp. 503–08. [G: U.S.]

Weisbrod, Burton A. Measuring Performance in Education: Comment. In *Moss, M., ed.,* 1973, pp. 428–33. [G: U.S.]

Young, Elmer, Jr. Corporate Social Responsibility to the Minority Community. In *Dierkes, M. and Bauer, R. A., eds.,* 1973, pp. 297–300. [G: U.S.]

Yuchtman, Ephraim. Reward Structure, the Quality of Work Environment, and Social Accounting. In *Dierkes, M. and Bauer, R. A., eds.,* 1973, pp. 183–90. [G: U.S.]

226 Productivity and Growth Indicators

2260 Productivity and Growth Indicators

Ahmad, Qazi Kholiquzzaman and Anwaruzzaman, Chowdhury. Productivity Trends in the Manufacturing Sector of Bangladesh: A Case Study of Selected Industries. *Bangladesh Econ. Rev.,* April 1973, *1*(2), pp. 119–48. [G: Bangladesh]

Ardolini, Charles W. Productivity Gains in 1972 in Selected Industries. *Mon. Lab. Rev.,* July 1973, *96*(7), pp. 43–45. [G: U.S.]

Asher, Ephraim and Kumar, T. Krishna. Capital-Labor Substitution and Technical Progress in Planned and Market Oriented Economies: A

Comparative Study. *Southern Econ. J.,* July 1973, *40*(1), pp. 103–09. [G: U.S.S.R.; Yugoslavia; Hungary; N. America; Israel]

Ayres, Robert U. and Kneese, Allen V. Economic and Ecological Effects of a Stationary Economy. In *Enthoven, A. C. and Freeman, A. M., III, eds.,* 1973, pp. 235–52.

Behrman, Jere R. Cyclical Sectoral Capacity Utilization in a Developing Economy. In *Eckaus, R. S. and Rosenstein-Rodan, P. N., eds.,* 1973, pp. 251–66. [G: Chile]

Bernolak, Imre. Is Growth Obsolete? Comment. In *Moss, M., ed.,* 1973, pp. 536–40. [G: U.S.]

Bhagwati, Jagdish N. and Hansen, Bent. Should Growth Rates Be Evaluated at International Prices? In *[Rosenstein-Rodan, P.],* 1973, pp. 53–68.

Boulding, Kenneth E. The Shadow of the Stationary State. In *Olson, M. and Landsberg, H. H., eds.,* 1973, pp. 89–101.

Brand, Horst. Productivity in Telephone Communications. *Mon. Lab. Rev.,* November 1973, *96*(11), pp. 3–9. [G: U.S.]

Brooks, Harvey. The Technology of Zero Growth. In *Olson, M. and Landsberg, H. H., eds.,* 1973, pp. 139–52.

Capdevielle, Patricia and Neef, Arthur. Productivity and Unit Labor Costs in 12 Industrial Countries. *Mon. Lab. Rev.,* November 1973, *96*(11), pp. 14–21.

Čáp, Václav. The Development of Effectiveness of the Czechoslovak Economy. *Czech. Econ. Digest.,* June 1973, (4), pp. 3–33. [G: Czechoslovakia]

Chacko, V. J. Problems of Statistical Methodology in Measuring Agricultural Growth. In *Ofori, I. M., ed.,* 1973, pp. 14–19.

Christensen, Laurits R. and Jorgenson, Dale W. Measuring Economic Performance in the Private Sector: Reply to Eisner. In *Moss, M., ed.,* 1973, pp. 349–50. [G: U.S.]

Christensen, Laurits R. and Jorgenson, Dale W. Measuring Economic Performance in the Private Sector. In *Moss, M., ed.,* 1973, pp. 233–338. [G: U.S.]

Christensen, Laurits R. and Jorgenson, Dale W. Measuring Economic Performance in the Private Sector: Reply to Kendrick. In *Moss, M., ed.,* 1973, pp. 350–51. [G: U.S.]

Clark, Peter B. and Foxley, Alejandro. Target Shooting with a Multisectoral Model. In *Eckaus, R. S. and Rosenstein-Rodan, P. N., eds.,* 1973, pp. 341–66. [G: Chile]

Cohn, Stanley H. Handbook of Soviet Social Science Data: Production. In *Mickiewicz, E., ed.,* 1973, pp. 91–99. [G: U.S.S.R.]

Cole, H. S. D. and Curnow, R. C. An Evaluation of the World Models. In *Cole, H. S. D., et al., eds.,* 1973, pp. 108–34.

Cole, H. S. D. The Structure of the World Models. In *Cole, H. S. D., et al., eds.,* 1973, pp. 14–32.

Day, Lincoln H. Social Consequences of Zero Economic Growth. In *Weintraub, A.; Schwartz, E. and Aronson, J. R., eds.,* 1973, pp. 116–40.

Denison, Edward F. Is Growth Obsolete? Comment. In *Moss, M., ed.,* 1973, pp. 546–48. [G: U.S.]

Eisner, Robert. Measuring Economic Performance in the Private Sector: Comment. In *Moss, M., ed.,* 1973, pp. 343–49. [G: U.S.]

Elkan, Walter. On the Apparent Benefits of Higher Productivity: An Arithmetical Illustration: Reply. *J. Devel. Stud.,* April 1973, *9*(3), pp. 452–53.

Erdös, T. Investments and Economic Growth. *Acta Oecon.,* 1973, *11*(4), pp. 281–303.

Freeman, Christopher. Malthus with a Computer. In *Cole, H. S. D., et al., eds.,* 1973, pp. 5–13.

Gerber, Abraham. Energy Supply as a Factor in Economic Growth. In *Weintraub, A.; Schwartz, E. and Aronson, J. R., eds.,* 1973, pp. 82–97. [G: U.S.]

Gillion, C. Econometric Models and Current Economic Issues. In *Deane, R. S., ed.,* 1972, pp. 67–73. [G: New Zealand]

Goldman, Marshall I. Growth and Environmental Problems of Noncapitalist Nations. In *Weintraub, A.; Schwartz, E. and Aronson, J. R., eds.,* 1973, pp. 98–115.

Greenwald, Carol S. A New Deflated Composite Index of Leading Indicators. *New Eng. Econ. Rev.,* July-August 1973, pp. 3–18. [G: U.S.]

Griliches, Zvi. Research Expenditures and Growth Accounting. In *Williams, B. R., ed.,* 1973, pp. 59–83. [G: U.S.]

Grossman, Michael and Fuchs, Victor R. Intersectoral Shifts and Aggregate Productivity Change. *Ann. Econ. Soc. Measure,* July 1973, *2*(3), pp. 227–43. [G: U.S.]

Haywood, E. The Deviation Cycle: A New Index of the Australian Business Cycle 1950-1973. *Australian Econ. Rev.,* 4th Quarter 1973, pp. 31–39. [G: Australia]

Hsia, Ronald. Technological Change in the Industrial Growth of Hong Kong. In *Williams, B. R., ed.,* 1973, pp. 335–53. [G: Hong Kong]

Ihrig, Károly. Agriculture's Contribution to the Growth of Capitalist Economies. In *Földi, T., ed.,* 1973, pp. 135–60.

Ireland, Norman J.; Briscoe, G. and Smyth, David J. Specification Bias and Short-run Returns to Labour: Some Evidence for the United Kingdom. *Rev. Econ. Statist.,* February 1973, *55*(1), pp. 23–27. [G: U.K.]

Johnson, Willard R. Should the Poor Buy No Growth? In *Olson, M. and Landsberg, H. H., eds.,* 1973, pp. 165–89. [G: U.S.]

Julien, P.-A. and Freeman, Christopher. The Capital and Industrial Output Sub-system. In *Cole, H. S. D., et al., eds.,* 1973, pp. 66–79.

Kendrick, John W. Measuring Economic Performance in the Private Sector: Comment. In *Moss, M., ed.,* 1973, pp. 338–43. [G: U.S.]

Kinsella, R. P. A Note on Bank Productivity in a Service Economy. *Rivista Int. Sci. Econ. Com.,* October 1973, *20*(10), pp. 985–94. [G: Ireland]

Klein, Lawrence R. and Long, Virginia. Capacity Utilization: Concept, Measurement, and Recent Estimates. *Brookings Pap. Econ. Act.,* 1973, (3), pp. 743–56. [G: U.S.]

Kuznets, Simon. Economic Capacity and Population Growth. In *Kuznets, S.,* 1973, pp. 49–93.

Kuznets, Simon. Population and Economic Growth. In *Kuznets, S.,* 1973, pp. 1–48.

Kuznets, Simon. Problems in Comparing Recent

Growth Rates for Developed and Less-Developed Countries. In *Kuznets, S.*, 1973, pp. 311–42.

Marstrand, Pauline K. and Pavitt, K. L. R. The Agricultural Sub-system. In *Cole, H. S. D., et al., eds.*, 1973, pp. 56–65.

Matthews, R. C. O. The Contribution of Science and Technology to Economic Development. In *Williams, B. R., ed.*, 1973, pp. 1–31. [G: U.S.; Canada; Europe; Japan]

McKean, Roland N. Growth vs. No Growth: An Evaluation. In *Olson, M. and Landsberg, H. H., eds.*, 1973, pp. 207–27.

Meyer, John R. Is Growth Obsolete? Comment. In *Moss, M., ed.*, 1973, pp. 548–54. [G: U.S.]

Mishan, Ezra J. Ills, Bads, and Disamenities: The Wages of Growth. In *Olson, M. and Landsberg, H. H., eds.*, 1973, pp. 63–87.

Nelson, Richard R. Recent Exercises in Growth Accounting: New Understanding or Dead End? *Amer. Econ. Rev.*, June 1973, *63*(3), pp. 462–68.

Nordhaus, William D. and Tobin, James. Is Growth Obsolete? In *Moss, M., ed.*, 1973, pp. 509–32. [G: U.S.]

Nordhaus, William D. and Tobin, James. Is Growth Obsolete? Reply to Denison and Usher. In *Moss, M., ed.*, 1973, pp. 554–63. [G: U.S.]

Nordhaus, William D. and Tobin, James. Is Growth Obsolete? Reply to Meyer. In *Moss, M., ed.*, 1973, pp. 563–64. [G: U.S.]

O'Loughlin, Carleen. What Is Agricultural Growth? In *Ofori, I. M., ed.*, 1973, pp. 7–13. [G: Central America; W. Africa]

Olson, Mancur. The No-Growth Society: Introduction. In *Olson, M. and Landsberg, H. H., eds.*, 1973, pp. 1–13.

Olson, Mancur; Landsberg, Hans H. and Fisher, Joseph L. The No-Growth Society: Epilogue. In *Olson, M. and Landsberg, H. H., eds.*, 1973, pp. 229–41.

Oshima, Keichi. Research and Development and Economic Growth in Japan. In *Williams, B. R., ed.*, 1973, pp. 310–23. [G: Japan]

Packard, Philip C. On the Apparent Benefits of Higher Productivity: An Arithmetical Illustration: A Comment. *J. Devel. Stud.*, April 1973, *9*(3), pp. 451–52.

Page, William. The Non-renewable Resources Sub-system. In *Cole, H. S. D., et al., eds.*, 1973, pp. 33–42.

Page, William. The Population Sub-system. In *Cole, H. S. D., et al., eds.*, 1973, pp. 43–55.

Perroux, François. The Growth of the French Economy 1946–1970 a First Assessment. *Écon. Appl.*, 1973, *26*(2–3–4), pp. 641–46. [G: France]

Perry, George L. Capacity in Manufacturing. *Brookings Pap. Econ. Act.*, 1973, (3), pp. 701–42. [G: U.S.]

Phelps Brown, E. H. Levels and Movements of Industrial Productivity and Real Wages Internationally Compared, 1860-1970. *Econ. J.*, March 1973, *83*(329), pp. 58–71. [G: Germany; Sweden; U.K.; U.S.; France]

Pinto, Aníbal and Kñakal, Jan. The Centre-Periphery System Twenty Years Later. *Soc. Econ. Stud.*, March 1973, *22*(1), pp. 34–89.

Poulson, Barry W. and Dowling, J. Malcolm, Jr. The Climacteric in U.S. Economic Growth. *Oxford Econ. Pap.*, November 1973, *25*(3), pp. 420–34. [G: U.S.]

Roberts, Marc J. On Reforming Economic Growth. In *Olson, M. and Landsberg, H. H., eds.*, 1973, pp. 119–37.

Singer, S. Fred. Is Growth Obsolete? Comment. In *Moss, M., ed.*, 1973, pp. 532–36. [G: U.S.]

Solow, Robert M. Some Evidence on the Short-Run Productivity Puzzle. In *[Rosenstein-Rodan, P.]*, 1973, pp. 316–25. [G: U.S.]

Teague, J. and Eilon, S. Productivity Measurement: A Brief Survey. *Appl. Econ.*, June 1973, *5*(2), pp. 133–45.

Usher, Dan. Is Growth Obsolete? Comment. In *Moss, M., ed.*, 1973, pp. 540–45. [G: U.S.]

Usher, Dan. An Imputation to the Measure of Economic Growth for Changes in Life Expectancy. In *Moss, M., ed.*, 1973, pp. 193–226. [G: Canada]

Williams, R. L. A Note on the Specification and Estimation of a Bias in the Measurement of the Size and Growth of Real GDP in Jamaica. *Soc. Econ. Stud.*, September 1973, *22*(3), pp. 384–94. [G: Jamaica]

Willis, Robert J. An Imputation to the Measure of Economic Growth for Changes in Life Expectancy: Comment. In *Moss, M., ed.*, 1973, pp. 226–32. [G: Canada]

Yotopoulos, Pan A. and Lau, Lawrence J. A Test for Relative Economic Efficiency: Some Further Results. *Amer. Econ. Rev.*, March 1973, *63*(1), pp. 214–23. [G: India]

Zeckhauser, Richard J. The Risks of Growth. In *Olson, M. and Landsberg, H. H., eds.*, 1973, pp. 103–18.

227 Prices

2270 Prices

Asaduzzaman, Md. The Seasonal Variation in Price of Rice: Bangladesh 1950–72. *Bangladesh Econ. Rev.*, April 1973, *1*(2), pp. 213–20. [G: Bangladesh]

Bahr, Richard C. Price Indexes by Size of City Show Increases Ranging from 7.6 to 8.9 Percent. *Mon. Lab. Rev.*, June 1973, *96*(6), pp. 54–55. [G: U.S.]

Bahr, Richard C. Second Quarter Prices Rise Faster in Smaller Urban Areas. *Mon. Lab. Rev.*, September 1973, *96*(9), pp. 73–74. [G: U.S.]

Bain, R. A. Factors Affecting Consumption and Prices of the Major Feed Grains in Australia. *Quart. Rev. Agr. Econ.*, July 1973, *26*(3), pp. 186–97. [G: Australia]

Barr, Terry N. and Gale, Hazen F. A Quarterly Forecasting Model for the Consumer Price Index for Food. *Agr. Econ. Res.*, January 1973, *25*(1), pp. 1–14. [G: U.S.]

Bechter, Dan M. and Pickett, Margaret S. The Wholesale and Consumer Price Indexes: What's the Connection? *Fed. Res. Bank Kansas City Rev.*, June 1973, pp. 3–9.

Behrman, Jere R. Price Determination in an Infla-

tionary Economy: The Dynamics of Chilean Inflation Revisited. In *Eckaus, R. S. and Rosenstein-Rodan, P. N., eds.*, 1973, pp. 369–97.
[G: Chile]

Bose, Swadesh R. The Price Situation in Bangladesh—A Preliminary Analysis. *Bangladesh Econ. Rev.*, July 1973, *1*(3), pp. 243–68. [G: Bangladesh]

Downes, Beverley. Purchase Taxes and Retail Prices in the United Kingdom. *Appl. Econ.*, September 1973, *5*(3), pp. 199–218. [G: U.K.]

Dunn, Robert M., Jr. Flexible Exchange Rates and Traded Goods Prices: The Role of Oligopoly Pricing in the Canadian Experience. In *Johnson, H. G. and Swoboda, A. K., eds.*, 1973, pp. 259–80.
[G: U.S.; Canada]

Epley, D. R. A Price Index for Life Insurance: Comment. *J. Risk Ins.*, December 1973, *40*(4), pp. 629.

Ewusi, Kodwo. The Rate of Inflation, Variation in Local Food Prices and the Effect of Transport Facilities on Local Food Prices in Ghana in the Sixties. In *Ofori, I. M., ed.*, 1973, pp. 278–91.
[G: Ghana]

Fethke, Gary C. and Belmont, William R. Buyers' Versus Sellers' Prices: An Econometric Investigation. *Nebr. J. Econ. Bus.*, Autumn 1973, *12*(4), pp. 37–50. [G: U.S.]

Gibson, William E. Price-Expectations Effects on Interest Rates: Reply. *J. Finance*, June 1973, *28* (3), pp. 751–53. [G: U.S.]

Gordon, Robert J. The Use of Unit Values to Measure Deviations of Transaction Prices from List Prices. *Rev. Income Wealth*, September 1973, *19*(3), pp. 267–69.

Gordon, Robert J. The Response of Wages and Prices to the First Two Years of Controls. *Brookings Pap. Econ. Act.*, 1973, (3), pp. 765–78. [G: U.S.]

Hasson, Joseph. The Impact of Dollar Devaluation on Domestic Prices. *J. Econ. Bus.*, Fall 1973, *26*(1), pp. 25–40. [G: U.S.]

Haworth, C. T. and Rasmussen, David W. Determinants of Metropolitan Cost of Living Variations. *Southern Econ. J.*, October 1973, *40*(2), pp. 183–92. [G: U.S.]

Helliwell, John F.; Sparks, Gordon and Frisch, Jack. The Supply Price of Capital in Macroeconomic Models. In *Powell, A. A. and Williams, R. A., eds.*, 1973, pp. 261–83. [G: Canada; Australia]

Holmes, R. A. The Inadequacy of Unit Value Indexes as Proxies for Canadian Industrial Selling Price Indexes. *Rev. Income Wealth*, September 1973, *19*(3), pp. 271–77. [G: Canada]

Klijn, Nico. The Effects of a 9.42 Per Cent Price Increase for Iron and Steel on Other Prices. *Australian Econ. Rev.*, 4th Quarter 1973, pp. 27–30.
[G: Australia]

Lenti, Libero. Business Cycles and Price Trend in Italy. *Rev. Econ. Cond. Italy*, May 1973, *27*(3), pp. 113–26. [G: Italy]

Lin, Cheyeh. A Price Index for Life Insurance: Reply. *J. Risk Ins.*, December 1973, *40*(4), pp. 630.

Lovell, Michael C. and Vogel, Robert C. A CPI–Futures Market. *J. Polit. Econ.*, July-August 1973, *81* (4), pp. 1009–12.

McCawley, Peter. Survey of Recent Developments. *Bull. Indonesian Econ. Stud.*, November 1973, *9* (3), pp. 1–27. [G: Indonesia]

McCollum, James F. Price-Expectations Effects on Interest Rates: Comment. *J. Finance*, June 1973, *28*(3), pp. 746–50. [G: U.S.]

Musgrave, John C. Alternative Measures of Price Change for GNP, 1970–73. *Surv. Curr. Bus.*, August 1973, *53*(8), pp. 15–17. [G: U.S.]

Nakayama, Toshiko. Price Increases Accelerate in First Quarter 1973. *Mon. Lab. Rev.*, June 1973, *96*(6), pp. 50–54. [G: U.S.]

Nakayama, Toshiko and Bahr, Richard C. New CPI by Size of City Shows Larger Increases in Big Areas. *Mon. Lab. Rev.*, March 1973, *96*(3), pp. 55–57. [G: U.S.]

Popkin, Joel. Prices in 1972: An Analysis of Changes During Phase 2. *Mon. Lab. Rev.*, February 1973, *96*(2), pp. 16–23. [G: U.S.]

Qureshi, Sarfraz K. Reliability of Pakistani Agricultural Price Data. *Pakistan Develop. Rev.*, Summer 1973, *12*(2), pp. 168–80. [G: Pakistan]

Rao, B. Bhaskara. Price Behaviour in India: A Note on Professor Raj's Model. *Indian Econ. Rev.*, October 1973, *8*(2), pp. 186–92. [G: India]

Ripley, Frank C. and Segal, Lydia. Price Determination in 395 Manufacturing Industries. *Rev. Econ. Statist.*, August 1973, *55*(3), pp. 263–71. [G: U.S.]

Roy, Sujit K. and Johnson, Phillip N. Econometric Models for Quarterly Shell Egg Prices. *Amer. J. Agr. Econ.*, May 1973, *55*(2), pp. 209–13.
[G: U.S.]

Schimmler, Harry. On National Accounts at Constant Prices. *Rev. Income Wealth*, December 1973, *19* (4), pp. 457–61.

Schnittker, John A. The 1972–73 Food Price Spiral. *Brookings Pap. Econ. Act.*, 1973, (2), pp. 498–507.
[G: U.S.]

Sevaldson, Per. Price Differentiation and Computation of National Accounts Figures at Constant Prices. *Rev. Income Wealth*, December 1973, *19* (4), pp. 453–56.

Stigler, George J. and Kindahl, James K. Industrial Prices, as Administered by Dr. Means. *Amer. Econ. Rev.*, September 1973, *63*(4), pp. 717–21.

Summers, Robert. International Price Comparisons Based Upon Incomplete Data. *Rev. Income Wealth*, March 1973, *19*(1), pp. 1–16.

Theil, Henri. Measuring the Quality of the Consumer's Basket. *De Economist*, July-August 1973, *121*(4), pp. 333–46. [G: Netherlands]

Thomas, David B. How Reliable Are Those Price and Employment Measures? *Fed. Res. Bank Bus. Rev. Phila.*, April 1973, pp. 17–22. [G: U.S.]

Triplett, Jack E. and Merchant, Stephen M. The CPI and the PCE Deflator: An Econometric Analysis of Two Price Measures. *Ann. Econ. Soc. Measure*, July 1973, *2*(3), pp. 263–82. [G: U.S.]

Triplett, Jack E. and Merchant, Stephen M. The CPI and the PCE Deflator: An Econometric Analysis of Two Price Measures: Reply. *Ann. Econ. Soc. Measure*, July 1973, *2*(3), pp. 287–88. [G: U.S.]

Verma, Krishnanand. Price Rise in India (1949–72). *Econ. Aff.*, June 1973, *18*(6), pp. 281–90.
[G: India]

Veverka, Ján. Strukturní model pro vypocty zmen velkoobchodních cen. (Structure Models for Calculating Wholesale Prices Changes. With English summary.) *Ekon.-Mat. Obzor*, 1973, *9*(3), pp. 260–74.

Williams, R. L. A Note on the Specification and Estimation of a Bias in the Measurement of the Size and Growth of Real GDP in Jamaica. *Soc. Econ. Stud.*, September 1973, *22*(3), pp. 384–94.
[G: Jamaica]

Yeats, Alexander J. An Evaluation of the Predictive Ability of the FRB Sensitive Price Index. *J. Amer. Statist. Assoc.*, December 1973, *68*(344), pp. 782–87.
[G: U.S.]

Young, Allan H. The CPI and the PCE Deflator: An Econometric Analysis of Two Price Measures: Comment. *Ann. Econ. Soc. Measure*, July 1973, *2* (3), pp. 283–86.
[G: U.S.]

228 Regional Statistics

2280 Regional Statistics

Bretzfelder, Robert B. Regional and State Personal Income: Second Quarter Developments. *Surv. Curr. Bus.*, October 1973, *53*(10), pp. 18–19, 44.
[G: U.S.]

Bretzfelder, Robert B. Regional and State Personal Income Developments. *Surv. Curr. Bus.*, January 1973, *53*(1), pp. 30–32.
[G: U.S.]

Bretzfelder, Robert B. Sensitivity of State and Regional Income to National Business Cycles. *Surv. Curr. Bus.*, April 1973, *53*(4), pp. 22–33.
[G: U.S.]

Brown, H. James. Shift and Share Projections Revisited: Reply. *J. Reg. Sci.*, April 1973, *13*(1), pp. 121.
[G: U.S.]

Divilov, S. Labor Resources and the Comparison of General Economic Indices by Union Republic. *Prob. Econ.*, March 1973, *15*(11), pp. 63–72.
[G: U.S.S.R.]

Floyd, Charles F. and Sirmans, C. F. Shift and Share Projections Revisited. *J. Reg. Sci.*, April 1973, *13* (1), pp. 115–20.
[G: U.S.]

Jonish, James E. and Kau, James B. State Differentials in Income Inequality. *Rev. Soc. Econ.*, October 1973, *31*(2), pp. 179–90.
[G: U.S.]

Kerr, Alex. Structure of Final Demand in Perth. *Econ. Rec.*, December 1973, *49*(128), pp. 505–17.
[G: Australia]

Nakayama, Toshiko and Warsky, D. Measuring Regional Price Change in Urban Areas. *Mon. Lab. Rev.*, October 1973, *96*(10), pp. 34–38.

Ousset, Jean and Nègre, Michel. Des comptes nationaux aux comptes régionaux. L'exemple des comptes de l'Agriculture. (Regional and National Accounts: The Example of French Agricultural Accounts. With English summary.) *Revue Écon.*, July 1973, *24*(4), pp. 549–87.
[G: France]

Schroeder, Gertrude E. Regional Differences in Incomes and Levels of Living in the USSR. In *Bandera, V. N. and Melnyk, Z. L., eds.*, 1973, pp. 167–95.
[G: U.S.S.R.]

Smith, Curtis R. Despite Damage by Agnes...District Economy Forges Ahead in '72. *Fed. Res. Bank*

Bus. Rev. Phila., February 1973, pp. 12–18.
[G: U.S.]

Vinod, H. D. Interregional Comparison of Production Structures. *J. Reg. Sci.*, August 1973, *13*(2), pp. 261–67.
[G: U.S.]

Wagener, Hans-Jürgen. Rules of Location and the Concept of Rationality: The Case of the USSR. In *Bandera, V. N. and Melnyk, Z. L., eds.*, 1973, pp. 63–103.
[G: U.S.S.R.]

229 Micro-data

2290 Micro-data

Aidenoff, Abraham. A Proposal for a System of Economic and Social Accounts: Comment. In *Moss, M., ed.*, 1973, pp. 153–59.
[G: U.S.]

Alcantara, Reinaldo and Prato, Anthony A. Returns to Scale and Input Elasticities for Sugarcane: The Case of Sao Paulo, Brazil. *Amer. J. Agr. Econ.*, Part I, November 1973, *55*(4), pp. 577–83.
[G: Brazil]

Aukrust, Odd and Nordbotten, Svein. Files of Individual Data and their Potentials for Social Research. *Rev. Income Wealth*, June 1973, *19*(2), pp. 189–201.
[G: Norway]

Battalio, Raymond C., et al. A Test of Consumer Demand Theory Using Observations of Individual Consumer Purchases. *Western Econ. J.*, December 1973, *11*(4), pp. 411–28.

Berney, Robert E. and Frerichs, Bernard H. Income Elasticities for State Tax Revenues: Techniques of Estimation and their Usefulness for Forecasting. *Public Finance Quart.*, October 1973, *1*(4), pp. 409–25.
[G: U.S.]

Carley, D. H. Silage-Concentrate Substitution; Effects on Milk Production and Income Over Feed Cost in DHIA Herds. *Amer. J. Agr. Econ.*, Part I, November 1973, *55*(4), pp. 641–46. [G: U.S.]

Denison, Edward F. A Proposal for a System of Economic and Social Accounts: Comment. In *Moss, M., ed.*, 1973, pp. 159–60.
[G: U.S.]

Ferber, Robert and Salazar-Carrillo, Jorge. Experience in Generating Micro Data in Latin America. In *Ayal, E. B., ed.*, 1973, pp. 84–100. [G: Latin America]

Friend, Irwin. Generating Micro Data in Less Developed Countries through Surveys: Some Experience in Asia: Comment. In *Ayal, E. B., ed.*, 1973, pp. 118–21.
[G: Taiwan; India]

Ghez, Gilbert R. The Measurement of Output of the Nonmarket Sector: The Evaluation of Housewives' Time: Comment. In *Moss, M., ed.*, 1973, pp. 190–92.
[G: U.S.; Israel]

Gronau, Reuben. The Measurement of Output of the Nonmarket Sector: The Evaluation of Housewives' Time. In *Moss, M., ed.*, 1973, pp. 163–90.
[G: U.S.; Israel]

Hammonds, T. M.; Yadav, R. and Vathana, C. The Elasticity of Demand for Hired Farm Labor. *Amer. J. Agr. Econ.*, May 1973, *55*(2), pp. 242–45.
[G: U.S.]

Hartle, Douglas G. A Proposal for a System of Economic and Social Accounts: Comment. In *Moss, M., ed.*, 1973, pp. 146–53.
[G: U.S.]

Kelly, Terence F. The Creation of Longitudinal Data

from Cross-Section Surveys: An Illustration from the Current Population Survey. *Ann. Econ. Soc. Measure,* April 1973, *2*(2), pp. 209–14.

Laird, Roy D. Handbook of Soviet Social Science Data: Agriculture. In *Mickiewicz, E., ed.,* 1973, pp. 65–90. [G: U.S.S.R.]

Lee, Maw Lin and Wallace, Richard L. Problems in Estimating Multiproduct Cost Functions: An Application to Hospitals. *Western Econ. J.,* September 1973, *11*(3), pp. 350–63. [G: U.S.]

Lim, David. A Note on Supply Response of Tin Producers, 1949–1969. *Malayan Econ. Rev.,* October 1973, *18*(2), pp. 50–59.

Lovell, C. A. Knox. Homotheticity and the Average Cost Function. *Western Econ. J.,* December 1973, *11*(4), pp. 506–13. [G: U.S.]

McClung, Nelson. Editing Census Microdata Files for Income and Wealth. *Ann. Econ. Soc. Measure,* April 1973, *2*(2), pp. 201–08. [G: U.S.]

McGee, John S. Economies of Size in Auto Body Manufacture. *J. Law Econ.,* October 1973, *16*(2), pp. 239–73. [G: U.S.; W. Europe]

Metwally, Mokhtar M. Economies of Size in Butter Production: The New Zealand Experience. *Econ. Anal. Pol.,* March 1973, *4*(1), pp. 33–44. [G: New Zealand]

Mueller, Eva. Generating Micro Data in Less Developed Countries through Surveys: Some Experience in Asia. In *Ayal, E. B., ed.,* 1973, pp. 101–18. [G: Taiwan; India]

Ofer, Gur. Returns to Scale in Retail Trade. *Rev. Income Wealth,* December 1973, *19*(4), pp. 363–84. [G: Israel]

Parikh, A. United States, European, and World Demand Functions for Coffee. *Amer. J. Agr. Econ.,* August 1973, *55*(3), pp. 490–94.

Rees, R. D. Optimum Plant Size in United Kingdom Industries: Some Survivor Estimates. *Economica, N.S.,* November 1973, *40*(160), pp. 394–401. [G: U.K.]

Rose-Ackerman, Susan. Used Cars as a Depreciating Asset. *Western Econ. J.,* December 1973, *11*(4), pp. 463–74. [G: U.S.]

Ruggles, Nancy and Ruggles, Richard. A Proposal for a System of Economic and Social Accounts. In *Moss, M., ed.,* 1973, pp. 111–46. [G: U.S.]

Smallhorn, P. J. Demand Elasticities for Raw Wool in Japan. *Quart. Rev. Agr. Econ.,* October 1973, *26*(4), pp. 253–62. [G: Japan]

Sudit, Ephraim F. Additive Nonhomogeneous Production Functions in Telecommunications. *Bell J. Econ. Manage. Sci.,* Autumn 1973, *4*(2), pp. 499–514.

Tryfos, Peter and Tryphonopoulos, N. Consumer Demand for Meat in Canada. *Amer. J. Agr. Econ.,* Part I, November 1973, *55*(4), pp. 647–52. [G: Canada]

Uselding, Paul and Juba, Bruce. Biased Technical Progress in American Manufacturing, 1839–1899. *Exploration Econ. Hist.,* Fall 1973, *11*(1), pp. 55–72. [G: U.S.]

Wells, Louis T., Jr. Economic Man and Engineering Man: Choice in a Low-Wage Country. *Public Policy,* Summer 1973, *21*(3), pp. 319–42. [G: Indonesia]

Wilkinson, R. K. The Income Elasticity of Demand

for Housing. *Oxford Econ. Pap.,* November 1973, *25*(3), pp. 361–77. [G: U.K.]

300 Domestic Monetary and Fiscal Theory and Institutions

310 DOMESTIC MONETARY AND FINANCIAL THEORY AND INSTITUTIONS

3100 General

Christian, James W. and Pagoulatos, Emilio. Domestic Financial Markets in Developing Economies: An Econometric Analysis. *Kyklos,* 1973, *26*(1), pp. 75–90.

311 Domestic Monetary and Financial Theory and Policy

3110 Monetary Theory and Policy

Ajayi, Simeon I. Money Supply Relationships when Government Debts are Held as Reserves. *Econ. Bull. Ghana, Sec. Ser.,* 1973, *3*(2), pp. 31–34.

Aliber, Robert Z. Speculation in the Flexible Exchange Re-Revisited: Reply. *Kyklos,* 1973, *26*(3), pp. 619–20. [G: France]

Allsbrook, Ogden O., Jr. and DeLorme, Charles D., Jr. Monetary Policy, Price Expectations, and the Case of a Positively-Sloped *IS* Curve. *Rivista Int. Sci. Econ. Com.,* March 1973, *20*(3), pp. 278–85.

Allsbrook, Ogden O., Jr. and DeLorme, Charles D., Jr. A Reconsideration of Interest Rates, Money Growth Rates, Inflation and the 'Ease' or 'Tightness' of Money: Comment. *Kyklos,* 1973, *26*(1), pp. 151–55.

Andersen, Leonall C. A Note on the Effects of Government Finance on Aggregate Demand for Goods and Services—A Reply. *Public Finance,* 1973, *28*(3–4), pp. 397–406.

Andersen, Leonall C. A Comparison of Stabilization Policies: 1966–67 and 1969–70. *J. Money, Credit, Banking,* Part I, February 1973, *5*(1), pp. 26–38. [G: U.S.]

Andersen, Leonall C. The State of the Monetarist Debate. *Fed. Res. Bank St. Louis Rev.,* September 1973, *55*(9), pp. 2–8. [G: U.S.]

Arcaini, Giuseppe. I presupposti del risparmio. (Savings Prerequisites. With English summary.) *Bancaria,* October 1973, *29*(10), pp. 1203–05. [G: Italy]

Arndt, Sven W. Policy Choices in an Open Economy: Some Dynamic Considerations. *J. Polit. Econ.,* July-August 1973, *81*(4), pp. 916–35.

Baltensperger, Ernst. Zur Rolle des Bankensystems in makroökonomischen Modellen. (The Role of the Banking System in Macroeconomic Models. With English summary.) *Kyklos,* 1973, *26*(4), pp. 787–803.

Basevi, G. Balances of Payments and Exchange Markets: A Lost Correspondence. *Europ. Econ. Rev.,* December 1973, *4*(4), pp. 309–28.

Boll, F. Multiplicatoren en economische politiek in verschillende wisselkoerssystemen. (Multipliers and Economic Policy under Various Exchange Rate Systems. With English summary.) *Tijdschr. Econ.*, 1973, *18*(3), pp. 381–427.

Brunner, Karl. The State of the Monetarist Debate: A Comment. *Fed. Res. Bank St. Louis Rev.*, September 1973, *55*(9), pp. 9, 12–14.

Brunner, Karl. A Diagrammatic Exposition of the Money Supply Process. *Schweiz. Z. Volkswirtsch. Statist.*, December 1973, *109*(4), pp. 481–533.

Brunner, Karl, et al. Fiscal and Monetary Policies in Moderate Inflation: Case Studies of Three Countries. *J. Money, Credit, Banking*, Part II, February 1973, *5*(1), pp. 313–53. **[G: U.S.; Germany; Italy]**

Budd, A. P. and Litzenberger, Robert H. Changes in the Supply of Money, the Firm's Market Value and Cost of Capital. *J. Finance*, March 1973, *28*(1), pp. 49–57.

Burns, Arthur F. Money Supply in the Conduct of Monetary Policy. *Fed. Res. Bull.*, November 1973, *59*(11), pp. 791–98. **[G: U.S.]**

Cebula, Richard J. and Chapin, Gene L. Bond Yields and the Lock-in Effect of Capital-Gains Taxation: A Pedagogical Note. *Rivista Int. Sci. Econ. Com.*, January 1973, *20*(1), pp. 83–89.

Chen, Chau-Nan. A Graphical Note on the Aggregative Effect of Payments of Interest on Deposits: Comment. *J. Money, Credit, Banking*, November 1973, *5*(4), pp. 985–87.

Chick, Victoria. Financial Counterparts of Saving and Investment and Inconsistency in Some Simple Macro Models. *Weltwirtsch. Arch.*, 1973, *109*(4), pp. 621–43.

Clinton, Kevin. Pitfalls in Financial Model Building: Comment. *Amer. Econ. Rev.*, December 1973, *63*(5), pp. 1003–04.

Davidson, Paul and Weintraub, Sidney. Money as Cause and Effect. *Econ. J.*, December 1973, *83*(332), pp. 1117–32.

Dellacasa, Giorgio. Teoria e politica monetaria nel pensiero di Milton Friedman. Parte Seconda (Milton Friedman and Modern Monetary Theory and Policy. With English summary.) *Econ. Int.*, February 1973, *26*(1), pp. 46–72.

Despres, Emile. Inflation and Development: Brazil. In *Despres, E.*, 1973, pp. 184–206. **[G: Brazil]**

Duggar, Jan W. and Beard, Thomas R. The Concept and Measurement of Defensive Open Market Operations. *Miss. Val. J. Bus. Econ.*, Spring 1973, *8*(3), pp. 29–38. **[G: U.S.]**

den Dunnen, Emile. Monetary Policy in the Netherlands. In *Holbik, K., ed.*, 1973, pp. 282–328. **[G: Netherlands]**

Feige, E. L., et al. The Roles of Money in an Economy and the Optimum Quantity of Money. *Economica, N.S.*, November 1973, *40*(160), pp. 416–31.

Fellner, William J. Employment Goals and Monetary-Fiscal Overexpansion. In *Cagan, P., et al.*, 1973, pp. 135–72. **[G: U.S.]**

Fried, Joel. Money, Exchange and Growth. *Western Econ. J.*, September 1973, *11*(3), pp. 285–301.

Gould, J. The Great Debasement and the Supply of Money. *Australian Econ. Hist. Rev.*, September 1973, *13*(2), pp. 177–89. **[G: U.K.]**

Grandmont, Jean-Michel and Laroque, Guy. Money

in the Pure Consumption Loan Model. *J. Econ. Theory*, August 1973, *6*(4), pp. 382–95.

Griffiths, Brian. Resource Efficiency, Monetary Policy and the Reform of the U.K. Banking System. *J. Money, Credit, Banking*, Part I, February 1973, *5*(1), pp. 61–77. **[G: U.K.]**

Grünärml, Frohmund. Demand Management—Illusion oder Realität? (Demand Management—Illusion or Reality? With English summary.) *Z. Wirtschaft. Sozialwissen.*, 1973, *93*(5), pp. 537–66.

Guitian, Manuel. Credit Versus Money as an Instrument of Control. *Int. Monet. Fund Staff Pap.*, November 1973, *20*(3), pp. 785–800.

Hadjimichalakis, Michael G. On the Effectiveness of Monetary Policy as a Stabilization Device. *Rev. Econ. Stud.*, October 1973, *40*(4), pp. 561–70.

Hahn, Frank H. On Transaction Costs, Inessential Sequence Economies and Money. *Rev. Econ. Stud.*, October 1973, *40*(4), pp. 449–61.

Havrilesky, Thomas M. Alternative Monetary Control Responses in a Stochastic Macro Model. *Quart. Rev. Econ. Bus.*, Spring 1973, *13*(1), pp. 37–48.

Hirshleifer, Jack. Exchange Theory: The Missing Chapter. *Western Econ. J.*, June 1973, *11*(2), pp. 129–46.

Howitt, P. W. Walras and Monetary Theory. *Western Econ. J.*, December 1973, *11*(4), pp. 487–99.

Ionescu, Eugen. Procesul economisirii la C.E.C. Tendinţe şi structuri. (The Process of Economizing with the Savings Bank—Trends and Structures. With English summary.) *Stud. Cercet. Econ.*, 1973, (4), pp. 65–71. **[G: Rumania]**

Johnson, Harry G. Monetary Theory and Monetary Policy. In *Johnson, H. G.*, 1973, pp. 77–87. **[G: U.S.; U.K.]**

Jones, J. C. H. and Laudadio, Leonard. Canadian Bank Mergers, the Public Interest and Public Policy. *Banca Naz. Lavoro Quart. Rev.*, June 1973, *105*, pp. 109–40. **[G: Canada]**

Jordan, Jerry L. Interest Rates and Monetary Growth. *Fed. Res. Bank St. Louis Rev.*, January 1973, *55*(1), pp. 2–11. **[G: U.S.]**

Kareken, John H.; Muench, Thomas and Wallace, Neil. Optimal Open Market Strategy: The Use of Information Variables. *Amer. Econ. Rev.*, March 1973, *63*(1), pp. 156–72. **[G: U.S.]**

Klein, Lawrence R. The State of the Monetarist Debate: A Comment. *Fed. Res. Bank St. Louis Rev.*, September 1973, *55*(9), pp. 9–12.

Korteweg, P. Over de beheersbaarheid van de geldhoeveelheid in Nederland. (The Supply and Controllability of Money in an Open Economy: The Dutch Case. With English summary.) *De Economist*, May-June 1973, *121*(3), pp. 273–99. **[G: Netherlands]**

Krainer, Robert E. Economic Structure and the Assignment Problem: A Contribution to the Theory of Macro-Economic Policy for Net Creditor Countries. *Can. J. Econ.*, May 1973, *6*(2), pp. 239–47.

Kumar, Rishi. Demand Policies and Internal-External Balance Under Fixed Exchange Rates—The Mundellian Assignment: A Reformulation and

Some Extensions. *Weltwirtsch. Arch.*, 1973, *109* (2), pp. 253–73.

Ladenson, Mark L. Pitfalls in Financial Model Building: Reply and Some Further Extensions. *Amer. Econ. Rev.*, December 1973, *63*(5), pp. 1005–08.

Laidler, David. Monetarist Policy Prescriptions and Their Background. *Manchester Sch. Econ. Soc. Stud.*, March 1973, *41*(1), pp. 59–71. [G: U.K.]

Laumas, Prem S. and Mohabhat, Khan A. Money and Economic Development. *Indian Econ. J.*, April-June 1973, *20*(4–5), pp. 619–29. [G: India]

Lee, Boyden E. The Euro-Dollar Multiplier. *J. Finance*, September 1973, *28*(4), pp. 867–74.
[G: U.S.; Europe]

Levin, Fred J. Examination of the Money-Stock Control Approach of Burger, Kalish, and Babb. *J. Money, Credit, Banking*, November 1973, *5*(4), pp. 924–38. [G: U.S.]

Lombra, Raymond E. and Torto, Raymond G. Federal Reserve "Defensive" Behavior and the Reverse Causation Argument. *Southern Econ. J.*, July 1973, *40*(1), pp. 47–55. [G: U.S.]

Marty, Alvin L. Growth, Satiety, and the Tax Revenue from Money Creation. *J. Polit. Econ.*, September-October 1973, *81*(5), pp. 1136–52.

Mathieson, Donald J. Traded Goods, Nontraded Goods, and the Balance of Payments. *Int. Econ. Rev.*, October 1973, *14*(3), pp. 615–24.

McLaughlin, Donald H. The Triumph Not the Twilight of Gold. In *Wiegand, G. C.*, ed., 1973, pp. 30–32.

Meiselman, David I. Simulations of Stabilization Policies for 1966–1970 *and* A Comparison of Stabilization Policies: 1966–67 and 1969–70: Comment. *J. Money, Credit, Banking*, Part I, February 1973, *5*(1), pp. 43–46. [G: U.S.]

Meiselman, David I. The Case Against the Case for Gold. In *Wiegand, G. C.*, ed., 1973, pp. 14–20.
[G: U.S.]

Miller, Marcus H. "Competition and Credit Control" and the Open Economy. *Manchester Sch. Econ. Soc. Stud.*, March 1973, *41*(1), pp. 123–40.
[G: U.K.]

Monissen, Hans G. Preise, Löhne und Beschäftigung in dynamischer Betrachtung: Eine einfache Exposition. (Prices, Wages and Employment in Dynamic Perspective: A Simple Exposition. With English summary.) *Kyklos*, 1973, *26*(3), pp. 545–58.

Morgan, E. Victor and Harrington, R. L. Reserve Assets and the Supply of Money. *Manchester Sch. Econ. Soc. Stud.*, March 1973, *41*(1), pp. 73–87.
[G: U.K.]

Morley, Samuel A. The Relationship Between Money, Income and Prices in the Short and Long Run. *J. Finance*, December 1973, *28*(5), pp. 1119–30.

Mullineaux, Donald J. Deposit-Rate Ceilings and Noncompetitive Bidding for U.S. Treasury Bills. *J. Money, Credit, Banking*, Part I, February 1973, *5*(1), pp. 201–12. [G: U.S.]

Niehans, Jürg. Veendorp on Optimal Payment Arrangements: Reply. *J. Money, Credit, Banking*, Part I, February 1973, *5*(1), pp. 213–14.

Nobay, A. R. The Bank of England, Monetary Policy and Monetary Theory in the United Kingdom,

1951-1971. *Manchester Sch. Econ. Soc. Stud.*, March 1973, *41*(1), pp. 43–58. [G: U.K.]

Okun, Arthur M. Rules and Roles for Fiscal and Monetary Policy. In *Reynolds, L. G.; Green, G. D. and Lewis, D. R.*, eds., 1973, pp. 62–80. [G: U.S.]

Olienyk, John and Fan, Liang-Shing. Inflation in a Growing Economy: A Monetaristic Elucidation. *Intermountain Econ. Rev.*, Fall 1973, *4*(2), pp. 75–76.

Parkin, Michael. The Discount Houses' Role in the Money Supply Control Process Under the "Competition and Credit Control" Regime. *Manchester Sch. Econ. Soc. Stud.*, March 1973, *41*(1), pp. 89–105. [G: U.K.]

Park, Yung C. The Transmission Process and the Relative Effectiveness of Monetary and Fiscal Policy in a Two-Sector Neoclassical Model. *J. Money, Credit, Banking*, May 1973, *5*(2), pp. 595–622.

Perlman, Morris. The Roles of Money in an Economy and the Optimum Quantity of Money: Reply. *Economica, N.S.*, November 1973, *40*(160), pp. 432–41.

Pippenger, John E. Speculation in the Flexible Exchange Re-Revisited. *Kyklos*, 1973, *26*(3), pp. 613–18. [G: France]

Puckett, Richard H. Monetary Policy Effectiveness: The Case of a Positively Sloped I-S Curve: Comment. *J. Finance*, December 1973, *28*(5), pp. 1362–64.

Rao, D. C. and Kaminow, Ira. Selective Credit Controls and the Real Investment Mix: A General Equilibrium Approach. *J. Finance*, December 1973, *28*(5), pp. 1103–18.

Rasche, Robert H. Simulations of Stabilization Policies for 1966–1970. *J. Money, Credit, Banking*, Part I, February 1973, *5*(1), pp. 1–25. [G: U.S.]

Ratchford, B. U. Interest Rates and Inflation. *Nebr. J. Econ. Bus.*, Spring 1973, *12*(2), pp. 45–54.

Rea, John D. Trends and Cycles in Money and Bank Credit. *Fed. Res. Bank Kansas City Rev.*, March 1973, pp. 3–9. [G: U.S.]

Roll, Richard. Assets, Money, and Commodity Price Inflation Under Uncertainty: Demand Theory. *J. Money, Credit, Banking*, November 1973, *5*(4), pp. 903–23.

Rosa, Jean-Jacques. Keynes or Fisher? Monetary Channels and the 1967 Reform. *Econ. Int.*, August-November 1973, *26*(3–4), pp. 433–50.
[G: France]

Santomero, Anthony M. A Note on Interest Rates and Prices in General Equilibrium. *J. Finance*, September 1973, *28*(4), pp. 997–1000.

Sargent, Thomas J. and Wallace, Neil. Rational Expectations and the Dynamics of Hyperinflation. *Int. Econ. Rev.*, June 1973, *14*(2), pp. 328–50.

Schmitt-Rink, Gerhard. Marktform und Geldschöpfungsmultiplikator. (Market Structure and Multiple Money Expansion. With English summary.) *Jahr. Nationalökon. Statist.*, December 1973, *188*(1), pp. 1–9.

Scott, James H., Jr. The Portfolio Balance Theory of the Expected Rate of Change of Prices: Comment. *Rev. Econ. Stud.*, October 1973, *40*(4), pp. 579–80.

Silber, William L. Monetary Policy Effectiveness: The Case of a Positively Sloped I-S Curve: Reply. *J. Finance,* December 1973, *28*(5), pp. 1365.

Silverman, Lester P. Credit Standards and Tight Money: Comment. *J. Money, Credit, Banking,* Part I, February 1973, *5*(1), pp. 221–23.

Starrett, David A. Inefficiency and the Demand for "Money" in a Sequence Economy. *Rev. Econ. Stud.,* October 1973, *40*(4), pp. 437–48.

Steindl, Frank G. Price Expectations and Interest Rates. *J. Money, Credit, Banking,* November 1973, *5*(4), pp. 939–49.

Steindl, Frank G. Money and Bonds as Giffen Goods. *Manchester Sch. Econ. Soc. Stud.,* December 1973, *41*(4), pp. 418–24.

Strydom, P. D. F. Some Observations on Monetary Policy. *S. Afr. J. Econ.,* September 1973, *41*(3), pp. 234–56. [G: S. Africa]

Swoboda, Alexander K. Monetary Policy under Fixed Exchange Rates: Effectiveness, the Speed of Adjustment and Proper Use. *Economica, N.S.,* May 1973, *40*(158), pp. 136–54.

Thore, Sten and Eriksen, Ib. Payment Clearing Networks. *Swedish J. Econ.,* June 1973, *75*(2), pp. 143–63.

Thygesen, Niels. Monetary Policy, Capital Flows and Internal Stability: Some Experiences from Large Industrial Countries. *Swedish J. Econ.,* March 1973, *75*(1), pp. 83–99. [G: W. Germany; Italy; Japan]

Tilly, Richard H. Zeitreihen zum Geldumlauf in Deutschland, 1870–1913. (Time Series Concerning the Aggregate Money Supply in Germany, 1870–1913. With English summary.) *Jahr. Nationalökon. Statist.,* May 1973, *187*(4), pp. 330–63. [G: Germany]

Vaciago, Giacomo. Monetary Analysis and Policy: An Aggregated Model for the Italian Economy. *Banca Naz. Lavoro Quart. Rev.,* June 1973, (105), pp. 84–108. [G: Italy]

Valentine, T. J. The Loan Supply Function of Australian Trading Banks: An Empirical Analysis. *Australian Econ. Pap.,* June 1973, *12*(20), pp. 57–69. [G: Australia]

Waud, Roger N. Index Bonds and Economic Stability. *Public Finance,* 1973, *28*(1), pp. 52–68.

Waud, Roger N. A Reconsideration of Interest Rates, Money Growth Rates, Inflation and the 'Ease' or 'Tightness' of Money: Reply. *Kyklos,* 1973, *26*(1), pp. 156–58.

Williams, Raburn and Miller, Roger LeRoy. A Note on the Effects of Government Finance on Aggregate Demand for Goods and Services. *Public Finance,* 1973, *28*(3–4), pp. 393–96.

3112 Monetary Theory; Empirical Studies

Adie, Douglas K. An International Comparison of the Quantity and Income-Expenditure Theories. *J. Amer. Statist. Assoc.,* March 1973, *68*(341), pp. 63–65.

Akerlof, George A. The Demand for Money: A General-Equilibirum Inventory-Theoretic Approach. *Rev. Econ. Stud.,* January 1973, *40*(1), pp. 115–30.

Arak, Marcelle and Spiro, Alan. A Theoretical Expla-

nation of the Interest Inelasticity of Money Demand. *Rev. Econ. Statist.,* November 1973, *55*(4), pp. 520–23. [G: U.S.]

Artis, M. J. Analysis of the Determination of the Stock of Money: Discussion. In *Parkin, M., ed.,* 1973, pp. 262–65.

Aschheim, Joseph. Neutral Money Reconsidered. *Banca Naz. Lavoro Quart. Rev.,* June 1973, *105,* pp. 75–83.

Asimakopulos, A. Keynes, Patinkin, Historical Time, and Equilibrium Analysis. *Can. J. Econ.,* May 1973, *6*(2), pp. 179–88.

Babeau, André. Economies d'échelle dans les encaisses monétaires des ménages: une série de tests empiriques. (Economies of Scale in the Households' Cash Balances. With English summary.) *Revue Écon.,* May 1973, *24*(3), pp. 401–41. [G: France]

Bain, A. D. Flow of Funds Analysis: Survey. *Econ. J.,* December 1973, *83*(332), pp. 1055–93.

Bechter, Dan M. Money and Inflation. *Fed. Res. Bank Kansas City Rev.,* July-August 1973, pp. 3–6. [G: U.S.]

Bellante, Donald M. The Relative Importance of Monetary and Fiscal Variables in Determining Price Level Movements: Comment. *J. Finance,* March 1973, *28*(1), pp. 188–90.

Billings, Brad and Tuccillo, John A. Determinants of the Money Multiplier: Comment. *Quart. Rev. Econ. Bus.,* Winter 1973, *13*(4), pp. 93–101. [G: U.S.]

Bolle, Michael. Geld, Wachstum und Beschäftigung. (Money, Growth and Employment. With English summary.) *Z. ges. Staatswiss.,* February 1973, *129*(1), pp. 1–22.

Bowden, Roger J. Some Implications of the Permanent-Income Hypothesis. *Rev. Econ. Stud.,* January 1973, *40*(1), pp. 33–37.

Brunner, Karl and Meltzer, Allan H. Mr. Hicks and the "Monetarists." *Economica, N.S.,* February 1973, *40*(157), pp. 44–59.

Cebula, Richard J. Expected Interest Rate Changes and Monetary Policy: A Brief Note. *Miss. Val. J. Bus. Econ.,* Spring 1973, *8*(3), pp. 71–76.

Christ, Carl F. Monetary and Fiscal Influences on U.S. Money Income, 1891–1970. *J. Money, Credit, Banking,* Part II, February 1973, *5*(1), pp. 279–300. [G: U.S.]

Clark, Carolyn. The Demand for Money and the Choice of a Permanent Income Estimate: Some Canadian Evidence, 1926-65. *J. Money, Credit, Banking,* August 1973, *5*(3), pp. 773–93. [G: Canada]

Clauretie, Terrence M. Interest Rates, the Business Demand for Funds, and the Residential Mortgage Market: A Sectoral Econometric Study. *J. Finance,* December 1973, *28*(5), pp. 1313–26. [G: U.S.]

Clinton, Kevin. The Demand for Money in Canada, 1955-70: Some Single-Equation Estimates and Stability Tests. *Can. J. Econ.,* February 1973, *6*(1), pp. 53–61. [G: Canada]

Clinton, Kevin. Interest Rate Expectations and the Demand for Money in Canada: Comment. *J. Finance,* March 1973, *28*(1), pp. 207–12. [G: Canada]

Cohan, Sandra B. The Determinants of Supply and Demand for Certificates of Deposit. *J. Money, Credit, Banking*, Part I, February 1973, *5*(1), pp. 100–12. **[G: U.S.]**

Dean, James W. and Tower, Edward. Internal and External Balance in an "Almost Classical" World: Rejoinder. *Western Econ. J.*, June 1973, *11*(2), pp. 240.

Dean, James W. and Tower, Edward. More on Internal and External Balance in an "Almost Classical" World. *Western Econ. J.*, June 1973, *11*(2), pp. 232–37.

Dewald, William G. The Term Structure of Interest Rates in Australia, 1952–1966. *Econ. Anal. Pol.*, September 1973, *4*(2), pp. 1–17. **[G: Australia]**

Dutton, Dean S. and Gramm, William P. Transactions Costs, the Wage Rate, and the Demand for Money. *Amer. Econ. Rev.*, September 1973, *63*(4), pp. 652–65. **[G: U.S.]**

Fase, M. M. G. A Principal Components Analysis of Market Interest Rates in the Netherlands, 1962–1970. *Europ. Econ. Rev.*, June 1973, *4*(2), pp. 107–34. **[G: Netherlands]**

Feige, E. L., et al. The Roles of Money in an Economy and the Optimum Quantity of Money. *Economica, N.S.*, November 1973, *40*(160), pp. 416–31.

Feldstein, Martin S. and Chamberlain, Gary. Multimarket Expectations and the Rate of Interest. *J. Money, Credit, Banking*, November 1973, *5*(4), pp. 873–902. **[G: U.S.]**

Fischer, Stanley. A Neoclassical Monetary Growth Model: Comment. *J. Money, Credit, Banking*, May 1973, *5*(2), pp. 704–06.

Fisher, Douglas. The Speculative Demand for Money: An Empirical Test. *Economica, N.S.*, May 1973, *40*(158), pp. 174–79. **[G: U.K.]**

Floyd, John E. Monetary and Fiscal Policy in a World of Capital Mobility: A Reply. *Rev. Econ. Stud.*, April 1973, *40*(2), pp. 299–303.

Frenkel, Jacob A. Elasticities and the Interest Parity Theory. *J. Polit. Econ.*, May-June 1973, *81*(3), pp. 741–47.

Fry, Maxwell J. Manipulating Demand for Money. In *Parkin, M., ed.*, 1973, pp. 371–85. **[G: Iran; Pakistan; Turkey]**

Gebauer, Wolfgang. The Theory of Monetarism. *Z. ges. Staatswiss.*, February 1973, *129*(1), pp. 23–45.

Gibson, William E. Price-Expectations Effects on Interest Rates: Reply. *J. Finance*, June 1973, *28*(3), pp. 751–53. **[G: U.S.]**

Gibson, William E. Interest Rates and Prices in the Long Run: A Study of the Gibson Paradox: Comment. *J. Money, Credit, Banking*, Part II, February 1973, *5*(1), pp. 450–53. **[G: U.S.]**

Gilbert, Gary G. Estimation of Liquidity Functions in the U.S. Economy. *Rivista Int. Sci. Econ. Com.*, February 1973, *20*(2), pp. 107–29. **[G: U.S.]**

Glahe, Fred R. A Permanent Restatement of the IS-LM Model. *Amer. Econ.*, Spring 1973, *17*(1), pp. 158–67.

Goldfeld, Stephen M. The Demand for Money Revisited. *Brookings Pap. Econ. Act.*, 1973, (3), pp. 577–638. **[G: U.S.]**

Goodhart, Charles. Analysis of the Determination of

the Stock of Money. In *Parkin, M., ed.*, 1973, pp. 243–61.

Gordon, Robert J. Interest Rates and Prices in the Long Run: A Study of the Gibson Paradox: Comment. *J. Money, Credit, Banking*, Part II, February 1973, *5*(1), pp. 460–63. **[G: U.S.]**

Grandmont, Jean-Michel and Younes, Yves. On the Efficiency of a Monetary Equilibrium. *Rev. Econ. Stud.*, April 1973, *40*(2), pp. 149–65.

Grandmont, Jean-Michel. On the Short-Run and Long-Run Demand for Money. *Europ. Econ. Rev.*, October 1973, *4*(3), pp. 265–87. **[G: France]**

Grandmont, Jean-Michel and Neel, Gérard. Sur les taux d'intérêt en France. (About Interest Rates in France. With English summary.) *Revue Écon.*, May 1973, *24*(3), pp. 460–72. **[G: France]**

Gray, Jean M. New Evidence on the Term Structure of Interest Rates: 1884–1900. *J. Finance*, June 1973, *28*(3), pp. 635–46. **[G: U.S.]**

Hahn, Frank H. On the Foundations of Monetary Theory. In *Parkin, M., ed.*, 1973, pp. 230–42.

Hamburger, Michael J. The Demand for Money in 1971: Was There a Shift? Comment. *J. Money, Credit, Banking*, May 1973, *5*(2), pp. 720–25.

Hanson, James S. and Vogel, Robert C. Inflation and Monetary Velocity in Latin America. *Rev. Econ. Statist.*, August 1973, *55*(3), pp. 365–70. **[G: Latin America]**

Harvey, C. E. On the Cost-Inflationary Impact of High Interest Rates: Reply. *J. Econ. Issues*, September 1973, *7*(3), pp. 514.

Haulman, Clyde A. A Structural Model of the Canadian Monetary Sector: Reply. *Southern Econ. J.*, April 1973, *39*(4), pp. 642–44. **[G: Canada]**

Hebert, Robert F. and Byrns, Ralph T. On the Cost-Inflationary Impact of High Interest Rates: Comment. *J. Econ. Issues*, September 1973, *7*(3), pp. 511–14.

Hendershott, Patric H. and Van Horne, James C. Expected Inflation Implied by Capital Market Rates. *J. Finance*, May 1973, *28*(2), pp. 301–14. **[G: U.S.]**

Hendershott, Patric H. Financial Disintermediation in a Macroeconomic Framework: Reply. *J. Finance*, September 1973, *28*(4), pp. 1033–34.

Hendershott, Patric H. Interest Rates and Prices in the Long Run: A Study of the Gibson Paradox: Comment. *J. Money, Credit, Banking*, Part II, February 1973, *5*(1), pp. 454–59. **[G: U.S.]**

Hendershott, Patric H. Monetary and Fiscal Influences on U.S. Money Income, 1891–1970: Comment. *J. Money, Credit, Banking*, Part II, February 1973, *5*(1), pp. 311–12. **[G: U.S.]**

Henderson, Dale W. and Sargent, Thomas J. Monetary and Fiscal Policy in a Two-Sector Aggregative Model. *Amer. Econ. Rev.*, June 1973, *63*(3), pp. 345–65.

Hess, Alan C. Household Demand for Durable Goods: The Influences of Rates of Return and Wealth. *Rev. Econ. Statist.*, February 1973, *55*(1), pp. 9–15. **[G: U.S.]**

Holzheu, Franz. Das Geld- und Kreditsystem als Variable im Wachstumsprozess. (The Monetary

System as a Variable in the Process of Growth. With English summary.) *Jahr. Nationalökon. Statist.*, January 1973, *187*(2), pp. 97–107.

Hopewell, Michael H. and Kaufman, George G. Bond Price Volatility and Term to Maturity: A Generalized Respecification. *Amer. Econ. Rev.*, September 1973, *63*(4), pp. 749–53.

Hosek, William R. Determinants of the Money Multiplier: Reply. *Quart. Rev. Econ. Bus.*, Winter 1973, *13*(4), pp. 101–02. [G: U.S.]

Humphrey, Thomas M. Empirical Tests of the Quantity Theory of Money in the United States, 1900–1930. *Hist. Polit. Econ.*, Fall 1973, *5*(2), pp. 285–316. [G: U.S.]

Humphrey, Thomas M. On the Monetary Economics of Chicagoans and Non-Chicagoans: Reply. *Southern Econ. J.*, January 1973, *39*(3), pp. 460–63.

Kane, Edward J. Politics and the Prime Rate: A Deceptive Solution. *Ohio State U. Bull. Bus. Res.*, June 1973, *48*(6), pp. 1–3, 5. [G: U.S.]

Kane, Edward J. Monetary and Fiscal Influence on U.S. Money Income, 1891–1970: Comment. *J. Money, Credit, Banking*, Part II, February 1973, *5*(1), pp. 301–03. [G: U.S.]

Karni, Edi. Transactions Costs and the Demand for Media of Exchange. *Western Econ. J.*, March 1973, *11*(1), pp. 71–80.

Karni, Edi. The Transactions Demand for Cash: Incorporation of the Value of Time into the Inventory Approach. *J. Polit. Econ.*, September-October 1973, *81*(5), pp. 1216–25.

Khan, Mohsin S. A Note on the Secular Behaviour of Velocity Within the Context of the Inventory-Theoretic Model of Demand for Money. *Manchester Sch. Econ. Soc. Stud.*, June 1973, *41*(2), pp. 207–13. [G: U.S.]

Klein, Benjamin. Income Velocity, Interest Rates, and the Money Supply Multiplier: A Reinterpretation of the Long-Term Evidence. *J. Money, Credit, Banking*, May 1973, *5*(2), pp. 656–67. [G: U.S.]

Kliman, M. L. and Oksanen, Ernest H. The Keynesian Demand-for-Money Function: Comment. *J. Money, Credit, Banking*, Part I, February 1973, *5*(1), pp. 215–20.

Kliman, M. L. The Permanent Income Hypothesis and the Firm's Demand for Money. *J. Econ. Bus.*, Winter 1973, *25*(2), pp. 89–92. [G: U.S.]

Kmenta, J. and Smith, Paul E. Autonomous Expenditures Versus Money Supply: An Application of Dynamic Multipliers. *Rev. Econ. Statist.*, August 1973, *55*(3), pp. 299–307. [G: U.S.]

Koot, Ronald S. Price Expectations and Monetary Adjustments in Latin America. *Schweiz. Z. Volkswirtsch. Statist.*, June 1973, *109*(2), pp. 223–32. [G: Latin America]

Laidler, David. The Influence of Money on Real Income and Inflation:—A Simple Model with some Empirical Tests for the United States 1953–72. *Manchester Sch. Econ. Soc. Stud.*, December 1973, *41*(4), pp. 367–95. [G: U.S.]

Laidler, David. Expectations, Adjustment, and the Dynamic Response of Income to Policy Changes. *J. Money, Credit, Banking*, Part I, February 1973, *5*(1), pp. 157–72.

Leijonhufvud, Axel. Effective Demand Failures. *Swedish J. Econ.*, March 1973, *75*(1), pp. 27–48.

LeRoy, Stephen F. Interest Rates and the Inflation Premium. *Fed. Res. Bank Kansas City Rev.*, May 1973, pp. 11–18.

Lucia, Joseph L. Money Market Strategy or Monetary Aggregates: An Analysis of Recent Federal Reserve Policy. *Econ. Soc. Rev.*, October 1973, *5*(1), pp. 31–45. [G: U.S.]

Macbeth, Thomas G. and Downey, Gerald F. The Monetary Consequences of Demand Deposit Creation by Mutual Savings Banks—The Commonwealth of Massachusetts Case. *Marquette Bus. Rev.*, Spring 1973, *17*(1), pp. 1–8. [G: U.S.]

Machlup, Fritz. Stateless Money. In *[Halm, G. N.]*, 1973, pp. 115–22.

Mammen, Thampy. Indian Money Market: An Econometric Study. *Int. Econ. Rev.*, February 1973, *14*(1), pp. 49–68. [G: India]

Marcis, Richard G. and Smith, V. Kerry. The Demand for Liquid Asset Balances by U.S. Manufacturing Corporations: 1959-1970. *J. Financial Quant. Anal.*, March 1973, *8*(2), pp. 207–18. [G: U.S.]

Marcis, Richard G. and Smith, V. Kerry. Monetary Activity and Interest Rates: A Spectral Analysis. *Quart. Rev. Econ. Bus.*, Summer 1973, *13*(2), pp. 69–82.

Mattfeldt, Harald. Zum Verhältnis verschiedener finanzieller Aktiva im Portefeuille inländischer Nichtbanken der BRD. (On the Relationship Between Different Financial Assets of Non-bank Portfolio Composition in Western Germany. With English summary.) *Jahr. Nationalökon. Statist.*, March 1973, *187*(3), pp. 237–44. [G: W. Germany]

McCallum, B. T. Friedman's Missing Equation: Another Approach. *Manchester Sch. Econ. Soc. Stud.*, September 1973, *41*(3), pp. 311–28. [G: U.S.]

McCollum, James F. Price-Expectations Effects on Interest Rates: Comment. *J. Finance*, June 1973, *28*(3), pp. 746–50. [G: U.S.]

McGregor, L. and Walters, A. A. Real Balances and Output: A Productivity Model of a Monetary Economy. In *Powell, A. A. and Williams, R. A.*, eds., 1973, pp. 233–59.

Mélitz, Jacques and Pardue, Morris. The Demand and Supply of Commercial Bank Loans. *J. Money, Credit, Banking*, May 1973, *5*(2), pp. 669–92. [G: U.S.]

Meltzer, Allan H. The Dollar as an International Money. *Banca Naz. Lavoro Quart. Rev.*, March 1973, (104), pp. 21–28.

Metzler, Lloyd A. The Structure of Taxes, Open-Market Operations, and the Rate of Interest. In *Metzler, L. A.*, 1973, pp. 345–62. [G: U.S.]

Metzler, Lloyd A. Wealth, Saving, and the Rate of Interest. In *Metzler, L. A.*, 1973, pp. 311–44.

Modigliani, Franco and Shiller, Robert J. Inflation, Rational Expectations and the Term Structure of Interest Rates. *Economica, N.S.*, February 1973, *40*(157), pp. 12–43.

de Montbrial, Thierry. Intertemporal General Equilibrium and Interest Rates Theory. *Écon. Appl.*, 1973, *26*(2–3–4), pp. 877–917.

Morishima, M. Optimal Transactions Demand for Money. In *Morishima, M., et al.*, 1973, pp. 271–84.

Morishima, M. Consumer Behaviour and Liquidity Preference. In *Morishima, M., et al.*, 1973, pp. 215–41.

Nobay, A. R. Manipulating Demand for Money: Discussion. In *Parkin, M., ed.*, 1973, pp. 386–88.
[G: Iran; Pakistan; Turkey]

Ostroy, Joseph M. The Informational Efficiency of Monetary Exchange. *Amer. Econ. Rev.*, September 1973, *63*(4), pp. 597–610.

Parkin, Michael. The 1973 Report of the President's Council of Economic Advisers: A Critique. *Amer. Econ. Rev.*, September 1973, *63*(4), pp. 535–45.
[G: U.S.]

Park, Yung C. The Role of Money in Stabilization Policy in Developing Countries. *Int. Monet. Fund Staff Pap.*, July 1973, *20*(2), pp. 379–418.

Patinkin, Don. On the Monetary Economics of Chicagoans and Non-Chicagoans: Comment. *Southern Econ. J.*, January 1973, *39*(3), pp. 454–59.

Perlman, Morris. The Roles of Money in an Economy and the Optimum Quantity of Money: Reply. *Economica, N.S.*, November 1973, *40*(160), pp. 432–41.

Pesek, Boris P. Equilibrium Level of Transaction Services of Money. *J. Finance*, June 1973, *28*(3), pp. 647–60.

Poole, William and Kornblith, Elinda B. F. The Friedman-Meiselman CMC Paper: New Evidence on an Old Controversy. *Amer. Econ. Rev.*, December 1973, *63*(5), pp. 908–17.

Puckett, Richard H. and Vroman, Susan B. Rules Versus Discretion: A Simulation Study. *J. Finance*, September 1973, *28*(4), pp. 853–65. [G: U.S.]

Purvis, Douglas D. Short-Run Dynamics in Models of Money and Growth. *Amer. Econ. Rev.*, March 1973, *63*(1), pp. 12–23.

Rao, Cherukuri U. The Demand for Liquid Asset Balances by U.S. Manufacturing Corporations: 1959-1970: Comment. *J. Financial Quant. Anal.*, March 1973, *8*(2), pp. 223–25.

Rasche, Robert H. A Comparative Static Analysis of Some Monetarist Propositions. *Fed. Res. Bank St. Louis Rev.*, December 1973, *55*(12), pp. 15–23.

Richardson, Dennis W. The Emerging Era of Electronic Money: Some Implications for Monetary Policy. *J. Bank Res.*, Winter 1973, *3*(4), pp. 261–64. [G: U.S.]

Rose, Hugh. Effective Demand in the Long Run. In *Mirrlees, J. A. and Stern, N. H., eds.*, 1973, pp. 25–47.

Rose, Peter S. and Hunt, Lacy H., II. The Relative Importance of Monetary and Fiscal Variables in Determining Price Level Movements: Reply. *J. Finance*, March 1973, *28*(1), pp. 191–93.

Rose, Peter S. and Fraser, Donald R. The Short-run Determinants of Loan Mix at Large Commercial Banks. *J. Econ. Bus.*, Fall 1973, *26*(1), pp. 1–9.
[G: U.S.]

Rousseaux, R. De liquiditeitenmassa in België en Nederland. (Currency in Belgium and the Netherlands. With English summary.) *Econ. Soc. Tijdschr.*, February 1973, *27*(1), pp. 73–89.
[G: Belgium; Netherlands]

Samuelson, Paul A. Monetarism Re-evaluated. In *Reynolds, L. G.; Green, G. D. and Lewis, D. R., eds.*, 1973, pp. 50–59. [G: U.S.]

Sargent, Thomas J. What Do Regressions of Interest on Inflation Show? *Ann. Econ. Soc. Measure*, July 1973, *2*(3), pp. 289–301.

Sargent, Thomas J. Interest Rates and Prices in the Long Run: A Study of the Gibson Paradox. *J. Money, Credit, Banking*, Part II, February 1973, *5*(1), pp. 385–449. [G: U.S.]

Sargent, Thomas J. "Rational Expectations": A Correction. *Brookings Pap. Econ. Act.*, 1973, (3), pp. 799–800.

Sargent, Thomas J. and Wallace, Neil. The Stability of Models of Money and Growth with Perfect Foresight. *Econometrica*, November 1973, *41*(6), pp. 1043–48.

Sargent, Thomas J. Rational Expectations, the Real Rate of Interest, and the Natural Rate of Unemployment. *Brookings Pap. Econ. Act.*, 1973, (2), pp. 429–72.

Saving, Thomas R. On the Neutrality of Money. *J. Polit. Econ.*, January-February 1973, *81*(1), pp. 98–119.

Sekine, Thomas T. Classical Monetary Theory and the Non-Optimality Theorem. *Z. Nationalökon.*, 1973, *33*(1–2), pp. 1–24.

Shapiro, A. A. Inflation, Lags, and the Demand for Money. *Int. Econ. Rev.*, February 1973, *14*(1), pp. 81–96. [G: U.S.]

Shapiro, Harold T. Monetary and Fiscal Influences on U.S. Money Income, 1891-1970: Comment. *J. Money, Credit, Banking*, Part II, February 1973, *5*(1), pp. 304–10. [G: U.S.]

Shiller, Robert J. Rational Expectations and the Term Structure of Interest Rates: Comment. *J. Money, Credit, Banking*, August 1973, *5*(3), pp. 856–60. [G: U.S.]

Shin, Kilman. The Rate of Interest and Inflation: An International Comparison. *Econ. Int.*, August-November 1973, *26*(3–4), pp. 603–22.

Short, Brock K. The Velocity of Money and *Per Capita* Income in Developing Economies: West Malaysia and Singapore. *J. Devel. Stud.*, January 1973, *9*(2), pp. 291–300. [G: Malaysia; Singapore]

Shubik, Martin. Commodity Money, Oligopoly, Credit and Bankruptcy in a General Equilibrium Model. *Western Econ. J.*, March 1973, *11*(1), pp. 24–38.

Shubik, Martin and Whitt, Ward. Fiat Money in an Economy with One Nondurable Good and No Credit (A Noncooperative Sequential Game). In *Blaquière, A., ed.*, 1973, pp. 401–48.

Silveira, Antonio M. Interest Rate and Rapid Inflation: The Evidence from the Brazilian Economy. *J. Money, Credit, Banking*, August 1973, *5*(3), pp. 794–805. [G: Brazil]

Silveira, Antonio M. The Demand for Money: The Evidence from the Brazilian Economy. *J. Money, Credit, Banking*, Part I, February 1973, *5*(1), pp. 113–40. [G: Brazil]

Silverberg, Stanley C. Deposit Costs and Bank Portfolio Policy. *J. Finance*, September 1973, *28*(4), pp. 881–95. [G: U.S.]

Sinkey, Joseph F., Jr. The Term Structure of Interest Rates: A Time-Series Test of the Kane Expected-Change Model of Interest-Rate Forecasting. *J. Money, Credit, Banking*, Part I, February 1973, *5*(1), pp. 192–200. [G: U.S.]

Smith, Lawrence B. and Winder, John W. L. Interest Rate Expectations and the Demand for Money in Canada: Reply. *J. Finance*, March 1973, *28*(1), pp. 213–14. [G: Canada]

Sommariva, A. Some Theoretical Implications of the Model of the Bank of Italy. *Tijdschr. Econ.*, 1973, *18*(2), pp. 207–34. [G: Italy]

Steindl, Frank G. A Structural Model of the Canadian Monetary Sector: Comment. *Southern Econ. J.*, April 1973, *39*(4), pp. 642. [G: Canada]

Struyk, Raymond J. Price Determinants in the Republic of Vietnam, 1966–1970. *Malayan Econ. Rev.*, April 1973, *18*(1), pp. 74–80. [G: S. Vietnam]

Sundrum, R. M. Money Supply and Prices: A Reinterpretation. *Bull. Indonesian Econ. Stud.*, November 1973, *9*(3), pp. 73–86. [G: Indonesia]

Talley, Ronald J. A "Real" Explanation of Interest Rate Movements. *Quart. Rev. Econ. Bus.*, Winter 1973, *13*(4), pp. 7–17. [G: U.S.]

Teriba, O. The Demand for Money in Nigeria. *Econ. Bull. Ghana, Sec. Ser.*, 1973, *3*(4), pp. 14–22. [G: Nigeria]

Uzawa, Hirofumi. Towards a Keynesian Model of Monetary Growth. In *Mirrlees, J. A. and Stern, N. H., eds.*, 1973, pp. 53–70.

Valentine, T. J. The Demand for Very Liquid Assets in Australia. *Australian Econ. Pap.*, December 1973, *12*(21), pp. 196–207. [G: Australia]

Van Belle, John J. Spot Rates, Forward Rates, and the Interest-Rate Differentials: Comment. *J. Money, Credit, Banking*, November 1973, *5*(4), pp. 997–99.

Van Eeckhoudt, M. Least Squares Construction of Yield Curves for Belgian Government Bonds (1955–1972): A Note. *Tijdschr. Econ.*, 1973, *18*(4), pp. 591–96. [G: Belgium]

Vernon, Jack. Financial Disintermediation in a Macroeconomic Framework: Comment. *J. Finance*, September 1973, *28*(4), pp. 1029–32.

Villanueva, Delano P. A Neoclassical Monetary Growth Model: Reply. *J. Money, Credit, Banking*, May 1973, *5*(2), pp. 707–12.

Vuchelen, Jozef. Likwiditeiten en de lange termijn rentevoet: een empirische studie. (With English summary.) *Cah. Écon. Bruxelles*, First Trimestre 1973, (57), pp. 53–81. [G: Belgium]

Wallich, Henry C. The Economics of an Automated Payment System. In *The Diebold Group, Inc.*, 1973, pp. 161–68. [G: U.S.]

Weinrobe, Maurice D. The Demand for Money by Six Non-Bank Financial Intermediaries. *Western Econ. J.*, June 1973, *11*(2), pp. 191–213. [G: U.S.]

Weston, J. Fred and Hoskins, W. Lee. Geographic Aspects of Market Structure and Performance in Banking. *J. Bus. Res.*, Summer 1973, *1*(1), pp. 31–42. [G: U.S.]

Wilford, W. T. and Villasuso, Juan M. The Velocity

of Money in Central America. *Bangladesh Econ. Rev.*, October 1973, *1*(4), pp. 375–86. [G: Central America]

Zahn, Frank and Hosek, William R. Impact of Trade Credit on the Velocity of Money and the Market Rate of Interest. *Southern Econ. J.*, October 1973, *40*(2), pp. 202–09. [G: U.S.]

Zelder, Raymond E.; Ross, Myron H. and Collery, Arnold. Internal and External Balance in an "Almost Classical" World: Reply. *Western Econ. J.*, June 1973, *11*(2), pp. 238–40.

Zellner, Arnold; Huang, David S. and Chau, L. C. Real Balances and the Demand for Money: Comment. *J. Polit. Econ.*, Part I, March-April 1973, *81*(2), pp. 485–87.

3116 Monetary Policy (including all central banking topics)

Acheson, Keith and Chant, John F. Bureaucratic Theory and the Choice of Central Bank Goals. *J. Money, Credit, Banking*, May 1973, *5*(2), pp. 637–55. [G: Canada]

Ahtiala, Pekka. Verotus, korkosäännöstely ja inflaatio säästövarojen allokoijina. (Taxation, Interest Rate Controls, and Inflation as Allocators of Saving. With English summary.) *Liiketaloudellinen Aikak.*, 1973, *22*(2), pp. 94–113. [G: Finland]

Anderson, Eric L. The Timing of Open Market Operations. *Miss. Val. J. Bus. Econ.*, Fall 1973, *9*(1), pp. 18–27. [G: U.S.]

Aschinger, F. E. The Eurocurrency Market and National Credit Policy. In *Henley, D. S., ed.*, 1973, pp. 217–22. [G: U.S.]

Balles, John J. Evaluating Money Market Conditions. *Fed. Res. Bank San Francisco Rev.*, September-October 1973, pp. 3–11. [G: U.S.]

Barber, G. Russell, Jr. The One Hundred Percent Reserve System. *Amer. Econ.*, Spring 1973, *17*(1), pp. 115–27. [G: U.S.]

Bareau, Paul. Bank Rate—Without the Mystique. *Irish Banking Rev.*, March 1973, pp. 13–18. [G: U.K.]

Benavie, Arthur and Poindexter, J. Carl, Jr. Deposit Ceilings and Monetary Policy. *Rev. Econ. Statist.*, November 1973, *55*(4), pp. 487–92. [G: U.S.]

Berman, Peter I. The Discount Facility and Staggered Reserve Periods. *Amer. Econ.*, Spring 1973, *17*(1), pp. 85–92. [G: U.S.]

Beyen, Karel H. Il finanziamento del commercio internazionale. (International Trade Finance. With English summary.) *Bancaria*, December 1973, *29*(12), pp. 1461–66.

Brahmananda, Palahalli Ramaiya. Commercial Banks as Development Agencies—Appraisal and Prospect. In *Simha, S. L. N., ed.*, 1973, pp. 208–22. [G: India]

Brahmananda, Palahalli Ramaiya. The Structural Efficiency of the Monetary System in India: An Appraisal. In *Simha, S. L. N., ed.*, 1973, pp. 322–30. [G: India]

Brimmer, Andrew F. Statements to Congress. *Fed. Res. Bull.*, June 1973, *59*(6), pp. 429–32. [G: U.S.]

Brimmer, Andrew F. Multi-National Banks and the Management of Monetary Policy in the United

States. *J. Finance*, May 1973, *28*(2), pp. 439–54.

Bucher, Jeffrey M. Statements to Congress. *Fed. Res. Bull.*, June 1973, *59*(6), pp. 420–25. [G: U.S.]

Burchardt, Michael. Die Koordination von Geld- und Fiskalpolitik bei festen Wechselkursen. (The Coordination of Monetary and Fiscal Policies under Fixed Exchange Rates. With English summary.) *Z. Wirtschaft. Sozialwissen.*, 1973, *93*(4), pp. 423–43.

Burke, William. RCPC's—Transitional Step. *Fed. Res. Bank San Francisco Rev.*, July-August 1973, pp. 11–15. [G: U.S.]

Burns, Arthur F. Statement to Congress. *Fed. Res. Bull.*, February 1973, *59*(2), pp. 81–85. [G: U.S.]

Burns, Arthur F. Statements to Congress. *Fed. Res. Bull.*, April 1973, *59*(4), pp. 280–85. [G: U.S.]

Burns, Arthur F. Statements to Congress. *Fed. Res. Bull.*, December 1973, *59*(12), pp. 879–83. [G: U.S.]

Burns, Arthur F. The Structure of Reserve Requirements. *Fed. Res. Bull.*, May 1973, *59*(5), pp. 339–43. [G: U.S.]

Burns, Arthur F. Money Supply in the Conduct of Monetary Policy. *Fed. Res. Bull.*, November 1973, *59*(11), pp. 791–98. [G: U.S.]

Burns, Arthur F. Statement to Congress. *Fed. Res. Bull.*, August 1973, *59*(8), pp. 567–73. [G: U.S.]

Burns, Arthur F. Some Problems of Central Banking. *Fed. Res. Bull.*, June 1973, *59*(6), pp. 417–19. [G: U.S.]

Burns, Arthur F. Objectives and Responsibilities of the Federal Reserve System. *Fed. Res. Bull.*, September 1973, *59*(9), pp. 655–57. [G: U.S.]

Burns, Arthur F. Statement to Congress. *Fed. Res. Bull.*, September 1973, *59*(9), pp. 658–64. [G: U.S.]

Burns, Arthur F. Letter on Monetary Policy to Senator William Proxmire. *Fed. Res. Bank St. Louis Rev.*, November 1973, *55*(11), pp. 15–22. [G: U.S.]

Burns, Joseph M. Academic Views on Improving the Federal Reserve Discount Mechanism: A Review Essay. *J. Money, Credit, Banking*, Part I, February 1973, *5*(1), pp. 47–60. [G: U.S.]

Cagan, Phillip. Controls and Monetary Policy, 1969–1973. In *Cagan, P., et al.*, 1973, pp. 1–34. [G: U.S.]

Carli, Guido. Riforma monetaria, bilancia dei pagamenti e liquidità interna. (Monetary Reform, Balance of Payments and Domestic Liquidity. With English summary.) *Bancaria*, January 1973, *29*(1), pp. 7–16.

Carli, Guido. Per la difesa del valore interno e del valore esterno della lira. (Defending the Internal and External Value of the Lira. With English summary.) *Bancaria*, November 1973, *29*(11), pp. 1338–41. [G: Italy]

Carlson, Keith M. The 1973 National Economic Plan: Slowing the Boom. *Fed. Res. Bank St. Louis Rev.*, March 1973, *55*(3), pp. 2–9. [G: U.S.]

Chant, John F. and Acheson, Keith. Mythology and Central Banking. *Kyklos*, 1973, *26*(2), pp. 362–79. [G: Canada]

Coats, Warren L., Jr. Regulation D and the Vault Cash Game. *J. Finance*, June 1973, *28*(3), pp. 601–07. [G: U.S.]

Coombs, Charles A. Treasury and Federal Reserve Foreign Exchange Operations: Interim Report. *Fed. Res. Bull.*, December 1973, *59*(12), pp. 871–73. [G: U.S.]

Coombs, Charles A. Treasury and Federal Reserve Foreign Exchange Operations. *Fed. Res. Bull.*, March 1973, *59*(3), pp. 142–63.

Courakis, Anthony S. Monetary Policy: Old Wisdom behind a New Facade. *Economica, N.S.*, February 1973, *40*(157), pp. 73–86. [G: U.K.]

Daane, J. Dewey. Statements to Congress. *Fed. Res. Bull.*, June 1973, *59*(6), pp. 425–29. [G: U.S.]

Dammann, Axel. Monetary Policy in Norway. In *Holbik, K., ed.*, 1973, pp. 329–74. [G: Norway]

Dasmahapatra, Rajkrishna. Recent Rise in Bank Rate in India and its Probable Consequences. *Econ. Aff.*, June 1973, *18*(6), pp. 299–304. [G: India]

Davis, E. W. and Yeomans, K. A. Competition and Credit Control: The Rubicon and Beyond. *Lloyds Bank Rev.*, January 1973, (107), pp. 44–55. [G: U.K.]

Desai, V. R. M. Trends and Progress of Busy Season 1972–73. *Econ. Aff.*, June 1973, *18*(6), pp. 275–80. [G: India]

Despres, Emile. Determining the Size of a Development Plan: Pakistan. In *Despres, E.*, 1973, pp. 99–132. [G: Pakistan]

Dickman, A. B. Exchequer Financing and the Money Supply. *S. Afr. J. Econ.*, June 1973, *41*(2), pp. 154–57. [G: S. Africa]

Dieterlen, Pierre and Durand, Huguette. Monetary Policy in France. In *Holbik, K., ed.*, 1973, pp. 117–60. [G: France]

Duesenberry, James S. Some Observations on Monetary Policy. *Brookings Pap. Econ. Act.*, 1973, (2), pp. 508–14. [G: U.S.]

Eastburn, David P. The Future Role of Interest Rates in Open Market Policy. *Fed. Res. Bank Bus. Rev. Phila.*, January 1973, pp. 3–7. [G: U.S.]

Eastburn, David P. Monetary Policy In a "New" Economy. *Fed. Res. Bank Bus. Rev. Phila.*, October 1973, pp. 3–6. [G: U.S.]

English, M. D. Macro-Economic Policy: Canada. In *Perkins, J. O. N., ed.*, 1973, pp. 57–93. [G: Canada]

Fand, David I. The Viability of Thrift Intermediaries as Financial Institutions. *Banca Naz. Lavoro Quart. Rev.*, September 1973, (106), pp. 235–68. [G: U.S.]

Ferrari, Alberto. Monetary Policy in Italy. In *Holbik, K., ed.*, 1973, pp. 214–45. [G: Italy]

Finet, Jacques. Monetary Policy in Belgium. In *Holbik, K., ed.*, 1973, pp. 39–69. [G: Belgium]

Ford, William F. and Tuccillo, John A. Monetary Policy Implications of the Hunt Commission Report. *Quart. Rev. Econ. Bus.*, Autumn 1973, *13*(3), pp. 93–103. [G: U.S.]

Gibson, William E. Fiscal and Monetary Policy: Opportunities and Problems. *Fed. Res. Bank St. Louis Rev.*, January 1973, *55*(1), pp. 14–18. [G: U.S.]

Goodhart, Charles A. E. Monetary Policy in the United Kingdom. In *Holbik, K., ed.*, 1973, pp. 465–524. [G: U.K.]

Griffiths, Brian. The Development of Restrictive Practices in the U.K. Monetary System. *Manchester Sch. Econ. Soc. Stud.*, March 1973, *41*(1), pp.

3–18. [G: U.K.]

Gupta, Suraj B. The Controversy over Differential Lending Rates for Banks: An Examination. *Indian Econ. Rev.,* April 1973, *8*(1), pp. 16–38. [G: India]

Gusen, P.; Havrilesky, Thomas M. and Weintraub, E. R. Potpourri: The Monetarist's Papers. *Intermountain Econ. Rev.,* Fall 1973, *4*(2), pp. 78–80.

Hansen, Bent. On the Effects of Fiscal and Monetary Policy: A Taxonomic Discussion. *Amer. Econ. Rev.,* September 1973, *63*(4), pp. 546–71. [G: U.S.]

Havrilesky, Thomas M.; Yohe, William P. and Schirm, David. The Economic Affiliations of Directors of Federal Reserve District Banks. *Soc. Sci. Quart.,* December 1973, *54*(3), pp. 608–22. [G: U.S.]

Holbik, Karel. Monetary Policy in Twelve Industrial Countries: Introduction. In *Holbik, K., ed.,* 1973, pp. xxi–xxvii.

Holland, Robert C. Statement to Congress. *Fed. Res. Bull.,* November 1973, *59*(11), pp. 799–803. [G: U.S.]

Holmes, Alan R. Open Market Operations in 1972. *Fed. Res. Bull.,* June 1973, *59*(6), pp. 405–16. [G: U.S.]

Iengar, H. V. R. Reform of the Indian Banking System: Proceedings of a Seminar: Inaugural Address. In *Simha, S. L. N., ed.,* 1973, pp. 5–14. [G: India]

Ishikawa, Tsuneo. Some Reflections on the "New Scheme for Monetary Control" by the Bank of Japan. *Kyoto Univ. Econ. Rev.,* April–October 1973, *43*(1–2), pp. 45–58. [G: Japan]

Jacobs, Donald P. and Phillips, Almarin. Overview of the Commission's Philosophy and Recommendations. In *Federal Reserve Bank of Boston,* 1973, pp. 9–20. [G: U.S.]

Johnson, Harry G. The Panamanian Monetary System. In *Johnson, H. G.,* 1973, pp. 223–28. [G: Panama]

Jordan, Jerry L. FOMC Policy Actions in 1972. *Fed. Res. Bank St. Louis Rev.,* March 1973, *55*(3), pp. 10–24. [G: U.S.]

Kalish, Lionel, III and Gilbert, R. Alton. The Influence of Bank Regulation of the Operating Efficiency of Commercial Banks. *J. Finance,* December 1973, *28*(5), pp. 1287–1301. [G: U.S.]

Kane, Edward J. The Central Bank as Big Brother: Comment. *J. Money, Credit, Banking,* November 1973, *5*(4), pp. 979–81. [G: U.S.]

Kane, Edward J. Simulations of Stabilization Policies for 1966–1970 *and* A Comparison of Stabilization Policies: 1966–67 and 1969–70: Comment. *J. Money, Credit, Banking,* Part I, February 1973, *5*(1), pp. 39–42. [G: U.S.]

Kukkonen, Pertti. Features of the Finnish Monetary Relationships: Comment. *Ekon. Samfundets Tidskr.,* 1973, *26*(2), pp. 123–31. [G: Finland]

Kurtz, Robert D. and Sinkey, Joseph F., Jr. Bank Disclosure Policy and Procedures, Adverse Publicity and Bank Deposit Flows. *J. Bank Res.,* Autumn 1973, *4*(3), pp. 177–84. [G: U.S.]

Lademann, John R. Monetary Policy in Switzerland. In *Holbik, K., ed.,* 1973, pp. 423–64. [G: Switzerland]

Largay, James A., III and West, Richard R. Margin Changes and Stock Price Behavior. *J. Polit. Econ.,* Part I, March-April 1973, *81*(2), pp. 328–39. [G: U.S.]

Lin, Steven A. Y. Effects of Monetary Policy and Credit Conditions on the Housing Sector. *Amer. Real Estate Urban Econ. Assoc. J.,* June 1973, *1*(1), pp. 8–30. [G: U.S.]

Lomax, David F. Reserve Assets and Competition and Credit Control. *Nat. Westminster Bank Quart. Rev.,* August 1973, pp. 36–46. [G: U.K.]

Lucia, Joseph L. Money Market Strategy or Monetary Aggregates: An Analysis of Recent Federal Reserve Policy. *Econ. Soc. Rev.,* October 1973, *5*(1), pp. 31–45. [G: U.S.]

Lybeck, Johan A. The Monetary Sector of the Bank of Finland's Quarterly Model: A Critical Comment. *Ekon. Samfundets Tidskr.,* 1973, *26*(2), pp. 117–21. [G: Finland]

Maccarone, Salvatore. Aspetti e problemi della riforma del protesto. (Problems of the Italian Reform of the Protest. With English summary.) *Bancaria,* August 1973, *29*(8), pp. 951–62. [G: Italy]

Mayne, Lucille S. The Deposit Reserve Requirement Recommendations of the Commission on Financial Structure & Regulation: An Analysis and Critique. *J. Bank Res.,* Spring 1973, *4*(1), pp. 41–51. [G: U.S.]

McKinnon, Ronald I. On Securing a Common Monetary Policy in Europe. *Banca Naz. Lavoro Quart. Rev.,* March 1973, (104), pp. 3–20. [G: E.E.C.]

Mélitz, Jacques. Une tentative d'explication de l'offre de monnaie en France. (The French Money Supply: An Attempted Explanation. With English summary.) *Revue Écon.,* September 1973, *24*(5), pp. 761–800. [G: France]

Mikitani, Ryoichi. Monetary Policy in Japan. In *Holbik, K., ed.,* 1973, pp. 246–81. [G: Japan]

Miller, Ervin. The Pains of Monetary Restraint. *Lloyds Bank Rev.,* July 1973, (109), pp. 36–51. [G: U.S.; U.K.]

Mitchell, George W. Statements to Congress. *Fed. Res. Bull.,* April 1973, *59*(4), pp. 276–80. [G: U.S.]

Mitchell, George W. Statement to Congress. *Fed. Res. Bull.,* October 1973, *59*(10), pp. 734–38. [G: U.S.]

Mitchell, George W. Statements to Congress. *Fed. Res. Bull.,* December 1973, *59*(12), pp. 874–78. [G: U.S.]

Moiola, David L. Regulation Q: A New Tool for Monetary Policy? *Intermountain Econ. Rev.,* Spring 1973, *4*(1), pp. 22–28. [G: U.S.]

Morgan, E. Victor. Regional Problems and Common Currencies. *Lloyds Bank Rev.,* October 1973, (110), pp. 19–30. [G: U.K.]

Mullineaux, Donald J. Deposit-Rate Ceilings and Noncompetitive Bidding for U.S. Treasury Bills. *J. Money, Credit, Banking,* Part I, February 1973, *5*(1), pp. 201–12. [G: U.S.]

Myhrman, Johan. An Analytical Treatment of Swedish Monetary Policy. *Swedish J. Econ.,* September 1973, *75*(3), pp. 221–37. [G: Sweden]

Niblack, William C. Operations of the Federal Reserve Bank of St. Louis—1972. *Fed. Res. Bank St.*

Louis Rev., February 1973, 55(2), pp. 17–19, 22–24. [G: U.S.]

Nieuwenhuysen, J. P. Macro-Economic Policy: South Africa. In Perkins, J. O. N., ed., 1973, pp. 130–76. [G: S. Africa]

Nissen, Anton. Revision of the Money Stock Measures and Member Bank Reserves and Deposits. Fed. Res. Bull., February 1973, 59(2), pp. 61–79. [G: U.S.]

Noyes, Guy E. The Multinational Firm: Bane or Boon?: Discussion. J. Finance, May 1973, 28(2), pp. 462–65.

Ølgaard, Anders. Føres der pengepolitik i Danmark? (Danish Monetary Policy—Does it Exist? With English summary.) Nationalokon. Tidsskr., 1973, 111(1), pp. 9–24. [G: Denmark]

Ossola, Rinaldo. Central Bank Interventions and Eurocurrency Markets. Banca Naz. Lavoro Quart. Rev., March 1973, (104), pp. 29–45.

Pandit, Shrikrishna A. Nationalization of the Banks in India. Finance Develop., March 1973, 10(1), pp. 32–37. [G: India]

Peeran, S. T. Control over Non-Banking Financial Intermediaries by the Reserve Bank. In Simha, S. L. N., ed., 1973, pp. 252–64. [G: India]

Perkins, J. O. N. and Nieuwenhuysen, J. P. Macro-Economic Policy: Australia. In Perkins, J. O. N., ed., 1973, pp. 17–56. [G: Australia]

Perkins, J. O. N. and Nieuwenhuysen, J. P. Macro-Economic Policies in the Four Countries. In Perkins, J. O. N., ed., 1973, pp. 177–208. [G: Australia; New Zealand; Canada; S. Africa]

Pesando, James E. and Smith, Lawrence B. Monetary Policy in Canada. In Holbik, K., ed., 1973, pp. 70–116. [G: Canada]

Puckett, Richard H. and Vroman, Susan B. Rules Versus Discretion: A Simulation Study. J. Finance, September 1973, 28(4), pp. 853–65. [G: U.S.]

Raman, A. Credit Planning—Role of the Reserve Bank of India. In Simha, S. L. N., ed., 1973, pp. 331–39. [G: India]

Rasminsky, Louis. Canadian Monetary Policy and the Problem of Inflation. In Moskoff, W., ed., 1973, pp. 56–62. [G: Canada]

Ray, Edward J. The Sources of Finance in West Germany. Z. ges. Staatswiss., October 1973, 129 (4), pp. 663–84. [G: W. Germany]

Richardson, Dennis W. The Emerging Era of Electronic Money: Some Implications for Monetary Policy. J. Bank Res., Winter 1973, 3(4), pp. 261–64. [G: U.S.]

Roe, Alan R. The Case for Flow of Funds and National Balance Sheet Accounts. Econ. J., June 1973, 83(330), pp. 399–420. [G: U.K.]

Rose, Peter S. The Impact of Policy Variables on Price-Level Movements. Miss. Val. J. Bus. Econ., Fall 1973, 9(1), pp. 1–11. [G: U.S.]

Rousseaux, R. De liquiditeitenmassa in België en Nederland. (Currency in Belgium and the Netherlands. With English summary.) Econ. Soc. Tijdschr., February 1973, 27(1), pp. 73–89. [G: Belgium; Netherlands]

Rowan, D. C. The Monetary System in the Fifties and Sixties. Manchester Sch. Econ. Soc. Stud., March 1973, 41(1), pp. 19–42. [G: U.K.]

Rowe, J. W. Macro-Economic Policy: New Zealand.

In Perkins, J. O. N., ed., 1973, pp. 94–129. [G: New Zealand]

Sacerdoti, Emilio. A Note on Monetary Policy when Banks Have Managerial Objectives. L'Industria, January-June 1973, (1–2), pp. 89–108.

Savona, Paolo. Mercato internazionale delle valute e mercato italiano delle obbligazioni. (International Exchange Market and Italian Bond Market. With English summary.) Bancaria, December 1973, 29(12), pp. 1467–73. [G: Italy]

Scarth, William M. The Effects on Stabilization Policy of Several Monetary Reform Proposals. J. Econ. Bus., Spring-Summer 1973, 25(3), pp. 154–58.

Scarth, William M. The Financing of Stabilization Policies: Evidence for the Canadian Economy. Can. J. Econ., August 1973, 6(3), pp. 301–18. [G: Canada]

Schlesinger, Helmut and Bockelmann, Horst. Monetary Policy in the Federal Republic of Germany. In Holbik, K., ed., 1973, pp. 161–213. [G: W. Germany]

Schmidt, Peter and Waud, Roger N. The Almon Lag Technique and the Monetary Versus Fiscal Policy Debate. J. Amer. Statist. Assoc., March 1973, 68 (341), pp. 11–19.

Sdralevich, Alberto and Monti, Mario. I modelli macroeconomici per la politica monetaria in Italia: aggregazione e realismo. (Macroeconomic Models for Monetary Policy in Italy: Aggregation and Realism. With English summary.) L'Industria, January-June 1973, (1–2), pp. 36–58. [G: Italy]

Silber, William L. Selective Credit Policies: A Survey. Banca Naz. Lavoro Quart. Rev., December 1973, (107), pp. 328–51. [G: U.S.]

Simha, S. L. N. Future of the Subsidiaries of the State Bank of India. In Simha, S. L. N., ed., 1973, pp. 189–202. [G: India]

Simha, S. L. N. Reform of the Central Banking System in India. In Simha, S. L. N., ed., 1973, pp. 309–21. [G: India]

Socher, Karl. Monetary Policy in Austria. In Holbik, K., ed., 1973, pp. 1–38. [G: Austria]

Vikbladh, Inge. Monetary Policy in Sweden. In Holbik, K., ed., 1973, pp. 375–422. [G: Sweden]

Wadsworth, J. E. The Banks and the Monetary System in the UK 1959–1971. In Wadsworth, J. E., ed., 1973, pp. 1–16. [G: U.K.]

Waud, Roger N. Proximate Targets and Monetary Policy. Econ. J., March 1973, 83(329), pp. 1–20.

Wilson, J. S. G. The Australian Money Market. Banca Naz. Lavoro Quart. Rev., March 1973, (104), pp. 46–69. [G: Australia]

Zecher, Richard. Short-run Monetary Adjustments in the Australian Economy, 1952–70. In Powell, A. A. and Williams, R. A., eds., 1973, pp. 335–48. [G: Australia]

312 Commercial Banking

3120 Commercial Banking

Addo, John Sackah. Savings Banks and Savings Facilities in African Countries: Ghana. In Alberici, A. and Baravelli, M., eds., 1973, pp. 37–39. [G: Ghana]

Aigner, Dennis J. On Estimation of an Econometric Model of Short-Run Bank Behaviour. *J. Econometrics*, October 1973, *1*(3), pp. 201–28.
[G: U.S.]

Arcucci, Francesco and Frediani, Lorenzo. Savings Banks and Savings Facilities in African Countries: Malawi. In *Alberici, A. and Baravelli, M., eds.*, 1973, pp. 55–59. [G: Malawi]

Areeda, Phillip E. The Bank Holding Company—A Superior Device for Expanding Activities? Discussion. In *Federal Reserve Bank of Boston*, 1973, pp. 88–93. [G: U.S.]

Argentarius. Sviluppi e problemi attuali del credito al consumo. (Development and Current Problems of Consumer Credit. With English summary.) *Bancaria*, January 1973, *29*(1), pp. 76–82.

Arunachalam, M. V. Role of Commercial Banks as Development Agencies. In *Simha, S. L. N., ed.*, 1973, pp. 223–29. [G: India]

Babingui, Denis. Savings Banks and Savings Facilities in African Countries: Congo Brazzaville. In *Alberici, A. and Baravelli, M., eds.*, 1973, pp. 19–21. [G: Congo Brazzaville]

Baker, Donald I. Chartering, Branching, and the Concentration Problem. In *Federal Reserve Bank of Boston*, 1973, pp. 21–39. [G: U.S.]

Baltensperger, Ernst. Optimal Bank Portfolios: The Liability Side. *Jahr. Nationalökon. Statist.*, January 1973, *187*(2), pp. 147–60.

Bates, Timothy. An Econometric Analysis of Lending to Black Businessmen. *Rev. Econ. Statist.*, August 1973, *55*(3), pp. 272–83. [G: U.S.]

Batra, Harish. Dynamic Interdependence in Demand for Savings Deposits. *J. Finance*, May 1973, *28*(2), pp. 507–14. [G: U.S.]

Belkhodja, Hassen. Savings Banks and Savings Facilities in African Countries: Tunisia. In *Alberici, A. and Baravelli, M., eds.*, 1973, pp. 115–20. [G: Tunisia]

Benston, George J. The Optimal Banking Structure: Theory and Evidence. *J. Bank Res.*, Winter 1973, *3*(4), pp. 220–37. [G: U.S.]

Berman, Peter I. The Discount Facility and Staggered Reserve Periods. *Amer. Econ.*, Spring 1973, *17*(1), pp. 85–92. [G: U.S.]

Beyen, Karel H. Il finanziamento del commercio internazionale. (International Trade Finance. With English summary.) *Bancaria*, December 1973, *29*(12), pp. 1461–66.

Bhat, M. V. The Role of Small Banks in the Commercial Banking System. In *Simha, S. L. N., ed.*, 1973, pp. 203–07. [G: India]

Birara, Jean. Savings Banks and Savings Facilities in African Countries: Rwanda. In *Alberici, A. and Baravelli, M., eds.*, 1973, pp. 81. [G: Rwanda]

Boubacar, Mamadou N'Diaye. Savings Banks and Savings Facilities in African Countries: Dahomey. In *Alberici, A. and Baravelli, M., eds.*, 1973, pp. 23–27. [G: Dahomey]

Boyd, John H. Bank Strategies in the Retail Demand Deposit Markets. *J. Bank Res.*, Summer 1973, *4*(2), pp. 111–21.

Bradley, Stephen P. and Crane, Dwight B. Management of Commercial Bank Government Security Portfolios: An Optimization Approach Under Un-

certainty. *J. Bank Res.*, Spring 1973, *4*(1), pp. 18–30.

Braemer, Pierre. Savings Banks and Savings Facilities in African Countries: Mauritania. In *Alberici, A. and Baravelli, M., eds.*, 1973, pp. 63–64.
[G: Mauritania]

Brahmananda, Palahalli Ramaiya. Commercial Banks as Development Agencies—Appraisal and Prospect. In *Simha, S. L. N., ed.*, 1973, pp. 208–22. [G: India]

Buonomo, Maurizio. Multinazionali e banche. (Multinational Firms and Banks. With English summary.) *Bancaria*, September 1973, *29*(9), pp. 1113–22.

Carnoy, Martin. Financial Institutions and Dependency. In *Bonilla, F. and Girling, R., eds.*, 1973, pp. 34–45. [G: U.S.]

Chase, Samuel B., Jr. The Bank Holding Company—A Superior Device for Expanding Activities? In *Federal Reserve Bank of Boston*, 1973, pp. 77–87. [G: U.S.]

Coates, Robert and Updegraff, David E. The Relationship between Organizational Size and the Administrative Component of Banks. *J. Bus.*, October 1973, *46*(4), pp. 576–88. [G: U.S.]

Coats, Warren L., Jr. Regulation D and the Vault Cash Game. *J. Finance*, June 1973, *28*(3), pp. 601–07. [G: U.S.]

Cohan, Sandra B. The Determinants of Supply and Demand for Certificates of Deposit. *J. Money, Credit, Banking*, Part I, February 1973, *5*(1), pp. 100–12. [G: U.S.]

Congo, M. Savings Banks and Savings Facilities in African Countries: Upper Volta. In *Alberici, A. and Baravelli, M., eds.*, 1973, pp. 125–28.
[G: Upper Volta]

Coste, Roger. Les entreprises financières en mutation face au commerce de l'épargne. (The Trade of Savings and the Change of Financial Firms. With English summary.) *Consommation*, January-March 1973, *20*(1), pp. 37–57. [G: France]

Cramer, Robert H. and Miller, Robert B. Development of a Deposit Forecasting Procedure for Use in Bank Financial Management. *J. Bank Res.*, Summer 1973, *4*(2), pp. 122–88.

Cyrnak, Anthony W. Member Bank Income, 1972. *Fed. Res. Bull.*, May 1973, *59*(5), pp. 329–35.
[G: U.S.]

Dammann, Axel. Monetary Policy in Norway. In *Holbik, K., ed.*, 1973, pp. 329–74. [G: Norway]

Daniel, Donnie L.; Longbrake, William A. and Murphy, Neil B. The Effect of Technology on Bank Economies of Scale for Demand Deposits. *J. Finance*, March 1973, *28*(1), pp. 131–46. [G: U.S.]

Darnell, Jerome C. Bank Mergers: Prices Paid to Marriage Partners. *Fed. Res. Bank Bus. Rev. Phila.*, July 1973, pp. 16–25. [G: U.S.]

Darnell, Jerome C. Banking Structure: What Does the Future Hold? *Fed. Res. Bank Bus. Rev. Phila.*, August 1973, pp. 3–9. [G: U.S.]

Dematté, Claudio. Savings Banks and Savings Facilities in African Countries: Mali. In *Alberici, A. and Baravelli, M., eds.*, 1973, pp. 61–62. [G: Mali]

Desai, V. R. M. Trends and Progress of Busy Season 1972–73. *Econ. Aff.*, June 1973, *18*(6), pp. 275–80.
[G: India]

Di Loreto, Sandro. Il problema dei costi nell'instituto di credito ordinario. Un tentativo di applicazione di procedimenti analitici di calcolo e di controllo-I. (The Cost Problem of Commercial Banks. An Attempt to Apply Analytical Calculation and Control Processes-I. With English summary.) *Bancaria,* July 1973, *29*(7), pp. 820–31.

Di Loreto, Sandro. Il problema dei costi nell'instituto di credito ordinario. Un tentativo di applicazione di procedimenti analitici di calcolo e di controllo-III. (The Cost Problem of Commercial Banks. An Attempt to Apply Analytical Calculation and Control Processes-III. With English summary.) *Bancaria,* September 1973, *29*(9), pp. 1094–1112.

Di Loreto, Sandro. Il problema dei costi nell'instituto di credito ordinario. Un tentativo di applicazione di procedimenti analitici di calcolo e di controllo-II. (The Cost Problem of Commercial Banks. An Attempt to Apply Analytical Calculation and Control Processes-II. With English summary.) *Bancaria,* August 1973, *29*(8), pp. 936–86.

Dince, Robert R. Finance and Banking: Refereed Papers II: Discussion. *J. Finance,* May 1973, *28*(2), pp. 541–44. [G: U.S.]

Dyson, Richard. Panorama dell'attività bancaria. (The Banking Spectrum. With English summary.) *Bancaria,* December 1973, *29*(12), pp. 1451–60. [G: U.K.]

Edwards, Franklin R. Advertising and Competition in Banking. *Antitrust Bull.,* Spring 1973, *18*(1), pp. 23–32. [G: U.S.]

Edwards, Franklin R. and Heggestad, Arnold A. Uncertainty, Market Structure, and Performance in Banking: The Galbraith-Caves Hypothesis and Managerial Motives in Banking. *Quart. J. Econ.,* August 1973, *87*(3), pp. 455–73. [G: U.S.]

Falco, James F. Section 7 of the Clayton Act and "Control" in Bank Holding Company Regulation. *Antitrust Bull.,* Winter 1973, *18*(4), pp. 715–41. [G: U.S.]

Falkenberg, John F. The Sources of Bank Profitability. *J. Bank Res.,* Summer 1973, *4*(2), pp. 105–10.

Fand, David I. The Viability of Thrift Intermediaries as Financial Institutions. *Banca Naz. Lavoro Quart. Rev.,* September 1973, (106), pp. 235–68. [G: U.S.]

Finet, Jacques. Monetary Policy in Belgium. In *Holbik, K., ed.,* 1973, pp. 39–69. [G: Belgium]

Ford, William F. and Tuccillo, John A. Monetary Policy Implications of the Hunt Commission Report. *Quart. Rev. Econ. Bus.,* Autumn 1973, *13*(3), pp. 93–103. [G: U.S.]

Formuzis, Peter. The Demand for Eurodollars and the Optimum Stock of Bank Liabilities. *J. Money, Credit, Banking,* August 1973, *5*(3), pp. 806–18. [G: U.S.]

Fraser, Donald R. and Rose, Peter S. Short-Run Bank Portfolio Behavior: An Examination of Selected Liquid Assets. *J. Finance,* May 1973, *28*(2), pp. 531–37. [G: U.S.]

Fry, Joseph N., et al. Customer Loyalty to Banks: A Longitudinal Study. *J. Bus.,* October 1973, *46*(4), pp. 517–25. [G: Canada]

Gado, Abdou. Savings Banks and Savings Facilities in African Countries: Niger. In *Alberici, A. and Baravelli, M., eds.,* 1973, pp. 77–79. [G: Niger]

Gilbert, Gary G. and Longbrake, William A. The Effects of Branching by Financial Institutions on Competition, Productive Efficiency and Stability: An Examination of the Evidence. *J. Bank Res.,* Autumn 1973, *4*(3), pp. 154–67. [G: U.S.]

Gilbert, R. Alton. Income and Expenses of Eighth District Member Banks. *Fed. Res. Bank St. Louis Rev.,* August 1973, *55*(8), pp. 16–22. [G: U.S.]

Goodhart, Charles A. E. Monetary Policy in the United Kingdom. In *Holbik, K., ed.,* 1973, pp. 465–524. [G: U.K.]

Griffiths, Brian. The Development of Restrictive Practices in the U.K. Monetary System. *Manchester Sch. Econ. Soc. Stud.,* March 1973, *41*(1), pp. 3–18. [G: U.K.]

Gupta, Suraj B. The Controversy over Differential Lending Rates for Banks: An Examination. *Indian Econ. Rev.,* April 1973, *8*(1), pp. 16–38. [G: India]

Gupta, Suraj B. Financial Progress, Banking Expansion, and Saving. *Indian Econ. J.,* April-June 1973, *20*(4–5), pp. 548–69.

Hall, George R. Expanded Powers for Depositary Financial Institutions: Discussion. In *Federal Reserve Bank of Boston,* 1973, pp. 72–76. [G: U.S.]

Harris, Duane G. Some Evidence on Differential Lending Practices at Commercial Banks. *J. Finance,* December 1973, *28*(5), pp. 1303–11. [G: U.S.]

Harris, Duane G. A Model of Bank Loan Term Adjustment. *Western Econ. J.,* December 1973, *11*(4), pp. 451–62.

Hatch, J. H. and Lewis, M. K. Economies of Scale in Australian Banking: Reply. *Econ. Rec.,* September 1973, *49*(127), pp. 481–84. [G: Australia]

Hempel, George H. and Kretschman, Stephen R. Comparative Performances of Portfolio Maturity Policies of Commercial Banks. *Miss. Val. J. Bus. Econ.,* Fall 1973, *9*(1), pp. 55–75. [G: U.S.]

Herman, Edward S. Expanded Powers for Depositary Financial Institutions: Discussion. In *Federal Reserve Bank of Boston,* 1973, pp. 64–71. [G: U.S.]

Herzi, Abdurahman Nur. Savings Banks and Savings Facilities in African Countries: Somalia. In *Alberici, A. and Baravelli, M., eds.,* 1973, pp. 93–96. [G: Somalia]

Hinderliter, Roger H. and Rockoff, Hugh. The Management of Reserves by Ante-bellum Banks in Eastern Financial Centers. *Exploration Econ. Hist.,* Fall 1973, *11*(1), pp. 37–53. [G: U.S.]

Horton, Alexander Romeo. Savings Banks and Savings Facilities in African Countries: Liberia. In *Alberici, A. and Baravelli, M., eds.,* 1973, pp. 47–48. [G: Liberia]

Iengar, H. V. R. Reform of the Indian Banking System: Proceedings of a Seminar: Inaugural Address. In *Simha, S. L. N., ed.,* 1973, pp. 5–14. [G: India]

Ikinda, Antoine. Savings Banks and Savings Facilities in African Countries: Gabon. In *Alberici, A. and Baravelli, M., eds.,* 1973, pp. 33–34. [G: Gabon]

Iwasa, Yoshizane. Banking in Japan. In *Moskoff, W.,*

ed., 1973, pp. 33–54.   [G: Japan]

Jacobs, Donald P. and Phillips, Almarin. Overview of the Commission's Philosophy and Recommendations. In *Federal Reserve Bank of Boston,* 1973, pp. 9–20.   [G: U.S.]

Johnson, A. S. C. Savings Banks and Savings Facilities in African Countries: Sierra Leone. In *Alberici, A. and Baravelli, M., eds.,* 1973, pp. 87–92.
                    [G: Sierra Leone]

Johnson, Herbert E. Strategic Planning for Banks. *J. Bank Res.,* Summer 1973, *4*(2), pp. 79–83.

Johnson, Rodney D. and Meinster, David R. An Analysis of Bank Holding Company Acquisitions: Some Methodological Issues. *J. Bank Res.,* Spring 1973, *4*(1), pp. 58–61.   [G: U.S.]

Jones, J. C. H. and Laudadio, Leonard. Canadian Bank Mergers, the Public Interest and Public Policy. *Banca Naz. Lavoro Quart. Rev.,* June 1973, *105,* pp. 109–40.   [G: Canada]

Kaatz, John R. and Tarpley, Fred A., Jr. Economies of Scale and Holding Company Affiliation in Banking: Comment. *Southern Econ. J.,* July 1973, *40*(1), pp. 140.

Kalish, Lionel, III and Gilbert, R. Alton. The Influence of Bank Regulation of the Operating Efficiency of Commercial Banks. *J. Finance,* December 1973, *28*(5), pp. 1287–1301.   [G: U.S.]

Kalish, Lionel, III and Gilbert, R. Alton. An Analysis of Efficiency of Scale and Organizational Form in Commercial Banking. *J. Ind. Econ.,* July 1973, *21* (3), pp. 293–307.   [G: U.S.]

Kamulegeya, Edric Spencer. Savings Banks and Savings Facilities in African Countries: Uganda. In *Alberici, A. and Baravelli, M., eds.,* 1973, pp. 121–24.   [G: Uganda]

Kane, Edward J. Politics and the Prime Rate: A Deceptive Solution. *Ohio State U. Bull. Bus. Res.,* June 1973, *48*(6), pp. 1–3, 5.   [G: U.S.]

Kansara, T. D. Reorganisation of the Banking System in India. In *Simha, S. L. N., ed.,* 1973, pp. 155–82.   [G: India]

Karani, Hiram. Savings Banks and Savings Facilities in African Countries: Kenya. In *Alberici, A. and Baravelli, M., eds.,* 1973, pp. 41–43.   [G: Kenya]

Kientz, Jean. Savings Banks and Savings Facilities in African Countries: Madagascar. In *Alberici, A. and Baravelli, M., eds.,* 1973, pp. 49–53.
                    [G: Madagascar]

Kinsella, R. P. A Note on Bank Productivity in a Service Economy. *Rivista Int. Sci. Econ. Com.,* October 1973, *20*(10), pp. 985–94.   [G: Ireland]

Klebaner, Benjamin J. Recent Changes in United States' Commercial Banking Structure in Perspective. *Antitrust Bull.,* Winter 1973, *18*(4), pp. 759–86.   [G: U.S.]

Knight, Malcolm. A Continuous Disequilibrium Econometric Model of the Domestic and International Portfolio Behaviour of the UK Banking System. In *Parkin, M., ed.,* 1973, pp. 266–90.
                    [G: U.K.]

Kongbo, Basile. Savings Banks and Savings Facilities in African Countries: Central African Republic. In *Alberici, A. and Baravelli, M., eds.,* 1973, pp. 7–10.   [G: Central African Rep.]

Kulshreshtha, S. N. Discriminating Credit Worthi-

ness of Canadian Prairie Farmers. *Can. J. Agr. Econ.,* July 1973, *21*(2), pp. 16–24.   [G: Canada]

Kurtz, Robert D. and Sinkey, Joseph F., Jr. Bank Disclosure Policy and Procedures, Adverse Publicity and Bank Deposit Flows. *J. Bank Res.,* Autumn 1973, *4*(3), pp. 177–84.   [G: U.S.]

Lademann, John R. Monetary Policy in Switzerland. In *Holbik, K., ed.,* 1973, pp. 423–64.   [G: Switzerland]

Laokole, Jean-Baptiste. Savings Banks and Savings Facilities in African Countries: Chad. In *Alberici, A. and Baravelli, M., eds.,* 1973, pp. 11–17.
                    [G: Chad]

Lapidus, Leonard. Chartering, Branching, and the Concentration Problem: Discussion. In *Federal Reserve Bank of Boston,* 1973, pp. 46–53.
                    [G: U.S.]

Lavely, Joe. Diversity of Interest Rates on Bank Savings Accounts. *Indiana Bus. Rev.,* September-October 1973, *48,* pp. 20–24.   [G: U.S.]

Lerner, Eugene M. The Bank Holding Company—A Superior Device for Expanding Activities? Discussion. In *Federal Reserve Bank of Boston,* 1973, pp. 94–97.   [G: U.S.]

Levy, Sidney J. Consumer Views of Bank Services. *J. Bank Res.,* Summer 1973, *4*(2), pp. 100–04.

Lifson, K. A. and Blackmarr, Brian R. Simulation and Optimization Models for Asset Deployment and Funds Sources Balancing Profit, Liquidity and Growth. *J. Bank Res.,* Autumn 1973, *4*(3), pp. 239–55.

Longbrake, William A. Computers and the Cost of Producing Banking Services: Planning and Control Considerations. *J. Bank Res.,* Autumn 1973, *4*(3), pp. 194–202.   [G: U.S.]

Longbrake, William A. Murphy's Method for Determining the Weights Assigned to Demand Deposit Items: A Clarification and Extension. *J. Bank Res.,* Summer 1973, *4*(2), pp. 139–44.

Long, Robert H. Planning for Tomorrow's Customer. *J. Bank Res.,* Summer 1973, *4*(2), pp. 93–99.

Lybecker, Martin E. Regulation of Bank Trust Department Investment Activities. *Yale Law J.,* April 1973, *82*(5), pp. 977–1002.   [G: U.S.]

Makin, John H. Identifying a Reserve Base for the Euro-Dollar System. *J. Finance,* June 1973, *28*(3), pp. 609–17.

Mandich, Donald R. International Loans: Profit Center or Loss Leader. In *Henley, D. S., ed.,* 1973, pp. 420–32.   [G: U.S.; U.K.]

Mankoubi, Bawa Sandani. Savings Banks and Savings Facilities in African Countries: Togo. In *Alberici, A. and Baravelli, M., eds.,* 1973, pp. 111–13.
                    [G: Togo]

Marchesini, Giambattista. Il ruolo del mercato del credito nel ciclo di produzione del reddito, I. (Role of the Credit Market in the Income Production Cycle, I. With English summary.) *Bancaria,* October 1973, *29*(10), pp. 1239–43.

Marchesini, Giambattista. Il ruolo del mercato del credito nel ciclo di produzione del reddito, II. (Role of the Credit Market in the Income Production Cycle, II. With English summary.) *Bancaria,* November 1973, *29*(11), pp. 1346–57.

Mathew, V. T. Restructuring of India's Banking Sys-

tem. In *Simha, S. L. N., ed.*, 1973, pp. 183–88.
[G: India]

Mattsson, Peter. Projektanalys. (Project Analysis. With English summary.) *Ekon. Samfundets Tidskr.*, 1973, 26(2), pp. 95–100. [G: Finland]

Mayne, Lucille S. The Deposit Reserve Requirement Recommendations of the Commission on Financial Structure & Regulation: An Analysis and Critique. *J. Bank Res.*, Spring 1973, 4(1), pp. 41–51. [G: U.S.]

M'Baye, M. Savings Banks and Savings Facilities in African Countries: Senegal. In *Alberici, A. and Baravelli, M., eds.*, 1973, pp. 83–86. [G: Senegal]

McAnaw, Richard. Bankers and Politicians: The Not So Strange Bedfellows. *Mich. Academician*, Spring 1973, 5(4), pp. 505–13. [G: U.S.]

McCall, Alan S. and Walker, David A. The Effects of Control Status on Commercial Bank Profitability. *J. Financial Quant. Anal.*, September 1973, 8(4), pp. 637–45. [G: U.S.]

McWilliams, James D. A Closer Look at Incentive Fees for Bank Managed Pension Funds. *J. Bank Res.*, Winter 1973, 3(4), pp. 238–46. [G: U.S.]

Mélitz, Jacques and Pardue, Morris. The Demand and Supply of Commercial Bank Loans. *J. Money, Credit, Banking*, May 1973, 5(2), pp. 669–92.
[G: U.S.]

Mélitz, Jacques. Une tentative d'explication de l'offre de monnaie en France. (The French Money Supply: An Attempted Explanation. With English summary.) *Revue Écon.*, September 1973, 24(5), pp. 761–800. [G: France]

Mikitani, Ryoichi. Monetary Policy in Japan. In *Holbik, K., ed.*, 1973, pp. 246–81. [G: Japan]

Mishra, G. P.; Tripathy, B. N. and Pandey, Ram Lala. Role of Banking in Financing Rural Credit. *Econ. Aff.*, July 1973, 18(7), pp. 313–25. [G: India]

Moag, Joseph M. Strategic Planning in Banks—A Behavioral Science Perspective. *J. Bank Res.*, Summer 1973, 4(2), pp. 84–92.

Mondanga, Emony. Savings Banks and Savings Facilities in African Countries: Zaire. In *Alberici, A. and Baravelli, M., eds.*, 1973, pp. 129–31.
[G: Zaire]

Mowry, Glenn K. Steps Toward a Less-Check Society. In *The Diebold Group, Inc.*, 1973, pp. 169–79. [G: U.S.]

Moyer, R. Charles and Sussna, Edward. Registered Bank Holding Company Acquisition: A Cross-Section Analysis. *J. Financial Quant. Anal.*, September 1973, 8(4), pp. 647–61. [G: U.S.]

Murphy, Neil B. The Implications of Econometric Analysis of Bank Cost Functions for Bank Planning. *J. Bank Res.*, Autumn 1973, 4(3), pp. 203–06.
[G: U.S.]

Musarra, Emanuele Parisi. Note sull'automazione elettronica per la gestione e la direzione aziendale bancaria. (Notes on the Electronic Automation for Bank Management. With English summary.) *Bancaria*, April 1973, 29(4), pp. 447–52. [G: Italy]

Narayanaswamy, S. Banking Organisation: The Need for Service Orientation. In *Simha, S. L. N., ed.*, 1973, pp. 230–37. [G: India]

Nelson, Jane. Swiss Banks. In *Moskoff, W., ed.*, 1973, pp. 28–33. [G: Switzerland]

Nesci, Vincenzo. Savings Banks and Savings Facilities in African Countries: Morocco. In *Alberici, A. and Baravelli, M., eds.*, 1973, pp. 69–76. [G: Morocco]

Nicholson, Edward A., Jr. and Litschert, Robert L. Long-Range Planning in Banking: Ten Cases in the U.S. and Britain. *J. Bank Res.*, Spring 1973, 4(1), pp. 31–40. [G: U.S.; U.K.]

Nlend, Emmanuel. Savings Banks and Savings Facilities in African Countries: Cameroon. In *Alberici, A. and Baravelli, M., eds.*, 1973, pp. 1–5.
[G: Cameroon]

Ølgaard, Anders. Føres der pengepolitik i Danmark? (Danish Monetary Policy—Does it Exist? With English summary.) *Nationalokon. Tidsskr.*, 1973, 111(1), pp. 9–24. [G: Denmark]

Onado, Marco and Porteri, Antonio. Savings Banks and Savings Facilities in African Countries: Lesotho. In *Alberici, A. and Baravelli, M., eds.*, 1973, pp. 45–46. [G: Lesotho]

Parkin, Michael. The Discount Houses' Role in the Money Supply Control Process Under the "Competition and Credit Control" Regime. *Manchester Sch. Econ. Soc. Stud.*, March 1973, 41(1), pp. 89–105. [G: U.K.]

Parkin, Michael. A Continuous Disequilibrium Econometric Model of the Domestic and International Portfolio Behaviour of the UK Banking System: Discussion. In *Parkin, M., ed.*, 1973, pp. 291–93. [G: U.K.]

Patman, Wright. Commercial Banks and Their Trust Activities. In *Andreano, R. L., ed.*, 1973, pp. R344–19. [G: U.S.]

Pejovich, Svetozar. The Banking System and the Investment Behavior of the Yugoslav Firm. In *Bornstein, M., ed.*, 1973, pp. 285–311. [G: Yugoslavia]

Portugués, Juan Marrero. Savings Banks and Savings Facilities in African Countries: Equatorial Guinea. In *Alberici, A. and Baravelli, M., eds.*, 1973, pp. 29–32. [G: Equatorial Guinea]

Pringle, John J. A Theory of the Banking Firm: Comment. *J. Money, Credit, Banking*, November 1973, 5(4), pp. 990–96.

Puckett, Richard H. Changes in Bank Lending Practices, 1972. *Fed. Res. Bull.*, July 1973, 59(7), pp. 501–05. [G: U.S.]

Quantius, Frances W. Commercial Banking and the Hunt Commission Report. *Ohio State U. Bull. Bus. Res.*, April 1973, 48(4), pp. 4–5, 8. [G: U.S.]

Rahman El Sheikh, Ahmed Abdel. Savings Banks and Savings Facilities in African Countries: Sudan. In *Alberici, A. and Baravelli, M., eds.*, 1973, pp. 97–101. [G: Sudan]

Raman, A. Expansion of Branches of Commercial Banks with Special Reference to 'Lead Bank' Scheme. In *Simha, S. L. N., ed.*, 1973, pp. 139–54.
[G: India]

Reid, Samuel Richardson. "The Bank Merger Act of 1960: A Decade After": Comment. *Antitrust Bull.*, Fall, 1973, 18(3), pp. 449–62. [G: U.S.]

Renda, Benedetto. Credito, risparmio e banche nelle prospettive dell'integrazione europea. (Credit, Savings and Bank Systems in the Perspective of

European Economic Integration. With English summary.) *Mondo Aperto*, February 1973, *27*(1), pp. 9–23.

Robertson, Ross M. Chartering, Branching, and the Concentration Problem: Discussion. In *Federal Reserve Bank of Boston*, 1973, pp. 40–45. [G: U.S.]

Robinson, Randall S. BANKMOD: An Interactive Simulation Aid for Bank Financial Planning. *J. Bank Res.*, Autumn 1973, *4*(3), pp. 212–24.

Rose, Peter S. and Fraser, Donald R. The Short-run Determinants of Loan Mix at Large Commercial Banks. *J. Econ. Bus.*, Fall 1973, *26*(1), pp. 1–9. [G: U.S.]

Ruozi, Roberto. Savings Banks and Savings Facilities in African Countries: Introduction. In *Alberici, A. and Baravelli, M., eds.*, 1973, pp. ix–xxiii. [G: Africa]

Rybczynski, T. M. The Merchant Banks. *Manchester Sch. Econ. Soc. Stud.*, March 1973, *41*(1), pp. 107–21. [G: U.K.]

Sacerdoti, Emilio. A Note on Monetary Policy when Banks Have Managerial Objectives. *L'Industria*, January-June 1973, (1–2), pp. 89–108.

Saraiya, R. G. Banking Commission's Approach to Its Task. In *Simha, S. L. N., ed.*, 1973, pp. 62–68. [G: India]

Saxena, D. N. Commercial Banks in the Current Development Strategy in India. In *Simha, S. L. N., ed.*, 1973, pp. 125–38. [G: India]

Schlesinger, Helmut and Bockelmann, Horst. Monetary Policy in the Federal Republic of Germany. In *Holbik, K., ed.*, 1973, pp. 161–213. [G: W. Germany]

Schmitt-Rink, Gerhard. Marktform und Geldschöpfungsmultiplikator. (Market Structure and Multiple Money Expansion. With English summary.) *Jahr. Nationalökon. Statist.*, December 1973, *188*(1), pp. 1–9.

Schweitzer, Stuart A. Economies of Scale and Holding Company Affiliation in Banking: Reply. *Southern Econ. J.*, July 1973, *40*(1), pp. 141–42.

Seiders, David. Credit-Card and Check-Credit Plans at Commercial Banks. *Fed. Res. Bull.*, September 1973, *59*(9), pp. 646–53. [G: U.S.]

Senghore, Alhagi A. J. Savings Banks and Savings Facilities in African Countries: Gambia. In *Alberici, A. and Baravelli, M., eds.*, 1973, pp. 35–36. [G: Gambia]

Shank, John K. Long Range Planning Systems: Achieving Both "Realism" and "Reach." *J. Bank Res.*, Autumn 1973, *4*(3), pp. 185–93.

Sidambaram, Mootoosamy. Savings Banks and Savings Facilities in African Countries: Mauritius. In *Alberici, A. and Baravelli, M., eds.*, 1973, pp. 65–67. [G: Mauritius]

Silveira, Antonio M. Interest Rate and Rapid Inflation: The Evidence from the Brazilian Economy. *J. Money, Credit, Banking*, August 1973, *5*(3), pp. 794–805. [G: Brazil]

Silverberg, Stanley C. Deposit Costs and Bank Portfolio Policy. *J. Finance*, September 1973, *28*(4), pp. 881–95. [G: U.S.]

Silverman, Lester P. Credit Standards and Tight Money: Comment. *J. Money, Credit, Banking*, Part I, February 1973, *5*(1), pp. 221–23.

Simha, S. L. N. Future of the Subsidiaries of the State Bank of India. In *Simha, S. L. N., ed.*, 1973, pp. 189–202. [G: India]

Simha, S. L. N. Evolution of Indian Banking. In *Simha, S. L. N., ed.*, 1973, pp. 20–43. [G: India]

Snider, Thomas E. The Effect of Merger on the Lending Behavior of Rural Unit Banks in Virginia. *J. Bank Res.*, Spring 1973, *4*(1), pp. 52–57. [G: U.S.]

Snider, William D. Building an On-Line Financial Planning Model. *J. Bank Res.*, Autumn 1973, *4*(3), pp. 232–38.

Socher, Karl. Monetary Policy in Austria. In *Holbik, K., ed.*, 1973, pp. 1–38. [G: Austria]

Şovei, George. Sistem informaţional bancar modern. (A Modern Banking Informational System. With English summary.) *Stud. Cercet. Econ.*, 1973, (4), pp. 127–40.

Spencer, Roger W. Strong Credit Demands, But No "Crunch" in Early 1973. *Fed. Res. Bank St. Louis Rev.*, June 1973, *55*(6), pp. 2–10. [G: U.S.]

Strayhorn, Martha. Changes in Time and Savings Deposits at Commercial Banks, July 1972–January 1973. *Fed. Res. Bull.*, April 1973, *59*(4), pp. 261–75. [G: U.S.]

Strayhorn, Martha. Changes in Time and Savings Deposits at Commercial Banks: April-July 1973. *Fed. Res. Bull.*, October 1973, *59*(10), pp. 724–30. [G: U.S.]

Strayhorn, Martha. Changes in Time and Savings Deposits, January-April 1973. *Fed. Res. Bull.*, July 1973, *59*(7), pp. 493–500. [G: U.S.]

Swamy, Dalip S. Optimum Interest Rates on Bank Deposits. *Indian Econ. J.*, April-June 1973, *20* (4–5), pp. 630–37.

Thomson, Michael R. Forecasting for Financial Planning. *J. Bank Res.*, Autumn 1973, *4*(3), pp. 225–31.

Thore, Sten and Eriksen, Ib. Payment Clearing Networks. *Swedish J. Econ.*, June 1973, *75*(2), pp. 143–63.

Valentine, T. J. The Loan Supply Function of Australian Trading Banks: An Empirical Analysis. *Australian Econ. Pap.*, June 1973, *12*(20), pp. 57–69. [G: Australia]

Verbrugge, James A. The Effects of Pledging Regulations on Bank Asset Composition. *J. Bank Res.*, Autumn 1973, *4*(3), pp. 168–76. [G: U.S.]

Verbrugge, James A. Idle Public Funds Policies: Some Additional Evidence. *Nebr. J. Econ. Bus.*, Spring 1973, *12*(2), pp. 9–19. [G: U.S.]

Vikbladh, Inge. Monetary Policy in Sweden. In *Holbik, K., ed.*, 1973, pp. 375–422. [G: Sweden]

Wadsworth, J. E. The Banks and the Monetary System in the UK 1959–1971. In *Wadsworth, J. E., ed.*, 1973, pp. 1–16. [G: U.K.]

Wallich, Henry C. The Economics of an Automated Payment System. In *The Diebold Group, Inc.*, 1973, pp. 161–68. [G: U.S.]

Wentz, John and Mazza, Gertrude. The Acquisitive Bank Holding Companies: A Bigger Role in Mortgage Banking. *Fed. Res. Bank Bus. Rev. Phila.*, October 1973, pp. 7–8. [G: U.S.]

Weston, J. Fred and Hoskins, W. Lee. Geographic Aspects of Market Structure and Performance in Banking. *J. Bus. Res.*, Summer 1973, *1*(1), pp.

31–42. [G: U.S.]

White, S. Douglass. Marketing in Bank: Philosophies and Actions. *J. Bank Res.*, Winter 1973, *3*(4), pp. 265–68. [G: U.S.]

Wille, Frank. Expanded Powers for Depositary Financial Institutions. In *Federal Reserve Bank of Boston*, 1973, pp. 55–63. [G: U.S.]

Wilson, J. S. G. The Australian Money Market. *Banca Naz. Lavoro Quart. Rev.*, March 1973, (104), pp. 46–69. [G: Australia]

Wilson, Ruth. Banking the Boom. *Fed. Res. Bank San Francisco Rev.*, May-June 1973, pp. 9–13. [G: U.S.]

Wilson, Ruth. Where the Money Came From. *Fed. Res. Bank San Francisco Rev.*, January-February 1973, pp. 9–11. [G: U.S.]

Wrightsman, Dwayne. On the Rationality of Compensating Balance Requirements. *Southern Econ. J.*, January 1973, *39*(3), pp. 427–30.

Yeats, Alexander J. An Analysis of the Effect of Mergers on Banking Market Structures. *J. Money, Credit, Banking*, May 1973, *5*(2), pp. 623–36. [G: U.S.]

Yeo, Edwin H., III. A Management View of Financial Planning or The Best Laid Schemes. *J. Bank Res.*, Autumn 1973, *4*(3), pp. 207–11.

Yona, Daniel A. N. Savings Banks and Savings Facilities in African Countries: Tanzania. In *Alberici, A. and Baravelli, M., eds.*, 1973, pp. 103–09. [G: Tanzania]

Zwick, Charles J. Strategic Planning and its Role in the Banking Environment of the Seventies. *J. Bank Res.*, Summer 1973, *4*(2), pp. 74–78.

313 Financial Markets

3130 General

Agmon, Tamir. Country Risk: The Significance of the Country Factor for Share-Price Movements in the United Kingdom, Germany, and Japan. *J. Bus.*, January 1973, *46*(1), pp. 24–32. [G: U.K.; W. Germany; Japan]

Ahtiala, Pekka. Rahoitusjärjestelmästä ja sen tehtävistä. (The Financial System and Its Functions. With English summary.) *Liiketaloudellinen Aikak.*, 1973, *22*(4), pp. 236–47.

Bain, A. D. Flow of Funds Analysis: Survey. *Econ. J.*, December 1973, *83*(332), pp. 1055–93.

Bicksler, James L. and Thorp, Edward O. The Capital Growth Model: An Empirical Investigation. *J. Financial Quant. Anal.*, March 1973, *8*(2), pp. 273–87.

Bierman, Harold, Jr. The Cost of Warrants. *J. Financial Quant. Anal.*, June 1973, *8*(3), pp. 499–503.

Blume, Marshall E. and Friend, Irwin. A New Look at the Capital Asset Pricing Model. *J. Finance*, March 1973, *28*(1), pp. 19–33. [G: U.S.]

Budd, A. P. and Litzenberger, Robert H. Changes in the Supply of Money, the Firm's Market Value and Cost of Capital. *J. Finance*, March 1973, *28*(1), pp. 49–57.

Burke, William. Higher Payout? *Fed. Res. Bank San Francisco Rev.*, July-August 1973, pp. 3–7. [G: U.S.]

Cheng, Pao L. and Deets, M. King. Systematic Risk and the Horizon Problem. *J. Financial Quant. Anal.*, March 1973, *8*(2), pp. 299–316. [G: U.S.]

De Alessi, Louis. Private Property and Dispersion of Ownership in Large Corporations. *J. Finance*, September 1973, *28*(4), pp. 839–51. [G: U.S.]

Dickman, A. B. The Financing of Industrial Development in South Africa. *S. Afr. J. Econ.*, December 1973, *41*(4), pp. 373–400. [G: S.Africa]

von Furstenberg, George M. The Equilibrium Spread Between Variable Rates and Fixed Rates on Long-Term Financing Instruments. *J. Financial Quant. Anal.*, December 1973, *8*(5), pp. 807–19.

Goldsmith, Raymond W. Basic Considerations. In *Goldsmith, R. W., ed.*, 1973, pp. 1–33. [G: U.S.]

Gonedes, Nicholas J. Evidence on the Information Content of Accounting Numbers: Accounting-Based and Market-Based Estimates of Systematic Risk. *J. Financial Quant. Anal.*, June 1973, *8*(3), pp. 407–43. [G: U.S.]

Gonzales, Nestor. The Capital Growth Model: An Empirical Investigation: Comment. *J. Financial Quant. Anal.*, March 1973, *8*(2), pp. 293–97.

Gray, Jean M. New Evidence on the Term Structure of Interest Rates: 1884–1900. *J. Finance*, June 1973, *28*(3), pp. 635–46. [G: U.S.]

Gupta, Suraj B. Financial Progress, Banking Expansion, and Saving. *Indian Econ. J.*, April-June 1973, *20*(4–5), pp. 548–69.

Hopewell, Michael H. and Kaufman, George G. Bond Price Volatility and Term to Maturity: A Generalized Respecification. *Amer. Econ. Rev.*, September 1973, *63*(4), pp. 749–53.

Jacob, Nancy L. Systematic Risk and the Horizon Problem: Comment. *J. Financial Quant. Anal.*, March 1973, *8*(2), pp. 351–54.

Klein, Michael A. The Economics of Security Divisibility and Financial Intermediation. *J. Finance*, September 1973, *28*(4), pp. 923–31.

LeRoy, Stephen F. Risk Aversion and the Martingale Property of Stock Prices. *Int. Econ. Rev.*, June 1973, *14*(2), pp. 436–46.

Merton, Robert C. An Intertemporal Capital Asset Pricing Model. *Econometrica*, September 1973, *41*(5), pp. 867–87.

Merton, Robert C. Theory of Rational Option Pricing. *Bell J. Econ. Manage. Sci.*, Spring 1973, *4*(1), pp. 141–83.

Prell, Michael J. How Well Do the Experts Forecast Interest Rates? *Fed. Res. Bank Kansas City Rev.*, September-October 1973, pp. 3–13. [G: U.S.]

Ragazzi, Giorgio. Theories of the Determinants of Direct Foreign Investment. *Int. Monet. Fund Staff Pap.*, July 1973, *20*(2), pp. 471–98. [G: U.S.]

Rosenberg, Barr and McKibben, Walt. The Prediction of Systematic and Specific Risk in Common Stocks. *J. Financial Quant. Anal.*, March 1973, *8*(2), pp. 317–33. [G: U.S.]

Rubinstein, Mark E. A Comparative Statics Analysis of Risk Premiums. *J. Bus.*, October 1973, *46*(4), pp. 605–15.

Rush, David F. The Interdependent Structure of Security Returns: Comment. *J. Financial Quant. Anal.*, March 1973, *8*(2), pp. 289–91.

Samuelson, Paul A. Proof that Properly Discounted

Present Values of Assets Vibrate Randomly. *Bell J. Econ. Manage. Sci.*, Autumn 1973, *4*(2), pp. 369–74.

Sarnat, Marshall. Purchasing Power Risk, Portfolio Analysis, and the Case for Index-Linked Bonds: Comment. *J. Money, Credit, Banking,* August 1973, *5*(3), pp. 836–45.

Schimmler, Jörg. Speculation, Profitability, and Price Stability—A Formal Approach. *Rev. Econ. Statist.,* February 1973, *55*(1), pp. 110–14.

Simkowitz, Michael A. and Logue, Dennis E. The Interdependent Structure of Security Returns. *J. Financial Quant. Anal.,* March 1973, *8*(2), pp. 259–72.

Stern, Ernest. Private Capital Markets for Development. In *[Halm, G. N.],* 1973, pp. 185–97.

Wai, U Tun and Patrick, Hugh T. Stock and Bond Issues and Capital Markets in Less Developed Countries. *Int. Monet. Fund Staff Pap.,* July 1973, *20*(2), pp. 253–317.

Wakoff, Gary I. On Shareholders' Indifference to the Proceeds Price in Preemptive Rights Offerings. *J. Financial Quant. Anal.,* December 1973, *8*(5), pp. 835–36.

Weil, Roman L. Macaulay's Duration: An Appreciation. *J. Bus.,* October 1973, *46*(4), pp. 589–92.

Wicke, Lutz. Zinserhöhungen bei festverzinslichen Wertpapieren während einer schleichdenden Inflation. (Are Increases in the Interest Rates of Fixed-Interest-Bearing Securities During a Creeping Inflation a Compensation for Losses of Real Value? With English summary.) *Z. Wirtschaft. Sozialwissen.,* 1973, *93*(5), pp. 567–85.

Wilson, J. S. G. The Australian Money Market. *Banca Naz. Lavoro Quart. Rev.,* March 1973, (104), pp. 46–69. [G: Australia]

3132 Financial Markets Studies and Regulation

Barnea, Amir and Downes, David H. A Reexamination of the Empirical Distribution of Stock Price Changes. *J. Amer. Statist. Assoc.,* June 1973, *68* (342), pp. 348–50. [G: U.S.]

Barnea, Amir and Logue, Dennis E. Stock-Market Based Measures of Corporate Diversification. *J. Ind. Econ.,* September 1973, *22*(1), pp. 51–60. [G: U.S.]

Beaver, William H. and Dukes, Roland E. Interperiod Tax Allocation and δ-Depreciation Methods: Some Empirical Results. *Accounting Rev.,* July 1973, *48*(3), pp. 549–59.

Benishay, Haskel. Market Preferences for Characteristics of Common Stocks. *Econ. J.,* March 1973, *83*(329), pp. 173–91.

Ben-Shahar, H. and Cukierman, A. The Term-Structure of Interest Rates and Expectations of Price Increase and Devaluation. *J. Finance,* June 1973, *28*(3), pp. 567–75. [G: Israel]

Benston, George J. Required Disclosure and the Stock Market: An Evaluation of the Securities Exchange Act of 1934. *Amer. Econ. Rev.,* March 1973, *63*(1), pp. 132–55. [G: U.S.]

Bernstein, Peter L. What Rate of Return Can You "Reasonably" Expect? *J. Finance,* May 1973, *28* (2), pp. 273–82. [G: U.S.]

Bhatia, Kul B. The Estimation of Accrued Capital

Gains on Individuals' Corporate Stock Holdings. *J. Amer. Statist. Assoc.,* March 1973, *68*(341), pp. 55–62.

Bildersee, John S. Some Aspects of the Performance of Non-Convertible Preferred Stocks. *J. Finance,* December 1973, *28*(5), pp. 1187–1201. [G: U.S.]

Bird, R. G. and Peirson, C. G. A Study of Convertible Notes Issued in Australia. *Australian Econ. Pap.,* June 1973, *12*(20), pp. 91–105. [G: Australia]

Black, Fischer and Scholes, Myron S. The Pricing of Options and Corporate Liabilities. *J. Polit. Econ.,* May-June 1973, *81*(3), pp. 637–54.

Blume, Marshall E. and Husic, Frank. Price, Beta, and Exchange Listing. *J. Finance,* May 1973, *28* (2), pp. 283–99. [G: U.S.]

Bolten, Steven. Treasury Bill Auction Procedures: An Empirical Investigation. *J. Finance,* June 1973, *28* (3), pp. 577–85. [G: U.S.]

Bolten, Steven. The Behavior of Convertible Debenture Premiums: Reply. *Miss. Val. J. Bus. Econ.,* Winter 1973-74, *9*(2), pp. 69–70.

Boone, Michael M. Management Accountants and the Securities Laws. *Manage. Account.,* June 1973, *54*(12), pp. 18–22.

Boudreaux, Kenneth J. Discounts and Premiums on Closed-End Mutual Funds: A Study in Valuation. *J. Finance,* May 1973, *28*(2), pp. 515–22. [G: U.S.]

Brennan, Michael J. An Approach to the Valuation of Uncertain Income Streams. *J. Finance,* June 1973, *28*(3), pp. 661–74.

Choi, Frederick D. S. Financial Disclosure and Entry to the European Capital Market. *J. Acc. Res.,* Autumn 1973, *11*(2), pp. 159–75.

Claessens, G. and Verheirstraeten, A. De technische analyse van het verloop van aandelenkoersen—met een toepassing op de beurs te Brussel. (With English summary.) *Tijdschr. Econ.,* 1973, *18*(4), pp. 647–81.

Clark, Peter K. A Subordinated Stochastic Process Model with Finite Variance for Speculative Prices. *Econometrica,* January 1973, *41*(1), pp. 135–55. [G: U.S.]

Cohen, Jacob and Miller, Richard K. A Flow-of-Funds Model of the Stock Market. *J. Econ. Bus.,* Winter 1973, *25*(2), pp. 71–82. [G: U.S.]

Cohen, Stanley and Smyth, David J. Some Determinants of Price/Earnings Ratios of Industrial Common Stock. *Quart. Rev. Econ. Bus.,* Winter 1973, *13*(4), pp. 49–60. [G: U.S.]

Conrad, Klaus and Jüttner, D. Johannes. Recent Behaviour of Stock Market Prices in Germany and the Random Walk Hypothesis. *Kyklos,* 1973, *26* (3), pp. 576–99. [G: W. Germany]

Cooper, Ronald L. An Econometric Forecasting Model of the Financial Sector of U.S. Households. *Appl. Econ.,* June 1973, *5*(2), pp. 101–17. [G: U.S.]

Dalrymple, Brent B. Risk Analysis Applied to Commodity Speculation. *J. Econ. Bus.,* Winter 1973, *25*(2), pp. 127–30.

Davis, E. G.; Dunn, D. M. and Williams, W. H. Ambiguities in the Cross-Section Analysis of Per Share Financial Data. *J. Finance,* December 1973, *28*(5), pp. 1241–48. [G: U.S.]

Dennis, Charles N. The Information Content of Daily Market Indicators: Comment. *J. Financial Quant. Anal.*, March 1973, *8*(2), pp. 193–94..

Dennis, Charles N. An Investigation Into the Effects of Independent Investor Relations Firms on Common Stock Prices. *J. Finance*, May 1973, *28* (2), pp. 373–80. [G: U.S.]

Downes, David H. and Dyckman, Thomas R. A Critical Look at the Efficient Market Empirical Research Literature As It Relates to Accounting Information. *Accounting Rev.*, April 1973, *48*(2), pp. 300–17.

Eastburn, David P. A Crunch in '73? *Fed. Res. Bank Bus. Rev. Phila.*, June 1973, pp. 3–6. [G: U.S.]

Eilbott, Peter. Estimates of the Market Value of the Outstanding Corporate Stock of All Domestic Corporations. In *Goldsmith, R. W., ed.*, 1973, pp. 429–55. [G: U.S.]

Emery, John T. The Information Content of Daily Market Indicators. *J. Financial Quant. Anal.*, March 1973, *8*(2), pp. 183–90. [G: U.S.]

Feldstein, Martin S. and Chamberlain, Gary. Multimarket Expectations and the Rate of Interest. *J. Money, Credit, Banking*, November 1973, *5*(4), pp. 873–902. [G: U.S.]

Finet, Jacques. Monetary Policy in Belgium. In *Holbik, K., ed.*, 1973, pp. 39–69. [G: Belgium]

Firth, Michael A. An Empirical Examination of the Applicability of Adopting the AICPA and NYSE Regulations and Free Share Distributions in the U.K. *J. Acc. Res.*, Spring 1973, *11*(1), pp. 16–24. [G: U.K.]

Fisher, Lawrence. Investment Characteristics of Common Stocks in Regulated and Unregulated Industries: A Comparative Study. In *Russell, M., ed.*, 1973, pp. 53–78. [G: U.S.]

Fleming, Robert M. How Risky Is the Market? *J. Bus.*, July 1973, *46*(3), pp. 404–24. [G: U.S.]

Forbes, Ronald. Finance and Banking: Refereed Papers II: Discussion. *J. Finance*, May 1973, *28*(2), pp. 539–41. [G: U.S.]

Foster, George. Stock Market Reaction to Estimates of Earnings per Share by Company Officials. *J. Acc. Res.*, Spring 1973, *11*(1), pp. 25–37. [G: U.S.]

Francis, Jack Clark. Economic Pressures Reshape America's Stock Markets. *Fed. Res. Bank Bus. Rev. Phila.*, June 1973, pp. 12–18. [G: U.S.]

Frankle, A. W. and Hawkins, Clark A. The Behavior of Convertible Debenture Premiums: Comment. *Miss. Val. J. Bus. Econ.*, Winter 1973-74, *9*(2), pp. 65–68.

Friend, Irwin. Mythodology in Finance. *J. Finance*, May 1973, *28*(2), pp. 257–72.

Friend, Irwin and Blume, Marshall E. Competitive Commissions on the New York Stock Exchange. *J. Finance*, September 1973, *28*(4), pp. 795–819. [G: U.S.]

Gentry, James A. Investment Characteristics of Common Stocks in Regulated and Unregulated Industries: A Comparative Study: Comment. In *Russell, M., ed.*, 1973, pp. 79–83. [G: U.S.]

Glyn, Andrew. The Stock Market Valuation of British Companies and the Cost of Capital 1955–69. *Oxford Econ. Pap.*, July 1973, *25*(2), pp. 213–40. [G: U.K.]

Goldsmith, Raymond W. The Position of Institutional Investors and of Corporate Stock in the National Balance Sheets and the Flow of Funds Accounts of the United States of America, 1952–68. In *Goldsmith, R. W., ed.*, 1973, pp. 91–164. [G: U.S.]

Goodhart, Charles A. E. Monetary Policy in the United Kingdom. In *Holbik, K., ed.*, 1973, pp. 465–524. [G: U.K.]

Gordon, Myron J. Causes and Predictions of Rates of Return on Stocks and Bonds: Discussion. *J. Finance*, May 1973, *28*(2), pp. 318–20. [G: U.S.]

Grier, Paul C. and Albin, Peter S. Nonrandom Price Changes in Association with Trading in Large Blocks. *J. Bus.*, July 1973, *46*(3), pp. 425–33. [G: U.S.]

Gunnelson, Jerald A. and Farris, Paul L. Use of Soybean Futures Markets by Large Processing Firms. *Agr. Econ. Res.*, April 1973, *25*(2), pp. 27–40. [G: U.S.]

Gup, Benton E. A Note on Stock Market Indicators and Stock Prices. *J. Financial Quant. Anal.*, September 1973, *8*(4), pp. 673–82. [G: U.S.]

Hagerman, Robert L. and Richmond, Richard D. Random Walks, Martingales and the OTC. *J. Finance*, September 1973, *28*(4), pp. 897–909. [G: U.S.]

Hagerman, Robert L. The Efficiency of the Market for Bank Stocks: An Empirical Test: Comment. *J. Money, Credit, Banking*, August 1973, *5*(3), pp. 846–55. [G: U.S.]

Halpern, Paul J. Empirical Estimates of the Amount and Distribution of Gains to Companies in Mergers. *J. Bus.*, October 1973, *46*(4), pp. 554–75. [G: U.S.]

Haugen, Robert A. and Wichern, Dean W. The Diametric Effects of the Capital Gains Tax on the Stability of Stock Prices. *J. Finance*, September 1973, *28*(4), pp. 987–96.

Hempel, George H. Quantitative Borrower Characteristics Associated with Defaults on Municipal General Obligations. *J. Finance*, May 1973, *28*(2), pp. 523–30. [G: U.S.]

Islam, Taherul. Structure of Futures Contract, Difference System and Hedging Effectiveness—An Economic Study of Bombay Cotton Futures Market. *Indian Econ. J.*, January-March 1973, *20*(3), pp. 479–99. [G: India]

Jarrett, Jeffrey E. Finance and Investment: Refereed Papers I: Discussion. *J. Finance*, May 1973, *28*(2), pp. 404–05. [G: U.S.]

Joehnk, Michael D. and Wert, James E. The Call-Risk Performance of the Discounted Seasoned Issue. *Miss. Val. J. Bus. Econ.*, Winter 1973-74, *9*(2), pp. 1–15. [G: U.S.]

Jordan, Ronald J. An Empirical Investigation of the Adjustment of Stock Prices to New Quarterly Earnings Information. *J. Financial Quant. Anal.*, September 1973, *8*(4), pp. 609–20. [G: U.S.]

Kichline, James L.; Laub, P. Michael and Stevens, Guy V. G. Obtaining the Yield on a Standard Bond from a Sample of Bonds with Heterogeneous Characteristics. *Fed. Res. Bull.*, May 1973, *59*(5), pp. 327–28. [G: U.S.]

Kichline, James L.; Laub, P. Michael and Deck, Beryl. Yields on Recently Offered Corporate

Bonds. *Fed. Res. Bull.*, May 1973, *59*(5), pp. 336–37. [G: U.S.]

Kiger, Jack E. An Empirical Test of Annual Earnings Projection Models Using Quarterly Data. *Miss. Val. J. Bus. Econ.*, Spring 1973, *8*(3), pp. 17–28. [G: U.S.]

Klemkosky, Robert C. and Petty, J. William. A Multivariate Analysis of Stock Price Variability. *J. Bus. Res.*, Summer 1973, *1*(1), pp. 1–10. [G: U.S.]

Knight, Malcolm. A Continuous Disequilibrium Econometric Model of the Domestic and International Portfolio Behaviour of the UK Banking System. In *Parkin, M., ed.*, 1973, pp. 266–90. [G: U.K.]

Kofi, Tetteh A. A Framework for Comparing the Efficiency of Futures Markets. *Amer. J. Agr. Econ.*, Part I, November 1973, *55*(4), pp. 584–94. [G: U.S.]

Largay, James A., III and West, Richard R. Margin Changes and Stock Price Behavior. *J. Polit. Econ.*, Part I, March-April 1973, *81*(2), pp. 328–39. [G: U.S.]

Largay, James A., III. 100% Margins: Combating Speculation in Individual Security Issues. *J. Finance*, September 1973, *28*(4), pp. 973–86. [G: U.S.]

Latané, Henry A. Cross-Section Regularities in Returns on Investment in Common Stocks. *J. Bus.*, October 1973, *46*(4), pp. 512–16. [G: U.S.]

Lee, Sang M. and Lerro, A. J. Optimizing the Portfolio Selection for Mutual Funds. *J. Finance*, December 1973, *28*(5), pp. 1087–1102. [G: U.S.]

Logue, Dennis E. Premia on Unseasoned Equity Issues. *J. Econ. Bus.*, Spring-Summer 1973, *25*(3), pp. 133–41.

Logue, Dennis E. and Merville, Larry J. General Model of Imperfect Capital Markets. *Southern Econ. J.*, October 1973, *40*(2), pp. 224–33.

Logue, Dennis E. On the Pricing of Unseasoned Equity Issues: 1965-1969. *J. Financial Quant. Anal.*, January 1973, *8*(1), pp. 91–103. [G: U.S.]

May, Robert G. and Sundem, Gary L. Cost of Information and Security Prices: Market Association Tests for Accounting Policy Decisions. *Accounting Rev.*, January 1973, *48*(1), pp. 80–94. [G: U.S.]

McCallum, John S. The Impact of the Capital Gains Tax on Bond Yields. *Nat. Tax J.*, December 1973, *26*(4), pp. 575–83. [G: Canada]

McDonald, John G. French Mutual Fund Performance: Evaluation of Internationally-Diversified Portfolios. *J. Finance*, December 1973, *28*(5), pp. 1161–80. [G: France]

McGowan, John J. The Supply of Equity Securities, 1952–68. In *Goldsmith, R. W., ed.*, 1973, pp. 165–203. [G: U.S.]

McIntyre, Edward V. Current-Cost Financial Statements and Common-Stock Investments Decisions. *Accounting Rev.*, July 1973, *48*(3), pp. 575–85. [G: U.S.]

Mendelson, Morris. The *Martin Report* and its Aftermath. *Bell J. Econ. Manage. Sci.*, Spring 1973, *4* (1), pp. 250–69. [G: U.S.]

Merrett, A. J. and Sykes, Allen. Return on Equities and Fixed Interest Securities: 1919–66. In *Lister, R. J., ed.*, 1973, pp. 28–38. [G: U.K.]

Meyers, Stephen L. The Stationarity Problem in the Use of the Market Model of Security Price Behavior. *Accounting Rev.*, April 1973, *48*(2), pp. 318–22. [G: U.S.]

Meyers, Stephen L. A Re-Examination of Market and Industry Factors in Stock Price Behavior. *J. Finance*, June 1973, *28*(3), pp. 695–705. [G: U.S.]

Mingat, Alain. Cheminements aléatoires et modèles systématiques d'intervention. Bourse des valeures de Paris. (Random Walk Changes and Buying and Selling Models. With English summary). *Consommation*, January-March 1973, *20*(1), pp. 77–96. [G: France]

Mott, Charles H. Forecast Disclosure. *Manage. Account.*, July 1973, *55*(1), pp. 17–18, 28.

Mueller, Willard F. Corporate Secrecy and the Need for Financial Disclosure. In *Haveman, R. H. and Hamrin, R. D., eds.*, 1973, pp. 283–91. [G: U.S.]

Mullineaux, Donald J. Interest-Rate Ceilings and the Treasury-Bill Market: Disintermediation and the Small Saver. *New Eng. Econ. Rev.*, July-August 1973, pp. 19–26. [G: U.S.]

Nielsen, James F. and Melicher, Ronald W. A Financial Analysis of Acquisition and Merger Premiums. *J. Financial Quant. Anal.*, March 1973, *8*(2), pp. 139–48. [G: U.S.]

Nielsen, James F. and Joehnk, Michael D. Further Evidence on the Effects of Block Transactions on Stock Price Fluctuations. *Miss. Val. J. Bus. Econ.*, Winter 1973-74, *9*(2), pp. 27–34. [G: U.S.]

O'Connor, Melvin C. On the Usefulness of Financial Ratios to Investors in Common Stock. *Accounting Rev.*, April 1973, *48*(2), pp. 339–52. [G: U.S.]

Officer, R. R. The Variability of the Market Factor of the New York Stock Exchange. *J. Bus.*, July 1973, *46*(3), pp. 434–53. [G: U.S.]

Oudet, Bruno A. The Variation of the Return of Stocks in Periods of Inflation. *J. Financial Quant. Anal.*, March 1973, *8*(2), pp. 247–58. [G: U.S.]

Painter, William H. An Analysis of Recent Proposals for Reform of Federal Securities Legislation. *Mich. Law Rev.*, August 1973, *71*(8), pp. 1576–1638. [G: U.S.]

Parkin, Michael. A Continuous Disequilibrium Econometric Model of the Domestic and International Portfolio Behaviour of the UK Banking System: Discussion. In *Parkin, M., ed.*, 1973, pp. 291–93. [G: U.K.]

Pelleri, Paolo. Fatti e tendenze del mese in Borsa. (Facts and Tendencies in the Month. With English summary.) *Bancaria*, January 1973, *29*(1), pp. 104–08. [G: Italy]

Pelleri, Paolo. Le borse estere nel 1972. (Foreign Stock Exchanges in 1972. With English summary.) *Bancaria*, February 1973, *29*(2), pp. 164–88.

Pelleri, Paolo. Le Borse italiane nel 1972. (Italian Stock Market in 1972. With English summary.) *Bancaria*, January 1973, *29*(1), pp. 40–75. [G: Italy]

Perlstein, William J. Revising the Private Placement Exemption. *Yale Law J.*, June 1973, *82*(7), pp. 1512–32. [G: U.S.]

Pesando, James E. and Smith, Lawrence B. Monetary Policy in Canada. In *Holbik, K., ed.*, 1973, pp.

70–116. [G: Canada]

Philippatos, George C. and Nawrocki, David N. The Behavior of Stock Market Aggregates: Evidence of Dependence on the American Stock Exchange. *J. Bus. Res.*, Fall 1973, *1*(2), pp. 102–14. [G: U.S.]

Philippatos, George C. and Nawrocki, David N. The Information Inaccuracy of Stock Market Forecasts: Some New Evidence of Dependence on the New York Stock Exchange. *J. Financial Quant. Anal.*, June 1973, *8*(3), pp. 445–58. [G: U.S.]

Pinches, George E. and Mingo, Kent A. A Multivariate Analysis of Industrial Bond Ratings. *J. Finance*, March 1973, *28*(1), pp. 1–18. [G: U.S.]

Pizzala, F. B. The Cost of Capital to the Private Sector: A Critique of Merrett and Sykes. In *Lister, R. J., ed.*, 1973, pp. 39–48. [G: U.K.]

Porter, Richard C. The Birth of a Bill Market. *J. Devel. Stud.*, April 1973, *9*(3), pp. 439–50. [G: Colombia]

Potter, Roger E. Characteristics of Two Groups of Investors. *Marquette Bus. Rev.*, Summer 1973, *17*(2), pp. 109–12. [G: U.S.]

Praetz, P. D. A Spectral Analysis of Australian Share Prices. *Australian Econ. Pap.*, June 1973, *12*(20), pp. 70–78. [G: Australia]

Reilly, Frank K. and Slaughter, William C. The Effect of Dual Markets on Common Stock Market Making. *J. Financial Quant. Anal.*, March 1973, *8*(2), pp. 167–82. [G: U.S.]

Reilly, Frank K. and Sherr, Lawrence A. The Shift Method: A Technique for Measuring the Differential Performance of Stocks. *Miss. Val. J. Bus. Econ.*, Fall 1973, *9*(1), pp. 28–40. [G: U.S.]

Reilly, Frank K. Further Evidence on Short-Run Results for New Issue Investors. *J. Financial Quant. Anal.*, January 1973, *8*(1), pp. 83–90. [G: U.S.]

Reilly, Frank K. and Drzycimski, Eugene F. Tests of Stock Market Efficiency Following Major Events. *J. Bus. Res.*, Summer 1973, *1*(1), pp. 57–72. [G: U.S.]

Richardson, Robert A. and Farris, Paul L. Farm Commodity Price Stabilization Through Futures Markets. *Amer. J. Agr. Econ.*, May 1973, *55*(2), pp. 225–30. [G: U.S.]

Ripley, Duncan M. Systematic Elements in the Linkage of National Stock Market Indices. *Rev. Econ. Statist.*, August 1973, *55*(3), pp. 356–61.

Roenfeldt, Rodney L. and Tuttle, Donald L. An Examination of the Discounts and Premiums of Closed-End Investment Companies. *J. Bus. Res.*, Fall 1973, *1*(2), pp. 129–40. [G: U.S.]

Rutz, A. Die Kurse schweizerischer Aktien im letzten Jahrzehnt. Regressionstechnische Bestimmung möglicher Einflussgrössen. (The Swiss Stock Market During the Last Decade. With English summary.) *Schweiz. Z. Volkswirtsch. Statist.*, June 1973, *109*(2), pp. 147–69. [G: Switzerland]

Sacerdoti, Emilio. Economic Effects of the New Treasury Bill Market in Italy. *Rivista Int. Sci. Econ. Com.*, July 1973, *20*(7), pp. 651–68. [G: Italy]

Sandor, Richard L. Innovation by an Exchange: A Case Study of the Development of the Plywood Futures Contract. *J. Law Econ.*, April 1973, *16*(1),

pp. 119–36. [G: U.S.]

Savona, Paolo. Mercato internazionale delle valute e mercato italiano delle obbligazioni. (International Exchange Market and Italian Bond Market. With English summary.) *Bancaria*, December 1973, *29*(12), pp. 1467–73. [G: Italy]

Schachter, Gustav and Cohen, Bruce. Influenze esterne sui mercati dei capitali degli Stati Uniti. (Foreign Influences on the U.S. Capital Markets. With English summary.) *Bancaria*, February 1973, *29*(2), pp. 156–63. [G: U.S.]

Scholes, Myron S. Causes and Predictions of Rates of Return on Stocks and Bonds: Discussion. *J. Finance*, May 1973, *28*(2), pp. 315–18. [G: U.S.]

Schwartz, Robert A. and Altman, Edward I. Volatility Behavior of Industrial Stock Price Indices. *J. Finance*, September 1973, *28*(4), pp. 957–71. [G: U.S.]

Sinkey, Joseph F., Jr. The Term Structure of Interest Rates: A Time-Series Test of the Kane Expected-Change Model of Interest-Rate Forecasting. *J. Money, Credit, Banking*, Part I, February 1973, *5*(1), pp. 192–200. [G: U.S.]

Soldofsky, Robert M. and Jennings, Edward H. Risk-Premium Curves: Empirical Evidence on Their Changing Position, 1950 to 1970. *Quart. Rev. Econ. Bus.*, Spring 1973, *13*(1), pp. 49–68. [G: U.S.]

Solnik, Bruno H. Note on the Validity of the Random Walk for European Stock Prices. *J. Finance*, December 1973, *28*(5), pp. 1151–59. [G: W. Europe]

Stevenson, Richard A. Brokerage Commissions and the Small Shareholder. *J. Bus. Res.*, Fall 1973, *1*(2), pp. 193–200. [G: U.S.]

Stevenson, Richard A. Odd-Lot Trading in the Stock Market and its Market Impact: Comment. *J. Financial Quant. Anal.*, June 1973, *8*(3), pp. 527–33.

Stewart, Samuel S., Jr. A Behavioral Model for Predicting Stock Prices. *J. Bus. Res.*, Fall 1973, *1*(2), pp. 173–82. [G: U.S.]

Strazheim, Mahlon R. The Demand for Corporate Stock in the Postwar Period. In *Goldsmith, R. W., ed.*, 1973, pp. 204–65. [G: U.S.]

Thompson, Howard E. and Thatcher, Lionel W. Required Rate of Return for Equity Capital Under Conditions of Growth and Consideration of Regulatory Lag. *Land Econ.*, May 1973, *49*(2), pp. 148–62.

Thompson, Howard E. A Note on the Value of Rights in Estimating the Investor Capitalization Rate. *J. Finance*, March 1973, *28*(1), pp. 157–60.

Van Eeckhoudt, M. Least Squares Construction of Yield Curves for Belgian Government Bonds (1955–1972): A Note. *Tijdschr. Econ.*, 1973, *18*(4), pp. 591–96. [G: Belgium]

Van Horne, James C. Implied Fixed Costs of Long-Term Debt Issues. *J. Financial Quant. Anal.*, December 1973, *8*(5), pp. 821–33. [G: U.S.]

Vanthienen, L. and Depre, F. Methodologie voor empirish onderzoek op de kapitaalmarkt. (With English summary.) *Tijdschr. Econ.*, 1973, *18*(4), pp. 629–46.

Walsh, Cornelius F. Does Listing Increase the Market Price of Common Stocks?: Comment. *J. Bus.*, October 1973, *46*(4), pp. 616–20. [G: U.S.]

Walter, James E. and Que, Agustin V. The Valuation of Convertible Bonds. *J. Finance*, June 1973, *28* (3), pp. 713–32. [G: U.S.]

Walters, Joan G. Finance and Banking: Refereed Papers II: Discussion. *J. Finance*, May 1973, *28*(2), pp. 538–39. [G: U.S.]

West, Richard R. Bond Ratings, Bond Yields and Financial Regulation: Some Findings. *J. Law Econ.*, April 1973, *16*(1), pp. 159–68. [G: U.S.]

Williams, John D. Security Exchange Packages Utilized in Mergers. *J. Econ. Bus.*, Spring-Summer 1973, *25*(3), pp. 187–90. [G: U.S.]

Winkler, Robert L. Bayesian Models for Forecasting Future Security Prices. *J. Financial Quant. Anal.*, June 1973, *8*(3), pp. 387–405.

Wood, William F. J. The Effect of Dual Markets on Common Stock Market Making: Comment. *J. Financial Quant. Anal.*, March 1973, *8*(2), pp. 191–92. [G: U.S.]

Wu, Hsiu-Kwang. Odd-Lot Trading in the Stock Market and its Market Impact: Reply. *J. Financial Quant. Anal.*, June 1973, *8*(3), pp. 535.

Wymer, C. R. A Continuous Disequilibrium Model of United Kingdom Financial Markets. In *Powell, A. A. and Williams, R. A., eds.*, 1973, pp. 301–34. [G: U.K.]

Zweig, Martin E. An Investor Expectations Stock Price Predictive Model Using Closed-End Fund Premiums. *J. Finance*, March 1973, *28*(1), pp. 67–78. [G: U.S.]

3135 Portfolio Selection: Theories and Studies

Allingham, M. G. and Morishima, M. Veblen Effects and Portfolio Selection. In *Morishima, M., et al.*, 1973, pp. 242–70.

Arnold, Donald F. and Humann, Thomas E. Earnings Per Share: An Empirical Test of the Market Parity and the Investment Value Methods. *Accounting Rev.*, January 1973, *48*(1), pp. 23–33. [G: U.S.]

Baltensperger, Ernst. Optimal Bank Portfolios: The Liability Side. *Jahr. Nationalökon. Statist.*, January 1973, *187*(2), pp. 147–60.

Ben-Zion, Uri and Balch, Michael. On the Analysis of Corporate Financial Theory under Uncertainty: A Comment. *Quart. J. Econ.*, May 1973, *87* (2), pp. 290–95.

Bernstein, Peter L. What Rate of Return Can You "Reasonably" Expect? *J. Finance*, May 1973, *28* (2), pp. 273–82. [G: U.S.]

Bicksler, James L.; Barnea, Amir and Babad, Jair. Portfolio Choice, the Horizon Problem and the Investment Opportunity Set. *Amer. Econ. Rev.*, May 1973, *63*(2), pp. 140–44.

Bierman, Harold, Jr. and Hass, Jerome E. Capital Budgeting Under Uncertainty: A Reformulation. *J. Finance*, March 1973, *28*(1), pp. 119–29.

Blume, Marshall E. and Husic, Frank. Price, Beta, and Exchange Listing. *J. Finance*, May 1973, *28* (2), pp. 283–99. [G: U.S.]

Bradley, Stephen P. and Crane, Dwight B. Management of Commercial Bank Government Security Portfolios: An Optimization Approach Under Un-

certainty. *J. Bank Res.*, Spring 1973, *4*(1), pp. 18–30.

Breen, William J. and Lerner, Eugene M. Corporate Financial Strategies and Market Measures of Risk and Return. *J. Finance*, May 1973, *28*(2), pp. 339–51. [G: U.S.]

Brumelle, Shelby L. and Schwab, Bernhard. Capital Budgeting with Uncertain Future Opportunities: A Markovian Approach. *J. Financial Quant. Anal.*, January 1973, *8*(1), pp. 111–22.

Cheng, Pao L. and Deets, M. King. Portfolio Returns and the Random Walk Theory: Reply. *J. Finance*, June 1973, *28*(3), pp. 742–45.

Chipman, John S. The Ordering of Portfolios in Terms of Mean and Variance. *Rev. Econ. Stud.*, April 1973, *40*(2), pp. 167–90.

Dince, Robert R. Finance and Banking: Refereed Papers II: Discussion. *J. Finance*, May 1973, *28*(2), pp. 541–44. [G: U.S.]

Dusak, Katherine. Futures Trading and Investor Returns: An Investigation of Commodity Market Risk Premiums. *J. Polit. Econ.*, November-December 1973, *81*(6), pp. 1387–1406.

Ellis, Dennis F. A Portfolio Selection Model—*à la* Arrow. *Amer. Econ.*, Spring 1973, *17*(1), pp. 103–14.

Elton, Edwin J. and Gruber, Martin J. Estimating the Dependence Structure of Share Prices—Implications for Portfolio Selection. *J. Finance*, December 1973, *28*(5), pp. 1203–32. [G: U.S.]

Falk, Haim and Ophir, Tsvi. The Influence of Differences in Accounting Policies on Investment Decisions. *J. Acc. Res.*, Spring 1973, *11*(1), pp. 108–16.

Falk, Haim and Ophir, Tsvi. The Effect of Risk on the Use of Financial Statements by Investment Decision-Makers: A Case Study. *Accounting Rev.*, April 1973, *48*(2), pp. 323–38. [G: Israel]

Fama, Eugene F. and MacBeth, James D. Risk, Return, and Equilibrium: Empirical Tests. *J. Polit. Econ.*, May-June 1973, *81*(3), pp. 607–36. [G: U.S.]

Fama, Eugene F. Risk, Return, and Portfolio Analysis: Reply. *J. Polit. Econ.*, May-June 1973, *81*(3), pp. 753–55.

Fama, Eugene F. A Note on the Market Model and the Two-Parameter Model. *J. Finance*, December 1973, *28*(5), pp. 1181–85.

Folks, William R., Jr. The Optimal Level of Forward Exchange Transactions. *J. Financial Quant. Anal.*, January 1973, *8*(1), pp. 105–10.

Fraser, Donald R. and Rose, Peter S. Short-Run Bank Portfolio Behavior: An Examination of Selected Liquid Assets. *J. Finance*, May 1973, *28*(2), pp. 531–37. [G: U.S.]

Gordon, Myron J. Causes and Predictions of Rates of Return on Stocks and Bonds: Discussion. *J. Finance*, May 1973, *28*(2), pp. 318–20. [G: U.S.]

Gray, M. R. and Parkin, Michael. Portfolio Diversification as Optimal Precautionary Behaviour. In *Morishima, M., et al.*, 1973, pp. 301–15.

Harris, Duane G. A Model of Bank Loan Term Adjustment. *Western Econ. J.*, December 1973, *11* (4), pp. 451–62.

Heckerman, Donald G. Portfolio Selection when Future Prices of Consumption Goods May Change:

Reply. *J. Finance*, December 1973, *28*(5), pp. 1361.

Heckerman, Donald G. On the Effects of Exchange Risk. *J. Int. Econ.*, November 1973, *3*(4), pp. 379–87.

Heintz, James A. Price-Level Restated Financial Statements and Investment Decision Making. *Accounting Rev.*, October 1973, *48*(4), pp. 679–89.

Hempel, George H. and Kretschman, Stephen R. Comparative Performances of Portfolio Maturity Policies of Commercial Banks. *Miss. Val. J. Bus. Econ.*, Fall 1973, *9*(1), pp. 55–75. [G: U.S.]

Herzog, John P. Natural Behavior Toward Risk and the Question of Value Determination: Comment. *J. Financial Quant. Anal.*, March 1973, *8*(2), pp. 357–59.

Hull, J.; Moore, P. G. and Thomas, H. Utility and its Measurement. *J. Roy. Statist. Soc.*, Part 2, 1973, *136*, pp. 226–47.

Huntsman, Blaine. Natural Behavior Toward Risk and the Question of Value Determination. *J. Financial Quant. Anal.*, March 1973, *8*(2), pp. 335–50.

Jean, William H. More on Multidimensional Portfolio Analysis. *J. Financial Quant. Anal.*, June 1973, *8*(3), pp. 475–90.

Kamoike, Osamu. Portfolio Selection when Future Prices of Consumption Goods May Change: Comment. *J. Finance*, December 1973, *28*(5), pp. 1357–60.

Klemkosky, Robert C. The Bias in Composite Performance Measures. *J. Financial Quant. Anal.*, June 1973, *8*(3), pp. 505–14.

Klevorick, Alvin K. A Note on "The Ordering of Portfolios in Terms of Mean and Variance." *Rev. Econ. Stud.*, April 1973, *40*(2), pp. 293–96.

Lee, Sang M. and Lerro, A. J. Optimizing the Portfolio Selection for Mutual Funds. *J. Finance*, December 1973, *28*(5), pp. 1087–1102.

Lessard, Donald R. International Portfolio Diversification: A Multivariate Analysis for a Group of Latin American Countries. *J. Finance*, June 1973, *28*(3), pp. 619–33. [G: Colombia; Chile; Brazil; Argentina]

Levy, Haim. The Demand for Assets Under Conditions of Risk. *J. Finance*, March 1973, *28*(1), pp. 79–96.

Levy, Haim. Stochastic Dominance, Efficiency Criteria, and Efficient Portfolios: The Multi-Period Case. *Amer. Econ. Rev.*, December 1973, *63*(5), pp. 986–94.

Levy, Haim. Stochastic Dominance Among Log-Normal Prospects. *Int. Econ. Rev.*, October 1973, *14*(3), pp. 601–14.

Mantripragada, K. Capital Management and Capital Theory: Discussion. *J. Finance*, May 1973, *28*(2), pp. 369–72. [G: U.S.]

Marinacos, George N. Big Board: Does it Really Increase Market Price? *Marquette Bus. Rev.*, Winter 1973, *17*(4), pp. 197–200. [G: U.S.]

Mayers, David. Nonmarketable Assets and the Determination of Capital Asset Prices in the Absence of a Riskless Asset. *J. Bus.*, April 1973, *46*(2), pp. 258–67.

McDonald, John G. and Baron, Donald C. Risk and Return on Short Positions in Common Stocks. *J.*

Finance, March 1973, *28*(1), pp. 97–107. [G: U.S.]

McEnally, Richard W. Some Portfolio-Relevant Risk Characteristics of Long-Term Marketable Securities. *J. Financial Quant. Anal.*, September 1973, *8*(4), pp. 565–85. [G: U.S.]

McGuigan, James R. and King, William R. Security Option Strategy under Risk Aversion: An Analysis. *J. Financial Quant. Anal.*, January 1973, *8*(1), pp. 1–15.

McLure, Charles E., Jr. Investment Life Insurance Versus Term Insurance and Separate Investment: A Determination of Expected-Return Equivalents: Comment. *J. Risk Ins.*, June 1973, *40*(2), pp. 291–93.

McQuown, J. A. Technical and Fundamental Analysis and Capital Market Theory. *J. Bank Res.*, Spring 1973, *4*(1), pp. 8–17.

Merton, Robert C. The Relationship Between Put and Call Option Prices: Comment. *J. Finance*, March 1973, *28*(1), pp. 183–84.

Miller, Marcus H. "Competition and Credit Control" and the Open Economy. *Manchester Sch. Econ. Soc. Stud.*, March 1973, *41*(1), pp. 123–40. [G: U.K.]

Morishima, M. A Two-Parametric 'Revealed-Preference' Theory of Portfolio Selection. In *Morishima, M., et al.*, 1973, pp. 287–300.

Neave, Edwin H. and Rorke, C. Harvey. Risk, Ruin, and Investment Analysis: Comment. *J. Financial Quant. Anal.*, June 1973, *8*(3), pp. 517–26.

O'Connor, Melvin C. On the Usefulness of Financial Ratios to Investors in Common Stock. *Accounting Rev.*, April 1973, *48*(2), pp. 339–52. [G: U.S.]

Oudet, Bruno A. and von Furstenberg, George M. The Valuation of Common Stocks During Periods of Inflation. *Z. Nationalökon.*, 1973, *33*(1–2), pp. 67–78. [G: U.S.]

Petersen, Russell J. Interindustry Estimation of General Price-level Impact on Financial Information. *Accounting Rev.*, January 1973, *48*(1), pp. 34–43. [G: U.S.]

Porter, R. Burr. An Empirical Comparison of Stochastic Dominance and Mean-Variance Portfolio Choice Criteria. *J. Financial Quant. Anal.*, September 1973, *8*(4), pp. 587–608. [G: U.S.]

Porter, R. Burr; Wart, James R. and Ferguson, Donald L. Efficient Algorithms for Conducting Stochastic Dominance Tests on Large Numbers of Portfolios. *J. Financial Quant. Anal.*, January 1973, *8*(1), pp. 71–81.

Pye, Gordon. Lifetime Portfolio Selection in Continuous Time for a Multiplicative Class of Utility Functions. *Amer. Econ. Rev.*, December 1973, *63*(5), pp. 1013–16.

Reints, William W. and Vandenberg, Pieter A. A Comment on the Risk Level Discriminatory Powers of the Wiesenberger Classifications. *J. Bus.*, April 1973, *46*(2), pp. 278–83.

Remaley, William A. Suboptimization in Mean-Variance Efficient Set Analysis. *J. Finance*, May 1973, *28*(2), pp. 397–403.

Roll, Richard. Evidence on the "Growth-Optimum" Model. *J. Finance*, June 1973, *28*(3), pp. 551–66. [G: U.S.]

Rubinstein, Mark E. The Fundamental Theorem of

Parameter-Preference Security Valuation. *J. Financial Quant. Anal.*, January 1973, *8*(1), pp. 61–69.

Rubinstein, Mark E. A Mean-Variance Synthesis of Corporate Financial Theory. *J. Finance*, March 1973, *28*(1), pp. 167–81.

Ryan, Terence M. The Demand for Financial Assets by the British Life Funds. *Oxford Bull. Econ. Statist.*, February 1973, *35*(1), pp. 61–67. [G: U.K.]

Ryan, Terence M. Security Prices as Markov Processes. *J. Financial Quant. Anal.*, January 1973, *8* (1), pp. 17–36.

Schilbred, Cornelius M. The Market Price of Risk. *Rev. Econ. Stud.*, April 1973, *40*(2), pp. 283–92. [G: Italy]

Scholes, Myron S. Causes and Predictions of Rates of Return on Stocks and Bonds: Discussion. *J. Finance*, May 1973, *28*(2), pp. 315–18. [G: U.S.]

Scott, David F., Jr. and Petty, J. William. An Analysis of Corporate Insider Trading Activity. *J. Econ. Bus.*, Fall 1973, *26*(1), pp. 19–24. [G: U.S.]

Sharpe, Ian G. A Quarterly Econometric Model of Portfolio Choice—Part I: Specification and Estimation Problems. *Econ. Rec.*, December 1973, *49* (128), pp. 518–33.

Silverberg, Stanley C. Deposit Costs and Bank Portfolio Policy. *J. Finance*, September 1973, *28*(4), pp. 881–95. [G: U.S.]

Silvers, J. B. An Alternative to the Yield Spread as a Measure of Risk. *J. Finance*, September 1973, *28* (4), pp. 933–55. [G: U.S.]

Soldofsky, Robert M. and Jennings, Edward H. Risk-Premium Curves: Empirical Evidence on Their Changing Position, 1950 to 1970. *Quart. Rev. Econ. Bus.*, Spring 1973, *13*(1), pp. 49–68. [G: U.S.]

Stewart, Samuel S., Jr. Shifts in Equity Composition and Market Performance. *Miss. Val. J. Bus. Econ.*, Fall 1973, *9*(1), pp. 12–17. [G: U.S.]

Stoll, Hans R. The Relationship Between Put and Call Option Prices: Reply. *J. Finance*, March 1973, *28*(1), pp. 185–87.

Stone, Bernell K. A Linear Programming Formulation of the General Portfolio Selection Problem. *J. Financial Quant. Anal.*, September 1973, *8*(4), pp. 621–36.

Tepper, Irwin. Revealed Preference Methods and the Pure Theory of the Cost of Capital. *J. Finance*, March 1973, *28*(1), pp. 35–48.

Treynor, Jack L. and Black, Fischer. How to Use Security Analysis to Improve Portfolio Selection. *J. Bus.*, January 1973, *46*(1), pp. 66–86.

Tsiang, S. C. Risk, Return, and Portfolio Analysis: Comment. *J. Polit. Econ.*, May-June 1973, *81*(3), pp. 748–52. [G: U.S.]

Vanthienen, L. Portfolio Theorie en Bedrijfsfinanciering. (With English summary.) *Tijdschr. Econ.*, 1973, *18*(4), pp. 597–627.

Vasicek, Oldrich A. A Note on Using Cross-Sectional Information in Bayesian Estimation of Security Betas. *J. Finance*, December 1973, *28*(5), pp. 1233–39.

Verbrugge, James A. The Effects of Pledging Regulations on Bank Asset Composition. *J. Bank Res.*, Autumn 1973, *4*(3), pp. 168–76. [G: U.S.]

Watts, Ross. The Information Content of Dividends. *J. Bus.*, April 1973, *46*(2), pp. 191–211. [G: U.S.]

Weber, Harry. God as Portfolio Manager. *J. Finance*, December 1973, *28*(5), pp. 1353–55.

West, Richard R. and Tinic, Seha M. Portfolio Returns and the Random Walk Theory: Comment. *J. Finance*, June 1973, *28*(3), pp. 733–41.

Zabel, Edward. Consumer Choice, Portfolio Decisions, and Transaction Costs. *Econometrica*, March 1973, *41*(2), pp. 321–35.

314 Financial Intermediaries

3140 Financial Intermediaries

Addo, John Sackah. Savings Banks and Savings Facilities in African Countries: Ghana. In *Alberici, A. and Baravelli, M., eds.*, 1973, pp. 37–39. [G: Ghana]

Arcucci, Francesco and Frediani, Lorenzo. Savings Banks and Savings Facilities in African Countries: Malawi. In *Alberici, A. and Baravelli, M., eds.*, 1973, pp. 55–59. [G: Malawi]

Babingui, Denis. Savings Banks and Savings Facilities in African Countries: Congo Brazzaville. In *Alberici, A. and Baravelli, M., eds.*, 1973, pp. 19–21. [G: Congo Brazzaville]

Bácskai, T. The Experience of Savings-Banks in Socialist Economies and its Applicability to Developing Countries. *Acta Oecon.*, 1973, *10*(2), pp. 201–16.

Barr, Joseph W. A Revised Regulatory Framework. In *Federal Reserve Bank of Boston*, 1973, pp. 205–08. [G: U.S.]

Belkhodja, Hassen. Savings Banks and Savings Facilities in African Countries: Tunisia. In *Alberici, A. and Baravelli, M., eds.*, 1973, pp. 115–20. [G: Tunisia]

Benston, George J. A Revised Regulatory Framework: Discussion. In *Federal Reserve Bank of Boston*, 1973, pp. 216–21. [G: U.S.]

Birara, Jean. Savings Banks and Savings Facilities in African Countries: Rwanda. In *Alberici, A. and Baravelli, M., eds.*, 1973, pp. 81. [G: Rwanda]

Boorman, John T. and Peterson, Manferd O. Instability of Savings Flows and Mortgage Lending by Financial Intermediaries. *Southern Econ. J.*, October 1973, *40*(2), pp. 297–312. [G: U.S.]

Boubacar, Mamadou N'Diaye. Savings Banks and Savings Facilities in African Countries: Dahomey. In *Alberici, A. and Baravelli, M., eds.*, 1973, pp. 23–27. [G: Dahomey]

Boyd, John H. Some Recent Developments in the Savings and Loan Deposit Markets. *J. Money, Credit, Banking*, August 1973, *5*(3), pp. 733–50. [G: U.S.]

Braemer, Pierre. Savings Banks and Savings Facilities in African Countries: Mauritania. In *Alberici, A. and Baravelli, M., eds.*, 1973, pp. 63–64. [G: Mauritania]

Congo, M. Savings Banks and Savings Facilities in African Countries: Upper Volta. In *Alberici, A. and Baravelli, M., eds.*, 1973, pp. 125–28. [G: Upper Volta]

Coste, Roger. Les entreprises financières en mutation face au commerce de l'épargne. (The Trade of Savings and the Change of Financial Firms. With English summary.) *Consommation,* January-March 1973, *20*(1), pp. 37–57.   [G: France]

Dammann, Axel. Monetary Policy in Norway. In *Holbik, K., ed.,* 1973, pp. 329–74.   [G: Norway]

Davidson, Paul. Inequality and the Double Bluff. *Ann. Amer. Acad. Polit. Soc. Sci.,* September 1973, *409,* pp. 24–33.

Dematté, Claudio. Savings Banks and Savings Facilities in African Countries: Mali. In *Alberici, A. and Baravelli, M., eds.,* 1973, pp. 61–62.   [G: Mali]

Dentzer, William T. A Revised Regulatory Framework: Discussion. In *Federal Reserve Bank of Boston,* 1973, pp. 209–15.   [G: U.S.]

Dran, John J., Jr. A Comparison of Credit Union Efficiency by Chartering Authority: An Ohio Case Study. *Marquette Bus. Rev.,* Fall 1973, *17*(3), pp. 155–65.   [G: U.S.]

Fand, David I. The Viability of Thrift Intermediaries as Financial Institutions. *Banca Naz. Lavoro Quart. Rev.,* September 1973, (106), pp. 235–68.   [G: U.S.]

Fisher, Thomas E. Il finanziamento del credito rateale in Gran Bretagna. (Instalment Credit Finance in the United Kingdom. With English summary.) *Bancaria,* January 1973, *29*(1), pp. 23–29.   [G: U.K.]

Ford, William F. and Tuccillo, John A. Monetary Policy Implications of the Hunt Commission Report. *Quart. Rev. Econ. Bus.,* Autumn 1973, *13*(3), pp. 93–103.   [G: U.S.]

Fortune, Peter. A Theory of Optimal Life Insurance: Development and Tests. *J. Finance,* June 1973, *28* (3), pp. 587–600.   [G: U.S.]

Gado, Abdou. Savings Banks and Savings Facilities in African Countries: Niger. In *Alberici, A. and Baravelli, M., eds.,* 1973, pp. 77–79.   [G: Niger]

Ghafari, R. Saving and Investment and the Effects of Financial Intermediaries on the Rate of Change of G.N.P. in Iran 1936–71. *Tahq. Eq.,* Winter & Spring 1973, *10*(29 & 30), pp. 50–79.   [G: Iran]

Gilleran, Robert T. Regulating Risk-Taking by Mutual Funds. *Yale Law J.,* May 1973, *82*(6), pp. 1305–24.

Goldsmith, Raymond W. Basic Considerations. In *Goldsmith, R. W., ed.,* 1973, pp. 1–33. [G: U.S.]

Goldsmith, Raymond W. The Position of Institutional Investors and of Corporate Stock in the National Balance Sheets and the Flow of Funds Accounts of the United States of America, 1952–68. In *Goldsmith, R. W., ed.,* 1973, pp. 91–164.   [G: U.S.]

Grebler, Leo. The Effect of FHLB Bond Operations on Savings Inflows at Savings and Loan Associations: Comment. *J. Finance,* March 1973, *28*(1), pp. 198–202.

Greene, Mark R. Should Variable Policy Loan Interest Rates be Adopted? *J. Risk Ins.,* December 1973, *40*(4), pp. 585–98.   [G: U.S.]

Hall, George R. Expanded Powers for Depositary Financial Institutions: Discussion. In *Federal Reserve Bank of Boston,* 1973, pp. 72–76. [G: U.S.]

Heim, Axel. L'attività degli istituti di credito rateale in Germania. (West German Instalment-Sales Financing Institutions. With English summary.) *Bancaria,* January 1973, *29*(1), pp. 30–39.   [G: W. Germany]

Hendershott, Patric H. Financial Disintermediation in a Macroeconomic Framework: Reply. *J. Finance,* September 1973, *28*(4), pp. 1033–34.

Herman, Edward S. Expanded Powers for Depositary Financial Institutions: Discussion. In *Federal Reserve Bank of Boston,* 1973, pp. 64–71.   [G: U.S.]

Herzi, Abdurahman Nur. Savings Banks and Savings Facilities in African Countries: Somalia. In *Alberici, A. and Baravelli, M., eds.,* 1973, pp. 93–96.   [G: Somalia]

Horton, Alexander Romeo. Savings Banks and Savings Facilities in African Countries: Liberia. In *Alberici, A. and Baravelli, M., eds.,* 1973, pp. 47–48.   [G: Liberia]

Ikinda, Antoine. Savings Banks and Savings Facilities in African Countries: Gabon. In *Alberici, A. and Baravelli, M., eds.,* 1973, pp. 33–34. [G: Gabon]

Iwasa, Yoshizane. Banking in Japan. In *Moskoff, W., ed.,* 1973, pp. 33–54.   [G: Japan]

Jacobs, Donald P. and Phillips, Almarin. Overview of the Commission's Philosophy and Recommendations. In *Federal Reserve Bank of Boston,* 1973, pp. 9–20.   [G: U.S.]

Johnson, A. S. C. Savings Banks and Savings Facilities in African Countries: Sierra Leone. In *Alberici, A. and Baravelli, M., eds.,* 1973, pp. 87–92.   [G: Sierra Leone]

Kalchbrenner, John H. A Summary of the Current Financial Intermediary, Mortgage, and Housing Sectors of the FRB-MIT-Penn Econometric Model. In *Ricks, R. B., ed.,* 1973, pp. 93–124.   [G: U.S.]

Kalyanasundaram, R. Regulation of Chit Funds. In *Simha, S. L. N., ed.,* 1973, pp. 279–83.   [G: India]

Kamulegeya, Edric Spencer. Savings Banks and Savings Facilities in African Countries: Uganda. In *Alberici, A. and Baravelli, M., eds.,* 1973, pp. 121–24.   [G: Uganda]

Kane, Edward J. Proposals for Rechanneling Funds to Meet Social Priorities: Discussion. In *Federal Reserve Bank of Boston,* 1973, pp. 190–98.   [G: U.S.]

Karani, Hiram. Savings Banks and Savings Facilities in African Countries: Kenya. In *Alberici, A. and Baravelli, M., eds.,* 1973, pp. 41–43. [G: Kenya]

Kaufman, George G. The Questionable Benefit of Variable-Rate Mortgages. *Quart. Rev. Econ. Bus.,* Autumn 1973, *13*(3), pp. 43–52.   [G: U.S.]

Kaufman, Herbert M. An Examination of the Financing of Federal Home Loan Bank Advances: A Comment. *Rev. Econ. Statist.,* May 1973, *55*(2), pp. 257–58.   [G: U.S.]

Kientz, Jean. Savings Banks and Savings Facilities in African Countries: Madagascar. In *Alberici, A. and Baravelli, M., eds.,* 1973, pp. 49–53.   [G: Madagascar]

Klein, Michael A. The Economics of Security Divisibility and Financial Intermediation. *J. Finance,* September 1973, *28*(4), pp. 923–31.

Kongbo, Basile. Savings Banks and Savings Facilities in African Countries: Central African Republic.

In *Alberici, A. and Baravelli, M., eds.*, 1973, pp. 7–10.   [G: Central African Rep.]

Kwon, Jene K. and Thornton, Richard M. The Effect of FHLB Bond Operations on Savings Inflows at Savings and Loan Associations: Reply. *J. Finance*, March 1973, *28*(1), pp. 203–06.

Kwon, Jene K. and Thornton, Richard M. An Examination of the Financing of Federal Home Loan Bank Advances: A Reply. *Rev. Econ. Statist.*, May 1973, *55*(2), pp. 258.   [G: U.S.]

Laokole, Jean-Baptiste. Savings Banks and Savings Facilities in African Countries: Chad. In *Alberici, A. and Baravelli, M., eds.*, 1973, pp. 11–17.
[G: Chad]

Macbeth, Thomas G. and Downey, Gerald F. The Monetary Consequences of Demand Deposit Creation by Mutual Savings Banks—The Commonwealth of Massachusetts Case. *Marquette Bus. Rev.*, Spring 1973, *17*(1), pp. 1–8. [G: U.S.]

Mankoubi, Bawa Sandani. Savings Banks and Savings Facilities in African Countries: Togo. In *Alberici, A. and Baravelli, M., eds.*, 1973, pp. 111–13.
[G: Togo]

Marchesini, Giambattista. Il ruolo del mercato del credito nel ciclo di produzione del reddito, II. (Role of the Credit Market in the Income Production Cycle, II. With English summary.) *Bancaria*, November 1973, *29*(11), pp. 1346–57.

Marchesini, Giambattista. Il ruolo del mercato del credito nel ciclo di produzione del reddito, I. (Role of the Credit Market in the Income Production Cycle, I. With English summary.) *Bancaria*, October 1973, *29*(10), pp. 1239–43.

M'Baye, M. Savings Banks and Savings Facilities in African Countries: Senegal. In *Alberici, A. and Baravelli, M., eds.*, 1973, pp. 83–86. [G: Senegal]

McDonald, John G. French Mutual Fund Performance: Evaluation of Internationally-Diversified Portfolios. *J. Finance*, December 1973, *28*(5), pp. 1161–80.   [G: France]

McWilliams, James D. A Closer Look at Incentive Fees for Bank Managed Pension Funds. *J. Bank Res.*, Winter 1973, *3*(4), pp. 238–46. [G: U.S.]

Mikitani, Ryoichi. Monetary Policy in Japan. In *Holbik, K., ed.*, 1973, pp. 246–81.   [G: Japan]

Mitchell, George W. Statements to Congress. *Fed. Res. Bull.*, April 1973, *59*(4), pp. 276–80.
[G: U.S.]

Mondanga, Emony. Savings Banks and Savings Facilities in African Countries: Zaire. In *Alberici, A. and Baravelli, M., eds.*, 1973, pp. 129–31.
[G: Zaire]

Murray, Roger F. Pension Funds: Newest Among Major Financial Institutions. *J. Bank Res.*, Winter 1973, *3*(4), pp. 247–60.   [G: U.S.]

Nagata, Ernest A. The Cost Structure of Consumer Finance Small-Loan Operations. *J. Finance*, December 1973, *28*(5), pp. 1327–37. [G: U.S.]

Nelson, Jane. Swiss Banks. In *Moskoff, W., ed.*, 1973, pp. 28–33.   [G: Switzerland]

Nesci, Vincenzo. Savings Banks and Savings Facilities in African Countries: Morocco. In *Alberici, A. and Baravelli, M., eds.*, 1973, pp. 69–76. [G: Morocco]

Nlend, Emmanuel. Savings Banks and Savings Facili-

ties in African Countries: Cameroon. In *Alberici, A. and Baravelli, M., eds.*, 1973, pp. 1–5.
[G: Cameroon]

Onado, Marco and Porteri, Antonio. Savings Banks and Savings Facilities in African Countries: Lesotho. In *Alberici, A. and Baravelli, M., eds.*, 1973, pp. 45–46.   [G: Lesotho]

Parthasarathy, L. S. Chit Funds: Commission's Report and Suggestions. In *Simha, S. L. N., ed.*, 1973, pp. 272–78.   [G: India]

Peeran, S. T. Control over Non-Banking Financial Intermediaries by the Reserve Bank. In *Simha, S. L. N., ed.*, 1973, pp. 252–64.   [G: India]

Peterson, Manferd O. Some Evidence on Intraregional Differences in Yields of Costs of Mortgage Lending. *Land Econ.*, February 1973, *49*(1), pp. 96–99.

Portugués, Juan Marrero. Savings Banks and Savings Facilities in African Countries: Equatorial Guinea. In *Alberici, A. and Baravelli, M., eds.*, 1973, pp. 29–32.   [G: Equatorial Guinea]

Puckett, A. Marshall. Consumer Financial Management and Financial Institution Response—A Two-Decade Perspective: Response. In *Sheldon, E. B., ed.*, 1973, pp. 363–67.   [G: U.S.]

Radhakrishnan, S. The Future Role of Some Non-Banking Financial Intermediaries. In *Simha, S. L. N., ed.*, 1973, pp. 265–71.   [G: India]

Rahman El Sheikh, Ahmed Abdel. Savings Banks and Savings Facilities in African Countries: Sudan. In *Alberici, A. and Baravelli, M., eds.*, 1973, pp. 97–101.   [G: Sudan]

Rettaroli, Riccardo. L'esperienza delle SICAV in Francia. (The SICAV Experience in France. With English summary.) *Bancaria*, April 1973, *29*(4), pp. 453–66.   [G: France]

Roenfeldt, Rodney L. and Tuttle, Donald L. An Examination of the Discounts and Premiums of Closed-End Investment Companies. *J. Bus. Res.*, Fall 1973, *1*(2), pp. 129–40.   [G: U.S.]

Ruozi, Roberto. Savings Banks and Savings Facilities in African Countries: Introduction. In *Alberici, A. and Baravelli, M., eds.*, 1973, pp. ix–xxiii.
[G: Africa]

Rybczynski, T. M. The Merchant Banks. *Manchester Sch. Econ. Soc. Stud.*, March 1973, *41*(1), pp. 107–21.   [G: U.K.]

Schott, Francis H. Consumer Financial Management and Financial Institution Response—A Two-Decade Perspective. In *Sheldon, E. B., ed.*, 1973, pp. 311–62.   [G: U.S.]

Senghore, Alhagi A. J. Savings Banks and Savings Facilities in African Countries: Gambia. In *Alberici, A. and Baravelli, M., eds.*, 1973, pp. 35–36.
[G: Gambia]

Shapiro, Eli. Proposals for Rechanneling Funds to Meet Social Priorities: Discussion. In *Federal Reserve Bank of Boston*, 1973, pp. 199–204.
[G: U.S.]

Shiralkar, S. S. Non-Banking Financial Intermediaries. In *Simha, S. L. N., ed.*, 1973, pp. 241–51.
[G: India]

Sidambaram, Mootoosamy. Savings Banks and Savings Facilities in African Countries: Mauritius. In *Alberici, A. and Baravelli, M., eds.*, 1973, pp. 65–67.   [G: Mauritius]

Silber, William L. A Model of Federal Home Loan Bank System and Federal National Mortgage Association Behavior. *Rev. Econ. Statist.,* August 1973, *55*(3), pp. 308–20. [G: U.S.]

Strazheim, Mahlon R. The Demand for Corporate Stock in the Postwar Period. In *Goldsmith, R. W., ed.,* 1973, pp. 204–65. [G: U.S.]

Thurow, Lester C. Proposals for Rechanneling Funds to Meet Social Priorities. In *Federal Reserve Bank of Boston,* 1973, pp. 179–89. [G: U.S.]

Tice, Helen Stone and Duff, Virginia A. Basic Statistical Data. In *Goldsmith, R. W., ed.,* 1973, pp. 269–342. [G: U.S.]

Tindale, L. V. D. New Era in Finance. In *Rybczynski, T. M., ed.,* 1973, pp. 96–105. [G: U.K.]

Trieschmann, James S. and Pinches, George E. A Multivariate Model for Predicting Financially Distressed P-L Insurers. *J. Risk Ins.,* September 1973, *40*(3), pp. 327–38. [G: U.S.]

Vachha, Homiar S. and Iyengar, Sampath S. Financial Institutions and Backward Regions: A Case Study of Gujarat. *Artha-Vikas,* January-July 1973, *9*(1–2), pp. 185–202. [G: India]

Van Horne, James C. The Effect of FHLB Bond Operations on Savings Inflows at Savings and Loan Associations: Comment. *J. Finance,* March 1973, *28*(1), pp. 194–97.

de la Vergne, Pierre. Le società finanziarie in Francia—Attività e regime giuridico. (Finance Companies in France: Activities and Juridical Regime. With English summary.) *Bancaria,* January 1973, *29*(1), pp. 17–22. [G: France]

Vernon, Jack. Financial Disintermediation in a Macroeconomic Framework: Comment. *J. Finance,* September 1973, *28*(4), pp. 1029–32.

Vikbladh, Inge. Monetary Policy in Sweden. In *Holbik, K., ed.,* 1973, pp. 375–422. [G: Sweden]

Wai, U Tun and Patrick, Hugh T. Stock and Bond Issues and Capital Markets in Less Developed Countries. *Int. Monet. Fund Staff Pap.,* July 1973, *20*(2), pp. 253–317.

Weinrobe, Maurice D. The Demand for Money by Six Non-Bank Financial Intermediaries. *Western Econ. J.,* June 1973, *11*(2), pp. 191–213. [G: U.S.]

Wille, Frank. Expanded Powers for Depositary Financial Institutions. In *Federal Reserve Bank of Boston,* 1973, pp. 55–63. [G: U.S.]

Yona, Daniel A. N. Savings Banks and Savings Facilities in African Countries: Tanzania. In *Alberici, A. and Baravelli, M., eds.,* 1973, pp. 103–09. [G: Tanzania]

Ziock, Richard W. A Realistic Profit Model for Individual Non-Participating Life Insurance. *J. Risk Ins.,* September 1973, *40*(3), pp. 357–73. [G: U.S.]

315 Credit to Business, Consumer, etc. (including mortgages)

3150 General

Dran, John J., Jr. A Comparison of Credit Union Efficiency by Chartering Authority: An Ohio Case Study. *Marquette Bus. Rev.,* Fall 1973, *17*(3), pp. 155–65. [G: U.S.]

Guitian, Manuel. Credit Versus Money as an Instrument of Control. *Int. Monet. Fund Staff Pap.,* November 1973, *20*(3), pp. 785–800.

Gupta, Suraj B. The Controversy over Differential Lending Rates for Banks: An Examination. *Indian Econ. Rev.,* April 1973, *8*(1), pp. 16–38. [G: India]

Harris, Duane G. Some Evidence on Differential Lending Practices at Commercial Banks. *J. Finance,* December 1973, *28*(5), pp. 1303–11. [G: U.S.]

Johnson, A. S. C. Savings Banks and Savings Facilities in African Countries: Sierra Leone. In *Alberici, A. and Baravelli, M., eds.,* 1973, pp. 87–92. [G: Sierra Leone]

Lehto, Sakari T. Nej till styrda kreditströmmar. ("No" to Directed Credit Flows. With English summary.) *Ekon. Samfundets Tidskr.,* 1973, *26* (2), pp. 101–03. [G: Finland]

Lomax, David F. Reserve Assets and Competition and Credit Control. *Nat. Westminster Bank Quart. Rev.,* August 1973, pp. 36–46. [G: U.K.]

Maragi, Mario. La problematica del prestito su pegno. (Pledge Loan Problems. With English summary.) *Bancaria,* July 1973, *29*(7), pp. 813–19.

Mattsson, Peter. Projektanalys. (Project Analysis. With English summary.) *Ekon. Samfundets Tidskr.,* 1973, *26*(2), pp. 95–100. [G: Finland]

Parkin, Michael. The Discount Houses' Role in the Money Supply Control Process Under the "Competition and Credit Control" Regime. *Manchester Sch. Econ. Soc. Stud.,* March 1973, *41*(1), pp. 89–105. [G: U.K.]

Penkava, Jaromír. Improvements of the Finance and Credit System in Czechoslovakia. *Czech. Econ. Digest.,* August 1973, (5), pp. 3–24. [G: Czechoslovakia]

Penner, Rudolph G. and Silber, William L. The Interaction Between Federal Credit Programs and the Impact on the Allocation of Credit. *Amer. Econ. Rev.,* December 1973, *63*(5), pp. 838–52. [G: U.S.]

Potác, Svatopluk. The Role of Credit in the Plan-Based Management of the Czechoslovak Economy. *Czech. Econ. Digest.,* September 1973, (6), pp. 63–104. [G: Czechoslovakia]

Rao, D. C. and Kaminow, Ira. Selective Credit Controls and the Real Investment Mix: A General Equilibrium Approach. *J. Finance,* December 1973, *28*(5), pp. 1103–18.

Ray, Edward J. The Sources of Finance in West Germany. *Z. ges. Staatswiss.,* October 1973, *129* (4), pp. 663–84. [G: W. Germany]

Riesz, M. The Main Issues of Credit Theory in the Past 25 Years. *Acta Oecon.,* 1973, *10*(2), pp. 233–46. [G: Hungary]

Rubinfeld, Daniel. Credit Ratings and the Market for General Obligation Municipal Bonds. *Nat. Tax J.,* March 1973, *26*(1), pp. 17–27. [G: U.S.]

Silber, William L. Selective Credit Policies: A Survey. *Banca Naz. Lavoro Quart. Rev.,* December 1973, (107), pp. 328–51. [G: U.S.]

Sommariva, A. Some Theoretical Implications of the Model of the Bank of Italy. *Tijdschr. Econ.,* 1973, *18*(2), pp. 207–34. [G: Italy]

Spencer, Roger W. Strong Credit Demands, But No

"Crunch" in Early 1973. *Fed. Res. Bank St. Louis Rev.*, June 1973, *55*(6), pp. 2–10. [G: U.S.]

Valentine, T. J. The Loan Supply Function of Australian Trading Banks: An Empirical Analysis. *Australian Econ. Pap.*, June 1973, *12*(20), pp. 57–69. [G: Australia]

de la Vergne, Pierre. Le società finanziarie in Francia—Attività e regime giuridico. (Finance Companies in France: Activities and Juridical Regime. With English summary.) *Bancaria*, January 1973, *29*(1), pp. 17–22. [G: France]

Vikbladh, Inge. Monetary Policy in Sweden. In *Holbik, K., ed.*, 1973, pp. 375–422. [G: Sweden]

3151 Consumer Finance

Argentarius. Sviluppi e problemi attuali del credito al consumo. (Development and Current Problems of Consumer Credit. With English summary.) *Bancaria*, January 1973, *29*(1), pp. 76–83.

Avio, Kenneth L. An Economic Rationale for Statutory Interest Rate Ceilings. *Quart. Rev. Econ. Bus.*, Autumn 1973, *13*(3), pp. 61–72.

Brimmer, Andrew F. Statements to Congress. *Fed. Res. Bull.*, June 1973, *59*(6), pp. 429–32. [G: U.S.]

Bucher, Jeffrey M. Statements to Congress. *Fed. Res. Bull.*, June 1973, *59*(6), pp. 420–25. [G: U.S.]

Burke, William. Buying on Time. *Fed. Res. Bank San Francisco Rev.*, March-April 1973, pp. 3–11. [G: U.S.]

Cooper, Ronald L. An Econometric Forecasting Model of the Financial Sector of U.S. Households. *Appl. Econ.*, June 1973, *5*(2), pp. 101–17. [G: U.S.]

Daane, J. Dewey. Statements to Congress. *Fed. Res. Bull.*, June 1973, *59*(6), pp. 425–29. [G: U.S.]

Fisher, Thomas E. Il finanziamento del credito rateale in Gran Bretagna. (Instalment Credit Finance in the United Kingdom. With English summary.) *Bancaria*, January 1973, *29*(1), pp. 23–29. [G: U.K.]

Heim, Axel. L'attività degli istituti di credito rateale in Germania. (West German Instalment-Sales Financing Institutions. With English summary.) *Bancaria*, January 1973, *29*(1), pp. 30–39. [G: W. Germany]

Nagata, Ernest A. The Cost Structure of Consumer Finance Small-Loan Operations. *J. Finance*, December 1973, *28*(5), pp. 1327–37. [G: U.S.]

Prell, Michael J. The Long-Run Growth of Consumer Installment Credit—Some Observations. *Fed. Res. Bank Kansas City Rev.*, February 1973, pp. 3–13. [G: U.S.]

Seiders, David. Credit-Card and Check-Credit Plans at Commercial Banks. *Fed. Res. Bull.*, September 1973, *59*(9), pp. 646–53. [G: U.S.]

Wallace, George J. The Logic of Consumer Credit Reform. *Yale Law J.*, January 1973, *82*(3), pp. 461–82. [G: U.S.]

3152 Mortgage Market

Anderson, Paul S. and Eisenmenger, Robert W. Impact of the Proposed New Financial Structure on Mortgage Markets. In *Federal Reserve Bank of Boston*, 1973, pp. 149–72. [G: U.S.]

Arcelus, Francisco and Meltzer, Allan H. The Markets for Housing and Housing Services: Reply. *J. Money, Credit, Banking*, November 1973, *5*(4), pp. 973–78. [G: U.S.]

Arcelus, Francisco and Meltzer, Allan H. The Markets for Housing and Housing Services. *J. Money, Credit, Banking*, Part I, February 1973, *5*(1), pp. 78–99. [G: U.S.]

Boorman, John T. and Peterson, Manferd O. Instability of Savings Flows and Mortgage Lending by Financial Intermediaries. *Southern Econ. J.*, October 1973, *40*(2), pp. 297–312. [G: U.S.]

Brady, Eugene A. An Econometric Analysis of the U.S. Residential Housing Market. In *Ricks, R. B., ed.*, 1973, pp. 1–47. [G: U.S.]

Burns, Arthur F. Statement to Congress. *Fed. Res. Bull.*, September 1973, *59*(9), pp. 658–64. [G: U.S.]

Clauretie, Terrence M. Interest Rates, the Business Demand for Funds, and the Residential Mortgage Market: A Sectoral Econometric Study. *J. Finance*, December 1973, *28*(5), pp. 1313–26. [G: U.S.]

Fair, Ray C. and Jaffee, Dwight M. The Implications of the Proposals of the Hunt Commission for the Mortgage and Housing Markets: An Empirical Study. In *Federal Reserve Bank of Boston*, 1973, pp. 99–148. [G: U.S.]

Fair, Ray C. Monthly Housing Starts. In *Ricks, R. B., ed.*, 1973, pp. 69–91. [G: U.S.]

Fand, David I. The Viability of Thrift Intermediaries as Financial Institutions. *Banca Naz. Lavoro Quart. Rev.*, September 1973, (106), pp. 235–68. [G: U.S.]

Fromm, Gary. Econometric Models of the Residential Construction Sector: A Comparison. In *Ricks, R. B., ed.*, 1973, pp. 125–55. [G: U.S.]

Gibson, William E. Protecting Homebuilding from Restrictive Credit Conditions. *Brookings Pap. Econ. Act.*, 1973, (3), pp. 647–91. [G: U.S.]

Goh, Chui Muah. A Note on Housing Finance in Singapore. *Malayan Econ. Rev.*, October 1973, *18*(2), pp. 37–42. [G: Singapore]

Huang, David S. Short-Run Instability in Single-Family Housing Starts. *J. Amer. Statist. Assoc.*, December 1973, *68*(344), pp. 788–92. [G: U.S.]

Johnston, Verle. Housing: On the Way Down? *Fed. Res. Bank San Francisco Rev.*, January-February 1973, pp. 3–8. [G: U.S.]

Kalchbrenner, John H. A Summary of the Current Financial Intermediary, Mortgage, and Housing Sectors of the FRB-MIT-Penn Econometric Model. In *Ricks, R. B., ed.*, 1973, pp. 93–124. [G: U.S.]

Kaufman, George G. The Questionable Benefit of Variable-Rate Mortgages. *Quart. Rev. Econ. Bus.*, Autumn 1973, *13*(3), pp. 43–52. [G: U.S.]

Lin, Steven A. Y. Effects of Monetary Policy and Credit Conditions on the Housing Sector. *Amer. Real Estate Urban Econ. Assoc. J.*, June 1973, *1*(1), pp. 8–30. [G: U.S.]

Osgood, Russell K. Mutual-to-Stock Conversions and the Federal Home Loan Bank Board. *Yale Law J.*, January 1973, *82*(3), pp. 559–72. [G: U.S.]

Penner, Rudolph G. and Silber, William L. The Interaction Between Federal Credit Programs and the Impact on the Allocation of Credit. *Amer.*

Econ. Rev., December 1973, *63*(5), pp. 838–52.
[G: U.S.]

Peterson, Manferd O. Some Evidence on Intraregional Differences in Yields of Costs of Mortgage Lending. *Land Econ.*, February 1973, *49*(1), pp. 96–99.

Plant, Kenneth M. The Secondary Mortgage Market: Problems and Prospects. *Indiana Bus. Rev.*, January-February 1973, *48*, pp. 1–7. [G: U.S.]

Rakes, G. K. A Numerical Credit Evaluation Model for Residential Mortgages. *Quart. Rev. Econ. Bus.*, Autumn 1973, *13*(3), pp. 73–84. [G: U.S.]

Sharpe, Ian G. A Mortgage Model: Some Theoretical and Empirical Results as Applied to Australian Savings Banks. *Australian Econ. Pap.*, December 1973, *12*(21), pp. 208–20. [G: Australia]

Silber, William L. A Model of Federal Home Loan Bank System and Federal National Mortgage Association Behavior. *Rev. Econ. Statist.*, August 1973, *55*(3), pp. 308–20. [G: U.S.]

Stone, Michael E. Federal Housing Policy: A Political-Economic Analysis. In *Pynoos, J.; Schafer, R. and Hartman, C. W., eds.*, 1973, pp. 423–33.
[G: U.S.]

Swan, Craig. The Markets for Housing and Housing Services: Comment. *J. Money, Credit, Banking*, November 1973, *5*(4), pp. 960–72. [G: U.S.]

Wallich, Henry C. Discussion of the Implications of the Proposals of the Hunt Commission for the Mortgage and Housing Markets: An Empirical Study and Impact of the Proposed New Financial Structure on Mortgage Markets. In *Federal Reserve Bank of Boston*, 1973, pp. 173–78.
[G: U.S.]

Wentz, John and Mazza, Gertrude. The Acquisitive Bank Holding Companies: A Bigger Role in Mortgage Banking. *Fed. Res. Bank Bus. Rev. Phila.*, October 1973, pp. 7–8. [G: U.S.]

3153 Business Credit

Arunachalam, M. V. Role of Commercial Banks as Development Agencies. In *Simha, S. L. N., ed.*, 1973, pp. 223–29. [G: India]

Bates, Timothy. An Econometric Analysis of Lending to Black Businessmen. *Rev. Econ. Statist.*, August 1973, *55*(3), pp. 272–83. [G: U.S.]

Berger, Paul D. and Harper, William K. Determination of an Optimal Revolving Credit Agreement. *J. Financial Quant. Anal.*, June 1973, *8*(3), pp. 491–97.

Brahmananda, Palahalli Ramaiya. Commercial Banks as Development Agencies—Appraisal and Prospect. In *Simha, S. L. N., ed.*, 1973, pp. 208–22. [G: India]

Cole, William A. and Wales, Stephen H., Sr. The Investment Credit. *Manage. Account.*, March 1973, *54*(9), pp. 13–16, 35.

Eastburn, David P. A Crunch in '73? *Fed. Res. Bank Bus. Rev. Phila.*, June 1973, pp. 3–6. [G: U.S.]

Ford, Allen. Selecting a Useful Life for the Investment Credit. *Manage. Account.*, April 1973, *54* (10), pp. 14–16.

Joshi, Nandini U. Bank Credit Policy for Export Incentives. *Indian Econ. J.*, April-June 1973, *20* (4–5), pp. 638–45. [G: India]

Mishra, G. P.; Tripathy, B. N. and Pandey, Ram Lala. Role of Banking in Financing Rural Credit. *Econ. Aff.*, July 1973, *18*(7), pp. 313–25. [G: India]

Waris, Klaus. Styrningen av kreditströmmarna. (Directing the Credit Flows. With English summary.) *Ekon. Samfundets Tidskr.*, 1973, *26*(2), pp. 87–94. [G: Finland]

320 FISCAL THEORY AND POLICY; PUBLIC FINANCE

3200 General

Harriss, C. Lowell. Government Spending & Land Values: Public Money & Private Gain: Introduction. In *Harriss, C. L., ed.*, 1973, pp. ix–xix.
[G: U.S.]

321 Fiscal Theory and Policy

3210 Fiscal Theory and Policy

Alchian, Armen A. and Demsetz, Harold. The Property Rights Paradigm. *J. Econ. Hist.*, March 1973, *33*(1), pp. 16–27.

Andersen, Leonall C. A Note on the Effects of Government Finance on Aggregate Demand for Goods and Services—A Reply. *Public Finance*, 1973, *28*(3–4), pp. 397–406.

Andersen, Leonall C. The State of the Monetarist Debate. *Fed. Res. Bank St. Louis Rev.*, September 1973, *55*(9), pp. 2–8. [G: U.S.]

Andersen, Palle Schelde. Built-in Flexibility and Sensitivity of the Personal Income Tax in Denmark. *Swedish J. Econ.*, March 1973, *75*(1), pp. 1–18.
[G: Denmark]

Arndt, Sven W. Policy Choices in an Open Economy: Some Dynamic Considerations. *J. Polit. Econ.*, July-August 1973, *81*(4), pp. 916–35.

Azzi, Corry F. and Cox, James C. Equity and Efficiency in Evaluation of Public Programs. *Quart. J. Econ.*, August 1973, *87*(3), pp. 495–502.

Ball, R. J. Investment Incentives. *Nat. Westminster Bank Quart. Rev.*, August 1973, pp. 22–35.
[G: U.K.]

Beenhakker, Henri L. Discounting Indices Proposed for Capital Investment Evaluation: A Further Examination. *Eng. Econ.*, April-May 1973, *18*(3), pp. 149–68.

Biehl, Dieter, et al. On the Cyclical Effects of Budgetary Policy from 1960 to 1970 in the Federal Republic of Germany. *Ger. Econ. Rev.*, 1973, *11* (4), pp. 273–91. [G: W. Germany]

Boll, F. Multiplicatoren en economische politiek in verschillende wisselkoerssystemen. (Multipliers and Economic Policy under Various Exchange Rate Systems. With English summary.) *Tijdschr. Econ.*, 1973, *18*(3), pp. 381–427.

Brittain, John A. Research on the Transmission of Material Wealth. *Amer. Econ. Rev.*, May 1973, *63* (2), pp. 335–45.

Brunner, Karl. The State of the Monetarist Debate: A Comment. *Fed. Res. Bank St. Louis Rev.*, September 1973, *55*(9), pp. 9, 12–14.

Brunner, Karl, et al. Fiscal and Monetary Policies in

Moderate Inflation: Case Studies of Three Countries. *J. Money, Credit, Banking,* Part II, February 1973, *5*(1), pp. 313–53. **[G: U.S.; Germany; Italy]**

Burns, Arthur F. Statement to Congress. *Fed. Res. Bull.,* March 1973, *59*(3), pp. 164–68.

Buttler, Friedrich. Explikative und normative Theorie der meritorishen Güter—eine Problemanalyse. (A Theory of Merit Goods. With English summary.) *Z. Wirtschaft. Sozialwissen.,* 1973, *93*(2), pp. 129–46.

Cebula, Richard J. Deficit Spending, Expectations, and Fiscal Policy Effectiveness. *Public Finance,* 1973, *28*(3–4), pp. 362–70.

Chelliah, Raja J. Significance of Alternative Concepts of Budget Deficit. *Int. Monet. Fund Staff Pap.,* November 1973, *20*(3), pp. 741–84.

Diamond, Peter A. Taxation and Public Production in a Growth Setting. In *Mirrlees, J. A. and Stern, N. H., eds.,* 1973, pp. 215–35.

Dorn, Dietmar. Marketing in der Staatswirtschaft. (Marketing in Public Economy. With English summary.) *Z. Wirtschaft. Sozialwissen.,* 1973, *93* (1), pp. 21–33.

Farioletti, Marius. Tax Administration Funding and Fiscal Policy. *Nat. Tax J.,* March 1973, *26*(1), pp. 1–16. **[G: U.S.]**

Foulon, Alain. Consommation des ménages et consommation publique "divisible": Structure, évolution et financement 1959–1969. (Private Consumption and Public "Divisible" Consumption: Structure, Evolution and Financement. 1959–1969. With English summary.) *Consommation,* April-June 1973, *20*(2), pp. 5–94. **[G: France]**

Gardner, Bernard and Richardson, Peter. The Fiscal Treatment of Shipping. *J. Ind. Econ.,* December 1973, *22*(2), pp. 95–117. **[G: U.K.]**

Grünärml, Frohmund. Demand Management—Illusion oder Realität? (Demand Management—Illusion or Reality? With English summary.) *Z. Wirtschaft. Sozialwissen.,* 1973, *93*(5), pp. 537–66.

Haller, Heinz. Die Berücksichtigung des Lebensunterhalts der Kinder und der Vorsorgeaufwendungen im Rahmen der Steuerreform—Zielsetzungen und Implikationen. (The Consideration of Family Expenses for Children and of Providence Expenditures in the Tax Reform. With English summary.) *Z. ges. Staatswiss.,* August 1973, *129*(3), pp. 504–34. **[G: Germany]**

Harriss, C. Lowell. Capital Needs, Savings, and Jobs. In *Tax Foundation, Inc.,* 1973, pp. 27–34. **[G: U.S.]**

Haveman, Robert H. Private Power and Federal Policy. In *Haveman, R. H. and Hamrin, R. D., eds.,* 1973, pp. 3–8. **[G: U.S.]**

Hebert, Robert F. and Byrns, Ralph T. On the Cost-Inflationary Impact of High Interest Rates: Comment. *J. Econ. Issues,* September 1973, *7*(3), pp. 511–14.

Hulett, Joe R. On the Use of Regression Analysis with a Qualitative Dependent Variable. *Public Finance Quart.,* July 1973, *1*(3), pp. 339–44.

Klein, Lawrence R. The State of the Monetarist De-

bate: A Comment. *Fed. Res. Bank St. Louis Rev.,* September 1973, *55*(9), pp. 9–12.

Krainer, Robert E. Economic Structure and the Assignment Problem: A Contribution to the Theory of Macro-Economic Policy for Net Creditor Countries. *Can. J. Econ.,* May 1973, *6*(2), pp. 239–47.

Kumar, Rishi. Demand Policies and Internal-External Balance Under Fixed Exchange Rates—The Mundellian Assignment: A Reformulation and Some Extensions. *Weltwirtsch. Arch.,* 1973, *109* (2), pp. 253–73.

Lloyd, P. J. Optimal Intervention in a Distortion-Ridden Open Economy. *Econ. Rec.,* September 1973, *49*(127), pp. 377–93.

Madden, Carl H. Is Our Tax System Making Us Second-Rate? Tax Reform: Savings and Consumption. *Nat. Tax J.,* September 1973, *26*(3), pp. 403–07. **[G: U.S.]**

Marty, Alvin L. Growth, Satiety, and the Tax Revenue from Money Creation. *J. Polit. Econ.,* September-October 1973, *81*(5), pp. 1136–52.

Mathieson, Donald J. Traded Goods, Nontraded Goods, and the Balance of Payments. *Int. Econ. Rev.,* October 1973, *14*(3), pp. 615–24.

McGuire, Martin. Notes on Grants-in-Aid and Economic Interactions among Governments. *Can. J. Econ.,* May 1973, *6*(2), pp. 207–21.

McGuire, Thomas. A Note on Lindahl's Voluntary Exchange Theory. *Public Finance,* 1973, *28*(1), pp. 94–97.

McKean, Roland N. Government and the Consumer. *Southern Econ. J.,* April 1973, *39*(4), pp. 481–89.

McKenzie, Richard B. The Micro and Macro Economic Effects of Changes in the Statutory Tax Rates. *Rev. Soc. Econ.,* April 1973, *31*(1), pp. 20–30.

Molitor, Bruno. Öffentliche Leistungen in verteilungspolitischer Sicht. (Social Goods and Income Redistribution. With English summary.) *Z. Wirtschaft. Sozialwissen.,* 1973, *93*(2), pp. 147–58.

Myers, Myron G.; Rogstad, Barry K. and Wehner, Harrison G. A Theoretical Evaluation of Alternative Subsidy Schemes for Regional Development. *Amer. J. Agr. Econ.,* May 1973, *55*(2), pp. 304–12.

Naouri, Jean-Charles. Le financement des investissements publics. Les deux taux d'actualisation et la charge morte du transfert fiscal. (Financing Public Expenditure and the Deadweight Loss of Fiscal Transfers. With English summary.) *Revue Écon.,* July 1973, *24*(4), pp. 588–618.

Ohtsuki, Yoshitaka. Public Investment and Economic Growth—Fiscal Policy and Resource Allocation. (In Japanese. With English summary.) *Econ. Stud. Quart.,* December 1973, *24*(3), pp. 16–30.

Okun, Arthur M. Rules and Roles for Fiscal and Monetary Policy. In *Reynolds, L. G.; Green, G. D. and Lewis, D. R., eds.,* 1973, pp. 62–80. **[G: U.S.]**

Ostrom, Vincent. The Work of the Contemporary Political Economists. In *Ostrom, V.,* 1973, pp. 48–73.

Park, Yung C. The Transmission Process and the Relative Effectiveness of Monetary and Fiscal Policy in a Two-Sector Neoclassical Model. *J. Money, Credit, Banking,* May 1973, *5*(2), pp. 595–622.

Polinsky, A. Mitchell. A Note on the Measurement of Incidence. *Public Finance Quart.,* April 1973, *1*(2), pp. 219–30.

Prest, Alan R. Public Finance: Backward Area or New Frontier? *Economica, N.S.,* May 1973, *40* (158), pp. 121–35. [G: U.K.]

Recktenwald, Horst Claus. From Public Finance to Public Economics. In *Rectenwald, H. C., ed.,* 1973, pp. 424–36.

Richelson, Jeffrey. A Note on Collective Goods and the Theory of Political Entrepreneurship. *Public Choice,* Fall 1973, *16,* pp. 73–75.

Roberts, Donald John. Existence of Lindahl Equilibrium with a Measure Space of Consumers. *J. Econ. Theory,* August 1973, *6*(4), pp. 355–81.

Ross, Miceal. Procedures for Integrated Regional Planning. I: The Background to Decentralisation. *Econ. Soc. Rev.,* July 1973, *4*(4), pp. 523–42. [G: Ireland]

Ruggeri, Giuseppe C. Automatic Stabilizers, Business Cycles, and Economic Growth. *Kyklos,* 1973, *26*(2), pp. 288–306. [G: U.S.]

Schultze, Charles L. Perverse Incentives and the Inefficiency of Government. In *Haveman, R. H. and Hamrin, R. D., eds.,* 1973, pp. 15–22. [G: U.S.]

Scott, Anthony. The Defense of Federalism, or, the Attack on Unitary Government. *Amer. Econ.,* Fall 1973, *17*(2), pp. 162–69.

Szeplaki, Leslie. Pricing and Taxation in a Marxian Two-Sector Model: A Brief Reflection. *J. Econ. Theory,* August 1973, *6*(4), pp. 404–08.

Varga, Gy. On the System of Preferences. *Acta Oecon.,* 1973, *10*(1), pp. 52–66. [G: Hungary]

Wagner, Antonin. Die Auswirkung der öffentlichen Haushalte auf den Konjunkturverlauf in der Schweiz, 1955–1970. (The Effects of Public Finance on Trade Cycles in Switzerland, 1955–1970. With English summary.) *Schweiz. Z. Volkswirtsch. Statist.,* March 1973, *109*(1), pp. 17–57. [G: Switzerland]

3212 Fiscal Theory; Empirical Studies Illustrating Fiscal Theory

Ahluwalia, Montek S. Taxes, Subsidies, and Employment. *Quart. J. Econ.,* August 1973, *87*(3), pp. 393–409.

Akin, John S.; Fields, Gary S. and Neenan, William B. A Socioeconomic Explanation of Demand for Public Goods. *Public Finance Quart.,* April 1973, *1*(2), pp. 169–89. [G: U.S.]

Andic, Fuat M. Fiscal Reform in Colombia: A Review Article. *Finanzarchiv,* 1973, *32*(1), pp. 160–66. [G: Colombia]

Aoki, Masanao. On Sufficient Conditions for Optimal Stabilization Policies. *Rev. Econ. Stud.,* January 1973, *40*(1), pp. 131–38.

Atkinson, A. B. How Progressive Should Income Tax Be? In *Parkin, M., ed.,* 1973, pp. 90–109.

Barlow, Joel. The Tax Law Bias Against Investment

in Production Facilities. *Nat. Tax J.,* September 1973, *26*(3), pp. 415–37. [G: U.S.]

Behrens, Jean and Smolensky, Eugene. Alternative Definitions of Income Redistribution. *Public Finance,* 1973, *28*(3–4), pp. 315–32.

Bergstrom, Theodore C. and Goodman, Robert P. Private Demands for Public Goods. *Amer. Econ. Rev.,* June 1973, *63*(3), pp. 280–96.

Bernhard, Richard H. Consumer Surplus as an Index of User Benefit from Public Expenditure. *Eng. Econ.,* October-November 1973, *19*(1), pp. 1–33.

Bish, Robert L. and O'Donoghue, Patrick D. Public Goods, Increasing Cost, and Monopsony: Reply. *J. Polit. Econ.,* January-February 1973, *81*(1), pp. 231–36.

Blinder, Alan S. Note: Can Income Tax Increases Be Inflationary? *Nat. Tax J.,* June 1973, *26*(2), pp. 295–301.

Boadway, Robin W.; Maital, Shlomo and Prachowny, Martin F. J. Optimal Tariffs, Optimal Taxes and Public Goods. *J. Public Econ.,* November 1973, *2* (4), pp. 391–403.

Boadway, Robin W. Similarities and Differences between Public Goods and Public Factors. *Public Finance,* 1973, *28*(3–4), pp. 245–58.

Booms, Bernard H. and Halldorson, James R. The Politics of Redistribution: A Reformulation. *Amer. Polit. Sci. Rev.,* September 1973, *67*(3), pp. 924–33. [G: U.S.]

Boskin, Michael J. Local Government Tax and Product Competition and the Optimal Provision of Public Goods. *J. Polit. Econ.,* January-February 1973, *81*(1), pp. 203–10.

Brannon, Gerard M. Death Taxes in a Structure of Progressive Taxes. *Nat. Tax J.,* September 1973, *26*(3), pp. 451–57.

Brechling, Frank. Announcement Effects of Profits Taxation: Discussion. In *Parkin, M., ed.,* 1973, pp. 33–34.

Broussalian, V. L. Discounting and the Evaluation of Public Investments: Reply. *Appl. Econ.,* September 1973, *5*(3), pp. 225–26.

Browning, Edgar K. Alternative Programs for Income Redistribution: The NIT and the NWT. *Amer. Econ. Rev.,* March 1973, *63*(1), pp. 38–49. [G: U.S.]

Canes, Michael E. Discounting and the Evaluation of Public Investments: Comment. *Appl. Econ.,* September 1973, *5*(3), pp. 219–23.

Carroll, Sidney L. A Note on Revenue Sharing and the Theory of Public Expenditures. *Public Choice,* Spring 1973, *14,* pp. 109–16.

Christ, Carl F. Monetary and Fiscal Influences on U.S. Money Income, 1891–1970. *J. Money, Credit, Banking,* Part II, February 1973, *5*(1), pp. 279–300. [G: U.S.]

Chung, Pham. Some Notes on the Assignment Problem. *Public Finance,* 1973, *28*(1), pp. 20–29.

Colwell, Peter F. and Lash, Nicholas A. Comparing Fiscal Indicators. *Rev. Econ. Statist.,* August 1973, *55*(3), pp. 321–26. [G: U.S.]

Covey, Richard B. Estate and Gift Taxation. *Nat. Tax J.,* September 1973, *26*(3), pp. 459–63. [G: U.S.]

Dean, James M. Redistribution and Tax Concessions

for Charitable Contributions. *Public Finance,* 1973, *28*(3–4), pp. 371–76.

Dean, James W. and Tower, Edward. Internal and External Balance in an "Almost Classical" World: Rejoinder. *Western Econ. J.,* June 1973, *11*(2), pp. 240.

Dean, James W. and Tower, Edward. More on Internal and External Balance in an "Almost Classical" World. *Western Econ. J.,* June 1973, *11*(2), pp. 232–37.

Demsetz, Harold. Joint Supply and Price Discrimination. *J. Law Econ.,* October 1973, *16*(2), pp. 389–405.

Demsetz, Harold. The Private Production of Public Goods: Reply. *J. Law Econ.,* October 1973, *16*(2), pp. 413–15.

DeSalvo, Joseph S. Effects of the Property Tax on Operating and Investment Decisions of Rental Property Owners: Reply. *Nat. Tax J.,* March 1973, *26*(1), pp. 129–31.

Dixon, Daryl A. The Full Employment Budget Surplus Concept as a Tool of Fiscal Analysis in the United States. *Int. Monet. Fund Staff Pap.,* March 1973, *20*(1), pp. 203–26.   [G: U.S.]

Downes, Beverley. Purchase Taxes and Retail Prices in the United Kingdom. *Appl. Econ.,* September 1973, *5*(3), pp. 199–218.   [G: U.K.]

Egozi, Mosheh. An Elementary Model of the Determination of the Level of Public Expenditure and the Distribution of the Tax Burden. *Public Finance,* 1973, *28*(3–4), pp. 259–79.

Ekelund, Robert B., Jr. and Hulett, Joe R. Joint Supply, the Taussig-Pigou Controversy, and the Competitive Provision of Public Goods. *J. Law Econ.,* October 1973, *16*(2), pp. 369–87.

Ellickson, Bryan. A Generalization of the Pure Theory of Public Goods. *Amer. Econ. Rev.,* June 1973, *63*(3), pp. 417–32.

Fisher, Anthony C. A Paradox in the Theory of Public Investment. *J. Public Econ.,* November 1973, *2*(4), pp. 405–07.

Floyd, John E. Monetary and Fiscal Policy in a World of Capital Mobility: A Reply. *Rev. Econ. Stud.,* April 1973, *40*(2), pp. 299–303.

Foulon, Alain; Hatchuel, Georges and Kende, Pierre. Un premier bilan de la redistribution des revenus en France; Les impôts et cotisations sociales à la charge des ménages en 1965. (Balance of the Redistribution of Incomes in France: Personal Taxes and Social Security Contributions in 1965. With English summary.) *Consommation,* October-December 1973, *20*(4), pp. 5–133.   [G: France]

Friedlaender, Ann F.; Swanson, Gerald J. and Due, John F. Estimating Sales Tax Revenue Changes in Response to Changes in Personal Income and Sales Tax Rates. *Nat. Tax J.,* March 1973, *26*(1), pp. 103–10.   [G: U.S.]

Friedlaender, Ann F. Macro Policy Goals in the Postwar Period: A Study in Revealed Preference. *Quart. J. Econ.,* February 1973, *87*(1), pp. 25–43.   [G: U.S.]

Galper, Harvey and Wendel, Helmut F. Time Lags in the Federal Expenditure Process and their Stabilization Implications. *Public Finance Quart.,* April 1973, *1*(2), pp. 123–46.   [G: U.S.]

Gandhi, Ved P. Tax Burden on Indian Agriculture. In *Wadhva, C. D., ed.,* 1973, pp. 340–45.   [G: India]

Ganter, Ralph. Zur Weiterwälzung spezieller Verbrauchsteuern. (On the Shifting of Specific Excise Taxes. With English summary.) *Jahr. Nationalökon. Statist.,* January 1973, *187*(2), pp. 108–27.

Garfinkel, Irwin. Is In-Kind Redistribution Efficient? *Quart. J. Econ.,* May 1973, *87*(2), pp. 320–30.

Ghosh, Ranen. The Public Sector and Economic Development in India–I. *Econ. Aff.,* January–February 1973, *18*(1-2), pp. 9–16, 89–94.   [G: India]

Gould, J. R. Meade on External Economies: Should the Beneficiaries Be Taxed? *J. Law Econ.,* April 1973, *16*(1), pp. 53–66.

Green, H. A. John. Public Sector Resource Allocation under Conditions of Risk: Discussion. In *Parkin, M., ed.,* 1973, pp. 137–38.

Grieson, Ronald E. Effects of the Property Tax on Operating and Investment Decisions of Rental Property Owners: A Note. *Nat. Tax J.,* March 1973, *26*(1), pp. 127–28.

Guadagni, Alieto A. La evaluación social de los proyectos industriales según "Guidelines for Project Evaluation" de Unido. (Social Evaluation of Industrial Projects According Unidó's "Guidelines for Project Evaluation." With English summary.) *Económica,* May-August 1973, *19*(2), pp. 165–83.

Hahn, Frank H. On Optimum Taxation. *J. Econ. Theory,* February 1973, *6*(1), pp. 96–106.

Harberger, Arnold C. On Measuring the Social Opportunity Cost of Public Funds. In *Harberger, A. C.,* 1973, pp. 94–122.

Harvey, C. E. On the Cost-Inflationary Impact of High Interest Rates: Reply. *J. Econ. Issues,* September 1973, *7*(3), pp. 514.

Head, John G. Public Goods and Multi-Level Government. In *[Hicks, U.],* 1973, pp. 20–43.

Head, John G. and Shoup, Carl S. Public, Private, and Ambiguous Goods Reconsidered. *Public Finance,* 1973, *28*(3–4), pp. 384–92.

Hendershott, Patric H. Monetary and Fiscal Influences on U.S. Money Income, 1891–1970: Comment. *J. Money, Credit, Banking,* Part II, February 1973, *5*(1), pp. 311–12.   [G: U.S.]

Henderson, Dale W. and Sargent, Thomas J. Monetary and Fiscal Policy in a Two-Sector Aggregative Model. *Amer. Econ. Rev.,* June 1973, *63*(3), pp. 345–65.

Hogan, Timothy D. and Shelton, Robert B. Interstate Tax Exportation and States' Fiscal Structures. *Nat. Tax J.,* December 1973, *26*(4), pp. 553–64.   [G: U.S.]

Husby, Ralph D. Impact of a Negative Income Tax on Aggregate Demand and Supply. *Western Econ. J.,* March 1973, *11*(1), pp. 111–17.

Idachaba, F. S. Marketing Boards as Potential Stabilizers of Government Revenues in Developing Countries: The Nigerian Experience. *Econ. Bull. Ghana, Sec. Ser.,* 1973, *3*(4), pp. 23–30.   [G: Nigeria]

Isard, Peter. The Effectiveness of Using the Tax System to Curb Inflationary Collective Bargains: An

Analysis of the Wallich-Weintraub Plan. *J. Polit. Econ.*, May-June 1973, *81*(3), pp. 729–40. [G: U.S.]

Jones, F. S. and Kubursi, A. A. A Programming Model of Government Expenditures. *Public Finance*, 1973, *28*(1), pp. 84–93.

Junankar, P. N. Analytics of Choice in Fiscal Policy: Discussion. In *Parkin, M., ed.*, 1973, pp. 369–70. [G: U.S.; New Zealand; U.K.]

Kahn, C. Harry. The Place of Consumption and Net-Worth Taxation in the Federal Tax Structure. In *Musgrave, R. A., ed.*, 1973, pp. 133–54. [G: U.S.]

Kane, Edward J. Monetary and Fiscal Influence on U.S. Money Income, 1891–1970: Comment. *J. Money, Credit, Banking*, Part II, February 1973, *5*(1), pp. 301–03. [G: U.S.]

Karageorgas, Dionysios. The Distribution of Tax Burden by Income Groups in Greece. *Econ. J.*, June 1973, *83*(330), pp. 436–48. [G: Greece]

Karageorgas, Dionysios. Taxation of Foreign Firms: Discriminative and Allocative Effects. *Public Finance Quart.*, July 1973, *1*(3), pp. 239–65.

Kau, Randall K. C. and Schler, Michael L. Inflation and the Federal Income Tax. *Yale Law J.*, March 1973, *82*(4), pp. 716–44. [G: U.S.]

Khan, Mohammad Zubair. The Responsiveness of Tax Yield to Increases in National Income. *Pakistan Develop. Rev.*, Winter 1973, *12*(4), pp. 416–32. [G: Pakistan]

Kmenta, J. and Smith, Paul E. Autonomous Expenditures Versus Money Supply: An Application of Dynamic Multipliers. *Rev. Econ. Statist.*, August 1973, *55*(3), pp. 299–307. [G: U.S.]

Kolm, Serge-Christophe. A Note on Optimum Tax Evasion. *J. Public Econ.*, July 1973, *2*(3), pp. 265–70.

Lemennicier, Bertrand. La contrainte budgétaire de l'Etat et l' "Optimal Policy Mix" en régime de change fixe et flexible. (The Optimal Policy Mix in a Fixed and Flexible Exchange Rate System Under the Constraint of Financing Monetary and Public Expenditure Policies. With English summary.) *Revue Écon.*, May 1973, *24*(3), pp. 473–504.

Levin, Jonathan. Government Finance and the Balance of Payments. In *[Halm, G. N.]*, 1973, pp. 199–210.

Lind, Robert C. Spatial Equilibrium, the Theory of Rents, and the Measurement of Benefits from Public Programs. *Quart. J. Econ.*, May 1973, *87*(2), pp. 188–207.

Maital, Shlomo. Public Goods and Income Distribution: Some Further Results. *Econometrica*, May 1973, *41*(3), pp. 561–68.

Mammen, Thampy. Indian Money Market: An Econometric Study. *Int. Econ. Rev.*, February 1973, *14*(1), pp. 49–68. [G: India]

Matthiessen, Lars. Index-tied Income Taxes and Economic Policy. *Swedish J. Econ.*, March 1973, *75*(1), pp. 49–66.

McKinnon, Ronald I. The Value-Added Tax and the Liberalization of Foreign Trade in Developing Economies: A Comment. *J. Econ. Lit.*, June 1973, *11*(2), pp. 520–24.

McLure, Charles E., Jr. Economic Effects of Taxing Value Added. In *Musgrave, R. A., ed.*, 1973, pp. 155–204. [G: U.S.]

McNees, Stephen K. Deductibility of Charitable Bequests. *Nat. Tax J.*, March 1973, *26*(1), pp. 79–98. [G: U.S.]

Metwally, Mohktar M. and Timmaiah, G. A Note on the Classical Utility Function for Purpose of the Theory of Taxation. *Finanzarchiv*, 1973, *31*(3), pp. 441–45.

Metzler, Lloyd A. Flexible Exchange Rates, the Transfer Problem, and the Balanced-Budget Theorem. In *Metzler, L. A.*, 1973, pp. 95–111.

Metzler, Lloyd A. Taxes and Subsidies in Leontief's Input-Output Model. In *Metzler, L. A.*, 1973, pp. 568–74.

Metzler, Lloyd A. The Structure of Taxes, Open-Market Operations, and the Rate of Interest. In *Metzler, L. A.*, 1973, pp. 345–62. [G: U.S.]

Mirrlees, James A. The Integration of Project and Sector Analysis: Discussion. In *Parkin, M., ed.*, 1973, pp. 167–69.

Modigliani, Franco. International Capital Movements, Fixed Parities, and Monetary and Fiscal Policies. In *[Rosenstein-Rodan, P.]*, 1973, pp. 239–53.

Mohring, Herbert and Maslove, Allan. The Optimal Provision of Public Goods: Yet Another Comment. *J. Polit. Econ.*, May-June 1973, *81*(3), pp. 778–85.

Negishi, Takashi. The Excess of Public Expenditures on Industries. *J. Public Econ.*, July 1973, *2*(3), pp. 231–40.

Neumann, Manfred J. M. On Public Expenditure and Taxation. *Public Finance*, 1973, *28*(3–4), pp. 377–83.

Nichols, Donald R. and Fielitz, Bruce D. Awareness of Marginal Income Tax Rates Among Taxpayers. *Miss. Val. J. Bus. Econ.*, Spring 1973, *8*(3), pp. 39–46. [G: U.S.]

Nishimura, Osamu. Transaction Activity and Optimal Taxation. *Econ. Stud. Quart.*, August 1973, *24*(2), pp. 16–25.

Nobukuni, Makoto and Fukuchi, Takao. The Economic Measurement of the Benefit of Public Transportation Investment. (In Japanese. With English summary.) *Econ. Stud. Quart.*, December 1973, *24*(3), pp. 43–53.

Ott, David J. and Ott, Attiat F. The Effect of Nonneutral Taxation on the Use of Capital by Sector. *J. Polit. Econ.*, July-August 1973, *81*(4), pp. 972–81. [G: U.S.]

Peacock, Alan. Cost-benefit Analysis and the Political Control of Public Investment. In *Wolfe, J. N., ed.*, 1973, pp. 17–29. [G: U.S.; U.K.]

Pechman, Joseph A. Responsiveness of the Federal Individual Income Tax to Changes in Income. *Brookings Pap. Econ. Act.*, 1973, (2), pp. 385–421. [G: U.S.]

Peston, Maurice. A Note on Tax Changes and Fluctuations in National Income. *J. Polit. Econ.*, November-December 1973, *81*(6), pp. 1467–70. [G: U.S.]

Peterson, George E. Welfare, Workfare, and Pareto Optimality. *Public Finance Quart.*, July 1973, *1*(3), pp. 323–38.

Phelps, Edmund S. Inflation in the Theory of Public Finance. *Swedish J. Econ.*, March 1973, *75*(1), pp. 67–82.

Phelps, Edmund S. Taxation of Wage Income for Economic Justice. *Quart. J. Econ.*, August 1973, *87*(3), pp. 331–54.

Poole, William and Kornblith, Elinda B. F. The Friedman-Meiselman CMC Paper: New Evidence on an Old Controversy. *Amer. Econ. Rev.*, December 1973, *63*(5), pp. 908–17.

Prest, Alan R. On the Distinction between Direct and Indirect Taxation. In *[Hicks, U.]*, 1973, pp. 44–56.

Price, R. W. R. Some Aspects of the Progressive Income Tax Structure in the UK. *Nat. Inst. Econ. Rev.*, August 1973, (65), pp. 52–63. **[G: U.K.]**

Rees, R. Public Sector Resource Allocation under Conditions of Risk. In *Parkin, M., ed.*, 1973, pp. 110–36.

Ribich, Thomas I. Soft Sell for Soft Drinks: An Excise Tax Problem. *Nat. Tax J.*, March 1973, *26*(1), pp. 115–17.

Rodgers, James D. Distributional Externalities and the Optimal Form of Income Transfers. *Public Finance Quart.*, July 1973, *1*(3), pp. 266–99.

Rose, Manfred. Das fiskalische Ziel der Besteuerung. (The Fiscal Goal of Taxation. With English summary.) *Kyklos*, 1973, *26*(4), pp. 815–40.

Rosenthal, Robert W. Taxation vs. Prohibition of an External Diseconomy by Direct Vote: A Game Theoretic Approach. *Int. Econ. Rev.*, June 1973, *14*(2), pp. 414–20.

Rürup, Bert. Handlungsverzögerungen diskretionärer Fiskalpolitik: Konstruktionsfehler oder Element rationaler Politik? (Decision Lags of Discretionary Fiscal Policy: Defects of Construction or Element of a Rational Policy. With English summary.) *Z. Wirtschaft. Sozialwissen.*, 1973, *93*(1), pp. 35–50.

Sadler, P. G. The Integration of Project and Sector Analysis. In *Parkin, M., ed.*, 1973, pp. 156–66.

Sandmo, Agnar. Public Goods and the Technology of Consumption. *Rev. Econ. Stud.*, October 1973, *40*(4), pp. 517–28.

Schleicher, Heinz. On European Social Rates of Discount: Survey. *Finanzarchiv*, 1973, *31*(3), pp. 434–40. **[G: W. Europe]**

Schmidt, Ádám. Equilibrium of the Budget and of the National Economy. In *Földi, T., ed.*, 1973, pp. 89–115.

Shapiro, David L. Can Public Investment Have a Positive Rate of Return? *J. Polit. Econ.*, Part I, March-April 1973, *81*(2), pp. 401–13. **[G: U.S.]**

Shapiro, Harold T. Monetary and Fiscal Influences on U.S. Money Income, 1891–1970: Comment. *J. Money, Credit, Banking*, Part II, February 1973, *5*(1), pp. 304–10. **[G: U.S.]**

Shapiro, Perry and Legler, John B. Estimating Tax Revenue Changes in Response to Changes in Tax Rates. *Nat. Tax J.*, March 1973, *26*(1), pp. 111–13.

Shibata, Hirofumi. Public Goods, Increasing Cost, and Monopsony: Comment. *J. Polit. Econ.*, January-February 1973, *81*(1), pp. 223–30.

Shoup, Carl S. Three Fiscal Reports on Colombia: A Review Article. *Nat. Tax J.*, March 1973, *26*(1), pp. 59–63. **[G: Colombia]**

Shoven, John B. and Whalley, John. General Equilibrium with Taxes: A Computational Procedure and an Existence Proof. *Rev. Econ. Stud.*, October 1973, *40*(4), pp. 475–89.

Skouras, Athanassios. On the Analysis of Property Tax Effects on Operating and Investment Decisions of Rental Property Owners. *Nat. Tax J.*, March 1973, *26*(1), pp. 123–25.

Steedman, Ian. Some Long-run Equilibrium Tax Theory. *Public Finance*, 1973, *28*(1), pp. 43–51.

Suman, H. N. P. S. Effect of Corporate Taxation on Saving and Capital Formation in Some Indian Industries. *Econ. Aff.*, November-December 1973, *18*(11–12), pp. 485–96. **[G: India]**

Sumner, M. T. Investment and Corporate Taxation. *J. Polit. Econ.*, July-August 1973, *81*(4), pp. 982–93. **[G: U.K.]**

Sumner, M. T. Announcement Effects of Profits Taxation. In *Parkin, M., ed.*, 1973, pp. 17–32.

Terre, Norbert C.; Warnke, Dale W. and Ameiss, Albert P. Cost/Benefit Analysis of Public Projects. *Manage. Account.*, January 1973, *54*(7), pp. 34–37.

Thompson, Earl A. The Private Production of Public Goods: Comment. *J. Law Econ.*, October 1973, *16*(2), pp. 407–12.

Topham, Neville. Micro-Economic Risk and the Social Rate of Discount. In *Parkin, M., ed.*, 1973, pp. 139–55.

Vitaliano, Donald F. A Reconsideration of Some Aspects of the Utility Sacrifice Rules of Taxation. *Public Finance Quart.*, January 1973, *1*(1), pp. 59–65.

Warr, Peter G. Savings Propensities and the Shadow Wage. *Economica, N.S.*, November 1973, *40*(160), pp. 410–15.

Weber, Wilhelm. Collective Goods and the Planning of Fiscal Programmes. In *Hicks, J. R. and Weber, W., eds.*, 1973, pp. 149–63.

West, E. G. The Bilateral Monopoly Theory of Public Goods: A Critique. *J. Polit. Econ.*, September-October 1973, *81*(5), pp. 1226–35.

Williams, Raburn and Miller, Roger LeRoy. A Note on the Effects of Government Finance on Aggregate Demand for Goods and Services. *Public Finance*, 1973, *28*(3–4), pp. 393–96.

Winch, David M. The Pure Theory of Non-Pure Goods. *Can. J. Econ.*, May 1973, *6*(2), pp. 149–63.

Wolfson, M. and Rayner, A. Analytics of Choice in Fiscal Policy. In *Parkin, M., ed.*, 1973, pp. 345–68. **[G: U.S.; New Zealand; U.K.]**

Young, Warren L. Compulsory Loans, Disposable Income, and Quarterly Consumption Behaviour in Israel: 1964–1969. *Finanzarchiv*, 1973, *32*(1), pp. 98–115. **[G: Israel]**

Zeckhauser, Richard J. Determining the Qualities of a Public Good—A Paradigm on Town Park Location. *Western Econ. J.*, March 1973, *11*(1), pp. 39–60.

Zelder, Raymond E.; Ross, Myron H. and Collery, Arnold. Internal and External Balance in an "Almost Classical" World: Reply. *Western Econ. J.*, June 1973, *11*(2), pp. 238–40.

3216 Fiscal Policy; Studies

Ahtiala, Pekka. Verotus, korkosäännöstely ja inflaatio säästövarojen allokoijina. (Taxation, Interest Rate Controls, and Inflation as Allocators of Saving. With English summary.) *Liiketaloudellinen Aikak.*, 1973, *22*(2), pp. 94–113. **[G: Finland]**

Andersen, Leonall C. A Comparison of Stabilization Policies: 1966–67 and 1969–70. *J. Money, Credit, Banking,* Part I, February 1973, *5*(1), pp. 26–38. [G: U.S.]

Biehl, Dieter, et al. Measuring the Demand Effects of Fiscal Policy. In *Giersch, H., ed.,* 1973, pp. 223–41. [G: W. Germany]

Blinder, Alan S. and Solow, Robert M. Does Fiscal Policy Matter? *J. Public Econ.,* November 1973, *2*(4), pp. 319–37. [G: U.S.]

Borpujari, Jitendra G. and Ter-Minassian, Teresa. The Weighted Budget Balance Approach to Fiscal Analysis: A Methodology and Some Case Studies. *Int. Monet. Fund Staff Pap.,* November 1973, *20*(3), pp. 801–31. [G: Italy]

Break, George F. Federal Tax Policy and the Private Saving Ratio. *Nat. Tax J.,* September 1973, *26*(3), pp. 409–14. [G: U.S.]

Burchardt, Michael. Die Koordination von Geld- und Fiskalpolitik bei festen Wechselkursen. (The Coordination of Monetary and Fiscal Policies under Fixed Exchange Rates. With English summary.) *Z. Wirtschaft. Sozialwissen.,* 1973, *93*(4), pp. 423–43.

Burger, Hendrik. Possible Concepts for Better Planning and Evaluating Fiscal Policy—Experiences in the Netherlands. In *Giersch, H., ed.,* 1973, pp. 210–22. [G: Netherlands]

Carlson, Keith M. The 1973 National Economic Plan: Slowing the Boom. *Fed. Res. Bank St. Louis Rev.,* March 1973, *55*(3), pp. 2–9. [G: U.S.]

Chiancone, Aldo. Il sistema svedese dei fondi di riserva per gli investimenti come strumento di stabilizzazione economica. (The Swedish System of Investment Funds as an Instrument of Stabilization Policy. With English summary.) *Rivista Int. Sci. Econ. Com.,* March 1973, *20*(3), pp. 242–66. [G: Sweden]

Despres, Emile. Determining the Size of a Development Plan: Pakistan. In *Despres, E.,* 1973, pp. 99–132. [G: Pakistan]

English, M. D. Macro-Economic Policy: Canada. In *Perkins, J. O. N., ed.,* 1973, pp. 57–93. [G: Canada]

von Furstenberg, George M. and Boughton, James M. Stabilization Goals and the Appropriateness of Fiscal Policy during the Eisenhower and Kennedy-Johnson Administrations. *Public Finance Quart.,* January 1973, *1*(1), pp. 5–28. [G: U.S.]

Gibson, William E. Fiscal and Monetary Policy: Opportunities and Problems. *Fed. Res. Bank St. Louis Rev.,* January 1973, *55*(1), pp. 14–18. [G: U.S.]

Hamdani, Daood H. Fiscal Measures Against Inflation and Unemployment in Canada: 1973 Budget and Other Developments. *Bull. Int. Fiscal Doc.,* June 1973, *27*(6), pp. 223–40. [G: Canada]

Hansen, Bent. On the Effects of Fiscal and Monetary Policy: A Taxonomic Discussion. *Amer. Econ. Rev.,* September 1973, *63*(4), pp. 546–71. [G: U.S.]

Heller, Walter W. Should the Government Share Its Tax Take? In *Rasmussen, D. W. and Haworth, C. T., eds.,* 1973, pp. 217–24. [G: U.S.]

Hicks, John R. [Sir] and Hicks, Ursula K. [Lady]. British Fiscal Policy. In *Giersch, H., ed.,* 1973, pp. 142–54. [G: U.K.]

Ishi, Hiromitsu. Cyclical Behavior of Government Receipts and Expenditures—A Case Study of Postwar Japan. *Hitotsubashi J. Econ.,* June 1973, *14*(1), pp. 56–83. [G: Japan]

Jetha, Nizar. Some Aspects of Domestic Financing of Central Government Expenditure: The Case of Kenya. In *[Hicks, U.],* 1973, pp. 95–139. [G: Kenya]

Kane, Edward J. Simulations of Stabilization Policies for 1966–1970 *and* A Comparison of Stabilization Policies: 1966–67 and 1969–70: Comment. *J. Money, Credit, Banking,* Part I, February 1973, *5*(1), pp. 39–42. [G: U.S.]

Kirschen, Etienne S. BENELUX Experience with Public Finance Instruments for Achieving the Objectives of Full Employment and Expansion. In *Giersch, H., ed.,* 1973, pp. 155–69. [G: Belgium; Netherlands]

Knauerhase, Ramon. A Survey of the Revenue Structure of the Kingdom of Saudi Arabia, 1961/62 to 1971/72. *Public Finance,* 1973, *28*(3–4), pp. 435–53. [G: Saudi Arabia]

Laidler, David. Expectations, Adjustment, and the Dynamic Response of Income to Policy Changes. *J. Money, Credit, Banking,* Part I, February 1973, *5*(1), pp. 157–72.

La Malfa, Ugo. Contenimento della spesa pubblica e lotta all'inflazione per una solida linea di stabilità. (Containment of Public Expenditure and Fight Against Inflation for Stability. With Engish summary.) *Bancaria,* November 1973, *29* (11), pp. 1342–45. [G: Italy]

Lent, George E.; Casanegra, Milka and Guerard, Michèle. The Value-Added Tax in Developing Countries. *Int. Monet. Fund Staff Pap.,* July 1973, *20*(2), pp. 318–78.

Maital, Shlomo. Targets, Tradeoffs, and Economic Policy: A Generalized Phillips Curve. *Public Finance Quart.,* January 1973, *1*(1), pp. 67–83.

Matthiessen, Lars. Recent Experience with Fiscal Policy in Sweden. In *Giersch, H., ed.,* 1973, pp. 170–87. [G: Sweden]

McCracken, Paul W. Federal Budget Discipline and National Priorities of the 1970's. In *Levy, M. E., ed.,* 1973, pp. 8–13. [G: U.S.]

McLure, Charles E., Jr. Gradualism and the New Economic Policy: Fiscal Economics in Transition. In *Cagan, P., et al.,* 1973, pp. 35–77. [G: U.S.]

Meiselman, David I. Simulations of Stabilization Policies for 1966–1970 *and* A Comparison of Stabilization Policies: 1966–67 and 1969–70: Comment. *J. Money, Credit, Banking,* Part I, February 1973, *5*(1), pp. 43–46. [G: U.S.]

Merz, C. M.; Gibson, T. A. and Seitz, C. Ward. Impact of the Space Shuttle Program on the National Economy. *Eng. Econ.,* January-February 1973, *18* (2), pp. 115–33. [G: U.S.]

Nieuwenhuysen, J. P. Macro-Economic Policy: South Africa. In *Perkins, J. O. N., ed.,* 1973, pp. 130–76. [G: S. Africa]

Peacock, Alan T. and Shaw, G. K. Fiscal Measures to Create Employment: The Indonesian Case. *Bull. Int. Fiscal Doc.,* November 1973, *27*(11), pp. 443–54. [G: Indonesia]

Pedersen, Peder J. Har finanspolitikken mistet sin effektivitet? (With English summary.) *Nationalokon. Tidsskr.*, 1973, *111*(3), pp. 327–41. [G: Denmark]

Perkins, J. O. N. and Nieuwenhuysen, J. P. Macro-Economic Policy: Australia. In *Perkins, J. O. N., ed.*, 1973, pp. 17–56. [G: Australia]

Perkins, J. O. N. and Nieuwenhuysen, J. P. Macro-Economic Policies in the Four Countries. In *Perkins, J. O. N., ed.*, 1973, pp. 177–208. [G: Australia; New Zealand; Canada; S. Africa]

Poindexter, J. Carl, Jr. and Jones, C. P. The Effect of Recent Tax Policy Changes on Manufacturing Investment. *Quart. Rev. Econ. Bus.*, Winter 1973, *13*(4), pp. 79–88. [G: U.S.]

Rasche, Robert H. Simulations of Stabilization Policies for 1966–1970. *J. Money, Credit, Banking*, Part I, February 1973, *5*(1), pp. 1–25. [G: U.S.]

Rose, Peter S. The Impact of Policy Variables on Price-Level Movements. *Miss. Val. J. Bus. Econ.*, Fall 1973, *9*(1), pp. 1–11. [G: U.S.]

Rowe, J. W. Macro-Economic Policy: New Zealand. In *Perkins, J. O. N., ed.*, 1973, pp. 94–129. [G: New Zealand]

Salant, Walter S. Some Intellectual Contributions of the Truman Council of Economic Advisers to Policy-Making. *Hist. Polit. Econ.*, Spring 1973, *5*(1), pp. 36–49.

Saulnier, Raymond J. Is a Tax Increase Inevitable? In *Tax Foundation, Inc.*, 1973, pp. 6–9. [G: U.S.]

Scarth, William M. The Financing of Stabilization Policies: Evidence for the Canadian Economy. *Can. J. Econ.*, August 1973, *6*(3), pp. 301–18. [G: Canada]

Schiff, Frank W. Alternative Tax and Spending Policies, 1971–1976. In *Giersch, H., ed.*, 1973, pp. 188–94. [G: U.S.]

Schmidt, Peter and Waud, Roger N. The Almon Lag Technique and the Monetary Versus Fiscal Policy Debate. *J. Amer. Statist. Assoc.*, March 1973, *68*(341), pp. 11–19.

Schüler, Manfred. Fiscal Policy in Recession: The German Experience. In *Giersch, H., ed.*, 1973, pp. 195–202. [G: W. Germany]

Sheehan, P. J. The Real Income Guarantee: A Fiscal Policy to Control Inflation. *Australian Econ. Rev.*, 4th Quarter 1973, pp. 9–14. [G: Australia]

Stammati, Gaetano. Italian Experience with Fiscal Policy. In *Giersch, H., ed.*, 1973, pp. 203–09. [G: Italy]

Stott, Alexander L. Capital Recovery in a World of Inflation. In *Tax Foundation, Inc.*, 1973, pp. 35–42. [G: U.S.]

Sumner, M. T. Recent Changes in Fiscal Investment Incentives: A Postscript. *Manchester Sch. Econ. Soc. Stud.*, June 1973, *41*(2), pp. 235–39. [G: U.K.]

Vitaliano, Donald F. The Payment of Interest on the Federal Debt and the Distribution of Income. *J. Econ. Bus.*, Spring-Summer 1973, *25*(3), pp. 175–86. [G: U.S.]

de Wit, Y. B. The *Kabupaten* Program. *Bull. Indonesian Econ. Stud.*, March 1973, *9*(1), pp. 65–85. [G: Indonesia]

322 National Government Expenditures and Budgeting

3220 General

Corwin, R. D. and Miller, S. M. A qui profite l'impôt? Mythes et réalités. (Taxation and its Beneficiaries: The Manipulation of Symbols. With English summary.) *Consommation*, January-March 1973, *20*(1), pp. 17–35. [G: U.S.]

Ott, David J., et al. Introduction and Summary of Findings. In *Ott, D. J., et al.*, 1973, pp. 1–9. [G: U.S.]

Waite, Charles A. and Wakefield, Joseph C. Federal Fiscal Programs. *Surv. Curr. Bus.*, February 1973, *53*(2), pp. 18–28, 40. [G: U.S.]

Weinberger, Caspar W. Expenditure Priorities and Budget Reform. In *Tax Foundation, Inc.*, 1973, pp. 57–59. [G: U.S.]

Young, Warren L. Compulsory Loans and Consumption-Savings Behaviour: Some Micro- and Macro-Economic Aspects. *Public Finance*, 1973, *28*(3–4), pp. 333–53. [G: Israel]

3221 National Government Expenditures

Adams, Earl W., Jr. and Spiro, Michael H. Reducing the Lags in Government Spending: An Empirical Analysis of Highway Construction. *Public Finance*, 1973, *28*(2), pp. 125–38. [G: U.S.]

Ball, Robert. Labor and Materials Required for Highway Construction. *Mon. Lab. Rev.*, June 1973, *96*(6), pp. 40–45. [G: U.S.]

Bromley, Daniel W. and Beattie, Bruce R. On the Incongruity of Program Objectives and Project Evaluation: An Example from the Reclamation Program. *Amer. J. Agr. Econ.*, August 1973, *55*(3), pp. 472–76. [G: U.S.]

Carlin, Alan. The Grand Canyon Controversy; or, How Reclamation Justifies the Unjustifiable. In *Enthoven, A. C. and Freeman, A. M., III, eds.*, 1973, pp. 263–70. [G: U.S.]

Chapman, Duane. Economic Aspects of a Nuclear Desalination Agro-Industrial Project in the United Arab Republic. *Amer. J. Agr. Econ.*, August 1973, *55*(3), pp. 433–40. [G: United Arab Republic]

Charles, K. J. Public Services and Poverty. *Econ. Aff.*, January–February 1973, *18*(1-2), pp. 74–80. [G: India]

Chester, T. E. Public Money in the Private Sector. *Nat. Westminster Bank Quart. Rev.*, May 1973, pp. 20–30. [G: U.K.]

Cohn, Elchanan. On the Ranking of Social Investments in Education: A Reply. *Public Finance*, 1973, *28*(3–4), pp. 431–34. [G: U.S.]

Enweze, Cyril. Structure of Public Expenditures in Selected Developing Countries: A Time Series Study. *Manchester Sch. Econ. Soc. Stud.*, December 1973, *41*(4), pp. 430–63.

Jones, F. S. and Kubursi, A. A. A Programming Model of Government Expenditures. *Public Finance*, 1973, *28*(1), pp. 84–93.

Jones, P. M. S. The Use of Cost-benefit Analysis as an Aid to Allocating Government Resources for Research and Development. In *Wolfe, J. N., ed.*,

1973, pp. 155–81. [G: U.K.]

Korb, Lawrence J. National Defense. In *Ott, D. J., et al.,* 1973, pp. 29–52. [G: U.S.]

Leonard, William N. Government in Political Economy. *Amer. Econ.,* Fall 1973, *17*(2), pp. 57–62. [G: U.S.]

Marshall, Harold Emory. Cost Sharing and Multiobjectives in Water Resource Development. *Water Resources Res.,* February 1973, *9*(1), pp. 1–10. [G: U.S.]

Mathews, Russell. Patterns of Educational Finance. *Australian Econ. Pap.,* December 1973, *12*(21), pp. 145–61. [G: Australia]

McLeod, Donald. Determinants of Jamaican Government Revenue Shares. *J. Devel. Stud.,* April 1973, *9*(3), pp. 427–37. [G: Jamaica]

Merewitz, Leonard. Cost Overruns in Public Works. In *Niskanen, W. A., et al., eds.,* 1973, pp. 277–95. [G: U.S.]

Miller, W. L. and Byers, D. M. Development and Display of Multiple-Objective Project Impacts. *Water Resources Res.,* February 1973, *9*(1), pp. 11–20. [G: U.S.]

Moore, Thomas Gale. Science, Technology, and Industry. In *Ott, D. J., et al.,* 1973, pp. 67–89. [G: U.S.]

Negishi, Takashi. The Excess of Public Expenditures on Industries. *J. Public Econ.,* July 1973, *2*(3), pp. 231–40.

Nwaneri, V. C. Income Distribution and Project Selection. *Finance Develop.,* September 1973, *10*(3), pp. 27–29, 33.

O'Neill, Dave M. Manpower. In *Ott, D. J., et al.,* 1973, pp. 153–70.

Ott, Attiat F. Education. In *Ott, D. J., et al.,* 1973, pp. 113–52. [G: U.S.]

Penner, Rudolph G. Health. In *Ott, D. J., et al.,* 1973, pp. 171–92. [G: U.S.]

Penner, Rudolph G. Housing and Community Development. In *Ott, D. J., et al.,* 1973, pp. 91–111. [G: U.S.]

Penner, Rudolph G.; Ott, David J. and Ott, Attiat F. Income Security. In *Ott, D. J., et al.,* 1973, pp. 193–214. [G: U.S.]

Reading, Don C. New Deal Activity and the States, 1933 to 1939. *J. Econ. Hist.,* December 1973, *33*(4), pp. 792–810. [G: U.S.]

Reich, Michael and Finkelhor, David. The Military-Industrial Complex. In *Reynolds, L. G.; Green, G. D. and Lewis, D. R., eds.,* 1973, pp. 334–46. [G: U.S.]

Rosenfeld, Barry D. The Displacement-Effect in the Growth of Canadian Government Expenditures. *Public Finance,* 1973, *28*(3–4), pp. 301–14. [G: Canada]

Schenker, Eric and Bunamo, Michael. A Study of the Corps of Engineers' Regional Pattern of Investments. *Southern Econ. J.,* April 1973, *39*(4), pp. 548–58. [G: U.S.]

Scotto di Carlo, Giovampietro. Programmi quinquennali di spesa pubblica. Il sistema inglese e quello italiano. (Five-Year Public Expenditure Programmes. The British and Italian Systems. With English summary.) *Bancaria,* July 1973, *29*(7), pp. 832–38. [G: Italy]

Trueger, Paul M. Contract Termination and Unab-

sorbed Overhead. *Manage. Account.,* February 1973, *54*(8), pp. 38–40.

Udis, Bernard. The Economic Consequences of Reduced Military Spending: Overview and Summary. In *Udis, B., ed.,* 1973, pp. 1–15. [G: U.S.]

Vasquez, Thomas and Ott, David J. Agriculture. In *Ott, D. J., et al.,* 1973, pp. 53–65. [G: U.S.]

Warr, Peter G. Savings Propensities and the Shadow Wage. *Economica, N.S.,* November 1973, *40*(160), pp. 410–15.

Ziderman, Adrian. On the Ranking of Social Investments in Education: A Comment. *Public Finance,* 1973, *28*(3–4), pp. 424–30. [G: U.S.]

3226 National Government Budgeting

Allison, Graham T. Organizational and Administrative Factors Affecting Shifts in Defense Expenditures. In *Udis, B., ed.,* 1973, pp. 289–35. [G: U.S.]

Andic, Fuat M. Fiscal Reform in Colombia: A Review Article. *Finanzarchiv,* 1973, *32*(1), pp. 160–66. [G: Colombia]

Arnell, J. C. Development of Program Budgeting in the Canadian Department of National Defense. In *Novick, D., ed.,* 1973, pp. 79–88. [G: Canada]

Battersby, J. R. Introduction and Development of Programme Budgeting in New Zealand. In *Novick, D., ed.,* 1973, pp. 129–38. [G: New Zealand]

Borpujari, Jitendra G. and Ter-Minassian, Teresa. The Weighted Budget Balance Approach to Fiscal Analysis: A Methodology and Some Case Studies. *Int. Monet. Fund Staff Pap.,* November 1973, *20*(3), pp. 801–31. [G: Italy]

Bravo, Jacques. L'expérience française des budgets de programmes. (The French Experiment in Program Budgeting. With English summary.) *Revue Écon.,* January 1973, *24*(1), pp. 1–65. [G: France]

Bridgeman, J. M. Planning-Programming-Budgeting in the United Kingdom Central Government. In *Novick, D., ed.,* 1973, pp. 89–95. [G: U.K.]

Brierley, J. D. Programme Budgeting in Education in the United Kingdom. In *Novick, D., ed.,* 1973, pp. 97–103. [G: U.K.]

Burns, Arthur F. Statement to Congress. *Fed. Res. Bull.,* March 1973, *59*(3), pp. 164–68.

Burns, Arthur F. Statement to Congress. *Fed. Res. Bull.,* March 1973, *59*(3), pp. 171–76. [G: U.S.]

Carlson, Jack W. Recent U.S. Federal Government Experience with Program Budgeting. In *Novick, D., ed.,* 1973, pp. 207–16. [G: U.S.]

Castello, Albert P. The Model Cities Program: An Application of PPBS. *Manage. Account.,* January 1973, *54*(7), pp. 29–33, 44. [G: U.S.]

Cebula, Richard J. Deficit Spending, Expectations, and Fiscal Policy Effectiveness. *Public Finance,* 1973, *28*(3–4), pp. 362–70.

Chelliah, Raja J. Significance of Alternative Concepts of Budget Deficit. *Int. Monet. Fund Staff Pap.,* November 1973, *20*(3), pp. 741–84.

Dickman, A. B. Exchequer Financing and the Money Supply. *S. Afr. J. Econ.,* June 1973, *41*(2), pp. 154–57. [G: S. Africa]

Dixon, Daryl A. The Full Employment Budget Surplus Concept as a Tool of Fiscal Analysis in the United States. *Int. Monet. Fund Staff Pap.*, March 1973, *20*(1), pp. 203–26.   [G: U.S.]

Fukushima, Yasuto. PPBS in the Japanese Government: Necessity, Preparation and Problems. In *Novick, D., ed.*, 1973, pp. 125–28.   [G: Japan]

Harlow, Robert L. On the Decline and Possible Fall of PPBS. *Public Finance Quart.*, January 1973, *1*(1), pp. 85–105.

Hayden, F. Gregory. Fiscal Federalism: Program Budgeting and the Multilevel Governmental Setting. *Nebr. J. Econ. Bus.*, Winter 1973, *12*(1), pp. 23–42.

Hellmuth, William F. The Federal Revenue System: Discussion. *J. Finance*, May 1973, *28*(2), pp. 496–99.   [G: U.S.]

Herring, S. G. Programme Budgeting in the Australian Federal Government. In *Novick, D., ed.*, 1973, pp. 55–60.   [G: Australia]

Hroneš, Václav. State Budgets for 1973. *Czech. Econ. Digest.*, May 1973, (3), pp. 25–51.   [G: Czechoslovakia]

Ishi, Hiromitsu. Cyclical Behavior of Government Receipts and Expenditures—A Case Study of Postwar Japan. *Hitotsubashi J. Econ.*, June 1973, *14*(1), pp. 56–83.   [G: Japan]

Krogh, D. C. The Budget and Industry. *S. Afr. J. Econ.*, June 1973, *41*(2), pp. 158–60.   [G: S. Africa]

Lachmann, L. M. The Budget and Inflation. *S. Afr. J. Econ.*, June 1973, *41*(2), pp. 146–49.   [G: S. Africa]

MacDonald, B. A. Program Budgeting in the Government of Canada: Origin and Progress. In *Novick, D., ed.*, 1973, pp. 71–78.   [G: Canada]

Martin, David A. Protecting the Fisc: Executive Impoundment and Congressional Power. *Yale Law J.*, July 1973, *82*(8), pp. 1636–58.   [G: U.S.]

Mathews, Russell. Budget Structure and Organisation in Developed and Developing Countries. In *[Hicks, U.]*, 1973, pp. 233–59.

Matzner, Egon and Vak, Karl. Program Budgeting in Austria: An Essay in Persuasion. In *Novick, D., ed.*, 1973, pp. 61–64.   [G: Austria]

McCawley, Peter. Survey of Recent Developments. *Bull. Indonesian Econ. Stud.*, November 1973, *9*(3), pp. 1–27.   [G: Indonesia]

Natchez, Peter B. and Bupp, Irvin C. Policy and Priority in the Budgetary Process. *Amer. Polit. Sci. Rev.*, September 1973, *67*(3), pp. 951–63.   [G: U.S.]

Novick, David. Brief History of Program Budgeting. In *Novick, D., ed.*, 1973, pp. 19–28.

Novick, David. Program Budgeting, 1971. In *Novick, D., ed.*, 1973, pp. 29–47.

O'Cofaigh, Thomas F. Programme Budgeting in Ireland. In *Novick, D., ed.*, 1973, pp. 119–24.   [G: Ireland]

Ott, David J. The Federal Revenue System: Discussion. *J. Finance*, May 1973, *28*(2), pp. 499–500.   [G: U.S.]

Ott, David J. The Budget Outlook: An Overview. In *Ott, D. J., et al.*, 1973, pp. 11–27.   [G: U.S.]

Packer, Arnold H. A Budget Structured to Reflect Economic Objectives. *J. Finance*, May 1973, *28*

(2), pp. 467–80.   [G: U.S.]

Poullet, E. The PPBS Experiment in Belgium. In *Novick, D., ed.*, 1973, pp. 65–69.   [G: Belgium]

Schmidt, Ádám. Equilibrium of the Budget and of the National Economy. In *Földi, T., ed.*, 1973, pp. 89–115.

Scotto di Carlo, Giovampietro. Effetto reddito ed effetto finanziario per la programmazione della politica di bilancio. (Income Effect and Financial Effect in the Planning of the Budget Policy. With English summary.) *L'Industria*, January-June 1973, (1–2), pp. 109–24.

Sinha, R. K. A Note on Central Budget 1973–74. *Econ. Aff.*, April 1973, *18*(4), pp. 190–96.   [G: India]

Stammati, Gaetano. Il coordinamento delle politiche di bilancio nella C.E.E. (Coordination of Budget Policies in E.E.C. With English summary.) *Bancaria*, February 1973, *29*(2), pp. 151–55.   [G: E.E.C.]

Surrey, Stanley S. Tax Expenditures and Tax Reform. In *Haveman, R. H. and Hamrin, R. D., eds.*, 1973, pp. 82–91.   [G: U.S.]

Weralski, Marian. Problems of Budgetary Policy in Socialist Planned Economies. In *[Hicks, U.]*, 1973, pp. 260–69.

Woodworth, Laurence N. Tax Reform—Past and Present. In *Tax Foundation, Inc.*, 1973, pp. 10–13.   [G: U.S.]

3228 National Government Debt Management

Bolten, Steven. Treasury Bill Auction Procedures: An Empirical Investigation. *J. Finance*, June 1973, *28*(3), pp. 577–85.   [G: U.S.]

Dobson, Steven W. The Term Structure of Interest Rates and the Maturity Composition of the Government Debt: The Canadian Case. *Can. J. Econ.*, August 1973, *6*(3), pp. 319–31.   [G: Canada]

Jetha, Nizar. Some Aspects of Domestic Financing of Central Government Expenditure: The Case of Kenya. In *[Hicks, U.]*, 1973, pp. 95–139.   [G: Kenya]

Vitaliano, Donald F. The Payment of Interest on the Federal Debt and the Distribution of Income. *J. Econ. Bus.*, Spring-Summer 1973, *25*(3), pp. 175–86.   [G: U.S.]

323 National Taxation and Subsidies

3230 National Taxation and Subsidies

Adam, Harold. Aspetti giuridici e fiscali delle società transnazionali nella C.E.E. (Legal and Taxation Aspects of the Transnational Corporations in the EEC. With English summary.) *Bancaria*, April 1973, *29*(4), pp. 495–500.   [G: Europe]

Ahmad, Rafiq. Incentive Taxation for Economic and Social Development. *Pakistan Econ. Soc. Rev.*, Summer 1973, *11*(2), pp. 154–66.   [G: Pakistan]

Akin, John S. Fiscal Capacity and the Estimation Method of the Advisory Commission on Intergovernmental Relations. *Nat. Tax J.*, June 1973, *26*(2), pp. 275–91.

Andersen, Palle Schelde. Built-in Flexibility and Sensitivity of the Personal Income Tax in Denmark.

Swedish J. Econ., March 1973, *75*(1), pp. 1–18.
[G: Denmark]

Andic, Fuat M. Fiscal Reform in Colombia: A Review Article. *Finanzarchiv*, 1973, *32*(1), pp. 160–66. [G: Colombia]

Andic, Suphan. Tax Problems of Developing Countries. *Finanzarchiv*, 1973, *32*(1), pp. 155–59.

Andrews, W. D. What's Fair About Death Taxes? *Nat. Tax J.*, September 1973, *26*(3), pp. 465–69.
[G: U.S.]

Atkinson, A. B. How Progressive Should Income Tax Be? In *Parkin, M., ed.*, 1973, pp. 90–109.

Azhar, B. A. Land Revenue Assessment: A Case Study. *Pakistan Develop. Rev.*, Autumn 1973, *12*(3), pp. 232–46. [G: Pakistan]

Azhar, B. A. Agricultural Taxation in West Pakistan. *Pakistan Econ. Soc. Rev.*, Autumn 1973, *11*(3), pp. 288–315. [G: Pakistan]

Azzi, Corry F. and Cox, James C. Equity and Efficiency in Evaluation of Public Programs. *Quart. J. Econ.*, August 1973, *87*(3), pp. 495–502.

Baer, Donald E. Income and Export Taxation of Agriculture in Costa Rica and Honduras. *J. Devel. Areas*, October 1973, *8*(1), pp. 39–53. [G: Costa Rica; Honduras]

Baker, R. Palmer, Jr. and Fritzhand, Gary I. United States Federal Income Taxation of Foreign-Flag Shipping Earnings. *Nat. Tax J.*, December 1973, *26*(4), pp. 537–51. [G: U.S.]

Bates, W. R.; Sexton, R. N. and Jackson, R. The Impact of Death Duties on the Rural Industries in Australia. *Quart. Rev. Agr. Econ.*, January 1973, *26*(1), pp. 25–43. [G: Australia]

Becker, Arthur P. The Distribution of Benefits and Costs of the Federally Subsidized Urban Renewal Programs. In *Harriss, C. L., ed.*, 1973, pp. 203–29.
[G: U.S.]

Behrens, John O. The Public and the Publicans Talk Taxes. *Nat. Tax J.*, June 1973, *26*(2), pp. 221–32.
[G: U.S.]

Beidleman, Carl R. Fixed Asset Depreciation Patterns: Market Based Evidence. *Z. ges. Staatswiss.*, October 1973, *129*(4), pp. 643–62. [G: U.S.]

Bhagwati, Jagdish N. and Dellalfar, William. The Brain Drain and Income Taxation. *World Devel.*, February 1973, *1*(1-2), pp. 94–101.

Bhargava, P. K. Problem of Pendency of Income-tax Appeals in India. *Bull. Int. Fiscal Doc.*, March 1973, *27*(3), pp. 95–103. [G: India]

Bird, Richard M. and De Wulf, Luc H. Taxation and Income Distribution in Latin America: A Critical Review of Empirical Studies. *Int. Monet. Fund Staff Pap.*, November 1973, *20*(3), pp. 639–82.
[G: Latin America]

Bittker, Boris I. Income Tax Deductions, Credits, and Subsidies for Personal Expenditures. *J. Law Econ.*, October 1973, *16*(2), pp. 193–213.
[G: U.S.]

Bittker, Boris I. Income Tax "Loopholes" and Political Rhetoric. *Mich. Law Rev.*, May 1973, *71*(6), pp. 1099–1128. [G: U.S.]

Blinder, Alan S. Note: Can Income Tax Increases Be Inflationary? *Nat. Tax J.*, June 1973, *26*(2), pp. 295–301.

Blum, Robert. Estate and Gift Taxation—Moderator's Remarks. *Nat. Tax J.*, September

1973, *26*(3), pp. 439–40. [G: U.S.]

Booms, Bernard H. and Halldorson, James R. The Politics of Redistribution: A Reformulation. *Amer. Polit. Sci. Rev.*, September 1973, *67*(3), pp. 924–33. [G: U.S.]

Boyle, Gerald J. Financing the Corporation for Public Television. *Nat. Tax J.*, June 1973, *26*(2), pp. 199–207. [G: U.S.]

Brannon, Gerard M. and Morss, Elliott R. The Tax Allowance for Dependents: Deductions versus Credits. *Nat. Tax J.*, December 1973, *26*(4), pp. 599–609. [G: U.S.]

Brannon, Gerard M. Death Taxes in a Structure of Progressive Taxes. *Nat. Tax J.*, September 1973, *26*(3), pp. 451–57.

Branson, William H. The Use of Variable Tax Rates for Stabilization Purposes. In *Musgrave, R. A., ed.*, 1973, pp. 267–85. [G: U.S.]

Brantner, Paul F. Taxation and the Multinational Firm. *Manage. Account.*, October 1973, *55*(4), pp. 11–16, 26. [G: U.S.]

Brazer, Harvey E. The Income Tax in the Federal Revenue System. In *Musgrave, R. A., ed.*, 1973, pp. 3–37. [G: U.S.]

Break, George F. Federal Tax Policy and the Private Saving Ratio. *Nat. Tax J.*, September 1973, *26*(3), pp. 409–14. [G: U.S.]

Briner, Ernst K. International Tax Management. *Manage. Account.*, February 1973, *54*(8), pp. 47–50.

Brinner, Roger. Inflation, Deferral and the Neutral Taxation of Capital Gains. *Nat. Tax J.*, December 1973, *26*(4), pp. 565–73. [G: U.S.]

Browne, K. M. Y. Transfer Duty: A Plea for Reform. *S. Afr. J. Econ.*, March 1973, *41*(1), pp. 26–33.
[G: S. Africa]

Browning, Edgar K. Social Insurance and Intergenerational Transfers. *J. Law Econ.*, October 1973, *16*(2), pp. 215–37. [G: U.S.]

Byrne, Robert F. and Spiro, Michael H. On Taxation as a Pollution Control Policy. *Swedish J. Econ.*, March 1973, *75*(1), pp. 105–09.

Cahoon, C. R. and Brown, William R. The Interstate Tax Dilemma—A Proposed Solution. *Nat. Tax J.*, June 1973, *26*(2), pp. 187–97. [G: U.S.]

Calhoun, Donald A. Oil and Gas Taxation. *Manage. Account.*, November 1973, *55*(5), pp. 21–24.
[G: U.S.]

Carman, Hoy F. and Youde, James G. Alternative Tax Treatment of Orchard Development Costs: Impacts on Producers, Middlemen, and Consumers. *Amer. J. Agr. Econ.*, May 1973, *55*(2), pp. 184–91. [G: U.S.]

Carroll, Mitchell B. The United States-Canada Income Tax Convention—Its Origin and Development. *Bull. Int. Fiscal Doc.*, April 1973, *27*(4), pp. 131–34. [G: U.S.; Canada]

Cebula, Richard J. and Chapin, Gene L. Bond Yields and the Lock-in Effect of Capital-Gains Taxation: A Pedagogical Note. *Rivista Int. Sci. Econ. Com.*, January 1973, *20*(1), pp. 83–89.

Chapman, Wayne E. Real Estate Tax Incentives. *Nat. Tax J.*, September 1973, *26*(3), pp. 389–93.
[G: U.S.]

Chaudhry, M. Ghaffar. The Problem of Agricultural Taxation in West Pakistan and an Alternative Solution. *Pakistan Develop. Rev.*, Summer 1973, *12* (2), pp. 93–122. [G: Pakistan]

Chiancone, Aldo. Il sistema svedese dei fondi di riserva per gli investimenti come strumento di stabilizzazione economica. (The Swedish System of Investment Funds as an Instrument of Stabilization Policy. With English summary.) *Rivista Int. Sci. Econ. Com.*, March 1973, *20*(3), pp. 242–66. [G: Sweden]

Cohen, Edwin S. Tax Simplification: Remarks. *Nat. Tax J.*, September 1973, *26*(3), pp. 311–15. [G: U.S.]

Cohen, Edwin S. The Administration's Tax Priorities. In *Tax Foundation, Inc.*, 1973, pp. 51–56. [G: U.S.]

Cole, William A. and Wales, Stephen H., Sr. The Investment Credit. *Manage. Account.*, March 1973, *54*(9), pp. 13–16, 35.

Collie, Marvin K. Estate and Gift Tax Revision. *Nat. Tax J.*, September 1973, *26*(3), pp. 441–49. [G: U.S.]

Corwin, R. D. and Miller, S. M. A qui profite l'impôt? Mythes et réalitiés. (Taxation and its Beneficiaries: The Manipulation of Symbols. With English summary.) *Consommation*, January-March 1973, *20*(1), pp. 17–35. [G: U.S.]

Cosciani, Cesare. La riforma delle imposte dirette: il problema del gettito. (Reform of Direct Taxes: Problem of Revenue. With English summary.) *Bancaria*, October 1973, *29*(10), pp. 1229–38. [G: Italy]

Covey, Richard B. Estate and Gift Taxation. *Nat. Tax J.*, September 1973, *26*(3), pp. 459–63. [G: U.S.]

Crumbley, D. Larry. Behavioral Implications of Taxation. *Accounting Rev.*, October 1973, *48*(4), pp. 759–63. [G: U.S.]

Dahlman, S. Roland. Joint Establishments in Sweden. *Bull. Int. Fiscal Doc.*, June 1973, *27*(6), pp. 241–44. [G: Sweden]

Daicoff, Darwin W. The Federal Revenue System: Discussion. *J. Finance*, May 1973, *28*(2), pp. 503–06. [G: U.S.]

David, Martin. Increased Taxation with Increased Acceptability—A Discussion of Net Worth Taxation as a Federal Revenue Alternative. *J. Finance*, May 1973, *28*(2), pp. 481–95. [G: U.S.]

Davis, Jeffrey. The Krzyzaniak and Musgrave Model—Some Further Comments. *Kyklos*, 1973, *26* (2), pp. 387–94.

Dean, James M. Redistribution and Tax Concessions for Charitable Contributions. *Public Finance*, 1973, *28*(3–4), pp. 371–76.

Dewald, William G. The High Employment Budget and Overwithholding in 1972. *Ohio State U. Bull. Bus. Res.*, March 1973, *48*(3), pp. 1–3, 7. [G: U.S.]

Douglas, Paul H. The Problem of Tax Loopholes (or: My Eighteen Years in a Quandary). In *Haveman, R. H. and Hamrin, R. D., eds.*, 1973, pp. 74–81. [G: U.S.]

Downes, Beverley. Purchase Taxes and Retail Prices in the United Kingdom. *Appl. Econ.*, September 1973, *5*(3), pp. 199–218. [G: U.K.]

Due, John F. The Case for the Use of the Retail Form of Sales Tax in Preference to the Value-Added Tax. In *Musgrave, R. A., ed.*, 1973, pp. 205–13. [G: U.S.]

Eapen, A. T. and Eapen, Ana N. Income Redistributive Effects of State and Local Fiscs: Connecticut, A Case Study. *Public Finance Quart.*, October 1973, *1*(4), pp. 372–87. [G: U.S.]

Egozi, Mosheh. An Elementary Model of the Determination of the Level of Public Expenditure and the Distribution of the Tax Burden. *Public Finance*, 1973, *28*(3–4), pp. 259–79.

Eisner, Robert. Tax Incentives for Investment. *Nat. Tax J.*, September 1973, *26*(3), pp. 397–401. [G: U.S.]

Farioletti, Marius. Tax Administration Funding and Fiscal Policy. *Nat. Tax J.*, March 1973, *26*(1), pp. 1–16. [G: U.S.]

Feldstein, Martin S. Tax Incentives, Corporate Saving, and Capital Accumulation in the United States. *J. Public Econ.*, April 1973, *2*(2), pp. 159–71. [G: U.S.]

Feldstein, Martin S. and Fane, George. Taxes, Corporate Dividend Policy and Personal Savings: The British Postwar Experience. *Rev. Econ. Statist.*, November 1973, *55*(4), pp. 399–411. [G: U.K.]

Feldstein, Martin S. On the Optimal Progressivity of the Income Tax. *J. Public Econ.*, November 1973, *2*(4), pp. 357–76.

Fiegehen, G. C. and Lansley, P. S. The Tax-Credit Proposals. *Nat. Inst. Econ. Rev.*, May 1973, (64), pp. 44–67. [G: U.K.]

Ford, Allen. Selecting a Useful Life for the Investment Credit. *Manage. Account.*, April 1973, *54* (10), pp. 14–16.

Foster, C. D. A Note on the Treatment of Taxation in Cost-benefit Analysis. In *Wolfe, J. N., ed.*, 1973, pp. 63–74. [G: U.K.]

Foulon, Alain; Hatchuel, Georges and Kende, Pierre. Un premier bilan de la redistribution des revenus en France; Les impôts et cotisations sociales à la charge des ménages en 1965. (Balance of the Redistribution of Incomes in France: Personal Taxes and Social Security Contributions in 1965. With English summary.) *Consommation*, October-December 1973, *20*(4), pp. 5–133. [G: France]

Franke, Jürgen F. A. W. Zur Besteuerung der Werbung. (With English summary.) *Kyklos*, 1973, *26* (2), pp. 337–61. [G: W. Germany]

Freeman, A. Myrick, III and Haveman, Robert H. Clean Rhetoric and Dirty Water. In *Enthoven, A. C. and Freeman, A. M., III, eds.*, 1973, pp. 122–37. [G: U.S.]

Freeman, Roger A. Tax Relief for the Homeowner? *Nat. Tax J.*, September 1973, *26*(3), pp. 485–90. [G: U.S.]

Gangadin, Victor J. A Brief Outline of the Imposition in Guyana of Income Tax, Corporation Tax, Capital Gains Tax, Withholding Tax and Property Tax with Special Reference to Foreign Corporations Operating in Guyana, Through a Branch Establishment or an Agency. *Bull. Int. Fiscal Doc.*, November 1973, *27*(11), pp. 455–63. [G: Guyana]

Ganter, Ralph. Zur Weiterwälzung spezieller Verbrauchsteuern. (On the Shifting of Specific Excise Taxes. With English summary.) *Jahr. Nationalö-*

kon. Statist., January 1973, *187*(2), pp. 108–27.

Gifford, William C., Jr. United States Tax Effects of Foreign Losses: A Symmetry Analysis. *Yale Law J.,* December 1973, *83*(2), pp. 312–56. [G: U.S.]

Gillum, Gary P. Capital Gains: Perennial Subject for Tax Reform Debate. *Fed. Res. Bank Bus. Rev. Phila.,* September 1973, pp. 3–11. [G: U.S.]

Ginsburg, Martin D. Tax Simplification—A Practitioner's View. *Nat. Tax J.,* September 1973, *26*(3), pp. 317–30. [G: U.S.]

Glennerster, Howard. A Tax Credit Scheme for Britain?—A Review of the British Government's Green Paper. *J. Human Res.,* Fall 1973, *8*(4), pp. 422–35. [G: U.K.]

Goddard, Frederick O. and Goffman, Irving J. The Public Financing of Non-Public Education. *Rev. Soc. Econ.,* October 1973, *31*(2), pp. 152–66. [G: U.S.]

Goldsmith, J. C. Developments in French T. V. A. The Abandonment of the So Called "Buffer Rule." *Bull. Int. Fiscal Doc.,* February 1973, *27* (2), pp. 61–66. [G: France]

Goodman, Wolfe D. Deemed Realizations Under the Canadian Income Tax Act. *Bull. Int. Fiscal Doc.,* July 1973, *27*(7), pp. 291–97. [G: Canada]

Goodman, Wolfe D. Canada: The Effect of Recent Death Tax Legislation on Non-Canadians. *Bull. Int. Fiscal Doc.,* October 1973, *27*(10), pp. 415–19. [G: Canada]

Griffin, Wade L. and Lacewell, Ronald D. Long-Run Implications of a Tax in Kind to Reduce Supply and Increase Income: Comment. *Amer. J. Agr. Econ.,* Part I, November 1973, *55*(4), pp. 670–74.

Guerard, Michèle. The Brazilian State Value-Added Tax. *Int. Monet. Fund Staff Pap.,* March 1973, *20* (1), pp. 118–69. [G: Brazil]

Hahn, Frank H. On Optimum Taxation. *J. Econ. Theory,* February 1973, *6*(1), pp. 96–106.

Haller, Heinz. Die Berücksichtigung des Lebensunterhalts der Kinder und der Vorsorgeaufwendungen im Rahmen der Steuerreform—Zielsetzungen und Implikationen. (The Consideration of Family Expenses for Children and of Providence Expenditures in the Tax Reform. With English summary.) *Z. ges. Staatswiss.,* August 1973, *129*(3), pp. 504–34. [G: Germany]

Hamdani, Daood H. Fiscal Measures Against Inflation and Unemployment in Canada: 1973 Budget and Other Developments. *Bull. Int. Fiscal Doc.,* June 1973, *27*(6), pp. 223–40. [G: Canada]

Hamid, Javed. The Problem of Agricultural Taxation in West Pakistan and an Alternative Solution: Comment. *Pakistan Develop. Rev.,* Autumn 1973, *12*(3), pp. 311–14. [G: Pakistan]

Harriss, C. Lowell. Capital Needs, Savings, and Jobs. In *Tax Foundation, Inc.,* 1973, pp. 27–34. [G: U.S.]

Heady, Earl O. Long-Run Implications of a Tax in Kind to Reduce Supply and Increase Income: Reply. *Amer. J. Agr. Econ.,* Part I, November 1973, *55*(4), pp. 675.

Heffernan, W. Joseph, Jr. Variations in Negative Tax Rates in Current Public Assistance Programs: An Example of Administrative Discretion. *J. Human Res.,* Supplement 1973, *8,* pp. 56–68. [G: U.S.]

Heimann, Fritz F. Foundations and Government: Perspectives for the Future. In *Heimann, F. F., ed.,* 1973, pp. 259–73. [G: U.S.]

Hellmuth, William F. The Federal Revenue System: Discussion. *J. Finance,* May 1973, *28*(2), pp. 496–99. [G: U.S.]

Heyding, Lawrence F. Corporate Reorganizations ("Rollovers") in Canada. *Bull. Int. Fiscal Doc.,* September 1973, *27*(9), pp. 363–71. [G: Canada]

Holloway, Ronald. More Gambling, Less Tax? *Lloyds Bank Rev.,* October 1973, (110), pp. 31–43. [G: U.K.]

Husby, Ralph D. Impact of a Negative Income Tax on Aggregate Demand and Supply. *Western Econ. J.,* March 1973, *11*(1), pp. 111–17.

Jain, Anil Kumar. Computation of Net Taxable Income for Assessment in India. *Bull. Int. Fiscal Doc.,* February 1973, *27*(2), pp. 47–58. [G: India]

Jain, Anil Kumar. Appellate Machinery for Income-Tax in India. *Bull. Int. Fiscal Doc.,* April 1973, *27* (4), pp. 135–42. [G: India]

Jain, Usha. India: A Review of Wealth Tax. *Bull. Int. Fiscal Doc.,* October 1973, *27*(10), pp. 421–28. [G: India]

Jao, Y. C. Tax Structure and Tax Burden in Taiwan. *Bull. Int. Fiscal Doc.,* March 1973, *27*(3), pp. 104–14. [G: Taiwan]

Jasinowski, Jerry J. The Economics of Federal Subsidy Programs. In *Harriss, C. L., ed.,* 1973, pp. 3–17. [G: U.S.]

Jasinowski, Jerry J. The Great Fiscal Unknown —Subsidies. *Amer. J. Econ. Soc.,* January 1973, *32* (1), pp. 1–16. [G: U.S.]

Jetha, Nizar. Some Aspects of Domestic Financing of Central Government Expenditure: The Case of Kenya. In *[Hicks, U.],* 1973, pp. 95–139. [G: Kenya]

Kahn, C. Harry. The Place of Consumption and Net-Worth Taxation in the Federal Tax Structure. In *Musgrave, R. A., ed.,* 1973, pp. 133–54. [G: U.S.]

Karageorgas, Dionysios. The Distribution of Tax Burden by Income Groups in Greece. *Econ. J.,* June 1973, *83*(330), pp. 436–48. [G: Greece]

Karageorgas, Dionysios. Taxation of Foreign Firms: Discriminative and Allocative Effects. *Public Finance Quart.,* July 1973, *1*(3), pp. 239–65.

Kau, Randall K. C. and Schler, Michael L. Inflation and the Federal Income Tax. *Yale Law J.,* March 1973, *82*(4), pp. 716–44. [G: U.S.]

Kerns, Waldon R. and Jansma, J. Dean. Financial Need Priorities for Awarding Construction Grants-in-Aid. *Growth Change,* January 1973, *4* (1), pp. 17–24. [G: U.S.]

Kesselman, Jonathan R. A Comprehensive Approach to Income Maintenance: Swift. *J. Public Econ.,* February 1973, *2*(1), pp. 59–88. [G: U.S.]

Khan, Mohammad Zubair. The Responsiveness of Tax Yield to Increases in National Income. *Pakistan Develop. Rev.,* Winter 1973, *12*(4), pp. 416–32. [G: Pakistan]

Khanna, Kailash C. India: The Finance Bill, 1973. *Bull. Int. Fiscal Doc.,* April 1973, *27*(4), pp.

143–45. [G: India]

Kinoshita, Kazuo. The Use of Tax Incentives for Export by Developed Countries—The Japanese Case. *Bull. Int. Fiscal Doc.*, July 1973, *27*(7), pp. 271–90. [G: Japan]

Knauerhase, Ramon. A Survey of the Revenue Structure of the Kingdom of Saudi Arabia, 1961/62 to 1971/72. *Public Finance*, 1973, *28*(3–4), pp. 435–53. [G: Saudi Arabia]

Kolm, Serge-Christophe. A Note on Optimum Tax Evasion. *J. Public Econ.*, July 1973, *2*(3), pp. 265–70.

Kottis, Athena P. and Kottis, George C. Who Benefits from Higher Education Subsidies. A Reconsideration. *Tijdschr. Econ.*, 1973, *18*(3), pp. 451–56.

Kristof, Frank S. The Role of State Housing Finance and Development Agencies in Future Federal Housing Programs. *Amer. Real Estate Urban Econ. Assoc. J.*, Fall 1973, *1*(2), pp. 53–72. [G: U.S.]

Kristof, Frank S. Federal Housing Policies: Subsidized Production, Filtration and Objectives: Part II. *Land Econ.*, May 1973, *49*(2), pp. 163–74. [G: U.S.]

Krzyzaniak, Marian. Benefit-Cost and Incidence Study of Transfers, Financed by Taxes on Profits, in a Growing Neoclassical Economy with Two Labor Inputs. *Public Finance*, 1973, *28*(2), pp. 151–77.

Krzyzaniak, Marian and Özmucur, Süleyman. The Distribution of Income and the Short-run Burden of Taxes in Turkey, 1968. *Finanzarchiv*, 1973, *32* (1), pp. 69–97. [G: Turkey]

Kurtz, Jerome. Real Estate Tax Shelter—A Postscript. *Nat. Tax J.*, September 1973, *26*(3), pp. 341–46. [G: U.S.]

Kust, Leonard E. Alternatives for New Federal Revenues. In *Tax Foundation, Inc.*, 1973, pp. 14–18. [G: U.S.]

Labovitz, John R. 1969 Tax Reforms Reconsidered. In *Heimann, F. F., ed.*, 1973, pp. 101–31. [G: U.S.]

Leino, Unto. Lähdevero. (Source Tax. With English summary.) *Liiketaloudellinen Aikak.*, 1973, *22* (2), pp. 131–40. [G: Finland]

Lent, George E. Taxation of Agricultural Income in Developing Countries. *Bull. Int. Fiscal Doc.*, August 1973, *27*(8), pp. 324–42.

Lent, George E.; Casanegra, Milka and Guerard, Michèle. The Value-Added Tax in Developing Countries. *Int. Monet. Fund Staff Pap.*, July 1973, *20*(2), pp. 318–78.

LeRoy, Stephen F. Property Tax Assessment: How Fair Is It? *Fed. Res. Bank Kansas City Rev.*, July-August 1973, pp. 7–16. [G: U.S.]

Lewis, Stephen R., Jr. Agricultural Taxation and Intersectoral Resource Transfers. *Food Res. Inst. Stud.*, 1973, *12*(2), pp. 93–114.

Lockner, Allyn O. and Kim, Han J. Circuit-Breakers on Farm-Property-Tax Overload: A Case Study. *Nat. Tax J.*, June 1973, *26*(2), pp. 233–40. [G: U.S.]

Lumb, H. C. Economic Incentives to Control Pollution. In *Reynolds, L. G.; Green, G. D. and Lewis, D. R., eds.*, 1973, pp. 220–30. [G: U.S.]

Madden, Carl H. Is Our Tax System Making Us Se-

cond-Rate? Tax Reform: Savings and Consumption. *Nat. Tax J.*, September 1973, *26*(3), pp. 403–07. [G: U.S.]

Manvel, Allen D. Tax Capacity Versus Tax Performance: Comment. *Nat. Tax J.*, June 1973, *26*(2), pp. 293–4.

Matthiessen, Lars. Index-tied Income Taxes and Economic Policy. *Swedish J. Econ.*, March 1973, *75* (1), pp. 49–66.

Maxwell, James A. Income Tax Discrimination Against the Renter. *Nat. Tax J.*, September 1973, *26*(3), pp. 491–97. [G: U.S.]

McCallum, John S. The Impact of the Capital Gains Tax on Bond Yields. *Nat. Tax J.*, December 1973, *26*(4), pp. 575–83. [G: Canada]

McDaniel, Paul R. Tax Shelters and Tax Policy. *Nat. Tax J.*, September 1973, *26*(3), pp. 353–88. [G: U.S.]

McKenzie, Richard B. The Micro and Macro Economic Effects of Changes in the Statutory Tax Rates. *Rev. Soc. Econ.*, April 1973, *31*(1), pp. 20–30.

McKinnon, Ronald I. The Value-Added Tax and the Liberalization of Foreign Trade in Developing Economies: A Comment. *J. Econ. Lit.*, June 1973, *11*(2), pp. 520–24.

McLure, Charles E., Jr. Economic Effects of Taxing Value Added. In *Musgrave, R. A., ed.*, 1973, pp. 155–204. [G: U.S.]

McNees, Stephen K. Tax Refunds and Consumer Spending. *New Eng. Econ. Rev.*, January-February 1973, pp. 3–11. [G: U.S.]

McNees, Stephen K. Deductibility of Charitable Bequests. *Nat. Tax J.*, March 1973, *26*(1), pp. 79–98. [G: U.S.]

Mercer, Lloyd J. Rates of Return and Government Subsidization of the Canadian Pacific Railway: An Alternate View. *Can. J. Econ.*, August 1973, *6*(3), pp. 428–37. [G: Canada]

Metwally, Mohktar M. and Timmaiah, G. A Note on the Classical Utility Function for Purpose of the Theory of Taxation. *Finanzarchiv*, 1973, *31*(3), pp. 441–45.

Meyer, Peter B. Differences in Taxation of Households: One Test of a Policy-Relevant Evaluative Technique. *Public Finance*, 1973, *28* (1), pp. 30–42. [G: Philippines]

Mikesell, John L. The Corporate Income Tax and Rate of Return in Privately Owned Utilities, 1948–1970. *Public Finance*, 1973, *28*(3–4), pp. 291–300. [G: U.S.]

Miura, Makoto. The Tax Appeals System in Japan. *Bull. Int. Fiscal Doc.*, January 1973, *27*(1), pp. 3–9. [G: Japan]

Moeller, John F. Development of a Microsimulation Model for Evaluating Economic Implications of Income Transfer and Tax Policies. *Ann. Econ. Soc. Measure*, April 1973, *2*(2), pp. 183–87.

Moore, Thomas Gale. Science, Technology, and Industry. In *Ott, D. J., et al.*, 1973, pp. 67–89. [G: U.S.]

Morawetz, David. Personal Income Taxes and Consumer Spending in the United Kingdom, 1958–69. *Public Finance*, 1973, *28*(2), pp. 178–95. [G: U.K.]

Motley, Brian. Sales versus Income Taxes: A Pedagogic Note. *Oxford Econ. Pap.*, July 1973, *25*(2), pp. 204–12.

Mullineaux, Donald J. Paying for Social Security: Is It Time To "Retire" the Payroll Tax? *Fed. Res. Bank Bus. Rev. Phila.*, April 1973, pp. 3–10.
[G: U.S.]

Munsche, Richard C. International Competition and Tax Reform. In *Tax Foundation, Inc.*, 1973, pp. 59–64.
[G: U.S.]

Nath, Shyam. On Moping of the Agricultural Surplus. *Econ. Aff.*, January–February 1973, *18*(1-2), pp. 81–85.

Nath, Shyam. Comparison of States' Tax Ratio, Marginal Tax Rate and Income Elasticity of Taxation. *Econ. Aff.*, April 1973, *18*(4), pp. 185–89, 196.
[G: India]

Nelson, Richard R. and Krashinsky, Michael. Two Major Issues of Public Policy: Public Subsidy and Organization of Supply. In *Young, D. R. and Nelson, R. R., eds.*, 1973, pp. 47–69.
[G: U.S.]

Nichols, Donald R. and Fielitz, Bruce D. Awareness of Marginal Income Tax Rates Among Taxpayers. *Miss. Val. J. Bus. Econ.*, Spring 1973, *8*(3), pp. 39–46.
[G: U.S.]

Nowotny, Ewald. On the Incidence of Real Estate Taxation. *Z. Nationalökon.*, 1973, *33*(1-2), pp. 133–60.

Okner, Benjamin A. The Federal Revenue System: Discussion. *J. Finance*, May 1973, *28*(2), pp. 500–03.
[G: U.S.]

Ott, David J. and Ott, Attiat F. The Effect of Nonneutral Taxation on the Use of Capital by Sector. *J. Polit. Econ.*, July-August 1973, *81*(4), pp. 972–81.
[G: U.S.]

Ott, David J. The Federal Revenue System: Discussion. *J. Finance*, May 1973, *28*(2), pp. 499–500.
[G: U.S.]

Packer, Arnold H. A Budget Structured to Reflect Economic Objectives. *J. Finance*, May 1973, *28*(2), pp. 467–80.
[G: U.S.]

Pasour, E. C., Jr. Real Property Taxes and Farm Real Estate Values: Incidence and Implications. *Amer. J. Agr. Econ.*, Part I, November 1973, *55*(4), pp. 549–56.
[G: U.S.]

Pechman, Joseph A. International Trends in the Distribution of Tax Burdens: Implications for Tax Policy. *Bull. Int. Fiscal Doc.*, December 1973, *27*(12), pp. 487–95.
[G: U.S.]

Pechman, Joseph A. The Rich, the Poor, and the Taxes They Pay. In *Reynolds, L. G.; Green, G. D. and Lewis, D. R., eds.*, 1973, pp. 260–82.
[G: U.S.]

Pechman, Joseph A. Responsiveness of the Federal Individual Income Tax to Changes in Income. *Brookings Pap. Econ. Act.*, 1973, (2), pp. 385–421.
[G: U.S.]

Pelkmans, Jacques. Government Aid to Industry in the Benelux Countries. In *Scaperlanda, A. E., ed.*, 1973, pp. 107–62.
[G: Benelux]

Peltzman, Sam. The Effect of Government Subsidies-in-Kind on Private Expenditures: The Case of Higher Education. *J. Polit. Econ.*, January-February 1973, *81*(1), pp. 1–27.
[G: U.S.]

Penner, Rudolph G. Health. In *Ott, D. J., et al.*, 1973, pp. 171–92.
[G: U.S.]

Penner, Rudolph G. Housing and Community De-velopment. In *Ott, D. J., et al.*, 1973, pp. 91–111.
[G: U.S.]

Penner, Rudolph G.; Ott, David J. and Ott, Attiat F. Income Security. In *Ott, D. J., et al.*, 1973, pp. 193–214.
[G: U.S.]

Pepper, H. W. T. Taxing Pollution. *Bull. Int. Fiscal Doc.*, May 1973, *27*(5), pp. 189–93.

Peston, Maurice. A Note on Tax Changes and Fluctuations in National Income. *J. Polit. Econ.*, November-December 1973, *81*(6), pp. 1467–70.
[G: U.S.]

Plowden, S. P. C. Indirect Taxation of Motorway and Alternative Consumption. *J. Transp. Econ. Policy*, September 1973, *7*(3), pp. 250–57.
[G: U.K.]

Poindexter, J. Carl, Jr. and Jones, C. P. The Effect of Recent Tax Policy Changes on Manufacturing Investment. *Quart. Rev. Econ. Bus.*, Winter 1973, *13*(4), pp. 79–88.
[G: U.S.]

Polanyi, George and Polanyi, Priscilla. Tax Credits: A Reverse Income Tax. *Nat. Westminster Bank Quart. Rev.*, February 1973, pp. 20–34.
[G: U.K.]

Pollock, Richard. The Effect of Alternative Regulatory Treatment of Tax Depreciation on Utility Tax Payments. *Nat. Tax J.*, March 1973, *26*(1), pp. 43–57.
[G: U.S.]

Prest, Alan R. Public Finance: Backward Area or New Frontier? *Economica, N.S.*, May 1973, *40*(158), pp. 121–35.
[G: U.K.]

Prest, Alan R. On the Distinction between Direct and Indirect Taxation. In *[Hicks, U.]*, 1973, pp. 44–56.

Price, R. W. R. Some Aspects of the Progressive Income Tax Structure in the UK. *Nat. Inst. Econ. Rev.*, August 1973, (65), pp. 52–63.
[G: U.K.]

Qureshi, Sarfraz K. The Problem of Agricultural Taxation in West Pakistan and an Alternative Solution: A Comment. *Pakistan Develop. Rev.*, Winter 1973, *12*(4), pp. 433–37.
[G: Pakistan]

Racster, Ronald L. and Howard, Robert. Evaluation of Multiple Subsidy Programs in a Local Market. *Amer. Real Estate Urban Econ. Assoc. J.*, Fall 1973, *1*(2), pp. 104–18.
[G: U.S.]

Raj, K. N. Direct Taxation of Agriculture. *Indian Econ. Rev.*, April 1973, *8*(1), pp. 1–15.
[G: India]

Raup, Phillip. Corporate Farming in the United States. *J. Econ. Hist.*, March 1973, *33*(1), pp. 274–90.
[G: U.S.]

Rein, Martin. Recent British Experience with Negative Income Tax. *J. Human Res.*, Supplement 1973, *8*, pp. 69–89.
[G: U.K.; U.S.]

Rejda, George E. and Shepler, Richard J. The Impact of Zero Population Growth on the OASDHI Program. *J. Risk Ins.*, September 1973, *40*(3), pp. 313–25.
[G: U.S.]

Renas, Steve. Work Effort and the Progressive Income Tax: A Note. *Tijdschr. Econ.*, 1973, *18*(3), pp. 441–43.

Rennie, Henry G. Federal Tax Policy and Fixed Capital Expenditures by Ohio's Electric Utilities. *Ohio State U. Bull. Bus. Res.*, July 1973, *48*(7), pp. 5–7.
[G: U.S.]

Renshaw, Edward F. A Note on Mass Transit Subsidies. *Nat. Tax J.*, December 1973, *26*(4), pp. 638–44.
[G: U.S.]

Rica, Narciso A. Some Reflections on Permanent Tributary Reform. *Bull. Int. Fiscal Doc.*, May 1973, *27*(5), pp. 179–88.

Richard, Enrique P. Treatment of Royalties in Tax Conventions Between Developed and Developing Countries. *Bull. Int. Fiscal Doc.*, October 1973, *27*(10), pp. 407–14.

Rolph, Earl R. Discriminating Effects of the Income Tax Treatment of Owner-Occupants. *Nat. Tax J.*, September 1973, *26*(3), pp. 471–84. [G: U.S.]

Rose, Louis A. The Development Value Tax. *Urban Stud.*, June 1973, *10*(2), pp. 271–75.

Ruebling, Charlotte E. A Value Added Tax and Factors Affecting Its Economic Impact. *Fed. Res. Bank St. Louis Rev.*, September 1973, *55*(9), pp. 15–19.

Rzhanitsina, L. Public Consumption Funds in the USSR. *Int. Lab. Rev.*, December 1973, *108*(6), pp. 516–35. [G: U.S.S.R.]

Sandford, C. T. Prospects for Wealth Taxes. *Nat. Westminster Bank Quart. Rev.*, November 1973, pp. 27–40. [G: U.K.]

Saulnier, Raymond J. Is a Tax Increase Inevitable? In *Tax Foundation, Inc.*, 1973, pp. 6–9. [G: U.S.]

Sazama, Geraldo W. and Davis, Harlan. Land Taxation and Land Reform. *Econ. Develop. Cult. Change*, Part I, July 1973, *21*(4), pp. 642–54. [G: Latin America]

Schechter, Henry B. Federally Subsidized Housing Program Benefits. In *Harriss, C. L., ed.*, 1973, pp. 31–63. [G: U.S.]

Shannon, John. Residential Property Tax Relief—A Federal Responsibility? *Nat. Tax J.*, September 1973, *26*(3), pp. 499–513. [G: U.S.]

Shaw, Gaylord. Government as Promoter, Sustainer, and Subsidizer of "Private Enterprise." In *Haveman, R. H. and Hamrin, R. D., eds.*, 1973, pp. 47–51. [G: U.S.]

Shoup, Carl S. Factors Bearing on an Assumed Choice between a Federal Retail-Sales Tax and a Federal Value-Added Tax. In *Musgrave, R. A., ed.*, 1973, pp. 215–26. [G: U.S.]

Shoup, Carl S. Three Fiscal Reports on Colombia: A Review Article. *Nat. Tax J.*, March 1973, *26*(1), pp. 59–63. [G: Colombia]

Silverstein, Leonard L. Federal Tax Policy for Tax Shelters. *Nat. Tax J.*, September 1973, *26*(3), pp. 347–51. [G: U.S.]

Singh, Balbir. Making Honesty the Best Policy. *J. Public Econ.*, July 1973, *2*(3), pp. 257–63.

Sinha, R. K. Report of the Committee on Taxation of Agricultural Wealth and Income—An Appraisal. *Econ. Aff.*, January–February 1973, *18*(1-2), pp. 17–28. [G: India]

Sinha, R. K. A Note on Central Budget 1973–74. *Econ. Aff.*, April 1973, *18*(4), pp. 190–96. [G: India]

Slitor, Richard E. Administrative Aspects of Expenditures Taxation. In *Musgrave, R. A., ed.*, 1973, pp. 227–63. [G: U.S.]

Smith, Dan Throop. Capital Gains and Losses in Income Taxation. In *Tax Foundation, Inc.*, 1973, pp. 43–47. [G: U.S.]

Snowbarger, Marvin and Kirk, John. A Cross-Sectional Model of Built-In Flexibility, 1954–1969.

Nat. Tax J., June 1973, *26*(2), pp. 241–49. [G: U.S.]

Spiro, Erwin. The 1973 Income Tax Changes in South Africa. *Bull. Int. Fiscal Doc.*, September 1973, *27*(9), pp. 372–78. [G: S. Africa]

Srinivasan, T. N. Tax Evasion: A Model. *J. Public Econ.*, November 1973, *2*(4), pp. 339–46.

Steedman, Ian. Some Long-run Equilibrium Tax Theory. *Public Finance*, 1973, *28*(1), pp. 43–51.

Stephenson, Charles M. Implications of PLLRC Tax Recommendations for Federal Hydro Projects and Power Facilities. *Land Econ.*, February 1973, *49*(1), pp. 67–75. [G: U.S.]

Stott, Alexander L. Capital Recovery in a World of Inflation. In *Tax Foundation, Inc.*, 1973, pp. 35–42. [G: U.S.]

Suliman, Ali A. Fiscal Incentives for Industrial Investment in the Sudan. *Bull. Int. Fiscal Doc.*, August 1973, *27*(8), pp. 315–23. [G: Sudan]

Suman, H. N. P. S. Effect of Corporate Taxation on Saving and Capital Formation in Some Indian Industries. *Econ. Aff.*, November-December 1973, *18*(11–12), pp. 485–96. [G: India]

Sunley, Emil M., Jr. Towards a More Neutral Investment Tax Credit. *Nat. Tax J.*, June 1973, *26*(2), pp. 209–20. [G: U.S.]

Surrey, Stanley S. Tax Expenditures and Tax Reform. In *Haveman, R. H. and Hamrin, R. D., eds.*, 1973, pp. 82–91. [G: U.S.]

Swan, Craig. Housing Subsidies and Housing Starts. *Amer. Real Estate Urban Econ. Assoc. J.*, Fall 1973, *1*(2), pp. 119–40. [G: U.S.]

Szakolczai, G. Capital Taxes, Self-Financing and Capital Transfer. *Acta Oecon.*, 1973, *10*(3–4), pp. 361–76. [G: Hungary]

Teeters, Nancy H. The Payroll Tax and Social-Security Finance. In *Musgrave, R. A., ed.*, 1973, pp. 87–112. [G: U.S.]

Tietenberg, Thomas H. Specific Taxes and the Control of Pollution: A General Equilibrium Analysis. *Quart. J. Econ.*, November 1973, *87*(4), pp. 503–22.

Todd, Ralph H. Evidence of Immediate Tax Shifting in U.S. Manufacturing, 1948–1967. *Nebr. J. Econ. Bus.*, Spring 1973, *12*(2), pp. 55–63. [G: U.S.]

Turner, John N. Canada: Bill C-222. *Bull. Int. Fiscal Doc.*, March 1973, *27*(3), pp. 87–94. [G: Canada]

Vanik, Charles A. Corporate Federal Tax Payments and Federal Subsidies to Corporations. In *Andreano, R. L., ed.*, 1973, pp. R340–23.

Vartholomeos, John. Corporate Taxes and the United States Balance of Trade: A Comment. *Nat. Tax J.*, December 1973, *26*(4), pp. 653–54.

Vitaliano, Donald F. A Reconsideration of Some Aspects of the Utility Sacrifice Rules of Taxation. *Public Finance Quart.*, January 1973, *1*(1), pp. 59–65.

Vitaliano, Donald F. The Payment of Interest on the Federal Debt and the Distribution of Income. *J. Econ. Bus.*, Spring-Summer 1973, *25*(3), pp. 175–86. [G: U.S.]

Weigner, Edward A. Tax Simplification. *Nat. Tax J.*, September 1973, *26*(3), pp. 337–39. [G: U.S.]

Weinrobe, Maurice D. Corporate Taxes and the

United States Balance of Trade: Reply. *Nat. Tax J.*, December 1973, *26*(4), pp. 655.

Weissler, Mark L. Snowmobiles and the Environment. *Yale Law J.*, March 1973, *82*(4), pp. 772–86.
[G: U.S.]

Welfeld, Irving H. Toward a New Federal Housing Policy. In *Grieson, R. E., ed.*, 1973, pp. 200–13.
[G: U.S.]

Wenders, John T. Corrective Taxes and Pollution Abatement. *J. Law Econ.*, October 1973, *16*(2), pp. 365–68.

Weralski, Marian. The New Structure of Turnover and Income Taxes in Poland. *Bull. Int. Fiscal Doc.*, December 1973, *27*(12), pp. 497–506.
[G: Poland]

White, Kenneth J. The Tax Structure and Discrimination Against Working Wives: A Comment. *Nat. Tax J.*, March 1973, *26*(1), pp. 119–22.

Wiegner, Edward A. Tax Simplification. *Nat. Tax J.*, September 1973, *26*(3), pp. 337–39. [G: U.S.]

Williams, David O., Jr. Simplification of the Federal Tax Laws for Corporations. *Nat. Tax J.*, September 1973, *26*(3), pp. 331–36. [G: U.S.]

Wisman, Jon D. and Sawers, Larry. Wealth Taxation for the United States. *J. Econ. Issues*, September 1973, *7*(3), pp. 417–36. [G: U.S.]

Wolk, Harry I. and Tearney, Michael G. Income Tax Allocation and Loss Carryforwards: Exploring Uncharted Ground. *Accounting Rev.*, April 1973, *48*(2), pp. 292–99.

Woods, W. Fred. Impact of Estate and Inheritance Taxes on U.S. Farms. *Agr. Finance Rev.*, July 1973, *34*, pp. 7–11. [G: U.S.]

Woods, W. Fred. Tax-Loss Farming. *Agr. Finance Rev.*, July 1973, *34*, pp. 24–30. [G: U.S.]

Woodworth, Laurence N. Tax Reform—Past and Present. In *Tax Foundation, Inc.*, 1973, pp. 10–13. [G: U.S.]

Zwick, David R. A Criticism of the Effluent Charge. In *Enthoven, A. C. and Freeman, A. M., III, eds.*, 1973, pp. 138–40. [G: U.S.]

324 State and Local Government Finance

3240 General

Ahlbrandt, Roger S., Jr. Efficiency in the Provision of Fire Services. *Public Choice*, Fall 1973, *16*, pp. 1–15. [G: U.S.]

Boskin, Michael J. Local Government Tax and Product Competition and the Optimal Provision of Public Goods. *J. Polit. Econ.*, January-February 1973, *81*(1), pp. 203–10.

Cooper, S. Kerry. Idle Cash Balances of State and Local Governments: An Estimation Technique. *Nebr. J. Econ. Bus.*, Spring 1973, *12*(2), pp. 21–33. [G: U.S.]

David, Wilfred L. Development from Below: Aspects of Local Government and Finance in a Developing Economy—Guyana. In *[Hicks, U.]*, 1973, pp. 304–27. [G: Guyana]

Dobson, L. Wayne. The Investment of Idle Public Funds: A Review of the Issues. *Nebr. J. Econ. Bus.*, Spring 1973, *12*(2), pp. 3–8. [G: U.S.]

Dobson, L. Wayne and Hollenhorst, Jerry. The Economics of Idle Public Funds Policies: A Reconsid-

eration: A Reply. *Nat. Tax J.*, December 1973, *26*(4), pp. 657–59.

Eapen, A. T. and Eapen, Ana N. Income Redistributive Effects of State and Local Fiscs: Connecticut, A Case Study. *Public Finance Quart.*, October 1973, *1*(4), pp. 372–87. [G: U.S.]

Ehrenberg, Ronald G. Municipal Government Structure, Unionization, and the Wages of Fire Fighters. *Ind. Lab. Relat. Rev.*, October 1973, *27*(1), pp. 36–48. [G: U.S.]

Gramlich, Edward M. and Galper, Harvy. State and Local Fiscal Behavior and Federal Grant Policy. *Brookings Pap. Econ. Act.*, 1973, (1), pp. 15–58.
[G: U.S.]

Hempel, George H. Wage and Price Controls for State and Local Governments: Their Effectiveness and the Potential Effects of Phase III. *Public Policy*, Summer 1973, *21*(3), pp. 425–36.
[G: U.S.]

Hempel, George H. An Evaluation of Municipal "Bankruptcy" Laws and Procedures. *J. Finance*, December 1973, *28*(5), pp. 1339–51. [G: U.S.]

Kessler, Robert P. and Hartman, Chester W. The Illusion and the Reality of Urban Renewal: A Case Study of San Francisco's Yerba Buena Center. *Land Econ.*, November 1973, *49*(4), pp. 440–53.
[G: U.S.]

Kiefer, Donald W. Compared to Other States, Indiana Taxes are Very High—Very Low—Neither of the Above. *Indiana Bus. Rev.*, January-February 1973, *48*, pp. 8–10. [G: U.S.]

Lotz, Jørgen R. Om refusioner eller generelle tilskud til kommunerne. (Grants-in-aid to Danish Local Governments—Matching or General? With English summary.) *Nationalokon. Tidsskr.*, 1973, *111*(2), pp. 205–20. [G: Denmark]

Mellor, Earl F. A Case Study: Costs and Benefits of Public Goods and Expenditures for a Ghetto. In *Boulding, K. E.; Pfaff, M. and Pfaff, A., eds.*, 1973, pp. 38–57. [G: U.S.]

Mikesell, John L. and Blair, John P. A Note on the Empirical Nature of the Taxpayer Rebellion. *Public Choice*, Fall 1973, *16*, pp. 43–50. [G: U.S.]

Raiff, Donald L. and Young, Richard M. Budget Surpluses for State and Local Governments: Undercutting Uncle Sam's Fiscal Stance? *Fed. Res. Bank Bus. Rev. Phila.*, March 1973, pp. 19–28.
[G: U.S.]

Rhodes, R. A. W. The European Community and British Public Administration: The Case of Local Government. *J. Common Market Stud.*, June 1973, *11*(4), pp. 263–75. [G: U.K.; E.E.C.]

Simon, Larry G. The School Finance Decisions: Collective Bargaining and Future Finance Systems. *Yale Law J.*, January 1973, *82*(3), pp. 409–60.
[G: U.S.]

Stern, David. Effects of Alternative State Aid Formulas on the Distribution of Public School Expenditures in Massachusetts. *Rev. Econ. Statist.*, February 1973, *55*(1), pp. 91–97. [G: U.S.]

Summers, Anita A. Equity in School Financing: The Courts Move In. *Fed. Res. Bank Bus. Rev. Phila.*, March 1973, pp. 3–13. [G: U.S.]

Thompson, Wilbur R. A Preface to Suburban Economics. In *Masotti, L. H. and Hadden, J. K., eds.*, 1973, pp. 409–30. [G: U.S.]

Toye, J. F. J. Structural Changes in the Government Sector of the Indian States, 1955-70. *J. Devel. Stud.*, January 1973, *9*(2), pp. 261–77. [G: India]

Verbrugge, James A. Idle Public Funds Policies: Some Additional Evidence. *Nebr. J. Econ. Bus.*, Spring 1973, *12*(2), pp. 9–19. [G: U.S.]

Watson, Ronald D. Lotteries: Can the Public and State Both Win? *Fed. Res. Bank Bus. Rev. Phila.*, July 1973, pp. 3–11. [G: U.S.]

Weissbourd, Bernard. The Satellite Community as Suburb. In *Masotti, L. H. and Hadden, J. K., eds.*, 1973, pp. 495–532. [G: U.S.]

Wirt, Frederick M. Financial and Desegregation Reform in Suburbia. In *Masotti, L. H. and Hadden, J. K., eds.*, 1973, pp. 457–88. [G: U.S.]

Zimmerman, Dennis. Expenditure-Tax Incidence Studies, Public Higher Education, and Equity. *Nat. Tax J.*, March 1973, *26*(1), pp. 65–70. [G: U.S.]

3241 State and Local Government Expenditures and Budgeting

Armstrong, R. H. R. Programme Budgeting in English Local Government. In *Novick, D., ed.*, 1973, pp. 105–10. [G: U.K.]

Aronson, J. Richard and Schwartz, Eli. Financing Public Goods and the Distribution of Population in a System of Local Governments. *Nat. Tax J.*, June 1973, *26*(2), pp. 137–60. [G: U.S.]

Barlow, Robin. Efficiency Aspects of Local School Finance: Reply. *J. Polit. Econ.*, January-February 1973, *81*(1), pp. 199–202. [G: U.S.]

Barzel, Yoram. Private Schools and Public School Finance. *J. Polit. Econ.*, January-February 1973, *81* (1), pp. 174–86. [G: U.S.]

Beck, Morris. Public Services in Metropolitan Areas of Australia. *Public Finance Quart.*, July 1973, *1* (3), pp. 307–22. [G: Australia]

Bergstrom, Theodore C. A Note on Efficient Taxation. *J. Polit. Econ.*, January-February 1973, *81*(1), pp. 187–91. [G: U.S.]

Bleakney, Thomas P. Problems and Issues in Public Employee Retirement Systems. *J. Risk Ins.*, March 1973, *40*(1), pp. 39–46. [G: U.S.]

Brierley, J. D. Programme Budgeting in Education in the United Kingdom. In *Novick, D., ed.*, 1973, pp. 97–103. [G: U.K.]

Cohn, Elchanan. On the Ranking of Social Investments in Education: A Reply. *Public Finance*, 1973, *28*(3–4), pp. 431–34. [G: U.S.]

Cook, Gail C. A. Effect of Metropolitan Government on Resource Allocation: The Case of Education in Toronto. *Nat. Tax J.*, December 1973, *26*(4), pp. 585–90. [G: Canada]

Crisman, R. E. W. State of Vermont, Program Budgeting, 1970. In *Novick, D., ed.*, 1973, pp. 181–84. [G: U.S.]

Derber, Milton, et al. Bargaining and Budget Making in Illinois Public Institutions. *Ind. Lab. Relat. Rev.*, October 1973, *27*(1), pp. 49–62. [G: U.S.]

Edelson, Noel M. Efficiency Aspects of Local School Finance: Comments and Extensions. *J. Polit. Econ.*, January-February 1973, *81*(1), pp. 158–73. [G: U.S.]

Ehrenberg, Ronald G. The Demand for State and Local Government Employees. *Amer. Econ. Rev.*, June 1973, *63*(3), pp. 366–79. [G: U.S.]

Firestine, Robert E. The Impact of Reapportionment Upon Local Government Aid Receipts within Large Metropolitan Areas. *Soc. Sci. Quart.*, September 1973, *54*(2), pp. 394–402. [G: U.S.]

Fleming, Thomas F., Jr. Manpower Impact of Purchases by State and Local Governments. *Mon. Lab. Rev.*, June 1973, *96*(6), pp. 33–39. [G: U.S.]

Gillespie, Hugh. Problems and Issues in Public Employee Retirement Systems: Discussion. *J. Risk Ins.*, March 1973, *40*(1), pp. 50–53. [G: U.S.]

Gilmer, Robert W. and Morgan, Daniel, Jr. The Equivalence of Flat Grants and Foundation Programs in State Education Aid Formulas. *Public Finance Quart.*, October 1973, *1*(4), pp. 437–47.

Greene, Kenneth V. Collective Decision-Making Models and the Measurement of Benefits in Fiscal Incidence Studies. *Nat. Tax J.*, June 1973, *26*(2), pp. 177–85.

Greenwood, Michael J. and Wadycki, Walter J. Crime Rates and Public Expenditures for Police Protection: Their Interaction. *Rev. Soc. Econ.*, October 1973, *31*(2), pp. 138–51. [G: U.S.]

Gylys, Julius A. Economic Analysis of Municipal and County Police Interdependence. In *Mattila, J. M. and Thompson, W. R., eds.*, 1973, pp. 151–63. [G: U.S.]

Hayes, Frederick O'R. Program Budgeting in the City of New York. In *Novick, D., ed.*, 1973, pp. 185–91. [G: U.S.]

Hight, Joseph E. and Pollock, Richard. Income Distribution Effects of Higher Education Expenditures in California, Florida and Hawaii. *J. Human Res.*, Summer 1973, *8*(3), pp. 318–30. [G: U.S.]

Hogan, Timothy D. and Shelton, Robert B. A Note on Barlow's Local School Finance. *J. Polit. Econ.*, January-February 1973, *81*(1), pp. 192–98. [G: U.S.]

Kirlin, John J. The Impact of Contract Services Arrangements on the Los Angeles Sheriff's Department and Law-Enforcement Services in Los Angeles County. *Public Policy*, Fall 1973, *21*(4), pp. 553–84. [G: U.S.]

Mehay, Stephen L. Police and Productivity: Can the Invisible Hand of Competition Extend the Long Arm of the Law? *Fed. Res. Bank Bus. Rev. Phila.*, May 1973, pp. 3–12. [G: U.S.]

Merewitz, Leonard. Cost Overruns in Public Works. In *Niskanen, W. A., et al., eds.*, 1973, pp. 277–95. [G: U.S.]

Miller, Stephen M. and Tabb, William K. A New Look at a Pure Theory of Local Expenditures. *Nat. Tax J.*, June 1973, *26*(2), pp. 161–76.

Mowitz, Robert J. Pennsylvania's Planning, Programming, Budgeting System. In *Novick, D., ed.*, 1973, pp. 169–80. [G: U.S.]

Murray, Barbara B. A Pure Theory of Local Expenditures Revisited. In *Mattila, J. M. and Thompson, W. R., eds.*, 1973, pp. 129–39.

Novick, David. Program Budgeting, 1971. In *Novick, D., ed.*, 1973, pp. 29–47.

Oates, Wallace E. The Effects of Property Taxes and Local Public Spending on Property Values: A

Reply and Yet Further Results. *J. Polit. Econ.*, July-August 1973, *81*(4), pp. 1004–08. [G: U.S.]

Ott, David J. The Budget Outlook: An Overview. In *Ott, D. J., et al.*, 1973, pp. 11–27. [G: U.S.]

Pollakowski, Henry O. The Effects of Property Taxes and Local Public Spending on Property Values: A Comment and Further Results. *J. Polit. Econ.*, July-August 1973, *81*(4), pp. 994–1003. [G: U.S.]

Ross, Kenneth H. Problems and Issues in Public Employee Retirement Systems: Discussion. *J. Risk Ins.*, March 1973, *40*(1), pp. 46–50. [G: U.S.]

Snyder, Wayne W. Are the Budgets of State and Local Governments Destabilizing? A Six Country Comparison. *Europ. Econ. Rev.*, June 1973, *4*(2), pp. 197–213.

Vogel, Ronald J. and Morrall, John F., III. The Impact of Medicaid on State and Local Health and Hospitals Expenditures, with Special Reference to Blacks. *J. Human Res.*, Spring 1973, *8*(2), pp. 202–11. [G: U.S.]

Weicher, John C. and Emerine, R. J., II. Econometric Analysis of State and Local Aggregate Expenditure Functions. *Public Finance*, 1973, *28*(1), pp. 69–83. [G: U.S.]

Ziderman, Adrian. On the Ranking of Social Investments in Education: A Comment. *Public Finance*, 1973, *28*(3–4), pp. 424–30. [G: U.S.]

3242 State and Local Government Taxation, Subsidies, and Revenue

Agapos, A. M. and Dunlap, Paul R. Elimination of Urban Blight Through Inverse Proportional Ad Valorem Property Taxation. *Amer. J. Econ. Soc.*, April 1973, *32*(2), pp. 143–52. [G: U.S.]

Atkinson, A. B. How Progressive Should Income Tax Be? In *Parkin, M., ed.*, 1973, pp. 90–109.

Bails, Dale. An Alternative: The Land Value Tax. *Amer. J. Econ. Soc.*, July 1973, *32*(3), pp. 283–94.

Barlev, Benzion. Location Effects of Intra-Area Tax Differentials. *Land Econ.*, February 1973, *49*(1), pp. 86–89.

Barlowe, Raleigh; Ahl, James G. and Bachman, Gordon. Use-Value Assessment Legislation in the United States. *Land Econ.*, May 1973, *49*(2), pp. 206–12. [G: U.S.]

Bentley, Philip. The Australian Local Government Tax Base: Revenue Potential. *Australian Econ. Pap.*, June 1973, *12*(20), pp. 21–35. [G: Australia]

Berney, Robert E. and Frerichs, Bernard H. Income Elasticities for State Tax Revenues: Techniques of Estimation and their Usefulness for Forecasting. *Public Finance Quart.*, October 1973, *1*(4), pp. 409–25. [G: U.S.]

Bohley, Peter. Der Nulltarif im Nahverkehr. (Free Transit in Metropolitan Areas. With English summary.) *Kyklos*, 1973, *26*(1), pp. 113–42.

Booms, Bernard H. and Hu, Teh-wei. Economic and Social Factors in the Provision of Urban Public Education. *Amer. J. Econ. Soc.*, January 1973, *32*(1), pp. 35–43. [G: U.S.]

Botha, D. J. J. Rating and Valuation. *S. Afr. J. Econ.*, March 1973, *41*(1), pp. 40–48. [G: S. Africa]

Briner, Ernst K. International Tax Management. *Manage. Account.*, February 1973, *54*(8), pp. 47–50.

Brown, Byron W. State Grants and Inequality of Opportunity in Education. In *Boulding, K. E.; Pfaff, M. and Pfaff, A., eds.*, 1973, pp. 208–25. [G: U.S.]

Cord, Steven. Revenue Sharing and Property Tax Reform. *Amer. J. Econ. Soc.*, October 1973, *32*(4), pp. 404. [G: U.S.]

Cord, Steven. How Land Value Taxation Would Affect Homeowners. *Amer. J. Econ. Soc.*, April 1973, *32*(2), pp. 153–54. [G: U.S.]

Downing, Paul B. User Charges and the Development of Urban Land. *Nat. Tax J.*, December 1973, *26*(4), pp. 631–37. [G: U.S.]

Elesh, David, et al. The New Jersey-Pennsylvania Experiment: A Field Study in Negative Taxation. In *Boulding, K. E.; Pfaff, M. and Pfaff, A., eds.*, 1973, pp. 181–201. [G: U.S.]

Fitch, Lyle C. Metropolitan Financial Problems. In *Grieson, R. E., ed.*, 1973, pp. 418–28. [G: U.S.]

Fortune, Peter. The Impact of Taxable Municipal Bonds: Policy Simulations with a Large Econometric Model. *Nat. Tax J.*, March 1973, *26*(1), pp. 29–42. [G: U.S.]

Freeman, A. Myrick, III and Haveman, Robert H. Clean Rhetoric and Dirty Water. In *Enthoven, A. C. and Freeman, A. M., III, eds.*, 1973, pp. 122–37. [G: U.S.]

Friedlaender, Ann F.; Swanson, Gerald J. and Due, John F. Estimating Sales Tax Revenue Changes in Response to Changes in Personal Income and Sales Tax Rates. *Nat. Tax J.*, March 1973, *26*(1), pp. 103–10. [G: U.S.]

Gaffney, Mason. Tax Reform to Release Land. In *Clawson, M., ed.*, 1973, pp. 115–51. [G: U.S.]

Gaffney, Mason. Land Rent, Taxation and Public Policy: Taxation and the Functions of Urban Land Rent. *Amer. J. Econ. Soc.*, January 1973, *32*(1), pp. 17–34.

Goetz, Charles J. The Revenue Potential of User-Related Charges in State and Local Governments. In *Musgrave, R. A., ed.*, 1973, pp. 113–29. [G: U.S.]

Grieson, Ronald E. Zoning, Housing Markets, and Urban Renewal: Introduction. In *Grieson, R. E., ed.*, 1973, pp. 133–48. [G: U.S.]

Guerard, Michèle. The Brazilian State Value-Added Tax. *Int. Monet. Fund Staff Pap.*, March 1973, *20*(1), pp. 118–69. [G: Brazil]

Hogan, Timothy D. and Shelton, Robert B. Interstate Tax Exportation and States' Fiscal Structures. *Nat. Tax J.*, December 1973, *26*(4), pp. 553–64. [G: U.S.]

Hyman, David N. and Pasour, E. C., Jr. Real Property Taxes, Local Public Services, and Residential Property Values. *Southern Econ. J.*, April 1973, *39*(4), pp. 601–11. [G: U.S.]

Hyman, David N. and Pasour, E. C., Jr. Note: Property Tax Differentials and Residential Rents in North Carolina. *Nat. Tax J.*, June 1973, *26*(2), pp. 303–07. [G: U.S.]

Jaffee, Bruce L. The Indiana Intangibles Tax: The Tax Nobody Pays? *Indiana Bus. Rev.*, July-August 1973, *48*, pp. 3–7. [G: U.S.]

Kerns, Waldon R. and Jansma, J. Dean. Financial Need Priorities for Awarding Construction Grants-in-Aid. *Growth Change,* January 1973, *4* (1), pp. 17–24. [G: U.S.]

Kiefer, Donald W. The 1973 Tax Package: The Effect on Local Governments. *Indiana Bus. Rev.,* September-October 1973, *48,* pp. 12–15. [G: U.S.]

Kiefer, Donald W. The 1973 Tax Package: Corporate Tax Restructuring. *Indiana Bus. Rev.,* July-August 1973, *48,* pp. 1–2. [G: U.S.]

Kiefer, Donald W. The 1973 Tax Package: The Sources of Property Tax Relief. *Indiana Bus. Rev.,* May-June 1973, *48,* pp. 21–23. [G: U.S.]

Ladd, Helen F. The Role of the Property Tax: A Reassessment. In *Musgrave, R. A., ed.,* 1973, pp. 39–86. [G: U.S.]

LeRoy, Stephen F. Property Tax Assessment: How Fair Is It? *Fed. Res. Bank Kansas City Rev.,* July-August 1973, pp. 7–16. [G: U.S.]

Lott, William F. and Miller, Stephen M. A Note on the Optimality Conditions for Excise Taxation. *Southern Econ. J.,* July 1973, *40*(1), pp. 122–23.

Lucier, Richard I. The Prediction of Public Choice Behavior in the Washington Tax Substitution Referendum. *Nat. Tax J.,* December 1973, *26*(4), pp. 625–30. [G: U.S.]

McLaren, J. Alec. An Income Tax Simulation Model for the State of Minnesota. *Nat. Tax J.,* March 1973, *26*(1), pp. 71–77. [G: U.S.]

Mitchell, William E. Equity Effects of Property Tax Relief for the Aged: The Circuit-Breaker Legislation. *Amer. J. Econ. Soc.,* October 1973, *32*(4), pp. 367–78. [G: U.S.]

Muller, Thomas. Income Redistribution Impact of State Grants to Public Schools: A Case Study of Delaware. In *Boulding, K. E.; Pfaff, M. and Pfaff, A., eds.,* 1973, pp. 226–45. [G: U.S.]

Nath, Shyam. Comparison of States' Tax Ratio, Marginal Tax Rate and Income Elasticity of Taxation. *Econ. Aff.,* April 1973, *18*(4), pp. 185–89, 196. [G: India]

Netzer, Dick. The Incidence of the Property Tax Revisited. *Nat. Tax J.,* December 1973, *26*(4), pp. 515–35. [G: U.S.]

Netzer, Dick. Effects of the Property Tax in Urban Areas. In *Pynoos, J.; Schafer, R. and Hartman, C. W., eds.,* 1973, pp. 510–22. [G: U.S.]

Oates, Wallace E. The Effects of Property Taxes and Local Public Spending on Property Values: A Reply and Yet Further Results. *J. Polit. Econ.,* July-August 1973, *81*(4), pp. 1004–08. [G: U.S.]

Olson, Edwin G. Determining Sample Size for State Tax Impact Studies. *Nat. Tax J.,* March 1973, *26* (1), pp. 99–102. [G: U.S.]

Ophek, Eli. On Samuelson's Analysis of Land Rent. *Amer. J. Econ. Soc.,* July 1973, *32*(3), pp. 306–10.

Paelinck, J. and Van Rompuy, P. Regionaal en sectoraal subsidiebeleid: Economische theorie en modellen. (Regional and Sectoral Subsidies—Economic Theory and Models. With English summary.) *Tijdschr. Econ.,* 1973, *18*(1), pp. 39–55. [G: Belgium]

Paglin, Morton and Fogarty, Michael. Equity and the Property Tax: A Reply. *Nat. Tax J.,* December 1973, *26*(4), pp. 651–52. [G: U.S.]

Pauly, Mark V. Income Redistribution as a Local Public Good. *J. Public Econ.,* February 1973, *2*(1), pp. 35–58.

Pechman, Joseph A. The Rich, the Poor, and the Taxes They Pay. In *Reynolds, L. G.; Green, G. D. and Lewis, D. R., eds.,* 1973, pp. 260–82. [G: U.S.]

Phares, Donald L. Impact of Spatial Tax Flows as Implicit Grants on State-Local Tax Incidence: With Reference to the Financing of Education. In *Boulding, K. E.; Pfaff, M. and Pfaff, A., eds.,* 1973, pp. 258–75. [G: U.S.]

Pollakowski, Henry O. The Effects of Property Taxes and Local Public Spending on Property Values: A Comment and Further Results. *J. Polit. Econ.,* July-August 1973, *81*(4), pp. 994–1003. [G: U.S.]

Reeves, H. Clyde. System Value Determination in the Assessment of Railroads for Property Taxation. *Nat. Tax J.,* March 1973, *26*(1), pp. 133–35.

Richman, Raymond L. The Capitalization of Property Taxes and Subsidies. In *Harriss, C. L., ed.,* 1973, pp. 19–27. [G: U.S.]

Rokoff, Gerald. Alternatives to the University Property Tax Exemption. *Yale Law J.,* November 1973, *83*(1), pp. 181–96.

Sabella, Edward M. Equity and the Property Tax: A Comment and an Alternative Conceptual Framework. *Nat. Tax J.,* December 1973, *26*(4), pp. 645–50. [G: U.S.]

de Seve, Charles W. Improved Pari-Mutual Taxation. *Nat. Tax J.,* December 1973, *26*(4), pp. 591–97. [G: U.S.]

Shannon, John. Residential Property Tax Relief—A Federal Responsibility? *Nat. Tax J.,* September 1973, *26*(3), pp. 499–513. [G: U.S.]

Shapiro, Perry and Legler, John B. Estimating Tax Revenue Changes in Response to Changes in Tax Rates. *Nat. Tax J.,* March 1973, *26*(1), pp. 111–13.

Skouras, Athanassios. On the Analysis of Property Tax Effects on Operating and Investment Decisions of Rental Property Owners. *Nat. Tax J.,* March 1973, *26*(1), pp. 123–25.

Stephenson, Charles M. Implications of PLLRC Tax Recommendations for Federal Hydro Projects and Power Facilities. *Land Econ.,* February 1973, *49*(1), pp. 67–75. [G: U.S.]

Szychowski, Mario L. Consideraciones analíticas respecto a un sistema alternativo del impuesto inmobiliario. (Analytical Considerations Regarding a System of Alternative Real Estate Tax. With English summary.) *Económica,* May-August 1973, *19*(2), pp. 201–16.

Waldauer, Charles. External Effects of Education Grants on Tax Base-Sharing Municipal Governments. In *Boulding, K. E.; Pfaff, M. and Pfaff, A., eds.,* 1973, pp. 246–58. [G: U.S.]

Webb, Lee. The Swindling of the Average Taxpayer: The Story of Taxes in Vermont. *Rev. Radical Polit. Econ.,* Summer 1973, *5*(2), pp. 18–46. [G: U.S.]

Williams, William V., et al. The Stability, Growth and Stabilizing Influence of State Taxes. *Nat. Tax J.,* June 1973, *26*(2), pp. 267–74. [G: U.S.]

3243 State and Local Government Borrowing

Dobson, Steven W. The Term Structure of Interest Rates and the Maturity Composition of the Government Debt: The Canadian Case. *Can. J. Econ.,* August 1973, *6*(3), pp. 319–31.   [G: Canada]

Forbes, Ronald. Finance and Banking: Refereed Papers II: Discussion. *J. Finance,* May 1973, *28*(2), pp. 539–41.   [G: U.S.]

Galper, Harvey and Peterson, George E. The Equity Effects of a Taxable Municipal Bond Subsidy. *Nat. Tax J.,* December 1973, *26*(4), pp. 611–24.   [G: U.S.]

Hempel, George H. Quantitative Borrower Characteristics Associated with Defaults on Municipal General Obligations. *J. Finance,* May 1973, *28*(2), pp. 523–30.   [G: U.S.]

Pruitt, Eleanor M. State and Local Borrowing Anticipations and Realizations. *Fed. Res. Bull.,* April 1973, *59*(4), pp. 257–60.   [G: U.S.]

Rubinfeld, Daniel. Credit Ratings and the Market for General Obligation Municipal Bonds. *Nat. Tax J.,* March 1973, *26*(1), pp. 17–27.   [G: U.S.]

325 Intergovernmental Financial Relationships

3250 Intergovernmental Financial Relationships

Akin, John S. Fiscal Capacity and the Estimation Method of the Advisory Commission on Intergovernmental Relations. *Nat. Tax J.,* June 1973, *26*(2), pp. 275–91.

Arnold, Mark R. Public Schools. In *Levitan, S. A., ed.,* 1973, pp. 21–51.   [G: U.S.]

Basu, Kalipada. Centre-States Financial Relations: A Critique. *Econ. Aff.,* May 1973, *18*(5), pp. 249–54.   [G: India]

Cahoon, C. R. and Brown, William R. The Interstate Tax Dilemma—A Proposed Solution. *Nat. Tax J.,* June 1973, *26*(2), pp. 187–97.   [G: U.S.]

Carroll, Mitchell B. The United States-Canada Income Tax Convention—Its Origin and Development. *Bull. Int. Fiscal Doc.,* April 1973, *27*(4), pp. 131–34.   [G: U.S.; Canada]

Carroll, Sidney L. A Note on Revenue Sharing and the Theory of Public Expenditures. *Public Choice,* Spring 1973, *14*, pp. 109–16.

Cohen, David K., et al. Revenue-Sharing as an Incentive Device: The Experience with Title I of the Elementary and Secondary Education Act. In *Stein, B. and Miller, S. M., eds.,* 1973, pp. 93–115.   [G: U.S.]

Courchene, Thomas J. and Beavis, David A. Federal-Provincial Tax Equalization: An Evaluation. *Can. J. Econ.,* November 1973, *6*(4), pp. 483–502.   [G: Canada]

Dales, Sophie R. Federal Grants to State and Local Governments. *Soc. Sec. Bull.,* June 1973, *36*(6), pp. 16–27.   [G: U.S.]

David, Wilfred L. Development from Below: Aspects of Local Government and Finance in a Developing Economy—Guyana. In *[Hicks, U.],* 1973, pp. 304–27.   [G: Guyana]

Dixon, John. The Changing Role of the Australian Commonwealth Grants Commission: A Reply. *Public Finance,* 1973, *28*(3–4), pp. 420–23.

Edwards, Clive T. Federal-State Financial Relations in Malaya. In *[Hicks, U.],* 1973, pp. 191–206.   [G: Malaysia]

Firestine, Robert E. The Impact of Reapportionment Upon Local Government Aid Receipts within Large Metropolitan Areas. *Soc. Sci. Quart.,* September 1973, *54*(2), pp. 394–402.   [G: U.S.]

Gramlich, Edward M. and Galper, Harvey. State and Local Fiscal Behavior and Federal Grant Policy. *Brookings Pap. Econ. Act.,* 1973, (1), pp. 15–58.   [G: U.S.]

Guerard, Michèle. The Brazilian State Value-Added Tax. *Int. Monet. Fund Staff Pap.,* March 1973, *20* (1), pp. 118–69.   [G: Brazil]

Hayden, F. Gregory. Fiscal Federalism: Program Budgeting and the Multilevel Governmental Setting. *Nebr. J. Econ. Bus.,* Winter 1973, *12*(1), pp. 23–42.

Heller, Walter W. Should the Government Share Its Tax Take? In *Rasmussen, D. W. and Haworth, C. T., eds.,* 1973, pp. 217–24.   [G: U.S.]

Heller, Walter W. Should the Government Share Its Tax Take? In *Reynolds, L. G.; Green, G. D. and Lewis, D. R., eds.,* 1973, pp. 417–24.   [G: U.S.]

Holland, David W. and Tweeten, Luther G. Human Capital Migration: Implications for Common School Finance. *Land Econ.,* August 1973, *49*(3), pp. 278–84.   [G: U.S.]

Hunter, J. S. H. Interstate Fiscal Equalization in the Federal Republic of Germany and Comparisons with Australia and Canada. *Australian Econ. Pap.,* June 1973, *12*(20), pp. 42–56.   [G: W. Germany; Australia; Canada]

James, Louis J. The Stimulation and Substitution Effects of Grants-In-Aid: A General Equilibrium Analysis. *Nat. Tax J.,* June 1973, *26*(2), pp. 251–65.

Levitan, Sar A. The Art of Giving Away Federal Dollars. In *Levitan, S. A., ed.,* 1973, pp. 1–20.   [G: U.S.]

Levitan, Sar A. The Payoff of the Federal Social Dollar. In *Levitan, S. A., ed.,* 1973, pp. 259–72.   [G: U.S.]

Levy, Michael E. and Torres, Juan. Grants and Revenue Sharing Abroad: Canada, Australia, West Germany. In *Moskoff, W., ed.,* 1973, pp. 4–21.   [G: Canada; W. Germany; Australia]

Lindholm, Richard W. State-Local School and Highway Expenditure Trends, 1965-1966 and 1969-1970. *Public Finance Quart.,* January 1973, *1*(1), pp. 29–34.   [G: U.S.]

Lotz, Jørgen R. Om refusioner eller generelle tilskud til kommunerne. (Grants-in-aid to Danish Local Governments—Matching or General? With English summary.) *Nationalokon. Tidsskr.,* 1973, *111*(2), pp. 205–20.   [G: Denmark]

Maxwell, James A. The New 1971 Federal-Provincial Fiscal Arrangements Act in Canada. *Econ. Rec.,* June 1973, *49*(126), pp. 306–10.   [G: Canada]

McGuire, Martin. Notes on Grants-in-Aid and Economic Interactions among Governments. *Can. J. Econ.,* May 1973, *6*(2), pp. 207–21.

Merriam, Robert E. The Impact of Federal Tax Reform on State-Local Revenues. In *Tax Foundation, Inc.*, 1973, pp. 19–21. [G: U.S.]

Ott, Attiat F. Education. In *Ott, D. J., et al.*, 1973, pp. 113–52. [G: U.S.]

Phares, Donald L. Impact of Spatial Tax Flows as Implicit Grants on State-Local Tax Incidence: With Reference to the Financing of Education. In *Boulding, K. E.; Pfaff, M. and Pfaff, A., eds.*, 1973, pp. 258–75. [G: U.S.]

Porter, David O. and Warner, David C. How Effective Are Grantor Controls?: The Case of Federal Aid to Education. In *Boulding, K. E.; Pfaff, M. and Pfaff, A., eds.*, 1973, pp. 276–302. [G: U.S.]

Pozen, Robert. The Financing of Local Housing Authorities: A Contract Approach for Public Corporations. *Yale Law J.*, May 1973, *82*(6), pp. 1208–27.

Raiff, Donald L. and Young, Richard M. Budget Surpluses for State and Local Governments: Undercutting Uncle Sam's Fiscal Stance? *Fed. Res. Bank Bus. Rev. Phila.*, March 1973, pp. 19–28. [G: U.S.]

Sastri, K. V. S. Federal Finance in Underdeveloped Countries. In *[Hicks, U.]*, 1973, pp. 207–29.

Scott, Anthony. The Defense of Federalism, or, the Attack on Unitary Government. *Amer. Econ.*, Fall 1973, *17*(2), pp. 162–69.

Starler, Norman H. and Thomas, Robert W. Intergovernmental Education Grants and the Efficiency of Resource Allocation in School Districts. *Appl. Econ.*, September 1973, *5*(3), pp. 181–92. [G: U.S.]

Stern, David. Effects of Alternative State Aid Formulas on the Distribution of Public School Expenditures in Massachusetts. *Rev. Econ. Statist.*, February 1973, *55*(1), pp. 91–97. [G: U.S.]

Thimmaiah, G. The Changing Role of the Australian Commonwealth Grants Commission: A Reexamination. *Public Finance*, 1973, *28*(3–4), pp. 407–19. [G: Australia]

Waldauer, Charles. Grant Structures and Their Effects on Aided Government Expenditures: An Indifference Curve Analysis. *Public Finance*, 1973, *28*(2), pp. 212–26.

Waldauer, Charles. External Effects of Education Grants on Tax Base-Sharing Municipal Governments. In *Boulding, K. E.; Pfaff, M. and Pfaff, A., eds.*, 1973, pp. 246–58. [G: U.S.]

Wentworth, Eric. Higher Education: The Reach Exceeds the Grasp. In *Levitan, S. A., ed.*, 1973, pp. 52–88. [G: U.S.]

400 International Economics

4000 General

Bergsten, C. Fred. The Future of the International Economic Order: An Agenda for Research. In *Bergsten, C. F., ed.*, 1973, pp. 1–59.

Howe, James W. The Developing Countries in a Changing International Economic Order: A Survey of Research Needs. In *Bergsten, C. F., ed.*, 1973, pp. 197–264.

410 INTERNATIONAL TRADE THEORY

411 International Trade Theory

4110 General

Ball, R. J. The Economic Models of Project LINK. In *Ball, R. J., ed.*, 1973, pp. 65–107. [G: W. Europe; N. America; Japan]

Balogh, T. and Balacs, P. Fact and Fancy in International Economic Relations. *World Devel.*, February 1973, *1*(1-2), pp. 76–92.

Batra, Raveendra N. Optimal Restrictions on Foreign Trade and Investment: Note. *Amer. Econ. Rev.*, December 1973, *63*(5), pp. 957–59.

Bhagwati, Jagdish N. and Hansen, Bent. A Theoretical Analysis of Smuggling. *Quart. J. Econ.*, May 1973, *87*(2), pp. 172–87.

Blattner, Niklaus. Domestic Competition and Foreign Trade: The Case of the Excess Capacity Barrier to Entry. *Z. Nationalökon.*, 1973, *33*(3–4), pp. 403–12.

Clark, Peter B. Uncertainty, Exchange Risk, and the Level of International Trade. *Western Econ. J.*, September 1973, *11*(3), pp. 302–13.

Courbis, Raymond. La théorie des "économies concurrencées" fondement du modèle FIFI. (The Theory of "Competitioned Economies" as a Basis of the Fifi Model. With English summary.) *Revue Écon.*, November 1973, *24*(6), pp. 905–22.

Hickman, Bert G. A General Linear Model of World Trade. In *Ball, R. J., ed.*, 1973, pp. 21–43.

Johnson, Harry G. Notes on the Welfare Effects of a Reversed Transfer. *Osaka Econ. Pap.*, March 1973, *21*(38), pp. 45–52.

Katrak, Homi. Human Skills, R and D and Scale Economies in the Exports of the United Kingdom and the United States. *Oxford Econ. Pap.*, November 1973, *25*(3), pp. 337–60. [G: U.K.; U.S.]

Khang, Chulsoon and Uekawa, Yasuo. The Production Possibility Set in a Model Allowing Interindustry Flows: The Necessary and Sufficient Conditions for its Strict Convexity. *J. Int. Econ.*, August 1973, *3*(3), pp. 283–90.

Klein, Lawrence R. and Van Peeterssen, A. Forecasting World Trade within Project LINK. In *Ball, R. J., ed.*, 1973, pp. 429–63. [G: Japan; N. America; W. Europe]

Leamer, Edward E. Empirically Weighted Indexes for Import Demand Functions. *Rev. Econ. Statist.*, November 1973, *55*(4), pp. 441–50.

Magnifico, Giovanni. The Theory of Optimum Currency Areas and European Monetary Unification. In *Magnifico, G.*, 1973, pp. 43–84. [G: E.E.C.]

Metzler, Lloyd A. A Multiple-Country Theory of Income Transfers. In *Metzler, L. A.*, 1973, pp. 545–67.

Metzler, Lloyd A. The Theory of International Trade. In *Metzler, L. A.*, 1973, pp. 1–49.

Parrinello, Sergio. Distribuzione, sviluppo e commercio internazionale. (Distribution, Growth and International Trade. With English summary.) *Econ. Int.*, May 1973, *26*(2), pp. 197–229.

Phan, Duc-Loï. Le modèle FIFI et la politique économique à moyen terme. (The Physico-Financial Model and the Medium Term Policy. With English summary.) *Revue Écon.*, November 1973, *24*(6), pp. 923–50. **[G: France]**

Reid, Frank J. Mundell on Growth and the Balance of Payments: A Note. *Can. J. Econ.*, November 1973, *6*(4), pp. 592–95.

Rhomberg, Rudolf R. Towards a General Trade Model. In *Ball, R. J., ed.*, 1973, pp. 9–20.

Scheffman, D. T. Some Remarks on the Net Production Possibilities Set in Models with Intermediate Goods. *J. Int. Econ.*, August 1973, *3*(3), pp. 291–95.

Smith, V. Kerry. International Trade Theory Without Homogeneity: A Comment. *Quart. J. Econ.*, May 1973, *87*(2), pp. 288–89.

Steedman, Ian and Metcalfe, J. S. On Foreign Trade. *Econ. Int.*, August-November 1973, *26*(3–4), pp. 516–28.

Steinherr, Alfred. Economic Policy in the Short Run under Fixed Exchange Rates. *Rech. Écon. Louvain*, December 1973, *39*(4), pp. 419–36.

Stewart, Frances. Trade and Technology. In *Streeten, P., ed.*, 1973, pp. 231–63.

Waelbroeck, J. The Methodology of Linkage. In *Ball, R. J., ed.*, 1973, pp. 45–61.

4112 Theory of International Trade: Prices, Comparative Advantage, etc.

Allen, Polly Reynolds. The Transfer Problem: A Note on the Terms in Which a Transfer is Expressed. *Econ. J.*, June 1973, *83*(330), pp. 516–19.

Aquino, Antonio. Alcune riflessioni sull'analisi dei fattori esplicativi della struttura degli scambi internazionali. (Some Considerations of the Analysis of the Explanatory Factors of the Pattern of International Trade. With English summary.) *Rivista Int. Sci. Econ. Com.*, October 1973, *20* (10), pp. 995–1012.

Askari, Hossein. A Note on the Empirical Testing of the Ricardian Theory of Comparative Advantage. *Southern Econ. J.*, July 1973, *40*(1), pp. 120–21.

Batra, Raveendra N. and Casas, Francisco R. Intermediate Products and the Pure Theory of International Trade: A Neo-Heckscher-Ohlin Framework. *Amer. Econ. Rev.*, June 1973, *63*(3), pp. 297–311.

Batra, Raveendra N. Nontraded Goods, Factor Market Distortions, and the Gains from Trade. *Amer. Econ. Rev.*, September 1973, *63*(4), pp. 706–13.

Berglas, Eitan and Razin, Assaf. A Trade Model with Variable Returns to Scale. *Econ. Rec.*, March 1973, *49*(125), pp. 126–34.

Berglas, Eitan and Razin, Assaf. Real Exchange Rate and Devaluation. *J. Int. Econ.*, May 1973, *3*(2), pp. 179–91.

Berry, R. Albert. Terms of Trade Fluctuations and the Income Instability of Factor Owners. *Economica, N.S.*, May 1973, *40*(158), pp. 187–94.

Bertrand, Trent J. Trade and Growth: A Comment. *J. Int. Econ.*, May 1973, *3*(2), pp. 193–95.

Bliss, C. J. Heterogeneous Capital and the Heckscher-Ohlin-Samuelson Theory of Trade: Discussion. In *Parkin, M., ed.*, 1973, pp. 61–64.

Casas, Francisco R. International Factor Movements in a Tariff-ridden World Economy. *Manchester Sch. Econ. Soc. Stud.*, June 1973, *41*(2), pp. 215–23.

Chang, Winston W. and Mayer, Wolfgang. Intermediate Goods in a General Equilibrium Trade Model. *Int. Econ. Rev.*, June 1973, *14*(2), pp. 447–59.

Coppock, D. J. Devaluation When Exports Have an Import Content: Reply. *Manchester Sch. Econ. Soc. Stud.*, December 1973, *41*(4), pp. 428–29.

Cuddy, J. D. A. A Note on Projections of International Trade Based on Coefficients of Trade Intensity. *Econ. J.*, December 1973, *83*(332), pp. 1222–35.

Deiss, Joseph. Les frais de transport et les termes de l'échange international. (Transport Costs and International Terms of Trade. With English summary.) *Schweiz. Z. Volkswirtsch. Statist.*, June 1973, *109*(2), pp. 201–22.

Demery, Lionel and Gorman, D. The Classical and Factor Proportions Trade Patterns:—A Note. *Manchester Sch. Econ. Soc. Stud.*, September 1973, *41*(3), pp. 343.

Dornbusch, Rudiger. Currency Depreciation, Hoarding, and Relative Prices. *J. Polit. Econ.*, July-August 1973, *81*(4), pp. 893–915.

Eleftheriou, T. The Classical and Factor Proportions Trade Patterns: Comment on a Note. *Manchester Sch. Econ. Soc. Stud.*, September 1973, *41*(3), pp. 345.

Erdilek, Asim. Shadow Prices, Unit Costs, Total Factor Costs and the Gains from Trade. *Indian Econ. J.*, July–September 1973, *21*(1), pp. 66–72.

Fløystad, Gunnar. Factor Price Equalization in Theory and Practice—A Study of Mainly Norwegian Data. *Weltwirtsch. Arch.*, 1973, *109*(4), pp. 554–78. **[G: E.E.C.; E.F.T.A.; Norway]**

Gray, H. Peter. Two-Way International Trade in Manufactures: A Theoretical Underpinning. *Weltwirtsch. Arch.*, 1973, *109*(1), pp. 19–39.

Heinemann, Hans-Joachim. Einige Bemerkungen zum Samuelson-Stolper Theorem und zur Theorie des Aussenhandelsgewinns. (Some Remarks on the Samuelson-Stolper Theorem and on the Theory of Gains by International Trade. With English summary.) *Jahr. Nationalökon. Statist.*, January 1973, *187*(2), pp. 134–46.

Hickman, Bert G. and Lau, Lawrence J. Elasticities of Substitution and Export Demands in a World Trade Model. *Europ. Econ. Rev.*, December 1973, *4*(4), pp. 347–80.

Hirsch, Seev and Lev, Baruch. Trade and Per Capita Income Differentials: A Test of the Burenstam-Linder Hypothesis. *World Devel.*, September 1973, *1*(9), pp. 11–17.

Holmes, James M. The Process of International Adjustment under Conditions of Full Employment: A Keynesian View Revised. *J. Polit. Econ.*, November-December 1973, *81*(6), pp. 1407–29.

Horiba, Y. Factor Proportions and the Structure of Interregional Trade: The Case of Japan. *Southern Econ. J.*, January 1973, *39*(3), pp. 381–88. **[G: Japan]**

Humphrey, Thomas M. Changing Views of Comparative Advantage. In *Henley, D. S., ed.,* 1973, pp. 18–24. [G: U.S.]

Ichikawa, Hiroya. Factor Proportions, Human Capital and Comparative Advantage. *Econ. Rec.,* March 1973, *49*(125), pp. 104–25. [G: Australia; New Zealand]

Ikemoto, K. Devaluation When Exports Have an Import Content: Comment. *Manchester Sch. Econ. Soc. Stud.,* December 1973, *41*(4), pp. 425–27.

Kemp, Murray C. Heterogeneous Capital Goods and Long-Run Stolper-Samuelson Theorems. *Australian Econ. Pap.,* December 1973, *12*(21), pp. 253–60.

Kemp, Murray C. and Liviatan, Nissan. Production and Trade Patterns under Uncertainty. *Econ. Rec.,* June 1973, *49*(126), pp. 215–27.

Kemp, Murray C. Trade Gains in a Pure Consumption-Loan Model. *Australian Econ. Pap.,* June 1973, *12*(20), pp. 124–26.

Kleinewefers, Henner. Leistungsbilanz, Wachstum und Transferproblem. (Balance of Current Business Transactions, Growth and Transfer Problems. With English summary.) *Weltwirtsch. Arch.,* 1973, *109*(1), pp. 40–58.

Klein, Roger W. A Dynamic Theory of Comparative Advantage. *Amer. Econ. Rev.,* March 1973, *63*(1), pp. 173–84. [G: U.S.]

Kojima, Kiyoshi. A Macroeconomic Approach to Foreign Direct Investment. *Hitotsubashi J. Econ.,* June 1973, *14*(1), pp. 1–21. [G: U.S.; Japan]

Kreinin, Mordechai E. Some Economic Consequences of Reverse Preferences. *J. Common Market Stud.,* March 1973, *11*(3), pp. 161–72. [G: Europe]

Kreinin, Mordechai E. A Further Note on the Export Elasticity of Substitution. *Can. J. Econ.,* November 1973, *6*(4), pp. 606–08.

Leontief, Wassily W. Explanatory Power of the Comparative Cost Theory of International Trade and Its Limits. In *[Tinbergen, J.],* 1973, pp. 153–60. [G: U.S.]

Magee, Stephen P. Factor Market Distortions, Production, and Trade: A Survey. *Oxford Econ. Pap.,* March 1973, *25*(1), pp. 1–43.

Maiti, Pradip. Factor Price Equalization Theorem in Linear Programming. *J. Int. Econ.,* November 1973, *3*(4), pp. 367–78.

Makower, H. The Pure Theory of International Trade: The Teaching of It. *Indian Econ. J.,* July–September 1973, *21*(1), pp. 1–18.

Mauer, Laurence Jay. Logical Consistency and Jacob Mosak's General Equilibrium in International Trade. *Indian Econ. J.,* July–September 1973, *21*(1), pp. 37–41.

McGilvray, James and Simpson, David. The Commodity Structure of Anglo-Irish Trade. *Rev. Econ. Statist.,* November 1973, *55*(4), pp. 451–58. [G: U.K.; Ireland]

Melvin, James R. and Warne, Robert D. Monopoly and the Theory of International Trade. *J. Int. Econ.,* May 1973, *3*(2), pp. 117–34.

Metcalfe, J. S. and Steedman, Ian. Heterogeneous Capital and the Heckscher-Ohlin-Samuelson Theory of Trade. In *Parkin, M., ed.,* 1973, pp. 50–60.

Metzler, Lloyd A. A Multiple-Region Theory of Income and Trade. In *Metzler, L. A.,* 1973, pp. 516–44.

Metzler, Lloyd A. Imported Raw Materials, the Transfer Problem, and the Concepts of Income. In *Metzler, L. A.,* 1973, pp. 70–94.

Metzler, Lloyd A. The Transfer Problem Reconsidered. In *Metzler, L. A.,* 1973, pp. 50–69.

Metzler, Lloyd A. Underemployment Equilibrium in International Trade. In *Metzler, L. A.,* 1973, pp. 258–74.

Mundell, Robert A. Uncommon Arguments for Common Currencies. In *Johnson, H. G. and Swoboda, A. K., eds.,* 1973, pp. 114–32.

Naqvi, Syed Nawab Haider. Pakistan's Export Possibilities. *Pakistan Develop. Rev.,* Spring 1973, *12*(1), pp. 1–30. [G: Pakistan]

Okuguchi, Koji. Magnification Effect in a Two-Good Model with Intermediate Inputs. *Z. Nationalökon.,* 1973, *33*(3–4), pp. 413–18.

Oliva, T. Extensions of Selected Graphical Techniques in International Economics: A Theoretical Approach. *Amer. Econ.,* Spring 1973, *17*(1), pp. 128–46.

Otani, Yoshihiko. Neo-Classical Technology Sets and Properties of Production Possibility Sets. *Econometrica,* July 1973, *41*(4), pp. 667–82.

Resnick, Stephen A. and Truman, Edwin M. An Empirical Examination of Bilateral Trade in Western Europe. *J. Int. Econ.,* November 1973, *3*(4), pp. 305–35. [G: W. Europe]

Richardson, J. David. Beyond (But Back To?) the Elasticity of Substitution in International Trade. *Europ. Econ. Rev.,* December 1973, *4*(4), pp. 381–92.

Sailors, Joel W.; Qureshi, Usman A. and Cross, Edward M. Empirical Verification of Linder's Trade Thesis. *Southern Econ. J.,* October 1973, *40*(2), pp. 262–68.

Samuelson, Paul A. Deadweight Loss in International Trade from the Profit Motive? In *[Halm, G. N.],* 1973, pp. 149–54.

Sanchez, Nicolas and Sweeney, Richard J. The Allocation of Tariff Revenues and Optimum Trade Distortion. With Empirical Applications to United States Sugar Policy. *Weltwirtsch. Arch.,* 1973, *109*(3), pp. 382–401. [G: U.S.]

Sandler, Todd M. The Rybczynski Theorem, the Gains from Trade and Non-Homogeneous Utility Functions. *Indian Econ. J.,* July–September 1973, *21*(1), pp. 19–32.

Schmitz, Andrew. Distortions and Product Specialization in International Trade. *Econ. Rec.,* June 1973, *49*(126), pp. 263–69.

Scully, Gerald W. Technical Progress, Factor Market Distortions, and the Pattern of Trade. *Econ. Int.,* February 1973, *26*(1), pp. 3–16.

Shinkai, Yoichi. The Accumulation of International Reserves under an Inflationary Pressure. *Z. Nationalökon.,* 1973, *33*(1–2), pp. 55–66.

Steedman, Ian and Metcalfe, J. S. The Non-Substitution Theorem and International Trade Theory. *Australian Econ. Pap.,* December 1973, *12*(21), pp. 267–69.

Tahmassebi, H. The General Equilibrium Analysis of Customs Union. *Tahq. Eq.,* Winter & Spring 1973, *10*(29 & 30), pp. 146–69.

Teubal, Morris. Comparative Advantage and Technological Change: The Learning by Doing Case. *J. Int. Econ.,* May 1973, *3*(2), pp. 161–77.

Uekawa, Yasuo; Kemp, Murray C. and Wegge, Leon L. P- and PN-Matrices, Minkowski- and Metzler-Matrices, and Generalizations of the Stolper-Samuelson and Samuelson-Rybczynski Theorems. *J. Int. Econ.,* February 1973, *3*(1), pp. 53–76.

Van Moeseke, P. and Rader, J. Trout. Heckscher-Ohlin Hypothesis and Scarce-Factor Theorems. *Tijdschr. Econ.,* 1973, *18*(3), pp. 445–50.

Warne, Robert D. Factor Intensity and the Heckscher-Ohlin Theorem in a Three-Factor, Three-Good Model. *Can. J. Econ.,* August 1973, *6*(3), pp. 369–75.

Warne, Robert D. The Heckscher-Ohlin Model with Three Factors and Two Goods. *Econ. Rec.,* June 1973, *49*(126), pp. 300–05.

4113 Theory of Protection

Bacha, Edmar. Preference for Industry and Commercial Policy Theory in Industrializing Countries. In *Eckaus, R. S. and Rosenstein-Rodan, P. N., eds.,* 1973, pp. 269–92.

Balassa, Bela. Policy Issues in Adjustment Assistance: The United States: Comment. In *Hughes, H., ed.,* 1973, pp. 180–86.

Baldwin, Robert and Mutti, John H. Policy Issues in Adjustment Assistance: The United States. In *Hughes, H., ed.,* 1973, pp. 149–77.   [G: U.S.]

Batra, Raveendra N. Effective Protection in General Equilibrium: A Geometrical Analysis. *Indian Econ. Rev.,* October 1973, *8*(2), pp. 125–47.

Berglas, Eitan and Razin, Assaf. Effective Protection and Decreasing Returns to Scale. *Amer. Econ. Rev.,* September 1973, *63*(4), pp. 733–37.

Berglas, Eitan and Razin, Assaf. A Trade Model with Variable Returns to Scale. *Econ. Rec.,* March 1973, *49*(125), pp. 126–34.

Bertrand, Trent J. Optional Tariff Policy Designed for Governmental Gain. *Can. J. Econ.,* May 1973, *6*(2), pp. 257–60.

Bhagwati, Jagdish N. and Srinivasan, T. N. Smuggling and Trade Policy. *J. Public Econ.,* November 1973, *2*(4), pp. 377–89.

Bhagwati, Jagdish N. and Srinivasan, T. N. The General Equilibrium Theory of Effective Protection and Resource Allocation. *J. Int. Econ.,* August 1973, *3*(3), pp. 259–81.

Bieri, Jurg and Schmitz, Andrew. Export Instability, Monopoly Power, and Welfare. *J. Int. Econ.,* November 1973, *3*(4), pp. 389–96.

Billings, Brad. Production Effects of Effective Rates of Protection. *J. Econ. Bus.,* Winter 1973, *25*(2), pp. 112–21.

Blackhurst, Richard. Estimating the Impact of Tariff Manipulation: The Excess Demand and Supply Approach. *Oxford Econ. Pap.,* March 1973, *25*(1), pp. 80–87.

Boadway, Robin W.; Maital, Shlomo and Prachowny, Martin F. J. Optimal Tariffs, Optimal Taxes and Public Goods. *J. Public Econ.,* November 1973, *2*(4), pp. 391–403.

Bruno, M. Protection and Tariff Change under General Equilibrium. *J. Int. Econ.,* August 1973, *3*(3), pp. 205–25.

Casas, Francisco R. Optimal Effective Protection in General Equilibrium. *Amer. Econ. Rev.,* September 1973, *63*(4), pp. 714–16.

Charles, David. The Tariff System and the Composition of Imports. *J. Polit. Econ.,* November-December 1973, *81*(6), pp. 1471–72.

Fløystad, Gunnar. The Impact on Allocation and Return to Labor and Capital of a Reduction of Customs Duties in the Developed Countries in Their Trade with Less Developed Countries. *Weltwirtsch. Arch.,* 1973, *109*(1), pp. 59–69.   [G: Norway]

Gray, H. Peter. Senile Industry Protection: A Proposal. *Southern Econ. J.,* April 1973, *39*(4), pp. 569–74.

Hinton, Deane. Policy Issues in Adjustment Assistance: The United States: Comment. In *Hughes, H., ed.,* 1973, pp. 177–80.

Johnson, D. Gale. What Difference Does Trade Make in World Community Welfare? In *Iowa State University Center for Agricultural and Rural Development,* 1973, pp. 49–68.   [G: E.E.C.; U.S.]

Johnson, Harry G. Optimum Tariffs and Retaliation. In *Farrell, M. J., ed.,* 1973, pp. 115–27.

Khang, Chulsoon. Factor Substitution in the Theory of Effective Protection: A General Equilibrium Analysis. *J. Int. Econ.,* August 1973, *3*(3), pp. 227–43.

Kuga, Kiyoshi. Tariff Retaliation and Policy Equilibrium. *J. Int. Econ.,* November 1973, *3*(4), pp. 351–66.

Lloyd, P. J. Optimal Intervention in a Distortion-Ridden Open Economy. *Econ. Rec.,* September 1973, *49*(127), pp. 377–93.

Marks, Peter A. A Further Note on Tariff vs. Subsidy. *Kyklos,* 1973, *26*(4), pp. 870–71.

Massel, M. S. Non-Tariff Barriers as an Obstacle to World Trade. In *Thorelli, H. B., ed.,* 1973, pp. 71–82.

Mauer, Laurence Jay and van de Gevel, A. J. W. Non-Tariff Distortions in International Trade: A Methodological Review. In *Scaperlanda, A. E., ed.,* 1973, pp. 47–69.

McCulloch, Rachel and Johnson, Harry G. A Note on Proportionally Distributed Quotas. *Amer. Econ. Rev.,* September 1973, *63*(4), pp. 726–32.

McCulloch, Rachel. When Are a Tariff and a Quota Equivalent? *Can. J. Econ.,* November 1973, *6*(4), pp. 503–11.

McKinnon, Ronald I. The Value-Added Tax and the Liberalization of Foreign Trade in Developing Economies: A Comment. *J. Econ. Lit.,* June 1973, *11*(2), pp. 520–24.

Metzler, Lloyd A. Tariffs, the Terms of Trade, and the Distribution of National Income. In *Metzler, L. A.,* 1973, pp. 159–97.

Metzler, Lloyd A. Tariffs, International Demand, and Domestic Prices. In *Metzler, L. A.,* 1973, pp. 198–208.

Okuguchi, Koji. Magnification Effect in a Two-Good

Model with Intermediate Inputs. *Z. Nationalökon.,* 1973, *33*(3–4), pp. 413–18.

Ozawa, Terutomo and McDonnell, C. F. On the Geometric Measurement of an Optimum Tariff. *Indian Econ. J.,* July–September 1973, *21*(1), pp. 33–36.

Pursell, G. and Snape, R. H. Economies of Scale, Price Discrimination and Exporting. *J. Int. Econ.,* February 1973, *3*(1), pp. 85–91.

Ray, Alok. Non-Traded Inputs and Effective Protection: A General Equilibrium Analysis. *J. Int. Econ.,* August 1973, *3*(3), pp. 245–57.

Sanchez, Nicolas and Sweeney, Richard J. The Allocation of Tariff Revenues and Optimum Trade Distortion. With Empirical Applications to United States Sugar Policy. *Weltwirtsch. Arch.,* 1973, *109*(3), pp. 382–401.   [G: U.S.]

Scitovszky, Tibor. A Reconsideration of the Theory of Tariffs. In *Farrell, M. J., ed.,* 1973, pp. 58–79.

Stern, Robert M. Tariffs and Other Measures of Trade Control: A Survey of Recent Developments. *J. Econ. Lit.,* September 1973, *11*(3), pp. 857–88.

4114 Theory of International Trade and Economic Development

Aboyade, Ojetunji. Developing Country Alternatives: Comment. In *Hughes, H., ed.,* 1973, pp. 140–48.

Adams, N. A. Trade as a Handmaiden of Growth: Comment. *Econ. J.,* March 1973, *83*(329), pp. 210–12.

Afzal, Mohammad and Mirakhor, Abbas. An Index of Export Performance as a Criterion of Export Policy for Developing Countries. *Pakistan Econ. Soc. Rev.,* Summer 1973, *11*(2), pp. 193–99.

Agarwala, R. An Econometric Test of Alternative Constraints on the Growth of Underdeveloped Countries: A Comment. *Rev. Econ. Statist.,* February 1973, *55*(1), pp. 132–33.

Bacha, Edmar. Developing Country Alternatives: Comment. In *Hughes, H., ed.,* 1973, pp. 137–40.

Batra, Raveendra N. and Casas, Francisco R. Economic Growth and International Trade in an Imperfect Market Setting. *Indian Econ. J.,* July–September 1973, *21*(1), pp. 57–65.

Bhagwati, Jagdish N. and Krueger, Anne O. Exchange Control, Liberalization, and Economic Development. *Amer. Econ. Rev.,* May 1973, *63* (2), pp. 419–27.

Cochrane, Willard W. Agricultural and Trade Developments in the Less Developed Countries. In *Iowa State University Center for Agricultural and Rural Development,* 1973, pp. 194–209.

Coen, Edward. Relative Growth Rates: The Experience of the Advanced Economies. *Banca Naz. Lavoro Quart. Rev.,* June 1973, *105,* pp. 158–76.

Corden, W. Max. Employment in the Industrialized Countries: Comment. In *Hughes, H., ed.,* 1973, pp. 125–27.

Crafts, N. F. R. Trade as a Handmaiden of Growth: An Alternative View. *Econ. J.,* September 1973, *83*(331), pp. 875–84.

Cukor, György. Industrial Development Strategy in

Developing Countries. In *Földi, T., ed.,* 1973, pp. 37–63.

Currie, Lauchlin. The Exchange Constraint on Development—A Partial Solution to the Problem: A Reply. *Econ. J.,* March 1973, *83*(329), pp. 207–10.

Deardorff, Alan V. The Gains from Trade in and out of Steady-state Growth. *Oxford Econ. Pap.,* July 1973, *25*(2), pp. 173–91.

Despres, Emile. Price Distortions and Development Planning: Pakistan. In *Despres, E.,* 1973, pp. 133–45.   [G: Pakistan]

Fane, George. Consistent Measures of Import Substitution. *Oxford Econ. Pap.,* July 1973, *25*(2), pp. 251–61.   [G: Pakistan]

Frank, Charles R., Jr. Trade, Investment and Labor, and the Changing International Division of Production: Comment. In *Hughes, H., ed.,* 1973, pp. 61–68.

Glezakos, Constantine. Export Instability and Economic Growth: A Statistical Verification. *Econ. Develop. Cult. Change,* Part I, July 1973, *21*(4), pp. 670–78.

Goldfinger, Nathaniel. Employment in the Industrialized Countries: Comment. In *Hughes, H., ed.,* 1973, pp. 117–24.

Haq, Mahbub. Developing Country Alternatives. In *Hughes, H., ed.,* 1973, pp. 128–37.

Haq, Mahbub. Industrialisation and Trade Policies in the 1970s: Developing Country Alternatives. In *Streeten, P., ed.,* 1973, pp. 93–102.

Healey, Derek T. Foreign Capital and Exports in Economic Development: The Experience of Eight Asian Countries. *Econ. Rec.,* September 1973, *49*(127), pp. 394–419.

Helleiner, Gerald K. Manufactured Exports from Less-Developed Countries and Multinational Firms. *Econ. J.,* March 1973, *83*(329), pp. 21–47.

Hoffmann, Lutz. Import Substitution—Export Expansion and Growth in an Open Developing Economy: The Case of West Malaysia. *Weltwirtsch. Arch.,* 1973, *109*(3), pp. 452–75.
          [G: W. Malaysia]

Hughes, Helen. Prospects for Partnership: Industrialization and Trade Policies in the 1970s: Summary and Conclusions. In *Hughes, H., ed.,* 1973, pp. 269–89.

Ikram, Khalid. Social Versus Private Profitability in Pakistan's Export of Manufactures. *Pakistan Develop. Rev.,* Summer 1973, *12*(2), pp. 156–67.
          [G: Pakistan]

Islam, Nurul. National Import Substitution and Inward-Looking Strategies: Policies of Less Developed Countries. In *Streeten, P., ed.,* 1973, pp. 76–92.

Iyoha, Milton Ame. The Optimal Balance-of-Payments Strategy of a Less Developed Country. *Econ. Rec.,* June 1973, *49*(126), pp. 270–79.

Johnson, Harry G. Trade, Investment and Labor, and the Changing International Division of Production. In *Hughes, H., ed.,* 1973, pp. 40–55.

Johnson, Harry G. International Trade and Economic Development. In *Streeten, P., ed.,* 1973, pp. 27–34.

Kapur, Basant K. Professor McKinnon's Model of Foreign Exchange Constraints in Economic Development: A Note. *Econ. J.*, March 1973, *83* (329), pp. 221–34.

Karlik, John. Trade, Investment and Labor, and the Changing International Division of Production: Comment. In *Hughes, H., ed.*, 1973, pp. 56–61.

Katrak, Homi. Commodity Concentration and Export Fluctuations: A Probability Analysis. *J. Devel. Stud.*, July 1973, *9*(4), pp. 556–65.

Khan, Mohsin S. The Effect of Growth on the Balance of Payments of Developing Countries: An Empirical Note. *Pakistan Econ. Soc. Rev.*, Autumn 1973, *11*(3), pp. 354–59.

Kravis, Irving B. Trade as a Handmaiden of Growth: Reply. *Econ. J.*, March 1973, *83*(329), pp. 212–17.

Kravis, Irving B. Trade as a Handmaiden of Growth: A Reply. *Econ. J.*, September 1973, *83*(331), pp. 885–89.

Leff, Nathaniel H. Tropical Trade and Development in the Nineteenth Century: The Brazilian Experience. *J. Polit. Econ.*, May-June 1973, *81*(3), pp. 678–96. **[G: Brazil]**

Lubitz, Raymond. Export-Led Growth in Industrial Economies. *Kyklos*, 1973, *26*(2), pp. 307–21.

Manfredini, Marialuisa. Il vantaggio comparato potenziale come principio-guida del processo di sviluppo. (On the Potential Comparative Advantage in International Trade: Theory and Evidence. With English summary.) *Rivista Int. Sci. Econ. Com.*, June 1973, *20*(6), pp. 546–65.

Matthews, R. C. O. Foreign Trade and British Economic Growth. *Scot. J. Polit. Econ.*, November 1973, *20*(3), pp. 195–209. **[G: U.K.]**

Melinte, T.; Horovicz, M. and Olteanu, I. World Market, Economic Cooperation and the Planning of the National Economy. In *Kiss, T., ed.*, 1973, pp. 127–33. **[G: Romania]**

Miles, Caroline. Employment in the Industrialized Countries. In *Hughes, H., ed.*, 1973, pp. 101–16.

Mitra, P. K. Rationale of Commercial Policy of Developing Countries. *Rivista Int. Sci. Econ. Com.*, February 1973, *20*(2), pp. 139–52.

Monroe, Wilbur F. The Contribution of Japanese Exports to Growth in Output. *Nebr. J. Econ. Bus.*, Winter 1973, *12*(1), pp. 11–21. **[G: Japan]**

Murray, Tracy. Preferential Tariffs for the LDCs. *Southern Econ. J.*, July 1973, *40*(1), pp. 35–46.

Murray, Tracy. How Helpful is the Generalised System of Preferences to Developing Countries? *Econ. J.*, June 1973, *83*(330), pp. 449–55.

Naseem, S. M. Import Substitution: A Survey of Concepts, Measures and Models. *Pakistan Develop. Rev.*, Spring 1973, *12*(1), pp. 31–47.

Patel, I. G. Some Reflections on Trade and Development. In *Streeten, P., ed.*, 1973, pp. 35–48.

Ranis, Gustav. The Exchange Constraint on Development—A Partial Solution to the Problem: A Comment. *Econ. J.*, March 1973, *83*(329), pp. 203–07.

Sachs, Ignacy. Outward-Looking Strategies: A Dangerous Illusion? In *Streeten, P., ed.*, 1973, pp. 51–61.

Schuster, Helmut. Direktinvestitionen und Zahlungsbilanz in Entwicklungsländern. (Direct Investment and the Balance of Payments in Developing Countries. With English summary.) *Z. Wirtschaft. Sozialwissen.*, 1973, *93*(2), pp. 190–96.

Sharpston, C. H. Competition and the Developing Countries. In *Rybczynski, T. M., ed.*, 1973, pp. 46–54.

Singh, Anoop. An Enquiry into the Nature and Implications of a Foreign Exchange Constraint on Development. *Indian Econ. J.*, October–December 1973, *21*(2), pp. 147–57.

Singh, Manmohan. Export Strategy for the Take-off. In *Wadhva, C. D., ed.*, 1973, pp. 394–406. **[G: India]**

Sreekantaradhya, B. S. Economic Integration Among Developing Countries with Special Reference to South-East Asia—I. *Econ. Aff.*, November-December 1973, *18*(11–12), pp. 483–84, 511–16. **[G: S.E.Asia]**

Streeten, Paul. Trade Strategies for Development: Some Themes for the Seventies. In *Streeten, P., ed.*, 1973, pp. 1–24.

Taylor, Lance and Bacha, Edmar. Growth and Trade Distortions in Chile, and Their Implications in Calculating the Shadow Price of Foreign Exchange. In *Eckaus, R. S. and Rosenstein-Rodan, P. N., eds.*, 1973, pp. 121–46. **[G: Chile]**

Taylor, Lance. Investment Project Analysis in Terms of a Model of Optical Growth: The Case of Chile. In *Eckaus, R. S. and Rosenstein-Rodan, P. N., eds.*, 1973, pp. 167–98. **[G: Chile]**

Teubal, Morris. Heavy and Light Industry in Economic Development. *Amer. Econ. Rev.*, September 1973, *63*(4), pp. 588–96.

Thoburn, J. T. Exports and Economic Growth in West Malaysia. *Oxford Econ. Pap.*, March 1973, *25*(1), pp. 88–111. **[G: Malaysia]**

Voivodas, Constantin S. Exports, Foreign Capital Inflow and Economic Growth. *J. Int. Econ.*, November 1973, *3*(4), pp. 337–49.

Walter, Ingo. Commonwealth Preferences in Retrospect: Some Policy Implications for the Developing Countries. *Econ. Bull. Ghana, Sec. Ser.*, 1973, *3*(4), pp. 3–13. **[G: U.K.]**

Weisskopf, Thomas E. An Econometric Test of Alternative Constraints on the Growth of Underdeveloped Countries: A Reply. *Rev. Econ. Statist.*, February 1973, *55*(1), pp. 133–34.

420 TRADE RELATIONS; COMMERCIAL POLICY; INTERNATIONAL ECONOMIC INTEGRATION

4200 General

Bell, Clive and Lehmann, David. The International Context of La Via Chilena. In *Zammit, J. A., ed.*, 1973, pp. 343–65. **[G: Chile; U.S.]**

Holzman, Franklyn D. Future East-West Economic Issues. In *Bergsten, C. F., ed.*, 1973, pp. 265–92.

Keohane, Robert O. and Nye, Joseph S. World Politics and the International Economic System. In *Bergsten, C. F., ed.*, 1973, pp. 115–79.

Onitiri, H. M. A. The International Aspects of Economic Independence. In *Ghai, D., ed.*, 1973, pp. 35–44. **[G: Africa]**

Vernon, Raymond. Rogue Elephant in the Forest: An

Appraisal of Transatlantic Relations. *Foreign Aff.*, April 1973, *51*(3), pp. 573–87. [G: U.S.; E.E.C.]

421 Trade Relations

4210 Trade Relations

Abboud, A. Robert. The Case Against Floating Rates and for a Stronger Dollar. In *Wiegand, G. C., ed.,* 1973, pp. 89–96. [G: U.S.]

Agosin, Manuel R. On the Third World's Narrowing Trade Gap: A Comment. *Oxford Econ. Pap.*, March 1973, *25*(1), pp. 133–40.

Aitken, Norman D. The Effect of the EEC and EFTA on European Trade: A Temporal Cross-Section Analysis. *Amer. Econ. Rev.*, December 1973, *63* (5), pp. 881–92. [G: E.E.C.; E.F.T.A.]

Aitken, Norman D. and Lowry, William R. A Cross-Sectional Study of the Effects of LAFTA and CACM on Latin American Trade. *J. Common Market Stud.,* June 1973, *11*(4), pp. 326–36. [G: Latin America]

Alamgir, Mohiuddin and Berlage, Lodewijk J. J. B. Foodgrain (Rice and Wheat) Demand, Import and Price Policy for Bangladesh. *Bangladesh Econ. Rev.,* January 1973, *1*(1), pp. 25–58. [G: Bangladesh]

Amid-hozour, Esmail and Somogyi, János. East-West Trade. *Finance Develop.,* June 1973, *10*(2), pp. 32–37.

Artus, Jacques R. The Short-Run Effects of Domestic Demand Pressure on Export Delivery Delays for Machinery. *J. Int. Econ.,* February 1973, *3*(1), pp. 21–36. [G: U.S.; U.K.; W. Germany]

Awad, M. Dilemmas in Economic Independence: Lessons from Sudan. In *Ghai, D., ed.,* 1973, pp. 205–31. [G: Sudan]

Ayob, Ahmad Mahzan and Prato, Anthony A. United States Import Demand and Prices of Natural Rubber. *Malayan Econ. Rev.,* April 1973, *18*(1), pp. 24–35. [G: U.S.]

Bale, Malcolm D. Full Employment, Trade Expansion, and Adjustment Assistance: Comment. *Southern Econ. J.,* July 1973, *40*(1), pp. 135–38.

Barkai, Haim. The European Economic Community Approach to Adjustment: Comment. In *Hughes, H., ed.,* 1973, pp. 217–22. [G: E.E.C.]

Basevi, G. Commodity Trade Equations in Project LINK. In *Ball, R. J., ed.,* 1973, pp. 227–81. [G: W. Europe; Japan; N. America]

Baumann, H. G. The Industrial Composition of U.S. Export and Subsidiary Sales to the Canadian Market: Note. *Amer. Econ. Rev.,* December 1973, *63* (5), pp. 1009–12. [G: U.S.]

Botero, Rodrigo. Relations with the United States: A Latin American View. In *Urquidi, V. L. and Thorp, R., eds.,* 1973, pp. 283–303. [G: U.S.; Latin America]

Braun, Ferdnand. The European Economic Community Approach to Adjustment. In *Hughes, H., ed.,* 1973, pp. 187–216. [G: E.E.C.]

Bronfenbrenner, Martin. Japanese-American Economic War? Some Further Reflections. *Quart. Rev. Econ. Bus.,* Autumn 1973, *13*(3), pp. 33–42. [G: Japan; U.S.]

Brown, Alan A. and Marer, Paul. Foreign Trade in the East European Reforms. In *Bornstein, M., ed.,* 1973, pp. 153–205. [G: E. Europe]

Carney, M. K. Agricultural Trade Intensity: The European Markets and the U.S. *Amer. J. Agr. Econ.,* Part I, November 1973, *55*(4), pp. 637–40.

Chenery, Hollis B. and Hughes, Helen. Industrialization and Trade Trends: Some Issues for the 1970s. In *Hughes, H., ed.,* 1973, pp. 3–31.

Chen, Tung-pi. Legal Aspects of Canadian Trade with the People's Republic of China. *Law Contemp. Probl.,* Summer-Autumn 1973, *38*(2), pp. 201–29. [G: Canada; China]

Christensen, Raymond P. and Goolsby, O. Halbert. U.S. Agricultural Trade and Balance of Payments. In *Iowa State University Center for Agricultural and Rural Development,* 1973, pp. 122–40. [G: U.S.]

Cochrane, James D. and Sloan, John W. LAFTA and the CACM: A Comparative Analysis of Integration in Latin America. *J. Devel. Areas,* October 1973, *8*(1), pp. 13–37. [G: Latin America]

Dahlstedt, Roy. Cycles in the Finnish Trade with the Soviet Union. *Liiketaloudellinen Aikak.,* 1973, *22* (1), pp. 63–66. [G: Finland]

Dell, Sidney. An Appraisal of UNCTAD III. *World Devel.,* May 1973, *1*(5), pp. 1–13.

Denny, David L. and Stein, Daniel D. Recent Developments in Trade between the U.S. and the P.-R.C.: A Legal and Economic Perspective. *Law Contemp. Probl.,* Summer-Autumn 1973, *38*(2), pp. 260–73. [G: China; U.S.]

Donges, Juergen B. Shaping Spain's Export Industry. *World Devel.,* September 1973, *1*(9), pp. 19–37. [G: Spain]

Donges, Juergen B. The European Economic Community Approach to Adjustment: Comment. In *Hughes, H., ed.,* 1973, pp. 222–27. [G: E.E.C.]

Dunning, John H. Multinational Enterprises and Trade Flows of Developing Countries. In *Streeten, P., ed.,* 1973, pp. 300–20.

Dunn, Robert M., Jr. Flexible Exchange Rates and Traded Goods Prices: The Role of Oligopoly Pricing in the Canadian Experience. In *Johnson, H. G. and Swoboda, A. K., eds.,* 1973, pp. 259–80. [G: U.S.; Canada]

Eldridge, D. P. and Saunders, N. C. Employment and Exports, 1963–72. *Mon. Lab. Rev.,* August 1973, *96*(8), pp. 16–27. [G: U.S.]

Erdilek, Asim. Foreign Trade, Domestic Production and Relative Prices—A Simulation Model for the United States and Japan. *Weltwirtsch. Arch.,* 1973, *109*(4), pp. 601–20. [G: U.S.; Japan]

Fan, Liang-Shing. The Economy and Foreign Trade of China. *Law Contemp. Probl.,* Summer-Autumn 1973, *38*(2), pp. 249–59. [G: China]

Farley, Noel J. J. Outward-looking Policies and Industrialization in a Small Economy: Some Notes on the Irish Case. *Econ. Develop. Cult. Change,* Part I, July 1973, *21*(4), pp. 610–28. [G: Ireland]

Finger, J. M. The Generalized Scheme of Preferences—Impact on the Donor Countries. *Bull. Econ. Res.,* May 1973, *25*(1), pp. 43–54.

Fried, Edward R. Foreign Economic Policy: The Search for a Strategy. In *Owen, H., ed.,* 1973, pp. 157–202. [G: U.S.]

Gately, Dermot. International Commodity Agreements: The Experience of Coffee and the Prospects for Cocoa. *Econ. Bull. Ghana, Sec. Ser.,* 1973, *3*(2), pp. 3–10.

Gianfranchi, Franco. Le nuove prospettive di cooperazione economica est-ovest in Europa. (New Prospects of East-West Economic Cooperation in Europe and the Role of the European Economic Community. With English summary.) *Mondo Aperto,* April 1973, *27*(2), pp. 112–21.

Giersch, Herbert. Some Neglected Aspects of Inflation in the World Economy. *Public Finance,* 1973, *28*(2), pp. 105–24.

Girgis, Maurice. Development and Trade Patterns in the Arab World. *Weltwirtsch. Arch.,* 1973, *109*(1), pp. 121–68.

Glynn, Sean and Lougheed, Alan L. A Comment on United States Economic Policy and the "Dollar Gap" of the 1920's. *Econ. Hist. Rev., 2nd Ser.,* November 1973, *26*(4), pp. 692–94.

Goldfinger, Nathaniel. An American Trade Union View of International Trade and Investment. In *Kujawa, D., ed.,* 1973, pp. 28–53. [G: U.S.]

Goodman, Richard J. United States Agricultural Trade in the Pacific Rim: Marketing Agricultural Products, Approaches, and Accomplishments. In *Canadian Agricultural Economics Society,* 1973, pp. 1–26. [G: U.S.; E. Asia]

Graham, Edward D. Special Interests and the Early China Trade. *Mich. Academician,* Fall 1973, *6*(2), pp. 233–42. [G: U.S.]

Graziosi, Dante. Italian Foreign Trade: Final Results for 1972 Short-Term Prospects. *Rev. Econ. Cond. Italy,* January-March 1973, *27*(1–2), pp. 29–42. [G: Italy]

Gregory, R. G. and Tearle, D. Product Differentiation and International Trade Flows: An Application of the "Hedonic" Regression Technique. *Australian Econ. Pap.,* June 1973, *12*(20), pp. 79–90. [G: Australia]

Grzybowski, Kazimierz. Control of U.S. Trade with China: An Overview. *Law Contemp. Probl.,* Summer-Autumn 1973, *38*(2), pp. 175–81. [G: China; U.S.]

Gwyer, G. D. Three International Commodity Agreements: The Experience of East Africa. *Econ. Develop. Cult. Change,* April 1973, *21*(3), pp. 465–76. [G: E. Africa]

Halder, A. and Richards, J. H. Structural Characteristics of India's Foreign Trade and its Effect on the Instability of Export Receipts. *Indian Econ. J.,* October–December 1973, *21*(2), pp. 132–46. [G: India]

Hallwood, C. P. The Impact of Foreign Aid Upon India's International Trade 1951-65. *Bull. Econ. Res.,* November 1973, *25*(2), pp. 129–45. [G: India]

Hazlewood, Arthur. State Trading and the East African Customs Union. *Oxford Bull. Econ. Statist.,* May 1973, *35*(2), pp. 75–89. [G: E. Africa]

Helliwell, John F., et al. Comprehensive Linkage of Large Models: Canada and the United States. In *Ball, R. J., ed.,* 1973, pp. 395–426. [G: Canada; U.S.]

Hickman, Bert G. and Lau, Lawrence J. Elasticities of Substitution and Export Demands in a World Trade Model. *Europ. Econ. Rev.,* December 1973, *4*(4), pp. 347–80.

Hickman, Bert G.; Klein, Lawrence R. and Rhomberg, Rudolf R. Background, Organization and Preliminary Results of Project LINK. In *Alexandrides, C. G., ed.,* 1973, pp. 19–56.

Hirsch, Seev and Lev, Baruch. Trade and Per Capita Income Differentials: A Test of the Burenstam-Linder Hypothesis. *World Devel.,* September 1973, *1*(9), pp. 11–17.

Hoffmann, Lutz. Import Substitution—Export Expansion and Growth in an Open Developing Economy: The Case of West Malaysia. *Weltwirtsch. Arch.,* 1973, *109*(3), pp. 452–75. [G: W. Malaysia]

Holland, I. Irving. Implications of the 1970 Timber Review for Trade in Timber Products. *Amer. J. Agr. Econ.,* December 1973, *55*(5), pp. 967–73. [G: U.S.]

Hsieh, C. Measuring the Effects of Trade Expansion on Employment: A Review of Some Research. *Int. Lab. Rev.,* January 1973, *107*(1), pp. 1–29.

Hsieh, C. Measuring the Effects of Trade Expansion on Employment: A Review of Some Research. *Int. Lab. Rev.,* January 1973, *107*(1), pp. 1–29.

Humphrey, Thomas M. Changing Views of Comparative Advantage. In *Henley, D. S., ed.,* 1973, pp. 18–24. [G: U.S.]

Ikram, Khalid. Devaluation and Export Price Competitiveness: A Note. *Pakistan Econ. Soc. Rev.,* Autumn 1973, *11*(3), pp. 349–53. [G: Pakistan]

Ikram, Khalid. Suspension of Interwing Trade: Structure and Growth of West Pakistan's Exports. *Pakistan Econ. Soc. Rev.,* Summer 1973, *11*(2), pp. 141–53. [G: Pakistan]

Ioanes, Raymond A. Trends and Structure of U.S. Agricultural Trade. In *Iowa State University Center for Agricultural and Rural Development,* 1973, pp. 87–102. [G: U.S.]

Jedel, Michael Jay and Stamm, John H. The Battle over Jobs: An Appraisal of Recent Publications on the Employment Effects of U.S. Multinational Corporations. In *Kujawa, D., ed.,* 1973, pp. 144–91. [G: U.S.]

Johns, B. L. Import Substitution and Export Potential—The Case of Manufacturing Industry in West Malaysia. *Australian Econ. Pap.,* December 1973, *12*(21), pp. 175–95. [G: Malaysia]

Josling, Tim. Domestic Farm Policies and International Trade in Agricultural Goods. In *Streeten, P., ed.,* 1973, pp. 264–78.

Juhár, Z. Commodity Trade in Consumer Goods. In *Kiss, T., ed.,* 1973, pp. 149–57. [G: CMEA]

Junz, Helen B. and Rhomberg, Rudolf R. Price Competitiveness in Export Trade Among Industrial Countries. *Amer. Econ. Rev.,* May 1973, *63*(2), pp. 412–18.

Kafka, Alexandre. Optimum Currency Areas and Latin America. In *Johnson, H. G. and Swoboda, A. K., eds.,* 1973, pp. 210–18. [G: Latin America; W. Europe; U.S.]

Kanamori, Hisao. II Giappone e l'Europa: Un'analisi economica. (Japan and Europe: An Economic Analysis. With English summary.) *Mondo Aperto,*

April 1973, *27*(2), pp. 122–26.   [G: Japan; W. Europe]

Kanet, Roger. Handbook of Soviet Social Science Data: International Interactions. In *Mickiewicz, E., ed.*, 1973, pp. 197–225.   [G: U.S.S.R.; C.M.E.A.]

Katrak, Homi. Human Skills, R and D and Scale Economies in the Exports of the United Kingdom and the United States. *Oxford Econ. Pap.*, November 1973, *25*(3), pp. 337–60.   [G: U.K.; U.S.]

Katrak, Homi. Commodity Concentration and Export Fluctuations: A Probability Analysis. *J. Devel. Stud.*, July 1973, *9*(4), pp. 556–65.

Kershner, Thomas R. The Growth of Trade and Competition: Japan's Exports to Pacific Asia, 1960-1969. *Amer. Econ.*, Spring 1973, *17*(1), pp. 93–101.   [G: Japan]

Kingston, Jerry L. Export Instability in Latin America: The Postwar Statistical Record. *J. Devel. Areas*, April 1973, *7*(3), pp. 381–95.   [G: Latin America]

Kojima, Kiyoshi. The Japanese Experience and Attitudes Toward Trade Adjustment. In *Hughes, H., ed.*, 1973, pp. 228–62.   [G: Japan]

Kojima, Kiyoshi. Reorganisation of North-South Trade: Japan's Foreign Economic Policy for the 1970s. *Hitotsubashi J. Econ.*, February 1973, *13*(2), pp. 1–28.   [G: Japan]

Korka, Mihai. Folosirea indicilor la măsurarea modificărilor structurale ale exportului. (The Use of Indices in Measuring the Structural Transformations of Export. With English summary.) *Stud. Cercet. Econ.*, 1973, (1), pp. 123–31.   [G: Rumania]

Koropeckyj, I. S. Technology and the Direction of Soviet Foreign Trade. *Rivista Int. Sci. Econ. Com.*, December 1973, *20*(12), pp. 1190–1208.   [G: U.S.S.R.]

Korth, Christopher M. and Selander, Sharon L. The China Market: Boom or Bust? In *Henley, D. S., ed.*, 1973, pp. 55–64.   [G: U.S.; China]

Kostál, Miroslav and Vesely, Zdenek. The Czechoslovak Socialist Republic and the Council for Mutual Economic Assistance. *Czech. Econ. Digest.*, August 1973, (5), pp. 25–43.   [G: Czechoslovakia]

Kreinin, Mordechai E. The Static Effects of EEC Enlargement on Trade Flows. *Southern Econ. J.*, April 1973, *39*(4), pp. 559–68.   [G: E.E.C.]

Kreinin, Mordechai E. Some Economic Consequences of Reverse Preferences. *J. Common Market Stud.*, March 1973, *11*(3), pp. 161–72.   [G: Europe]

Kreinin, Mordechai E. A Further Note on the Export Elasticity of Substitution. *Can. J. Econ.*, November 1973, *6*(4), pp. 606–08.

Kroese, C. E. Dutch Trade with the People's Republic of China. *Law Contemp. Probl.*, Summer-Autumn 1973, *38*(2), pp. 230–39.   [G: China; Netherlands]

Labys, Walter C. A Lauric Oil Exports Model Based on Capital Stock Supply Adjustment. *Malayan Econ. Rev.*, April 1973, *18*(1), pp. 1–10.   [G: Philippines; Ceylon; Indonesia]

Lermer, George. Evidence from Trade Data Regarding the Rationalizing of Canadian Industry. *Can. J. Econ.*, May 1973, *6*(2), pp. 248–56.   [G: Canada]

Luey, Paul. Discrepancies in Trade Statistics: Rejoinder. *Malayan Econ. Rev.*, October 1973, *18*(2), pp. 79–81.

Mackie, Arthur B. Patterns of World Agricultural Trade. In *Iowa State University Center for Agricultural and Rural Development*, 1973, pp. 69–86.

Maizels, Alfred. Recent Trends in Latin America's Exports to the Industrialised Countries. In *Urquidi, V. L. and Thorp, R., eds.*, 1973, pp. 35–52.   [G: Latin America]

Mathur, A. B. L. India's Terms of Trade with U.S.A. 1951–52 to 1968–69. *Indian Econ. J.*, October–December 1973, *21*(2), pp. 73–90.   [G: India; U.S.]

McGilvray, James and Simpson, David. The Commodity Structure of Anglo-Irish Trade. *Rev. Econ. Statist.*, November 1973, *55*(4), pp. 451–58.   [G: U.K.; Ireland]

Moriguchi, C. and Tatemoto, M. An Econometric Analysis of a Bilateral Model of International Economic Activity: Japan and U.S.A. In *Ball, R. J., ed.*, 1973, pp. 367–93.   [G: Japan; U.S.]

Moriguchi, C. Forecasting and Simulation Analysis of the World Economy. *Amer. Econ. Rev.*, May 1973, *63*(2), pp. 402–09.

Murray, Tracy and Edgmand, Michael R. Full Employment, Trade Expansion, and Adjustment Assistance: Reply. *Southern Econ. J.*, July 1973, *40*(1), pp. 138–39.

Myrdal, Gunnar. Politics and Economics in International Relations. In *Myrdal, G.*, 1973, pp. 167–81.

Namiki, Nobuyoshi. Future of the Economic Relations Between Japan and the European Community. *Rivista Int. Sci. Econ. Com.*, August-September 1973, *20*(8–9), pp. 758–85.   [G: Japan; E.E.C.]

Naranjo, John and Porter, Richard C. The Impact of the Commonwealth Preference System on the Exports of Latin America to the United Kingdom. *J. Devel. Stud.*, July 1973, *9*(4), pp. 581–97.   [G: U.K.; Latin America]

Naya, Seiji. Fluctuations in Export Earnings and Economic Patterns of Asian Countries. *Econ. Develop. Cult. Change*, Part I, July 1973, *21*(4), pp. 629–41.   [G: Asia]

Nayyar, Deepak. An Analysis of the Stagnation in India's Cotton Textile Exports During the Sixties. *Oxford Bull. Econ. Statist.*, February 1973, *35*(1), pp. 1–19.   [G: India]

Nove, Alec. Great Britain and Latin American Economic Development. In *Urquidi, V. L. and Thorp, R., eds.*, 1973, pp. 331–66.   [G: U.K.; Latin America]

Ohlin, Göran. Industrialization and Trade Trends: Some Issues for the 1970s: Comment. In *Hughes, H., ed.*, 1973, pp. 32–34.

Ouattara, Alassane D. Trade Effects of the Association of African Countries with the European Economic Community. *Int. Monet. Fund Staff Pap.*, July 1973, *20*(2), pp. 499–543.   [G: E.E.C.; Africa]

Palánkai, T. and Veress, P. Effect of the United Kingdom's Entry Into the Common Market on Anglo-Hungarian Relations. *Acta Oecon.*, 1973, *10*(1), pp. 81–94.

Pertot, Vladimir. Eastern European Trade and Financial Relations with Latin America. In *Urquidi, V. L. and Thorp, R., eds.*, 1973, pp. 400–419. [G: E. Europe; Latin America]

Peterson, Peter G. The Russian Economy and Its Trade Potential. In *Henley, D. S., ed.*, 1973, pp. 25–38. [G: U.S.S.R.; U.S.]

Pinto, Aníbal and Kñakal, Jan. The Centre-Periphery System Twenty Years Later. *Soc. Econ. Stud.*, March 1973, *22*(1), pp. 34–89.

Radhu, Ghulam M. Trade Between East and West Pakistan at World Prices, 1960/61–1969/70. *Pakistan Develop. Rev.*, Summer 1973, *12*(2), pp. 148–55. [G: Pakistan]

Ramsey, J. A. East-West Business Cooperation: The Twain Meet. In *Thorelli, H. B., ed.*, 1973, pp. 58–63. [G: E. Europe]

Resnick, Stephen A. and Truman, Edwin M. An Empirical Examination of Bilateral Trade in Western Europe. *J. Int. Econ.*, November 1973, *3*(4), pp. 305–35. [G: W. Europe]

Reynolds, Clark W. Relations with Latin America: An American View. In *Urquidi, V. L. and Thorp, R., eds.*, 1973, pp. 235–82. [G: U.S.; Latin America]

Richardson, J. David. Beyond (But Back To?) the Elasticity of Substitution in International Trade. *Europ. Econ. Rev.*, December 1973, *4*(4), pp. 381–92.

Rothschild, Kurt W. Military Expenditure, Exports and Growth. *Kyklos*, 1973, *26*(4), pp. 804–14. [G: O.E.C.D.]

Savost'ianov, V. V. Factors Determining the Effectiveness of Socialist Foreign Trade. *Prob. Econ.*, September 1973, *16*(5), pp. 94–105. [G: U.S.S.R.]

Savost'ianov, V. V. Quantitative Estimation of the Factors in Foreign Trade. *Matekon*, Winter 1973-74, *10*(2), pp. 26–35. [G: U.S.S.R.]

Saxe, Jo. The Japanese Experience and Attitudes Toward Trade Adjustment: Comment. In *Hughes, H., ed.*, 1973, pp. 266–68. [G: Japan]

Schaeffer, Maurice. The European Economic Community and Latin American Development. In *Urquidi, V. L. and Thorp, R., eds.*, 1973, pp. 313–30. [G: E.E.C.; Latin America]

Schloctern, F. J. M. Meyer Zu and Yajima, Akira. The OECD Trade Model 1970 Version. In *Alexandrides, C. G., ed.*, 1973, pp. 57–78.

Seevers, G. L. and Keeton, W. R. Interrelationships between the Levels of U.S. Exports and Imports. In *Iowa State University Center for Agricultural and Rural Development*, 1973, pp. 111–21. [G: U.S.]

Sellekaerts, Willy. How Meaningful are Empirical Studies on Trade Creation and Diversion? *Weltwirtsch. Arch.*, 1973, *109*(4), pp. 519–53. [G: E.E.C.]

Sharma, K. C. Indo-East European Trade—A Perspective. *Indian Econ. J.*, October–December 1973, *21*(2), pp. 91–106. [G: E. Europe]

Sharma, M. L. Exports of Engineering Goods—Retrospect and Prospects. *Econ. Aff.*, January–February 1973, *18*(1-2), pp. 39–40, 73. [G: India]

Shastiko, B. M. and Shiryaev, Y. S. Interrelations with Non-Socialist Markets. In *Kiss, T., ed.*, 1973, pp. 159–65. [G: CMEA]

Shinkai, Yoichi. Problems in the Estimation of Price Elasticities of Exports and Imports: A Survey. (In Japanese. With English summary.) *Econ. Stud. Quart.*, August 1973, *24*(2), pp. 31–39.

Singh, H. P. Export of Spices. *Econ. Aff.*, March 1973, *18*(3), pp. 131–42. [G: India]

Stein, L. On the Third World's Narrowing Trade Gap: A Rejoinder. *Oxford Econ. Pap.*, March 1973, *25*(1), pp. 141–44.

Streeten, Paul. Industrialization and Trade Trends: Some Issues for the 1970s: Comment. In *Hughes, H., ed.*, 1973, pp. 35–39.

Studenmund, A. H. A Cross-Sectional Analysis of the Law of Declining International Trade. *Western Econ. J.*, December 1973, *11*(4), pp. 481–86.

Sun, Nai-Ching and Bunamo, Michael C. Competition for Handling U.S. Foreign Trade Cargoes: The Port of New York's Experience. *Econ. Geogr.*, April 1973, *49*(2), pp. 156–62. [G: U.S.]

Taplin, G. B. A Model of World Trade. In *Ball, R. J., ed.*, 1973, pp. 177–223.

Teigeiro, José D. and Elson, R. Anthony. The Export Promotion System and the Growth of Minor Exports in Colombia. *Int. Monet. Fund Staff Pap.*, July 1973, *20*(2), pp. 419–70. [G: Colombia]

Tharakan, Mathew. India's Diamond Trade with Belgium. A Case-Study in "Cross-Hauling." *Econ. Soc. Tijdschr.*, February 1973, *27*(1), pp. 39–56. [G: India; Belgium]

Tharakan, Mathew. Indian Exports of Selected Primary Products and Semi-Manufactures to European Community. Problems and Prospects. *Tijdschr. Econ.*, 1973, *18*(2), pp. 235–61. [G: India]

Thoburn, J. T. Exports and the Malaysian Engineering Industry: A Case Study of Backward Linkage. *Oxford Bull. Econ. Statist.*, May 1973, *35*(2), pp. 91–117. [G: Malaya]

Trejo Reyes, Saúl. EXPORTA, A Multi-Sector Model for Optimal Growth and Export Policies. In *Goreux, L. M. and Manne, A. S., eds.*, 1973, pp. 179–95. [G: Mexico]

Tsuchiya, Masaya. Recent Developments in Sino-Japanese Trade. *Law Contemp. Probl.*, Summer-Autumn 1973, *38*(2), pp. 240–48. [G: China; Japan]

Tyler, Geoffrey and Neiss, Hubert. Problems and Prospects in East-West Trade. *Finance Develop.*, September 1973, *10*(3), pp. 24–26.

Tyler, William G. Manufactured Export Promotion in a Semi-Industrialized Economy: The Brazilian Case. *J. Devel. Stud.*, October 1973, *10*(1), pp. 3–15. [G: Brazil]

Újhelyi, T. Foreign Trade in Agricultural and Food Products—The Hungarian National Economy and the World Market. *Acta Oecon.*, 1973, *11*(1), pp. 3–18. [G: Hungary]

Valdés E., Alberto. Trade Policy and Its Effect on the External Agricultural Trade of Chile 1945–1965. *Amer. J. Agr. Econ.*, May 1973, *55*(2), pp. 154–64. [G: Chile]

Vartholomeos, John. Corporate Taxes and the

United States Balance of Trade: A Comment. *Nat. Tax J.,* December 1973, *26*(4), pp. 653–54.

Wall, David. The Japanese Experience and Attitudes Toward Trade Adjustment: Comment. In *Hughes, H., ed.,* 1973, pp. 263–66. [G: Japan]

Walter, Ingo. The Pollution Content of American Trade. *Western Econ. J.,* March 1973, *11*(1), pp. 61–70. [G: U.S.]

Wang, Kenneth. Foreign Trade Policy and Apparatus of the People's Republic of China. *Law Contemp. Probl.,* Summer-Autumn 1973, *38*(2), pp. 182–200. [G: China]

Watanabe, Tamao and Ogawa, Kazuo. Introduction to Japan-China Trade. *Chinese Econ. Stud.,* Fall 1973, *7*(1), pp. 3–137. [G: Japan; China]

Weinrobe, Maurice D. Corporate Taxes and the United States Balance of Trade: Reply. *Nat. Tax J.,* December 1973, *26*(4), pp. 655.

Welch, Wilford. The Business Outlook for Southeast Asia. *Harvard Bus. Rev.,* May-June 1973, *51*(3), pp. 72–84. [G: S.E. Asia]

Wilford, W. T. and Christou, G. A Sectoral Analysis of Disaggregated Trade Flows in the Central American Common Market 1962–1970. *J. Common Market Stud.,* December 1973, *12*(2), pp. 159–75. [G: Central America]

Wilson, A. G. Examination of Alternative Methods, Approaches, and Programs for Production and Market Stabilization with Particular Reference to the Pacific Rim Market. In *Canadian Agricultural Economics Society,* 1973, pp. 98–140. [G: Canada; E. Asia]

Wolf, Charles, Jr. and Weinschrott, David. International Transactions and Regionalism: Distinguishing "Insiders" from "Outsiders." *Amer. Econ. Rev.,* May 1973, *63*(2), pp. 52–60.

422 Commercial Policy

4220 Commercial Policy and Trade Regulations; Empirical Studies

Aboyade, Ojetunji. Advancing Tropical African Development: A Defence of Inward-Looking Strategy. In *Streeten, P., ed.,* 1973, pp. 62–75. [G: Africa]

Afzal, Mohammad and Mirakhor, Abbas. An Index of Export Performance as a Criterion of Export Policy for Developing Countries. *Pakistan Econ. Soc. Rev.,* Summer 1973, *11*(2), pp. 193–99.

Akins, James E. The Oil Crisis: This Time the Wolf Is Here. *Foreign Aff.,* April 1973, *51*(3), pp. 462–90.

Alamgir, Mohiuddin and Berlage, Lodewijk J. J. B. Foodgrain (Rice and Wheat) Demand, Import and Price Policy for Bangladesh. *Bangladesh Econ. Rev.,* January 1973, *1*(1), pp. 25–58. [G: Bangladesh]

Amacher, Ryan C.; Tollison, Robert D. and Willett, Thomas D. Import Controls on Foreign Oil: Comment. *Amer. Econ. Rev.,* December 1973, *63*(5), pp. 1031–34.

Anyanwu, Enoch A. The Contribution of Finance to Industrial Development: The Nigerian Experience. In *[Hicks, U.],* 1973, pp. 59–94. [G: Nigeria]

Arndt, Sven W. The Role of World Trade Policy: The View from the Advanced Countries. In *Urquidi, V. L. and Thorp, R., eds.,* 1973, pp. 88–106.

Baack, Bennett D. and Ray, Edward J. Tariff Policy and Comparative Advantage in the Iron and Steel Industry: 1870–1929. *Exploration Econ. Hist.,* Fall 1973, *11*(1), pp. 3–23. [G: U.S.]

Bacha, Edmar. Preference for Industry and Commercial Policy Theory in Industrializing Countries. In *Eckaus, R. S. and Rosenstein-Rodan, P. N., eds.,* 1973, pp. 269–92.

Baer, Donald E. Income and Export Taxation of Agriculture in Costa Rica and Honduras. *J. Devel. Areas,* October 1973, *8*(1), pp. 39–53. [G: Costa Rica; Honduras]

Balassa, Bela. Tariffs and Trade Policy in the Andean Common Market. *J. Common Market Stud.,* December 1973, *12*(2), pp. 176–95. [G: South America]

Balassa, Bela. Policy Issues in Adjustment Assistance: The United States: Comment. In *Hughes, H., ed.,* 1973, pp. 180–86.

Baldwin, Robert and Mutti, John H. Policy Issues in Adjustment Assistance: The United States. In *Hughes, H., ed.,* 1973, pp. 149–77. [G: U.S.]

Bale, Malcolm D. Full Employment, Trade Expansion, and Adjustment Assistance: Comment. *Southern Econ. J.,* July 1973, *40*(1), pp. 135–38.

Barger, Harold. International Liquidity and International Trade: Comment. In *Wiegand, G. C., ed.,* 1973, pp. 97–98. [G: U.S.]

Bergsten, C. Fred. Future Directions for U.S. Trade. *Amer. J. Agr. Econ.,* May 1973, *55*(2), pp. 280–88. [G: U.S.]

Bhatia, Rattan J. Import Programming in Ghana— 1966-69. *Finance Develop.,* March 1973, *10*(1), pp. 20–24. [G: Ghana]

Bieri, Jurg and Schmitz, Andrew. Export Instability, Monopoly Power, and Welfare. *J. Int. Econ.,* November 1973, *3*(4), pp. 389–96.

Blackhurst, Richard. Estimating the Impact of Tariff Manipulation: The Excess Demand and Supply Approach. *Oxford Econ. Pap.,* March 1973, *25*(1), pp. 80–87.

Boarman, Patrick M. Healing the Rift Between the U.S. and Europe. *Calif. Manage. Rev.,* Fall 1973, *16*(1), pp. 76–85. [G: U.S.; Europe]

Botha, D. J. J. On Tariff Policy: The Formative Years. *S. Afr. J. Econ.,* December 1973, *41*(4), pp. 321–55. [G: S.Africa]

Brada, Josef C. The Allocative Efficiency of Centrally Planned Foreign Trade: A Programming Approach to the Czech Case. *Europ. Econ. Rev.,* December 1973, *4*(4), pp. 329–46. [G: Czechoslovakia]

Brandis, R. Buford. The National Need for an Integrated Trade Policy: The Textile Example. In *Iowa State University Center for Agricultural and Rural Development,* 1973, pp. 155–65. [G: U.S.]

Bronfenbrenner, Martin. Japanese-American Economic War? Some Further Reflections. *Quart. Rev. Econ. Bus.,* Autumn 1973, *13*(3), pp. 33–42. [G: Japan; U.S.]

Brown, Alan A. and Marer, Paul. Foreign Trade in the East European Reforms. In *Bornstein, M., ed.,* 1973, pp. 153–205. [G: E. Europe]

Cain, Neville. Political Economy and the Tariff: Australia in the 1920s. *Australian Econ. Pap.,* June 1973, *12*(20), pp. 1–20. [G: Australia]

Cateora, P. R. and Hess, J. M. Pricing in International Markets. In *Thorelli, H. B., ed.,* 1973, pp. 209–21.

Channon, J. W. Role of Provincial Governments in Export Market Development. In *Canadian Agricultural Economics Society,* 1973, pp. 49–57. [G: Canada]

Chenery, Hollis B. and Hughes, Helen. Industrialization and Trade Trends: Some Issues for the 1970s. In *Hughes, H., ed.,* 1973, pp. 3–31.

Chen, Tung-pi. Legal Aspects of Canadian Trade with the People's Republic of China. *Law Contemp. Probl.,* Summer-Autumn 1973, *38*(2), pp. 201–29. [G: Canada; China]

Cicchetti, Charles J. and Gillen, William J. The Mandatory Oil Import Quota Program: A Consideration of Economic Efficiency and Equity. *Natural Res. J.,* July 1973, *13*(3), pp. 399–430. [G: U.S.]

Cochrane, James D. and Sloan, John W. LAFTA and the CACM: A Comparative Analysis of Integration in Latin America. *J. Devel. Areas,* October 1973, *8*(1), pp. 13–37. [G: Latin America]

Corden, W. Max. Employment in the Industrialized Countries: Comment. In *Hughes, H., ed.,* 1973, pp. 125–27.

Curzon, Gerard and Curzon, Victoria. GATT and NTD's. In *Scaperlanda, A. E., ed.,* 1973, pp. 283–97.

Dawson, R. M. Canadian Trade and Tariff Policy as it Relates to the Pacific Rim. In *Canadian Agricultural Economics Society,* 1973, pp. 43–48. [G: Canada; Oceania]

Dekker, P. G. Economische oorlogvoering. Enige opmerkingen over boycot en embargo. (Economic Warfare: A Note on Boycott and Embargo. With English summary.) *De Economist,* July-August 1973, *121*(4), pp. 387–402.

Denny, David L. and Stein, Daniel D. Recent Developments in Trade between the U.S. and the P.-R.C.: A Legal and Economic Perspective. *Law Contemp. Probl.,* Summer-Autumn 1973, *38*(2), pp. 260–73. [G: China; U.S.]

Despres, Emile. The Significance of the European Common Market to the American Economy. In *Despres, E.,* 1973, pp. 60–86. [G: U.S.; E.E.C.]

Diebold, John. Business, Government and Science: The Need for a Fresh Look. *Foreign Aff.,* April 1973, *51*(3), pp. 555–72. [G: U.S.]

Doganis, Rigas. Air Transport—A Case Study in International Regulation. *J. Transp. Econ. Policy,* May 1973, *7*(2), pp. 109–33.

Donges, Juergen B. Shaping Spain's Export Industry. *World Devel.,* September 1973, *1*(9), pp. 19–37. [G: Spain]

Dorling, M. J. Extending the Production-Distribution Model to Handle International Competition in Agriculture. *Can. J. Agr. Econ.,* February 1973, *21*(1), pp. 57–62.

Due, Jean M. and Gehring, Donald C. Jamaica's Strategy for Import Substitution of Vegetables in the 1960's. *Ill. Agr. Econ.,* January 1973, *13*(1), pp. 20–26. [G: Jamaica]

Dunning, John H. Multinational Enterprises and Trade Flows of Developing Countries. In *Streeten, P., ed.,* 1973, pp. 300–20.

Dunn, Robert M., Jr. Canada and Its Economic Discontents. *Foreign Aff.,* October 1973, *52*(1), pp. 119–40. [G: Canada]

Dutta, Amita. Migration in a Trading Economy. *J. Devel. Stud.,* October 1973, *10*(1), pp. 79–91. [G: Ceylon]

Edwards, C. D. The World of Antitrust. In *Thorelli, H. B., ed.,* 1973, pp. 89–103. [G: U.S.]

Fan, Liang-Shing. The Economy and Foreign Trade of China. *Law Contemp. Probl.,* Summer-Autumn 1973, *38*(2), pp. 249–59. [G: China]

Farley, Noel J. J. Outward-looking Policies and Industrialization in a Small Economy: Some Notes on the Irish Case. *Econ. Develop. Cult. Change,* Part I, July 1973, *21*(4), pp. 610–28. [G: Ireland]

Finger, J. M. The Generalized Scheme of Preferences—Impact on the Donor Countries. *Bull. Econ. Res.,* May 1973, *25*(1), pp. 43–54.

Fløystad, Gunnar. The Impact on Allocation and Return to Labor and Capital of a Reduction of Customs Duties in the Developed Countries in Their Trade with Less Developed Countries. *Weltwirtsch. Arch.,* 1973, *109*(1), pp. 59–69. [G: Norway]

Frankena, Mark. Marketing Characteristics and Prices of Exports of Engineering Goods from India. *Oxford Econ. Pap.,* March 1973, *25*(1), pp. 127–32. [G: India]

Fried, Edward R. Foreign Economic Policy: The Search for a Strategy. In *Owen, H., ed.,* 1973, pp. 157–202. [G: U.S.]

Gamache, Adrian E. The Influence of U.S. Trade Policy on Forest Products Trade. *Amer. J. Agr. Econ.,* December 1973, *55*(5), pp. 983–88. [G: U.S.]

Gately, Dermot. International Commodity Agreements: The Experience of Coffee and the Prospects for Cocoa. *Econ. Bull. Ghana, Sec. Ser.,* 1973, *3*(2), pp. 3–10.

Geiger, Theodore. Toward a World of Trading Blocs? In *Henley, D. S., ed.,* 1973, pp. 6–17. [G: W. Europe; Japan; U.S.]

Ghai, Dharam P. The Association Agreement between the European Economic Community and the Partner States of the East African Community. *J. Common Market Stud.,* September 1973, *12*(1), pp. 78–103. [G: E. Africa; E.E.C.]

Giltinan, John W. Customs Drawback. *Manage. Account.,* April 1973, *54*(10), pp. 23–27.

Glassburner, Bruce. The January 1973 Tariff Revision. *Bull. Indonesian Econ. Stud.,* November 1973, *9*(3), pp. 103–08. [G: Indonesia]

Glynn, Sean and Lougheed, Alan L. A Comment on United States Economic Policy and the "Dollar Gap" of the 1920's. *Econ. Hist. Rev., 2nd Ser.,* November 1973, *26*(4), pp. 692–94.

Golbert, Albert S. Pitfalls of DISC. *Manage. Account.,* July 1973, *55*(1), pp. 52–55. [G: U.S.]

Goldfinger, Nathaniel. Employment in the Industrialized Countries: Comment. In *Hughes, H., ed.,* 1973, pp. 117–24.

Goldman, Marshall I. Who Profits More from U.S.-Soviet Trade? *Harvard Bus. Rev.,* November-

December 1973, *51*(6), pp. 79–87. [G: U.S.; U.S.S.R.]

Graham, Philip L., Jr.; Hermann, Donald H. G. and Marcus, Sumner. Section 7 of the Clayton Act and Mergers Involving Foreign Interests. In *Henley, D. S., ed.,* 1973, pp. 155–84. [G: U.S.]

Gray, H. Peter. Senile Industry Protection: A Proposal. *Southern Econ. J.,* April 1973, *39*(4), pp. 569–74.

Gregory, R. G. and Tearle, D. Product Differentiation and International Trade Flows: An Application of the "Hedonic" Regression Technique. *Australian Econ. Pap.,* June 1973, *12*(20), pp. 79–90. [G: Australia]

Grubel, Herbert G. The Case for Optimum Exchange Rate Stability. *Weltwirtsch. Arch.,* 1973, *109*(3), pp. 351–81.

Grzybowski, Kazimierz. Control of U.S. Trade with China: An Overview. *Law Contemp. Probl.,* Summer-Autumn 1973, *38*(2), pp. 175–81. [G: China; U.S.]

Guisinger, Stephen. The Rise of the Multinational Corporation and United States Trade Policy. *Soc. Sci. Quart.,* December 1973, *54*(3), pp. 552–67. [G: U.S.]

Gwyer, G. D. Three International Commodity Agreements: The Experience of East Africa. *Econ. Develop. Cult. Change,* April 1973, *21*(3), pp. 465–76. [G: E. Africa]

Hamilton, Richard E. Canada's "Exportable Surplus" Natural Gas Policy: A Theoretical Analysis. *Land Econ.,* August 1973, *49*(3), pp. 251–59. [G: Canada]

Handke, Werner. Die Neue Aussenwirtschaftspolitik der USA. (The 'New Foreign Economic Policy' of the USA. With English summary.) *Z. ges. Staatswiss.,* May 1973, *129*(2), pp. 312–32. [G: U.S.]

Hartke, Vance. A Foreign Trade and Investment Policy for the 1970s. In *Kujawa, D., ed.,* 1973, pp. 54–71. [G: U.S.]

Hathaway, Dale E. Trade Restrictions and U.S. Consumers. In *Iowa State University Center for Agricultural and Rural Development,* 1973, pp. 103–10. [G: U.S.]

Hay, George A. Import Controls on Foreign Oil: Reply. *Amer. Econ. Rev.,* December 1973, *63*(5), pp. 1035–36.

Hazlewood, Arthur. State Trading and the East African Customs Union. *Oxford Bull. Econ. Statist.,* May 1973, *35*(2), pp. 75–89. [G: E. Africa]

Heaver, Trevor D. The Structure of Liner Conference Rates. *J. Ind. Econ.,* July 1973, *21*(3), pp. 257–65.

Heitmann, G. United States Oil Import Quotas and the Price of Foreign Oil. *J. Ind. Econ.,* July 1973, *21*(3), pp. 266–71. [G: U.S.]

Hinton, Deane. Policy Issues in Adjustment Assistance: The United States: Comment. In *Hughes, H., ed.,* 1973, pp. 177–80.

Hoffmann, Lutz. Import Substitution—Export Expansion and Growth in an Open Developing Economy: The Case of West Malaysia. *Weltwirtsch. Arch.,* 1973, *109*(3), pp. 452–75. [G: W. Malaysia]

Hosono, Akio. Japanese Economic Relations with Latin America: Prospects and Possible Lines of Action. In *Urquidi, V. L. and Thorp, R., eds.,* 1973, pp. 374–95. [G: Japan; Latin America]

van Houten, Jan F. Assembly Industries in the Caribbean. *Finance Develop.,* June 1973, *10*(2), pp. 19–22, 37. [G: Caribbean]

Hughes, Helen. Prospects for Partnership: Industrialization and Trade Policies in the 1970s: Summary and Conclusions. In *Hughes, H., ed.,* 1973, pp. 269–89.

Ikram, Khalid. Devaluation and Export Price Competitiveness: A Note. *Pakistan Econ. Soc. Rev.,* Autumn 1973, *11*(3), pp. 349–53. [G: Pakistan]

Ikram, Khalid. Social Versus Private Profitability in Pakistan's Export of Manufactures. *Pakistan Develop. Rev.,* Summer 1973, *12*(2), pp. 156–67. [G: Pakistan]

Ikram, Khalid. Suspension of Interwing Trade: Structure and Growth of West Pakistan's Exports. *Pakistan Econ. Soc. Rev.,* Summer 1973, *11*(2), pp. 141–53. [G: Pakistan]

Isard, Peter. Employment Impacts of Textile Imports and Investment: A Vintage-Capital Model. *Amer. Econ. Rev.,* June 1973, *63*(3), pp. 402–16. [G: U.S.]

Iyoha, Milton Ame. The Optimal Balance-of-Payments Strategy of a Less Developed Country. *Econ. Rec.,* June 1973, *49*(126), pp. 270–79.

Jedel, Michael Jay and Stamm, John H. The Battle over Jobs: An Appraisal of Recent Publications on the Employment Effects of U.S. Multinational Corporations. In *Kujawa, D., ed.,* 1973, pp. 144–91. [G: U.S.]

Johansson, B. O. Den nya GATT-rundan—en lösning av de handelspolitiska problemen. (The New GATT Negotiations—A Solution to the Commercial Policy Program? With English summary.) *Ekon. Samfundets Tidskr.,* 1973, *26*(3), pp. 167–76.

Johns, B. L. Import Substitution and Export Potential—The Case of Manufacturing Industry in West Malaysia. *Australian Econ. Pap.,* December 1973, *12*(21), pp. 175–95. [G: Malaysia]

Johnson, D. Gale. What Difference Does Trade Make in World Community Welfare? In *Iowa State University Center for Agricultural and Rural Development,* 1973, pp. 49–68. [G: E.E.C.; U.S.]

Johnson, D. Gale. The Impact of Freer Trade on North American Agriculture. *Amer. J. Agr. Econ.,* May 1973, *55*(2), pp. 294–99. [G: U.S.; Canada]

Joshi, Nandini U. Bank Credit Policy for Export Incentives. *Indian Econ. J.,* April-June 1973, *20* (4–5), pp. 638–45. [G: India]

Josling, Tim. Domestic Farm Policies and International Trade in Agricultural Goods. In *Streeten, P., ed.,* 1973, pp. 264–78.

Kanamori, Hisao. Il Giappone e l'Europa: Un'analisi economica. (Japan and Europe: An Economic Analysis. With English summary.) *Mondo Aperto,* April 1973, *27*(2), pp. 122–26. [G: Japan; W. Europe]

Kindleberger, Charles P. Restrictions on Direct Investment in Host Countries. In *[Rosenstein-Rodan, P.],* 1973, pp. 201–09.

Kinoshita, Kazuo. The Use of Tax Incentives for Export by Developed Countries—The Japanese

Case. *Bull. Int. Fiscal Doc.*, July 1973, *27*(7), pp. 271–90. [G: Japan]

Kojima, Kiyoshi. The Japanese Experience and Attitudes Toward Trade Adjustment. In *Hughes, H., ed.*, 1973, pp. 228–62. [G: Japan]

Kojima, Kiyoshi. Reorganisation of North-South Trade: Japan's Foreign Economic Policy for the 1970s. *Hitotsubashi J. Econ.*, February 1973, *13* (2), pp. 1–28. [G: Japan]

Korovkin, G. Scientific-Technical Progress and Trade. *Prob. Econ.*, November 1973, *16*(7), pp. 84–101. [G: U.S.S.R.]

Krasner, Stephen D. Manipulating International Commodity Markets: Brazilian Coffee Policy 1906 to 1962. *Public Policy*, Fall 1973, *21*(4), pp. 493–523. [G: Brazil]

Kreinin, Mordechai E. Disaggregated Import Demand Functions—Further Results. *Southern Econ. J.*, July 1973, *40*(1), pp. 19–25.

Kressler, Peter R. Investment Barriers Facing the United States Automotive Industry in the Japanese Market. *Ohio State U. Bull. Bus. Res.*, September 1973, *48*(9), pp. 1–3. [G: U.S.; Japan]

Kroese, C. E. Dutch Trade with the People's Republic of China. *Law Contemp. Probl.*, Summer-Autumn 1973, *38*(2), pp. 230–39. [G: China; Netherlands]

Lermer, George. Evidence from Trade Data Regarding the Rationalizing of Canadian Industry. *Can. J. Econ.*, May 1973, *6*(2), pp. 248–56. [G: Canada]

Leung, David T. W. The Concept of Effective Subsidy and its Application to the Canadian Flour Milling Industry. *Can. J. Agr. Econ.*, February 1973, *21*(1), pp. 1–9. [G: Canada]

van Lith, Jan A. Government Procurement in the Benelux Countries. In *Scaperlanda, A. E., ed.*, 1973, pp. 163–90. [G: Benelux]

Luttrell, Clifton B. The Russian Wheat Deal—Hindsight vs. Foresight. *Fed. Res. Bank St. Louis Rev.*, October 1973, *55*(10), pp. 2–9. [G: U.S.]

Macario, Santiago P. The Role of World Trade Policy: A Latin American Viewpoint. In *Urquidi, V. L. and Thorp, R., eds.*, 1973, pp. 58–87. [G: Latin America]

Maitra, Priyatosh. Relative Effects of Import Substitution in New Zealand. *Econ. Aff.*, May 1973, *18* (5), pp. 213–16, 234–40. [G: New Zealand]

Malmgren, Harald B. The Impact of the Developed Countries. In *Streeten, P., ed.*, 1973, pp. 123–42.

Massel, M. S. Non-Tariff Barriers as an Obstacle to World Trade. In *Thorelli, H. B., ed.*, 1973, pp. 71–82.

Mayer, Leo V. Regional Effects of Alternative Trade Policies. In *Iowa State University Center for Agricultural and Rural Development*, 1973, pp. 166–83. [G: U.S.]

McCulloch, Rachel and Johnson, Harry G. A Note on Proportionally Distributed Quotas. *Amer. Econ. Rev.*, September 1973, *63*(4), pp. 726–32.

Meany, George. A Trade Policy for America. In *Reynolds, L. G.; Green, G. D. and Lewis, D. R., eds.*, 1973, pp. 443–51. [G: U.S.]

Meier, G. M. The Impact of the Developed Countries. In *Streeten, P., ed.*, 1973, pp. 105–22.

Melinte, T.; Horovicz, M. and Olteanu, I. World

Market, Economic Cooperation and the Planning of the National Economy. In *Kiss, T., ed.*, 1973, pp. 127–33. [G: Romania]

Miles, Caroline. Employment in the Industrialized Countries. In *Hughes, H., ed.*, 1973, pp. 101–16.

Morawetz, David. Harmonization of Economic Policies in a Free Trade Area: The Andean Group. *Weltwirtsch. Arch.*, 1973, *109*(4), pp. 579–600. [G: Latin America]

Morawetz, David. Harmonization of Economic Policies in Customs Unions: The Andean Group. *J. Common Market Stud.*, June 1973, *11*(4), pp. 294–313. [G: Latin America]

Munsche, Richard C. International Competition and Tax Reform. In *Tax Foundation, Inc.*, 1973, pp. 59–64. [G: U.S.]

Murray, Tracy. E.E.C. Enlargement and Preference for the Developing Countries. *Econ. J.*, September 1973, *83*(331), pp. 853–57.

Murray, Tracy and Edgmand, Michael R. Full Employment, Trade Expansion, and Adjustment Assistance: Reply. *Southern Econ. J.*, July 1973, *40* (1), pp. 138–39.

Murray, Tracy. Preferential Tariffs for the LDCs. *Southern Econ. J.*, July 1973, *40*(1), pp. 35–46.

Murray, Tracy. How Helpful is the Generalised System of Preferences to Developing Countries? *Econ. J.*, June 1973, *83*(330), pp. 449–55.

Namiki, Nobuyoshi. Future of the Economic Relations Between Japan and the European Community. *Rivista Int. Sci. Econ. Com.*, August-September 1973, *20*(8–9), pp. 758–85. [G: Japan; E.E.C.]

Naranjo, John and Porter, Richard C. The Impact of the Commonwealth Preference System on the Exports of Latin America to the United Kingdom. *J. Devel. Stud.*, July 1973, *9*(4), pp. 581–97. [G: U.K.; Latin America]

Naseem, S. M. and Berendsen, B. S. M. On Two Formulae for Calculating the Effective Rate of Protection. *Pakistan Develop. Rev.*, Summer 1973, *12*(2), pp. 189–93.

Neu, Axel and Glismann, Hans H. Quantitative Aspects of Nontariff Distortions of Trade in the Federal Republic of Germany. In *Scaperlanda, A. E., ed.*, 1973, pp. 193–253. [G: Germany]

Norwood, Bernard. The Next World Trade Negotiations. In *[Halm, G. N.]*, 1973, pp. 125–48.

Ohlin, Göran. Industrialization and Trade Trends: Some Issues for the 1970s: Comment. In *Hughes, H., ed.*, 1973, pp. 32–34.

Ouattara, Alassane D. Trade Effects of the Association of African Countries with the European Economic Community. *Int. Monet. Fund Staff Pap.*, July 1973, *20*(2), pp. 499–543. [G: E.E.C.; Africa]

Oyejide, T. Ademola. Tariff Protection and Industrialization via Import Substitution: An Empirical Analysis of the Nigerian Experience. *Econ. Bull. Ghana, Sec. Ser.*, 1973, *3*(3), pp. 20–27. [G: Nigeria]

Oyejide, T. Ademola. Tariff Protection and Industrialization via Import Substitution: An Empirical Analysis of the Nigerian Experience. *Bangladesh Econ. Rev.*, October 1973, *1*(4), pp. 331–40. [G: Nigeria]

Park, Sung-Jo. Ökonomische und politische Zielkonflikte in der Gestaltung des kommunistischen Aussenhandels: Autarkie und Pragmatismus in der Aussenwirtschaftspolitik der Volksrepublik China. (Autarky and Pragmatism in the Foreign Trade Policy of the People's Republic of China. With English summary.) *Z. Wirtschaft. Sozialwissen.*, 1973, *93*(5), pp. 587–600. **[G: China]**

Parzych, Kenneth M. The U.S. Balance-of-Payments: A Restructuring of Commercial Policy. *Rivista Int. Sci. Econ. Com.*, December 1973, *20*(12), pp. 1179–89. **[G: U.S.]**

Pavliuchenko, V. Some Problems in the Long-Term Planning of Purchases of Licenses. *Prob. Econ.*, March 1973, *15*(11), pp. 92–98. **[G: U.S.S.R.]**

Pertot, Vladimir. Eastern European Trade and Financial Relations with Latin America. In *Urquidi, V. L. and Thorp, R., eds.*, 1973, pp. 400–419. **[G: E. Europe; Latin America]**

Petersen, Gustav H. Latin America: Benign Neglect Is Not Enough. *Foreign Aff.*, April 1973, *51*(3), pp. 598–607. **[G: U.S.; Latin America]**

Pinder, John. The Community and the Developing Countries: Associates and Outsiders. *J. Common Market Stud.*, September 1973, *12*(1), pp. 53–77. **[G: E.E.C.]**

Polaczek, S. and Zdanowicz, J. Subsidy, Taxation and Foreign Trade. In *Kiss, T., ed.*, 1973, pp. 221–26. **[G: CMEA]**

Rees, Richard D. World Wheat Production and Trade. *Fed. Res. Bank Kansas City Rev.*, June 1973, pp. 10–16.

Reynolds, Clark W. Relations with Latin America: An American View. In *Urquidi, V. L. and Thorp, R., eds.*, 1973, pp. 235–82. **[G: U.S.; Latin America]**

Robertson, David. Multilateral Trade Negotiations. *Nat. Westminster Bank Quart. Rev.*, February 1973, pp. 46–58.

Rogers, Christopher D. Gli accordi internazionali per le materie prime. (The International Agreements on Raw Materials. With English summary.) *Mondo Aperto*, December 1973, *27*(6), pp. 415–28.

Rogers, Christopher D. International Commodity Agreements. *Lloyds Bank Rev.*, April 1973, (108), pp. 33–47.

Rose, Sanford. U.S. Foreign Trade: There's No Need to Panic. In *Reynolds, L. G.; Green, G. D. and Lewis, D. R., eds.*, 1973, pp. 452–62. **[G: U.S.]**

Russell, Robert William. Political Distortions in Trade Negotiations among Industrialized Countries. In *Scaperlanda, A. E., ed.*, 1973, pp. 299–317.

Sanchez, Nicolas and Sweeney, Richard J. The Allocation of Tariff Revenues and Optimum Trade Distortion. With Empirical Applications to United States Sugar Policy. *Weltwirtsch. Arch.*, 1973, *109*(3), pp. 382–401. **[G: U.S.]**

Saxe, Jo. The Japanese Experience and Attitudes Toward Trade Adjustment: Comment. In *Hughes, H., ed.*, 1973, pp. 266–68. **[G: Japan]**

Scaperlanda, Anthony E. E.E.C. NTD's and Developing Economies. In *Scaperlanda, A. E., ed.*, 1973, pp. 255–80. **[G: E.E.C.; Africa]**

Scaperlanda, Anthony E. Perspectives and Implica-

tions. In *Scaperlanda, A. E., ed.*, 1973, pp. 17–45. **[G: E.E.C.]**

Scheinberg, Stephen. Invitation to Empire: Tariffs and American Economic Expansion in Canada. *Bus. Hist. Rev.*, Summer 1973, *47*(2), pp. 218–38. **[G: Canada]**

Schneider, J. W. Intra-Benelux NTD's. In *Scaperlanda, A. E., ed.*, 1973, pp. 73–106. **[G: Benelux]**

Schnittker, John A. Prospects for Freer Agricultural Trade. *Amer. J. Agr. Econ.*, May 1973, *55*(2), pp. 289–93.

Schurr, Samuel. Minerals Trade and International Relations. In *Bergsten, C. F., ed.*, 1973, pp. 181–96.

Seevers, G. L. and Keeton, W. R. Interrelationships between the Levels of U.S. Exports and Imports. In *Iowa State University Center for Agricultural and Rural Development*, 1973, pp. 111–21. **[G: U.S.]**

Seifer, Daniel M. Foreign Steel and U.S. Jobs, Trade, Environment, and Safety. *Ohio State U. Bull. Bus. Res.*, March 1973, *48*(3), pp. 4–7. **[G: U.S.]**

Sharpston, C. H. Competition and the Developing Countries. In *Rybczynski, T. M., ed.*, 1973, pp. 46–54.

Sorenson, Vernon L. Contradictions in U.S. Trade Policy. In *Iowa State University Center for Agricultural and Rural Development*, 1973, pp. 184–93. **[G: U.S.]**

Staelin, Charles. Indian Export Incentives: A Critical View. *Indian Econ. J.*, October–December 1973, *21*(2), pp. 107–23. **[G: India]**

Stern, Robert M. Tariffs and Other Measures of Trade Control: A Survey of Recent Developments. *J. Econ. Lit.*, September 1973, *11*(3), pp. 857–88.

Streeten, Paul. Industrialization and Trade Trends: Some Issues for the 1970s: Comment. In *Hughes, H., ed.*, 1973, pp. 35–39.

Suliman, Ali A. Fiscal Incentives for Industrial Investment in the Sudan. *Bull. Int. Fiscal Doc.*, August 1973, *27*(8), pp. 315–23. **[G: Sudan]**

Swidrowski, Jozef. Export Controls and Export Promotion. *S. Afr. J. Econ.*, March 1973, *41*(1), pp. 49–59.

Talbot, Ross B. Effect of Domestic Political Groups and Forces on U.S. Trade Policy. In *Iowa State University Center for Agricultural and Rural Development*, 1973, pp. 141–54. **[G: U.S.]**

Taylor, James R. Industrialization of the Mexican Border Region. *N. Mex. Bus.*, March 1973, *26*(3), pp. 3–9. **[G: U.S.; Mexico]**

Taylor, Lance and Bacha, Edmar. Growth and Trade Distortions in Chile, and Their Implications in Calculating the Shadow Price of Foreign Exchange. In *Eckaus, R. S. and Rosenstein-Rodan, P. N., eds.*, 1973, pp. 121–46. **[G: Chile]**

Teigeiro, José D. and Elson, R. Anthony. The Export Promotion System and the Growth of Minor Exports in Colombia. *Int. Monet. Fund Staff Pap.*, July 1973, *20*(2), pp. 419–70. **[G: Colombia]**

Teigeiro, José D. and Elson, R. Anthony. Export Incentives in Colombia. *Finance Develop.*, December 1973, *10*(4), pp. 30–33. **[G: Colombia]**

Tharakan, Mathew. Indian Exports of Selected Pri-

mary Products and Semi-Manufactures to European Community. Problems and Prospects. *Tijdschr. Econ.*, 1973, *18*(2), pp. 235–61.
[G: India]

Thoburn, J. T. Exports and the Malaysian Engineering Industry: A Case Study of Backward Linkage. *Oxford Bull. Econ. Statist.*, May 1973, *35*(2), pp. 91–117. [G: Malaya]

Tontz, Robert L. U.S. Trade Policy: Background and Historical Trends. In *Iowa State University Center for Agricultural and Rural Development*, 1973, pp. 17–48. [G: U.S.]

Tower, Edward. Commercial Policy Under Fixed and Flexible Exchange Rates. *Quart. J. Econ.*, August 1973, *87*(3), pp. 436–54.

Trejo Reyes, Saúl. EXPORTA, A Multi-Sector Model for Optimal Growth and Export Policies. In *Goreux, L. M. and Manne, A. S., eds.*, 1973, pp. 179–95. [G: Mexico]

Tsuchiya, Masaya. Recent Developments in Sino-Japanese Trade. *Law Contemp. Probl.*, Summer-Autumn 1973, *38*(2), pp. 240–48. [G: China; Japan]

Tumlir, Jan. Trade Negotiations in the Field of Manufactures. In *Streeten, P., ed.*, 1973, pp. 279–99.

Tyler, William G. Manufactured Export Promotion in a Semi-Industrialized Economy: The Brazilian Case. *J. Devel. Stud.*, October 1973, *10*(1), pp. 3–15. [G: Brazil]

Valdés E., Alberto. Trade Policy and Its Effect on the External Agricultural Trade of Chile 1945–1965. *Amer. J. Agr. Econ.*, May 1973, *55*(2), pp. 154–64. [G: Chile]

Van Lam, Ngo. The Pursuit of Growth and Stability Through Taxation of Agricultural Exports: Thailand's Experience: A Comment. *Public Finance*, 1973, *28*(2), pp. 227–32. [G: Thailand]

Van Roy, Edward. Ngo Van Lam on the Rice Premium: A Rejoinder. *Public Finance*, 1973, *28* (2), pp. 233–36.

Wall, David. The Japanese Experience and Attitudes Toward Trade Adjustment: Comment. In *Hughes, H., ed.*, 1973, pp. 263–66. [G: Japan]

Walter, Ingo. Commonwealth Preferences in Retrospect: Some Policy Implications for the Developing Countries. *Econ. Bull. Ghana, Sec. Ser.*, 1973, *3*(4), pp. 3–13. [G: U.K.]

Walter, Ingo. Environmental Management and the International Economic Order. In *Bergsten, C. F., ed.*, 1973, pp. 293–346.

Wang, Kenneth. Foreign Trade Policy and Apparatus of the People's Republic of China. *Law Contemp. Probl.*, Summer-Autumn 1973, *38*(2), pp. 182–200. [G: China]

Watanabe, Tamao and Ogawa, Kazuo. Introduction to Japan-China Trade. *Chinese Econ. Stud.*, Fall 1973, *7*(1), pp. 3–137. [G: Japan; China]

Witthans, Fred. Estimates of Effective Rates of Protection for United States Industries in 1967. *Rev. Econ. Statist.*, August 1973, *55*(3), pp. 362–64. [G: U.S.]

Wolf, Thomas A. A Note on the Restrictive Effect of Unilateral United States Export Controls. *J. Polit. Econ.*, January-February 1973, *81*(1), pp. 219–22. [G: U.S.]

423 Economic Integration

4230 General

Ausch, S. Plan, Market and Socialist Integration. In *Kiss, T., ed.*, 1973, pp. 63–76. [G: CMEA]

Balassa, Bela. Implications for Integration of the World Economy: Comment. In *Krause, L. B. and Salant, W. S., eds.*, 1973, pp. 266–69. [G: U.S.; Europe]

Bautina, N. Problems of Equivalence. In *Kiss, T., ed.*, 1973, pp. 191–95. [G: CMEA]

Bhagwati, Jagdish N. Trade Diverting Customs Unions and Welfare Improvement: A Reply. *Econ. J.*, September 1973, *83*(331), pp. 895–97.

Bogomolov, O. The International Market of the CMEA Countries. In *Kiss, T., ed.*, 1973, pp. 31–36. [G: CMEA]

Carney, M. K. Agricultural Trade Intensity: The European Markets and the U.S. *Amer. J. Agr. Econ.*, Part I, November 1973, *55*(4), pp. 637–40.

Chalupski, Z. Characteristics of the Socialist International Market. In *Kiss, T., ed.*, 1973, pp. 57–62.

Cooper, Richard N. Implications for Integration of the World Economy. In *Krause, L. B. and Salant, W. S., eds.*, 1973, pp. 250–66. [G: U.S.; Europe]

Corden, W. Max. The Adjustment Problem. In *Krause, L. B. and Salant, W. S., eds.*, 1973, pp. 159–84. [G: U.S.; E.E.C.]

Csikós-Nagy, B. Mutual Advantages in the Economic Cooperation. In *Kiss, T., ed.*, 1973, pp. 179–90. [G: CMEA]

Diebold, William, Jr. Implications for Integration of the World Economy: Comment. In *Krause, L. B. and Salant, W. S., eds.*, 1973, pp. 269–75. [G: U.S.; Europe]

Gianfranchi, Franco. Le nuove prospettive di cooperazione economica est-ovest in Europa. (New Prospects of East-West Economic Cooperation in Europe and the Role of the European Economic Community. With English summary.) *Mondo Aperto*, April 1973, *27*(2), pp. 112–21.

Gilbert, Gary G. Investment Planning for Latin American Economic Integration. *J. Common Market Stud.*, June 1973, *11*(4), pp. 314–25. [G: Latin America]

Girvan, Norman. The Development of Dependency Economics in the Caribbean and Latin America: Review and Comparison. *Soc. Econ. Stud.*, March 1973, *22*(1), pp. 1–33. [G: Caribbean; Latin America]

Gitelson, Susan A. Can the U.N. Be an Effective Catalyst for Regional Integration? The Case of the East African Community. *J. Devel. Areas*, October 1973, *8*(1), pp. 65–82. [G: E. Africa]

Gräbig, G. Planned Use of Commodity and Money Relations. In *Kiss, T., ed.*, 1973, pp. 197–202. [G: CMEA]

Gregg, Robert W. The UN Regional Economic Commissions and Integration in the Underdeveloped Regions. In *Falk, R. A. and Mendlovitz, S. H., eds.*, 1973, pp. 308–27.

Hamouz, Frantisek. Implementation of the Comprehensive Program of Socialist Economic Integration. *Czech. Econ. Digest.*, December 1973, (8), pp. 3–46.

Ingram, James C. The Adjustment Problem: Comment. In *Krause, L. B. and Salant, W. S., eds.,* 1973, pp. 184–91. [G: U.S.; E.E.C.]

Isaev, B. L. A Matrix Balance of Socialist Economic Integration. *Matekon,* Fall 1973, *10*(1), pp. 93–116.

Iumin, M. N. The Mongolian People's Republic in the System of International Socialist Economic Integration. *Chinese Econ. Stud.,* Winter 1973–74, *7*(2), pp. 92–105. [G: Mongolia]

Josling, Tim. The Common Agricultural Policy of the European Economic Community. In *Krauss, M. B., ed.,* 1973, pp. 267–96. [G: E.E.C.]

Kádár, B. Small-Sized Developing Countries in the Regional Arrangements. *Acta Oecon.,* 1973, *10*(2), pp. 217–31.

Kirman, Alan P. Trade Diverting Customs Unions and Welfare Improvement: A Comment. *Econ. J.,* September 1973, *83*(331), pp. 890–94.

Kiss, T. The Development of the Forms of Economic Relations in the CMEA Integration. In *Kiss, T., ed.,* 1973, pp. 109–26. [G: CMEA]

Kohlhase, Norbert. The European Community: A New Actor in a Changing International Pattern. *Intermountain Econ. Rev.,* Fall 1973, *4*(2), pp. 70–74. [G: E.E.C.]

Korbonski, Andrzej. Theory and Practice of Regional Integration: The Case of Comecon. In *Falk, R. A. and Mendlovitz, S. H., eds.,* 1973, pp. 152–77. [G: E. Europe]

Kövér, K. International Monetary Systems and Foreign Exchange Systems. In *Kiss, T., ed.,* 1973, pp. 213–19. [G: CMEA]

Krauss, Melvyn B. The Economics of Integration: Introduction. In *Krauss, M. B., ed.,* 1973, pp. 11–29. [G: E.E.C.]

Lindberg, Leon N. and Scheingold, Stuart A. The Future of the European Community: Equilibrium and Beyond. In *Falk, R. A. and Mendlovitz, S. H., eds.,* 1973, pp. 435–54. [G: E.E.C.]

Lyutov, A. Economic Integration and the Socialist International Market. In *Kiss, T., ed.,* 1973, pp. 49–55. [G: CMEA]

Magnifico, Giovanni. European Monetary Integration. In *Magnifico, G.,* 1973, pp. 199–222. [G: E.E.C.]

Magnifico, Giovanni. Further Considerations on the New Approach to European Monetary Unification. In *Magnifico, G.,* 1973, pp. 85–136. [G: E.E.C.]

McKinnon, Ronald I. On Securing a Common Monetary Policy in Europe. *Banca Naz. Lavoro Quart. Rev.,* March 1973, (104), pp. 3–20. [G: E.E.C.]

Morawetz, David. Harmonization of Economic Policies in Customs Unions: The Andean Group. *J. Common Market Stud.,* June 1973, *11*(4), pp. 294–313. [G: Latin America]

Murphy, J. Carter. The Adjustment Problem: Comment. In *Krause, L. B. and Salant, W. S., eds.,* 1973, pp. 191–97. [G: U.S.; E.E.C.]

Nye, Joseph S. Regional Institutions. In *Falk, R. A. and Mendlovitz, S. H., eds.,* 1973, pp. 78–93.

Pécsi, K. Capital Movements and Joint Undertakings. In *Kiss, T., ed.,* 1973, pp. 227–34. [G: CMEA]

Perroux, François. Multinational Investments and the Analysis of Development and Integration Poles. *Écon. Soc.,* May-June 1973, *7*(5–6), pp. 831–68.

Polaczek, S. and Zdanowicz, J. Subsidy, Taxation and Foreign Trade. In *Kiss, T., ed.,* 1973, pp. 221–26. [G: CMEA]

Rédei, J. The System of Foreign Trade Agreements. In *Kiss, T., ed.,* 1973, pp. 167–75. [G: CMEA]

Russett, Bruce M. International Regions and the International System. In *Falk, R. A. and Mendlovitz, S. H., eds.,* 1973, pp. 182–208.

Scheingold, Stuart A. Domestic and International Consequences of Regional Integration. In *Falk, R. A. and Mendlovitz, S. H., eds.,* 1973, pp. 133–51. [G: W. Europe]

Sreekantaradhya, B. S. Economic Integration Among Developing Countries with Special Reference to South-East Asia—I. *Econ. Aff.,* November-December 1973, *18*(11–12), pp. 483–84, 511–16. [G: S.E.Asia]

Steeger, H. Cooperation in Planning. In *Kiss, T., ed.,* 1973, pp. 37–40. [G: CMEA]

Tardos, M. Necessity of Direct Connections between Productive Enterprises and Difficulties of Their Development in the Foreign Trade between CMEA Countries. (In Russian. With English summary.) *Acta Oecon.,* 1973, *11*(4), pp. 369–80.

Tarnovsky, I. O. The Role of Market in the Socialist Economic Integration. In *Kiss, T., ed.,* 1973, pp. 41–48. [G: CMEA]

Wadhva, Charan D. Asian Regional Economic Cooperation in Indian Perspective. In *Wadhva, C. D., ed.,* 1973, pp. 478–96. [G: India; E.C.A.F.E.]

Walter, Ingo. Commonwealth Preferences in Retrospect: Some Policy Implications for the Developing Countries. *Econ. Bull. Ghana, Sec. Ser.,* 1973, *3*(4), pp. 3–13. [G: U.K.]

Wesolowski, J. Monetary and Financial Relations. In *Kiss, T., ed.,* 0000, pp. 203–11. [G: CMEA]

Wilcsek, J. Interrelations between the National Economic Management Systems and the Socialist International Market Mechanism. In *Kiss, T., ed.,* 1973, pp. 99–107. [G: CMEA]

4232 Theory of Economic Integration

Akkihal, R. G. Locational Effects in the Theory of Customs Unions and Welfare Analysis. *Indian Econ. J.,* July–September 1973, *21*(1), pp. 42–56.

Balassa, Bela. Regional Integration of Trade: Policies of Less Developed Countries. In *Streeten, P., ed.,* 1973, pp. 176–86.

Behrman, Jack N. Can the Multinational Enterprise Gain Acceptability through Industrial Integration? In *Fayerweather, J., ed.,* 1973, pp. 27–38.

Green, R. H. Economic Independence and Economic Co-operation. In *Ghai, D., ed.,* 1973, pp. 45–87. [G: Africa]

Grubel, Herbert G. The Theory of Optimum Regional Associations. In *Johnson, H. G. and Swoboda, A. K., eds.,* 1973, pp. 99–113.

Haas, Ernst B. The Study of Regional Integration: Reflections on the Joy and Anguish of Pretheorizing. In *Falk, R. A. and Mendlovitz, S. H., eds.,* 1973, pp. 103–32.

Henig, Stanley. From External Relations to Foreign Policy: An Introductory Note. *J. Common Market Stud.,* September 1973, *12*(1), pp. 1–6. [G: E.E.C.]

Hoffmeyer, Erik. Hvor meget vil den økonomiske og monetære union binde vor økonomiske politik? (To What Extent will Our Economic Policy Be Bound by the European Economic and Monetary Union? With English summary.) *Nationalokon. Tidsskr.,* 1973, *111*(1), pp. 144–53.

Magnifico, Giovanni. The Theory of Optimum Currency Areas and European Monetary Unification. In *Magnifico, G.,* 1973, pp. 43–84. [G: E.E.C.]

Tahmassebi, H. The General Equilibrium Analysis of Customs Union. *Tahq. Eq.,* Winter & Spring 1973, *10*(29 & 30), pp. 146–69.

Yalem, Ronald. Theories of Regionalism. In *Falk, R. A. and Mendlovitz, S. H., eds.,* 1973, pp. 218–31.

4233 Economic Integration: Policy and Empirical Studies

Adam, Harold. Aspetti giuridici e fiscali delle società transnazionali nella C.E.E. (Legal and Taxation Aspects of the Transnational Corporations in the EEC. With English summary.) *Bancaria,* April 1973, *29*(4), pp. 495–500. [G: Europe]

Ahmad, Jaleel. Regional Allocation of Industrial Capacity in the Latin American Free Trade Association. In *Pollock, D. H. and Ritter, A. R. M., eds.,* 1973, pp. 58–69. [G: LAFTA]

Aitken, Norman D. The Effect of the EEC and EFTA on European Trade: A Temporal Cross-Section Analysis. *Amer. Econ. Rev.,* December 1973, *63*(5), pp. 881–92. [G: E.E.C.; E.F.T.A.]

Aitken, Norman D. and Lowry, William R. A Cross-Sectional Study of the Effects of LAFTA and CACM on Latin American Trade. *J. Common Market Stud.,* June 1973, *11*(4), pp. 326–36. [G: Latin America]

Argy, Victor and Hodjera, Zoran. Financial Integration and Interest Rate Linkages in Industrial Countries, 1958-71. *Int. Monet. Fund Staff Pap.,* March 1973, *20*(1), pp. 1–77.

Bailey, Richard. Britain and a Community Energy Policy. *Nat. Westminster Bank Quart. Rev.,* November 1973, pp. 5–15. [G: U.K.; E.E.C.]

Balassa, Bela. Planning and Programming in the European Common Market. *Europ. Econ. Rev.,* October 1973, *4*(3), pp. 217–33. [G: E.E.C.]

Balassa, Bela. Tariffs and Trade Policy in the Andean Common Market. *J. Common Market Stud.,* December 1973, *12*(2), pp. 176–95. [G: South America]

Balassa, Bela. Regional Policies and the Environment in the European Common Market. *Weltwirtsch. Arch.,* 1973, *109*(3), pp. 402–17. [G: E.E.C.]

Balassa, Bela. Industrial Policy in the European Common Market. *Banca Naz. Lavoro Quart. Rev.,* December 1973, (107), pp. 311–27. [G: E.E.C.]

Barkai, Haim. The European Economic Community Approach to Adjustment: Comment. In *Hughes, H., ed.,* 1973, pp. 217–22. [G: E.E.C.]

Bechtold, Peter K. New Attempts at Arab Cooperation: The Federation of Arab Republics, 1971–? *Middle East J.,* Spring 1973, *27*(2), pp. 152–72.

Bernstein, Edward M. Narrowing the Exchange Rate Bands: Comment. In *Krause, L. B. and Salant, W. S., eds.,* 1973, pp. 97–105. [G: U.S.; E.E.C.]

Bloomfield, Arthur I. The Historical Setting. In *Krause, L. B. and Salant, W. S., eds.,* 1973, pp. 1–30. [G: E.E.C.]

Boni, Milena. Il problema della localizzazione industriale. L'Europa occidentale: recenti esperienze e prospettive. (The Problem of Industrial Localization. Western Europe: Recent Experiences and Prospectives. With English summary.) *L'Impresa,* 1973, *15*(2), pp. 100–04. [G: E.E.C.]

Borlenghi, Erminio. Il progetto per un'area forte nella Francia di sud-est. (The Project for a Strong Area in South-East France. With English summary.) *L'Impresa,* 1973, *15*(2), pp. 105–12. [G: France]

Braun, Ferdnand. The European Economic Community Approach to Adjustment. In *Hughes, H., ed.,* 1973, pp. 187–216. [G: E.E.C.]

van Buren Cleveland, Harold. Implications for Private Capital Markets: Comment. In *Krause, L. B. and Salant, W. S., eds.,* 1973, pp. 141–49. [G: U.S.; E.E.C.]

Carbaugh, Robert J. An Expanded EEC: Implications for the United States. *Intermountain Econ. Rev.,* Spring 1973, *4*(1), pp. 81–89. [G: U.S.]

Cochrane, James D. and Sloan, John W. LAFTA and the CACM: A Comparative Analysis of Integration in Latin America. *J. Devel. Areas,* October 1973, *8*(1), pp. 13–37. [G: Latin America]

Cohen, Benjamin J. The Historical Setting: Comment. In *Krause, L. B. and Salant, W. S., eds.,* 1973, pp. 30–33. [G: E.E.C.]

Cooper, Richard N. European Monetary Unification and the International Monetary System. In *Krauss, M. B., ed.,* 1973, pp. 215–35. [G: E.E.C.]

Curzon, Gerard and Curzon, Victoria. European Integration: Lessons for the Developing World. In *Streeten, P., ed.,* 1973, pp. 189–97. [G: E.E.C.; E.F.T.A.]

Dahrendorf, Ralf. The Foreign Trade Policy of the EEC. In *Henley, D. S., ed.,* 1973, pp. 1–5. [G: E.E.C.]

Dell, Sidney. Regional Groupings and Developing Countries. In *Streeten, P., ed.,* 1973, pp. 198–215. [G: E.E.C.; E.F.T.A.]

Despres, Emile. The Significance of the European Common Market to the American Economy. In *Despres, E.,* 1973, pp. 60–86. [G: U.S.; E.E.C.]

Diaz-Alejandro, Carlos. The Andean Common Market: Gestation and Outlook. In *Eckaus, R. S. and Rosenstein-Rodan, P. N., eds.,* 1973, pp. 293–326. [G: Bolivia; Colombia; Chile; Ecuador; Peru]

Dietz, John. Enforcement of Anti-Trust Laws in the EEC. In *Henley, D. S., ed.,* 1973, pp. 185–213.

Donges, Juergen B. The European Economic Community Approach to Adjustment: Comment. In *Hughes, H., ed.,* 1973, pp. 222–27. [G: E.E.C.]

Ezra, Derek. Regional Policy in the European Community. *Nat. Westminster Bank Quart. Rev.,* August 1973, pp. 8–21. [G: Europe]

Fellner, William J. Narrowing the Exchange Rate Bands: Comment. In *Krause, L. B. and Salant, W. S., eds.*, 1973, pp. 105–08. [G: U.S.; E.E.C.]

Ferrari, Alberto. Integrazione monetaria europea e movimenti internazionali dei capitali. (European Monetary Integration and International Capital Movements. With English summary.) *Bancaria*, May 1973, 29(5), pp. 563–67. [G: E.E.C.]

Gavrilov, V. Improving the Economic Collaboration of Socialist Countries. *Prob. Econ.*, October 1973, 16(6), pp. 93–103. [G: E. Europe]

Geiger, Theodore. Toward a World of Trading Blocs? In *Henley, D. S., ed.*, 1973, pp. 6–17. [G: W. Europe; Japan; U.S.]

Geiger, Theodore. The Political Context: Comment. In *Krause, L. B. and Salant, W. S., eds.*, 1973, pp. 62–69. [G: E.E.C.]

Ghai, Dharam P. The Association Agreement between the European Economic Community and the Partner States of the East African Community. *J. Common Market Stud.*, September 1973, 12(1), pp. 78–103. [G: E. Africa; E.E.C.]

Giersch, Herbert. Competitive Pressures in an Enlarged EEC. In *Rybczynski, T. M., ed.*, 1973, pp. 1–17. [G: E.E.C.]

Ginsburgh, Victor A. The Common Market Economies: Interdependence or Independence. *Europ. Econ. Rev.*, October 1973, 4(3), pp. 289–91. [G: E.E.C.]

Goodwin, G. L. A European Community Foreign Policy? *J. Common Market Stud.*, September 1973, 12(1), pp. 7–27. [G: E.E.C.]

Grant, W. P. British Employers' Associations and the Enlarged Community. *J. Common Market Stud.*, June 1973, 11(4), pp. 276–86. [G: E.E.C.; U.K.]

Haberler, Gottfried. The Historical Setting: Comment. In *Krause, L. B. and Salant, W. S., eds.*, 1973, pp. 33–36. [G: E.E.C.]

Hazlewood, Arthur. State Trading and the East African Customs Union. *Oxford Bull. Econ. Statist.*, May 1973, 35(2), pp. 75–89. [G: E. Africa]

Henig, Stanley. New Institutions for European Integration. *J. Common Market Stud.*, December 1973, 12(2), pp. 129–37. [G: E.E.C.]

Hirsch, Seev. The Impact of European Integration on Trade with Developing Countries: Empirical Evidence and Policy Implications. In *Streeten, P., ed.*, 1973, pp. 216–30. [G: E.E.C.; E.F.T.A.]

Holzheu, Franz. Zur Problematik der Bandbreiteneinengung in der Europäischen Wirtschaftsgemeinschaft. (On the Problem of Narrowing the Exchange Rate Margins within the EEC. With English summary.) *Z. Wirtschaft. Sozialwissen.*, 1973, 93(2), pp. 159–89. [G: E.E.C.]

Inozemtsev, N. Main Tasks in the Coordination of the National Economic Plans of COMECON Countries. *Prob. Econ.*, October 1973, 16(6), pp. 20–35. [G: E. Europe]

Johnson, Harry G. Narrowing the Exchange Rate Bands. In *Krause, L. B. and Salant, W. S., eds.*, 1973, pp. 78–97. [G: U.S.; E.E.C.]

Johnson, Harry G. Problems of European Monetary Union. In *Krauss, M. B., ed.*, 1973, pp. 188–200. [G: E.E.C.]

Johnson, Harry G. The Exchange-Rate Question for a United Europe. In *Krauss, M. B., ed.*, 1973, pp. 201–14. [G: E.E.C.]

Juhár, Z. Commodity Trade in Consumer Goods. In *Kiss, T., ed.*, 1973, pp. 149–57. [G: CMEA]

Kanet, Roger. Handbook of Soviet Social Science Data: International Interactions. In *Mickiewicz, E., ed.*, 1973, pp. 197–225. [G: U.S.S.R.; C.M.E.A.]

Kazakevich, L. and Shishankov, V. Economic Collaboration Between the USSR and the Socialist Countries. *Prob. Econ.*, October 1973, 16(6), pp. 72–92. [G: E. Europe; U.S.S.R.]

Kenen, Peter B. Implications for International Reserves: Comment. In *Krause, L. B. and Salant, W. S., eds.*, 1973, pp. 236–47. [G: E.E.C.; U.S.]

Kindleberger, Charles P. Implications for Private Capital Markets: Comment. In *Krause, L. B. and Salant, W. S., eds.*, 1973, pp. 149–54. [G: U.S.; E.E.C.]

Kormnov, Iu. International Economic Organizations and Their Role in the Collaboration of COMECON Countries. *Prob. Econ.*, October 1973, 16(6), pp. 36–54. [G: E. Europe]

Kormnov, Y. International Industrial Specialization. In *Kiss, T., ed.*, 1973, pp. 143–48. [G: CMEA]

Kostál, Miroslav and Vesely, Zdenek. The Czechoslovak Socialist Republic and the Council for Mutual Economic Assistance. *Czech. Econ. Digest.*, August 1973, (5), pp. 25–43. [G: Czechoslovakia]

Krause, Lawrence B. Implications for Private Capital Markets. In *Krause, L. B. and Salant, W. S., eds.*, 1973, pp. 114–41. [G: U.S.; E.E.C.]

Kreinin, Mordechai E. The Static Effects of EEC Enlargement on Trade Flows. *Southern Econ. J.*, April 1973, 39(4), pp. 559–68. [G: E.E.C.]

Kreinin, Mordechai E. Some Economic Consequences of Reverse Preferences. *J. Common Market Stud.*, March 1973, 11(3), pp. 161–72. [G: Europe]

Landry, David M. U.S. Policy and Lessons Learned from the Central American Economic Integration Experience. *Southern Quart.*, July 1973, 11(4), pp. 297–308. [G: Central America]

van Lith, Jan A. Government Procurement in the Benelux Countries. In *Scaperlanda, A. E., ed.*, 1973, pp. 163–90. [G: Benelux]

Machlup, Fritz. Implications for International Reserves: Comment. In *Krause, L. B. and Salant, W. S., eds.*, 1973, pp. 247–49. [G: E.E.C.; U.S.]

Magnifico, Giovanni. European Monetary Unification for Balanced Growth: A New Approach. In *Magnifico, G.*, 1973, pp. 1–42. [G: E.E.C.]

Magnifico, Giovanni. Towards a European Money and Capital Market. In *Magnifico, G.*, 1973, pp. 137–98. [G: E.E.C.]

Mayer, Leo V. Regional Effects of Alternative Trade Policies. In *Iowa State University Center for Agricultural and Rural Development*, 1973, pp. 166–83. [G: U.S.]

McKinnon, Ronald I. The Dual Currency System Revisited. In *Johnson, H. G. and Swoboda, A. K., eds.*, 1973, pp. 85–90. [G: U.S.; Canada; Japan; W. Europe]

Moncarz, Raul. Monetary Aspects of the Central American Common Market. *J. Common Market*

Stud., December 1973, *12*(2), pp. 196–204.
[G: Central America]

Morawetz, David. Harmonization of Economic Policies in a Free Trade Area: The Andean Group. *Weltwirtsch. Arch.*, 1973, *109*(4), pp. 579–600.
[G: Latin America]

Morgan, E. Victor. Regional Problems and Common Currencies. *Lloyds Bank Rev.*, October 1973, (110), pp. 19–30. [G: U.K.]

Morse, Edward L. The Political Context: Comment. In *Krause, L. B. and Salant, W. S., eds.*, 1973, pp. 55–62. [G: E.E.C.]

Moser, Claus A. and Beesley, I. B. United Kingdom Official Statistics and the European Communities. *J. Roy. Statist. Soc.*, Part 4, 1973, *136*, pp. 539–72.
[G: U.K.; E.E.C.]

Murray, Tracy. E.E.C. Enlargement and Preference for the Developing Countries. *Econ. J.*, September 1973, *83*(331), pp. 853–57.

Mytelka, Lynn Krieger. Foreign Aid and Regional Integration: The UDEAC Case. *J. Common Market Stud.*, December 1973, *12*(2), pp. 138–58.
[G: Africa]

Nye, Joseph S. The Political Context. In *Krause, L. B. and Salant, W. S., eds.*, 1973, pp. 37–55.
[G: E.E.C.]

Oslizlok, J. S. Community Regional Policy. *Irish Banking Rev.*, December 1973, pp. 15–22.
[G: E.E.C.]

Ouattara, Alassane D. Trade Effects of the Association of African Countries with the European Economic Community. *Int. Monet. Fund Staff Pap.*, July 1973, *20*(2), pp. 499–543. [G: E.E.C.; Africa]

Palánkai, T. and Veress, P. Effect of the United Kingdom's Entry Into the Common Market on Anglo-Hungarian Relations. *Acta Oecon.*, 1973, *10*(1), pp. 81–94.

Pazos, Felipe. Regional Integration of Trade Among Less Developed Countries. In *Streeten, P., ed.*, 1973, pp. 145–75. [G: CACM; LAFTA]

Pinder, John. The Community and the Developing Countries: Associates and Outsiders. *J. Common Market Stud.*, September 1973, *12*(1), pp. 53–77.
[G: E.E.C.]

Rainoni, Antonio. Monetary Cooperation and the International Monetary System. In *Holbik, K., ed.*, 1973, pp. 525–71.

Renda, Benedetto. Credito, risparmio e banche nelle prospettive dell'integrazione europea. (Credit, Savings and Bank Systems in the Perspective of European Economic Integration. With English summary.) *Mondo Aperto*, February 1973, *27*(1), pp. 9–23.

Rhodes, R. A. W. The European Community and British Public Administration: The Case of Local Government. *J. Common Market Stud.*, June 1973, *11*(4), pp. 263–75. [G: U.K.; E.E.C.]

Richards, Vincent A. E. Development Prospects in the Commonwealth Caribbean in the 1970s. In *Pollock, D. H. and Ritter, A. R. M., eds.*, 1973, pp. 269–86. [G: Caribbean]

Rybakov, O. Some Organizational and Methodological Problems Relating to the Elaboration of Long-Range Plans for Collaboration Between the USSR and Socialist Countries. *Prob. Econ.*, October

1973, *16*(6), pp. 3–19. [G: E. Europe; U.S.S.R.]

Rybakov, O. Improvements in Planning Methods of Collaboration Among COMECON Countries. *Prob. Econ.*, March 1973, *15*(11), pp. 3–20.
[G: COMECON]

Salant, Walter S. Implications for International Reserves. In *Krause, L. B. and Salant, W. S., eds.*, 1973, pp. 203–36. [G: E.E.C.; U.S.]

Sassen, E. M. J. A. Ensuring Fair Competition in the European Community. In *Thorelli, H. B., ed.*, 1973, pp. 104–15. [G: E.E.C.]

Savost'ianov, V. V. Factors Determining the Effectiveness of Socialist Foreign Trade. *Prob. Econ.*, September 1973, *16*(5), pp. 94–105. [G: U.S.S.R.]

Scaperlanda, Anthony E. Perspectives and Implications. In *Scaperlanda, A. E., ed.*, 1973, pp. 17–45.
[G: E.E.C.]

Schneider, J. W. Intra-Benelux NTD's. In *Scaperlanda, A. E., ed.*, 1973, pp. 73–106. [G: Benelux]

Schwartz, Ivo E. Creating a Common Market for Insurance: Harmonization of EEC Insurance Legislation. *Antitrust Bull.*, Spring 1973, *18*(1), pp. 103–16.

Secchi, Carlo. Il rinnovo della associazione tra la CEE e i SAMA e le tendenze della politica comunitaria verso i paesi sottosviluppati. (The Renewal of the Association Between the EEC and the AASM and the Prospects of the Community Policy Towards Underdeveloped Countries. With English summary.) *Rivista Int. Sci. Econ. Com.*, November 1973, *20*(11), pp. 1081–1108. [G: E.E.C.; Africa]

Seligson, Mitchell A. Transactions and Community Formation: Fifteen Years of Growth and Stagnation in Central America. *J. Common Market Stud.*, March 1973, *11*(3), pp. 173–90. [G: Central America]

Sellekaerts, Willy. How Meaningful are Empirical Studies on Trade Creation and Diversion? *Weltwirtsch. Arch.*, 1973, *109*(4), pp. 519–53.
[G: E.E.C.]

Shastiko, B. M. and Shiryaev, Y. S. Interrelations with Non-Socialist Markets. In *Kiss, T., ed.*, 1973, pp. 159–65. [G: CMEA]

Shiriaev, Iu. Developing Scientific Foundations for Joint Planning Activity of COMECON Countries. *Prob. Econ.*, October 1973, *16*(6), pp. 55–71.
[G: E. Europe]

Soldaczuk, J. Trade and Cooperation among CMEA Member Countries. In *Kiss, T., ed.*, 1973, pp. 137–42. [G: CMEA]

Soloveytchik, George. Nordic Uncertainties and Realities. *Nat. Westminster Bank Quart. Rev.*, May 1973, pp. 31–45. [G: Norway; Sweden; Iceland; Denmark; Finland]

Stammati, Gaetano. Il coordinamento delle politiche di bilancio nella C.E.E. (Coordination of Budget Policies in E.E.C. With English summary.) *Bancaria*, February 1973, *29*(2), pp. 151–55.
[G: E.E.C.]

Stern, Robert M. Tariffs and Other Measures of Trade Control: A Survey of Recent Developments. *J. Econ. Lit.*, September 1973, *11*(3), pp. 857–88.

Stoutjesdijk, A. LDC Regional Markets: Do They

Work? In *Thorelli, H. B., ed.*, 1973, pp. 47–57.

Triffin, Robert. The Collapse of the International Monetary System: Structural Causes and Remedies. *De Economist*, July-August 1973, *121*(4), pp. 362–74.   [G: E.E.C.; U.S.]

Tulloch, Peter. Developing Countries and the Enlargement of the EEC. In *Dinwiddy, B., ed.*, 1973, pp. 88–111.   [G: E.E.C.]

Van Rompuy, E. De stop-go cyclus en de Europese monetaire integratie. (The Stop-go Cycle and the European Monetary Integration. With English summary.) *Tijdschr. Econ.*, 1973, *18*(3), pp. 457–79.   [G: U.K.; Europe]

Vlerick, André. Unione Monetaria Europea. (The European Monetary Union. With English summary.) *Mondo Aperto*, June-August 1973, *27*(3–4), pp. 224–35.   [G: Europe]

Wallace, Helen and Wallace, William. The Impact of Community Membership on the British Machinery of Government. *J. Common Market Stud.*, June 1973, *11*(4), pp. 243–62.   [G: U.K.]

Wallace, William. British External Relations and the European Community: The Changing Context of Foreign Policy-Making. *J. Common Market Stud.*, September 1973, *12*(1), pp. 28–52.   [G: E.E.C.]

Wilford, W. T. The Central American Common Market: Trade Patterns After a Decade of Union. *Nebr. J. Econ. Bus.*, Summer 1973, *12*(3), pp. 3–22.   [G: Central America]

Wilford, W. T. and Christou, G. A Sectoral Analysis of Disaggregated Trade Flows in the Central American Common Market 1962–1970. *J. Common Market Stud.*, December 1973, *12*(2), pp. 159–75.   [G: Central America]

Wolf, Charles, Jr. and Weinschrott, David. International Transactions and Regionalism: Distinguishing "Insiders" from "Outsiders." *Amer. Econ. Rev.*, May 1973, *63*(2), pp. 52–60.

Zakheim, Dov S. Britain and the EEC-Opinion Poll Data 1970–72. *J. Common Market Stud.*, March 1973, *11*(3), pp. 191–233.   [G: U.K.]

430 BALANCE OF PAYMENTS; INTERNATIONAL FINANCE

4300 General

Haberler, Gottfried. International Aspects of U.S. Inflation. In *Cagan, P., et al.*, 1973, pp. 79–105.   [G: U.S.]

Holzman, Franklyn D. Future East-West Economic Issues. In *Bergsten, C. F., ed.*, 1973, pp. 265–92.

Moriguchi, C. Forecasting and Simulation Analysis of the World Economy. *Amer. Econ. Rev.*, May 1973, *63*(2), pp. 402–09.

Wallich, Henry C. Reconstructing Humpty Dumpty. In *Henley, D. S., ed.*, 1973, pp. 145–51.   [G: U.S.]

431 Balance of Payments; Mechanisms of Adjustment; Exchange Rates

4310 General

Aliber, Robert Z. Japanese Growth and the Equilibrium Foreign Exchange Value of the Yen. *South-*

ern Econ. J., January 1973, *39*(3), pp. 406–18.   [G: Japan]

Aliber, Robert Z. Speculation in the Flexible Exchange Re-Revisited: Reply. *Kyklos*, 1973, *26*(3), pp. 619–20.   [G: France]

Aliber, Robert Z. Gold, SDR's, and Central Bank Swaps. *J. Money, Credit, Banking*, August 1973, *5*(3), pp. 819–25.

Allen, William R. For Want of an International Adjustment Mechanism. *Soc. Sci. Quart.*, June 1973, *54*(1), pp. 140–45.

Areskoug, Kaj. Foreign-Capital Utilization and Economic Policies in Developing Countries. *Rev. Econ. Statist.*, May 1973, *55*(2), pp. 182–89.

Argy, Victor and Hodjera, Zoran. Financial Integration and Interest Rate Linkages in Industrial Countries, 1958-71. *Int. Monet. Fund Staff Pap.*, March 1973, *20*(1), pp. 1–77.

Askari, Hossein; Bizien, Yves and Hossain, Ekram. The Success of Some Devaluations and Revaluations in the Post-War Era. *Econ. Int.*, August-November 1973, *26*(3–4), pp. 471–91.

Balassa, Bela. Two Arguments for Fixed Rates: Comment. In *Johnson, H. G. and Swoboda, A. K., eds.*, 1973, pp. 40–45.

Balassa, Bela. A Plan for a European Currency: Comment. In *Johnson, H. G. and Swoboda, A. K., eds.*, 1973, pp. 173–77.

Bame, Jack J. U.S. Balance of Payments Developments: First Quarter 1973. *Surv. Curr. Bus.*, June 1973, *53*(6), pp. 17–23, 53–55.   [G: U.S.]

Barger, Harold. International Liquidity and International Trade: Comment. In *Wiegand, G. C., ed.*, 1973, pp. 97–98.   [G: U.S.]

Basevi, G. Balances of Payments and Exchange Markets: A Lost Correspondence. *Europ. Econ. Rev.*, December 1973, *4*(4), pp. 309–28.

Benoit, Emile. Structural Causes of Recent International Disequilibrium—A Preliminary Note. In *Wiegand, G. C., ed.*, 1973, pp. 63–69.

Boarman, Patrick M. International Trade and National Autonomy. In *Wiegand, G. C., ed.*, 1973, pp. 77–88.

Bodner, David E. The Role of Central Bank Swaps in the International Monetary System. In *Wiegand, G. C., ed.*, 1973, pp. 100–06.   [G: U.S.]

Bromwich, Michael. The Effects of Sterling Devaluation on International Trade. In *Moskoff, W., ed.*, 1973, pp. 231–38.   [G: U.K.]

Brown, Alan A. and Marer, Paul. Foreign Trade in the East European Reforms. In *Bornstein, M., ed.*, 1973, pp. 153–205.   [G: E. Europe]

Burns, Arthur F. Statement to Congress. *Fed. Res. Bull.*, March 1973, *59*(3), pp. 164–68.

Burns, Arthur F. Statement to Congress. *Fed. Res. Bull.*, July 1973, *59*(7), pp. 508–12.   [G: U.S.]

Camu, Louis. I movimenti dei capitali a breve termine. (Short-Term Capital Movements. With English summary.) *Bancaria*, July 1973, *29*(7), pp. 807–12.

Despres, Emile. Britain's Foreign Exchange Policy. In *Despres, E.*, 1973, pp. 3–12.

Despres, Emile. Germany's Exchange Control Mechanism. In *Despres, E.*, 1973, pp. 13–27.

Despres, Emile. The Mechanism for Adjustment in International Payments—The Lessons of Postwar Experience. In *Despres, E.,* 1973, pp. 45–59.

den Dunnen, Emile. Monetary Policy in the Netherlands. In *Holbik, K., ed.,* 1973, pp. 282–328.
[G: Netherlands]

English, M. D. Macro-Economic Policy: Canada. In *Perkins, J. O. N., ed.,* 1973, pp. 57–93. [G: Canada]

Floyd, John E. Monetary and Fiscal Policy in a World of Capital Mobility: A Reply. *Rev. Econ. Stud.,* April 1973, *40*(2), pp. 299–303.

Frank, Helmut J. and Wells, Donald A. United States Oil Imports: Implications for the Balance of Payments. *Natural Res. J.,* July 1973, *13*(3), pp. 431–47. [G: U.S.]

Frank, Helmut J. and Wells, Donald A. United States Oil Imports: Implications for the Balance of Payments. *Natural Res. J.,* July 1973, *13*(3), pp. 431–47. [G: U.S.]

Fried, Edward R. The Military and the Balance of Payments. *Ann. Amer. Acad. Polit. Soc. Sci.,* March 1973, *406,* pp. 80–85. [G: U.S.]

Grubel, Herbert. The Optimum Stability of Exchange Rates: A Southeast Asian Payments Union. In *Grubel, H. G. and Morgan, T., eds.,* 1973, pp. 77–92. [G: S.E. Asia]

Haberler, Gottfried. Two Arguments for Fixed Rates: Comment. In *Johnson, H. G. and Swoboda, A. K., eds.,* 1973, pp. 35–39.

Johnson, Harry G. The International Monetary Crisis of 1971. *J. Bus.,* January 1973, *46*(1), pp. 11–23.

Johnson, Harry G. Secular Inflation and the International Monetary System. *J. Money, Credit, Banking,* Part II, February 1973, *5*(1), pp. 509–19.

Kahn, Richard F. [Lord]. The International Monetary System. *Amer. Econ. Rev.,* May 1973, *63*(2), pp. 181–88.

Kenen, Peter B. Implications for International Reserves: Comment. In *Krause, L. B. and Salant, W. S., eds.,* 1973, pp. 236–47. [G: E.E.C.; U.S.]

Kindleberger, Charles P. Money Illusion and Foreign Exchange. In *[Halm, G. N.],* 1973, pp. 51–63.

Kövér, K. International Monetary Systems and Foreign Exchange Systems. In *Kiss, T., ed.,* 1973, pp. 213–19. [G: CMEA]

Lademann, John R. Monetary Policy in Switzerland. In *Holbik, K., ed.,* 1973, pp. 423–64. [G: Switzerland]

Laffer, Arthur B. Two Arguments for Fixed Rates. In *Johnson, H. G. and Swoboda, A. K., eds.,* 1973, pp. 25–34.

Machlup, Fritz. Implications for International Reserves: Comment. In *Krause, L. B. and Salant, W. S., eds.,* 1973, pp. 247–49. [G: E.E.C.; U.S.]

Machlup, Fritz. Exchange Rate Flexibility: A Variety of Choices. In *Wiegand, G. C., ed.,* 1973, pp. 110–26.

Magnifico, Giovanni. European Monetary Integration. In *Magnifico, G.,* 1973, pp. 199–222. [G: E.E.C.]

Magnifico, Giovanni. European Monetary Unification for Balanced Growth: A New Approach. In *Magnifico, G.,* 1973, pp. 1–42. [G: E.E.C.]

Magnifico, Giovanni. Further Considerations on the New Approach to European Monetary Unification. In *Magnifico, G.,* 1973, pp. 85–136.
[G: E.E.C.]

Magnifico, Giovanni. The Theory of Optimum Currency Areas and European Monetary Unification. In *Magnifico, G.,* 1973, pp. 43–84. [G: E.E.C.]

McKinnon, Ronald I. The Monetary Approach to Exchange-Rate Policy in Less Developed Countries. In *Grubel, H. G. and Morgan, T., eds.,* 1973, pp. 67–75.

Metzler, Lloyd A. Flexible Exchange Rates and the Theory of Employment. In *Metzler, L. A.,* 1973, pp. 275–307.

Metzler, Lloyd A. The Theory of International Trade. In *Metzler, L. A.,* 1973, pp. 1–49.

Miller, Etienne and Smith, Gordon P. International Travel, Passenger Fares, and Other Transportation in the U.S. Balance of Payments: 1972. *Surv. Curr. Bus.,* June 1973, *53*(6), pp. 12–16, 56.
[G: U.S.]

Miller, Marcus H. "Competition and Credit Control" and the Open Economy. *Manchester Sch. Econ. Soc. Stud.,* March 1973, *41*(1), pp. 123–40.
[G: U.K.]

Modigliani, Franco. International Capital Movements, Fixed Parities, and Monetary and Fiscal Policies. In *[Rosenstein-Rodan, P.],* 1973, pp. 239–53.

Mundell, Robert A. A Plan for a European Currency. In *Johnson, H. G. and Swoboda, A. K., eds.,* 1973, pp. 143–72. [G: W. Europe; U.S.]

Naqvi, Syed Nawab Haider. The Balance-of-Payments Problems in Developing Countries. *Pakistan Develop. Rev.,* Autumn 1973, *12*(3), pp. 259–72.

Needham, Douglas. Monetary and Fiscal Policy under Fixed Exchange Rates: Comment. *Swedish J. Econ.,* March 1973, *75*(1), pp. 112–18.

Niehans, Jürg. The Flexibility of the Gold-Exchange Standard. In *Johnson, H. G. and Swoboda, A. K., eds.,* 1973, pp. 46–64. [G: U.S.]

Nieuwenhuysen, J. P. Macro-Economic Policy: South Africa. In *Perkins, J. O. N., ed.,* 1973, pp. 130–76. [G: S. Africa]

Parry, Thomas G. The International Firm and National Economic Policy: A Survey of Some Issues. *Econ. J.,* December 1973, *83*(332), pp. 1201–21.

Perkins, J. O. N. and Nieuwenhuysen, J. P. Macro-Economic Policy: Australia. In *Perkins, J. O. N., ed.,* 1973, pp. 17–56. [G: Australia]

Perkins, J. O. N. and Nieuwenhuysen, J. P. Macro-Economic Policies in the Four Countries. In *Perkins, J. O. N., ed.,* 1973, pp. 177–208. [G: Australia; New Zealand; Canada; S. Africa]

Pesando, James E. and Smith, Lawrence B. Monetary Policy in Canada. In *Holbik, K., ed.,* 1973, pp. 70–116. [G: Canada]

Pippenger, John E. Speculation in the Flexible Exchange Re-Revisited. *Kyklos,* 1973, *26*(3), pp. 613–18. [G: France]

Pippenger, John E. Balance-of-Payments Deficits: Measurement and Interpretation. *Fed. Res. Bank St. Louis Rev.,* November 1973, *55*(11), pp. 6–14.
[G: U.S.]

Pippenger, John E. and Phillips, Llad. Stabilization of the Canadian Dollar: 1952–1960. *Econometrica,* September 1973, *41*(5), pp. 797–815.
[G: Canada]

Polaczek, S. and Zdanowicz, J. Subsidy, Taxation and

Foreign Trade. In *Kiss, T., ed.*, 1973, pp. 221–26.
[G: CMEA]

Ranuwihardjo, Sukadji. Exchange Rate Experience and Policy in Indonesia Since World War II. In *Grubel, H. G. and Morgan, T., eds.*, 1973, pp. 41–53. [G: Indonesia]

Reynolds, Clark W. Relations with Latin America: An American View. In *Urquidi, V. L. and Thorp, R., eds.*, 1973, pp. 235–82. [G: U.S.; Latin America]

Rowan, D. C. The Monetary System in the Fifties and Sixties. *Manchester Sch. Econ. Soc. Stud.*, March 1973, *41*(1), pp. 19–42. [G: U.K.]

Rowe, J. W. Macro-Economic Policy: New Zealand. In *Perkins, J. O. N., ed.*, 1973, pp. 94–129. [G: New Zealand]

Roxas, Sixto K. Exchange Rate Experience and Policy in the Philippines Since World War II. In *Grubel, H. G. and Morgan, T., eds.*, 1973, pp. 55–66. [G: Philippines]

Salant, Walter S. Implications for International Reserves. In *Krause, L. B. and Salant, W. S., eds.*, 1973, pp. 203–36. [G: E.E.C.; U.S.]

Shinkai, Yoichi. The Accumulation of International Reserves under an Inflationary Pressure. *Z. Nationalökon.*, 1973, *33*(1–2), pp. 55–66.

Socher, Karl. Monetary Policy in Austria. In *Holbik, K., ed.*, 1973, pp. 1–38. [G: Austria]

Triffin, Robert. The Collapse of the International Monetary System. In *Wiegand, G. C., ed.*, 1973, pp. 46–55. [G: U.S.; E.E.C.]

Tyler, William G. Exchange Rate Flexibility under Conditions of Endemic Inflation: A Case Study of the Recent Brazilian Experience. In *[Halm, G. N.]*, 1973, pp. 19–49. [G: Brazil]

Wallich, Henry C. Why Fixed Rates? *Soc. Sci. Quart.*, June 1973, *54*(1), pp. 146–51.

Willett, Thomas D. Secular Inflation and the International Monetary System: Comment. *J. Money, Credit, Banking*, Part II, February 1973, *5*(1), pp. 520–23.

Williamson, John. Payments Objectives and Economic Welfare. *Int. Monet. Fund Staff Pap.*, November 1973, *20*(3), pp. 573–90.

Zweig, Michael. Foreign Investment and the Aggregate Balance of Payments for Underdeveloped Countries. *Rev. Radical Polit. Econ.*, Spring 1973, *5*(1), pp. 13–18.

4312 Balance of Payments and Adjustment Mechanisms: Theory

Aghevli, B. B. and Borts, G. H. The Stability and Equilibrium of the Balance of Payments under a Fixed Exchange Rate. *J. Int. Econ.*, February 1973, *3*(1), pp. 1–20.

Almonacid, Ruben and Guitian, Manuel. The Optimal Rate of Devaluation. In *Johnson, H. G. and Swoboda, A. K., eds.*, 1973, pp. 281–97.

Amano, A. International Capital Movements: Theory and Estimation. In *Ball, R. J., ed.*, 1973, pp. 283–327. [G: Japan]

Arndt, Sven W. Joint Balance: Capital Mobility and the Monetary System of a Currency Area. In *Johnson, H. G. and Swoboda, A. K., eds.*, 1973, pp. 196–209.

Bandera, V. N. Interdependence between Interregional and International Payments: The Balance of Payments of Ukraine. In *Bandera, V. N. and Melnyk, Z. L., eds.*, 1973, pp. 132–53. [G: U.S.S.R.]

Boll, F. Multiplicatoren en economische politiek in verschillende wisselkoerssystemen. (Multipliers and Economic Policy under Various Exchange Rate Systems. With English summary.) *Tijdschr. Econ.*, 1973, *18*(3), pp. 381–427.

Britto, Ronald and Heller, H. Robert. International Adjustment and Optimal Reserves. *Int. Econ. Rev.*, February 1973, *14*(1), pp. 182–95.

Chen, Chau-Nan. The Monetary Effect of Devaluation: An Alternative Interpretation of the Cooper Paradox. *Western Econ. J.*, December 1973, *11*(4), pp. 475–80.

Chen, Chau-Nan. Diversified Currency Holdings and Flexible Exchange Rates. *Quart. J. Econ.*, February 1973, *87*(1), pp. 96–111.

Claassen, Emil-Maria. Alternative Policies to Achieve Internal and External Equilibrium: A Graphical Overview. *Z. Nationalökon.*, 1973, *33* (1–2), pp. 127–31.

Coppock, D. J. Devaluation When Exports Have an Import Content: Reply. *Manchester Sch. Econ. Soc. Stud.*, December 1973, *41*(4), pp. 428–29.

Dean, James W. and Tower, Edward. Internal and External Balance in an "Almost Classical" World: Rejoinder. *Western Econ. J.*, June 1973, *11*(2), pp. 240.

Dean, James W. and Tower, Edward. More on Internal and External Balance in an "Almost Classical" World. *Western Econ. J.*, June 1973, *11*(2), pp. 232–37.

Dornbusch, Rudiger. Devaluation, Money, and Nontraded Goods. *Amer. Econ. Rev.*, December 1973, *63*(5), pp. 871–80.

Fink, William H. Dollar Surplus and Devaluation. *Rivista Int. Sci. Econ. Com.*, July 1973, *20*(7), pp. 625–39.

Gerakis, Andreas S. Budgetary Implications of a Devaluation. *Finance Develop.*, March 1973, *10* (1), pp. 7–11.

Ghosh, Sukesh K. Speculative Capital Movement and Financial Policy in Interacting Economies. *Indian Econ. J.*, April–June 1973, *20*(4–5), pp. 581–603.

Hodjera, Zoran. International Short-Term Capital Movements: A Survey of Theory and Empirical Analysis. *Int. Monet. Fund Staff Pap.*, November 1973, *20*(3), pp. 683–740.

Ikemoto, K. Devaluation When Exports Have an Import Content: Comment. *Manchester Sch. Econ. Soc. Stud.*, December 1973, *41*(4), pp. 425–27.

Johnson, Harry G. Notes on the Welfare Effects of a Reversed Transfer. *Osaka Econ. Pap.*, March 1973, *21*(38), pp. 45–52.

Johnson, Harry G. Problems of Stabilization Policy in an Integrated World Economy. In *Johnson, H. G.*, 1973, pp. 338–52.

Johnson, Harry G. The Monetary Approach to Balance-of-Payments Theory. In *Johnson, H. G.*, 1973, pp. 229–49.

Kahn, Richard F. [Lord]. SDRs and Aid. *Lloyds Bank Rev.*, October 1973, (110), pp. 1–18.

Kaufmann, Hugo M. International Liquidity and Balance-of-Payments Adjustments: A Reinterpretation. *Econ. Int.*, August-November 1973, *26* (3–4), pp. 592–602.

Kleinewefers, Henner. Leistungsbilanz, Wachstum und Transferproblem. (Balance of Current Business Transactions, Growth and Transfer Problems. With English summary.) *Weltwirtsch. Arch.*, 1973, *109*(1), pp. 40–58.

Kumar, Rishi. Demand Policies and Internal-External Balance Under Fixed Exchange Rates—The Mundellian Assignment: A Reformulation and Some Extensions. *Weltwirtsch. Arch.*, 1973, *109* (2), pp. 253–73.

Levin, Jonathan. Government Finance and the Balance of Payments. In *[Halm, G. N.]*, 1973, pp. 199–210.

Lindbeck, Assar. Research on Internal Adjustment to External Disturbances: A European View. In *Bergsten, C. F., ed.*, 1973, pp. 61–74.

Mathieson, Donald J. Traded Goods, Nontraded Goods, and the Balance of Payments. *Int. Econ. Rev.*, October 1973, *14*(3), pp. 615–24.

Metzler, Lloyd A. Flexible Exchange Rates, the Transfer Problem, and the Balanced-Budget Theorem. In *Metzler, L. A.*, 1973, pp. 95–111.

Modigliani, Franco and Askari, Hossein. The International Transfer of Capital and the Propagation of Domestic Disturbances Under Alternative Payment Systems. *Banca Naz. Lavoro Quart. Rev.*, December 1973, (107), pp. 295–310.

Pippenger, John E. The Determination of the Stock of Reserves and the Balance of Payments in a Neo-Keynesian Model: Comment. *J. Money, Credit, Banking*, May 1973, *5*(2), pp. 713–19.

Prachowny, Martin F. J. The Effectiveness of Stabilization Policy in a Small Open Economy. *Weltwirtsch. Arch.*, 1973, *109*(2), pp. 214–31.

Reid, Frank J. Mundell on Growth and the Balance of Payments: A Note. *Can. J. Econ.*, November 1973, *6*(4), pp. 592–95.

Roper, Don E. Implications of the Gold-Exchange Standard for Balance of Payments Adjustment. *Econ. Int.*, August-November 1973, *26*(3–4), pp. 413–32.

Sacchetti, Ugo. Sharing the Burden of International Adjustment. *Banca Naz. Lavoro Quart. Rev.*, June 1973, (105), pp. 141–57.

Sandler, Todd M. Exchange Rate Systems, the Marginal Efficiency of Investment and Foreign Direct Capital Movements: A Comment. *Kyklos*, 1973, *26*(4), pp. 866–68.

Sellekaerts, Willy and Sellekaerts, Brigette. Balance of Payments Deficits, the Adjustment Cost and the Optimum Level of International Reserves. *Weltwirtsch. Arch.*, 1973, *109*(1), pp. 1–18.

Shinkai, Yoichi. A Model of Imported Inflation. *J. Polit. Econ.*, July-August 1973, *81*(4), pp. 962–71.

Stern, Robert M. Research on Internal Adjustment to External Economic Disturbances: An American View. In *Bergsten, C. F., ed.*, 1973, pp. 75–92.

Swoboda, Alexander K. Policy Conflict, Inconsistent Goals, and the Coordination of Economic Policies. In *Johnson, H. G. and Swoboda, A. K., eds.*, 1973, pp. 133–42.

Thygesen, Niels. Monetary Policy, Capital Flows and Internal Stability: Some Experiences from Large Industrial Countries. *Swedish J. Econ.*, March 1973, *75*(1), pp. 83–99. **[G: W. Germany; Italy; Japan]**

Williams, Harold R. Exchange Rate Systems, the Marginal Efficiency of Investment and Foreign Direct Capital Movements: Reply. *Kyklos*, 1973, *26*(4), pp. 869.

Williamson, John. Stability, Resource Transfers and Income Distribution. In *Wiegand, G. C., ed.*, 1973, pp. 73–76.

Williamson, John. Another Case of Profitable Destabilising Speculation. *J. Int. Econ.*, February 1973, *3*(1), pp. 77–83.

Williamson, John. Surveys in Applied Economics: International Liquidity. *Econ. J.*, September 1973, *83*(331), pp. 685–746.

Zelder, Raymond E.; Ross, Myron H. and Collery, Arnold. Internal and External Balance in an "Almost Classical" World: Reply. *Western Econ. J.*, June 1973, *11*(2), pp. 238–40.

4313 Balance of Payments and Adjustment Mechanisms: Studies

Agosin, Manuel R. On the Third World's Narrowing Trade Gap: A Comment. *Oxford Econ. Pap.*, March 1973, *25*(1), pp. 133–40.

Arndt, H. W. and Sundrum, R. M. Foreign Capital and Indonesian Economic Growth: A Comment. *Bull. Indonesian Econ. Stud.*, July 1973, *9*(2), pp. 90–95. **[G: Indonesia]**

Arndt, H. W. Survey of Recent Developments. *Bull. Indonesian Econ. Stud.*, July 1973, *9*(2), pp. 1–27. **[G: Indonesia]**

Artus, Jacques R. and Rhomberg, Rudolf R. A Multilateral Exchange Rate Model. *Int. Monet. Fund Staff Pap.*, November 1973, *20*(3), pp. 591–611.

Bach, Christopher L. Foreign Exchange and U.S. Balance-of-Payments Developments in 1972 and Early 1973. *Fed. Res. Bank St. Louis Rev.*, April 1973, *55*(4), pp. 14–20. **[G: U.S.]**

Balogh, T. and Balacs, P. Fact and Fancy in International Economic Relations. *World Devel.*, March-April 1973, *1*(3–4), pp. 71–105.

Bame, Jack J. U.S. Balance of Payments Developments: Third Quarter and First Nine Months of 1973. *Surv. Curr. Bus.*, December 1973, *53*(12), pp. 33–40, 56. **[G: U.S.]**

Bame, Jack J. U.S. Balance of Payments Developments: First Quarter 1973. *Surv. Curr. Bus.*, June 1973, *53*(6), pp. 17–23, 53–55. **[G: U.S.]**

Bartolomei, José A. Políticas de esterilización del superavit o déficit de la balanza de pagos: la experiencia alemana entre 1958 y 1968. (Policies of Neutralizing the Effects of a Surplus or a Deficit in a Balance of Payments: The German Experience Between the Years 1958–1968. With English summary.) *Económica*, January-April 1973, *19*(1), pp. 3–44. **[G: W. Germany]**

Bell, Geoffrey. The United Kingdom and International Capital Flows. *Aussenwirtschaft*, March-June 1973, *28*(1–2), pp. 74–82. **[G: U.K.]**

Benoit, Emile. Balance of Payments Impact of a Vietnam Disengagement. In *Udis, B., ed.,* 1973, pp. 211–23. [G: U.S.]

Ben-Shahar, H. and Cukierman, A. The Term-Structure of Interest Rates and Expectations of Price Increase and Devaluation. *J. Finance,* June 1973, *28*(3), pp. 567–75. [G: Israel]

Bergsten, C. Fred. The Multinational Firm: Bane or Boon?: Discussion. *J. Finance,* May 1973, *28*(2), pp. 457–62. [G: Canada]

Carli, Guido. Per la difesa del valore interno e del valore esterno della lira. (Defending the Internal and External Value of the Lira. With English summary.) *Bancaria,* November 1973, *29*(11), pp. 1338–41. [G: Italy]

Casey, William J., Jr. Internationalization of Capital Markets. In *Wiegand, G. C., ed.,* 1973, pp. 132–38. [G: U.S.]

Christensen, Raymond P. and Goolsby, O. Halbert. U.S. Agricultural Trade and Balance of Payments. In *Iowa State University Center for Agricultural and Rural Development,* 1973, pp. 122–40. [G: U.S.]

Chugh, Ram L. Interest Sensitivity of Short-Term Capital Movements Between Canada and the United States: A Stock-Adjustment Analysis. *Econ. Int.,* August-November 1973, *26*(3–4), pp. 579–91. [G: U.S.; Canada]

Despres, Emile. American Aid and Western European Recovery. In *Despres, E.,* 1973, pp. 28–38. [G: W. Europe]

Despres, Emile. Capital Movements, Gold, and Balance of Payments. In *Despres, E.,* 1973, pp. 209–12. [G: U.S.]

Despres, Emile. Financing of Development: Malaysia. In *Despres, E.,* 1973, pp. 154–83. [G: Malaysia]

Despres, Emile. Gold—Where to from Here? In *Despres, E.,* 1973, pp. 279–86. [G: U.S.]

Despres, Emile. The Significance of the European Common Market to the American Economy. In *Despres, E.,* 1973, pp. 60–86. [G: U.S.; E.E.C.]

Despres, Emile. Western Europe's Long-Term Balance-of-Payments Problem. In *Despres, E.,* 1973, pp. 39–44. [G: W. Europe]

Donnelly, John T. External Financing and Short-Term Consequences of External Debt Servicing for Brazilian Economic Development, 1947-1968. *J. Devel. Areas,* April 1973, *7*(3), pp. 411–29. [G: Brazil]

Ferrari, Alberto. Integrazione monetaria europea e movimenti internazionali dei capitali, II. (European Monetary Integration and International Capital Movements, II. With English summary.) *Bancaria,* June 1973, *29*(6), pp. 688–95.

Ferrari, Alberto. Integrazione monetaria europea e movimenti internazionali dei capitali. (European Monetary Integration and International Capital Movements. With English summary.) *Bancaria,* May 1973, *29*(5), pp. 563–67. [G: E.E.C.]

Formuzis, Peter. The Demand for Eurodollars and the Optimum Stock of Bank Liabilities. *J. Money, Credit, Banking,* August 1973, *5*(3), pp. 806–18. [G: U.S.]

Gillespie, Robert W. and Rushing, Philip J. Expenditure Switching vs. Altering Absorption: An Empirical Approach. *Southern Econ. J.,* July 1973, *40* (1), pp. 26–34.

Grassman, Sven. A Fundamental Symmetry in International Payment Patterns. *J. Int. Econ.,* May 1973, *3*(2), pp. 105–16. [G: Sweden]

Harris, C. Lowell. Monetary and Incomes Policies: Comment. In *Wiegand, G. C., ed.,* 1973, pp. 155–56. [G: U.S.]

Harrod, Roy [Sir]. A British View of American Monetary Problems. In *Wiegand, G. C., ed.,* 1973, pp. 152–54. [G: U.S.]

Helbling, Hans H. U.S. Balance-of-Payments Developments During 1973. *Fed. Res. Bank St. Louis Rev.,* December 1973, *55*(12), pp. 11–14. [G: U.S.]

Hodjera, Zoran. International Short-Term Capital Movements: A Survey of Theory and Empirical Analysis. *Int. Monet. Fund Staff Pap.,* November 1973, *20*(3), pp. 683–740.

Howle, Edward S. On Revaluations versus Devaluations. *Amer. Econ. Rev.,* December 1973, *63*(5), pp. 918–28.

Kafka, Alexandre. Adjustment Under the Bretton Woods Code with Special Reference to the Less Developed Countries. In *[Rosenstein-Rodan, P.],* 1973, pp. 210–38.

Kawata, Fukuo. An Analysis of the Brazilian Balance of Payments, 1960–1972. *Kobe Econ. Bus. Rev.,* 1973, *20,* pp. 1–21. [G: Brazil]

Khan, Mohsin S. The Effect of Growth on the Balance of Payments of Developing Countries: An Empirical Note. *Pakistan Econ. Soc. Rev.,* Autumn 1973, *11*(3), pp. 354–59.

Kohn, Donald L. Capital Flows in a Foreign Exchange Crisis. *Fed. Res. Bank Kansas City Rev.,* February 1973, pp. 14–23. [G: U.S.]

Korka, Mihai. Evoluţia comerţului invizibil al ţărilor în curs de dezvoltare. (The Evolution of the Invisible Trade of the Developing Countries. With English summary.) *Stud. Cercet. Econ.,* 1973, (4), pp. 177–92.

MacDougall, Donald. Indian Balance of Payments. In *Wadhva, C. D., ed.,* 1973, pp. 430–38. [G: India]

Magnani, Livio. Considerazioni sui flussi e sulle disponibilità. (Money Flows and Assets Formation. With English summary.) *Bancaria,* January 1973, *29*(1), pp. 83–103. [G: Italy]

Magnani, Livio. I recenti avvenimenti monetari internazionali. (The Recent International Monetary Events. With English summary.) *Bancaria,* February 1973, *29*(2), pp. 189–92.

Masera, Francesco. Autonomous Capital Movements: The Italian Experience in the Past Decade. *Aussenwirtschaft,* March-June 1973, *28* (1–2), pp. 83–106. [G: Italy]

Masera, Francesco. I movimenti di capitali autonomi nell'esperienza italiana degli ultimi dieci anni. (Autonomous Movements of Capital Within the Range of Italian Experience During the Last Ten Years. With English summary.) *Bancaria,* June 1973, *29*(6), pp. 696–707. [G: Italy]

Matthews, R. C. O. Foreign Trade and British Economic Growth. *Scot. J. Polit. Econ.,* November 1973, *20*(3), pp. 195–209. [G: U.K.]

McClam, Warren D. The Control of Capital Movements: Comparative Policy Developments in the United States and Japan. *Aussenwirtschaft*, March-June 1973, *28*(1–2), pp. 107–29. [G: Japan; U.S.]

Meinander, Nils. The Finnmark Devaluation—Implications and Follow-Up Measures. In *Moskoff, W., ed.*, 1973, pp. 224–31. [G: Finland]

Mendelson, Morris. The Eurobond Market: A Prospective Review. In *Henley, D. S., ed.*, 1973, pp. 223–39. [G: U.S.; E.E.C.]

Miller, Etienne and Smith, Gordon P. International Travel, Passenger Fares, and Other Transportation in the U.S. Balance of Payments: 1972. *Surv. Curr. Bus.*, June 1973, *53*(6), pp. 12–16, 56. [G: U.S.]

Moncarz, Raul. Monetary Aspects of the Central American Common Market. *J. Common Market Stud.*, December 1973, *12*(2), pp. 196–204. [G: Central America]

Murray, Tracy and Ginman, Peter J. Will Devaluation Improve the US Trade Deficit? *Kyklos*, 1973, *26*(4), pp. 844–48. [G: U.S.]

Naito, Takeshi. Japan's Changing Role. In *Wiegand, G. C., ed.*, 1973, pp. 139–42. [G: Japan]

Papandreou, Andreas G. The Multinational Firm: Bane or Boon?: Discussion. *J. Finance*, May 1973, *28*(2), pp. 455–57. [G: Canada]

Parrish, Evelyn M. U.S. Balance of Payments Developments: Fourth Quarter and Year 1972. *Surv. Curr. Bus.*, March 1973, *53*(3), pp. 22–30, 52. [G: U.S.]

Parzych, Kenneth M. The U.S. Balance-of-Payments: A Restructuring of Commercial Policy. *Rivista Int. Sci. Econ. Com.*, December 1973, *20*(12), pp. 1179–89. [G: U.S.]

Ranuzzi de Bianchi, Paolo. Le società multinazionali e la bilancia dei pagamenti americana. (Multinational Companies and the American Balance of Payments. With English summary.) *Bancaria*, September 1973, *29*(9), pp. 1090–93.

Reierson, Roy L. International Financial Markets: Problems and Prospects. In *Levy, M. E., ed.*, 1973, pp. 24–36. [G: U.S.]

Safarian, A. E. Perspectives on Foreign Direct Investment from the Viewpoint of a Capital Receiving Country. *J. Finance*, May 1973, *28*(2), pp. 419–38. [G: Canada]

Salant, Walter S. The Post-Devaluation Weakness of the Dollar. *Brookings Pap. Econ. Act.*, 1973, (2), pp. 481–97. [G: U.S.]

Samuels, Nathaniel. National Policies, the Balance of Payments and the Role of the Dollar. In *Levy, M. E., ed.*, 1973, pp. 37–44. [G: U.S.]

Savona, Paolo. Mercato internazionale delle valute e mercato italiano delle obbligazioni. (International Exchange Market and Italian Bond Market. With English summary.) *Bancaria*, December 1973, *29*(12), pp. 1467–73. [G: Italy]

Sawyer, J. A. The Invisible Components of the Current Account of the Balance of International Payments. In *Ball, R. J., ed.*, 1973, pp. 329–63. [G: W. Europe; N. America; Japan]

Schachter, Gustav and Cohen, Bruce. Influenze esterne sui mercati dei capitali degli Stati Uniti. (Foreign Influences on the U.S. Capital Markets. With English summary.) *Bancaria*, February

1973, *29*(2), pp. 156–63. [G: U.S.]

Sood, James H. The Computer Manufacturing Industry and the U.S. Balance of Payments. *Calif. Manage. Rev.*, Winter 1973, *16*(2), pp. 37–43. [G: U.S.]

Stein, L. On the Third World's Narrowing Trade Gap: A Rejoinder. *Oxford Econ. Pap.*, March 1973, *25*(1), pp. 141–44.

Strout, Alan M. Foreign Capital and Indonesian Economic Growth. *Bull. Indonesian Econ. Stud.*, July 1973, *9*(2), pp. 77–90. [G: Indonesia]

Strout, Alan M. Foreign Capital and Indonesian Economic Growth: A Reply. *Bull. Indonesian Econ. Stud.*, July 1973, *9*(2), pp. 96–99. [G: Indonesia]

Vernon, Raymond. U.S. Direct Investment in Canada: Consequences for the U.S. Economy. *J. Finance*, May 1973, *28*(2), pp. 407–17. [G: Canada; U.S.]

Wiegand, G. C. America and the International Monetary Crisis. In *Wiegand, G. C., ed.*, 1973, pp. 56–62. [G: U.S.]

Zecher, Richard. Short-run Monetary Adjustments in the Australian Economy, 1952–70. In *Powell, A. A. and Williams, R. A., eds.*, 1973, pp. 335–48. [G: Australia]

4314 Exchange Rates and Markets

Abboud, A. Robert. The Case Against Floating Rates and for a Stronger Dollar. In *Wiegand, G. C., ed.*, 1973, pp. 89–96. [G: U.S.]

Aliber, Robert Z. The Interest Rate Parity Theorem: A Reinterpretation. *J. Polit. Econ.*, November-December 1973, *81*(6), pp. 1451–59.

Artus, Jacques R. and Rhomberg, Rudolf R. A Multilateral Exchange Rate Model. *Int. Monet. Fund Staff Pap.*, November 1973, *20*(3), pp. 591–611.

Bacha, Edmar and Taylor, Lance. Foreign Exchange Shadow Prices: A Critical Review of Current Theories. In *Eckaus, R. S. and Rosenstein-Rodan, P. N., eds.*, 1973, pp. 3–29.

Balassa, Bela. Just How Misleading are Official Exchange Rate Conversions?: Comment. *Econ. J.*, December 1973, *83*(332), pp. 1258–67.

Balogh, T. and Balacs, P. Fact and Fancy in International Economic Relations. *World Devel.*, March-April 1973, *1*(3–4), pp. 71–105.

Barker, C. Austin. Alternative Monetary Proposals. In *Wiegand, G. C., ed.*, 1973, pp. 179–82. [G: U.S.]

Bautista, Romeo M. Devaluation and Employment in a Labor-Surplus Economy: The Philippines. *Econ. Int.*, August-November 1973, *26*(3–4), pp. 543–59. [G: Philippines]

Berglas, Eitan and Razin, Assaf. Real Exchange Rate and Devaluation. *J. Int. Econ.*, May 1973, *3*(2), pp. 179–91.

Bernstein, Edward M. Narrowing the Exchange Rate Bands: Comment. In *Krause, L. B. and Salant, W. S., eds.*, 1973, pp. 97–105. [G: U.S.; E.E.C.]

Bhagwati, Jagdish N. and Krueger, Anne O. Exchange Control, Liberalization, and Economic Development. *Amer. Econ. Rev.*, May 1973, *63*(2), pp. 419–27.

Bhagwati, Jagdish N. The Case for Devaluation. In *Wadhva, C. D., ed.,* 1973, pp. 457–61. [G: India]

Bichi, C. Devalorizarea dolarului, un nou episod în adîncirea crizei sistemului valutar interoccidental. (The Devaluation of the Dollar, a New Episode in the Deepening of the Crisis of the Western Currency System. With English summary.) *Stud. Cercet. Econ.,* 1973, (3), pp. 153–64. [G: U.S.]

Burns, Arthur F. Statement to Congress. *Fed. Res. Bull.,* March 1973, *59*(3), pp. 168–71. [G: U.S.]

Burns, Arthur F. Statements to Congress. *Fed. Res. Bull.,* December 1973, *59*(12), pp. 879–83. [G: U.S.]

Coombs, Charles A. Treasury and Federal Reserve Foreign Exchange Operations: Interim Report. *Fed. Res. Bull.,* December 1973, *59*(12), pp. 871–73. [G: U.S.]

Corden, W. Max. The Adjustment Problem. In *Krause, L. B. and Salant, W. S., eds.,* 1973, pp. 159–84. [G: U.S.; E.E.C.]

Courchene, Thomas J. The Price-Specie-Flow Mechanism and the Gold-Exchange Standard: Some Exploratory Empiricism Relating to the Endogeneity of Country Money Balances. In *Johnson, H. G. and Swoboda, A. K., eds.,* 1973, pp. 65–84. [G: U.S.; Europe; Japan; Australia]

Dale, William B. The International Monetary Fund and Greater Flexibility of Exchange Rates. In *[Halm, G. N.],* 1973, pp. 3–17.

David, Paul A. Just How Misleading are Official Exchange Rate Conversions?: Reply. *Econ. J.,* December 1973, *83*(332), pp. 1267–76.

Dornbusch, Rudiger. Currency Depreciation, Hoarding, and Relative Prices. *J. Polit. Econ.,* July-August 1973, *81*(4), pp. 893–915.

Dunn, Robert M., Jr. Flexible Exchange Rates and Traded Goods Prices: The Role of Oligopoly Pricing in the Canadian Experience. In *Johnson, H. G. and Swoboda, A. K., eds.,* 1973, pp. 259–80. [G: U.S.; Canada]

Ethier, Wilfred. International Trade and the Forward Exchange Market. *Amer. Econ. Rev.,* June 1973, *63*(3), pp. 494–503.

Fellner, William J. Controlled Floating and the Confused Issue of Money Illusion. *Banca Naz. Lavoro Quart. Rev.,* September 1973, (106), pp. 206–34.

Fellner, William J. Narrowing the Exchange Rate Bands: Comment. In *Krause, L. B. and Salant, W. S., eds.,* 1973, pp. 105–08. [G: U.S.; E.E.C.]

Folks, William R., Jr. The Optimal Level of Forward Exchange Transactions. *J. Financial Quant. Anal.,* January 1973, *8*(1), pp. 105–10.

Frenkel, Jacob A. Elasticities and the Interest Parity Theory. *J. Polit. Econ.,* May-June 1973, *81*(3), pp. 741–47.

Fried, Joel. Inflation-unemployment Trade-offs under Fixed and Floating Exchange Rates. *Can. J. Econ.,* February 1973, *6*(1), pp. 43–52.

Giersch, Herbert. On the Desirable Degree of Flexibility of Exchange Rates. *Weltwirtsch. Arch.,* 1973, *109*(2), pp. 191–213.

Goldstein, Henry N. On the Neutrality of Forward Market Intervention. *Weltwirtsch. Arch.,* 1973, *109*(4), pp. 688–700.

Goodhart, Charles A. E. Monetary Policy in the United Kingdom. In *Holbik, K., ed.,* 1973, pp. 465–524. [G: U.K.]

Grubel, Herbert G. Forward Exchange Market Intervention is not Necessarily Neutral. *Weltwirtsch. Arch.,* 1973, *109*(4), pp. 704–06.

Grubel, Herbert G. The Case for Optimum Exchange Rate Stability. *Weltwirtsch. Arch.,* 1973, *109*(3), pp. 351–81.

Haberler, Gottfried. Prospects for the Dollar Standard. In *[Halm, G. N.],* 1973, pp. 65–80.

Halm, George N. Reforming the Par-Value System. *Weltwirtsch. Arch.,* 1973, *109*(2), pp. 171–90.

Hasson, Joseph. The Impact of Dollar Devaluation on Domestic Prices. *J. Econ. Bus.,* Fall 1973, *26*(1), pp. 25–40. [G: U.S.]

Heckerman, Donald G. On the Effects of Exchange Risk. *J. Int. Econ.,* November 1973, *3*(4), pp. 379–87.

Hirsch, Fred. The Politics of World Money. In *Henley, D. S., ed.,* 1973, pp. 132–41.

Holzheu, Franz. Zur Problematik der Bandbreiteneinengung in der Europäischen Wirtschaftsgemeinschaft. (On the Problem of Narrowing the Exchange Rate Margins within the EEC. With English summary.) *Z. Wirtschaft. Sozialwissen.,* 1973, *93*(2), pp. 159–89. [G: E.E.C.]

Horsefield, J. Keith. Proposals for Using Objective Indicators as a Guide to Exchange Rate Changes: A Historical Comment. *Int. Monet. Fund Staff Pap.,* November 1973, *20*(3), pp. 832–37.

Igawa, Kazuhiro. Assets Choice and Optimal International Reserves. *Kobe Econ. Bus. Rev.,* 1973, *20,* pp. 79–88.

Ingram, James C. The Adjustment Problem: Comment. In *Krause, L. B. and Salant, W. S., eds.,* 1973, pp. 184–91. [G: U.S.; E.E.C.]

Johnson, Harry G. Narrowing the Exchange Rate Bands. In *Krause, L. B. and Salant, W. S., eds.,* 1973, pp. 78–97. [G: U.S.; E.E.C.]

Johnson, Harry G. The Exchange-Rate Question for a United Europe. In *Krauss, M. B., ed.,* 1973, pp. 201–14. [G: E.E.C.]

Junz, Helen B. and Rhomberg, Rudolf R. Price Competitiveness in Export Trade Among Industrial Countries. *Amer. Econ. Rev.,* May 1973, *63* (2), pp. 412–18.

Lieftinck, Pieter. To Float or Not to Float. *Finance Develop.,* December 1973, *10*(4), pp. 27–29, 41–42.

MacDonald, A. S. Exchange Rates for National Expenditure on Research and Development. *Econ. J.,* June 1973, *83*(330), pp. 477–94.

Machlup, Fritz. Exchange-Rate Flexibility. *Banca Naz. Lavoro Quart. Rev.,* September 1973, (106), pp. 183–205.

Magee, Stephen P. Currency Contracts, Pass-through, and Devaluation. *Brookings Pap. Econ. Act.,* 1973, (1), pp. 303–23. [G: U.S.]

Masera, Francesco. European Fund for Monetary Cooperation: Objectives and Operating Guidelines. *Banca Naz. Lavoro Quart. Rev.,* September 1973, (106), pp. 269–86. [G: E.E.C.]

Meiselman, David I. The Case Against the Case for

Gold. In *Wiegand, G. C., ed.*, 1973, pp. 14–20. [G: U.S.]

Merican, Malik Ali. Exchange Rate Experience and Policy in Malaysia Since World War II. In *Grubel, H. G. and Morgan, T., eds.*, 1973, pp. 19–29. [G: Malaysia]

Metzler, Lloyd A. Exchange Rates and the International Monetary Fund. In *Metzler, L. A.*, 1973, pp. 112–58.

Moore, George S. The Monetary Crisis—From a Banker's Point of View. In *Wiegand, G. C., ed.*, 1973, pp. 35–38. [G: U.S.]

Mundell, Robert A. Uncommon Arguments for Common Currencies. In *Johnson, H. G. and Swoboda, A. K., eds.*, 1973, pp. 114–32.

Murphy, J. Carter. The Adjustment Problem: Comment. In *Krause, L. B. and Salant, W. S., eds.*, 1973, pp. 191–97. [G: U.S.; E.E.C.]

Nugent, Jeffrey B. Exchange-Rate Movements and Economic Development in the Late Nineteenth Century. *J. Polit. Econ.*, September-October 1973, *81*(5), pp. 1110–35.

Pippenger, John E. The Case for Freely Fluctuating Exchange Rates: Some Evidence. *Western Econ. J.*, September 1973, *11*(3), pp. 314–26.

Rasaputram, Warnasena. Exchange Rate Experience and Policy in Sri Lanka (Ceylon) Since World War II. In *Grubel, H. G. and Morgan, T., eds.*, 1973, pp. 9–18. [G: Sri Lanka]

Reese, K. The Soviet Ruble and Comecon Countries. *S. Afr. J. Econ.*, June 1973, *41*(2), pp. 134–45. [G: U.S.S.R.]

Reimann, Guenter. Floating Rates and the Market Place. In *Wiegand, G. C., ed.*, 1973, pp. 160–68. [G: U.S.; W. Germany]

Roethenmund, Otto. The Dollar Problem from the Point of View of a Swiss Banker. In *Wiegand, G. C., ed.*, 1973, pp. 127–30. [G: U.S.]

de Roos, F. Floating Exchange Rates. *S. Afr. J. Econ.*, June 1973, *41*(2), pp. 111–33.

de Roos, F. Zwevende wisselkoersen. (Fluctuating Exchange Rates. With English summary.) *De Economist*, January-February 1973, *121*(1), pp. 1–28.

Rose, Klaus and Bender, Dieter. Flexible Wechselkurse und Inflationsimport. (Flexible Exchange Rates and Import of Inflation. With English summary.) *Jahr. Nationalökon. Statist.*, August 1973, *187*(6), pp. 481–506.

Rosendale, Phyllis B. The Short-Run Pricing Policies of Some British Engineering Exporters. *Nat. Inst. Econ. Rev.*, August 1973, (65), pp. 44–51. [G: U.K.]

Ross, Russell and Tower, Edward. More on the Neutrality of Forward Market Intervention. *Weltwirtsch. Arch.*, 1973, *109*(4), pp. 701–03.

Salant, Walter S. The Post-Devaluation Weakness of the Dollar. *Brookings Pap. Econ. Act.*, 1973, (2), pp. 481–97. [G: U.S.]

Sanittanont, Sura. Exchange Rate Experience and Policy in Thailand Since World War II. In *Grubel, H. G. and Morgan, T., eds.*, 1973, pp. 31–40. [G: Thailand]

Shapiro, Alan C. Optimal Inventory and Credit-Granting Strategies under Inflation and Devaluation. *J. Financial Quant. Anal.*, January 1973, *8* (1), pp. 37–46.

Shinkai, Yoichi. Problems in the Estimation of Price Elasticities of Exports and Imports: A Survey. (In Japanese. With English summary.) *Econ. Stud. Quart.*, August 1973, *24*(2), pp. 31–39.

Steinherr, Alfred. Economic Policy in the Short Run under Fixed Exchange Rates. *Rech. Écon. Louvain*, December 1973, *39*(4), pp. 419–36.

Stokes, Houston H. Spot Speculation, Forward Speculation, and Arbitrage: Comment. *Amer. Econ. Rev.*, December 1973, *63*(5), pp. 995–98.

Swoboda, Alexander K. Monetary Policy under Fixed Exchange Rates: Effectiveness, the Speed of Adjustment and Proper Use. *Economica, N.S.*, May 1973, *40*(158), pp. 136–54.

Tarasanar, Hsiung. Recent Developments on the Gold Front. *Fed. Res. Bank Bus. Rev. Phila.*, November 1973, pp. 12–13.

Taylor, Lance and Bacha, Edmar. Growth and Trade Distortions in Chile, and Their Implications in Calculating the Shadow Price of Foreign Exchange. In *Eckaus, R. S. and Rosenstein-Rodan, P. N., eds.*, 1973, pp. 121–46. [G: Chile]

Taylor, Lance. Neoclassical Projections of Foreign Exchange Needs in Chile. In *Eckaus, R. S. and Rosenstein-Rodan, P. N., eds.*, 1973, pp. 327–40. [G: Chile]

Thomas, Lloyd B. Speculation in the Flexible Exchange Revisited—Another View. *Kyklos*, 1973, *26*(1), pp. 143–50. [G: U.S.; France; Canada; Spain]

Thomas, Lloyd B. Behavior of Flexible Exchange Rates: Additional Tests from the Post-World War I Episode. *Southern Econ. J.*, October 1973, *40*(2), pp. 167–82.

Tower, Edward. Commercial Policy Under Fixed and Flexible Exchange Rates. *Quart. J. Econ.*, August 1973, *87*(3), pp. 436–54.

Tsiang, S. C. Spot Speculation, Forward Speculation, and Arbitrage: A Clarification and Reply. *Amer. Econ. Rev.*, December 1973, *63*(5), pp. 999–1002.

Underwood, Trevor G. Analysis of Proposals for Using Objective Indicators as a Guide to Exchange Rate Changes. *Int. Monet. Fund Staff Pap.*, March 1973, *20*(1), pp. 100–17.

Van Belle, John J. Spot Rates, Forward Rates, and the Interest-Rate Differentials: Comment. *J. Money, Credit, Banking*, November 1973, *5*(4), pp. 997–99.

Van Belle, John J. A Neglected Aspect of the Modern Theory of Forward Exchange. *Southern Econ. J.*, July 1973, *40*(1), pp. 117–19.

Van Oenen, Richard. Exchange Rate Experience in Southeast Asia. In *Grubel, H. G. and Morgan, T., eds.*, 1973, pp. 1–7. [G: S.E. Asia]

Williams, Harold R. Resource Allocation under Alternative Exchange Rate Systems: Reply. *Southern Econ. J.*, April 1973, *39*(4), pp. 651.

Williams, Harold R. Exchange Rate Systems, the Marginal Efficiency of Investment, and Foreign Direct Capital Movements. *Kyklos*, 1973, *26*(1), pp. 58–74.

Williamson, John. Another Case of Profitable Destabilising Speculation. *J. Int. Econ.*, February 1973, *3*(1), pp. 77–83.

Wood, Geoffrey E. Resource Allocation under Alternative Exchange Rate Systems: A Comment. *Southern Econ. J.*, April 1973, *39*(4), pp. 650–51.

432 International Monetary Arrangements

4320 International Monetary Arrangements

Adler, John H. The External Debt Problem. In *Lewis, J. P. and Kapur, I., eds.*, 1973, pp. 111–22.

Aliber, Robert Z. The Impact of External Markets for National Currencies on Central Bank Reserves. In *Johnson, H. G. and Swoboda, A. K., eds.*, 1973, pp. 178–95. [G: U.S.; W. Europe]

Aliber, Robert Z. Gold, SDR's, and Central Bank Swaps. *J. Money, Credit, Banking*, August 1973, 5(3), pp. 819–25.

Allen, William R. For Want of an International Adjustment Mechanism. *Soc. Sci. Quart.*, June 1973, 54(1), pp. 140–45.

Andersen, Stig. The World Bank and the United Nations: Comment. In *Lewis, J. P. and Kapur, I., eds.*, 1973, pp. 139–41.

Argy, Victor and Hodjera, Zoran. Financial Integration and Interest Rate Linkages in Industrial Countries, 1958-71. *Int. Monet. Fund Staff Pap.*, March 1973, 20(1), pp. 1–77.

Arndt, Sven W. Joint Balance: Capital Mobility and the Monetary System of a Currency Area. In *Johnson, H. G. and Swoboda, A. K., eds.*, 1973, pp. 196–209.

Aschinger, F. E. The Eurocurrency Market and National Credit Policy. In *Henley, D. S., ed.*, 1973, pp. 217–22. [G: U.S.]

Bailey, Norman A. The Monetary System and the Businessman: Comment. In *Wiegand, G. C., ed.*, 1973, pp. 158–59. [G: U.S.]

Bailey, Richard. European Community in a World Context. *Irish Banking Rev.*, June 1973, pp. 16–22. [G: W. Europe]

Balassa, Bela. Implications for Integration of the World Economy: Comment. In *Krause, L. B. and Salant, W. S., eds.*, 1973, pp. 266–69. [G: U.S.; Europe]

Balassa, Bela. A Plan for a European Currency: Comment. In *Johnson, H. G. and Swoboda, A. K., eds.*, 1973, pp. 173–77.

Balogh, T. and Balacs, P. Fact and Fancy in International Economic Relations. *World Devel.*, March-April 1973, 1(3–4), pp. 71–105.

Barattieri, Vittorio. La riforma del sistema monetario internazionale. (Reform of the International Monetary System. With English summary.) *Bancaria*, May 1973, 29(5), pp. 568–78.

Barger, Harold. International Liquidity and International Trade: Comment. In *Wiegand, G. C., ed.*, 1973, pp. 97–98. [G: U.S.]

Barker, C. Austin. Alternative Monetary Proposals. In *Wiegand, G. C., ed.*, 1973, pp. 179–82. [G: U.S.]

Bauer, Peter. Inflation, SDRs and AID. *Lloyds Bank Rev.*, July 1973, (109), pp. 31–35.

Benoit, Emile. Structural Causes of Recent International Disequilibrium—A Preliminary Note. In *Wiegand, G. C., ed.*, 1973, pp. 63–69.

Bergsten, C. Fred. Implications for U.S. Policy toward Europe: Comment. In *Krause, L. B. and Salant, W. S., eds.*, 1973, pp. 286–92. [G: U.S.; E.E.C.]

Bergsten, C. Fred. Convertibility for the Dollar and International Monetary Reform. In *[Halm, G. N.]*,

1973, pp. 99–114. [G: U.S.]

Bernstein, Edward M. Narrowing the Exchange Rate Bands: Comment. In *Krause, L. B. and Salant, W. S., eds.*, 1973, pp. 97–105. [G: U.S.; E.E.C.]

Beyen, Karel H. Il finanziamento del commercio internazionale. (International Trade Finance. With English summary.) *Bancaria*, December 1973, 29(12), pp. 1461–66.

Bichi, C. Devalorizarea dolarului, un nou episod în adîncirea crizei sistemului valutar interoccidental. (The Devaluation of the Dollar, a New Episode in the Deepening of the Crisis of the Western Currency System. With English summary.) *Stud. Cercet. Econ.*, 1973, (3), pp. 153–64. [G: U.S.]

Bloomfield, Arthur I. The Historical Setting. In *Krause, L. B. and Salant, W. S., eds.*, 1973, pp. 1–30. [G: E.E.C.]

Boarman, Patrick M. International Trade and National Autonomy. In *Wiegand, G. C., ed.*, 1973, pp. 77–88.

Boarman, Patrick M. Healing the Rift Between the U.S. and Europe. *Calif. Manage. Rev.*, Fall 1973, 16(1), pp. 76–85. [G: U.S.; Europe]

Bodner, David E. The Role of Central Bank Swaps in the International Monetary System. In *Wiegand, G. C., ed.*, 1973, pp. 100–06. [G: U.S.]

Bowie, Robert R. Implications for U.S. Policy toward Europe: Comment. In *Krause, L. B. and Salant, W. S., eds.*, 1973, pp. 292–95. [G: U.S.; E.E.C.]

Brimmer, Andrew F. Multi-National Banks and the Management of Monetary Policy in the United States. *J. Finance*, May 1973, 28(2), pp. 439–54.

van Buren Cleveland, Harold. Implications for Private Capital Markets: Comment. In *Krause, L. B. and Salant, W. S., eds.*, 1973, pp. 141–49. [G: U.S.; E.E.C.]

Burns, Arthur F. Statement to Congress. *Fed. Res. Bull.*, March 1973, 59(3), pp. 164–68.

Burns, Arthur F. Statement to Congress. *Fed. Res. Bull.*, March 1973, 59(3), pp. 176–78.

Burns, Arthur F. Statements to Congress. *Fed. Res. Bull.*, December 1973, 59(12), pp. 879–83. [G: U.S.]

Burns, Arthur F. Statement to Congress. *Fed. Res. Bull.*, July 1973, 59(7), pp. 508–12. [G: U.S.]

Burns, Arthur F. Some Essentials of International Monetary Reform. In *Henley, D. S., ed.*, 1973, pp. 127–31.

Carli, Guido. Riforma monetaria, bilancia dei pagamenti e liquidità interna. (Monetary Reform, Balance of Payments and Domestic Liquidity. With English summary.) *Bancaria*, January 1973, 29(1), pp. 7–16.

Carli, Guido. Crisi monetaria internazionale e politica di ripresa economica-I. (Policies Designed to Overcome the International Monetary Crisis and to Support the Economic Recovery in Italy-I. With English summary.) *Bancaria*, May 1973, 29(5), pp. 543–62. [G: Italy]

Carli, Guido. Intervento all'assemblea del Fondo Monetario. (Statement at the Meeting of the International Monetary Fund. With English summary.) *Bancaria*, August 1973, 29(8), pp. 947–50.

Clark, Russell J. The Importance of Being Confident. *Nat. Westminster Bank Quart. Rev.*, August 1973, pp. 2–7.

Cohen, Benjamin J. The Future Role of Sterling. *Nat. Westminster Bank Quart. Rev.*, May 1973, pp. 6–19.   [G: U.K.]

Cohen, Benjamin J. The Historical Setting: Comment. In *Krause, L. B. and Salant, W. S., eds.*, 1973, pp. 30–33.   [G: E.E.C.]

Coker, David and Kay, John. The Fund Meeting. *Finance Develop.*, December 1973, *10*(4), pp. 37–40.

Cooper, Richard N. Implications for Integration of the World Economy. In *Krause, L. B. and Salant, W. S., eds.*, 1973, pp. 250–66. [G: U.S.; Europe]

Cooper, Richard N. European Monetary Unification and the International Monetary System. In *Krauss, M. B., ed.*, 1973, pp. 215–35.   [G: E.E.C.]

Corden, W. Max. The Adjustment Problem. In *Krause, L. B. and Salant, W. S., eds.*, 1973, pp. 159–84.   [G: U.S.; E.E.C.]

Dale, William B. The International Monetary Fund and Greater Flexibility of Exchange Rates. In *[Halm, G. N.]*, 1973, pp. 3–17.

Davis, Steven I. A Buyer's Market in Eurodollars. *Harvard Bus. Rev.*, May-June 1973, *51*(3), pp. 119–30.

Dell, Sidney. An Appraisal of UNCTAD III. *World Devel.*, May 1973, *1*(5), pp. 1–13.

Demuth, Richard H. Relations with Other Multilateral Agencies. In *Lewis, J. P. and Kapur, I., eds.*, 1973, pp. 133–38.

Despres, Emile. A Proposal for Strengthening the Dollar. In *Despres, E.*, 1973, pp. 213–35.
                                                      [G: U.S.]

Despres, Emile. Capital Movements, Gold, and Balance of Payments. In *Despres, E.*, 1973, pp. 209–12.   [G: U.S.]

Despres, Emile. Financing of Development: Malaysia. In *Despres, E.*, 1973, pp. 154–83.
                                                [G: Malaysia]

Despres, Emile. Gold—Where to from Here? In *Despres, E.*, 1973, pp. 279–86.   [G: U.S.]

Despres, Emile. International Financial Intermediation. In *Despres, E.*, 1973, pp. 257–65.

Despres, Emile. The Dollar and World Liquidity: A Minority View. In *Despres, E.*, 1973, pp. 266–78.
                                          [G: U.S.; W. Europe]

Despres, Emile. Toward the Demonetization of Gold. In *Despres, E.*, 1973, pp. 236–56.

Diebold, William, Jr. Implications for Integration of the World Economy: Comment. In *Krause, L. B. and Salant, W. S., eds.*, 1973, pp. 269–75.
                                              [G: U.S.; Europe]

Diz, Adolfo. L'inflazione e il sistema monetario internazionale: Intervento. (Inflation and the International Monetary System: Discussion. With English summary.) *Bancaria*, October 1973, *29*(10), pp. 1220–24.

Economides, Chris. Earned International Reserve Units: The Catalyst of Two Complementary World Problems—the Monetary and Development. *World Devel.*, March-April 1973, *1*(3–4), pp. 49–69.

Emminger, Otmar. L'inflazione e il sistema monetario internazionale. (Inflation and the International Monetary System. With English summary.) *Bancaria*, October 1973, *29*(10), pp. 1206–19.

Exter, John. Toward a New World Monetary System. In *Wiegand, G. C., ed.*, 1973, pp. 186–98.

Fekete, Janos. L'inflazione e il sistema monetario internazionale: Intervento. (Inflation and the International Monetary System: Discussion. With English summary.) *Bancaria*, October 1973, *29* (10), pp. 1225–28.

Fellner, William J. Controlled Floating and the Confused Issue of Money Illusion. *Banca Naz. Lavoro Quart. Rev.*, September 1973, (106), pp. 206–34.

Fellner, William J. Narrowing the Exchange Rate Bands: Comment. In *Krause, L. B. and Salant, W. S., eds.*, 1973, pp. 105–08.   [G: U.S.; E.E.C.]

Ferrari, Alberto. Integrazione monetaria europea e movimenti internazionali dei capitali. (European Monetary Integration and International Capital Movements. With English summary.) *Bancaria*, May 1973, *29*(5), pp. 563–67.   [G: E.E.C.]

Ferrari, Alberto. Integrazione monetaria europea e movimenti internazionali dei capitali, II. (European Monetary Integration and International Capital Movements, II. With English summary.) *Bancaria*, June 1973, *29*(6), pp. 688–95.

Fieleke, Norman S. International Economic Reform. *New Eng. Econ. Rev.*, January-February 1973, pp. 19–27.   [G: U.S.]

Formuzis, Peter. The Demand for Eurodollars and the Optimum Stock of Bank Liabilities. *J. Money, Credit, Banking*, August 1973, *5*(3), pp. 806–18.
                                                      [G: U.S.]

Frank, Charles R., Jr. Debt Adjustment: The Tyranny of Bankers, Brokers, and Bondholders: Comment. In *Lewis, J. P. and Kapur, I., eds.*, 1973, pp. 123–30.

Fried, Edward R. Foreign Economic Policy: The Search for a Strategy. In *Owen, H., ed.*, 1973, pp. 157–202.   [G: U.S.]

Fried, Edward R. Implications for U.S. Policy toward Europe: Comment. In *Krause, L. B. and Salant, W. S., eds.*, 1973, pp. 283–86.   [G: U.S.; E.E.C.]

Friedman, Irving S. International Monetary System: 1973 Reforming in a Hurricane. *Banca Naz. Lavoro Quart. Rev.*, December 1973, (107), pp. 352–74.

Fujita, Masahiro. International Money Flow and the Multinational Corporations. *Kobe Econ. Bus. Rev.*, 1973, *20*, pp. 22–36.   [G: Japan; U.S.]

Furth, J. Herbert. International Dollar Liquidity and the Eurodollar Market. *De Economist*, July-August 1973, *121*(4), pp. 347–61.   [G: U.S.]

Gaines, Tilford. International Monetary Arrangements. In *Reynolds, L. G.; Green, G. D. and Lewis, D. R., eds.*, 1973, pp. 474–84.

Gaud, William S. High Profile, Better Target: Comment. In *Lewis, J. P. and Kapur, I., eds.*, 1973, pp. 53–56.

Geesey, Ronald E. International Competition in the Provision of Financial Services. In *Rybczynski, T. M., ed.*, 1973, pp. 37–45. [G: U.S.; U.K.; E.E.C.]

Geiger, Theodore. Toward a World of Trading Blocs? In *Henley, D. S., ed.*, 1973, pp. 6–17.   [G: W. Europe; Japan; U.S.]

Geiger, Theodore. The Political Context: Comment. In *Krause, L. B. and Salant, W. S., eds.*, 1973, pp. 62–69. [G: E.E.C.]

Gordenker, Leon. International Economic Diplomacy: Comment. In *Lewis, J. P. and Kapur, I., eds.,* 1973, pp. 143–46.

Gräbig, G. Planned Use of Commodity and Money Relations. In *Kiss, T., ed.,* 1973, pp. 197–202. [G: CMEA]

Grassman, Sven. A Fundamental Symmetry in International Payment Patterns. *J. Int. Econ.,* May 1973, *3*(2), pp. 105–16. [G: Sweden]

Grubel, Herbert G. The Optimum Stability of Exchange Rates: A Southeast Asian Payments Union. In *Grubel, H. G. and Morgan, T., eds.,* 1973, pp. 77–92. [G: S.E. Asia]

Grubel, Herbert G. The Case for Optimum Exchange Rate Stability. *Weltwirtsch. Arch.,* 1973, *109*(3), pp. 351–81.

Grubel, Herbert G. The Theory of Optimum Regional Associations. In *Johnson, H. G. and Swoboda, A. K., eds.,* 1973, pp. 99–113.

Guggenheim, Thomas. Some Early Views on Monetary Integration. In *Johnson, H. G. and Swoboda, A. K., eds.,* 1973, pp. 93–98.

Haberler, Gottfried. The Historical Setting: Comment. In *Krause, L. B. and Salant, W. S., eds.,* 1973, pp. 33–36. [G: E.E.C.]

Halm, George N. Reforming the Par-Value System. *Weltwirtsch. Arch.,* 1973, *109*(2), pp. 171–90.

ul Haq, Mahbub. The Transfer of Resources: Comment. In *Lewis, J. P. and Kapur, I., eds.,* 1973, pp. 83–87.

Hazlitt, Henry. The Problem and Its Solution. In *Wiegand, G. C., ed.,* 1973, pp. 170–78. [G: U.S.]

Heller, H. Robert. The Costs and Benefits of the Dollar as a Reserve Currency: Discussion. *Amer. Econ. Rev.,* May 1973, *63*(2), pp. 212–14.

Helliwell, John F. Dollars as Reserve Assets: What Next? *Amer. Econ. Rev.,* May 1973, *63*(2), pp. 206–11.

Henderson, P. D. Terms and Flexibility of Bank Lending. In *Lewis, J. P. and Kapur, I., eds.,* 1973, pp. 65–76.

Hirsch, Fred. The Politics of World Money. In *Henley, D. S., ed.,* 1973, pp. 132–41.

Hoffman, Michael L. The Challenges of the 1970s and the Present Institutional Structure. In *Lewis, J. P. and Kapur, I., eds.,* 1973, pp. 13–19.

Hoffmeyer, Erik. Hvor meget vil den økonomiske og monetære union binde vor økonomiske politik? (To What Extent will Our Economic Policy Be Bound by the European Economic and Monetary Union? With English summary.) *Nationalokon. Tidsskr.,* 1973, *111*(1), pp. 144–53.

Hosono, Akio. Japanese Economic Relations with Latin America: Prospects and Possible Lines of Action. In *Urquidi, V. L. and Thorp, R., eds.,* 1973, pp. 374–95. [G: Japan; Latin America]

Humphrey, Don D. The Case for Gold. In *[Halm, G. N.],* 1973, pp. 81–98.

Ingram, James C. The Adjustment Problem: Comment. In *Krause, L. B. and Salant, W. S., eds.,* 1973, pp. 184–91. [G: U.S.; E.E.C.]

Johnson, Elizabeth S. and Johnson, Harry G. Keynes, the Wider Band, and the Crawling Peg. *J. Money, Credit, Banking,* November 1973, *5*(4), pp. 988–89.

Johnson, Harry G. Narrowing the Exchange Rate Bands. In *Krause, L. B. and Salant, W. S., eds.,* 1973, pp. 78–97. [G: U.S.; E.E.C.]

Johnson, Harry G. Problems of European Monetary Union. In *Krauss, M. B., ed.,* 1973, pp. 188–200. [G: E.E.C.]

Johnson, Harry G. The Exchange-Rate Question for a United Europe. In *Krauss, M. B., ed.,* 1973, pp. 201–14. [G: E.E.C.]

Johnson, Harry G. Efficiency in International Money Supply. In *Johnson, H. G.,* 1973, pp. 271–76.

Johnson, Harry G. Problems of European Monetary Union. In *Johnson, H. G.,* 1973, pp. 312–24. [G: E.E.C.]

Johnson, Harry G. Problems of Stabilization Policy in an Integrated World Economy. In *Johnson, H. G.,* 1973, pp. 338–52.

Johnson, Harry G. The International Monetary Crisis of 1971. In *Johnson, H. G.,* 1973, pp. 353–61.

Johnson, Harry G. The Panamanian Monetary System. In *Johnson, H. G.,* 1973, pp. 223–28. [G: Panama]

Johnson, Harry G. Secular Inflation and the International Monetary System. *J. Money, Credit, Banking,* Part II, February 1973, *5*(1), pp. 509–19.

Kafka, Alexandre. Optimum Currency Areas and Latin America. In *Johnson, H. G. and Swoboda, A. K., eds.,* 1973, pp. 210–18. [G: Latin America; W. Europe; U.S.]

Kahn, Richard F. [Lord]. The International Monetary System. *Amer. Econ. Rev.,* May 1973, *63*(2), pp. 181–88.

Kahn, Richard F. [Lord]. SDRs and Aid. *Lloyds Bank Rev.,* October 1973, (110), pp. 1–18.

Kaufmann, Hugo M. International Liquidity and Balance-of-Payments Adjustments: A Reinterpretation. *Econ. Int.,* August–November 1973, *26* (3–4), pp. 592–602.

Kemmerer, Donald L. The Role of Gold in the Past Century. In *Wiegand, G. C., ed.,* 1973, pp. 3–13.

Kenen, Peter B. Convertibility and Consolidation: A Survey of Options for Reform. *Amer. Econ. Rev.,* May 1973, *63*(2), pp. 189–98.

Kenen, Peter B. Implications for International Reserves: Comment. In *Krause, L. B. and Salant, W. S., eds.,* 1973, pp. 236–47. [G: E.E.C.; U.S.]

Kindleberger, Charles P. Implications for Private Capital Markets: Comment. In *Krause, L. B. and Salant, W. S., eds.,* 1973, pp. 149–54. [G: U.S.; E.E.C.]

Kirschen, Etienne S. Le seigneuriage externe américain. Son origine, son coût pour l'Europe, et quelques ripostes possibles. (With English summary.) *Cah. Écon. Bruxelles,* 3rd Trimestre 1973, (59), pp. 345–84.

Knapp, J. Burke. Determination of Priorities and the Allocation of Resources. In *Lewis, J. P. and Kapur, I., eds.,* 1973, pp. 37–51.

Knight, Malcolm. A Continuous Disequilibrium Econometric Model of the Domestic and International Portfolio Behaviour of the UK Banking System. In *Parkin, M., ed.,* 1973, pp. 266–90. [G: U.K.]

Kohn, Donald L. Capital Flows in a Foreign Exchange Crisis. *Fed. Res. Bank Kansas City Rev.,* February 1973, pp. 14–23. [G: U.S.]

König, Wolfgang. International Financial Institutions and Latin American Development. In *Urquidi, V. L. and Thorp, R., eds.*, 1973, pp. 116–63. [G: Latin America]

Kövér, K. International Monetary Systems and Foreign Exchange Systems. In *Kiss, T., ed.*, 1973, pp. 213–19. [G: CMEA]

Krause, Lawrence B. Implications for Private Capital Markets. In *Krause, L. B. and Salant, W. S., eds.*, 1973, pp. 114–41. [G: U.S.; E.E.C.]

Lalwani, K. C. International Monetary System: Present Position and Future Outlook. *Econ. Aff.*, January–February 1973, *18*(1-2), pp. 29–38.

Lee, Boyden E. The Euro-Dollar Multiplier. *J. Finance*, September 1973, *28*(4), pp. 867–74. [G: U.S.; Europe]

Levy, Michael E. Major Economic Issues of the 1970's. In *Levy, M. E., ed.*, 1973, pp. 1–5. [G: U.S.]

Lewis, John P. and Kapur, Ishan. The World Bank Group, Multilateral Aid, and the 1970s. In *Lewis, J. P. and Kapur, I., eds.*, 1973, pp. 1–11.

Lewis, John P. Grants, Loans, and Local-Cost Financing: Comment. In *Lewis, J. P. and Kapur, I., eds.*, 1973, pp. 77–81.

Lieftinck, Pieter. To Float or Not to Float. *Finance Develop.*, December 1973, *10*(4), pp. 27–29, 41–42.

Machlup, Fritz. Implications for International Reserves: Comment. In *Krause, L. B. and Salant, W. S., eds.*, 1973, pp. 247–49. [G: E.E.C.; U.S.]

Machlup, Fritz. Stateless Money. In *[Halm, G. N.]*, 1973, pp. 115–22.

Machlup, Fritz. Exchange-Rate Flexibility. *Banca Naz. Lavoro Quart. Rev.*, September 1973, (106), pp. 183–205.

Magnani, Livio. I recenti avvenimenti monetari internazionali. (The Recent International Monetary Events. With English summary.) *Bancaria*, February 1973, *29*(2), pp. 189–92.

Magnifico, Giovanni. European Monetary Integration. In *Magnifico, G.*, 1973, pp. 199–222. [G: E.E.C.]

Magnifico, Giovanni. European Monetary Unification for Balanced Growth: A New Approach. In *Magnifico, G.*, 1973, pp. 1–42. [G: E.E.C.]

Magnifico, Giovanni. Further Considerations on the New Approach to European Monetary Unification. In *Magnifico, G.*, 1973, pp. 85–136. [G: E.E.C.]

Magnifico, Giovanni. The Theory of Optimum Currency Areas and European Monetary Unification. In *Magnifico, G.*, 1973, pp. 43–84. [G: E.E.C.]

Magnifico, Giovanni. Towards a European Money and Capital Market. In *Magnifico, G.*, 1973, pp. 137–98. [G: E.E.C.]

Magnifico, Giovanni. The European and International Currency Problem. *Banca Naz. Lavoro Quart. Rev.*, December 1973, (107), pp. 375–95.

Makin, John H. Identifying a Reserve Base for the Euro-Dollar System. *J. Finance*, June 1973, *28*(3), pp. 609–17.

Marzola, Pier L. Indicazioni verso l'aumento del prezzo ufficiale dell'oro per la ricostruzione del sistema monetario internazionale. (Towards a Rise of the Official Price of Gold as a Means to Rebuild the International Monetary System. With English summary.) *Rivista Int. Sci. Econ. Com.*, December 1973, *20*(12), pp. 1157–78.

Masera, Francesco. European Fund for Monetary Cooperation: Objectives and Operating Guidelines. *Banca Naz. Lavoro Quart. Rev.*, September 1973, (106), pp. 269–86. [G: E.E.C.]

McCracken, Paul W. Domestic Economic Policy and Convertibility. *Amer. Econ. Rev.*, May 1973, *63*(2), pp. 199–205.

McKinnon, Ronald I. The Dual Currency System Revisited. In *Johnson, H. G. and Swoboda, A. K., eds.*, 1973, pp. 85–90. [G: U.S.; Canada; Japan; W. Europe]

McKinnon, Ronald I. On Securing a Common Monetary Policy in Europe. *Banca Naz. Lavoro Quart. Rev.*, March 1973, (104), pp. 3–20. [G: E.E.C.]

Medow, Paul. Towards a Reexamination of Ragnar Frisch's Proposal for a Multilateral Trade Clearing Agency in the Light of International Program Budgeting. *Amer. Econ.*, Fall 1973, *17*(2), pp. 51–55.

Meltzer, Allan H. The Dollar as an International Money. *Banca Naz. Lavoro Quart. Rev.*, March 1973, (104), pp. 21–28.

Mendelson, Morris. The Eurobond Market: A Prospective Review. In *Henley, D. S., ed.*, 1973, pp. 223–39. [G: U.S.; E.E.C.]

Merk, Gerhard. Möglichkeiten einer vindikativen Devisenterminpolitik der Zentralbank. (The Possibilities of Vindicative Forward Exchange Policy of the Central Bank. With English summary.) *Z. Wirtschaft. Sozialwissen.*, 1973, *93*(3), pp. 323–40. [G: W. Germany]

Metzler, Lloyd A. Exchange Rates and the International Monetary Fund. In *Metzler, L. A.*, 1973, pp. 112–58.

Mohammed, Azizali F. and Saccomanni, Fabrizio. Short-Term Banking and Euro-Currency Credits to Developing Countries. *Int. Monet. Fund Staff Pap.*, November 1973, *20*(3), pp. 612–38.

Moore, George S. The Monetary Crisis—From a Banker's Point of View. In *Wiegand, G. C., ed.*, 1973, pp. 35–38. [G: U.S.]

Morse, C. J. La crisi monetaria del 1971 e gli insegnamenti da trarne. Intervento. (The Monetary Crisis of 1971. The Lessons to be Learned. With English summary.) *Bancaria*, March 1973, *29*(3), pp. 314–18.

Morse, Edward L. The Political Context: Comment. In *Krause, L. B. and Salant, W. S., eds.*, 1973, pp. 55–62. [G: E.E.C.]

Mundell, Robert A. The Monetary Consequences of Jacques Rueff: Review Article. *J. Bus.*, July 1973, *46*(3), pp. 384–95.

Mundell, Robert A. A Plan for a European Currency. In *Johnson, H. G. and Swoboda, A. K., eds.*, 1973, pp. 143–72. [G: W. Europe; U.S.]

Mundell, Robert A. Uncommon Arguments for Common Currencies. In *Johnson, H. G. and Swoboda, A. K., eds.*, 1973, pp. 114–32.

Murphy, J. Carter. The Adjustment Problem: Comment. In *Krause, L. B. and Salant, W. S., eds.*, 1973, pp. 191–97. [G: U.S.; E.E.C.]

Neumann, Manfred J. M. Special Drawing Rights

and Inflation. *Weltwirtsch. Arch.*, 1973, *109*(2), pp. 232–52.

Noyes, Guy E. The Multinational Firm: Bane or Boon?: Discussion. *J. Finance*, May 1973, *28*(2), pp. 462–65.

Nye, Joseph S. The Political Context. In *Krause, L. B. and Salant, W. S., eds.*, 1973, pp. 37–55. [G: E.E.C.]

Ossola, Rinaldo. Central Bank Interventions and Eurocurrency Markets. *Banca Naz. Lavoro Quart. Rev.*, March 1973, (104), pp. 29–45.

Parkin, Michael. A Continuous Disequilibrium Econometric Model of the Domestic and International Portfolio Behaviour of the UK Banking System: Discussion. In *Parkin, M., ed.*, 1973, pp. 291–93. [G: U.K.]

Patel, I. G. La crisi monetaria del 1971 e gli insegnamenti da trarne. Intervento. (The Monetary Crisis of 1971. The Lessons to be Learned. With English summary.) *Bancaria*, March 1973, *29*(3), pp. 319–25.

Polasek, M. IMF Special Drawing Rights and Economic Aid to Less Developed Countries. *Econ. Rec.*, September 1973, *49*(127), pp. 358–76.

Portman, Heinz. Special Drawing Rights and the Monetary System, An Interim Report. In *Henley, D. S., ed.*, 1973, pp. 142–44.

Portmann, Heinz. Il ruolo dei diritti speciali di prelievo nel sistema monetario internazionale-II. (Role of Special Drawing Rights in the International Monetary System-II. With English summary.) *Bancaria*, April 1973, *29*(4), pp. 437–46.

Portmann, Heinz. Il ruolo dei diritti speciali di prelievo nel sistema monetario internazionale-I. (Role of Special Drawing Rights in the International Monetary System-I. With English summary.) *Bancaria*, March 1973, *29*(3), pp. 326–32.

Rainoni, Antonio. Monetary Cooperation and the International Monetary System. In *Holbik, K., ed.*, 1973, pp. 525–71.

Reierson, Roy L. International Financial Markets: Problems and Prospects. In *Levy, M. E., ed.*, 1973, pp. 24–36. [G: U.S.]

Reimann, Guenter. Floating Rates and the Market Place. In *Wiegand, G. C., ed.*, 1973, pp. 160–68. [G: U.S.; W. Germany]

Reuss, Henry S. A Congressional View of the World's Monetary Problems. In *Wiegand, G. C., ed.*, 1973, pp. 145–50. [G: U.S.]

Reynolds, Clark W. Relations with Latin America: An American View. In *Urquidi, V. L. and Thorp, R., eds.*, 1973, pp. 235–82. [G: U.S.; Latin America]

Richardson, Richard W. The Raising of Resources: Comment. In *Lewis, J. P. and Kapur, I., eds.*, 1973, pp. 57–63. [G: U.S.]

Rueff, Jacques. The Lessons of Bretton Woods. In *Wiegand, G. C., ed.*, 1973, pp. 39–44. [G: U.S.]

Rueff, Jacques and Carli, Guido. Dibattito sulla riforma del sistema monetario internazionale. (Debate on the Reform of the International Monetary System. With English summary.) *Bancaria*, August 1973, *29*(8), pp. 935–46.

Rueff, Jacques. Prolegomeni a qualsiasi riforma del sistema monetario internazionale. (Prolegomena to Any Reform Concerning the International

Monetary System. With English summary.) *Bancaria*, June 1973, *29*(6), pp. 679–87.

Rugina, Anghel N. A Reorganization Plan of the International Monetary Fund as Oriented Toward Conditions of Stable Equilibrium. *Econ. Int.*, August-November 1973, *26*(3–4), pp. 451–67.

Sacchetti, Ugo. Sharing the Burden of International Adjustment. *Banca Naz. Lavoro Quart. Rev.*, June 1973, (105), pp. 141–57.

Salant, Walter S. Implications for International Reserves. In *Krause, L. B. and Salant, W. S., eds.*, 1973, pp. 203–36. [G: E.E.C.; U.S.]

Salin, Edgar. Die EWG im Koma. (EEC—A Fainting Patient. With English summary.) *Kyklos*, 1973, *26*(4), pp. 723–35. [G: E.E.C.]

Samuelson, Paul A. Interrogativi un po' eretici sui meccanismi monetari internazionali. (Heretical Doubts about the International Monetary Mechanisms. With English summary.) *Bancaria*, April 1973, *29*(4), pp. 423–29.

Sennholz, Hans F. Make Peace with Gold. In *Wiegand, G. C., ed.*, 1973, pp. 21–27. [G: U.S.]

Steib, Steve B. The Demand for Euro-Dollar Borrowings by U.S. Banks. *J. Finance*, September 1973, *28*(4), pp. 875–79. [G: U.S.; Europe]

Swoboda, Alexander K. Policy Conflict, Inconsistent Goals, and the Coordination of Economic Policies. In *Johnson, H. G. and Swoboda, A. K., eds.*, 1973, pp. 133–42.

Thomas, Lloyd B. Behavior of Flexible Exchange Rates: Additional Tests from the Post-World War I Episode. *Southern Econ. J.*, October 1973, *40*(2), pp. 167–82.

Tobin, James. Payments Imbalances and the Demand for International Reserves: A Theoretic and Empiric Inquiry. *Econ. Int.*, August-November 1973, *26*(3–4), pp. 529–39.

Trenton, R. W. Successor to Bretton Woods. *Rivista Int. Sci. Econ. Com.*, December 1973, *20*(12), pp. 1140–56.

Trezise, Philip H. Implications for U.S. Policy toward Europe. In *Krause, L. B. and Salant, W. S., eds.*, 1973, pp. 276–83. [G: U.S.; E.E.C.]

Triffin, Robert. The Collapse of the International Monetary System: Structural Causes and Remedies. *De Economist*, July-August 1973, *121*(4), pp. 362–74. [G: E.E.C.; U.S.]

Triffin, Robert. La crisi del sistema monetario internazionale: cause strutturali e rimedi. (The Collapse of the International Monetary System: Structural Causes and Remedies. With English summary.) *Bancaria*, April 1973, *29*(4), pp. 430–36.

Triffin, Robert. The Collapse of the International Monetary System. In *Wiegand, G. C., ed.*, 1973, pp. 46–55. [G: U.S.; E.E.C.]

Triffin, Robert. The International Monetary Chaos and the Way Out. *J. Common Market Stud.*, September 1973, *12*(1), pp. 104–17.

Van Rompuy, E. De stop-go cyclus en de Europese monetaire integratie. (The Stop-go Cycle and the European Monetary Integration. With English summary.) *Tijdschr. Econ.*, 1973, *18*(3), pp. 457–79. [G: U.K.; Europe]

Vinney, Les C. Credit Creation in the Eurodollar

Market: An Unresolved Issue. *Rivista Int. Sci. Econ. Com.*, January 1973, *20*(1), pp. 33–47.

Vlerick, André. Unione Monetaria Europea. (The European Monetary Union. With English summary.) *Mondo Aperto,* June-August 1973, *27*(3–4), pp. 224–35. **[G: Europe]**

Wallich, Henry C. Why Fixed Rates? *Soc. Sci. Quart.*, June 1973, *54*(1), pp. 146–51.

Wallich, Henry C. La crisi monetaria del 1971 e gli insegnamenti da trarne. (The Monetary Crisis of 1971. The Lessons to be Learned. With English summary.) *Bancaria,* March 1973, *29*(3), pp. 295–313.

Wesolowski, J. Monetary and Financial Relations. In *Kiss, T., ed.*, 0000, pp. 203–11. **[G: CMEA]**

Wiegand, G. C. America and the International Monetary Crisis. In *Wiegand, G. C., ed.,* 1973, pp. 56–62. **[G: U.S.]**

Wiegand, G. C. Whither the World? In *Wiegand, G. C., ed.,* 1973, pp. iii–vii. **[G: U.S.]**

Willett, Thomas D. Secular Inflation and the International Monetary System: Comment. *J. Money, Credit, Banking,* Part II, February 1973, *5*(1), pp. 520–23.

Williamson, John. Stability, Resource Transfers and Income Distribution. In *Wiegand, G. C., ed.,* 1973, pp. 73–76.

Williamson, John. Surveys in Applied Economics: International Liquidity. *Econ. J.,* September 1973, *83*(331), pp. 685–746.

Wilson, Ewen M. The Gold Standard and Monetary Reform. *S. Afr. J. Econ.,* March 1973, *41*(1), pp. 17–25.

Wittich, Günter and Shiratori, Masaki. The Snake in the Tunnel. *Finance Develop.,* June 1973, *10*(2), pp. 9–13, 38.

440 INTERNATIONAL INVESTMENT AND FOREIGN AID

441 International Investment and Capital Markets

4410 Theory of International Investment and Capital Flows

Agmon, Tamir. Country Risk: The Significance of the Country Factor for Share-Price Movements in the United Kingdom, Germany, and Japan. *J. Bus.,* January 1973, *46*(1), pp. 24–32. **[G: U.K.; W. Germany; Japan]**

Allen, Polly Reynolds. A Portfolio Approach to International Capital Flows. *J. Int. Econ.,* May 1973, *3* (2), pp. 135–60.

Amano, A. International Capital Movements: Theory and Estimation. In *Ball, R. J., ed.,* 1973, pp. 283–327. **[G: Japan]**

Arndt, Sven W. Policy Choices in an Open Economy: Some Dynamic Considerations. *J. Polit. Econ.,* July-August 1973, *81*(4), pp. 916–35.

Bade, Robin. Optimal Foreign Investment and International Trade. *Econ. Rec.,* March 1973, *49*(125), pp. 62–75.

Chudnovsky, Daniel. Endeudamiento y rentabilidad en empresas multinacionales. (Gearing and Prof-

itability in Multinational Enterprises. With English summary.) *Económica,* September-December 1973, *19*(3), pp. 245–63.

Cohn, Richard A. and Pringle, John J. Imperfections in International Financial Markets: Implications for Risk Premia and the Cost of Capital to Firms. *J. Finance,* March 1973, *28*(1), pp. 59–66.

Dobrotă, Niță and Stan, Sorin. Investițiile și creditele internaționale—componente importante ale circuitului economic mondial. (International Investments and Credits—Important Components of the World Economic Circulation. With English summary.) *Stud. Cercet. Econ.,* 1973, (4), pp. 149–65.

Dunning, John H. Multinational Enterprises and Domestic Capital Formation. *Manchester Sch. Econ. Soc. Stud.,* September 1973, *41*(3), pp. 283–310.

Ghosh, Sukesh K. Speculative Capital Movement and Financial Policy in Interacting Economies. *Indian Econ. J.,* April-June 1973, *20*(4–5), pp. 581–603.

Hymer, Stephen. Effects of Policies Encouraging Foreign Joint Ventures in Developing Countries: Comment. In *Ayal, E. B., ed.,* 1973, pp. 177–80.

Kindleberger, Charles P. Restrictions on Direct Investment in Host Countries. In *[Rosenstein-Rodan, P.],* 1973, pp. 201–09.

Kojima, Kiyoshi. A Macroeconomic Approach to Foreign Direct Investment. *Hitotsubashi J. Econ.,* June 1973, *14*(1), pp. 1–21. **[G: U.S.; Japan]**

Lubitz, Raymond. Export-Led Growth in Industrial Economies. *Kyklos,* 1973, *26*(2), pp. 307–21.

Modigliani, Franco and Askari, Hossein. The International Transfer of Capital and the Propagation of Domestic Disturbances Under Alternative Payment Systems. *Banca Naz. Lavoro Quart. Rev.,* December 1973, (107), pp. 295–310.

Modigliani, Franco. International Capital Movements, Fixed Parities, and Monetary and Fiscal Policies. In *[Rosenstein-Rodan, P.],* 1973, pp. 239–53.

Naqvi, Syed Nawab Haider. The Balance-of-Payments Problems in Developing Countries. *Pakistan Develop. Rev.,* Autumn 1973, *12*(3), pp. 259–72.

Ragazzi, Giorgio. Theories of the Determinants of Direct Foreign Investment. *Int. Monet. Fund Staff Pap.,* July 1973, *20*(2), pp. 471–98. **[G: U.S.]**

Rose, Klaus and Bender, Dieter. Flexible Wechselkurse und Inflationsimport. (Flexible Exchange Rates and Import of Inflation. With English summary.) *Jahr. Nationalökon. Statist.,* August 1973, *187*(6), pp. 481–506.

Sandler, Todd M. Exchange Rate Systems, the Marginal Efficiency of Investment and Foreign Direct Capital Movements: A Comment. *Kyklos,* 1973, *26*(4), pp. 866–68.

Schuster, Helmut. Direktinvestitionen und Zahlungsbilanz in Entwicklungsländern. (Direct Investment and the Balance of Payments in Developing Countries. With English summary.) *Z. Wirtschaft. Sozialwissen.,* 1973, *93*(2), pp. 190–96.

Van Long, Ngo. On a Paradox in the Theory of International Capital Movements. *Econ. Rec.*, September 1973, *49*(127), pp. 440–46.

Vernon, Raymond. A Program of Research on Foreign Direct Investment. In *Bergsten, C. F., ed.*, 1973, pp. 93–113.

Voivodas, Constantin S. Exports, Foreign Capital Inflow and Economic Growth. *J. Int. Econ.*, November 1973, *3*(4), pp. 337–49.

Wells, Louis T., Jr. Effects of Policies Encouraging Foreign Joint Ventures in Developing Countries. In *Ayal, E. B., ed.*, 1973, pp. 149–77.

Williams, Harold R. Exchange Rate Systems, the Marginal Efficiency of Investment, and Foreign Direct Capital Movements. *Kyklos*, 1973, *26*(1), pp. 58–74.

Williams, Harold R. Exchange Rate Systems, the Marginal Efficiency of Investment and Foreign Direct Capital Movements: Reply. *Kyklos*, 1973, *26*(4), pp. 869.

Zweig, Michael. Foreign Investment and the Aggregate Balance of Payments for Underdeveloped Countries. *Rev. Radical Polit. Econ.*, Spring 1973, *5*(1), pp. 13–18.

4412 International Investment and Capital Flows: Studies

Anyanwu, Enoch A. The Contribution of Finance to Industrial Development: The Nigerian Experience. In *[Hicks, U.]*, 1973, pp. 59–94. [G: Nigeria]

Areskoug, Kaj. Foreign-Capital Utilization and Economic Policies in Developing Countries. *Rev. Econ. Statist.*, May 1973, *55*(2), pp. 182–89.

Argy, Victor and Hodjera, Zoran. Financial Integration and Interest Rate Linkages in Industrial Countries, 1958-71. *Int. Monet. Fund Staff Pap.*, March 1973, *20*(1), pp. 1–77.

Arndt, H. W. and Sundrum, R. M. Foreign Capital and Indonesian Economic Growth: A Comment. *Bull. Indonesian Econ. Stud.*, July 1973, *9*(2), pp. 90–95. [G: Indonesia]

Bagchi, Amiya Kumar. Foreign Capital and Economic Development in India: A Schematic View. In *Gough, K. and Sharma, H. P., eds.*, 1973, pp. 43–76. [G: India]

Balbach, Anatol. Foreign Investment in the United States—A Danger to Our Welfare and Sovereignty? *Fed. Res. Bank St. Louis Rev.*, October 1973, *55*(10), pp. 10–13. [G: U.S.]

Ballon, Robert J. Japan's Investment Overseas. *Aussenwirtschaft*, September-December 1973, *28* (3/4), pp. 128–53. [G: Japan]

Barber, Clarence L. Presidential Address: A Sense of Proportion. *Can. J. Econ.*, November 1973, *6* (4), pp. 467–82.

Belli, R. David; Allnutt, Smith W. and Murad, Howard. Property, Plant, and Equipment Expenditures by Majority-Owned Foreign Affiliates of U.S. Companies: Revised Estimates for 1966–72 and Projections for 1973 and 1974. *Surv. Curr. Bus.*, December 1973, *53*(12), pp. 19–32. [G: U.S.]

van Buren Cleveland, Harold. Implications for Private Capital Markets: Comment. In *Krause, L. B.*

and Salant, W. S., eds., 1973, pp. 141–49. [G: U.S.; E.E.C.]

Carbaugh, Robert J. An Expanded EEC: Implications for the United States. *Intermountain Econ. Rev.*, Spring 1973, *4*(1), pp. 81–89. [G: U.S.]

Cardoso, Fernando Henrique. Associated-Dependent Development: Theoretical and Practical Implications. In *Stepan, A., ed.*, 1973, pp. 142–76. [G: Brazil]

Casey, William J., Jr. Internationalization of Capital Markets. In *Wiegand, G. C., ed.*, 1973, pp. 132–38. [G: U.S.]

Colonna di Paliano, Guido. International Private Investment Problems: European Community—United States. *Aussenwirtschaft*, September-December 1973, *28*(3/4), pp. 110–27. [G: E.E.C.; U.S.]

Donnelly, John T. External Financing and Short-Term Consequences of External Debt Servicing for Brazilian Economic Development, 1947-1968. *J. Devel. Areas*, April 1973, *7*(3), pp. 411–29. [G: Brazil]

Dunning, John H. The Determinants of International Production. *Oxford Econ. Pap.*, November 1973, *25*(3), pp. 289–336. [G: U.S.; U.K.]

Dunn, Robert M., Jr. Canada and Its Economic Discontents. *Foreign Aff.*, October 1973, *52*(1), pp. 119–40. [G: Canada]

Ekblom, H. E. European Direct Investments in the United States. *Harvard Bus. Rev.*, July-August 1973, *51*(4), pp. 16–26, 146–50.

Ffrench-Davis, Ricardo. Foreign Investment in Latin America: Recent Trends and Prospects. In *Urquidi, V. L. and Thorp, R., eds.*, 1973, pp. 169–89. [G: Latin America]

Fujita, Masahiro. International Money Flow and the Multinational Corporations. *Kobe Econ. Bus. Rev.*, 1973, *20*, pp. 22–36. [G: Japan; U.S.]

Gibson, J. Douglas. Canada's Declaration of Less Dependence. *Harvard Bus. Rev.*, September-October 1973, *51*(5), pp. 69–79. [G: Canada]

Goldfinger, Nathaniel. An American Trade Union View of International Trade and Investment. In *Kujawa, D., ed.*, 1973, pp. 28–53. [G: U.S.]

Goldsmith, Raymond W. The Position of Institutional Investors and of Corporate Stock in the National Balance Sheets and the Flow of Funds Accounts of the United States of America, 1952–68. In *Goldsmith, R. W., ed.*, 1973, pp. 91–164. [G: U.S.]

Grayson, Leslie E. The Role of Suppliers' Credits in the Industrialization of Ghana. *Econ. Develop. Cult. Change*, April 1973, *21*(3), pp. 477–99. [G: Ghana]

Hartke, Vance. A Foreign Trade and Investment Policy for the 1970s. In *Kujawa, D., ed.*, 1973, pp. 54–71. [G: U.S.]

Hawkins, Robert G. American Labor and the Multinational Corporation: Foreword. In *Kujawa, D., ed.*, 1973, pp. vi–xvii. [G: U.S.]

Healey, Derek T. Foreign Capital and Exports in Economic Development: The Experience of Eight Asian Countries. *Econ. Rec.*, September 1973, *49*(127), pp. 394–419.

Herring, Richard and Willett, Thomas D. The Relationship Between U.S. Direct Investment at

Home and Abroad. *Rivista Int. Sci. Econ. Com.*, January 1973, *20*(1), pp. 72–82. [G: U.S.]

Hoya, Thomas W. The Office of Foreign Direct Investments and East-West Joint Ventures. In *Henley, D. S., ed.*, 1973, pp. 95–98. [G: U.S.]

Jedel, Michael Jay and Stamm, John H. The Battle over Jobs: An Appraisal of Recent Publications on the Employment Effects of U.S. Multinational Corporations. In *Kujawa, D., ed.*, 1973, pp. 144–91. [G: U.S.]

Keohane, Robert O. and Ooms, Van Doorn. The Multinational Enterprise and World Political Economy. In *Henley, D. S., ed.*, 1973, pp. 241–77. [G: U.S.]

Killick, Tony. The Benefits of Foreign Direct Investment and Its Alternatives: An Empirical Exploration. *J. Devel. Stud.*, January 1973, *9*(2), pp. 301–16. [G: Sierra Leone]

Kindleberger, Charles P. Implications for Private Capital Markets: Comment. In *Krause, L. B. and Salant, W. S., eds.*, 1973, pp. 149–54. [G: U.S.; E.E.C.]

Klaasen, Thomas A. Regional Comparative Advantage in the United States. *J. Reg. Sci.*, April 1973, *13*(1), pp. 97–105. [G: U.S.]

Knapp, J. Burke. Determination of Priorities and the Allocation of Resources. In *Lewis, J. P. and Kapur, I., eds.*, 1973, pp. 37–51.

Kojima, Kiyoshi. The Japanese Experience and Attitudes Toward Trade Adjustment. In *Hughes, H., ed.*, 1973, pp. 228–62. [G: Japan]

Kojima, Kiyoshi. Reorganisation of North-South Trade: Japan's Foreign Economic Policy for the 1970s. *Hitotsubashi J. Econ.*, February 1973, *13* (2), pp. 1–28. [G: Japan]

Krause, Lawrence B. Implications for Private Capital Markets. In *Krause, L. B. and Salant, W. S., eds.*, 1973, pp. 114–41. [G: U.S.; E.E.C.]

Kressler, Peter R. Investment Barriers Facing the United States Automotive Industry in the Japanese Market. *Ohio State U. Bull. Bus. Res.*, September 1973, *48*(9), pp. 1–3. [G: U.S.; Japan]

Leftwich, Robert B. and Boyke, Robert. Foreign Direct Investments in the United States in 1972. *Surv. Curr. Bus.*, August 1973, *53*(8), pp. 50–51. [G: U.S.]

Leftwich, Robert B. Foreign Direct Investments in the United States, 1962–71. *Surv. Curr. Bus.*, February 1973, *53*(2), pp. 29–40. [G: U.S.]

Lessard, Donald R. International Portfolio Diversification: A Multivariate Analysis for a Group of Latin American Countries. *J. Finance*, June 1973, *28*(3), pp. 619–33. [G: Colombia; Chile; Brazil; Argentina]

McCawley, Peter. Survey of Recent Developments. *Bull. Indonesian Econ. Stud.*, November 1973, *9* (3), pp. 1–27. [G: Indonesia]

Mendelson, Morris. The Eurobond Market: A Prospective Review. In *Henley, D. S., ed.*, 1973, pp. 223–39. [G: U.S.; E.E.C.]

Miller, Norman C. and Whitman, Marina v. N. Alternative Theories and Tests of U.S. Short-Term Foreign Investment. *J. Finance*, December 1973, *28* (5), pp. 1131–50. [G: U.S.]

Miller, Robert R. and Weigel, Dale R. Factors Affecting Resource Transfer Through Direct Investment. In *Alexandrides, C. G., ed.*, 1973, pp. 129–44. [G: U.S.; Brazil]

Naito, Takeshi. Japan's Changing Role. In *Wiegand, G. C., ed.*, 1973, pp. 139–42. [G: Japan]

Namiki, Nobuyoshi. Future of the Economic Relations Between Japan and the European Community. *Rivista Int. Sci. Econ. Com.*, August-September 1973, *20*(8–9), pp. 758–85. [G: Japan; E.E.C.]

Nove, Alec. Great Britain and Latin American Economic Development. In *Urquidi, V. L. and Thorp, R., eds.*, 1973, pp. 331–66. [G: U.K.; Latin America]

Ogren, Kenneth E. Exports of U.S. Capital and Technology and International Political Conflicts. In *Iowa State University Center for Agricultural and Rural Development*, 1973, pp. 210–24. [G: U.S.]

Pécsi, K. Capital Movements and Joint Undertakings. In *Kiss, T., ed.*, 1973, pp. 227–34. [G: CMEA]

Polk, Judd. International Perspectives on World Companies. In *Alexandrides, C. G., ed.*, 1973, pp. 261–71. [G: U.S.]

Polk, Judd. The New International Production. *World Devel.*, May 1973, *1*(5), pp. 15–20.

Ragazzi, Giorgio. Theories of the Determinants of Direct Foreign Investment. *Int. Monet. Fund Staff Pap.*, July 1973, *20*(2), pp. 471–98. [G: U.S.]

Reynolds, Clark W. Relations with Latin America: An American View. In *Urquidi, V. L. and Thorp, R., eds.*, 1973, pp. 235–82. [G: U.S.; Latin America]

Riley, J. C. Dutch Investment in France, 1781–1787. *J. Econ. Hist.*, December 1973, *33*(4), pp. 732–60. [G: Netherlands; France]

Ruckdeschel, Frederic Brill. The Determinants of a Direct Investment Outflow with Emphasis on the Supply of Funds. *Fed. Res. Bull.*, June 1973, *59*(6), pp. 403–04. [G: U.S.]

Saxe, Jo. The Japanese Experience and Attitudes Toward Trade Adjustment: Comment. In *Hughes, H., ed.*, 1973, pp. 266–68. [G: Japan]

Scaperlanda, Anthony E. and Mauer, Laurence Jay. The Impact of Controls on United States Direct Foreign Investment in the European Economic Community. *Southern Econ. J.*, January 1973, *39* (3), pp. 419–23. [G: E.E.C.; U.S.]

Schachter, Gustav and Cohen, Bruce. Influenze esterne sui mercati dei capitali degli Stati Uniti. (Foreign Influences on the U.S. Capital Markets. With English summary.) *Bancaria*, February 1973, *29*(2), pp. 156–63. [G: U.S.]

Schaeffer, Maurice. The European Economic Community and Latin American Development. In *Urquidi, V. L. and Thorp, R., eds.*, 1973, pp. 313–30. [G: E.E.C.; Latin America]

Scholl, Russell B. The International Investment Position of the United States: Developments in 1972. *Surv. Curr. Bus.*, August 1973, *53*(8), pp. 18–23. [G: U.S.]

Stern, Ernest. Private Capital Markets for Development. In *[Halm, G. N.]*, 1973, pp. 185–97.

Strout, Alan M. Foreign Capital and Indonesian Economic Growth: A Reply. *Bull. Indonesian Econ.*

Stud., July 1973, *9*(2), pp. 96–99. [**G: Indonesia**]

Strout, Alan M. Foreign Capital and Indonesian Economic Growth. *Bull. Indonesian Econ. Stud.*, July 1973, *9*(2), pp. 77–90. [**G: Indonesia**]

Sunkel, Osvaldo. Transnational Capitalism and National Disintegration in Latin America. *Soc. Econ. Stud.*, March 1973, *22*(1), pp. 132–76. [**G: Latin America**]

Teplin, Mary F. U.S. International Transactions in Royalties and Fees: Their Relationship to the Transfer of Technology. *Surv. Curr. Bus.*, December 1973, *53*(12), pp. 14–18. [**G: U.S.**]

Vaitsos, Constantine V. Strategic Choices in the Commercialization of Technology: The Point of View of Developing Countries. *Int. Soc. Sci. J.*, 1973, *25*(3), pp. 370–86.

Wall, David. The Japanese Experience and Attitudes Toward Trade Adjustment: Comment. In *Hughes, H., ed.*, 1973, pp. 263–66. [**G: Japan**]

Willmore, L. N. Direct Foreign Investment and Industrial Entrepreneurship in Central America. In *Pollock, D. H. and Ritter, A. R. M., eds.*, 1973, pp. 287–300. [**G: Central America**]

442 International Business

4420 International Business; Management and Policies; Economic Imperialism and Host Country Policies

Abboud, A. Robert. The Case Against Floating Rates and for a Stronger Dollar. In *Wiegand, G. C., ed.*, 1973, pp. 89–96. [**G: U.S.**]

Abegglen, James C. and Rapp, William V. Japanese Managerial Behavior and "Excessive Competition." In *Henley, D. S., ed.*, 1973, pp. 65–82. [**G: Japan**]

Adam, Harold. Aspetti giuridici e fiscali delle società transnazionali nella C.E.E. (Legal and Taxation Aspects of the Transnational Corporations in the EEC. With English summary.) *Bancaria*, April 1973, *29*(4), pp. 495–500. [**G: Europe**]

Adler, Michael. The Valuation and Financing of the Multi-National Firm: Comment. *Kyklos*, 1973, *26*(4), pp. 849–51.

Ajiferuke, Musbau and Boddewyn, J. J. Socioeconomic Indicators in Comparative Management. In *Alexandrides, C. G., ed.*, 1973, pp. 163–72.

Alexandrides, C. G. A Methodology for Computerization. In *Alexandrides, C. G., ed.*, 1973, pp. 185–93.

Amadeo, Eduardo P. Algunas ideas para un nuevo enfoque de la teoría del "ciclo del producto". (Some Ideas for a New Approach on the Theory of the "Product Cycle". With English summary.) *Económica*, May-August 1973, *19*(2), pp. 135–45.

Amin, Samir. Underdevelopment and Dependence in Black Africa—Their Historical Origins and Contemporary Forms. *Soc. Econ. Stud.*, March 1973, *22*(1), pp. 177–96. [**G: Africa**]

Amuzegar, Jahangir. The Oil Story: Facts, Fiction and Fair Play. *Foreign Aff.*, July 1973, *51*(4), pp. 676–89.

Antin, P. The Nestlé Product Manager as Demigod. In *Thorelli, H. B., ed.*, 1973, pp. 290–300.

Arrate, Jorge. The Nationalization of Copper. In *Zammit, J. A., ed.*, 1973, pp. 145–50. [**G: Chile**]

Arrighi, Giovanni and Saul, John S. Nationalism and Revolution in Sub-Saharan Africa. In *Arrighi, G. and Saul, J. S.*, 1973, pp. 44–102. [**G: S. Africa; Rhodesia; U.S.**]

Babson, Steve. The Multinational Corporation and Labor. *Rev. Radical Polit. Econ.*, Spring 1973, *5*(1), pp. 19–36. [**G: U.S.**]

Bagchi, Amiya Kumar. Foreign Capital and Economic Development in India: A Schematic View. In *Gough, K. and Sharma, H. P., eds.*, 1973, pp. 43–76. [**G: India**]

Ballon, Robert J. Japan's Investment Overseas. *Aussenwirtschaft*, September-December 1973, *28*(3/4), pp. 128–53. [**G: Japan**]

Barber, Arthur. Emerging New Power: The World Corporation. In *Andreano, R. L., ed.*, 1973, pp. R333–05.

Bates, Thomas H. Management and the Multinational Business Environment. *Calif. Manage. Rev.*, Spring 1973, *15*(3), pp. 37–45.

Beeth, G. Distributors—Finding and Keeping the Good Ones. In *Thorelli, H. B., ed.*, 1973, pp. 273–79.

Behrman, Jack N. Can the Multinational Enterprise Gain Acceptability through Industrial Integration? In *Fayerweather, J., ed.*, 1973, pp. 27–38.

Bell, Clive and Lehmann, David. The International Context of La Via Chilena. In *Zammit, J. A., ed.*, 1973, pp. 343–65. [**G: Chile; U.S.**]

Belli, R. David; Allnutt, Smith W. and Murad, Howard. Property, Plant, and Equipment Expenditures by Majority-Owned Foreign Affiliates of U.S. Companies: Revised Estimates for 1966–72 and Projections for 1973 and 1974. *Surv. Curr. Bus.*, December 1973, *53*(12), pp. 19–32. [**G: U.S.**]

Belli, R. David. Plant and Equipment Expenditures of U.S.-Owned Foreign Affiliates: Revised Estimates for 1972 and 1973. *Surv. Curr. Bus.*, March 1973, *53*(3), pp. 45–52. [**G: U.S.**]

Bergsten, C. Fred. The Multinational Firm: Bane or Boon?: Discussion. *J. Finance*, May 1973, *28*(2), pp. 457–62. [**G: Canada**]

Bergsten, C. Fred. The Role of the Multinational Corporation: Comment. In *Hughes, H., ed.*, 1973, pp. 90–95.

Black, R. D. Collison. Emigrazione e colonizzazione. (Emigration and Colonization. With English summary.) *Rivista Int. Sci. Econ. Com.*, November 1973, *20*(11), pp. 1071–80. [**G: U.K.; Ireland**]

Blake, David H. Government, Politics, and the Multinational Enterprise. In *Fayerweather, J., ed.*, 1973, pp. 63–83.

Boddewyn, J. J. The External Affairs Function in American Multinational Corporations. In *Fayerweather, J., ed.*, 1973, pp. 49–62. [**G: U.S.**]

Boddewyn, J. J. External Affairs at Four Levels in U.S. Multinationals. *Ind. Relat.*, May 1973, *12*(2), pp. 239–47. [**G: U.S.**]

Brantner, Paul F. Taxation and the Multinational Firm. *Manage. Account.*, October 1973, *55*(4), pp. 11–16, 26. [**G: U.S.**]

Brimmer, Andrew F. Multi-National Banks and the Management of Monetary Policy in the United

States. *J. Finance*, May 1973, *28*(2), pp. 439–54.

Briner, Ernst K. International Tax Management. *Manage. Account.*, February 1973, *54*(8), pp. 47–50.

Buonomo, Maurizio. Multinazionali e banche. (Multinational Firms and Banks. With English summary.) *Bancaria*, September 1973, *29*(9), pp. 1113–22.

Calhoun, Donald A. Computing DISC Profits. *Manage. Account.*, June 1973, *54*(12), pp. 45–46. [G: U.S.]

Carbaugh, Robert J. An Expanded EEC: Implications for the United States. *Intermountain Econ. Rev.*, Spring 1973, *4*(1), pp. 81–89. [G: U.S.]

Cardoso, Fernando Henrique. Associated-Dependent Development: Theoretical and Practical Implications. In *Stepan, A., ed.*, 1973, pp. 142–76. [G: Brazil]

Cardoso, Fernando Henrique. Imperialism and Dependency in Latin America. In *Bonilla, F. and Girling, R., eds.*, 1973, pp. 7–16.

Carnoy, Martin. Financial Institutions and Dependency. In *Bonilla, F. and Girling, R., eds.*, 1973, pp. 34–45. [G: U.S.]

Cateora, P. R. and Hess, J. M. Pricing in International Markets. In *Thorelli, H. B., ed.*, 1973, pp. 209–21.

Cebula, Richard J. and Kohn, Robert M. Foreign Capital and Steady-State Growth in Developing Economies. *Pakistan Econ. Soc. Rev.*, Winter 1973, *11*(4), pp. 378–82.

Chudnovsky, Daniel. Endeudamiento y rentabilidad en empresas multinacionales. (Gearing and Profitability in Multinational Enterprises. With English summary.) *Económica*, September-December 1973, *19*(3), pp. 245–63.

Coelho, Philip R. P. The Profitability of Imperialism: The British Experience in the West Indies 1768-1772. *Exploration Econ. Hist.*, Spring 1973, *10*(3), pp. 253–80. [G: U.K.]

Cohen, Benjamin I. Comparative Behavior of Foreign and Domestic Export Firms in a Developing Economy. *Rev. Econ. Statist.*, May 1973, *55*(2), pp. 190–97. [G: S. Korea]

Colonna di Paliano, Guido. International Private Investment Problems: European Community—United States. *Aussenwirtschaft*, September-December 1973, *28*(3/4), pp. 110–27. [G: E.E.C.; U.S.]

Copp, Robert. Ford Motor Co. as a Multinational Employer. *Mon. Lab. Rev.*, August 1973, *96*(8), pp. 58–61.

Curtin, William J. The Multinational Corporation and Transnational Collective Bargaining. In *Kujawa, D., ed.*, 1973, pp. 192–222. [G: U.S.]

Dahlstedt, Roy. Muuttujavalinnasta monikansallisen yrityksen käyttäytymismalleissa. (On the Selection of Variables for Descriptive Models of Multinational Firms. With English summary.) *Liiketaloudellinen Aikak.*, 1973, *22*(2), pp. 127–30.

Daniels, John D. and Arpan, Jeffrey. Comparative Home Country Influences on Management Practices Abroad. In *Henley, D. S., ed.*, 1973, pp. 409–19. [G: Canada; W. Europe; U.S.]

De La Vinelle, Duquesne. Aspetti economici sociali

e culturali delle multinazionali. (Socio-Economic Features of Multinational Enterprises. With English summary.) *Mondo Aperto*, December 1973, *27*(6), pp. 397–414.

Dietz, John. Enforcement of Anti-Trust Laws in the EEC. In *Henley, D. S., ed.*, 1973, pp. 185–213. [G: E.E.C.]

Drucker, Peter F. Global Management. In *The Conference Board*, 1973, pp. 228–74.

Duncan, M. W. Union Carbide: A Case Study in Sales to Eastern Europe. In *Thorelli, H. B., ed.*, 1973, pp. 64–70. [G: E. Europe]

Dunning, John H. Multinational Enterprises and Domestic Capital Formation. *Manchester Sch. Econ. Soc. Stud.*, September 1973, *41*(3), pp. 283–310.

Dunning, John H. Multinational Enterprises and Trade Flows of Developing Countries. In *Streeten, P., ed.*, 1973, pp. 300–20.

Dunning, John H. The Determinants of International Production. *Oxford Econ. Pap.*, November 1973, *25*(3), pp. 289–336. [G: U.S.; U.K.]

Dunn, Robert M., Jr. Canada and Its Economic Discontents. *Foreign Aff.*, October 1973, *52*(1), pp. 119–40. [G: Canada]

Edwards, C. D. The World of Antitrust. In *Thorelli, H. B., ed.*, 1973, pp. 89–103. [G: U.S.]

Ekblom, H. E. European Direct Investments in the United States. *Harvard Bus. Rev.*, July-August 1973, *51*(4), pp. 16–26, 146–50.

Farmer, David H. Source Decision Making in the Multinational Company Environment. In *Henley, D. S., ed.*, 1973, pp. 474–86.

Fayerweather, John and Kapoor, Ashok. Simulated International Business Negotiations. In *Alexandrides, C. G., ed.*, 1973, pp. 5–18.

Fayerweather, John. Attitudes Affecting International Business-Government Affairs. In *Fayerweather, J., ed.*, 1973, pp. 5–16.

Fayerweather, John; Blake, David H. and Murray, J. Alex. Perspectives for the Future. In *Fayerweather, J., ed.*, 1973, pp. 95–123.

Fernandez, Raul A. The Border Industrial Program on the United States-Mexico Border. *Rev. Radical Polit. Econ.*, Spring 1973, *5*(1), pp. 37–52. [G: U.S.; Mexico]

Franko, Lawrence G. Strategy + Structure − Frustration = the Experiences of European Firms in America. In *Henley, D. S., ed.*, 1973, pp. 83–94. [G: W. Europe; U.S.]

Fujita, Masahiro. International Money Flow and the Multinational Corporations. *Kobe Econ. Bus. Rev.*, 1973, *20*, pp. 22–36. [G: Japan; U.S.]

Furtado, Celso. The Concept of External Dependence in the Study of Underdevelopment. In *Wilber, C. K., ed.*, 1973, pp. 118–23.

Gagliani, Giorgio. Note sulle imprese multinazionali e l'occupazione. (Notes on Multinational Firms and Employment. With English summary.) *Bancaria*, September 1973, *29*(9), pp. 1081–89.

Gangadin, Victor J. A Brief Outline of the Imposition in Guyana of Income Tax, Corporation Tax, Capital Gains Tax, Withholding Tax and Property Tax with Special Reference to Foreign Corporations Operating in Guyana, Through a Branch Establishment or an Agency. *Bull. Int. Fiscal Doc.*,

November 1973, *27*(11), pp. 455–63. [G: Guyana]

Gedicks, Al. The Nationalization of Copper in Chile: Antecedents and Consequences. *Rev. Radical Polit. Econ.*, Fall 1973, *5*(3), pp. 1–25. [G: Chile]

Geesey, Ronald E. International Competition in the Provision of Financial Services. In *Rybczynski, T. M., ed.*, 1973, pp. 37–45. [G: U.S.; U.K.; E.E.C.]

Gennard, John and Steuer, M. D. The Industrial Relations of Foreign Owned Subsidiaries in the United Kingdom. In *Henley, D. S., ed.*, 1973, pp. 301–17. [G: U.K.]

Gibson, J. Douglas. Canada's Declaration of Less Dependence. *Harvard Bus. Rev.*, September-October 1973, *51*(5), pp. 69–79. [G: Canada]

Girling, Robert. Dependency, Technology and Development. In *Bonilla, F. and Girling, R., eds.*, 1973, pp. 46–62.

Gitman, Lawrence J. A Multinational Firm Investment Model. *J. Econ. Bus.*, Fall 1973, *26*(1), pp. 41–48.

Goldfinger, Nathaniel. An American Trade Union View of International Trade and Investment. In *Kujawa, D., ed.*, 1973, pp. 28–53. [G: U.S.]

Goodnow, James D. and Hansz, James E. Environmental Determinants of Overseas Market Entry Strategies. In *Alexandrides, C. G., ed.*, 1973, pp. 195–215. [G: U.S.]

Graham, Philip L., Jr.; Hermann, Donald H. G. and Marcus, Sumner. Section 7 of the Clayton Act and Mergers Involving Foreign Interests. In *Henley, D. S., ed.*, 1973, pp. 155–84. [G: U.S.]

Guisinger, Stephen. The Rise of the Multinational Corporation and United States Trade Policy. *Soc. Sci. Quart.*, December 1973, *54*(3), pp. 552–67. [G: U.S.]

Hadari, Yitzhak. The Structure of the Private Multinational Enterprise. *Mich. Law Rev.*, March 1973, *71*(4), pp. 729–806.

Hartke, Vance. A Foreign Trade and Investment Policy for the 1970s. In *Kujawa, D., ed.*, 1973, pp. 54–71. [G: U.S.]

Hawkins, Robert G. American Labor and the Multinational Corporation: Foreword. In *Kujawa, D., ed.*, 1973, pp. vi–xvii. [G: U.S.]

Helfgott, Roy B. Multinational Corporations and Manpower Utilization in Developing Nations. *J. Devel. Areas*, January 1973, *7*(2), pp. 235–46. [G: U.S.; Latin America]

Helleiner, Gerald K. Manufactured Exports from Less-Developed Countries and Multinational Firms. *Econ. J.*, March 1973, *83*(329), pp. 21–47.

Helleiner, Gerry. The Role of the Multinational Corporation: Comment. In *Hughes, H., ed.*, 1973, pp. 95–100.

Henley, Donald S. Multinational Marketing: Present Position and Future Challenges. In *Henley, D. S., ed.*, 1973, pp. 337–54. [G: U.S.]

Heyding, Lawrence F. Corporate Reorganizations ("Rollovers") in Canada. *Bull. Int. Fiscal Doc.*, September 1973, *27*(9), pp. 363–71. [G: Canada]

Hochmut, M. S. How Americans Manage Germans. In *Henley, D. S., ed.*, 1973, pp. 390–94. [G: U.S.; W. Germany]

Hoya, Thomas W. The Office of Foreign Direct In-

vestments and East-West Joint Ventures. In *Henley, D. S., ed.*, 1973, pp. 95–98. [G: U.S.]

Hymer, Stephen. Effects of Policies Encouraging Foreign Joint Ventures in Developing Countries: Comment. In *Ayal, E. B., ed.*, 1973, pp. 177–80.

Hymer, Stephen. The Multinational Corporation and Uneven Development. In *Andreano, R. L., ed.*, 1973, pp. R335–04.

Ikeda, Y. Distribution Innovation in Japan and the Role Played by General Trading Companies. In *Thorelli, H. B., ed.*, 1973, pp. 237–43. [G: Japan]

Inostroza, Alfonso. The World Bank and Imperialism. In *Wilber, C. K., ed.*, 1973, pp. 152–57. [G: Chile]

Jedel, Michael Jay and Stamm, John H. The Battle over Jobs: An Appraisal of Recent Publications on the Employment Effects of U.S. Multinational Corporations. In *Kujawa, D., ed.*, 1973, pp. 144–91. [G: U.S.]

Kapoor, Ashok. The Negotiation Era and the Multinational Enterprise. In *Fayerweather, J., ed.*, 1973, pp. 85–93.

Karageorgas, Dionysios. Taxation of Foreign Firms: Discriminative and Allocative Effects. *Public Finance Quart.*, July 1973, *1*(3), pp. 239–65.

Keegan, Warren J. Multinational Marketing Control. In *Alexandrides, C. G., ed.*, 1973, pp. 243–60.

Keegan, W. J. Headquarters Involvement in Multinational Marketing. In *Thorelli, H. B., ed.*, 1973, pp. 283–89.

Keegan, W. J. Five Strategies for Multinational Marketing. In *Thorelli, H. B., ed.*, 1973, pp. 195–203. [G: U.S.; W. Europe]

Keohane, Robert O. and Ooms, Van Doorn. The Multinational Enterprise and World Political Economy. In *Henley, D. S., ed.*, 1973, pp. 241–77. [G: U.S.]

Kindleberger, Charles P. Restrictions on Direct Investment in Host Countries. In *[Rosenstein-Rodan, P.]*, 1973, pp. 201–09.

Klein, Roger W. A Dynamic Theory of Comparative Advantage. *Amer. Econ. Rev.*, March 1973, *63*(1), pp. 173–84. [G: U.S.]

Kojima, Kiyoshi. A Macroeconomic Approach to Foreign Direct Investment. *Hitotsubashi J. Econ.*, June 1973, *14*(1), pp. 1–21. [G: U.S.; Japan]

Krainer, Robert E. The Valuation and Financing of the Multi-National Firm: Reply and Some Extensions. *Kyklos*, 1973, *26*(4), pp. 857–65.

Kraseman, Thomas W. and Barker, Betty L. Employment and Payroll Costs of U.S. Multinational Companies. *Surv. Curr. Bus.*, October 1973, *53*(10), pp. 36–44. [G: U.S.]

Kujawa, Duane. Foreign Sourcing Decisions and the Duty to Bargain under the NLRA. In *Kujawa, D., ed.*, 1973, pp. 223–69. [G: U.S.]

Lall, Sanjaya. Transfer-Pricing by Multinational Manufacturing Firms. *Oxford Bull. Econ. Statist.*, August 1973, *35*(3), pp. 173–95. [G: U.S.; U.K.; Colombia]

Lamont, Douglas F. Joining Forces with Foreign State Enterprises. *Harvard Bus. Rev.*, July-August 1973, *51*(4), pp. 68–79.

Ludlow, Nicholas. China Trade. In *Henley, D. S., ed.*,

1973, pp. 39–54. [G: U.S.; China]

Lupo, Leonard A. Worldwide Sales by U.S. Multinational Companies. *Surv. Curr. Bus.*, January 1973, *53*(1), pp. 33–39. [G: U.S.]

Maier, Heribert. The International Free Trade Union Movement and International Corporations. In *Kujawa, D., ed.*, 1973, pp. 8–27. [G: U.S.]

Malizia, Emil. Imperialism Reconsidered. *Rev. Radical Polit. Econ.*, Summer 1973, *5*(2), pp. 87–92.

Malysiak, James T. Toward a Substantive Private International Law of Trademarks: The Lessons of the *Carl Zeiss* Litigation. *Yale Law J.*, April 1973, *82*(5), pp. 1072–91.

Martyn, Howe. Multinational Corporations in a Nationalistic World. In *Andreano, R. L., ed.*, 1973, pp. R332–06.

Mason, R. Hal. The Multinational Firm and the Cost of Technology to Developing Countries. *Calif. Manage. Rev.*, Summer 1973, *15*(4), pp. 5–13. [G: Latin America; Europe; Canada]

Mason, R. Hal. Some Observations on the Choice of Technology by Multinational Firms in Developing Countries. *Rev. Econ. Statist.*, August 1973, *55* (3), pp. 349–55. [G: Mexico; Philippines; U.S.]

Miller, Robert R. and Weigel, Dale R. Factors Affecting Resource Transfer Through Direct Investment. In *Alexandrides, C. G., ed.*, 1973, pp. 129–44. [G: U.S.; Brazil]

Moyer, R. International Market Analysis. In *Thorelli, H. B., ed.*, 1973, pp. 162–79.

Müller, Ronald. The Multinational Corporation and the Underdevelopment of the Third World. In *Wilber, C. K., ed.*, 1973, pp. 124–51. [G: S. America]

Munsche, Richard C. International Competition and Tax Reform. In *Tax Foundation, Inc.*, 1973, pp. 59–64. [G: U.S.]

Noyes, Guy E. The Multinational Firm: Bane or Boon?: Discussion. *J. Finance*, May 1973, *28*(2), pp. 462–65.

O'Brien of Lothbury [Lord]. Le imprese multinazionali. (Multinational Enterprises. With English summary.) *Bancaria*, September 1973, *29*(9), pp. 1075–80.

Ogram, Ernest W., Jr. The Multinational Corporation in the Future. In *Alexandrides, C. G., ed.*, 1973, pp. 273–83.Ogren, Kenneth E. Exports of U.S. Capital and Technology and International Political Conflicts. In *Iowa State University Center for Agricultural and Rural Development*, 1973, pp. 210–24. [G: U.S.]

Papandreou, Andreas G. The Multinational Firm: Bane or Boon?: Discussion. *J. Finance*, May 1973, *28*(2), pp. 455–57. [G: Canada]

Papandreou, Andreas G. The Multinational Corporation. *Amer. Econ.*, Fall 1973, *17*(2), pp. 154–60. [G: U.S.]

Parry, Thomas G. The International Firm and National Economic Policy: A Survey of Some Issues. *Econ. J.*, December 1973, *83*(332), pp. 1201–21.

Penrose, Edith. International Patenting and the Less-Developed Countries. *Econ. J.*, September 1973, *83*(331), pp. 768–86.

Perlmutter, Howard V. Super-Giant Firms in the Future. In *Andreano, R. L., ed.*, 1973, pp. R336–07.

Philip, Kjeld. Nogle bemærkninger om kriterier for u-landsbistand. (With English summary.) *Nationalokon. Tidsskr.*, 1973, *111*(3), pp. 342–60.

Polk, Judd. The International Corporation. In *Andreano, R. L., ed.*, 1973, pp. R334–08. [G: U.S.]

Polk, Judd. American Labor and the U.S. Multinational Enterprise in an Emerging World Economy. In *Kujawa, D., ed.*, 1973, pp. 270–85. [G: U.S.]

Polk, Judd. International Perspectives on World Companies. In *Alexandrides, C. G., ed.*, 1973, pp. 261–71. [G: U.S.]

Polk, Judd. The New International Production. *World Devel.*, May 1973, *1*(5), pp. 15–20.

Prasad, S. Benjamin. Comparative Management Models: Structure and Research Potential. In *Alexandrides, C. G., ed.*, 1973, pp. 145–61.

Radhu, Ghulam M. Some Aspects of Direct Foreign Private Investment in Pakistan. *Pakistan Develop. Rev.*, Spring 1973, *12*(1), pp. 68–80. [G: Pakistan]

Radhu, Ghulam M. Transfer of Technical Know-How Through Multinational Corporations in Pakistan. *Pakistan Develop. Rev.*, Winter 1973, *12* (4), pp. 361–74. [G: Pakistan]

Ramsey, J. A. East-West Business Cooperation: The Twain Meet. In *Thorelli, H. B., ed.*, 1973, pp. 58–63. [G: E. Europe]

Ranuzzi de Bianchi, Paolo. Le società multinazionali e la bilancia dei pagamenti americana. (Multinational Companies and the American Balance of Payments. With English summary.) *Bancaria*, September 1973, *29*(9), pp. 1090–93.

Richard, Enrique P. Treatment of Royalties in Tax Conventions Between Developed and Developing Countries. *Bull. Int. Fiscal Doc.*, October 1973, *27*(10), pp. 407–14.

Robbins, Sidney M. and Stobaugh, Robert B. The Bent Measuring Stick for Foreign Subsidiaries. *Harvard Bus. Rev.*, September-October 1973, *51* (5), pp. 80–88.

Roberts, Paul Craig and Rabushka, Alvin. A Diagrammatic Exposition of an Economic Theory of Imperialism. *Public Choice*, Spring 1973, *14*, pp. 101–07.

Robinson, Derek. Trade Unions and Multinational Companies. In *Robinson, D.*, 1973, pp. 158–84.

Robinson, Richard D. From Multinational Corporation to World Government? In *Alexandrides, C. G., ed.*, 1973, pp. 285–93. [G: Japan; W. Europe; U.S.]

Robinson, Richard D. Beyond the Multinational Corporation. In *Fayerweather, J., ed.*, 1973, pp. 17–26. [G: U.S.]

Robinson, Richard D. The Engagement of Host Government Interests upon the Entry of Foreign Business. In *Fayerweather, J., ed.*, 1973, pp. 39–48.

Rosendale, Phyllis B. The Short-Run Pricing Policies of Some British Engineering Exporters. *Nat. Inst. Econ. Rev.*, August 1973, (65), pp. 44–51. [G: U.K.]

Rossitch, Eugene and Meckler, Jack M. Foreign Currency Exposure Control. *Manage. Account.*, July 1973, *55*(1), pp. 29–37.

Rutenberg, David P. Maneuvering Liquid Assets in a Multinational Company: Formulation and Deterministic Solution Procedures. In *Alexandrides, C. G., ed.,* 1973, pp. 109–28.

Ryans, J. K., Jr. Is It Too Soon to Put a Tiger in Every Tank? In *Thorelli, H. B., ed.,* 1973, pp. 227–36.

Safarian, A. E. Perspectives on Foreign Direct Investment from the Viewpoint of a Capital Receiving Country. *J. Finance,* May 1973, *28*(2), pp. 419–38. **[G: Canada]**

Salmi, Timo. Monikansallinen yritys tarkasteltuna matemaattisen optimointimallin avulla. (Some Aspects of Production and Profit Adjustment in the Multinational Firm. With English summary.) *Liiketaloudellinen Aikak.,* 1973, *22*(2), pp. 114–26.

Schmidt, Benicio Viero. Dependency and the Multinational Corporation. In *Bonilla, F. and Girling, R., eds.,* 1973, pp. 17–33. **[G: U.S.; Latin America]**

Schollhammer, Hans. Organization Structures of Multinational Corporations. In *Henley, D. S., ed.,* 1973, pp. 445–65. **[G: W. Germany; Switzerland; France; U.S.; U.K.]**

Schollhammer, Hans. Le strutture organizzative delle aziende multinazionali. (Organizational Structures of Multinational Companies. With English summary.) *Mondo Aperto,* October 1973, *27*(5), pp. 321–40.

Schultze, Charles L. The Economic Content of National Security Policy. *Foreign Aff.,* April 1973, *51* (3), pp. 522–40. **[G: U.S.]**

Schwendiman, John S. Strategic and Long Range Planning in the International Firm. In *Alexandrides, C. G., ed.,* 1973, pp. 173–84.

Sethi, S. Prakash and Holton, Richard H. Country Typologies for the Multinational Corporation: A New Basic Approach. *Calif. Manage. Rev.,* Spring 1973, *15*(3), pp. 105–18.

Severn, Alan K. The Financing of the Multi-National Firm: Comment. *Kyklos,* 1973, *26*(4), pp. 852–56.

Shapiro, Alan C. Optimal Inventory and Credit-Granting Strategies under Inflation and Devaluation. *J. Financial Quant. Anal.,* January 1973, *8* (1), pp. 37–46.

Shapiro, Alan C. Management Science Models for Multicurrency Cash Management. In *Alexandrides, C. G., ed.,* 1973, pp. 93–107.

Sharman, Ben. Multinational Corporations and Trade Unions. *Mon. Lab. Rev.,* August 1973, *96* (8), pp. 56–58.

Shulman, J. S. Transfer Pricing in the Multinational Firm. In *Thorelli, H. B., ed.,* 1973, pp. 312–22.

Sirota, David. The Multinational Corporation: Management Myths. In *Henley, D. S., ed.,* 1973, pp. 466–73.

Standing, Guy and Taira, Koji. Labor Market Effects of Multinational Enterprises in Latin America. *Nebr. J. Econ. Bus.,* Autumn 1973, *12*(4), pp. 103–17. **[G: Latin America]**

Stobaugh, Robert B., et al. U.S. Multinational Enterprises and the U.S. Economy. In *Kujawa, D., ed.,* 1973, pp. 82–126. **[G: U.S.]**

Stone, P. The Massive Market for Simplicity. In *Thorelli, H. B., ed.,* 1973, pp. 204–08. **[G: U.K.]**

Sunkel, Osvaldo. The Pattern of Latin American Dependence. In *Urquidi, V. L. and Thorp, R., eds.,* 1973, pp. 3–25. **[G: U.S.; Latin America]**

Sunkel, Osvaldo. Transnational Capitalism and National Disintegration in Latin America. *Soc. Econ. Stud.,* March 1973, *22*(1), pp. 132–76. **[G: Latin America]**

Thackray, John. International Banking: What's Behind Its Rage to Innovate? In *Henley, D. S., ed.,* 1973, pp. 433–41.

Thorelli, Hans B. International Marketing Strategy: Introduction. In *Thorelli, H. B., ed.,* 1973, pp. 11–19.

Thorelli, Hans B. International Marketing: An Ecologic View. In *Thorelli, H. B., ed.,* 1973, pp. 23–40.

Thorelli, Hans B. Simulating International Business Operations. In *Alexandrides, C. G., ed.,* 1973, pp. 1–4.

Tisdell, Clement A. The Australian Research Subsidy to Overseas Firms and Other Aspects of the Distribution of Research Grants. *Econ. Rec.,* June 1973, *49*(126), pp. 194–214. **[G: Australia]**

de la Torre, Jose, Jr.; Stobaugh, Robert B. and Telesio, Piero. U.S. Multinational Enterprises and Changes in the Skill Composition of U.S. Employment. In *Kujawa, D., ed.,* 1973, pp. 127–43. **[G: U.S.]**

Uri, Pierre. The Role of the Multinational Corporation. In *Hughes, H., ed.,* 1973, pp. 69–90.

Vernon, Raymond. A Program of Research on Foreign Direct Investment. In *Bergsten, C. F., ed.,* 1973, pp. 93–113.

Vernon, Raymond. U.S. Direct Investment in Canada: Consequences for the U.S. Economy. *J. Finance,* May 1973, *28*(2), pp. 407–17. **[G: Canada; U.S.]**

Vilas, Carlos M. Aspectos del desarrollo de las corporaciones multinacionales en Argentina. (Aspects of Multinational Corporations Development in Argentina. With English summary.) *Económica,* September-December 1973, *19*(3), pp. 331–68. **[G: Argentina]**

Weisskopf, Thomas E. Dependence and Imperialism in India. *Rev. Radical Polit. Econ.,* Spring 1973, *5*(1), pp. 53–96. **[G: India]**

Wells, Louis T., Jr. Effects of Policies Encouraging Foreign Joint Ventures in Developing Countries. In *Ayal, E. B., ed.,* 1973, pp. 149–77.

West, Robert LeRoy. Economic Dependence and Policy in Developing Countries. In *[Halm, G. N.],* 1973, pp. 157–83.

Widing, J. William, Jr. Reorganizing Your Worldwide Business. *Harvard Bus. Rev.,* May-June 1973, *51*(3), pp. 153–60.

Willmore, L. N. Direct Foreign Investment and Industrial Entrepreneurship in Central America. In *Pollock, D. H. and Ritter, A. R. M., eds.,* 1973, pp. 287–300. **[G: Central America]**

443 International Aid

4430 International Aid

Abbott, George C. Two Concepts of Foreign Aid. *World Devel.,* September 1973, *1*(9), pp. 1–10. **[G: U.S.; U.K.]**

Adler, John H. Development and Income Distribution. *Finance Develop.,* September 1973, *10*(3), pp. 2–5.

Adler, John H. The External Debt Problem. In *Lewis, J. P. and Kapur, I., eds.*, 1973, pp. 111–22.

Andersen, Stig. The World Bank and the United Nations: Comment. In *Lewis, J. P. and Kapur, I., eds.*, 1973, pp. 139–41.

Arndt, H. W. and Sundrum, R. M. Foreign Capital and Indonesian Economic Growth: A Comment. *Bull. Indonesian Econ. Stud.*, July 1973, *9*(2), pp. 90–95. [G: Indonesia]

Asher, Robert E. The Leopard's Spots. In *Lewis, J. P. and Kapur, I., eds.*, 1973, pp. 21–26.

Bagchi, Amiya Kumar. Foreign Capital and Economic Development in India: A Schematic View. In *Gough, K. and Sharma, H. P., eds.*, 1973, pp. 43–76. [G: India]

Bailey, Richard. European Community in a World Context. *Irish Banking Rev.*, June 1973, pp. 16–22. [G: W. Europe]

Bardhan, Pranab K. On Terms of Foreign Borrowing. *Amer. Econ. Rev.*, June 1973, *63*(3), pp. 458–61.

Bauer, Peter. Inflation, SDRs and AID. *Lloyds Bank Rev.*, July 1973, (109), pp. 31–35.

Bhattacharya, Debesh. Foreign Aid and Economic Development. *Econ. Aff.*, January–February 1973, *18*(1-2), pp. 41–53.

Botero, Rodrigo. Relations with the United States: A Latin American View. In *Urquidi, V. L. and Thorp, R., eds.*, 1973, pp. 283–303. [G: U.S.; Latin America]

Brecher, Michael. Images, Process and Feedback in Foreign Policy: Israel's Decision on German Reparations. *Amer. Polit. Sci. Rev.*, March 1973, *67*(1), pp. 73–102. [G: Israel; Germany]

Cargill, I. P. M. Efforts to Influence Recipient Performance: Case Study of India. In *Lewis, J. P. and Kapur, I., eds.*, 1973, pp. 89–95. [G: India]

Chenery, Hollis B. and Carter, Nicholas G. Foreign Assistance and Development Performance, 1960-1970. *Amer. Econ. Rev.*, May 1973, *63*(2), pp. 459–68.

Costa, E. The World Food Programme and Employment: Ten Years of Multilateral Food Aid for Development. *Int. Lab. Rev.*, March 1973, *107*(3), pp. 209–21.

Crouch, Robert L. Economic Development, Foreign Aid and Neoclassical Growth. *J. Devel. Stud.*, April 1973, *9*(3), pp. 353–64.

Decker, Robert L. The Saving Gap and Foreign Aid. *Intermountain Econ. Rev.*, Fall 1973, *4*(2), pp. 45–54.

Dell, Sidney. An Appraisal of UNCTAD III. *World Devel.*, May 1973, *1*(5), pp. 1–13.

Demuth, Richard H. Relations with Other Multilateral Agencies. In *Lewis, J. P. and Kapur, I., eds.*, 1973, pp. 133–38.

Despres, Emile. American Aid and Western European Recovery. In *Despres, E.*, 1973, pp. 28–38. [G: W. Europe]

Eichberg, Henning. "Entwicklungshilfe" Verhaltensumformung nach europäischem Modell? ("Assistance" for Underdeveloped Countries—Transformation of Behaviour According to Western Patterns? With English summary.) *Z. Wirtschaft. Sozialwissen.*, 1973, *93*(6), pp. 641–70.

Feldstein, Martin S. Cost-Benefit Analysis in Developing Countries: The Evaluation of Projects Financed by Aid and External Loans. In *[Hicks, U.]*, 1973, pp. 3–19.

Frank, Charles R., Jr. Debt Adjustment: The Tyranny of Bankers, Brokers, and Bondholders: Comment. In *Lewis, J. P. and Kapur, I., eds.*, 1973, pp. 123–30.

Fried, Edward R. Foreign Economic Policy: The Search for a Strategy. In *Owen, H., ed.*, 1973, pp. 157–202. [G: U.S.]

Gaud, William S. High Profile, Better Target: Comment. In *Lewis, J. P. and Kapur, I., eds.*, 1973, pp. 53–56.

van Geet, Dick. Netherlands Aid Performance and Development Policy. In *Dinwiddy, B., ed.*, 1973, pp. 73–87. [G: Netherlands]

Gordenker, Leon. International Economic Diplomacy: Comment. In *Lewis, J. P. and Kapur, I., eds.*, 1973, pp. 143–46.

Griffin, Keith. The Effect of Aid and Other Resource Transfers on Savings and Growth in Less-Developed Countries: A Comment. *Econ. J.*, September 1973, *83*(331), pp. 863–66.

Hallwood, C. P. The Impact of Foreign Aid Upon India's International Trade 1951-65. *Bull. Econ. Res.*, November 1973, *25*(2), pp. 129–45. [G: India]

ul Haq, Mahbub. The Transfer of Resources: Comment. In *Lewis, J. P. and Kapur, I., eds.*, 1973, pp. 83–87.

Harberger, Arnold C. Issues Concerning Capital Assistance to Less-Developed Countries. In *Harberger, A. C.*, 1973, pp. 311–23. [G: U.S.]

Healey, Derek T. Foreign Capital and Exports in Economic Development: The Experience of Eight Asian Countries. *Econ. Rec.*, September 1973, *49*(127), pp. 394–419.

Henderson, P. D. Terms and Flexibility of Bank Lending. In *Lewis, J. P. and Kapur, I., eds.*, 1973, pp. 65–76.

Hirschman, Albert O. The Organization and Functions of Foreign Aid: Reply. *Econ. Develop. Cult. Change*, Part I, July 1973, *21*(4), pp. 714–16.

Hoffman, Michael L. The Challenges of the 1970s and the Present Institutional Structure. In *Lewis, J. P. and Kapur, I., eds.*, 1973, pp. 13–19.

Howe, James W. and Hunter, Robert. United States Aid Performance and Development Policy. In *Dinwiddy, B., ed.*, 1973, pp. 57–72. [G: U.S.]

Hunter, Guy. Development—The Search for a New Strategy. In *Dinwiddy, B., ed.*, 1973, pp. 112–34.

Inostroza, Alfonso. The World Bank and Imperialism. In *Wilber, C. K., ed.*, 1973, pp. 152–57. [G: Chile]

Jaguaribe, Helio. Foreign Technical Assistance and National Development. In *Thurber, C. E. and Graham, L. S., eds.*, 1973, pp. 109–29.

Jha, L. K. Leaning Against Open Doors? Comment. In *Lewis, J. P. and Kapur, I., eds.*, 1973, pp. 97–101.

Kahn, Richard F. [Lord]. The International Monetary System. *Amer. Econ. Rev.*, May 1973, *63*(2), pp. 181–88.

Kahn, Richard F. [Lord]. SDRs and Aid. *Lloyds Bank Rev.*, October 1973, (110), pp. 1–18.

Kanet, Roger. Handbook of Soviet Social Science Data: International Interactions. In *Mickiewicz, E., ed.*, 1973, pp. 197–225.   [G: U.S.S.R.; C.M.E.A.]

Klein, Thomas M. Economic Aid Through Debt Relief. *Finance Develop.*, September 1973, *10*(3), pp. 17–20, 34–35.

Knapp, J. Burke. Determination of Priorities and the Allocation of Resources. In *Lewis, J. P. and Kapur, I., eds.*, 1973, pp. 37–51.

Kojima, Kiyoshi. Reorganisation of North-South Trade: Japan's Foreign Economic Policy for the 1970s. *Hitotsubashi J. Econ.*, February 1973, *13* (2), pp. 1–28.   [G: Japan]

Kokulinsky, Detlef and Park, Sung-Jo. Die Entwicklungshilfe als ein aussenpolitisches Instrument der Volksrepublik China. (Development Aid as Instrument of Foreign Policy of the People's Republic of China. With English summary.) *Z. ges. Staatswiss.*, August 1973, *129*(3), pp. 559–72.   [G: China]

König, Wolfgang. International Financial Institutions and Latin American Development. In *Urquidi, V. L. and Thorp, R., eds.*, 1973, pp. 116–63.   [G: Latin America]

Korka, Mihai. Evoluția comerțului invizibil al țărilor în curs de dezvoltare. (The Evolution of the Invisible Trade of the Developing Countries. With English summary.) *Stud. Cercet. Econ.*, 1973, (4), pp. 177–92.

Lewis, John P. and Kapur, Ishan. The World Bank Group, Multilateral Aid, and the 1970s. In *Lewis, J. P. and Kapur, I., eds.*, 1973, pp. 1–11.

Lewis, John P. Grants, Loans, and Local-Cost Financing: Comment. In *Lewis, J. P. and Kapur, I., eds.*, 1973, pp. 77–81.

Louis, R. Co-operative Development Centres. *Int. Lab. Rev.*, June 1973, *107*(6), pp. 539–51.

Mandich, Donald R. International Loans: Profit Center or Loss Leader. In *Henley, D. S., ed.*, 1973, pp. 420–32.   [G: U.S.; U.K.]

Maynard, Geoffrey. Special Drawing Rights and Development Aid. *J. Devel. Stud.*, July 1973, *9*(4), pp. 518–43.

Mohammed, Azizali F. and Saccomanni, Fabrizio. Short-Term Banking and Euro-Currency Credits to Developing Countries. *Int. Monet. Fund Staff Pap.*, November 1973, *20*(3), pp. 612–38.

Montrie, Charles. The Organization and Functions of Foreign Aid. *Econ. Develop. Cult. Change*, Part I, July 1973, *21*(4), pp. 697–713.

Murray, Tracy. E.E.C. Enlargement and Preference for the Developing Countries. *Econ. J.*, September 1973, *83*(331), pp. 853–57.

Murray, Tracy. Preferential Tariffs for the LDCs. *Southern Econ. J.*, July 1973, *40*(1), pp. 35–46.

Mytelka, Lynn Krieger. Foreign Aid and Regional Integration: The UDEAC Case. *J. Common Market Stud.*, December 1973, *12*(2), pp. 138–58.   [G: Africa]

Newlyn, Walter T. The Effect of Aid and Other Resource Transfers on Savings and Growth in Less-Developed Countries: A Comment. *Econ. J.*, September 1973, *83*(331), pp. 867–69.

Ng, Yew-Kwang. Optimal Terms of Foreign Assistance: Comment. *J. Polit. Econ.*, Part I, March-April 1973, *81*(2), pp. 488–90.

Ohman, Carl I. An Integrated Radicalism: Comment. In *Lewis, J. P. and Kapur, I., eds.*, 1973, pp. 27–34.

Okita, Saburo. Possible Modifications in Development Aid Policy. In *Berg, A.; Scrimshaw, N. S. and Call, D. L., eds.*, 1973, pp. 207–09.

Pandit, Shrikrishna A. IMF Resident Representatives. *Finance Develop.*, September 1973, *10*(3), pp. 30–33.

Papanek, Gustav F. Aid, Foreign Private Investment, Savings, and Growth in Less Developed Countries. *J. Polit. Econ.*, January-February 1973, *81*(1), pp. 120–30.

Papanek, Gustav F. The Effect of Aid and Other Resource Transfers on Savings and Growth in Less-Developed Countries: A Reply. *Econ. J.*, September 1973, *83*(331), pp. 870–74.

Petersen, Gustav H. Latin America: Benign Neglect Is Not Enough. *Foreign Aff.*, April 1973, *51*(3), pp. 598–607.   [G: U.S.; Latin America]

Polasek, M. IMF Special Drawing Rights and Economic Aid to Less Developed Countries. *Econ. Rec.*, September 1973, *49*(127), pp. 358–76.

Reid, Escott. McNamara's World Bank. *Foreign Aff.*, July 1973, *51*(4), pp. 794–810.

Richardson, Richard W. The Raising of Resources: Comment. In *Lewis, J. P. and Kapur, I., eds.*, 1973, pp. 57–63.   [G: U.S.]

Ripman, Hugh B. Project Supervision. *Finance Develop.*, June 1973, *10*(2), pp. 14–18.

Rogers, Christopher D. Gli accordi internazionali per le materie prime. (The International Agreements on Raw Materials. With English summary.) *Mondo Aperto*, December 1973, *27*(6), pp. 415–28.

Rogers, Christopher D. International Commodity Agreements. *Lloyds Bank Rev.*, April 1973, (108), pp. 33–47.

Sankaran, Sundaram. Population and the World Bank. *Finance Develop.*, December 1973, *10*(4), pp. 18–21, 41.

Schaeffer, Maurice. The European Economic Community and Latin American Development. In *Urquidi, V. L. and Thorp, R., eds.*, 1973, pp. 313–30.   [G: E.E.C.; Latin America]

Schmitt, Hans O. Development and Assistance: The View from Bretton Woods. *Public Policy*, Fall 1973, *21*(4), pp. 585–600.   [G: U.S.]

Secchi, Carlo. Il rinnovo della associazione tra la CEE e i SAMA e le tendenze della politica comunitaria verso i paesi sottosviluppati. (The Renewal of the Association Between the EEC and the AASM and the Prospects of the Community Policy Towards Underdeveloped Countries. With English summary.) *Rivista Int. Sci. Econ. Com.*, November 1973, *20*(11), pp. 1081–1108.   [G: E.E.C.; Africa]

Sharma, R. K. Grant Element in External Assistance to India. *Indian Econ. J.*, October–December 1973, *21*(2), pp. 124–31.   [G: India]

Shivnan, Martin. The Bank Group Meeting. *Finance Develop.*, December 1973, *10*(4), pp. 34–37.

Stoner, James A. F. and Aram, John D. Effectiveness of Two Technical Assistance Efforts in Differing

Environments. *J. Devel. Stud.,* July 1973, *9*(4), pp. 508–17.

Strout, Alan M. Foreign Capital and Indonesian Economic Growth: A Reply. *Bull. Indonesian Econ. Stud.,* July 1973, *9*(2), pp. 96–99. **[G: Indonesia]**

Strout, Alan M. Foreign Capital and Indonesian Economic Growth. *Bull. Indonesian Econ. Stud.,* July 1973, *9*(2), pp. 77–90. **[G: Indonesia]**

Tulloch, Peter. Developing Countries and the Enlargement of the EEC. In *Dinwiddy, B., ed.,* 1973, pp. 88–111. **[G: E.E.C.]**

de Vries, Barend A. The Plight of Small Countries. *Finance Develop.,* September 1973, *10*(3), pp. 6–8, 34.

Weisskopf, Thomas E. Dependence and Imperialism in India. *Rev. Radical Polit. Econ.,* Spring 1973, *5*(1), pp. 53–96. **[G: India]**

Williams, Maurice J. A Bilateral Viewpoint: Comment. In *Lewis, J. P. and Kapur, I., eds.,* 1973, pp. 103–08. **[G: India]**

Wittkopf, Eugene R. Foreign Aid and United Nations Votes: A Comparative Study. *Amer. Polit. Sci. Rev.,* September 1973, *67*(3), pp. 868–88.

500 Administration; Business Finance; Marketing; Accounting

510 ADMINISTRATION

511 Organization and Decision Theory

5110 Organization and Decision Theory

Ackoff, Russell L. The Nature and Content of Planning. In *Klein, W. H. and Murphy, D. C., eds.,* 1973, pp. 202–23.

Allen, Louis A. Who Speaks Management? *Calif. Manage. Rev.,* Summer 1973, *15*(4), pp. 22–27.

Allison, Graham T. Organizational and Administrative Factors Affecting Shifts in Defense Expenditures. In *Udis, B., ed.,* 1973, pp. 289–35. **[G: U.S.]**

Anshen, Melvin and Guth, William D. Strategies for Research in Policy Formulation. *J. Bus.,* October 1973, *46*(4), pp. 499–511.

Ansoff, H. Igor and Hayes, Robert L. Roles of Models in Corporate Decision Making. In *Ross, M., ed.,* 1973, pp. 131–62.

Anthony, Robert N. Characteristics of Management Control Systems. In *Thomas, W. E., Jr., ed.,* 1973, pp. 27–42.

Aubin, Jean-Pierre. Multi-Games and Decentralization in Management. In *Cochrane, J. L. and Zeleny, M., eds.,* 1973, pp. 313–26.

Bienaymé, Alain. Les processus de croissance des entreprises sont-ils déterminés ou indéterminés? (Why Growth Rates of Business Firms Differ? With English summary.) *Revue Écon.,* March 1973, *24*(2), pp. 216–34.

Boehlje, Michael. Optimization and Decision Models: The Use of Statistical Search Procedures. *Can. J. Agr. Econ.,* July 1973, *21*(2), pp. 43–53.

Boulding, Kenneth E. Intersects: The Peculiar Or-

ganizations. In *The Conference Board,* 1973, pp. 179–201. **[G: U.S.]**

Boulding, Kenneth E. The Ethnics of Rational Decision. In *Haynes, W. W.; Coyne, T. J. and Osborne, D. K., eds.,* 1973, pp. 8–17.

Brough, B. M. Information Systems for Decision and Control: Discussant 1. In *Ross, M., ed.,* 1973, pp. 183–84.

Burke, Ronald J. Effects of Organizational Experience on Managerial Attitudes and Beliefs: A Better Press for Managers. *J. Bus. Res.,* Summer 1973, *1*(1), pp. 21–30.

Burns, Tom and Meeker, L. D. A Mathematical Model of Multi-Dimensional Evaluation, Decision-Making, and Social Interaction. In *Cochrane, J. L. and Zeleny, M., eds.,* 1973, pp. 141–63.

Calkins, Robert D. The Decision Process in Administration. In *Thomas, W. E., Jr., ed.,* 1973, pp. 142–50.

Caplan, Edwin H. Behavioral Assumptions of Management Accounting. In *Thomas, W. E., Jr., ed.,* 1973, pp. 76–96.

de Carbonnel, Francois E. and Dorrance, Roy G. Information Sources for Planning Decisions. *Calif. Manage. Rev.,* Summer 1973, *15*(4), pp. 42–53.

Carlson, C. E. Om företagsekonomiska beslut. (Decision in Business Economics. With English summary.) *Ekon. Samfundets Tidskr.,* January 1973, *26*(1), pp. 21–31.

Clifford, Donald K., Jr. Growth Pains of the Threshold Company. *Harvard Bus. Rev.,* September-October 1973, *51*(5), pp. 143–54. **[G: U.S.]**

Cohen, Kalman J. and Cyert, Richard M. Strategy: Formulation, Implementation, and Monitoring. *J. Bus.,* July 1973, *46*(3), pp. 349–67.

Collins, David C. Applications of Multiple Criterial Evaluation to Decision Aiding. In *Cochrane, J. L. and Zeleny, M., eds.,* 1973, pp. 477–505. **[G: U.S.]**

Crawford, Robert G. Implications of Learning for Economic Models of Uncertainty. *Int. Econ. Rev.,* October 1973, *14*(3), pp. 587–600.

Davis, B. E.; Caccappolo, G. J. and Chaudry, M. A. An Econometric Planning Model for American Telephone and Telegraph Company. *Bell J. Econ. Manage. Sci.,* Spring 1973, *4*(1), pp. 29–56. **[G: U.S.]**

Dinkelbach, Werner and Isermann, Heinz. On Decision Making under Multiple Criteria and under Incomplete Information. In *Cochrane, J. L. and Zeleny, M., eds.,* 1973, pp. 302–12.

Donovan, J. F. Information Systems for Decision and Control: Discussant 2. In *Ross, M., ed.,* 1973, pp. 185–88.

Dorcey, Anthony H. J. Effluent Charges, Information Generation and Bargaining Behavior. *Natural Res. J.,* January 1973, *13*(1), pp. 118–33.

Drinkwater, David A. Management Theory and the Budgeting Process. *Manage. Account.,* June 1973, *54*(12), pp. 15–17.

Dyer, James S. An Empirical Investigation of a Man-Machine Interactive Approach to the Solution of the Multiple Criteria Problem. In *Cochrane, J. L. and Zeleny, M., eds.,* 1973, pp. 202–16.

Easton, Allan. One-of-a-Kind Decisions Involving

Weighted Multiple Objectives and Disparate Alternatives. In *Cochrane, J. L. and Zeleny, M., eds.*, 1973, pp. 657–67.

Ebert, Ronald J. and Piehl, DeWayne. Time Horizon: A Concept for Management. *Calif. Manage. Rev.*, Summer 1973, *15*(4), pp. 35–41.

Etzioni, Amitai. Societal Turnability: A Theoretical Treatment. In *Udis, B., ed.*, 1973, pp. 337–80. [G: U.S.]

Farris, George F.; Senner, Eldon E. and Butterfield, D. Anthony. Trust, Culture, and Organizational Behavior. *Ind. Relat.*, May 1973, *12*(2), pp. 144–57.

Fazel, Hassan. Optimization and Decision Models. *Can. J. Agr. Econ.*, July 1973, *21*(2), pp. 54–58.

Foss, Laurence. Managerial Strategy for the Future: Theory Z Management. *Calif. Manage. Rev.*, Spring 1973, *15*(3), pp. 68–81.

Fox, Irving K. and Wible, Lyman. Information Generation and Communication to Establish Environmental Quality Objectives. *Natural Res. J.*, January 1973, *13*(1), pp. 134–49. [G: U.S.]

Gregory, K. and Russell, C. SIMPREP, A Computer Model for Coal Preparation. In *Ross, M., ed.*, 1973, pp. 379–89. [G: U.K.]

Gross, Bertram M. What Are Your Organization's Objectives? A General-Systems Approach to Planning. In *Klein, W. H. and Murphy, D. C., eds.*, 1973, pp. 106–29.

Groves, Theodore. Incentives in Teams. *Econometrica*, July 1973, *41*(4), pp. 617–31.

Guthrie, Art. Middle Managers and MIS: An Attitude Survey. *J. Econ. Bus.*, Fall 1973, *26*(1), pp. 58–66.

Hampton, J. M.; Moore, P. G. and Thomas, H. Subjective Probability and Its Measurement. *J. Roy. Statist. Soc.*, Part 1, 1973, *136*, pp. 21–42.

Heller, Frank A. Leadership, Decision Making, and Contingency Theory. *Ind. Relat.*, May 1973, *12* (2), pp. 183–99. [G: S. America]

Helman, Amir and Shechter, Mordechai. Collective Decision-Making in a Kibbutz: A Case Study. *Public Finance*, 1973, *28*(2), pp. 139–50. [G: Israel]

Helmer, Jean-Yves. Essai sur la croissance de l'entreprise. (Essay on Firm Growth. With English summary.) *Revue Écon.*, March 1973, *24*(2), pp. 235–72.

Hertz, David B. Planning under Uncertainty. In *Ross, M., ed.*, 1973, pp. 103–22.

Hindman, William R. and Kettering, Floyd F., Jr. Integrated MIS: A Case Study. *Manage. Account.*, August 1973, *55*(2), pp. 20–27.

Hull, J.; Moore, P. G. and Thomas, H. Utility and its Measurement. *J. Roy. Statist. Soc.*, Part 2, 1973, *136*, pp. 226–47.

Hurst, David B. Constructing an Adaptive Strategy for a National Newspaper. In *Ross, M., ed.*, 1973, pp. 275–89. [G: U.K.]

Ijiri, Yuji. A Historical Cost Approach to Aggregation of Multiple Goals. In *Cochrane, J. L. and Zeleny, M., eds.*, 1973, pp. 395–405.

Ingram, Helen M. Information Channels and Environmental Decision Making. *Natural Res. J.*, January 1973, *13*(1), pp. 150–69.

Jain, Tribhowan N. Alternative Methods of Accounting and Decision Making: A Psycho-linguistical Analysis. *Accounting Rev.*, January 1973, *48*(1), pp. 95–104.

Johnsen, Erik. Behavioral Science Models: Discussant 1. In *Ross, M., ed.*, 1973, pp. 265–67.

Johnson, Herbert E. Strategic Planning for Banks. *J. Bank Res.*, Summer 1973, *4*(2), pp. 79–83.

Kall, Peter. Planning under Uncertainty: Discussant 1. In *Ross, M., ed.*, 1973, pp. 123–26.

Kazmann, Raphael G. Democratic Organization: A Preliminary Mathematical Model. *Public Choice*, Fall 1973, *16*, pp. 17–26.

Kerr, Steven. Ability- and Willingness-to-Leave as Moderators of Relationships Between Task and Leader Variables and Satisfaction. *J. Bus. Res.*, Fall 1973, *1*(2), pp. 115–28.

Klein, Walter H. and Murphy, David C. Policy: Concepts in Organizational Guidance: Introduction. In *Klein, W. H. and Murphy, D. C., eds.*, 1973, pp. 1–12.

Koopman, Bernard Osgood. Recent US Advances in OR Theory. In *Ross, M., ed.*, 1973, pp. 561–70. [G: U.S.]

Krishnamoorthy, M. and Sudarsana Rao, J. Some Characteristics of Project Duration for a Class of Stochastic Activity Networks. In *Ross, M., ed.*, 1973, pp. 509–18.

Krouse, Clement G. Experimental Decision-Making in the Theory of the Firm. In *Weston, J. F. and Ornstein, S. I., eds.*, 1973, pp. 129–38.

Kroužek, Jan. Průmyslová dynamika—systémová disciplína zaměřená na komplexní zkoumáni dynamického chování systémů. (Industrial Dynamics—An Experimental Method for Study of Behaviour of Management Control Systems. With English summary.) *Ekon.-Mat. Obzor*, 1973, *9*(2), pp. 184–200.

Lea, Richard B. Comments on Mock's Concepts of Information Value. *Accounting Rev.*, April 1973, *48*(2), pp. 389–93.

de Leeuw, C. G. OR Aspects of a Management Information System. In *Ross, M., ed.*, 1973, pp. 465–74.

Levine, Kenneth C. Corporate Modeling of a Life Insurance Company: A Developmental Game Plan. *J. Risk Ins.*, December 1973, *40*(4), pp. 555–64.

Liao, Shu S. Responsibility Centers. *Manage. Account.*, July 1973, *55*(1), pp. 46–48.

Lindström, Caj-Gunnar. Om beslutsplanering. (Decision Planning. With English summary.) *Ekon. Samfundets Tidskr.*, January 1973, *26*(1), pp. 32–38.

Long, Robert H. Planning for Tomorrow's Customer. *J. Bank Res.*, Summer 1973, *4*(2), pp. 93–99.

Lord, William B. and Warner, Maurice L. Aggregates and Externalities: Information Needs for Public Natural Resource Decision-Making. *Natural Res. J.*, January 1973, *13*(1), pp. 106–17.

Lundstedt, Sven. Using Information Theory in Administrative Systems. *Ohio State U. Bull. Bus. Res.*, February 1973, *48*(2), pp. 1–3, 6–7.

MacCrimmon, Kenneth R. An Overview of Multiple Objective Decision Making. In *Cochrane, J. L. and Zeleny, M., eds.*, 1973, pp. 18–44.

Martin, Donald L. Legal Constraints and the Choice of Organizational Form. *Amer. Econ. Rev.*, May

1973, *63*(2), pp. 326–34.   [G: Netherlands]

Mascarenhas, R. C. A Conceptual Framework for Understanding Autonomy for Public Enterprises in India. In *Henley, D. S., ed.,* 1973, pp. 395–405.   [G: India]

Massy, William F. Issues in the Development of Information Systems. In *Britt, S. H. and Boyd, H. W., Jr., eds.,* 1973, pp. 647–55.

Mehr, Robert I. and Forbes, Stephen W. The Risk Management Decision in the Total Business Setting. *J. Risk Ins.,* September 1973, *40*(3), pp. 389–401.

Meisel, William S. Tradeoff Decisions in Multiple Criteria Decision Making. In *Cochrane, J. L. and Zeleny, M., eds.,* 1973, pp. 461–76.

Melman, Seymour. Industrial Efficiency under Managerial vs. Cooperative Decision-Making: A Comparative Study of Manufacturing Enterprises in Israel. In *Wilber, C. K., ed.,* 1973, pp. 240–57.   [G: Israel]

Minnehan, Robert F. Multiple Objectives and Multigroup Decision Making in Physical Design Situations. In *Cochrane, J. L. and Zeleny, M., eds.,* 1973, pp. 506–16.   [G: U.S.]

Mintzberg, Henry. Strategy-Making in Three Modes. *Calif. Manage. Rev.,* Winter 1973, *16*(2), pp. 44–53.

Moag, Joseph M. Strategic Planning in Banks—A Behavioral Science Perspective. *J. Bank Res.,* Summer 1973, *4*(2), pp. 84–92.

Mock, Theodore J. Concepts of Information Value and Accounting: A Reply. *Accounting Rev.,* April 1973, *48*(2), pp. 394–97.

Mock, Theodore J. The Value of Budget Information. *Accounting Rev.,* July 1973, *48*(3), pp. 520–34.   [G: U.S.]

Mockler, Robert J. The Systems Approach to Business Organization and Decision Making. In *Klein, W. H. and Murphy, D. C., eds.,* 1973, pp. 28–33.

Mohr, Lawrence B. The Concept of Organizational Goal. *Amer. Polit. Sci. Rev.,* June 1973, *67*(2), pp. 470–81.

Mott, Charles H. Forecast Disclosure. *Manage. Account.,* July 1973, *55*(1), pp. 17–18, 28.

Müller-Merbach, Heiner. Operational Research '72: Summing Up. In *Ross, M., ed.,* 1973, pp. 713–18.

Neuberger, Egon and James, Estelle. The Yugoslav Self-Managed Enterprise: A Systemic Approach. In *Bornstein, M., ed.,* 1973, pp. 245–84.   [G: Yugoslavia]

Nichols, Charles and Wittman, Donald A. Cheating and Control. *Public Choice,* Spring 1973, *14,* pp. 137–42.

Palda, Kristian S. Production Functions and Performance Evaluation. In *Palda, K. S., ed.,* 1973, pp. 34–42.

Palmerio, Giovanni. Contributo alla teoria dello sviluppo dell'impresa. (A Contribution to the Theory of the Growth of the Firm. With English summary.) *L'Industria,* January–June 1973, (1–2), pp. 59–88.

Pauly, Mark V. Public Utilities and the Theory of Power: Comment. In *Russell, M., ed.,* 1973, pp. 27–33.

Pfeiffer, W. and Staudt, E. The Integration of Technological Prediction into Management Systems by Improvement of Forecasting Analysis. In *Blohm, H. and Steinbuch, K., eds.,* 1973, pp. 105–14.

Pierre, Joseph C. La gestion des ressources humaines: une approche intégrée et prévisionnelle. (The Management of Human Resources: An Integrated and Planned Approach. With English summary.) *Ann. Sci. Écon. Appl.,* 1973–1974, (1), pp. 17–45.

Pintilie, C. Concepte de bază ale ştiinţei conducerii societăţii socialiste, a ramurilor şi unităţilor lor componente. (Basic Concepts of the Science of Management of the Socialist Society, of their Component Branches and Units. With English summary.) *Stud. Cercet. Econ.,* 1973, (2), pp. 73–87.

Pittman, Clarence R. Organizational Behavior and the Management Accountant. *Manage. Account.,* July 1973, *55*(1), pp. 25–28.

Roberts, Karlene H. A Symposium: Cross-national Organizational Research: Overview. *Ind. Relat.,* May 1973, *12*(2), pp. 137–43.

di Roccaferrera, Giuseppe M. Ferrero. Behavioral Aspects of Decision Making Under Multiple Goals. In *Cochrane, J. L. and Zeleny, M., eds.,* 1973, pp. 635–56.

Ross, Miceal. Systems and Management: A Review. *Econ. Soc. Rev.,* April 1973, *4*(3), pp. 365–94.

Rowe, A. J. and Bahr, F. R. A Heuristic Approach to Managerial Problem Solving. *J. Econ. Bus.,* Spring–Summer 1973, *25*(3), pp. 159–63.

Roy, Bernard. How Outranking Relation Helps Multiple Criteria Decision Making. In *Cochrane, J. L. and Zeleny, M., eds.,* 1973, pp. 179–201.

Ruefli, Timothy W. Linked Multi-Criteria Decision Models. In *Cochrane, J. L. and Zeleny, M., eds.,* 1973, pp. 406–15.

Ruh, Robert A.; Wallace, Roger L. and Frost, Carl F. Management Attitudes and the Scanlon Plan. *Ind. Relat.,* October 1973, *12*(3), pp. 282–88.

Rychlewski, Eugeniusz. The Investment System of a Socialist Economy. *Eastern Europ. Econ.,* Fall 1973, *12*(1), pp. 3–44.   [G: Poland]

Samuels, Warren J. Public Utilities and the Theory of Power. In *Russell, M., ed.,* 1973, pp. 1–27.

Schollhammer, Hans. Organization Structures of Multinational Corporations. In *Henley, D. S., ed.,* 1973, pp. 445–65.   [G: W. Germany; Switzerland; France; U.S.; U.K.]

Schollhammer, Hans. Le strutture organizzative delle aziende multinazionali. (Organizational Structures of Multinational Companies. With English summary.) *Mondo Aperto,* October 1973, *27*(5), pp. 321–40.

Scholl, Robert. Managing the Scientific Mind. *Manage. Account.,* September 1973, *55*(3), pp. 48–50.

Schonberger, Richard J. A Taxonomy of Systems Management. *Nebr. J. Econ. Bus.,* Spring 1973, *12*(2), pp. 35–44.

Schonberger, Richard J. Management Information Systems in Insurance: Comment. *J. Risk Ins.,* June 1973, *40*(2), pp. 294–96.

Schwartz, Lawrence E. Uncertainty Reduction Over Time in the Theory of Multiattributed Utility. In *Cochrane, J. L. and Zeleny, M., eds.,* 1973, pp. 108–23.

Shamin, A.; Dubinkin, V. and Smirtiukov, V. Structural Analysis of the Network of Scientific Organizations. *Prob. Econ.*, December 1973, *16*(8), pp. 44–55.

Shank, John K. Long Range Planning Systems: Achieving Both "Realism" and "Reach." *J. Bank Res.*, Autumn 1973, *4*(3), pp. 185–93.

Shell, Richard L. and Stelzer, David F. Systems Analysis: Aid to Decision Making. In *Klein, W. H. and Murphy, D. C., eds.*, 1973, pp. 34–39.

Shocker, Allan D. and Sethi, S. Prakash. An Approach to Incorporating Societal Preferences in Developing Corporate Action Strategies. *Calif. Manage. Rev.*, Summer 1973, *15*(4), pp. 97–105.

Sollenberger, Harold and Arens, Alvin A. Assessing Information Systems Projects. *Manage. Account.*, September 1973, *55*(3), pp. 37–42.

Şovei, George. Sistem informaţional bancar modern. (A Modern Banking Informational System. With English summary.) *Stud. Cercet. Econ.*, 1973, (4), pp. 127–40.

Steiner, Gary A. The Creative Organization. In *Britt, S. H. and Boyd, H. W., Jr., eds.*, 1973, pp. 45–60.

Stern, Louis W.; Sternthal, Brian and Craig, C. Samuel. Managing Conflict in Distribution Channels: A Laboratory Study. *J. Marketing Res.*, May 1973, *10*(2), pp. 169–79.

Straus, Alexis K. Role of Models in Corporate Decision Making: Discussant 2. In *Ross, M., ed.*, 1973, pp. 167–69.

Stringer, John. Behavioral Science Models. In *Ross, M., ed.*, 1973, pp. 253–63.

Suzumura, Kotaro. The Economic Theory of Organization and Planning: A Review Article. *Econ. Stud. Quart.*, April 1973, *24*(1), pp. 33–51.

Szeplaki, Leslie. Elements of Risk and Information in Business Decisions: Principles and Methodology. *Rivista Int. Sci. Econ. Com.*, April 1973, *20* (4), pp. 358–70.

Teodorescu, N. Mathematical Modelling of Cybernetic Systems. In *Hawkes, N., ed.*, 1973, pp. 182–94.

Thirlby, G. F. The Economist's Description of Business Behaviour. In *Buchanan, J. M. and Thirlby, G. F., eds.*, 1973, pp. 201–24.

Tobin, Norman. Planning under Uncertainty: Discussant 2. In *Ross, M., ed.*, 1973, pp. 127–29.

Verbist, Daniel. La gestion prévisionnelle des ressources humaines. (The Planning and Forecasting of Human Resources. With English summary.) *Ann. Sci. Écon. Appl.*, 1973–1974, (1), pp. 81–104.

Vesper, Karl H. and Sayeki, Yutaka. A Quantitative Approach for Policy Analysis. *Calif. Manage. Rev.*, Spring 1973, *15*(3), pp. 119–26.

Vlček, Jaroslav. K teorii informačních systémů. (On a Theory of Information Systems. With English summary.) *Ekon.-Mat. Obzor*, 1973, *9*(4), pp. 361–80.

Webster, Frederick E., Jr. Does Business Misunderstand Consumerism? *Harvard Bus. Rev.*, September-October 1973, *51*(5), pp. 89–97.

Wedekind, H. Information Systems for Decision and Control. In *Ross, M., ed.*, 1973, pp. 171–82.

Weston, J. Fred. Pricing Behavior of Large Firms. In *Weston, J. F. and Ornstein, S. I., eds.*, 1973, pp. 143–55.

Williamson, Oliver E. Markets and Hierarchies: Some Elementary Considerations. *Amer. Econ. Rev.*, May 1973, *63*(2), pp. 316–25.

Wotruba, Thomas R. and Breeden, Joseph S. The Ideal Company Image and Self-Image Congruence. *J. Bus. Res.*, Fall 1973, *1*(2), pp. 165–72.

Young, A. Behavioral Science Models: Discussant 2. In *Ross, M., ed.*, 1973, pp. 269–72.

Young, Stanley. Organization as a Total System. In *Klein, W. H. and Murphy, D. C., eds.*, 1973, pp. 16–27.

Zadeh, Lotfi, A. Outline of a New Approach to the Analysis of Complex Systems and Decision Processes. In *Cochrane, J. L. and Zeleny, M., eds.*, 1973, pp. 686–725.

Zannetos, Zenon S. Some Thoughts on Internal Control Systems of the Firm. In *Thomas, W. E., Jr., ed.*, 1973, pp. 2–15.

Zwick, Charles J. Strategic Planning and its Role in the Banking Environment of the Seventies. *J. Bank Res.*, Summer 1973, *4*(2), pp. 74–78.

512 Managerial Economics

5120 Managerial Economics

Ackoff, Russell L. The Nature and Content of Planning. In *Klein, W. H. and Murphy, D. C., eds.*, 1973, pp. 202–23.

Aldrich, Carole A. and Morton, Thomas E. A Note on Bayesian Modification of the Failure Rate Function. *J. Amer. Statist. Assoc.*, June 1973, *68* (342), pp. 483–84.

Bellas, Carl J. and Samli, A. Coskun. Improving New Product Planning with GERT Simulation. *Calif. Manage. Rev.*, Summer 1973, *15*(4), pp. 14–21.

Boyd, John H. Bank Strategies in the Retail Demand Deposit Markets. *J. Bank Res.*, Summer 1973, *4* (2), pp. 111–21.

Brans, J. P.; Leclercq, M. and Hansen, P. An Algorithm for Optimal Reloading of Pressurized Water Reactors. In *Ross, M., ed.*, 1973, pp. 417–28.

Briskin, Lawrence E. Establishing a Generalized Multi-Attribute Utility Function. In *Cochrane, J. L. and Zeleny, M., eds.*, 1973, pp. 236–45.

Buchan, Joseph F. Why Scientific Inventory Management Has Proved Useful. In *Thomas, W. E., Jr., ed.*, 1973, pp. 392–400.

Burt, David N. Stretching Your Building Dollar. *Calif. Manage. Rev.*, Summer 1973, *15*(4), pp. 54–60.

Carter, E. Eugene. A Simultaneous Equation Approach to Financial Planning: Comment. *J. Finance*, September 1973, *28*(4), pp. 1035–38.

Čepelák, Vladimír. Simulační model železniční vlečky. (Simulation Model of a Railway Siding. With English summary.) *Ekon.-Mat. Obzor*, 1973, *9*(4), pp. 450–57.

Chasteen, Lanny G. Implicit Factors in the Evaluation of Lease vs. Buy Alternatives. *Accounting Rev.*, October 1973, *48*(4), pp. 764–67.

Chobot, Michal. Stochasticky prístup k cieľovému programovaniu. (Stochastic Approaches to Goal Programming. With English summary.) *Ekon.-Mat. Obzor*, 1973, *9*(3), pp. 305–19.

Coates, Robert and Updegraff, David E. The Relationship between Organizational Size and the Administrative Component of Banks. *J. Bus.,* October 1973, *46*(4), pp. 576–88. [G: U.S.]

Collier, Roger J. Simulation of Computer Systems: An Introduction. *Manage. Account.,* May 1973, *54* (11), pp. 45–47.

Conley, Patrick. Experience Curves as a Planning Tool. In *Britt, S. H. and Boyd, H. W., Jr., eds.,* 1973, pp. 257–68.

Cotter, Richard V. A General Model for Accounts-Receivable Analysis and Control: Comment. *J. Financial Quant. Anal.,* March 1973, *8*(2), pp. 219–21.

Cramer, Robert H. and Miller, Robert B. Development of a Deposit Forecasting Procedure for Use in Bank Financial Management. *J. Bank Res.,* Summer 1973, *4*(2), pp. 122–38.

Crowston, Wallace B. and Kleindorfer, Paul R. Coordinating Multi-Project Networks. In *Cochrane, J. L. and Zeleny, M., eds.,* 1973, pp. 668–85.

Cyert, Richard M. Managerial Personnel Considerations. In *The Diebold Group, Inc.,* 1973, pp. 103–10.

Davis, Mark W. Cash Flow Analysis for Feedlot Operations. *Manage. Account.,* June 1973, *54*(12), pp. 38–41.

Dearden, John. The Impact of Computers on Corporation Management. In *The Diebold Group, Inc.,* 1973, pp. 11–18.

Douglas, Patricia P. Finance and Investment: Refereed Papers I: Discussion. *J. Finance,* May 1973, *28* (2), pp. 405–06. [G: U.S.]

Drucker, Peter F. Information as a Management Resource. In *The Diebold Group, Inc.,* 1973, pp. 31–39.

Drucker, Peter F. Personnel and Organizational Changes in the Decade Ahead. In *The Diebold Group, Inc.,* 1973, pp. 95–102.

Eichner, Alfred S. A Theory of the Determination of the Mark-up Under Oligopoly. *Econ. J.,* December 1973, *83*(332), pp. 1184–1200.

Flamholtz, Eric. The Role of Human Resource Accounting in Social Accounting. In *Dierkes, M. and Bauer, R. A., eds.,* 1973, pp. 166–82.

Formánek, Karel. Příspěvek k teorii nepravidelnosti dodávek. (Contribution to the Theory of Irregular Supplies. With English summary.) *Ekon.-Mat. Obzor,* 1973, *9*(1), pp. 30–50.

Foster, F. G. Stochastic Processes. In *Ross, M., ed.,* 1973, pp. 223–39.

Frankel, Marvin. Pricing Decisions Under Unknown Demand. *Kyklos,* 1973, *26*(1), pp. 1–24.

Fraquelli, Giovanni. La matrice applicata alle previsioni aziendali. (Business Applications of the Matrix Input-Output for Forecasting Analyses. With English summary.) *L'Impresa,* 1973, *15*(3–4), pp. 273–77.

Frigero, Piercarlo. I modelli macroeconomici di sviluppo come strumento operativo per l'impresa. (Models of Economic Growth as an Operative Instrument of the Firm. With English summary.) *L'Impresa,* 1973, *15*(3–4), pp. 233–39.

Gaynor, Edwin W. Use of Control Charts in Cost Control. In *Thomas, W. E., Jr., ed.,* 1973, pp. 306–16.

Goodman, Richard A. A System Diagram of the Functions of a Manager. In *Thomas, W. E., Jr., ed.,* 1973, pp. 43–59.

Goodman, Richard A. A System Diagram of the Functions of a Manager. In *Klein, W. H. and Murphy, D. C., eds.,* 1973, pp. 50–61.

Grayson, C. Jackson, Jr. Management Science and Business Practice. *Harvard Bus. Rev.,* July-August 1973, *51*(4), pp. 41–48.

Greer, Howard Clark. Cost Factors in Price Making. In *Thomas, W. E., Jr., ed.,* 1973, pp. 201–23.

Gregory, K. and Russell, C. SIMPREP, A Computer Model for Coal Preparation. In *Ross, M., ed.,* 1973, pp. 379–89. [G: U.K.]

Hanke, Steve H. and Davis, Robert K. Potential for Marginal Cost Pricing in Water Resource Management. *Water Resources Res.,* August 1973, *9* (4), pp. 808–25.

Hanold, Terrance. Management Perspective on an Advanced Information System. In *The Diebold Group, Inc.,* 1973, pp. 271–97. [G: U.S.]

Harris, William T., Jr. and Chapin, Wayne R. Joint Product Costing. *Manage. Account.,* April 1973, *54*(10), pp. 43–47.

Hartley, Ronald V. A Note on Quadratic Programming in a Case of Joint Production: A Reply. *Accounting Rev.,* October 1973, *48*(4), pp. 771–74.

Hawes, D. M. Operational Gaming in the Planning of the Geologically Troubled Colliery. In *Ross, M., ed.,* 1973, pp. 405–16. [G: U.K.]

Heine, Rolf. Simulation of a Computer-Controlled Conveyance System for Air Passengers' Luggage. In *Ross, M., ed.,* 1973, pp. 373–78. [G: W. Germany]

Hochman, Eitan; Hochman, Oded and Razin, Assaf. Demand for Investment in Productive and Financial Capital. *Europ. Econ. Rev.,* April 1973, *4* (1), pp. 67–83.

Holstrum, Gary L. and Sauls, Eugene H. The Opportunity Cost Transfer Price. *Manage. Account.,* May 1973, *54*(11), pp. 29–33.

Ijiri, Yuji and Itami, Hiroyuki. Quadratic Cost-Volume Relationship and Timing of Demand Information. *Accounting Rev.,* October 1973, *48*(4), pp. 724–37.

Jackson, Raymond. Peak Load Pricing Model of an Electric Utility Using Pumped Storage. *Water Resources Res.,* June 1973, *9*(3), pp. 556–62.

Jarrett, Jeffrey E. An Abandonment Decision Model. *Eng. Econ.,* October-November 1973, *19*(1), pp. 35–46.

Jensen, Daniel L. Hartley's Demand-Price Analysis in a Case of Joint Production: A Comment. *Accounting Rev.,* October 1973, *48*(4), pp. 768–70.

Jensen, Daniel L. A Computer Experiment on Alternative Methods of Allocating Capacity Cost. *Quart. Rev. Econ. Bus.,* Summer 1973, *13*(2), pp. 21–31.

Jensen, Daniel L. A Computer Model for the Generation of System and Component Load Curves. *Eng. Econ.,* July-August 1973, *18*(4), pp. 243–56.

Jhabvala, Firdaus. The Optimal Allocation of Resources in a Decentralized Model. *Eng. Econ.,* April-May 1973, *18*(3), pp. 169–89.

Kaplan, Robert S. Variable and Self-Service Costs in Reciprocal Allocation Models. *Accounting Rev.,* October 1973, *48*(4), pp. 738–48.

Keeney, Ralph L. A Decision Analysis with Multiple Objectives: the Mexico City Airport. *Bell J. Econ. Manage. Sci.,* Spring 1973, *4*(1), pp. 101–17. [G: Mexico]

Kichline, James L.; Laub, P. Michael and Deck, Beryl. Yields on Recently Offered Corporate Bonds. *Fed. Res. Bull.,* May 1973, *59*(5), pp. 336–37. [G: U.S.]

Kolmin, Frank W. and Cerullo, Michael J. Measuring Productivity and Efficiency. *Manage. Account.,* November 1973, *55*(5), pp. 32–34.

Kraemer, Svend A. Warehouse Location and Allocation Problems Solved by Mathematical Programming Methods. In *Ross, M., ed.,* 1973, pp. 541–49.

Krouse, Clement G. On the Theory of Optimal Investment, Dividends, and Growth in the Firm. *Amer. Econ. Rev.,* June 1973, *63*(3), pp. 269–79.

Kroužek, Jan. Průmyslová dynamika—systémová disciplína zaměřená na komplexní zkoumáni dynamického chování systémů. (Industrial Dynamics—An Experimental Method for Study of Behaviour of Management Control Systems. With English summary.) *Ekon.-Mat. Obzor,* 1973, *9*(2), pp. 184–200.

Lee, Alec M. Stochastic Processes: Discussant 1. In *Ross, M., ed.,* 1973, pp. 241–43.

de Leeuw, C. G. OR Aspects of a Management Information System. In *Ross, M., ed.,* 1973, pp. 465–74.

LeKashman, Raymond and Stolle, John F. The Total Cost Approach to Distribution. In *Britt, S. H. and Boyd, H. W., Jr., eds.,* 1973, pp. 441–58.

Lewellen, Wilbur G. and Edmister, Robert O. A General Model for Accounts-Receivable Analysis and Control. *J. Financial Quant. Anal.,* March 1973, *8*(2), pp. 195–206.

Lifson, K. A. and Blackmarr, Brian R. Simulation and Optimization Models for Asset Deployment and Funds Sources Balancing Profit, Liquidity and Growth. *J. Bank Res.,* Autumn 1973, *4*(3), pp. 239–55.

Lindström, Caj-Gunnar. Företagsekonomin som vetenskapsgren och undervisnings disciplin. (Business Economics as a Branch of Science and Educational Discipline. With English summary.) *Ekon. Samfundets Tidskr.,* 1973, *26*(3), pp. 201–10.

Machol, Robert E. New Applications and Trends in OR in the US. In *Ross, M., ed.,* 1973, pp. 571–78. [G: U.S.]

Maixner, Ladislav. Optimalizace kapacit zásobníků pružné automatické linky. (Optimalization of the Size of Magazines in an Elastic Production Line. With English summary.) *Ekon.-Mat. Obzor,* 1973, *9*(2), pp. 150–66.

Marangoni, Giandemetrio. Problemi d'ordinamento e decisioni aziendali. (Scheduling Problems and Firm Decisions. With English summary.) *Rivista Int. Sci. Econ. Com.,* November 1973, *20*(11), pp. 1116–26.

Massy, William F. Issues in the Development of Information Systems. In *Britt, S. H. and Boyd, H. W., Jr., eds.,* 1973, pp. 647–55.

Miles, Raymond E. and Vergin, Roger C. Behavioral Properties of Variance Controls. In *Thomas, W. E., Jr., ed.,* 1973, pp. 325–39.

Monarchi, David E.; Kisiel, Chester C. and Duckstein, Lucien. Interactive Multiobjective Programming in Water Resources: A Case Study. *Water Resources Res.,* August 1973, *9*(4), pp. 837–50.

Müller-Oehring, H. Determining the Coal Wagon Requirements in the Rhenish Lignite Mines. In *Ross, M., ed.,* 1973, pp. 391–404. [G: W. Germany]

Murdick, Robert G. The Long-Range Planning Matrix. In *Klein, W. H. and Murphy, D. C., eds.,* 1973, pp. 234–41.

Murphy, Neil B. The Implications of Econometric Analysis of Bank Cost Functions for Bank Planning. *J. Bank Res.,* Autumn 1973, *4*(3), pp. 203–06. [G: U.S.]

Naert, Philippe A. Measuring Performance in a Decentralized Firm with Interrelated Divisions: Profit Center Versus Cost Center. *Eng. Econ.,* January-February 1973, *18*(2), pp. 99–114.

Niculescu, I. N. Folosirea metodei probelor curente în analiza procesului tehnologic. (Using the Method of Current Samples in Analysing the Technological Process. With English summary.) *Stud. Cercet. Econ.,* 1973, (4), pp. 73–87.

Onsi, Mohamed. Factor Analysis of Behavioral Variables Affecting Budgetary Slack. *Accounting Rev.,* July 1973, *48*(3), pp. 535–48. [G: U.S.]

Papandreou, Andreas G. The Multinational Corporation. *Amer. Econ.,* Fall 1973, *17*(2), pp. 154–60. [G: U.S.]

Pettway, Richard H. Integer Programming in Capital Budgeting: A Note on Computational Experience. *J. Financial Quant. Anal.,* September 1973, *8*(4), pp. 665–72.

Plowman, E. Grosvenor. The Logistics of Industrial Distribution. In *The Diebold Group, Inc.,* 1973, pp. 128–33.

Psoinos, D. P. and Xirokostas, D. A. A Dynamic Programming Approach to Establishing Teaching Posts in a Centralized Educational System. In *Ross, M., ed.,* 1973, pp. 315–23.

Robinson, Randall S. BANKMOD: An Interactive Simulation Aid for Bank Financial Planning. *J. Bank Res.,* Autumn 1973, *4*(3), pp. 212–24.

Ross, Miceal. Systems and Management: A Review. *Econ. Soc. Rev.,* April 1973, *4*(3), pp. 365–94.

Ross, Myron H. Probability, Games, Regret and Investment Criteria. *Eng. Econ.,* April-May 1973, *18*(3), pp. 191–98.

Ruiz-Palá, Ernesto and Avila Beloso, Carlos. Stochastic Processes: Discussant 2. In *Ross, M., ed.,* 1973, pp. 245–51.

Rupli, R. G. How to Improve Profits Through Simulation. *Manage. Account.,* November 1973, *55*(5), pp. 16–20.

Sabel, Hermann. On Pricing New Products. *Ger. Econ. Rev.,* 1973, *11*(4), pp. 292–311.

Schonberger, Richard J. A Taxonomy of Systems Management. *Nebr. J. Econ. Bus.,* Spring 1973, *12*(2), pp. 35–44.

Shimada, Toshiro. Industrial Dynamics Model of a Japanese University. In *Ross, M., ed.,* 1973, pp. 303–14. [G: Japan]

Slacik, Karl F. What Can You, the Financial Executive, Do About Customer Service? In *Thomas, W. E., Jr., ed.,* 1973, pp. 130–40.

Smalls, Isaac S. Hospital Cost Controls. *Manage. Account.,* March 1973, *54*(9), pp. 17–20.

Snooks, G. D. The Growth Process of the Firm: A Case Study. *Australian Econ. Pap.,* December 1973, *12*(21), pp. 162–74. [G: Australia]

Sobek, Robert S. A Manager's Primer on Forecasting. *Harvard Bus. Rev.,* May-June 1973, *51*(3), pp. 6–28, 181–83. [G: U.S.]

Squire, Lyn. Some Aspects of Optimal Pricing for Telecommunications. *Bell J. Econ. Manage. Sci.,* Autumn 1973, *4*(2), pp. 515–25.

Teague, J. and Eilon, S. Productivity Measurement: A Brief Survey. *Appl. Econ.,* June 1973, *5*(2), pp. 133–45.

Thirlby, G. F. The Ruler. In *Buchanan, J. M. and Thirlby, G. F., eds.,* 1973, pp. 163–98.

Thompson, Charles W. N. and Rath, Gustave J. Planning Solutions Aided by Management and Systems Technology. *Ann. Amer. Acad. Polit. Soc. Sci.,* January 1973, *405*, pp. 151–62.

Tobin, Norman and Butfield, Terry. The Implementation of OR Models in Planning Procedures. In *Ross, M., ed.,* 1973, pp. 363–72.

Troie, L. Cu privire la eficienţa cheltuielilor cu reparaţiile şi întreţinerea utilajelor de producţie. (Considerations on the Efficiency of Expenses for the Repair and Maintenance of Production Equipment. With English summary.) *Stud. Cercet. Econ.,* 1973, (2), pp. 99–115.

Van Mechelen, C. and Heirman, W. Receptselective en receptcreatie in de vleeswarenindustrie met behulp van lineaire programmering. (Selection and Creation of Recipes. The Application of Linear Programming in the Meat Industry. With English summary.) *Econ. Soc. Tijdschr.,* August 1973, *27*(4), pp. 411–21.

Vesper, Karl H. and Sayeki, Yutaka. A Quantitative Approach for Policy Analysis. *Calif. Manage. Rev.,* Spring 1973, *15*(3), pp. 119–26.

Warren, James M. and Shelton, John P. A Simultaneous Equation Approach to Financial Planning: Reply. *J. Finance,* September 1973, *28*(4), pp. 1039–42.

Weston, J. Fred. ROI Planning and Control as a Dynamic Management System. In *Weston, J. F. and Ornstein, S. I., eds.,* 1973, pp. 107–15.

Wettstein, Jürg. Operations Research in the Swiss Telecommunication Services. In *Ross, M., ed.,* 1973, pp. 475–81. [G: Switzerland]

Wilson, Charles J. The Operating Lease and the Risk of Obsolescence. *Manage. Account.,* December 1973, *55*(6), pp. 41–44.

Yarrow, G. K. Managerial Utility Maximization under Uncertainty. *Economica, N.S.,* May 1973, *40* (158), pp. 155–73.

513 Business and Public Administration

5130 Business and Public Administration

Ahmad, Muneer. The Political Context of Civil Service Reorganization in Pakistan. *Pakistan Econ. Soc. Rev.,* Summer 1973, *11*(2), pp. 167–92. [G: Pakistan]

Ajiferuke, Musbau and Boddewyn, J. J. Socioeconomic Indicators in Comparative Management. In *Alexandrides, C. G., ed.,* 1973, pp. 163–72.

Allison, Graham T. Organizational and Administrative Factors Affecting Shifts in Defense Expenditures. In *Udis, B., ed.,* 1973, pp. 289–35. [G: U.S.]

Ameiss, Albert P., et al. Program Management in Missouri's Division of Mental Health. *Manage. Account.,* August 1973, *55*(2), pp. 31–34. [G: U.S.]

Ansoff, H. Igor. Management in Transition. In *The Conference Board,* 1973, pp. 22–63. [G: U.S.]

Armstrong, R. H. R. Programme Budgeting in English Local Government. In *Novick, D., ed.,* 1973, pp. 105–10. [G: U.K.]

Bates, Thomas H. Management and the Multinational Business Environment. *Calif. Manage. Rev.,* Spring 1973, *15*(3), pp. 37–45.

Battersby, J. R. Introduction and Development of Programme Budgeting in New Zealand. In *Novick, D., ed.,* 1973, pp. 129–38. [G: New Zealand]

Becker, Theodore M. and Stern, Robert N. Professionalism, Professionalization, and Bias in the Commercial Human Relations Consulting Operation: A Survey Analysis. *J. Bus.,* April 1973, *46*(2), pp. 230–57. [G: U.S.]

Bodenstab, Charles J. Exception Reports for Management Action. In *Thomas, W. E., Jr., ed.,* 1973, pp. 317–24.

Boeninger, Edgardo. The Role of the University in the Training of Personnel for Public Administration: A Latin American Perspective. In *Thurber, C. E. and Graham, L. S., eds.,* 1973, pp. 188–94. [G: Latin America]

Boulding, Kenneth E. Intersects: The Peculiar Organizations. In *The Conference Board,* 1973, pp. 179–201. [G: U.S.]

Bowen, Charles P., Jr. Let's Put Realism into Management Development. *Harvard Bus. Rev.,* July-August 1973, *51*(4), pp. 80–87.

Bower, Marvin and Walton, C. Lee, Jr. Gearing a Business to the Future. In *The Conference Board,* 1973, pp. 93–148. [G: U.S.]

Bréaud, Patrick and Gorgorin, Jean-Louis. An Appraisal of Program Budgeting in France. In *Novick, D., ed.,* 1973, pp. 111–18. [G: France]

Bridgeman, J. M. Planning-Programming-Budgeting in the United Kingdom Central Government. In *Novick, D., ed.,* 1973, pp. 89–95. [G: U.K.]

Buchele, Robert B. How to Evaluate a Firm. In *Klein, W. H. and Murphy, D. C., eds.,* 1973, pp. 322–34.

Burt, David N. Stretching Your Building Dollar. *Calif. Manage. Rev.,* Summer 1973, *15*(4), pp. 54–60.

Calkins, Robert D. The Decision Process in Administration. In *Thomas, W. E., Jr., ed.,* 1973, pp. 142–50.

Cannon, Mark W. Interactive Training Techniques for Improving Public Service in Latin America. In *Thurber, C. E. and Graham, L. S., eds.,* 1973, pp. 148–87. [G: Latin America]

Carey, William D. New Perspectives on Governance. In *The Conference Board,* 1973, pp. 64–92. [G: U.S.]

Carlson, Jack W. Recent U.S. Federal Government Experience with Program Budgeting. In *Novick, D., ed.*, 1973, pp. 207–16. **[G: U.S.]**

Cheek, Logan M. Cost Effectiveness Comes to the Personnel Function. *Harvard Bus. Rev.*, May-June 1973, *51*(3), pp. 96–105.

Cook, Gail C. A. Metropolitan Government: The Significance of Context and Form. In *Mattila, J. M. and Thompson, W. R., eds.*, 1973, pp. 164–74. **[G: Canada]**

Cox, Steven R. and Shauger, Donald. Executive Compensation, Firm Sales, and Profitability. *Intermountain Econ. Rev.*, Spring 1973, *4*(1), pp. 29–39. **[G: U.S.]**

Crisman, R. E. W. State of Vermont, Program Budgeting, 1970. In *Novick, D., ed.*, 1973, pp. 181–84. **[G: U.S.]**

Cross, Hershner. General Organization Structure and Functions. In *Weston, J. F. and Ornstein, S. I., eds.*, 1973, pp. 117–21.

Dean, Joel. Profit Performance Measurement of Division Managers. In *Thomas, W. E., Jr., ed.*, 1973, pp. 428–35.

Dearden, John. 'Time Span' in Management Control. In *Thomas, W. E., Jr., ed.*, 1973, pp. 340–53.

Desai, Satish. Professional-Pool Concept for Company Groups. *Marquette Bus. Rev.*, Spring 1973, *17*(1), pp. 30–34.

Di Nuzzo, Vincenzo. Come affrontare il problema della "corporate image." (How to Approach the Problem of "Corporate Image." With English summary.) *L'Impresa*, 1973, *15*(9–10), pp. 527–37.

Dolphin, Robert. Made in Japan. *Ohio State U. Bull. Bus. Res.*, September 1973, *48*(9), pp. 4–7. **[G: Japan]**

Drucker, Peter F. Global Management. In *The Conference Board*, 1973, pp. 228–74.

Drucker, Peter F. Personnel and Organizational Changes in the Decade Ahead. In *The Diebold Group, Inc.*, 1973, pp. 95–102.

Edie, Leslie C., et al. Urban Planning. In *Ross, M., ed.*, 1973, pp. 599–615. **[G: U.S.]**

Falkenberg, John F. The Sources of Bank Profitability. *J. Bank Res.*, Summer 1973, *4*(2), pp. 105–10.

Farmer, David H. Source Decision Making in the Multinational Company Environment. In *Henley, D. S., ed.*, 1973, pp. 474–86.

Flamholtz, Eric. Human Resource Accounting: Its Role in Management Planning and Control. *Econ. Soc. Tijdschr.*, February 1973, *27*(1), pp. 3–22.

Folsom, Donald J. A Control Guide for Computer Systems. *Manage. Account.*, August 1973, *55*(2), pp. 49–55.

Fukushima, Yasuto. PPBS in the Japanese Government: Necessity, Preparation and Problems. In *Novick, D., ed.*, 1973, pp. 125–28. **[G: Japan]**

Ginzberg, Eli. Challenge and Resolution. In *Ginzberg, E. and Yohalem, A. M., eds.*, 1973, pp. 140–52. **[G: U.S.]**

Glueck, William F. and Kavran, Dragoljub. The Yugoslav Management System. In *Henley, D. S., ed.*, 1973, pp. 375–89. **[G: Yugoslavia]**

Goldston, Eli. Executive Sabbaticals: About to Take Off? *Harvard Bus. Rev.*, September-October 1973, *51*(5), pp. 57–68. **[G: U.S.]**

Graham, Lawrence S. Evaluations and Recommendations. In *Thurber, C. E. and Graham, L. S., eds.*, 1973, pp. 425–42. **[G: Latin America]**

Green, Thad B. and Cotlar, Morton. An Evaluation of a Novel Business Simulation Technique for Management Development. *J. Bus.*, April 1973, *46*(2), pp. 212–29.

Greenstreet, D. K. Public Administration: A Comparative Analysis of the 1950 Colonial Ten-Year Development Plan and the 1951 'Nkrumah' Development Plan of the Gold Coast (Ghana) *Econ. Bull. Ghana, Sec. Ser.*, 1973, *3*(4), pp. 31–55. **[G: Ghana]**

Green, Thad B. and Cotlar, Morton. An Evaluation of a Novel Business Simulation Technique for Management Development. *J. Bus.*, April 1973, *46*(2), pp. 212–29.

Groves, Roderick T. The Venezuelan Administrative Reform Movement, 1958–1963. In *Thurber, C. E. and Graham, L. S., eds.*, 1973, pp. 47–80. **[G: Venezuela]**

Guerreiro-Ramos, Alberto. The New Ignorance and the Future of Public Administration in Latin America. In *Thurber, C. E. and Graham, L. S., eds.*, 1973, pp. 382–422. **[G: Latin America]**

Gunn, Lewis A. Government, Technology, and Planning in Britain. In *Edge, D. O. and Wolfe, J. N., eds.*, 1973, pp. 161–79. **[G: U.K.]**

Gylys, Julius A. Economic Analysis of Municipal and County Police Interdependence. In *Mattila, J. M. and Thompson, W. R., eds.*, 1973, pp. 151–63. **[G: U.S.]**

Half, Robert. Gamesmanship in Salary Management. *Manage. Account.*, March 1973, *54*(9), pp. 56–57.

Hanold, Terrance. Management Perspective on an Advanced Information System. In *The Diebold Group, Inc.*, 1973, pp. 271–97. **[G: U.S.]**

Harper, Edwin L.; Kramer, Fred A. and Rouse, Andrew M. Personnel Limitations of "Instant Analysis." In *Novick, D., ed.*, 1973, pp. 201–05.

Hayes, Frederick O'R. Program Budgeting in the City of New York. In *Novick, D., ed.*, 1973, pp. 185–91. **[G: U.S.]**

Hearle, Edward F. R. EDP Systems in State and Local Governments. In *The Diebold Group, Inc.*, 1973, pp. 134–39. **[G: U.S.]**

Hees, Marc. Système de travail et principe de qualification. (The Work System and Qualification. With English summary.) *Ann. Sci. Écon. Appl.*, 1973–1974, (1), pp. 67–79.

Heller, Frank A. Leadership, Decision Making, and Contingency Theory. *Ind. Relat.*, May 1973, *12*(2), pp. 183–99. **[G: S. America]**

Herring, S. G. Programme Budgeting in the Australian Federal Government. In *Novick, D., ed.*, 1973, pp. 55–60. **[G: Australia]**

Herwitz, Paul S. Evaluation of Programmers. In *The Diebold Group, Inc.*, 1973, pp. 213–22.

Hitch, Charles J. Program Planning and Budgeting: Its Origin and Potential Applications. In *The Diebold Group, Inc.*, 1973, pp. 55–62. **[G: U.S.]**

Hoselitz, Bert F. Dominance and Achievement in Entrepreneurial Personalities: Comment. In *Ayal, E. B., ed.*, 1973, pp. 145–48. **[G: U.S.]**

Howard, Godfrey G. Anatomy of a Hospital Trustee. *Harvard Bus. Rev.*, May-June 1973, *51*(3), pp. 65–71.

Howell, Robert A. Managing by Objectives—A Three-Stage System. In *Klein, W. H. and Murphy, D. C., eds.,* 1973, pp. 139–43.

Jaspan, Norman. The $8 Billion Rip-off. *Manage. Account.,* June 1973, *54*(12), pp. 49–50. [G: U.S.]

Johnson, Howard G. Key Item Control. In *Thomas, W. E., Jr., ed.,* 1973, pp. 296–305.

Jones, Edward W., Jr. What it's Like to be a Black Manager. *Harvard Bus. Rev.,* July-August 1973, *51*(4), pp. 108–16.

Jones, Ken. Employee Directors in Steel. In *Tivey, L., ed.,* 1973, pp. 298–302. [G: U.K.]

Kohvakka, Liisa. Kvantitatiivinen henkilöstösuunnittelu. (Quantitative Personnel Planning. With English summary.) *Liiketaloudellinen Aikak.,* 1973, *22*(2), pp. 141–57.

Lamphere, Robert J. Program Budgeting at John Hancock Life Insurance. In *Novick, D., ed.,* 1973, pp. 151–60. [G: U.S.]

Leontief, Wassily W. Input-Output Analysis in Business Planning. In *The Diebold Group, Inc.,* 1973, pp. 78–83.

Lewellen, Wilbur G. and Lanser, Howard P. Executive Pay Preferences. *Harvard Bus. Rev.,* September-October 1973, *51*(5), pp. 115–22. [G: U.S.]

Lewin, David. Public Employment Relations: Confronting the Issues. *Ind. Relat.,* October 1973, *12* (3), pp. 309–21. [G: U.S.]

Longbrake, William A. Computers and the Cost of Producing Banking Services: Planning and Control Considerations. *J. Bank Res.,* Autumn 1973, *4*(3), pp. 194–202. [G: U.S.]

Luoma, Väinö. Yritys ja yhteiskunta. (The Enterprise and Society: The Social Responsibility of Management in Outline. With English summary.) *Liiketaloudellinen Aikak.,* 1973, *22*(1), pp. 18–28.

MacDonald, B. A. Program Budgeting in the Government of Canada: Origin and Progress. In *Novick, D., ed.,* 1973, pp. 71–78. [G: Canada]

Matzner, Egon and Vak, Karl. Program Budgeting in Austria: An Essay in Persuasion. In *Novick, D., ed.,* 1973, pp. 61–64. [G: Austria]

May, Paul A. The Budgeting Process. *Manage. Account.,* January 1973, *54*(7), pp. 19–25.

Mazis, Michael B. and Green, Robert. Implementing Social Responsibility. In *Klein, W. H. and Murphy, D. C., eds.,* 1973, pp. 296–304.

McHale, John and McHale, Magda Cordell. Management: The Larger Perspective. In *The Conference Board,* 1973, pp. 298–370. [G: U.S.]

McKitterick, John B. Resource Allocation in the General Electric Company. In *Weston, J. F. and Ornstein, S. I., eds.,* 1973, pp. 123–27.

Mee, John F. Management Philosophy for Professional Executives. In *Klein, W. H. and Murphy, D. C., eds.,* 1973, pp. 43–49.

Miller, S. M. On Not Abusing Incentives. In *Stein, B. and Miller, S. M., eds.,* 1973, pp. 199–204.

Mowitz, Robert J. Pennsylvania's Planning, Programming, Budgeting System. In *Novick, D., ed.,* 1973, pp. 169–80. [G: U.S.]

Mulholland, William D., Jr. Financial Simulation in Long–Range Project Planning. In *The Diebold Group, Inc.,* 1973, pp. 43–54. [G: U.S.]

Murdick, Robert G. Nature of Planning and Plans. In *Klein, W. H. and Murphy, D. C., eds.,* 1973, pp. 224–33.

Musarra, Emanuele Parisi. Note sull'automazione elettronica per la gestione e la direzione aziendale bancaria. (Notes on the Electronic Automation for Bank Management. With English summary.) *Bancaria,* April 1973, *29*(4), pp. 447–52. [G: Italy]

Newman, William H. Shaping the Master Strategy of Your Firm. In *Klein, W. H. and Murphy, D. C., eds.,* 1973, pp. 174–85. [G: U.S.]

Nicholson, Edward A., Jr. and Litschert, Robert L. Long-Range Planning in Banking: Ten Cases in the U.S. and Britain. *J. Bank Res.,* Spring 1973, *4* (1), pp. 31–40. [G: U.S.; U.K.]

Nolan, Richard L. Computer Data Bases: The Future is Now. *Harvard Bus. Rev.,* September-October 1973, *51*(5), pp. 98–114.

Novick, David. Brief History of Program Budgeting. In *Novick, D., ed.,* 1973, pp. 19–28.

Novick, David. Evaluating Program Budgeting in the 1960s. In *Novick, D., ed.,* 1973, pp. 49–53.

Novick, David. Program Budgeting, 1971. In *Novick, D., ed.,* 1973, pp. 29–47.

Novick, David. What Program Budgeting Is and Is Not. In *Novick, D., ed.,* 1973, pp. 5–17.

O'Cofaigh, Thomas F. Programme Budgeting in Ireland. In *Novick, D., ed.,* 1973, pp. 119–24. [G: Ireland]

Oehm, J. Kent. Controlling Professional Manpower Costs. *Manage. Account.,* March 1973, *54*(9), pp. 31–35.

Ostrom, Vincent. The Crisis of Confidence. In *Ostrom, V.,* 1973, pp. 1–22.

Ostrom, Vincent. The Work of the Contemporary Political Economists. In *Ostrom, V.,* 1973, pp. 48–73.

Parrish, Charles J. Bureaucracy, Democracy, and Development: Some Considerations Based on the Chilean Case. In *Thurber, C. E. and Graham, L. S., eds.,* 1973, pp. 229–59. [G: Chile]

Petras, James F. Cuba: Fourteen Years of Revolutionary Government. In *Thurber, C. E. and Graham, L. S., eds.,* 1973, pp. 281–93. [G: Cuba]

Pierre, Joseph C. La gestion des ressources humaines: une approche intégrée et prévisionnelle. (The Management of Human Resources: An Integrated and Planned Approach. With English summary.) *Ann. Sci. Écon. Appl.,* 1973–1974, (1), pp. 17–45.

Poullet, E. The PPBS Experiment in Belgium. In *Novick, D., ed.,* 1973, pp. 65–69. [G: Belgium]

Prasad, S. Benjamin. Comparative Management Models: Structure and Research Potential. In *Alexandrides, C. G., ed.,* 1973, pp. 145–61.

Rauscher, Walter J. The Implementation and Impact of SABRE: American Airlines. In *The Diebold Group, Inc.,* 1973, pp. 265–70. [G: U.S.]

Reddington, Donald A. Control Methods for Small Business. *Manage. Account.,* September 1973, *55* (3), pp. 15–17, 26.

Reilley, Ewing W. Planning the Strategy of the Business. In *Klein, W. H. and Murphy, D. C., eds.,* 1973, pp. 166–73.

Rieder, George A. Performance Review—A Mixed Bag. *Harvard Bus. Rev.*, July-August 1973, *51*(4), pp. 61–67.

Robbins, Sidney M. and Stobaugh, Robert B. The Bent Measuring Stick for Foreign Subsidiaries. *Harvard Bus. Rev.*, September-October 1973, *51* (5), pp. 80–88.

Roberts, C. A. Reorganization of the National Coal Board. In *Tivey, L., ed.*, 1973, pp. 242–48. [G: U.K.]

Roberts, R. W. and Schmitt, R. W. Program Budgeting R and D at General Electric. In *Novick, D., ed.*, 1973, pp. 139–50. [G: U.S.]

Robie, Edward A. Challenge to Management. In *Ginzberg, E. and Yohalem, A. M., eds.*, 1973, pp. 9–29. [G: U.S.]

Robinson, James W. and Turner, James T. An Empirical Investigation of the Theory Y Management—Theory X Union Hypothesis. *Miss. Val. J. Bus. Econ.*, Spring 1973, *8*(3), pp. 77–84.

Rosenbloom, Richard S. The *Real* Productivity Crisis is in Government. *Harvard Bus. Rev.*, September-October 1973, *51*(5), pp. 156–64. [G: U.S.]

Scioli, Frank P., Jr. and Cook, Thomas J. Experimental Design in Policy Impact Analysis. *Soc. Sci. Quart.*, September 1973, *54*(2), pp. 271–80.

Sellekaerts, Willy. The Soviet Managerial Evolution. *Marquette Bus. Rev.*, Summer 1973, *17*(2), pp. 84–97. [G: U.S.S.R.]

Sethi, Narendra K. The Japanese Managerial Scene: An Introductory View. *Marquette Bus. Rev.*, Winter 1973, *17*(4), pp. 201–06. [G: Japan]

Shawcross, Hartley William [Lord]. The Structure of Public Company Boards. In *Allen, G. C., et al.*, 1973, pp. 45–54. [G: U.K.]

Sherwood, Frank P. Technical Assistance for Education in Public Administration: Lessons of Experience. In *Thurber, C. E. and Graham, L. S., eds.*, 1973, pp. 195–226. [G: U.S.; Brazil]

Siegel, Gilbert B. Brazil: Diffusion and Centralization of Power. In *Thurber, C. E. and Graham, L. S., eds.*, 1973, pp. 362–81. [G: Brazil]

Silber, Sigmund. The Common Data-Base: Defining Its Role in the Information System. In *The Diebold Group, Inc.*, 1973, pp. 63–77.

Simon, William. Management and Man. In *The Conference Board*, 1973, pp. 275–97.

Sisco, Anthony F., Jr. Overhead Variance Analysis and Corrective Action. *Manage. Account.*, October 1973, *55*(4), pp. 45–47, 51.

Snider, William D. Building an On-Line Financial Planning Model. *J. Bank Res.*, Autumn 1973, *4*(3), pp. 232–38.

Starr, Martin K. Productivity is the USA's Problem. *Calif. Manage. Rev.*, Winter 1973, *16*(2), pp. 32–36. [G: U.S.]

Steiner, George A. Long-Range Planning: Concept and Implementation. In *Klein, W. H. and Murphy, D. C., eds.*, 1973, pp. 242–49.

Steiner, George A. Approaches to Long-Range Planning for Small Business. In *Klein, W. H. and Murphy, D. C., eds.*, 1973, pp. 250–63.

Stitelman, Leonard. The "Base Data-Cluster" Concept: A Regional Approach to a Governmental Information Network. *Mich. Academician*, Spring 1973, *5*(4), pp. 435–40. [G: U.S.]

Stolk, William C. Beyond Profitability: A Proposal for Managing the Corporation's Public Business. In *Klein, W. H. and Murphy, D. C., eds.*, 1973, pp. 305–07.

Strangert, Per. Budget Simulation: A Tool for Adaptive Planning. In *Ross, M., ed.*, 1973, pp. 491–97.

Sutton, C. J. Management Behaviour and a Theory of Diversification. *Scot. J. Polit. Econ.*, February 1973, *20*(1), pp. 27–42.

Tannenbaum, Robert and Schmidt, Warren H. How to Choose a Leadership Pattern. *Harvard Bus. Rev.*, May-June 1973, *51*(3), pp. 162–80.

Thirlby, G. F. The Ruler. In *Buchanan, J. M. and Thirlby, G. F., eds.*, 1973, pp. 163–98.

Thomson, Michael R. Forecasting for Financial Planning. *J. Bank Res.*, Autumn 1973, *4*(3), pp. 225–31.

Thurber, Clarence E. Islands of Development: A Political and Social Approach to Development Administration in Latin America. In *Thurber, C. E. and Graham, L. S., eds.*, 1973, pp. 15–46. [G: Latin America]

Trist, Eric. A Socio-Technical Critique of Scientific Management. In *Edge, D. O. and Wolfe, J. N., eds.*, 1973, pp. 95–116.

Tsaklanganos, Angelos A. Informal Organization: A Managerial Myth Revisited. *Marquette Bus. Rev.*, Winter 1973, *17*(4), pp. 167–73.

Tyran, Michael R. A Financial Projection Plan. *Manage. Account.*, July 1973, *55*(1), pp. 19–23, 28.

Vais, T. The Topic of an International Symposium: Labor Resources in COMECON Nations. *Prob. Econ.*, July 1973, *16*(3), pp. 77–86. [G: U.S.S.R.]

Vanneman, Reeve D. Dominance and Achievement in Entrepreneurial Personalities. In *Ayal, E. B., ed.*, 1973, pp. 122–45. [G: U.S.]

Vanni, Lido. Immagine aziendale e politica del personale. (Company Image and Personnel Policy. With English summary.) *L'Impresa*, 1973, *15* (9–10), pp. 549–60.

Vendig, Richard E. A Three-Part Transfer Price. *Manage. Account.*, September 1973, *55*(3), pp. 33–36.

Verbist, Daniel. La gestion prévisionnelle des ressources humaines. (The Planning and Forecasting of Human Resources. With English summary.) *Ann. Sci. Écon. Appl.*, 1973–1974, (1), pp. 81–104.

Weaver, Jerry L. Bureaucracy during a Period of Social Change: The Case of Guatemala. In *Thurber, C. E. and Graham, L. S., eds.*, 1973, pp. 314–61. [G: Guatemala]

Weigand, Robert E. The Problems of Managing Reciprocity. *Calif. Manage. Rev.*, Fall 1973, *16*(1), pp. 40–48.

White, Harold C. A Leadership Audit. *Manage. Account.*, August 1973, *55*(2), pp. 39–41.

Whyte, William F. Organizations for the Future. In *Somers, G. G., ed.*, 1973, pp. 129–40. [G: U.S.]

Widing, J. William, Jr. Reorganizing Your Worldwide Business. *Harvard Bus. Rev.*, May-June 1973, *51*(3), pp. 153–60.

Wright, Chester. Recruiting and Developing PPB Staff. In *Novick, D., ed.*, 1973, pp. 193–200.

Yeo, Edwin H., III. A Management View of Financial

Planning or The Best Laid Schemes. *J. Bank Res.,* Autumn 1973, *4*(3), pp. 207–11.

Yoder, Dale. Personnel Administration. In *Somers, G. G., ed.,* 1973, pp. 141–56. [G: U.S.]

Young, Ralph. An Exploratory Analysis of Demand for the Public Library Lending Service. *Appl. Econ.,* June 1973, *5*(2), pp. 119–32. [G: U.K.]

514 Goals and Objectives of Firms

5140 Goals and Objectives of Firms

Ackerman, Robert W. How Companies Respond to Social Demands. *Harvard Bus. Rev.,* July-August 1973, *51*(4), pp. 88–98.

Ackoff, Russell L. The Nature and Content of Planning. In *Klein, W. H. and Murphy, D. C., eds.,* 1973, pp. 202–23.

Andrews, Frederick. New Box Score. In *Klein, W. H. and Murphy, D. C., eds.,* 1973, pp. 310–18. [G: U.S.]

Andrews, Kenneth R. Can the Best Corporations be Made Moral? *Harvard Bus. Rev.,* May-June 1973, *51*(3), pp. 57–64.

Arrow, Kenneth J. Social Responsibility and Economic Efficiency. *Public Policy,* Summer 1973, *21*(3), pp. 303–17.

Balassa, Bela. The Firm in the New Economic Mechanism in Hungary. In *Bornstein, M., ed.,* 1973, pp. 347–72. [G: Hungary]

Barker, Robinson F. The Businessman's Role. *Manage. Account.,* February 1973, *54*(8), pp. 15–16, 25.

Bass, Bernard M. and Eldridge, Larry D. Accelerated Managers' Objectives in Twelve Countries. *Ind. Relat.,* May 1973, *12*(2), pp. 158–71.

Bauer, Raymond A. The Corporate Social Audit: Getting on the Learning Curve. *Calif. Manage. Rev.,* Fall 1973, *16*(1), pp. 5–10.

Bernthal, Wilmar F. Value Perspectives in Management Decisions. In *Klein, W. H. and Murphy, D. C., eds.,* 1973, pp. 277–83.

Bienaymé, Alain. Les processus de croissance des entreprises sont-ils déterminés ou indéterminés? (Why Growth Rates of Business Firms Differ? With English summary.) *Revue Écon.,* March 1973, *24*(2), pp. 216–34.

Bilkey, Warren J. Empirical Evidence Regarding Business Goals. In *Cochrane, J. L. and Zeleny, M., eds.,* 1973, pp. 613–34. [G: El Salvador; Costa Rica; U.S.]

Boettinger, Henry M. The Management Challenge. In *The Conference Board,* 1973, pp. 1–21.

Boudreaux, Kenneth J. 'Managerialism' and Risk-Return Performance. *Southern Econ. J.,* January 1973, *39*(3), pp. 366–72. [G: U.S.]

Boulding, Kenneth E. The Future Corporation and Public Attitudes. In *Boulding, K. E.,* 1973, pp. 175–93. [G: U.S.]

Bower, Marvin and Walton, C. Lee, Jr. Gearing a Business to the Future. In *The Conference Board,* 1973, pp. 93–148. [G: U.S.]

Bradshaw, T. F. Corporate Social Reform: An Ex-

ecutive's Viewpoint. *Calif. Manage. Rev.,* Summer 1973, *15*(4), pp. 85–89.

Brechling, Frank. Announcement Effects of Profits Taxation: Discussion. In *Parkin, M., ed.,* 1973, pp. 33–34.

Burck, Gilbert. The Myths and Realities of Corporate Pricing. In *Britt, S. H. and Boyd, H. W., Jr., eds.,* 1973, pp. 345–57. [G: U.S.]

Butcher, Bernard L. The Program Management Approach to the Corporate Social Audit. *Calif. Manage. Rev.,* Fall 1973, *16*(1), pp. 11–16.

Cannon, Peter. The Principles of Business Relations. In *Allen, G. C., et al.,* 1973, pp. 55–59. [G: U.K.]

Cox, Steven R. and Shauger, Donald. Executive Compensation, Firm Sales, and Profitability. *Intermountain Econ. Rev.,* Spring 1973, *4*(1), pp. 29–39. [G: U.S.]

Cravens, David W. and Hills, Gerald E. Consumerism: A Perspective for Business. In *Murray, B. B., ed.,* 1973, pp. 233–42. [G: U.S.]

Dalton, James A. and Esposito, Louis. The Impact of Liquidity on Merger Activity. *Quart. Rev. Econ. Bus.,* Spring 1973, *13*(1), pp. 15–26. [G: U.S.]

Davies, J. R. On the Sales Maximization Hypothesis: A Comment. *J. Ind. Econ.,* April 1973, *21*(2), pp. 200–02.

Davis, Keith. Can Business Afford to Ignore Social Responsibilities? In *Klein, W. H. and Murphy, D. C., eds.,* 1973, pp. 270–76.

Day, George S. The Role of the Consumer in the Corporate Social Audit. In *Dierkes, M. and Bauer, R. A., eds.,* 1973, pp. 117–29.

Dierkes, Meinolf, et al. Social Pressure and Business Actions. In *Dierkes, M. and Bauer, R. A., eds.,* 1973, pp. 57–92. [G: U.S.]

Epstein, Edwin M. Dimensions of Corporate Power, Pt. 1. *Calif. Manage. Rev.,* Winter 1973, *16*(2), pp. 9–23. [G: U.S.]

Fabris, Giampaolo. La "corporate image": per una ridefinizione del problema. (The "Corporate Image": A Redefinition. With English summary.) *L'Impresa,* 1973, *15*(9–10), pp. 538–47.

Finkelstein, Larry. Concepts for Reporting on Corporations' Community Involvement. In *Dierkes, M. and Bauer, R. A., eds.,* 1973, pp. 219–24. [G: U.S.]

Gastil, Raymond D. Social Accounting versus Social Responsibility. In *Dierkes, M. and Bauer, R. A., eds.,* 1973, pp. 93–106.

Geneen, Harold S. and Judelson, David N. Additional Data on ITT and Gulf and Western. In *Andreano, R. L., ed.,* 1973, pp. R331–42. [G: U.S.]

Geneen, Harold S. Statement on ITT Policy and Conglomerates. In *Andreano, R. L., ed.,* 1973, pp. R329–13. [G: U.S.]

Goetz, Billy E. The Management of Objectives. *Manage. Account.,* August 1973, *55*(2), pp. 35–38.

Granof, Michael H. Financial Evaluation of Labor Contracts. *Manage. Account.,* July 1973, *55*(1), pp. 38–42, 45.

Gray, Daniel H. Methodology: One Approach to the Corporate Social Audit. *Calif. Manage. Rev.,* Summer 1973, *15*(4), pp. 106–09.

Grochow, Jerrold M. Corporate Social Reform: A

Young Person's Viewpoint. *Calif. Manage. Rev.,* Summer 1973, *15*(4), pp. 74–77.

Gross, Bertram M. What Are Your Organization's Objectives? A General-Systems Approach to Planning. In *Klein, W. H. and Murphy, D. C., eds.,* 1973, pp. 106–29.

Hague, D. C. Competition and the U.K. Industry. In *Rybczynski, T. M., ed.,* 1973, pp. 78–95.
[G: U.K.]

Helmer, Jean-Yves. Essai sur la croissance de l'entreprise. (Essay on Firm Growth. With English summary.) *Revue Écon.,* March 1973, *24*(2), pp. 235–72.

Ijiri, Yuji. A Historical Cost Approach to Aggregation of Multiple Goals. In *Cochrane, J. L. and Zeleny, M., eds.,* 1973, pp. 395–405.

Kamerschen, David R. Further Thoughts on Separation of Ownership and Control. *Rivista Int. Sci. Econ. Com.,* February 1973, *20*(2), pp. 179–83.

Kaye, William G. Take in a New Partner—The Consumer. In *Murray, B. B., ed.,* 1973, pp. 243–48.
[G: U.S.]

Killough, Larry N. and Souders, Thomas L. A Goal Programming Model for Public Accounting Firms. *Accounting Rev.,* April 1973, *48*(2), pp. 268–79.

Krouse, Clement G. Experimental Decision-Making in the Theory of the Firm. In *Weston, J. F. and Ornstein, S. I., eds.,* 1973, pp. 129–38.

Lawler, Edward E., III. Quality of Working Life and Social Accounts. In *Dierkes, M. and Bauer, R. A., eds.,* 1973, pp. 154–65. [G: U.S.]

Levin, Samuel M. Economic Aspects of Modern Speed. In *Levin, S. M.,* 1973, pp. 65–77.
[G: U.S.]

Luthans, Fred and Hodgetts, Richard M. Determining a Social-Responsibility Strategy. In *Klein, W. H. and Murphy, D. C., eds.,* 1973, pp. 292–95.

Mason, R. Hal; Harris, Jerome and McLoughlin, John. Corporate Strategy: A Point of View. In *Klein, W. H. and Murphy, D. C., eds.,* 1973, pp. 158–65.

Mathias, Robert A. An Approach Toward Corporate Social Measures. In *Dierkes, M. and Bauer, R. A., eds.,* 1973, pp. 285–91.

Mazis, Michael B. and Green, Robert. Implementing Social Responsibility. In *Klein, W. H. and Murphy, D. C., eds.,* 1973, pp. 296–304.

McGuire, Joseph W. The Social Responsibility of the Corporation. In *Klein, W. H. and Murphy, D. C., eds.,* 1973, pp. 284–91.

Monsen, R. Joseph. Is Social Accounting a Mirage? In *Dierkes, M. and Bauer, R. A., eds.,* 1973, pp. 107–10.

Moore, Philip W. Corporate Social Reform: An Activist's Viewpoint. *Calif. Manage. Rev.,* Summer 1973, *15*(4), pp. 90–96.

Murdick, Robert G. The Long-Range Planning Matrix. In *Klein, W. H. and Murphy, D. C., eds.,* 1973, pp. 234–41.

Neuberger, Egon and James, Estelle. The Yugoslav Self-Managed Enterprise: A Systemic Approach. In *Bornstein, M., ed.,* 1973, pp. 245–84. [G: Yugoslavia]

Newman, William H. Basic Objectives Which Shape the Character of a Company. In *Klein, W. H. and* *Murphy, D. C., eds.,* 1973, pp. 85–97. [G: U.S.]

Newman, William H. Shaping the Master Strategy of Your Firm. In *Klein, W. H. and Murphy, D. C., eds.,* 1973, pp. 174–85. [G: U.S.]

Nolan, Joseph T. The Social Audit: One Corporation's Experience. In *Dierkes, M. and Bauer, R. A., eds.,* 1973, pp. 292–96. [G: U.S.]

O'Donnell, Cyril. Planning Objectives. In *Klein, W. H. and Murphy, D. C., eds.,* 1973, pp. 98–105.

Osteryoung, Jerome S. Multiple Goals in the Capital Budgeting Decision. In *Cochrane, J. L. and Zeleny, M., eds.,* 1973, pp. 447–57.

Palmer, John P. The Profit Variability Effects of the Managerial Enterprise. *Western Econ. J.,* June 1973, *11*(2), pp. 228–31.

Peel, David A. Some Implications of Utility Maximizing Firms: A Note. *Bull. Econ. Res.,* November 1973, *25*(2), pp. 148–51.

Pen, Jan. Business Against the Consumer. In *Reynolds, L. G.; Green, G. D. and Lewis, D. R., eds.,* 1973, pp. 190–200.

Peterson, Peter G. The Art of Managing Change. In *The Diebold Group, Inc.,* 1973, pp. 3–10.
[G: U.S.]

Pickle, Hal B. and Rungeling, Brian S. Empirical Investigation of Entrepreneurial Goals and Customer Satisfaction. *J. Bus.,* April 1973, *46*(2), pp. 268–73. [G: U.S.]

Reilley, Ewing W. Planning the Strategy of the Business. In *Klein, W. H. and Murphy, D. C., eds.,* 1973, pp. 166–73.

Richman, Barry. New Paths to Corporate Social Responsibility. *Calif. Manage. Rev.,* Spring 1973, *15*(3), pp. 20–36.

Shawcross, Hartley William [Lord]. The Structure of Public Company Boards. In *Allen, G. C., et al.,* 1973, pp. 45–54. [G: U.K.]

Steiner, George A. Long-Range Planning: Concept and Implementation. In *Klein, W. H. and Murphy, D. C., eds.,* 1973, pp. 242–49.

Steiner, George A. Approaches to Long-Range Planning for Small Business. In *Klein, W. H. and Murphy, D. C., eds.,* 1973, pp. 250–63.

Stewart, Samuel S., Jr. Share Price Maximization: A Tool for Management Decision-Making. *Calif. Manage. Rev.,* Winter 1973, *16*(2), pp. 54–58.

Stolk, William C. Beyond Profitability: A Proposal for Managing the Corporation's Public Business. In *Klein, W. H. and Murphy, D. C., eds.,* 1973, pp. 305–07.

Sumner, M. T. Announcement Effects of Profits Taxation. In *Parkin, M., ed.,* 1973, pp. 17–32.

Sutton, C. J. Management Behaviour and a Theory of Diversification. *Scot. J. Polit. Econ.,* February 1973, *20*(1), pp. 27–42.

Townsend, Harry. Big Business and Competition. In *Rybczynski, T. M., ed.,* 1973, pp. 68–77.

Vance, Jack O. The Anatomy of a Corporate Strategy. In *Klein, W. H. and Murphy, D. C., eds.,* 1973, pp. 150–57. [G: U.S.]

Votaw, Dow. Corporate Social Reform: An Educator's Viewpoint. *Calif. Manage. Rev.,* Summer 1973, *15*(4), pp. 67–73.

Votaw, Dow. Genius Becomes Rare: A Comment on the Doctrine of Social Responsibility Pt. II. *Calif. Manage. Rev.,* Spring 1973, *15*(3), pp. 5–19.

Weiss, E. B. The Corporate Deaf Ear. In *Murray, B. B., ed.*, 1973, pp. 260–70. [G: U.S.]

Wetherell, David. Nuovi orientamenti della "company image." (New Directions for the "Company Image." With English summary.) *L'Impresa*, 1973, *15*(9–10), pp. 562–67.

Worcester, Robert M. Il valore della "corporate image." (The Value of Corporate Image. With English summary.) *L'Impresa*, 1973, *15*(9–10), pp. 522–26.

Yarrow, G. K. Managerial Utility Maximization under Uncertainty. *Economica, N.S.*, May 1973, *40* (158), pp. 155–73.

Young, Elmer, Jr. Corporate Social Responsibility to the Minority Community. In *Dierkes, M. and Bauer, R. A., eds.*, 1973, pp. 297–300. [G: U.S.]

Zwick, Charles J. Strategic Planning and its Role in the Banking Environment of the Seventies. *J. Bank Res.*, Summer 1973, *4*(2), pp. 74–78.

520 BUSINESS FINANCE AND INVESTMENT

5200 Business Finance and Investment

Abegglen, James C. and Rapp, William V. Japanese Managerial Behavior and "Excessive Competition." In *Henley, D. S., ed.*, 1973, pp. 65–82. [G: Japan]

Levy, Haim and Arditti, Fred D. Valuation, Leverage, and the Cost of Capital in the Case of Depreciable Assets. *J. Finance*, June 1973, *28*(3), pp. 687–93.

Reinhardt, U. E. Break-Even Analysis for Lockheed's Tri Star: An Application of Financial Theory. *J. Finance*, September 1973, *28*(4), pp. 821–38. [G: U.S.]

521 Business Finance

5210 Business Finance

Adler, Michael. The Valuation and Financing of the Multi-National Firm: Comment. *Kyklos*, 1973, *26* (4), pp. 849–51.

Aigner, Dennis J. and Sprenkle, C. M. On Optimal Financing of Cyclical Cash Needs. *J. Finance*, December 1973, *28*(5), pp. 1249–54.

Alberts, W. W. and Archer, S. H. Some Evidence on the Effect of Company Size on the Cost of Equity Capital. *J. Financial Quant. Anal.*, March 1973, *8*(2), pp. 229–42. [G: U.S.]

Altman, Edward I. Predicting Railroad Bankruptcies in America. *Bell J. Econ. Manage. Sci.*, Spring 1973, *4*(1), pp. 184–211. [G: U.S.]

Arditti, Fred D. The Weighted Average Cost of Capital: Some Questions on its Definition, Interpretation, and Use. *J. Finance*, September 1973, *28*(4), pp. 1001–07.

Baker, Samuel H. Risk, Leverage, and Profitability: An Industry Analysis. *Rev. Econ. Statist.*, November 1973, *55*(4), pp. 503–07. [G: U.S.]

Bates, Timothy. An Econometric Analysis of Lending to Black Businessmen. *Rev. Econ. Statist.*, August 1973, *55*(3), pp. 272–83. [G: U.S.]

Baumol, William J., et al. Efficiency of Corporate Investment: A Reply. *Rev. Econ. Statist.*, February 1973, *55*(1), pp. 128–31.

Benston, George J. Required Disclosure and the Stock Market: An Evaluation of the Securities Exchange Act of 1934. *Amer. Econ. Rev.*, March 1973, *63*(1), pp. 132–55. [G: U.S.]

Ben-Zion, Uri and Balch, Michael. On the Analysis of Corporate Financial Theory under Uncertainty: A Comment. *Quart. J. Econ.*, May 1973, *87* (2), pp. 290–95.

Berger, Paul D. and Harper, William K. Determination of an Optimal Revolving Credit Agreement. *J. Financial Quant. Anal.*, June 1973, *8*(3), pp. 491–97.

Bierman, Harold, Jr. The Cost of Warrants. *J. Financial Quant. Anal.*, June 1973, *8*(3), pp. 499–503.

Bird, R. G. and Peirson, C. G. A Study of Convertible Notes Issued in Australia. *Australian Econ. Pap.*, June 1973, *12*(20), pp. 91–105. [G: Australia]

Breen, William J. and Lerner, Eugene M. Corporate Financial Strategies and Market Measures of Risk and Return. *J. Finance*, May 1973, *28*(2), pp. 339–51. [G: U.S.]

Brumelle, Shelby L. and Schwab, Bernhard. Capital Budgeting with Uncertain Future Opportunities: A Markovian Approach. *J. Financial Quant. Anal.*, January 1973, *8*(1), pp. 111–22.

Carleton, Willard T.; Dick, Charles L., Jr. and Downes, David H. Financial Policy Models: Theory and Practice. *J. Financial Quant. Anal.*, December 1973, *8*(5), pp. 691–709.

Carter, E. Eugene. A Simultaneous Equation Approach to Financial Planning: Comment. *J. Finance*, September 1973, *28*(4), pp. 1035–38.

Churchill, Gilbert A., Jr. and Hunt, Shelby D. Sources of Funds and Franchisee Success. *J. Bus. Res.*, Fall 1973, *1*(2), pp. 157–64. [G: U.S.]

Cohen, Stanley and Smyth, David J. Some Determinants of Price/Earnings Ratios of Industrial Common Stock. *Quart. Rev. Econ. Bus.*, Winter 1973, *13*(4), pp. 49–60. [G: U.S.]

Daniels, John D. and Arpan, Jeffrey. Comparative Home Country Influences on Management Practices Abroad. In *Henley, D. S., ed.*, 1973, pp. 409–19. [G: Canada; W. Europe; U.S.]

Davis, B. E.; Caccappolo, G. J. and Chaudry, M. A. An Econometric Planning Model for American Telephone and Telegraph Company. *Bell J. Econ. Manage. Sci.*, Spring 1973, *4*(1), pp. 29–56. [G: U.S.]

Davis, E. G.; Dunn, D. M. and Williams, W. H. Ambiguities in the Cross-Section Analysis of Per Share Financial Data. *J. Finance*, December 1973, *28*(5), pp. 1241–48. [G: U.S.]

De Alessi, Louis. Private Property and Dispersion of Ownership in Large Corporations. *J. Finance*, September 1973, *28*(4), pp. 839–51. [G: U.S.]

Dickman, A. B. The Financing of Industrial Development in South Africa. *S. Afr. J. Econ.*, December 1973, *41*(4), pp. 373–400. [G: S.Africa]

Drucker, Peter F. The Computer's Contribution to Financial Management. In *The Diebold Group, Inc.*, 1973, pp. 118–27.

Elton, Edwin J. and Gruber, Martin J. Asset Selection with Changing Capital Structure. *J. Financial Quant. Anal.*, June 1973, *8*(3), pp. 459–74.

Fama, Eugene F. A Note on the Market Model and the Two-Parameter Model. *J. Finance,* December 1973, *28*(5), pp. 1181–85.

Feldstein, Martin S. and Fane, George. Taxes, Corporate Dividend Policy and Personal Savings: The British Postwar Experience. *Rev. Econ. Statist.,* November 1973, *55*(4), pp. 399–411. **[G: U.K.]**

Florence, Gary A. Electric Utility Bond Financing. *Manage. Account.,* June 1973, *54*(12), pp. 35–37, 41.

Friend, Irwin and Husic, Frank. Efficiency of Corporate Investment. *Rev. Econ. Statist.,* February 1973, *55*(1), pp. 122–27.

Friend, Irwin. Mythodology in Finance. *J. Finance,* May 1973, *28*(2), pp. 257–72.

von Furstenberg, George M. The Equilibrium Spread Between Variable Rates and Fixed Rates on Long-Term Financing Instruments. *J. Financial Quant. Anal.,* December 1973, *8*(5), pp. 807–19.

Gershefski, George W. The Development of the Sun Oil Co. Corporate Financial Model. In *Thomas, W. E., Jr., ed.,* 1973, pp. 226–36. **[G: U.S.]**

Glyn, Andrew. The Stock Market Valuation of British Companies and the Cost of Capital 1955–69. *Oxford Econ. Pap.,* July 1973, *25*(2), pp. 213–40. **[G: U.K.]**

Goudzwaard, Maurice B. Some Evidence on the Effect of Company Size on the Cost of Equity Capital: Comment. *J. Financial Quant. Anal.,* March 1973, *8*(2), pp. 243–45.

Gupta, Manak C. Optimal Financing Policy for a Firm with Uncertain Fund Requirements. *J. Financial Quant. Anal.,* December 1973, *8*(5), pp. 731–47.

Gustafson, Dale R. Perspectives on Life Insurance Financial Reporting: Discussion. *J. Risk Ins.,* March 1973, *40*(1), pp. 22–25. **[G: U.S.]**

Hagen, Kare P. Optimal Dividend Policies and Corporate Growth. *Swedish J. Econ.,* September 1973, *75*(3), pp. 238–48.

Hemmings, Dan B. Leverage, Dividend Policy and the Cost of Capital: Comment. *J. Finance,* December 1973, *28*(5), pp. 1366–70.

Inselbag, Isik. Financing Decisions and the Theory of the Firm. *J. Financial Quant. Anal.,* December 1973, *8*(5), pp. 763–76.

Jaffee, Bruce L. Depreciation in a Simple Regulatory Model. *Bell J. Econ. Manage. Sci.,* Spring 1973, *4*(1), pp. 338–42.

Joehnk, Michael D. and Wert, James E. The Call-Risk Performance of the Discounted Seasoned Issue. *Miss. Val. J. Bus. Econ.,* Winter 1973-74, *9*(2), pp. 1–15. **[G: U.S.]**

Jones, Reginald H. The Challenge of Capital Attraction. *Manage. Account.,* June 1973, *54*(12), pp. 52–53, 58.

Jordan, Ronald J. An Empirical Investigation of the Adjustment of Stock Prices to New Quarterly Earnings Information. *J. Financial Quant. Anal.,* September 1973, *8*(4), pp. 609–20. **[G: U.S.]**

Kellog, Martin N. Analysis and Control of a Cash Flow System. In *Thomas, W. E., Jr., ed.,* 1973, pp. 420–27.

Kiger, Jack E. An Empirical Test of Annual Earnings Projection Models Using Quarterly Data. *Miss.*

Val. J. Bus. Econ., Spring 1973, *8*(3), pp. 17–28. **[G: U.S.]**

Krainer, Robert E. The Valuation and Financing of the Multi-National Firm: Reply and Some Extensions. *Kyklos,* 1973, *26*(4), pp. 857–65.

Kraus, Alan and Litzenberger, Robert H. A State-Preference Model of Optimal Financial Leverage. *J. Finance,* September 1973, *28*(4), pp. 911–22.

Kraus, Alan. The Bond Refunding Decision in an Efficient Market. *J. Financial Quant. Anal.,* December 1973, *8*(5), pp. 793–806.

Krouse, Clement G. and Lee, Wayne Y. Optimal Equity Financing of the Corporation. *J. Financial Quant. Anal.,* September 1973, *8*(4), pp. 539–63.

Krouse, Clement G. On the Theory of Optimal Investment, Dividends, and Growth in the Firm. *Amer. Econ. Rev.,* June 1973, *63*(3), pp. 269–79.

Lerner, Eugene M. Simulating a Cash Budget. In *Thomas, W. E., Jr., ed.,* 1973, pp. 266–78.

Lewellen, Wilbur G. and Racette, George A. Convertible Debt Financing. *J. Financial Quant. Anal.,* December 1973, *8*(5), pp. 777–92.

Lister, R. J. Financing an Acquisition. In *Lister, R. J., ed.,* 1973, pp. 186–200.

Litzenberger, Robert H.; Joy, O. Maurice and Jones, Charles P. Leverage and the Valuation of Risk Assets: An Empirical Test. *J. Financial Quant. Anal.,* March 1973, *8*(2), pp. 227. **[G: U.S.]**

Logue, Dennis E. On the Pricing of Unseasoned Equity Issues: 1965-1969. *J. Financial Quant. Anal.,* January 1973, *8*(1), pp. 91–103. **[G: U.S.]**

Lotti, Eraldo. L'eccedenza industriale. Analisi e calcola dell'incidenza delle anomalie del processo produttivo sull'eccedenza industriale. (Industrial Surplus. Analysis of Calculations of the Effect of Irregularities of the Productive Process of the Industrial Surplus. With English summary.) *L'Impresa,* 1973, *15*(3–4), pp. 245–51.

Mantripragada, K. Capital Management and Capital Theory: Discussion. *J. Finance,* May 1973, *28*(2), pp. 369–72. **[G: U.S.]**

Marinacos, George N. Big Board: Does it Really Increase Market Price? *Marquette Bus. Rev.,* Winter 1973, *17*(4), pp. 197–200.

Mastrapasqua, Frank and Bolten, Steven. A Note on Financial Analyst Evaluation. *J. Finance,* June 1973, *28*(3), pp. 707–12.

McGowan, John J. The Supply of Equity Securities, 1952–68. In *Goldsmith, R. W., ed.,* 1973, pp. 165–203. **[G: U.S.]**

McKeown, James C. A Brief Exploration of the Goal Congruence of Net Realizable Value. *Accounting Rev.,* April 1973, *48*(2), pp. 386–88.

Mehr, Robert I. and Forbes, Stephen W. The Risk Management Decision in the Total Business Setting. *J. Risk Ins.,* September 1973, *40*(3), pp. 389–401.

Melnik, A. and Pollatschek, M. A. Debt Capacity, Diversification and Conglomerate Mergers. *J. Finance,* December 1973, *28*(5), pp. 1163–73.

Merville, Larry J. and Tavis, Lee A. Optimal Working Capital Policies: A Chance-Constrained Programming Approach. *J. Financial Quant. Anal.,* January 1973, *8*(1), pp. 47–59.

Monroe, Robert J. Financial Characteristics of

Merged Firms: A Multivariate Analysis: Comment. *J. Financial Quant. Anal.*, March 1973, 8 (2), pp. 163–65.

Myers, Stewart C. A Simple Model of Firm Behavior Under Regulation and Uncertainty. *Bell J. Econ. Manage. Sci.*, Spring 1973, *4*(1), pp. 304–15.

Nielsen, James F. and Melicher, Ronald W. A Financial Analysis of Acquisition and Merger Premiums. *J. Financial Quant. Anal.*, March 1973, *8*(2), pp. 139–48. [G: U.S.]

Osborn, Richards C. The Supply of Equity Capital by the SBICs. *Quart. Rev. Econ. Bus.*, Spring 1973, *13*(1), pp. 69–86. [G: U.S.]

Pinches, George E.; Mingo, Kent A. and Caruthers, J. Kent. The Stability of Financial Patterns in Industrial Organizations. *J. Finance*, May 1973, *28* (2), pp. 389–96. [G: U.S.]

Pizzala, F. B. The Cost of Capital to the Private Sector: A Critique of Merrett and Sykes. In *Lister, R. J., ed.*, 1973, pp. 39–48. [G: U.K.]

Posnak, Robert L. Perspectives on Life Insurance Financial Reporting. *J. Risk Ins.*, March 1973, *40* (1), pp. 7–22. [G: U.S.]

Rabe, B. Financiële modellen als beleidsinstrument in de onderneming. (Financial Models as Management Tools. With English summary.) *Econ. Soc. Tijdschr.*, April 1973, *27*(2), pp. 173–80.

Racette, George A. Earnings Retention, New Capital and the Growth of the Firm: A Comment. *Rev. Econ. Statist.*, February 1973, *55*(1), pp. 127–28.

Reilly, Raymond R. and Wecker, William E. On the Weighted Average Cost of Capital. *J. Financial Quant. Anal.*, January 1973, *8*(1), pp. 123–26.

Rubinstein, Mark E. The Fundamental Theorem of Parameter-Preference Security Valuation. *J. Financial Quant. Anal.*, January 1973, *8*(1), pp. 61–69.

Rubinstein, Mark E. A Mean-Variance Synthesis of Corporate Financial Theory. *J. Finance*, March 1973, *28*(1), pp. 167–81.

Rubinstein, Mark E. Corporate Financial Policy in Segmented Securities Markets. *J. Financial Quant. Anal.*, December 1973, *8*(5), pp. 749–61.

Rutenberg, David P. Maneuvering Liquid Assets in a Multinational Company: Formulation and Deterministic Solution Procedures. In *Alexandrides, C. G., ed.*, 1973, pp. 109–28.

Sethi, Suresh P. A Note on Modeling Simple Dynamic Cash Balance Problems. *J. Financial Quant. Anal.*, September 1973, *8*(4), pp. 685–87.

Severn, Alan K. The Financing of the Multi-National Firm: Comment. *Kyklos*, 1973, *26*(4), pp. 852–56.

Shapiro, Alan C. Optimal Inventory and Credit-Granting Strategies under Inflation and Devaluation. *J. Financial Quant. Anal.*, January 1973, *8* (1), pp. 37–46.

Shapiro, Alan C. Management Science Models for Multicurrency Cash Management. In *Alexandrides, C. G., ed.*, 1973, pp. 93–107.

Smith, Keith V. A Financial Analysis of Acquisition and Merger Premiums: Comment. *J. Financial Quant. Anal.*, March 1973, *8*(2), pp. 159–62.

Stevens, Donald L. Financial Characteristics of Merged Firms: A Multivariate Analysis. *J. Financial Quant. Anal.*, March 1973, *8*(2), pp. 149–58. [G: U.S.]

Stewart, Samuel S., Jr. Share Price Maximization: A Tool for Management Decision-Making. *Calif. Manage. Rev.*, Winter 1973, *16*(2), pp. 54–58.

Stiglitz, Joseph E. Taxation, Corporate Financial Policy, and the Cost of Capital. *J. Public Econ.*, February 1973, *2*(1), pp. 1–34.

Stone, Bernell K. Cash Planning and Credit-Line Determination with a Financial Statement Simulator: A Case Report on Short-Term Financial Planning. *J. Financial Quant. Anal.*, December 1973, *8*(5), pp. 711–29.

Thompson, Howard E. and Thatcher, Lionel W. Required Rate of Return for Equity Capital Under Conditions of Growth and Consideration of Regulatory Lag. *Land Econ.*, May 1973, *49*(2), pp. 148–62.

Tyran, Michael R. A Financial Projection Plan. *Manage. Account.*, July 1973, *55*(1), pp. 19–23, 28.

Van Horne, James C. Implied Fixed Costs of Long-Term Debt Issues. *J. Financial Quant. Anal.*, December 1973, *8*(5), pp. 821–33. [G: U.S.]

Vanthienen, L. and Depre, F. Methodologie voor empirish onderzoek op de kapitaalmarkt. (With English summary.) *Tijdschr. Econ.*, 1973, *18*(4), pp. 629–46.

Vanthienen, L. Portfolio Theorie en Bedrijfsfinanciering. (With English summary.) *Tijdschr. Econ.*, 1973, *18*(4), pp. 597–627.

Wakoff, Gary I. On Shareholders' Indifference to the Proceeds Price in Preemptive Rights Offerings. *J. Financial Quant. Anal.*, December 1973, *8*(5), pp. 835–36.

Warren, James M. and Shelton, John P. A Simultaneous Equation Approach to Financial Planning: Reply. *J. Finance*, September 1973, *28*(4), pp. 1039–42.

Watts, Ross. The Information Content of Dividends. *J. Bus.*, April 1973, *46*(2), pp. 191–211. [G: U.S.]

Weber, John A. A Note on Keeping Abreast of Developments in the Field of Finance. *J. Finance*, March 1973, *28*(1), pp. 161–65. [G: U.S.]

Weil, Roman L. Macaulay's Duration: An Appreciation. *J. Bus.*, October 1973, *46*(4), pp. 589–92.

Wemelsfelder, J. Kapitaalvoorzieningsproblemen in een op arbeiderszelfbestuur gebaseerde industrie. Het voorbeeld van Joegoslavië. (Problems of Financing Labor-Managed Firms: The Case of Yugo-Slavia. With English summary.) *De Economist*, March-April 1973, *121*(2), pp. 122–56. [G: Yugoslavia]

Wendt, Paul F. New Techniques in Financing Real Estate. *Amer. Real Estate Urban Econ. Assoc. J.*, June 1973, *1*(1), pp. 140–57.

Wiar, Robert C. Economic Implications of Multiple Rates of Return in the Leveraged Lease Context. *J. Finance*, December 1973, *28*(5), pp. 1275–86.

Winkle, Gary M. Perspectives on Life Insurance Financial Reporting: Discussion. *J. Risk Ins.*, March 1973, *40*(1), pp. 25–30. [G: U.S.]

Winklevoss, Howard E. and Zelten, Robert A. An Empirical Analysis of Mutual Life Insurance Company Surplus. *J. Risk Ins.*, September 1973, *40*(3), pp. 403–25. [G: U.S.]

Wyman, Harold E. Financial Lease Evaluation Under Conditions of Uncertainty. *Accounting Rev.*, July 1973, *48*(3), pp. 489–93.

Zaloom, Victor A. On the Proper Use of Compound Interest Factors—A Technical Note. *Eng. Econ.*, July-August 1973, *18*(4), pp. 257–64.

522 Business Investment

5220 Business Investment

Adelson, R. M. Discounted Cash Flow—The Other Point of View. In *Lister, R. J., ed.*, 1973, pp. 92–105.

Ahmed, S. Basheer. Optimal Equipment Replacement Policy: An Empirical Study. *J. Transp. Econ. Policy*, January 1973, *7*(1), pp. 71–79.

Andriano, Angelo. Un procedimento analitico per la quantificazione degli smobilizzi. (An Analytical Procedure to Quantify Disinvestments. With English summary.) *L'Impresa*, 1973, *15*(3–4), pp. 240–43.

Arditti, Fred D.; Grinold, Richard C. and Levy, Haim. The Investment-Consumption Decision under Capital Rationing: An Efficient Set Analysis. *Rev. Econ. Stud.*, July 1973, *40*(3), pp. 367–76.

Baker, C. B. Capital Budgeting and Financial Management in Linear Programming Models. In *Judge, G. G. and Takayama, T., eds.*, 1973, pp. 688–705.

Balloni, Valeriano. Le decisioni di investimento. Risultati di interviste con dirigenti industriali inglesi. (Investment Decisions: Interviews with English Businessmen. With English summary.) *L'Impresa*, 1973, *15*(3–4), pp. 278–81. [G: U.K.]

Ball, R. J. Investment Incentives. *Nat. Westminster Bank Quart. Rev.*, August 1973, pp. 22–35.
[G: U.K.]

Barlow, Joel. The Tax Law Bias Against Investment in Production Facilities. *Nat. Tax J.*, September 1973, *26*(3), pp. 415–37. [G: U.S.]

Baumol, William J., et al. Efficiency of Corporate Investment: A Reply. *Rev. Econ. Statist.*, February 1973, *55*(1), pp. 128–31.

Beenhakker, Henri L. Discounting Indices Proposed for Capital Investment Evaluation: A Further Examination. *Eng. Econ.*, April-May 1973, *18*(3), pp. 149–68.

Belli, R. David; Allnutt, Smith W. and Murad, Howard. Property, Plant, and Equipment Expenditures by Majority-Owned Foreign Affiliates of U.S. Companies: Revised Estimates for 1966–72 and Projections for 1973 and 1974. *Surv. Curr. Bus.*, December 1973, *53*(12), pp. 19–32.
[G: U.S.]

Belli, R. David. Plant and Equipment Expenditures of U.S.-Owned Foreign Affiliates: Revised Estimates for 1972 and 1973. *Surv. Curr. Bus.*, March 1973, *53*(3), pp. 45–52. [G: U.S.]

Bennett, J. W. and Leather, J. Investment Cut-off Rates for a Public Company. *Econ. Rec.*, June 1973, *49*(126), pp. 228–40.

Bierman, Harold, Jr. and Hass, Jerome E. Capital Budgeting Under Uncertainty: A Reformulation. *J. Finance*, March 1973, *28*(1), pp. 119–29.

Bierman, Harold, Jr. Analysis of the Lease-or-Buy Decision: Comment. *J. Finance*, September 1973, *28*(4), pp. 1019–21.

Bitar, Sergio and Trivelli, Hugo. The Cost of Capital in the Chilean Economy. In *Eckaus, R. S. and Rosenstein-Rodan, P. N., eds.*, 1973, pp. 147–65.
[G: Chile]

Boddy, Raford and Gort, Michael. Capital Expenditures and Capital Stocks. *Ann. Econ. Soc. Measure*, July 1973, *2*(3), pp. 245–61. [G: U.S.]

Bodkin, Ronald G. and Murthy, K. S. R. The Orders-Shipments Mechanism in Canadian Producer Goods Industries. *J. Amer. Statist. Assoc.*, June 1973, *68*(342), pp. 297–305. [G: Canada]

Boudreaux, Kenneth J. 'Managerialism' and Risk-Return Performance. *Southern Econ. J.*, January 1973, *39*(3), pp. 366–72. [G: U. S.]

Bower, Richard S. and Lessard, Donald R. An Operational Approach to Risk-Screening. *J. Finance*, May 1973, *28*(2), pp. 321–37. [G: U.S.]

Brechling, Frank. Announcement Effects of Profits Taxation: Discussion. In *Parkin, M., ed.*, 1973, pp. 33–34.

Brennan, Michael J. An Approach to the Valuation of Uncertain Income Streams. *J. Finance*, June 1973, *28*(3), pp. 661–74.

Brief, Richard P. and Owen, Joel. Present Value Models and the Multi-Asset Problem. *Accounting Rev.*, October 1973, *48*(4), pp. 690–95.

Budd, A. P. and Litzenberger, Robert H. Changes in the Supply of Money, the Firm's Market Value and Cost of Capital. *J. Finance*, March 1973, *28*(1), pp. 49–57.

Burrows, Paul and Godfrey, Leslie G. Identifying and Estimating the Parameters of a Symmetrical Model of Inventory Investment. *Appl. Econ.*, September 1973, *5*(3), pp. 193–97.

Candler, Wilfred V. Linear Programming in Capital Budgeting with Multiple Goals. In *Cochrane, J. L. and Zeleny, M., eds.*, 1973, pp. 416–28.

Chang, John C. and Holt, Charles C. Optimal Investment Orders Under Uncertainty and Dynamic Costs: Theory and Estimates. *Southern Econ. J.*, April 1973, *39*(4), pp. 508–25. [G: U.S.]

Clark, Robert A.; Jantorni, Joan M. and Gann, Robert R. Analysis of the Lease-or-Buy Decision: Comment. *J. Finance*, September 1973, *28*(4), pp. 1015–16.

Cohn, Richard A. and Pringle, John J. Imperfections in International Financial Markets: Implications for Risk Premia and the Cost of Capital to Firms. *J. Finance*, March 1973, *28*(1), pp. 59–66.

Colberg, Marshall R. and King, James P. Theory of Production Abandonment. *Rivista Int. Sci. Econ. Com.*, October 1973, *20*(10), pp. 961–72.

Cole, William A. and Wales, Stephen H., Sr. The Investment Credit. *Manage. Account.*, March 1973, *54*(9), pp. 13–16, 35.

Davenport, Michael. Leverage and the Cost of Capital: Reply. *Economica, N.S.*, August 1973, *40*(159), pp. 321.

Durand, David. Indices of Profitability as Aids to Judgment in Capital Budgeting. *J. Bank Res.*, Winter 1973, *3*(4), pp. 200–19.

Edwards, James B. Adjusted DCF Rate of Return. *Manage. Account.*, January 1973, *54*(7), pp. 45–49.

Eisner, Robert. Tax Incentives for Investment. *Nat. Tax J.*, September 1973, *26*(3), pp. 397–401.
[G: U.S.]

Elliott, J. W. Theories of Corporate Investment Behavior Revisited. *Amer. Econ. Rev.*, March 1973, *63*(1), pp. 195–207. [G: U.S.]

Elton, Edwin J. Capital Management and Capital Theory: Discussion. *J. Finance*, May 1973, *28*(2), pp. 368–69. [G: U.S.]

Elton, Edwin J. and Gruber, Martin J. Asset Selection with Changing Capital Structure. *J. Financial Quant. Anal.*, June 1973, *8*(3), pp. 459–74.

de Faro, Clovis. A Sufficient Condition for a Unique Nonnegative Internal Rate of Return: Comment. *J. Financial Quant. Anal.*, September 1973, *8*(4), pp. 683–84.

Fawthrop, R. A. Underlying Problems in Discounted Cash Flow. In *Lister, R. J., ed.,* 1973, pp. 106–29.

Fisher, Lawrence. Investment Characteristics of Common Stocks in Regulated and Unregulated Industries: A Comparative Study. In *Russell, M., ed.,* 1973, pp. 53–78. [G: U.S.]

Forbes, Stephen W. Further Studies of Property-Liability Return Adequacy: Reply. *J. Risk Ins.*, September 1973, *40*(3), pp. 460–62.

Ford, Allen. Selecting a Useful Life for the Investment Credit. *Manage. Account.*, April 1973, *54* (10), pp. 14–16.

Forsyth, John D. and Laughhunn, D. J. Capital Rationing in the Face of Multiple Organizational Objectives. In *Cochrane, J. L. and Zeleny, M., eds.,* 1973, pp. 439–46.

Fremgen, James M. Capital Budgeting Practices: A Survey. *Manage. Account.*, May 1973, *54*(11), pp. 19–25. [G: U.S.]

Friend, Irwin and Husic, Frank. Efficiency of Corporate Investment. *Rev. Econ. Statist.*, February 1973, *55*(1), pp. 122–27.

Gardner, Bernard and Richardson, Peter. The Fiscal Treatment of Shipping. *J. Ind. Econ.*, December 1973, *22*(2), pp. 95–117. [G: U.K.]

Gentry, James A. Investment Characteristics of Common Stocks in Regulated and Unregulated Industries: A Comparative Study: Comment. In *Russell, M., ed.,* 1973, pp. 79–83. [G: U.S.]

Gitman, Lawrence J. A Multinational Firm Investment Model. *J. Econ. Bus.*, Fall 1973, *26*(1), pp. 41–48.

Goetz, Billy E. A Note on Discounted Cash Flow Examples: A Reply. *Accounting Rev.*, January 1973, *48*(1), pp. 135–36.

Gould, John P. and Waud, Roger N. The Neoclassical Model of Investment Behavior: Another View. *Int. Econ. Rev.*, February 1973, *14*(1), pp. 33–48.

Grant, L. C. Monitoring Capital Investments. In *Thomas, W. E., Jr., ed.,* 1973, pp. 379–90.

Grossman, Steven D. A Test of Speed of Adjustment in Manufacturing Inventory Investment. *Quart. Rev. Econ. Bus.*, Autumn 1973, *13*(3), pp. 21–32.
[G: U.S.]

Gupta, Manak C. On Intra-Firm Resource Allocation Under Risk. *Eng. Econ.*, July-August 1973, *18* (4), pp. 229–42.

Harriss, C. Lowell. Capital Needs, Savings, and Jobs. In *Tax Foundation, Inc.,* 1973, pp. 27–34.
[G: U.S.]

Hartman, Richard. Adjustment Costs, Price and Wage Uncertainty, and Investment. *Rev. Econ. Stud.*, April 1973, *40*(2), pp. 259–67.

Hemmings, Dan B. Leverage and the Cost of Capital: A Comment. *Economica, N.S.*, August 1973, *40*(159), pp. 316–20.

Hempenius, A. L. On the Specification of Risk Aversion in an Expenditure Equation. *De Economist,* July-August 1973, *121*(4), pp. 375–86.

Herring, Richard and Willett, Thomas D. The Relationship Between U.S. Direct Investment at Home and Abroad. *Rivista Int. Sci. Econ. Com.,* January 1973, *20*(1), pp. 72–82. [G: U.S.]

Heubes, Jürgen. Investitionsverhalten in der Industrie der Bundesrepublik Deutschland 1950–1970. (Investment Behavior in the West-German Industry 1950–1970. With English summary.) *Z. ges. Staatswiss.*, October 1973, *129*(4), pp. 685–701. [G: W. Germany]

Hochman, Eitan; Hochman, Oded and Razin, Assaf. Demand for Investment in Productive and Financial Capital. *Europ. Econ. Rev.*, April 1973, *4* (1), pp. 67–83.

Inselbag, Isik. Financing Decisions and the Theory of the Firm. *J. Financial Quant. Anal.*, December 1973, *8*(5), pp. 763–76.

Jain, Chaman L. and Migliaro, Alfonso. Optimum Customer Investment Criteria in Mail Order Operation. *Rivista Int. Sci. Econ. Com.*, May 1973, *20*(5), pp. 470–78.

Jarkovsky, Vladimír. The Dynamic Determination of Economically Efficient Capital Investment and New Technology. *Eastern Europ. Econ.*, Summer 1973, *11*(4), pp. 86–112. [G: Czechoslovakia]

Jarrett, Jeffrey E. An Abandonment Decision Model. *Eng. Econ.*, October-November 1973, *19*(1), pp. 35–46.

Johnson, Keith B. and Hazuka, Thomas B. The NPV-IRR Debate in Lease Analysis. *Miss. Val. J. Bus. Econ.*, Winter 1973-74, *9*(2), pp. 16–26.

Johnson, Robert W. and Lewellen, Wilbur G. Analysis of the Lease-or-Buy Decision: Reply. *J. Finance*, September 1973, *28*(4), pp. 1024–28.

Johnson, Rodney D. and Klein, Richard H. A Further Note on the Analysis of Capital Investment Alternatives: Reply. *Miss. Val. J. Bus. Econ.*, Fall 1973, *9*(1), pp. 91–93.

Jorgenson, Dale W. Technology and Decision Rules in the Theory of Investment Behavior. *Quart. J. Econ.*, November 1973, *87*(4), pp. 523–43.

Joyce, Jon M. Cost of Capital and Inventory Investment: Further Evidence. *Southern Econ. J.*, October 1973, *40*(2), pp. 323–29. [G: U.S.]

Joy, O. Maurice and Bradley, Jerry O. A Note on Sensitivity Analysis of Rates of Return. *J. Finance,* December 1973, *28*(5), pp. 1255–61.

Katano, Hikoji. Estimation of Investment Allocation Ratios of Japanese Economy: 1960–1969. *Kobe Econ. Bus. Rev.,* 1973, *20*, pp. 37–50. [G: Japan]

Khachaturov, T. Improving the Methods of Determining the Effectiveness of Capital Investments. *Prob. Econ.*, September 1973, *16*(5), pp. 3–30.
[G: U.S.S.R.]

Klammer, Thomas. The Association of Capital Budgeting Techniques with Firm Performance. *Ac-*

counting Rev., April 1973, *48*(2), pp. 353–64.
[G: U.S.]

Kostenko, M. V. On Choosing the Ratio Between the Norm of Effectiveness and the Discount Coefficient. *Matekon*, Spring 1973, *9*(3), pp. 3–5.

Krouse, Clement G. On the Theory of Optimal Investment, Dividends, and Growth in the Firm. *Amer. Econ. Rev.*, June 1973, *63*(3), pp. 269–79.

Latham, R. W. and Peel, David A. A Comment on Adjustments Costs and the Flexible Accelerator. *Rech. Écon. Louvain*, September 1973, *39*(3), pp. 371–76.

Leftwich, Robert B. Foreign Direct Investments in the United States, 1962–71. *Surv. Curr. Bus.*, February 1973, *53*(2), pp. 29–40. [G: U.S.]

Lev, Baruch and Orgler, Yair E. Analysis of the Lease-or-Buy Decision: Comment. *J. Finance*, September 1973, *28*(4), pp. 1022–23.

Lindström, Caj-Gunnar. Om beslutsplanering. (Decision Planning. With English summary.) *Ekon. Samfundets Tidskr.*, January 1973, *26*(1), pp. 32–38.

Littrell, Earl K., III. A Note on Discounted Cash Flow Examples. *Accounting Rev.*, January 1973, *48*(1), pp. 132–34.

Litzenberger, Robert H. and Joy, O. Maurice. Inter-Industry Profitability Under Uncertainty. *Western Econ. J.*, September 1973, *11*(3), pp. 338–49.
[G: U.S.]

Litzenberger, Robert H.; Joy, O. Maurice and Jones, Charles P. Leverage and the Valuation of Risk Assets: An Empirical Test. *J. Financial Quant. Anal.*, March 1973, *8*(2), pp. 227. [G: U.S.]

Lorange, Peter and Norman, Victor D. Risk Preference in Scandinavian Shipping. *Appl. Econ.*, March 1973, *5*(1), pp. 49–59. [G: Scandinavia]

Lusztig, Peter. Analysis of the Lease-or-Buy Decision: Comment. *J. Finance*, September 1973, *28*(4), pp. 1017–18.

Maass, Randal O. and Hutchins, Robert C. Measurement of Multicompany Diversification. *J. Econ. Bus.*, Fall 1973, *26*(1), pp. 74–77. [G: U.S.]

Maccini, Louis J. On Optimal Delivery Lags. *J. Econ. Theory*, April 1973, *6*(2), pp. 107–25.

Maccini, Louis J. Delivery Lags and the Demand for Investment. *Rev. Econ. Stud.*, April 1973, *40*(2), pp. 269–81.

Mantripragada, K. Capital Management and Capital Theory: Discussion. *J. Finance*, May 1973, *28*(2), pp. 369–72. [G: U.S.]

McEnally, Richard W. and Tavis, Lee A. Further Studies of Property-Liability Return Adequacy: Comment. *J. Risk Ins.*, September 1973, *40*(3), pp. 453–60.

McGuigan, James R. and King, William R. Security Option Strategy under Risk Aversion: An Analysis. *J. Financial Quant. Anal.*, January 1973, *8*(1), pp. 1–15.

Megyeri, E. Optimal Utilization of Enterprise Funds and Some Problems of Measuring Effectiveness. *Acta Oecon.*, 1973, *11*(4), pp. 347–67. [G: Hungary]

Melicher, Ronald W. and Rush, David F. The Performance of Conglomerate Firms: Recent Risk and Return Experience. *J. Finance*, May 1973, *28*(2), pp. 381–88. [G: U.S.]

Mercer, Lloyd J. Rates of Return and Government Subsidization of the Canadian Pacific Railway: An Alternate View. *Can. J. Econ.*, August 1973, *6*(3), pp. 428–37. [G: Canada]

Merville, Larry J. and Tavis, Lee A. A Generalized Model for Capital Investment. *J. Finance*, March 1973, *28*(1), pp. 109–18.

Moore, Basil J. Some Macroeconomic Consequences of Corporate Equities. *Can. J. Econ.*, November 1973, *6*(4), pp. 529–44.

Mortensen, Dale T. Generalized Costs of Adjustment and Dynamic Factor Demand Theory. *Econometrica*, July 1973, *41*(4), pp. 657–65.

Öhqvist, Henrik. Kapitalets produktivitet i industriföretag. (Capital Productivity in Industrial Enterprise. With English summary.) *Ekon. Samfundets Tidskr.*, 1973, *26*(3), pp. 159–66.

Osborn, Richards C. The Supply of Equity Capital by the SBICs. *Quart. Rev. Econ. Bus.*, Spring 1973, *13*(1), pp. 69–86. [G: U.S.]

Osteryoung, Jerome S. Multiple Goals in the Capital Budgeting Decision. In *Cochrane, J. L. and Zeleny, M., eds.*, 1973, pp. 447–57.

Pejovich, Svetozar. The Banking System and the Investment Behavior of the Yugoslav Firm. In *Bornstein, M., ed.*, 1973, pp. 285–311. [G: Yugoslavia]

Petrei, Amalio H. Rates of Return to Physical Capital in Manufacturing Industries in Argentina. *Oxford Econ. Pap.*, November 1973, *25*(3), pp. 378–404. [G: Argentina]

Pettway, Richard H. Integer Programming in Capital Budgeting: A Note on Computational Experience. *J. Financial Quant. Anal.*, September 1973, *8*(4), pp. 665–72.

Poindexter, J. Carl, Jr. and Jones, C. P. The Effect of Recent Tax Policy Changes on Manufacturing Investment. *Quart. Rev. Econ. Bus.*, Winter 1973, *13*(4), pp. 79–88. [G: U.S.]

Porter, R. Burr; Wart, James R. and Ferguson, Donald L. Efficient Algorithms for Conducting Stochastic Dominance Tests on Large Numbers of Portfolios. *J. Financial Quant. Anal.*, January 1973, *8*(1), pp. 71–81.

Racette, George A. Earnings Retention, New Capital and the Growth of the Firm: A Comment. *Rev. Econ. Statist.*, February 1973, *55*(1), pp. 127–28.

Reilly, Frank K. Further Evidence on Short-Run Results for New Issue Investors. *J. Financial Quant. Anal.*, January 1973, *8*(1), pp. 83–90.
[G: U.S.]

Robichek, Alexander A.; Higgins, Robert C. and Kinsman, Michael. The Effect of Leverage on the Cost of Equity Capital of Electric Utility Firms. *J. Finance*, May 1973, *28*(2), pp. 353–67.
[G: U.S.]

Rooney, Robert F. Descartes' Rule and Multiple Internal Rates of Return. *Western Econ. J.*, June 1973, *11*(2), pp. 241.

Ross, Myron H. Probability, Games, Regret and Investment Criteria. *Eng. Econ.*, April–May 1973, *18*(3), pp. 191–98.

Salamon, Gerald L. Models of the Relationship between the Accounting and Internal Rate of Return: An Examination of the Methodology. *J. Acc. Res.*, Autumn 1973, *11*(2), pp. 296–303.

Sankar, U. Investment Behavior in the U.S. Telephone Industry—1949 to 1968. *Bell J. Econ. Manage. Sci.*, Autumn 1973, *4*(2), pp. 665–78.
[G: U.S.]

Scherer, Frederic M. Investment Variability, Seller Concentration, and Plant Scale Economies. *J. Ind. Econ.*, December 1973, *22*(2), pp. 157–60.
[G: U.S.]

Sher, William. An Alternative Proof of the B-M Theorem on the Existence of the Firm's Optimal Capital Structure. *Quart. J. Econ.*, August 1973, *87*(3), pp. 474–81.

Smith, Vernon L. Depreciation, Market Valuations and Investment Theory. In *Haynes, W. W.; Coyne, T. J. and Osborne, D. K., eds.*, 1973, pp. 375–82.

Solomon, Martin B., Jr. Uncertainty and Its Effect on Capital Investment Analysis. In *Haynes, W. W.; Coyne, T. J. and Osborne, D. K., eds.*, 1973, pp. 408–13.

Ştirbu, Cornelia and Condurache, Gheorghe. Determinarea timpului optim de înlocuire a unei linii tehnologice du sudură de la Uzina metalurgică—Iaşi. (Determining the Optimum Time for Replacing a Welding Technological Line at the Jassy Metallurgical Works. With English summary.) *Stud. Cercet. Econ.*, 1973, (4), pp. 89–98.
[G: Rumania]

Stone, Bernell K. A General Class of Three-Parameter Risk Measures. *J. Finance,* June 1973, *28*(3), pp. 675–85.

Stott, Alexander L. Capital Recovery in a World of Inflation. In *Tax Foundation, Inc.*, 1973, pp. 35–42.
[G: U.S.]

Sumner, M. T. Investment and Corporate Taxation. *J. Polit. Econ.*, July-August 1973, *81*(4), pp. 982–93.
[G: U.K.]

Sumner, M. T. Announcement Effects of Profits Taxation. In *Parkin, M., ed.*, 1973, pp. 17–32.

Sundblom, Dan J. Investeringsbeslutets systematik. (Classification of Investment Decision. With English summary.) *Ekon. Samfundets Tidskr.*, 1973, *26*(3), pp. 177–200.

Talonen, Pentti. Näkökohtia yrityksen kasvusta ja kannattavuudesta. Osa II. (Growth and Profitability of the Firm. Part II. With English summary.) *Liiketaloudellinen Aikak.*, 1973, *22*(4), pp. 248–62.

Tapiero, Charles S. and Leinekugel-Le-Cocq, Armand R. Investissements, utilisation de capacité productive et amortissement: politiques optimales. (Investments, Capacity Utilization and Depreciation: Optimal Policies. With English summary.) *Revue Écon.*, May 1973, *24*(3), pp. 442–59.

Tepper, Irwin. Revealed Preference Methods and the Pure Theory of the Cost of Capital. *J. Finance,* March 1973, *28*(1), pp. 35–48.

Thompson, Richard G.; Callen, Richard W. and Wolken, Lawrence C. A Stochastic Investment Model for a Survival Conscious Fishing Firm. In *Sokoloski, A. A., ed.*, 1973, pp. 112–20. [G: U.S.]

Thompson, Russell G., et al. A Stochastic Investment Model for a Survival Conscious Firm Applied to Shrimp Fishing. *Appl. Econ.*, June 1973, *5*(2), pp. 75–87.

Thrun, Walter J., Sr. A Systems Approach to Cash Flow Determination. *Manage. Account.*, February 1973, *54*(8), pp. 29–31.

Treischmann, James S. Further Studies of Property-Liability Return Adequacy: Reply. *J. Risk Ins.*, September 1973, *40*(3), pp. 462–64.

Trivedi, P. K. Retail Inventory Investment Behaviour. *J. Econometrics*, March 1973, *1*(1), pp. 61–80.
[G: U.K.]

Vandenberg, Pieter A. A Further Note on the Analysis of Capital Investment Alternatives: Comment. *Miss. Val. J. Bus. Econ.*, Fall 1973, *9*(1), pp. 88–90.

Vatter, William J. Capital Budget Formulae. In *Thomas, W. E., Jr., ed.*, 1973, pp. 176–200.

Venieris, Yiannis P. Sales Expectations, Inventory Fluctuations, and Price Behavior. *Southern Econ. J.*, October 1973, *40*(2), pp. 246–61. [G: U.S.]

Volkov, A. M. and Senchagov, V. K. Problems of Depreciation and Its Reflection in the Input-Output Balance. *Matekon*, Spring 1973, *9*(3), pp. 55–66.

Weingartner, H. Martin. Some New Views on the Payback Period and Capital Budgeting Decisions. In *Haynes, W. W.; Coyne, T. J. and Osborne, D. K., eds.*, 1973, pp. 393–407.

Weston, J. Fred. Pricing Behavior of Large Firms. In *Weston, J. F. and Ornstein, S. I., eds.*, 1973, pp. 143–55.

Whitmore, G. A. and Amey, Lloyd R. Capital Budgeting under Rationing: Comments on the Lusztig and Schwab Procedure. *J. Financial Quant. Anal.*, January 1973, *8*(1), pp. 127–35.

Wiar, Robert C. Economic Implications of Multiple Rates of Return in the Leveraged Lease Context. *J. Finance*, December 1973, *28*(5), pp. 1275–86.

Williams, Fred E. On the Evaluation of Intertemporal Outcomes. In *Cochrane, J. L. and Zeleny, M., eds.*, 1973, pp. 429–38.

Woodward, John T. Investment Programs and Sales Expectations for 1973. *Surv. Curr. Bus.*, March 1973, *53*(3), pp. 16–21. [G: U.S.]

Woodward, John T. 1973 Plant and Equipment Expenditure Programs. *Surv. Curr. Bus.*, June 1973, *53*(6), pp. 8–11. [G: U.S.]

Woodward, John T. Capital Spending Expected to Rise Through First Half of 1974. *Surv. Curr. Bus.*, December 1973, *53*(12), pp. 9–13. [G: U.S.]

530 MARKETING

531 Marketing and Advertising

5310 Marketing and Advertising

Alexandrides, C. G. A Methodology for Computerization. In *Alexandrides, C. G., ed.*, 1973, pp. 185–93.

Amadeo, Eduardo P. Algunas ideas para un nuevo enfoque de la teoría del "ciclo del producto". (Some Ideas for a New Approach on the Theory of the "Product Cycle". With English summary.) *Económica*, May-August 1973, *19*(2), pp. 135–45.

Anderson, Rolph E. Consumer Dissatisfaction: The Effect of Disconfirmed Expectancy on Perceived Product Performance. *J. Marketing Res.*, February 1973, *10*(1), pp. 38–44.

Antin, P. The Nestlé Product Manager as Demigod. In *Thorelli, H. B., ed.*, 1973, pp. 290–300.

Bass, Frank M. and Wilkie, William L. A Comparative Analysis of Attitudinal Predictions of Brand Preference. *J. Marketing Res.*, August 1973, *10*(3), pp. 262–69.

Beckwith, Neil E. and Lehmann, Donald R. The Importance of Differential Weights in Multiple Attribute Models of Consumer Attitude. *J. Marketing Res.*, May 1973, *10*(2), pp. 141–45.

Beckwith, Neil E. Concerning the Logical Consistency of Multivariate Market Share Models. *J. Marketing Res.*, August 1973, *10*(3), pp. 341–44.

Bell, Carolyn Shaw. Middle-Class Action and the Ghetto Consumer. *J. Econ. Issues,* June 1973, *7*(2), pp. 245–57.   [G: U.S.]

Berhold, Marvin. Multiple Criteria Decision Making in Consumer Behavior. In *Cochrane, J. L. and Zeleny, M., eds.*, 1973, pp. 570–76.

Berruti, Giuseppe. Il "merchandising" un nuovo aspetto del rapporto fra industria e distribuzione. ("Merchandising": A New Aspect of the Relations between Industry and Distribution. With English summary.) *L'Impresa*, 1973, *15*(9–10), pp. 628–30.

Bettman, James R. Perceived Risk and Its Components: A Model and Empirical Test. *J. Marketing Res.*, May 1973, *10*(2), pp. 184–90.   [G: U.S.]

Bettman, James R. Perceived Price and Product Perceptual Variables. *J. Marketing Res.*, February 1973, *10*(1), pp. 100–02.

Bieda, John C. and Kassarjian, Harold H. An Overview of Market Segmentation. In *Britt, S. H. and Boyd, H. W., Jr., eds.*, 1973, pp. 209–17.

Bievert, Bernd. Sociomarketing and the Quality of Life. In *Dierkes, M. and Bauer, R. A., eds.*, 1973, pp. 142–48.

Bither, Stewart W. and Wright, Peter L. The Self-Confidence-Advertising Response Relationship: A Function of Situational Distraction. *J. Marketing Res.*, May 1973, *10*(2), pp. 146–52.

Blattberg, Robert C. and Sen, Subrata K. An Evaluation of the Application of Minimum Chi-Square Procedures to Stochastic Models of Brand Choice. *J. Marketing Res.*, November 1973, *10*(4), pp. 421–27.

Boddewyn, J. J. and Hollander, Stanley C. Public Policy Toward Retailing: Introduction. In *Boddewyn, J. J. and Hollander, S. C., eds.*, 1972, pp. 1–9.

Boddewyn, J. J. and Hollander, Stanley C. Public Policy Toward Retailing: Conclusions. In *Boddewyn, J. J. and Hollander, S. C., eds.*, 1972, pp. 431–52.

Bogart, Leo. Comment on Silk and Geiger. *J. Marketing Res.*, May 1973, *10*(2), pp. 219–20.

Bogart, Leo and Lehman, Charles. What Makes a Brand Name Familiar? *J. Marketing Res.*, February 1973, *10*(1), pp. 17–22.   [G: U.S.]

Braccaioli-Alberti, Enzo. Il mercato dei mezzi pubblicitari in Italia. (The Market of Advertising Media in Italy. With English summary.) *L'Impresa*, 1973, *15*(5–6), pp. 347–51.   [G: Italy]

Brigida, Franco. L'immagine di impresa e di prodotto come strumento di commercializzazione. (Company and Product Image as Marketing Tools. With English summary.) *L'Impresa*, 1973, *15*(9–10), pp. 569–77.   [G: Italy]

Brioschi, Edoardo T. Per una politica di comunicazione nell'azienda. (For a Policy of Communication in the Firm. With English summary.) *L'Impresa*, 1973, *15*(5–6), pp. 325–32.

Browne, William G. Problems—The Planning Process in Marketing. *Marquette Bus. Rev.*, Fall 1973, *17*(3), pp. 149–54.

Brown, Robert G. A Model for Measuring the Influence of Promotion on Inventory and Consumer Demand. *J. Marketing Res.*, November 1973, *10*(4), pp. 380–89.

Brozen, Yale. In Defense of Advertising. In *Murray, B. B., ed.*, 1973, pp. 341–51.   [G: U.S.]

Bruce, Grady D.; Witt, Robert E. and Martin, Warren S. Interpersonal Orientation and Innovative Behavior. *Miss. Val. J. Bus. Econ.*, Winter 1973-74, *9*(2), pp. 35–42.

Burck, Gilbert. The Myths and Realities of Corporate Pricing. In *Britt, S. H. and Boyd, H. W., Jr., eds.*, 1973, pp. 345–57.   [G: U.S.]

Cardozo, Richard N. Segmenting the Industrial Market. In *Britt, S. H. and Boyd, H. W., Jr., eds.*, 1973, pp. 239–54.

Charlton, P. and Ehrenberg, A. S. C. McConnell's Experimental Brand Choice Data. *J. Marketing Res.*, August 1973, *10*(3), pp. 302–07.

Chatfield, C. and Goodhardt, G. J. A Consumer Purchasing Model with Erlang Inter-Purchase Times. *J. Amer. Statist. Assoc.*, December 1973, *68*(344), pp. 828–35.

Clarke, Darral G. Sales-Advertising Cross-Elasticities and Advertising Competition. *J. Marketing Res.*, August 1973, *10*(3), pp. 250–61.

Conley, Patrick. Experience Curves as a Planning Tool. In *Britt, S. H. and Boyd, H. W., Jr., eds.*, 1973, pp. 257–68.

Cortellazzo, Sandro. Aspetti metodologici nelle ricerche sulla "corporate image." (Methodological Aspects of "Corporate Image" Research. With English summary.) *L'Impresa*, 1973, *15*(9–10), pp. 579–88.

David, Michel. I dodici tratti caratteristici dell'ipermercato alla francese. (Twelve Characteristics of the French Hypermarket. With English summary.) *L'Impresa*, 1973, *15*(9–10), pp. 634–39.   [G: France]

Dawson, Lyndon E., Jr. and Moore, Charles T. Psychometric Measures of Inter-Media Advertising Effectiveness: A Case Study. *Marquette Bus. Rev.*, Summer 1973, *17*(2), pp. 73–83.   [G: U.S.]

Dietz, Stephens. Get More Out of Your Brand Management. *Harvard Bus. Rev.*, July-August 1973, *51*(4), pp. 127–36.

Dodds, Wellesley. An Application of the Bass Model in Long-Term New Product Forecasting. *J. Marketing Res.*, August 1973, *10*(3), pp. 308–11.   [G: U.S.]

Donnelly, James H., Jr. and Etzel, Michael J. Degrees of Product Newness and Early Trial. *J. Mar-*

keting Res., August 1973, *10*(3), pp. 295–300. [G: U.S.]

Edwards, Franklin R. Advertising and Competition in Banking. *Antitrust Bull.*, Spring 1973, *18*(1), pp. 23–32. [G: U.S.]

Eeckhoudt, Louis R. The "Dorfman-Steiner" Rule: The Intertemporal Case: A Reply. *Z. Nationalökon.*, 1973, *33*(3–4), pp. 431–34.

Engwall, Lars. Business Behavior: The Cigarette Case. *Marquette Bus. Rev.*, Summer 1973, *17*(2), pp. 59–72. [G: U.S.]

Epps, Thomas W. An Econometric Analysis of the Effectiveness of the U.S. Army's 1971 Paid Advertising Campaign. *Appl. Econ.*, December 1973, *5* (4), pp. 261–69. [G: U.S.]

Eskin, Gerald J. Dynamic Forecasts of New Product Demand Using a Depth of Repeat Model. *J. Marketing Res.*, May 1973, *10*(2), pp. 115–29. [G: U.S.]

Fabris, Giampaolo. I valori della pubblicità. (The Value of Advertising. With English summary.) *L'Impresa*, 1973, *15*(5–6), pp. 333–45.

Ferber, Robert. Family Decision Making and Economic Behavior: A Review. In *Sheldon, E. B., ed.*, 1973, pp. 29–61.

Franke, Jürgen F. A. W. Advertising and Collusion in Oligopoly. *Jahr. Nationalökon. Statist.*, December 1973, *188*(1), pp. 33–50.

Franke, Jürgen F. A. W. Zur Besteuerung der Werbung. (With English summary.) *Kyklos*, 1973, *26* (2), pp. 337–61. [G: W. Germany]

Fry, Joseph N., et al. Customer Loyalty to Banks: A Longitudinal Study. *J. Bus.*, October 1973, *46*(4), pp. 517–25. [G: Canada]

Gardner, David M. The Package, Legislation, and the Shopper—Customer Behavior Should Determine Regulations. In *Murray, B. B., ed.*, 1973, pp. 200–207. [G: U.S.]

Gerbotto, Gianni. Ricerche tecnico-commerciali. (Technical-Commercial Research. With English summary.) *L'Impresa*, 1973, *15*(1), pp. 44–47.

Giddens, Paul H. Historical Origins of the Adoption of the Exxon Name and Trademark. *Bus. Hist. Rev.*, Autumn 1973, *47*(3), pp. 353–66. [G: U.S.]

Grashof, John F. Supermarket Chain Product Addition and Deletion Decisions: A Case Study. *Marquette Bus. Rev.*, Fall 1973, *17*(3), pp. 120–28. [G: U.S.]

Greeno, Daniel W.; Sommers, Montrose S. and Kernan, Jerome B. Personality and Implicit Behavior Patterns. *J. Marketing Res.*, February 1973, *10*(1), pp. 63–69. [G: U.S.]

Green, Paul E. On the Analysis of Interactions in Marketing Research Data. *J. Marketing Res.*, November 1973, *10*(4), pp. 410–20.

Green, Paul E. Multidimensional Scaling and Conjoint Measurement in the Study of Choice Among Multiattribute Alternatives. In *Cochrane, J. L. and Zeleny, M., eds.*, 1973, pp. 577–609.

Green, Paul E.; Wind, Yoram and Jain, Arun K. Analyzing Free-Response Data in Marketing Research. *J. Marketing Res.*, February 1973, *10*(1), pp. 45–52.

Greer, Douglas F. Advertising and Market Concentration: Reply. *Southern Econ. J.*, January 1973, *39* (3), pp. 451–53.

Greer, Douglas F. Some Case History Evidence on

the Advertising-Concentration Relationship. *Antitrust Bull.*, Summer 1973, *18*(2), pp. 307–32. [G: U.S.]

Grønhaug, Kjell. Buying Experience and Buying Purpose. *Ekon. Samfundets Tidskr.*, 1973, *26*(4), pp. 247–54. [G: Finland]

Heeler, Roger M.; Kearney, Michael J. and Mehaffey, Bruce J. Modeling Supermarket Product Selection. *J. Marketing Res.*, February 1973, *10* (1), pp. 34–37.

Henley, Donald S. Multinational Marketing: Present Position and Future Challenges. In *Henley, D. S., ed.*, 1973, pp. 337–54. [G: U.S.]

Herniter, Jerome D. An Entropy Model of Brand Purchase Behavior. *J. Marketing Res.*, November 1973, *10*(4), pp. 361–75.

Holland, Charles W. and Cravens, David W. Fractional Factorial Experimental Designs in Marketing Research. *J. Marketing Res.*, August 1973, *10* (3), pp. 270–76.

Hostiuck, K. Tim and Kurtz, David L. Alderson's Functionalism and the Development of Marketing Theory. *J. Bus. Res.*, Fall 1973, *1*(2), pp. 141–56.

Hustad, Thomas P. and Pessemier, Edgar A. Will the Real Consumer Activist Please Stand Up: An Examination of Consumers' Opinions About Marketing Practices. *J. Marketing Res.*, August 1973, *10*(3), pp. 319–24. [G: U.S.]

Ireland, Norman J. The "Dorfman-Steiner" Rule and Bandwagon Effects. *Z. Nationalökon.*, 1973, *33*(3–4), pp. 427–30.

Isakson, Hans R. and Maurizi, Alex R. The Consumer Economics of Unit Pricing. *J. Marketing Res.*, August 1973, *10*(3), pp. 277–85. [G: U.S.]

Jääskeläinen, Veikko and Kervinen, Esko. Designing Retail Outlets with Markov Chains and Mathematical Programming. *Liiketaloudellinen Aikak.*, 1973, *22*(2), pp. 83–93.

Jacoby, Jacob and Kyner, David B. Brand Loyalty vs. Repeat Purchasing Behavior. *J. Marketing Res.*, February 1973, *10*(1), pp. 1–9. [G: U.S.]

Jain, Chaman L. and Migliaro, Alfonso. Optimum Customer Investment Criteria in Mail Order Operation. *Rivista Int. Sci. Econ. Com.*, May 1973, *20*(5), pp. 470–78.

Jentz, Gaylord A. Federal Regulation of Advertising. In *Murray, B. B., ed.*, 1973, pp. 328–40. [G: U.S.]

Jentz, Gaylord A. Federal Regulation of Advertising. In *Britt, S. H. and Boyd, H. W., Jr., eds.*, 1973, pp. 585–97. [G: U.S.]

Johansson, Johny K. A Generalized Logistic Function with an Application to the Effect of Advertising. *J. Amer. Statist. Assoc.*, December 1973, *68* (344), pp. 824–27.

Jolson, Marvin A. New Product Planning in an Age of Future Consciousness. *Calif. Manage. Rev.*, Fall 1973, *16*(1), pp. 25–33.

Kaye, William G. Take in a New Partner—The Consumer. In *Murray, B. B., ed.*, 1973, pp. 243–48. [G: U.S.]

Keegan, Warren J. Multinational Marketing Control. In *Alexandrides, C. G., ed.*, 1973, pp. 243–60.

Keegan, W. J. Five Strategies for Multinational Marketing. In *Thorelli, H. B., ed.*, 1973, pp. 195–203. [G: U.S.; W. Europe]

Kensicki, Peter R. and Richmond, David. Consumerism and Automobile Insurance. *J. Risk Ins.*, June 1973, *40*(2), pp. 209–17. [G: U.S.]

Kinnear, Thomas C. and Taylor, James R. The Effect of Ecological Concern on Brand Perceptions. *J. Marketing Res.*, May 1973, *10*(2), pp. 191–97. [G: U.S.]

Kjaer-Hansen, Max. Revolution i konsumenternas varuförsörjning. (Revolution in Consumer Goods Supply. With English summary.) *Ekon. Samfundets Tidskr.*, January 1973, *26*(1), pp. 3–15.

Kotler, Philip. Marketing Mix Decisions for New Products. In *Palda, K. S., ed.*, 1973, pp. 160–68.

Kraft, Frederic B.; Granbois, Donald H. and Summers, John O. Brand Evaluation and Brand Choice: A Longitudinal Study. *J. Marketing Res.*, August 1973, *10*(3), pp. 235–41. [G: U.S.]

Lavia, Alberto. Ricerche sui flussi distributivi. (Research on the Distributive Fluctuations. With English summary.) *L'Impresa*, 1973, *15*(1), pp. 36–40.

Lehtinen, Uolevi. On Some Possibilities of Taking Risk into Account in a Brand Choice Model. *Liiketaloudellinen Aikak.*, 1973, *22*(4), pp. 272–77.

LeKashman, Raymond and Stolle, John F. The Total Cost Approach to Distribution. In *Britt, S. H. and Boyd, H. W., Jr., eds.*, 1973, pp. 441–58.

Lev, Baruch. The RAS Method for Two-Dimensional Forecasts. *J. Marketing Res.*, May 1973, *10*(2), pp. 153–59.

Levy, Sidney J. Consumer Views of Bank Services. *J. Bank Res.*, Summer 1973, *4*(2), pp. 100–04.

Luni, Paolo. La "società d'acquisti": premessa per una nuova e più rapida evoluzione del settore distributivo. (The "Purchasing Company": Ideas for New and Rapid Developments in the Distribution Sector. With English summary.) *L'Impresa*, 1973, *15*(9–10), pp. 631–33.

MacKay, David B. A Spectral Analysis of the Frequency of Supermarket Visits. *J. Marketing Res.*, February 1973, *10*(1), pp. 84–90. [G: U.S.]

MacKay, David B. Spatial Measurement of Retail Store Demand. *J. Marketing Res.*, November 1973, *10*(4), pp. 447–53.

Main, Jeremy. Industry Still Has Something to Learn About Congress. In *Murray, B. B., ed.*, 1973, pp. 192–99. [G: U.S.]

Mandell, Lewis. The Changing Role of the American Consumer. In *Britt, S. H. and Boyd, H. W., Jr., eds.*, 1973, pp. 190–95. [G: U.S.]

Mann, H. Michael; Henning, John A. and Meehan, James W., Jr. Advertising and Market Concentration: Comment. *Southern Econ. J.*, January 1973, *39*(3), pp. 448–51.

Marsiglia, Alessandro. Considerazioni metodologiche. (Research on Distribution: Methodological Considerations. With English summary.) *L'Impresa*, 1973, *15*(1), pp. 53–58.

Marvulli, Roberto. Il messaggio pubblicitario sulla stampa quotidiana: un esame quantitativo. (An Analysis of the Quantitative Importance of the Advertising Message on the Daily Newspapers. With English summary.) *L'Impresa*, 1973, *15* (5–6), pp. 353–58.

Mason, Joseph Barry and Mayer, Morris L. Insights into the Image Determinants of Fashion Specialty Outlets. *J. Bus. Res.*, Summer 1973, *1*(1), pp. 73–80. [G: U.S.]

Mazis, Michael B.; Settle, Robert B. and Leslie, Dennis C. Elimination of Phosphate Detergents and Psychological Reactance. *J. Marketing Res.*, November 1973, *10*(4), pp. 390–95. [G: U.S.]

McDonald, Charles L. An Empirical Examination of the Reliability of Published Predictions of Future Earnings. *Accounting Rev.*, July 1973, *48*(3), pp. 502–10. [G: U.S.]

Mehr, Robert I. Consumerism and Automobile Insurance: Discussion. *J. Risk Ins.*, June 1973, *40*(2), pp. 217–20. [G: U.S.]

Metwally, Mohktar M. Australian Advertising Expenditure and its Relation to Demand. *Econ. Rec.*, June 1973, *49*(126), pp. 290–99. [G: Australia]

Metwally, Mohktar M. Economic Strategies of Firms Facing Asymptotic Demand: A Case Study. *Appl. Econ.*, December 1973, *5*(4), pp. 271–80. [G: Australia]

Monroe, Kent B. Buyers' Subjective Perceptions of Price. *J. Marketing Res.*, February 1973, *10*(1), pp. 70–80.

Moran, R. Allen. Cooperative Advertising: An Alternative Interpretation of Price Discrimination. *Calif. Manage. Rev.*, Summer 1973, *15*(4), pp. 61–63. [G: U.S.]

Moyer, R. International Market Analysis. In *Thorelli, H. B., ed.*, 1973, pp. 162–79.

Myers, John G. Measuring and Monitoring the Impact of Advertising. In *Dierkes, M. and Bauer, R. A., eds.*, 1973, pp. 130–41.

Naert, Philippe A. and Bultez, Alain. Logically Consistent Market Share Models. *J. Marketing Res.*, August 1973, *10*(3), pp. 334–40.

Nakanishi, Masao. Advertising and Promotion Effects on Consumer Response to New Products. *J. Marketing Res.*, August 1973, *10*(3), pp. 242–49.

Newman, Joseph W. and Werbel, Richard A. Multivariate Analysis of Brand Loyalty for Major Household Appliances. *J. Marketing Res.*, November 1973, *10*(4), pp. 404–09. [G: U.S.]

Olshavsky, Richard W. Customer-Salesman Interaction in Appliance Retailing. *J. Marketing Res.*, May 1973, *10*(2), pp. 208–12.

Ostlund, Lyman E. A Further Caution: It's Innovativeness Overlap. *J. Marketing Res.*, May 1973, *10* (2), pp. 225–26.

Oxenfeldt, Alfred R., et al. Attitudes and Pricing. In *Britt, S. H. and Boyd, H. W., Jr., eds.*, 1973, pp. 372–86.

Patrucco, Carlo. Dimensione sociale del fenomeno distributivo commerciale. (The Social Dimensions of the Distributive Phenomenon. With English summary.) *L'Impresa*, 1973, *15*(1), pp. 24–26.

Patrucco, Carlo. Ricerche geo-commerciali. (Geo-Commercial Research. With English summary.) *L'Impresa*, 1973, *15*(1), pp. 40–44.

Patrucco, Carlo. Le imprese commerciali di fronte all'evoluzione strutturale del loro settore. (Trade Companies and the Developing Structures of their Sector. With English summary.) *L'Impresa*, 1973, *15*(9–10), pp. 619–22.

Paul, Robert J. Psychographics, Demographics and Affluence—Predictors of Individual Decision Patterns? *Marquette Bus. Rev.*, Fall 1973, *17*(3),

pp. 144–48. [G: U.S.]

Peel, David A. The Non-uniqueness of the Dorfman-Steiner Condition: A Note. *Economica, N.S.,* May 1973, *40*(158), pp. 208–09.

Pen, Jan. Business Against the Consumer. In *Reynolds, L. G.; Green, G. D. and Lewis, D. R., eds.,* 1973, pp. 190–200.

Perry, Arnon. Heredity, Personality Traits, Product Attitude, and Product Consumption—An Exploratory Study. *J. Marketing Res.,* November 1973, *10*(4), pp. 376–79.

Peters, Michael P. and Venkatesan, M. Exploration of Variables Inherent in Adopting an Industrial Product. *J. Marketing Res.,* August 1973, *10*(3), pp. 312–15. [G: U.S.]

Peterson, Robert A. and Sharpe, Louis K. Market Segmentation: Product Usage Patterns and Psychographic Configurations. *J. Bus. Res.,* Summer 1973, *1*(1), pp. 11–20.

Peterson, Robert A. A Note on Optimal Adopter Category Determination. *J. Marketing Res.,* August 1973, *10*(3), pp. 325–29. [G: U.S.]

Peterson, Robert A. and Cagley, James W. The Effect of Shelf Space Upon Sales of Branded Products: An Appraisal. *J. Marketing Res.,* February 1973, *10*(1), pp. 103–04.

Peters, William H. Income and Occupation as Explanatory Variables: Their Power Combined vs. Separate. *J. Bus. Res.,* Summer 1973, *1*(1), pp. 81–89. [G: U.S.]

Petrini, Bart F. and Grub, Phillip D. Product Management in High Technology Defense Industry Marketing. *Calif. Manage. Rev.,* Spring 1973, *15* (3), pp. 138–46.

Petrof, John V. Minority Representation in French Advertising. *Marquette Bus. Rev.,* Spring 1973, *17* (1), pp. 9–12. [G: France]

Ravazzi, Giancarlo. Evoluzione delle strutture commerciali: analisi funzionale e indicazioni prospettiche. (Development of Distribution Structures: A Functional Analysis and Prospects. With English summary.) *L'Impresa,* 1973, *15*(9–10), pp. 607–17.

Ravazzi, Giancarlo. La conoscenza come fattore di razionalizzazione del sistema distributivo-commerciale. (Knowledge As a Factor of Rationalization of the Distributive System. With English summary.) *L'Impresa,* 1973, *15*(1), pp. 12–19.

Riesz, Peter C. Size versus Price, or Another Vote for Tonypandy. *J. Bus.,* July 1973, *46*(3), pp. 396–403. [G: U.S.]

Rossi, Aldo. Pubblicità industriale per l' agricoltura. (Industrial Advertising for Agriculture. With English summary.) *L'Impresa,* 1973, *15*(5–6), pp. 359–64.

Rühl, G. Forecasting in Goods' Transport and Market Behaviour. In *Blohm, H. and Steinbuch, K., eds.,* 1973, pp. 91–102.

Ryans, J. K., Jr. Is It Too Soon to Put a Tiger in Every Tank? In *Thorelli, H. B., ed.,* 1973, pp. 227–36.

Särkisilta, Martti. Markkinoinnin informaatiojärjestelmän rakenne ja kehittämisen pääsuuntaviivat. (The Structure of a Marketing Information System and Main Lines for Development. With English summary.) *Liiketaloudellinen Aikak.,* 1973, *22*(1), pp. 3–17.

Savoré, Carlo. Nuovi problemi delle imprese di produzione di fronte all'evoluzione delle strutture commerciali. (New Problems of Manufacturing Companies and the Development of Distributive Structures. With English summary.) *L'Impresa,* 1973, *15*(9–10), pp. 623–26.

Savoré, Carlo. Ricerche aziendali. (Firm Research. With English summary.) *L'Impresa,* 1973, *15*(1), pp. 48–49.

Sawyer, Alan G. The Effects of Repetition of Refutational and Supportive Advertising Appeals. *J. Marketing Res.,* February 1973, *10*(1), pp. 23–33. [G: U.S.]

Scanlon, Paul D. Anti-Competitive Advertising and the FTC: A Ban on Oligopoly-Creating-Ads? In *Murray, B. B., ed.,* 1973, pp. 363–69. [G: U.S.]

Scanlon, Paul D. Oligopoly and Deceptive Advertising: The Cereal Industry Affair. In *Murray, B. B., ed.,* 1973, pp. 125–34.

Scheidell, John M. The Price Reducing Potential of Advertising. *Southern Econ. J.,* April 1973, *39*(4), pp. 535–43.

Schlissel, Martin R. Promotional Strategy in a High-Technology Industry. *J. Econ. Bus.,* Fall 1973, *26* (1), pp. 67–73. [G: U.S.]

Schnabel, Morton. A Model of Cigarette Advertising. *Antitrust Bull.,* Spring 1973, *18*(1), pp. 33–43. [G: U.S.]

Scott, Walter Giorgio. Proposta per una ricerca sui costi di distribuzione commerciale. (Proposal for Research on the Distribution Costs Met by Firms. With English summary.) *L'Impresa,* 1973, *15*(1), pp. 50–52.

Shafer, Ronald G. A Food Chain Recruits a Consumer Advocate to Shape Its Policies. In *Murray, B. B., ed.,* 1973, pp. 274–78. [G: U.S.]

Shapiro, Benson P. Price Reliance: Existence and Sources. *J. Marketing Res.,* August 1973, *10*(3), pp. 286–94. [G: U.S.]

Shapiro, Benson P. Marketing for Nonprofit Organizations. *Harvard Bus. Rev.,* September-October 1973, *51*(5), pp. 123–32.

Sheth, Jagdish N. A Review of Buyer Behavior. In *Britt, S. H. and Boyd, H. W., Jr., eds.,* 1973, pp. 126–68.

Silk, Alvin J. Testing the Inverse Ad Size-Selective Exposure Hypothesis: Clarifying Bogart. *J. Marketing Res.,* May 1973, *10*(2), pp. 221–23.

Slacik, Karl F. What Can You, the Financial Executive, Do About Customer Service? In *Thomas, W. E., Jr., ed.,* 1973, pp. 130–40.

Soldi, Costantino. Ricerche economiche. (Economic Research. With English summary.) *L'Impresa,* 1973, *15*(1), pp. 32–36.

Staelin, Richard and Turner, Ronald E. Error in Judgmental Sales Forecasts: Theory and Results. *J. Marketing Res.,* February 1973, *10*(1), pp. 10–16. [G: U.S.]

Stelu, Şerban. Circuitul economic al ambalajelor. (The Economic Circuit of Packings. With English summary.) *Stud. Cercet. Econ.,* 1973, (2), pp. 157–69.

Stern, Louis W.; Sternthal, Brian and Craig, C. Samuel. Managing Conflict in Distribution Channels: A Laboratory Study. *J. Marketing Res.,* May 1973, *10*(2), pp. 169–79.

Stone, Alan. The F.T.C. and Advertising Regulation: An Examination of Agency Failure. *Public Policy,* Spring 1973, *21*(2), pp. 203–34. [G: U.S.]

Stone, Gary K. Life Insurance Sales Practices on the College Campus. *J. Risk Ins.,* June 1973, *40*(2), pp. 167–79. [G: U.S.]

Szybillo, George J. and Heslin, Richard. Resistence to Persuasion: Inoculation Theory in a Marketing Context. *J. Marketing Res.,* November 1973, *10* (4), pp. 396–403.

Tatham, Ronald L. and Dornoff, Ronald J. A Cautionary Note on Innovative Overlap. *J. Marketing Res.,* May 1973, *10*(2), pp. 224–25.

Thorelli, Hans B. International Marketing Strategy: Introduction. In *Thorelli, H. B., ed.,* 1973, pp. 11–19.

Thorelli, Hans B. International Marketing: An Ecologic View. In *Thorelli, H. B., ed.,* 1973, pp. 23–40.

Tsurumi, Hiroki. A Comparison of Alternative Optimal Models of Advertising Expenditures: Stock Adjustment vs. Control Theoretic Approaches. *Rev. Econ. Statist.,* May 1973, *55*(2), pp. 156–68. [G: Japan]

Vergnano, Franco. La conoscenza di base: ricerche strutturali e funzionali. (The Basic Knowledge: Structural and Functional Research. With English summary.) *L'Impresa,* 1973, *15*(1), pp. 28–32.

Vergnano, Franco. Determinazione dello stanziamento pubblicitario. Una bibliografia e un commento introduttivo. (A Determination of the Advertising Budget. A Bibliography and Preliminary Notes. With English summary.) *L'Impresa,* 1973, *15*(5–6), pp. 365–72.

Vernon, John M. and Nourse, Robert E. M. Profit Rates and Market Structure of Advertising Intensive Firms. *J. Ind. Econ.,* September 1973, *22*(1), pp. 1–20. [G: U.S.]

Vinson, Donald E. The Marketing Concept: an Examination. *Rivista Int. Sci. Econ. Com.,* March 1973, *20*(3), pp. 291–95.

Webb, Don R. and Darling, John R. The Post-Use Problem—A Response from Management. *J. Bus. Res.,* Summer 1973, *1*(1), pp. 49–56.

Weigand, Robert E. The Problems of Managing Reciprocity. *Calif. Manage. Rev.,* Fall 1973, *16*(1), pp. 40–48.

Weiss, E. B. The Corporate Deaf Ear. In *Murray, B. B., ed.,* 1973, pp. 260–70. [G: U.S.]

Wetherell, David. Nuovi orientamenti della "company image." (New Directions for the "Company Image." With English summary.) *L'Impresa,* 1973, *15*(9–10), pp. 562–67.

Wilder, Ronald P. Public Utility Advertising: Some Observations. *Land Econ.,* November 1973, *49* (4), pp. 458–62. [G: U.S.]

Wilkie, William L. and Pessemier, Edgar A. Issues in Marketing's Use of Multi-Attribute Attitude Models. *J. Marketing Res.,* November 1973, *10*(4), pp. 428–41.

Winer, Leon. The Effect of Product Sales Quotas on Sales Force Productivity. *J. Marketing Res.,* May 1973, *10*(2), pp. 180–83. [G: U.S.]

Winter, Frederick W. A Laboratory Experiment of Individual Attitude Response to Advertising Exposure. *J. Marketing Res.,* May 1973, *10*(2), pp. 130–40. [G: U.S.]

Worcester, Robert M. Il valore della "corporate image." (The Value of Corporate Image. With English summary.) *L'Impresa,* 1973, *15*(9–10), pp. 522–26.

Wright, Peter L. The Cognitive Processes Mediating Acceptance of Advertising. *J. Marketing Res.,* February 1973, *10*(1), pp. 53–62. [G: U.S.]

Wyckham, Robert G. and Stewart, Max D. Public Policy Toward Retailing: Canada. In *Boddewyn, J. J. and Hollander, S. C., eds.,* 1972, pp. 81–99. [G: Canada]

540 ACCOUNTING

541 Accounting

5410 Accounting

Anthony, Robert N. Accounting for the Cost of Equity. *Harvard Bus. Rev.,* November-December 1973, *51*(6), pp. 88–102.

Bailey, Andrew D., Jr. A Dynamic Programming Approach to the Analysis of Different Costing Methods in Accounting for Inventories. *Accounting Rev.,* July 1973, *48*(3), pp. 560–74.

Bailey, F. A. A Note on Pert/Cost Resource Allocation. In *Thomas, W. E., Jr., ed.,* 1973, pp. 264–65.

Bashan, O., et al. Laspeyres Indexes for Variance Analysis in Cost Accounting. *Accounting Rev.,* October 1973, *48*(4), pp. 790–93.

Bauer, Raymond A. The Future of Corporate Social Accounting. In *Dierkes, M. and Bauer, R. A., eds.,* 1973, pp. 389–405. [G: U.S.]

Bauer, Raymond A. The Corporate Social Audit: Getting on the Learning Curve. *Calif. Manage. Rev.,* Fall 1973, *16*(1), pp. 5–10.

Beaver, William H. and Dukes, Roland E. Interperiod Tax Allocation and δ-Depreciation Methods: Some Empirical Results. *Accounting Rev.,* July 1973, *48*(3), pp. 549–59.

Beidleman, Carl R. Income Smoothing: The Role of Management. *Accounting Rev.,* October 1973, *48* (4), pp. 653–67. [G: U.S.]

Beidleman, Carl R. Fixed Asset Depreciation Patterns: Market Based Evidence. *Z. ges. Staatswiss.,* October 1973, *129*(4), pp. 643–62. [G: U.S.]

Benston, George J. Multiple Regression Analysis of Cost Behavior. In *Palda, K. S., ed.,* 1973, pp. 84–97.

Bilderbeek, J. Financieel-economische indices ten behoeve van de bedrijfsbeoordeling. (Financial-economic Indices for Management Auditing. With English summary.) *Econ. Soc. Tijdschr.,* April 1973, *27*(2), pp. 141–55. [G: U.S.]

Boone, Michael M. Management Accountants and the Securities Laws. *Manage. Account.,* June 1973, *54*(12), pp. 18–22.

Brantner, Paul F. Accounting for Land Development Companies. *Manage. Account.,* August 1973, *55*(2), pp. 15–19.

Brenner, Vincent C. Critical Characteristics for a Pragmatic Concept of Income. *Marquette Bus. Rev.,* Winter 1973, *17*(4), pp. 188–96.

Brief, Richard P. and Owen, Joel. A Reformulation

of the Estimation Problem. *J. Acc. Res.*, Spring 1973, *11*(1), pp. 1–15.

Brinkman, Donald R. Minimizing the Loss of Investment Tax Credits. *Manage. Account.*, January 1973, *54*(7), pp. 38–40.

Brummet, R. Lee. Total Performance Measurement. *Manage. Account.*, November 1973, *55*(5), pp. 11–15.

Brummet, R. Lee. Nonfinancial Measures in Social Accounts. In *Dierkes, M. and Bauer, R. A., eds.*, 1973, pp. 345–50.

Butcher, Bernard L. The Program Management Approach. In *Dierkes, M. and Bauer, R. A., eds.*, 1973, pp. 276–84. [G: U.S.]

Butcher, Bernard L. The Program Management Approach to the Corporate Social Audit. *Calif. Manage. Rev.*, Fall 1973, *16*(1), pp. 11–16.

Calhoun, Donald A. Computing DISC Profits. *Manage. Account.*, June 1973, *54*(12), pp. 45–46. [G: U.S.]

Calhoun, Donald A. Oil and Gas Taxation. *Manage. Account.*, November 1973, *55*(5), pp. 21–24. [G: U.S.]

Călin, O. and Văduva, I. Folosirea metodelor matematice în contabilitate. (Utilization of Mathematical Models in Book-keeping. With English summary.) *Stud. Cercet. Econ.*, 1973, (2), pp. 139–56.

Călin, Oprea and Ciucur, Elena. Rolul prețului de cost în cadrul sistemului informațional economic al întreprinderii. (The Role of the Cost Price in the Economic Informational System of the Enterprise. With English summary.) *Stud. Cercet. Econ.*, 1973, (4), pp. 111–26.

Caplan, Edwin H. Behavioral Assumptions of Management Accounting. In *Thomas, W. E., Jr., ed.*, 1973, pp. 76–96.

Carleton, Bette N. The Status of Women in Accounting. *Manage. Account.*, September 1973, *55*(3), pp. 59–62. [G: U.S.]

Choi, Frederick D. S. Financial Disclosure and Entry to the European Capital Market. *J. Acc. Res.*, Autumn 1973, *11*(2), pp. 159–75.

Clark, John J. and Elgers, Pieter. Forecasted Income Statements: An Investor Perspective. *Accounting Rev.*, October 1973, *48*(4), pp. 668–78.

Coase, R. H. Business Organization and the Accountant. In *Buchanan, J. M. and Thirlby, G. F., eds.*, 1973, pp. 95–132.

Cohen, Jeffrey M. Accounting for Modular Housing Manufacturers. *Manage. Account.*, September 1973, *55*(3), pp. 11–14.

Colantoni, C. S.; Cooper, W. W. and Dietzer, H. J. Budgetary Disclosure and Social Accounting. In *Dierkes, M. and Bauer, R. A., eds.*, 1973, pp. 365–86.

Corbin, Donald A. Guidelines for Reporting Corporate Environmental Impact. In *Dierkes, M. and Bauer, R. A., eds.*, 1973, pp. 321–26.

Corcoran, A. Wayne and Leininger, Wayne E. Stochastic Process Costing Models. *Accounting Rev.*, January 1973, *48*(1), pp. 105–14.

Cote, Joseph T. The Concept of Materiality. *Manage. Account.*, December 1973, *55*(6), pp. 17–22.

Cotter, Richard V. A General Model for Accounts-Receivable Analysis and Control: Comment. *J. Fi-*nancial *Quant. Anal.*, March 1973, *8*(2), pp. 219–21.

Crumbley, D. Larry. Introducing Probabilities and Present Value Analysis into Taxation: A Reply. *Accounting Rev.*, July 1973, *48*(3), pp. 595–97.

Crum, William F. Interim Reports: Do They Meet MAP Standards? *Manage. Account.*, May 1973, *54* (11), pp. 26–28.

De Coorde, F. and Reyns, C. Accountancy versus Management. (In Flemish. With English summary.) *Econ. Soc. Tijdschr.*, June 1973, *27*(3), pp. 277–86.

De Lembre, E. De cash-flow. (Cash-Flow. With English summary.) *Econ. Soc. Tijdschr.*, February 1973, *27*(1), pp. 23–38.

Demski, Joel S. Rational Choice of Accounting Method for a Class of Partnerships. *J. Acc. Res.*, Autumn 1973, *11*(2), pp. 176–90.

Dickhaut, John W. Alternative Information Structures and Probability Revisions. *Accounting Rev.*, January 1973, *48*(1), pp. 61–79.

Di Loreto, Sandro. Il problema dei costi nell'instituto di credito ordinario. Un tentativo di applicazione di procedimenti analitici di calcolo e di controllo-I. (The Cost Problem of Commercial Banks. An Attempt to Apply Analytical Calculation and Control Processes-I. With English summary.) *Bancaria*, July 1973, *29*(7), pp. 820–31.

Di Loreto, Sandro. Il problema dei costi nell'instituto di credito ordinario. Un tentativo di applicazione di procedimenti analitici di calcolo e di controllo-III. (The Cost Problem of Commercial Banks. An Attempt to Apply Analytical Calculation and Control Processes-III. With English summary.) *Bancaria*, September 1973, *29*(9), pp. 1094–1112.

Di Loreto, Sandro. Il problema dei costi nell'instituto di credito ordinario. Un tentativo di applicazione di procedimenti analitici di calcolo e di controllo-II. (The Cost Problem of Commercial Banks. An Attempt to Apply Analytical Calculation and Control Processes-II. With English summary.) *Bancaria*, August 1973, *29*(8), pp. 936–86.

Dopuch, N. and Ronen, J. The Effects of Alternative Inventory Valuation Methods—An Experimental Study. *J. Acc. Res.*, Autumn 1973, *11*(2), pp. 191–211.

Downes, David H. and Dyckman, Thomas R. A Critical Look at the Efficient Market Empirical Research Literature As It Relates to Accounting Information. *Accounting Rev.*, April 1973, *48*(2), pp. 300–17.

Drobny, Neil L. Social Accounting in Environmental Planning. In *Dierkes, M. and Bauer, R. A., eds.*, 1973, pp. 248–59. [G: U.S.]

Edey, Harold. The Public Company and the Shareholders. In *Allen, G. C., et al.*, 1973, pp. 29–38.

Edwards, R. S. The Rationale of Cost Accounting. In *Buchanan, J. M. and Thirlby, G. F., eds.*, 1973, pp. 71–92.

Elliott-Jones, M. F. Matrix Methods in Corporate Social Accounting. In *Dierkes, M. and Bauer, R. A., eds.*, 1973, pp. 351–64.

Enthoven, Adolf J. H. Standardized Accountancy and Economic Development. *Finance Develop.*, March 1973, *10*(1), pp. 28–31.

Falk, Haim and Ophir, Tsvi. The Influence of Differences in Accounting Policies on Investment Decisions. *J. Acc. Res.*, Spring 1973, *11*(1), pp. 108–16.

Fekrat, M. Ali. Absorption Costing and Fixed Factors of Production: A Reply. *Accounting Rev.*, January 1973, *48*(1), pp. 130–31.

Ferrara, William L. Responsibility Accounting—A Basic Control Concept. In *Thomas, W. E., Jr., ed.*, 1973, pp. 60–71.

Firth, Michael A. An Empirical Examination of the Applicability of Adopting the AICPA and NYSE Regulations and Free Share Distributions in the U.K. *J. Acc. Res.*, Spring 1973, *11*(1), pp. 16–24.
[G: U.K.]

Francis, M. E. Accounting and the Evaluation of Social Programs: A Critical Comment. *Accounting Rev.*, April 1973, *48*(2), pp. 245–57.

Friberg, Ronald A. Probabilistic Depreciation with a Varying Salvage Value. *Accounting Rev.*, January 1973, *48*(1), pp. 50–60.

Goetz, Billy E. A Note on Discounted Cash Flow Examples: A Reply. *Accounting Rev.*, January 1973, *48*(1), pp. 135–36.

Golbert, Albert S. Pitfalls of DISC. *Manage. Account.*, July 1973, *55*(1), pp. 52–55. [G: U.S.]

Gonedes, Nicholas J. Properties of Accounting Numbers: Models and Tests. *J. Acc. Res.*, Autumn 1973, *11*(2), pp. 212–37.

Gordon, Lawrence A. and Cook, Henry, Jr. Absorption Costing an Fixed Factors of Production. *Accounting Rev.*, January 1973, *48*(1), pp. 128–29.

Gray, Daniel H. One Way to Go about Inventing Social Accounting. In *Dierkes, M. and Bauer, R. A., eds.*, 1973, pp. 315–20.

Gustafson, Dale R. Perspectives on Life Insurance Financial Reporting: Discussion. *J. Risk Ins.*, March 1973, *40*(1), pp. 22–25. [G: U.S.]

Harris, William T., Jr. and Chapin, Wayne R. Joint Product Costing. *Manage. Account.*, April 1973, *54*(10), pp. 43–47.

Hartley, Ronald V. A Note on Quadratic Programming in a Case of Joint Production: A Reply. *Accounting Rev.*, October 1973, *48*(4), pp. 771–74.

Hensler, Emil J., Jr. Accounting for Small Nonprofit Organizations. *Manage. Account.*, January 1973, *54*(7), pp. 41–44.

Hirschman, R. W. Direct Costing and the Law. In *Thomas, W. E., Jr., ed.*, 1973, pp. 504–15.
[G: U.S.]

Ijiri, Yuji. A Historical Cost Approach to Aggregation of Multiple Goals. In *Cochrane, J. L. and Zeleny, M., eds.*, 1973, pp. 395–405.

Jaedicke, Robert K. and Robichek, Alexander A. Cost-Volume-Profit Analysis Under Conditions of Uncertainty. In *Thomas, W. E., Jr., ed.*, 1973, pp. 279–93.

Jain, Tribhowan N. Alternative Methods of Accounting and Decision Making: A Psycho-linguistical Analysis. *Accounting Rev.*, January 1973, *48*(1), pp. 95–104.

Jenkins, Glenn P. The Measurement of Rates of Return and Taxation from Private Capital in Canada. In *Niskanen, W. A., et al., eds.*, 1973, pp. 211–45. [G: Canada]

Jenkins, William L. Nonprofit Hospital Accounting System. *Manage. Account.*, June 1973, *54*(12), pp. 23–27.

Jensen, Daniel L. Hartley's Demand-Price Analysis in a Case of Joint Production: A Comment. *Accounting Rev.*, October 1973, *48*(4), pp. 768–70.

Jones, James W. Accounting Practices in Ship Chandlery. *Manage. Account.*, August 1973, *55*(2), pp. 28–30, 34.

Kaplan, Robert S. Statistical Sampling in Auditing with Auxiliary Information Estimators. *J. Acc. Res.*, Autumn 1973, *11*(2), pp. 238–58.

Keller, I. Wayne. Concepts, Standards, and Rules. *Manage. Account.*, May 1973, *54*(11), pp. 13–15, 25.

Kolmin, Frank W. and Cerullo, Michael J. Measuring Productivity and Efficiency. *Manage. Account.*, November 1973, *55*(5), pp. 32–34.

Lamson, Robert W. Corporate Accounting for Environmental Effects. In *Dierkes, M. and Bauer, R. A., eds.*, 1973, pp. 230–47.

Largay, James A., III. Microeconomic Foundations of Variable Costing. *Accounting Rev.*, January 1973, *48*(1), pp. 115–19.

Lea, Richard B. Comments on Mock's Concepts of Information Value. *Accounting Rev.*, April 1973, *48*(2), pp. 389–93.

Lerner, Eugene M. Simulating a Cash Budget. In *Thomas, W. E., Jr., ed.*, 1973, pp. 266–78.

Lewellen, Wilbur G. and Edmister, Robert O. A General Model for Accounts-Receivable Analysis and Control. *J. Financial Quant. Anal.*, March 1973, *8*(2), pp. 195–206.

Littrell, Earl K., III. A Note on Discounted Cash Flow Examples. *Accounting Rev.*, January 1973, *48*(1), pp. 132–34.

Lyon, George C. Fixed Characteristics of Variable Costs. *Manage. Account.*, October 1973, *55*(4), pp. 27–30.

Mathias, Robert A. An Approach Toward Corporate Social Measures. In *Dierkes, M. and Bauer, R. A., eds.*, 1973, pp. 285–91.

May, Robert G. and Sundem, Gary L. Cost of Information and Security Prices: Market Association Tests for Accounting Policy Decisions. *Accounting Rev.*, January 1973, *48*(1), pp. 80–94.
[G: U.S.]

McDonald, Charles L. An Empirical Examination of the Reliability of Published Predictions of Future Earnings. *Accounting Rev.*, July 1973, *48*(3), pp. 502–10. [G: U.S.]

McElyea, Steward D. Auditing Corporate Social Impact in a Period of Rising Social Concern. In *Dierkes, M. and Bauer, R. A., eds.*, 1973, pp. 308–14.

McGrail, George R. and Furlong, Daniel R. Absorption Break-Even. *Manage. Account.*, October 1973, *55*(4), pp. 31–35.

McIntyre, Edward V. Current-Cost Financial Statements and Common-Stock Investments Decisions. *Accounting Rev.*, July 1973, *48*(3), pp. 575–85. [G: U.S.]

McKeown, James C. A Brief Exploration of the Goal Congruence of Net Realizable Value. *Accounting Rev.*, April 1973, *48*(2), pp. 386–88.

Meimaroglou, M. C. Break-Even Analysis with Stepwise Varying Marginal Costs and Revenues. In *Haynes, W. W.; Coyne, T. J. and Osborne, D. K., eds.*, 1973, pp. 250–63.

Meyers, Stephen L. An Examination of the Relationship Between Interperiod Tax Allocation and

Present-Value Depreciation. *Accounting Rev.,* January 1973, *48*(1), pp. 44–49.   [G: U.S.]

Miller, Jerry D. Accounting for Warrants and Convertible Bonds. *Manage. Account.,* January 1973, *54*(7), pp. 26–28.

Miller, Malcolm C. Goodwill—An Aggregation Issue. *Accounting Rev.,* April 1973, *48*(2), pp. 280–91.

Mock, Theodore J. Concepts of Information Value and Accounting: A Reply. *Accounting Rev.,* April 1973, *48*(2), pp. 394–97.

Moyer, R. Charles and Mastrapasqua, Frank. Socioeconomic Accounting and External Diseconomies: A Comment. *Accounting Rev.,* January 1973, *48*(1), pp. 126–27.

Nakano, Isao. Homomorphism and Business Income Measurement. *Kobe Econ. Bus. Rev.,* 1973, *20,* pp. 61–77.

Nolan, Joseph T. The Social Audit: One Corporation's Experience. In *Dierkes, M. and Bauer, R. A., eds.,* 1973, pp. 292–96.   [G: U.S.]

Nurnberg, Hugo. A Strange Animal. *J. Acc. Res.,* Autumn 1973, *11*(2), pp. 331–33.

Ophir, Tsvi. Introducing Probabilities and Present Value Analysis into Taxation: A Comment. *Accounting Rev.,* July 1973, *48*(3), pp. 594.

Oţoiu, Alexandrina. Cu privire la metodele de evidenţă a cheltuielilor de producţie şi de calculaţie a preţului de cost. (On the Concept and Classification of the Accounts Keeping Methods of Production Expenses and of Cost Price Calculation. With English summary.) *Stud. Cercet. Econ.,* 1973, (1), pp. 141–49.

Paton, W. A. and Littleton, A. C. An Introduction to Corporate Accounting Standards. In *Thomas, W. E., Jr., ed.,* 1973, pp. 446–53.   [G: U.S.]

Petersen, Russell J. Price-Level Changes and Company Wealth. *Manage. Account.,* February 1973, *54*(8), pp. 17–20.

Petri, Enrico. Holding Gains and Losses as Cost Savings: A Comment on *Supplementary Statement No. 2* on Inventory Valuation. *Accounting Rev.,* July 1973, *48*(3), pp. 483–88.

Posnak, Robert L. Perspectives on Life Insurance Financial Reporting. *J. Risk Ins.,* March 1973, *40* (1), pp. 7–22.   [G: U.S.]

Reddington, Donald A. Control Methods for Small Business. *Manage. Account.,* September 1973, *55* (3), pp. 15–17, 26.

Riley, Kevin. Productive Hours Analysis for a Small Shop. *Manage. Account.,* January 1973, *54*(7), pp. 17–18.

Ristea, Mihai. Conceptul de operativitate în sistemul informaţional contabil. (The Concept of Efficiency in the Book-keeping Information System. With English summary.) *Stud. Cercet. Econ.,* 1973, (4), pp. 99–109.

Rossitch, Eugene and Meckler, Jack M. Foreign Currency Exposure Control. *Manage. Account.,* July 1973, *55*(1), pp. 29–37.

Ross, W. R. Pert/Cost Resource Allocation Procedure. In *Thomas, W. E., Jr., ed.,* 1973, pp. 249–63.

Salamon, Gerald L. Models of the Relationship between the Accounting and Internal Rate of Return: An Examination of the Methodology. *J. Acc. Res.,* Autumn 1973, *11*(2), pp. 296–303.

Scott, William R. A Bayesian Approach to Asset Valuation and Audit Size. *J. Acc. Res.,* Autumn 1973, *11*(2), pp. 304–30.

Shwayder, Keith R. Two "Wrongs" Making a "Right." *J. Acc. Res.,* Autumn 1973, *11*(2), pp. 259–72.

Sorter, G. H. and Horngren, Charles T. Asset Recognition and Economic Attributes—The Relevant Costing Approach. In *Thomas, W. E., Jr., ed.,* 1973, pp. 461–74.

Talonen, Pentti. Näkökohtia yrityksen kasvusta ja kannattavuudesta. Osa II. (Growth and Profitability of the Firm. Part II. With English summary.) *Liiketaloudellinen Aikak.,* 1973, *22*(4), pp. 248–62.

Thirlby, G. F. The Subjective Theory of Value and Accounting 'Cost'. In *Buchanan, J. M. and Thirlby, G. F., eds.,* 1973, pp. 135–61.

Toan, Arthur B., Jr. Publicly Reporting on Corporate Social Impact. In *Dierkes, M. and Bauer, R. A., eds.,* 1973, pp. 327–44.   [G: U.S.]

Ureel, William L. Nuclear Fuel Accounting. *Manage. Account.,* July 1973, *55*(1), pp. 14–16, 24.   [G: U.S.]

Vatter, William J. Limitations of Overhead Allocation. In *Thomas, W. E., Jr., ed.,* 1973, pp. 484–503.

Vendig, Richard E. A Three-Part Transfer Price. *Manage. Account.,* September 1973, *55*(3), pp. 33–36.

Wilson, David A. A Note on "Environmental Complexity and Financial Reports" *Accounting Rev.,* July 1973, *48*(3), pp. 586–88.

Winkle, Gary M. Perspectives on Life Insurance Financial Reporting: Discussion. *J. Risk Ins.,* March 1973, *40*(1), pp. 25–30.   [G: U.S.]

Wolk, Harry I. and Tearney, Michael G. Income Tax Allocation and Loss Carryforwards: Exploring Uncharted Ground. *Accounting Rev.,* April 1973, *48*(2), pp. 292–99.

Wyman, Harold E. Financial Lease Evaluation Under Conditions of Uncertainty. *Accounting Rev.,* July 1973, *48*(3), pp. 489–93.

Yu, Seongjae and Neter, John. A Stochastic Model of the Internal Control System. *J. Acc. Res.,* Autumn 1973, *11*(2), pp. 273–95.

Ziock, Richard W. A Realistic Profit Model for Individual Non-Participating Life Insurance. *J. Risk Ins.,* September 1973, *40*(3), pp. 357–73.   [G: U.S.]

600 Industrial Organization; Technological Change; Industry Studies

610 INDUSTRIAL ORGANIZATION AND PUBLIC POLICY

611 Industrial Organization and Market Structure

6110 Industrial Organization and Market Structure

Abegglen, James C. and Rapp, William V. Japanese Managerial Behavior and "Excessive Competition." In *Henley, D. S., ed.,* 1973, pp. 65–82.   [G: Japan]

Aberle, Gerd. Reaktionshypothesen in Oligopolmodellen und oligopolistisches Marktverhalten. (Reaction Hypotheses in Oligopoly Models and Oligopolistic Market Behavior. With English summary.) *Z. ges. Staatswiss.,* August 1973, *129*(3), pp. 454–77.

Abrams, Samuel K. Association Participation in Government Standard-Setting—How an Association Can Avoid Antitrust Liability. *Antitrust Bull.,* Summer 1973, *18*(2), pp. 281–90. [G: U.S.]

Allen, G. C. Competition and Mergers. In *Allen, G. C., et al.,* 1973, pp. 1–10. [G: U.K.]

Amjad, Rashid. Growth, Profitability and Savings of Quoted Public Limited Companies 1964–70. *Pakistan Econ. Soc. Rev.,* Winter 1973, *11*(4), pp. 417–42. [G: Pakistan]

Andersen, Per. Økonomisk overlevelse i et stokastisk marked. (The Behaviour of a Monopolist Who Seeks Economic Survival in a Stochastic Market. With English summary.) *Nationalokon. Tidsskr.,* 1973, *111*(2), pp. 266–76.

Balogh, T. and Balacs, P. Fact and Fancy in International Economic Relations. *World Devel.,* February 1973, *1*(1-2), pp. 76–92.

Barnea, Amir and Logue, Dennis E. Stock-Market Based Measures of Corporate Diversification. *J. Ind. Econ.,* September 1973, *22*(1), pp. 51–60. [G: U.S.]

Baron, David P. Limit Pricing, Potential Entry, and Barriers to Entry. *Amer. Econ. Rev.,* September 1973, *63*(4), pp. 666–74.

Beesley, Michael E. Mergers and Economic Welfare. In *Allen, G. C., et al.,* 1973, pp. 71–80.

Bergson, Abram. On Monopoly Welfare Losses. *Amer. Econ. Rev.,* December 1973, *63*(5), pp. 853–70.

Blattner, Niklaus. Domestic Competition and Foreign Trade: The Case of the Excess Capacity Barrier to Entry. *Z. Nationalökon.,* 1973, *33*(3–4), pp. 403–12.

Boyle, Stanley E. The Average Concentration Ratio: An Inappropriate Measure of Industry Structure. *J. Polit. Econ.,* Part I, March-April 1973, *81*(2), pp. 414–26. [G: U.S.]

Brozen, Yale. Concentration and Profits: Does Concentration Matter? In *Weston, J. F. and Ornstein, S. I., eds.,* 1973, pp. 59–70. [G: U.S.]

Burney, Anthony [Sir]. Take-Overs: Aims and Objects. In *Allen, G. C., et al.,* 1973, pp. 11–19. [G: U.K.]

Cannon, C. M. Size of Establishments in Manufacturing: A Comment. *Econ. J.,* September 1973, *83* (331), pp. 898–99.

Clarke, Darral G. Sales-Advertising Cross-Elasticities and Advertising Competition. *J. Marketing Res.,* August 1973, *10*(3), pp. 250–61.

Clearwaters, Keith I. Trade Associations and the Antitrust Laws—A View from the Justice Department. *Antitrust Bull.,* Summer 1973, *18*(2), pp. 233–42. [G: U.S.]

Conn, Robert L. Performance of Conglomerate Firms: Comment. *J. Finance,* June 1973, *28*(3), pp. 754–58.

Culyer, Anthony J. Pareto, Peacock and Rowley, and Policy Towards Natural Monopoly: Comment. *J. Public Econ.,* February 1973, *2*(1), pp. 89–95.

Dalton, James A. and Esposito, Louis. The Impact of Liquidity on Merger Activity. *Quart. Rev. Econ. Bus.,* Spring 1973, *13*(1), pp. 15–26. [G: U.S.]

Dalton, James A. Administered Inflation and Business Pricing: Another Look. *Rev. Econ. Statist.,* November 1973, *55*(4), pp. 516–19. [G: U.S.]

Darnell, Jerome C. Bank Mergers: Prices Paid to Marriage Partners. *Fed. Res. Bank Bus. Rev. Phila.,* July 1973, pp. 16–25. [G: U.S.]

De Alessi, Louis. Private Property and Dispersion of Ownership in Large Corporations. *J. Finance,* September 1973, *28*(4), pp. 839–51. [G: U.S.]

Demsetz, Harold. Industry Structure, Market Rivalry, and Public Policy. *J. Law Econ.,* April 1973, *16*(1), pp. 1–9. [G: U.S.]

Denenberg, Herbert S. and Cummins, J. David. Insurance and Reciprocity: Reply. *J. Risk Ins.,* March 1973, *40*(1), pp. 141–42. [G: U.S.]

Dixon, Donald F. Economic Effects of Exclusive Dealing and Ownership Control: The U.K. Petrol Case Revisited. *Antitrust Bull.,* Summer 1973, *18* (2), pp. 375–90. [G: U.K.]

Duetsch, Larry L. Elements of Market Structure and the Extent of Suboptimal Capacity. *Southern Econ. J.,* October 1973, *40*(2), pp. 216–23. [G: U.S.]

Edwards, Franklin R. Advertising and Competition in Banking. *Antitrust Bull.,* Spring 1973, *18*(1), pp. 23–32. [G: U.S.]

Edwards, Franklin R. and Heggestad, Arnold A. Uncertainty, Market Structure, and Performance in Banking: The Galbraith-Caves Hypothesis and Managerial Motives in Banking. *Quart. J. Econ.,* August 1973, *87*(3), pp. 455–73. [G: U.S.]

Eeckhoudt, Louis R. The "Dorfman-Steiner" Rule: The Intertemporal Case: A Reply. *Z. Nationalökon.,* 1973, *33*(3–4), pp. 431–34.

Elzinga, Kenneth G. and Hogarty, Thomas F. The Problem of Geographic Market Delineation in Antimerger Suits. *Antitrust Bull.,* Spring 1973, *18* (1), pp. 45–81. [G: U.S.]

Engwall, Lars. Business Behavior: The Cigarette Case. *Marquette Bus. Rev.,* Summer 1973, *17*(2), pp. 59–72. [G: U.S.]

Farris, Paul L. Market Growth and Concentration Change in U.S. Manufacturing Industries. *Antitrust Bull.,* Summer 1973, *18*(2), pp. 291–305. [G: U.S.]

Fellman, Steven John. What Services Must a Trade Association Render to Non-members? *Antitrust Bull.,* Summer 1973, *18*(2), pp. 167–79. [G: U.S.]

Filippi, Enrico. Finanza italiana: Analisi di un caso di fusione (FINGEST/SALSI) (Italian Finance: Analysis of a Case of Merger (FINGEST/SALSI). With English summary.) *L'Impresa,* 1973, *15* (3–4), pp. 225–31. [G: Italy]

Fisher, Franklin M. Stability and Competitive Equilibrium in Two Models of Search and Individual Price Adjustment. *J. Econ. Theory,* October 1973, *6*(5), pp. 446–70.

Formby, John P. On Revenue Maximizing Duopoly. *J. Ind. Econ.,* July 1973, *21*(3), pp. 272–92.

Franke, Jürgen F. A. W. Advertising and Collusion in Oligopoly. *Jahr. Nationalökon. Statist.,* December 1973, *188*(1), pp. 33–50.

Franke, Jürgen F. A. W. Marktmacht und Inflation.

(Market Power and Inflation. With English summary.) *Z. Wirtschaft. Sozialwissen.*, 1973, *93*(3), pp. 285–305.

Frugali, Fabio. Situation and Prospects of Small and Medium-Sized Industry in Italy. *Rev. Econ. Cond. Italy*, November 1973, *27*(6), pp. 397–409. [G: Italy]

Galbraith, John Kenneth. Controls or Competition—What's at Issue? Comment. *Rev. Econ. Statist.*, November 1973, *55*(4), pp. 524.

Gannon, Colin A. Central Concentration in Simple Spatial Duopoly: Some Behavioral and Functional Conditions. *J. Reg. Sci.*, December 1973, *13*(3), pp. 357–75.

Gannon, Colin A. Optimization of Market Share in Spatial Competition. *Southern Econ. J.*, July 1973, *40*(1), pp. 66–79.

Geneen, Harold S. and Judelson, David N. Additional Data on ITT and Gulf and Western. In *Andreano, R. L., ed.*, 1973, pp. R331–42. [G: U.S.]

Geneen, Harold S. Statement on ITT Policy and Conglomerates. In *Andreano, R. L., ed.*, 1973, pp. R329–13. [G: U.S.]

George, Kenneth D. The Changing Structure of Industry in the United Kingdom. In *Rybczynski, T. M., ed.*, 1973, pp. 55–67. [G: U.K.]

Goldberg, Lawrence G. The Effect of Conglomerate Mergers on Competition. *J. Law Econ.*, April 1973, *16*(1), pp. 137–58. [G: U.S.]

Goodnow, James D. and Hansz, James E. Environmental Determinants of Overseas Market Entry Strategies. In *Alexandrides, C. G., ed.*, 1973, pp. 195–215. [G: U.S.]

Greenhut, M. L. and Ohta, H. Spatial Configurations and Competitive Equilibrium. *Weltwirtsch. Arch.*, 1973, *109*(1), pp. 87–104.

Green, Mark J. The High Cost of Monopoly. In *Andreano, R. L., ed.*, 1973, pp. R325–05. [G: U.S.]

Green, Mark J. and Moore, Beverly C., Jr. Winter's Discontent: Market Failure and Consumer Welfare. *Yale Law J.*, April 1973, *82*(5), pp. 903–19. [G: U.S.]

Greer, Douglas F. Advertising and Market Concentration: Reply. *Southern Econ. J.*, January 1973, *39*(3), pp. 451–53. [G: U.S.]

Greer, Douglas F. Some Case History Evidence on the Advertising-Concentration Relationship. *Antitrust Bull.*, Summer 1973, *18*(2), pp. 307–32. [G: U.S.]

Guerci, Carlo M. Nuovi miti sulla grande impresa? (New Myths on the Big Firm? With English summary.) *L'industria, N. S.*, 1973, (1), pp. 91–101. [G: Italy]

Gutowski, Armin. Theoretical Approaches to a Concept of Supplier's Power. *Ger. Econ. Rev.*, 1973, *11*(3), pp. 193–215.

Halpern, Paul J. Empirical Estimates of the Amount and Distribution of Gains to Companies in Mergers. *J. Bus.*, October 1973, *46*(4), pp. 554–75. [G: U.S.]

Halverson, James T. Expanded Roles for Trade Associations. *Antitrust Bull.*, Summer 1973, *18*(2), pp. 221–31. [G: U.S.]

Hauptmann, Harry and Seifert, Hans G. Ein Oligopolspiel mit wirksamen Kapazitätsschranken. (An Oligopoly Game with Effective Capacity Bounds.

With English summary.) *Jahr. Nationalökon. Statist.*, December 1973, *188*(1), pp. 51–64.

Herdzina, Klaus. Markstruktur und Wettbewerb. (Market Structure and Competition. On Definition Patterns of Workable Competition. With English summary.) *Z. Wirtschaft. Sozialwissen.*, 1973, *93*(3), pp. 267–84.

Herold, Arthur L. What Can an Association Do to Meet Foreign Competition? *Antitrust Bull.*, Summer 1973, *18*(2), pp. 181–90. [G: U.S.]

Hexter, J. L. and Snow, John W. Entropy, Lorenz Curves, and Some Comments on Size Inequality Among the Largest U.S. Corporations. *Nebr. J. Econ. Bus.*, Winter 1973, *12*(1), pp. 43–50. [G: U.S.]

Hibdon, James E., et al. Market Areas in Spatial Duopoly. *Rivista Int. Sci. Econ. Com.*, March 1973, *20*(3), pp. 267–77.

Hindley, Brian. Take-Overs: 'Victims' and 'Victors' In *Allen, G. C., et al.*, 1973, pp. 21–28.

Holtermann, Sally E. Market Structure and Economic Performance in U.K. Manufacturing Industry. *J. Ind. Econ.*, December 1973, *22*(2), pp. 119–39. [G: U.K.]

Horowitz, David and Erlich, Reese. Big Brother as a Holding Company. In *Andreano, R. L., ed.*, 1973, pp. R330–15. [G: U.S.]

House, William J. Market Structure and Industry Performance: The Case of Kenya. *Oxford Econ. Pap.*, November 1973, *25*(3), pp. 405–19. [G: Kenya]

Howe, M. A Study of Trade Association Price Fixing. *J. Ind. Econ.*, July 1973, *21*(3), pp. 236–56. [G: U.K.]

Hu, Sheng Cheng. On the Incentive to Invent: A Clarificatory Note. *J. Law Econ.*, April 1973, *16*(1), pp. 169–77.

Imel, Blake and Helmberger, Peter. Estimation of Structure-Profit Relationships: Reply. *Amer. Econ. Rev.*, September 1973, *63*(4), pp. 768–69. [G: U.S.]

Intriligator, Michael D., et al. Conceptual Framework of an Econometric Model of Industrial Organization. In *Weston, J. F. and Ornstein, S. I., eds.*, 1973, pp. 23–55. [G: U.S.]

Ireland, Norman J. The "Dorfman-Steiner" Rule and Bandwagon Effects. *Z. Nationalökon.*, 1973, *33*(3–4), pp. 427–30.

Jacquemin, Alex P. and Cardon de Lichtbuer, Michel. Size Structure, Stability and Performance of the Largest British and EEC Firms. *Europ. Econ. Rev.*, December 1973, *4*(4), pp. 393–408. [G: U.K.; E.E.C.]

Joelson, Mark R. Protective Legislation v. Our Competitive System: The Dilemma and the Role of the Trade Association. *Antitrust Bull.*, Summer 1973, *18*(2), pp. 255–70. [G: U.S.]

Johnson, Ramon E. Conglomerate Firms in Perspective: Comment. *Intermountain Econ. Rev.*, Fall 1973, *4*(2), pp. 67–69. [G: U.S.]

Johnson, Rodney D. and Meinster, David R. An Analysis of Bank Holding Company Acquisitions: Some Methodological Issues. *J. Bank Res.*, Spring 1973, *4*(1), pp. 58–61. [G: U.S.]

Jones, J. C. H.; Laudadio, Leonard and Percy, M. Market Structure and Profitability in Canadian

Manufacturing Industry: Some Cross-Section Results. *Can. J. Econ.*, August 1973, *6*(3), pp. 356–68. [G: Canada]

Kalish, Lionel, III and Gilbert, R. Alton. An Analysis of Efficiency of Scale and Organizational Form in Commercial Banking. *J. Ind. Econ.*, July 1973, *21*(3), pp. 293–307. [G: U.S.]

Kamerschen, David R. Further Thoughts on Separation of Ownership and Control. *Rivista Int. Sci. Econ. Com.*, February 1973, *20*(2), pp. 179–83.

Kerton, Robert R. Price Effects of Market Power in the Canadian Newspaper Industry. *Can. J. Econ.*, November 1973, *6*(4), pp. 602–06. [G: Canada]

Knowles, James C. The Rockefeller Financial Group. In *Andreano, R. L., ed.*, 1973, pp. M343–59. [G: U.S.]

Koch, James V. Market Structure and Industry Growth: Reply. *Miss. Val. J. Bus. Econ.*, Fall 1973, *9*(1), pp. 87. [G: U.S.]

Laiken, S. N. Financial Performance of Merging Firms in a Virtually Unconstrained Legal Environment. *Antitrust Bull.*, Winter 1973, *18*(4), pp. 827–51. [G: Canada]

Leibenstein, Harvey. Competition and X-Efficiency: Reply. *J. Polit. Econ.*, May-June 1973, *81*(3), pp. 765–77.

Levhari, David and Peles, Yoram. Market Structure, Quality and Durability. *Bell J. Econ. Manage. Sci.*, Spring 1973, *4*(1), pp. 235–48.

Lotti, Eraldo. Nuove tecniche di organizzazione della produzione. Estensione di alcuni concetti di Ragnar Frisch. (New Techniques of Industrial Organization. An Extension of Some Ideas of Ragnar Frisch. With English summary.) *L'Impresa*, 1973, *15*(11–12), pp. 701–08.

Louis, R. Co-operative Development Centres. *Int. Lab. Rev.*, June 1973, *107*(6), pp. 539–51.

Maass, Randal O. and Hutchins, Robert C. Measurement of Multicompany Diversification. *J. Econ. Bus.*, Fall 1973, *26*(1), pp. 74–77. [G: U.S.]

MacPhee, Craig R. Insurance and Reciprocity: Comment. *J. Risk Ins.*, March 1973, *40*(1), pp. 139–41. [G: U.S.]

Madden, Carl H. Controls or Competition—What's at Issue? Reply. *Rev. Econ. Statist.*, November 1973, *55*(4), pp. 524–25.

Mann, H. Michael. Concentration, Barriers to Entry, and Rates of Return Revisited: A Reply. *J. Ind. Econ.*, April 1973, *21*(2), pp. 203–04.

Mann, H. Michael; Henning, John A. and Meehan, James W., Jr. Advertising and Market Concentration: Comment. *Southern Econ. J.*, January 1973, *39*(3), pp. 448–51.

Mansfield, Edwin. Determinants of the Speed of Application of New Technology. In *Williams, B. R., ed.*, 1973, pp. 199–216. [G: U.S.]

Marfels, Christian. Whither Industrial Organization? *Z. Nationalökon.*, 1973, *33*(3–4), pp. 435–45.

Marfels, Christian. Relevant Market and Concentration: The Case of the U.S. Automobile Industry. *Jahr. Nationalökon. Statist.*, March 1973, *187*(3), pp. 209–17. [G: U.S.]

Markham, Jesse W. The Conglomerate Firm: A Factual Analysis. In *Weston, J. F. and Ornstein, S. I., eds.*, 1973, pp. 185–201. [G: U.S.]

McFetridge, Donald G. Market Structure and Price-Cost Margins: An Analysis of the Canadian Manufacturing Sector. *Can. J. Econ.*, August 1973, *6*(3), pp. 344–55. [G: Canada]

McFetridge, Donald G. The Determinants of Pricing Behaviour: A Study of the Canadian Cotton Textile Industry. *J. Ind. Econ.*, December 1973, *22*(2), pp. 141–52. [G: Canada]

Meehan, James W., Jr. and Duchesneau, Thomas D. The Critical Level of Concentration: An Empirical Analysis. *J. Ind. Econ.*, September 1973, *22*(1), pp. 21–36. [G: U.S.]

Melicher, Ronald W. and Rush, David F. The Performance of Conglomerate Firms: Recent Risk and Return Experience. *J. Finance*, May 1973, *28*(2), pp. 381–88. [G: U.S.]

Melnik, A. and Pollatschek, M. A. Debt Capacity, Diversification and Conglomerate Mergers. *J. Finance*, December 1973, *28*(5), pp. 1163–73. [G: U.S.]

Metwally, Mohktar M. Entry Gap in New Zealand Markets for Manufactured Consumer Goods. *Econ. Rec.*, December 1973, *49*(128), pp. 575–87. [G: New Zealand]

Metwally, Mohktar M. Economic Strategies of Firms Facing Asymptotic Demand: A Case Study. *Appl. Econ.*, December 1973, *5*(4), pp. 271–80. [G: Australia]

Moran, R. Allen. Cooperative Advertising: An Alternative Interpretation of Price Discrimination. *Calif. Manage. Rev.*, Summer 1973, *15*(4), pp. 61–63. [G: U.S.]

Moyer, R. Charles and Sussna, Edward. Registered Bank Holding Company Acquisition: A Cross-Section Analysis. *J. Financial Quant. Anal.*, September 1973, *8*(4), pp. 647–61. [G: U.S.]

Nibale, Gianfranco. Distribuzione automobilistica e dimensione d'impresa. (Automobile Distribution and Business Size. With English summary.) *Rivista Int. Sci. Econ. Com.*, October 1973, *20*(10), pp. 1013–24. [G: U.S.]

Nielsen, James F. and Melicher, Ronald W. A Financial Analysis of Acquisition and Merger Premiums. *J. Financial Quant. Anal.*, March 1973, *8*(2), pp. 139–48. [G: U.S.]

Ornstein, Stanley I. Market Structure and Industry Growth: Comment. *Miss. Val. J. Bus. Econ.*, Fall 1973, *9*(1), pp. 83–86. [G: U.S.]

Ornstein, Stanley I. Concentration and Profits. In *Weston, J. F. and Ornstein, S. I., eds.*, 1973, pp. 87–102. [G: U.S.]

Ornstein, Stanley I., et al. Determinants of Market Structure. *Southern Econ. J.*, April 1973, *39*(4), pp. 612–25. [G: U.S.]

Owen, Bruce M. Newspaper and Television Station Joint Ownership. *Antitrust Bull.*, Winter 1973, *18*(4), pp. 787–807. [G: U.S.]

Palmer, John P. The Profit-Performance Effects of the Separation of Ownership from Control in Large U.S. Industrial Corporations. *Bell J. Econ. Manage. Sci.*, Spring 1973, *4*(1), pp. 293–303. [G: U.S.]

Papadia, Francesco. Nota sugli indici di concentrazione. (Essays on the Indexes of Concentration. With English summary.) *L'Impresa*, 1973, *15*(3–4), pp. 265–72.

Peacock, Alan T. and Rowley, Charles K. Welfare Economics and the Public Regulation of Natural

Monopoly: Reply. *J. Public Econ.*, February 1973, *2*(1), pp. 97–100.

Prescott, Edward C. Market Structure and Monopoly Profits: A Dynamic Theory. *J. Econ. Theory*, December 1973, *6*(6), pp. 546–57.

Primeaux, Walter J. Price Variability and Price Discrimination: A Case Study. *Marquette Bus. Rev.*, Spring 1973, *17*(1), pp. 25–29. [G: U.S.]

Pryor, Frederic L. Size of Establishments in Manufacturing: A Reply. *Econ. J.*, September 1973, *83* (331), pp. 900.

Rhoades, Stephen A. and Cleaver, Joe M. The Nature of the Concentration—Price/Cost Margin Relationship for 352 Manufacturing Industries: 1967. *Southern Econ. J.*, July 1973, *40*(1), pp. 90–102. [G: U.S.]

Rhoades, Stephen A. The Concentration-Profitability Relationship: Policy Implications and Some Empirical Evidence. *Antitrust Bull.*, Summer 1973, *18*(2), pp. 333–54. [G: U.S.]

Rhoades, Stephen A. The Effect of Diversification on Industry Profit Performance in 241 Manufacturing Industries: 1963. *Rev. Econ. Statist.*, May 1973, *55*(2), pp. 146–55. [G: U.S.]

Ripley, Frank C. and Segal, Lydia. Price Determination in 395 Manufacturing Industries. *Rev. Econ. Statist.*, August 1973, *55*(3), pp. 263–71. [G: U.S.]

Robbins, Lionel [Lord]. Summing Up: Mergers and the Legal Framework. In *Allen, G. C., et al.*, 1973, pp. 81–84.

Ross, Stephen A. and Wachter, Michael L. Wage Determination, Inflation, and the Industrial Structure. *Amer. Econ. Rev.*, September 1973, *63* (4), pp. 675–92.

Savoré, Carlo. Nuovi problemi delle imprese di produzione di fronte all'evoluzione delle strutture commerciali. (New Problems of Manufacturing Companies and the Development of Distributive Structures. With English summary.) *L'Impresa*, 1973, *15*(9–10), pp. 623–26.

Sawhney, Pawan K. and Sawhney, Bansi L. Capacity-Utilization, Concentration, and Price-Cost Margins: Results on Indian Industries. *J. Ind. Econ.*, April 1973, *21*(2), pp. 145–53. [G: India]

Scanlon, Paul D. Anti-Competitive Advertising and the FTC: A Ban on Oligopoly-Creating-Ads? In *Murray, B. B., ed.*, 1973, pp. 363–69. [G: U.S.]

Scanlon, Paul D. Oligopoly and Deceptive Advertising: The Cereal Industry Affair. In *Murray, B. B., ed.*, 1973, pp. 125–34.

Scherer, Frederic M. Investment Variability, Seller Concentration, and Plant Scale Economies. *J. Ind. Econ.*, December 1973, *22*(2), pp. 157–60. [G: U.S.]

Scherer, Frederic M. The Determinants of Industrial Plant Sizes in Six Nations. *Rev. Econ. Statist.*, May 1973, *55*(2), pp. 135–45. [G: Sweden; N. America; France; U.K.; W. Germany]

Schmalensee, Richard. A Note on the Theory of Vertical Integration. *J. Polit. Econ.*, Part I, March-April 1973, *81*(2), pp. 442–49.

Schnabel, Morton. A Model of Cigarette Advertising. *Antitrust Bull.*, Spring 1973, *18*(1), pp. 33–43. [G: U.S.]

Schwartzman, David. Competition and Efficiency: Comment. *J. Polit. Econ.*, May-June 1973, *81*(3), pp. 756–64.

Schwartzman, David. The Cost-Elasticity of Demand and Industry Boundaries: Coal, Oil, Gas, and Uranium. *Antitrust Bull.*, Fall, 1973, *18*(3), pp. 483–507. [G: U.S.]

Selander, Stephen E. Is Annual Style Change in the Automobile Industry an Unfair Method of Competition? A Rebuttal. *Yale Law J.*, March 1973, *82* (4), pp. 691–710.

Sellekaerts, Willy and Lesage, Richard. A Reformulation and Empirical Verification of the Administered Prices Inflation Hypothesis: The Canadian Case. *Southern Econ. J.*, January 1973, *39*(3), pp. 345–60. [G: Canada]

Shaw, R. W. Investment and Competition from Boom to Recession: A Case Study in the Processes of Competition—The Dry Cleaning Industry. *J. Ind. Econ.*, July 1973, *21*(3), pp. 308–24. [G: U.K.]

Sheehan, Robert. Proprietors in the World of Big Business. In *Andreano, R. L., ed.*, 1973, pp. R342–06. [G: U.S.]

Sichel, Werner. Vertical Integration as a Dynamic Industry Concept. *Antitrust Bull.*, Fall, 1973, *18* (3), pp. 463–82.

Snell, Bradford C. Is Annual Style Change in the Automobile Industry an Unfair Method of Competition? A Reply. *Yale Law J.*, March 1973, *82*(4), pp. 711–14.

Snider, Thomas E. The Effect of Merger on the Lending Behavior of Rural Unit Banks in Virginia. *J. Bank Res.*, Spring 1973, *4*(1), pp. 52–57. [G: U.S.]

Sorenson, L. Orlo. Rail-barge Competition in Transporting Winter Wheat. *Amer. J. Agr. Econ.*, December 1973, *55*(5), pp. 814–19. [G: U.S.]

Stevens, Donald L. Financial Characteristics of Merged Firms: A Multivariate Analysis. *J. Financial Quant. Anal.*, March 1973, *8*(2), pp. 149–58. [G: U.S.]

Stigler, George J. and Kindahl, James K. Industrial Prices, as Administered by Dr. Means. *Amer. Econ. Rev.*, September 1973, *63*(4), pp. 717–21.

Sweezy, Paul M. and Magdoff, Harry. The Merger Movement: A Study in Power. In *Andreano, R. L., ed.*, 1973, pp. R328–19. [G: U.S.]

Tokita, Tadahiko. Behavior of Oligopolistic Firm and Market Adjustment—A Short Run Macroeconomic Approach. (In Japanese.) *Econ. Stud. Quart.*, April 1973, *24*(1), pp. 9–17.

Townsend, Robert C. America Inc.: A Review. In *Andreano, R. L., ed.*, 1973, pp. R326–05. [G: U.S.]

Tsurumi, Hiroki. A Comparison of Alternative Optimal Models of Advertising Expenditures: Stock Adjustment vs. Control Theoretic Approaches. *Rev. Econ. Statist.*, May 1973, *55*(2), pp. 156–68. [G: Japan]

Vernon, John M. and McElroy, Marjorie B. Estimation of Structure-Profit Relationships: Comment. *Amer. Econ. Rev.*, September 1973, *63*(4), pp. 763–67. [G: U.S.]

Vernon, John M. and Nourse, Robert E. M. Profit Rates and Market Structure of Advertising Intensive Firms. *J. Ind. Econ.*, September 1973, *22*(1), pp. 1-20. [G: U.S.]

Waite, David. The Economic Significance of Small Firms. *J. Ind. Econ.*, April 1973, *21*(2), pp. 154-66. [G: U.K.]

Weston, J. Fred and Mansinghka, Surendra K. Performance of Conglomerate Firms: Reply. *J. Finance*, June 1973, *28*(3), pp. 759.

Weston, J. Fred. Conglomerate Firm in Perspective. *Intermountain Econ. Rev.*, Spring 1973, *4*(1), pp. 1-13. [G: U.S.]

Weston, J. Fred and Ornstein, Stanley I. Trends and Causes of Concentration—A Survey. In *Weston, J. F. and Ornstein, S. I., eds.*, 1973, pp. 3-21. [G: U.S.]

Weston, J. Fred. Large Firms and Economic Performance. In *Weston, J. F. and Ornstein, S. I., eds.*, 1973, pp. 225-46. [G: U.S.]

Weston, J. Fred and Mansinghka, Surendra K. Tests of the Efficiency Performance of Conglomerate Firms. In *Weston, J. F. and Ornstein, S. I., eds.*, 1973, pp. 203-24. [G: U.S.]

White, Daniel L. and Walker, Michael C. First Degree Price Discrimination and Profit Maximization. *Southern Econ. J.*, October 1973, *40*(2), pp. 313-18.

Williams, C. Arthur, Jr. and Whitman, Andrew F. Open Competition Rating Laws and Price Competition. *J. Risk Ins.*, December 1973, *40*(4), pp. 483-96. [G: U.S.]

Williams, John D. Security Exchange Packages Utilized in Mergers. *J. Econ. Bus.*, Spring-Summer 1973, *25*(3), pp. 187-90. [G: U.S.]

Winter, Ralph K., Jr. Economic Regulation vs. Competition: Ralph Nader and Creeping Capitalism. *Yale Law J.*, April 1973, *82*(5), pp. 890-902. [G: U.S.]

Worcester, Dean A., Jr. New Estimates of the Welfare Loss to Monopoly, United States: 1956-1969. *Southern Econ. J.*, October 1973, *40*(2), pp. 234-45. [G: U.S.]

Yeats, Alexander J. An Analysis of the Effect of Mergers on Banking Market Structures. *J. Money, Credit, Banking*, May 1973, *5*(2), pp. 623-36. [G: U.S.]

612 Public Policy Towards Monopoly and Competition

6120 Public Policy Towards Monopoly and Competition

Abrams, Samuel K. Association Participation in Government Standard-Setting—How an Association Can Avoid Antitrust Liability. *Antitrust Bull.*, Summer 1973, *18*(2), pp. 281-90. [G: U.S.]

Allen, G. C. Competition and Mergers. In *Allen, G. C., et al.*, 1973, pp. 1-10. [G: U.K.]

Anderson, Dole A. Public Policy Toward Retailing: Thailand. In *Boddewyn, J. J. and Hollander, S. C., eds.*, 1972, pp. 297-310. [G: Thailand]

Aspin, Les. A Solution to the Energy Crisis: The Case for Increased Competition. *Ann. Amer. Acad. Polit. Soc. Sci.*, November 1973, *410*, pp. 154-68. [G: U.S.]

Balassa, Bela. Industrial Policy in the European Common Market. *Banca Naz. Lavoro Quart.*

Rev., December 1973, (107), pp. 311-27. [G: E.E.C.]

Barber, Clarence L. The Farm Machinery Industry: Reconciling the Interests of the Farmer, the Industry, and the General Public. *Amer. J. Agr. Econ.*, December 1973, *55*(5), pp. 820-28. [G: Canada]

Beesley, Michael E. Regulation of Taxis. *Econ. J.*, March 1973, *83*(329), pp. 150-72. [G: U.K.]

Beesley, Michael E. Mergers and Economic Welfare. In *Allen, G. C., et al.*, 1973, pp. 71-80.

Bhatt, V. V. Monopoly and Public Policy. In *Wadhva, C. D., ed.*, 1973, pp. 188-98. [G: India]

Bishop, Richard C. Limitation of Entry in the United States Fishing Industry: An Economic Appraisal of a Proposed Policy. *Land Econ.*, November 1973, *49*(4), pp. 381-90. [G: U.S.]

Bliss, Michael. Another Anti-Trust Tradition: Canadian Anti-Combines Policy, 1889-1910. *Bus. Hist. Rev.*, Summer 1973, *47*(2), pp. 177-88. [G: Canada]

Boddewyn, J. J. Public Policy Toward Retailing: Belgium. In *Boddewyn, J. J. and Hollander, S. C., eds.*, 1972, pp. 37-62. [G: Belgium]

Boddewyn, J. J. and Hollander, Stanley C. Public Policy Toward Retailing: Introduction. In *Boddewyn, J. J. and Hollander, S. C., eds.*, 1972, pp. 1-9.

Boddewyn, J. J. and Hollander, Stanley C. Public Policy Toward Retailing: Conclusions. In *Boddewyn, J. J. and Hollander, S. C., eds.*, 1972, pp. 431-52.

Borgsdorf, C. W. The Virtually Unconstrained Legal Environment for Mergers in Canada. *Antitrust Bull.*, Winter 1973, *18*(4), pp. 809-25. [G: Canada]

Brebbia, John Henry. The Role of Advisory Opinions and the Business Review Procedure. *Antitrust Bull.*, Summer 1973, *18*(2), pp. 191-219. [G: U.S.]

Christensen, Gary L. A View from the National Cable Television Association. In *Park, R. E., ed.*, 1973, pp. 15-18. [G: U.S.]

Clearwaters, Keith I. Trade Associations and the Antitrust Laws—A View from the Justice Department. *Antitrust Bull.*, Summer 1973, *18*(2), pp. 233-42. [G: U.S.]

Cohen, Alain-Gérard. Tunisia: Reforming the Commercial Structure. In *Boddewyn, J. J. and Hollander, S. C., eds.*, 1972, pp. 311-25. [G: Tunisia]

Comanor, William S. The View of an Academic Consultant. In *Park, R. E., ed.*, 1973, pp. 31-34. [G: U.S.]

Cortesse, Pierre. Public Policy Toward Retailing: France. In *Boddewyn, J. J. and Hollander, S. C., eds.*, 1972, pp. 117-43. [G: France]

Curran, R. J. Public Policy Toward Retailing: Ireland. In *Boddewyn, J. J. and Hollander, S. C., eds.*, 1972, pp. 167-90. [G: Ireland]

Darby, Michael R. and Karni, Edi. Free Competition and the Optimal Amount of Fraud. *J. Law Econ.*, April 1973, *16*(1), pp. 67-88.

Denenberg, Herbert S. and Cummins, J. David. Insurance and Reciprocity: Reply. *J. Risk Ins.*,

March 1973, *40*(1), pp. 141–42.   [G: U.S.]

Dietz, John. Enforcement of Anti-Trust Laws in the EEC. In *Henley, D. S., ed.*, 1973, pp. 185–213.   [G: E.E.C.]

Dimling, John A., Jr. A View from the National Association of Broadcasters. In *Park, R. E., ed.*, 1973, pp. 19–29.   [G: U.S.]

Dixon, Donald F. Economic Effects of Exclusive Dealing and Ownership Control: The U.K. Petrol Case Revisited. *Antitrust Bull.*, Summer 1973, *18* (2), pp. 375–90.   [G: U.K.]

Dixon, Donald F. Public Policy Toward Retailing: Australia. In *Boddewyn, J. J. and Hollander, S. C., eds.*, 1972, pp. 11–35.   [G: Australia]

Eckert, Ross D. On the Incentives of Regulators: The Case of Taxicabs. *Public Choice*, Spring 1973, *14*, pp. 83–99.   [G: U.S.]

Edwards, C. D. The World of Antitrust. In *Thorelli, H. B., ed.*, 1973, pp. 89–103.   [G: U.S.]

El-Hodiri, Mohamed and Takayama, Akira. Behavior of the Firm Under Regulatory Constraint: Clarifications. *Amer. Econ. Rev.*, March 1973, *63*(1), pp. 235–37.

Elzinga, Kenneth G. and Hogarty, Thomas F. The Problem of Geographic Market Delineation in Antimerger Suits. *Antitrust Bull.*, Spring 1973, *18* (1), pp. 45–81.   [G: U.S.]

Epstein, Barbara. The Illusory Conflict Between Antidumping and Antitrust. *Antitrust Bull.*, Spring 1973, *18*(1), pp. 1–22.   [G: U.S.]

Falco, James F. Section 7 of the Clayton Act and "Control" in Bank Holding Company Regulation. *Antitrust Bull.*, Winter 1973, *18*(4), pp. 715–41.   [G: U.S.]

Fellman, Steven John. What Services Must a Trade Association Render to Non-members? *Antitrust Bull.*, Summer 1973, *18*(2), pp. 167–79.   [G: U.S.]

Fraser, Ian. Balance Sheet on Take-Overs. In *Allen, G. C., et al.*, 1973, pp. 61–70.   [G: U.K.]

Gibbons, Hugh. The "Market Share" Theory of Damages in Private Enforcement Cases. *Antitrust Bull.*, Winter 1973, *18*(4), pp. 742–58.   [G: U.S.]

Goldberg, Lawrence G. The Effect of Conglomerate Mergers on Competition. *J. Law Econ.*, April 1973, *16*(1), pp. 137–58.   [G: U.S.]

Goldberg, Victor and Moirao, Sharon. Limit Pricing and Potential Competition. *J. Polit. Econ.*, November-December 1973, *81*(6), pp. 1460–66.

Goodwin, Kenneth R. Another View from the Federal Communications Commission. In *Park, R. E., ed.*, 1973, pp. 43–56.   [G: U.S.]

Graham, Philip L., Jr.; Hermann, Donald H. G. and Marcus, Sumner. Section 7 of the Clayton Act and Mergers Involving Foreign Interests. In *Henley, D. S., ed.*, 1973, pp. 155–84.   [G: U.S.]

Green, Mark J. The High Cost of Monopoly. In *Andreano, R. L., ed.*, 1973, pp. R325–05. [G: U.S.]

Green, Mark J. and Moore, Beverly C., Jr. The Nader Antitrust Report: A Tale of Two Critics. *Antitrust Bull.*, Fall, 1973, *18*(3), pp. 551–79. [G: U.S.]

Green, Mark J. and Nader, Ralph. Economic Regulation vs. Competition: Uncle Sam the Monopoly Man. *Yale Law J.*, April 1973, *82*(5), pp. 871–89.   [G: U.S.]

Green, Mark J. and Moore, Beverly C., Jr. Winter's

Discontent: Market Failure and Consumer Welfare. *Yale Law J.*, April 1973, *82*(5), pp. 903–19.   [G: U.S.]

Haccou, J. F. and Lübbers, P. J. M. Public Policy Toward Retailing: The Netherlands. In *Boddewyn, J. J. and Hollander, S. C., eds.*, 1972, pp. 245–70.   [G: Netherlands]

Hale, Rosemary D. Cement Mergers—Market Dispersion and Conglomerate Entry. *Marquette Bus. Rev.*, Summer 1973, *17*(2), pp. 98–108. [G: U.S.]

Halverson, James T. Expanded Roles for Trade Associations. *Antitrust Bull.*, Summer 1973, *18*(2), pp. 221–31.   [G: U.S.]

Hamburger, Polia Lerner. Public Policy Toward Retailing: Brazil. In *Boddewyn, J. J. and Hollander, S. C., eds.*, 1972, pp. 63–79.   [G: Brazil]

Herold, Arthur L. What Can an Association Do to Meet Foreign Competition? *Antitrust Bull.*, Summer 1973, *18*(2), pp. 181–90.   [G: U.S.]

Hollander, Stanley C. Public Policy Toward Retailing: United States of America. In *Boddewyn, J. J. and Hollander, S. C., eds.*, 1972, pp. 367–403.   [G: U.S.]

Hoppmann, Erich. Zur ökonomischen Begründung von Ausnahmebereichen. Zugleich eine Bemerkung zum Diskussionsbeitrag von M. Tolksdorf "Hoppmanns neoklassische Wettbewerbstheorie als Grundlage der Wettbewerbspolitik." (Note on the Economic Reasons for Exceptions to Competitive Policy. Comment on M. Tolksdorf's "Hoppmann's Neoclassic Theory of a Competition as a Basis for Competition Policy." With English summary.) *Jahr. Nationalökon. Statist.*, January 1973, *187*(2), pp. 161–69.

Howe, Geoffrey [Sir]. Public Policy on Mergers and Monopolies. In *Allen, G. C., et al.*, 1973, pp. 39–44.   [G: U.K.]

Izraeli, Dov. Public Policy Toward Retailing: Israel. In *Boddewyn, J. J. and Hollander, S. C., eds.*, 1972, pp. 191–211.   [G: Israel]

Joelson, Mark R. Protective Legislation v. Our Competitive System: The Dilemma and the Role of the Trade Association. *Antitrust Bull.*, Summer 1973, *18*(2), pp. 255–70.   [G: U.S.]

Jones, J. C. H. and Laudadio, Leonard. Canadian Bank Mergers, the Public Interest and Public Policy. *Banca Naz. Lavoro Quart. Rev.*, June 1973, *105*, pp. 109–40.   [G: Canada]

Jones, Mary Gardiner. Social Responsibility: The Regulator's View. *Calif. Manage. Rev.*, Summer 1973, *15*(4), pp. 78–84.   [G: U.S.]

Keen, E. A. Limited Entry: The Case of the Japanese Tuna Fishery. In *Sokoloski, A. A., ed.*, 1973, pp. 146–58.   [G: Japan]

Laiken, S. N. Financial Performance of Merging Firms in a Virtually Unconstrained Legal Environment. *Antitrust Bull.*, Winter 1973, *18*(4), pp. 827–51.   [G: Canada]

Lamont, Douglas F. Public Policy Toward Retailing: Mexico. In *Boddewyn, J. J. and Hollander, S. C., eds.*, 1972, pp. 229–44.   [G: Mexico]

Lanzillotti, Robert F. and Blair, Roger D. Automobile Pollution, Externalities and Public Policy. *Antitrust Bull.*, Fall, 1973, *18*(3), pp. 431–47.   [G: U.S.]

Laumer, Helmut. Public Policy Toward Retailing: Uganda. In *Boddewyn, J. J. and Hollander, S. C., eds.*, 1972, pp. 327–36.   [G: Uganda]

Lawlor, Reed C. Copyright and Patent Protection for Computer Programs. In *The Diebold Group, Inc.*, 1973, pp. 204–12.   [G: U.S.]

Lindblad, Sven and Hallencreutz, Ingrid. Public Policy Toward Retailing: Sweden. In *Boddewyn, J. J. and Hollander, S. C., eds.*, 1972, pp. 283–95.   [G: Sweden]

Loevinger, Lee. The Closed Mind Strikes Again. *Antitrust Bull.*, Fall, 1973, *18*(3), pp. 581–87.   [G: U.S.]

Long, William F.; Schramm, Richard and Tollison, Robert D. The Economic Determinants of Antitrust Activity. *J. Law Econ.*, October 1973, *16*(2), pp. 351–64.   [G: U.S.]

MacPhee, Craig R. Insurance and Reciprocity: Comment. *J. Risk Ins.*, March 1973, *40*(1), pp. 139–41.   [G: U.S.]

Martin, Donald L. Legal Constraints and the Choice of Organizational Form. *Amer. Econ. Rev.*, May 1973, *63*(2), pp. 326–34.   [G: Netherlands]

McClelland, W. G. Public Policy Toward Retailing: The United Kingdom. In *Boddewyn, J. J. and Hollander, S. C., eds.*, 1972, pp. 351–66.   [G: U.K.]

Mestmäcker, Ernst-Joachim. Wettbewerbspolitik in der Industriegesellschaft. (Policy of Competition in the Industrial Society. With English summary.) *Z. ges. Staatswiss.*, February 1973, *129*(1), pp. 89–101.   [G: W. Germany]

Miller, Roger LeRoy. The Closed Enterprise System Opened Up. *Antitrust Bull.*, Fall, 1973, *18*(3), pp. 589–606.   [G: U.S.]

Moran, R. Allen. Cooperative Advertising: An Alternative Interpretation of Price Discrimination. *Calif. Manage. Rev.*, Summer 1973, *15*(4), pp. 61–63.   [G: U.S.]

Morris, John P. In the Wake of the Flood. *Law Contemp. Probl.*, Winter-Spring 1973, *38*(1), pp. 85–98.   [G: U.S.]

Mueller, Willard F. Corporate Secrecy and the Need for Financial Disclosure. In *Haveman, R. H. and Hamrin, R. D., eds.*, 1973, pp. 283–91. [G: U.S.]

Mulaney, Charles W., Jr. Gasoline Marketing and the Robinson-Patman Act. *Yale Law J.*, July 1973, *82*(8), pp. 1706–18.   [G: U.S.]

Nader, Ralph. Efficiency and Regulatory Policy: Issues of Compliance, Disclosure, and Accountability. In *Haveman, R. H. and Hamrin, R. D., eds.*, 1973, pp. 267–72.   [G: U.S.]

Nader, Ralph, et al. Government Secrecy and the People's Right to Know. In *Haveman, R. H. and Hamrin, R. D., eds.*, 1973, pp. 273–82. [G: U.S.]

Noll, Roger G. and Rivlin, Lewis A. Regulating Prices in Competitive Markets. *Yale Law J.*, June 1973, *82*(7), pp. 1426–34.   [G: U.S.]

Noll, Roger G. Selling Research to Regulatory Agencies. In *Park, R. E., ed.*, 1973, pp. 63–69.   [G: U.S.]

Owen, Bruce M. A View from the President's Office of Telecommunications Policy. In *Park, R. E., ed.*, 1973, pp. 3–14.   [G: U.S.]

Park, Rolla Edward. A Bayesian Framework for Thinking about the Role of Analysis. In *Park, R. E., ed.*, 1973, pp. 57–61.   [G: U.S.]

Park, Rolla Edward. The Role of Analysis in Regulatory Decisionmaking: The Case of Cable Television: Conclusion. In *Park, R. E., ed.*, 1973,

pp. 71–78.   [G: U.S.]

Pengilley, Warren. The Register of Trade Practices Agreements—How Relevant Is It? *Econ. Anal. Pol.*, September 1973, *4*(2), pp. 18–42.   [G: Australia]

Pengilley, Warren. Australian Experience of Antitrust Regulation—A Vindication of the Per Se Approach. *Antitrust Bull.*, Summer 1973, *18*(2), pp. 355–74.   [G: Australia]

Penrose, Edith. International Patenting and the Less-Developed Countries. *Econ. J.*, September 1973, *83*(331), pp. 768–86.

Phlips, Louis. Illusions in Testing for Administered Prices: A Reply. *J. Ind. Econ.*, April 1973, *21*(2), pp. 196–99.

Posner, Richard A. Report on the Federal Trade Commission. In *Murray, B. B., ed.*, 1973, pp. 102–15.   [G: U.S.]

Pressman, Israel and Carol, Arthur. Behavior of the Firm Under Regulatory Constraint: Reply. *Amer. Econ. Rev.*, March 1973, *63*(1), pp. 238.

Reid, Samuel Richardson. "The Bank Merger Act of 1960: A Decade After": Comment. *Antitrust Bull.*, Fall, 1973, *18*(3), pp. 449–62. [G: U.S.]

Rhoades, Stephen A. The Concentration-Profitability Relationship: Policy Implications and Some Empirical Evidence. *Antitrust Bull.*, Summer 1973, *18*(2), pp. 333–54.   [G: U.S.]

Robbins, Lionel [Lord]. Summing Up: Mergers and the Legal Framework. In *Allen, G. C., et al.*, 1973, pp. 81–84.

Ross, Howard N. Illusions in Testing for Administered Prices. *J. Ind. Econ.*, April 1973, *21*(2), pp. 187–95.

Sassen, E. M. J. A. Ensuring Fair Competition in the European Community. In *Thorelli, H. B., ed.*, 1973, pp. 104–15.   [G: E.E.C.]

Scanlon, Paul D. Anti-Competitive Advertising and the FTC: A Ban on Oligopoly-Creating-Ads? In *Murray, B. B., ed.*, 1973, pp. 363–69. [G: U.S.]

Schmidtchen, Dieter. Für eine konsequente Wettbewerbspolitik und über die Wege dorthin: Bemerkungen zum Wettbewerbsverständnis des Sachverständigenrates. (Consequent Competition Policy and the Ways Towards It: Remarks on the Understanding of Competition of the German Council of Economic Experts. With English summary.) *Z. ges. Staatswiss.*, February 1973, *129*(1), pp. 102–22.   [G: W. Germany]

Shaffer, Richard A. More Antitrust Suits Are Filed by States, Firms, Private Parties. In *Murray, B. B., ed.*, 1973, pp. 228–32.   [G: U.S.]

Skolnikoff, Eugene B. La tecnologia e la politica mondiale. (Technology and World Politics. With English summary.) *Mondo Aperto*, April 1973, *27*(2), pp. 101–11.

Soldner, Helmut. Public Policy Toward Retailing: West Germany. In *Boddewyn, J. J. and Hollander, S. C., eds.*, 1972, pp. 405–29. [G: W. Germany]

Stahl, Sheldon W. and Harshbarger, C. Edward. Free Enterprise Revisited—A Look at Economic Concentration. *Fed. Res. Bank Kansas City Rev.*, March 1973, pp. 10–16.   [G: U.S.]

Stone, Alan. The F.T.C. and Advertising Regulation: An Examination of Agency Failure. *Public Policy*, Spring 1973, *21*(2), pp. 203–34.   [G: U.S.]

Tolksdorf, Michael. Zur ökonomischen Begründung

von Ausnahmebereichen. Bemerkungen zu E. Hoppmanns Erwiderung. (Economic Reasons for Exceptions to Competitive Policy Norms—A Comment to Hoppmanns Article. With English summary.) *Jahr. Nationalökon. Statist.*, August 1973, *187*(6), pp. 543–49.

Tucker, William H. Regulatory Constraint: The Need for a New Look. In *The Diebold Group, Inc.*, 1973, pp. 113–17. [G: U.S.]

Van Cise, J. G. The Supreme Court and the Antitrust Laws: 1972–1973. *Antitrust Bull.*, Winter 1973, *18*(4), pp. 691–714. [G: U.S.]

Wadhva, Charan D. New Industrial Licensing Policy: An Appraisal. In *Wadhva, C. D., ed.*, 1973, pp. 199–215. [G: India]

Wasserstein, Bruce. British Merger Policy from an American Perspective. *Yale Law J.*, March 1973, *82*(4), pp. 656–90. [G: U.S.; U.K.]

Webbink, Douglas W. A View from the Federal Communications Commission. In *Park, R. E., ed.*, 1973, pp. 35–41. [G: U.S.]

Werner, Ray O. Buyer's Inducement of Discriminatory Prices Under the Robinson-Patman Act. *Nebr. J. Econ. Bus.*, Summer 1973, *12*(3), pp. 37–42. [G: U.S.]

Williams, C. Arthur, Jr. and Whitman, Andrew F. Open Competition Rating Laws and Price Competition. *J. Risk Ins.*, December 1973, *40*(4), pp. 483–96. [G: U.S.]

Winter, Ralph K., Jr. Economic Regulation vs. Competition: Ralph Nader and Creeping Capitalism. *Yale Law J.*, April 1973, *82*(5), pp. 890–902. [G: U.S.]

Worcester, Dean A., Jr. New Estimates of the Welfare Loss to Monopoly, United States: 1956–1969. *Southern Econ. J.*, October 1973, *40*(2), pp. 234–45. [G: U.S.]

Wyckham, Robert G. and Stewart, Max D. Public Policy Toward Retailing: Canada. In *Boddewyn, J. J. and Hollander, S. C., eds.*, 1972, pp. 81–99. [G: Canada]

Yoshino, Michael Y. Japan: Rationalizing the Retail Structure. In *Boddewyn, J. J. and Hollander, S. C., eds.*, 1972, pp. 213–27. [G: Japan]

613 Public Utilities and Government Regulation of Other Industries in the Private Sector

6130 Public Utilities and Government Regulation of Other Industries in the Private Sector

Aislabie, Colin S. Payment by Use in Urban Water Supply. In *Aislabie, C., ed.*, 1973, pp. 1–18. [G: Australia]

Allen, Howard P. Electric Utilities: Can They Meet Future Power Needs? *Ann. Amer. Acad. Polit. Soc. Sci.*, November 1973, *410*, pp. 86–96. [G: U.S.]

Artle, Roland and Averous, Christian P. The Telephone System as a Public Good: Static and Dynamic Aspects. *Bell J. Econ. Manage. Sci.*, Spring 1973, *4*(1), pp. 89–100.

Atkinson, A. B. and Waverman, L. Resource Allocation and the Regulated Firm: Comment. *Bell J.*

Econ. Manage. Sci., Spring 1973, *4*(1), pp. 283–87.

Bailey, Elizabeth E. Resource Allocation and the Regulated Firm: Comment on the Comments. *Bell J. Econ. Manage. Sci.*, Spring 1973, *4*(1), pp. 288–92.

Baumol, William J. and Walton, Alfred G. Full Costing, Competition and Regulatory Practice. *Yale Law J.*, March 1973, *82*(4), pp. 639–55. [G: U.S.]

Bell, A. R. Industrial Electricity Consumption—An Example of an Intermediate Good. *J. Ind. Econ.*, April 1973, *21*(2), pp. 95–109. [G: U.K.]

Besen, Stanley M. and Soligo, Ronald. The Economics of the Network-Affiliate Relationship in the Television Broadcasting Industry. *Amer. Econ. Rev.*, June 1973, *63*(3), pp. 259–68.

Brainard, Calvin H. Massachusetts Loss Experience Under No-Fault in 1971: Analysis and Implications. *J. Risk Ins.*, March 1973, *40*(1), pp. 95–101. [G: U.S.]

Collins, William H. Comparative Performance of Combinations and Separately Managed Electric Utilities. *Southern Econ. J.*, July 1973, *40*(1), pp. 80–89. [G: U.S.]

Conard, Alfred F. An Overview of the Laws of Corporations. *Mich. Law Rev.*, March 1973, *71*(4), pp. 621–90. [G: U.S.]

Culyer, Anthony J. Pareto, Peacock and Rowley, and Policy Towards Natural Monopoly: Comment. *J. Public Econ.*, February 1973, *2*(1), pp. 89–95.

Davis, E. G. A Dynamic Model of the Regulated Firm with a Price Adjustment Mechanism. *Bell J. Econ. Manage. Sci.*, Spring 1973, *4*(1), pp. 270–82.

Elliott, Ralph D. Economic Study of the Effect of Municipal Sewer Surcharges on Industrial Wastes and Water Usage. *Water Resources Res.*, October 1973, *9*(5), pp. 1121–31. [G: U.S.]

Emery, E. David. Regulated Utilities and Equipment Manufacturers' Conspiracies in the Electrical Power Industry. *Bell J. Econ. Manage. Sci.*, Spring 1973, *4*(1), pp. 322–37. [G: U.S.]

Florence, Gary A. Electric Utility Bond Financing. *Manage. Account.*, June 1973, *54*(12), pp. 35–37, 41.

Greene, Mark R. Should Variable Policy Loan Interest Rates be Adopted? *J. Risk Ins.*, December 1973, *40*(4), pp. 585–98. [G: U.S.]

Greene, Robert L. Peak Load Pricing: An Application. *Quart. Rev. Econ. Bus.*, Autumn 1973, *13*(3), pp. 105–14.

Green, Harold P. Nuclear Power: Risk, Liability, and Indemnity. *Mich. Law Rev.*, january 1973, *71*(3), pp. 479–510. [G: U.S.]

Harberger, Arnold C. Marginal Cost Pricing and Social Investment Criteria for Electricity Undertakings. In *Harberger, A. C.*, 1973, pp. 233–47.

Horn, Carl E. Practical Economics of Public Utility Regulation: An Application to Pipelines: Comment. In *Russell, M., ed.*, 1973, pp. 47–51. [G: U.S.]

Huxley, S. J. A Note on the Economics of Retail Trading Hours. *Econ. Anal. Pol.*, March 1973, *4* (1), pp. 17–22. [G: Australia]

Jaffee, Bruce L. Depreciation in a Simple Regulatory

Model. *Bell J. Econ. Manage. Sci.*, Spring 1973, *4* (1), pp. 338–42.

Johnson, Leland L. Behavior of the Firm Under Regulatory Constraint: A Reassessment. *Amer. Econ. Rev.*, May 1973, *63*(2), pp. 90–97.

Johnson, Nicholas. Economic Analysis and Regulatory Decisions. In *Haveman, R. H. and Hamrin, R. D., eds.*, 1973, pp. 261–66. [G: U.S.]

Johnson, Nicholas and Dystel, John J. A Day in the Life: The Federal Communications Commission. *Yale Law J.*, July 1973, *82*(8), pp. 1575–1634. [G: U.S.]

Joskow, Paul L. Pricing Decisions of Regulated Firms: A Behavioral Approach. *Bell J. Econ. Manage. Sci.*, Spring 1973, *4*(1), pp. 118–40.

Joskow, Paul L. Cartels, Competition and Regulation in the Property-Liability Insurance Industry. *Bell J. Econ. Manage. Sci.*, Autumn 1973, *4*(2), pp. 375–427. [G: U.S.]

Keeton, Robert E. Beyond Current Reforms in Automobile Reparations. *J. Risk Ins.*, March 1973, *40* (1), pp. 31–37. [G: U.S.]

Klevorick, Alvin K. The Behavior of a Firm Subject to Stochastic Regulatory Review. *Bell J. Econ. Manage. Sci.*, Spring 1973, *4*(1), pp. 57–88.

Kohlmeier, Louis M. The Regulators and the Regulated. In *Haveman, R. H. and Hamrin, R. D., eds.*, 1973, pp. 256–60. [G: U.S.]

Koller, Roland H., II. Why Regulate Utilities? To Control Price Discrimination. *J. Law Econ.*, April 1973, *16*(1), pp. 191–92.

Landon, John H. Pricing in Combined Gas and Electric Utilities: A Second Look. *Antitrust Bull.*, Spring 1973, *18*(1), pp. 83–98. [G: U.S.]

Levhari, David and Peles, Yoram. Market Structure, Quality and Durability. *Bell J. Econ. Manage. Sci.*, Spring 1973, *4*(1), pp. 235–48.

Levin, Harvey J. Television's Second Chance: A Retrospective Look at the Sloan Cable Commission. *Bell J. Econ. Manage. Sci.*, Spring 1973, *4*(1), pp. 343–65. [G: U.S.]

Long, Stanley G. Public Utility Regulation: Structure and Performance: Comment. In *Russell, M., ed.*, 1973, pp. 105–07. [G: U.S.]

MacAvoy, Paul W. and Pindyck, Robert S. Alternative Regulatory Policies for Dealing with the Natural Gas Shortage. *Bell J. Econ. Manage. Sci.*, Autumn 1973, *4*(2), pp. 454–98. [G: U.S.]

MacAvoy, Paul W. and Noll, Roger G. Relative Prices on Regulated Transactions of the Natural Gas Pipelines. *Bell J. Econ. Manage. Sci.*, Spring 1973, *4*(1), pp. 212–34. [G: U.S.]

Marchand, M. G. The Economic Principles of Telephone Rates Under a Budgetary Constraint. *Rev. Econ. Stud.*, October 1973, *40*(4), pp. 507–15.

McKie, James W. Public Utility Regulation: Structure and Performance. In *Russell, M., ed.*, 1973, pp. 85–105. [G: U.S.]

McNicol, David L. The Comparative Statics Properties of the Theory of the Regulated Firm. *Bell J. Econ. Manage. Sci.*, Autumn 1973, *4*(2), pp. 428–53.

Mikesell, John L. and Seifried, Edmond J. Rates of Return in Public and Private Enterprise: Electric Utilities in the United States. *Miss. Val. J. Bus. Econ.*, Fall 1973, *9*(1), pp. 41–54. [G: U.S.]

Mikesell, John L. The Corporate Income Tax and Rate of Return in Privately Owned Utilities, 1948–1970. *Public Finance*, 1973, *28*(3–4), pp. 291–300. [G: U.S.]

Miller, James C., III. The Optimal Pricing of Freight in Combination Aircraft. *J. Transp. Econ. Policy*, September 1973, *7*(3), pp. 258–68. [G: U.S.]

Murry, Donald A. Practical Economics of Public Utility Regulation: An Application to Pipelines. In *Russell, M., ed.*, 1973, pp. 35–47. [G: U.S.]

Myers, Stewart C. A Simple Model of Firm Behavior Under Regulation and Uncertainty. *Bell J. Econ. Manage. Sci.*, Spring 1973, *4*(1), pp. 304–15.

Noll, Roger G. and Rivlin, Lewis A. Regulating Prices in Competitive Markets. *Yale Law J.*, June 1973, *82*(7), pp. 1426–34. [G: U.S.]

Owen, Bruce M. Pricing in Combined Gas and Electric Utilities: Reply. *Antitrust Bull.*, Spring 1973, *18*(1), pp. 99. [G: U.S.]

Palmer, John P. A Further Analysis of Provincial Trucking Regulation. *Bell J. Econ. Manage. Sci.*, Autumn 1973, *4*(2), pp. 655–64. [G: Canada]

Pauly, Mark V. Public Utilities and the Theory of Power: Comment. In *Russell, M., ed.*, 1973, pp. 27–33.

Peacock, Alan T. and Rowley, Charles K. Welfare Economics and the Public Regulation of Natural Monopoly: Reply. *J. Public Econ.*, February 1973, *2*(1), pp. 97–100.

Peltzman, Sam. An Evaluation of Consumer Protection Legislation: The 1962 Drug Amendments. *J. Polit. Econ.*, September-October 1973, *81*(5), pp. 1049–91. [G: U.S.]

Pollock, Richard. The Effect of Alternative Regulatory Treatment of Tax Depreciation on Utility Tax Payments. *Nat. Tax J.*, March 1973, *26*(1), pp. 43–57. [G: U.S.]

Rennie, Henry G. Federal Tax Policy and Fixed Capital Expenditures by Ohio's Electric Utilities. *Ohio State U. Bull. Bus. Res.*, July 1973, *48*(7), pp. 5–7. [G: U.S.]

Robichek, Alexander A.; Higgins, Robert C. and Kinsman, Michael. The Effect of Leverage on the Cost of Equity Capital of Electric Utility Firms. *J. Finance*, May 1973, *28*(2), pp. 353–67. [G: U.S.]

Rose, Marshall. Market Problems in the Distribution of Emission Rights. *Water Resources Res.*, October 1973, *9*(5), pp. 1132–44.

Russell, Milton. Introduction: The Political Economy of Public Utilities. In *Russell, M., ed.*, 1973, pp. xix–xxviii.

Samuels, Warren J. Public Utilities and the Theory of Power. In *Russell, M., ed.*, 1973, pp. 1–27.

Sankar, U. Investment Behavior in the U.S. Telephone Industry—1949 to 1968. *Bell J. Econ. Manage. Sci.*, Autumn 1973, *4*(2), pp. 665–78. [G: U.S.]

Schwartz, Ivo E. Creating a Common Market for Insurance: Harmonization of EEC Insurance Legislation. *Antitrust Bull.*, Spring 1973, *18*(1), pp. 103–16.

Shepherd, William G. Entry as a Substitute for Regulation. *Amer. Econ. Rev.*, May 1973, *63*(2), pp. 98–105.

Stanley, Kenneth B. International Telecommunica-

tions Industry: Interdependence of Market Structure and Performance Under Regulation. *Land Econ.*, November 1973, *49*(4), pp. 391–403.
[G: U.S.]

Swidler, Joseph C. The Challenge to State Regulation Agencies: The Experience of New York State. *Ann. Amer. Acad. Polit. Soc. Sci.*, November 1973, *410*, pp. 106–19. [G: U.S.]

Thompson, Howard E. and Thatcher, Lionel W. Required Rate of Return for Equity Capital Under Conditions of Growth and Consideration of Regulatory Lag. *Land Econ.*, May 1973, *49*(2), pp. 148–62.

Thomson, Herbert F. Policy Alternatives for Ohio's Electric Power Industry. *Ohio State U. Bull. Bus. Res.*, December 1973, *48*(12), pp. 1–5. [G: U.S.]

Tybout, Richard A. Prices, Costs, and the Energy Crisis. *Ohio State U. Bull. Bus. Res.*, June 1973, *48*(6), pp. 4–8. [G: U.S.]

Tyler, George R. and Hoffer, George E. Reform of the Non-Commercial Vehicle Liability Insurance Market. *J. Risk Ins.*, December 1973, *40*(4), pp. 565–74. [G: U.S.]

Van Horne, James C. Implied Fixed Costs of Long-Term Debt Issues. *J. Financial Quant. Anal.*, December 1973, *8*(5), pp. 821–33. [G: U.S.]

Watters, Gil. A New Decision for Urban Investment and Pricing Decisions. In *Aislabie, C., ed.*, 1973, pp. 177–78.

Webbink, Douglas W. Regulation, Profits and Entry in the Television Broadcasting Industry. *J. Ind. Econ.*, April 1973, *21*(2), pp. 167–76. [G: U.S.]

Wilder, Ronald P. Public Utility Advertising: Some Observations. *Land Econ.*, November 1973, *49*(4), pp. 458–62. [G: U.S.]

Witt, Robert Charles. Pricing Problems in Automobile Insurance: An Economic Analysis. *J. Risk Ins.*, March 1973, *40*(1), pp. 75–93. [G: U.S.]

614 Public Enterprises

6140 Public Enterprises

Arrate, Jorge. The Nationalization of Copper. In *Zammit, J. A., ed.*, 1973, pp. 145–50. [G: Chile]

Balassa, Bela. The Firm in the New Economic Mechanism in Hungary. In *Bornstein, M., ed.*, 1973, pp. 347–72. [G: Hungary]

Bennett, J. W. and Leather, J. Investment Cut-off Rates for a Public Company. *Econ. Rec.*, June 1973, *49*(126), pp. 228–40.

Brown, Gardner, Jr. and Johnson, M. Bruce. Welfare-Maximizing Price and Output with Stochastic Demand: Reply. *Amer. Econ. Rev.*, March 1973, *63*(1), pp. 230–31.

Edwards, Ronald [Sir]. The Status Agreement in Electricity. In *Tivey, L., ed.*, 1973, pp. 284–98.
[G: U.K.]

Fuller, Stephen S. Social and Economic Factors in Federal Building Location Decisions. *Growth Change*, April 1973, *4*(2), pp. 43–48. [G: U.S.]

Glueck, William F. and Kavran, Dragoljub. The Yugoslav Management System. In *Henley, D. S., ed.*, 1973, pp. 375–89. [G: Yugoslavia]

Jhabvala, Firdaus. A Model of Motivation in State Enterprises in Underdeveloped Economies. *Indian Econ. Rev.*, October 1973, *8*(2), pp. 172–85.

Jones, Ken. Employee Directors in Steel. In *Tivey, L., ed.*, 1973, pp. 298–302. [G: U.K.]

Keeney, Ralph L. A Decision Analysis with Multiple Objectives: the Mexico City Airport. *Bell J. Econ. Manage. Sci.*, Spring 1973, *4*(1), pp. 101–17.
[G: Mexico]

Lamont, Douglas F. Joining Forces with Foreign State Enterprises. *Harvard Bus. Rev.*, July-August 1973, *51*(4), pp. 68–79.

Mascarenhas, R. C. A Conceptual Framework for Understanding Autonomy for Public Enterprises in India. In *Henley, D. S., ed.*, 1973, pp. 395–405.
[G: India]

Neuberger, Egon and James, Estelle. The Yugoslav Self-Managed Enterprise: A Systemic Approach. In *Bornstein, M., ed.*, 1973, pp. 245–84. [G: Yugoslavia]

Pejovich, Svetozar. The Banking System and the Investment Behavior of the Yugoslav Firm. In *Bornstein, M., ed.*, 1973, pp. 285–311. [G: Yugoslavia]

Pyrke, Richard. The Growth of Efficiency. In *Tivey, L., ed.*, 1973, pp. 121–26. [G: U.K.]

Roberts, C. A. Reorganization of the National Coal Board. In *Tivey, L., ed.*, 1973, pp. 242–48.
[G: U.K.]

Stephenson, Charles M. Implications of PLLRC Tax Recommendations for Federal Hydro Projects and Power Facilities. *Land Econ.*, February 1973, *49*(1), pp. 67–75. [G: U.S.]

Tivey, Leonard. British Nationalization in the 1960s. In *Tivey, L., ed.*, 1973, pp. 11–17. [G: U.K.]

Visscher, Michael L. Welfare-Maximizing Price and Output with Stochastic Demand: Comment. *Amer. Econ. Rev.*, March 1973, *63*(1), pp. 224–29.

Wattles, George M. The Rates and Costs of the United States Postal Service. *J. Law Econ.*, April 1973, *16*(1), pp. 89–117. [G: U.S.]

615 Economics of Transportation

6150 Economics of Transportation

Abelson, P. W. Quantification of Road User Costs: A Comment with Special Reference to Thailand. *J. Transp. Econ. Policy*, January 1973, *7*(1), pp. 80–97. [G: Thailand]

Adams, Earl W., Jr. and Spiro, Michael H. Reducing the Lags in Government Spending: An Empirical Analysis of Highway Construction. *Public Finance*, 1973, *28*(2), pp. 125–38. [G: U.S.]

Altman, Edward I. Predicting Railroad Bankruptcies in America. *Bell J. Econ. Manage. Sci.*, Spring 1973, *4*(1), pp. 184–211. [G: U.S.]

Annable, James E., Jr. The ICC, the IBT, and the Cartelization of the American Trucking Industry. *Quart. Rev. Econ. Bus.*, Summer 1973, *13*(2), pp. 33–47. [G: U.S.]

Baker, R. Palmer, Jr. and Fritzhand, Gary I. United States Federal Income Taxation of Foreign-Flag Shipping Earnings. *Nat. Tax J.*, December 1973, *26*(4), pp. 537–51. [G: U.S.]

Ball, Robert. Labor and Materials Required for Highway Construction. *Mon. Lab. Rev.,* June 1973, *96* (6), pp. 40–45. [G: U.S.]

Baum, Herbert J. Free Public Transport. *J. Transp. Econ. Policy,* January 1973, *7*(1), pp. 3–19. [G: W. Germany]

Bierman, Harold, Jr. and Thomas, L. Joseph. Airline Overbooking Strategies and Bumping Procedures. *Public Policy,* Fall 1973, *21*(4), pp. 601–06.

Black, William R. Toward a Factorial Ecology of Flows. *Econ. Geogr.,* January 1973, *49*(1), pp. 59–67. [G: U.S.]

Brandes, Ove. Models for Domestic Air Travel Fares. *Swedish J. Econ.,* September 1973, *75*(3), pp. 249–56. [G: Sweden]

Bucksar, Richard G. The White Pass and Yukon Railway: Past, Present and Future. *Mich. Academician,* Winter 1973, *5*(3), pp. 315–23. [G: Canada]

Carroll, Joseph L. and Bronzini, Michael S. Waterway Transportation Simulation Models: Development and Application. *Water Resources Res.,* February 1973, *9*(1), pp. 51–63.

Čepelák, Vladimír. Simulační model železničního vlečky. (Simulation Model of a Railway Siding. With English summary.) *Ekon.-Mat. Obzor,* 1973, *9*(4), pp. 450–57.

Cesario, Frank J. A Generalized Trip Distribution Model. *J. Reg. Sci.,* August 1973, *13*(2), pp. 233–47. [G: U.S.]

Coles, O. B. An Economic Comparison of Urban Railways and Express Bus Services: Comment. *J. Transp. Econ. Policy,* September 1973, *7*(3), pp. 295–97. [G: U.K.]

Collins, David C. Applications of Multiple Criterial Evaluation to Decision Aiding. In *Cochrane, J. L. and Zeleny, M., eds.,* 1973, pp. 477–505. [G: U.S.]

Crowley, Ronald W. A Case Study of the Effects of an Airport on Land Values. *J. Transp. Econ. Policy,* May 1973, *7*(2), pp. 144–52. [G: Canada]

Crvcanin, Milan. Application de modèles intégrés à la planification des systèmes de transports de la région lausannoise. (Integrated Models Used in Lausanne Area Transportation Study. With English summary.) *Schweiz. Z. Volkswirtsch. Statist.,* September 1973, *109*(3), pp. 357–73. [G: Switzerland]

Cunningham, Roger A. Billboard Control under the Highway Beautification Act of 1965. *Mich. Law Rev.,* June 1973, *71*(7), pp. 1295–1374.

De Bruyne, L. De Antwerpse luchthavenbehoeften 1970–1980. (The Air Transport Needs of Antwerp. With English summary.) *Econ. Soc. Tijdschr.,* June 1973, *27*(3), pp. 227–43. [G: Belgium]

Dodgson, J. S. External Effects and Secondary Benefits in Road Investment Appraisal. *J. Transp. Econ. Policy,* May 1973, *7*(2), pp. 169–85.

Doganis, Rigas. Air Transport—A Case Study in International Regulation. *J. Transp. Econ. Policy,* May 1973, *7*(2), pp. 109–33.

Dramais, A. The Influence of Road Characteristics on Road Accidents in Belgium: An Econometric Approach. *Europ. Econ. Rev.,* October 1973, *4*(3), pp. 293–306. [G: Belgium]

Edwards, C. B. A Cost-Benefit Analysis of the Concorde Project: Comment. *J. Transp. Econ. Policy,* September 1973, *7*(3), pp. 300–01. [G: U.K.]

Evans, Alan W. On the Theory of the Valuation and Allocation of Time: Reply. *Scot. J. Polit. Econ.,* February 1973, *20*(1), pp. 73–74.

Fitzgerald, E. V. K. and Aneuryn-Evans, G. B. The Economics of Airport Development and Control. *J. Transp. Econ. Policy,* September 1973, *7*(3), pp. 269–82. [G: U.K.]

Flemming, J. S. On the Theory of the Valuation and Allocation of Time: Some Comments. *Scot. J. Polit. Econ.,* February 1973, *20*(1), pp. 65–71.

Franco, G. Robert. The Wage Subsidy Index in the Merchant Marine Act of 1970. *J. Transp. Econ. Policy,* September 1973, *7*(3), pp. 283–90. [G: U.S.]

Frankena, Mark. Income Distributional Effects of Urban Transit Subsidies. *J. Transp. Econ. Policy,* September 1973, *7*(3), pp. 215–30. [G: Canada]

Gardner, Bernard and Richardson, Peter. The Fiscal Treatment of Shipping. *J. Ind. Econ.,* December 1973, *22*(2), pp. 95–117. [G: U.K.]

Garrison, W. L. Fragments on Future Transportation Policy and Programs. *Econ. Geogr.,* April 1973, *49*(2), pp. 95–102.

Gauthier, Howard L. The Appalachian Development Highway System: Development for Whom? *Econ. Geogr.,* April 1973, *49*(2), pp. 103–08. [G: U.S.]

Gazis, Denos C. Mathematical Modelling of Some Social and Environmental Problems. In *Hawkes, N., ed.,* 1973, pp. 52–59. [G: U.S.]

Goldberg, Joseph P. Longshoremen and the Modernisation of Cargo Handling in the United States. *Int. Lab. Rev.,* March 1973, *107*(3), pp. 253–79. [G: U.S.]

Gordon, I. R. and Edwards, S. L. Holiday Trip Generation. *J. Transp. Econ. Policy,* May 1973, *7*(2), pp. 153–68. [G: U.K.]

Gourvish, Terence R. A British Business Elite: The Chief Executive Managers of the Railway Industry, 1850–1922. *Bus. Hist. Rev.,* Autumn 1973, *47*(3), pp. 289–316. [G: U.K.]

Graf, Hans G. Zukünftige Verkehrsentwicklung in der Schweiz. (Future Development of Traffic in Switzerland. With English summary.) *Schweiz. Z. Volkswirtsch. Statist.,* September 1973, *109*(3), pp. 341–55. [G: Switzerland]

Guedry, L. J. An Application of a Multi-Commodity Transportation Model to the U.S. Feed Grain Economy. In *Judge, G. G. and Takayama, T., eds.,* 1973, pp. 243–60. [G: U.S.]

Harberger, Arnold C. Cost-Benefit Analysis of Transportation Projects. In *Harberger, A. C.,* 1973, pp. 248–79.

Haveman, Robert H. and Stephan, Paula. White Elephants, Waterways, and the Transportation Act of 1966. In *Haveman, R. H. and Hamrin, R. D., eds.,* 1973, pp. 220–25. [G: U.S.]

Haveman, Robert H. The Ex Post Evaluation of Navigation Improvements. In *Niskanen, W. A., et al., eds.,* 1973, pp. 249–76. [G: U.S.]

Heath, J. B. and Oulton, W. N. A Cost-benefit Study of Alternative Runway Investments at Edinburgh

(Turnhouse) Airport. In *Wolfe, J. N., ed.,* 1973, pp. 117–39. [G: U.K.]

Heaver, Trevor D. The Structure of Liner Conference Rates. *J. Ind. Econ.,* July 1973, *21*(3), pp. 257–65.

Heinrich, K. On Forecasting New Techniques in Passenger Transport. In *Blohm, H. and Steinbuch, K., eds.,* 1973, pp. 67–72. [G: W. Germany]

Horton, Frank E.; Louviere, Jordan and Reynolds, David R. Mass Transit Utilization: Individual Response Data Inputs. *Econ. Geogr.,* April 1973, *49* (2), pp. 122–33. [G: U.S.]

Hurst, Michael E. Eliot. Transportation and the Societal Framework. *Econ. Geogr.,* April 1973, *49*(2), pp. 163–80.

Jagers, Peter. How Many People Pay Their Tram Fares? *J. Amer. Statist. Assoc.,* December 1973, *68* (344), pp. 801–04. [G: Sweden]

Johnson, G. P. and Steiner, H. M. Evaluating Social Roads in Mexico. *J. Transp. Econ. Policy,* January 1973, *7*(1), pp. 98–101. [G: Mexico]

Jones, James W. Accounting Practices in Ship Chandlery. *Manage. Account.,* August 1973, *55*(2), pp. 28–30, 34.

Jürgensen, Harald. Problems of Investment Planning in the Transport Field. *Ger. Econ. Rev.,* 1973, *11*(1), pp. 1–13.

Keeney, Ralph L. A Decision Analysis with Multiple Objectives: the Mexico City Airport. *Bell J. Econ. Manage. Sci.,* Spring 1973, *4*(1), pp. 101–17. [G: Mexico]

King, L. J.; Casetti, Emilio and Kissling, C. C. Optimal Transportation Patterns of Single Commodities in Capacitated Networks. In *Judge, G. G. and Takayama, T., eds.,* 1973, pp. 225–42. [G: U.S.; New Zealand]

Kohlmeier, Louis M. The Federal Highway Program. In *Haveman, R. H. and Hamrin, R. D., eds.,* 1973, pp. 226–30. [G: U.S.]

Kolsen, H. M. The Victorian Land Transport Inquiry. *Econ. Rec.,* September 1973, *49*(127), pp. 464–80. [G: Australia]

Koshal, Rajindar K. A Possible Production Function for Indian Railway System—A Comment. *Indian Econ. Rev.,* April 1973, *8*(1), pp. 85–89. [G: India]

Lindholm, Richard W. State-Local School and Highway Expenditure Trends, 1965-1966 and 1969-1970. *Public Finance Quart.,* January 1973, *1*(1), pp. 29–34. [G: U.S.]

Littlechild, S. C. Myopic Investment Rules and Toll Charges in a Transport Network. *J. Transp. Econ. Policy,* May 1973, *7*(2), pp. 194–204.

Lorange, Peter and Norman, Victor D. Risk Preference in Scandinavian Shipping. *Appl. Econ.,* March 1973, *5*(1), pp. 49–59. [G: Scandinavia]

Martin, Donald L. Some Economics of Job Rights in the Longshore Industry. *J. Econ. Bus.,* Winter 1973, *25*(2), pp. 93–100. [G: U.S.]

Mason, Joseph Barry. Along the Interstate: Highway Interchange Land Use Development. *Growth Change,* October 1973, *4*(4), pp. 38–43. [G: U.S.]

Mayer, Harold M. Some Geographic Aspects of Technological Change in Maritime Transporta-

tion. *Econ. Geogr.,* April 1973, *49*(2), pp. 145–55. [G: U.S.]

McDonough, Carol C. The Demand for Commuter Rail Transport. *J. Transp. Econ. Policy,* May 1973, *7*(2), pp. 134–43. [G: U.S.]

Mercer, Lloyd J. Rates of Return and Government Subsidization of the Canadian Pacific Railway: An Alternate View. *Can. J. Econ.,* August 1973, *6*(3), pp. 428–37. [G: Canada]

Mestelman, Stuart. Highway User Fees and Vehicle Transport Modes: An Old Rule Defended. *J. Polit. Econ.,* May-June 1973, *81*(3), pp. 786–95.

Miller, James C., III. The Optimal Pricing of Freight in Combination Aircraft. *J. Transp. Econ. Policy,* September 1973, *7*(3), pp. 258–68. [G: U.S.]

Moore, Thomas Gale. Science, Technology, and Industry. In *Ott, D. J., et al.,* 1973, pp. 67–89. [G: U.S.]

Morris, Stuart. Stalled Professionalism: The Recruitment of Railway Officials in the United States, 1885–1940. *Bus. Hist. Rev.,* Autumn 1973, *47*(3), pp. 317–34. [G: U.S.]

Nobukuni, Makoto and Fukuchi, Takao. The Economic Measurement of the Benefit of Public Transportation Investment. (In Japanese. With English summary.) *Econ. Stud. Quart.,* December 1973, *24*(3), pp. 43–53.

Ody, J. G. Economics of Change in Road Passenger Transport: Comment. *J. Transp. Econ. Policy,* September 1973, *7*(3), pp. 291–92. [G: U.K.]

Palmer, John P. A Further Analysis of Provincial Trucking Regulation. *Bell J. Econ. Manage. Sci.,* Autumn 1973, *4*(2), pp. 655–64. [G: Canada]

Pattison, John C. Some Aspects of Price Discrimination in the Airline Industry. *J. Econ. Issues,* March 1973, *7*(1), pp. 136–47.

Plessas, Demetrius J. Airplane Noise: Some Analytic and Policy Perspectives. *Land Econ.,* February 1973, *49*(1), pp. 14–21. [G: U.S.]

Plowden, S. P. C. Indirect Taxation of Motorway and Alternative Consumption. *J. Transp. Econ. Policy,* September 1973, *7*(3), pp. 250–57. [G: U.K.]

Polenske, Karen R. An Analysis of United States Commodity Freight Shipments. In *Judge, G. G. and Takayama, T., eds.,* 1973, pp. 163–79. [G: U.S.]

Rapping, Leonard A. U.S. Maritime Policy: Subsidizing Waste and Inefficiency. In *Haveman, R. H. and Hamrin, R. D., eds.,* 1973, pp. 215–19. [G: U.S.]

Reinhardt, U. E. Break-Even Analysis for Lockheed's Tri Star: An Application of Financial Theory. *J. Finance,* September 1973, *28*(4), pp. 821–38. [G: U.S.]

Rhys, D. G. Economics of Change in Road Passenger Transport: Rejoinder. *J. Transp. Econ. Policy,* September 1973, *7*(3), pp. 292–93. [G: U.K.]

Rühl, G. Forecasting in Goods' Transport and Market Behaviour. In *Blohm, H. and Steinbuch, K., eds.,* 1973, pp. 91–102.

Scherer, Frederic M. The Determinants of Industrial Plant Sizes in Six Nations. *Rev. Econ. Statist.,* May 1973, *55*(2), pp. 135–45. [G: Sweden; N. America; France; U.K.; W. Germany]

Schleicher, Heinz. On European Social Rates of Discount: Survey. *Finanzarchiv,* 1973, *31*(3), pp. 434–40. [G: W. Europe]

Schlichthaber, Roland. Verkehrsplanung in der Agglomeration aus der Sicht eines Ökonomen. (Traffic Planning in Agglomerations from the Economist's Point of View. With English summary.) *Schweiz. Z. Volkswirtsch. Statist.*, September 1973, *109*(3), pp. 375–84.

Scott, Donald E. Takings and the Public Interest in Railroad Reorganization. *Yale Law J.*, April 1973, *82*(5), pp. 1004–22.

Segelhorst, Elbert W. and Kirkus, Larry D. Parking Bias in Transit Choice. *J. Transp. Econ. Policy*, January 1973, *7*(1), pp. 58–70. [G: U.S.]

Seneca, Rosalind S. Inherent Advantage, Costs, and Resource Allocation in the Transportation Industry. *Amer. Econ. Rev.*, December 1973, *63*(5), pp. 945–56.

Smith, Edward. An Economic Comparison of Urban Railways and Express Bus Services. *J. Transp. Econ. Policy*, January 1973, *7*(1), pp. 20–31. [G: U.K.]

Smith, Edward. An Economic Comparison of Urban Railways and Express Bus Services: Rejoinder. *J. Transp. Econ. Policy*, September 1973, *7*(3), pp. 297–99. [G: U.K.]

Smithies, Richard M. The Changing Demand for Air Transport: The North Atlantic Case. *J. Transp. Econ. Policy*, September 1973, *7*(3), pp. 231–49.

Sorenson, L. Orlo. Rail-barge Competition in Transporting Winter Wheat. *Amer. J. Agr. Econ.*, December 1973, *55*(5), pp. 814–19. [G: U.S.]

Sprenger, Rolf-Ulrich. Zur Problematik der Treffsicherheit von langfristigen Verkehrsvorausschätzungen—Methodische Ansätze ter Treffsicherheitsanalyse und ihr Aussagewert für die prognostische Praxis. (Notes on Testing the Accuracy of Long-Term Traffic Forecasts. With English summary.) *Ifo-Studien*, January 1973, *19*(1/2), pp. 17–57. [G: W. Germany]

Squire, Lyn. Optimal Feeder Roads in Developing Countries: The Case of Thailand. *J. Devel. Stud.*, January 1973, *9*(2), pp. 279–90. [G: Thailand]

Stern, Martin O. and Ayres, Robert U. Transportation Outlays: Who Pays and Who Benefits? In *Harriss, C. L., ed.*, 1973, pp. 117–54. [G: U.S.]

Stutz, Frederick P. Distance and Network Effects on Urban Social Travel Fields. *Econ. Geogr.*, April 1973, *49*(2), pp. 134–44. [G: U.S.]

Sun, Nai-Ching and Bunamo, Michael C. Competition for Handling U.S. Foreign Trade Cargoes: The Port of New York's Experience. *Econ. Geogr.*, April 1973, *49*(2), pp. 156–62. [G: U.S.]

Susuki, Shigemichi. A Method of Planning Yard Pass Trains on a General Network. In *Ross, M., ed.*, 1973, pp. 353–61.

Szpigel, Bernardo. Optimal Train Scheduling on a Single Track Railway. In *Ross, M., ed.*, 1973, pp. 343–52. [G: Brazil]

Tobin, Norman and Butfield, Terry. The Implementation of OR Models in Planning Procedures. In *Ross, M., ed.*, 1973, pp. 363–72.

Tyrchniewicz, Edward W. and Tosterud, Robert J. A Model for Rationalizing the Canadian Grain Transportation and Handling System on a Regional Basis. *Amer. J. Agr. Econ.*, December 1973, *55*(5), pp. 805–13. [G: Canada]

Van der Tak, Herman G. and Ray, Anandarup. The Economic Benefits of Road Transport Projects. In *Niskanen, W. A., et al., eds.*, 1973, pp. 132–73.

Walgreen, John A.; Rastatter, E. H. and Moore, Arnold B. The Economics of the United States Supersonic Transport. *J. Transp. Econ. Policy*, May 1973, *7*(2), pp. 186–93. [G: U.S.]

Walters, A. A. Investments in Airports and the Economist's Role: John F. Kennedy International Airport: An Example and Some Comparisons. In *Wolfe, J. N., ed.*, 1973, pp. 140–54. [G: U.S.]

Waters, W. G., II and Hildebrand, D. G. Road Costs and Government Revenues from Heavy Vehicles in Canada. *Can. J. Econ.*, November 1973, *6*(4), pp. 608–12. [G: Canada]

Watson, P. and Mansfield, N. The Valuation of Time in Cost-benefit Studies. In *Wolfe, J. N., ed.*, 1973, pp. 222–32. [G: U.K.]

White, P. R. An Economic Comparison of Urban Railways and Express Bus Services: Comment. *J. Transp. Econ. Policy*, September 1973, *7*(3), pp. 294–95. [G: U.K.]

Woodward, Robert S. The Iso-Outlay Function and Variable Transport Costs. *J. Reg. Sci.*, December 1973, *13*(3), pp. 349–55.

Woolley, P. K. A Cost-Benefit Analysis of the Concorde Project: Rejoinder. *J. Transp. Econ. Policy*, September 1973, *7*(3), pp. 301–02. [G: U.K.]

Yamamoto, Hiromasa. Available Jobs and Employment in Japanese Foreign-Going Shipping. *Kobe Econ. Bus. Rev.*, 1973, *20*(20), pp. 51–59. [G: Japan]

620 ECONOMICS OF TECHNOLOGICAL CHANGE

621 Technological Change; Innovation; Research and Development

6210 General

Aujac, H. A New Approach to Technological Forecasting in French National Planning. In *Williams, B. R., ed.*, 1973, pp. 96–115. [G: France]

Ault, David E. On the Importance of Lags in Technology: An Empirical Test. *Rivista Int. Sci. Econ. Com.*, October 1973, *20*(10), pp. 945–60.

Ayres, Robert U. and Kneese, Allen V. Economic and Ecological Effects of a Stationary Economy. In *Enthoven, A. C. and Freeman, A. M., III, eds.*, 1973, pp. 235–52.

Balázsy, S. Financial Regulating System and Technical Development. *Acta Oecon.*, 1973, *10*(3–4), pp. 315–38. [G: Hungary]

Bechhofer, Frank. The Relationship between Technology and Shop-Floor Behaviour: A Less Heated Look at a Controversy. In *Edge, D. O. and Wolfe, J. N., eds.*, 1973, pp. 121–42.

Bhaduri, Amit. A Study in Agricultural Backwardness under Semi-Feudalism. *Econ. J.*, March 1973, *83*(329), pp. 120–37. [G: India]

Booms, Bernard H. Impact of Urban Market Structure on the Level of Inventive Activity in Cities in the Early Nineteen Hundreds. *Land Econ.*, August 1973, *49*(3), pp. 318–25. [G: U.S.]

Brooks, Harvey. Technology Assessment as a Process. *Int. Soc. Sci. J.,* 1973, *25*(3), pp. 247–56. **[G: U.S.]**

Büti, G. Technological Pre-assessment as the Partner of Macroeconomic Forecasting. In *Blohm, H. and Steinbuch, K., eds.,* 1973, pp. 133–38.

Cooper, Charles. Choice of Techniques and Technological Change as Problems in Political Economy. *Int. Soc. Sci. J.,* 1973, *25*(3), pp. 293–304.

Dathe, H. M. Cybernetic Models as Aids in Normative Forecasting. In *Blohm, H. and Steinbuch, K., eds.,* 1973, pp. 39–53.

Davidson, Martin J. Technological Risk Assumption Corporations: Reply. *J. Econ. Issues,* March 1973, *7*(1), pp. 124–30.

Davies, R. W. Research, Development, and Innovation in the Soviet Economy, 1968–1970. In *Edge, D. O. and Wolfe, J. N., eds.,* 1973, pp. 241–61. **[G: U.S.S.R.]**

Dobrov, Gennady M. Science Policy and Assessment in the Soviet Union. *Int. Soc. Sci. J.,* 1973, *25*(3), pp. 305–25. **[G: U.S.S.R.]**

Edge, D. O. Technological Metaphor. In *Edge, D. O. and Wolfe, J. N., eds.,* 1973, pp. 31–59.

Ferrer-Pacces, F. M. Una ricerca (da 5 milioni di $) interrotta. (A Discontinued Research (worth $5 millions.) With English summary.) *L'Impresa,* 1973, *15*(7–8), pp. 418–24.

Fisher, Franklin M. and Temin, Peter. Returns to Scale in Research and Development: What Does the Schumpeterian Hypothesis Imply? *J. Polit. Econ.,* January-February 1973, *81*(1), pp. 56–70.

Freeman, Christopher. A Study of Success and Failure in Industrial Innovation. In *Williams, B. R., ed.,* 1973, pp. 227–45. **[G: U.K.]**

Freivalds, John. Bringing Space Down to Earth: Space Age Technology Transfer and the Developing Countries. *J. Devel. Areas,* October 1973, *8*(1), pp. 83–92.

Gewald, K. The Delphi Method as an Instrument of Technological Forecasting—Practical Experience. In *Blohm, H. and Steinbuch, K., eds.,* 1973, pp. 13–17.

Girling, Robert. Dependency, Technology and Development. In *Bonilla, F. and Girling, R., eds.,* 1973, pp. 46–62.

Gliazer, L. The Economics of Science and the Science of Economics. *Prob. Econ.,* December 1973, *16*(8), pp. 22–43.

Globerman, Steven. Technological Risk Assumption Corporations. *J. Econ. Issues,* March 1973, *7*(1), pp. 119–24.

Goering, R. W. Critical Comments on Technological Research into the Future. In *Blohm, H. and Steinbuch, K., eds.,* 1973, pp. 151–55.

Gotsch, Carl H. Tractor Mechanisation and Rural Development in Pakistan. *Int. Lab. Rev.,* February 1973, *107*(2), pp. 133–66. **[G: Pakistan]**

Griliches, Zvi. Research Expenditures and Growth Accounting. In *Williams, B. R., ed.,* 1973, pp. 59–83. **[G: U.S.]**

Gunn, Lewis A. Government, Technology, and Planning in Britain. In *Edge, D. O. and Wolfe, J. N., eds.,* 1973, pp. 161–79. **[G: U.K.]**

Hennings, U.; Hüber, R. P. O. and Stanke, F. Delphi Interrogation Concerning Future Possibilities of the Employment of Robots. In *Blohm, H. and Steinbuch, K., eds.,* 1973, pp. 19–28.

Hetman, François. Steps in Technology Assessment. *Int. Soc. Sci. J.,* 1973, *25*(3), pp. 257–72.

Hoffmann, H.-J. Survey of the Methods used in Technological Forecasting. In *Blohm, H. and Steinbuch, K., eds.,* 1973, pp. 3–12.

Hu, Sheng Cheng. On the Incentive to Invent: A Clarificatory Note. *J. Law Econ.,* April 1973, *16*(1), pp. 169–77.

Katz, Jorge M. Industrial Growth, Royalty Payments and Local Expenditure on Research and Development. In *Urquidi, V. L. and Thorp, R., eds.,* 1973, pp. 197–224. **[G: Argentina]**

Kay, Harry. The Effect of Technology in Educational Structure. In *Edge, D. O. and Wolfe, J. N., eds.,* 1973, pp. 143–57.

Kennedy, Charles and Thirlwall, A. P. Technological Change and the Distribution of Income: A Belated Comment. *Int. Econ. Rev.,* October 1973, *14*(3), pp. 780–84.

Khachaturov, T. S. Development of Science and Technology in the U.S.S.R. In *Williams, B. R., ed.,* 1973, pp. 147–68. **[G: U.S.S.R.]**

Kishida, Junnosuke. Technology Assessment in Japan. *Int. Soc. Sci. J.,* 1973, *25*(3), pp. 326–35. **[G: Japan]**

Koropeckyj, I. S. Technology and the Direction of Soviet Foreign Trade. *Rivista Int. Sci. Econ. Com.,* December 1973, *20*(12), pp. 1190–1208. **[G: U.S.S.R.]**

Korovkin, G. Scientific-Technical Progress and Trade. *Prob. Econ.,* November 1973, *16*(7), pp. 84–101. **[G: U.S.S.R.]**

Lakhtin, G. The Subject of the Economics of Science. *Prob. Econ.,* December 1973, *16*(8), pp. 3–21.

Lapan, Harvey and Bardhan, Pranab K. Localized Technical Progress and Transfer of Technology and Economic Development. *J. Econ. Theory,* December 1973, *6*(6), pp. 585–95.

Leitenberg, Milton. The Dynamics of Military Technology Today. *Int. Soc. Sci. J.,* 1973, *25*(3), pp. 336–57.

Mansfield, Edwin. Determinants of the Speed of Application of New Technology. In *Williams, B. R., ed.,* 1973, pp. 199–216. **[G: U.S.]**

Mansfield, Edwin. The Production and Application of New Technology by American Business Firms. In *Edge, D. O. and Wolfe, J. N., eds.,* 1973, pp. 199–221. **[G: U.S.]**

Mason, R. Hal. The Multinational Firm and the Cost of Technology to Developing Countries. *Calif. Manage. Rev.,* Summer 1973, *15*(4), pp. 5–13. **[G: Latin America; Europe; Canada]**

Medford, Derek. Il controllo dei processi technologici. (The Control of Technological Processes. With English summary.) *L'Impresa,* 1973, *15*(7–8), pp. 439–44.

Mitchell, Jeremy. The Consumer Movement and Technological Change. *Int. Soc. Sci. J.,* 1973, *25*(3), pp. 358–69.

Morgenthaler, George W. Guiding Technological Development. In *Ross, M., ed.,* 1973, pp. 617–40.

Nabseth, Lars. The Diffusion of Innovations in Swedish Industry. In *Williams, B. R., ed.,* 1973, pp. 256–80.   [G: Sweden]

Nelson, Richard R. and Winter, Sidney G. Toward an Evolutionary Theory of Economic Capabilities. *Amer. Econ. Rev.*, May 1973, *63*(2), pp. 440–49.

Oldham, C. H. G. Science and Technology Policies. In *Oksenberg, M., ed.*, 1973, pp. 80–94.   [G: China]

Pfeiffer, W. and Staudt, E. The Integration of Technological Prediction into Management Systems by Improvement of Forecasting Analysis. In *Blohm, H. and Steinbuch, K., eds.*, 1973, pp. 105–14.

Postan, M. M. Why Was Science Backward in the Middle Ages? In *Postan, M. M. (I)*, 1973, pp. 81–86.   [G: W. Europe]

Ropohl, G. The Use of Systems Technology and Morphological Method in Technological Forecasting. In *Blohm, H. and Steinbuch, K., eds.*, 1973, pp. 29–38.

Ropohl, G. Technological Forecasting: Between Speculation and Science. In *Blohm, H. and Steinbuch, K., eds.*, 1973, pp. 157–69.

Sachs, Ignacy. Development, Environment and Technology Assessment. *Int. Soc. Sci. J.*, 1973, *25*(3), pp. 273–83.

Schumacher, D. Technological Forecasting and Political Planning. In *Blohm, H. and Steinbuch, K., eds.*, 1973, pp. 145–49.

Shell, Karl. Inventive Activity, Industrial Organisation and Economic Growth. In *Mirrlees, J. A. and Stern, N. H., eds.*, 1973, pp. 77–96.

Simmons, Harvey. System Dynamics and Technocracy. In *Cole, H. S. D., et al., eds.*, 1973, pp. 192–208.

Skolnikoff, Eugene B. La tecnologia e la politica mondiale. (Technology and World Politics. With English summary.) *Mondo Aperto*, April 1973, *27*(2), pp. 101–11.

Steinbuch, K. Technological Forecasting in Practice: Conclusion. In *Blohm, H. and Steinbuch, K., eds.*, 1973, pp. 171–72.

Stöber, G. J. Technological Forecasting and Technology Policy. In *Blohm, H. and Steinbuch, K., eds.*, 1973, pp. 139–44.

Teplin, Mary F. U.S. International Transactions in Royalties and Fees: Their Relationship to the Transfer of Technology. *Surv. Curr. Bus.*, December 1973, *53*(12), pp. 14–18.   [G: U.S.]

Tinbergen, Jan. Exhaustion and Technological Development: A Macro-Dynamic Policy Model. *Z. Nationalökon.*, 1973, *33*(3–4), pp. 213–34.

Toffler, Alvin. "Soft Models", Hard Data, and Social Reality. In *Hawkes, N., ed.*, 1973, pp. 195–204.

Trapeznikov, V. Scientific-Technical Progress and the Effectiveness of Science. *Prob. Econ.*, August 1973, *16*(4), pp. 23–46.   [G: U.S.S.R.]

Vaitsos, Constantine V. Strategic Choices in the Commercialization of Technology: The Point of View of Developing Countries. *Int. Soc. Sci. J.*, 1973, *25*(3), pp. 370–86.

6211 Technological Change and Innovation

Asher, Ephraim and Kumar, T. Krishna. Capital-Labor Substitution and Technical Progress in Planned and Market Oriented Economies: A Comparative Study. *Southern Econ. J.*, July 1973, *40*(1), pp. 103–09.   [G: U.S.S.R.; Yugoslavia; Hungary; N. America; Israel]

Audouin, Maurice. Application of Computers to Distribution in the Newspaper and Publishing Industries. In *The Diebold Group, Inc.*, 1973, pp. 314–24.

Bardhan, Pranab K. More on Putty-Clay. *Int. Econ. Rev.*, February 1973, *14*(1), pp. 211–22.

Barkai, Haim and Levhari, David. The Impact of Experience on Kibbutz Farming. *Rev. Econ. Statist.*, February 1973, *55*(1), pp. 56–63.   [G: Israel]

Barraclough, Solon and Schatan, Jacobo. Technological Policy and Agricultural Development. *Land Econ.*, May 1973, *49*(2), pp. 175–94.   [G: Latin America]

Beer, Stafford. Adaptations in Systems: The Human Approach. In *The Diebold Group, Inc.*, 1973, pp. 19–30.

Bodenhöfer, Hans-Joachim. X-Effizienz, Innovations-Effizienz und wirtschaftliches Wachstum. (X-Efficiency, Innovation Efficiency, and Economic Growth. With English summary.) *Z. Wirtschaft. Sozialwissen.*, 1973, *93*(6), pp. 671–86.

Bosworth, Derek L. Changes in the Quality of Inventive Output and Patent Based Indices of Technological Change. *Bull. Econ. Res.*, November 1973, *25*(2), pp. 95–103.   [G: U.K.]

Brown, Alan A.; Licari, J. A. and Neuberger, Egon. A Dynamic CES Production Function Interpretation of Hungarian Growth. *Acta Oecon.*, 1973, *11*(4), pp. 305–24.   [G: Hungary]

Brown, Lawrence A. and Lentnek, Barry. Innovation Diffusion in a Developing Economy: A Mesoscale View. *Econ. Develop. Cult. Change*, January 1973, *21*(2), pp. 274–92.   [G: Mexico]

Craven, John. Stability in a Two-Sector Model with Induced Bias. *Econ. J.*, September 1973, *83*(331), pp. 858–62.

Diebold, John. Computers in Publishing. In *The Diebold Group, Inc.*, 1973, pp. 298–309.

Dixit, Avinash K. Comparative Dynamics from the Point of View of the Dual. In *Parkin, M., ed.*, 1973, pp. 35–46.

Donaldson, G. F. and McInerney, J. P. Changing Machinery Technology and Agricultural Adjustment. *Amer. J. Agr. Econ.*, December 1973, *55*(5), pp. 829–39.

Galbraith, John Kenneth. Technology in the Developed Economy. In *Williams, B. R., ed.*, 1973, pp. 39–47.

Gatovskiy, L. M. Estimating the National Economic Effect of a New Technology. In *Williams, B. R., ed.*, 1973, pp. 125–39.

Grayson, C. Jackson, Jr. Education and Technology. In *The Diebold Group, Inc.*, 1973, pp. 180–88.

Gregory, R. G. and James, Denis W. Do New Factories Embody Best Practice Technology? *Econ. J.*, December 1973, *83*(332), pp. 1133–55.   [G: Australia]

Hale, Carl W. Impact of Technological Change on Urban Market Areas, Land Values, and Land Uses. *Land Econ.*, August 1973, *49*(3), pp. 351–56.

Hammond, P. J. Comparative Dynamics from the

Point of View of the Dual: Discussion. In *Parkin, M., ed.*, 1973, pp. 47–49.

Hanieski, John F. Technological Change as the Optimization of a Multidimensional Product. In *Cochrane, J. L. and Zeleny, M., eds.*, 1973, pp. 550–69.

Hayami, Yujiro and Ruttan, Vernon W. Induced Innovation in Agricultural Development. In *Ayal, E. B., ed.*, 1973, pp. 181–208. [G: U.S.; Japan]

Hayami, Yujiro and Ruttan, Vernon W. Professor Rosenberg and the Direction of Technological Change: Comment. *Econ. Develop. Cult. Change*, January 1973, *21*(2), pp. 352–55.

Heilbroner, Robert L. Men and Machines in Perspective. In *Reynolds, L. G.; Green, G. D. and Lewis, D. R., eds.*, 1973, pp. 100–109. [G: U.S.]

Holzheu, Franz. Das Geld- und Kreditsystem als Variable im Wachstumsprozess. (The Monetary System as a Variable in the Process of Growth. With English summary.) *Jahr. Nationalökon. Statist.*, January 1973, *187*(2), pp. 97–107.

Hsia, Ronald. Technological Change in the Industrial Growth of Hong Kong. In *Williams, B. R., ed.*, 1973, pp. 335–53. [G: Hong Kong]

Ishikawa, Tsuneo. Conceptualization of Learning by Doing: A Note on Paul David's "Learning by Doing and . . . the Ante-Bellum United States Cotton Textile Industry." *J. Econ. Hist.*, December 1973, *33*(4), pp. 851–61. [G: U.S.]

Ivanov, N. How Many Specialists are Needed? *Prob. Econ.*, August 1973, *16*(4), pp. 63–81.

Jaeger, Klaus. Ein einfaches monetäres Wachstumsmodell mit Produkt- und Prozessinnovationen. (A Simple Monetary Growth Model with Product and Process Innovations. With English summary.) *Z. ges. Staatswiss.*, August 1973, *129*(3), pp. 409–44.

de Janvry, Alain. A Socioeconomic Model of Induced Innovations for Argentine Agricultural Development. *Quart. J. Econ.*, August 1973, *87*(3), pp. 410–435. [G: Argentina]

Kennedy, Charles. A Generalisation of the Theory of Induced Bias in Technical Progress. *Econ. J.*, March 1973, *83*(329), pp. 48–57.

Kislev, Yoav and Shchori-Bachrach, Nira. The Process of an Innovation Cycle. *Amer. J. Agr. Econ.*, February 1973, *55*(1), pp. 28–37. [G: Israel]

Kranzberg, Melvin. Can Technological Progress Continue to Provide for the Future? In *Weintraub, A.; Schwartz, E. and Aronson, J. R., eds.*, 1973, pp. 62–81.

Leibenstein, Harvey. Notes on X-Efficiency and Technical Progress. In *Ayal, E. B., ed.*, 1973, pp. 18–38.

Lekvall, Per and Wahlbin, Clas. A Study of Some Assumptions Underlying Innovation Diffusion Functions. *Swedish J. Econ.*, December 1973, *75*(4), pp. 362–77.

McFadden, Daniel. On the Existence of Optimal Development Programmes in Infinite-Horizon Economies. In *Mirrlees, J. A. and Stern, N. H., eds.*, 1973, pp. 260–82.

Meacci, Ferdinando. Protezione dell'ambiente, aumento dei coefficienti tecnici e preferenze collettive. (Environmental Protection, Increase in Technical Coefficients and Collective Prefer-

ences. With English summary.) *Econ. Int.*, August-November 1973, *26*(3–4), pp. 393–412.

Müller, Jens. Appropriate Technology and Technological Dualism. In *Institute for Development Research*, 1973, pp. 161–76.

Nordhaus, William D. Some Skeptical Thoughts on the Theory of Induced Innovation. *Quart. J. Econ.*, May 1973, *87*(2), pp. 208–19.

Palda, Kristian S. Production Functions and Performance Evaluation. In *Palda, K. S., ed.*, 1973, pp. 34–42.

Penrose, Edith. International Patenting and the Less-Developed Countries. *Econ. J.*, September 1973, *83*(331), pp. 768–86.

Peterson, Peter G. The Art of Managing Change. In *The Diebold Group, Inc.*, 1973, pp. 3–10. [G: U.S.]

Radhu, Ghulam M. Transfer of Technical Know-How Through Multinational Corporations in Pakistan. *Pakistan Develop. Rev.*, Winter 1973, *12*(4), pp. 361–74. [G: Pakistan]

Rasmussen, Jon A. Applications of a Model of Endogenous Technical Change to US Industry Data. *Rev. Econ. Stud.*, April 1973, *40*(2), pp. 225–38. [G: U.S.]

Rosenberg, Nathan. The Direction of Technological Change: Reply. *Econ. Develop. Cult. Change*, January 1973, *21*(2), pp. 356–57.

Rubinshtein, M. Scientific and Technical Progress and Planned Price Formation. *Prob. Econ.*, July 1973, *16*(3), pp. 22–36. [G: U.S.S.R.]

Shen, T. Y. Technology Diffusion, Substitution, and X-Efficiency. *Econometrica*, March 1973, *41*(2), pp. 263–84. [G: U.S.]

Sjaastad, Larry A. Notes on X-Efficiency and Technical Progress: Comment. In *Ayal, E. B., ed.*, 1973, pp. 38–40.

Sláma, Jiří and Vogel, Heinrich. Zur Verbreitung neuer Technologien in der UdSSR—eine Fallstudie: das Oxygenblasstahlverfahren. (Diffusion of New Technologies in the USSR—the Case of Oxygene-Steel. With English summary.) *Jahr. Nationalökon. Statist.*, March 1973, *187*(3), pp. 245–61. [G: U.S.S.R.]

Snooks, G. D. The Growth Process of the Firm: A Case Study. *Australian Econ. Pap.*, December 1973, *12*(21), pp. 162–74. [G: Australia]

Solow, Robert M. Technology and Unemployment. In *Reynolds, L. G.; Green, G. D. and Lewis, D. R., eds.*, 1973, pp. 89–99.

Srivastava, Uma K. and Heady, Earl O. Technological Change and Relative Factor Shares in Indian Agriculture: An Empirical Analysis. *Amer. J. Agr. Econ.*, August 1973, *55*(3), pp. 509–14. [G: India]

Srivastava, Uma K.; Nagadevara, Vishnuprasad and Heady, Earl O. Resource Productivity, Returns to Scale and Farm Size in Indian Agriculture: Some Recent Evidence. *Australian J. Agr. Econ.*, April 1973, *17*(1), pp. 43–57. [G: India]

Swan, Philip L. The International Diffusion of an Innovation. *J. Ind. Econ.*, September 1973, *22*(1), pp. 61–69.

Teubal, Morris. Comparative Advantage and Technological Change: The Learning by Doing Case. *J. Int. Econ.*, May 1973, *3*(2), pp. 161–77.

Thomson, Roy Herbert [Lord]. Modernization of Newspaper Techniques. In *The Diebold Group, Inc.*, 1973, pp. 310–13.

Tomescu, Gh. I. Tendințe și resorturi ale automatizării în capitalism. (Trends and Spheres of Automation in Capitalism. With English summary.) *Stud. Cercet. Econ.*, 1973, (4), pp. 167–76.

Yeung, Patrick. Induced Innovation in Agricultural Development: Comment. In *Ayal, E. B., ed.*, 1973, pp. 208–11.

Zeisel, Rose N. Modernization and Manpower in Textile Mills. *Mon. Lab. Rev.*, June 1973, *96*(6), pp. 18–25. [G: U.S.]

Zinam, Oleg. Impact of Modernization on USSR: Two Revolutions in Conflict. *Econ. Int.*, May 1973, *26*(2), pp. 283–302. [G: U.S.S.R.]

6212 Research and Development

Angilley, Alan S. Returns to Scale in Research in the Ethical Pharmaceutical Industry: Some Further Empirical Evidence. *J. Ind. Econ.*, December 1973, *22*(2), pp. 81–93. [G: U.K.]

Arditti, Fred D. and Sandor, Richard L. A Note on Variable Patent Life. *J. Ind. Econ.*, April 1973, *21*(2), pp. 177–83. [G: U.S.]

Bobrow, Davis B. Military Research and Development: Implications for the Civil Sector. *Ann. Amer. Acad. Polit. Soc. Sci.*, March 1973, *406*, pp. 117–28. [G: U.S.]

Bradbury, F. R. Changes in the Chemical Industry. In *Edge, D. O. and Wolfe, J. N., eds.*, 1973, pp. 181–95. [G: U.K.]

Branch, Ben. Research and Development and Its Relation to Sales Growth. *J. Econ. Bus.*, Winter 1973, *25*(2), pp. 107–11. [G: U.S.]

Brankamp, K. and Kremeier, A. Effect of Technological Development upon Substitution Processes. In *Blohm, H. and Steinbuch, K., eds.*, 1973, pp. 121–32.

Cartwright, R. Wayne and Candler, Wilfred V. Mathematical Analysis to Optimise Acquisition of Research Funds. *Can. J. Agr. Econ.*, February 1973, *21*(1), pp. 10–26.

Duetsch, Larry L. Research Performance in the Ethical Drug Industry. *Marquette Bus. Rev.*, Fall 1973, *17*(3), pp. 129–43.

Evenson, Robert E. and Kislev, Yoav. Research and Productivity in Wheat and Maize. *J. Polit. Econ.*, November-December 1973, *81*(6), pp. 1309–29.

Freeman, Christopher. The International Science Race. In *Edge, D. O. and Wolfe, J. N., eds.*, 1973, pp. 231–38.

Globerman, Steven. Market Structure and R&D in Canadian Manufacturing Industries. *Quart. Rev. Econ. Bus.*, Summer 1973, *13*(2), pp. 59–67. [G: Canada]

Grabowski, Henry G. and Baxter, Nevins D. Rivalry in Industrial Research and Development. *J. Ind. Econ.*, July 1973, *21*(3), pp. 209–35. [G: U.S.]

Hurtado, Hernán and Piñeiro, Martín. Rentabilidad potencial de la investigación ganadera: Una estimación empírica. (Rateable of Livestock Research: An Empirical Estimation. With English summary.) *Económica*, May-August 1973, *19*(2),

pp. 185–200. [G: Argentina]

Jones, P. M. S. The Use of Cost-benefit Analysis as an Aid to Allocating Government Resources for Research and Development. In *Wolfe, J. N., ed.*, 1973, pp. 155–81. [G: U.K.]

Katrak, Homi. Human Skills, R and D and Scale Economies in the Exports of the United Kingdom and the United States. *Oxford Econ. Pap.*, November 1973, *25*(3), pp. 337–60. [G: U.K.; U.S.]

Klein, Roger W. A Dynamic Theory of Comparative Advantage. *Amer. Econ. Rev.*, March 1973, *63*(1), pp. 173–84. [G: U.S.]

Leonard, William N. Research and Development in Industrial Growth: Reply. *J. Polit. Econ.*, September-October 1973, *81*(5), pp. 1249–52.

MacDonald, A. S. Exchange Rates for National Expenditure on Research and Development. *Econ. J.*, June 1973, *83*(330), pp. 477–94.

Matthews, R. C. O. The Contribution of Science and Technology to Economic Development. In *Williams, B. R., ed.*, 1973, pp. 1–31. [G: U.S.; Canada; Europe; Japan]

Moore, Thomas Gale. Science, Technology, and Industry. In *Ott, D. J., et al.*, 1973, pp. 67–89. [G: U.S.]

Nekola, Jiří and Vrba, Josef. Optimalizace rozsahu výkumné a vývojové činnosti na základě produkčni funkce. (The Optimization of the Level of Research and Development Activity on the Basis of the Production Function. With English summary.) *Ekon.-Mat. Obzor*, 1973, *9*(1), pp. 51–67.

Nussbaumer, Adolf. Financing the Generation of New Science and Technology. In *Williams, B. R., ed.*, 1973, pp. 169–89. [G: Austria]

Oshima, Keichi. Research and Development and Economic Growth in Japan. In *Williams, B. R., ed.*, 1973, pp. 310–23. [G: Japan]

Pellicanò, Giuseppe. Research, Technological Innovation and Management in Italy. *Rev. Econ. Cond. Italy*, November 1973, *27*(6), pp. 381–96. [G: Italy]

Roberts, R. W. and Schmitt, R. W. Program Budgeting R and D at General Electric. In *Novick, D., ed.*, 1973, pp. 139–50. [G: U.S.]

Romacker, B. Problems of Product Planning. In *Blohm, H. and Steinbuch, K., eds.*, 1973, pp. 115–19.

Sargent, J. R. The Distribution of Scientific Manpower. In *Williams, B. R., ed.*, 1973, pp. 360–74. [G: U.K.]

Seetzen, J. and Ferrari, A. La ricerca innovazionale in USA e in Europa. (Results of Innovation Research in USA and Europe. With English summary.) *L'Impresa*, 1973, *15*(7–8), pp. 425–32.

Shamin, A.; Dubinkin, V. and Smirtiukov, V. Structural Analysis of the Network of Scientific Organizations. *Prob. Econ.*, December 1973, *16*(8), pp. 44–55.

Shaw, John A. and Leet, Don R. Research and Development and Productivity Change in the U.S., 1948–1968. *J. Ind. Econ.*, December 1973, *22*(2), pp. 153–55. [G: U.S.]

Shumway, C. Richard. Allocation of Scarce Resources to Agricultural Research: Review of

Methodology. *Amer. J. Agr. Econ.*, Part I, November 1973, *55*(4), pp. 557–66.

Thomas, H. The Assessment of Project Worth with Applications to Research and Development. In *Wolfe, J. N., ed.*, 1973, pp. 88–114.

Tilton, John E. Research and Development in Industrial Growth: Comment. *J. Polit. Econ.*, September-October 1973, *81*(5), pp. 1245–48.

Tisdell, Clement A. The Australian Research Subsidy to Overseas Firms and Other Aspects of the Distribution of Research Grants. *Econ. Rec.*, June 1973, *49*(126), pp. 194–214. [G: Australia]

Trickŏvic, Vidosav. Science Policy and Development Strategy in Developing Countries. In *Williams, B. R., ed.*, 1973, pp. 287–99.

Udis, Bernard and Weidenbaum, Murray L. The Many Dimensions of the Military Effort. In *Udis, B., ed.*, 1973, pp. 17–57. [G: U.S.]

von Weizsäcker, C. C. Notes on Endogenous Growth of Productivity. In *Mirrlees, J. A. and Stern, N. H., eds.*, 1973, pp. 101–10.

Williams, B. R. The Basis of Science Policy in Market Economies. In *Williams, B. R., ed.*, 1973, pp. 416–31.

Williams, B. R. Science and Technology in Economic Growth: Introduction. In *Williams, B. R., ed.*, 1973, pp. xi–xvii.

Wolfe, J. N. Cost Escalation in Research and Development Activities. In *Edge, D. O. and Wolfe, J. N., eds.*, 1973, pp. 225–30.

630 INDUSTRY STUDIES

6300 General

Alagh, Yoginder K. and Pathak, Pravin G. Industrial Development in Gujarat: Regional Structure and Policies. *Artha-Vikas*, January-July 1973, *9*(1–2), pp. 143–84. [G: India]

Ardolini, Charles W. Productivity Gains in 1972 in Selected Industries. *Mon. Lab. Rev.*, July 1973, *96*(7), pp. 43–45. [G: U.S.]

Belli, R. David; Allnutt, Smith W. and Murad, Howard. Property, Plant, and Equipment Expenditures by Majority-Owned Foreign Affiliates of U.S. Companies: Revised Estimates for 1966–72 and Projections for 1973 and 1974. *Surv. Curr. Bus.*, December 1973, *53*(12), pp. 19–32. [G: U.S.]

Bitar, Sergio and Trivelli, Hugo. The Cost of Capital in the Chilean Economy. In *Eckaus, R. S. and Rosenstein-Rodan, P. N., eds.*, 1973, pp. 147–65. [G: Chile]

Boddy, Raford and Gort, Michael. Capital Expenditures and Capital Stocks. *Ann. Econ. Soc. Measure*, July 1973, *2*(3), pp. 245–61. [G: U.S.]

Cohen, Stanley and Smyth, David J. Some Determinants of Price/Earnings Ratios of Industrial Common Stock. *Quart. Rev. Econ. Bus.*, Winter 1973, *13*(4), pp. 49–60. [G: U.S.]

Comanor, William S. Racial Discrimination in American Industry. *Economica, N.S.*, November 1973, *40*(160), pp. 363–78.

Cumberland, John H. Dimensions of the Impact of Reduced Military Expenditures on Industries, Regions, and Communities. In *Udis, B., ed.*, 1973, pp. 79–147. [G: U.S.]

Davies, S. W. and Scott, T. W. K. Forecasting Industrial Production. *Nat. Inst. Econ. Rev.*, November 1973, (66), pp. 54–68. [G: U.K.]

Desai, Padma. Soviet Industrial Production: Estimates of Gross Outputs by Branches and Groups. *Oxford Bull. Econ. Statist.*, May 1973, *35*(2), pp. 153–71. [G: U.S.S.R.]

Donges, Juergen B. Shaping Spain's Export Industry. *World Devel.*, September 1973, *1*(9), pp. 19–37. [G: Spain]

Elliott, J. W. Theories of Corporate Investment Behavior Revisited. *Amer. Econ. Rev.*, March 1973, *63*(1), pp. 195–207. [G: U.S.]

Farooq, Ghazi M. Economic Growth and Changes in the Industrial Structure of Income and Labor Force in Pakistan. *Econ. Develop. Cult. Change*, January 1973, *21*(2), pp. 293–308. [G: Pakistan]

Fløystad, Gunnar. Factor Price Equalization in Theory and Practice—A Study of Mainly Norwegian Data. *Weltwirtsch. Arch.*, 1973, *109*(4), pp. 554–78. [G: E.E.C.; E.F.T.A.; Norway]

Freeman, Christopher. A Study of Success and Failure in Industrial Innovation. In *Williams, B. R., ed.*, 1973, pp. 227–45. [G: U.K.]

Frugali, Fabio. Situation and Prospects of Small and Medium-Sized Industry in Italy. *Rev. Econ. Cond. Italy*, November 1973, *27*(6), pp. 397–409. [G: Italy]

Gellner, Christopher G. A 25-Year Look at Employment as Measured by Two Surveys. *Mon. Lab. Rev.*, July 1973, *96*(7), pp. 14–23. [G: U.S.]

George, Kenneth D. The Changing Structure of Industry in the United Kingdom. In *Rybczynski, T. M., ed.*, 1973, pp. 55–67. [G: U.K.]

Hedges, Janice Neipert. Absence from Work: A Look at Some National Data. *Mon. Lab. Rev.*, July 1973, *96*(7), pp. 24–30. [G: U.S.]

Heubes, Jürgen. Investitionsverhalten in der Industrie der Bundesrepublik Deutschland 1950–1970. (Investment Behavior in the West-German Industry 1950–1970. With English summary.) *Z. ges. Staatswiss.*, October 1973, *129*(4), pp. 685–701. [G: W. Germany]

Hodgens, Evan L. Survivor's Pensions: An Emerging Employee Benefit. *Mon. Lab. Rev.*, July 1973, *96*(7), pp. 31–34. [G: U.S.]

Iudina, E. and Oleinik, I. Structural Changes in the Economies of Socialist Countries. *Prob. Econ.*, March 1973, *15*(11), pp. 21–43. [G: U.S.S.R.]

Jenkins, Glenn P. The Measurement of Rates of Return and Taxation from Private Capital in Canada. In *Niskanen, W. A., et al., eds.*, 1973, pp. 211–45. [G: Canada]

Katano, Hikoji. Estimation of Investment Allocation Ratios of Japanese Economy: 1960–1969. *Kobe Econ. Bus. Rev.*, 1973, *20*, pp. 37–50. [G: Japan]

Klijn, Nico. The Effects of a 9.42 Per Cent Price Increase for Iron and Steel on Other Prices. *Australian Econ. Rev.*, 4th Quarter 1973, pp. 27–30. [G: Australia]

Koch, James V. Market Structure and Industry Growth: Reply. *Miss. Val. J. Bus. Econ.*, Fall 1973, *9*(1), pp. 87. [G: U.S.]

Kossov, V. V. Relationships in the Development of

Industries. *Matekon,* Spring 1973, *9*(3), pp. 89–108.

Kux, Jaroslav. Comparative Study of Labour Productivity in Industry Between Czechoslovakia, Hungary, France and Austria. *Czech. Econ. Digest.,* November 1973, (7), pp. 74–95. [G: Czechoslavakia; Hungary; France; Austria]

Lermer, George. Evidence from Trade Data Regarding the Rationalizing of Canadian Industry. *Can. J. Econ.,* May 1973, *6*(2), pp. 248–56. [G: Canada]

Litzenberger, Robert H. and Joy, O. Maurice. Inter-Industry Profitability Under Uncertainty. *Western Econ. J.,* September 1973, *11*(3), pp. 338–49. [G: U.S.]

McGowan, John J. The Supply of Equity Securities, 1952–68. In *Goldsmith, R. W., ed.,* 1973, pp. 165–203. [G: U.S.]

Narayana, N. Changing Pattern of Indian Industries in the Plan Period 1950–70. *Econ. Aff.,* July 1973, *18*(7), pp. 338–46. [G: India]

Ornstein, Stanley I. Market Structure and Industry Growth: Comment. *Miss. Val. J. Bus. Econ.,* Fall 1973, *9*(1), pp. 83–86. [G: U.S.]

Ornstein, Stanley I., et al. Determinants of Market Structure. *Southern Econ. J.,* April 1973, *39*(4), pp. 612–25. [G: U.S.]

Rice, G. Randolph. Poverty and Industrial Growth Patterns: Some Cross-State Evidence. *J. Reg. Sci.,* December 1973, *13*(3), pp. 377–84. [G: U.S.]

Ritz, Philip M. and Roberts, Eugene P. Industry Inventory Requirements: An Input-Output Analysis. *Surv. Curr. Bus.,* November 1973, *53*(11), pp. 15–22. [G: U.S.]

Scheper, W. and Reichenbach, H. Die Entwicklung der Anteile der Wirtschaftsbereiche am Bruttoinlandsprodukt—Eine Strukturprognose. (The Development of the Sectoral Shares of Production in Gross National Product. A Forecast of the Production Structure. With English summary) *Weltwirtsch. Arch.,* 1973, *109*(2), pp. 291–320. [G: W. Germany]

Schwartz, Robert A. and Altman, Edward I. Volatility Behavior of Industrial Stock Price Indices. *J. Finance,* September 1973, *28*(4), pp. 957–71. [G: U.S.]

Stigler, George J. The Economies of Scale. In *Haynes, W. W.; Coyne, T. J. and Osborne, D. K., eds.,* 1973, pp. 232–49. [G: U.S.]

Stobaugh, Robert B., et al. U.S. Multinational Enterprises and the U.S. Economy. In *Kujawa, D., ed.,* 1973, pp. 82–126. [G: U.S.]

Suman, H. N. P. S. Effect of Corporate Taxation on Saving and Capital Formation in Some Indian Industries. *Econ. Aff.,* November-December 1973, *18*(11–12), pp. 485–96. [G: India]

Swamy, Subramanian. Economic Growth in China and India, 1952–1970: A Comparative Appraisal. *Econ. Develop. Cult. Change,* Part II, July 1973, *21*(4), pp. 1–84. [G: China; India]

Thoburn, J. T. Exports and the Malaysian Engineering Industry: A Case Study of Backward Linkage. *Oxford Bull. Econ. Statist.,* May 1973, *35*(2), pp. 91–117. [G: Malaya]

Wagstaff, H. R. Employment Multipliers in Rural Scotland. *Scot. J. Polit. Econ.,* November 1973, *20*

(3), pp. 239–61. [G: U.K.]

Weidenbaum, Murray L. Industrial Adjustments to Military Expenditure Shifts and Cutbacks. In *Udis, B., ed.,* 1973, pp. 253–87. [G: U.S.]

Woodward, John T. Capital Spending Expected to Rise Through First Half of 1974. *Surv. Curr. Bus.,* December 1973, *53*(12), pp. 9–13. [G: U.S.]

631 Industry Studies: Manufacturing

6310 General

Ahmad, Qazi Kholiquzzaman and Anwaruzzaman, Chowdhury. Productivity Trends in the Manufacturing Sector of Bangladesh: A Case Study of Selected Industries. *Bangladesh Econ. Rev.,* April 1973, *1*(2), pp. 119–48. [G: Bangladesh]

Amjad, Rashid. Growth, Profitability and Savings of Quoted Public Limited Companies 1964–70. *Pakistan Econ. Soc. Rev.,* Winter 1973, *11*(4), pp. 417–42. [G: Pakistan]

Asher, Ephraim and Kumar, T. Krishna. Capital-Labor Substitution and Technical Progress in Planned and Market Oriented Economies: A Comparative Study. *Southern Econ. J.,* July 1973, *40*(1), pp. 103–09. [G: U.S.S.R.; Yugoslavia; Hungary; N. America; Israel]

Azizur Rahman, A. N. M. Elasticities of Substitution in Manufacturing Industries of Bangladesh: An International Comparison. *Bangladesh Econ. Rev.,* April 1973, *1*(2), pp. 173–85. [G: Bangladesh]

Bain, A. D. and Evans, J. D. Price Formation and Profits: Explanatory and Forecasting Models of Manufacturing Industry Profits in the U.K. *Oxford Bull. Econ. Statist.,* November 1973, *35*(4), pp. 295–308. [G: U.K.]

Baker, Samuel H. Risk, Leverage, and Profitability: An Industry Analysis. *Rev. Econ. Statist.,* November 1973, *55*(4), pp. 503–07. [G: U.S.]

Beidleman, Carl R. Income Smoothing: The Role of Management. *Accounting Rev.,* October 1973, *48*(4), pp. 653–67. [G: U.S.]

Bell, Donald R. Prevalence of Private Retirement Plans in Manufacturing. *Mon. Lab. Rev.,* September 1973, *96*(9), pp. 29–32. [G: U.S.]

Bell, R. T. Some Aspects of Industrial Decentralization in South Africa. *S. Afr. J. Econ.,* December 1973, *41*(4), pp. 401–31. [G: S. Africa]

Berndt, Ernst R. and Christensen, Laurits R. The Translog Function and the Substitution of Equipment, Structures, and Labor in U.S. Manufacturing 1929–68. *J. Econometrics,* March 1973, *1*(1), pp. 81–113. [G: U.S.]

Bodkin, Ronald G. and Murthy, K. S. R. The Orders-Shipments Mechanism in Canadian Producer Goods Industries. *J. Amer. Statist. Assoc.,* June 1973, *68*(342), pp. 297–305. [G: Canada]

Boyle, Stanley E. The Average Concentration Ratio: An Inappropriate Measure of Industry Structure. *J. Polit. Econ.,* Part I, March-April 1973, *81*(2), pp. 414–26. [G: U.S.]

Branch, Ben. Research and Development and Its Relation to Sales Growth. *J. Econ. Bus.,* Winter 1973, *25*(2), pp. 107–11. [G: U.S.]

Brite, Robert L. Scale and the Elasticity of Substitution in Cross-Section Production Functions. *J. Econ. Bus.*, Winter 1973, *25*(2), pp. 101–06. [G: U.S.]

Brozen, Yale. Concentration and Profits: Does Concentration Matter? In *Weston, J. F. and Ornstein, S. I., eds.*, 1973, pp. 59–70. [G: U.S.]

Burley, H. T. Production Functions for Australian Manufacturing Industries. *Rev. Econ. Statist.*, February 1973, *55*(1), pp. 118–22. [G: Australia]

Carlson, John A. The Production Lag. *Amer. Econ. Rev.*, March 1973, *63*(1), pp. 73–86. [G: U.S.]

Chandrasekar, Krishnamurti. U.S. and French Productivity in 19 Manufacturing Industries. *J. Ind. Econ.*, April 1973, *21*(2), pp. 110–25. [G: U.S.; France]

Chang, John C. and Holt, Charles C. Optimal Investment Orders Under Uncertainty and Dynamic Costs: Theory and Estimates. *Southern Econ. J.*, April 1973, *39*(4), pp. 508–25. [G: U.S.]

Chenery, Hollis B. and Hughes, Helen. Industrialization and Trade Trends: Some Issues for the 1970s. In *Hughes, H., ed.*, 1973, pp. 3–31.

Christian, Charles M. and Bennett, Sari J. Industrial Relocations from the Black Community of Chicago. *Growth Change*, April 1973, *4*(2), pp. 14–20. [G: U.S.]

Clark, C. Scott. Labor Hoarding in Durable Goods Industries. *Amer. Econ. Rev.*, December 1973, *63*(5), pp. 811–24. [G: U.S.]

Clifford, Donald K., Jr. Growth Pains of the Threshold Company. *Harvard Bus. Rev.*, September-October 1973, *51*(5), pp. 143–54. [G: U.S.]

Dadi, M. M. Labour's Share in Indian Industry: Theory and Fact. *Indian Econ. J.*, January-March 1973, *20*(3), pp. 500–14. [G: India]

Dalton, James A. and Esposito, Louis. The Impact of Liquidity on Merger Activity. *Quart. Rev. Econ. Bus.*, Spring 1973, *13*(1), pp. 15–26. [G: U.S.]

Dixon, R. J. Regional Specialisation and Trade in the United Kingdom: A Test of Some Hypotheses. *Scot. J. Polit. Econ.*, June 1973, *20*(2), pp. 159–70. [G: U.K.]

Dowling, J. Malcolm, Jr. Wage Determination in Two-Digit Manufacturing Industries: Theory, Test, and Forecast. *Quart. Rev. Econ. Bus.*, Spring 1973, *13*(1), pp. 27–36. [G: U.S.]

Duetsch, Larry L. Elements of Market Structure and the Extent of Suboptimal Capacity. *Southern Econ. J.*, October 1973, *40*(2), pp. 216–23. [G: U.S.]

Edmonson, Nathan. Capacity Utilization in Major Materials Industries. *Fed. Res. Bull.*, August 1973, *59*(8), pp. 564–66. [G: U.S.]

Fane, George. Consistent Measures of Import Substitution. *Oxford Econ. Pap.*, July 1973, *25*(2), pp. 251–61. [G: Pakistan]

Farley, Noel J. J. Outward-looking Policies and Industrialization in a Small Economy: Some Notes on the Irish Case. *Econ. Develop. Cult. Change*, Part I, July 1973, *21*(4), pp. 610–28. [G: Ireland]

Farris, Paul L. Market Growth and Concentration Change in U.S. Manufacturing Industries. *Antitrust Bull.*, Summer 1973, *18*(2), pp. 291–305. [G: U.S.]

Freund, James L. A Note on Short Period Changes in Earned Income in Manufacturing Among Urban Areas. *J. Reg. Sci.*, August 1973, *13*(2), pp. 279–89. [G: U.S.]

Fry, Fred L. More on the Causes of Quits in Manufacturing. *Mon. Lab. Rev.*, June 1973, *96*(6), pp. 48–49. [G: U.S.]

Gábor, Ottó and Gede, Miklós. Role of the Engineering Industries in the Development of the Hungarian Economy and in the Transformation of the Economic Structure. *Eastern Europ. Econ.*, Fall 1973, *12*(1), pp. 82–104. [G: Hungary]

Garrison, Charles B. and Paulson, Albert S. An Entropy Measure of the Geographic Concentration of Economic Activity. *Econ. Geogr.*, October 1973, *49*(4), pp. 319–24. [G: U.S.]

Globerman, Steven. Market Structure and R&D in Canadian Manufacturing Industries. *Quart. Rev. Econ. Bus.*, Summer 1973, *13*(2), pp. 59–67. [G: Canada]

Grabowski, Henry G. and Baxter, Nevins D. Rivalry in Industrial Research and Development. *J. Ind. Econ.*, July 1973, *21*(3), pp. 209–35. [G: U.S.]

Gregory, R. G. and James, Denis W. Do New Factories Embody Best Practice Technology? *Econ. J.*, December 1973, *83*(332), pp. 1133–55. [G: Australia]

Grossman, Steven D. A Test of Speed of Adjustment in Manufacturing Inventory Investment. *Quart. Rev. Econ. Bus.*, Autumn 1973, *13*(3), pp. 21–32. [G: U.S.]

Helfgott, Roy B. Multinational Corporations and Manpower Utilization in Developing Nations. *J. Devel. Areas*, January 1973, *7*(2), pp. 235–46. [G: U.S.; Latin America]

Hoffmann, Lutz. Import Substitution—Export Expansion and Growth in an Open Developing Economy: The Case of West Malaysia. *Weltwirtsch. Arch.*, 1973, *109*(3), pp. 452–75. [G: W. Malaysia]

Holtermann, Sally E. Market Structure and Economic Performance in U.K. Manufacturing Industry. *J. Ind. Econ.*, December 1973, *22*(2), pp. 119–39. [G: U.K.]

House, William J. Market Structure and Industry Performance: The Case of Kenya. *Oxford Econ. Pap.*, November 1973, *25*(3), pp. 405–19. [G: Kenya]

Hsia, Ronald. Technological Change in the Industrial Growth of Hong Kong. In *Williams, B. R., ed.*, 1973, pp. 335–53. [G: Hong Kong]

Ikram, Khalid. Social Versus Private Profitability in Pakistan's Export of Manufactures. *Pakistan Develop. Rev.*, Summer 1973, *12*(2), pp. 156–67. [G: Pakistan]

Ireland, Norman J.; Briscoe, G. and Smyth, David J. Specification Bias and Short-run Returns to Labour: Some Evidence for the United Kingdom. *Rev. Econ. Statist.*, February 1973, *55*(1), pp. 23–27. [G: U.K.]

Jacquemin, Alex P. and Cardon de Lichtbuer, Michel. Size Structure, Stability and Performance of the Largest British and EEC Firms. *Europ. Econ. Rev.*, December 1973, *4*(4), pp. 393–408. [G: U.K.; E.E.C.]

James, Franklin J., Jr. and Hughes, James W. The

Process of Employment Location Change: An Empirical Analysis. *Land Econ.*, November 1973, *49*(4), pp. 404–13. [G: U.S.]

Johns, B. L. Import Substitution and Export Potential—The Case of Manufacturing Industry in West Malaysia. *Australian Econ. Pap.*, December 1973, *12*(21), pp. 175–95. [G: Malaysia]

Jones, J. C. H.; Laudadio, Leonard and Percy, M. Market Structure and Profitability in Canadian Manufacturing Industry: Some Cross-Section Results. *Can. J. Econ.*, August 1973, *6*(3), pp. 356–68. [G: Canada]

Katrak, Homi. Human Skills, R and D and Scale Economies in the Exports of the United Kingdom and the United States. *Oxford Econ. Pap.*, November 1973, *25*(3), pp. 337–60. [G: U.K.; U.S.]

Katz, Jorge M. Industrial Growth, Royalty Payments and Local Expenditure on Research and Development. In *Urquidi, V. L. and Thorp, R., eds.*, 1973, pp. 197–224. [G: Argentina]

Klammer, Thomas. The Association of Capital Budgeting Techniques with Firm Performance. *Accounting Rev.*, April 1973, *48*(2), pp. 353–64. [G: U.S.]

Klein, Lawrence R. and Long, Virginia. Capacity Utilization: Concept, Measurement, and Recent Estimates. *Brookings Pap. Econ. Act.*, 1973, (3), pp. 743–56. [G: U.S.]

Kliman, M. L. The Permanent Income Hypothesis and the Firm's Demand for Money. *J. Econ. Bus.*, Winter 1973, *25*(2), pp. 89–92. [G: U.S.]

Lall, Sanjaya. Transfer-Pricing by Multinational Manufacturing Firms. *Oxford Bull. Econ. Statist.*, August 1973, *35*(3), pp. 173–95. [G: U.S.; U.K.; Colombia]

Lovell, C. A. Knox. Technology and Specification Error. *Southern Econ. J.*, July 1973, *40*(1), pp. 110–16. [G: U.S.]

Lovell, C. A. Knox. Estimation and Prediction with CES and VES Production Functions. *Int. Econ. Rev.*, October 1973, *14*(3), pp. 676–92. [G: U.S.]

Lovell, C. A. Knox and Moroney, J. R. Estimating the Elasticity of Substitution: A Correction and Some Further Results. *Southern Econ. J.*, January 1973, *39*(3), pp. 437–41.

Mabogunje, Akin L. Manufacturing and the Geography of Development in Tropical Africa. *Econ. Geogr.*, January 1973, *49*(1), pp. 1–20. [G: Africa]

Maitra, Priyatosh. Relative Effects of Import Substitution in New Zealand. *Econ. Aff.*, May 1973, *18* (5), pp. 213–16, 234–40. [G: New Zealand]

Marcis, Richard G. and Smith, V. Kerry. The Demand for Liquid Asset Balances by U.S. Manufacturing Corporations: 1959-1970. *J. Financial Quant. Anal.*, March 1973, *8*(2), pp. 207–18. [G: U.S.]

Mason, R. Hal. Some Observations on the Choice of Technology by Multinational Firms in Developing Countries. *Rev. Econ. Statist.*, August 1973, *55* (3), pp. 349–55. [G: Mexico; Philippines; U.S.]

McFetridge, Donald G. Market Structure and Price-Cost Margins: An Analysis of the Canadian Manufacturing Sector. *Can. J. Econ.*, August 1973, *6*(3), pp. 344–55. [G: Canada]

Meehan, James W., Jr. and Duchesneau, Thomas D. The Critical Level of Concentration: An Empirical Analysis. *J. Ind. Econ.*, September 1973, *22*(1), pp. 21–36. [G: U.S.]

Merz, C. M.; Gibson, T. A. and Seitz, C. Ward. Impact of the Space Shuttle Program on the National Economy. *Eng. Econ.*, January-February 1973, *18* (2), pp. 115–33. [G: U.S.]

Metwally, Mohktar M. Entry Gap in New Zealand Markets for Manufactured Consumer Goods. *Econ. Rec.*, December 1973, *49*(128), pp. 575–87. [G: New Zealand]

Neu, Axel and Glismann, Hans H. Quantitative Aspects of Nontariff Distortions of Trade in the Federal Republic of Germany. In *Scaperlanda, A. E., ed.*, 1973, pp. 193–253. [G: Germany]

Nishioka, Hisao and Krumme, Gunter. Location Conditions, Factors and Decisions: An Evaluation of Selected Location Surveys. *Land Econ.*, May 1973, *49*(2), pp. 195–205. [G: Japan; U.S.]

Nussbaumer, Adolf. Financing the Generation of New Science and Technology. In *Williams, B. R., ed.*, 1973, pp. 169–89. [G: Austria]

Ohlin, Göran. Industrialization and Trade Trends: Some Issues for the 1970s: Comment. In *Hughes, H., ed.*, 1973, pp. 32–34.

Oshima, Keichi. Research and Development and Economic Growth in Japan. In *Williams, B. R., ed.*, 1973, pp. 310–23. [G: Japan]

Palmer, John P. The Profit-Performance Effects of the Separation of Ownership from Control in Large U.S. Industrial Corporations. *Bell J. Econ. Manage. Sci.*, Spring 1973, *4*(1), pp. 293–303. [G: U.S.]

Panic, M. and Close, R. E. Profitability of British Manufacturing Industry. *Lloyds Bank Rev.*, July 1973, (109), pp. 17–30. [G: U.K.]

Pepson, Robert P. Job Vacancies, Hires, Quits, and Layoffs in Manufacturing, 1972. *Mon. Lab. Rev.*, April 1973, *96*(4), pp. 66–68. [G: U.S.]

Perry, George L. Capacity in Manufacturing. *Brookings Pap. Econ. Act.*, 1973, (3), pp. 701–42. [G: U.S.]

Petrei, Amalio H. Rates of Return to Physical Capital in Manufacturing Industries in Argentina. *Oxford Econ. Pap.*, November 1973, *25*(3), pp. 378–404. [G: Argentina]

Poindexter, J. Carl, Jr. and Jones, C. P. The Effect of Recent Tax Policy Changes on Manufacturing Investment. *Quart. Rev. Econ. Bus.*, Winter 1973, *13*(4), pp. 79–88. [G: U.S.]

Radhu, Ghulam M. Some Aspects of Direct Foreign Private Investment in Pakistan. *Pakistan Develop. Rev.*, Spring 1973, *12*(1), pp. 68–80. [G: Pakistan]

Rasmussen, Jon A. Applications of a Model of Endogenous Technical Change to US Industry Data. *Rev. Econ. Stud.*, April 1973, *40*(2), pp. 225–38. [G: U.S.]

Rawski, Thomas G. Chinese Industrial Production, 1952-1971. *Rev. Econ. Statist.*, May 1973, *55*(2), pp. 169–81. [G: China]

Rees, R. D. Optimum Plant Size in United Kingdom Industries: Some Survivor Estimates. *Economica, N.S.*, November 1973, *40*(160), pp. 394–401. [G: U.K.]

Rhoades, Stephen A. and Cleaver, Joe M. The Nature of the Concentration—Price/Cost Margin Relationship for 352 Manufacturing Industries: 1967. *Southern Econ. J.,* July 1973, *40*(1), pp. 90–102. [G: U.S.]

Rhoades, Stephen A. The Concentration-Profitability Relationship: Policy Implications and Some Empirical Evidence. *Antitrust Bull.,* Summer 1973, *18*(2), pp. 333–54. [G: U.S.]

Rhoades, Stephen A. The Effect of Diversification on Industry Profit Performance in 241 Manufacturing Industries: 1963. *Rev. Econ. Statist.,* May 1973, *55*(2), pp. 146–55. [G: U.S.]

Ripley, Frank C. and Segal, Lydia. Price Determination in 395 Manufacturing Industries. *Rev. Econ. Statist.,* August 1973, *55*(3), pp. 263–71. [G: U.S.]

Rosendale, Phyllis B. The Short-Run Pricing Policies of Some British Engineering Exporters. *Nat. Inst. Econ. Rev.,* August 1973, (65), pp. 44–51. [G: U.K.]

Rowley, J. C. R. and Wilton, D. A. Quarterly Models of Wage Determination Some New Efficient Estimates. *Amer. Econ. Rev.,* June 1973, *63*(3), pp. 380–89. [G: Canada]

Ryan, Terence M. C.E.S. Production Functions in British Manufacturing Industry: A Cross-section Study. *Oxford Econ. Pap.,* July 1973, *25*(2), pp. 241–50. [G: U.K.]

Sawhney, Pawan K. and Sawhney, Bansi L. Capacity-Utilization, Concentration, and Price-Cost Margins: Results on Indian Industries. *J. Ind. Econ.,* April 1973, *21*(2), pp. 145–53. [G: India]

Sawyer, M. C. The Earnings of Manual Workers: A Cross-Section Analysis. *Scot. J. Polit. Econ.,* June 1973, *20*(2), pp. 141–57. [G: U.K.]

Scherer, Frederic M. Investment Variability, Seller Concentration, and Plant Scale Economies. *J. Ind. Econ.,* December 1973, *22*(2), pp. 157–60. [G: U.S.]

Scherer, Frederic M. The Determinants of Industrial Plant Sizes in Six Nations. *Rev. Econ. Statist.,* May 1973, *55*(2), pp. 135–45. [G: Sweden; N. America; France; U.K.; W. Germany]

Shaw, John A. and Leet, Don R. Research and Development and Productivity Change in the U.S., 1948–1968. *J. Ind. Econ.,* December 1973, *22*(2), pp. 153–55. [G: U.S.]

Shen, T. Y. Technology Diffusion, Substitution, and X-Efficiency. *Econometrica,* March 1973, *41*(2), pp. 263–84. [G: U.S.]

Spandau, Arnt. Cross-Section Production Functions and Income-Shares in South African Industry. *S. Afr. J. Econ.,* September 1973, *41*(3), pp. 208–33. [G: S. Africa]

Sreenivas, M. A. Prices, Money Wages and Real Output: A Case Study of Indian Manufacturing Sector. *Indian Econ. J.,* April-June 1973, *20*(4–5), pp. 604–18. [G: India]

Stigler, George J. The Kinky Oligopoly Demand Curve and Rigid Prices. In *Haynes, W. W.; Coyne, T. J. and Osborne, D. K., eds.,* 1973, pp. 281–99. [G: U.S.]

Stoikov, Vladimir. Size of Firm, Worker Earnings, and Human Capital: The Case of Japan. *Ind. Lab. Relat. Rev.,* July 1973, *26*(4), pp. 1095–1106. [G: Japan]

Stoikov, Vladimir. The Structure of Earnings in Japanese Manufacturing Industries: A Human-Capital Approach. *J. Polit. Econ.,* Part I, March-April 1973, *81*(2), pp. 340–55. [G: Japan]

Streeten, Paul. Industrialization and Trade Trends: Some Issues for the 1970s: Comment. In *Hughes, H., ed.,* 1973, pp. 35–39.

Swan, Philip L. Decentralization and the Growth of Urban Manufacturing Employment. *Land Econ.,* May 1973, *49*(2), pp. 212–16. [G: U.S.]

Syrquin, Moshe. Efficient Input Frontiers for the Manufacturing Sector in Mexico 1965–1980. *Int. Econ. Rev.,* October 1973, *14*(3), pp. 657–75. [G: Mexico]

Tisdell, Clement A. The Australian Research Subsidy to Overseas Firms and Other Aspects of the Distribution of Research Grants. *Econ. Rec.,* June 1973, *49*(126), pp. 194–214. [G: Australia]

Todd, Ralph H. Evidence of Immediate Tax Shifting in U.S. Manufacturing, 1948–1967. *Nebr. J. Econ. Bus.,* Spring 1973, *12*(2), pp. 55–63. [G: U.S.]

de la Torre, Jose, Jr.; Stobaugh, Robert B. and Telesio, Piero. U.S. Multinational Enterprises and Changes in the Skill Composition of U.S. Employment. In *Kujawa, D., ed.,* 1973, pp. 127–43. [G: U.S.]

Tumlir, Jan. Trade Negotiations in the Field of Manufactures. In *Streeten, P., ed.,* 1973, pp. 279–99.

Tyler, William G. Manufactured Export Promotion in a Semi-Industrialized Economy: The Brazilian Case. *J. Devel. Stud.,* October 1973, *10*(1), pp. 3–15. [G: Brazil]

Uselding, Paul and Juba, Bruce. Biased Technical Progress in American Manufacturing, 1839–1899. *Exploration Econ. Hist.,* Fall 1973, *11*(1), pp. 55–72. [G: U.S.]

Verma, Pramod. Regional Wages and Economic Development: A Case Study of Manufacturing Wages in India, 1950–1960. *J. Devel. Stud.,* October 1973, *10*(1), pp. 16–32. [G: India]

Vernon, John M. and Nourse, Robert E. M. Profit Rates and Market Structure of Advertising Intensive Firms. *J. Ind. Econ.,* September 1973, *22*(1), pp. 1–20. [G: U.S.]

Waldorf, William H. Quality of Labor in Manufacturing. *Rev. Econ. Statist.,* August 1973, *55*(3), pp. 284–90. [G: U.S.]

Walter, Emil J. Technologische, wirtschaftliche und soziale Aspekte der wachsenden Bedeutung der Schichtarbeit. (Technological, Economic and Social Aspects of the Growing Importance of Shift Work. With English summary.) *Schweiz. Z. Volkswirtsch. Statist.,* March 1973, *109*(1), pp. 69–89. [G: Switzerland]

Wells, Louis T., Jr. Economic Man and Engineering Man: Choice in a Low-Wage Country. *Public Policy,* Summer 1973, *21*(3), pp. 319–42. [G: Indonesia]

Wells, Louis T., Jr. Men and Machines in Indonesia's Light Manufacturing Industries. *Bull. Indonesian Econ. Stud.,* November 1973, *9*(3), pp. 62–72. [G: Indonesia]

Weston, J. Fred and Ornstein, Stanley I. Trends and Causes of Concentration—A Survey. In *Weston, J. F. and Ornstein, S. I., eds.,* 1973, pp. 3–21.
[G: U.S.]

Witte, Ann Dryden. Employment in the Manufacturing Sector of Developing Economies: A Study of Mexico and Peru. *J. Devel. Stud.,* October 1973, *10*(1), pp. 33–49. [G: Mexico; Peru]

Witthans, Fred. Estimates of Effective Rates of Protection for United States Industries in 1967. *Rev. Econ. Statist.,* August 1973, *55*(3), pp. 362–64.
[G: U.S.]

Wolkowitz, Benjamin. Estimation of a Set of Homothetic Production Functions: A Time Series Analysis of American Postwar Manufacturing. *Southern Econ. J.,* April 1973, *39*(4), pp. 626–37.
[G: U.S.]

Woodfield, Alan. Biased Efficiency Growth and the Declining Relative Share of Labor in New Zealand Manufacturing. *Southern Econ. J.,* January 1973, *39*(3), pp. 373–80. [G: New Zealand]

6312 Metals (iron, steel, and other)

Abe, Masatoshi A. Dynamic Micro-economic Models of Production, Investment and Technological Change of the U.S. and Japanese Iron and Steel Industries. In *Judge, G. G. and Takayama, T., eds.,* 1973, pp. 345–67. [G: U.S.; Japan]

Ault, David E. On the Importance of Lags in Technology: An Empirical Test. *Rivista Int. Sci. Econ. Com.,* October 1973, *20*(10), pp. 945–60.

Ault, David E. The Continued Deterioration of the Competitive Ability of the U.S. Steel Industry: The Development of Continuous Casting. *Western Econ. J.,* March 1973, *11*(1), pp. 89–97.
[G: U.S.]

Baack, Bennett D. and Ray, Edward J. Tariff Policy and Comparative Advantage in the Iron and Steel Industry: 1870–1929. *Exploration Econ. Hist.,* Fall 1973, *11*(1), pp. 3–23. [G: U.S.]

Bralove, Mary. Does Your Paprika Get Up Off the Plate and Just Walk Away? In *Murray, B. B., ed.,* 1973, pp. 86–88. [G: U.S.]

Carey, John L. Productivity in the Steel Foundries Industry. *Mon. Lab. Rev.,* May 1973, *96*(5), pp. 8–11. [G: U.S.]

Day, Richard H. and Nelson, Jon P. A Class of Dynamic Models for Describing and Projecting Industrial Development. *J. Econometrics,* June 1973, *1*(2), pp. 155–90. [G: U.S.; Japan]

Fernández de la Garza, Guillermo and Manne, Alan S. ENERGETICOS, A Process Analysis of the Energy Sectors. In *Goreux, L. M. and Manne, A. S., eds.,* 1973, pp. 233–75. [G: Mexico]

Guntermann, Karl L. Air Pollution Control in the Secondary Aluminum Industry. *Land Econ.,* August 1973, *49*(3), pp. 285–93. [G: U.S.]

Hyde, Charles K. The Adoption of the Hot Blast by the British Iron Industry: A Reinterpretation. *Exploration Econ. Hist.,* Spring 1973, *10*(3), pp. 281–93. [G: U.K.]

Hyde, Charles K. The Adoption of Coke-Smelting by the British Iron Industry, 1709–1790. *Exploration Econ. Hist.,* Summer 1973, *10*(4), pp. 397–418. [G: U.K.]

Jones, Ken. Employee Directors in Steel. In *Tivey, L., ed.,* 1973, pp. 298–302. [G: U.K.]

Joskow, Paul L. and McKelvey, Edward F. The Fogel-Engerman Iron Model: A Clarifying Note. *J. Polit. Econ.,* September-October 1973, *81*(5), pp. 1236–40.

Nelson, Jon P. An Interregional Recursive Programming Model of the U.S. Iron and Steel Industry. In *Judge, G. G. and Takayama, T., eds.,* 1973, pp. 368–93. [G: U.S.]

Seifer, Daniel M. Foreign Steel and U.S. Jobs, Trade, Environment, and Safety. *Ohio State U. Bull. Bus. Res.,* March 1973, *48*(3), pp. 4–7. [G: U.S.]

Sláma, Jiří and Vogel, Heinrich. Zur Verbreitung neuer Technologien in der UdSSR—eine Fallstudie: das Oxygenblasstahlverfahren. (Diffusion of New Technologies in the USSR—the Case of Oxygene-Steel. With English summary.) *Jahr. Nationalökon. Statist.,* March 1973, *187*(3), pp. 245–61. [G: U.S.S.R.]

6313 Machinery (tools, electrical equipment, and appliances)

Artus, Jacques R. The Short-Run Effects of Domestic Demand Pressure on Export Delivery Delays for Machinery. *J. Int. Econ.,* February 1973, *3*(1), pp. 21–36. [G: U.S.; U.K.; W. Germany]

Barber, Clarence L. The Farm Machinery Industry: Reconciling the Interests of the Farmer, the Industry, and the General Public. *Amer. J. Agr. Econ.,* December 1973, *55*(5), pp. 820–28.
[G: Canada]

Barlow, Joel. The Tax Law Bias Against Investment in Production Facilities. *Nat. Tax J.,* September 1973, *26*(3), pp. 415–37. [G: U.S.]

Emery, E. David. Regulated Utilities and Equipment Manufacturers' Conspiracies in the Electrical Power Industry. *Bell J. Econ. Manage. Sci.,* Spring 1973, *4*(1), pp. 322–37. [G: U.S.]

Gregory, R. G. and Tearle, D. Product Differentiation and International Trade Flows: An Application of the "Hedonic" Regression Technique. *Australian Econ. Pap.,* June 1973, *12*(20), pp. 79–90. [G: Australia]

Joshi, Nandini U. Bank Credit Policy for Export Incentives. *Indian Econ. J.,* April-June 1973, *20* (4–5), pp. 638–45. [G: India]

Leue, G. Transformation of Technical Forecasts into Market Predictions for the Computer Industry. In *Blohm, H. and Steinbuch, K., eds.,* 1973, pp. 73–78. [G: W. Germany]

Mansfield, Edwin. Determinants of the Speed of Application of New Technology. In *Williams, B. R., ed.,* 1973, pp. 199–216. [G: U.S.]

Mares, Miroslav and Hrbek, Antonín. Prognostické ekonometrické modely strojírenstvi. (Prognostic Econometric Models of Machine Industry. With English summary.) *Ekon.-Mat. Obzor,* 1973, *9*(3), pp. 241–59. [G: Czechoslovakia]

Novara, Francesco. Job Enrichment in the Olivetti Company. *Int. Lab. Rev.,* October 1973, *108*(4), pp. 283–94. [G: Italy]

Schlissel, Martin R. Promotional Strategy in a High-

Technology Industry. *J. Econ. Bus.*, Fall 1973, *26* (1), pp. 67–73. [G: U.S.]

Smith, R. J. Medium-Term Forecasts Reassessed: IV. Domestic Appliances. *Nat. Inst. Econ. Rev.*, May 1973, (64), pp. 68–83. [G: U.K.]

Sood, James H. The Computer Manufacturing Industry and the U.S. Balance of Payments. *Calif. Manage. Rev.*, Winter 1973, *16*(2), pp. 37–43. [G: U.S.]

Sultan, Ralph. Product Line Pricing and Technological Change: The Case of Sophisticated Electrical Machinery. In *Weston, J. F. and Ornstein, S. I., eds.*, 1973, pp. 163–79. [G: U.S.]

6314 Transportation and Communication Equipment

Ahern, William R., Jr. Health Effects of Automotive Air Pollution. In *Jacoby, H. D., et al.*, 1973, pp. 139–74. [G: U.S.]

Ahern, William R., Jr. Measuring the Value of Emissions Reductions. In *Jacoby, H. D., et al.*, 1973, pp. 175–205. [G: U.S.]

Appleman, Jack M. Testing and Maintenance of In-Use Vehicles. In *Jacoby, H. D., et al.*, 1973, pp. 113–37. [G: U.S.]

Barksdale, Hiram C. and Guffey, Hugh J., Jr. A Cross-Spectral Analysis of Motor Vehicle Sales and Registrations. *Swedish J. Econ.*, September 1973, *75*(3), pp. 266–77. [G: U.S.]

Ellison, A. P. and Stafford, E. M. The Order Delivery Lag in the World's Civil Aircraft Industry. *Appl. Econ.*, March 1973, *5*(1), pp. 19–34.

George, P. J. and Oksanen, Ernest H. Saturation in the Automobile Market in the Late Twenties: Some Further Results. *Exploration Econ. Hist.*, Fall 1973, *11*(1), pp. 73–85. [G: U.S.]

Gibson, Charles H. Volvo Increases Productivity Through Job Enrichment. *Calif. Manage. Rev.*, Summer 1973, *15*(4), pp. 64–66. [G: Sweden]

Jacoby, Henry D. and Steinbruner, John D. Salvaging the Federal Attempt to Control Auto Pollution. *Public Policy*, Winter 1973, *21*(1), pp. 1–48. [G: U.S.]

Jacoby, Henry D. and Steinbruner, John D. Advanced Technology and the Problem of Implementation. In *Jacoby, H. D., et al.*, 1973, pp. 49–61. [G: U.S.]

Jacoby, Henry D. and Steinbruner, John D. Policy Analysis and the Public Sector. In *Jacoby, H. D., et al.*, 1973, pp. 1–8. [G: U.S.]

Jacoby, Henry D. and Steinbruner, John D. Policy Options and Predicted Outcomes. In *Jacoby, H. D., et al.*, 1973, pp. 27–47. [G: U.S.]

Jacoby, Henry D. and Steinbruner, John D. The Context of Current Policy Discussions. In *Jacoby, H. D., et al.*, 1973, pp. 9–26. [G: U.S.]

Kressler, Peter R. Investment Barriers Facing the United States Automotive Industry in the Japanese Market. *Ohio State U. Bull. Bus. Res.*, September 1973, *48*(9), pp. 1–3. [G: U.S.; Japan]

Lanzillotti, Robert F. and Blair, Roger D. Automobile Pollution, Externalities and Public Policy. *Antitrust Bull.*, Fall, 1973, *18*(3), pp. 431–47. [G: U.S.]

Lovell, C. A. Knox. Homotheticity and the Average

Cost Function. *Western Econ. J.*, December 1973, *11*(4), pp. 506–13. [G: U.S.]

Marfels, Christian. Relevant Market and Concentration: The Case of the U.S. Automobile Industry. *Jahr. Nationalökon. Statist.*, March 1973, *187*(3), pp. 209–17. [G: U.S.]

McGee, John S. Economies of Size in Auto Body Manufacture. *J. Law Econ.*, October 1973, *16*(2), pp. 239–73. [G: U.S.; W. Europe]

Nibale, Gianfranco. Distribuzione automobilistica e dimensione d'impresa. (Automobile Distribution and Business Size. With English summary.) *Rivista Int. Sci. Econ. Com.*, October 1973, *20* (10), pp. 1013–24. [G: U.S.]

Perline, Martin M. and Presley, Ronald W. Mobility of Unemployed Engineers: A Case Study. *Mon. Lab. Rev.*, May 1973, *96*(5), pp. 41–43. [G: U.S.]

Reinhardt, U. E. Break-Even Analysis for Lockheed's Tri Star: An Application of Financial Theory. *J. Finance*, September 1973, *28*(4), pp. 821–38. [G: U.S.]

Remes Lenicov, Jorge L. Algunos resultados de la política desarrollista (1958–64): el caso de la industria automotriz. (Some Results of the Development Policy 1958–64; the Case of the Automobile Industry. With English summary.) *Económica*, September-December 1973, *19*(3), pp. 293–329. [G: Argentina]

di Ruffia, Rodolfo B. Situation and Prospects of the Motor Industry in Italy. *Rev. Econ. Cond. Italy*, January-March 1973, *27*(1–2), pp. 43–52. [G: Italy]

Selander, Stephen E. Is Annual Style Change in the Automobile Industry an Unfair Method of Competition? A Rebuttal. *Yale Law J.*, March 1973, *82* (4), pp. 691–710.

Smith, P. Seasonal Fluctuations in the Motor Vehicle Industry: A Comment. *J. Ind. Econ.*, April 1973, *21*(2), pp. 184–86. [G: U.K.]

Snell, Bradford C. Is Annual Style Change in the Automobile Industry an Unfair Method of Competition? A Reply. *Yale Law J.*, March 1973, *82*(4), pp. 711–14.

Vinod, H. D. Interregional Comparison of Production Structures. *J. Reg. Sci.*, August 1973, *13*(2), pp. 261–67. [G: U.S.]

Weinstein, Milton C. and Clark, Ian D. Emissions Measurement and the Testing of New Vehicles. In *Jacoby, H. D., et al.*, 1973, pp. 63–111. [G: U.S.]

6315 Chemicals, Drugs, Plastics, Ceramics, Glass, and Rubber

Angilley, Alan S. Returns to Scale in Research in the Ethical Pharmaceutical Industry: Some Further Empirical Evidence. *J. Ind. Econ.*, December 1973, *22*(2), pp. 81–93. [G: U.K.]

Ayob, Ahmad Mahzan and Prato, Anthony A. United States Import Demand and Prices of Natural Rubber. *Malayan Econ. Rev.*, April 1973, *18*(1), pp. 24–35. [G: U.S.]

Bradbury, F. R. Changes in the Chemical Industry. In *Edge, D. O. and Wolfe, J. N., eds.*, 1973, pp. 181–95. [G: U.K.]

Clark, Peter B.; Foxley, Alejandro and Jul, Anna

Maria. Project Evaluation within a Macroeconomic Framework. In *Eckaus, R. S. and Rosenstein-Rodan, P. N., eds.*, 1973, pp. 199–226. [G: Chile]

Duetsch, Larry L. Research Performance in the Ethical Drug Industry. *Marquette Bus. Rev.*, Fall 1973, *17*(3), pp. 129–43.

Finke, Jeffrey. Nitrogen Fertilizer: Price Levels and Sales in Illinois, 1945–1971. *Ill. Agr. Econ.*, January 1973, *13*(1), pp. 34–40. [G: U.S.]

Hale, Rosemary D. Cement Mergers—Market Dispersion and Conglomerate Entry. *Marquette Bus. Rev.*, Summer 1973, *17*(2), pp. 98–108. [G: U.S.]

Levhari, David and Sheshinski, Eytan. Experience and Productivity in the Israel Diamond Industry. *Econometrica*, March 1973, *41*(2), pp. 239–53. [G: Israel]

Metwally, Mohktar M. Economic Strategies of Firms Facing Asymptotic Demand: A Case Study. *Appl. Econ.*, December 1973, *5*(4), pp. 271–80. [G: Australia]

Moretti, Giovanni. The Italian Plastic Materials Industry. *Rev. Econ. Cond. Italy*, May 1973, *27*(3), pp. 162–77. [G: Italy]

Peltzman, Sam. An Evaluation of Consumer Protection Legislation: The 1962 Drug Amendments. *J. Polit. Econ.*, September-October 1973, *81*(5), pp. 1049–91. [G: U.S.]

Swan, Philip L. The International Diffusion of an Innovation. *J. Ind. Econ.*, September 1973, *22*(1), pp. 61–69.

Tsurumi, Hiroki and Tsurumi, Yoshi. An Econometric Model of a Japanese Pharmaceutical Company. In *Palda, K. S., ed.*, 1973, pp. 290–315. [G: Japan]

Tsurumi, Hiroki. A Comparison of Alternative Optimal Models of Advertising Expenditures: Stock Adjustment vs. Control Theoretic Approaches. *Rev. Econ. Statist.*, May 1973, *55*(2), pp. 156–68. [G: Japan]

6316 Textiles, Leather, and Clothing

Ahmad, Qazi Kholiquzzaman. A Note on Capacity Utilization in the Jute Manufacturing Industry of Bangladesh. *Bangladesh Econ. Rev.*, January 1973, *1*(1), pp. 103–14. [G: Bangladesh]

Aujac, H. A New Approach to Technological Forecasting in French National Planning. In *Williams, B. R., ed.*, 1973, pp. 96–115. [G: France]

Bellani, Felice F. Medium-Term Evolution of the Italian Cotton Industry. *Rev. Econ. Cond. Italy*, September 1973, *27*(5), pp. 313–25. [G: Italy]

Brandis, R. Buford. The National Need for an Integrated Trade Policy: The Textile Example. In *Iowa State University Center for Agricultural and Rural Development*, 1973, pp. 155–65. [G: U.S.]

Bush, Joseph C. Pay Increases in Footwear Lag Behind Other Industries. *Mon. Lab. Rev.*, June 1973, *96*(6), pp. 57–58. [G: U.S.]

Doyle, Philip M. Wages in Dress Manufacturing Vary Widely by Area. *Mon. Lab. Rev.*, March 1973, *96*(3), pp. 57–58. [G: U.S.]

Fløystad, Gunnar. The Impact on Allocation and Return to Labor and Capital of a Reduction of Customs Duties in the Developed Countries in Their Trade with Less Developed Countries. *Welt-wirtsch. Arch.*, 1973, *109*(1), pp. 59–69. [G: Norway]

Isard, Peter. Employment Impacts of Textile Imports and Investment: A Vintage-Capital Model. *Amer. Econ. Rev.*, June 1973, *63*(3), pp. 402–16. [G: U.S.]

Martelli, Antonio. Transformazioni tecnologiche nell'industria tessile: implicazioni economiche e sociali. (Technological Changes in the Textile Industry: Economical and Social Implications. With English summary.) *L'Impresa*, 1973, *15*(7–8), pp. 434–38.

Mazumdar, D. Labour Supply in Early Industrialization: the Case of the Bombay Textile Industry. *Econ. Hist. Rev.*, 2nd Ser., August 1973, *26*(3), pp. 477–96. [G: India]

McFetridge, Donald G. The Determinants of Pricing Behaviour: A Study of the Canadian Cotton Textile Industry. *J. Ind. Econ.*, December 1973, *22*(2), pp. 141–52. [G: Canada]

Nayyar, Deepak. An Analysis of the Stagnation in India's Cotton Textile Exports During the Sixties. *Oxford Bull. Econ. Statist.*, February 1973, *35*(1), pp. 1–19. [G: India]

Oțoiu, Alexandrina. Probleme ale calculației prețului de cost în industria de încălțăminte. (Problems of the Calculation of the Cost Price in the Footwear Industry. With English summary.) *Stud. Cercet. Econ.*, 1973, (3), pp. 121–39. [G: Rumania]

Paraskevopoulos, Christos C. Shifts in Industry Employment, Population Size and the Wage Structure: An Analysis of Two National Industries. In *Mattila, J. M. and Thompson, W. R., eds.*, 1973, pp. 105–25. [G: U.S.]

Ridzon, Donald S. Occupational Pay in Shirt Manufacturing. *Mon. Lab. Rev.*, January 1973, *96*(1), pp. 60–61. [G: U.S.]

Stanciu, Ion E. Eficiența economică a diversificării produselor textile. (The Economic Efficiency of the Diversification of Textile Products. With English summary.) *Stud. Cercet. Econ.*, 1973, (4), pp. 141–48. [G: Rumania]

Ursachi, I. Probleme ale planificării productivității muncii în întreprinderile industriei textile. (Problems of the Planning of Labour Productivity in the Enterprises of the Textile Industry. With English summary.) *Stud. Cercet. Econ.*, 1973, (3), pp. 41–50. [G: Rumania]

Zeisel, Rose N. Modernization and Manpower in Textile Mills. *Mon. Lab. Rev.*, June 1973, *96*(6), pp. 18–25. [G: U.S.]

6317 Forest Products, Building Materials, and Paper

Apsey, T. M.; Garton, M. M. and Hajdu, C. Economic Trends in the Canadian Forest Products Industry. *Amer. J. Agr. Econ.*, December 1973, *55*(5), pp. 974–82. [G: Canada]

Damachi, Ukandi G. Industrial Relations in the Sapele Timber Industry: The Development of Collective Bargaining. In *Damachi, U. G. and Seibel, H. D., eds.*, 1973, pp. 98–118. [G: Nigeria]

Davis, Lawrence S.; Thompson, Emmett F. and Richards, Douglas F. The South's Third Forest: A Critique. *Land Econ.*, February 1973, *49*(1), pp. 105–09. [G: U.S.]

Day, C. L. Changes in Rates of Return: A Cross-Section Study. *Oxford Bull. Econ. Statist.*, May 1973, *35*(2), pp. 135–52. [G: U.K.]

Diaz-Alejandro, Carlos. Labour Productivity and Other Characteristics of Cement Plants—An International Comparison. In *[Rosenstein-Rodan, P.]*, 1973, pp. 283–315. [G: Latin America]

Ferguson, Ian S. Forecasting the Future for Timber. *Australian J. Agr. Econ.*, December 1973, *17*(3), pp. 159–69. [G: Australia]

Gamache, Adrian E. The Influence of U.S. Trade Policy on Forest Products Trade. *Amer. J. Agr. Econ.*, December 1973, *55*(5), pp. 983–88. [G: U.S.]

Granata, Dale. Survey Highlights Occupational Pay Differences in Furniture Industry. *Mon. Lab. Rev.*, June 1973, *96*(6), pp. 58–60. [G: U.S.]

Herman, Arthur S. Productivity in the Paints and Allied Products Industry. *Mon. Lab. Rev.*, November 1973, *96*(11), pp. 10–13. [G: U.S.]

Holland, I. Irving. Implications of the 1970 Timber Review for Trade in Timber Products. *Amer. J. Agr. Econ.*, December 1973, *55*(5), pp. 967–73. [G: U.S.]

Moruzzi, Paolo. Situation and Prospects of the Furniture Industry in Italy. *Rev. Econ. Cond. Italy*, September 1973, *27*(5), pp. 326–35. [G: Italy]

Nabseth, Lars. The Diffusion of Innovations in Swedish Industry. In *Williams, B. R., ed.*, 1973, pp. 256–80. [G: Sweden]

Robinowitz, Robert S. and Riche, Martha F. Productivity in the Ready-Mixed Concrete Industry. *Mon. Lab. Rev.*, May 1973, *96*(5), pp. 12–15. [G: U.S.]

Snooks, G. D. The Growth Process of the Firm: A Case Study. *Australian Econ. Pap.*, December 1973, *12*(21), pp. 162–74. [G: Australia]

6318 Food Processing (excluding agribusiness), Tobacco, and Beverages

Atkinson, A. B. and Skegg, J. L. Anti-Smoking Publicity and the Demand for Tobacco in the U.K. *Manchester Sch. Econ. Soc. Stud.*, September 1973, *41*(3), pp. 265–82. [G: U.K.]

Doyle, Philip M. Wages and Productivity Rise in Flour Mills as Employment Declines. *Mon. Lab. Rev.*, October 1973, *96*(10), pp. 51–52. [G: U.S.]

Engwall, Lars. Business Behavior: The Cigarette Case. *Marquette Bus. Rev.*, Summer 1973, *17*(2), pp. 59–72. [G: U.S.]

Farris, Paul L. Changes in Number and Size Distribution of U.S. Soybean Processing Firms. *Amer. J. Agr. Econ.*, August 1973, *55*(3), pp. 495–99. [G: U.S.]

Greer, Douglas F. Some Case History Evidence on the Advertising-Concentration Relationship. *Antitrust Bull.*, Summer 1973, *18*(2), pp. 307–32. [G: U.S.]

Gruebele, J. W. Measures of Efficiency in Milk Plant Operations. *Ill. Agr. Econ.*, July 1973, *13*(2), pp. 38–43. [G: U.S.]

Leung, David T. W. The Concept of Effective Subsidy and its Application to the Canadian Flour Milling Industry. *Can. J. Agr. Econ.*, February 1973, *21*(1), pp. 1–9. [G: Canada]

Leunis, J. V. and Vandenborre, R. J. An Interregional Analysis of the United States Soybean Industry. In *Judge, G. G. and Takayama, T., eds.*, 1973, pp. 274–97. [G: U.S.]

Mann, Jitendar S. A Dynamic Model of the U.S. Tobacco Economy. *Agr. Econ. Res.*, July 1973, *25*(3), pp. 81–92. [G: U.S.]

Metwally, Mokhtar M. Economies of Size in Butter Production: The New Zealand Experience. *Econ. Anal. Pol.*, March 1973, *4*(1), pp. 33–44. [G: New Zealand]

Michetti, Ambrogio. The Mineral Water and Spa Industry in Italy. *Rev. Econ. Cond. Italy*, November 1973, *27*(6), pp. 410–20. [G: Italy]

Ridzon, Donald S. Wages and Productivity Rise as Employment Falls in Cigar Plants. *Mon. Lab. Rev.*, June 1973, *96*(6), pp. 56–57. [G: U.S.]

Scanlon, Paul D. Oligopoly and Deceptive Advertising: The Cereal Industry Affair. In *Murray, B. B., ed.*, 1973, pp. 125–34.

Schnabel, Morton. A Model of Cigarette Advertising. *Antitrust Bull.*, Spring 1973, *18*(1), pp. 33–43. [G: U.S.]

632 Industry Studies: Extractive Industries

6320 General

Akins, James E. International Cooperative Efforts in Energy Supply. *Ann. Amer. Acad. Polit. Soc. Sci.*, November 1973, *410*, pp. 75–85.

Aspin, Les. A Solution to the Energy Crisis: The Case for Increased Competition. *Ann. Amer. Acad. Polit. Soc. Sci.*, November 1973, *410*, pp. 154–68. [G: U.S.]

Bailey, Richard. Britain and a Community Energy Policy. *Nat. Westminster Bank Quart. Rev.*, November 1973, pp. 5–15. [G: U.K.; E.E.C.]

Blainey, Geoffrey. A Theory of Mineral Discovery: A Rejoinder. *Econ. Hist. Rev.*, 2nd Ser., August 1973, *26*(3), pp. 506–09. [G: Australia]

Gehman, Clayton. U.S. Energy Supplies and Uses. *Fed. Res. Bull.*, December 1973, *59*(12), pp. 847–70A. [G: U.S.]

Kähr, Walter. Die Entwicklung des Energieverbrauchs der Schweiz im Zeitraum 1950 bis 1970 und Vorschau auf das Jahr 2000. (The Development of the Energy Consumption in the Period 1950–1970, with a Forecast for the Year 2000. With English summary.) *Schweiz. Z. Volkswirtsch. Statist.*, September 1973, *109*(3), pp. 385–410. [G: Switzerland]

McGee, Dean A. Assessing the "Energy Crisis"—Problems and Prospects. *Fed. Res. Bank Kansas City Rev.*, September-October 1973, pp. 14–20. [G: U.S.]

Morissey, M. J. and Burt, R. A Theory of Mineral Discovery: A Note. *Econ. Hist. Rev.*, 2nd Ser., August 1973, *26*(3), pp. 497–505. [G: Australia]

Nordhaus, William D. The Allocation of Energy Resources. *Brookings Pap. Econ. Act.*, 1973, (3), pp. 529–70. [G: U.S.]

Schwartzman, David. The Cost-Elasticity of Demand and Industry Boundaries: Coal, Oil, Gas, and Uranium. *Antitrust Bull.*, Fall, 1973, *18*(3), pp. 483–507. [G: U.S.]

Swidler, Joseph C. The Challenge to State Regulation Agencies: The Experience of New York State. *Ann. Amer. Acad. Polit. Soc. Sci.*, November 1973, *410*, pp. 106–19. [G: U.S.]

6322 Mining (metal, coal, and other nonmetallic minerals)

Arrate, Jorge. The Nationalization of Copper. In *Zammit, J. A., ed.*, 1973, pp. 145–50. [G: Chile]

Barnsby, G. J. The Standard of Living in the Black Country in the Nineteenth Century: A Rejoinder. *Econ. Hist. Rev., 2nd Ser.*, August 1973, *26*(3), pp. 514–16. [G: U.K.]

Christenson, C. L. and Andrews, W. H. Coal Mine Injury Rates in Two Eras of Federal Control. *J. Econ. Issues*, March 1973, *7*(1), pp. 61–82. [G: U.S.]

Day, Richard H. and Nelson, Jon P. A Class of Dynamic Models for Describing and Projecting Industrial Development. *J. Econometrics*, June 1973, *1*(2), pp. 155–90. [G: U.S.; Japan]

Fenske, G. A. and Main, T. R. N. Labour and the Gold Mines. *S. Afr. J. Econ.*, September 1973, *41*(3), pp. 298–304. [G: S. Africa]

Gedicks, Al. The Nationalization of Copper in Chile: Antecedents and Consequences. *Rev. Radical Polit. Econ.*, Fall 1973, *5*(3), pp. 1–25. [G: Chile]

Graebner, William. The Coal-Mine Operator and Safety: A Study of Business Reform in the Progressive Period. *Labor Hist.*, Fall 1973, *14*(4), pp. 483–505. [G: U.S.]

Gregory, K. and Russell, C. SIMPREP, A Computer Model for Coal Preparation. In *Ross, M., ed.*, 1973, pp. 379–89. [G: U.K.]

Griffin, Colin P. The Standard of Living in the Black Country in the Nineteenth Century: A Comment. *Econ. Hist. Rev., 2nd Ser.*, August 1973, *26*(3), pp. 510–13. [G: U.K.]

Harvey, Charles. International Corporations and Economic Independence: A View from Zambia. In *Ghai, D., ed.*, 1973, pp. 176–89. [G: Zambia]

Hawes, D. M. Operational Gaming in the Planning of the Geologically Troubled Colliery. In *Ross, M., ed.*, 1973, pp. 405–16. [G: U.K.]

Henry, John P., Jr. and Schmidt, Richard A. Coal: Still Old Reliable? *Ann. Amer. Acad. Polit. Soc. Sci.*, November 1973, *410*, pp. 35–51. [G: U.S.]

Horn, Carl E. Practical Economics of Public Utility Regulation: An Application to Pipelines: Comment. In *Russell, M., ed.*, 1973, pp. 47–51. [G: U.S.]

Lim, David. A Note on Supply Response of Tin Producers, 1949–1969. *Malayan Econ. Rev.*, October 1973, *18*(2), pp. 50–59.

Müller-Oehring, H. Determining the Coal Wagon Requirements in the Rhenish Lignite Mines. In *Ross, M., ed.*, 1973, pp. 391–404. [G: W. Germany]

Murry, Donald A. Practical Economics of Public Utility Regulation: An Application to Pipelines. In *Russell, M., ed.*, 1973, pp. 35–47. [G: U.S.]

Ratcliffe, Anne E. Labour in the South African Gold Mines. (Review article). *S. Afr. J. Econ.*, September 1973, *41*(3), pp. 257–67. [G: S. Africa]

Roberts, C. A. Reorganization of the National Coal Board. In *Tivey, L., ed.*, 1973, pp. 242–48. [G: U.K.]

Vedovato, Giuseppe. Situation and Prospects of the Italian Extractive Industry. *Rev. Econ. Cond. Italy*, July 1973, *27*(4), pp. 225–35. [G: Italy]

Wilson, I. H.; Robertson, B. C. and Ellis, P. L. Rock Phosphate Mining in North West Queensland—A Cost-Benefit Analysis. *Econ. Anal. Pol.*, March 1973, *4*(1), pp. 23–32. [G: Australia]

6323 Oil, Gas, and Other Fuels

Akins, James E. The Oil Crisis: This Time the Wolf Is Here. *Foreign Aff.*, April 1973, *51*(3), pp. 462–90.

Amuzegar, Jahangir. The Oil Story: Facts, Fiction and Fair Play. *Foreign Aff.*, July 1973, *51*(4), pp. 676–89.

Arthur, W. Brian. The Elasticity of Demand for Petrol in Ireland: Comment. *Econ. Soc. Rev.*, October 1973, *5*(1), pp. 105–10. [G: Ireland]

Atwood, Janet. Energy Resources in New Mexico. *N. Mex. Bus.*, May 1973, *26*(5), pp. 3–10. [G: U.S.]

Bataillie, M. Naar een nieuwe petroleumcrisis? (Towards a New Oil Crisis? With English summary.) *Econ. Soc. Tijdschr.*, April 1973, *27*(2), pp. 129–40.

Bradley, Paul G. Increasing Scarcity: The Case of Energy Resources. *Amer. Econ. Rev.*, May 1973, *63*(2), pp. 119–25.

Burke, William. Oil From the Artic. *Fed. Res. Bank San Francisco Rev.*, September-October 1973, pp. 13–21. [G: U.S.]

Cicchetti, Charles J. and Freeman, A. Myrick, III. The Trans-Alaska Pipeline: An Economic Analysis of Alternatives. In *Enthoven, A. C. and Freeman, A. M., III, eds.*, 1973, pp. 271–84. [G: U.S.]

Cicchetti, Charles J. and Gillen, William J. The Mandatory Oil Import Quota Program: A Consideration of Economic Efficiency and Equity. *Natural Res. J.*, July 1973, *13*(3), pp. 399–430. [G: U.S.]

Dixon, Donald F. Economic Effects of Exclusive Dealing and Ownership Control: The U.K. Petrol Case Revisited. *Antitrust Bull.*, Summer 1973, *18*(2), pp. 375–90. [G: U.K.]

Eslami, M. The World Energy Crisis and Iranian Strategy. *Tahq. Eq.*, Winter & Spring 1973, *10*(29 & 30), pp. 17–49. [G: Iran]

Evan, Harry Zvi. Comparing Conditions of Work by Collective Agreement Analysis: A Case Study of the Petroleum Industry. *Int. Lab. Rev.*, July 1973, *108*(1), pp. 59–75.

Frank, Helmut J. and Schanz, John J., Jr. The Future of American Oil and Natural Gas. *Ann. Amer. Acad. Polit. Soc. Sci.*, November 1973, *410*, pp. 24–34. [G: U.S.]

Hamilton, Richard E. Canada's "Exportable Surplus" Natural Gas Policy: A Theoretical Analysis. *Land Econ.*, August 1973, *49*(3), pp. 251–59. [G: Canada]

MacAvoy, Paul W. and Pindyck, Robert S. Alternative Regulatory Policies for Dealing with the Natural Gas Shortage. *Bell J. Econ. Manage. Sci.*, Autumn 1973, *4*(2), pp. 454–98. [G: U.S.]

MacAvoy, Paul W. and Noll, Roger G. Relative Prices on Regulated Transactions of the Natural Gas Pipelines. *Bell J. Econ. Manage. Sci.*, Spring

1973, *4*(1), pp. 212–34. [G: U.S.]

Massetti, C. Les incertitudes quantitatives et qualitatives des prévisions du bilan et de l'approvisionnement énergétique européen: ses implications pour l'industrie pétrolière. (The Quantitative and Qualitative Uncertainties of Forecasting the European Energy Balance and Supply: Its Implications for the Mineral Oil Industry. With English summary.) *Schweiz. Z. Volkswirtsch. Statist.*, September 1973, *109*(3), pp. 411–20. [G: Europe]

Miller, Edward. Some Implications of Land Ownership Patterns for Petroleum Policy. *Land Econ.*, November 1973, *49*(4), pp. 414–23. [G: U.S.]

O'Riordan, W. K. Elasticity of Demand for Petrol in Ireland: Reply. *Econ. Soc. Rev.*, October 1973, *5* (1), pp. 111–12. [G: Ireland]

Personick, Martin E. Earnings Rise as Employment Dips in Petroleum and Gas. *Mon. Lab. Rev.*, August 1973, *96*(8), pp. 68–70. [G: U.S.]

Robinson, Colin and Crook, Elizabeth M. Is There a World Energy Crisis? *Nat. Westminster Bank Quart. Rev.*, May 1973, pp. 46–60.

Schurr, Samuel. Minerals Trade and International Relations. In *Bergsten, C. F., ed.*, 1973, pp. 181–96.

Tybout, Richard A. Prices, Costs, and the Energy Crisis. *Ohio State U. Bull. Bus. Res.*, June 1973, *48*(6), pp. 4–8. [G: U.S.]

Wilson, Carroll L. A Plan for Energy Independence. *Foreign Aff.*, July 1973, *51*(4), pp. 657–75. [G: U.S.]

633 Industry Studies: Distributive Trades

6330 General

Dacey, Michael F. A Central Focus Cluster Process for Urban Dispersion. *J. Reg. Sci.*, April 1973, *13* (1), pp. 77–89.

Fog, Bjarke. A Danish Study of the Distribution Process. *L'Impresa*, 1973, *15*(1), pp. 59–64. [G: Denmark]

Patrucco, Carlo. Dimensione sociale del fenomeno distributivo commerciale. (The Social Dimensions of the Distributive Phenomenon. With English summary.) *L'Impresa*, 1973, *15*(1), pp. 24–26.

Ravazzi, Giancarlo. La conoscenza come fattore di razionalizzazione del sistema distributivo-commerciale. (Knowledge As a Factor of Rationalization of the Distributive System. With English summary.) *L'Impresa*, 1973, *15*(1), pp. 12–19.

Soldi, Costantino. Ricerche economiche. (Economic Research. With English summary.) *L'Impresa*, 1973, *15*(1), pp. 32–36.

Vergnano, Franco. La conoscenza di base: ricerche strutturali e funzionali. (The Basic Knowledge: Structural and Functional Research. With English summary.) *L'Impresa*, 1973, *15*(1), pp. 28–32.

6332 Wholesale Trade

Cassady, Ralph, Jr. and Barker, F. David. Price Formation and Decision-Making in Covent Garden Market, London. *Calif. Manage. Rev.*, Fall 1973, *16*(1), pp. 86–94. [G: U.K.]

David, Michel. I dodici tratti caratteristici dell'iper-

mercato alla francese. (Twelve Characteristics of the French Hypermarket. With English summary.) *L'Impresa*, 1973, *15*(9–10), pp. 634–39. [G: France]

Ikeda, Y. Distribution Innovation in Japan and the Role Played by General Trading Companies. In *Thorelli, H. B., ed.*, 1973, pp. 237–43. [G: Japan]

Lisandru, N. Necesitatea verigii comerciale cu ridicata în organizarea circulaţiei mărfurilor. (The Necessity of a Wholesale Trade Link in Organizing the Circulation of Goods. With English summary.) *Stud. Cercet. Econ.*, 1973, (1), pp. 133–39.

6333 Retail Trade

Allen, Tom C. and Duvall, Richard M. Determinants of Property Loss Ratios in The Retail Industry. *J. Risk Ins.*, June 1973, *40*(2), pp. 181–90. [G: U.S.]

Anderson, Dole A. Public Policy Toward Retailing: Thailand. In *Boddewyn, J. J. and Hollander, S. C., eds.*, 1972, pp. 297–310. [G: Thailand]

Bartlett, Roland W. Are Supermarkets Charging Consumers Too Much for Handling Milk? *Ill. Agr. Econ.*, July 1973, *13*(2), pp. 1–5. [G: U.S.]

Boddewyn, J. J. Public Policy Toward Retailing: Belgium. In *Boddewyn, J. J. and Hollander, S. C., eds.*, 1972, pp. 37–62. [G: Belgium]

Boddewyn, J. J. and Hollander, Stanley C. Public Policy Toward Retailing: Introduction. In *Boddewyn, J. J. and Hollander, S. C., eds.*, 1972, pp. 1–9.

Boddewyn, J. J. and Hollander, Stanley C. Public Policy Toward Retailing: Conclusions. In *Boddewyn, J. J. and Hollander, S. C., eds.*, 1972, pp. 431–52.

Bogart, Leo. The Future of Retailing. *Harvard Bus. Rev.*, November-December 1973, *51*(6), pp. 16–32, 176. [G: U.S.]

Cohen, Alain-Gérard. Tunisia: Reforming the Commercial Structure. In *Boddewyn, J. J. and Hollander, S. C., eds.*, 1972, pp. 311–25. [G: Tunisia]

Cortesse, Pierre. Public Policy Toward Retailing: France. In *Boddewyn, J. J. and Hollander, S. C., eds.*, 1972, pp. 117–43. [G: France]

Cottrell, James L. Forecasting in Multi-Outlet Businesses. *Manage. Account.*, April 1973, *54*(10), pp. 17–22, 30.

Curran, R. J. Public Policy Toward Retailing: Ireland. In *Boddewyn, J. J. and Hollander, S. C., eds.*, 1972, pp. 167–90. [G: Ireland]

Dixon, Donald F. Public Policy Toward Retailing: Australia. In *Boddewyn, J. J. and Hollander, S. C., eds.*, 1972, pp. 11–35. [G: Australia]

Donaldson, Loraine and Strangways, Raymond S. Can Ghetto Groceries Price Competitively and Make a Profit? *J. Bus.*, January 1973, *46*(1), pp. 61–65. [G: U.S.]

Douglas, Susan P. Public Planning of Retail Location in France and Great Britain. In *Boddewyn, J. J. and Hollander, S. C., eds.*, 1972, pp. 145–65. [G: France; U.K.]

Friedman, Judith J. Variations in the Level of Central Business District Retail Activity Among

Large U.S. Cities: 1954 and 1967. *Land Econ.,* August 1973, *49*(3), pp. 326–35. [G: U.S.]

George, Kenneth D. and Ward, Terry. Productivity Growth in the Retail Trade. *Oxford Bull. Econ. Statist.,* February 1973, *35*(1), pp. 31–47. [G: U.K.]

Goldman, Marshall I. Public Policy Toward Retailing: USSR. In *Boddewyn, J. J. and Hollander, S. C., eds.,* 1972, pp. 337–49. [G: U.S.S.R.]

Gruebele, J. W. and Miller, James J. Effects of the Use of Spot Cases in the Sale of Selected Dairy Products in Retail Food Chains. *Ill. Agr. Econ.,* July 1973, *13*(2), pp. 44–48. [G: U.S.]

Haccou, J. F. and Lübbers, P. J. M. Public Policy Toward Retailing: The Netherlands. In *Boddewyn, J. J. and Hollander, S. C., eds.,* 1972, pp. 245–70. [G: Netherlands]

Haines, George H., Jr.; Simon, Leonard S. and Alexis, Marcus. An Analysis of Central City Neighborhood Food Trading Areas: A Reply. *J. Reg. Sci.,* August 1973, *13*(2), pp. 301. [G: U.S.]

Hamburger, Polia Lerner. Public Policy Toward Retailing: Brazil. In *Boddewyn, J. J. and Hollander, S. C., eds.,* 1972, pp. 63–79. [G: Brazil]

Heeler, Roger M.; Kearney, Michael J. and Mehaffey, Bruce J. Modeling Supermarket Product Selection. *J. Marketing Res.,* February 1973, *10*(1), pp. 34–37.

Hellman, Daryl A. An Analysis of Central City Neighborhood Food Trading Areas: A Comment. *J. Reg. Sci.,* August 1973, *13*(2), pp. 299. [G: U.S.]

Hollander, Stanley C. Public Policy Toward Retailing: United States of America. In *Boddewyn, J. J. and Hollander, S. C., eds.,* 1972, pp. 367–403. [G: U.S.]

Hunt, Shelby D. Experimental Determinants of Franchisee Success. *J. Econ. Bus.,* Fall 1973, *26*(1), pp. 81–83. [G: U.S.]

Huxley, S. J. A Note on the Economics of Retail Trading Hours. *Econ. Anal. Pol.,* March 1973, *4*(1), pp. 17–22. [G: Australia]

Izraeli, Dov. Public Policy Toward Retailing: Israel. In *Boddewyn, J. J. and Hollander, S. C., eds.,* 1972, pp. 191–211. [G: Israel]

Jääskeläinen, Veikko and Kervinen, Esko. Designing Retail Outlets with Markov Chains and Mathematical Programming. *Liiketaloudellinen Aikak.,* 1973, *22*(2), pp. 83–93.

Kjaer-Hansen, Max. Revolution i konsumenternas varuförsörjning. (Revolution in Consumer Goods Supply. With English summary.) *Ekon. Samfundets Tidskr.,* January 1973, *26*(1), pp. 3–15.

Kunreuther, Howard. Why the Poor May Pay More for Food: Theoretical and Empirical Evidence. *J. Bus.,* July 1973, *46*(3), pp. 368–83. [G: U.S.]

Lamont, Douglas F. Public Policy Toward Retailing: Mexico. In *Boddewyn, J. J. and Hollander, S. C., eds.,* 1972, pp. 229–44. [G: Mexico]

Laumer, Helmut. Public Policy Toward Retailing: Uganda. In *Boddewyn, J. J. and Hollander, S. C., eds.,* 1972, pp. 327–36. [G: Uganda]

Lebédel, Claude. Public Policy Toward Retailing: East Germany. In *Boddewyn, J. J. and Hollander, S. C., eds.,* 1972, pp. 101–15. [G: E. Germany]

Lindblad, Sven and Hallencreutz, Ingrid. Public Policy Toward Retailing: Sweden. In *Boddewyn,*

J. J. and Hollander, S. C., eds., 1972, pp. 283–95. [G: Sweden]

MacKay, David B. A Spectral Analysis of the Frequency of Supermarket Visits. *J. Marketing Res.,* February 1973, *10*(1), pp. 84–90. [G: U.S.]

MacKay, David B. Spatial Measurement of Retail Store Demand. *J. Marketing Res.,* November 1973, *10*(4), pp. 447–53.

Mason, Joseph Barry and Mayer, Morris L. Insights into the Image Determinants of Fashion Specialty Outlets. *J. Bus. Res.,* Summer 1973, *1*(1), pp. 73–80. [G: U.S.]

Masson, Robert Tempest. Costs of Search and Racial Price Discrimination. *Western Econ. J.,* June 1973, *11*(2), pp. 167–86.

McClelland, W. G. Public Policy Toward Retailing: The United Kingdom. In *Boddewyn, J. J. and Hollander, S. C., eds.,* 1972, pp. 351–66. [G: U.K.]

Ofer, Gur. Returns to Scale in Retail Trade. *Rev. Income Wealth,* December 1973, *19*(4), pp. 363–84. [G: Israel]

Olshavsky, Richard W. Customer-Salesman Interaction in Appliance Retailing. *J. Marketing Res.,* May 1973, *10*(2), pp. 208–12.

Personick, Martin E. Meat Department Workers Register Top Wage Rates in Grocery Stores. *Mon. Lab. Rev.,* May 1973, *96*(5), pp. 47–49. [G: U.S.]

Primeaux, Walter J. Price Variability and Price Discrimination: A Case Study. *Marquette Bus. Rev.,* Spring 1973, *17*(1), pp. 25–29. [G: U.S.]

Robinson, R. V. F. and Hebden, J. The Influence of Price and Trading Stamps on Retail Petrol Sales. *J. Ind. Econ.,* September 1973, *22*(1), pp. 37–50. [G: U.K.]

Scanlon, Paul D. Oligopoly and Deceptive Advertising: The Cereal Industry Affair. In *Murray, B. B., ed.,* 1973, pp. 125–34.

Shafer, Ronald G. A Food Chain Recruits a Consumer Advocate to Shape Its Policies. In *Murray, B. B., ed.,* 1973, pp. 274–78. [G: U.S.]

Soldner, Helmut. Public Policy Toward Retailing: West Germany. In *Boddewyn, J. J. and Hollander, S. C., eds.,* 1972, pp. 405–29. [G: W. Germany]

Stabler, J. C. and Williams, P. R. The Changing Structure of the Central Place Hierarchy. *Land Econ.,* November 1973, *49*(4), pp. 454–58. [G: Canada]

Sturdivant, Frederick D. and Wilhelm, Walter T. Poverty, Minorities, and Consumer Exploitation. In *Murray, B. B., ed.,* 1973, pp. 447–54. [G: U.S.]

Thomas, Brian. The Structure of Retailing and Economies of Scale. *Bull. Econ. Res.,* November 1973, *25*(2), pp. 122–28. [G: U.K.]

Trivedi, P. K. Retail Inventory Investment Behaviour. *J. Econometrics,* March 1973, *1*(1), pp. 61–80. [G: U.K.]

Walters, J., Jr. Public Policy Toward Retailing: Poland. In *Boddewyn, J. J. and Hollander, S. C., eds.,* 1972, pp. 271–82. [G: Poland]

Wyckham, Robert G. and Stewart, Max D. Public Policy Toward Retailing: Canada. In *Boddewyn, J. J. and Hollander, S. C., eds.,* 1972, pp. 81–99. [G: Canada]

Yoshino, Michael Y. Japan: Rationalizing the Retail

Structure. In *Boddewyn, J. J. and Hollander, S. C.*, eds., 1972, pp. 213–27. [G: Japan]

634 Industry Studies: Construction

6340 Construction

Adams, Earl W., Jr. and Spiro, Michael H. Reducing the Lags in Government Spending: An Empirical Analysis of Highway Construction. *Public Finance*, 1973, 28(2), pp. 125–38. [G: U.S.]

Adams, Earl W., Jr. and Spiro, Michael H. Labor Force Adjustment in the Construction Trades. *J. Econ. Bus.*, Fall 1973, 26(1), pp. 78–80. [G: U.S.]

Ball, Robert. Labor and Materials Required for Highway Construction. *Mon. Lab. Rev.*, June 1973, 96(6), pp. 40–45. [G: U.S.]

Cohen, Jeffrey M. Accounting for Modular Housing Manufacturers. *Manage. Account.*, September 1973, 55(3), pp. 11–14.

Grebler, Leo. Growing Scale of Real Estate Firms and Projects. *Amer. Real Estate Urban Econ. Assoc. J.*, June 1973, 1(1), pp. 107–22.

Hodgins, Cyril D. and Tanner, J. Ernest. Forecasting Non-residential Building Construction. *Can. J. Econ.*, February 1973, 6(1), pp. 79–89. [G: Canada]

Huang, David S. Short-Run Instability in Single-Family Housing Starts. *J. Amer. Statist. Assoc.*, December 1973, 68(344), pp. 788–92. [G: U.S.]

Maurizi, Alex R. Minority Membership in Apprenticeship Programs in the Construction Trades: Reply. *Ind. Lab. Relat. Rev.*, October 1973, 27(1), pp. 100–102.

Miles, Barbara L. and Robinson, Thomas R. Residential Construction Boom, 1970–73. *Surv. Curr. Bus.*, May 1973, 53(5), pp. 14–22. [G: U.S.]

Robinowitz, Robert S. and Riche, Martha F. Productivity in the Ready-Mixed Concrete Industry. *Mon. Lab. Rev.*, May 1973, 96(5), pp. 12–15. [G: U.S.]

Sims, Christopher A. Efficiency in the Construction Industry. In *Pynoos, J.; Schafer, R. and Hartman, C. W.*, eds., 1973, pp. 329–42. [G: U.S.]

Stegman, Michael A. Reducing the Cost of New Construction. In *Pynoos, J.; Schafer, R. and Hartman, C. W.*, eds., 1973, pp. 372–75. [G: U.S.]

Strauss, George. Minority Membership in Apprenticeship Programs in the Construction Trades: Comment. *Ind. Lab. Relat. Rev.*, October 1973, 27(1), pp. 93–99.

Ujázy, Karol. An Analysis of the Situation in Capital Construction. *Czech. Econ. Digest.*, November 1973, (7), pp. 3–55. [G: Czechoslovakia]

635 Industry Studies: Services and Related Industries

6350 General

Denison, Edward F. The Shift to Services and the Rate of Productivity Change. *Surv. Curr. Bus.*, October 1973, 53(10), pp. 20–35. [G: U.S.]

Komarov, V. The Service Sphere and Its Structure. *Prob. Econ.*, July 1973, 16(3), pp. 3–21. [G: U.S.S.R.]

Nelson, Ralph L. Estimates of Balance Sheets and Income Statements of Foundations and Colleges and Universities. In *Goldsmith, R. W.*, ed., 1973, pp. 378–91. [G: U.S.]

Personick, Martin E. Shorter Workweeks Dampen Earnings Gains in Contract Cleaning Services. *Mon. Lab. Rev.*, March 1973, 96(3), pp. 53–55. [G: U.S.]

Rutgaizer, V. A Comprehensive Plan for the Development of the Service Sector. *Prob. Econ.*, September 1973, 16(5), pp. 41–59. [G: U.S.S.R.]

6352 Electrical, Communication, and Information Services

Allen, Howard P. Electric Utilities: Can They Meet Future Power Needs? *Ann. Amer. Acad. Polit. Soc. Sci.*, November 1973, 410, pp. 86–96. [G: U.S.]

Altman, Edward I. Predicting Railroad Bankruptcies in America. *Bell J. Econ. Manage. Sci.*, Spring 1973, 4(1), pp. 184–211. [G: U.S.]

Anderson, Kent P. Residential Demand for Electricity: Econometric Estimates for California and the United States. *J. Bus.*, October 1973, 46(4), pp. 526–53. [G: U.S.]

Artle, Roland and Averous, Christian P. The Telephone System as a Public Good: Static and Dynamic Aspects. *Bell J. Econ. Manage. Sci.*, Spring 1973, 4(1), pp. 89–100.

Audouin, Maurice. Application of Computers to Distribution in the Newspaper and Publishing Industries. In *The Diebold Group, Inc.*, 1973, pp. 314–24.

Bell, A. R. Industrial Electricity Consumption—An Example of an Intermediate Good. *J. Ind. Econ.*, April 1973, 21(2), pp. 95–109. [G: U.K.]

Besen, Stanley M. and Soligo, Ronald. The Economics of the Network-Affiliate Relationship in the Television Broadcasting Industry. *Amer. Econ. Rev.*, June 1973, 63(3), pp. 259–68.

Bower, Richard S. Market Changes in the Computer Services Industry. *Bell J. Econ. Manage. Sci.*, Autumn 1973, 4(2), pp. 539–90. [G: U.S.]

Brand, Horst. Productivity in Telephone Communications. *Mon. Lab. Rev.*, November 1973, 96(11), pp. 3–9. [G: U.S.]

Brans, J. P.; Leclercq, M. and Hansen, P. An Algorithm for Optimal Reloading of Pressurized Water Reactors. In *Ross, M.*, ed., 1973, pp. 417–28.

Burnham, John B. Societal Values in Power Generation. In *Dierkes, M. and Bauer, R. A.*, eds., 1973, pp. 260–70. [G: U.S.]

Christensen, Gary L. A View from the National Cable Television Association. In *Park, R. E.*, ed., 1973, pp. 15–18. [G: U.S.]

Collier, Roger J. Simulation of Computer Systems: An Introduction. *Manage. Account.*, May 1973, 54(11), pp. 45–47.

Comanor, William S. The View of an Academic Consultant. In *Park, R. E.*, ed., 1973, pp. 31–34. [G: U.S.]

Diebold, John. Computers in Publishing. In *The Diebold Group, Inc.,* 1973, pp. 298–309.

Dimling, John A., Jr. A View from the National Association of Broadcasters. In *Park, R. E., ed.,* 1973, pp. 19–29. [G: U.S.]

Doyle, Philip M. Wages of Telephone and Telegraph Workers Showed Rapid Rise. *Mon. Lab. Rev.,* September 1973, *96*(9), pp. 75–76.

Edwards, Ronald [Sir]. The Status Agreement in Electricity. In *Tivey, L., ed.,* 1973, pp. 284–98. [G: U.K.]

Emery, E. David. Regulated Utilities and Equipment Manufacturers' Conspiracies in the Electrical Power Industry. *Bell J. Econ. Manage. Sci.,* Spring 1973, *4*(1), pp. 322–37. [G: U.S.]

Fernández de la Garza, Guillermo; Manne, Alan S. and Valencia, José Alberto. Multi-Level Planning for Electric Power Projects. In *Goreux, L. M. and Manne, A. S., eds.,* 1973, pp. 197–231. [G: Mexico]

Forsyth, John D. and Laughhunn, D. J. Capital Rationing in the Face of Multiple Organizational Objectives. In *Cochrane, J. L. and Zeleny, M., eds.,* 1973, pp. 439–46.

Goddard, Haynes C. Analysis of Social Production Functions: The Public Library. *Public Finance Quart.,* April 1973, *1*(2), pp. 191–204. [G: U.S.]

Goodwin, Kenneth R. Another View from the Federal Communications Commission. In *Park, R. E., ed.,* 1973, pp. 43–56. [G: U.S.]

Harberger, Arnold C. Marginal Cost Pricing and Social Investment Criteria for Electricity Undertakings. In *Harberger, A. C.,* 1973, pp. 233–47.

Heine, Rolf. Simulation of a Computer-Controlled Conveyance System for Air Passengers' Luggage. In *Ross, M., ed.,* 1973, pp. 373–78. [G: W. Germany]

Herwitz, Paul S. Evaluation of Programmers. In *The Diebold Group, Inc.,* 1973, pp. 213–22.

Hochberg, Philip and Horowitz, Ira. Broadcasting and CATV: The Beauty and the Bane of Major College Football. *Law Contemp. Probl.,* Winter-Spring 1973, *38*(1), pp. 112–28. [G: U.S.]

Hollander, Gayle D. Handbook of Soviet Social Science Data: Communications. In *Mickiewicz, E., ed.,* 1973, pp. 175–96. [G: U.S.S.R.]

Hurst, David B. Constructing an Adaptive Strategy for a National Newspaper. In *Ross, M., ed.,* 1973, pp. 275–89. [G: U.K.]

Jackson, Raymond. Peak Load Pricing Model of an Electric Utility Using Pumped Storage. *Water Resources Res.,* June 1973, *9*(3), pp. 556–62.

Jensen, Daniel L. A Computer Experiment on Alternative Methods of Allocating Capacity Cost. *Quart. Rev. Econ. Bus.,* Summer 1973, *13*(2), pp. 21–31.

Johnson, Nicholas. Economic Analysis and Regulatory Decisions. In *Haveman, R. H. and Hamrin, R. D., eds.,* 1973, pp. 261–66. [G: U.S.]

Jones, Malcolm M. The FCC Inquiry and the Data Communications User. In *The Diebold Group, Inc.,* 1973, pp. 233–38. [G: U.S.]

Kerton, Robert R. Price Effects of Market Power in the Canadian Newspaper Industry. *Can. J. Econ.,* November 1973, *6*(4), pp. 602–06. [G: Canada]

Lawlor, Reed C. Copyright and Patent Protection for Computer Programs. In *The Diebold Group, Inc.,* 1973, pp. 204–12. [G: U.S.]

Levin, Harvey J. Television's Second Chance: A Retrospective Look at the Sloan Cable Commission. *Bell J. Econ. Manage. Sci.,* Spring 1973, *4*(1), pp. 343–65. [G: U.S.]

Lubin, John Francis. Failures in the Procurement of Data Processing Equipment. In *The Diebold Group, Inc.,* 1973, pp. 199–203.

Marks, Leonard H. A Communications Satellite System for the United States. In *The Diebold Group, Inc.,* 1973, pp. 153–60. [G: U.S.]

Martin, Donald L. Legal Constraints and the Choice of Organizational Form. *Amer. Econ. Rev.,* May 1973, *63*(2), pp. 326–34. [G: Netherlands]

McKitterick, John B. Resource Allocation in the General Electric Company. In *Weston, J. F. and Ornstein, S. I., eds.,* 1973, pp. 123–27.

Owen, Bruce M. A View from the President's Office of Telecommunications Policy. In *Park, R. E., ed.,* 1973, pp. 3–14. [G: U.S.]

Owen, Bruce M. Newspaper and Television Station Joint Ownership. *Antitrust Bull.,* Winter 1973, *18* (4), pp. 787–807. [G: U.S.]

Park, Rolla Edward. The Role of Analysis in Regulatory Decisionmaking: The Case of Cable Television: Conclusion. In *Park, R. E., ed.,* 1973, pp. 71–78. [G: U.S.]

Perlman, Mark. On the Classification of Economics Material. *J. Econ. Lit.,* September 1973, *11*(3), pp. 898–99.

Rauscher, Walter J. The Implementation and Impact of SABRE: American Airlines. In *The Diebold Group, Inc.,* 1973, pp. 265–70. [G: U.S.]

Riesz, Peter C. Size versus Price, or Another Vote for Tonypandy. *J. Bus.,* July 1973, *46*(3), pp. 396–403. [G: U.S.]

Ross, Charles R. Electricity as a Social Force. *Ann. Amer. Acad. Polit. Soc. Sci.,* January 1973, *405*, pp. 47–54. [G: U.S.]

Sankar, U. Investment Behavior in the U.S. Telephone Industry—1949 to 1968. *Bell J. Econ. Manage. Sci.,* Autumn 1973, *4*(2), pp. 665–78. [G: U.S.]

Schubert, A. Eugene. Organizing to Supply Nuclear Energy. In *Weston, J. F. and Ornstein, S. I., eds.,* 1973, pp. 157–62. [G: U.S.]

Smith, Bruce W. Analysis of the Location of Coal-Fired Power Plants in the Eastern United States. *Econ. Geogr.,* July 1973, *49*(3), pp. 243–50. [G: U.S.]

Squire, Lyn. Some Aspects of Optimal Pricing for Telecommunications. *Bell J. Econ. Manage. Sci.,* Autumn 1973, *4*(2), pp. 515–25.

Stanley, Kenneth B. International Telecommunications Industry: Interdependence of Market Structure and Performance Under Regulation. *Land Econ.,* November 1973, *49*(4), pp. 391–403. [G: U.S.]

Sudit, Ephraim F. Additive Nonhomogeneous Production Functions in Telecommunications. *Bell J. Econ. Manage. Sci.,* Autumn 1973, *4*(2), pp. 499–514.

Thomson, Herbert F. Policy Alternatives for Ohio's Electric Power Industry. *Ohio State U. Bull. Bus. Res.,* December 1973, *48*(12), pp. 1–5. [G: U.S.]

Thomson, Roy Herbert [Lord]. Modernization of Newspaper Techniques. In *The Diebold Group, Inc.,* 1973, pp. 310–13.

Ureel, William L. Nuclear Fuel Accounting. *Manage. Account.,* July 1973, *55*(1), pp. 14–16, 24. [G: U.S.]

Webbink, Douglas W. A View from the Federal Communications Commission. In *Park, R. E., ed.,* 1973, pp. 35–41. [G: U.S.]

Webbink, Douglas W. Regulation, Profits and Entry in the Television Broadcasting Industry. *J. Ind. Econ.,* April 1973, *21*(2), pp. 167–76. [G: U.S.]

Wettstein, Jürg. Operations Research in the Swiss Telecommunication Services. In *Ross, M., ed.,* 1973, pp. 475–81. [G: Switzerland]

Young, H. Peyton and Thompson, Russell G. Forecasting Water Use for Electric Power Generation. *Water Resources Res.,* August 1973, *9*(4), pp. 800–07.

Young, Ralph. An Exploratory Analysis of Demand for the Public Library Lending Service. *Appl. Econ.,* June 1973, *5*(2), pp. 119–32. [G: U.K.]

6353 Personal Services

Jackson, Emma. The Present System of Publicly Supported Day Care. In *Young, D. R. and Nelson, R. R., eds.,* 1973, pp. 21–46. [G: U.S.]

Johnson, Harry G. The Economics of Undertaking. In *Johnson, H. G. and Weisbrod, B. A., eds.,* 1973, pp. 35–39.

Nelson, Richard R. and Krashinsky, Michael. The Demand and Supply of Extra-Family Day Care. In *Young, D. R. and Nelson, R. R., eds.,* 1973, pp. 9–20. [G: U.S.]

Nelson, Richard R. and Krashinsky, Michael. Two Major Issues of Public Policy: Public Subsidy and Organization of Supply. In *Young, D. R. and Nelson, R. R., eds.,* 1973, pp. 47–69. [G: U.S.]

Shaw, R. W. Investment and Competition from Boom to Recession: A Case Study in the Processes of Competition—The Dry Cleaning Industry. *J. Ind. Econ.,* July 1973, *21*(3), pp. 308–24. [G: U.K.]

Young, Dennis and Jackson, Emma. Public Policy for Day Care of Young Children: Introduction. In *Young, D. R. and Nelson, R. R., eds.,* 1973, pp. 1–8. [G: U.S.]

Zamoff, Richard and Lyle, Jerolyn R. Planning and Evaluation of Day Care at the Community Level. In *Young, D. R. and Nelson, R. R., eds.,* 1973, pp. 71–90. [G: U.S.]

6354 Business and Legal Services

Woo, H. Nam and Barckley, Robert. Sources of Cost Differentials in Higher Education: The Case of California State Colleges. *Malayan Econ. Rev.,* October 1973, *18*(2), pp. 68–78. [G: U.S.]

6355 Repair Services

Bylin, James E. An Agency in California Is Model in Campaign to Curb Repair Frauds. In *Murray, B. B., ed.,* 1973, pp. 56–59. [G: U.S.]

6356 Insurance

Allen, Tom C. and Duvall, Richard M. Determinants of Property Loss Ratios in The Retail Industry. *J. Risk Ins.,* June 1973, *40*(2), pp. 181–90. [G: U.S.]

Belth, Joseph M. Credit Life Insurance Prices. *J. Risk Ins.,* March 1973, *40*(1), pp. 115–27. [G: U.S.]

Berekson, Leonard L. Birth Order, Anxiety, Affiliation and the Purchase of Life Insurance: Reply. *J. Risk Ins.,* December 1973, *40*(4), pp. 646–48.

Bickelhaupt, David L. The Future of ARIA: Discussion. *J. Risk Ins.,* March 1973, *40*(1), pp. 109–14. [G: U.S.]

Brainard, Calvin H. Massachusetts Loss Experience Under No-Fault in 1971: Analysis and Implications. *J. Risk Ins.,* March 1973, *40*(1), pp. 95–101. [G: U.S.]

Braverman, Jerome D. and Hartman, Gerald R. The Process of Classifying Drivers: A Suggestion for Insurance Ratemaking: Comment. *J. Risk Ins.,* March 1973, *40*(1), pp. 143–46.

Brightman, Harvey J. and Dorfman, Mark S. Birth Order, Anxiety, Affiliation and the Purchase of Life Insurance: Comment. *J. Risk Ins.,* December 1973, *40*(4), pp. 643–46.

Caramela, Edward J. Staffing and Pay Changes in Life Insurance Companies. *Mon. Lab. Rev.,* August 1973, *96*(8), pp. 66–68. [G: U.S.]

Cummins, J. David. An Econometric Model of the Life Insurance Sector of the U. S. Economy. *J. Risk Ins.,* December 1973, *40*(4), pp. 533–54. [G: U.S.]

Denenberg, Herbert S. and Cummins, J. David. Insurance and Reciprocity: Reply. *J. Risk Ins.,* March 1973, *40*(1), pp. 141–42. [G: U.S.]

Duker, Jacob M. and Hughes, Charles E. The Black-Owned Life Insurance Company: Issues and Recommendations. *J. Risk Ins.,* June 1973, *40*(2), pp. 221–30. [G: U.S.]

Duvall, Richard M. and Allen, Tom C. Least Cost Deductible Decisions. *J. Risk Ins.,* December 1973, *40*(4), pp. 497–508.

Epley, D. R. A Price Index for Life Insurance: Comment. *J. Risk Ins.,* December 1973, *40*(4), pp. 629.

Fischer, Stanley. A Life Cycle Model of Life Insurance Purchases. *Int. Econ. Rev.,* February 1973, *14*(1), pp. 132–52.

Fitzgerald, John F., Jr. Demutualization of Mutual Property and Liability Insurers. *J. Risk Ins.,* December 1973, *40*(4), pp. 575–84. [G: U.S.]

Forbes, Stephen W. Further Studies of Property-Liability Return Adequacy: Reply. *J. Risk Ins.,* September 1973, *40*(3), pp. 460–62.

Forsythe, Graeme A. Rural and Urban Flood Insurance: A Review. In *Aislabie, C., ed.,* 1973, pp. 68–77.

Fortune, Peter. A Theory of Optimal Life Insurance: Development and Tests. *J. Finance,* June 1973, *28*(3), pp. 587–600. [G: U.S.]

Greene, Mark R. Should Variable Policy Loan Interest Rates be Adopted? *J. Risk Ins.,* December 1973, *40*(4), pp. 585–98. [G: U.S.]

Greene, Mark R. A Note on Loading Charges for Variable Annuities. *J. Risk Ins.,* September 1973,

40(3), pp. 473–78. [G: U.S.]

Gustafson, Dale R. Perspectives on Life Insurance Financial Reporting: Discussion. *J. Risk Ins.,* March 1973, *40*(1), pp. 22–25. [G: U.S.]

Hedges, Bob A. On the Skinning of Cats. *J. Risk Ins.,* March 1973, *40*(1), pp. 1–6.

Herrick, Kenneth W. Auto Accidents and Alcohol in Great Britain—An Analysis. *J. Risk Ins.,* March 1973, *40*(1), pp. 55–73. [G: U.K.]

Ingraham, Harold G., Jr. Problems in Agents' Compensation. *J. Risk Ins.,* June 1973, *40*(2), pp. 191–208. [G: U.S.]

Joskow, Paul L. Cartels, Competition and Regulation in the Property-Liability Insurance Industry. *Bell J. Econ. Manage. Sci.,* Autumn 1973, *4*(2), pp. 375–427. [G: U.S.]

Keeton, Robert E. Beyond Current Reforms in Automobile Reparations. *J. Risk Ins.,* March 1973, *40*(1), pp. 31–37. [G: U.S.]

Kensicki, Peter R. and Richmond, David. Consumerism and Automobile Insurance. *J. Risk Ins.,* June 1973, *40*(2), pp. 209–17. [G: U.S.]

Kroncke, Charles O. The Process of Classifying Drivers: A Suggestion for Insurance Ratemaking: Reply. *J. Risk Ins.,* March 1973, *40*(1), pp. 147–48.

Lamphere, Robert J. Program Budgeting at John Hancock Life Insurance. In *Novick, D., ed.,* 1973, pp. 151–60. [G: U.S.]

Levine, Kenneth C. Corporate Modeling of a Life Insurance Company: A Developmental Game Plan. *J. Risk Ins.,* December 1973, *40*(4), pp. 555–64.

Lin, Cheyeh. A Price Index for Life Insurance: Reply. *J. Risk Ins.,* December 1973, *40*(4), pp. 630.

MacPhee, Craig R. Insurance and Reciprocity: Comment. *J. Risk Ins.,* March 1973, *40*(1), pp. 139–41. [G: U.S.]

McEnally, Richard W. and Tavis, Lee A. Further Studies of Property-Liability Return Adequacy: Comment. *J. Risk Ins.,* September 1973, *40*(3), pp. 453–60.

McLure, Charles E., Jr. Investment Life Insurance Versus Term Insurance and Separate Investment: A Determination of Expected-Return Equivalents: Comment. *J. Risk Ins.,* June 1973, *40*(2), pp. 291–93.

Mehr, Robert I. Consumerism and Automobile Insurance: Discussion. *J. Risk Ins.,* June 1973, *40*(2), pp. 217–20. [G: U.S.]

Meyer, Richard L. and Power, Fred B. Total Insurance Costs and the Frequency of Premium Payments. *J. Risk Ins.,* December 1973, *40*(4), pp. 599–605.

Mueller, Marjorie Smith. Private Health Insurance in 1971: Health Care Services, Enrollment, and Finances. *Soc. Sec. Bull.,* February 1973, *36*(2), pp. 3–22. [G: U.S.]

Neumann, Seev. Ownership and Performance: Stock and Mutual Life Insurance Companies: Comment. *J. Risk Ins.,* December 1973, *40*(4), pp. 631–35.

Posnak, Robert L. Perspectives on Life Insurance Financial Reporting. *J. Risk Ins.,* March 1973, *40*(1), pp. 7–22. [G: U.S.]

Pritchett, S. Travis. Operating Expenses of Life Insurers, 1961–70: Implications for Economies of Size. *J. Risk Ins.,* June 1973, *40*(2), pp. 157–65. [G: U.S.]

Puth, Robert C. From Enforced Segregation to Integration: Market Factors in the Development of a Negro Life Insurance. In *[Williamson, H. F.],* 1973, pp. 280–301. [G: U.S.]

Scheel, William C. A Critique of the Interest-Adjusted Net Cost Index. *J. Risk Ins.,* June 1973, *40*(2), pp. 245–61.

Schonberger, Richard J. Management Information Systems in Insurance: Comment. *J. Risk Ins.,* June 1973, *40*(2), pp. 294–96.

Schwartz, Ivo E. Creating a Common Market for Insurance: Harmonization of EEC Insurance Legislation. *Antitrust Bull.,* Spring 1973, *18*(1), pp. 103–16.

Spiller, Richard. Ownership and Performance: Stock and Mutual Life Insurance Companies: Reply. *J. Risk Ins.,* December 1973, *40*(4), pp. 635–38.

Stone, Gary K. Life Insurance Sales Practices on the College Campus. *J. Risk Ins.,* June 1973, *40*(2), pp. 167–79. [G: U.S.]

Stone, James M. A Theory of Capacity and the Insurance of Catastrophe Risks (Part II) *J. Risk Ins.,* September 1973, *40*(3), pp. 339–55.

Stone, James M. A Theory of Capacity and the Insurance of Catastrophe Risks (Part I) *J. Risk Ins.,* June 1973, *40*(2), pp. 231–43.

Syron, Richard F. Administered Prices and the Market Reaction: The Case of Urban Core Property Insurance. *J. Finance,* March 1973, *28*(1), pp. 147–56. [G: U.S.]

Treischmann, James S. Further Studies of Property-Liability Return Adequacy: Reply. *J. Risk Ins.,* September 1973, *40*(3), pp. 462–64.

Trieschmann, James S. and Pinches, George E. A Multivariate Model for Predicting Financially Distressed P-L Insurers. *J. Risk Ins.,* September 1973, *40*(3), pp. 327–38. [G: U.S.]

Tyler, George R. and Hoffer, George E. Reform of the Non-Commercial Vehicle Liability Insurance Market. *J. Risk Ins.,* December 1973, *40*(4), pp. 565–74. [G: U.S.]

Williams, C. Arthur, Jr. and Whitman, Andrew F. Open Competition Rating Laws and Price Competition. *J. Risk Ins.,* December 1973, *40*(4), pp. 483–96. [G: U.S.]

Williams, Harold M. The Future of ARIA. *J. Risk Ins.,* March 1973, *40*(1), pp. 103–09. [G: U.S.]

Winkle, Gary M. Perspectives on Life Insurance Financial Reporting: Discussion. *J. Risk Ins.,* March 1973, *40*(1), pp. 25–30. [G: U.S.]

Winklevoss, Howard E. and Zelten, Robert A. An Empirical Analysis of Mutual Life Insurance Company Surplus. *J. Risk Ins.,* September 1973, *40*(3), pp. 403–25. [G: U.S.]

Witt, Robert Charles. Pricing Problems in Automobile Insurance: An Economic Analysis. *J. Risk Ins.,* March 1973, *40*(1), pp. 75–93. [G: U.S.]

Witt, Robert Charles. Pricing and Underwriting Risk in Automobile Insurance: A Probabilistic View. *J. Risk Ins.,* December 1973, *40*(4), pp. 509–31. [G: U.S.]

Ziock, Richard W. A Realistic Profit Model for In-

dividual Non-Participating Life Insurance. *J. Risk Ins.,* September 1973, *40*(3), pp. 357–73.
[G: U.S.]

6357 Real Estate

Brantner, Paul F. Accounting for Land Development Companies. *Manage. Account.,* August 1973, *55*(2), pp. 15–19.

Carliner, Geoffrey. Income Elasticity of Housing Demand. *Rev. Econ. Statist.,* November 1973, *55*(4), pp. 528–32. [G: U.S.]

Collard, David. Exclusion by Estate Agents—An Analysis. *Appl. Econ.,* December 1973, *5*(4), pp. 281–88.

Dahlman, S. Roland. Joint Establishments in Sweden. *Bull. Int. Fiscal Doc.,* June 1973, *27*(6), pp. 241–44. [G: Sweden]

Fisher, Ernest M. Speculative Development of Residential Land and Residential Structures during the 1920's and the 1960's and 1970's. *Amer. Real Estate Urban Econ. Assoc. J.,* June 1973, *1*(1), pp. 123–39. [G: U.S.]

Kristof, Frank S. Federal Housing Policies: Subsidized Production, Filtration and Objectives: Part II. *Land Econ.,* May 1973, *49*(2), pp. 163–74.
[G: U.S.]

Pyhrr, Stephen A. A Computer Simulation Model to Measure the Risk in Real Estate Investment. *Amer. Real Estate Urban Econ. Assoc. J.,* June 1973, *1*(1), pp. 48–78.

Rothman, Jack. The Ghetto Makers. In *Pynoos, J.; Schafer, R. and Hartman, C. W., eds.,* 1973, pp. 274–78. [G: U.S.]

Wendt, Paul F. New Techniques in Financing Real Estate. *Amer. Real Estate Urban Econ. Assoc. J.,* June 1973, *1*(1), pp. 140–57.

6358 Entertainment, Recreation, Tourism

Askari, Hossein. Demand for Travel to Europe by American Citizens. *Econ. Int.,* May 1973, *26*(2), pp. 305–17. [G: U.S.]

Gordon, I. R. and Edwards, S. L. Holiday Trip Generation. *J. Transp. Econ. Policy,* May 1973, *7*(2), pp. 153–68. [G: U.K.]

Harrop, Jeffrey. On the Economics of the Tourist Boom. *Bull. Econ. Res.,* May 1973, *25*(1), pp. 55–72. [G: U.K.]

Hochberg, Philip and Horowitz, Ira. Broadcasting and CATV: The Beauty and the Bane of Major College Football. *Law Contemp. Probl.,* Winter-Spring 1973, *38*(1), pp. 112–28. [G: U.S.]

Koch, James V. A Troubled Cartel: The NCAA. *Law Contemp. Probl.,* Winter-Spring 1973, *38*(1), pp. 135–50. [G: U.S.]

Levin, Harvey J. Television's Second Chance: A Retrospective Look at the Sloan Cable Commission. *Bell J. Econ. Manage. Sci.,* Spring 1973, *4*(1), pp. 343–65. [G: U.S.]

Li, Wen L.; Smith, Gerald W. and Udell, Jonathan. The Gambling Business in the U.S.A. *Ohio State U. Bull. Bus. Res.,* April 1973, *48*(4), pp. 1–3, 6–7.
[G: U.S.]

Lowell, Cym H. Collective Bargaining and the Professional Team Sport Industry. *Law Contemp.*

Probl., Winter-Spring 1973, *38*(1), pp. 3–41.
[G: U.S.]

Lucero, Maryetta. New Mexico Travel Service Training Program. *N. Mex. Bus.,* March 1973, *26*(3), pp. 10–12. [G: U.S.]

Moorhouse, John C. Censorship, Revenue, and X-Rated Movie Taxes. *Quart. Rev. Econ. Bus.,* Summer 1973, *13*(2), pp. 83–89. [G: U.S.]

Morris, John P. In the Wake of the Flood. *Law Contemp. Probl.,* Winter-Spring 1973, *38*(1), pp. 85–98. [G: U.S.]

O'Riordan, T. An Analysis of the Use and Management of Campgrounds in British Columbia Provincial Parks. *Econ. Geogr.,* October 1973, *49*(4), pp. 298–308. [G: Canada]

Pérez, Louis A., Jr. Aspects of Underdevelopment: Tourism in the West Indies. *Sci. Soc.,* Winter 1973–1974, *37*(4), pp. 473–80. [G: W. Indies]

Quirk, James. An Economic Analysis of Team Movements in Professional Sports. *Law Contemp. Probl.,* Winter-Spring 1973, *38*(1), pp. 42–66.
[G: U.S.]

Ryan, Allan J. Medical Practices in Sports. *Law Contemp. Probl.,* Winter-Spring 1973, *38*(1), pp. 99–111. [G: U.S.]

Scully, Gerald W. Economic Discrimination in Professional Sports. *Law Contemp. Probl.,* Winter-Spring 1973, *38*(1), pp. 67–84. [G: U.S.]

de Seve, Charles W. Improved Pari-Mutual Taxation. *Nat. Tax J.,* December 1973, *26*(4), pp. 591–97. [G: U.S.]

Taylor, Frank F. The Tourist Industry in Jamaica, 1919–1939. *Soc. Econ. Stud.,* June 1973, *22*(2), pp. 205–28. [G: Jamaica]

Wise, Gordon L. The Business of Major League Baseball as a Spectator Sport. *Ohio State U. Bull. Bus. Res.,* October 1973, *48*(10), pp. 1–3, 6–7.
[G: U.S.]

640 ECONOMIC CAPACITY

641 Economic Capacity

6410 Economic Capacity

Ahmad, Qazi Kholiquzzaman. A Note on Capacity Utilization in the Jute Manufacturing Industry of Bangladesh. *Bangladesh Econ. Rev.,* January 1973, *1*(1), pp. 103–14. [G: Bangladesh]

Behrman, Jere R. Cyclical Sectoral Capacity Utilization in a Developing Economy. In *Eckaus, R. S. and Rosenstein-Rodan, P. N., eds.,* 1973, pp. 251–66. [G: Chile]

Duetsch, Larry L. Elements of Market Structure and the Extent of Suboptimal Capacity. *Southern Econ. J.,* October 1973, *40*(2), pp. 216–23.
[G: U.S.]

Eckaus, Richard S. Absorptive Capacity as a Constraint Due to Maturation Processes. In *[Rosenstein-Rodan, P.],* 1973, pp. 79–108.

Edmonson, Nathan. Capacity Utilization in Major Materials Industries. *Fed. Res. Bull.,* August 1973, *59*(8), pp. 564–66. [G: U.S.]

Klein, Lawrence R. and Long, Virginia. Capacity Utilization: Concept, Measurement, and Recent Estimates. *Brookings Pap. Econ. Act.*, 1973, (3), pp. 743–56. [G: U.S.]

Perry, George L. Capacity in Manufacturing. *Brookings Pap. Econ. Act.*, 1973, (3), pp. 701–42. [G: U.S.]

Sawhney, Pawan K. and Sawhney, Bansi L. Capacity-Utilization, Concentration, and Price-Cost Margins: Results on Indian Industries. *J. Ind. Econ.*, April 1973, *21*(2), pp. 145–53. [G: India]

Solow, Robert M. Technology and Unemployment. In *Reynolds, L. G.; Green, G. D. and Lewis, D. R., eds.*, 1973, pp. 89–99.

Stigler, George J. The Economies of Scale. In *Haynes, W. W.; Coyne, T. J. and Osborne, D. K., eds.*, 1973, pp. 232–49. [G: U.S.]

Stone, James M. A Theory of Capacity and the Insurance of Catastrophe Risks (Part II) *J. Risk Ins.*, September 1973, *40*(3), pp. 339–55.

Stone, James M. A Theory of Capacity and the Insurance of Catastrophe Risks (Part I) *J. Risk Ins.*, June 1973, *40*(2), pp. 231–43.

700 Agriculture; Natural Resources

710 AGRICULTURE

7100 Agriculture

Adegboye, R. O. and Abidogun, A. Contribution of Part-Time Farming to Rural Development in Ibadan Area, Western Nigeria. In *Ofori, I. M., ed.*, 1973, pp. 158–63. [G: Nigeria]

Azhar, B. A. Land Revenue Assessment: A Case Study. *Pakistan Develop. Rev.*, Autumn 1973, *12* (3), pp. 232–46. [G: Pakistan]

Bardhan, Kalpana and Bardhan, Pranab K. The Green Revolution and Socio-Economic Tensions: The Case of India. *Int. Soc. Sci. J.*, 1973, *25*(3), pp. 285–92. [G: India]

Bardhan, Pranab K. 'Green Revolution' and Agricultural Labourers. In *Wadhva, C. D., ed.*, 1973, pp. 346–61. [G: India]

Bardhan, Pranab K. A Model of Growth of Capitalism in a Dual Agrarian Economy. In *[Rosenstein-Rodan, P.]*, 1973, pp. 109–17.

Barkin, David P. Cuban Agriculture: A Strategy of Economic Development. In *Barkin, D. P. and Manitzas, N. R., eds.*, 1973, pp. R261–21. [G: Cuba]

Barraclough, Solon and Schatan, Jacobo. Technological Policy and Agricultural Development. *Land Econ.*, May 1973, *49*(2), pp. 175–94. [G: Latin America]

Bassoco, Luz María and Rendón, Teresa. The Technology Set and Data Base for CHAC. In *Goreux, L. M. and Manne, A. S., eds.*, 1973, pp. 339–71. [G: Mexico]

Bassoco, Luz María, et al. A Programming Model of an Agricultural District. In *Goreux, L. M. and Manne, A. S., eds.*, 1973, pp. 401–16. [G: Mexico]

Beale, Calvin L. Migration Patterns of Minorities in the United States. *Amer. J. Agr. Econ.*, December 1973, *55*(5), pp. 938–46. [G: U.S.]

Behrman, Jere R. Aggregative Market Responses in

Developing Agriculture: The Postwar Chilean Experience. In *Eckaus, R. S. and Rosenstein-Rodan, P. N., eds.*, 1973, pp. 229–50. [G: Chile]

Bertram, Gordon W. The Relevance of the Wheat Boom in Canadian Economic Growth. *Can. J. Econ.*, November 1973, *6*(4), pp. 545–66. [G: Canada]

Bhati, U. N. Farmers' Technical Knowledge and Income—A Case Study of Padi Farmers of West Malaysia. *Malayan Econ. Rev.*, April 1973, *18*(1), pp. 36–47. [G: Malaya]

Boesen, Jannik. Peasants and Coffee Export. In *Institute for Development Research*, 1973, pp. 79–100.

Breimyer, Harold F. Public Sector Research and Education and the Agribusiness Complex: Unholy Alliance or Socially Beneficial Partnership? Discussion. *Amer. J. Agr. Econ.*, December 1973, *55* (5), pp. 993–96. [G: U.S.]

Breimyer, Harold F. Man, Physical Resources, and Economic Organization. *Amer. J. Agr. Econ.*, February 1973, *55*(1), pp. 1–9.

Brown, Lawrence A. and Lentnek, Barry. Innovation Diffusion in a Developing Economy: A Mesoscale View. *Econ. Develop. Cult. Change*, January 1973, *21*(2), pp. 274–92. [G: Mexico]

Burns, E. O. Random Thoughts on Some Problems of Professional Communication. *Australian J. Agr. Econ.*, August 1973, *17*(2), pp. 93–103.

Carlin, Thomas A. and Smith, Allen G. A New Approach in Accounting for Our Nation's Farm Income. *Agr. Finance Rev.*, July 1973, *34*, pp. 1–6. [G: U.S.]

Carney, M. K. Agricultural Trade Intensity: The European Markets and the U.S. *Amer. J. Agr. Econ.*, Part I, November 1973, *55*(4), pp. 637–40.

Chattopadhyay, Paresh. Some Trends in India's Economic Development. In *Gough, K. and Sharma, H. P., eds.*, 1973, pp. 103–29. [G: India]

Cochrane, Willard W. Agricultural and Trade Developments in the Less Developed Countries. In *Iowa State University Center for Agricultural and Rural Development*, 1973, pp. 194–209.

Connor, Larry J. Michigan State's Curricula in Agricultural Economics. *Amer. J. Agr. Econ.*, Part II, November 1973, *55*(4), pp. 752–54. [G: U.S.]

Corea, Gamani. Economic Planning, the Green Revolution and the 'Food Drive' in Ceylon. In *[Hicks, U.]*, 1973, pp. 273–303. [G: Ceylon]

Csendes, Béla. Development Trends of Hungarian Agriculture. In *Földi, T., ed.*, 1973, pp. 117–34. [G: Hungary]

Daroesman, Ruth. An Economic Survey of Bali. *Bull. Indonesian Econ. Stud.*, November 1973, *9*(3), pp. 28–61. [G: Indonesia]

De Boer, John. Sacred Cows: Comment. *Amer. J. Agr. Econ.*, May 1973, *55*(2), pp. 341–42. [G: India]

Duloy, John H.; Kutcher, Gary P. and Norton, Roger D. Investment and Employment Alternatives in the Agricultural District Model. In *Goreux, L. M. and Manne, A. S., eds.*, 1973, pp. 417–33. [G: Mexico]

Epstein, T. Scarlett. The Dimensions of Rural Development. In *Epstein, T. S. and Penny, D. H., eds.*, 1973, pp. 241–51.

Fortt, J. M. and Hougham, D. A. Environment,

Population and Economic History. In *Richards, A. I.; Sturrock, F. and Fortt, J. M., eds.,* 1973, pp. 17–46.   [G: Uganda]

de Gaay Fortman, B. Rural Development in an Age of Survival. *De Economist,* March-April 1973, *121* (2), pp. 157–71.

Gotsch, Carl H. Tractor Mechanisation and Rural Development in Pakistan. *Int. Lab. Rev.,* February 1973, *107*(2), pp. 133–66.   [G: Pakistan]

Gray, Roger W. Agricultural Economics: An Orientation for the 70s. *Food Res. Inst. Stud.,* 1973, *12* (2), pp. 169–75.

Gray, Roger W. The Rebirth of Agricultural Economics? *Food Res. Inst. Stud.,* 1973, *12*(3), pp. 253–58.

Green, W. A. The Planter Class and the British West Indian Sugar Production, before and after Emancipation. *Econ. Hist. Rev., 2nd Ser.,* August 1973, *26*(3), pp. 448–63.   [G: Caribbean]

Grove, Ernest W. Use of the Arithmetic Mean in Farm Policy. *Amer. J. Agr. Econ.,* May 1973, *55* (2), pp. 344–45.

Gyenes, A. Re-stratification of the Agricultural Population in Hungary. *Acta Oecon.,* 1973, *11*(1), pp. 33–49.   [G: Hungary]

Hathaway, Dale E. Public Sector Research and Education and the Agribusiness Complex: Unholy Alliance or Socially Beneficial Partnership? Summary of the Discussion. *Amer. J. Agr. Econ.,* December 1973, *55*(5), pp. 1002.   [G: U.S.]

Hathaway, Dale E. Public Sector Research and Education and the Agribusiness Complex: Unholy Alliance or Socially Beneficial Partnership? *Amer. J. Agr. Econ.,* December 1973, *55*(5), pp. 993.
[G: U.S.]

Hildreth, R. J.; Krause, Kenneth R. and Nelson, Paul E., Jr. Organization and Control of the U.S. Food and Fiber Sector. *Amer. J. Agr. Econ.,* December 1973, *55*(5), pp. 851–59.   [G: U.S.]

Holland, I. Irving. Implications of the 1970 Timber Review for Trade in Timber Products. *Amer. J. Agr. Econ.,* December 1973, *55*(5), pp. 967–73.
[G: U.S.]

Horvat, Branko. The Postwar Evolution of Yugoslav Agricultural Organization: Interaction of Ideology, Practice, and Results. *Eastern Europ. Econ.,* Winter 1973-74, *12*(2), pp. 3–106.   [G: Yugoslavia]

Hougham, D. A. and Mafeje, Archie. Sampling and Field-work Methods. In *Richards, A. I.; Sturrock, F. and Fortt, J. M., eds.,* 1973, pp. 95–123.
[G: Uganda]

Hsien, Ju-kao. Education in Line and Policies Promotes Agricultural Development. *Chinese Econ. Stud.,* Winter 1973–74, *7*(2), pp. 18–26.
[G: China]

Ihrig, Károly. Agriculture's Contribution to the Growth of Capitalist Economies. In *Földi, T., ed.,* 1973, pp. 135–60.

Jabbar, M. A. Agriculture in Economic Development: The Competitive Approach Versus Soviet Control. *Can. J. Agr. Econ.,* February 1973, *21*(1), pp. 63–64.   [G: Canada; U.S.S.R.]

Jarvis, Lovell S. Un ejemplo del uso de modelos económicos para la construcción de datos no disponibles: la estimación de la existencia de vacunos desagregado en Argentina 1937–1967. (An

Example of the Use of Economics Models for the Construction of Unavailable Data. The Appreciation of the Existence of Disaggregated Cattle in Argentina—1937–1967. With English summary.) *Económica,* January-April 1973, *19*(1), pp. 71–117.   [G: Argentina]

Klippenstein, D. H. and Ironside, R. G. Farmers' Attitudes Toward Farm-Based Recreational Facilities in Alberta. *Can. J. Agr. Econ.,* November 1973, *21*(3), pp. 23–33.   [G: Canada]

Komló, L. The Industrialization and Integration of Agriculture in a Socialist Country. *Acta Oecon.,* 1973, *10*(1), pp. 67–79.

Lefeber, Louis. Income Distribution and Agricultural Development. In *[Rosenstein-Rodan, P.],* 1973, pp. 133–51.   [G: India]

Lockwood, Brian and Moulik, T. K. Seeds of Development in a Delhi Village. In *Epstein, T. S. and Penny, D. H., eds.,* 1973, pp. 157–72. [G: India]

Luttrell, Clifton B. The Russian Wheat Deal—Hindsight vs. Foresight. *Fed. Res. Bank St. Louis Rev.,* October 1973, *55*(10), pp. 2–9.   [G: U.S.]

Macourt, M. P. A. An Exploratory Compartive Study of Catholic and Protestant Farmers in the Republic of Ireland. *Econ. Soc. Rev.,* July 1973, *4*(4), pp. 511–22.   [G: Ireland]

Marstrand, Pauline K. and Pavitt, K. L. R. The Agricultural Sub-system. In *Cole, H. S. D., et al., eds.,* 1973, pp. 56–65.

McCalla, Alex F. Public Sector Research and Education and the Agribusiness Complex: Unholy Alliance or Socially Beneficial Partnership? Discussion. *Amer. J. Agr. Econ.,* December 1973, *55*(5), pp. 999–1002.   [G: U.S.]

McCawley, Peter. Survey of Recent Developments. *Bull. Indonesian Econ. Stud.,* November 1973, *9* (3), pp. 1–27.   [G: Indonesia]

Mehren, George. Public Sector Research and Education and the Agribusiness Complex: Unholy Alliance or Socially Beneficial Partnership? Discussion. *Amer. J. Agr. Econ.,* December 1973, *55*(5), pp. 997–99.   [G: U.S.]

Mellor, John W. Accelerated Growth in Agricultural Production and the Intersectoral Transfer of Resources. *Econ. Develop. Cult. Change,* October 1973, *22*(1), pp. 1–16.   [G: Taiwan; India]

Muller, Peter O. Trend Surfaces of American Agricultural Patterns: A Macro-Thünian Analysis. *Econ. Geogr.,* July 1973, *49*(3), pp. 228–42.
[G: U.S.]

Nukunya, G. K. Land Tenure and Agricultural Development in the Anloga Area of the Volta Region. In *Ofori, I. M., ed.,* 1973, pp. 101–06.
[G: Ghana]

Okwuosa, E. A. The Problem of Demand in Relation to Policy for Agricultural Development. In *Ofori, I. M., ed.,* 1973, pp. 20–25.   [G: Nigeria]

O'Loughlin, Carleen. What Is Agricultural Growth? In *Ofori, I. M., ed.,* 1973, pp. 7–13. [G: Central America; W. Africa]

Oluwasanmi, H. A. West African Agricultural Development in the '60's. In *Ofori, I. M., ed.,* 1973, pp. 1–6.   [G: Sierra Leone; Nigeria; Ghana]

Parker, Edith H. New Directions in Agricultural Economics Curricula, University of California, Davis. *Amer. J. Agr. Econ.,* Part II, November 1973, *55*(4), pp. 748–49.   [G: U.S.]

Pasour, E. C., Jr. Economic Growth and Agriculture: An Evaluation of the Compensation Principle. *Amer. J. Agr. Econ.,* Part I, November 1973, *55*(4), pp. 611–16.

Pathak, Mahesh T.; Desai, Mahendra D. and Charan, A. S. Development of Agriculture in Backward Regions of Gujarat: Facts and Issues. *Artha-Vikas,* January-July 1973, *9*(1–2), pp. 100–38. [G: India]

Patrick, George F. and Kehrberg, Earl W. Costs and Returns of Education in Five Agricultural Areas of Eastern Brazil. *Amer. J. Agr. Econ.,* May 1973, *55*(2), pp. 145–53. [G: Brazil]

Penny, David H. and Singarimbun, Masri. Economic Activity among the Karo Batak of Indonesia: A Case Study in Economic Change. In *Epstein, T. S. and Penny, D. H., eds.,* 1973, pp. 86–113. [G: Indonesia]

Perelman, Michael A. Mechanization and the Division of Labor in Agriculture. *Amer. J. Agr. Econ.,* August 1973, *55*(3), pp. 523–26.

Perelman, Michael A. Sacred Cows: Response. *Amer. J. Agr. Econ.,* May 1973, *55*(2), pp. 342–43. [G: India]

Perkins, Brian B. Farm Income and Labour Mobility. *Amer. J. Agr. Econ.,* December 1973, *55*(5), pp. 913–20. [G: Canada]

Perkins, Dwight H. Development of Agriculture. In *Oksenberg, M., ed.,* 1973, pp. 55–67. [G: China]

Plaxico, James S. and Ray, Daryll E. Implications for Agricultural Economists. *Amer. J. Agr. Econ.,* August 1973, *55*(3), pp. 399–403. [G: U.S.]

Qureshi, Sarfraz K. Reliability of Pakistani Agricultural Price Data. *Pakistan Develop. Rev.,* Summer 1973, *12*(2), pp. 168–80. [G: Pakistan]

Richards, A. I. Characteristics of the Selected Farmers—A Summary. In *Richards, A. I.; Sturrock, F. and Fortt, J. M., eds.,* 1973, pp. 271–88. [G: Uganda]

Richards, A. I. Some Conclusions. In *Richards, A. I.; Sturrock, F. and Fortt, J. M., eds.,* 1973, pp. 289–305. [G: Uganda]

Richards, A. I. Subsistence to Commercial Farming in Present-Day Buganda: An Economic and Anthropological Survey: Introduction. In *Richards, A. I.; Sturrock, F. and Fortt, J. M., eds.,* 1973, pp. 1–13. [G: Uganda]

Richards, A. I. The Traditional Administrative Structure and the Agricultural Development of Buganda. In *Richards, A. I.; Sturrock, F. and Fortt, J. M., eds.,* 1973, pp. 47–65. [G: Uganda]

Richter, Joseph J. Constitutional and Institutional Constraints in Agriculture and Agricultural Policy. *Can. J. Agr. Econ.,* February 1973, *21*(1), pp. 49–56. [G: Canada]

Robertson, A. F. Bugerere—A Country Case History: The Successful Commercial Farmer in an Immigrant Society. In *Richards, A. I.; Sturrock, F. and Fortt, J. M., eds.,* 1973, pp. 232–68. [G: Uganda]

Robinson, Joan. Chinese Agricultural Communes. In *Wilber, C. K., ed.,* 1973, pp. 209–15. [G: China]

Rourke, B. E. and Obeng, F. A. Seasonality in the Employment of Casual Agricultural Labour in Ghana. *Econ. Bull. Ghana, Sec. Ser.,* 1973, *3*(3), pp. 3–13. [G: Ghana]

Saul, John S. and Woods, Roger. Appendix: African Peasantries. In *Arrighi, G. and Saul, J. S.,* 1973, pp. 406–16. [G: Tanzania; Rhodesia]

Saxena, P. S. and Dubey, R. M. Rural Unemployment: A Direct Approach. *Econ. Aff.,* June 1973, *18*(6), pp. 265–74, 304. [G: India]

Sharma, Hari P. The Green Revolution in India: Prelude to a Red One? In *Gough, K. and Sharma, H. P., eds.,* 1973, pp. 77–102. [G: India]

Sharples, Jerry and Prindle, Allen. Income Characteristics of Farm Families in the Corn Belt. *Agr. Finance Rev.,* July 1973, *34,* pp. 12–17. [G: U.S.]

Sigurdson, Jon. Rural Economic Planning. In *Oksenberg, M., ed.,* 1973, pp. 68–79. [G: China]

Singh, I. Recursive Programming Models of Agricultural Development. In *Judge, G. G. and Takayama, T., eds.,* 1973, pp. 394–416. [G: India]

Sinha, R. K. Report of the Committee on Taxation of Agricultural Wealth and Income—An Appraisal. *Econ. Aff.,* January–February 1973, *18*(1-2), pp. 17–28. [G: India]

Sjo, John; Orazem, Frank and Biere, Arlo. Undergraduate Program Revision at Kansas State University. *Amer. J. Agr. Econ.,* Part I, November 1973, *55*(4), pp. 604–10. [G: U.S.]

Smith, Glenn R. Has Social Science Research at the Experiment Stations Increased in Line with Society's Needs and Congressional Intent? *Amer. J. Agr. Econ.,* Part I, November 1973, *55*(4), pp. 667–69.

Squire, Lyn. Optimal Feeder Roads in Developing Countries: The Case of Thailand. *J. Devel. Stud.,* January 1973, *9*(2), pp. 279–90. [G: Thailand]

Storey, David A. and Christensen, Robert L. Graduate Programs in Agricultural Economics: Results of a Survey. *Amer. J. Agr. Econ.,* February 1973, *55*(1), pp. 61–64. [G: U.S.; Canada]

Storgaard, Birgit. A Delayed Proletarianization of Peasants. In *Institute for Development Research,* 1973, pp. 103–25. [G: Tanzania]

Sturrock, Ford. The Comparative Viewpoint. In *Richards, A. I.; Sturrock, F. and Fortt, J. M., eds.,* 1973, pp. 306–19. [G: Uganda]

Waters, Alan Rufus. Migration, Remittances, and the Cash Constraint in African Smallholder Economic Development. *Oxford Econ. Pap.,* November 1973, *25*(3), pp. 435–54. [G: Africa]

Weisgerber, P. The Impact of Wealth Benefits on Farm Returns in the Wheat Area. *Agr. Finance Rev.,* July 1973, *34,* pp. 31–34. [G: U.S.]

Wills, Walter J. SIU's Curriculum in Agricultural Economics. *Amer. J. Agr. Econ.,* Part II, November 1973, *55*(4), pp. 750–51. [G: U.S.]

Woods, W. Fred. Tax-Loss Farming. *Agr. Finance Rev.,* July 1973, *34,* pp. 24–30. [G: U.S.]

711 Agricultural Supply and Demand Analysis

7110 Agricultural Supply and Demand Analysis

Alamgir, Mohiuddin and Berlage, Lodewijk J. J. B. Estimation of Income Elasticity of Demand for Foodgrain in Bangladesh from Cross Section

Data: A Skeptical View. *Bangladesh Econ. Rev.,* October 1973, *1*(4), pp. 387–408. [G: Bangladesh]

Alamgir, Mohiuddin and Berlage, Lodewijk J. J. B. Foodgrain (Rice and Wheat) Demand, Import and Price Policy for Bangladesh. *Bangladesh Econ. Rev.,* January 1973, *1*(1), pp. 25–58. [G: Bangladesh]

Alcantara, Reinaldo and Prato, Anthony A. Returns to Scale and Input Elasticities for Sugarcane: The Case of Sao Paulo, Brazil. *Amer. J. Agr. Econ.,* Part I, November 1973, *55*(4), pp. 577–83. [G: Brazil]

Ambegaonkar, L. V.; Ashturkar, B. W. and Choudhuri, S. D. Response of Irrigated M35-1 Rabi Jowar to Levels of Nitrogen. *Econ. Aff.,* June 1973, *18*(6), pp. 261–64. [G: India]

Anderson, Jock R. Sparse Data, Climatic Variability, and Yield Uncertainty in Response Analysis. *Amer. J. Agr. Econ.,* February 1973, *55*(1), pp. 77–82. [G: Australia]

Anderson, Jock R. and Powell, R. A. Economics of Size in Australian Farming. *Australian J. Agr. Econ.,* April 1973, *17*(1), pp. 1–16. [G: Australia]

Apsey, T. M.; Garton, M. M. and Hajdu, C. Economic Trends in the Canadian Forest Products Industry. *Amer. J. Agr. Econ.,* December 1973, *55* (5), pp. 974–82. [G: Canada]

Asaduzzaman, Md. The Seasonal Variation in Price of Rice: Bangladesh 1950–72. *Bangladesh Econ. Rev.,* April 1973, *1*(2), pp. 213–20. [G: Bangladesh]

Ayob, Ahmad Mahzan and Prato, Anthony A. United States Import Demand and Prices of Natural Rubber. *Malayan Econ. Rev.,* April 1973, *18*(1), pp. 24–35. [G: U.S.]

Azhar, B. A.; Chaudhry, M. Ghaffar and Shafique, M. A Model for Forecasting Wheat Production in the Punjab. *Pakistan Develop. Rev.,* Winter 1973, *12* (4), pp. 407–15. [G: Pakistan]

Bain, R. A. Factors Affecting Consumption and Prices of the Major Feed Grains in Australia. *Quart. Rev. Agr. Econ.,* July 1973, *26*(3), pp. 186–97. [G: Australia]

Bazlova, A. Improving Purchase Prices on Agricultural Output. *Prob. Econ.,* July 1973, *16*(3), pp. 37–58. [G: U.S.S.R.]

Berry, R. Albert. Land Distribution, Income Distribution, and the Productive Efficiency of Colombian Agriculture. *Food Res. Inst. Stud.,* 1973, *12* (3), pp. 199–232. [G: Colombia]

Bhaduri, Amit. A Study in Agricultural Backwardness under Semi-Feudalism. *Econ. J.,* March 1973, *83*(329), pp. 120–37. [G: India]

Bickel, Blaine W. Meeting Consumer Demand for Beef—From Ranch to Roast. *Fed. Res. Bank Kansas City Rev.,* April 1973, pp. 12–19. [G: U.S.]

Buchholz, H. E. Pricing and Allocation Models Applied to Problems of Interregional Trade and Location of Industries. In *Judge, G. G. and Takayama, T., eds.,* 1973, pp. 298–306. [G: W. Germany]

Carley, D. H. Silage-Concentrate Substitution; Effects on Milk Production and Income Over Feed Cost in DHIA Herds. *Amer. J. Agr. Econ.,* Part I,

November 1973, *55*(4), pp. 641–46. [G: U.S.]

Carman, Hoy F. and Youde, James G. Alternative Tax Treatment of Orchard Development Costs: Impacts on Producers, Middlemen, and Consumers. *Amer. J. Agr. Econ.,* May 1973, *55*(2), pp. 184–91. [G: U.S.]

Chacko, V. J. Problems of Statistical Methodology in Measuring Agricultural Growth. In *Ofori, I. M., ed.,* 1973, pp. 14–19.

Cheung, Steven N. S. The Fable of the Bees: An Economic Investigation. *J. Law Econ.,* April 1973, *16*(1), pp. 11–33. [G: U.S.]

Christensen, Raymond P. and Goolsby, O. Halbert. U.S. Agricultural Trade and Balance of Payments. In *Iowa State University Center for Agricultural and Rural Development,* 1973, pp. 122–40. [G: U.S.]

Cline, William R. Interrelationships Between Agricultural Strategy and Rural Income Distribution. *Food Res. Inst. Stud.,* 1973, *12*(2), pp. 139–57.

Clottey, St. John A. Increasing Ghana's Meat Output through Improvement in Ruminant Production. In *Ofori, I. M., ed.,* 1973, pp. 231–39. [G: Ghana]

Collier, William L. and Soentoro, Gunawan Wiradi. Recent Changes in Rice Harvesting Methods: Some Serious Social Implications. *Bull. Indonesian Econ. Stud.,* July 1973, *9*(2), pp. 36–45. [G: Indonesia]

Colwell, J. D. Assessments of the Relative Values of Compound Nitrogen-Phosphorus Fertilizers for Wheat Production. *Australian J. Agr. Econ.,* December 1973, *17*(3), pp. 189–99. [G: Australia]

Craddock, W. J. The Agricultural Production Plant —What Can It Accomplish in Output and Stability? In *Canadian Agricultural Economics Society,* 1973, pp. 82–97. [G: Canada]

Cuskaden, Charles M. Labor Productivity in Apple Harvesting. *Amer. J. Agr. Econ.,* Part I, November 1973, *55*(4), pp. 633–36. [G: U.S.]

Dadson, J. A. Farm Size and the Modernization of Agriculture in Ghana. In *Ofori, I. M., ed.,* 1973, pp. 193–202. [G: Ghana]

Davidson, B. R. The Relationship Between the Price of Wool and the Relative Profitability of Sheep and Cattle Grazing in Australia and its Possible Effect on the Future Supplies of Wool and Beef. *Rev. Marketing Agr. Econ.,* March 1973, *41*(1), pp. 3–19. [G: Australia]

Davison, Cecil W. and Martin, Neil R., Jr. Sensitivity of Beef Quantity and Prices—1980 Preview. *Ill. Agr. Econ.,* July 1973, *13*(2), pp. 33–37. [G: U.S.]

Day, Richard H. Recursive Programming Models: A Brief Introduction. In *Judge, G. G. and Takayama, T., eds.,* 1973, pp. 329–44. [G: U.S.]

Decanio, Stephen. Cotton "Overproduction" in Late Nineteenth-Century Southern Agriculture. *J. Econ. Hist.,* September 1973, *33*(3), pp. 608–33.

Dietrich, J. Kimball and Gutierrez, Alfredo D. An Evaluation of Short-Term Forecasts of Coffee and Cocoa. *Amer. J. Agr. Econ.,* February 1973, *55*(1), pp. 93–99.

Donaldson, G. F. and McInerney, J. P. Changing

Machinery Technology and Agricultural Adjustment. *Amer. J. Agr. Econ.*, December 1973, *55*(5), pp. 829–39.

Dorling, M. J. Extending the Production-Distribution Model to Handle International Competition in Agriculture. *Can. J. Agr. Econ.*, February 1973, *21*(1), pp. 57–62.

Douglas, J. J. A Note on the Use of a Modified Input-Output Multiplier for Land Use Evaluation. *Australian J. Agr. Econ.*, April 1973, *17*(1), pp. 68–72. **[G: Australia]**

Due, Jean M. Experience with Mechanised Agriculture in Ghana and Sierra Leone Rice Production. In *Ofori, I. M., ed.*, 1973, pp. 203–16. **[G: Sierra Leone]**

Duloy, John H. and Norton, Roger D. CHAC, A Programming Model of Mexican Agriculture. In *Goreux, L. M. and Manne, A. S., eds.*, 1973, pp. 291–337. **[G: Mexico]**

Eldridge, D. P. and Saunders, N. C. Employment and Exports, 1963–72. *Mon. Lab. Rev.*, August 1973, *96*(8), pp. 16–27. **[G: U.S.]**

Evenson, Robert E. and Kislev, Yoav. Research and Productivity in Wheat and Maize. *J. Polit. Econ.*, November-December 1973, *81*(6), pp. 1309–29.

Farris, Paul L. Changes in Number and Size Distribution of U.S. Soybean Processing Firms. *Amer. J. Agr. Econ.*, August 1973, *55*(3), pp. 495–99. **[G: U.S.]**

Finke, Jeffrey and Swanson, E. R. Diversification in Illinois Crop Production: 1938–1970. *Ill. Agr. Econ.*, January 1973, *13*(1), pp. 8–11. **[G: U.S.]**

Firch, Robert S. Adjustments in a Slowly Declining U.S. Cotton Production Industry. *Amer. J. Agr. Econ.*, December 1973, *55*(5), pp. 892–902. **[G: U.S.]**

Freebairn, J. W. Some Estimates of Supply and Inventory Response Functions for the Cattle and Sheep Sector of New South Wales. *Rev. Marketing Agr. Econ.*, June and September 1973, *41*(2–3), pp. 53–90. **[G: Australia]**

Ghosh, Arabinda. Size-Structure, Productivity and Growth: A Case Study of West Bengal Agriculture. *Bangladesh Econ. Rev.*, January 1973, *1*(1), pp. 59–70. **[G: India]**

Girdlestone, J. N. and Parsons, S. A. The Regional Supply Pattern of Beef Cattle for Slaughter in Queensland. *Quart. Rev. Agr. Econ.*, January 1973, *26*(1), pp. 44–60. **[G: Australia]**

Green, Richard; Hassan, Zuhair A. and Johnson, Stanley R. An Alternative Method for Pricing Pork Carcasses. *Can. J. Agr. Econ.*, November 1973, *21*(3), pp. 1–5. **[G: Canada]**

Guedry, L. J. An Application of a Multi-Commodity Transportation Model to the U.S. Feed Grain Economy. In *Judge, G. G. and Takayama, T., eds.*, 1973, pp. 243–60. **[G: U.S.]**

Guise, J. W. B. and Aggrey-Mensah, W. An Evaluation of Policy Alternatives Facing Australian Banana Producers. In *Judge, G. G. and Takayama, T., eds.*, 1973, pp. 519–35. **[G: Australia]**

Guither, Harold D. Extension Education in Bargaining Among Midwest Livestock and Grain Producers. *Amer. J. Agr. Econ.*, February 1973, *55*(1), pp. 58–60. **[G: U.S.]**

Haizel, K. A. Ecological Problems of Agricultural Production in West Africa. In *Ofori, I. M., ed.*, 1973, pp. 82–90. **[G: W. Africa]**

Hall, Darwin C. and Norgaard, Richard B. On the Timing and Application of Pesticides. *Amer. J. Agr. Econ.*, May 1973, *55*(2), pp. 198–201.

Hammonds, T. M.; Yadav, R. and Vathana, C. The Elasticity of Demand for Hired Farm Labor. *Amer. J. Agr. Econ.*, May 1973, *55*(2), pp. 242–45. **[G: U.S.]**

Harris, Duane G. Harvesting a Record Corn Crop. *Fed. Res. Bank Bus. Rev. Phila.*, October 1973, pp. 9–14. **[G: U.S.]**

Harshbarger, C. Edward and Doll, Raymond J. Farm Prices and Food Prices: The Relevant Issues. *Fed. Res. Bank Kansas City Rev.*, May 1973, pp. 3–10. **[G: U.S.]**

Hassan, Zuhair A.; Finley, Robert M. and Johnson, Stanley R. The Demand for Food in the United States. *Appl. Econ.*, December 1973, *5*(4), pp. 233–48. **[G: U.S.]**

Hayami, Yujiro and Ruttan, Vernon W. Induced Innovation in Agricultural Development. In *Ayal, E. B., ed.*, 1973, pp. 181–208. **[G: U.S.; Japan]**

Hayami, Yujiro and Peterson, Willis. Social Return to Public Information Services: Statistical Reporting of U.S. Farm Commodities: Reply. *Amer. Econ. Rev.*, December 1973, *63*(5), pp. 1020–21. **[G: U.S.]**

Hoogvliet, W. The Australian Sheep Industry Survey 1971–72: Summary of Results and Recent Changes in the Structure and Economic Situation of the Industry. *Quart. Rev. Agr. Econ.*, July 1973, *26*(3), pp. 171–85. **[G: Australia]**

Hoogvliet, W. Production Adjustments and Productivity in the Australian Sheep Industry. *Quart. Rev. Agr. Econ.*, October 1973, *26*(4), pp. 239–52. **[G: Australia]**

Hossain, Mahabub and Quddus, M. A. Some Economic Aspects of Jute Production in Bangladesh —An Inter-District Study. *Bangladesh Econ. Rev.*, July 1973, *1*(3), pp. 269–96. **[G: Bangladesh]**

Hurtado, Hernán and Piñeiro, Martín. Rentabilidad potencial de la investigación ganadera: Una estimación empírica. (Rateable of Livestock Research: An Empirical Estimation. With English summary.) *Económica*, May-August 1973, *19*(2), pp. 185–200. **[G: Argentina]**

Hussain, Sayed M. Price Incentives for the Production of High Yielding Mexican Varieties of Wheat: A Rejoinder. *Pakistan Develop. Rev.*, Summer 1973, *12*(2), pp. 194–97. **[G: Pakistan]**

Jacobson, Robert E. and Walker, Francis E. Efficiency Considerations in Butterfat Differential and Component Pricing of Milk. *Amer. J. Agr. Econ.*, May 1973, *55*(2), pp. 214–16.

Jelavich, Mark S. Distributed Lag Estimation of Harmonic Motion in the Hog Market. *Amer. J. Agr. Econ.*, May 1973, *55*(2), pp. 223–24. **[G: U.S.]**

Johl, S. S. Green Revolution and What Next. *Econ. Aff.*, September-October 1973, *18*(9–10), pp. 405–13. **[G: India]**

Judge, G. G.; Havlicek, J. and Rizek, R. L. A Spatial Analysis of the U.S. Livestock Economy. In *Judge, G. G. and Takayama, T., eds.*, 1973, pp. 261–73. **[G: U.S.]**

Kaur, Surinderjit and Tagat, R. G. India's Green Revolution: Socio-Economic and Political Implications. *Econ. Aff.,* September-October 1973, *18*(9–10), pp. 414–27, 433. **[G: India]**

Khan, Mahmood H. "Green Revolution" or "Technocratic Euphoria." Some Problems of Rapid Agricultural Change in Asia. *Econ. Int.,* February 1973, *26*(1), pp. 119–34. **[G: Asia]**

Kim, S. Rural-Urban Migration and Technological Changes in the Agriculture of a Developing Country. *Econ. Rec.,* March 1973, *49*(125), pp. 15–23.

Köhler, Walter. Konkurrenzgleichgewicht und Zollwirkung am Brotmarkt. (Equilibrium under Conditions of Competition and Effects of Duties in the Baker's Market. With English summary.) *Jahr. Nationalökon. Statist.,* March 1973, *187*(3), pp. 218–36.

Kolawole, M. I. The Reform of Commodity Marketing Boards in Nigeria: An Analysis of New Producer Price Policy. *Econ. Bull. Ghana, Sec. Ser.,* 1973, *3*(3), pp. 14–19. **[G: Nigeria]**

Kottke, Marvin W. Allocation of Milk Through Space and Time in a Competitively-Mixed Dairy Industry. In *Judge, G. G. and Takayama, T., eds.,* 1973, pp. 557–78. **[G: U.S.]**

Krishna, Raj. A Note on the Elasticity of the Marketable Surplus of a Subsistence Crop. In *Wadhva, C. D., ed.,* 1973, pp. 313–18.

Kulshreshtha, S. N. and Wilson, A. G. A Harmonic Analysis of Cattle and Hog Cycles in Canada. *Can. J. Agr. Econ.,* November 1973, *21*(3), pp. 34–45. **[G: Canada]**

Kuznets, Simon. Economic Capacity and Population Growth. In *Kuznets, S.,* 1973, pp. 49–93.

Labys, Walter C. A Lauric Oil Exports Model Based on Capital Stock Supply Adjustment. *Malayan Econ. Rev.,* April 1973, *18*(1), pp. 1–10. **[G: Philippines; Ceylon; Indonesia]**

Lacci, Livio. Agriculture's Contribution to the Gross National Product in Italy. *Rev. Econ. Cond. Italy,* July 1973, *27*(4), pp. 236–50. **[G: Italy]**

Laird, Roy D. Handbook of Soviet Social Science Data: Agriculture. In *Mickiewicz, E., ed.,* 1973, pp. 65–90. **[G: U.S.S.R.]**

Lau, Lawrence J. and Yotopoulos, Pan A. Micro Functions in a Macro Model: An Application to Agricultural Employment and Development Strategies. In *Ayal, E. B., ed.,* 1973, pp. 212–40. **[G: India]**

Leunis, J. V. and Vandenborre, R. J. An Interregional Analysis of the United States Soybean Industry. In *Judge, G. G. and Takayama, T., eds.,* 1973, pp. 274–97. **[G: U.S.]**

Loyns, R. M. A. and Lu, W. F. A Cross-Section and Time-Series Analysis of Canadian Egg Demand. *Can. J. Agr. Econ.,* July 1973, *21*(2), pp. 1–15. **[G: Canada]**

Mackie, Arthur B. Patterns of World Agricultural Trade. In *Iowa State University Center for Agricultural and Rural Development,* 1973, pp. 69–86.

McCumstie, R. F. The New South Wales Beef Cattle Industry: A Summary of BAE Survey Results, 1968–69 to 1970–71. *Quart. Rev. Agr. Econ.,* April 1973, *26*(2), pp. 117–39. **[G: Australia]**

McShane, R. W. The Influence of Financial Factors on Household Meat Consumption. *Rev. Marketing Agr. Econ.,* March 1973, *41*(1), pp. 20–29. **[G: Australia]**

Miller, Bill R. and Masters, Gene C. A Short-Run Price Prediction Model for Eggs. *Amer. J. Agr. Econ.,* August 1973, *55*(3), pp. 484–89. **[G: U.S.]**

Miller, S. F. and Halter, A. N. Systems-Simulation in a Practical Policy-Making Setting: The Venezuelan Cattle Industry. *Amer. J. Agr. Econ.,* August 1973, *55*(3), pp. 420–32. **[G: Venezuela]**

Miller, Thomas A. Economic Adjustment Research for Policy Guidance: An Example from Agriculture. In *Judge, G. G. and Takayama, T., eds.,* 1973, pp. 65–88. **[G: U.S.]**

Newell, William H. The Agricultural Revolution in Nineteenth-Century France. *J. Econ. Hist.,* December 1973, *33*(4), pp. 697–731. **[G: France]**

Nowshirvani, Vahid F. A Note on the Elasticity of the Marketable Surplus of a Subsistence Crop—A Comment. In *Wadhva, C. D., ed.,* 1973, pp. 319–22.

Olayide, S. Olajuwon. Some Aspects of Beef Production in Nigeria. In *Ofori, I. M., ed.,* 1973, pp. 240–50. **[G: Nigeria]**

Oni, S. A. An Econometric Analysis of Western Nigerian Cocoa Output Response Relations. *Econ. Bull. Ghana, Sec. Ser.,* 1973, *3*(1), pp. 27–38. **[G: Nigeria]**

Pal, D. N. Agrarian Revolution. *Econ. Aff.,* September-October 1973, *18*(9–10), pp. 439–49. **[G: India]**

Pal, Sasanka Shekhar. Productivity of Farm Labour in the Context of Rural Unemployment (A Case Study of 79 Farms in a Village) *Econ. Aff.,* May 1973, *18*(5), pp. 241–48. **[G: India]**

Pandey, V. K. and Takayama, T. Temporal Equilibrium Analysis of Rice and Wheat in India. In *Judge, G. G. and Takayama, T., eds.,* 1973, pp. 579–96. **[G: India]**

Pant, S. P. and Takayama, T. An Investigation of Agricultural Planning Models: A Case Study of the Indian's Food Economy. In *Judge, G. G. and Takayama, T., eds.,* 1973, pp. 597–623. **[G: India]**

Papadopoulos, C. Factors Determining Australian Saleyard Prices for Beef Cattle. *Quart. Rev. Agr. Econ.,* July 1973, *26*(3), pp. 159–70. **[G: Australia]**

Parikh, A. United States, European, and World Demand Functions for Coffee. *Amer. J. Agr. Econ.,* August 1973, *55*(3), pp. 490–94.

Pliska, Stanley R. Supply of Storage Theory and Commodity Equilibrium Prices with Stochastic Production. *Amer. J. Agr. Econ.,* Part I, November 1973, *55*(4), pp. 653–58.

Prato, Anthony A. Milk Demand, Supply, and Price Relationships, 1950–1968. *Amer. J. Agr. Econ.,* May 1973, *55*(2), pp. 217–22. **[G: U.S.]**

Prosser, P. B. The Market for Beef in Japan. *Quart. Rev. Agr. Econ.,* April 1973, *26*(2), pp. 67–89. **[G: Japan]**

Purvis, Malcolm J. The New Varieties Under Dryland Conditions: Mexican Wheats In Tunisia.

Amer. J. Agr. Econ., February 1973, *55*(1), pp. 54–57. **[G: Tunisia]**

Rees, Richard D. World Wheat Production and Trade. *Fed. Res. Bank Kansas City Rev.*, June 1973, pp. 10–16.

Reid, G. K. R. and Thomas, D. A. Pastoral Production, Stocking Rate and Seasonal Conditions. *Quart. Rev. Agr. Econ.*, October 1973, *26*(4), pp. 217–27. **[G: Australia]**

Rochin, Refugio I. A Study of Bangladesh Farmers' Experiences with IR-20 Rice Variety and Complementary Production Inputs. *Bangladesh Econ. Rev.*, January 1973, *1*(1), pp. 71–94. **[G: Bangladesh]**

Roy, Sujit K. and Johnson, Phillip N. Econometric Models for Quarterly Shell Egg Prices. *Amer. J. Agr. Econ.*, May 1973, *55*(2), pp. 209–13. **[G: U.S.]**

Ryan, James G. Some Implications of Rice Price and Policy Changes for Irrigated Farms. *Rev. Marketing Agr. Econ.*, June and September 1973, *41* (2–3), pp. 39–52. **[G: Australia]**

Ryan, Mary E. and Abel, Martin E. Oats and Barley Acreage Response to Government Programs. *Agr. Econ. Res.*, October 1973, *25*(4), pp. 105–14. **[G: U.S.]**

Ryan, Mary E. and Abel, Martin E. Supply Response of U.S. Sorghum Acreage to Government Programs. *Agr. Econ. Res.*, April 1973, *25*(2), pp. 45–55. **[G: U.S.]**

Salkin, Jay S. The Optimal Level of Production in Generalized Production Functions an Application to South Vietnamese Rice Production. *Malayan Econ. Rev.*, October 1973, *18*(2), pp. 60–67. **[G: S. Vietnam]**

Sandhu, H. S. and Gupta, J. R. Adoption and Performance of Recommended Practices—A Comparative Study of Two Villages in Ludhiana District. *Econ. Aff.*, August 1973, *18*(8), pp. 389–94. **[G: India]**

Schmitz, Andrew and Bawden, D. Lee. A Spatial Price Analysis of the World Wheat Economy: Some Long-Run Predictions. In *Judge, G. G. and Takayama, T., eds.,* 1973, pp. 488–516.

Schnittker, John A. The 1972–73 Food Price Spiral. *Brookings Pap. Econ. Act.*, 1973, (2), pp. 498–507. **[G: U.S.]**

Shand, R. T. The Spectrum of Cash Crop Participation in New Guinea Villages. In *Epstein, T. S. and Penny, D. H., eds.,* 1973, pp. 69–85. **[G: New Guinea]**

Singh, Balwinder; Rangi, P. S. and Sankhayan, P. L. Relative Contributions of Area and Productivity in Increasing Production of Major Foodgrain Crops in Panjab (1960–61 to 1969–70) *Econ. Aff.*, March 1973, *18*(3), pp. 124–30. **[G: India]**

Singh, H. P. Export of Spices. *Econ. Aff.*, March 1973, *18*(3), pp. 131–42. **[G: India]**

Smallhorn, P. J. Demand Elasticities for Raw Wool in Japan. *Quart. Rev. Agr. Econ.*, October 1973, *26*(4), pp. 253–62. **[G: Japan]**

Smith, Blair J. Dynamic Programming of the Dairy Cow Replacement Program. *Amer. J. Agr. Econ.*, February 1973, *55*(1), pp. 100–04.

Smith, Lawrence N. and Scherr, Bruce A. Social Return to Public Information Services: Statistical

Reporting of U.S. Farm Commodities: Comment. *Amer. Econ. Rev.*, December 1973, *63*(5), pp. 1017–19. **[G: U.S.]**

Smyth, David J. Effect of Public Price Forecasts on Market Price Variation: A Stochastic Cobweb Example. *Amer. J. Agr. Econ.*, February 1973, *55*(1), pp. 83–88.

Spencer, Dustan S. C. Rice Production and Marketing in Sierra Leone. In *Ofori, I. M., ed.,* 1973, pp. 217–30. **[G: Sierra Leone]**

Srinivasan, M. Problems of Inputs (With Special Reference to Water and Fertilisers) in Indian Agriculture. *Econ. Aff.*, September-October 1973, *18*(9–10), pp. 466–74. **[G: India]**

Srivastava, Uma K. and Heady, Earl O. Technological Change and Relative Factor Shares in Indian Agriculture: An Empirical Analysis. *Amer. J. Agr. Econ.*, August 1973, *55*(3), pp. 509–14. **[G: India]**

Srivastava, Uma K.; Nagadevara, Vishnuprasad and Heady, Earl O. Resource Productivity, Returns to Scale and Farm Size in Indian Agriculture: Some Recent Evidence. *Australian J. Agr. Econ.*, April 1973, *17*(1), pp. 43–57. **[G: India]**

Standen, B. J. Where Are the Markets for Farm Poplar on the North Coast? *Rev. Marketing Agr. Econ.*, June and September 1973, *41*(2–3), pp. 91–92. **[G: Australia]**

Suslov, I. Technical Progress and Effectiveness of Agriculture. *Prob. Econ.*, January 1973, *15*(9), pp. 47–60. **[G: U.S.S.R.]**

Swamy, Subramanian. Economic Growth in China and India, 1952–1970: A Comparative Appraisal. *Econ. Develop. Cult. Change*, Part II, July 1973, *21*(4), pp. 1–84. **[G: China; India]**

Swanson, E. R.; Taylor, C. R. and Welch, L. F. Economically Optimal Levels of Nitrogen Fertilizer for Corn: An Analysis Based on Experimental Data, 1966–71. *Ill. Agr. Econ.*, July 1973, *13*(2), pp. 16–25. **[G: U.S.]**

Syed, Hasan A. Demand for and Supply of Pulses in the Punjab. *Pakistan Econ. Soc. Rev.*, Winter 1973, *11*(4), pp. 363–77. **[G: Pakistan]**

Taylor, C. R. and Swanson, E. R. Experimental Nitrogen Response Functions, Actual Farm Experience and Policy Analysis. *Ill. Agr. Econ.*, July 1973, *13*(2), pp. 26–32. **[G: U.S.]**

Taylor, C. R. An Analysis of Nitrate Concentrations in Illinois Streams. *Ill. Agr. Econ.*, January 1973, *13*(1), pp. 12–19. **[G: U.S.]**

Timmer, C. Peter. Choice of Technique in Rice Milling in Java. *Bull. Indonesian Econ. Stud.*, July 1973, *9*(2), pp. 57–76. **[G: Indonesia]**

Tryfos, Peter and Tryphonopoulos, N. Consumer Demand for Meat in Canada. *Amer. J. Agr. Econ.*, Part I, November 1973, *55*(4), pp. 647–52. **[G: Canada]**

Tryfos, Peter. The Determinants of Prices and Employment in the Canadian Meat Industry. *Can. J. Agr. Econ.*, July 1973, *21*(2), pp. 25–42. **[G: Canada]**

Vasquez, Thomas and Ott, David J. Agriculture. In *Ott, D. J., et al.,* 1973, pp. 53–65. **[G: U.S.]**

Weinschenck, G.; Henrichsmeyer, W. and Hanf, C. H. Experiences with Multi-Commodity Models in Regional Analysis. In *Judge, G. G. and*

Takayama, T., eds., 1973, pp. 307–26. [G: W. Germany]

Wickens, M. R. and Greenfield, J. N. The Econometrics of Agricultural Supply: An Application to the World Coffee Market. *Rev. Econ. Statist.*, November 1973, *55*(4), pp. 433–40.

Wills, Ian R. and Lloyd, A. G. Economic Theory and Sheep-Cattle Combinations. *Australian J. Agr. Econ.*, April 1973, *17*(1), pp. 58–67. [G: Australia]

Wong, John. Agricultural Production and Socialist Transformation in China: Two Decades After. *Malayan Econ. Rev.*, October 1973, *18*(2), pp. 1–15. [G: China]

Yeung, Patrick. Induced Innovation in Agricultural Development: Comment. In *Ayal, E. B., ed.*, 1973, pp. 208–11.

Yotopoulos, Pan A. Agricultural and Factory Processes: Implications for Empirical Research. *Food Res. Inst. Stud.*, 1973, *12*(2), pp. 159–67.

Young, Ralph and Crestani, I. Productivity Change and Farm Income. *Quart. Rev. Agr. Econ.*, July 1973, *26*(3), pp. 198–214. [G: Australia]

Zusman, P.; Melamed, A. and Katzir, I. A Spatial Analysis of the EEC Trade Policies in the Market for Winter Oranges. In *Judge, G. G. and Takayama, T., eds.*, 1973, pp. 464–87. [G: E.E.C.]

712 Agricultural Situation and Outlook

7120 Agricultural Situation and Outlook

Alderfer, Evan B. Changing Times on Pennsylvania Farms. *Fed. Res. Bank Bus. Rev. Phila.*, May 1973, pp. 18–26. [G: U.S.]

Arndt, H. W. Survey of Recent Developments. *Bull. Indonesian Econ. Stud.*, July 1973, *9*(2), pp. 1–27. [G: Indonesia]

Barraclough, Solon. The Structure and Problems of the Chilean Agrarian Sector. In *Zammit, J. A., ed.*, 1973, pp. 115–22. [G: Chile]

Barraza, Luciano and Solís, Leopoldo. Agricultural Policies and the Role of the Sectoral Model. In *Goreux, L. M. and Manne, A. S., eds.*, 1973, pp. 463–75. [G: Mexico]

Bickel, Blaine W. Meeting Consumer Demand for Beef—From Ranch to Roast. *Fed. Res. Bank Kansas City Rev.*, April 1973, pp. 12–19. [G: U.S.]

Bonnen, James T. Implications for Agricultural Policy. *Amer. J. Agr. Econ.*, August 1973, *55*(3), pp. 391–98. [G: U.S.]

Chen, Dean. Horn of Plenty. *Fed. Res. Bank San Francisco Rev.*, March-April 1973, pp. 12–16. [G: U.S.]

Craddock, W. J. The Agricultural Production Plant —What Can It Accomplish in Output and Stability? In *Canadian Agricultural Economics Society,* 1973, pp. 82–97. [G: Canada]

Drtina, František. International Position of Czechoslovak Agriculture. *Czech. Econ. Digest.*, June 1973, (4), pp. 57–76. [G: Czechoslovakia]

Duloy, John H. and Norton, Roger D. CHAC Results: Economic Alternatives for Mexican Agriculture. In *Goreux, L. M. and Manne, A. S., eds.,* 1973, pp. 373–99. [G: Mexico]

Harshbarger, C. Edward. A Look at 1973: Agriculture Has a Tough Act to Follow. *Fed. Res. Bank Kansas City Rev.*, January 1973, pp. 3–10. [G: U.S.]

Harshbarger, C. Edward. 1974 Agricultural Outlook: How High the Summit? *Fed. Res. Bank Kansas City Rev.*, December 1973, pp. 12–20. [G: U.S.]

Heady, Earl O. Fundamental Issues in Trade of Farm Commodities. In *Iowa State University Center for Agricultural and Rural Development,* 1973, pp. 3–16. [G: U.S.]

Hoogvliet, W. Recent Developments in the Victorian Lamb Industry: An Economic Survey, 1968–69 to 1970–71, Preliminary Results. *Quart. Rev. Agr. Econ.*, April 1973, *26*(2), pp. 100–16. [G: Australia]

Hunter, Guy. The Food Research Institute's Fiftieth Anniversary Conference, Strategies for Agricultural Development in the 1970s. *Food Res. Inst. Stud.*, 1973, *12*(1), pp. 3–72.

Ioanes, Raymond A. Trends and Structure of U.S. Agricultural Trade. In *Iowa State University Center for Agricultural and Rural Development,* 1973, pp. 87–102. [G: U.S.]

de Janvry, Alain. A Socioeconomic Model of Induced Innovations for Argentine Agricultural Development. *Quart. J. Econ.*, August 1973, *87*(3), pp. 410–435. [G: Argentina]

Johl, S. S. Green Revolution and What Next. *Econ. Aff.*, September-October 1973, *18*(9–10), pp. 405–13. [G: India]

Khan, Dilawar Ali and Ali, Chaudhari Haider. Income Impact of the Green Revolution. *Pakistan Econ. Soc. Rev.*, Spring 1973, *11*(1), pp. 67–82. [G: Pakistan]

Luttrell, Clifton B. Food and Agriculture in 1973. *Fed. Res. Bank St. Louis Rev.*, May 1973, *55*(5), pp. 11–16. [G: U.S.]

Mahadevan, P. Nutrition and Agriculture. In *Berg, A.; Scrimshaw, N. S. and Call, D. L., eds.,* 1973, pp. 150–53.

McCumstie, R. F. The New South Wales Beef Cattle Industry: A Summary of BAE Survey Results, 1968–69 to 1970–71. *Quart. Rev. Agr. Econ.*, April 1973, *26*(2), pp. 117–39. [G: Australia]

Mercer, Lloyd J. Corporate Farming in the United States: Discussion. *J. Econ. Hist.*, March 1973, *33*(1), pp. 291–95.

Passell, Peter. Corporate Farming in the United States: Discussion. *J. Econ. Hist.*, March 1973, *33*(1), pp. 296–98.

Raup, Phillip. Corporate Farming in the United States. *J. Econ. Hist.*, March 1973, *33*(1), pp. 274–90. [G: U.S.]

Richter, Joseph J. Discussion: The Position of an Importer of Canadian Agricultural Products: Marketing Requirements for Pacific Rim Markets. In *Canadian Agricultural Economics Society,* 1973, pp. 38–42. [G: Canada; Japan]

Rochin, Refugio I. A Study of Bangladesh Farmers' Experiences with IR-20 Rice Variety and Complementary Production Inputs. *Bangladesh Econ. Rev.*, January 1973, *1*(1), pp. 71–94. [G: Bangladesh]

Schmitz, Andrew and Bawden, D. Lee. A Spatial Price Analysis of the World Wheat Economy:

Some Long-Run Predictions. In *Judge, G. G. and Takayama, T., eds.*, 1973, pp. 488–516.

Sturgess, Ian. The Prospects of UK Cereal Surpluses. *Nat. Westminster Bank Quart. Rev.*, February 1973, pp. 35–45. [G: U.K.]

Újhelyi, T. Foreign Trade in Agricultural and Food Products—The Hungarian National Economy and the World Market. *Acta Oecon.*, 1973, *11*(1), pp. 3–18. [G: Hungary]

Umemoto, H. E. Marketing Requirements for the Pacific Rim: The Position of an Importer. In *Canadian Agricultural Economics Society*, 1973, pp. 27–37. [G: Canada; Japan]

Williams, S. W. Potential of Soybeans as Food in India. *Ill. Agr. Econ.*, January 1973, *13*(1), pp. 1–7. [G: India]

713 Agricultural Policy, Domestic and International

7130 Agricultural Policy, Domestic and International

Abkin, M. H., et al. System Simulation of Agricultural Development: Some Nigerian Policy Comparisons. *Amer. J. Agr. Econ.*, August 1973, *55*(3), pp. 404–19. [G: Nigeria]

Anker, Desmond L. W. Rural Development Problems and Strategies. *Int. Lab. Rev.*, December 1973, *108*(6), pp. 461–84.

Austman, H. H. Agricultural Economists Responding to an Expanding Clientele. *Amer. J. Agr. Econ.*, December 1973, *55*(5), pp. 989–92. [G: Canada]

Avramescu, P. Coordonate ale intensificării aviculturii în cooperativele agricole de producție. (Coordinates of the Intensification of Poultry Farming in the Agricultural Production Cooperatives. With English summary.) *Stud. Cercet. Econ.*, 1973, (3), pp. 51–72. [G: Rumania]

Azhar, B. A. Agricultural Taxation in West Pakistan. *Pakistan Econ. Soc. Rev.*, Autumn 1973, *11*(3), pp. 288–315. [G: Pakistan]

Baer, Donald E. Income and Export Taxation of Agriculture in Costa Rica and Honduras. *J. Devel. Areas*, October 1973, *8*(1), pp. 39–53. [G: Costa Rica; Honduras]

Ballinger, Roy A. The Benefits and Burdens of the United States Sugar Quota System. In *Harriss, C. L., ed.*, 1973, pp. 105–13. [G: U.S.]

Barraza, Luciano and Solís, Leopoldo. Agricultural Policies and the Role of the Sectoral Model. In *Goreux, L. M. and Manne, A. S., eds.*, 1973, pp. 463–75. [G: Mexico]

Bazlova, A. Improving Purchase Prices on Agricultural Output. *Prob. Econ.*, July 1973, *16*(3), pp. 37–58. [G: U.S.S.R.]

Bergsten, C. Fred. Future Directions for U.S. Trade. *Amer. J. Agr. Econ.*, May 1973, *55*(2), pp. 280–88. [G: U.S.]

Berlage, Lodewijk J. J. B. An Application of Dynamic Programming Models to Foodgrain Import and Storage Policy in Bangladesh. *Bangladesh Econ. Rev.*, October 1973, *1*(4), pp. 341–74. [G: Bangladesh]

Bonnen, James T. Implications for Agricultural Policy. *Amer. J. Agr. Econ.*, August 1973, *55*(3), pp. 391–98. [G: U.S.]

Boulding, Kenneth E. Agricultural Organizations and Policies: A Personal Evaluation. In *Boulding, K. E.*, 1973, pp. 161–73. [G: U.S.]

Boulding, Kenneth E. Parity, Charity, and Clarity. In *Boulding, K. E.*, 1973, pp. 121–25. [G: U.S.]

Boxley, Robert F. and Anderson, William D. The Incidence of Benefits from Commodity Price-Support Programs: A Case Study of Tobacco. In *Harriss, C. L., ed.*, 1973, pp. 79–103. [G: U.S.]

Bradley, Michael E. Incentives and Labour Supply on Soviet Collective Farms: Reply. *Can. J. Econ.*, August 1973, *6*(3), pp. 438–42.

Brandow, G. E. Conflicts and Consistencies in the Agricultural Policies of the United States and Canada. *Amer. J. Agr. Econ.*, December 1973, *55* (5), pp. 778–84. [G: U.S.; Canada]

Browning, Thomas L. and Reinsel, Edward I. Distribution of Farm Program Payments by Income of Sole Proprietors. *Agr. Econ. Res.*, April 1973, *25* (2), pp. 41–44. [G: U.S.]

Cameron, Norman. Incentives and Labour Supply on Soviet Collective Farms: Rejoinder. *Can. J. Econ.*, August 1973, *6*(3), pp. 442–44.

Campbell, Keith. The State Marketing Board—Relic or Prototype? *Australian J. Agr. Econ.*, December 1973, *17*(3), pp. 179–88. [G: Australia]

Carman, Hoy F. and Youde, James G. Alternative Tax Treatment of Orchard Development Costs: Impacts on Producers, Middlemen, and Consumers. *Amer. J. Agr. Econ.*, May 1973, *55*(2), pp. 184–91. [G: U.S.]

Channon, J. W. Role of Provincial Governments in Export Market Development. In *Canadian Agricultural Economics Society*, 1973, pp. 49–57. [G: Canada]

Chapman, R. and Foley, K. A Note on Losses from Price Stabilization. *Australian J. Agr. Econ.*, August 1973, *17*(2), pp. 140–43. [G: Australia]

Chaudhry, M. Ghaffar. The Problem of Agricultural Taxation in West Pakistan and an Alternative Solution. *Pakistan Develop. Rev.*, Summer 1973, *12* (2), pp. 93–122. [G: Pakistan]

Chonchol, Jacques. The Agrarian Policy of the Popular Government. In *Zammit, J. A., ed.*, 1973, pp. 107–14. [G: Chile]

Ch'ün, An. The Basic Problem in the Development of Agriculture Lies in the Line. *Chinese Econ. Stud.*, Winter 1973–74, *7*(2), pp. 7–17. [G: China]

Cline, William R. Interrelationships Between Agricultural Strategy and Rural Income Distribution. *Food Res. Inst. Stud.*, 1973, *12*(2), pp. 139–57.

Dadson, J. A. Farm Size and the Modernization of Agriculture in Ghana. In *Ofori, I. M., ed.*, 1973, pp. 193–202. [G: Ghana]

Dawson, R. M. Canadian Trade and Tariff Policy as it Relates to the Pacific Rim. In *Canadian Agricultural Economics Society*, 1973, pp. 43–48. [G: Canada; Oceania]

Dixon, Orani; Dixon, Peter and Miranowski, John. Insecticide Requirements in an Efficient Agricultural Sector. *Rev. Econ. Statist.*, November 1973,

55(4), pp. 423–32. [G: U.S.]

Due, Jean M. and Gehring, Donald C. Jamaica's Strategy for Import Substitution of Vegetables in the 1960's. *Ill. Agr. Econ.*, January 1973, *13*(1), pp. 20–26. [G: Jamaica]

Duloy, John H. and Norton, Roger D. CHAC Results: Economic Alternatives for Mexican Agriculture. In *Goreux, L. M. and Manne, A. S., eds.*, 1973, pp. 373–99. [G: Mexico]

Fiorentino, Raúl and Dean, Geral. Política agraria para la economía yerbatera como contribución al desarrollo agrícola misionero, un enfoque estructural. (Agricultural Policy for the Argentine Yerba Mate Industry and the Small Farm Sector of Misiones, a Structural Approach. With English summary.) *Económica*, September-December 1973, *19*(3), pp. 265–91. [G: Argentina]

Firch, Robert S. Adjustments in a Slowly Declining U.S. Cotton Production Industry. *Amer. J. Agr. Econ.*, December 1973, *55*(5), pp. 892–902. [G: U.S.]

Freebairn, J. W. The Value of Information Provided by a Uniform Grading System. *Australian J. Agr. Econ.*, August 1973, *17*(2), pp. 127–39.

Gandhi, Ved P. Tax Burden on Indian Agriculture. In *Wadhva, C. D., ed.*, 1973, pp. 340–45. [G: India]

Gilson, J. C. A Canadian View of Conflicts and Consistencies in the Agricultural Policies of Canada and the United States. *Amer. J. Agr. Econ.*, December 1973, *55*(5), pp. 785–90. [G: U.S.; Canada]

Griffin, Keith. Policy Options for Rural Development. *Oxford Bull. Econ. Statist.*, November 1973, *35*(4), pp. 239–74.

Griffin, Wade L. and Lacewell, Ronald D. Long-Run Implications of a Tax in Kind to Reduce Supply and Increase Income: Comment. *Amer. J. Agr. Econ.*, Part I, November 1973, *55*(4), pp. 670–74.

Guise, J. W. B. and Aggrey-Mensah, W. An Evaluation of Policy Alternatives Facing Australian Banana Producers. In *Judge, G. G. and Takayama, T., eds.*, 1973, pp. 519–35. [G: Australia]

Hamid, Javed. The Problem of Agricultural Taxation in West Pakistan and an Alternative Solution: Comment. *Pakistan Develop. Rev.*, Autumn 1973, *12*(3), pp. 311–14. [G: Pakistan]

Harris, Gene. Some Aspects of Decentralisation and the Formulation and Implementation of Agricultural Policy in Ghana. In *Ofori, I. M., ed.*, 1973, pp. 177–92. [G: Ghana]

Heady, Earl O. Fundamental Issues in Trade of Farm Commodities. In *Iowa State University Center for Agricultural and Rural Development*, 1973, pp. 3–16. [G: U.S.]

Heady, Earl O. Long-Run Implications of a Tax in Kind to Reduce Supply and Increase Income: Reply. *Amer. J. Agr. Econ.*, Part I, November 1973, *55*(4), pp. 675.

Heady, Earl O. and Madsen, Howard C. National and Interregional Models of Water Demand for Land Use and Agricultural Policies. In *Judge, G. G. and Takayama, T., eds.*, 1973, pp. 651–75. [G: U.S.]

Heady, Earl O., et al. National and Interregional Models of Water Demand, Land Use, and Agricul-

tural Policies. *Water Resources Res.*, August 1973, *9*(4), pp. 777–91. [G: U.S.]

Hiscocks, Geoffrey A. The Role of the Federal Government in Export Market Development. In *Canadian Agricultural Economics Society*, 1973, pp. 69–81. [G: Canada]

Houck, James P. Some Aspects of Income Stabilization for Primary Producers. *Australian J. Agr. Econ.*, December 1973, *17*(3), pp. 200–15. [G: Australia]

Hunter, Guy. Agricultural Administration and Institutions. *Food Res. Inst. Stud.*, 1973, *12*(3), pp. 233–51.

Hunter, Guy. The Food Research Institute's Fiftieth Anniversary Conference, Strategies for Agricultural Development in the 1970s. *Food Res. Inst. Stud.*, 1973, *12*(1), pp. 3–72.

Hussain, Sayed M. Price Incentives for the Production of High Yielding Mexican Varieties of Wheat: A Rejoinder. *Pakistan Develop. Rev.*, Summer 1973, *12*(2), pp. 194–97. [G: Pakistan]

Johnson, D. Gale. What Difference Does Trade Make in World Community Welfare? In *Iowa State University Center for Agricultural and Rural Development*, 1973, pp. 49–68. [G: E.E.C.; U.S.]

Johnson, D. Gale. The Impact of Freer Trade on North American Agriculture. *Amer. J. Agr. Econ.*, May 1973, *55*(2), pp. 294–99. [G: U.S.; Canada]

Johnson, D. Gale. Government and Agricultural Adjustment. *Amer. J. Agr. Econ.*, December 1973, *55*(5), pp. 860–67.

Josling, Tim. Domestic Farm Policies and International Trade in Agricultural Goods. In *Streeten, P., ed.*, 1973, pp. 264–78.

Josling, Tim. The Common Agricultural Policy of the European Economic Community. In *Krauss, M. B., ed.*, 1973, pp. 267–96. [G: E.E.C.]

Just, Richard E. A Methodology for Investigating the Importance of Government Intervention in Farmers' Decisions. *Amer. J. Agr. Econ.*, August 1973, *55*(3), pp. 441–52. [G: U.S.]

Kahn, Mahmood A. and Kahn, Dilawar A. Rural Development Strategy and Need for Institution Building at Village Level. *Pakistan Econ. Soc. Rev.*, Winter 1973, *11*(4), pp. 383–402. [G: Pakistan]

Karcz, Jerzy F. Agricultural Reform in Eastern Europe. In *Bornstein, M., ed.*, 1973, pp. 207–43. [G: E. Europe]

Kaur, Surinderjit and Tagat, R. G. India's Green Revolution: Socio-Economic and Political Implications. *Econ. Aff.*, September-October 1973, *18*(9–10), pp. 414–27, 433. [G: India]

Khan, Mahmood H. "Green Revolution" or "Technocratic Euphoria." Some Problems of Rapid Agricultural Change in Asia. *Econ. Int.*, February 1973, *26*(1), pp. 119–34. [G: Asia]

Kolawole, M. I. The Reform of Commodity Marketing Boards in Nigeria: An Analysis of New Producer Price Policy. *Econ. Bull. Ghana, Sec. Ser.*, 1973, *3*(3), pp. 14–19. [G: Nigeria]

Kriesel, Herbert C. and Hedley, Douglas D. Planners as Factors in Agricultural Growth. In *Ofori, I. M., ed.*, 1973, pp. 33–41.

Krishna, Raj. Government Operations in Foodgrains. In *Wadhva, C. D., ed.*, 1973, pp. 323–39. [G: India]

Lau, Lawrence J. and Yotopoulos, Pan A. Micro Functions in a Macro Model: An Application to Agricultural Employment and Development Strategies. In *Ayal, E. B., ed.*, 1973, pp. 212–40. [G: India]

Lent, George E. Taxation of Agricultural Income in Developing Countries. *Bull. Int. Fiscal Doc.*, August 1973, *27*(8), pp. 324–42.

Lewis, Stephen R., Jr. Agricultural Taxation and Intersectoral Resource Transfers. *Food Res. Inst. Stud.*, 1973, *12*(2), pp. 93–114.

Lissner, Will. Developing Agriculture in Low Income Countries. *Amer. J. Econ. Soc.*, October 1973, *32*(4), pp. 436–38.

Lockner, Allyn O. and Kim, Han J. Circuit-Breakers on Farm-Property-Tax Overload: A Case Study. *Nat. Tax J.*, June 1973, *26*(2), pp. 233–40. [G: U.S.]

Mafeje, Archie. Agrarian Revolution and the Land Question in Buganda. In *Institute for Development Research*, 1973, pp. 127–54. [G: Uganda; U.K.]

Manogaran, Chelvadurai. Economic Feasibility of Irrigating Southern Pipes. *Water Resources Res.*, December 1973, *9*(6), pp. 1485–96. [G: U.S.]

Márton, J. The Vertical Integration of the Hungarian Food Economy. *Acta Oecon.*, 1973, *11*(1), pp. 81–96. [G: Hungary]

Mayer, Leo V. Regional Effects of Alternative Trade Policies. In *Iowa State University Center for Agricultural and Rural Development*, 1973, pp. 166–83. [G: U.S.]

Miller, S. F. and Halter, A. N. Systems-Simulation in a Practical Policy-Making Setting: The Venezuelan Cattle Industry. *Amer. J. Agr. Econ.*, August 1973, *55*(3), pp. 420–32. [G: Venezuela]

Miller, Thomas A. Economic Adjustment Research for Policy Guidance: An Example from Agriculture. In *Judge, G. G. and Takayama, T., eds.*, 1973, pp. 65–88. [G: U.S.]

Nath, Shyam. On Moping of the Agricultural Surplus. *Econ. Aff.*, January–February 1973, *18*(1-2), pp. 81–85.

Nath, Vishwa. Progress of New Agricultural Strategy in India. *Econ. Aff.*, September-October 1973, *18* (9–10), pp. 450–54. [G: India]

Nondasuta, Amorn. Suggested Components of Intervention Programs. In *Berg, A.; Scrimshaw, N. S. and Call, D. L., eds.*, 1973, pp. 223–28.

Norman, D. W. and Simmons, E. B. Determination of Relevant Research Priorities for Farm Development in West Africa. In *Ofori, I. M., ed.*, 1973, pp. 42–48.

Ogren, Kenneth E. Exports of U.S. Capital and Technology and International Political Conflicts. In *Iowa State University Center for Agricultural and Rural Development*, 1973, pp. 210–24. [G: U.S.]

Plaunt, Darrel H. Agricultural Development Policies and Programs in Canada. *Amer. J. Agr. Econ.*, December 1973, *55*(5), pp. 903–12. [G: Canada]

Prybyla, Jan S. Soviet Economic Reforms in Agriculture. *Weltwirtsch. Arch.*, 1973, *109*(4), pp. 644–87. [G: U.S.S.R.]

Qureshi, Sarfraz K. The Problem of Agricultural Tax-

ation in West Pakistan and an Alternative Solution: A Comment. *Pakistan Develop. Rev.*, Winter 1973, *12*(4), pp. 433–37. [G: Pakistan]

Raj, K. N. Direct Taxation of Agriculture. *Indian Econ. Rev.*, April 1973, *8*(1), pp. 1–15. [G: India]

Raup, Phillip. Corporate Farming in the United States. *J. Econ. Hist.*, March 1973, *33*(1), pp. 274–90. [G: U.S.]

Rees, Richard D. World Wheat Production and Trade. *Fed. Res. Bank Kansas City Rev.*, June 1973, pp. 10–16.

Richards, A. I. Government Policy and the Commercial Farmer. In *Richards, A. I.; Sturrock, F. and Fortt, J. M., eds.*, 1973, pp. 85–92. [G: Uganda]

Richardson, Robert A. and Farris, Paul L. Farm Commodity Price Stabilization Through Futures Markets. *Amer. J. Agr. Econ.*, May 1973, *55*(2), pp. 225–30. [G: U.S.]

Richter, Joseph J. Discussion: The Position of an Importer of Canadian Agricultural Products: Marketing Requirements for Pacific Rim Markets. In *Canadian Agricultural Economics Society*, 1973, pp. 38–42. [G: Canada; Japan]

Robertson, David. Multilateral Trade Negotiations. *Nat. Westminster Bank Quart. Rev.*, February 1973, pp. 46–58.

Ryan, Mary E. and Abel, Martin E. Oats and Barley Acreage Response to Government Programs. *Agr. Econ. Res.*, October 1973, *25*(4), pp. 105–14. [G: U.S.]

Ryan, Mary E. and Abel, Martin E. Supply Response of U.S. Sorghum Acreage to Government Programs. *Agr. Econ. Res.*, April 1973, *25*(2), pp. 45–55. [G: U.S.]

Schnittker, John A. Prospects for Freer Agricultural Trade. *Amer. J. Agr. Econ.*, May 1973, *55*(2), pp. 289–93.

Schultze, Charles L. U.S. Farm Policy: Who Gets the Benefits. In *Haveman, R. H. and Hamrin, R. D., eds.*, 1973, pp. 182–90. [G: U.S.]

Smith, Douglas V. Opportunity for Village Development: The Tanks of Bangladesh. *Bangladesh Econ. Rev.*, July 1973, *1*(3), pp. 297–308. [G: Bangladesh]

Smith, Theodore Reynolds. Community Development and Agrarian Reform in the East Asian Setting. *Amer. J. Econ. Soc.*, January 1973, *32*(1), pp. 73–86. [G: E. Asia]

Sorenson, Vernon L. Contradictions in U.S. Trade Policy. In *Iowa State University Center for Agricultural and Rural Development*, 1973, pp. 184–93. [G: U.S.]

Taylor, C. R. and Swanson, E. R. Experimental Nitrogen Response Functions, Actual Farm Experience and Policy Analysis. *Ill. Agr. Econ.*, July 1973, *13*(2), pp. 26–32. [G: U.S.]

Thorbecke, Erik. Sector Analysis and Models of Agriculture in Developing Countries. *Food Res. Inst. Stud.*, 1973, *12*(1), pp. 73–89.

Tisdell, Clement A. A Comment on Losses from Stabilization. *Australian J. Agr. Econ.*, August 1973, *17*(2), pp. 144–45. [G: Australia]

Tontz, Robert L. U.S. Trade Policy: Background and Historical Trends. In *Iowa State University Center for Agricultural and Rural Development*,

1973, pp. 17–48. [G: U.S.]

Trant, G. I. Adjustment Problems and Policies Within a Framework of Political Economy. *Amer. J. Agr. Econ.*, December 1973, *55*(5), pp. 888–91. [G: Canada; U.S.]

Tulloch, Peter. Developing Countries and the Enlargement of the EEC. In *Dinwiddy, B., ed.,* 1973, pp. 88–111. [G: E.E.C.]

Umemoto, H. E. Marketing Requirements for the Pacific Rim: The Position of an Importer. In *Canadian Agricultural Economics Society,* 1973, pp. 27–37. [G: Canada; Japan]

Valdés E., Alberto. Trade Policy and Its Effect on the External Agricultural Trade of Chile 1945–1965. *Amer. J. Agr. Econ.*, May 1973, *55*(2), pp. 154–64. [G: Chile]

Van Lam, Ngo. The Pursuit of Growth and Stability Through Taxation of Agricultural Exports: Thailand's Experience: A Comment. *Public Finance,* 1973, *28*(2), pp. 227–32. [G: Thailand]

Van Roy, Edward. Ngo Van Lam on the Rice Premium: A Rejoinder. *Public Finance,* 1973, *28* (2), pp. 233–36.

Vercruijsse, E. V. W. and Boyd, T. A. Evaluation of an Extension Programme in Agriculture. In *Ofori, I. M., ed.,* 1973, pp. 57–66. [G: Ghana]

Wilson, A. G. Examination of Alternative Methods, Approaches, and Programs for Production and Market Stabilization with Particular Reference to the Pacific Rim Market. In *Canadian Agricultural Economics Society,* 1973, pp. 98–140. [G: Canada; E. Asia]

Wong, John. Agricultural Production and Socialist Transformation in China: Two Decades After. *Malayan Econ. Rev.*, October 1973, *18*(2), pp. 1–15. [G: China]

Yung-kuei, Ch'en. On Scientific Farming. *Chinese Econ. Stud.*, Summer 1973, *6*(4), pp. 56–74. [G: China]

Zusman, P.; Melamed, A. and Katzir, I. A Spatial Analysis of the EEC Trade Policies in the Market for Winter Oranges. In *Judge, G. G. and Takayama, T., eds.,* 1973, pp. 464–87. [G: E.E.C.]

714 Agricultural Finance

7140 Agricultural Finance

Chari, T. S. K. Rural Banks—A Good Link between Farmers and Banks. (Co-operative and Commercial Banks). In *Simha, S. L. N., ed.,* 1973, pp. 92–105. [G: India]

Fettig, L. P.; Ogut, Soner and Baker, C. B. Effects of Financing and Employment Alternatives on a Modern Farm Village in Turkey. *Ill. Agr. Econ.,* July 1973, *13*(2), pp. 12–15. [G: Turkey]

Huff, H. B. and MacAulay, T. G. Summing Components of Real Capital Gains. *Amer. J. Agr. Econ.,* February 1973, *55*(1), pp. 69–72. [G: U.S.]

Kanakasabai, R. Role of the Co-operative Banks in the Rural Sector. In *Simha, S. L. N., ed.,* 1973, pp. 85–91. [G: India]

Kansara, T. D. Reorganisation of the Banking System in India. In *Simha, S. L. N., ed.,* 1973, pp. 155–82. [G: India]

Krishnaswamy, S. Y. Banking in the Rural Sector. In *Simha, S. L. N., ed.,* 1973, pp. 71–84. [G: India]

Kulshreshtha, S. N. Discriminating Credit Worthiness of Canadian Prairie Farmers. *Can. J. Agr. Econ.,* July 1973, *21*(2), pp. 16–24. [G: Canada]

Melichar, Emanuel. Financing Agriculture: Demand for and Supply of Farm Capital and Credit. *Amer. J. Agr. Econ.,* May 1973, *55*(2), pp. 313–25. [G: U.S.]

Mishra, G. P.; Tripathy, B. N. and Pandey, Ram Lala. Role of Banking in Financing Rural Credit. *Econ. Aff.,* July 1973, *18*(7), pp. 313–25. [G: India]

Opoku-Owusu, K. Problems in the Provision of Institutional Finance for Agricultural Development in Ghana. In *Ofori, I. M., ed.,* 1973, pp. 164–76. [G: Ghana]

Rice, E. B. and Dalrymple, Dana G. Review of Small Farmer Credit in Developing Nations. *Agr. Finance Rev.,* July 1973, *34,* pp. 35–37.

Rudamoorthy, B. Financing Agriculture in Backward Regions. *Artha-Vikas,* January-July 1973, *9* (1–2), pp. 139–42. [G: India]

Saraiya, R. G. Reform of the Indian Banking System: Proceedings of a Seminar: Introductory Address. In *Simha, S. L. N., ed.,* 1973, pp. 15–19. [G: India]

Sheth, V. K. Organizational Structure for Agricultural Credit. In *Simha, S. L. N., ed.,* 1973, pp. 106–14. [G: India]

Snider, Thomas E. The Effect of Merger on the Lending Behavior of Rural Unit Banks in Virginia. *J. Bank Res.,* Spring 1973, *4*(1), pp. 52–57. [G: U.S.]

Stanbridge, R. J. Sources and Uses of Funds in the New Zealand Farm Sector. *Australian J. Agr. Econ.,* April 1973, *17*(1), pp. 17–32. [G: New Zealand]

Thirunarayanan, R. Functional Efficiency of Rural Banks. In *Simha, S. L. N., ed.,* 1973, pp. 115–21. [G: India]

Waters, Alan Rufus. Migration, Remittances, and the Cash Constraint in African Smallholder Economic Development. *Oxford Econ. Pap.,* November 1973, *25*(3), pp. 435–54. [G: Africa]

Young, Ralph. Institutional Credit in the Rural Sector: An Exploratory Analysis of Demand and Supply. *Quart. Rev. Agr. Econ.,* October 1973, *26*(4), pp. 228–38. [G: Australia]

715 Agricultural Marketing and Agribusiness

7150 Agricultural Marketing; Cooperatives

Anthonio, Q. B. O. Problems of Marketing Agricultural Produce with Special Reference to Foodstuffs in Nigeria. In *Ofori, I. M., ed.,* 1973, pp. 251–62. [G: Nigeria]

Breimyer, Harold F. The Economics of Agricultural Marketing: A Survey. *Rev. Marketing Agr. Econ.,* December 1973, *41*(4), pp. 115–65.

Campbell, Keith. The State Marketing Board—Relic or Prototype? *Australian J. Agr. Econ.,* December 1973, *17*(3), pp. 179–88. [G: Australia]

Channon, J. W. Role of Provincial Governments in Export Market Development. In *Canadian*

Agricultural Economics Society, 1973, pp. 49–57.
[G: Canada]

Child, A. J. E. The Private Trader in Export Market Development. In *Canadian Agricultural Economics Society*, 1973, pp. 58–68. [G: Canada]

Ewusi, Kodwo. The Rate of Inflation, Variation in Local Food Prices and the Effect of Transport Facilities on Local Food Prices in Ghana in the Sixties. In *Ofori, I. M., ed.*, 1973, pp. 278–91.
[G: Ghana]

Fowler, Loretta. The Arapahoe Ranch: An Experiment in Cultural Change and Economic Development. *Econ. Develop. Cult. Change*, April 1973, *21*(3), pp. 446–64. [G: U.S.]

Ghadiri-Asli, B. The Experience of Rural Co-operatives and Co-operative Unions in Iran. *Tahq. Eq.*, Winter & Spring 1973, *10*(29 & 30), pp. 80–105.
[G: Iran]

Goodman, Richard J. United States Agricultural Trade in the Pacific Rim: Marketing Agricultural Products, Approaches, and Accomplishments. In *Canadian Agricultural Economics Society*, 1973, pp. 1–26. [G: U.S.; E. Asia]

Gruebele, J. W. and Miller, James J. Effects of the Use of Spot Cases in the Sale of Selected Dairy Products in Retail Food Chains. *Ill. Agr. Econ.*, July 1973, *13*(2), pp. 44–48. [G: U.S.]

Harshbarger, C. Edward and Doll, Raymond J. Farm Prices and Food Prices: The Relevant Issues. *Fed. Res. Bank Kansas City Rev.*, May 1973, pp. 3–10. [G: U.S.]

Hiscocks, Geoffrey A. The Role of the Federal Government in Export Market Development. In *Canadian Agricultural Economics Society*, 1973, pp. 69–81. [G: Canada]

Houck, James P. Some Aspects of Income Stabilization for Primary Producers. *Australian J. Agr. Econ.*, December 1973, *17*(3), pp. 200–15.
[G: Australia]

Kanakasabai, R. Role of the Co-operative Banks in the Rural Sector. In *Simha, S. L. N., ed.*, 1973, pp. 85–91. [G: India]

Kansara, T. D. Reorganisation of the Banking System in India. In *Simha, S. L. N., ed.*, 1973, pp. 155–82. [G: India]

Kolawole, M. I. The Reform of Commodity Marketing Boards in Nigeria: An Analysis of New Producer Price Policy. *Econ. Bull. Ghana, Sec. Ser.*, 1973, *3*(3), pp. 14–19. [G: Nigeria]

Koll, Michael. The Western Nigerian Cooperative Administration: An Obstacle to Development. In *Damachi, U. G. and Seibel, H. D., eds.*, 1973, pp. 40–50. [G: Nigeria]

Kracht, Uwe. Marketing Unconventional Protein-Rich Foods—One Form of Nutrition Intervention. In *Berg, A.; Scrimshaw, N. S. and Call, D. L., eds.*, 1973, pp. 213–16.

Krishna, Raj. A Note on the Elasticity of the Marketable Surplus of a Subsistence Crop. In *Wadhva, C. D., ed.*, 1973, pp. 313–18.

Lee, T.-C. and Seaver, S. K. A Positive Model of Spatial Equilibrium with Special Reference to the Broiler Markets. In *Judge, G. G. and Takayama, T., eds.*, 1973, pp. 443–63. [G: U.S.]

Lytle, P. W. and Hill, Lowell D. Opportunities for New Investment in Country Elevator Facilities.

Ill. Agr. Econ., July 1973, *13*(2), pp. 6–11.
[G: U.S.]

Manoff, Richard K. The Mass Media Contribution to Intervention Programs. In *Berg, A.; Scrimshaw, N. S. and Call, D. L., eds.*, 1973, pp. 217–22.

Márton, J. The Vertical Integration of the Hungarian Food Economy. *Acta Oecon.*, 1973, *11*(1), pp. 81–96. [G: Hungary]

Menzies, Merril W. Grain Marketing Methods in Canada—The Theory, Assumptions, and Approach. *Amer. J. Agr. Econ.*, December 1973, *55* (5), pp. 791–99. [G: Canada]

Nowshirvani, Vahid F. A Note on the Elasticity of the Marketable Surplus of a Subsistence Crop—A Comment. In *Wadhva, C. D., ed.*, 1973, pp. 319–22.

Nyanteng, V. K. and van Apeldoorn, G. J. Some Development Implications of Farmers' Problems in Marketing Their Foodcrops. In *Ofori, I. M., ed.*, 1973, pp. 263–77. [G: Ghana]

Purcell, Wayne D. An Approach to Research on Vertical Coordination: The Beef System in Oklahoma. *Amer. J. Agr. Econ.*, February 1973, *55* (1), pp. 65–68. [G: U.S.]

Richter, Joseph J. Discussion: The Position of an Importer of Canadian Agricultural Products: Marketing Requirements for Pacific Rim Markets. In *Canadian Agricultural Economics Society*, 1973, pp. 38–42. [G: Canada; Japan]

Rossi, Aldo. Pubblicità industriale per l' agricoltura. (Industrial Advertising for Agriculture. With English summary.) *L'Impresa*, 1973, *15*(5–6), pp. 359–64.

Saraiya, R. G. Reform of the Indian Banking System: Proceedings of a Seminar: Introductory Address. In *Simha, S. L. N., ed.*, 1973, pp. 15–19.
[G: India]

Sasaki, Kozo. Spatial Equilibrium Analysis of Livestock Products in Eastern Japan. In *Judge, G. G. and Takayama, T., eds.*, 1973, pp. 419–42.
[G: Japan]

Schruben, Leonard W. Grain Marketing Methods in the U.S.A.—The Theory, Assumptions, and Approach. *Amer. J. Agr. Econ.*, December 1973, *55* (5), pp. 800–04. [G: U.S.]

Simmons, G. H. An Evaluation of Use of Grab Samples in the Appraisal of Wool for Store Handling. *Quart. Rev. Agr. Econ.*, April 1973, *26*(2), pp. 89–99.

Smith, Gordon W. Marketing and Economic Development: A Brazilian Case Study, 1930–70. *Food Res. Inst. Stud.*, 1973, *12*(3), pp. 179–98.
[G: Brazil]

Sorenson, L. Orlo. Rail-barge Competition in Transporting Winter Wheat. *Amer. J. Agr. Econ.*, December 1973, *55*(5), pp. 814–19. [G: U.S.]

Spencer, Dustan S. C. Rice Production and Marketing in Sierra Leone. In *Ofori, I. M., ed.*, 1973, pp. 217–30. [G: Sierra Leone]

Szabó, I. Economic Associations of Farming Cooperatives. *Acta Oecon.*, 1973, *11*(1), pp. 51–64.
[G: Hungary]

Tyrchniewicz, Edward W. and Tosterud, Robert J. A Model for Rationalizing the Canadian Grain Transportation and Handling System on a Regional Basis. *Amer. J. Agr. Econ.*, December 1973,

55(5), pp. 805–13. [G: Canada]

Umemoto, H. E. Marketing Requirements for the Pacific Rim: The Position of an Importer. In *Canadian Agricultural Economics Society*, 1973, pp. 27–37. [G: Canada; Japan]

Wilson, A. G. Examination of Alternative Methods, Approaches, and Programs for Production and Market Stabilization with Particular Reference to the Pacific Rim Market. In *Canadian Agricultural Economics Society*, 1973, pp. 98–140.
[G: Canada; E. Asia]

7151 Agribusiness

Bazlova, A. Improving Purchase Prices on Agricultural Output. *Prob. Econ.*, July 1973, *16*(3), pp. 37–58. [G: U.S.S.R.]

Breimyer, Harold F. Public Sector Research and Education and the Agribusiness Complex: Unholy Alliance or Socially Beneficial Partnership? Discussion. *Amer. J. Agr. Econ.*, December 1973, *55*(5), pp. 993–96. [G: U.S.]

Buchholz, H. E. Pricing and Allocation Models Applied to Problems of Interregional Trade and Location of Industries. In *Judge, G. G. and Takayama, T., eds.*, 1973, pp. 298–306. [G: W. Germany]

Cameron, Norman. Incentives and Labour Supply on Soviet Collective Farms: Rejoinder. *Can. J. Econ.*, August 1973, *6*(3), pp. 442–44.

Davis, Mark W. Cash Flow Analysis for Feedlot Operations. *Manage. Account.*, June 1973, *54*(12), pp. 38–41.

Gunnelson, Jerald A. and Farris, Paul L. Use of Soybean Futures Markets by Large Processing Firms. *Agr. Econ. Res.*, April 1973, *25*(2), pp. 27–40.
[G: U.S.]

Hathaway, Dale E. Public Sector Research and Education and the Agribusiness Complex: Unholy Alliance or Socially Beneficial Partnership? Summary of the Discussion. *Amer. J. Agr. Econ.*, December 1973, *55*(5), pp. 1002. [G: U.S.]

Hathaway, Dale E. Public Sector Research and Education and the Agribusiness Complex: Unholy Alliance or Socially Beneficial Partnership? *Amer. J. Agr. Econ.*, December 1973, *55*(5), pp. 993.
[G: U.S.]

Makeenko, M. and Khalitov, R. Agroindustrial Associations and Their Effectiveness: Based on the Example of the Moldavian SSR. *Prob. Econ.*, January 1973, *15*(9), pp. 71–89. [G: U.S.S.R.]

McCalla, Alex F. Public Sector Research and Education and the Agribusiness Complex: Unholy Alliance or Socially Beneficial Partnership? Discussion. *Amer. J. Agr. Econ.*, December 1973, *55*(5), pp. 999–1002. [G: U.S.]

Mehren, George. Public Sector Research and Education and the Agribusiness Complex: Unholy Alliance or Socially Beneficial Partnership? Discussion. *Amer. J. Agr. Econ.*, December 1973, *55*(5), pp. 997–99. [G: U.S.]

Mercer, Lloyd J. Corporate Farming in the United States: Discussion. *J. Econ. Hist.*, March 1973, *33*(1), pp. 291–95.

Morozov, F. Structural Problems in the Formation of an Agroindustrial Complex. *Prob. Econ.*, September 1973, *16*(5), pp. 72–93. [G: U.S.S.R.]

Passell, Peter. Corporate Farming in the United States: Discussion. *J. Econ. Hist.*, March 1973, *33*(1), pp. 296–98.

Raup, Phillip. Corporate Farming in the United States. *J. Econ. Hist.*, March 1973, *33*(1), pp. 274–90. [G: U.S.]

Scoville, Orlin J. The Agribusiness Sector—An Important Link in Economic Growth Models. *Amer. J. Agr. Econ.*, August 1973, *55*(3), pp. 520–23.

716 Farm Management

7160 Farm Management; Allocative Efficiency

Adegboye, R. O. and Abidogun, A. Contribution of Part-Time Farming to Rural Development in Ibadan Area, Western Nigeria. In *Ofori, I. M., ed.*, 1973, pp. 158–63. [G: Nigeria]

Ang, James S. Reliability of Using the Mean Absolute Deviation to Derive Efficient E, V Farm Plans: Comment. *Amer. J. Agr. Econ.*, Part I, November 1973, *55*(4), pp. 675–77.

Bardhan, Pranab K. Size, Productivity, and Returns to Scale: An Analysis of Farm-Level Data in Indian Agriculture. *J. Polit. Econ.*, November-December 1973, *81*(6), pp. 1370–86.

Barkai, Haim and Levhari, David. The Impact of Experience on Kibbutz Farming. *Rev. Econ. Statist.*, February 1973, *55*(1), pp. 56–63. [G: Israel]

Beker, Víctor A. Algunos factores que afectan la asignación de recursos entre agricultura y ganadería. (Some Factors Affecting Resource Allocation Between Crop and Beef Production. With English summary.) *Económica*, May-August 1973, *19*(2), pp. 146–56.

Boehlje, Michael; Eidman, Vernon and Walker, Odell. An Approach to Farm Management Education. *Amer. J. Agr. Econ.*, May 1973, *55*(2), pp. 192–97.

Bradley, Michael E. Incentives and Labour Supply on Soviet Collective Farms: Reply. *Can. J. Econ.*, August 1973, *6*(3), pp. 438–42.

Chen, Joyce T. Quadratic Programming for Least-Cost Feed Formulations Under Probabilistic Protein Constraints. *Amer. J. Agr. Econ.*, May 1973, *55*(2), pp. 175–83.

Chen, Joyce T. Separable Programming for Considering Risk in Farm Planning: Comment. *Amer. J. Agr. Econ.*, February 1973, *55*(1), pp. 115–17.

Ching, C. T. K. A Note on the Stability of Firm Size Distribution Functions for Western Cattle Ranches. *Amer. J. Agr. Econ.*, August 1973, *55*(3), pp. 500–02. [G: U.S.]

Colwell, J. D. Assessments of the Relative Values of Compound Nitrogen-Phosphorus Fertilizers for Wheat Production. *Australian J. Agr. Econ.*, December 1973, *17*(3), pp. 189–99. [G: Australia]

Dalton, G. E. Adaptation of Farm Management Theory to the Problems of the Small-Scale Farmer in West Africa. In *Ofori, I. M., ed.*, 1973, pp. 114–29.
[G: Ghana; Nigeria]

Dent, J. B. and Pearse, R. A. Operations Research, Agricultural Research and Agricultural Practice. In *Ross, M., ed.*, 1973, pp. 641–53.

Due, Jean M. Experience with Mechanised Agriculture in Ghana and Sierra Leone Rice Production. In *Ofori, I. M., ed.,* 1973, pp. 203–16. [G: Sierra Leone]

Eisgruber, Ludwig M. Managerial Information and Decision Systems in the U.S.A.: Historical Developments, Current Status, and Major Issues. *Amer. J. Agr. Econ.,* December 1973, *55*(5), pp. 930–37. [G: U.S.]

Fekete, F. The Major Social and Economic Features of Co-operative Farming in Hungary. *Acta Oecon.,* 1973, *11*(1), pp. 19–32. [G: Hungary]

Fettig, L. P.; Ogut, Soner and Baker, C. B. Effects of Financing and Employment Alternatives on a Modern Farm Village in Turkey. *Ill. Agr. Econ.,* July 1973, *13*(2), pp. 12–15. [G: Turkey]

Frăţilă, Gh. Optimizarea repartiţiei teritoriale a îngrăşămintelor chimice. (Optimizing the Territorial Distribution of Chemical Fertilizers. With English summary.) *Stud. Cercet. Econ.,* 1973, (3), pp. 99–104.

Helmers, Glenn A.; Lentz, Gary W. and Kendrick, James G. Specialization and Flexibility Considerations in a Polyperiod Firm Investment Model. *Can. J. Agr. Econ.,* February 1973, *21*(1), pp. 41–48. [G: U.S.]

Hill, Lowell D. and Kau, Paul. Application of Multivariate Probit to a Threshold Model of Grain Dryer Purchasing Decisions. *Amer. J. Agr. Econ.,* February 1973, *55*(1), pp. 19–27. [G: U.S.]

Hougham, D. A. and Sturrock, Ford. The Farms —Present-day Organisation. In *Richards, A. I.; Sturrock, F. and Fortt, J. M., eds.,* 1973, pp. 150–78. [G: Uganda]

Huang, Yukon. On Some Determinants of Farm Size Across Countries. *Amer. J. Agr. Econ.,* February 1973, *55*(1), pp. 89–92.

Kennedy, J. O. S., et al. Optimal Fertilizer Carryover and Crop Recycling Policies for a Tropical Grain Crop. *Australian J. Agr. Econ.,* August 1973, *17*(2), pp. 104–13. [G: Australia]

Khan, Dilawar Ali and Ali, Chaudhari Haider. Income Impact of the Green Revolution. *Pakistan Econ. Soc. Rev.,* Spring 1973, *11*(1), pp. 67–82. [G: Pakistan]

Komló, L. The Industrialization and Integration of Agriculture in a Socialist Country. *Acta Oecon.,* 1973, *10*(1), pp. 67–79.

Krause, Kenneth R. Joint Ventures and Family Labor Sized Farms. *Amer. J. Agr. Econ.,* Part I, November 1973, *55*(4), pp. 628–32. [G: U.S.]

Lee, George E. and Nicholson, Raymond C. Managerial Information (Recording, Data, and Decision) Systems in Canada. *Amer. J. Agr. Econ.,* December 1973, *55*(5), pp. 921–29. [G: Canada]

Lytle, P. W. and Hill, Lowell D. The Optimum Combination of Resources Within and Among Country Elevators. *Amer. J. Agr. Econ.,* May 1973, *55*(2), pp. 202–08. [G: U.S.]

Maddock, Thomas, III. Management Model as a Tool for Studying the Worth of Data. *Water Resources Res.,* April 1973, *9*(2), pp. 270–80.

Mafeje, Archie and Richards, A. I. The Commercial Farmer and His Labour Supply. In *Richards, A. I.; Sturrock, F. and Fortt, J. M., eds.,* 1973, pp. 179–97. [G: Uganda]

Mauldon, R. G. Financial Control within Commercial Family Farms. *Australian J. Agr. Econ.,* April 1973, *17*(1), pp. 33–42. [G: Australia]

McKay, L. E. Some Aspects of Diversification of Production in the Pastoral Zone of the Australian Sheep Industry. *Quart. Rev. Agr. Econ.,* April 1973, *26*(2), pp. 140–48. [G: Australia]

Norman, D. W. Crop Mixtures under Indigenous Conditions in the Northern Part of Nigeria. In *Ofori, I. M., ed.,* 1973, pp. 130–44. [G: Nigeria]

Pasternak, Hanoch and Passy, Ury. Bicriterion Functions in Annual Activity Planning. In *Ross, M., ed.,* 1973, pp. 325–41. [G: Israel]

Pozdniakova, N. On the Distribution of Incomes on Collective Farms. *Prob. Econ.,* January 1973, *15* (9), pp. 90–100. [G: U.S.S.R.]

Reid, G. K. R. and Thomas, D. A. Pastoral Production, Stocking Rate and Seasonal Conditions. *Quart. Rev. Agr. Econ.,* October 1973, *26*(4), pp. 217–27. [G: Australia]

Ryan, Timothy J. An Empirical Investigation of the Harvest Operation Using Systems Simulation. *Australian J. Agr. Econ.,* August 1973, *17*(2), pp. 114–26.

Scott, John T., Jr. and Chen, C. T. Expected Changes in Farm Organization When Industry Moves into a Rural Area. *Ill. Agr. Econ.,* January 1973, *13*(1), pp. 41–47. [G: U.S.]

Shumway, C. Richard. Allocation of Scarce Resources to Agricultural Research: Review of Methodology. *Amer. J. Agr. Econ.,* Part I, November 1973, *55*(4), pp. 557–66.

Smith, Blair J. Dynamic Programming of the Dairy Cow Replacement Program. *Amer. J. Agr. Econ.,* February 1973, *55*(1), pp. 100–04.

Strickland, Roger P., Jr. Alternative Analyses of Farm Growth. *Agr. Econ. Res.,* October 1973, *25* (4), pp. 99–104.

Sycheva, L. Economic Foundations of an Optimal Combination of Accumulation and Consumption on Collective Farms. *Prob. Econ.,* February 1973, *15*(10), pp. 46–61. [G: U.S.S.R.]

Thomas, Wayne, et al. Separable Programming for Considering Risk in Farm Planning: Reply. *Amer. J. Agr. Econ.,* February 1973, *55*(1), pp. 117–18.

Thomson, K. J. and Hazell, P. B. R. Reliability of Using the Mean Absolute Deviation to Derive Efficient E, V Farm Plans: Reply. *Amer. J. Agr. Econ.,* Part I, November 1973, *55*(4), pp. 677–78.

Todd, M. and Freestone, R. The Effect on Store Costs of a Trial Method for Rehandling Bulk-Class Wools: A Preliminary Analysis. *Quart. Rev. Agr. Econ.,* October 1973, *26*(4), pp. 263–76. [G: Australia]

Utami, Widya and Ihalauw, John. Some Consequences of Small Farm Size. *Bull. Indonesian Econ. Stud.,* July 1973, *9*(2), pp. 46–56. [G: Indonesia]

Verkhovskii, B. S. Optimal Redistribution of Water Resources. *Matekon,* Summer 1973, *9*(4), pp. 95–101.

Wagenbuur, H. T. M. Labour and Development: An Analysis of the Time Budget of Lime Farmers in Southern Ghana. In *Ofori, I. M., ed.,* 1973, pp. 145–57. [G: Ghana]

Weisgerber, P. The Impact of Wealth Benefits on

Farm Returns in the Wheat Area. *Agr. Finance Rev.*, July 1973, *34*, pp. 31–34. [G: U.S.]

Williams, Willard F. Another Look at Economies of Size of Cattle Feeding. *Can. J. Agr. Econ.*, February 1973, *21*(1), pp. 65.

Wills, Ian R. and Lloyd, A. G. Economic Theory and Sheep-Cattle Combinations. *Australian J. Agr. Econ.*, April 1973, *17*(1), pp. 58–67. [G: Australia]

Yotopoulos, Pan A. and Lau, Lawrence J. A Test for Relative Economic Efficiency: Some Further Results. *Amer. Econ. Rev.*, March 1973, *63*(1), pp. 214–23. [G: India]

717 Land Reform and Land Use

7170 General

Afzal, Mohammad. Implications of the Green Revolution for Land Use Patterns and Relative Crop Profitability Under Domestic and International Prices. *Pakistan Develop. Rev.*, Summer 1973, *12*(2), pp. 135–47. [G: Pakistan]

Anker, Desmond L. W. Rural Development Problems and Strategies. *Int. Lab. Rev.*, December 1973, *108*(6), pp. 461–84.

Azhar, B. A. Land Revenue Assessment: A Case Study. *Pakistan Develop. Rev.*, Autumn 1973, *12*(3), pp. 232–46. [G: Pakistan]

Benneh, G. Land Tenure and Land Use Systems in the Forest-Savannah Contact Zone in Ghana: A Case-Study. In *Ofori, I. M., ed.*, 1973, pp. 107–13. [G: Ghana]

Fettig, L. P.; Ogut, Soner and Baker, C. B. Effects of Financing and Employment Alternatives on a Modern Farm Village in Turkey. *Ill. Agr. Econ.*, July 1973, *13*(2), pp. 12–15. [G: Turkey]

Fortt, J. M. Land Tenure and the Emergence of Large Scale Farming. In *Richards, A. I.; Sturrock, F. and Fortt, J. M., eds.*, 1973, pp. 66–84. [G: Uganda]

Gofman, K. G., et al. Optimal Land Management. *Matekon*, Spring 1973, *9*(3), pp. 71–88.

Griffin, Keith. Policy Options for Rural Development. *Oxford Bull. Econ. Statist.*, November 1973, *35*(4), pp. 239–74.

Hougham, D. A. The Farms—Origin and Growth. In *Richards, A. I.; Sturrock, F. and Fortt, J. M., eds.*, 1973, pp. 124–49. [G: Uganda]

Hunter, Guy. The Food Research Institute's Fiftieth Anniversary Conference, Strategies for Agricultural Development in the 1970s. *Food Res. Inst. Stud.*, 1973, *12*(1), pp. 3–72.

Jensen, Robert G. Regional Pricing and the Economic Evaluation of Land in Soviet Agriculture. In *Bandera, V. N. and Melnyk, Z. L., eds.*, 1973, pp. 305–27. [G: U.S.S.R.]

Kangayappan, Kumar. Some Policy Issues in Mitigating Poverty in India. *Land Econ.*, February 1973, *49*(1), pp. 76–81. [G: India]

Newell, William H. The Agricultural Revolution in Nineteenth-Century France. *J. Econ. Hist.*, December 1973, *33*(4), pp. 697–731. [G: France]

Ofori, I. M. Land Tenure Interactions and Land Use Patterns in Ghanaian Agriculture: Some Basic

Theoretical Considerations. In *Ofori, I. M., ed.*, 1973, pp. 91–100. [G: Ghana]

Pal, D. N. Agrarian Revolution. *Econ. Aff.*, September-October 1973, *18*(9–10), pp. 439–49. [G: India]

Sazama, Geraldo W. and Davis, Harlan. Land Taxation and Land Reform. *Econ. Develop. Cult. Change*, Part I, July 1973, *21*(4), pp. 642–54. [G: Latin America]

Sinha, J. N. Agrarian Reforms and Employment in Densely Populated Agrarian Economies: A Dissenting View. *Int. Lab. Rev.*, November 1973, *108*(5), pp. 395–421. [G: Japan; India]

Smith, Theodore Reynolds. Community Development and Agrarian Reform in the East Asian Setting. *Amer. J. Econ. Soc.*, January 1973, *32*(1), pp. 73–86. [G: E. Asia]

7171 Land Ownership and Tenure; Land Reform

Adams, Dale W. The Economics of Land Reform. *Food Res. Inst. Stud.*, 1973, *12*(2), pp. 133–38.

Berry, R. Albert. Land Distribution, Income Distribution, and the Productive Efficiency of Colombian Agriculture. *Food Res. Inst. Stud.*, 1973, *12*(3), pp. 199–232. [G: Colombia]

Blankstein, Charles S. and Zuvekas, Clarence, Jr. Agrarian Reform in Ecuador: An Evaluation of Past Efforts and the Development of a New Approach. *Econ. Develop. Cult. Change*, October 1973, *22*(1), pp. 73–94. [G: Ecuador]

Chakravorty, S. K. Tenant Farmers in Changing Agriculture of West Bengal. *Econ. Aff.*, September-October 1973, *18*(9–10), pp. 428–33. [G: India]

Chonchol, Jacques. The Agrarian Policy of the Popular Government. In *Zammit, J. A., ed.*, 1973, pp. 107–14. [G: Chile]

Cline, William R. Interrelationships Between Agricultural Strategy and Rural Income Distribution. *Food Res. Inst. Stud.*, 1973, *12*(2), pp. 139–57.

Delgado, Oscar. Revolution, Reform, Conservatism: Three Types of Agrarian Structure. In *Wilber, C. K., ed.*, 1973, pp. 173–86. [G: Latin America]

Findley, Roger W. Problems Faced by Colombia's Agrarian Reform Institute in Acquiring and Distributing Land. In *Scott, R. E., ed.*, 1973, pp. 122–92. [G: Colombia]

Gyenes, A. Re-stratification of the Agricultural Population in Hungary. *Acta Oecon.*, 1973, *11*(1), pp. 33–49. [G: Hungary]

Higgs, Robert. Race, Tenure, and Resource Allocation in Southern Agriculture, 1910. *J. Econ. Hist.*, March 1973, *33*(1), pp. 149–69. [G: U.S.]

Huang, Yukon. Risk, Entrepreneurship, and Tenancy. *J. Polit. Econ.*, September-October 1973, *81*(5), pp. 1241–44. [G: India]

Kehal, H. S. Role of Land Reforms in Punjab's Agricultural Development. *Econ. Aff.*, September-October 1973, *18*(9–10), pp. 434–38, 454. [G: India]

Koo, Anthony Y. C. Towards a More General Model of Land Tenancy and Reform. *Quart. J. Econ.*, November 1973, *87*(4), pp. 567–80.

McLennan, Marshall S. Land Tenure in the Philip-

pines, An Heterogeneous Heritage. *Mich. Academician,* Summer 1973, *6*(1), pp. 17–27.
[G: Philippines]

Miller, Edward. Some Implications of Land Ownership Patterns for Petroleum Policy. *Land Econ.,* November 1973, *49*(4), pp. 414–23. [G: U.S.]

Mishra, G. P. Land Reform and Changing Structure of Indian Agriculture. *Econ. Aff.,* September-October 1973, *18*(9–10), pp. 455–65, 476.
[G: India]

Mishra, G. P. Planning and Land Reform Policy in India. *Econ. Aff.,* May 1973, *18*(5), pp. 217–33.
[G: India]

Nukunya, G. K. Land Tenure and Agricultural Development in the Anloga Area of the Volta Region. In *Ofori, I. M., ed.,* 1973, pp. 101–06.
[G: Ghana]

Reid, Joseph D. Sharecropping as an Understandable Market Response—The Post-Bellum South. *J. Econ. Hist.,* March 1973, *33*(1), pp. 106–30.
[G: U.S.]

Singh, Pritam. Land to the Landless. *Econ. Aff.,* July 1973, *18*(7), pp. 326–37. [G: India]

Warriner, Doreen. Results of Land Reform in Asian and Latin American Countries. *Food Res. Inst. Stud.,* 1973, *12*(2), pp. 115–31. [G: Asia; Latin America]

Woods, W. Fred. Impact of Estate and Inheritance Taxes on U.S. Farms. *Agr. Finance Rev.,* July 1973, *34,* pp. 7–11. [G: U.S.]

Wright, Gavin. Race, Tenure, and Resource Allocation in Southern Agriculture, 1910: Discussion. *J. Econ. Hist.,* March 1973, *33*(1), pp. 170–76.
[G: U.S.]

Zaman, M. Raquibuz. Sharecropping and Economic Efficiency in Bangladesh. *Bangladesh Econ. Rev.,* April 1973, *1*(2), pp. 149–72. [G: Bangladesh]

7172 Land Development; Land Use; Irrigation Policy

Acquaye, D. K. Some Problems in the Use of West African Soils. In *Ofori, I. M., ed.,* 1973, pp. 67–70.
[G: W. Africa]

Alessio, Frank J. A Neo-Classical Land Use Model: The Influence of Externalities. *Swedish J. Econ.,* December 1973, *75*(4), pp. 414–19.

Alonso, William. A Theory of the Urban Land Market. In *Grieson, R. E., ed.,* 1973, pp. 45–55.

Benet, I. and Góczán, L. A Pilot Study on the Valuation of Land. (In Russian. With English summary.) *Acta Oecon.,* 1973, *11*(2–3), pp. 191–209.
[G: Hungary]

Benneh, G. Water Requirements and Limitations Imposed on Agricultural Development in Northern Ghana. In *Ofori, I. M., ed.,* 1973, pp. 71–81.
[G: Ghana]

Bromley, Daniel W. and Beattie, Bruce R. On the Incongruity of Program Objectives and Project Evaluation: An Example from the Reclamation Program. *Amer. J. Agr. Econ.,* August 1973, *55*(3), pp. 472–76. [G: U.S.]

Butterworth, Douglas. Squatters or Suburbanites? The Growth of Shantytowns in Oaxaca, Mexico. In *Scott, R. E., ed.,* 1973, pp. 209–32. [G: Mexico]

Chapman, Duane. Economic Aspects of a Nuclear Desalination Agro-Industrial Project in the United Arab Republic. *Amer. J. Agr. Econ.,* August 1973, *55*(3), pp. 433–40. [G: United Arab Republic]

Cline, William R. Cost-Benefit Analysis of Irrigation Projects in Northeastern Brazil. *Amer. J. Agr. Econ.,* Part I, November 1973, *55*(4), pp. 622–27.
[G: Brazil]

Cobb, Gary D. Evolving Water Policies in the United States. *Amer. J. Agr. Econ.,* December 1973, *55*(5), pp. 1003–07. [G: U.S.]

Costonis, John J. Development Rights Transfer: An Exploratory Essay. *Yale Law J.,* November 1973, *83*(1), pp. 75–128.

Crowley, Ronald W. A Case Study of the Effects of an Airport on Land Values. *J. Transp. Econ. Policy,* May 1973, *7*(2), pp. 144–52. [G: Canada]

Day, John C. A Linear Programming Approach to Floodplain Land Use Planning in Urban Areas. *Amer. J. Agr. Econ.,* May 1973, *55*(2), pp. 165–74.

Dean, Gerald W., et al. Programming Model for Evaluating Economic and Financial Feasibility of Irrigation Projects with Extended Development Periods. *Water Resources Res.,* June 1973, *9*(3), pp. 546–55.

Dolan, Edwin G. Preserving the Wilderness—Public Interest or Special Interest? In *Reynolds, L. G.; Green, G. D. and Lewis, D. R., eds.,* 1973, pp. 231–42. [G: U.S.]

Douglas, J. J. A Note on the Use of a Modified Input-Output Multiplier for Land Use Evaluation. *Australian J. Agr. Econ.,* April 1973, *17*(1), pp. 68–72.
[G: Australia]

Dudley, Norman J. and Burt, Oscar R. Stochastic Reservoir Management and System Design for Irrigation. *Water Resources Res.,* June 1973, *9*(3), pp. 507–22.

Forsythe, Graeme A. Rural and Urban Flood Insurance: A Review. In *Aislabie, C., ed.,* 1973, pp. 68–77.

Gisser, Micha and Mercado, Abraham. Economic Aspects of Ground Water Resources and Replacement Flows in Semiarid Agricultural Areas. *Amer. J. Agr. Econ.,* August 1973, *55*(3), pp. 461–66.

González Villarreal, Fernando J. Mexican National Water Plan: Organization and Preliminary Assessment. *Amer. J. Agr. Econ.,* December 1973, *55*(5), pp. 1008–16. [G: Mexico]

Gordon, Peter and Lande, Paul S. The Pricing of Goods and Agricultural Land in Multiregional General Equilibrium: Comment. *Southern Econ. J.,* July 1973, *40*(1), pp. 143–44.

Guha, Sabita. Economics of Deep-Tubewell Irrigation. *Econ. Aff.,* June 1973, *18*(6), pp. 291–98.
[G: India]

Hartwick, John M. The Pricing of Goods and Agricultural Land in Multiregional General Equilibrium: Reply. *Southern Econ. J.,* July 1973, *40* (1), pp. 144–45.

Heady, Earl O. and Madsen, Howard C. National and Interregional Models of Water Demand for Land Use and Agricultural Policies. In *Judge, G. G. and Takayama, T., eds.,* 1973, pp. 651–75.
[G: U.S.]

Heady, Earl O., et al. National and Interregional Models of Water Demand, Land Use, and Agricultural Policies. *Water Resources Res.,* August 1973, *9*(4), pp. 777–91. [G: U.S.]

Helmers, Glenn A.; Lentz, Gary W. and Kendrick, James G. Specialization and Flexibility Considerations in a Polyperiod Firm Investment Model. *Can. J. Agr. Econ.,* February 1973, *21*(1), pp. 41–48. [G: U.S.]

Hougham, D. A. and Sturrock, Ford. The Farms —Present-day Organisation. In *Richards, A. I.; Sturrock, F. and Fortt, J. M., eds.,* 1973, pp. 150–78. [G: Uganda]

Hyslop, John D. Project Selection and Macroeconomic Objectives: Comment. *Amer. J. Agr. Econ.,* February 1973, *55*(1), pp. 105–07.

Klinefelter, Danny A. Factors Affecting Farmland Values in Illinois. *Ill. Agr. Econ.,* January 1973, *13*(1), pp. 27–33. [G: U.S.]

Lansford, Robert R.; Clevenger, Thomas S. and Gorman, William D. Economic Planning for the Navajo Indian Irrigation Project. *N. Mex. Bus.,* April 1973, *26*(4), pp. 3–8. [G: U.S.]

Loboda, I. On Certain Ways of Restructuring the Countryside. *Prob. Econ.,* January 1973, *15*(9), pp. 61–70. [G: U.S.S.R.]

Maddock, Thomas, III. Management Model as a Tool for Studying the Worth of Data. *Water Resources Res.,* April 1973, *9*(2), pp. 270–80.

Manogaran, Chelvadurai. Economic Feasibility of Irrigating Southern Pipes. *Water Resources Res.,* December 1973, *9*(6), pp. 1485–96. [G: U.S.]

Mason, Joseph Barry. Along the Interstate: Highway Interchange Land Use Development. *Growth Change,* October 1973, *4*(4), pp. 38–43. [G: U.S.]

McGaughey, Stephen E. Project Selection and Macroeconomic Objectives: Reply. *Amer. J. Agr. Econ.,* February 1973, *55*(1), pp. 107–09.

Parvin, D. W., Jr. Estimation of Irrigation Response from Time-Series Data on Nonirrigated Crops. *Amer. J. Agr. Econ.,* February 1973, *55*(1), pp. 73–76. [G: U.S.]

Pasour, E. C., Jr. Real Property Taxes and Farm Real Estate Values: Incidence and Implications. *Amer. J. Agr. Econ.,* Part I, November 1973, *55*(4), pp. 549–56. [G: U.S.]

Ryan, James G. Some Implications of Rice Price and Policy Changes for Irrigated Farms. *Rev. Marketing Agr. Econ.,* June and September 1973, *41* (2–3), pp. 39–52. [G: Australia]

Sandhu, H. S. and Gupta, J. R. Adoption and Performance of Recommended Practices—A Comparative Study of Two Villages in Ludhiana District. *Econ. Aff.,* August 1973, *18*(8), pp. 389–94. [G: India]

Smith, Douglas V. Opportunity for Village Development: The Tanks of Bangladesh. *Bangladesh Econ. Rev.,* July 1973, *1*(3), pp. 297–308. [G: Bangladesh]

Srinivasan, M. Problems of Inputs (With Special Reference to Water and Fertilisers) in Indian Agriculture. *Econ. Aff.,* September-October 1973, *18*(9–10), pp. 466–74. [G: India]

Winfield, Gerald F. The Impact of Urbanization on Agricultural Processes. *Ann. Amer. Acad. Polit. Soc. Sci.,* January 1973, *405*, pp. 65–74. [G: U.S.]

Yaron, D. and Olian, A. Application of Dynamic Programming in Markov Chains to the Evaluation of Water Quality in Irrigation. *Amer. J. Agr. Econ.,* August 1973, *55*(3), pp. 467–71.

718 Rural Economics

7180 Rural Economics

Afzal, Mohammad; Hashmi, M. Iqbal and Nizami, N. H. Marriage Patterns in a Rural Agglomeration. *Pakistan Develop. Rev.,* Autumn 1973, *12*(3), pp. 273–82. [G: Pakistan]

Bardhan, Pranab K. 'Green Revolution' and Agricultural Labourers. In *Wadhva, C. D., ed.,* 1973, pp. 346–61. [G: India]

Bates, W. R.; Sexton, R. N. and Jackson, R. The Impact of Death Duties on the Rural Industries in Australia. *Quart. Rev. Agr. Econ.,* January 1973, *26*(1), pp. 25–43. [G: Australia]

Belshaw, D. G. R. The Role of Agricultural Economics in University Economics Teaching in Africa. In *Livingstone, I., et al., eds.,* 1973, pp. 119–29. [G: Africa]

Bieker, Richard F. and Anschel, Kurt R. Estimating Educational Production Functions for Rural High Schools: Some Findings. *Amer. J. Agr. Econ.,* August 1973, *55*(3), pp. 515–19. [G: U.S.]

Cain, Glen G. Economics of the Size of North Carolina Rural Families: Comment. *J. Polit. Econ.,* Part II, March-April 1973, *81*(2), pp. S123–27. [G: U.S.]

Carlin, Thomas A. Economic Position of Farm Families When Money Income and Net Worth are Combined. *Agr. Econ. Res.,* July 1973, *25*(3), pp. 61–70. [G: U.S.]

Carlin, Thomas A. and Reinsel, Edward I. Combining Income and Wealth: An Analysis of Farm Family "Well-Being." *Amer. J. Agr. Econ.,* February 1973, *55*(1), pp. 38–44. [G: U.S.]

Chaudhry, M. Ghaffar. Rural Income Distribution in Pakistan in the Green Revolution Perspective. *Pakistan Develop. Rev.,* Autumn 1973, *12*(3), pp. 247–58. [G: Pakistan]

Cline, William R. Interrelationships Between Agricultural Strategy and Rural Income Distribution. *Food Res. Inst. Stud.,* 1973, *12*(2), pp. 139–57.

Dent, J. B. and Pearse, R. A. Operations Research, Agricultural Research and Agricultural Practice. In *Ross, M., ed.,* 1973, pp. 641–53.

Derban, L. A. K. The Impact of Health and Nutrition on Agricultural Production in West Africa. In *Ofori, I. M., ed.,* 1973, pp. 26–32. [G: W. Africa]

Dovring, Folke. Distribution of Farm Size and Income: Analysis by Exponential Functions. *Land Econ.,* May 1973, *49*(2), pp. 133–47. [G: U.S.]

Gardner, Bruce. Economics of the Size of North Carolina Rural Families. *J. Polit. Econ.,* Part II, March-April 1973, *81*(2), pp. S99–122. [G: U.S.]

Griffin, Keith. Policy Options for Rural Development. *Oxford Bull. Econ. Statist.*, November 1973, *35*(4), pp. 239–74.

Hougham, D. A. and Sturrock, Ford. The Farms —Present-day Organisation. In *Richards, A. I.; Sturrock, F. and Fortt, J. M., eds.,* 1973, pp. 150–78. [G: Uganda]

Kahn, Mahmood A. and Kahn, Dilawar A. Rural Development Strategy and Need for Institution Building at Village Level. *Pakistan Econ. Soc. Rev.,* Winter 1973, *11*(4), pp. 383–402. [G: Pakistan]

Khin, Maung Kyi, et al. Process of Communication in Modernisation of Rural Society: A Survey Report on Two Burmese Villages. *Malayan Econ. Rev.,* April 1973, *18*(1), pp. 55–73. [G: Burma]

Leal de Araujo, Lucila. Extension of Social Security to Rural Workers in Mexico. *Int. Lab. Rev.,* October 1973, *108*(4), pp. 295–312. [G: Mexico]

Mafeje, Archie. The Farmers—Economic and Social Differentiation. In *Richards, A. I.; Sturrock, F. and Fortt, J. M., eds.,* 1973, pp. 198–231. [G: Uganda]

Mathew, T. I. Social Security for the Rural Population: A Study of Some Social Services in Selected Rural Areas of India. *Int. Lab. Rev.,* October 1973, *108*(4), pp. 313–28. [G: India]

Mikesell, James J. Mobile Homes: An Important New Element in Rural Housing. *Agr. Finance Rev.,* July 1973, *34*, pp. 18–23. [G: U.S.]

Mosher, A. T. Higher Education in the Rural Social Sciences. *Amer. J. Agr. Econ.,* Part II, November 1973, *55*(4), pp. 711–19.

Schreiner, Dean; Muncrief, George and Davis, Bob. Solid Waste Management for Rural Areas: Analysis of Costs and Service Requirements. *Amer. J. Agr. Econ.,* Part I, November 1973, *55*(4), pp. 567–76. [G: U.S.]

Schroeder, Gertrude E. Regional Differences in Incomes and Levels of Living in the USSR. In *Bandera, V. N. and Melnyk, Z. L., eds.,* 1973, pp. 167–95. [G: U.S.S.R.]

Schultze, Charles L. U.S. Farm Policy: Who Gets the Benefits. In *Haveman, R. H. and Hamrin, R. D., eds.,* 1973, pp. 182–90. [G: U.S.]

Scott, John T., Jr. and Chen, C. T. Expected Changes in Farm Organization When Industry Moves into a Rural Area. *Ill. Agr. Econ.,* January 1973, *13*(1), pp. 41–47. [G: U.S.]

Silcock, T. H. Rationality, Fluency and Impersonality in Rural Thailand. In *Epstein, T. S. and Penny, D. H., eds.,* 1973, pp. 203–15. [G: Thailand]

Srikantan, K. S. Regional and Rural-Urban Socio-Demographic Differences in Turkey. *Middle East J.,* Summer 1973, *27*(3), pp. 275–300. [G: Turkey]

Steckle, Jean. Changes in Food Use Patterns: Some Aspects of Household Enumeration in Measuring Levels of Living through Studies in Depth. In *Ofori, I. M., ed.,* 1973, pp. 49–56. [G: Ghana]

Tefertiller, K. R. Rural Development in an Urban Age. *Amer. J. Agr. Econ.,* December 1973, *55*(5), pp. 771–77. [G: U.S.]

Tweeten, Luther G. Emerging Issues for Sparsely Populated Areas and Regions Under a National Growth Policy. *Amer. J. Agr. Econ.,* December 1973, *55*(5), pp. 840–50. [G: U.S.]

Walter, John P. The City as a Source of Regional Economic Disparity in Latin America. *Rev. Soc. Econ.,* April 1973, *31*(1), pp. 66–84. [G: Latin America]

Waters, Alan Rufus. Migration, Remittances, and the Cash Constraint in African Smallholder Economic Development. *Oxford Econ. Pap.,* November 1973, *25*(3), pp. 435–54. [G: Africa]

White, Fred and Tweeten, Luther G. Optimal School District Size Emphasizing Rural Areas. *Amer. J. Agr. Econ.,* February 1973, *55*(1), pp. 45–53. [G: U.S.]

Woods, Roger. Interdisciplinary Courses and Professional Training in East African Universities. In *Livingstone, I., et al., eds.,* 1973, pp. 105–17. [G: E. Africa]

Wrigley, Robert L., Jr. Small Cities Can Help to Revitalize Rural Areas. *Ann. Amer. Acad. Polit. Soc. Sci.,* January 1973, *405*, pp. 55–64. [G: U.S.]

720 NATURAL RESOURCES

721 Natural Resources

7210 General

Adam, Paul. Practical Problems of Constructing Bioeconomic Models for Fishery Management. In *Sokoloski, A. A., ed.,* 1973, pp. 96–103.

Alemany, Ricardo; Fernandez, Pedro and Pousa, Aurora G. Algorithm for Solving a Class of Linear Programing Problems Related to Reservoir Management and Design. *Water Resources Res.,* October 1973, *9*(5), pp. 1227–34.

Anderson, F. M., et al. Simulation Experiments to Evaluate Alternative Hunting Strategies for a Deer Population. In *Sokoloski, A. A., ed.,* 1973, pp. 121–32.

Apsey, T. M.; Garton, M. M. and Hajdu, C. Economic Trends in the Canadian Forest Products Industry. *Amer. J. Agr. Econ.,* December 1973, *55* (5), pp. 974–82. [G: Canada]

Ayres, Robert U. and Kneese, Allen V. Economic and Ecological Effects of a Stationary Economy. In *Enthoven, A. C. and Freeman, A. M., III, eds.,* 1973, pp. 235–52.

Bahl, Roy W.; Coelen, Stephen P. and Warford, Jeremy J. Land Value Increments as a Measure of the Net Benefits of Urban Water Supply Projects in Developing Countries: Theory and Measurement. In *Harriss, C. L., ed.,* 1973, pp. 171–88.

Bell, Frederick W.; Carlson, Ernest W. and Waugh, Frederick V. Production from the Sea. In *Sokoloski, A. A., ed.,* 1973, pp. 72–91. [G: U.S.]

Bell, Frederick W. and Fullenbaum, Richard F. The Regional Impact of Resource Management. In *Mattila, J. M. and Thompson, W. R., eds.,* 1973, pp. 11–26. [G: U.S.]

Bishop, Richard C. Limitation of Entry in the United States Fishing Industry: An Economic Appraisal of a Proposed Policy. *Land Econ.,* November 1973, *49*(4), pp. 381–90. [G: U.S.]

Borovskikh, B. Urgent Problems in Planning the

Reproduction of Natural Resources. *Prob. Econ.,* November 1973, *16*(7), pp. 3–23.

Bradley, Paul G. Increasing Scarcity: The Case of Energy Resources. *Amer. Econ. Rev.,* May 1973, *63*(2), pp. 119–25.

Brown, Gardner, Jr. and Hammack, Judd. Dynamic Economic Management of Migratory Waterfowl. *Rev. Econ. Statist.,* February 1973, *55*(1), pp. 73–82. [G: U.S.]

Carlin, Alan. The Grand Canyon Controversy; or, How Reclamation Justifies the Unjustifiable. In *Enthoven, A. C. and Freeman, A. M., III, eds.,* 1973, pp. 263–70. [G: U.S.]

Carlson, Ernest W. Cross Section Production Functions for North Atlantic Groundfish and Tropical Tuna Seine Fisheries. In *Sokoloski, A. A., ed.,* 1973, pp. 42–56. [G: U.S.]

Carroll, Joseph L. and Bronzini, Michael S. Waterway Transportation Simulation Models: Development and Application. *Water Resources Res.,* February 1973, *9*(1), pp. 51–63.

Cassidy, P. A. Commonality, Fishery Resources, Potential and Policy: Comment. *Amer. J. Agr. Econ.,* August 1973, *55*(3), pp. 526–29. [G: U.S.]

Cicchetti, Charles J., et al. Benefits or Costs? An Assessment of the Water Resources Council's Proposed Principles and Standards. In *Niskanen, W. A., et al., eds.,* 1973, pp. 431–46. [G: U.S.]

Cloud, Preston. Mineral Resources in Fact and Fancy. In *Daly, H. E., ed.,* 1973, pp. 50–75.

Coale, Ansley J. Man and His Environment. In *Enthoven, A. C. and Freeman, A. M., III, eds.,* 1973, pp. 155–65. [G: U.S.]

Cobb, Gary D. Evolving Water Policies in the United States. *Amer. J. Agr. Econ.,* December 1973, *55*(5), pp. 1003–07. [G: U.S.]

Cohon, Jared L. and Marks, David H. Multiobjective Screening Models and Water Resource Investment. *Water Resources Res.,* August 1973, *9*(4), pp. 826–36.

Common, Michael S. and Pearce, David W. Adaptive Mechanisms, Growth, and the Environment: The Case of Natural Resources. *Can. J. Econ.,* August 1973, *6*(3), pp. 289–300.

Crabb, Peter. Urban Water Catchments: Some Illustrations of Resource Allocation and Conflict Regulation. In *Aislabie, C., ed.,* 1973, pp. 19–33. [G: Australia]

Crutchfield, James A. Economic, Political, and Social Barriers to Efficiency in Selected Pacific Coast Fisheries. In *Sokoloski, A. A., ed.,* 1973, pp. 28–38. [G: U.S.]

Curtis, Christopher C. Managing Federal Lands: Replacing the Multiple Use System. *Yale Law J.,* March 1973, *82*(4), pp. 787–805. [G: U.S.]

Daicoff, Darwin W. Capitalization of the Benefits of Water Resource Development. In *Harriss, C. L., ed.,* 1973, pp. 189–99. [G: U.S.]

Darby, Michael R. Paper Recycling and the Stock of Trees. *J. Polit. Econ.,* September-October 1973, *81*(5), pp. 1253–55.

Davidson, A. T. National Water Policy: The Canadian Experience. *Amer. J. Agr. Econ.,* December 1973, *55*(5), pp. 1017–21. [G: Canada]

Davis, Lawrence S.; Thompson, Emmett F. and Rich-ards, Douglas F. The South's Third Forest: A Critique. *Land Econ.,* February 1973, *49*(1), pp. 105–09. [G: U.S.]

Davis, Robert K. and Hanke, Steve H. Conventional and Unconventional Alternatives for Water Supply Management. *Water Resources Res.,* August 1973, *9*(4), pp. 861–70.

DeCoursey, Donn G. Application of Discriminant Analysis in Design Review. *Water Resources Res.,* February 1973, *9*(1), pp. 93–102.

Dee, Norbert, et al. An Environmental Evaluation System for Water Resource Planning. *Water Resources Res.,* June 1973, *9*(3), pp. 523–35.

Dickinson, Neal J. Water Development and Urban Development in Africa. In *Aislabie, C., ed.,* 1973, pp. 34–48. [G: Rhodesia]

Eastman, John and ReVelle, Charles. Linear Decision Rule in Reservoir Management and Design: 3. Direct Capacity Determination and Intraseasonal Constraints. *Water Resources Res.,* February 1973, *9*(1), pp. 29–42.

Evans, Raymond W. G. Some Aspects of Urban Water Supply in Victoria. In *Aislabie, C., ed.,* 1973, pp. 61–67. [G: Australia]

Ferguson, Ian S. Forecasting the Future for Timber. *Australian J. Agr. Econ.,* December 1973, *17*(3), pp. 159–69. [G: Australia]

Fischer, David W. Some Social and Economic Aspects of Marine Resource Development. *Amer. J. Econ. Soc.,* April 1973, *32*(2), pp. 113–27.

Fisher, Joseph L. and Ridker, Ronald G. Population Growth, Resource Availability and Environmental Quality. *Amer. Econ. Rev.,* May 1973, *63*(2), pp. 79–87. [G: U.S.]

Forster, Bruce A. and Logan, John. The Welfare Economics of Water Resource Allocation Over Time: Comment. *Appl. Econ.,* March 1973, *5*(1), pp. 61–68.

Frank, Helmut J. and Schanz, John J., Jr. The Future of American Oil and Natural Gas. *Ann. Amer. Acad. Polit. Soc. Sci.,* November 1973, *410,* pp. 24–34. [G: U.S.]

Gaffney, Mason. The Water Giveaway: A Critique of Federal Water Policy. In *Haveman, R. H. and Hamrin, R. D., eds.,* 1973, pp. 191–97. [G: U.S.]

Gazis, Denos C. Mathematical Modelling of Some Social and Environmental Problems. In *Hawkes, N., ed.,* 1973, pp. 52–59. [G: U.S.]

Gisser, Micha and Mercado, Abraham. Economic Aspects of Ground Water Resources and Replacement Flows in Semiarid Agricultural Areas. *Amer. J. Agr. Econ.,* August 1973, *55*(3), pp. 461–66.

González Villarreal, Fernando J. Mexican National Water Plan: Organization and Preliminary Assessment. *Amer. J. Agr. Econ.,* December 1973, *55*(5), pp. 1008–16. [G: Mexico]

Gopalakrishnan, Chennat. Doctrine of Prior Appropriation and Its Impact on Water Development: A Critical Survey. *Amer. J. Econ. Soc.,* January 1973, *32*(1), pp. 61–72. [G: U.S.]

Gordon, Scott. Today's Apocalypses and Yesterday's. *Amer. Econ. Rev.,* May 1973, *63*(2), pp. 106–10.

Guise, J. W. B. and Flinn, J. C. Allocation and Pricing of Water Resources. In *Judge, G. G. and*

Takayama, T., eds., 1973, pp. 536–56. **[G: Australia]**

Hamilton, Richard E. Canada's "Exportable Surplus" Natural Gas Policy: A Theoretical Analysis. *Land Econ.*, August 1973, *49*(3), pp. 251–59. **[G: Canada]**

Hanke, Steve H. and Davis, Robert K. Potential for Marginal Cost Pricing in Water Resource Management. *Water Resources Res.*, August 1973, *9*(4), pp. 808–25.

Harberger, Arnold C. Costs and Benefits of the Ullum Dam Project: An Analytical Framework and an Empirical Exploration. In *Harberger, A. C.*, 1973, pp. 280–310. **[G: Argentina]**

Haveman, Robert H. Efficiency and Equity in Natural Resource and Environmental Policy. *Amer. J. Agr. Econ.*, December 1973, *55*(5), pp. 868–78.

Haveman, Robert H. The Ex Post Evaluation of Navigation Improvements. In *Niskanen, W. A., et al., eds.*, 1973, pp. 249–76. **[G: U.S.]**

Heady, Earl O. and Madsen, Howard C. National and Interregional Models of Water Demand for Land Use and Agricultural Policies. In *Judge, G. G. and Takayama, T., eds.*, 1973, pp. 651–75. **[G: U.S.]**

Heady, Earl O., et al. National and Interregional Models of Water Demand, Land Use, and Agricultural Policies. *Water Resources Res.*, August 1973, *9*(4), pp. 777–91. **[G: U.S.]**

Holland, I. Irving. Implications of the 1970 Timber Review for Trade in Timber Products. *Amer. J. Agr. Econ.*, December 1973, *55*(5), pp. 967–73. **[G: U.S.]**

Holmsen, Andreas A. Management of the Peruvian Anchoveta Resource. In *Sokoloski, A. A., ed.*, 1973, pp. 106–11. **[G: Peru]**

Huq, A. M. A Study of the Socioeconomic Impact of Changes in the Harvesting Labor Force in the Maine Lobster Industry. In *Sokoloski, A. A., ed.*, 1973, pp. 159–73. **[G: U.S.]**

Ingram, Helen M. The Political Economy of Regional Water Institutions. *Amer. J. Agr. Econ.*, February 1973, *55*(1), pp. 10–18. **[G: U.S.]**

Kane, Julius; Vertinsky, Ilan and Thomson, William. KSIM: A Methodology for Interactive Resource Policy Simulation. *Water Resources Res.*, February 1973, *9*(1), pp. 65–79.

Keen, E. A. Limited Entry: The Case of the Japanese Tuna Fishery. In *Sokoloski, A. A., ed.*, 1973, pp. 146–58. **[G: Japan]**

Kevern, Niles R. Education and Research Needs in Natural Resources: The Role of the Large State University. *Mich. Academician*, Winter 1973, *5*(3), pp. 367–71.

Kleinpeter, M. Technological Forecasting in the Energy Industry. In *Blohm, H. and Steinbuch, K., eds.*, 1973, pp. 83–90.

Kneese, Allen V. Economics and the Quality of the Environment: Some Empirical Experiences. In *Enthoven, A. C. and Freeman, A. M., III, eds.*, 1973, pp. 72–87. **[G: U.S.]**

Kneese, Allen V. and Bower, Blair T. The Delaware Estuary Study: Effluent Charges, Least-Cost Treatment, and Efficiency. In *Enthoven, A. C. and Freeman, A. M., III, eds.*, 1973, pp. 112–21. **[G: U.S.]**

Krutilla, John V. Some Environmental Effects of Economic Development. In *Enthoven, A. C. and Freeman, A. M., III, eds.*, 1973, pp. 253–62.

LeClerc, Guy and Marks, David H. Determination of the Discharge Policy for Existing Reservoir Networks under Differing Objectives. *Water Resources Res.*, October 1973, *9*(5), pp. 1155–65. **[G: Canada]**

Lewis, William Cris. Public Investment Impacts and Regional Economic Growth. *Water Resources Res.*, August 1973, *9*(4), pp. 851–60.

Lim, David. A Note on Supply Response of Tin Producers, 1949–1969. *Malayan Econ. Rev.*, October 1973, *18*(2), pp. 50–59.

Loehman, Edna and Whinston, A. Reply to Forster and Logan. *Appl. Econ.*, March 1973, *5*(1), pp. 69–73.

Malenbaum, Wilfred. World Resources for the Year 2000. *Ann. Amer. Acad. Polit. Soc. Sci.*, July 1973, *408*, pp. 30–46.

Marshall, Harold Emory. Cost Sharing and Multiobjectives in Water Resource Development. *Water Resources Res.*, February 1973, *9*(1), pp. 1–10. **[G: U.S.]**

McCalden, Gerald. Towards a Model for Prediction of Residential Water Use. In *Aislabie, C., ed.*, 1973, pp. 99–113. **[G: Australia]**

McGee, Dean A. Assessing the "Energy Crisis"—Problems and Prospects. *Fed. Res. Bank Kansas City Rev.*, September-October 1973, pp. 14–20. **[G: U.S.]**

Miller, W. L. and Byers, D. M. Development and Display of Multiple-Objective Project Impacts. *Water Resources Res.*, February 1973, *9*(1), pp. 11–20. **[G: U.S.]**

Minnehan, Robert F. Multiple Objectives and Multigroup Decision Making in Physical Design Situations. In *Cochrane, J. L. and Zeleny, M., eds.*, 1973, pp. 506–16. **[G: U.S.]**

Monarchi, David E.; Kisiel, Chester C. and Duckstein, Lucien. Interactive Multiobjective Programming in Water Resources: A Case Study. *Water Resources Res.*, August 1973, *9*(4), pp. 837–50.

Moncur, James E. T. Opportunity Costs of a Transbasin Diversion: 2. The Columbia River Basin. *Water Resources Res.*, February 1973, *9*(1), pp. 43–49. **[G: U.S.]**

Moore, Thomas Gale. Science, Technology, and Industry. In *Ott, D. J., et al.*, 1973, pp. 67–89. **[G: U.S.]**

Morin, Thomas L. Pathology of a Dynamic Programming Sequencing Algorithm. *Water Resources Res.*, October 1973, *9*(5), pp. 1178–85.

Morissey, M. J. and Burt, R. A Theory of Mineral Discovery: A Note. *Econ. Hist. Rev., 2nd Ser.*, August 1973, *26*(3), pp. 497–505. **[G: Australia]**

Morse, Chandler. Natural Resources as a Constraint on Economic Growth: Discussion. *Amer. Econ. Rev.*, May 1973, *63*(2), pp. 126–28.

Müller, Paul. Protection of the Environment in Agriculture and Forestry. *Ger. Econ. Rev.*, 1973, *11*(1), pp. 77–88. **[G: W. Germany]**

O'Rourke, A. Desmond. Commonality, Fishery Resources, Potential and Policy: Reply. *Amer. J. Agr.*

Econ., August 1973, *55*(3), pp. 530–31. [G: U.S.]

Page, William. The Non-renewable Resources Subsystem. In *Cole, H. S. D., et al., eds.,* 1973, pp. 33–42.

Pattison, Allan. The Economics of Data Collection Systems. In *Aislabie, C., ed.,* 1973, pp. 119–44. [G: Australia]

Paulson, Albert S. and Garrison, Charles B. Entropy as a Measure of the Areal Concentration of Water-Oriented Industry. *Water Resources Res.,* April 1973, *9*(2), pp. 263–69.

Pigram, John J. J. Urban-Rural Conflicts in Urban Water Supply. In *Aislabie, C., ed.,* 1973, pp. 145–54. [G: Australia]

Pontecorvo, Giulio. On the Utility of Bioeconomic Models for Fisheries Management. In *Sokoloski, A. A., ed.,* 1973, pp. 12–22. [G: U.S.]

Pullinger, Barry F. A Method of Analysis of Residential Water Demand and Its Relation to Management. In *Aislabie, C., ed.,* 1973, pp. 155–70. [G: Australia]

Regev, Uri and Schwartz, Aba. Optimal Path of Interregional Investment and Allocation of Water. *Water Resources Res.,* April 1973, *9*(2), pp. 251–62.

Rettig, R. Bruce. Multiple Objectives for Marine Resource Management. In *Sokoloski, A. A., ed.,* 1973, pp. 23–27. [G: U.S.]

Rich, Jack. Natural Resources and External Economies: Regulation of the Pacific Halibut Fishery. In *Sokoloski, A. A., ed.,* 1973, pp. 65–71. [G: U.S.]

Rosenberg, Nathan. Innovative Responses to Materials Shortages. *Amer. Econ. Rev.,* May 1973, *63*(2), pp. 111–18.

Schurr, Samuel. Minerals Trade and International Relations. In *Bergsten, C. F., ed.,* 1973, pp. 181–96.

Segura, Edilberto L. Optimal Fishing Effort in the Peruvian Anchoveta Fishery. In *Sokoloski, A. A., ed.,* 1973, pp. 57–64. [G: Peru]

Sharpe, Ron. Models for Allocation of Water Resources. In *Aislabie, C., ed.,* 1973, pp. 171–76.

Smetherman, Bobbie B. and Smetherman, Robert M. Peruvian Fisheries: Conservation and Development. *Econ. Develop. Cult. Change,* January 1973, *21*(2), pp. 338–51. [G: Peru]

Smith, Herbert L. The Natural Christmas Tree Industry. *Manage. Account.,* December 1973, *55*(6), pp. 9–11, 27. [G: U.S.]

Sokoloski, Adam A. The Status of Fisheries Management Research: An Overview. In *Sokoloski, A. A., ed.,* 1973, pp. 1–6. [G: U.S.]

Stevens, Joe B. and Mattox, Bruce W. Augmentation of Salmon Stocks through Artificial Propagation: Methods and Implications. In *Sokoloski, A. A., ed.,* 1973, pp. 133–45. [G: U.S.]

Stever, Guyford. Impact of Space on World Development. *World Devel.,* February 1973, *1*(1-2), pp. 116–21.

Stroup, Richard and Baden, John. Externality, Property Rights, and the Management of our National Forests. *J. Law Econ.,* October 1973, *16*(2), pp. 303–12. [G: U.S.]

Surrey, A. J. and Bromley, A. J. Energy Resources. In *Cole, H. S. D., et al., eds.,* 1973, pp. 90–107.

Swidler, Joseph C. The Challenge to State Regulation Agencies: The Experience of New York State. *Ann. Amer. Acad. Polit. Soc. Sci.,* November 1973, *410*, pp. 106–19. [G: U.S.]

Thompson, Richard G.; Callen, Richard W. and Wolken, Lawrence C. A Stochastic Investment Model for a Survival Conscious Fishing Firm. In *Sokoloski, A. A., ed.,* 1973, pp. 112–20. [G: U.S.]

Thompson, Russell G. Some Suggestions for the Development of a Bioeconomic Theory of the Fishery. In *Sokoloski, A. A., ed.,* 1973, pp. 92–95.

Thompson, Russell G. and Young, H. Peyton. Forecasting Water Use for Policy Making: A Review. *Water Resources Res.,* August 1973, *9*(4), pp. 792–99.

Tinbergen, Jan. Exhaustion and Technological Development: A Macro-Dynamic Policy Model. *Z. Nationalökon.,* 1973, *33*(3–4), pp. 213–34.

Tisdell, Clement A. Kangaroos: The Economic Management of a Common-Property Resource Involving Interdependence of Production. *Econ. Anal. Pol.,* September 1973, *4*(2), pp. 59–75. [G: Australia]

Van Meir, Lawrence W. Problems in Implementing New Fishery Management Programs. In *Sokoloski, A. A., ed.,* 1973, pp. 9–11. [G: U.S.]

Verkhovskii, B. S. Optimal Redistribution of Water Resources. *Matekon,* Summer 1973, *9*(4), pp. 95–101.

Vianelli, Silvio. Problemi economici e programmazione ecologica per la difesa dell'uomo e del suo ambiente. (Economic Problems and Environmental Planning for the Defense of Mankind and its Habitat. With English summary.) *Mondo Aperto,* June-August 1973, *27*(3–4), pp. 185–223.

Vousden, Neil. Basic Theoretical Issues of Resource Depletion. *J. Econ. Theory,* April 1973, *6*(2), pp. 126–43.

Ward, Robert C. and Vanderholm, Dale H. Cost-Effectiveness Methodologies for Data Acquisition in Water Quality Management. *Water Resources Res.,* June 1973, *9*(3), pp. 536–45. [G: U.S.]

Wiener, Anthony J. The Future of Economic Activity. *Ann. Amer. Acad. Polit. Soc. Sci.,* July 1973, *408*, pp. 47–61.

Windsor, James S. Optimization Model for the Operation of Flood Control Systems. *Water Resources Res.,* October 1973, *9*(5), pp. 1219–26.

Young, H. Peyton and Thompson, Russell G. Least-Cost Allocation and Valuation Model for Water Resources. *Water Resources Res.,* October 1973, *9*(5), pp. 1186–95.

7211 Recreational Aspects of Natural Resources

Brown, William G. and Nawas, Farid. Impact of Aggregation on the Estimation of Outdoor Recreation Demand Functions. *Amer. J. Agr. Econ.,* May 1973, *55*(2), pp. 246–49. [G: U.S.]

Darling, Arthur H. Measuring Benefits Generated by Urban Water Parks. *Land Econ.,* February 1973, *49*(1), pp. 22–34. [G: U.S.]

David, F. J. L. Floodplain Lands for Parks and Recreation: A Case Study of Milwaukee. *Land Econ.,* May 1973, *49*(2), pp. 221–26. [G: U.S.]

Ditton, Robert B. and Goodale, Thomas L. Water Quality Perception and the Recreational Uses of Green Bay, Lake Michigan. *Water Resources Res.,* June 1973, *9*(3), pp. 569–79. [G: U.S.]

Gaumnitz, Jack E.; Swinth, Robert L. and Tollefson, John O. Simulation of Water Recreation Users' Decisions. *Land Econ.,* August 1973, *49*(3), pp. 269–77.

Holman, Mary A. and Bennett, James T. Determinants of Use of Water-Based Recreational Facilities. *Water Resources Res.,* October 1973, *9*(5), pp. 1208–18. [G: U.S.]

Jaakson, Reiner. Factor Analysis of Shoreline Physiography and Perception of Water Level Drawdown by Reservoir Shoreline Residents. *Water Resources Res.,* February 1973, *9*(1), pp. 81–92.

Klippenstein, D. H. and Ironside, R. G. Farmers' Attitudes Toward Farm-Based Recreational Facilities in Alberta. *Can. J. Agr. Econ.,* November 1973, *21*(3), pp. 23–33. [G: Canada]

O'Riordan, T. An Analysis of the Use and Management of Campgrounds in British Columbia Provincial Parks. *Econ. Geogr.,* October 1973, *49*(4), pp. 298–308. [G: Canada]

Weicher, John C. and Zerbst, Robert H. The Externalities of Neighborhood Parks: An Empirical Investigation. *Land Econ.,* February 1973, *49*(1), pp. 99–105.

Weissler, Mark L. Snowmobiles and the Environment. *Yale Law J.,* March 1973, *82*(4), pp. 772–86. [G: U.S.]

722 Conservation and Pollution

7220 Conservation and Pollution

Ahern, William R., Jr. Health Effects of Automotive Air Pollution. In *Jacoby, H. D., et al.,* 1973, pp. 139–74. [G: U.S.]

Ahern, William R., Jr. Measuring the Value of Emissions Reductions. In *Jacoby, H. D., et al.,* 1973, pp. 175–205. [G: U.S.]

Akins, James E. International Cooperative Efforts in Energy Supply. *Ann. Amer. Acad. Polit. Soc. Sci.,* November 1973, *410,* pp. 75–85.

Alchian, Armen A. and Demsetz, Harold. The Property Rights Paradigm. *J. Econ. Hist.,* March 1973, *33*(1), pp. 16–27.

Alekseev, V. Protection of the Natural Environment (Economic Aspect) *Prob. Econ.,* November 1973, *16*(7), pp. 24–35.

Alessio, Frank J. Multiple Criteria in Environmental Control: Use of Economic Maximization Rules to Determine Relative Standards. In *Cochrane, J. L. and Zeleny, M., eds.,* 1973, pp. 544–49.

Appleman, Jack M. Testing and Maintenance of In-Use Vehicles. In *Jacoby, H. D., et al.,* 1973, pp. 113–37. [G: U.S.]

d'Arge, R. C. and Kogiku, K. C. Economic Growth and the Environment. *Rev. Econ. Stud.,* January 1973, *40*(1), pp. 61–77.

Bailey, Richard. Britain and a Community Energy Policy. *Nat. Westminster Bank Quart. Rev.,* November 1973, pp. 5–15. [G: U.K.; E.E.C.]

Bandurski, Bruce Lord. Ecology and Economics —Partners for Productivity. *Ann. Amer. Acad.*

Polit. Soc. Sci., January 1973, *405,* pp. 75–94. [G: U.S.]

Banks, F. E. Growth and Pollution. *Ekon. Samfundets Tidskr.,* 1973, *26*(2), pp. 67–74.

Barnett, Andy H. and Yandle, Bruce, Jr. Allocating Environmental Resources. *Public Finance,* 1973, *28*(1), pp. 11–19.

Baroutsis, A. Paul and Horton, Joseph. An Economic Strategy for Environmental Quality. In *Gabriel, R. A. and Cohen, S. H., eds.,* 1973, pp. 61–93. [G: U.S.]

Bergstrom, Theodore C. The Use of Markets to Control Pollution. *Rech. Écon. Louvain,* December 1973, *39*(4), pp. 403–18.

Blair, Roger D. Problems of Pollution Standards: The Clean Air Act of 1970. *Land Econ.,* August 1973, *49*(3), pp. 260–68. [G: U.S.]

Boulding, Kenneth E. Environment and Economics. In *Boulding, K. E.,* 1973, pp. 569–79.

Boulding, Kenneth E. The Economics of Energy. *Ann. Amer. Acad. Polit. Soc. Sci.,* November 1973, *410,* pp. 120–26.

Brown, Lester. Rich Countries and Poor in a Finite, Interdependent World. In *Olson, M. and Landsberg, H. H., eds.,* 1973, pp. 153–64.

Brown, Lowell S., et al. Are There Real Limits to Growth?—A Reply to Beckerman. *Oxford Econ. Pap.,* November 1973, *25*(3), pp. 455–60.

Buchanan, James M. The Institutional Structure of Externality. *Public Choice,* Spring 1973, *14,* pp. 69–82.

Burke, William. Oil From the Artic. *Fed. Res. Bank San Francisco Rev.,* September-October 1973, pp. 13–21. [G: U.S.]

Burnham, John B. Societal Values in Power Generation. In *Dierkes, M. and Bauer, R. A., eds.,* 1973, pp. 260–70. [G: U.S.]

Byrne, Robert F. and Spiro, Michael H. On Taxation as a Pollution Control Policy. *Swedish J. Econ.,* March 1973, *75*(1), pp. 105–09.

Caldwell, Lynton K. Energy and Environment: The Bases for Public Policies. *Ann. Amer. Acad. Polit. Soc. Sci.,* November 1973, *410,* pp. 127–38.

Carlin, Alan. The Grand Canyon Controversy; or, How Reclamation Justifies the Unjustifiable. In *Enthoven, A. C. and Freeman, A. M., III, eds.,* 1973, pp. 263–70. [G: U.S.]

Cebula, Richard J. and Vedder, Richard K. A Note on Migration, Economic Opportunity, and the Quality of Life. *J. Reg. Sci.,* August 1973, *13*(2), pp. 205–11. [G: U.S.]

Cicchetti, Charles J. and Freeman, A. Myrick, III. The Trans-Alaska Pipeline: An Economic Analysis of Alternatives. In *Enthoven, A. C. and Freeman, A. M., III, eds.,* 1973, pp. 271–84. [G: U.S.]

Clark, Colin W. Profit Maximization and the Extinction of Animal Species. *J. Polit. Econ.,* July-August 1973, *81*(4), pp. 950–61.

Clough, Donald J. Environmental Pollution. In *Ross, M., ed.,* 1973, pp. 685–99.

Coale, Ansley J. Man and His Environment. In *Enthoven, A. C. and Freeman, A. M., III, eds.,* 1973, pp. 155–65. [G: U.S.]

Cohen, Sylvan H. The Politics of Urban Renewal and the Politics of Ecology. In *Gabriel, R. A. and Cohen, S. H., eds.,* 1973, pp. 171–91. [G: U.S.]

Collins, David C. Applications of Multiple Criterial Evaluation to Decision Aiding. In *Cochrane, J. L. and Zeleny, M., eds.*, 1973, pp. 477–505. [G: U.S.]

Common, Michael S. and Pearce, David W. Adaptive Mechanisms, Growth, and the Environment: The Case of Natural Resources. *Can. J. Econ.*, August 1973, *6*(3), pp. 289–300.

Corbin, Donald A. Guidelines for Reporting Corporate Environmental Impact. In *Dierkes, M. and Bauer, R. A., eds.*, 1973, pp. 321–26.

Costonis, John J. Development Rights Transfer: An Exploratory Essay. *Yale Law J.*, November 1973, *83*(1), pp. 75–128.

Coughlin, Robert E. and Hammer, Thomas R. Estimating the Benefits of Stream Valley and Open Space Preservation Projects. In *Harriss, C. L., ed.*, 1973, pp. 155–70. [G: U.S.]

Cramton, Roger C. and Berg, Richard K. On Leading a Horse to Water: NEPA and the Federal Bureaucracy. *Mich. Law Rev.*, january 1973, *71*(3), pp. 511–36. [G: U.S.]

Cunningham, Roger A. Billboard Control under the Highway Beautification Act of 1965. *Mich. Law Rev.*, June 1973, *71*(7), pp. 1295–1374.

Daly, George A. and Giertz, Fred J. Pollution Abatement, Pareto Optimality, and the Market Mechanism. In *Boulding, K. E.; Pfaff, M. and Pfaff, A., eds.*, 1973, pp. 350–58.

Darby, Michael R. Paper Recycling and the Stock of Trees. *J. Polit. Econ.*, September-October 1973, *81*(5), pp. 1253–55.

Davies, J. Clarence, III. Standard-Setting. In *Enthoven, A. C. and Freeman, A. M., III, eds.*, 1973, pp. 107–11. [G: U.S.]

De Bruyne, L. De Antwerpse luchthavenbehoeften 1970–1980. (The Air Transport Needs of Antwerp. With English summary.) *Econ. Soc. Tijdschr.*, June 1973, *27*(3), pp. 227–43. [G: Belgium]

Dee, Norbert, et al. An Environmental Evaluation System for Water Resource Planning. *Water Resources Res.*, June 1973, *9*(3), pp. 523–35.

Ditwiler, C. Dirck. Environmental Perceptions and Policy Misconceptions. *Amer. J. Agr. Econ.*, August 1973, *55*(3), pp. 477–83.

Dixon, John M. A Multidisciplinary Policy Decision Model for Water Pollution. In *Aislabie, C., ed.*, 1973, pp. 49–60. [G: Australia]

Dixon, Orani; Dixon, Peter and Miranowski, John. Insecticide Requirements in an Efficient Agricultural Sector. *Rev. Econ. Statist.*, November 1973, *55*(4), pp. 423–32. [G: U.S.]

Doggett, Kathleen M. and Friedman, Donald J. Legislation for Clean Air: An Indoor Front. *Yale Law J.*, April 1973, *82*(5), pp. 1040–54.

Dolan, Edwin G. Preserving the Wilderness—Public Interest or Special Interest? In *Reynolds, L. G.; Green, G. D. and Lewis, D. R., eds.*, 1973, pp. 231–42. [G: U.S.]

Dorcey, Anthony H. J. Effluent Charges, Information Generation and Bargaining Behavior. *Natural Res. J.*, January 1973, *13*(1), pp. 118–33.

Dorfman, Robert. Economics of Pollution: Discussion. *Amer. Econ. Rev.*, May 1973, *63*(2), pp. 253–56.

Drobny, Neil L. Social Accounting in Environmental Planning. In *Dierkes, M. and Bauer, R. A., eds.*, 1973, pp. 248–59. [G: U.S.]

Dunlap, Riley E.; Gale, Richard P. and Rutherford, Brent M. Concern for Environmental Rights Among College Students. *Amer. J. Econ. Soc.*, January 1973, *32*(1), pp. 45–60. [G: U.S.]

Elliott, Ralph D. Economic Study of the Effect of Municipal Sewer Surcharges on Industrial Wastes and Water Usage. *Water Resources Res.*, October 1973, *9*(5), pp. 1121–31. [G: U.S.]

England, Richard and Bluestone, Barry. Ecology and Social Conflict. In *Daly, H. E., ed.*, 1973, pp. 190–214. [G: U.S.]

Ethridge, Don. The Inclusion of Wastes in the Theory of the Firm. *J. Polit. Econ.*, November-December 1973, *81*(6), pp. 1430–41.

Evans, Michael K. A Forecasting Model Applied to Pollution Control Costs. *Amer. Econ. Rev.*, May 1973, *63*(2), pp. 244–52.

Fedorenko, N. and Gofman, K. G. Problems of Optimization in the Planning and Control of the Environment. *Prob. Econ.*, April 1973, *15*(12), pp. 37–51. [G: U.S.S.R.]

Fedorov, E. Urgent Problems in the Interaction Between Society and the Environment. *Prob. Econ.*, May 1973, *16*(1), pp. 70–90.

Ferrar, Terry A. Progressive Taxation as a Policy for Water Quality Management. *Water Resources Res.*, June 1973, *9*(3), pp. 563–68.

Fisher, Anthony C. Environmental Externalities and the Arrow-Lind Public Investment Theorem. *Amer. Econ. Rev.*, September 1973, *63*(4), pp. 722–25.

Fisher, Joseph L. and Ridker, Ronald G. Population Growth, Resource Availability and Environmental Quality. *Amer. Econ. Rev.*, May 1973, *63*(2), pp. 79–87. [G: U.S.]

Forster, Bruce A. Optimal Consumption Planning in a Polluted Environment. *Econ. Rec.*, December 1973, *49*(128), pp. 534–45.

Forster, Bruce A. and Logan, John. The Welfare Economics of Water Resource Allocation Over Time: Comment. *Appl. Econ.*, March 1973, *5*(1), pp. 61–68.

Forster, Bruce A. Optimal Capital Accumulation in a Polluted Environment. *Southern Econ. J.*, April 1973, *39*(4), pp. 544–47.

Fox, Irving K. and Wible, Lyman. Information Generation and Communication to Establish Environmental Quality Objectives. *Natural Res. J.*, January 1973, *13*(1), pp. 134–49. [G: U.S.]

Frech, H. E., III. Pricing of Pollution: The Coase Theorem in the Long Run. *Bell J. Econ. Manage. Sci.*, Spring 1973, *4*(1), pp. 316–19.

Freeman, A. Myrick, III and Haveman, Robert H. Clean Rhetoric and Dirty Water. In *Enthoven, A. C. and Freeman, A. M., III, eds.*, 1973, pp. 122–37. [G: U.S.]

Freeman, A. Myrick, III. Income Distribution and Environmental Quality. In *Enthoven, A. C. and Freeman, A. M., III, eds.*, 1973, pp. 100–06. [G: U.S.]

Freeman, A. Myrick, III. Grants and Environmental Policy. In *Boulding, K. E.; Pfaff, M. and Pfaff, A., eds.*, 1973, pp. 309–17. [G: U.S.]

Freeman, S. David. Is There an Energy Crisis? An Overview. *Ann. Amer. Acad. Polit. Soc. Sci.*,

November 1973, *410*, pp. 1–10.   [G: U.S.]

Gabriel, Richard A. The Moral Basis of Ecology. In *Gabriel, R. A. and Cohen, S. H., eds.*, 1973, pp. 19–31.   [G: U.S.]

Gifford, Adam, Jr. Pollution, Technology, and Economic Growth. *Southern Econ. J.*, October 1973, *40*(2), pp. 210–15.

Gopalakrishnan, Chennat. The Economics of Water Transfer. *Amer. J. Econ. Soc.*, October 1973, *32*(4), pp. 395–403.   [G: U.S.]

Gould, Bernard W. Sampling Errors in Flood Damage Estimates. In *Aislabie, C., ed.*, 1973, pp. 82–98.

Green, Harold P. Nuclear Power: Risk, Liability, and Indemnity. *Mich. Law Rev.*, January 1973, *71*(3), pp. 479–510.   [G: U.S.]

Guicciardi, Diego. Industry and Ecological Problems in Italy. *Rev. Econ. Cond. Italy*, September 1973, *27*(5), pp. 305–12.   [G: Italy]

Guntermann, Karl L. Air Pollution Control in the Secondary Aluminum Industry. *Land Econ.*, August 1973, *49*(3), pp. 285–93.   [G: U.S.]

Hannon, Bruce M. An Energy Standard of Value. *Ann. Amer. Acad. Polit. Soc. Sci.*, November 1973, *410*, pp. 139–53.   [G: U.S.]

Hardesty, John; Clement, Norris C. and Jencks, Clinton E. Ecological Conflicts: A Reply. *Rev. Radical Polit. Econ.*, Summer 1973, *5*(2), pp. 95–102.

Haveman, Robert H. Efficiency and Equity in Natural Resource and Environmental Policy. *Amer. J. Agr. Econ.*, December 1973, *55*(5), pp. 868–78.

Haveman, Robert H. Common Property, Congestion, and Environmental Pollution. *Quart. J. Econ.*, May 1973, *87*(2), pp. 278–87.

Havrilesky, Thomas M. Technological Innovativeness, the Grants Economy, and the Ecological Crisis. In *Boulding, K. E.; Pfaff, M. and Pfaff, A., eds.*, 1973, pp. 317–39.   [G: U.S.]

Haworth, Joan G. Externalities and the City. In *Rasmussen, D. W. and Haworth, C. T., eds.*, 1973, pp. 28–30.   [G: U.S.]

Heilbroner, Robert L. Ecological Armageddon. In *Enthoven, A. C. and Freeman, A. M., III, eds.*, 1973, pp. 176–85.

Henderson, Hazel. Ecologists versus Economists. *Harvard Bus. Rev.*, July-August 1973, *51*(4), pp. 28–36, 152–57.

Herfindahl, Orris C. and Kneese, Allen V. Measuring Social and Economic Change: Benefits and Costs of Environmental Pollution. In *Moss, M., ed.*, 1973, pp. 441–503.   [G: U.S.]

Hitch, Charles J. The Environment: A New Challenge for Operations Research. In *Ross, M., ed.*, 1973, pp. 29–39.

Housley, Carl B. Water Pollution Solutions in a Costless and Frictionless Legal System. *Southern Quart.*, October 1973, *12*(1), pp. 15–31.

Howards, Irving. The Comparative Case: Environmental Problems in Israel. In *Gabriel, R. A. and Cohen, S. H., eds.*, 1973, pp. 129–53. [G: Israel]

Hufbauer, G. C. Environmental Quality, Income Distribution, and Factor Mobility: The Consequences of Local Action. *J. Econ. Issues*, June 1973, *7*(2), pp. 323–35.

Iliff, Neil. Is There a World Environmental Crisis? In *Robinson, J., ed.*, 1973, pp. 117–24.

Ingram, Helen M. Information Channels and Environmental Decision Making. *Natural Res. J.*, January 1973, *13*(1), pp. 150–69.

Jacoby, Henry D. and Steinbruner, John D. Salvaging the Federal Attempt to Control Auto Pollution. *Public Policy*, Winter 1973, *21*(1), pp. 1–48.   [G: U.S.]

Jacoby, Henry D. and Steinbruner, John D. Advanced Technology and the Problem of Implementation. In *Jacoby, H. D., et al.*, 1973, pp. 49–61.   [G: U.S.]

Jacoby, Henry D. and Steinbruner, John D. Policy Analysis and the Public Sector. In *Jacoby, H. D., et al.*, 1973, pp. 1–8.   [G: U.S.]

Jacoby, Henry D. and Steinbruner, John D. Policy Options and Predicted Outcomes. In *Jacoby, H. D., et al.*, 1973, pp. 27–47.   [G: U.S.]

Jacoby, Henry D. and Steinbruner, John D. The Context of Current Policy Discussions. In *Jacoby, H. D., et al.*, 1973, pp. 9–26.   [G: U.S.]

Jones, Charles O. Air Pollution and Contemporary Environmental Politics. *Growth Change*, July 1973, *4*(3), pp. 22–27.   [G: U.S.]

Kassirov, L. Rent Relationships in the Economic Mechanism of Social Production. *Prob. Econ.*, November 1973, *16*(7), pp. 36–58.

Kinnear, Thomas C. and Taylor, James R. The Effect of Ecological Concern on Brand Perceptions. *J. Marketing Res.*, May 1973, *10*(2), pp. 191–97.   [G: U.S.]

Kinnersley, D. J. Water Pollution. In *Robinson, J., ed.*, 1973, pp. 134–55.   [G: U.K.]

Klevorick, Alvin K. and Kramer, Gerald H. Social Choice on Pollution Management: The Genossenschaften. *J. Public Econ.*, April 1973, *2*(2), pp. 101–46.   [G: W. Germany]

Kneese, Allen V. Water Quality Management by Regional Authorities in the Ruhr Area with Special Emphasis on the Role of Cost Assessment. In *Grieson, R. E., ed.*, 1973, pp. 251–71.   [G: W. Germany]

Kneese, Allen V.; Ayres, Robert U. and d'Arge, Ralph C. Economics and the Environment: A Materials Balance Approach. In *Enthoven, A. C. and Freeman, A. M., III, eds.*, 1973, pp. 25–36.

Kneese, Allen V. Economics and the Quality of the Environment: Some Empirical Experiences. In *Enthoven, A. C. and Freeman, A. M., III, eds.*, 1973, pp. 72–87.   [G: U.S.]

Kneese, Allen V. and Bower, Blair T. The Delaware Estuary Study: Effluent Charges, Least-Cost Treatment, and Efficiency. In *Enthoven, A. C. and Freeman, A. M., III, eds.*, 1973, pp. 112–21.   [G: U.S.]

Kneese, Allen V. and Mäler, Karl-Göran. Bribes and Charges in Pollution Control: An Aspect of the Coase Controversy. *Natural Res. J.*, October 1973, *13*(4), pp. 705–16.

Kolm, Serge-Christophe. Les pollués doivent-ils payer? (With English summary.) *Kyklos*, 1973, *26*(2), pp. 322–36.

Krier, James E. and Montgomery, W. David. Resource Allocation, Information Cost and the Form of Government Intervention. *Natural Res. J.*, January 1973, *13*(1), pp. 89–105.

Kuipers, S. K. and Nentjes, A. Pollution in a Neo-Classical World: The Classics Rehabilitated? *De*

Economist, January-February 1973, *121*(1), pp. 52–67.

Lamson, Robert W. Corporate Accounting for Environmental Effects. In *Dierkes, M. and Bauer, R. A., eds.,* 1973, pp. 230–47.

Lanzillotti, Robert F. and Blair, Roger D. Automobile Pollution, Externalities and Public Policy. *Antitrust Bull.,* Fall, 1973, *18*(3), pp. 431–47. [G: U.S.]

Lave, Lester B. and Seskin, Eugene P. Air Pollution and Human Health. In *Enthoven, A. C. and Freeman, A. M., III, eds.,* 1973, pp. 88–99. [G: U.S.]

Lave, Lester B. and Seskin, Eugene P. An Analysis of the Association Between U.S. Mortality and Air Pollution. *J. Amer. Statist. Assoc.,* June 1973, *68* (342), pp. 284–90. [G: U.S.]

Leduc, Edgar and Baccanari, Samuel M. Interlocal Governmental Relations in Air Pollution Abatement. In *Gabriel, R. A. and Cohen, S. H., eds.,* 1973, pp. 113–28. [G: U.S.]

Lee, Norman. Interactions between Economic and Eco-systems. In *Robinson, J., ed.,* 1973, pp. 125–33.

Levy, Yvonne. Pollution Control: Two Industries. *Fed. Res. Bank San Francisco Rev.,* January-February 1973, pp. 12–20. [G: U.S.]

Lieber, Harvey and Rosinoff, Bruce. Evaluating the State's Role in Water Pollution Control. *Amer. Real Estate Urban Econ. Assoc. J.,* Fall 1973, *1*(2), pp. 73–87. [G: U.S.]

Lord, William B. and Warner, Maurice L. Aggregates and Externalities: Information Needs for Public Natural Resource Decision-Making. *Natural Res. J.,* January 1973, *13*(1), pp. 106–17.

Lumb, H. C. Economic Incentives to Control Pollution. In *Reynolds, L. G.; Green, G. D. and Lewis, D. R., eds.,* 1973, pp. 220–30. [G: U.S.]

Manchester, Harland. Refuse is Reusable. In *Moskoff, W., ed.,* 1973, pp. 242–48. [G: W. Europe]

Marstrand, Pauline K. and Sinclair, T. C. The Pollution Sub-system. In *Cole, H. S. D., et al., eds.,* 1973, pp. 80–89.

Mathur, Vijay K. Models of Air Pollution Damage Control in a Region. In *Mattila, J. M. and Thompson, W. R., eds.,* 1973, pp. 27–40.

Meacci, Ferdinando. Protezione dell'ambiente, aumento dei coefficienti tecnici e preferenze collettive. (Environmental Protection, Increase in Technical Coefficients and Collective Preferences. With English summary.) *Econ. Int.,* August-November 1973, *26*(3–4), pp. 393–412.

Mellanby, Kenneth. The Biological Effects of Pollution—An Ecological Problem. In *Robinson, J., ed.,* 1973, pp. 189–99. [G: U.K.]

Metcalf, Lee. The Vested Oracles: How Industry Regulates Government. In *Haveman, R. H. and Hamrin, R. D., eds.,* 1973, pp. 52–59. [G: U.S.]

Morton, Rogers C. B. The Nixon Administration Energy Policy. *Ann. Amer. Acad. Polit. Soc. Sci.,* November 1973, *410,* pp. 65–74. [G: U.S.]

Moyer, R. Charles and Mastrapasqua, Frank. Socioeconomic Accounting and External Diseconomies: A Comment. *Accounting Rev.,* January 1973, *48*(1), pp. 126–27.

Myrdal, Gunnar. Economics of an Improved Environment. *World Devel.,* February 1973, *1*(1-2), pp. 102–14.

Näslund, Bertil. Pollution and the Value of Time. *Europ. Econ. Rev.,* June 1973, *4*(2), pp. 181–96.

Nordhaus, William D. World Dynamics: Measurement Without Data. *Econ. J.,* December 1973, *83* (332), pp. 1156–83.

Oldham, James C. Organized Labor, the Environment, and the Taft-Hartley Act. *Mich. Law Rev.,* April 1973, *71*(5), pp. 935–1040. [G: U.S.]

Orleans, Leo A. and Suttmeier, Richard P. The Mao Ethic and Environmental Quality. In *Wilber, C. K., ed.,* 1973, pp. 258–65. [G: China]

Page, Talbot. Failure of Bribes and Standards for Pollution Abatement. *Natural Res. J.,* October 1973, *13*(4), pp. 677–704.

Pajestka, Jøzef. Need for Greater World-Wide Rationality. In *[Tinbergen, J.],* 1973, pp. 273–83.

Pepper, H. W. T. Taxing Pollution. *Bull. Int. Fiscal Doc.,* May 1973, *27*(5), pp. 189–93.

Plessas, Demetrius J. Airplane Noise: Some Analytic and Policy Perspectives. *Land Econ.,* February 1973, *49*(1), pp. 14–21. [G: U.S.]

Ramey, James T. The Promise of Nuclear Energy. *Ann. Amer. Acad. Polit. Soc. Sci.,* November 1973, *410,* pp. 11–23. [G: U.S.]

Randers, Jørgen and Meadows, Dennis L. System Simulation to Test Environmental Policy: A Sample Study of DDT Movement in the Environment. In *Hawkes, N., ed.,* 1973, pp. 96–143.

Reay, J. S. S. Air Pollution. In *Robinson, J., ed.,* 1973, pp. 156–74. [G: U.K.]

Reed, Laurance. Policy Issues. In *Robinson, J., ed.,* 1973, pp. 175–88. [G: U.K.]

Roberts, Marc J. On Reforming Economic Growth. In *Olson, M. and Landsberg, H. H., eds.,* 1973, pp. 119–37.

Robinson, Colin and Crook, Elizabeth M. Is There a World Energy Crisis? *Nat. Westminster Bank Quart. Rev.,* May 1973, pp. 46–60.

Rohrlich, George F. The Potential of *Social* Ecology for Economic Science. *Rev. Soc. Econ.,* April 1973, *31*(1), pp. 31–39.

Rose-Ackerman, Susan. Effluent Charges: A Critique. *Can. J. Econ.,* November 1973, *6*(4), pp. 512–28.

Rose, Marshall. Market Problems in the Distribution of Emission Rights. *Water Resources Res.,* October 1973, *9*(5), pp. 1132–44.

Ruff, Larry E. The Economic Common Sense of Pollution. In *Enthoven, A. C. and Freeman, A. M., III, eds.,* 1973, pp. 37–53. [G: U.S.]

Russell, Clifford S. Application of Microeconomic Models to Regional Environmental Quality Management. *Amer. Econ. Rev.,* May 1973, *63*(2), pp. 236–43.

Sacco, John F. Local Government and Air Quality Problems: A Study of Problem Solving Approaches. In *Gabriel, R. A. and Cohen, S. H., eds.,* 1973, pp. 32–60. [G: U.S.]

Sachs, Ignacy. Development, Environment and Technology Assessment. *Int. Soc. Sci. J.,* 1973, *25* (3), pp. 273–83.

Saini, Krishan G. and Neece, Roger N. Poverty versus Pollution: Is There a Choice? *Indian Econ. J.,* January-March 1973, *20*(3), pp. 452–68.

Salgo, Harvey. The Obsolescence of Growth: Capitalism and the Environmental Crisis. *Rev. Radical Polit. Econ.*, Fall 1973, *5*(3), pp. 26–45.

Savage, Paul L. The Ecological Bind: The Political Imperative. In *Gabriel, R. A. and Cohen, S. H., eds.*, 1973, pp. 192–211.

Schmid, A. Allan. The Role of Grants, Exchange, and Property Rights in Environmental Policy. In *Boulding, K. E.; Pfaff, M. and Pfaff, A., eds.*, 1973, pp. 340–49. [G: U.S.]

Schneider, Jan. New Perspectives on International Environmental Law. *Yale Law J.*, July 1973, *82* (8), pp. 1659–80.

Schreiner, Dean; Muncrief, George and Davis, Bob. Solid Waste Management for Rural Areas: Analysis of Costs and Service Requirements. *Amer. J. Agr. Econ.*, Part I, November 1973, *55*(4), pp. 567–76. [G: U.S.]

Schweikert, H. Zur Planung der Energieversorgung in städtischen Agglomerationen. (The Planning of Distribution of Energy in Urban Areas. With English summary.) *Schweiz. Z. Volkswirtsch. Statist.*, September 1973, *109*(3), pp. 421–39.

Seagraves, James A. On Appraising Environmental Institutions. *Amer. J. Agr. Econ.*, Part I, November 1973, *55*(4), pp. 617–21.

Seskin, Eugene P. Residential Choice and Air Pollution: A General Equilibrium Model. *Amer. Econ. Rev.*, December 1973, *63*(5), pp. 960–67.

Siebert, Horst. Environment and Regional Growth. *Z. Nationalökon.*, 1973, *33*(1–2), pp. 79–85.

Sinclair, T. C. Environmentalism: A la recherche du temps perdu—bien perdu? In *Cole, H. S. D., et al., eds.*, 1973, pp. 175–91.

Stelzer, Irwin M. and Netschert, Bruce C. Energy and the Environment in New York State: A Balancing of Needs. *Amer. Econ.*, Fall 1973, *17*(2), pp. 143–47. [G: U.S.]

Strong, Maurice F. One Year after Stockholm: An Ecological Approach to Management. *Foreign Aff.*, July 1973, *51*(4), pp. 690–707.

Strotz, Robert H. and Wright, Colin. Externalities, Welfare Economics, and Environmental Problems. In *Boulding, K. E.; Pfaff, M. and Pfaff, A., eds.*, 1973, pp. 359–73.

Stroup, Richard and Baden, John. Externality, Property Rights, and the Management of our National Forests. *J. Law Econ.*, October 1973, *16*(2), pp. 303–12. [G: U.S.]

Swanson, E. R. and Narayanan, A. V. S. Evaluation of the Effect of Alternative Agricultural Systems on Water Quality: A Linear Programming Approach. In *Judge, G. G. and Takayama, T., eds.*, 1973, pp. 676–87. [G: U.S.]

Swidler, Joseph C. The Challenge to State Regulation Agencies: The Experience of New York State. *Ann. Amer. Acad. Polit. Soc. Sci.*, November 1973, *410*, pp. 106–19. [G: U.S.]

Szucs, Ferenc K. The Impact of Electoral Systems on Environmental Amelioration: A Comparative Study of London and Liege. In *Gabriel, R. A. and Cohen, S. H., eds.*, 1973, pp. 154–70. [G: U.K.; Belgium]

Taylor, C. R. An Analysis of Nitrate Concentrations in Illinois Streams. *Ill. Agr. Econ.*, January 1973, *13*(1), pp. 12–19. [G: U.S.]

Thomann, Robert V. Effect of Longitudinal Dispersion on Dynamic Water Quality Response of Streams and Rivers. *Water Resources Res.*, April 1973, *9*(2), pp. 355–66.

Tietenberg, Thomas H. Controlling Pollution by Price and Standard Systems: A General Equilibrium Analysis. *Swedish J. Econ.*, June 1973, *75*(2), pp. 193–203.

Tietenberg, Thomas H. Specific Taxes and the Control of Pollution: A General Equilibrium Analysis. *Quart. J. Econ.*, November 1973, *87*(4), pp. 503–22.

Tybout, Richard A. Pricing of Pollution: The Coase Theorem in the Long Run: Reply. *Bell J. Econ. Manage. Sci.*, Spring 1973, *4*(1), pp. 320–21.

Tybout, Richard A. Prices, Costs, and the Energy Crisis. *Ohio State U. Bull. Bus. Res.*, June 1973, *48*(6), pp. 4–8. [G: U.S.]

Vianelli, Silvio. Problemi economici e programmazione ecologica per la difesa dell'uomo e del suo ambiente. (Economic Problems and Environmental Planning for the Defense of Mankind and its Habitat. With English summary.) *Mondo Aperto*, June-August 1973, *27*(3–4), pp. 185–223.

Vickrey, William. Measuring Social and Economic Change: Benefits and Costs of Environmental Pollution: Comment. In *Moss, M., ed.*, 1973, pp. 503–08. [G: U.S.]

Walter, Ingo. Environmental Management and the International Economic Order. In *Bergsten, C. F., ed.*, 1973, pp. 293–346.

Walter, Ingo. The Pollution Content of American Trade. *Western Econ. J.*, March 1973, *11*(1), pp. 61–70. [G: U.S.]

Watson, William D., Jr. Stochastic Operating Characteristics and Cost Functions of Electrostatic Precipitators. *Eng. Econ.*, January-February 1973, *18*(2), pp. 79–98.

Webb, Don R. and Darling, John R. The Post-Use Problem—A Response from Management. *J. Bus. Res.*, Summer 1973, *1*(1), pp. 49–56.

Wedin, Dick. Externalities and Open Field Burning: A Case Study. *Amer. J. Agr. Econ.*, December 1973, *55*(5), pp. 1026–29. [G: U.S.]

Weinrobe, Maurice D. Accounting for Pollution: Pollution Abatement and the National Product. *Land Econ.*, May 1973, *49*(2), pp. 115–21.

Weinstein, Milton C. and Clark, Ian D. Emissions Measurement and the Testing of New Vehicles. In *Jacoby, H. D., et al.*, 1973, pp. 63–111. [G: U.S.]

Wenders, John T. Corrective Taxes and Pollution Abatement. *J. Law Econ.*, October 1973, *16*(2), pp. 365–68.

Whitney, J. B. R. Ecology and Environmental Control. In *Oksenberg, M., ed.*, 1973, pp. 95–109. [G: China]

Wieand, Kenneth F. Air Pollution and Property Values: A Study of the St. Louis Area. *J. Reg. Sci.*, April 1973, *13*(1), pp. 91–95. [G: U.S.]

Winch, David M. The Pure Theory of Non-Pure Goods. *Can. J. Econ.*, May 1973, *6*(2), pp. 149–63.

Winfield, Gerald F. The Impact of Urbanization on Agricultural Processes. *Ann. Amer. Acad. Polit. Soc. Sci.*, January 1973, *405*, pp. 65–74. [G: U.S.]

Young, H. Peyton and Thompson, Russell G. Least-

Cost Allocation and Valuation Model for Water Resources. *Water Resources Res.*, October 1973, *9*(5), pp. 1186–95.

Zwick, David R. A Criticism of the Effluent Charge. In *Enthoven, A. C. and Freeman, A. M., III, eds.*, 1973, pp. 138–40. **[G: U.S.]**

Zwick, David R. and Benstock, Marcy. Water Wasteland: Conclusions and Recommendations. In *Enthoven, A. C. and Freeman, A. M., III, eds.*, 1973, pp. 141–44. **[G: U.S.]**

Zwintz, Richard. Der Abwasserkoeffizient der Industrie und ihrer Gruppen. (The Waste Water Coefficient of the Industrial Activities. With English summary.) *Z. ges. Staatswiss.*, October 1973, *129*(4), pp. 714–37. **[G: W. Germany]**

Capel, R. E. and Pandey, R. K. Evaluating Demand for Deer Hunting: A Comparison of Methods. *Can. J. Agr. Econ.*, November 1973, *21*(3), pp. 6–14. **[G: Canada]**

723 Energy

7230 Energy

Akins, James E. International Cooperative Efforts in Energy Supply. *Ann. Amer. Acad. Polit. Soc. Sci.*, November 1973, *410*, pp. 75–85.

Allen, Howard P. Electric Utilities: Can They Meet Future Power Needs? *Ann. Amer. Acad. Polit. Soc. Sci.*, November 1973, *410*, pp. 86–96. **[G: U.S.]**

Amuzegar, Jahangir. The Oil Story: Facts, Fiction and Fair Play. *Foreign Aff.*, July 1973, *51*(4), pp. 676–89.

Aspin, Les. A Solution to the Energy Crisis: The Case for Increased Competition. *Ann. Amer. Acad. Polit. Soc. Sci.*, November 1973, *410*, pp. 154–68. **[G: U.S.]**

Atwood, Janet. Energy Resources in New Mexico. *N. Mex. Bus.*, May 1973, *26*(5), pp. 3–10. **[G: U.S.]**

Bailey, Richard. Britain and a Community Energy Policy. *Nat. Westminster Bank Quart. Rev.*, November 1973, pp. 5–15. **[G: U.K.; E.E.C.]**

Bataillie, M. Naar een nieuwe petroleumcrisis? (Towards a New Oil Crisis? With English summary.) *Econ. Soc. Tijdschr.*, April 1973, *27*(2), pp. 129–40.

Boulding, Kenneth E. The Economics of Energy. *Ann. Amer. Acad. Polit. Soc. Sci.*, November 1973, *410*, pp. 120–26.

Bradley, Paul G. Increasing Scarcity: The Case of Energy Resources. *Amer. Econ. Rev.*, May 1973, *63*(2), pp. 119–25.

Burke, William. Buying on Time. *Fed. Res. Bank San Francisco Rev.*, March–April 1973, pp. 3–11. **[G: U.S.]**

Caldwell, Lynton K. Energy and Environment: The Bases for Public Policies. *Ann. Amer. Acad. Polit. Soc. Sci.*, November 1973, *410*, pp. 127–38.

Calhoun, Donald A. Oil and Gas Taxation. *Manage. Account.*, November 1973, *55*(5), pp. 21–24. **[G: U.S.]**

Cicchetti, Charles J. and Gillen, William J. The Mandatory Oil Import Quota Program: A Consideration of Economic Efficiency and Equity. *Natural Res. J.*, July 1973, *13*(3), pp. 399–430. **[G: U.S.]**

Erlenkotter, Donald. Sequencing of Interdependent Hydroelectric Projects. *Water Resources Res.*, February 1973, *9*(1), pp. 21–27.

Eslami, M. The World Energy Crisis and Iranian Strategy. *Tahq. Eq.*, Winter & Spring 1973, *10*(29 & 30), pp. 17–49. **[G: Iran]**

Fernández de la Garza, Guillermo and Manne, Alan S. ENERGETICOS, A Process Analysis of the Energy Sectors. In *Goreux, L. M. and Manne, A. S., eds.*, 1973, pp. 233–75. **[G: Mexico]**

Frank, Helmut J. and Wells, Donald A. United States Oil Imports: Implications for the Balance of Payments. *Natural Res. J.*, July 1973, *13*(3), pp. 431–47. **[G: U.S.]**

Frank, Helmut J. and Schanz, John J., Jr. The Future of American Oil and Natural Gas. *Ann. Amer. Acad. Polit. Soc. Sci.*, November 1973, *410*, pp. 24–34. **[G: U.S.]**

Freeman, S. David. Is There an Energy Crisis? An Overview. *Ann. Amer. Acad. Polit. Soc. Sci.*, November 1973, *410*, pp. 1–10. **[G: U.S.]**

Gehman, Clayton. U.S. Energy Supplies and Uses. *Fed. Res. Bull.*, December 1973, *59*(12), pp. 847–70A. **[G: U.S.]**

Gerber, Abraham. Energy Supply as a Factor in Economic Growth. In *Weintraub, A.; Schwartz, E. and Aronson, J. R., eds.*, 1973, pp. 82–97. **[G: U.S.]**

Green, Harold P. Nuclear Power: Risk, Liability, and Indemnity. *Mich. Law Rev.*, january 1973, *71*(3), pp. 479–510. **[G: U.S.]**

Hamilton, Richard E. Canada's "Exportable Surplus" Natural Gas Policy: A Theoretical Analysis. *Land Econ.*, August 1973, *49*(3), pp. 251–59. **[G: Canada]**

Hannon, Bruce M. An Energy Standard of Value. *Ann. Amer. Acad. Polit. Soc. Sci.*, November 1973, *410*, pp. 139–53. **[G: U.S.]**

Heitmann, G. United States Oil Import Quotas and the Price of Foreign Oil. *J. Ind. Econ.*, July 1973, *21*(3), pp. 266–71. **[G: U.S.]**

Henry, John P., Jr. and Schmidt, Richard A. Coal: Still Old Reliable? *Ann. Amer. Acad. Polit. Soc. Sci.*, November 1973, *410*, pp. 35–51. **[G: U.S.]**

Löf, George O. G. Solar Energy: An Infinite Source of Clean Energy. *Ann. Amer. Acad. Polit. Soc. Sci.*, November 1973, *410*, pp. 52–64.

MacAvoy, Paul W. and Pindyck, Robert S. Alternative Regulatory Policies for Dealing with the Natural Gas Shortage. *Bell J. Econ. Manage. Sci.*, Autumn 1973, *4*(2), pp. 454–98. **[G: U.S.]**

Malenbaum, Wilfred. World Resources for the Year 2000. *Ann. Amer. Acad. Polit. Soc. Sci.*, July 1973, *408*, pp. 30–46.

McGee, Dean A. Assessing the "Energy Crisis"—Problems and Prospects. *Fed. Res. Bank Kansas City Rev.*, September–October 1973, pp. 14–20. **[G: U.S.]**

McLean, John G. The United States Energy Outlook and Its Implications for National Policy. *Ann. Amer. Acad. Polit. Soc. Sci.*, November 1973, *410*, pp. 97–105. **[G: U.S.]**

Morse, Chandler. Natural Resources as a Constraint on Economic Growth: Discussion. *Amer. Econ. Rev.*, May 1973, *63*(2), pp. 126–28.

Morton, Rogers C. B. The Nixon Administration

Energy Policy. *Ann. Amer. Acad. Polit. Soc. Sci.*, November 1973, *410*, pp. 65–74. [G: U.S.]

Nordhaus, William D. The Allocation of Energy Resources. *Brookings Pap. Econ. Act.*, 1973, (3), pp. 529–70. [G: U.S.]

Ramey, James T. The Promise of Nuclear Energy. *Ann. Amer. Acad. Polit. Soc. Sci.*, November 1973, *410*, pp. 11–23. [G: U.S.]

Robinson, Colin and Crook, Elizabeth M. Is There a World Energy Crisis? *Nat. Westminster Bank Quart. Rev.*, May 1973, pp. 46–60.

Ross, Charles R. Electricity as a Social Force. *Ann. Amer. Acad. Polit. Soc. Sci.*, January 1973, *405*, pp. 47–54. [G: U.S.]

Schubert, A. Eugene. Organizing to Supply Nuclear Energy. In *Weston, J. F. and Ornstein, S. I., eds.*, 1973, pp. 157–62. [G: U.S.]

Schweikert, H. Zur Planung der Energieversorgung in städtischen Agglomerationen. (The Planning of Distribution of Energy in Urban Areas. With English summary.) *Schweiz. Z. Volkswirtsch. Statist.*, September 1973, *109*(3), pp. 421–39.

Surrey, A. J. and Bromley, A. J. Energy Resources. In *Cole, H. S. D., et al., eds.*, 1973, pp. 90–107.

Thomson, Herbert F. Policy Alternatives for Ohio's Electric Power Industry. *Ohio State U. Bull. Bus. Res.*, December 1973, *48*(12), pp. 1–5. [G: U.S.]

Tybout, Richard A. Prices, Costs, and the Energy Crisis. *Ohio State U. Bull. Bus. Res.*, June 1973, *48*(6), pp. 4–8. [G: U.S.]

Vousden, Neil. Basic Theoretical Issues of Resource Depletion. *J. Econ. Theory*, April 1973, *6*(2), pp. 126–43.

Wilson, Carroll L. A Plan for Energy Independence. *Foreign Aff.*, July 1973, *51*(4), pp. 657–75. [G: U.S.]

Young, H. Peyton and Thompson, Russell G. Forecasting Water Use for Electric Power Generation. *Water Resources Res.*, August 1973, *9*(4), pp. 800–07.

730 ECONOMIC GEOGRAPHY

731 Economic Geography

7310 Economic Geography

Alonso, William. A Theory of the Urban Land Market. In *Grieson, R. E., ed.*, 1973, pp. 45–55.

Benneh, G. Water Requirements and Limitations Imposed on Agricultural Development in Northern Ghana. In *Ofori, I. M., ed.*, 1973, pp. 71–81. [G: Ghana]

Borlenghi, Erminio. Il progetto per un'area forte nella Francia di sud-est. (The Project for a Strong Area in South-East France. With English summary.) *L'Impresa*, 1973, *15*(2), pp. 105–12. [G: France]

Buchholz, H. E. Pricing and Allocation Models Applied to Problems of Interregional Trade and Location of Industries. In *Judge, G. G. and Takayama, T., eds.*, 1973, pp. 298–306. [G: W. Germany]

Chapman, G. P. The Spatial Organization of the

Population of the United States and England and Wales. *Econ. Geogr.*, October 1973, *49*(4), pp. 325–43. [G: U.S.; U.K.]

Ernst, Robert T. and Hugg, Lawrence. Institutional Growth and Community Fragmentation: An Inner City Example. *Mich. Academician*, Fall 1973, *6*(2), pp. 179–91. [G: U.S.]

Friedmann, John. The Role of Cities in National Development. In *Friedmann, J.*, 1973, pp. 21–39.

Friedmann, John. Problems of Spatial Development in the Capital Region of Chile. In *Friedmann, J.*, 1973, pp. 187–226. [G: Chile]

Friedmann, John, et al. Towards a National Urbanization Policy. In *Friedmann, J.*, 1973, pp. 153–86.

Friedmann, John, et al. Urbanization and National Development: A Comparative Analysis. In *Friedmann, J.*, 1973, pp. 65–90.

Garrison, Charles B. and Paulson, Albert S. An Entropy Measure of the Geographic Concentration of Economic Activity. *Econ. Geogr.*, October 1973, *49*(4), pp. 319–24. [G: U.S.]

Guedry, L. J. An Application of a Multi-Commodity Transportation Model to the U.S. Feed Grain Economy. In *Judge, G. G. and Takayama, T., eds.*, 1973, pp. 243–60. [G: U.S.]

Haizel, K. A. Ecological Problems of Agricultural Production in West Africa. In *Ofori, I. M., ed.*, 1973, pp. 82–90. [G: W. Africa]

Hartnett, Harry D. A Locational Analysis of Manufacturing Plants within the City of Chicago: 1959–1968. *Amer. Real Estate Urban Econ. Assoc. J.*, June 1973, *1*(1), pp. 31–47. [G: U.S.]

Holmes, J. C. An Ordinal Method of Evaluation: A Rejoinder. *Urban Stud.*, February 1973, *10*(1), pp. 101–04.

Hurst, Michael E. Eliot. Transportation and the Societal Framework. *Econ. Geogr.*, April 1973, *49*(2), pp. 163–80.

Judge, G. G.; Havlicek, J. and Rizek, R. L. A Spatial Analysis of the U.S. Livestock Economy. In *Judge, G. G. and Takayama, T., eds.*, 1973, pp. 261–73. [G: U.S.]

Kamarck, Andrew M. Climate and Economic Development. *Finance Develop.*, June 1973, *10*(2), pp. 2–8.

Kettle, Peter and Whitbread, Michael. An Ordinal Method of Evaluation: A Comment. *Urban Stud.*, February 1973, *10*(1), pp. 95–99.

Mabogunje, Akin L. Manufacturing and the Geography of Development in Tropical Africa. *Econ. Geogr.*, January 1973, *49*(1), pp. 1–20. [G: Africa]

Muller, Peter O. Trend Surfaces of American Agricultural Patterns: A Macro-Thünian Analysis. *Econ. Geogr.*, July 1973, *49*(3), pp. 228–42. [G: U.S.]

Nishioka, Hisao and Krumme, Gunter. Location Conditions, Factors and Decisions: An Evaluation of Selected Location Surveys. *Land Econ.*, May 1973, *49*(2), pp. 195–205. [G: Japan; U.S.]

Papageorgiou, G. J. The Impact of the Environment upon the Spatial Distribution of Population and Land Values. *Econ. Geogr.*, July 1973, *49*(3), pp. 251–56.

Parr, John B. Structure and Size in the Urban System

of Lösch. *Econ. Geogr.,* July 1973, *49*(3), pp. 185–212.

Smith, Bruce W. Analysis of the Location of Coal-Fired Power Plants in the Eastern United States. *Econ. Geogr.,* July 1973, *49*(3), pp. 243–50.
[G: U.S.]

Solow, Robert M. On Equilibrium Models of Urban Location. In *Parkin, M., ed.,* 1973, pp. 2–16.

Takeuchi, Keiichi. Tendenze recenti degli studi di geografia economica in Giappone. (Recent Trends in the Studies of Economic Geography in Japan. With English summary.) *Rivista Int. Sci. Econ. Com.,* August-September 1973, *20*(8–9), pp. 918–26.
[G: Japan]

di Vallega, Adalberto. Aree industriali in Piemonte connesse con i porti liguri. (Industrial Areas in Pedemont Connected with Ligurian Harbors. With English summary.) *L'Impresa,* 1973, *15* (5–6), pp. 317–22.

Webber, M. J. and Symanski, Richard. Periodic Markets: An Economic Location Analysis. *Econ. Geogr.,* July 1973, *49*(3), pp. 213–27.

800 Manpower; Labor; Population

810 MANPOWER TRAINING AND ALLOCATION; LABOR FORCE AND SUPPLY

811 Manpower Training and Development

8110 Manpower Training and Development

Ahamad, Bashir and Blaug, Mark. The Practice of Manpower Forecasting: Introduction. In *Ahamad, B. and Blaug, M., eds.,* 1973, pp. 1–25.

Ahamad, Bashir and Blaug, Mark. The Practice of Manpower Forecasting: Conclusions. In *Ahamad, B. and Blaug, M., eds.,* 1973, pp. 310–23.

Alamgir, Mohiuddin. Some Theoretical Issues in Manpower and Educational Planning. *Bangladesh Econ. Rev.,* April 1973, *1*(2), pp. 199–212.

Aronson, Robert L. Current Issues in Manpower Planning. In *Aronson, R. L., ed.,* 1973, pp. 1–13.
[G: U.S.]

Baher, G. H. A Planning Model for the Educational Requirements of Economic Development: The Case of Iran. *Tahq. Eq.,* Winter & Spring 1973, *10* (29 & 30), pp. 170–205.
[G: Iran]

Barkin, Solomon. Changing Profile of European Manpower Policies. In *Somers, G. G., ed.,* 1973, pp. 83–100.
[G: W. Europe]

Bauer, David. Low Unemployment Rates Abroad. In *Moskoff, W., ed.,* 1973, pp. 76–85.

Blaug, Mark. Manpower Forecasting for All Occupations: Thailand. In *Ahamad, B. and Blaug, M., eds.,* 1973, pp. 106–30.

Boeninger, Edgardo. The Role of the University in the Training of Personnel for Public Administration: A Latin American Perspective. In *Thurber, C. E. and Graham, L. S., eds.,* 1973, pp. 188–94.
[G: Latin America]

Bosanquet, Nicholas and Doeringer, Peter B. Is There a Dual Labour Market in Great Britain? *Econ. J.,* June 1973, *83*(330), pp. 421–35.
[G: U.K.]

Bowen, Charles P., Jr. Let's Put Realism into Management Development. *Harvard Bus. Rev.,* July-August 1973, *51*(4), pp. 80–87.

Bowlby, Roger L. and Schriver, William R. Academic Ability and Rates of Return to Vocational Training. *Ind. Lab. Relat. Rev.,* April 1973, *26*(3), pp. 980–90.

Boye-Møller, Monica. Language Training for Immigrant Workers in Sweden. *Int. Lab. Rev.,* December 1973, *108*(6), pp. 505–15.
[G: Sweden]

Bradley, Iver E.; Mangum, Garth L. and Robson, R. Thayne. Impact of Manpower Programs upon Employment and Earnings. In *Mangum, G. L. and Robson, R. T., eds.,* 1973, pp. 227–59.
[G: U.S.]

Bradley, Iver E.; Mangum, Garth L. and Robson, R. Thayne. Total Impact of Manpower Programs. In *Mangum, G. L. and Robson, R. T., eds.,* 1973, pp. 260–93.
[G: U.S.]

Brehmer, Ekhard and Bradford, Maxwell R. Incomes and Labor Market Policies in Sweden. *Finance Develop.,* September 1973, *10*(3), pp. 21–23, 35.
[G: Sweden]

Calkins, Hugh. Breaking Down the Fiscal Barriers to Career Education. In *McClure, L. and Buan, C., eds.,* 1973, pp. 247–55.
[G: U.S.]

Cannon, Mark W. Interactive Training Techniques for Improving Public Service in Latin America. In *Thurber, C. E. and Graham, L. S., eds.,* 1973, pp. 148–87.
[G: Latin America]

Champagne, Jean. Adapting Jobs to People: Experiments at Alcan. *Mon. Lab. Rev.,* April 1973, *96*(4), pp. 49–51.
[G: Canada]

Christoffel, Pamela and Celio, Mary Beth. A Benefit-Cost Analysis of the Upward Bound Program: A Comment. *J. Human Res.,* Winter 1973, *8*(1), pp. 110–15.
[G: U.S.]

Cleary, T. Anne. New Directions for Career Planning. In *McClure, L. and Buan, C., eds.,* 1973, pp. 39–53.
[G: U.S.]

Conly, Sonia. Success and Failure in the Work Incentive Program. *Growth Change,* October 1973, *4* (4), pp. 16–23.
[G: U.S.]

Damachi, Ukandi G. Manpower in Nigeria. In *Damachi, U. G. and Seibel, H. D., eds.,* 1973, pp. 81–97.
[G: Nigeria]

Davenport, Lawrence F. Career Education and the Black Student. In *McClure, L. and Buan, C., eds.,* 1973, pp. 177–84.
[G: U.S.]

Davis, Donald L. A Pedagogical Tool for Manpower Analysis. *Intermountain Econ. Rev.,* Spring 1973, *4*(1), pp. 40–52.

Davis, Otto A., et al. An Empirical Study of the NAB-JOBS Program. *Public Policy,* Spring 1973, *21*(2), pp. 235–62.
[G: U.S.]

Dowding, A. E. An Introduction to Vocational Training Using Modules of Employable Skills. *Int. Lab. Rev.,* June 1973, *107*(6), pp. 553–57.

Drouet, Pierre. Systematic Evaluation of Vocational Training Programmes in Latin America. *Int. Lab. Rev.,* April 1973, *107*(4), pp. 339–57.
[G: Latin America]

Duscha, Julius. Manpower Training: Turning the Unskilled Into Productive Workers. In *Levitan, S. A., ed.,* 1973, pp. 89–118.
[G: U.S.]

Eichner, Alfred S. Manpower Planning and Economic Planning: The Two Perspectives. In *Aronson, R. L., ed.*, 1973, pp. 65–80. [G: U.S.]

Evans, Graham J. and Lindley, Robert M. The Use of RAS and Related Models in Manpower Forecasting. *Econ. Planning*, 1973, *13*(1–2), pp. 53–73. [G: U.K.]

Gallardo, Lloyd. Development of Bay Area Manpower Institutions. In *Mangum, G. L. and Robson, R. T., eds.*, 1973, pp. 154–75. [G: U.S.]

Gallardo, Lloyd. Evaluating Bay Area Manpower Programs. In *Mangum, G. L. and Robson, R. T., eds.*, 1973, pp. 176–201. [G: U.S.]

Gallardo, Lloyd. Institutional Impact of Bay Area Manpower Programs. In *Mangum, G. L. and Robson, R. T., eds.*, 1973, pp. 202–24. [G: U.S.]

Gannicott, Kenneth and Blaug, Mark. Manpower Forecasting for All Occupations: The United States. In *Ahamad, B. and Blaug, M., eds.*, 1973, pp. 48–76. [G: U.S.]

Garms, Walter I. Reply to "A Benefit-Cost Analysis of the Upward Bound Program: A Comment." *J. Human Res.*, Winter 1973, *8*(1), pp. 115–18. [G: U.S.]

Ghazalah, I. A. and Pejovich, Svetozar. The Economics of Vocational and Technical Education: A Report on Three Studies. *Rev. Soc. Econ.*, October 1973, *31*(2), pp. 191–98. [G: U.S.]

Goldstein, Jon H. The Effectiveness of Manpower Training Programs: A Review of Research on the Impact on the Poor. In *Niskanen, W. A., et al., eds.*, 1973, pp. 338–73. [G: U.S.]

Goldston, Eli. Executive Sabbaticals: About to Take Off? *Harvard Bus. Rev.*, September-October 1973, *51*(5), pp. 57–68. [G: U.S.]

Green, Alfred L. The Future of Manpower Planning: Discussion. In *Aronson, R. L., ed.*, 1973, pp. 99–102. [G: U.S.]

Gunderson, Morley. Determinants of Individual Success in On-the-Job Training. *J. Human Res.*, Fall 1973, *8*(4), pp. 472–84. [G: Canada]

Haber, Lawrence D. Social Planning for Disability. *J. Human Res.*, Supplement 1973, *8*, pp. 33–55. [G: U.S.]

Harbison, Frederick H. Human Resources and the Development of Modernizing Nations. In *Somers, G. G., ed.*, 1973, pp. 177–86.

Helfgott, Roy B. Multinational Corporations and Manpower Utilization in Developing Nations. *J. Devel. Areas*, January 1973, *7*(2), pp. 235–46. [G: U.S.; Latin America]

Hinchliffe, Keith. Manpower Forecasting for All Occupations: Nigeria. In *Ahamad, B. and Blaug, M., eds.*, 1973, pp. 131–56. [G: Nigeria]

Holtmann, A. G. Skill Obsolescence and Training: Reply. *Southern Econ. J.*, April 1973, *39*(4), pp. 648–49.

Horowitz, Morris A. and Herrnstadt, Irwin L. Boston's Manpower Institutions. In *Mangum, G. L. and Robson, R. T., eds.*, 1973, pp. 23–48. [G: U.S.]

Horowitz, Morris A. and Herrnstadt, Irwin L. Institutional and Labor Market Impact of Manpower Programs. In *Mangum, G. L. and Robson, R. T., eds.*, 1973, pp. 76–92. [G: U.S.]

Horowitz, Morris A. and Herrnstadt, Irwin L. Training and Jobs for Boston's Disadvantaged. In *Man-gum, G. L. and Robson, R. T., eds.*, 1973, pp. 49–75. [G: U.S.]

Hughes, James J. In Defence of the Industrial Training Act. *J. Ind. Econ.*, April 1973, *21*(2), pp. 126–44. [G: U.K.]

Hughes, James J. Britain's Training Act: A Manpower Revolution? *Ind. Relat.*, October 1973, *12* (3), pp. 352–53. [G: U.K.]

Ivanova, R. Concerning the Development of the Eastern Regions and Their Manpower Supply. *Prob. Econ.*, June 1973, *16*(2), pp. 26–41. [G: U.S.S.R.]

Keesing, Donald B. and Manne, Alan S. Manpower Projections. In *Goreux, L. M. and Manne, A. S., eds.*, 1973, pp. 55–83. [G: Mexico]

Khomelianskii, B. The Sphere of Social and Economic Services and the Reproduction of Aggregate Labor Power. *Prob. Econ.*, June 1973, *16*(2), pp. 55–67. [G: U.S.S.R.]

Klarman, Herbert E. Approaches to Health Manpower Analysis, with Special Reference to Physicians. *Amer. Econ.*, Fall 1973, *17*(2), pp. 137–42.

Krevnevich, V. The Manpower Needs of the National Economy and Vocational Guidance of Youth. *Prob. Econ.*, June 1973, *16*(2), pp. 68–83. [G: U.S.S.R.]

Levitan, Sar A. Manpower Programs for a Healthier Economy. In *Ulman, L., ed.*, 1973, pp. 102–16. [G: U.S.]

Levitan, Sar A. and Marwick, David. Work and Training for Relief Recipients. *J. Human Res.*, Supplement 1973, *8*, pp. 5–18. [G: U.S.]

Lewis, Morgan V. and Cohn, Elchanan. Recruiting and Retaining Participants in a Manpower Program. *Ind. Lab. Relat. Rev.*, January 1973, *26*(2), pp. 842–50. [G: U.S.]

Lipsky, David B. Employer Role in Hard-Core Trainee Success. *Ind. Relat.*, May 1973, *12*(2), pp. 125–36. [G: U.S.]

Lovell, Malcolm R., Jr. The Politics of Manpower Planning. In *Aronson, R. L., ed.*, 1973, pp. 14–22. [G: U.S.]

Lucero, Maryetta. New Mexico Travel Service Training Program. *N. Mex. Bus.*, March 1973, *26*(3), pp. 10–12. [G: U.S.]

Mangum, Garth L. Manpower Programs as Career Education. In *McClure, L. and Buan, C., eds.*, 1973, pp. 129–41. [G: U.S.]

Mangum, Garth L. and Robson, R. Thayne. Metropolitan Impact of Manpower Programs: A Four-City Comparison: Introduction. In *Mangum, G. L. and Robson, R. T., eds.*, 1973, pp. 1–5. [G: U.S.]

Martinoli, Gino. Formazione dei quadri e "stages" all'estero. (Cadres Training and "Stages" abroad. With English summary.) *L'Impresa*, 1973, *15*(2), pp. 147–56.

Maurizi, Alex R. Minority Membership in Apprenticeship Programs in the Construction Trades: Reply. *Ind. Lab. Relat. Rev.*, October 1973, *27*(1), pp. 100–102.

van der Merwe, P. J. Manpower Policy in South Africa. *Finance Trade Rev.*, December 1972-June 1973, *10*(2–3), pp. 73–135. [G: S. Africa]

Myers, Charles A. Manpower Policies in the U.S. In *Somers, G. G., ed.*, 1973, pp. 72–82. [G: U.S.]

Nowacek, Charles G. Organizing Manpower Delivery Systems in Big Cities: Discussion. In *Aronson, R. L., ed.*, 1973, pp. 44–50. [G: U.S.]

Olivier, R. and Sabolo, Y. Simultaneous Planning of Employment, Production and Education. *Int. Lab. Rev.*, April 1973, *107*(4), pp. 359–72. [G: Peru]

O'Neill, Dave M. Manpower. In *Ott, D. J., et al.*, 1973, pp. 153–70.

Ord, H. W. The Employment of Economists in Africa. In *Livingstone, I., et al., eds.*, 1973, pp. 147–51. [G: Africa]

Parnes, Herbert S. The Role of Forecasting and Planning Manpower Programs: Discussion. In *Aronson, R. L., ed.*, 1973, pp. 62–64. [G: U.S.]

Pohlman, Jerry E. A Trade-off Analysis of Job Creation vs. Welfare. *J. Econ. Bus.*, Spring-Summer 1973, *25*(3), pp. 168–74. [G: U.S.]

Psacharopoulos, George. Manpower Forecasting for all Occupations: France. In *Ahamad, B. and Blaug, M., eds.*, 1973, pp. 106–30. [G: France]

Psacharopoulos, George. Substitution Assumptions versus Empirical Evidence in Manpower Planning. *De Economist*, November-December 1973, *121*(6), pp. 609–25. [G: Greece]

Rehnberg, Bertil. Active Manpower Policy in Sweden. In *Moskoff, W., ed.*, 1973, pp. 85–91. [G: Sweden]

Reubens, Beatrice G. Manpower Training in Japan. *Mon. Lab. Rev.*, September 1973, *96*(9), pp. 16–24. [G: Japan]

Richardson, Reed C. Delivery Systems for Manpower Services. In *Mangum, G. L. and Robson, R. T., eds.*, 1973, pp. 100–119. [G: U.S.]

Richardson, Reed C. Skills and Jobs for Denver's Disadvantaged. In *Mangum, G. L. and Robson, R. T., eds.*, 1973, pp. 120–33. [G: U.S.]

Richardson, Reed C. The Impact of Denver's Manpower Programs. In *Mangum, G. L. and Robson, R. T., eds.*, 1973, pp. 134–43. [G: U.S.]

Rogers, David. Organizing Manpower Delivery Systems in Big Cities. In *Aronson, R. L., ed.*, 1973, pp. 24–44. [G: U.S.]

Roomkin, Myron. Economic Effects of Basic Education for Adults: The Milwaukee MDTA Experience. *Quart. Rev. Econ. Bus.*, Spring 1973, *13*(1), pp. 87–96. [G: U.S.]

Ruttenberg, Stanley H. The Future of Manpower Planning. In *Aronson, R. L., ed.*, 1973, pp. 85–99. [G: U.S.]

Sargent, J. R. The Distribution of Scientific Manpower. In *Williams, B. R., ed.*, 1973, pp. 360–74. [G: U.K.]

Scoville, James G. The Role of Forecasting and Planning Manpower Programs. In *Aronson, R. L., ed.*, 1973, pp. 51–62. [G: U.S.]

Shearer, John C. High-Level Human Resources in Latin American Development. In *Thurber, C. E. and Graham, L. S., eds.*, 1973, pp. 133–47. [G: U.S.; S. America]

Sherwood, Frank P. Technical Assistance for Education in Public Administration: Lessons of Experience. In *Thurber, C. E. and Graham, L. S., eds.*, 1973, pp. 195–226. [G: U.S.; Brazil]

Shipunov, V. Effectiveness of Vocational-Technical Training of Workers. *Prob. Econ.*, August 1973, *16*

(4), pp. 82–94. [G: U.S.S.R.]

Skraly, Emile B. Manpower Planning and Economic Planning: The Two Perspectives: Discussion. In *Aronson, R. L., ed.*, 1973, pp. 80–84. [G: U.S.]

Smith, Ralph E. Manpower Programs and Unemployment Statistics. *Mon. Lab. Rev.*, April 1973, *96*(4), pp. 63–65. [G: U.S.]

Sorkin, Alan. Manpower Programs for American Indians. *J. Econ. Bus.*, Fall 1973, *26*(1), pp. 49–57. [G: U.S.]

Strauss, George. Minority Membership in Apprenticeship Programs in the Construction Trades: Comment. *Ind. Lab. Relat. Rev.*, October 1973, *27*(1), pp. 93–99. [G: U.S.]

Su, Teddy T. Skill Obsolescence and Training: Comment. *Southern Econ. J.*, April 1973, *39*(4), pp. 645–48.

Thurow, Lester C. Redistributional Aspects of Manpower Training Programs. In *Ulman, L., ed.*, 1973, pp. 83–101. [G: U.S.]

Trąmpczyński, Bolesław. Co-operatives of the Disabled in Poland. *Int. Lab. Rev.*, November 1973, *108*(5), pp. 423–37. [G: Poland]

Voronov, O. Paid Educational Leave in the USSR. *Int. Lab. Rev.*, June 1973, *107*(6), pp. 529–38. [G: U.S.S.R.]

Wingate, Livingston L. The Politics of Manpower Planning: Discussion. In *Aronson, R. L., ed.*, 1973, pp. 22–23. [G: U.S.]

Ziderman, Adrian and Driver, C. A Markov Chain Model of the Benefits of Participating in Government Training Schemes. *Manchester Sch. Econ. Soc. Stud.*, December 1973, *41*(4), pp. 401–17. [G: U.K.]

812 Occupation

8120 Occupation

Ahamad, Bashir and Blaug, Mark. The Practice of Manpower Forecasting: Introduction. In *Ahamad, B. and Blaug, M., eds.*, 1973, pp. 1–25.

Armstrong, William. Management Training for Statisticians and Opportunities to Enter Top Management. *J. Roy. Statist. Soc.*, Part 1, 1973, *136*, pp. 95–99.

Bartholomew, D. J. Post-experience Training for Statisticians. *J. Roy. Statist. Soc.*, Part 1, 1973, *136*, pp. 65–70.

Bezdek, Roger H. and Getzel, Barry. Education and Job Training of Scientists and Engineers. *Mon. Lab. Rev.*, November 1973, *96*(11), pp. 54–55.

Boddy, Francis M. The Market for Economists. *Amer. J. Agr. Econ.*, Part II, November 1973, *55*(4), pp. 720–24. [G: U.S.]

Bouwsma, William J. Lawyers in Early Modern Culture. *Amer. Hist. Rev.*, April 1973, *78*(2), pp. 303–27. [G: Europe]

Boyd, Monica. Occupational Mobility and Fertility in Metropolitan Latin America. *Demography*, February 1973, *10*(1), pp. 1–17. [G: Latin America]

Carol, Arthur. Stochastic Dominance and 'The Economic Rationale of Occupational Choice': Reply. *Ind. Lab. Relat. Rev.*, April 1973, *26*(3), pp. 1001. [G: U.S.]

Comanor, William S. Racial Discrimination in American Industry. *Economica, N.S.*, November 1973, *40*(160), pp. 363–78.

Craft, James A. Racial and Occupational Aspects of Public Employment Service Placements. *Quart. Rev. Econ. Bus.*, Autumn 1973, *13*(3), pp. 53–60. [G: U.S.]

Desai, Satish. Professional-Pool Concept for Company Groups. *Marquette Bus. Rev.*, Spring 1973, *17*(1), pp. 30–34.

Ehrenberg, Ronald G. Municipal Government Structure, Unionization, and the Wages of Fire Fighters. *Ind. Lab. Relat. Rev.*, October 1973, *27* (1), pp. 36–48. [G: U.S.]

Granata, Dale. Survey Highlights Occupational Pay Differences in Furniture Industry. *Mon. Lab. Rev.*, June 1973, *96*(6), pp. 58–60. [G: U.S.]

Hall, Robert E. and Kasten, Richard A. The Relative Occupational Success of Blacks and Whites. *Brookings Pap. Econ. Act.*, 1973, (3), pp. 781–95. [G: U.S.]

Healy, M. J. R. Varieties of Statistician. *J. Roy. Statist. Soc.*, Part 1, 1973, *136*, pp. 71–74.

Hedges, Janice Neipert. Absence from Work: A Look at Some National Data. *Mon. Lab. Rev.*, July 1973, *96*(7), pp. 24–30. [G: U.S.]

Hellman, Daryl A. The Spatial Distribution of Unemployment by Occupation: A Further Note. *J. Reg. Sci.*, December 1973, *13*(3), pp. 463–66. [G: U.S.]

Helmberger, John D. The Market for Agricultural Economists. *Amer. J. Agr. Econ.*, Part II, November 1973, *55*(4), pp. 725–34. [G: U.S.]

Hufbauer, G. C. Occupational Trends and Social Mobility in the West Punjab. *Pakistan Econ. Soc. Rev.*, Spring 1973, *11*(1), pp. 83–103. [G: India]

Hulin, Charles L. Worker Background and Job Satisfaction: Reply. *Ind. Lab. Relat. Rev.*, January 1973, *26*(2), pp. 853–55.

Hurd, Richard W. Equilibrium Vacancies in a Labor Market Dominated by Non-Profit Firms: The "Shortage" of Nurses. *Rev. Econ. Statist.*, May 1973, *55*(2), pp. 234–40. [G: U.S.]

Hussain, Mazhar and Butt, Abdul Rauf. Projections of Job Opportunities for Natural Scientists and Mathematicians in West Pakistan. *Pakistan Econ. Soc. Rev.*, Summer 1973, *11*(2), pp. 200–06. [G: Pakistan]

King, Allan G. Stochastic Dominance and 'The Economic Rationale of Occupational Choice': Comment. *Ind. Lab. Relat. Rev.*, April 1973, *26*(3), pp. 996–1000. [G: U.S.]

Koch, James V. and Chizmar, John F. The Influence of Teaching and Other Factors Upon Absolute Salaries and Salary Increments at Illinois State University. *J. Econ. Educ.*, Fall 1973, *5*(1), pp. 27–34. [G: U.S.]

Lahne, Herbert J. Blacksmiths and Welders: Identity and Phenomenal Change: Comment. *Ind. Lab. Relat. Rev.*, January 1973, *26*(2), pp. 860–62.

Leonard, Walter J. The Development of the Black Bar. *Ann. Amer. Acad. Polit. Soc. Sci.*, May 1973, *407*, pp. 134–43.

Link, Charles R. The Quantity and Quality of Education and Their Influence on Earnings: The Case of Chemical Engineers. *Rev. Econ. Statist.*, May 1973, *55*(2), pp. 241–47. [G: U.S.]

Lipsky, David B. and Drotning, John E. The Influence of Collective Bargaining on Teachers' Salaries in New York State. *Ind. Lab. Relat. Rev.*, October 1973, *27*(1), pp. 18–35. [G: U.S.]

Lüttichau, Knud. Pengelønsudviklingen for fire udvalgte fag for Danmark i mellemkrigstiden. (With English summary.) *Nationalokon. Tidsskr.*, 1973, *111*(3), pp. 382–96. [G: Denmark]

Mantell, Edmund H. Labor Markets for Engineers of Differing Ability and Education. *Ind. Lab. Relat. Rev.*, October 1973, *27*(1), pp. 63–73. [G: U.S.]

Mattila, J. Peter. The Effects of Extending Minimum Wages to Cover Household Maids. *J. Human Res.*, Summer 1973, *8*(3), pp. 365–82. [G: U.S.]

Mergen, Bernard. Blacksmiths and Welders: Identity and Phenomenal Change: Reply. *Ind. Lab. Relat. Rev.*, January 1973, *26*(2), pp. 862–64.

Moore, P. G. Relationship between Statisticians and Other Numerate Professions. *J. Roy. Statist. Soc.*, Part 1, 1973, *136*, pp. 89–94.

Moser, Claus A. Staffing in the Government Statistical Service. *J. Roy. Statist. Soc.*, Part 1, 1973, *136*, pp. 75–88.

Oehm, J. Kent. Controlling Professional Manpower Costs. *Manage. Account.*, March 1973, *54*(9), pp. 31–35.

Oohashi, Ryuken. Working Class in the Present World—Statistics and Their Meaning. *Kyoto Univ. Econ. Rev.*, April–October 1973, *43*(1–2), pp. 1–29.

Palmer, John P. and Palomba, Neil A. Skill Differentials and their Determinants. *Amer. Econ.*, Fall 1973, *17*(2), pp. 130–36. [G: U.S.]

Parsons, Donald O. Quit Rates Over Time: A Search and Information Approach. *Amer. Econ. Rev.*, June 1973, *63*(3), pp. 390–401. [G: U.S.]

Phillips, Bruce D. The Spatial Distribution of Unemployment by Occupation: Reply. *J. Reg. Sci.*, December 1973, *13*(3), pp. 471. [G: U.S.]

Ramanujam, M. S. Requirements of Technical Manpower in India: 1965–66 to 1980–81. *Indian Econ. Rev.*, October 1973, *8*(2), pp. 101–24. [G: India]

Reynaud, Paul and Zarca, Bernard. Les leçons d'une enquête sur les petits commerçants âgés (Action sociale et transformation du milieu sociologique). (The Lessons of a Survey of Old Small Shop-keepers. (Social Policy and Change of Social Settings.) With English summary.) *Consommation*, January–March 1973, *20*(1), pp. 59–76. [G: France]

Richardson, Harry W. The Spatial Distribution of Unemployment by Occupation: A Comment. *J. Reg. Sci.*, December 1973, *13*(3), pp. 467–69. [G: U.S.]

Ridzon, Donald S. Occupational Pay in Shirt Manufacturing. *Mon. Lab. Rev.*, January 1973, *96*(1), pp. 60–61. [G: U.S.]

Rosenthal, Neal H. Projected Changes in Occupations. *Mon. Lab. Rev.*, December 1973, *96*(12), pp. 18–26. [G: U.S.]

Rugh, William. Emergence of a New Middle Class in Saudi Arabia. *Middle East J.*, Winter 1973, *27* (1), pp. 7–20. [G: Saudi Arabia]

Schmalen, Helmut. Rationale individuelle Berufswahl und die langfristige Entwicklung des Arbeitsmarktes. (Rational Individual Choice of Professions and the Long-Term Development of the Labor Market. With English summary.) *Z. ges. Staatswiss.*, May 1973, *129*(2), pp. 292–311.

Schuler, Randall. Worker Background and Job Satisfaction: Comment. *Ind. Lab. Relat. Rev.*, January 1973, *26*(2), pp. 851–53.

Shepard, Jon M. Specialization, Autonomy, and Job Satisfaction. *Ind. Relat.*, October 1973, *12*(3), pp. 274–81. [G: U.S.]

Shepard, Jon M. Worker Background and Job Satisfaction: Reply. *Ind. Lab. Relat. Rev.*, January 1973, *26*(2), pp. 856–59.

Siegfried, John J. and White, Kenneth J. Financial Rewards to Research and Teaching: A Case Study of Academic Economists. *Amer. Econ. Rev.*, May 1973, *63*(2), pp. 309–15. [G: U.S.]

Sorkin, Alan L. On The Occupational Status of Women, 1870–1970. *Amer. J. Econ. Soc.*, July 1973, *32*(3), pp. 235–43. [G: U.S.]

Taubman, Paul J. Occupational Coding. *Ann. Econ. Soc. Measure*, January 1973, *2*(1), pp. 71–87. [G: U.S.]

Thompson, Edward. International Protection of Performers' Rights: Some Current Problems. *Int. Lab. Rev.*, April 1973, *107*(4), pp. 303–14.

Thompson, Mark and Cairnie, James. Compulsory Arbitration: The Case of British Columbia Teachers. *Ind. Lab. Relat. Rev.*, October 1973, *27*(1), pp. 3–17. [G: Canada]

Workman, Randy L. Ohio's Women Workers. *Ohio State U. Bull. Bus. Res.*, August 1973, *48*(8), pp. 4–6. [G: U.S.]

813 Labor Force

8130 General

Ahamad, Bashir. Manpower Forecasting for All Occupations: Canada. In *Ahamad, B. and Blaug, M., eds.*, 1973, pp. 26–47. [G: Canada]

Barkin, Solomon. Changing Profile of European Manpower Policies. In *Somers, G. G., ed.*, 1973, pp. 83–100. [G: W. Europe]

Beg, M. Afzal. A Review of Labour Force Participation Rates in Pakistan. *Pakistan Develop. Rev.*, Winter 1973, *12*(4), pp. 393–406. [G: Pakistan]

Bergonzini, Luciano. Professionalità femminile e lavoro a domicilio: Questioni generali ed esiti di un'indagine statistica in alcuni comuni dell'Emilia-Romagna. (Women's Professional Status and Work at Home: Some General Questions and Some Results of a Statistical Inquiry in a Few Municipalities of the Emilia-Romagna Region (Italy). With English summary.) *Statistica*, October-December 1973, *33*(4), pp. 492–546. [G: Italy]

Bezdek, Roger H. Interindustry Manpower Analysis: Theoretical Potential and Empirical Problems. *Amer. Econ.*, Spring 1973, *17*(1), pp. 147–53.

Bhagwat, Avinash. Main Features of the Employment Problem in Developing Countries. *Int. Monet. Fund Staff Pap.*, March 1973, *20*(1), pp. 78–99.

Bulgaru, Mircea. Modificări în structura social-profe-

sională a populaţiei României în anii Republicii. (Changes in the Social-Professional Structure of Romania's Population in the Years of the Republic. With English summary.) *Stud. Cercet. Econ.*, 1973, (1), pp. 5–11. [G: Rumania]

Clague, Ewan. Developments in Labor Statistics. In *Somers, G. G., ed.*, 1973, pp. 37–46. [G: U.S.]

Coen, Robert M. Labor Force and Unemployment in the 1920's and 1930's: A Re-examination Based on Postwar Experience. *Rev. Econ. Statist.*, February 1973, *55*(1), pp. 46–55. [G: U.S.]

Coen, Robert M. Labor Force and Unemployment in the 1920's and 1930's: Reply. *Rev. Econ. Statist.*, November 1973, *55*(4), pp. 527–28. [G: U.S.]

Damachi, Ukandi G. Manpower in Nigeria. In *Damachi, U. G. and Seibel, H. D., eds.*, 1973, pp. 81–97. [G: Nigeria]

Denton, Frank T. A Simulation Model of Month-to-Month Labor Force Movement in Canada. *Int. Econ. Rev.*, June 1973, *14*(2), pp. 293–311. [G: Canada]

Dvorák, Jiří and Jezek, Tomás. Some Problems of Strain in the Manpower Balances. *Eastern Europ. Econ.*, Summer 1973, *11*(4), pp. 60–85. [G: Czechoslovakia]

Farooq, Ghazi M. Economic Growth and Changes in the Industrial Structure of Income and Labor Force in Pakistan. *Econ. Develop. Cult. Change*, January 1973, *21*(2), pp. 293–308. [G: Pakistan]

Flaim, Paul O. Employment Developments in the First Half of 1973. *Mon. Lab. Rev.*, September 1973, *96*(9), pp. 25–28. [G: U.S.]

Flaim, Paul O. Discouraged Workers and Changes in Unemployment. *Mon. Lab. Rev.*, March 1973, *96*(3), pp. 8–16. [G: U.S.]

Gannicott, Kenneth and Blaug, Mark. Manpower Forecasting for All Occupations: The United States. In *Ahamad, B. and Blaug, M., eds.*, 1973, pp. 48–76. [G: U.S.]

Gilroy, Curtis L. Job Losers, Leavers, and Entrants: Traits and Trends. *Mon. Lab. Rev.*, August 1973, *96*(8), pp. 3–15. [G: U.S.]

Gordon, Robert A. Some Macroeconomic Aspects of Manpower Policy. In *Ulman, L., ed.*, 1973, pp. 14–50. [G: U.S.]

Green, Gloria P. and Stinson, John F. Changes in the Employment Situation in 1972. *Mon. Lab. Rev.*, February 1973, *96*(2), pp. 24–34. [G: U.S.]

Gregory, R. G. and Sheehan, P. J. The Cyclical Sensitivity of Labour Force Participation Rates. *Australian Econ. Rev.*, 2nd Quarter 1973, pp. 9–20. [G: Australia]

Gronau, Reuben. The Intrafamily Allocation of Time: The Value of the Housewives' Time. *Amer. Econ. Rev.*, September 1973, *63*(4), pp. 634–51. [G: U.S.]

Harbison, Frederick H. Human Resources and the Development of Modernizing Nations. In *Somers, G. G., ed.*, 1973, pp. 177–86.

Hayghe, Howard. Labor Force Activity of Married Women. *Mon. Lab. Rev.*, April 1973, *96*(4), pp. 31–36. [G: U.S.]

Ivanov, N. How Many Specialists are Needed? *Prob. Econ.*, August 1973, *16*(4), pp. 63–81.

Johnston, Denis F. Education of Workers: Projections to 1990. *Mon. Lab. Rev.*, November 1973, *96*(11), pp. 22–31.

Johnston, Denis F. Population and Labor Force Projections. *Mon. Lab. Rev.*, December 1973, *96*(12), pp. 8–17. **[G: U.S.]**

Johnston, Denis F. The U.S. Labor Force: Projections to 1990. *Mon. Lab. Rev.*, July 1973, *96*(7), pp. 3–13. **[G: U.S.]**

Keesing, Donald B. and Manne, Alan S. Manpower Projections. In *Goreux, L. M. and Manne, A. S., eds.*, 1973, pp. 55–83. **[G: Mexico]**

Kraft, Arthur and Kraft, John. A Cross-Section Comparison of How Individuals Allocate Time: 1960 Versus 1970. *Nebr. J. Econ. Bus.*, Autumn 1973, *12*(4), pp. 51–68. **[G: U.S.]**

Kraft, Arthur. Preference Orderings as Determinants of the Labor Force Behavior of Married Women. *Western Econ. J.*, September 1973, *11*(3), pp. 270–84. **[G: U.S.]**

Landsberger, Michael. Children's Age as a Factor Affecting the Simultaneous Determination of Consumption and Labor Supply. *Southern Econ. J.*, October 1973, *40*(2), pp. 279–88. **[G: U.S.; Israel]**

Lebergott, Stanley. A New Technique for Time Series? Comment. *Rev. Econ. Statist.*, November 1973, *55*(4), pp. 525–27.

Melson, Robert. Political Dilemmas of Nigerian Labor. In *Damachi, U. G. and Seibel, H. D., eds.*, 1973, pp. 119–37. **[G: Nigeria]**

Michelotti, Kopp. Young Workers: In School and Out. *Mon. Lab. Rev.*, September 1973, *96*(9), pp. 11–15. **[G: U.S.]**

Mujahid, G. B. S. "Disguised" Unemployment Once Again: East Pakistan, 1951–1961: Comment. *Amer. J. Agr. Econ.*, February 1973, *55*(1), pp. 118–19. **[G: Pakistan]**

Oohashi, Ryuken. Working Class in the Present World—Statistics and Their Meaning. *Kyoto Univ. Econ. Rev.*, April–October 1973, *43*(1–2), pp. 1–29.

Pompermayer, Malori J. Dependency and Unemployment: Some Issues. In *Bonilla, F. and Girling, R., eds.*, 1973, pp. 63–82.

Psacharopoulos, George. Manpower Forecasting for all Occupations: France. In *Ahamad, B. and Blaug, M., eds.*, 1973, pp. 106–30. **[G: France]**

Ramanujam, M. S. Requirements of Technical Manpower in India: 1965–66 to 1980–81. *Indian Econ. Rev.*, October 1973, *8*(2), pp. 101–24. **[G: India]**

Reynolds, Lloyd G. Labor in Less Developed Economies. In *Somers, G. G., ed.*, 1973, pp. 165–76.

Robinson, Warren C. "Disguised" Unemployment Once Again: East Pakistan, 1951–1961: Reply. *Amer. J. Agr. Econ.*, February 1973, *55*(1), pp. 120. **[G: Pakistan]**

Robinson, Warren C. and Pawakaranond, Lamduan. Manpower Imbalances in Thailand: Comment. *Western Econ. J.*, September 1973, *11*(3), pp. 375–79. **[G: Thailand]**

Rosenblum, Marc. The Great Labor Force Projection Debate: Implications for 1980. *Amer. Econ.*, Fall 1973, *17*(2), pp. 122–29. **[G: U.S.]**

Seibel, H. Dieter. The Process of Adaptation to Wage Labor. In *Damachi, U. G. and Seibel, H. D., eds.*, 1973, pp. 3–10. **[G: Africa]**

Sobol, Marion G. A Dynamic Analysis of Labor Force Participation of Married Women of Childbearing Age. *J. Human Res.*, Fall 1973, *8*(4), pp. 497–505. **[G: U.S.]**

Spencer, Byron G. Determinants of the Labour Force Participation of Married Women: A Micro-Study of Toronto Households. *Can. J. Econ.*, May 1973, *6*(2), pp. 222–38. **[G: Canada]**

Swisher, Idella G. The Disabled and the Decline in Men's Labor Force Participation. *Mon. Lab. Rev.*, November 1973, *96*(11), pp. 53. **[G: U.S.]**

Toms, Miroslav. The Labor Force and Relations Within the Production Process. *Eastern Europ. Econ.*, Summer 1973, *11*(4), pp. 3–59. **[G: Czechoslovakia]**

de la Torre, Jose, Jr.; Stobaugh, Robert B. and Telesio, Piero. U.S. Multinational Enterprises and Changes in the Skill Composition of U.S. Employment. In *Kujawa, D., ed.*, 1973, pp. 127–43. **[G: U.S.]**

Workman, Randy L. Ohio's Women Workers. *Ohio State U. Bull. Bus. Res.*, August 1973, *48*(8), pp. 4–6. **[G: U.S.]**

Young, Anne M. The High School Class of 1972: More at Work, Fewer in College. *Mon. Lab. Rev.*, June 1973, *96*(6), pp. 26–32. **[G: U.S.]**

Young, Anne M. Going Back to School at 35. *Mon. Lab. Rev.*, October 1973, *96*(10), pp. 39–42. **[G: U.S.]**

Young, Anne M. Children of Working Mothers. *Mon. Lab. Rev.*, April 1973, *96*(4), pp. 37–40. **[G: U.S.]**

8131 Agriculture

Gyenes, A. Re-stratification of the Agricultural Population in Hungary. *Acta Oecon.*, 1973, *11*(1), pp. 33–49. **[G: Hungary]**

Huq, A. M. A Study of the Socioeconomic Impact of Changes in the Harvesting Labor Force in the Maine Lobster Industry. In *Sokoloski, A. A., ed.*, 1973, pp. 159–73. **[G: U.S.]**

Jackson, Dudley and Turner, H. A. How to Provide More Employment in a Labour-Surplus Economy. *Int. Lab. Rev.*, April 1973, *107*(4), pp. 315–38. **[G: Morocco]**

Lantsev, M. Progress in Social Security for Agricultural Workers in the USSR. *Int. Lab. Rev.*, March 1973, *107*(3), pp. 239–52. **[G: U.S.S.R.]**

Leal de Araujo, Lucila. Extension of Social Security to Rural Workers in Mexico. *Int. Lab. Rev.*, October 1973, *108*(4), pp. 295–312. **[G: Mexico]**

Mafeje, Archie and Richards, A. I. The Commercial Farmer and His Labour Supply. In *Richards, A. I.; Sturrock, F. and Fortt, J. M., eds.*, 1973, pp. 179–97. **[G: Uganda]**

Mujahid, G. B. S. The Measurement of Disguised Unemployment: A Comment. *Can. J. Econ.*, February 1973, *6*(1), pp. 128–29. **[G: India]**

8132 Manufacturing

Walter, Emil J. Technologische, wirtschaftliche und soziale Aspekte der wachsenden Bedeutung der Schichtarbeit. (Technological, Economic and Social Aspects of the Growing Importance of Shift

Work. With English summary.) *Schweiz. Z. Volkswirtsch. Statist.*, March 1973, *109*(1), pp. 69–89. [G: Switzerland]

8134 Professional

Ahamad, Bashir. Manpower Forecasting for Single Occupations: Doctors in the United States, Britain and Canada. In *Ahamad, B. and Blaug, M., eds.*, 1973, pp. 285–309. [G: U.S.; U.K.; Canada]

Ahamad, Bashir. Manpower Forecasting for Single Occupations: Teachers in England and Wales. In *Ahamad, B. and Blaug, M., eds.*, 1973, pp. 261–84. [G: U.K.]

Bishop, Christine E. Manpower Policy and the Supply of Nurses. *Ind. Relat.*, February 1973, *12*(1), pp. 86–94. [G: U.S.]

Blitz, Rudolph C. and Ow, Chin Hock. A Cross-Sectional Analysis of Women's Participation in the Professions. *J. Polit. Econ.*, January-February 1973, *81*(1), pp. 131–44. [G: U.S.]

Corry, B. A. Some Aspects of University Teachers' Labour Market in the UK: Discussion. In *Parkin, M., ed.*, 1973, pp. 212–13. [G: U.K.]

Davis, Carlton G. Traditional Graduate Admission Standards as Constraints to Increasing the Supply of Black Professional Agriculturalists: The Florida Experience. *Amer. J. Agr. Econ.*, December 1973, *55*(5), pp. 952–66. [G: U.S.]

Gannicott, Kenneth and Blaug, Mark. Manpower Forecasting for Single Occupations: Scientists and Engineers in Britain. In *Ahamad, B. and Blaug, M., eds.*, 1973, pp. 240–60. [G: U.K.]

Gannicott, Kenneth. Manpower Forecasting for Single Occupations: Engineers in Sweden. In *Ahamad, B. and Blaug, M., eds.*, 1973, pp. 201–39. [G: Sweden]

Gramm, Wendy Lee. The Labor Force Decision of Married Female Teachers: A Discriminant Analysis Approach. *Rev. Econ. Statist.*, August 1973, *55*(3), pp. 341–48. [G: U.S.]

Metcalf, David. Some Aspects of University Teachers' Labour Market in the UK. In *Parkin, M., ed.*, 1973, pp. 192–211. [G: U.K.]

Ord, H. W. The Employment of Economists in Africa. In *Livingstone, I., et al., eds.*, 1973, pp. 147–51. [G: Africa]

Perline, Martin M. and Presley, Ronald W. Mobility of Unemployed Engineers: A Case Study. *Mon. Lab. Rev.*, May 1973, *96*(5), pp. 41–43. [G: U.S.]

Sen, Amartya K. Brain Drain: Causes and Effects. In *Williams, B. R., ed.*, 1973, pp. 385–404. [G: U.S.]

Woodhall, Maureen. Manpower Forecasting for Single Occupations: Engineers in India. In *Ahamad, B. and Blaug, M., eds.*, 1973, pp. 157–200. [G: India]

8135 Government Employees

Daicoff, Darwin W. The Adjustment of DOD Civilian and Military Personnel. In *Udis, B., ed.*, 1973, pp. 167–77. [G: U.S.]

Ehrenberg, Ronald G. The Demand for State and Local Government Employees. *Amer. Econ. Rev.*, June 1973, *63*(3), pp. 366–79. [G: U.S.]

Pisano, Paolo G. International Manual on Collective Bargaining for Public Employees: Italy. In *Kaye, S. P. and Marsh, A., eds.*, 1973, pp. 210–63. [G: Italy]

Weaver, Jerry L. Bureaucracy during a Period of Social Change: The Case of Guatemala. In *Thurber, C. E. and Graham, L. S., eds.*, 1973, pp. 314–61. [G: Guatemala]

8136 Construction

Adams, Earl W., Jr. and Spiro, Michael H. Labor Force Adjustment in the Construction Trades. *J. Econ. Bus.*, Fall 1973, *26*(1), pp. 78–80. [G: U.S.]

Foster, Howard G. The Labor Market in Nonunion Construction. *Ind. Lab. Relat. Rev.*, July 1973, *26*(4), pp. 1071–85. [G: U.S.]

Franklin, William S. A Comparison of Formally and Informally Trained Journeymen in Construction. *Ind. Lab. Relat. Rev.*, July 1973, *26*(4), pp. 1086–94. [G: U.S.]

Hammerman, Herbert. Minorities in Construction Referral Unions—Revisited. *Mon. Lab. Rev.*, May 1973, *96*(5), pp. 43–46. [G: U.S.]

Lewin, David. Wage Parity and the Supply of Police and Firemen. *Ind. Relat.*, February 1973, *12*(1), pp. 77–85. [G: U.S.]

Madden, Carl H. Construction Wages: The Great Consumer Robbery. In *Reynolds, L. G.; Green, C. D. and Lewis, D. R., eds.*, 1973, pp. 18–23. [G: U.S.]

Maurizi, Alex R. Minority Membership in Apprenticeship Programs in the Construction Trades: Reply. *Ind. Lab. Relat. Rev.*, October 1973, *27*(1), pp. 100–102.

Strauss, George. Minority Membership in Apprenticeship Programs in the Construction Trades: Comment. *Ind. Lab. Relat. Rev.*, October 1973, *27*(1), pp. 93–99.

820 LABOR MARKETS; PUBLIC POLICY

821 Theory of Labor Markets and Leisure

8210 Theory of Labor Markets and Leisure: Empirical Studies Illustrating Theories

Ahluwalia, Montek S. Taxes, Subsidies, and Employment. *Quart. J. Econ.*, August 1973, *87*(3), pp. 393–409.

Alexis, Marcus. A Theory of Labor Market Discrimination with Interdependent Utilities. *Amer. Econ. Rev.*, May 1973, *63*(2), pp. 296–302.

Annable, James E., Jr. and Fruitman, Frederick H. An Earnings Function for High-Level Manpower. *Ind. Lab. Relat. Rev.*, July 1973, *26*(4), pp. 1107–21.

Bacon, Robert. The Phillips Curve: Another Forerunner. *Economica, N.S.*, August 1973, *40*(159), pp. 314–15.

Barbash, Jack. Consumption Values of Trade Unions. *J. Econ. Issues*, June 1973, *7*(2), pp. 289–301.

Barzel, Yoram and McDonald, Richard J. Assets,

Subsistence, and The Supply Curve of Labor. *Amer. Econ. Rev.*, September 1973, *63*(4), pp. 621–33. [G: U.S.]

Barzel, Yoram. The Determination of Daily Hours and Wages. *Quart. J. Econ.*, May 1973, *87*(2), pp. 220–38.

Beare, John B. Wage and Price Change Relationships in Post-War Canada. *Can. J. Econ.*, May 1973, *6*(2), pp. 260–65. [G: Canada]

Behrman, Jere R. and Mujica, Jorge G. A Study of Quarterly Nominal Wage Change Determination in an Inflationary Developing Economy. In *Eckaus, R. S. and Rosenstein-Rodan, P. N., eds.*, 1973, pp. 399–416. [G: Chile]

Ben-Porath, Yoram. Labor-Force Participation Rates and the Supply of Labor. *J. Polit. Econ.*, May-June 1973, *81*(3), pp. 697–704.

Bergmann, Barbara R. Combining Microsimulation and Regression: A "Prepared" Regression of Poverty Incidence on Unemployment and Growth. *Econometrica*, September 1973, *41*(5), pp. 955–63.

Block, M. K. and Heineke, J. M. The Allocation of Effort under Uncertainty: The Case of Risk-averse Behavior. *J. Polit. Econ.*, Part I, March-April 1973, *81*(2), pp. 376–85.

Boelaert, Remi. Unemployment-Inflation Trade-Offs in EEC–Countries. *Weltwirtsch. Arch.*, 1973, *109* (3), pp. 418–51. [G: E.E.C.]

Bosanquet, Nicholas and Doeringer, Peter B. Is There a Dual Labour Market in Great Britain? *Econ. J.*, June 1973, *83*(330), pp. 421–35. [G: U.K.]

Bradley, Michael E. Incentives and Labour Supply on Soviet Collective Farms: Reply. *Can. J. Econ.*, August 1973, *6*(3), pp. 438–42.

Brechling, Frank. Wage Inflation and the Structure of Regional Unemployment. *J. Money, Credit, Banking*, Part II, February 1973, *5*(1), pp. 355–79.

Browning, Edgar K. Alternative Programs for Income Redistribution: The NIT and the NWT. *Amer. Econ. Rev.*, March 1973, *63*(1), pp. 38–49. [G: U.S.]

Brownlee, Oswald. The Effects of Inflation on the Distribution of Economic Welfare: Comment. *J. Money, Credit, Banking*, Part II, February 1973, *5*(1), pp. 505–06. [G: U.S.]

Brunner, Karl, et al. Fiscal and Monetary Policies in Moderate Inflation: Case Studies of Three Countries. *J. Money, Credit, Banking*, Part II, February 1973, *5*(1), pp. 313–53. [G: U.S.; Germany; Italy]

Butler, Arthur and Kim, Kye. The Dynamics of Wage Structures. *Southern Econ. J.*, April 1973, *39*(4), pp. 588–600. [G: U.S.]

Cameron, Norman. Incentives and Labour Supply in Co-operative Enterprises. *Can. J. Econ.*, February 1973, *6*(1), pp. 16–22. [G: U.S.S.R.]

Cameron, Norman. Incentives and Labour Supply on Soviet Collective Farms: Rejoinder. *Can. J. Econ.*, August 1973, *6*(3), pp. 442–44.

Cheng, Juei Ming. On the Stability of Equilibrium of the Manufacturing Market Structure. *Rivista Int. Sci. Econ. Com.*, February 1973, *20*(2), pp. 184–89.

Chiplin, B. and Sloane, P. J. Real and Money Wages Revisited. *Appl. Econ.*, December 1973, *5*(4), pp. 289–304. [G: U.K.]

Clark, Colin. The Marginal Utility of Income. *Oxford Econ. Pap.*, July 1973, *25*(2), pp. 145–59.

Clark, C. Scott. Labor Hoarding in Durable Goods Industries. *Amer. Econ. Rev.*, December 1973, *63* (5), pp. 811–24. [G: U.S.]

Corden, W. Max. Employment in the Industrialized Countries: Comment. In *Hughes, H., ed.*, 1973, pp. 125–27.

Correa, H. An Econometric Model of Supply, Demand and Wages of Educated Workers. In *Judge, G. G. and Takayama, T., eds.*, 1973, pp. 706–23. [G: U.S.]

Craine, Roger. On the Service Flow from Labour. *Rev. Econ. Stud.*, January 1973, *40*(1), pp. 39–46.

Crossley, J. R. A Mixed Strategy for Labour Economists. *Scot. J. Polit. Econ.*, November 1973, *20*(3), pp. 211–38. [G: U.K.]

Dadi, M. M. Labour's Share in Indian Industry: Theory and Fact. *Indian Econ. J.*, January-March 1973, *20*(3), pp. 500–14. [G: India]

Das, A. C. and Banerjee, R. M. Theoretical Approach for Measuring Intensity of Unemployment. *Econ. Aff.*, November-December 1973, *18* (11–12), pp. 497–502.

Davis, Donald L. A Pedogogical Tool for Manpower Analysis. *Intermountain Econ. Rev.*, Spring 1973, *4*(1), pp. 40–52.

Desai, Meghnad. Growth Cycles and Inflation in a Model of the Class Struggle. *J. Econ. Theory*, December 1973, *6*(6), pp. 527–45.

Donner, Arthur W. and Lazar, Fred. Some Comments on the Canadian Phillips Curve. *Economica, N.S.*, May 1973, *40*(158), pp. 195–207. [G: Canada]

Donner, Arthur W. and Lazar, Fred. An Econometric Study of Segmented Labor Markets and the Structure of Unemployment: The Canadian Experience. *Int. Econ. Rev.*, June 1973, *14*(2), pp. 312–27. [G: Canada]

Dougherty, Christopher and Selowsky, Marcelo. Measuring the Effects of the Misallocation of Labour. *Rev. Econ. Statist.*, August 1973, *55*(3), pp. 386–90. [G: Colombia]

Duncan, Otis Dudley and Featherman, David L. Psychological and Cultural Factors in the Process of Occupational Achievement. In *Goldberger, A. S. and Duncan, O. D., eds.*, 1973, pp. 229–53. [G: U.S.]

Dutton, Dean S. and Gramm, William P. Transactions Costs, the Wage Rate, and the Demand for Money. *Amer. Econ. Rev.*, September 1973, *63*(4), pp. 652–65. [G: U.S.]

Emmerij, Louis. Education and Employment: Some Preliminary Findings and Thoughts. *Int. Lab. Rev.*, January 1973, *107*(1), pp. 31–42.

Evans, Alan W. On the Theory of the Valuation and Allocation of Time: Reply. *Scot. J. Polit. Econ.*, February 1973, *20*(1), pp. 73–74.

Fellner, William J. Controlled Floating and the Confused Issue of Money Illusion. *Banca Naz. Lavoro Quart. Rev.*, September 1973, (106), pp. 206–34.

Fellner, William J. Employment Goals and Monetary-Fiscal Overexpansion. In *Cagan, P., et al.*,

1973, pp. 135–72. [G: U.S.]

Flanagan, Robert J. Segmented Market Theories and Racial Discrimination. *Ind. Relat.,* October 1973, *12*(3), pp. 253–73. [G: U.S.]

Flanagan, Robert J. The U.S. Phillips Curve and International Unemployment Rate Differentials. *Amer. Econ. Rev.,* March 1973, *63*(1), pp. 114–31. [G: U.S.]

Flanders, Dwight P. and Anderson, Peggy Engelhardt. Sex Discrimination in Employment: Theory and Practice. *Ind. Lab. Relat. Rev.,* April 1973, *26*(3), pp. 938–55. [G: U.S.]

Flemming, J. S. On the Theory of the Valuation and Allocation of Time: Some Comments. *Scot. J. Polit. Econ.,* February 1973, *20*(1), pp. 65–71.

Foran, Terry G. Unionism and Wage Differentials. *Southern Econ. J.,* October 1973, *40*(2), pp. 269–78. [G: U.S.]

Gallaway, Lowell E. and Cebula, Richard J. Differentials and Indeterminacy in Wage Rate Analysis: An Empirical Note. *Ind. Lab. Relat. Rev.,* April 1973, *26*(3), pp. 991–95.

Gilbert, Ronald D. Okun's Law: Some Additional Evidence. *Nebr. J. Econ. Bus.,* Winter 1973, *12*(1), pp. 51–60. [G: U.S.]

Godfrey, Leslie G. and Taylor, Jim. Earnings Changes in the United Kingdom, 1954–70: Excess Labour Supply, Expected Inflation and Union Influence. *Oxford Bull. Econ. Statist.,* August 1973, *35*(3), pp. 197–216. [G: U.K.]

Goldfarb, Robert S. A Model of Wage Setting and Wage Diversity in Local Labor Markets. *Western Econ. J.,* March 1973, *11*(1), pp. 98–110.

Goldfinger, Nathaniel. Employment in the Industrialized Countries: Comment. In *Hughes, H., ed.,* 1973, pp. 117–24.

Gordon, Robert A. Some Macroeconomic Aspects of Manpower Policy. In *Ulman, L., ed.,* 1973, pp. 14–50. [G: U.S.]

Gordon, Robert J. The Welfare Cost of Higher Unemployment. *Brookings Pap. Econ. Act.,* 1973, (1), pp. 133–95. [G: U.S.]

Gronau, Reuben. The Intrafamily Allocation of Time: The Value of the Housewives' Time. *Amer. Econ. Rev.,* September 1973, *63*(4), pp. 634–51. [G: U.S.]

Gronau, Reuben. The Effect of Children on the Housewife's Value of Time. *J. Polit. Econ.,* Part II, March-April 1973, *81*(2), pp. S168–99. [G: U.S.]

Grossman, Herschel I. Aggregate Demand, Job Search, and Employment. *J. Polit. Econ.,* November-December 1973, *81*(6), pp. 1353–69.

Grossman, Michael. Unemployment and Consumption: Note. *Amer. Econ. Rev.,* March 1973, *63*(1), pp. 208–13. [G: U.S.]

Hall, Robert E. The Effect of Children on the Housewife's Value of Time: Comment. *J. Polit. Econ.,* Part II, March-April 1973, *81*(2), pp. S200–01. [G: U.S.]

Hamdani, Daood H. Fiscal Measures Against Inflation and Unemployment in Canada: 1973 Budget and Other Developments. *Bull. Int. Fiscal Doc.,* June 1973, *27*(6), pp. 223–40. [G: Canada]

Hart, R. A. The Role of Overtime Working in the Recent Wage Inflation Process. *Bull. Econ. Res.,* May 1973, *25*(1), pp. 73–87. [G: U.K.]

Hedrick, Charles L. Expectations and the Labor Supply. *Amer. Econ. Rev.,* December 1973, *63*(5), pp. 968–74. [G: U.S.]

Herman, Bohuslav. Unemployment and the International Division of Labour. In *Judge, G. G. and Takayama, T., eds.,* 1973, pp. 89–115.

Higgins, Benjamin. Trade-Off Curves and Regional Gaps. In *[Rosenstein-Rodan, P.],* 1973, pp. 152–77. [G: Canada]

Higgins, Benjamin. The Employment Problem in Development. In *Ayal, E. B., ed.,* 1973, pp. 241–75.

Holt, Charles C. Wage Inflation and the Structure of Regional Unemployment: Comment. *J. Money, Credit, Banking,* Part II, February 1973, *5*(1), pp. 380–81.

Holt, Charles C., et al. Manpower Policies to Reduce Inflation and Unemployment. In *Ulman, L., ed.,* 1973, pp. 51–82. [G: U.S.]

Hoselitz, Bert F. The Development of a Labor Market in the Process of Economic Growth. In *Sturmthal, A. and Scoville, J. G., eds.,* 1973, pp. 34–57.

Isard, Peter. The Effectiveness of Using the Tax System to Curb Inflationary Collective Bargains: An Analysis of the Wallich-Weintraub Plan. *J. Polit. Econ.,* May-June 1973, *81*(3), pp. 729–40. [G: U.S.]

Jackson, Mark and Jones, E. B. Unemployment and Occupational Wage Changes in Local Labor Markets. *Ind. Lab. Relat. Rev.,* July 1973, *26*(4), pp. 1135–45. [G: U.S.]

Johnson, Stanley R. and Smith, Paul E. The Phillips Curve, Expectations, and Stability. *Quart. Rev. Econ. Bus.,* Autumn 1973, *13*(3), pp. 85–91.

Johnston, J. and Timbrell, M. Empirical Tests of a Bargaining Theory of Wage Rate Determination. *Manchester Sch. Econ. Soc. Stud.,* June 1973, *41* (2), pp. 141–67. [G: U.K.]

Jones, Ethel B. and Barnes, William F. Robbins, Hicks, Buchanan and the Backward Bending Labor Supply Curve. *Miss. Val. J. Bus. Econ.,* Fall 1973, *9*(1), pp. 76–82.

Kaliski, S. F. and Smith, D. C. Inflation, Unemployment and Incomes Policy. *Can. J. Econ.,* November 1973, *6*(4), pp. 574–91. [G: Canada]

Kesselman, Jonathan R. Incentive Effects of Transfer Systems Once Again. *J. Human Res.,* Winter 1973, *8*(1), pp. 119–29. [G: U.S.]

Kessel, Reuben A. The Effects of Inflation on the Distribution of Economic Welfare: Comment. *J. Money, Credit, Banking,* Part II, February 1973, *5*(1), pp. 507–08. [G: U.S.]

Knight, J. B. and Mabro, Robert. On the Determination of the General Wage Level: A Rejoinder. *Econ. J.,* June 1973, *83*(330), pp. 520–22.

Koshal, Rajindar K. and Gallaway, Lowell E. The Phillips Curve: An International Phenomenon. *Rivista Int. Sci. Econ. Com.,* July 1973, *20*(7), pp. 669–80.

Kraft, Arthur and Kraft, John. A Cross-Section Comparison of How Individuals Allocate Time: 1960 Versus 1970. *Nebr. J. Econ. Bus.,* Autumn 1973, *12*(4), pp. 51–68. [G: U.S.]

Kraft, Arthur. Preference Orderings as Determinants of the Labor Force Behavior of Married

Women. *Western Econ. J.,* September 1973, *11*(3), pp. 270–84. [G: U.S.]

Kymn, Kern O. A Note on Logical Inconsistencies of the Kennedy Wage-Price Guidelines. *Southern Econ. J.,* January 1973, *39*(3), pp. 434–36.

Laidler, David. Simultaneous Fluctuations in Prices and Output—A Business Cycle Approach. *Economica, N.S.,* February 1973, *40*(157), pp. 60–72.

Lal, Deepak. Employment, Income Distribution and a Poverty Redressal Index. *World Devel.,* March-April 1973, *1*(3–4), pp. 121–25.

Lal, Deepak. Disutility of Effort, Migration, and the Shadow Wage-rate. *Oxford Econ. Pap.,* March 1973, *25*(1), pp. 112–26.

Lécaillon, Jacques and Botalla-Gambetta, Brigitte. Inflation, répartition et chômage dans la France contemporaine. (Inflation, Distribution and Unemployment in Today's France. With English summary.) *Revue Écon.,* May 1973, *24*(3), pp. 373–400. [G: France]

Leff, Nathaniel H. The Employment Problem in Development: Comment. In *Ayal, E. B., ed.,* 1973, pp. 275–77.

Leijonhufvud, Axel and Buchanan, James M. The Backbending Supply Curve of Labor: Comment on Buchanan, with His Reply. *Hist. Polit. Econ.,* Spring 1973, *5*(1), pp. 261–67.

Leslie, D. G. A Note on the Regional Distribution of Unemployment. *Oxford Bull. Econ. Statist.,* August 1973, *35*(3), pp. 233–37.

Levitan, S. A. and Taggart, R. Employment-Earnings Inadequacy: A Measure of Welfare. *Mon. Lab. Rev.,* October 1973, *96*(10), pp. 19–27. [G: U.S.]

Lindauer, John. Stabilization Inflation and the Inflation-Unemployment Trade-off. *Indian Econ. J.,* April-June 1973, *20*(4–5), pp. 541–47.

Lucas, Robert E., Jr. Wage Inflation and the Structure of Regional Unemployment: Comment. *J. Money, Credit, Banking,* Part II, February 1973, *5*(1), pp. 382–84.

Lüttichau, Knud. Kvartalsresultater for pengeløns-aendringens determinanter for Danmark i mellem-og efter-krigstiden. (Quarterly Results Concerning the Determinants of Changes in Money Wage Rates in Denmark in the Interwar and Post–war Period. With English summary.) *Nationalokon. Tidsskr.,* 1973, *111*(1), pp. 92–111. [G: Denmark]

Maital, Shlomo. Targets, Tradeoffs, and Economic Policy: A Generalized Phillips Curve. *Public Finance Quart.,* January 1973, *1*(1), pp. 67–83.

Martin, Donald L. Some Economics of Job Rights in the Longshore Industry. *J. Econ. Bus.,* Winter 1973, *25*(2), pp. 93–100. [G: U.S.]

McCain, Roger A. The Cost of Supervision and the Quality of Labor: A Determinant of X-Inefficiency. *Miss. Val. J. Bus. Econ.,* Spring 1973, *8*(3), pp. 1–16.

McCormick, B. J. Trade Unions and Wage Inflation in the UK: A Reappraisal: Discussion. In *Parkin, M., ed.,* 1973, pp. 328–29. [G: U.K.]

Meidner, Rudolf and Andersson, Rolf. The Overall Impact of an Active Labor Market Policy in Sweden. In *Ulman, L., ed.,* 1973, pp. 117–58. [G: Sweden]

Metcalf, David. Pay Dispersion, Information, and Returns to Search in a Professional Labour Market. *Rev. Econ. Stud.,* October 1973, *40*(4), pp. 491–505. [G: U.K.]

Miles, Caroline. Employment in the Industrialized Countries. In *Hughes, H., ed.,* 1973, pp. 101–16.

Miller, Herman P. Measuring Subemployment in Poverty Areas of Large U.S. Cities. *Mon. Lab. Rev.,* October 1973, *96*(10), pp. 10–18. [G: U.S.]

Minami, Ryoshin. Wage Adjustments in Postwar Japan: An Alternative Approach to the Phillips-Lipsey Curve. *Hitotsubashi J. Econ.,* June 1973, *14*(1), pp. 44–55. [G: Japan]

Modigliani, Franco and Tarantelli, Ezio. A Generalization of the Phillips Curve for a Developing Country. *Rev. Econ. Stud.,* April 1973, *40*(2), pp. 203–23. [G: Italy]

Mohindru, Rajesh K. The Structural Unemployment Controversy Revisited. *J. Econ. Bus.,* Winter 1973, *25*(2), pp. 122–26. [G: U.S.]

Monissen, Hans G. Preise, Löhne und Beschäftigung in dynamischer Betrachtung: Eine einfache Exposition. (Prices, Wages and Employment in Dynamic Perspective: A Simple Exposition. With English summary.) *Kyklos,* 1973, *26*(3), pp. 545–58.

Mouly, Jean. Prices, Wages, Unemployment: Inflation in Contemporary Economic Theory. *Int. Lab. Rev.,* October 1973, *108*(4), pp. 329–43.

Mulvey, C. and Trevithick, J. A. Trade Unions and Wage Inflation. *Econ. Soc. Rev.,* January 1973, *4* (2), pp. 209–29.

Neild, P. G. The Construction and Estimation of a Coherent Labour-Market System. *Australian Econ. Pap.,* June 1973, *12*(20), pp. 106–23. [G: New Zealand]

Nelson, Phillip. The Elasticity of Labor Supply to the Individual Firm. *Econometrica,* September 1973, *41*(5), pp. 853–66.

Nordhaus, William D. The Effects of Inflation on the Distribution of Economic Welfare. *J. Money, Credit, Banking,* Part II, February 1973, *5*(1), pp. 465–504. [G: U.S.]

O'Brien, James M. Inflation and Unemployment: The Great Debate. *Fed. Res. Bank Bus. Rev. Phila.,* January 1973, pp. 13–18. [G: U.S.]

Okun, Arthur M. Upward Mobility in a High-pressure Economy. *Brookings Pap. Econ. Act.,* 1973, (1), pp. 207–52. [G: U.S.]

Olivier, R. and Sabolo, Y. Simultaneous Planning of Employment, Production and Education. *Int. Lab. Rev.,* April 1973, *107*(4), pp. 359–72. [G: Peru]

Packer, Arnold H. and Park, Seong H. Distortions in Relative Wages and Shifts in the Phillips Curve. *Rev. Econ. Statist.,* February 1973, *55*(1), pp. 16–22. [G: U.S.]

Parkin, Michael. The Short-Run and Long-Run Trade-Offs Between Inflation and Unemployment in Australia. *Australian Econ. Pap.,* December 1973, *12*(21), pp. 127–44. [G: Australia]

Pedersen, Peder J. Har finanspolitikken mistet sin effektivitet? (With English summary.) *Nationalokon. Tidsskr.,* 1973, *111*(3), pp. 327–41. [G: Denmark]

Perlman, Mark. Consumption Values of Trade Unions: Comment. *J. Econ. Issues,* June 1973, *7*(2), pp. 303–05.

Perry, George L. The Success of Anti-Inflation Policies in the United States. *J. Money, Credit, Banking,* Part II, February 1973, *5*(1), pp. 569–93. [G: U.S.]

Phelps, Edmund S. Optimal Stabilization Paths: Comment. *J. Money, Credit, Banking,* Part II, February 1973, *5*(1), pp. 563–65.

Piore, Michael J. Fragments of a "Sociological" Theory of Wages. *Amer. Econ. Rev.,* May 1973, *63*(2), pp. 377–84.

Purdy, D. L. and Zis, G. Trade Unions and Wage Inflation in the UK: A Reappraisal. In *Parkin, M., ed.,* 1973, pp. 294–327. [G: U.K.]

Reich, Michael; Gordon, David M. and Edwards, Richard C. A Theory of Labor Market Segmentation. *Amer. Econ. Rev.,* May 1973, *63*(2), pp. 359–65.

Renas, Steve. Work Effort and the Progressive Income Tax: A Note. *Tijdschr. Econ.,* 1973, *18*(3), pp. 441–43.

Robinson, Derek. Forecasting Manpower Requirements: The Functioning of the Labour Market in Practice. In *Robinson, D.,* 1973, pp. 205–18.

Rose, Hugh. Optimal Stabilization Paths: Comment. *J. Money, Credit, Banking,* Part II, February 1973, *5*(1), pp. 566–67.

Ross, Stephen A. and Wachter, Michael L. Wage Determination, Inflation, and the Industrial Structure. *Amer. Econ. Rev.,* September 1973, *63*(4), pp. 675–92.

Rowley, J. C. R. and Wilton, D. A. Quarterly Models of Wage Determination Some New Efficient Estimates. *Amer. Econ. Rev.,* June 1973, *63*(3), pp. 380–89. [G: Canada]

Rowley, J. C. R. and Wilton, D. A. The Empirical Sensitivity of the Phillips Curve. *Amer. Econ.,* Fall 1973, *17*(2), pp. 90–112. [G: U.S.]

Rowley, J. C. R. and Wilton, D. A. Wage Determination: The Use of Instrumental Assumptions. *Int. Econ. Rev.,* June 1973, *14*(2), pp. 525–29.

Salop, S. C. Systematic Job Search and Unemployment. *Rev. Econ. Stud.,* April 1973, *40*(2), pp. 191–201.

Salop, S. C. Wage Differentials in a Dynamic Theory of the Firm. *J. Econ. Theory,* August 1973, *6*(4), pp. 321–44.

Sargent, Thomas J. "Rational Expectations": A Correction. *Brookings Pap. Econ. Act.,* 1973, (3), pp. 799–800.

Sargent, Thomas J. Rational Expectations, the Real Rate of Interest, and the Natural Rate of Unemployment. *Brookings Pap. Econ. Act.,* 1973, (2), pp. 429–72.

Sato, Ryuzo and Koizumi, Tetsunori. On the Elasticities of Substitution and Complementarity. *Oxford Econ. Pap.,* March 1973, *25*(1), pp. 44–56.

Scarfe, B. L. A Model of the Inflation Cycle in a Small Open Economy. *Oxford Econ. Pap.,* July 1973, *25*(2), pp. 192–203.

Schmalen, Helmut. Rationale individuelle Berufswahl und die langfristige Entwicklung des Arbeitsmarktes. (Rational Individual Choice of Professions and the Long-Term Development of the Labor Market. With English summary.) *Z. ges. Staatswiss.,* May 1973, *129*(2), pp. 292–311.

Scitovsky, Tibor. Inequalities: Open and Hidden, Measured and Immeasurable. *Ann. Amer. Acad. Polit. Soc. Sci.,* September 1973, *409*, pp. 112–19.

Seton, Francis. Shadow Wages in Chile. In *Eckaus, R. S. and Rosenstein-Rodan, P. N., eds.,* 1973, pp. 49–119. [G: Chile]

Sharot, T. Unemployment Dispersion as a Determinant of Wage Inflation in the U.K. 1925–66—A Note. *Manchester Sch. Econ. Soc. Stud.,* June 1973, *41*(2), pp. 225–28. [G: U.K.]

Solow, Robert M. What Happened to Full Employment? *Quart. Rev. Econ. Bus.,* Summer 1973, *13*(2), pp. 7–20. [G: U.S.]

Solow, Robert M. Technology and Unemployment. In *Reynolds, L. G.; Green, G. D. and Lewis, D. R., eds.,* 1973, pp. 89–99.

Spence, A. Michael. Job Market Signaling. *Quart. J. Econ.,* August 1973, *87*(3), pp. 355–74.

Sreenivas, M. A. Prices, Money Wages and Real Output: A Case Study of Indian Manufacturing Sector. *Indian Econ. J.,* April-June 1973, *20*(4–5), pp. 604–18. [G: India]

Stein, Jerome L. and Infante, Ettore F. Optimal Stabilization Paths. *J. Money, Credit, Banking,* Part II, February 1973, *5*(1), pp. 525–62.

Steinmann, Gunter. Lohnentwicklung und Beschäftigungsgrad: Die Neuauflage der Kontroverse zwischen der Keynesschen und der neoklassischen Theorie bei der Diskussion um die Phillips-Kurve. (Wages and the Rate of Employment. With English summary.) *Weltwirtsch. Arch.,* 1973, *109*(1), pp. 105–20.

Stiglitz, Joseph E. Approaches to the Economics of Discrimination. *Amer. Econ. Rev.,* May 1973, *63*(2), pp. 287–95.

Stolz, Peter. Flexibilitätsspielräume im Einsatz des Arbeitspotentials und bedarfsorientierte Modelle der Bildungsökonomie. (Manpower Forecasts and the Problem of Flexible Relationships between Educational Qualifications and Occupations. With English summary.) *Z. Wirtschaft. Sozialwissen.,* 1973, *93*(1), pp. 3–20.

Streeten, Paul. An Institutional Critique of Development Concepts. In *Livingstone, I., et al., eds.,* 1973, pp. 82–94.

Thirlwall, A. P. The Recent "Shift" in the U.S. Phillips Curve. *Ind. Relat.,* October 1973, *12*(3), pp. 297–306. [G: U.S.]

Thomas, R. B. On the Definition of 'Shortages' in Administered Labour Markets. *Manchester Sch. Econ. Soc. Stud.,* June 1973, *41*(2), pp. 169–86. [G: U.K.]

Thomas, R. L. Unemployment Dispersion as a Determinant of Wage Inflation in the U.K. 1925–66—A Rejoinder. *Manchester Sch. Econ. Soc. Stud.,* June 1973, *41*(2), pp. 229–33. [G: U.K.]

Tinbergen, Jan. Actual, Feasible and Optimal Income Inequality in a Three-Level Education Model. *Ann. Amer. Acad. Polit. Soc. Sci.,* September 1973, *409*, pp. 156–62. [G: Netherlands]

Tinbergen, Jan. Labour with Different Types of Skills and Jobs as Production Factors. *De Economist,* May-June 1973, *121*(3), pp. 213–24.

Tuckwell, R. H. The Wage-Price Link. *Econ. Anal.*

Pol., September 1973, *4*(2), pp. 76–87.   [G: Australia]

Tullock, Gordon. Inflation and Unemployment: The Discussion Continued: Comment. *J. Money, Credit, Banking*, August 1973, *5*(3), pp. 826–35.

Turner, H. A. and Jackson, D. A. S. A Riposte to Knight and Mabro. *Econ. J.*, June 1973, *83*(330), pp. 523–25.

Ulman, Lloyd. Introduction: The Problems in Policy Context. In *Ulman, L., ed.*, 1973, pp. 1–13.
[G: U.S.; Sweden]

Vietorisz, Thomas and Harrison, Bennett. Labor Market Segmentation: Positive Feedback and Divergent Development. *Amer. Econ. Rev.*, May 1973, *63*(2), pp. 366–76.

Votey, Harold L., Jr. The Choice of Technique and a Growing Real Wage. *Indian Econ. Rev.*, April 1973, *8*(1), pp. 81–84.   [G: 1132]

Wales, Terence J. Estimation of a Labor Supply Curve for Self-Employed Business Proprietors. *Int. Econ. Rev.*, February 1973, *14*(1), pp. 69–80.
[G: U.S.]

Whipple, David. A Generalized Theory of Job Search. *J. Polit. Econ.*, September-October 1973, *81*(5), pp. 1170–88.

822 Public Policy; Role of Government

8220 General

Aaron, Benjamin. Legal Framework of Industrial Relations. In *Somers, G. G., ed.*, 1973, pp. 101–10.
[G: U.S.]

Adams, Arvil V. Evaluating the Success of the EEOC Compliance Process. *Mon. Lab. Rev.*, May 1973, *96*(5), pp. 26–29.   [G: U.S.]

Adie, Douglas K. and Gallaway, Lowell. The Minimum Wage and Teenage Unemployment: A Comment. *Western Econ. J.*, December 1973, *11*(4), pp. 525–28.   [G: U.S.]

Barkin, Solomon. Changing Profile of European Manpower Policies. In *Somers, G. G., ed.*, 1973, pp. 83–100.   [G: W. Europe]

Bradley, Iver E.; Mangum, Garth L. and Robson, R. Thayne. Total Impact of Manpower Programs. In *Mangum, G. L. and Robson, R. T., eds.*, 1973, pp. 260–93.   [G: U.S.]

Brown, Douglass V. The Role of the NLRB. In *Somers, G. G., ed.*, 1973, pp. 111–17.   [G: U.S.]

Burki, Shahid J. Employment Creating Urban Public Works Programmes: Outline of a Strategy. *Pakistan Develop. Rev.*, Autumn 1973, *12*(3), pp. 293–310.

Cook, Carvin. Federal Employment Standards Legislation. *Mon. Lab. Rev.*, January 1973, *96*(1), pp. 50–51.   [G: U.S.]

Davis, Otto A., et al. An Empirical Study of the NAB-JOBS Program. *Public Policy*, Spring 1973, *21*(2), pp. 235–62.   [G: U.S.]

Epstein, E. and Monat, J. Labour Contracting and Its Regulation: II. *Int. Lab. Rev.*, June 1973, *107*(6), pp. 513–28.

Fisher, Robert W. Labor in a Year of Economic Stabilization. *Mon. Lab. Rev.*, January 1973, *96*(1), pp. 17–26.   [G: U.S.]

Fusfeld, Daniel R. A Living Wage. *Ann. Amer. Acad. Polit. Soc. Sci.*, September 1973, *409*,

pp. 34–41.   [G: U.S.]

Gallardo, Lloyd. Institutional Impact of Bay Area Manpower Programs. In *Mangum, G. L. and Robson, R. T., eds.*, 1973, pp. 202–24.   [G: U.S.]

Gannicott, Kenneth and Blaug, Mark. Manpower Forecasting for All Occupations: The United States. In *Ahamad, B. and Blaug, M., eds.*, 1973, pp. 48–76.   [G: U.S.]

Grossman, Jonathan. The Origin of the U.S. Department of Labor. *Mon. Lab. Rev.*, March 1973, *96*(3), pp. 3–7.   [G: U.S.]

Gupta, M. L. Outflow of High-Level Manpower from the Philippines, with Special Reference to the Period 1965-71. *Int. Lab. Rev.*, February 1973, *107*(2), pp. 167–91.   [G: Philippines]

Haber, William. Employment Policies. In *Somers, G. G., ed.*, 1973, pp. 56–64.   [G: U.S.]

Hassan, M. F. Unemployment in Latin America: Causes and Remedies. *Amer. J. Econ. Soc.*, April 1973, *32*(2), pp. 179–90.   [G: Latin America]

Herrick, Neal Q. Government Approaches to the Humanization of Work. *Mon. Lab. Rev.*, April 1973, *96*(4), pp. 52–54.   [G: U.S.]

Hildebrand, George H. The Declining Importance of the General Unemployment Rate for Future Employment Policy. In *Somers, G. G., ed.*, 1973, pp. 65–71.   [G: U.S.]

Ivanov, S. A. New Codification of Soviet Labour Law. *Int. Lab. Rev.*, August-September 1973, *108*(2–3), pp. 143–61.   [G: U.S.S.R.]

Lester, Richard A. Manipulation of the Labor Market. In *Somers, G. G., ed.*, 1973, pp. 47–55.
[G: U.S.]

Matiukha, I. The Rise in Living Standards of Working People in the USSR. *Prob. Econ.*, September 1973, *16*(5), pp. 60–71.   [G: U.S.S.R.]

Meidner, Rudolf and Andersson, Rolf. The Overall Impact of an Active Labor Market Policy in Sweden. In *Ulman, L., ed.*, 1973, pp. 117–58.
[G: Sweden]

van der Merwe, P. J. Manpower Policy in South Africa. *Finance Trade Rev.*, December 1972-June 1973, *10*(2–3), pp. 73–135.   [G: S. Africa]

Oldham, James C. Organized Labor, the Environment, and the Taft-Hartley Act. *Mich. Law Rev.*, April 1973, *71*(5), pp. 935–1040.   [G: U.S.]

Popovici, Otilia. Perfecționarea remunerării muncii. (Improving the Pay for Work. With English summary.) *Stud. Cercet. Econ.*, 1973, (2), pp. 117–26.
[G: Rumania]

Rehnberg, Bertil. Active Manpower Policy in Sweden. In *Moskoff, W., ed.*, 1973, pp. 85–91.
[G: Sweden]

Richardson, Reed C. The Impact of Denver's Manpower Programs. In *Mangum, G. L. and Robson, R. T., eds.*, 1973, pp. 134–43.   [G: U.S.]

Roomkin, Myron. Economic Effects of Basic Education for Adults: The Milwaukee MDTA Experience. *Quart. Rev. Econ. Bus.*, Spring 1973, *13*(1), pp. 87–96.   [G: U.S.]

Rosenthal, Albert J. Employment Discrimination and the Law. *Ann. Amer. Acad. Polit. Soc. Sci.*, May 1973, *407*, pp. 91–101.   [G: U.S.]

Steenkamp, W. F. J. Labour and Management in Manufacturing Development. *S. Afr. J. Econ.*, December 1973, *41*(4), pp. 438–51.   [G: S.Africa]

Takagi, Tadao. Il problema salariale in Giappone. (Wage Problems in Japan. With English summary.) *Rivista Int. Sci. Econ. Com.,* August-September 1973, *20*(8–9), pp. 804–38. [G: Japan]

Taylor, George W. Collective Bargaining in the Public Sector. In *Somers, G. G., ed.,* 1973, pp. 27–35. [G: U.S.]

Tuller, S. Mark. New Standards for Domination and Support under Section 8(a)(2). *Yale Law J.,* January 1973, *82*(3), pp. 510–32. [G: U.S.]

Weissbrodt, Sylvia R. Changes in State Labor Laws in 1972. *Mon. Lab. Rev.,* January 1973, *96*(1), pp. 27–36. [G: U.S.]

Wilson, Thomas. Pensions, Inflation and Growth. *Lloyds Bank Rev.,* April 1973, (108), pp. 1–17. [G: U.K.]

Wollheim, Richard. John Stuart Mill and the Limits of State Action. *Soc. Res.,* Spring 1973, *40*(1), pp. 1–30.

8221 Wages and Hours

Adie, Douglas K. Teen-Age Unemployment and Real Federal Minimum Wages. *J. Polit. Econ.,* Part I, March-April 1973, *81*(2), pp. 435–41. [G: U.S.]

Annable, James E., Jr. and Fruitman, Frederick H. An Earnings Function for High-Level Manpower. *Ind. Lab. Relat. Rev.,* July 1973, *26*(4), pp. 1107–21.

Fisher, Alan A. The Minimum Wage and Teenage Unemployment: A Comment on the Literature. *Western Econ. J.,* December 1973, *11*(4), pp. 514–24. [G: U.S.]

Fusfeld, Daniel R. A Living Wage. *Ann. Amer. Acad. Polit. Soc. Sci.,* September 1973, *409,* pp. 34–41. [G: U.S.]

Greenwald, Carol S. Maternity Leave Policy. *New Eng. Econ. Rev.,* January-February 1973, pp. 13–18. [G: U.S.]

Hedges, Janice Neipert. New Patterns for Working Time. *Mon. Lab. Rev.,* February 1973, *96*(2), pp. 3–8. [G: U.S.; W. Europe]

Katz, Arnold. Teenage Employment Effects of State Minimum Wages. *J. Human Res.,* Spring 1973, *8*(2), pp. 250–56. [G: U.S.]

Lovell, Michael C. The Minimum Wage Reconsidered. *Western Econ. J.,* December 1973, *11*(4), pp. 529–37. [G: U.S.]

Mattila, J. Peter. The Effects of Extending Minimum Wages to Cover Household Maids. *J. Human Res.,* Summer 1973, *8*(3), pp. 365–82. [G: U.S.]

Steindl, Frank G. The Appeal of Minimum Wage Laws and the Invisible Hand in Government. *Public Choice,* Spring 1973, *14,* pp. 133–36.

Zucker, Albert. Minimum Wages and the Long-run Elasticity of Demand for Low-Wage Labor. *Quart. J. Econ.,* May 1973, *87*(2), pp. 267–77. [G: U.S.]

8222 Workmen's Compensation

Anderson, Maxine. Broad Accident Compensation Law Enacted in New Zealand. *Mon. Lab. Rev.,* August 1973, *96*(8), pp. 77–78. [G: New Zealand]

Johnson, Florence C. Changes in Workmen's Compensation Laws in 1972. *Mon. Lab. Rev.,* January

1973, *96*(1), pp. 45–49. [G: U.S.]

Lees, Dennis and Doherty, Neil. Compensation for Personal Injury. *Lloyds Bank Rev.,* April 1973, (108), pp. 18–32. [G: U.K.]

Malisoff, Harry. Beyond the Limits of State Workmen's Compensation: Comment. *J. Risk Ins.,* June 1973, *40*(2), pp. 287–90.

8223 Factory Act and Safety Legislation

Christenson, C. L. and Andrews, W. H. Coal Mine Injury Rates in Two Eras of Federal Control. *J. Econ. Issues,* March 1973, *7*(1), pp. 61–82. [G: U.S.]

Collier, Joe. Inspection and Enforcement at the Workplace. *Mon. Lab. Rev.,* August 1973, *96*(8), pp. 35–42. [G: U.S.]

Foulkes, Fred K. Learning to Live with OSHA. *Harvard Bus. Rev.,* November-December 1973, *51* (6), pp. 57–67. [G: U.S.]

Goff, Phoebe H. Disabled-Worker Beneficiaries Under OASDHI: Regional and State Patterns. *Soc. Sec. Bull.,* September 1973, *36*(9), pp. 3–23. [G: U.S.]

Graebner, William. The Coal-Mine Operator and Safety: A Study of Business Reform in the Progressive Period. *Labor Hist.,* Fall 1973, *14*(4), pp. 483–505. [G: U.S.]

Greenberg, L. The Enforcement of Occupational Safety Legislation. *Int. Lab. Rev.,* May 1973, *107* (5), pp. 425–40.

Hohn, Herbert M. Research to Determine What's Dangerous. *Mon. Lab. Rev.,* August 1973, *96*(8), pp. 48–52. [G: U.S.]

Inzana, John T. The New Survey of Occupational Injuries and Illnesses. *Mon. Lab. Rev.,* August 1973, *96*(8), pp. 53–55. [G: U.S.]

Kirkpatrick, Elizabeth K. No-Fault Accident Compensation in New Zealand. *Soc. Sec. Bull.,* September 1973, *36*(9), pp. 25–29. [G: New Zealand]

Lawler, Edward E., III. Quality of Working Life and Social Accounts. In *Dierkes, M. and Bauer, R. A., eds.,* 1973, pp. 154–65. [G: U.S.]

Schmidt, Herbert. Governmental Regulations and Quality of Work Environment. In *Dierkes, M. and Bauer, R. A., eds.,* 1973, pp. 191–211. [G: Germany]

Seymour, Sally. Forging a Partnership with the States. *Mon. Lab. Rev.,* August 1973, *96*(8), pp. 28–34. [G: U.S.]

Tavela, John. If a Citation is Appealed. *Mon. Lab. Rev.,* August 1973, *96*(8), pp. 43–47. [G: U.S.]

8224 Unemployment Insurance

Hickey, Joseph A. State Unemployment Insurance Laws: Status Report. *Mon. Lab. Rev.,* January 1973, *96*(1), pp. 37–44. [G: U.S.]

Rosow, Jerome M. Work Requirements in Welfare and Unemployment Insurance. *Mon. Lab. Rev.,* April 1973, *96*(4), pp. 56–57. [G: U.S.]

8225 Employment Services

Balassa, Bela. Policy Issues in Adjustment Assistance: The United States: Comment. In *Hughes, H., ed.,* 1973, pp. 180–86.

Baldwin, Robert and Mutti, John H. Policy Issues in Adjustment Assistance: The United States. In *Hughes, H., ed.,* 1973, pp. 149–77. [G: U.S.]

Barkai, Haim. The European Economic Community Approach to Adjustment: Comment. In *Hughes, H., ed.,* 1973, pp. 217–22. [G: E.E.C.]

Braun, Ferdnand. The European Economic Community Approach to Adjustment. In *Hughes, H., ed.,* 1973, pp. 187–216. [G: E.E.C.]

Caffè, Federico. Considerazioni sul problema della disoccupazione in Italia. (On Unemployment in Italy. With English summary.) *Rivista Int. Sci. Econ. Com.,* January 1973, *20*(1), pp. 6–17. [G: Italy]

Craft, James A. Racial and Occupational Aspects of Public Employment Service Placements. *Quart. Rev. Econ. Bus.,* Autumn 1973, *13*(3), pp. 53–60. [G: U.S.]

Donges, Juergen B. The European Economic Community Approach to Adjustment: Comment. In *Hughes, H., ed.,* 1973, pp. 222–27. [G: E.E.C.]

Epstein, E. and Monat, J. Labour Contracting and Its Regulation: II. *Int. Lab. Rev.,* June 1973, *107*(6), pp. 513–28.

Epstein, E. and Monat, J. Labour Contracting and Its Regulation: I. *Int. Lab. Rev.,* May 1973, *107*(5), pp. 451–70.

Gallardo, Lloyd. Development of Bay Area Manpower Institutions. In *Mangum, G. L. and Robson, R. T., eds.,* 1973, pp. 154–75. [G: U.S.]

Gallardo, Lloyd. Evaluating Bay Area Manpower Programs. In *Mangum, G. L. and Robson, R. T., eds.,* 1973, pp. 176–201. [G: U.S.]

Hinton, Deane. Policy Issues in Adjustment Assistance: The United States: Comment. In *Hughes, H., ed.,* 1973, pp. 177–80.

Horowitz, Morris A. and Herrnstadt, Irwin L. Boston's Manpower Institutions. In *Mangum, G. L. and Robson, R. T., eds.,* 1973, pp. 23–48. [G: U.S.]

Horowitz, Morris A. and Herrnstadt, Irwin L. Institutional and Labor Market Impact of Manpower Programs. In *Mangum, G. L. and Robson, R. T., eds.,* 1973, pp. 76–92. [G: U.S.]

Horowitz, Morris A. and Herrnstadt, Irwin L. Training and Jobs for Boston's Disadvantaged. In *Mangum, G. L. and Robson, R. T., eds.,* 1973, pp. 49–75. [G: U.S.]

Levitan, Sar A. Manpower Programs for a Healthier Economy. In *Ulman, L., ed.,* 1973, pp. 102–16. [G: U.S.]

Myers, Charles A. Manpower Policies in the U.S. In *Somers, G. G., ed.,* 1973, pp. 72–82. [G: U.S.]

O'Neill, Dave M. Manpower. In *Ott, D. J., et al.,* 1973, pp. 153–70.

Richardson, Reed C. Delivery Systems for Manpower Services. In *Mangum, G. L. and Robson, R. T., eds.,* 1973, pp. 100–119. [G: U.S.]

Valticos, Nicolas. Temporary Work Agencies and International Labour Standards. *Int. Lab. Rev.,* January 1973, *107*(1), pp. 43–56.

Veldkamp, Gérard M. J. and Raetsen, M. J. E. H. Temporary Work Agencies and Western European Social Legislation. *Int. Lab. Rev.,* February 1973, *107*(2), pp. 117–31. [G: Sweden; Denmark; Belgium; W. Germany; Netherlands]

Williams, T. David and Ntim, S. M. Public Employ-ment Centres as a Source of Data on Unemployment in Ghana. *Econ. Bull. Ghana, Sec. Ser.,* 1973, *3*(1), pp. 16–26. [G: Ghana]

8226 Employment in Public Sector

Ahmad, Muneer. The Political Context of Civil Service Reorganization in Pakistan. *Pakistan Econ. Soc. Rev.,* Summer 1973, *11*(2), pp. 167–92. [G: Pakistan]

Anderman, Steven D. International Manual on Collective Bargaining for Public Employees: Sweden. In *Kaye, S. P. and Marsh, A., eds.,* 1973, pp. 264–99. [G: Sweden]

Bleakney, Thomas P. Problems and Issues in Public Employee Retirement Systems. *J. Risk Ins.,* March 1973, *40*(1), pp. 39–46. [G: U.S.]

Brinkmann, Gerhard. Die Diskriminierung der Nicht-Juristen im allgemeinen höheren Verwaltungsdienst der Bundesrepublik Deutschland. (The Discrimination of Non-lawyers in the General Higher Civil Service of the German Federal Republic. With English summary.) *Z. ges. Staatswiss.,* February 1973, *129*(1), pp. 150–67. [G: W. Germany; U.S.]

Ehrenberg, Ronald G. Heterogeneous Labor, Minimum Hiring Standards, and Job Vacancies in Public Employment. *J. Polit. Econ.,* November-December 1973, *81*(6), pp. 1442–50. [G: U.S.]

Ehrenberg, Ronald G. The Demand for State and Local Government Employees. *Amer. Econ. Rev.,* June 1973, *63*(3), pp. 366–79. [G: U.S.]

Gallardo, Lloyd. Evaluating Bay Area Manpower Programs. In *Mangum, G. L. and Robson, R. T., eds.,* 1973, pp. 176–201. [G: U.S.]

Gillespie, Hugh. Problems and Issues in Public Employee Retirement Systems: Discussion. *J. Risk Ins.,* March 1973, *40*(1), pp. 50–53. [G: U.S.]

Horowitz, Morris A. and Herrnstadt, Irwin L. Training and Jobs for Boston's Disadvantaged. In *Mangum, G. L. and Robson, R. T., eds.,* 1973, pp. 49–75. [G: U.S.]

Jackson, Dudley and Turner, H. A. How to Provide More Employment in a Labour-Surplus Economy. *Int. Lab. Rev.,* April 1973, *107*(4), pp. 315–38. [G: Morocco]

Kochan, Thomas A. Correlates of State Public Employee Bargaining Laws. *Ind. Relat.,* October 1973, *12*(3), pp. 322–37. [G: U.S.]

Lewin, David. Public Employment Relations: Confronting the Issues. *Ind. Relat.,* October 1973, *12*(3), pp. 309–21. [G: U.S.]

Myers, Charles A. Manpower Policies in the U.S. In *Somers, G. G., ed.,* 1973, pp. 72–82. [G: U.S.]

Ross, Kenneth H. Problems and Issues in Public Employee Retirement Systems: Discussion. *J. Risk Ins.,* March 1973, *40*(1), pp. 46–50. [G: U.S.]

Staudohar, Paul D. The Emergence of Hawaii's Public Employment Law. *Ind. Relat.,* October 1973, *12*(3), pp. 338–51. [G: U.S.]

Stern, James L. Bargaining and Arbitration in the British Civil Service. *Mon. Lab. Rev.,* August 1973, *96*(8), pp. 61–63. [G: U.K.]

Thomas, R. B. On the Definition of 'Shortages' in Administered Labour Markets. *Manchester Sch.*

Econ. Soc. Stud., June 1973, *41*(2), pp. 169–86.
[G: U.K.]

823 Labor Mobility; National and International Migration

8230 Labor Mobility; National and International Migration

Baraquin, Yves and Jobert, Annette. Les immigrés: Réflexions sur leur insertion sociale et leur intégration juridique. (Immigrants: Their Social Insertion and Juridical Integration. With English summary.) *Consommation*, July-September 1973, *20*(3), pp. 83–97.

Beale, Calvin L. Migration Patterns of Minorities in the United States. *Amer. J. Agr. Econ.*, December 1973, *55*(5), pp. 938–46. [G: U.S.]

Bhagwati, Jagdish N. and Dellalfar, William. The Brain Drain and Income Taxation. *World Devel.*, February 1973, *1*(1-2), pp. 94–101.

Black, R. D. Collison. Emigrazione e colonizzazione. (Emigration and Colonization. With English summary.) *Rivista Int. Sci. Econ. Com.*, November 1973, *20*(11), pp. 1071–80. [G: U.K.; Ireland]

Boye-Møller, Monica. Language Training for Immigrant Workers in Sweden. *Int. Lab. Rev.*, December 1973, *108*(6), pp. 505–15. [G: Sweden]

Brawner, Marlyn R. Migration and Educational Achievement of Mexican Americans. *Soc. Sci. Quart.*, March 1973, *53*(4), pp. 727–37. [G: U.S.]

Brechling, Frank. Wage Inflation and the Structure of Regional Unemployment. *J. Money, Credit, Banking*, Part II, February 1973, *5*(1), pp. 355–79.

Burki, Shahid J. Employment Creating Urban Public Works Programmes: Outline of a Strategy. *Pakistan Develop. Rev.*, Autumn 1973, *12*(3), pp. 293–310.

Cebula, Richard J. On Migration, Migration Costs, and Wage Differentials, with Special Reference to the United States. *Schweiz. Z. Volkswirtsch. Statist.*, March 1973, *109*(1), pp. 59–68. [G: U.S.]

Cebula, Richard J. and Gatons, Paul K. Interregional Factor Prices and Mobility. *Pakistan Econ. Soc. Rev.*, Summer 1973, *11*(2), pp. 207–14. [G: U.S.]

Cebula, Richard J.; Kohn, Robert M. and Vedder, Richard K. Some Determinants of Interstate Migration of Blacks, 1965–1970. *Western Econ. J.*, December 1973, *11*(4), pp. 500–05. [G: U.S.]

Cebula, Richard J. and Vedder, Richard K. A Note on Migration, Economic Opportunity, and the Quality of Life. *J. Reg. Sci.*, August 1973, *13*(2), pp. 205–11. [G: U.S.]

Cebula, Richard J.; Kohn, Robert M. and Gallaway, Lowell E. Determinants of Net Migration to SMSA's, 1960–1970. *Miss. Val. J. Bus. Econ.*, Winter 1973-74, *9*(2), pp. 59–64. [G: U.S.]

Conroy, J. D. Urbanization in Papua New Guinea: A Development Constraint. *Econ. Rec.*, March 1973, *49*(125), pp. 76–88. [G: New Guinea]

Dutta, Amita. Migration in a Trading Economy. *J. Devel. Stud.*, October 1973, *10*(1), pp. 79–91. [G: Ceylon]

Eastman, Clyde, et al. Labor Mobility in Northcentral New Mexico. *N. Mex. Bus.*, June 1973, *26*(6), pp. 3–9. [G: U.S.]

Elovikov, L. A. Ways of Creating Social and Economic Conditions for the Reproduction of Labor Power in the New Regions of the West Siberian Plains. *Prob. Econ.*, June 1973, *16*(2), pp. 42–54. [G: U.S.S.R.]

Evsiukov, Iu. Migration of the Population from the Countryside to the City (Problems of Analysis and Forecasting). *Prob. Econ.*, June 1973, *16*(2), pp. 14–25. [G: U.S.S.R.]

Frank, Charles R., Jr. Trade, Investment and Labor, and the Changing International Division of Production: Comment. In *Hughes, H., ed.*, 1973, pp. 61–68.

Gallaway, Lowell E. and Cebula, Richard J. Differentials and Indeterminacy in Wage Rate Analysis: An Empirical Note. *Ind. Lab. Relat. Rev.*, April 1973, *26*(3), pp. 991–95.

Gallaway, Lowell E.; Rydén, Rune and Vedder, Richard K. Internal Labor Migration in Sweden, 1967. *Swedish J. Econ.*, September 1973, *75*(3), pp. 257–65. [G: Sweden]

Ghai, Yash and Ghai, Dharam P. The Asian Minorities of East and Central Africa. In *Whitaker, B., ed.*, 1973, pp. 24–72. [G: Africa]

Godfrey, E. M. Economic Variables and Rural-Urban Migration: Some Thoughts on the Todaro Hypothesis. *J. Devel. Stud.*, October 1973, *10*(1), pp. 66–78.

Greenwood, Michael J. The Geographic Mobility of College Graduates. *J. Human Res.*, Fall 1973, *8*(4), pp. 506–15. [G: U.S.]

Gupta, M. L. Outflow of High-Level Manpower from the Philippines, with Special Reference to the Period 1965-71. *Int. Lab. Rev.*, February 1973, *107*(2), pp. 167–91. [G: Philippines]

Haran, E. G. P. and Vining, Daniel R., Jr. A Modified Yule-Simon Model Allowing for Intercity Migration and Accounting for the Observed Form of the Size Distribution of Cities. *J. Reg. Sci.*, December 1973, *13*(3), pp. 421–37. [G: U.S.]

Haynes, Kingsley E.; Poston, Dudley L., Jr. and Schnirring, Paul. Intermetropolitan Migration in High and Low Opportunity Areas: Indirect Tests of the Distance and Intervening Opportunities Hypotheses. *Econ. Geogr.*, January 1973, *49*(1), pp. 68–73.

Holland, David W. and Tweeten, Luther G. Human Capital Migration: Implications for Common School Finance. *Land Econ.*, August 1973, *49*(3), pp. 278–84. [G: U.S.]

Holt, Charles C. Wage Inflation and the Structure of Regional Unemployment: Comment. *J. Money, Credit, Banking*, Part II, February 1973, *5*(1), pp. 380–81.

Johnson, Harry G. Trade, Investment and Labor, and the Changing International Division of Production. In *Hughes, H., ed.*, 1973, pp. 40–55.

Kao, Charles H. C. and Lee, Jae Won. An Empirical Analysis of China's Brain Drain into the United States. *Econ. Develop. Cult. Change*, April 1973, *21*(3), pp. 500–13. [G: China; U.S.]

Karlik, John. Trade, Investment and Labor, and the Changing International Division of Production:

Comment. In *Hughes, H., ed.*, 1973, pp. 56–61.

Kim, S. Rural-Urban Migration and Technological Changes in the Agriculture of a Developing Country. *Econ. Rec.*, March 1973, *49*(125), pp. 15–23.

Kohn, Robert M. On Migration, Migration Costs, and Wage Differentials: A Comment. *Schweiz. Z. Volkswirtsch. Statist.*, December 1973, *109*(4), pp. 603–04. [G: U.S.]

Laber, Gene. Human Capital in Southern Migration. *J. Human Res.*, Spring 1973, *8*(2), pp. 223–41. [G: U.S.]

Ladenkov, V. N. Studies of Migration of Skilled Personnel in Agriculture. *Prob. Econ.*, February 1973, *15*(10), pp. 62–80. [G: U.S.S.R.]

Lal, Deepak. Disutility of Effort, Migration, and the Shadow Wage-rate. *Oxford Econ. Pap.*, March 1973, *25*(1), pp. 112–26.

Leuschner, Dieter. Volkswirtschaftliche Kosten und Erträge der Beschäftigung ausländischer Arbeitnehmer. (With English summary.) *Z. ges. Staatswiss.*, October 1973, *129*(4), pp. 702–13. [G: W. Germany]

Levi, J. F. S. Migration from the Land and Urban Unemployment in Sierra Leone. *Oxford Bull. Econ. Statist.*, November 1973, *35*(4), pp. 309–26. [G: Sierra Leone]

Levy, Mildred B. and Wadycki, Walter J. The Influence of Family and Friends on Geographic Labor Mobility: An International Comparison. *Rev. Econ. Statist.*, May 1973, *55*(2), pp. 198–203. [G: Venezuela]

Long, Larry H. New Estimates of Migration Expectancy in the United States. *J. Amer. Statist. Assoc.*, March 1973, *68*(341), pp. 37–43. [G: U.S.]

Lubell, Harold. Urban Development and Employment in Calcutta. *Int. Lab. Rev.*, July 1973, *108* (1), pp. 25–41. [G: India]

Lucas, Robert E., Jr. Wage Inflation and the Structure of Regional Unemployment: Comment. *J. Money, Credit, Banking*, Part II, February 1973, *5*(1), pp. 382–84.

Mas-Colell, Andreu and Razin, Assaf. A Model of Intersectoral Migration and Growth. *Oxford Econ. Pap.*, March 1973, *25*(1), pp. 72–79.

van der Merwe, P. J. Manpower Policy in South Africa. *Finance Trade Rev.*, December 1972-June 1973, *10*(2–3), pp. 73–135. [G: S. Africa]

Miller, Edward. Return and Nonreturn In-Migration. *Growth Change*, January 1973, *4*(1), pp. 3–9. [G: U.S.]

Miller, Edward. The Flight of the Native Born. *Growth Change*, October 1973, *4*(4), pp. 10–15. [G: U.S.]

Miller, Edward. Is Out-Migration Affected by Economic Conditions? *Southern Econ. J.*, January 1973, *39*(3), pp. 396–405. [G: U. S.]

Morrison, Peter A. A Demographic Assessment of New Cities and Growth Centers as Population Redistribution Strategies. *Public Policy*, Summer 1973, *21*(3), pp. 367–82. [G: U.S.]

Niemi, Albert W., Jr. Returns to Educated Blacks Resulting from Southern Outmigration. *Southern Econ. J.*, October 1973, *40*(2), pp. 330–32. [G: U.S.]

Oh, Tai K. Estimating the Migration of U.S.-

Educated Manpower from Asia to the United States. *Soc. Econ. Stud.*, September 1973, *22*(3), pp. 335–57. [G: Asia; U.S.]

Perkins, Brian B. Farm Income and Labour Mobility. *Amer. J. Agr. Econ.*, December 1973, *55*(5), pp. 913–20. [G: Canada]

Raymond, Richard. The Interregional Brain Drain and Public Education. *Growth Change*, July 1973, *4*(3), pp. 28–34. [G: U.S.]

Riew, John. Migration and Public Policy. *J. Reg. Sci.*, April 1973, *13*(1), pp. 65–76.

Roche, D. J. D., et al. Some Determinants of Labour Mobility in Northern Ireland. *Econ. Soc. Rev.*, October 1973, *5*(1), pp. 59–73. [G: Ireland]

Schwartz, Aba. Interpreting the Effect of Distance on Migration. *J. Polit. Econ.*, September-October 1973, *81*(5), pp. 1153–69. [G: U.S.]

Sen, Amartya K. Brain Drain: Causes and Effects. In *Williams, B. R., ed.*, 1973, pp. 385–404. [G: U.S.]

Shearer, John C. High-Level Human Resources in Latin American Development. In *Thurber, C. E. and Graham, L. S., eds.*, 1973, pp. 133–47. [G: U.S.; S. America]

Sommers, Paul M. and Suits, Daniel B. Analysis of Net Interstate Migration. *Southern Econ. J.*, October 1973, *40*(2), pp. 193–201. [G: U.S.]

Songre, Ambroise. Mass Emigration from Upper Volta: The Facts and Implications. *Int. Lab. Rev.*, August-September 1973, *108*(2–3), pp. 209–25. [G: Upper Volta]

Stewart, Charles T. and Benson, Virginia. Job Migration Linkages Between Smaller SMSAs and Their Hinterlands. *Land Econ.*, November 1973, *49*(4), pp. 432–39. [G: U.S.]

Taqieddin, Nureddin and Gardner, B. Delworth. Net Migration and Population Distribution in the State of Utah. *Intermountain Econ. Rev.*, Fall 1973, *4*(2), pp. 32–44. [G: U.S.]

Truu, M. L. Some Effects of Regional Migration. *S. Afr. J. Econ.*, June 1973, *41*(2), pp. 98–110. [G: S. Africa]

Vandendries, René. Internal Migration and Economic Development in Peru. In *Scott, R. E., ed.*, 1973, pp. 193–207. [G: Peru]

Völker, Gottfried E. Impact of Turkish Labour Migration on the Economy of the Federal Republic of Germany. *Ger. Econ. Rev.*, 1973, *11*(1), pp. 61–77. [G: W. Germany]

Waters, Alan Rufus. Migration, Remittances, and the Cash Constraint in African Smallholder Economic Development. *Oxford Econ. Pap.*, November 1973, *25*(3), pp. 435–54. [G: Africa]

Whitehouse, F. Douglas. Demographic Aspects of Regional Economic Development in the USSR. In *Bandera, V. N. and Melnyk, Z. L., eds.*, 1973, pp. 154–66. [G: U.S.S.R.]

Zimmer, Basil G. Residential Mobility and Housing. *Land Econ.*, August 1973, *49*(3), pp. 344–50. [G: U.S.]

824 Labor Market Studies, Wages, Employment

8240 General

Bauer, David. Low Unemployment Rates Abroad. In *Moskoff, W., ed.*, 1973, pp. 76–85.

Behrman, Jere R. and Mujica, Jorge G. A Study of Quarterly Nominal Wage Change Determination in an Inflationary Developing Economy. In *Eckaus, R. S. and Rosenstein-Rodan, P. N., eds.*, 1973, pp. 399–416. [G: Chile]

Bergmann, Barbara R. and Adelman, Irma. The 1973 Report of the President's Council of Economic Advisers: The Economic Role of Women. *Amer. Econ. Rev.*, September 1973, *63*(4), pp. 509–14. [G: U.S.]

Bosanquet, Nicholas and Doeringer, Peter B. Is There a Dual Labour Market in Great Britain? *Econ. J.*, June 1973, *83*(330), pp. 421–35. [G: U.K.]

Cherry, Robert. Class Struggle and the Nature of the Working Class. *Rev. Radical Polit. Econ.*, Summer 1973, *5*(2), pp. 47–86. [G: U.S.]

Comanor, William S. Racial Discrimination in American Industry. *Economica, N.S.*, November 1973, *40*(160), pp. 363–78.

Dadi, M. M. Labour's Share in Indian Industry: Theory and Fact. *Indian Econ. J.*, January-March 1973, *20*(3), pp. 500–14. [G: India]

Daly, Herman E. Electric Power, Employment, and Economic Growth: A Case Study in Growthmania. In *Daly, H. E., ed.*, 1973, pp. 252–77. [G: U.S.]

Davies, David G. A Critical Discussion of I.L.O. Report on Employment in Kenya. *Pakistan Develop. Rev.*, Autumn 1973, *12*(3), pp. 283–92. [G: Kenya]

Davis, Otto A., et al. An Empirical Study of the NAB-JOBS Program. *Public Policy*, Spring 1973, *21*(2), pp. 235–62. [G: U.S.]

Divilov, S. Labor Resources and the Comparison of General Economic Indices by Union Republic. *Prob. Econ.*, March 1973, *15*(11), pp. 63–72. [G: U.S.S.R.]

Dougherty, Christopher and Selowsky, Marcelo. Measuring the Effects of the Misallocation of Labour. *Rev. Econ. Statist.*, August 1973, *55*(3), pp. 386–90. [G: Colombia]

Durbin, Elizabeth. Work and Welfare: The Case of Aid to Families with Dependent Children. *J. Human Res.*, Supplement 1973, *8*, pp. 103–25. [G: U.S.]

Epstein, E. and Monat, J. Labour Contracting and Its Regulation: I. *Int. Lab. Rev.*, May 1973, *107*(5), pp. 451–70.

Estey, Marten. Wage Stabilization Policy and the Nixon Administration. In *Cagan, P., et al.*, 1973, pp. 107–33. [G: U.S.]

Evans, E. W. and Galambos, P. Work Stoppages in the United Kingdom 1965–70: A Quantitative Study. *Bull. Econ. Res.*, May 1973, *25*(1), pp. 22–42. [G: U.K.]

Evans, Robert, Jr. Education Levels and Unemployment in Asian Countries. *Mon. Lab. Rev.*, November 1973, *96*(11), pp. 58–59. [G: Asia]

Fellner, William J. Employment Goals and Monetary-Fiscal Overexpansion. In *Cagan, P., et al.*, 1973, pp. 135–72. [G: U.S.]

Fisher, Robert W. Labor in a Year of Economic Stabilization. *Mon. Lab. Rev.*, January 1973, *96*(1), pp. 17–26. [G: U.S.]

Flaim, Paul O. Employment Developments in the First Half of 1973. *Mon. Lab. Rev.*, September 1973, *96*(9), pp. 25–28. [G: U.S.]

Flanagan, Robert J. Racial Wage Discrimination and Employment Segregation. *J. Human Res.*, Fall 1973, *8*(4), pp. 456–71. [G: U.S.]

Freeman, Richard B. Decline of Labor Market Discrimination and Economic Analysis. *Amer. Econ. Rev.*, May 1973, *63*(2), pp. 280–86.

Godfrey, Leslie G. and Taylor, Jim. Earnings Changes in the United Kingdom, 1954–70: Excess Labour Supply, Expected Inflation and Union Influence. *Oxford Bull. Econ. Statist.*, August 1973, *35*(3), pp. 197–216. [G: U.K.]

Gramm, Wendy Lee. The Labor Force Decision of Married Female Teachers: A Discriminant Analysis Approach. *Rev. Econ. Statist.*, August 1973, *55*(3), pp. 341–48. [G: U.S.]

Green, Gloria P. and Stinson, John F. Changes in the Employment Situation in 1972. *Mon. Lab. Rev.*, February 1973, *96*(2), pp. 24–34. [G: U.S.]

Hall, Robert E. and Kasten, Richard A. The Relative Occupational Success of Blacks and Whites. *Brookings Pap. Econ. Act.*, 1973, (3), pp. 781–95. [G: U.S.]

Hamblin, Mary and Prell, Michael J. Income of Men and Women: Why Do They Differ? *Fed. Res. Bank Kansas City Rev.*, April 1973, pp. 3–11. [G: U.S.]

Hause, John C. Enlistment Rates for Military Service and Unemployment. *J. Human Res.*, Winter 1973, *8*(1), pp. 98–109. [G: U.S.]

Hedrick, Charles L. Expectations and the Labor Supply. *Amer. Econ. Rev.*, December 1973, *63*(5), pp. 968–74. [G: U.S.]

Héthy, Lajos and Makó, Csaba. Incentive Problems in the Centrally Planned Economy of Hungary. *Ind. Lab. Relat. Rev.*, January 1973, *26*(2), pp. 767–77. [G: Hungary]

Hsieh, C. Measuring the Effects of Trade Expansion on Employment: A Review of Some Research. *Int. Lab. Rev.*, January 1973, *107*(1), pp. 1–29.

Hsieh, C. Measuring the Effects of Trade Expansion on Employment: A Review of Some Research. *Int. Lab. Rev.*, January 1973, *107*(1), pp. 1–29.

Jackson, Dudley and Turner, H. A. How to Provide More Employment in a Labour-Surplus Economy. *Int. Lab. Rev.*, April 1973, *107*(4), pp. 315–38. [G: Morocco]

Kaplan, H. Roy. How Do Workers View Their Work in America? *Mon. Lab. Rev.*, June 1973, *96*(6), pp. 46–48. [G: U.S.]

Kasper, H. Measuring the Labour Market Costs of Housing Dislocation. *Scot. J. Polit. Econ.*, June 1973, *20*(2), pp. 85–106. [G: U.K.]

Klein, Deborah P. Exploring the Adequacy of Employment. *Mon. Lab. Rev.*, October 1973, *96*(10), pp. 3–9. [G: U.S.]

Kotek, Miloslav. Employment Trends in Czechoslovakia. *Czech. Econ. Digest.*, August 1973, (5), pp. 44–63. [G: Czechoslovakia]

Lee, Ronald. Population in Preindustrial England: An Econometric Analysis. *Quart. J. Econ.*, November 1973, *87*(4), pp. 581–607. [G: U.K.]

Levitan, S. A. and Taggart, R. Employment-Earnings Inadequacy: A Measure of Welfare. *Mon. Lab. Rev.*, October 1973, *96*(10), pp. 19–27. [G: U.S.]

Levitan, Sar A. and Johnston, William B. Job Redesign, Reform, Enrichment: Exploring the Limitations. *Mon. Lab. Rev.,* July 1973, *96*(7), pp. 35–41. [G: U.S.]

Mabry, Bevars D. The Economics of Fringe Benefits. *Ind. Relat.,* February 1973, *12*(1), pp. 95–106.

Matiukha, I. The Rise in Living Standards of Working People in the USSR. *Prob. Econ.,* September 1973, *16*(5), pp. 60–71. [G: U.S.S.R.]

McCormick, B. J. Trade Unions and Wage Inflation in the UK: A Reappraisal: Discussion. In *Parkin, M., ed.,* 1973, pp. 328–29. [G: U.K.]

Michelotti, Kopp. Young Workers: In School and Out. *Mon. Lab. Rev.,* September 1973, *96*(9), pp. 11–15. [G: U.S.]

Mohindru, Rajesh K. The Structural Unemployment Controversy Revisited. *J. Econ. Bus.,* Winter 1973, *25*(2), pp. 122–26. [G: U.S.]

Mulvey, C. and Trevithick, J. A. Trade Unions and Wage Inflation. *Econ. Soc. Rev.,* January 1973, *4*(2), pp. 209–29.

Okun, Arthur M. Upward Mobility in a High-pressure Economy. *Brookings Pap. Econ. Act.,* 1973, (1), pp. 207–52. [G: U.S.]

Pang, Eng Fong. A Note on Labour Underutilization in Singapore. *Malayan Econ. Rev.,* April 1973, *18*(1), pp. 15–23. [G: Singapore]

Paraskevopoulos, Christos C. The Impact of Regional Wage Differentials. *Growth Change,* April 1973, *4*(2), pp. 40–42. [G: U.S.]

Parkin, Michael. The Short-Run and Long-Run Trade-Offs Between Inflation and Unemployment in Australia. *Australian Econ. Pap.,* December 1973, *12*(21), pp. 127–44. [G: Australia]

Personick, Martin E. Earnings Rise as Employment Dips in Petroleum and Gas. *Mon. Lab. Rev.,* August 1973, *96*(8), pp. 68–70. [G: U.S.]

Powell, C. Randall. The Indiana MBA: Where Is He? *Indiana Bus. Rev.,* July-August 1973, *48*, pp. 8–11. [G: U.S.]

Purdy, D. L. and Zis, G. Trade Unions and Wage Inflation in the UK: A Reappraisal. In *Parkin, M., ed.,* 1973, pp. 294–327. [G: U.K.]

Quinn, Robert P., et al. Evaluating Working Conditions in America. *Mon. Lab. Rev.,* November 1973, *96*(11), pp. 32–41. [G: U.S.]

Randall, J. N. Shift-Share Analysis as a Guide to the Employment Performance of West Central Scotland. *Scot. J. Polit. Econ.,* February 1973, *20*(1), pp. 1–26. [G: U.K.]

Ridzon, Donald S. Wages and Productivity Rise as Employment Falls in Cigar Plants. *Mon. Lab. Rev.,* June 1973, *96*(6), pp. 56–57. [G: U.S.]

Ryscavage, P. M. and Mellor, Earl F. The Economic Situation of Spanish Americans. *Mon. Lab. Rev.,* April 1973, *96*(4), pp. 3–9. [G: U.S.]

Sawhill, Isabel V. The Economics of Discrimination Against Women: Some New Findings. *J. Human Res.,* Summer 1973, *8*(3), pp. 383–96. [G: U.S.]

Shea, John R. Welfare Mothers: Barriers to Labor Force Entry. *J. Human Res.,* Supplement 1973, *8*, pp. 90–102. [G: U.S.]

Sheppard, Harold L. Asking the Right Questions on Job Satisfaction. *Mon. Lab. Rev.,* April 1973, *96*(4), pp. 51–52. [G: U.S.]

Singer, Hans and Jolly, Richard. Unemployment in an African Setting: Lessons of the Employment Strategy Mission to Kenya. *Int. Lab. Rev.,* February 1973, *107*(2), pp. 103–15. [G: Kenya]

Smith, Curtis R. Will the Four-Day Week Work? *Fed. Res. Bank Bus. Rev. Phila.,* August 1973, pp. 14–21.

Sorkin, Alan L. On The Occupational Status of Women, 1870–1970. *Amer. J. Econ. Soc.,* July 1973, *32*(3), pp. 235–43. [G: U.S.]

Toms, Miroslav. The Labor Force and Relations Within the Production Process. *Eastern Europ. Econ.,* Summer 1973, *11*(4), pp. 3–59. [G: Czechoslovakia]

Wales, Terence J. Estimation of a Labor Supply Curve for Self-Employed Business Proprietors. *Int. Econ. Rev.,* February 1973, *14*(1), pp. 69–80. [G: U.S.]

Walter, Emil J. Technologische, wirtschaftliche und soziale Aspekte der wachsenden Bedeutung der Schichtarbeit. (Technological, Economic and Social Aspects of the Growing Importance of Shift Work. With English summary.) *Schweiz. Z. Volkswirtsch. Statist.,* March 1973, *109*(1), pp. 69–89. [G: Switzerland]

Winpisinger, William W. Job Enrichment: A Union View. *Mon. Lab. Rev.,* April 1973, *96*(4), pp. 54–56. [G: U.S.]

Wool, Harold. What's Wrong with Work in America?—A Review Essay. *Mon. Lab. Rev.,* March 1973, *96*(3), pp. 38–44. [G: U.S.]

8241 Specific Labor Market Studies

Bardhan, Pranab K. 'Green Revolution' and Agricultural Labourers. In *Wadhva, C. D., ed.,* 1973, pp. 346–61. [G: India]

Bergonzini, Luciano. Professionalità femminile e lavoro a domicilio: Questioni generali ed esiti di un'indagine statistica in alcuni comuni dell'Emilia-Romagna. (Women's Professional Status and Work at Home: Some General Questions and Some Results of a Statistical Inquiry in a Few Municipalities of the Emilia-Romagna Region (Italy). With English summary.) *Statistica,* October-December 1973, *33*(4), pp. 492–546. [G: Italy]

Bishop, Christine E. Manpower Policy and the Supply of Nurses. *Ind. Relat.,* February 1973, *12*(1), pp. 86–94. [G: U.S.]

Boddy, Francis M. The Market for Economists. *Amer. J. Agr. Econ.,* Part II, November 1973, *55*(4), pp. 720–24. [G: U.S.]

Bradley, Iver E.; Mangum, Garth L. and Robson, R. Thayne. Impact of Manpower Programs upon Employment and Earnings. In *Mangum, G. L. and Robson, R. T., eds.,* 1973, pp. 227–59. [G: U.S.]

Christensen, Andrea. White-collar Pay Up 5.4 Percent. *Mon. Lab. Rev.,* October 1973, *96*(10), pp. 53–55. [G: U.S.]

Coelho, Philip R. P. and Ghali, Moheb A. The End of the North-South Wage Differential: Reply. *Amer. Econ. Rev.,* September 1973, *63*(4), pp. 757–62. [G: U.S.]

Corry, B. A. Some Aspects of University Teachers' Labour Market in the UK: Discussion. In *Parkin,*

M., ed., 1973, pp. 212–13.   [G: U.K.]

Doyle, Philip M. Wages and Productivity Rise in Flour Mills as Employment Declines. *Mon. Lab. Rev.*, October 1973, *96*(10), pp. 51–52.
[G: U.S.]

Early, John F. Factors Affecting Trends in Real Spendable Earnings. *Mon. Lab. Rev.*, May 1973, *96*(5), pp. 16–19.   [G: U.S.]

Eaton, B. Curtis. The Individual and the Defense Mass-Layoff. In *Udis, B., ed.*, 1973, pp. 179–209.
[G: U.S.]

Fenske, G. A. and Main, T. R. N. Labour and the Gold Mines. *S. Afr. J. Econ.*, September 1973, *41* (3), pp. 298–304.   [G: S. Africa]

Fettig, L. P.; Ogut, Soner and Baker, C. B. Effects of Financing and Employment Alternatives on a Modern Farm Village in Turkey. *Ill. Agr. Econ.*, July 1973, *13*(2), pp. 12–15.   [G: Turkey]

Gallardo, Lloyd. Institutional Impact of Bay Area Manpower Programs. In *Mangum, G. L. and Robson, R. T., eds.*, 1973, pp. 202–24. [G: U.S.]

Gregory, Paul. A Model of Socialist Industrial Wage Differentials: The Case of East Germany. *Quart. J. Econ.*, February 1973, *87*(1), pp. 132–37.
[G: E. Germany; W. Germany]

Hammonds, T. M.; Yadav, R. and Vathana, C. The Elasticity of Demand for Hired Farm Labor. *Amer. J. Agr. Econ.*, May 1973, *55*(2), pp. 242–45.
[G: U.S.]

Helmberger, John D. The Market for Agricultural Economists. *Amer. J. Agr. Econ.*, Part II, November 1973, *55*(4), pp. 725–34.   [G: U.S.]

Huq, A. M. A Study of the Socioeconomic Impact of Changes in the Harvesting Labor Force in the Maine Lobster Industry. In *Sokoloski, A. A., ed.*, 1973, pp. 159–73.   [G: U.S.]

Katz, David A. Faculty Salaries, Promotion, and Productivity at a Large University. *Amer. Econ. Rev.*, June 1973, *63*(3), pp. 469–77.

Lacci, Livio. Agriculture's Contribution to the Gross National Product in Italy. *Rev. Econ. Cond. Italy*, July 1973, *27*(4), pp. 236–50.   [G: Italy]

Ladenson, Mark L. The End of the North-South Wage Differential: Comment. *Amer. Econ. Rev.*, September 1973, *63*(4), pp. 754–56.   [G: U.S.]

Leslie, D. G. A Note on the Regional Distribution of Unemployment. *Oxford Bull. Econ. Statist.*, August 1973, *35*(3), pp. 233–37.

Lubell, Harold. Urban Development and Employment in Calcutta. *Int. Lab. Rev.*, July 1973, *108* (1), pp. 25–41.   [G: India]

Metcalf, David. Some Aspects of University Teachers' Labour Market in the UK. In *Parkin, M., ed.*, 1973, pp. 192–211.   [G: U.K.]

Metcalf, David. Pay Dispersion, Information, and Returns to Search in a Professional Labour Market. *Rev. Econ. Stud.*, October 1973, *40*(4), pp. 491–505.   [G: U.K.]

Miller, Herman P. Measuring Subemployment in Poverty Areas of Large U.S. Cities. *Mon. Lab. Rev.*, October 1973, *96*(10), pp. 10–18. [G: U.S.]

Oh, Tai K. Estimating the Migration of U.S.-Educated Manpower from Asia to the United States. *Soc. Econ. Stud.*, September 1973, *22*(3), pp. 335–57.   [G: Asia; U.S.]

Paraskevopoulos, Christos C. Shifts in Industry Em-

ployment, Population Size and the Wage Structure: An Analysis of Two National Industries. In *Mattila, J. M. and Thompson, W. R., eds.*, 1973, pp. 105–25.   [G: U.S.]

Paulson, Albert S. and Garrison, Charles B. Entropy as a Measure of the Areal Concentration of Water-Oriented Industry. *Water Resources Res.*, April 1973, *9*(2), pp. 263–69.

Perrella, Vera C. Employment of Recent College Graduates. *Mon. Lab. Rev.*, February 1973, *96*(2), pp. 41–50.   [G: U.S.]

Personick, Martin E. Meat Department Workers Register Top Wage Rates in Grocery Stores. *Mon. Lab. Rev.*, May 1973, *96*(5), pp. 47–49. [G: U.S.]

Psacharopoulos, George and Williams, Gareth. Public Sector Earnings and Educational Planning. *Int. Lab. Rev.*, July 1973, *108*(1), pp. 43–57.
[G: Iran]

Ratcliffe, Anne E. Labour in the South African Gold Mines. (Review article). *S. Afr. J. Econ.*, September 1973, *41*(3), pp. 257–67.   [G: S. Africa]

Richardson, Reed C. The Impact of Denver's Manpower Programs. In *Mangum, G. L. and Robson, R. T., eds.*, 1973, pp. 134–43.   [G: U.S.]

Scoville, James G. Pre-Industrial Industrial Relations: The Case of Afghanistan. In *Sturmthal, A. and Scoville, J. G., eds.*, 1973, pp. 199–227.
[G: Afghanistan]

Shanahan, James L. Mis-Match in the Supply of and Demand for Low Skill Jobs in the Inner City. In *Mattila, J. M. and Thompson, W. R., eds.*, 1973, pp. 192–205.

Shore, Arnold R. and Scott, Robert A. Work Response and Family Composition Changes in a Negative Income Tax Experiment: Preliminary Mid-Experiment Results. In *Sheldon, E. B., ed.*, 1973, pp. 233–63.   [G: U.S.]

Siegel, Philip H. The Location of Industry and Job Participation: An Econometric Study. *Econ. Aff.*, January–February 1973, *18*(1-2), pp. 54–58.
[G: U.S.]

Strober, Myra H. Economic Development and the Hierachy of Earnings. *Ind. Relat.*, February 1973, *12*(1), pp. 65–76.

Susman, Gerald I. Job Enlargement: Effects of Culture on Worker Responses. *Ind. Relat.*, February 1973, *12*(1), pp. 1–15.   [G: U.S.]

Tideman, T. Nicolaus. Defining Area Distress in Unemployment. *Public Policy*, Fall 1973, *21*(4), pp. 441–92.   [G: U.S.]

Till, Thomas. The Extent of Industrialization in Southern Nonmetro Labor Markets in the 1960's. *J. Reg. Sci.*, December 1973, *13*(3), pp. 453–61.
[G: U.S.]

Tryfos, Peter. The Determinants of Prices and Employment in the Canadian Meat Industry. *Can. J. Agr. Econ.*, July 1973, *21*(2), pp. 25–42.   [G: Canada]

Wagstaff, H. R. Employment Multipliers in Rural Scotland. *Scot. J. Polit. Econ.*, November 1973, *20* (3), pp. 239–61.   [G: U.K.]

Whipple, Daniel S. Employment Among the Poor of Six Central Cities. *Mon. Lab. Rev.*, October 1973, *96*(10), pp. 52–53.   [G: U.S.]

de Willebois, J. L. J. M. van Der Does. A Workshop for Married Women in Part-Time Employment:

Implications of an Experiment in the Netherlands. In *Moskoff, W., ed.*, 1973, pp. 302–22.

[G: Netherlands]

8242 Wage and Fringe Benefit Studies

Barzel, Yoram. The Determination of Daily Hours and Wages. *Quart. J. Econ.*, May 1973, 87(2), pp. 220–38.

Bell, Donald R. Prevalence of Private Retirement Plans in Manufacturing. *Mon. Lab. Rev.*, September 1973, 96(9), pp. 29–32. [G: U.S.]

Bleakney, Thomas P. Problems and Issues in Public Employee Retirement Systems. *J. Risk Ins.*, March 1973, 40(1), pp. 39–46. [G: U.S.]

Blinder, Alan S. Wage Discrimination: Reduced Form and Structural Estimates. *J. Human Res.*, Fall 1973, 8(4), pp. 436–55. [G: U.S.]

Bush, Joseph C. Pay Increases in Footwear Lag Behind Other Industries. *Mon. Lab. Rev.*, June 1973, 96(6), pp. 57–58. [G: U.S.]

Butler, Arthur and Kim, Kye. The Dynamics of Wage Structures. *Southern Econ. J.*, April 1973, 39(4), pp. 588–600. [G: U.S.]

Caramela, Edward J. Staffing and Pay Changes in Life Insurance Companies. *Mon. Lab. Rev.*, August 1973, 96(8), pp. 66–68. [G: U.S.]

Cebula, Richard J. On Migration, Migration Costs, and Wage Differentials, with Special Reference to the United States. *Schweiz. Z. Volkswirtsch. Statist.*, March 1973, 109(1), pp. 59–68. [G: U.S.]

Chiplin, B. and Sloane, P. J. Real and Money Wages Revisited. *Appl. Econ.*, December 1973, 5(4), pp. 289–304. [G: U.K.]

Creagan, James F. Rise of Prices and Pay Adjustments in Italy. *Mon. Lab. Rev.*, July 1973, 96(7), pp. 47–48. [G: Italy]

Davis, Harry E. Pension Provisions Affecting the Employment of Older Workers. *Mon. Lab. Rev.*, April 1973, 96(4), pp. 41–45. [G: U.S.]

Dowling, J. Malcolm, Jr. Wage Determination in Two-Digit Manufacturing Industries: Theory, Test, and Forecast. *Quart. Rev. Econ. Bus.*, Spring 1973, 13(1), pp. 27–36. [G: U.S.]

Doyle, Philip M. Wages of Telephone and Telegraph Workers Showed Rapid Rise. *Mon. Lab. Rev.*, September 1973, 96(9), pp. 75–76.

Doyle, Philip M. Wages in Dress Manufacturing Vary Widely by Area. *Mon. Lab. Rev.*, March 1973, 96(3), pp. 57–58. [G: U.S.]

Ehrenberg, Ronald G. Municipal Government Structure, Unionization, and the Wages of Fire Fighters. *Ind. Lab. Relat. Rev.*, October 1973, 27 (1), pp. 36–48. [G: U.S.]

Evan, Harry Zvi. Comparing Conditions of Work by Collective Agreement Analysis: A Case Study of the Petroleum Industry. *Int. Lab. Rev.*, July 1973, 108(1), pp. 59–75.

Ewusi, Kodwo. Changes in Distribution of Earnings of Africans in Recorded Employment in Uganda. *Econ. Bull. Ghana, Sec. Ser.*, 1973, 3(1), pp. 39–49. [G: Uganda]

Ferber, Robert and Salazar-Carrillo, Jorge. Experience in Generating Micro Data in Latin America.

In *Ayal, E. B., ed.*, 1973, pp. 84–100. [G: Latin America]

Foegen, J. H. The High Cost of Innovative Employee Benefits. *Calif. Manage. Rev.*, Spring 1973, 15(3), pp. 100–04. [G: U.S.]

Franco, G. Robert. The Wage Subsidy Index in the Merchant Marine Act of 1970. *J. Transp. Econ. Policy*, September 1973, 7(3), pp. 283–90. [G: U.S.]

Freeman, Richard B. Changes in the Labor Market for Black Americans, 1948–72. *Brookings Pap. Econ. Act.*, 1973, (1), pp. 67–120. [G: U.S.]

Fremr, Jiří. Wage Developments in the Czechoslovak National Economy Since 1945, and Wage Trends in the 5th Five-Year Plan. *Czech. Econ. Digest.*, September 1973, (6), pp. 105–19. [G: Czechoslovakia]

Freund, James L. A Note on Short Period Changes in Earned Income in Manufacturing Among Urban Areas. *J. Reg. Sci.*, August 1973, 13(2), pp. 279–89. [G: U.S.]

Gillespie, Hugh. Problems and Issues in Public Employee Retirement Systems: Discussion. *J. Risk Ins.*, March 1973, 40(1), pp. 50–53. [G: U.S.]

Goldfarb, Robert S. A Model of Wage Setting and Wage Diversity in Local Labor Markets. *Western Econ. J.*, March 1973, 11(1), pp. 98–110.

Gordon, Robert J. The Response of Wages and Prices to the First Two Years of Controls. *Brookings Pap. Econ. Act.*, 1973, (3), pp. 765–78. [G: U.S.]

Granata, Dale. Survey Highlights Occupational Pay Differences in Furniture Industry. *Mon. Lab. Rev.*, June 1973, 96(6), pp. 58–60. [G: U.S.]

Greenwald, Carol S. Maternity Leave Policy. *New Eng. Econ. Rev.*, January-February 1973, pp. 13–18. [G: U.S.]

Hamilton, Mary Townsend. Sex and Income Inequality among the Employed. *Ann. Amer. Acad. Polit. Soc. Sci.*, September 1973, 409, pp. 42–52. [G: U.S.]

Hanushek, Eric A. Regional Differences in the Structure of Earnings. *Rev. Econ. Statist.*, May 1973, 55 (2), pp. 204–13. [G: U.S.]

Hart, R. A. The Role of Overtime Working in the Recent Wage Inflation Process. *Bull. Econ. Res.*, May 1973, 25(1), pp. 73–87. [G: U.K.]

Hodgens, Evan L. Survivor's Pensions: An Emerging Employee Benefit. *Mon. Lab. Rev.*, July 1973, 96 (7), pp. 31–34. [G: U.S.]

Houff, James N. Improving Area Wage Survey Indexes. *Mon. Lab. Rev.*, January 1973, 96(1), pp. 52–57. [G: U.S.]

Jackson, Mark and Jones, E. B. Unemployment and Occupational Wage Changes in Local Labor Markets. *Ind. Lab. Relat. Rev.*, July 1973, 26(4), pp. 1135–45. [G: U.S.]

Jedel, Michael Jay and Stamm, John H. The Battle over Jobs: An Appraisal of Recent Publications on the Employment Effects of U.S. Multinational Corporations. In *Kujawa, D., ed.*, 1973, pp. 144–91. [G: U.S.]

Johnston, J. and Timbrell, M. Empirical Tests of a Bargaining Theory of Wage Rate Determination. *Manchester Sch. Econ. Soc. Stud.*, June 1973, 41 (2), pp. 141–67. [G: U.K.]

Kesselman, Jonathan R. Incentive Effects of Trans-

824 Labor Market Studies, Wages, Employment

fer Systems Once Again. *J. Human Res.*, Winter 1973, *8*(1), pp. 119–29. [G: U.S.]

Koch, James V. and Chizmar, John F. The Influence of Teaching and Other Factors Upon Absolute Salaries and Salary Increments at Illinois State University. *J. Econ. Educ.*, Fall 1973, *5*(1), pp. 27–34. [G: U.S.]

Kohn, Robert M. On Migration, Migration Costs, and Wage Differentials: A Comment. *Schweiz. Z. Volkswirtsch. Statist.*, December 1973, *109*(4), pp. 603–04. [G: U.S.]

Kolodrubetz, Walter W. Employee-Benefit Plans, 1971. *Soc. Sec. Bull.*, April 1973, *36*(4), pp. 27–33. [G: U.S.]

Kolodrubetz, Walter W. Private Retirement Benefits and Relationship to Earnings: Survey of New Beneficiaries. *Soc. Sec. Bull.*, May 1973, *36*(5), pp. 16–37. [G: U.S.]

Kolodrubetz, Walter W. and Landay, Donald M. Coverage and Vesting of Full-Time Employees Under Private Retirement Plans. *Soc. Sec. Bull.*, November 1973, *36*(11), pp. 20–36. [G: U.S.]

Lewellen, Wilbur G. and Lanser, Howard P. Executive Pay Preferences. *Harvard Bus. Rev.*, September-October 1973, *51*(5), pp. 115–22. [G: U.S.]

Lewin, David. Wage Parity and the Supply of Police and Firemen. *Ind. Relat.*, February 1973, *12*(1), pp. 77–85. [G: U.S.]

Link, Charles R. The Quantity and Quality of Education and Their Influence on Earnings: The Case of Chemical Engineers. *Rev. Econ. Statist.*, May 1973, *55*(2), pp. 241–47. [G: U.S.]

Lipsky, David B. and Drotning, John E. The Influence of Collective Bargaining on Teachers' Salaries in New York State. *Ind. Lab. Relat. Rev.*, October 1973, *27*(1), pp. 18–35. [G: U.S.]

Lüttichau, Knud. Kvartalsresultater for pengelønsaendringens determinanter for Danmark i mellem-og efter-krigstiden. (Quarterly Results Concerning the Determinants of Changes in Money Wage Rates in Denmark in the Interwar and Post–war Period. With English summary.) *Nationalokon. Tidsskr.*, 1973, *111*(1), pp. 92–111. [G: Denmark]

Lüttichau, Knud. Pengelønsudviklingen for fire udvalgte fag for Danmark i mellemkrigstiden. (With English summary.) *Nationalokon. Tidsskr.*, 1973, *111*(3), pp. 382–96. [G: Denmark]

Lüttichau, Knud. Pengelønsudviklingen for fire udvalgte fag for Danmark i efterkrigstiden. (The Changes in the Wage Rates for Four Trades in Denmark in the Post-War Period. With English summary.) *Nationalokon. Tidsskr.*, 1973, *111*(2), pp. 242–65. [G: Denmark]

Malkiel, Burton G. and Malkiel, Judith A. Male-Female Pay Differentials in Professional Employment. *Amer. Econ. Rev.*, September 1973, *63*(4), pp. 693–705. [G: U.S.]

Marsh, Robert M. and Mannari, Hiroshi. Pay and Social Structure in a Japanese Firm. *Ind. Relat.*, February 1973, *12*(1), pp. 16–32. [G: Japan]

Mitchell, D. J. B. and Azevedo, R. A Pay Board Assessment of Wage Controls. *Mon. Lab. Rev.*, April 1973, *96*(4), pp. 21–23. [G: U.S.]

Mogull, Robert G. Football Salaries and Race: Some Empirical Evidence. *Ind. Relat.*, February 1973,

12(1), pp. 109–12. [G: U.S.]

Morgenstern, Richard D. Direct and Indirect Effects on Earnings of Schooling and Socio-Economic Background. *Rev. Econ. Statist.*, May 1973, *55*(2), pp. 225–33. [G: U.S.]

Packer, Arnold H. and Park, Seong H. Distortions in Relative Wages and Shifts in the Phillips Curve. *Rev. Econ. Statist.*, February 1973, *55*(1), pp. 16–22. [G: U.S.]

Personick, Martin E. Shorter Workweeks Dampen Earnings Gains in Contract Cleaning Services. *Mon. Lab. Rev.*, March 1973, *96*(3), pp. 53–55. [G: U.S.]

Phelps Brown, E. H. Levels and Movements of Industrial Productivity and Real Wages Internationally Compared, 1860-1970. *Econ. J.*, March 1973, *83*(329), pp. 58–71. [G: Germany; Sweden; U.K.; U.S.; France]

Raveed, Sion and Renforth, William C. Shifting World Wage Rates: What Do They Mean for Indiana? *Indiana Bus. Rev.*, September-October 1973, *48*, pp. 15–19. [G: U.S.]

Ridzon, Donald S. Occupational Pay in Shirt Manufacturing. *Mon. Lab. Rev.*, January 1973, *96*(1), pp. 60–61. [G: U.S.]

Robinson, Derek. Capital-Sharing Schemes. In *Robinson, D.*, 1973, pp. 137–57.

Robinson, Derek. Trade Union Views on Workers' Negotiated Savings Plans for Capital Formation. In *Robinson, D.*, 1973, pp. 76–104. [G: W. Europe]

Robinson, Derek. Workers' Savings Plans for Capital Formation in Germany. In *Robinson, D.*, 1973, pp. 105–36. [G: W. Germany]

Ross, Kenneth H. Problems and Issues in Public Employee Retirement Systems: Discussion. *J. Risk Ins.*, March 1973, *40*(1), pp. 46–50. [G: U.S.]

Rowley, J. C. R. and Wilton, D. A. Quarterly Models of Wage Determination Some New Efficient Estimates. *Amer. Econ. Rev.*, June 1973, *63*(3), pp. 380–89. [G: Canada]

Saunders, Robert J. and Coccari, Ronald L. Racial Earnings Differentials: Some Economic Factors. *Amer. J. Econ. Soc.*, July 1973, *32*(3), pp. 225–33. [G: U.S.]

Sawyer, M. C. The Earnings of Manual Workers: A Cross-Section Analysis. *Scot. J. Polit. Econ.*, June 1973, *20*(2), pp. 141–57. [G: U.K.]

Schmenner, Roger W. The Determination of Municipal Employee Wages. *Rev. Econ. Statist.*, February 1973, *55*(1), pp. 83–90. [G: U.S.]

Schroeder, Gertrude E. Regional Differences in Incomes and Levels of Living in the USSR. In *Bandera, V. N. and Melnyk, Z. L.*, eds., 1973, pp. 167–95. [G: U.S.S.R.]

Sharot, T. Unemployment Dispersion as a Determinant of Wage Inflation in the U.K., 1925–1966 —A Note. *Manchester Sch. Econ. Soc. Stud.*, June 1973, *41* (2), pp. 225–28.

Sheifer, Victor J. Reconciling Labor Department and Stabilization Agency Wage Data. *Mon. Lab. Rev.*, April 1973, *96*(4), pp. 24–30. [G: U.S.]

Siegfried, John J. and White, Kenneth J. Financial Rewards to Research and Teaching: A Case Study of Academic Economists. *Amer. Econ. Rev.*, May

334

1973, *63*(2), pp. 309–15.   [G: U.S.]

Siegfried, John J. and White, Kenneth J. Teaching and Publishing as Determinants of Academic Salaries. *J. Econ. Educ.,* Spring 1973, *4*(2), pp. 90–99.
[G: U.S.]

Standing, Guy and Taira, Koji. Labor Market Effects of Multinational Enterprises in Latin America. *Nebr. J. Econ. Bus.,* Autumn 1973, *12*(4), pp. 103–17.   [G: Latin America]

Stoikov, Vladimir. Size of Firm, Worker Earnings, and Human Capital: The Case of Japan. *Ind. Lab. Relat. Rev.,* July 1973, *26*(4), pp. 1095–1106.
[G: Japan]

Stoikov, Vladimir. The Structure of Earnings in Japanese Manufacturing Industries: A Human-Capital Approach. *J. Polit. Econ.,* Part I, March-April 1973, *81*(2), pp. 340–55.   [G: Japan]

Struyk, Raymond J. Explaining Variations in the Hourly Wage Rates of Urban Minority Group Females. *J. Human Res.,* Summer 1973, *8*(3), pp. 349–64.   [G: U.S.]

Sussman, Zvi. The Determination of Wages for Unskilled Labor in the Advanced Sector of the Dual Economy of Mandatory Palestine. *Econ. Develop. Cult. Change,* October 1973, *22*(1), pp. 95–113.
[G: Israel]

Takagi, Tadao. Il problema salariale in Giappone. (Wage Problems in Japan. With English summary.) *Rivista Int. Sci. Econ. Com.,* August-September 1973, *20*(8–9), pp. 804–38.   [G: Japan]

Talbot, Joseph E., Jr. Wage Changes and Bargaining Gains in 1972. *Mon. Lab. Rev.,* April 1973, *96*(4), pp. 17–20.   [G: U.S.]

Thomas, R. L. Unemployment Dispersion as a Determinant of Wage Inflation in the U.K. 1925–66—A Rejoinder. *Manchester Sch. Econ. Soc. Stud.,* June 1973, *41*(2), pp. 229–33.   [G: U.K.]

Verma, Pramod. Regional Wages and Economic Development: A Case Study of Manufacturing Wages in India, 1950–1960. *J. Devel. Stud.,* October 1973, *10*(1), pp. 16–32.   [G: India]

Voronov, O. Paid Educational Leave in the USSR. *Int. Lab. Rev.,* June 1973, *107*(6), pp. 529–38.
[G: U.S.S.R.]

Wilkinson, R. K. and Burkitt, B. Wage Determination and Trade Unions. *Scot. J. Polit. Econ.,* June 1973, *20*(2), pp. 107–22.   [G: U.K.]

Wilson, Thomas. Pensions, Inflation and Growth. In *Robinson, J., ed.,* 1973, pp. 88–114.   [G: W. Europe]

Wilson, Thomas. Pensions, Inflation and Growth. *Lloyds Bank Rev.,* April 1973, (108), pp. 1–17.
[G: U.K.]

8243 Employment Studies; Unemployment and Vacancies

Adams, Arvil V. Title VII and Fair Employment in Ohio: Guidelines to Action. *Ohio State U. Bull. Bus. Res.,* May 1973, *48*(5), pp. 1-7.   [G: U.S.]

Adie, Douglas K. Teen-Age Unemployment and Real Federal Minimum Wages. *J. Polit. Econ.,* Part I, March-April 1973, *81*(2), pp. 435–41.
[G: U.S.]

Ahmed, Iftikhar. Sectoral Employment Response in an Input-Output Framework: The Case of Bangladesh. *Bangladesh Econ. Rev.,* July 1973, *1*(3), pp. 317–23.   [G: Bangladesh]

Ball, Robert. Labor and Materials Required for Highway Construction. *Mon. Lab. Rev.,* June 1973, *96* (6), pp. 40–45.   [G: U.S.]

Bell, Frederick W. and Fullenbaum, Richard F. The Regional Impact of Resource Management. In *Mattila, J. M. and Thompson, W. R., eds.,* 1973, pp. 11–26.   [G: U.S.]

Bhagwat, Avinash. Main Features of the Employment Problem in Developing Countries. *Int. Monet. Fund Staff Pap.,* March 1973, *20*(1), pp. 78–99.

Biderman, Albert D. Where Do They Go from Here?—Retired Military in America. *Ann. Amer. Acad. Polit. Soc. Sci.,* March 1973, *406*, pp. 146–61.   [G: U.S.]

Blandy, Richard and Wery, René. Population and Employment Growth: Bachue-1. *Int. Lab. Rev.,* May 1973, *107*(5), pp. 441–49.

Blankart, Beat. Arbeitskräftenachfrage im Konjunkturablauf—das Problem des temporären Hortens von Arbeitskräften. (The Demand for Labour During Business Cycles—the Problem of Short-Term Labour Hoarding. With English summary.) *Schweiz. Z. Volkswirtsch. Statist.,* June 1973, *109* (2), pp. 171–85.

Bradshaw, Thomas F. Jobseeking Methods Used by Unemployed Workers. *Mon. Lab. Rev.,* February 1973, *96*(2), pp. 35–40.   [G: U.S.]

Carroll, Stephen J. and Rolph, John E. A Stochastic Model of Discrimination in the Labor Market. *Econometrica,* January 1973, *41*(1), pp. 97–108.

Chiswick, Barry R. Racial Discrimination in the Labor Market: A Test of Alternative Hypotheses. *J. Polit. Econ.,* November-December 1973, *81*(6), pp. 1330–52.   [G: U.S.]

Clark, C. Scott. Labor Hoarding in Durable Goods Industries. *Amer. Econ. Rev.,* December 1973, *63* (5), pp. 811–24.   [G: U.S.]

Coen, Robert M. Labor Force and Unemployment in the 1920's and 1930's: A Re-examination Based on Postwar Experience. *Rev. Econ. Statist.,* February 1973, *55*(1), pp. 46–55.   [G: U.S.]

Coen, Robert M. Labor Force and Unemployment in the 1920's and 1930's: Reply. *Rev. Econ. Statist.,* November 1973, *55*(4), pp. 527–28.   [G: U.S.]

Costa, E. Maximising Employment in Labour-intensive Development Programmes. *Int. Lab. Rev.,* November 1973, *108*(5), pp. 371–94.

Cumberland, John H. Dimensions of the Impact of Reduced Military Expenditures on Industries, Regions, and Communities. In *Udis, B., ed.,* 1973, pp. 79–147.   [G: U.S.]

Denton, Frank T. A Simulation Model of Month-to-Month Labor Force Movement in Canada. *Int. Econ. Rev.,* June 1973, *14*(2), pp. 293–311.
[G: Canada]

Donner, Arthur W. and Lazar, Fred. An Econometric Study of Segmented Labor Markets and the Structure of Unemployment: The Canadian Experience. *Int. Econ. Rev.,* June 1973, *14*(2), pp. 312–27.   [G: Canada]

Dyer, Lee D. Job Search Success of Middle-Aged Managers and Engineers. *Ind. Lab. Relat. Rev.*, April 1973, *26*(3), pp. 969–79. [G: U.S.]

Ehrenberg, Ronald G. Heterogeneous Labor, Minimum Hiring Standards, and Job Vacancies in Public Employment. *J. Polit. Econ.*, November-December 1973, *81*(6), pp. 1442–50. [G: U.S.]

Ehrenberg, Ronald G. The Demand for State and Local Government Employees. *Amer. Econ. Rev.*, June 1973, *63*(3), pp. 366–79. [G: U.S.]

Eldridge, D. P. and Saunders, N. C. Employment and Exports, 1963–72. *Mon. Lab. Rev.*, August 1973, *96*(8), pp. 16–27. [G: U.S.]

Flaim, Paul O. Discouraged Workers and Changes in Unemployment. *Mon. Lab. Rev.*, March 1973, *96*(3), pp. 8–16. [G: U.S.]

Flanagan, Robert J. The U.S. Phillips Curve and International Unemployment Rate Differentials. *Amer. Econ. Rev.*, March 1973, *63*(1), pp. 114–31. [G: U.S.]

Fleming, Thomas F., Jr. Manpower Impact of Purchases by State and Local Governments. *Mon. Lab. Rev.*, June 1973, *96*(6), pp. 33–39. [G: U.S.]

Flowers, Vincent S. and Hughes, Charles L. Why Employees Stay. *Harvard Bus. Rev.*, July-August 1973, *51*(4), pp. 49–60. [G: U.S.]

Foster, J. I. The Behaviour of Unemployment and Unfilled Vacancies: Great Britain, 1958–1971—A Comment. *Econ. J.*, March 1973, *83*(329), pp. 192–201. [G: U.K.]

Fry, Fred L. More on the Causes of Quits in Manufacturing. *Mon. Lab. Rev.*, June 1973, *96*(6), pp. 48–49. [G: U.S.]

Gaston, Robert J. Labor Market Conditions and Employer Hiring Standards: Reply. *Ind. Relat.*, May 1973, *12*(2), pp. 250–51.

Gastwirth, Joseph L. Estimating the Number of "Hidden Unemployed" *Mon. Lab. Rev.*, March 1973, *96*(3), pp. 17–26. [G: U.S.]

Gellner, Christopher G. A 25-Year Look at Employment as Measured by Two Surveys. *Mon. Lab. Rev.*, July 1973, *96*(7), pp. 14–23. [G: U.S.]

Gellner, Christopher G. Where Unemployment Was Heaviest in 1972. *Mon. Lab. Rev.*, August 1973, *96*(8), pp. 65–66. [G: U.S.]

Gilbert, R. Alton. Employment Growth in St. Louis. *Fed. Res. Bank St. Louis Rev.*, August 1973, *55*(8), pp. 9–15. [G: U.S.]

Gilbert, Ronald D. Okun's Law: Some Additional Evidence. *Nebr. J. Econ. Bus.*, Winter 1973, *12*(1), pp. 51–60. [G: U.S.]

Gilroy, Curtis L. Job Losers, Leavers, and Entrants: Traits and Trends. *Mon. Lab. Rev.*, August 1973, *96*(8), pp. 3–15. [G: U.S.]

Gordon, Robert J. The Welfare Cost of Higher Unemployment. *Brookings Pap. Econ. Act.*, 1973, (1), pp. 133–95. [G: U.S.]

Gotsch, Carl H. Tractor Mechanisation and Rural Development in Pakistan. *Int. Lab. Rev.*, February 1973, *107*(2), pp. 133–66. [G: Pakistan]

Gujarati, Damodar. The Behaviour of Unemployment and Unfilled Vacancies: Great Britain, 1958–1971—A Reply. *Econ. J.*, March 1973, *83* (329), pp. 201–03. [G: U.K.]

Hart, R. A. Employment Creation in the Development Areas: A Reply. *Scot. J. Polit. Econ.*, June 1973, *20*(2), pp. 171–73.

Hassan, M. F. Unemployment in Latin America: Causes and Remedies. *Amer. J. Econ. Soc.*, April 1973, *32*(2), pp. 179–90. [G: Latin America]

Hedges, Janice Neipert. Absence from Work: A Look at Some National Data. *Mon. Lab. Rev.*, July 1973, *96*(7), pp. 24–30. [G: U.S.]

Heilbroner, Robert L. Men and Machines in Perspective. In *Reynolds, L. G.; Green, G. D. and Lewis, D. R., eds.*, 1973, pp. 100–109. [G: U.S.]

Hellman, Daryl A. The Spatial Distribution of Unemployment by Occupation: A Further Note. *J. Reg. Sci.*, December 1973, *13*(3), pp. 463–66. [G: U.S.]

van Houten, Jan F. Assembly Industries in the Caribbean. *Finance Develop.*, June 1973, *10*(2), pp. 19–22, 37. [G: Caribbean]

Hurd, Richard W. Equilibrium Vacancies in a Labor Market Dominated by Non-Profit Firms: The "Shortage" of Nurses. *Rev. Econ. Statist.*, May 1973, *55*(2), pp. 234–40. [G: U.S.]

Isard, Peter. Employment Impacts of Textile Imports and Investment: A Vintage-Capital Model. *Amer. Econ. Rev.*, June 1973, *63*(3), pp. 402–16. [G: U.S.]

Joshi, Nandini U. Estimating Future Unemployment of Graduates. *Bangladesh Econ. Rev.*, October 1973, *1*(4), pp. 409–24. [G: India]

Katz, Arnold. Teenage Employment Effects of State Minimum Wages. *J. Human Res.*, Spring 1973, *8* (2), pp. 250–56. [G: U.S.]

Kraseman, Thomas W. and Barker, Betty L. Employment and Payroll Costs of U.S. Multinational Companies. *Surv. Curr. Bus.*, October 1973, *53* (10), pp. 36–44. [G: U.S.]

Lebergott, Stanley. A New Technique for Time Series? Comment. *Rev. Econ. Statist.*, November 1973, *55*(4), pp. 525–27.

Leigh, Duane E. and Rawlins, V. Lane. On the Stability of Relative Black-White Unemployment. *Mon. Lab. Rev.*, May 1973, *96*(5), pp. 30–32. [G: U.S.]

Levi, J. F. S. Migration from the Land and Urban Unemployment in Sierra Leone. *Oxford Bull. Econ. Statist.*, November 1973, *35*(4), pp. 309–26. [G: Sierra Leone]

Lyle, Jerolyn R. Factors Affecting the Job Status of Workers with Spanish Surnames. *Mon. Lab. Rev.*, April 1973, *96*(4), pp. 10–16. [G: U.S.]

MacKay, R. R. Employment Creation: A Resurrection. *Scot. J. Polit. Econ.*, June 1973, *20*(2), pp. 175–77.

Meidner, Rudolf and Andersson, Rolf. The Overall Impact of an Active Labor Market Policy in Sweden. In *Ulman, L., ed.*, 1973, pp. 117–58. [G: Sweden]

Mincer, Jacob. Determining Who Are the "Hidden Unemployed." *Mon. Lab. Rev.*, March 1973, *96* (3), pp. 27–30. [G: U.S.]

Neild, P. G. The Construction and Estimation of a Coherent Labour-Market System. *Australian Econ. Pap.*, June 1973, *12*(20), pp. 106–23. [G: New Zealand]

Olivier, R. and Sabolo, Y. Simultaneous Planning of Employment, Production and Education. *Int.*

Lab. Rev., April 1973, *107*(4), pp. 359–72.
[G: Peru]

Parsons, Donald O. Quit Rates Over Time: A Search and Information Approach. *Amer. Econ. Rev.*, June 1973, *63*(3), pp. 390–401. [G: U.S.]

Pepson, Robert P. Job Vacancies, Hires, Quits, and Layoffs in Manufacturing, 1972. *Mon. Lab. Rev.*, April 1973, *96*(4), pp. 66–68. [G: U.S.]

Phillips, Bruce D. The Spatial Distribution of Unemployment by Occupation: Reply. *J. Reg. Sci.*, December 1973, *13*(3), pp. 471. [G: U.S.]

Polzin, Paul E. Urban Employment Models: Estimation and Interpretation. *Land Econ.*, May 1973, *49*(2), pp. 226–32. [G: U.S.]

Pompermayer, Malori J. Dependency and Unemployment: Some Issues. In *Bonilla, F. and Girling, R., eds.*, 1973, pp. 63–82.

Prodromidis, Kyprianos P. and Lianos, Theodore P. City Size and Patterns of Employment Structure. In *Mattila, J. M. and Thompson, W. R., eds.*, 1973, pp. 91–104. [G: U.S.]

Richardson, Harry W. The Spatial Distribution of Unemployment by Occupation: A Comment. *J. Reg. Sci.*, December 1973, *13*(3), pp. 467–69. [G: U.S.]

Richards, P. J. Job Mobility and Unemployment in the Ceylon Urban Labour Market. *Oxford Bull. Econ. Statist.*, February 1973, *35*(1), pp. 49–59. [G: Ceylon]

Rosen, Carol. Hidden Unemployment and Related Issues. *Mon. Lab. Rev.*, March 1973, *96*(3), pp. 31–37. [G: U.S.]

Rourke, B. E. and Obeng, F. A. Seasonality in the Employment of Casual Agricultural Labour in Ghana. *Econ. Bull. Ghana, Sec. Ser.*, 1973, *3*(3), pp. 3–13. [G: Ghana]

Saxena, P. S. and Dubey, R. M. Rural Unemployment: A Direct Approach. *Econ. Aff.*, June 1973, *18*(6), pp. 265–74, 304. [G: India]

Scully, Gerald W. and Gallaway, Lowell E. A Spectral Analysis of the Demographic Structure of American Unemployment. *J. Bus.*, January 1973, *46*(1), pp. 87–102. [G: U.S.]

Sharot, T. Unemployment Dispersion as a Determinant of Wage Inflation in the U.K. 1925–66—A Note. *Manchester Sch. Econ. Soc. Stud.*, June 1973, *41*(2), pp. 225–28. [G: U.K.]

Sinha, J. N. Agrarian Reforms and Employment in Densely Populated Agrarian Economies: A Dissenting View. *Int. Lab. Rev.*, November 1973, *108* (5), pp. 395–421. [G: Japan; India]

Smith, P. Seasonal Fluctuations in the Motor Vehicle Industry: A Comment. *J. Ind. Econ.*, April 1973, *21*(2), pp. 184–86. [G: U.K.]

Smith, Robert S. Labor Market Conditions and Employer Hiring Standards: Comment. *Ind. Relat.*, May 1973, *12*(2), pp. 248–49.

Sufrin, Sidney C. and Wagner, Abraham. U.S. Employment and Growth in the Immediate Future: A Guess. *Rivista Int. Sci. Econ. Com.*, January 1973, *20*(1), pp. 63–71. [G: U.S.]

Swan, Philip L. Decentralization and the Growth of Urban Manufacturing Employment. *Land Econ.*, May 1973, *49*(2), pp. 212–16. [G: U.S.]

Thomas, David B. How Reliable Are Those Price and Employment Measures? *Fed. Res. Bank Bus.*

Rev. Phila., April 1973, pp. 17–22. [G: U.S.]

Thomas, R. B. On the Definition of 'Shortages' in Administered Labour Markets. *Manchester Sch. Econ. Soc. Stud.*, June 1973, *41*(2), pp. 169–86. [G: U.K.]

Thomas, R. L. Unemployment Dispersion as a Determinant of Wage Inflation in the U.K. 1925–66—A Rejoinder. *Manchester Sch. Econ. Soc. Stud.*, June 1973, *41*(2), pp. 229–33. [G: U.K.]

Thorbecke, Erik. The Employment Problem: A Critical Evaluation of Four ILO Comprehensive Country Reports. *Int. Lab. Rev.*, May 1973, *107* (5), pp. 393–423. [G: Colombia; Sri Lanka; Kenya; Iran]

Tideman, T. Nicolaus. Defining Area Distress in Unemployment. *Public Policy*, Fall 1973, *21*(4), pp. 441–92. [G: U.S.]

de la Torre, Jose, Jr.; Stobaugh, Robert B. and Telesio, Piero. U.S. Multinational Enterprises and Changes in the Skill Composition of U.S. Employment. In *Kujawa, D., ed.*, 1973, pp. 127–43. [G: U.S.]

Williams, T. David and Ntim, S. M. Public Employment Centres as a Source of Data on Unemployment in Ghana. *Econ. Bull. Ghana, Sec. Ser.*, 1973, *3*(1), pp. 16–26. [G: Ghana]

Witte, Ann Dryden. Employment in the Manufacturing Sector of Developing Economies: A Study of Mexico and Peru. *J. Devel. Stud.*, October 1973, *10*(1), pp. 33–49. [G: Mexico; Peru]

de Wit, Y. B. The *Kabupaten* Program. *Bull. Indonesian Econ. Stud.*, March 1973, *9*(1), pp. 65–85. [G: Indonesia]

Yamamoto, Hiromasa. Available Jobs and Employment in Japanese Foreign-Going Shipping. *Kobe Econ. Bus. Rev.*, 1973, *20*(20), pp. 51–59. [G: Japan]

Zucker, Albert. Minimum Wages and the Long-run Elasticity of Demand for Low-Wage Labor. *Quart. J. Econ.*, May 1973, *87*(2), pp. 267–77. [G: U.S.]

825 Labor Productivity

8250 Labor Productivity

Abramovitz, Moses and David, Paul A. Economic Growth in America: Historical Parables and Realities. *De Economist*, May-June 1973, *121*(3), pp. 251–72. [G: U.S.]

Barkai, Haim and Levhari, David. The Impact of Experience on Kibbutz Farming. *Rev. Econ. Statist.*, February 1973, *55*(1), pp. 56–63. [G: Israel]

Bellante, Donald M. A Florida Example: Measuring the Productivity Loss from Labor Force Disability. *Growth Change*, January 1973, *4*(1), pp. 38–42. [G: U.S.]

Birkin, Stanley J. and Ford, James S. The Quantity/Quality Dilemma: The Impact of a Zero Defects Program. In *Cochrane, J. L. and Zeleny, M., eds.*, 1973, pp. 517–29. [G: U.S.]

Brand, Horst. Productivity in Telephone Communications. *Mon. Lab. Rev.*, November 1973, *96*(11), pp. 3–9. [G: U.S.]

Burloiu, P. Considerații privind îmbunătățirea

măsurării productivității muncii. (Considerations on Improving the Measuring of Labour Productivity. With English summary.) *Stud. Cercet. Econ.*, 1973, (2), pp. 47–53.

Capdevielle, Patricia and Neef, Arthur. Productivity and Unit Labor Costs in 12 Industrial Countries. *Mon. Lab. Rev.*, November 1973, *96*(11), pp. 14–21.

Carey, John L. Productivity in the Steel Foundries Industry. *Mon. Lab. Rev.*, May 1973, *96*(5), pp. 8–11. [G: U.S.]

Chandrasekar, Krishnamurti. U.S. and French Productivity in 19 Manufacturing Industries. *J. Ind. Econ.*, April 1973, *21*(2), pp. 110–25.
[G: U.S.; France]

Ciucur, Dumitru and Gavrilă, I. Aspecte ale gîndirii economice burgheze contemporane privind munca productivă. (Aspects of the Contemporary Bourgeois Economic Thinking on Productive Labor. With English summary.) *Stud. Cercet. Econ.*, 1973, (1), pp. 151–61.

Constantinescu, N. N. Cîteva probleme ale teoriei și practicii în domeniul productivității muncii. (Some Problems of the Theory and Practice in the Field of Labour Productivity. With English summary.) *Stud. Cercet. Econ.*, 1973, (1), pp. 27–34.

Craine, Roger. On the Service Flow from Labour. *Rev. Econ. Stud.*, January 1973, *40*(1), pp. 39–46.

Denison, Edward F. The Shift to Services and the Rate of Productivity Change. *Surv. Curr. Bus.*, October 1973, *53*(10), pp. 20–35. [G: U.S.]

Diaz-Alejandro, Carlos. Labour Productivity and Other Characteristics of Cement Plants—An International Comparison. In *[Rosenstein-Rodan, P.]*, 1973, pp. 283–315. [G: Latin America]

Doyle, Philip M. Wages and Productivity Rise in Flour Mills as Employment Declines. *Mon. Lab. Rev.*, October 1973, *96*(10), pp. 51–52. [G: U.S.]

Eisenberg, William M. and Fulco, Lawrence J. Productivity and Costs in the Private Economy, 1972. *Mon. Lab. Rev.*, May 1973, *96*(5), pp. 3–7.
[G: U.S.]

Elkan, Walter. On the Apparent Benefits of Higher Productivity: An Arithmetical Illustration: Reply. *J. Devel. Stud.*, April 1973, *9*(3), pp. 452–53.

Gavrilă, Tatiana. Organizarea științifică a producției și a muncii—factor dinamizator al productivității muncii. (The Scientific Organization of Production and Labour—A Stimulating Factor of Labour Productivity. With English summary.) *Stud. Cercet. Econ.*, 1973, (3), pp. 29–39.

George, Kenneth D. and Ward, Terry. Productivity Growth in the Retail Trade. *Oxford Bull. Econ. Statist.*, February 1973, *35*(1), pp. 31–47.
[G: U.K.]

Gibson, Charles H. Volvo Increases Productivity Through Job Enrichment. *Calif. Manage. Rev.*, Summer 1973, *15*(4), pp. 64–66. [G: Sweden]

Gregory, R. G. and James, Denis W. Do New Factories Embody Best Practice Technology? *Econ. J.*, December 1973, *83*(332), pp. 1133–55. [G: Australia]

Gruebele, J. W. Measures of Efficiency in Milk Plant Operations. *Ill. Agr. Econ.*, July 1973, *13*(2), pp. 38–43. [G: U.S.]

Herman, Arthur S. Productivity in the Paints and

Allied Products Industry. *Mon. Lab. Rev.*, November 1973, *96*(11), pp. 10–13. [G: U.S.]

Ireland, Norman J.; Briscoe, G. and Smyth, David J. Specification Bias and Short-run Returns to Labour: Some Evidence for the United Kingdom. *Rev. Econ. Statist.*, February 1973, *55*(1), pp. 23–27. [G: U.K.]

Khachaturov, T. Improving the Methods of Determining the Effectiveness of Capital Investments. *Prob. Econ.*, September 1973, *16*(5), pp. 3–30.
[G: U.S.S.R.]

Khromov, P. Labor Productivity and Accumulation. *Prob. Econ.*, February 1973, *15*(10), pp. 30–45.
[G: U.S.S.R.]

Konius, A. A. Commensuration of Labor by Means of an Input-Output Table. *Matekon*, Summer 1973, *9*(4), pp. 31–42.

Kuipers, S. K. The Positive Relation Between Average Labour Productivity and Labour Intensity. *Z. Nationalökon.*, 1973, *33*(1–2), pp. 115–26.

Kux, Jaroslav. Comparative Study of Labour Productivity in Industry Between Czechoslovakia, Hungary, France and Austria. *Czech. Econ. Digest.*, November 1973, (7), pp. 74–95. [G: Czechoslavakia; Hungary; France; Austria]

Levhari, David and Sheshinski, Eytan. Experience and Productivity in the Israel Diamond Industry. *Econometrica*, March 1973, *41*(2), pp. 239–53.
[G: Israel]

Malenbaum, Wilfred. A Note on the Poor Nation Situation. In *Berg, A.; Scrimshaw, N. S. and Call, D. L., eds.*, 1973, pp. 81–86.

Packard, Philip C. On the Apparent Benefits of Higher Productivity: An Arithmetical Illustration: A Comment. *J. Devel. Stud.*, April 1973, *9*(3), pp. 451–52.

Pal, Sasanka Shekhar. Productivity of Farm Labour in the Context of Rural Unemployment (A Case Study of 79 Farms in a Village) *Econ. Aff.*, May 1973, *18*(5), pp. 241–48. [G: India]

Paraskevopoulos, Christos C. Shifts in Industry Employment, Population Size and the Wage Structure: An Analysis of Two National Industries. In *Mattila, J. M. and Thompson, W. R., eds.*, 1973, pp. 105–25. [G: U.S.]

Phelps Brown, E. H. Levels and Movements of Industrial Productivity and Real Wages Internationally Compared, 1860-1970. *Econ. J.*, March 1973, *83*(329), pp. 58–71. [G: Germany; Sweden; U.K.; U.S.; France]

Porta, Pier Luigi. Patterns of Association of Output and Employment in the Industrially Advanced Countries. *Rivista Int. Sci. Econ. Com.*, May 1973, *20*(5), pp. 449–69.

Robinowitz, Robert S. and Riche, Martha F. Productivity in the Ready-Mixed Concrete Industry. *Mon. Lab. Rev.*, May 1973, *96*(5), pp. 12–15.
[G: U.S.]

Robinson, Derek. Productivity Bargaining. In *Robinson, D.*, 1973, pp. 185–204.

Sandu, C. and Popescu, C. Corelația între creșterea productivității muncii și salariul mediu și influența ei asupra mărimii prețului de cost și a rentabilității. (The Correlation Between the Increase of Labour Productivity and the Average Wage and Its Influence on the Proportion of the Cost

Price and of Profitableness. With English summary.) *Stud. Cercet. Econ.*, 1973, (1), pp. 35–42.

Selowsky, Marcelo. An Attempt to Estimate Rates of Return to Investment in Infant Nutrition. In *Niskanen, W. A., et al., eds.*, 1973, pp. 410–28.
[G: Chile]

Slezak, Lester. Effects of Changes in Payment System on Productivity in Sweden. *Mon. Lab. Rev.*, March 1973, *96*(3), pp. 51–52. [G: Sweden]

Solow, Robert M. Some Evidence on the Short-Run Productivity Puzzle. In *[Rosenstein-Rodan, P.]*, 1973, pp. 316–25. [G: U.S.]

Spornic, Aneta. Influența factorilor social-politici asupra creșterii productivității muncii. (The Influence of Social-Political Factors on the Increase of Labour Productivity. With English summary.) *Stud. Cercet. Econ.*, 1973, (2), pp. 55–62.

Starr, Martin K. Productivity is the USA's Problem. *Calif. Manage. Rev.*, Winter 1973, *16*(2), pp. 32–36. [G: U.S.]

Ursachi, I. Probleme ale planificării productivității muncii în întreprinderile industriei textile. (Problems of the Planning of Labour Productivity in the Enterprises of the Textile Industry. With English summary.) *Stud. Cercet. Econ.*, 1973, (3), pp. 41–50. [G: Rumania]

Vais, T. The Topic of an International Symposium: Labor Resources in COMECON Nations. *Prob. Econ.*, July 1973, *16*(3), pp. 77–86. [G: U.S.S.R.]

Vasil'ev, V. F. Some Properties of the Application of Mathematical Methods to Develop Labor Norms. *Matekon*, Winter 1973-74, *10*(2), pp. 64–73.

Waldorf, William H. Quality of Labor in Manufacturing. *Rev. Econ. Statist.*, August 1973, *55*(3), pp. 284–90. [G: U.S.]

Whitehouse, F. Douglas. Demographic Aspects of Regional Economic Development in the USSR. In *Bandera, V. N. and Melnyk, Z. L., eds.*, 1973, pp. 154–66. [G: U.S.S.R.]

826 Labor Markets: Demographic Characteristics

8260 Labor Markets: Demographic Characteristics

Adie, Douglas K. Teen-Age Unemployment and Real Federal Minimum Wages. *J. Polit. Econ.*, Part I, March-April 1973, *81*(2), pp. 435–41.
[G: U.S.]

Anderson, Roy C. Black Employment in the Securities Industry. *Ind. Relat.*, February 1973, *12*(1), pp. 107–08. [G: U.S.]

Bergonzini, Luciano. Professionalità femminile e lavoro a domicilio: Questioni generali ed esiti di un'indagine statistica in alcuni comuni dell'Emilia-Romagna. (Women's Professional Status and Work at Home: Some General Questions and Some Results of a Statistical Inquiry in a Few Municipalities of the Emilia-Romagna Region (Italy). With English summary.) *Statistica*, October-December 1973, *33*(4), pp. 492–546. [G: Italy]

Bradley, Iver E.; Mangum, Garth L. and Robson, R. Thayne. Impact of Manpower Programs upon

Employment and Earnings. In *Mangum, G. L. and Robson, R. T., eds.*, 1973, pp. 227–59.
[G: U.S.]

Carleton, Bette N. The Status of Women in Accounting. *Manage. Account.*, September 1973, *55*(3), pp. 59–62. [G: U.S.]

Davis, Harry E. Pension Provisions Affecting the Employment of Older Workers. *Mon. Lab. Rev.*, April 1973, *96*(4), pp. 41–45. [G: U.S.]

Denton, Frank T. A Simulation Model of Month-to-Month Labor Force Movement in Canada. *Int. Econ. Rev.*, June 1973, *14*(2), pp. 293–311.
[G: Canada]

Dickinson, Katherine P. and Dickinson, Jonathan G. Labor Force Participation of Wives: The Effects of Components of Husbands' Income. In *Mandell, L., et al., eds.*, 1973, pp. 233–52. [G: U.S.]

Dodge, Norton T. Women in the Soviet Economy. In *Moskoff, W., ed.*, 1973, pp. 290–302. [G: U.S.S.R.]

Donner, Arthur W. and Lazar, Fred. An Econometric Study of Segmented Labor Markets and the Structure of Unemployment: The Canadian Experience. *Int. Econ. Rev.*, June 1973, *14*(2), pp. 312–27. [G: Canada]

Fisher, Alan A. The Minimum Wage and Teenage Unemployment: A Comment on the Literature. *Western Econ. J.*, December 1973, *11*(4), pp. 514–24. [G: U.S.]

Fisher, Robert W. Labor in a Year of Economic Stabilization. *Mon. Lab. Rev.*, January 1973, *96*(1), pp. 17–26. [G: U.S.]

Gagala, Ken. The Dual Urban Labor Market: Blacks and Whites. *Amer. Econ.*, Spring 1973, *17*(1), pp. 51–59.

Gordon, Robert A. Some Macroeconomic Aspects of Manpower Policy. In *Ulman, L., ed.*, 1973, pp. 14–50. [G: U.S.]

Grad, Susan. Relative Importance of Income Sources of the Aged. *Soc. Sec. Bull.*, August 1973, *36*(8), pp. 37–45. [G: U.S.]

Gramm, Wendy Lee. The Labor Force Decision of Married Female Teachers: A Discriminant Analysis Approach. *Rev. Econ. Statist.*, August 1973, *55*(3), pp. 341–48. [G: U.S.]

Gwartney, James and Stroup, Richard. Measurement of Employment Discrimination According to Sex. *Southern Econ. J.*, April 1973, *39*(4), pp. 575–87.
[G: U.S.]

Haber, Sheldon. Trends in Work Rates of White Females, 1890 to 1950. *Ind. Lab. Relat. Rev.*, July 1973, *26*(4), pp. 1122–34. [G: U.S.]

Hayghe, Howard. Labor Force Activity of Married Women. *Mon. Lab. Rev.*, April 1973, *96*(4), pp. 31–36. [G: U.S.]

Hufbauer, G. C. Occupational Trends and Social Mobility in the West Punjab. *Pakistan Econ. Soc. Rev.*, Spring 1973, *11*(1), pp. 83–103. [G: India]

Johnston, Denis F. Education of Workers: Projections to 1990. *Mon. Lab. Rev.*, November 1973, *96*(11), pp. 22–31.

Katz, Arnold. Teenage Employment Effects of State Minimum Wages. *J. Human Res.*, Spring 1973, *8* (2), pp. 250–56. [G: U.S.]

Kotliar, A. and Kirpa, I. Demographic Aspects of Employment in Cities with Differing Industrial

Structures. *Prob. Econ.*, April 1973, *15*(12), pp. 73–85. [G: U.S.S.R.]

Kraft, Arthur and Kraft, John. A Cross-Section Comparison of How Individuals Allocate Time: 1960 Versus 1970. *Nebr. J. Econ. Bus.*, Autumn 1973, *12*(4), pp. 51–68. [G: U.S.]

Kraft, Arthur. Preference Orderings as Determinants of the Labor Force Behavior of Married Women. *Western Econ. J.*, September 1973, *11*(3), pp. 270–84. [G: U.S.]

Kreps, Juanita. The Sources of Inequality. In *Ginzberg, E. and Yohalem, A. M., eds.*, 1973, pp. 85–96. [G: U.S.]

Kuhn, James W. An Economist's View of Women's Work. In *Ginzberg, E. and Yohalem, A. M., eds.*, 1973, pp. 63–68. [G: U.S.]

Michelotti, Kopp. Young Workers: In School and Out. *Mon. Lab. Rev.*, September 1973, *96*(9), pp. 11–15. [G: U.S.]

Mogull, Robert G. Football Salaries and Race: Some Empirical Evidence. *Ind. Relat.*, February 1973, *12*(1), pp. 109–12. [G: U.S.]

Nicholson, Edward A., Jr. and Roderick, Roger D. Correlates of Job Attitudes Among Young Women. *Nebr. J. Econ. Bus.*, Autumn 1973, *12*(4), pp. 77–89. [G: U.S.]

Oaxaca, Ronald. Male-Female Wage Differentials in Urban Labor Markets. *Int. Econ. Rev.*, October 1973, *14*(3), pp. 693–709. [G: U.S.]

Oppenheimer, Valerie K. A Sociologist's Skepticism. In *Ginzberg, E. and Yohalem, A. M., eds.*, 1973, pp. 30–38. [G: U.S.]

Park, Rosemary. Like Their Fathers Instead. In *Ginzberg, E. and Yohalem, A. M., eds.*, 1973, pp. 39–57. [G: U.S.]

Rasmussen, David W. Changes in the Relative Income of Nonwhite Males, 1948–1970. In *Rasmussen, D. W. and Haworth, C. T., eds.*, 1973, pp. 81–86. [G: U.S.]

Robie, Edward A. Challenge to Management. In *Ginzberg, E. and Yohalem, A. M., eds.*, 1973, pp. 9–29. [G: U.S.]

Ryscavage, P. M. and Mellor, Earl F. The Economic Situation of Spanish Americans. *Mon. Lab. Rev.*, April 1973, *96*(4), pp. 3–9. [G: U.S.]

Scully, Gerald W. and Gallaway, Lowell E. A Spectral Analysis of the Demographic Structure of American Unemployment. *J. Bus.*, January 1973, *46*(1), pp. 87–102. [G: U.S.]

Shanahan, James L. Mis-Match in the Supply of and Demand for Low Skill Jobs in the Inner City. In *Mattila, J. M. and Thompson, W. R., eds.*, 1973, pp. 192–205. [G: U.S.]

Shepherd, William G. and Levin, Sharon G. Managerial Discrimination in Large Firms. *Rev. Econ. Statist.*, November 1973, *55*(4), pp. 412–22. [G: U.S.]

Sherman, Sally R. Assets on the Threshold of Retirement. *Soc. Sec. Bull.*, August 1973, *36*(8), pp. 3–17. [G: U.S.]

Sobol, Marion G. A Dynamic Analysis of Labor Force Participation of Married Women of Childbearing Age. *J. Human Res.*, Fall 1973, *8*(4), pp. 497–505. [G: U.S.]

Spencer, Byron G. Determinants of the Labour Force Participation of Married Women: A Micro-

Study of Toronto Households. *Can. J. Econ.*, May 1973, *6*(2), pp. 222–38. [G: Canada]

Steger, Wilbur A. Economic and Social Costs of Residential Segregation. In *Clawson, M., ed.*, 1973, pp. 83–113. [G: U.S.]

Struyk, Raymond J. Explaining Variations in the Hourly Wage Rates of Urban Minority Group Females. *J. Human Res.*, Summer 1973, *8*(3), pp. 349–64. [G: U.S.]

Wallace, Phyllis. Sex Discrimination: Some Societal Constraints on Upward Mobility for Women Executives. In *Ginzberg, E. and Yohalem, A. M., eds.*, 1973, pp. 69–84. [G: U.S.]

de Willebois, J. L. J. M. van Der Does. A Workshop for Married Women in Part-Time Employment: Implications of an Experiment in the Netherlands. In *Moskoff, W., ed.*, 1973, pp. 302–22. [G: Netherlands]

Young, Anne M. Children of Working Mothers. *Mon. Lab. Rev.*, April 1973, *96*(4), pp. 37–40. [G: U.S.]

830 TRADE UNIONS; COLLECTIVE BARGAINING; LABOR–MANAGEMENT RELATIONS

831 Trade Unions

8310 Trade Unions

Anderman, Steven D. International Manual on Collective Bargaining for Public Employees: Sweden. In *Kaye, S. P. and Marsh, A., eds.*, 1973, pp. 264–99. [G: Sweden]

Anderson, Arvid and Kaye, Seymour P. International Manual on Collective Bargaining for Public Employees: The United States. In *Kaye, S. P. and Marsh, A., eds.*, 1973, pp. 3–66. [G: U.S.]

Aussieker, Bill and Garbarino, Joseph W. Measuring Faculty Unionism: Quantity and Quality. *Ind. Relat.*, May 1973, *12*(2), pp. 117–24. [G: U.S.]

Baker, Mary Roys. Anglo-Massachusetts Trade Union Roots, 1130–1790. *Labor Hist.*, Summer 1973, *14*(3), pp. 352–96. [G: U.S.; U.K.]

Barbash, Jack. Consumption Values of Trade Unions. *J. Econ. Issues*, June 1973, *7*(2), pp. 289–301.

Barkin, Solomon. Trade Unions and Consumerism. *J. Econ. Issues*, June 1973, *7*(2), pp. 317–21.

Chaison, Gary N. Unit Size and Union Success in Representation Elections. *Mon. Lab. Rev.*, February 1973, *96*(2), pp. 51–52. [G: U.S.]

Cole, David L. The Effect of Labor Relations. In *The Diebold Group, Inc.*, 1973, pp. 239–49. [G: U.S.]

Copp, Robert. Ford Motor Co. as a Multinational Employer. *Mon. Lab. Rev.*, August 1973, *96*(8), pp. 58–61.

Curtin, William J. The Multinational Corporation and Transnational Collective Bargaining. In *Kujawa, D., ed.*, 1973, pp. 192–222. [G: U.S.]

Dubin, Robert. Attachment to Work and Union Militancy. *Ind. Relat.*, February 1973, *12*(1), pp. 51–64.

Dubinsky, Irwin. Trade Union Discrimination in the

Pittsburgh Construction Industry. In *Pynoos, J.; Schafer, R. and Hartman, C. W., eds.,* 1973, pp. 376–91. [G: U.S.]

Ehrenberg, Ronald G. Municipal Government Structure, Unionization, and the Wages of Fire Fighters. *Ind. Lab. Relat. Rev.,* October 1973, *27* (1), pp. 36–48. [G: U.S.]

Fink, Gary M. The Rejection of Voluntarism. *Ind. Lab. Relat. Rev.,* January 1973, *26*(2), pp. 805–19. [G: U.S.]

Foner, Philip S. An Early Trades Union and Its Fate. *Labor Hist.,* Summer 1973, *14*(3), pp. 423–24. [G: U.S.]

Foran, Terry G. Unionism and Wage Differentials. *Southern Econ. J.,* October 1973, *40*(2), pp. 269–78. [G: U.S.]

Form, William H. Job vs. Political Unionism: A Cross-national Comparison. *Ind. Relat.,* May 1973, *12*(2), pp. 224–38.

Franklin, William S. A Comparison of Formally and Informally Trained Journeymen in Construction. *Ind. Lab. Relat. Rev.,* July 1973, *26*(4), pp. 1086–94. [G: U.S.]

Gaul, Dieter. International Manual on Collective Bargaining for Public Employees: Federal Republic of Germany. In *Kaye, S. P. and Marsh, A., eds.,* 1973, pp. 171–209. [G: W. Germany]

Ghali, Moheb A. On Measuring "Third Party" Effects of a Strike. *Western Econ. J.,* June 1973, *11* (2), pp. 214–27. [G: U.S.]

Ginger, Ray. American Workers: Views From the Left. *Labor Hist.,* Summer 1973, *14*(3), pp. 425–28. [G: U.S.]

Goldfinger, Nathaniel. An American Trade Union View of International Trade and Investment. In *Kujawa, D., ed.,* 1973, pp. 28–53. [G: U.S.]

Gould, William B. Black Workers Inside the House of Labor. *Ann. Amer. Acad. Polit. Soc. Sci.,* May 1973, *407*, pp. 78–90. [G: U.S.]

Hall, W. Clayton and Carroll, Norman E. The Effect of Teachers' Organizations on Salaries and Class Size. *Ind. Lab. Relat. Rev.,* January 1973, *26*(2), pp. 834–41. [G: U.S.]

Hamilton, Richard F. Trends in Labor Union Voting Behavior, 1948-1968: Comment. *Ind. Relat.,* February 1973, *12*(1), pp. 113–15. [G: U.S.]

Hammerman, Herbert. Minorities in Construction Referral Unions—Revisited. *Mon. Lab. Rev.,* May 1973, *96*(5), pp. 43–46. [G: U.S.]

Hu, Sheng Cheng. Capital Mobility and the Effects of Unionization. *Southern Econ. J.,* April 1973, *39* (4), pp. 526–34.

Kawada, Hisashi and Komatsu, Ryuji. Post-War Labor Movements in Japan. In *Sturmthal, A. and Scoville, J. G., eds.,* 1973, pp. 123–48. [G: Japan]

Kaye, Seymour P. Summary of Comparative Public Policies and Procedures. In *Kaye, S. P. and Marsh, A., eds.,* 1973, pp. 300–321. [G: U.S.; W. Europe]

Kayode, M. O. The Management of Trade Union Finances in Nigeria. In *Damachi, U. G. and Seibel, H. D., eds.,* 1973, pp. 138–46. [G: Nigeria]

Kilby, Peter. Trade Unionism in Nigeria, 1938–66. In *Sturmthal, A. and Scoville, J. G., eds.,* 1973, pp. 228–58. [G: Nigeria]

Kleinhenz, Gerhard. Interessenverbände und sozialstaatliche Wirtschaftspolitik. (Interest Groups and Economic Policy. With English summary.) *Z. Wirtschaft. Sozialwissen.,* 1973, *93*(3), pp. 307–21.

Kritzberg, Barry. An Unfinished Chapter in White-Collar Unionism: The Formative Years of the Chicago Newspaper Guild. *Labor Hist.,* Summer 1973, *14*(3), pp. 397–413. [G: U.S.]

Kujawa, Duane. Foreign Sourcing Decisions and the Duty to Bargain under the NLRA. In *Kujawa, D., ed.,* 1973, pp. 223–69. [G: U.S.]

Lahne, Herbert J. Blacksmiths and Welders: Identity and Phenomenal Change: Comment. *Ind. Lab. Relat. Rev.,* January 1973, *26*(2), pp. 860–62.

Levin, Samuel M. Social Implications of Factory Labor. In *Levin, S. M.,* 1973, pp. 3–13. [G: U.S.]

Lösche, Peter. Stages in the Evolution of the German Labor Movement. In *Sturmthal, A. and Scoville, J. G., eds.,* 1973, pp. 101–22. [G: Germany]

Madden, Carl H. Construction Wages: The Great Consumer Robbery. In *Reynolds, L. G.; Green, G. D. and Lewis, D. R., eds.,* 1973, pp. 18–23. [G: U.S.]

Maier, Heribert. The International Free Trade Union Movement and International Corporations. In *Kujawa, D., ed.,* 1973, pp. 8–27. [G: U.S.]

McCormick, B. J. Trade Unions and Wage Inflation in the UK: A Reappraisal: Discussion. In *Parkin, M., ed.,* 1973, pp. 328–29. [G: U.K.]

McLaughlin, Doris B. The Second Battle of Battle Creek—The Open Shop Movement in the Early Twentieth Century. *Labor Hist.,* Summer 1973, *14*(3), pp. 323–39. [G: U.S.]

Mergen, Bernard. Blacksmiths and Welders: Identity and Phenomenal Change: Reply. *Ind. Lab. Relat. Rev.,* January 1973, *26*(2), pp. 862–64.

Meyers, Frederic. Public Employee Unions: The French Experience. *Ind. Relat.,* February 1973, *12*(1), pp. 33–50. [G: France]

Mulvey, C. and Trevithick, J. A. Trade Unions and Wage Inflation. *Econ. Soc. Rev.,* January 1973, *4* (2), pp. 209–29.

Näslund, Bertil. Labor Power and Income Distribution. *Swedish J. Econ.,* June 1973, *75*(2), pp. 128–42.

Odewahn, Charles A. and Krislov, Joseph. Contract Rejections: Testing the Explanatory Hypotheses. *Ind. Relat.,* October 1973, *12*(3), pp. 289–96. [G: U.S.]

Oldham, James C. Organized Labor, the Environment, and the Taft-Hartley Act. *Mich. Law Rev.,* April 1973, *71*(5), pp. 935–1040. [G: U.S.]

Pásara, Luís and Santistevan, Jorge. "Industrial Communities" and Trade Unions in Peru: A Preliminary Analysis. *Int. Lab. Rev.,* August-September 1973, *108*(2–3), pp. 127–42. [G: Peru]

Pen, Jan. Trade Union Attitudes Toward Central Wage Policy: Remarks on the Dutch Experience. In *Sturmthal, A. and Scoville, J. G., eds.,* 1973, pp. 259–82. [G: Netherlands]

Perlman, Mark. Consumption Values of Trade Unions: Comment. *J. Econ. Issues,* June 1973, *7*(2), pp. 303–05.

Pisano, Paolo G. International Manual on Collective Bargaining for Public Employees: Italy. In *Kaye,*

S. P. and Marsh, A., eds., 1973, pp. 210–63.
[G: Italy]

Polk, Judd. American Labor and the U.S. Multinational Enterprise in an Emerging World Economy. In *Kujawa, D., ed.,* 1973, pp. 270–85.
[G: U.S.]

Purdy, D. L. and Zis, G. Trade Unions and Wage Inflation in the UK: A Reappraisal. In *Parkin, M., ed.,* 1973, pp. 294–327.
[G: U.K.]

Reisler, Mark. Mexican Unionization in California Agriculture, 1927–1936. *Labor Hist.,* Fall 1973, *14*(4), pp. 562–79.
[G: U.S.]

Robinson, Derek. Industrial Relations Aspects of Incomes Policies. In *Robinson, D.,* 1973, pp. 42–75.

Robinson, Derek. Trade Union Views on Workers' Negotiated Savings Plans for Capital Formation. In *Robinson, D.,* 1973, pp. 76–104.
[G: W. Europe]

Robinson, Derek. Trade Unions and Multinational Companies. In *Robinson, D.,* 1973, pp. 158–84.

Sánchez, Carlos E. and Arnaudo, Aldo A. The Economic Power of Argentine Manufacturing Labor Unions. In *Sturmthal, A. and Scoville, J. G., eds.,* 1973, pp. 178–98.
[G: Argentina]

Scoville, James G. Some Determinants of the Structure of Labor Movements. In *Sturmthal, A. and Scoville, J. G., eds.,* 1973, pp. 58–78.
[G: U.S.; U.K.]

Sharman, Ben. Multinational Corporations and Trade Unions. *Mon. Lab. Rev.,* August 1973, *96*(8), pp. 56–58.

Taft, Philip. Internal Union Structure and Functions. In *Somers, G. G., ed.,* 1973, pp. 1–9. [G: U.S.]

Tuller, S. Mark. New Standards for Domination and Support under Section 8(a)(2). *Yale Law J.,* January 1973, *82*(3), pp. 510–32.
[G: U.S.]

Warne, Clinton L. The Consumer Movement and the Labor Movement. *J. Econ. Issues,* June 1973, *7*(2), pp. 307–16.

Wilkinson, R. K. and Burkitt, B. Wage Determination and Trade Unions. *Scot. J. Polit. Econ.,* June 1973, *20*(2), pp. 107–22.
[G: U.K.]

832 Collective Bargaining

8320 General

Aaron, Benjamin. Legal Framework of Industrial Relations. In *Somers, G. G., ed.,* 1973, pp. 101–10.
[G: U.S.]

Bairstow, Frances. Canada's Discontent with Strikes Prompts Interest in Arbitration. *Mon. Lab. Rev.,* August 1973, *96*(8), pp. 63–64. [G: Canada]

Burke, Donald R. and Rubin, Lester. Is Contract Rejection a Major Collective Bargaining Problem? *Ind. Lab. Relat. Rev.,* January 1973, *26*(2), pp. 820–33.
[G: U.S.]

Ciller, Ozer U. Pricing Employment Contracts. *Manage. Account.,* November 1973, *55*(5), pp. 29–31.

Di Noto, M. J. A Sequential Decision Model of Bargaining: Comment. *Western Econ. J.,* September 1973, *11*(3), pp. 371–74.

Dunlop, John T. Structure of Collective Bargaining. In *Somers, G. G., ed.,* 1973, pp. 10–18. [G: U.S.]

Evan, Harry Zvi. Comparing Conditions of Work by Collective Agreement Analysis: A Case Study of the Petroleum Industry. *Int. Lab. Rev.,* July 1973, *108*(1), pp. 59–75.

Ferrer-Pacces, F. M. Strategia sindacale. Verso lo sfondamento delle linee di difesa tattica. (Trade Unions Strategy. Towards the Breaking of Tactical Defense Lines. With English summary.) *L'Impresa,* 1973, *15*(11–12), pp. 656–58. [G: Italy]

Garbarino, Joseph W. The British Experiment with Industrial Relations Reform. *Ind. Lab. Relat. Rev.,* January 1973, *26*(2), pp. 793–804. [G: U.K.]

Hamermesh, Daniel S. Who "Wins" in Wage Bargaining? *Ind. Lab. Relat. Rev.,* July 1973, *26*(4), pp. 1146–49. [G: U.S.]

Harnett, Donald L. and Hamner, W. Clay. The Value of Information in Bargaining. *Western Econ. J.,* March 1973, *11*(1), pp. 81–88.

Högberg, Gunnar. Recent Trends in Collective Bargaining in Sweden. *Int. Lab. Rev.,* March 1973, *107*(3), pp. 223–38. [G: Sweden]

Isard, Peter. The Effectiveness of Using the Tax System to Curb Inflationary Collective Bargains: An Analysis of the Wallich-Weintraub Plan. *J. Polit. Econ.,* May-June 1973, *81*(3), pp. 729–40.
[G: U.S.]

Ivanov, S. A. New Codification of Soviet Labour Law. *Int. Lab. Rev.,* August-September 1973, *108* (2–3), pp. 143–61. [G: U.S.S.R.]

Larson, David and Bolton, Lena W. Calendar of Wage Increases and Negotiations for 1973. *Mon. Lab. Rev.,* January 1973, *96*(1), pp. 3–16.
[G: U.S.]

Lester, Richard A. Manipulation of the Labor Market. In *Somers, G. G., ed.,* 1973, pp. 47–55.
[G: U.S.]

Odewahn, Charles A. and Krislov, Joseph. The Relationship Between Union Contract Rejections and the Business Cycle—A Theoretical Approach. *Nebr. J. Econ. Bus.,* Summer 1973, *12*(3), pp. 23–36.

Robinson, Derek. Industrial Relations Aspects of Incomes Policies. In *Robinson, D.,* 1973, pp. 42–75.

Robinson, Derek. Productivity Bargaining. In *Robinson, D.,* 1973, pp. 185–204.

Seitz, Peter. Mandatory Contract Arbitration: A Viable Process or Not, It Works (Sometimes). *Ind. Lab. Relat. Rev.,* April 1973, *26*(3), pp. 1009–12.

Sturmthal, Adolf. Industrial Relations Strategies. In *Sturmthal, A. and Scoville, J. G., eds.,* 1973, pp. 1–33. [G: U.S.; U.K.]

Talbot, Joseph E., Jr. Wage Changes and Bargaining Gains in 1972. *Mon. Lab. Rev.,* April 1973, *96*(4), pp. 17–20. [G: U.S.]

Weiller, Augusto. Arbitrato e programmazione. (Arbitration and Planning. With English summary.) *Bancaria,* December 1973, *29*(12), pp. 1474–80.

8321 Collective Bargaining in the Private Sector

Benson, Charles S. Collective Bargaining in Higher Education. *Mon. Lab. Rev.,* May 1973, *96*(5), pp. 33–34. [G: U.S.]

Bolton, Lena W. Bargaining Ahead: Major Contracts Expiring in 1974. *Mon. Lab. Rev.,* December 1973, *96*(12), pp. 43–51. [G: U.S.]

Chamberlain, Neil W. Collective Bargaining in the Private Sector. In *Somers, G. G., ed.,* 1973,

pp. 19–26. [G: U.S.]

Curtin, William J. The Multinational Corporation and Transnational Collective Bargaining. In *Kujawa, D., ed.*, 1973, pp. 192–222. [G: U.S.]

Damachi, Ukandi G. Industrial Relations in the Sapele Timber Industry: The Development of Collective Bargaining. In *Damachi, U. G. and Seibel, H. D., eds.*, 1973, pp. 98–118. [G: Nigeria]

Granof, Michael H. Financial Evaluation of Labor Contracts. *Manage. Account.*, July 1973, *55*(1), pp. 38–42, 45.

Henle, Peter. Reverse Collective Bargaining? A Look at Some Union Concession Situations. *Ind. Lab. Relat. Rev.*, April 1973, *26*(3), pp. 956–68. [G: U.S.]

Hodgens, Evan L. Survivor's Pensions: An Emerging Employee Benefit. *Mon. Lab. Rev.*, July 1973, *96* (7), pp. 31–34. [G: U.S.]

Kawada, Hisashi and Komatsu, Ryuji. Post-War Labor Movements in Japan. In *Sturmthal, A. and Scoville, J. G., eds.*, 1973, pp. 123–48. [G: Japan]

Kilby, Peter. Trade Unionism in Nigeria, 1938–66. In *Sturmthal, A. and Scoville, J. G., eds.*, 1973, pp. 228–58. [G: Nigeria]

Kujawa, Duane. Foreign Sourcing Decisions and the Duty to Bargain under the NLRA. In *Kujawa, D., ed.*, 1973, pp. 223–69. [G: U.S.]

Lowell, Cym H. Collective Bargaining and the Professional Team Sport Industry. *Law Contemp. Probl.*, Winter-Spring 1973, *38*(1), pp. 3–41. [G: U.S.]

Maier, Heribert. The International Free Trade Union Movement and International Corporations. In *Kujawa, D., ed.*, 1973, pp. 8–27. [G: U.S.]

Martin, Donald L. Some Economics of Job Rights in the Longshore Industry. *J. Econ. Bus.*, Winter 1973, *25*(2), pp. 93–100. [G: U.S.]

Oldham, James C. Organized Labor, the Environment, and the Taft-Hartley Act. *Mich. Law Rev.*, April 1973, *71*(5), pp. 935–1040. [G: U.S.]

Thompson, Duane E. and Borglum, Richard P. A Case Study of Employee Attitudes and Labor Unrest. *Ind. Lab. Relat. Rev.*, October 1973, *27*(1), pp. 74–83. [G: U.S.]

Veldkamp, Gérard M. J. and Raetsen, M. J. E. H. Temporary Work Agencies and Western European Social Legislation. *Int. Lab. Rev.*, February 1973, *107*(2), pp. 117–31. [G: Sweden; Denmark; Belgium; W. Germany; Netherlands]

8322 Collective Bargaining in the Public Sector

Anderman, Steven D. International Manual on Collective Bargaining for Public Employees: Sweden. In *Kaye, S. P. and Marsh, A., eds.*, 1973, pp. 264–99. [G: Sweden]

Anderson, Arvid and Kaye, Seymour P. International Manual on Collective Bargaining for Public Employees: The United States. In *Kaye, S. P. and Marsh, A., eds.*, 1973, pp. 3–66. [G: U.S.]

Derber, Milton, et al. Bargaining and Budget Making in Illinois Public Institutions. *Ind. Lab. Relat. Rev.*, October 1973, *27*(1), pp. 49–62. [G: U.S.]

Døhlem, Bjarne. The Report of Norwegian Public Collective Bargaining. In *Kaye, S. P. and Marsh, A., eds.*, 1973, pp. 350–64. [G: Norway]

Edwards, Harry T. The Emerging Duty to Bargain in the Public Sector. *Mich. Law Rev.*, April 1973, *71*(5), pp. 885–934. [G: U.S.]

Edwards, Ronald [Sir]. The Status Agreement in Electricity. In *Tivey, L., ed.*, 1973, pp. 284–98. [G: U.K.]

Ehrenberg, Ronald G. Municipal Government Structure, Unionization, and the Wages of Fire Fighters. *Ind. Lab. Relat. Rev.*, October 1973, *27* (1), pp. 36–48. [G: U.S.]

Gaul, Dieter. International Manual on Collective Bargaining for Public Employees: Federal Republic of Germany. In *Kaye, S. P. and Marsh, A., eds.*, 1973, pp. 171–209. [G: W. Germany]

Goldenberg, Shirley B. Public Sector Bargaining: The Canadian Experience. *Mon. Lab. Rev.*, May 1973, *96*(5), pp. 34–36. [G: Canada]

Kaye, Seymour P. Summary of Comparative Public Policies and Procedures. In *Kaye, S. P. and Marsh, A., eds.*, 1973, pp. 300–321. [G: U.S.; W. Europe]

Kochan, Thomas A. Correlates of State Public Employee Bargaining Laws. *Ind. Relat.*, October 1973, *12*(3), pp. 322–37. [G: U.S.]

Lewin, David. Wage Parity and the Supply of Police and Firemen. *Ind. Relat.*, February 1973, *12*(1), pp. 77–85. [G: U.S.]

Lewin, David. Public Employment Relations: Confronting the Issues. *Ind. Relat.*, October 1973, *12* (3), pp. 309–21. [G: U.S.]

Lipsky, David B. and Drotning, John E. The Influence of Collective Bargaining on Teachers' Salaries in New York State. *Ind. Lab. Relat. Rev.*, October 1973, *27*(1), pp. 18–35. [G: U.S.]

Marsh, Arthur I. International Manual on Collective Bargaining for Public Employees: Great Britain. In *Kaye, S. P. and Marsh, A., eds.*, 1973, pp. 128–70. [G: U.K.]

Meyers, Frederic. Public Employee Unions: The French Experience. *Ind. Relat.*, February 1973, *12*(1), pp. 33–50. [G: France]

Nelson, Richard R. Collective Bargaining Agreements in the Federal Service. *Mon. Lab. Rev.*, September 1973, *96*(9), pp. 76–78.

Pisano, Paolo G. International Manual on Collective Bargaining for Public Employees: Italy. In *Kaye, S. P. and Marsh, A., eds.*, 1973, pp. 210–63. [G: Italy]

Schmenner, Roger W. The Determination of Municipal Employee Wages. *Rev. Econ. Statist.*, February 1973, *55*(1), pp. 83–90. [G: U.S.]

Seidman, Joel and Staudohar, Paul D. The Hawaii Public Employment Relations Act: A Critical Analysis. *Ind. Lab. Relat. Rev.*, April 1973, *26*(3), pp. 919–37. [G: U.S.]

Simon, Larry G. The School Finance Decisions: Collective Bargaining and Future Finance Systems. *Yale Law J.*, January 1973, *82*(3), pp. 409–60. [G: U.S.]

Somerhausen, Marc. International Manual on Collective Bargaining for Public Employees: Belgium. In *Kaye, S. P. and Marsh, A., eds.*, 1973, pp. 67–127. [G: Belgium]

Staudohar, Paul D. The Emergence of Hawaii's Public Employment Law. *Ind. Relat.*, October 1973, *12*(3), pp. 338–51. [G: U.S.]

Stern, James L. Bargaining and Arbitration in the

British Civil Service. *Mon. Lab. Rev.*, August 1973, *96*(8), pp. 61–63. [G: U.K.]

Taylor, George W. Collective Bargaining in the Public Sector. In *Somers, G. G., ed.*, 1973, pp. 27–35. [G: U.S.]

Thompson, Mark and Cairnie, James. Compulsory Arbitration: The Case of British Columbia Teachers. *Ind. Lab. Relat. Rev.*, October 1973, *27*(1), pp. 3–17. [G: Canada]

Witney, Fred. Final-Offer Arbitration: The Indianapolis Experience. *Mon. Lab. Rev.*, May 1973, *96*(5), pp. 20–25. [G: U.S.]

Zack, Arnold M. Meeting the Rising Cost of Public Sector Settlements. *Mon. Lab. Rev.*, May 1973, *96* (5), pp. 38–40. [G: U.S.]

Zagoria, Sam. Resolving Impasses by Public Referendum. *Mon. Lab. Rev.*, May 1973, *96*(5), pp. 36–38. [G: U.S.]

833 Labor–Management Relations

8330 General

Aaron, Benjamin. Legal Framework of Industrial Relations. In *Somers, G. G., ed.*, 1973, pp. 101–10. [G: U.S.]

Atkinson, A. B. Worker Management and the Modern Industrial Enterprise. *Quart. J. Econ.*, August 1973, *87*(3), pp. 375–92.

Becker, James F. Class Structure and Conflict in the Managerial Phase: II. *Sci. Soc.*, Winter 1973–1974, *37*(4), pp. 437–53.

Cascioli, Ettore. Analisi statistica della conflittualità nel mercato del lavoro. (Statistical Analysis of Labor Disputes According to the 1965–67 Italian Experience. With English summary.) *Rivista Int. Sci. Econ. Com.*, July 1973, *20*(7), pp. 681–93. [G: Italy]

Champagne, Jean. Adapting Jobs to People: Experiments at Alcan. *Mon. Lab. Rev.*, April 1973, *96*(4), pp. 49–51. [G: Canada]

Cole, David L. The Effect of Labor Relations. In *The Diebold Group, Inc.*, 1973, pp. 239–49. [G: U.S.]

Dolphin, Robert. Made in Japan. *Ohio State U. Bull. Bus. Res.*, September 1973, *48*(9), pp. 4–7. [G: Japan]

Dubin, Robert. Attachment to Work and Union Militancy. *Ind. Relat.*, February 1973, *12*(1), pp. 51–64.

Evans, E. W. and Galambos, P. Work Stoppages in the United Kingdom 1965–70: A Quantitative Study. *Bull. Econ. Res.*, May 1973, *25*(1), pp. 22–42. [G: U.K.]

Fisher, Robert W. When Workers are Discharged—An Overview. *Mon. Lab. Rev.*, June 1973, *96* (6), pp. 4–17. [G: U.S.]

Flowers, Vincent S. and Hughes, Charles L. Why Employees Stay. *Harvard Bus. Rev.*, July-August 1973, *51*(4), pp. 49–60. [G: U.S.]

Furubotn, Eirik G. and Pejovich, Svetozar. Property Rights, Economic Decentralization, and the Evolution of the Yugoslav Firm, 1965–1972. *J. Law Econ.*, October 1973, *16*(2), pp. 275–302. [G: Yugoslavia]

Garbarino, Joseph W. The British Experiment with Industrial Relations Reform. *Ind. Lab. Relat.*

Rev., January 1973, *26*(2), pp. 793–804. [G: U.K.]

Joffe, Paul L. French Labor Relations: A Functional Analysis. *Yale Law J.*, March 1973, *82*(4), pp. 806–28. [G: France]

Kaplan, H. Roy. How *Do* Workers View Their Work in America? *Mon. Lab. Rev.*, June 1973, *96*(6), pp. 46–48. [G: U.S.]

Lester, Richard A. Manipulation of the Labor Market. In *Somers, G. G., ed.*, 1973, pp. 47–55. [G: U.S.]

Levin, Samuel M. Social Implications of Factory Labor. In *Levin, S. M.*, 1973, pp. 3–13. [G: U.S.]

Levin, Samuel M. Thoughts on Industrial Democracy. In *Levin, S. M.*, 1973, pp. 143–56. [G: U.S.]

van der Merwe, P. J. Manpower Policy in South Africa. *Finance Trade Rev.*, December 1972-June 1973, *10*(2–3), pp. 73–135. [G: S. Africa]

Mire, Joseph. European Workers' Participation in Management. *Mon. Lab. Rev.*, February 1973, *96* (2), pp. 9–15. [G: Europe]

Quinn, Robert P., et al. Evaluating Working Conditions in America. *Mon. Lab. Rev.*, November 1973, *96*(11), pp. 32–41. [G: U.S.]

Roberts, Karlene H. A Symposium: Cross-national Organizational Research: Overview. *Ind. Relat.*, May 1973, *12*(2), pp. 137–43.

Robinson, James W. and Turner, James T. An Empirical Investigation of the Theory Y Management—Theory X Union Hypothesis. *Miss. Val. J. Bus. Econ.*, Spring 1973, *8*(3), pp. 77–84.

Soutar, Douglas. A Forward Look at Labor-Management Relations within the Framework of a Free Enterprise System. In *Somers, G. G., ed.*, 1973, pp. 157–63. [G: U.S.]

Steenkamp, W. F. J. Labour and Management in Manufacturing Development. *S. Afr. J. Econ.*, December 1973, *41*(4), pp. 438–51. [G: S.Africa]

Susman, Gerald I. Job Enlargement: Effects of Culture on Worker Responses. *Ind. Relat.*, February 1973, *12*(1), pp. 1–15. [G: U.S.]

Winpisinger, William W. Job Enrichment: A Union View. *Mon. Lab. Rev.*, April 1973, *96*(4), pp. 54–56. [G: U.S.]

Wyer, Rolfe. Learning Curve Techniques for Direct Labor Management. In *Thomas, W. E., Jr., ed.*, 1973, pp. 370–78.

Young, Edwin. Personnel Relations in Non-Profit Institutions. In *Somers, G. G., ed.*, 1973, pp. 198–204. [G: U.S.]

Yuchtman, Ephraim. Reward Structure, the Quality of Work Environment, and Social Accounting. In *Dierkes, M. and Bauer, R. A., eds.*, 1973, pp. 183–90. [G: U.S.]

Županov, Josip. Two Patterns of Conflict Management in Industry. *Ind. Relat.*, May 1973, *12*(2), pp. 213–23. [G: U.S.; Yugoslavia]

8331 Labor–Management Relations in Private Sector

Birkin, Stanley J. and Ford, James S. The Quantity/ Quality Dilemma: The Impact of a Zero Defects Program. In *Cochrane, J. L. and Zeleny, M., eds.*,

1973, pp. 517–29. [G: U.S.]

Chamberlain, Neil W. Collective Bargaining in the Private Sector. In *Somers, G. G., ed.*, 1973, pp. 19–26. [G: U.S.]

Copp, Robert. Ford Motor Co. as a Multinational Employer. *Mon. Lab. Rev.*, August 1973, *96*(8), pp. 58–61.

Damachi, Ukandi G. Industrial Relations in the Sapele Timber Industry: The Development of Collective Bargaining. In *Damachi, U. G. and Seibel, H. D., eds.*, 1973, pp. 98–118. [G: Nigeria]

Gagliani, Giorgio. Note sulle imprese multinazionali e l'occupazione. (Notes on Multinational Firms and Employment. With English summary.) *Bancaria*, September 1973, *29*(9), pp. 1081–89.

Gennard, John and Steuer, M. D. The Industrial Relations of Foreign Owned Subsidiaries in the United Kingdom. In *Henley, D. S., ed.*, 1973, pp. 301–17. [G: U.K.]

Ghali, Moheb A. On Measuring "Third Party" Effects of a Strike. *Western Econ. J.*, June 1973, *11*(2), pp. 214–27. [G: U.S.]

Goldberg, Joseph P. Longshoremen and the Modernisation of Cargo Handling in the United States. *Int. Lab. Rev.*, March 1973, *107*(3), pp. 253–79. [G: U.S.]

Jaeger, Klaus. Zur Problematik der Gewinnbeteiligung der Arbeitnehmer als Mittel der Vermögenspolitik. (Profit-Sharing as an Instrument of Ownership Policy. With English summary.) *Z. Wirtschaft. Sozialwissen.*, 1973, *93*(6), pp. 687–707. [G: W. Germany]

Krusius-Ahrenberg, Lolo. Kring företagsdemokratin i tyska förbundsrepubliken. (On Industrial Democracy in the Federal Republic of Germany. With English summary.) *Ekon. Samfundets Tidskr.*, 1973, *26*(4), pp. 270–99. [G: W. Germany]

Levitan, Sar A. and Johnston, William B. Job Redesign, Reform, Enrichment: Exploring the Limitations. *Mon. Lab. Rev.*, July 1973, *96*(7), pp. 35–41. [G: U.S.]

Maier, Heribert. The International Free Trade Union Movement and International Corporations. In *Kujawa, D., ed.*, 1973, pp. 8–27. [G: U.S.]

Novara, Francesco. Job Enrichment in the Olivetti Company. *Int. Lab. Rev.*, October 1973, *108*(4), pp. 283–94. [G: Italy]

Orr, John A. The Rise and Fall of Steel's Human Relations Committee. *Labor Hist.*, Winter 1973, *14*(1), pp. 69–81. [G: U.S.]

Polk, Judd. American Labor and the U.S. Multinational Enterprise in an Emerging World Economy. In *Kujawa, D., ed.*, 1973, pp. 270–85. [G: U.S.]

Rosner, M., et al. Worker Participation and Influence in Five Countries. *Ind. Relat.*, May 1973, *12*(2), pp. 200–12. [G: U.S.; Italy; Austria; Israel; Yugoslavia]

Scoville, James G. Pre-Industrial Industrial Relations: The Case of Afghanistan. In *Sturmthal, A. and Scoville, J. G., eds.*, 1973, pp. 199–227. [G: Afghanistan]

Thompson, Duane E. and Borglum, Richard P. A Case Study of Employee Attitudes and Labor Un-

rest. *Ind. Lab. Relat. Rev.*, October 1973, *27*(1), pp. 74–83. [G: U.S.]

8332 Labor–Management Relations in Public Sector

Adam, Jan. The Incentive System in the USSR: The Abortive Reform of 1965. *Ind. Lab. Relat. Rev.*, October 1973, *27*(1), pp. 84–92. [G: U.S.S.R.]

Anderman, Steven D. International Manual on Collective Bargaining for Public Employees: Sweden. In *Kaye, S. P. and Marsh, A., eds.*, 1973, pp. 264–99. [G: Sweden]

Anderson, Arvid and Kaye, Seymour P. International Manual on Collective Bargaining for Public Employees: The United States. In *Kaye, S. P. and Marsh, A., eds.*, 1973, pp. 3–66. [G: U.S.]

Brown, Emily Clark. Fundamental Soviet Labor Legislation. *Ind. Lab. Relat. Rev.*, January 1973, *26*(2), pp. 778–92. [G: U.S.S.R.]

Gaul, Dieter. International Manual on Collective Bargaining for Public Employees: Federal Republic of Germany. In *Kaye, S. P. and Marsh, A., eds.*, 1973, pp. 171–209. [G: W. Germany]

Héthy, Lajos and Makó, Csaba. Incentive Problems in the Centrally Planned Economy of Hungary. *Ind. Lab. Relat. Rev.*, January 1973, *26*(2), pp. 767–77. [G: Hungary]

Jones, Ken. Employee Directors in Steel. In *Tivey, L., ed.*, 1973, pp. 298–302. [G: U.K.]

Kaye, Seymour P. Summary of Comparative Public Policies and Procedures. In *Kaye, S. P. and Marsh, A., eds.*, 1973, pp. 300–321. [G: U.S.; W. Europe]

Marsh, Arthur I. International Manual on Collective Bargaining for Public Employees: Great Britain. In *Kaye, S. P. and Marsh, A., eds.*, 1973, pp. 128–70. [G: U.K.]

Pisano, Paolo G. International Manual on Collective Bargaining for Public Employees: Italy. In *Kaye, S. P. and Marsh, A., eds.*, 1973, pp. 210–63. [G: Italy]

Somerhausen, Marc. International Manual on Collective Bargaining for Public Employees: Belgium. In *Kaye, S. P. and Marsh, A., eds.*, 1973, pp. 67–127. [G: Belgium]

Thompson, Mark and Cairnie, James. Compulsory Arbitration: The Case of British Columbia Teachers. *Ind. Lab. Relat. Rev.*, October 1973, *27*(1), pp. 3–17. [G: Canada]

Vais, T. The Topic of an International Symposium: Labor Resources in COMECON Nations. *Prob. Econ.*, July 1973, *16*(3), pp. 77–86. [G: U.S.S.R.]

840 DEMOGRAPHIC ECONOMICS

841 Demographic Economics

8410 Demographic Economics

Abramson, Fredric David. High Foetal Mortality and Birth Intervals. *Population Stud.*, July 1973, *27*(2), pp. 235–42. [G: U.S.]

Afzal, Mohammad. 1972 Census: Population—Expected and Actual. *Pakistan Develop. Rev.*, Summer 1973, *12*(2), pp. 123–34. [G: Pakistan]

Afzal, Mohammad; Hashmi, M. Iqbal and Nizami, N. H. Marriage Patterns in a Rural Agglomeration. *Pakistan Develop. Rev.*, Autumn 1973, *12*(3), pp. 273–82. [G: Pakistan]

Afzal, Mohammad; Bean, Lee L. and Hussain, Imtiazuddin. Muslim Marriages: Age, Mehr and Social Status. *Pakistan Develop. Rev.*, Spring 1973, *12*(1), pp. 48–61. [G: Pakistan]

Ahmad, Muneer. Requirements of an Organisational Structure for a Broad Based Population Programme. *Pakistan Econ. Soc. Rev.*, Autumn 1973, *11*(3), pp. 277–87. [G: Pakistan]

Allen, Jodie T. A Guide to the 1960–1971 Current Population Survey Files. *Ann. Econ. Soc. Measure*, April 1973, *2*(2), pp. 189–99. [G: U.S.]

Alonso, William. The Mirage of New Towns. In *Grieson, R. E., ed.*, 1973, pp. 213–28. [G: U.S.]

Alvírez, David. The Effects of Formal Church Affiliation and Religiosity on the Fertility Patterns of Mexican-American Catholics. *Demography*, February 1973, *10*(1), pp. 19–36. [G: U.S.]

Anderson, Otto. Dødelighedsforholdene i Danmark 1735–1839. (Mortality Conditions in Denmark 1735–1839. With English summary.) *Nationalokon. Tidsskr.*, 1973, *111*(2), pp. 277–305. [G: Denmark]

Appleby, Andrew B. Disease or Famine? Mortality in Cumberland and Westmorland, 1580–1640. *Econ. Hist. Rev.*, 2nd Ser., August 1973, *26*(3), pp. 403–32. [G: U.K.]

Ashenfelter, Orley. Child Quality and the Demand for Children: Comment. *J. Polit. Econ.*, Part II, March-April 1973, *81*(2), pp. S96–98. [G: U.S.]

Balakrishnan, T. R. A Cost Benefit Analysis of the Barbados Family Planning Programme. *Population Stud.*, July 1973, *27*(2), pp. 353–64. [G: Barbados]

Baldwin, George B. "Population Policy in Developed Countries" *Finance Develop.*, December 1973, *10*(4), pp. 3–7.

Baraquin, Yves and Jobert, Annette. Les immigrés: Réflexions sur leur insertion sociale et leur intégration juridique. (Immigrants: Their Social Insertion and Juridical Integration. With English summary.) *Consommation*, July-September 1973, *20*(3), pp. 83–97.

Bauman, Karl E. and Udry, J. Richard. The Difference in Unwanted Births between Blacks and Whites. *Demography*, August 1973, *10*(3), pp. 315–28. [G: U.S.]

Bean, Frank D. Components of Income and Expected Family Size Among Mexican Americans. *Soc. Sci. Quart.*, June 1973, *54*(1), pp. 103–16. [G: U.S.]

Beaver, M. W. Population, Infant Mortality and Milk. *Population Stud.*, July 1973, *27*(2), pp. 243–54. [G: U.S.]

Becker, Gary S. A Theory of Marriage: Part I. *J. Polit. Econ.*, July-August 1973, *81*(4), pp. 813–46.

Becker, Gary S. and Lewis, H. Gregg. On the Interaction between the Quantity and Quality of Children. *J. Polit. Econ.*, Part II, March-April 1973, *81*(2), pp. S279–88.

Ben-Porath, Yoram. Economic Analysis of Fertility in Israel: Point and Counterpoint. *J. Polit. Econ.*, Part II, March-April 1973, *81*(2), pp. S202–33. [G: Israel]

Betti, G. and Bettuzzi, G. La concentrazione della popolazione sparsa relativa in Emilia-Romagna e nel Veneto. (The Concentration of Relative Population Spread in the Countryside in the Italian Regions of Emilia-Romagna and Veneto. With English summary.) *Statistica*, April-June 1973, *33*(2), pp. 169–239. [G: Italy]

Bhagwat, Avinash. Main Features of the Employment Problem in Developing Countries. *Int. Monet. Fund Staff Pap.*, March 1973, *20*(1), pp. 78–99.

Biswas, Suddhendu. A Note on the Generalization of William Brass's Model. *Demography*, August 1973, *10*(3), pp. 459–67. [G: U.S.]

Blake, Judith and Das Gupta, Prithwis. The Fallacy of the Five Million Women: A Re-Estimate: Rejoinder. *Demography*, November 1973, *10*(4), pp. 679–84.

Blandy, Richard and Wery, René. Population and Employment Growth: Bachue-1. *Int. Lab. Rev.*, May 1973, *107*(5), pp. 441–49.

Blumenfeld, Hans. Growth Rate Comparisons: Soviet Union and German Democratic Republic. *Land Econ.*, May 1973, *49*(2), pp. 122–32. [G: U.S.S.R.; E. Germany]

Borus, Michael E. and Nestel, Gilbert. Response Bias in Reports of Father's Education and Socioeconomic Status. *J. Amer. Statist. Assoc.*, December 1973, *68*(344), pp. 816–20. [G: U.S.]

Bowen, Ian. "Nature's Feast" Today. *Finance Develop.*, December 1973, *10*(4), pp. 13–17.

Boyd, Monica. Occupational Mobility and Fertility in Metropolitan Latin America. *Demography*, February 1973, *10*(1), pp. 1–17. [G: Latin America]

Bradshaw, Benjamin S. and Bean, Frank D. Trends in the Fertility of Mexican Americans, 1950-1970. *Soc. Sci. Quart.*, March 1973, *53*(4), pp. 688–96. [G: U.S.]

Brown, George H. Census Projections: 1970 to 1985. *Manage. Account.*, January 1973, *54*(7), pp. 11–14. [G: U.S.]

Brown, Lester. Rich Countries and Poor in a Finite, Interdependent World. In *Olson, M. and Landsberg, H. H., eds.*, 1973, pp. 153–64.

Burki, Shahid J. Rapid Population Growth and Urbanization: The Case of Pakistan. *Pakistan Econ. Soc. Rev.*, Autumn 1973, *11*(3), pp. 239–76. [G: Pakistan]

Bzhilianskii, Iu. Political and Economic Problems of Population Under Socialism. *Prob. Econ.*, April 1973, *15*(12), pp. 52–72. [G: U.S.S.R.]

Cain, Glen G. Economics of the Size of North Carolina Rural Families: Comment. *J. Polit. Econ.*, Part II, March-April 1973, *81*(2), pp. S123–27. [G: U.S.]

Caldwell, J. C. and Ware, H. The Evolution of Family Planning in Australia. *Population Stud.*, March 1973, *27*(1), pp. 7–31. [G: Australia]

Cebula, Richard J. On Migration, Migration Costs, and Wage Differentials, with Special Reference to the United States. *Schweiz. Z. Volkswirtsch.*

Statist., March 1973, *109*(1), pp. 59–68. [G: U.S.]

Cebula, Richard J. and Vedder, Richard K. A Note on Migration, Economic Opportunity, and the Quality of Life. *J. Reg. Sci.*, August 1973, *13*(2), pp. 205–11. [G: U.S.]

Cebula, Richard J.; Kohn, Robert M. and Gallaway, Lowell E. Determinants of Net Migration to SMSA's, 1960–1970. *Miss. Val. J. Bus. Econ.*, Winter 1973-74, *9*(2), pp. 59–64. [G: U.S.]

Chapman, G. P. The Spatial Organization of the Population of the United States and England and Wales. *Econ. Geogr.*, October 1973, *49*(4), pp. 325–43. [G: U.S.; U.K.]

Chen, Lihsin. Population Planning in China. *Pakistan Econ. Soc. Rev.*, Autumn 1973, *11*(3), pp. 231–38. [G: China]

Chen, Martin K. The G Index for Program Priority. In *Berg, R. L., ed.*, 1973, pp. 28–34. [G: U.S.]

Coale, Ansley J. Man and His Environment. In *Enthoven, A. C. and Freeman, A. M., III, eds.*, 1973, pp. 155–65. [G: U.S.]

Coale, Ansley J. Age Composition in the Absence of Mortality and in Other Odd Circumstances. *Demography*, November 1973, *10*(4), pp. 537–42.

Cochrane, Susan Hill. Population and Development: A More General Model. *Econ. Develop. Cult. Change*, April 1973, *21*(3), pp. 409–22.

Cohen, Alvin. Population Problems—Myths and Realities: A Comment. *Econ. Develop. Cult. Change*, October 1973, *22*(1), pp. 137–39.

Cutright, Phillips. The Fallacy of the Five Million Women: A Re-Estimate: A Reaction. *Demography*, November 1973, *10*(4), pp. 663–72.

Cutright, Phillips and Galle, Omer. The Effect of Illegitimacy on U.S. General Fertility Rates and Population Growth. *Population Stud.*, November 1973, *27*(3), pp. 515–26. [G: U.S.]

Das Gupta, Prithwis. Growth of U.S. Population, 1940–1971, in the Light of an Interactive Two-Sex Model. *Demography*, November 1973, *10*(4), pp. 543–65. [G: U.S.]

Davis, Kingsley. Zero Population Growth: The Goal and the Means. In *Olson, M. and Landsberg, H. H., eds.*, 1973, pp. 15–30.

Davis, T. L. F. Fertility Differentials among the Tribal Groups of Sierra Leone. *Population Stud.*, November 1973, *27*(3), pp. 501–14. [G: Sierra Leone]

DeJong, Gordon F. and Donnelly, William L. Public Welfare and Migration. *Soc. Sci. Quart.*, September 1973, *54*(2), pp. 329–44. [G: U.S.]

Dell'Atti, Angelo. Un nuovo modello logistico per la rappresentazione dei fenomeni sociali. (A New Logistic Model for the Representation of Social Phenomena. With English summary.) *Rivista Int. Sci. Econ. Com.*, May 1973, *20*(5), pp. 479–82. [G: Italy]

Denton, Frank T. and Spencer, Byron G. A Simulation Analysis of the Effects of Population Change on a Neoclassical Economy. *J. Polit. Econ.*, Part I, March-April 1973, *81*(2), pp. 356–75. [G: Canada]

Derban, L. A. K. The Impact of Health and Nutrition on Agricultural Production in West Africa. In

Ofori, I. M., ed., 1973, pp. 26–32. [G: W. Africa]

De Tray, Dennis N. Child Quality and the Demand for Children. *J. Polit. Econ.*, Part II, March-April 1973, *81*(2), pp. S70–95. [G: U.S.]

Dyke, Bennett and MacCluer, Jean W. Estimation of Vital Rates by Means of Monte Carlo Simulation. *Demography*, August 1973, *10*(3), pp. 383–403. [G: U.S.]

Eason, Warren W. Handbook of Soviet Social Science Data: Demography. In *Mickiewicz, E., ed.*, 1973, pp. 49–63. [G: U.S.S.R.]

Easterlin, Richard A. Relative Economic Status and the American Fertility Swing. In *Sheldon, E. B., ed.*, 1973, pp. 170–223. [G: U.S.]

Ehrlich, Paul R. and Holdren, John P. Impact of Population Growth. In *Daly, H. E., ed.*, 1973, pp. 76–89.

Enke, Stephen. Economic Consequences of Rapid Population Growth: A Reply. *Econ. J.*, March 1973, *83*(329), pp. 219–21.

Evsiukov, Iu. Migration of the Population from the Countryside to the City (Problems of Analysis and Forecasting). *Prob. Econ.*, June 1973, *16*(2), pp. 14–25. [G: U.S.S.R.]

Farid, S. M. On the Pattern of Cohort Fertility. *Population Stud.*, March 1973, *27*(1), pp. 159–68. [G: U.K.]

Festy, Patrick. Canada, United States, Australia and New Zealand: Nuptiality Trends. *Population Stud.*, November 1973, *27*(3), pp. 479–92. [G: New Zealand; Canada; U.S.; Australia]

Fisher, Joseph L. and Ridker, Ronald G. Population Growth, Resource Availability and Environmental Quality. *Amer. Econ. Rev.*, May 1973, *63*(2), pp. 79–87. [G: U.S.]

Forst, Brian E. An Analysis of Alternative Periodic Health Examination Strategies. In *Niskanen, W. A., et al., eds.*, 1973, pp. 393–409. [G: U.S.]

Fortt, J. M. and Hougham, D. A. Environment, Population and Economic History. In *Richards, A. I.; Sturrock, F. and Fortt, J. M., eds.*, 1973, pp. 17–46. [G: Uganda]

Freedman, Ronald. Social and Economic Factors in Hong Kong's Fertility Decline: A Comment. *Population Stud.*, November 1973, *27*(3), pp. 589–95. [G: Hong Kong]

Friedlander, Dov. Demographic Patterns and Socioeconomic Characteristics of the Coal-mining Population in England and Wales in the Nineteenth Century. *Econ. Develop. Cult. Change*, October 1973, *22*(1), pp. 39–51. [G: U.K.]

Friedmann, John, et al. Towards a National Urbanization Policy. In *Friedmann, J.*, 1973, pp. 153–86.

Gale, Stephen. Explanation Theory and Models of Migration. *Econ. Geogr.*, July 1973, *49*(3), pp. 257–74.

Gardner, Bruce. Economics of the Size of North Carolina Rural Families. *J. Polit. Econ.*, Part II, March-April 1973, *81*(2), pp. S99–122. [G: U.S.]

Gardner, M. J. Using the Environment to Explain and Predict Mortality. *J. Roy. Statist. Soc.*, Part 3 1973, *136*, pp. 421–40. [G: U.K.]

Gehan, Edmund A. and Siddiqui, M. M. Simple Regression Methods for Survival Time Studies. *J.*

Amer. Statist. Assoc., December 1973, *68*(344), pp. 848–56.

Gholl, Joseph E. and Zachariah, K. C. Toward the Year 2000. *Finance Develop.*, December 1973, *10* (4), pp. 22–26.

Gibson, Campbell. Urbanization in New Zealand: A Comparative Analysis. *Demography*, February 1973, *10*(1), pp. 71–84.   [G: New Zealand]

Glantz, Frederic B. Migration and Economic Opportunity: The Case of the Poor. *New Eng. Econ. Rev.*, March-April 1973, pp. 14–17.   [G: U.S.]

Glenn, Norval D. Suburbanization in the United States Since World War II. In *Masotti, L. H. and Hadden, J. K., eds.*, 1973, pp. 51–78.   [G: U.S.]

Glick, Paul C. and Norton, Arthur J. Perspectives on the Recent Upturn in Divorce and Remarriage. *Demography*, August 1973, *10*(3), pp. 301–14.   [G: U.S.]

Godfrey, E. M. Economic Variables and Rural-Urban Migration: Some Thoughts on the Todaro Hypothesis. *J. Devel. Stud.*, October 1973, *10*(1), pp. 66–78.

Goldberger, Arthur S. Dependency Rates and Savings Rates: Further Comment. *Amer. Econ. Rev.*, March 1973, *63*(1), pp. 232–33.

Goodhart, C. B. On the Incidence of Illegal Abortion: A Reply. *Population Stud.*, July 1973, *27*(2), pp. 207–33.   [G: U.K.]

Greenwood, Michael J. The Geographic Mobility of College Graduates. *J. Human Res.*, Fall 1973, *8*(4), pp. 506–15.   [G: U.S.]

Gregory, Paul; Campbell, John and Cheng, Benjamin. Differences in Fertility Determinants: Developed and Developing Countries. *J. Devel. Stud.*, January 1973, *9*(2), pp. 233–41.

Grindstaff, Carl F. and Ebanks, G. Edward. Male Sterilization as a Contraceptive Method in Canada: An Empirical Study. *Population Stud.*, November 1973, *27*(3), pp. 443–55. [G: Canada]

Guest, Avery M. Urban Growth and Population Densities. *Demography*, February 1973, *10*(1), pp. 53–69.   [G: U.S.]

Gupta, Biswatosh Sen. The Birth Table and Its Construction for Belgium. *J. Amer. Statist. Assoc.*, March 1973, *68*(341), pp. 44–45.   [G: Belgium]

Hahn, Harlan. Ethnic Minorities: Politics and the Family in Suburbia. In *Masotti, L. H. and Hadden, J. K., eds.*, 1973, pp. 185–205.   [G: U.S.]

Hall, M.-Françoise. Population Growth: U.S. and Latin American Views: An Interpretation of the Response of the United States and Latin America to the Latin American Population Growth. *Population Stud.*, November 1973, *27*(3), pp. 415–29.
     [G: Latin America]

Hamblin, Mary and Prell, Michael J. Income of Men and Women: Why Do They Differ? *Fed. Res. Bank Kansas City Rev.*, April 1973, pp. 3–11.
     [G: U.S.]

Hanson, John R., III. Economic Consequences of Rapid Population Growth: A Comment. *Econ. J.*, March 1973, *83*(329), pp. 217–19.

Hardin, Garrett. The Tragedy of the Commons. In *Daly, H. E., ed.*, 1973, pp. 133–48.

Hardin, Garrett. The Tragedy of the Commons. In *Enthoven, A. C. and Freeman, A. M., III, eds.*, 1973, pp. 1–13.

Hardoy, Jorge E. Spatial Structure and Society in Revolutionary Cuba. In *Barkin, D. P. and Manitzas, N. R., eds.*, 1973, pp. M265–16.   [G: Cuba]

Harewood, Jack. Changes in the Use of Birth Control Methods. *Population Stud.*, March 1973, *27*(1), pp. 33–57.   [G: Trinidad; Tobago]

Hauser, Jürg. Reorganisation der Familienplanung in der Dritten Welt. (Reorganizing Family Planning Policies in LDC's. With English summary.) *Schweiz. Z. Volkswirtsch. Statist.*, March 1973, *109*(1), pp. 1–16.

Hawkins, E. K. A Family View of Population Questions. *Finance Develop.*, December 1973, *10*(4), pp. 8–12.

Hayghe, Howard. Labor Force Activity of Married Women. *Mon. Lab. Rev.*, April 1973, *96*(4), pp. 31–36.   [G: U.S.]

Haynes, Kingsley E.; Poston, Dudley L., Jr. and Schnirring, Paul. Intermetropolitan Migration in High and Low Opportunity Areas: Indirect Tests of the Distance and Intervening Opportunities Hypotheses. *Econ. Geogr.*, January 1973, *49*(1), pp. 68–73.

Heilbroner, Robert L. Ecological Armageddon. In *Enthoven, A. C. and Freeman, A. M., III, eds.*, 1973, pp. 176–85.

Hendershot, Gerry E. Population Size, Military Power, and Antinatal Policy. *Demography*, November 1973, *10*(4), pp. 517–24.

Hernández, José; Estrada, Leo and Alvírez, David. Census Data and the Problem of Conceptually Defining the Mexican American Population. *Soc. Sci. Quart.*, March 1973, *53*(4), pp. 671–87.
     [G: U.S.]

Hieser, R. O. The Economic Consequences of Zero Population Growth. *Econ. Rec.*, June 1973, *49* (126), pp. 241–62.

Higgs, Robert. Mortality in Rural America, 1870-1920: Estimates and Conjectures. *Exploration Econ. Hist.*, Winter 1973, *10*(2), pp. 177–95.
     [G: U.S.]

Hill, Reuben and Klein, David M. Toward a Research Agenda and Theoretical Synthesis. In *Sheldon, E. B., ed.*, 1973, pp. 371–404. [G: U.S.]

Holdren, John P. Population and the American Predicament: The Case against Complacency. In *Olson, M. and Landsberg, H. H., eds.*, 1973, pp. 31–43.   [G: U.S.]

Hughes, James C. Population Estimates for Small Area Decision-Makers. In *Gabriel, R. A. and Cohen, S. H., eds.*, 1973, pp. 94–112.   [G: U.S.]

Hume, Ian M. Migrant Workers in Europe. *Finance Develop.*, March 1973, *10*(1), pp. 2–6.   [G: W. Europe]

Hunter, Guy. The Food Research Institute's Fiftieth Anniversary Conference, Strategies for Agricultural Development in the 1970s. *Food Res. Inst. Stud.*, 1973, *12*(1), pp. 3–72.

Isbister, John. Birth Control, Income Redistribution, and the Rate of Saving: The Case of Mexico. *Demography*, February 1973, *10*(1), pp. 85–98.
     [G: Mexico]

James, William H. The Fecundability of U.S. Women. *Population Stud.*, November 1973, *27* (3), pp. 493–500.   [G: U.S.]

Janowitz, Barbara S. Cross-Section Studies as Predictors of Trends in Birth Rates: A Note on Ekanem's Results. *Demography*, August 1973, *10*(3), pp. 479–81.

Janowitz, Barbara S. The Effects of Demographic Factors on Age Composition and the Implications for Per Capita Income. *Demography*, November 1973, *10*(4), pp. 507–15.   [G: U.S.]

Janowitz, Barbara S. An Econometric Analysis of Trends in Fertility Rates. *J. Devel. Stud.*, April 1973, *9*(3), pp. 413–25.

Johnson, D. Gale. Economics of Population: Discussion. *Amer. Econ. Rev.*, May 1973, *63*(2), pp. 88–89.

Johnson, J. Timothy; Tan Boon Ann and Corsa, Leslie. Assessment of Family Planning Programme Effects on Births: Preliminary Results Obtained through Direct Matching of Birth and Programme Acceptor Records. *Population Stud.*, March 1973, *27*(1), pp. 85–96.   [G: Malaysia]

Johnston, Denis F. Population and Labor Force Projections. *Mon. Lab. Rev.*, December 1973, *96*(12), pp. 8–17.   [G: U.S.]

Jones, H. J. M.; Lawson, H. B. and Newman, D. Population Census: Some Recent British Developments in Methodology. *J. Roy. Statist. Soc.*, Part 4, 1973, *136*, pp. 505–20.   [G: U.K.]

Kasnacich, Johannes. Le più importanti prospettive macro-economiche del mondo attuale. (The Main Macro-Economic Perspectives of World Development. With English summary.) *Mondo Aperto*, February 1973, *27*(1), pp. 1–8.

Katouzian, M. A. A Two-Sector Model of Population, Growth and Economic Development (1). *Tahq. Eq.*, Summer & Autumn 1973, *10*(31&32), pp. 60–79.

Katz, Sidney, et al. Measuring the Health Status of Populations. In *Berg, R. L., ed.*, 1973, pp. 39–51.   [G: U.S.]

Keller, Suzanne. The Future Role of Women. *Ann. Amer. Acad. Polit. Soc. Sci.*, July 1973, *408*, pp. 1–12.   [G: U.S.]

Kelley, Allen C. Relative Economic Status and the American Fertility Swing: Response. In *Sheldon, E. B., ed.*, 1973, pp. 224–27.

Kelley, Allen C. Population Growth, the Dependency Rate, and the Pace of Economic Development. *Population Stud.*, November 1973, *27*(3), pp. 405–14.

Kende, Pierre; Detourbet, Christine and Debache, Joëlle. Vers une description du mode de vie au moyen d'indicateurs. (Towards a Description of Life Styles Through Indicators. With English summary.) *Consommation*, April-June 1973, *20*(2), pp. 117–30.   [G: Netherlands]

Kerr, Clark. Educational Changes: Potential Impacts on Industrial Relations. In *Somers, G. G., ed.*, 1973, pp. 187–97.   [G: U.S.]

Keyfitz, Nathan. Individual Mobility in a Stationary Population. *Population Stud.*, July 1973, *27*(2), pp. 335–52.   [G: U.S.]

Keyfitz, Nathan. The Long-term Prospect for Indonesian Population. *Bull. Indonesian Econ. Stud.*, March 1973, *9*(1), pp. 107–09.   [G: Indonesia]

Khalifa, Atef M. A Proposed Explanation of the Fertility Gap Differentials by Socio-Economic Status

and Modernity: The Case of Egypt. *Population Stud.*, November 1973, *27*(3), pp. 431–42.   [G: Egypt]

Khan, Masihur Rahman. Bangladesh Population During First Five Year Plan Period (1973–78): An Estimate. *Bangladesh Econ. Rev.*, April 1973, *1*(2), pp. 186–98.   [G: Bangladesh]

Klein, Ira. Death in India, 1871–1921. *J. Asian Stud.*, August 1973, *32*(4), pp. 639–59.   [G: India]

Kleinman, David S. Fertility Variation and Resources in Rural India (1961) *Econ. Develop. Cult. Change*, Part I, July 1973, *21*(4), pp. 679–96.   [G: India]

Knodel, John and Prachuabmoh, Visid. Desired Family Size in Thailand: Are the Responses Meaningful? *Demography*, November 1973, *10*(4), pp. 619–37.   [G: Thailand]

Kobrin, Frances E. Household Headship and its Changes in the United States, 1940–1960, 1970. *J. Amer. Statist. Assoc.*, December 1973, *68*(344), pp. 793–800.   [G: U.S.]

Kohn, Robert M. On Migration, Migration Costs, and Wage Differentials: A Comment. *Schweiz. Z. Volkswirtsch. Statist.*, December 1973, *109*(4), pp. 603–04.   [G: U.S.]

Kotliar, A. and Kirpa, I. Demographic Aspects of Employment in Cities with Differing Industrial Structures. *Prob. Econ.*, April 1973, *15*(12), pp. 73–85.   [G: U.S.S.R.]

Kuznets, Simon. Economic Capacity and Population Growth. In *Kuznets, S.*, 1973, pp. 49–93.

Kuznets, Simon. Population and Economic Growth. In *Kuznets, S.*, 1973, pp. 1–48.

Landsberger, Michael. Children's Age as a Factor Affecting the Simultaneous Determination of Consumption and Labor Supply. *Southern Econ. J.*, October 1973, *40*(2), pp. 279–88.   [G: U.S.; Israel]

Laslett, Peter and Oosterveen, Karla. Long-term Trends in Bastardy in England: A Study of the Illegitimacy Figures in the Parish Registers and in the Reports of the Registrar General, 1561–1960. *Population Stud.*, July 1973, *27*(2), pp. 255–86.   [G: U.K.]

Lave, Lester B. and Seskin, Eugene P. Air Pollution and Human Health. In *Enthoven, A. C. and Freeman, A. M., III, eds.*, 1973, pp. 88–99. [G: U.S.]

Lave, Lester B. and Seskin, Eugene P. An Analysis of the Association Between U.S. Mortality and Air Pollution. *J. Amer. Statist. Assoc.*, June 1973, *68*(342), pp. 284–90.   [G: U.S.]

Lee, Ronald. Population in Preindustrial England: An Econometric Analysis. *Quart. J. Econ.*, November 1973, *87*(4), pp. 581–607.   [G: U.K.]

Leff, Nathaniel H. Dependency Rates and Savings Rates: Reply. *Amer. Econ. Rev.*, March 1973, *63*(1), pp. 234.

Levine, Daniel S. and Yett, Donald E. A Method for Constructing Proxy Measures of Health Status. In *Berg, R. L., ed.*, 1973, pp. 12–22.   [G: U.S.]

Levy, Mildred B. and Wadycki, Walter J. The Influence of Family and Friends on Geographic Labor Mobility: An International Comparison. *Rev. Econ. Statist.*, May 1973, *55*(2), pp. 198–203.   [G: Venezuela]

Lewis, H. Gregg. Economic Analysis of Fertility in

Israel: Point and Counterpoint: Comment. *J. Polit. Econ.*, Part II, March-April 1973, *81*(2), pp. S234–37.   [G: Israel]

Li, Wen L. Temporal and Spatial Analysis of Fertility Decline in Taiwan. *Population Stud.*, March 1973, *27*(1), pp. 97–104.   [G: Taiwan]

Loebner, Hugh and Driver, Edwin D. Differential Fertility in Central India: A Path Analysis. *Demography*, August 1973, *10*(3), pp. 329–50.   [G: India]

Lombardo, Enzo. La costruzione delle tavole ridotte di mortalità. (The Construction of Abridged Life Tables. With English summary.) *Statistica*, July-September 1973, *33*(3), pp. 437–54.   [G: Italy]

Long, Larry H. New Estimates of Migration Expectancy in the United States. *J. Amer. Statist. Assoc.*, March 1973, *68*(341), pp. 37–43.   [G: U.S.]

Lubell, Harold. Urban Development and Employment in Calcutta. *Int. Lab. Rev.*, July 1973, *108*(1), pp. 25–41.   [G: India]

Lugovskaia, L. Current Problems of Urbanization. *Prob. Econ.*, May 1973, *16*(1), pp. 91–99.
[G: U.S.S.R.]

Macura, Milos. World Population Prospects and Policies. *Econ. Bull. Ghana, Sec. Ser.*, 1973, *3*(2), pp. 22–30.

Marckwardt, Albert M. Evaluation of an Experimental Short Interview Form Designed to Collect Fertility Data: The Case of Peru. *Demography*, November 1973, *10*(4), pp. 639–57.   [G: Peru]

Marshall, Harvey. Suburban Life Styles: A Contribution to the Debate. In *Masotti, L. H. and Hadden, J. K., eds.*, 1973, pp. 123–48.   [G: U.S.]

Martin, Randolph C. Spatial Distribution of Population: Cities and Suburbs. *J. Reg. Sci.*, August 1973, *13*(2), pp. 269–78.   [G: U.S.]

Mayer, Kurt B. Die jüdische Bevölkerung der Schweiz. (The Jewish Population of Switzerland. With English summary.) *Schweiz. Z. Volkswirtsch. Statist.*, March 1973, *109*(1), pp. 91–100.
[G: Switzerland]

Mazur, D. Peter. Fertility and Economic Dependency of Soviet Women. *Demography*, February 1973, *10*(1), pp. 37–51.   [G: U.S.S.R.]

Mazur, D. Peter. Relation of Marriage and Education to Fertility in the U.S.S.R. *Population Stud.*, March 1973, *27*(1), pp. 105–15.   [G: U.S.S.R.]

McCann, James C. A More Accurate Short Method of Approximating Lotka's *r*.. *Demography*, November 1973, *10*(4), pp. 567–70.

Michael, Robert T. Education and the Derived Demand for Children. *J. Polit. Econ.*, Part II, March-April 1973, *81*(2), pp. S128–64.   [G: U.S.]

Miller, Edward. Return and Nonreturn In-Migration. *Growth Change*, January 1973, *4*(1), pp. 3–9.
[G: U.S.]

Miller, Edward. The Flight of the Native Born. *Growth Change*, October 1973, *4*(4), pp. 10–15.
[G: U.S.]

Miller, Edward. Is Out-Migration Affected by Economic Conditions? *Southern Econ. J.*, January 1973, *39*(3), pp. 396–405.   [G: U. S.]

Milne, Robin G. Family Planning in Malta. *Population Stud.*, July 1973, *27*(2), pp. 373–86.   [G: Malta]

Mitra, S. and Romaniuk, A. Pearsonian Type I Curve and Its Fertility Projection Potentials. *Demography*, August 1973, *10*(3), pp. 351–65.   [G: Canada]

Mitra, S. On the Efficiency of the Estimates of Life Table Functions. *Demography*, August 1973, *10*(3), pp. 421–26.

Mizrahi, Andrée; Mizrahi, Arié and Rösch, Georges. Un indicateur de morbidité. (An Indicator of Morbidity. With English summary.) *Consommation*, July-September 1973, *20*(3), pp. 7–55.   [G: France]

Morrison, Peter A. A Demographic Assessment of New Cities and Growth Centers as Population Redistribution Strategies. *Public Policy*, Summer 1973, *21*(3), pp. 367–82.   [G: U.S.]

Murray, Janet. Family Structure in the Preretirement Years. *Soc. Sec. Bull.*, October 1973, *36*(10), pp. 25–45.   [G: U.S.]

Nag, Moni. Anthropology and Population: Problems and Perspectives. *Population Stud.*, March 1973, *27*(1), pp. 59–68.

Nerlove, Marc and Schultz, T. Paul. Love and Life between the Censuses. In *Goldberger, A. S. and Duncan, O. D., eds.*, 1973, pp. 317–23.
[G: U.S.]

Olson, Mancur. The No-Growth Society: Introduction. In *Olson, M. and Landsberg, H. H., eds.*, 1973, pp. 1–13.

Onaka, Alvin T. and Yaukey, David. Reproductive Time Lost Due to Sexual Union Dissolution in San José, Costa Rica. *Population Stud.*, November 1973, *27*(3), pp. 457–65.   [G: Costa Rica]

Osborn, Richard Warren. The Fallacy of the Five Million Women: A Re-Estimate: Further Reactions. *Demography*, November 1973, *10*(4), pp. 673–77.

Pack, Janet Rothenberg. Determinants of Migration to Central Cities. *J. Reg. Sci.*, August 1973, *13*(2), pp. 249–60.   [G: U.S.]

Page, William. Population Forecasting. In *Cole, H. S. D., et al., eds.*, 1973, pp. 159–74.

Page, William. The Population Sub-system. In *Cole, H. S. D., et al., eds.*, 1973, pp. 43–55.

Parish, William L., Jr. Internal Migration and Modernization: The European Case. *Econ. Develop. Cult. Change*, Part I, July 1973, *21*(4), pp. 591–609.   [G: Europe]

Pendleton, William W. Blacks in Suburbs. In *Masotti, L. H. and Hadden, J. K., eds.*, 1973, pp. 171–84.   [G: U.S.]

Perline, Martin M. and Presley, Ronald W. Mobility of Unemployed Engineers: A Case Study. *Mon. Lab. Rev.*, May 1973, *96*(5), pp. 41–43.   [G: U.S.]

Piché, Victor and George, M. V. Estimates of Vital Rates for the Canadian Indians, 1960–1970. *Demography*, August 1973, *10*(3), pp. 367–82.
[G: Canada]

Pickard, Jerome P. Growth of Urbanized Population in the United States: Past, Present, and Future. In *Rasmussen, D. W. and Haworth, C. T., eds.*, 1973, pp. 5–15.   [G: U.S.]

Pitchford, J. D. The Optimum Population and Growth: A Closer Look. *J. Econ. Theory*, February 1973, *6*(1), pp. 94–95.

Pittenger, Donald B. An Exponential Model of Female Sterility. *Demography*, February 1973,

10(1), pp. 113–21.

Rao, S. L. N. On Long-Term Mortality Trends in the United States, 1850–1968. *Demography*, August 1973, *10*(3), pp. 405–19. [G: U.S.]

Reid, Margaret G. Education and the Derived Demand for Children: Comment. *J. Polit. Econ.*, Part II, March-April 1973, *81*(2), pp. S165–67. [G: U.S.]

Rejda, George E. and Shepler, Richard J. The Impact of Zero Population Growth on the OASDHI Program. *J. Risk Ins.*, September 1973, *40*(3), pp. 313–25. [G: U.S.]

Retherford, Robert D. Cigarette Smoking and Widowhood in the United States. *Population Stud.*, July 1973, *27*(2), pp. 193–206. [G: U.S.]

Ritchey, P. Neal. The Fertility of Negroes without Southern Rural Experience: A Re-examination of the 1960 GAF Study Findings with 1967 SEO Data. *Population Stud.*, March 1973, *27*(1), pp. 127–34. [G: U.S.]

Roberts, Robert E. Modernization and Infant Mortality in Mexico. *Econ. Develop. Cult. Change*, Part I, July 1973, *21*(4), pp. 655–69. [G: Mexico]

Romaniuk, A. A Three Parameter Model for Birth Projections. *Population Stud.*, November 1973, *27*(3), pp. 467–78. [G: Canada]

Roy, René. Demography and Economic Growth: Income Distribution and Way of Life. In *[Tinbergen, J.]*, 1973, pp. 257–71.

Ruzicka, L. T. Length of Working Life for Australian Males: 1933–66. *Econ. Rec.*, June 1973, *49*(126), pp. 280–89. [G: Australia]

Ryder, Norman B. A New Approach to the Economic Theory of Fertility Behavior: Comment. *J. Polit. Econ.*, Part II, March-April 1973, *81*(2), pp. S65–69. [G: U.S.]

Ryder, Norman B. Two Cheers for ZPG. In *Olson, M. and Landsberg, H. H., eds.*, 1973, pp. 45–62. [G: U.S.]

Ryder, Norman B. A Critique of the National Fertility Study. *Demography*, November 1973, *10*(4), pp. 495–506. [G: U.S.]

Salaff, Janet W. Mortality Decline in the People's Republic of China and the United States. *Population Stud.*, November 1973, *27*(3), pp. 551–76. [G: U.S.; China]

Sandler, Todd M. and Hogan, Timothy D. The Optimum Population and Growth: A Further Look. *J. Econ. Theory*, December 1973, *6*(6), pp. 582–84.

Sankaran, Sundaram. Population and the World Bank. *Finance Develop.*, December 1973, *10*(4), pp. 18–21, 41.

Schnaiberg, Allan. The Concept and Measurement of Child Dependency: An Approach to Family Formation Analysis. *Population Stud.*, March 1973, *27*(1), pp. 69–84.

Schultz, Theodore W. The Value of Children: An Economic Perspective. *J. Polit. Econ.*, Part II, March-April 1973, *81*(2), pp. S2–13.

Schultz, T. Paul. Explanation of Birth Rate Changes over Space and Time: A Study of Taiwan. *J. Polit. Econ.*, Part II, March-April 1973, *81*(2), pp. S238–74. [G: Taiwan]

Schultz, T. Paul. A Preliminary Survey of Economic Analyses of Fertility. *Amer. Econ. Rev.*, May 1973, *63*(2), pp. 71–78.

Schwartz, Aba. Interpreting the Effect of Distance on Migration. *J. Polit. Econ.*, September-October 1973, *81*(5), pp. 1153–69. [G: U.S.]

Selowsky, Marcelo. An Attempt to Estimate Rates of Return to Investment in Infant Nutrition. In *Niskanen, W. A., et al., eds.*, 1973, pp. 410–28. [G: Chile]

Shantakumar, G. A Note on the Recent Increase in Fertility in Singapore. *Malayan Econ. Rev.*, October 1973, *18*(2), pp. 43–49. [G: Singapore]

Shore, Arnold R. and Scott, Robert A. Work Response and Family Composition Changes in a Negative Income Tax Experiment: Preliminary Mid-Experiment Results. In *Sheldon, E. B., ed.*, 1973, pp. 233–63. [G: U.S.]

Shorter, Edward. Female Emancipation, Birth Control, and Fertility in European History. *Amer. Hist. Rev.*, June 1973, *78*(3), pp. 605–40. [G: Europe]

Singer, S. Fred. Is There an Optimum Level of Population? In *Weintraub, A.; Schwartz, E. and Aronson, J. R., eds.*, 1973, pp. 154–64. [G: U.S.]

Sirken, Monroe G. Design of Household Sample Surveys to Test Death Registration Completeness. *Demography*, August 1973, *10*(3), pp. 469–78.

Sommers, Paul M. and Suits, Daniel B. Analysis of Net Interstate Migration. *Southern Econ. J.*, October 1973, *40*(2), pp. 193–201. [G: U.S.]

Songre, Ambroise. Mass Emigration from Upper Volta: The Facts and Implications. *Int. Lab. Rev.*, August-September 1973, *108*(2–3), pp. 209–25. [G: Upper Volta]

Southey, Clive. Peasants, Procreation, and Pensions: Note. *Amer. Econ. Rev.*, December 1973, *63*(5), pp. 983–85.

Speare, Alden, Jr.; Speare, Mary C. and Lin, Hui-Sheng. Urbanization, Non-Familial Work, Education, and Fertility in Taiwan. *Population Stud.*, July 1973, *27*(2), pp. 323–34. [G: Taiwan]

Srikantan, K. S. Regional and Rural-Urban Socio-Demographic Differences in Turkey. *Middle East J.*, Summer 1973, *27*(3), pp. 275–300. [G: Turkey]

Stokes, C. Shannon. Family Structure and Socio-economic Differentials in Fertility. *Population Stud.*, July 1973, *27*(2), pp. 295–304. [G: U.S.]

Stone, Richard. Economic and Demographic Accounts and the Distribution of Income. *Acta Oecon.*, 1973, *11*(2–3), pp. 165–76.

Studer, Tobias. Untersuchungen über das Wachstum der Schweizer Städte. (Investigations Upon the Growth of Swiss Towns. With English summary.) *Schweiz. Z. Volkswirtsch. Statist.*, June 1973, *109*(2), pp. 187–99. [G: Switzerland]

Sufrin, Sidney C. and Wagner, Abraham. U.S. Employment and Growth in the Immediate Future: A Guess. *Rivista Int. Sci. Econ. Com.*, January 1973, *20*(1), pp. 63–71. [G: U.S.]

Sullivan, Jeremiah M. The Influence of Cause-Specific Mortality Conditions on the Age Pattern of Mortality with Special Reference to Taiwan. *Population Stud.*, March 1973, *27*(1), pp. 135–58. [G: Taiwan]

Sundquist, James L. Where Shall They Live? In *Rasmussen, D. W. and Haworth, C. T., eds.*, 1973, pp. 247–59. [G: U.S.]

Taqieddin, Nureddin and Gardner, B. Delworth. Net Migration and Population Distribution in the State of Utah. *Intermountain Econ. Rev.*, Fall 1973, *4*(2), pp. 32–44. [G: U.S.]

Taylor, Carl E. Nutrition and Population. In *Berg, A.; Scrimshaw, N. S. and Call, D. L., eds.*, 1973, pp. 74–80.

Terhune, Kenneth W. and Kaufman, Sol. The Family Size Utility Function. *Demography*, November 1973, *10*(4), pp. 599–618. [G: U.S.]

Thomas, George. Regional Migration Patterns and Poverty Among the Aged in the South. *J. Human Res.*, Winter 1973, *8*(1), pp. 73–84. [G: U.S.]

Titmuss, R. and Titmuss, K. Parents' Revolt, 1942. In *Tranter, N. L., ed.*, 1973, pp. 155–62. [G: U.K.]

Tobin, James. Explanation of Birth Rate Changes over Space and Time: A Study of Taiwan: Comment. *J. Polit. Econ.*, Part II, March-April 1973, *81*(2), pp. S275–78. [G: Taiwan]

Truu, M. L. Some Effects of Regional Migration. *S. Afr. J. Econ.*, June 1973, *41*(2), pp. 98–110. [G: S. Africa]

Tyree, Andrea. Mobility Ratios and Association in Mobility Tables. *Population Stud.*, November 1973, *27*(3), pp. 577–88.

Udry, J. Richard; Bauman, Karl E. and Chase, Charles L. Population Growth Rates in Perfect Contraceptive Populations. *Population Stud.*, July 1973, *27*(2), pp. 365–71.

Usher, Dan. An Imputation to the Measure of Economic Growth for Changes in Life Expectancy. In *Moss, M., ed.*, 1973, pp. 193–226. [G: Canada]

Vandendries, René. Internal Migration and Economic Development in Peru. In *Scott, R. E., ed.*, 1973, pp. 193–207. [G: Peru]

Van Der Tak, Jean and Gendell, Murray. The Size and Structure of Residential Families, Guatemala City, 1964. *Population Stud.*, July 1973, *27*(2), pp. 305–22. [G: Guatemala]

Veevers, J. E. Estimating the Incidence and Prevalence of Birth Orders: A Technique Using Census Data. *Demography*, August 1973, *10*(3), pp. 447–58. [G: U.S.]

Venieris, Yiannis P.; Sebold, Frederick D. and Harper, Richard D. The Impact of Economic, Technological and Demographic Factors on Aggregate Births. *Rev. Econ. Statist.*, November 1973, *55*(4), pp. 493–97. [G: U.S.]

Vermishev, K. The Stimulation of Population Growth. *Prob. Econ.*, June 1973, *16*(2), pp. 3–13. [G: U.S.S.R.]

Weisbord, Robert G. Birth Control and the Black American: A Matter of Genocide? *Demography*, November 1973, *10*(4), pp. 571–90. [G: U.S.]

White, Desmond A. Some Aspects of Recent In-Migration to the Albuquerque Area. *N. Mex. Bus.*, April 1973, *26*(4), pp. 9–14. [G: U.S.]

Whitehouse, F. Douglas. Demographic Aspects of Regional Economic Development in the USSR. In *Bandera, V. N. and Melnyk, Z. L., eds.*, 1973, pp. 154–66. [G: U.S.S.R.]

Wilkinson, Maurice. An Econometric Analysis of Fertility in Sweden, 1870–1965. *Econometrica*, July 1973, *41*(4), pp. 633–42.

Willis, Robert J. An Imputation to the Measure of Economic Growth for Changes in Life Expectancy: Comment. In *Moss, M., ed.*, 1973, pp. 226–32. [G: Canada]

Willis, Robert J. A New Approach to the Economic Theory of Fertility Behavior. *J. Polit. Econ.*, Part II, March-April 1973, *81*(2), pp. S14–64. [G: U.S.]

Wilson, Franklin D. and Bumpass, Larry. The Prediction of Fertility among Catholics: A Longitudinal Analysis. *Demography*, November 1973, *10* (4), pp. 591–97. [G: U.S.]

Young, Anne M. Going Back to School at 35. *Mon. Lab. Rev.*, October 1973, *96*(10), pp. 39–42. [G: U.S.]

Yunker, James A. A Statistical Estimate of Optimum Population in the United States. *Nebr. J. Econ. Bus.*, Winter 1973, *12*(1), pp. 3–10. [G: U.S.]

Zahn, Frank. A Test of the Escape from the Persistence of Backwardness. *J. Devel. Stud.*, April 1973, *9*(3), pp. 403–11. [G: Japan]

850 HUMAN CAPITAL

851 Human Capital

8510 Human Capital

Annable, James E., Jr. and Fruitman, Frederick H. An Earnings Function for High-Level Manpower. *Ind. Lab. Relat. Rev.*, July 1973, *26*(4), pp. 1107–21.

Baher, G. H. A Planning Model for the Educational Requirements of Economic Development: The Case of Iran. *Tahq. Eq.*, Winter & Spring 1973, *10* (29 & 30), pp. 170–205. [G: Iran]

Barg, Benjamin. Nutrition and National Development. In *Berg, A.; Scrimshaw, N. S. and Call, D. L., eds.*, 1973, pp. 49–69.

Becker, Gary S. A Theory of Marriage: Part I. *J. Polit. Econ.*, July-August 1973, *81*(4), pp. 813–46.

Bhagwati, Jagdish N. Education, Class Structure and Income Equality. *World Devel.*, May 1973, *1*(5), pp. 21–36. [G: India]

Bhati, U. N. Farmers' Technical Knowledge and Income—A Case Study of Padi Farmers of West Malaysia. *Malayan Econ. Rev.*, April 1973, *18*(1), pp. 36–47. [G: Malaya]

Bieker, Richard F. and Anschel, Kurt R. Estimating Educational Production Functions for Rural High Schools: Some Findings. *Amer. J. Agr. Econ.*, August 1973, *55*(3), pp. 515–19. [G: U.S.]

Blaug, Mark. Manpower Forecasting for All Occupations: Thailand. In *Ahamad, B. and Blaug, M., eds.*, 1973, pp. 106–30.

Boulding, Kenneth E. Human Resource Development as a Learning Process. In *Boulding, K. E.*, 1973, pp. 339–49.

Boulding, Kenneth E. The Misallocation of Intellectual Resources. In *Boulding, K. E.*, 1973, pp. 195–200.

Bowlby, Roger L. and Schriver, William R. Academic Ability and Rates of Return to Vocational Training. *Ind. Lab. Relat. Rev.*, April 1973, *26*(3), pp. 980–90.

Christoffel, Pamela and Celio, Mary Beth. A Benefit-Cost Analysis of the Upward Bound Program: A Comment. *J. Human Res.*, Winter 1973, *8*(1), pp. 110–15. [G: U.S.]

Comay, Yochanan; Melnik, A. and Pollatschek, M. A. The Option Value of Education and the Optimal Path for Investment in Human Capital. *Int. Econ. Rev.*, June 1973, *14*(2), pp. 421–35. [G: U.S.]

Correa, H. An Econometric Model of Supply, Demand and Wages of Educated Workers. In *Judge, G. G. and Takayama, T., eds.*, 1973, pp. 706–23. [G: U.S.]

Crean, John F. Forgone Earnings and the Demand for Education: Some Empirical Evidence. *Can. J. Econ.*, February 1973, *6*(1), pp. 23–42. [G: Canada]

Davis, Joseph M. Health and the Education-Earnings Relationship. *Mon. Lab. Rev.*, April 1973, *96*(4), pp. 61–63.

Deaglio, Mario. Differenze di instruzione e differenze di retribuzione in una società ugualitaria. (Education and Pay Structures in an Egalitarian Society. With English summary.) *L'Industria*, January-June 1973, (1–2), pp. 134–75.

Eckaus, Richard S. Estimation of the Returns to Education with Hourly Standardized Incomes. *Quart. J. Econ.*, February 1973, *87*(1), pp. 121–31. [G: U.S.]

Eden, Philip. Estimating U.S. Human Capital Loss in Southeast Asia: Reply. *J. Human Res.*, Fall 1973, *8*(4), pp. 526–27. [G: U.S.]

Edwards, Edgar O. and Todaro, Michael P. Educational Demand and Supply in the Context of Growing Unemployment in Less Developed Countries. *World Devel.*, March-April 1973, *1*(3–4), pp. 107–117.

Eichner, Alfred S. Manpower Planning and Economic Planning: The Two Perspectives. In *Aronson, R. L., ed.*, 1973, pp. 65–80. [G: U.S.]

Eisner, Robert. Tax Incentives for Investment. *Nat. Tax J.*, September 1973, *26*(3), pp. 397–401. [G: U.S.]

Emmerij, Louis. Education and Employment: Some Preliminary Findings and Thoughts. *Int. Lab. Rev.*, January 1973, *107*(1), pp. 31–42.

Flamholtz, Eric. Human Resource Accounting: Its Role in Management Planning and Control. *Econ. Soc. Tijdschr.*, February 1973, *27*(1), pp. 3–22.

Flamholtz, Eric. The Role of Human Resource Accounting in Social Accounting. In *Dierkes, M. and Bauer, R. A., eds.*, 1973, pp. 166–82.

Garms, Walter I. Reply to "A Benefit-Cost Analysis of the Upward Bound Program: A Comment." *J. Human Res.*, Winter 1973, *8*(1), pp. 115–18. [G: U.S.]

Ghazalah, I. A. and Pejovich, Svetozar. The Economics of Vocational and Technical Education: A Report on Three Studies. *Rev. Soc. Econ.*, October 1973, *31*(2), pp. 191–98. [G: U.S.]

Griliches, Zvi and Mason, William M. Education, Income, and Ability. In *Goldberger, A. S. and Duncan, O. D., eds.*, 1973, pp. 285–316. [G: U.S.]

Gronau, Reuben. The Effect of Children on the Housewife's Value of Time. *J. Polit. Econ.*, Part II, March-April 1973, *81*(2), pp. S168–99. [G: U.S.]

Gustman, Alan L. On the Appropriate Model for Analyzing Investment in Human Capital Where the Capital Market is Imperfect. *Rev. Income Wealth*, September 1973, *19*(3), pp. 303–05.

Gustman, Alan L. On Estimating the Rate of Return to Education. *Appl. Econ.*, June 1973, *5*(2), pp. 89–99.

Haley, William J. Human Capital: The Choice Between Investment and Income. *Amer. Econ. Rev.*, December 1973, *63*(5), pp. 929–44. [G: U.S.]

Hall, Robert E. The Effect of Children on the Housewife's Value of Time: Comment. *J. Polit. Econ.*, Part II, March-April 1973, *81*(2), pp. S200–01. [G: U.S.]

Hanushek, Eric A. Regional Differences in the Structure of Earnings. *Rev. Econ. Statist.*, May 1973, *55*(2), pp. 204–13. [G: U.S.]

Harbison, Frederick H. Human Resources and the Development of Modernizing Nations. In *Somers, G. G., ed.*, 1973, pp. 177–86.

Hewlett, Sylvia-Ann. Rates of Return to Education in Urban Brazil. *Pakistan Econ. Soc. Rev.*, Winter 1973, *11*(4), pp. 403–16. [G: Brazil]

Hoerr, O. D. Education, Income and Equity in Malaysia. *Econ. Develop. Cult. Change*, January 1973, *21*(2), pp. 247–73. [G: Malaysia]

Hoffer, Stefan N. Private Rates of Return to Higher Education for Women. *Rev. Econ. Statist.*, November 1973, *55*(4), pp. 482–86. [G: U.S.]

Holland, David W. and Tweeten, Luther G. Human Capital Migration: Implications for Common School Finance. *Land Econ.*, August 1973, *49*(3), pp. 278–84. [G: U.S.]

Holtmann, A. G. Skill Obsolescence and Training: Reply. *Southern Econ. J.*, April 1973, *39*(4), pp. 648–49.

Holtmann, A. G. The Timing of Investments in Human Capital: A Case in Education. *Public Finance Quart.*, July 1973, *1*(3), pp. 300–06. [G: U.S.]

Johnson, George E. and Stafford, Frank P. Social Returns to Quantity and Quality of Schooling. *J. Human Res.*, Spring 1973, *8*(2), pp. 139–55. [G: U.S.]

Joshi, Nandini U. Validity of International Comparisons of Relationship between Economic Development and Human Resource Development. *Indian Econ. Rev.*, April 1973, *8*(1), pp. 90–92.

Kazmi, Aqdas Ali. Education and Supply of Manpower in Pakistan. *Pakistan Econ. Soc. Rev.*, Spring 1973, *11*(1), pp. 125–39. [G: Pakistan]

Keesing, Donald B. and Manne, Alan S. Manpower Projections. In *Goreux, L. M. and Manne, A. S., eds.*, 1973, pp. 55–83. [G: Mexico]

Kerr, Clark. Educational Changes: Potential Impacts on Industrial Relations. In *Somers, G. G., ed.*, 1973, pp. 187–97. [G: U.S.]

Kiker, B. F. and Cochrane, James L. War and Human Capital in Western Economic Analysis. *Hist. Polit. Econ.*, Fall 1973, *5*(2), pp. 375–98.

Knapp, Charles B. A Human Capital Approach to the Burden of the Military Draft. *J. Human Res.*, Fall 1973, *8*(4), pp. 485–96. [G: U.S.]

Konius, A. A. Commensuration of Labor by Means of an Input-Output Table. *Matekon*, Summer 1973, *9*(4), pp. 31–42.

Kottis, Athena P. and Kottis, George C. Who Benefits from Higher Education Subsidies: A Reconsideration. *Econ. Int.*, August-November 1973, *26* (3–4), pp. 492–501.

Laber, Gene. Human Capital in Southern Migration. *J. Human Res.*, Spring 1973, *8*(2), pp. 223–41. [G: U.S.]

Layard, Richard. Denison and the Contribution of Education to National Income Growth: A Comment. *J. Polit. Econ.*, July-August 1973, *81*(4), pp. 1013–16.

Levy-Garboua, Louis. Rémunère-t-on les études? (Does Schooling Pay? With English summary.) *Consommation*, July-September 1973, *20*(3), pp. 57–81. [G: France]

Lindsay, Cotton M. Real Returns to Medical Education. *J. Human Res.*, Summer 1973, *8*(3), pp. 331–48. [G: U.S.]

Link, Charles R. The Quantity and Quality of Education and Their Influence on Earnings: The Case of Chemical Engineers. *Rev. Econ. Statist.*, May 1973, *55*(2), pp. 241–47. [G: U.S.]

Magnusson, Leif. Cost-Benefit Analysis of Investment in Higher Education: Some Swedish Results. *Swedish J. Econ.*, June 1973, *75*(2), pp. 119–27. [G: Sweden]

Malenbaum, Wilfred. A Note on the Poor Nation Situation. In *Berg, A.; Scrimshaw, N. S. and Call, D. L., eds.*, 1973, pp. 81–86.

Mantell, Edmund H. Labor Markets for Engineers of Differing Ability and Education. *Ind. Lab. Relat. Rev.*, October 1973, *27*(1), pp. 63–73. [G: U.S.]

Mathews, Russell. Patterns of Educational Finance. *Australian Econ. Pap.*, December 1973, *12*(21), pp. 145–61. [G: Australia]

Matthews, R. C. O. The Contribution of Science and Technology to Economic Development. In *Williams, B. R., ed.*, 1973, pp. 1–31. [G: U.S.; Canada; Europe; Japan]

Metcalf, David. The Rate of Return to Investing in a Doctorate: A Case Study. *Scot. J. Polit. Econ.*, February 1973, *20*(1), pp. 43–51. [G: U.K.]

Michael, Robert T. Education in Nonmarket Production. *J. Polit. Econ.*, Part I, March-April 1973, *81*(2), pp. 306–27. [G: U.S.]

Moreh, J. Human Capital: Deterioration and Net Investment. *Rev. Income Wealth*, September 1973, *19*(3), pp. 279–302. [G: U.S.]

Morgenstern, Richard D. Direct and Indirect Effects on Earnings of Schooling and Socio-Economic Background. *Rev. Econ. Statist.*, May 1973, *55*(2), pp. 225–33. [G: U.S.]

Morse, Wayne J. A Note on the Relationship Between Human Assets and Human Capital. *Accounting Rev.*, July 1973, *48*(3), pp. 589–93.

Munro, Donald J. Man, State, and School. In *Oksenberg, M., ed.*, 1973, pp. 121–43. [G: China]

Niemi, Albert W., Jr. Returns to Educated Blacks Resulting from Southern Outmigration. *Southern Econ. J.*, October 1973, *40*(2), pp. 330–32. [G: U.S.]

Orosel, Gerhard O. A Linear Growth Model Including Education. *Z. Nationalökon.*, 1973, *33*(3–4), pp. 251–79.

Patrick, George F. and Kehrberg, Earl W. Costs and Returns of Education in Five Agricultural Areas of Eastern Brazil. *Amer. J. Agr. Econ.*, May 1973, *55*(2), pp. 145–53. [G: Brazil]

Perl, Lewis J. Family Background, Secondary School Expenditure, and Student Ability. *J. Human Res.*, Spring 1973, *8*(2), pp. 156–80. [G: U.S.]

Psacharopoulos, George. Substitution Assumptions versus Empirical Evidence in Manpower Planning. *De Economist*, November-December 1973, *121*(6), pp. 609–25. [G: Greece]

Ryder, Norman B. A New Approach to the Economic Theory of Fertility Behavior: Comment. *J. Polit. Econ.*, Part II, March-April 1973, *81*(2), pp. S65–69. [G: U.S.]

Saunders, Robert J. and Coccari, Ronald L. Racial Earnings Differentials: Some Economic Factors. *Amer. J. Econ. Soc.*, July 1973, *32*(3), pp. 225–33. [G: U.S.]

Schofield, Roger. Dimensions of Illiteracy, 1750–1850. *Exploration Econ. Hist.*, Summer 1973, *10* (4), pp. 437–54. [G: U.K.]

Schultz, Theodore W. The Value of Children: An Economic Perspective. *J. Polit. Econ.*, Part II, March-April 1973, *81*(2), pp. S2–13.

Selowsky, Marcelo and Taylor, Lance. The Economics of Malnourished Children: An Example of Disinvestment in Human Capital. *Econ. Develop. Cult. Change*, October 1973, *22*(1), pp. 17–30. [G: Chile]

Selowsky, Marcelo. An Attempt to Estimate Rates of Return to Investment in Infant Nutrition. In *Niskanen, W. A., et al., eds.*, 1973, pp. 410–28. [G: Chile]

Shearer, John C. High-Level Human Resources in Latin American Development. In *Thurber, C. E. and Graham, L. S., eds.*, 1973, pp. 133–47. [G: U.S.; S. America]

Skraly, Emile B. Manpower Planning and Economic Planning: The Two Perspectives: Discussion. In *Aronson, R. L., ed.*, 1973, pp. 80–84. [G: U.S.]

Sorkin, Alan. Manpower Programs for American Indians. *J. Econ. Bus.*, Fall 1973, *26*(1), pp. 49–57. [G: U.S.]

Stoikov, Vladimir. Size of Firm, Worker Earnings, and Human Capital: The Case of Japan. *Ind. Lab. Relat. Rev.*, July 1973, *26*(4), pp. 1095–1106. [G: Japan]

Stoikov, Vladimir. Recurrent Education: Some Neglected Economic Issues. *Int. Lab. Rev.*, August-September 1973, *108*(2–3), pp. 187–208.

Stoikov, Vladimir. The Structure of Earnings in Japanese Manufacturing Industries: A Human-Capital Approach. *J. Polit. Econ.*, Part I, March-April 1973, *81*(2), pp. 340–55. [G: Japan]

Stolz, Peter. Flexibilitätsspielräume im Einsatz des Arbeitspotentials und bedarfsorientierte Modelle der Bildungsökonomie. (Manpower Forecasts and the Problem of Flexible Relationships between

Educational Qualifications and Occupations. With English summary.) *Z. Wirtschaft. Sozialwissen.*, 1973, *93*(1), pp. 3–20.

Stone, Richard. Economic and Demographic Accounts and the Distribution of Income. *Acta Oecon.*, 1973, *11*(2–3), pp. 165–76.

Sundaram, K. Education and Class Structure: Further Evidence from India. *World Devel.*, May 1973, *1*(5), pp. 37–40.　　　　[G: India]

Su, Teddy T. Skill Obsolescence and Training: Comment. *Southern Econ. J.*, April 1973, *39*(4), pp. 645–48.

Taubman, Paul J. and Wales, Terence J. Higher Education, Mental Ability, and Screening. *J. Polit. Econ.*, January-February 1973, *81*(1), pp. 28–55. [G: U.S.]

Thurow, Lester C. Redistributional Aspects of Manpower Training Programs. In *Ulman, L., ed.*, 1973, pp. 83–101.　　　　[G: U.S.]

Voronov, O. Paid Educational Leave in the USSR. *Int. Lab. Rev.*, June 1973, *107*(6), pp. 529–38. [G: U.S.S.R.]

Wales, Terence J. The Effect of College Quality on Earnings: Results from the NBER-Thorndike Data. *J. Human Res.*, Summer 1973, *8*(3), pp. 306–17.　　　　[G: U.S.]

Weintraub, Andrew. The Economics of Lincoln's Proposal for Compensated Emancipation. *Amer. J. Econ. Soc.*, April 1973, *32*(2), pp. 171–77. [G: U.S.]

Welch, Finis. Black-White Differences in Returns to Schooling. *Amer. Econ. Rev.*, December 1973, *63* (5), pp. 893–907.　　　　[G: U.S.]

Willis, Robert J. A New Approach to the Economic Theory of Fertility Behavior. *J. Polit. Econ.*, Part II, March-April 1973, *81*(2), pp. S14–64. [G: U.S.]

Wilson, Douglas. The Economic Analysis of Malnutrition. In *Berg, A.; Scrimshaw, N. S. and Call, D. L., eds.*, 1973, pp. 129–44.

Windham, Douglas M. The Economics of Education: A Survey. In *Chamberlain, N. W., ed.*, 1973, pp. 159–217.　　　　[G: U.S.]

Wolf, Charles, Jr. Heresies About Time: Wasted Time, Double-Duty Time, and Past Time. *Quart. J. Econ.*, November 1973, *87*(4), pp. 661–67.

de Wolff, P. and van Slijpe, A. R. D. The Relation Between Income, Intelligence, Education and Social Background. *Europ. Econ. Rev.*, October 1973, *4*(3), pp. 235–64.　　　　[G: Sweden]

Zhamin, V. Forecasting the Level of Education. *Prob. Econ.*, March 1973, *15*(11), pp. 73–91. [G: U.S.S.R.]

Ziderman, Adrian and Driver, C. A Markov Chain Model of the Benefits of Participating in Government Training Schemes. *Manchester Sch. Econ. Soc. Stud.*, December 1973, *41*(4), pp. 401–17. [G: U.K.]

Ziderman, Adrian. Does it Pay to Take a Degree? *Oxford Econ. Pap.*, July 1973, *25*(2), pp. 262–74. [G: U.K.]

Ziderman, Adrian. Estimating U.S. Human Capital Loss in Southeast Asia: Comment. *J. Human Res.*, Fall 1973, *8*(4), pp. 524–26.　　　　[G: U.S.]

Ziderman, Adrian. Rates of Return on Investment in

Education: Recent Results for Britain. *J. Human Res.*, Winter 1973, *8*(1), pp. 85–97.　　　[G: U.K.]

900 Welfare Programs; Consumer Economics; Urban and Regional Economics

910 WELFARE, HEALTH, AND EDUCATION

911 General Welfare Programs

9110 General Welfare Programs

Ackerman, Bruce. More on Slum Housing and Redistribution Policy: A Reply to Professor Komesar. *Yale Law J.*, May 1973, *82*(6), pp. 1194–1207.

Breimyer, Harold F. An Analysis of the Market for Food Stamps: Comment. *Amer. J. Agr. Econ.*, February 1973, *55*(1), pp. 110–12.　　[G: U.S.]

Browning, Edgar K. Alternative Programs for Income Redistribution: The NIT and the NWT. *Amer. Econ. Rev.*, March 1973, *63*(1), pp. 38–49. [G: U.S.]

Brown, J. Douglas. Social Security in the Years Ahead. In *Somers, G. G., ed.*, 1973, pp. 118–27. [G: U.S.]

Bryant, W. Keith. An Analysis of the Market for Food Stamps: Reply. *Amer. J. Agr. Econ.*, February 1973, *55*(1), pp. 112–15.　　　　[G: U.S.]

Byrne, Dennis M. Some Preliminary Results of Income-Maintenance Experiments. *Nebr. J. Econ. Bus.*, Autumn 1973, *12*(4), pp. 23–35. [G: U.S.]

Dales, Sophie R. Federal Grants to State and Local Governments. *Soc. Sec. Bull.*, June 1973, *36*(6), pp. 16–27.　　　　[G: U.S.]

DeJong, Gordon F. and Donnelly, William L. Public Welfare and Migration. *Soc. Sci. Quart.*, September 1973, *54*(2), pp. 329–44.　　[G: U.S.]

Durbin, Elizabeth. Work and Welfare: The Case of Aid to Families with Dependent Children. *J. Human Res.*, Supplement 1973, *8*, pp. 103–25. [G: U.S.]

Edmonds, Juliet. Child Care and Family Services in Barbados. *Soc. Econ. Stud.*, June 1973, *22*(2), pp. 229–48.　　　　[G: Barbados]

Elesh, David, et al. The New Jersey-Pennsylvania Experiment: A Field Study in Negative Taxation. In *Boulding, K. E.; Pfaff, M. and Pfaff, A., eds.*, 1973, pp. 181–201.　　　　[G: U.S.]

Feagin, Joe R. Issues in Welfare Research: A Critical Overview. *Soc. Sci. Quart.*, September 1973, *54* (2), pp. 321–28.　　　　[G: U.S.]

Fiegehen, G. C. and Lansley, P. S. The Tax-Credit Proposals. *Nat. Inst. Econ. Rev.*, May 1973, (64), pp. 44–67.　　　　[G: U.K.]

Foley, Duncan K. A Primer on Negative Taxation. In *Grieson, R. E., ed.*, 1973, pp. 297–312. [G: U.S.]

Friedman, Richard E. Private Foundation-Government Relationships. In *Heimann, F. F., ed.*, 1973, pp. 163–91.　　　　[G: U.S.]

Fusfeld, Daniel R. Transfer Payments and the Ghetto Economy. In *Boulding, K. E.; Pfaff, M. and Pfaff, A., eds.*, 1973, pp. 78–92.　　[G: U.S.]

Galatin, Malcolm. A Comparison of the Benefits of the Food-Stamp Program, Free Food Stamps, and an Equivalent Cash Payment. *Public Policy,* Spring 1973, *21*(2), pp. 291–302.   [G: U.S.]

Garfinkel, Irwin and Masters, Stanley H. Two Income Maintenance Plans, Work Incentives and the Closure of the Poverty Gap: Comment. *Ind. Lab. Relat. Rev.,* April 1973, *26*(3), pp. 1002–04.   [G: U.S.]

Glantz, Frederic B. Migration and Economic Opportunity: The Case of the Poor. *New Eng. Econ. Rev.,* March-April 1973, pp. 14–17.   [G: U.S.]

Glennerster, Howard. A Tax Credit Scheme for Britain?—A Review of the British Government's Green Paper. *J. Human Res.,* Fall 1973, *8*(4), pp. 422–35.   [G: U.K.]

Grieson, Ronald E. Poverty: Introduction. In *Grieson, R. E., ed.,* 1973, pp. 273–85.   [G: U.S.]

Haber, Lawrence D. Social Planning for Disability. *J. Human Res.,* Supplement 1973, *8,* pp. 33–55.   [G: U.S.]

Hausman, Leonard J. The Politics of a Guaranteed Income: The Nixon Administration and the Family Assistance Plan—A Review Article. *J. Human Res.,* Fall 1973, *8*(4), pp. 411–21. [G: U.S.]

Heffernan, W. Joseph, Jr. Variations in Negative Tax Rates in Current Public Assistance Programs: An Example of Administrative Discretion. *J. Human Res.,* Supplement 1973, *8,* pp. 56–68. [G: U.S.]

Hiemstra, Stephen J. An Analysis of the Market for Food Stamps: Comment. *Amer. J. Agr. Econ.,* February 1973, *55*(1), pp. 109–10.   [G: U.S.]

Hill, C. Russell. Two Income Maintenance Plans, Work Incentives and the Closure of the Poverty Gap: Reply. *Ind. Lab. Relat. Rev.,* April 1973, *26* (3), pp. 1005–08.   [G: U.S.]

Husby, Ralph D. Impact of a Negative Income Tax on Aggregate Demand and Supply. *Western Econ. J.,* March 1973, *11*(1), pp. 111–17.

Husby, Ralph D. Work Incentives and the Cost Effectiveness of Income Maintenance Programs. *Quart. Rev. Econ. Bus.,* Spring 1973, *13*(1), pp. 7–13.   [G: U.S.]

Jackson, Emma. The Present System of Publicly Supported Day Care. In *Young, D. R. and Nelson, R. R., eds.,* 1973, pp. 21–46.   [G: U.S.]

Johnson, Warren A. The Guaranteed Income as an Environmental Measure. In *Daly, H. E., ed.,* 1973, pp. 175–89.   [G: U.S.]

Kesselman, Jonathan R. Incentive Effects of Transfer Systems Once Again. *J. Human Res.,* Winter 1973, *8*(1), pp. 119–29.   [G: U.S.]

Kesselman, Jonathan R. A Comprehensive Approach to Income Maintenance: Swift. *J. Public Econ.,* February 1973, *2*(1), pp. 59–88. [G: U.S.]

Komesar, Neil K. Return to Slumville: A Critique of the Ackerman Analysis of Housing Code Enforcement and the Poor. *Yale Law J.,* May 1973, *82*(6), pp. 1175–93.

Kottis, Athena P. Community Effects of an Income Maintenance Plan: A Theoretical Exploration. In *Mattila, J. M. and Thompson, W. R., eds.,* 1973, pp. 41–57.   [G: U.S.]

Levitan, Sar A. and Marwick, David. Work and Training for Relief Recipients. *J. Human Res.,* Supplement 1973, *8,* pp. 5–18.   [G: U.S.]

Lynn, Mary and Kotz, Nick. You Are What You Eat: Feeding D.C.'s Hungry. In *Levitan, S. A., ed.,* 1973, pp. 143–74.   [G: U.S.]

Mathew, T. I. Social Security for the Rural Population: A Study of Some Social Services in Selected Rural Areas of India. *Int. Lab. Rev.,* October 1973, *108*(4), pp. 313–28.   [G: India]

Moeller, John F. Development of a Microsimulation Model for Evaluating Economic Implications of Income Transfer and Tax Policies. *Ann. Econ. Soc. Measure,* April 1973, *2*(2), pp. 183–87.

Nelson, Richard R. and Young, Dennis. National Day Care Policy. In *Young, D. R. and Nelson, R. R., eds.,* 1973, pp. 91–103.   [G: U.S.]

Nelson, Richard R. and Krashinsky, Michael. Two Major Issues of Public Policy: Public Subsidy and Organization of Supply. In *Young, D. R. and Nelson, R. R., eds.,* 1973, pp. 47–69.   [G: U.S.]

Penner, Rudolph G.; Ott, David J. and Ott, Attiat F. Income Security. In *Ott, D. J., et al.,* 1973, pp. 193–214.   [G: U.S.]

Pfaff, Anita B. Transfer Payments to Large Metropolitan Poverty Areas: Their Distributive and Poverty-Reducing Effects. In *Boulding, K. E.; Pfaff, M. and Pfaff, A., eds.,* 1973, pp. 93–130.   [G: U.S.]

Pohlman, Jerry E. A Trade-off Analysis of Job Creation vs. Welfare. *J. Econ. Bus.,* Spring-Summer 1973, *25*(3), pp. 168–74.   [G: U.S.]

Raskin, Barbara. The AFDC Numbers Game. In *Levitan, S. A., ed.,* 1973, pp. 119–42.   [G: U.S.]

Reich, Utz-Peter. Die theoretischen Grundlagen des SPD-Langzeitprogramms. (Theoretical Framework of the SPD-Long-Term-Program. With English summary.) *Z. Wirtschaft. Sozialwissen.,* 1973, *93*(5), pp. 513–35.   [G: W. Germany]

Rein, Martin. Recent British Experience with Negative Income Tax. *J. Human Res.,* Supplement 1973, *8,* pp. 69–89.   [G: U.K.; U.S.]

Rein, Martin. Work Incentives and Welfare Reform in Britain and the United States. In *Stein, B. and Miller, S. M., eds.,* 1973, pp. 151–95.   [G: U.S.; U.K.]

Rosow, Jerome M. Work Requirements in Welfare and Unemployment Insurance. *Mon. Lab. Rev.,* April 1973, *96*(4), pp. 56–57.   [G: U.S.]

Rzhanitsina, L. Public Consumption Funds in the USSR. *Int. Lab. Rev.,* December 1973, *108*(6), pp. 516–35.   [G: U.S.S.R.]

Schiller, Bradley R. Moving from Welfare to Workfare. *Public Policy,* Winter 1973, *21*(1), pp. 125–33.   [G: U.S.]

Schiller, Bradley R. Empirical Studies of Welfare Dependency: A Survey. *J. Human Res.,* Supplement 1973, *8,* pp. 19–32.   [G: U.S.]

Seidman, Bert. Welfare Reform Should Mean the Welfare of Children. *Mon. Lab. Rev.,* April 1973, *96*(4), pp. 57–59.   [G: U.S.]

Shea, John R. Welfare Mothers: Barriers to Labor Force Entry. *J. Human Res.,* Supplement 1973, *8,* pp. 90–102.   [G: U.S.]

Shore, Arnold R. and Scott, Robert A. Work Response and Family Composition Changes in a Negative Income Tax Experiment: Preliminary Mid-Experiment Results. In *Sheldon, E. B., ed.,* 1973, pp. 233–63.   [G: U.S.]

Thurow, Lester C. The Political Economy of Income Redistribution Policies. *Ann. Amer. Acad. Polit. Soc. Sci.*, September 1973, *409*, pp. 146–55. [G: U.S.]

Trąmpczyński, Bolesław. Co-operatives of the Disabled in Poland. *Int. Lab. Rev.*, November 1973, *108*(5), pp. 423–37. [G: Poland]

Winegarden, C. R. Welfare 'Explosion': Determinants of the Size and Recent Growth of the AFDC Population. *Amer. J. Econ. Soc.*, July 1973, *32*(3), pp. 245–56. [G: U.S.]

Young, Dennis and Jackson, Emma. Public Policy for Day Care of Young Children: Introduction. In *Young, D. R. and Nelson, R. R., eds.*, 1973, pp. 1–8. [G: U.S.]

912 Economics of Education

9120 Economics of Education

Abelle, Barnie E. The Teaching-Learning Implications of Educational Technology. *J. Risk Ins.*, December 1973, *40*(4), pp. 607–15.

Ahamad, Bashir. Manpower Forecasting for Single Occupations: Teachers in England and Wales. In *Ahamad, B. and Blaug, M., eds.*, 1973, pp. 261–84. [G: U.K.]

Alamgir, Mohiuddin. Some Theoretical Issues in Manpower and Educational Planning. *Bangladesh Econ. Rev.*, April 1973, *1*(2), pp. 199–212.

Arnold, Mark R. Public Schools. In *Levitan, S. A., ed.*, 1973, pp. 21–51. [G: U.S.]

Arrow, Kenneth J. Higher Education as a Filter. *J. Public Econ.*, July 1973, *2*(3), pp. 193–216.

Aussieker, Bill and Garbarino, Joseph W. Measuring Faculty Unionism: Quantity and Quality. *Ind. Relat.*, May 1973, *12*(2), pp. 117–24. [G: U.S.]

Barlow, Robin. Efficiency Aspects of Local School Finance: Reply. *J. Polit. Econ.*, January-February 1973, *81*(1), pp. 199–202. [G: U.S.]

Barzel, Yoram. Private Schools and Public School Finance. *J. Polit. Econ.*, January-February 1973, *81*(1), pp. 174–86. [G: U.S.]

Bellin, Seymour S. and Bellin, Shirley S. Teacher Incentives Tied to Pupil Performance: A Strategy for Educational Accountability. In *Stein, B. and Miller, S. M., eds.*, 1973, pp. 117–48. [G: U.S.]

Benson, Charles S. Collective Bargaining in Higher Education. *Mon. Lab. Rev.*, May 1973, *96*(5), pp. 33–34.

Bergstrom, Theodore C. A Note on Efficient Taxation. *J. Polit. Econ.*, January-February 1973, *81*(1), pp. 187–91. [G: U.S.]

Bhagwati, Jagdish N. Education, Class Structure and Income Equality. *World Devel.*, May 1973, *1*(5), pp. 21–36. [G: India]

Blaug, Mark. University Efficiency and University Finance: Discussion. In *Parkin, M., ed.*, 1973, pp. 189–91.

Boehlje, Michael; Eidman, Vernon and Walker, Odell. An Approach to Farm Management Education. *Amer. J. Agr. Econ.*, May 1973, *55*(2), pp. 192–97.

Booms, Bernard H. and Hu, Teh-wei. Economic and Social Factors in the Provision of Urban Public Education. *Amer. J. Econ. Soc.*, January 1973, *32*(1), pp. 35–43. [G: U.S.]

Borus, Michael E. and Nestel, Gilbert. Response Bias in Reports of Father's Education and Socioeconomic Status. *J. Amer. Statist. Assoc.*, December 1973, *68*(344), pp. 816–20. [G: U.S.]

Boulding, Kenneth E. Factors Affecting the Future Demand for Education. In *Boulding, K. E.*, 1973, pp. 503–31. [G: U.S.]

Boulding, Kenneth E. The University as an Economic and Social Unit. In *Boulding, K. E.*, 1973, pp. 413–27.

Bourgeois, Lawrence L. and Schlenker, Jon A. Family Assistance to Married University Students. *Southern Quart.*, January 1973, *11*(2), pp. 147–55. [G: U.S.]

Brierley, J. D. Programme Budgeting in Education in the United Kingdom. In *Novick, D., ed.*, 1973, pp. 97–103. [G: U.K.]

Brown, Byron W. State Grants and Inequality of Opportunity in Education. In *Boulding, K. E.; Pfaff, M. and Pfaff, A., eds.*, 1973, pp. 208–25. [G: U.S.]

Brown, Francis J. Economic Crisis in Private Education: Whither Now? *Rev. Soc. Econ.*, April 1973, *31*(1), pp. 93–97. [G: U.S.]

Brownrigg, M. The Economic Impact of a New University. *Scot. J. Polit. Econ.*, June 1973, *20*(2), pp. 123–39. [G: U.K.]

Calkins, Hugh. Breaking Down the Fiscal Barriers to Career Education. In *McClure, L. and Buan, C., eds.*, 1973, pp. 247–55. [G: U.S.]

Cleary, T. Anne. New Directions for Career Planning. In *McClure, L. and Buan, C., eds.*, 1973, pp. 39–53. [G: U.S.]

Cohen, David K., et al. Revenue-Sharing as an Incentive Device: The Experience with Title I of the Elementary and Secondary Education Act. In *Stein, B. and Miller, S. M., eds.*, 1973, pp. 93–115. [G: U.S.]

Cohn, Elchanan. On the Ranking of Social Investments in Education: A Reply. *Public Finance*, 1973, *28*(3–4), pp. 431–34. [G: U.S.]

Comay, Yochanan; Melnik, A. and Pollatschek, M. A. The Option Value of Education and the Optimal Path for Investment in Human Capital. *Int. Econ. Rev.*, June 1973, *14*(2), pp. 421–35. [G: U.S.]

Cook, Gail C. A. and Stager, David A. A. Contingent Repayment Student Finance: The Problem of Non-Participants in the Labour Force. *Ann. Econ. Soc. Measure*, January 1973, *2*(1), pp. 65–67. [G: U.S.]

Cook, Gail C. A. Effect of Metropolitan Government on Resource Allocation: The Case of Education in Toronto. *Nat. Tax J.*, December 1973, *26*(4), pp. 585–90. [G: Canada]

Costin, Frank; Greenough, William T. and Menges, Robert J. Student Ratings of College Teaching: Reliability, Validity, and Usefulness. *J. Econ. Educ.*, Fall 1973, *5*(1), pp. 51–53.

Crean, John F. Forgone Earnings and the Demand for Education: Some Empirical Evidence. *Can. J. Econ.*, February 1973, *6*(1), pp. 23–42. [G: Canada]

Curtis, William H. Application of the Concept to School District Decision-Making. In *Novick, D., ed.*, 1973, pp. 161–67.   [G: U.S.]

Daley, Thelma T. Career Development: A Cooperative Thrust of the School and Its Community. In *McClure, L. and Buan, C., eds.*, 1973, pp. 85–92. [G: U.S.]

Deaglio, Mario. Differenze di instruzione e differenze di retribuzione in una società ugualitaria. (Education and Pay Structures in an Egalitarian Society. With English summary.) *L'Industria,* January-June 1973, (1–2), pp. 134–75.

Dresch, Stephen P. Contingent Repayment Student Finance: The Problem of Non-Participants in the Labour Force: Reply. *Ann. Econ. Soc. Measure,* January 1973, *2*(1), pp. 69. [G: U.S.]

Edelson, Noel M. Efficiency Aspects of Local School Finance: Comments and Extensions. *J. Polit. Econ.,* January-February 1973, *81*(1), pp. 158–73. [G: U.S.]

Evans, Robert, Jr. Education Levels and Unemployment in Asian Countries. *Mon. Lab. Rev.,* November 1973, *96*(11), pp. 58–59. [G: Asia]

Evans, Rupert N. and Galloway, Joel D. Verbal Ability and Socioeconomic Status of 9th and 12th Grade College Preparatory, General, and Vocational Students. *J. Human Res.,* Winter 1973, *8*(1), pp. 24–36. [G: U.S.]

Freiden, Alan and Staaf, Robert J. Scholastic Choice: An Economic Model of Student Behavior. *J. Human Res.,* Summer 1973, *8*(3), pp. 396–404. [G: U.S.]

Frey, Donald E. The Distribution of Educational Resources in Large American Cities: Comment. *J. Human Res.,* Fall 1973, *8*(4), pp. 516–18. [G: U.S.]

Garfinkel, Irwin and Gramlich, Edward M. A Statistical Analysis of the OEO Experiment in Educational Performance Contracting. *J. Human Res.,* Summer 1973, *8*(3), pp. 275–305. [G: U.S.]

Ghazalah, I. A. and Pejovich, Svetozar. The Economics of Vocational and Technical Education: A Report on Three Studies. *Rev. Soc. Econ.,* October 1973, *31*(2), pp. 191–98. [G: U.S.]

Gilmer, Robert W. and Morgan, Daniel, Jr. The Equivalence of Flat Grants and Foundation Programs in State Education Aid Formulas. *Public Finance Quart.,* October 1973, *1*(4), pp. 437–47.

Goddard, Frederick O. and Goffman, Irving J. The Public Financing of Non-Public Education. *Rev. Soc. Econ.,* October 1973, *31*(2), pp. 152–66. [G: U.S.]

Goetz, Charles J.; Tucker, James F. and Weber, Warren E. Student Incentive Payments and Academic Achievement: An Empirical Test. *Soc. Sci. Quart.,* June 1973, *54*(1), pp. 159–67. [G: U.S.]

Green, R. H. University Economics in Anglophonic Africa: A Modest Critique from a Consumer Viewpoint. In *Livingstone, I., et al., eds.,* 1973, pp. 137–46. [G: Africa]

Griffin, James B. The Economics of Education: Social Benefits and Costs. In *Mattila, J. M. and Thompson, W. R., eds.,* 1973, pp. 140–50. [G: U.S.]

Griliches, Zvi. Measuring Performance in Education: Comment. In *Moss, M., ed.,* 1973, pp. 433–35. [G: U.S.]

Gustman, Alan L. and Pidot, George B., Jr. Interactions Between Educational Spending and Student

Enrollment. *J. Human Res.,* Winter 1973, *8*(1), pp. 3–23. [G: U.S.]

Hall, W. Clayton and Carroll, Norman E. The Effect of Teachers' Organizations on Salaries and Class Size. *Ind. Lab. Relat. Rev.,* January 1973, *26*(2), pp. 834–41. [G: U.S.]

Hambor, John C.; Phillips, Llad and Votey, Harold L., Jr. High School Inputs and Their Contribution to School Performance: A Comment. *J. Human Res.,* Spring 1973, *8*(2), pp. 260–63. [G: U.S.]

Hambor, John C.; Phillips, Llad and Votey, Harold L., Jr. Optimal Community Educational Attainment: A Simultaneous Equation Approach. *Rev. Econ. Statist.,* February 1973, *55*(1), pp. 98–103. [G: U.S.]

Hanushek, Eric A. The High Cost of Graduate Education in the Military. *Public Policy,* Fall 1973, *21*(4), pp. 525–52. [G: U.S.]

Hendon, William S. Property Values, Schools, and Park-School Combinations. *Land Econ.,* May 1973, *49*(2), pp. 216–18. [G: U.S.]

Hight, Joseph E. and Pollock, Richard. Income Distribution Effects of Higher Education Expenditures in California, Florida and Hawaii. *J. Human Res.,* Summer 1973, *8*(3), pp. 318–30. [G: U.S.]

Hogan, Timothy D. and Shelton, Robert B. A Note on Barlow's Local School Finance. *J. Polit. Econ.,* January-February 1973, *81*(1), pp. 192–98. [G: U.S.]

Holland, David W. and Tweeten, Luther G. Human Capital Migration: Implications for Common School Finance. *Land Econ.,* August 1973, *49*(3), pp. 278–84. [G: U.S.]

Johnson, George E. and Stafford, Frank P. Social Returns to Quantity and Quality of Schooling. *J. Human Res.,* Spring 1973, *8*(2), pp. 139–55. [G: U.S.]

Johnson, Harry G. The Economics of Student Protest. In *Johnson, H. G. and Weisbrod, B. A., eds.,* 1973, pp. 3–7.

Johnston, Denis F. Education of Workers: Projections to 1990. *Mon. Lab. Rev.,* November 1973, *96*(11), pp. 22–31.

Joshi, Nandini U. Estimating Future Unemployment of Graduates. *Bangladesh Econ. Rev.,* October 1973, *1*(4), pp. 409–24. [G: India]

King, Allan G. A Comment on Bowles' Model of Educational Planning. *Econ. Planning,* 1973, *13*(1–2), pp. 131–35.

Koch, James V. and Chizmar, John F. The Influence of Teaching and Other Factors Upon Absolute Salaries and Salary Increments at Illinois State University. *J. Econ. Educ.,* Fall 1973, *5*(1), pp. 27–34. [G: U.S.]

Koshal, Rajindar K. The Future of Higher Education in the State of Ohio: An Econometric Approach. *Ohio State U. Bull. Bus. Res.,* November 1973, *48*(11), pp. 1–3, 5. [G: U.S.]

Kottis, Athena P. and Kottis, George C. Who Benefits from Higher Education Subsidies. A Reconsideration. *Tijdschr. Econ.,* 1973, *18*(3), pp. 451–56.

Latham, Robert J. Operating Expenditures and Sponsored Research at U.S. Medical Schools: Comment. *J. Human Res.,* Fall 1973, *8*(4), pp. 519–22. [G: U.S.]

Layard, Richard and Jackman, Richard. University

Efficiency and University Finance. In *Parkin, M., ed.*, 1973, pp. 170–88.

Lazarcik, Gregor. Defense, Education and Health Expenditures and Their Relation to GNP in Eastern Europe, 1960-1970. *Amer. Econ.*, Spring 1973, *17*(1), pp. 29–34. [G: E. Europe]

Levy-Garboua, Louis. Rémunère-t-on les études? (Does Schooling Pay? With English summary.) *Consommation*, July-September 1973, *20*(3), pp. 57–81. [G: France]

Lindholm, Richard W. State-Local School and Highway Expenditure Trends, 1965-1966 and 1969-1970. *Public Finance Quart.*, January 1973, *1*(1), pp. 29–34. [G: U.S.]

Lumsden, Keith G. Summary of an Analysis of Student Evaluations of Faculty and Courses. *J. Econ. Educ.*, Fall 1973, *5*(1), pp. 54–56.

Lu, Yao-Chi and Tweeten, Luther G. The Impact of Busing on Student Achievement. *Growth Change*, October 1973, *4*(4), pp. 44–46. [G: U.S.]

Machlis, Peter David. The Distributional Effects of Public Higher Education in New York City. *Public Finance Quart.*, January 1973, *1*(1), pp. 35–57. [G: U.S.]

Magnusson, Leif. Cost-Benefit Analysis of Investment in Higher Education: Some Swedish Results. *Swedish J. Econ.*, June 1973, *75*(2), pp. 119–27. [G: Sweden]

Mathews, Russell. Patterns of Educational Finance. *Australian Econ. Pap.*, December 1973, *12*(21), pp. 145–61. [G: Australia]

Michael, Robert T. Education in Nonmarket Production. *J. Polit. Econ.*, Part I, March-April 1973, *81*(2), pp. 306–27. [G: U.S.]

Mirus, Rolf. Some Implications of Student Evaluation of Teachers. *J. Econ. Educ.*, Fall 1973, *5*(1), pp. 35–46.

Moor, R. Carl. The Economic Efficiency of Mixed Financing of Education in Economic Space. *Public Finance Quart.*, October 1973, *1*(4), pp. 399–408.

Morgenstern, Richard D. Direct and Indirect Effects on Earnings of Schooling and Socio-Economic Background. *Rev. Econ. Statist.*, May 1973, *55*(2), pp. 225–33. [G: U.S.]

Muller, Thomas. Income Redistribution Impact of State Grants to Public Schools: A Case Study of Delaware. In *Boulding, K. E.; Pfaff, M. and Pfaff, A., eds.*, 1973, pp. 226–45. [G: U.S.]

Nouri, Clement J. Comparative Job Attitudes—Iraqui and American Students. *Marquette Bus. Rev.*, Spring 1973, *17*(1), pp. 13–24. [G: U.S.; Iraq]

Olivier, R. and Sabolo, Y. Simultaneous Planning of Employment, Production and Education. *Int. Lab. Rev.*, April 1973, *107*(4), pp. 359–72. [G: Peru]

Ott, Attiat F. Education. In *Ott, D. J., et al.*, 1973, pp. 113–52. [G: U.S.]

Owen, John D. The Distribution of Educational Resources in Large American Cities: Reply. *J. Human Res.*, Fall 1973, *8*(4), pp. 518–19.

Peltzman, Sam. The Effect of Government Subsidies-in-Kind on Private Expenditures: The Case of Higher Education. *J. Polit. Econ.*, January-February 1973, *81*(1), pp. 1–27. [G: U.S.]

Perl, Lewis J. Family Background, Secondary School Expenditure, and Student Ability. *J. Human Res.*, Spring 1973, *8*(2), pp. 156–80. [G: U.S.]

Phares, Donald L. Impact of Spatial Tax Flows as Implicit Grants on State-Local Tax Incidence: With Reference to the Financing of Education. In *Boulding, K. E.; Pfaff, M. and Pfaff, A., eds.*, 1973, pp. 258–75. [G: U.S.]

Pool, A. Jonathan, et al. Handbook of Soviet Social Science Data: Education. In *Mickiewicz, E., ed.*, 1973, pp. 137–58. [G: U.S.S.R.]

Porter, David O. and Warner, David C. How Effective Are Grantor Controls?: The Case of Federal Aid to Education. In *Boulding, K. E.; Pfaff, M. and Pfaff, A., eds.*, 1973, pp. 276–302. [G: U.S.]

Psacharopoulos, George and Williams, Gareth. Public Sector Earnings and Educational Planning. *Int. Lab. Rev.*, July 1973, *108*(1), pp. 43–57. [G: Iran]

Psacharopoulos, George. A Note on the Demand for Enrollment in Higher Education. *De Economist*, September-October 1973, *121*(5), pp. 521–25. [G: U.S.]

Psoinos, D. P. and Xirokostas, D. A. A Dynamic Programming Approach to Establishing Teaching Posts in a Centralized Educational System. In *Ross, M., ed.*, 1973, pp. 315–23.

Raymond, Richard. The Interregional Brain Drain and Public Education. *Growth Change*, July 1973, *4*(3), pp. 28–34. [G: U.S.]

Rivlin, Alice M. Measuring Performance in Education. In *Moss, M., ed.*, 1973, pp. 411–28. [G: U.S.]

Rodin, Miriam and Rodin, Burton. Student Evaluations of Teachers. *J. Econ. Educ.*, Fall 1973, *5*(1), pp. 5–21.

Schultz, Theodore W. The Value of Children: An Economic Perspective. *J. Polit. Econ.*, Part II, March-April 1973, *81*(2), pp. S2–13.

Shapiro, David. Economy of Scale as a Cost Factor in the Operation of School Districts in Alberta. *Can. J. Econ.*, February 1973, *6*(1), pp. 114–21. [G: Canada]

Shimada, Toshiro. Industrial Dynamics Model of a Japanese University. In *Ross, M., ed.*, 1973, pp. 303–14. [G: Japan]

Simon, Larry G. The School Finance Decisions: Collective Bargaining and Future Finance Systems. *Yale Law J.*, January 1973, *82*(3), pp. 409–60. [G: U.S.]

Sims, Edwin C., Jr. and Pinches, George E. Factors Related to the Performance of College Endowment Funds. *J. Econ. Bus.*, Spring-Summer 1973, *25*(3), pp. 198–205. [G: U.S.]

Singell, Larry D. and Yordon, Wesley J. Incentives for More Efficient Education: The Development of a Model. In *Stein, B. and Miller, S. M., eds.*, 1973, pp. 71–91. [G: U.S.]

Soper, John C. Soft Research on a Hard Subject: Student Evaluations Reconsidered. *J. Econ. Educ.*, Fall 1973, *5*(1), pp. 22–26.

Southwick, Lawrence, Jr. The Higher Education Industry: Forecasts to 1990. *Rev. Soc. Econ.*, April 1973, *31*(1), pp. 1–19. [G: U.S.]

Speare, Alden, Jr.; Speare, Mary C. and Lin, Hui-

Sheng. Urbanization, Non-Familial Work, Education, and Fertility in Taiwan. *Population Stud.*, July 1973, *27*(2), pp. 323–34.   [G: Taiwan]

Staaf, Robert J. and Tullock, Gordon. Education and Equality. *Ann. Amer. Acad. Polit. Soc. Sci.*, September 1973, *409*, pp. 125–34.

Starler, Norman H. and Thomas, Robert W. Intergovernmental Education Grants and the Efficiency of Resource Allocation in School Districts. *Appl. Econ.*, September 1973, *5*(3), pp. 181–92.   [G: U.S.]

Stern, David. Effects of Alternative State Aid Formulas on the Distribution of Public School Expenditures in Massachusetts. *Rev. Econ. Statist.*, February 1973, *55*(1), pp. 91–97.   [G: U.S.]

Stiglitz, Joseph E. Education and Inequality. *Ann. Amer. Acad. Polit. Soc. Sci.*, September 1973, *409*, pp. 135–45.   [G: U.S.]

Stoikov, Vladimir. Recurrent Education: Some Neglected Economic Issues. *Int. Lab. Rev.*, August-September 1973, *108*(2–3), pp. 187–208.

Summers, Anita A. Equity in School Financing: The Courts Move In. *Fed. Res. Bank Bus. Rev. Phila.*, March 1973, pp. 3–13.   [G: U.S.]

Sundaram, K. Education and Class Structure: Further Evidence from India. *World Devel.*, May 1973, *1*(5), pp. 37–40.   [G: India]

Terleckyj, Nestor E. Measuring Performance in Education: Comment. In *Moss, M., ed.*, 1973, pp. 435–37.   [G: U.S.]

Tollison, Robert D. and Willett, Thomas D. The University and the Price System. *J. Econ. Bus.*, Spring-Summer 1973, *25*(3), pp. 191–97.   [G: U.S.]

Tuckman, Howard P. Local Colleges and the Demand for Higher Education: The Enrollment Inducing Effects of Location. *Amer. J. Econ. Soc.*, July 1973, *32*(3), pp. 257–68.   [G: U.S.]

Villard, Henry H. Some Reflections on Student Evaluation of Teaching. *J. Econ. Educ.*, Fall 1973, *5*(1), pp. 47–50.

Voronov, O. Paid Educational Leave in the USSR. *Int. Lab. Rev.*, June 1973, *107*(6), pp. 529–38.   [G: U.S.S.R.]

Wales, Terence J. The Effect of College Quality on Earnings: Results from the NBER-Thorndike Data. *J. Human Res.*, Summer 1973, *8*(3), pp. 306–17.   [G: U.S.]

Wales, Terence J. The Effect of School and District Size on Education Costs in British Columbia. *Int. Econ. Rev.*, October 1973, *14*(3), pp. 710–20.   [G: Canada]

Weisbrod, Burton A. Measuring Performance in Education: Comment. In *Moss, M., ed.*, 1973, pp. 428–33.   [G: U.S.]

Wentworth, Eric. Higher Education: The Reach Exceeds the Grasp. In *Levitan, S. A., ed.*, 1973, pp. 52–88.   [G: U.S.]

White, Fred and Tweeten, Luther G. Optimal School District Size Emphasizing Rural Areas. *Amer. J. Agr. Econ.*, February 1973, *55*(1), pp. 45–53.   [G: U.S.]

Willard, Norman, Jr. Relating the Concept and Content to the Consumers. In *McClure, L. and Buan, C., eds.*, 1973, pp. 193–203.   [G: U.S.]

Windham, Douglas M. The Economics of Education:

A Survey. In *Chamberlain, N. W., ed.*, 1973, pp. 159–217.   [G: U.S.]

Wing, Paul. Operating Expenditures and Sponsored Research at U.S. Medical Schools: Reply. *J. Human Res.*, Fall 1973, *8*(4), pp. 522–24. [G: U.S.]

Wirt, Frederick M. Financial and Desegregation Reform in Suburbia. In *Masotti, L. H. and Hadden, J. K., eds.*, 1973, pp. 457–88.   [G: U.S.]

Young, Anne M. Going Back to School at 35. *Mon. Lab. Rev.*, October 1973, *96*(10), pp. 39–42.
        [G: U.S.]

Young, Edwin. Personnel Relations in Non-Profit Institutions. In *Somers, G. G., ed.*, 1973, pp. 198–204.   [G: U.S.]

Zhamin, V. Economic Progress and the Development of Higher Education. *Prob. Econ.*, August 1973, *16*(4), pp. 47–62.   [G: U.S.S.R.]

Ziderman, Adrian. On the Ranking of Social Investments in Education: A Comment. *Public Finance*, 1973, *28*(3–4), pp. 424–30.   [G: U.S.]

Zimmerman, Dennis. Expenditure-Tax Incidence Studies, Public Higher Education, and Equity. *Nat. Tax J.*, March 1973, *26*(1), pp. 65–70.
        [G: U.S.]

913 Economics of Health

9130 Economics of Health

Ahamad, Bashir. Manpower Forecasting for Single Occupations: Doctors in the United States, Britain and Canada. In *Ahamad, B. and Blaug, M., eds.*, 1973, pp. 285–309. [G: U.S.; U.K.; Canada]

Ahern, William R., Jr. Health Effects of Automotive Air Pollution. In *Jacoby, H. D., et al.*, 1973, pp. 139–74.   [G: U.S.]

Ahern, William R., Jr. Measuring the Value of Emissions Reductions. In *Jacoby, H. D., et al.*, 1973, pp. 175–205.   [G: U.S.]

Ameiss, Albert P., et al. Program Management in Missouri's Division of Mental Health. *Manage. Account.*, August 1973, *55*(2), pp. 31–34.
        [G: U.S.]

Atkinson, A. B. and Skegg, J. L. Anti-Smoking Publicity and the Demand for Tobacco in the U.K. *Manchester Sch. Econ. Soc. Stud.*, September 1973, *41*(3), pp. 265–82.   [G: U.K.]

Ault, David E. and Johnson, Thomas E., Jr. Probabilistic Models Applied to Hospital Planning. *Growth Change*, April 1973, *4*(2), pp. 7–13.

Ball, Robert M. Social Security Amendments of 1972: Summary and Legislative History. *Soc. Sec. Bull.*, March 1973, *36*(3), pp. 3–25.

Barg, Benjamin. Nutrition and National Development. In *Berg, A.; Scrimshaw, N. S. and Call, D. L., eds.*, 1973, pp. 49–69.

Beaver, M. W. Population, Infant Mortality and Milk. *Population Stud.*, July 1973, *27*(2), pp. 243–54.
        [G: U.S.]

Béhar, Moisés. The Importance of Accurate Measures of Malnutrition. In *Berg, A.; Scrimshaw, N. S. and Call, D. L., eds.*, 1973, pp. 145–49.

Bekele, Maaza. Nutrition, Planning, and Development. In *Berg, A.; Scrimshaw, N. S. and Call, D. L., eds.*, 1973, pp. 22–28.

Bengoa, J. M. Significance of Malnutrition and Priorities for Its Prevention. In *Berg, A.; Scrimshaw, N. S. and Call, D. L., eds.*, 1973, pp. 103–28.

Berdit, Martin and Williamson, John W. Function Limitation Scale for Measuring Health Outcomes. In *Berg, R. L., ed.*, 1973, pp. 59–65. **[G: U.S.]**

Berg, Alan and Muscat, Robert. Nutrition Program Planning: An Approach. In *Berg, A.; Scrimshaw, N. S. and Call, D. L., eds.*, 1973, pp. 247–74.

Berg, Robert L. Establishing the Values of Various Conditions of Life for a Health Status Index. In *Berg, R. L., ed.*, 1973, pp. 120–26. **[G: U.S.]**

Bishop, Christine E. Manpower Policy and the Supply of Nurses. *Ind. Relat.*, February 1973, *12*(1), pp. 86–94. **[G: U.S.]**

Boulding, Kenneth E. The Concept of Need for Health Services. In *Boulding, K. E.*, 1973, pp. 277–98.

Brinker, Paul A. and Murdock, E. Wayne. Children of the Severely Injured. *J. Human Res.*, Spring 1973, *8*(2), pp. 242–49. **[G: U.S.]**

Bush, J. W.; Chen, M. M. and Patrick, D. L. Health Status Index in Cost Effectiveness: Analysis of PKU Program. In *Berg, R. L., ed.*, 1973, pp. 172–93. **[G: U.S.]**

Call, David L. and Levinson, F. James. A Systematic Approach to Nutrition Intervention Programs. In *Berg, A.; Scrimshaw, N. S. and Call, D. L., eds.*, 1973, pp. 165–97.

Cantwell, J.; Lenehan, B. and O'Farrell, J. Improving the Performance of a Local Authority Ambulance Service. In *Ross, M., ed.*, 1973, pp. 443–53. **[G: Ireland]**

Chen, Martin K. The G Index for Program Priority. In *Berg, R. L., ed.*, 1973, pp. 28–34. **[G: U.S.]**

Chester, T. E. Health Service Reorganized. *Nat. Westminster Bank Quart. Rev.*, November 1973, pp. 41–54. **[G: U.K.]**

Chirikos, Thomas N. Health Service Employment in Ohio. *Ohio State U. Bull. Bus. Res.*, January 1973, *48*(1), pp. 4–5, 8. **[G: U.S.]**

Cohen, Harold A. Cost Functions of Hospital Diagnostic Procedures: A Possible Argument for Diagnostic Centers. *J. Econ. Bus.*, Winter 1973, *25*(2), pp. 83–88. **[G: U.S.]**

Collins, David C. Applications of Multiple Criterial Evaluation to Decision Aiding. In *Cochrane, J. L. and Zeleny, M., eds.*, 1973, pp. 477–505. **[G: U.S.]**

Cooper, Barbara S. and Worthington, Nancy L. Age Differences in Medical Care Spending, Fiscal Year 1972. *Soc. Sec. Bull.*, May 1973, *36*(5), pp. 3–15. **[G: U.S.]**

Cooper, Barbara S. and Worthington, Nancy L. National Health Expenditures, 1929-72. *Soc. Sec. Bull.*, January 1973, *36*(1), pp. 3–19, 40. **[G: U.S.]**

Cooper, Michael H. and Culyer, Anthony J. The Economics of Giving and Selling Blood. In *Alchian, A. A., et al.*, 1973, pp. 109–43.

Davis, Joseph M. Health and the Education-Earnings Relationship. *Mon. Lab. Rev.*, April 1973, *96*(4), pp. 61–63.

Davis, Karen. Hospital Costs and the Medicare Program. *Soc. Sec. Bull.*, August 1973, *36*(8), pp. 18–36. **[G: U.S.]**

Davis, Karen. Theories of Hospital Inflation: Some

Empirical Evidence. *J. Human Res.*, Spring 1973, *8*(2), pp. 181–201. **[G: U.S.]**

Derban, L. A. K. The Impact of Health and Nutrition on Agricultural Production in West Africa. In *Ofori, I. M., ed.*, 1973, pp. 26–32. **[G: W. Africa]**

Dramais, A. The Influence of Road Characteristics on Road Accidents in Belgium: An Econometric Approach. *Europ. Econ. Rev.*, October 1973, *4*(3), pp. 293–306. **[G: Belgium]**

Edmonds, Juliet. Child Care and Family Services in Barbados. *Soc. Econ. Stud.*, June 1973, *22*(2), pp. 229–48. **[G: Barbados]**

Ehrlich, George E. Health Challenges of the Future. *Ann. Amer. Acad. Polit. Soc. Sci.*, July 1973, *408*, pp. 70–82. **[G: U.S.]**

Ellwood, Paul M., Jr. and Herbert, Michael E. Health Care: Should Industry Buy It or Sell It? *Harvard Bus. Rev.*, July-August 1973, *51*(4), pp. 99–107.

Evans, R. G.; Parish, E. M. A. and Sully, Floyd. Medical Productivity, Scale Effects, and Demand Generation. *Can. J. Econ.*, August 1973, *6*(3), pp. 376–93. **[G: Canada]**

Feldstein, Martin S. The Welfare Loss of Excess Health Insurance. *J. Polit. Econ.*, Part I, March-April 1973, *81*(2), pp. 251–80. **[G: U.S.]**

Feldstein, Martin S. An Econometric Model of the Medicare System: Reply. *Quart. J. Econ.*, August 1973, *87*(3), pp. 490–94. **[G: U.S.]**

Field, Mark G. Handbook of Soviet Social Science Data: Health. In *Mickiewicz, E., ed.*, 1973, pp. 101–18. **[G: U.S.S.R.]**

Fisher, Paul. Major Social Security Issues: Japan, 1972. *Soc. Sec. Bull.*, March 1973, *36*(3), pp. 26–38. **[G: Japan]**

Flook, E. Evelyn and Sanazaro, Paul J. Health Services Research: Origins and Milestones. In *Flook, E. E. and Sanazaro, P. J., eds.*, 1973, pp. 1–81. **[G: U.S.]**

Forst, Brian E. Quantifying the Patient's Preferences. In *Berg, R. L., ed.*, 1973, pp. 209–20.

Forst, Brian E. An Analysis of Alternative Periodic Health Examination Strategies. In *Niskanen, W. A., et al., eds.*, 1973, pp. 393–409. **[G: U.S.]**

Ginor, Fanny. Importance of the Nutrition Component in Economic Planning. In *Berg, A.; Scrimshaw, N. S. and Call, D. L., eds.*, 1973, pp. 275–81.

Ginsburgh, Paul B. and Manheim, Larry M. Insurance, Copayment, and Health Services Utilization: A Critical Review. *J. Econ. Bus.*, Spring-Summer 1973, *25*(3), pp. 142–53. **[G: U.S.]**

Gordon, Wendell. Institutionalized Consumption Patterns in Underdeveloped Countries. *J. Econ. Issues*, June 1973, *7*(2), pp. 267–87.

Griffith, John R.; Hancock, Walton M. and Munson, Fred C. Practical Ways to Contain Hospital Costs. *Harvard Bus. Rev.*, November-December 1973, *51*(6), pp. 131–39.

Haanes-Olsen, Leif. Dental Insurance in Sweden. *Soc. Sec. Bull.*, December 1973, *36*(12), pp. 20–22. **[G: Sweden]**

Holtmann, A. G. The Size and Distribution of Benefits from U.S. Medical Research: The Case of Eliminating Cancer and Heart Disease. *Public Fi-*

nance, 1973, *28*(3–4), pp. 354–61. [G: U.S.]

Horowitz, Loucele A. Medical Care Price Changes Under the Economic Stabilization Program. *Soc. Sec. Bull.,* June 1973, *36*(6), pp. 28–32. [G: U.S.]

Howard, Godfrey G. Anatomy of a Hospital Trustee. *Harvard Bus. Rev.,* May-June 1973, *51*(3), pp. 65–71.

Hurd, Richard W. Equilibrium Vacancies in a Labor Market Dominated by Non-Profit Firms: The "Shortage" of Nurses. *Rev. Econ. Statist.,* May 1973, *55*(2), pp. 234–40. [G: U.S.]

In Sang Song. Some Conceptual and Administrative Difficulties in Nutrition Planning. In *Berg, A.; Scrimshaw, N. S. and Call, D. L., eds.,* 1973, pp. 290–92.

Ireland, Marilyn J. The Legal Framework of the Market for Blood. In *Alchian, A. A., et al.,* 1973, pp. 171–78. [G: U.S.]

Ireland, Thomas R. and Koch, James V. Blood and American Social Attitudes. In *Alchian, A. A., et al.,* 1973, pp. 145–55. [G: U.S.]

Jelliffe, Derrick B. Nutrition, National Development, and Planning: Summation. In *Berg, A.; Scrimshaw, N. S. and Call, D. L., eds.,* 1973, pp. 378–85.

Jenkins, William L. Nonprofit Hospital Accounting System. *Manage. Account.,* June 1973, *54*(12), pp. 23–27.

Johnson, David B. The US Market in Blood. In *Alchian, A. A., et al.,* 1973, pp. 157–67. [G: U.S.; U.K.]

Joy, Leonard. Nutrition Intervention Programs: Identification and Selection. In *Berg, A.; Scrimshaw, N. S. and Call, D. L., eds.,* 1973, pp. 198–206.

Jul, Mogens. Importance of Project Preparation and Evaluation. In *Berg, A.; Scrimshaw, N. S. and Call, D. L., eds.,* 1973, pp. 210–12.

Kamien, Morton I. and Schwartz, Nancy L. Payment Plans and the Efficient Delivery of Health Care Services. *J. Risk Ins.,* September 1973, *40*(3), pp. 427–36.

Katz, Sidney, et al. Measuring the Health Status of Populations. In *Berg, R. L., ed.,* 1973, pp. 39–51. [G: U.S.]

Klarman, Herbert E. Approaches to Health Manpower Analysis, with Special Reference to Physicians. *Amer. Econ.,* Fall 1973, *17*(2), pp. 137–42.

Kneppreth, Norwood P., et al. Techniques for the Assessment of Worth. In *Berg, R. L., ed.,* 1973, pp. 228–39.

Kracht, Uwe. Marketing Unconventional Protein-Rich Foods—One Form of Nutrition Intervention. In *Berg, A.; Scrimshaw, N. S. and Call, D. L., eds.,* 1973, pp. 213–16.

Křikava, L.; Mašek, J. and Malek, P. The Czech Experience in Nutrition Improvement. In *Berg, A.; Scrimshaw, N. S. and Call, D. L., eds.,* 1973, pp. 329–34. [G: Czechoslovakia]

Latham, Michael C. A Historical Perspective. In *Berg, A.; Scrimshaw, N. S. and Call, D. L., eds.,* 1973, pp. 313–28.

Latham, Robert J. Operating Expenditures and Sponsored Research at U.S. Medical Schools: Comment. *J. Human Res.,* Fall 1973, *8*(4), pp. 519–22. [G: U.S.]

Lave, Judith R.; Lave, Lester B. and Morton, Thomas E. Sources and Uses of Paramedical Personnel. In *Stein, B. and Miller, S. M., eds.,* 1973, pp. 37–68. [G: U.S.]

Lave, Lester B. and Seskin, Eugene P. Air Pollution and Human Health. In *Enthoven, A. C. and Freeman, A. M., III, eds.,* 1973, pp. 88–99. [G: U.S.]

Lazarcik, Gregor. Defense, Education and Health Expenditures and Their Relation to GNP in Eastern Europe, 1960-1970. *Amer. Econ.,* Spring 1973, *17*(1), pp. 29–34. [G: E. Europe]

Lee, Maw Lin and Wallace, Richard L. Problems in Estimating Multiproduct Cost Functions: An Application to Hospitals. *Western Econ. J.,* September 1973, *11*(3), pp. 350–63. [G: U.S.]

Lees, Dennis and Doherty, Neil. Compensation for Personal Injury. *Lloyds Bank Rev.,* April 1973, (108), pp. 18–32. [G: U.K.]

Leveson, Irving. Cost-Benefit Analysis and Program Target Populations: The Narcotics Addiction Treatment Case. *Amer. J. Econ. Soc.,* April 1973, *32*(2), pp. 129–42. [G: U.S.]

Levine, Daniel S. and Yett, Donald E. A Method for Constructing Proxy Measures of Health Status. In *Berg, R. L., ed.,* 1973, pp. 12–22. [G: U.S.]

Lindsay, Cotton M. Real Returns to Medical Education. *J. Human Res.,* Summer 1973, *8*(3), pp. 331–48. [G: U.S.]

Mahadevan, P. Nutrition and Agriculture. In *Berg, A.; Scrimshaw, N. S. and Call, D. L., eds.,* 1973, pp. 150–53.

Malenbaum, Wilfred. A Note on the Poor Nation Situation. In *Berg, A.; Scrimshaw, N. S. and Call, D. L., eds.,* 1973, pp. 81–86.

Manoff, Richard K. The Mass Media Contribution to Intervention Programs. In *Berg, A.; Scrimshaw, N. S. and Call, D. L., eds.,* 1973, pp. 217–22.

Meeker, Edward. Allocation of Resources to Health Revisited. *J. Human Res.,* Spring 1973, *8*(2), pp. 257–59. [G: U.S.]

Mellor, John W. Nutrition and Economic Growth. In *Berg, A.; Scrimshaw, N. S. and Call, D. L., eds.,* 1973, pp. 70–73.

Miller, James E. Guidelines for Selecting a Health Status Index: Suggested Criteria. In *Berg, R. L., ed.,* 1973, pp. 243–46.

Mitra, Asok. The Nutrition Movement in India. In *Berg, A.; Scrimshaw, N. S. and Call, D. L., eds.,* 1973, pp. 357–65. [G: India]

Moore, John R., Jr. Planning an Efficient Regional Health System. In *Stein, B. and Miller, S. M., eds.,* 1973, pp. 13–35. [G: U.S.]

Mueller, Marjorie Smith. Private Health Insurance in 1971: Health Care Services, Enrollment, and Finances. *Soc. Sec. Bull.,* February 1973, *36*(2), pp. 3–22. [G: U.S.]

Nathan, Robert R. Focusing Attention on Nutrition in Development Planning. In *Berg, A.; Scrimshaw, N. S. and Call, D. L., eds.,* 1973, pp. 282–84.

Newhouse, Joseph P. The Economics of Group Practice. *J. Human Res.,* Winter 1973, *8*(1), pp. 37–56. [G: U.S.]

Nondasuta, Amorn. Suggested Components of Intervention Programs. In *Berg, A.; Scrimshaw, N. S. and Call, D. L., eds.,* 1973, pp. 223–28.

Nour, Mohamed A. Planning Priorities in Nutrition

and Development. In *Berg, A.; Scrimshaw, N. S. and Call, D. L., eds.*, 1973, pp. 87–90.

Oiso, Toshio. Nutrition in National Development: The Japanese Experience. In *Berg, A.; Scrimshaw, N. S. and Call, D. L., eds.*, 1973, pp. 366–69. [G: Japan]

Okita, Saburo. Possible Modifications in Development Aid Policy. In *Berg, A.; Scrimshaw, N. S. and Call, D. L., eds.*, 1973, pp. 207–09.

Orita, Sadao. National Nutrition Survey in Japan. In *Berg, A.; Scrimshaw, N. S. and Call, D. L., eds.*, 1973, pp. 293–98. [G: Japan]

Paez-Franco, Jaime. The National Nutrition Program in Colombia. In *Berg, A.; Scrimshaw, N. S. and Call, D. L., eds.*, 1973, pp. 335–56. [G: Colombia]

Pauly, Mark V. and Redisch, Michael. The Not-For-Profit Hospital as a Physicians' Cooperative. *Amer. Econ. Rev.*, March 1973, *63*(1), pp. 87–99. [G: U.S.]

Peel, Evelyn and Scharff, Jack. Impact of Cost-Sharing on Use of Ambulatory Services Under Medicare, 1969. *Soc. Sec. Bull.*, October 1973, *36*(10), pp. 3–24. [G: U.S.]

Penner, Rudolph G. Health. In *Ott, D. J., et al.*, 1973, pp. 171–92. [G: U.S.]

Petrovsky, Boris. Progress in Public Health in the USSR, 1917–1967. In *Moskoff, W., ed.*, 1973, pp. 260–71. [G: U.S.S.R.]

Pettengill, Julian. The Financial Position of Private Community Hospitals, 1961–71. *Soc. Sec. Bull.*, November 1973, *36*(11), pp. 3–19. [G: U.S.]

Piro, Paula A. and Lutins, Theodore. Utilization and Reimbursements under Medicare for 1967 and 1968 Decedents. *Soc. Sec. Bull.*, May 1973, *36*(5), pp. 37–41, 58. [G: U.S.]

Povey, George; Uyeno, Dean and Vertinsky, Ilan. Social Impact Index for Evaluation of Regional Resource Allocation. In *Berg, R. L., ed.*, 1973, pp. 104–14. [G: U.S.]

Prato, Anthony A. A Proposal for Reducing Nutrient Deficiencies with Economical Diets. *Can. J. Agr. Econ.*, November 1973, *21*(3), pp. 15–22.

Price, Daniel N. Cash Benefits for Short-Term Sickness, 1948-71. *Soc. Sec. Bull.*, January 1973, *36*(1), pp. 20–29. [G: U.S.]

Pyle, Gerald F. Measles as an Urban Health Problem: The Akron Example. *Econ. Geogr.*, October 1973, *49*(4), pp. 344–56. [G: U.S.]

Retherford, Robert D. Cigarette Smoking and Widowhood in the United States. *Population Stud.*, July 1973, *27*(2), pp. 193–206. [G: U.S.]

Rifkin, Susan B. and Kaplinsky, Raphael. Health Strategy and Development Planning: Lessons from the People's Republic of China. *J. Devel. Stud.*, January 1973, *9*(2), pp. 213–32. [G: China]

Roemer, Milton J. Development of Medical Services under Social Security in Latin America. *Int. Lab. Rev.*, July 1973, *108*(1), pp. 1–23. [G: Latin America]

Rosett, Richard N. and Huang, Lien-fu. The Effect of Health Insurance on the Demand for Medical Care. *J. Polit. Econ.*, Part I, March-April 1973, *81* (2), pp. 281–305. [G: U.S.]

Rosser, Rachel and Watts, Vincent. Health and Welfare Systems. In *Ross, M., ed.*, 1973, pp. 655–69.

Rud, Jon. Freedom of Employment and Maintenance of Public Services: A Study of Obligatory Service for Dentists in Norway. In *Moskoff, W., ed.*, 1973, pp. 271–88. [G: Norway]

Rueda-Williamson, Roberto. Top Priority Programs in National Development Plans. In *Berg, A.; Scrimshaw, N. S. and Call, D. L., eds.*, 1973, pp. 285–89.

Ruffin, Roy J. and Leigh, Duane E. Charity, Competition, and the Pricing of Doctors' Services. *J. Human Res.*, Spring 1973, *8*(2), pp. 212–22.

Russell, Louise B. The Impact of the Extended-Care Facility Benefit on Hospital Use and Reimbursements Under Medicare. *J. Human Res.*, Winter 1973, *8*(1), pp. 57–72. [G: U.S.]

Russell, Louise B. An Econometric Model of the Medicare System: Comment. *Quart. J. Econ.*, August 1973, *87*(3), pp. 482–89. [G: U.S.]

Ryan, Allan J. Medical Practices in Sports. *Law Contemp. Probl.*, Winter-Spring 1973, *38*(1), pp. 99–111. [G: U.S.]

Sai, F. T. Problems in Nutrition and Diagnosis and Planning. In *Berg, A.; Scrimshaw, N. S. and Call, D. L., eds.*, 1973, pp. 154–58.

Salaff, Janet W. Mortality Decline in the People's Republic of China and the United States. *Population Stud.*, November 1973, *27*(3), pp. 551–76. [G: U.S.; China]

Salsbury, A. J. Medical Evidence: Blood Donation and the Australia Antigen. In *Alchian, A. A., et al.*, 1973, pp. 179–91. [G: Australia]

Sanazaro, Paul J. Federal Health Services R&D Under the Auspices of the National Center for Health Services Research and Development. In *Flook, E. E. and Sanazaro, P. J., eds.*, 1973, pp. 150–83. [G: U.S.]

Selowsky, Marcelo. An Attempt to Estimate Rates of Return to Investment in Infant Nutrition. In *Niskanen, W. A., et al., eds.*, 1973, pp. 410–28. [G: Chile]

Short, John H. Is Health Care an Economic Commodity? *Intermountain Econ. Rev.*, Spring 1973, *4*(1), pp. 14–21.

Sidel, Victor W. Medicine and Public Health. In *Oksenberg, M., ed.*, 1973, pp. 110–20. [G: China]

Simanis, Joseph G. Medical Care Expenditures in Seven Countries. *Soc. Sec. Bull.*, March 1973, *36* (3), pp. 39–42.

Skinner, Douglas E. and Yett, Donald E. Debility Index for Long-term-care Patients. In *Berg, R. L., ed.*, 1973, pp. 69–81. [G: U.S.]

Sullivan, Jeremiah M. The Influence of Cause-Specific Mortality Conditions on the Age Pattern of Mortality with Special Reference to Taiwan. *Population Stud.*, March 1973, *27*(1), pp. 135–58. [G: Taiwan]

Swanston, David. Poverty and Poor Health. In *Levitan, S. A., ed.*, 1973, pp. 175–97. [G: U.S.]

Taylor, Carl E. Nutrition and Population. In *Berg, A.; Scrimshaw, N. S. and Call, D. L., eds.*, 1973, pp. 74–80.

Taylor, Ryland A. Resource Misallocation in Hospital Care: Comment. *Rev. Soc. Econ.*, October

1973, *31*(2), pp. 199–201.

Taylor, Vincent D. Incentives for Inefficiency in Medicare and Medicaid. In *Haveman, R. H. and Hamrin, R. D., eds.,* 1973, pp. 238–42. [G: U.S.]

Torrance, George W.; Sackett, David L. and Thomas, Warren H. Utility Maximization Model for Program Evaluation: A Demonstration Application. In *Berg, R. L., ed.,* 1973, pp. 156–64. [G: U.S.]

Torrance, George W. A Generalized Cost-Effectiveness Model for Health Planning. In *Ross, M., ed.,* 1973, pp. 455–64.

Tracy, Martin B. Sweden: Cash Maternity Benefits for Fathers. *Soc. Sec. Bull.,* November 1973, *36* (11), pp. 37–39. [G: Sweden]

Valdes, Nelson P. "Health and Revolution in Cuba": An Addendum. *Sci. Soc.,* Winter 1973–1974, *37* (4), pp. 481. [G: Cuba]

Van Langendonck, Jozef. The European Experience in Social Health Insurance. *Soc. Sec. Bull.,* July 1973, *36*(7), pp. 21–30. [G: E.E.C.]

Vertinsky, Ilan and Uyeno, Dean. Demand for Health Services and the Theory of Time Allocation. *Appl. Econ.,* December 1973, *5*(4), pp. 249–60.

Vogel, Ronald J. and Morrall, John F., III. The Impact of Medicaid on State and Local Health and Hospitals Expenditures, with Special Reference to Blacks. *J. Human Res.,* Spring 1973, *8*(2), pp. 202–11. [G: U.S.]

Weaver, Jerry L. Mexican American Health Care Behavior: A Critical Review of the Literature. *Soc. Sci. Quart.,* June 1973, *54*(1), pp. 85–102. [G: U.S.]

Weaver, Jerry L. Health Care Costs as a Political Issue: Comparative Responses of Chicanos and Anglos. *Soc. Sci. Quart.,* March 1973, *53*(4), pp. 846–54. [G: U.S.]

West, P. A. Allocation and Equity in the Public Sector: The Hospital Revenue Allocation Formula. *Appl. Econ.,* September 1973, *5*(3), pp. 153–66. [G: U.K.]

Whitmore, G. A. Health State Preferences and the Social Choice. In *Berg, R. L., ed.,* 1973, pp. 135–45.

Wilford, W. T. Nutrition Levels and Economic Growth: Some Empirical Measures. *J. Econ. Issues,* September 1973, *7*(3), pp. 437–58.

Wilson, Douglas. The Economic Analysis of Malnutrition. In *Berg, A.; Scrimshaw, N. S. and Call, D. L., eds.,* 1973, pp. 129–44.

Wing, Paul. Operating Expenditures and Sponsored Research at U.S. Medical Schools: Reply. *J. Human Res.,* Fall 1973, *8*(4), pp. 522–24. [G: U.S.]

Zeckhauser, Richard J. Coverage for Catastrophic Illness. *Public Policy,* Spring 1973, *21*(2), pp. 149–72. [G: U.S.]

914 Economics of Poverty

9140 Economics of Poverty

Bardhan, Pranab K. 'Green Revolution' and Agricultural Labourers. In *Wadhva, C. D., ed.,* 1973, pp. 346–61. [G: India]

Berton, Lee. Aiding the Poor. In *Murray, B. B., ed.,*

1973, pp. 420–25. [G: U.S.]

Brown, J. Douglas. Social Security in the Years Ahead. In *Somers, G. G., ed.,* 1973, pp. 118–27. [G: U.S.]

Byrne, Dennis M. Some Preliminary Results of Income-Maintenance Experiments. *Nebr. J. Econ. Bus.,* Autumn 1973, *12*(4), pp. 23–35. [G: U.S.]

Charles, K. J. Public Services and Poverty. *Econ. Aff.,* January–February 1973, *18*(1-2), pp. 74–80. [G: India]

Christoffel, Pamela and Celio, Mary Beth. A Benefit-Cost Analysis of the Upward Bound Program: A Comment. *J. Human Res.,* Winter 1973, *8*(1), pp. 110–15. [G: U.S.]

Davies, David G. A Critical Discussion of I.L.O. Report on Employment in Kenya. *Pakistan Develop. Rev.,* Autumn 1973, *12*(3), pp. 283–92. [G: Kenya]

Downs, Anthony. Who are the Urban Poor? In *Grieson, R. E., ed.,* 1973, pp. 285–88. [G: U.S.]

Elesh, David. Poverty Theories and Income Maintenance: Validity and Policy Relevance. *Soc. Sci. Quart.,* September 1973, *54*(2), pp. 359–73.

Elesh, David, et al. The New Jersey-Pennsylvania Experiment: A Field Study in Negative Taxation. In *Boulding, K. E.; Pfaff, M. and Pfaff, A., eds.,* 1973, pp. 181–201. [G: U.S.]

Fiegehen, G. C. and Lansley, P. S. The Tax-Credit Proposals. *Nat. Inst. Econ. Rev.,* May 1973, (64), pp. 44–67. [G: U.K.]

Foley, Duncan K. A Primer on Negative Taxation. In *Grieson, R. E., ed.,* 1973, pp. 297–312. [G: U.S.]

Friedman, Lawrence M. Public Housing and the Poor. In *Pynoos, J.; Schafer, R. and Hartman, C. W., eds.,* 1973, pp. 448–59. [G: U.S.]

Fried, Marc and Gleicher, Peggy. Some Sources of Residential Satisfaction in an Urban Slum. In *Rasmussen, D. W. and Haworth, C. T., eds.,* 1973, pp. 150–59. [G: U.S.]

Fusfeld, Daniel R. A Living Wage. *Ann. Amer. Acad. Polit. Soc. Sci.,* September 1973, *409*, pp. 34–41. [G: U.S.]

Fusfeld, Daniel R. Transfer Payments and the Ghetto Economy. In *Boulding, K. E.; Pfaff, M. and Pfaff, A., eds.,* 1973, pp. 78–92. [G: U.S.]

Galatin, Malcolm. A Comparison of the Benefits of the Food-Stamp Program, Free Food Stamps, and an Equivalent Cash Payment. *Public Policy,* Spring 1973, *21*(2), pp. 291–302. [G: U.S.]

Gallardo, Lloyd. Development of Bay Area Manpower Institutions. In *Mangum, G. L. and Robson, R. T., eds.,* 1973, pp. 154–75. [G: U.S.]

Gallardo, Lloyd. Evaluating Bay Area Manpower Programs. In *Mangum, G. L. and Robson, R. T., eds.,* 1973, pp. 176–201. [G: U.S.]

Gallardo, Lloyd. Institutional Impact of Bay Area Manpower Programs. In *Mangum, G. L. and Robson, R. T., eds.,* 1973, pp. 202–24. [G: U.S.]

Garfinkel, Irwin and Masters, Stanley H. Two Income Maintenance Plans, Work Incentives and the Closure of the Poverty Gap: Comment. *Ind. Lab. Relat. Rev.,* April 1973, *26*(3), pp. 1002–04. [G: U.S.]

Garfinkel, Irwin. A Skeptical Note on "The Optimality" of Wage Subsidy Programs. *Amer. Econ. Rev.*, June 1973, *63*(3), pp. 447–53.

Garms, Walter I. Reply to "A Benefit-Cost Analysis of the Upward Bound Program: A Comment." *J. Human Res.*, Winter 1973, *8*(1), pp. 115–18. [G: U.S.]

Glantz, Frederic B. Migration and Economic Opportunity: The Case of the Poor. *New Eng. Econ. Rev.*, March-April 1973, pp. 14–17. [G: U.S.]

Glennerster, Howard. A Tax Credit Scheme for Britain?—A Review of the British Government's Green Paper. *J. Human Res.*, Fall 1973, *8*(4), pp. 422–35. [G: U.K.]

Goldstein, Jon H. The Effectiveness of Manpower Training Programs: A Review of Research on the Impact on the Poor. In *Niskanen, W. A., et al., eds.*, 1973, pp. 338–73. [G: U.S.]

Grieson, Ronald E. Poverty: Introduction. In *Grieson, R. E., ed.*, 1973, pp. 273–85. [G: U.S.]

Haber, Lawrence D. Social Planning for Disability. *J. Human Res.*, Supplement 1973, *8*, pp. 33–55. [G: U.S.]

Hausman, Leonard J. The Politics of a Guaranteed Income: The Nixon Administration and the Family Assistance Plan—A Review Article. *J. Human Res.*, Fall 1973, *8*(4), pp. 411–21. [G: U.S.]

Hill, C. Russell. Two Income Maintenance Plans, Work Incentives and the Closure of the Poverty Gap: Reply. *Ind. Lab. Relat. Rev.*, April 1973, *26* (3), pp. 1005–08. [G: U.S.]

Horowitz, Morris A. and Herrnstadt, Irwin L. Training and Jobs for Boston's Disadvantaged. In *Mangum, G. L. and Robson, R. T., eds.*, 1973, pp. 49–75. [G: U.S.]

Husby, Ralph D. Work Incentives and the Cost Effectiveness of Income Maintenance Programs. *Quart. Rev. Econ. Bus.*, Spring 1973, *13*(1), pp. 7–13. [G: U.S.]

Jackson, Carolyn and Velten, Terri. Residence, Race, and Age of Poor Families in 1966. In *Rasmussen, D. W. and Haworth, C. T., eds.*, 1973, pp. 53–71. [G: U.S.]

Johnson, Willard R. Should the Poor Buy No Growth? In *Olson, M. and Landsberg, H. H., eds.*, 1973, pp. 165–89. [G: U.S.]

Kangayappan, Kumar. Some Policy Issues in Mitigating Poverty in India. *Land Econ.*, February 1973, *49*(1), pp. 76–81. [G: India]

Kesselman, Jonathan R. A Comprehensive Approach to Income Maintenance: Swift. *J. Public Econ.*, February 1973, *2*(1), pp. 59–88. [G: U.S.]

Kilpatrick, Robert W. The Income Elasticity of the Poverty Line. *Rev. Econ. Statist.*, August 1973, *55* (3), pp. 327–32. [G: U.S.]

Kottis, Athena P. and Kottis, George C. Average Propensity to Spend Inside the Ghetto Areas: Comment. *J. Reg. Sci.*, April 1973, *13*(1), pp. 123–25. [G: U.S.]

Kunreuther, Howard. Why the Poor May Pay More for Food: Theoretical and Empirical Evidence. *J. Bus.*, July 1973, *46*(3), pp. 368–83. [G: U.S.]

Leveson, Irving. Strategies against Urban Poverty. In *Boulding, K. E.; Pfaff, M. and Pfaff, A., eds.*, 1973, pp. 130–59. [G: U.S.]

Lynn, Mary and Kotz, Nick. You Are What You Eat:

Feeding D.C.'s Hungry. In *Levitan, S. A., ed.*, 1973, pp. 143–74. [G: U.S.]

McCall, David B. Profit: Spur for Solving Social Ills. *Harvard Bus. Rev.*, May-June 1973, *51*(3), pp. 46–54, 180–82. [G: U.S.]

McCloskey, Donald N. New Perspectives on the Old Poor Law. *Exploration Econ. Hist.*, Summer 1973, *10*(4), pp. 419–36. [G: U.K.]

McCormick, James A. A Look at Poverty in New Mexico Through the 1970 Census. *N. Mex. Bus.*, June 1973, *26*(6), pp. 10–16. [G: U.S.]

Metcalf, Charles E. Making Inferences from Controlled Income Maintenance Experiments. *Amer. Econ. Rev.*, June 1973, *63*(3), pp. 478–83.

Meyer, John R. and Kain, John F. Transportation and Poverty. In *Grieson, R. E., ed.*, 1973, pp. 323–35. [G: U.S.]

Miller, Herman P. Measuring Subemployment in Poverty Areas of Large U.S. Cities. *Mon. Lab. Rev.*, October 1973, *96*(10), pp. 10–18. [G: U.S.]

Oakland, W. H.; Sparrow, Frederick T. and Stettler, H. Louis, III. More on Ghetto Multipliers. *J. Reg. Sci.*, April 1973, *13*(1), pp. 127–28. [G: U.S.]

O'Neill, Dave M. Manpower. In *Ott, D. J., et al.*, 1973, pp. 153–70.

Pfaff, Anita B. Transfer Payments to Large Metropolitan Poverty Areas: Their Distributive and Poverty-Reducing Effects. In *Boulding, K. E.; Pfaff, M. and Pfaff, A., eds.*, 1973, pp. 93–130. [G: U.S.]

Polanyi, George and Polanyi, Priscilla. Tax Credits: A Reverse Income Tax. *Nat. Westminster Bank Quart. Rev.*, February 1973, pp. 20–34. [G: U.K.]

Potgieter, J. F. The Poverty Datum Line. *S. Afr. J. Econ.*, June 1973, *41*(2), pp. 161–63. [G: S. Africa]

Rice, G. Randolph. Poverty and Industrial Growth Patterns: Some Cross-State Evidence. *J. Reg. Sci.*, December 1973, *13*(3), pp. 377–84. [G: U.S.]

Richards, Louise G. Consumer Practices of the Poor. In *Murray, B. B., ed.*, 1973, pp. 426–41.

Richardson, Reed C. Delivery Systems for Manpower Services. In *Mangum, G. L. and Robson, R. T., eds.*, 1973, pp. 100–119. [G: U.S.]

Richardson, Reed C. Skills and Jobs for Denver's Disadvantaged. In *Mangum, G. L. and Robson, R. T., eds.*, 1973, pp. 120–33. [G: U.S.]

Schafer, Robert and Field, Charles G. Section 235 of the National Housing Act: Homeownership for Low-income Families? In *Pynoos, J.; Schafer, R. and Hartman, C. W., eds.*, 1973, pp. 460–71. [G: U.S.]

Scheuren, Frederick J. Ransacking CPS Tabulations: Applications of the Log Linear Model to Poverty Statistics. *Ann. Econ. Soc. Measure*, April 1973, *2* (2), pp. 159–82. [G: U.S.]

Schiller, Bradley R. Empirical Studies of Welfare Dependency: A Survey. *J. Human Res.*, Supplement 1973, *8*, pp. 19–32. [G: U.S.]

Schlenker, Robert E. Optimal Mechanisms for Income Transfer: Note. *Amer. Econ. Rev.*, June 1973, *63*(3), pp. 454–57.

Selowsky, Marcelo and Taylor, Lance. The Economics of Malnourished Children: An Example of Disinvestment in Human Capital. *Econ. Develop.*

Cult. Change, October 1973, *22*(1), pp. 17–30. [G: Chile]

Singer, Dan and Walzer, Norman. The Distribution of Income in Large Urban Areas. *Nebr. J. Econ. Bus.,* Autumn 1973, *12*(4), pp. 91–101. [G: U.S.]

Smolensky, Eugene. Poverty, Propinquity and Policy. *Ann. Amer. Acad. Polit. Soc. Sci.,* September 1973, *409,* pp. 120–24. [G: U.S.]

Stockdale, Jerry D. Human Potential: A Perspective on Poverty and Quality of Life. *Growth Change,* October 1973, *4*(4), pp. 24–28.

Sturdivant, Frederick D. Rationality and Racism in the Ghetto Marketplace. *Soc. Sci. Quart.,* September 1973, *54*(2), pp. 380–83. [G: U.S.]

Sturdivant, Frederick D. and Wilhelm, Walter T. Poverty, Minorities, and Consumer Exploitation. In *Murray, B. B., ed.,* 1973, pp. 447–54. [G: U.S.]

Swanston, David. Poverty and Poor Health. In *Levitan, S. A., ed.,* 1973, pp. 175–97. [G: U.S.]

Swanston, Walterene. Community Organizations: The Voice of the Poor. In *Levitan, S. A., ed.,* 1973, pp. 198–225. [G: U.S.]

Thomas, George. Regional Migration Patterns and Poverty Among the Aged in the South. *J. Human Res.,* Winter 1973, *8*(1), pp. 73–84. [G: U.S.]

Thurow, Lester C. The Political Economy of Income Redistribution Policies. *Ann. Amer. Acad. Polit. Soc. Sci.,* September 1973, *409,* pp. 146–55. [G: U.S.]

Tussing, A. Dale. Poverty Research and Policy Analysis in the United States: Implications for Ireland. *Econ. Soc. Rev.,* October 1973, *5*(1), pp. 75–98. [G: U.S.; Ireland]

Van Til, Sally Bould and Van Til, Jon. The Lower Class and the Future of Inequality. *Growth Change,* January 1973, *4*(1), pp. 10–16. [G: U.S.]

Wachtel, Howard M. Theses on Poverty and Inequality. *Amer. Econ.,* Fall 1973, *17*(2), pp. 17–22.

Whipple, Daniel S. Employment Among the Poor of Six Central Cities. *Mon. Lab. Rev.,* October 1973, *96*(10), pp. 52–53. [G: U.S.]

Williams, Walter E. Why the Poor Pay More: An Alternative Explanation. *Soc. Sci. Quart.,* September 1973, *54*(2), pp. 375–79.

Winegarden, C. R. Welfare 'Explosion': Determinants of the Size and Recent Growth of the AFDC Population. *Amer. J. Econ. Soc.,* July 1973, *32*(3), pp. 245–56. [G: U.S.]

Young, Richard M. Inflation and the Distribution of Income and Wealth: Are the Poor Really Hurt? *Fed. Res. Bank Bus. Rev. Phila.,* September 1973, pp. 16–25. [G: U.S.]

915 Social Security

9150 Social Security (public superannuation and survivors benefits)

Ball, Robert M. Social Security Amendments of 1972: Summary and Legislative History. *Soc. Sec. Bull.,* March 1973, *36*(3), pp. 3–25.

Brown, J. Douglas. Social Security in the Years

Ahead. In *Somers, G. G., ed.,* 1973, pp. 118–27. [G: U.S.]

Browning, Edgar K. Social Insurance and Intergenerational Transfers. *J. Law Econ.,* October 1973, *16*(2), pp. 215–37. [G: U.S.]

Fisher, Paul. Major Social Security Issues: Japan, 1972. *Soc. Sec. Bull.,* March 1973, *36*(3), pp. 26–38. [G: Japan]

Foulon, Alain; Hatchuel, Georges and Kende, Pierre. Un premier bilan de la redistribution des revenus en France; Les impôts et cotisations sociales à la charge des ménages en 1965. (Balance of the Redistribution of Incomes in France: Personal Taxes and Social Security Contributions in 1965. With English summary.) *Consommation,* October-December 1973, *20*(4), pp. 5–133. [G: France]

Geary, R. C. Are Ireland's Social Security Payments Too Small? A Note. *Econ. Soc. Rev.,* April 1973, *4*(3), pp. 343–48. [G: Ireland]

Geary, R. C. Are Ireland's Social Security Payments too Small? Rejoinder. *Econ. Soc. Rev.,* October 1973, *5*(1), pp. 123–26. [G: Ireland]

Goff, Phoebe H. Disabled-Worker Beneficiaries Under OASDHI: Regional and State Patterns. *Soc. Sec. Bull.,* September 1973, *36*(9), pp. 3–23. [G: U.S.]

Grad, Susan. Relative Importance of Income Sources of the Aged. *Soc. Sec. Bull.,* August 1973, *36*(8), pp. 37–45. [G: U.S.]

Greene, Mark R. A Note on Loading Charges for Variable Annuities. *J. Risk Ins.,* September 1973, *40*(3), pp. 473–78. [G: U.S.]

Horlick, Max. Social Security Revisions in Spain. *Soc. Sec. Bull.,* April 1973, *36*(4), pp. 36–39. [G: Spain]

Horlick, Max. Switzerland: Compulsory Private Pensions. *Soc. Sec. Bull.,* October 1973, *36*(10), pp. 46–47, 49. [G: Switzerland]

Horlick, Max. Supplemental Security Income for the Aged: Foreign Experience. *Soc. Sec. Bull.,* December 1973, *36*(12), pp. 3–12. [G: W. Europe]

Kolodrubetz, Walter W. Private Retirement Benefits and Relationship to Earnings: Survey of New Beneficiaries. *Soc. Sec. Bull.,* May 1973, *36*(5), pp. 16–37. [G: U.S.]

Lantsev, M. Progress in Social Security for Agricultural Workers in the USSR. *Int. Lab. Rev.,* March 1973, *107*(3), pp. 239–52. [G: U.S.S.R.]

Leal de Araujo, Lucila. Extension of Social Security to Rural Workers in Mexico. *Int. Lab. Rev.,* October 1973, *108*(4), pp. 295–312. [G: Mexico]

Mathew, T. I. Social Security for the Rural Population: A Study of Some Social Services in Selected Rural Areas of India. *Int. Lab. Rev.,* October 1973, *108*(4), pp. 313–28. [G: India]

Mullineaux, Donald J. Paying for Social Security: Is It Time To "Retire" the Payroll Tax? *Fed. Res. Bank Bus. Rev. Phila.,* April 1973, pp. 3–10. [G: U.S.]

Murray, Janet. Family Structure in the Preretirement Years. *Soc. Sec. Bull.,* October 1973, *36*(10), pp. 25–45. [G: U.S.]

Niessen, A. M. Twelfth Valuation of the Railroad Retirement System: A Summary View. *Soc. Sec.*

Bull., December 1973, *36*(12), pp. 13–19.
[G: U.S.]

O'Hagan, John and O'Higgins, Michael. Are Ireland's Social Security Payments too Small? Comment. *Econ. Soc. Rev.*, October 1973, *5*(1), pp. 113–21. [G: Ireland]

Penner, Rudolph G.; Ott, David J. and Ott, Attiat F. Income Security. In *Ott, D. J., et al.*, 1973, pp. 193–214. [G: U.S.]

Rejda, George E. and Shepler, Richard J. The Impact of Zero Population Growth on the OASDHI Program. *J. Risk Ins.*, September 1973, *40*(3), pp. 313–25. [G: U.S.]

Reno, Virginia. Women Newly Entitled to Retired-Worker Benefits: Survey of New Beneficiaries. *Soc. Sec. Bull.*, April 1973, *36*(4), pp. 3–26.
[G: U.S.]

Rubin, Leonard. Late Entitlement to Retirement Benefits: Findings from the Survey of New Beneficiaries. *Soc. Sec. Bull.*, July 1973, *36*(7), pp. 3–20. [G: U.S.]

Schmähl, Winfried. Zur Struktur von Rentenleistungen. (On the Structure of Pensions. With English summary.) *Z. ges. Staatswiss.*, February 1973, *129* (1), pp. 123–49. [G: W. Germany]

Schmulowitz, Jack. Recovery and Benefit Termination: Program Experience of Disabled-Worker Beneficiaries. *Soc. Sec. Bull.*, June 1973, *36*(6), pp. 3–15. [G: U.S.]

Schmulowitz, Jack. Spanish-Surnamed OASDI Beneficiaries in the Southwest. *Soc. Sec. Bull.*, April 1973, *36*(4), pp. 33–36. [G: U.S.]

Sherman, Sally R. Assets on the Threshold of Retirement. *Soc. Sec. Bull.*, August 1973, *36*(8), pp. 3–17. [G: U.S.]

Staples, Thomas G. Supplemental Security Income: The Aged Eligible. *Soc. Sec. Bull.*, July 1973, *36* (7), pp. 31–35. [G: U.S.]

Taylor, Vincent D. Incentives for Inefficiency in Medicare and Medicaid. In *Haveman, R. H. and Hamrin, R. D., eds.*, 1973, pp. 238–42. [G: U.S.]

Teeters, Nancy H. The Payroll Tax and Social-Security Finance. In *Musgrave, R. A., ed.*, 1973, pp. 87–112. [G: U.S.]

Tracy, Martin B. Proposed Pension Reform in United Kingdom, 1972. *Soc. Sec. Bull.*, August 1973, *36*(8), pp. 45–49. [G: U.K.]

Treitel, Ralph. Recovery of Disabled After Trust Fund Financing of Rehabilitation. *Soc. Sec. Bull.*, February 1973, *36*(2), pp. 23–31. [G: U.S.]

Veldkamp, Gérard M. J. The Coherence of Social Security Policy. *Int. Lab. Rev.*, November 1973, *108*(5), pp. 357–69.

Wang, Gisela C. Flexible Retirement Feature of German Pension Reform. *Soc. Sec. Bull.*, July 1973, *36*(7), pp. 36–39, 41. [G: W. Germany]

Weil, Roman L. Annuitants Can Afford CREF's Projecting Earnings at a Rate Larger Than 4 Percent. *J. Risk Ins.*, September 1973, *40*(3), pp. 465–72.

Wilson, Thomas. Pensions, Inflation and Growth. *Lloyds Bank Rev.*, April 1973, (108), pp. 1–17.
[G: U.K.]

Winklevoss, Howard E. An Explanatory Analysis of the Insurable Value Concept. *J. Risk Ins.*, September 1973, *40*(3), pp. 437–42.

9160 Economics of Crime

Anderson, Annelise. Organized Crime: Comment. In *Rottenberg, S., ed.*, 1973, pp. 167–71.

Avio, Kenneth L. An Economic Analysis of Criminal Corrections: The Canadian Case. *Can. J. Econ.*, May 1973, *6*(2), pp. 164–78. [G: Canada]

Bailey, William C. Motives of Criminals: Comment. In *Rottenberg, S., ed.*, 1973, pp. 39–55. [G: U.S.]

Blair, Roger D. and Vogel, Ronald J. Heroin Addiction and Urban Crime. *Public Finance Quart.*, October 1973, *1*(4), pp. 457–66.

Brito, Dagobert L. Organized Crime: Comment. In *Rottenberg, S., ed.*, 1973, pp. 175–78.

Brown, William W. and Reynolds, Morgan O. Crime and "Punishment": Risk Implications. *J. Econ. Theory*, October 1973, *6*(5), pp. 508–14.

Buchanan, James M. A Defense of Organized Crime? In *Rottenberg, S., ed.*, 1973, pp. 119–32.

Carr-Hill, R. A. and Stern, Nicholas H. An Econometric Model of the Supply and Control of Recorded Offences in England and Wales. *J. Public Econ.*, November 1973, *2*(4), pp. 289–318.
[G: U.K.]

Cassidy, R. Gordon. Crime Prevention and Control. In *Ross, M., ed.*, 1973, pp. 671–84.

Clague, Christopher. Legal Strategies for Dealing with Heroin Addiction. *Amer. Econ. Rev.*, May 1973, *63*(2), pp. 263–69.

Cobb, William E. Theft and the Two Hypotheses. In *Rottenberg, S., ed.*, 1973, pp. 19–30. [G: U.S.]

Culyer, Anthony J. Should Social Policy Concern Itself with Drug "Abuse"? *Public Finance Quart.*, October 1973, *1*(4), pp. 449–56.

Ehrlich, Isaac. Participation in Illegitimate Activities: A Theoretical and Empirical Investigation. *J. Polit. Econ.*, May-June 1973, *81*(3), pp. 521–65.
[G: U.S.]

Fernandez, Raul A. The Problem of Heroin Addiction and Radical Political Economy. *Amer. Econ. Rev.*, May 1973, *63*(2), pp. 257–62.

Gibbs, Jack P. Does Punishment Deter? Comment. In *Rottenberg, S., ed.*, 1973, pp. 112–16.

Greenwood, Michael J. and Wadycki, Walter J. Crime Rates and Public Expenditures for Police Protection: Their Interaction. *Rev. Soc. Econ.*, October 1973, *31*(2), pp. 138–51. [G: U.S.]

Gunning, J. Patrick, Jr. How Profitable Is Burglary? In *Rottenberg, S., ed.*, 1973, pp. 35–38. [G: U.S.]

Gylys, Julius A. Economic Analysis of Municipal and County Police Interdependence. In *Mattila, J. M. and Thompson, W. R., eds.*, 1973, pp. 151–63.
[G: U.S.]

Holahan, John. The Economics of Control of the Illegal Supply of Heroin. *Public Finance Quart.*, October 1973, *1*(4), pp. 467–77.

Ireland, Thomas R. Organized Crime: Comment. In *Rottenberg, S., ed.*, 1973, pp. 171–75.

Kaslow, Florence. Evolution of Theory and Policy on Inner City Delinquency. *Growth Change*, October 1973, *4*(4), pp. 29–37. [G: U.S.]

Kirlin, John J. The Impact of Contract Services Arrangements on the Los Angeles Sheriff's Department and Law-Enforcement Services in Los

Angeles County. *Public Policy,* Fall 1973, *21*(4), pp. 553–84. [G: U.S.]

Klein, Benjamin. Does Punishment Deter? Comment. In *Rottenberg, S., ed.,* 1973, pp. 106–12.

Krohm, Gregory C. An Alternative View of the Returns to Burglary. *Western Econ. J.,* September 1973, *11*(3), pp. 364–67. [G: U.S.]

Krohm, Gregory C. Does Punishment Deter? Comment. In *Rottenberg, S., ed.,* 1973, pp. 103–05.

Krohm, Gregory C. The Pecuniary Incentives of Property Crime. In *Rottenberg, S., ed.,* 1973, pp. 31–34. [G: U.S.]

Logan, Charles H. Motives of Criminals: Comment. In *Rottenberg, S., ed.,* 1973, pp. 55–58. [G: U.S.]

Magaddino, Joseph P. Crime, Victim Compensation, and the Supply of Offenses. *Public Policy,* Summer 1973, *21*(3), pp. 437–40.

Mehay, Stephen L. Police and Productivity: Can the Invisible Hand of Competition Extend the Long Arm of the Law? *Fed. Res. Bank Bus. Rev. Phila.,* May 1973, pp. 3–12. [G: U.S.]

Moore, Mark H. Policies to Achieve Discrimination on the Effective Price of Heroin. *Amer. Econ. Rev.,* May 1973, *63*(2), pp. 270–77.

Ostrom, Elinor and Parks, Roger B. Suburban Police Departments: Too Many and Too Small? In *Masotti, L. H. and Hadden, J. K., eds.,* 1973, pp. 367–402. [G: U.S.]

Phillips, Llad. Crime Control: The Case for Deterrence. In *Rottenberg, S., ed.,* 1973, pp. 65–84.

Prohaska, Charles R. and Taylor, Walton. Minimizing Losses in a Hostile Environment: The Costs of Defending One's Castle. *J. Risk Ins.,* September 1973, *40*(3), pp. 375–87.

Rottenberg, Simon. The Economics of Crime and Punishment: Introduction. In *Rottenberg, S., ed.,* 1973, pp. 1–8.

Rubin, Paul H. The Economic Theory of the Criminal Firm. In *Rottenberg, S., ed.,* 1973, pp. 155–66.

Seagraves, James A. Economics of Heroin: Discussion. *Amer. Econ. Rev.,* May 1973, *63*(2), pp. 278–79.

Sesnowitz, Michael. The Returns to Burglary: An Alternative to the Alternative. *Western Econ. J.,* September 1973, *11*(3), pp. 368–70. [G: U.S.]

Sjoquist, David Lawrence. Property Crime and Economic Behavior: Some Empirical Results. *Amer. Econ. Rev.,* June 1973, *63*(3), pp. 439–46.

Skogh, Göran. A Note on Gary Becker's "Crime and Punishment: An Economic Approach." *Swedish J. Econ.,* September 1973, *75*(3), pp. 305–11.

Zalba, Serapio R. Motives of Criminals: Comment. In *Rottenberg, S., ed.,* 1973, pp. 58–62. [G: U.S.]

917 Economics of Discrimination

9170 Economics of Discrimination

Adams, Arvil V. Title VII and Fair Employment in Ohio: Guidelines to Action. *Ohio State U. Bull. Bus. Res.,* May 1973, *48*(5), pp. 1–7. [G: U.S.]

Adams, Arvil V. Evaluating the Success of the EEOC Compliance Process. *Mon. Lab. Rev.,* May 1973, *96*(5), pp. 26–29. [G: U.S.]

Alexis, Marcus. A Theory of Labor Market Discrimi-

nation with Interdependent Utilities. *Amer. Econ. Rev.,* May 1973, *63*(2), pp. 296–302.

Alvarez, Rodolfo. The Psycho-Historical and Socioeconomic Development of the Chicano Community in the United States. *Soc. Sci. Quart.,* March 1973, *53*(4), pp. 920–42. [G: U.S.]

Anderson, Roy C. Black Employment in the Securities Industry. *Ind. Relat.,* February 1973, *12*(1), pp. 107–08. [G: U.S.]

Astin, Helen S. Women's Studies in American Colleges and Universities. *Int. Soc. Sci. J.,* 1973, *25*(3), pp. 389–400. [G: U.S.]

Babcock, Richard F. Exclusionary Zoning: A Code Phrase for a Notable Legal Struggle. In *Masotti, L. H. and Hadden, J. K., eds.,* 1973, pp. 313–28. [G: U.S.]

Bailey, Ronald. Economic Aspects of the Black Internal Colony. In *Bonilla, F. and Girling, R., eds.,* 1973, pp. 161–88. [G: U.S.]

Bates, Timothy. An Econometric Analysis of Lending to Black Businessmen. *Rev. Econ. Statist.,* August 1973, *55*(3), pp. 272–83. [G: U.S.]

Bates, Timothy. The Potential of Black Capitalism. *Public Policy,* Winter 1973, *21*(1), pp. 135–48. [G: U.S.]

Beale, Calvin L. Migration Patterns of Minorities in the United States. *Amer. J. Agr. Econ.,* December 1973, *55*(5), pp. 938–46. [G: U.S.]

Bell, Carolyn Shaw. Middle-Class Action and the Ghetto Consumer. *J. Econ. Issues,* June 1973, *7*(2), pp. 245–57. [G: U.S.]

Bergmann, Barbara R. and Adelman, Irma. The 1973 Report of the President's Council of Economic Advisers: The Economic Role of Women. *Amer. Econ. Rev.,* September 1973, *63*(4), pp. 509–14. [G: U.S.]

Berton, Lee. Aiding the Poor. In *Murray, B. B., ed.,* 1973, pp. 420–25. [G: U.S.]

Blinder, Alan S. Wage Discrimination: Reduced Form and Structural Estimates. *J. Human Res.,* Fall 1973, *8*(4), pp. 436–55. [G: U.S.]

Blitz, Rudolph C. and Ow, Chin Hock. A Cross-Sectional Analysis of Women's Participation in the Professions. *J. Polit. Econ.,* January-February 1973, *81*(1), pp. 131–44. [G: U.S.]

Bowles, Samuel. Understanding Unequal Economic Opportunity. *Amer. Econ. Rev.,* May 1973, *63*(2), pp. 346–56.

Boyle, M. Barbara. Equal Opportunity for Women is Smart Business. *Harvard Bus. Rev.,* May-June 1973, *51*(3), pp. 85–95.

Brawner, Marlyn R. Migration and Educational Achievement of Mexican Americans. *Soc. Sci. Quart.,* March 1973, *53*(4), pp. 727–37. [G: U.S.]

Carleton, Bette N. The Status of Women in Accounting. *Manage. Account.,* September 1973, *55*(3), pp. 59–62. [G: U.S.]

Carroll, Stephen J. and Rolph, John E. A Stochastic Model of Discrimination in the Labor Market. *Econometrica,* January 1973, *41*(1), pp. 97–108.

Chiswick, Barry R. Racial Discrimination in the Labor Market: A Test of Alternative Hypotheses. *J. Polit. Econ.,* November-December 1973, *81*(6), pp. 1330–52. [G: U.S.]

Collard, David. Exclusion by Estate Agents—An

Analysis. *Appl. Econ.*, December 1973, *5*(4), pp. 281–88.

Collard, David. Price and Prejudice in the Housing Market. *Econ. J.*, June 1973, *83*(330), pp. 510–15.

Comanor, William S. Racial Discrimination in American Industry. *Economica, N.S.*, November 1973, *40*(160), pp. 363–78.

Craft, James A. Racial and Occupational Aspects of Public Employment Service Placements. *Quart. Rev. Econ. Bus.*, Autumn 1973, *13*(3), pp. 53–60. [G: U.S.]

Davenport, Lawrence F. Career Education and the Black Student. In *McClure, L. and Buan, C., eds.*, 1973, pp. 177–84. [G: U.S.]

Davis, Carlton G. Traditional Graduate Admission Standards as Constraints to Increasing the Supply of Black Professional Agriculturalists: The Florida Experience. *Amer. J. Agr. Econ.*, December 1973, *55*(5), pp. 952–66. [G: U.S.]

Davis, Harry E. Pension Provisions Affecting the Employment of Older Workers. *Mon. Lab. Rev.*, April 1973, *96*(4), pp. 41–45. [G: U.S.]

Donaldson, Loraine and Strangways, Raymond S. Can Ghetto Groceries Price Competitively and Make a Profit? *J. Bus.*, January 1973, *46*(1), pp. 61–65. [G: U.S.]

Dubinsky, Irwin. Trade Union Discrimination in the Pittsburgh Construction Industry. In *Pynoos, J.; Schafer, R. and Hartman, C. W., eds.*, 1973, pp. 376–91. [G: U.S.]

Duker, Jacob M. and Hughes, Charles E. The Black-Owned Life Insurance Company: Issues and Recommendations. *J. Risk Ins.*, June 1973, *40*(2), pp. 221–30. [G: U.S.]

Farbman, Michael. Income Concentration in the Southern United States. *Rev. Econ. Statist.*, August 1973, *55*(3), pp. 333–40. [G: U.S.]

Felice, Lawrence G. Mexican American Self-Concept and Educational Achievement: The Effects of Ethnic Isolation and Socioeconomic Deprivation. *Soc. Sci. Quart.*, March 1973, *53*(4), pp. 716–26. [G: U.S.]

Fessler, Daniel Wm. Casting the Courts in a Land Use Reform Effort: A Starring Role or a Supporting Part? In *Clawson, M., ed.*, 1973, pp. 175–203. [G: U.S.]

Flanagan, Robert J. Segmented Market Theories and Racial Discrimination. *Ind. Relat.*, October 1973, *12*(3), pp. 253–73. [G: U.S.]

Flanagan, Robert J. Racial Wage Discrimination and Employment Segregation. *J. Human Res.*, Fall 1973, *8*(4), pp. 456–71. [G: U.S.]

Flanders, Dwight P. and Anderson, Peggy Engelhardt. Sex Discrimination in Employment: Theory and Practice. *Ind. Lab. Relat. Rev.*, April 1973, *26*(3), pp. 938–55. [G: U.S.]

Flores, Guillermo V. and Bailey, Ronald. Internal Colonialism and Racial Minorities in the U.S.: An Overview. In *Bonilla, F. and Girling, R., eds.*, 1973, pp. 149–60. [G: U.S.]

Flores, Guillermo V. Race and Culture in the Black Colony: Keeping the Chicano in His Place. In *Bonilla, F. and Girling, R., eds.*, 1973, pp. 189–223.

Freeman, Richard B. Changes in the Labor Market for Black Americans, 1948–72. *Brookings Pap.*

Econ. Act., 1973, (1), pp. 67–120. [G: U.S.]

Freeman, Richard B. Decline of Labor Market Discrimination and Economic Analysis. *Amer. Econ. Rev.*, May 1973, *63*(2), pp. 280–86.

Fretz, C. F. and Hayman, Joanne. Progress for Women—Men are Still More Equal. *Harvard Bus. Rev.*, September-October 1973, *51*(5), pp. 133–42. [G: U.S.]

Frey, Donald E. The Distribution of Educational Resources in Large American Cities: Comment. *J. Human Res.*, Fall 1973, *8*(4), pp. 516–18. [G: U.S.]

Gagala, Ken. The Dual Urban Labor Market: Blacks and Whites. *Amer. Econ.*, Spring 1973, *17*(1), pp. 51–59.

Gallardo, Lloyd. Development of Bay Area Manpower Institutions. In *Mangum, G. L. and Robson, R. T., eds.*, 1973, pp. 154–75. [G: U.S.]

Gallardo, Lloyd. Evaluating Bay Area Manpower Programs. In *Mangum, G. L. and Robson, R. T., eds.*, 1973, pp. 176–201. [G: U.S.]

Gallardo, Lloyd. Institutional Impact of Bay Area Manpower Programs. In *Mangum, G. L. and Robson, R. T., eds.*, 1973, pp. 202–24. [G: U.S.]

Gelb, Betsy D. and Enis, Ben M. Affirmative Action in Housing and Beyond. *Calif. Manage. Rev.*, Winter 1973, *16*(2), pp. 24–31. [G: U.S.]

Ghai, Yash and Ghai, Dharam P. The Asian Minorities of East and Central Africa. In *Whitaker, B., ed.*, 1973, pp. 24–72. [G: Africa]

Ginzberg, Eli. Challenge and Resolution. In *Ginzberg, E. and Yohalem, A. M., eds.*, 1973, pp. 140–52.

Glantz, Frederic B. and Delaney, Nancy J. Changes in Nonwhite Residential Patterns in Large Metropolitan Areas, 1960 and 1970. *New Eng. Econ. Rev.*, March-April 1973, pp. 2–13. [G: U.S.]

Goldstein, Gerald S. and Moses, Leon N. A Survey of Urban Economics. *J. Econ. Lit.*, June 1973, *11*(2), pp. 471–515.

Gould, William B. Black Workers Inside the House of Labor. *Ann. Amer. Acad. Polit. Soc. Sci.*, May 1973, *407*, pp. 78–90. [G: U.S.]

Gwartney, James and Stroup, Richard. Measurement of Employment Discrimination According to Sex. *Southern Econ. J.*, April 1973, *39*(4), pp. 575–87. [G: U.S.]

Hall, Robert E. and Kasten, Richard A. The Relative Occupational Success of Blacks and Whites. *Brookings Pap. Econ. Act.*, 1973, (3), pp. 781–95. [G: U.S.]

Hamblin, Mary and Prell, Michael J. Income of Men and Women: Why Do They Differ? *Fed. Res. Bank Kansas City Rev.*, April 1973, pp. 3–11. [G: U.S.]

Hamilton, Mary Townsend. Sex and Income Inequality among the Employed. *Ann. Amer. Acad. Polit. Soc. Sci.*, September 1973, *409*, pp. 42–52. [G: U.S.]

Hammerman, Herbert. Minorities in Construction Referral Unions—Revisited. *Mon. Lab. Rev.*, May 1973, *96*(5), pp. 43–46. [G: U.S.]

Hemley, David D. and Ozawa, Terutomo. Intra-Racial and Minority Inter-Racial Discrimination. *J. Econ. Bus.*, Spring-Summer 1973, *25*(3), pp. 206–07.

Higgs, Robert. Race, Tenure, and Resource Allocation in Southern Agriculture, 1910. *J. Econ. Hist.,* March 1973, *33*(1), pp. 149–69.   [G: U.S.]

Hoffer, Stefan N. Private Rates of Return to Higher Education for Women. *Rev. Econ. Statist.,* November 1973, *55*(4), pp. 482–86.   [G: U.S.]

Horowitz, Morris A. and Herrnstadt, Irwin L. Boston's Manpower Institutions. In *Mangum, G. L. and Robson, R. T., eds.,* 1973, pp. 23–48.
          [G: U.S.]

Horowitz, Morris A. and Herrnstadt, Irwin L. Training and Jobs for Boston's Disadvantaged. In *Mangum, G. L. and Robson, R. T., eds.,* 1973, pp. 49–75.   [G: U.S.]

Jackson, Raymond. Job-Discrimination and the Use of Bonuses. *Amer. J. Econ. Soc.,* October 1973, *32* (4), pp. 351–66.   [G: U.S.]

Jones, Edward W., Jr. What it's Like to be a Black Manager. *Harvard Bus. Rev.,* July-August 1973, *51*(4), pp. 108–16.

Jonish, James E. and Kau, James B. Measures of Discrimination in Occupational and Income Levels. *Miss. Val. J. Bus. Econ.,* Spring 1973, *8*(3), pp. 59–70.   [G: U.S.]

Kain, John F. Effect of Housing Market Segregation on Urban Development. In *Pynoos, J.; Schafer, R. and Hartman, C. W., eds.,* 1973, pp. 251–66.
          [G: U.S.]

Kalachek, Edward D. Ghetto Dwellers, Transportation and Employment. In *Rasmussen, D. W. and Haworth, C. T., eds.,* 1973, pp. 72–80. [G: U.S.]

Keller, Suzanne. The Future Role of Women. *Ann. Amer. Acad. Polit. Soc. Sci.,* July 1973, *408,* pp. 1–12.   [G: U.S.]

King, A. Thomas and Mieszkowski, Peter. Racial Discrimination, Segregation, and the Price of Housing. *J. Polit. Econ.,* May-June 1973, *81*(3), pp. 590–606.   [G: U.S.]

Kleinhenz, Gerhard. Interessenverbände und sozialstaatliche Wirtschaftspolitik. (Interest Groups and Economic Policy. With English summary.) *Z. Wirtschaft. Sozialwissen.,* 1973, *93*(3), pp. 307–21.

Kreps, Juanita. The Sources of Inequality. In *Ginzberg, E. and Yohalem, A. M., eds.,* 1973, pp. 85–96.   [G: U.S.]

Kuhn, James W. An Economist's View of Women's Work. In *Ginzberg, E. and Yohalem, A. M., eds.,* 1973, pp. 63–68.   [G: U.S.]

Leibowitz, Arleen. Intergenerational Determinants of Individual Incomes: Discussion. *Amer. Econ. Rev.,* May 1973, *63*(2), pp. 357–58.

Leonard, Walter J. The Development of the Black Bar. *Ann. Amer. Acad. Polit. Soc. Sci.,* May 1973, *407,* pp. 134–43.

Lipsky, David B. Employer Role in Hard-Core Trainee Success. *Ind. Relat.,* May 1973, *12*(2), pp. 125–36.   [G: U.S.]

Lyle, Jerolyn R. Factors Affecting the Job Status of Workers with Spanish Surnames. *Mon. Lab. Rev.,* April 1973, *96*(4), pp. 10–16.   [G: U.S.]

Malkiel, Burton G. and Malkiel, Judith A. Male-Female Pay Differentials in Professional Employment. *Amer. Econ. Rev.,* September 1973, *63*(4), pp. 693–705.   [G: U.S.]

Masson, Robert Tempest. Costs of Search and Racial

Price Discrimination. *Western Econ. J.,* June 1973, *11*(2), pp. 167–86.

Maurizi, Alex R. Minority Membership in Apprenticeship Programs in the Construction Trades: Reply. *Ind. Lab. Relat. Rev.,* October 1973, *27*(1), pp. 100–102.

Mogull, Robert G. Football Salaries and Race: Some Empirical Evidence. *Ind. Relat.,* February 1973, *12*(1), pp. 109–12.   [G: U.S.]

Morgenstern, Richard D. Direct and Indirect Effects on Earnings of Schooling and Socio-Economic Background. *Rev. Econ. Statist.,* May 1973, *55*(2), pp. 225–33.   [G: U.S.]

Morsell, John A. Ethnic Relations of the Future. *Ann. Amer. Acad. Polit. Soc. Sci.,* July 1973, *408,* pp. 83–93.   [G: U.S.]

Moskow, Michael H. Government in the Lead. In *Ginzberg, E. and Yohalem, A. M., eds.,* 1973, pp. 125–32.   [G: U.S.]

Oaxaca, Ronald. Male-Female Wage Differentials in Urban Labor Markets. *Int. Econ. Rev.,* October 1973, *14*(3), pp. 693–709.   [G: U.S.]

Owen, John D. The Distribution of Educational Resources in Large American Cities: Reply. *J. Human Res.,* Fall 1973, *8*(4), pp. 518–19.

Park, Rosemary. Like Their Fathers Instead. In *Ginzberg, E. and Yohalem, A. M., eds.,* 1973, pp. 39–57.   [G: U.S.]

Piven, Frances Fox and Cloward, Richard A. The Case Against Urban Desegregation. In *Pynoos, J.; Schafer, R. and Hartman, C. W., eds.,* 1973, pp. 97–107.   [G: U.S.]

Polk, Lon. The Radical Paradigm and Urban Economics. In *Mattila, J. M. and Thompson, W. R., eds.,* 1973, pp. 206–23.   [G: U.S.]

Poston, Dudley L., Jr. and Alvírez, David. On the Cost of Being a Mexican American Worker. *Soc. Sci. Quart.,* March 1973, *53*(4), pp. 697–709.
          [G: U.S.]

Puth, Robert C. From Enforced Segregation to Integration: Market Factors in the Development of a Negro Life Insurance. In *[Williamson, H. F.],* 1973, pp. 280–301.   [G: U.S.]

Rabin, Yale. Highways as a Barrier to Equal Access. *Ann. Amer. Acad. Polit. Soc. Sci.,* May 1973, *407,* pp. 63–77.   [G: U.S.]

Rasmussen, David W. Changes in the Relative Income of Nonwhite Males, 1948–1970. In *Rasmussen, D. W. and Haworth, C. T., eds.,* 1973, pp. 81–86.   [G: U.S.]

Richardson, Reed C. Skills and Jobs for Denver's Disadvantaged. In *Mangum, G. L. and Robson, R. T., eds.,* 1973, pp. 120–33.   [G: U.S.]

Rosenthal, Albert J. Employment Discrimination and the Law. *Ann. Amer. Acad. Polit. Soc. Sci.,* May 1973, *407,* pp. 91–101.   [G: U.S.]

Rothman, Jack. The Ghetto Makers. In *Pynoos, J.; Schafer, R. and Hartman, C. W., eds.,* 1973, pp. 274–78.   [G: U.S.]

Rubinowitz, Leonard S. A Question of Choice: Access of the Poor and the Black to Suburban Housing. In *Masotti, L. H. and Hadden, J. K., eds.,* 1973, pp. 329–66.   [G: U.S.]

Ryscavage, P. M. and Mellor, Earl F. The Economic Situation of Spanish Americans. *Mon. Lab. Rev.,* April 1973, *96*(4), pp. 3–9.   [G: U.S.]

Saunders, Robert J. and Coccari, Ronald L. Racial Earnings Differentials: Some Economic Factors. *Amer. J. Econ. Soc.,* July 1973, *32*(3), pp. 225–33. [G: U.S.]

Sawhill, Isabel V. The Economics of Discrimination Against Women: Some New Findings. *J. Human Res.,* Summer 1973, *8*(3), pp. 383–96. [G: U.S.]

Scully, Gerald W. Economic Discrimination in Professional Sports. *Law Contemp. Probl.,* Winter-Spring 1973, *38*(1), pp. 67–84. [G: U.S.]

Shea, John R. Welfare Mothers: Barriers to Labor Force Entry. *J. Human Res.,* Supplement 1973, *8*, pp. 90–102. [G: U.S.]

Shepherd, William G. and Levin, Sharon G. Managerial Discrimination in Large Firms. *Rev. Econ. Statist.,* November 1973, *55*(4), pp. 412–22. [G: U.S.]

Singer, Dan and Walzer, Norman. The Distribution of Income in Large Urban Areas. *Nebr. J. Econ. Bus.,* Autumn 1973, *12*(4), pp. 91–101. [G: U.S.]

Singer, Neil M. Federal Aid to Minority Business: Survey and Critique. *Soc. Sci. Quart.,* September 1973, *54*(2), pp. 292–305. [G: U.S.]

Sorkin, Alan L. On The Occupational Status of Women, 1870–1970. *Amer. J. Econ. Soc.,* July 1973, *32*(3), pp. 235–43. [G: U.S.]

Steger, Wilbur A. Economic and Social Costs of Residential Segregation. In *Clawson, M., ed.,* 1973, pp. 83–113. [G: U.S.]

Stiglitz, Joseph E. Approaches to the Economics of Discrimination. *Amer. Econ. Rev.,* May 1973, *63* (2), pp. 287–95.

Strauss, George. Minority Membership in Apprenticeship Programs in the Construction Trades: Comment. *Ind. Lab. Relat. Rev.,* October 1973, *27*(1), pp. 93–99.

Struyk, Raymond J. Explaining Variations in the Hourly Wage Rates of Urban Minority Group Females. *J. Human Res.,* Summer 1973, *8*(3), pp. 349–64. [G: U.S.]

Sturdivant, Frederick D. Rationality and Racism in the Ghetto Marketplace. *Soc. Sci. Quart.,* September 1973, *54*(2), pp. 380–83. [G: U.S.]

Sturdivant, Frederick D. and Wilhelm, Walter T. Poverty, Minorities, and Consumer Exploitation. In *Murray, B. B., ed.,* 1973, pp. 447–54. [G: U.S.]

Sutch, Richard and Ransom, Roger. The Ex-Slave in the Post-Bellum South: A Study of the Economic Impact of Racism in a Market Environment. *J. Econ. Hist.,* March 1973, *33*(1), pp. 131–48. [G: U.S.]

Syron, Richard F. Administered Prices and the Market Reaction: The Case of Urban Core Property Insurance. *J. Finance,* March 1973, *28*(1), pp. 147–56. [G: U.S.]

Tabb, William K. Black Power–Green Power. In *Reynolds, L. G.; Green, G. D. and Lewis, D. R., eds.,* 1973, pp. 284–99. [G: U.S.]

Tatalovich, Anne. John Stuart Mill: The Subjection of Women: An Analysis. *Southern Quart.,* October 1973, *12*(1), pp. 87–105.

Thurow, Lester C. Discrimination. In *Grieson, R. E., ed.,* 1973, pp. 341–63. [G: U.S.]

Vogel, Ronald J. and Morrall, John F., III. The Impact of Medicaid on State and Local Health and Hospitals Expenditures, with Special Reference to Blacks. *J. Human Res.,* Spring 1973, *8*(2), pp. 202–11. [G: U.S.]

Wallace, Phyllis. Sex Discrimination: Some Societal Constraints on Upward Mobility for Women Executives. In *Ginzberg, E. and Yohalem, A. M., eds.,* 1973, pp. 69–84. [G: U.S.]

Weaver, Robert C. Housing and Associated Problems of Minorities. In *Clawson, M., ed.,* 1973, pp. 49–81. [G: U.S.]

Weissbourd, Bernard. The Satellite Community as Suburb. In *Masotti, L. H. and Hadden, J. K., eds.,* 1973, pp. 495–532. [G: U.S.]

Welch, Finis. Black-White Differences in Returns to Schooling. *Amer. Econ. Rev.,* December 1973, *63* (5), pp. 893–907. [G: U.S.]

Whitehead, Carlton J. and King, Albert S. Differences in Managers' Attitudes Toward Mexican and Non-Mexican Americans in Organizational Authority Relations. *Soc. Sci. Quart.,* March 1973, *53*(4), pp. 760–71. [G: U.S.]

White, Kenneth J. The Tax Structure and Discrimination Against Working Wives: A Comment. *Nat. Tax J.,* March 1973, *26*(1), pp. 119–22.

Williams, J. Allen, Jr.; Beeson, Peter G. and Johnson, David R. Some Factors Associated with Income Among Mexican Americans. *Soc. Sci. Quart.,* March 1973, *53*(4), pp. 710–15. [G: U.S.]

Wirt, Frederick M. Financial and Desegregation Reform in Suburbia. In *Masotti, L. H. and Hadden, J. K., eds.,* 1973, pp. 457–88. [G: U.S.]

Workman, Randy L. Ohio's Women Workers. *Ohio State U. Bull. Bus. Res.,* August 1973, *48*(8), pp. 4–6. [G: U.S.]

Wright, Gavin. Race, Tenure, and Resource Allocation in Southern Agriculture, 1910: Discussion. *J. Econ. Hist.,* March 1973, *33*(1), pp. 170–76. [G: U.S.]

Young, Elmer, Jr. Corporate Social Responsibility to the Minority Community. In *Dierkes, M. and Bauer, R. A., eds.,* 1973, pp. 297–300. [G: U.S.]

920 CONSUMER ECONOMICS

921 Consumer Economics; Levels and Standards of Living

9210 General

Anderson, Rolph E. Consumer Dissatisfaction: The Effect of Disconfirmed Expectancy on Perceived Product Performance. *J. Marketing Res.,* February 1973, *10*(1), pp. 38–44.

Anthony, William P. and Nosari, Eldon J. A Test of the Permanent Income Hypothesis. *J. Bus. Res.,* Summer 1973, *1*(1), pp. 43–48. [G: U.S.]

Barkin, Solomon. Trade Unions and Consumerism. *J. Econ. Issues,* June 1973, *7*(2), pp. 317–21.

Beckwith, Neil E. and Lehmann, Donald R. The Importance of Differential Weights in Multiple Attribute Models of Consumer Attitude. *J. Marketing Res.,* May 1973, *10*(2), pp. 141–45.

Burress, Glenn E. Who First Proposed the Habit Persistence Hypothesis: Keynes or Duesenberry and Modigliani. *Indian Econ. J.*, January-March 1973, *20*(3), pp. 472–78.

Bymers, Gwen J. Consumerism: Origin and Research Implications: Response. In *Sheldon, E. B., ed.*, 1973, pp. 295–304. **[G: U.S.]**

Curtin, Richard T. Index Construction: An Appraisal of the Index of Consumer Sentiment. In *Mandell, L., et al., eds.*, 1973, pp. 253–61. **[G: U.S.]**

Diwan, Romesh K. Are We Saving Enough for Our Plans? In *Wadhva, C. D., ed.*, 1973, pp. 163–78. **[G: India]**

Early, John F. Factors Affecting Trends in Real Spendable Earnings. *Mon. Lab. Rev.*, May 1973, *96*(5), pp. 16–19. **[G: U.S.]**

Erdös, P. On the Returns Principle of Pricing. *Acta Oecon.*, 1973, *11*(4), pp. 417–25.

Evans, Alan W. On the Theory of the Valuation and Allocation of Time: Reply. *Scot. J. Polit. Econ.*, February 1973, *20*(1), pp. 73–74.

Ferber, Robert. Family Decision Making and Economic Behavior: A Review. In *Sheldon, E. B., ed.*, 1973, pp. 29–61.

Ferber, Robert. Consumer Economics, A Survey. *J. Econ. Lit.*, December 1973, *11*(4), pp. 1303–42.

Flemming, J. S. On the Theory of the Valuation and Allocation of Time: Some Comments. *Scot. J. Polit. Econ.*, February 1973, *20*(1), pp. 65–71.

Gørtz, Erik and Vibe-Pedersen, J. Livsindkomstberegninger og deres betydning. (Calculation and Significance of Lifetime Incomes. With English summary.) *Nationalokon. Tidsskr.*, 1973, *111*(1), pp. 25–59. **[G: Denmark]**

Hanlon, Richard A. Differences in Reporting Family Income. *Mon. Lab. Rev.*, April 1973, *96*(4), pp. 46–48. **[G: U.S.]**

Hathaway, Dale E. Trade Restrictions and U.S. Consumers. In *Iowa State University Center for Agricultural and Rural Development*, 1973, pp. 103–10. **[G: U.S.]**

Herniter, Jerome D. An Entropy Model of Brand Purchase Behavior. *J. Marketing Res.*, November 1973, *10*(4), pp. 361–75.

Hill, Reuben and Klein, David M. Understanding Family Consumption: Common Ground for Integrating Uncommon Disciplinary Perspectives. In *Sheldon, E. B., ed.*, 1973, pp. 1–22. **[G: U.S.]**

Hill, Reuben and Klein, David M. Toward a Research Agenda and Theoretical Synthesis. In *Sheldon, E. B., ed.*, 1973, pp. 371–404. **[G: U.S.]**

Hoch, Róbert and Kovács, Ilona. Changes in Income and Consumer Prices Affecting Demand. In *Földi, T., ed.*, 1973, pp. 65–88. **[G: Europe; U.S.; Canada]**

Hulett, Joe R. On the Use of Regression Analysis with a Qualitative Dependent Variable. *Public Finance Quart.*, July 1973, *1*(3), pp. 339–44.

Hustad, Thomas P. and Pessemier, Edgar A. Will the Real Consumer Activist Please Stand Up: An Examination of Consumers' Opinions About Marketing Practices. *J. Marketing Res.*, August 1973, *10*(3), pp. 319–24. **[G: U.S.]**

Isbister, John. Birth Control, Income Redistribution, and the Rate of Saving: The Case of Mexico. *Demography*, February 1973, *10*(1), pp. 85–98. **[G: Mexico]**

Jones, Mary Gardiner. The Consumer Interest: The Role of Public Policy. *Calif. Manage. Rev.*, Fall 1973, *16*(1), pp. 17–24. **[G: U.S.]**

Katona, George; Strumpel, Burkhard and Zahn, E. The Sociocultural Environment. In *Thorelli, H. B., ed.*, 1973, pp. 135–45. **[G: U.S.; W. Germany; U.K.; Italy]**

Katona, George. Cognitive Processes in Learning: Reactions to Inflation and Change in Taxes. In *Mandell, L., et al., eds.*, 1973, pp. 183–203. **[G: U.S.]**

Kjaer-Hansen, Max. Revolution i konsumenternas varuförsörjning. (Revolution in Consumer Goods Supply. With English summary.) *Ekon. Samfundets Tidskr.*, January 1973, *26*(1), pp. 3–15.

Mandell, Lewis. The Changing Role of the American Consumer. In *Britt, S. H. and Boyd, H. W., Jr., eds.*, 1973, pp. 190–95. **[G: U.S.]**

Masson, Robert Tempest. Costs of Search and Racial Price Discrimination. *Western Econ. J.*, June 1973, *11*(2), pp. 167–86.

Maynes, E. Scott. Consumerism: Origin and Research Implications. In *Sheldon, E. B., ed.*, 1973, pp. 270–94. **[G: U.S.]**

McKean, Roland N. Government and the Consumer. *Southern Econ. J.*, April 1973, *39*(4), pp. 481–89.

Meyer, Richard L. and Power, Fred B. Total Insurance Costs and the Frequency of Premium Payments. *J. Risk Ins.*, December 1973, *40*(4), pp. 599–605.

Mitchell, Jeremy. The Consumer Movement and Technological Change. *Int. Soc. Sci. J.*, 1973, *25*(3), pp. 358–69.

Monroe, Kent B. Buyers' Subjective Perceptions of Price. *J. Marketing Res.*, February 1973, *10*(1), pp. 70–80.

Morawetz, David. Personal Income Taxes and Consumer Spending in the United Kingdom, 1958–69. *Public Finance*, 1973, *28*(2), pp. 178–95. **[G: U.K.]**

Nasta, Eliza and Vasilescu, Floarea. Considerații asupra metodologiei de calcul a coeficientului elasticității. (Considerations of the Methodology of Calculating the Elasticity Coefficient. With English summary.) *Stud. Cercet. Econ.*, 1973, (1), pp. 99–109.

Paroush, Jacob. Efficient Purchasing Behavior and Order Relations in Consumption. *Kyklos*, 1973, *26*(1), pp. 91–112.

Paul, Robert J. Psychographics, Demographics and Affluence—Predictors of Individual Decision Patterns? *Marquette Bus. Rev.*, Fall 1973, *17*(3), pp. 144–48. **[G: U.S.]**

Pickering, J. F.; Harrison, J. A. and Cohen, C. D. Identification and Measurment of Consumer Confidence: Methodology and Some Preliminary Results. *J. Roy. Statist. Soc.*, Part 1, 1973, *136*, pp. 43–63. **[G: U.K.]**

Powell, A. A. An ELES Consumption Function for the United States. *Econ. Rec.*, September 1973, *49*(127), pp. 337–57. **[G: U.S.]**

Prato, Anthony A. A Proposal for Reducing Nutrient Deficiencies with Economical Diets. *Can. J. Agr. Econ.*, November 1973, *21*(3), pp. 15–22.

Reinhardt, Paul G. A Theory of Household Grocery

Inventory Holdings. *Kyklos*, 1973, *26*(3), pp. 497–511.

Richards, Louise G. Consumer Practices of the Poor. In *Murray, B. B., ed.*, 1973, pp. 426–41.

Richardson, Lee. Consumers in the Federal Decision-Making Process. *Calif. Manage. Rev.*, Winter 1973, *16*(2), pp. 79–84. [G: U.S.]

Rose-Ackerman, Susan. Used Cars as a Depreciating Asset. *Western Econ. J.*, December 1973, *11*(4), pp. 463–74. [G: U.S.]

Scitovsky, Tibor. Notes on the Producer Society. *De Economist*, May-June 1973, *121*(3), pp. 225–50.

Segal, David R. and Felson, Marcus. Social Stratification and Family Economic Behavior. In *Sheldon, E. B., ed.*, 1973, pp. 143–64. [G: U.S.]

Shapiro, Benson P. Price Reliance: Existence and Sources. *J. Marketing Res.*, August 1973, *10*(3), pp. 286–94. [G: U.S.]

Smith, James D. New Perspectives in Government Data Distribution: The Current Population Survey. *Ann. Econ. Soc. Measure*, April 1973, *2*(2), pp. 131–39. [G: U.S.]

Stone, Richard. Personal Spending and Saving in Postwar Britain. In *[Tinbergen, J.]*, 1973, pp. 75–98. [G: U.K.]

Strumpel, Burkhard; Schmiedeskamp, Jay and Schwartz, M. Susan. The Function of Consumer Attitude Data Beyond Econometric Forecasts. In *Mandell, L., et al., eds.*, 1973, pp. 263–88. [G: U.S.]

Sundrum, R. M. Consumer Expenditure Patterns: An Analysis of the Socio-Economic Surveys. *Bull. Indonesian Econ. Stud.*, March 1973, *9*(1), pp. 86–106. [G: Indonesia]

Surrey, A. J. and Bromley, A. J. Energy Resources. In *Cole, H. S. D., et al., eds.*, 1973, pp. 90–107.

Warne, Clinton L. The Consumer Movement and the Labor Movement. *J. Econ. Issues*, June 1973, *7*(2), pp. 307–16.

Webster, Frederick E., Jr. Does Business Misunderstand Consumerism? *Harvard Bus. Rev.*, September-October 1973, *51*(5), pp. 89–97.

Wilson, William J. Consumer Reality and Corporate Image. *Calif. Manage. Rev.*, Winter 1973, *16*(2), pp. 85–90.

Worcester, Robert M. Il valore della "corporate image." (The Value of Corporate Image. With English summary.) *L'Impresa*, 1973, *15*(9–10), pp. 522–26.

9211 Living Standards Studies and Composition of Over-all Expenditures

Azfar, Javaid. The Distribution of Income in Pakistan—1966–67. *Pakistan Econ. Soc. Rev.*, Spring 1973, *11*(1), pp. 40–66. [G: Pakistan]

Baerwaldt, Nancy A. and Morgan, James N. Trends in Inter-Family Transfers. In *Mandell, L., et al., eds.*, 1973, pp. 205–32. [G: U.S.]

Bowles, Samuel. Understanding Unequal Economic Opportunity. *Amer. Econ. Rev.*, May 1973, *63*(2), pp. 346–56.

Brackett, Jean. Urban Family Budgets Updated to Autumn 1972. *Mon. Lab. Rev.*, August 1973, *96*(8), pp. 70–76. [G: U.S.]

Brittain, John A. Research on the Transmission of

Material Wealth. *Amer. Econ. Rev.*, May 1973, *63*(2), pp. 335–45.

Caceres, Luis R. Consumption Functions for Latin America. *Intermountain Econ. Rev.*, Fall 1973, *4*(2), pp. 55–65. [G: Latin America]

Creedy, John. A Problem in the Estimation of Double-Log Engel Curves. *Oxford Bull. Econ. Statist.*, August 1973, *35*(3), pp. 217–22. [G: U.K.]

Feldstein, Martin S. and Fane, George. Taxes, Corporate Dividend Policy and Personal Savings: The British Postwar Experience. *Rev. Econ. Statist.*, November 1973, *55*(4), pp. 399–411. [G: U.K.]

Ferber, Robert and Salazar-Carrillo, Jorge. Experience in Generating Micro Data in Latin America. In *Ayal, E. B., ed.*, 1973, pp. 84–100. [G: Latin America]

Fishlow, Albert. Comparative Consumption Patterns, the Extent of the Market, and Alternative Development Strategies. In *Ayal, E. B., ed.*, 1973, pp. 41–80. [G: U.S.; U.K.; France]

Gedney, Frances S. Retired Couple's Budget Updated to Autumn 1972. *Mon. Lab. Rev.*, October 1973, *96*(10), pp. 45–50. [G: U.S.]

Goldberger, Arthur S. Dependency Rates and Savings Rates: Further Comment. *Amer. Econ. Rev.*, March 1973, *63*(1), pp. 232–33.

Grossman, Michael. Unemployment and Consumption: Note. *Amer. Econ. Rev.*, March 1973, *63*(1), pp. 208–13. [G: U.S.]

Haworth, C. T. and Rasmussen, David W. Determinants of Metropolitan Cost of Living Variations. *Southern Econ. J.*, October 1973, *40*(2), pp. 183–92. [G: U.S.]

Hempenius, A. L. On the Specification of Risk Aversion in an Expenditure Equation. *De Economist*, July-August 1973, *121*(4), pp. 375–86.

Henderson, A. M. The Cost of a Family. In *Farrell, M. J., ed.*, 1973, pp. 93–114. [G: U.K.]

Johnson, Björn and Meuller, Anders. Interactions of Consumption and Metropolitan Growth. *Swedish J. Econ.*, September 1973, *75*(3), pp. 278–88. [G: Sweden]

Keen, Howard, Jr. Urban Family Budgets: The Philadelphia Scene. *Fed. Res. Bank Bus. Rev. Phila.*, September 1973, pp. 12–15. [G: U.S.]

Khandker, R. H. Distribution of Income and Wealth in Pakistan. *Pakistan Econ. Soc. Rev.*, Spring 1973, *11*(1), pp. 1–39. [G: Pakistan]

Kilpatrick, Robert W. The Income Elasticity of the Poverty Line. *Rev. Econ. Statist.*, August 1973, *55*(3), pp. 327–32. [G: U.S.]

Kottis, Athena P. and Kottis, George C. Average Propensity to Spend Inside the Ghetto Areas: Comment. *J. Reg. Sci.*, April 1973, *13*(1), pp. 123–25. [G: U.S.]

Kovács, J. Simplified Model for Level-of-Planning-Consistency Control. *Acta Oecon.*, 1973, *11*(2–3), pp. 177–90.

Leff, Nathaniel H. Dependency Rates and Savings Rates: Reply. *Amer. Econ. Rev.*, March 1973, *63*(1), pp. 234.

Leibowitz, Arleen. Intergenerational Determinants of Individual Incomes: Discussion. *Amer. Econ. Rev.*, May 1973, *63*(2), pp. 357–58.

Levin, A. Problems in the Control of Consumer Demand. *Prob. Econ.*, December 1973, *16*(8), pp. 81–104. [G: U.S.S.R.]

Lluch, Constantino. The Extended Linear Expenditure System. *Europ. Econ. Rev.*, April 1973, *4*(1), pp. 21–32.

McNees, Stephen K. Tax Refunds and Consumer Spending. *New Eng. Econ. Rev.*, January-February 1973, pp. 3–11. [G: U.S.]

Mikesell, Raymond F. and Zinser, James E. The Nature of the Savings Function in Developing Countries: A Survey of the Theoretical and Empirical Literature. *J. Econ. Lit.*, March 1973, *11*(1), pp. 1–26.

Nasse, Ph. Un système complet de fonctions de demande: Les équations de Fourgeaud et Nataf. *Econometrica*, November 1973, *41*(6), pp. 1137–58. [G: France]

Odling-Smee, J. C. Personal Saving Revisited: More Statistics, Fewer Facts. *Oxford Bull. Econ. Statist.*, February 1973, *35*(1), pp. 21–29. [G: U.K.]

Pesaran, M. Hashem. An Alternative Econometric Approach to the Permanent Income Hypothesis: An International Comparison: A Comment. *Rev. Econ. Statist.*, May 1973, *55*(2), pp. 259–61.

Pfaff, Martin. Economic Life-Styles, Values, and Subjective Welfare—An Empirical Approach: Response. In *Sheldon, E. B., ed.*, 1973, pp. 126–38. [G: U.S.]

Popkin, Joel. Prices in 1972: An Analysis of Changes During Phase 2. *Mon. Lab. Rev.*, February 1973, *96*(2), pp. 16–23. [G: U.S.]

Puckett, A. Marshall. Consumer Financial Management and Financial Institution Response—A Two-Decade Perspective: Response. In *Sheldon, E. B., ed.*, 1973, pp. 363–67. [G: U.S.]

Rao, B. Bhaskara. An Alternative Econometric Approach to the Permanent Income Hypothesis: An International Comparison: A Comment. *Rev. Econ. Statist.*, May 1973, *55*(2), pp. 261.

Sadan, Ezra and Tropp, Zvi. Consumption Function Analysis in a Communal Household: Cross Section and Time Series. *Rev. Econ. Statist.*, November 1973, *55*(4), pp. 475–81. [G: Israel]

Schott, Francis H. Consumer Financial Management and Financial Institution Response—A Two-Decade Perspective. In *Sheldon, E. B., ed.*, 1973, pp. 311–62. [G: U.S.]

Singh, Balvir and Nagar, A. L. Determination of Consumer Unit Scales. *Econometrica*, March 1973, *41*(2), pp. 347–55.

Strazheim, Mahlon R. The Demand for Corporate Stock in the Postwar Period. In *Goldsmith, R. W., ed.*, 1973, pp. 204–65. [G: U.S.]

Strumpel, Burkhard. Economic Life-Styles, Values, and Subjective Welfare—An Empirical Approach. In *Sheldon, E. B., ed.*, 1973, pp. 69–125. [G: U.S.]

Theil, Henri. Measuring the Quality of the Consumer's Basket. *De Economist*, July-August 1973, *121*(4), pp. 333–46. [G: Netherlands]

Vakil, Firouz. Indian Saving Behavior: A Reconciliation of Time Series and Cross Section Evidence. *Rev. Income Wealth*, September 1973, *19*(3), pp. 307–23. [G: India]

Vakil, Firouz. The Propensity to Consume Permanent Income in India. *Econ. Develop. Cult.*

Change, April 1973, *21*(3), pp. 514–21. [G: India]

Vuchelen, Jozef. Gezinsbesparingen in inflatie: een mogelijke benadering voor de Belgische ervaring. (With English summary.) *Cah. Écon. Bruxelles*, 3rd Trimestre 1973, (59), pp. 413–42. [G: Belgium]

van der Werf, D. Ein Beitrag zur Problematik der Konsumfunktion in der Bundesrepublik Deutschland. (A Contribution to the Problem of Consumption Function in the German Federal Republic. With English summary.) *Weltwirtsch. Arch.*, 1973, *109*(2), pp. 274–90. [G: W. Germany]

Wilford, W. T. Nutrition Levels and Economic Growth: Some Empirical Measures. *J. Econ. Issues*, September 1973, *7*(3), pp. 437–58.

Williamson, Jeffrey G. Comparative Consumption Patterns, the Extent of the Market, and Alternative Development Strategies: Comment. In *Ayal, E. B., ed.*, 1973, pp. 80–83. [G: U.S.; U.K.; France]

Young, Warren L. Compulsory Loans, Disposable Income, and Quarterly Consumption Behaviour in Israel: 1964–1969. *Finanzarchiv*, 1973, *32*(1), pp. 98–115. [G: Israel]

Zellner, Arnold and Williams, Anne D. Bayesian Analysis of the Federal Reserve–MIT–Penn Model's Almon Lag Consumption Function. *J. Econometrics*, October 1973, *1*(3), pp. 267–99. [G: U.S.]

9212 Expenditure Patterns and Consumption of Expenditure on Specific Items

Adamu, S. O. Socio-Economic Characteristics in Consumer Expenditure Patterns: An Application of Analysis of Covariance. *Econ. Bull. Ghana, Sec. Ser.*, 1973, *3*(2), pp. 11–21. [G: Nigeria]

Alamgir, Mohiuddin and Berlage, Lodewijk J. J. B. Estimation of Income Elasticity of Demand for Foodgrain in Bangladesh from Cross Section Data: A Skeptical View. *Bangladesh Econ. Rev.*, October 1973, *1*(4), pp. 387–408. [G: Bangladesh]

Anderson, Kent P. Residential Demand for Electricity: Econometric Estimates for California and the United States. *J. Bus.*, October 1973, *46*(4), pp. 526–53. [G: U.S.]

Arthur, W. Brian. The Elasticity of Demand for Petrol in Ireland: Comment. *Econ. Soc. Rev.*, October 1973, *5*(1), pp. 105–10. [G: Ireland]

Askari, Hossein. Demand for Travel to Europe by American Citizens. *Econ. Int.*, May 1973, *26*(2), pp. 305–17. [G: U.S.]

Atkinson, A. B. and Skegg, J. L. Anti-Smoking Publicity and the Demand for Tobacco in the U.K. *Manchester Sch. Econ. Soc. Stud.*, September 1973, *41*(3), pp. 265–82. [G: U.K.]

Bain, R. A. Factors Affecting Consumption and Prices of the Major Feed Grains in Australia. *Quart. Rev. Agr. Econ.*, July 1973, *26*(3), pp. 186–97. [G: Australia]

Barr, Terry N. and Gale, Hazen F. A Quarterly Forecasting Model for the Consumer Price Index for Food. *Agr. Econ. Res.*, January 1973, *25*(1),

pp. 1–14. [G: U.S.]

Basmann, R. L.; Battalio, Raymond C. and Kagel, John H. Comment on R. P. Byron's "The Restricted Aitken Estimation of Sets of Demand Relations." *Econometrica*, March 1973, *41*(2), pp. 365–70.

Battalio, Raymond C., et al. A Test of Consumer Demand Theory Using Observations of Individual Consumer Purchases. *Western Econ. J.*, December 1973, *11*(4), pp. 411–28.

Bechdolt, Burley V., Jr. Cross-Sectional Travel Demand Functions: US Visitors to Hawaii, 1961–70. *Quart. Rev. Econ. Bus.*, Winter 1973, *13*(4), pp. 37–47. [G: U.S.]

Bell, Carolyn Shaw. Middle-Class Action and the Ghetto Consumer. *J. Econ. Issues,* June 1973, *7*(2), pp. 245–57. [G: U.S.]

Berekson, Leonard L. Birth Order, Anxiety, Affiliation and the Purchase of Life Insurance: Reply. *J. Risk Ins.*, December 1973, *40*(4), pp. 646–48.

Bettman, James R. Perceived Price and Product Perceptual Variables. *J. Marketing Res.*, February 1973, *10*(1), pp. 100–02.

Bogart, Leo and Lehman, Charles. What Makes a Brand Name Familiar? *J. Marketing Res.*, February 1973, *10*(1), pp. 17–22. [G: U.S.]

Bonus, Holger. Quasi-Engel Curves, Diffusion, and the Ownership of Major Consumer Durables. *J. Polit. Econ.*, May-June 1973, *81*(3), pp. 655–77. [G: W. Germany]

Brightman, Harvey J. and Dorfman, Mark S. Birth Order, Anxiety, Affiliation and the Purchase of Life Insurance: Comment. *J. Risk Ins.*, December 1973, *40*(4), pp. 643–46.

Brobst, Robert W. and Wrighton, Fred M. The Income Elasticity of Housing: A Cross-Sectional Analysis of New Orleans. *Miss. Val. J. Bus. Econ.*, Winter 1973-74, *9*(2), pp. 43–58. [G: U.S.]

Byron, R. P. The Restricted Aitken Estimation of Sets of Demand Relations: Reply. *Econometrica*, March 1973, *41*(2), pp. 371–74.

Carliner, Geoffrey. Income Elasticity of Housing Demand. *Rev. Econ. Statist.*, November 1973, *55*(4), pp. 528–32. [G: U.S.]

Casey, Michael G. An Application of the Samuelson-Stone Linear Expenditure System to Food Consumption in Ireland. *Econ. Soc. Rev.*, April 1973, *4*(3), pp. 309–42. [G: Ireland]

Chatfield, C. and Goodhardt, G. J. A Consumer Purchasing Model with Erlang Inter-Purchase Times. *J. Amer. Statist. Assoc.*, December 1973, *68*(344), pp. 828–35.

Cramer, J. S. Interaction of Income and Price in Consumer Demand. *Int. Econ. Rev.*, June 1973, *14*(2), pp. 351–63. [G: Sweden; Netherlands; U.K.]

Dodds, Wellesley. An Application of the Bass Model in Long-Term New Product Forecasting. *J. Marketing Res.*, August 1973, *10*(3), pp. 308–11. [G: U.S.]

Donnelly, James H., Jr. and Etzel, Michael J. Degrees of Product Newness and Early Trial. *J. Marketing Res.*, August 1973, *10*(3), pp. 295–300. [G: U.S.]

Gamaletsos, Theodore. Further Analysis of Cross-Country Comparison of Consumer Expenditure Patterns. *Europ. Econ. Rev.*, April 1973, *4*(1), pp. 1–20. [G: O.E.C.D.]

Geary, P. T. The Demand for Petrol and Tobacco in Ireland: A Comment. *Econ. Soc. Rev.*, January 1973, *4*(2), pp. 201–07. [G: Ireland]

Greeno, Daniel W.; Sommers, Montrose S. and Kernan, Jerome B. Personality and Implicit Behavior Patterns. *J. Marketing Res.*, February 1973, *10*(1), pp. 63–69. [G: U.S.]

Grønhaug, Kjell. Buying Experience and Buying Purpose. *Ekon. Samfundets Tidskr.*, 1973, *26*(4), pp. 247–54. [G: Finland]

Hamilton, David. What Has Evolutionary Economics to Contribute to Consumption Theory? *J. Econ. Issues*, June 1973, *7*(2), pp. 197–207.

Hess, Alan C. Household Demand for Durable Goods: The Influences of Rates of Return and Wealth. *Rev. Econ. Statist.*, February 1973, *55*(1), pp. 9–15. [G: U.S.]

Ingham, Barbara M. Ghana Cocoa Farmers—Income, Expenditure Relationships. *J. Devel. Stud.*, April 1973, *9*(3), pp. 365–72. [G: Ghana]

Isakson, Hans R. and Maurizi, Alex R. The Consumer Economics of Unit Pricing. *J. Marketing Res.*, August 1973, *10*(3), pp. 277–85. [G: U.S.]

Jacoby, Jacob and Kyner, David B. Brand Loyalty vs. Repeat Purchasing Behavior. *J. Marketing Res.*, February 1973, *10*(1), pp. 1–9. [G: U.S.]

Janáček, K. Estimating the Aggregate Macroeconomic Consumption Function in Czechoslovakia. *Eastern Europ. Econ.*, Spring 1973, *11*(3), pp. 74–107. [G: Czechoslovakia]

Kinnear, Thomas C. and Taylor, James R. The Effect of Ecological Concern on Brand Perceptions. *J. Marketing Res.*, May 1973, *10*(2), pp. 191–97. [G: U.S.]

Kraft, Frederic B.; Granbois, Donald H. and Summers, John O. Brand Evaluation and Brand Choice: A Longitudinal Study. *J. Marketing Res.*, August 1973, *10*(3), pp. 235–41. [G: U.S.]

Kunreuther, Howard. Why the Poor May Pay More for Food: Theoretical and Empirical Evidence. *J. Bus.*, July 1973, *46*(3), pp. 368–83. [G: U.S.]

Lehtinen, Uolevi. On Some Possibilities of Taking Risk into Account in a Brand Choice Model. *Liiketaloudellinen Aikak.*, 1973, *22*(4), pp. 272–77.

Mazis, Michael B.; Settle, Robert B. and Leslie, Dennis C. Elimination of Phosphate Detergents and Psychological Reactance. *J. Marketing Res.*, November 1973, *10*(4), pp. 390–95. [G: U.S.]

McCalden, Gerald. Towards a Model for Prediction of Residential Water Use. In *Aislabie, C., ed.*, 1973, pp. 99–113. [G: Australia]

McShane, R. W. The Influence of Financial Factors on Household Meat Consumption. *Rev. Marketing Agr. Econ.*, March 1973, *41*(1), pp. 20–29. [G: Australia]

Metwally, Mohktar M. Australian Advertising Expenditure and its Relation to Demand. *Econ. Rec.*, June 1973, *49*(126), pp. 290–99. [G: Australia]

Moyer, R. International Market Analysis. In *Thorelli, H. B., ed.*, 1973, pp. 162–79.

Nakanishi, Masao. Advertising and Promotion Effects on Consumer Response to New Products. *J. Marketing Res.*, August 1973, *10*(3), pp. 242–49.

Nakao, Takeo. An Examination of Duesenberry's Hypothesis on the Growth of Demand for the New Product. (In Japanese.) *Econ. Stud. Quart.*, April 1973, *24*(1), pp. 18–32.

Newman, Joseph W. and Werbel, Richard A. Multivariate Analysis of Brand Loyalty for Major Household Appliances. *J. Marketing Res.*, November 1973, *10*(4), pp. 404–09. [G: U.S.]

Onigkeit, Dietmar. Zur Berechnung von Einkommenselastizitäten für Prognosen. (The Computation of Income Elasticities for Forecasts. With English summary.) *Schweiz. Z. Volkswirtsch. Statist.*, December 1973, *109*(4), pp. 597–602.

O'Riordan, W. K. Elasticity of Demand for Petrol in Ireland: Reply. *Econ. Soc. Rev.*, October 1973, *5* (1), pp. 111–12. [G: Ireland]

Parks, Richard W. and Barten, Anton P. A Cross-Country Comparison of the Effects of Prices, Income and Population Composition on Consumption Patterns. *Econ. J.*, September 1973, *83*(331), pp. 834–52.

Peaker, A. Holiday Spending by the British at Home and Abroad. *Nat. Westminster Bank Quart. Rev.*, August 1973, pp. 47–55. [G: U.K.]

Perry, Arnon. Heredity, Personality Traits, Product Attitude, and Product Consumption—An Exploratory Study. *J. Marketing Res.*, November 1973, *10*(4), pp. 376–79.

Peters, William H. Income and Occupation as Explanatory Variables: Their Power Combined vs. Separate. *J. Bus. Res.*, Summer 1973, *1*(1), pp. 81–89. [G: U.S.]

Prochaska, Fred J. and Schrimper, R. A. Opportunity Cost of Time and Other Socioeconomic Effects on Away-From-Home Food Consumption. *Amer. J. Agr. Econ.*, Part I, November 1973, *55*(4), pp. 595–603. [G: U.S.]

Prosser, P. B. The Market for Beef in Japan. *Quart. Rev. Agr. Econ.*, April 1973, *26*(2), pp. 67–89. [G: Japan]

Pullinger, Barry F. A Method of Analysis of Residential Water Demand and Its Relation to Management. In *Aislabie, C., ed.*, 1973, pp. 155–70. [G: Australia]

Rugg, Donald. The Choice of Journey Destination: A Theoretical and Empirical Analysis. *Rev. Econ. Statist.*, February 1973, *55*(1), pp. 64–72. [G: U.S.]

Sawyer, Alan G. The Effects of Repetition of Refutational and Supportive Advertising Appeals. *J. Marketing Res.*, February 1973, *10*(1), pp. 23–33. [G: U.S.]

Smith, R. J. Medium-Term Forecasts Reassessed: IV. Domestic Appliances. *Nat. Inst. Econ. Rev.*, May 1973, (64), pp. 68–83. [G: U.K.]

Steckle, Jean. Changes in Food Use Patterns: Some Aspects of Household Enumeration in Measuring Levels of Living through Studies in Depth. In *Ofori, I. M., ed.*, 1973, pp. 49–56. [G: Ghana]

Straszheim, Mahlon R. Estimation of the Demand for Urban Housing Services from Household Interview Data. *Rev. Econ. Statist.*, February 1973, *55*(1), pp. 1–8. [G: U.S.]

Syed, Hasan A. Demand for and Supply of Pulses in the Punjab. *Pakistan Econ. Soc. Rev.*, Winter 1973, *11*(4), pp. 363–77. [G: Pakistan]

Wilkinson, R. K. The Income Elasticity of Demand for Housing. *Oxford Econ. Pap.*, November 1973, *25*(3), pp. 361–77. [G: U.K.]

Winter, Frederick W. A Laboratory Experiment of Individual Attitude Response to Advertising Exposure. *J. Marketing Res.*, May 1973, *10*(2), pp. 130–40. [G: U.S.]

Wykoff, Frank C. A User Cost Approach to New Automobile Purchases. *Rev. Econ. Stud.*, July 1973, *40*(3), pp. 377–90. [G: U.S.]

9213 Consumer Protection

Avio, Kenneth L. An Economic Rationale for Statutory Interest Rate Ceilings. *Quart. Rev. Econ. Bus.*, Autumn 1973, *13*(3), pp. 61–72.

Bartlett, Roland W. Are Supermarkets Charging Consumers Too Much for Handling Milk? *Ill. Agr. Econ.*, July 1973, *13*(2), pp. 1–5. [G: U.S.]

Berton, Lee. Aiding the Poor. In *Murray, B. B., ed.*, 1973, pp. 420–25. [G: U.S.]

Birmingham, Robert L. The Consumer as King: The Economics of Precarious Sovereignty. In *Murray, B. B., ed.*, 1973, pp. 212–24. [G: U.S.]

Boone, Louis E. and Kurtz, David L. The Consumer Versus Holder-in-Due-Course Doctrine. *Ohio State U. Bull. Bus. Res.*, August 1973, *48*(8), pp. 1–3, 6. [G: U.S.]

Bralove, Mary. Does Your Paprika Get Up Off the Plate and Just Walk Away? In *Murray, B. B., ed.*, 1973, pp. 86–88. [G: U.S.]

Brimmer, Andrew F. Statements to Congress. *Fed. Res. Bull.*, June 1973, *59*(6), pp. 429–32. [G: U.S.]

Brozen, Yale. In Defense of Advertising. In *Murray, B. B., ed.*, 1973, pp. 341–51. [G: U.S.]

Bucher, Jeffrey M. Statements to Congress. *Fed. Res. Bull.*, June 1973, *59*(6), pp. 420–25. [G: U.S.]

Burditt, George M. Fair Packaging and Labeling—the Cost to Consumers. In *Murray, B. B., ed.*, 1973, pp. 208–11. [G: U.S.]

Bylin, James E. An Agency in California Is Model in Campaign to Curb Repair Frauds. In *Murray, B. B., ed.*, 1973, pp. 56–59. [G: U.S.]

Cravens, David W. and Hills, Gerald E. Consumerism: A Perspective for Business. In *Murray, B. B., ed.*, 1973, pp. 233–42. [G: U.S.]

Daane, J. Dewey. Statements to Congress. *Fed. Res. Bull.*, June 1973, *59*(6), pp. 425–29. [G: U.S.]

Darby, Michael R. and Karni, Edi. Free Competition and the Optimal Amount of Fraud. *J. Law Econ.*, April 1973, *16*(1), pp. 67–88.

Day, George S. The Role of the Consumer in the Corporate Social Audit. In *Dierkes, M. and Bauer, R. A., eds.*, 1973, pp. 117–29.

Dixon, Donald F. Public Policy Toward Retailing: Australia. In *Boddewyn, J. J. and Hollander, S. C., eds.*, 1972, pp. 11–35. [G: Australia]

Gardner, David M. The Package, Legislation, and the Shopper—Customer Behavior Should Determine Regulations. In *Murray, B. B., ed.*, 1973, pp. 200–207. [G: U.S.]

Givens, Richard A. Product Safety Standard-Making Powers Under the Consumer Product Safety Act. *Antitrust Bull.*, Summer 1973, *18*(2), pp. 243–53. [G: U.S.]

Green, Mark J. and Moore, Beverly C., Jr. Winter's Discontent: Market Failure and Consumer Welfare. *Yale Law J.,* April 1973, *82*(5), pp. 903–19. [G: U.S.]

Jentz, Gaylord A. Federal Regulation of Advertising. In *Murray, B. B., ed.,* 1973, pp. 328–40. [G: U.S.]

Jentz, Gaylord A. Federal Regulation of Advertising. In *Britt, S. H. and Boyd, H. W., Jr., eds.,* 1973, pp. 585–97. [G: U.S.]

Johnson, Lyndon B. The American Consumer. In *Murray, B. B., ed.,* 1973, pp. 60–67. [G: U.S.]

Jones, Mary Gardiner. Social Responsibility: The Regulator's View. *Calif. Manage. Rev.,* Summer 1973, *15*(4), pp. 78–84. [G: U.S.]

Kaye, William G. Take in a New Partner—The Consumer. In *Murray, B. B., ed.,* 1973, pp. 243–48. [G: U.S.]

Kensicki, Peter R. and Richmond, David. Consumerism and Automobile Insurance. *J. Risk Ins.,* June 1973, *40*(2), pp. 209–17. [G: U.S.]

Kirkpatrick, Miles W., et al. The ABA Report on the FTC: Consumer Protection or Consumer Exploitation. In *Murray, B. B., ed.,* 1973, pp. 98–101. [G: U.S.]

MacGregor, James. Skeptical Consumers, Tough Regulators Spur a New Candor in Ads. In *Murray, B. B., ed.,* 1973, pp. 310–15. [G: U.S.]

Main, Jeremy. Industry Still Has Something to Learn About Congress. In *Murray, B. B., ed.,* 1973, pp. 192–99. [G: U.S.]

Mehr, Robert I. Consumerism and Automobile Insurance: Discussion. *J. Risk Ins.,* June 1973, *40*(2), pp. 217–20. [G: U.S.]

Moore, Beverly C., Jr. Product Safety—Who Should Absorb the Cost? In *Britt, S. H. and Boyd, H. W., Jr., eds.,* 1973, pp. 340–44. [G: U.S.]

Murray, Barbara B. Consumerism: The Eternal Triangle: Introduction. In *Murray, B. B., ed.,* 1973, pp. xi–xvii. [G: U.S.]

Murray, Barbara B. Major Federal Consumer Protection Laws, 1906–1970. In *Murray, B. B., ed.,* 1973, pp. 78–85. [G: U.S.]

Nader, Ralph. A Case for More Consumer Protection. In *Reynolds, L. G.; Green, G. D. and Lewis, D. R., eds.,* 1973, pp. 181–89. [G: U.S.]

Nader, Ralph. The Great American Gyp. In *Murray, B. B., ed.,* 1973, pp. 39–51. [G: U.S.]

Nicosia, Francesco M. Consumer Behavior: Can Economics and Behavioral Science Converge? *Calif. Manage. Rev.,* Winter 1973, *16*(2), pp. 71–78.

Nixon, Richard M. Consumer Protection. In *Murray, B. B., ed.,* 1973, pp. 68–77. [G: U.S.]

Oi, Walter Y. The Economics of Product Safety. *Bell J. Econ. Manage. Sci.,* Spring 1973, *4*(1), pp. 3–28.

Peltzman, Sam. An Evaluation of Consumer Protection Legislation: The 1962 Drug Amendments. *J. Polit. Econ.,* September-October 1973, *81*(5), pp. 1049–91. [G: U.S.]

Posner, Richard A. Report on the Federal Trade Commission. In *Murray, B. B., ed.,* 1973, pp. 102–15. [G: U.S.]

Proxmire, William. Qualifications for FTC Chairmanship: Competence, Concern, and Consumer Confidence. In *Murray, B. B., ed.,* 1973,

pp. 92–97. [G: U.S.]

Scanlon, Paul D. Anti-Competitive Advertising and the FTC: A Ban on Oligopoly-Creating-Ads? In *Murray, B. B., ed.,* 1973, pp. 363–69. [G: U.S.]

Scanlon, Paul D. Oligopoly and Deceptive Advertising: The Cereal Industry Affair. In *Murray, B. B., ed.,* 1973, pp. 125–34.

Shafer, Ronald G. Consumers in Court. In *Murray, B. B., ed.,* 1973, pp. 373–77. [G: U.S.]

Shafer, Ronald G. A Food Chain Recruits a Consumer Advocate to Shape Its Policies. In *Murray, B. B., ed.,* 1973, pp. 274–78. [G: U.S.]

Shaffer, Richard A. Consumers Gripe That Credit Reporting Law Doesn't Always Work. In *Murray, B. B., ed.,* 1973, pp. 138–42. [G: U.S.]

Warne, Clinton L. The Consumer Movement and the Labor Movement. *J. Econ. Issues,* June 1973, *7*(2), pp. 307–16.

Wyckham, Robert G. and Stewart, Max D. Public Policy Toward Retailing: Canada. In *Boddewyn, J. J. and Hollander, S. C., eds.,* 1972, pp. 81–99. [G: Canada]

930 URBAN ECONOMICS

9300 General

Goldstein, Gerald S. and Moses, Leon N. A Survey of Urban Economics. *J. Econ. Lit.,* June 1973, *11*(2), pp. 471–515.

931 Urban Economics and Public Policy

9310 Urban Economics and Public Policy

Adams, Carolyn. Political Accommodation in the Metropolis. *Growth Change,* July 1973, *4*(3), pp. 10–15. [G: Sweden]

Agapos, A. M. and Dunlap, Paul R. Elimination of Urban Blight Through Inverse Proportional Ad Valorem Property Taxation. *Amer. J. Econ. Soc.,* April 1973, *32*(2), pp. 143–52. [G: U.S.]

Ahlbrandt, Roger S., Jr. Efficiency in the Provision of Fire Services. *Public Choice,* Fall 1973, *16,* pp. 1–15. [G: U.S.]

Aislabie, Colin S. Payment by Use in Urban Water Supply. In *Aislabie, C., ed.,* 1973, pp. 1–18. [G: Australia]

Alonso, William. The Mirage of New Towns. In *Grieson, R. E., ed.,* 1973, pp. 213–28. [G: U.S.]

Alonso, William. Urban Zero Population Growth. In *Olson, M. and Landsberg, H. H., eds.,* 1973, pp. 191–206. [G: U.S.]

Archer, R. W. Land Speculation and Scattered Development; Failures in the Urban-Fringe Land Market. *Urban Stud.,* October 1973, *10*(3), pp. 367–72. [G: U.S.]

Aronson, J. Richard and Schwartz, Eli. Financing Public Goods and the Distribution of Population in a System of Local Governments. *Nat. Tax J.,* June 1973, *26*(2), pp. 137–60. [G: U.S.]

Averous, Christian P. and Lee, Douglass B., Jr. Land Allocation and Transportation Pricing in a Mixed Economy. *J. Reg. Sci.,* August 1973, *13*(2), pp. 173–85.

Babcock, Richard F. Exclusionary Zoning: A Code

Phrase for a Notable Legal Struggle. In *Masotti, L. H. and Hadden, J. K., eds.*, 1973, pp. 313–28.
[G: U.S.]

Bahl, Roy W.; Coelen, Stephen P. and Warford, Jeremy J. Land Value Increments as a Measure of the Net Benefits of Urban Water Supply Projects in Developing Countries: Theory and Measurement. In *Harriss, C. L., ed.*, 1973, pp. 171–88.

Bails, Dale. An Alternative: The Land Value Tax. *Amer. J. Econ. Soc.*, July 1973, *32*(3), pp. 283–94.

Banfield, Edward C. A Critical View of the Urban Crisis. *Ann. Amer. Acad. Polit. Soc. Sci.*, January 1973, *405*, pp. 7–14. [G: U.S.]

Barlev, Benzion. Location Effects of Intra-Area Tax Differentials. *Land Econ.*, February 1973, *49*(1), pp. 86–89.

Barlowe, Raleigh; Ahl, James G. and Bachman, Gordon. Use-Value Assessment Legislation in the United States. *Land Econ.*, May 1973, *49*(2), pp. 206–12. [G: U.S.]

Becker, Arthur P. The Distribution of Benefits and Costs of the Federally Subsidized Urban Renewal Programs. In *Harriss, C. L., ed.*, 1973, pp. 203–29.
[G: U.S.]

Beck, Morris. Public Services in Metropolitan Areas of Australia. *Public Finance Quart.*, July 1973, *1* (3), pp. 307–22. [G: Australia]

Bell, Carolyn Shaw. Middle-Class Action and the Ghetto Consumer. *J. Econ. Issues*, June 1973, *7*(2), pp. 245–57. [G: U.S.]

Bernstein, Samuel J. and Mellon, W. Giles. Multi-Dimensional Considerations in the Evaluation of Urban Policy. In *Cochrane, J. L. and Zeleny, M., eds.*, 1973, pp. 530–43. [G: U.S.]

Blair, Roger D. and Vogel, Ronald J. Heroin Addiction and Urban Crime. *Public Finance Quart.*, October 1973, *1*(4), pp. 457–66.

Booms, Bernard H. Impact of Urban Market Structure on the Level of Inventive Activity in Cities in the Early Nineteen Hundreds. *Land Econ.*, August 1973, *49*(3), pp. 318–25. [G: U.S.]

von Böventer, Edwin. City Size Systems: Theoretical Issues, Empirical Regularities and Planning Guides. *Urban Stud.*, June 1973, *10*(2), pp. 145–62.

Boyes, William J. and Peseau, Dennis E. On Optimization in Models of Urban Land Use Densities: Comment. *J. Reg. Sci.*, April 1973, *13*(1), pp. 129–33.

Braby, R. H. Urban Growth and Policy: A Multi-Nodal Approach. *Econ. Anal. Pol.*, September 1973, *4*(2), pp. 43–58. [G: Australia]

Brackett, Jean. Urban Family Budgets Updated to Autumn 1972. *Mon. Lab. Rev.*, August 1973, *96* (8), pp. 70–76. [G: U.S.]

Bradley, Iver E.; Mangum, Garth L. and Robson, R. Thayne. Impact of Manpower Programs upon Employment and Earnings. In *Mangum, G. L. and Robson, R. T., eds.*, 1973, pp. 227–59.
[G: U.S.]

Bradley, Iver E.; Mangum, Garth L. and Robson, R. Thayne. Total Impact of Manpower Programs. In *Mangum, G. L. and Robson, R. T., eds.*, 1973, pp. 260–93. [G: U.S.]

Brewer, Garry D. and Hall, Owen P., Jr. Policy Analysis by Computer Simulation: The Need for Ap-

praisal. *Public Policy*, Summer 1973, *21*(3), pp. 343–65.

Bromley, David G. and Smith, Joel. The Historical Significance of Annexation as a Social Process. *Land Econ.*, August 1973, *49*(3), pp. 294–309.
[G: U.S.]

Burki, Shahid J. Rapid Population Growth and Urbanization: The Case of Pakistan. *Pakistan Econ. Soc. Rev.*, Autumn 1973, *11*(3), pp. 239–76.
[G: Pakistan]

Burki, Shahid J. Employment Creating Urban Public Works Programmes: Outline of a Strategy. *Pakistan Develop. Rev.*, Autumn 1973, *12*(3), pp. 293–310.

Callahan, John J. Evaluation of Metropolitan Conflict and Cooperation. *Amer. Real Estate Urban Econ. Assoc. J.*, Fall 1973, *1*(2), pp. 141–51.
[G: U.S.]

Casetti, Emilio. Urban Land Value Functions: Equilibrium Versus Optimality. *Econ. Geogr.*, October 1973, *49*(4), pp. 357–65.

Clawson, Marion and Perloff, Harvey S. Alternatives for Future Urban Land Policy. In *Clawson, M., ed.*, 1973, pp. 221–39. [G: U.S.]

Clemente, Frank and Sturgis, Richard B. Population Size and Industrial Diversification: A Rejoinder. *Urban Stud.*, October 1973, *10*(3), pp. 397.
[G: U.S.]

Cohen, Sylvan H. The Politics of Urban Renewal and the Politics of Ecology. In *Gabriel, R. A. and Cohen, S. H., eds.*, 1973, pp. 171–91. [G: U.S.]

Comay, Yochanan and Kirschenbaum, Alan. The Israeli New Town: An Experiment at Population Redistribution. *Econ. Develop. Cult. Change*, October 1973, *22*(1), pp. 124–34. [G: Israel]

Cord, Steven. Revenue Sharing and Property Tax Reform. *Amer. J. Econ. Soc.*, October 1973, *32*(4), pp. 404. [G: U.S.]

Crabb, Peter. Urban Water Catchments: Some Illustrations of Resource Allocation and Conflict Regulation. In *Aislabie, C., ed.*, 1973, pp. 19–33.
[G: Australia]

Crowley, Ronald W. Reflections and Further Evidence on Population Size and Industrial Diversification. *Urban Stud.*, February 1973, *10*(1), pp. 91–94. [G: Canada]

Czamanski, Stan. A Model of Urban Land Allocation. *Growth Change*, January 1973, *4*(1), pp. 43–48.

Dacey, Michael F. A Central Focus Cluster Process for Urban Dispersion. *J. Reg. Sci.*, April 1973, *13* (1), pp. 77–89.

Daicoff, Darwin W. The Community Impact of Military Installations. In *Udis, B., ed.*, 1973, pp. 149–66. [G: U.S.]

Dajani, Jarir S. Cost Studies of Urban Public Services. *Land Econ.*, November 1973, *49*(4), pp. 479–83.

Daly, M. T. and Webber, M. J. The Growth of the Firm Within the City. *Urban Stud.*, October 1973, *10*(3), pp. 303–17. [G: Australia]

Darling, Arthur H. Measuring Benefits Generated by Urban Water Parks. *Land Econ.*, February 1973, *49*(1), pp. 22–34. [G: U.S.]

David, F. J. L. Floodplain Lands for Parks and Recreation: A Case Study of Milwaukee. *Land Econ.*, May 1973, *49*(2), pp. 221–26. [G: U.S.]

Davis, Otto A. and Whinston, Andrew B. The Economics of Urban Renewal. In *Grieson, R. E., ed.,* 1973, pp. 163–77.

Day, John C. A Linear Programming Approach to Floodplain Land Use Planning in Urban Areas. *Amer. J. Agr. Econ.,* May 1973, *55*(2), pp. 165–74.

De Bruyne, L. De Antwerpse luchthavenbehoeften 1970–1980. (The Air Transport Needs of Antwerp. With English summary.) *Econ. Soc. Tijdschr.,* June 1973, *27*(3), pp. 227–43. [G: Belgium]

Dickinson, Neal J. Water Development and Urban Development in Africa. In *Aislabie, C., ed.,* 1973, pp. 34–48. [G: Rhodesia]

Dixit, Avinash K. The Optimum Factory Town. *Bell J. Econ. Manage. Sci.,* Autumn 1973, *4*(2), pp. 637–51.

Domański, Ryszard. Structure, Law of Motion, and Optimal Path of Growth of Complex Urban Systems. *Econ. Geogr.,* January 1973, *49*(1), pp. 37–46.

Douglas, Susan P. Public Planning of Retail Location in France and Great Britain. In *Boddewyn, J. J. and Hollander, S. C., eds.,* 1972, pp. 145–65. [G: France; U.K.]

Downes, Bryan T. Problem-solving in Suburbia: The Basis for Political Conflict. In *Masotti, L. H. and Hadden, J. K., eds.,* 1973, pp. 281–312. [G: U.S.]

Downing, Paul B. User Charges and the Development of Urban Land. *Nat. Tax J.,* December 1973, *26*(4), pp. 631–37. [G: U.S.]

Downing, Paul B. Factors Affecting Commercial Land Values: An Empirical Study of Milwaukee, Wisconsin. *Land Econ.,* February 1973, *49*(1), pp. 44–56. [G: U.S.]

Downs, Anthony. Who are the Urban Poor? In *Grieson, R. E., ed.,* 1973, pp. 285–88. [G: U.S.]

Downs, Anthony. Evaluating Efficiency and Equity in Federal Urban Programs. In *Haveman, R. H. and Hamrin, R. D., eds.,* 1973, pp. 231–37. [G: U.S.]

Dyckman, John. The Changing Uses of the City. In *Rasmussen, D. W. and Haworth, C. T., eds.,* 1973, pp. 31–50.

Edie, Leslie C., et al. Urban Planning. In *Ross, M., ed.,* 1973, pp. 599–615. [G: U.S.]

Eichler, Edward and Kaplan, Marshall. New Communities. In *Pynoos, J.; Schafer, R. and Hartman, C. W., eds.,* 1973, pp. 523–31. [G: U.S.]

Ernst, Robert T. and Hugg, Lawrence. Institutional Growth and Community Fragmentation: An Inner City Example. *Mich. Academician,* Fall 1973, *6*(2), pp. 179–91. [G: U.S.]

Evans, Alan W. The Location of the Headquarters of Industrial Companies. *Urban Stud.,* October 1973, *10*(3), pp. 387–95. [G: U.K.; U.S.]

Evans, Raymond W. G. Some Aspects of Urban Water Supply in Victoria. In *Aislabie, C., ed.,* 1973, pp. 61–67. [G: Australia]

Fessler, Daniel Wm. Casting the Courts in a Land Use Reform Effort: A Starring Role or a Supporting Part? In *Clawson, M., ed.,* 1973, pp. 175–203. [G: U.S.]

Fitch, Lyle C. Metropolitan Financial Problems. In *Grieson, R. E., ed.,* 1973, pp. 418–28. [G: U.S.]

Forsythe, Graeme A. Rural and Urban Flood Insurance: A Review. In *Aislabie, C., ed.,* 1973, pp. 68–77.

Foster, C. D. and Whitehead, C. M. E. The Layfield Report on the Greater London Development Plan. *Economica, N.S.,* November 1973, *40*(160), pp. 442–54. [G: U.K.]

Freund, James L. A Note on Short Period Changes in Earned Income in Manufacturing Among Urban Areas. *J. Reg. Sci.,* August 1973, *13*(2), pp. 279–89. [G: U.S.]

Frick, Andreas; Kiener, Urs and Vieli, Klaus. Bodenpreise und Stadtentwicklung. Eine empirische Untersuchung. (Land Prices and Urban Development. With English summary.) *Schweiz. Z. Volkswirtsch. Statist.,* March 1973, *109*(1), pp. 101–15.

Friedman, Judith J. Variations in the Level of Central Business District Retail Activity Among Large U.S. Cities: 1954 and 1967. *Land Econ.,* August 1973, *49*(3), pp. 326–35. [G: U.S.]

Friedmann, John. National Urbanization Policy: Scope and Objectives. In *Friedmann, J.,* 1973, pp. 133–38.

Friedmann, John. The Urban-Regional Frame for National Development. In *Friedmann, J.,* 1973, pp. 139–51.

Friedmann, John, et al. Towards a National Urbanization Policy. In *Friedmann, J.,* 1973, pp. 153–86.

Fusfeld, Daniel R. Transfer Payments and the Ghetto Economy. In *Boulding, K. E.; Pfaff, M. and Pfaff, A., eds.,* 1973, pp. 78–92. [G: U.S.]

Gabriel, Richard A. The Moral Basis of Ecology. In *Gabriel, R. A. and Cohen, S. H., eds.,* 1973, pp. 19–31. [G: U.S.]

Gaffney, Mason. Tax Reform to Release Land. In *Clawson, M., ed.,* 1973, pp. 115–51. [G: U.S.]

Gaffney, Mason. Land Rent, Taxation and Public Policy: Taxation and the Functions of Urban Land Rent. *Amer. J. Econ. Soc.,* January 1973, *32*(1), pp. 17–34.

Gallardo, Lloyd. Development of Bay Area Manpower Institutions. In *Mangum, G. L. and Robson, R. T., eds.,* 1973, pp. 154–75. [G: U.S.]

Gallardo, Lloyd. Evaluating Bay Area Manpower Programs. In *Mangum, G. L. and Robson, R. T., eds.,* 1973, pp. 176–201. [G: U.S.]

Gallardo, Lloyd. Institutional Impact of Bay Area Manpower Programs. In *Mangum, G. L. and Robson, R. T., eds.,* 1973, pp. 202–24. [G: U.S.]

Gans, Herbert J. The Failure of Urban Renewal: A Critique and Some Proposals. In *Rasmussen, D. W. and Haworth, C. T., eds.,* 1973, pp. 160–67. [G: U.S.]

Ganz, Alexander and O'Brien, Thomas. The City: Sandbox, Reservation, or Dynamo? *Public Policy,* Winter 1973, *21*(1), pp. 107–23. [G: U.S.]

Garvey, John, Jr. What Can Europe Teach Us About Urban Growth? In *Moskoff, W., ed.,* 1973, pp. 339–48. [G: W. Europe]

Gerlach, Knut and Liepmann, Peter. Industrialisierung und Siedlungsstruktur—Bemerkungen zum regionalpolitischen Programm einer aktiven Sanierung der bayerischen Rückstandsgebiete. (Industrialization and Settlement Structure—Remarks on the Regional Program of the Promotion of Less Developed Regions in Bavaria. With English summary.) *Jahr. Nationalökon. Stat-*

ist., August 1973, *187*(6), pp. 507–21.   [G: W. Germany]

Gibson, Campbell. Urbanization in New Zealand: A Comparative Analysis. *Demography*, February 1973, *10*(1), pp. 71–84.   [G: New Zealand]

Gilbert, R. Alton. Employment Growth in St. Louis. *Fed. Res. Bank St. Louis Rev.*, August 1973, *55*(8), pp. 9–15.   [G: U.S.]

Glenn, Norval D. Suburbanization in the United States Since World War II. In *Masotti, L. H. and Hadden, J. K., eds.*, 1973, pp. 51–78.   [G: U.S.]

Gould, Bernard W. Sampling Errors in Flood Damage Estimates. In *Aislabie, C., ed.*, 1973, pp. 82–98.

Greene, Kenneth V. Collective Decision-Making Models and the Measurement of Benefits in Fiscal Incidence Studies. *Nat. Tax J.*, June 1973, *26*(2), pp. 177–85.

Grieson, Ronald E. Zoning, Housing Markets, and Urban Renewal: Introduction. In *Grieson, R. E., ed.*, 1973, pp. 133–48.   [G: U.S.]

Grigsby, William G. Real Estate and Urban Land Economics: Illusions of Progress? *Amer. Real Estate Urban Econ. Assoc. J.*, June 1973, *1*(1), pp. 4–7.

Guest, Avery M. Urban Growth and Population Densities. *Demography*, February 1973, *10*(1), pp. 53–69.   [G: U.S.]

Haccou, J. F. and Lübbers, P. J. M. Public Policy Toward Retailing: The Netherlands. In *Boddewyn, J. J. and Hollander, S. C., eds.*, 1972, pp. 245–70.   [G: Netherlands]

Hahn, Harlan. Ethnic Minorities: Politics and the Family in Suburbia. In *Masotti, L. H. and Hadden, J. K., eds.*, 1973, pp. 185–205.   [G: U.S.]

Haines, George H., Jr.; Simon, Leonard S. and Alexis, Marcus. An Analysis of Central City Neighborhood Food Trading Areas: A Reply. *J. Reg. Sci.*, August 1973, *13*(2), pp. 301.   [G: U.S.]

Hale, Carl W. Impact of Technological Change on Urban Market Areas, Land Values, and Land Uses. *Land Econ.*, August 1973, *49*(3), pp. 351–56.

Ham, Euiyoung. Urbanization and Asian Lifestyles. *Ann. Amer. Acad. Polit. Soc. Sci.*, January 1973, *405*, pp. 104–13.   [G: Asia]

Hansen, Niles M. Urbanism and Regional Disparities in Developed Countries. *Rev. Soc. Econ.*, April 1973, *31*(1), pp. 54–65.

Hansen, Niles M. A Growth Center Strategy for the United States. In *Rasmussen, D. W. and Haworth, C. T., eds.*, 1973, pp. 267–82.   [G: U.S.]

Haran, E. G. P. and Vining, Daniel R., Jr. A Modified Yule-Simon Model Allowing for Intercity Migration and Accounting for the Observed Form of the Size Distribution of Cities. *J. Reg. Sci.*, December 1973, *13*(3), pp. 421–37.   [G: U.S.]

Haworth, Joan G. Externalities and the City. In *Rasmussen, D. W. and Haworth, C. T., eds.*, 1973, pp. 28–30.   [G: U.S.]

Hellman, Daryl A. An Analysis of Central City Neighborhood Food Trading Areas: A Comment. *J. Reg. Sci.*, August 1973, *13*(2), pp. 299.   [G: U.S.]

Hendon, William S. Property Values, Schools, and Park-School Combinations. *Land Econ.*, May 1973, *49*(2), pp. 216–18.   [G: U.S.]

Heyman, Ira Michael. Legal Assaults on Municipal Land Use Regulation. In *Clawson, M., ed.*, 1973, pp. 153–74.   [G: U.S.]

Horowitz, Morris A. and Herrnstadt, Irwin L. Boston's Manpower Institutions. In *Mangum, G. L. and Robson, R. T., eds.*, 1973, pp. 23–48.   [G: U.S.]

Horowitz, Morris A. and Herrnstadt, Irwin L. Institutional and Labor Market Impact of Manpower Programs. In *Mangum, G. L. and Robson, R. T., eds.*, 1973, pp. 76–92.   [G: U.S.]

Horowitz, Morris A. and Herrnstadt, Irwin L. Training and Jobs for Boston's Disadvantaged. In *Mangum, G. L. and Robson, R. T., eds.*, 1973, pp. 49–75.   [G: U.S.]

Huttman, John P. and Huttman, Elizabeth D. Dutch and British New Towns: Self-Containment and Socioeconomic Balance. *Growth Change*, January 1973, *4*(1), pp. 30–37.   [G: U.K.; Netherlands]

Jaffee, Bruce L. Population Density as a Measure of City Size. *Indiana Bus. Rev.*, May-June 1973, *48*, pp. 15–18.   [G: U.S.]

Kalachek, Edward D. Ghetto Dwellers, Transportation and Employment. In *Rasmussen, D. W. and Haworth, C. T., eds.*, 1973, pp. 72–80.   [G: U.S.]

Kasper, H. Measuring the Labour Market Costs of Housing Dislocation. *Scot. J. Polit. Econ.*, June 1973, *20*(2), pp. 85–106.   [G: U.K.]

Kass, Roy. A Functional Classification of Metropolitan Communities. *Demography*, August 1973, *10* (3), pp. 427–45.   [G: U.S.]

Kessler, Robert P. and Hartman, Chester W. The Illusion and the Reality of Urban Renewal: A Case Study of San Francisco's Yerba Buena Center. *Land Econ.*, November 1973, *49*(4), pp. 440–53.   [G: U.S.]

Kinsey, David N. The French Z.U.P. Technique of Urban Development. In *Moskoff, W., ed.*, 1973, pp. 324–38.   [G: France]

Kirlin, John J. The Impact of Contract Services Arrangements on the Los Angeles Sheriff's Department and Law-Enforcement Services in Los Angeles County. *Public Policy*, Fall 1973, *21*(4), pp. 553–84.   [G: U.S.]

Kottis, Athena P. and Kottis, George C. Average Propensity to Spend Inside the Ghetto Areas: Comment. *J. Reg. Sci.*, April 1973, *13*(1), pp. 123–25.   [G: U.S.]

Kottis, George Christopher. New Towns and the Problem of "Optimum" City Size: A Critique. In *Mattila, J. M. and Thompson, W. R., eds.*, 1973, pp. 71–90.

Lasuén, J. R. Urbanisation and Development—the Temporal Interaction between Geographical and Sectoral Clusters. *Urban Stud.*, June 1973, *10*(2), pp. 163–88.

Leduc, Edgar and Baccanari, Samuel M. Interlocal Governmental Relations in Air Pollution Abatement. In *Gabriel, R. A. and Cohen, S. H., eds.*, 1973, pp. 113–28.   [G: U.S.]

Legey, L.; Ripper, M. and Varaiya, P. Effects of Congestion on the Shape of a City. *J. Econ. Theory*, April 1973, *6*(2), pp. 162–79.

Lever, William F. A Markov Approach to the Optimal Size of Cities in England and Wales. *Urban*

Stud., October 1973, *10*(3), pp. 353–65. [G: U.K.]

Leveson, Irving. Strategies against Urban Poverty. In *Boulding, K. E.; Pfaff, M. and Pfaff, A., eds.,* 1973, pp. 130–59. [G: U.S.]

Levi, J. F. S. Migration from the Land and Urban Unemployment in Sierra Leone. *Oxford Bull. Econ. Statist.,* November 1973, *35*(4), pp. 309–26. [G: Sierra Leone]

Livesey, D. A. Optimum City Size: A Minimum Congestion Cost Approach. *J. Econ. Theory,* April 1973, *6*(2), pp. 144–61.

Loewenstein, Louis K. and McGrath, Dorn C., Jr. The Planning Imperative in America's Future. *Ann. Amer. Acad. Polit. Soc. Sci.,* January 1973, *405,* pp. 15–24. [G: U.S.]

Long, Norton E. The City as Reservation. In *Rasmussen, D. W. and Haworth, C. T., eds.,* 1973, pp. 229–44.

Lubell, Harold. Urban Development and Employment in Calcutta. *Int. Lab. Rev.,* July 1973, *108*(1), pp. 25–41. [G: India]

Lugovskaia, L. Current Problems of Urbanization. *Prob. Econ.,* May 1973, *16*(1), pp. 91–99. [G: U.S.S.R.]

Lynch, Edward. Propositions for Planning New Towns in Venezuela. *J. Devel. Areas,* July 1973, *7*(4), pp. 549–70. [G: Venezuela]

Mabogunje, Akin L. Manufacturing and the Geography of Development in Tropical Africa. *Econ. Geogr.,* January 1973, *49*(1), pp. 1–20. [G: Africa]

Mangum, Garth L. and Robson, R. Thayne. Metropolitan Impact of Manpower Programs: A Four-City Comparison: Introduction. In *Mangum, G. L. and Robson, R. T., eds.,* 1973, pp. 1–5. [G: U.S.]

Martin, Randolph C. Spatial Distribution of Population: Cities and Suburbs. *J. Reg. Sci.,* August 1973, *13*(2), pp. 269–78. [G: U.S.]

Masotti, Louis H. Epilogue: Suburbia in the Seventies . . . and Beyond. In *Masotti, L. H. and Hadden, J. K., eds.,* 1973, pp. 533–42. [G: U.S.]

Masotti, Louis H. Prologue: Suburbia Reconsidered—Myth and Counter-Myth. In *Masotti, L. H. and Hadden, J. K., eds.,* 1973, pp. 15–22. [G: U.S.]

Mattila, John M. A Metropolitan Income Determination Model and the Estimation of Metropolitan Income Multipliers. *J. Reg. Sci.,* April 1973, *13*(1), pp. 1–16. [G: U.S.]

McCall, David B. Profit: Spur for Solving Social Ills. *Harvard Bus. Rev.,* May-June 1973, *51*(3), pp. 46–54, 180–82. [G: U.S.]

McElroy, Jerome L. and Singell, Larry D. Some Structural Contours of the Recent Urban Crisis: An Empirical Analysis of the Social and Economic Conditions of Riot and Non-Riot Cities. In *Mattila, J. M. and Thompson, W. R., eds.,* 1973, pp. 177–91. [G: U.S.]

McKean, Roland N. An Outsider Looks at Urban Economics. *Urban Stud.,* February 1973, *10*(1), pp. 19–37.

Mellor, Earl F. A Case Study: Costs and Benefits of Public Goods and Expenditures for a Ghetto. In *Boulding, K. E.; Pfaff, M. and Pfaff, A., eds.,* 1973,

pp. 38–57. [G: U.S.]

Mera, Koichi. On the Urban Agglomeration and Economic Efficiency. *Econ. Develop. Cult. Change,* January 1973, *21*(2), pp. 309–24.

Meyer, Eugene L. Urban Renewal and Housing: Rhetoric and Realtiy. In *Levitan, S. A., ed.,* 1973, pp. 226–58. [G: U.S.]

Meyer, John R. Knocking Down the Straw Men. In *Rasmussen, D. W. and Haworth, C. T., eds.,* 1973, pp. 190–98. [G: U.S.]

Meyer, John R. and Kain, John F. Transportation and Poverty. In *Grieson, R. E., ed.,* 1973, pp. 323–35. [G: U.S.]

Miller, Stephen M. and Tabb, William K. A New Look at a Pure Theory of Local Expenditures. *Nat. Tax J.,* June 1973, *26*(2), pp. 161–76.

Mills, Edwin S. and MacKinnon, James. Notes on the New Urban Economics. *Bell J. Econ. Manage. Sci.,* Autumn 1973, *4*(2), pp. 593–601.

Mirrlees, James A. A Comment on Some Uses of Mathematical Models in Urban Economics: Rejoinder—II. *Urban Stud.,* June 1973, *10*(2), pp. 267–69.

Mishan, Ezra J. The Nature of External Diseconomies. In *Grieson, R. E., ed.,* 1973, pp. 234–44.

Mollenkopf, John and Pynoos, Jon. Boardwalk and Park Place: Property Ownership, Political Structure, and Housing Policy at the Local Level. In *Pynoos, J.; Schafer, R. and Hartman, C. W., eds.,* 1973, pp. 55–74. [G: U.S.]

Money, W. J. The Need to Sustain a Viable System of Local Democracy. *Urban Stud.,* October 1973, *10*(3), pp. 319–33.

Morrison, Peter A. A Demographic Assessment of New Cities and Growth Centers as Population Redistribution Strategies. *Public Policy,* Summer 1973, *21*(3), pp. 367–82. [G: U.S.]

Mott, George Fox. Communicative Turbulence in Urban Dynamics—Media, Education, and Planning. *Ann. Amer. Acad. Polit. Soc. Sci.,* January 1973, *405,* pp. 114–30. [G: U.S.]

Mumphrey, Anthony J. and Seley, John. Simulation Approaches to Locational Conflicts. *Econ. Geogr.,* January 1973, *49*(1), pp. 21–36.

Murray, Barbara B. A Pure Theory of Local Expenditures Revisited. In *Mattila, J. M. and Thompson, W. R., eds.,* 1973, pp. 129–39.

Niedercorn, John H. A Negative Exponential Model of Urban Land Use Densities and Its Implications for Metropolitan Development: Reply. *J. Reg. Sci.,* April 1973, *13*(1), pp. 139–40.

Nowacek, Charles G. Organizing Manpower Delivery Systems in Big Cities: Discussion. In *Aronson, R. L., ed.,* 1973, pp. 44–50. [G: U.S.]

Oakland, W. H.; Sparrow, Frederick T. and Stettler, H. Louis, III. More on Ghetto Multipliers. *J. Reg. Sci.,* April 1973, *13*(1), pp. 127–28. [G: U.S.]

Oron, Yitzhak; Pines, David and Sheshinski, Eytan. Optimum vs. Equilibrium Land Use Pattern and Congestion Toll. *Bell J. Econ. Manage. Sci.,* Autumn 1973, *4*(2), pp. 619–36.

Ostrom, Elinor and Parks, Roger B. Suburban Police Departments: Too Many and Too Small? In *Masotti, L. H. and Hadden, J. K., eds.,* 1973, pp. 367–402. [G: U.S.]

Owen, Carol and Witton, Ronald A. National Division and Mobilization: A Reinterpretation of Primacy. *Econ. Develop. Cult. Change,* January 1973, *21*(2), pp. 325–37.

Papageorgiou, G. J. The Impact of the Environment upon the Spatial Distribution of Population and Land Values. *Econ. Geogr.,* July 1973, *49*(3), pp. 251–56.

Parr, John B. and Suzuki, Keisuke. Settlement Populations and the Lognormal Distribution. *Urban Stud.,* October 1973, *10*(3), pp. 335–52. [G: U.S.]

Parr, John B. Structure and Size in the Urban System of Lösch. *Econ. Geogr.,* July 1973, *49*(3), pp. 185–212.

Perloff, Harvey S. The Development of Urban Economics in the United States. *Urban Stud.,* October 1973, *10*(3), pp. 289–301. [G: U.S.]

Pickard, Jerome P. Growth of Urbanized Population in the United States: Past, Present, and Future. In *Rasmussen, D. W. and Haworth, C. T., eds.,* 1973, pp. 5–15. [G: U.S.]

Plessas, Demetrius J. Airplane Noise: Some Analytic and Policy Perspectives. *Land Econ.,* February 1973, *49*(1), pp. 14–21. [G: U.S.]

Polk, Lon. The Radical Paradigm and Urban Economics. In *Mattila, J. M. and Thompson, W. R., eds.,* 1973, pp. 206–23. [G: U.S.]

Polzin, Paul E. Urban Employment Models: Estimation and Interpretation. *Land Econ.,* May 1973, *49*(2), pp. 226–32. [G: U.S.]

Prodromidis, Kyprianos P. and Lianos, Theodore P. City Size and Patterns of Employment Structure. In *Mattila, J. M. and Thompson, W. R., eds.,* 1973, pp. 91–104. [G: U.S.]

Prud'homme, Rémy. Costs and Financing of Urban Development in France. *Urban Stud.,* June 1973, *10*(2), pp. 189–98. [G: France]

Rabin, Yale. Highways as a Barrier to Equal Access. *Ann. Amer. Acad. Polit. Soc. Sci.,* May 1973, *407,* pp. 63–77. [G: U.S.]

Ratford, Bruce E. A Note on Niedercorn's Negative Exponential Model of Urban Land Use. *J. Reg. Sci.,* April 1973, *13*(1), pp. 135–38.

Redcliff, M. R. Squatter Settlements in Latin American Cities: The Response from Government. *J. Devel. Stud.,* October 1973, *10*(1), pp. 92–109. [G: S. America]

Reps, John W. Public Land, Urban Development Policy, and the American Planning Tradition. In *Clawson, M., ed.,* 1973, pp. 15–48. [G: U.S.]

Richards, P. J. Job Mobility and Unemployment in the Ceylon Urban Labour Market. *Oxford Bull. Econ. Statist.,* February 1973, *35*(1), pp. 49–59. [G: Ceylon]

Richardson, Harry W. A Comment on Some Uses of Mathematical Models in Urban Economics. *Urban Stud.,* June 1973, *10*(2), pp. 259–66.

Richardson, Harry W. A Comment on Some Uses of Mathematical Models in Urban Economics: Reply to Solow and Mirrlees. *Urban Stud.,* June 1973, *10*(2), pp. 269–70.

Richardson, Harry W. A Guide to Urban Economics Texts: A Review Article. *Urban Stud.,* October 1973, *10*(3), pp. 399–405.

Richardson, Reed C. Delivery Systems for Manpower Services. In *Mangum, G. L. and Robson,*

R. T., eds., 1973, pp. 100–119. [G: U.S.]

Richardson, Reed C. Skills and Jobs for Denver's Disadvantaged. In *Mangum, G. L. and Robson, R. T., eds.,* 1973, pp. 120–33. [G: U.S.]

Richardson, Reed C. The Impact of Denver's Manpower Programs. In *Mangum, G. L. and Robson, R. T., eds.,* 1973, pp. 134–43. [G: U.S.]

Riley, John G. "Gammaville": An Optimal Town. *J. Econ. Theory,* October 1973, *6*(5), pp. 471–82.

Rogers, David. Organizing Manpower Delivery Systems in Big Cities. In *Aronson, R. L., ed.,* 1973, pp. 24–44. [G: U.S.]

Rose, Louis A. The Development Value Tax. *Urban Stud.,* June 1973, *10*(2), pp. 271–75.

Rothenberg, Jerome. Spatial Economics: Discussion. *Amer. Econ. Rev.,* May 1973, *63*(2), pp. 67–70.

Rueter, Frederick H. Externalities in Urban Property Markets: An Empirical Test of the Zoning Ordinance of Pittsburgh. *J. Law Econ.,* October 1973, *16*(2), pp. 313–49. [G: U.S.]

Sacco, John F. Local Government and Air Quality Problems: A Study of Problem Solving Approaches. In *Gabriel, R. A. and Cohen, S. H., eds.,* 1973, pp. 32–60. [G: U.S.]

Sadove, Robert. Urban Needs of Developing Countries. *Finance Develop.,* June 1973, *10*(2), pp. 26–31.

Schweikert, H. Zur Planung der Energieversorgung in städtischen Agglomerationen. (The Planning of Distribution of Energy in Urban Areas. With English summary.) *Schweiz. Z. Volkswirtsch. Statist.,* September 1973, *109*(3), pp. 421–39.

Seskin, Eugene P. Residential Choice and Air Pollution: A General Equilibrium Model. *Amer. Econ. Rev.,* December 1973, *63*(5), pp. 960–67.

Shanahan, James L. Mis-Match in the Supply of and Demand for Low Skill Jobs in the Inner City. In *Mattila, J. M. and Thompson, W. R., eds.,* 1973, pp. 192–205. [G: U.S.]

Sharpe, Ron. Models for Allocation of Water Resources. In *Aislabie, C., ed.,* 1973, pp. 171–76.

Shefer, Daniel. Localization Economies in SMSA'S: A Production Function Analysis. *J. Reg. Sci.,* April 1973, *13*(1), pp. 55–64. [G: U.S.]

Sheshinski, Eytan. Congestion and the Optimum City Size. *Amer. Econ. Rev.,* May 1973, *63*(2), pp. 61–66.

Solow, Robert M. A Comment on Some Uses of Mathematical Models in Urban Economics: Rejoinder—I. *Urban Stud.,* June 1973, *10*(2), pp. 267.

Speare, Alden, Jr.; Speare, Mary C. and Lin, Hui-Sheng. Urbanization, Non-Familial Work, Education, and Fertility in Taiwan. *Population Stud.,* July 1973, *27*(2), pp. 323–34. [G: Taiwan]

Stanfield, J. Ronald and Mullendore, Walter E. A Suggested Form of Benefit-Cost Analysis for an Evaluation of Urban Renewal Projects. *Land Econ.,* February 1973, *49*(1), pp. 81–86.

Sternlieb, George. The City as Sandbox. In *Rasmussen, D. W. and Haworth, C. T., eds.,* 1973, pp. 125–32. [G: U.S.]

Stern, Nicholas. Homogeneous Utility Functions and Equality in "The Optimum Town." A Note. *Swedish J. Econ.,* June 1973, *75*(2), pp. 204–07.

Stitelman, Leonard. The "Base Data-Cluster" Concept: A Regional Approach to a Governmental Information Network. *Mich. Academician,* Spring 1973, *5*(4), pp. 435–40. [G: U.S.]

Sussna, Stephen. Residential Densities or a Fool's Paradise. *Land Econ.,* February 1973, *49*(1), pp. 1–13. [G: U.S.]

Swan, Philip L. Decentralization and the Growth of Urban Manufacturing Employment. *Land Econ.,* May 1973, *49*(2), pp. 212–16. [G: U.S.]

Swanston, Walterene. Community Organizations: The Voice of the Poor. In *Levitan, S. A., ed.,* 1973, pp. 198–225. [G: U.S.]

Syron, Richard F. Administered Prices and the Market Reaction: The Case of Urban Core Property Insurance. *J. Finance,* March 1973, *28*(1), pp. 147–56. [G: U.S.]

Thompson, Charles W. N. and Rath, Gustave J. Planning Solutions Aided by Management and Systems Technology. *Ann. Amer. Acad. Polit. Soc. Sci.,* January 1973, *405*, pp. 151–62.

Thompson, Wilbur R. A Preface to Suburban Economics. In *Masotti, L. H. and Hadden, J. K., eds.,* 1973, pp. 409–30. [G: U.S.]

Thompson, Wilbur R. The City as a Distorted Price System. In *Grieson, R. E., ed.,* 1973, pp. 4–14.

Van Cleef, Eugene. The Economic Relation Between Cities and Their Immediate Environments. *Ohio State U. Bull. Bus. Res.,* November 1973, *48*(11), pp. 4, 6–7. [G: U.S.]

Walter, John P. The City as a Source of Regional Economic Disparity in Latin America. *Rev. Soc. Econ.,* April 1973, *31*(1), pp. 66–84. [G: Latin America]

Watters, Gil. A New Decision for Urban Investment and Pricing Decisions. In *Aislabie, C., ed.,* 1973, pp. 177–78.

Weicher, John C. and Zerbst, Robert H. The Externalities of Neighborhood Parks: An Empirical Investigation. *Land Econ.,* February 1973, *49*(1), pp. 99–105.

Weicher, John C. A Test of Jane Jacobs' Theory of Successful Neighborhoods. *J. Reg. Sci.,* April 1973, *13*(1), pp. 29–40. [G: U.S.]

Weissbourd, Bernard. The Satellite Community as Suburb. In *Masotti, L. H. and Hadden, J. K., eds.,* 1973, pp. 495–532. [G: U.S.]

Wilkinson, R. K. House Prices and the Measurement of Externalities. *Econ. J.,* March 1973, *83*(329), pp. 72–86.

Wilson, James Q. The War on Cities. In *Rasmussen, D. W. and Haworth, C. T., eds.,* 1973, pp. 16–27. [G: U.S.]

Wingo, Lowdon. The Quality of Life: Toward a Microeconomic Definition. *Urban Stud.,* February 1973, *10*(1), pp. 3–18.

932 Housing Economics

9320 Housing Economics (including nonurban housing)

Achtenberg, Emily Paradise. The Social Utility of Rent Control. In *Pynoos, J.; Schafer, R. and Hartman, C. W., eds.,* 1973, pp. 434–47. [G: U.S.]

Ackerman, Bruce. More on Slum Housing and Redis-

tribution Policy: A Reply to Professor Komesar. *Yale Law J.,* May 1973, *82*(6), pp. 1194–1207.

Anderson, Paul S. and Eisenmenger, Robert W. Impact of the Proposed New Financial Structure on Mortgage Markets. In *Federal Reserve Bank of Boston,* 1973, pp. 149–72. [G: U.S.]

Antosenkov, E. G. The Availability of Housing and Personnel Turnover. *Prob. Econ.,* July 1973, *16*(3), pp. 59–76. [G: U.S.S.R.]

Arcelus, Francisco and Meltzer, Allan H. The Markets for Housing and Housing Services: Reply. *J. Money, Credit, Banking,* November 1973, *5*(4), pp. 973–78. [G: U.S.]

Arcelus, Francisco and Meltzer, Allan H. The Markets for Housing and Housing Services. *J. Money, Credit, Banking,* Part I, February 1973, *5*(1), pp. 78–99. [G: U.S.]

Atkinson, L. J. Factors Affecting the Purchase Value of New Houses. In *Haynes, W. W.; Coyne, T. J. and Osborne, D. K., eds.,* 1973, pp. 85–112. [G: U.S.]

Babcock, Richard F. and Callies, David L. Ecology and Housing: Virtues in Conflict. In *Clawson, M., ed.,* 1973, pp. 205–20. [G: U.S.]

von Ball, Michael J. Recent Empirical Work on the Determinants of Relative House Prices. *Urban Stud.,* June 1973, *10*(2), pp. 213–33. [G: U.S.; U.K.]

Barlev, Benzion. Location Effects of Intra-Area Tax Differentials. *Land Econ.,* February 1973, *49*(1), pp. 86–89.

Baxter, Gary L. Indiana Housing Cycle: 1973 Forecast. *Indiana Bus. Rev.,* May-June 1973, *48*, pp. 10–12. [G: U.S.]

Bellush, Jewel and Hausknecht, Murray. Public Housing: The Contexts of Failure. In *Pynoos, J.; Schafer, R. and Hartman, C. W., eds.,* 1973, pp. 114–18. [G: U.S.]

Bloch, Ben W. and Pilgrim, John D. A Reappraisal of Some Factors Associated with Fluctuations in the United States in the Interwar Period. *Southern Econ. J.,* January 1973, *39*(3), pp. 327–44. [G: U. S.]

Boorman, John T. and Peterson, Manferd O. Instability of Savings Flows and Mortgage Lending by Financial Intermediaries. *Southern Econ. J.,* October 1973, *40*(2), pp. 297–312. [G: U.S.]

Boyes, William J. and Peseau, Dennis E. On Optimization in Models of Urban Land Use Densities: Comment. *J. Reg. Sci.,* April 1973, *13*(1), pp. 129–33.

Bradford, David F. and Kelejian, Harry H. An Econometric Model of the Flight to the Suburbs. *J. Polit. Econ.,* May-June 1973, *81*(3), pp. 566–89. [G: U.S.]

Brady, Eugene A. An Econometric Analysis of the U.S. Residential Housing Market. In *Ricks, R. B., ed.,* 1973, pp. 1–47. [G: U.S.]

Branfman, Eric J.; Cohen, Benjamin I. and Trubek, David M. Measuring the Invisible Wall: Land Use Controls and the Residential Patterns of the Poor. *Yale Law J.,* January 1973, *82*(3), pp. 483–508. [G: U.S.]

Brobst, Robert W. and Wrighton, Fred M. The Income Elasticity of Housing: A Cross-Sectional Analysis of New Orleans. *Miss. Val. J. Bus. Econ.,*

Winter 1973-74, *9*(2), pp. 43–58. [G: U.S.]

Burnham, James B. Housing Starts in 1966 and 1969: A Comparison Using an Econometric Model. In *Ricks, R. B., ed.,* 1973, pp. 49–67. [G: U.S.]

Byatt, I. C. R.; Holmans, A. E. and Laidler, David. Income and the Demand for Housing: Some Evidence for Great Britain. In *Parkin, M., ed.,* 1973, pp. 65–84. [G: U.K.]

Carliner, Geoffrey. Income Elasticity of Housing Demand. *Rev. Econ. Statist.,* November 1973, *55*(4), pp. 528–32. [G: U.S.]

Chapman, Wayne E. Real Estate Tax Incentives. *Nat. Tax J.,* September 1973, *26*(3), pp. 389–93. [G: U.S.]

Clauretie, Terrence M. Interest Rates, the Business Demand for Funds, and the Residential Mortgage Market: A Sectoral Econometric Study. *J. Finance,* December 1973, *28*(5), pp. 1313–26. [G: U.S.]

Collard, David. Exclusion by Estate Agents—An Analysis. *Appl. Econ.,* December 1973, *5*(4), pp. 281–88.

Collard, David. Price and Prejudice in the Housing Market. *Econ. J.,* June 1973, *83*(330), pp. 510–15.

Cord, Steven. How Land Value Taxation Would Affect Homeowners. *Amer. J. Econ. Soc.,* April 1973, *32*(2), pp. 153–54. [G: U.S.]

Currie, Lauchlin. The Exchange Constraint on Development—A Partial Solution to the Problem: A Reply. *Econ. J.,* March 1973, *83*(329), pp. 207–10.

DeSalvo, Joseph S. Effects of the Property Tax on Operating and Investment Decisions of Rental Property Owners: Reply. *Nat. Tax J.,* March 1973, *26*(1), pp. 129–31.

Doling, J. F. A Two-Stage Model of Tenure Choice in the Housing Market. *Urban Stud.,* June 1973, *10*(2), pp. 199–211. [G: U.K.]

Eichler, Edward and Kaplan, Marshall. New Communities. In *Pynoos, J.; Schafer, R. and Hartman, C. W., eds.,* 1973, pp. 523–31. [G: U.S.]

English, John. Oatlands: An Area of Twilight Housing in Glasgow. *Urban Stud.,* October 1973, *10*(3), pp. 381–86. [G: U.K.]

Estrup, Jørgen. Er marxistisk økonomi et alternativ? —En analyse af et aktuelt forsøg. (Marxian Economic Theory and the Housing Problem: A Review Article. With English summary.) *Nationalokon. Tidsskr.,* 1973, *111*(1), pp. 165–80. [G: Denmark]

Fair, Ray C. and Jaffee, Dwight M. The Implications of the Proposals of the Hunt Commission for the Mortgage and Housing Markets: An Empirical Study. In *Federal Reserve Bank of Boston,* 1973, pp. 99–148. [G: U.S.]

Fair, Ray C. Monthly Housing Starts. In *Ricks, R. B., ed.,* 1973, pp. 69–91. [G: U.S.]

Field, Charles G. Evaluating the Administrative Delivery of Housing Goals. *Amer. Real Estate Urban Econ. Assoc. J.,* Fall 1973, *1*(2), pp. 21–34. [G: U.S.]

Fisher, Ernest M. Evaluation of National Housing Goals. *Amer. Real Estate Urban Econ. Assoc. J.,* Fall 1973, *1*(2), pp. 5–20.

Fisher, Ernest M. Speculative Development of Residential Land and Residential Structures during the 1920's and the 1960's and 1970's. *Amer. Real Estate Urban Econ. Assoc. J.,* June 1973, *1*(1), pp. 123–39. [G: U.S.]

Foster, C. D. and Whitehead, C. M. E. The Layfield Report on the Greater London Development Plan. *Economica, N.S.,* November 1973, *40*(160), pp. 442–54. [G: U.K.]

Frankenhoff, Charles. The Economics of a Popular Housing Policy. *Land Econ.,* August 1973, *49*(3), pp. 336–43.

Freeman, Roger A. Tax Relief for the Homeowner? *Nat. Tax J.,* September 1973, *26*(3), pp. 485–90. [G: U.S.]

Friedman, Lawrence M. Public Housing and the Poor. In *Pynoos, J.; Schafer, R. and Hartman, C. W., eds.,* 1973, pp. 448–59. [G: U.S.]

Fried, Marc and Gleicher, Peggy. Some Sources of Residential Satisfaction in an Urban Slum. In *Rasmussen, D. W. and Haworth, C. T., eds.,* 1973, pp. 150–59.

Fromm, Gary. Econometric Models of the Residential Construction Sector: A Comparison. In *Ricks, R. B., ed.,* 1973, pp. 125–55. [G: U.S.]

Gans, Herbert J. The Failure of Urban Renewal: A Critique and Some Proposals. In *Rasmussen, D. W. and Haworth, C. T., eds.,* 1973, pp. 160–67. [G: U.S.]

Garrity, Paul G. Redesigning Landlord-Tenant Law for an Urban Society. In *Pynoos, J.; Schafer, R. and Hartman, C. W., eds.,* 1973, pp. 75–86. [G: U.S.]

Gazis, Denos C. Mathematical Modelling of Some Social and Environmental Problems. In *Hawkes, N., ed.,* 1973, pp. 52–59. [G: U.S.]

Gelb, Betsy D. and Enis, Ben M. Affirmative Action in Housing and Beyond. *Calif. Manage. Rev.,* Winter 1973, *16*(2), pp. 24–31. [G: U.S.]

Gibson, William E. Protecting Homebuilding from Restrictive Credit Conditions. *Brookings Pap. Econ. Act.,* 1973, (3), pp. 647–91. [G: U.S.]

Glantz, Frederic B. and Delaney, Nancy J. Changes in Nonwhite Residential Patterns in Large Metropolitan Areas, 1960 and 1970. *New Eng. Econ. Rev.,* March-April 1973, pp. 2–13. [G: U.S.]

Glazer, Nathan. The Bias of American Housing Policy. In *Pynoos, J.; Schafer, R. and Hartman, C. W., eds.,* 1973, pp. 405–22. [G: U.S.]

Goh, Chui Muah. A Note on Housing Finance in Singapore. *Malayan Econ. Rev.,* October 1973, *18*(2), pp. 37–42. [G: Singapore]

Grebler, Leo. Growing Scale of Real Estate Firms and Projects. *Amer. Real Estate Urban Econ. Assoc. J.,* June 1973, *1*(1), pp. 107–22.

Grieson, Ronald E. Poverty: Introduction. In *Grieson, R. E., ed.,* 1973, pp. 273–85. [G: U.S.]

Grieson, Ronald E. Zoning, Housing Markets, and Urban Renewal: Introduction. In *Grieson, R. E., ed.,* 1973, pp. 133–48. [G: U.S.]

Grieson, Ronald E. Effects of the Property Tax on Operating and Investment Decisions of Rental Property Owners: A Note. *Nat. Tax J.,* March 1973, *26*(1), pp. 127–28.

Grieson, Ronald E. The Supply of Rental Housing: Comment. *Amer. Econ. Rev.,* June 1973, *63*(3), pp. 433–36.

Hartman, Chester W. The Politics of Housing. In

Pynoos, J.; Schafer, R. and Hartman, C. W., eds., 1973, pp. 119–28. **[G: U.S.]**

Hoffman, Manfred. Sozialistische Mietenpolitik in der DDR. (Socialist Policy of Housing Rents in the DDR. With English summary.) *Z. ges. Staatswiss.,* May 1973, *129*(2), pp. 246–91. **[G: Germany]**

Hoffman, Manfred. Genossenschaftlicher Wohnungsbau in der DDR. (Cooperative House Construction in the GDR. With English summary.) *Jahr. Nationalökon. Statist.,* August 1973, *187*(6), pp. 522–42. **[G: E. Germany]**

Huang, David S. Short-Run Instability in Single-Family Housing Starts. *J. Amer. Statist. Assoc.,* December 1973, *68*(344), pp. 788–92. **[G: U.S.]**

Hyman, David N. and Pasour, E. C., Jr. Real Property Taxes, Local Public Services, and Residential Property Values. *Southern Econ. J.,* April 1973, *39* (4), pp. 601–11. **[G: U.S.]**

Hyman, David N. and Pasour, E. C., Jr. Note: Property Tax Differentials and Residential Rents in North Carolina. *Nat. Tax J.,* June 1973, *26*(2), pp. 303–07. **[G: U.S.]**

Ingram, Gregory K. and Kain, John F. A Simple Model of Housing Production and the Abandonment Problem. *Amer. Real Estate Urban Econ. Assoc. J.,* June 1973, *1*(1), pp. 79–106. **[G: U.S.]**

Johnston, Verle. Housing: On the Way Down? *Fed. Res. Bank San Francisco Rev.,* January-February 1973, pp. 3–8. **[G: U.S.]**

Kain, John F. Effect of Housing Market Segregation on Urban Development. In *Pynoos, J.; Schafer, R. and Hartman, C. W., eds.,* 1973, pp. 251–66. **[G: U.S.]**

Kalchbrenner, John H. A Summary of the Current Financial Intermediary, Mortgage, and Housing Sectors of the FRB-MIT-Penn Econometric Model. In *Ricks, R. B., ed.,* 1973, pp. 93–124. **[G: U.S.]**

Kasper, H. Measuring the Labour Market Costs of Housing Dislocation. *Scot. J. Polit. Econ.,* June 1973, *20*(2), pp. 85–106. **[G: U.K.]**

Keyes, Langley C., Jr. The Boston Rehabilitation Program. In *Pynoos, J.; Schafer, R. and Hartman, C. W., eds.,* 1973, pp. 472–83. **[G: U.S.]**

King, A. Thomas and Mieszkowski, Peter. Racial Discrimination, Segregation, and the Price of Housing. *J. Polit. Econ.,* May-June 1973, *81*(3), pp. 590–606. **[G: U.S.]**

Komesar, Neil K. Return to Slumville: A Critique of the Ackerman Analysis of Housing Code Enforcement and the Poor. *Yale Law J.,* May 1973, *82*(6), pp. 1175–93.

Kosoff, Allen. Incentives for Urban Apartment Construction. *Amer. J. Econ. Soc.,* July 1973, *32*(3), pp. 295–305.

Kristof, Frank S. The Role of State Housing Finance and Development Agencies in Future Federal Housing Programs. *Amer. Real Estate Urban Econ. Assoc. J.,* Fall 1973, *1*(2), pp. 53–72. **[G: U.S.]**

Kristof, Frank S. Federal Housing Policies: Subsidized Production, Filtration and Objectives: Part II. *Land Econ.,* May 1973, *49*(2), pp. 163–74. **[G: U.S.]**

Lapping, Mark B. The Emergence of Federal Public Housing: Atlanta's Techwood Project. *Amer. J.*

Econ. Soc., October 1973, *32*(4), pp. 379–86. **[G: U.S.]**

de Leeuw, Frank and Ekanem, Nkanta F. Time Lags in the Rental Housing Market. *Urban Stud.,* February 1973, *10*(1), pp. 39–68. **[G: U.S.]**

de Leeuw, Frank and Ekanem, Nkanta F. The Supply of Rental Housing: Reply. *Amer. Econ. Rev.,* June 1973, *63*(3), pp. 437–38.

LeRoy, Stephen F. Property Tax Assessment: How Fair Is It? *Fed. Res. Bank Kansas City Rev.,* July-August 1973, pp. 7–16. **[G: U.S.]**

Lilley, William, III. The Homebuilders' Lobby. In *Pynoos, J.; Schafer, R. and Hartman, C. W., eds.,* 1973, pp. 30–48. **[G: U.S.]**

Lin, Steven A. Y. Effects of Monetary Policy and Credit Conditions on the Housing Sector. *Amer. Real Estate Urban Econ. Assoc. J.,* June 1973, *1*(1), pp. 8–30. **[G: U.S.]**

Marcuse, Peter. The Rise of Tenant Organizations. In *Pynoos, J.; Schafer, R. and Hartman, C. W., eds.,* 1973, pp. 49–54. **[G: U.S.]**

Marcus, Morton J. The Indiana Housing Market: An Alternative View. *Indiana Bus. Rev.,* May-June 1973, *48*, pp. 13–14. **[G: U.S.]**

Maxwell, James A. Income Tax Discrimination Against the Renter. *Nat. Tax J.,* September 1973, *26*(3), pp. 491–97. **[G: U.S.]**

Meyer, Eugene L. Urban Renewal and Housing: Rhetoric and Realtiy. In *Levitan, S. A., ed.,* 1973, pp. 226–58. **[G: U.S.]**

Mikesell, James J. Mobile Homes: An Important New Element in Rural Housing. *Agr. Finance Rev.,* July 1973, *34*, pp. 18–23. **[G: U.S.]**

Miller, L. Charles, Jr. The Economics of Housing Code Enforcement. *Land Econ.,* February 1973, *49*(1), pp. 92–96.

Mollenkopf, John and Pynoos, Jon. Boardwalk and Park Place: Property Ownership, Political Structure, and Housing Policy at the Local Level. In *Pynoos, J.; Schafer, R. and Hartman, C. W., eds.,* 1973, pp. 55–74. **[G: U.S.]**

Morton, Henry W. Handbook of Soviet Social Science Data: Housing. In *Mickiewicz, E., ed.,* 1973, pp. 119–35. **[G: U.S.S.R.]**

Muth, Richard F. The Determinants of Dwelling-Unit Condition. In *Pynoos, J.; Schafer, R. and Hartman, C. W., eds.,* 1973, pp. 239–50. **[G: U.S.]**

Muth, Richard F. Capital and Current Expenditures in the Production of Housing. In *Harriss, C. L., ed.,* 1973, pp. 65–78. **[G: U.S.]**

Nelson, Robert H. Accessibility and Rent: Applying Becker's "Time Price" Concept to the Theory of Residential Location. *Urban Stud.,* February 1973, *10*(1), pp. 83–86.

Netzer, Dick. The Incidence of the Property Tax Revisited. *Nat. Tax J.,* December 1973, *26*(4), pp. 515–35. **[G: U.S.]**

Netzer, Dick. Effects of the Property Tax in Urban Areas. In *Pynoos, J.; Schafer, R. and Hartman, C. W., eds.,* 1973, pp. 510–22. **[G: U.S.]**

Nicholson, R. J. and Topham, N. Step-wise Regression and Principal Components Analysis in Estimating a Relationship in an Econometric Model. *Manchester Sch. Econ. Soc. Stud.,* June 1973, *41* (2), pp. 187–205.

Nicholson, R. J. Income and the Demand for Housing: Some Evidence for Great Britain: Discussion. In *Parkin, M., ed.*, 1973, pp. 85–88. [G: U.K.]

Niedercorn, John H. A Negative Exponential Model of Urban Land Use Densities and Its Implications for Metropolitan Development: Reply. *J. Reg. Sci.*, April 1973, *13*(1), pp. 139–40.

Nowotny, Ewald. On the Incidence of Real Estate Taxation. *Z. Nationalökon.*, 1973, *33*(1–2), pp. 133–60.

Ogur, Jonathan D. Higher Education and Housing: The Impact of Colleges and Universities on Local Rental Housing Markets. *Amer. J. Econ. Soc.*, October 1973, *32*(4), pp. 387–94. [G: U.S.]

Onibokun, Adepoju. Forces Shaping the Physical Environment of Cities in the Developing Countries: The Ibadan Case. *Land Econ.*, November 1973, *49*(4), pp. 424–31. [G: Nigeria]

Penner, Rudolph G. and Silber, William L. The Interaction Between Federal Credit Programs and the Impact on the Allocation of Credit. *Amer. Econ. Rev.*, December 1973, *63*(5), pp. 838–52. [G: U.S.]

Penner, Rudolph G. Housing and Community Development. In *Ott, D. J., et al.*, 1973, pp. 91–111. [G: U.S.]

Peterson, Manferd O. Some Evidence on Intra-regional Differences in Yields of Costs of Mortgage Lending. *Land Econ.*, February 1973, *49*(1), pp. 96–99.

Piven, Frances Fox and Cloward, Richard A. The Case Against Urban Desegregation. In *Pynoos, J.; Schafer, R. and Hartman, C. W., eds.*, 1973, pp. 97–107. [G: U.S.]

Pollock, Richard. Supply of Residential Construction: A Cross-Section Examination of Recent Housing Market Behavior. *Land Econ.*, February 1973, *49*(1), pp. 57–66. [G: U.S.]

Pozen, Robert. The Financing of Local Housing Authorities: A Contract Approach for Public Corporations. *Yale Law J.*, May 1973, *82*(6), pp. 1208–27.

Pynoos, Jon; Schafer, Robert and Hartman, Chester W. Housing Urban America: Introduction. In *Pynoos, J.; Schafer, R. and Hartman, C. W., eds.*, 1973, pp. 1–12. [G: U.S.]

Racster, Ronald L. and Howard, Robert. Evaluation of Multiple Subsidy Programs in a Local Market. *Amer. Real Estate Urban Econ. Assoc. J.*, Fall 1973, *1*(2), pp. 104–18. [G: U.S.]

Ranis, Gustav. The Exchange Constraint on Development—A Partial Solution to the Problem: A Comment. *Econ. J.*, March 1973, *83*(329), pp. 203–07.

Ratford, Bruce E. A Note on Niedercorn's Negative Exponential Model of Urban Land Use. *J. Reg. Sci.*, April 1973, *13*(1), pp. 135–38.

Riley, Kathleen M. An Estimate of the Age Distribution of the Dwelling Stock in Great Britain. *Urban Stud.*, October 1973, *10*(3), pp. 373–79. [G: U.K.]

Rolph, Earl R. Discriminating Effects of the Income Tax Treatment of Owner-Occupants. *Nat. Tax J.*, September 1973, *26*(3), pp. 471–84. [G: U.S.]

Rothman, Jack. The Ghetto Makers. In *Pynoos, J.; Schafer, R. and Hartman, C. W., eds.*, 1973,

pp. 274–78. [G: U.S.]

Rubinowitz, Leonard S. A Question of Choice: Access of the Poor and the Black to Suburban Housing. In *Masotti, L. H. and Hadden, J. K., eds.*, 1973, pp. 329–66. [G: U.S.]

Rueter, Frederick H. Externalities in Urban Property Markets: An Empirical Test of the Zoning Ordinance of Pittsburgh. *J. Law Econ.*, October 1973, *16*(2), pp. 313–49. [G: U.S.]

Sadove, Robert. Urban Needs of Developing Countries. *Finance Develop.*, June 1973, *10*(2), pp. 26–31.

Schafer, Robert and Field, Charles G. Section 235 of the National Housing Act: Homeownership for Low-income Families? In *Pynoos, J.; Schafer, R. and Hartman, C. W., eds.*, 1973, pp. 460–71. [G: U.S.]

Schechter, Henry B. Federally Subsidized Housing Program Benefits. In *Harriss, C. L., ed.*, 1973, pp. 31–63. [G: U.S.]

Schwirian, Kent P. and Bleda, Sharon E. Ecological and Socio-Economic Factors in Neighborhood Housing Conditions: The Case of the Cleveland Metropolitan Area. *Ohio State U. Bull. Bus. Res.*, January 1973, *48*(1), pp. 1–3, 6–7. [G: U.S.]

Shannon, John. Residential Property Tax Relief—A Federal Responsibility? *Nat. Tax J.*, September 1973, *26*(3), pp. 499–513. [G: U.S.]

Shuman, Howard E. Federal Housing Policy and the HUD Bureaucracy. In *Haveman, R. H. and Hamrin, R. D., eds.*, 1973, pp. 243–49. [G: U.S.]

Silber, William L. A Model of Federal Home Loan Bank System and Federal National Mortgage Association Behavior. *Rev. Econ. Statist.*, August 1973, *55*(3), pp. 308–20. [G: U.S.]

Skouras, Athanassios. On the Analysis of Property Tax Effects on Operating and Investment Decisions of Rental Property Owners. *Nat. Tax J.*, March 1973, *26*(1), pp. 123–25.

Slater, Paul B. Spatial and Temporal Effects in Residential Sales Prices. *J. Amer. Statist. Assoc.*, September 1973, *68*(343), pp. 554–61. [G: U.S.]

Smith, Lawrence B. Evaluating National Housing Criteria in Canada. *Amer. Real Estate Urban Econ. Assoc. J.*, Fall 1973, *1*(2), pp. 35–51. [G: Canada]

Solomon, Arthur P. Housing and Public Policy Analysis. In *Pynoos, J.; Schafer, R. and Hartman, C. W., eds.*, 1973, pp. 558–77. [G: U.S.]

Steger, Wilbur A. Economic and Social Costs of Residential Segregation. In *Clawson, M., ed.*, 1973, pp. 83–113. [G: U.S.]

Stegman, Michael A. Private Participation in Low-income Housing. In *Pynoos, J.; Schafer, R. and Hartman, C. W., eds.*, 1973, pp. 532–35. [G: U.S.]

Stoddard, Ellwyn R. The Adjustment of Mexican American Barrio Families to Forced Housing Relocation. *Soc. Sci. Quart.*, March 1973, *53*(4), pp. 749–59. [G: U.S.]

Stokes, Charles J. How the General Accounting Office Evaluates Urban Housing Policies: An Analysis of Criteria and Procedures. *Amer. Real Estate Urban Econ. Assoc. J.*, Fall 1973, *1*(2), pp. 88–103. [G: U.S.]

Stone, Michael E. Federal Housing Policy: A Political-Economic Analysis. In *Pynoos, J.; Schafer, R. and Hartman, C. W., eds.*, 1973, pp. 423–33. [G: U.S.]

Straszheim, Mahlon R. Estimation of the Demand for Urban Housing Services from Household Interview Data. *Rev. Econ. Statist.*, February 1973, *55*(1), pp. 1–8. [G: U.S.]

Stull, William J. A Note on Residential Bid Price Curves. *J. Reg. Sci.*, April 1973, *13*(1), pp. 107–13.

Sugden, Robert and Williams, Alan. The Location Choices of Students in Lodgings and Flats. *Urban Stud.*, February 1973, *10*(1), pp. 87–90. [G: U.K.]

Sussna, Stephen. Residential Densities or a Fool's Paradise. *Land Econ.*, February 1973, *49*(1), pp. 1–13. [G: U.S.]

Swan, Craig. Housing Subsidies and Housing Starts. *Amer. Real Estate Urban Econ. Assoc. J.*, Fall 1973, *1*(2), pp. 119–40. [G: U.S.]

Swan, Craig. The Markets for Housing and Housing Services: Comment. *J. Money, Credit, Banking*, November 1973, *5*(4), pp. 960–72. [G: U.S.]

Wallich, Henry C. Discussion of the Implications of the Proposals of the Hunt Commission for the Mortgage and Housing Markets: An Empirical Study and Impact of the Proposed New Financial Structure on Mortgage Markets. In *Federal Reserve Bank of Boston*, 1973, pp. 173–78. [G: U.S.]

Weaver, Robert C. Housing and Associated Problems of Minorities. In *Clawson, M., ed.*, 1973, pp. 49–81. [G: U.S.]

Weicher, John C. A Test of Jane Jacobs' Theory of Successful Neighborhoods. *J. Reg. Sci.*, April 1973, *13*(1), pp. 29–40. [G: U.S.]

Welfeld, Irving H. Toward a New Federal Housing Policy. In *Grieson, R. E., ed.*, 1973, pp. 200–13. [G: U.S.]

Welfeld, Irving H. Toward a New Federal Housing Policy. In *Pynoos, J.; Schafer, R. and Hartman, C. W., eds.*, 1973, pp. 543–47. [G: U.S.]

Whitehead, C. M. E. Inflation and the New Housing Market. *Oxford Bull. Econ. Statist.*, November 1973, *35*(4), pp. 275–93. [G: U.K.]

Wilkinson, R. K. House Prices and the Measurement of Externalities. *Econ. J.*, March 1973, *83*(329), pp. 72–86.

Wilkinson, R. K. The Income Elasticity of Demand for Housing. *Oxford Econ. Pap.*, November 1973, *25*(3), pp. 361–77. [G: U.K.]

Winger, Alan R. Some Internal Determinants of Upkeep Spending by Urban Home-Owners. *Land Econ.*, November 1973, *49*(4), pp. 474–79. [G: U.S.]

Zimmer, Basil G. Residential Mobility and Housing. *Land Econ.*, August 1973, *49*(3), pp. 344–50. [G: U.S.]

933 Urban Transportation Economics

9330 Urban Transportation Economics

Abelson, P. W. Quantification of Road User Costs: A Comment with Special Reference to Thailand. *J. Transp. Econ. Policy*, January 1973, *7*(1), pp. 80–97. [G: Thailand]

Abe, Masatoshi A. The Peak Load Pricing Problem in Urban Transportation. *Econ. Stud. Quart.*, December 1973, *24*(3), pp. 54–62.

Averous, Christian P. and Lee, Douglass B., Jr. Land Allocation and Transportation Pricing in a Mixed Economy. *J. Reg. Sci.*, August 1973, *13*(2), pp. 173–85.

Baum, Herbert J. Free Public Transport. *J. Transp. Econ. Policy*, January 1973, *7*(1), pp. 3–19. [G: W. Germany]

Beesley, Michael E. and Dalvi, M. Q. The Journey to Work and Cost-benefit Analysis. In *Wolfe, J. N., ed.*, 1973, pp. 195–221. [G: U.K.]

Beesley, Michael E. Regulation of Taxis. *Econ. J.*, March 1973, *83*(329), pp. 150–72. [G: U.K.]

Bohley, Peter. Der Nulltarif im Nahverkehr. (Free Transit in Metropolitan Areas. With English summary.) *Kyklos*, 1973, *26*(1), pp. 113–42.

Borukhov, Eli. City Size and Transportation Costs. *J. Polit. Econ.*, September-October 1973, *81*(5), pp. 1205–15.

Cesario, Frank J. A Generalized Trip Distribution Model. *J. Reg. Sci.*, August 1973, *13*(2), pp. 233–47. [G: U.S.]

Coles, O. B. An Economic Comparison of Urban Railways and Express Bus Services: Comment. *J. Transp. Econ. Policy*, September 1973, *7*(3), pp. 295–97. [G: U.K.]

Downing, Paul B. Factors Affecting Commercial Land Values: An Empirical Study of Milwaukee, Wisconsin. *Land Econ.*, February 1973, *49*(1), pp. 44–56. [G: U.S.]

Eckert, Ross D. On the Incentives of Regulators: The Case of Taxicabs. *Public Choice*, Spring 1973, *14*, pp. 83–99. [G: U.S.]

Faure, Robert. Mathematical Models in the Design and Operation of Public Transport Systems. In *Hawkes, N., ed.*, 1973, pp. 41–50. [G: France]

Foster, C. D. A Note on the Treatment of Taxation in Cost-benefit Analysis. In *Wolfe, J. N., ed.*, 1973, pp. 63–74. [G: U.K.]

Frankena, Mark. Income Distributional Effects of Urban Transit Subsidies. *J. Transp. Econ. Policy*, September 1973, *7*(3), pp. 215–30. [G: Canada]

Garrison, W. L. Fragments on Future Transportation Policy and Programs. *Econ. Geogr.*, April 1973, *49*(2), pp. 95–102.

Gazis, Denos C. Mathematical Modelling of Some Social and Environmental Problems. In *Hawkes, N., ed.*, 1973, pp. 52–59. [G: U.S.]

Heinrich, K. On Forecasting New Techniques in Passenger Transport. In *Blohm, H. and Steinbuch, K., eds.*, 1973, pp. 67–72. [G: W. Germany]

Horton, Frank E.; Louviere, Jordan and Reynolds, David R. Mass Transit Utilization: Individual Response Data Inputs. *Econ. Geogr.*, April 1973, *49*(2), pp. 122–33. [G: U.S.]

Hurst, Michael E. Eliot. Transportation and the Societal Framework. *Econ. Geogr.*, April 1973, *49*(2), pp. 163–80.

Kalachek, Edward D. Ghetto Dwellers, Transportation and Employment. In *Rasmussen, D. W. and Haworth, C. T., eds.*, 1973, pp. 72–80. [G: U.S.]

Kraft, Gerald. Free Transit Revisited. *Public Policy*, Winter 1973, *21*(1), pp. 79–105. [G: U.S.]

Kutter, Eckhard. A Model for Individual Travel Behaviour. *Urban Stud.*, June 1973, *10*(2), pp. 235–58.

Mantell, Edmund H. Suboptimal Land Use Induced by Transportation Planning for New Towns. *Land Econ.*, February 1973, *49*(1), pp. 89–92.

McDonough, Carol C. The Demand for Commuter Rail Transport. *J. Transp. Econ. Policy*, May 1973, *7*(2), pp. 134–43. [G: U.S.]

McKay, Roberta V. Commuting Patterns of Inner-City Residents. *Mon. Lab. Rev.*, November 1973, *96*(11), pp. 43–48. [G: U.S.]

Meyer, John R. Knocking Down the Straw Men. In *Rasmussen, D. W. and Haworth, C. T., eds.*, 1973, pp. 190–98. [G: U.S.]

Meyer, John R. and Kain, John F. Transportation and Poverty. In *Grieson, R. E., ed.*, 1973, pp. 323–35. [G: U.S.]

Mumphrey, Anthony J. and Wolpert, Julian. Equity Considerations and Concessions in the Siting of Public Facilities. *Econ. Geogr.*, April 1973, *49*(2), pp. 109–21. [G: U.S.]

Pearce, David and Nash, Christopher. The Evaluation of Urban Motorway Schemes: A Case Study—Southampton. *Urban Stud.*, June 1973, *10*(2), pp. 129–43.

Rabin, Yale. Highways as a Barrier to Equal Access. *Ann. Amer. Acad. Polit. Soc. Sci.*, May 1973, *407*, pp. 63–77. [G: U.S.]

Renshaw, Edward F. A Note on Mass Transit Subsidies. *Nat. Tax J.*, December 1973, *26*(4), pp. 638–44. [G: U.S.]

Segelhorst, Elbert W. and Kirkus, Larry D. Parking Bias in Transit Choice. *J. Transp. Econ. Policy*, January 1973, *7*(1), pp. 58–70. [G: U.S.]

Shoup, Donald C. Cost Effectiveness of Urban Traffic Law Enforcement. *J. Transp. Econ. Policy*, January 1973, *7*(1), pp. 32–57. [G: U.S.]

Slater, Paul B. Spatial and Temporal Effects in Residential Sales Prices. *J. Amer. Statist. Assoc.*, September 1973, *68*(343), pp. 554–61. [G: U.S.]

Slavin, Richard H. and Devine, Edward J. Multi-Discipline Design Teams for Transportation Facilities. *Land Econ.*, August 1973, *49*(3), pp. 241–50.

Smith, Edward. An Economic Comparison of Urban Railways and Express Bus Services. *J. Transp. Econ. Policy*, January 1973, *7*(1), pp. 20–31. [G: U.K.]

Smith, Edward. An Economic Comparison of Urban Railways and Express Bus Services: Rejoinder. *J. Transp. Econ. Policy*, September 1973, *7*(3), pp. 297–99. [G: U.K.]

Solow, Robert M. Congestion Cost and the Use of Land for Streets. *Bell J. Econ. Manage. Sci.*, Autumn 1973, *4*(2), pp. 602–18.

Stern, Martin O. and Ayres, Robert U. Transportation Outlays: Who Pays and Who Benefits? In *Harriss, C. L., ed.*, 1973, pp. 117–54. [G: U.S.]

Stutz, Frederick P. Distance and Network Effects on Urban Social Travel Fields. *Econ. Geogr.*, April 1973, *49*(2), pp. 134–44. [G: U.S.]

White, P. R. An Economic Comparison of Urban Railways and Express Bus Services: Comment. *J. Transp. Econ. Policy*, September 1973, *7*(3), pp. 294–95. [G: U.K.]

940 REGIONAL ECONOMICS

941 Regional Economics

9410 General

Allegri, Vincenzo. La politica industriale delle Regioni. (The Industrial Policy of the Italian Regions. With English summary.) *L'industria, N. S.*, 1973, (1), pp. 15–24. [G: Italy]

Alonso, William. The Mirage of New Towns. In *Grieson, R. E., ed.*, 1973, pp. 213–28. [G: U.S.]

Aronson, J. Richard and Schwartz, Eli. Financing Public Goods and the Distribution of Population in a System of Local Governments. *Nat. Tax J.*, June 1973, *26*(2), pp. 137–60. [G: U.S.]

Balassa, Bela. Regional Policies and the Environment in the European Common Market. *Weltwirtsch. Arch.*, 1973, *109*(3), pp. 402–17. [G: E.E.C.]

Bandera, V. N. and Melnyk, Z. Lew. The Soviet Economy in Regional Perspective: Introduction. In *Bandera, V. N. and Melnyk, Z. L., eds.*, 1973, pp. xvii–xxi. [G: U.S.S.R.]

Billon, S. A. Centralization of Authority and Regional Management. In *Bandera, V. N. and Melnyk, Z. L., eds.*, 1973, pp. 214–34. [G: U.S.S.R.]

Blohm, Margareta and Ohlsson, Ingvar. Experience in Measurement of Welfare Components and their Regional Implications. *Rev. Income Wealth*, June 1973, *19*(2), pp. 167–88. [G: Sweden]

von Böventer, Edwin. City Size Systems: Theoretical Issues, Empirical Regularities and Planning Guides. *Urban Stud.*, June 1973, *10*(2), pp. 145–62.

Brownrigg, M. The Regional Income Multiplier: An Attempt to Complete the Model: A Correction. *Scot. J. Polit. Econ.*, June 1973, *20*(2), pp. 193.

Comay, Yochanan and Kirschenbaum, Alan. The Israeli New Town: An Experiment at Population Redistribution. *Econ. Develop. Cult. Change*, October 1973, *22*(1), pp. 124–34. [G: Israel]

Conroy, Michael E. Rejection of Growth Center Strategy in Latin American Regional Development Planning. *Land Econ.*, November 1973, *49*(4), pp. 371–80. [G: Latin America]

Cook, Gail C. A. Metropolitan Government: The Significance of Context and Form. In *Mattila, J. M. and Thompson, W. R., eds.*, 1973, pp. 164–74. [G: Canada]

Cooper, Leon. N-Dimensional Location Models: An Application to Cluster Analysis. *J. Reg. Sci.*, April 1973, *13*(1), pp. 41–54.

Crvcanin, Milan. Application de modèles intégrés à la planification des systèmes de transports de la région lausannoise. (Integrated Models Used in Lausanne Area Transportation Study. With English summary.) *Schweiz. Z. Volkswirtsch. Statist.*, September 1973, *109*(3), pp. 357–73. [G: Switzerland]

Dellepiane, Nicola. Localizzazione delle attività interne: metodi quantitativi di ottimizzazione. (Locating facilities: Optimizing Techniques. With English summary.) *L'Impresa*, 1973, *15*(2), pp. 157–63.

Dorling, M. J. Extending the Production-Distribution Model to Handle International Competition in Agriculture. *Can. J. Agr. Econ.*, February 1973, *21*(1), pp. 57–62.

Elovikov, L. A. Ways of Creating Social and Economic Conditions for the Reproduction of Labor Power in the New Regions of the West Siberian Plains. *Prob. Econ.*, June 1973, *16*(2), pp. 42–54. [G: U.S.S.R.]

Elzinga, Kenneth G. and Hogarty, Thomas F. The Problem of Geographic Market Delineation in Antimerger Suits. *Antitrust Bull.*, Spring 1973, *18*(1), pp. 45–81. [G: U.S.]

Ezra, Derek. Regional Policy in the European Community. *Nat. Westminster Bank Quart. Rev.*, August 1973, pp. 8–21. [G: Europe]

Ferrara, Reno. Le concentrazioni economico-spaziali nelle decisioni localizzative degli impianti. (Industrial Linkages in the Decisions Taken for the Localization of Installations. With English summary.) *L'Impresa*, 1973, *15*(2), pp. 123–27.

Fitch, Lyle C. Metropolitan Financial Problems. In *Grieson, R. E., ed.*, 1973, pp. 418–28. [G: U.S.]

Foster, C. D. and Whitehead, C. M. E. The Layfield Report on the Greater London Development Plan. *Economica, N.S.*, November 1973, *40*(160), pp. 442–54. [G: U.K.]

Friedmann, John. Education for Regional Planning in Developing Countries. In *Friedmann, J.*, 1973, pp. 299–309.

Friedmann, John. Hyperurbanization and National Development in Chile. In *Friedmann, J.*, 1973, pp. 91–114. [G: Chile]

Friedmann, John. Problems of Spatial Development in the Capital Region of Chile. In *Friedmann, J.*, 1973, pp. 187–226. [G: Chile]

Friedmann, John. Social Dimensions of Urban Development. In *Friedmann, J.*, 1973, pp. 115–29. [G: Chile]

Friedmann, John. The Implementation of Regional Development Policies: Lessons of Experience. In *Friedmann, J.*, 1973, pp. 235–54.

Friedmann, John. The Urban-Regional Frame for National Development. In *Friedmann, J.*, 1973, pp. 139–51.

Friedmann, John and Stöhr, Walter. The Uses of Regional Science: Policy Planning in Chile. In *Friedmann, J.*, 1973, pp. 255–74. [G: Chile]

Friedmann, John, et al. Towards a National Urbanization Policy. In *Friedmann, J.*, 1973, pp. 153–86.

Fuller, Stephen S. Social and Economic Factors in Federal Building Location Decisions. *Growth Change*, April 1973, *4*(2), pp. 43–48. [G: U.S.]

Fulton, Richard M. Interregional Development and Urban Tribalism in Africa: Comment. *Growth Change*, April 1973, *4*(2), pp. 38–39. [G: Africa]

Garrison, Charles B. and Paulson, Albert S. An Entropy Measure of the Geographic Concentration of Economic Activity. *Econ. Geogr.*, October 1973, *49*(4), pp. 319–24. [G: U.S.]

Genovese, Nicola M. and Sobbrio, Giuseppe. Regional Inequality and the Market Mechanism: Comment. *Kyklos*, 1973, *26*(3), pp. 621–23. [G: Italy]

Goldstein, Gerald S. and Moses, Leon N. A Survey of Urban Economics. *J. Econ. Lit.*, June 1973, *11*(2), pp. 471–515.

Hamilton, F. E. Ian. Spatial Dimensions of Soviet Economic Decision Making. In *Bandera, V. N. and Melnyk, Z. L., eds.*, 1973, pp. 235–60. [G: U.S.S.R.]

Hansen, Niles M. Urbanism and Regional Disparities in Developed Countries. *Rev. Soc. Econ.*, April 1973, *31*(1), pp. 54–65.

Hansen, Niles M. A Growth Center Strategy for the United States. In *Rasmussen, D. W. and Haworth, C. T., eds.*, 1973, pp. 267–82. [G: U.S.]

Haveman, Robert H. The Ex Post Evaluation of Navigation Improvements. In *Niskanen, W. A., et al., eds.*, 1973, pp. 249–76. [G: U.S.]

Hibdon, James E., et al. Market Areas in Spatial Duopoly. *Rivista Int. Sci. Econ. Com.*, March 1973, *20*(3), pp. 267–77.

Hoffmann, Pavel. Methodological Aspects of Prognoses in the Regional Development of the National Economy. *Czech. Econ. Digest.*, November 1973, (7), pp. 56–73. [G: Czechoslovakia]

Holmes, J. C. An Ordinal Method of Evaluation: A Rejoinder. *Urban Stud.*, February 1973, *10*(1), pp. 101–04.

Holubnychy, Vsevolod. Spatial Efficiency in the Soviet Economy. In *Bandera, V. N. and Melnyk, Z. L., eds.*, 1973, pp. 1–44. [G: U.S.S.R.]

Hurst, Michael E. Eliot. Transportation and the Societal Framework. *Econ. Geogr.*, April 1973, *49*(2), pp. 163–80.

Ingram, Helen M. The Political Economy of Regional Water Institutions. *Amer. J. Agr. Econ.*, February 1973, *55*(1), pp. 10–18. [G: U.S.]

Jensen, Robert G. Regional Pricing and the Economic Evaluation of Land in Soviet Agriculture. In *Bandera, V. N. and Melnyk, Z. L., eds.*, 1973, pp. 305–27. [G: U.S.S.R.]

Jensen, Rodney C. Aspects of The Spatial Dimension in Economics. *Econ. Anal. Pol.*, March 1973, *4*(1), pp. 1–16.

Johnson, Björn and Meuller, Anders. Interactions of Consumption and Metropolitan Growth. *Swedish J. Econ.*, September 1973, *75*(3), pp. 278–88. [G: Sweden]

Johnson, G. P. and Steiner, H. M. Evaluating Social Roads in Mexico. *J. Transp. Econ. Policy*, January 1973, *7*(1), pp. 98–101. [G: Mexico]

Joshi, N. D. Review of the Policy for the Development of Backward Regions in India. *Artha-Vikas*, January-July 1973, *9*(1–2), pp. 11–24. [G: India]

Joshi, V. H. The Concept of Regional Analysis: Its Application to the Study of the Development of Backward Regions. *Artha-Vikas*, January-July 1973, *9*(1–2), pp. 64–68.

Kale, J. D. Attracting Industries to Backward Areas. *Artha-Vikas*, January-July 1973, *9*(1–2), pp. 245–48. [G: India]

Kettle, Peter and Whitbread, Michael. An Ordinal Method of Evaluation: A Comment. *Urban Stud.*, February 1973, *10*(1), pp. 95–99.

Klaasen, Thomas A. Regional Comparative Advantage in the United States. *J. Reg. Sci.*, April 1973, *13*(1), pp. 97–105. [G: U.S.]

Kotzenberg, H. R. P. A. The Policy and Programme for the Decentralisation of Industry in South

Africa. *Finance Trade Rev.,* December 1973, *10* (4), pp. 137–67. [G: S. Africa]

Lahikainen, Pekka. Finnish Regional Development Policy. In *Moskoff, W., ed.,* 1973, pp. 140–44. [G: Finland]

Lasuén, J. R. Urbanisation and Development—the Temporal Interaction between Geographical and Sectoral Clusters. *Urban Stud.,* June 1973, *10*(2), pp. 163–88.

Lever, William F. A Markov Approach to the Optimal Size of Cities in England and Wales. *Urban Stud.,* October 1973, *10*(3), pp. 353–65. [G: U.K.]

Loboda, I. On Certain Ways of Restructuring the Countryside. *Prob. Econ.,* January 1973, *15*(9), pp. 61–70. [G: U.S.S.R.]

Lynch, Edward. Propositions for Planning New Towns in Venezuela. *J. Devel. Areas,* July 1973, *7*(4), pp. 549–70. [G: Venezuela]

McKee, David L. Regional Inequality and the Market Mechanism: Comment. *Kyklos,* 1973, *26*(3), pp. 624–26. [G: Italy]

Metwally, Mohktar M. and Jensen, Rodney C. A Note on the Measurement of Regional Income Dispersion. *Econ. Develop. Cult. Change,* October 1973, *22*(1), pp. 135–36.

Meyer, John R.; Kain, John F. and Wohl, Martin. Economic Change and the City: A Qualitative Evaluation and Some Hypotheses. In *Grieson, R. E., ed.,* 1973, pp. 55–72. [G: U.S.]

Mirrlees, James A. A Comment on Some Uses of Mathematical Models in Urban Economics: Rejoinder—II. *Urban Stud.,* June 1973, *10*(2), pp. 267–69.

Moor, R. Carl. The Economic Efficiency of Mixed Financing of Education in Economic Space. *Public Finance Quart.,* October 1973, *1*(4), pp. 399–408.

Moore, John R., Jr. Planning an Efficient Regional Health System. In *Stein, B. and Miller, S. M., eds.,* 1973, pp. 13–35. [G: U.S.]

Morrison, Peter A. A Demographic Assessment of New Cities and Growth Centers as Population Redistribution Strategies. *Public Policy,* Summer 1973, *21*(3), pp. 367–82. [G: U.S.]

Myers, Myron G.; Rogstad, Barry K. and Wehner, Harrison G. A Theoretical Evaluation of Alternative Subsidy Schemes for Regional Development. *Amer. J. Agr. Econ.,* May 1973, *55*(2), pp. 304–12.

Nobukuni, Makoto and Fukuchi, Takao. The Economic Measurement of the Benefit of Public Transportation Investment. (In Japanese. With English summary.) *Econ. Stud. Quart.,* December 1973, *24*(3), pp. 43–53.

Nuttall, T. The Industry Act and Regional Policy. *Nat. Westminster Bank Quart. Rev.,* November 1973, pp. 55–68. [G: U.K.]

Nye, Richard C. The Indiana Economic Forum. *Indiana Bus. Rev.,* May-June 1973, *48*, pp. 19–20. [G: U.S.]

Oslizlok, J. S. Community Regional Policy. *Irish Banking Rev.,* December 1973, pp. 15–22. [G: E.E.C.]

Owen, Carol and Witton, Ronald A. National Division and Mobilization: A Reinterpretation of Primacy. *Econ. Develop. Cult. Change,* January 1973, *21*(2), pp. 325–37.

Oza, Ghanshyambhai. Inaugural Speech. *Artha-Vikas,* January-July 1973, *9*(1–2), pp. 5–10. [G: India]

Paraskevopoulos, Christos C. Shifts in Industry Employment, Population Size and the Wage Structure: An Analysis of Two National Industries. In *Mattila, J. M. and Thompson, W. R., eds.,* 1973, pp. 105–25. [G: U.S.]

Paraskevopoulos, Christos C. The Impact of Regional Wage Differentials. *Growth Change,* April 1973, *4*(2), pp. 40–42. [G: U.S.]

Parr, John B. and Suzuki, Keisuke. Settlement Populations and the Lognormal Distribution. *Urban Stud.,* October 1973, *10*(3), pp. 335–52. [G: U.S.]

Patankar, H. R. Some Observations about Efficacy of Financial Incentives on Industrial Development in Backward Districts. *Artha-Vikas,* January-July 1973, *9*(1–2), pp. 220–29. [G: India]

Patel, V. G. Promotion of Entrepreneurship and Regional Development. *Artha-Vikas,* January-July 1973, *9*(1–2), pp. 214–19.

Pathak, H. N. Developing Entrepreneurship in Backward Regions. *Artha-Vikas,* January-July 1973, *9*(1–2), pp. 47–54. [G: India]

Pathak, Mahesh T. Development of Backward Areas: Problems and Prospects. *Artha-Vikas,* January-July 1973, *9*(1–2), pp. 25–46. [G: India]

Patrucco, Carlo. Ricerche geo-commerciali. (Geo-Commercial Research. With English summary.) *L'Impresa,* 1973, *15*(1), pp. 40–44.

Patterson, D. Jeanne. Indiana's Regions: How Delimited? *Indiana Bus. Rev.,* January-February 1973, *48*, pp. 10–20. [G: U.S.]

Perloff, Harvey S. The Development of Urban Economics in the United States. *Urban Stud.,* October 1973, *10*(3), pp. 289–301. [G: U.S.]

Perroux, François. Multinational Investments and the Analysis of Development and Integration Poles. *Écon. Soc.,* May-June 1973, *7*(5–6), pp. 831–68.

Peterson, Manferd O. Some Evidence on Intraregional Differences in Yields of Costs of Mortgage Lending. *Land Econ.,* February 1973, *49*(1), pp. 96–99.

Polzin, Paul E. Urban Employment Models: Estimation and Interpretation. *Land Econ.,* May 1973, *49*(2), pp. 226–32. [G: U.S.]

Richardson, Harry W. A Comment on Some Uses of Mathematical Models in Urban Economics: Reply to Solow and Mirrlees. *Urban Stud.,* June 1973, *10*(2), pp. 269–70.

Richardson, Harry W. A Comment on Some Uses of Mathematical Models in Urban Economics. *Urban Stud.,* June 1973, *10*(2), pp. 259–66.

Ross, Miceal. Procedures for Integrated Regional Planning. I: The Background to Decentralisation. *Econ. Soc. Rev.,* July 1973, *4*(4), pp. 523–42. [G: Ireland]

Rudamoorthy, B. Financing Agriculture in Backward Regions. *Artha-Vikas,* January-July 1973, *9* (1–2), pp. 139–42. [G: India]

Russell, Clifford S. Application of Microeconomic Models to Regional Environmental Quality Management. *Amer. Econ. Rev.,* May 1973, *63*(2), pp. 236–43.

Salvatore, Dominick. Regional Inequality and the

Market Mechanism: Reply. *Kyklos*, 1973, *26*(3), pp. 627–33. [G: Italy]

Sawicki, David S. Studies of Aggregated Areal Data: Problems of Statistical Inference. *Land Econ.*, February 1973, *49*(1), pp. 109–14. [G: U.S.]

Schlichthaber, Roland. Verkehrsplanung in der Agglomeration aus der Sicht eines Ökonomen. (Traffic Planning in Agglomerations from the Economist's Point of View. With English summary.) *Schweiz. Z. Volkswirtsch. Statist.*, September 1973, *109*(3), pp. 375–84.

Siebert, Horst. Environment and Regional Growth. *Z. Nationalökon.*, 1973, *33*(1–2), pp. 79–85.

Solow, Robert M. A Comment on Some Uses of Mathematical Models in Urban Economics: Rejoinder—I. *Urban Stud.*, June 1973, *10*(2), pp. 267.

Sun, Nai-Ching and Bunamo, Michael C. Competition for Handling U.S. Foreign Trade Cargoes: The Port of New York's Experience. *Econ. Geogr.*, April 1973, *49*(2), pp. 156–62. [G: U.S.]

Takeuchi, Keiichi. Tendenze recenti degli studi di geografia economica in Giappone. (Recent Trends in the Studies of Economic Geography in Japan. With English summary.) *Rivista Int. Sci. Econ. Com.*, August-September 1973, *20*(8–9), pp. 918–26. [G: Japan]

Tefertiller, K. R. Rural Development in an Urban Age. *Amer. J. Agr. Econ.*, December 1973, *55*(5), pp. 771–77. [G: U.S.]

Thomas, George. Regional Migration Patterns and Poverty Among the Aged in the South. *J. Human Res.*, Winter 1973, *8*(1), pp. 73–84. [G: U.S.]

Tideman, T. Nicolaus. Defining Area Distress in Unemployment. *Public Policy*, Fall 1973, *21*(4), pp. 441–92. [G: U.S.]

Tweeten, Luther G. Emerging Issues for Sparsely Populated Areas and Regions Under a National Growth Policy. *Amer. J. Agr. Econ.*, December 1973, *55*(5), pp. 840–50. [G: U.S.]

Wagener, Hans-Jürgen. Rules of Location and the Concept of Rationality: The Case of the USSR. In *Bandera, V. N. and Melnyk, Z. L., eds.*, 1973, pp. 63–103. [G: U.S.S.R.]

Waters, Alan Rufus. Interregional Development and Urban Tribalism in Africa. *Growth Change*, April 1973, *4*(2), pp. 30–37. [G: Africa]

Weicher, John C. A Test of Jane Jacobs' Theory of Successful Neighborhoods. *J. Reg. Sci.*, April 1973, *13*(1), pp. 29–40. [G: U.S.]

Wolf, Charles, Jr. and Weinschrott, David. International Transactions and Regionalism: Distinguishing "Insiders" from "Outsiders." *Amer. Econ. Rev.*, May 1973, *63*(2), pp. 52–60.

Woroniak, Alexander. Regional Aspects of Soviet Planning and Industrial Organization. In *Bandera, V. N. and Melnyk, Z. L., eds.*, 1973, pp. 261–304. [G: U.S.S.R.]

9411 Theory of Regional Economics

Adhvaryu, J. H. Area Development and the Theory of Multiplier. *Artha-Vikas*, January-July 1973, *9*(1–2), pp. 55–63.

Aganbegian, A. G. and Bagrinovsky, K. A. Problem-Complexes in Optimal Planning. *Acta Oecon.*, 1973, *10*(1), pp. 21–27.

Alessio, Frank J. A Neo-Classical Land Use Model: The Influence of Externalities. *Swedish J. Econ.*, December 1973, *75*(4), pp. 414–19.

Alessio, Frank J. Multiple Criteria in Environmental Control: Use of Economic Maximization Rules to Determine Relative Standards. In *Cochrane, J. L. and Zeleny, M., eds.*, 1973, pp. 544–49.

Alonso, William. A Theory of the Urban Land Market. In *Grieson, R. E., ed.*, 1973, pp. 45–55.

Brechling, Frank. Wage Inflation and the Structure of Regional Unemployment. *J. Money, Credit, Banking*, Part II, February 1973, *5*(1), pp. 355–79.

Collier, George A., Jr. On the Size and Spacing of Growth Centers: Comment. *Growth Change*, October 1973, *4*(4), pp. 47–48.

Colwell, Peter F. Florence, Gini, and Mr. Lorenz: Consider the Possibilities. In *Mattila, J. M. and Thompson, W. R., eds.*, 1973, pp. 58–68.

Dacey, Michael F. A Central Focus Cluster Process for Urban Dispersion. *J. Reg. Sci.*, April 1973, *13*(1), pp. 77–89.

Dökmeci, Vedia F. An Optimization Model for a Hierarchical Spatial System. *J. Reg. Sci.*, December 1973, *13*(3), pp. 439–51.

Eaton, B. Curtis. Comment on "Duopoly and Space." *Can. J. Econ.*, February 1973, *6*(1), pp. 124–27.

Emerson, David L. Optimum Firm Location and the Theory of Production. *J. Reg. Sci.*, December 1973, *13*(3), pp. 335–47.

Friedmann, John. A Theory of Polarized Development. In *Friedmann, J.*, 1973, pp. 41–64.

Friedmann, John. The Role of Cities in National Development. In *Friedmann, J.*, 1973, pp. 21–39.

Friedmann, John, et al. Urbanization and National Development: A Comparative Analysis. In *Friedmann, J.*, 1973, pp. 65–90.

Fujita, Masahisa. Optimum Growth in Two-Region, Two-Good Space Systems: The Final State Problem. *J. Reg. Sci.*, December 1973, *13*(3), pp. 385–407.

Gannon, Colin A. Central Concentration in Simple Spatial Duopoly: Some Behavioral and Functional Conditions. *J. Reg. Sci.*, December 1973, *13*(3), pp. 357–75.

Gannon, Colin A. Optimization of Market Share in Spatial Competition. *Southern Econ. J.*, July 1973, *40*(1), pp. 66–79.

Greenhut, M. L. and Ohta, H. Spatial Configurations and Competitive Equilibrium. *Weltwirtsch. Arch.*, 1973, *109*(1), pp. 87–104.

Hale, Carl W. Impact of Technological Change on Urban Market Areas, Land Values, and Land Uses. *Land Econ.*, August 1973, *49*(3), pp. 351–56.

Hartnett, Harry D. A Locational Analysis of Manufacturing Plants within the City of Chicago: 1959–1968. *Amer. Real Estate Urban Econ. Assoc. J.*, June 1973, *1*(1), pp. 31–47. [G: U.S.]

Hartwick, John M. and Hartwick, Philip G. Reply to Comment by B. C. Eaton. *Can. J. Econ.*, February 1973, *6*(1), pp. 127–28.

Hartwick, John M. Lösch's Theorem on Hexagonal Market Areas. *J. Reg. Sci.*, August 1973, *13*(2), pp. 213–21.

Higgins, Benjamin. Trade-Off Curves and Regional Gaps. In *[Rosenstein-Rodan, P.]*, 1973, pp. 152–77. [G: Canada]

Holt, Charles C. Wage Inflation and the Structure of Regional Unemployment: Comment. *J. Money, Credit, Banking*, Part II, February 1973, *5*(1), pp. 380–81.

Koropeckyj, I. S. Regional Resource Allocation, Growth, and Income Inequality under Socialism. In *Bandera, V. N. and Melnyk, Z. L., eds.*, 1973, pp. 45–62. [G: E. Europe]

Kottis, Athena P. Community Effects of an Income Maintenance Plan: A Theoretical Exploration. In *Mattila, J. M. and Thompson, W. R., eds.*, 1973, pp. 41–57. [G: U.S.]

Legey, L.; Ripper, M. and Varaiya, P. Effects of Congestion on the Shape of a City. *J. Econ. Theory*, April 1973, *6*(2), pp. 162–79.

Lewis, William Cris. Public Investment Impacts and Regional Economic Growth. *Water Resources Res.*, August 1973, *9*(4), pp. 851–60.

Lind, Robert C. Spatial Equilibrium, the Theory of Rents, and the Measurement of Benefits from Public Programs. *Quart. J. Econ.*, May 1973, *87* (2), pp. 188–207.

Livesey, D. A. Optimum City Size: A Minimum Congestion Cost Approach. *J. Econ. Theory*, April 1973, *6*(2), pp. 144–61.

Lucas, Robert E., Jr. Wage Inflation and the Structure of Regional Unemployment: Comment. *J. Money, Credit, Banking*, Part II, February 1973, *5*(1), pp. 382–84.

Mattila, John M. A Metropolitan Income Determination Model and the Estimation of Metropolitan Income Multipliers. *J. Reg. Sci.*, April 1973, *13*(1), pp. 1–16. [G: U.S.]

Nelson, Robert H. Accessibility and Rent: Applying Becker's "Time Price" Concept to the Theory of Residential Location. *Urban Stud.*, February 1973, *10*(1), pp. 83–86.

Oakland, W. H.; Sparrow, Frederick T. and Stettler, H. Louis, III. More on Ghetto Multipliers. *J. Reg. Sci.*, April 1973, *13*(1), pp. 127–28. [G: U.S.]

Odland, J.; Casetti, Emilio and King, L. J. Testing Hypotheses of Polarized Growth Within a Central Place Hierarchy. *Econ. Geogr.*, January 1973, *49*(1), pp. 74–79.

Richardson, Harry W. A Markov Chain Model of Interregional Savings and Capital Growth. *J. Reg. Sci.*, April 1973, *13*(1), pp. 17–27.

Riew, John. Migration and Public Policy. *J. Reg. Sci.*, April 1973, *13*(1), pp. 65–76.

Sakashita, Noboru and Kamoike, Osamu. National Growth and Regional Income Inequality: A Consistent Model. *Int. Econ. Rev.*, June 1973, *14*(2), pp. 372–82.

Solow, Robert M. On Equilibrium Models of Urban Location. In *Parkin, M., ed.*, 1973, pp. 2–16.

Stull, William J. A Note on Residential Bid Price Curves. *J. Reg. Sci.*, April 1973, *13*(1), pp. 107–13.

Tiebout, Charles M. A Method of Determining Incomes and Their Variation in Small Regions. In *Grieson, R. E., ed.*, 1973, pp. 19–25.

Van der Tak, Herman G. and Ray, Anandarup. The Economic Benefits of Road Transport Projects. In *Niskanen, W. A., et al., eds.*, 1973, pp. 132–73.

Webber, M. J. and Symanski, Richard. Periodic Markets: An Economic Location Analysis. *Econ. Geogr.*, July 1973, *49*(3), pp. 213–27.

Woodward, Robert S. The Iso-Outlay Function and Variable Transport Costs. *J. Reg. Sci.*, December 1973, *13*(3), pp. 349–55.

Zinam, Oleg. The Dilemma of Specialization versus Autarky in the USSR: Issues and Solutions. In *Bandera, V. N. and Melnyk, Z. L., eds.*, 1973, pp. 196–213. [G: U.S.S.R.]

9412 Regional Economic Studies

Ahlbrandt, Roger S., Jr. Efficiency in the Provision of Fire Services. *Public Choice*, Fall 1973, *16*, pp. 1–15. [G: U.S.]

Alagh, Yoginder K. and Pathak, Pravin G. Industrial Development in Gujarat: Regional Structure and Policies. *Artha-Vikas*, January-July 1973, *9*(1–2), pp. 143–84. [G: India]

Alderfer, Evan B. Changing Times on Pennsylvania Farms. *Fed. Res. Bank Bus. Rev. Phila.*, May 1973, pp. 18–26. [G: U.S.]

Archer, R. W. Land Speculation and Scattered Development; Failures in the Urban-Fringe Land Market. *Urban Stud.*, October 1973, *10*(3), pp. 367–72. [G: U.S.]

Arndt, H. W. Regional Income Estimates. *Bull. Indonesian Econ. Stud.*, November 1973, *9*(3), pp. 87–102. [G: Indonesia]

Atwood, Janet. Energy Resources in New Mexico. *N. Mex. Bus.*, May 1973, *26*(5), pp. 3–10. [G: U.S.]

Azfar, Javaid. The Distribution of Income in Pakistan—1966–67. *Pakistan Econ. Soc. Rev.*, Spring 1973, *11*(1), pp. 40–66. [G: Pakistan]

Bandera, V. N. Interdependence between Interregional and International Payments: The Balance of Payments of Ukraine. In *Bandera, V. N. and Melnyk, Z. L., eds.*, 1973, pp. 132–53. [G: U.S.S.R.]

Bauch, Vlastislav. The Effect of the Economic Policy of the Communist Party of Czechoslovakia on the Material Situation of the Population of Slovakia. *Czech. Econ. Digest.*, June 1973, (4), pp. 34–56. [G: Czechoslovakia]

Baxter, Gary L. Indiana Housing Cycle: 1973 Forecast. *Indiana Bus. Rev.*, May-June 1973, *48*, pp. 10–12. [G: U.S.]

Beck, E. M.; Dotson, Louis and Summers, Gene F. Effects of Industrial Development on Heads of Households. *Growth Change*, July 1973, *4*(3), pp. 16–19. [G: U.S.]

Bell, R. T. Some Aspects of Industrial Decentralization in South Africa. *S. Afr. J. Econ.*, December 1973, *41*(4), pp. 401–31. [G: S. Africa]

Bergonzini, Luciano. Professionalità femminile e lavoro a domicilio: Questioni generali ed esiti di un'indagine statistica in alcuni comuni dell'Emilia-Romagna. (Women's Professional Status and Work at Home: Some General Questions and Some Results of a Statistical Inquiry in a Few Municipalities of the Emilia-Romagna Region (Italy). With English summary.) *Statistica*, October-December 1973, *33*(4), pp. 492–546. [G: Italy]

Berry, Brian J. L. and Cohen, Yehoshua S. Decentralization of Commerce and Industry: The Restructuring of Metropolitan America. In *Masotti, L. H. and Hadden, J. K., eds.*, 1973, pp. 431–55. [G: U.S.]

Biggs, Joseph R. Emigration of Industry from Ohio. *Ohio State U. Bull. Bus. Res.*, February 1973, *48* (2), pp. 4–7. [G: U.S.]

Black, William R. Toward a Factorial Ecology of Flows. *Econ. Geogr.*, January 1973, *49*(1), pp. 59–67. [G: U.S.]

Blake, C. The Gains from Regional Policy. In *Wolfe, J. N., ed.*, 1973, pp. 185–94. [G: U.K.]

Boesen, Jannik. Peasants and Coffee Export. In *Institute for Development Research*, 1973, pp. 79–100.

Boni, Milena. Il problema della localizzazione industriale. L'Europa occidentale: recenti esperienze e prospettive. (The Problem of Industrial Localization. Western Europe: Recent Experiences and Prospectives. With English summary.) *L'Impresa*, 1973, *15*(2), pp. 100–04. [G: E.E.C.]

Bradley, Iver E.; Mangum, Garth L. and Robson, R. Thayne. Impact of Manpower Programs upon Employment and Earnings. In *Mangum, G. L. and Robson, R. T., eds.*, 1973, pp. 227–59. [G: U.S.]

Bretzfelder, Robert B. Sensitivity of State and Regional Income to National Business Cycles. *Surv. Curr. Bus.*, April 1973, *53*(4), pp. 22–33. [G: U.S.]

Bretzfelder, Robert B. State and Regional Personal Income, 1959–1972. *Surv. Curr. Bus.*, August 1973, *53*(8), pp. 39–49. [G: U.S.]

Bromley, Daniel W. and Beattie, Bruce R. On the Incongruity of Program Objectives and Project Evaluation: An Example from the Reclamation Program. *Amer. J. Agr. Econ.*, August 1973, *55*(3), pp. 472–76. [G: U.S.]

Brownrigg, M. The Economic Impact of a New University. *Scot. J. Polit. Econ.*, June 1973, *20*(2), pp. 123–39. [G: U.K.]

Burki, Shahid J. Rapid Population Growth and Urbanization: The Case of Pakistan. *Pakistan Econ. Soc. Rev.*, Autumn 1973, *11*(3), pp. 239–76. [G: Pakistan]

Cebula, Richard J. and Gatons, Paul K. Interregional Factor Prices and Mobility. *Pakistan Econ. Soc. Rev.*, Summer 1973, *11*(2), pp. 207–14. [G: U.S.]

Cebula, Richard J.; Kohn, Robert M. and Vedder, Richard K. Some Determinants of Interstate Migration of Blacks, 1965–1970. *Western Econ. J.*, December 1973, *11*(4), pp. 500–05. [G: U.S.]

Cebula, Richard J. The City as a Source of Regional Economic Disparity in Latin America: Comment. *Rev. Soc. Econ.*, April 1973, *31*(1), pp. 85–88. [G: Latin America]

Cebula, Richard J. and Vedder, Richard K. A Note on Migration, Economic Opportunity, and the Quality of Life. *J. Reg. Sci.*, August 1973, *13*(2), pp. 205–11. [G: U.S.]

Cebula, Richard J.; Kohn, Robert M. and Gallaway, Lowell E. Determinants of Net Migration to SMSA's, 1960–1970. *Miss. Val. J. Bus. Econ.*, Winter 1973-74, *9*(2), pp. 59–64. [G: U.S.]

Cesario, Frank J. A Generalized Trip Distribution Model. *J. Reg. Sci.*, August 1973, *13*(2), pp. 233–47. [G: U.S.]

Chakravorty, S. K. Tenant Farmers in Changing Agriculture of West Bengal. *Econ. Aff.*, September-October 1973, *18*(9–10), pp. 428–33. [G: India]

Chapman, G. P. The Spatial Organization of the Population of the United States and England and Wales. *Econ. Geogr.*, October 1973, *49*(4), pp. 325–43. [G: U.S.; U.K.]

Christian, Charles M. and Bennett, Sari J. Industrial Relocations from the Black Community of Chicago. *Growth Change*, April 1973, *4*(2), pp. 14–20. [G: U.S.]

Clemente, Frank. Effects of Industrial Development on Heads of Households: Comment. *Growth Change*, July 1973, *4*(3), pp. 20–21. [G: U.S.]

Clemente, Frank and Sturgis, Richard B. Population Size and Industrial Diversification: A Rejoinder. *Urban Stud.*, October 1973, *10*(3), pp. 397. [G: U.S.]

Crowley, Ronald W. Reflections and Further Evidence on Population Size and Industrial Diversification. *Urban Stud.*, February 1973, *10*(1), pp. 91–94. [G: Canada]

Crowley, Ronald W. A Case Study of the Effects of an Airport on Land Values. *J. Transp. Econ. Policy*, May 1973, *7*(2), pp. 144–52. [G: Canada]

Dahyabhai, Indulal. Industrial Development of Backward Areas in Gujarat. *Artha-Vikas*, January-July 1973, *9*(1–2), pp. 240–44. [G: India]

Daly, M. T. and Webber, M. J. The Growth of the Firm Within the City. *Urban Stud.*, October 1973, *10*(3), pp. 303–17. [G: Australia]

Daroesman, Ruth. An Economic Survey of Bali. *Bull. Indonesian Econ. Stud.*, November 1973, *9*(3), pp. 28–61. [G: Indonesia]

De Castro, Tina. Gli insediamenti industriali: documentazione. (Industrial Localization. With English summary.) *L'Impresa*, 1973, *15*(2), pp. 132–44. [G: Italy]

Dematteis, Giuseppe. Politica regionale e scelte aziendali nella localizzazione delle industrie in Gran Bretagna. (Regional Politics and Firm Selections in the Localization of Industry in Great Britain. With English summary.) *L'Impresa*, 1973, *15* (2), pp. 113–22. [G: U.K.]

Dixon, Orani; Dixon, Peter and Miranowski, John. Insecticide Requirements in an Efficient Agricultural Sector. *Rev. Econ. Statist.*, November 1973, *55*(4), pp. 423–32. [G: U.S.]

Dixon, R. J. Regional Specialisation and Trade in the United Kingdom: A Test of Some Hypotheses. *Scot. J. Polit. Econ.*, June 1973, *20*(2), pp. 159–70. [G: U.K.]

Eastman, Clyde, et al. Labor Mobility in Northcentral New Mexico. *N. Mex. Bus.*, June 1973, *26*(6), pp. 3–9. [G: U.S.]

Epley, D. R. Construction of Income and Employment Indexes as a Test of Base Theory. *Land Econ.*, August 1973, *49*(3), pp. 365–67. [G: U.S.]

Evans, Alan W. The Location of the Headquarters of Industrial Companies. *Urban Stud.*, October 1973, *10*(3), pp. 387–95. [G: U.K.; U.S.]

Farbman, Michael. Income Concentration in the Southern United States. *Rev. Econ. Statist.*, August 1973, *55*(3), pp. 333–40. [G: U.S.]

Fowler, Loretta. The Arapahoe Ranch: An Experiment in Cultural Change and Economic Development. *Econ. Develop. Cult. Change,* April 1973, *21*(3), pp. 446–64. [G: U.S.]

Freund, James L. A Note on Short Period Changes in Earned Income in Manufacturing Among Urban Areas. *J. Reg. Sci.,* August 1973, *13*(2), pp. 279–89. [G: U.S.]

Friedman, Judith J. Variations in the Level of Central Business District Retail Activity Among Large U.S. Cities: 1954 and 1967. *Land Econ.,* August 1973, *49*(3), pp. 326–35. [G: U.S.]

Friedmann, John. An Approach to the Development of New Core Regions: The Guayana Program in a Regional Perspective. In *Friedmann, J.,* 1973, pp. 273–86. [G: Venezuela]

Gallardo, Lloyd. The San Francisco-Oakland Bay Area. In *Mangum, G. L. and Robson, R. T., eds.,* 1973, pp. 147–53. [G: U.S.]

Gallaway, Lowell E. and Cebula, Richard J. Differentials and Indeterminacy in Wage Rate Analysis: An Empirical Note. *Ind. Lab. Relat. Rev.,* April 1973, *26*(3), pp. 991–95.

Garnaut, Ross and Manning, Chris M. An Economic Survey of West Irian, Part II. *Bull. Indonesian Econ. Stud.,* March 1973, *9*(1), pp. 30–64. [G: Indonesia]

Gauthier, Howard L. The Appalachian Development Highway System: Development for Whom? *Econ. Geogr.,* April 1973, *49*(2), pp. 103–08. [G: U.S.]

Gerlach, Knut and Liepmann, Peter. Industrialisierung und Siedlungsstruktur—Bemerkungen zum regionalpolitischen Programm einer aktiven Sanierung der bayerischen Rückstandsgebiete. (Industrialization and Settlement Structure—Remarks on the Regional Program of the Promotion of Less Developed Regions in Bavaria. With English summary.) *Jahr. Nationalökon. Statist.,* August 1973, *187*(6), pp. 507–21. [G: W. Germany]

Ghali, Moheb A. Exports, Investment, and Regional Growth. *Southern Econ. J.,* October 1973, *40*(2), pp. 289–96. [G: U.S.]

Glenn, Norval D. Suburbanization in the United States Since World War II. In *Masotti, L. H. and Hadden, J. K., eds.,* 1973, pp. 51–78. [G: U.S.]

Goff, Phoebe H. Disabled-Worker Beneficiaries Under OASDHI: Regional and State Patterns. *Soc. Sec. Bull.,* September 1973, *36*(9), pp. 3–23. [G: U.S.]

Gohil, B. K. Provision of Infrastructure in Gujarat. *Artha-Vikas,* January-July 1973, *9*(1–2), pp. 69–99. [G: India]

Greenwood, Michael J. The Geographic Mobility of College Graduates. *J. Human Res.,* Fall 1973, *8*(4), pp. 506–15. [G: U.S.]

Grossman, Howard J. Regional Development Districts: A Case Study of Northeastern Pennsylvania. *Growth Change,* October 1973, *4*(4), pp. 4–9. [G: U.S.]

Gupta, S. The Role of the Public Sector in Reducing Regional Income Disparity in Indian Plans. *J. Devel. Stud.,* January 1973, *9*(2), pp. 243–60. [G: India]

Gupta, Satyadev and Lal, Prem. Inter-Regional Transfer of Real Resources: A Case Study of Pakistan, 1948–70. *Indian Econ. Rev.,* April 1973, *8*(1), pp. 39–60. [G: Pakistan]

Hale, Carl W. Growth Centers, Regional Spread Effects, and National Economic Growth. *J. Econ. Bus.,* Fall 1973, *26*(1), pp. 10–18. [G: U.S.]

Hanushek, Eric A. Regional Differences in the Structure of Earnings. *Rev. Econ. Statist.,* May 1973, *55*(2), pp. 204–13. [G: U.S.]

Haran, E. G. P. and Vining, Daniel R., Jr. A Modified Yule-Simon Model Allowing for Intercity Migration and Accounting for the Observed Form of the Size Distribution of Cities. *J. Reg. Sci.,* December 1973, *13*(3), pp. 421–37. [G: U.S.]

Harberger, Arnold C. Costs and Benefits of the Ullum Dam Project: An Analytical Framework and an Empirical Exploration. In *Harberger, A. C.,* 1973, pp. 280–310. [G: Argentina]

Hardoy, Jorge E. Spatial Structure and Society in Revolutionary Cuba. In *Barkin, D. P. and Manitzas, N. R., eds.,* 1973, pp. M265–16. [G: Cuba]

Hart, R. A. Employment Creation in the Development Areas: A Reply. *Scot. J. Polit. Econ.,* June 1973, *20*(2), pp. 171–73.

Harvey, Andrew S. Spatial Variation of Export Employment Multipliers: A Cross-Section Analysis. *Land Econ.,* November 1973, *49*(4), pp. 469–74. [G: Canada]

Haworth, C. T. and Rasmussen, David W. Determinants of Metropolitan Cost of Living Variations. *Southern Econ. J.,* October 1973, *40*(2), pp. 183–92. [G: U.S.]

Hayward, Jack. The Prospects for British Regional Policy in the EEC Context. *J. Common Market Stud.,* June 1973, *11*(4), pp. 287–93. [G: E.E.C.; U.K.]

Horiba, Y. Factor Proportions and the Structure of Interregional Trade: The Case of Japan. *Southern Econ. J.,* January 1973, *39*(3), pp. 381–88. [G: Japan]

Horowitz, Morris A. and Herrnstadt, Irwin L. The Old, the New, and the Other Boston. In *Mangum, G. L. and Robson, R. T., eds.,* 1973, pp. 9–22. [G: U.S.]

Horwitz, Bertrand and Whitehouse, F. Douglas. Soviet Land Value and Enterprise Location. *Land Econ.,* May 1973, *49*(2), pp. 233–37. [G: U.S.S.R.]

Hossain, Mahabub and Quddus, M. A. Some Economic Aspects of Jute Production in Bangladesh—An Inter-District Study. *Bangladesh Econ. Rev.,* July 1973, *1*(3), pp. 269–96. [G: Bangladesh]

Ivanova, R. Concerning the Development of the Eastern Regions and Their Manpower Supply. *Prob. Econ.,* June 1973, *16*(2), pp. 26–41. [G: U.S.S.R.]

Jackson, Carolyn and Velten, Terri. Residence, Race, and Age of Poor Families in 1966. In *Rasmussen, D. W. and Haworth, C. T., eds.,* 1973, pp. 53–71. [G: U.S.]

Jackson, Mark and Jones, E. B. Unemployment and Occupational Wage Changes in Local Labor Markets. *Ind. Lab. Relat. Rev.,* July 1973, *26*(4), pp. 1135–45. [G: U.S.]

James, Franklin J., Jr. and Hughes, James W. A Test of Shift and Share Analysis as a Predictive Device.

J. Reg. Sci., August 1973, *13*(2), pp. 223–31.
[G: U.S.]

James, Franklin J., Jr. and Hughes, James W. The Process of Employment Location Change: An Empirical Analysis. *Land Econ.*, November 1973, *49*(4), pp. 404–13. [G: U.S.]

Johnston, Verle; Levy, Yvonne and Chen, Dean. Boom in the West. *Fed. Res. Bank San Francisco Rev.*, May-June 1973, pp. 3–8. [G: U.S.]

Jones, David E. and Miller, Paul B. Regional Growth and Industrial Change in Ohio: A Shift-Share Analysis. *Ohio State U. Bull. Bus. Res.*, July 1973, *48*(7), pp. 1–4, 8. [G: U.S.]

Jonish, James E. and Kau, James B. State Differentials in Income Inequality. *Rev. Soc. Econ.*, October 1973, *31*(2), pp. 179–90. [G: U.S.]

Kariel, Herbert G. and Vaselenak, Michael J. Waves of Spatial Diffusion Reconsidered: Comment. *J. Reg. Sci.*, August 1973, *13*(2), pp. 291–95.

Keen, Howard, Jr. Pennsylvania's Economy: Cyclically Sensitive and Secularly Sluggish. *Fed. Res. Bank Bus. Rev. Phila.*, August 1973, pp. 10–13. [G: U.S.]

Kehal, H. S. Role of Land Reforms in Punjab's Agricultural Development. *Econ. Aff.*, September-October 1973, *18*(9–10), pp. 434–38, 454. [G: India]

Kerr, Alex. Structure of Final Demand in Perth. *Econ. Rec.*, December 1973, *49*(128), pp. 505–17. [G: Australia]

Khan, Dilawar Ali and Ali, Chaudhari Haider. Income Impact of the Green Revolution. *Pakistan Econ. Soc. Rev.*, Spring 1973, *11*(1), pp. 67–82. [G: Pakistan]

Khandker, R. H. Distribution of Income and Wealth in Pakistan. *Pakistan Econ. Soc. Rev.*, Spring 1973, *11*(1), pp. 1–39. [G: Pakistan]

Khin, Maung Kyi, et al. Process of Communication in Modernisation of Rural Society: A Survey Report on Two Burmese Villages. *Malayan Econ. Rev.*, April 1973, *18*(1), pp. 55–73. [G: Burma]

King, L. J.; Casetti, Emilio and Kissling, C. C. Optimal Transportation Patterns of Single Commodities in Capacitated Networks. In *Judge, G. G. and Takayama, T., eds.*, 1973, pp. 225–42. [G: U.S.; New Zealand]

Kneese, Allen V. Water Quality Management by Regional Authorities in the Ruhr Area with Special Emphasis on the Role of Cost Assessment. In *Grieson, R. E., ed.*, 1973, pp. 251–71. [G: W. Germany]

Kneese, Allen V. and Bower, Blair T. The Delaware Estuary Study: Effluent Charges, Least-Cost Treatment, and Efficiency. In *Enthoven, A. C. and Freeman, A. M., III, eds.*, 1973, pp. 112–21. [G: U.S.]

Koshal, Rajindar K. The Future of Higher Education in the State of Ohio: An Econometric Approach. *Ohio State U. Bull. Bus. Res.*, November 1973, *48* (11), pp. 1–3, 5. [G: U.S.]

de Leeuw, Frank and Ekanem, Nkanta F. Time Lags in the Rental Housing Market. *Urban Stud.*, February 1973, *10*(1), pp. 39–68. [G: U.S.]

Lell, Hans-Joachim. Integrated Regional Development. *Finance Develop.*, June 1973, *10*(2), pp. 23–25, 38.

Leslie, D. G. A Note on the Regional Distribution of Unemployment. *Oxford Bull. Econ. Statist.*, August 1973, *35*(3), pp. 233–37.

Lever, William F. Cyclical Changes in Factors Affecting Industrial Location. *Land Econ.*, May 1973, *49*(2), pp. 218–21. [G: U.K.]

Levy, Yvonne. Recovery in Washington. *Fed. Res. Bank San Francisco Rev.*, September-October 1973, pp. 22–28. [G: U.S.]

Lytle, P. W. and Hill, Lowell D. Opportunities for New Investment in Country Elevator Facilities. *Ill. Agr. Econ.*, July 1973, *13*(2), pp. 6–11. [G: U.S.]

MacKay, R. R. Employment Creation: A Resurrection. *Scot. J. Polit. Econ.*, June 1973, *20*(2), pp. 175–77.

Mangum, Garth L. and Robson, R. Thayne. Metropolitan Impact of Manpower Programs: A Four-City Comparison: Introduction. In *Mangum, G. L. and Robson, R. T., eds.*, 1973, pp. 1–5. [G: U.S.]

Manogaran, Chelvadurai. Economic Feasibility of Irrigating Southern Pipes. *Water Resources Res.*, December 1973, *9*(6), pp. 1485–96. [G: U.S.]

Marcus, Morton J. The Indiana Housing Market: An Alternative View. *Indiana Bus. Rev.*, May-June 1973, *48*, pp. 13–14. [G: U.S.]

McCormick, James A. A Look at Poverty in New Mexico Through the 1970 Census. *N. Mex. Bus.*, June 1973, *26*(6), pp. 10–16. [G: U.S.]

McGregor, John R. Terre Haute, The "No Grow" Industrial Center. *Indiana Bus. Rev.*, March-April 1973, *48*, pp. 14–18. [G: U.S.]

Melnyk, Z. Lew. Regional Contribution to Capital Formation in the USSR: The Case of the Ukrainian Republic. In *Bandera, V. N. and Melnyk, Z. L., eds.*, 1973, pp. 104–31. [G: U.S.S.R.]

Moore, Barry and Rhodes, John. Evaluating the Effects of British Regional Economic Policy. *Econ. J.*, March 1973, *83*(329), pp. 87–110. [G: U.K.]

Morgan, E. Victor. Regional Problems and Common Currencies. *Lloyds Bank Rev.*, October 1973, (110), pp. 19–30. [G: U.K.]

Morrill, Richard L. Waves of Spatial Diffusion: Reply. *J. Reg. Sci.*, August 1973, *13*(2), pp. 297.

Morrill, Richard L. On the Size and Spacing of Growth Centers. *Growth Change*, April 1973, *4* (2), pp. 21–24. [G: U.S.]

Mumphrey, Anthony J. and Wolpert, Julian. Equity Considerations and Concessions in the Siting of Public Facilities. *Econ. Geogr.*, April 1973, *49*(2), pp. 109–21. [G: U.S.]

Murie, A. S., et al. A Survey of Industrial Movement in Northern Ireland between 1965 and 1969. *Econ. Soc. Rev.*, January 1973, *4*(2), pp. 231–44. [G: U.K.]

Nishioka, Hisao and Krumme, Gunter. Location Conditions, Factors and Decisions: An Evaluation of Selected Location Surveys. *Land Econ.*, May 1973, *49*(2), pp. 195–205. [G: Japan; U.S.]

Nunnally, Nelson and Pollina, Ronald. Recent Trends in Industrial Park Location in the Chicago Metropolitan Area. *Land Econ.*, August 1973, *49* (3), pp. 356–61. [G: U.S.]

O'Neill, Helen. Regional Planning in Ireland—The Case for Concentration. *Irish Banking Rev.*, September 1973, pp. 9–20. [G: Ireland]

Onibokun, Adepoju. Forces Shaping the Physical Environment of Cities in the Developing Countries: The Ibadan Case. *Land Econ.*, November 1973, *49*(4), pp. 424–31. [G: Nigeria]

Ousset, Jean and Nègre, Michel. Des comptes nationaux aux comptes régionaux. L'exemple des comptes de l'Agriculture. (Regional and National Accounts: The Example of French Agricultural Accounts. With English summary.) *Revue Écon.*, July 1973, *24*(4), pp. 549–87. [G: France]

Pack, Janet Rothenberg. Determinants of Migration to Central Cities. *J. Reg. Sci.*, August 1973, *13*(2), pp. 249–60. [G: U.S.]

Parr, John B. and Suzuki, Keisuke. Settlement Populations and the Lognormal Distribution. *Urban Stud.*, October 1973, *10*(3), pp. 335–52. [G: U.S.]

Pathak, Mahesh T.; Desai, Mahendra D. and Charan, A. S. Development of Agriculture in Backward Regions of Gujarat: Facts and Issues. *Artha-Vikas*, January-July 1973, *9*(1–2), pp. 100–38. [G: India]

Paulson, Albert S. and Garrison, Charles B. Entropy as a Measure of the Areal Concentration of Water-Oriented Industry. *Water Resources Res.*, April 1973, *9*(2), pp. 263–69.

Pearce, David and Nash, Christopher. The Evaluation of Urban Motorway Schemes: A Case Study—Southampton. *Urban Stud.*, June 1973, *10*(2), pp. 129–43.

Persky, Joseph. The Dominance of the Rural-Industrial South, 1900–1930. *J. Reg. Sci.*, December 1973, *13*(3), pp. 409–19. [G: U.S.]

Pfaff, Anita B. Transfer Payments to Large Metropolitan Poverty Areas: Their Distributive and Poverty-Reducing Effects. In *Boulding, K. E.; Pfaff, M. and Pfaff, A., eds.*, 1973, pp. 93–130. [G: U.S.]

Pickard, Jerome P. Growth of Urbanized Population in the United States: Past, Present, and Future. In *Rasmussen, D. W. and Haworth, C. T., eds.*, 1973, pp. 5–15. [G: U.S.]

Pigram, John J. J. Urban-Rural Conflicts in Urban Water Supply. In *Aislabie, C., ed.*, 1973, pp. 145–54. [G: Australia]

Pinkerton, James R. The Changing Class Composition of Cities and Suburbs. *Land Econ.*, November 1973, *49*(4), pp. 462–69. [G: U.S.]

Prud'homme, Rémy. Costs and Financing of Urban Development in France. *Urban Stud.*, June 1973, *10*(2), pp. 189–98. [G: France]

Rao, M. R. S. N. Proposed Role of GIIC in Industrialisation of Backward Districts. *Artha-Vikas*, January-July 1973, *9*(1–2), pp. 230–39. [G: India]

Raveed, Sion and Renforth, William C. Shifting World Wage Rates: What Do They Mean for Indiana? *Indiana Bus. Rev.*, September-October 1973, *48*, pp. 15–19. [G: U.S.]

Regev, Uri and Schwartz, Aba. Optimal Path of Interregional Investment and Allocation of Water. *Water Resources Res.*, April 1973, *9*(2), pp. 251–62.

Reid, G. K. R. and Thomas, D. A. Pastoral Production, Stocking Rate and Seasonal Conditions. *Quart. Rev. Agr. Econ.*, October 1973, *26*(4), pp. 217–27. [G: Australia]

Renaud, Bertrand M. Conflicts Between National Growth and Regional Income Equality in a Rapidly Growing Economy: The Case of Korea. *Econ. Develop. Cult. Change*, April 1973, *21*(3), pp. 429–45. [G: S. Korea]

Rice, G. Randolph. Poverty and Industrial Growth Patterns: Some Cross-State Evidence. *J. Reg. Sci.*, December 1973, *13*(3), pp. 377–84. [G: U.S.]

Richardson, Reed C. The Economic, Social, and Political Environment. In *Mangum, G. L. and Robson, R. T., eds.*, 1973, pp. 95–99. [G: U.S.]

Ringrose, David R. The Impact of a New Capital City: Madrid, Toledo, and New Castile, 1560–1660. *J. Econ. Hist.*, December 1973, *33*(4), pp. 761–91. [G: Spain]

Robertson, Ross M., et al. The Uncertain Outlook for 1974. *Indiana Bus. Rev.*, November-December 1973, *48*, pp. 3–15. [G: U.S.]

Robinson, Albert J. A Planned New Town: The Canberra Experiment. *Land Econ.*, August 1973, *49*(3), pp. 362–65. [G: Australia]

Sandhu, H. S. and Gupta, J. R. Adoption and Performance of Recommended Practices—A Comparative Study of Two Villages in Ludhiana District. *Econ. Aff.*, August 1973, *18*(8), pp. 389–94. [G: India]

Saraceno, Pasquale. The Process of Industrialization of an Overpopulated Agricultural Area—The Italian Experience. In *[Rosenstein-Rodan, P.]*, 1973, pp. 185–98. [G: Italy]

Schenker, Eric and Bunamo, Michael. A Study of the Corps of Engineers' Regional Pattern of Investments. *Southern Econ. J.*, April 1973, *39*(4), pp. 548–58. [G: U.S.]

Scherer, Frederic M. The Determinants of Industrial Plant Sizes in Six Nations. *Rev. Econ. Statist.*, May 1973, *55*(2), pp. 135–45. [G: Sweden; N. America; France; U.K.; W. Germany]

Schroeder, Gertrude E. Regional Differences in Incomes and Levels of Living in the USSR. In *Bandera, V. N. and Melnyk, Z. L., eds.*, 1973, pp. 167–95. [G: U.S.S.R.]

Schulenberg, T. W. Indiana's Regions: Emerging Policy and Management. *Indiana Bus. Rev.*, March-April 1973, *48*, pp. 19–24. [G: U.S.]

Schwartz, Aba. Interpreting the Effect of Distance on Migration. *J. Polit. Econ.*, September-October 1973, *81*(5), pp. 1153–69. [G: U.S.]

Semple, R. Keith. Recent Trends in the Spatial Concentration of Corporate Headquarters. *Econ. Geogr.*, October 1973, *49*(4), pp. 309–18. [G: U.S.]

Shah, Anil C. and Patel, V. G. An Integrated Strategy for Backward Districts Industrial Development. *Artha-Vikas*, January-July 1973, *9*(1–2), pp. 203–13. [G: India]

Sharman, F. A. A Network Analysis of Airport Accessibility in South Hampshire: A Comment. *J. Transp. Econ. Policy*, January 1973, *7*(1), pp. 102–03. [G: U.K.]

Shefer, Daniel. Localization Economies in SMSA'S: A Production Function Analysis. *J. Reg. Sci.*, April 1973, *13*(1), pp. 55–64. [G: U.S.]

Siegel, Philip H. The Location of Industry and Job Participation: An Econometric Study. *Econ. Aff.*, January–February 1973, *18*(1-2), pp. 54–58. [G: U.S.]

Singh, Balwinder; Rangi, P. S. and Sankhayan, P. L. Relative Contributions of Area and Productivity in Increasing Production of Major Foodgrain Crops in Panjab (1960–61 to 1969–70) *Econ. Aff.*, March 1973, *18*(3), pp. 124–30. [G: India]

Smith, Bruce W. Analysis of the Location of Coal-Fired Power Plants in the Eastern United States. *Econ. Geogr.*, July 1973, *49*(3), pp. 243–50. [G: U.S.]

Smith, Curtis R. Despite Damage by Agnes...District Economy Forges Ahead in '72. *Fed. Res. Bank Bus. Rev. Phila.*, February 1973, pp. 12–18. [G: U.S.]

Stabler, J. C. and Williams, P. R. The Changing Structure of the Central Place Hierarchy. *Land Econ.*, November 1973, *49*(4), pp. 454–58. [G: Canada]

Stewart, Charles T. and Benson, Virginia. Job Migration Linkages Between Smaller SMSAs and Their Hinterlands. *Land Econ.*, November 1973, *49*(4), pp. 432–39. [G: U.S.]

Storgaard, Birgit. A Delayed Proletarianization of Peasants. In *Institute for Development Research*, 1973, pp. 103–25. [G: Tanzania]

Swanson, E. R.; Taylor, C. R. and Welch, L. F. Economically Optimal Levels of Nitrogen Fertilizer for Corn: An Analysis Based on Experimental Data, 1966–71. *Ill. Agr. Econ.*, July 1973, *13*(2), pp. 16–25. [G: U.S.]

Tagliacarne, Guglielmo. The Regions Twenty Years Later: Socio-Economic Dynamics of the Regions Between 1951 and 1971. *Rev. Econ. Cond. Italy*, May 1973, *27*(3), pp. 127–61. [G: Italy]

Taqieddin, Nureddin and Gardner, B. Delworth. Net Migration and Population Distribution in the State of Utah. *Intermountain Econ. Rev.*, Fall 1973, *4*(2), pp. 32–44. [G: U.S.]

Taylor, James R. Industrialization of the Mexican Border Region. *N. Mex. Bus.*, March 1973, *26*(3), pp. 3–9. [G: U.S.; Mexico]

Thomson, Herbert F. Policy Alternatives for Ohio's Electric Power Industry. *Ohio State U. Bull. Bus. Res.*, December 1973, *48*(12), pp. 1–5. [G: U.S.]

Till, Thomas. The Extent of Industrialization in Southern Nonmetro Labor Markets in the 1960's. *J. Reg. Sci.*, December 1973, *13*(3), pp. 453–61. [G: U.S.]

Truu, M. L. Some Effects of Regional Migration. *S. Afr. J. Econ.*, June 1973, *41*(2), pp. 98–110. [G: S. Africa]

Vachha, Homiar S. and Iyengar, Sampath S. Financial Institutions and Backward Regions: A Case Study of Gujarat. *Artha-Vikas*, January-July 1973, *9*(1–2), pp. 185–202. [G: India]

di Vallega, Adalberto. Aree industriali in Piemonte connesse con i porti liguri. (Industrial Areas in Pedemont Connected with Ligurian Harbors. With English summary.) *L'Impresa*, 1973, *15* (5–6), pp. 317–22.

Ventriglia, Ferdinando. Results and Prospects of the Policy for Southern Italy. *Rev. Econ. Cond. Italy*, January-March 1973, *27*(1–2), pp. 5–28. [G: Italy]

Verma, Pramod. Regional Wages and Economic Development: A Case Study of Manufacturing Wages in India, 1950–1960. *J. Devel. Stud.*, October 1973, *10*(1), pp. 16–32. [G: India]

Vinod, H. D. Interregional Comparison of Production Structures. *J. Reg. Sci.*, August 1973, *13*(2), pp. 261–67. [G: U.S.]

Voet, James R. Current Economic Developments. *N. Mex. Bus.*, May 1973, *26*(5), pp. 11–20. [G: U.S.]

Voet, James R. Current Economic Developments in New Mexico: Business Conditions Monthly Summary and Economic Indicators. *N. Mex. Bus.*, June 1973, *26*(6), pp. 17, 26–27. [G: U.S.]

Wagstaff, H. R. Employment Multipliers in Rural Scotland. *Scot. J. Polit. Econ.*, November 1973, *20* (3), pp. 239–61. [G: U.K.]

Walter, John P. The City as a Source of Regional Economic Disparity in Latin America. *Rev. Soc. Econ.*, April 1973, *31*(1), pp. 66–84. [G: Latin America]

Walters, A. A. Investments in Airports and the Economist's Role: John F. Kennedy International Airport: An Example and Some Comparisons. In *Wolfe, J. N., ed.*, 1973, pp. 140–54. [G: U.S.]

Weinand, Herbert C. Some Spatial Aspects of Economic Development in Nigeria. *J. Devel. Areas*, January 1973, *7*(2), pp. 247–63. [G: Nigeria]

White, Desmond A. Some Aspects of Recent In-Migration to the Albuquerque Area. *N. Mex. Bus.*, April 1973, *26*(4), pp. 9–14. [G: U.S.]

White, Fred and Tweeten, Luther G. Optimal School District Size Emphasizing Rural Areas. *Amer. J. Agr. Econ.*, February 1973, *55*(1), pp. 45–53. [G: U.S.]

Whitehouse, F. Douglas. Demographic Aspects of Regional Economic Development in the USSR. In *Bandera, V. N. and Melnyk, Z. L., eds.*, 1973, pp. 154–66. [G: U.S.S.R.]

Widner, Ralph R. Evaluating the Administration of the Appalachian Regional Development Program. *Growth Change*, January 1973, *4*(1), pp. 25–29. [G: U.S.]

Wieand, Kenneth F. Air Pollution and Property Values: A Study of the St. Louis Area. *J. Reg. Sci.*, April 1973, *13*(1), pp. 91–95. [G: U.S.]

Wilson, Ruth. Banking the Boom. *Fed. Res. Bank San Francisco Rev.*, May-June 1973, pp. 9–13. [G: U.S.]

Wrigley, Robert L., Jr. Small Cities Can Help to Revitalize Rural Areas. *Ann. Amer. Acad. Polit. Soc. Sci.*, January 1973, *405*, pp. 55–64. [G: U.S.]

Ylä-Anttila, Pekka. Infrastruktuuri ja teollisuuden kehitys. (Overhead Capital and Industrial Development. With English summary.) *Liiketaloudellinen Aikak.*, 1973, *22*(4), pp. 278–87.

Zink, Lee B. The New Mexico Economy in 1972 and 1973. *N. Mex. Bus.*, January-February 1973, *26* (1-2), pp. 3–7. [G: U.S.]

9413 Regional Economic Models and Forecasts

Ault, David E. and Johnson, Thomas E., Jr. Probabilistic Models Applied to Hospital Planning. *Growth Change*, April 1973, *4*(2), pp. 7–13.

Azhar, B. A.; Chaudhry, M. Ghaffar and Shafique, M. A Model for Forecasting Wheat Production in the Punjab. *Pakistan Develop. Rev.*, Winter 1973, *12* (4), pp. 407–15. [G: Pakistan]

Bagrinovsky, K. A. A System of Models for Central Planning. In *Hawkes, N., ed.*, 1973, pp. 21–30. [G: U.S.S.R.]

Bassoco, Luz María, et al. A Programming Model of an Agricultural District. In *Goreux, L. M. and Manne, A. S., eds.*, 1973, pp. 401–16. [G: Mexico]

Bell, Frederick W. and Fullenbaum, Richard F. The Regional Impact of Resource Management. In *Mattila, J. M. and Thompson, W. R., eds.*, 1973, pp. 11–26. [G: U.S.]

Boyes, William J. and Peseau, Dennis E. On Optimization in Models of Urban Land Use Densities: Comment. *J. Reg. Sci.*, April 1973, *13*(1), pp. 129–33.

Brown, H. James. Shift and Share Projections Revisited: Reply. *J. Reg. Sci.*, April 1973, *13*(1), pp. 121. [G: U.S.]

Buchholz, H. E. Pricing and Allocation Models Applied to Problems of Interregional Trade and Location of Industries. In *Judge, G. G. and Takayama, T., eds.*, 1973, pp. 298–306. [G: W. Germany]

Cicchetti, Charles J., et al. Benefits or Costs? An Assessment of the Water Resources Council's Proposed Principles and Standards. In *Niskanen, W. A., et al., eds.*, 1973, pp. 431–46. [G: U.S.]

Costa, P. and Piasentin, U. A Dynamic Simulation Model of the Urban Development of Venice. In *Hawkes, N., ed.*, 1973, pp. 144–54. [G: Italy]

Crow, Robert Thomas. A Nationally-Linked Regional Econometric Model. *J. Reg. Sci.*, August 1973, *13*(2), pp. 187–204. [G: U.S.]

Cumberland, John H. Dimensions of the Impact of Reduced Military Expenditures on Industries, Regions, and Communities. In *Udis, B., ed.*, 1973, pp. 79–147. [G: U.S.]

Czamanski, Stan. Linkages between Industries in Urban-Regional Complexes. In *Judge, G. G. and Takayama, T., eds.*, 1973, pp. 180–204. [G: U.S.]

Dagenais, Marcel G. Un modèle annuel de prévision pour l'économie du Québec. (An Annual Forecasting Model of the Quebec Economy. With English summary.) *Can. J. Econ.*, February 1973, *6*(1), pp. 62–78. [G: Canada]

Day, Richard H. Recursive Programming Models: A Brief Introduction. In *Judge, G. G. and Takayama, T., eds.*, 1973, pp. 329–44. [G: U.S.]

Edie, Leslie C., et al. Urban Planning. In *Ross, M., ed.*, 1973, pp. 599–615. [G: U.S.]

Fernández de la Garza, Guillermo; Manne, Alan S. and Valencia, José Alberto. Multi-Level Planning for Electric Power Projects. In *Goreux, L. M. and Manne, A. S., eds.*, 1973, pp. 197–231. [G: Mexico]

Floyd, Charles F. and Sirmans, C. F. Shift and Share Projections Revisited. *J. Reg. Sci.*, April 1973, *13*(1), pp. 115–20. [G: U.S.]

Gofman, K. G., et al. Optimal Land Management. *Matekon*, Spring 1973, *9*(3), pp. 71–88.

Gordon, Peter and Lande, Paul S. The Pricing of Goods and Agricultural Land in Multiregional General Equilibrium: Comment. *Southern Econ. J.*, July 1973, *40*(1), pp. 143–44.

Guedry, L. J. An Application of a Multi-Commodity Transportation Model to the U.S. Feed Grain Economy. In *Judge, G. G. and Takayama, T., eds.*, 1973, pp. 243–60. [G: U.S.]

Hartwick, John M. The Pricing of Goods and Agricultural Land in Multiregional General Equilibrium: Reply. *Southern Econ. J.*, July 1973, *40*(1), pp. 144–45.

Heady, Earl O., et al. National and Interregional Models of Water Demand, Land Use, and Agricultural Policies. *Water Resources Res.*, August 1973, *9*(4), pp. 777–91. [G: U.S.]

Hellman, Daryl A. The Spatial Distribution of Unemployment by Occupation: A Further Note. *J. Reg. Sci.*, December 1973, *13*(3), pp. 463–66. [G: U.S.]

Hughes, James C. Population Estimates for Small Area Decision-Makers. In *Gabriel, R. A. and Cohen, S. H., eds.*, 1973, pp. 94–112. [G: U.S.]

Jones, Lonnie L. and Mustafa, Gholam. RIMLOC: A Computer Algorithm for Regional Input-Output Analyses. *Ann. Econ. Soc. Measure*, July 1973, *2*(3), pp. 313–16.

Judge, G. G.; Havlicek, J. and Rizek, R. L. A Spatial Analysis of the U.S. Livestock Economy. In *Judge, G. G. and Takayama, T., eds.*, 1973, pp. 261–73. [G: U.S.]

Kottke, Marvin W. Allocation of Milk Through Space and Time in a Competitively-Mixed Dairy Industry. In *Judge, G. G. and Takayama, T., eds.*, 1973, pp. 557–78. [G: U.S.]

Kutcher, Gary P. On Decomposing Price-Endogenous Models. In *Goreux, L. M. and Manne, A. S., eds.*, 1973, pp. 499–519. [G: Mexico]

Lee, T.-C. and Seaver, S. K. A Positive Model of Spatial Equilibrium with Special Reference to the Broiler Markets. In *Judge, G. G. and Takayama, T., eds.*, 1973, pp. 443–63. [G: U.S.]

Leunis, J. V. and Vandenborre, R. J. An Interregional Analysis of the United States Soybean Industry. In *Judge, G. G. and Takayama, T., eds.*, 1973, pp. 274–97. [G: U.S.]

Maki, Wilbur R. and Angus, James E. Development Planning. In *Judge, G. G. and Takayama, T., eds.*, 1973, pp. 43–64.

Mathur, Vijay K. Models of Air Pollution Damage Control in a Region. In *Mattila, J. M. and Thompson, W. R., eds.*, 1973, pp. 27–40.

Mattila, John M. A Metropolitan Income Determination Model and the Estimation of Metropolitan Income Multipliers. *J. Reg. Sci.*, April 1973, *13*(1), pp. 1–16. [G: U.S.]

Nakayama, Toshiko and Warsky, D. Measuring Regional Price Change in Urban Areas. *Mon. Lab. Rev.*, October 1973, *96*(10), pp. 34–38.

Nelson, Jon P. An Interregional Recursive Programming Model of the U.S. Iron and Steel Industry. In *Judge, G. G. and Takayama, T., eds.*, 1973, pp. 368–93. [G: U.S.]

Niedercorn, John H. A Negative Exponential Model of Urban Land Use Densities and Its Implications for Metropolitan Development: Reply. *J. Reg. Sci.*, April 1973, *13*(1), pp. 139–40.

Paelinck, J. and Van Rompuy, P. Regionaal en sectoraal subsidiebeleid: Economische theorie en modellen. (Regional and Sectoral Subsidies—Economic Theory and Models. With English summary.) *Tijdschr. Econ.*, 1973, *18*(1), pp. 39–55. [G: Belgium]

Pant, S. P. and Takayama, T. An Investigation of Agricultural Planning Models: A Case Study of the Indian's Food Economy. In *Judge, G. G. and Takayama, T., eds.,* 1973, pp. 597–623. [G: India]

Phillips, Bruce D. The Spatial Distribution of Unemployment by Occupation: Reply. *J. Reg. Sci.,* December 1973, *13*(3), pp. 471. [G: U.S.]

Polenske, Karen R. An Analysis of United States Commodity Freight Shipments. In *Judge, G. G. and Takayama, T., eds.,* 1973, pp. 163–79. [G: U.S.]

Povey, George; Uyeno, Dean and Vertinsky, Ilan. Social Impact Index for Evaluation of Regional Resource Allocation. In *Berg, R. L., ed.,* 1973, pp. 104–14. [G: U.S.]

Presman, L. S. A Model of Industrial Location. *Matekon,* Spring 1973, *9*(3), pp. 6–21.

Randall, J. N. Shift-Share Analysis as a Guide to the Employment Performance of West Central Scotland. *Scot. J. Polit. Econ.,* February 1973, *20*(1), pp. 1–26. [G: U.K.]

Ratford, Bruce E. A Note on Niedercorn's Negative Exponential Model of Urban Land Use. *J. Reg. Sci.,* April 1973, *13*(1), pp. 135–38.

Richardson, Harry W. A Markov Chain Model of Interregional Savings and Capital Growth. *J. Reg. Sci.,* April 1973, *13*(1), pp. 17–27.

Richardson, Harry W. The Spatial Distribution of Unemployment by Occupation: A Comment. *J. Reg. Sci.,* December 1973, *13*(3), pp. 467–69. [G: U.S.]

Riefler, Roger F. Interregional Input-Output: A State of the Arts Survey. In *Judge, G. G. and Takayama, T., eds.,* 1973, pp. 133–62.

Sasaki, Kozo. Spatial Equilibrium Analysis of Livestock Products in Eastern Japan. In *Judge, G. G. and Takayama, T., eds.,* 1973, pp. 419–42. [G: Japan]

Sebestyén, Joseph. On Models of Planning Regional Development in Hungary. In *Judge, G. G. and Takayama, T., eds.,* 1973, pp. 26–42. [G: Hungary]

Studer, Tobias. Untersuchungen über das Wachstum der Schweizer Städte. (Investigations Upon the Growth of Swiss Towns. With English summary.) *Schweiz. Z. Volkswirtsch. Statist.,* June 1973, *109* (2), pp. 187–99. [G: Switzerland]

Tyrchniewicz, Edward W. and Tosterud, Robert J. A Model for Rationalizing the Canadian Grain Transportation and Handling System on a Regional Basis. *Amer. J. Agr. Econ.,* December 1973, *55*(5), pp. 805–13. [G: Canada]

Weinschenck, G.; Henrichsmeyer, W. and Hanf, C. H. Experiences with Multi-Commodity Models in Regional Analysis. In *Judge, G. G. and Takayama, T., eds.,* 1973, pp. 307–26. [G: W. Germany]

Author Index of Articles in Current Periodicals, Collective Volumes, and Government Documents

Abbreviated titles for journals are the same as those used in the *Journal of Economic Literature*. Full titles of journals may be found on pages xi–xv.

Books have been identified by author or editor (noted *ed.*). In rare cases where two books by the same author appear, volumes are distinguished by I or II after the name. In some cases there appear two books by the same person, once as author, once as editor. These may be distinguished by *ed.* noted for the edited volume. Full titles and bibliographic references for books may be found on pages xvi–xxiii.

Aaron, Benjamin. Legal Framework of Industrial Relations. In *Somers, G. G., ed.,* 1973, pp. 101–10.

Abbott, George C. Two Concepts of Foreign Aid. *World Devel.,* September 1973, *1*(9), pp. 1–10.

Abboud, A. Robert. The Case Against Floating Rates and for a Stronger Dollar. In *Wiegand, G. C., ed.,* 1973, pp. 89–96.

Abdalla, Ismail-Sabry. Economic Independence Through Socialism: The Egyptian Approach. In *Ghai, D., ed.,* 1973, pp. 190–204.

Abdullah, Abu A. The Success Story That Wasn't— "Development Policy II: The Pakistan Experience." *Bangladesh Econ. Rev.,* July 1973, *1*(3), pp. 309–16.

Abe, Masatoshi A. Dynamic Micro-economic Models of Production, Investment and Technological Change of the U.S. and Japanese Iron and Steel Industries. In *Judge, G. G. and Takayama, T., eds.,* 1973, pp. 345–67.

—— The Peak Load Pricing Problem in Urban Transportation. *Econ. Stud. Quart.,* December 1973, *24*(3), pp. 54–62.

Abegglen, James C. and Rapp, William V. Japanese Managerial Behavior and "Excessive Competition." In *Henley, D. S., ed.,* 1973, pp. 65–82.

Abel, Martin E. and Ryan, Mary E. Oats and Barley Acreage Response to Government Programs. *Agr. Econ. Res.,* October 1973, *25*(4), pp. 105–14.

—— **and Ryan, Mary E.** Supply Response of U.S. Sorghum Acreage to Government Programs. *Agr. Econ. Res.,* April 1973, *25*(2), pp. 45–55.

Abelle, Barnie E. The Teaching-Learning Implications of Educational Technology. *J. Risk Ins.,* December 1973, *40*(4), pp. 607–15.

Abelson, P. W. Quantification of Road User Costs: A Comment with Special Reference to Thailand. *J. Transp. Econ. Policy,* January 1973, *7*(1), pp. 80–97.

Aberle, Gerd. Reaktionshypothesen in Oligopolmodellen und oligopolistisches Marktverhalten. (Reaction Hypotheses in Oligopoly Models and Oligopolistic Market Behavior. With English summary.) *Z. ges. Staatswiss.,* August 1973, *129*(3), pp. 454–77.

Abidogun, A. and Adegboye, R. O. Contribution of Part-Time Farming to Rural Development in Ibadan Area, Western Nigeria. In *Ofori, I. M., ed.,* 1973, pp. 158–63.

Abkin, M. H., et al. System Simulation of Agricultural Development: Some Nigerian Policy Comparisons. *Amer. J. Agr. Econ.,* August 1973, *55*(3), pp. 404–19.

Aboyade, Ojetunji. Advancing Tropical African Development: A Defence of Inward-Looking Strategy. In *Streeten, P., ed.,* 1973, pp. 62–75.

—— Developing Country Alternatives: Comment. In *Hughes, H., ed.,* 1973, pp. 140–48.

Abrahams, Paul P. Brandeis and Lamont on Finance Capitalism. *Bus. Hist. Rev.,* Spring 1973, *47*(1), pp. 72–94.

Abramovitz, Moses and David, Paul A. Economic Growth in America: Historical Parables and Realities. *De Economist,* May-June 1973, *121*(3), pp. 251–72.

—— **and David, Paul A.** Reinterpreting Economic Growth: Parables and Realities. *Amer. Econ. Rev.,* May 1973, *63*(2), pp. 428–39.

Abrams, Samuel K. Association Participation in Government Standard-Setting—How an Association Can Avoid Antitrust Liability. *Antitrust Bull.,* Summer 1973, *18*(2), pp. 281–90.

Abramson, Fredric David. High Foetal Mortality and Birth Intervals. *Population Stud.,* July 1973, *27*(2), pp. 235–42.

Acheson, Keith and Chant, John F. Bureaucratic Theory and the Choice of Central Bank Goals. *J. Money, Credit, Banking,* May 1973, *5*(2), pp. 637–55.

—— **and Chant, John F.** Mythology and Central Banking. *Kyklos,* 1973, *26*(2), pp. 362–79.

Acheson, T. W. Changing Social Origins of the Canadian Industrial Elite, 1880–1910. *Bus. Hist. Rev.,* Summer 1973, *47*(2), pp. 189–217.

Achtenberg, Emily Paradise. The Social Utility of Rent Control. In *Pynoos, J.; Schafer, R. and Hartman, C. W., eds.,* 1973, pp. 434–47.

Ackerman, Bruce. More on Slum Housing and Redistribution Policy: A Reply to Professor Komesar. *Yale Law J.,* May 1973, *82*(6), pp. 1194–1207.

Ackerman, Robert W. How Companies Respond to Social Demands. *Harvard Bus. Rev.,* July-August 1973, *51*(4), pp. 88–98.

Ackoff, Russell L. The Nature and Content of Planning. In *Klein, W. H. and Murphy, D. C., eds.,* 1973, pp. 202–23.

Acquaye, D. K. Some Problems in the Use of West African Soils. In *Ofori, I. M., ed.,* 1973, pp. 67–70.

Adam, Harold. Aspetti giuridici e fiscali delle società transnazionali nella C.E.E. (Legal and Taxation Aspects of the Transnational Corporations in the EEC. With English summary.) *Bancaria,* April 1973, *29*(4), pp. 495–500.

Adam, Jan. The Incentive System in the USSR: The Abortive Reform of 1965. *Ind. Lab. Relat. Rev.,* October 1973, *27*(1), pp. 84–92.

Adam, Paul. Practical Problems of Constructing Bioeconomic Models for Fishery Management. In *Sokoloski, A. A., ed.,* 1973, pp. 96–103.

Adamec, Štefan. Problémy ekonometrie a rozhodovania. (Problems of Econometrics and Decision. With English summary.) *Ekon.-Mat. Obzor,* 1973, *9*(1), pp. 84–91.

Adams, Arvil V. Evaluating the Success of the EEOC Compliance Process. *Mon. Lab. Rev.,* May 1973, *96*(5), pp. 26–29.

―――― Title VII and Fair Employment in Ohio: Guidelines to Action. *Ohio State U. Bull. Bus. Res.,* May 1973, *48*(5), pp. 1–7.

Adams, Carolyn. Political Accommodation in the Metropolis. *Growth Change,* July 1973, *4*(3), pp. 10–15.

Adams, Curtis; Ramsett, David E. and Johnson, Jerry D. Some Evidence on the Value of Instructors in Teaching Economic Principles. *J. Econ. Educ.,* Fall 1973, *5*(1), pp. 57–62.

Adams, Dale W. The Economics of Land Reform. *Food Res. Inst. Stud.,* 1973, *12*(2), pp. 133–38.

Adams, Donald R., Jr. Wage Rates in the Iron Industry: Comment. *Exploration Econ. Hist.,* Fall 1973, *11*(1), pp. 89–94.

Adams, Earl W., Jr. and Spiro, Michael H. Labor Force Adjustment in the Construction Trades. *J. Econ. Bus.,* Fall 1973, *26*(1), pp. 78–80.

―――― **and Spiro, Michael H.** Reducing the Lags in Government Spending: An Empirical Analysis of Highway Construction. *Public Finance,* 1973, *28* (2), pp. 125–38.

Adams, F. Gerard; Clavijo, Fernando and Orsi, Renzo. A Macroeconomic Model of Belgium: Anelise. *Rech. Écon. Louvain,* September 1973, *39*(3), pp. 303–26.

Adams, N. A. Trade as a Handmaiden of Growth: Comment. *Econ. J.,* March 1973, *83*(329), pp. 210–12.

Adamu, S. O. Socio-Economic Characteristics of Consumer Expenditure Patterns: An Application of Analysis of Covariance. *Econ. Bull. Ghana, Sec. Ser.,* 1973, *3*(2), pp. 11–21.

Addo, John Sackah. Savings Banks and Savings Facilities in African Countries: Ghana. In *Alberici, A. and Baravelli, M., eds.,* 1973, pp. 37–39.

Adegboye, R. O. and Abidogun, A. Contribution of Part-Time Farming to Rural Development in Ibadan Area, Western Nigeria. In *Ofori, I. M., ed.,* 1973, pp. 158–63.

Adelman, Irma. Planning for Social Equity. In *[Tinbergen, J.],* 1973, pp. 181–200.

―――― Social and Economic Development at the Micro Level—A Tentative Hypothesis. In *Ayal, E. B., ed.,* 1973, pp. 3–13.

―――― **and Bergmann, Barbara R.** The 1973 Report of the President's Council of Economic Advisers: The Economic Role of Women. *Amer. Econ. Rev.,* September 1973, *63*(4), pp. 509–14.

Adelson, R. M. Discounted Cash Flow—The Other Point of View. In *Lister, R. J., ed.,* 1973, pp. 92–105.

Adhvaryu, J. H. Area Development and the Theory of Multiplier. *Artha-Vikas,* January-July 1973, *9* (1–2), pp. 55–63.

Adie, Douglas K. An International Comparison of the Quantity and Income-Expenditure Theories.

J. Amer. Statist. Assoc., March 1973, *68*(341), pp. 63–65.

―――― Teen-Age Unemployment and Real Federal Minimum Wages. *J. Polit. Econ.,* Part I, March-April 1973, *81*(2), pp. 435–41.

―――― **and Gallaway, Lowell.** The Minimum Wage and Teenage Unemployment: A Comment. *Western Econ. J.,* December 1973, *11*(4), pp. 525–28.

Adler, John H. Development and Income Distribution. *Finance Develop.,* September 1973, *10*(3), pp. 2–5.

―――― The External Debt Problem. In *Lewis, J. P. and Kapur, I., eds.,* 1973, pp. 111–22.

―――― The World Bank's Concept of Development —An In-House Dogmengeschichte. In *[Rosenstein-Rodan, P.],* 1973, pp. 30–50.

Adler, Michael. The Valuation and Financing of the Multi-National Firm: Comment. *Kyklos,* 1973, *26* (4), pp. 849–51.

Aduddell, Robert and Cain, Louis. Location and Collusion in the Meat Packing Industry. In *[Williamson, H. F.],* 1973, pp. 85–117.

Ady, P. On Economic Advice to Developing Countries. *World Devel.,* February 1973, *1*(1-2), pp. 64–75.

Afifi, A. A. and Malkovich, J. F. On Tests for Multivariate Normality. *J. Amer. Statist. Assoc.,* March 1973, *68*(341), pp. 176–79.

Afriat, S. N. On a System of Inequalities in Demand Analysis: An Extension of the Classical Method. *Int. Econ. Rev.,* June 1973, *14*(2), pp. 460–72.

―――― A Theorem on Shadow Prices. *Econometrica,* November 1973, *41*(6), pp. 1197–99.

Afzal, Mohammad. Implications of the Green Revolution for Land Use Patterns and Relative Crop Profitability Under Domestic and International Prices. *Pakistan Develop. Rev.,* Summer 1973, *12* (2), pp. 135–47.

―――― 1972 Census: Population—Expected and Actual. *Pakistan Develop. Rev.,* Summer 1973, *12* (2), pp. 123–34.

――――; **Bean, Lee L. and Hussain, Imtiazuddin.** Muslim Marriages: Age, Mehr and Social Status. *Pakistan Develop. Rev.,* Spring 1973, *12*(1), pp. 48–61.

――――; **Hashmi, M. Iqbal and Nizami, N. H.** Marriage Patterns in a Rural Agglomeration. *Pakistan Develop. Rev.,* Autumn 1973, *12*(3), pp. 273–82.

―――― **and Mirakhor, Abbas.** An Index of Export Performance as a Criterion of Export Policy for Developing Countries. *Pakistan Econ. Soc. Rev.,* Summer 1973, *11*(2), pp. 193–99.

Aganbegian, A. G. and Bagrinovsky, K. A. Problem-Complexes in Optimal Planning. *Acta Oecon.,* 1973, *10*(1), pp. 21–27.

Agapos, A. M. and Dunlap, Paul R. Elimination of Urban Blight Through Inverse Proportional Ad Valorem Property Taxation. *Amer. J. Econ. Soc.,* April 1973, *32*(2), pp. 143–52.

Agarwala, R. An Econometric Test of Alternative Constraints on the Growth of Underdeveloped Countries: A Comment. *Rev. Econ. Statist.,* February 1973, *55*(1), pp. 132–33.

Aggarwal, R. C. Socio-Economic Objectives of Fifth Plan—A Critique. *Econ. Aff.,* April 1973, *18*(4), pp. 153–63.

Aggrey-Mensah, W. and Guise, J. W. B. An Evaluation of Policy Alternatives Facing Australian Banana Producers. In *Judge, G. G. and Takayama, T., eds.*, 1973, pp. 519–35.

Aghevli, B. B. and Borts, G. H. The Stability and Equilibrium of the Balance of Payments under a Fixed Exchange Rate. *J. Int. Econ.*, February 1973, *3*(1), pp. 1–20.

Agmon, Tamir. Country Risk: The Significance of the Country Factor for Share-Price Movements in the United Kingdom, Germany, and Japan. *J. Bus.*, January 1973, *46*(1), pp. 24–32.

Agnati, Achille. Dal calcolo dell'opinione nei preclassici all'analisi economica dell'esogeneità. (From the Calculus of Consent in the Preclassics to the Economic Analysis of Exogeneity. With English summary.) *Rivista Int. Sci. Econ. Com.*, February 1973, *20*(2), pp. 153–78.

Agosin, Manuel R. On the Third World's Narrowing Trade Gap: A Comment. *Oxford Econ. Pap.*, March 1973, *25*(1), pp. 133–40.

Ågren, Anders. Extensions of the Fix-Point Method I. The GEID Estimator and the Fractional Fix-Point Method. *Écon. Appl.*, 1973, *26*(2–3–4), pp. 561–82.

Aguda, Oluwadare. The State and the Economy in the Sudan: From a Political Scientist's Point of View. *J. Devel. Areas*, April 1973, *7*(3), pp. 431–48.

Ahamad, Bashir. Manpower Forecasting for All Occupations: Canada. In *Ahamad, B. and Blaug, M., eds.*, 1973, pp. 26–47.

––––– Manpower Forecasting for Single Occupations: Doctors in the United States, Britain and Canada. In *Ahamad, B. and Blaug, M., eds.*, 1973, pp. 285–309.

––––– Manpower Forecasting for Single Occupations: Teachers in England and Wales. In *Ahamad, B. and Blaug, M., eds.*, 1973, pp. 261–84.

––––– and Blaug, Mark. The Practice of Manpower Forecasting: Conclusions. In *Ahamad, B. and Blaug, M., eds.*, 1973, pp. 310–23.

––––– and Blaug, Mark. The Practice of Manpower Forecasting: Introduction. In *Ahamad, B. and Blaug, M., eds.*, 1973, pp. 1–25.

Ahern, William R., Jr. Health Effects of Automotive Air Pollution. In *Jacoby, H. D., et al.*, 1973, pp. 139–74.

––––– Measuring the Value of Emissions Reductions. In *Jacoby, H. D., et al.*, 1973, pp. 175–205.

Ahl, James G.; Bachman, Gordon and Barlowe, Raleigh. Use-Value Assessment Legislation in the United States. *Land Econ.*, May 1973, *49*(2), pp. 206–12.

Ahlbrandt, Roger S., Jr. Efficiency in the Provision of Fire Services. *Public Choice*, Fall 1973, *16*, pp. 1–15.

Ahluwalia, Montek S. Taxes, Subsidies, and Employment. *Quart. J. Econ.*, August 1973, *87*(3), pp. 393–409.

Ahmad, Jaleel. Regional Allocation of Industrial Capacity in the Latin American Free Trade Association. In *Pollock, D. H. and Ritter, A. R. M., eds.*, 1973, pp. 58–69.

Ahmad, Meekal A. The Cobb-Douglas Production Function: A Comment. *Pakistan Econ. Soc. Rev.*, Summer 1973, *11*(2), pp. 219–26.

–––––; Flesher, John and Over, Mead. An Econometric Test of a Zero Elasticity of Substitution Production Function for Pakistan. *Pakistan Econ. Soc. Rev.*, Winter 1973, *11*(4), pp. 443–53.

Ahmad, Muneer. The Political Context of Civil Service Reorganization in Pakistan. *Pakistan Econ. Soc. Rev.*, Summer 1973, *11*(2), pp. 167–92.

––––– Requirements of an Organisational Structure for a Broad Based Population Programme. *Pakistan Econ. Soc. Rev.*, Autumn 1973, *11*(3), pp. 277–87.

Ahmad, Qazi Kholiquzzaman. A Note on Capacity Utilization in the Jute Manufacturing Industry of Bangladesh. *Bangladesh Econ. Rev.*, January 1973, *1*(1), pp. 103–14.

––––– and Anwaruzzaman, Chowdhury. Productivity Trends in the Manufacturing Sector of Bangladesh: A Case Study of Selected Industries. *Bangladesh Econ. Rev.*, April 1973, *1*(2), pp. 119–48.

Ahmad, Rafiq. Incentive Taxation for Economic and Social Development. *Pakistan Econ. Soc. Rev.*, Summer 1973, *11*(2), pp. 154–66.

––––– South Asian Developmental Crisis. *Pakistan Develop. Rev.*, Summer 1973, *12*(2), pp. 181–88.

Ahmed, Feroz. The Structural Matrix of the Struggle in Bangladesh. In *Gough, K. and Sharma, H. P., eds.*, 1973, pp. 419–48.

Ahmed, Iftikhar. Sectoral Employment Response in an Input-Output Framework: The Case of Bangladesh. *Bangladesh Econ. Rev.*, July 1973, *1*(3), pp. 317–23.

Ahmed, S. Basheer. Optimal Equipment Replacement Policy: An Empirical Study. *J. Transp. Econ. Policy*, January 1973, *7*(1), pp. 71–79.

Ahtiala, Pekka. Rahoitusjärjestelmästä ja sen tehtävistä. (The Financial System and Its Functions. With English summary.) *Liiketaloudellinen Aikak.*, 1973, *22*(4), pp. 236–47.

––––– Verotus, korkosäännöstely ja inflaatio säästövarojen allokoijina. (Taxation, Interest Rate Controls, and Inflation as Allocators of Saving. With English summary.) *Liiketaloudellinen Aikak.*, 1973, *22*(2), pp. 94–113.

Aidenoff, Abraham. A Proposal for a System of Economic and Social Accounts: Comment. In *Moss, M., ed.*, 1973, pp. 153–59.

Aigner, Dennis J. An Errors-In-Variables Model in Which Least Squares Is Consistent. *Int. Econ. Rev.*, February 1973, *14*(1), pp. 256–57.

––––– On Estimation of an Econometric Model of Short-Run Bank Behaviour. *J. Econometrics*, October 1973, *1*(3), pp. 201–28.

––––– Regression With a Binary Independent Variable Subject to Errors of Observation. *J. Econometrics*, March 1973, *1*(1), pp. 49–59.

––––– and Goldfeld, Stephen M. Simulation and Aggregation: A Reconsideration. *Rev. Econ. Statist.*, February 1973, *55*(1), pp. 114–18.

––––– and Sprenkle, C. M. On Optimal Financing of Cyclical Cash Needs. *J. Finance*, December 1973, *28*(5), pp. 1249–54.

Aislabie, Colin S. Payment by Use in Urban Water Supply. In *Aislabie, C., ed.*, 1973, pp. 1–18.

Aitken, Norman D. The Effect of the EEC and EFTA on European Trade: A Temporal Cross-Section Analysis. *Amer. Econ. Rev.*, December 1973, *63* (5), pp. 881–92.

—— **and Lowry, William R.** A Cross-Sectional Study of the Effects of LAFTA and CACM on Latin American Trade. *J. Common Market Stud.*, June 1973, *11*(4), pp. 326–36.

Ajayi, Simeon I. Money Supply Relationships when Government Debts are Held as Reserves. *Econ. Bull. Ghana, Sec. Ser.*, 1973, *3*(2), pp. 31–34.

Ajiferuke, Musbau and Boddewyn, J. J. Socioeconomic Indicators in Comparative Management. In *Alexandrides, C. G., ed.*, 1973, pp. 163–72.

Akerlof, George A. The Demand for Money: A General-Equilibirum Inventory-Theoretic Approach. *Rev. Econ. Stud.*, January 1973, *40*(1), pp. 115–30.

Akhtar, M. A. The Stationary State of Ricardo and Malthus: Comment. *Intermountain Econ. Rev.*, Spring 1973, *4*(1), pp. 77–79.

Akin, John S. Fiscal Capacity and the Estimation Method of the Advisory Commission on Intergovernmental Relations. *Nat. Tax J.*, June 1973, *26*(2), pp. 275–91.

——; **Fields, Gary S. and Neenan, William B.** A Socioeconomic Explanation of Demand for Public Goods. *Public Finance Quart.*, April 1973, *1*(2), pp. 169–89.

Akins, James E. International Cooperative Efforts in Energy Supply. *Ann. Amer. Acad. Polit. Soc. Sci.*, November 1973, *410*, pp. 75–85.

—— The Oil Crisis: This Time the Wolf Is Here. *Foreign Aff.*, April 1973, *51*(3), pp. 462–90.

Akkihal, R. G. Locational Effects in the Theory of Customs Unions and Welfare Analysis. *Indian Econ. J.*, July–September 1973, *21*(1), pp. 42–56.

Alagh, Yoginder K. and Pathak, Pravin G. Industrial Development in Gujarat: Regional Structure and Policies. *Artha-Vikas*, January-July 1973, *9*(1–2), pp. 143–84.

Alamgir, Mohiuddin. Some Theoretical Issues in Manpower and Educational Planning. *Bangladesh Econ. Rev.*, April 1973, *1*(2), pp. 199–212.

—— **and Berlage, Lodewijk J. J. B.** Estimation of Income Elasticity of Demand for Foodgrain in Bangladesh from Cross Section Data: A Skeptical View. *Bangladesh Econ. Rev.*, October 1973, *1*(4), pp. 387–408.

—— **and Berlage, Lodewijk J. J. B.** Foodgrain (Rice and Wheat) Demand, Import and Price Policy for Bangladesh. *Bangladesh Econ. Rev.*, January 1973, *1*(1), pp. 25–58.

Alberts, W. W. and Archer, S. H. Some Evidence on the Effect of Company Size on the Cost of Equity Capital. *J. Financial Quant. Anal.*, March 1973, *8*(2), pp. 229–42.

Albin, Peter S. and Grier, Paul C. Nonrandom Price Changes in Association with Trading in Large Blocks. *J. Bus.*, July 1973, *46*(3), pp. 425–33.

Alcantara, Reinaldo and Prato, Anthony A. Returns to Scale and Input Elasticities for Sugarcane: The Case of Sao Paulo, Brazil. *Amer. J. Agr. Econ.*, Part I, November 1973, *55*(4), pp. 577–83.

Alchian, Armen A. and Allen, William R. The Pure Economics of Giving. In *Alchian, A. A., et al.*, 1973, pp. 3–13.

—— **and Demsetz, Harold.** The Property Rights Paradigm. *J. Econ. Hist.*, March 1973, *33*(1), pp. 16–27.

—— **and Klein, Benjamin.** On a Correct Measure of Inflation. *J. Money, Credit, Banking*, Part I, February 1973, *5*(1), pp. 173–91.

Alderfer, Evan B. Changing Times on Pennsylvania Farms. *Fed. Res. Bank Bus. Rev. Phila.*, May 1973, pp. 18–26.

Aldrich, Carole A. and Morton, Thomas E. A Note on Bayesian Modification of the Failure Rate Function. *J. Amer. Statist. Assoc.*, June 1973, *68* (342), pp. 483–84.

Aldrich, Mark. Flexible Exchange Rates, Northern Expansion, and the Market for Southern Cotton: 1866–1879. *J. Econ. Hist.*, June 1973, *33*(2), pp. 399–416.

Alekseev, V. Protection of the Natural Environment (Economic Aspect) *Prob. Econ.*, November 1973, *16*(7), pp. 24–35.

Alemany, Ricardo; Fernandez, Pedro and Pousa, Aurora G. Algorithm for Solving a Class of Linear Programing Problems Related to Reservoir Management and Design. *Water Resources Res.*, October 1973, *9*(5), pp. 1227–34.

Alessio, Frank J. Multiple Criteria in Environmental Control: Use of Economic Maximization Rules to Determine Relative Standards. In *Cochrane, J. L. and Zeleny, M., eds.*, 1973, pp. 544–49.

—— A Neo-Classical Land Use Model: The Influence of Externalities. *Swedish J. Econ.*, December 1973, *75*(4), pp. 414–19.

Alexandrides, C. G. A Methodology for Computerization. In *Alexandrides, C. G., ed.*, 1973, pp. 185–93.

Alexis, Marcus. A Theory of Labor Market Discrimination with Interdependent Utilities. *Amer. Econ. Rev.*, May 1973, *63*(2), pp. 296–302.

——; **Haines, George H., Jr. and Simon, Leonard S.** An Analysis of Central City Neighborhood Food Trading Areas: A Reply. *J. Reg. Sci.*, August 1973, *13*(2), pp. 301.

Ali, Chaudhari Haider and Khan, Dilawar Ali. Income Impact of the Green Revolution. *Pakistan Econ. Soc. Rev.*, Spring 1973, *11*(1), pp. 67–82.

Aliber, Robert Z. Gold, SDR's, and Central Bank Swaps. *J. Money, Credit, Banking*, August 1973, *5*(3), pp. 819–25.

—— The Impact of External Markets for National Currencies on Central Bank Reserves. In *Johnson, H. G. and Swoboda, A. K., eds.*, 1973, pp. 178–95.

—— The Interest Rate Parity Theorem: A Reinterpretation. *J. Polit. Econ.*, November-December 1973, *81*(6), pp. 1451–59.

—— Japanese Growth and the Equilibrium Foreign Exchange Value of the Yen. *Southern Econ. J.*, January 1973, *39*(3), pp. 406–18.

—— Speculation in the Flexible Exchange Re-Revisited: Reply. *Kyklos*, 1973, *26*(3), pp. 619–20.

Allais, Maurice. Inequality and Civilizations. *Soc. Sci. Quart.*, December 1973, *54*(3), pp. 508–24.

Allegri, Vincenzo. La politica industriale delle Regioni. (The Industrial Policy of the Italian Regions. With English summary.) *L'industria, N. S.*, 1973, (1), pp. 15–24.

Allen, G. C. Competition and Mergers. In *Allen, G. C., et al.,* 1973, pp. 1–10.

Allen, Howard P. Electric Utilities: Can They Meet Future Power Needs? *Ann. Amer. Acad. Polit. Soc. Sci.,* November 1973, *410,* pp. 86–96.

Allen, Jodie T. A Guide to the 1960–1971 Current Population Survey Files. *Ann. Econ. Soc. Measure,* April 1973, *2*(2), pp. 189–99.

Allen, Louis A. Who Speaks Management? *Calif. Manage. Rev.,* Summer 1973, *15*(4), pp. 22–27.

Allen, Polly Reynolds. A Portfolio Approach to International Capital Flows. *J. Int. Econ.,* May 1973, *3*(2), pp. 135–60.

_____ The Transfer Problem: A Note on the Terms in Which a Transfer is Expressed. *Econ. J.,* June 1973, *83*(330), pp. 516–19.

Allen, R. G. D. The Statistician and the British Library of Political and Economic Science. *J. Roy. Statist. Soc.,* Part 2, 1973, *136,* pp. 255–57.

Allen, Tom C. and Duvall, Richard M. Determinants of Property Loss Ratios in The Retail Industry. *J. Risk Ins.,* June 1973, *40*(2), pp. 181–90.

_____ and Duvall, Richard M. Least Cost Deductible Decisions. *J. Risk Ins.,* December 1973, *40*(4), pp. 497–508.

Allen, William R. For Want of an International Adjustment Mechanism. *Soc. Sci. Quart.,* June 1973, *54*(1), pp. 140–45.

_____ The Interpretation of Mercantilist Economics: Some Historiographical Problems: Rearguard Response. *Hist. Polit. Econ.,* Fall 1973, *5*(2), pp. 496–98.

_____ and Alchian, Armen A. The Pure Economics of Giving. In *Alchian, A. A., et al.,* 1973, pp. 3–13.

Allende, Salvador. The Chilean Road to Socialism. In *Zammit, J. A., ed.,* 1973, pp. 17–25.

Allingham, M. G. and Morishima, M. Qualitative Economics and Comparative Statics. In *Morishima, M., et al.,* 1973, pp. 3–69.

_____ and Morishima, M. Veblen Effects and Portfolio Selection. In *Morishima, M., et al.,* 1973, pp. 242–70.

Allison, Graham T. Organizational and Administrative Factors Affecting Shifts in Defense Expenditures. In *Udis, B., ed.,* 1973, pp. 289–35.

Allnutt, Smith W.; Murad, Howard and Belli, R. David. Property, Plant, and Equipment Expenditures by Majority-Owned Foreign Affiliates of U.S. Companies: Revised Estimates for 1966–72 and Projections for 1973 and 1974. *Surv. Curr. Bus.,* December 1973, *53*(12), pp. 19–32.

Allsbrook, Ogden O., Jr. Keynes's Involuntary Unemployment Equilibrium: An Alternative View. *S. Afr. J. Econ.,* March 1973, *41*(1), pp. 60–66.

_____ and DeLorme, Charles D., Jr. Monetary Policy, Price Expectations, and the Case of a Positively-Sloped *IS* Curve. *Rivista Int. Sci. Econ. Com.,* March 1973, *20*(3), pp. 278–85.

_____ and DeLorme, Charles D., Jr. A Reconsideration of Interest Rates, Money Growth Rates, Inflation and the 'Ease' or 'Tightness' of Money: Comment. *Kyklos,* 1973, *26*(1), pp. 151–55.

Almon, Clopper. Programs and Methods for Input-Output Analysis—A Preview. *Ann. Econ. Soc. Measure,* July 1973, *2*(3), pp. 307–08.

Almonacid, Ruben and Guitian, Manuel. The Optimal Rate of Devaluation. In *Johnson, H. G. and Swoboda, A. K., eds.,* 1973, pp. 281–97.

Alonso, William. The Mirage of New Towns. In *Grieson, R. E., ed.,* 1973, pp. 213–28.

_____ A Theory of the Urban Land Market. In *Grieson, R. E., ed.,* 1973, pp. 45–55.

_____ Urban Zero Population Growth. In *Olson, M. and Landsberg, H. H., eds.,* 1973, pp. 191–206.

Alterman, Jack. An Overview of BLS Projections. *Mon. Lab. Rev.,* December 1973, *96*(12), pp. 3–7.

Altman, Edward I. Predicting Railroad Bankruptcies in America. *Bell J. Econ. Manage. Sci.,* Spring 1973, *4*(1), pp. 184–211.

_____ and Schwartz, Robert A. Volatility Behavior of Industrial Stock Price Indices. *J. Finance,* September 1973, *28*(4), pp. 957–71.

Alvarez, Rodolfo. The Psycho-Historical and Socioeconomic Development of the Chicano Community in the United States. *Soc. Sci. Quart.,* March 1973, *53*(4), pp. 920–42.

Alvírez, David. The Effects of Formal Church Affiliation and Religiosity on the Fertility Patterns of Mexican-American Catholics. *Demography,* February 1973, *10*(1), pp. 19–36.

_____; Hernández, José and Estrada, Leo. Census Data and the Problem of Conceptually Defining the Mexican American Population. *Soc. Sci. Quart.,* March 1973, *53*(4), pp. 671–87.

_____ and Poston, Dudley L., Jr. On the Cost of Being a Mexican American Worker. *Soc. Sci. Quart.,* March 1973, *53*(4), pp. 697–709.

Amacher, Ryan C.; Tollison, Robert D. and Willett, Thomas D. Import Controls on Foreign Oil: Comment. *Amer. Econ. Rev.,* December 1973, *63*(5), pp. 1031–34.

Amadeo, Eduardo P. Algunas ideas para un nuevo enfoque de la teoría del "ciclo del producto". (Some Ideas for a New Approach on the Theory of the "Product Cycle". With English summary.) *Económica,* May-August 1973, *19*(2), pp. 135–45.

Amano, A. International Capital Movements: Theory and Estimation. In *Ball, R. J., ed.,* 1973, pp. 283–327.

Ambegaonkar, L. V.; Ashturkar, B. W. and Choudhuri, S. D. Response of Irrigated M35–1 Rabi Jowar to Levels of Nitrogen. *Econ. Aff.,* June 1973, *18*(6), pp. 261–64.

Ameiss, Albert P., et al. Program Management in Missouri's Division of Mental Health. *Manage. Account.,* August 1973, *55*(2), pp. 31–34.

_____; Terre, Norbert C. and Warnke, Dale W. Cost/Benefit Analysis of Public Projects. *Manage. Account.,* January 1973, *54*(7), pp. 34–37.

Amemiya, Takeshi. Generalized Least Squares with an Estimated Autocovariance Matrix. *Econometrica,* July 1973, *41*(4), pp. 723–32.

_____ Regression Analysis when the Dependent Variable is Truncated Normal. *Econometrica,* November 1973, *41*(6), pp. 997–1016.

_____ Regression Analysis When the Variance of the Dependent Variable Is Proportional to the Square of Its Expectation. *J. Amer. Statist. Assoc.,* December 1973, *68*(344), pp. 928–34.

Ames, Edward. The Emerging Theory of Comparative Economic Systems. *Amer. Econ.,* Spring 1973, *17*(1), pp. 22–28.

Amey, Lloyd R. and Whitmore, G. A. Capital Budgeting under Rationing: Comments on the Lusztig and Schwab Procedure. *J. Financial Quant. Anal.,* January 1973, *8*(1), pp. 127–35.

Amid-hozour, Esmail and Somogyi, János. East-West Trade. *Finance Develop.,* June 1973, *10*(2), pp. 32–37.

Amin, Samir. The Place of Economic History in the Teaching of Economics in Africa. In *Livingstone, I., et al., eds.,* 1973, pp. 101–03.

_____ Underdevelopment and Dependence in Black Africa—Their Historical Origins and Contemporary Forms. *Soc. Econ. Stud.,* March 1973, *22*(1), pp. 177–96.

Amjad, Rashid. Growth, Profitability and Savings of Quoted Public Limited Companies 1964–70. *Pakistan Econ. Soc. Rev.,* Winter 1973, *11*(4), pp. 417–42.

Amoroso, Luigi. The Work of Vilfredo Pareto. In *Rectenwald, H. C., ed.,* 1973, pp. 307–10.

Amuzegar, Jahangir. The Oil Story: Facts, Fiction and Fair Play. *Foreign Aff.,* July 1973, *51*(4), pp. 676–89.

Anderman, Steven D. International Manual on Collective Bargaining for Public Employees: Sweden. In *Kaye, S. P. and Marsh, A., eds.,* 1973, pp. 264–99.

Andersen, Leonall C. A Comparison of Stabilization Policies: 1966–67 and 1969–70. *J. Money, Credit, Banking,* Part I, February 1973, *5*(1), pp. 26–38.

_____ A Note on the Effects of Government Finance on Aggregate Demand for Goods and Services—A Reply. *Public Finance,* 1973, *28*(3–4), pp. 397–406.

_____ The State of the Monetarist Debate. *Fed. Res. Bank St. Louis Rev.,* September 1973, *55*(9), pp. 2–8.

Andersen, Palle Schelde. Automatic Stabilization in Static and Dynamic Models. *Nationalokon. Tidsskr.,* 1973, *111*(1), pp. 60–85.

_____ Built-in Flexibility and Sensitivity of the Personal Income Tax in Denmark. *Swedish J. Econ.,* March 1973, *75*(1), pp. 1–18.

Andersen, Per. Økonomisk overlevelse i et stokastisk marked. (The Behaviour of a Monopolist Who Seeks Economic Survival in a Stochastic Market. With English summary.) *Nationalokon. Tidsskr.,* 1973, *111*(2), pp. 266–76.

Andersen, Stig. The World Bank and the United Nations: Comment. In *Lewis, J. P. and Kapur, I., eds.,* 1973, pp. 139–41.

Anderson, Annelise. Organized Crime: Comment. In *Rottenberg, S., ed.,* 1973, pp. 167–71.

Anderson, Arvid and Kaye, Seymour P. International Manual on Collective Bargaining for Public Employees: The United States. In *Kaye, S. P. and Marsh, A., eds.,* 1973, pp. 3–66.

Anderson, Dole A. Public Policy Toward Retailing: Thailand. In *Boddewyn, J. J. and Hollander, S. C., eds.,* 1972, pp. 297–310.

Anderson, Eric L. The Timing of Open Market Operations. *Miss. Val. J. Bus. Econ.,* Fall 1973, *9*(1), pp. 18–27.

Anderson, F. M., et al. Simulation Experiments to Evaluate Alternative Hunting Strategies for a Deer Population. In *Sokoloski, A. A., ed.,* 1973, pp. 121–32.

Anderson, Jock R. Risk Aversion and Polynomial Preference. *Australian Econ. Pap.,* December 1973, *12*(21), pp. 261–62.

_____ Sparse Data, Climatic Variability, and Yield Uncertainty in Response Analysis. *Amer. J. Agr. Econ.,* February 1973, *55*(1), pp. 77–82.

_____ **and Powell, R. A.** Economics of Size in Australian Farming. *Australian J. Agr. Econ.,* April 1973, *17*(1), pp. 1–16.

Anderson, Kent P. Residential Demand for Electricity: Econometric Estimates for California and the United States. *J. Bus.,* October 1973, *46*(4), pp. 526–53.

Anderson, Maxine. Broad Accident Compensation Law Enacted in New Zealand. *Mon. Lab. Rev.,* August 1973, *96*(8), pp. 77–78.

Anderson, Otto. Dødelighedsforholdene i Danmark 1735–1839. (Mortality Conditions in Denmark 1735–1839. With English summary.) *Nationalokon. Tidsskr.,* 1973, *111*(2), pp. 277–305.

Anderson, Paul S. and Eisenmenger, Robert W. Impact of the Proposed New Financial Structure on Mortgage Markets. In *Federal Reserve Bank of Boston,* 1973, pp. 149–72.

Anderson, Peggy Engelhardt and Flanders, Dwight P. Sex Discrimination in Employment: Theory and Practice. *Ind. Lab. Relat. Rev.,* April 1973, *26* (3), pp. 938–55.

Anderson, Robert J., Jr. A Nesting Theorem on Efficiency of Bayesian or Mixed Regression Model Estimators. *Int. Econ. Rev.,* October 1973, *14*(3), pp. 789–90.

Anderson, Rolph E. Consumer Dissatisfaction: The Effect of Disconfirmed Expectancy on Perceived Product Performance. *J. Marketing Res.,* February 1973, *10*(1), pp. 38–44.

Anderson, Roy C. Black Employment in the Securities Industry. *Ind. Relat.,* February 1973, *12*(1), pp. 107–08.

Anderson, Terry L. and Reed, Clyde G. An Economic Explanation of English Agricultural Organization in the Twelfth and Thirteenth Centuries: Comment. *Econ. Hist. Rev., 2nd Ser.,* February 1973, *26*(1), pp. 134–37.

_____ **and Thomas, Robert Paul.** White Population, Labor Force and Extensive Growth of the New England Economy in the Seventeenth Century. *J. Econ. Hist.,* September 1973, *33*(3), pp. 634–67.

Anderson, T. W. and Sawa, Takamitsu. Distributions of Estimates of Coefficients of a Single Equation in a Simultaneous System and Their Asymptotic Expansions. *Econometrica,* July 1973, *41*(4), pp. 683–714.

Anderson, William D. and Boxley, Robert F. The Incidence of Benefits from Commodity Price-Support Programs: A Case Study of Tobacco. In *Harriss, C. L., ed.,* 1973, pp. 79–103.

Anderson, W. T., Jr. and Sharpe, L. K. The New American Marketplace: Life-Style in Revolution. In *Thorelli, H. B., ed.,* 1973, pp. 146–53.

Andersson, Rolf and Meidner, Rudolf. The Overall Impact of an Active Labor Market Policy in Sweden. In *Ulman, L., ed.,* 1973, pp. 117–58.

Andic, Fuat M. Fiscal Reform in Colombia: A Review Article. *Finanzarchiv*, 1973, *32*(1), pp. 160–66.

Andic, Suphan. Tax Problems of Developing Countries. *Finanzarchiv*, 1973, *32*(1), pp. 155–59.

Andreano, Ralph. A Note on the Horatio Alger Legend: Statistical Studies of the Nineteenth–Century American Business Elite. In *[Williamson, H. F.]*, 1973, pp. 227–46.

Andrews, Frank M. Social Indicators and Socioeconomic Development. *J. Devel. Areas*, October 1973, *8*(1), pp. 3–12.

Andrews, Frederick. New Box Score. In *Klein, W. H. and Murphy, D. C., eds.*, 1973, pp. 310–18.

Andrews, Kenneth R. Can the Best Corporations be Made Moral? *Harvard Bus. Rev.*, May-June 1973, *51*(3), pp. 57–64.

Andrews, W. D. What's Fair About Death Taxes? *Nat. Tax J.*, September 1973, *26*(3), pp. 465–69.

Andrews, W. H. and Christenson, C. L. Coal Mine Injury Rates in Two Eras of Federal Control. *J. Econ. Issues*, March 1973, *7*(1), pp. 61–82.

Andriano, Angelo. Un procedimento analitico per la quantificazione degli smobilizzi. (An Analytical Procedure to Quantify Disinvestments. With English summary.) *L'Impresa*, 1973, *15*(3–4), pp. 240–43.

Aneuryn-Evans, G. B. and Fitzgerald, E. V. K. The Economics of Airport Development and Control. *J. Transp. Econ. Policy*, September 1973, *7*(3), pp. 269–82.

Ang, James S. Reliability of Using the Mean Absolute Deviation to Derive Efficient E, V Farm Plans: Comment. *Amer. J. Agr. Econ.*, Part I, November 1973, *55*(4), pp. 675–77.

Angilley, Alan S. Returns to Scale in Research in the Ethical Pharmaceutical Industry: Some Further Empirical Evidence. *J. Ind. Econ.*, December 1973, *22*(2), pp. 81–93.

Angus, James E. and Maki, Wilbur R. Development Planning. In *Judge, G. G. and Takayama, T., eds.*, 1973, pp. 43–64.

Anker, Desmond L. W. Rural Development Problems and Strategies. *Int. Lab. Rev.*, December 1973, *108*(6), pp. 461–84.

Annable, James E., Jr. The ICC, the IBT, and the Cartelization of the American Trucking Industry. *Quart. Rev. Econ. Bus.*, Summer 1973, *13*(2), pp. 33–47.

_____ and Fruitman, Frederick H. An Earnings Function for High-Level Manpower. *Ind. Lab. Relat. Rev.*, July 1973, *26*(4), pp. 1107–21.

Anschel, Kurt R. and Bieker, Richard F. Estimating Educational Production Functions for Rural High Schools: Some Findings. *Amer. J. Agr. Econ.*, August 1973, *55*(3), pp. 515–19.

Anshen, Melvin and Guth, William D. Strategies for Research in Policy Formulation. *J. Bus.*, October 1973, *46*(4), pp. 499–511.

Ansoff, H. Igor. Management in Transition. In *The Conference Board*, 1973, pp. 22–63.

_____ and Hayes, Robert L. Roles of Models in Corporate Decision Making. In *Ross, M., ed.*, 1973, pp. 131–62.

Anthonio, Q. B. O. Problems of Marketing Agricultural Produce with Special Reference to Food-

stuffs in Nigeria. In *Ofori, I. M., ed.*, 1973, pp. 251–62.

Anthony, Robert N. Accounting for the Cost of Equity. *Harvard Bus. Rev.*, November-December 1973, *51*(6), pp. 88–102.

_____ Characteristics of Management Control Systems. In *Thomas, W. E., Jr., ed.*, 1973, pp. 27–42.

Anthony, William P. and Nosari, Eldon J. A Test of the Permanent Income Hypothesis. *J. Bus. Res.*, Summer 1973, *1*(1), pp. 43–48.

Antin, P. The Nestlé Product Manager as Demigod. In *Thorelli, H. B., ed.*, 1973, pp. 290–300.

Antosenkov, E. G. The Availability of Housing and Personnel Turnover. *Prob. Econ.*, July 1973, *16*(3), pp. 59–76.

Anwaruzzaman, Chowdhury and Ahmad, Qazi Kholiquzzaman. Productivity Trends in the Manufacturing Sector of Bangladesh: A Case Study of Selected Industries. *Bangladesh Econ. Rev.*, April 1973, *1*(2), pp. 119–48.

Anyanwu, Enoch A. The Contribution of Finance to Industrial Development: The Nigerian Experience. In *[Hicks, U.]*, 1973, pp. 59–94.

Aoki, Masanao. Approximation Scheme for Evaluating Some Terminal Capital Stock. *J. Econ. Theory*, June 1973, *6*(3), pp. 317–19.

_____ On Sufficient Conditions for Optimal Stabilization Policies. *Rev. Econ. Stud.*, January 1973, *40*(1), pp. 131–38.

van Apeldoorn, G. J. and Nyanteng, V. K. Some Development Implications of Farmers' Problems in Marketing Their Foodcrops. In *Ofori, I. M., ed.*, 1973, pp. 263–77.

Appleby, Andrew B. Disease or Famine? Mortality in Cumberland and Westmorland, 1580–1640. *Econ. Hist. Rev., 2nd Ser.*, August 1973, *26*(3), pp. 403–32.

Appleman, Jack M. Testing and Maintenance of In-Use Vehicles. In *Jacoby, H. D., et al.*, 1973, pp. 113–37.

Apsey, T. M.; Garton, M. M. and Hajdu, C. Economic Trends in the Canadian Forest Products Industry. *Amer. J. Agr. Econ.*, December 1973, *55*(5), pp. 974–82.

Aquino, Antonio. Alcune riflessioni sull'analisi dei fattori esplicativi della struttura degli scambi internazionali. (Some Considerations of the Analysis of the Explanatory Factors of the Pattern of International Trade. With English summary.) *Rivista Int. Sci. Econ. Com.*, October 1973, *20*(10), pp. 995–1012.

Ara, Kenjiro. Some Notes on Utility Function. *Hitotsubashi J. Econ.*, February 1973, *13*(2), pp. 37–42.

Arak, Marcelle and Spiro, Alan. A Theoretical Explanation of the Interest Inelasticity of Money Demand. *Rev. Econ. Statist.*, November 1973, *55*(4), pp. 520–23.

Aram, John D. and Stoner, James A. F. Effectiveness of Two Technical Assistance Efforts in Differing Environments. *J. Devel. Stud.*, July 1973, *9*(4), pp. 508–17.

Arcaini, Giuseppe. I presupposti del risparmio. (Savings Prerequisites. With English summary.) *Bancaria*, October 1973, *29*(10), pp. 1203–05.

Arcelus, Francisco and Meltzer, Allan H. The Markets for Housing and Housing Services. *J. Money,*

Credit, Banking, Part I, February 1973, *5*(1), pp. 78–99.

———— The Markets for Housing and Housing Services: Reply. *J. Money, Credit, Banking,* November 1973, *5*(4), pp. 973–78.

Archer, R. W. Land Speculation and Scattered Development; Failures in the Urban-Fringe Land Market. *Urban Stud.,* October 1973, *10*(3), pp. 367–72.

Archer, S. H. and Alberts, W. W. Some Evidence on the Effect of Company Size on the Cost of Equity Capital. *J. Financial Quant. Anal.,* March 1973, *8*(2), pp. 229–42.

Arcucci, Francesco and Frediani, Lorenzo. Savings Banks and Savings Facilities in African Countries: Malawi. In *Alberici, A. and Baravelli, M., eds.,* 1973, pp. 55–59.

Arditti, Fred D. The Weighted Average Cost of Capital: Some Questions on its Definition, Interpretation, and Use. *J. Finance,* September 1973, *28*(4), pp. 1001–07.

————; **Grinold, Richard C. and Levy, Haim.** The Investment-Consumption Decision under Capital Rationing: An Efficient Set Analysis. *Rev. Econ. Stud.,* July 1973, *40*(3), pp. 367–76.

———— **and Levy, Haim.** Valuation, Leverage, and the Cost of Capital in the Case of Depreciable Assets. *J. Finance,* June 1973, *28*(3), pp. 687–93.

———— **and Sandor, Richard L.** A Note on Variable Patent Life. *J. Ind. Econ.,* April 1973, *21*(2), pp. 177–83.

Ardolini, Charles W. Productivity Gains in 1972 in Selected Industries. *Mon. Lab. Rev.,* July 1973, *96* (7), pp. 43–45.

Areeda, Phillip E. The Bank Holding Company—A Superior Device for Expanding Activities? Discussion. In *Federal Reserve Bank of Boston,* 1973, pp. 88–93.

Arens, Alvin A. and Sollenberger, Harold. Assessing Information Systems Projects. *Manage. Account.,* September 1973, *55*(3), pp. 37–42.

Areskoug, Kaj. Foreign-Capital Utilization and Economic Policies in Developing Countries. *Rev. Econ. Statist.,* May 1973, *55*(2), pp. 182–89.

d'Arge, Ralph C. Coase Theorem Symposium. *Natural Res. J.,* October 1973, *13*(4), pp. 557–60.

———— **and Hunt, E. K.** On Lemmings and Other Acquisitive Animals: Propositions on Consumption. *J. Econ. Issues,* June 1973, *7*(2), pp. 337–53.

————; **Kneese, Allen V. and Ayres, Robert U.** Economics and the Environment: A Materials Balance Approach. In *Enthoven, A. C. and Freeman, A. M., III, eds.,* 1973, pp. 25–36.

———— **and Kogiku, K. C.** Economic Growth and the Environment. *Rev. Econ. Stud.,* January 1973, *40* (1), pp. 61–77.

Argentarius. Sviluppi e problemi attuali del credito al consumo. (Development and Current Problems of Consumer Credit. With English summary.) *Bancaria,* January 1973, *29*(1), pp. 76–82.

Argy, Victor and Hodjera, Zoran. Financial Integration and Interest Rate Linkages in Industrial Countries, 1958-71. *Int. Monet. Fund Staff Pap.,* March 1973, *20*(1), pp. 1–77.

Armstrong, Christopher and Nelles, H. V. Private Property in Peril: Ontario Businessmen and the Federal System, 1898–1911. *Bus. Hist. Rev.,* Summer 1973, *47*(2), pp. 158–76.

Armstrong, R. H. R. Programme Budgeting in English Local Government. In *Novick, D., ed.,* 1973, pp. 105–10.

Armstrong, William. Management Training for Statisticians and Opportunities to Enter Top Management. *J. Roy. Statist. Soc.,* Part 1, 1973, *136,* pp. 95–99.

Arnaudo, Aldo A. and Sánchez, Carlos E. The Economic Power of Argentine Manufacturing Labor Unions. In *Sturmthal, A. and Scoville, J. G., eds.,* 1973, pp. 178–98.

Arndt, H. W. Development Economics Before 1945. In *[Rosenstein-Rodan, P.],* 1973, pp. 13–29.

———— Inflation: New Policy Prescriptions. *Australian Econ. Rev.,* 3rd Quarter 1973, pp. 41–48.

———— Regional Income Estimates. *Bull. Indonesian Econ. Stud.,* November 1973, *9*(3), pp. 87–102.

———— Survey of Recent Developments. *Bull. Indonesian Econ. Stud.,* July 1973, *9*(2), pp. 1–27.

———— **and Sundrum, R. M.** Foreign Capital and Indonesian Economic Growth: A Comment. *Bull. Indonesian Econ. Stud.,* July 1973, *9*(2), pp. 90–95.

Arndt, Sven W. Joint Balance: Capital Mobility and the Monetary System of a Currency Area. In *Johnson, H. G. and Swoboda, A. K., eds.,* 1973, pp. 196–209.

———— Policy Choices in an Open Economy: Some Dynamic Considerations. *J. Polit. Econ.,* July-August 1973, *81*(4), pp. 916–35.

———— The Role of World Trade Policy: The View from the Advanced Countries. In *Urquidi, V. L. and Thorp, R., eds.,* 1973, pp. 88–106.

Arnell, J. C. Development of Program Budgeting in the Canadian Department of National Defense. In *Novick, D., ed.,* 1973, pp. 79–88.

Arnold, Donald F. and Humann, Thomas E. Earnings Per Share: An Empirical Test of the Market Parity and the Investment Value Methods. *Accounting Rev.,* January 1973, *48*(1), pp. 23–33.

Arnold, Mark R. Public Schools. In *Levitan, S. A., ed.,* 1973, pp. 21–51.

Aronson, J. Richard and Schwartz, Eli. Financing Public Goods and the Distribution of Population in a System of Local Governments. *Nat. Tax J.,* June 1973, *26*(2), pp. 137–60.

Aronson, Robert L. Current Issues in Manpower Planning. In *Aronson, R. L., ed.,* 1973, pp. 1–13.

Arora, Swarnjit S. Error Components Regression Models and Their Applications. *Ann. Econ. Soc. Measure,* October 1973, *2*(4), pp. 451–61.

Arpan, Jeffrey and Daniels, John D. Comparative Home Country Influences on Management Practices Abroad. In *Henley, D. S., ed.,* 1973, pp. 409–19.

Arrate, Jorge. The Nationalization of Copper. In *Zammit, J. A., ed.,* 1973, pp. 145–50.

Arrighi, Giovanni. The Political Economy of Rhodesia. In *Arrighi, G. and Saul, J. S.,* 1973, pp. 336–77.

———— **and Saul, John S.** Nationalism and Revolution in Sub-Saharan Africa. In *Arrighi, G. and Saul, J. S.,* 1973, pp. 44–102.

_____ and Saul, John S. Socialism and Economic Development in Tropical Africa. In *Arrighi, G. and Saul, J. S.*, 1973, pp. 11–43.

Arrow, Kenneth J. Higher Education as a Filter. *J. Public Econ.*, July 1973, *2*(3), pp. 193–216.

_____ Rawls's Principle of Just Saving. *Swedish J. Econ.*, December 1973, *75*(4), pp. 323–35.

_____ Social Responsibility and Economic Efficiency. *Public Policy*, Summer 1973, *21*(3), pp. 303–17.

_____ and Starrett, David A. Cost- and Demand-theoretical Approaches to the Theory of Price Determination. In *Hicks, J. R. and Weber, W., eds.*, 1973, pp. 129–48.

Arthur, W. Brian. The Elasticity of Demand for Petrol in Ireland: Comment. *Econ. Soc. Rev.*, October 1973, *5*(1), pp. 105–10.

Artis, M. J. Analysis of the Determination of the Stock of Money: Discussion. In *Parkin, M., ed.*, 1973, pp. 262–65.

Artle, Roland and Averous, Christian P. The Telephone System as a Public Good: Static and Dynamic Aspects. *Bell J. Econ. Manage. Sci.*, Spring 1973, *4*(1), pp. 89–100.

Artus, Jacques R. The Short-Run Effects of Domestic Demand Pressure on Export Delivery Delays for Machinery. *J. Int. Econ.*, February 1973, *3*(1), pp. 21–36.

_____ and Rhomberg, Rudolf R. A Multilateral Exchange Rate Model. *Int. Monet. Fund Staff Pap.*, November 1973, *20*(3), pp. 591–611.

Arunachalam, M. V. Role of Commercial Banks as Development Agencies. In *Simha, S. L. N., ed.*, 1973, pp. 223–29.

Asaduzzaman, Md. The Seasonal Variation in Price of Rice: Bangladesh 1950–72. *Bangladesh Econ. Rev.*, April 1973, *1*(2), pp. 213–20.

Aschheim, Joseph. Neutral Money Reconsidered. *Banca Naz. Lavoro Quart. Rev.*, June 1973, *105*, pp. 75–83.

Aschinger, F. E. The Eurocurrency Market and National Credit Policy. In *Henley, D. S., ed.*, 1973, pp. 217–22.

Aschoff, John; Simon, Julian L. and Puig, Carlos M. A Duopoly Simulation and Richer Theory: An End to Cournot. *Rev. Econ. Stud.*, July 1973, *40*(3), pp. 353–66.

Ashenfelter, Orley. Child Quality and the Demand for Children: Comment. *J. Polit. Econ.*, Part II, March-April 1973, *81*(2), pp. S96–98.

Asher, Ephraim. Consumers Time-Preferences and Welfare Economics under Socialism. *Scot. J. Polit. Econ.*, November 1973, *20*(3), pp. 283–90.

_____ and Kumar, T. Krishna. Capital-Labor Substitution and Technical Progress in Planned and Market Oriented Economies: A Comparative Study. *Southern Econ. J.*, July 1973, *40*(1), pp. 103–09.

Asher, Robert. Radicalism and Reform: State Insurance of Workmen's Compensation in Minnesota, 1910-1933. *Labor Hist.*, Winter 1973, *14*(1), pp. 19–41.

Asher, Robert E. The Leopard's Spots. In *Lewis, J. P. and Kapur, I., eds.*, 1973, pp. 21–26.

Ashturkar, B. W.; Choudhuri, S. D. and Ambegaonkar, L. V. Response of Irrigated M35-1 Rabi Jo-

war to Levels of Nitrogen. *Econ. Aff.*, June 1973, *18*(6), pp. 261–64.

Asimakopulos, A. Keynes, Patinkin, Historical Time, and Equilibrium Analysis. *Can. J. Econ.*, May 1973, *6*(2), pp. 179–88.

Askari, Hossein. Demand for Travel to Europe by American Citizens. *Econ. Int.*, May 1973, *26*(2), pp. 305–17.

_____ A Note on the Empirical Testing of the Ricardian Theory of Comparative Advantage. *Southern Econ. J.*, July 1973, *40*(1), pp. 120–21.

_____; Bizien, Yves and Hossain, Ekram. The Success of Some Devaluations and Revaluations in the Post-War Era. *Econ. Int.*, August-November 1973, *26*(3–4), pp. 471–91.

_____ and Modigliani, Franco. The International Transfer of Capital and the Propagation of Domestic Disturbances Under Alternative Payment Systems. *Banca Naz. Lavoro Quart. Rev.*, December 1973, (107), pp. 295–310.

Aspin, Les. A Solution to the Energy Crisis: The Case for Increased Competition. *Ann. Amer. Acad. Polit. Soc. Sci.*, November 1973, *410*, pp. 154–68.

Astin, Helen S. Women's Studies in American Colleges and Universities. *Int. Soc. Sci. J.*, 1973, *25*(3), pp. 389–400.

Astiz, Carlos A. The Military Establishment as a Political Elite: The Peruvian Case. In *Pollock, D. H. and Ritter, A. R. M., eds.*, 1973, pp. 203–29.

Atkinson, A. B. How Progressive Should Income Tax Be? In *Parkin, M., ed.*, 1973, pp. 90–109.

_____ Worker Management and the Modern Industrial Enterprise. *Quart. J. Econ.*, August 1973, *87*(3), pp. 375–92.

_____ and Skegg, J. L. Anti-Smoking Publicity and the Demand for Tobacco in the U.K. *Manchester Sch. Econ. Soc. Stud.*, September 1973, *41*(3), pp. 265–82.

_____ and Waverman, L. Resource Allocation and the Regulated Firm: Comment. *Bell J. Econ. Manage. Sci.*, Spring 1973, *4*(1), pp. 283–87.

Atkinson, L. J. Factors Affecting the Purchase Value of New Houses. In *Haynes, W. W.; Coyne, T. J. and Osborne, D. K., eds.*, 1973, pp. 85–112.

Atlas, Z. Profits and Profitability as Criteria of the Effectiveness of Production. *Prob. Econ.*, December 1973, *16*(8), pp. 56–80.

Atwood, Janet. Energy Resources in New Mexico. *N. Mex. Bus.*, May 1973, *26*(5), pp. 3–10.

Aubin, Jean-Pierre. Multi-Games and Decentralization in Management. In *Cochrane, J. L. and Zeleny, M., eds.*, 1973, pp. 313–26.

Audouin, Maurice. Application of Computers to Distribution in the Newspaper and Publishing Industries. In *The Diebold Group, Inc.*, 1973, pp. 314–24.

Aufhauser, R. Keith. Slavery and Scientific Management. *J. Econ. Hist.*, December 1973, *33*(4), pp. 811–24.

Aujac, H. A New Approach to Technological Forecasting in French National Planning. In *Williams, B. R., ed.*, 1973, pp. 96–115.

Aukrust, Odd and Nordbotten, Svein. Files of Individual Data and their Potentials for Social Research. *Rev. Income Wealth*, June 1973, *19*(2), pp. 189–201.

Ault, David E. The Continued Deterioration of the Competitive Ability of the U.S. Steel Industry: The Development of Continuous Casting. *Western Econ. J.,* March 1973, *11*(1), pp. 89–97.

———— On the Importance of Lags in Technology: An Empirical Test. *Rivista Int. Sci. Econ. Com.,* October 1973, *20*(10), pp. 945–60.

———— **and Johnson, Thomas E., Jr.** Probabilistic Models Applied to Hospital Planning. *Growth Change,* April 1973, *4*(2), pp. 7–13.

Aumann, Robert J. Disadvantageous Monopolies. *J. Econ. Theory,* February 1973, *6*(1), pp. 1–11.

Ausch, S. Plan, Market and Socialist Integration. In *Kiss, T., ed.,* 1973, pp. 63–76.

Aussieker, Bill and Garbarino, Joseph W. Measuring Faculty Unionism: Quantity and Quality. *Ind. Relat.,* May 1973, *12*(2), pp. 117–24.

Auster, Richard and Silver, Morris. Collective Goods and Collective Decision Mechanisms. *Public Choice,* Spring 1973, *14,* pp. 1–17.

Austman, H. H. Agricultural Economists Responding to an Expanding Clientele. *Amer. J. Agr. Econ.,* December 1973, *55*(5), pp. 989–92.

Averous, Christian P. and Artle, Roland. The Telephone System as a Public Good: Static and Dynamic Aspects. *Bell J. Econ. Manage. Sci.,* Spring 1973, *4*(1), pp. 89–100.

———— **and Lee, Douglass B., Jr.** Land Allocation and Transportation Pricing in a Mixed Economy. *J. Reg. Sci.,* August 1973, *13*(2), pp. 173–85.

Avila Beloso, Carlos and Ruiz-Palá, Ernesto. Stochastic Processes: Discussant 2. In *Ross, M., ed.,* 1973, pp. 245–51.

Avio, Kenneth L. An Economic Analysis of Criminal Corrections: The Canadian Case. *Can. J. Econ.,* May 1973, *6*(2), pp. 164–78.

———— An Economic Rationale for Statutory Interest Rate Ceilings. *Quart. Rev. Econ. Bus.,* Autumn 1973, *13*(3), pp. 61–72.

Avramescu, P. Coordonate ale intensificării aviculturii în cooperativele agricole de producţie. (Coordinates of the Intensification of Poultry Farming in the Agricultural Production Cooperatives. With English summary.) *Stud. Cercet. Econ.,* 1973, (3), pp. 51–72.

Awad, M. Dilemmas in Economic Independence: Lessons from Sudan. In *Ghai, D., ed.,* 1973, pp. 205–31.

Axelsson, Runo. The Economic Postulate of Rationality—Some Methodological Views. *Swedish J. Econ.,* September 1973, *75*(3), pp. 289–95.

Ayal, Eliezer B. Micro Aspects of Development: Introduction. In *Ayal, E. B., ed.,* 1973, pp. xix–xxxi.

Ayers, C. E. and Burger, David H. In Memoriam. *Amer. J. Econ. Soc.,* July 1973, *32*(3), pp. 335–36.

Ayob, Ahmad Mahzan and Prato, Anthony A. United States Import Demand and Prices of Natural Rubber. *Malayan Econ. Rev.,* April 1973, *18*(1), pp. 24–35.

Ayres, Robert U.; d'Arge, Ralph C. and Kneese, Allen V. Economics and the Environment: A Materials Balance Approach. In *Enthoven, A. C. and Freeman, A. M., III, eds.,* 1973, pp. 25–36.

———— **and Kneese, Allen V.** Economic and Ecological Effects of a Stationary Economy. In *Enthoven, A. C. and Freeman, A. M., III, eds.,* 1973, pp. 235–52.

———— **and Stern, Martin O.** Transportation Outlays: Who Pays and Who Benefits? In *Harriss, C. L., ed.,* 1973, pp. 117–54.

Azevedo, R. and Mitchell, D. J. B. A Pay Board Assessment of Wage Controls. *Mon. Lab. Rev.,* April 1973, *96*(4), pp. 21–23.

Azfar, Javaid. The Distribution of Income in Pakistan—1966–67. *Pakistan Econ. Soc. Rev.,* Spring 1973, *11*(1), pp. 40–66.

Azhar, B. A. Agricultural Taxation in West Pakistan. *Pakistan Econ. Soc. Rev.,* Autumn 1973, *11*(3), pp. 288–315.

———— An Econometric Analysis of Price Behaviour in Pakistan. *Pakistan Develop. Rev.,* Winter 1973, *12*(4), pp. 375–92.

———— Land Revenue Assessment: A Case Study. *Pakistan Develop. Rev.,* Autumn 1973, *12*(3), pp. 232–46.

———— **; Chaudhry, M. Ghaffar and Shafique, M.** A Model for Forecasting Wheat Production in the Punjab. *Pakistan Develop. Rev.,* Winter 1973, *12*(4), pp. 407–15.

Azizur Rahman, A. N. M. Elasticities of Substitution in Manufacturing Industries of Bangladesh: An International Comparison. *Bangladesh Econ. Rev.,* April 1973, *1*(2), pp. 173–85.

Azzi, Corry F. and Cox, James C. Equity and Efficiency in Evaluation of Public Programs. *Quart. J. Econ.,* August 1973, *87*(3), pp. 495–502.

Baack, Bennett D. and Ray, Edward J. Tariff Policy and Comparative Advantage in the Iron and Steel Industry: 1870–1929. *Exploration Econ. Hist.,* Fall 1973, *11*(1), pp. 3–23.

Babad, Jair; Bicksler, James L. and Barnea, Amir. Portfolio Choice, the Horizon Problem and the Investment Opportunity Set. *Amer. Econ. Rev.,* May 1973, *63*(2), pp. 140–44.

Babcock, Richard F. Exclusionary Zoning: A Code Phrase for a Notable Legal Struggle. In *Masotti, L. H. and Hadden, J. K., eds.,* 1973, pp. 313–28.

———— **and Callies, David L.** Ecology and Housing: Virtues in Conflict. In *Clawson, M., ed.,* 1973, pp. 205–20.

Babeau, André. Economies d'échelle dans les encaisses monétaires des ménages: une série de tests empiriques. (Economies of Scale in the Households' Cash Balances. With English summary.) *Revue Écon.,* May 1973, *24*(3), pp. 401–41.

Babingui, Denis. Savings Banks and Savings Facilities in African Countries: Congo Brazzaville. In *Alberici, A. and Baravelli, M., eds.,* 1973, pp. 19–21.

Babson, Steve. The Multinational Corporation and Labor. *Rev. Radical Polit. Econ.,* Spring 1973, *5*(1), pp. 19–36.

Baccanari, Samuel M. and Leduc, Edgar. Interlocal Governmental Relations in Air Pollution Abatement. In *Gabriel, R. A. and Cohen, S. H., eds.,* 1973, pp. 113–28.

Bach, Christopher L. Foreign Exchange and U.S. Balance-of-Payments Developments in 1972 and Early 1973. *Fed. Res. Bank St. Louis Rev.,* April 1973, *55*(4), pp. 14–20.

Bach, G. L. An Agenda for Improving the Teaching of Economics. *Amer. Econ. Rev.,* May 1973, *63*(2), pp. 303–08.

Bacha, Edmar. Developing Country Alternatives:

Comment. In *Hughes, H., ed.*, 1973, pp. 137–40.

───── Preference for Industry and Commercial Policy Theory in Industrializing Countries. In *Eckaus, R. S. and Rosenstein-Rodan, P. N., eds.*, 1973, pp. 269–92.

───── and Taylor, Lance. Foreign Exchange Shadow Prices: A Critical Review of Current Theories. In *Eckaus, R. S. and Rosenstein-Rodan, P. N., eds.*, 1973, pp. 3–29.

───── and Taylor, Lance. Growth and Trade Distortions in Chile, and Their Implications in Calculating the Shadow Price of Foreign Exchange. In *Eckaus, R. S. and Rosenstein-Rodan, P. N., eds.*, 1973, pp. 121–46.

Bachman, Gordon; Barlowe, Raleigh and Ahl, James G. Use-Value Assessment Legislation in the United States. *Land Econ.*, May 1973, *49*(2), pp. 206–12.

Bacon, Robert. The Phillips Curve: Another Forerunner. *Economica, N.S.*, August 1973, *40*(159), pp. 314–15.

Bácskai, T. The Experience of Savings-Banks in Socialist Economies and its Applicability to Developing Countries. *Acta Oecon.*, 1973, *10*(2), pp. 201–16.

Bade, Robin. Optimal Foreign Investment and International Trade. *Econ. Rec.*, March 1973, *49* (125), pp. 62–75.

Baden, John and Stroup, Richard. Externality, Property Rights, and the Management of our National Forests. *J. Law Econ.*, October 1973, *16*(2), pp. 303–12.

Baer, Donald E. Income and Export Taxation of Agriculture in Costa Rica and Honduras. *J. Devel. Areas*, October 1973, *8*(1), pp. 39–53.

Baer, Werner and Villela, Annibal V. Industrial Growth and Industrialization: Revisions in the Stages of Brazil's Economic Development. *J. Devel. Areas*, January 1973, *7*(2), pp. 217–34.

Baerwaldt, Nancy A. and Morgan, James N. Trends in Inter-Family Transfers. In *Mandell, L., et al., eds.*, 1973, pp. 205–32.

Bagchi, Amiya Kumar. Foreign Capital and Economic Development in India: A Schematic View. In *Gough, K. and Sharma, H. P., eds.*, 1973, pp. 43–76.

Bagrinovsky, K. A. A System of Models for Central Planning. In *Hawkes, N., ed.*, 1973, pp. 21–30.

───── and Aganbegian, A. G. Problem-Complexes in Optimal Planning. *Acta Oecon.*, 1973, *10*(1), pp. 21–27.

Baher, G. H. A Planning Model for the Educational Requirements of Economic Development: The Case of Iran. *Tahq. Eq.*, Winter & Spring 1973, *10* (29 & 30), pp. 170–205.

Bahl, Roy W.; Coelen, Stephen P. and Warford, Jeremy J. Land Value Increments as a Measure of the Net Benefits of Urban Water Supply Projects in Developing Countries: Theory and Measurement. In *Harriss, C. L., ed.*, 1973, pp. 171–88.

Bahr, F. R. and Rowe, A. J. A Heuristic Approach to Managerial Problem Solving. *J. Econ. Bus.*, Spring-Summer 1973, *25*(3), pp. 159–63.

Bahr, Richard C. Price Indexes by Size of City Show Increases Ranging from 7.6 to 8.9 Percent. *Mon. Lab. Rev.*, June 1973, *96*(6), pp. 54–55.

───── Second Quarter Prices Rise Faster in Smaller

Urban Areas. *Mon. Lab. Rev.*, September 1973, *96*(9), pp. 73–74.

───── and Nakayama, Toshiko. New CPI by Size of City Shows Larger Increases in Big Areas. *Mon. Lab. Rev.*, March 1973, *96*(3), pp. 55–57.

Bailey, Andrew D., Jr. A Dynamic Programming Approach to the Analysis of Different Costing Methods in Accounting for Inventories. *Accounting Rev.*, July 1973, *48*(3), pp. 560–74.

Bailey, Elizabeth E. Resource Allocation and the Regulated Firm: Comment on the Comments. *Bell J. Econ. Manage. Sci.*, Spring 1973, *4*(1), pp. 288–92.

Bailey, F. A. A Note on Pert/Cost Resource Allocation. In *Thomas, W. E., Jr., ed.*, 1973, pp. 264–65.

Bailey, Norman A. The Monetary System and the Businessman: Comment. In *Wiegand, G. C., ed.*, 1973, pp. 158–59.

Bailey, Richard. Britain and a Community Energy Policy. *Nat. Westminster Bank Quart. Rev.*, November 1973, pp. 5–15.

───── European Community in a World Context. *Irish Banking Rev.*, June 1973, pp. 16–22.

Bailey, Ronald. Economic Aspects of the Black Internal Colony. In *Bonilla, F. and Girling, R., eds.*, 1973, pp. 161–88.

───── and Flores, Guillermo V. Internal Colonialism and Racial Minorities in the U.S.: An Overview. In *Bonilla, F. and Girling, R., eds.*, 1973, pp. 149–60.

Bailey, William C. Motives of Criminals: Comment. In *Rottenberg, S., ed.*, 1973, pp. 39–55.

Bails, Dale. An Alternative: The Land Value Tax. *Amer. J. Econ. Soc.*, July 1973, *32*(3), pp. 283–94.

Bain, A. D. Flow of Funds Analysis: Survey. *Econ. J.*, December 1973, *83*(332), pp. 1055–93.

───── and Evans, J. D. Price Formation and Profits: Explanatory and Forecasting Models of Manufacturing Industry Profits in the U.K. *Oxford Bull. Econ. Statist.*, November 1973, *35*(4), pp. 295–308.

Bain, R. A. Factors Affecting Consumption and Prices of the Major Feed Grains in Australia. *Quart. Rev. Agr. Econ.*, July 1973, *26*(3), pp. 186–97.

Bairstow, Frances. Canada's Discontent with Strikes Prompts Interest in Arbitration. *Mon. Lab. Rev.*, August 1973, *96*(8), pp. 63–64.

Bǎjan, Ana. Verificarea existenței legăturilor statistice prin metoda distribuțiilor condiționate și prin analiza dispersională. (Verifying the Existence of Statistical Connections Through the Method of Conditioned Distributions and Through the Dispersional Analysis. With English summary.) *Stud. Cercet. Econ.*, 1973, (1), pp. 77–97.

Baker, A. R. H. Field Systems of Southeast England. In *Baker, A. R. H. and Butlin, R. A., eds.*, 1973, pp. 377–429.

───── and Butlin, R. A. Studies of Field Systems in the British Isles: Conclusion: Problems and Perspectives. In *Baker, A. R. H. and Butlin, R. A., eds.*, 1973, pp. 619–56.

───── and Butlin, R. A. Studies of Field Systems in the British Isles: Introduction: Materials and Methods. In *Baker, A. R. H. and Butlin, R. A., eds.*, 1973, pp. 1–40.

Baker, C. B. Capital Budgeting and Financial Management in Linear Programming Models. **In** *Judge, G. G. and Takayama, T., eds.*, 1973, pp. 688–705.

_____; **Fettig, L. P. and Ogut, Soner.** Effects of Financing and Employment Alternatives on a Modern Farm Village in Turkey. *Ill. Agr. Econ.*, July 1973, *13*(2), pp. 12–15.

Baker, Donald I. Chartering, Branching, and the Concentration Problem. **In** *Federal Reserve Bank of Boston*, 1973, pp. 21–39.

Baker, Mary Roys. Anglo-Massachusetts Trade Union Roots, 1130–1790. *Labor Hist.*, Summer 1973, *14*(3), pp. 352–96.

Baker, Robert P. Labor History, Social Science, and the Concept of the Working Class. *Labor Hist.*, Winter 1973, *14*(1), pp. 98–105.

Baker, R. Palmer, Jr. and Fritzhand, Gary I. United States Federal Income Taxation of Foreign-Flag Shipping Earnings. *Nat. Tax J.*, December 1973, *26*(4), pp. 537–51.

Baker, Samuel H. Risk, Leverage, and Profitability: An Industry Analysis. *Rev. Econ. Statist.*, November 1973, *55*(4), pp. 503–07.

Balacs, P. and Balogh, T. Fact and Fancy in International Economic Relations. *World Devel.*, February 1973, *1*(1-2), pp. 76–92.

_____ **and Balogh, T.** Fact and Fancy in International Economic Relations. *World Devel.*, March-April 1973, *1*(3–4), pp. 71–105.

Balakrishnan, T. R. A Cost Benefit Analysis of the Barbados Family Planning Programme. *Population Stud.*, July 1973, *27*(2), pp. 353–64.

Balassa, Á. Economic Growth, Equilibrium and Efficiency in the Present Stage of Development. *Acta Oecon.*, 1973, *10*(3–4), pp. 339–60.

Balassa, Bela. The Firm in the New Economic Mechanism in Hungary. **In** *Bornstein, M., ed.*, 1973, pp. 347–72.

_____ Implications for Integration of the World Economy: Comment. **In** *Krause, L. B. and Salant, W. S., eds.*, 1973, pp. 266–69.

_____ Industrial Policy in the European Common Market. *Banca Naz. Lavoro Quart. Rev.*, December 1973, (107), pp. 311–27.

_____ Just How Misleading are Official Exchange Rate Conversions?: Comment. *Econ. J.*, December 1973, *83*(332), pp. 1258–67.

_____ A Plan for a European Currency: Comment. **In** *Johnson, H. G. and Swoboda, A. K., eds.*, 1973, pp. 173–77.

_____ Planning and Programming in the European Common Market. *Europ. Econ. Rev.*, October 1973, *4*(3), pp. 217–33.

_____ Policy Issues in Adjustment Assistance: The United States: Comment. **In** *Hughes, H., ed.*, 1973, pp. 180–86.

_____ Regional Integration of Trade: Policies of Less Developed Countries. **In** *Streeten, P., ed.*, 1973, pp. 176–86.

_____ Regional Policies and the Environment in the European Common Market. *Weltwirtsch. Arch.*, 1973, *109*(3), pp. 402–17.

_____ Tariffs and Trade Policy in the Andean Common Market. *J. Common Market Stud.*, December 1973, *12*(2), pp. 176–95.

_____ Two Arguments for Fixed Rates: Comment.

In *Johnson, H. G. and Swoboda, A. K., eds.*, 1973, pp. 40–45.

Balázsy, S. Financial Regulating System and Technical Development. *Acta Oecon.*, 1973, *10*(3–4), pp. 315–38.

Balbach, Anatol. Foreign Investment in the United States—A Danger to Our Welfare and Sovereignty? *Fed. Res. Bank St. Louis Rev.*, October 1973, *55*(10), pp. 10–13.

Balch, Michael and Ben-Zion, Uri. On the Analysis of Corporate Financial Theory under Uncertainty: A Comment. *Quart. J. Econ.*, May 1973, *87* (2), pp. 290–95.

Baldwin, George B. "Population Policy in Developed Countries" *Finance Develop.*, December 1973, *10*(4), pp. 3–7.

Baldwin, Robert and Mutti, John H. Policy Issues in Adjustment Assistance: The United States. **In** *Hughes, H., ed.*, 1973, pp. 149–77.

Bale, Malcolm D. Full Employment, Trade Expansion, and Adjustment Assistance: Comment. *Southern Econ. J.*, July 1973, *40*(1), pp. 135–38.

Balestra, Pietro. Best Quadratic Unbiased Estimators of the Variance-Covariance Matrix in Normal Regression. *J. Econometrics*, March 1973, *1*(1), pp. 17–28.

Balintfy, Joseph L. and Goodman, Seymour S. Socio-Economic Factors in Income Inequality: A Log-Normal Hypothesis. *Z. Nationalökon.*, 1973, *33* (3–4), pp. 389–402.

von Ball, Michael J. Recent Empirical Work on the Determinants of Relative House Prices. *Urban Stud.*, June 1973, *10*(2), pp. 213–33.

Ball, R. J. The Economic Models of Project LINK. **In** *Ball, R. J., ed.*, 1973, pp. 65–107.

_____ Investment Incentives. *Nat. Westminster Bank Quart. Rev.*, August 1973, pp. 22–35.

Ball, Robert. Labor and Materials Required for Highway Construction. *Mon. Lab. Rev.*, June 1973, *96*(6), pp. 40–45.

Ball, Robert M. Social Security Amendments of 1972: Summary and Legislative History. *Soc. Sec. Bull.*, March 1973, *36*(3), pp. 3–25.

Balles, John J. Evaluating Money Market Conditions. *Fed. Res. Bank San Francisco Rev.*, September-October 1973, pp. 3–11.

Ballinger, Roy A. The Benefits and Burdens of the United States Sugar Quota System. **In** *Harriss, C. L., ed.*, 1973, pp. 105–13.

Ballon, Robert J. Japan's Investment Overseas. *Aussenwirtschaft*, September-December 1973, *28* (3/4), pp. 128–53.

Balloni, Valeriano. Le decisioni di investimento. Risultati di interviste con dirigenti industriali inglesi. (Investment Decisions: Interviews with English Businessmen. With English summary.) *L'Impresa*, 1973, *15*(3–4), pp. 278–81.

Balogh, T. and Balacs, P. Fact and Fancy in International Economic Relations. *World Devel.*, March-April 1973, *1*(3–4), pp. 71–105.

_____ **and Balacs, P.** Fact and Fancy in International Economic Relations. *World Devel.*, February 1973, *1*(1-2), pp. 76–92.

Balquière, Austin and Caussin, Pierre. Differential Games with Time Lag. **In** *Blaquière, A., ed.*, 1973, pp. 151–78.

Baltensperger, Ernst. Optimal Bank Portfolios: The Liability Side. *Jahr. Nationalökon. Statist.*, January 1973, *187*(2), pp. 147–60.

_____ Zur Rolle des Bankensystems in makroökonomischen Modellen. (The Role of the Banking System in Macroeconomic Models. With English summary.) *Kyklos*, 1973, *26*(4), pp. 787–803.

Bambrick, Susan. Australian Price Levels, 1890–1970. *Australian Econ. Hist. Rev.*, March 1973, *13*(1), pp. 57–71.

Bame, Jack J. U.S. Balance of Payments Developments: First Quarter 1973. *Surv. Curr. Bus.*, June 1973, *53*(6), pp. 17–23, 53–55.

_____ U.S. Balance of Payments Developments: Third Quarter and First Nine Months of 1973. *Surv. Curr. Bus.*, December 1973, *53*(12), pp. 33–40, 56.

Bandera, V. N. Interdependence between Interregional and International Payments: The Balance of Payments of Ukraine. In *Bandera, V. N. and Melnyk, Z. L., eds.*, 1973, pp. 132–53.

_____ **and Melnyk, Z. Lew.** The Soviet Economy in Regional Perspective: Introduction. In *Bandera, V. N. and Melnyk, Z. L., eds.*, 1973, pp. xvii–xxi.

Bandurski, Bruce Lord. Ecology and Economics—Partners for Productivity. *Ann. Amer. Acad. Polit. Soc. Sci.*, January 1973, *405*, pp. 75–94.

Banerjee, B. P. A Working Plan for Programming and Sustaining the Growth of Small Scale Industries around Calcutta, India. In *Ross, M., ed.*, 1973, pp. 483–89.

Banerjee, R. M. and Das, A. C. Theoretical Approach for Measuring Intensity of Unemployment. *Econ. Aff.*, November-December 1973, *18*(11–12), pp. 497–502.

Banfield, Edward C. A Critical View of the Urban Crisis. *Ann. Amer. Acad. Polit. Soc. Sci.*, January 1973, *405*, pp. 7–14.

Banke, Niels. Kommentarer til Karl Marx's mindesten. (On Marxian Economics. With English summary.) *Nationalokon. Tidsskr.*, 1973, *111*(1), pp. 112–43.

Banks, F. E. Growth and Pollution. *Ekon. Samfundets Tidskr.*, 1973, *26*(2), pp. 67–74.

_____ A Note on Stochastic Programming in a Development Plan. *Kyklos*, 1973, *26*(2), pp. 395–98.

_____ On Optimal Transformation Frontier. *Tahq. Eq.*, Summer & Autumn 1973, *10*(31&32), pp. 80–83.

Bannister, Robert C., Jr. William Graham Sumner's Social Darwinism: A Recommendation. *Hist. Polit. Econ.*, Spring 1973, *5*(1), pp. 89–109.

Baraquin, Yves and Jobert, Annette. Les immigrés: Réflexions sur leur insertion sociale et leur intégration juridique. (Immigrants: Their Social Insertion and Juridical Integration. With English summary.) *Consommation*, July-September 1973, *20*(3), pp. 83–97.

Barattieri, Vittorio. La riforma del sistema monetario internazionale. (Reform of the International Monetary System. With English summary.) *Bancaria*, May 1973, *29*(5), pp. 568–78.

Barbash, Jack. Consumption Values of Trade Unions. *J. Econ. Issues*, June 1973, *7*(2), pp. 289–301.

Barber, Arthur. Emerging New Power: The World Corporation. In *Andreano, R. L., ed.*, 1973, pp. R333–05.

Barber, Clarence L. The Farm Machinery Industry: Reconciling the Interests of the Farmer, the Industry, and the General Public. *Amer. J. Agr. Econ.*, December 1973, *55*(5), pp. 820–28.

_____ Presidential Address: A Sense of Proportion. *Can. J. Econ.*, November 1973, *6*(4), pp. 467–82.

Barber, G. Russell, Jr. The One Hundred Percent Reserve System. *Amer. Econ.*, Spring 1973, *17*(1), pp. 115–27.

Barckley, Robert and Woo, H. Nam. Sources of Cost Differentials in Higher Education: The Case of California State Colleges. *Malayan Econ. Rev.*, October 1973, *18*(2), pp. 68–78.

Bardhan, Kalpana and Bardhan, Pranab K. The Green Revolution and Socio-Economic Tensions: The Case of India. *Int. Soc. Sci. J.*, 1973, *25*(3), pp. 285–92.

Bardhan, Pranab K. A Model of Growth of Capitalism in a Dual Agrarian Economy. In *[Rosenstein-Rodan, P.]*, 1973, pp. 109–17.

_____ More on Putty-Clay. *Int. Econ. Rev.*, February 1973, *14*(1), pp. 211–22.

_____ 'Green Revolution' and Agricultural Labourers. In *Wadhva, C. D., ed.*, 1973, pp. 346–61.

_____ On Terms of Foreign Borrowing. *Amer. Econ. Rev.*, June 1973, *63*(3), pp. 458–61.

_____ Size, Productivity, and Returns to Scale: An Analysis of Farm-Level Data in Indian Agriculture. *J. Polit. Econ.*, November-December 1973, *81*(6), pp. 1370–86.

_____ **and Bardhan, Kalpana.** The Green Revolution and Socio-Economic Tensions: The Case of India. *Int. Soc. Sci. J.*, 1973, *25*(3), pp. 285–92.

_____ **and Lapan, Harvey.** Localized Technical Progress and Transfer of Technology and Economic Development. *J. Econ. Theory*, December 1973, *6*(6), pp. 585–95.

Bareau, Paul. Bank Rate—Without the Mystique. *Irish Banking Rev.*, March 1973, pp. 13–18.

Barg, Benjamin. Nutrition and National Development. In *Berg, A.; Scrimshaw, N. S. and Call, D. L., eds.*, 1973, pp. 49–69.

Barger, Harold. International Liquidity and International Trade: Comment. In *Wiegand, G. C., ed.*, 1973, pp. 97–98.

Barkai, Haim. The European Economic Community Approach to Adjustment: Comment. In *Hughes, H., ed.*, 1973, pp. 217–22.

_____ The Macro-Economics of Tsarist Russia in the Industrialization Era: Monetary Developments, the Balance of Payments and the Gold Standard. *J. Econ. Hist.*, June 1973, *33*(2), pp. 339–71.

_____ **and Levhari, David.** The Impact of Experience on Kibbutz Farming. *Rev. Econ. Statist.*, February 1973, *55*(1), pp. 56–63.

Barker, Betty L. and Kraseman, Thomas W. Employment and Payroll Costs of U.S. Multinational Companies. *Surv. Curr. Bus.*, October 1973, *53*(10), pp. 36–44.

Barker, C. Austin. Alternative Monetary Proposals. In *Wiegand, G. C., ed.*, 1973, pp. 179–82.

Barker, F. David and Cassady, Ralph, Jr. Price Formation and Decision-Making in Covent Garden Market, London. *Calif. Manage. Rev.*, Fall 1973, *16*(1), pp. 86–94.

Barker, Robinson F. The Businessman's Role. *Manage. Account.*, February 1973, *54*(8), pp. 15–16, 25.

Barkin, David P. Cuban Agriculture: A Strategy of Economic Development. In *Barkin, D. P. and Manitzas, N. R., eds.*, 1973, pp. R261–21.

Barkin, Solomon. Changing Profile of European Manpower Policies. In *Somers, G. G., ed.*, 1973, pp. 83–100.

_____ Trade Unions and Consumerism. *J. Econ. Issues*, June 1973, *7*(2), pp. 317–21.

Barksdale, Hiram C. and Guffey, Hugh J., Jr. A Cross-Spectral Analysis of Motor Vehicle Sales and Registrations. *Swedish J. Econ.*, September 1973, *75*(3), pp. 266–77.

Barlev, Benzion. Location Effects of Intra-Area Tax Differentials. *Land Econ.*, February 1973, *49*(1), pp. 86–89.

Barlow, Colin. The Socio-Economic Response to Different Institutional Structure. In *Epstein, T. S. and Penny, D. H., eds.*, 1973, pp. 193–202.

Barlow, Joel. The Tax Law Bias Against Investment in Production Facilities. *Nat. Tax J.*, September 1973, *26*(3), pp. 415–37.

Barlow, Robin. Efficiency Aspects of Local School Finance: Reply. *J. Polit. Econ.*, January-February 1973, *81*(1), pp. 199–202.

Barlowe, Raleigh; Ahl, James G. and Bachman, Gordon. Use-Value Assessment Legislation in the United States. *Land Econ.*, May 1973, *49*(2), pp. 206–12.

Barnea, Amir; Babad, Jair and Bicksler, James L. Portfolio Choice, the Horizon Problem and the Investment Opportunity Set. *Amer. Econ. Rev.*, May 1973, *63*(2), pp. 140–44.

_____ and Downes, David H. A Reexamination of the Empirical Distribution of Stock Price Changes. *J. Amer. Statist. Assoc.*, June 1973, *68* (342), pp. 348–50.

_____ and Logue, Dennis E. Stock-Market Based Measures of Corporate Diversification. *J. Ind. Econ.*, September 1973, *22*(1), pp. 51–60.

Barnes, William F. and Jones, Ethel B. Robbins, Hicks, Buchanan and the Backward Bending Labor Supply Curve. *Miss. Val. J. Bus. Econ.*, Fall 1973, *9*(1), pp. 76–82.

Barnett, Andy H. and Yandle, Bruce, Jr. Allocating Environmental Resources. *Public Finance*, 1973, *28*(1), pp. 11–19.

Barnett, William A. The Effects of Consumer Bliss on Welfare Economics. *J. Econ. Issues*, March 1973, *7*(1), pp. 29–45.

Barnsby, G. J. The Standard of Living in the Black Country in the Nineteenth Century: A Rejoinder. *Econ. Hist. Rev.*, 2nd Ser., August 1973, *26*(3), pp. 514–16.

Baron, David P. Limit Pricing, Potential Entry, and Barriers to Entry. *Amer. Econ. Rev.*, September 1973, *63*(4), pp. 666–74.

_____ Point Estimation and Risk Preferences. *J. Amer. Statist. Assoc.*, December 1973, *68*(344), pp. 944–50.

_____ Stochastic Programming and Risk Aversion.

In *Cochrane, J. L. and Zeleny, M., eds.*, 1973, pp. 124–38.

Baron, Donald C. and McDonald, John G. Risk and Return on Short Positions in Common Stocks. *J. Finance*, March 1973, *28*(1), pp. 97–107.

Baroutsis, A. Paul and Horton, Joseph. An Economic Strategy for Environmental Quality. In *Gabriel, R. A. and Cohen, S. H., eds.*, 1973, pp. 61–93.

Barr, Joseph W. A Revised Regulatory Framework. In *Federal Reserve Bank of Boston*, 1973, pp. 205–08.

Barr, Terry N. and Gale, Hazen F. A Quarterly Forecasting Model for the Consumer Price Index for Food. *Agr. Econ. Res.*, January 1973, *25*(1), pp. 1–14.

Barraclough, Solon. The Structure and Problems of the Chilean Agrarian Sector. In *Zammit, J. A., ed.*, 1973, pp. 115–22.

_____ and Schatan, Jacobo. Technological Policy and Agricultural Development. *Land Econ.*, May 1973, *49*(2), pp. 175–94.

Barraza, Luciano and Solís, Leopoldo. Agricultural Policies and the Role of the Sectoral Model. In *Goreux, L. M. and Manne, A. S., eds.*, 1973, pp. 463–75.

Barro, Robert J. The Control of Politicians: An Economic Model. *Public Choice*, Spring 1973, *14*, pp. 19–42.

Barsby, Steven L. Great Spurts and the Experience of Non-European Countries. *J. Econ. Issues*, September 1973, *7*(3), pp. 459–74.

Barták, Rudolf and Hynar, Ladislav. Optimální cesty. (Optimal Routes. With English summary.) *Ekon.-Mat. Obzor*, 1973, *9*(2), pp. 167–83.

Barten, Anton P. and Parks, Richard W. A Cross-Country Comparison of the Effects of Prices, Income and Population Composition on Consumption Patterns. *Econ. J.*, September 1973, *83*(331), pp. 834–52.

Barth, James R. and Bennett, James T. Astronomics: A New Approach to Economics? *J. Polit. Econ.*, November-December 1973, *81*(6), pp. 1473–75.

Bartholomew, D. J. Post-experience Training for Statisticians. *J. Roy. Statist. Soc.*, Part 1, 1973, *136*, pp. 65–70.

Bartlett, Roland W. Are Supermarkets Charging Consumers Too Much for Handling Milk? *Ill. Agr. Econ.*, July 1973, *13*(2), pp. 1–5.

Bartolomei, José A. Políticas de esterilización del superavit o déficit de la balanza de pagos: la experiencia alemana entre 1958 y 1968. (Policies of Neutralizing the Effects of a Surplus or a Deficit in a Balance of Payments: The German Experience Between the Years 1958–1968. With English summary.) *Económica*, January-April 1973, *19*(1), pp. 3–44.

Barton, David M. Constitutional Choice and Simple Majority Rule: Comment. *J. Polit. Econ.*, Part I, March-April 1973, *81*(2), pp. 471–79.

Bartsch, William H. Notes on Developing Countries and their Statistics: Comment. *Rev. Income Wealth*, June 1973, *19*(2), pp. 211–12.

Barwick, Diane. Coranderrk and Cumeroogunga: Pioneers and Policy. In *Epstein, T. S. and Penny, D. H., eds.*, 1973, pp. 11–68.

Barzel, Yoram. The Determination of Daily Hours

and Wages. *Quart. J. Econ.*, May 1973, *87*(2), pp. 220–38.

――― Private Schools and Public School Finance. *J. Polit. Econ.*, January-February 1973, *81*(1), pp. 174–86.

――― **and McDonald, Richard J.** Assets, Subsistence, and The Supply Curve of Labor. *Amer. Econ. Rev.*, September 1973, *63*(4), pp. 621–33.

――― **and Silberberg, Eugene.** Is the Act of Voting Rational? *Public Choice*, Fall 1973, *16*, pp. 51–58.

Basevi, G. Balances of Payments and Exchange Markets: A Lost Correspondence. *Europ. Econ. Rev.*, December 1973, *4*(4), pp. 309–28.

――― Commodity Trade Equations in Project LINK. In *Ball, R. J., ed.*, 1973, pp. 227–81.

Bashan, O., et al. Laspeyres Indexes for Variance Analysis in Cost Accounting. *Accounting Rev.*, October 1973, *48*(4), pp. 790–93.

Basmann, R. L.; Battalio, Raymond C. and Kagel, John H. Comment on R. P. Byron's "The Restricted Aitken Estimation of Sets of Demand Relations." *Econometrica*, March 1973, *41*(2), pp. 365–70.

――― **and Richardson, D. H.** The Exact Finite Sample Distribution of a Non-Consistent Structural Variance Estimator. *Econometrica*, January 1973, *41*(1), pp. 41–58.

Bass, Bernard M. and Eldridge, Larry D. Accelerated Managers' Objectives in Twelve Countries. *Ind. Relat.*, May 1973, *12*(2), pp. 158–71.

Bass, Frank M. and Wilkie, William L. A Comparative Analysis of Attitudinal Predictions of Brand Preference. *J. Marketing Res.*, August 1973, *10*(3), pp. 262–69.

Bassin, William M. A Bayesian Optimal Overhaul Interval Model for the Weibull Restoration Process Case. *J. Amer. Statist. Assoc.*, September 1973, *68*(343), pp. 575–78.

Bassoco, Luz María, et al. A Programming Model of an Agricultural District. In *Goreux, L. M. and Manne, A. S., eds.*, 1973, pp. 401–16.

――― **and Rendón, Teresa.** The Technology Set and Data Base for CHAC. In *Goreux, L. M. and Manne, A. S., eds.*, 1973, pp. 339–71.

Basu, Kalipada. Centre-States Financial Relations: A Critique. *Econ. Aff.*, May 1973, *18*(5), pp. 249–54.

Bataillie, M. Naar een nieuwe petroleumcrisis? (Towards a New Oil Crisis? With English summary.) *Econ. Soc. Tijdschr.*, April 1973, *27*(2), pp. 129–40.

Bates, Thomas H. Management and the Multinational Business Environment. *Calif. Manage. Rev.*, Spring 1973, *15*(3), pp. 37–45.

Bates, Timothy. An Econometric Analysis of Lending to Black Businessmen. *Rev. Econ. Statist.*, August 1973, *55*(3), pp. 272–83.

――― The Economic Origins of Political Power in America. In *Haveman, R. H. and Hamrin, R. D., eds.*, 1973, pp. 26–32.

――― The Potential of Black Capitalism. *Public Policy*, Winter 1973, *21*(1), pp. 135–48.

Bates, W. R.; Sexton, R. N. and Jackson, R. The Impact of Death Duties on the Rural Industries in Australia. *Quart. Rev. Agr. Econ.*, January 1973, *26*(1), pp. 25–43.

Batra, Harish. Dynamic Interdependence in Demand for Savings Deposits. *J. Finance*, May 1973, *28*(2), pp. 507–14.

Batra, Raveendra N. Effective Protection in General Equilibrium: A Geometrical Analysis. *Indian Econ. Rev.*, October 1973, *8*(2), pp. 125–47.

――― Nontraded Goods, Factor Market Distortions, and the Gains from Trade. *Amer. Econ. Rev.*, September 1973, *63*(4), pp. 706–13.

――― Optimal Restrictions on Foreign Trade and Investment: Note. *Amer. Econ. Rev.*, December 1973, *63*(5), pp. 957–59.

――― **and Casas, Francisco R.** Intermediate Products and the Pure Theory of International Trade: A Neo-Heckscher-Ohlin Framework. *Amer. Econ. Rev.*, June 1973, *63*(3), pp. 297–311.

――― **and Casas, Francisco R.** Economic Growth and International Trade in an Imperfect Market Setting. *Indian Econ. J.*, July–September 1973, *21*(1), pp. 57–65.

Battalio, Raymond C., et al. A Test of Consumer Demand Theory Using Observations of Individual Consumer Purchases. *Western Econ. J.*, December 1973, *11*(4), pp. 411–28.

――― **; Hulett, Joe R. and Kagel, John H.** A Comment on J. J. Siegfried's "The Publishing of Economic Papers and Its Impact on Graduate Faculty Ratings, 1960-1969." *J. Econ. Lit.*, March 1973, *11*(1), pp. 68–70.

――― **; Kagel, John H. and Basmann, R. L.** Comment on R. P. Byron's "The Restricted Aitken Estimation of Sets of Demand Relations." *Econometrica*, March 1973, *41*(2), pp. 365–70.

Battersby, J. R. Introduction and Development of Programme Budgeting in New Zealand. In *Novick, D., ed.*, 1973, pp. 129–38.

Battese, George E. and Fuller, Wayne A. Transformations for Estimation of Linear Models with Nested-Error Structure. *J. Amer. Statist. Assoc.*, September 1973, *68*(343), pp. 626–32.

Bauch, Vlastislav. The Effect of the Economic Policy of the Communist Party of Czechoslovakia on the Material Situation of the Population of Slovakia. *Czech. Econ. Digest.*, June 1973, (4), pp. 34–56.

Baudier, Edmond. Competitive Equilibrium in a Game. *Econometrica*, November 1973, *41*(6), pp. 1049–68.

Bauer, David. Low Unemployment Rates Abroad. In *Moskoff, W., ed.*, 1973, pp. 76–85.

Bauer, Peter. Inflation, SDRs and AID. *Lloyds Bank Rev.*, July 1973, (109), pp. 31–35.

Bauer, Raymond A. The Corporate Social Audit: Getting on the Learning Curve. *Calif. Manage. Rev.*, Fall 1973, *16*(1), pp. 5–10.

――― The Future of Corporate Social Accounting. In *Dierkes, M. and Bauer, R. A., eds.*, 1973, pp. 389–405.

――― The State of the Art of Social Auditing. In *Dierkes, M. and Bauer, R. A., eds.*, 1973, pp. 3–40.

Baum, Herbert J. Free Public Transport. *J. Transp. Econ. Policy*, January 1973, *7*(1), pp. 3–19.

Bauman, Karl E.; Chase, Charles L. and Udry, J. Richard. Population Growth Rates in Perfect Contraceptive Populations. *Population Stud.*, July 1973, *27*(2), pp. 365–71.

――― **and Udry, J. Richard.** The Difference in Unwanted Births between Blacks and Whites. *Demography,* August 1973, *10*(3), pp. 315–28.

Baumann, H. G. The Industrial Composition of U.S. Export and Subsidiary Sales to the Canadian Market: Note. *Amer. Econ. Rev.,* December 1973, *63* (5), pp. 1009–12.

Baumol, William J. Income and Substitution Effects in the Linder Theorem. *Quart. J. Econ.,* November 1973, *87*(4), pp. 629–33.

_____ Values vs. Prices: What Marx "Really" Meant. *Amer. Econ.,* Fall 1973, *17*(2), pp. 63–71.

_____, et al. Efficiency of Corporate Investment: A Reply. *Rev. Econ. Statist.,* February 1973, *55*(1), pp. 128–31.

_____ and Walton, Alfred G. Full Costing, Competition and Regulatory Practice. *Yale Law J.,* March 1973, *82*(4), pp. 639–55.

Bautina, N. Problems of Equivalence. In *Kiss, T., ed.,* 1973, pp. 191–95.

Bautista, Romeo M. Devaluation and Employment in a Labor-Surplus Economy: The Philippines. *Econ. Int.,* August-November 1973, *26*(3–4), pp. 543–59.

Bawden, D. Lee. The Neglected Human Factor. *Amer. J. Agr. Econ.,* December 1973, *55*(5), pp. 879–87.

_____ and Schmitz, Andrew. A Spatial Price Analysis of the World Wheat Economy: Some Long-Run Predictions. In *Judge, G. G. and Takayama, T., eds.,* 1973, pp. 488–516.

Baxter, Gary L. Indiana Housing Cycle: 1973 Forecast. *Indiana Bus. Rev.,* May-June 1973, *48,* pp. 10–12.

Baxter, J. L. Inflation in the Context of Relative Deprivation and Social Justice. *Scot. J. Polit. Econ.,* November 1973, *20*(3), pp. 263–82.

Baxter, Nevins D. and Grabowski, Henry G. Rivalry in Industrial Research and Development. *J. Ind. Econ.,* July 1973, *21*(3), pp. 209–35.

Bazlova, A. Improving Purchase Prices on Agricultural Output. *Prob. Econ.,* July 1973, *16*(3), pp. 37–58.

Beale, Calvin L. Migration Patterns of Minorities in the United States. *Amer. J. Agr. Econ.,* December 1973, *55*(5), pp. 938–46.

Bealer, Robert C. and Sofranko, Andrew J. Modernization Balance, Imbalance, and Domestic Instability. *Econ. Develop. Cult. Change,* October 1973, *22*(1), pp. 52–72.

Bean, Frank D. Components of Income and Expected Family Size Among Mexican Americans. *Soc. Sci. Quart.,* June 1973, *54*(1), pp. 103–16.

_____ and Bradshaw, Benjamin S. Trends in the Fertility of Mexican Americans, 1950-1970. *Soc. Sci. Quart.,* March 1973, *53*(4), pp. 688–96.

Bean, Lee L.; Hussain, Imtiazuddin and Afzal, Mohammad. Muslim Marriages: Age, Mehr and Social Status. *Pakistan Develop. Rev.,* Spring 1973, *12*(1), pp. 48–61.

Bean, Richard. War and the Birth of the Nation State. *J. Econ. Hist.,* March 1973, *33*(1), pp. 203–21.

Beard, Thomas R. and Duggar, Jan W. The Concept and Measurement of Defensive Open Market Operations. *Miss. Val. J. Bus. Econ.,* Spring 1973, *8*(3), pp. 29–38.

Beare, John B. Wage and Price Change Relationships in Post-War Canada. *Can. J. Econ.,* May 1973, *6*(2), pp. 260–65.

Beattie, Bruce R. and Bromley, Daniel W. On the Incongruity of Program Objectives and Project Evaluation: An Example from the Reclamation Program. *Amer. J. Agr. Econ.,* August 1973, *55*(3), pp. 472–76.

Beauchamp, John J.; Frome, Edward L. and Kutner, Michael H. Regression Analysis of Poisson-Distributed Data. *J. Amer. Statist. Assoc.,* December 1973, *68*(344), pp. 935–40.

Beaver, M. W. Population, Infant Mortality and Milk. *Population Stud.,* July 1973, *27*(2), pp. 243–54.

Beaver, William H. and Dukes, Roland E. Interperiod Tax Allocation and δ-Depreciation Methods: Some Empirical Results. *Accounting Rev.,* July 1973, *48*(3), pp. 549–59.

Beavis, David A. and Courchene, Thomas J. Federal-Provincial Tax Equalization: An Evaluation. *Can. J. Econ.,* November 1973, *6*(4), pp. 483–502.

Bechdolt, Burley V., Jr. Cross-Sectional Travel Demand Functions: US Visitors to Hawaii, 1961–70. *Quart. Rev. Econ. Bus.,* Winter 1973, *13*(4), pp. 37–47.

Bechhofer, Frank. The Relationship between Technology and Shop-Floor Behaviour: A Less Heated Look at a Controversy. In *Edge, D. O. and Wolfe, J. N., eds.,* 1973, pp. 121–42.

Bechter, Dan M. Money and Inflation. *Fed. Res. Bank Kansas City Rev.,* July-August 1973, pp. 3–6.

_____ and Pickett, Margaret S. The Wholesale and Consumer Price Indexes: What's the Connection? *Fed. Res. Bank Kansas City Rev.,* June 1973, pp. 3–9.

Bechtold, Peter K. New Attempts at Arab Cooperation: The Federation of Arab Republics, 1971–? *Middle East J.,* Spring 1973, *27*(2), pp. 152–72.

Beck, E. M.; Dotson, Louis and Summers, Gene F. Effects of Industrial Development on Heads of Households. *Growth Change,* July 1973, *4*(3), pp. 16–19.

Beck, Jiř and Nachtigal, Vladimír. K problematice systému makroekonomických modelů v podmínkách ČSSR. (Problems of a System of Macroeconomic Models in the Conditions of Czechoslovakia. With English summary.) *Ekon.-Mat. Obzor,* 1973, *9*(1), pp. 13–29.

Beck, Morris. Public Services in Metropolitan Areas of Australia. *Public Finance Quart.,* July 1973, *1* (3), pp. 307–22.

Becker, Arthur P. The Distribution of Benefits and Costs of the Federally Subsidized Urban Renewal Programs. In *Harriss, C. L., ed.,* 1973, pp. 203–29.

Becker, Gary S. A Theory of Marriage: Part I. *J. Polit. Econ.,* July-August 1973, *81*(4), pp. 813–46.

_____ and Lewis, H. Gregg. On the Interaction between the Quantity and Quality of Children. *J. Polit. Econ.,* Part II, March-April 1973, *81*(2), pp. S279–88.

_____ and Michael, Robert T. On the New Theory of Consumer Behavior. *Swedish J. Econ.,* December 1973, *75*(4), pp. 378–96.

Becker, James F. Class Structure and Conflict in the

Managerial Phase: I. *Sci. Soc.*, Fall 1973, *37*(3), pp. 259–77.

———— Class Structure and Conflict in the Managerial Phase: II. *Sci. Soc.*, Winter 1973–1974, *37*(4), pp. 437–53.

Becker, Theodore M. and Stern, Robert N. Professionalism, Professionalization, and Bias in the Commercial Human Relations Consulting Operation: A Survey Analysis. *J. Bus.*, April 1973, *46*(2), pp. 230–57.

Becker, William H. American Manufacturers and Foreign Markets, 1870–1900: Business Historians and the "New Economic Determinists." *Bus. Hist. Rev.*, Winter 1973, *47*(4), pp. 466–81.

von Beckerath, Erwin. The Work of Gustav von Schmoller. In *Rectenwald, H. C., ed.*, 1973, pp. 275–78.

Beckwith, Neil E. Concerning the Logical Consistency of Multivariate Market Share Models. *J. Marketing Res.*, August 1973, *10*(3), pp. 341–44.

———— **and Lehmann, Donald R.** The Importance of Differential Weights in Multiple Attribute Models of Consumer Attitude. *J. Marketing Res.*, May 1973, *10*(2), pp. 141–45.

Becsky, Gy. An Analysis of the Economic Growth in Developed Capitalist Countries: Comment and Criticism. *Acta Oecon.*, 1973, *11*(2–3), pp. 247–62.

Beenhakker, Henri L. Discounting Indices Proposed for Capital Investment Evaluation: A Further Examination. *Eng. Econ.*, April-May 1973, *18*(3), pp. 149–68.

Beer, Stafford. Adaptations in Systems: The Human Approach. In *The Diebold Group, Inc.*, 1973, pp. 19–30.

Beesley, I. B. and Moser, Claus A. United Kingdom Official Statistics and the European Communities. *J. Roy. Statist. Soc.*, Part 4, 1973, *136*, pp. 539–72.

Beesley, Michael E. Mergers and Economic Welfare. In *Allen, G. C., et al.*, 1973, pp. 71–80.

———— Regulation of Taxis. *Econ. J.*, March 1973, *83* (329), pp. 150–72.

———— **and Dalvi, M. Q.** The Journey to Work and Cost-benefit Analysis. In *Wolfe, J. N., ed.*, 1973, pp. 195–221.

Beeson, Peter G.; Johnson, David R. and Williams, J. Allen, Jr. Some Factors Associated with Income Among Mexican Americans. *Soc. Sci. Quart.*, March 1973, *53*(4), pp. 710–15.

Beeth, G. Distributors—Finding and Keeping the Good Ones. In *Thorelli, H. B., ed.*, 1973, pp. 273–79.

Beg, M. Afzal. A Review of Labour Force Participation Rates in Pakistan. *Pakistan Develop. Rev.*, Winter 1973, *12*(4), pp. 393–406.

Béhar, Moisés. The Importance of Accurate Measures of Malnutrition. In *Berg, A.; Scrimshaw, N. S. and Call, D. L., eds.*, 1973, pp. 145–49.

Behrens, Jean and Smolensky, Eugene. Alternative Definitions of Income Redistribution. *Public Finance*, 1973, *28*(3–4), pp. 315–32.

Behrens, John O. The Public and the Publicans Talk Taxes. *Nat. Tax J.*, June 1973, *26*(2), pp. 221–32.

Behrman, Jack N. Can the Multinational Enterprise Gain Acceptability through Industrial Integration? In *Fayerweather, J., ed.*, 1973, pp. 27–38.

Behrman, Jere R. Aggregative Market Responses in

Developing Agriculture: The Postwar Chilean Experience. In *Eckaus, R. S. and Rosenstein-Rodan, P. N., eds.*, 1973, pp. 229–50.

———— Cyclical Sectoral Capacity Utilization in a Developing Economy. In *Eckaus, R. S. and Rosenstein-Rodan, P. N., eds.*, 1973, pp. 251–66.

———— Price Determination in an Inflationary Economy: The Dynamics of Chilean Inflation Revisited. In *Eckaus, R. S. and Rosenstein-Rodan, P. N., eds.*, 1973, pp. 369–97.

———— **and Mujica, Jorge G.** A Study of Quarterly Nominal Wage Change Determination in an Inflationary Developing Economy. In *Eckaus, R. S. and Rosenstein-Rodan, P. N., eds.*, 1973, pp. 399–416.

Beidleman, Carl R. Fixed Asset Depreciation Patterns: Market Based Evidence. *Z. ges. Staatswiss.*, October 1973, *129*(4), pp. 643–62.

———— Income Smoothing: The Role of Management. *Accounting Rev.*, October 1973, *48*(4), pp. 653–67.

Bekele, Maaza. Nutrition, Planning, and Development. In *Berg, A.; Scrimshaw, N. S. and Call, D. L., eds.*, 1973, pp. 22–28.

Beker, Víctor A. Algunos factores que afectan la asignación de recursos entre agricultura y ganadería. (Some Factors Affecting Resource Allocation Between Crop and Beef Production. With English summary.) *Económica*, May-August 1973, *19*(2), pp. 146–56.

Belen'kii, V. Z.; Volkonskii, V. A. and Pavlov, N. V. Dynamic Input-Output Models in Planning and Price Calculations and Economic Analysis. *Matekon*, Winter 1973-74, *10*(2), pp. 74–101.

Belfiglio, Valentine J. India's Economic Relations with Nepal 1947–1967. *Econ. Int.*, August-November 1973, *26*(3–4), pp. 560–78.

Belkhodja, Hassen. Savings Banks and Savings Facilities in African Countries: Tunisia. In *Alberici, A. and Baravelli, M., eds.*, 1973, pp. 115–20.

Bell, A. R. Industrial Electricity Consumption—An Example of an Intermediate Good. *J. Ind. Econ.*, April 1973, *21*(2), pp. 95–109.

Bell, Carolyn Shaw. Middle-Class Action and the Ghetto Consumer. *J. Econ. Issues*, June 1973, *7*(2), pp. 245–57.

Bell, Clive and Lehmann, David. The International Context of La Via Chilena. In *Zammit, J. A., ed.*, 1973, pp. 343–65.

Bell, D. J.; Brenneman, Ronald and Steedman, Ian. A Control Theory Analysis of a Finite Optimum Savings Program in a Two-Sector Model. *Int. Econ. Rev.*, June 1973, *14*(2), pp. 520–24.

Bell, Donald R. Prevalence of Private Retirement Plans in Manufacturing. *Mon. Lab. Rev.*, September 1973, *96*(9), pp. 29–32.

Bell, Frederick W.; Carlson, Ernest W. and Waugh, Frederick V. Production from the Sea. In *Sokoloski, A. A., ed.*, 1973, pp. 72–91.

———— **and Fullenbaum, Richard F.** The Regional Impact of Resource Management. In *Mattila, J. M. and Thompson, W. R., eds.*, 1973, pp. 11–26.

Bell, Geoffrey. The United Kingdom and International Capital Flows. *Aussenwirtschaft*, March-June 1973, *28*(1–2), pp. 74–82.

Bell, R. T. Some Aspects of Industrial Decentralization in South Africa. *S. Afr. J. Econ.,* December 1973, *41*(4), pp. 401–31.

Bellani, Felice F. Medium-Term Evolution of the Italian Cotton Industry. *Rev. Econ. Cond. Italy,* September 1973, *27*(5), pp. 313–25.

Bellante, Donald M. A Florida Example: Measuring the Productivity Loss from Labor Force Disability. *Growth Change,* January 1973, *4*(1), pp. 38–42.

_____ The Relative Importance of Monetary and Fiscal Variables in Determining Price Level Movements: Comment. *J. Finance,* March 1973, *28*(1), pp. 188–90.

Bellas, Carl J. and Samli, A. Coskun. Improving New Product Planning with GERT Simulation. *Calif. Manage. Rev.,* Summer 1973, *15*(4), pp. 14–21.

Belli, R. David. Plant and Equipment Expenditures of U.S.-Owned Foreign Affiliates: Revised Estimates for 1972 and 1973. *Surv. Curr. Bus.,* March 1973, *53*(3), pp. 45–52.

_____; **Allnutt, Smith W. and Murad, Howard.** Property, Plant, and Equipment Expenditures by Majority-Owned Foreign Affiliates of U.S. Companies: Revised Estimates for 1966–72 and Projections for 1973 and 1974. *Surv. Curr. Bus.,* December 1973, *53*(12), pp. 19–32.

Bellin, Seymour S. and Bellin, Shirley S. Teacher Incentives Tied to Pupil Performance: A Strategy for Educational Accountability. In *Stein, B. and Miller, S. M., eds.,* 1973, pp. 117–48.

Bellin, Shirley S. and Bellin, Seymour S. Teacher Incentives Tied to Pupil Performance: A Strategy for Educational Accountability. In *Stein, B. and Miller, S. M., eds.,* 1973, pp. 117–48.

Bellush, Jewel and Hausknecht, Murray. Public Housing: The Contexts of Failure. In *Pynoos, J.; Schafer, R. and Hartman, C. W., eds.,* 1973, pp. 114–18.

Belmont, William R. and Fethke, Gary C. Buyers' Versus Sellers' Prices: An Econometric Investigation. *Nebr. J. Econ. Bus.,* Autumn 1973, *12*(4), pp. 37–50.

Belshaw, D. G. R. The Role of Agricultural Economics in University Economics Teaching in Africa. In *Livingstone, I., et al., eds.,* 1973, pp. 119–29.

Belsley, David A. The Applicability of the Kalman Filter in the Determination of Systematic Parameter Variation. *Ann. Econ. Soc. Measure,* October 1973, *2*(4), pp. 531–33.

_____ On the Determination of Systematic Parameter Variation in the Linear Regression Model. *Ann. Econ. Soc. Measure,* October 1973, *2*(4), pp. 487–94.

_____ The Relative Power of the τ-Test: A Furthering Comment. *Rev. Econ. Statist.,* February 1973, *55*(1), pp. 132.

_____ A Test for Systematic Variation in Regression Coefficients. *Ann. Econ. Soc. Measure,* October 1973, *2*(4), pp. 495–99.

_____ **and Kuh, Edwin.** Time-Varying Parameter Structures: An Overview. *Ann. Econ. Soc. Measure,* October 1973, *2*(4), pp. 375–79.

Belth, Joseph M. Credit Life Insurance Prices. *J. Risk Ins.,* March 1973, *40*(1), pp. 115–27.

Benavie, Arthur. Imports in Macroeconomic Models.

Int. Econ. Rev., June 1973, *14*(2), pp. 530–32.

_____ **and Poindexter, J. Carl, Jr.** Deposit Ceilings and Monetary Policy. *Rev. Econ. Statist.,* November 1973, *55*(4), pp. 487–92.

Bender, Dieter and Rose, Klaus. Flexible Wechselkurse und Inflationsimport. (Flexible Exchange Rates and Import of Inflation. With English summary.) *Jahr. Nationalökon. Statist.,* August 1973, *187*(6), pp. 481–506.

Bendix, Reinhard. Max Weber: Career and Personal Orientation. In *Rectenwald, H. C., ed.,* 1973, pp. 341–47.

Benet, I. and Góczán, L. A Pilot Study on the Valuation of Land. (In Russian. With English summary.) *Acta Oecon.,* 1973, *11*(2–3), pp. 191–209.

Bengoa, J. M. Significance of Malnutrition and Priorities for Its Prevention. In *Berg, A.; Scrimshaw, N. S. and Call, D. L., eds.,* 1973, pp. 103–28.

Benishay, Haskel. Market Preferences for Characteristics of Common Stocks. *Econ. J.,* March 1973, *83*(329), pp. 173–91.

Ben-Israel, Adi and Stern, Ronald J. On Linear Optimal Control Problems with Multiple Quadratic Criteria. In *Cochrane, J. L. and Zeleny, M., eds.,* 1973, pp. 366–72.

Benneh, G. Land Tenure and Land Use Systems in the Forest-Savannah Contact Zone in Ghana: A Case-Study. In *Ofori, I. M., ed.,* 1973, pp. 107–13.

_____ Water Requirements and Limitations Imposed on Agricultural Development in Northern Ghana. In *Ofori, I. M., ed.,* 1973, pp. 71–81.

Bennett, James T. and Barth, James R. Astronomics: A New Approach to Economics? *J. Polit. Econ.,* November-December 1973, *81*(6), pp. 1473–75.

_____ **and Holman, Mary A.** Determinants of Use of Water-Based Recreational Facilities. *Water Resources Res.,* October 1973, *9*(5), pp. 1208–18.

Bennett, J. W. and Leather, J. Investment Cut-off Rates for a Public Company. *Econ. Rec.,* June 1973, *49*(126), pp. 228–40.

Bennett, Sari J. and Christian, Charles M. Industrial Relocations from the Black Community of Chicago. *Growth Change,* April 1973, *4*(2), pp. 14–20.

Benoit, Emile. Balance of Payments Impact of a Vietnam Disengagement. In *Udis, B., ed.,* 1973, pp. 211–23.

_____ Cutting Back Military Spending: The Vietnam Withdrawal and the Recession. *Ann. Amer. Acad. Polit. Soc. Sci.,* March 1973, *406*, pp. 73–79.

_____ Structural Causes of Recent International Disequilibrium—A Preliminary Note. In *Wiegand, G. C., ed.,* 1973, pp. 63–69.

Ben-Porath, Yoram. Economic Analysis of Fertility in Israel: Point and Counterpoint. *J. Polit. Econ.,* Part II, March-April 1973, *81*(2), pp. S202–33.

_____ Labor-Force Participation Rates and the Supply of Labor. *J. Polit. Econ.,* May-June 1973, *81*(3), pp. 697–704.

Ben-Shahar, H. and Cukierman, A. The Term-Structure of Interest Rates and Expectations of Price Increase and Devaluation. *J. Finance,* June 1973, *28*(3), pp. 567–75.

Benson, Charles S. Collective Bargaining in Higher Education. *Mon. Lab. Rev.,* May 1973, *96*(5), pp. 33–34.

Benson, Virginia and Stewart, Charles T. Job Migration Linkages Between Smaller SMSAs and Their Hinterlands. *Land Econ.*, November 1973, *49*(4), pp. 432–39.

Benstock, Marcy and Zwick, David R. Water Wasteland: Conclusions and Recommendations. In *Enthoven, A. C. and Freeman, A. M., III, eds.*, 1973, pp. 141–44.

Benston, George J. Multiple Regression Analysis of Cost Behavior. In *Palda, K. S., ed.*, 1973, pp. 84–97.

_____ The Optimal Banking Structure: Theory and Evidence. *J. Bank Res.*, Winter 1973, *3*(4), pp. 220–37.

_____ Required Disclosure and the Stock Market: An Evaluation of the Securities Exchange Act of 1934. *Amer. Econ. Rev.*, March 1973, *63*(1), pp. 132–55.

_____ A Revised Regulatory Framework: Discussion. In *Federal Reserve Bank of Boston*, 1973, pp. 216–21.

Bentley, Philip. The Australian Local Government Tax Base: Revenue Potential. *Australian Econ. Pap.*, June 1973, *12*(20), pp. 21–35.

Ben-Zion, Uri and Balch, Michael. On the Analysis of Corporate Financial Theory under Uncertainty: A Comment. *Quart. J. Econ.*, May 1973, *87*(2), pp. 290–95.

Berdit, Martin and Williamson, John W. Function Limitation Scale for Measuring Health Outcomes. In *Berg, R. L., ed.*, 1973, pp. 59–65.

Berekson, Leonard L. Birth Order, Anxiety, Affiliation and the Purchase of Life Insurance: Reply. *J. Risk Ins.*, December 1973, *40*(4), pp. 646–48.

Berendsen, B. S. M. and Naseem, S. M. On Two Formulae for Calculating the Effective Rate of Protection. *Pakistan Develop. Rev.*, Summer 1973, *12*(2), pp. 189–93.

Berg, Alan and Muscat, Robert. Nutrition Program Planning: An Approach. In *Berg, A.; Scrimshaw, N. S. and Call, D. L., eds.*, 1973, pp. 247–74.

Berg, Richard K. and Cramton, Roger C. On Leading a Horse to Water: NEPA and the Federal Bureaucracy. *Mich. Law Rev.*, january 1973, *71*(3), pp. 511–36.

Berg, Robert L. Establishing the Values of Various Conditions of Life for a Health Status Index. In *Berg, R. L., ed.*, 1973, pp. 120–26.

Berg, Sanford V. The CPS Viewed from the Outside. *Ann. Econ. Soc. Measure*, April 1973, *2*(2), pp. 99–104.

_____ Interdependent Tastes and Fashion Behavior. *Quart. Rev. Econ. Bus.*, Summer 1973, *13*(2), pp. 49–58.

Bergendorff, Hans G.; Clark, Peter B. and Taylor, Lance. Welfare Gains from Optimization in Dynamic Planning Models. *Econ. Planning*, 1973, *13*(1–2), pp. 75–90.

Berger, Agnes and Gold, Ruth Z. Note on Cochran's Q-Test for the Comparison of Correlated Proportions. *J. Amer. Statist. Assoc.*, December 1973, *68*(344), pp. 989–93.

Berger, Paul D. and Harper, William K. Determination of an Optimal Revolving Credit Agreement. *J. Financial Quant. Anal.*, June 1973, *8*(3), pp. 491–97.

Berglas, Eitan and Razin, Assaf. Effective Protection and Decreasing Returns to Scale. *Amer. Econ. Rev.*, September 1973, *63*(4), pp. 733–37.

_____ and Razin, Assaf. Real Exchange Rate and Devaluation. *J. Int. Econ.*, May 1973, *3*(2), pp. 179–91.

_____ and Razin, Assaf. A Trade Model with Variable Returns to Scale. *Econ. Rec.*, March 1973, *49*(125), pp. 126–34.

Bergmann, Barbara R. Combining Microsimulation and Regression: A "Prepared" Regression of Poverty Incidence on Unemployment and Growth. *Econometrica*, September 1973, *41*(5), pp. 955–63.

_____ and Adelman, Irma. The 1973 Report of the President's Council of Economic Advisers: The Economic Role of Women. *Amer. Econ. Rev.*, September 1973, *63*(4), pp. 509–14.

Bergonzini, Luciano. Professionalità femminile e lavoro a domicilio: Questioni generali ed esiti di un'indagine statistica in alcuni comuni dell-'Emilia-Romagna. (Women's Professional Status and Work at Home: Some General Questions and Some Results of a Statistical Inquiry in a Few Municipalities of the Emilia-Romagna Region (Italy). With English summary.) *Statistica*, October-December 1973, *33*(4), pp. 492–546.

Bergson, Abram. On Monopoly Welfare Losses. *Amer. Econ. Rev.*, December 1973, *63*(5), pp. 853–70.

Bergsten, C. Fred. Convertibility for the Dollar and International Monetary Reform. In *[Halm, G. N.]*, 1973, pp. 99–114.

_____ Future Directions for U.S. Trade. *Amer. J. Agr. Econ.*, May 1973, *55*(2), pp. 280–88.

_____ The Future of the International Economic Order: An Agenda for Research. In *Bergsten, C. F., ed.*, 1973, pp. 1–59.

_____ Implications for U.S. Policy toward Europe: Comment. In *Krause, L. B. and Salant, W. S., eds.*, 1973, pp. 286–92.

_____ The Multinational Firm: Bane or Boon?: Discussion. *J. Finance*, May 1973, *28*(2), pp. 457–62.

_____ The Role of the Multinational Corporation: Comment. In *Hughes, H., ed.*, 1973, pp. 90–95.

Bergström, Reinhold. Investigations of the Fix-Point and Iterative Instrumental Variables Methods. Convergence Properties, Comparative Studies and Applications. *Écon. Appl.*, 1973, *26*(2–3–4), pp. 505–35.

Bergstrom, Theodore C. A Note on Efficient Taxation. *J. Polit. Econ.*, January-February 1973, *81*(1), pp. 187–91.

_____ The Use of Markets to Control Pollution. *Rech. Écon. Louvain*, December 1973, *39*(4), pp. 403–18.

_____ and Goodman, Robert P. Private Demands for Public Goods. *Amer. Econ. Rev.*, June 1973, *63*(3), pp. 280–96.

Berhold, Marvin. Multiple Criteria Decision Making in Consumer Behavior. In *Cochrane, J. L. and Zeleny, M., eds.*, 1973, pp. 570–76.

Berlage, Lodewijk J. J. B. An Application of Dynamic Programming Models to Foodgrain Import and Storage Policy in Bangladesh. *Bangladesh Econ. Rev.*, October 1973, *1*(4), pp. 341–74.

—— and Alamgir, Mohiuddin. Estimation of Income Elasticity of Demand for Foodgrain in Bangladesh from Cross Section Data: A Skeptical View. *Bangladesh Econ. Rev.*, October 1973, *1*(4), pp. 387–408.

—— and Alamgir, Mohiuddin. Foodgrain (Rice and Wheat) Demand, Import and Price Policy for Bangladesh. *Bangladesh Econ. Rev.*, January 1973, *1*(1), pp. 25–58.

Berlin, Isaiah. Karl Marx: His Life and Environment. In *Rectenwald, H. C., ed.*, 1973, pp. 223–38.

Berman, Peter I. The Discount Facility and Staggered Reserve Periods. *Amer. Econ.*, Spring 1973, *17*(1), pp. 85–92.

Berndt, Ernst R. and Christensen, Laurits R. The Internal Structure of Functional Relationships: Separability, Substitution and Aggregation. *Rev. Econ. Stud.*, July 1973, *40*(3), pp. 403–10.

—— and Christensen, Laurits R. The Translog Function and the Substitution of Equipment, Structures, and Labor in U.S. Manufacturing 1929–68. *J. Econometrics*, March 1973, *1*(1), pp. 81–113.

Berney, Robert E. and Frerichs, Bernard H. Income Elasticities for State Tax Revenues: Techniques of Estimation and their Usefulness for Forecasting. *Public Finance Quart.*, October 1973, *1*(4), pp. 409–25.

Bernhard, Richard H. Consumer Surplus as an Index of User Benefit from Public Expenditure. *Eng. Econ.*, October-November 1973, *19*(1), pp. 1–33.

Bernholz, Peter. Logrolling, Arrow Paradox and Cyclical Majorities. *Public Choice*, Summer 1973, *15*, pp. 87–95.

—— and Faber, Malte. A Note on Stackelberg's Hypothesis Concerning a Relationship between the Price of Land, the Real Rate of Interest and Impatience to Consume. *Z. Nationalökon.*, 1973, *33*(3–4), pp. 375–88.

—— and Faber, Malte. Technical Productivity of Roundabout Processes and Positive Rate of Interest. A Capital Model with Depreciation and n-Period Horizon. *Z. ges. Staatswiss.*, February 1973, *129*(1), pp. 46–61.

Bernolak, Imre. Is Growth Obsolete? Comment. In *Moss, M., ed.*, 1973, pp. 536–40.

Bernstein, Edward M. Narrowing the Exchange Rate Bands: Comment. In *Krause, L. B. and Salant, W. S., eds.*, 1973, pp. 97–105.

Bernstein, Peter L. What Rate of Return Can You "Reasonably" Expect? *J. Finance*, May 1973, *28*(2), pp. 273–82.

Bernstein, Samuel J. and Mellon, W. Giles. Multi-Dimensional Considerations in the Evaluation of Urban Policy. In *Cochrane, J. L. and Zeleny, M., eds.*, 1973, pp. 530–43.

Bernthal, Wilmar F. Value Perspectives in Management Decisions. In *Klein, W. H. and Murphy, D. C., eds.*, 1973, pp. 277–83.

Berruti, Giuseppe. Il "merchandising" un nuovo aspetto del rapporto fra industria e distribuzione. ("Merchandising": A New Aspect of the Relations between Industry and Distribution. With English summary.) *L'Impresa*, 1973, *15*(9–10), pp. 628–30.

Berry, Brian J. L. and Cohen, Yehoshua S. Decen-

tralization of Commerce and Industry: The Restructuring of Metropolitan America. In *Masotti, L. H. and Hadden, J. K., eds.*, 1973, pp. 431–55.

Berry, R. Albert. Land Distribution, Income Distribution, and the Productive Efficiency of Colombian Agriculture. *Food Res. Inst. Stud.*, 1973, *12*(3), pp. 199–232.

—— Terms of Trade Fluctuations and the Income Instability of Factor Owners. *Economica, N.S.*, May 1973, *40*(158), pp. 187–94.

Berry, Robert and Niskanen, William. The 1973 Economic Report of the President. *J. Money, Credit, Banking*, May 1973, *5*(2), pp. 693–703.

Bertolino, Alberto. Un problema fondamentale per lo sviluppo economico: la formazione dei quadri tecnico-economici. (A Basic Problem for Economic Development: The Formation of Technico-economic Personnel. With English summary.) *Rivista Int. Sci. Econ. Com.*, February 1973, *20*(2), pp. 130–38.

Berton, Lee. Aiding the Poor. In *Murray, B. B., ed.*, 1973, pp. 420–25.

Bertram, Gordon W. The Relevance of the Wheat Boom in Canadian Economic Growth. *Can. J. Econ.*, November 1973, *6*(4), pp. 545–66.

Bertrand, Trent J. Optional Tariff Policy Designed for Governmental Gain. *Can. J. Econ.*, May 1973, *6*(2), pp. 257–60.

—— Trade and Growth: A Comment. *J. Int. Econ.*, May 1973, *3*(2), pp. 193–95.

Besen, Stanley M. and Soligo, Ronald. The Economics of the Network-Affiliate Relationship in the Television Broadcasting Industry. *Amer. Econ. Rev.*, June 1973, *63*(3), pp. 259–68.

Betancourt, Roger R. Increasing Risk and Nonseparable Utility Functions. *J. Econ. Theory*, December 1973, *6*(6), pp. 575–81.

Betti, G. and Bettuzzi, G. La concentrazione della popolazione sparsa relativa in Emilia-Romagna e nel Veneto. (The Concentration of Relative Population Spread in the Countryside in the Italian Regions of Emilia-Romagna and Veneto. With English summary.) *Statistica*, April-June 1973, *33*(2), pp. 169–239.

Bettman, James R. Perceived Price and Product Perceptual Variables. *J. Marketing Res.*, February 1973, *10*(1), pp. 100–02.

—— Perceived Risk and Its Components: A Model and Empirical Test. *J. Marketing Res.*, May 1973, *10*(2), pp. 184–90.

Bettuzzi, G. and Betti, G. La concentrazione della popolazione sparsa relativa in Emilia-Romagna e nel Veneto. (The Concentration of Relative Population Spread in the Countryside in the Italian Regions of Emilia-Romagna and Veneto. With English summary.) *Statistica*, April-June 1973, *33*(2), pp. 169–239.

Betz, Horst. The Pattern of Economic Reform in East Germany: Return to Increased Centralization? *Econ. Int.*, May 1973, *26*(2), pp. 318–28.

Bevin, J. H. and Livingstone, I. Economic History and Economics Teaching. In *Livingstone, I., et al., eds.*, 1973, pp. 95–100.

Bewley, Truman F. Edgeworth's Conjecture. *Econometrica*, May 1973, *41*(3), pp. 425–54.

—— The Equality of the Core and the Set of Equilibria in Economies with Infinitely Many Commodities and a Continuum of Agents. *Int. Econ. Rev.*, June 1973, *14*(2), pp. 383–94.

Beyen, Karel H. Il finanziamento del commercio internazionale. (International Trade Finance. With English summary.) *Bancaria,* December 1973, *29*(12), pp. 1461–66.

Bezdek, Roger H. Interindustry Manpower Analysis: Theoretical Potential and Empirical Problems. *Amer. Econ.,* Spring 1973, *17*(1), pp. 147–53.

_____ **and Getzel, Barry.** Education and Job Training of Scientists and Engineers. *Mon. Lab. Rev.,* November 1973, *96*(11), pp. 54–55.

Bhaduri, Amit. A Study in Agricultural Backwardness under Semi-Feudalism. *Econ. J.,* March 1973, *83*(329), pp. 120–37.

Bhagwat, Avinash. Main Features of the Employment Problem in Developing Countries. *Int. Monet. Fund Staff Pap.,* March 1973, *20*(1), pp. 78–99.

Bhagwati, Jagdish N. The Case for Devaluation. In *Wadhva, C. D., ed.,* 1973, pp. 457–61.

_____ Education, Class Structure and Income Equality. *World Devel.,* May 1973, *1*(5), pp. 21–36.

_____ Trade Diverting Customs Unions and Welfare Improvement: A Reply. *Econ. J.,* September 1973, *83*(331), pp. 895–97.

_____ **and Dellalfar, William.** The Brain Drain and Income Taxation. *World Devel.,* February 1973, *1*(1-2), pp. 94–101.

_____ **and Hansen, Bent.** Should Growth Rates Be Evaluated at International Prices? In *[Rosenstein-Rodan, P.],* 1973, pp. 53–68.

_____ **and Hansen, Bent.** A Theoretical Analysis of Smuggling. *Quart. J. Econ.,* May 1973, *87*(2), pp. 172–87.

_____ **and Krueger, Anne O.** Exchange Control, Liberalization, and Economic Development. *Amer. Econ. Rev.,* May 1973, *63*(2), pp. 419–27.

_____ **and Srinivasan, T. N.** The General Equilibrium Theory of Effective Protection and Resource Allocation. *J. Int. Econ.,* August 1973, *3*(3), pp. 259–81.

_____ **and Srinivasan, T. N.** Smuggling and Trade Policy. *J. Public Econ.,* November 1973, *2*(4), pp. 377–89.

Bhalla, A. S. A Disaggregative Approach to Employment in LDCs. *J. Devel. Stud.,* October 1973, *10*(1), pp. 50–65.

Bhansali, R. J. A Monte Carlo Comparison of the Regression Method and the Spectral Methods of Prediction. *J. Amer. Statist. Assoc.,* September 1973, *68*(343), pp. 621–25.

Bharadwaj, V. P. and Dave, P. K. An Empirical Test of Kaldor's Macro Model of Income Distribution for Indian Economy. *Indian Econ. J.,* January-March 1973, *20*(3), pp. 515–20.

Bhargava, P. K. Problem of Pendency of Income-tax Appeals in India. *Bull. Int. Fiscal Doc.,* March 1973, *27*(3), pp. 95–103.

Bhat, M. V. The Role of Small Banks in the Commercial Banking System. In *Simha, S. L. N., ed.,* 1973, pp. 203–07.

Bhati, U. N. Farmers' Technical Knowledge and Income—A Case Study of Padi Farmers of West

Malaysia. *Malayan Econ. Rev.,* April 1973, *18*(1), pp. 36–47.

Bhatia, Kul B. The Estimation of Accrued Capital Gains on Individuals' Corporate Stock Holdings. *J. Amer. Statist. Assoc.,* March 1973, *68*(341), pp. 55–62.

_____ **and Frankena, Mark.** Canadian Contributions to Economics Journals, 1968-1972. *Can. J. Econ.,* February 1973, *6*(1), pp. 121–24.

Bhatia, Rattan J. Import Programming in Ghana—1966-69. *Finance Develop.,* March 1973, *10*(1), pp. 20–24.

Bhatt, V. V. Monopoly and Public Policy. In *Wadhva, C. D., ed.,* 1973, pp. 188–98.

Bhattacharya, Debesh. A Critical Survey of Indian Planning and its Achievements. *Econ. Aff.,* March 1973, *18*(3), pp. 105–23.

_____ Foreign Aid and Economic Development. *Econ. Aff.,* January–February 1973, *18*(1-2), pp. 41–53.

Bhattacharya, Rabindra Nath and Majumdar, Mukul. Random Exchange Economies. *J. Econ. Theory,* February 1973, *6*(1), pp. 37–67.

Bhattacharya, Sourin. Separate Treatment of Demand and Supply Lags and Stability of Multiplier Processes. *Indian Econ. J.,* April-June 1973, *20* (4–5), pp. 570–80.

Bianchi, Andrés. Notes on the Theory of Latin American Economic Development. *Soc. Econ. Stud.,* March 1973, *22*(1), pp. 96–121.

Bichi, C. Devalorizarea dolarului, un nou episod în adîncirea crizei sistemului valutar interoccidental. (The Devaluation of the Dollar, a New Episode in the Deepening of the Crisis of the Western Currency System. With English summary.) *Stud. Cercet. Econ.,* 1973, (3), pp. 153–64.

_____ Inflația în țările capitaliste și apologia ei. (Inflation in the Capitalist Countries and its Apology. With English summary.) *Stud. Cercet. Econ.,* 1973, (1), pp. 163–79.

Bickel, Blaine W. Meeting Consumer Demand for Beef—From Ranch to Roast. *Fed. Res. Bank Kansas City Rev.,* April 1973, pp. 12–19.

Bickelhaupt, David L. The Future of ARIA: Discussion. *J. Risk Ins.,* March 1973, *40*(1), pp. 109–14.

Bicksler, James L.; Barnea, Amir and Babad, Jair. Portfolio Choice, the Horizon Problem and the Investment Opportunity Set. *Amer. Econ. Rev.,* May 1973, *63*(2), pp. 140–44.

_____ **and Thorp, Edward O.** The Capital Growth Model: An Empirical Investigation. *J. Financial Quant. Anal.,* March 1973, *8*(2), pp. 273–87.

Biderman, Albert D. Where Do They Go from Here?—Retired Military in America. *Ann. Amer. Acad. Polit. Soc. Sci.,* March 1973, *406,* pp. 146–61.

Bieda, John C. and Kassarjian, Harold H. An Overview of Market Segmentation. In *Britt, S. H. and Boyd, H. W., Jr., eds.,* 1973, pp. 209–17.

Bieda, K. Copernicus as an Economist. *Econ. Rec.,* March 1973, *49*(125), pp. 89–103.

Biehl, Dieter, et al. Measuring the Demand Effects of Fiscal Policy. In *Giersch, H., ed.,* 1973, pp. 223–41.

_____, **et al.** On the Cyclical Effects of Budgetary Policy from 1960 to 1970 in the Federal Republic of Germany. *Ger. Econ. Rev.*, 1973, *11*(4), pp. 273–91.

Bieker, Richard F. and Anschel, Kurt R. Estimating Educational Production Functions for Rural High Schools: Some Findings. *Amer. J. Agr. Econ.*, August 1973, *55*(3), pp. 515–19.

Bienaymé, Alain. Les processus de croissance des entreprises sont-ils déterminés ou indéterminés? (Why Growth Rates of Business Firms Differ? With English summary.) *Revue Écon.*, March 1973, *24*(2), pp. 216–34.

Biere, Arlo; Sjo, John and Orazem, Frank. Undergraduate Program Revision at Kansas State University. *Amer. J. Agr. Econ.*, Part I, November 1973, *55*(4), pp. 604–10.

Bieri, Jurg and Schmitz, Andrew. Export Instability, Monopoly Power, and Welfare. *J. Int. Econ.*, November 1973, *3*(4), pp. 389–96.

Bierman, Harold, Jr. Analysis of the Lease-or-Buy Decision: Comment. *J. Finance*, September 1973, *28*(4), pp. 1019–21.

‑‑‑‑‑‑ The Cost of Warrants. *J. Financial Quant. Anal.*, June 1973, *8*(3), pp. 499–503.

‑‑‑‑‑‑ **and Hass, Jerome E.** Capital Budgeting Under Uncertainty: A Reformulation. *J. Finance*, March 1973, *28*(1), pp. 119–29.

‑‑‑‑‑‑ **and Thomas, L. Joseph.** Airline Overbooking Strategies and Bumping Procedures. *Public Policy*, Fall 1973, *21*(4), pp. 601–06.

Bievert, Bernd. Sociomarketing and the Quality of Life. In *Dierkes, M. and Bauer, R. A., eds.*, 1973, pp. 142–48.

Biggs, Joseph R. Emigration of Industry from Ohio. *Ohio State U. Bull. Bus. Res.*, February 1973, *48* (2), pp. 4–7.

Bilderbeek, J. Financieel-economische indices ten behoeve van de bedrijfsbeoordeling. (Financial-economic Indices for Management Auditing. With English summary.) *Econ. Soc. Tijdschr.*, April 1973, *27*(2), pp. 141–55.

Bildersee, John S. Some Aspects of the Performance of Non-Convertible Preferred Stocks. *J. Finance*, December 1973, *28*(5), pp. 1187–1201.

Bilkey, Warren J. Empirical Evidence Regarding Business Goals. In *Cochrane, J. L. and Zeleny, M., eds.*, 1973, pp. 613–34.

Billings, Brad. Production Effects of Effective Rates of Protection. *J. Econ. Bus.*, Winter 1973, *25*(2), pp. 112–21.

‑‑‑‑‑‑ **and Tuccillo, John A.** Determinants of the Money Multiplier: Comment. *Quart. Rev. Econ. Bus.*, Winter 1973, *13*(4), pp. 93–101.

Billon, S. A. Centralization of Authority and Regional Management. In *Bandera, V. N. and Melnyk, Z. L., eds.*, 1973, pp. 214–34.

Birara, Jean. Savings Banks and Savings Facilities in African Countries: Rwanda. In *Alberici, A. and Baravelli, M., eds.*, 1973, pp. 81.

Bird, R. G. and Peirson, C. G. A Study of Convertible Notes Issued in Australia. *Australian Econ. Pap.*, June 1973, *12*(20), pp. 91–105.

Bird, Richard M. and De Wulf, Luc H. Taxation and Income Distribution in Latin America: A Critical Review of Empirical Studies. *Int. Monet. Fund Staff Pap.*, November 1973, *20*(3), pp. 639–82.

Birdsall, William C. and Goldstein, Jon H. The Ef-

fect of Interest-Rate Changes on Consumption Allocation Over Time. *Int. Econ. Rev.*, June 1973, *14*(2), pp. 487–92.

Birkin, Stanley J. and Ford, James S. The Quantity/Quality Dilemma: The Impact of a Zero Defects Program. In *Cochrane, J. L. and Zeleny, M., eds.*, 1973, pp. 517–29.

Birmingham, Robert L. The Consumer as King: The Economics of Precarious Sovereignty. In *Murray, B. B., ed.*, 1973, pp. 212–24.

Birnberg, Thomas and Resnick, Stephen A. A Model of the Trade and Government Sectors in Colonial Economies. *Amer. Econ. Rev.*, September 1973, *63*(4), pp. 572–87.

Bish, Robert L. and O'Donoghue, Patrick D. Public Goods, Increasing Cost, and Monopsony: Reply. *J. Polit. Econ.*, January-February 1973, *81*(1), pp. 231–36.

Bishop, Christine E. Manpower Policy and the Supply of Nurses. *Ind. Relat.*, February 1973, *12*(1), pp. 86–94.

Bishop, Richard C. Limitation of Entry in the United States Fishing Industry: An Economic Appraisal of a Proposed Policy. *Land Econ.*, November 1973, *49*(4), pp. 381–90.

Bisogno, Paolo and Forti, Augusto. International Seminar on Trends in Mathematical Modelling: Introduction. In *Hawkes, N., ed.*, 1973, pp. 1–7.

Biswas, Suddhendu. A Note on the Generalization of William Brass's Model. *Demography*, August 1973, *10*(3), pp. 459–67.

Bitar, Sergio and Trivelli, Hugo. The Cost of Capital in the Chilean Economy. In *Eckaus, R. S. and Rosenstein-Rodan, P. N., eds.*, 1973, pp. 147–65.

Bither, Stewart W. and Wright, Peter L. The Self-Confidence-Advertising Response Relationship: A Function of Situational Distraction. *J. Marketing Res.*, May 1973, *10*(2), pp. 146–52.

Bittker, Boris I. Income Tax Deductions, Credits, and Subsidies for Personal Expenditures. *J. Law Econ.*, October 1973, *16*(2), pp. 193–213.

‑‑‑‑‑‑ Income Tax "Loopholes" and Political Rhetoric. *Mich. Law Rev.*, May 1973, *71*(6), pp. 1099–1128.

‑‑‑‑‑‑ Should Foundations Be Third-Class Charities? In *Heimann, F. F., ed.*, 1973, pp. 132–62.

Bizien, Yves; Hossain, Ekram and Askari, Hossein. The Success of Some Devaluations and Revaluations in the Post-War Era. *Econ. Int.*, August-November 1973, *26*(3–4), pp. 471–91.

Black, Fischer and Scholes, Myron S. The Pricing of Options and Corporate Liabilities. *J. Polit. Econ.*, May-June 1973, *81*(3), pp. 637–54.

‑‑‑‑‑‑ **and Treynor, Jack L.** How to Use Security Analysis to Improve Portfolio Selection. *J. Bus.*, January 1973, *46*(1), pp. 66–86.

Black, R. D. Collinson. The Irish Experience in Relation to the Theory and Policy of Economic Development. In *Youngson, A. J., ed.*, 1973, pp. 192–210.

Black, R. D. Collison. Emigrazione e colonizzazione. (Emigration and Colonization. With English summary.) *Rivista Int. Sci. Econ. Com.*, November 1973, *20*(11), pp. 1071–80.

‑‑‑‑‑‑ Libero scambio e imperialismo nel pensiero e nella politica economica dei classici inglesi.

(Free Trade and Imperialism in English Classical Economic Thought and Policy. With English summary.) *Rivista Int. Sci. Econ. Com.*, July 1973, *20*(7), pp. 640–49.

Black, William R. Toward a Factorial Ecology of Flows. *Econ. Geogr.*, January 1973, *49*(1), pp. 59–67.

Blackaby, F. T. Incomes and Inflation. In *Robinson, J., ed.*, 1973, pp. 55–70.

Blackford, Mansel G. Banking and Bank Legislation in California, 1890–1915. *Bus. Hist. Rev.*, Winter 1973, *47*(4), pp. 482–507.

Blackhurst, Richard. Estimating the Impact of Tariff Manipulation: The Excess Demand and Supply Approach. *Oxford Econ. Pap.*, March 1973, *25*(1), pp. 80–87.

Blackmarr, Brian R. and Lifson, K. A. Simulation and Optimization Models for Asset Deployment and Funds Sources Balancing Profit, Liquidity and Growth. *J. Bank Res.*, Autumn 1973, *4*(3), pp. 239–55.

Blackorby, Charles, et al. Consistent Intertemporal Decision Making. *Rev. Econ. Stud.*, April 1973, *40*(2), pp. 239–48.

Blainey, Geoffrey. A Theory of Mineral Discovery: A Rejoinder. *Econ. Hist. Rev., 2nd Ser.*, August 1973, *26*(3), pp. 506–09.

Blair, John P. and Mikesell, John L. A Note on the Empirical Nature of the Taxpayer Rebellion. *Public Choice*, Fall 1973, *16*, pp. 43–50.

Blair, Roger D. Problems of Pollution Standards: The Clean Air Act of 1970. *Land Econ.*, August 1973, *49*(3), pp. 260–68.

────── **and Lanzillotti, Robert F.** Automobile Pollution, Externalities and Public Policy. *Antitrust Bull.*, Fall, 1973, *18*(3), pp. 431–47.

────── **and Vogel, Ronald J.** Heroin Addiction and Urban Crime. *Public Finance Quart.*, October 1973, *1*(4), pp. 457–66.

Blake, C. The Gains from Regional Policy. In *Wolfe, J. N., ed.*, 1973, pp. 185–94.

Blake, David H. Government, Politics, and the Multinational Enterprise. In *Fayerweather, J., ed.*, 1973, pp. 63–83.

────── **; Murray, J. Alex and Fayerweather, John.** Perspectives for the Future. In *Fayerweather, J., ed.*, 1973, pp. 95–123.

Blake, Judith and Das Gupta, Prithwis. The Fallacy of the Five Million Women: A Re-Estimate: Rejoinder. *Demography*, November 1973, *10*(4), pp. 679–84.

Blandy, Richard and Wery, René. Population and Employment Growth: Bachue-1. *Int. Lab. Rev.*, May 1973, *107*(5), pp. 441–49.

Blankart, Beat. Arbeitskräftenachfrage im Konjunkturablauf—das Problem des temporären Hortens von Arbeitskräften. (The Demand for Labour During Business Cycles—the Problem of Short-Term Labour Hoarding. With English summary.) *Schweiz. Z. Volkswirtsch. Statist.*, June 1973, *109*(2), pp. 171–85.

Blankstein, Charles S. and Zuvekas, Clarence, Jr. Agrarian Reform in Ecuador: An Evaluation of Past Efforts and the Development of a New Approach. *Econ. Develop. Cult. Change*, October 1973, *22*(1), pp. 73–94.

Blaquière, Austin and Caussin, Pierre. Further Geometric Aspects of Differential Games. In *Blaquière, A., ed.*, 1973, pp. 101–49.

────── **; Juricek, Libuska and Wiese, Karl E.** Geometry of Pareto Equilibria in N-Person Differential Games. In *Blaquière, A., ed.*, 1973, pp. 271–310.

Blattberg, Robert C. Evaluation of the Power of the Durbin-Watson Statistic for Non-First Order Serial Correlation Alternatives. *Rev. Econ. Statist.*, November 1973, *55*(4), pp. 508–15.

────── **and Sen, Subrata K.** An Evaluation of the Application of Minimum Chi-Square Procedures to Stochastic Models of Brand Choice. *J. Marketing Res.*, November 1973, *10*(4), pp. 421–27.

Blattner, Niklaus. Domestic Competition and Foreign Trade: The Case of the Excess Capacity Barrier to Entry. *Z. Nationalökon.*, 1973, *33*(3–4), pp. 403–12.

Blaug, Mark. Manpower Forecasting for All Occupations: Thailand. In *Ahamad, B. and Blaug, M., eds.*, 1973, pp. 106–30.

────── University Efficiency and University Finance: Discussion. In *Parkin, M., ed.*, 1973, pp. 189–91.

────── **and Ahamad, Bashir.** The Practice of Manpower Forecasting: Conclusions. In *Ahamad, B. and Blaug, M., eds.*, 1973, pp. 310–23.

────── **and Ahamad, Bashir.** The Practice of Manpower Forecasting: Introduction. In *Ahamad, B. and Blaug, M., eds.*, 1973, pp. 1–25.

────── **and Gannicott, Kenneth.** Manpower Forecasting for All Occupations: The United States. In *Ahamad, B. and Blaug, M., eds.*, 1973, pp. 48–76.

────── **and Gannicott, Kenneth.** Manpower Forecasting for Single Occupations: Scientists and Engineers in Britain. In *Ahamad, B. and Blaug, M., eds.*, 1973, pp. 240–60.

Bleakney, Thomas P. Problems and Issues in Public Employee Retirement Systems. *J. Risk Ins.*, March 1973, *40*(1), pp. 39–46.

Bleda, Sharon E. and Schwirian, Kent P. Ecological and Socio-Economic Factors in Neighborhood Housing Conditions: The Case of the Cleveland Metropolitan Area. *Ohio State U. Bull. Bus. Res.*, January 1973, *48*(1), pp. 1–3, 6–7.

Blicksilver, Jack. The Life Insurance Company of Georgia: The Formative Years, 1891–1918. In *[Williamson, H. F.]*, 1973, pp. 248–79.

Bliemel, Friedhelm. Theil's Forecast Accuracy Coefficient: A Clarification. *J. Marketing Res.*, November 1973, *10*(4), pp. 444–46.

Blin, Jean-Marie. A Further Procedure for Ordering an Input-output Matrix: Some Empirical Evidence. *Econ. Planning*, 1973, *13*(1–2), pp. 121–29.

────── The General Concept of Multidimensional Consistency: Some Algebraic Aspects of the Aggregation Problem. In *Cochrane, J. L. and Zeleny, M., eds.*, 1973, pp. 164–78.

────── Intransitive Social Orderings and the Probability of the Condorcet Effect. *Kyklos*, 1973, *26*(1), pp. 25–35.

Blinder, Alan S. A Model of Inherited Wealth. *Quart. J. Econ.*, November 1973, *87*(4), pp. 608–26.

────── Note: Can Income Tax Increases Be Inflationary? *Nat. Tax J.*, June 1973, *26*(2), pp. 295–301.

────── Wage Discrimination: Reduced Form and

Structural Estimates. *J. Human Res.,* Fall 1973, *8* (4), pp. 436–55.

_____ and Solow, Robert M. Does Fiscal Policy Matter? *J. Public Econ.,* November 1973, *2*(4), pp. 319–37.

Bliss, C. J. Heterogeneous Capital and the Heckscher-Ohlin-Samuelson Theory of Trade: Discussion. In *Parkin, M., ed.,* 1973, pp. 61–64.

Bliss, Michael. Another Anti-Trust Tradition: Canadian Anti-Combines Policy, 1889–1910. *Bus. Hist. Rev.,* Summer 1973, *47*(2), pp. 177–88.

Blitz, Rudolph C. and Ow, Chin Hock. A Cross-Sectional Analysis of Women's Participation in the Professions. *J. Polit. Econ.,* January-February 1973, *81*(1), pp. 131–44.

Bloch, Ben W. and Pilgrim, John D. A Reappraisal of Some Factors Associated with Fluctuations in the United States in the Interwar Period. *Southern Econ. J.,* January 1973, *39*(3), pp. 327–44.

Block, M. K. and Heineke, J. M. The Allocation of Effort under Uncertainty: The Case of Risk-averse Behavior. *J. Polit. Econ.,* Part I, March-April 1973, *81*(2), pp. 376–85.

Blohm, Margareta and Ohlsson, Ingvar. Experience in Measurement of Welfare Components and their Regional Implications. *Rev. Income Wealth,* June 1973, *19*(2), pp. 167–88.

Blomqvist, A. G. Hypothesis Tests and Confidence Intervals for Steady-State Coefficients in Models with Lagged Dependent Variables: Some Notes in Fieller's Method. *Oxford Bull. Econ. Statist.,* February 1973, *35*(1), pp. 69–74.

Bloomfield, Arthur I. The Historical Setting. In *Krause, L. B. and Salant, W. S., eds.,* 1973, pp. 1–30.

Bluestone, Barry and England, Richard. Ecology and Social Conflict. In *Daly, H. E., ed.,* 1973, pp. 190–214.

Blum, Robert. Estate and Gift Taxation— Moderator's Remarks. *Nat. Tax J.,* September 1973, *26*(3), pp. 439–40.

Blume, Marshall E. and Friend, Irwin. Competitive Commissions on the New York Stock Exchange. *J. Finance,* September 1973, *28*(4), pp. 795–819.

_____ and Friend, Irwin A New Look at the Capital Asset Pricing Model. *J. Finance,* March 1973, *28* (1), pp. 19–33.

_____ and Husic, Frank. Price, Beta, and Exchange Listing. *J. Finance,* May 1973, *28*(2), pp. 283–99.

Blumenfeld, Hans. Growth Rate Comparisons: Soviet Union and German Democratic Republic. *Land Econ.,* May 1973, *49*(2), pp. 122–32.

Boadway, Robin W. Similarities and Differences between Public Goods and Public Factors. *Public Finance,* 1973, *28*(3–4), pp. 245–58.

_____; Maital, Shlomo and Prachowny, Martin F. J. Optimal Tariffs, Optimal Taxes and Public Goods. *J. Public Econ.,* November 1973, *2*(4), pp. 391–403.

Boarman, Patrick M. Healing the Rift Between the U.S. and Europe. *Calif. Manage. Rev.,* Fall 1973, *16*(1), pp. 76–85.

_____ International Trade and National Autonomy. In *Wiegand, G. C., ed.,* 1973, pp. 77–88.

Bobrow, Davis B. Military Research and Development: Implications for the Civil Sector. *Ann.*

Amer. Acad. Polit. Soc. Sci., March 1973, *406,* pp. 117–28.

Bock, M. E.; Judge, G. G. and Yancey, T. A. Properties of Estimators After Preliminary Tests of Significance When Stochastic Restrictions Are Used in Regression. *J. Econometrics,* March 1973, *1*(1), pp. 29–47.

_____; Judge, G. G. and Yancey, T. A. Some Comments on Estimation in Regression After Preliminary Tests of Significance. *J. Econometrics,* June 1973, *1*(2), pp. 191–200.

_____; Yancey, T. A. and Judge, G. G. The Statistical Consequences of Preliminary Test Estimators in Regression. *J. Amer. Statist. Assoc.,* March 1973, *68*(341), pp. 109–16.

_____; Yancey, T. A. and Judge, G. G. Wallace's Weak Mean Square Error Criterion for Testing Linear Restrictions in Regression: A Tighter Bound. *Econometrica,* November 1973, *41*(6), pp. 1203–06.

Bockelmann, Horst and Schlesinger, Helmut. Monetary Policy in the Federal Republic of Germany. In *Holbik, K., ed.,* 1973, pp. 161–213.

Boddewyn, J. J. External Affairs at Four Levels in U.S. Multinationals. *Ind. Relat.,* May 1973, *12*(2), pp. 239–47.

_____ The External Affairs Function in American Multinational Corporations. In *Fayerweather, J., ed.,* 1973, pp. 49–62.

_____ Public Policy Toward Retailing: Belgium. In *Boddewyn, J. J. and Hollander, S. C., eds.,* 1972, pp. 37–62.

_____ and Ajiferuke, Musbau. Socioeconomic Indicators in Comparative Management. In *Alexandrides, C. G., ed.,* 1973, pp. 163–72.

_____ and Hollander, Stanley C. Public Policy Toward Retailing: Conclusions. In *Boddewyn, J. J. and Hollander, S. C., eds.,* 1972, pp. 431–52.

_____ and Hollander, Stanley C. Public Policy Toward Retailing: Introduction. In *Boddewyn, J. J. and Hollander, S. C., eds.,* 1972, pp. 1–9.

Boddy, Francis M. The Market for Economists. *Amer. J. Agr. Econ.,* Part II, November 1973, *55* (4), pp. 720–24.

Boddy, Raford and Gort, Michael. Capital Expenditures and Capital Stocks. *Ann. Econ. Soc. Measure,* July 1973, *2*(3), pp. 245–61.

Bodenhöfer, Hans-Joachim. X-Effizienz, Innovations-Effizienz und wirtschaftliches Wachstum. (X-Efficiency, Innovation Efficiency, and Economic Growth. With English summary.) *Z. Wirtschaft. Sozialwissen.,* 1973, *93*(6), pp. 671–86.

Bodenstab, Charles J. Exception Reports for Management Action. In *Thomas, W. E., Jr., ed.,* 1973, pp. 317–24.

Bodin, Lennart. Extensions of the Fix-Point Method II: The Recursive Fix-Point Method. *Écon. Appl.,* 1973, *26*(2–3–4), pp. 583–607.

Bodkin, Ronald G. Econometric Models: Discussion. *Amer. Econ. Rev.,* May 1973, *63*(2), pp. 410–11.

_____ and Murthy, K. S. R. The Orders-Shipments Mechanism in Canadian Producer Goods Industries. *J. Amer. Statist. Assoc.,* June 1973, *68*(342), pp. 297–305.

Bodner, David E. The Role of Central Bank Swaps

in the International Monetary System. **In** *Wiegand, G. C., ed.,* 1973, pp. 100–06.

Boehlje, Michael. Optimization and Decision Models: The Use of Statistical Search Procedures. *Can. J. Agr. Econ.,* July 1973, *21*(2), pp. 43–53.

———; **Eidman, Vernon and Walker, Odell.** An Approach to Farm Management Education. *Amer. J. Agr. Econ.,* May 1973, *55*(2), pp. 192–97.

Boehm, E. A. Australia's Economic Depression of the 1930s. *Econ. Rec.,* December 1973, *49*(128), pp. 606–23.

Boehm, Volker. Firms and Market Equilibria in a Private Ownership Economy. *Z. Nationalökon.,* 1973, *33*(1–2), pp. 87–102.

——— On Cores and Equilibria of Productive Economies with a Measure Space of Consumers: An Example. *J. Econ. Theory,* August 1973, *6*(4), pp. 409–12.

Boelaert, Remi. Unemployment-Inflation Trade-Offs in EEC–Countries. *Weltwirtsch. Arch.,* 1973, *109* (3), pp. 418–51.

Boeninger, Edgardo. The Role of the University in the Training of Personnel for Public Administration: A Latin American Perspective. **In** *Thurber, C. E. and Graham, L. S., eds.,* 1973, pp. 188–94.

Boesen, Jannik. Peasants and Coffee Export. **In** *Institute for Development Research,* 1973, pp. 79–100.

Boettinger, Henry M. The Management Challenge. **In** *The Conference Board,* 1973, pp. 1–21.

Bogart, Leo. Comment on Silk and Geiger. *J. Marketing Res.,* May 1973, *10*(2), pp. 219–20.

——— The Future of Retailing. *Harvard Bus. Rev.,* November-December 1973, *51*(6), pp. 16–32, 176.

——— **and Lehman, Charles.** What Makes a Brand Name Familiar? *J. Marketing Res.,* February 1973, *10*(1), pp. 17–22.

Bogomolov, O. The International Market of the CMEA Countries. **In** *Kiss, T., ed.,* 1973, pp. 31–36.

Bogucka, Maria. Amsterdam and the Baltic in the First Half of the Seventeenth Century. *Econ. Hist. Rev., 2nd Ser.,* August 1973, *26*(3), pp. 433–47.

Bohi, Douglas R. Profit Performance in the Defense Industry. *J. Polit. Econ.,* May-June 1973, *81*(3), pp. 721–28.

Bohley, Peter. Der Nulltarif im Nahverkehr. (Free Transit in Metropolitan Areas. With English summary.) *Kyklos,* 1973, *26*(1), pp. 113–42.

Bohman, J. and Bohman, M. K. The Neoclassical Theory of Technical Progress: Note. *Amer. Econ. Rev.,* June 1973, *63*(3), pp. 490–93.

Bohman, M. K. and Bohman, J. The Neoclassical Theory of Technical Progress: Note. *Amer. Econ. Rev.,* June 1973, *63*(3), pp. 490–93.

Boll, F. Multiplicatoren en economische politiek in verschillende wisselkoerssystemen. (Multipliers and Economic Policy under Various Exchange Rate Systems. With English summary.) *Tijdschr. Econ.,* 1973, *18*(3), pp. 381–427.

Bolle, Michael. Geld, Wachstum und Beschäftigung. (Money, Growth and Employment. With English summary.) *Z. ges. Staatswiss.,* February 1973, *129* (1), pp. 1–22.

Bolten, Steven. The Behavior of Convertible Deben-

ture Premiums: Reply. *Miss. Val. J. Bus. Econ.,* Winter 1973-74, *9*(2), pp. 69–70.

——— Treasury Bill Auction Procedures: An Empirical Investigation. *J. Finance,* June 1973, *28*(3), pp. 577–85.

——— **and Mastrapasqua, Frank.** A Note on Financial Analyst Evaluation. *J. Finance,* June 1973, *28* (3), pp. 707–12.

Bolton, G. C. Louis Hartz. *Australian Econ. Hist. Rev.,* September 1973, *13*(2), pp. 168–76.

Bolton, Lena W. Bargaining Ahead: Major Contracts Expiring in 1974. *Mon. Lab. Rev.,* December 1973, *96*(12), pp. 43–51.

——— **and Larson, David.** Calendar of Wage Increases and Negotiations for 1973. *Mon. Lab. Rev.,* January 1973, *96*(1), pp. 3–16.

Bombach, Gottfried. Problemstellungen, Methoden und Grenzen mittelfristiger Wirtschafts- und Finanzplanung. (Problems, Methods and Limits of Medium-Termed Economic and Financial Planning. With English summary.) *Schweiz. Z. Volkswirtsch. Statist.,* September 1973, *109*(3), pp. 293–316.

Bonar, James. Malthus and His Work. **In** *Rectenwald, H. C., ed.,* 1973, pp. 83–89.

Boni, Milena. Il problema della localizzazione industriale. L'Europa occidentale: recenti esperienze e prospettive. (The Problem of Industrial Localization. Western Europe: Recent Experiences and Prospectives. With English summary.) *L'Impresa,* 1973, *15*(2), pp. 100–04.

Bonnaud, Jean-Jacques and Pagé, Jean-Pierre. L'utilisation d'un modèle de simulation économique dans la procédure de préparation du VIe Plan (1970–1975). (The Utilisation of a Mathematical Economic Model in the Process of Elaboration of the French VIth Plan (1970–1975). With English summary.) *Revue Écon.,* November 1973, *24*(6), pp. 988–1025.

Bonnen, James T. Implications for Agricultural Policy. *Amer. J. Agr. Econ.,* August 1973, *55*(3), pp. 391–98.

Bonus, Holger. Quasi-Engel Curves, Diffusion, and the Ownership of Major Consumer Durables. *J. Polit. Econ.,* May-June 1973, *81*(3), pp. 655–77.

Booms, Bernard H. Impact of Urban Market Structure on the Level of Inventive Activity in Cities in the Early Nineteen Hundreds. *Land Econ.,* August 1973, *49*(3), pp. 318–25.

——— **and Halldorson, James R.** The Politics of Redistribution: A Reformulation. *Amer. Polit. Sci. Rev.,* September 1973, *67*(3), pp. 924–33.

——— **and Hu, Teh-wei.** Economic and Social Factors in the Provision of Urban Public Education. *Amer. J. Econ. Soc.,* January 1973, *32*(1), pp. 35–43.

Boone, Louis E. and Kurtz, David L. The Consumer Versus Holder-in-Due-Course Doctrine. *Ohio State U. Bull. Bus. Res.,* August 1973, *48*(8), pp. 1–3, 6.

Boone, Michael M. Management Accountants and the Securities Laws. *Manage. Account.,* June 1973, *54*(12), pp. 18–22.

Boorman, John T. and Peterson, Manferd O. Instability of Savings Flows and Mortgage Lending by

Financial Intermediaries. *Southern Econ. J.,* October 1973, *40*(2), pp. 297–312.

Borch, Karl. The Place of Uncertainty in the Theories of the Austrian School. In *Hicks, J. R. and Weber, W., eds.,* 1973, pp. 61–74.

_____ Uncertainty and Indifference Curves—A Correction. *Rev. Econ. Stud.,* January 1973, *40*(1), pp. 141.

Borglin, Anders. Price Characterization of Stable Allocations in Exchange Economies with Externalities. *J. Econ. Theory,* October 1973, *6*(5), pp. 483–94.

Borglum, Richard P. and Thompson, Duane E. A Case Study of Employee Attitudes and Labor Unrest. *Ind. Lab. Relat. Rev.,* October 1973, *27*(1), pp. 74–83.

Borgsdorf, C. W. The Virtually Unconstrained Legal Environment for Mergers in Canada. *Antitrust Bull.,* Winter 1973, *18*(4), pp. 809–25.

Borlenghi, Erminio. Il progetto per un'area forte nella Francia di sud-est. (The Project for a Strong Area in South-East France. With English summary.) *L'Impresa,* 1973, *15*(2), pp. 105–12.

Bornstein, Morris. Plan and Market: Economic Reform in Eastern Europe: Introduction. In *Bornstein, M., ed.,* 1973, pp. 1–22.

Borovskikh, B. Urgent Problems in Planning the Reproduction of Natural Resources. *Prob. Econ.,* November 1973, *16*(7), pp. 3–23.

Borpujari, Jitendra G. and Ter-Minassian, Teresa. The Weighted Budget Balance Approach to Fiscal Analysis: A Methodology and Some Case Studies. *Int. Monet. Fund Staff Pap.,* November 1973, *20*(3), pp. 801–31.

Borts, G. H. and Aghevli, B. B. The Stability and Equilibrium of the Balance of Payments under a Fixed Exchange Rate. *J. Int. Econ.,* February 1973, *3*(1), pp. 1–20.

Borukhov, Eli. City Size and Transportation Costs. *J. Polit. Econ.,* September-October 1973, *81*(5), pp. 1205–15.

Borus, Michael E. and Nestel, Gilbert. Response Bias in Reports of Father's Education and Socioeconomic Status. *J. Amer. Statist. Assoc.,* December 1973, *68*(344), pp. 816–20.

Bosanquet, Nicholas and Doeringer, Peter B. Is There a Dual Labour Market in Great Britain? *Econ. J.,* June 1973, *83*(330), pp. 421–35.

Bose, Swadesh R. The Price Situation in Bangladesh—A Preliminary Analysis. *Bangladesh Econ. Rev.,* July 1973, *1*(3), pp. 243–68.

Boskin, Michael J. Local Government Tax and Product Competition and the Optimal Provision of Public Goods. *J. Polit. Econ.,* January-February 1973, *81*(1), pp. 203–10.

Bossons, John. The Distribution of Assets Among Individuals of Different Age and Wealth. In *Goldsmith, R. W., ed.,* 1973, pp. 394–428.

Bosworth, Barry. The Current Inflation: Malign Neglect? *Brookings Pap. Econ. Act.,* 1973, (1), pp. 263–83.

Bosworth, Derek L. Changes in the Quality of Inventive Output and Patent Based Indices of Technological Change. *Bull. Econ. Res.,* November 1973, *25*(2), pp. 95–103.

Botalla-Gambetta, Brigitte and Lécaillon, Jacques.

Inflation, répartition et chômage dans la France contemporaine. (Inflation, Distribution and Unemployment in Today's France. With English summary.) *Revue Écon.,* May 1973, *24*(3), pp. 373–400.

Botero, Rodrigo. Relations with the United States: A Latin American View. In *Urquidi, V. L. and Thorp, R., eds.,* 1973, pp. 283–303.

Botez, Mihai C. and Moldovan, Roman. Correlation Between Forecasting and Action—An Essential Feature in Planning. *Revue Roumaine Sci. Soc. Serie Sci. Econ.,* 1973, *17*(1), pp. 41–52.

Botha, D. J. J. On Tariff Policy: The Formative Years. *S. Afr. J. Econ.,* December 1973, *41*(4), pp. 321–55.

_____ Rating and Valuation. *S. Afr. J. Econ.,* March 1973, *41*(1), pp. 40–48.

_____ A School of Economic Studies. *S. Afr. J. Econ.,* September 1973, *41*(3), pp. 281–90.

Boubacar, Mamadou N'Diaye. Savings Banks and Savings Facilities in African Countries: Dahomey. In *Alberici, A. and Baravelli, M., eds.,* 1973, pp. 23–27.

Bouckaert, L. François Perroux en de verruiming van het economisch denken. (The Economic Thought of F. Perroux. With English summary.) *Tijdschr. Econ.,* 1973, *18*(1), pp. 9–37.

Boudreaux, Kenneth J. Discounts and Premiums on Closed-End Mutual Funds: A Study in Valuation. *J. Finance,* May 1973, *28*(2), pp. 515–22.

_____ 'Managerialism' and Risk-Return Performance. *Southern Econ. J.,* January 1973, *39*(3), pp. 366–72.

Boughton, James M. and von Furstenberg, George M. Stabilization Goals and the Appropriateness of Fiscal Policy during the Eisenhower and Kennedy-Johnson Administrations. *Public Finance Quart.,* January 1973, *1*(1), pp. 5–28.

Boulding, Kenneth E. Agricultural Organizations and Policies: A Personal Evaluation. In *Boulding, K. E.,* 1973, pp. 161–73.

_____ America's Economy: The Qualified Uproarious Success. In *Boulding, K. E.,* 1973, pp. 361–81.

_____ Business and Economic Systems. In *Boulding, K. E.,* 1973, pp. 429–47.

_____ Can We Control Inflation in a Garrison State? In *Boulding, K. E.,* 1973, pp. 1–24.

_____ The Changing Framework of American Capitalism. In *Boulding, K. E.,* 1973, pp. 251–56.

_____ The Concept of Need for Health Services. In *Boulding, K. E.,* 1973, pp. 277–98.

_____ Economic Progress as a Goal in Economic Life. In *Boulding, K. E.,* 1973, pp. 53–86.

_____ Economics and the Behavioral Sciences: A Desert Frontier? In *Boulding, K. E.,* 1973, pp. 105–20.

_____ Economics as a Social Science. In *Boulding, K. E.,* 1973, pp. 25–40.

_____ The Economics of Energy. *Ann. Amer. Acad. Polit. Soc. Sci.,* November 1973, *410,* pp. 120–26.

_____ Environment and Economics. In *Boulding, K. E.,* 1973, pp. 569–79.

_____ Equality and Conflict. *Ann. Amer. Acad. Polit. Soc. Sci.,* September 1973, *409,* pp. 1–8.

_____ The Ethnics of Rational Decision. In *Haynes,*

W. W.; Coyne, T. J. and Osborne, D. K., eds., 1973, pp. 8–17.

——— Factors Affecting the Future Demand for Education. In Boulding, K. E., 1973, pp. 503–31.

——— The Formation of Values as a Process in Human Learning. In Boulding, K. E., 1973, pp. 457–66.

——— Fun and Games with the Gross National Product—The Role of Misleading Indicators in Social Policy. In Reynolds, L. G.; Green, G. D. and Lewis, D. R., eds., 1973, pp. 112–22.

——— Fun and Games with the Gross National Product: The Role of Misleading Indicators in Social Policy. In Boulding, K. E., 1973, pp. 467–82.

——— The Future Corporation and Public Attitudes. In Boulding, K. E., 1973, pp. 175–93.

——— Human Resource Development as a Learning Process. In Boulding, K. E., 1973, pp. 339–49.

——— The Impact of the Defense Industry on the Structure of the American Economy. In Udis, B., ed., 1973, pp. 225–52.

——— Intersects: The Peculiar Organizations. In The Conference Board, 1973, pp. 179–201.

——— Is Scarcity Dead? In Boulding, K. E., 1973, pp. 311–21.

——— Man as a Commodity. In Boulding, K. E., 1973, pp. 587–603.

——— The Misallocation of Intellectual Resources. In Boulding, K. E., 1973, pp. 195–200.

——— The Misallocation of Intellectual Resources in Economics. In Boulding, K. E., 1973, pp. 533–52.

——— The Need for Reform of National Income Statistics. In Boulding, K. E., 1973, pp. 581–86.

——— Parity, Charity, and Clarity. In Boulding, K. E., 1973, pp. 121–25.

——— The Public Image of American Economic Institutions. In Boulding, K. E., 1973, pp. 127–45.

——— Religious Foundations of Economic Progress. In Boulding, K. E., 1973, pp. 41–51.

——— The Role of Economics in the Establishment of Stable Peace. In Boulding, K. E., 1973, pp. 407–11.

——— The Scientific-Military-Industrial Complex. In Boulding, K. E., 1973, pp. 351–60.

——— The Shadow of the Stationary State. In Olson, M. and Landsberg, H. H. eds., 1973, pp. 89–101.

——— The Skills of the Economist. In Rectenwald, H. C., ed., 1973, pp. 415–24.

——— Some Questions on the Measurement and Evaluation of Organization. In Boulding, K. E., 1973, pp. 147–59.

——— The University as an Economic and Social Unit. In Boulding, K. E., 1973, pp. 413–27.

——— War Industry and the American Economy. In Boulding, K. E., 1973, pp. 483–501.

Bourgeois, Lawrence L. and Schlenker, Jon A. Family Assistance to Married University Students. Southern Quart., January 1973, 11(2), pp. 147–55.

Bourgoignie, Th. Overheid en bedrijfsleven/3 La réglementation des prix en Belgique. (Price Regulation in Belgium. With English summary.) Econ. Soc. Tijdschr., August 1973, 27(4), pp. 387–400.

Bousquet, Georges-Henri. Vilfredo Pareto. In Rectenwald, H. C., ed., 1973, pp. 297–306.

Bouvier, Leon F. A Survey of Population Textbooks. Demography, November 1973, 10(4), pp. 685–92.

Bouwsma, William J. Lawyers in Early Modern Culture. Amer. Hist. Rev., April 1973, 78(2), pp. 303–27.

von Böventer, Edwin. City Size Systems: Theoretical Issues, Empirical Regularities and Planning Guides. Urban Stud., June 1973, 10(2), pp. 145–62.

Bowden, Roger J. Note on Coefficient Restrictions in Estimating Sets of Demand Relations. Econometrica, May 1973, 41(3), pp. 575–79.

——— Some Implications of the Permanent-Income Hypothesis. Rev. Econ. Stud., January 1973, 40(1), pp. 33–37.

——— The Theory of Parametric Identification. Econometrica, November 1973, 41(6), pp. 1069–74.

Bowen, Charles P., Jr. Let's Put Realism into Management Development. Harvard Bus. Rev., July-August 1973, 51(4), pp. 80–87.

Bowen, Ian. "Nature's Feast" Today. Finance Develop., December 1973, 10(4), pp. 13–17.

Bowen, John and Hinshaw, Elton. Inflation and Stagnation in Brazil: Comment. Econ. Develop. Cult. Change, April 1973, 21(3), pp. 522–25.

Bower, Blair T. and Kneese, Allen V. The Delaware Estuary Study: Effluent Charges, Least-Cost Treatment, and Efficiency. In Enthoven, A. C. and Freeman, A. M., III, eds., 1973, pp. 112–21.

Bower, Marvin and Walton, C. Lee, Jr. Gearing a Business to the Future. In The Conference Board, 1973, pp. 93–148.

Bower, Richard S. Market Changes in the Computer Services Industry. Bell J. Econ. Manage. Sci., Autumn 1973, 4(2), pp. 539–90.

——— and Lessard, Donald R. An Operational Approach to Risk-Screening. J. Finance, May 1973, 28(2), pp. 321–37.

Bowie, Robert R. Implications for U.S. Policy toward Europe: Comment. In Krause, L. B. and Salant, W. S., eds., 1973, pp. 292–95.

Bowlby, Roger L. and Schriver, William R. Academic Ability and Rates of Return to Vocational Training. Ind. Lab. Relat. Rev., April 1973, 26(3), pp. 980–90.

Bowles, Samuel. Understanding Unequal Economic Opportunity. Amer. Econ. Rev., May 1973, 63(2), pp. 346–56.

Bowsher, Norman N. 1973—A Year of Inflation. Fed. Res. Bank St. Louis Rev., December 1973, 55(12), pp. 2–11.

Box, G. E. P. and Jenkins, G. M. Some Comments on a Paper by Chatfield and Prothero and on a Review by Kendall. J. Roy. Statist. Soc., Part 3 1973, 136, pp. 337–52.

Boxley, Robert F. and Anderson, William D. The Incidence of Benefits from Commodity Price-Support Programs: A Case Study of Tobacco. In Harriss, C. L., ed., 1973, pp. 79–103.

Boyd, John H. Bank Strategies in the Retail Demand Deposit Markets. J. Bank Res., Summer 1973, 4(2), pp. 111–21.

——— Some Recent Developments in the Savings and Loan Deposit Markets. J. Money, Credit, Banking, August 1973, 5(3), pp. 733–50.

Boyd, Monica. Occupational Mobility and Fertility in Metropolitan Latin America. *Demography,* February 1973, *10*(1), pp. 1–17.

Boyd, T. A. and Vercruijsse, E. V. W. Evaluation of an Extension Programme in Agriculture. In *Ofori, I. M., ed.,* 1973, pp. 57–66.

Boye-Møller, Monica. Language Training for Immigrant Workers in Sweden. *Int. Lab. Rev.,* December 1973, *108*(6), pp. 505–15.

Boyes, William J. and Peseau, Dennis E. On Optimization in Models of Urban Land Use Densities: Comment. *J. Reg. Sci.,* April 1973, *13*(1), pp. 129–33.

Boyke, Robert and Leftwich, Robert B. Foreign Direct Investments in the United States in 1972. *Surv. Curr. Bus.,* August 1973, *53*(8), pp. 50–51.

Boyle, Gerald J. Financing the Corporation for Public Television. *Nat. Tax J.,* June 1973, *26*(2), pp. 199–207.

Boyle, M. Barbara. Equal Opportunity for Women is Smart Business. *Harvard Bus. Rev.,* May-June 1973, *51*(3), pp. 85–95.

Boyle, Stanley E. The Average Concentration Ratio: An Inappropriate Measure of Industry Structure. *J. Polit. Econ.,* Part I, March-April 1973, *81*(2), pp. 414–26.

Braby, R. H. Urban Growth and Policy: A Multi-Nodal Approach. *Econ. Anal. Pol.,* September 1973, *4*(2), pp. 43–58.

Braccaioli-Alberti, Enzo. Il mercato dei mezzi pubblicitari in Italia. (The Market of Advertising Media in Italy. With English summary.) *L'Impresa,* 1973, *15*(5–6), pp. 347–51.

Brackett, Jean. Urban Family Budgets Updated to Autumn 1972. *Mon. Lab. Rev.,* August 1973, *96* (8), pp. 70–76.

Brada, Josef C. The Allocative Efficiency of Centrally Planned Foreign Trade: A Programming Approach to the Czech Case. *Europ. Econ. Rev.,* December 1973, *4*(4), pp. 329–46.

——— The Microallocative Impact of the Hungarian Economic Reform of 1968: Some Evidence from the Export Sector. *Econ. Planning,* 1973, *13*(1–2), pp. 1–14.

Bradburn, Norman M. and Sudman, Seymour. Effects of Time and Memory Factors on Response in Surveys. *J. Amer. Statist. Assoc.,* December 1973, *68*(344), pp. 805–15.

Bradbury, F. R. Changes in the Chemical Industry. In *Edge, D. O. and Wolfe, J. N., eds.,* 1973, pp. 181–95.

Bradford, David F. and Kelejian, Harry H. An Econometric Model of the Flight to the Suburbs. *J. Polit. Econ.,* May-June 1973, *81*(3), pp. 566–89.

Bradford, Maxwell R. and Brehmer, Ekhard. Incomes and Labor Market Policies in Sweden. *Finance Develop.,* September 1973, *10*(3), pp. 21–23, 35.

Bradley, Edwin L. The Equivalence of Maximum Likelihood and Weighted Least Squares Estimates in the Exponential Family. *J. Amer. Statist. Assoc.,* March 1973, *68*(341), pp. 199–200.

Bradley, Iver E.; Mangum, Garth L. and Robson, R. Thayne. Impact of Manpower Programs upon Employment and Earnings. In *Mangum, G. L. and Robson, R. T., eds.,* 1973, pp. 227–59.

———; **Mangum, Garth L. and Robson, R. Thayne.** Total Impact of Manpower Programs. In *Mangum, G. L. and Robson, R. T., eds.,* 1973, pp. 260–93.

Bradley, Jerry O. and Joy, O. Maurice. A Note on Sensitivity Analysis of Rates of Return. *J. Finance,* December 1973, *28*(5), pp. 1255–61.

Bradley, Michael E. Incentives and Labour Supply on Soviet Collective Farms: Reply. *Can. J. Econ.,* August 1973, *6*(3), pp. 438–42.

Bradley, Paul G. Increasing Scarcity: The Case of Energy Resources. *Amer. Econ. Rev.,* May 1973, *63*(2), pp. 119–25.

Bradley, Stephen P. and Crane, Dwight B. Management of Commercial Bank Government Security Portfolios: An Optimization Approach Under Uncertainty. *J. Bank Res.,* Spring 1973, *4*(1), pp. 18–30.

Bradshaw, Benjamin S. and Bean, Frank D. Trends in the Fertility of Mexican Americans, 1950-1970. *Soc. Sci. Quart.,* March 1973, *53*(4), pp. 688–96.

Bradshaw, T. F. Corporate Social Reform: An Executive's Viewpoint. *Calif. Manage. Rev.,* Summer 1973, *15*(4), pp. 85–89.

Bradshaw, Thomas F. Jobseeking Methods Used by Unemployed Workers. *Mon. Lab. Rev.,* February 1973, *96*(2), pp. 35–40.

Brady, Eugene A. An Econometric Analysis of the U.S. Residential Housing Market. In *Ricks, R. B., ed.,* 1973, pp. 1–47.

———, **et al.** The Outlook: A Reevaluation of the Forecast for 1973. *Indiana Bus. Rev.,* May-June 1973, *48,* pp. 1–9.

Braemer, Pierre. Savings Banks and Savings Facilities in African Countries: Mauritania. In *Alberici, A. and Baravelli, M., eds.,* 1973, pp. 63–64.

Brahmananda, Palahalli Ramaiya. A. C. Pigou. In *Rectenwald, H. C., ed.,* 1973, pp. 358–67.

——— Commercial Banks as Development Agencies—Appraisal and Prospect. In *Simha, S. L. N., ed.,* 1973, pp. 208–22.

——— The Structural Efficiency of the Monetary System in India: An Appraisal. In *Simha, S. L. N., ed.,* 1973, pp. 322–30.

Brainard, Calvin H. Massachusetts Loss Experience Under No-Fault in 1971: Analysis and Implications. *J. Risk Ins.,* March 1973, *40*(1), pp. 95–101.

Bralove, Mary. Does Your Paprika Get Up Off the Plate and Just Walk Away? In *Murray, B. B., ed.,* 1973, pp. 86–88.

Bramble, William J.; Wiley, David E. and Schmidt, William H. Studies of a Class of Covariance Structure Models. *J. Amer. Statist. Assoc.,* June 1973, *68*(342), pp. 317–23.

Branch, Ben. Research and Development and Its Relation to Sales Growth. *J. Econ. Bus.,* Winter 1973, *25*(2), pp. 107–11.

Brand, Horst. Productivity in Telephone Communications. *Mon. Lab. Rev.,* November 1973, *96*(11), pp. 3–9.

Brand, S. S. Economic Development as a Policy Objective. *Finance Trade Rev.,* December 1973, *10* (4), pp. 168–75.

Brandes, Ove. Models for Domestic Air Travel Fares. *Swedish J. Econ.,* September 1973, *75*(3), pp. 249–56.

Brandis, R. Buford. The National Need for an Integrated Trade Policy: The Textile Example. In *Iowa State University Center for Agricultural and Rural Development*, 1973, pp. 155–65.

Brandow, G. E. Conflicts and Consistencies in the Agricultural Policies of the United States and Canada. *Amer. J. Agr. Econ.*, December 1973, *55* (5), pp. 778–84.

_____ A Discussion of the 1973 Economic Report of the President: The Food Price Problem. *Amer. J. Agr. Econ.*, August 1973, *55*(3), pp. 385–90.

Branfman, Eric J.; Cohen, Benjamin I. and Trubek, David M. Measuring the Invisible Wall: Land Use Controls and the Residential Patterns of the Poor. *Yale Law J.*, January 1973, *82*(3), pp. 483–508.

Brankamp, K. and Kremeier, A. Effect of Technological Development upon Substitution Processes. In *Blohm, H. and Steinbuch, K., eds.*, 1973, pp. 121–32.

Brannon, Gerard M. Death Taxes in a Structure of Progressive Taxes. *Nat. Tax J.*, September 1973, *26*(3), pp. 451–57.

_____ and Morss, Elliott R. The Tax Allowance for Dependents: Deductions versus Credits. *Nat. Tax J.*, December 1973, *26*(4), pp. 599–609.

Brans, J. P.; Leclercq, M. and Hansen, P. An Algorithm for Optimal Reloading of Pressurized Water Reactors. In *Ross, M., ed.*, 1973, pp. 417–28.

Branson, William H. The Use of Variable Tax Rates for Stabilization Purposes. In *Musgrave, R. A., ed.*, 1973, pp. 267–85.

Brantner, Paul F. Accounting for Land Development Companies. *Manage. Account.*, August 1973, *55*(2), pp. 15–19.

_____ Taxation and the Multinational Firm. *Manage. Account.*, October 1973, *55*(4), pp. 11–16, 26.

Braun, Ferdnand. The European Economic Community Approach to Adjustment. In *Hughes, H., ed.*, 1973, pp. 187–216.

Braverman, E. M. A Production Model with Disequilibrium Prices. *Matekon*, Fall 1973, *10*(1), pp. 40–64.

Braverman, Jerome D. and Hartman, Gerald R. The Process of Classifying Drivers: A Suggestion for Insurance Ratemaking: Comment. *J. Risk Ins.*, March 1973, *40*(1), pp. 143–46.

Bravo, Jacques. L'expérience française des budgets de programmes. (The French Experiment in Program Budgeting. With English summary.) *Revue Écon.*, January 1973, *24*(1), pp. 1–65.

Brawner, Marlyn R. Migration and Educational Achievement of Mexican Americans. *Soc. Sci. Quart.*, March 1973, *53*(4), pp. 727–37.

Brazer, Harvey E. The Income Tax in the Federal Revenue System. In *Musgrave, R. A., ed.*, 1973, pp. 3–37.

Break, George F. Federal Tax Policy and the Private Saving Ratio. *Nat. Tax J.*, September 1973, *26*(3), pp. 409–14.

Bréaud, Patrick and Gorgorin, Jean-Louis. An Appraisal of Program Budgeting in France. In *Novick, D., ed.*, 1973, pp. 111–18.

Brebbia, John Henry. The Role of Advisory Opinions and the Business Review Procedure. *Antitrust Bull.*, Summer 1973, *18*(2), pp. 191–219.

Brecher, Michael. Images, Process and Feedback in Foreign Policy: Israel's Decision on German Reparations. *Amer. Polit. Sci. Rev.*, March 1973, *67*(1), pp. 73–102.

Brechling, Frank. Announcement Effects of Profits Taxation: Discussion. In *Parkin, M., ed.*, 1973, pp. 33–34.

_____ Wage Inflation and the Structure of Regional Unemployment. *J. Money, Credit, Banking*, Part II, February 1973, *5*(1), pp. 355–79.

Breeden, Joseph S. and Wotruba, Thomas R. The Ideal Company Image and Self-Image Congruence. *J. Bus. Res.*, Fall 1973, *1*(2), pp. 165–72.

Breen, William J. and Lerner, Eugene M. Corporate Financial Strategies and Market Measures of Risk and Return. *J. Finance*, May 1973, *28*(2), pp. 339–51.

Brehmer, Ekhard and Bradford, Maxwell R. Incomes and Labor Market Policies in Sweden. *Finance Develop.*, September 1973, *10*(3), pp. 21–23, 35.

Breimyer, Harold F. An Analysis of the Market for Food Stamps: Comment. *Amer. J. Agr. Econ.*, February 1973, *55*(1), pp. 110–12.

_____ The Economics of Agricultural Marketing: A Survey. *Rev. Marketing Agr. Econ.*, December 1973, *41*(4), pp. 115–65.

_____ Man, Physical Resources, and Economic Organization. *Amer. J. Agr. Econ.*, February 1973, *55*(1), pp. 1–9.

_____ Public Sector Research and Education and the Agribusiness Complex: Unholy Alliance or Socially Beneficial Partnership? Discussion. *Amer. J. Agr. Econ.*, December 1973, *55*(5), pp. 993–96.

Breit, William. The Development of Clarence Ayres's Theoretical Institutionalism. *Soc. Sci. Quart.*, September 1973, *54*(2), pp. 244–57.

Brems, Hans. Nature and Neoclassical Growth. *Ekon. Samfundets Tidskr.*, January 1973, *26*(1), pp. 16–20.

Brennan, Geoffrey. Pareto Desirable Redistribution: The Non-Altruistic Dimension. *Public Choice*, Spring 1973, *14*, pp. 43–67.

_____ Pareto Desirable Redistribution: The Case of Malice and Envy. *J. Public Econ.*, April 1973, *2*(2), pp. 173–83.

_____ and Walsh, Cliff. Pareto-Optimal Redistribution Reconsidered. *Public Finance Quart.*, April 1973, *1*(2), pp. 147–68.

Brennan, Michael J. An Approach to the Valuation of Uncertain Income Streams. *J. Finance*, June 1973, *28*(3), pp. 661–74.

Brenneman, Ronald; Steedman, Ian and Bell, D. J. A Control Theory Analysis of a Finite Optimum Savings Program in a Two-Sector Model. *Int. Econ. Rev.*, June 1973, *14*(2), pp. 520–24.

Brenner, Vincent C. Critical Characteristics for a Pragmatic Concept of Income. *Marquette Bus. Rev.*, Winter 1973, *17*(4), pp. 188–96.

Bressler, Barry. Family Size and Income Inequality. *Amer. Econ.*, Fall 1973, *17*(2), pp. 113–21.

Bretzfelder, Robert B. Regional and State Personal Income Developments. *Surv. Curr. Bus.*, January 1973, *53*(1), pp. 30–32.

_____ Regional and State Personal Income: Second

Quarter Developments. *Surv. Curr. Bus.*, October 1973, *53*(10), pp. 18–19, 44.

—— Sensitivity of State and Regional Income to National Business Cycles. *Surv. Curr. Bus.*, April 1973, *53*(4), pp. 22–33.

—— State and Regional Personal Income, 1959–1972. *Surv. Curr. Bus.*, August 1973, *53*(8), pp. 39–49.

Brewer, Garry D. and Hall, Owen P., Jr. Policy Analysis by Computer Simulation: The Need for Appraisal. *Public Policy*, Summer 1973, *21*(3), pp. 343–65.

Brewer, K. R. W. Some Consequences of Temporal Aggregation and Systematic Sampling for ARMA and ARMAX Models. *J. Econometrics*, June 1973, *1*(2), pp. 133–54.

Brewster, Havelock. Economic Dependence: A Quantitative Interpretation. *Soc. Econ. Stud.*, March 1973, *22*(1), pp. 90–95.

Bridbury, A. R. The Black Death. *Econ. Hist. Rev.*, *2nd Ser.*, November 1973, *26*(4), pp. 577–92.

Bridgeman, J. M. Planning-Programming-Budgeting in the United Kingdom Central Government. In *Novick, D., ed.*, 1973, pp. 89–95.

Brief, Richard P. and Owen, Joel. Present Value Models and the Multi-Asset Problem. *Accounting Rev.*, October 1973, *48*(4), pp. 690–95.

—— and Owen, Joel. A Reformulation of the Estimation Problem. *J. Acc. Res.*, Spring 1973, *11*(1), pp. 1–15.

Brierley, J. D. Programme Budgeting in Education in the United Kingdom. In *Novick, D., ed.*, 1973, pp. 97–103.

Brightman, Harvey J. and Dorfman, Mark S. Birth Order, Anxiety, Affiliation and the Purchase of Life Insurance: Comment. *J. Risk Ins.*, December 1973, *40*(4), pp. 643–46.

Brigida, Franco. L'immagine di impresa e di prodotto come strumento di commercializzazione. (Company and Product Image as Marketing Tools. With English summary.) *L'Impresa*, 1973, *15*(9–10), pp. 569–77.

Brim, Orville G., Jr. Do We Know What We Are Doing? In *Heimann, F. F., ed.*, 1973, pp. 216–58.

Brimmer, Andrew F. Multi-National Banks and the Management of Monetary Policy in the United States. *J. Finance*, May 1973, *28*(2), pp. 439–54.

—— Statements to Congress. *Fed. Res. Bull.*, June 1973, *59*(6), pp. 429–32.

Briner, Ernst K. International Tax Management. *Manage. Account.*, February 1973, *54*(8), pp. 47–50.

Brinker, Paul A. and Murdock, E. Wayne. Children of the Severely Injured. *J. Human Res.*, Spring 1973, *8*(2), pp. 242–49.

Brinkman, Donald R. Minimizing the Loss of Investment Tax Credits. *Manage. Account.*, January 1973, *54*(7), pp. 38–40.

Brinkmann, Gerhard. Die Diskriminierung der Nicht-Juristen im allgemeinen höheren Verwaltungsdienst der Bundesrepublik Deutschland. (The Discrimination of Non-lawyers in the General Higher Civil Service of the German Federal Republic. With English summary.) *Z. ges. Staatswiss.*, February 1973, *129*(1), pp. 150–67.

Brinner, Roger. Inflation, Deferral and the Neutral Taxation of Capital Gains. *Nat. Tax J.*, December 1973, *26*(4), pp. 565–73.

Brioschi, Edoardo T. Per una politica di comunicazione nell'azienda. (For a Policy of Communication in the Firm. With English summary.) *L'Impresa*, 1973, *15*(5–6), pp. 325–32.

Briscoe, G.; Smyth, David J. and Ireland, Norman J. Specification Bias and Short-run Returns to Labour: Some Evidence for the United Kingdom. *Rev. Econ. Statist.*, February 1973, *55*(1), pp. 23–27.

Briskin, Lawrence E. Establishing a Generalized Multi-Attribute Utility Function. In *Cochrane, J. L. and Zeleny, M., eds.*, 1973, pp. 236–45.

Brite, Robert L. Scale and the Elasticity of Substitution in Cross-Section Production Functions. *J. Econ. Bus.*, Winter 1973, *25*(2), pp. 101–06.

Brito, Dagobert L. Estimation, Prediction and Economic Control. *Int. Econ. Rev.*, October 1973, *14*(3), pp. 646–52.

—— Organized Crime: Comment. In *Rottenberg, S., ed.*, 1973, pp. 175–78.

—— and Williamson, Jeffrey G. Skilled Labor and Nineteenth Century Anglo-American Managerial Behavior. *Exploration Econ. Hist.*, Spring 1973, *10*(3), pp. 235–51.

Brits, R. N. Inflation and Capital Growth in South Africa, 1963–1972. *S. Afr. J. Econ.*, September 1973, *41*(3), pp. 291–97.

Brittain, John A. Research on the Transmission of Material Wealth. *Amer. Econ. Rev.*, May 1973, *63*(2), pp. 335–45.

Britto, Ronald. Some Recent Developments in the Theory of Economic Growth: An Interpretation. *J. Econ. Lit.*, December 1973, *11*(4), pp. 1343–66.

—— and Heller, H. Robert. International Adjustment and Optimal Reserves. *Int. Econ. Rev.*, February 1973, *14*(1), pp. 182–95.

Brobst, Robert W. and Wrighton, Fred M. The Income Elasticity of Housing: A Cross-Sectional Analysis of New Orleans. *Miss. Val. J. Bus. Econ.*, Winter 1973-74, *9*(2), pp. 43–58.

Brock, William A. Some Results on the Uniqueness of Steady States in Multisector Models of Optimum Growth when Future Utilities are Discounted. *Int. Econ. Rev.*, October 1973, *14*(3), pp. 535–59.

—— and Mirman, Leonard J. Optimal Economic Growth and Uncertainty: The No Discounting Case. *Int. Econ. Rev.*, October 1973, *14*(3), pp. 560–73.

Brody, Richard A. and Page, Benjamin I. Indifference, Alienation and Rational Decisions: The Effects of Candidate Evaluations on Turnout and the Vote. *Public Choice*, Summer 1973, *15*, pp. 1–17.

Broeze, Frank J. A. The New Economic History, the Navigation Acts, and the Continental Tobacco Market, 1770–90. *Econ. Hist. Rev.*, *2nd Ser.*, November 1973, *26*(4), pp. 668–78.

Bromley, A. J. and Surrey, A. J. Energy Resources. In *Cole, H. S. D., et al., eds.*, 1973, pp. 90–107.

Bromley, Daniel W. and Beattie, Bruce R. On the Incongruity of Program Objectives and Project

Evaluation: An Example from the Reclamation Program. *Amer. J. Agr. Econ.*, August 1973, *55*(3), pp. 472–76.

Bromley, David G. and Smith, Joel. The Historical Significance of Annexation as a Social Process. *Land Econ.*, August 1973, *49*(3), pp. 294–309.

Bromwich, Michael. The Effects of Sterling Devaluation on International Trade. In *Moskoff, W., ed.*, 1973, pp. 231–38.

Bronfenbrenner, Martin. Equality and Equity. *Ann. Amer. Acad. Polit. Soc. Sci.*, September 1973, *409*, pp. 9–23.

———— Japanese-American Economic War? Some Further Reflections. *Quart. Rev. Econ. Bus.*, Autumn 1973, *13*(3), pp. 33–42.

———— On "Let-'er-Rip" Inflation Policy. *Southern Econ. J.*, January 1973, *39*(3), pp. 424–26.

———— "Samuelson and Marx": Reply. *J. Econ. Lit.*, December 1973, *11*(4), pp. 1367.

———— Samuelson, Marx, and Their Latest Critics. *J. Econ. Lit.*, March 1973, *11*(1), pp. 58–63.

———— A Skeptical View of Radical Economics. *Amer. Econ.*, Fall 1973, *17*(2), pp. 4–8.

———— What the Radical Economists Are Saying. *Harvard Bus. Rev.*, September-October 1973, *51* (5), pp. 26–38, 166–68.

Bronsard, Camille. The Computational Economics of Jacques Lesourne. *J. Public Econ.*, July 1973, *2*(3), pp. 271–80.

———— **and Lacroix, Robert.** L'équilbre du consommateur en économie monétaire. (Consumer Equilibrium in a Monetary Economy. With English summary.) *Can. J. Econ.*, August 1973, *6*(3), pp. 332–43.

Bronzini, Michael S. and Carroll, Joseph L. Waterway Transportation Simulation Models: Development and Application. *Water Resources Res.*, February 1973, *9*(1), pp. 51–63.

Brook, Richard and Wallace, T. D. A Note on Extraneous Information in Regression. *J. Econometrics*, October 1973, *1*(3), pp. 315–16.

Brooks, Harvey. Technology Assessment as a Process. *Int. Soc. Sci. J.*, 1973, *25*(3), pp. 247–56.

———— The Technology of Zero Growth. In *Olson, M. and Landsberg, H. H., eds.*, 1973, pp. 139–52.

Brough, B. M. Information Systems for Decision and Control: Discussant 1. In *Ross, M., ed.*, 1973, pp. 183–84.

Broussalian, V. L. Discounting and the Evaluation of Public Investments: Reply. *Appl. Econ.*, September 1973, *5*(3), pp. 225–26.

Brown, Alan A.; Licari, J. A. and Neuberger, Egon. A Dynamic CES Production Function Interpretation of Hungarian Growth. *Acta Oecon.*, 1973, *11* (4), pp. 305–24.

———— **and Marer, Paul.** Foreign Trade in the East European Reforms. In *Bornstein, M., ed.*, 1973, pp. 153–205.

Brown, Byron W. State Grants and Inequality of Opportunity in Education. In *Boulding, K. E.; Pfaff, M. and Pfaff, A., eds.*, 1973, pp. 208–25.

Brown, Charles; Fane, George and Medoff, James. The Income Distribution as a Pure Public Good: Comment. *Quart. J. Econ.*, May 1973, *87*(2), pp. 296–303.

Brown, Douglass V. The Role of the NLRB. In *Somers, G. G., ed.*, 1973, pp. 111–17.

Brown, Emily Clark. Fundamental Soviet Labor Legislation. *Ind. Lab. Relat. Rev.*, January 1973, *26*(2), pp. 778–92.

Brown, Francis J. Economic Crisis in Private Education: Whither Now? *Rev. Soc. Econ.*, April 1973, *31*(1), pp. 93–97.

Brown, Gardner, Jr. and Hammack, Judd. Dynamic Economic Management of Migratory Waterfowl. *Rev. Econ. Statist.*, February 1973, *55*(1), pp. 73–82.

———— **and Johnson, M. Bruce.** Welfare-Maximizing Price and Output with Stochastic Demand: Reply. *Amer. Econ. Rev.*, March 1973, *63*(1), pp. 230–31.

Brown, George H. Census Projections: 1970 to 1985. *Manage. Account.*, January 1973, *54*(7), pp. 11–14.

Brown, H. James. Shift and Share Projections Revisited: Reply. *J. Reg. Sci.*, April 1973, *13*(1), pp. 121.

Brown, J. Douglas. Social Security in the Years Ahead. In *Somers, G. G., ed.*, 1973, pp. 118–27.

Brown, Kenneth M. Welfare Implications of Congestion in Public Goods. *Rev. Soc. Econ.*, April 1973, *31*(1), pp. 89–92.

———— **and Zech, Charles E.** Welfare Effects of Announcing Election Forecasts. *Public Choice*, Spring 1973, *14*, pp. 117–23.

Brown, Lawrence A. and Lentnek, Barry. Innovation Diffusion in a Developing Economy: A Mesoscale View. *Econ. Develop. Cult. Change*, January 1973, *21*(2), pp. 274–92.

Brown, Lester. Rich Countries and Poor in a Finite, Interdependent World. In *Olson, M. and Landsberg, H. H., eds.*, 1973, pp. 153–64.

Brown, Lowell S., et al. Are There Real Limits to Growth?—A Reply to Beckerman. *Oxford Econ. Pap.*, November 1973, *25*(3), pp. 455–60.

Brown, Murray. Toward an Econometric Accommodation of the Capital-Intensity-Perversity Phenomenon. *Econometrica*, September 1973, *41* (5), pp. 937–54.

Brown, Robert G. A Model for Measuring the Influence of Promotion on Inventory and Consumer Demand. *J. Marketing Res.*, November 1973, *10* (4), pp. 380–89.

Brown, William G. and Nawas, Farid. Impact of Aggregation on the Estimation of Outdoor Recreation Demand Functions. *Amer. J. Agr. Econ.*, May 1973, *55*(2), pp. 246–49.

Brown, William R. and Cahoon, C. R. The Interstate Tax Dilemma—A Proposed Solution. *Nat. Tax J.*, June 1973, *26*(2), pp. 187–97.

Brown, William W. and Reynolds, Morgan O. Crime and "Punishment": Risk Implications. *J. Econ. Theory*, October 1973, *6*(5), pp. 508–14.

———— **and Reynolds, Morgan O.** Debt Peonage Reexamined. *J. Econ. Hist.*, December 1973, *33*(4), pp. 862–71.

Browne, K. M. Y. Transfer Duty: A Plea for Reform. *S. Afr. J. Econ.*, March 1973, *41*(1), pp. 26–33.

Browne, William G. Problems—The Planning Process in Marketing. *Marquette Bus. Rev.*, Fall 1973, *17*(3), pp. 149–54.

Browning, Edgar K. Alternative Programs for Income Redistribution: The NIT and the NWT. *Amer. Econ. Rev.*, March 1973, *63*(1), pp. 38–49.

―――― Social Insurance and Intergenerational Transfers. *J. Law Econ.*, October 1973, *16*(2), pp. 215–37.

Browning, Thomas L. and Reinsel, Edward I. Distribution of Farm Program Payments by Income of Sole Proprietors. *Agr. Econ. Res.*, April 1973, *25* (2), pp. 41–44.

Brownlee, Oswald. The Effects of Inflation on the Distribution of Economic Welfare: Comment. *J. Money, Credit, Banking*, Part II, February 1973, *5*(1), pp. 505–06.

Brownrigg, M. The Economic Impact of a New University. *Scot. J. Polit. Econ.*, June 1973, *20*(2), pp. 123–39.

―――― The Regional Income Multiplier: An Attempt to Complete the Model: A Correction. *Scot. J. Polit. Econ.*, June 1973, *20*(2), pp. 193.

Brozen, Yale. Concentration and Profits: Does Concentration Matter? In *Weston, J. F. and Ornstein, S. I.*, eds., 1973, pp. 59–70.

―――― In Defense of Advertising. In *Murray, B. B.*, ed., 1973, pp. 341–51.

Bruce, Grady D.; Witt, Robert E. and Martin, Warren S. Interpersonal Orientation and Innovative Behavior. *Miss. Val. J. Bus. Econ.*, Winter 1973-74, *9*(2), pp. 35–42.

Brumelle, Shelby L. and Schwab, Bernhard. Capital Budgeting with Uncertain Future Opportunities: A Markovian Approach. *J. Financial Quant. Anal.*, January 1973, *8*(1), pp. 111–22.

Brummet, R. Lee. Nonfinancial Measures in Social Accounts. In *Dierkes, M. and Bauer, R. A.*, eds., 1973, pp. 345–50.

―――― Total Performance Measurement. *Manage. Account.*, November 1973, *55*(5), pp. 11–15.

Brunner, Karl. A Diagrammatic Exposition of the Money Supply Process. *Schweiz. Z. Volkswirtsch. Statist.*, December 1973, *109*(4), pp. 481–533.

―――― The State of the Monetarist Debate: A Comment. *Fed. Res. Bank St. Louis Rev.*, September 1973, *55*(9), pp. 9, 12–14.

――――, **et al.** Fiscal and Monetary Policies in Moderate Inflation: Case Studies of Three Countries. *J. Money, Credit, Banking*, Part II, February 1973, *5*(1), pp. 313–53.

―――― and **Meltzer, Allan H.** Mr. Hicks and the "Monetarists." *Economica*, N.S., February 1973, *40*(157), pp. 44–59.

Bruno, M. Protection and Tariff Change under General Equilibrium. *J. Int. Econ.*, August 1973, *3*(3), pp. 205–25.

Bruyn-Hundt, M. Naar de meetbaarheid van een rechtvaardige verdeling van de helft voor de helft. (An Approach to the Measurement of Just Distribution of One Half for One Half. With English summary.) *De Economist*, November-December 1973, *121*(6), pp. 626–28, 29.

Bryant, W. Keith. An Analysis of the Market for Food Stamps: Reply. *Amer. J. Agr. Econ.*, February 1973, *55*(1), pp. 112–15.

Bryson, Phillip J. Dynamic Price Planning in Com-

mand Systems: A Partial Equilibrium Approach. *Weltwirtsch. Arch.*, 1973, *109*(3), pp. 495–513.

Bubnov, Iu. T. Modeling the Distribution and Adjustment to the Annual Production Program. *Matekon*, Fall 1973, *10*(1), pp. 83–92.

Buchan, Joseph F. Why Scientific Inventory Management Has Proved Useful. In *Thomas, W. E., Jr.*, ed., 1973, pp. 392–400.

Buchanan, James M. The Coase Theorem and the Theory of the State. *Natural Res. J.*, October 1973, *13*(4), pp. 579–94.

―――― A Defense of Organized Crime? In *Rottenberg, S.*, ed., 1973, pp. 119–32.

―――― The Institutional Structure of Externality. *Public Choice*, Spring 1973, *14*, pp. 69–82.

―――― Introduction: L.S.E. Cost Theory in Retrospect. In *Buchanan, J. M. and Thirlby, G. F.*, eds., 1973, pp. 1–16.

―――― and **Goetz, Charles J.** External Diseconomies in Competitive Supply: Reply. *Amer. Econ. Rev.*, September 1973, *63*(4), pp. 745–48.

―――― and **Leijonhufvud, Axel.** The Backbending Supply Curve of Labor: Comment on Buchanan, with His Reply. *Hist. Polit. Econ.*, Spring 1973, *5* (1), pp. 261–67.

Buchanan, R. H. Field Systems of Ireland. In *Baker, A. R. H. and Butlin, R. A.*, eds., 1973, pp. 580–618.

Buchele, Robert B. How to Evaluate a Firm. In *Klein, W. H. and Murphy, D. C.*, eds., 1973, pp. 322–34.

Bucher, Jeffrey M. Statements to Congress. *Fed. Res. Bull.*, June 1973, *59*(6), pp. 420–25.

Buchholz, H. E. Pricing and Allocation Models Applied to Problems of Interregional Trade and Location of Industries. In *Judge, G. G. and Takayama, T.*, eds., 1973, pp. 298–306.

Bucksar, Richard G. The White Pass and Yukon Railway: Past, Present and Future. *Mich. Academician*, Winter 1973, *5*(3), pp. 315–23.

Budd, A. P. and Litzenberger, Robert H. Changes in the Supply of Money, the Firm's Market Value and Cost of Capital. *J. Finance*, March 1973, *28*(1), pp. 49–57.

Bulgaru, Mircea. Modificări în structura social-profesională a populaţiei României în anii Republicii. (Changes in the Social-Professional Structure of Romania's Population in the Years of the Republic. With English summary.) *Stud. Cercet. Econ.*, 1973, (1), pp. 5–11.

―――― Unele probleme ale integrării învăţămîntului cu cercetarea şi producţia. (Problems of the Integration of Economic Education into Scientific Research and Production. With English summary.) *Stud. Cercet. Econ.*, 1973, (2), pp. 33–46.

Bultez, Alain and Naert, Philippe A. Logically Consistent Market Share Models. *J. Marketing Res.*, August 1973, *10*(3), pp. 334–40.

Bumpass, Larry and Wilson, Franklin D. The Prediction of Fertility among Catholics: A Longitudinal Analysis. *Demography*, November 1973, *10* (4), pp. 591–97.

Bunamo, Michael and Schenker, Eric. A Study of the Corps of Engineers' Regional Pattern of Investments. *Southern Econ. J.*, April 1973, *39*(4), pp. 548–58.

Bunamo, Michael C. and Sun, Nai-Ching. Competition for Handling U.S. Foreign Trade Cargoes: The Port of New York's Experience. *Econ. Geogr.,* April 1973, *49*(2), pp. 156–62.

Buonomo, Maurizio. Multinazionali e banche. (Multinational Firms and Banks. With English summary.) *Bancaria,* September 1973, *29*(9), pp. 1113–22.

Bupp, Irvin C. and Natchez, Peter B. Policy and Priority in the Budgetary Process. *Amer. Polit. Sci. Rev.,* September 1973, *67*(3), pp. 951–63.

Burchardt, Michael. Die Koordination von Geld- und Fiskalpolitik bei festen Wechselkursen. (The Coordination of Monetary and Fiscal Policies under Fixed Exchange Rates. With English summary.) *Z. Wirtschaft. Sozialwissen.,* 1973, *93*(4), pp. 423–43.

Burck, Gilbert. The Myths and Realities of Corporate Pricing. In *Britt, S. H. and Boyd, H. W., Jr., eds.,* 1973, pp. 345–57.

Burditt, George M. Fair Packaging and Labeling— the Cost to Consumers. In *Murray, B. B., ed.,* 1973, pp. 208–11.

van Buren Cleveland, Harold. Implications for Private Capital Markets: Comment. In *Krause, L. B. and Salant, W. S., eds.,* 1973, pp. 141–49.

Burger, Albert E. Relative Movements in Wages and Profits. *Fed. Res. Bank St. Louis Rev.,* February 1973, *55*(2), pp. 8–16.

Burger, David H. and Ayers, C. E. In Memoriam. *Amer. J. Econ. Soc.,* July 1973, *32*(3), pp. 335–36.

Burger, Hendrik. Possible Concepts for Better Planning and Evaluating Fiscal Policy—Experiences in the Netherlands. In *Giersch, H., ed.,* 1973, pp. 210–22.

Burke, Donald R. and Rubin, Lester. Is Contract Rejection a Major Collective Bargaining Problem? *Ind. Lab. Relat. Rev.,* January 1973, *26*(2), pp. 820–33.

Burke, Ronald J. Effects of Organizational Experience on Managerial Attitudes and Beliefs: A Better Press for Managers. *J. Bus. Res.,* Summer 1973, *1*(1), pp. 21–30.

Burke, William. Buying on Time. *Fed. Res. Bank San Francisco Rev.,* March-April 1973, pp. 3–11.

_____ Higher Payout? *Fed. Res. Bank San Francisco Rev.,* July-August 1973, pp. 3–7.

_____ Oil From the Artic. *Fed. Res. Bank San Francisco Rev.,* September-October 1973, pp. 13–21.

_____ RCPC's—Transitional Step. *Fed. Res. Bank San Francisco Rev.,* July-August 1973, pp. 11–15.

Burki, Shahid J. Employment Creating Urban Public Works Programmes: Outline of a Strategy. *Pakistan Develop. Rev.,* Autumn 1973, *12*(3), pp. 293–310.

_____ Rapid Population Growth and Urbanization: The Case of Pakistan. *Pakistan Econ. Soc. Rev.,* Autumn 1973, *11*(3), pp. 239–76.

Burkitt, B. and Wilkinson, R. K. Wage Determination and Trade Unions. *Scot. J. Polit. Econ.,* June 1973, *20*(2), pp. 107–22.

Burks, R. V. The Political Implications of Economic Reform. In *Bornstein, M., ed.,* 1973, pp. 373–402.

Burley, H. T. Production Functions for Australian Manufacturing Industries. *Rev. Econ. Statist.,* February 1973, *55*(1), pp. 118–22.

Burloiu, P. Considerații privind îmbunătățirea

măsurării productivității muncii. (Considerations on Improving the Measuring of Labour Productivity. With English summary.) *Stud. Cercet. Econ.,* 1973, (2), pp. 47–53.

Burmeister, Edwin, et al. The "Saddlepoint Property" and the Structure of Dynamic Heterogeneous Capital Good Models. *Econometrica,* January 1973, *41*(1), pp. 79–95.

Burness, H. Stuart. Impatience and the Preference for Advancement in the Timing of Satisfactions. *J. Econ. Theory,* October 1973, *6*(5), pp. 495–507.

Burney, Anthony [Sir]. Take-Overs: Aims and Objects. In *Allen, G. C., et al.,* 1973, pp. 11–19.

Burnham, James B. Housing Starts in 1966 and 1969: A Comparison Using an Econometric Model. In *Ricks, R. B., ed.,* 1973, pp. 49–67.

Burnham, John B. Societal Values in Power Generation. In *Dierkes, M. and Bauer, R. A., eds.,* 1973, pp. 260–70.

Burns, Arthur F. Letter on Monetary Policy to Senator William Proxmire. *Fed. Res. Bank St. Louis Rev.,* November 1973, *55*(11), pp. 15–22.

_____ Money Supply in the Conduct of Monetary Policy. *Fed. Res. Bull.,* November 1973, *59*(11), pp. 791–98.

_____ Objectives and Responsibilities of the Federal Reserve System. *Fed. Res. Bull.,* September 1973, *59*(9), pp. 655–57.

_____ Some Essentials of International Monetary Reform. In *Henley, D. S., ed.,* 1973, pp. 127–31.

_____ Some Problems of Central Banking. *Fed. Res. Bull.,* June 1973, *59*(6), pp. 417–19.

_____ Statement to Congress. *Fed. Res. Bull.,* July 1973, *59*(7), pp. 508–12.

_____ Statement to Congress. *Fed. Res. Bull.,* September 1973, *59*(9), pp. 658–64.

_____ Statement to Congress. *Fed. Res. Bull.,* August 1973, *59*(8), pp. 567–73.

_____ Statement to Congress. *Fed. Res. Bull.,* March 1973, *59*(3), pp. 164–68.

_____ Statement to Congress. *Fed. Res. Bull.,* February 1973, *59*(2), pp. 81–85.

_____ Statement to Congress. *Fed. Res. Bull.,* March 1973, *59*(3), pp. 168–71.

_____ Statement to Congress. *Fed. Res. Bull.,* March 1973, *59*(3), pp. 176–78.

_____ Statement to Congress. *Fed. Res. Bull.,* March 1973, *59*(3), pp. 171–76.

_____ Statements to Congress. *Fed. Res. Bull.,* April 1973, *59*(4), pp. 280–85.

_____ Statements to Congress. *Fed. Res. Bull.,* December 1973, *59*(12), pp. 879–83.

_____ The Structure of Reserve Requirements. *Fed. Res. Bull.,* May 1973, *59*(5), pp. 339–43.

Burns, E. O. Random Thoughts on Some Problems of Professional Communication. *Australian J. Agr. Econ.,* August 1973, *17*(2), pp. 93–103.

Burns, Joseph M. Academic Views on Improving the Federal Reserve Discount Mechanism: A Review Essay. *J. Money, Credit, Banking,* Part I, February 1973, *5*(1), pp. 47–60.

Burns, M. E. A Note on the Choice of Data in Econometric Studies. *Econ. Rec.,* March 1973, *49* (125), pp. 24–30.

Burns, Michael E. A Note on the Concept and Measure of Consumer's Surplus. *Amer. Econ. Rev.*, June 1973, *63*(3), pp. 335–44.

Burns, Tom and Meeker, L. D. A Mathematical Model of Multi-Dimensional Evaluation, Decision-Making, and Social Interaction. In *Cochrane, J. L. and Zeleny, M., eds.*, 1973, pp. 141–63.

Burress, Glenn E. A More General Theory of the Short-Run Consumption Function and Recent Data. *Nebr. J. Econ. Bus.*, Autumn 1973, *12*(4), pp. 7–22.

_____ Who First Proposed the Habit Persistence Hypothesis: Keynes or Duesenberry and Modigliani. *Indian Econ. J.*, January-March 1973, *20* (3), pp. 472–78.

Burrows, Paul and Godfrey, Leslie G. Identifying and Estimating the Parameters of a Symmetrical Model of Inventory Investment. *Appl. Econ.*, September 1973, *5*(3), pp. 193–97.

Burstein, Herman. Close Approximations of Percentage Points of the Chi-Square Distribution and Poisson Confidence Limits. *J. Amer. Statist. Assoc.*, September 1973, *68*(343), pp. 581–84.

Burt, David N. Stretching Your Building Dollar. *Calif. Manage. Rev.*, Summer 1973, *15*(4), pp. 54–60.

Burt, Oscar R. and Dudley, Norman J. Stochastic Reservoir Management and System Design for Irrigation. *Water Resources Res.*, June 1973, *9*(3), pp. 507–22.

Burt, R. and Morissey, M. J. A Theory of Mineral Discovery: A Note. *Econ. Hist. Rev., 2nd Ser.*, August 1973, *26*(3), pp. 497–505.

Buse, R. C. Increasing Response Rates in Mailed Questionnaires? *Amer. J. Agr. Econ.*, August 1973, *55*(3), pp. 503–08.

Bush, Joseph C. Pay Increases in Footwear Lag Behind Other Industries. *Mon. Lab. Rev.*, June 1973, *96*(6), pp. 57–58.

Bush, J. W.; Chen, M. M. and Patrick, D. L. Health Status Index in Cost Effectiveness: Analysis of PKU Program. In *Berg, R. L., ed.*, 1973, pp. 172–93.

Bush, Winston C. Population and Mill's Peasant-Proprietor Economy. *Hist. Polit. Econ.*, Spring 1973, *5*(1), pp. 110–20.

Butcher, Bernard L. The Program Management Approach. In *Dierkes, M. and Bauer, R. A., eds.*, 1973, pp. 276–84.

_____ The Program Management Approach to the Corporate Social Audit. *Calif. Manage. Rev.*, Fall 1973, *16*(1), pp. 11–16.

Butfield, Terry and Tobin, Norman. The Implementation of OR Models in Planning Procedures. In *Ross, M., ed.*, 1973, pp. 363–72.

Büti, G. Technological Pre-assessment as the Partner of Macroeconomic Forecasting. In *Blohm, H. and Steinbuch, K., eds.*, 1973, pp. 133–38.

Butler, Arthur and Kim, Kye. The Dynamics of Wage Structures. *Southern Econ. J.*, April 1973, *39*(4), pp. 588–600.

Butlin, R. A. Field Systems of Northumberland and Durham. In *Baker, A. R. H. and Butlin, R. A., eds.*, 1973, pp. 93–144.

_____ and Baker, A. R. H. Studies of Field Systems in the British Isles: Conclusion: Problems and Perspectives. In *Baker, A. R. H. and Butlin, R. A., eds.*, 1973, pp. 619–56.

_____ and Baker, A. R. H. Studies of Field Systems in the British Isles: Introduction: Materials and Methods. In *Baker, A. R. H. and Butlin, R. A., eds.*, 1973, pp. 1–40.

Butt, Abdul Rauf and Hussain, Mazhar. Projections of Job Opportunities for Natural Scientists and Mathematicians in West Pakistan. *Pakistan Econ. Soc. Rev.*, Summer 1973, *11*(2), pp. 200–06.

Butterfield, D. Anthony; Farris, George F. and Senner, Eldon E. Trust, Culture, and Organizational Behavior. *Ind. Relat.*, May 1973, *12*(2), pp. 144–57.

Butterworth, Douglas. Squatters or Suburbanites? The Growth of Shantytowns in Oaxaca, Mexico. In *Scott, R. E., ed.*, 1973, pp. 209–32.

Buttler, Friedrich. Explikative und normative Theorie der meritorishen Güter—eine Problemanalyse. (A Theory of Merit Goods. With English summary.) *Z. Wirtschaft. Sozialwissen.*, 1973, *93* (2), pp. 129–46.

Byatt, I. C. R.; Holmans, A. E. and Laidler, David. Income and the Demand for Housing: Some Evidence for Great Britain. In *Parkin, M., ed.*, 1973, pp. 65–84.

Byers, D. M. and Miller, W. L. Development and Display of Multiple-Objective Project Impacts. *Water Resources Res.*, February 1973, *9*(1), pp. 11–20.

Bylin, James E. An Agency in California Is Model in Campaign to Curb Repair Frauds. In *Murray, B. B., ed.*, 1973, pp. 56–59.

Bymers, Gwen J. Consumerism: Origin and Research Implications: Response. In *Sheldon, E. B., ed.*, 1973, pp. 295–304.

Byrne, Dennis M. Some Preliminary Results of Income-Maintenance Experiments. *Nebr. J. Econ. Bus.*, Autumn 1973, *12*(4), pp. 23–35.

Byrne, Robert F. and Spiro, Michael H. On Taxation as a Pollution Control Policy. *Swedish J. Econ.*, March 1973, *75*(1), pp. 105–09.

Byrns, Ralph T. and Hebert, Robert F. On the Cost-Inflationary Impact of High Interest Rates: Comment. *J. Econ. Issues*, September 1973, *7*(3), pp. 511–14.

Byron, R. P. The Restricted Aitken Estimation of Sets of Demand Relations: Reply. *Econometrica*, March 1973, *41*(2), pp. 371–74.

Bzhilianskii, Iu. Political and Economic Problems of Population Under Socialism. *Prob. Econ.*, April 1973, *15*(12), pp. 52–72.

Caccappolo, G. J.; Chaudry, M. A. and Davis, B. E. An Econometric Planning Model for American Telephone and Telegraph Company. *Bell J. Econ. Manage. Sci.*, Spring 1973, *4*(1), pp. 29–56.

Caceres, Luis R. Consumption Functions for Latin America. *Intermountain Econ. Rev.*, Fall 1973, *4* (2), pp. 55–65.

Cacy, J. A. and Miller, Glenn H., Jr. Business and Financial Outlook—A Promising 1973. *Fed. Res. Bank Kansas City Rev.*, January 1973, pp. 11–20.

_____ and Stahl, Sheldon W. For 1974—An Uncertain Outlook. *Fed. Res. Bank Kansas City Rev.*, December 1973, pp. 3–11.

Caffè, Federico. Considerazioni sul problema della disoccupazione in Italia. (On Unemployment in Italy. With English summary.) *Rivista Int. Sci. Econ. Com.*, January 1973, *20*(1), pp. 6–17.

Cagan, Phillip. Controls and Monetary Policy, 1969–1973. In *Cagan, P., et al.,* 1973, pp. 1–34.

Cagley, James W. and Peterson, Robert A. The Effect of Shelf Space Upon Sales of Branded Products: An Appraisal. *J. Marketing Res.,* February 1973, *10*(1), pp. 103–04.

Cahoon, C. R. and Brown, William R. The Interstate Tax Dilemma—A Proposed Solution. *Nat. Tax J.,* June 1973, *26*(2), pp. 187–97.

Cain, Glen G. Economics of the Size of North Carolina Rural Families: Comment. *J. Polit. Econ.,* Part II, March-April 1973, *81*(2), pp. S123–27.

Cain, Louis and Aduddell, Robert. Location and Collusion in the Meat Packing Industry. In *[Williamson, H. F.],* 1973, pp. 85–117.

Cain, Neville. Political Economy and the Tariff: Australia in the 1920s. *Australian Econ. Pap.,* June 1973, *12*(20), pp. 1–20.

Cairnie, James and Thompson, Mark. Compulsory Arbitration: The Case of British Columbia Teachers. *Ind. Lab. Relat. Rev.,* October 1973, *27*(1), pp. 3–17.

Caldwell, J. C. and Ware, H. The Evolution of Family Planning in Australia. *Population Stud.,* March 1973, *27*(1), pp. 7–31.

Caldwell, Lynton K. Energy and Environment: The Bases for Public Policies. *Ann. Amer. Acad. Polit. Soc. Sci.,* November 1973, *410,* pp. 127–38.

Calhoun, Donald A. Computing DISC Profits. *Manage. Account.,* June 1973, *54*(12), pp. 45–46.

—— Oil and Gas Taxation. *Manage. Account.,* November 1973, *55*(5), pp. 21–24.

Călin, Oprea and Văduva, I. Folosirea metodelor matematice în contabilitate. (Utilization of Mathematical Models in Book-keeping. With English summary.) *Stud. Cercet. Econ.,* 1973, (2), pp. 139–56.

—— **and Ciucur, Elena.** Rolul preţului de cost în cadrul sistemului informaţional economic al întreprinderii. (The Role of the Cost Price in the Economic Informational System of the Enterprise. With English summary.) *Stud. Cercet. Econ.,* 1973, (4), pp. 111–26.

Calkins, Hugh. Breaking Down the Fiscal Barriers to Career Education. In *McClure, L. and Buan, C., eds.,* 1973, pp. 247–55.

Calkins, Robert D. The Decision Process in Administration. In *Thomas, W. E., Jr., ed.,* 1973, pp. 142–50.

Call, David L. and Levinson, F. James. A Systematic Approach to Nutrition Intervention Programs. In *Berg, A.; Scrimshaw, N. S. and Call, D. L., eds.,* 1973, pp. 165–97.

Callahan, John J. Evaluation of Metropolitan Conflict and Cooperation. *Amer. Real Estate Urban Econ. Assoc. J.,* Fall 1973, *1*(2), pp. 141–51.

Callen, Richard W.; Wolken, Lawrence C. and Thompson, Richard G. A Stochastic Investment Model for a Survival Conscious Fishing Firm. In *Sokoloski, A. A., ed.,* 1973, pp. 112–20.

Callies, David L. and Babcock, Richard F. Ecology and Housing: Virtues in Conflict. In *Clawson, M., ed.,* 1973, pp. 205–20.

Cameron, Norman. Incentives and Labour Supply in Co-operative Enterprises. *Can. J. Econ.,* February 1973, *6*(1), pp. 16–22.

—— Incentives and Labour Supply on Soviet Collective Farms: Rejoinder. *Can. J. Econ.,* August 1973, *6*(3), pp. 442–44.

Campbell, Donald E. Social Choice and Intensity of Preference. *J. Polit. Econ.,* January-February 1973, *81*(1), pp. 211–18.

Campbell, John; Cheng, Benjamin and Gregory, Paul. Differences in Fertility Determinants: Developed and Developing Countries. *J. Devel. Stud.,* January 1973, *9*(2), pp. 233–41.

Campbell, Keith. The State Marketing Board—Relic or Prototype? *Australian J. Agr. Econ.,* December 1973, *17*(3), pp. 179–88.

Camu, Louis. I movimenti dei capitali a breve termine. (Short-Term Capital Movements. With English summary.) *Bancaria,* July 1973, *29*(7), pp. 807–12.

Candler, Wilfred V. Linear Programming in Capital Budgeting with Multiple Goals. In *Cochrane, J. L. and Zeleny, M., eds.,* 1973, pp. 416–28.

—— **and Cartwright, R. Wayne.** Mathematical Analysis to Optimise Acquisition of Research Funds. *Can. J. Agr. Econ.,* February 1973, *21*(1), pp. 10–26.

——; **Cartwright, R. Wayne and Penn, J. B.** The Substitution of Analytic for Simulation Algorithms: Comment. *Amer. J. Agr. Econ.,* May 1973, *55*(2), pp. 235–39.

Canes, Michael E. Discounting and the Evaluation of Public Investments: Comment. *Appl. Econ.,* September 1973, *5*(3), pp. 219–23.

Cannon, C. M. Size of Establishments in Manufacturing: A Comment. *Econ. J.,* September 1973, *83* (331), pp. 898–99.

Cannon, Mark W. Interactive Training Techniques for Improving Public Service in Latin America. In *Thurber, C. E. and Graham, L. S., eds.,* 1973, pp. 148–87.

Cannon, Peter. The Principles of Business Relations. In *Allen, G. C., et al.,* 1973, pp. 55–59.

Canterbery, E. R. and Tuckman, Howard P. The Income Distribution as a Pure Public Good: Comment. *Quart. J. Econ.,* May 1973, *87*(2), pp. 304–10.

Cantwell, J.; Lenehan, B. and O'Farrell, J. Improving the Performance of a Local Authority Ambulance Service. In *Ross, M., ed.,* 1973, pp. 443–53.

Čáp, Václav. The Development of Effectiveness of the Czechoslovak Economy. *Czech. Econ. Digest.,* June 1973, (4), pp. 3–33.

Capdevielle, Patricia and Neef, Arthur. Productivity and Unit Labor Costs in 12 Industrial Countries. *Mon. Lab. Rev.,* November 1973, *96*(11), pp. 14–21.

Capel, R. E. and Pandey, R. K. Evaluating Demand for Deer Hunting: A Comparison of Methods. *Can. J. Agr. Econ.,* November 1973, *21*(3), pp. 6–14.

Caplan, Edwin H. Behavioral Assumptions of Management Accounting. In *Thomas, W. E., Jr., ed.,* 1973, pp. 76–96.

Caramela, Edward J. Staffing and Pay Changes in Life Insurance Companies. *Mon. Lab. Rev.,* August 1973, *96*(8), pp. 66–68.

Carbaugh, Robert J. An Expanded EEC: Implications for the United States. *Intermountain Econ. Rev.,* Spring 1973, *4*(1), pp. 81–89.

de Carbonnel, Francois E. and Dorrance, Roy G. Information Sources for Planning Decisions. *Calif. Manage. Rev.*, Summer 1973, *15*(4), pp. 42–53.

Cardon de Lichtbuer, Michel and Jacquemin, Alex P. Size Structure, Stability and Performance of the Largest British and EEC Firms. *Europ. Econ. Rev.*, December 1973, *4*(4), pp. 393–408.

Cardoso, Fernando Henrique. Associated-Dependent Development: Theoretical and Practical Implications. In *Stepan, A., ed.,* 1973, pp. 142–76.

_____ Imperialism and Dependency in Latin America. In *Bonilla, F. and Girling, R., eds.,* 1973, pp. 7–16.

Cardozo, Richard N. Segmenting the Industrial Market. In *Britt, S. H. and Boyd, H. W., Jr., eds.,* 1973, pp. 239–54.

Carey, John L. Productivity in the Steel Foundries Industry. *Mon. Lab. Rev.,* May 1973, *96*(5), pp. 8–11.

Carey, William D. New Perspectives on Governance. In *The Conference Board,* 1973, pp. 64–92.

Cargill, I. P. M. Efforts to Influence Recipient Performance: Case Study of India. In *Lewis, J. P. and Kapur, I., eds.,* 1973, pp. 89–95.

Carleton, Bette N. The Status of Women in Accounting. *Manage. Account.,* September 1973, *55*(3), pp. 59–62.

Carleton, Willard T.; Dick, Charles L., Jr. and Downes, David H. Financial Policy Models: Theory and Practice. *J. Financial Quant. Anal.,* December 1973, *8*(5), pp. 691–709.

Carley, D. H. Silage-Concentrate Substitution; Effects on Milk Production and Income Over Feed Cost in DHIA Herds. *Amer. J. Agr. Econ.,* Part I, November 1973, *55*(4), pp. 641–46.

Carli, Guido. Crisi monetaria internazionale e politica di ripresa economica-I. (Policies Designed to Overcome the International Monetary Crisis and to Support the Economic Recovery in Italy-I. With English summary.) *Bancaria,* May 1973, *29*(5), pp. 543–62.

_____ Intervento all'assemblea del Fondo Monetario. (Statement at the Meeting of the International Monetary Fund. With English summary.) *Bancaria,* August 1973, *29*(8), pp. 947–50.

_____ Per la difesa del valore interno e del valore esterno della lira. (Defending the Internal and External Value of the Lira. With English summary.) *Bancaria,* November 1973, *29*(11), pp. 1338–41.

_____ Riforma monetaria, bilancia dei pagamenti e liquidità interna. (Monetary Reform, Balance of Payments and Domestic Liquidity. With English summary.) *Bancaria,* January 1973, *29*(1), pp. 7–16.

_____ and Rueff, Jacques. Dibattito sulla riforma del sistema monetario internazionale. (Debate on the Reform of the International Monetary System. With English summary.) *Bancaria,* August 1973, *29*(8), pp. 935–46.

Carlin, Alan. The Grand Canyon Controversy; or, How Reclamation Justifies the Unjustifiable. In *Enthoven, A. C. and Freeman, A. M., III, eds.,* 1973, pp. 263–70.

Carlin, Thomas A. Economic Position of Farm Families When Money Income and Net Worth are Combined. *Agr. Econ. Res.,* July 1973, *25*(3), pp. 61–70.

_____ and Reinsel, Edward I. Combining Income and Wealth: An Analysis of Farm Family "Well-Being." *Amer. J. Agr. Econ.,* February 1973, *55* (1), pp. 38–44.

_____ and Smith, Allen G. A New Approach in Accounting for Our Nation's Farm Income. *Agr. Finance Rev.,* July 1973, *34*, pp. 1–6.

Carliner, Geoffrey. Income Elasticity of Housing Demand. *Rev. Econ. Statist.,* November 1973, *55*(4), pp. 528–32.

Carlson, C. E. Om företagsekonomiska beslut. (Decision in Business Economics. With English summary.) *Ekon. Samfundets Tidskr.,* January 1973, *26*(1), pp. 21–31.

Carlson, Ernest W. Cross Section Production Functions for North Atlantic Groundfish and Tropical Tuna Seine Fisheries. In *Sokoloski, A. A., ed.,* 1973, pp. 42–56.

_____; Waugh, Frederick V. and Bell, Frederick W. Production from the Sea. In *Sokoloski, A. A., ed.,* 1973, pp. 72–91.

Carlson, Jack W. Recent U.S. Federal Government Experience with Program Budgeting. In *Novick, D., ed.,* 1973, pp. 207–16.

Carlson, John A. The Production Lag. *Amer. Econ. Rev.,* March 1973, *63*(1), pp. 73–86.

Carlson, Keith M. The 1973 National Economic Plan: Slowing the Boom. *Fed. Res. Bank St. Louis Rev.,* March 1973, *55*(3), pp. 2–9.

Carman, Hoy F. and Youde, James G. Alternative Tax Treatment of Orchard Development Costs: Impacts on Producers, Middlemen, and Consumers. *Amer. J. Agr. Econ.,* May 1973, *55*(2), pp. 184–91.

Carney, M. K. Agricultural Trade Intensity: The European Markets and the U.S. *Amer. J. Agr. Econ.,* Part I, November 1973, *55*(4), pp. 637–40.

Carnoy, Martin. Financial Institutions and Dependency. In *Bonilla, F. and Girling, R., eds.,* 1973, pp. 34–45.

Carol, Arthur. Stochastic Dominance and 'The Economic Rationale of Occupational Choice': Reply. *Ind. Lab. Relat. Rev.,* April 1973, *26*(3), pp. 1001.

_____ and Pressman, Israel. Behavior of the Firm Under Regulatory Constraint: Reply. *Amer. Econ. Rev.,* March 1973, *63*(1), pp. 238.

Carosso, Vincent P. The Wall Street Money Trust from Pujo through Medina. *Bus. Hist. Rev.,* Winter 1973, *47*(4), pp. 421–37.

Carpenter, Kenneth E. and Redlich, Fritz. Research Possibilities in the History of Political Economy Through a Bibliography of Translations. *Hist. Polit. Econ.,* Spring 1973, *5*(1), pp. 268–83.

Carr-Hill, R. A. and Stern, Nicholas H. An Econometric Model of the Supply and Control of Recorded Offences in England and Wales. *J. Public Econ.,* November 1973, *2*(4), pp. 289–318.

Carroll, Joseph L. and Bronzini, Michael S. Waterway Transportation Simulation Models: Development and Application. *Water Resources Res.,* February 1973, *9*(1), pp. 51–63.

Carroll, Mitchell B. The United States-Canada Income Tax Convention—Its Origin and Development. *Bull. Int. Fiscal Doc.*, April 1973, *27*(4), pp. 131–34.

Carroll, Norman E. and Hall, W. Clayton. The Effect of Teachers' Organizations on Salaries and Class Size. *Ind. Lab. Relat. Rev.*, January 1973, *26*(2), pp. 834–41.

Carroll, Sidney L. A Note on Revenue Sharing and the Theory of Public Expenditures. *Public Choice*, Spring 1973, *14,* pp. 109–16.

Carroll, Stephen J. and Rolph, John E. A Stochastic Model of Discrimination in the Labor Market. *Econometrica*, January 1973, *41*(1), pp. 97–108.

Carson, Carol S. Inventory-Sales Ratios in Manufacturing and Trade, 1961–72. *Surv. Curr. Bus.*, February 1973, *53*(2), pp. 41–48.

Carter, E. Eugene. A Simultaneous Equation Approach to Financial Planning: Comment. *J. Finance*, September 1973, *28*(4), pp. 1035–38.

Carter, Nicholas G. and Chenery, Hollis B. Foreign Assistance and Development Performance, 1960-1970. *Amer. Econ. Rev.*, May 1973, *63*(2), pp. 459–68.

Carter, R. A. L. Least Squares as an Exploratory Estimator. *Can. J. Econ.*, February 1973, *6*(1), pp. 108–14.

Cartwright, R. Wayne and Candler, Wilfred V. Mathematical Analysis to Optimise Acquisition of Research Funds. *Can. J. Agr. Econ.*, February 1973, *21*(1), pp. 10–26.

———; **Penn, J. B. and Candler, Wilfred V.** The Substitution of Analytic for Simulation Algorithms: Comment. *Amer. J. Agr. Econ.*, May 1973, *55*(2), pp. 235–39.

Caruthers, J. Kent; Pinches, George E. and Mingo, Kent A. The Stability of Financial Patterns in Industrial Organizations. *J. Finance*, May 1973, *28* (2), pp. 389–96.

Casanegra, Milka; Guerard, Michèle and Lent, George E. The Value-Added Tax in Developing Countries. *Int. Monet. Fund Staff Pap.*, July 1973, *20*(2), pp. 318–78.

Casas, Francisco R. International Factor Movements in a Tariff-ridden World Economy. *Manchester Sch. Econ. Soc. Stud.*, June 1973, *41*(2), pp. 215–23.

——— Optimal Effective Protection in General Equilibrium. *Amer. Econ. Rev.*, September 1973, *63*(4), pp. 714–16.

——— **and Batra, Raveendra N.** Intermediate Products and the Pure Theory of International Trade: A Neo-Heckscher-Ohlin Framework. *Amer. Econ. Rev.*, June 1973, *63*(3), pp. 297–311.

——— **and Batra, Raveendra N.** Economic Growth and International Trade in an Imperfect Market Setting. *Indian Econ. J.*, July–September 1973, *21* (1), pp. 57–65.

Cascioli, Ettore. Analisi statistica della conflittualità nel mercato del lavoro. (Statistical Analysis of Labor Disputes According to the 1965–67 Italian Experience. With English summary.) *Rivista Int. Sci. Econ. Com.*, July 1973, *20*(7), pp. 681–93.

Case, James. Differential Trading Games. In *Blaquière, A., ed.*, 1973, pp. 377–400.

Casetti, Emilio. Urban Land Value Functions: Equilibrium Versus Optimality. *Econ. Geogr.*, October 1973, *49*(4), pp. 357–65.

———; **King, L. J. and Odland, J.** Testing Hypotheses of Polarized Growth Within a Central Place Hierarchy. *Econ. Geogr.*, January 1973, *49*(1), pp. 74–79.

———; **Kissling, C. C. and King, L. J.** Optimal Transportation Patterns of Single Commodities in Capacitated Networks. In *Judge, G. G. and Takayama, T., eds.*, 1973, pp. 225–42.

Casey, Michael G. An Application of the Samuelson-Stone Linear Expenditure System to Food Consumption in Ireland. *Econ. Soc. Rev.*, April 1973, *4*(3), pp. 309–42.

Casey, William J., Jr. Internationalization of Capital Markets. In *Wiegand, G. C., ed.*, 1973, pp. 132–38.

Cass, David. On the Wicksellian Point-Input, Point-Output Model of Capital Accumulation: A Modern View (or, Neoclassicism Slightly Vindicated). *J. Polit. Econ.*, January-February 1973, *81*(1), pp. 71–97.

Cassady, Ralph, Jr. and Barker, F. David. Price Formation and Decision-Making in Covent Garden Market, London. *Calif. Manage. Rev.*, Fall 1973, *16*(1), pp. 86–94.

Cassidy, P. A. Commonality, Fishery Resources, Potential and Policy: Comment. *Amer. J. Agr. Econ.*, August 1973, *55*(3), pp. 526–29.

Cassidy, R. Gordon. Crime Prevention and Control. In *Ross, M., ed.*, 1973, pp. 671–84.

Casson, M. C. Linear Regression with Error in the Deflating Variable. *Econometrica*, July 1973, *41* (4), pp. 751–59.

Casstevens, Harold T., II; Marz, Roger H. and Casstevens, Thomas W. The Hunting of the Paradox. *Public Choice*, Summer 1973, *15,* pp. 97–102.

Casstevens, Thomas W.; Casstevens, Harold T., II and Marz, Roger H. The Hunting of the Paradox. *Public Choice*, Summer 1973, *15,* pp. 97–102.

Castello, Albert P. The Model Cities Program: An Application of PPBS. *Manage. Account.*, January 1973, *54*(7), pp. 29–33, 44.

Catanese, Anthony James. Planning in a State of Siege: The Colombia Experience. *Land Econ.*, February 1973, *49*(1), pp. 35–43.

Cateora, P. R. and Hess, J. M. Pricing in International Markets. In *Thorelli, H. B., ed.*, 1973, pp. 209–21.

Cauas, Jorge. Short-Term Economic Policy. In *[Rosenstein-Rodan, P.],* 1973, pp. 118–30.

Caussin, Pierre and Balquière, Austin. Differential Games with Time Lag. In *Blaquière, A., ed.*, 1973, pp. 151–78.

——— **and Blaquière, Austin.** Further Geometric Aspects of Differential Games. In *Blaquière, A., ed.*, 1973, pp. 101–49.

Cazenave, Philippe and Morrisson, Christian. Fonctions d'utilité interdépendantes et théorie de la redistribution en économie de production. (Interdependent Utility Functions and Redistribution Theory in a Production Economy. With English summary.) *Revue Écon.*, September 1973, *24*(5), pp. 725–60.

Cebula, Richard J. The City as a Source of Regional Economic Disparity in Latin America: Comment. *Rev. Soc. Econ.*, April 1973, *31*(1), pp. 85–88.

——— Deficit Spending, Expectations, and Fiscal

Policy Effectiveness. *Public Finance*, 1973, *28* (3–4), pp. 362–70.

――― Expected Interest Rate Changes and Monetary Policy: A Brief Note. *Miss. Val. J. Bus. Econ.*, Spring 1973, *8*(3), pp. 71–76.

――― On Migration, Migration Costs, and Wage Differentials, with Special Reference to the United States. *Schweiz. Z. Volkswirtsch. Statist.*, March 1973, *109*(1), pp. 59–68.

――― and Chapin, Gene L. Bond Yields and the Lock-in Effect of Capital-Gains Taxation: A Pedagogical Note. *Rivista Int. Sci. Econ. Com.*, January 1973, *20*(1), pp. 83–89.

――― and Gallaway, Lowell E. Differentials and Indeterminacy in Wage Rate Analysis: An Empirical Note. *Ind. Lab. Relat. Rev.*, April 1973, *26* (3), pp. 991–95.

――― and Gatons, Paul K. Interregional Factor Prices and Mobility. *Pakistan Econ. Soc. Rev.*, Summer 1973, *11*(2), pp. 207–14.

――― and Kohn, Robert M. Foreign Capital and Steady-State Growth in Developing Economies. *Pakistan Econ. Soc. Rev.*, Winter 1973, *11*(4), pp. 378–82.

―――; Kohn, Robert M. and Gallaway, Lowell E. Determinants of Net Migration to SMSA's, 1960–1970. *Miss. Val. J. Bus. Econ.*, Winter 1973-74, *9* (2), pp. 59–64.

―――; Kohn, Robert M. and Vedder, Richard K. Some Determinants of Interstate Migration of Blacks, 1965–1970. *Western Econ. J.*, December 1973, *11*(4), pp. 500–05.

――― and Vedder, Richard K. A Note on Migration, Economic Opportunity, and the Quality of Life. *J. Reg. Sci.*, August 1973, *13*(2), pp. 205–11.

Celio, Mary Beth and Christoffel, Pamela. A Benefit-Cost Analysis of the Upward Bound Program: A Comment. *J. Human Res.*, Winter 1973, *8*(1), pp. 110–15.

Čepelák, Vladimír. Simulační model železniční vlečky. (Simulation Model of a Railway Siding. With English summary.) *Ekon.-Mat. Obzor*, 1973, *9*(4), pp. 450–57.

Cerny, Martin. Preference Relations and Order-Preserving Functons. *Ekon.-Mat. Obzor*, 1973, *9* (3), pp. 275–91.

Cerullo, Michael J. and Kolmin, Frank W. Measuring Productivity and Efficiency. *Manage. Account.*, November 1973, *55*(5), pp. 32–34.

Cesario, Frank J. A Generalized Trip Distribution Model. *J. Reg. Sci.*, August 1973, *13*(2), pp. 233–47.

Chacko, V. J. Problems of Statistical Methodology in Measuring Agricultural Growth. In *Ofori, I. M., ed.*, 1973, pp. 14–19.

Chaison, Gary N. Unit Size and Union Success in Representation Elections. *Mon. Lab. Rev.*, February 1973, *96*(2), pp. 51–52.

Chakravarty, Sukhamoy. Theory of Development Planning: An Appraisal. In *[Tinbergen, J.]*, 1973, pp. 163–79.

――― and Lefeber, Louis. An Optimising Planning Model. In *Wadhva, C. D., ed.*, 1973, pp. 51–77.

Chakravorty, S. K. Tenant Farmers in Changing Agriculture of West Bengal. *Econ. Aff.*, September-October 1973, *18*(9–10), pp. 428–33.

Chalupski, Z. Characteristics of the Socialist International Market. In *Kiss, T., ed.*, 1973, pp. 57–62.

Chamberlain, Gary and Feldstein, Martin S. Multimarket Expectations and the Rate of Interest. *J. Money, Credit, Banking*, November 1973, *5*(4), pp. 873–902.

Chamberlain, Neil W. Collective Bargaining in the Private Sector. In *Somers, G. G., ed.*, 1973, pp. 19–26.

Chambers, J. D. The Vale of Trent, 1957. In *Tranter, N. L., ed.*, 1973, pp. 122–26.

Champagne, Jean. Adapting Jobs to People: Experiments at Alcan. *Mon. Lab. Rev.*, April 1973, *96*(4), pp. 49–51.

Chand, Sheetal. Period Analysis and Continuous Analysis in Patinkin's Macroeconomic Model—A Critical Note. *J. Econ. Theory*, October 1973, *6*(5), pp. 520–24.

Chandavarkar, Anand G. How Relevant is Finance for Development? *Finance Develop.*, September 1973, *10*(3), pp. 14–16.

Chandler, Alfred D., Jr. Decision Making and Modern Institutional Change. *J. Econ. Hist.*, March 1973, *33*(1), pp. 1–15.

Chandrasekar, Krishnamurti. U.S. and French Productivity in 19 Manufacturing Industries. *J. Ind. Econ.*, April 1973, *21*(2), pp. 110–25.

Chang, John C. and Holt, Charles C. Optimal Investment Orders Under Uncertainty and Dynamic Costs: Theory and Estimates. *Southern Econ. J.*, April 1973, *39*(4), pp. 508–25.

Chang, Winston W. Intermediate Products, Aggregation, and Economic Growth. *Southern Econ. J.*, July 1973, *40*(1), pp. 56–65.

――― and Mayer, Wolfgang. Intermediate Goods in a General Equilibrium Trade Model. *Int. Econ. Rev.*, June 1973, *14*(2), pp. 447–59.

Channon, J. W. Role of Provincial Governments in Export Market Development. In *Canadian Agricultural Economics Society*, 1973, pp. 49–57.

Chant, John F. and Acheson, Keith. Bureaucratic Theory and the Choice of Central Bank Goals. *J. Money, Credit, Banking*, May 1973, *5*(2), pp. 637–55.

――― and Acheson, Keith. Mythology and Central Banking. *Kyklos*, 1973, *26*(2), pp. 362–79.

Chapin, Gene L. and Cebula, Richard J. Bond Yields and the Lock-in Effect of Capital-Gains Taxation: A Pedagogical Note. *Rivista Int. Sci. Econ. Com.*, January 1973, *20*(1), pp. 83–89.

Chapin, Wayne R. and Harris, William T., Jr. Joint Product Costing. *Manage. Account.*, April 1973, *54*(10), pp. 43–47.

Chapman, Duane. Economic Aspects of a Nuclear Desalination Agro-Industrial Project in the United Arab Republic. *Amer. J. Agr. Econ.*, August 1973, *55*(3), pp. 433–40.

Chapman, G. P. The Spatial Organization of the Population of the United States and England and Wales. *Econ. Geogr.*, October 1973, *49*(4), pp. 325–43.

Chapman, R. and Foley, K. A Note on Losses from Price Stabilization. *Australian J. Agr. Econ.*, August 1973, *17*(2), pp. 140–43.

Chapman, Wayne E. Real Estate Tax Incentives. *Nat. Tax J.*, September 1973, *26*(3), pp. 389–93.

Charan, A. S.; Pathak, Mahesh T. and Desai, Mahendra D. Development of Agriculture in Backward Regions of Gujarat: Facts and Issues. *Artha-Vikas*, January-July 1973, *9*(1–2), pp. 100–38.

Chari, T. S. K. Rural Banks—A Good Link between Farmers and Banks. (Co-operative and Commercial Banks). In *Simha, S. L. N., ed.*, 1973, pp. 92–105.

Charles, David. The Tariff System and the Composition of Imports. *J. Polit. Econ.*, November-December 1973, *81*(6), pp. 1471–72.

Charles, K. J. Public Services and Poverty. *Econ. Aff.*, January–February 1973, *18*(1-2), pp. 74–80.

Charlton, P. and Ehrenberg, A. S. C. McConnell's Experimental Brand Choice Data. *J. Marketing Res.*, August 1973, *10*(3), pp. 302–07.

Chase, Charles L.; Udry, J. Richard and Bauman, Karl E. Population Growth Rates in Perfect Contraceptive Populations. *Population Stud.*, July 1973, *27*(2), pp. 365–71.

Chase, Samuel B., Jr. The Bank Holding Company—A Superior Device for Expanding Activities? In *Federal Reserve Bank of Boston*, 1973, pp. 77–87.

Chasteen, Lanny G. Implicit Factors in the Evaluation of Lease vs. Buy Alternatives. *Accounting Rev.*, October 1973, *48*(4), pp. 764–67.

Chatfield, C. and Goodhardt, G. J. A Consumer Purchasing Model with Erlang Inter-Purchase Times. *J. Amer. Statist. Assoc.*, December 1973, *68*(344), pp. 828–35.

_____ **and Prothero, D. L.** Box-Jenkins Seasonal Forecasting: Problems in a Case-study. *J. Roy. Statist. Soc.*, Part 3 1973, *136*, pp. 295–315.

Chattopadhyay, Paresh. Some Trends in India's Economic Development. In *Gough, K. and Sharma, H. P., eds.*, 1973, pp. 103–29.

Chau, L. C.; Zellner, Arnold and Huang, David S. Real Balances and the Demand for Money: Comment. *J. Polit. Econ.*, Part I, March-April 1973, *81*(2), pp. 485–87.

Chaudhry, M. Ghaffar. The Problem of Agricultural Taxation in West Pakistan and an Alternative Solution. *Pakistan Develop. Rev.*, Summer 1973, *12*(2), pp. 93–122.

_____ Rural Income Distribution in Pakistan in the Green Revolution Perspective. *Pakistan Develop. Rev.*, Autumn 1973, *12*(3), pp. 247–58.

_____; **Shafique, M. and Azhar, B. A.** A Model for Forecasting Wheat Production in the Punjab. *Pakistan Develop. Rev.*, Winter 1973, *12*(4), pp. 407–15.

Chaudry, M. A.; Davis, B. E. and Caccappolo, G. J. An Econometric Planning Model for American Telephone and Telegraph Company. *Bell J. Econ. Manage. Sci.*, Spring 1973, *4*(1), pp. 29–56.

Chaudry, M. Anwar. An Econometric Approach to Saving Analysis. *Pakistan Develop. Rev.*, Autumn 1973, *12*(3), pp. 200–31.

Cheek, Logan M. Cost Effectiveness Comes to the Personnel Function. *Harvard Bus. Rev.*, May-June 1973, *51*(3), pp. 96–105.

Chelliah, Raja J. Significance of Alternative Concepts of Budget Deficit. *Int. Monet. Fund Staff Pap.*, November 1973, *20*(3), pp. 741–84.

Chen, Chau-Nan. Diversified Currency Holdings and Flexible Exchange Rates. *Quart. J. Econ.*, February 1973, *87*(1), pp. 96–111.

_____ A Graphical Note on the Aggregative Effect of Payments of Interest on Deposits: Comment. *J. Money, Credit, Banking*, November 1973, *5*(4), pp. 985–87.

_____ The Monetary Effect of Devaluation: An Alternative Interpretation of the Cooper Paradox. *Western Econ. J.*, December 1973, *11*(4), pp. 475–80.

Chen, C. T. and Scott, John T., Jr. Expected Changes in Farm Organization When Industry Moves into a Rural Area. *Ill. Agr. Econ.*, January 1973, *13*(1), pp. 41–47.

Chen, Dean. Horn of Plenty. *Fed. Res. Bank San Francisco Rev.*, March-April 1973, pp. 12–16.

_____; **Johnston, Verle and Levy, Yvonne.** Boom in the West. *Fed. Res. Bank San Francisco Rev.*, May-June 1973, pp. 3–8.

Chen, Joyce T. Quadratic Programming for Least-Cost Feed Formulations Under Probabilistic Protein Constraints. *Amer. J. Agr. Econ.*, May 1973, *55*(2), pp. 175–83.

_____ Separable Programming for Considering Risk in Farm Planning: Comment. *Amer. J. Agr. Econ.*, February 1973, *55*(1), pp. 115–17.

Chen, Lihsin. Population Planning in China. *Pakistan Econ. Soc. Rev.*, Autumn 1973, *11*(3), pp. 231–38.

Chen, Martin K. The G Index for Program Priority. In *Berg, R. L., ed.*, 1973, pp. 28–34.

Chen, M. M.; Patrick, D. L. and Bush, J. W. Health Status Index in Cost Effectiveness: Analysis of PKU Program. In *Berg, R. L., ed.*, 1973, pp. 172–93.

Chen, Nai-Ruenn. Economic Structure of Traditional China. In *Meskill, J., ed.*, 1973, pp. 463–81.

Chen, Tung-pi. Legal Aspects of Canadian Trade with the People's Republic of China. *Law Contemp. Probl.*, Summer-Autumn 1973, *38*(2), pp. 201–29.

Chenery, Hollis B. and Carter, Nicholas G. Foreign Assistance and Development Performance, 1960-1970. *Amer. Econ. Rev.*, May 1973, *63*(2), pp. 459–68.

_____ **and Hughes, Helen.** Industrialization and Trade Trends: Some Issues for the 1970s. In *Hughes, H., ed.*, 1973, pp. 3–31.

Cheng, Benjamin; Gregory, Paul and Campbell, John. Differences in Fertility Determinants: Developed and Developing Countries. *J. Devel. Stud.*, January 1973, *9*(2), pp. 233–41.

Cheng, Juei Ming. On the Stability of Equilibrium of the Manufacturing Market Structure. *Rivista Int. Sci. Econ. Com.*, February 1973, *20*(2), pp. 184–89.

Cheng, Pao L. and Deets, M. King. Portfolio Returns and the Random Walk Theory: Reply. *J. Finance*, June 1973, *28*(3), pp. 742–45.

_____ **and Deets, M. King.** Systematic Risk and the Horizon Problem. *J. Financial Quant. Anal.*, March 1973, *8*(2), pp. 299–316.

Chernov, Iu. P. Problems of Fractional Programming with Linear, Separable, and Quadratic Functions. *Matekon*, Spring 1973, *9*(3), pp. 22–40.

Cherry, Robert. Class Struggle and the Nature of the

Working Class. *Rev. Radical Polit. Econ.,* Summer 1973, *5*(2), pp. 47–86.

Chervak, Iu. Iu. On the Problem of Constructing Supplementary Constraints in Gomory's Integer Linear Programming Method. *Matekon,* Winter 1973-74, *10*(2), pp. 52–55.

Chester, T. E. Health Service Reorganized. *Nat. Westminster Bank Quart. Rev.,* November 1973, pp. 41–54.

_____ Public Money in the Private Sector. *Nat. Westminster Bank Quart. Rev.,* May 1973, pp. 20–30.

Cheung, Steven N. S. The Fable of the Bees: An Economic Investigation. *J. Law Econ.,* April 1973, *16*(1), pp. 11–33.

Chiancone, Aldo. Il sistema svedese dei fondi di riserva per gli investimenti come strumento di stabilizzazione economica. (The Swedish System of Investment Funds as an Instrument of Stabilization Policy. With English summary.) *Rivista Int. Sci. Econ. Com.,* March 1973, *20*(3), pp. 242–66.

Chiang, Alpha C. A Simple Generalization of the Kaldor-Pasinetti Theory of Profit Rate and Income Distribution. *Economica, N.S.,* August 1973, *40*(159), pp. 311–13.

Chick, Victoria. Financial Counterparts of Saving and Investment and Inconsistency in Some Simple Macro Models. *Weltwirtsch. Arch.,* 1973, *109* (4), pp. 621–43.

Child, A. J. E. The Private Trader in Export Market Development. In *Canadian Agricultural Economics Society,* 1973, pp. 58–68.

Ching, C. T. K. A Note on the Stability of Firm Size Distribution Functions for Western Cattle Ranches. *Amer. J. Agr. Econ.,* August 1973, *55*(3), pp. 500–02.

Chiplin, B. and Sloane, P. J. Real and Money Wages Revisited. *Appl. Econ.,* December 1973, *5*(4), pp. 289–304.

Chipman, John S. The Ordering of Portfolios in Terms of Mean and Variance. *Rev. Econ. Stud.,* April 1973, *40*(2), pp. 167–90.

_____ **and Moore, James C.** Aggregate Demand, Real National Income, and the Compensation Principle. *Int. Econ. Rev.,* February 1973, *14*(1), pp. 153–81.

Chirikos, Thomas N. Health Service Employment in Ohio. *Ohio State U. Bull. Bus. Res.,* January 1973, *48*(1), pp. 4–5, 8.

Chiswick, Barry R. Racial Discrimination in the Labor Market: A Test of Alternative Hypotheses. *J. Polit. Econ.,* November-December 1973, *81*(6), pp. 1330–52.

Chizmar, John F. and Koch, James V. The Influence of Teaching and Other Factors Upon Absolute Salaries and Salary Increments at Illinois State University. *J. Econ. Educ.,* Fall 1973, *5*(1), pp. 27–34.

Chobot, Michal. Stochasticky prístup k ciel'ovému programovaniu. (Stochastic Approaches to Goal Programming. With English summary.) *Ekon.-Mat. Obzor,* 1973, *9*(3), pp. 305–19.

Choi, Frederick D. S. Financial Disclosure and Entry to the European Capital Market. *J. Acc. Res.,* Autumn 1973, *11*(2), pp. 159–75.

Chonchol, Jacques. The Agrarian Policy of the Popular Government. In *Zammit, J. A., ed.,* 1973, pp. 107–14.

Chong, Fei Wan and Chung, N. H. Paul. The Currency Reform of the Straits Settlements and Malay States: Misunderstood Intention. *Malayan Econ. Rev.,* April 1973, *18*(1), pp. 48–54.

Choucri, Nazil. Applications of Econometric Analysis to Forecasting in International Relations. *Peace Sci. Soc.,* 1973, *21*, pp. 15–39.

Choudhuri, S. D.; Ambegaonkar, L. V. and Ashturkar, B. W. Response of Irrigated M35–1 Rabi Jowar to Levels of Nitrogen. *Econ. Aff.,* June 1973, *18*(6), pp. 261–64.

Chow, Gregory C. Effect of Uncertainty on Optimal Control Policies. *Int. Econ. Rev.,* October 1973, *14*(3), pp. 632–45.

_____ Multiperiod Predictions from Stochastic Difference Equations by Bayesian Methods. *Econometrica,* January 1973, *41*(1), pp. 109–18.

_____ On the Computation of Full-Information Maximum Likelihood Estimates for Nonlinear Equation Systems. *Rev. Econ. Statist.,* February 1973, *55*(1), pp. 104–09.

_____ Problems of Economic Policy from the Viewpoint of Optimal Control. *Amer. Econ. Rev.,* December 1973, *63*(5), pp. 825–37.

_____ **and Fair, Ray C.** Maximum Likelihood Estimation of Linear Equation Systems with Auto-Regressive Residuals. *Ann. Econ. Soc. Measure,* January 1973, *2*(1), pp. 17–28.

Christ, Carl F. Monetary and Fiscal Influences on U.S. Money Income, 1891–1970. *J. Money, Credit, Banking,* Part II, February 1973, *5*(1), pp. 279–300.

_____ The 1973 Report of the President's Council of Economic Advisers: A Review. *Amer. Econ. Rev.,* September 1973, *63*(4), pp. 515–26.

Christensen, Andrea. White-collar Pay Up 5.4 Percent. *Mon. Lab. Rev.,* October 1973, *96*(10), pp. 53–55.

Christensen, Gary L. A View from the National Cable Television Association. In *Park, R. E., ed.,* 1973, pp. 15–18.

Christensen, Laurits R. Simultaneous Statistical Inference in the Normal Multiple Linear Regression Model. *J. Amer. Statist. Assoc.,* June 1973, *68* (342), pp. 457–61.

_____ **and Berndt, Ernst R.** The Internal Structure of Functional Relationships: Separability, Substitution and Aggregation. *Rev. Econ. Stud.,* July 1973, *40*(3), pp. 403–10.

_____ **and Berndt, Ernst R.** The Translog Function and the Substitution of Equipment, Structures, and Labor in U.S. Manufacturing 1929–68. *J. Econometrics,* March 1973, *1*(1), pp. 81–113.

_____ **and Jorgenson, Dale W.** Measuring Economic Performance in the Private Sector. In *Moss, M., ed.,* 1973, pp. 233–338.

_____ **and Jorgenson, Dale W.** Measuring Economic Performance in the Private Sector: Reply to Kendrick. In *Moss, M., ed.,* 1973, pp. 350–51.

_____ **and Jorgenson, Dale W.** Measuring Economic Performance in the Private Sector: Reply to Eisner. In *Moss, M., ed.,* 1973, pp. 349–50.

_____ **and Jorgenson, Dale W.** U.S. Income, Saving,

and Wealth, 1929–1969. *Rev. Income Wealth,* December 1973, *19*(4), pp. 329–62.

———; Jorgenson, Dale W. and Lau, Lawrence J. Transcendental Logarithmic Production Frontiers. *Rev. Econ. Statist.,* February 1973, *55*(1), pp. 28–45.

Christensen, Raymond P. and Goolsby, O. Halbert. U.S. Agricultural Trade and Balance of Payments. In *Iowa State University Center for Agricultural and Rural Development,* 1973, pp. 122–40.

Christensen, Robert L. and Storey, David A. Graduate Programs in Agricultural Economics: Results of a Survey. *Amer. J. Agr. Econ.,* February 1973, *55*(1), pp. 61–64.

Christenson, C. L. and Andrews, W. H. Coal Mine Injury Rates in Two Eras of Federal Control. *J. Econ. Issues,* March 1973, *7*(1), pp. 61–82.

Christian, Charles M. and Bennett, Sari J. Industrial Relocations from the Black Community of Chicago. *Growth Change,* April 1973, *4*(2), pp. 14–20.

Christian, James W. and Pagoulatos, Emilio. Domestic Financial Markets in Developing Economies: An Econometric Analysis. *Kyklos,* 1973, *26*(1), pp. 75–90.

Christoffel, Pamela and Celio, Mary Beth. A Benefit-Cost Analysis of the Upward Bound Program: A Comment. *J. Human Res.,* Winter 1973, *8*(1), pp. 110–15.

Christou, G. and Wilford, W. T. A Sectoral Analysis of Disaggregated Trade Flows in the Central American Common Market 1962–1970. *J. Common Market Stud.,* December 1973, *12*(2), pp. 159–75.

Chudnovsky, Daniel. Endeudamiento y rentabilidad en empresas multinacionales. (Gearing and Profitability in Multinational Enterprises. With English summary.) *Económica,* September-December 1973, *19*(3), pp. 245–63.

Chugh, Ram L. Interest Sensitivity of Short-Term Capital Movements Between Canada and the United States: A Stock-Adjustment Analysis. *Econ. Int.,* August-November 1973, *26*(3–4), pp. 579–91.

Ch'ün, An. The Basic Problem in the Development of Agriculture Lies in the Line. *Chinese Econ. Stud.,* Winter 1973–74, *7*(2), pp. 7–17.

Chung, N. H. Paul and Chong, Fei Wan. The Currency Reform of the Straits Settlements and Malay States: Misunderstood Intention. *Malayan Econ. Rev.,* April 1973, *18*(1), pp. 48–54.

Chung, Pham. A Note on a Standard Theorem of Welfare Economics. *Indian Econ. J.,* January-March 1973, *20*(3), pp. 440–44.

——— A Note on the Optimal Product Mix in a Centrally Planned Economy. *J. Polit. Econ.,* Part I, March-April 1973, *81*(2), pp. 427–34.

——— Some Notes on the Assignment Problem. *Public Finance,* 1973, *28*(1), pp. 20–29.

Churchill, Gilbert A., Jr. and Hunt, Shelby D. Sources of Funds and Franchisee Success. *J. Bus. Res.,* Fall 1973, *1*(2), pp. 157–64.

Cicchetti, Charles J., et al. Benefits or Costs? An Assessment of the Water Resources Council's Proposed Principles and Standards. In *Niskanen, W. A., et al., eds.,* 1973, pp. 431–46.

——— and Freeman, A. Myrick, III. The Trans-Alaska Pipeline: An Economic Analysis of Alternatives. In *Enthoven, A. C. and Freeman, A. M., III, eds.,* 1973, pp. 271–84.

——— and Gillen, William J. The Mandatory Oil Import Quota Program: A Consideration of Economic Efficiency and Equity. *Natural Res. J.,* July 1973, *13*(3), pp. 399–430.

Cichetti, Charles J. and Smith, V. Kerry. Interdependent Consumer Decisions: A Production Function Approach. *Australian Econ. Pap.,* December 1973, *12*(21), pp. 239–52.

Ciletti, Michael D. Differential Games with Information Time Lag. In *Blaquière, A., ed.,* 1973, pp. 179–268.

Ciller, Ozer U. Pricing Employment Contracts. *Manage. Account.,* November 1973, *55*(5), pp. 29–31.

Ciucur, Dumitru and Gavrilă, Ilie. Aspecte ale gîndirii economice burgheze contemporane privind munca productivă. (Aspects of the Contemporary Bourgeois Economic Thinking on Productive Labor. With English summary.) *Stud. Cercet. Econ.,* 1973, (1), pp. 151–61.

——— and Gavrilă, Ilie. Competența economică a muncitorului modern din țara noastră. (The Economic Competence of the Modern Worker in Our Country. With English summary.) *Stud. Cercet. Econ.,* 1973, (4), pp. 15–23.

Ciucur, Elena and Călin, Oprea. Rolul prețului de cost în cadrul sistemului informațional economic al întreprinderii. (The Role of the Cost Price in the Economic Informational System of the Enterprise. With English summary.) *Stud. Cercet. Econ.,* 1973, (4), pp. 111–26.

Claassen, Emil-Maria. Alternative Policies to Achieve Internal and External Equilibrium: A Graphical Overview. *Z. Nationalökon.,* 1973, *33* (1–2), pp. 127–31.

Claessens, G. and Verheirstraeten, A. De technische analyse van het verloop van aandelenkoersen—met een toepassing op de beurs te Brussel. (With English summary.) *Tijdschr. Econ.,* 1973, *18*(4), pp. 647–81.

Clague, Christopher. Legal Strategies for Dealing with Heroin Addiction. *Amer. Econ. Rev.,* May 1973, *63*(2), pp. 263–69.

Clague, Ewan. Developments in Labor Statistics. In *Somers, G. G., ed.,* 1973, pp. 37–46.

Clark, Carolyn. The Demand for Money and the Choice of a Permanent Income Estimate: Some Canadian Evidence, 1926-65. *J. Money, Credit, Banking,* August 1973, *5*(3), pp. 773–93.

Clark, Colin. The Marginal Utility of Income. *Oxford Econ. Pap.,* July 1973, *25*(2), pp. 145–59.

Clark, Colin W. Profit Maximization and the Extinction of Animal Species. *J. Polit. Econ.,* July-August 1973, *81*(4), pp. 950–61.

Clark, C. Scott. Labor Hoarding in Durable Goods Industries. *Amer. Econ. Rev.,* December 1973, *63* (5), pp. 811–24.

Clark, Duncan W. Politics and Health Services Research: A Cameo Study of Policy in the Health Services in the 1930's. In *Flook, E. E. and Sanazaro, P. J., eds.,* 1973, pp. 109–25.

Clark, Ian D. and Weinstein, Milton C. Emissions

Measurement and the Testing of New Vehicles. In *Jacoby, H. D., et al.*, 1973, pp. 63–111.

Clark, John J. and Elgers, Pieter. Forecasted Income Statements: An Investor Perspective. *Accounting Rev.*, October 1973, 48(4), pp. 668–78.

Clark, Peter B. Uncertainty, Exchange Risk, and the Level of International Trade. *Western Econ. J.*, September 1973, 11(3), pp. 302–13.

———— **and Foxley, Alejandro.** Target Shooting with a Multisectoral Model. In *Eckaus, R. S. and Rosenstein-Rodan, P. N., eds.*, 1973, pp. 341–66.

————; **Foxley, Alejandro and Jul, Anna Maria.** Project Evaluation within a Macroeconomic Framework. In *Eckaus, R. S. and Rosenstein-Rodan, P. N., eds.*, 1973, pp. 199–226.

————; **Taylor, Lance and Bergendorff, Hans G.** Welfare Gains from Optimization in Dynamic Planning Models. *Econ. Planning*, 1973, 13(1–2), pp. 75–90.

Clark, Peter K. A Subordinated Stochastic Process Model with Finite Variance for Speculative Prices. *Econometrica*, January 1973, 41(1), pp. 135–55.

Clark, Robert A.; Jantorni, Joan M. and Gann, Robert R. Analysis of the Lease-or-Buy Decision: Comment. *J. Finance*, September 1973, 28(4), pp. 1015–16.

Clark, Russell J. The Importance of Being Confident. *Nat. Westminster Bank Quart. Rev.*, August 1973, pp. 2–7.

Clarke, Darral G. Sales-Advertising Cross-Elasticities and Advertising Competition. *J. Marketing Res.*, August 1973, 10(3), pp. 250–61.

Clauretie, Terrence M. Interest Rates, the Business Demand for Funds, and the Residential Mortgage Market: A Sectoral Econometric Study. *J. Finance*, December 1973, 28(5), pp. 1313–26.

Clavijo, Fernando; Orsi, Renzo and Adams, F. Gerard. A Macroeconomic Model of Belgium: Anelise. *Rech. Écon. Louvain*, September 1973, 39(3), pp. 303–26.

Clawson, Marion and Perloff, Harvey S. Alternatives for Future Urban Land Policy. In *Clawson, M., ed.*, 1973, pp. 221–39.

Clayton, James L. The Ultimate Cost of the Vietnam Conflict. In *Haveman, R. H. and Hamrin, R. D., eds.*, 1973, pp. 107–11.

Clearwaters, Keith I. Trade Associations and the Antitrust Laws—A View from the Justice Department. *Antitrust Bull.*, Summer 1973, 18(2), pp. 233–42.

Cleary, T. Anne. New Directions for Career Planning. In *McClure, L. and Buan, C., eds.*, 1973, pp. 39–53.

Cleaver, Joe M. and Rhoades, Stephen A. The Nature of the Concentration—Price/Cost Margin Relationship for 352 Manufacturing Industries: 1967. *Southern Econ. J.*, July 1973, 40(1), pp. 90–102.

Clement, Norris C.; Jencks, Clinton E. and Hardesty, John. Ecological Conflicts: A Reply. *Rev. Radical Polit. Econ.*, Summer 1973, 5(2), pp. 95–102.

Clemente, Frank. Effects of Industrial Development on Heads of Households: Comment. *Growth Change*, July 1973, 4(3), pp. 20–21.

———— **and Sturgis, Richard B.** Population Size and

Industrial Diversification: A Rejoinder. *Urban Stud.*, October 1973, 10(3), pp. 397.

Cleur, Eugene M. A Simulation Study on the Powers of Three Tests for Serial Correlation in the Errors from Least Squares Analysis. *Statistica*, April-June 1973, 33(2), pp. 285–300.

Clevenger, Thomas S.; Gorman, William D. and Lansford, Robert R. Economic Planning for the Navajo Indian Irrigation Project. *N. Mex. Bus.*, April 1973, 26(4), pp. 3–8.

Clifford, Donald K., Jr. Growth Pains of the Threshold Company. *Harvard Bus. Rev.*, September-October 1973, 51(5), pp. 143–54.

Cline, William R. Cost-Benefit Analysis of Irrigation Projects in Northeastern Brazil. *Amer. J. Agr. Econ.*, Part I, November 1973, 55(4), pp. 622–27.

———— Interrelationships Between Agricultural Strategy and Rural Income Distribution. *Food Res. Inst. Stud.*, 1973, 12(2), pp. 139–57.

Clinton, Kevin. The Demand for Money in Canada, 1955-70: Some Single-Equation Estimates and Stability Tests. *Can. J. Econ.*, February 1973, 6(1), pp. 53–61.

———— Interest Rate Expectations and the Demand for Money in Canada: Comment. *J. Finance*, March 1973, 28(1), pp. 207–12.

———— Pitfalls in Financial Model Building: Comment. *Amer. Econ. Rev.*, December 1973, 63(5), pp. 1003–04.

Close, R. E. and Panic, M. Profitability of British Manufacturing Industry. *Lloyds Bank Rev.*, July 1973, (109), pp. 17–30.

Clottey, St. John A. Increasing Ghana's Meat Output through Improvement in Ruminant Production. In *Ofori, I. M., ed.*, 1973, pp. 231–39.

Cloud, Preston. Mineral Resources in Fact and Fancy. In *Daly, H. E., ed.*, 1973, pp. 50–75.

Clough, Donald J. Environmental Pollution. In *Ross, M., ed.*, 1973, pp. 685–99.

Cloward, Richard A. and Piven, Frances Fox. The Case Against Urban Desegregation. In *Pynoos, J.; Schafer, R. and Hartman, C. W., eds.*, 1973, pp. 97–107.

Clower, Robert W. Snarks, Quarks, and Other Fictions. In *[Williamson, H. F.]*, 1973, pp. 3–14.

———— **and Leijonhufvud, Axel.** Say's Principle, What it Means and Doesn't Mean: Part I. *Intermountain Econ. Rev.*, Fall 1973, 4(2), pp. 1–16.

Coale, Ansley J. Age Composition in the Absence of Mortality and in Other Odd Circumstances. *Demography*, November 1973, 10(4), pp. 537–42.

———— Man and His Environment. In *Enthoven, A. C. and Freeman, A. M., III, eds.*, 1973, pp. 155–65.

Coase, R. H. Business Organization and the Accountant. In *Buchanan, J. M. and Thirlby, G. F., eds.*, 1973, pp. 95–132.

Coates, Robert and Updegraff, David E. The Relationship between Organizational Size and the Administrative Component of Banks. *J. Bus.*, October 1973, 46(4), pp. 576–88.

Coats, A. W. The Interpretation of Mercantilist Economics: Some Historiographical Problems. *Hist. Polit. Econ.*, Fall 1973, 5(2), pp. 485–95.

Coats, Warren L., Jr. Regulation D and the Vault Cash Game. *J. Finance*, June 1973, 28(3), pp. 601–07.

Cobb, Gary D. Evolving Water Policies in the United States. *Amer. J. Agr. Econ.*, December 1973, *55*(5), pp. 1003–07.

Cobb, William E. Theft and the Two Hypotheses. In *Rottenberg, S., ed.*, 1973, pp. 19–30.

Coccari, Ronald L. and Saunders, Robert J. Racial Earnings Differentials: Some Economic Factors. *Amer. J. Econ. Soc.*, July 1973, *32*(3), pp. 225–33.

Cochrane, James D. and Sloan, John W. LAFTA and the CACM: A Comparative Analysis of Integration in Latin America. *J. Devel. Areas*, October 1973, *8*(1), pp. 13–37.

Cochrane, James L. Ricardo on the Rate of Profit and Distributive Shares: Comment. *Indian Econ. J.*, January-March 1973, *20*(3), pp. 521–22.

────── **and Kiker, B. F.** War and Human Capital in Western Economic Analysis. *Hist. Polit. Econ.*, Fall 1973, *5*(2), pp. 375–98.

────── **and Zeleny, Milan.** A Priori and A Posteriori Goals in Macroeconomic Policy Making. In *Cochrane, J. L. and Zeleny, M., eds.*, 1973, pp. 373–91.

Cochrane, Susan Hill. Population and Development: A More General Model. *Econ. Develop. Cult. Change*, April 1973, *21*(3), pp. 409–22.

Cochrane, Willard W. Agricultural and Trade Developments in the Less Developed Countries. In *Iowa State University Center for Agricultural and Rural Development*, 1973, pp. 194–209.

Cockerell, Hugh. The History of British and American Fire Marks: Comment. *J. Risk Ins.*, December 1973, *40*(4), pp. 639–41.

Coddington, Alan. Bargaining as a Decision Process. *Swedish J. Econ.*, December 1973, *75*(4), pp. 397–405.

────── Economists and Policy. *Nat. Westminster Bank Quart. Rev.*, February 1973, pp. 59–68.

Coelen, Stephen P.; Warford, Jeremy J. and Bahl, Roy W. Land Value Increments as a Measure of the Net Benefits of Urban Water Supply Projects in Developing Countries: Theory and Measurement. In *Harriss, C. L., ed.*, 1973, pp. 171–88.

Coelho, Philip R. P. The Profitability of Imperialism: The British Experience in the West Indies 1768-1772. *Exploration Econ. Hist.*, Spring 1973, *10*(3), pp. 253–80.

────── **and Ghali, Moheb A.** The End of the North-South Wage Differential: Reply. *Amer. Econ. Rev.*, September 1973, *63*(4), pp. 757–62.

Coen, Edward. Relative Growth Rates: The Experience of the Advanced Economies. *Banca Naz. Lavoro Quart. Rev.*, June 1973, *105*, pp. 158–76.

Coen, Robert M. Labor Force and Unemployment in the 1920's and 1930's: Reply. *Rev. Econ. Statist.*, November 1973, *55*(4), pp. 527–28.

────── Labor Force and Unemployment in the 1920's and 1930's: A Re-examination Based on Postwar Experience. *Rev. Econ. Statist.*, February 1973, *55*(1), pp. 46–55.

Coffey, Robert E. and Nanus, Burt. Future-Oriented Business Education. *Calif. Manage. Rev.*, Summer 1973, *15*(4), pp. 28–34.

Cogger, Kenneth O. Specification Analysis. *J. Amer. Statist. Assoc.*, December 1973, *68*(344), pp. 899–905.

Cohan, Sandra B. The Determinants of Supply and Demand for Certificates of Deposit. *J. Money,* *Credit, Banking,* Part I, February 1973, *5*(1), pp. 100–12.

Cohen, Alain-Gérard. Tunisia: Reforming the Commercial Structure. In *Boddewyn, J. J. and Hollander, S. C., eds.*, 1972, pp. 311–25.──

Cohen, Alvin. Population Problems—Myths and Realities: A Comment. *Econ. Develop. Cult. Change*, October 1973, *22*(1), pp. 137–39.

Cohen, Benjamin I. Comparative Behavior of Foreign and Domestic Export Firms in a Developing Economy. *Rev. Econ. Statist.*, May 1973, *55*(2), pp. 190–97.

────── **; Trubek, David M. and Branfman, Eric J.** Measuring the Invisible Wall: Land Use Controls and the Residential Patterns of the Poor. *Yale Law J.*, January 1973, *82*(3), pp. 483–508.

Cohen, Benjamin J. The Future Role of Sterling. *Nat. Westminster Bank Quart. Rev.*, May 1973, pp. 6–19.

────── The Historical Setting: Comment. In *Krause, L. B. and Salant, W. S., eds.*, 1973, pp. 30–33.

Cohen, Bruce and Schachter, Gustav. Influenze esterne sui mercati dei capitali degli Stati Uniti. (Foreign Influences on the U.S. Capital Markets. With English summary.) *Bancaria*, February 1973, *29*(2), pp. 156–63.

Cohen, C. D.; Pickering, J. F. and Harrison, J. A. Identification and Measurment of Consumer Confidence: Methodology and Some Preliminary Results. *J. Roy. Statist. Soc.*, Part 1, 1973, *136*, pp. 43–63.

Cohen, David K., et al. Revenue-Sharing as an Incentive Device: The Experience with Title I of the Elementary and Secondary Education Act. In *Stein, B. and Miller, S. M., eds.*, 1973, pp. 93–115.

Cohen, Edwin S. The Administration's Tax Priorities. In *Tax Foundation, Inc.*, 1973, pp. 51–56.

────── Tax Simplification: Remarks. *Nat. Tax J.*, September 1973, *26*(3), pp. 311–15.

Cohen, Harold A. Cost Functions of Hospital Diagnostic Procedures: A Possible Argument for Diagnostic Centers. *J. Econ. Bus.*, Winter 1973, *25*(2), pp. 83–88.

Cohen, Jacob and Miller, Richard K. A Flow-of-Funds Model of the Stock Market. *J. Econ. Bus.*, Winter 1973, *25*(2), pp. 71–82.

Cohen, Jeffrey M. Accounting for Modular Housing Manufacturers. *Manage. Account.*, September 1973, *55*(3), pp. 11–14.

Cohen, Kalman J. and Cyert, Richard M. Strategy: Formulation, Implementation, and Monitoring. *J. Bus.*, July 1973, *46*(3), pp. 349–67.

Cohen, Malcolm; Gillingham, Robert and Heien, Dale. A Monte Carlo Study of Complex Finite Distributed Lag Structures. *Ann. Econ. Soc. Measure*, January 1973, *2*(1), pp. 53–63.

Cohen, Stanley and Smyth, David J. Some Determinants of Price/Earnings Ratios of Industrial Common Stock. *Quart. Rev. Econ. Bus.*, Winter 1973, *13*(4), pp. 49–60.

Cohen, Sylvan H. The Politics of Urban Renewal and the Politics of Ecology. In *Gabriel, R. A. and Cohen, S. H., eds.*, 1973, pp. 171–91.

Cohen, Yehoshua S. and Berry, Brian J. L. Decentralization of Commerce and Industry: The Restructuring of Metropolitan America. In *Masotti,*

L. H. and Hadden, J. K., eds., 1973, pp. 431–55.

Cohn, Elchanan. On the Ranking of Social Investments in Education: A Reply. *Public Finance*, 1973, *28*(3–4), pp. 431–34.

_____ **and Lewis, Morgan V.** Recruiting and Retaining Participants in a Manpower Program. *Ind. Lab. Relat. Rev.*, January 1973, *26*(2), pp. 842–50.

Cohn, Richard A. and Pringle, John J. Imperfections in International Financial Markets: Implications for Risk Premia and the Cost of Capital to Firms. *J. Finance*, March 1973, *28*(1), pp. 59–66.

Cohn, Stanley H. Handbook of Soviet Social Science Data: Production. In *Mickiewicz, E., ed.*, 1973, pp. 91–99.

Cohon, Jared L. and Marks, David H. Multiobjective Screening Models and Water Resource Investment. *Water Resources Res.*, August 1973, *9*(4), pp. 826–36.

Coker, David and Kay, John. The Fund Meeting. *Finance Develop.*, December 1973, *10*(4), pp. 37–40.

Colantoni, C. S.; Cooper, W. W. and Dietzer, H. J. Budgetary Disclosure and Social Accounting. In *Dierkes, M. and Bauer, R. A., eds.*, 1973, pp. 365–86.

Colberg, Marshall R. and King, James P. Theory of Production Abandonment. *Rivista Int. Sci. Econ. Com.*, October 1973, *20*(10), pp. 961–72.

Cole, David L. The Effect of Labor Relations. In *The Diebold Group, Inc.*, 1973, pp. 239–49.

Cole, H. S. D. The Structure of the World Models. In *Cole, H. S. D., et al., eds.*, 1973, pp. 14–32.

_____ **and Curnow, R. C.** An Evaluation of the World Models. In *Cole, H. S. D., et al., eds.*, 1973, pp. 108–34.

Cole, W. A. Eighteenth-Century Economic Growth Revisited. *Exploration Econ. Hist.*, Summer 1973, *10*(4), pp. 327–48.

_____ **and Deane, Phyllis.** British Economic Growth, 1967. In *Tranter, N. L., ed.*, 1973, pp. 127–35.

Cole, William A. and Wales, Stephen H., Sr. The Investment Credit. *Manage. Account.*, March 1973, *54*(9), pp. 13–16, 35.

Coleman, D. C. Gentlemen and Players. *Econ. Hist. Rev., 2nd Ser.*, February 1973, *26*(1), pp. 92–116.

Coles, O. B. An Economic Comparison of Urban Railways and Express Bus Services: Comment. *J. Transp. Econ. Policy*, September 1973, *7*(3), pp. 295–97.

Collard, David. Exclusion by Estate Agents—An Analysis. *Appl. Econ.*, December 1973, *5*(4), pp. 281–88.

_____ Léon Walras and the Cambridge Caricature. *Econ. J.*, June 1973, *83*(330), pp. 465–76.

_____ Price and Prejudice in the Housing Market. *Econ. J.*, June 1973, *83*(330), pp. 510–15.

Collery, Arnold; Zelder, Raymond E. and Ross, Myron H. Internal and External Balance in an "Almost Classical" World: Reply. *Western Econ. J.*, June 1973, *11*(2), pp. 238–40.

Collie, Marvin K. Estate and Gift Tax Revision. *Nat. Tax J.*, September 1973, *26*(3), pp. 441–49.

Collier, George A., Jr. On the Size and Spacing of Growth Centers: Comment. *Growth Change*, October 1973, *4*(4), pp. 47–48.

Collier, Joe. Inspection and Enforcement at the Workplace. *Mon. Lab. Rev.*, August 1973, *96*(8), pp. 35–42.

Collier, Roger J. Simulation of Computer Systems: An Introduction. *Manage. Account.*, May 1973, *54*(11), pp. 45–47.

Collier, William L. and Soentoro, Gunawan Wiradi. Recent Changes in Rice Harvesting Methods: Some Serious Social Implications. *Bull. Indonesian Econ. Stud.*, July 1973, *9*(2), pp. 36–45.

Collins, David C. Applications of Multiple Criterial Evaluation to Decision Aiding. In *Cochrane, J. L. and Zeleny, M., eds.*, 1973, pp. 477–505.

Collins, William H. Comparative Performance of Combinations and Separately Managed Electric Utilities. *Southern Econ. J.*, July 1973, *40*(1), pp. 80–89.

Colonna di Paliano, Guido. International Private Investment Problems: European Community —United States. *Aussenwirtschaft*, September-December 1973, *28*(3/4), pp. 110–27.

Colwell, J. D. Assessments of the Relative Values of Compound Nitrogen-Phosphorus Fertilizers for Wheat Production. *Australian J. Agr. Econ.*, December 1973, *17*(3), pp. 189–99.

Colwell, Peter F. Florence, Gini, and Mr. Lorenz: Consider the Possibilities. In *Mattila, J. M. and Thompson, W. R., eds.*, 1973, pp. 58–68.

_____ **and Lash, Nicholas A.** Comparing Fiscal Indicators. *Rev. Econ. Statist.*, August 1973, *55*(3), pp. 321–26.

Comanor, William S. Racial Discrimination in American Industry. *Economica, N.S.*, November 1973, *40*(160), pp. 363–78.

_____ The View of an Academic Consultant. In *Park, R. E., ed.*, 1973, pp. 31–34.

Comay, Yochanan and Kirschenbaum, Alan. The Israeli New Town: An Experiment at Population Redistribution. *Econ. Develop. Cult. Change*, October 1973, *22*(1), pp. 124–34.

_____; **Melnik, A. and Pollatschek, M. A.** The Option Value of Education and the Optimal Path for Investment in Human Capital. *Int. Econ. Rev.*, June 1973, *14*(2), pp. 421–35.

Common, Michael S. and Pearce, David W. Adaptive Mechanisms, Growth, and the Environment: The Case of Natural Resources. *Can. J. Econ.*, August 1973, *6*(3), pp. 289–300.

Conacher, H. M. Causes of the Fall of Agricultural Prices between 1875 and 1895. In *Perry, P. J., ed.*, 1973, pp. 18–29.

Conard, Alfred F. An Overview of the Laws of Corporations. *Mich. Law Rev.*, March 1973, *71*(4), pp. 621–90.

Condurache, Gheorghe and Ştirbu, Cornelia. Determinarea timpului optim de înlocuire a unei linii tehnologice du sudură de la Uzina metalurgică—Iaşi. (Determining the Optimum Time for Replacing a Welding Technological Line at the Jassy Metallurgical Works. With English summary.) *Stud. Cercet. Econ.*, 1973, (4), pp. 89–98.

Congdon, Timothy G. Why Has Inflation Accelerated? *Nat. Westminster Bank Quart. Rev.*, February 1973, pp. 6–19.

Congo, M. Savings Banks and Savings Facilities in

African Countries: Upper Volta. In *Alberici, A. and Baravelli, M., eds.*, 1973, pp. 125–28.

Conley, Patrick. Experience Curves as a Planning Tool. In *Britt, S. H. and Boyd, H. W., Jr., eds.*, 1973, pp. 257–68.

Conlisk, John. Choice of Response Functional Form in Designing Subsidy Experiments. *Econometrica*, July 1973, *41*(4), pp. 643–56.

—— Quick Stability Checks and Matrix Norms. *Economica, N.S.*, November 1973, *40*(160), pp. 402–09.

Conly, Sonia. Success and Failure in the Work Incentive Program. *Growth Change*, October 1973, *4*(4), pp. 16–23.

Conn, Robert L. Performance of Conglomerate Firms: Comment. *J. Finance*, June 1973, *28*(3), pp. 754–58.

Connor, Larry J. Michigan State's Curricula in Agricultural Economics. *Amer. J. Agr. Econ.*, Part II, November 1973, *55*(4), pp. 752–54.

Conrad, A. H. and Meyer, John R. The Economics of Slavery in the Antebellum South. In *Temin, P., ed.*, 1973, pp. 339–97.

Conrad, Klaus and Jüttner, D. Johannes. Recent Behaviour of Stock Market Prices in Germany and the Random Walk Hypothesis. *Kyklos*, 1973, *26*(3), pp. 576–99.

Conroy, J. D. Urbanization in Papua New Guinea: A Development Constraint. *Econ. Rec.*, March 1973, *49*(125), pp. 76–88.

Conroy, Michael E. Rejection of Growth Center Strategy in Latin American Regional Development Planning. *Land Econ.*, November 1973, *49*(4), pp. 371–80.

Constantinescu, N. N. Cadrul economic, social și politic în care a apărut Manifestul Partidului Comunist. (The Economic, Social and Political Background Against which the Manifesto of the Communist Party was Published. With English summary.) *Stud. Cercet. Econ.*, 1973, (2), pp. 25–32.

—— Cîteva probleme ale teoriei și practicii în domeniul productivității muncii. (Some Problems of the Theory and Practice in the Field of Labour Productivity. With English summary.) *Stud. Cercet. Econ.*, 1973, (1), pp. 27–34.

Contini, Bruno; Hughes, G. David and Juhasz, Joseph B. The Influence of Personality on the Bargaining Process. *J. Bus.*, October 1973, *46*(4), pp. 593–604.

Conway, William J. Economic Dominants and Community Power: A Reputational and Decisional Analysis. *Amer. J. Econ. Soc.*, July 1973, *32*(3), pp. 269–82.

Cook, Carvin. Federal Employment Standards Legislation. *Mon. Lab. Rev.*, January 1973, *96*(1), pp. 50–51.

Cook, Gail C. A. Effect of Metropolitan Government on Resource Allocation: The Case of Education in Toronto. *Nat. Tax J.*, December 1973, *26*(4), pp. 585–90.

—— Metropolitan Government: The Significance of Context and Form. In *Mattila, J. M. and Thompson, W. R., eds.*, 1973, pp. 164–74.

—— and Stager, David A. A. Contingent Repayment Student Finance: The Problem of Non-Par-

ticipants in the Labour Force. *Ann. Econ. Soc. Measure*, January 1973, *2*(1), pp. 65–67.

Cook, Henry, Jr. and Gordon, Lawrence A. Absorption Costing an Fixed Factors of Production. *Accounting Rev.*, January 1973, *48*(1), pp. 128–29.

Cook, Thomas J. and Scioli, Frank P., Jr. Experimental Design in Policy Impact Analysis. *Soc. Sci. Quart.*, September 1973, *54*(2), pp. 271–80.

Cooley, Thomas F. and Prescott, Edward C. An Adaptive Regression Model. *Int. Econ. Rev.*, June 1973, *14*(2), pp. 364–71.

—— and Prescott, Edward C. Systematic (Non-Random) Variation Models Varying Parameter Regression: A Theory and Some Applications. *Ann. Econ. Soc. Measure*, October 1973, *2*(4), pp. 463–73.

—— and Prescott, Edward C. Tests of an Adaptive Regression Model. *Rev. Econ. Statist.*, May 1973, *55*(2), pp. 248–56.

Coombs, Charles A. Treasury and Federal Reserve Foreign Exchange Operations. *Fed. Res. Bull.*, March 1973, *59*(3), pp. 142–63.

—— Treasury and Federal Reserve Foreign Exchange Operations: Interim Report. *Fed. Res. Bull.*, December 1973, *59*(12), pp. 871–73.

Cooper, Barbara S. and Worthington, Nancy L. Age Differences in Medical Care Spending, Fiscal Year 1972. *Soc. Sec. Bull.*, May 1973, *36*(5), pp. 3–15.

—— and Worthington, Nancy L. National Health Expenditures, 1929-72. *Soc. Sec. Bull.*, January 1973, *36*(1), pp. 3–19, 40.

Cooper, Charles. Choice of Techniques and Technological Change as Problems in Political Economy. *Int. Soc. Sci. J.*, 1973, *25*(3), pp. 293–304.

Cooper, J. Phillip. Time-Varying Regression Coefficients: A Mixed Estimation Approach and Operational Limitations of the General Markov Structure. *Ann. Econ. Soc. Measure*, October 1973, *2*(4), pp. 525–30.

—— and Fischer, Stanley. Stabilization Policy and Lags. *J. Polit. Econ.*, July-August 1973, *81*(4), pp. 847–77.

—— and Fischer, Stanley. The Use of the Secant Method in Econometric Models. *J. Bus.*, April 1973, *46*(2), pp. 274–77.

Cooper, Leon. N-Dimensional Location Models: An Application to Cluster Analysis. *J. Reg. Sci.*, April 1973, *13*(1), pp. 41–54.

Cooper, Michael H. and Culyer, Anthony J. The Economics of Giving and Selling Blood. In *Alchian, A. A., et al.*, 1973, pp. 109–43.

Cooper, Richard N. European Monetary Unification and the International Monetary System. In *Krauss, M. B., ed.*, 1973, pp. 215–35.

—— Implications for Integration of the World Economy. In *Krause, L. B. and Salant, W. S., eds.*, 1973, pp. 250–66.

Cooper, Ronald L. An Econometric Forecasting Model of the Financial Sector of U.S. Households. *Appl. Econ.*, June 1973, *5*(2), pp. 101–17.

Cooper, S. Kerry. Idle Cash Balances of State and Local Governments: An Estimation Technique. *Nebr. J. Econ. Bus.*, Spring 1973, *12*(2), pp. 21–33.

Cooper, W. W.; Dietzer, H. J. and Colantoni, C. S. Budgetary Disclosure and Social Accounting. In

Dierkes, M. and Bauer, R. A., eds., 1973, pp. 365–86.

Copp, Robert. Ford Motor Co. as a Multinational Employer. *Mon. Lab. Rev.,* August 1973, *96*(8), pp. 58–61.

Coppock, D. J. Devaluation When Exports Have an Import Content: Reply. *Manchester Sch. Econ. Soc. Stud.,* December 1973, *41*(4), pp. 428–29.

Coppock, J. T. Agricultural Changes in the Chilterns, 1875–1900. In *Perry, P. J., ed.,* 1973, pp. 56–76.

Corbin, Donald A. Guidelines for Reporting Corporate Environmental Impact. In *Dierkes, M. and Bauer, R. A., eds.,* 1973, pp. 321–26.

Corcoran, A. Wayne and Leininger, Wayne E. Stochastic Process Costing Models. *Accounting Rev.,* January 1973, *48*(1), pp. 105–14.

Cord, Steven. How Land Value Taxation Would Affect Homeowners. *Amer. J. Econ. Soc.,* April 1973, *32*(2), pp. 153–54.

—— Revenue Sharing and Property Tax Reform. *Amer. J. Econ. Soc.,* October 1973, *32*(4), pp. 404.

Corden, W. Max. The Adjustment Problem. In *Krause, L. B. and Salant, W. S., eds.,* 1973, pp. 159–84.

—— Employment in the Industrialized Countries: Comment. In *Hughes, H., ed.,* 1973, pp. 125–27.

Corea, Gamani. Economic Planning, the Green Revolution and the 'Food Drive' in Ceylon. In *[Hicks, U.],* 1973, pp. 273–303.

Cornwall, Richard R. A Note on Using Profit Functions to Aggregate Production Functions. *Int. Econ. Rev.,* June 1973, *14*(2), pp. 511–19.

Correa, H. An Econometric Model of Supply, Demand and Wages of Educated Workers. In *Judge, G. G. and Takayama, T., eds.,* 1973, pp. 706–23.

Corry, B. A. Some Aspects of University Teachers' Labour Market in the UK: Discussion. In *Parkin, M., ed.,* 1973, pp. 212–13.

Corsa, Leslie; Johnson, J. Timothy and Tan Boon Ann. Assessment of Family Planning Programme Effects on Births: Preliminary Results Obtained through Direct Matching of Birth and Programme Acceptor Records. *Population Stud.,* March 1973, *27*(1), pp. 85–96.

Cortellazzo, Sandro. Aspetti metodologici nelle ricerche sulla "corporate image." (Methodological Aspects of "Corporate Image" Research. With English summary.) *L'Impresa,* 1973, *15*(9–10), pp. 579–88.

Cortesse, Pierre. Public Policy Toward Retailing: France. In *Boddewyn, J. J. and Hollander, S. C., eds.,* 1972, pp. 117–43.

Corti, G. Risk, Uncertainty and Cost Benefit: Some Notes on Practical Difficulties for Project Appraisals. In *Wolfe, J. N., ed.,* 1973, pp. 75–87.

Corwin, R. D. and Miller, S. M. A qui profite l'impôt? Mythes et réalitiés. (Taxation and its Beneficiaries: The Manipulation of Symbols. With English summary.) *Consommation,* January-March 1973, *20*(1), pp. 17–35.

Cosciani, Cesare. La riforma delle imposte dirette: il problema del gettito. (Reform of Direct Taxes: Problem of Revenue. With English summary.) *Bancaria,* October 1973, *29*(10), pp. 1229–38.

Costa, E. Maximising Employment in Labour-intensive Development Programmes. *Int. Lab. Rev.,* November 1973, *108*(5), pp. 371–94.

—— The World Food Programme and Employment: Ten Years of Multilateral Food Aid for Development. *Int. Lab. Rev.,* March 1973, *107*(3), pp. 209–21.

Costa, P. and Piasentin, U. A Dynamic Simulation Model of the Urban Development of Venice. In *Hawkes, N., ed.,* 1973, pp. 144–54.

Costache, Sandu and Popescu, Constantin. Coordonate ale echilibrului dezvoltării economico-sociale în profil de ramură şi teritorial. (Coordinates of the Equilibrium of Economic-Social Development as Regards Branch and Territory. With English summary.) *Stud. Cercet. Econ.,* 1973, (4), pp. 25–38.

Coste, Roger. Inflation et processus de décision. (Inflation and Decision Making Process. With English summary.) *Consommation,* April-June 1973, *20*(2), pp. 95–116.

—— Les entreprises financières en mutation face au commerce de l'épargne. (The Trade of Savings and the Change of Financial Firms. With English summary.) *Consommation,* January-March 1973, *20*(1), pp. 37–57.

Costin, Frank; Greenough, William T. and Menges, Robert J. Student Ratings of College Teaching: Reliability, Validity, and Usefulness. *J. Econ. Educ.,* Fall 1973, *5*(1), pp. 51–53.

Costonis, John J. Development Rights Transfer: An Exploratory Essay. *Yale Law J.,* November 1973, *83*(1), pp. 75–128.

Cote, Joseph T. The Concept of Materiality. *Manage. Account.,* December 1973, *55*(6), pp. 17–22.

Cote, R.; Manson, A. R. and Hader, R. J. Minimum Bias Approximation of a General Regression Model. *J. Amer. Statist. Assoc.,* September 1973, *68*(343), pp. 633–38.

Cotlar, Morton and Green, Thad B. An Evaluation of a Novel Business Simulation Technique for Management Development. *J. Bus.,* April 1973, *46*(2), pp. 212–29.

Cotter, Richard V. A General Model for Accounts-Receivable Analysis and Control: Comment. *J. Financial Quant. Anal.,* March 1973, *8*(2), pp. 219–21.

Cottrell, James L. Forecasting in Multi-Outlet Businesses. *Manage. Account.,* April 1973, *54*(10), pp. 17–22, 30.

Coughlin, Robert E. and Hammer, Thomas R. Estimating the Benefits of Stream Valley and Open Space Preservation Projects. In *Harriss, C. L., ed.,* 1973, pp. 155–70.

Courakis, Anthony S. Monetary Policy: Old Wisdom behind a New Facade. *Economica, N.S.,* February 1973, *40*(157), pp. 73–86.

Courbis, Raymond. La théorie des "économies concurrencées" fondement du modèle FIFI. (The Theory of "Competitioned Economies" as a Basis of the Fifi Model. With English summary.) *Revue Écon.,* November 1973, *24*(6), pp. 905–22.

—— Les méthodes de planification française: évolution et perspectives. (The Methods of French Planification: Evolution and Perspectives. With English summary.) *Schweiz. Z. Volkswirtsch. Statist.,* September 1973, *109*(3), pp. 317–40.

_____ and Pagé, Jean-Pierre. Techniques de projection macro-économique et choix du Plan français. (Macro-Economic Forecasting Techniques and Decision Making in the French Planning System. With English summary.) *Revue Écon.*, November 1973, *24*(6), pp. 951–87.

Courchene, Thomas J. The Price-Specie-Flow Mechanism and the Gold-Exchange Standard: Some Exploratory Empiricism Relating to the Endogeneity of Country Money Balances. In *Johnson, H. G. and Swoboda, A. K., eds.*, 1973, pp. 65–84.

_____ and Beavis, David A. Federal-Provincial Tax Equalization: An Evaluation. *Can. J. Econ.*, November 1973, *6*(4), pp. 483–502.

Court, R. H. Efficient Estimation of the Reduced Form from Incomplete Econometric Models. *Rev. Econ. Stud.*, July 1973, *40*(3), pp. 411–17.

Covey, Richard B. Estate and Gift Taxation. *Nat. Tax J.*, September 1973, *26*(3), pp. 459–63.

Cox, James C. Properties of Functions which are Solutions to Maximization Problems. *J. Econ. Theory*, August 1973, *6*(4), pp. 396–98.

_____ A Theorem on Additively-Separable, Quasi-Concave Functions. *J. Econ. Theory*, April 1973, *6*(2), pp. 210–12.

_____ and Azzi, Corry F. Equity and Efficiency in Evaluation of Public Programs. *Quart. J. Econ.*, August 1973, *87*(3), pp. 495–502.

Cox, R. C. W. The Old Centre of Croydon: Victorian Decay and Redevelopment. In *Everitt, A., ed.*, 1973, pp. 184–212.

Cox, Steven R. and Shauger, Donald. Executive Compensation, Firm Sales, and Profitability. *Intermountain Econ. Rev.*, Spring 1973, *4*(1), pp. 29–39.

Crabb, Peter. Urban Water Catchments: Some Illustrations of Resource Allocation and Conflict Regulation. In *Aislabie, C., ed.*, 1973, pp. 19–33.

Craddock, W. J. The Agricultural Production Plant —What Can It Accomplish in Output and Stability? In *Canadian Agricultural Economics Society*, 1973, pp. 82–97.

Craft, James A. Racial and Occupational Aspects of Public Employment Service Placements. *Quart. Rev. Econ. Bus.*, Autumn 1973, *13*(3), pp. 53–60.

Crafts, N. F. R. Trade as a Handmaiden of Growth: An Alternative View. *Econ. J.*, September 1973, *83*(331), pp. 875–84.

Craig, C. Samuel; Stern, Louis W. and Sternthal, Brian. Managing Conflict in Distribution Channels: A Laboratory Study. *J. Marketing Res.*, May 1973, *10*(2), pp. 169–79.

Craine, Roger. On the Service Flow from Labour. *Rev. Econ. Stud.*, January 1973, *40*(1), pp. 39–46.

Cramer, J. S. Interaction of Income and Price in Consumer Demand. *Int. Econ. Rev.*, June 1973, *14*(2), pp. 351–63.

Cramer, Robert H. and Miller, Robert B. Development of a Deposit Forecasting Procedure for Use in Bank Financial Management. *J. Bank Res.*, Summer 1973, *4*(2), pp. 122–38.

Cramton, Roger C. and Berg, Richard K. On Leading a Horse to Water: NEPA and the Federal Bureaucracy. *Mich. Law Rev.*, january 1973, *71*(3), pp. 511–36.

Crane, Dwight B. and Bradley, Stephen P. Management of Commercial Bank Government Security Portfolios: An Optimization Approach Under Uncertainty. *J. Bank Res.*, Spring 1973, *4*(1), pp. 18–30.

Craven, John. Stability in a Two-Sector Model with Induced Bias. *Econ. J.*, September 1973, *83*(331), pp. 858–62.

Cravens, David W. and Hills, Gerald E. Consumerism: A Perspective for Business. In *Murray, B. B., ed.*, 1973, pp. 233–42.

_____ and Holland, Charles W. Fractional Factorial Experimental Designs in Marketing Research. *J. Marketing Res.*, August 1973, *10*(3), pp. 270–76.

Crawford, Robert G. Implications of Learning for Economic Models of Uncertainty. *Int. Econ. Rev.*, October 1973, *14*(3), pp. 587–600.

Creagan, James F. Rise of Prices and Pay Adjustments in Italy. *Mon. Lab. Rev.*, July 1973, *96*(7), pp. 47–48.

Crean, John F. Forgone Earnings and the Demand for Education: Some Empirical Evidence. *Can. J. Econ.*, February 1973, *6*(1), pp. 23–42.

Creedy, John. A Problem in the Estimation of Double-Log Engel Curves. *Oxford Bull. Econ. Statist.*, August 1973, *35*(3), pp. 217–22.

Crestani, I. and Young, Ralph. Productivity Change and Farm Income. *Quart. Rev. Agr. Econ.*, July 1973, *26*(3), pp. 198–214.

Crisman, R. E. W. State of Vermont, Program Budgeting, 1970. In *Novick, D., ed.*, 1973, pp. 181–84.

de Cristofaro, Rodolfo. Il confronto tra varianze nell'inferenza bayesiana. (A Bayesian Approach to the Comparison of Variances. With English summary.) *Statistica*, October-December 1973, *33*(4), pp. 547–59.

_____ Probabilità delle ipotesi e loro accettazione. (Probability of Hypotheses and their Acceptance. With English summary.) *Statistica*, January-March 1973, *33*(1), pp. 13–40.

Crocker, Thomas D. Contractual Choice. *Natural Res. J.*, October 1973, *13*(4), pp. 561–77.

Crook, Elizabeth M. and Robinson, Colin. Is There a World Energy Crisis? *Nat. Westminster Bank Quart. Rev.*, May 1973, pp. 46–60.

Crook, Frederick W. Collective Farms in Communist China. *Mon. Lab. Rev.*, March 1973, *96*(3), pp. 45–50.

Cross, Edward M.; Sailors, Joel W. and Qureshi, Usman A. Empirical Verification of Linder's Trade Thesis. *Southern Econ. J.*, October 1973, *40*(2), pp. 262–68.

Cross, Hershner. General Organization Structure and Functions. In *Weston, J. F. and Ornstein, S. I., eds.*, 1973, pp. 117–21.

Cross, John G. A Stochastic Learning Model of Economic Behavior. *Quart. J. Econ.*, May 1973, *87*(2), pp. 239–66.

Crossley, J. R. A Mixed Strategy for Labour Economists. *Scot. J. Polit. Econ.*, November 1973, *20*(3), pp. 211–38.

Crotty, James R. Specification Error in Macro-Econometric Models: The Influence of Policy Goals. *Amer. Econ. Rev.*, December 1973, *63*(5), pp. 1025–30.

Crouch, Robert L. Economic Development, Foreign

Aid and Neoclassical Growth. *J. Devel. Stud.,* April 1973, *9*(3), pp. 353–64.

———— A New Approach to the Monetisation of Neoclassical Growth Models. In *Powell, A. A. and Williams, R. A., eds.,* 1973, pp. 285–99.

Crouzet, F. Western Europe and Great Britain: 'Catching Up' in the First Half of the Nineteenth Century. In *Youngson, A. J., ed.,* 1973, pp. 98–125.

Crow, Robert Thomas. A Nationally-Linked Regional Econometric Model. *J. Reg. Sci.,* August 1973, *13*(2), pp. 187–204.

Crowley, Ronald W. A Case Study of the Effects of an Airport on Land Values. *J. Transp. Econ. Policy,* May 1973, *7*(2), pp. 144–52.

———— Reflections and Further Evidence on Population Size and Industrial Diversification. *Urban Stud.,* February 1973, *10*(1), pp. 91–94.

Crowston, Wallace B. and Kleindorfer, Paul R. Coordinating Multi-Project Networks. In *Cochrane, J. L. and Zeleny, M., eds.,* 1973, pp. 668–85.

Crum, William F. Interim Reports: Do They Meet MAP Standards? *Manage. Account.,* May 1973, *54* (11), pp. 26–28.

Crumbley, D. Larry. Behavioral Implications of Taxation. *Accounting Rev.,* October 1973, *48*(4), pp. 759–63.

———— Introducing Probabilities and Present Value Analysis into Taxation: A Reply. *Accounting Rev.,* July 1973, *48*(3), pp. 595–97.

Crutchfield, James A. Economic, Political, and Social Barriers to Efficiency in Selected Pacific Coast Fisheries. In *Sokoloski, A. A., ed.,* 1973, pp. 28–38.

Crvcanin, Milan. Application de modèles intégrés à la planification des systèmes de transports de la région lausannoise. (Integrated Models Used in Lausanne Area Transportation Study. With English summary.) *Schweiz. Z. Volkswirtsch. Statist.,* September 1973, *109*(3), pp. 357–73.

Csendes, Béla. Development Trends of Hungarian Agriculture. In *Földi, T., ed.,* 1973, pp. 117–34.

Csernok, Attila; Ehrlich, Eva and Szilágyi, Gyorgy. Numerical Results of an International Comparison of Infrastructure Development Over the Last 100 Years. *Europ. Econ. Rev.,* April 1973, *4*(1), pp. 63–65.

Csikós-Nagy, B. Mutual Advantages in the Economic Cooperation. In *Kiss, T., ed.,* 1973, pp. 179–90.

Cuddy, J. D. A. A Note on Projections of International Trade Based on Coefficients of Trade Intensity. *Econ. J.,* December 1973, *83*(332), pp. 1222–35.

Cuénod, Michel. Identification Procedures for Dynamic Systems. In *Ross, M., ed.,* 1973, pp. 75–100.

Cukierman, A. and Ben-Shahar, H. The Term-Structure of Interest Rates and Expectations of Price Increase and Devaluation. *J. Finance,* June 1973, *28*(3), pp. 567–75.

Cukor, György. Industrial Development Strategy in Developing Countries. In *Földi, T., ed.,* 1973, pp. 37–63.

Culyer, Anthony J. Pareto, Peacock and Rowley, and Policy Towards Natural Monopoly: Comment. *J. Public Econ.,* February 1973, *2*(1), pp. 89–95.

———— Quids without Quos—A Praxeological Ap-

proach. In *Alchian, A. A., et al.,* 1973, pp. 33–61.

———— Should Social Policy Concern Itself with Drug "Abuse"? *Public Finance Quart.,* October 1973, *1*(4), pp. 449–56.

———— and Cooper, Michael H. The Economics of Giving and Selling Blood. In *Alchian, A. A., et al.,* 1973, pp. 109–43.

Cumberland, John H. Dimensions of the Impact of Reduced Military Expenditures on Industries, Regions, and Communities. In *Udis, B., ed.,* 1973, pp. 79–147.

Cummins, J. David. An Econometric Model of the Life Insurance Sector of the U. S. Economy. *J. Risk Ins.,* December 1973, *40*(4), pp. 533–54.

———— and Denenberg, Herbert S. Insurance and Reciprocity: Reply. *J. Risk Ins.,* March 1973, *40* (1), pp. 141–42.

Cunningham, Roger A. Billboard Control under the Highway Beautification Act of 1965. *Mich. Law Rev.,* June 1973, *71*(7), pp. 1295–1374.

Curnow, R. C. and Cole, H. S. D. An Evaluation of the World Models. In *Cole, H. S. D., et al., eds.,* 1973, pp. 108–34.

Curran, R. J. Public Policy Toward Retailing: Ireland. In *Boddewyn, J. J. and Hollander, S. C., eds.,* 1972, pp. 167–90.

Currie, Lauchlin. The Exchange Constraint on Development—A Partial Solution to the Problem: A Reply. *Econ. J.,* March 1973, *83*(329), pp. 207–10.

Curtin, Richard T. Index Construction: An Appraisal of the Index of Consumer Sentiment. In *Mandell, L., et al., eds.,* 1973, pp. 253–61.

Curtin, William J. The Multinational Corporation and Transnational Collective Bargaining. In *Kujawa, D., ed.,* 1973, pp. 192–222.

Curtis, Christopher C. Managing Federal Lands: Replacing the Multiple Use System. *Yale Law J.,* March 1973, *82*(4), pp. 787–805.

Curtis, William H. Application of the Concept to School District Decision-Making. In *Novick, D., ed.,* 1973, pp. 161–67.

Curzon, Gerard and Curzon, Victoria. European Integration: Lessons for the Developing World. In *Streeten, P., ed.,* 1973, pp. 189–97.

———— and Curzon, Victoria. GATT and NTD's. In *Scaperlanda, A. E., ed.,* 1973, pp. 283–97.

Curzon, Victoria and Curzon, Gerard. European Integration: Lessons for the Developing World. In *Streeten, P., ed.,* 1973, pp. 189–97.

———— and Curzon, Gerard. GATT and NTD's. In *Scaperlanda, A. E., ed.,* 1973, pp. 283–97.

Cuskaden, Charles M. Labor Productivity in Apple Harvesting. *Amer. J. Agr. Econ.,* Part I, November 1973, *55*(4), pp. 633–36.

Cutright, Phillips. The Fallacy of the Five Million Women: A Re-Estimate: A Reaction. *Demography,* November 1973, *10*(4), pp. 663–72.

———— and Galle, Omer. The Effect of Illegitimacy on U.S. General Fertility Rates and Population Growth. *Population Stud.,* November 1973, *27* (3), pp. 515–26.

Cyert, Richard M. Managerial Personnel Considerations. In *The Diebold Group, Inc.,* 1973, pp. 103–10.

———— and Cohen, Kalman J. Strategy: Formulation,

Implementation, and Monitoring. *J. Bus.*, July 1973, *46*(3), pp. 349–67.

――――― and DeGroot, Morris H. An Analysis of Cooperation and Learning in a Duopoly Context. *Amer. Econ. Rev.*, March 1973, *63*(1), pp. 24–37.

Cyrnak, Anthony W. Member Bank Income, 1972. *Fed. Res. Bull.*, May 1973, *59*(5), pp. 329–35.

Czamanski, Stan. Linkages between Industries in Urban-Regional Complexes. In *Judge, G. G. and Takayama, T., eds.*, 1973, pp. 180–204.

――――― A Model of Urban Land Allocation. *Growth Change*, January 1973, *4*(1), pp. 43–48.

Daane, J. Dewey. Statements to Congress. *Fed. Res. Bull.*, June 1973, *59*(6), pp. 425–29.

Dacey, Michael F. A Central Focus Cluster Process for Urban Dispersion. *J. Reg. Sci.*, April 1973, *13*(1), pp. 77–89.

Dadayan, V. S. Economic Forecasting and Scientific and Technical Progress. *Amer. Econ.*, Fall 1973, *17*(2), pp. 49–50.

Dadi, M. M. Labour's Share in Indian Industry: Theory and Fact. *Indian Econ. J.*, January-March 1973, *20*(3), pp. 500–14.

Dadson, J. A. Farm Size and the Modernization of Agriculture in Ghana. In *Ofori, I. M., ed.*, 1973, pp. 193–202.

Daems, H. Consumption and Savings Decisions Under Uncertainty: A Numerical Example. *Tijdschr. Econ.*, 1973, *18*(3), pp. 429–40.

Daff, Trevor. The Establishment of Ironmaking at Scunthorpe 1858-77. *Bull. Econ. Res.*, November 1973, *25*(2), pp. 104–21.

Dagenais, Marcel G. Un modèle annuel de prévision pour l'économie du Québec. (An Annual Forecasting Model of the Quebec Economy. With English summary.) *Can. J. Econ.*, February 1973, *6*(1), pp. 62–78.

――――― The Use of Incomplete Observations in Multiple Regression Analysis: A Generalized Least Squares Approach. *J. Econometrics*, December 1973, *1*(4), pp. 317–28.

Dagli, Ates, et al. Microdata Processing Package. *Ann. Econ. Soc. Measure*, July 1973, *2*(3), pp. 303–05.

Dagnino Pastore, José M. and de Pablo, Juan C. Sobre la restricción de ahorro-inversión en los modelos de dos brechas. (On the Savings Constraint in Two Gap Models. With English summary.) *Económica*, May-August 1973, *19*(2), pp. 157–64.

Dahlman, S. Roland. Joint Establishments in Sweden. *Bull. Int. Fiscal Doc.*, June 1973, *27*(6), pp. 241–44.

Dahlstedt, Roy. Cycles in the Finnish Trade with the Soviet Union. *Liiketaloudellinen Aikak.*, 1973, *22*(1), pp. 63–66.

――――― Muuttujavalinnasta monikansallisen yrityksen käyttäytymismalleissa. (On the Selection of Variables for Descriptive Models of Multinational Firms. With English summary.) *Liiketaloudellinen Aikak.*, 1973, *22*(2), pp. 127–30.

Dahmén, Erik. Inflation: Economics or Politics? *Nat. Westminster Bank Quart. Rev.*, November 1973, pp. 16–26.

Dahrendorf, Ralf. The Foreign Trade Policy of the EEC. In *Henley, D. S., ed.*, 1973, pp. 1–5.

Dahyabhai, Indulal. Industrial Development of Backward Areas in Gujarat. *Artha-Vikas,* January-July 1973, *9*(1–2), pp. 240–44.

Daicoff, Darwin W. The Adjustment of DOD Civilian and Military Personnel. In *Udis, B., ed.*, 1973, pp. 167–77.

――――― Capitalization of the Benefits of Water Resource Development. In *Harriss, C. L., ed.*, 1973, pp. 189–99.

――――― The Community Impact of Military Installations. In *Udis, B., ed.*, 1973, pp. 149–66.

――――― The Federal Revenue System: Discussion. *J. Finance*, May 1973, *28*(2), pp. 503–06.

Dajani, Jarir S. Cost Studies of Urban Public Services. *Land Econ.*, November 1973, *49*(4), pp. 479–83.

D'Albergo, Ernesto. "Relativizzazione" di un teorema. (On the Relativity of a Theorem. With English summary.) *Econ. Int.*, February 1973, *26*(1), pp. 35–45.

Dale, William B. The International Monetary Fund and Greater Flexibility of Exchange Rates. In *[Halm, G. N.]*, 1973, pp. 3–17.

Dales, Sophie R. Federal Grants to State and Local Governments. *Soc. Sec. Bull.*, June 1973, *36*(6), pp. 16–27.

Daley, Thelma T. Career Development: A Cooperative Thrust of the School and Its Community. In *McClure, L. and Buan, C., eds.*, 1973, pp. 85–92.

Dalrymple, Brent B. Risk Analysis Applied to Commodity Speculation. *J. Econ. Bus.*, Winter 1973, *25*(2), pp. 127–30.

Dalrymple, Dana G. and Rice, E. B. Review of Small Farmer Credit in Developing Nations. *Agr. Finance Rev.*, July 1973, *34*, pp. 35–37.

Dalton, G. E. Adaptation of Farm Management Theory to the Problems of the Small-Scale Farmer in West Africa. In *Ofori, I. M., ed.*, 1973, pp. 114–29.

Dalton, James A. Administered Inflation and Business Pricing: Another Look. *Rev. Econ. Statist.*, November 1973, *55*(4), pp. 516–19.

――――― and Esposito, Louis. The Impact of Liquidity on Merger Activity. *Quart. Rev. Econ. Bus.*, Spring 1973, *13*(1), pp. 15–26.

Dalvi, M. Q. and Beesley, Michael E. The Journey to Work and Cost-benefit Analysis. In *Wolfe, J. N., ed.*, 1973, pp. 195–221.

Daly, George A. and Giertz, Fred J. Pollution Abatement, Pareto Optimality, and the Market Mechanism. In *Boulding, K. E.; Pfaff, M. and Pfaff, A., eds.*, 1973, pp. 350–58.

Daly, Herman E. Electric Power, Employment, and Economic Growth: A Case Study in Growthmania. In *Daly, H. E., ed.*, 1973, pp. 252–77.

――――― The Steady-State Economy: Toward a Political Economy of Biophysical Equilibrium and Moral Growth. In *Daly, H. E., ed.*, 1973, pp. 149–74.

――――― Toward a Steady-State Economy: Introduction. In *Daly, H. E., ed.*, 1973, pp. 1–29.

Daly, M. T. and Webber, M. J. The Growth of the Firm Within the City. *Urban Stud.*, October 1973, *10*(3), pp. 303–17.

Damachi, Ukandi G. Industrial Relations in the Sapele Timber Industry: The Development of

Collective Bargaining. In *Damachi, U. G. and Seibel, H. D., eds.*, 1973, pp. 98–118.

────── Manpower in Nigeria. In *Damachi, U. G. and Seibel, H. D., eds.*, 1973, pp. 81–97.

Dammann, Axel. Monetary Policy in Norway. In *Holbik, K., ed.*, 1973, pp. 329–74.

Danciu, Constantin and Mănescu, Gheorghe. Istoria contemporană a României şi reprezentarea viitorului. (The Contemporary History of Romania and the Representation of the Future. With English summary.) *Stud. Cercet. Econ.*, 1973, (3), pp. 5–18.

Daniel, Donnie L.; Longbrake, William A. and Murphy, Neil B. The Effect of Technology on Bank Economies of Scale for Demand Deposits. *J. Finance*, March 1973, *28*(1), pp. 131–46.

Daniels, John D. and Arpan, Jeffrey. Comparative Home Country Influences on Management Practices Abroad. In *Henley, D. S., ed.*, 1973, pp. 409–19.

Danø, Sven and Rasmussen, Nørregaard. Ragnar Frisch. *Nationalokon. Tidsskr.*, 1973, *111*(1), pp. 5–8.

Darby, Michael R. Paper Recycling and the Stock of Trees. *J. Polit. Econ.*, September-October 1973, *81*(5), pp. 1253–55.

────── **and Karni, Edi.** Free Competition and the Optimal Amount of Fraud. *J. Law Econ.*, April 1973, *16*(1), pp. 67–88.

Darling, Arthur H. Measuring Benefits Generated by Urban Water Parks. *Land Econ.*, February 1973, *49*(1), pp. 22–34.

Darling, John R. and Webb, Don R. The Post-Use Problem—A Response from Management. *J. Bus. Res.*, Summer 1973, *1*(1), pp. 49–56.

Darnell, Jerome C. Bank Mergers: Prices Paid to Marriage Partners. *Fed. Res. Bank Bus. Rev. Phila.*, July 1973, pp. 16–25.

────── Banking Structure: What Does the Future Hold? *Fed. Res. Bank Bus. Rev. Phila.*, August 1973, pp. 3–9.

────── Relaxed Controls: A Bigger Year for Corporate Treasurers in '73? *Fed. Res. Bank Bus. Rev. Phila.*, February 1973, pp. 3–11.

Daroesman, Ruth. An Economic Survey of Bali. *Bull. Indonesian Econ. Stud.*, November 1973, 9 (3), pp. 28–61.

Darvas, Gy. Major Implications of Long-Term Planning on the Fifth Five-Year Plan. *Acta Oecon.*, 1973, *11*(2–3), pp. 149–63.

Das, A. C. and Banerjee, R. M. Theoretical Approach for Measuring Intensity of Unemployment. *Econ. Aff.*, November-December 1973, *18* (11–12), pp. 497–502.

Dasgupta, Partha; Sen, Amartya K. and Starrett, David. Notes on the Measurement of Inequality. *J. Econ. Theory*, April 1973, *6*(2), pp. 180–87.

Das Gupta, Prithwis. Growth of U.S. Population, 1940–1971, in the Light of an Interactive Two-Sex Model. *Demography*, November 1973, *10*(4), pp. 543–65.

────── **and Blake, Judith.** The Fallacy of the Five Million Women: A Re-Estimate: Rejoinder. *Demography*, November 1973, *10*(4), pp. 679–84.

Dasmahapatra, Rajkrishna. Recent Rise in Bank Rate in India and its Probable Consequences. *Econ. Aff.*, June 1973, *18*(6), pp. 299–304.

Dathe, H. M. Cybernetic Models as Aids in Normative Forecasting. In *Blohm, H. and Steinbuch, K., eds.*, 1973, pp. 39–53.

Daub, Mervin. On the Accuracy of Canadian Short-term Economic Forecasts. *Can. J. Econ.*, February 1973, *6*(1), pp. 90–107.

Dave, P. K. and Bharadwaj, V. P. An Empirical Test of Kaldor's Macro Model of Income Distribution for Indian Economy. *Indian Econ. J.*, January-March 1973, *20*(3), pp. 515–20.

Davenport, Lawrence F. Career Education and the Black Student. In *McClure, L. and Buan, C., eds.*, 1973, pp. 177–84.

Davenport, Michael. Leverage and the Cost of Capital: Reply. *Economica, N.S.*, August 1973, *40*(159), pp. 321.

David, F. J. L. Floodplain Lands for Parks and Recreation: A Case Study of Milwaukee. *Land Econ.*, May 1973, *49*(2), pp. 221–26.

David, Martin. Increased Taxation with Increased Acceptability—A Discussion of Net Worth Taxation as a Federal Revenue Alternative. *J. Finance*, May 1973, *28*(2), pp. 481–95.

David, Michel. I dodici tratti caratteristici dell'ipermercato alla francese. (Twelve Characteristics of the French Hypermarket. With English summary.) *L'Impresa*, 1973, *15*(9–10), pp. 634–39.

David, Paul A. Just How Misleading are Official Exchange Rate Conversions?: Reply. *Econ. J.*, December 1973, *83*(332), pp. 1267–76.

────── The 'Horndal Effect' in Lowell, 1834-1856: A Short-run Learning Curve for Integrated Cotton Textile Mills. *Exploration Econ. Hist.*, Winter 1973, *10*(2), pp. 131–50.

────── **and Abramovitz, Moses.** Economic Growth in America: Historical Parables and Realities. *De Economist*, May-June 1973, *121*(3), pp. 251–72.

────── **and Abramovitz, Moses.** Reinterpreting Economic Growth: Parables and Realities. *Amer. Econ. Rev.*, May 1973, *63*(2), pp. 428–39.

David, Wilfred L. Development from Below: Aspects of Local Government and Finance in a Developing Economy—Guyana. In *[Hicks, U.]*, 1973, pp. 304–27.

Davidson, A. T. National Water Policy: The Canadian Experience. *Amer. J. Agr. Econ.*, December 1973, *55*(5), pp. 1017–21.

Davidson, B. R. The Relationship Between the Price of Wool and the Relative Profitability of Sheep and Cattle Grazing in Australia and its Possible Effect on the Future Supplies of Wool and Beef. *Rev. Marketing Agr. Econ.*, March 1973, *41*(1), pp. 3–19.

Davidson, Martin J. Technological Risk Assumption Corporations: Reply. *J. Econ. Issues*, March 1973, *7*(1), pp. 124–30.

Davidson, Paul. Inequality and the Double Bluff. *Ann. Amer. Acad. Polit. Soc. Sci.*, September 1973, *409*, pp. 24–33.

────── **and Weintraub, Sidney.** Money as Cause and Effect. *Econ. J.*, December 1973, *83*(332), pp. 1117–32.

Davies, David G. A Critical Discussion of I.L.O. Report on Employment in Kenya. *Pakistan Develop. Rev.*, Autumn 1973, *12*(3), pp. 283–92.

Davies, J. Clarence, III. Standard-Setting. In *En-*

thoven, A. C. and Freeman, A. M., III, eds., 1973, pp. 107–11.

Davies, J. R. On the Sales Maximization Hypothesis: A Comment. *J. Ind. Econ.,* April 1973, *21*(2), pp. 200–202.

Davies, M. Field Systems of South Wales. In *Baker, A. R. H. and Butlin, R. A., eds.,* 1973, pp. 480–529.

Davies, R. W. Research, Development, and Innovation in the Soviet Economy, 1968–1970. In *Edge, D. O. and Wolfe, J. N., eds.,* 1973, pp. 241–61.

Davies, S. W. and Scott, T. W. K. Forecasting Industrial Production. *Nat. Inst. Econ. Rev.,* November 1973, (66), pp. 54–68.

Davis, B. E.; Caccappolo, G. J. and Chaudry, M. A. An Econometric Planning Model for American Telephone and Telegraph Company. *Bell J. Econ. Manage. Sci.,* Spring 1973, *4*(1), pp. 29–56.

Davis, Bob; Schreiner, Dean and Muncrief, George. Solid Waste Management for Rural Areas: Analysis of Costs and Service Requirements. *Amer. J. Agr. Econ.,* Part I, November 1973, *55*(4), pp. 567–76.

Davis, Carlton G. Traditional Graduate Admission Standards as Constraints to Increasing the Supply of Black Professional Agriculturalists: The Florida Experience. *Amer. J. Agr. Econ.,* December 1973, *55*(5), pp. 952–66.

Davis, Donald L. A Pedogogical Tool for Manpower Analysis. *Intermountain Econ. Rev.,* Spring 1973, *4*(1), pp. 40–52.

Davis, E. G. A Dynamic Model of the Regulated Firm with a Price Adjustment Mechanism. *Bell J. Econ. Manage. Sci.,* Spring 1973, *4*(1), pp. 270–82.

_____; **Dunn, D. M. and Williams, W. H.** Ambiguities in the Cross-Section Analysis of Per Share Financial Data. *J. Finance,* December 1973, *28*(5), pp. 1241–48.

Davis, E. W. and Yeomans, K. A. Competition and Credit Control: The Rubicon and Beyond. *Lloyds Bank Rev.,* January 1973, (107), pp. 44–55.

Davis, Harlan and Sazama, Geraldo W. Land Taxation and Land Reform. *Econ. Develop. Cult. Change,* Part I, July 1973, *21*(4), pp. 642–54.

Davis, Harry E. Pension Provisions Affecting the Employment of Older Workers. *Mon. Lab. Rev.,* April 1973, *96*(4), pp. 41–45.

Davis, Jeffrey. The Krzyzaniak and Musgrave Model—Some Further Comments. *Kyklos,* 1973, *26*(2), pp. 387–94.

Davis, Joseph M. Health and the Education-Earnings Relationship. *Mon. Lab. Rev.,* April 1973, *96*(4), pp. 61–63.

Davis, Karen. Hospital Costs and the Medicare Program. *Soc. Sec. Bull.,* August 1973, *36*(8), pp. 18–36.

_____ Theories of Hospital Inflation: Some Empirical Evidence. *J. Human Res.,* Spring 1973, *8*(2), pp. 181–201.

Davis, Keith. Can Business Afford to Ignore Social Responsibilities? In *Klein, W. H. and Murphy, D. C., eds.,* 1973, pp. 270–76.

Davis, Kingsley. Zero Population Growth: The Goal and the Means. In *Olson, M. and Landsberg, H. H., eds.,* 1973, pp. 15–30.

Davis, Lance E. Secular Price Change in Historical Perspective: Comment. *J. Money, Credit, Bank-*

ing, Part II, February 1973, *5*(1), pp. 270–73.

Davis, Lawrence S.; Thompson, Emmett F. and Richards, Douglas F. The South's Third Forest: A Critique. *Land Econ.,* February 1973, *49*(1), pp. 105–09.

Davis, Mark W. Cash Flow Analysis for Feedlot Operations. *Manage. Account.,* June 1973, *54*(12), pp. 38–41.

Davis, Otto A., et al. An Empirical Study of the NAB-JOBS Program. *Public Policy,* Spring 1973, *21*(2), pp. 235–62.

_____ **and Whinston, Andrew B.** The Economics of Urban Renewal. In *Grieson, R. E., ed.,* 1973, pp. 163–77.

Davis, Robert K. and Hanke, Steve H. Conventional and Unconventional Alternatives for Water Supply Management. *Water Resources Res.,* August 1973, *9*(4), pp. 861–70.

_____ Potential for Marginal Cost Pricing in Water Resource Management. *Water Resources Res.,* August 1973, *9*(4), pp. 808–25.

Davis, Steven I. A Buyer's Market in Eurodollars. *Harvard Bus. Rev.,* May-June 1973, *51*(3), pp. 119–30.

Davis, T. L. F. Fertility Differentials among the Tribal Groups of Sierra Leone. *Population Stud.,* November 1973, *27*(3), pp. 501–14.

Davison, Cecil W. and Martin, Neil R., Jr. Sensitivity of Beef Quantity and Prices—1980 Preview. *Ill. Agr. Econ.,* July 1973, *13*(2), pp. 33–37.

Dawson, Lyndon E., Jr. and Moore, Charles T. Psychometric Measures of Inter-Media Advertising Effectiveness: A Case Study. *Marquette Bus. Rev.,* Summer 1973, *17*(2), pp. 73–83.

Dawson, R. M. Canadian Trade and Tariff Policy as it Relates to the Pacific Rim. In *Canadian Agricultural Economics Society,* 1973, pp. 43–48.

Day, C. L. Changes in Rates of Return: A Cross-Section Study. *Oxford Bull. Econ. Statist.,* May 1973, *35*(2), pp. 135–52.

Day, George S. The Role of the Consumer in the Corporate Social Audit. In *Dierkes, M. and Bauer, R. A., eds.,* 1973, pp. 117–29.

Day, John C. A Linear Programming Approach to Floodplain Land Use Planning in Urban Areas. *Amer. J. Agr. Econ.,* May 1973, *55*(2), pp. 165–74.

Day, Lincoln H. Social Consequences of Zero Economic Growth. In *Weintraub, A.; Schwartz, E. and Aronson, J. R., eds.,* 1973, pp. 116–40.

_____ A Survey of Population Textbooks. *Demography,* November 1973, *10*(4), pp. 693–96.

Day, Richard H. Recursive Programming Models: A Brief Introduction. In *Judge, G. G. and Takayama, T., eds.,* 1973, pp. 329–44.

_____ **and Nelson, Jon P.** A Class of Dynamic Models for Describing and Projecting Industrial Development. *J. Econometrics,* June 1973, *1*(2), pp. 155–90.

_____ **and Robinson, Stephen M.** Economic Decisions with L** Utility. In *Cochrane, J. L. and Zeleny, M., eds.,* 1973, pp. 84–92.

Dayananda, R. A. and Evans, I. G. Bayesian Acceptance-Sampling Schemes for Two-Sided Tests of the Mean of a Normal Distribution of Known Variance. *J. Amer. Statist. Assoc.,* March 1973, *68*(341), pp. 131–36.

Deagle, Edwin A., Jr. Contemporary Professionalism and Future Military Leadership. *Ann. Amer. Acad. Polit. Soc. Sci.,* March 1973, *406,* pp. 162–70.

Deaglio, Mario. Differenze di instruzione e differenze di retribuzione in una società ugualitaria. (Education and Pay Structures in an Egalitarian Society. With English summary.) *L'Industria,* January-June 1973, (1–2), pp. 134–75.

De Alessi, Louis. Private Property and Dispersion of Ownership in Large Corporations. *J. Finance,* September 1973, *28*(4), pp. 839–51.

Dean, Geral and Fiorentino, Raúl. Política agraria para la economía yerbatera como contribución al desarrollo agrícola misionero, un enfoque estructural. (Agricultural Policy for the Argentine Yerba Mate Industry and the Small Farm Sector of Misiones, a Structural Approach. With English summary.) *Económica,* September-December 1973, *19*(3), pp. 265–91.

Dean, Gerald W., et al. Programming Model for Evaluating Economic and Financial Feasibility of Irrigation Projects with Extended Development Periods. *Water Resources Res.,* June 1973, *9*(3), pp. 546–55.

Dean, James M. Redistribution and Tax Concessions for Charitable Contributions. *Public Finance,* 1973, *28*(3–4), pp. 371–76.

Dean, James W. and Tower, Edward. Internal and External Balance in an "Almost Classical" World: Rejoinder. *Western Econ. J.,* June 1973, *11*(2), pp. 240.

——— **and Tower, Edward.** More on Internal and External Balance in an "Almost Classical" World. *Western Econ. J.,* June 1973, *11*(2), pp. 232–37.

Dean, Joel. Profit Performance Measurement of Division Managers. In *Thomas, W. E., Jr., ed.,* 1973, pp. 428–35.

Deane, Phyllis. The Role of Capital in the Industrial Revolution. *Exploration Econ. Hist.,* Summer 1973, *10*(4), pp. 349–64.

——— **and Cole, W. A.** British Economic Growth, 1967. In *Tranter, N. L., ed.,* 1973, pp. 127–35.

Deane, R. S. Macroeconometric Model Simulation: Contexts and Uses. In *Deane, R. S., ed.,* 1972, pp. 7–12.

——— Macroeconometric Relationships within New Zealand: A Preliminary Examination. In *Powell, A. A. and Williams, R. A., eds.,* 1973, pp. 85–114.

———; **Lumsden, M. A. and Sturm, A. B.** Some Simulation Experiments with a New Zealand Model. In *Deane, R. S., ed.,* 1972, pp. 15–64.

Dearden, John. 'Time Span' in Management Control. In *Thomas, W. E., Jr., ed.,* 1973, pp. 340–53.

——— The Impact of Computers on Corporation Management. In *The Diebold Group, Inc.,* 1973, pp. 11–18.

Deardorff, Alan V. The Gains from Trade in and out of Steady-state Growth. *Oxford Econ. Pap.,* July 1973, *25*(2), pp. 173–91.

Debache, Joëlle; Kende, Pierre and Detourbet, Christine. Vers une description du mode de vie au moyen d'indicateurs. (Towards a Description of Life Styles Through Indicators. With English summary.) *Consommation,* April-June 1973, *20* (2), pp. 117–30.

De Boer, John. Sacred Cows: Comment. *Amer. J. Agr. Econ.,* May 1973, *55*(2), pp. 341–42.

De Bruyne, L. De Antwerpse luchthavenbehoeften 1970–1980. (The Air Transport Needs of Antwerp. With English summary.) *Econ. Soc. Tijdschr.,* June 1973, *27*(3), pp. 227–43.

Decanio, Stephen. Cotton "Overproduction" in Late Nineteenth-Century Southern Agriculture. *J. Econ. Hist.,* September 1973, *33*(3), pp. 608–33.

De Castro, Tina. Gli insediamenti industriali: documentazione. (Industrial Localization. With English summary.) *L'Impresa,* 1973, *15*(2), pp. 132–44.

Deck, Beryl; Kichline, James L. and Laub, P. Michael. Yields on Recently Offered Corporate Bonds. *Fed. Res. Bull.,* May 1973, *59*(5), pp. 336–37.

Decker, Robert L. The Saving Gap and Foreign Aid. *Intermountain Econ. Rev.,* Fall 1973, *4*(2), pp. 45–54.

——— Success and Attrition Characteristics in Graduate Studies. *J. Econ. Educ.,* Spring 1973, *4* (2), pp. 130–37.

De Coorde, F. and Reyns, C. Accountancy versus Management. (In Flemish. With English summary.) *Econ. Soc. Tijdschr.,* June 1973, *27*(3), pp. 277–86.

DeCoursey, Donn G. Application of Discriminant Analysis in Design Review. *Water Resources Res.,* February 1973, *9*(1), pp. 93–102.

Dee, Norbert, et al. An Environmental Evaluation System for Water Resource Planning. *Water Resources Res.,* June 1973, *9*(3), pp. 523–35.

Deets, M. King and Cheng, Pao L. Portfolio Returns and the Random Walk Theory: Reply. *J. Finance,* June 1973, *28*(3), pp. 742–45.

——— **and Cheng, Pao L.** Systematic Risk and the Horizon Problem. *J. Financial Quant. Anal.,* March 1973, *8*(2), pp. 299–316.

De Gregori, Thomas R. Prodigality or Parsimony: The False Dilemma in Economic Development Theory. *J. Econ. Issues,* June 1973, *7*(2), pp. 259–66.

DeGroot, Morris H. Doing What Comes Naturally: Interpreting a Tail Area as a Posterior Probability or as a Likelihood Ratio. *J. Amer. Statist. Assoc.,* December 1973, *68*(344), pp. 966–69.

——— **and Cyert, Richard M.** An Analysis of Cooperation and Learning in a Duopoly Context. *Amer. Econ. Rev.,* March 1973, *63*(1), pp. 24–37.

Deiss, Joseph. Les frais de transport et les termes de l'échange international. (Transport Costs and International Terms of Trade. With English summary.) *Schweiz. Z. Volkswirtsch. Statist.,* June 1973, *109*(2), pp. 201–22.

DeJong, Gordon F. and Donnelly, William L. Public Welfare and Migration. *Soc. Sci. Quart.,* September 1973, *54*(2), pp. 329–44.

Dekker, P. G. Economische oorlogvoering. Enige opmerkingen over boycot en embargo. (Economic Warfare: A Note on Boycott and Embargo. With English summary.) *De Economist,* July-August 1973, *121*(4), pp. 387–402.

Delaney, Nancy J. and Glantz, Frederic B. Changes in Nonwhite Residential Patterns in Large Metropolitan Areas, 1960 and 1970. *New Eng. Econ. Rev.,* March-April 1973, pp. 2–13.

De La Vinelle, Duquesne. Aspetti economici sociali e culturali delle multinazionali. (Socio-Economic

Features of Multinational Enterprises. With English summary.) *Mondo Aperto,* December 1973, *27*(6), pp. 397–414.

Deleau, Michel; Guesnerie, Roger and Malgrange, Pierre. Planification, incertitude et politique économique. L'operation Optimix. Une procédure formalisée d'adaptation du Plan à l'aléa. (Planning Uncertainty and Economic Policy. A Formalized Procedure: "Optimix." With English summary.) *Revue Écon.,* September 1973, *24*(5), pp. 801–36.

_____; **Guesnerie, Roger and Malgrange, Pierre.** Planification, incertitude et politique économique. II—L'opération Optimix: Résultats numériques. (Planning, Uncertainty and Economic Policy. II—Optimix Operation: Numerical Results. With English summary.) *Revue Écon.,* November 1973, *24*(6), pp. 1072–1103.

De Lembre, E. De cash-flow. (Cash-Flow. With English summary.) *Econ. Soc. Tijdschr.,* February 1973, *27*(1), pp. 23–38.

Delgado, Oscar. Revolution, Reform, Conservatism: Three Types of Agrarian Structure. In *Wilber, C. K., ed.,* 1973, pp. 173–86.

Dell, Sidney. An Appraisal of UNCTAD III. *World Devel.,* May 1973, *1*(5), pp. 1–13.

_____ Regional Groupings and Developing Countries. In *Streeten, P., ed.,* 1973, pp. 198–215.

Dellacasa, Giorgio. Teoria e politica monetaria nel pensiero di Milton Friedman. Parte Seconda (Milton Friedman and Modern Monetary Theory and Policy. With English summary.) *Econ. Int.,* February 1973, *26*(1), pp. 46–72.

Dellalfar, William and Bhagwati, Jagdish N. The Brain Drain and Income Taxation. *World Devel.,* February 1973, *1*(1-2), pp. 94–101.

Dell'Amore, Giordano. Attualità del risparmio e insegnamenti della storia della Cassa di Risparmio delle Provincie Lombarde. (The Present Need for Saving and the Lessons from the History of the Cassa di Risparmio delle Provincie Lombarde. With English summary.) *Bancaria,* November 1973, *29*(11), pp. 1329–37.

Dell'Atti, Angelo. Un nuovo modello logistico per la rappresentazione dei fenomeni sociali. (A New Logistic Model for the Representation of Social Phenomena. With English summary.) *Rivista Int. Sci. Econ. Com.,* May 1973, *20*(5), pp. 479–82.

Dellepiane, Nicola. Localizzazione delle attività interne: metodi quantitativi di ottimizzazione. (Locating facilities: Optimizing Techniques. With English summary.) *L'Impresa,* 1973, *15*(2), pp. 157–63.

DeLorme, Charles D., Jr. and Allsbrook, Ogden O., Jr. Monetary Policy, Price Expectations, and the Case of a Positively-Sloped *IS* Curve. *Rivista Int. Sci. Econ. Com.,* March 1973, *20*(3), pp. 278–85.

_____ **and Allsbrook, Ogden O., Jr.** A Reconsideration of Interest Rates, Money Growth Rates, Inflation and the 'Ease' or 'Tightness' of Money: Comment. *Kyklos,* 1973, *26*(1), pp. 151–55.

Dematté, Claudio. Savings Banks and Savings Facilities in African Countries: Mali. In *Alberici, A. and Baravelli, M., eds.,* 1973, pp. 61–62.

Dematteis, Giuseppe. Politica regionale e scelte aziendali nella localizzazione delle industrie in Gran Bretagna. (Regional Politics and Firm Selec-

tions in the Localization of Industry in Great Britain. With English summary.) *L'Impresa,* 1973, *15*(2), pp. 113–22.

Demery, David and Demery, Lionel. Cross-Section Evidence for Balanced and Unbalanced Growth. *Rev. Econ. Statist.,* November 1973, *55*(4), pp. 459–64.

Demery, Lionel and Demery, David. Cross-Section Evidence for Balanced and Unbalanced Growth. *Rev. Econ. Statist.,* November 1973, *55*(4), pp. 459–64.

_____ **and Gorman, D.** The Classical and Factor Proportions Trade Patterns:—A Note. *Manchester Sch. Econ. Soc. Stud.,* September 1973, *41*(3), pp. 343.

Demsetz, Harold. Industry Structure, Market Rivalry, and Public Policy. *J. Law Econ.,* April 1973, *16*(1), pp. 1–9.

_____ Joint Supply and Price Discrimination. *J. Law Econ.,* October 1973, *16*(2), pp. 389–405.

_____ The Private Production of Public Goods: Reply. *J. Law Econ.,* October 1973, *16*(2), pp. 413–15.

_____ **and Alchian, Armen A.** The Property Rights Paradigm. *J. Econ. Hist.,* March 1973, *33*(1), pp. 16–27.

Demski, Joel S. Rational Choice of Accounting Method for a Class of Partnerships. *J. Acc. Res.,* Autumn 1973, *11*(2), pp. 176–90.

Demuth, Richard H. Relations with Other Multilateral Agencies. In *Lewis, J. P. and Kapur, I., eds.,* 1973, pp. 133–38.

Denenberg, Herbert S. and Cummins, J. David. Insurance and Reciprocity: Reply. *J. Risk Ins.,* March 1973, *40*(1), pp. 141–42.

Denison, Edward F. Is Growth Obsolete? Comment. In *Moss, M., ed.,* 1973, pp. 546–48.

_____ A Proposal for a System of Economic and Social Accounts: Comment. In *Moss, M., ed.,* 1973, pp. 159–60.

_____ The Shift to Services and the Rate of Productivity Change. *Surv. Curr. Bus.,* October 1973, *53*(10), pp. 20–35.

Dennis, Charles N. An Investigation Into the Effects of Independent Investor Relations Firms on Common Stock Prices. *J. Finance,* May 1973, *28*(2), pp. 373–80.

_____ The Information Content of Daily Market Indicators: Comment. *J. Financial Quant. Anal.,* March 1973, *8*(2), pp. 193–94..

Denny, David L. and Stein, Daniel D. Recent Developments in Trade between the U.S. and the P.R.C.: A Legal and Economic Perspective. *Law Contemp. Probl.,* Summer-Autumn 1973, *38*(2), pp. 260–73.

Dent, J. B. and Pearse, R. A. Operations Research, Agricultural Research and Agricultural Practice. In *Ross, M., ed.,* 1973, pp. 641–53.

Denton, Frank T. A Simulation Model of Month-to-Month Labor Force Movement in Canada. *Int. Econ. Rev.,* June 1973, *14*(2), pp. 293–311.

_____ **and Oksanen, Ernest H.** Data Revisions and Forecasting Accuracy: An Econometric Analysis Based on Preliminary and Revised National Accounting Estimates. *Rev. Income Wealth,* December 1973, *19*(4), pp. 437–52.

_____ **and Spencer, Byron G.** A Simulation Analysis

of the Effects of Population Change on a Neoclassical Economy. *J. Polit. Econ.*, Part I, March-April 1973, *81*(2), pp. 356–75.

Dentzer, William T. A Revised Regulatory Framework: Discussion. In *Federal Reserve Bank of Boston*, 1973, pp. 209–15.

Depre, F. and Vanthienen, L. Methodologie voor empirish onderzoek op de kapitaalmarkt. (With English summary.) *Tijdschr. Econ.*, 1973, *18*(4), pp. 629–46.

Derban, L. A. K. The Impact of Health and Nutrition on Agricultural Production in West Africa. In *Ofori, I. M., ed.*, 1973, pp. 26–32.

Derber, Milton. Some Further Thoughts on the Historical Study of Industrial Democracy. *Labor Hist.*, Fall 1973, *14*(4), pp. 599–611.

——, et al. Bargaining and Budget Making in Illinois Public Institutions. *Ind. Lab. Relat. Rev.*, October 1973, *27*(1), pp. 49–62.

Desai, Mahendra D.; Charan, A. S. and Pathak, Mahesh T. Development of Agriculture in Backward Regions of Gujarat: Facts and Issues. *Artha-Vikas*, January-July 1973, *9*(1–2), pp. 100–38.

Desai, Meghnad. Growth Cycles and Inflation in a Model of the Class Struggle. *J. Econ. Theory*, December 1973, *6*(6), pp. 527–45.

Desai, Padma. Soviet Industrial Production: Estimates of Gross Outputs by Branches and Groups. *Oxford Bull. Econ. Statist.*, May 1973, *35*(2), pp. 153–71.

—— Third World Social Scientists in Santiago. *World Devel.*, September 1973, *1*(9), pp. 57–65.

Desai, Satish. Professional-Pool Concept for Company Groups. *Marquette Bus. Rev.*, Spring 1973, *17*(1), pp. 30–34.

Desai, V. R. M. Trends and Progress of Busy Season 1972–73. *Econ. Aff.*, June 1973, *18*(6), pp. 275–80.

DeSalvo, Joseph S. Effects of the Property Tax on Operating and Investment Decisions of Rental Property Owners: Reply. *Nat. Tax J.*, March 1973, *26*(1), pp. 129–31.

Deschamps, Robert. Risk Aversion and Demand Functions. *Econometrica*, May 1973, *41*(3), pp. 455–65.

Despres, Emile. American Aid and Western European Recovery. In *Despres, E.*, 1973, pp. 28–38.

—— Britain's Foreign Exchange Policy. In *Despres, E.*, 1973, pp. 3–12.

—— Capital Movements, Gold, and Balance of Payments. In *Despres, E.*, 1973, pp. 209–12.

—— Determining the Size of a Development Plan: Pakistan. In *Despres, E.*, 1973, pp. 99–132.

—— Dimensions and Dilemmas of Economic Development. In *Despres, E.*, 1973, pp. 89–98.

—— The Dollar and World Liquidity: A Minority View. In *Despres, E.*, 1973, pp. 266–78.

—— Financing of Development: Malaysia. In *Despres, E.*, 1973, pp. 154–83.

—— Germany's Exchange Control Mechanism. In *Despres, E.*, 1973, pp. 13–27.

—— Gold—Where to from Here? In *Despres, E.*, 1973, pp. 279–86.

—— Inflation and Development: Brazil. In *Despres, E.*, 1973, pp. 184–206.

—— International Financial Intermediation. In *Despres, E.*, 1973, pp. 257–65.

—— The Mechanism for Adjustment in International Payments—The Lessons of Postwar Experience. In *Despres, E.*, 1973, pp. 45–59.

—— Price Distortions and Development Planning: Pakistan. In *Despres, E.*, 1973, pp. 133–45.

—— A Proposal for Strengthening the Dollar. In *Despres, E.*, 1973, pp. 213–35.

—— The Significance of the European Common Market to the American Economy. In *Despres, E.*, 1973, pp. 60–86.

—— Toward the Demonetization of Gold. In *Despres, E.*, 1973, pp. 236–56.

—— The Welfare State and Development Expenditure: Pakistan. In *Despres, E.*, 1973, pp. 146–53.

—— Western Europe's Long-Term Balance-of-Payments Problem. In *Despres, E.*, 1973, pp. 39–44.

Detourbet, Christine; Debache, Joëlle and Kende, Pierre. Vers une description du mode de vie au moyen d'indicateurs. (Towards a Description of Life Styles Through Indicators. With English summary.) *Consommation*, April-June 1973, *20* (2), pp. 117–30.

De Tray, Dennis N. Child Quality and the Demand for Children. *J. Polit. Econ.*, Part II, March-April 1973, *81*(2), pp. S70–95.

Devine, Edward J. and Slavin, Richard H. Multi-Discipline Design Teams for Transportation Facilities. *Land Econ.*, August 1973, *49*(3), pp. 241–50.

Devore, Jay L. Reconstructing a Noisy Markov Chain. *J. Amer. Statist. Assoc.*, June 1973, *68*(342), pp. 394–98.

—— Reconstructing a Noisy Markov Chain Using Near-Neighbor Rules. *J. Amer. Statist. Assoc.*, September 1973, *68*(343), pp. 599–602.

Dewald, William G. The High Employment Budget and Overwithholding in 1972. *Ohio State U. Bull. Bus. Res.*, March 1973, *48*(3), pp. 1–3, 7.

—— The Term Structure of Interest Rates in Australia, 1952–1966. *Econ. Anal. Pol.*, September 1973, *4*(2), pp. 1–17.

Dewey, Donald. Imperfect Competition: Dewey and Heuss: Reply. *Weltwirtsch. Arch.*, 1973, *109* (3), pp. 517–18.

De Wulf, Luc H. and Bird, Richard M. Taxation and Income Distribution in Latin America: A Critical Review of Empirical Studies. *Int. Monet. Fund Staff Pap.*, November 1973, *20*(3), pp. 639–82.

Dhrymes, Phoebus J. Restricted and Unrestricted Reduced Forms: Asymptotic Distribution and Relative Efficiency. *Econometrica*, January 1973, *41*(1), pp. 119–34.

—— A Simple Proof of the Asymptotic Efficiency of 3SLS Relative to 2SLS Estimators. *Western Econ. J.*, June 1973, *11*(2), pp. 187–90.

—— Small Sample and Asymptotic Relations Between Maximum Likelihood and Three Stage Least Squares Estimators. *Econometrica*, March 1973, *41*(2), pp. 357–64.

Diamond, Peter A. Consumption Externalities and Imperfect Corrective Pricing. *Bell J. Econ. Manage. Sci.*, Autumn 1973, *4*(2), pp. 526–38.

—— Taxation and Public Production in a Growth Setting. In *Mirrlees, J. A. and Stern, N. H., eds.*, 1973, pp. 215–35.

—— **and Mirrlees, James A.** Aggregate Production

with Consumption Externalities. *Quart. J. Econ.,* February 1973, *87*(1), pp. 1–24.

Diaz-Alejandro, Carlos. The Andean Common Market: Gestation and Outlook. In *Eckaus, R. S. and Rosenstein-Rodan, P. N., eds.,* 1973, pp. 293–326.

———— Labour Productivity and Other Characteristics of Cement Plants—An International Comparison. In *[Rosenstein-Rodan, P.],* 1973, pp. 283–315.

Dick, Charles L., Jr.; Downes, David H. and Carleton, Willard T. Financial Policy Models: Theory and Practice. *J. Financial Quant. Anal.,* December 1973, *8*(5), pp. 691–709.

Dickhaut, John W. Alternative Information Structures and Probability Revisions. *Accounting Rev.,* January 1973, *48*(1), pp. 61–79.

Dickinson, Jonathan G. and Dickinson, Katherine P. Labor Force Participation of Wives: The Effects of Components of Husbands' Income. In *Mandell, L., et al., eds.,* 1973, pp. 233–52.

Dickinson, Katherine P. and Dickinson, Jonathan G. Labor Force Participation of Wives: The Effects of Components of Husbands' Income. In *Mandell, L., et al., eds.,* 1973, pp. 233–52.

Dickinson, Neal J. Water Development and Urban Development in Africa. In *Aislabie, C., ed.,* 1973, pp. 34–48.

Dickman, A. B. Exchequer Financing and the Money Supply. *S. Afr. J. Econ.,* June 1973, *41*(2), pp. 154–57.

———— The Financing of Industrial Development in South Africa. *S. Afr. J. Econ.,* December 1973, *41*(4), pp. 373–400.

Diebold, John. Business, Government and Science: The Need for a Fresh Look. *Foreign Aff.,* April 1973, *51*(3), pp. 555–72.

———— Computers in Publishing. In *The Diebold Group, Inc.,* 1973, pp. 298–309.

Diebold, William, Jr. Implications for Integration of the World Economy: Comment. In *Krause, L. B. and Salant, W. S., eds.,* 1973, pp. 269–75.

Diéguez, Héctor L. and Porto, Alberto. Un modelo simple de equilibrio general: cambio tecnológico. (A Simple Model of General Equilibrium Technological Change. With English summary.) *Económica,* January-April 1973, *19*(1), pp. 45–69.

Dierkes, Meinolf, et al. Social Pressure and Business Actions. In *Dierkes, M. and Bauer, R. A., eds.,* 1973, pp. 57–92.

Dieterlen, Pierre and Durand, Huguette. Monetary Policy in France. In *Holbik, K., ed.,* 1973, pp. 117–60.

Dietrich, J. Kimball and Gutierrez, Alfredo D. An Evaluation of Short-Term Forecasts of Coffee and Cocoa. *Amer. J. Agr. Econ.,* February 1973, *55*(1), pp. 93–99.

Dietz, James L. Paradise Reswitched. *Rev. Radical Polit. Econ.,* Summer 1973, *5*(2), pp. 1–17.

Dietz, John. Enforcement of Anti-Trust Laws in the EEC. In *Henley, D. S., ed.,* 1973, pp. 185–213.

Dietz, Stephens. Get More Out of Your Brand Management. *Harvard Bus. Rev.,* July-August 1973, *51*(4), pp. 127–36.

Dietzer, H. J.; Colantoni, C. S. and Cooper, W. W. Budgetary Disclosure and Social Accounting. In *Dierkes, M. and Bauer, R. A., eds.,* 1973, pp. 365–86.

Diewert, W. E. Afriat and Revealed Preference Theory. *Rev. Econ. Stud.,* July 1973, *40*(3), pp. 419–25.

———— Functional Forms for Profit and Transformation Functions. *J. Econ. Theory,* June 1973, *6*(3), pp. 284–316.

Dillard, Dudley. Capitalism. In *Wilber, C. K., ed.,* 1973, pp. 60–67.

Di Loreto, Sandro. Il problema dei costi nell'instituto di credito ordinario. Un tentativo di applicazione di procedimenti analitici di calcolo e di controllo–III. (The Cost Problem of Commercial Banks. An Attempt to Apply Analytical Calculation and Control Processes-III. With English summary.) *Bancaria,* September 1973, *29*(9), pp. 1094–1112.

———— Il problema dei costi nell'instituto di credito ordinario. Un tentativo di applicazione di procedimenti analitici di calcolo e di controllo–II. (The Cost Problem of Commercial Banks. An Attempt to Apply Analytical Calculation and Control Processes–II. With English summary.) *Bancaria,* August 1973, *29*(8), pp. 936–86.

———— Il problema dei costi nell'instituto di credito ordinario. Un tentativo di applicazione di procedimenti analitici di calcolo e di controllo-I. (The Cost Problem of Commercial Banks. An Attempt to Apply Analytical Calculation and Control Processes-I. With English summary.) *Bancaria,* July 1973, *29*(7), pp. 820–31.

Dimling, John A., Jr. A View from the National Association of Broadcasters. In *Park, R. E., ed.,* 1973, pp. 19–29.

Dince, Robert R. Finance and Banking: Refereed Papers II: Discussion. *J. Finance,* May 1973, *28*(2), pp. 541–44.

Dinkelbach, Werner and Isermann, Heinz. On Decision Making under Multiple Criteria and under Incomplete Information. In *Cochrane, J. L. and Zeleny, M., eds.,* 1973, pp. 302–12.

Di Noto, M. J. A Sequential Decision Model of Bargaining: Comment. *Western Econ. J.,* September 1973, *11*(3), pp. 371–74.

Di Nuzzo, Vincenzo. Come affrontare il problema della "corporate image." (How to Approach the Problem of "Corporate Image." With English summary.) *L'Impresa,* 1973, *15*(9–10), pp. 527–37.

Ditton, Robert B. and Goodale, Thomas L. Water Quality Perception and the Recreational Uses of Green Bay, Lake Michigan. *Water Resources Res.,* June 1973, *9*(3), pp. 569–79.

Ditwiler, C. Dirck. Environmental Perceptions and Policy Misconceptions. *Amer. J. Agr. Econ.,* August 1973, *55*(3), pp. 477–83.

Divilov, S. Labor Resources and the Comparison of General Economic Indices by Union Republic. *Prob. Econ.,* March 1973, *15*(11), pp. 63–72.

Diwan, Romesh K. Are We Saving Enough for Our Plans? In *Wadhva, C. D., ed.,* 1973, pp. 163–78.

Dixit, Avinash K. Comparative Dynamics from the Point of View of the Dual. In *Parkin, M., ed.,* 1973, pp. 35–46.

———— Models of Dual Economies. In *Mirrlees, J. A. and Stern, N. H., eds.,* 1973, pp. 325–52.

———— The Optimum Factory Town. *Bell J. Econ. Manage. Sci.,* Autumn 1973, *4*(2), pp. 637–51.

Dixon, Daryl A. The Full Employment Budget Surplus Concept as a Tool of Fiscal Analysis in the United States. *Int. Monet. Fund Staff Pap.*, March 1973, *20*(1), pp. 203–26.

Dixon, Donald F. Economic Effects of Exclusive Dealing and Ownership Control: The U.K. Petrol Case Revisited. *Antitrust Bull.*, Summer 1973, *18* (2), pp. 375–90.

――― Public Policy Toward Retailing: Australia. In *Boddewyn, J. J. and Hollander, S. C., eds.*, 1972, pp. 11–35.

Dixon, John. The Changing Role of the Australian Commonwealth Grants Commission: A Reply. *Public Finance*, 1973, *28*(3–4), pp. 420–23.

Dixon, John M. A Multidisciplinary Policy Decision Model for Water Pollution. In *Aislabie, C., ed.*, 1973, pp. 49–60.

Dixon, Orani; Dixon, Peter and Miranowski, John. Insecticide Requirements in an Efficient Agricultural Sector. *Rev. Econ. Statist.*, November 1973, *55*(4), pp. 423–32.

Dixon, Peter; Miranowski, John and Dixon, Orani. Insecticide Requirements in an Efficient Agricultural Sector. *Rev. Econ. Statist.*, November 1973, *55*(4), pp. 423–32.

Dixon, R. J. Regional Specialisation and Trade in the United Kingdom: A Test of Some Hypotheses. *Scot. J. Polit. Econ.*, June 1973, *20*(2), pp. 159–70.

Diz, Adolfo. L'inflazione e il sistema monetario internazionale: Intervento. (Inflation and the International Monetary System: Discussion. With English summary.) *Bancaria*, October 1973, *29* (10), pp. 1220–24.

Dobrescu, Em. Models of Proportions Between the Investment Fund and the Consumption Fund for Forecasting the Development of the Rumanian Economy. *Eastern Europ. Econ.*, Spring 1973, *11* (3), pp. 50–73.

Dobrotă, Niță. Principalele caracteristici ale unei țări în curs de dezvoltare. (The Main Characteristics of a Developing Country. With English summary.) *Stud. Cercet. Econ.*, 1973, (1), pp. 13–26.

――― **and Stan, Sorin.** Investițiile și creditele internaționale—componente importante ale circuitului economic mondial. (International Investments and Credits—Important Components of the World Economic Circulation. With English summary.) *Stud. Cercet. Econ.*, 1973, (4), pp. 149–65.

Dobrov, Gennady M. Science Policy and Assessment in the Soviet Union. *Int. Soc. Sci. J.*, 1973, *25*(3), pp. 305–25.

Dobson, L. Wayne. The Investment of Idle Public Funds: A Review of the Issues. *Nebr. J. Econ. Bus.*, Spring 1973, *12*(2), pp. 3–8.

――― **and Hollenhorst, Jerry.** The Economics of Idle Public Funds Policies: A Reconsideration: A Reply. *Nat. Tax J.*, December 1973, *26*(4), pp. 657–59.

Dobson, R. B. Admissions to the Freedom of the City of York in the Later Middle Ages. *Econ. Hist. Rev., 2nd Ser.*, February 1973, *26*(1), pp. 1–22.

Dobson, Steven W. The Term Structure of Interest Rates and the Maturity Composition of the Government Debt: The Canadian Case. *Can. J. Econ.*, August 1973, *6*(3), pp. 319–31.

Dodds, Wellesley. An Application of the Bass Model

in Long-Term New Product Forecasting. *J. Marketing Res.*, August 1973, *10*(3), pp. 308–11.

Dodge, Norton T. Women in the Soviet Economy. In *Moskoff, W., ed.*, 1973, pp. 290–302.

Dodgson, J. S. External Effects and Secondary Benefits in Road Investment Appraisal. *J. Transp. Econ. Policy*, May 1973, *7*(2), pp. 169–85.

Doeksen, Gerald A. and Little, Charles H. Measurement of Leakage by the Use of an Input-Output Model: Reply. *Amer. J. Agr. Econ.*, Part I, November 1973, *55*(4), pp. 682.

Doeringer, Peter B. and Bosanquet, Nicholas. Is There a Dual Labour Market in Great Britain? *Econ. J.*, June 1973, *83*(330), pp. 421–35.

Doganis, Rigas. Air Transport—A Case Study in International Regulation. *J. Transp. Econ. Policy*, May 1973, *7*(2), pp. 109–33.

Doggett, Kathleen M. and Friedman, Donald J. Legislation for Clean Air: An Indoor Front. *Yale Law J.*, April 1973, *82*(5), pp. 1040–54.

Doherty, Neil and Lees, Dennis. Compensation for Personal Injury. *Lloyds Bank Rev.*, April 1973, (108), pp. 18–32.

Døhlen, Bjarne. The Report of Norwegian Public Collective Bargaining. In *Kaye, S. P. and Marsh, A., eds.*, 1973, pp. 350–64.

Dökmeci, Vedia F. An Optimization Model for a Hierarchical Spatial System. *J. Reg. Sci.*, December 1973, *13*(3), pp. 439–51.

Dolan, Edwin G. Preserving the Wilderness—Public Interest or Special Interest? In *Reynolds, L. G.; Green, G. D. and Lewis, D. R., eds.*, 1973, pp. 231–42.

Doling, J. F. A Two-Stage Model of Tenure Choice in the Housing Market. *Urban Stud.*, June 1973, *10*(2), pp. 199–211.

Doll, Raymond J. and Harshbarger, C. Edward. Farm Prices and Food Prices: The Relevant Issues. *Fed. Res. Bank Kansas City Rev.*, May 1973, pp. 3–10.

Dolphin, Robert. Made in Japan. *Ohio State U. Bull. Bus. Res.*, September 1973, *48*(9), pp. 4–7.

Domański, Ryszard. Structure, Law of Motion, and Optimal Path of Growth of Complex Urban Systems. *Econ. Geogr.*, January 1973, *49*(1), pp. 37–46.

Donaldson, G. F. and McInerney, J. P. Changing Machinery Technology and Agricultural Adjustment. *Amer. J. Agr. Econ.*, December 1973, *55*(5), pp. 829–39.

Donaldson, Loraine and Strangways, Raymond S. Can Ghetto Groceries Price Competitively and Make a Profit? *J. Bus.*, January 1973, *46*(1), pp. 61–65.

Donges, Juergen B. The European Economic Community Approach to Adjustment: Comment. In *Hughes, H., ed.*, 1973, pp. 222–27.

――― Shaping Spain's Export Industry. *World Devel.*, September 1973, *1*(9), pp. 19–37.

Donna, Giorgio. Modelli di sviluppo per una teoria dinamica dell'impresa. (Models of Development for a Dynamic Theory of the Firm. With English summary.) *L'Impresa*, 1973, *15*(3–4), pp. 253–64.

Donnelly, James H., Jr. and Etzel, Michael J. Degrees of Product Newness and Early Trial. *J. Marketing Res.*, August 1973, *10*(3), pp. 295–300.

Donnelly, John T. External Financing and Short-Term Consequences of External Debt Servicing for Brazilian Economic Development, 1947-1968. *J. Devel. Areas,* April 1973, *7*(3), pp. 411–29.

Donnelly, William L. and DeJong, Gordon F. Public Welfare and Migration. *Soc. Sci. Quart.,* September 1973, *54*(2), pp. 329–44.

Donner, Arthur W. and Lazar, Fred. An Econometric Study of Segmented Labor Markets and the Structure of Unemployment: The Canadian Experience. *Int. Econ. Rev.,* June 1973, *14*(2), pp. 312–27.

_____ **and Lazar, Fred.** Some Comments on the Canadian Phillips Curve. *Economica, N.S.,* May 1973, *40*(158), pp. 195–207.

Donovan, J. F. Information Systems for Decision and Control: Discussant 2. In *Ross, M., ed.,* 1973, pp. 185–88.

Dopuch, N. and Ronen, J. The Effects of Alternative Inventory Valuation Methods—An Experimental Study. *J. Acc. Res.,* Autumn 1973, *11*(2), pp. 191–211.

Dorcey, Anthony H. J. Effluent Charges, Information Generation and Bargaining Behavior. *Natural Res. J.,* January 1973, *13*(1), pp. 118–33.

Dore, Ronald P. L'effetto di sviluppo ritardato e il Giappone. (Late Development Effect and Japan. With English summary.) *Rivista Int. Sci. Econ. Com.,* August-September 1973, *20*(8–9), pp. 738–57.

Dorfman, Joseph. Source and Impact of Veblen. In *Rectenwald, H. C., ed.,* 1973, pp. 333–38.

Dorfman, Mark S. and Brightman, Harvey J. Birth Order, Anxiety, Affiliation and the Purchase of Life Insurance: Comment. *J. Risk Ins.,* December 1973, *40*(4), pp. 643–46.

Dorfman, Robert. Economics of Pollution: Discussion. *Amer. Econ. Rev.,* May 1973, *63*(2), pp. 253–56.

_____ Wassily Leontief's Contribution to Economics. *Swedish J. Econ.,* December 1973, *75*(4), pp. 430–49.

Dorling, M. J. Extending the Production-Distribution Model to Handle International Competition in Agriculture. *Can. J. Agr. Econ.,* February 1973, *21*(1), pp. 57–62.

Dorn, Dietmar. Marketing in der Staatswirtschaft. (Marketing in Public Economy. With English summary.) *Z. Wirtschaft. Sozialwissen.,* 1973, *93*(1), pp. 21–33.

Dornbusch, Rudiger. Currency Depreciation, Hoarding, and Relative Prices. *J. Polit. Econ.,* July-August 1973, *81*(4), pp. 893–915.

_____ Devaluation, Money, and Nontraded Goods. *Amer. Econ. Rev.,* December 1973, *63*(5), pp. 871–80.

_____ **and Frenkel, Jacob A.** Inflation and Growth: Alternative Approaches. *J. Money, Credit, Banking,* Part I, February 1973, *5*(1), pp. 141–56.

Dornoff, Ronald J. and Tatham, Ronald L. A Cautionary Note on Innovative Overlap. *J. Marketing Res.,* May 1973, *10*(2), pp. 224–25.

Dorrance, Roy G. and de Carbonnel, Francois E. Information Sources for Planning Decisions. *Calif. Manage. Rev.,* Summer 1973, *15*(4), pp. 42–53.

Dotson, Louis; Summers, Gene F. and Beck, E. M. Effects of Industrial Development on Heads of Households. *Growth Change,* July 1973, *4*(3), pp. 16–19.

Dougherty, Christopher and Selowsky, Marcelo. Measuring the Effects of the Misallocation of Labour. *Rev. Econ. Statist.,* August 1973, *55*(3), pp. 386–90.

Douglas, Aaron J. Stochastic Returns and the Theory of the Firm. *Amer. Econ. Rev.,* May 1973, *63*(2), pp. 129–33.

Douglas, Evan J. Price Strategy Duopoly with Product Variation: Comment. *Kyklos,* 1973, *26*(3), pp. 608–11.

_____ Price Variation Duopoly with Differentiated Products: A Note. *J. Econ. Theory,* December 1973, *6*(6), pp. 618–20.

Douglas, J. J. A Note on the Use of a Modified Input-Output Multiplier for Land Use Evaluation. *Australian J. Agr. Econ.,* April 1973, *17*(1), pp. 68–72.

Douglas, Patricia P. Finance and Investment: Refereed Papers I: Discussion. *J. Finance,* May 1973, *28*(2), pp. 405–06.

Douglas, Paul H. The Problem of Tax Loopholes (or: My Eighteen Years in a Quandary). In *Haveman, R. H. and Hamrin, R. D., eds.,* 1973, pp. 74–81.

Douglas, Susan P. Public Planning of Retail Location in France and Great Britain. In *Boddewyn, J. J. and Hollander, S. C., eds.,* 1972, pp. 145–65.

Dovring, Folke. Distribution of Farm Size and Income: Analysis by Exponential Functions. *Land Econ.,* May 1973, *49*(2), pp. 133–47.

Dowding, A. E. An Introduction to Vocational Training Using Modules of Employable Skills. *Int. Lab. Rev.,* June 1973, *107*(6), pp. 553–57.

Dowling, J. Malcolm, Jr. Wage Determination in Two-Digit Manufacturing Industries: Theory, Test, and Forecast. *Quart. Rev. Econ. Bus.,* Spring 1973, *13*(1), pp. 27–36.

_____ **and Poulson, Barry W.** The Climacteric in U.S. Economic Growth. *Oxford Econ. Pap.,* November 1973, *25*(3), pp. 420–34.

Downes, Beverley. Purchase Taxes and Retail Prices in the United Kingdom. *Appl. Econ.,* September 1973, *5*(3), pp. 199–218.

Downes, Bryan T. Problem-solving in Suburbia: The Basis for Political Conflict. In *Masotti, L. H. and Hadden, J. K., eds.,* 1973, pp. 281–312.

Downes, David H. and Barnea, Amir. A Reexamination of the Empirical Distribution of Stock Price Changes. *J. Amer. Statist. Assoc.,* June 1973, *68*(342), pp. 348–50.

_____; **Carleton, Willard T. and Dick, Charles L., Jr.** Financial Policy Models: Theory and Practice. *J. Financial Quant. Anal.,* December 1973, *8*(5), pp. 691–709.

_____ **and Dyckman, Thomas R.** A Critical Look at the Efficient Market Empirical Research Literature As It Relates to Accounting Information. *Accounting Rev.,* April 1973, *48*(2), pp. 300–17.

Downey, Gerald F. and Macbeth, Thomas G. The Monetary Consequences of Demand Deposit Creation by Mutual Savings Banks—The Commonwealth of Massachusetts Case. *Marquette Bus. Rev.,* Spring 1973, *17*(1), pp. 1–8.

Downing, Paul B. Factors Affecting Commercial

──────; Friedlaender, Ann F. and Swanson, Gerald J. Estimating Sales Tax Revenue Changes in Response to Changes in Personal Income and Sales Tax Rates. *Nat. Tax J.*, March 1973, *26*(1), pp. 103–10.

Duesenberry, James S. Some Observations on Monetary Policy. *Brookings Pap. Econ. Act.*, 1973, (2), pp. 508–14.

Duetsch, Larry L. Elements of Market Structure and the Extent of Suboptimal Capacity. *Southern Econ. J.*, October 1973, *40*(2), pp. 216–23.

────── Research Performance in the Ethical Drug Industry. *Marquette Bus. Rev.*, Fall 1973, *17*(3), pp. 129–43.

Duff, Virginia A. and Tice, Helen Stone. Basic Statistical Data. In *Goldsmith, R. W., ed.*, 1973, pp. 269–342.

Duggar, Jan W. and Beard, Thomas R. The Concept and Measurement of Defensive Open Market Operations. *Miss. Val. J. Bus. Econ.*, Spring 1973, *8*(3), pp. 29–38.

Duker, Jacob M. and Hughes, Charles E. The Black-Owned Life Insurance Company: Issues and Recommendations. *J. Risk Ins.*, June 1973, *40*(2), pp. 221–30.

Dukes, Roland E. and Beaver, William H. Interperiod Tax Allocation and δ-Depreciation Methods: Some Empirical Results. *Accounting Rev.*, July 1973, *48*(3), pp. 549–59.

Duloy, John H.; Kutcher, Gary P. and Norton, Roger D. Investment and Employment Alternatives in the Agricultural District Model. In *Goreux, L. M. and Manne, A. S., eds.*, 1973, pp. 417–33.

────── and Norton, Roger D. CHAC Results: Economic Alternatives for Mexican Agriculture. In *Goreux, L. M. and Manne, A. S., eds.*, 1973, pp. 373–99.

────── and Norton, Roger D. CHAC, A Programming Model of Mexican Agriculture. In *Goreux, L. M. and Manne, A. S., eds.*, 1973, pp. 291–337.

────── and Norton, Roger D. Linking the Agricultural Model and the Economy-Wide Model. In *Goreux, L. M. and Manne, A. S., eds.*, 1973, pp. 435–61.

Dumitru, Georgeta and Fundătură, D. Îmbunătățirea utilizării extensive a fondurilor fixe. (Improving the Extensive Use of Productive Fixed Assets. With English summary.) *Stud. Cercet. Econ.*, 1973, (1), pp. 53–64.

────── and Purcărea, M. Eficiența economică a diversificării producției industriale. (The Economic Efficiency of the Diversification of Industrial Production. With English summary.) *Stud. Cercet. Econ.*, 1973, (2), pp. 63–71.

DuMouchel, William H. Stable Distributions in Statistical Inference: 1. Symmetric Stable Distributions Compared to Other Symmetric Long-Tailed Distributions. *J. Amer. Statist. Assoc.*, June 1973, *68*(342), pp. 469–77.

Duncan, M. W. Union Carbide: A Case Study in Sales to Eastern Europe. In *Thorelli, H. B., ed.*, 1973, pp. 64–70.

Duncan, Otis Dudley and Featherman, David L. Psychological and Cultural Factors in the Process of Occupational Achievement. In *Goldberger, A. S. and Duncan, O. D., eds.*, 1973, pp. 229–53.

Dunlap, Paul R. and Agapos, A. M. Elimination of Urban Blight Through Inverse Proportional Ad Valorem Property Taxation. *Amer. J. Econ. Soc.*, April 1973, *32*(2), pp. 143–52.

Dunlap, Riley E.; Gale, Richard P. and Rutherford, Brent M. Concern for Environmental Rights Among College Students. *Amer. J. Econ. Soc.*, January 1973, *32*(1), pp. 45–60.

Dunlop, John T. Structure of Collective Bargaining. In *Somers, G. G., ed.*, 1973, pp. 10–18.

Dunn, D. M.; Williams, W. H. and Davis, E. G. Ambiguities in the Cross-Section Analysis of Per Share Financial Data. *J. Finance*, December 1973, *28*(5), pp. 1241–48.

Dunn, Robert M., Jr. Canada and Its Economic Discontents. *Foreign Aff.*, October 1973, *52*(1), pp. 119–40.

────── Flexible Exchange Rates and Traded Goods Prices: The Role of Oligopoly Pricing in the Canadian Experience. In *Johnson, H. G. and Swoboda, A. K., eds.*, 1973, pp. 259–80.

den Dunnen, Emile. Monetary Policy in the Netherlands. In *Holbik, K., ed.*, 1973, pp. 282–328.

Dunning, John H. The Determinants of International Production. *Oxford Econ. Pap.*, November 1973, *25*(3), pp. 289–336.

────── Multinational Enterprises and Domestic Capital Formation. *Manchester Sch. Econ. Soc. Stud.*, September 1973, *41*(3), pp. 283–310.

────── Multinational Enterprises and Trade Flows of Developing Countries. In *Streeten, P., ed.*, 1973, pp. 300–20.

Durand, David. Indices of Profitability as Aids to Judgment in Capital Budgeting. *J. Bank Res.*, Winter 1973, *3*(4), pp. 200–19.

Durand, Huguette and Dieterlen, Pierre. Monetary Policy in France. In *Holbik, K., ed.*, 1973, pp. 117–60.

Durbin, Elizabeth. Work and Welfare: The Case of Aid to Families with Dependent Children. *J. Human Res.*, Supplement 1973, *8*, pp. 103–25.

Dusak, Katherine. Futures Trading and Investor Returns: An Investigation of Commodity Market Risk Premiums. *J. Polit. Econ.*, November-December 1973, *81*(6), pp. 1387–1406.

Duscha, Julius. Manpower Training: Turning the Unskilled Into Productive Workers. In *Levitan, S. A., ed.*, 1973, pp. 89–118.

Dutta, Amita. Migration in a Trading Economy. *J. Devel. Stud.*, October 1973, *10*(1), pp. 79–91.

Dutta, M. and Sharma, P. L. Alternative Estimators and Predictive Power of Alternative Estimators: An Econometric Model of Puerto Rico. *Rev. Econ. Statist.*, August 1973, *55*(3), pp. 381–85.

Dutton, Dean S. and Gramm, William P. Transactions Costs, the Wage Rate, and the Demand for Money. *Amer. Econ. Rev.*, September 1973, *63*(4), pp. 652–65.

Duvall, Richard M. and Allen, Tom C. Determinants of Property Loss Ratios in The Retail Industry. *J. Risk Ins.*, June 1973, *40*(2), pp. 181–90.

────── and Allen, Tom C. Least Cost Deductible Decisions. *J. Risk Ins.*, December 1973, *40*(4), pp. 497–508.

Dvorák, Jirí and Jezek, Tomás. Some Problems of

Strain in the Manpower Balances. *Eastern Europ. Econ.*, Summer 1973, *11*(4), pp. 60–85.

Dyckman, John. The Changing Uses of the City. In *Rasmussen, D. W. and Haworth, C. T., eds.*, 1973, pp. 31–50.

Dyckman, Thomas R. and Downes, David H. A Critical Look at the Efficient Market Empirical Research Literature As It Relates to Accounting Information. *Accounting Rev.*, April 1973, *48*(2), pp. 300–17.

Dyer, Alan R. Discrimination Procedures for Separate Families of Hypotheses. *J. Amer. Statist. Assoc.*, December 1973, *68*(344), pp. 970–74.

Dyer, James S. An Empirical Investigation of a Man-Machine Interactive Approach to the Solution of the Multiple Criteria Problem. In *Cochrane, J. L. and Zeleny, M., eds.*, 1973, pp. 202–16.

Dyer, Lee D. Job Search Success of Middle-Aged Managers and Engineers. *Ind. Lab. Relat. Rev.*, April 1973, *26*(3), pp. 969–79.

Dyke, Bennett and MacCluer, Jean W. Estimation of Vital Rates by Means of Monte Carlo Simulation. *Demography*, August 1973, *10*(3), pp. 383–403.

Dyson, Lowell K. The Southern Tenant Farmers Union and Depression Politics. *Polit. Sci. Quart.*, June 1973, *88*(2), pp. 230–52.

Dyson, Richard. Panorama dell'attività bancaria. (The Banking Spectrum. With English summary.) *Bancaria*, December 1973, *29*(12), pp. 1451–60.

Dystel, John J. and Johnson, Nicholas. A Day in the Life: The Federal Communications Commission. *Yale Law J.*, July 1973, *82*(8), pp. 1575–1634.

Eapen, Ana N. and Eapen, A. T. Income Redistributive Effects of State and Local Fiscs: Connecticut, A Case Study. *Public Finance Quart.*, October 1973, *1*(4), pp. 372–87.

Eapen, A. T. and Eapen, Ana N. Income Redistributive Effects of State and Local Fiscs: Connecticut, A Case Study. *Public Finance Quart.*, October 1973, *1*(4), pp. 372–87.

Early, John F. Factors Affecting Trends in Real Spendable Earnings. *Mon. Lab. Rev.*, May 1973, *96*(5), pp. 16–19.

Eason, Warren W. Handbook of Soviet Social Science Data: Demography. In *Mickiewicz, E., ed.*, 1973, pp. 49–63.

Eastburn, David P. A Crunch in '73? *Fed. Res. Bank Bus. Rev. Phila.*, June 1973, pp. 3–6.

—— The Future Role of Interest Rates in Open Market Policy. *Fed. Res. Bank Bus. Rev. Phila.*, January 1973, pp. 3–7.

—— Monetary Policy In a "New" Economy. *Fed. Res. Bank Bus. Rev. Phila.*, October 1973, pp. 3–6.

Easterlin, Richard A. Relative Economic Status and the American Fertility Swing. In *Sheldon, E. B., ed.*, 1973, pp. 170–223.

Eastman, Clyde, et al. Labor Mobility in Northcentral New Mexico. *N. Mex. Bus.*, June 1973, *26*(6), pp. 3–9.

Eastman, John and ReVelle, Charles. Linear Decision Rule in Reservoir Management and Design: 3. Direct Capacity Determination and Intraseasonal Constraints. *Water Resources Res.*, February 1973, *9*(1), pp. 29–42.

Easton, Allan. One-of-a-Kind Decisions Involving Weighted Multiple Objectives and Disparate Alternatives. In *Cochrane, J. L. and Zeleny, M., eds.*, 1973, pp. 657–67.

Eaton, B. Curtis. Comment on "Duopoly and Space." *Can. J. Econ.*, February 1973, *6*(1), pp. 124–27.

—— The Individual and the Defense Mass-Layoff. In *Udis, B., ed.*, 1973, pp. 179–209.

Ebanks, G. Edward and Grindstaff, Carl F. Male Sterilization as a Contraceptive Method in Canada: An Empirical Study. *Population Stud.*, November 1973, *27*(3), pp. 443–55.

Ebbeler, Donald H. Measuring the Permanent Component of a Series for Serially Correlated Observations. *J. Amer. Statist. Assoc.*, September 1973, *68*(343), pp. 579–80.

—— A Note on Large-Sample Approximations in Lognormal Linear Models. *J. Amer. Statist. Assoc.*, March 1973, *68*(341), pp. 231.

—— On the Measurement of the Permanent Component of a Series. *J. Amer. Statist. Assoc.*, June 1973, *68*(342), pp. 343–47.

—— **and McDonald, James B.** An Analysis of the Properties of the Exact Finite Sample Distribution of a Nonconsistent GCL Structural Variance Estimator. *Econometrica,* January 1973, *41*(1), pp. 59–65.

Ebert, Ronald J. and Piehl, DeWayne. Time Horizon: A Concept for Management. *Calif. Manage. Rev.*, Summer 1973, *15*(4), pp. 35–41.

Eckaus, Richard S. Absorptive Capacity as a Constraint Due to Maturation Processes. In *[Rosenstein-Rodan, P.]*, 1973, pp. 79–108.

—— The Chinese Economy at the Present Juncture: Discussion. *Amer. Econ. Rev.*, May 1973, *63*(2), pp. 233–34.

—— Estimation of the Returns to Education with Hourly Standardized Incomes. *Quart. J. Econ.*, February 1973, *87*(1), pp. 121–31.

Eckel, Dieter. Probleme der Erfolgsmessung der Wirtschaftspolitik. (Problems of Evaluation of Macro-Economic-Policy. With English summary.) *Z. ges. Staatswiss.*, May 1973, *129*(2), pp. 375–84.

Eckert, Ross D. On the Incentives of Regulators: The Case of Taxicabs. *Public Choice*, Spring 1973, *14*, pp. 83–99.

Eckstein, Otto. Instability in the Private and Public Sectors. *Swedish J. Econ.*, March 1973, *75*(1), pp. 19–26.

Economides, Chris. Earned International Reserve Units: The Catalyst of Two Complementary World Problems—the Monetary and Development. *World Devel.*, March-April 1973, *1*(3–4), pp. 49–69.

Edde, Richard. Production, Income and Expenditure. *S. Afr. J. Econ.*, September 1973, *41*(3), pp. 268–80.

Edelson, Noel M. Efficiency Aspects of Local School Finance: Comments and Extensions. *J. Polit. Econ.*, January-February 1973, *81*(1), pp. 158–73.

Eden, Philip. Estimating U.S. Human Capital Loss in Southeast Asia: Reply. *J. Human Res.*, Fall 1973, *8*(4), pp. 526–27.

Edey, Harold. The Public Company and the Shareholders. In *Allen, G. C., et al.*, 1973, pp. 29–38.

Edge, D. O. Technological Metaphor. In *Edge, D. O. and Wolfe, J. N., eds.*, 1973, pp. 31–59.

Edgerton, David L. The Combined Use of Predictors and Taylor Series in Nonlinear Interdependent Systems. *Écon. Appl.*, 1973, *26*(2–3–4), pp. 537–59.

Edgmand, Michael R. and Murray, Tracy. Full Employment, Trade Expansion, and Adjustment Assistance: Reply. *Southern Econ. J.*, July 1973, *40* (1), pp. 138–39.

Edie, Leslie C., et al. Urban Planning. In *Ross, M., ed.*, 1973, pp. 599–615.

Edmister, Robert O. and Lewellen, Wilbur G. A General Model for Accounts-Receivable Analysis and Control. *J. Financial Quant. Anal.*, March 1973, *8*(2), pp. 195–206.

Edmonds, Juliet. Child Care and Family Services in Barbados. *Soc. Econ. Stud.*, June 1973, *22*(2), pp. 229–48.

Edmonson, Nathan. Capacity Utilization in Major Materials Industries. *Fed. Res. Bull.*, August 1973, *59*(8), pp. 564–66.

Edwards, C. B. A Cost-Benefit Analysis of the Concorde Project: Comment. *J. Transp. Econ. Policy,* September 1973, *7*(3), pp. 300–01.

Edwards, C. D. The World of Antitrust. In *Thorelli, H. B., ed.*, 1973, pp. 89–103.

Edwards, Clive T. Federal-State Financial Relations in Malaya. In *[Hicks, U.],* 1973, pp. 191–206.

Edwards, Edgar O. and Todaro, Michael P. Educational Demand and Supply in the Context of Growing Unemployment in Less Developed Countries. *World Devel.*, March-April 1973, *1* (3–4), pp. 107–117.

Edwards, Franklin R. Advertising and Competition in Banking. *Antitrust Bull.*, Spring 1973, *18*(1), pp. 23–32.

_____ **and Heggestad, Arnold A.** Uncertainty, Market Structure, and Performance in Banking: The Galbraith-Caves Hypothesis and Managerial Motives in Banking. *Quart. J. Econ.*, August 1973, *87* (3), pp. 455–73.

Edwards, Harry T. The Emerging Duty to Bargain in the Public Sector. *Mich. Law Rev.*, April 1973, *71*(5), pp. 885–934.

Edwards, James B. Adjusted DCF Rate of Return. *Manage. Account.*, January 1973, *54*(7), pp. 45–49.

Edwards, Richard C.; Reich, Michael and Gordon, David M. A Theory of Labor Market Segmentation. *Amer. Econ. Rev.*, May 1973, *63*(2), pp. 359–65.

Edwards, Ronald [Sir]. The Status Agreement in Electricity. In *Tivey, L., ed.*, 1973, pp. 284–98.

Edwards, R. S. The Rationale of Cost Accounting. In *Buchanan, J. M. and Thirlby, G. F., eds.*, 1973, pp. 71–92.

Edwards, S. L. and Gordon, I. R. Holiday Trip Generation. *J. Transp. Econ. Policy*, May 1973, *7*(2), pp. 153–68.

Eeckhoudt, Louis R. The "Dorfman-Steiner" Rule: The Intertemporal Case: A Reply. *Z. Nationalökon.*, 1973, *33*(3–4), pp. 431–34.

Efron, Bradley and Morris, Carl. Stein's Estimation Rule and Its Competitors—An Empirical Bayes Approach. *J. Amer. Statist. Assoc.*, March 1973, *68* (341), pp. 117–30.

Egozi, Mosheh. An Elementary Model of the Determination of the Level of Public Expenditure and the Distribution of the Tax Burden. *Public Finance*, 1973, *28*(3–4), pp. 259–79.

Ehrenberg, A. S. C. and Charlton, P. McConnell's Experimental Brand Choice Data. *J. Marketing Res.*, August 1973, *10*(3), pp. 302–07.

Ehrenberg, Ronald G. The Demand for State and Local Government Employees. *Amer. Econ. Rev.*, June 1973, *63*(3), pp. 366–79.

_____ Heterogeneous Labor, Minimum Hiring Standards, and Job Vacancies in Public Employment. *J. Polit. Econ.*, November-December 1973, *81*(6), pp. 1442–50.

_____ Municipal Government Structure, Unionization, and the Wages of Fire Fighters. *Ind. Lab. Relat. Rev.*, October 1973, *27*(1), pp. 36–48.

Ehrlich, Cyril. Building and Caretaking: Economic Policy in British Tropical Africa, 1890–1960. *Econ. Hist. Rev., 2nd Ser.*, November 1973, *26*(4), pp. 649–67.

Ehrlich, Eva; Szilágyi, Gyorgy and Csernok, Attila. Numerical Results of an International Comparison of Infrastructure Development Over the Last 100 Years. *Europ. Econ. Rev.*, April 1973, *4*(1), pp. 63–65.

Ehrlich, George E. Health Challenges of the Future. *Ann. Amer. Acad. Polit. Soc. Sci.*, July 1973, *408*, pp. 70–82.

Ehrlich, Isaac. Participation in Illegitimate Activities: A Theoretical and Empirical Investigation. *J. Polit. Econ.*, May-June 1973, *81*(3), pp. 521–65.

Ehrlich, Paul R. and Holdren, John P. Impact of Population Growth. In *Daly, H. E., ed.*, 1973, pp. 76–89.

Eichberg, Henning. "Entwicklungshilfe" Verhaltensumformung nach europäischem Modell? ("Assistance" for Underdeveloped Countries—Transformation of Behaviour According to Western Patterns? With English summary.) *Z. Wirtschaft. Sozialwissen.*, 1973, *93*(6), pp. 641–70.

Eichler, Edward and Kaplan, Marshall. New Communities. In *Pynoos, J.; Schafer, R. and Hartman, C. W., eds.*, 1973, pp. 523–31.

Eichner, Alfred S. Manpower Planning and Economic Planning: The Two Perspectives. In *Aronson, R. L., ed.*, 1973, pp. 65–80.

_____ A Theory of the Determination of the Markup Under Oligopoly. *Econ. J.*, December 1973, *83* (332), pp. 1184–1200.

Eidel'man, M. The New Ex Post Interbranch Balance of Production and Distribution of Output in the National Economy of the USSR. *Prob. Econ.*, May 1973, *16*(1), pp. 3–34.

Eidman, Vernon; Walker, Odell and Boehlje, Michael. An Approach to Farm Management Education. *Amer. J. Agr. Econ.*, May 1973, *55*(2), pp. 192–97.

Eilbott, Peter. Estimates of the Market Value of the Outstanding Corporate Stock of All Domestic Corporations. In *Goldsmith, R. W., ed.*, 1973, pp. 429–55.

Eilon, S. and Teague, J. Productivity Measurement: A Brief Survey. *Appl. Econ.*, June 1973, *5*(2), pp. 133–45.

Eisenberg, William M. and Fulco, Lawrence J. Productivity and Costs in the Private Economy, 1972. *Mon. Lab. Rev.*, May 1973, *96*(5), pp. 3–7.

Eisenmenger, Robert W. and Anderson, Paul S. Impact of the Proposed New Financial Structure on Mortgage Markets. In *Federal Reserve Bank of Boston*, 1973, pp. 149–72.

Eisgruber, Ludwig M. Managerial Information and Decision Systems in the U.S.A.: Historical Developments, Current Status, and Major Issues. *Amer. J. Agr. Econ.*, December 1973, *55*(5), pp. 930–37.

Eisner, Mark and Pindyck, Robert S. A Generalized Approach to Estimation as Implemented in the TROLL/1 System. *Ann. Econ. Soc. Measure*, January 1973, *2*(1), pp. 29–51.

Eisner, Robert. A Framework for the Measurement of Economic and Social Performance: Comment. In *Moss, M., ed.*, 1973, pp. 99–102.

———— Measuring Economic Performance in the Private Sector: Comment. In *Moss, M., ed.*, 1973, pp. 343–49.

———— Tax Incentives for Investment. *Nat. Tax J.*, September 1973, *26*(3), pp. 397–401.

Ekanem, Nkanta F. and de Leeuw, Frank. The Supply of Rental Housing: Reply. *Amer. Econ. Rev.*, June 1973, *63*(3), pp. 437–38.

———— **and de Leeuw, Frank.** Time Lags in the Rental Housing Market. *Urban Stud.*, February 1973, *10*(1), pp. 39–68.

Ekblom, H. E. European Direct Investments in the United States. *Harvard Bus. Rev.*, July-August 1973, *51*(4), pp. 16–26, 146–50.

Ekelund, Robert B., Jr. and Hebert, Robert F. Public Economics at the Ecole des Ponts et Chaussées: 1830–1850. *J. Public Econ.*, July 1973, *2*(3), pp. 241–56.

———— **and Hooks, Donald L.** Ellet, Dupuit, and Lardner: On Nineteenth Century Engineers and Economic Analysis. *Nebr. J. Econ. Bus.*, Summer 1973, *12*(3), pp. 43–52.

———— **and Hulett, Joe R.** Joint Supply, the Taussig-Pigou Controversy, and the Competitive Provision of Public Goods. *J. Law Econ.*, October 1973, *16*(2), pp. 369–87.

———— **and Olsen, Emilie S.** Comte, Mill, and Cairnes: The Positivist-Empiricist Interlude in Late Classical Economics. *J. Econ. Issues*, September 1973, *7*(3), pp. 383–416.

Eldridge, D. P. and Saunders, N. C. Employment and Exports, 1963–72. *Mon. Lab. Rev.*, August 1973, *96*(8), pp. 16–27.

Eldridge, Larry D. and Bass, Bernard M. Accelerated Managers' Objectives in Twelve Countries. *Ind. Relat.*, May 1973, *12*(2), pp. 158–71.

Eleftheriou, T. The Classical and Factor Proportions Trade Patterns: Comment on a Note. *Manchester Sch. Econ. Soc. Stud.*, September 1973, *41*(3), pp. 345.

Elesh, David. Poverty Theories and Income Maintenance: Validity and Policy Relevance. *Soc. Sci. Quart.*, September 1973, *54*(2), pp. 359–73.

————, **et al.** The New Jersey-Pennsylvania Experiment: A Field Study in Negative Taxation. In *Boulding, K. E.; Pfaff, M. and Pfaff, A., eds.*, 1973, pp. 181–201.

Elgers, Pieter and Clark, John J. Forecasted Income Statements: An Investor Perspective. *Accounting Rev.*, October 1973, *48*(4), pp. 668–78.

El-Hodiri, Mohamed and Takayama, Akira. Behavior of the Firm Under Regulatory Constraint:

Clarifications. *Amer. Econ. Rev.*, March 1973, *63*(1), pp. 235–37.

Elkan, Walter. On the Apparent Benefits of Higher Productivity: An Arithmetical Illustration: Reply. *J. Devel. Stud.*, April 1973, *9*(3), pp. 452–53.

Ellenberg, Jonas H. The Joint Distribution of the Standardized Least Squares Residuals from a General Linear Regression. *J. Amer. Statist. Assoc.*, December 1973, *68*(344), pp. 941–43.

Ellickson, Bryan. A Generalization of the Pure Theory of Public Goods. *Amer. Econ. Rev.*, June 1973, *63*(3), pp. 417–32.

Elliott, G. Field Systems of Northwest England. In *Baker, A. R. H. and Butlin, R. A., eds.*, 1973, pp. 42–92.

Elliott, J. W. A Direct Comparison of Short-Run GNP Forecasting Models. *J. Bus.*, January 1973, *46*(1), pp. 33–60.

———— Theories of Corporate Investment Behavior Revisited. *Amer. Econ. Rev.*, March 1973, *63*(1), pp. 195–207.

Elliott, Ralph D. Economic Study of the Effect of Municipal Sewer Surcharges on Industrial Wastes and Water Usage. *Water Resources Res.*, October 1973, *9*(5), pp. 1121–31.

Elliott-Jones, M. F. Matrix Methods in Corporate Social Accounting. In *Dierkes, M. and Bauer, R. A., eds.*, 1973, pp. 351–64.

Ellis, Dennis F. A Portfolio Selection Model—*à la* Arrow. *Amer. Econ.*, Spring 1973, *17*(1), pp. 103–14.

Ellis, P. L.; Wilson, I. H. and Robertson, B. C. Rock Phosphate Mining in North West Queensland—A Cost-Benefit Analysis. *Econ. Anal. Pol.*, March 1973, *4*(1), pp. 23–32.

Ellison, A. P. and Stafford, E. M. The Order Delivery Lag in the World's Civil Aircraft Industry. *Appl. Econ.*, March 1973, *5*(1), pp. 19–34.

Ellman, Michael. Bonus Formulae and Soviet Managerial Performance: A Further Comment. *Southern Econ. J.*, April 1973, *39*(4), pp. 652–53.

Ellwood, Paul M., Jr. and Herbert, Michael E. Health Care: Should Industry Buy It or Sell It? *Harvard Bus. Rev.*, July-August 1973, *51*(4), pp. 99–107.

Elovikov, L. A. Ways of Creating Social and Economic Conditions for the Reproduction of Labor Power in the New Regions of the West Siberian Plains. *Prob. Econ.*, June 1973, *16*(2), pp. 42–54.

Elson, R. Anthony and Teigeiro, José D. Export Incentives in Colombia. *Finance Develop.*, December 1973, *10*(4), pp. 30–33.

———— The Export Promotion System and the Growth of Minor Exports in Colombia. *Int. Monet. Fund Staff Pap.*, July 1973, *20*(2), pp. 419–70.

Elton, Edwin J. Capital Management and Capital Theory: Discussion. *J. Finance*, May 1973, *28*(2), pp. 368–69.

———— **and Gruber, Martin J.** Asset Selection with Changing Capital Structure. *J. Financial Quant. Anal.*, June 1973, *8*(3), pp. 459–74.

———— **and Gruber, Martin J.** Estimating the Dependence Structure of Share Prices—Implications for Portfolio Selection. *J. Finance*, December 1973, *28*(5), pp. 1203–32.

Elzinga, Kenneth G. and Hogarty, Thomas F. The

Problem of Geographic Market Delineation in Antimerger Suits. *Antitrust Bull.*, Spring 1973, *18*(1), pp. 45–81.

Emdin, G. and Starostin, S. The Five-Year Plan and the Soviet Way of Life. *Prob. Econ.*, February 1973, *15*(10), pp. 81–103.

Emerine, R. J., II and Weicher, John C. Econometric Analysis of State and Local Aggregate Expenditure Functions. *Public Finance*, 1973, *28*(1), pp. 69–83.

Emerson, David L. Optimum Firm Location and the Theory of Production. *J. Reg. Sci.*, December 1973, *13*(3), pp. 335–47.

Emery, E. David. Regulated Utilities and Equipment Manufacturers' Conspiracies in the Electrical Power Industry. *Bell J. Econ. Manage. Sci.*, Spring 1973, *4*(1), pp. 322–37.

Emery, John T. The Information Content of Daily Market Indicators. *J. Financial Quant. Anal.*, March 1973, *8*(2), pp. 183–90.

Emmerij, Louis. Education and Employment: Some Preliminary Findings and Thoughts. *Int. Lab. Rev.*, January 1973, *107*(1), pp. 31–42.

Emminger, Otmar. L'inflazione e il sistema monetario internazionale. (Inflation and the International Monetary System. With English summary.) *Bancaria*, October 1973, *29*(10), pp. 1206–19.

Enache, Constantin. Unele probleme ale reproducţiei forţei de muncă în socialism. (Some Problems of the Reproduction of Labour in Socialism. With English summary.) *Stud. Cercet. Econ.*, 1973, (4), pp. 5–13.

Engerman, Stanley. Some Considerations Relating to Property Rights in Man. *J. Econ. Hist.*, March 1973, *33*(1), pp. 43–65.

England, Richard and Bluestone, Barry. Ecology and Social Conflict. In *Daly, H. E., ed.*, 1973, pp. 190–214.

English, John. Oatlands: An Area of Twilight Housing in Glasgow. *Urban Stud.*, October 1973, *10*(3), pp. 381–86.

English, M. D. Macro-Economic Policy: Canada. In *Perkins, J. O. N., ed.*, 1973, pp. 57–93.

Engwall, Lars. Business Behavior: The Cigarette Case. *Marquette Bus. Rev.*, Summer 1973, *17*(2), pp. 59–72.

Enis, Ben M. and Gelb, Betsy D. Affirmative Action in Housing and Beyond. *Calif. Manage. Rev.*, Winter 1973, *16*(2), pp. 24–31.

Enke, Stephen. Economic Consequences of Rapid Population Growth: A Reply. *Econ. J.*, March 1973, *83*(329), pp. 219–21.

Enthoven, Adolf J. H. Standardized Accountancy and Economic Development. *Finance Develop.*, March 1973, *10*(1), pp. 28–31.

Enweze, Cyril. Structure of Public Expenditures in Selected Developing Countries: A Time Series Study. *Manchester Sch. Econ. Soc. Stud.*, December 1973, *41*(4), pp. 430–63.

Enzer, Selwyn. Applications of Futures Research to Society's Problems. In *Hawkes, N., ed.*, 1973, pp. 243–87.

Epley, D. R. Construction of Income and Employment Indexes as a Test of Base Theory. *Land Econ.*, August 1973, *49*(3), pp. 365–67.

———— A Price Index for Life Insurance: Comment. *J. Risk Ins.*, December 1973, *40*(4), pp. 629.

Epps, Thomas W. An Econometric Analysis of the Effectiveness of the U.S. Army's 1971 Paid Advertising Campaign. *Appl. Econ.*, December 1973, *5*(4), pp. 261–69.

Epstein, Barbara. The Illusory Conflict Between Antidumping and Antitrust. *Antitrust Bull.*, Spring 1973, *18*(1), pp. 1–22.

Epstein, E. and Monat, J. Labour Contracting and Its Regulation: I. *Int. Lab. Rev.*, May 1973, *107*(5), pp. 451–70.

———— **and Monat, J.** Labour Contracting and Its Regulation: II. *Int. Lab. Rev.*, June 1973, *107*(6), pp. 513–28.

Epstein, Edwin M. Dimensions of Corporate Power, Pt. 1. *Calif. Manage. Rev.*, Winter 1973, *16*(2), pp. 9–23.

Epstein, T. Scarlett. The Dimensions of Rural Development. In *Epstein, T. S. and Penny, D. H., eds.*, 1973, pp. 241–51.

———— Economic Development and Social Change in South India and New Guinea. In *Epstein, T. S. and Penny, D. H., eds.*, 1973, pp. 131–55.

Erdilek, Asim. Foreign Trade, Domestic Production and Relative Prices—A Simulation Model for the United States and Japan. *Weltwirtsch. Arch.*, 1973, *109*(4), pp. 601–20.

———— Shadow Prices, Unit Costs, Total Factor Costs and the Gains from Trade. *Indian Econ. J.*, July–September 1973, *21*(1), pp. 66–72.

Erdös, P. On the Returns Principle of Pricing. *Acta Oecon.*, 1973, *11*(4), pp. 417–25.

Erdös, T. Investments and Economic Growth. *Acta Oecon.*, 1973, *11*(4), pp. 281–303.

Eriksen, Ib and Thore, Sten. Payment Clearing Networks. *Swedish J. Econ.*, June 1973, *75*(2), pp. 143–63.

Erlenkotter, Donald. Sequencing of Interdependent Hydroelectric Projects. *Water Resources Res.*, February 1973, *9*(1), pp. 21–27.

Erlich, Reese and Horowitz, David. Big Brother as a Holding Company. In *Andreano, R. L., ed.*, 1973, pp. R330–15.

Ernle, [Lord]. The Great Depression and Recovery, 1874–1914. In *Perry, P. J., ed.*, 1973, pp. 1–17.

Ernst, Robert T. and Hugg, Lawrence. Institutional Growth and Community Fragmentation: An Inner City Example. *Mich. Academician*, Fall 1973, *6*(2), pp. 179–91.

Escobedo, Gilberto. The Response of the Mexican Economy to Policy Actions. *Fed. Res. Bank St. Louis Rev.*, June 1973, *55*(6), pp. 15–23.

Eskin, Gerald J. Dynamic Forecasts of New Product Demand Using a Depth of Repeat Model. *J. Marketing Res.*, May 1973, *10*(2), pp. 115–29.

Eslami, M. The World Energy Crisis and Iranian Strategy. *Tahq. Eq.*, Winter & Spring 1973, *10*(29 & 30), pp. 17–49.

Espenshade, Thomas J. A Note on the Population of Seventeenth Century London: Comment. *Demography*, November 1973, *10*(4), pp. 659–60.

Esposito, Louis and Dalton, James A. The Impact of Liquidity on Merger Activity. *Quart. Rev. Econ. Bus.*, Spring 1973, *13*(1), pp. 15–26.

Estey, Marten. Wage Stabilization Policy and the

Nixon Administration. In *Cagan, P., et al.*, 1973, pp. 107–33.

Estrada, Leo; Alvírez, David and Hernández, José. Census Data and the Problem of Conceptually Defining the Mexican American Population. *Soc. Sci. Quart.*, March 1973, *53*(4), pp. 671–87.

Estrup, Jørgen. Er marxistisk økonomi et alternativ? —En analyse af et aktuelt forsøg. (Marxian Economic Theory and the Housing Problem: A Review Article. With English summary.) *Nationalokon. Tidsskr.*, 1973, *111*(1), pp. 165–80.

Ethier, Wilfred. International Trade and the Forward Exchange Market. *Amer. Econ. Rev.*, June 1973, *63*(3), pp. 494–503.

Ethridge, Don. The Inclusion of Wastes in the Theory of the Firm. *J. Polit. Econ.*, November-December 1973, *81*(6), pp. 1430–41.

Etzel, Michael J. and Donnelly, James H., Jr. Degrees of Product Newness and Early Trial. *J. Marketing Res.*, August 1973, *10*(3), pp. 295–300.

Etzioni, Amitai. Societal Turnability: A Theoretical Treatment. In *Udis, B., ed.*, 1973, pp. 337–80.

Evan, Harry Zvi. Comparing Conditions of Work by Collective Agreement Analysis: A Case Study of the Petroleum Industry. *Int. Lab. Rev.*, July 1973, *108*(1), pp. 59–75.

Evans, Alan W. The Location of the Headquarters of Industrial Companies. *Urban Stud.*, October 1973, *10*(3), pp. 387–95.

_____ On the Theory of the Valuation and Allocation of Time: Reply. *Scot. J. Polit. Econ.*, February 1973, *20*(1), pp. 73–74.

Evans, Dennis A. The Influence of Computers on the Teaching of Statistics. *J. Roy. Statist. Soc.*, Part 2, 1973, *136*, pp. 153–90.

Evans, E. W. and Galambos, P. Work Stoppages in the United Kingdom 1965–70: A Quantitative Study. *Bull. Econ. Res.*, May 1973, *25*(1), pp. 22–42.

Evans, Graham J. and Lindley, Robert M. The Use of RAS and Related Models in Manpower Forecasting. *Econ. Planning*, 1973, *13*(1–2), pp. 53–73.

Evans, I. G. and Dayananda, R. A. Bayesian Acceptance-Sampling Schemes for Two-Sided Tests of the Mean of a Normal Distribution of Known Variance. *J. Amer. Statist. Assoc.*, March 1973, *68* (341), pp. 131–36.

Evans, J. D. and Bain, A. D. Price Formation and Profits: Explanatory and Forecasting Models of Manufacturing Industry Profits in the U.K. *Oxford Bull. Econ. Statist.*, November 1973, *35*(4), pp. 295–308.

Evans, John P. and Steuer, Ralph E. Generating Efficient Extreme Points in Linear Multiple Objective Programming: Two Algorithms and Computing Experience. In *Cochrane, J. L. and Zeleny, M., eds.*, 1973, pp. 349–65.

Evans, John S. and Leathers, Charles G. Thorstein Veblen and the New Industrial State. *Hist. Polit. Econ.*, Fall 1973, *5*(2), pp. 420–37.

Evans, Michael K. A Forecasting Model Applied to Pollution Control Costs. *Amer. Econ. Rev.*, May 1973, *63*(2), pp. 244–52.

Evans, Raymond W. G. Some Aspects of Urban Water Supply in Victoria. In *Aislabie, C., ed.*, 1973, pp. 61–67.

Evans, R. G.; Parish, E. M. A. and Sully, Floyd. Medical Productivity, Scale Effects, and Demand Generation. *Can. J. Econ.*, August 1973, *6*(3), pp. 376–93.

Evans, Robert, Jr. Education Levels and Unemployment in Asian Countries. *Mon. Lab. Rev.*, November 1973, *96*(11), pp. 58–59.

Evans, Rupert N. and Galloway, Joel D. Verbal Ability and Socioeconomic Status of 9th and 12th Grade College Preparatory, General, and Vocational Students. *J. Human Res.*, Winter 1973, *8*(1), pp. 24–36.

Evenson, Robert E. and Kislev, Yoav. Research and Productivity in Wheat and Maize. *J. Polit. Econ.*, November-December 1973, *81*(6), pp. 1309–29.

Everitt, Alan. The English Urban Inn, 1560–1760. In *Everitt, A., ed.*, 1973, pp. 91–137.

_____ Perspectives in English Urban History: Introduction. In *Everitt, A., ed.*, 1973, pp. 1–15.

_____ Town and Country in Victorian Leicestershire: The Role of the Village Carrier. In *Everitt, A., ed.*, 1973, pp. 213–40.

Evsiukov, Iu. Migration of the Population from the Countryside to the City (Problems of Analysis and Forecasting). *Prob. Econ.*, June 1973, *16*(2), pp. 14–25.

Ewusi, Kodwo. Changes in Distribution of Earnings of Africans in Recorded Employment in Uganda. *Econ. Bull. Ghana, Sec. Ser.*, 1973, *3*(1), pp. 39–49.

_____ The Rate of Inflation, Variation in Local Food Prices and the Effect of Transport Facilities on Local Food Prices in Ghana in the Sixties. In *Ofori, I. M., ed.*, 1973, pp. 278–91.

Exter, John. Toward a New World Monetary System. In *Wiegand, G. C., ed.*, 1973, pp. 186–98.

Ezra, Derek. Regional Policy in the European Community. *Nat. Westminster Bank Quart. Rev.*, August 1973, pp. 8–21.

Faber, Malte. Einstimmigkeitsregel und Einkommensumverteilung. (Rule of Unanimity and Income Redistribution. With English summary.) *Kyklos*, 1973, *26*(1), pp. 36–57.

_____ and Bernholz, Peter. A Note on Stackelberg's Hypothesis Concerning a Relationship between the Price of Land, the Real Rate of Interest and Impatience to Consume. *Z. Nationalökon.*, 1973, *33*(3–4), pp. 375–88.

_____ and Bernholz, Peter. Technical Productivity of Roundabout Processes and Positive Rate of Interest. A Capital Model with Depreciation and n-Period Horizon. *Z. ges. Staatswiss.*, February 1973, *129*(1), pp. 46–61.

Fabricant, Solomon. The Perennial Problem of Economic Stability. *Amer. Econ.*, Fall 1973, *17*(2), pp. 85–89.

Fabris, Giampaolo. I valori della pubblicità. (The Value of Advertising. With English summary.) *L'Impresa*, 1973, *15*(5–6), pp. 333–45.

_____ La "corporate image": per una ridefinizione del problema. (The "Corporate Image": A Redefinition. With English summary.) *L'Impresa*, 1973, *15*(9–10), pp. 538–47.

Fabrycy, Mark Z. Economic Theory and Multicollinearity. *Amer. Econ.*, Spring 1973, *17*(1), pp. 81–84.

Fach, Wolfgang. Über einige Schwierigkeiten der Neuen Politischen Ökonomie: Das Beispiel der Koalitionstheorie. (Some Difficulties of the New Political Economy: The Example of the Coalition Theory. With English summary.) *Z. ges. Staatswiss.,* May 1973, *129*(2), pp. 347–74.

Fair, Ray C. A Comparison of Alternative Estimators of Macroeconomic Models. *Int. Econ. Rev.,* June 1973, *14*(2), pp. 261–77.

―――― Monthly Housing Starts. In *Ricks, R. B., ed.,* 1973, pp. 69–91.

―――― **and Chow, Gregory C.** Maximum Likelihood Estimation of Linear Equation Systems with Auto-Regressive Residuals. *Ann. Econ. Soc. Measure,* January 1973, *2*(1), pp. 17–28.

―――― **and Jaffee, Dwight M.** The Implications of the Proposals of the Hunt Commission for the Mortgage and Housing Markets: An Empirical Study. In *Federal Reserve Bank of Boston,* 1973, pp. 99–148.

Falco, James F. Section 7 of the Clayton Act and "Control" in Bank Holding Company Regulation. *Antitrust Bull.,* Winter 1973, *18*(4), pp. 715–41.

Faliva, Mario. Stimatori lineari ottimali dei parametri in un modello di regressione lineare con vincoli di diseguaglianza sui parametri. (An Optimal Linear Estimator of Parameters in the Linear Regression Model with Inequality Constraints. With English summary.) *Statistica,* July-September 1973, *33*(3), pp. 363–94.

Falk, Haim and Ophir, Tsvi. The Effect of Risk on the Use of Financial Statements by Investment Decision-Makers: A Case Study. *Accounting Rev.,* April 1973, *48*(2), pp. 323–38.

―――― The Influence of Differences in Accounting Policies on Investment Decisions. *J. Acc. Res.,* Spring 1973, *11*(1), pp. 108–16.

Falkenberg, John F. The Sources of Bank Profitability. *J. Bank Res.,* Summer 1973, *4*(2), pp. 105–10.

Fama, Eugene F. A Note on the Market Model and the Two-Parameter Model. *J. Finance,* December 1973, *28*(5), pp. 1181–85.

―――― Risk, Return, and Portfolio Analysis: Reply. *J. Polit. Econ.,* May-June 1973, *81*(3), pp. 753–55.

―――― **and MacBeth, James D.** Risk, Return, and Equilibrium: Empirical Tests. *J. Polit. Econ.,* May-June 1973, *81*(3), pp. 607–36.

Fan, Liang-Shing. The Economy and Foreign Trade of China. *Law Contemp. Probl.,* Summer-Autumn 1973, *38*(2), pp. 249–59.

―――― **and Olienyk, John.** Inflation in a Growing Economy: A Monetaristic Elucidation. *Intermountain Econ. Rev.,* Fall 1973, *4*(2), pp. 75–76.

Fand, David I. The Viability of Thrift Intermediaries as Financial Institutions. *Banca Naz. Lavoro Quart. Rev.,* September 1973, (106), pp. 235–68.

Fane, George. Consistent Measures of Import Substitution. *Oxford Econ. Pap.,* July 1973, *25*(2), pp. 251–61.

―――― **and Feldstein, Martin S.** Taxes, Corporate Dividend Policy and Personal Savings: The British Postwar Experience. *Rev. Econ. Statist.,* November 1973, *55*(4), pp. 399–411.

―――― **; Medoff, James and Brown, Charles.** The Income Distribution as a Pure Public Good: Com-

ment. *Quart. J. Econ.,* May 1973, *87*(2), pp. 296–303.

Farbman, Michael. Income Concentration in the Southern United States. *Rev. Econ. Statist.,* August 1973, *55*(3), pp. 333–40.

Farebrother, R. W. Simplified Samuelson Conditions for Cubic and Quartic Equations. *Manchester Sch. Econ. Soc. Stud.,* December 1973, *41*(4), pp. 396–400.

Farid, S. M. On the Pattern of Cohort Fertility. *Population Stud.,* March 1973, *27*(1), pp. 159–68.

Farioletti, Marius. Tax Administration Funding and Fiscal Policy. *Nat. Tax J.,* March 1973, *26*(1), pp. 1–16.

Farley, Noel J. J. Outward-looking Policies and Industrialization in a Small Economy: Some Notes on the Irish Case. *Econ. Develop. Cult. Change,* Part I, July 1973, *21*(4), pp. 610–28.

Farmer, David H. Source Decision Making in the Multinational Company Environment. In *Henley, D. S., ed.,* 1973, pp. 474–86.

de Faro, Clovis. A Sufficient Condition for a Unique Nonnegative Internal Rate of Return: Comment. *J. Financial Quant. Anal.,* September 1973, *8*(4), pp. 683–84.

Farooq, Ghazi M. Economic Growth and Changes in the Industrial Structure of Income and Labor Force in Pakistan. *Econ. Develop. Cult. Change,* January 1973, *21*(2), pp. 293–308.

Farrar, Marjorie M. Preclusive Purchases: Politics and Economic Warfare in France during the First World War. *Econ. Hist. Rev., 2nd Ser.,* February 1973, *26*(1), pp. 117–33.

Farris, George F.; Senner, Eldon E. and Butterfield, D. Anthony. Trust, Culture, and Organizational Behavior. *Ind. Relat.,* May 1973, *12*(2), pp. 144–57.

Farris, Paul L. Changes in Number and Size Distribution of U.S. Soybean Processing Firms. *Amer. J. Agr. Econ.,* August 1973, *55*(3), pp. 495–99.

―――― Market Growth and Concentration Change in U.S. Manufacturing Industries. *Antitrust Bull.,* Summer 1973, *18*(2), pp. 291–305.

―――― **and Gunnelson, Jerald A.** Use of Soybean Futures Markets by Large Processing Firms. *Agr. Econ. Res.,* April 1973, *25*(2), pp. 27–40.

―――― **and Richardson, Robert A.** Farm Commodity Price Stabilization Through Futures Markets. *Amer. J. Agr. Econ.,* May 1973, *55*(2), pp. 225–30.

Fase, M. M. G. A Principal Components Analysis of Market Interest Rates in the Netherlands, 1962–1970. *Europ. Econ. Rev.,* June 1973, *4*(2), pp. 107–34.

―――― **; Koning, J. and Volgenant, A. F.** An Experimental Look at Seasonal Adjustment. *De Economist,* September-October 1973, *121*(5), pp. 441–80.

Faure, Robert. Mathematical Models in the Design and Operation of Public Transport Systems. In *Hawkes, N., ed.,* 1973, pp. 41–50.

Fawthrop, R. A. Underlying Problems in Discounted Cash Flow. In *Lister, R. J., ed.,* 1973, pp. 106–29.

Fayerweather, John. Attitudes Affecting International Business-Government Affairs. In *Fayerweather, J., ed.,* 1973, pp. 5–16.

―――― **; Blake, David H. and Murray, J. Alex.** Perspectives for the Future. In *Fayerweather, J., ed.*, 1973, pp. 95–123.

_____ **and Kapoor, Ashok.** Simulated International Business Negotiations. In *Alexandrides, C. G., ed.*, 1973, pp. 5–18.

Fazel, Hassan. Optimization and Decision Models. *Can. J. Agr. Econ.*, July 1973, *21*(2), pp. 54–58.

Feagin, Joe R. Issues in Welfare Research: A Critical Overview. *Soc. Sci. Quart.*, September 1973, *54*(2), pp. 321–28.

Featherman, David L. and Duncan, Otis Dudley. Psychological and Cultural Factors in the Process of Occupational Achievement. In *Goldberger, A. S. and Duncan, O. D., eds.*, 1973, pp. 229–53.

Fedorenko, N. On the Elaboration of a System of Optimal Functioning of the Socialist Economy. *Prob. Econ.*, January 1973, *15*(9), pp. 3–27.

_____ **and Gofman, K. G.** Problems of Optimization in the Planning and Control of the Environment. *Prob. Econ.*, April 1973, *15*(12), pp. 37–51.

Fedorenko, Nicolai P. Methodological Aspects of Forecasting Long-Term Socio-Economic Development. *Amer. Econ.*, Fall 1973, *17*(2), pp. 46–48.

Fedorenko, N. P. The Present Stage and Future Prospects for the Creation of Automatic Control Systems for Industrial Enterprise. *Matekon*, Fall 1973, *10*(1), pp. 24–39.

Fedorov, E. Urgent Problems in the Interaction Between Society and the Environment. *Prob. Econ.*, May 1973, *16*(1), pp. 70–90.

Feige, E. L., et al. The Roles of Money in an Economy and the Optimum Quantity of Money. *Economica, N.S.*, November 1973, *40*(160), pp. 416–31.

Feiwel, George R. The Dynamics of Perpetuation: Some Observations on the Efficacy of Soviet Economic Reforms. *Econ. Int.*, May 1973, *26*(2), pp. 233–61.

_____ Growth, Planning, Price Mechanism and Consumer Sovereignty. *Rivista Int. Sci. Econ. Com.*, November 1973, *20*(11), pp. 1041–70.

Fekete, F. The Major Social and Economic Features of Co-operative Farming in Hungary. *Acta Oecon.*, 1973, *11*(1), pp. 19–32.

Fekete, Janos. L'inflazione e il sistema monetario internazionale: Intervento. (Inflation and the International Monetary System: Discussion. With English summary.) *Bancaria*, October 1973, *29*(10), pp. 1225–28.

Fekrat, M. Ali. Absorption Costing and Fixed Factors of Production: A Reply. *Accounting Rev.*, January 1973, *48*(1), pp. 130–31.

Felderer, Bernhard. Der Zusammenhang zwischen Allokation von Produktionsfaktoren und wirtschaftlichem Wachstum. (The Relation of Factor Allocation and Economic Growth. With English summary.) *Z. ges. Staatswiss.*, October 1973, *129*(4), pp. 589–600.

Feldman, Allan M. Bilateral Trading, Processes, Pairwise Optimality, and Pareto Optimality. *Rev. Econ. Stud.*, October 1973, *40*(4), pp. 463–73.

Feldstein, Martin S. An Econometric Model of the Medicare System: Reply. *Quart. J. Econ.*, August 1973, *87*(3), pp. 490–94.

_____ Cost-Benefit Analysis in Developing Countries: The Evaluation of Projects Financed by Aid

and External Loans. In *[Hicks, U.]*, 1973, pp. 3–19.

_____ Multicollinearity and the Mean Square Error of Alternative Estimators. *Econometrica*, March 1973, *41*(2), pp. 337–46.

_____ On the Optimal Progressivity of the Income Tax. *J. Public Econ.*, November 1973, *2*(4), pp. 357–76.

_____ Tax Incentives, Corporate Saving, and Capital Accumulation in the United States. *J. Public Econ.*, April 1973, *2*(2), pp. 159–71.

_____ The Welfare Loss of Excess Health Insurance. *J. Polit. Econ.*, Part I, March-April 1973, *81*(2), pp. 251–80.

_____ **and Chamberlain, Gary.** Multimarket Expectations and the Rate of Interest. *J. Money, Credit, Banking*, November 1973, *5*(4), pp. 873–902.

_____ **and Fane, George.** Taxes, Corporate Dividend Policy and Personal Savings: The British Postwar Experience. *Rev. Econ. Statist.*, November 1973, *55*(4), pp. 399–411.

Felice, Lawrence G. Mexican American Self-Concept and Educational Achievement: The Effects of Ethnic Isolation and Socioeconomic Deprivation. *Soc. Sci. Quart.*, March 1973, *53*(4), pp. 716–26.

Feller, Irwin. Determinants of the Composition of Urban Inventions. *Econ. Geogr.*, January 1973, *49*(1), pp. 47–58.

Fellman, Steven John. What Services Must a Trade Association Render to Non-members? *Antitrust Bull.*, Summer 1973, *18*(2), pp. 167–79.

Fellner, William J. Controlled Floating and the Confused Issue of Money Illusion. *Banca Naz. Lavoro Quart. Rev.*, September 1973, (106), pp. 206–34.

_____ Employment Goals and Monetary-Fiscal Overexpansion. In *Cagan, P., et al.*, 1973, pp. 135–72.

_____ Narrowing the Exchange Rate Bands: Comment. In *Krause, L. B. and Salant, W. S., eds.*, 1973, pp. 105–08.

Felson, Marcus and Segal, David R. Social Stratification and Family Economic Behavior. In *Sheldon, E. B., ed.*, 1973, pp. 143–64.

Fenske, G. A. and Main, T. R. N. Labour and the Gold Mines. *S. Afr. J. Econ.*, September 1973, *41*(3), pp. 298–304.

Ferber, Robert. Consumer Economics, A Survey. *J. Econ. Lit.*, December 1973, *11*(4), pp. 1303–42.

_____ Family Decision Making and Economic Behavior: A Review. In *Sheldon, E. B., ed.*, 1973, pp. 29–61.

_____ **and Salazar-Carrillo, Jorge.** Experience in Generating Micro Data in Latin America. In *Ayal, E. B., ed.*, 1973, pp. 84–100.

Ferejohn, John and Page, Talbot. A Note on "Voting or a Price System in a Competitive Market Structure." *Amer. Polit. Sci. Rev.*, March 1973, *67*(1), pp. 157–60.

Ferghali, Salwa Ali S. and Tintner, Gerhard. A Note on Stochastic Programming in a Development Plan: Reply. *Kyklos*, 1973, *26*(2), pp. 399–401.

Ferguson, C. E. The Specialization Gap: Barton, Ricardo, and Hollander. *Hist. Polit. Econ.*, Spring 1973, *5*(1), pp. 1–13.

_____ **and Maurice, S. Charles.** Factor Demand Elasticity under Monopoly and Monopsony. *Economica, N.S.*, May 1973, *40*(158), pp. 180–86.

Ferguson, Donald L.; Porter, R. Burr and Wart, James R. Efficient Algorithms for Conducting Stochastic Dominance Tests on Large Numbers of Portfolios. *J. Financial Quant. Anal.,* January 1973, *8*(1), pp. 71–81.

Ferguson, Ian S. Forecasting the Future for Timber. *Australian J. Agr. Econ.,* December 1973, *17*(3), pp. 159–69.

Fernandez, Pedro; Pousa, Aurora G. and Alemany, Ricardo. Algorithm for Solving a Class of Linear Programing Problems Related to Reservoir Management and Design. *Water Resources Res.,* October 1973, *9*(5), pp. 1227–34.

Fernandez, Raul A. The Border Industrial Program on the United States-Mexico Border. *Rev. Radical Polit. Econ.,* Spring 1973, *5*(1), pp. 37–52.

_____ The Problem of Heroin Addiction and Radical Political Economy. *Amer. Econ. Rev.,* May 1973, *63*(2), pp. 257–62.

Fernández de la Garza, Guillermo and Manne, Alan S. ENERGETICOS, A Process Analysis of the Energy Sectors. In *Goreux, L. M. and Manne, A. S., eds.,* 1973, pp. 233–75.

_____; **Manne, Alan S. and Valencia, José Alberto.** Multi-Level Planning for Electric Power Projects. In *Goreux, L. M. and Manne, A. S., eds.,* 1973, pp. 197–231.

Fernando, T. D. H.; Sengupta, S. Sankar and Podrebarac, Michael L. Probabilities of Optima in Multi-Objective Linear Programmes. In *Cochrane, J. L. and Zeleny, M., eds.,* 1973, pp. 217–35.

Ferrar, Terry A. Progressive Taxation as a Policy for Water Quality Management. *Water Resources Res.,* June 1973, *9*(3), pp. 563–68.

Ferrara, Reno. Le concentrazioni economico-spaziali nelle decisioni localizzative degli impianti. (Industrial Linkages in the Decisions Taken for the Localization of Installations. With English summary.) *L'Impresa,* 1973, *15*(2), pp. 123–27.

Ferrara, William L. Responsibility Accounting—A Basic Control Concept. In *Thomas, W. E., Jr., ed.,* 1973, pp. 60–71.

Ferrari, A. and Seetzen, J. La ricerca innovazionale in USA e in Europa. (Results of Innovation Research in USA and Europe. With English summary.) *L'Impresa,* 1973, *15*(7–8), pp. 425–32.

Ferrari, Alberto. Integrazione monetaria europea e movimenti internazionali dei capitali. (European Monetary Integration and International Capital Movements. With English summary.) *Bancaria,* May 1973, *29*(5), pp. 563–67.

_____ Integrazione monetaria europea e movimenti internazionali dei capitali, II. (European Monetary Integration and International Capital Movements, II. With English summary.) *Bancaria,* June 1973, *29*(6), pp. 688–95.

_____ Monetary Policy in Italy. In *Holbik, K., ed.,* 1973, pp. 214–45.

Ferrer-Pacces, F. M. La rivincita dei gamma. (Gamma's Revenge. With English summary.) *L'Impresa,* 1973, *15*(5–6), pp. 305–08.

_____ Strategia sindacale. Verso lo sfondamento delle linee di difesa tattica. (Trade Unions Strategy. Towards the Breaking of Tactical Defense Lines. With English summary.) *L'Impresa,* 1973, *15*(11–12), pp. 656–58.

_____ Teoria senza ricerca. (Theory Without Research. With English summary.) *L'Impresa,* 1973, *15*(3–4), pp. 187–89.

_____ Una ricerca (da 5 milioni di $) interrotta. (A Discontinued Research (worth $5 millions.) With English summary.) *L'Impresa,* 1973, *15*(7–8), pp. 418–24.

Ferrier, R. W. The Armenians and the East India Company in Persia in the Seventeenth and Early Eighteenth Centuries. *Econ. Hist. Rev., 2nd Ser.,* February 1973, *26*(1), pp. 38–62.

Fessler, Daniel Wm. Casting the Courts in a Land Use Reform Effort: A Starring Role or a Supporting Part? In *Clawson, M., ed.,* 1973, pp. 175–203.

Festy, Patrick. Canada, United States, Australia and New Zealand: Nuptiality Trends. *Population Stud.,* November 1973, *27*(3), pp. 479–92.

Fethke, Gary C. and Belmont, William R. Buyers' Versus Sellers' Prices: An Econometric Investigation. *Nebr. J. Econ. Bus.,* Autumn 1973, *12*(4), pp. 37–50.

Fetscher, Iring. Karl Marx on Human Nature. *Soc. Res.,* Autumn 1973, *40*(3), pp. 443–67.

Fettig, L. P.; Ogut, Soner and Baker, C. B. Effects of Financing and Employment Alternatives on a Modern Farm Village in Turkey. *Ill. Agr. Econ.,* July 1973, *13*(2), pp. 12–15.

Ffrench-Davis, Ricardo. Foreign Investment in Latin America: Recent Trends and Prospects. In *Urquidi, V. L. and Thorp, R., eds.,* 1973, pp. 169–89.

Fiegehen, G. C. and Lansley, P. S. The Tax-Credit Proposals. *Nat. Inst. Econ. Rev.,* May 1973, (64), pp. 44–67.

Field, Charles G. Evaluating the Administrative Delivery of Housing Goals. *Amer. Real Estate Urban Econ. Assoc. J.,* Fall 1973, *1*(2), pp. 21–34.

_____ **and Schafer, Robert.** Section 235 of the National Housing Act: Homeownership for Low-income Families? In *Pynoos, J.; Schafer, R. and Hartman, C. W., eds.,* 1973, pp. 460–71.

Field, Mark G. Handbook of Soviet Social Science Data: Health. In *Mickiewicz, E., ed.,* 1973, pp. 101–18.

Fields, Gary S.; Neenan, William B. and Akin, John S. A Socioeconomic Explanation of Demand for Public Goods. *Public Finance Quart.,* April 1973, *1*(2), pp. 169–89.

Fieleke, Norman S. International Economic Reform. *New Eng. Econ. Rev.,* January-February 1973, pp. 19–27.

Fielitz, Bruce D. and Nichols, Donald R. Awareness of Marginal Income Tax Rates Among Taxpayers. *Miss. Val. J. Bus. Econ.,* Spring 1973, *8*(3), pp. 39–46.

Figueroa, Luis. Participation under the Popular Unity Government. In *Zammit, J. A., ed.,* 1973, pp. 187–91.

Filippi, Enrico. Finanza italiana: Analisi di un caso di fusione (FINGEST/SALSI) (Italian Finance: Analysis of a Case of Merger (FINGEST/SALSI). With English summary.) *L'Impresa,* 1973, *15* (3–4), pp. 225–31.

Findley, Roger W. Problems Faced by Colombia's Agrarian Reform Institute in Acquiring and Distributing Land. In *Scott, R. E., ed.*, 1973, pp. 122–92.

Fine, Kit. Conditions for the Existence of Cycles Under Majority and Non-Minority Rules. *Econometrica*, September 1973, *41*(5), pp. 889–99.

Finet, Jacques. Monetary Policy in Belgium. In *Holbik, K., ed.*, 1973, pp. 39–69.

Finger, J. M. The Generalized Scheme of Preferences—Impact on the Donor Countries. *Bull. Econ. Res.*, May 1973, *25*(1), pp. 43–54.

Fink, Gary M. The Rejection of Voluntarism. *Ind. Lab. Relat. Rev.*, January 1973, *26*(2), pp. 805–19.

Fink, William H. Dollar Surplus and Devaluation. *Rivista Int. Sci. Econ. Com.*, July 1973, *20*(7), pp. 625–39.

Finke, Jeffrey. Nitrogen Fertilizer: Price Levels and Sales in Illinois, 1945–1971. *Ill. Agr. Econ.*, January 1973, *13*(1), pp. 34–40.

—— **and Swanson, E. R.** Diversification in Illinois Crop Production: 1938–1970. *Ill. Agr. Econ.*, January 1973, *13*(1), pp. 8–11.

Finkelhor, David and Reich, Michael. The Military-Industrial Complex. In *Reynolds, L. G.; Green, G. D. and Lewis, D. R., eds.*, 1973, pp. 334–46.

Finkelstein, Larry. Concepts for Reporting on Corporations' Community Involvement. In *Dierkes, M. and Bauer, R. A., eds.*, 1973, pp. 219–24.

Finley, Robert M.; Johnson, Stanley R. and Hassan, Zuhair A. The Demand for Food in the United States. *Appl. Econ.*, December 1973, *5*(4), pp. 233–48.

Finney, B. R. Big-men, Half-men and Trader-chiefs: Entrepreneurial Styles in Australian New Guinea and French Polynesia. In *Epstein, T. S. and Penny, D. H., eds.*, 1973, pp. 114–30.

Fiorentino, Raúl and Dean, Geral. Política agraria para la economía yerbatera como contribución al desarrollo agrícola misionero, un enfoque estructural. (Agricultural Policy for the Argentine Yerba Mate Industry and the Small Farm Sector of Misiones, a Structural Approach. With English summary.) *Económica*, September-December 1973, *19*(3), pp. 265–91.

Firch, Robert S. Adjustments in a Slowly Declining U.S. Cotton Production Industry. *Amer. J. Agr. Econ.*, December 1973, *55*(5), pp. 892–902.

Firestine, Robert E. The Impact of Reapportionment Upon Local Government Aid Receipts within Large Metropolitan Areas. *Soc. Sci. Quart.*, September 1973, *54*(2), pp. 394–402.

Firth, Michael A. An Empirical Examination of the Applicability of Adopting the AICPA and NYSE Regulations and Free Share Distributions in the U.K. *J. Acc. Res.*, Spring 1973, *11*(1), pp. 16–24.

Fischer, David W. Some Social and Economic Aspects of Marine Resource Development. *Amer. J. Econ. Soc.*, April 1973, *32*(2), pp. 113–27.

Fischer, Dietrich. Kosten-Nutzen-Analysen. (Cost-Benefit-Analyses. With English summary.) *Z. ges. Staatswiss.*, May 1973, *129*(2), pp. 230–45.

Fischer, Stanley. A Life Cycle Model of Life Insurance Purchases. *Int. Econ. Rev.*, February 1973, *14*(1), pp. 132–52.

—— A Neoclassical Monetary Growth Model:

Comment. *J. Money, Credit, Banking*, May 1973, *5*(2), pp. 704–06.

—— **and Cooper, J. Phillip.** Stabilization Policy and Lags. *J. Polit. Econ.*, July-August 1973, *81*(4), pp. 847–77.

—— **and Cooper, J. Phillip.** The Use of the Secant Method in Econometric Models. *J. Bus.*, April 1973, *46*(2), pp. 274–77.

Fishburn, Peter C. Bernoullian Utilities for Multiple-Factor Situations. In *Cochrane, J. L. and Zeleny, M., eds.*, 1973, pp. 47–61.

—— A Mixture-Set Axiomatization of Conditional Subjective Expected Utility. *Econometrica*, January 1973, *41*(1), pp. 1–25.

—— Summation Social Choice Functions. *Econometrica*, November 1973, *41*(6), pp. 1183–96.

—— Transitive Binary Social Choices and Intraprofile Conditions. *Econometrica*, July 1973, *41*(4), pp. 603–15.

Fisher, Alan A. The Minimum Wage and Teenage Unemployment: A Comment on the Literature. *Western Econ. J.*, December 1973, *11*(4), pp. 514–24.

Fisher, Anthony C. Environmental Externalities and the Arrow-Lind Public Investment Theorem. *Amer. Econ. Rev.*, September 1973, *63*(4), pp. 722–25.

—— A Paradox in the Theory of Public Investment. *J. Public Econ.*, November 1973, *2*(4), pp. 405–07.

Fisher, Douglas. The Speculative Demand for Money: An Empirical Test. *Economica, N.S.*, May 1973, *40*(158), pp. 174–79.

Fisher, Ernest M. Evaluation of National Housing Goals. *Amer. Real Estate Urban Econ. Assoc. J.*, Fall 1973, *1*(2), pp. 5–20.

—— Speculative Development of Residential Land and Residential Structures during the 1920's and the 1960's and 1970's. *Amer. Real Estate Urban Econ. Assoc. J.*, June 1973, *1*(1), pp. 123–39.

Fisher, Franklin M. Stability and Competitive Equilibrium in Two Models of Search and Individual Price Adjustment. *J. Econ. Theory*, October 1973, *6*(5), pp. 446–70.

—— **and Temin, Peter.** Returns to Scale in Research and Development: What Does the Schumpeterian Hypothesis Imply? *J. Polit. Econ.*, January-February 1973, *81*(1), pp. 56–70.

Fisher, Joseph L.; Olson, Mancur and Landsberg, Hans H. The No-Growth Society: Epilogue. In *Olson, M. and Landsberg, H. H., eds.*, 1973, pp. 229–41.

—— **and Ridker, Ronald G.** Population Growth, Resource Availability and Environmental Quality. *Amer. Econ. Rev.*, May 1973, *63*(2), pp. 79–87.

Fisher, Lawrence. Investment Characteristics of Common Stocks in Regulated and Unregulated Industries: A Comparative Study. In *Russell, M., ed.*, 1973, pp. 53–78.

Fisher, Lloyd and Van Ness, John W. Admissible Discriminant Analysis. *J. Amer. Statist. Assoc.*, September 1973, *68*(343), pp. 603–07.

Fisher, Paul. Major Social Security Issues: Japan, 1972. *Soc. Sec. Bull.*, March 1973, *36*(3), pp. 26–38.

Fisher, Robert W. Labor in a Year of Economic Stabilization. *Mon. Lab. Rev.*, January 1973, *96*(1), pp. 17–26.

_____ When Workers are Discharged—An Overview. *Mon. Lab. Rev.*, June 1973, *96*(6), pp. 4–17.

Fisher, Thomas E. Il finanziamento del credito rateale in Gran Bretagna. (Instalment Credit Finance in the United Kingdom. With English summary.) *Bancaria*, January 1973, *29*(1), pp. 23–29.

Fishlow, Albert. Comparative Consumption Patterns, the Extent of the Market, and Alternative Development Strategies. In *Ayal, E. B., ed.*, 1973, pp. 41–80.

_____ Some Reflections on Post-1964 Brazilian Economic Policy. In *Stepan, A., ed.*, 1973, pp. 69–118.

Fishman, L. The Rate of Interest in a State of Economic Flux: Discussion. In *Parkin, M., ed.*, 1973, pp. 343–44.

Fisk, E. K. and Honeybone, D. Belshaw's 'Emergent Fijian Enterprise' after Ten Years. In *Epstein, T. S. and Penny, D. H., eds.*, 1973, pp. 173–92.

Fitch, Lyle C. Metropolitan Financial Problems. In *Grieson, R. E., ed.*, 1973, pp. 418–28.

Fitts, John. Testing for Autocorrelation in the Autoregressive Moving Average Error Model. *J. Econometrics*, December 1973, *1*(4), pp. 363–76.

Fitzgerald, A. Ernest. Golden Fleece. In *Haveman, R. H. and Hamrin, R. D., eds.*, 1973, pp. 166–74.

Fitzgerald, E. V. K. and Aneuryn-Evans, G. B. The Economics of Airport Development and Control. *J. Transp. Econ. Policy*, September 1973, *7*(3), pp. 269–82.

Fitzgerald, John F., Jr. Demutualization of Mutual Property and Liability Insurers. *J. Risk Ins.*, December 1973, *40*(4), pp. 575–84.

FitzGerald, V. W. Dynamic Properties of a Non-Linear Econometric Model. In *Powell, A. A. and Williams, R. A., eds.*, 1973, pp. 169–93.

_____ and Higgins, C. I. An Econometric Model of the Australian Economy. *J. Econometrics*, October 1973, *1*(3), pp. 229–65.

Flaim, Paul O. Discouraged Workers and Changes in Unemployment. *Mon. Lab. Rev.*, March 1973, *96*(3), pp. 8–16.

_____ Employment Developments in the First Half of 1973. *Mon. Lab. Rev.*, September 1973, *96*(9), pp. 25–28.

Flakierski, H. The Polish Economic Reform of 1970. *Can. J. Econ.*, February 1973, *6*(1), pp. 1–15.

Flamholtz, Eric. Human Resource Accounting: Its Role in Management Planning and Control. *Econ. Soc. Tijdschr.*, February 1973, *27*(1), pp. 3–22.

_____ The Role of Human Resource Accounting in Social Accounting. In *Dierkes, M. and Bauer, R. A., eds.*, 1973, pp. 166–82.

Flanagan, John C. Inputs to Social Accounts Gained from Studies of Individuals' Quality of Life. In *Dierkes, M. and Bauer, R. A., eds.*, 1973, pp. 50–56.

Flanagan, Robert J. Racial Wage Discrimination and Employment Segregation. *J. Human Res.*, Fall 1973, *8*(4), pp. 456–71.

_____ Segmented Market Theories and Racial Discrimination. *Ind. Relat.*, October 1973, *12*(3), pp. 253–73.

_____ The U.S. Phillips Curve and International Unemployment Rate Differentials. *Amer. Econ. Rev.*, March 1973, *63*(1), pp. 114–31.

Flanders, Dwight P. and Anderson, Peggy Engelhardt. Sex Discrimination in Employment: Theory and Practice. *Ind. Lab. Relat. Rev.*, April 1973, *26*(3), pp. 938–55.

Fleck, F. H., et al. The Cost-function of a CES-Production Function. *Rivista Int. Sci. Econ. Com.*, January 1973, *20*(1), pp. 18–32.

Fleming, Robert M. How Risky Is the Market? *J. Bus.*, July 1973, *46*(3), pp. 404–24.

Fleming, Thomas F., Jr. Manpower Impact of Purchases by State and Local Governments. *Mon. Lab. Rev.*, June 1973, *96*(6), pp. 33–39.

Flemming, J. S. The Consumption Function when Capital Markets are Imperfect: The Permanent Income Hypothesis Reconsidered. *Oxford Econ. Pap.*, July 1973, *25*(2), pp. 160–72.

_____ On the Theory of the Valuation and Allocation of Time: Some Comments. *Scot. J. Polit. Econ.*, February 1973, *20*(1), pp. 65–71.

Flesher, John; Over, Mead and Ahmad, Meekal A. An Econometric Test of a Zero Elasticity of Substitution Production Function for Pakistan. *Pakistan Econ. Soc. Rev.*, Winter 1973, *11*(4), pp. 443–53.

Fletcher, T. W. Lancashire Livestock Farming during the Great Depression. In *Perry, P. J., ed.*, 1973, pp. 77–108.

Flinn, J. C. and Guise, J. W. B. Allocation and Pricing of Water Resources. In *Judge, G. G. and Takayama, T., eds.*, 1973, pp. 536–56.

Flook, E. Evelyn and Sanazaro, Paul J. Health Services Research: Origins and Milestones. In *Flook, E. E. and Sanazaro, P. J., eds.*, 1973, pp. 1–81.

Florence, Gary A. Electric Utility Bond Financing. *Manage. Account.*, June 1973, *54*(12), pp. 35–37, 41.

Flores, Guillermo V. Race and Culture in the Black Colony: Keeping the Chicano in His Place. In *Bonilla, F. and Girling, R., eds.*, 1973, pp. 189–223.

_____ and Bailey, Ronald. Internal Colonialism and Racial Minorities in the U.S.: An Overview. In *Bonilla, F. and Girling, R., eds.*, 1973, pp. 149–60.

Flowers, Vincent S. and Hughes, Charles L. Why Employees Stay. *Harvard Bus. Rev.*, July-August 1973, *51*(4), pp. 49–60.

Floyd, Charles F. and Sirmans, C. F. Shift and Share Projections Revisited. *J. Reg. Sci.*, April 1973, *13*(1), pp. 115–20.

Floyd, John E. Monetary and Fiscal Policy in a World of Capital Mobility: A Reply. *Rev. Econ. Stud.*, April 1973, *40*(2), pp. 299–303.

Fløystad, Gunnar. Factor Price Equalization in Theory and Practice—A Study of Mainly Norwegian Data. *Weltwirtsch. Arch.*, 1973, *109*(4), pp. 554–78.

_____ The Impact on Allocation and Return to Labor and Capital of a Reduction of Customs Duties in the Developed Countries in Their Trade with Less Developed Countries. *Weltwirtsch. Arch.*, 1973, *109*(1), pp. 59–69.

_____ A Note on Estimating the Elasticity of Substitution Between Labour and Capital from Norwegian Time Series Data. *Swedish J. Econ.*, March 1973, *75*(1), pp. 100–04.

Foegen, J. H. The High Cost of Innovative Employee Benefits. *Calif. Manage. Rev.*, Spring 1973, *15*(3), pp. 100–04.

Fog, Bjarke. A Danish Study of the Distribution Process. *L'Impresa*, 1973, *15*(1), pp. 59–64.

Fogarty, Michael and Paglin, Morton. Equity and the Property Tax: A Reply. *Nat. Tax J.*, December 1973, *26*(4), pp. 651–52.

Fogarty, Robert S. Oneida: A Utopian Search for Religious Security. *Labor Hist.*, Spring 1973, *14* (2), pp. 202–27.

Foley, Duncan K. A Primer on Negative Taxation. In *Grieson, R. E., ed.*, 1973, pp. 297–312.

Foley, K. and Chapman, R. A Note on Losses from Price Stabilization. *Australian J. Agr. Econ.*, August 1973, *17*(2), pp. 140–43.

Foley, V. An Origin of the *Tableau Économique*. *Hist. Polit. Econ.*, Spring 1973, *5*(1), pp. 121–50.

Folks, William R., Jr. The Optimal Level of Forward Exchange Transactions. *J. Financial Quant. Anal.*, January 1973, *8*(1), pp. 105–10.

Folsom, Donald J. A Control Guide for Computer Systems. *Manage. Account.*, August 1973, *55*(2), pp. 49–55.

Folsom, Ralph E., et al. The Two Alternate Questions Randomized Response Model for Human Surveys. *J. Amer. Statist. Assoc.*, September 1973, *68*(343), pp. 525–30.

Foner, Philip S. An Early Trades Union and Its Fate. *Labor Hist.*, Summer 1973, *14*(3), pp. 423–24.

Foran, Terry G. Unionism and Wage Differentials. *Southern Econ. J.*, October 1973, *40*(2), pp. 269–78.

Forbes, Ronald. Finance and Banking: Refereed Papers II: Discussion. *J. Finance*, May 1973, *28*(2), pp. 539–41.

Forbes, Stephen W. Further Studies of Property-Liability Return Adequacy: Reply. *J. Risk Ins.*, September 1973, *40*(3), pp. 460–62.

———— **and Mehr, Robert I.** The Risk Management Decision in the Total Business Setting. *J. Risk Ins.*, September 1973, *40*(3), pp. 389–401.

Ford, Allen. Selecting a Useful Life for the Investment Credit. *Manage. Account.*, April 1973, *54* (10), pp. 14–16.

Ford, James S. and Birkin, Stanley J. The Quantity/ Quality Dilemma: The Impact of a Zero Defects Program. In *Cochrane, J. L. and Zeleny, M., eds.*, 1973, pp. 517–29.

Ford, William F. and Tuccillo, John A. Monetary Policy Implications of the Hunt Commission Report. *Quart. Rev. Econ. Bus.*, Autumn 1973, *13*(3), pp. 93–103.

Form, William H. Job vs. Political Unionism: A Cross-national Comparison. *Ind. Relat.*, May 1973, *12*(2), pp. 224–38.

Formánek, Karel. Příspěvek k teorii nepravidelnosti dodávek. (Contribution to the Theory of Irregular Supplies. With English summary.) *Ekon.-Mat. Obzor*, 1973, *9*(1), pp. 30–50.

Formby, John P. A Clarification of Rent Theory: Reply. *Southern Econ. J.*, July 1973, *40*(1), pp. 131–34.

———— On Revenue Maximizing Duopoly. *J. Ind. Econ.*, July 1973, *21*(3), pp. 272–92.

Formuzis, Peter. The Demand for Eurodollars and the Optimum Stock of Bank Liabilities. *J. Money, Credit, Banking*, August 1973, *5*(3), pp. 806–18.

Forst, Brian E. An Analysis of Alternative Periodic Health Examination Strategies. In *Niskanen, W. A., et al., eds.*, 1973, pp. 393–409.

———— Quantifying the Patient's Preferences. In *Berg, R. L., ed.*, 1973, pp. 209–20.

Forster, Bruce A. Optimal Consumption Planning in a Polluted Environment. *Econ. Rec.*, December 1973, *49*(128), pp. 534–45.

———— Optimal Capital Accumulation in a Polluted Environment. *Southern Econ. J.*, April 1973, *39* (4), pp. 544–47.

———— **and Logan, John.** The Welfare Economics of Water Resource Allocation Over Time: Comment. *Appl. Econ.*, March 1973, *5*(1), pp. 61–68.

Forsyth, John D. and Laughhunn, D. J. Capital Rationing in the Face of Multiple Organizational Objectives. In *Cochrane, J. L. and Zeleny, M., eds.*, 1973, pp. 439–46.

Forsythe, Alan B., et al. A Stopping Rule for Variable Selection in Multiple Regression. *J. Amer. Statist. Assoc.*, March 1973, *68*(341), pp. 75–77.

Forsythe, Graeme A. Rural and Urban Flood Insurance: A Review. In *Aislabie, C., ed.*, 1973, pp. 68–77.

Forti, Augusto and Bisogno, Paolo. International Seminar on Trends in Mathematical Modelling: Introduction. In *Hawkes, N., ed.*, 1973, pp. 1–7.

Fortt, J. M. Land Tenure and the Emergence of Large Scale Farming. In *Richards, A. I.; Sturrock, F. and Fortt, J. M., eds.*, 1973, pp. 66–84.

———— **and Hougham, D. A.** Environment, Population and Economic History. In *Richards, A. I.; Sturrock, F. and Fortt, J. M., eds.*, 1973, pp. 17–46.

Fortune, Peter. The Impact of Taxable Municipal Bonds: Policy Simulations with a Large Econometric Model. *Nat. Tax J.*, March 1973, *26*(1), pp. 29–42.

———— A Theory of Optimal Life Insurance: Development and Tests. *J. Finance*, June 1973, *28*(3), pp. 587–600.

Foss, Laurence. Managerial Strategy for the Future: Theory Z Management. *Calif. Manage. Rev.*, Spring 1973, *15*(3), pp. 68–81.

Foster, C. D. A Note on the Treatment of Taxation in Cost-benefit Analysis. In *Wolfe, J. N., ed.*, 1973, pp. 63–74.

———— **and Whitehead, C. M. E.** The Layfield Report on the Greater London Development Plan. *Economica, N.S.*, November 1973, *40*(160), pp. 442–54.

Foster, F. G. Stochastic Processes. In *Ross, M., ed.*, 1973, pp. 223–39.

Foster, George. Stock Market Reaction to Estimates of Earnings per Share by Company Officials. *J. Acc. Res.*, Spring 1973, *11*(1), pp. 25–37.

Foster, Howard G. The Labor Market in Nonunion Construction. *Ind. Lab. Relat. Rev.*, July 1973, *26* (4), pp. 1071–85.

Foster, J. I. The Behaviour of Unemployment and Unfilled Vacancies: Great Britain, 1958–1971—A

Comment. *Econ. J.*, March 1973, *83*(329), pp. 192–201.

Foulkes, Fred K. Learning to Live with OSHA. *Harvard Bus. Rev.*, November-December 1973, *51* (6), pp. 57–67.

Foulon, Alain. Consommation des ménages et consommation publique "divisible": Structure, évolution et financement 1959–1969. (Private Consumption and Public "Divisible" Consumption: Structure, Evolution and Financement. 1959–1969. With English summary.) *Consommation*, April-June 1973, *20*(2), pp. 5–94.

———; **Hatchuel, Georges and Kende, Pierre.** Un premier bilan de la redistribution des revenus en France; Les impôts et cotisations sociales à la charge des ménages en 1965. (Balance of the Redistribution of Incomes in France: Personal Taxes and Social Security Contributions in 1965. With English summary.) *Consommation*, October-December 1973, *20*(4), pp. 5–133.

Fowler, Loretta. The Arapahoe Ranch: An Experiment in Cultural Change and Economic Development. *Econ. Develop. Cult. Change*, April 1973, *21*(3), pp. 446–64.

Fox, Irving K. and Wible, Lyman. Information Generation and Communication to Establish Environmental Quality Objectives. *Natural Res. J.*, January 1973, *13*(1), pp. 134–49.

Fox, Karl A. and Van Moeseke, Paul. Derivation and Implications of a Scalar Measure of Social Income. In *[Tinbergen, J.]*, 1973, pp. 21–40.

Foxley, Alejandro and Clark, Peter B. Target Shooting with a Multisectoral Model. In *Eckaus, R. S. and Rosenstein-Rodan, P. N., eds.*, 1973, pp. 341–66.

———; **Jul, Anna Maria and Clark, Peter B.** Project Evaluation within a Macroeconomic Framework. In *Eckaus, R. S. and Rosenstein-Rodan, P. N., eds.*, 1973, pp. 199–226.

Franchet, Yves; Inman, Richard A. and Manne, Alan S. Numerical Data for Multi-Sector Planning. In *Goreux, L. M. and Manne, A. S., eds.*, 1973, pp. 85–106.

Francis, Darryl R. Economic Issues in 1974. *Fed. Res. Bank St. Louis Rev.*, October 1973, *55*(10), pp. 14–19.

——— The Problem of Re-Entry to a High-Employment Economy: An Address. *Fed. Res. Bank St. Louis Rev.*, June 1973, *55*(6), pp. 11–14.

——— The Usefulness of Applied Econometrics to the Policymaker: An Address. *Fed. Res. Bank St. Louis Rev.*, May 1973, *55*(5), pp. 7–10.

Francis, Gary. On the Obligation to Publish and the Nature of URPE Literature. *Rev. Radical Polit. Econ.*, Summer 1973, *5*(2), pp. 93–94.

Francis, Ivor. A Comparison of Several Analysis of Variance Programs. *J. Amer. Statist. Assoc.*, December 1973, *68*(344), pp. 860–65.

Francis, Jack Clark. Economic Pressures Reshape America's Stock Markets. *Fed. Res. Bank Bus. Rev. Phila.*, June 1973, pp. 12–18.

——— Has the Inventory Cycle Lost Its Oomph? *Fed. Res. Bank Bus. Rev. Phila.*, February 1973, pp. 19–27.

Francis, M. E. Accounting and the Evaluation of

Social Programs: A Critical Comment. *Accounting Rev.*, April 1973, *48*(2), pp. 245–57.

Franco, G. Robert. A Model of French Post-War Inflation. *Econ. Int.*, May 1973, *26*(2), pp. 329–48.

——— The Wage Subsidy Index in the Merchant Marine Act of 1970. *J. Transp. Econ. Policy*, September 1973, *7*(3), pp. 283–90.

Frank, Charles R., Jr. Debt Adjustment: The Tyranny of Bankers, Brokers, and Bondholders: Comment. In *Lewis, J. P. and Kapur, I., eds.*, 1973, pp. 123–30.

——— Trade, Investment and Labor, and the Changing International Division of Production: Comment. In *Hughes, H., ed.*, 1973, pp. 61–68.

Frank, Helmut J. and Schanz, John J., Jr. The Future of American Oil and Natural Gas. *Ann. Amer. Acad. Polit. Soc. Sci.*, November 1973, *410*, pp. 24–34.

——— **and Wells, Donald A.** United States Oil Imports: Implications for the Balance of Payments. *Natural Res. J.*, July 1973, *13*(3), pp. 431–47.

Franke, Jürgen F. A. W. Advertising and Collusion in Oligopoly. *Jahr. Nationalökon. Statist.*, December 1973, *188*(1), pp. 33–50.

——— Marktmacht und Inflation. (Market Power and Inflation. With English summary.) *Z. Wirtschaft. Sozialwissen.*, 1973, *93*(3), pp. 285–305.

——— Zur Besteuerung der Werbung. (With English summary.) *Kyklos*, 1973, *26*(2), pp. 337–61.

Frankel, Marvin. Pricing Decisions Under Unknown Demand. *Kyklos*, 1973, *26*(1), pp. 1–24.

Frankel, S. Herbert. Economic Change in Africa in Historical Perspective. In *Youngson, A. J., ed.*, 1973, pp. 211–28.

Frankena, Mark. Income Distributional Effects of Urban Transit Subsidies. *J. Transp. Econ. Policy*, September 1973, *7*(3), pp. 215–30.

——— Marketing Characteristics and Prices of Exports of Engineering Goods from India. *Oxford Econ. Pap.*, March 1973, *25*(1), pp. 127–32.

——— **and Bhatia, Kul B.** Canadian Contributions to Economics Journals, 1968-1972. *Can. J. Econ.*, February 1973, *6*(1), pp. 121–24.

Frankenhoff, Charles. The Economics of a Popular Housing Policy. *Land Econ.*, August 1973, *49*(3), pp. 336–43.

Frankle, A. W. and Hawkins, Clark A. The Behavior of Convertible Debenture Premiums: Comment. *Miss. Val. J. Bus. Econ.*, Winter 1973-74, *9*(2), pp. 65–68.

Franklin, William S. A Comparison of Formally and Informally Trained Journeymen in Construction. *Ind. Lab. Relat. Rev.*, July 1973, *26*(4), pp. 1086–94.

Franko, Lawrence G. Strategy + Structure − Frustration = the Experiences of European Firms in America. In *Henley, D. S., ed.*, 1973, pp. 83–94.

Fraquelli, Giovanni. La matrice applicata alle previsioni aziendali. (Business Applications of the Matrix Input-Output for Forecasting Analyses. With English summary.) *L'Impresa*, 1973, *15*(3–4), pp. 273–77.

Fraser, Donald R. and Rose, Peter S. Short-Run Bank Portfolio Behavior: An Examination of Selected

Liquid Assets. *J. Finance*, May 1973, *28*(2), pp. 531–37.

———— and Rose, Peter S. The Short-run Determinants of Loan Mix at Large Commercial Banks. *J. Econ. Bus.*, Fall 1973, *26*(1), pp. 1–9.

Fraser, Ian. Balance Sheet on Take-Overs. In *Allen, G. C., et al.*, 1973, pp. 61–70.

Frăţilă, Gh. Optimizarea repartiţiei teritoriale a îngrăşămintelor chimice. (Optimizing the Territorial Distribution of Chemical Fertilizers. With English summary.) *Stud. Cercet. Econ.*, 1973, (3), pp. 99–104.

Frazer, William J., Jr. An Assessment of the Impact of the Computer. *Schweiz. Z. Volkswirtsch. Statist.*, December 1973, *109*(4), pp. 579–95.

Frech, H. E., III. Pricing of Pollution: The Coase Theorem in the Long Run. *Bell J. Econ. Manage. Sci.*, Spring 1973, *4*(1), pp. 316–19.

———— The Public Choice Theory of Murray N. Rothbard, A Modern Anarchist. *Public Choice*, Spring 1973, *14*, pp. 143–54.

Frediani, Lorenzo and Arcucci, Francesco. Savings Banks and Savings Facilities in African Countries: Malawi. In *Alberici, A. and Baravelli, M., eds.*, 1973, pp. 55–59.

Freebairn, J. W. Some Estimates of Supply and Inventory Response Functions for the Cattle and Sheep Sector of New South Wales. *Rev. Marketing Agr. Econ.*, June and September 1973, *41* (2–3), pp. 53–90.

———— The Value of Information Provided by a Uniform Grading System. *Australian J. Agr. Econ.*, August 1973, *17*(2), pp. 127–39.

Freedman, Ronald. Social and Economic Factors in Hong Kong's Fertility Decline: A Comment. *Population Stud.*, November 1973, *27*(3), pp. 589–95.

Freeman, A. Myrick, III. Grants and Environmental Policy. In *Boulding, K. E.; Pfaff, M. and Pfaff, A., eds.*, 1973, pp. 309–17.

———— Income Distribution and Environmental Quality. In *Enthoven, A. C. and Freeman, A. M., III, eds.*, 1973, pp. 100–06.

———— and Cicchetti, Charles J. The Trans-Alaska Pipeline: An Economic Analysis of Alternatives. In *Enthoven, A. C. and Freeman, A. M., III, eds.*, 1973, pp. 271–84.

———— and Haveman, Robert H. Clean Rhetoric and Dirty Water. In *Enthoven, A. C. and Freeman, A. M., III, eds.*, 1973, pp. 122–37.

Freeman, Christopher. The International Science Race. In *Edge, D. O. and Wolfe, J. N., eds.*, 1973, pp. 231–38.

———— Malthus with a Computer. In *Cole, H. S. D., et al., eds.*, 1973, pp. 5–13.

———— A Study of Success and Failure in Industrial Innovation. In *Williams, B. R., ed.*, 1973, pp. 227–45.

———— and Julien, P.-A. The Capital and Industrial Output Sub-system. In *Cole, H. S. D., et al., eds.*, 1973, pp. 66–79.

Freeman, Richard B. Changes in the Labor Market for Black Americans, 1948–72. *Brookings Pap. Econ. Act.*, 1973, (1), pp. 67–120.

———— Decline of Labor Market Discrimination and

Economic Analysis. *Amer. Econ. Rev.*, May 1973, *63*(2), pp. 280–86.

Freeman, Roger A. Tax Relief for the Homeowner? *Nat. Tax J.*, September 1973, *26*(3), pp. 485–90.

Freeman, S. David. Is There an Energy Crisis? An Overview. *Ann. Amer. Acad. Polit. Soc. Sci.*, November 1973, *410*, pp. 1–10.

Freestone, R. and Todd, M. The Effect on Store Costs of a Trial Method for Rehandling Bulk-Class Wools: A Preliminary Analysis. *Quart. Rev. Agr. Econ.*, October 1973, *26*(4), pp. 263–76.

Freiden, Alan. A Program for the Estimation of Dymanic Economic Relations from a Time Series of Cross Sections. *Ann. Econ. Soc. Measure*, January 1973, *2*(1), pp. 89–91.

———— and Staaf, Robert J. Scholastic Choice: An Economic Model of Student Behavior. *J. Human Res.*, Summer 1973, *8*(3), pp. 396–404.

Freire, Paulo. Pedagogy of the Oppressed. In *Wilber, C. K., ed.*, 1973, pp. 410–26.

Freivalds, John. Bringing Space Down to Earth: Space Age Technology Transfer and the Developing Countries. *J. Devel. Areas*, October 1973, *8*(1), pp. 83–92.

Fremgen, James M. Capital Budgeting Practices: A Survey. *Manage. Account.*, May 1973, *54*(11), pp. 19–25.

Fremr, Jiří. Wage Developments in the Czechoslovak National Economy Since 1945, and Wage Trends in the 5th Five-Year Plan. *Czech. Econ. Digest.*, September 1973, (6), pp. 105–19.

French, Christopher J. Eighteenth-Century Shipping Tonnage Measurements. *J. Econ. Hist.*, June 1973, *33*(2), pp. 434–43.

Frenkel, Jacob A. Elasticities and the Interest Parity Theory. *J. Polit. Econ.*, May-June 1973, *81*(3), pp. 741–47.

———— and Dornbusch, Rudiger. Inflation and Growth: Alternative Approaches. *J. Money, Credit, Banking*, Part I, February 1973, *5*(1), pp. 141–56.

Frerichs, Bernard H. and Berney, Robert E. Income Elasticities for State Tax Revenues: Techniques of Estimation and their Usefulness for Forecasting. *Public Finance Quart.*, October 1973, *1*(4), pp. 409–25.

Fretz, C. F. and Hayman, Joanne. Progress for Women—Men are Still More Equal. *Harvard Bus. Rev.*, September-October 1973, *51*(5), pp. 133–42.

Freund, James L. A Note on Short Period Changes in Earned Income in Manufacturing Among Urban Areas. *J. Reg. Sci.*, August 1973, *13*(2), pp. 279–89.

Frey, Bruno S. Interactions Between Preferences and Consumption in Economic Development. *Scot. J. Polit. Econ.*, February 1973, *20*(1), pp. 53–64.

———— and Frey, Rene L. The Economic Theory of Politics: A Survey of German Contributions. *Public Choice*, Fall 1973, *16*, pp. 81–89.

Frey, Donald E. The Distribution of Educational Resources in Large American Cities: Comment. *J. Human Res.*, Fall 1973, *8*(4), pp. 516–18.

Frey, Helmuth E. The Treatment of Import Duties

in National Accounts, A Comment on A. L. Gaathon: Exchange Rate Problems in National Accounting of Developing Countries. *Rev. Income Wealth,* June 1973, *19*(2), pp. 203–05.

Frey, Rene L. and Frey, Bruno S. The Economic Theory of Politics: A Survey of German Contributions. *Public Choice,* Fall 1973, *16,* pp. 81–89.

Friberg, Ronald A. Probabilistic Depreciation with a Varying Salvage Value. *Accounting Rev.,* January 1973, *48*(1), pp. 50–60.

Frick, Andreas; Kiener, Urs and Vieli, Klaus. Bodenpreise und Stadtentwicklung. Eine empirische Untersuchung. (Land Prices and Urban Development. With English summary.) *Schweiz. Z. Volkswirtsch. Statist.,* March 1973, *109*(1), pp. 101–15.

Fried, Edward R. Foreign Economic Policy: The Search for a Strategy. In *Owen, H., ed.,* 1973, pp. 157–202.

———— Implications for U.S. Policy toward Europe: Comment. In *Krause, L. B. and Salant, W. S., eds.,* 1973, pp. 283–86.

———— The Military and the Balance of Payments. *Ann. Amer. Acad. Polit. Soc. Sci.,* March 1973, *406,* pp. 80–85.

Fried, Joel. Inflation-unemployment Trade-offs under Fixed and Floating Exchange Rates. *Can. J. Econ.,* February 1973, *6*(1), pp. 43–52.

———— Money, Exchange and Growth. *Western Econ. J.,* September 1973, *11*(3), pp. 285–301.

Fried, Marc and Gleicher, Peggy. Some Sources of Residential Satisfaction in an Urban Slum. In *Rasmussen, D. W. and Haworth, C. T., eds.,* 1973, pp. 150–59.

Friedlaender, Ann F. Macro Policy Goals in the Postwar Period: A Study in Revealed Preference. *Quart. J. Econ.,* February 1973, *87*(1), pp. 25–43.

————; **Swanson, Gerald J. and Due, John F.** Estimating Sales Tax Revenue Changes in Response to Changes in Personal Income and Sales Tax Rates. *Nat. Tax J.,* March 1973, *26*(1), pp. 103–10.

Friedlander, Dov. Demographic Patterns and Socioeconomic Characteristics of the Coal-mining Population in England and Wales in the Nineteenth Century. *Econ. Develop. Cult. Change,* October 1973, *22*(1), pp. 39–51.

Friedman, Donald J. and Doggett, Kathleen M. Legislation for Clean Air: An Indoor Front. *Yale Law J.,* April 1973, *82*(5), pp. 1040–54.

Friedman, Irving S. Dilemmas of the Developing Countries—The Sword of Damocles. *Finance Develop.,* March 1973, *10*(1), pp. 12–15, 37.

———— International Monetary System: 1973 Reforming in a Hurricane. *Banca Naz. Lavoro Quart. Rev.,* December 1973, (107), pp. 352–74.

Friedman, James W. Concavity of Production Functions and Non-Increasing Returns to Scale. *Econometrica,* September 1973, *41*(5), pp. 981–84.

———— A Non-cooperative Equilibrium for Supergames: A Correction. *Rev. Econ. Stud.,* July 1973, *40*(3), pp. 435.

———— On Reaction Function Equilibria. *Int. Econ. Rev.,* October 1973, *14*(3), pp. 721–34.

Friedman, Judith J. Variations in the Level of Central Business District Retail Activity Among

Large U.S. Cities: 1954 and 1967. *Land Econ.,* August 1973, *49*(3), pp. 326–35.

Friedman, Lawrence M. Public Housing and the Poor. In *Pynoos, J.; Schafer, R. and Hartman, C. W., eds.,* 1973, pp. 448–59.

Friedman, M. and Schwartz, Anna J. The Panic of 1907 and Banking Reform in Its Wake. In *Temin, P., ed.,* 1973, pp. 315–35.

Friedman, Philip. Suggestions for the Analysis of Qualitative Dependent Variables. *Public Finance Quart.,* July 1973, *1*(3), pp. 345–55.

Friedman, Richard E. Private Foundation-Government Relationships. In *Heimann, F. F., ed.,* 1973, pp. 163–91.

Friedman, Yoram and Theil, Henri. Regional Per Capita Incomes and Income Inequalities: Point Estimates and Their Standard Errors. *J. Amer. Statist. Assoc.,* September 1973, *68*(343), pp. 531–39.

Friedmann, John. An Approach to the Development of New Core Regions: The Guayana Program in a Regional Perspective. In *Friedmann, J.,* 1973, pp. 273–86.

———— Education for Regional Planning in Developing Countries. In *Friedmann, J.,* 1973, pp. 299–309.

———— Hyperurbanization and National Development in Chile. In *Friedmann, J.,* 1973, pp. 91–114.

———— The Implementation of Regional Development Policies: Lessons of Experience. In *Friedmann, J.,* 1973, pp. 235–54.

———— National Urbanization Policy: Scope and Objectives. In *Friedmann, J.,* 1973, pp. 133–38.

———— Problems of Spatial Development in the Capital Region of Chile. In *Friedmann, J.,* 1973, pp. 187–226.

———— The Role of Cities in National Development. In *Friedmann, J.,* 1973, pp. 21–39.

———— Social Dimensions of Urban Development. In *Friedmann, J.,* 1973, pp. 115–29.

———— A Theory of Polarized Development. In *Friedmann, J.,* 1973, pp. 41–64.

———— The Urban-Regional Frame for National Development. In *Friedmann, J.,* 1973, pp. 139–51.

————, **et al.** Towards a National Urbanization Policy. In *Friedmann, J.,* 1973, pp. 153–86.

————, **et al.** Urbanization and National Development: A Comparative Analysis. In *Friedmann, J.,* 1973, pp. 65–90.

———— **and Stöhr, Walter.** The Uses of Regional Science: Policy Planning in Chile. In *Friedmann, J.,* 1973, pp. 255–71.

Friend, Irwin. Generating Micro Data in Less Developed Countries through Surveys: Some Experience in Asia: Comment. In *Ayal, E. B., ed.,* 1973, pp. 118–21.

———— Mythodology in Finance. *J. Finance,* May 1973, *28*(2), pp. 257–72.

———— **and Blume, Marshall E.** Competitive Commissions on the New York Stock Exchange. *J. Finance,* September 1973, *28*(4), pp. 795–819.

———— **and Blume, Marshall E.** A New Look at the Capital Asset Pricing Model. *J. Finance,* March 1973, *28*(1), pp. 19–33.

_____ **and Husic, Frank.** Efficiency of Corporate Investment. *Rev. Econ. Statist.*, February 1973, *55*(1), pp. 122–27.

Frigero, Piercarlo. I modelli macroeconomici di sviluppo come strumento operativo per l'impresa. (Models of Economic Growth as an Operative Instrument of the Firm. With English summary.) *L'Impresa*, 1973, *15*(3–4), pp. 233–39.

Frisch, Jack; Helliwell, John F. and Sparks, Gordon. The Supply Price of Capital in Macroeconomic Models. In *Powell, A. A. and Williams, R. A., eds.*, 1973, pp. 261–83.

Friss, István. Objective Conditions of the Economy and the Extent of Centralization and Decentralization. *Acta Oecon.*, 1973, *10*(3–4), pp. 303–14.

_____ On Long–Term National Economic Planning. In *Földi, T., ed.*, 1973, pp. 9–36.

_____ Practical Experiences of the Economic Reform in Hungary. *Eastern Europ. Econ.*, Spring 1973, *11*(3), pp. 3–26.

Fritzhand, Gary I. and Baker, R. Palmer, Jr. United States Federal Income Taxation of Foreign-Flag Shipping Earnings. *Nat. Tax J.*, December 1973, *26*(4), pp. 537–51.

Froehlich, B. R. A Note on Some Monte Carlo Results on Non-Negative Variance Estimators for a Random Coefficient Regression Model. *Amer. J. Agr. Econ.*, May 1973, *55*(2), pp. 231–34.

_____ Some Estimators for a Random Coefficient Regression Model. *J. Amer. Statist. Assoc.*, June 1973, *68*(342), pp. 329–35.

Frome, Edward L.; Kutner, Michael H. and Beauchamp, John J. Regression Analysis of Poisson-Distributed Data. *J. Amer. Statist. Assoc.*, December 1973, *68*(344), pp. 935–40.

Fromm, Gary. Econometric Models of the Residential Construction Sector: A Comparison. In *Ricks, R. B., ed.*, 1973, pp. 125–55.

_____ Implications to and from Economic Theory in Models of Complex Systems. *Amer. J. Agr. Econ.*, May 1973, *55*(2), pp. 259–71.

_____ **and Klein, Lawrence R.** A Comparison of Eleven Econometric Models of the United States. *Amer. Econ. Rev.*, May 1973, *63*(2), pp. 385–93.

_____ **and Schink, George R.** Aggregation and Econometric Models. *Int. Econ. Rev.*, February 1973, *14*(1), pp. 1–32.

Frosini, Benito Vittorio. Su alcune diseguaglianze concernenti lo scarto medio assoluto. (On Some Inequalities Concerning Mean Deviation. With English summary.) *Statistica*, January-March 1973, *33*(1), pp. 41–61.

Frost, Carl F.; Ruh, Robert A. and Wallace, Roger L. Management Attitudes and the Scanlon Plan. *Ind. Relat.*, October 1973, *12*(3), pp. 282–88.

Frugali, Fabio. Situation and Prospects of Small and Medium-Sized Industry in Italy. *Rev. Econ. Cond. Italy*, November 1973, *27*(6), pp. 397–409.

Fruitman, Frederick H. and Annable, James E., Jr. An Earnings Function for High-Level Manpower. *Ind. Lab. Relat. Rev.*, July 1973, *26*(4), pp. 1107–21.

Fry, Fred L. More on the Causes of Quits in Manufacturing. *Mon. Lab. Rev.*, June 1973, *96*(6), pp. 48–49.

Fry, Joseph N., et al. Customer Loyalty to Banks: A Longitudinal Study. *J. Bus.*, October 1973, *46*(4), pp. 517–25.

Fry, Maxwell J. Manipulating Demand for Money. In *Parkin, M., ed.*, 1973, pp. 371–85.

Frye, Jerry K. Rhetorical Strategies Employed by Henry George and His Followers. *Amer. J. Econ. Soc.*, October 1973, *32*(4), pp. 405–20.

Fuchs, Claudio J. and Landsberger, Henry A. "Revolution of Rising Expectations" or "Traditional Life Ways"? A Study of Income Aspirations in a Developing Country. *Econ. Develop. Cult. Change*, January 1973, *21*(2), pp. 212–26.

Fuchs, Tomáš and Prič, Jozef. Meranie intenzity ekonomického rastu metódou úplne dynamizovanej substitučnej produkčnej funkcie Cobb-Douglasovho typu. (Measuring the Intensity of Economic Growth by the Method of Totally Dynamised Cobb-Douglas Type Production Function. With English summary.) *Ekon.-Mat. Obzor*, 1973, *9*(4), pp. 381–92.

Fuchs, Victor R. and Grossman, Michael. Intersectoral Shifts and Aggregate Productivity Change. *Ann. Econ. Soc. Measure*, July 1973, *2*(3), pp. 227–43.

Fujita, Masahiro. International Money Flow and the Multinational Corporations. *Kobe Econ. Bus. Rev.*, 1973, *20*, pp. 22–36.

Fujita, Masahisa. Optimum Growth in Two-Region, Two-Good Space Systems: The Final State Problem. *J. Reg. Sci.*, December 1973, *13*(3), pp. 385–407.

Fukuchi, Takao and Nobukuni, Makoto. The Economic Measurement of the Benefit of Public Transportation Investment. (In Japanese. With English summary.) *Econ. Stud. Quart.*, December 1973, *24*(3), pp. 43–53.

Fukushima, Yasuto. PPBS in the Japanese Government: Necessity, Preparation and Problems. In *Novick, D., ed.*, 1973, pp. 125–28.

Fulco, Lawrence J. and Eisenberg, William M. Productivity and Costs in the Private Economy, 1972. *Mon. Lab. Rev.*, May 1973, *96*(5), pp. 3–7.

Fullenbaum, Richard F. and Bell, Frederick W. The Regional Impact of Resource Management. In *Mattila, J. M. and Thompson, W. R., eds.*, 1973, pp. 11–26.

Fuller, Stephen S. Social and Economic Factors in Federal Building Location Decisions. *Growth Change*, April 1973, *4*(2), pp. 43–48.

Fuller, Wayne A. and Battese, George E. Transformations for Estimation of Linear Models with Nested-Error Structure. *J. Amer. Statist. Assoc.*, September 1973, *68*(343), pp. 626–32.

_____ **and Gallant, A. R.** Fitting Segmented Polynomial Regression Models Whose Join Points Have to Be Estimated. *J. Amer. Statist. Assoc.*, March 1973, *68*(341), pp. 144–47.

Fulton, Richard M. Interregional Development and Urban Tribalism in Africa: Comment. *Growth Change*, April 1973, *4*(2), pp. 38–39.

Fundătură, D. and Dumitru, Georgeta. Îmbunătățirea utilizării extensive a fondurilor fixe. (Improving the Extensive Use of Productive Fixed Assets. With English summary.) *Stud. Cercet. Econ.*, 1973, (1), pp. 53–64.

Furlong, Daniel R. and McGrail, George R. Absorption Break-Even. *Manage. Account.*, October 1973, *55*(4), pp. 31–35.

von Furstenberg, George M. The Equilibrium Spread Between Variable Rates and Fixed Rates on Long-Term Financing Instruments. *J. Financial Quant. Anal.*, December 1973, *8*(5), pp. 807–19.

_____ Welfare Maximization: Samuelson's Analysis with Public and Private Goods. *Public Finance Quart.*, October 1973, *1*(4), pp. 426–36.

_____ **and Boughton, James M.** Stabilization Goals and the Appropriateness of Fiscal Policy during the Eisenhower and Kennedy-Johnson Administrations. *Public Finance Quart.*, January 1973, *1*(1), pp. 5–28.

_____ **and Oudet, Bruno A.** The Valuation of Common Stocks During Periods of Inflation. *Z. Nationalökon.*, 1973, *33*(1–2), pp. 67–78.

_____ **and Spulber, Nicolas.** Is There an Economic System Based on Sovereignty of Each Consumer? *Z. Nationalökon.*, 1973, *33*(3–4), pp. 361–74.

Furtado, Celso. Adventures of a Brazilian Economist. *Int. Soc. Sci. J.*, 1973, *25*(1–2), pp. 28–38.

_____ The Brazilian 'Model' *Soc. Econ. Stud.*, March 1973, *22*(1), pp. 122–31.

_____ The Brazilian "Model" of Development. In *Wilber, C. K., ed.*, 1973, pp. 297–306.

_____ The Concept of External Dependence in the Study of Underdevelopment. In *Wilber, C. K., ed.*, 1973, pp. 118–23.

Furth, J. Herbert. International Dollar Liquidity and the Eurodollar Market. *De Economist*, July-August 1973, *121*(4), pp. 347–61.

Furubotn, Eirik G. and Pejovich, Svetozar. Property Rights, Economic Decentralization, and the Evolution of the Yugoslav Firm, 1965–1972. *J. Law Econ.*, October 1973, *16*(2), pp. 275–302.

Fusfeld, Daniel R. A Living Wage. *Ann. Amer. Acad. Polit. Soc. Sci.*, September 1973, *409*, pp. 34–41.

_____ Transfer Payments and the Ghetto Economy. In *Boulding, K. E.; Pfaff, M. and Pfaff, A., eds.*, 1973, pp. 78–92.

_____ Types of Radicalism in American Economics. *Amer. Econ. Rev.*, May 1973, *63*(2), pp. 145–51.

Gaathon, A. L. Exchange Rate Problems in National Accounting of Developing Countries: Reply. *Rev. Income Wealth*, June 1973, *19*(2), pp. 207–09.

de Gaay Fortman, B. Rural Development in an Age of Survival. *De Economist*, March-April 1973, *121*(2), pp. 157–71.

_____ The Teaching of Microeconomics. In *Livingstone, I., et al., eds.*, 1973, pp. 73–77.

Gabisch, Günter. Optimal Growth in the Two-Sector Neoclassical Growth Model. *Z. Nationalökon.*, 1973, *33*(3–4), pp. 419–26.

Gábor, Ottó and Gede, Miklós. Role of the Engineering Industries in the Development of the Hungarian Economy and in the Transformation of the Economic Structure. *Eastern Europ. Econ.*, Fall 1973, *12*(1), pp. 82–104.

Gabriel, Richard A. The Moral Basis of Ecology. In *Gabriel, R. A. and Cohen, S. H., eds.*, 1973, pp. 19–31.

Gács, János and Lackó, Mária. A Study of Planning Behaviour on the National-Economic Level: An Attempt at Analysing a Few Correlations Based on Hungarian Data. *Econ. Planning*, 1973, *13*(1–2), pp. 91–119.

Gadgil, D. R. Planning without a Policy Frame. In *Wadhva, C. D., ed.*, 1973, pp. 94–107.

Gado, Abdou. Savings Banks and Savings Facilities in African Countries: Niger. In *Alberici, A. and Baravelli, M., eds.*, 1973, pp. 77–79.

Gadó, O. Plan and Regulators in the Hungarian Economic Management. In *Kiss, T., ed.*, 1973, pp. 79–98.

Gaffney, Mason. Land Rent, Taxation and Public Policy: Taxation and the Functions of Urban Land Rent. *Amer. J. Econ. Soc.*, January 1973, *32*(1), pp. 17–34.

_____ Tax Reform to Release Land. In *Clawson, M., ed.*, 1973, pp. 115–51.

_____ The Water Giveaway: A Critique of Federal Water Policy. In *Haveman, R. H. and Hamrin, R. D., eds.*, 1973, pp. 191–97.

Gagala, Ken. The Dual Urban Labor Market: Blacks and Whites. *Amer. Econ.*, Spring 1973, *17*(1), pp. 51–59.

Gagliani, Giorgio. Note sulle imprese multinazionali e l'occupazione. (Notes on Multinational Firms and Employment. With English summary.) *Bancaria*, September 1973, *29*(9), pp. 1081–89.

Gaines, Tilford. International Monetary Arrangements. In *Reynolds, L. G.; Green, G. D. and Lewis, D. R., eds.*, 1973, pp. 474–84.

Galambos, P. and Evans, E. W. Work Stoppages in the United Kingdom 1965–70: A Quantitative Study. *Bull. Econ. Res.*, May 1973, *25*(1), pp. 22–42.

Galatin, Malcolm. A Comparison of the Benefits of the Food-Stamp Program, Free Food Stamps, and an Equivalent Cash Payment. *Public Policy*, Spring 1973, *21*(2), pp. 291–302.

_____ A True Price Index When the Consumer Saves. *Amer. Econ. Rev.*, March 1973, *63*(1), pp. 185–94.

Galbraith, John Kenneth. Controls or Competition—What's at Issue? Comment. *Rev. Econ. Statist.*, November 1973, *55*(4), p. 524.

_____ Military Power and the Military Budget. In *Haveman, R. H. and Hamrin, R. D., eds.*, 1973, pp. 112–16.

_____ Power and the Useful Economist. *Amer. Econ. Rev.*, March 1973, *63*(1), pp. 1–11.

_____ Technology in the Developed Economy. In *Williams, B. R., ed.*, 1973, pp. 39–47.

_____ The Theory of Social Balance. In *Reynolds, L. G.; Green, G. D. and Lewis, D. R., eds.*, 1973, pp. 304–14.

Gale, David. Pure Exchange Equilibrium of Dynamic Economic Models. *J. Econ. Theory*, February 1973, *6*(1), pp. 12–36.

Gale, Hazen F. and Barr, Terry N. A Quarterly Forecasting Model for the Consumer Price Index for Food. *Agr. Econ. Res.*, January 1973, *25*(1), pp. 1–14.

Gale, Richard P.; Rutherford, Brent M. and Dunlap, Riley E. Concern for Environmental Rights Among College Students. *Amer. J. Econ. Soc.*, January 1973, *32*(1), pp. 45–60.

Gale, Stephen. Explanation Theory and Models of

Migration. *Econ. Geogr.,* July 1973, *49*(3), pp. 257–74.

Gallant, A. R. and Fuller, Wayne A. Fitting Segmented Polynomial Regression Models Whose Join Points Have to Be Estimated. *J. Amer. Statist. Assoc.,* March 1973, *68*(341), pp. 144–47.

Gallardo, Lloyd. Development of Bay Area Manpower Institutions. In *Mangum, G. L. and Robson, R. T., eds.,* 1973, pp. 154–75.

——— Evaluating Bay Area Manpower Programs. In *Mangum, G. L. and Robson, R. T., eds.,* 1973, pp. 176–201.

——— Institutional Impact of Bay Area Manpower Programs. In *Mangum, G. L. and Robson, R. T., eds.,* 1973, pp. 202–24.

——— The San Francisco-Oakland Bay Area. In *Mangum, G. L. and Robson, R. T., eds.,* 1973, pp. 147–53.

Gallaway, Lowell and Adie, Douglas K. The Minimum Wage and Teenage Unemployment: A Comment. *Western Econ. J.,* December 1973, *11*(4), pp. 525–28.

Gallaway, Lowell E. and Cebula, Richard J. Differentials and Indeterminacy in Wage Rate Analysis: An Empirical Note. *Ind. Lab. Relat. Rev.,* April 1973, *26*(3), pp. 991–95.

———; Cebula, Richard J. and Kohn, Robert M. Determinants of Net Migration to SMSA's, 1960–1970. *Miss. Val. J. Bus. Econ.,* Winter 1973-74, *9*(2), pp. 59–64.

——— and Koshal, Rajindar K. The Phillips Curve: An International Phenomenon. *Rivista Int. Sci. Econ. Com.,* July 1973, *20*(7), pp. 669–80.

———; Rydén, Rune and Vedder, Richard K. Internal Labor Migration in Sweden, 1967. *Swedish J. Econ.,* September 1973, *75*(3), pp. 257–65.

——— and Scully, Gerald W. A Spectral Analysis of the Demographic Structure of American Unemployment. *J. Bus.,* January 1973, *46*(1), pp. 87–102.

Galle, Omer and Cutright, Phillips. The Effect of Illegitimacy on U.S. General Fertility Rates and Population Growth. *Population Stud.,* November 1973, *27*(3), pp. 515–26.

Gallik, Dimitri, M. and Treml, Vladimir G. Teaching the History of Economic Thought in the USSR. *Hist. Polit. Econ.,* Spring 1973, *5*(1), pp. 215–42.

Galloway, Joel D. and Evans, Rupert N. Verbal Ability and Socioeconomic Status of 9th and 12th Grade College Preparatory, General, and Vocational Students. *J. Human Res.,* Winter 1973, *8*(1), pp. 24–36.

Galper, Harvey and Gramlich, Edward M. State and Local Fiscal Behavior and Federal Grant Policy. *Brookings Pap. Econ. Act.,* 1973, (1), pp.15–58.

——— and Peterson, George E. The Equity Effects of a Taxable Municipal Bond Subsidy. *Nat. Tax J.,* December 1973, *26*(4), pp. 611–24.

——— and Wendel, Helmut F. Time Lags in the Federal Expenditure Process and their Stabilization Implications. *Public Finance Quart.,* April 1973, *1*(2), pp. 123–46.

Gamache, Adrian E. The Influence of U.S. Trade Policy on Forest Products Trade. *Amer. J. Agr. Econ.,* December 1973, *55*(5), pp. 983–88.

Gamaletsos, Theodore. Further Analysis of Cross-Country Comparison of Consumer Expenditure Patterns. *Europ. Econ. Rev.,* April 1973, *4*(1), pp. 1–20.

Gandenberger, Otto. Konkurrenzinformation und Wettbewerb. (Information Among Competitors in Respect to Competition. With English summary.) *Jahr. Nationalökon. Statist.,* December 1973, *188*(1), pp. 10–32.

Gandhi, Ved P. Tax Burden on Indian Agriculture. In *Wadhva, C. D., ed.,* 1973, pp. 340–45.

Gangadin, Victor J. A Brief Outline of the Imposition in Guyana of Income Tax, Corporation Tax, Capital Gains Tax, Withholding Tax and Property Tax with Special Reference to Foreign Corporations Operating in Guyana, Through a Branch Establishment or an Agency. *Bull. Int. Fiscal Doc.,* November 1973, *27*(11), pp. 455–63.

Gangulee, Srilata. Rising Real Wages and the Growth of Industrial Output in India, 1946-61. *Amer. Econ.,* Spring 1973, *17*(1), pp. 154–57.

Gann, Robert R.; Clark, Robert A. and Jantorni, Joan M. Analysis of the Lease-or-Buy Decision: Comment. *J. Finance,* September 1973, *28*(4), pp. 1015–16.

Gannicott, Kenneth. Manpower Forecasting for Single Occupations: Engineers in Sweden. In *Ahamad, B. and Blaug, M., eds.,* 1973, pp. 201–39.

——— and Blaug, Mark. Manpower Forecasting for All Occupations: The United States. In *Ahamad, B. and Blaug, M., eds.,* 1973, pp. 48–76.

——— and Blaug, Mark. Manpower Forecasting for Single Occupations: Scientists and Engineers in Britain. In *Ahamad, B. and Blaug, M., eds.,* 1973, pp. 240–60.

Gannon, Colin A. Central Concentration in Simple Spatial Duopoly: Some Behavioral and Functional Conditions. *J. Reg. Sci.,* December 1973, *13*(3), pp. 357–75.

——— Optimization of Market Share in Spatial Competition. *Southern Econ. J.,* July 1973, *40*(1), pp. 66–79.

Gans, Herbert J. The Failure of Urban Renewal: A Critique and Some Proposals. In *Rasmussen, D. W. and Haworth, C. T., eds.,* 1973, pp. 160–67.

Ganter, Ralph. Zur Weiterwälzung spezieller Verbrauchsteuern. (On the Shifting of Specific Excise Taxes. With English summary.) *Jahr. Nationalökon. Statist.,* January 1973, *187*(2), pp. 108–27.

Ganz, Alexander and O'Brien, Thomas. The City: Sandbox, Reservation, or Dynamo? *Public Policy,* Winter 1973, *21*(1), pp. 107–23.

Gapinski, James H. Growth Parameters and Neoclassical Estimates: Effect of an Adaptive Wage-Expectation Scheme. *Southern Econ. J.,* January 1973, *39*(3), pp. 431–33.

——— Putty-Clay Capital and Small-Sample Properties of Neoclassical Estimators. *J. Polit. Econ.,* January-February 1973, *81*(1), pp. 145–57.

Garbarino, Joseph W. The British Experiment with Industrial Relations Reform. *Ind. Lab. Relat. Rev.,* January 1973, *26*(2), pp. 793–804.

——— and Aussieker, Bill. Measuring Faculty Unionism: Quantity and Quality. *Ind. Relat.,* May 1973, *12*(2), pp. 117–24.

Garcés, Joán E. The Popular Unity Government's Workers' Participation Model: Some Conditioning Factors. In *Zammit, J. A., ed.*, 1973, pp. 181–86.

Gardezi, Hassan N. Neocolonial Alliances and the Crisis of Pakistan. In *Gough, K. and Sharma, H. P., eds.*, 1973, pp. 130–44.

Gardini, Attilio and Pezzoli, Ettore. Relazioni statistiche di un semplice modello aggregativo dell'economia italiana (1951–1970). (Some Statistical Relationships in a Simple Aggregate Model of the Italian Economy (1951–1970).) With English summary.) *Statistica*, April-June 1973, *33*(2), pp. 241–73.

———— **and Pezzoli, Ettore.** Soluzione e qualche simulazione di un semplice modello statistico aggregato dell'economia italiana (1952–1970). (Solution and Some Simulations of a Simple Aggregate Model of the Italian Economy (1952–1970). With English summary.) *Statistica*, July-September 1973, *33*(3), pp. 429–36.

Gardner, B. Delworth and Taqieddin, Nureddin. Net Migration and Population Distribution in the State of Utah. *Intermountain Econ. Rev.*, Fall 1973, *4*(2), pp. 32–44.

Gardner, Bernard and Richardson, Peter. The Fiscal Treatment of Shipping. *J. Ind. Econ.*, December 1973, *22*(2), pp. 95–117.

Gardner, Bruce. Economics of the Size of North Carolina Rural Families. *J. Polit. Econ.*, Part II, March-April 1973, *81*(2), pp. S99–122.

Gardner, David M. The Package, Legislation, and the Shopper—Customer Behavior Should Determine Regulations. In *Murray, B. B., ed.*, 1973, pp. 200–207.

Gardner, M. J. Using the Environment to Explain and Predict Mortality. *J. Roy. Statist. Soc.*, Part 3 1973, *136*, pp. 421–40.

Garfinkel, Irwin. Is In-Kind Redistribution Efficient? *Quart. J. Econ.*, May 1973, *87*(2), pp. 320–30.

———— A Skeptical Note on "The Optimality" of Wage Subsidy Programs. *Amer. Econ. Rev.*, June 1973, *63*(3), pp. 447–53.

———— **and Gramlich, Edward M.** A Statistical Analysis of the OEO Experiment in Educational Performance Contracting. *J. Human Res.*, Summer 1973, *8*(3), pp. 275–305.

———— **and Masters, Stanley H.** Two Income Maintenance Plans, Work Incentives and the Closure of the Poverty Gap: Comment. *Ind. Lab. Relat. Rev.*, April 1973, *26*(3), pp. 1002–04.

Garms, Walter I. Reply to "A Benefit-Cost Analysis of the Upward Bound Program: A Comment." *J. Human Res.*, Winter 1973, *8*(1), pp. 115–18.

Garnaut, Ross and Manning, Chris M. An Economic Survey of West Irian, Part II. *Bull. Indonesian Econ. Stud.*, March 1973, *9*(1), pp. 30–64.

Garrabe, Michel. Échange, transferts et préférences éthiques. (Exchange, Transfers and Ethical Preferences. With English summary.) *Public Finance*, 1973, *28*(3–4), pp. 280–90.

Garraty, John A. The New Deal, National Socialism and the Great Depression. *Amer. Hist. Rev.*, October 1973, *78*(4), pp. 907–44.

Garreton, Oscar. Some Preliminary Facts about the Management and Organization of the Industrial Sector. In *Zammit, J. A., ed.*, 1973, pp. 63–68.

Garrison, Charles B. and Paulson, Albert S. An En-

tropy Measure of the Geographic Concentration of Economic Activity. *Econ. Geogr.*, October 1973, *49*(4), pp. 319–24.

———— Entropy as a Measure of the Areal Concentration of Water-Oriented Industry. *Water Resources Res.*, April 1973, *9*(2), pp. 263–69.

Garrison, W. L. Fragments on Future Transportation Policy and Programs. *Econ. Geogr.*, April 1973, *49*(2), pp. 95–102.

Garrity, Paul G. Redesigning Landlord-Tenant Law for an Urban Society. In *Pynoos, J.; Schafer, R. and Hartman, C. W., eds.*, 1973, pp. 75–86.

Garton, M. M.; Hajdu, C. and Apsey, T. M. Economic Trends in the Canadian Forest Products Industry. *Amer. J. Agr. Econ.*, December 1973, *55* (5), pp. 974–82.

Garvey, John, Jr. What Can Europe Teach Us About Urban Growth? In *Moskoff, W., ed.*, 1973, pp. 339–48.

Gasparini, Innocenzo. Prospettive e problemi dell'economia giapponese. (Prospects and Problems of Japanese Economy. With English summary.) *Rivista Int. Sci. Econ. Com.*, August-September 1973, *20*(8–9), pp. 730–37.

Gastil, Raymond D. Social Accounting versus Social Responsibility. In *Dierkes, M. and Bauer, R. A., eds.*, 1973, pp. 93–106.

Gaston, Robert J. Labor Market Conditions and Employer Hiring Standards: Reply. *Ind. Relat.*, May 1973, *12*(2), pp. 250–51.

Gastwirth, Joseph L. Estimating the Number of "Hidden Unemployed" *Mon. Lab. Rev.*, March 1973, *96*(3), pp. 17–26.

Gately, Dermot. International Commodity Agreements: The Experience of Coffee and the Prospects for Cocoa. *Econ. Bull. Ghana, Sec. Ser.*, 1973, *3*(2), pp. 3–10.

Gatons, Paul K. and Cebula, Richard J. Interregional Factor Prices and Mobility. *Pakistan Econ. Soc. Rev.*, Summer 1973, *11*(2), pp. 207–14.

Gatovskiy, L. M. Estimating the National Economic Effect of a New Technology. In *Williams, B. R., ed.*, 1973, pp. 125–39.

Gaud, William S. High Profile, Better Target: Comment. In *Lewis, J. P. and Kapur, I., eds.*, 1973, pp. 53–56.

Gaul, Dieter. International Manual on Collective Bargaining for Public Employees: Federal Republic of Germany. In *Kaye, S. P. and Marsh, A., eds.*, 1973, pp. 171–209.

Gaumnitz, Jack E.; Swinth, Robert L. and Tollefson, John O. Simulation of Water Recreation Users' Decisions. *Land Econ.*, August 1973, *49*(3), pp. 269–77.

Gauthier, Howard L. The Appalachian Development Highway System: Development for Whom? *Econ. Geogr.*, April 1973, *49*(2), pp. 103–08.

Gavrilă, Ilie and Ciucur, Dumitru. Aspecte ale gîndirii economice burgheze contemporane privind munca productivă. (Aspects of the Contemporary Bourgeois Economic Thinking on Productive Labor. With English summary.) *Stud. Cercet. Econ.*, 1973, (1), pp. 151–61.

———— **and Ciucur, Dumitru.** Competenţa economică a muncitorului modern din ţara noastră. (The Economic Competence of the Modern

Worker in Our Country. With English summary.) *Stud. Cercet. Econ.*, 1973, (4), pp. 15–23.

Gavrilă, Tatiana. Organizarea ştiinţifică a producţiei şi a muncii—factor dinamizator al productivităţii muncii. (The Scientific Organization of Production and Labour—A Stimulating Factor of Labour Productivity. With English summary.) *Stud. Cercet. Econ.*, 1973, (3), pp. 29–39.

Gavrilov, V. Improving the Economic Collaboration of Socialist Countries. *Prob. Econ.*, October 1973, *16*(6), pp. 93–103.

Gaynor, Edwin W. Use of Control Charts in Cost Control. In *Thomas, W. E., Jr., ed.*, 1973, pp. 306–16.

Gazis, Denos C. Mathematical Modelling of Some Social and Environmental Problems. In *Hawkes, N., ed.*, 1973, pp. 52–59.

Geary, P. T. The Demand for Petrol and Tobacco in Ireland: A Comment. *Econ. Soc. Rev.*, January 1973, *4*(2), pp. 201–07.

———— **and Morishima, M.** Demand and Supply under Separability. In *Morishima, M., et al.*, 1973, pp. 87–147.

Geary, R. C. Are Ireland's Social Security Payments too Small? Rejoinder. *Econ. Soc. Rev.*, October 1973, *5*(1), pp. 123–26.

———— Are Ireland's Social Security Payments Too Small? A Note. *Econ. Soc. Rev.*, April 1973, *4*(3), pp. 343–48.

———— Identification of Cause and Effect in Simple Least Squares Regression. *Econ. Soc. Rev.*, October 1973, *5*(1), pp. 1–6.

———— A Method of Estimating the Elements of an Interindustry Matrix Knowing the Row and Column Totals. *Econ. Soc. Rev.*, July 1973, *4*(4), pp. 477–85.

———— Reflections on National Accounting. *Rev. Income Wealth*, September 1973, *19*(3), pp. 221–51.

Gebauer, Wolfgang. The Theory of Monetarism. *Z. ges. Staatswiss.*, February 1973, *129*(1), pp. 23–45.

Gede, Miklós and Gábor, Ottó. Role of the Engineering Industries in the Development of the Hungarian Economy and in the Transformation of the Economic Structure. *Eastern Europ. Econ.*, Fall 1973, *12*(1), pp. 82–104.

Gedicks, Al. The Nationalization of Copper in Chile: Antecedents and Consequences. *Rev. Radical Polit. Econ.*, Fall 1973, *5*(3), pp. 1–25.

Gedney, Frances S. Retired Couple's Budget Updated to Autumn 1972. *Mon. Lab. Rev.*, October 1973, *96*(10), pp. 45–50.

Geesey, Ronald E. International Competition in the Provision of Financial Services. In *Rybczynski, T. M., ed.*, 1973, pp. 37–45.

van Geet, Dick. Netherlands Aid Performance and Development Policy. In *Dinwiddy, B., ed.*, 1973, pp. 73–87.

Gehan, Edmund A. and Siddiqui, M. M. Simple Regression Methods for Survival Time Studies. *J. Amer. Statist. Assoc.*, December 1973, *68*(344), pp. 848–56.

Gehman, Clayton. U.S. Energy Supplies and Uses. *Fed. Res. Bull.*, December 1973, *59*(12), pp. 847–70A.

Gehring, Donald C. and Due, Jean M. Jamaica's Strategy for Import Substitution of Vegetables in

the 1960's. *Ill. Agr. Econ.*, January 1973, *13*(1), pp. 20–26.

Geiger, Theodore. The Political Context: Comment. In *Krause, L. B. and Salant, W. S., eds.*, 1973, pp. 62–69.

———— Toward a World of Trading Blocs? In *Henley, D. S., ed.*, 1973, pp. 6–17.

Geisel, Martin S. Bayesian Comparisons of Simple Macroeconomic Models. *J. Money, Credit, Banking*, August 1973, *5*(3), pp. 751–72.

Gelb, Betsy D. and Enis, Ben M. Affirmative Action in Housing and Beyond. *Calif. Manage. Rev.*, Winter 1973, *16*(2), pp. 24–31.

Gellner, Christopher G. Where Unemployment Was Heaviest in 1972. *Mon. Lab. Rev.*, August 1973, *96*(8), pp. 65–66.

———— A 25-Year Look at Employment as Measured by Two Surveys. *Mon. Lab. Rev.*, July 1973, *96*(7), pp. 14–23.

Gelting, Jørgen H. Boligbyggeri kontra anden investering. (Residential Construction and other Investment. With English summary.) *Nationaløkon. Tidsskr.*, 1973, *111*(1), pp. 86–91.

Gendell, Murray and Van Der Tak, Jean. The Size and Structure of Residential Families, Guatemala City, 1964. *Population Stud.*, July 1973, *27*(2), pp. 305–22.

Geneen, Harold S. Statement on ITT Policy and Conglomerates. In *Andreano, R. L., ed.*, 1973, pp. R329–13.

———— **and Judelson, David N.** Additional Data on ITT and Gulf and Western. In *Andreano, R. L., ed.*, 1973, pp. R331–42.

Gennard, John and Steuer, M. D. The Industrial Relations of Foreign Owned Subsidiaries in the United Kingdom. In *Henley, D. S., ed.*, 1973, pp. 301–17.

Genovese, Nicola M. and Sobbrio, Giuseppe. Regional Inequality and the Market Mechanism: Comment. *Kyklos*, 1973, *26*(3), pp. 621–23.

Gentles, Ian. The Sales of Crown Lands During the English Revolution. *Econ. Hist. Rev.*, 2nd Ser., November 1973, *26*(4), pp. 614–35.

Gentry, James A. Investment Characteristics of Common Stocks in Regulated and Unregulated Industries: A Comparative Study: Comment. In *Russell, M., ed.*, 1973, pp. 79–83.

George, Kenneth D. The Changing Structure of Industry in the United Kingdom. In *Rybczynski, T. M., ed.*, 1973, pp. 55–67.

———— **and Ward, Terry.** Productivity Growth in the Retail Trade. *Oxford Bull. Econ. Statist.*, February 1973, *35*(1), pp. 31–47.

George, M. V. and Piché, Victor. Estimates of Vital Rates for the Canadian Indians, 1960–1970. *Demography*, August 1973, *10*(3), pp. 367–82.

George, P. J. and Oksanen, Ernest H. Saturation in the Automobile Market in the Late Twenties: Some Further Results. *Exploration Econ. Hist.*, Fall 1973, *11*(1), pp. 73–85.

Georgescu-Roegen, Nicholas. The Entropy Law and the Economic Problem. In *Daly, H. E., ed.*, 1973, pp. 37–49.

Gerakis, Andreas S. Budgetary Implications of a Devaluation. *Finance Develop.*, March 1973, *10* (1), pp. 7–11.

Gerber, Abraham. Energy Supply as a Factor in Economic Growth. In *Weintraub, A.; Schwartz, E. and Aronson, J. R., eds.*, 1973, pp. 82–97.

Gerbotto, Gianni. Ricerche tecnico-commerciali. (Technical-Commercial Research. With English summary.) *L'Impresa*, 1973, *15*(1), pp. 44–47.

Gerlach, Knut and Liepmann, Peter. Industrialisierung und Siedlungsstruktur—Bemerkungen zum regionalpolitischen Programm einer aktiven Sanierung der bayerischen Rückstandsgebiete. (Industrialization and Settlement Structure—Remarks on the Regional Program of the Promotion of Less Developed Regions in Bavaria. With English summary.) *Jahr. Nationalökon. Statist.*, August 1973, *187*(6), pp. 507–21.

Gershefski, George W. The Development of the Sun Oil Co. Corporate Financial Model. In *Thomas, W. E., Jr., ed.*, 1973, pp. 226–36.

Getzel, Barry and Bezdek, Roger H. Education and Job Training of Scientists and Engineers. *Mon. Lab. Rev.*, November 1973, *96*(11), pp. 54–55.

van de Gevel, A. J. W. and Mauer, Laurence Jay. Non-Tariff Distortions in International Trade: A Methodological Review. In *Scaperlanda, A. E., ed.*, 1973, pp. 47–69.

Gewald, K. The Delphi Method as an Instrument of Technological Forecasting—Practical Experience. In *Blohm, H. and Steinbuch, K., eds.*, 1973, pp. 13–17.

Ghadiri-Asli, B. The Experience of Rural Co-operatives and Co-operative Unions in Iran. *Tahq. Eq.*, Winter & Spring 1973, *10*(29 & 30), pp. 80–105.

Ghafari, R. An Analysis of von Newmann "General Equilibrium." *Tahq. Eq.*, Summer & Autumn 1973, *10*(31&32), pp. 84–103.

_____ Saving and Investment and the Effects of Financial Intermediaries on the Rate of Change of G.N.P. in Iran 1936–71. *Tahq. Eq.*, Winter & Spring 1973, *10*(29 & 30), pp. 50–79.

Ghai, Dharam P. The Association Agreement between the European Economic Community and the Partner States of the East African Community. *J. Common Market Stud.*, September 1973, *12*(1), pp. 78–103.

_____ The Concept and Strategies of Economic Independence. In *Ghai, D., ed.*, 1973, pp. 9–34.

_____ and Ghai, Yash. The Asian Minorities of East and Central Africa. In *Whitaker, B., ed.*, 1973, pp. 24–72.

Ghai, Yash and Ghai, Dharam P. The Asian Minorities of East and Central Africa. In *Whitaker, B., ed.*, 1973, pp. 24–72.

Ghali, Moheb A. Exports, Investment, and Regional Growth. *Southern Econ. J.*, October 1973, *40*(2), pp. 289–96.

_____ On Measuring "Third Party" Effects of a Strike. *Western Econ. J.*, June 1973, *11*(2), pp. 214–27.

_____ and Coelho, Philip R. P. The End of the North-South Wage Differential: Reply. *Amer. Econ. Rev.*, September 1973, *63*(4), pp. 757–62.

Ghazalah, I. A. and Pejovich, Svetozar. The Economics of Vocational and Technical Education: A Report on Three Studies. *Rev. Soc. Econ.*, October 1973, *31*(2), pp. 191–98.

Ghez, Gilbert R. The Measurement of Output of the Nonmarket Sector: The Evaluation of House-

wives' Time: Comment. In *Moss, M., ed.*, 1973, pp. 190–92.

Gholl, Joseph E. and Zachariah, K. C. Toward the Year 2000. *Finance Develop.*, December 1973, *10*(4), pp. 22–26.

Ghosh, Arabinda. Size-Structure, Productivity and Growth: A Case Study of West Bengal Agriculture. *Bangladesh Econ. Rev.*, January 1973, *1*(1), pp. 59–70.

Ghosh, Ranen. The Public Sector and Economic Development in India–I. *Econ. Aff.*, January–February 1973, *18*(1-2), pp. 9–16, 89–94.

Ghosh, Sukesh K. Speculative Capital Movement and Financial Policy in Interacting Economies. *Indian Econ. J.*, April-June 1973, *20*(4–5), pp. 581–603.

Ghuge, V. B. Critique of Development Planning in India. *Econ. Aff.*, August 1973, *18*(8), pp. 357–71.

Gianfranchi, Franco. Le nuove prospettive di cooperazione economica est-ovest in Europa. (New Prospects of East-West Economic Cooperation in Europe and the Role of the European Economic Community. With English summary.) *Mondo Aperto*, April 1973, *27*(2), pp. 112–21.

Gibbard, Allan. Manipulation of Voting Schemes: A General Result. *Econometrica*, July 1973, *41*(4), pp. 587–601.

Gibbons, Hugh. The "Market Share" Theory of Damages in Private Enforcement Cases. *Antitrust Bull.*, Winter 1973, *18*(4), pp. 742–58.

Gibbs, Jack P. Does Punishment Deter? Comment. In *Rottenberg, S., ed.*, 1973, pp. 112–16.

Gibson, Campbell. Urbanization in New Zealand: A Comparative Analysis. *Demography*, February 1973, *10*(1), pp. 71–84.

Gibson, Charles H. Volvo Increases Productivity Through Job Enrichment. *Calif. Manage. Rev.*, Summer 1973, *15*(4), pp. 64–66.

Gibson, J. Douglas. Canada's Declaration of Less Dependence. *Harvard Bus. Rev.*, September-October 1973, *51*(5), pp. 69–79.

Gibson, Norman. Economic Conditions and Policy in Northern Ireland. *Econ. Soc. Rev.*, April 1973, *4*(3), pp. 349–64.

Gibson, T. A.; Seitz, C. Ward and Merz, C. M. Impact of the Space Shuttle Program on the National Economy. *Eng. Econ.*, January-February 1973, *18*(2), pp. 115–33.

Gibson, William E. Fiscal and Monetary Policy: Opportunities and Problems. *Fed. Res. Bank St. Louis Rev.*, January 1973, *55*(1), pp. 14–18.

_____ Interest Rates and Prices in the Long Run: A Study of the Gibson Paradox: Comment. *J. Money, Credit, Banking*, Part II, February 1973, *5*(1), pp. 450–53.

_____ Price-Expectations Effects on Interest Rates: Reply. *J. Finance*, June 1973, *28*(3), pp. 751–53.

_____ Protecting Homebuilding from Restrictive Credit Conditions. *Brookings Pap. Econ. Act.*, 1973, (3), pp. 647–91.

Giddens, Paul H. Historical Origins of the Adoption of the Exxon Name and Trademark. *Bus. Hist. Rev.*, Autumn 1973, *47*(3), pp. 353–66.

Giersch, Herbert. Competitive Pressures in an Enlarged EEC. In *Rybczynski, T. M., ed.*, 1973, pp. 1–17.

_____ On the Desirable Degree of Flexibility of Exchange Rates. *Weltwirtsch. Arch.*, 1973, *109*(2), pp. 191–213.

―――― Some Neglected Aspects of Inflation in the World Economy. *Public Finance*, 1973, *28*(2), pp. 105–24.

Giertz, Fred J. and Daly, George A. Pollution Abatement, Pareto Optimality, and the Market Mechanism. In *Boulding, K. E.; Pfaff, M. and Pfaff, A., eds.*, 1973, pp. 350–58.

Gifford, Adam, Jr. Pollution, Technology, and Economic Growth. *Southern Econ. J.*, October 1973, *40*(2), pp. 210–15.

―――― **and Stone, Courtenay C.** Externalities, Liability and the Coase Theorem: A Mathematical Analysis. *Western Econ. J.*, September 1973, *11* (3), pp. 260–69.

Gifford, William C., Jr. United States Tax Effects of Foreign Losses: A Symmetry Analysis. *Yale Law J.*, December 1973, *83*(2), pp. 312–56.

Gilbert, Gary G. Estimation of Liquidity Functions in the U.S. Economy. *Rivista Int. Sci. Econ. Com.*, February 1973, *20*(2), pp. 107–29.

―――― Investment Planning for Latin American Economic Integration. *J. Common Market Stud.*, June 1973, *11*(4), pp. 314–25.

―――― **and Longbrake, William A.** The Effects of Branching by Financial Institutions on Competition, Productive Efficiency and Stability: An Examination of the Evidence. *J. Bank Res.*, Autumn 1973, *4*(3), pp. 154–67.

Gilbert, R. Alton. Employment Growth in St. Louis. *Fed. Res. Bank St. Louis Rev.*, August 1973, *55*(8), pp. 9–15.

―――― Income and Expenses of Eighth District Member Banks. *Fed. Res. Bank St. Louis Rev.*, August 1973, *55*(8), pp. 16–22.

―――― **and Kalish, Lionel, III.** An Analysis of Efficiency of Scale and Organizational Form in Commercial Banking. *J. Ind. Econ.*, July 1973, *21*(3), pp. 293–307.

―――― **and Kalish, Lionel, III.** The Influence of Bank Regulation of the Operating Efficiency of Commercial Banks. *J. Finance*, December 1973, *28*(5), pp. 1287–1301.

Gilbert, Ronald D. Okun's Law: Some Additional Evidence. *Nebr. J. Econ. Bus.*, Winter 1973, *12*(1), pp. 51–60.

Giles, D. E. A. A Note on Some Recent Developments in Large–Model Estimation. In *Deane, R. S., ed.*, 1972, pp. 89–92.

―――― The Structural Stability of the Reserve Bank Model. In *Deane, R. S., ed.*, 1972, pp. 75–86.

Gillen, William J. and Cicchetti, Charles J. The Mandatory Oil Import Quota Program: A Consideration of Economic Efficiency and Equity. *Natural Res. J.*, July 1973, *13*(3), pp. 399–430.

Gilleran, Robert T. Regulating Risk-Taking by Mutual Funds. *Yale Law J.*, May 1973, *82*(6), pp. 1305–24.

Gillespie, Hugh. Problems and Issues in Public Employee Retirement Systems: Discussion. *J. Risk Ins.*, March 1973, *40*(1), pp. 50–53.

Gillespie, Robert W. and Rushing, Philip J. Expenditure Switching vs. Altering Absorption: An Empirical Approach. *Southern Econ. J.*, July 1973, *40* (1), pp. 26–34.

Gillingham, Robert; Heien, Dale and Cohen, Mal-

colm. A Monte Carlo Study of Complex Finite Distributed Lag Structures. *Ann. Econ. Soc. Measure,* January 1973, *2*(1), pp. 53–63.

Gillion, C. Econometric Models and Current Economic Issues. In *Deane, R. S., ed.*, 1972, pp. 67–73.

Gillum, Gary P. Capital Gains: Perennial Subject for Tax Reform Debate. *Fed. Res. Bank Bus. Rev. Phila.*, September 1973, pp. 3–11.

Gilmer, Robert W. and Morgan, Daniel, Jr. The Equivalence of Flat Grants and Foundation Programs in State Education Aid Formulas. *Public Finance Quart.*, October 1973, *1*(4), pp. 437–47.

Gilroy, Curtis L. Job Losers, Leavers, and Entrants: Traits and Trends. *Mon. Lab. Rev.*, August 1973, *96*(8), pp. 3–15.

Gilson, J. C. A Canadian View of Conflicts and Consistencies in the Agricultural Policies of Canada and the United States. *Amer. J. Agr. Econ.*, December 1973, *55*(5), pp. 785–90.

Giltinan, John W. Customs Drawback. *Manage. Account.*, April 1973, *54*(10), pp. 23–27.

Ginger, Ray. American Workers: Views From the Left. *Labor Hist.*, Summer 1973, *14*(3), pp. 425–28.

Ginman, Peter J. and Murray, Tracy. Will Devaluation Improve the US Trade Deficit? *Kyklos*, 1973, *26*(4), pp. 844–48.

Ginor, Fanny. Importance of the Nutrition Component in Economic Planning. In *Berg, A.; Scrimshaw, N. S. and Call, D. L., eds.*, 1973, pp. 275–81.

Ginsberg, William. Concavity and Quasiconcavity in Economics. *J. Econ. Theory*, December 1973, *6* (6), pp. 596–605.

Ginsburg, Martin D. Tax Simplification—A Practitioner's View. *Nat. Tax J.*, September 1973, *26*(3), pp. 317–30.

Ginsburgh, Paul B. and Manheim, Larry M. Insurance, Copayment, and Health Services Utilization: A Critical Review. *J. Econ. Bus.*, Spring-Summer 1973, *25*(3), pp. 142–53.

Ginsburgh, Victor A. The Common Market Economies: Interdependence or Independence. *Europ. Econ. Rev.*, October 1973, *4*(3), pp. 289–91.

Gintzburger, Alphonse A. Psychoanalysis of a Case of Stagnation. *Econ. Develop. Cult. Change,* January 1973, *21*(2), pp. 227–46.

Ginzberg, Eli. Challenge and Resolution. In *Ginzberg, E. and Yohalem, A. M., eds.*, 1973, pp. 140–52.

Girdlestone, J. N. and Parsons, S. A. The Regional Supply Pattern of Beef Cattle for Slaughter in Queensland. *Quart. Rev. Agr. Econ.*, January 1973, *26*(1), pp. 44–60.

Girgis, Maurice. Development and Trade Patterns in the Arab World. *Weltwirtsch. Arch.*, 1973, *109* (1), pp. 121–68.

Girling, Robert. Dependency and Persistent Income Inequality. In *Bonilla, F. and Girling, R., eds.*, 1973, pp. 83–101.

―――― Dependency, Technology and Development. In *Bonilla, F. and Girling, R., eds.*, 1973, pp. 46–62.

Girvan, Norman. The Development of Dependency Economics in the Caribbean and Latin America: Review and Comparison. *Soc. Econ. Stud.*, March 1973, *22*(1), pp. 1–33.

Gisser, Micha and Mercado, Abraham. Economic

Aspects of Ground Water Resources and Replacement Flows in Semiarid Agricultural Areas. *Amer. J. Agr. Econ.,* August 1973, *55*(3), pp. 461–66.

Gitelman, H. M. No Irish Need Apply: Patterns of and Responses to Ethnic Discrimination in the Labor Market. *Labor Hist.,* Winter 1973, *14*(1), pp. 56–68.

_____ Perspectives on American Industrial Violence. *Bus. Hist. Rev.,* Spring 1973, *47*(1), pp. 1–23.

Gitelson, Susan A. Can the U.N. Be an Effective Catalyst for Regional Integration? The Case of the East African Community. *J. Devel. Areas,* October 1973, *8*(1), pp. 65–82.

Gitman, Lawrence J. A Multinational Firm Investment Model. *J. Econ. Bus.,* Fall 1973, *26*(1), pp. 41–48.

Givens, Richard A. Product Safety Standard-Making Powers Under the Consumer Product Safety Act. *Antitrust Bull.,* Summer 1973, *18*(2), pp. 243–53.

Glahe, Fred R. A Permanent Restatement of the IS-LM Model. *Amer. Econ.,* Spring 1973, *17*(1), pp. 158–67.

Glantz, Frederic B. Migration and Economic Opportunity: The Case of the Poor. *New Eng. Econ. Rev.,* March-April 1973, pp. 14–17.

_____ **and Delaney, Nancy J.** Changes in Nonwhite Residential Patterns in Large Metropolitan Areas, 1960 and 1970. *New Eng. Econ. Rev.,* March-April 1973, pp. 2–13.

Glassburner, Bruce. The January 1973 Tariff Revision. *Bull. Indonesian Econ. Stud.,* November 1973, *9*(3), pp. 103–08.

_____ **and Riedel, James.** Economic Development Lessons from Hong Kong: A Reply. *Econ. Rec.,* December 1973, *49*(128), pp. 637–43.

Glazer, Nathan. The Bias of American Housing Policy. In *Pynoos, J.; Schafer, R. and Hartman, C. W., eds.,* 1973, pp. 405–22.

Gleicher, Peggy and Fried, Marc. Some Sources of Residential Satisfaction in an Urban Slum. In *Rasmussen, D. W. and Haworth, C. T., eds.,* 1973, pp. 150–59.

Glenn, Norval D. Suburbanization in the United States Since World War II. In *Masotti, L. H. and Hadden, J. K., eds.,* 1973, pp. 51–78.

Glennerster, Howard. A Tax Credit Scheme for Britain?—A Review of the British Government's Green Paper. *J. Human Res.,* Fall 1973, *8*(4), pp. 422–35.

Glezakos, Constantine. Export Instability and Economic Growth: A Statistical Verification. *Econ. Develop. Cult. Change,* Part I, July 1973, *21*(4), pp. 670–78.

Gliazer, L. The Economics of Science and the Science of Economics. *Prob. Econ.,* December 1973, *16*(8), pp. 22–43.

Glick, Paul C. and Norton, Arthur J. Perspectives on the Recent Upturn in Divorce and Remarriage. *Demography,* August 1973, *10*(3), pp. 301–14.

Glismann, Hans H. and Neu, Axel. Quantitative Aspects of Nontariff Distortions of Trade in the Federal Republic of Germany. In *Scaperlanda, A. E., ed.,* 1973, pp. 193–253.

Globerman, Steven. Market Structure and R&D in

Canadian Manufacturing Industries. *Quart. Rev. Econ. Bus.,* Summer 1973, *13*(2), pp. 59–67.

_____ Technological Risk Assumption Corporations. *J. Econ. Issues,* March 1973, *7*(1), pp. 119–24.

Glückaufová, Dagmar and Turková, Dana. Některá rozšíření metody zobecněných horních mezí. (Some Extensions of Generalized Upper Bounding Technique. With English summary.) *Ekon.-Mat. Obzor,* 1973, *9*(4), pp. 423–49.

Glueck, William F. and Kavran, Dragoljub. The Yugoslav Management System. In *Henley, D. S., ed.,* 1973, pp. 375–89.

Glycopantis, D. On the Relative Stability and Optimality of Consumption in Aggregative Growth Models: A Critical Analysis. *Economica, N.S.,* August 1973, *40*(159), pp. 283–90.

Glyn, Andrew. The Stock Market Valuation of British Companies and the Cost of Capital 1955–69. *Oxford Econ. Pap.,* July 1973, *25*(2), pp. 213–40.

Glynn, Sean and Lougheed, Alan L. A Comment on United States Economic Policy and the "Dollar Gap" of the 1920's. *Econ. Hist. Rev., 2nd Ser.,* November 1973, *26*(4), pp. 692–94.

Góczán, L. and Benet, I. A Pilot Study on the Valuation of Land. (In Russian. With English summary.) *Acta Oecon.,* 1973, *11*(2–3), pp. 191–209.

Goddard, Frederick O. Consumer Welfare and Product Differentiation: Reply. *Quart. Rev. Econ. Bus.,* Summer 1973, *13*(2), pp. 92–94.

_____ **and Goffman, Irving J.** The Public Financing of Non-Public Education. *Rev. Soc. Econ.,* October 1973, *31*(2), pp. 152–66.

Goddard, Haynes C. Analysis of Social Production Functions: The Public Library. *Public Finance Quart.,* April 1973, *1*(2), pp. 191–204.

Godfrey, E. M. Economic Variables and Rural-Urban Migration: Some Thoughts on the Todaro Hypothesis. *J. Devel. Stud.,* October 1973, *10*(1), pp. 66–78.

Godfrey, Leslie G. A Note on the Treatment of Serial Correlation. *Can. J. Econ.,* November 1973, *6*(4), pp. 567–73.

_____ **and Burrows, Paul.** Identifying and Estimating the Parameters of a Symmetrical Model of Inventory Investment. *Appl. Econ.,* September 1973, *5*(3), pp. 193–97.

_____ **and Taylor, Jim.** Earnings Changes in the United Kingdom, 1954–70: Excess Labour Supply, Expected Inflation and Union Influence. *Oxford Bull. Econ. Statist.,* August 1973, *35*(3), pp. 197–216.

Goering, R. W. Critical Comments on Technological Research into the Future. In *Blohm, H. and Steinbuch, K., eds.,* 1973, pp. 151–55.

Goetz, Billy E. The Management of Objectives. *Manage. Account.,* August 1973, *55*(2), pp. 35–38.

_____ A Note on Discounted Cash Flow Examples: A Reply. *Accounting Rev.,* January 1973, *48*(1), pp. 135–36.

Goetz, Charles J. The Revenue Potential of User-Related Charges in State and Local Governments. In *Musgrave, R. A., ed.,* 1973, pp. 113–29.

_____ **and Buchanan, James M.** External Diseconomies in Competitive Supply: Reply. *Amer. Econ. Rev.,* September 1973, *63*(4), pp. 745–48.

_____; **Tucker, James F. and Weber, Warren E.** Student Incentive Payments and Academic

Achievement: An Empirical Test. *Soc. Sci. Quart.*, June 1973, *54*(1), pp. 159–67.

Goff, Phoebe H. Disabled-Worker Beneficiaries Under OASDHI: Regional and State Patterns. *Soc. Sec. Bull.*, September 1973, *36*(9), pp. 3–23.

Goffman, Irving J. and Goddard, Frederick O. The Public Financing of Non-Public Education. *Rev. Soc. Econ.*, October 1973, *31*(2), pp. 152–66.

Gofman, K. G., et al. Optimal Land Management. *Matekon*, Spring 1973, *9*(3), pp. 71–88.

_____ **and Fedorenko, N.** Problems of Optimization in the Planning and Control of the Environment. *Prob. Econ.*, April 1973, *15*(12), pp. 37–51.

Goh, Chui Muah. A Note on Housing Finance in Singapore. *Malayan Econ. Rev.*, October 1973, *18* (2), pp. 37–42.

Gohil, B. K. Provision of Infrastructure in Gujarat. *Artha-Vikas*, January-July 1973, *9*(1–2), pp. 69–99.

Golbert, Albert S. Pitfalls of DISC. *Manage. Account.*, July 1973, *55*(1), pp. 52–55.

Gold, Ruth Z. and Berger, Agnes. Note on Cochran's Q-Test for the Comparison of Correlated Proportions. *J. Amer. Statist. Assoc.*, December 1973, *68* (344), pp. 989–93.

Goldberg, Joseph P. Longshoremen and the Modernisation of Cargo Handling in the United States. *Int. Lab. Rev.*, March 1973, *107*(3), pp. 253–79.

Goldberg, Lawrence G. The Effect of Conglomerate Mergers on Competition. *J. Law Econ.*, April 1973, *16*(1), pp. 137–58.

Goldberg, Robert D. and Dresch, Stephen P. IDIOM: An Inter-Industry, National-Regional Policy Evaluation Model. *Ann. Econ. Soc. Measure*, July 1973, *2*(3), pp. 323–56.

Goldberg, Victor and Moirao, Sharon. Limit Pricing and Potential Competition. *J. Polit. Econ.*, November-December 1973, *81*(6), pp. 1460–66.

Goldberger, Arthur S. Correlations Between Binary Outcomes and Probabilistic Predictions. *J. Amer. Statist. Assoc.*, March 1973, *68*(341), pp. 84.

_____ Dependency Rates and Savings Rates: Further Comment. *Amer. Econ. Rev.*, March 1973, *63* (1), pp. 232–33.

_____ Efficient Estimation in Overidentified Models: A Interpretive Analysis. In *Goldberger, A. S. and Duncan, O. D., eds.*, 1973, pp. 131–52.

_____ Structural Equation Models: An Overview. In *Goldberger, A. S. and Duncan, O. D., eds.*, 1973, pp. 1–18.

Goldenberg, Shirley B. Public Sector Bargaining: The Canadian Experience. *Mon. Lab. Rev.*, May 1973, *96*(5), pp. 34–36.

Goldfarb, Robert S. A Model of Wage Setting and Wage Diversity in Local Labor Markets. *Western Econ. J.*, March 1973, *11*(1), pp. 98–110.

Goldfeld, Stephen M. The Demand for Money Revisited. *Brookings Pap. Econ. Act.*, 1973, (3), pp. 577–638.

_____ **and Aigner, Dennis J.** Simulation and Aggregation: A Reconsideration. *Rev. Econ. Statist.*, February 1973, *55*(1), pp. 114–18.

_____ **and Quandt, Richard E.** The Estimation of Structural Shifts by Switching Regressions. *Ann. Econ. Soc. Measure*, October 1973, *2*(4), pp. 475–85.

_____ **and Quandt, Richard E.** A Markov Model for Switching Regressions. *J. Econometrics*, March 1973, *1*(1), pp. 3–15.

Goldfinger, Nathaniel. An American Trade Union View of International Trade and Investment. In *Kujawa, D., ed.*, 1973, pp. 28–53.

_____ Employment in the Industrialized Countries: Comment. In *Hughes, H., ed.*, 1973, pp. 117–24.

Goldin, Claudia Dale. The Economics of Emancipation. *J. Econ. Hist.*, March 1973, *33*(1), pp. 66–85.

Goldman, Marshall I. Growth and Environmental Problems of Noncapitalist Nations. In *Weintraub, A.; Schwartz, E. and Aronson, J. R., eds.*, 1973, pp. 98–115.

_____ Public Policy Toward Retailing: USSR. In *Boddewyn, J. J. and Hollander, S. C., eds.*, 1972, pp. 337–49.

_____ Who Profits More from U.S.-Soviet Trade? *Harvard Bus. Rev.*, November-December 1973, *51*(6), pp. 79–87.

Goldsmith, J. C. Developments in French T. V. A. The Abandonment of the So Called "Buffer Rule." *Bull. Int. Fiscal Doc.*, February 1973, *27* (2), pp. 61–66.

Goldsmith, Raymond W. Basic Considerations. In *Goldsmith, R. W., ed.*, 1973, pp. 1–33.

_____ The Historical Background: Financial Institutions as Investors in Corporate Stock Before 1952. In *Goldsmith, R. W., ed.*, 1973, pp. 34–90.

_____ The Position of Institutional Investors and of Corporate Stock in the National Balance Sheets and the Flow of Funds Accounts of the United States of America, 1952–68. In *Goldsmith, R. W., ed.*, 1973, pp. 91–164.

Goldstein, Gerald S. and Moses, Leon N. A Survey of Urban Economics. *J. Econ. Lit.*, June 1973, *11* (2), pp. 471–515.

Goldstein, Henry N. On the Neutrality of Forward Market Intervention. *Weltwirtsch. Arch.*, 1973, *109*(4), pp. 688–700.

Goldstein, Jon H. The Effectiveness of Manpower Training Programs: A Review of Research on the Impact on the Poor. In *Niskanen, W. A., et al., eds.*, 1973, pp. 338–73.

_____ **and Birdsall, William C.** The Effect of Interest-Rate Changes on Consumption Allocation Over Time. *Int. Econ. Rev.*, June 1973, *14*(2), pp. 487–92.

Goldstein, Melvyn C. The Circulation of Estates in Tibet: Reincarnation, Land and Politics. *J. Asian Stud.*, May 1973, *32*(3), pp. 445–55.

Goldston, Eli. Executive Sabbaticals: About to Take Off? *Harvard Bus. Rev.*, September-October 1973, *51*(5), pp. 57–68.

Gonce, R. A. Natural Law and Ludwig von Mises' Praxeology and Economic Science. *Southern Econ. J.*, April 1973, *39*(4), pp. 490–507.

Gonedes, Nicholas J. Evidence on the Information Content of Accounting Numbers: Accounting-Based and Market-Based Estimates of Systematic Risk. *J. Financial Quant. Anal.*, June 1973, *8*(3), pp. 407–43.

_____ Properties of Accounting Numbers: Models and Tests. *J. Acc. Res.*, Autumn 1973, *11*(2), pp. 212–37.

Gonzales, Nestor. The Capital Growth Model: An

Empirical Investigation: Comment. *J. Financial Quant. Anal.*, March 1973, *8*(2), pp. 293–97.

González Villarreal, Fernando J. Mexican National Water Plan: Organization and Preliminary Assessment. *Amer. J. Agr. Econ.*, December 1973, *55*(5), pp. 1008–16.

Good, David F. Backwardness and the Role of Banking in Nineteenth-Century European Industrialization. *J. Econ. Hist.*, December 1973, *33*(4), pp. 845–50.

Goodale, Thomas L. and Ditton, Robert B. Water Quality Perception and the Recreational Uses of Green Bay, Lake Michigan. *Water Resources Res.*, June 1973, *9*(3), pp. 569–79.

Goodeve, Charles [Sir]. The Critical Path to Growth. In *Ross, M., ed.*, 1973, pp. 21–27.

Goodhardt, G. J. and Chatfield, C. A Consumer Purchasing Model with Erlang Inter-Purchase Times. *J. Amer. Statist. Assoc.*, December 1973, *68*(344), pp. 828–35.

Goodhart, C. B. On the Incidence of Illegal Abortion: A Reply. *Population Stud.*, July 1973, *27*(2), pp. 207–33.

Goodhart, Charles. Analysis of the Determination of the Stock of Money. In *Parkin, M., ed.*, 1973, pp. 243–61.

Goodhart, Charles A. E. Monetary Policy in the United Kingdom. In *Holbik, K., ed.*, 1973, pp. 465–524.

Goodman, Richard A. A System Diagram of the Functions of a Manager. In *Klein, W. H. and Murphy, D. C., eds.*, 1973, pp. 50–61.

––––––– A System Diagram of the Functions of a Manager. In *Thomas, W. E., Jr., ed.*, 1973, pp. 43–59.

Goodman, Richard J. United States Agricultural Trade in the Pacific Rim: Marketing Agricultural Products, Approaches, and Accomplishments. In *Canadian Agricultural Economics Society*, 1973, pp. 1–26.

Goodman, Robert P. and Bergstrom, Theodore C. Private Demands for Public Goods. *Amer. Econ. Rev.*, June 1973, *63*(3), pp. 280–96.

Goodman, Seymour S. and Balintfy, Joseph L. Socio-Economic Factors in Income Inequality: A Log-Normal Hypothesis. *Z. Nationalökon.*, 1973, *33*(3–4), pp. 389–402.

Goodman, Wolfe D. Canada: The Effect of Recent Death Tax Legislation on Non-Canadians. *Bull. Int. Fiscal Doc.*, October 1973, *27*(10), pp. 415–19.

––––––– Deemed Realizations Under the Canadian Income Tax Act. *Bull. Int. Fiscal Doc.*, July 1973, *27*(7), pp. 291–97.

Goodnow, James D. and Hansz, James E. Environmental Determinants of Overseas Market Entry Strategies. In *Alexandrides, C. G., ed.*, 1973, pp. 195–215.

Goodwin, G. L. A European Community Foreign Policy? *J. Common Market Stud.*, September 1973, *12*(1), pp. 7–27.

Goodwin, Kenneth R. Another View from the Federal Communications Commission. In *Park, R. E., ed.*, 1973, pp. 43–56.

Goolsby, O. Halbert and Christensen, Raymond P. U.S. Agricultural Trade and Balance of Payments.

In *Iowa State University Center for Agricultural and Rural Development*, 1973, pp. 122–40.

Gootzeit, Michael J. The Corn Laws and Wage Adjustment in a Short-Run Ricardian Model. *Hist. Polit. Econ.*, Spring 1973, *5*(1), pp. 50–71.

Gopalakrishnan, Chennat. Doctrine of Prior Appropriation and Its Impact on Water Development: A Critical Survey. *Amer. J. Econ. Soc.*, January 1973, *32*(1), pp. 61–72.

––––––– The Economics of Water Transfer. *Amer. J. Econ. Soc.*, October 1973, *32*(4), pp. 395–403.

Gordenker, Leon. International Economic Diplomacy: Comment. In *Lewis, J. P. and Kapur, I., eds.*, 1973, pp. 143–46.

Gordon, David M.; Edwards, Richard C. and Reich, Michael. A Theory of Labor Market Segmentation. *Amer. Econ. Rev.*, May 1973, *63*(2), pp. 359–65.

Gordon, I. R. and Edwards, S. L. Holiday Trip Generation. *J. Transp. Econ. Policy*, May 1973, *7*(2), pp. 153–68.

Gordon, Lawrence A. and Cook, Henry, Jr. Absorption Costing an Fixed Factors of Production. *Accounting Rev.*, January 1973, *48*(1), pp. 128–29.

Gordon, Myron J. Causes and Predictions of Rates of Return on Stocks and Bonds: Discussion. *J. Finance*, May 1973, *28*(2), pp. 318–20.

Gordon, Nancy M. Ex Ante and Ex Post Substitutability in Economic Growth. *Int. Econ. Rev.*, June 1973, *14*(2), pp. 497–510.

Gordon, Peter and Lande, Paul S. The Pricing of Goods and Agricultural Land in Multiregional General Equilibrium: Comment. *Southern Econ. J.*, July 1973, *40*(1), pp. 143–44.

Gordon, Robert A. An Explicit Estimation of the Prevalence of Commitment to a Training School, to Age 18, by Race and by Sex. *J. Amer. Statist. Assoc.*, September 1973, *68*(343), pp. 547–53.

––––––– Some Macroeconomic Aspects of Manpower Policy. In *Ulman, L., ed.*, 1973, pp. 14–50.

Gordon, Robert J. Interest Rates and Prices in the Long Run: A Study of the Gibson Paradox: Comment. *J. Money, Credit, Banking*, Part II, February 1973, *5*(1), pp. 460–63.

––––––– The Response of Wages and Prices to the First Two Years of Controls. *Brookings Pap. Econ. Act.*, 1973, (3), pp. 765–78.

––––––– The Use of Unit Values to Measure Deviations of Transaction Prices from List Prices. *Rev. Income Wealth*, September 1973, *19*(3), pp. 267–69.

––––––– The Welfare Cost of Higher Unemployment. *Brookings Pap. Econ. Act.*, 1973, (1), pp. 133–95.

Gordon, Scott. Today's Apocalypses and Yesterday's. *Amer. Econ. Rev.*, May 1973, *63*(2), pp. 106–10.

––––––– The Wage-Fund Controversy: The Second Round. *Hist. Polit. Econ.*, Spring 1973, *5*(1), pp. 14–35.

Gordon, Wendell. Institutionalized Consumption Patterns in Underdeveloped Countries. *J. Econ. Issues*, June 1973, *7*(2), pp. 267–87.

Goreux, Louis M. Comparative Analysis of the Programming Models. In *Goreux, L. M. and Manne, A. S., eds.*, 1973, pp. 15–33.

––––––– The Problem of Interdependence. In *Goreux, L. M. and Manne, A. S., eds.*, 1973, pp. 35–54.

––––––– and Manne, Alan S. Multi-Level Planning:

Case Studies in Mexico: Introduction. In *Goreux, L. M. and Manne, A. S., eds.*, 1973, pp. 1–14.

Gorgorin, Jean-Louis and Bréaud, Patrick. An Appraisal of Program Budgeting in France. In *Novick, D., ed.*, 1973, pp. 111–18.

Gorman, D. and Demery, Lionel. The Classical and Factor Proportions Trade Patterns:—A Note. *Manchester Sch. Econ. Soc. Stud.*, September 1973, *41*(3), pp. 343.

Gorman, William D.; Lansford, Robert R. and Clevenger, Thomas S. Economic Planning for the Navajo Indian Irrigation Project. *N. Mex. Bus.*, April 1973, *26*(4), pp. 3–8.

Gort, Michael and Boddy, Raford. Capital Expenditures and Capital Stocks. *Ann. Econ. Soc. Measure,* July 1973, *2*(3), pp. 245–61.

Gørtz, Erik and Vibe-Pedersen, J. Livsindkomstberegninger og deres betydning. (Calculation and Significance of Lifetime Incomes. With English summary.) *Nationalokon. Tidsskr.*, 1973, *111*(1), pp. 25–59.

Gotsch, Carl H. Tractor Mechanisation and Rural Development in Pakistan. *Int. Lab. Rev.*, February 1973, *107*(2), pp. 133–66.

Gottinger, Hans-Werner. Conditional Utility. *Z. Nationalökon.*, 1973, *33*(3–4), pp. 315–24.

———— Toward a Fuzzy Reasoning in the Behavioral Sciences. *Ekon.-Mat. Obzor*, 1973, *9*(4), pp. 404–22.

Gottsegen, Jack J. GNP by Major Industry, 1972. *Surv. Curr. Bus.*, April 1973, *53*(4), pp. 19–21.

Goudzwaard, Maurice B. Some Evidence on the Effect of Company Size on the Cost of Equity Capital: Comment. *J. Financial Quant. Anal.*, March 1973, *8*(2), pp. 243–45.

Gough, Kathleen. Imperialism and Revolutionary Potential in South Asia. In *Gough, K. and Sharma, H. P., eds.*, 1973, pp. 3–42.

Gould, Bernard W. Sampling Errors in Flood Damage Estimates. In *Aislabie, C., ed.*, 1973, pp. 82–98.

Gould, J. The Great Debasement and the Supply of Money. *Australian Econ. Hist. Rev.*, September 1973, *13*(2), pp. 177–89.

Gould, John P. and Waud, Roger N. The Neoclassical Model of Investment Behavior: Another View. *Int. Econ. Rev.*, February 1973, *14*(1), pp. 33–48.

Gould, J. R. Meade on External Economies: Should the Beneficiaries Be Taxed? *J. Law Econ.*, April 1973, *16*(1), pp. 53–66.

Gould, William B. Black Workers Inside the House of Labor. *Ann. Amer. Acad. Polit. Soc. Sci.*, May 1973, *407*, pp. 78–90.

Goulet, Denis. "Development" . . . or Liberation? In *Wilber, C. K., ed.*, 1973, pp. 354–61.

Gourvish, Terence R. A British Business Elite: The Chief Executive Managers of the Railway Industry, 1850–1922. *Bus. Hist. Rev.*, Autumn 1973, *47*(3), pp. 289–316.

Gräbig, G. Planned Use of Commodity and Money Relations. In *Kiss, T., ed.*, 1973, pp. 197–202.

Grabowski, Henry G. and Baxter, Nevins D. Rivalry in Industrial Research and Development. *J. Ind. Econ.*, July 1973, *21*(3), pp. 209–35.

Grad, Susan. Relative Importance of Income Sources of the Aged. *Soc. Sec. Bull.*, August 1973, *36*(8), pp. 37–45.

Grady, Jesse C. Texas A&M's Curriculum. *Amer. J. Agr. Econ.*, Part II, November 1973, *55*(4), pp. 755–56.

Graebner, William. The Coal-Mine Operator and Safety: A Study of Business Reform in the Progressive Period. *Labor Hist.*, Fall 1973, *14*(4), pp. 483–505.

Graeser, Paul. Imperfect Competition: Dewey and Heuss: Comment. *Weltwirtsch. Arch.*, 1973, *109*(3), pp. 514–16.

Graf, Hans G. Zukünftige Verkehrsentwicklung in der Schweiz. (Future Development of Traffic in Switzerland. With English summary.) *Schweiz. Z. Volkswirtsch. Statist.*, September 1973, *109*(3), pp. 341–55.

Graham, Edward D. Special Interests and the Early China Trade. *Mich. Academician*, Fall 1973, *6*(2), pp. 233–42.

Graham, Lawrence S. Evaluations and Recommendations. In *Thurber, C. E. and Graham, L. S., eds.*, 1973, pp. 425–42.

Graham, Philip L., Jr.; Hermann, Donald H. G. and Marcus, Sumner. Section 7 of the Clayton Act and Mergers Involving Foreign Interests. In *Henley, D. S., ed.*, 1973, pp. 155–84.

Gramlich, Edward M. and Galper, Harvey. State and Local Fiscal Behavior and Federal Grant Policy. *Brookings Pap. Econ. Act.*, 1973, (1), pp. 15–58.

———— and Garfinkel, Irwin. A Statistical Analysis of the OEO Experiment in Educational Performance Contracting. *J. Human Res.*, Summer 1973, *8*(3), pp. 275–305.

Gramm, Warren S. Industrial Capitalism and the Breakdown of the Liberal Rule of Law. *J. Econ. Issues*, December 1973, *7*(4), pp. 577–603.

———— Natural Selection in Economic Thought: Ideology, Power, and the Keynesian Counterrevolution. *J. Econ. Issues*, March 1973, *7*(1), pp. 1–27.

Gramm, Wendy Lee. The Labor Force Decision of Married Female Teachers: A Discriminant Analysis Approach. *Rev. Econ. Statist.*, August 1973, *55*(3), pp. 341–48.

Gramm, William P. and Dutton, Dean S. Transactions Costs, the Wage Rate, and the Demand for Money. *Amer. Econ. Rev.*, September 1973, *63*(4), pp. 652–65.

Grampp, William D. Classical Economics and Its Moral Critics. *Hist. Polit. Econ.*, Fall 1973, *5*(2), pp. 359–74.

Granata, Dale. Survey Highlights Occupational Pay Differences in Furniture Industry. *Mon. Lab. Rev.*, June 1973, *96*(6), pp. 58–60.

Granbois, Donald H.; Summers, John O. and Kraft, Frederic B. Brand Evaluation and Brand Choice: A Longitudinal Study. *J. Marketing Res.*, August 1973, *10*(3), pp. 235–41.

Grandmont, Jean-Michel. On the Short-Run and Long-Run Demand for Money. *Europ. Econ. Rev.*, October 1973, *4*(3), pp. 265–87.

———— and Laroque, Guy. Money in the Pure Consumption Loan Model. *J. Econ. Theory*, August 1973, *6*(4), pp. 382–95.

———— and Neel, Gérard. Sur les taux d'intérêt en France. (About Interest Rates in France. With English summary.) *Revue Écon.*, May 1973, *24*(3), pp. 460–72.

———— and Younes, Yves. On the Efficiency of a

Monetary Equilibrium. *Rev. Econ. Stud.*, April 1973, *40*(2), pp. 149–65.

Granger, C. W. J. On the Properties of Forecasts Used in Optimal Economic Policy Decisions. *J. Public Econ.*, November 1973, *2*(4), pp. 347–56.

_____ **and Newbold, P.** Some Comments on the Evaluation of Economic Forecasts. *Appl. Econ.*, March 1973, *5*(1), pp. 35–47.

Granick, David. A Management Model of East European, Centrally-Planned Economies. *Europ. Econ. Rev.*, June 1973, *4*(2), pp. 135–61.

Granof, Michael H. Financial Evaluation of Labor Contracts. *Manage. Account.*, July 1973, *55*(1), pp. 38–42, 45.

Grant, C. H. Political Sequel to Alcan Nationalization in Guyana: The International Aspects. *Soc. Econ. Stud.*, June 1973, *22*(2), pp. 249–71.

Grant, L. C. Monitoring Capital Investments. In *Thomas, W. E., Jr., ed.*, 1973, pp. 379–90.

Grant, W. P. British Employers' Associations and the Enlarged Community. *J. Common Market Stud.*, June 1973, *11*(4), pp. 276–86.

Grashof, John F. Supermarket Chain Product Addition and Deletion Decisions: A Case Study. *Marquette Bus. Rev.*, Fall 1973, *17*(3), pp. 120–28.

Grassini, Maurizio. The Transformation Matrix in the Linear Statistical Model with Serially Correlated Errors Generated by Autoregressive Schemes. *Statistica*, July-September 1973, *33*(3), pp. 395–407.

Grassman, Sven. A Fundamental Symmetry in International Payment Patterns. *J. Int. Econ.*, May 1973, *3*(2), pp. 105–16.

Gray, Daniel H. Methodology: One Approach to the Corporate Social Audit. *Calif. Manage. Rev.*, Summer 1973, *15*(4), pp. 106–09.

_____ One Way to Go about Inventing Social Accounting. In *Dierkes, M. and Bauer, R. A., eds.*, 1973, pp. 315–20.

Gray, H. Peter. Senile Industry Protection: A Proposal. *Southern Econ. J.*, April 1973, *39*(4), pp. 569–74.

_____ Two-Way International Trade in Manufactures: A Theoretical Underpinning. *Weltwirtsch. Arch.*, 1973, *109*(1), pp. 19–39.

Gray, Jean M. New Evidence on the Term Structure of Interest Rates: 1884–1900. *J. Finance*, June 1973, *28*(3), pp. 635–46.

Gray, M. R. and Parkin, Michael. Portfolio Diversification as Optimal Precautionary Behaviour. In *Morishima, M., et al.*, 1973, pp. 301–15.

Gray, Roger W. Agricultural Economics: An Orientation for the 70s. *Food Res. Inst. Stud.*, 1973, *12*(2), pp. 169–75.

_____ The Rebirth of Agricultural Economics? *Food Res. Inst. Stud.*, 1973, *12*(3), pp. 253–58.

Grayson, C. Jackson, Jr. Education and Technology. In *The Diebold Group, Inc.*, 1973, pp. 180–88.

_____ Let's Get Back to the Competitive Market System. *Harvard Bus. Rev.*, November-December 1973, *51*(6), pp. 103–12.

_____ Management Science and Business Practice. *Harvard Bus. Rev.*, July-August 1973, *51*(4), pp. 41–48.

Grayson, Leslie E. The Role of Suppliers' Credits in the Industrialization of Ghana. *Econ. Develop. Cult. Change*, April 1973, *21*(3), pp. 477–99.

Graziosi, Dante. Italian Foreign Trade: Final Results for 1972 Short-Term Prospects. *Rev. Econ. Cond. Italy*, January-March 1973, *27*(1–2), pp. 29–42.

Grebler, Leo. The Effect of FHLB Bond Operations on Savings Inflows at Savings and Loan Associations: Comment. *J. Finance*, March 1973, *28*(1), pp. 198–202.

_____ Growing Scale of Real Estate Firms and Projects. *Amer. Real Estate Urban Econ. Assoc. J.*, June 1973, *1*(1), pp. 107–22.

Green, Alfred L. The Future of Manpower Planning: Discussion. In *Aronson, R. L., ed.*, 1973, pp. 99–102.

Green, Gloria P. and Stinson, John F. Changes in the Employment Situation in 1972. *Mon. Lab. Rev.*, February 1973, *96*(2), pp. 24–34.

Green, H. A. John. Public Sector Resource Allocation under Conditions of Risk: Discussion. In *Parkin, M., ed.*, 1973, pp. 137–38.

Green, Harold P. Nuclear Power: Risk, Liability, and Indemnity. *Mich. Law Rev.*, january 1973, *71*(3), pp. 479–510.

Green, Jerry R. Temporary General Equilibrium in a Sequential Trading Model with Spot and Futures Transactions. *Econometrica*, November 1973, *41*(6), pp. 1103–23.

Green, Mark J. The High Cost of Monopoly. In *Andreano, R. L., ed.*, 1973, pp. R325–05.

_____ **and Moore, Beverly C., Jr.** The Nader Antitrust Report: A Tale of Two Critics. *Antitrust Bull.*, Fall, 1973, *18*(3), pp. 551–79.

_____ **and Moore, Beverly C., Jr.** Winter's Discontent: Market Failure and Consumer Welfare. *Yale Law J.*, April 1973, *82*(5), pp. 903–19.

_____ **and Nader, Ralph.** Economic Regulation vs. Competition: Uncle Sam the Monopoly Man. *Yale Law J.*, April 1973, *82*(5), pp. 871–89.

Green, Paul E. Multidimensional Scaling and Conjoint Measurement in the Study of Choice Among Multiattribute Alternatives. In *Cochrane, J. L. and Zeleny, M., eds.*, 1973, pp. 577–609.

_____ On the Analysis of Interactions in Marketing Research Data. *J. Marketing Res.*, November 1973, *10*(4), pp. 410–20.

_____; **Wind, Yoram and Jain, Arun K.** Analyzing Free-Response Data in Marketing Research. *J. Marketing Res.*, February 1973, *10*(1), pp. 45–52.

Green, R. H. Economic Independence and Economic Co-operation. In *Ghai, D., ed.*, 1973, pp. 45–87.

_____ University Economics in Anglophonic Africa: A Modest Critique from a Consumer Viewpoint. In *Livingstone, I., et al., eds.*, 1973, pp. 137–46.

Green, Richard; Hassan, Zuhair and Johnson, Stanley R. Price and Income Flexibilities and the Double Logarithmic Demand System: Comment. *Amer. J. Agr. Econ.*, Part I, November 1973, *55*(4), pp. 678–79.

_____; **Hassan, Zuhair A. and Johnson, Stanley R.** An Alternative Method for Pricing Pork Carcasses. *Can. J. Agr. Econ.*, November 1973, *21*(3), pp. 1–5.

Green, Robert and Mazis, Michael B. Implementing Social Responsibility. In *Klein, W. H. and Murphy, D. C., eds.*, 1973, pp. 296–304.

Green, Thad B. and Cotlar, Morton. An Evaluation of a Novel Business Simulation Technique for

Management Development. *J. Bus.*, April 1973, *46*(2), pp. 212–29.

Green, W. A. The Planter Class and the British West Indian Sugar Production, before and after Emancipation. *Econ. Hist. Rev., 2nd Ser.*, August 1973, *26*(3), pp. 448–63.

Greenberg, L. The Enforcement of Occupational Safety Legislation. *Int. Lab. Rev.*, May 1973, *107* (5), pp. 425–40.

Greene, Kenneth V. Attitudes Toward Risk and the Relative Size of the Public Sector. *Public Finance Quart.*, April 1973, *1*(2), pp. 205–18.

———— Collective Decision-Making Models and the Measurement of Benefits in Fiscal Incidence Studies. *Nat. Tax J.*, June 1973, *26*(2), pp. 177–85.

———— Inheritance Unjustified? *J. Law Econ.*, October 1973, *16*(2), pp. 417–19.

———— **and Newlon, Daniel H.** Economic Factors Affecting the Likelihood of a Switch to a Volunteer Army. *Public Finance Quart.*, October 1973, *1*(4), pp. 388–98.

———— **and Newlon, Daniel H.** The Pareto Optimality of Eliminating a Lottery Draft. *Quart. Rev. Econ. Bus.*, Winter 1973, *13*(4), pp. 61–70.

Greene, Mark R. A Note on Loading Charges for Variable Annuities. *J. Risk Ins.*, September 1973, *40*(3), pp. 473–78.

———— Should Variable Policy Loan Interest Rates be Adopted? *J. Risk Ins.*, December 1973, *40*(4), pp. 585–98.

Greene, Robert L. Peak Load Pricing: An Application. *Quart. Rev. Econ. Bus.*, Autumn 1973, *13*(3), pp. 105–14.

Greenfield, J. N. and Wickens, M. R. The Econometrics of Agricultural Supply: An Application to the World Coffee Market. *Rev. Econ. Statist.*, November 1973, *55*(4), pp. 433–40.

Greenhut, M. L. and Ohta, H. Spatial Configurations and Competitive Equilibrium. *Weltwirtsch. Arch.*, 1973, *109*(1), pp. 87–104.

Greeno, Daniel W.; Sommers, Montrose S. and Kernan, Jerome B. Personality and Implicit Behavior Patterns. *J. Marketing Res.*, February 1973, *10*(1), pp. 63–69.

Greenough, William T.; Menges, Robert J. and Costin, Frank. Student Ratings of College Teaching: Reliability, Validity, and Usefulness. *J. Econ. Educ.*, Fall 1973, *5*(1), pp. 51–53.

Greenstreet, D. K. Public Administration: A Comparative Analysis of the 1950 Colonial Ten-Year Development Plan and the 1951 'Nkrumah' Development Plan of the Gold Coast (Ghana) *Econ. Bull. Ghana, Sec. Ser.*, 1973, *3*(4), pp. 31–55.

Greenwald, Carol S. Maternity Leave Policy. *New Eng. Econ. Rev.*, January-February 1973, pp. 13–18.

———— A New Deflated Composite Index of Leading Indicators. *New Eng. Econ. Rev.*, July-August 1973, pp. 3–18.

Greenwood, Michael J. The Geographic Mobility of College Graduates. *J. Human Res.*, Fall 1973, *8*(4), pp. 506–15.

———— **and Wadycki, Walter J.** Crime Rates and Public Expenditures for Police Protection: Their Interaction. *Rev. Soc. Econ.*, October 1973, *31*(2), pp. 138–51.

Greer, Douglas F. Advertising and Market Concentration: Reply. *Southern Econ. J.*, January 1973, *39* (3), pp. 451–53.

———— Some Case History Evidence on the Advertising-Concentration Relationship. *Antitrust Bull.*, Summer 1973, *18*(2), pp. 307–32.

Greer, Howard Clark. Cost Factors in Price Making. In *Thomas, W. E., Jr., ed.*, 1973, pp. 201–23.

Gregg, Robert W. The UN Regional Economic Commissions and Integration in the Underdeveloped Regions. In *Falk, R. A. and Mendlovitz, S. H., eds.*, 1973, pp. 308–27.

Gregory, Gene. Japan Enters the Technetronic Age. *Econ. Rec.*, March 1973, *49*(125), pp. 1–14.

Gregory, K. and Russell, C. SIMPREP, A Computer Model for Coal Preparation. In *Ross, M., ed.*, 1973, pp. 379–89.

Gregory, Paul. A Model of Socialist Industrial Wage Differentials: The Case of East Germany. *Quart. J. Econ.*, February 1973, *87*(1), pp. 132–37.

————**; Campbell, John and Cheng, Benjamin.** Differences in Fertility Determinants: Developed and Developing Countries. *J. Devel. Stud.*, January 1973, *9*(2), pp. 233–41.

Gregory, R. G. and James, Denis W. Do New Factories Embody Best Practice Technology? *Econ. J.*, December 1973, *83*(332), pp. 1133–55.

———— **and Sheehan, P. J.** The Cyclical Sensitivity of Labour Force Participation Rates. *Australian Econ. Rev.*, 2nd Quarter 1973, pp. 9–20.

———— **and Tearle, D.** Product Differentiation and International Trade Flows: An Application of the "Hedonic" Regression Technique. *Australian Econ. Pap.*, June 1973, *12*(20), pp. 79–90.

Grenville, Stephen. Survey of Recent Developments. *Bull. Indonesian Econ. Stud.*, March 1973, *9*(1), pp. 1–29.

Grether, D. M. and Maddala, G. S. Errors in Variables and Serially Correlated Disturbances in Distributed Lag Models. *Econometrica*, March 1973, *41*(2), pp. 255–62.

Grier, Paul C. and Albin, Peter S. Nonrandom Price Changes in Association with Trading in Large Blocks. *J. Bus.*, July 1973, *46*(3), pp. 425–33.

Grieson, Ronald E. Effects of the Property Tax on Operating and Investment Decisions of Rental Property Owners: A Note. *Nat. Tax J.*, March 1973, *26*(1), pp. 127–28.

———— Poverty: Introduction. In *Grieson, R. E., ed.*, 1973, pp. 273–85.

———— The Supply of Rental Housing: Comment. *Amer. Econ. Rev.*, June 1973, *63*(3), pp. 433–36.

———— Zoning, Housing Markets, and Urban Renewal: Introduction. In *Grieson, R. E., ed.*, 1973, pp. 133–48.

Griffin, Colin P. The Standard of Living in the Black Country in the Nineteenth Century: A Comment. *Econ. Hist. Rev., 2nd Ser.*, August 1973, *26*(3), pp. 510–13.

Griffin, James B. The Economics of Education: Social Benefits and Costs. In *Mattila, J. M. and Thompson, W. R., eds.*, 1973, pp. 140–50.

Griffin, Keith. The Effect of Aid and Other Resource Transfers on Savings and Growth in Less-Developed Countries: A Comment. *Econ. J.*, September 1973, *83*(331), pp. 863–66.

_____ Policy Options for Rural Development. *Oxford Bull. Econ. Statist.*, November 1973, *35*(4), pp. 239–74.

_____ Underdevelopment in History. In *Wilber, C. K., ed.*, 1973, pp. 68–81.

_____ Underdevelopment in Theory. In *Wilber, C. K., ed.*, 1973, pp. 15–25.

Griffin, Wade L. and Lacewell, Ronald D. Long-Run Implications of a Tax in Kind to Reduce Supply and Increase Income: Comment. *Amer. J. Agr. Econ.*, Part I, November 1973, *55*(4), pp. 670–74.

Griffith, G. Talbot. Population Problems in the Age of Malthus, 1967. In *Tranter, N. L., ed.*, 1973, pp. 208–10.

Griffith, John R.; Hancock, Walton M. and Munson, Fred C. Practical Ways to Contain Hospital Costs. *Harvard Bus. Rev.*, November-December 1973, *51*(6), pp. 131–39.

Griffiths, Brian. The Development of Restrictive Practices in the U.K. Monetary System. *Manchester Sch. Econ. Soc. Stud.*, March 1973, *41*(1), pp. 3–18.

_____ Resource Efficiency, Monetary Policy and the Reform of the U.K. Banking System. *J. Money, Credit, Banking*, Part I, February 1973, *5*(1), pp. 61–77.

Grigsby, William G. Real Estate and Urban Land Economics: Illusions of Progress? *Amer. Real Estate Urban Econ. Assoc. J.*, June 1973, *1*(1), pp. 4–7.

Griliches, Zvi. Measuring Performance in Education: Comment. In *Moss, M., ed.*, 1973, pp. 433–35.

_____ Research Expenditures and Growth Accounting. In *Williams, B. R., ed.*, 1973, pp. 59–83.

_____ **and Mason, William M.** Education, Income, and Ability. In *Goldberger, A. S. and Duncan, O. D., eds.*, 1973, pp. 285–316.

Grindstaff, Carl F. and Ebanks, G. Edward. Male Sterilization as a Contraceptive Method in Canada: An Empirical Study. *Population Stud.*, November 1973, *27*(3), pp. 443–55.

Grinold, Richard C.; Levy, Haim and Arditti, Fred D. The Investment-Consumption Decision under Capital Rationing: An Efficient Set Analysis. *Rev. Econ. Stud.*, July 1973, *40*(3), pp. 367–76.

Grochow, Jerrold M. Corporate Social Reform: A Young Person's Viewpoint. *Calif. Manage. Rev.*, Summer 1973, *15*(4), pp. 74–77.

Groenewegen, P. D. A Note on the Origin of the Phrase, "Supply and Demand". *Econ. J.*, June 1973, *83*(330), pp. 505–09.

Gronau, Reuben. The Effect of Children on the Housewife's Value of Time. *J. Polit. Econ.*, Part II, March-April 1973, *81*(2), pp. S168–99.

_____ The Intrafamily Allocation of Time: The Value of the Housewives' Time. *Amer. Econ. Rev.*, September 1973, *63*(4), pp. 634–51.

_____ The Measurement of Output of the Nonmarket Sector: The Evaluation of Housewives' Time. In *Moss, M., ed.*, 1973, pp. 163–90.

Grønhaug, Kjell. Buying Experience and Buying Purpose. *Ekon. Samfundets Tidskr.*, 1973, *26*(4), pp. 247–54.

Gros-Pietro, Gian M. Produzione industriale e teoria economica. (Industrial Production and Economic Theory. With English summary.) *L'Impresa*, 1973, *15*(3–4), pp. 209–21.

Gross, Bertram M. What Are Your Organization's Objectives? A General-Systems Approach to Planning. In *Klein, W. H. and Murphy, D. C., eds.*, 1973, pp. 106–29.

Grossman, Herschel I. Aggregate Demand, Job Search, and Employment. *J. Polit. Econ.*, November-December 1973, *81*(6), pp. 1353–69.

Grossman, Howard J. Regional Development Districts: A Case Study of Northeastern Pennsylvania. *Growth Change*, October 1973, *4*(4), pp. 4–9.

Grossman, Jonathan. The Origin of the U.S. Department of Labor. *Mon. Lab. Rev.*, March 1973, *96*(3), pp. 3–7.

_____ Wage and Price Controls During the American Revolution. *Mon. Lab. Rev.*, September 1973, *96*(9), pp. 3–10.

_____ Who is the Father of Labor Day? *Labor Hist.*, Fall 1973, *14*(4), pp. 612–23.

Grossman, Michael. Unemployment and Consumption: Note. *Amer. Econ. Rev.*, March 1973, *63*(1), pp. 208–13.

_____ **and Fuchs, Victor R.** Intersectoral Shifts and Aggregate Productivity Change. *Ann. Econ. Soc. Measure*, July 1973, *2*(3), pp. 227–43.

Grossman, Steven D. A Test of Speed of Adjustment in Manufacturing Inventory Investment. *Quart. Rev. Econ. Bus.*, Autumn 1973, *13*(3), pp. 21–32.

Grove, Ernest W. Evaluating Performance in the Public Sector: Comment. In *Moss, M., ed.*, 1973, pp. 394–97.

_____ Use of the Arithmetic Mean in Farm Policy. *Amer. J. Agr. Econ.*, May 1973, *55*(2), pp. 344–45.

Groves, Roderick T. The Venezuelan Administrative Reform Movement, 1958–1963. In *Thurber, C. E. and Graham, L. S., eds.*, 1973, pp. 47–80.

Groves, Theodore. Incentives in Teams. *Econometrica*, July 1973, *41*(4), pp. 617–31.

Groza, Maria and Iovanelli, Marcela. Activizarea şi conducerea politică a maselor țărănești de către Partidul Comunist Român în procesul înfăptuirii sarcinilor desăvârșirii revoluției burghezo-democratice. (The Activation and the Political Leadership of the Peasant Masses by the Romanian Communist Party in the Fulfilment of the Targets of the Completion of the Bourgeois-Democratic Revolution. With English summary.) *Stud. Cercet. Econ.*, 1973, (3), pp. 19–28.

Grub, Phillip D. and Petrini, Bart F. Product Management in High Technology Defense Industry Marketing. *Calif. Manage. Rev.*, Spring 1973, *15*(3), pp. 138–46.

Grubel, Herbert G. The Optimum Stability of Exchange Rates: A Southeast Asian Payments Union. In *Grubel, H. G. and Morgan, T., eds.*, 1973, pp. 77–92.

_____ The Case for Optimum Exchange Rate Stability. *Weltwirtsch. Arch.*, 1973, *109*(3), pp. 351–81.

_____ Forward Exchange Market Intervention is not Necessarily Neutral. *Weltwirtsch. Arch.*, 1973, *109*(4), pp. 704–06.

_____ The Theory of Optimum Regional Associations. In *Johnson, H. G. and Swoboda, A. K., eds.*, 1973, pp. 99–113.

Gruber, Martin J. and Elton, Edwin J. Asset Selection with Changing Capital Structure. *J. Financial Quant. Anal.*, June 1973, *8*(3), pp. 459–74.

────── Estimating the Dependence Structure of Share Prices—Implications for Portfolio Selection. *J. Finance*, December 1973, *28*(5), pp. 1203–32.

Gruchy, Allan G. Law, Politics, and Institutional Economics. *J. Econ. Issues*, December 1973, *7*(4), pp. 623–43.

Gruebele, J. W. Measures of Efficiency in Milk Plant Operations. *Ill. Agr. Econ.*, July 1973, *13*(2), pp. 38–43.

────── and Miller, James J. Effects of the Use of Spot Cases in the Sale of Selected Dairy Products in Retail Food Chains. *Ill. Agr. Econ.*, July 1973, *13*(2), pp. 44–48.

Grünärml, Frohmund. Demand Management—Illusion oder Realität? (Demand Management—Illusion or Reality? With English summary.) *Z. Wirtschaft. Sozialwissen.*, 1973, *93*(5), pp. 537–66.

Grundmann, Helge E. Towards a More Applicable Economic Theory. In *Livingstone, I., et al., eds.*, 1973, pp. 59–65.

Grzybowski, Kazimierz. Control of U.S. Trade with China: An Overview. *Law Contemp. Probl.*, Summer-Autumn 1973, *38*(2), pp. 175–81.

Guadagni, Alieto A. La evaluación social de los proyectos industriales según "Guidelines for Project Evaluation" de Unido. (Social Evaluation of Industrial Projects According Unidó's "Guidelines for Project Evaluation." With English summary.) *Económica*, May-August 1973, *19*(2), pp. 165–83.

Guarnieri, Raymond L. Short-Run Supply. *Southern Econ. J.*, July 1973, *40*(1), pp. 9–11.

────── A Suggestion for Rigorizing the Theory of Prediction. *Western Econ. J.*, June 1973, *11*(2), pp. 147–49.

Guedry, L. J. An Application of a Multi-Commodity Transportation Model to the U.S. Feed Grain Economy. In *Judge, G. G. and Takayama, T., eds.*, 1973, pp. 243–60.

Guerard, Michèle. The Brazilian State Value-Added Tax. *Int. Monet. Fund Staff Pap.*, March 1973, *20*(1), pp. 118–69.

────── ; Lent, George E. and Casanegra, Milka. The Value-Added Tax in Developing Countries. *Int. Monet. Fund Staff Pap.*, July 1973, *20*(2), pp. 318–78.

Guerci, Carlo M. Nuovi miti sulla grande impresa? (New Myths on the Big Firm? With English summary.) *L'industria, N. S.*, 1973, (1), pp. 91–101.

Guerreiro-Ramos, Alberto. The New Ignorance and the Future of Public Administration in Latin America. In *Thurber, C. E. and Graham, L. S., eds.*, 1973, pp. 382–422.

Guesnerie, Roger; Malgrange, Pierre and Deleau, Michel. Planification, incertitude et politique économique. II—L'opération Optimix: Résultats numériques. (Planning, Uncertainty and Economic Policy. II—Optimix Operation: Numerical Results. With English summary.) *Revue Écon.*, November 1973, *24*(6), pp. 1072–1103.

────── ; Malgrange, Pierre and Deleau, Michel.

Planification, incertitude et politique économique. L'operation Optimix. Une procédure formalisée d'adaptation du Plan à l'aléa. (Planning Uncertainty and Economic Policy. A Formalized Procedure: "Optimix." With English summary.) *Revue Écon.*, September 1973, *24*(5), pp. 801–36.

Guest, Avery M. Urban Growth and Population Densities. *Demography*, February 1973, *10*(1), pp. 53–69.

Guffey, Hugh J., Jr. and Barksdale, Hiram C. A Cross-Spectral Analysis of Motor Vehicle Sales and Registrations. *Swedish J. Econ.*, September 1973, *75*(3), pp. 266–77.

Guggenheim, Thomas. Some Early Views on Monetary Integration. In *Johnson, H. G. and Swoboda, A. K., eds.*, 1973, pp. 93–98.

Guha, Sabita. Economics of Deep-Tubewell Irrigation. *Econ. Aff.*, June 1973, *18*(6), pp. 291–98.

Guicciardi, Diego. Industry and Ecological Problems in Italy. *Rev. Econ. Cond. Italy*, September 1973, *27*(5), pp. 305–12.

Guilkey, David K. and Schmidt, Peter. Estimation of Seemingly Unrelated Regressions with Vector Autoregressive Errors. *J. Amer. Statist. Assoc.*, September 1973, *68*(343), pp. 642–47.

Guise, J. W. B. and Aggrey-Mensah, W. An Evaluation of Policy Alternatives Facing Australian Banana Producers. In *Judge, G. G. and Takayama, T., eds.*, 1973, pp. 519–35.

────── and Flinn, J. C. Allocation and Pricing of Water Resources. In *Judge, G. G. and Takayama, T., eds.*, 1973, pp. 536–56.

Guisinger, Stephen. The Rise of the Multinational Corporation and United States Trade Policy. *Soc. Sci. Quart.*, December 1973, *54*(3), pp. 552–67.

Guither, Harold D. Extension Education in Bargaining Among Midwest Livestock and Grain Producers. *Amer. J. Agr. Econ.*, February 1973, *55*(1), pp. 58–60.

Guitian, Manuel. Credit Versus Money as an Instrument of Control. *Int. Monet. Fund Staff Pap.*, November 1973, *20*(3), pp. 785–800.

────── and Almonacid, Ruben. The Optimal Rate of Devaluation. In *Johnson, H. G. and Swoboda, A. K., eds.*, 1973, pp. 281–97.

Gujarati, Damodar. The Behaviour of Unemployment and Unfilled Vacancies: Great Britain, 1958–1971—A Reply. *Econ. J.*, March 1973, *83*(329), pp. 201–03.

Gunderson, Gerald. Southern Ante-bellum Income Reconsidered. *Exploration Econ. Hist.*, Winter 1973, *10*(2), pp. 151–76.

Gunderson, Morley. Determinants of Individual Success in On-the-Job Training. *J. Human Res.*, Fall 1973, *8*(4), pp. 472–84.

Gunn, Lewis A. Government, Technology, and Planning in Britain. In *Edge, D. O. and Wolfe, J. N., eds.*, 1973, pp. 161–79.

Gunnelson, Jerald A. and Farris, Paul L. Use of Soybean Futures Markets by Large Processing Firms. *Agr. Econ. Res.*, April 1973, *25*(2), pp. 27–40.

Gunning, J. Patrick, Jr. How Profitable Is Burglary? In *Rottenberg, S., ed.*, 1973, pp. 35–38.

Guntermann, Karl L. Air Pollution Control in the Secondary Aluminum Industry. *Land Econ.*, August 1973, *49*(3), pp. 285–93.

Gup, Benton E. A Note on Stock Market Indicators and Stock Prices. *J. Financial Quant. Anal.*, September 1973, *8*(4), pp. 673–82.

Gupta, Biswatosh Sen. The Birth Table and Its Construction for Belgium. *J. Amer. Statist. Assoc.*, March 1973, *68*(341), pp. 44–45.

Gupta, J. R. and Sandhu, H. S. Adoption and Performance of Recommended Practices—A Comparative Study of Two Villages in Ludhiana District. *Econ. Aff.*, August 1973, *18*(8), pp. 389–94.

Gupta, Manak C. On Intra-Firm Resource Allocation Under Risk. *Eng. Econ.*, July-August 1973, *18*(4), pp. 229–42.

_____ Optimal Financing Policy for a Firm with Uncertain Fund Requirements. *J. Financial Quant. Anal.*, December 1973, *8*(5), pp. 731–47.

Gupta, M. L. Outflow of High-Level Manpower from the Philippines, with Special Reference to the Period 1965-71. *Int. Lab. Rev.*, February 1973, *107*(2), pp. 167–91.

Gupta, Rajendra K. Social Welfare Functions. *Indian Econ. J.*, January-March 1973, *20*(3), pp. 414–30.

Gupta, S. The Role of the Public Sector in Reducing Regional Income Disparity in Indian Plans. *J. Devel. Stud.*, January 1973, *9*(2), pp. 243–60.

Gupta, Satyadev and Lal, Prem. Inter-Regional Transfer of Real Resources: A Case Study of Pakistan, 1948-70. *Indian Econ. Rev.*, April 1973, *8*(1), pp. 39–60.

Gupta, Suraj B. The Controversy over Differential Lending Rates for Banks: An Examination. *Indian Econ. Rev.*, April 1973, *8*(1), pp. 16–38.

_____ Financial Progress, Banking Expansion, and Saving. *Indian Econ. J.*, April-June 1973, *20*(4–5), pp. 548–69.

Gurley, John W. Maoist Economic Development: The New Man in the New China. In *Wilber, C. K., ed.*, 1973, pp. 307–19.

Gusen, P.; Havrilesky, Thomas M. and Weintraub, E. R. Potpourri: The Monetarist's Papers. *Intermountain Econ. Rev.*, Fall 1973, *4*(2), pp. 78–80.

Gustafson, Dale R. Perspectives on Life Insurance Financial Reporting: Discussion. *J. Risk Ins.*, March 1973, *40*(1), pp. 22–25.

Gustman, Alan L. On Estimating the Rate of Return to Education. *Appl. Econ.*, June 1973, *5*(2), pp. 89–99.

_____ On the Appropriate Model for Analyzing Investment in Human Capital Where the Capital Market is Imperfect. *Rev. Income Wealth*, September 1973, *19*(3), pp. 303–05.

_____ and Pidot, George B., Jr. Interactions Between Educational Spending and Student Enrollment. *J. Human Res.*, Winter 1973, *8*(1), pp. 3–23.

Güth, Werner. Zur wohlfahrtsökonomischen Bedeutung marktwirtschaftlicher Verhandlungsgleichgewichte. (Welfare Economic Meaning of Market Economies' Competitive Equilibrium. With English summary.) *Z. ges. Staatswiss.*, August 1973, *129*(3), pp. 445–53.

Guth, William D. and Anshen, Melvin. Strategies for Research in Policy Formulation. *J. Bus.*, October 1973, *46*(4), pp. 499–511.

Guthrie, Art. Middle Managers and MIS: An Attitude

Survey. *J. Econ. Bus.*, Fall 1973, *26*(1), pp. 58–66.

Gutierrez, Alfredo D. and Dietrich, J. Kimball. An Evaluation of Short-Term Forecasts of Coffee and Cocoa. *Amer. J. Agr. Econ.*, February 1973, *55*(1), pp. 93–99.

Gutman, Herbert G. Work, Culture, and Society in Industrializing America, 1815-1919. *Amer. Hist. Rev.*, June 1973, *78*(3), pp. 531–88.

Gutowski, Armin. Theoretical Approaches to a Concept of Supplier's Power. *Ger. Econ. Rev.*, 1973, *11*(3), pp. 193–215.

Gwartney, James and Silberman, Jonathan. Distribution of Costs and Benefits and the Significance of Collective Decision Rules. *Soc. Sci. Quart.*, December 1973, *54*(3), pp. 568–78.

_____ and Stroup, Richard. Measurement of Employment Discrimination According to Sex. *Southern Econ. J.*, April 1973, *39*(4), pp. 575–87.

Gwyer, G. D. Three International Commodity Agreements: The Experience of East Africa. *Econ. Develop. Cult. Change*, April 1973, *21*(3), pp. 465–76.

Gyenes, A. Re-stratification of the Agricultural Population in Hungary. *Acta Oecon.*, 1973, *11*(1), pp. 33–49.

Gylys, Julius A. Economic Analysis of Municipal and County Police Interdependence. In *Mattila, J. M. and Thompson, W. R., eds.*, 1973, pp. 151–63.

Haanes-Olsen, Leif. Dental Insurance in Sweden. *Soc. Sec. Bull.*, December 1973, *36*(12), pp. 20–22.

Haas, Ernst B. The Study of Regional Integration: Reflections on the Joy and Anguish of Pretheorizing. In *Falk, R. A. and Mendlovitz, S. H., eds.*, 1973, pp. 103–32.

Habakkuk, H. J. American and British Technology in the Nineteenth Century, 1962. In *Tranter, N. L., ed.*, 1973, pp. 136–40.

Haber, Lawrence D. Social Planning for Disability. *J. Human Res.*, Supplement 1973, *8*, pp. 33–55.

Haber, Sheldon. Trends in Work Rates of White Females, 1890 to 1950. *Ind. Lab. Relat. Rev.*, July 1973, *26*(4), pp. 1122–34.

Haber, William. Employment Policies. In *Somers, G. G., ed.*, 1973, pp. 56–64.

Haberler, Gottfried. The Historical Setting: Comment. In *Krause, L. B. and Salant, W. S., eds.*, 1973, pp. 33–36.

_____ International Aspects of U.S. Inflation. In *Cagan, P., et al.*, 1973, pp. 79–105.

_____ Joseph Alois Schumpeter. In *Rectenwald, H. C., ed.*, 1973, pp. 370–93.

_____ Prospects for the Dollar Standard. In *[Halm, G. N.]*, 1973, pp. 65–80.

_____ Two Arguments for Fixed Rates: Comment. In *Johnson, H. G. and Swoboda, A. K., eds.*, 1973, pp. 35–39.

Habermas, Jürgen. What Does a Crisis Mean Today? Legitimation Problems in Late Capitalism. *Soc. Res.*, Winter 1973, *40*(4), pp. 643–67.

Habibagahi, Hamid and Quirk, James. Hicksian Stability and Walras' Law. *Rev. Econ. Stud.*, April 1973, *40*(2), pp. 249–58.

Haccou, J. F. and Lübbers, P. J. M. Public Policy Toward Retailing: The Netherlands. In *Bod-*

dewyn, J. J. and Hollander, S. C., eds., 1972, pp. 245–70.

Hadari, Yitzhak. The Structure of the Private Multinational Enterprise. *Mich. Law Rev.,* March 1973, *71*(4), pp. 729–806.

Hader, R. J.; Cote, R. and Manson, A. R. Minimum Bias Approximation of a General Regression Model. *J. Amer. Statist. Assoc.,* September 1973, *68*(343), pp. 633–38.

Hadjimichalakis, Michael G. On the Effectiveness of Monetary Policy as a Stabilization Device. *Rev. Econ. Stud.,* October 1973, *40*(4), pp. 561–70.

Hagen, Everett E. Economic Growth with Unlimited Foreign Exchange and No Technical Progress. In *[Rosenstein-Rodan, P.],* 1973, pp. 69–78.

Hagen, Kare P. Optimal Dividend Policies and Corporate Growth. *Swedish J. Econ.,* September 1973, *75*(3), pp. 238–48.

Hagerman, Robert L. The Efficiency of the Market for Bank Stocks: An Empirical Test: Comment. *J. Money, Credit, Banking,* August 1973, *5*(3), pp. 846–55.

_____ **and Richmond, Richard D.** Random Walks, Martingales and the OTC. *J. Finance,* September 1973, *28*(4), pp. 897–909.

Hagger, A. J. and Rayner, P. J. The Excess Demand for Commodities in Australia, 1950–51 to 1968–69. *Econ. Rec.,* June 1973, *49*(126), pp. 161–93.

el-Hag Musa, Omar. Reconciliation, Rehabilitation and Development Efforts in Southern Sudan. *Middle East J.,* Winter 1973, *27*(1), pp. 1–6.

Hague, D. C. Competition and the U.K. Industry. In *Rybczynski, T. M., ed.,* 1973, pp. 78–95.

Hahn, Frank H. On Optimum Taxation. *J. Econ. Theory,* February 1973, *6*(1), pp. 96–106.

_____ On Some Equilibrium Paths. In *Mirrlees, J. A. and Stern, N. H., eds.,* 1973, pp. 193–206.

_____ On the Foundations of Monetary Theory. In *Parkin, M., ed.,* 1973, pp. 230–42.

_____ On Transaction Costs, Inessential Sequence Economies and Money. *Rev. Econ. Stud.,* October 1973, *40*(4), pp. 449–61.

_____ The Winter of our Discontent. *Economica,* N.S., August 1973, *40*(159), pp. 322–30.

Hahn, Harlan. Ethnic Minorities: Politics and the Family in Suburbia. In *Masotti, L. H. and Hadden, J. K., eds.,* 1973, pp. 185–205.

Haig, Bryan D. The Treatment of Banks in the Social Accounts. *Econ. Rec.,* December 1973, *49*(128), pp. 624–28.

_____ The Treatment of Stock Appreciation in the Measurement of National Income. *Rev. Income Wealth,* December 1973, *19*(4), pp. 429–36.

Haines, George H., Jr.; Simon, Leonard S. and Alexis, Marcus. An Analysis of Central City Neighborhood Food Trading Areas: A Reply. *J. Reg. Sci.,* August 1973, *13*(2), pp. 301.

Haites, Erik F. and Mak, James. The Decline of Steamboating on the Ante-bellum Western Rivers: Some New Evidence and An Alternative Hypothesis. *Exploration Econ. Hist.,* Fall 1973, *11*(1), pp. 25–36.

Haizel, K. A. Ecological Problems of Agricultural Production in West Africa. In *Ofori, I. M., ed.,* 1973, pp. 82–90.

Hajdu, C.; Apsey, T. M. and Garton, M. M. Economic Trends in the Canadian Forest Products Industry. *Amer. J. Agr. Econ.,* December 1973, *55*(5), pp. 974–82.

Halabuk, L. Estimation and Structure of the Second Econometric Model of Hungary. *Matekon,* Summer 1973, *9*(4), pp. 43–66.

Halder, A. and Richards, J. H. Structural Characteristics of India's Foreign Trade and its Effect on the Instability of Export Receipts. *Indian Econ. J.,* October–December 1973, *21*(2), pp. 132–46.

Hale, Carl W. Growth Centers, Regional Spread Effects, and National Economic Growth. *J. Econ. Bus.,* Fall 1973, *26*(1), pp. 10–18.

_____ Impact of Technological Change on Urban Market Areas, Land Values, and Land Uses. *Land Econ.,* August 1973, *49*(3), pp. 351–56.

_____ United States' Economic Development, the Business Cycle, and Industrial Complementarity. *Miss. Val. J. Bus. Econ.,* Spring 1973, *8*(3), pp. 47–58.

Hale, Rosemary D. Cement Mergers—Market Dispersion and Conglomerate Entry. *Marquette Bus. Rev.,* Summer 1973, *17*(2), pp. 98–108.

Haley, William J. Human Capital: The Choice Between Investment and Income. *Amer. Econ. Rev.,* December 1973, *63*(5), pp. 929–44.

Half, Robert. Gamesmanship in Salary Management. *Manage. Account.,* March 1973, *54*(9), pp. 56–57.

Hall, Darwin C. and Norgaard, Richard B. On the Timing and Application of Pesticides. *Amer. J. Agr. Econ.,* May 1973, *55*(2), pp. 198–201.

Hall, George R. Expanded Powers for Depository Financial Institutions: Discussion. In *Federal Reserve Bank of Boston,* 1973, pp. 72–76.

Hall, M.-Françoise. Population Growth: U.S. and Latin American Views: An Interpretation of the Response of the United States and Latin America to the Latin American Population Growth. *Population Stud.,* November 1973, *27*(3), pp. 415–29.

Hall, Owen P., Jr. and Brewer, Garry D. Policy Analysis by Computer Simulation: The Need for Appraisal. *Public Policy,* Summer 1973, *21*(3), pp. 343–65.

Hall, Robert E. The Effect of Children on the Housewife's Value of Time: Comment. *J. Polit. Econ.,* Part II, March-April 1973, *81*(2), pp. S200–01.

_____ The Specification of Technology with Several Kinds of Output. *J. Polit. Econ.,* July-August 1973, *81*(4), pp. 878–92.

_____ **and Kasten, Richard A.** The Relative Occupational Success of Blacks and Whites. *Brookings Pap. Econ. Act.,* 1973, (3), pp. 781–95.

Hall, W. Clayton and Carroll, Norman E. The Effect of Teachers' Organizations on Salaries and Class Size. *Ind. Lab. Relat. Rev.,* January 1973, *26*(2), pp. 834–41.

Halldorson, James R. and Booms, Bernard H. The Politics of Redistribution: A Reformulation. *Amer. Polit. Sci. Rev.,* September 1973, *67*(3), pp. 924–33.

Hallencreutz, Ingrid and Lindblad, Sven. Public Policy Toward Retailing: Sweden. In *Boddewyn, J. J. and Hollander, S. C., eds.,* 1972, pp. 283–95.

Haller, Heinz. Die Berücksichtigung des Lebensunterhalts der Kinder und der Vorsorgeaufwendungen im Rahmen der Steuerreform—Zielsetzungen und Implikationen. (The Consideration of Family Expenses for Children and of Providence Expenditures in the Tax Reform. With English summary.) *Z. ges. Staatswiss.*, August 1973, *129* (3), pp. 504–34.

Hallwood, C. P. The Impact of Foreign Aid Upon India's International Trade 1951-65. *Bull. Econ. Res.*, November 1973, *25*(2), pp. 129–45.

Halm, George N. Reforming the Par-Value System. *Weltwirtsch. Arch.*, 1973, *109*(2), pp. 171–90.

Halpern, Elkan F. Polynomial Regression from a Bayesian Approach. *J. Amer. Statist. Assoc.*, March 1973, *68*(341), pp. 137–43.

Halpern, Paul J. Empirical Estimates of the Amount and Distribution of Gains to Companies in Mergers. *J. Bus.*, October 1973, *46*(4), pp. 554–75.

Halter, A. N. and Miller, S. F. Systems-Simulation in a Practical Policy-Making Setting: The Venezuelan Cattle Industry. *Amer. J. Agr. Econ.*, August 1973, *55*(3), pp. 420–32.

Halverson, James T. Expanded Roles for Trade Associations. *Antitrust Bull.*, Summer 1973, *18*(2), pp. 221–31.

Ham, Euiyoung. Urbanization and Asian Lifestyles. *Ann. Amer. Acad. Polit. Soc. Sci.*, January 1973, *405*, pp. 104–13.

Hamada, Koichi. A Simple Majority Rule on the Distribution of Income. *J. Econ. Theory*, June 1973, *6*(3), pp. 243–64.

Hamblin, Mary and Prell, Michael J. Income of Men and Women: Why Do They Differ? *Fed. Res. Bank Kansas City Rev.*, April 1973, pp. 3–11.

Hambor, John C.; Phillips, Llad and Votey, Harold L., Jr. High School Inputs and Their Contribution to School Performance: A Comment. *J. Human Res.*, Spring 1973, *8*(2), pp. 260–63.

—— Optimal Community Educational Attainment: A Simultaneous Equation Approach. *Rev. Econ. Statist.*, February 1973, *55*(1), pp. 98–103.

Hamburger, Michael J. The Demand for Money in 1971: Was There a Shift? Comment. *J. Money, Credit, Banking*, May 1973, *5*(2), pp. 720–25.

Hamburger, Polia Lerner. Public Policy Toward Retailing: Brazil. In *Boddewyn, J. J. and Hollander, S. C., eds.*, 1972, pp. 63–79.

Hamdani, Daood H. Fiscal Measures Against Inflation and Unemployment in Canada: 1973 Budget and Other Developments. *Bull. Int. Fiscal Doc.*, June 1973, *27*(6), pp. 223–40.

Hamermesh, Daniel S. Price and Quantity Adjustment in Factor Markets. *Western Econ. J.*, March 1973, *11*(1), pp. 118–25.

—— Who "Wins" in Wage Bargaining? *Ind. Lab. Relat. Rev.*, July 1973, *26*(4), pp. 1146–49.

Hamid, Javed. The Problem of Agricultural Taxation in West Pakistan and an Alternative Solution: Comment. *Pakistan Develop. Rev.*, Autumn 1973, *12*(3), pp. 311–14.

Hamilton, David. What Has Evolutionary Economics to Contribute to Consumption Theory? *J. Econ. Issues*, June 1973, *7*(2), pp. 197–207.

Hamilton, F. E. Ian. Spatial Dimensions of Soviet Economic Decision Making. In *Bandera, V. N. and Melnyk, Z. L., eds.*, 1973, pp. 235–60.

Hamilton, Mary Townsend. Sex and Income Inequality among the Employed. *Ann. Amer. Acad. Polit. Soc. Sci.*, September 1973, *409*, pp. 42–52.

Hamilton, Richard E. Canada's "Exportable Surplus" Natural Gas Policy: A Theoretical Analysis. *Land Econ.*, August 1973, *49*(3), pp. 251–59.

Hamilton, Richard F. Trends in Labor Union Voting Behavior, 1948-1968: Comment. *Ind. Relat.*, February 1973, *12*(1), pp. 113–15.

Hammack, Judd and Brown, Gardner, Jr. Dynamic Economic Management of Migratory Waterfowl. *Rev. Econ. Statist.*, February 1973, *55*(1), pp. 73–82.

Hammer, Peter L. Some Developments in 0–1 Programming. In *Ross, M., ed.*, 1973, pp. 551–54.

Hammer, Thomas R. and Coughlin, Robert E. Estimating the Benefits of Stream Valley and Open Space Preservation Projects. In *Harriss, C. L., ed.*, 1973, pp. 155–70.

Hammerman, Herbert. Minorities in Construction Referral Unions—Revisited. *Mon. Lab. Rev.*, May 1973, *96*(5), pp. 43–46.

Hammersley, G. The Charcoal Iron Industry and its Fuel, 1540-1750. *Econ. Hist. Rev., 2nd Ser.*, November 1973, *26*(4), pp. 593–613.

Hammond, Peter J. and Mirrlees, James A. Agreeable Plans. In *Mirrlees, J. A. and Stern, N. H., eds.*, 1973, pp. 283–99.

Hammond, P. J. Comparative Dynamics from the Point of View of the Dual: Discussion. In *Parkin, M., ed.*, 1973, pp. 47–49.

Hammonds, T. M.; Yadav, R. and Vathana, C. The Elasticity of Demand for Hired Farm Labor. *Amer. J. Agr. Econ.*, May 1973, *55*(2), pp. 242–45.

Hamner, W. Clay and Harnett, Donald L. The Value of Information in Bargaining. *Western Econ. J.*, March 1973, *11*(1), pp. 81–88.

Hamouz, Frantisek. Implementation of the Comprehensive Program of Socialist Economic Integration. *Czech. Econ. Digest.*, December 1973, (8), pp. 3–46.

Hampton, J. M.; Moore, P. G. and Thomas, H. Subjective Probability and Its Measurement. *J. Roy. Statist. Soc.*, Part 1, 1973, *136*, pp. 21–42.

Han, Chien-Pai. Double Sampling with Partial Information on Auxiliary Variables. *J. Amer. Statist. Assoc.*, December 1973, *68*(344), pp. 914–18.

Hancock, Walton M.; Munson, Fred C. and Griffith, John R. Practical Ways to Contain Hospital Costs. *Harvard Bus. Rev.*, November-December 1973, *51*(6), pp. 131–39.

Handke, Werner. Die Neue Aussenwirtschaftspolitik der USA. (The 'New Foreign Economic Policy' of the USA. With English summary.) *Z. ges. Staatswiss.*, May 1973, *129*(2), pp. 312–32.

Hanf, C. H.; Weinschenck, G. and Henrichsmeyer, W. Experiences with Multi-Commodity Models in Regional Analysis. In *Judge, G. G. and Takayama, T., eds.*, 1973, pp. 307–26.

Hanieski, John F. Technological Change as the Optimization of a Multidimensional Product. In *Cochrane, J. L. and Zeleny, M., eds.*, 1973, pp. 550–69.

Hanke, Steve H. and Davis, Robert K. Conventional

and Unconventional Alternatives for Water Supply Management. *Water Resources Res.*, August 1973, *9*(4), pp. 861–70.

―――― Potential for Marginal Cost Pricing in Water Resource Management. *Water Resources Res.*, August 1973, *9*(4), pp. 808–25.

Hanlon, Richard A. Differences in Reporting Family Income. *Mon. Lab. Rev.*, April 1973, *96*(4), pp. 46–48.

Hannan, E. J. and Terrell, R. D. Multiple Equation Systems with Stationary Errors. *Econometrica*, March 1973, *41*(2), pp. 299–320.

Hannon, Bruce M. An Energy Standard of Value. *Ann. Amer. Acad. Polit. Soc. Sci.*, November 1973, *410*, pp. 139–53.

Hanold, Terrance. Management Perspective on an Advanced Information System. In *The Diebold Group, Inc.*, 1973, pp. 271–97.

Hansen, Bent. On the Effects of Fiscal and Monetary Policy: A Taxonomic Discussion. *Amer. Econ. Rev.*, September 1973, *63*(4), pp. 546–71.

―――― Simulation of Fiscal, Monetary and Exchange Policy in a Primitive Economy: Afghanistan. In *[Tinbergen, J.]*, 1973, pp. 215–37.

―――― **and Bhagwati, Jagdish N.** Should Growth Rates Be Evaluated at International Prices? In *[Rosenstein-Rodan, P.]*, 1973, pp. 53–68.

―――― **and Bhagwati, Jagdish N.** A Theoretical Analysis of Smuggling. *Quart. J. Econ.*, May 1973, *87* (2), pp. 172–87.

Hansen, Gerd and Staudte, Axel. Eine empirische Überprüfung der Permanent-Income-Hypothese: Eine Erwiderung auf H. Drost. (An Empirical Reexamination of the Permanent Income Hypothesis: A Comment. With English summary.) *Jahr. Nationalökon. Statist.*, March 1973, *187*(3), pp. 269–81.

Hansen, Niles M. A Growth Center Strategy for the United States. In *Rasmussen, D. W. and Haworth, C. T., eds.*, 1973, pp. 267–82.

―――― Urbanism and Regional Disparities in Developed Countries. *Rev. Soc. Econ.*, April 1973, *31* (1), pp. 54–65.

Hansen, P.; Brans, J. P. and Leclercq, M. An Algorithm for Optimal Reloading of Pressurized Water Reactors. In *Ross, M., ed.*, 1973, pp. 417–28.

Hansen, Thomas J. and Prince, Barry L. The Paradox of Voting: An Elementary Solution for the Case of Three Alternatives. *Public Choice*, Summer 1973, *15*, pp. 103–17.

Hansen, W. Lee. Readings on Effective Teaching. *J. Econ. Educ.*, Fall 1973, *5*(1), pp. 63–67.

Hanson, James S. and Vogel, Robert C. Inflation and Monetary Velocity in Latin America. *Rev. Econ. Statist.*, August 1973, *55*(3), pp. 365–70.

Hanson, John R., III. Economic Consequences of Rapid Population Growth: A Comment. *Econ. J.*, March 1973, *83*(329), pp. 217–19.

Hansz, James E. and Goodnow, James D. Environmental Determinants of Overseas Market Entry Strategies. In *Alexandrides, C. G., ed.*, 1973, pp. 195–215.

Hanushek, Eric A. The High Cost of Graduate Education in the Military. *Public Policy*, Fall 1973, *21* (4), pp. 525–52.

―――― Regional Differences in the Structure of Earnings. *Rev. Econ. Statist.*, May 1973, *55*(2), pp. 204–13.

Haq, Mahbub. The Crisis in Development Strategies. In *Wilber, C. K., ed.*, 1973, pp. 367–72.

―――― Developing Country Alternatives. In *Hughes, H., ed.*, 1973, pp. 128–37.

―――― Employment in the 1970's: A New Perspective. In *Wilber, C. K., ed.*, 1973, pp. 266–72.

―――― Industrialisation and Trade Policies in the 1970s: Developing Country Alternatives. In *Streeten, P., ed.*, 1973, pp. 93–102.

―――― The Transfer of Resources: Comment. In *Lewis, J. P. and Kapur, I., eds.*, 1973, pp. 83–87.

Haran, E. G. P. and Vining, Daniel R., Jr. A Modified Yule-Simon Model Allowing for Intercity Migration and Accounting for the Observed Form of the Size Distribution of Cities. *J. Reg. Sci.*, December 1973, *13*(3), pp. 421–37.

Harberger, Arnold C. Cost-Benefit Analysis of Transportation Projects. In *Harberger, A. C.*, 1973, pp. 248–79.

―――― Costs and Benefits of the Ullum Dam Project: An Analytical Framework and an Empirical Exploration. In *Harberger, A. C.*, 1973, pp. 280–310.

―――― Issues Concerning Capital Assistance to Less-Developed Countries. In *Harberger, A. C.*, 1973, pp. 311–23.

―――― Marginal Cost Pricing and Social Investment Criteria for Electricity Undertakings. In *Harberger, A. C.*, 1973, pp. 233–47.

―――― On Estimating the Rate of Return to Capital in Colombia. In *Harberger, A. C.*, 1973, pp. 132–56.

―――― On Measuring the Social Opportunity Cost of Public Funds. In *Harberger, A. C.*, 1973, pp. 94–122.

―――― Survey of Literature on Cost-Benefit Analysis for Industrial Project Evaluation. In *Harberger, A. C.*, 1973, pp. 23–69.

Harbison, Frederick H. Human Resources and the Development of Modernizing Nations. In *Somers, G. G., ed.*, 1973, pp. 177–86.

Harbury, C. D. and McMahon, P. C. Inheritance and the Characteristics of Top Wealth Leavers in Britain. *Econ. J.*, September 1973, *83*(331), pp. 810–33.

Harcourt, G. C. The Rate of Profits in Equilibrium Growth Models: A Review Article. *J. Polit. Econ.*, September-October 1973, *81*(5), pp. 1261–77.

Hardaker, J. B. and Tanago, A. G. Assessment of the Output of a Stochastic Decision Model. *Australian J. Agr. Econ.*, December 1973, *17*(3), pp. 170–78.

Hardesty, John; Clement, Norris C. and Jencks, Clinton E. Ecological Conflicts: A Reply. *Rev. Radical Polit. Econ.*, Summer 1973, *5*(2), pp. 95–102.

Hardin, Garrett. The Tragedy of the Commons. In *Enthoven, A. C. and Freeman, A. M., III, eds.*, 1973, pp. 1–13.

―――― The Tragedy of the Commons. In *Daly, H. E., ed.*, 1973, pp. 133–48.

Hardoy, Jorge E. Spatial Structure and Society in Revolutionary Cuba. In *Barkin, D. P. and Manitzas, N. R., eds.*, 1973, pp. M265–16.

Harewood, Jack. Changes in the Use of Birth Control Methods. *Population Stud.*, March 1973, *27* (1), pp. 33–57.

Harley, C. K. On the Persistence of Old Techniques: The Case of North American Wooden Shipbuilding. *J. Econ. Hist.*, June 1973, *33*(2), pp. 372–98.

Harlow, Robert L. On the Decline and Possible Fall of PPBS. *Public Finance Quart.*, January 1973, *1* (1), pp. 85–105.

Harnett, Donald L. and Hamner, W. Clay. The Value of Information in Bargaining. *Western Econ. J.*, March 1973, *11*(1), pp. 81–88.

Harper, Edwin L.; Kramer, Fred A. and Rouse, Andrew M. Personnel Limitations of "Instant Analysis." In *Novick, D., ed.*, 1973, pp. 201–05.

Harper, Richard D.; Venieris, Yiannis P. and Sebold, Frederick D. The Impact of Economic, Technological and Demographic Factors on Aggregate Births. *Rev. Econ. Statist.*, November 1973, *55*(4), pp. 493–97.

Harper, William K. and Berger, Paul D. Determination of an Optimal Revolving Credit Agreement. *J. Financial Quant. Anal.*, June 1973, *8*(3), pp. 491–97.

Harrington, R. L. and Morgan, E. Victor. Reserve Assets and the Supply of Money. *Manchester Sch. Econ. Soc. Stud.*, March 1973, *41*(1), pp. 73–87.

Harris, C. Lowell. Monetary and Incomes Policies: Comment. In *Wiegand, G. C., ed.*, 1973, pp. 155–56.

Harris, Donald J. Capital, Distribution, and the Aggregate Production Function. *Amer. Econ. Rev.*, March 1973, *63*(1), pp. 100–13.

Harris, Duane G. Harvesting a Record Corn Crop. *Fed. Res. Bank Bus. Rev. Phila.*, October 1973, pp. 9–14.

———— A Model of Bank Loan Term Adjustment. *Western Econ. J.*, December 1973, *11*(4), pp. 451–62.

———— Some Evidence on Differential Lending Practices at Commercial Banks. *J. Finance*, December 1973, *28*(5), pp. 1303–11.

Harris, Gene. Some Aspects of Decentralisation and the Formulation and Implementation of Agricultural Policy in Ghana. In *Ofori, I. M., ed.*, 1973, pp. 177–92.

Harris, Jerome; McLoughlin, John and Mason, R. Hal. Corporate Strategy: A Point of View. In *Klein, W. H. and Murphy, D. C., eds.*, 1973, pp. 158–65.

Harris, John R. Entrepreneurship and Economic Development. In *[Williamson, H. F.]*, 1973, pp. 141–72.

Harris, William T., Jr. and Chapin, Wayne R. Joint Product Costing. *Manage. Account.*, April 1973, *54*(10), pp. 43–47.

Harrison, Bennett and Vietorisz, Thomas. Labor Market Segmentation: Positive Feedback and Divergent Development. *Amer. Econ. Rev.*, May 1973, *63*(2), pp. 366–76.

Harrison, J. A.; Cohen, C. D. and Pickering, J. F. Identification and Measurment of Consumer Confidence: Methodology and Some Preliminary Results. *J. Roy. Statist. Soc.*, Part 1, 1973, *136*, pp. 43–63.

Harriss, C. Lowell. Capital Needs, Savings, and Jobs. In *Tax Foundation, Inc.*, 1973, pp. 27–34.

———— Government Spending & Land Values: Public Money & Private Gain: Introduction. In *Harriss, C. L., ed.*, 1973, pp. ix–xix.

Harrod, Roy [Sir]. A British View of American Monetary Problems. In *Wiegand, G. C., ed.*, 1973, pp. 152–54.

Harrop, Jeffrey. On the Economics of the Tourist Boom. *Bull. Econ. Res.*, May 1973, *25*(1), pp. 55–72.

Harshbarger, C. Edward. A Look at 1973: Agriculture Has a Tough Act to Follow. *Fed. Res. Bank Kansas City Rev.*, January 1973, pp. 3–10.

———— 1974 Agricultural Outlook: How High the Summit? *Fed. Res. Bank Kansas City Rev.*, December 1973, pp. 12–20.

———— and Doll, Raymond J. Farm Prices and Food Prices: The Relevant Issues. *Fed. Res. Bank Kansas City Rev.*, May 1973, pp. 3–10.

———— and Stahl, Sheldon W. Free Enterprise Revisited—A Look at Economic Concentration. *Fed. Res. Bank Kansas City Rev.*, March 1973, pp. 10–16.

Hart, Jeffrey. Foundations and Social Activism: A Critical View. In *Heimann, F. F., ed.*, 1973, pp. 43–57.

Hart, R. A. Employment Creation in the Development Areas: A Reply. *Scot. J. Polit. Econ.*, June 1973, *20*(2), pp. 171–73.

———— The Role of Overtime Working in the Recent Wage Inflation Process. *Bull. Econ. Res.*, May 1973, *25*(1), pp. 73–87.

Hartke, Vance. A Foreign Trade and Investment Policy for the 1970s. In *Kujawa, D., ed.*, 1973, pp. 54–71.

Hartle, Douglas G. A Proposal for a System of Economic and Social Accounts: Comment. In *Moss, M., ed.*, 1973, pp. 146–53.

Hartley, H. O. and Jayatillake, K. S. E. Estimation for Linear Models with Unequal Variances. *J. Amer. Statist. Assoc.*, March 1973, *68*(341), pp. 189–92.

———— and Sielken, R. L., Jr. Two Linear Programming Algorithms for Unbiased Estimation of Linear Models. *J. Amer. Statist. Assoc.*, September 1973, *68*(343), pp. 639–41.

Hartley, Michael J. and Revankar, Nagesh S. An Independence Test and Conditional Unbiased Predictions in the Context of Simultaneous Equation Systems. *Int. Econ. Rev.*, October 1973, *14* (3), pp. 625–31.

Hartley, Ronald V. A Note on Quadratic Programming in a Case of Joint Production: A Reply. *Accounting Rev.*, October 1973, *48*(4), pp. 771–74.

Hartman, Chester W. The Politics of Housing. In *Pynoos, J.; Schafer, R. and Hartman, C. W., eds.*, 1973, pp. 119–28.

———— and Kessler, Robert P. The Illusion and the Reality of Urban Renewal: A Case Study of San Francisco's Yerba Buena Center. *Land Econ.*, November 1973, *49*(4), pp. 440–53.

———— ; Pynoos, Jon and Schafer, Robert. Housing Urban America: Introduction. In *Pynoos, J.; Schafer, R. and Hartman, C. W., eds.*, 1973, pp. 1–12.

Hartman, Gerald R. and Braverman, Jerome D. The Process of Classifying Drivers: A Suggestion for

Insurance Ratemaking: Comment. *J. Risk Ins.*, March 1973, *40*(1), pp. 143–46.

Hartman, Richard. Adjustment Costs, Price and Wage Uncertainty, and Investment. *Rev. Econ. Stud.*, April 1973, *40*(2), pp. 259–67.

Hartnett, Harry D. A Locational Analysis of Manufacturing Plants within the City of Chicago: 1959–1968. *Amer. Real Estate Urban Econ. Assoc. J.*, June 1973, *1*(1), pp. 31–47.

Hartwell, R. M. Good Old Economic History. *J. Econ. Hist.*, March 1973, *33*(1), pp. 28–40.

Hartwick, John M. Lösch's Theorem on Hexagonal Market Areas. *J. Reg. Sci.*, August 1973, *13*(2), pp. 213–21.

_____ The Pricing of Goods and Agricultural Land in Multiregional General Equilibrium: Reply. *Southern Econ. J.*, July 1973, *40*(1), pp. 144–45.

_____ and Hartwick, Philip G. Reply to Comment by B. C. Eaton. *Can. J. Econ.*, February 1973, *6*(1), pp. 127–28.

Hartwick, Philip G. and Hartwick, John M. Reply to Comment by B. C. Eaton. *Can. J. Econ.*, February 1973, *6*(1), pp. 127–28.

Harvey, Andrew S. Spatial Variation of Export Employment Multipliers: A Cross-Section Analysis. *Land Econ.*, November 1973, *49*(4), pp. 469–74.

Harvey, C. E. On the Cost-Inflationary Impact of High Interest Rates: Reply. *J. Econ. Issues*, September 1973, *7*(3), pp. 514.

Harvey, Charles. International Corporations and Economic Independence: A View from Zambia. In *Ghai, D., ed.,* 1973, pp. 176–89.

_____ Mathematics and the Teaching of Economics. In *Livingstone, I., et al., eds.,* 1973, pp. 131–36.

Hashmi, M. Iqbal; Nizami, N. H. and Afzal, Mohammad. Marriage Patterns in a Rural Agglomeration. *Pakistan Develop. Rev.*, Autumn 1973, *12*(3), pp. 273–82.

Hass, Jerome E. and Bierman, Harold, Jr. Capital Budgeting Under Uncertainty: A Reformulation. *J. Finance*, March 1973, *28*(1), pp. 119–29.

Hassan, M. F. Unemployment in Latin America: Causes and Remedies. *Amer. J. Econ. Soc.*, April 1973, *32*(2), pp. 179–90.

Hassan, Zuhair; Johnson, Stanley R. and Green, Richard. Price and Income Flexibilities and the Double Logarithmic Demand System: Comment. *Amer. J. Agr. Econ.*, Part I, November 1973, *55*(4), pp. 678–79.

_____; Finley, Robert M. and Johnson, Stanley R. The Demand for Food in the United States. *Appl. Econ.*, December 1973, *5*(4), pp. 233–48.

_____; Johnson, Stanley R. and Green, Richard. An Alternative Method for Pricing Pork Carcasses. *Can. J. Agr. Econ.*, November 1973, *21*(3), pp. 1–5.

Hasson, Joseph. The Impact of Dollar Devaluation on Domestic Prices. *J. Econ. Bus.*, Fall 1973, *26*(1), pp. 25–40.

Hatanaka, Michio. On the Existence and the Approximation Formulae for the Moments of the *k*-Class Estimators. *Econ. Stud. Quart.*, August 1973, *24*(2), pp. 1–15.

Hatch, J. H. and Lewis, M. K. Economies of Scale in Australian Banking: Reply. *Econ. Rec.*, September 1973, *49*(127), pp. 481–84.

Hatchuel, Georges; Kende, Pierre and Foulon, Alain. Un premier bilan de la redistribution des revenus en France; Les impôts et cotisations sociales à la charge des ménages en 1965. (Balance of the Redistribution of Incomes in France: Personal Taxes and Social Security Contributions in 1965. With English summary.) *Consommation*, October-December 1973, *20*(4), pp. 5–133.

Hathaway, Dale E. Public Sector Research and Education and the Agribusiness Complex: Unholy Alliance or Socially Beneficial Partnership? Summary of the Discussion. *Amer. J. Agr. Econ.*, December 1973, *55*(5), pp. 1002.

_____ Public Sector Research and Education and the Agribusiness Complex: Unholy Alliance or Socially Beneficial Partnership? *Amer. J. Agr. Econ.*, December 1973, *55*(5), pp. 993.

_____ Trade Restrictions and U.S. Consumers. In *Iowa State University Center for Agricultural and Rural Development*, 1973, pp. 103–10.

Hatta, Tatsuo. A Note on a Theorem in "Value and Capital." *Western Econ. J.*, June 1973, *11*(2), pp. 164–66.

Haugen, Robert A. and Wichern, Dean W. The Diametric Effects of the Capital Gains Tax on the Stability of Stock Prices. *J. Finance*, September 1973, *28*(4), pp. 987–96.

Haulman, Clyde A. A Structural Model of the Canadian Monetary Sector: Reply. *Southern Econ. J.*, April 1973, *39*(4), pp. 642–44.

Haun, Kathryn A. and Hsia, Tao-tai. Laws of the People's Republic of China on Industrial and Intellectual Property. *Law Contemp. Probl.*, Summer-Autumn 1973, *38*(2), pp. 274–91.

Hauptmann, Harry and Seifert, Hans G. Ein Oligopolspiel mit wirksamen Kapazitätsschranken. (An Oligopoly Game with Effective Capacity Bounds. With English summary.) *Jahr. Nationalökon. Statist.*, December 1973, *188*(1), pp. 51–64.

Hause, John C. Enlistment Rates for Military Service and Unemployment. *J. Human Res.*, Winter 1973, *8*(1), pp. 98–109.

Hauser, Jürg. Reorganisation der Familienplanung in der Dritten Welt. (Reorganizing Family Planning Policies in LDC's. With English summary.) *Schweiz. Z. Volkswirtsch. Statist.*, March 1973, *109*(1), pp. 1–16.

Hausknecht, Murray and Bellush, Jewel. Public Housing: The Contexts of Failure. In *Pynoos, J.; Schafer, R. and Hartman, C. W., eds.,* 1973, pp. 114–18.

Hausman, Leonard J. The Politics of a Guaranteed Income: The Nixon Administration and the Family Assistance Plan—A Review Article. *J. Human Res.*, Fall 1973, *8*(4), pp. 411–21.

Haveman, Robert H. Common Property, Congestion, and Environmental Pollution. *Quart. J. Econ.*, May 1973, *87*(2), pp. 278–87.

_____ Efficiency and Equity in Natural Resource and Environmental Policy. *Amer. J. Agr. Econ.*, December 1973, *55*(5), pp. 868–78.

_____ The Ex Post Evaluation of Navigation Improvements. In *Niskanen, W. A., et al., eds.,* 1973, pp. 249–76.

_____ Private Power and Federal Policy. In *Haveman, R. H. and Hamrin, R. D., eds.,* 1973, pp. 3–8.

_____ and Freeman, A. Myrick, III. Clean Rhetoric and Dirty Water. In *Enthoven, A. C. and Freeman, A. M., III, eds.*, 1973, pp. 122–37.

_____ and Stephan, Paula. White Elephants, Waterways, and the Transportation Act of 1966. In *Haveman, R. H. and Hamrin, R. D., eds.*, 1973, pp. 220–25.

Havlicek, J.; Rizek, R. L. and Judge, G. G. A Spatial Analysis of the U.S. Livestock Economy. In *Judge, G. G. and Takayama, T., eds.*, 1973, pp. 261–73.

Havrilesky, Thomas M. Alternative Monetary Control Responses in a Stochastic Macro Model. *Quart. Rev. Econ. Bus.*, Spring 1973, *13*(1), pp. 37–48.

_____ Legitimating the Corporate State. *Amer. Econ.*, Spring 1973, *17*(1), pp. 169–73.

_____ Technological Innovativeness, the Grants Economy, and the Ecological Crisis. In *Boulding, K. E.; Pfaff, M. and Pfaff, A., eds.*, 1973, pp. 317–39.

_____; Weintraub, E. R. and Gusen, P. Potpourri: The Monetarist's Papers. *Intermountain Econ. Rev.*, Fall 1973, *4*(2), pp. 78–80.

_____; Yohe, William P. and Schirm, David. The Economic Affiliations of Directors of Federal Reserve District Banks. *Soc. Sci. Quart.*, December 1973, *54*(3), pp. 608–22.

Hawes, D. M. Operational Gaming in the Planning of the Geologically Troubled Colliery. In *Ross, M., ed.*, 1973, pp. 405–16.

Hawke, G. R. The Government and the Depression of the 1930s in New Zealand: An Essay Towards a Revision. *Australian Econ. Hist. Rev.*, March 1973, *13*(1), pp. 72–95.

Hawkins, Clark A. and Frankle, A. W. The Behavior of Convertible Debenture Premiums: Comment. *Miss. Val. J. Bus. Econ.*, Winter 1973-74, *9*(2), pp. 65–68.

_____ and Weber, Jean E. The Estimation of Constant Elasticities: Reply. *Southern Econ. J.*, January 1973, *39*(3), pp. 445–47.

Hawkins, E. K. A Family View of Population Questions. *Finance Develop.*, December 1973, *10*(4), pp. 8–12.

Hawkins, Robert G. American Labor and the Multinational Corporation: Foreword. In *Kujawa, D., ed.*, 1973, pp. vi–xvii.

Haworth, C. T. and Rasmussen, David W. Determinants of Metropolitan Cost of Living Variations. *Southern Econ. J.*, October 1973, *40*(2), pp. 183–92.

Haworth, Joan G. Externalities and the City. In *Rasmussen, D. W. and Haworth, C. T., eds.*, 1973, pp. 28–30.

Hay, George A. Import Controls on Foreign Oil: Reply. *Amer. Econ. Rev.*, December 1973, *63*(5), pp. 1035–36.

_____ and McGowan, John J. External Diseconomies in Competitive Supply: Comment. *Amer. Econ. Rev.*, September 1973, *63*(4), pp. 738–40.

Hayami, Yujiro and Peterson, Willis. Social Return to Public Information Services: Statistical Reporting of U.S. Farm Commodities: Reply. *Amer. Econ. Rev.*, December 1973, *63*(5), pp. 1020–21.

_____ and Ruttan, Vernon W. Induced Innovation

in Agricultural Development. In *Ayal, E. B., ed.*, 1973, pp. 181–208.

_____ and Ruttan, Vernon W. Professor Rosenberg and the Direction of Technological Change: Comment. *Econ. Develop. Cult. Change*, January 1973, *21*(2), pp. 352–55.

Hayasaka, Tadashi. Dr. Yasuma Takada in the History of Economics in Japan. (In Japanese. With English summary.) *Econ. Stud. Quart.*, August 1973, *24*(2), pp. 46–60.

Hayden, F. Gregory. Fiscal Federalism: Program Budgeting and the Multilevel Governmental Setting. *Nebr. J. Econ. Bus.*, Winter 1973, *12*(1), pp. 23–42.

von Hayek, F. A. Economics and Knowledge. In *Buchanan, J. M. and Thirlby, G. F., eds.*, 1973, pp. 43–68.

_____ The Place of Menger's Grundsatze in the History of Economic Thought. In *Hicks, J. R. and Weber, W., eds.*, 1973, pp. 1–14.

Hayes, Frederick O'R. Program Budgeting in the City of New York. In *Novick, D., ed.*, 1973, pp. 185–91.

Hayes, Robert L. and Ansoff, H. Igor. Roles of Models in Corporate Decision Making. In *Ross, M., ed.*, 1973, pp. 131–62.

Hayghe, Howard. Labor Force Activity of Married Women. *Mon. Lab. Rev.*, April 1973, *96*(4), pp. 31–36.

Hayman, Joanne and Fretz, C. F. Progress for Women—Men are Still More Equal. *Harvard Bus. Rev.*, September-October 1973, *51*(5), pp. 133–42.

Haynes, Kingsley E.; Poston, Dudley L., Jr. and Schnirring, Paul. Intermetropolitan Migration in High and Low Opportunity Areas: Indirect Tests of the Distance and Intervening Opportunities Hypotheses. *Econ. Geogr.*, January 1973, *49*(1), pp. 68–73.

Haythorne, George V. Prices and Incomes Policy: The Canadian Experience, 1969–1972. *Int. Lab. Rev.*, December 1973, *108*(6), pp. 485–503.

Hayward, Jack. The Prospects for British Regional Policy in the EEC Context. *J. Common Market Stud.*, June 1973, *11*(4), pp. 287–93.

Haywood, E. The Deviation Cycle: A New Index of the Australian Business Cycle 1950-1973. *Australian Econ. Rev.*, 4th Quarter 1973, pp. 31–39.

Hazell, P. B. R. and Thomson, K. J. Reliability of Using the Mean Absolute Deviation to Derive Efficient *E, V* Farm Plans: Reply. *Amer. J. Agr. Econ.*, Part I, November 1973, *55*(4), pp. 677–78.

Hazlewood, Arthur. State Trading and the East African Customs Union. *Oxford Bull. Econ. Statist.*, May 1973, *35*(2), pp. 75–89.

Hazlitt, Henry. The Problem and Its Solution. In *Wiegand, G. C., ed.*, 1973, pp. 170–78.

Hazuka, Thomas B. and Johnson, Keith B. The NPV-IRR Debate in Lease Analysis. *Miss. Val. J. Bus. Econ.*, Winter 1973-74, *9*(2), pp. 16–26.

Head, John G. Public Goods and Multi-Level Government. In *[Hicks, U.]*, 1973, pp. 20–43.

_____ and Shoup, Carl S. Public, Private, and Ambiguous Goods Reconsidered. *Public Finance*, 1973, *28*(3–4), pp. 384–92.

Heady, Earl O. Fundamental Issues in Trade of

Farm Commodities. In *Iowa State University Center for Agricultural and Rural Development,* 1973, pp. 3–16.

―――― Long-Run Implications of a Tax in Kind to Reduce Supply and Increase Income: Reply. *Amer. J. Agr. Econ.,* Part I, November 1973, *55*(4), pp. 675.

――――, et al. National and Interregional Models of Water Demand, Land Use, and Agricultural Policies. *Water Resources Res.,* August 1973, *9*(4), pp. 777–91.

―――― and Madsen, Howard C. National and Interregional Models of Water Demand for Land Use and Agricultural Policies. In *Judge, G. G. and Takayama, T., eds.,* 1973, pp. 651–75.

―――― and Srivastava, Uma K. Technological Change and Relative Factor Shares in Indian Agriculture: An Empirical Analysis. *Amer. J. Agr. Econ.,* August 1973, *55*(3), pp. 509–14.

――――; Srivastava, Uma K. and Nagadevara, Vishnuprasad. Resource Productivity, Returns to Scale and Farm Size in Indian Agriculture: Some Recent Evidence. *Australian J. Agr. Econ.,* April 1973, *17*(1), pp. 43–57.

Heal, Felicity. The Tudors and Church Lands: Economic Problems of the Bishopric of Ely during the Sixteenth Century. *Econ. Hist. Rev., 2nd Ser.,* May 1973, *26*(2), pp. 198–217.

Heal, Geoffrey M. and Ryder, Harl E., Jr. Optimum Growth with Intertemporally Dependent Preferences. *Rev. Econ. Stud.,* January 1973, *40*(1), pp. 1–33.

Healey, Derek T. Foreign Capital and Exports in Economic Development: The Experience of Eight Asian Countries. *Econ. Rec.,* September 1973, *49*(127), pp. 394–419.

Healy, M. J. R. Varieties of Statistician. *J. Roy. Statist. Soc.,* Part 1, 1973, *136,* pp. 71–74.

Hearle, Edward F. R. EDP Systems in State and Local Governments. In *The Diebold Group, Inc.,* 1973, pp. 134–39.

Heath, J. B. and Oulton, W. N. A Cost-benefit Study of Alternative Runway Investments at Edinburgh (Turnhouse) Airport. In *Wolfe, J. N., ed.,* 1973, pp. 117–39.

Heaver, Trevor D. The Structure of Liner Conference Rates. *J. Ind. Econ.,* July 1973, *21*(3), pp. 257–65.

Hebden, J. and Robinson, R. V. F. The Influence of Price and Trading Stamps on Retail Petrol Sales. *J. Ind. Econ.,* September 1973, *22*(1), pp. 37–50.

Hebert, Robert F. Wage Cobwebs and Cobweb-Type Phenomena: An Early French Formulation. *Western Econ. J.,* December 1973, *11*(4), pp. 394–403.

―――― and Byrns, Ralph T. On the Cost-Inflationary Impact of High Interest Rates: Comment. *J. Econ. Issues,* September 1973, *7*(3), pp. 511–14.

―――― and Ekelund, Robert B., Jr. Public Economics at the Ecole des Ponts et Chaussées: 1830–1850. *J. Public Econ.,* July 1973, *2*(3), pp. 241–56.

Hecht, Jacqueline. The Life of François Quesnay. In *Rectenwald, H. C., ed.,* 1973, pp. 1–11.

Heckerman, Donald G. On the Effects of Exchange Risk. *J. Int. Econ.,* November 1973, *3*(4), pp. 379–87.

―――― Portfolio Selection when Future Prices of Consumption Goods May Change: Reply. *J. Finance,* December 1973, *28*(5), pp. 1361.

Hedges, Bob A. On the Skinning of Cats. *J. Risk Ins.,* March 1973, *40*(1), pp. 1–6.

Hedges, Janice Neipert. Absence from Work: A Look at Some National Data. *Mon. Lab. Rev.,* July 1973, *96*(7), pp. 24–30.

―――― New Patterns for Working Time. *Mon. Lab. Rev.,* February 1973, *96*(2), pp. 3–8.

Hedley, Douglas D. and Kriesel, Herbert C. Planners as Factors in Agricultural Growth. In *Ofori, I. M., ed.,* 1973, pp. 33–41.

Hedrick, Charles L. Expectations and the Labor Supply. *Amer. Econ. Rev.,* December 1973, *63*(5), pp. 968–74.

Heeler, Roger M.; Kearney, Michael J. and Mehaffey, Bruce J. Modeling Supermarket Product Selection. *J. Marketing Res.,* February 1973, *10*(1), pp. 34–37.

Hees, Marc. Système de travail et principe de qualification. (The Work System and Qualification. With English summary.) *Ann. Sci. Écon. Appl.,* 1973–1974, (1), pp. 67–79.

Heffernan, W. Joseph, Jr. Variations in Negative Tax Rates in Current Public Assistance Programs: An Example of Administrative Discretion. *J. Human Res.,* Supplement 1973, *8,* pp. 56–68.

Heggestad, Arnold A. and Edwards, Franklin R. Uncertainty, Market Structure, and Performance in Banking: The Galbraith-Caves Hypothesis and Managerial Motives in Banking. *Quart. J. Econ.,* August 1973, *87*(3), pp. 455–73.

Heien, Dale; Cohen, Malcolm and Gillingham, Robert. A Monte Carlo Study of Complex Finite Distributed Lag Structures. *Ann. Econ. Soc. Measure,* January 1973, *2*(1), pp. 53–63.

――――; Matthews, Jim and Womack, Abner. A Methods Note on the Gauss-Seidel Algorithm for Solving Econometric Models. *Agr. Econ. Res.,* July 1973, *25*(3), pp. 71–80.

Heilbroner, Robert L. Ecological Armageddon. In *Enthoven, A. C. and Freeman, A. M., III, eds.,* 1973, pp. 176–85.

―――― Economics as a "Value-Free" Science. *Soc. Res.,* Spring 1973, *40*(1), pp. 129–43.

―――― Men and Machines in Perspective. In *Reynolds, L. G.; Green, G. D. and Lewis, D. R., eds.,* 1973, pp. 100–109.

Heim, Axel. L'attività degli istituti di credito rateale in Germania. (West German Instalment-Sales Financing Institutions. With English summary.) *Bancaria,* January 1973, *29*(1), pp. 30–39.

Heimann, Fritz F. Foundations and Government: Perspectives for the Future. In *Heimann, F. F., ed.,* 1973, pp. 259–73.

Heine, Rolf. Simulation of a Computer-Controlled Conveyance System for Air Passengers' Luggage. In *Ross, M., ed.,* 1973, pp. 373–78.

Heineke, J. M. and Block, M. K. The Allocation of Effort under Uncertainty: The Case of Risk-averse Behavior. *J. Polit. Econ.,* Part I, March-April 1973, *81*(2), pp. 376–85.

Heinemann, Hans-Joachim. Einige Bemerkungen zum Samuelson-Stolper Theorem und zur Theorie des Aussenhandelsgewinns. (Some Remarks on the Samuelson-Stolper Theorem and on the Theory of Gains by International Trade. With English summary.) *Jahr. Nationalökon. Statist.,* January 1973, *187*(2), pp. 134–46.

—— Leistungsbilanzsalden, Wirtschaftswachstum und Konsummöglichkeiten. (Current Account, Economic Growth, and Consumption. With English summary.) *Ifo-Studien,* January 1973, *19* (1/2), pp. 1–16.

Heinrich, K. On Forecasting New Techniques in Passenger Transport. In *Blohm, H. and Steinbuch, K., eds.,* 1973, pp. 67–72.

Heintz, James A. Price-Level Restated Financial Statements and Investment Decision Making. *Accounting Rev.,* October 1973, *48*(4), pp. 679–89.

Heirman, W. and Van Mechelen, C. Receptselective en receptcreatie in de vleeswarenindustrie met behulp van lineaire programmering. (Selection and Creation of Recipes. The Application of Linear Programming in the Meat Industry. With English summary.) *Econ. Soc. Tijdschr.,* August 1973, *27*(4), pp. 411–21.

Heitmann, G. United States Oil Import Quotas and the Price of Foreign Oil. *J. Ind. Econ.,* July 1973, *21*(3), pp. 266–71.

Helbling, Hans H. U.S. Balance-of-Payments Developments During 1973. *Fed. Res. Bank St. Louis Rev.,* December 1973, *55*(12), pp. 11–14.

Helfgott, Roy B. Multinational Corporations and Manpower Utilization in Developing Nations. *J. Devel. Areas,* January 1973, *7*(2), pp. 235–46.

Helleiner, Gerald K. Manufactured Exports from Less-Developed Countries and Multinational Firms. *Econ. J.,* March 1973, *83*(329), pp. 21–47.

Helleiner, Gerry. The Role of the Multinational Corporation: Comment. In *Hughes, H., ed.,* 1973, pp. 95–100.

Heller, Frank A. Leadership, Decision Making, and Contingency Theory. *Ind. Relat.,* May 1973, *12* (2), pp. 183–99.

Heller, H. Robert. The Costs and Benefits of the Dollar as a Reserve Currency: Discussion. *Amer. Econ. Rev.,* May 1973, *63*(2), pp. 212–14.

—— **and Britto, Ronald.** International Adjustment and Optimal Reserves. *Int. Econ. Rev.,* February 1973, *14*(1), pp. 182–95.

Heller, Walter W. Should the Government Share Its Tax Take? In *Reynolds, L. G.; Green, G. D. and Lewis, D. R., eds.,* 1973, pp. 417–24.

—— Should the Government Share Its Tax Take? In *Rasmussen, D. W. and Haworth, C. T., eds.,* 1973, pp. 217–24.

Helliwell, John F. Dollars as Reserve Assets: What Next? *Amer. Econ. Rev.,* May 1973, *63*(2), pp. 206–11.

——, et al. Comprehensive Linkage of Large Models: Canada and the United States. In *Ball, R. J., ed.,* 1973, pp. 395–426.

——, et al. Some Features and Uses of the Canadian Quarterly Model RDX2. In *Powell, A. A. and Williams, R. A., eds.,* 1973, pp. 27–47.

——; **Sparks, Gordon and Frisch, Jack.** The Supply Price of Capital in Macroeconomic Models. In *Powell, A. A. and Williams, R. A., eds.,* 1973, pp. 261–83.

Hellman, Daryl A. An Analysis of Central City

Neighborhood Food Trading Areas: A Comment. *J. Reg. Sci.,* August 1973, *13*(2), pp. 299.

—— The Spatial Distribution of Unemployment by Occupation: A Further Note. *J. Reg. Sci.,* December 1973, *13*(3), pp. 463–66.

Hellmuth, William F. The Federal Revenue System: Discussion. *J. Finance,* May 1973, *28*(2), pp. 496–99.

Helman, Amir and Shechter, Mordechai. Collective Decision-Making in a Kibbutz: A Case Study. *Public Finance,* 1973, *28*(2), pp. 139–50.

Helmberger, John D. The Market for Agricultural Economists. *Amer. J. Agr. Econ.,* Part II, November 1973, *55*(4), pp. 725–34.

Helmberger, Peter and Imel, Blake. Estimation of Structure-Profit Relationships: Reply. *Amer. Econ. Rev.,* September 1973, *63*(4), pp. 768–69.

Helmer, Jean-Yves. Essai sur la croissance de l'entreprise. (Essay on Firm Growth. With English summary.) *Revue Écon.,* March 1973, *24*(2), pp. 235–72.

Helmer, Olaf. The Role of Futures Research in Societal Modelling. In *Hawkes, N., ed.,* 1973, pp. 9–13.

Helmers, Glenn A.; Lentz, Gary W. and Kendrick, James G. Specialization and Flexibility Considerations in a Polyperiod Firm Investment Model. *Can. J. Agr. Econ.,* February 1973, *21*(1), pp. 41–48.

Helmstädter, Ernst. The Long-Run Movement of the Capital-Output Ratio and of Labour's Share. In *Mirrlees, J. A. and Stern, N. H., eds.,* 1973, pp. 3–17.

Hemley, David D. and Ozawa, Terutomo. Intra-Racial and Minority Inter-Racial Discrimination. *J. Econ. Bus.,* Spring-Summer 1973, *25*(3), pp. 206–07.

Hemmings, Dan B. Leverage and the Cost of Capital: A Comment. *Economica, N.S.,* August 1973, *40*(159), pp. 316–20.

—— Leverage, Dividend Policy and the Cost of Capital: Comment. *J. Finance,* December 1973, *28*(5), pp. 1366–70.

Hempel, George H. An Evaluation of Municipal "Bankruptcy" Laws and Procedures. *J. Finance,* December 1973, *28*(5), pp. 1339–51.

—— Quantitative Borrower Characteristics Associated with Defaults on Municipal General Obligations. *J. Finance,* May 1973, *28*(2), pp. 523–30.

—— Wage and Price Controls for State and Local Governments: Their Effectiveness and the Potential Effects of Phase III. *Public Policy,* Summer 1973, *21*(3), pp. 425–36.

—— **and Kretschman, Stephen R.** Comparative Performances of Portfolio Maturity Policies of Commercial Banks. *Miss. Val. J. Bus. Econ.,* Fall 1973, *9*(1), pp. 55–75.

Hempenius, A. L. On the Specification of Risk Aversion in an Expenditure Equation. *De Economist,* July-August 1973, *121*(4), pp. 375–86.

Hendershot, Gerry E. Population Size, Military Power, and Antinatal Policy. *Demography,* November 1973, *10*(4), pp. 517–24.

Hendershott, Patric H. Financial Disintermediation in a Macroeconomic Framework: Reply. *J. Finance,* September 1973, *28*(4), pp. 1033–34.

_____ Interest Rates and Prices in the Long Run: A Study of the Gibson Paradox: Comment. *J. Money, Credit, Banking*, Part II, February 1973, *5*(1), pp. 454–59.

_____ Monetary and Fiscal Influences on U.S. Money Income, 1891–1970: Comment. *J. Money, Credit, Banking*, Part II, February 1973, *5*(1), pp. 311–12.

_____ and Van Horne, James C. Expected Inflation Implied by Capital Market Rates. *J. Finance*, May 1973, *28*(2), pp. 301–14.

Henderson, A. M. The Cost of a Family. In *Farrell, M. J., ed.*, 1973, pp. 93–114.

Henderson, Dale W. and Sargent, Thomas J. Monetary and Fiscal Policy in a Two-Sector Aggregative Model. *Amer. Econ. Rev.*, June 1973, *63*(3), pp. 345–65.

Henderson, Hazel. Ecologists versus Economists. *Harvard Bus. Rev.*, July-August 1973, *51*(4), pp. 28–36, 152–57.

Henderson, James P. William Whewell's Mathematical Statements of Price Flexibility, Demand Elasticity and the Giffen Paradox. *Manchester Sch. Econ. Soc. Stud.*, September 1973, *41*(3), pp. 329–42.

Henderson, J. F. and Norton, W. E. The Structure of a Model of the Australian Economy. In *Powell, A. A. and Williams, R. A., eds.*, 1973, pp. 49–83.

Henderson, John. A Putty-Clay Growth Model with Induced Technical Change. *Amer. Econ.*, Spring 1973, *17*(1), pp. 13–20.

Henderson, P. D. Terms and Flexibility of Bank Lending. In *Lewis, J. P. and Kapur, I., eds.*, 1973, pp. 65–76.

Hendon, William S. Property Values, Schools, and Park-School Combinations. *Land Econ.*, May 1973, *49*(2), pp. 216–18.

Hendry, D. F. On Asymptotic Theory and Finite Sample Experiments. *Economica, N.S.*, May 1973, *40*(158), pp. 210–17.

Henig, Stanley. From External Relations to Foreign Policy: An Introductory Note. *J. Common Market Stud.*, September 1973, *12*(1), pp. 1–6.

_____ New Institutions for European Integration. *J. Common Market Stud.*, December 1973, *12*(2), pp. 129–37.

Henle, Peter. Reverse Collective Bargaining? A Look at Some Union Concession Situations. *Ind. Lab. Relat. Rev.*, April 1973, *26*(3), pp. 956–68.

Henley, Donald S. Multinational Marketing: Present Position and Future Challenges. In *Henley, D. S., ed.*, 1973, pp. 337–54.

Henning, John A.; Meehan, James W., Jr. and Mann, H. Michael. Advertising and Market Concentration: Comment. *Southern Econ. J.*, January 1973, *39*(3), pp. 448–51.

_____ and Sufrin, Sidney C. Japan: Steady State or Explosion. *Rivista Int. Sci. Econ. Com.*, August-September 1973, *20*(8–9), pp. 786–93.

Hennings, U.; Hüber, R. P. O. and Stanke, F. Delphi Interrogation Concerning Future Possibilities of the Employment of Robots. In *Blohm, H. and Steinbuch, K., eds.*, 1973, pp. 19–28.

Henrichsmeyer, W.; Hanf, C. H. and Weinschenck, G. Experiences with Multi-Commodity Models

in Regional Analysis. In *Judge, G. G. and Takayama, T., eds.*, 1973, pp. 307–26.

Henry, E. W. A Note on the Logarithmic Transformation of the RAS. *Econ. Soc. Rev.*, July 1973, *4*(4), pp. 487–92.

_____ Relative Efficiency of RAS Versus Least Squares Methods of Updating Input-Output Structures, as Adjudged by Application to Irish Data. *Econ. Soc. Rev.*, October 1973, *5*(1), pp. 7–29.

Henry, John P., Jr. and Schmidt, Richard A. Coal: Still Old Reliable? *Ann. Amer. Acad. Polit. Soc. Sci.*, November 1973, *410*, pp. 35–51.

Henry, Neil W. Measurement Models for Continuous and Discrete Variables. In *Goldberger, A. S. and Duncan, O. D., eds.*, 1973, pp. 51–67.

Hensler, Emil J., Jr. Accounting for Small Nonprofit Organizations. *Manage. Account.*, January 1973, *54*(7), pp. 41–44.

Herberg, Horst. On the Convexity of the Production Possibility Set under General Production Conditions. *Z. ges. Staatswiss.*, May 1973, *129*(2), pp. 205–14.

Herbert, Michael E. and Ellwood, Paul M., Jr. Health Care: Should Industry Buy It or Sell It? *Harvard Bus. Rev.*, July-August 1973, *51*(4), pp. 99–107.

Herbst, Anthony F. and Wu, Joseph S. K. Some Evidence of Subsidization: The U.S. Trucking Industry, 1900–1920. *J. Econ. Hist.*, June 1973, *33*(2), pp. 417–33.

Herdzina, Klaus. Marktstruktur und Wettbewerb. (Market Structure and Competition. On Definition Patterns of Workable Competition. With English summary.) *Z. Wirtschaft. Sozialwissen.*, 1973, *93*(3), pp. 267–84.

Herfindahl, Orris C. and Kneese, Allen V. Measuring Social and Economic Change: Benefits and Costs of Environmental Pollution. In *Moss, M., ed.*, 1973, pp. 441–503.

Herman, Arthur S. Productivity in the Paints and Allied Products Industry. *Mon. Lab. Rev.*, November 1973, *96*(11), pp. 10–13.

Herman, Bohuslav. On the Choice of the Optimal Industry—A Check of a Controversy. *Weltwirtsch. Arch.*, 1973, *109*(1), pp. 70–86.

_____ Unemployment and the International Division of Labour. In *Judge, G. G. and Takayama, T., eds.*, 1973, pp. 89–115.

Herman, Edward S. Expanded Powers for Depositary Financial Institutions: Discussion. In *Federal Reserve Bank of Boston*, 1973, pp. 64–71.

Hermann, Donald H.; Marcus, Sumner and Graham, Philip L., Jr. Section 7 of the Clayton Act and Mergers Involving Foreign Interests. In *Henley, D. S., ed.*, 1973, pp. 155–84.

Hernández, José; Estrada, Leo and Alvírez, David. Census Data and the Problem of Conceptually Defining the Mexican American Population. *Soc. Sci. Quart.*, March 1973, *53*(4), pp. 671–87.

Herniter, Jerome D. An Entropy Model of Brand Purchase Behavior. *J. Marketing Res.*, November 1973, *10*(4), pp. 361–75.

Herold, Arthur L. What Can an Association Do to Meet Foreign Competition? *Antitrust Bull.*, Summer 1973, *18*(2), pp. 181–90.

Herrick, Kenneth W. Auto Accidents and Alcohol in Great Britain—An Analysis. *J. Risk Ins.*, March 1973, *40*(1), pp. 55–73.

Herrick, Neal Q. Government Approaches to the Humanization of Work. *Mon. Lab. Rev.*, April 1973, *96*(4), pp. 52–54.

Herring, Richard and Willett, Thomas D. The Relationship Between U.S. Direct Investment at Home and Abroad. *Rivista Int. Sci. Econ. Com.*, January 1973, *20*(1), pp. 72–82.

Herring, S. G. Programme Budgeting in the Australian Federal Government. In *Novick, D., ed.,* 1973, pp. 55–60.

Herrnstadt, Irwin L. and Horowitz, Morris A. Boston's Manpower Institutions. In *Mangum, G. L. and Robson, R. T., eds.,* 1973, pp. 23–48.

_____ Institutional and Labor Market Impact of Manpower Programs. In *Mangum, G. L. and Robson, R. T., eds.,* 1973, pp. 76–92.

_____ The Old, the New, and the Other Boston. In *Mangum, G. L. and Robson, R. T., eds.,* 1973, pp. 9–22.

_____ Training and Jobs for Boston's Disadvantaged. In *Mangum, G. L. and Robson, R. T., eds.,* 1973, pp. 49–75.

Hertz, David B. Planning under Uncertainty. In *Ross, M., ed.,* 1973, pp. 103–22.

Herwitz, Paul S. Evaluation of Programmers. In *The Diebold Group, Inc.,* 1973, pp. 213–22.

Herzberger, Hans G. Ordinal Preference and Rational Choice. *Econometrica*, March 1973, *41*(2), pp. 187–237.

Herzi, Abdurahman Nur. Savings Banks and Savings Facilities in African Countries: Somalia. In *Alberici, A. and Baravelli, M., eds.,* 1973, pp. 93–96.

Herzog, John P. Natural Behavior Toward Risk and the Question of Value Determination: Comment. *J. Financial Quant. Anal.*, March 1973, *8*(2), pp. 357–59.

Herzog, Philippe. À propos de la notion d'économie publique. (Reflexions on Public Economy Notion. With English summary.) *Revue Écon.*, January 1973, *24*(1), pp. 139–62.

Heslin, Richard and Szybillo, George J. Resistence to Persuasion: Inoculation Theory in a Marketing Context. *J. Marketing Res.*, November 1973, *10* (4), pp. 396–403.

Hess, Alan C. Household Demand for Durable Goods: The Influences of Rates of Return and Wealth. *Rev. Econ. Statist.*, February 1973, *55*(1), pp. 9–15.

Hess, Carroll V. Workshop Summary and Evaluation. *Amer. J. Agr. Econ.*, Part II, November 1973, *55*(4), pp. 767–69.

Hess, J. M. and Cateora, P. R. Pricing in International Markets. In *Thorelli, H. B., ed.,* 1973, pp. 209–21.

Heston, Alan. A Comparison of Some Short-Cut Methods of Estimating Real Product Per Capita. *Rev. Income Wealth*, March 1973, *19*(1), pp. 79–104.

Hetényi, I. and Drecin, J. Some Thoughts Concerning the Future of our Planning. (In Russian. With English summary.) *Acta Oecon.*, 1973, *11*(2–3), pp. 129–48.

Héthy, Lajos and Makó, Csaba. Incentive Problems in the Centrally Planned Economy of Hungary. *Ind. Lab. Relat. Rev.*, January 1973, *26*(2), pp. 767–77.

Hetman, François. Steps in Technology Assessment. *Int. Soc. Sci. J.,* 1973, *25*(3), pp. 257–72.

Heubes, Jürgen. Investitionsverhalten in der Industrie der Bundesrepublik Deutschland 1950–1970. (Investment Behavior in the West-German Industry 1950–1970. With English summary.) *Z. ges. Staatswiss.*, October 1973, *129*(4), pp. 685–701.

_____ Zyklisches Wachstum. (Cyclical Growth. With English summary.) *Z. ges. Staatswiss.*, February 1973, *129*(1), pp. 62–88.

Heuss, Theodor. Friedrich List. In *Rectenwald, H. C., ed.,* 1973, pp. 157–65.

Hewlett, Sylvia-Ann. Rates of Return to Education in Urban Brazil. *Pakistan Econ. Soc. Rev.*, Winter 1973, *11*(4), pp. 403–16.

Hexter, J. L. and Snow, John W. Entropy, Lorenz Curves, and Some Comments on Size Inequality Among the Largest U.S. Corporations. *Nebr. J. Econ. Bus.*, Winter 1973, *12*(1), pp. 43–50.

Heyding, Lawrence F. Corporate Reorganizations ("Rollovers") in Canada. *Bull. Int. Fiscal Doc.*, September 1973, *27*(9), pp. 363–71.

Heyman, Ira Michael. Legal Assaults on Municipal Land Use Regulation. In *Clawson, M., ed.,* 1973, pp. 153–74.

Hibdon, James E., et al. Market Areas in Spatial Duopoly. *Rivista Int. Sci. Econ. Com.*, March 1973, *20*(3), pp. 267–77.

Hickey, Joseph A. State Unemployment Insurance Laws: Status Report. *Mon. Lab. Rev.*, January 1973, *96*(1), pp. 37–44.

Hickman, Bert G. A General Linear Model of World Trade. In *Ball, R. J., ed.,* 1973, pp. 21–43.

_____; Klein, Lawrence R. and Rhomberg, Rudolf R. Background, Organization and Preliminary Results of Project LINK. In *Alexandrides, C. G., ed.,* 1973, pp. 19–56.

_____ and Lau, Lawrence J. Elasticities of Substitution and Export Demands in a World Trade Model. *Europ. Econ. Rev.*, December 1973, *4*(4), pp. 347–80.

Hicks, John R. [Sir]. The Austrian Theory of Capital and Its Rebirth in Modern Economics. In *Hicks, J. R. and Weber, W., eds.,* 1973, pp. 190–206.

_____ The Mainspring of Economic Growth. *Swedish J. Econ.*, December 1973, *75*(4), pp. 336–48.

_____ Recollections and Documents. *Economica*, N.S., February 1973, *40*(157), pp. 2–11.

_____ and Hicks, Ursula K. [Lady]. British Fiscal Policy. In *Giersch, H., ed.,* 1973, pp. 142–54.

_____ and Recktenwald, Horst Claus. Walras's Economic System. In *Rectenwald, H. C., ed.,* 1973, pp. 261–65.

Hicks, Ursula K. [Lady] and Hicks, John R. [Sir]. British Fiscal Policy. In *Giersch, H., ed.,* 1973, pp. 142–54.

Hiemstra, Stephen J. An Analysis of the Market for Food Stamps: Comment. *Amer. J. Agr. Econ.*, February 1973, *55*(1), pp. 109–10.

Hieser, R. O. The Economic Consequences of Zero Population Growth. *Econ. Rec.*, June 1973, *49* (126), pp. 241–62.

Higgins, Benjamin. The Employment Problem in Development. In *Ayal, E. B., ed.,* 1973, pp. 241–75.

_____ Profits and Planning in Developing Countries. *Écon. Appl.,* 1973, *26*(1), pp. 5–32.

_____ Trade-Off Curves and Regional Gaps. In *[Rosenstein-Rodan, P.],* 1973, pp. 152–77.

Higgins, C. I. A Wage-Price Sector for a Quarterly Australian Model. In *Powell, A. A. and Williams, R. A., eds.,* 1973, pp. 115–47.

_____ and FitzGerald, V. W. An Econometric Model of the Australian Economy. *J. Econometrics,* October 1973, *1*(3), pp. 229–65.

Higgins, Richard S. and Morrison, Clarence C. A Further Note on Distributional Equality. *Southern Econ. J.,* January 1973, *39*(3), pp. 442–43.

_____ and Morrison, Clarence C. A Note on Comparative Statics Analysis in Equality Constrained Models. *Southern Econ. J.,* April 1973, *39*(4), pp. 638–41.

Higgins, Robert C.; Kinsman, Michael and Robichek, Alexander A. The Effect of Leverage on the Cost of Equity Capital of Electric Utility Firms. *J. Finance,* May 1973, *28*(2), pp. 353–67.

Higgs, Robert. Mortality in Rural America, 1870-1920: Estimates and Conjectures. *Exploration Econ. Hist.,* Winter 1973, *10*(2), pp. 177–95.

_____ Race, Tenure, and Resource Allocation in Southern Agriculture, 1910. *J. Econ. Hist.,* March 1973, *33*(1), pp. 149–69.

Hight, Joseph E. and Pollock, Richard. Income Distribution Effects of Higher Education Expenditures in California, Florida and Hawaii. *J. Human Res.,* Summer 1973, *8*(3), pp. 318–30.

Higman, B. W. Household Structure and Fertility on Jamaican Slave Plantations: A Nineteenth-Century Example. *Population Stud.,* November 1973, *27*(3), pp. 527–50.

Hildebrand, D. G. and Waters, W. G., II. Road Costs and Government Revenues from Heavy Vehicles in Canada. *Can. J. Econ.,* November 1973, *6*(4), pp. 608–12.

Hildebrand, George H. The Declining Importance of the General Unemployment Rate for Future Employment Policy. In *Somers, G. G., ed.,* 1973, pp. 65–71.

Hildenbrand, Werner and Kirman, Alan P. Size Removes Inequity. *Rev. Econ. Stud.,* July 1973, *40*(3), pp. 305–19.

_____; Schmeidler, David and Zamir, Shmuel. Existence of Approximate Equilibria and Cores. *Econometrica,* November 1973, *41*(6), pp. 1159–66.

Hildreth, R. J.; Krause, Kenneth R. and Nelson, Paul E., Jr. Organization and Control of the U.S. Food and Fiber Sector. *Amer. J. Agr. Econ.,* December 1973, *55*(5), pp. 851–59.

Hill, C. Russell. Two Income Maintenance Plans, Work Incentives and the Closure of the Poverty Gap: Reply. *Ind. Lab. Relat. Rev.,* April 1973, *26*(3), pp. 1005–08.

Hill, Lowell D. and Kau, Paul. Application of Multivariate Probit to a Threshold Model of Grain Dryer Purchasing Decisions. *Amer. J. Agr. Econ.,* February 1973, *55*(1), pp. 19–27.

_____ and Lytle, P. W. Opportunities for New Investment in Country Elevator Facilities. *Ill. Agr. Econ.,* July 1973, *13*(2), pp. 6–11.

_____ and Lytle, P. W. The Optimum Combination of Resources Within and Among Country Elevators. *Amer. J. Agr. Econ.,* May 1973, *55*(2), pp. 202–08.

Hill, Reuben and Klein, David M. Toward a Research Agenda and Theoretical Synthesis. In *Sheldon, E. B., ed.,* 1973, pp. 371–404.

_____ and Klein, David M. Understanding Family Consumption: Common Ground for Integrating Uncommon Disciplinary Perspectives. In *Sheldon, E. B., ed.,* 1973, pp. 1–22.

Hillinger, Claude. Sales Maximization as an Explanation of Near Pareto Optimality of the U.S. Economy. *Jahr. Nationalökon. Statist.,* May 1973, *187*(4), pp. 364–67.

Hills, Gerald E. and Cravens, David W. Consumerism: A Perspective for Business. In *Murray, B. B., ed.,* 1973, pp. 233–42.

Hinchliffe, Keith. Manpower Forecasting for All Occupations: Nigeria. In *Ahamad, B. and Blaug, M., eds.,* 1973, pp. 131–56.

Hinderliter, Roger H. and Rockoff, Hugh. The Management of Reserves by Ante-bellum Banks in Eastern Financial Centers. *Exploration Econ. Hist.,* Fall 1973, *11*(1), pp. 37–53.

Hindley, Brian. Take-Overs: 'Victims' and 'Victors' In *Allen, G. C., et al.,* 1973, pp. 21–28.

Hindman, William R. and Kettering, Floyd F., Jr. Integrated MIS: A Case Study. *Manage. Account.,* August 1973, *55*(2), pp. 20–27.

Hines, Lawrence G. Precursors to Benefit-Cost Analysis in Early United States Public Investment Projects. *Land Econ.,* August 1973, *49*(3), pp. 310–17.

Hinshaw, Elton and Bowen, John. Inflation and Stagnation in Brazil: Comment. *Econ. Develop. Cult. Change,* April 1973, *21*(3), pp. 522–25.

Hinton, Deane. Policy Issues in Adjustment Assistance: The United States: Comment. In *Hughes, H., ed.,* 1973, pp. 177–80.

Hiromatsu, Takeshi and Sawa, Takamitsu. Minimax Regret Significance Points for a Preliminary Test in Regression Analysis. *Econometrica,* November 1973, *41*(6), pp. 1093–1101.

Hirsch, Albert A. The BEA Quarterly Model as a Forecasting Instrument. *Surv. Curr. Bus.,* August 1973, *53*(8), pp. 24–38, 52.

Hirsch, Fred. The Politics of World Money. In *Henley, D. S., ed.,* 1973, pp. 132–41.

Hirsch, Seev. The Impact of European Integration on Trade with Developing Countries: Empirical Evidence and Policy Implications. In *Streeten, P., ed.,* 1973, pp. 216–30.

_____ and Lev, Baruch. Trade and Per Capita Income Differentials: A Test of the Burenstam-Linder Hypothesis. *World Devel.,* September 1973, *1*(9), pp. 11–17.

Hirschman, Albert O. An Alternative Explanation of Contemporary Harriedness. *Quart. J. Econ.,* November 1973, *87*(4), pp. 634–37.

_____ The Organization and Functions of Foreign Aid: Reply. *Econ. Develop. Cult. Change,* Part I, July 1973, *21*(4), pp. 714–16.

_____ and Rothschild, Michael. The Changing Tolerance for Income Inequality in the Course of

Economic Development; with a Mathematical Appendix. *Quart. J. Econ.*, November 1973, *87*(4), pp. 544–66.

Hirschman, R. W. Direct Costing and the Law. In *Thomas, W. E., Jr., ed.*, 1973, pp. 504–15.

Hirshleifer, Jack. Exchange Theory: The Missing Chapter. *Western Econ. J.*, June 1973, *11*(2), pp. 129–46.

—— Where Are We in the Theory of Information? *Amer. Econ. Rev.*, May 1973, *63*(2), pp. 31–39.

Hiscocks, Geoffrey A. The Role of the Federal Government in Export Market Development. In *Canadian Agricultural Economics Society*, 1973, pp. 69–81.

Hitch, Charles J. The Environment: A New Challenge for Operations Research. In *Ross, M., ed.*, 1973, pp. 29–39.

—— Program Planning and Budgeting: Its Origin and Potential Applications. In *The Diebold Group, Inc.*, 1973, pp. 55–62.

Hjalmarsson, Lennart. Optimal Structural Change and Related Concepts. *Swedish J. Econ.*, June 1973, *75*(2), pp. 176–92.

Hoch, Róbert and Kovács, Ilona. Changes in Income and Consumer Prices Affecting Demand. In *Földi, T., ed.*, 1973, pp. 65–88.

Hochberg, Philip and Horowitz, Ira. Broadcasting and CATV: The Beauty and the Bane of Major College Football. *Law Contemp. Probl.*, Winter-Spring 1973, *38*(1), pp. 112–28.

Hochman, Eitan; Hochman, Oded and Razin, Assaf. Demand for Investment in Productive and Financial Capital. *Europ. Econ. Rev.*, April 1973, *4*(1), pp. 67–83.

Hochman, Harold M. and Rodgers, James D. Brennan and Walsh Reconsidered. (Mutt and Jeff Ride Again.) *Public Finance Quart.*, October 1973, *1*(4), pp. 359–71.

—— and Rodgers, James D. Utility Interdependence and Income Transfers through Charity. In *Boulding, K. E.; Pfaff, M. and Pfaff, A., eds.*, 1973, pp. 63–77.

——; Rodgers, James D. and Tullock, Gordon. The Income Distribution as a Pure Public Good: Comment. *Quart. J. Econ.*, May 1973, *87*(2), pp. 311–15.

Hochman, Oded; Razin, Assaf and Hochman, Eitan. Demand for Investment in Productive and Financial Capital. *Europ. Econ. Rev.*, April 1973, *4*(1), pp. 67–83.

Hochmut, M. S. How Americans Manage Germans. In *Henley, D. S., ed.*, 1973, pp. 390–94.

Hochwald, Werner. *The Idea of Progress:* A Review Article. *J. Econ. Issues*, March 1973, *7*(1), pp. 47–59.

Hodgens, Evan L. Survivor's Pensions: An Emerging Employee Benefit. *Mon. Lab. Rev.*, July 1973, *96*(7), pp. 31–34.

Hodgetts, Richard M. and Luthans, Fred. Determining a Social-Responsibility Strategy. In *Klein, W. H. and Murphy, D. C., eds.*, 1973, pp. 292–95.

Hodgins, Cyril D. and Tanner, J. Ernest. Forecasting Non-residential Building Construction. *Can. J. Econ.*, February 1973, *6*(1), pp. 79–89.

Hodjera, Zoran. International Short-Term Capital Movements: A Survey of Theory and Empirical Analysis. *Int. Monet. Fund Staff Pap.*, November 1973, *20*(3), pp. 683–740.

—— and Argy, Victor. Financial Integration and Interest Rate Linkages in Industrial Countries, 1958-71. *Int. Monet. Fund Staff Pap.*, March 1973, *20*(1), pp. 1–77.

Hoerr, O. D. Education, Income and Equity in Malaysia. *Econ. Develop. Cult. Change*, January 1973, *21*(2), pp. 247–73.

Hoffer, George E. and Tyler, George R. Reform of the Non-Commercial Vehicle Liability Insurance Market. *J. Risk Ins.*, December 1973, *40*(4), pp. 565–74.

Hoffer, Stefan N. Private Rates of Return to Higher Education for Women. *Rev. Econ. Statist.*, November 1973, *55*(4), pp. 482–86.

Hoffman, Manfred. Genossenschaftlicher Wohnungsbau in der DDR. (Cooperative House Construction in the GDR. With English summary.) *Jahr. Nationalökon. Statist.*, August 1973, *187*(6), pp. 522–42.

—— Sozialistische Mietenpolitik in der DDR. (Socialist Policy of Housing Rents in the DDR. With English summary.) *Z. ges. Staatswiss.*, May 1973, *129*(2), pp. 246–91.

Hoffman, Michael L. The Challenges of the 1970s and the Present Institutional Structure. In *Lewis, J. P. and Kapur, I., eds.*, 1973, pp. 13–19.

Hoffmann, H.-J. Survey of the Methods used in Technological Forecasting. In *Blohm, H. and Steinbuch, K., eds.*, 1973, pp. 3–12.

Hoffmann, Lutz. Import Substitution—Export Expansion and Growth in an Open Developing Economy: The Case of West Malaysia. *Weltwirtsch. Arch.*, 1973, *109*(3), pp. 452–75.

Hoffmann, Pavel. Methodological Aspects of Prognoses in the Regional Development of the National Economy. *Czech. Econ. Digest.*, November 1973, (7), pp. 56–73.

Hoffmeyer, Erik. Hvor meget vil den økonomiske og monetære union binde vor økonomiske politik? (To What Extent will Our Economic Policy Be Bound by the European Economic and Monetary Union? With English summary.) *Nationalokon. Tidsskr.*, 1973, *111*(1), pp. 144–53.

Hogan, Timothy D. Rankings of Ph.D. Programs in Economics and the Relative Publishing Performance of their Ph.D.'s: The Experience of the 1960's. *Western Econ. J.*, December 1973, *11*(4), pp. 429–50.

—— and Sandler, Todd M. The Optimum Population and Growth: A Further Look. *J. Econ. Theory*, December 1973, *6*(6), pp. 582–84.

—— and Shelton, Robert B. Interstate Tax Exportation and States' Fiscal Structures. *Nat. Tax J.*, December 1973, *26*(4), pp. 553–64.

—— and Shelton, Robert B. A Note on Barlow's Local School Finance. *J. Polit. Econ.*, January-February 1973, *81*(1), pp. 192–98.

Hogarty, Thomas F. and Elzinga, Kenneth G. The Problem of Geographic Market Delineation in Antimerger Suits. *Antitrust Bull.*, Spring 1973, *18*(1), pp. 45–81.

Högberg, Gunnar. Recent Trends in Collective Bargaining in Sweden. *Int. Lab. Rev.*, March 1973, *107*(3), pp. 223–38.

Hohn, Herbert M. Research to Determine What's Dangerous. *Mon. Lab. Rev.*, August 1973, *96*(8), pp. 48–52.

Holahan, John. The Economics of Control of the Illegal Supply of Heroin. *Public Finance Quart.*, October 1973, *1*(4), pp. 467–77.

Holbik, Karel. Monetary Policy in Twelve Industrial Countries: Introduction. In *Holbik, K., ed.*, 1973, pp. xxi–xxvii.

_____ The Tasks and Problems of Marxism in Chile's Economy. *Z. ges. Staatswiss.*, May 1973, *129*(2), pp. 333–46.

Holden, Daina. The Institute's Short Term Forecasting Procedures. *Australian Econ. Rev.*, 2nd Quarter 1973, pp. 45–56.

Holdren, John P. Population and the American Predicament: The Case against Complacency. In *Olson, M. and Landsberg, H. H., eds.*, 1973, pp. 31–43.

_____ and Ehrlich, Paul R. Impact of Population Growth. In *Daly, H. E., ed.*, 1973, pp. 76–89.

Holešovský, Václav. Planning and the Market in the Czechoslovak Reform. In *Bornstein, M., ed.*, 1973, pp. 313–45.

Holland, Charles W. and Cravens, David W. Fractional Factorial Experimental Designs in Marketing Research. *J. Marketing Res.*, August 1973, *10*(3), pp. 270–76.

Holland, David W. and Tweeten, Luther G. Human Capital Migration: Implications for Common School Finance. *Land Econ.*, August 1973, *49*(3), pp. 278–84.

Holland, I. Irving. Implications of the 1970 Timber Review for Trade in Timber Products. *Amer. J. Agr. Econ.*, December 1973, *55*(5), pp. 967–73.

Holland, Paul W. Computer Research Center for Economics and Management Science: The Data-Analysis Project (March 1973) *Ann. Econ. Soc. Measure*, April 1973, *2*(2), pp. 221–24.

Holland, Robert C. Statement to Congress. *Fed. Res. Bull.*, November 1973, *59*(11), pp. 799–803.

Hollander, Gayle D. Handbook of Soviet Social Science Data: Communications. In *Mickiewicz, E., ed.*, 1973, pp. 175–96.

Hollander, Samuel. Ricardo's Analysis of the Profit Rate, 1813–15. *Economica, N.S.*, August 1973, *40*(159), pp. 260–82.

Hollander, Stanley C. Public Policy Toward Retailing: United States of America. In *Boddewyn, J. J. and Hollander, S. C., eds.*, 1972, pp. 367–403.

_____ and Boddewyn, J. J. Public Policy Toward Retailing: Conclusions. In *Boddewyn, J. J. and Hollander, S. C., eds.*, 1972, pp. 431–52.

_____ and Boddewyn, J. J. Public Policy Toward Retailing: Introduction. In *Boddewyn, J. J. and Hollander, S. C., eds.*, 1972, pp. 1–9.

Hollenhorst, Jerry and Dobson, L. Wayne. The Economics of Idle Public Funds Policies: A Reconsideration: A Reply. *Nat. Tax J.*, December 1973, *26*(4), pp. 657–59.

Holloway, Ronald. More Gambling, Less Tax? *Lloyds Bank Rev.*, October 1973, (110), pp. 31–43.

Holman, Mary A. and Bennett, James T. Determinants of Use of Water-Based Recreational Facilities. *Water Resources Res.*, October 1973, *9*(5), pp. 1208–18.

Holmans, A. E.; Laidler, David and Byatt, I. C. R. Income and the Demand for Housing: Some Evidence for Great Britain. In *Parkin, M., ed.*, 1973, pp. 65–84.

Holmes, Alan R. Open Market Operations in 1972. *Fed. Res. Bull.*, June 1973, *59*(6), pp. 405–16.

Holmes, James M. The Process of International Adjustment under Conditions of Full Employment: A Keynesian View Revised. *J. Polit. Econ.*, November-December 1973, *81*(6), pp. 1407–29.

Holmes, J. C. An Ordinal Method of Evaluation: A Rejoinder. *Urban Stud.*, February 1973, *10*(1), pp. 101–04.

Holmes, R. A. The Inadequacy of Unit Value Indexes as Proxies for Canadian Industrial Selling Price Indexes. *Rev. Income Wealth*, September 1973, *19*(3), pp. 271–77.

Holmlund, Bertil. Om postulatens status i ekonomisk teori. (The Status of Postulates in Economic Theory. With English summary.) *Ekon. Samfundets Tidskr.*, 1973, *26*(4), pp. 255–69.

Holmsen, Andreas A. Management of the Peruvian Anchoveta Resource. In *Sokoloski, A. A., ed.*, 1973, pp. 106–11.

Holstrum, Gary L. and Sauls, Eugene H. The Opportunity Cost Transfer Price. *Manage. Account.*, May 1973, *54*(11), pp. 29–33.

Holt, Charles C. Wage Inflation and the Structure of Regional Unemployment: Comment. *J. Money, Credit, Banking*, Part II, February 1973, *5*(1), pp. 380–81.

_____ and Chang, John C. Optimal Investment Orders Under Uncertainty and Dynamic Costs: Theory and Estimates. *Southern Econ. J.*, April 1973, *39*(4), pp. 508–25.

_____, et al. Manpower Policies to Reduce Inflation and Unemployment. In *Ulman, L., ed.*, 1973, pp. 51–82.

Holtermann, Sally E. Market Structure and Economic Performance in U.K. Manufacturing Industry. *J. Ind. Econ.*, December 1973, *22*(2), pp. 119–39.

Holtmann, A. G. The Size and Distribution of Benefits from U.S. Medical Research: The Case of Eliminating Cancer and Heart Disease. *Public Finance*, 1973, *28*(3–4), pp. 354–61.

_____ Skill Obsolescence and Training: Reply. *Southern Econ. J.*, April 1973, *39*(4), pp. 648–49.

_____ The Timing of Investments in Human Capital: A Case in Education. *Public Finance Quart.*, July 1973, *1*(3), pp. 300–06.

Holton, Richard H. and Sethi, S. Prakash. Country Typologies for the Multinational Corporation: A New Basic Approach. *Calif. Manage. Rev.*, Spring 1973, *15*(3), pp. 105–18.

Holub, H. W. and Kuhbier, P. Ein ungleichgewichtiges Modell des Wachstums und der Einkommensverteilung mit endogenen Strukturänderungen. (A Disequilibrated Model of Growth and Income Distribution with Endogenous Structural Change. With English summary.) *Jahr. Nationalökon. Statist.*, May 1973, *187*(4), pp. 289–300.

Holubnychy, Vsevolod. Spatial Efficiency in the

Soviet Economy. In *Bandera, V. N. and Melnyk, Z. L., eds.*, 1973, pp. 1–44.

Holzheu, Franz. Das Geld- und Kreditsystem als Variable im Wachstumsprozess. (The Monetary System as a Variable in the Process of Growth. With English summary.) *Jahr. Nationalökon. Statist.*, January 1973, *187*(2), pp. 97–107.

_____ Zur Problematik der Bandbreiteneinengung in der Europäischen Wirtschaftsgemeinschaft. (On the Problem of Narrowing the Exchange Rate Margins within the EEC. With English summary.) *Z. Wirtschaft. Sozialwissen.*, 1973, *93*(2), pp. 159–89.

Holzman, Franklyn D. Future East-West Economic Issues. In *Bergsten, C. F., ed.*, 1973, pp. 265–92.

Homma, Masaaki. A Dynamic Pigovian Policy Under Production Externalities. *Econ. Stud. Quart.*, August 1973, *24*(2), pp. 26–30.

Honeybone, D. and Fisk, E. K. Belshaw's 'Emergent Fijian Enterprise' after Ten Years. In *Epstein, T. S. and Penny, D. H., eds.*, 1973, pp. 173–92.

Hoogvliet, W. The Australian Sheep Industry Survey 1971–72: Summary of Results and Recent Changes in the Structure and Economic Situation of the Industry. *Quart. Rev. Agr. Econ.*, July 1973, *26*(3), pp. 171–85.

_____ Production Adjustments and Productivity in the Australian Sheep Industry. *Quart. Rev. Agr. Econ.*, October 1973, *26*(4), pp. 239–52.

_____ Recent Developments in the Victorian Lamb Industry: An Economic Survey, 1968–69 to 1970–71, Preliminary Results. *Quart. Rev. Agr. Econ.*, April 1973, *26*(2), pp. 100–16.

Hooks, Donald L. and Ekelund, Robert B., Jr. Ellet, Dupuit, and Lardner: On Nineteenth Century Engineers and Economic Analysis. *Nebr. J. Econ. Bus.*, Summer 1973, *12*(3), pp. 43–52.

Hopewell, Michael H. and Kaufman, George G. Bond Price Volatility and Term to Maturity: A Generalized Respecification. *Amer. Econ. Rev.*, September 1973, *63*(4), pp. 749–53.

Hoppmann, Erich. Zur ökonomischen Begründung von Ausnahmebereichen. Zugleich eine Bemerkung zum Diskussionsbeitrag von M. Tolksdorf "Hoppmanns neoklassische Wettbewerbstheorie als Grundlage der Wettbewerbspolitik." (Note on the Economic Reasons for Exceptions to Competitive Policy. Comment on M. Tolksdorf's "Hoppmann's Neoclassic Theory of a Competition as a Basis for Competition Policy." With English summary.) *Jahr. Nationalökon. Statist.*, January 1973, *187*(2), pp. 161–69.

Horiba, Y. Factor Proportions and the Structure of Interregional Trade: The Case of Japan. *Southern Econ. J.*, January 1973, *39*(3), pp. 381–88.

Horja, Gavril and Nasta, Eliza. Conţinutul şi funcţiile contractelor economice în etapa actuală. (The Content and Functions of the Economic Contracts in the Present Stage. With English summary.) *Stud. Cercet. Econ.*, 1973, (4), pp. 47–53.

Horlick, Max. Social Security Revisions in Spain. *Soc. Sec. Bull.*, April 1973, *36*(4), pp. 36–39.

_____ Supplemental Security Income for the Aged: Foreign Experience. *Soc. Sec. Bull.*, December 1973, *36*(12), pp. 3–12.

_____ Switzerland: Compulsory Private Pensions.

Soc. Sec. Bull., October 1973, *36*(10), pp. 46–47, 49.

Horn, Carl E. Practical Economics of Public Utility Regulation: An Application to Pipelines: Comment. In *Russell, M., ed.*, 1973, pp. 47–51.

Horngren, Charles T. and Sorter, G. H. Asset Recognition and Economic Attributes—The Relevant Costing Approach. In *Thomas, W. E., Jr., ed.*, 1973, pp. 461–74.

Horovicz, M.; Olteanu, I. and Melinte, T. World Market, Economic Cooperation and the Planning of the National Economy. In *Kiss, T., ed.*, 1973, pp. 127–33.

Horowitz, David and Erlich, Reese. Big Brother as a Holding Company. In *Andreano, R. L., ed.*, 1973, pp. R330–15.

Horowitz, Ira and Hochberg, Philip. Broadcasting and CATV: The Beauty and the Bane of Major College Football. *Law Contemp. Probl.*, Winter-Spring 1973, *38*(1), pp. 112–28.

Horowitz, Loucele A. Medical Care Price Changes Under the Economic Stabilization Program. *Soc. Sec. Bull.*, June 1973, *36*(6), pp. 28–32.

Horowitz, Morris A. and Herrnstadt, Irwin L. Boston's Manpower Institutions. In *Mangum, G. L. and Robson, R. T., eds.*, 1973, pp. 23–48.

_____ Institutional and Labor Market Impact of Manpower Programs. In *Mangum, G. L. and Robson, R. T., eds.*, 1973, pp. 76–92.

_____ The Old, the New, and the Other Boston. In *Mangum, G. L. and Robson, R. T., eds.*, 1973, pp. 9–22.

_____ Training and Jobs for Boston's Disadvantaged. In *Mangum, G. L. and Robson, R. T., eds.*, 1973, pp. 49–75.

Horsefield, J. Keith. Proposals for Using Objective Indicators as a Guide to Exchange Rate Changes: A Historical Comment. *Int. Monet. Fund Staff Pap.*, November 1973, *20*(3), pp. 832–37.

Horton, Alexander Romeo. Savings Banks and Savings Facilities in African Countries: Liberia. In *Alberici, A. and Baravelli, M., eds.*, 1973, pp. 47–48.

Horton, Frank E.; Louviere, Jordan and Reynolds, David R. Mass Transit Utilization: Individual Response Data Inputs. *Econ. Geogr.*, April 1973, *49*(2), pp. 122–33.

Horton, Joseph and Baroutsis, A. Paul. An Economic Strategy for Environmental Quality. In *Gabriel, R. A. and Cohen, S. H., eds.*, 1973, pp. 61–93.

Horvat, Branko. Fixed Capital Cost, Depreciation Multiplier and the Rate of Interest. *Europ. Econ. Rev.*, June 1973, *4*(2), pp. 163–79.

_____ Labour-Time Prices of Production and the Transformation Problem in a Socialist Economy. *Kyklos*, 1973, *26*(4), pp. 762–86.

_____ The Postwar Evolution of Yugoslav Agricultural Organization: Interaction of Ideology, Practice, and Results. *Eastern Europ. Econ.*, Winter 1973-74, *12*(2), pp. 3–106.

_____ Real Fixed Capital Costs Under Steady Growth. *Europ. Econ. Rev.*, April 1973, *4*(1), pp. 85–103.

Horwitz, Bertrand and Whitehouse, F. Douglas. Soviet Land Value and Enterprise Location. *Land Econ.*, May 1973, *49*(2), pp. 233–37.

Hosek, William R. Determinants of the Money Multiplier: Reply. *Quart. Rev. Econ. Bus.*, Winter 1973, *13*(4), pp. 101–02.

_____ **and Zahn, Frank.** Impact of Trade Credit on the Velocity of Money and the Market Rate of Interest. *Southern Econ. J.*, October 1973, *40*(2), pp. 202–09.

Hoselitz, Bert F. The Development of a Labor Market in the Process of Economic Growth. In *Sturmthal, A. and Scoville, J. G., eds.*, 1973, pp. 34–57.

_____ Dominance and Achievement in Entrepreneurial Personalities: Comment. In *Ayal, E. B., ed.*, 1973, pp. 145–48.

Hoskins, W. Lee and Weston, J. Fred. Geographic Aspects of Market Structure and Performance in Banking. *J. Bus. Res.*, Summer 1973, *1*(1), pp. 31–42.

Hosono, Akio. Japanese Economic Relations with Latin America: Prospects and Possible Lines of Action. In *Urquidi, V. L. and Thorp, R., eds.*, 1973, pp. 374–95.

Hossain, Ekram; Askari, Hossein and Bizien, Yves. The Success of Some Devaluations and Revaluations in the Post-War Era. *Econ. Int.*, August-November 1973, *26*(3–4), pp. 471–91.

Hossain, Mahabub and Quddus, M. A. Some Economic Aspects of Jute Production in Bangladesh—An Inter-District Study. *Bangladesh Econ. Rev.*, July 1973, *1*(3), pp. 269–96.

Hostiuck, K. Tim and Kurtz, David L. Alderson's Functionalism and the Development of Marketing Theory. *J. Bus. Res.*, Fall 1973, *1*(2), pp. 141–56.

Hou, Chi-Ming. Economic Trends in Modern China. In *Meskill, J., ed.*, 1973, pp. 483–513.

Houck, James P. Price and Income Flexibilities and the Double Logarithmic Demand System: Reply. *Amer. J. Agr. Econ.*, Part I, November 1973, *55*(4), pp. 679–80.

_____ Some Aspects of Income Stabilization for Primary Producers. *Australian J. Agr. Econ.*, December 1973, *17*(3), pp. 200–15.

Houff, James N. Improving Area Wage Survey Indexes. *Mon. Lab. Rev.*, January 1973, *96*(1), pp. 52–57.

Hougham, D. A. The Farms—Origin and Growth. In *Richards, A. I.; Sturrock, F. and Fortt, J. M., eds.*, 1973, pp. 124–49.

_____ **and Fortt, J. M.** Environment, Population and Economic History. In *Richards, A. I.; Sturrock, F. and Fortt, J. M., eds.*, 1973, pp. 17–46.

_____ **and Mafeje, Archie.** Sampling and Fieldwork Methods. In *Richards, A. I.; Sturrock, F. and Fortt, J. M., eds.*, 1973, pp. 95–123.

_____ **and Sturrock, Ford.** The Farms—Present-day Organisation. In *Richards, A. I.; Sturrock, F. and Fortt, J. M., eds.*, 1973, pp. 150–78.

House, William J. Market Structure and Industry Performance: The Case of Kenya. *Oxford Econ. Pap.*, November 1973, *25*(3), pp. 405–19.

Housley, Carl B. Water Pollution Solutions in a Costless and Frictionless Legal System. *Southern Quart.*, October 1973, *12*(1), pp. 15–31.

van Houten, Jan F. Assembly Industries in the Caribbean. *Finance Develop.*, June 1973, *10*(2), pp. 19–22, 37.

Howard, Godfrey G. Anatomy of a Hospital Trustee. *Harvard Bus. Rev.*, May-June 1973, *51*(3), pp. 65–71.

Howard, Robert and Racster, Ronald L. Evaluation of Multiple Subsidy Programs in a Local Market. *Amer. Real Estate Urban Econ. Assoc. J.*, Fall 1973, *1*(2), pp. 104–18.

Howards, Irving. The Comparative Case: Environmental Problems in Israel. In *Gabriel, R. A. and Cohen, S. H., eds.*, 1973, pp. 129–53.

Howe, Geoffrey [Sir]. Public Policy on Mergers and Monopolies. In *Allen, G. C., et al.*, 1973, pp. 39–44.

Howe, James W. The Developing Countries in a Changing International Economic Order: A Survey of Research Needs. In *Bergsten, C. F., ed.*, 1973, pp. 197–264.

_____ **and Hunter, Robert.** United States Aid Performance and Development Policy. In *Dinwiddy, B., ed.*, 1973, pp. 57–72.

Howe, M. A Study of Trade Association Price Fixing. *J. Ind. Econ.*, July 1973, *21*(3), pp. 236–56.

Howell, Robert A. Managing by Objectives—A Three-Stage System. In *Klein, W. H. and Murphy, D. C., eds.*, 1973, pp. 139–43.

Howitt, P. W. Walras and Monetary Theory. *Western Econ. J.*, December 1973, *11*(4), pp. 487–99.

Howle, Edward S. On Revaluations versus Devaluations. *Amer. Econ. Rev.*, December 1973, *63*(5), pp. 918–28.

Howson, Susan. "A Dear Money Man"?: Keynes on Monetary Policy, 1920. *Econ. J.*, June 1973, *83* (330), pp. 456–64.

Hoya, Thomas W. The Office of Foreign Direct Investments and East-West Joint Ventures. In *Henley, D. S., ed.*, 1973, pp. 95–98.

Hrbek, Antonín and Mares, Miroslav. Prognostické ekonometrické modely strojírenstvi. (Prognostic Econometric Models of Machine Industry. With English summary.) *Ekon.-Mat. Obzor*, 1973, *9*(3), pp. 241–59.

Hroneš, Václav. State Budgets for 1973. *Czech. Econ. Digest.*, May 1973, (3), pp. 25–51.

Hsaio-wen, Kung. We Must Keep Count: In Refutation of "Statistics Is Useless." *Chinese Econ. Stud.*, Spring 1973, *6*(3), pp. 32–38.

Hsia, Ronald. Technological Change in the Industrial Growth of Hong Kong. In *Williams, B. R., ed.*, 1973, pp. 335–53.

Hsia, Tao-tai and Haun, Kathryn A. Laws of the People's Republic of China on Industrial and Intellectual Property. *Law Contemp. Probl.*, Summer-Autumn 1973, *38*(2), pp. 274–91.

Hsieh, C. Measuring the Effects of Trade Expansion on Employment: A Review of Some Research. *Int. Lab. Rev.*, January 1973, *107*(1), pp. 1–29.

_____ Measuring the Effects of Trade Expansion on Employment: A Review of Some Research. *Int. Lab. Rev.*, January 1973, *107*(1), pp. 1–29.

Hsien, Ju-kao. Education in Line and Policies Promotes Agricultural Development. *Chinese Econ. Stud.*, Winter 1973–74, *7*(2), pp. 18–26.

Hsü, King-yi. Agrarian Policies of the Chinese Communists: Extraction of Rural Resources During the Kiangsi Period. *Mich. Academician*, Spring 1973, *5*(4), pp. 515–28.

Hu, Sheng Cheng. Capital Mobility and the Effects of Unionization. *Southern Econ. J.,* April 1973, *39* (4), pp. 526–34.

_____ On the Incentive to Invent: A Clarificatory Note. *J. Law Econ.,* April 1973, *16*(1), pp. 169–77.

Hu, Teh-wei and Booms, Bernard H. Economic and Social Factors in the Provision of Urban Public Education. *Amer. J. Econ. Soc.,* January 1973, *32* (1), pp. 35–43.

Huang, Cliff J. Normality of Disturbance Terms and Specification of the Production Functional Forms. *Southern Econ. J.,* July 1973, *40*(1), pp. 12–18.

Huang, David S. Short-Run Instability in Single-Family Housing Starts. *J. Amer. Statist. Assoc.,* December 1973, *68*(344), pp. 788–92.

_____; **Chau, L. C. and Zellner, Arnold.** Real Balances and the Demand for Money: Comment. *J. Polit. Econ.,* Part I, March-April 1973, *81*(2), pp. 485–87.

Huang, Lien-fu and Rosett, Richard N. The Effect of Health Insurance on the Demand for Medical Care. *J. Polit. Econ.,* Part I, March-April 1973, *81* (2), pp. 281–305.

Huang, Yukon. On Some Determinants of Farm Size Across Countries. *Amer. J. Agr. Econ.,* February 1973, *55*(1), pp. 89–92.

_____ Risk, Entrepreneurship, and Tenancy. *J. Polit. Econ.,* September-October 1973, *81*(5), pp. 1241–44.

Hüber, R. P. O.; Stanke, F. and Hennings, U. Delphi Interrogation Concerning Future Possibilities of the Employment of Robots. In *Blohm, H. and Steinbuch, K., eds.,* 1973, pp. 19–28.

Hueckel, Glenn. War and the British Economy, 1793–1815: A General Equilibrium Analysis. *Exploration Econ. Hist.,* Summer 1973, *10*(4), pp. 365–96.

Hufbauer, G. C. Environmental Quality, Income Distribution, and Factor Mobility: The Consequences of Local Action. *J. Econ. Issues,* June 1973, *7*(2), pp. 323–35.

_____ Occupational Trends and Social Mobility in the West Punjab. *Pakistan Econ. Soc. Rev.,* Spring 1973, *11*(1), pp. 83–103.

Huff, H. B. and MacAulay, T. G. Summing Components of Real Capital Gains. *Amer. J. Agr. Econ.,* February 1973, *55*(1), pp. 69–72.

Hugg, Lawrence and Ernst, Robert T. Institutional Growth and Community Fragmentation: An Inner City Example. *Mich. Academician,* Fall 1973, *6*(2), pp. 179–91.

Hughes, Charles E. and Duker, Jacob M. The Black-Owned Life Insurance Company: Issues and Recommendations. *J. Risk Ins.,* June 1973, *40*(2), pp. 221–30.

Hughes, Charles L. and Flowers, Vincent S. Why Employees Stay. *Harvard Bus. Rev.,* July-August 1973, *51*(4), pp. 49–60.

Hughes, G. David; Juhasz, Joseph B. and Contini, Bruno. The Influence of Personality on the Bargaining Process. *J. Bus.,* October 1973, *46*(4), pp. 593–604.

Hughes, Helen. Prospects for Partnership: Industrialization and Trade Policies in the 1970s: Sum-mary and Conclusions. In *Hughes, H., ed.,* 1973, pp. 269–89.

_____ **and Chenery, Hollis B.** Industrialization and Trade Trends: Some Issues for the 1970s. In *Hughes, H., ed.,* 1973, pp. 3–31.

Hughes, James C. Population Estimates for Small Area Decision-Makers. In *Gabriel, R. A. and Cohen, S. H., eds.,* 1973, pp. 94–112.

Hughes, James J. Britain's Training Act: A Man-power Revolution? *Ind. Relat.,* October 1973, *12* (3), pp. 352–53.

_____ In Defence of the Industrial Training Act. *J. Ind. Econ.,* April 1973, *21*(2), pp. 126–44.

Hughes, James W. and James, Franklin J., Jr. The Process of Employment Location Change: An Empirical Analysis. *Land Econ.,* November 1973, *49*(4), pp. 404–13.

_____ **and James, Franklin J., Jr.** A Test of Shift and Share Analysis as a Predictive Device. *J. Reg. Sci.,* August 1973, *13*(2), pp. 223–31.

Hughes, Jonathan R. T. Business Enterprise and Economic Change: Comment. In *[Williamson, H. F.],* 1973, pp. 304–20.

Hulett, Joe R. On the Use of Regression Analysis with a Qualitative Dependent Variable. *Public Finance Quart.,* July 1973, *1*(3), pp. 339–44.

_____ **and Ekelund, Robert B., Jr.** Joint Supply, the Taussig-Pigou Controversy, and the Competitive Provision of Public Goods. *J. Law Econ.,* October 1973, *16*(2), pp. 369–87.

_____; **Kagel, John H. and Battalio, Raymond C.** A Comment on J. J. Siegfried's "The Publishing of Economic Papers and Its Impact on Graduate Faculty Ratings, 1960-1969." *J. Econ. Lit.,* March 1973, *11*(1), pp. 68–70.

Hulin, Charles L. Worker Background and Job Satis-faction: Reply. *Ind. Lab. Relat. Rev.,* January 1973, *26*(2), pp. 853–55.

Hull, J.; Moore, P. G. and Thomas, H. Utility and its Measurement. *J. Roy. Statist. Soc.,* Part 2, 1973, *136,* pp. 226–47.

Hulten, Charles R. Divisia Index Numbers. *Econometrica,* November 1973, *41*(6), pp. 1017–25.

Humann, Thomas E. and Arnold, Donald F. Earn-ings Per Share: An Empirical Test of the Market Parity and the Investment Value Methods. *Accounting Rev.,* January 1973, *48*(1), pp. 23–33.

Hume, Ian M. Migrant Workers in Europe. *Finance Develop.,* March 1973, *10*(1), pp. 2–6.

Humphrey, Don D. The Case for Gold. In *[Halm, G. N.],* 1973, pp. 81–98.

Humphrey, Thomas M. Changing Views of Com-parative Advantage. In *Henley, D. S., ed.,* 1973, pp. 18–24.

_____ Empirical Tests of the Quantity Theory of Money in the United States, 1900–1930. *Hist. Polit. Econ.,* Fall 1973, *5*(2), pp. 285–316.

_____ On the Monetary Economics of Chicagoans and Non-Chicagoans: Reply. *Southern Econ. J.,* January 1973, *39*(3), pp. 460–63.

Hunt, E. K. and d'Arge, Ralph C. On Lemmings and Other Acquisitive Animals: Propositions on Con-sumption. *J. Econ. Issues,* June 1973, *7*(2), pp. 337–53.

Hunt, Lacy H., II and Rose, Peter S. The Relative

Importance of Monetary and Fiscal Variables in Determining Price Level Movements: Reply. *J. Finance*, March 1973, *28*(1), pp. 191–93.

Hunt, Shelby D. Experimental Determinants of Franchisee Success. *J. Econ. Bus.*, Fall 1973, *26*(1), pp. 81–83.

—— **and Churchill, Gilbert A., Jr.** Sources of Funds and Franchisee Success. *J. Bus. Res.*, Fall 1973, *1*(2), pp. 157–64.

Hunt, Verl F. The Glass Bead Game of Orthodox Economics: Reply. *Intermountain Econ. Rev.*, Spring 1973, *4*(1), pp. 74–76.

Hunter, Guy. Agricultural Administration and Institutions. *Food Res. Inst. Stud.*, 1973, *12*(3), pp. 233–51.

—— Development—The Search for a New Strategy. In *Dinwiddy, B., ed.*, 1973, pp. 112–34.

—— The Food Research Institute's Fiftieth Anniversary Conference, Strategies for Agricultural Development in the 1970s. *Food Res. Inst. Stud.*, 1973, *12*(1), pp. 3–72.

Hunter, J. S. H. Interstate Fiscal Equalization in the Federal Republic of Germany and Comparisons with Australia and Canada. *Australian Econ. Pap.*, June 1973, *12*(20), pp. 42–56.

Hunter, Robert and Howe, James W. United States Aid Performance and Development Policy. In *Dinwiddy, B., ed.*, 1973, pp. 57–72.

Huntsman, Blaine. Natural Behavior Toward Risk and the Question of Value Determination. *J. Financial Quant. Anal.*, March 1973, *8*(2), pp. 335–50.

Huq, A. M. A Study of the Socioeconomic Impact of Changes in the Harvesting Labor Force in the Maine Lobster Industry. In *Sokoloski, A. A., ed.*, 1973, pp. 159–73.

Hurd, Richard W. Equilibrium Vacancies in a Labor Market Dominated by Non-Profit Firms: The "Shortage" of Nurses. *Rev. Econ. Statist.*, May 1973, *55*(2), pp. 234–40.

Hurst, David B. Constructing an Adaptive Strategy for a National Newspaper. In *Ross, M., ed.*, 1973, pp. 275–89.

Hurst, Michael E. Eliot. Transportation and the Societal Framework. *Econ. Geogr.*, April 1973, *49*(2), pp. 163–80.

Hurtado, Hernán and Piñeiro, Martín. Rentabilidad potencial de la investigación ganadera: Una estimación empírica. (Rateable of Livestock Research: An Empirical Estimation. With English summary.) *Económica*, May-August 1973, *19*(2), pp. 185–200.

Hurwicz, Leonid. The Design of Mechanisms for Resource Allocation. *Amer. Econ. Rev.*, May 1973, *63*(2), pp. 1–30.

—— **and Reiter, Stanley.** On the Boundedness of the Feasible Set Without Convexity Assumptions. *Int. Econ. Rev.*, October 1973, *14*(3), pp. 580–86.

Husain, Ishrat. Mechanics of Development Planning in Pakistan: A Suggested Framework. *Pakistan Econ. Soc. Rev.*, Winter 1973, *11*(4), pp. 454–62.

Husák, Gustáv. From the Report of the Central Committee Presidium of the Communist Party of Czechoslovakia on the Implementation of the Decisions of the 14th Congress of the Communist Party of Czechoslovakia. *Czech. Econ. Digest.*, May 1973, (3), pp. 3–24.

Husby, Ralph D. Impact of a Negative Income Tax on Aggregate Demand and Supply. *Western Econ. J.*, March 1973, *11*(1), pp. 111–17.

—— Work Incentives and the Cost Effectiveness of Income Maintenance Programs. *Quart. Rev. Econ. Bus.*, Spring 1973, *13*(1), pp. 7–13.

Husic, Frank and Blume, Marshall E. Price, Beta, and Exchange Listing. *J. Finance*, May 1973, *28*(2), pp. 283–99.

—— **and Friend, Irwin.** Efficiency of Corporate Investment. *Rev. Econ. Statist.*, February 1973, *55*(1), pp. 122–27.

Hussain, Imtiazuddin; Afzal, Mohammad and Bean, Lee L. Muslim Marriages: Age, Mehr and Social Status. *Pakistan Develop. Rev.*, Spring 1973, *12*(1), pp. 48–61.

Hussain, Mazhar and Butt, Abdul Rauf. Projections of Job Opportunities for Natural Scientists and Mathematicians in West Pakistan. *Pakistan Econ. Soc. Rev.*, Summer 1973, *11*(2), pp. 200–06.

Hussain, Sayed M. Price Incentives for the Production of High Yielding Mexican Varieties of Wheat: A Rejoinder. *Pakistan Develop. Rev.*, Summer 1973, *12*(2), pp. 194–97.

Hustad, Thomas P. and Pessemier, Edgar A. Will the Real Consumer Activist Please Stand Up: An Examination of Consumers' Opinions About Marketing Practices. *J. Marketing Res.*, August 1973, *10*(3), pp. 319–24.

Huszár, J. and Mandel, M. The Investment Decision-Making System in Hungary. *Eastern Europ. Econ.*, Spring 1973, *11*(3), pp. 27–49.

Hutchins, Robert C. and Maass, Randal O. Measurement of Multicompany Diversification. *J. Econ. Bus.*, Fall 1973, *26*(1), pp. 74–77.

Hutchison, T. W. *The Collected Writings of John Maynard Keynes*, Volumes I–VI and XV–XVI. *Econ. Hist. Rev.*, 2nd Ser., February 1973, pp. 141–52.

—— Some Themes from Investigations into Method. In *Hicks, J. R. and Weber, W., eds.*, 1973, pp. 15–37.

Huttman, Elizabeth D. and Huttman, John P. Dutch and British New Towns: Self-Containment and Socioeconomic Balance. *Growth Change*, January 1973, *4*(1), pp. 30–37.

Huttman, John P. and Huttman, Elizabeth D. Dutch and British New Towns: Self-Containment and Socioeconomic Balance. *Growth Change*, January 1973, *4*(1), pp. 30–37.

Huxley, S. J. A Note on the Economics of Retail Trading Hours. *Econ. Anal. Pol.*, March 1973, *4*(1), pp. 17–22.

Hyde, Charles K. The Adoption of Coke-Smelting by the British Iron Industry, 1709–1790. *Exploration Econ. Hist.*, Summer 1973, *10*(4), pp. 397–418.

—— The Adoption of the Hot Blast by the British Iron Industry: A Reinterpretation. *Exploration Econ. Hist.*, Spring 1973, *10*(3), pp. 281–93.

Hyer, Leon A. and Tate, Merle W. Inaccuracy of the X^2 Test of Goodness of Fit when Expected Frequencies Are Small. *J. Amer. Statist. Assoc.*, December 1973, *68*(344), pp. 836–41.

Hyman, David N. and Pasour, E. C., Jr. Real Property Taxes, Local Public Services, and Residential Property Values. *Southern Econ. J.,* April 1973, *39* (4), pp. 601–11.

———— and Pasour, E. C., Jr. Note: Property Tax Differentials and Residential Rents in North Carolina. *Nat. Tax J.,* June 1973, *26*(2), pp. 303–07.

Hymans, Saul H. On the Use of Leading Indicators to Predict Cyclical Turning Points. *Brookings Pap. Econ. Act.,* 1973, (2), pp. 339–75.

Hymer, Stephen. Effects of Policies Encouraging Foreign Joint Ventures in Developing Countries: Comment. In *Ayal, E. B., ed.,* 1973, pp. 177–80.

———— The Multinational Corporation and Uneven Development. In *Andreano, R. L., ed.,* 1973, pp. R335–04.

Hynar, Ladislav and Barták, Rudolf. Optimální cesty. (Optimal Routes. With English summary.) *Ekon.-Mat. Obzor,* 1973, *9*(2), pp. 167–83.

Hyslop, John D. Project Selection and Macroeconomic Objectives: Comment. *Amer. J. Agr. Econ.,* February 1973, *55*(1), pp. 105–07.

Ianovskii, V. S. The Problem of Economic Integration of Enterprises in Industry Production Associations and the Optimization of Current Planning. *Matekon,* Fall 1973, *10*(1), pp. 65–82.

Ibarra, Jose. Some Aspects of the Popular Unity's Development Model. In *Zammit, J. A., ed.,* 1973, pp. 57–62.

Ichikawa, Hiroya. Factor Proportions, Human Capital and Comparative Advantage. *Econ. Rec.,* March 1973, *49*(125), pp. 104–25.

Idachaba, F. S. Marketing Boards as Potential Stabilizers of Government Revenues in Developing Countries: The Nigerian Experience. *Econ. Bull. Ghana, Sec. Ser.,* 1973, *3*(4), pp. 23–30.

Iengar, H. V. R. Reform of the Indian Banking System: Proceedings of a Seminar: Inaugural Address. In *Simha, S. L. N., ed.,* 1973, pp. 5–14.

Igawa, Kazuhiro. Assets Choice and Optimal International Reserves. *Kobe Econ. Bus. Rev.,* 1973, *20,* pp. 79–88.

Ihalauw, John and Utami, Widya. Some Consequences of Small Farm Size. *Bull. Indonesian Econ. Stud.,* July 1973, *9*(2), pp. 46–56.

Ihrig, Károly. Agriculture's Contribution to the Growth of Capitalist Economies. In *Földi, T., ed.,* 1973, pp. 135–60.

Ijiri, Yuji. A Historical Cost Approach to Aggregation of Multiple Goals. In *Cochrane, J. L. and Zeleny, M., eds.,* 1973, pp. 395–405.

———— and Itami, Hiroyuki. Quadratic Cost-Volume Relationship and Timing of Demand Information. *Accounting Rev.,* October 1973, *48*(4), pp. 724–37.

Ike, Nobutaka. Economic Growth and Intergenerational Change in Japan. *Amer. Polit. Sci. Rev.,* December 1973, *67*(4), pp. 1194–1203.

Ikeda, Y. Distribution Innovation in Japan and the Role Played by General Trading Companies. In *Thorelli, H. B., ed.,* 1973, pp. 237–43.

Ikemoto, K. Devaluation When Exports Have an Import Content: Comment. *Manchester Sch. Econ. Soc. Stud.,* December 1973, *41*(4), pp. 425–27.

Ikinda, Antoine. Savings Banks and Savings Facilities in African Countries: Gabon. In *Alberici, A. and Baravelli, M., eds.,* 1973, pp. 33–34.

Ikonicoff, Moïses. Technologie et modèle de consommation dans le Tiers-Monde. (Technology and Consumption Patterns in Under-Developed Countries. With English summary.) *Revue Écon.,* July 1973, *24*(4), pp. 619–40.

Ikram, Khalid. Devaluation and Export Price Competitiveness: A Note. *Pakistan Econ. Soc. Rev.,* Autumn 1973, *11*(3), pp. 349–53.

———— Social Versus Private Profitability in Pakistan's Export of Manufactures. *Pakistan Develop. Rev.,* Summer 1973, *12*(2), pp. 156–67.

———— Suspension of Interwing Trade: Structure and Growth of West Pakistan's Exports. *Pakistan Econ. Soc. Rev.,* Summer 1973, *11*(2), pp. 141–53.

Iliff, Neil. Is There a World Environmental Crisis? In *Robinson, J., ed.,* 1973, pp. 117–24.

Illich, Ivan. Outwitting the "Developed" Countries. In *Wilber, C. K., ed.,* 1973, pp. 401–09.

Imel, Blake and Helmberger, Peter. Estimation of Structure-Profit Relationships: Reply. *Amer. Econ. Rev.,* September 1973, *63*(4), pp. 768–69.

Inada, Ken-Ichi and Kuga, Kiyoshi. Limitations of the "Coase Theorem" on Liability Rules. *J. Econ. Theory,* December 1973, *6*(6), pp. 606–13.

Inagaki, M. Intertemporal National Optimality and Temporal Social Preferences. In *Mirrlees, J. A. and Stern, N. H., eds.,* 1973, pp. 241–54.

Infante, Ettore F. and Stein, Jerome L. Optimal Growth with Robust Feedback Control. *Rev. Econ. Stud.,* January 1973, *40*(1), pp. 47–60.

———— and Stein, Jerome L. Optimal Stabilization Paths. *J. Money, Credit, Banking,* Part II, February 1973, *5*(1), pp. 525–62.

Ingham, Barbara M. Ghana Cocoa Farmers—Income, Expenditure Relationships. *J. Devel. Stud.,* April 1973, *9*(3), pp. 365–72.

Ingraham, Harold G., Jr. Problems in Agents' Compensation. *J. Risk Ins.,* June 1973, *40*(2), pp. 191–208.

Ingram, Gregory K. and Kain, John F. A Simple Model of Housing Production and the Abandonment Problem. *Amer. Real Estate Urban Econ. Assoc. J.,* June 1973, *1*(1), pp. 79–106.

Ingram, Helen M. Information Channels and Environmental Decision Making. *Natural Res. J.,* January 1973, *13*(1), pp. 150–69.

———— The Political Economy of Regional Water Institutions. *Amer. J. Agr. Econ.,* February 1973, *55* (1), pp. 10–18.

Ingram, James C. The Adjustment Problem: Comment. In *Krause, L. B. and Salant, W. S., eds.,* 1973, pp. 184–91.

Inman, Richard A.; Manne, Alan S. and Franchet, Yves. Numerical Data for Multi-Sector Planning. In *Goreux, L. M. and Manne, A. S., eds.,* 1973, pp. 85–106.

Inostroza, Alfonso. The World Bank and Imperialism. In *Wilber, C. K., ed.,* 1973, pp. 152–57.

Inozemtsev, N. Main Tasks in the Coordination of the National Economic Plans of COMECON Countries. *Prob. Econ.,* October 1973, *16*(6), pp. 20–35.

In Sang Song. Some Conceptual and Administrative

Difficulties in Nutrition Planning. In *Berg, A.; Scrimshaw, N. S. and Call, D. L., eds.*, 1973, pp. 290–92.

Inselbag, Isik. Financing Decisions and the Theory of the Firm. *J. Financial Quant. Anal.*, December 1973, *8*(5), pp. 763–76.

Intriligator, Michael D. A Probabilistic Model of Social Choice. *Rev. Econ. Stud.*, October 1973, *40*(4), pp. 553–60.

———, et al. Conceptual Framework of an Econometric Model of Industrial Organization. In *Weston, J. F. and Ornstein, S. I., eds.*, 1973, pp. 23–55.

——— and **Kalman, Peter J.** Generalized Comparative Statics with Applications to Consumer Theory and Producer Theory. *Int. Econ. Rev.*, June 1973, *14*(2), pp. 473–86.

Inzana, John T. The New Survey of Occupational Injuries and Illnesses. *Mon. Lab. Rev.*, August 1973, *96*(8), pp. 53–55.

Ioanes, Raymond A. Trends and Structure of U.S. Agricultural Trade. In *Iowa State University Center for Agricultural and Rural Development*, 1973, pp. 87–102.

Ionescu, Eugen. Procesul economisirii la C.E.C. Tendințe și structuri. (The Process of Economizing with the Savings Bank—Trends and Structures. With English summary.) *Stud. Cercet. Econ.*, 1973, (4), pp. 65–71.

Iovanelli, Marcela and Groza, Maria. Activizarea și conducerea politică a maselor țărănești de către Partidul Comunist Român în procesul înfăptuirii sarcinilor desăvîrșirii revoluției burghezo-democratice. (The Activation and the Political Leadership of the Peasant Masses by the Romanian Communist Party in the Fulfilment of the Targets of the Completion of the Bourgeois-Democratic Revolution. With English summary.) *Stud. Cercet. Econ.*, 1973, (3), pp. 19–28.

Ireland, Marilyn J. The Legal Framework of the Market for Blood. In *Alchian, A. A., et al.*, 1973, pp. 171–78.

Ireland, Norman J. The "Dorfman-Steiner" Rule and Bandwagon Effects. *Z. Nationalökon.*, 1973, *33*(3–4), pp. 427–30.

———; **Briscoe, G. and Smyth, David J.** Specification Bias and Short-run Returns to Labour: Some Evidence for the United Kingdom. *Rev. Econ. Statist.*, February 1973, *55*(1), pp. 23–27.

Ireland, Thomas R. The Calculus of Philanthropy. In *Alchian, A. A., et al.*, 1973, pp. 63–78.

——— Inheritance Justified: Comment. *J. Law Econ.*, October 1973, *16*(2), pp. 421–22.

——— Micropolitics and Macroeconomics: Discussion. *Amer. Econ. Rev.*, May 1973, *63*(2), pp. 179–80.

——— Organized Crime: Comment. In *Rottenberg, S., ed.*, 1973, pp. 171–75.

——— and **Koch, James V.** Blood and American Social Attitudes. In *Alchian, A. A., et al.*, 1973, pp. 145–55.

Ironside, R. G. and Klippenstein, D. H. Farmers' Attitudes Toward Farm-Based Recreational Facilities in Alberta. *Can. J. Agr. Econ.*, November 1973, *21*(3), pp. 23–33.

Isaac, J. E. Incomes Policy: Unnecessary? Undesirable? Impracticable? *Australian Econ. Rev.*, 1st Quarter 1973, pp. 41–50.

Isaacs, Rufus. Some Fundamentals of Differential Games. In *Blaquière, A., ed.*, 1973, pp. 1–42.

Isaev, B. L. A Matrix Balance of Socialist Economic Integration. *Matekon*, Fall 1973, *10*(1), pp. 93–116.

Isakson, Hans R. and Maurizi, Alex R. The Consumer Economics of Unit Pricing. *J. Marketing Res.*, August 1973, *10*(3), pp. 277–85.

Isard, Peter. The Effectiveness of Using the Tax System to Curb Inflationary Collective Bargains: An Analysis of the Wallich-Weintraub Plan. *J. Polit. Econ.*, May-June 1973, *81*(3), pp. 729–40.

——— Employment Impacts of Textile Imports and Investment: A Vintage-Capital Model. *Amer. Econ. Rev.*, June 1973, *63*(3), pp. 402–16.

Isard, Walter and Liossatos, Panagis. Social Injustice and Optimal Space-Time Development. *J. Peace Sci.*, Autumn 1973, *1*(1), pp. 69–93.

Isbister, John. Birth Control, Income Redistribution, and the Rate of Saving: The Case of Mexico. *Demography*, February 1973, *10*(1), pp. 85–98.

Isermann, Heinz and Dinkelbach, Werner. On Decision Making under Multiple Criteria and under Incomplete Information. In *Cochrane, J. L. and Zeleny, M., eds.*, 1973, pp. 302–12.

Ishi, Hiromitsu. Cyclical Behavior of Government Receipts and Expenditures—A Case Study of Postwar Japan. *Hitotsubashi J. Econ.*, June 1973, *14*(1), pp. 56–83.

Ishikawa, Tsuneo. Conceptualization of Learning by Doing: A Note on Paul David's "Learning by Doing and . . . the Ante-Bellum United States Cotton Textile Industry." *J. Econ. Hist.*, December 1973, *33*(4), pp. 851–61.

——— Some Reflections on the "New Scheme for Monetary Control" by the Bank of Japan. *Kyoto Univ. Econ. Rev.*, April–October 1973, *43*(1–2), pp. 45–58.

Islam, Nurul. National Import Substitution and Inward-Looking Strategies: Policies of Less Developed Countries. In *Streeten, P., ed.*, 1973, pp. 76–92.

Islam, Taherul. Structure of Futures Contract, Difference System and Hedging Effectiveness—An Economic Study of Bombay Cotton Futures Market. *Indian Econ. J.*, January-March 1973, *20*(3), pp. 479–99.

Israel, Joachim. Om marknadsekonomins förträfflighet: en sociologisk analys. (The functioning of the market economy: A Critical Analysis from a Sociological Point of View. With English summary.) *Nationalokon. Tidsskr.*, 1973, *111*(2), pp. 221–41.

Itami, Hiroyuki and Ijiri, Yuji. Quadratic Cost-Volume Relationship and Timing of Demand Information. *Accounting Rev.*, October 1973, *48*(4), pp. 724–37.

Iudina, E. and Oleinik, I. Structural Changes in the Economies of Socialist Countries. *Prob. Econ.*, March 1973, *15*(11), pp. 21–43.

Iumin, M. N. The Mongolian People's Republic in the System of International Socialist Economic Integration. *Chinese Econ. Stud.*, Winter 1973–74, *7*(2), pp. 92–105.

Ivanov, N. How Many Specialists are Needed? *Prob. Econ.*, August 1973, *16*(4), pp. 63–81.

Ivanov, S. A. New Codification of Soviet Labour Law. *Int. Lab. Rev.*, August-September 1973, *108* (2–3), pp. 143–61.

Ivanova, R. Concerning the Development of the Eastern Regions and Their Manpower Supply. *Prob. Econ.*, June 1973, *16*(2), pp. 26–41.

Iwasa, Yoshizane. Banking in Japan. In *Moskoff, W., ed.*, 1973, pp. 33–54.

Iyengar, Sampath S. and Vachha, Homiar S. Financial Institutions and Backward Regions: A Case Study of Gujarat. *Artha-Vikas,* January-July 1973, *9*(1–2), pp. 185–202.

Iyoha, Milton Ame. Inflation and "Openness" in Less Developed Economies: A Cross-Country Analysis. *Econ. Develop. Cult. Change*, October 1973, *22*(1), pp. 31–38.

_____ The Optimal Balance-of-Payments Strategy of a Less Developed Country. *Econ. Rec.*, June 1973, *49*(126), pp. 270–79.

Izraeli, Dov. Public Policy Toward Retailing: Israel. In *Boddewyn, J. J. and Hollander, S. C., eds.*, 1972, pp. 191–211.

Jaakson, Reiner. Factor Analysis of Shoreline Physiography and Perception of Water Level Drawdown by Reservoir Shoreline Residents. *Water Resources Res.*, February 1973, *9*(1), pp. 81–92.

Jääskeläinen, Veikko and Kervinen, Esko. Designing Retail Outlets with Markov Chains and Mathematical Programming. *Liiketaloudellinen Aikak.*, 1973, *22*(2), pp. 83–93.

Jabbar, M. A. Agriculture in Economic Development: The Competitive Approach Versus Soviet Control. *Can. J. Agr. Econ.*, February 1973, *21*(1), pp. 63–64.

Jackman, Richard and Layard, Richard. University Efficiency and University Finance. In *Parkin, M., ed.*, 1973, pp. 170–88.

Jackson, Carolyn and Velten, Terri. Residence, Race, and Age of Poor Families in 1966. In *Rasmussen, D. W. and Haworth, C. T., eds.*, 1973, pp. 53–71.

Jackson, D. A. S. and Turner, H. A. A Riposte to Knight and Mabro. *Econ. J.*, June 1973, *83*(330), pp. 523–25.

Jackson, Dudley and Turner, H. A. How to Provide More Employment in a Labour-Surplus Economy. *Int. Lab. Rev.*, April 1973, *107*(4), pp. 315–38.

Jackson, Emma. The Present System of Publicly Supported Day Care. In *Young, D. R. and Nelson, R. R., eds.*, 1973, pp. 21–46.

_____ and **Young, Dennis.** Public Policy for Day Care of Young Children: Introduction. In *Young, D. R. and Nelson, R. R., eds.*, 1973, pp. 1–8.

Jackson, Mark and Jones, E. B. Unemployment and Occupational Wage Changes in Local Labor Markets. *Ind. Lab. Relat. Rev.*, July 1973, *26*(4), pp. 1135–45.

Jackson, R.; Bates, W. R. and Sexton, R. N. The Impact of Death Duties on the Rural Industries in Australia. *Quart. Rev. Agr. Econ.*, January 1973, *26*(1), pp. 25–43.

Jackson, Raymond. Job-Discrimination and the Use of Bonuses. *Amer. J. Econ. Soc.*, October 1973, *32* (4), pp. 351–66.

_____ Peak Load Pricing Model of an Electric Utility Using Pumped Storage. *Water Resources Res.*, June 1973, *9*(3), pp. 556–62.

Jacob, Nancy L. Systematic Risk and the Horizon Problem: Comment. *J. Financial Quant. Anal.*, March 1973, *8*(2), pp. 351–54.

Jacobs, Donald P. and Phillips, Almarin. Overview of the Commission's Philosophy and Recommendations. In *Federal Reserve Bank of Boston*, 1973, pp. 9–20.

Jacobson, Robert E. and Walker, Francis E. Efficiency Considerations in Butterfat Differential and Component Pricing of Milk. *Amer. J. Agr. Econ.*, May 1973, *55*(2), pp. 214–16.

Jacoby, Henry D. and Steinbruner, John D. Advanced Technology and the Problem of Implementation. In *Jacoby, H. D., et al.*, 1973, pp. 49–61.

_____ and **Steinbruner, John D.** The Context of Current Policy Discussions. In *Jacoby, H. D., et al.*, 1973, pp. 9–26.

_____ and **Steinbruner, John D.** Policy Analysis and the Public Sector. In *Jacoby, H. D., et al.*, 1973, pp. 1–8.

_____ and **Steinbruner, John D.** Policy Options and Predicted Outcomes. In *Jacoby, H. D., et al.*, 1973, pp. 27–47.

_____ and **Steinbruner, John D.** Salvaging the Federal Attempt to Control Auto Pollution. *Public Policy*, Winter 1973, *21*(1), pp. 1–48.

Jacoby, Jacob and Kyner, David B. Brand Loyalty vs. Repeat Purchasing Behavior. *J. Marketing Res.*, February 1973, *10*(1), pp. 1–9.

Jacquemin, Alex P. and Cardon de Lichtbuer, Michel. Size Structure, Stability and Performance of the Largest British and EEC Firms. *Europ. Econ. Rev.*, December 1973, *4*(4), pp. 393–408.

Jaedicke, Robert K. and Robichek, Alexander A. Cost-Volume-Profit Analysis Under Conditions of Uncertainty. In *Thomas, W. E., Jr., ed.*, 1973, pp. 279–93.

Jaeger, Klaus. Ein einfaches monetäres Wachstumsmodell mit Produkt- und Prozessinnovationen. (A Simple Monetary Growth Model with Product and Process Innovations. With English summary.) *Z. ges. Staatswiss.*, August 1973, *129*(3), pp. 409–44.

_____ Income Distribution, Value of Capital, and Two Notions of the Wage-Profit Trade-Off: Comment. *Oxford Econ. Pap.*, July 1973, *25*(2), pp. 286–88.

_____ Sparverhalten und Vermögenspolitik in neoklassischen und generelleren Modellen. (Savings Behaviour and Distribution of Wealth in Neoclassical and More General Models. With English summary.) *Jahr. Nationalökon. Statist.*, March 1973, *187*(3), pp. 193–208.

_____ Zur Problematik der Gewinnbeteiligung der Arbeitnehmer als Mittel der Vermögenspolitik. (Profit-Sharing as an Instrument of Ownership Policy. With English summary.) *Z. Wirtschaft. Sozialwissen.*, 1973, *93*(6), pp. 687–707.

Jaffe, A. J. Notes on Developing Countries and their Statistics: Reply. *Rev. Income Wealth,* June 1973, *19*(2), pp. 213–14.

Jaffé, William. Léon Walras. In *Rectenwald, H. C., ed.,* 1973, pp. 253–61.

Jaffee, Bruce L. Depreciation in a Simple Regulatory Model. *Bell J. Econ. Manage. Sci.,* Spring 1973, *4*(1), pp. 338–42.

———— The Indiana Intangibles Tax: The Tax Nobody Pays? *Indiana Bus. Rev.,* July-August 1973, *48,* pp. 3–7.

———— Population Density as a Measure of City Size. *Indiana Bus. Rev.,* May-June 1973, *48,* pp. 15–18.

Jaffee, Dwight M. and Fair, Ray C. The Implications of the Proposals of the Hunt Commission for the Mortgage and Housing Markets: An Empirical Study. In *Federal Reserve Bank of Boston,* 1973, pp. 99–148.

Jagers, Peter. How Many People Pay Their Tram Fares? *J. Amer. Statist. Assoc.,* December 1973, *68*(344), pp. 801–04.

Jago, Charles. The Influence of Debt on the Relations between Crown and Aristocracy in Seventeenth-Century Castile. *Econ. Hist. Rev., 2nd Ser.,* May 1973, *26*(2), pp. 218–36.

Jaguaribe, Helio. Foreign Technical Assistance and National Development. In *Thurber, C. E. and Graham, L. S., eds.,* 1973, pp. 109–29.

Jahoda, Marie. A Postscript on Social Change. In *Cole, H. S. D., et al., eds.,* 1973, pp. 209–15.

Jain, Anil Kumar. Appellate Machinery for Income-Tax in India. *Bull. Int. Fiscal Doc.,* April 1973, *27*(4), pp. 135–42.

———— Computation of Net Taxable Income for Assessment in India. *Bull. Int. Fiscal Doc.,* February 1973, *27*(2), pp. 47–58.

Jain, Arun K.; Green, Paul E. and Wind, Yoram. Analyzing Free-Response Data in Marketing Research. *J. Marketing Res.,* February 1973, *10*(1), pp. 45–52.

Jain, Chaman L. and Migliaro, Alfonso. Optimum Customer Investment Criteria in Mail Order Operation. *Rivista Int. Sci. Econ. Com.,* May 1973, *20*(5), pp. 470–78.

Jain, Tribhowan N. Alternative Methods of Accounting and Decision Making: A Psycho-linguistical Analysis. *Accounting Rev.,* January 1973, *48*(1), pp. 95–104.

Jain, Usha. India: A Review of Wealth Tax. *Bull. Int. Fiscal Doc.,* October 1973, *27*(10), pp. 421–28.

James, Denis W. and Gregory, R. G. Do New Factories Embody Best Practice Technology? *Econ. J.,* December 1973, *83*(332), pp. 1133–55.

James, Estelle and Neuberger, Egon. The Yugoslav Self-Managed Enterprise: A Systemic Approach. In *Bornstein, M., ed.,* 1973, pp. 245–84.

James, Franklin J., Jr. and Hughes, James W. The Process of Employment Location Change: An Empirical Analysis. *Land Econ.,* November 1973, *49*(4), pp. 404–13.

———— and Hughes, James W. A Test of Shift and Share Analysis as a Predictive Device. *J. Reg. Sci.,* August 1973, *13*(2), pp. 223–31.

James, H. Thomas. Perspectives on Internal Functioning of Foundations. In *Heimann, F. F., ed.,* 1973, pp. 192–215.

James, Louis J. The Stimulation and Substitution Effects of Grants-In-Aid: A General Equilibrium Analysis. *Nat. Tax J.,* June 1973, *26*(2), pp. 251–65.

James, William H. The Fecundability of U.S. Women. *Population Stud.,* November 1973, *27*(3), pp. 493–500.

Jamison, Dean T. and Lau, Lawrence J. Semiorders and the Theory of Choice. *Econometrica,* September 1973, *41*(5), pp. 901–12.

Janáček, K. Estimating the Aggregate Macroeconomic Consumption Function in Czechoslovakia. *Eastern Europ. Econ.,* Spring 1973, *11*(3), pp. 74–107.

Janowitz, Barbara S. An Econometric Analysis of Trends in Fertility Rates. *J. Devel. Stud.,* April 1973, *9*(3), pp. 413–25.

———— Cross-Section Studies as Predictors of Trends in Birth Rates: A Note on Ekanem's Results. *Demography,* August 1973, *10*(3), pp. 479–81.

———— The Effects of Demographic Factors on Age Composition and the Implications for Per Capita Income. *Demography,* November 1973, *10*(4), pp. 507–15.

Janowitz, Morris. The Social Demography of the All-Volunteer Armed Force. *Ann. Amer. Acad. Polit. Soc. Sci.,* March 1973, *406,* pp. 86–93.

Jansen, M. A. Problems of International Comparisons of National Accounting Aggregates Between Countries with Different Economic Systems. *Rev. Income Wealth,* March 1973, *19*(1), pp. 69–77.

Jansma, J. Dean and Kerns, Waldon R. Financial Need Priorities for Awarding Construction Grants-in-Aid. *Growth Change,* January 1973, *4*(1), pp. 17–24.

Jantorni, Joan M.; Gann, Robert R. and Clark, Robert A. Analysis of the Lease-or-Buy Decision: Comment. *J. Finance,* September 1973, *28*(4), pp. 1015–16.

de Janvry, Alain. A Socioeconomic Model of Induced Innovations for Argentine Agricultural Development. *Quart. J. Econ.,* August 1973, *87*(3), pp. 410–435.

Jao, Y. C. Tax Structure and Tax Burden in Taiwan. *Bull. Int. Fiscal Doc.,* March 1973, *27*(3), pp. 104–14.

Jarkovsky, Vladimír. The Dynamic Determination of Economically Efficient Capital Investment and New Technology. *Eastern Europ. Econ.,* Summer 1973, *11*(4), pp. 86–112.

Jarrett, Jeffrey E. An Abandonment Decision Model. *Eng. Econ.,* October-November 1973, *19*(1), pp. 35–46.

———— Finance and Investment: Refereed Papers I: Discussion. *J. Finance,* May 1973, *28*(2), pp. 404–05.

Jarvis, Lovell S. Un ejemplo del uso de modelos económicos para la construcción de datos no disponibles: la estimación de la existencia de vacunos desagregado en Argentina 1937–1967. (An Example of the Use of Economics Models for the Construction of Unavailable Data. The Appreciation of the Existence of Disaggregated Cattle in Argentina—1937–1967. With English summary.) *Económica,* January-April 1973, *19*(1), pp. 71–117.

Jasinowski, Jerry J. The Economics of Federal Subsidy Programs. In *Harriss, C. L., ed.*, 1973, pp. 3–17.

———— The Great Fiscal Unknown—Subsidies. *Amer. J. Econ. Soc.*, January 1973, *32*(1), pp. 1–16.

Jaspan, Norman. The $8 Billion Rip-off. *Manage. Account.*, June 1973, *54*(12), pp. 49–50.

Jastrow, Robert. The Purpose of the Lunar Landing. In *The Diebold Group, Inc.*, 1973, pp. 143–52.

Jaszi, George. A Framework for the Measurement of Economic and Social Performance: Comment. In *Moss, M., ed.*, 1973, pp. 84–99.

Jayatillake, K. S. E. and Hartley, H. O. Estimation for Linear Models with Unequal Variances. *J. Amer. Statist. Assoc.*, March 1973, *68*(341), pp. 189–92.

Jean, William H. More on Multidimensional Portfolio Analysis. *J. Financial Quant. Anal.*, June 1973, *8*(3), pp. 475–90.

Jedel, Michael Jay and Stamm, John H. The Battle over Jobs: An Appraisal of Recent Publications on the Employment Effects of U.S. Multinational Corporations. In *Kujawa, D., ed.*, 1973, pp. 144–91.

Jelavich, Mark S. Distributed Lag Estimation of Harmonic Motion in the Hog Market. *Amer. J. Agr. Econ.*, May 1973, *55*(2), pp. 223–24.

Jelliffe, Derrick B. Nutrition, National Development, and Planning: Summation. In *Berg, A.; Scrimshaw, N. S. and Call, D. L., eds.*, 1973, pp. 378–85.

Jencks, Clinton E.; Hardesty, John and Clement, Norris C. Ecological Conflicts: A Reply. *Rev. Radical Polit. Econ.*, Summer 1973, *5*(2), pp. 95–102.

Jenkins, Glenn P. The Measurement of Rates of Return and Taxation from Private Capital in Canada. In *Niskanen, W. A., et al., eds.*, 1973, pp. 211–45.

Jenkins, G. M. and Box, G. E. P. Some Comments on a Paper by Chatfield and Prothero and on a Review by Kendall. *J. Roy. Statist. Soc.*, Part 3 1973, *136*, pp. 337–52.

Jenkins, William L. Nonprofit Hospital Accounting System. *Manage. Account.*, June 1973, *54*(12), pp. 23–27.

Jennergren, L. Peter. An Optimal Sampling Policy for a Matched Sampling Problem. *J. Amer. Statist. Assoc.*, March 1973, *68*(341), pp. 148–50.

———— A Price Schedules Decomposition Algorithm for Linear Programming Problems. *Econometrica*, September 1973, *41*(5), pp. 965–80.

Jennings, Edward H. and Soldofsky, Robert M. Risk-Premium Curves: Empirical Evidence on Their Changing Position, 1950 to 1970. *Quart. Rev. Econ. Bus.*, Spring 1973, *13*(1), pp. 49–68.

Jensen, Daniel L. A Computer Experiment on Alternative Methods of Allocating Capacity Cost. *Quart. Rev. Econ. Bus.*, Summer 1973, *13*(2), pp. 21–31.

———— A Computer Model for the Generation of System and Component Load Curves. *Eng. Econ.*, July-August 1973, *18*(4), pp. 243–56.

———— Hartley's Demand-Price Analysis in a Case of Joint Production: A Comment. *Accounting Rev.*, October 1973, *48*(4), pp. 768–70.

Jensen, Robert G. Regional Pricing and the Eco-

nomic Evaluation of Land in Soviet Agriculture. In *Bandera, V. N. and Melnyk, Z. L., eds.*, 1973, pp. 305–27.

Jensen, Rodney C. Aspects of The Spatial Dimension in Economics. *Econ. Anal. Pol.*, March 1973, *4*(1), pp. 1–16.

———— and Metwally, Mohktar M. A Note on the Measurement of Regional Income Dispersion. *Econ. Develop. Cult. Change*, October 1973, *22* (1), pp. 135–36.

Jentz, Gaylord A. Federal Regulation of Advertising. In *Britt, S. H. and Boyd, H. W., Jr., eds.*, 1973, pp. 585–97.

———— Federal Regulation of Advertising. In *Murray, B. B., ed.*, 1973, pp. 328–40.

Jeremy, David J. British Textile Technology Transmission to the United States: The Philadelphia Region Experience, 1770-1820. *Bus. Hist. Rev.*, Spring 1973, *47*(1), pp. 24–52.

Jetha, Nizar. Some Aspects of Domestic Financing of Central Government Expenditure: The Case of Kenya. In *[Hicks, U.]*, 1973, pp. 95–139.

Jezek, Tomás and Dvorák, Jiri. Some Problems of Strain in the Manpower Balances. *Eastern Europ. Econ.*, Summer 1973, *11*(4), pp. 60–85.

Jha, L. K. Leaning Against Open Doors? Comment. In *Lewis, J. P. and Kapur, I., eds.*, 1973, pp. 97–101.

Jhabvala, Firdaus. A Model of Motivation in State Enterprises in Underdeveloped Economies. *Indian Econ. Rev.*, October 1973, *8*(2), pp. 172–85.

———— The Optimal Allocation of Resources in a Decentralized Model. *Eng. Econ.*, April-May 1973, *18*(3), pp. 169–89.

Jhunjhunwala, Bharat. Hypothetical Compensation: Is it Relevant? *Indian Econ. J.*, January-March 1973, *20*(3), pp. 445–51.

Jobert, Annette and Baraquin, Yves. Les immigrés: Réflexions sur leur insertion sociale et leur intégration juridique. (Immigrants: Their Social Insertion and Juridical Integration. With English summary.) *Consommation*, July-September 1973, *20*(3), pp. 83–97.

Joehnk, Michael D. and Nielsen, James F. Further Evidence on the Effects of Block Transactions on Stock Price Fluctuations. *Miss. Val. J. Bus. Econ.*, Winter 1973-74, *9*(2), pp. 27–34.

———— and Wert, James E. The Call-Risk Performance of the Discounted Seasoned Issue. *Miss. Val. J. Bus. Econ.*, Winter 1973-74, *9*(2), pp. 1–15.

Joelson, Mark R. Protective Legislation v. Our Competitive System: The Dilemma and the Role of the Trade Association. *Antitrust Bull.*, Summer 1973, *18*(2), pp. 255–70.

Joffe, Paul L. French Labor Relations: A Functional Analysis. *Yale Law J.*, March 1973, *82*(4), pp. 806–28.

Johansen, Leif. Targets and Instruments under Uncertainty. In *[Tinbergen, J.]*, 1973, pp. 3–20.

Johansson, B. O. Den nya GATT-rundan—en lösning av de handelspolitiska problemen. (The New GATT Negotiations—A Solution to the Commercial Policy Program? With English summary.) *Ekon. Samfundets Tidskr.*, 1973, *26*(3), pp. 167–76.

Johansson, Johny K. A Generalized Logistic Function with an Application to the Effect of Advertising. *J. Amer. Statist. Assoc.*, December 1973, *68* (344), pp. 824–27.

Johl, S. S. Green Revolution and What Next. *Econ. Aff.*, September-October 1973, *18*(9–10), pp. 405–13.

Johnpoll, Bernard K. Manuscript Sources in American Radicalism. *Labor Hist.*, Winter 1973, *14*(1), pp. 92–97.

Johns, B. L. Import Substitution and Export Potential—The Case of Manufacturing Industry in West Malaysia. *Australian Econ. Pap.*, December 1973, *12*(21), pp. 175–95.

Johnsen, Erik. Behavioral Science Models: Discussant 1. In *Ross, M., ed.*, 1973, pp. 265–67.

Johnson, A. S. C. Savings Banks and Savings Facilities in African Countries: Sierra Leone. In *Alberici, A. and Baravelli, M., eds.*, 1973, pp. 87–92.

Johnson, Björn and Meuller, Anders. Interactions of Consumption and Metropolitan Growth. *Swedish J. Econ.*, September 1973, *75*(3), pp. 278–88.

Johnson, David B. The Charity Market: Theory and Practice. In *Alchian, A. A., et al.*, 1973, pp. 79–106.

_____ Meade, Bees and Externalities. *J. Law Econ.*, April 1973, *16*(1), pp. 35–52.

_____ The US Market in Blood. In *Alchian, A. A., et al.*, 1973, pp. 157–67.

Johnson, David R.; Williams, J. Allen, Jr. and Beeson, Peter G. Some Factors Associated with Income Among Mexican Americans. *Soc. Sci. Quart.*, March 1973, *53*(4), pp. 710–15.

Johnson, D. Gale. Economics of Population: Discussion. *Amer. Econ. Rev.*, May 1973, *63*(2), pp. 88–89.

_____ Government and Agricultural Adjustment. *Amer. J. Agr. Econ.*, December 1973, *55*(5), pp. 860–67.

_____ The Impact of Freer Trade on North American Agriculture. *Amer. J. Agr. Econ.*, May 1973, *55*(2), pp. 294–99.

_____ What Difference Does Trade Make in World Community Welfare? In *Iowa State University Center for Agricultural and Rural Development*, 1973, pp. 49–68.

Johnson, Dudley D. Properties of Alternative Seasonal Adjustment Techniques: A Comment on the OMB Model. *J. Bus.*, April 1973, *46*(2), pp. 284–303.

Johnson, Elizabeth S. The Collected Writings of John Maynard Keynes: Some Visceral Reactions. In *Parkin, M., ed.*, 1973, pp. 216–27.

_____ John Maynard Keynes: Scientist or Politician? In *Robinson, J., ed.*, 1973, pp. 12–25.

_____ and Johnson, Harry G. Keynes, the Wider Band, and the Crawling Peg. *J. Money, Credit, Banking*, November 1973, *5*(4), pp. 988–89.

Johnson, Florence C. Changes in Workmen's Compensation Laws in 1972. *Mon. Lab. Rev.*, January 1973, *96*(1), pp. 45–49.

Johnson, George E. and Stafford, Frank P. Social Returns to Quantity and Quality of Schooling. *J. Human Res.*, Spring 1973, *8*(2), pp. 139–55.

Johnson, G. P. and Steiner, H. M. Evaluating Social Roads in Mexico. *J. Transp. Econ. Policy*, January 1973, *7*(1), pp. 98–101.

Johnson, Harold B., Jr. A Preliminary Inquiry into Money, Prices, and Wages in Rio de Janeiro, 1763–1823. In *Alden, D., ed.*, 1973, pp. 231–83.

Johnson, Harry G. The Economics of Student Protest. In *Johnson, H. G. and Weisbrod, B. A., eds.*, 1973, pp. 3–7.

_____ The Economics of Undertaking. In *Johnson, H. G. and Weisbrod, B. A., eds.*, 1973, pp. 35–39.

_____ Efficiency in International Money Supply. In *Johnson, H. G.*, 1973, pp. 271–76.

_____ The Exchange-Rate Question for a United Europe. In *Krauss, M. B., ed.*, 1973, pp. 201–14.

_____ The Glass Bead Game of Orthodox Economics: Comment. *Intermountain Econ. Rev.*, Spring 1973, *4*(1), pp. 72–73.

_____ Inflation: A 'Monetarist' View. In *Johnson, H. G.*, 1973, pp. 325–37.

_____ The International Monetary Crisis of 1971. In *Johnson, H. G.*, 1973, pp. 353–61.

_____ The International Monetary Crisis of 1971. *J. Bus.*, January 1973, *46*(1), pp. 11–23.

_____ International Trade and Economic Development. In *Streeten, P., ed.*, 1973, pp. 27–34.

_____ Keynes and the Keynesians. In *Johnson, H. G.*, 1973, pp. 70–76.

_____ The Monetary Approach to Balance-of-Payments Theory. In *Johnson, H. G.*, 1973, pp. 229–49.

_____ Monetary Theory and Monetary Policy. In *Johnson, H. G.*, 1973, pp. 77–87.

_____ Narrowing the Exchange Rate Bands. In *Krause, L. B. and Salant, W. S., eds.*, 1973, pp. 78–97.

_____ Notes on the Welfare Effects of a Reversed Transfer. *Osaka Econ. Pap.*, March 1973, *21*(38), pp. 45–52.

_____ Optimum Tariffs and Retaliation. In *Farrell, M. J., ed.*, 1973, pp. 115–27.

_____ The Panamanian Monetary System. In *Johnson, H. G.*, 1973, pp. 223–28.

_____ Problems of European Monetary Union. In *Johnson, H. G.*, 1973, pp. 312–24.

_____ Problems of European Monetary Union. In *Krauss, M. B., ed.*, 1973, pp. 188–200.

_____ Problems of Stabilization Policy in an Integrated World Economy. In *Johnson, H. G.*, 1973, pp. 338–52.

_____ Secular Inflation and the International Monetary System. *J. Money, Credit, Banking*, Part II, February 1973, *5*(1), pp. 509–19.

_____ Some Micro-Economic Reflections on Income and Wealth Inequalities. *Ann. Amer. Acad. Polit. Soc. Sci.*, September 1973, *409*, pp. 53–60.

_____ Trade, Investment and Labor, and the Changing International Division of Production. In *Hughes, H., ed.*, 1973, pp. 40–55.

_____ and Johnson, Elizabeth S. Keynes, the Wider Band, and the Crawling Peg. *J. Money, Credit, Banking*, November 1973, *5*(4), pp. 988–89.

_____ and McCulloch, Rachel. A Note on Proportionally Distributed Quotas. *Amer. Econ. Rev.*, September 1973, *63*(4), pp. 726–32.

_____; Skouras, Thanos and Krauss, Melvyn B. On the Shape and Location of the Production Possibility Curve. *Economica, N.S.*, August 1973, *40* (159), pp. 305–10.

Johnson, Harry M. The History of British and American Fire Marks: Reply. *J. Risk Ins.,* December 1973, *40*(4), pp. 641–42.

Johnson, Herbert E. Strategic Planning for Banks. *J. Bank Res.,* Summer 1973, *4*(2), pp. 79–83.

Johnson, Howard G. Key Item Control. In *Thomas, W. E., Jr., ed.,* 1973, pp. 296–305.

Johnson, Jerry D.; Adams, Curtis and Ramsett, David E. Some Evidence on the Value of Instructors in Teaching Economic Principles. *J. Econ. Educ.,* Fall 1973, *5*(1), pp. 57–62.

Johnson, J. Timothy; Tan Boon Ann and Corsa, Leslie. Assessment of Family Planning Programme Effects on Births: Preliminary Results Obtained through Direct Matching of Birth and Programme Acceptor Records. *Population Stud.,* March 1973, *27*(1), pp. 85–96.

Johnson, Keith B. and Hazuka, Thomas B. The NPV-IRR Debate in Lease Analysis. *Miss. Val. J. Bus. Econ.,* Winter 1973-74, *9*(2), pp. 16–26.

Johnson, K. H. and Lyon, H. L. Experimental Evidence on Combining Cross-Section and Time Series Information. *Rev. Econ. Statist.,* November 1973, *55*(4), pp. 465–74.

Johnson, Leland L. Behavior of the Firm Under Regulatory Constraint: A Reassessment. *Amer. Econ. Rev.,* May 1973, *63*(2), pp. 90–97.

Johnson, Lyndon B. The American Consumer. In *Murray, B. B., ed.,* 1973, pp. 60–67.

Johnson, M. Bruce and Brown, Gardner, Jr. Welfare-Maximizing Price and Output with Stochastic Demand: Reply. *Amer. Econ. Rev.,* March 1973, *63*(1), pp. 230–31.

Johnson, Nicholas. Economic Analysis and Regulatory Decisions. In *Haveman, R. H. and Hamrin, R. D., eds.,* 1973, pp. 261–66.

_____ **and Dystel, John J.** A Day in the Life: The Federal Communications Commission. *Yale Law J.,* July 1973, *82*(8), pp. 1575–1634.

Johnson, Phillip N. and Roy, Sujit K. Econometric Models for Quarterly Shell Egg Prices. *Amer. J. Agr. Econ.,* May 1973, *55*(2), pp. 209–13.

Johnson, Ramon E. Conglomerate Firms in Perspective: Comment. *Intermountain Econ. Rev.,* Fall 1973, *4*(2), pp. 67–69.

Johnson, Robert W. and Lewellen, Wilbur G. Analysis of the Lease-or-Buy Decision: Reply. *J. Finance,* September 1973, *28*(4), pp. 1024–28.

Johnson, Rodney D. and Klein, Richard H. A Further Note on the Analysis of Capital Investment Alternatives: Reply. *Miss. Val. J. Bus. Econ.,* Fall 1973, *9*(1), pp. 91–93.

_____ **and Meinster, David R.** An Analysis of Bank Holding Company Acquisitions: Some Methodological Issues. *J. Bank Res.,* Spring 1973, *4*(1), pp. 58–61.

Johnson, Stanley R.; Green, Richard and Hassan, Zuhair. Price and Income Flexibilities and the Double Logarithmic Demand System: Comment. *Amer. J. Agr. Econ.,* Part I, November 1973, *55*(4), pp. 678–79.

_____ **; Green, Richard and Hassan, Zuhair A.** An Alternative Method for Pricing Pork Carcasses. *Can. J. Agr. Econ.,* November 1973, *21*(3), pp. 1–5.

_____ **; Hassan, Zuhair A. and Finley, Robert M.** The Demand for Food in the United States. *Appl. Econ.,* December 1973, *5*(4), pp. 233–48.

_____ **and Smith, Paul E.** The Phillips Curve, Expectations, and Stability. *Quart. Rev. Econ. Bus.,* Autumn 1973, *13*(3), pp. 85–91.

Johnson, Thomas E., Jr. and Ault, David E. Probabilistic Models Applied to Hospital Planning. *Growth Change,* April 1973, *4*(2), pp. 7–13.

Johnson, Warren A. The Guaranteed Income as an Environmental Measure. In *Daly, H. E., ed.,* 1973, pp. 175–89.

Johnson, Willard R. Should the Poor Buy No Growth? In *Olson, M. and Landsberg, H. H., eds.,* 1973, pp. 165–89.

Johnston, Denis F. Education of Workers: Projections to 1990. *Mon. Lab. Rev.,* November 1973, *96*(11), pp. 22–31.

_____ Population and Labor Force Projections. *Mon. Lab. Rev.,* December 1973, *96*(12), pp. 8–17.

_____ The U.S. Labor Force: Projections to 1990. *Mon. Lab. Rev.,* July 1973, *96*(7), pp. 3–13.

Johnston, J. and Timbrell, M. Empirical Tests of a Bargaining Theory of Wage Rate Determination. *Manchester Sch. Econ. Soc. Stud.,* June 1973, *41*(2), pp. 141–67.

Johnston, Verle. Housing: On the Way Down? *Fed. Res. Bank San Francisco Rev.,* January-February 1973, pp. 3–8.

_____ **; Levy, Yvonne and Chen, Dean.** Boom in the West. *Fed. Res. Bank San Francisco Rev.,* May-June 1973, pp. 3–8.

Johnston, William B. and Levitan, Sar A. Job Redesign, Reform, Enrichment: Exploring the Limitations. *Mon. Lab. Rev.,* July 1973, *96*(7), pp. 35–41.

Jolly, Richard and Singer, Hans. Unemployment in an African Setting: Lessons of the Employment Strategy Mission to Kenya. *Int. Lab. Rev.,* February 1973, *107*(2), pp. 103–15.

Jolson, Marvin A. New Product Planning in an Age of Future Consciousness. *Calif. Manage. Rev.,* Fall 1973, *16*(1), pp. 25–33.

Jones, Charles O. Air Pollution and Contemporary Environmental Politics. *Growth Change,* July 1973, *4*(3), pp. 22–27.

Jones, Charles P.; Litzenberger, Robert H. and Joy, O. Maurice. Leverage and the Valuation of Risk Assets: An Empirical Test. *J. Financial Quant. Anal.,* March 1973, *8*(2), pp. 227.

_____ **and Poindexter, J. Carl, Jr.** The Effect of Recent Tax Policy Changes on Manufacturing Investment. *Quart. Rev. Econ. Bus.,* Winter 1973, *13*(4), pp. 79–88.

Jones, David E. and Miller, Paul B. Regional Growth and Industrial Change in Ohio: A Shift-Share Analysis. *Ohio State U. Bull. Bus. Res.,* July 1973, *48*(7), pp. 1–4, 8.

Jones, E. B. and Jackson, Mark. Unemployment and Occupational Wage Changes in Local Labor Markets. *Ind. Lab. Relat. Rev.,* July 1973, *26*(4), pp. 1135–45.

Jones, Edward W., Jr. What it's Like to be a Black Manager. *Harvard Bus. Rev.,* July-August 1973, *51*(4), pp. 108–16.

Jones, Eric L. The Fashion Manipulators: Consumer

Tastes and British Industries, 1660–1800. **In** *[Williamson, H. F.]*, 1973, pp. 198–226.

Jones, Ethel B. and Barnes, William F. Robbins, Hicks, Buchanan and the Backward Bending Labor Supply Curve. *Miss. Val. J. Bus. Econ.*, Fall 1973, *9*(1), pp. 76–82.

Jones, F. S. and Kubursi, A. A. A Programming Model of Government Expenditures. *Public Finance*, 1973, *28*(1), pp. 84–93.

Jones, G. R. J. Field Systems of North Wales. **In** *Baker, A. R. H. and Butlin, R. A., eds.,* 1973, pp. 430–79.

Jones, H. J. M.; Lawson, H. B. and Newman, D. Population Census: Some Recent British Developments in Methodology. *J. Roy. Statist. Soc.*, Part 4, 1973, *136*, pp. 505–20.

Jones, James W. Accounting Practices in Ship Chandlery. *Manage. Account.*, August 1973, *55*(2), pp. 28–30, 34.

Jones, J. C. H. and Laudadio, Leonard. Canadian Bank Mergers, the Public Interest and Public Policy. *Banca Naz. Lavoro Quart. Rev.*, June 1973, *105*, pp. 109–40.

———; **Laudadio, Leonard and Percy, M.** Market Structure and Profitability in Canadian Manufacturing Industry: Some Cross-Section Results. *Can. J. Econ.*, August 1973, *6*(3), pp. 356–68.

Jones, Ken. Employee Directors in Steel. **In** *Tivey, L., ed.,* 1973, pp. 298–302.

Jones, Lonnie L. and Mustafa, Gholam. RIMLOC: A Computer Algorithm for Regional Input-Output Analyses. *Ann. Econ. Soc. Measure,* July 1973, *2*(3), pp. 313–16.

Jones, Malcolm M. The FCC Inquiry and the Data Communications User. **In** *The Diebold Group, Inc.,* 1973, pp. 233–38.

Jones, Mary Gardiner. The Consumer Interest: The Role of Public Policy. *Calif. Manage. Rev.*, Fall 1973, *16*(1), pp. 17–24.

——— Social Responsibility: The Regulator's View. *Calif. Manage. Rev.*, Summer 1973, *15*(4), pp. 78–84.

Jones, P. M. S. The Use of Cost-benefit Analysis as an Aid to Allocating Government Resources for Research and Development. **In** *Wolfe, J. N., ed.,* 1973, pp. 155–81.

Jones, Reginald H. The Challenge of Capital Attraction. *Manage. Account.*, June 1973, *54*(12), pp. 52–53, 58.

Jones, S. R. H. Price Associations and Competition in the British Pin Industry, 1814–40. *Econ. Hist. Rev., 2nd Ser.*, May 1973, *26*(2), pp. 237–53.

Jonish, James E. and Kau, James B. Measures of Discrimination in Occupational and Income Levels. *Miss. Val. J. Bus. Econ.*, Spring 1973, *8*(3), pp. 59–70.

——— **and Kau, James B.** State Differentials in Income Inequality. *Rev. Soc. Econ.*, October 1973, *31*(2), pp. 179–90.

Jonson, P. D. Our Current Inflationary Experience. *Australian Econ. Rev.*, 2nd Quarter 1973, pp. 21–26.

——— **and Mahoney, D. M.** Price Expectations in Australia. *Econ. Rec.*, March 1973, *49*(125), pp. 50–61.

Jordan, Jerry L. FOMC Policy Actions in 1972. *Fed. Res. Bank St. Louis Rev.*, March 1973, *55*(3), pp. 10–24.

——— Interest Rates and Monetary Growth. *Fed. Res. Bank St. Louis Rev.*, January 1973, *55*(1), pp. 2–11.

Jordan, Ronald J. An Empirical Investigation of the Adjustment of Stock Prices to New Quarterly Earnings Information. *J. Financial Quant. Anal.*, September 1973, *8*(4), pp. 609–20.

Jöreskog, Karl G. A General Method for Estimating a Linear Structural Equation System. **In** *Goldberger, A. S. and Duncan, O. D., eds.,* 1973, pp. 85–112.

Jorgenson, Dale W. Technology and Decision Rules in the Theory of Investment Behavior. *Quart. J. Econ.*, November 1973, *87*(4), pp. 523–43.

——— **and Christensen, Laurits R.** Measuring Economic Performance in the Private Sector: Reply to Kendrick. **In** *Moss, M., ed.,* 1973, pp. 350–51.

——— **and Christensen, Laurits R.** Measuring Economic Performance in the Private Sector: Reply to Eisner. **In** *Moss, M., ed.,* 1973, pp. 349–50.

——— **and Christensen, Laurits R.** Measuring Economic Performance in the Private Sector. **In** *Moss, M., ed.,* 1973, pp. 233–338.

——— **and Christensen, Laurits R.** U.S. Income, Saving, and Wealth, 1929–1969. *Rev. Income Wealth*, December 1973, *19*(4), pp. 329–62.

———; **Lau, Lawrence J. and Christensen, Laurits R.** Transcendental Logarithmic Production Frontiers. *Rev. Econ. Statist.*, February 1973, *55*(1), pp. 28–45.

Joshi, Nandini U. Bank Credit Policy for Export Incentives. *Indian Econ. J.*, April-June 1973, *20* (4–5), pp. 638–45.

——— Estimating Future Unemployment of Graduates. *Bangladesh Econ. Rev.*, October 1973, *1*(4), pp. 409–24.

——— Validity of International Comparisons of Relationship between Economic Development and Human Resource Development. *Indian Econ. Rev.*, April 1973, *8*(1), pp. 90–92.

Joshi, N. D. Review of the Policy for the Development of Backward Regions in India. *Artha-Vikas*, January-July 1973, *9*(1–2), pp. 11–24.

Joshi, V. H. The Concept of Regional Analysis: Its Application to the Study of the Development of Backward Regions. *Artha-Vikas*, January-July 1973, *9*(1–2), pp. 64–68.

Joskow, Paul L. Cartels, Competition and Regulation in the Property-Liability Insurance Industry. *Bell J. Econ. Manage. Sci.*, Autumn 1973, *4*(2), pp. 375–427.

——— Pricing Decisions of Regulated Firms: A Behavioral Approach. *Bell J. Econ. Manage. Sci.*, Spring 1973, *4*(1), pp. 118–40.

——— **and McKelvey, Edward F.** The Fogel-Engerman Iron Model: A Clarifying Note. *J. Polit. Econ.*, September-October 1973, *81*(5), pp. 1236–40.

Josling, Tim. The Common Agricultural Policy of the European Economic Community. **In** *Krauss, M. B., ed.,* 1973, pp. 267–96.

——— Domestic Farm Policies and International Trade in Agricultural Goods. **In** *Streeten, P., ed.,* 1973, pp. 264–78.

Joxe, Alain. Is the 'Chilean Road to Socialism'

Blocked? In *Zammit, J. A., ed.*, 1973, pp. 223–36.

Joy, Leonard. Nutrition Intervention Programs: Identification and Selection. In *Berg, A.; Scrimshaw, N. S. and Call, D. L., eds.*, 1973, pp. 198–206.

Joy, O. Maurice and Bradley, Jerry O. A Note on Sensitivity Analysis of Rates of Return. *J. Finance,* December 1973, *28*(5), pp. 1255–61.

_____; **Jones, Charles P. and Litzenberger, Robert H.** Leverage and the Valuation of Risk Assets: An Empirical Test. *J. Financial Quant. Anal.,* March 1973, *8*(2), pp. 227.

_____ **and Litzenberger, Robert H.** Inter-Industry Profitability Under Uncertainty. *Western Econ. J.,* September 1973, *11*(3), pp. 338–49.

Joyce, Jon M. Cost of Capital and Inventory Investment: Further Evidence. *Southern Econ. J.,* October 1973, *40*(2), pp. 323–29.

Juba, Bruce and Uselding, Paul. Biased Technical Progress in American Manufacturing, 1839–1899. *Exploration Econ. Hist.,* Fall 1973, *11*(1), pp. 55–72.

Judelson, David N. and Geneen, Harold S. Additional Data on ITT and Gulf and Western. In *Andreano, R. L., ed.*, 1973, pp. R331–42.

Judge, G. G.; Bock, M. E. and Yancey, T. A. The Statistical Consequences of Preliminary Test Estimators in Regression. *J. Amer. Statist. Assoc.,* March 1973, *68*(341), pp. 109–16.

_____; **Bock, M. E. and Yancey, T. A.** Wallace's Weak Mean Square Error Criterion for Testing Linear Restrictions in Regression: A Tighter Bound. *Econometrica,* November 1973, *41*(6), pp. 1203–06.

_____; **Havlicek, J. and Rizek, R. L.** A Spatial Analysis of the U.S. Livestock Economy. In *Judge, G. G. and Takayama, T., eds.*, 1973, pp. 261–73.

_____; **Yancey, T. A. and Bock, M. E.** Properties of Estimators After Preliminary Tests of Significance When Stochastic Restrictions Are Used in Regression. *J. Econometrics,* March 1973, *1*(1), pp. 29–47.

_____; **Yancey, T. A. and Bock, M. E.** Some Comments on Estimation in Regression After Preliminary Tests of Significance. *J. Econometrics,* June 1973, *1*(2), pp. 191–200.

Juhár, Z. Commodity Trade in Consumer Goods. In *Kiss, T., ed.*, 1973, pp. 149–73.

Juhasz, Joseph B.; Contini, Bruno and Hughes, G. David. The Influence of Personality on the Bargaining Process. *J. Bus.,* October 1973, *46*(4), pp. 593–604.

Jul, Anna Maria; Clark, Peter B. and Foxley, Alejandro. Project Evaluation within a Macroeconomic Framework. In *Eckaus, R. S. and Rosenstein-Rodan, P. N., eds.*, 1973, pp. 199–226.

Jul, Mogens. Importance of Project Preparation and Evaluation. In *Berg, A.; Scrimshaw, N. S. and Call, D. L., eds.*, 1973, pp. 210–12.

Julien, P.-A. and Freeman, Christopher. The Capital and Industrial Output Sub-system. In *Cole, H. S. D., et al., eds.*, 1973, pp. 66–79.

Junankar, P. N. Analytics of Choice in Fiscal Policy: Discussion. In *Parkin, M., ed.*, 1973, pp. 369–70.

Junz, Helen B. and Rhomberg, Rudolf R. Price Competitiveness in Export Trade Among Industrial Countries. *Amer. Econ. Rev.,* May 1973, *63*(2), pp. 412–18.

Jürgensen, Harald. Problems of Investment Planning in the Transport Field. *Ger. Econ. Rev.,* 1973, *11*(1), pp. 1–13.

Juricek, Libuska. Games with Coalitions. In *Blaquière, A., ed.*, 1973, pp. 311–44.

_____; **Wiese, Karl E. and Blaquière, Austin.** Geometry of Pareto Equilibria in N-Person Differential Games. In *Blaquière, A., ed.*, 1973, pp. 271–310.

Just, Richard E. A Methodology for Investigating the Importance of Government Intervention in Farmers' Decisions. *Amer. J. Agr. Econ.,* August 1973, *55*(3), pp. 441–52.

Juster, F. Thomas. A Framework for the Measurement of Economic and Social Performance. In *Moss, M., ed.*, 1973, pp. 25–84.

_____ A Framework for the Measurement of Economic and Social Performance: Reply. In *Moss, M., ed.*, 1973, pp. 105–09.

Jüttner, D. Johannes and Conrad, Klaus. Recent Behaviour of Stock Market Prices in Germany and the Random Walk Hypothesis. *Kyklos,* 1973, *26*(3), pp. 576–99.

Kaatz, John R. and Tarpley, Fred A., Jr. Economies of Scale and Holding Company Affiliation in Banking: Comment. *Southern Econ. J.,* July 1973, *40*(1), pp. 140.

Kádár, B. Small-Sized Developing Countries in the Regional Arrangements. *Acta Oecon.,* 1973, *10*(2), pp. 217–31.

Kafka, Alexandre. Adjustment Under the Bretton Woods Code with Special Reference to the Less Developed Countries. In *[Rosenstein-Rodan, P.],* 1973, pp. 210–38.

_____ Optimum Currency Areas and Latin America. In *Johnson, H. G. and Swoboda, A. K., eds.*, 1973, pp. 210–18.

Kagel, John H.; Basmann, R. L. and Battalio, Raymond C. Comment on R. P. Byron's "The Restricted Aitken Estimation of Sets of Demand Relations." *Econometrica,* March 1973, *41*(2), pp. 365–70.

_____; **Battalio, Raymond C. and Hulett, Joe R.** A Comment on J. J. Siegfried's "The Publishing of Economic Papers and Its Impact on Graduate Faculty Ratings, 1960-1969." *J. Econ. Lit.,* March 1973, *11*(1), pp. 68–70.

Kahan, Arcadius. Notes on Serfdom in Western and Eastern Europe. *J. Econ. Hist.,* March 1973, *33*(1), pp. 86–99.

Kahn, C. Harry. The Place of Consumption and Net-Worth Taxation in the Federal Tax Structure. In *Musgrave, R. A., ed.*, 1973, pp. 133–54.

Kahn, Dilawar A. and Kahn, Mahmood A. Rural Development Strategy and Need for Institution Building at Village Level. *Pakistan Econ. Soc. Rev.,* Winter 1973, *11*(4), pp. 383–402.

Kahn, Mahmood A. and Kahn, Dilawar A. Rural Development Strategy and Need for Institution Building at Village Level. *Pakistan Econ. Soc. Rev.,* Winter 1973, *11*(4), pp. 383–402.

Kahn, Richard F. [Lord]. The International Monetary System. *Amer. Econ. Rev.,* May 1973, *63*(2), pp. 181–88.

_____ SDRs and Aid. *Lloyds Bank Rev.*, October 1973, (110), pp. 1–18.

Kähr, Walter. Die Entwicklung des Energieverbrauchs der Schweiz im Zeitraum 1950 bis 1970 und Vorschau auf das Jahr 2000. (The Development of the Energy Consumption in the Period 1950–1970, with a Forecast for the Year 2000. With English summary.) *Schweiz. Z. Volkswirtsch. Statist.*, September 1973, *109*(3), pp. 385–410.

Kain, John F. Effect of Housing Market Segregation on Urban Development. In *Pynoos, J.; Schafer, R. and Hartman, C. W., eds.*, 1973, pp. 251–66.

_____ and Ingram, Gregory K. A Simple Model of Housing Production and the Abandonment Problem. *Amer. Real Estate Urban Econ. Assoc. J.*, June 1973, *1*(1), pp. 79–106.

_____ and Meyer, John R. Transportation and Poverty. In *Grieson, R. E., ed.*, 1973, pp. 323–35.

_____; Wohl, Martin and Meyer, John R. Economic Change and the City: A Qualitative Evaluation and Some Hypotheses. In *Grieson, R. E., ed.*, 1973, pp. 55–72.

Kaiser, Henry F. and Stefansky, Wilhelmine. Note on Discrete Approximations. *J. Amer. Statist. Assoc.*, March 1973, *68*(341), pp. 232–34.

Kaiyama, Michihiro. On the Growth Model of a Dual Economy. (In Japanese. With English summary.) *Econ. Stud. Quart.*, December 1973, *24*(3), pp. 1–15.

Kakwani, N. C. and Podder, N. On the Estimation of Lorenz Curves from Grouped Observations. *Int. Econ. Rev.*, June 1973, *14*(2), pp. 278–92.

Kalachek, Edward D. Ghetto Dwellers, Transportation and Employment. In *Rasmussen, D. W. and Haworth, C. T., eds.*, 1973, pp. 72–80.

Kalchbrenner, John H. A Summary of the Current Financial Intermediary, Mortgage, and Housing Sectors of the FRB-MIT-Penn Econometric Model. In *Ricks, R. B., ed.*, 1973, pp. 93–124.

Kale, J. D. Attracting Industries to Backward Areas. *Artha-Vikas*, January-July 1973, *9*(1–2), pp. 245–48.

Kalish, Lionel, III and Gilbert, R. Alton. An Analysis of Efficiency of Scale and Organizational Form in Commercial Banking. *J. Ind. Econ.*, July 1973, *21*(3), pp. 293–307.

_____ and Gilbert, R. Alton. The Influence of Bank Regulation of the Operating Efficiency of Commercial Banks. *J. Finance*, December 1973, *28*(5), pp. 1287–1301.

Kaliski, S. F. and Smith, D. C. Inflation, Unemployment and Incomes Policy. *Can. J. Econ.*, November 1973, *6*(4), pp. 574–91.

Kall, Peter. Planning under Uncertainty: Discussant 1. In *Ross, M., ed.*, 1973, pp. 123–26.

Kalman, Peter J. and Intriligator, Michael D. Generalized Comparative Statics with Applications to Consumer Theory and Producer Theory. *Int. Econ. Rev.*, June 1973, *14*(2), pp. 473–86.

Kalyanasundaram, R. Regulation of Chit Funds. In *Simha, S. L. N., ed.*, 1973, pp. 279–83.

Kamarck, Andrew M. Climate and Economic Development. *Finance Develop.*, June 1973, *10*(2), pp. 2–8.

Kamau, C. M. Localising Capitalism: The Kenya Experience. In *Ghai, D., ed.*, 1973, pp. 153–75.

Kamerschen, David R. Further Thoughts on Separation of Ownership and Control. *Rivista Int. Sci. Econ. Com.*, February 1973, *20*(2), pp. 179–83.

_____ A Reaffirmation of Marginal Productivity Theory. *Rivista Int. Sci. Econ. Com.*, March 1973, *20*(3), pp. 286–90.

Kamien, Morton I. and Schwartz, Nancy L. Payment Plans and the Efficient Delivery of Health Care Services. *J. Risk Ins.*, September 1973, *40*(3), pp. 427–36.

_____; Schwartz, Nancy L. and Roberts, Donald John. Exclusion, Externalities, and Public Goods. *J. Public Econ.*, July 1973, *2*(3), pp. 217–30.

Kaminow, Ira and Rao, D. C. Selective Credit Controls and the Real Investment Mix: A General Equilibrium Approach. *J. Finance*, December 1973, *28*(5), pp. 1103–18.

Kamoike, Osamu. Portfolio Selection when Future Prices of Consumption Goods May Change: Comment. *J. Finance*, December 1973, *28*(5), pp. 1357–60.

_____ and Sakashita, Noboru. National Growth and Regional Income Inequality: A Consistent Model. *Int. Econ. Rev.*, June 1973, *14*(2), pp. 372–82.

Kamulegeya, Edric Spencer. Savings Banks and Savings Facilities in African Countries: Uganda. In *Alberici, A. and Baravelli, M., eds.*, 1973, pp. 121–24.

Kanakasabai, R. Role of the Co-operative Banks in the Rural Sector. In *Simha, S. L. N., ed.*, 1973, pp. 85–91.

Kanamori, Hisao. Il Giappone e l'Europa: Un'analisi economica. (Japan and Europe: An Economic Analysis. With English summary.) *Mondo Aperto*, April 1973, *27*(2), pp. 122–26.

Kane, Edward J. The Central Bank as Big Brother: Comment. *J. Money, Credit, Banking*, November 1973, *5*(4), pp. 979–81.

_____ Monetary and Fiscal Influence on U.S. Money Income, 1891–1970: Comment. *J. Money, Credit, Banking*, Part II, February 1973, *5*(1), pp. 301–03.

_____ Politics and the Prime Rate: A Deceptive Solution. *Ohio State U. Bull. Bus. Res.*, June 1973, *48*(6), pp. 1–3, 5.

_____ Proposals for Rechanneling Funds to Meet Social Priorities: Discussion. In *Federal Reserve Bank of Boston*, 1973, pp. 190–98.

_____ Simulations of Stabilization Policies for 1966–1970 *and* A Comparison of Stabilization Policies: 1966–67 and 1969–70: Comment. *J. Money, Credit, Banking*, Part I, February 1973, *5*(1), pp. 39–42.

Kane, Julius; Vertinsky, Ilan and Thomson, William. KSIM: A Methodology for Interactive Resource Policy Simulation. *Water Resources Res.*, February 1973, *9*(1), pp. 65–79.

Kane, N. Stephen. Bankers and Diplomats: The Diplomacy of the Dollar in Mexico, 1921–1924. *Bus. Hist. Rev.*, Autumn 1973, *47*(3), pp. 335–52.

Kanet, Roger. Handbook of Soviet Social Science Data: International Interactions. In *Mickiewicz, E., ed.*, 1973, pp. 197–225.

Kangayappan, Kumar. Some Policy Issues in Mitigating Poverty in India. *Land Econ.*, February 1973, *49*(1), pp. 76–81.

Kansara, T. D. Reorganisation of the Banking System in India. In *Simha, S. L. N., ed.*, 1973, pp. 155–82.

Kao, Charles H. C. and Lee, Jae Won. An Empirical Analysis of China's Brain Drain into the United States. *Econ. Develop. Cult. Change*, April 1973, *21*(3), pp. 500–13.

Kaplan, G. A. Some Problems of Control by Minimum Mean-Square Deviation from Goals. *Matekon*, Summer 1973, *9*(4), pp. 3–9.

Kaplan, H. Roy. How *Do* Workers View Their Work in America? *Mon. Lab. Rev.*, June 1973, *96*(6), pp. 46–48.

Kaplan, Marshall and Eichler, Edward. New Communities. In *Pynoos, J.; Schafer, R. and Hartman, C. W., eds.*, 1973, pp. 523–31.

Kaplan, Robert S. Statistical Sampling in Auditing with Auxiliary Information Estimators. *J. Acc. Res.*, Autumn 1973, *11*(2), pp. 238–58.

—— Variable and Self-Service Costs in Reciprocal Allocation Models. *Accounting Rev.*, October 1973, *48*(4), pp. 738–48.

Kaplinsky, Raphael and Rifkin, Susan B. Health Strategy and Development Planning: Lessons from the People's Republic of China. *J. Devel. Stud.*, January 1973, *9*(2), pp. 213–32.

Kapoor, Ashok. The Negotiation Era and the Multinational Enterprise. In *Fayerweather, J., ed.*, 1973, pp. 85–93.

—— **and Fayerweather, John.** Simulated International Business Negotiations. In *Alexandrides, C. G., ed.*, 1973, pp. 5–18.

Kapteyn, Arie and van Praag, Bernard M. S. Further Evidence on the Individual Welfare Function of Income: An Empirical Investigation in The Netherlands. *Europ. Econ. Rev.*, April 1973, *4*(1), pp. 33–62.

Kapur, Basant K. Professor McKinnon's Model of Foreign Exchange Constraints in Economic Development: A Note. *Econ. J.*, March 1973, *83*(329), pp. 221–34.

Kapur, Ishan and Lewis, John P. The World Bank Group, Multilateral Aid, and the 1970s. In *Lewis, J. P. and Kapur, I., eds.*, 1973, pp. 1–11.

Karageorgas, Dionysios. The Distribution of Tax Burden by Income Groups in Greece. *Econ. J.*, June 1973, *83*(330), pp. 436–48.

—— Taxation of Foreign Firms: Discriminative and Allocative Effects. *Public Finance Quart.*, July 1973, *1*(3), pp. 239–65.

Karani, Hiram. Savings Banks and Savings Facilities in African Countries: Kenya. In *Alberici, A. and Baravelli, M., eds.*, 1973, pp. 41–43.

Karcz, Jerzy F. Agricultural Reform in Eastern Europe. In *Bornstein, M., ed.*, 1973, pp. 207–43.

Kareken, John H.; Muench, Thomas and Wallace, Neil. Optimal Open Market Strategy: The Use of Information Variables. *Amer. Econ. Rev.*, March 1973, *63*(1), pp. 156–72.

Kariel, Herbert G. and Vaselenak, Michael J. Waves of Spatial Diffusion Reconsidered: Comment. *J. Reg. Sci.*, August 1973, *13*(2), pp. 291–95.

Karlik, John. Trade, Investment and Labor, and the Changing International Division of Production: Comment. In *Hughes, H., ed.*, 1973, pp. 56–61.

Karni, Edi. Transactions Costs and the Demand for Media of Exchange. *Western Econ. J.*, March 1973, *11*(1), pp. 71–80.

—— The Transactions Demand for Cash: Incorporation of the Value of Time into the Inventory Approach. *J. Polit. Econ.*, September-October 1973, *81*(5), pp. 1216–25.

—— **and Darby, Michael R.** Free Competition and the Optimal Amount of Fraud. *J. Law Econ.*, April 1973, *16*(1), pp. 67–88.

Karsten, Siegfried G. Dialetics and the Evolution of Economic Thought. *Hist. Polit. Econ.*, Fall 1973, *5*(2), pp. 399–419.

Kaslow, Florence. Evolution of Theory and Policy on Inner City Delinquency. *Growth Change*, October 1973, *4*(4), pp. 29–37.

Kasnacich, Johannes. Le più importanti prospettive macro-economiche del mondo attuale. (The Main Macro-Economic Perspectives of World Development. With English summary.) *Mondo Aperto*, February 1973, *27*(1), pp. 1–8.

Kasper, H. Measuring the Labour Market Costs of Housing Dislocation. *Scot. J. Polit. Econ.*, June 1973, *20*(2), pp. 85–106.

Kass, Roy. A Functional Classification of Metropolitan Communities. *Demography*, August 1973, *10*(3), pp. 427–45.

Kassarjian, Harold H. and Bieda, John C. An Overview of Market Segmentation. In *Britt, S. H. and Boyd, H. W., Jr., eds.*, 1973, pp. 209–17.

Kassirov, L. Rent Relationships in the Economic Mechanism of Social Production. *Prob. Econ.*, November 1973, *16*(7), pp. 36–58.

Kasten, Richard A. and Hall, Robert E. The Relative Occupational Success of Blacks and Whites. *Brookings Pap. Econ. Act.*, 1973, (3), pp. 781–95.

Katano, Hikoji. Estimation of Investment Allocation Ratios of Japanese Economy: 1960–1969. *Kobe Econ. Bus. Rev.*, 1973, *20*, pp. 37–50.

Katona, George. Cognitive Processes in Learning: Reactions to Inflation and Change in Taxes. In *Mandell, L., et al., eds.*, 1973, pp. 183–203.

——; **Strumpel, Burkhard and Zahn, E.** The Sociocultural Environment. In *Thorelli, H. B., ed.*, 1973, pp. 135–45.

Katouzian, M. A. A Two-Sector Model of Population, Growth and Economic Development (1). *Tahq. Eq.*, Summer & Autumn 1973, *10*(31&32), pp. 60–79.

Katrak, Homi. Commodity Concentration and Export Fluctuations: A Probability Analysis. *J. Devel. Stud.*, July 1973, *9*(4), pp. 556–65.

—— Human Skills, R and D and Scale Economies in the Exports of the United Kingdom and the United States. *Oxford Econ. Pap.*, November 1973, *25*(3), pp. 337–60.

Katsenelinboigen, A. I. On the Various Methods of Describing the Socialist Economy. *Matekon*, Winter 1973-74, *10*(2), pp. 3–25.

Katz, Arnold. Teenage Employment Effects of State Minimum Wages. *J. Human Res.*, Spring 1973, *8*(2), pp. 250–56.

Katz, David A. Faculty Salaries, Promotion, and Productivity at a Large University. *Amer. Econ. Rev.*, June 1973, *63*(3), pp. 469–77.

Katz, Jorge M. Industrial Growth, Royalty Payments and Local Expenditure on Research and Development. In *Urquidi, V. L. and Thorp, R., eds.*, 1973, pp. 197–224.

Katz, Sidney, et al. Measuring the Health Status of

Populations. In *Berg, R. L., ed.*, 1973, pp. 39–51.

Katzir, I.; Zusman, P. and Melamed, A. A Spatial Analysis of the EEC Trade Policies in the Market for Winter Oranges. In *Judge, G. G. and Takayama, T., eds.*, 1973, pp. 464–87.

Kau, James B. and Jonish, James E. Measures of Discrimination in Occupational and Income Levels. *Miss. Val. J. Bus. Econ.*, Spring 1973, *8*(3), pp. 59–70.

——— **and Jonish, James E.** State Differentials in Income Inequality. *Rev. Soc. Econ.*, October 1973, *31*(2), pp. 179–90.

Kau, Paul and Hill, Lowell D. Application of Multivariate Probit to a Threshold Model of Grain Dryer Purchasing Decisions. *Amer. J. Agr. Econ.*, February 1973, *55*(1), pp. 19–27.

Kau, Randall K. C. and Schler, Michael L. Inflation and the Federal Income Tax. *Yale Law J.*, March 1973, *82*(4), pp. 716–44.

Kaufman, George G. The Questionable Benefit of Variable-Rate Mortgages. *Quart. Rev. Econ. Bus.*, Autumn 1973, *13*(3), pp. 43–52.

——— **and Hopewell, Michael H.** Bond Price Volatility and Term to Maturity: A Generalized Respecification. *Amer. Econ. Rev.*, September 1973, *63*(4), pp. 749–53.

Kaufman, G. M. and King, Benjamin. A Bayesian Analysis of Nonresponse in Dichotomous Processes. *J. Amer. Statist. Assoc.*, September 1973, *68* (343), pp. 670–78.

Kaufman, Herbert M. An Examination of the Financing of Federal Home Loan Bank Advances: A Comment. *Rev. Econ. Statist.*, May 1973, *55*(2), pp. 257–58.

Kaufman, Richard F. A Profile of the Military-Industrial Complex. In *Haveman, R. H. and Hamrin, R. D., eds.*, 1973, pp. 135–44.

Kaufman, Sol and Terhune, Kenneth W. The Family Size Utility Function. *Demography*, November 1973, *10*(4), pp. 599–618.

Kaufmann, Hugo M. International Liquidity and Balance-of-Payments Adjustments: A Reinterpretation. *Econ. Int.*, August-November 1973, *26* (3–4), pp. 592–602.

Kaur, Surinderjit and Tagat, R. G. India's Green Revolution: Socio-Economic and Political Implications. *Econ. Aff.*, September-October 1973, *18*(9–10), pp. 414–27, 433.

Kaushil, S. The Case of Adam Smith's Value Analysis. *Oxford Econ. Pap.*, March 1973, *25*(1), pp. 60–71.

Kavran, Dragoljub and Glueck, William F. The Yugoslav Management System. In *Henley, D. S., ed.*, 1973, pp. 375–89.

Kawada, Hisashi and Komatsu, Ryuji. Post-War Labor Movements in Japan. In *Sturmthal, A. and Scoville, J. G., eds.*, 1973, pp. 123–48.

Kawata, Fukuo. An Analysis of the Brazilian Balance of Payments, 1960–1972. *Kobe Econ. Bus. Rev.*, 1973, *20*, pp. 1–21.

Kay, Harry. The Effect of Technology in Educational Structure. In *Edge, D. O. and Wolfe, J. N., eds.*, 1973, pp. 143–57.

Kay, John and Coker, David. The Fund Meeting. *Finance Develop.*, December 1973, *10*(4), pp. 37–40.

Kaye, Seymour P. Summary of Comparative Public Policies and Procedures. In *Kaye, S. P. and Marsh, A., eds.*, 1973, pp. 300–321.

——— **and Anderson, Arvid.** International Manual on Collective Bargaining for Public Employees: The United States. In *Kaye, S. P. and Marsh, A., eds.*, 1973, pp. 3–66.

Kaye, William G. Take in a New Partner—The Consumer. In *Murray, B. B., ed.*, 1973, pp. 243–48.

Kayode, M. O. The Management of Trade Union Finances in Nigeria. In *Damachi, U. G. and Seibel, H. D., eds.*, 1973, pp. 138–46.

Kazakevich, L. and Shishankov, V. Economic Collaboration Between the USSR and the Socialist Countries. *Prob. Econ.*, October 1973, *16*(6), pp. 72–92.

Kazakova, M. F. A "Branches-Bounds" Type Method for the Generalized Knapsack Problem. *Matekon*, Spring 1973, *9*(3), pp. 47–54.

Kazmann, Raphael G. Democratic Organization: A Preliminary Mathematical Model. *Public Choice*, Fall 1973, *16*, pp. 17–26.

Kazmi, Aqdas Ali. Cobb-Douglas Production Function: A Reply. *Pakistan Econ. Soc. Rev.*, Summer 1973, *11*(2), pp. 227–29.

——— Education and Supply of Manpower in Pakistan. *Pakistan Econ. Soc. Rev.*, Spring 1973, *11*(1), pp. 125–39.

Kearney, Michael J.; Mehaffey, Bruce J. and Heeler, Roger M. Modeling Supermarket Product Selection. *J. Marketing Res.*, February 1973, *10*(1), pp. 34–37.

Keegan, Warren J. Multinational Marketing Control. In *Alexandrides, C. G., ed.*, 1973, pp. 243–60.

Keegan, W. J. Five Strategies for Multinational Marketing. In *Thorelli, H. B., ed.*, 1973, pp. 195–203.

——— Headquarters Involvement in Multinational Marketing. In *Thorelli, H. B., ed.*, 1973, pp. 283–89.

Keen, E. A. Limited Entry: The Case of the Japanese Tuna Fishery. In *Sokoloski, A. A., ed.*, 1973, pp. 146–58.

Keen, Howard, Jr. Pennsylvania's Economy: Cyclically Sensitive and Secularly Sluggish. *Fed. Res. Bank Bus. Rev. Phila.*, August 1973, pp. 10–13.

——— Urban Family Budgets: The Philadelphia Scene. *Fed. Res. Bank Bus. Rev. Phila.*, September 1973, pp. 12–15.

Keeney, Ralph L. Concepts of Independence in Multiattribute Utility Theory. In *Cochrane, J. L. and Zeleny, M., eds.*, 1973, pp. 62–71.

——— A Decision Analysis with Multiple Objectives: the Mexico City Airport. *Bell J. Econ. Manage. Sci.*, Spring 1973, *4*(1), pp. 101–17.

——— Risk Independence and Multiattributed Utility Functions. *Econometrica*, January 1973, *41* (1), pp. 27–34.

Keesing, Donald B. and Manne, Alan S. Manpower Projections. In *Goreux, L. M. and Manne, A. S., eds.*, 1973, pp. 55–83.

Keeton, Robert E. Beyond Current Reforms in Automobile Reparations. *J. Risk Ins.*, March 1973, *40* (1), pp. 31–37.

Keeton, W. R. and Seevers, G. L. Interrelationships between the Levels of U.S. Exports and Imports.

In *Iowa State University Center for Agricultural and Rural Development*, 1973, pp. 111–21.

Kehal, H. S. Role of Land Reforms in Punjab's Agricultural Development. *Econ. Aff.,* September-October 1973, *18*(9–10), pp. 434–38, 454.

Kehrberg, Earl W. and Patrick, George F. Costs and Returns of Education in Five Agricultural Areas of Eastern Brazil. *Amer. J. Agr. Econ.,* May 1973, *55*(2), pp. 145–53.

Keiding, Hans. Equilibrium in Economies with Non-Marketed Goods. *Swedish J. Econ.,* December 1973, *75*(4), pp. 349–61.

Kelejian, Harry H. Information Lost in Aggregation: A Bayesian Approach—A Further Note. *Econometrica,* March 1973, *41*(2), pp. 375.

——— **and Bradford, David F.** An Econometric Model of the Flight to the Suburbs. *J. Polit. Econ.,* May-June 1973, *81*(3), pp. 566–89.

Keller, I. Wayne. Concepts, Standards, and Rules. *Manage. Account.,* May 1973, *54*(11), pp. 13–15, 25.

Keller, Robert R. Estimates of National Income and Product, 1919–1941: The Best of All Possible Worlds. *Exploration Econ. Hist.,* Fall 1973, *11*(1), pp. 87–88.

——— Factor Income Distribution in the United States during the 1920's: A Reexamination of Fact and Theory. *J. Econ. Hist.,* March 1973, *33*(1), pp. 252–73.

Keller, Suzanne. The Future Role of Women. *Ann. Amer. Acad. Polit. Soc. Sci.,* July 1973, *408,* pp. 1–12.

Kelley, Allen C. Individualizing Education through the Use of Technology in Higher Education. *J. Econ. Educ.,* Spring 1973, *4*(2), pp. 77–89.

——— Population Growth, the Dependency Rate, and the Pace of Economic Development. *Population Stud.,* November 1973, *27*(3), pp. 405–14.

——— Relative Economic Status and the American Fertility Swing: Response. In *Sheldon, E. B., ed.,* 1973, pp. 224–27.

——— **and Williamson, Jeffrey G.** Modeling Economic Development and General Equilibrium Histories. *Amer. Econ. Rev.,* May 1973, *63*(2), pp. 450–58.

——— **and Williamson, Jeffrey G.** Sources of Growth Methodology in Low-Income Countries: A Critique. *Quart. J. Econ.,* February 1973, *87*(1), pp. 138–47.

Kellog, Martin N. Analysis and Control of a Cash Flow System. In *Thomas, W. E., Jr., ed.,* 1973, pp. 420–27.

Kelly, Terence F. The Creation of Longitudinal Data from Cross-Section Surveys: An Illustration from the Current Population Survey. *Ann. Econ. Soc. Measure,* April 1973, *2*(2), pp. 209–14.

Kemmerer, Donald L. The Role of Gold in the Past Century. In *Wiegand, G. C., ed.,* 1973, pp. 3–13.

Kemp, Murray C. Heterogeneous Capital Goods and Long-Run Stolper-Samuelson Theorems. *Australian Econ. Pap.,* December 1973, *12*(21), pp. 253–60.

——— Trade Gains in a Pure Consumption-Loan Model. *Australian Econ. Pap.,* June 1973, *12*(20), pp. 124–26.

——— **and Liviatan, Nissan.** Production and Trade

Patterns under Uncertainty. *Econ. Rec.,* June 1973, *49*(126), pp. 215–27.

———; **Wegge, Leon L. and Uekawa, Yasuo.** P- and PN-Matrices, Minkowski- and Metzler-Matrices, and Generalizations of the Stolper-Samuelson and Samuelson-Rybczynski Theorems. *J. Int. Econ.,* February 1973, *3*(1), pp. 53–76.

Kendall, M. G. A Computer Method of Analysing the Structure of Behavioural Models. In *Hawkes, N., ed.,* 1973, pp. 170–77.

Kende, Pierre; Detourbet, Christine and Debache, Joëlle. Vers une description du mode de vie au moyen d'indicateurs. (Towards a Description of Life Styles Through Indicators. With English summary.) *Consommation,* April-June 1973, *20*(2), pp. 117–30.

———; **Foulon, Alain and Hatchuel, Georges.** Un premier bilan de la redistribution des revenus en France; Les impôts et cotisations sociales à la charge des ménages en 1965. (Balance of the Redistribution of Incomes in France: Personal Taxes and Social Security Contributions in 1965. With English summary.) *Consommation,* October-December 1973, *20*(4), pp. 5–133.

Kendrick, James G. Techniques for Motivating Students. *Amer. J. Agr. Econ.,* Part II, November 1973, *55*(4), pp. 762–66.

———; **Helmers, Glenn A. and Lentz, Gary W.** Specialization and Flexibility Considerations in a Polyperiod Firm Investment Model. *Can. J. Agr. Econ.,* February 1973, *21*(1), pp. 41–48.

Kendrick, John W. Measuring Economic Performance in the Private Sector: Comment. In *Moss, M., ed.,* 1973, pp. 338–43.

Kenen, Peter B. Convertibility and Consolidation: A Survey of Options for Reform. *Amer. Econ. Rev.,* May 1973, *63*(2), pp. 189–98.

——— Implications for International Reserves: Comment. In *Krause, L. B. and Salant, W. S., eds.,* 1973, pp. 236–47.

Kenessey, Zoltan and Kravis, Irving B. Output and Prices in the International Comparison Project. *Rev. Income Wealth,* March 1973, *19*(1), pp. 49–67.

Kenneally, James J. Women and Trade Unions, 1870-1920: The Quandary of the Reformer. *Labor Hist.,* Winter 1973, *14*(1), pp. 42–55.

Kennedy, Charles. The Death-rate of 'Tractors' and the Rate of Depreciation. *Oxford Econ. Pap.,* March 1973, *25*(1), pp. 57–59.

——— A Generalisation of the Theory of Induced Bias in Technical Progress. *Econ. J.,* March 1973, *83*(329), pp. 48–57.

——— **and Thirlwall, A. P.** Technological Change and the Distribution of Income: A Belated Comment. *Int. Econ. Rev.,* October 1973, *14*(3), pp. 780–84.

Kennedy, J. O. S., et al. Optimal Fertilizer Carryover and Crop Recycling Policies for a Tropical Grain Crop. *Australian J. Agr. Econ.,* August 1973, *17*(2), pp. 104–13.

Kennedy, M. C. Employment Policy: What Went Wrong? In *Robinson, J., ed.,* 1973, pp. 71–87.

Kenny, David A. Cross-lagged and Synchronous Common Factors in Panel Data. In *Goldberger, A. S. and Duncan, O. D., eds.,* 1973, pp. 153–65.

Kensicki, Peter R. and Richmond, David. Consumerism and Automobile Insurance. *J. Risk Ins.*, June 1973, *40*(2), pp. 209–17.

Keohane, Robert O. and Nye, Joseph S. World Politics and the International Economic System. In *Bergsten, C. F., ed.*, 1973, pp. 115–79.

—— **and Ooms, Van Doorn.** The Multinational Enterprise and World Political Economy. In *Henley, D. S., ed.*, 1973, pp. 241–77.

Keren, Michael. Concentration Amid Devolution in East Germany's Reforms. In *Bornstein, M., ed.*, 1973, pp. 123–51.

Kernan, Jerome B.; Greeno, Daniel W. and Sommers, Montrose S. Personality and Implicit Behavior Patterns. *J. Marketing Res.*, February 1973, *10*(1), pp. 63–69.

Kerns, Waldon R. and Jansma, J. Dean. Financial Need Priorities for Awarding Construction Grants-in-Aid. *Growth Change*, January 1973, *4*(1), pp. 17–24.

Kerr, Alex. Structure of Final Demand in Perth. *Econ. Rec.*, December 1973, *49*(128), pp. 505–17.

Kerr, Clark. Educational Changes: Potential Impacts on Industrial Relations. In *Somers, G. G., ed.*, 1973, pp. 187–97.

Kerr, Steven. Ability- and Willingness-to-Leave as Moderators of Relationships Between Task and Leader Variables and Satisfaction. *J. Bus. Res.*, Fall 1973, *1*(2), pp. 115–28.

Kershner, Thomas R. The Growth of Trade and Competition: Japan's Exports to Pacific Asia, 1960-1969. *Amer. Econ.*, Spring 1973, *17*(1), pp. 93–101.

Kerton, Robert R. Price Effects of Market Power in the Canadian Newspaper Industry. *Can. J. Econ.*, November 1973, *6*(4), pp. 602–06.

Kervinen, Esko and Jääskeläinen, Veikko. Designing Retail Outlets with Markov Chains and Mathematical Programming. *Liiketaloudellinen Aikak.*, 1973, *22*(2), pp. 83–93.

Kessel, Reuben A. The Effects of Inflation on the Distribution of Economic Welfare: Comment. *J. Money, Credit, Banking*, Part II, February 1973, *5*(1), pp. 507–08.

Kesselman, Jonathan R. A Comprehensive Approach to Income Maintenance: Swift. *J. Public Econ.*, February 1973, *2*(1), pp. 59–88.

—— Incentive Effects of Transfer Systems Once Again. *J. Human Res.*, Winter 1973, *8*(1), pp. 119–29.

Kessler, Robert P. and Hartman, Chester W. The Illusion and the Reality of Urban Renewal: A Case Study of San Francisco's Yerba Buena Center. *Land Econ.*, November 1973, *49*(4), pp. 440–53.

Kettering, Floyd F., Jr. and Hindman, William R. Integrated MIS: A Case Study. *Manage. Account.*, August 1973, *55*(2), pp. 20–27.

Kettle, Peter and Whitbread, Michael. An Ordinal Method of Evaluation: A Comment. *Urban Stud.*, February 1973, *10*(1), pp. 95–99.

Kevern, Niles R. Education and Research Needs in Natural Resources: The Role of the Large State University. *Mich. Academician*, Winter 1973, 5(3), pp. 367–71.

Keyes, Langley C., Jr. The Boston Rehabilitation Program. In *Pynoos, J.; Schafer, R. and Hartman, C. W., eds.*, 1973, pp. 472–83.

Keyfitz, Nathan. Individual Mobility in a Stationary Population. *Population Stud.*, July 1973, *27*(2), pp. 335–52.

—— The Long-term Prospect for Indonesian Population. *Bull. Indonesian Econ. Stud.*, March 1973, *9*(1), pp. 107–09.

Keynes, John Maynard. Alfred Marshall. In *Rectenwald, H. C., ed.*, 1973, pp. 280–93.

Khachaturov, T. Improving the Methods of Determining the Effectiveness of Capital Investments. *Prob. Econ.*, September 1973, *16*(5), pp. 3–30.

Khachaturov, T. S. Development of Science and Technology in the U.S.S.R. In *Williams, B. R., ed.*, 1973, pp. 147–68.

Khalifa, Atef M. A Proposed Explanation of the Fertility Gap Differentials by Socio-Economic Status and Modernity: The Case of Egypt. *Population Stud.*, November 1973, *27*(3), pp. 431–42.

Khalitov, R. and Makeenko, M. Agroindustrial Associations and Their Effectiveness: Based on the Example of the Moldavian SSR. *Prob. Econ.*, January 1973, *15*(9), pp. 71–89.

Khan, Dilawar Ali and Ali, Chaudhari Haider. Income Impact of the Green Revolution. *Pakistan Econ. Soc. Rev.*, Spring 1973, *11*(1), pp. 67–82.

Khan, Mahmood H. "Green Revolution" or "Technocratic Euphoria." Some Problems of Rapid Agricultural Change in Asia. *Econ. Int.*, February 1973, *26*(1), pp. 119–34.

Khan, Masihur Rahman. Bangladesh Population During First Five Year Plan Period (1973–78): An Estimate. *Bangladesh Econ. Rev.*, April 1973, *1*(2), pp. 186–98.

Khan, Mohammad Zubair. The Responsiveness of Tax Yield to Increases in National Income. *Pakistan Develop. Rev.*, Winter 1973, *12*(4), pp. 416–32.

Khan, Mohsin S. The Effect of Growth on the Balance of Payments of Developing Countries: An Empirical Note. *Pakistan Econ. Soc. Rev.*, Autumn 1973, *11*(3), pp. 354–59.

—— A Note on the Secular Behaviour of Velocity Within the Context of the Inventory-Theoretic Model of Demand for Money. *Manchester Sch. Econ. Soc. Stud.*, June 1973, *41*(2), pp. 207–13.

Khandker, R. H. Distribution of Income and Wealth in Pakistan. *Pakistan Econ. Soc. Rev.*, Spring 1973, *11*(1), pp. 1–39.

Khang, Chulsoon. Factor Substitution in the Theory of Effective Protection: A General Equilibrium Analysis. *J. Int. Econ.*, August 1973, *3*(3), pp. 227–43.

—— **and Uekawa, Yasuo.** The Production Possibility Set in a Model Allowing Interindustry Flows: The Necessary and Sufficient Conditions for its Strict Convexity. *J. Int. Econ.*, August 1973, *3*(3), pp. 283–90.

Khanna, Kailash C. India: The Finance Bill, 1973. *Bull. Int. Fiscal Doc.*, April 1973, *27*(4), pp. 143–45.

Khin, Maung Kyi, et al. Process of Communication in Modernisation of Rural Society: A Survey Report on Two Burmese Villages. *Malayan Econ. Rev.*, April 1973, *18*(1), pp. 55–73.

Khomelianskii, B. The Sphere of Social and Economic Services and the Reproduction of Aggregate Labor Power. *Prob. Econ.*, June 1973, *16*(2), pp. 55–67.

Khromov, P. Labor Productivity and Accumulation. *Prob. Econ.*, February 1973, *15*(10), pp. 30–45.

Kibaki, M. Economic Independence: A Survey of Issues. In *Ghai, D., ed.*, 1973, pp. 3–8.

Kichline, James L.; Laub, P. Michael and Deck, Beryl. Yields on Recently Offered Corporate Bonds. *Fed. Res. Bull.*, May 1973, *59*(5), pp. 336–37.

_____; Laub, P. Michael and Stevens, Guy V. G. Obtaining the Yield on a Standard Bond from a Sample of Bonds with Heterogeneous Characteristics. *Fed. Res. Bull.*, May 1973, *59*(5), pp. 327–28.

Kiefer, Donald W. Compared to Other States, Indiana Taxes are Very High—Very Low—Neither of the Above. *Indiana Bus. Rev.*, January-February 1973, *48*, pp. 8–10.

_____ The 1973 Tax Package: Corporate Tax Restructuring. *Indiana Bus. Rev.*, July-August 1973, *48*, pp. 1–2.

_____ The 1973 Tax Package: The Effect on Local Governments. *Indiana Bus. Rev.*, September-October 1973, *48*, pp. 12–15.

_____ The 1973 Tax Package: The Sources of Property Tax Relief. *Indiana Bus. Rev.*, May-June 1973, *48*, pp. 21–23.

Kiener, Urs; Vieli, Klaus and Frick, Andreas. Bodenpreise und Stadtentwicklung. Eine empirische Untersuchung. (Land Prices and Urban Development. With English summary.) *Schweiz. Z. Volkswirtsch. Statist.*, March 1973, *109*(1), pp. 101–15.

Kientz, Jean. Savings Banks and Savings Facilities in African Countries: Madagascar. In *Alberici, A. and Baravelli, M., eds.*, 1973, pp. 49–53.

Kiger, Jack E. An Empirical Test of Annual Earnings Projection Models Using Quarterly Data. *Miss. Val. J. Bus. Econ.*, Spring 1973, *8*(3), pp. 17–28.

Kiker, B. F. and Cochrane, James L. War and Human Capital in Western Economic Analysis. *Hist. Polit. Econ.*, Fall 1973, *5*(2), pp. 375–98.

Kilby, Peter. Trade Unionism in Nigeria, 1938–66. In *Sturmthal, A. and Scoville, J. G., eds.*, 1973, pp. 228–58.

Killick, Tony. The Benefits of Foreign Direct Investment and Its Alternatives: An Empirical Exploration. *J. Devel. Stud.*, January 1973, *9*(2), pp. 301–16.

Killough, Larry N. and Souders, Thomas L. A Goal Programming Model for Public Accounting Firms. *Accounting Rev.*, April 1973, *48*(2), pp. 268–79.

Kilpatrick, Robert W. The Income Elasticity of the Poverty Line. *Rev. Econ. Statist.*, August 1973, *55* (3), pp. 327–32.

Kim, Han J. and Lockner, Allyn O. Circuit-Breakers on Farm-Property-Tax Overload: A Case Study. *Nat. Tax J.*, June 1973, *26*(2), pp. 233–40.

Kim, Kye and Butler, Arthur. The Dynamics of Wage Structures. *Southern Econ. J.*, April 1973, *39*(4), pp. 588–600.

Kim, S. Rural-Urban Migration and Technological Changes in the Agriculture of a Developing Country. *Econ. Rec.*, March 1973, *49*(125), pp. 15–23.

Kim, Young Chin. Choice in the Lottery-Insurance Situation Augmented-Income Approach. *Quart. J. Econ.*, February 1973, *87*(1), pp. 148–56.

Kindahl, James K. and Stigler, George J. Industrial Prices, as Administered by Dr. Means. *Amer. Econ. Rev.*, September 1973, *63*(4), pp. 717–21.

Kindleberger, Charles P. Implications for Private Capital Markets: Comment. In *Krause, L. B. and Salant, W. S., eds.*, 1973, pp. 149–54.

_____ Money Illusion and Foreign Exchange. In *[Halm, G. N.]*, 1973, pp. 51–63.

_____ Restrictions on Direct Investment in Host Countries. In *[Rosenstein-Rodan, P.]*, 1973, pp. 201–09.

King, Albert S. and Whitehead, Carlton J. Differences in Managers' Attitudes Toward Mexican and Non-Mexican Americans in Organizational Authority Relations. *Soc. Sci. Quart.*, March 1973, *53*(4), pp. 760–71.

King, Allan G. A Comment on Bowles' Model of Educational Planning. *Econ. Planning*, 1973, *13* (1–2), pp. 131–35.

_____ Stochastic Dominance and 'The Economic Rationale of Occupational Choice': Comment. *Ind. Lab. Relat. Rev.*, April 1973, *26*(3), pp. 996–1000.

King, A. Thomas and Mieszkowski, Peter. Racial Discrimination, Segregation, and the Price of Housing. *J. Polit. Econ.*, May-June 1973, *81*(3), pp. 590–606.

King, Benjamin and Kaufman, G. M. A Bayesian Analysis of Nonresponse in Dichotomous Processes. *J. Amer. Statist. Assoc.*, September 1973, *68* (343), pp. 670–78.

King, James P. and Colberg, Marshall R. Theory of Production Abandonment. *Rivista Int. Sci. Econ. Com.*, October 1973, *20*(10), pp. 961–72.

King, L. J.; Casetti, Emilio and Kissling, C. C. Optimal Transportation Patterns of Single Commodities in Capacitated Networks. In *Judge, G. G. and Takayama, T., eds.*, 1973, pp. 225–42.

_____; Odland, J. and Casetti, Emilio. Testing Hypotheses of Polarized Growth Within a Central Place Hierarchy. *Econ. Geogr.*, January 1973, *49* (1), pp. 74–79.

King, William R. and McGuigan, James R. Security Option Strategy under Risk Aversion: An Analysis. *J. Financial Quant. Anal.*, January 1973, *8*(1), pp. 1–15.

Kingston, Jerry L. Export Instability in Latin America: The Postwar Statistical Record. *J. Devel. Areas*, April 1973, *7*(3), pp. 381–95.

Kinnear, Thomas C. and Taylor, James R. The Effect of Ecological Concern on Brand Perceptions. *J. Marketing Res.*, May 1973, *10*(2), pp. 191–97.

Kinnersley, D. J. Water Pollution. In *Robinson, J., ed.*, 1973, pp. 134–55.

Kinoshita, Kazuo. The Use of Tax Incentives for Export by Developed Countries—The Japanese Case. *Bull. Int. Fiscal Doc.*, July 1973, *27*(7), pp. 271–90.

Kinsella, R. P. A Note on Bank Productivity in a Service Economy. *Rivista Int. Sci. Econ. Com.*, October 1973, *20*(10), pp. 985–94.

Kinsey, David N. The French Z.U.P. Technique of Urban Development. In *Moskoff, W., ed.,* 1973, pp. 324–38.

Kinsman, Michael; Robichek, Alexander A. and Higgins, Robert C. The Effect of Leverage on the Cost of Equity Capital of Electric Utility Firms. *J. Finance,* May 1973, *28*(2), pp. 353–67.

Kirby, M. W. The Control of Competition in the British Coal Mining Industry in the Thirties. *Econ. Hist. Rev., 2nd Ser.,* May 1973, *26*(2), pp. 273–84.

Kirk, John and Snowbarger, Marvin. A Cross-Sectional Model of Built-In Flexibility, 1954–1969. *Nat. Tax J.,* June 1973, *26*(2), pp. 241–49.

Kirkpatrick, Elizabeth K. No-Fault Accident Compensation in New Zealand. *Soc. Sec. Bull.,* September 1973, *36*(9), pp. 25–29.

Kirkpatrick, Miles W., et al. The ABA Report on the FTC: Consumer Protection or Consumer Exploitation. In *Murray, B. B., ed.,* 1973, pp. 98–101.

Kirkus, Larry D. and Segelhorst, Elbert W. Parking Bias in Transit Choice. *J. Transp. Econ. Policy,* January 1973, *7*(1), pp. 58–70.

Kirlin, John J. The Impact of Contract Services Arrangements on the Los Angeles Sheriff's Department and Law-Enforcement Services in Los Angeles County. *Public Policy,* Fall 1973, *21*(4), pp. 553–84.

Kirman, Alan P. Trade Diverting Customs Unions and Welfare Improvement: A Comment. *Econ. J.,* September 1973, *83*(331), pp. 890–94.

_____ **and Hildenbrand, Werner.** Size Removes Inequity. *Rev. Econ. Stud.,* July 1973, *40*(3), pp. 305–19.

Kirpa, I. and Kotliar, A. Demographic Aspects of Employment in Cities with Differing Industrial Structures. *Prob. Econ.,* April 1973, *15*(12), pp. 73–85.

Kirschen, Etienne S. BENELUX Experience with Public Finance Instruments for Achieving the Objectives of Full Employment and Expansion. In *Giersch, H., ed.,* 1973, pp. 155–69.

_____ Le seigneuriage externe américain. Son origine, son coût pour l'Europe, et quelques ripostes possibles. (With English summary.) *Cah. Écon. Bruxelles,* 3rd Trimestre 1973, (59), pp. 345–84.

Kirschenbaum, Alan and Comay, Yochanan. The Israeli New Town: An Experiment at Population Redistribution. *Econ. Develop. Cult. Change,* October 1973, *22*(1), pp. 124–34.

Kishida, Junnosuke. Technology Assessment in Japan. *Int. Soc. Sci. J.,* 1973, *25*(3), pp. 326–35.

Kisiel, Chester C.; Duckstein, Lucien and Monarchi, David E. Interactive Multiobjective Programming in Water Resources: A Case Study. *Water Resources Res.,* August 1973, *9*(4), pp. 837–50.

Kislev, Yoav and Evenson, Robert E. Research and Productivity in Wheat and Maize. *J. Polit. Econ.,* November-December 1973, *81*(6), pp. 1309–29.

_____ **and Shchori-Bachrach, Nira.** The Process of an Innovation Cycle. *Amer. J. Agr. Econ.,* February 1973, *55*(1), pp. 28–37.

Kiss, T. The Development of the Forms of Economic Relations in the CMEA Integration. In *Kiss, T., ed.,* 1973, pp. 109–26.

Kissling, C. C.; King, L. J. and Casetti, Emilio. Optimal Transportation Patterns of Single Commodities in Capacitated Networks. In *Judge, G. G. and Takayama, T., eds.,* 1973, pp. 225–42.

Kittrell, Edward R. Wakefield's Scheme of Systematic Colonization and Classical Economics. *Amer. J. Econ. Soc.,* January 1973, *32*(1), pp. 87–111.

Kjaer-Hansen, Max. Revolution i konsumenternas varuförsörjning. (Revolution in Consumer Goods Supply. With English summary.) *Ekon. Samfundets Tidskr.,* January 1973, *26*(1), pp. 3–15.

Klaasen, Thomas A. Regional Comparative Advantage in the United States. *J. Reg. Sci.,* April 1973, *13*(1), pp. 97–105.

Klacek, Jan and Toms, Miroslav. Prognostický model pro krátké období. (A Short-Run Forecasting Model. With English summary.) *Ekon.-Mat. Obzor,* 1973, *9*(1), pp. 68–83.

Klammer, Thomas. The Association of Capital Budgeting Techniques with Firm Performance. *Accounting Rev.,* April 1973, *48*(2), pp. 353–64.

Klarman, Herbert E. Approaches to Health Manpower Analysis, with Special Reference to Physicians. *Amer. Econ.,* Fall 1973, *17*(2), pp. 137–42.

Klebaner, Benjamin J. Recent Changes in United States' Commercial Banking Structure in Perspective. *Antitrust Bull.,* Winter 1973, *18*(4), pp. 759–86.

Kleiman, Ephraim. An Early Modern Hebrew Textbook of Economics. *Hist. Polit. Econ.,* Fall 1973, *5*(2), pp. 339–58.

Klein, Benjamin. Does Punishment Deter? Comment. In *Rottenberg, S., ed.,* 1973, pp. 106–12.

_____ Income Velocity, Interest Rates, and the Money Supply Multiplier: A Reinterpretation of the Long-Term Evidence. *J. Money, Credit, Banking,* May 1973, *5*(2), pp. 656–67.

_____ **and Alchian, Armen A.** On a Correct Measure of Inflation. *J. Money, Credit, Banking,* Part I, February 1973, *5*(1), pp. 173–91.

Klein, David M. and Hill, Reuben. Toward a Research Agenda and Theoretical Synthesis. In *Sheldon, E. B., ed.,* 1973, pp. 371–404.

_____ **and Hill, Reuben.** Understanding Family Consumption: Common Ground for Integrating Uncommon Disciplinary Perspectives. In *Sheldon, E. B., ed.,* 1973, pp. 1–22.

Klein, Deborah P. Exploring the Adequacy of Employment. *Mon. Lab. Rev.,* October 1973, *96*(10), pp. 3–9.

Klein, Ira. Death in India, 1871–1921. *J. Asian Stud.,* August 1973, *32*(4), pp. 639–59.

Klein, Lawrence R. The State of the Monetarist Debate: A Comment. *Fed. Res. Bank St. Louis Rev.,* September 1973, *55*(9), pp. 9–12.

_____ The Treatment of Undersized Samples in Econometrics. In *Powell, A. A. and Williams, R. A., eds.,* 1973, pp. 3–26.

_____ **and Fromm, Gary.** A Comparison of Eleven Econometric Models of the United States. *Amer. Econ. Rev.,* May 1973, *63*(2), pp. 385–93.

_____ **and Long, Virginia.** Capacity Utilization: Concept, Measurement, and Recent Estimates. *Brookings Pap. Econ. Act.,* 1973, (3), pp. 743–56.

_____ **and Mori, Kei.** The Impact of Disarmament on Aggregate Economic Activity: An Econometric Analysis. In *Udis, B., ed.*, 1973, pp. 59–77.

———; **Rhomberg, Rudolf R. and Hickman, Bert G.** Background, Organization and Preliminary Results of Project LINK. In *Alexandrides, C. G., ed.*, 1973, pp. 19–56.

——— and **Van Peeterssen, A.** Forecasting World Trade within Project LINK. In *Ball, R. J., ed.*, 1973, pp. 429–63.

Klein, Michael A. The Economics of Security Divisibility and Financial Intermediation. *J. Finance,* September 1973, *28*(4), pp. 923–31.

Klein, Philip A. Demand Theory and the Economist's Propensity to Assume. *J. Econ. Issues,* June 1973, *7*(2), pp. 209–39.

Klein, Richard H. and Johnson, Rodney D. A Further Note on the Analysis of Capital Investment Alternatives: Reply. *Miss. Val. J. Bus. Econ.,* Fall 1973, *9*(1), pp. 91–93.

Klein, Roger W. A Dynamic Theory of Comparative Advantage. *Amer. Econ. Rev.,* March 1973, *63*(1), pp. 173–84.

——— K-Class Estimators: The Optimum Normalization for Finite Samples. *J. Amer. Statist. Assoc.,* June 1973, *68*(342), pp. 445–51.

Klein, Thomas M. Economic Aid Through Debt Relief. *Finance Develop.,* September 1973, *10*(3), pp. 17–20, 34–35.

Klein, Walter H. and Murphy, David C. Policy: Concepts in Organizational Guidance: Introduction. In *Klein, W. H. and Murphy, D. C., eds.,* 1973, pp. 1–12.

Kleindorfer, Paul R. and Crowston, Wallace B. Coordinating Multi-Project Networks. In *Cochrane, J. L. and Zeleny, M., eds.,* 1973, pp. 668–85.

Kleinewefers, Henner. Leistungsbilanz, Wachstum und Transferproblem. (Balance of Current Business Transactions, Growth and Transfer Problems. With English summary.) *Weltwirtsch. Arch.,* 1973, *109*(1), pp. 40–58.

Kleinhenz, Gerhard. Interessenverbände und sozialstaatliche Wirtschaftspolitik. (Interest Groups and Economic Policy. With English summary.) *Z. Wirtschaft. Sozialwissen.,* 1973, *93*(3), pp. 307–21.

Kleinman, David S. Fertility Variation and Resources in Rural India (1961) *Econ. Develop. Cult. Change,* Part I, July 1973, *21*(4), pp. 679–96.

Kleinpeter, M. Technological Forecasting in the Energy Industry. In *Blohm, H. and Steinbuch, K., eds.,* 1973, pp. 83–90.

Klema, Virginia. A Note on Matrix Factorization. *Ann. Econ. Soc. Measure,* July 1973, *2*(3), pp. 317–22.

Klemkosky, Robert C. The Bias in Composite Performance Measures. *J. Financial Quant. Anal.,* June 1973, *8*(3), pp. 505–14.

——— and **Petty, J. William.** A Multivariate Analysis of Stock Price Variability. *J. Bus. Res.,* Summer 1973, *1*(1), pp. 1–10.

Klevorick, Alvin K. The Behavior of a Firm Subject to Stochastic Regulatory Review. *Bell J. Econ. Manage. Sci.,* Spring 1973, *4*(1), pp. 57–88.

——— A Note on "The Ordering of Portfolios in Terms of Mean and Variance." *Rev. Econ. Stud.,* April 1973, *40*(2), pp. 293–96.

——— and **Kramer, Gerald H.** Social Choice on Pol-

lution Management: The Genossenschaften. *J. Public Econ.,* April 1973, *2*(2), pp. 101–46.

Klijn, Nico. The Effects of a 9.42 Per Cent Price Increase for Iron and Steel on Other Prices. *Australian Econ. Rev.,* 4th Quarter 1973, pp. 27–30.

Kliman, M. L. The Permanent Income Hypothesis and the Firm's Demand for Money. *J. Econ. Bus.,* Winter 1973, *25*(2), pp. 89–92.

——— and **Oksanen, Ernest H.** The Keynesian Demand-for-Money Function: Comment. *J. Money, Credit, Banking,* Part I, February 1973, *5*(1), pp. 215–20.

Klinefelter, Danny A. Factors Affecting Farmland Values in Illinois. *Ill. Agr. Econ.,* January 1973, *13*(1), pp. 27–33.

Klippenstein, D. H. and Ironside, R. G. Farmers' Attitudes Toward Farm-Based Recreational Facilities in Alberta. *Can. J. Agr. Econ.,* November 1973, *21*(3), pp. 23–33.

Klotz, Benjamin P. Oscillatory Growth in Three Nations. *J. Amer. Statist. Assoc.,* September 1973, *68*(343), pp. 562–67.

——— and **Neal, Larry.** Spectral and Cross-Spectral Analysis of the Long-Swing Hypothesis. *Rev. Econ. Statist.,* August 1973, *55*(3), pp. 291–98.

Kmenta, J. and Oberhofer, W. Estimation of Standard Errors of the Characteristic Roots of a Dynamic Econometric Model. *Econometrica,* January 1973, *41*(1), pp. 171–77.

——— and **Smith, Paul E.** Autonomous Expenditures Versus Money Supply: An Application of Dynamic Multipliers. *Rev. Econ. Statist.,* August 1973, *55*(3), pp. 299–307.

Kñakal, Jan and Pinto, Aníbal. The Centre-Periphery System Twenty Years Later. *Soc. Econ. Stud.,* March 1973, *22*(1), pp. 34–89.

Knapp, Charles B. A Human Capital Approach to the Burden of the Military Draft. *J. Human Res.,* Fall 1973, *8*(4), pp. 485–96.

Knapp, J. Burke. Determination of Priorities and the Allocation of Resources. In *Lewis, J. P. and Kapur, I., eds.,* 1973, pp. 37–51.

Knapp, John. Economics or Political Economy? *Lloyds Bank Rev.,* January 1973, (107), pp. 19–43.

Knauerhase, Ramon. A Survey of the Revenue Structure of the Kingdom of Saudi Arabia, 1961/62 to 1971/72. *Public Finance,* 1973, *28*(3–4), pp. 435–53.

Kneese, Allen V. Economics and the Quality of the Environment: Some Empirical Experiences. In *Enthoven, A. C. and Freeman, A. M., III, eds.,* 1973, pp. 72–87.

——— Water Quality Management by Regional Authorities in the Ruhr Area with Special Emphasis on the Role of Cost Assessment. In *Grieson, R. E., ed.,* 1973, pp. 251–71.

——— and **Ayres, Robert U.** Economic and Ecological Effects of a Stationary Economy. In *Enthoven, A. C. and Freeman, A. M., III, eds.,* 1973, pp. 235–52.

———; **Ayres, Robert U. and d'Arge, Ralph C.** Economics and the Environment: A Materials Balance Approach. In *Enthoven, A. C. and Freeman, A. M., III, eds.,* 1973, pp. 25–36.

——— and **Bower, Blair T.** The Delaware Estuary Study: Effluent Charges, Least-Cost Treatment, and Efficiency. In *Enthoven, A. C. and Freeman, A. M., III, eds.*, 1973, pp. 112–21.

_____ and Herfindahl, Orris C. Measuring Social and Economic Change: Benefits and Costs of Environmental Pollution. In *Moss, M., ed.*, 1973, pp. 441–503.

_____ and Mäler, Karl-Göran. Bribes and Charges in Pollution Control: An Aspect of the Coase Controversy. *Natural Res. J.*, October 1973, *13*(4), pp. 705–16.

Kneppreth, Norwood P., et al. Techniques for the Assessment of Worth. In *Berg, R. L., ed.*, 1973, pp. 228–39.

Knight, J. B. and Mabro, Robert. On the Determination of the General Wage Level: A Rejoinder. *Econ. J.*, June 1973, *83*(330), pp. 520–22.

Knight, Malcolm. A Continuous Disequilibrium Econometric Model of the Domestic and International Portfolio Behaviour of the UK Banking System. In *Parkin, M., ed.*, 1973, pp. 266–90.

Knodel, John and Prachuabmoh, Visid. Desired Family Size in Thailand: Are the Responses Meaningful? *Demography*, November 1973, *10*(4), pp. 619–37.

Knowles, James C. The Rockefeller Financial Group. In *Andreano, R. L., ed.*, 1973, pp. M343–59.

Kobrin, Frances E. Household Headship and its Changes in the United States, 1940–1960, 1970. *J. Amer. Statist. Assoc.*, December 1973, *68*(344), pp. 793–800.

Koch, Gary G. An Alternative Approach to Multivariate Response Error Models for Sample Survey Data with Applications to Estimators Involving Subclass Means. *J. Amer. Statist. Assoc.*, December 1973, *68*(344), pp. 906–13.

Koch, James V. Market Structure and Industry Growth: Reply. *Miss. Val. J. Bus. Econ.*, Fall 1973, *9*(1), pp. 87.

_____ A Troubled Cartel: The NCAA. *Law Contemp. Probl.*, Winter-Spring 1973, *38*(1), pp. 135–50.

_____ and Chizmar, John F. The Influence of Teaching and Other Factors Upon Absolute Salaries and Salary Increments at Illinois State University. *J. Econ. Educ.*, Fall 1973, *5*(1), pp. 27–34.

_____ and Ireland, Thomas R. Blood and American Social Attitudes. In *Alchian, A. A., et al.*, 1973, pp. 145–55.

Kochan, Thomas A. Correlates of State Public Employee Bargaining Laws. *Ind. Relat.*, October 1973, *12*(3), pp. 322–37.

Koenig, Gilbert. Affectation des ressources et système de conscription en France. (Allocation of Resources and Draft System in France. With English summary.) *Revue Écon.*, January 1973, *24*(1), pp. 66–108.

Kofi, Tetteh A. A Framework for Comparing the Efficiency of Futures Markets. *Amer. J. Agr. Econ.*, Part I, November 1973, *55*(4), pp. 584–94.

Kogiku, K. C. and d'Arge, R. C. Economic Growth and the Environment. *Rev. Econ. Stud.*, January 1973, *40*(1), pp. 61–77.

Köhler, Walter. Konkurrenzgleichgewicht und Zollwirkung am Brotmarkt. (Equilibrium under Conditions of Competition and Effects of Duties in the Baker's Market. With English summary.) *Jahr. Nationalökon. Statist.*, March 1973, *187*(3), pp. 218–36.

Kohlhase, Norbert. The European Community: A New Actor in a Changing International Pattern. *Intermountain Econ. Rev.*, Fall 1973, *4*(2), pp. 70–74.

Kohlmeier, Louis M. The Federal Highway Program. In *Haveman, R. H. and Hamrin, R. D., eds.*, 1973, pp. 226–30.

_____ The Regulators and the Regulated. In *Haveman, R. H. and Hamrin, R. D., eds.*, 1973, pp. 256–60.

Kohn, Donald L. Capital Flows in a Foreign Exchange Crisis. *Fed. Res. Bank Kansas City Rev.*, February 1973, pp. 14–23.

Kohn, Robert M. On Migration, Migration Costs, and Wage Differentials: A Comment. *Schweiz. Z. Volkswirtsch. Statist.*, December 1973, *109*(4), pp. 603–04.

_____ and Cebula, Richard J. Foreign Capital and Steady-State Growth in Developing Economies. *Pakistan Econ. Soc. Rev.*, Winter 1973, *11*(4), pp. 378–82.

_____; Gallaway, Lowell E. and Cebula, Richard J. Determinants of Net Migration to SMSA's, 1960–1970. *Miss. Val. J. Bus. Econ.*, Winter 1973-74, *9* (2), pp. 59–64.

_____; Vedder, Richard K. and Cebula, Richard J. Some Determinants of Interstate Migration of Blacks, 1965–1970. *Western Econ. J.*, December 1973, *11*(4), pp. 500–05.

Kohvakka, Liisa. Kvantitatiivinen henkilöstösuunnittelu. (Quantitative Personnel Planning. With English summary.) *Liiketaloudellinen Aikak.*, 1973, *22*(2), pp. 141–57.

Koizumi, Tetsunori and Sato, Ryuzo. On the Elasticities of Substitution and Complementarity. *Oxford Econ. Pap.*, March 1973, *25*(1), pp. 44–56.

_____ and Sato, Ryuzo. The Production Function and the Theory of Distributive Shares. *Amer. Econ. Rev.*, June 1973, *63*(3), pp. 484–89.

_____ and Sato, Ryuzo. Relative Shares and Elasticities Simplified: Reply. *Amer. Econ. Rev.*, September 1973, *63*(4), pp. 772.

Kojima, Kiyoshi. The Japanese Experience and Attitudes Toward Trade Adjustment. In *Hughes, H., ed.*, 1973, pp. 228–62.

_____ A Macroeconomic Approach to Foreign Direct Investment. *Hitotsubashi J. Econ.*, June 1973, *14*(1), pp. 1–21.

_____ Reorganisation of North-South Trade: Japan's Foreign Economic Policy for the 1970s. *Hitotsubashi J. Econ.*, February 1973, *13*(2), pp. 1–28.

Kokulinsky, Detlef and Park, Sung-Jo. Die Entwicklungshilfe als ein aussenpolitisches Instrument der Volksrepublik China. (Development Aid as Instrument of Foreign Policy of the People's Republic of China. With English summary.) *Z. ges. Staatswiss.*, August 1973, *129*(3), pp. 559–72.

Kolawole, M. I. The Reform of Commodity Marketing Boards in Nigeria: An Analysis of New Producer Price Policy. *Econ. Bull. Ghana, Sec. Ser.*, 1973, *3*(3), pp. 14–19.

Kolb, Fredric R. The Stationary State of Ricardo and

Malthus: Reply. *Intermountain Econ. Rev.,* Spring 1973, *4*(1), pp. 80.

Koll, Michael. The Western Nigerian Cooperative Administration: An Obstacle to Development. In *Damachi, U. G. and Seibel, H. D., eds.,* 1973, pp. 40–50.

Koller, Roland H., II. Inheritance Justified: Comment. *J. Law Econ.,* October 1973, *16*(2), pp. 423–24.

_____ Why Regulate Utilities? To Control Price Discrimination. *J. Law Econ.,* April 1973, *16*(1), pp. 191–92.

Kolm, Serge-Christophe. Les pollués doivent-ils payer? (With English summary.) *Kyklos,* 1973, *26* (2), pp. 322–36.

_____ A Note on Optimum Tax Evasion. *J. Public Econ.,* July 1973, *2*(3), pp. 265–70.

Kolmin, Frank W. and Cerullo, Michael J. Measuring Productivity and Efficiency. *Manage. Account.,* November 1973, *55*(5), pp. 32–34.

Kolodrubetz, Walter W. Employee-Benefit Plans, 1971. *Soc. Sec. Bull.,* April 1973, *36*(4), pp. 27–33.

_____ Private Retirement Benefits and Relationship to Earnings: Survey of New Beneficiaries. *Soc. Sec. Bull.,* May 1973, *36*(5), pp. 16–37.

_____ **and Landay, Donald M.** Coverage and Vesting of Full-Time Employees Under Private Retirement Plans. *Soc. Sec. Bull.,* November 1973, *36*(11), pp. 20–36.

Kolsen, H. M. The Victorian Land Transport Inquiry. *Econ. Rec.,* September 1973, *49*(127), pp. 464–80.

Komarov, V. The Service Sphere and Its Structure. *Prob. Econ.,* July 1973, *16*(3), pp. 3–21.

Komatsu, Ryuji and Kawada, Hisashi. Post-War Labor Movements in Japan. In *Sturmthal, A. and Scoville, J. G., eds.,* 1973, pp. 123–48.

Komesar, Neil K. Return to Slumville: A Critique of the Ackerman Analysis of Housing Code Enforcement and the Poor. *Yale Law J.,* May 1973, *82*(6), pp. 1175–93.

Komin, A. Problems in the Methodology and Practice of Planned Price Formation. *Prob. Econ.,* May 1973, *16*(1), pp. 35–49.

Komiya, Ryutaro. A Note on Professor Mahalanobis' Model of Indian Economic Planning. In *Wadhva, C. D., ed.,* 1973, pp. 32–41.

Komló, L. The Industrialization and Integration of Agriculture in a Socialist Country. *Acta Oecon.,* 1973, *10*(1), pp. 67–79.

Kongbo, Basile. Savings Banks and Savings Facilities in African Countries: Central African Republic. In *Alberici, A. and Baravelli, M., eds.,* 1973, pp. 7–10.

König, Wolfgang. International Financial Institutions and Latin American Development. In *Urquidi, V. L. and Thorp, R., eds.,* 1973, pp. 116–63.

Koning, J.; Volgenant, A. F. and Fase, M. M. G. An Experimental Look at Seasonal Adjustment. *De Economist,* September-October 1973, *121*(5), pp. 441–80.

Konius, A. A. Commensuration of Labor by Means of an Input-Output Table. *Matekon,* Summer 1973, *9*(4), pp. 31–42.

Koo, Anthony Y. C. Towards a More General Model of Land Tenancy and Reform. *Quart. J. Econ.,* November 1973, *87*(4), pp. 567–80.

_____ **and Smith, Victor E.** A General Consumption Technology in New Demand Theory. *Western Econ. J.,* September 1973, *11*(3), pp. 243–59.

Koopman, Bernard Osgood. Recent US Advances in OR Theory. In *Ross, M., ed.,* 1973, pp. 561–70.

Koopmans, Tjalling C. Some Observations on 'Optimal' Economic Growth and Exhaustible Resources. In *[Tinbergen, J.],* 1973, pp. 239–55.

Koot, Ronald S. Price Expectations and Monetary Adjustments in Latin America. *Schweiz. Z. Volkswirtsch. Statist.,* June 1973, *109*(2), pp. 223–32.

Korb, Lawrence J. National Defense. In *Ott, D. J., et al.,* 1973, pp. 29–52.

Korbonski, Andrzej. Theory and Practice of Regional Integration: The Case of Comecon. In *Falk, R. A. and Mendlovitz, S. H., eds.,* 1973, pp. 152–77.

Koriagin, A. Problems of the Theory of Socialist Reproduction. *Prob. Econ.,* January 1973, *15*(9), pp. 28–46.

Korka, Mihai. Evoluția comerțului invizibil al țărilor în curs de dezvoltare. (The Evolution of the Invisible Trade of the Developing Countries. With English summary.) *Stud. Cercet. Econ.,* 1973, (4), pp. 177–92.

_____ Folosirea indicilor la măsurarea modificărilor structurale ale exportului. (The Use of Indices in Measuring the Structural Transformations of Export. With English summary.) *Stud. Cercet. Econ.,* 1973, (1), pp. 123–31.

Kormnov, Iu. International Economic Organizations and Their Role in the Collaboration of COMECON Countries. *Prob. Econ.,* October 1973, *16*(6), pp. 36–54.

Kormnov, Y. International Industrial Specialization. In *Kiss, T., ed.,* 1973, pp. 143–48.

Kornai, János. Some Intersectoral and Intemporal Choice Problems: Hungarian Experiences in Long-Term Planning. In *[Tinbergen, J.],* 1973, pp. 201–13.

_____ Thoughts on Multi-Level Planning Systems. In *Goreux, L. M. and Manne, A. S., eds.,* 1973, pp. 521–51.

_____ **and Martos, Béla.** Autonomous Control of the Economic System. *Econometrica,* May 1973, *41* (3), pp. 509–28.

Kornblith, Elinda B. F. and Poole, William. The Friedman-Meiselman CMC Paper: New Evidence on an Old Controversy. *Amer. Econ. Rev.,* December 1973, *63*(5), pp. 908–17.

Koropeckyj, I. S. Regional Resource Allocation, Growth, and Income Inequality under Socialism. In *Bandera, V. N. and Melnyk, Z. L., eds.,* 1973, pp. 45–62.

_____ Technology and the Direction of Soviet Foreign Trade. *Rivista Int. Sci. Econ. Com.,* December 1973, *20*(12), pp. 1190–1208.

Korovkin, G. Scientific-Technical Progress and Trade. *Prob. Econ.,* November 1973, *16*(7), pp. 84–101.

Korteweg, P. Over de beheersbaarheid van de geldhoeveelheid in Nederland. (The Supply and Controllability of Money in an Open Economy: The Dutch Case. With English summary.) *De*

Economist, May-June 1973, *121*(3), pp. 273–99.

Korth, Christopher M. and Selander, Sharon L. The China Market: Boom or Bust? In *Henley, D. S., ed.,* 1973, pp. 55–64.

Koshal, Manjulika and Koshal, Rajindar K. Gandhi's Influence on Indian Economic Planning: A Critical Analysis. *Amer. J. Econ. Soc.,* July 1973, *32*(3), pp. 311–30.

_____ **and Koshal, Rajindar K.** Gandhian Economic Philosophy. *Amer. J. Econ. Soc.,* April 1973, *32*(2), pp. 191–209.

Koshal, Rajindar K. The Future of Higher Education in the State of Ohio: An Econometric Approach. *Ohio State U. Bull. Bus. Res.,* November 1973, *48* (11), pp. 1–3, 5.

_____ A Possible Production Function for Indian Railway System—A Comment. *Indian Econ. Rev.,* April 1973, *8*(1), pp. 85–89.

_____ **and Gallaway, Lowell E.** The Phillips Curve: An International Phenomenon. *Rivista Int. Sci. Econ. Com.,* July 1973, *20*(7), pp. 669–80.

_____ **and Koshal, Manjulika.** Gandhi's Influence on Indian Economic Planning: A Critical Analysis. *Amer. J. Econ. Soc.,* July 1973, *32*(3), pp. 311–30.

_____ **and Koshal, Manjulika.** Gandhian Economic Philosophy. *Amer. J. Econ. Soc.,* April 1973, *32*(2), pp. 191–209.

Kosoff, Allen. Incentives for Urban Apartment Construction. *Amer. J. Econ. Soc.,* July 1973, *32*(3), pp. 295–305.

Kossov, V. V. Relationships in the Development of Industries. *Matekon,* Spring 1973, *9*(3), pp. 89–108.

Kostál, Miroslav and Vesely, Zdenek. The Czechoslovak Socialist Republic and the Council for Mutual Economic Assistance. *Czech. Econ. Digest.,* August 1973, (5), pp. 25–43.

Kostenko, M. V. On Choosing the Ratio Between the Norm of Effectiveness and the Discount Coefficient. *Matekon,* Spring 1973, *9*(3), pp. 3–5.

Kotek, Miloslav. Employment Trends in Czechoslovakia. *Czech. Econ. Digest.,* August 1973, (5), pp. 44–63.

Kotler, Philip. Marketing Mix Decisions for New Products. In *Palda, K. S., ed.,* 1973, pp. 160–68.

Kotliar, A. and Kirpa, I. Demographic Aspects of Employment in Cities with Differing Industrial Structures. *Prob. Econ.,* April 1973, *15*(12), pp. 73–85.

Kotov, V. Prices: The Instrument of National Economic Planning and the Basis of the Value Indices of the Plan. *Prob. Econ.,* May 1973, *16*(1), pp. 50–69.

Kottis, Athena P. Community Effects of an Income Maintenance Plan: A Theoretical Exploration. In *Mattila, J. M. and Thompson, W. R., eds.,* 1973, pp. 41–57.

_____ **and Kottis, George C.** Average Propensity to Spend Inside the Ghetto Areas: Comment. *J. Reg. Sci.,* April 1973, *13*(1), pp. 123–25.

_____ **and Kottis, George C.** Who Benefits from Higher Education Subsidies. A Reconsideration. *Tijdschr. Econ.,* 1973, *18*(3), pp. 451–56.

_____ **and Kottis, George C.** Who Benefits from Higher Education Subsidies: A Reconsideration.

Econ. Int., August-November 1973, *26*(3–4), pp. 492–501.

Kottis, George C. New Towns and the Problem of "Optimum" City Size: A Critique. In *Mattila, J. M. and Thompson, W. R., eds.* 1973, pp. 71–90.

_____ **and Kottis, Athena P.** Average Propensity to Spend Inside the Ghetto Areas: Comment. *J. Reg. Sci.,* April 1973, *13*(1), pp. 123–25.

_____ **and Kottis, Athena P.** Who Benefits from Higher Education Subsidies. A Reconsideration. *Tijdschr. Econ.,* 1973, *18*(3), pp. 451–56.

_____ **and Kottis, Athena P.** Who Benefits from Higher Education Subsidies: A Reconsideration. *Econ. Int.,* August-November 1973, *26*(3–4), pp. 492–501.

Kottke, Marvin W. Allocation of Milk Through Space and Time in a Competitively-Mixed Dairy Industry. In *Judge, G. G. and Takayama, T., eds.,* 1973, pp. 557–78.

Kotz, Nick and Lynn, Mary. You Are What You Eat: Feeding D.C.'s Hungry. In *Levitan, S. A., ed.,* 1973, pp. 143–74.

Kotzenberg, H. R. P. A. The Policy and Programme for the Decentralisation of Industry in South Africa. *Finance Trade Rev.,* December 1973, *10* (4), pp. 137–67.

Kovács, Ilona and Hoch, Róbert. Changes in Income and Consumer Prices Affecting Demand. In *Földi, T., ed.,* 1973, pp. 65–88.

Kovács, J. Simplified Model for Level-of-Planning-Consistency Control. *Acta Oecon.,* 1973, *11*(2–3), pp. 177–90.

Kövér, K. International Monetary Systems and Foreign Exchange Systems. In *Kiss, T., ed.,* 1973, pp. 213–19.

Kovyzhenko, V. Problems in Reducing Complex Labor to Simple Labor in Marxist Political Economy. *Prob. Econ.,* August 1973, *16*(4), pp. 3–22.

Kowal, Lubomyr M. The Market and Business Cycle Theories of M. I. Tugan-Baranovsky. *Rivista Int. Sci. Econ. Com.,* April 1973, *20*(4), pp. 305–34.

Kracht, Uwe. Marketing Unconventional Protein-Rich Foods—One Form of Nutrition Intervention. In *Berg, A.; Scrimshaw, N. S. and Call, D. L., eds.,* 1973, pp. 213–16.

Kraemer, Helena C. Improved Approximation to the Non-Null Distribution of the Correlation Coefficient. *J. Amer. Statist. Assoc.,* December 1973, *68*(344), pp. 1004–08.

Kraemer, Svend A. Warehouse Location and Allocation Problems Solved by Mathematical Programming Methods. In *Ross, M., ed.,* 1973, pp. 541–49.

Kraft, Arthur. Preference Orderings as Determinants of the Labor Force Behavior of Married Women. *Western Econ. J.,* September 1973, *11*(3), pp. 270–84.

_____ **and Kraft, John.** A Cross-Section Comparison of How Individuals Allocate Time: 1960 Versus 1970. *Nebr. J. Econ. Bus.,* Autumn 1973, *12*(4), pp. 51–68.

Kraft, Frederic B.; Granbois, Donald H. and Summers, John O. Brand Evaluation and Brand Choice: A Longitudinal Study. *J. Marketing Res.,* August 1973, *10*(3), pp. 235–41.

Kraft, Gerald. Free Transit Revisited. *Public Policy,* Winter 1973, *21*(1), pp. 79–105.

Kraft, John and Kraft, Arthur. A Cross-Section Comparison of How Individuals Allocate Time: 1960 Versus 1970. *Nebr. J. Econ. Bus.*, Autumn 1973, *12*(4), pp. 51–68.

Krainer, Robert E. Economic Structure and the Assignment Problem: A Contribution to the Theory of Macro-Economic Policy for Net Creditor Countries. *Can. J. Econ.*, May 1973, *6*(2), pp. 239–47.

────── The Valuation and Financing of the Multi-National Firm: Reply and Some Extensions. *Kyklos*, 1973, *26*(4), pp. 857–65.

Kramer, Fred A.; Rouse, Andrew M. and Harper, Edwin L. Personnel Limitations of "Instant Analysis." In *Novick, D.*, ed., 1973, pp. 201–05.

Kramer, Gerald H. On a Class of Equilibrium Conditions for Majority Rule. *Econometrica*, March 1973, *41*(2), pp. 285–97.

────── and Klevorick, Alvin K. Social Choice on Pollution Management: The Genossenschaften. *J. Public Econ.*, April 1973, *2*(2), pp. 101–46.

Kranzberg, Melvin. Can Technological Progress Continue to Provide for the Future? In *Weintraub, A.; Schwartz, E. and Aronson, J. R.*, eds., 1973, pp. 62–81.

Kraseman, Thomas W. Statistics and Analysis. *Mon. Lab. Rev.*, January 1973, *96*(1), pp. 58–59.

────── and Barker, Betty L. Employment and Payroll Costs of U.S. Multinational Companies. *Surv. Curr. Bus.*, October 1973, *53*(10), pp. 36–44.

Krashinsky, Michael and Nelson, Richard R. The Demand and Supply of Extra-Family Day Care. In *Young, D. R. and Nelson, R. R.*, eds., 1973, pp. 9–20.

────── and Nelson, Richard R. Two Major Issues of Public Policy: Public Subsidy and Organization of Supply. In *Young, D. R. and Nelson, R. R.*, eds., 1973, pp. 47–69.

Krasner, Stephen D. Manipulating International Commodity Markets: Brazilian Coffee Policy 1906 to 1962. *Public Policy*, Fall 1973, *21*(4), pp. 493–523.

Kraus, Alan. The Bond Refunding Decision in an Efficient Market. *J. Financial Quant. Anal.*, December 1973, *8*(5), pp. 793–806.

────── and Litzenberger, Robert H. A State-Preference Model of Optimal Financial Leverage. *J. Finance*, September 1973, *28*(4), pp. 911–22.

Krause, Kenneth R. Joint Ventures and Family Labor Sized Farms. *Amer. J. Agr. Econ.*, Part I, November 1973, *55*(4), pp. 628–32.

──────; Nelson, Paul E., Jr. and Hildreth, R. J. Organization and Control of the U.S. Food and Fiber Sector. *Amer. J. Agr. Econ.*, December 1973, *55*(5), pp. 851–59.

Krause, Lawrence B. Implications for Private Capital Markets. In *Krause, L. B. and Salant, W. S.*, eds., 1973, pp. 114–41.

Krauss, Melvyn B. The Economics of Integration: Introduction. In *Krauss, M. B.*, ed., 1973, pp. 11–29.

──────; Johnson, Harry G. and Skouras, Thanos. On the Shape and Location of the Production Possibility Curve. *Economica*, N.S., August 1973, *40*(159), pp. 305–10.

Kravis, Irving B. Trade as a Handmaiden of Growth: A Reply. *Econ. J.*, September 1973, *83*(331), pp. 885–89.

────── Trade as a Handmaiden of Growth: Reply. *Econ. J.*, March 1973, *83*(329), pp. 212–17.

────── A World of Unequal Incomes. *Ann. Amer. Acad. Polit. Soc. Sci.*, September 1973, *409*, pp. 61–80.

────── and Kenessey, Zoltan. Output and Prices in the International Comparison Project. *Rev. Income Wealth*, March 1973, *19*(1), pp. 49–67.

Kreinin, Mordechai E. The Static Effects of EEC Enlargement on Trade Flows. *Southern Econ. J.*, April 1973, *39*(4), pp. 559–68.

────── Disaggregated Import Demand Functions —Further Results. *Southern Econ. J.*, July 1973, *40*(1), pp. 19–25.

────── A Further Note on the Export Elasticity of Substitution. *Can. J. Econ.*, November 1973, *6*(4), pp. 606–08.

────── Some Economic Consequences of Reverse Preferences. *J. Common Market Stud.*, March 1973, *11*(3), pp. 161–72.

Krelle, Wilhelm. Dynamics of the Utility Function. In *Hicks, J. R. and Weber, W.*, eds., 1973, pp. 92–128.

────── and Siebke, Jürgen. Vermögensverteilung und Vermögenspolitik in der Bundesrepublik Deutschland. Ein Überblick. (Distribution of Wealth and Policy of Wealth Distribution in the Federal Republic of Germany. A Survey. With English summary.) *Z. ges. Staatswiss.*, August 1973, *129*(3), pp. 478–503.

Kremeier, A. and Brankamp, K. Effect of Technological Development upon Substitution Processes. In *Blohm, H. and Steinbuch, K.*, eds., 1973, pp. 121–32.

Kreps, Clifton H., Jr. Statistics for Public Policy Formation: New Needs. *Nebr. J. Econ. Bus.*, Winter 1973, *12*(1), pp. 61–63.

Kreps, Juanita. The Sources of Inequality. In *Ginzberg, E. and Yohalem, A. M.*, eds., 1973, pp. 85–96.

Kresl, Peter Karl. Nikolai Bukharin on Economic Imperialism. *Rev. Radical Polit. Econ.*, Spring 1973, *5*(1), pp. 3–12.

Kressler, Peter R. Investment Barriers Facing the United States Automotive Industry in the Japanese Market. *Ohio State U. Bull. Bus. Res.*, September 1973, *48*(9), pp. 1–3.

Kretschman, Stephen R. and Hempel, George H. Comparative Performances of Portfolio Maturity Policies of Commercial Banks. *Miss. Val. J. Bus. Econ.*, Fall 1973, *9*(1), pp. 55–75.

Krevnevich, V. The Manpower Needs of the National Economy and Vocational Guidance of Youth. *Prob. Econ.*, June 1973, *16*(2), pp. 68–83.

Krier, James E. and Montgomery, W. David. Resource Allocation, Information Cost and the Form of Government Intervention. *Natural Res. J.*, January 1973, *13*(1), pp. 89–105.

Kriesel, Herbert C. and Hedley, Douglas D. Planners as Factors in Agricultural Growth. In *Ofori, I. M.*, ed., 1973, pp. 33–41.

Křikava, L.; Mašek, J. and Malek, P. The Czech Experience in Nutrition Improvement. In *Berg,*

A.; Scrimshaw, N. S. and Call, D. L., eds., 1973, pp. 329–34.

Krishna, Raj. Government Operations in Foodgrains. In *Wadhva, C. D., ed.*, 1973, pp. 323–39.

———— A Note on the Elasticity of the Marketable Surplus of a Subsistence Crop. In *Wadhva, C. D., ed.*, 1973, pp. 313–18.

Krishnamoorthy, M. and Sudarsana Rao, J. Some Characteristics of Project Duration for a Class of Stochastic Activity Networks. In *Ross, M., ed.*, 1973, pp. 509–18.

Krishnaswamy, S. Y. Banking in the Rural Sector. In *Simha, S. L. N., ed.*, 1973, pp. 71–84.

Krislov, Joseph and Odewahn, Charles A. Contract Rejections: Testing the Explanatory Hopotheses. *Ind. Relat.*, October 1973, *12*(3), pp. 289–96.

———— **and Odewahn, Charles A.** The Relationship Between Union Contract Rejections and the Business Cycle—A Theoretical Approach. *Nebr. J. Econ. Bus.*, Summer 1973, *12*(3), pp. 23–36.

Kristof, Frank S. Federal Housing Policies: Subsidized Production, Filtration and Objectives: Part II. *Land Econ.*, May 1973, *49*(2), pp. 163–74.

———— The Role of State Housing Finance and Development Agencies in Future Federal Housing Programs. *Amer. Real Estate Urban Econ. Assoc. J.*, Fall 1973, *1*(2), pp. 53–72.

Kritzberg, Barry. An Unfinished Chapter in White-Collar Unionism: The Formative Years of the Chicago Newspaper Guild. *Labor Hist.*, Summer 1973, *14*(3), pp. 397–413.

Krivenkov, Iu. P. A Production Model with Circulating Capital. *Matekon*, Summer 1973, *9*(4), pp. 67–79.

Kroese, C. E. Dutch Trade with the People's Republic of China. *Law Contemp. Probl.*, Summer-Autumn 1973, *38*(2), pp. 230–39.

Krogh, D. C. The Budget and Industry. *S. Afr. J. Econ.*, June 1973, *41*(2), pp. 158–60.

Krohm, Gregory C. An Alternative View of the Returns to Burglary. *Western Econ. J.*, September 1973, *11*(3), pp. 364–67.

———— Does Punishment Deter? Comment. In *Rottenberg, S., ed.*, 1973, pp. 103–05.

———— The Pecuniary Incentives of Property Crime. In *Rottenberg, S., ed.*, 1973, pp. 31–34.

Kroncke, Charles O. The Process of Classifying Drivers: A Suggestion for Insurance Ratemaking: Reply. *J. Risk Ins.*, March 1973, *40*(1), pp. 147–48.

Krouse, Clement G. Experimental Decision-Making in the Theory of the Firm. In *Weston, J. F. and Ornstein, S. I., eds.*, 1973, pp. 129–38.

———— On the Theory of Optimal Investment, Dividends, and Growth in the Firm. *Amer. Econ. Rev.*, June 1973, *63*(3), pp. 269–79.

———— **and Lee, Wayne Y.** Optimal Equity Financing of the Corporation. *J. Financial Quant. Anal.*, September 1973, *8*(4), pp. 539–63.

Kroužek, Jan. Průmyslová dynamika—systémová disciplína zaměřená na komplexní zkoumáni dynamického chování systémů. (Industrial Dynamics—An Experimental Method for Study of Behaviour of Management Control Systems. With English summary.) *Ekon.-Mat. Obzor,* 1973, *9*(2), pp. 184–200.

Krueger, Anne O. and Bhagwati, Jagdish N. Exchange Control, Liberalization, and Economic Development. *Amer. Econ. Rev.*, May 1973, *63* (2), pp. 419–27.

Krumme, Gunter and Nishioka, Hisao. Location Conditions, Factors and Decisions: An Evaluation of Selected Location Surveys. *Land Econ.*, May 1973, *49*(2), pp. 195–205.

Krusius-Ahrenberg, Lolo. Kring företagsdemokratin i tyska förbundsrepubliken. (On Industrial Democracy in the Federal Republic of Germany. With English summary.) *Ekon. Samfundets Tidskr.*, 1973, *26*(4), pp. 270–99.

Krutilla, John V. Some Environmental Effects of Economic Development. In *Enthoven, A. C. and Freeman, A. M., III, eds.*, 1973, pp. 253–62.

Krzyzaniak, Marian. Benefit-Cost and Incidence Study of Transfers, Financed by Taxes on Profits, in a Growing Neoclassical Economy with Two Labor Inputs. *Public Finance*, 1973, *28*(2), pp. 151–77.

———— **and Özmucur, Süleyman.** The Distribution of Income and the Short-run Burden of Taxes in Turkey, 1968. *Finanzarchiv*, 1973, *32*(1), pp. 69–97.

Kubursi, A. A. and Jones, F. S. A Programming Model of Government Expenditures. *Public Finance*, 1973, *28*(1), pp. 84–93.

Kuga, Kiyoshi. More about Joint Production. *Int. Econ. Rev.*, February 1973, *14*(1), pp. 196–210.

———— Tariff Retaliation and Policy Equilibrium. *J. Int. Econ.*, November 1973, *3*(4), pp. 351–66.

———— **and Inada, Ken-Ichi.** Limitations of the "Coase Theorem" on Liability Rules. *J. Econ. Theory,* December 1973, *6*(6), pp. 606–13.

Kuh, Edwin and Belsley, David A. Time-Varying Parameter Structures: An Overview. *Ann. Econ. Soc. Measure*, October 1973, *2*(4), pp. 375–79.

Kuhbier, P. and Holub, H. W. Ein ungleichgewichtiges Modell des Wachstums und der Einkommensverteilung mit endogenen Strukturänderungen. (A Disequiliberated Model of Growth and Income Distribution with Endogenous Structural Change. With English summary.) *Jahr. Nationalökon. Statist.*, May 1973, *187*(4), pp. 289–300.

Kuhn, James W. An Economist's View of Women's Work. In *Ginzberg, E. and Yohalem, A. M., eds.*, 1973, pp. 63–68.

Kuipers, S. K. A Demand and Supply Model of Economic Growth. *De Economist,* November-December 1973, *121*(6), pp. 553–608.

———— The Positive Relation Between Average Labour Productivity and Labour Intensity. *Z. Nationalökon.*, 1973, *33*(1–2), pp. 115–26.

———— **and Nentjes, A.** Pollution in a Neo-Classical World: The Classics Rehabilitated? *De Economist,* January-February 1973, *121*(1), pp. 52–67.

Kujawa, Duane. Foreign Sourcing Decisions and the Duty to Bargain under the NLRA. In *Kujawa, D., ed.*, 1973, pp. 223–69.

Kukkonen, Pertti. Features of the Finnish Monetary Relationships: Comment. *Ekon. Samfundets Tidskr.*, 1973, *26*(2), pp. 123–31.

Kulldorff, Gunnar and Vännman, Kerstin. Estimation of the Location and Scale Parameters of a Pareto Distribution by Linear Functions of Order

Statistics. *J. Amer. Statist. Assoc.*, March 1973, *68* (341), pp. 218–27.

Kulshreshtha, S. N. Discriminating Credit Worthiness of Canadian Prairie Farmers. *Can. J. Agr. Econ.*, July 1973, *21*(2), pp. 16–24.

———— **and Wilson, A. G.** A Harmonic Analysis of Cattle and Hog Cycles in Canada. *Can. J. Agr. Econ.*, November 1973, *21*(3), pp. 34–45.

Kumar, Rishi. Demand Policies and Internal-External Balance Under Fixed Exchange Rates—The Mundellian Assignment: A Reformulation and Some Extensions. *Weltwirtsch. Arch.*, 1973, *109* (2), pp. 253–73.

Kumar, T. Krishna and Asher, Ephraim. Capital-Labor Substitution and Technical Progress in Planned and Market Oriented Economies: A Comparative Study. *Southern Econ. J.*, July 1973, *40*(1), pp. 103–09.

Küng, Emil. Economics on the Way into the 21st Century. *Nebr. J. Econ. Bus.*, Summer 1973, *12*(3), pp. 53–63.

Kunreuther, Howard. Why the Poor May Pay More for Food: Theoretical and Empirical Evidence. *J. Bus.*, July 1973, *46*(3), pp. 368–83.

Kurabayashi, Yoshimasa. Use of National Accounts as a Basis of Economic Data System. *Hitotsubashi J. Econ.*, June 1973, *14*(1), pp. 22–43.

Kurtz, David L. and Boone, Louis E. The Consumer Versus Holder-in-Due-Course Doctrine. *Ohio State U. Bull. Bus. Res.*, August 1973, *48*(8), pp. 1–3, 6.

———— **and Hostiuck, K. Tim.** Alderson's Functionalism and the Development of Marketing Theory. *J. Bus. Res.*, Fall 1973, *1*(2), pp. 141–56.

Kurtz, Jerome. Real Estate Tax Shelter—A Postscript. *Nat. Tax J.*, September 1973, *26*(3), pp. 341–46.

Kurtz, Robert D. and Sinkey, Joseph F., Jr. Bank Disclosure Policy and Procedures, Adverse Publicity and Bank Deposit Flows. *J. Bank Res.*, Autumn 1973, *4*(3), pp. 177–84.

Kushner, Harvey W. and Urken, Arnold B. Measuring Power in Voting Bodies. *Public Choice*, Summer 1973, *15*, pp. 77–85.

Kust, Leonard E. Alternatives for New Federal Revenues. In *Tax Foundation, Inc.*, 1973, pp. 14–18.

Kutcher, Gary P. On Decomposing Price-Endogenous Models. In *Goreux, L. M. and Manne, A. S., eds.*, 1973, pp. 499–519.

————; **Norton, Roger D. and Duloy, John H.** Investment and Employment Alternatives in the Agricultural District Model. In *Goreux, L. M. and Manne, A. S., eds.*, 1973, pp. 417–33.

Kutner, Michael H.; Beauchamp, John J. and Frome, Edward L. Regression Analysis of Poisson-Distributed Data. *J. Amer. Statist. Assoc.*, December 1973, *68*(344), pp. 935–40.

Kutscher, Ronald E. Projections of GNP, Income, Output, and Employment. *Mon. Lab. Rev.*, December 1973, *96*(12), pp. 27–42.

Kutter, Eckhard. A Model for Individual Travel Behaviour. *Urban Stud.*, June 1973, *10*(2), pp. 235–58.

Kux, Jaroslav. Comparative Study of Labour Productivity in Industry Between Czechoslo-

vakia, Hungary, France and Austria. *Czech. Econ. Digest.*, November 1973, (7), pp. 74–95.

Kuznets, Simon. Data for Quantitative Economic Analysis: Problems of Demand and Supply. In *Kuznets, S.*, 1973, pp. 243–62.

———— Economic Capacity and Population Growth. In *Kuznets, S.*, 1973, pp. 49–93.

———— The Measurement of Economic and Social Performance: Concluding Remarks. In *Moss, M., ed.*, 1973, pp. 579–92.

———— Modern Economic Growth: Findings and Reflections. *Amer. Econ. Rev.*, June 1973, *63*(3), pp. 247–58.

———— Modern Economic Growth: Findings and Reflections. In *Kuznets, S.*, 1973, pp. 165–84.

———— Notes on Stage of Economic Growth as a System Determinant. In *Kuznets, S.*, 1973, pp. 212–42.

———— Population and Economic Growth. In *Kuznets, S.*, 1973, pp. 1–48.

———— Problems in Comparing Recent Growth Rates for Developed and Less-Developed Countries. In *Kuznets, S.*, 1973, pp. 311–42.

Kwon, Jene K. and Thornton, Richard M. An Examination of the Financing of Federal Home Loan Bank Advances: A Reply. *Rev. Econ. Statist.*, May 1973, *55*(2), pp. 258.

———— The Effect of FHLB Bond Operations on Savings Inflows at Savings and Loan Associations: Reply. *J. Finance*, March 1973, *28*(1), pp. 203–06.

Kymn, Kern O. A Note on Logical Inconsistencies of the Kennedy Wage-Price Guidelines. *Southern Econ. J.*, January 1973, *39*(3), pp. 434–36.

Kyner, David B. and Jacoby, Jacob. Brand Loyalty vs. Repeat Purchasing Behavior. *J. Marketing Res.*, February 1973, *10*(1), pp. 1–9.

Laber, Gene. Human Capital in Southern Migration. *J. Human Res.*, Spring 1973, *8*(2), pp. 223–41.

Labia, N. A Neo-Classical Growth Model. *S. Afr. J. Econ.*, June 1973, *41*(2), pp. 164–66.

Labovitz, John R. 1969 Tax Reforms Reconsidered. In *Heimann, F. F., ed.*, 1973, pp. 101–31.

Labys, Walter C. A Lauric Oil Exports Model Based on Capital Stock Supply Adjustment. *Malayan Econ. Rev.*, April 1973, *18*(1), pp. 1–10.

Lacaze, Dominique. Prix duaux et prix du marché. Une théorie du producteur. (Dual Prices and Market Prices: A Theory of the Producer. With English summary.) *Revue Écon.*, March 1973, *24*(2), pp. 273–305.

Lacci, Livio. Agriculture's Contribution to the Gross National Product in Italy. *Rev. Econ. Cond. Italy*, July 1973, *27*(4), pp. 236–50.

Lacewell, Ronald D. and Griffin, Wade L. Long-Run Implications of a Tax in Kind to Reduce Supply and Increase Income: Comment. *Amer. J. Agr. Econ.*, Part I, November 1973, *55*(4), pp. 670–74.

Lachmann, L. M. The Budget and Inflation. *S. Afr. J. Econ.*, June 1973, *41*(2), pp. 146–49.

———— Sir John Hicks as a Neo-Austrian. *S. Afr. J. Econ.*, September 1973, *41*(3), pp. 195–207.

Lackó, Mária and Gács, János. A Study of Planning Behaviour on the National-Economic Level: An Attempt at Analysing a Few Correlations Based on Hungarian Data. *Econ. Planning*, 1973, *13* (1–2), pp. 91–119.

Lacroix, Robert and Bronsard, Camille. L'équilbre du consommateur en économie monétaire. (Consumer Equilibrium in a Monetary Economy. With English summary.) *Can. J. Econ.*, August 1973, *6* (3), pp. 332–43.

Ladd, Helen F. The Role of the Property Tax: A Reassessment. In *Musgrave, R. A., ed.*, 1973, pp. 39–86.

Lademann, John R. Monetary Policy in Switzerland. In *Holbik, K., ed.*, 1973, pp. 423–64.

Ladenkov, V. N. Studies of Migration of Skilled Personnel in Agriculture. *Prob. Econ.*, February 1973, *15*(10), pp. 62–80.

Ladenson, Mark L. The End of the North-South Wage Differential: Comment. *Amer. Econ. Rev.*, September 1973, *63*(4), pp. 754–56.

_____ Pitfalls in Financial Model Building: Reply and Some Further Extensions. *Amer. Econ. Rev.*, December 1973, *63*(5), pp. 1005–08.

Laevaert, W. Het Plan 1971–1975 Procedure, doelstellingen en draagwijdte. (The 1971–1975 Plan: Procedures, Aims and Significance. With English summary.) *Econ. Soc. Tijdschr.*, April 1973, *27*(2), pp. 157–71.

Laffer, Arthur B. Two Arguments for Fixed Rates. In *Johnson, H. G. and Swoboda, A. K., eds.*, 1973, pp. 25–34.

Lagos, Ricardo. The Historical Background to the Present Economic Situation in Chile. In *Zammit, J. A., ed.*, 1973, pp. 41–45.

Lahikainen, Pekka. Finnish Regional Development Policy. In *Moskoff, W., ed.*, 1973, pp. 140–44.

Lahne, Herbert J. Blacksmiths and Welders: Identity and Phenomenal Change: Comment. *Ind. Lab. Relat. Rev.*, January 1973, *26*(2), pp. 860–62.

Laibman, David. Values and Prices of Production: The Political Economy of the Transformation Problem. *Sci. Soc.*, Winter 1973–1974, *37*(4), pp. 404–36.

Laidler, David. The Current Inflation—The Problem of Explanation and the Problem of Policy. In *Robinson, J., ed.*, 1973, pp. 37–54.

_____ Expectations, Adjustment, and the Dynamic Response of Income to Policy Changes. *J. Money, Credit, Banking*, Part I, February 1973, *5*(1), pp. 157–72.

_____ The Influence of Money on Real Income and Inflation:—A Simple Model with some Empirical Tests for the United States 1953–72. *Manchester Sch. Econ. Soc. Stud.*, December 1973, *41*(4), pp. 367–95.

_____ Monetarist Policy Prescriptions and Their Background. *Manchester Sch. Econ. Soc. Stud.*, March 1973, *41*(1), pp. 59–71.

_____ Simultaneous Fluctuations in Prices and Output—A Business Cycle Approach. *Economica, N.S.*, February 1973, *40*(157), pp. 60–72.

_____; Byatt, I. C. R. and Holmans, A. E. Income and the Demand for Housing: Some Evidence for Great Britain. In *Parkin, M., ed.*, 1973, pp. 65–84.

Laiken, S. N. Financial Performance of Merging Firms in a Virtually Unconstrained Legal Environment. *Antitrust Bull.*, Winter 1973, *18*(4), pp. 827–51.

Laing, N. F. Technological Uncertainty and the Pure *Ex Ante* Theory of the Allocation of Resources.

Australian Econ. Pap., December 1973, *12*(21), pp. 221–38.

_____ A Theory of Employment Fluctuations in the Full Employment Zone. *Econ. Rec.*, December 1973, *49*(128), pp. 546–59.

Laird, Roy D. Handbook of Soviet Social Science Data: Agriculture. In *Mickiewicz, E., ed.*, 1973, pp. 65–90.

Lakhtin, G. The Subject of the Economics of Science. *Prob. Econ.*, December 1973, *16*(8), pp. 3–21.

Lal, Deepak. Disutility of Effort, Migration, and the Shadow Wage-rate. *Oxford Econ. Pap.*, March 1973, *25*(1), pp. 112–26.

_____ Employment, Income Distribution and a Poverty Redressal Index. *World Devel.*, March-April 1973, *1*(3–4), pp. 121–25.

Lal, Prem and Gupta, Satyadev. Inter-Regional Transfer of Real Resources: A Case Study of Pakistan, 1948–70. *Indian Econ. Rev.*, April 1973, *8*(1), pp. 39–60.

Lall, Sanjaya. Transfer-Pricing by Multinational Manufacturing Firms. *Oxford Bull. Econ. Statist.*, August 1973, *35*(3), pp. 173–95.

Lalwani, K. C. International Monetary System: Present Position and Future Outlook. *Econ. Aff.*, January–February 1973, *18*(1-2), pp. 29–38.

La Malfa, Ugo. Contenimento della spesa pubblica e lotta all'inflazione per una solida linea di stabilità. (Containment of Public Expenditure and Fight Against Inflation for Stability. With Engish summary.) *Bancaria*, November 1973, *29* (11), pp. 1342–45.

Lamb, Robert. Adam Smith's Concept of Alienation. *Oxford Econ. Pap.*, July 1973, *25*(2), pp. 275–85.

Lambelet, John C. Towards a Dynamic Two-Theater Model of the East-West Arms Race. *J. Peace Sci.*, Autumn 1973, *1*(1), pp. 1–38.

Lamont, Douglas F. Joining Forces with Foreign State Enterprises. *Harvard Bus. Rev.*, July-August 1973, *51*(4), pp. 68–79.

_____ Public Policy Toward Retailing: Mexico. In *Boddewyn, J. J. and Hollander, S. C., eds.*, 1972, pp. 229–44.

Lamphere, Robert J. Program Budgeting at John Hancock Life Insurance. In *Novick, D., ed.*, 1973, pp. 151–60.

Lampman, Robert J. Measured Inequality of Income: What Does It Mean and What Can It Tell Us? *Ann. Amer. Acad. Polit. Soc. Sci.*, September 1973, *409*, pp. 81–91.

Lamson, Robert W. Corporate Accounting for Environmental Effects. In *Dierkes, M. and Bauer, R. A., eds.*, 1973, pp. 230–47.

Lancaster, Kelvin. The Dynamic Inefficiency of Capitalism. *J. Polit. Econ.*, September-October 1973, *81*(5), pp. 1092–1109.

_____ Politically Feasible Income Redistribution in a Democracy. *Amer. Econ.*, Fall 1973, *17*(2), pp. 79–84.

Land, Charles E. Standard Confidence Limits for Linear Functions of the Normal Mean and Variance. *J. Amer. Statist. Assoc.*, December 1973, *68* (344), pp. 960–63.

Land, Kenneth C. Identification, Parameter Estimation, and Hypothesis Testing in Recursive Sociological Models. In *Goldberger, A. S. and Duncan, O. D., eds.*, 1973, pp. 19–49.

Landay, Donald M. and Kolodrubetz, Walter W. Coverage and Vesting of Full-Time Employees Under Private Retirement Plans. *Soc. Sec. Bull.*, November 1973, *36*(11), pp. 20–36.

Lande, Paul S. and Gordon, Peter. The Pricing of Goods and Agricultural Land in Multiregional General Equilibrium: Comment. *Southern Econ. J.*, July 1973, *40*(1), pp. 143–44.

Landon, John H. Pricing in Combined Gas and Electric Utilities: A Second Look. *Antitrust Bull.*, Spring 1973, *18*(1), pp. 83–98.

Landry, David M. U.S. Policy and Lessons Learned from the Central American Economic Integration Experience. *Southern Quart.*, July 1973, *11*(4), pp. 297–308.

Landsberg, Hans H.; Fisher, Joseph L. and Olson, Mancur. The No-Growth Society: Epilogue. In *Olson, M. and Landsberg, H. H., eds.*, 1973, pp. 229–41.

Landsberger, Henry A. and Fuchs, Claudio J. "Revolution of Rising Expectations" or "Traditional Life Ways"? A Study of Income Aspirations in a Developing Country. *Econ. Develop. Cult. Change*, January 1973, *21*(2), pp. 212–26.

Landsberger, Michael. Children's Age as a Factor Affecting the Simultaneous Determination of Consumption and Labor Supply. *Southern Econ. J.*, October 1973, *40*(2), pp. 279–88.

Lane, Elizabeth and Mighell, Ronald L. Writing and the Economic Researcher. *Agr. Econ. Res.*, January 1973, *25*(1), pp. 15–20.

Lange, O. Mr. Lerner's "Note on Socialist Economics." In *Farrell, M. J., ed.*, 1973, pp. 44–45.

Lanser, Howard P. and Lewellen, Wilbur G. Executive Pay Preferences. *Harvard Bus. Rev.*, September-October 1973, *51*(5), pp. 115–22.

Lansford, Robert R.; Clevenger, Thomas S. and Gorman, William D. Economic Planning for the Navajo Indian Irrigation Project. *N. Mex. Bus.*, April 1973, *26*(4), pp. 3–8.

Lansley, P. S. and Fiegehen, G. C. The Tax-Credit Proposals. *Nat. Inst. Econ. Rev.*, May 1973, (64), pp. 44–67.

Lantsev, M. Progress in Social Security for Agricultural Workers in the USSR. *Int. Lab. Rev.*, March 1973, *107*(3), pp. 239–52.

Lanzillotti, Robert F. and Blair, Roger D. Automobile Pollution, Externalities and Public Policy. *Antitrust Bull.*, Fall, 1973, *18*(3), pp. 431–47.

Laokole, Jean-Baptiste. Savings Banks and Savings Facilities in African Countries: Chad. In *Alberici, A. and Baravelli, M., eds.*, 1973, pp. 11–17.

Lapan, Harvey and Bardhan, Pranab K. Localized Technical Progress and Transfer of Technology and Economic Development. *J. Econ. Theory*, December 1973, *6*(6), pp. 585–95.

Lapidus, Leonard. Chartering, Branching, and the Concentration Problem: Discussion. In *Federal Reserve Bank of Boston*, 1973, pp. 46–53.

Lapping, Mark B. The Emergence of Federal Public Housing: Atlanta's Techwood Project. *Amer. J. Econ. Soc.*, October 1973, *32*(4), pp. 379–86.

Largay, James A., III. Microeconomic Foundations of Variable Costing. *Accounting Rev.*, January 1973, *48*(1), pp. 115–19.

_____ 100% Margins: Combating Speculation in Individual Security Issues. *J. Finance*, September 1973, *28*(4), pp. 973–86.

_____ and **West, Richard R.** Margin Changes and Stock Price Behavior. *J. Polit. Econ.*, Part I, March-April 1973, *81*(2), pp. 328–39.

Larnac, Pierre-Marie. Retards moyens et multiplicateurs dynamiques. (Mean Lags and Dynamic Multipliers. With English summary.) *Revue Écon.*, July 1973, *24*(4), pp. 646–64.

Laroque, Guy and Grandmont, Jean-Michel. Money in the Pure Consumption Loan Model. *J. Econ. Theory*, August 1973, *6*(4), pp. 382–95.

Larson, David and Bolton, Lena W. Calendar of Wage Increases and Negotiations for 1973. *Mon. Lab. Rev.*, January 1973, *96*(1), pp. 3–16.

Lash, Nicholas A. and Colwell, Peter F. Comparing Fiscal Indicators. *Rev. Econ. Statist.*, August 1973, *55*(3), pp. 321–26.

Laslett, Peter and Oosterveen, Karla. Long-term Trends in Bastardy in England: A Study of the Illegitimacy Figures in the Parish Registers and in the Reports of the Registrar General, 1561–1960. *Population Stud.*, July 1973, *27*(2), pp. 255–86.

Lasuén, J. R. Urbanisation and Development—the Temporal Interaction between Geographical and Sectoral Clusters. *Urban Stud.*, June 1973, *10*(2), pp. 163–88.

Latané, Henry A. Cross-Section Regularities in Returns on Investment in Common Stocks. *J. Bus.*, October 1973, *46*(4), pp. 512–16.

Latham, Michael C. A Historical Perspective. In *Berg, A.; Scrimshaw, N. S. and Call, D. L., eds.*, 1973, pp. 313–28.

Latham, Robert J. Operating Expenditures and Sponsored Research at U.S. Medical Schools: Comment. *J. Human Res.*, Fall 1973, *8*(4), pp. 519–22.

Latham, R. W. and Peel, David A. A Comment on Adjustments Costs and the Flexible Accelerator. *Rech. Écon. Louvain*, September 1973, *39*(3), pp. 371–76.

La Tourette, John E. Capital and Output in Postwar Canada. *Amer. Econ.*, Spring 1973, *17*(1), pp. 70–80.

_____ Public and Private Capital and the Capital Coefficient in Canada: Reply. *Quart. Rev. Econ. Bus.*, Spring 1973, *13*(1), pp. 100–04.

Lau, Lawrence J.; Christensen, Laurits R. and Jorgenson, Dale W. Transcendental Logarithmic Production Frontiers. *Rev. Econ. Statist.*, February 1973, *55*(1), pp. 28–45.

_____ and **Hickman, Bert G.** Elasticities of Substitution and Export Demands in a World Trade Model. *Europ. Econ. Rev.*, December 1973, *4*(4), pp. 347–80.

_____ and **Jamison, Dean T.** Semiorders and the Theory of Choice. *Econometrica*, September 1973, *41*(5), pp. 901–12.

_____ and **Yotopoulos, Pan A.** Micro Functions in a Macro Model: An Application to Agricultural Employment and Development Strategies. In *Ayal, E. B., ed.*, 1973, pp. 212–40.

_____ and **Yotopoulos, Pan A.** A Test for Relative Economic Efficiency: Some Further Results. *Amer. Econ. Rev.*, March 1973, *63*(1), pp. 214–23.

Laub, P. Michael; Deck, Beryl and Kichline, James L. Yields on Recently Offered Corporate Bonds. *Fed. Res. Bull.*, May 1973, *59*(5), pp. 336–37.

_____; **Stevens, Guy V. G. and Kichline, James L.** Obtaining the Yield on a Standard Bond from a Sample of Bonds with Heterogeneous Characteristics. *Fed. Res. Bull.*, May 1973, *59*(5), pp. 327–28.

Laudadio, Leonard. Teilhard de Chardin on Technological Progress. *Rev. Soc. Econ.*, October 1973, *31*(2), pp. 167–78.

_____ and **Jones, J. C. H.** Canadian Bank Mergers, the Public Interest and Public Policy. *Banca Naz. Lavoro Quart. Rev.*, June 1973, *105*, pp. 109–40.

_____; **Percy, M. and Jones, J. C. H.** Market Structure and Profitability in Canadian Manufacturing Industry: Some Cross-Section Results. *Can. J. Econ.*, August 1973, *6*(3), pp. 356–68.

Lăudatu, Alexandra. Determinarea capacității efective optime de producție în unitățile de construcții-montaj. (Determining the Best Effective Production Capacity in the Building-Assemblage Units. With English summary.) *Stud. Cercet. Econ.*, 1973, (2), pp. 89–98.

Läufer, Nikolaus K. A. Marktungleichgewichte und die Nichtoptimalität neutralen Revisionsverhaltens. (Market Disequilibria and the Nonoptimality of Neutral Revision Behaviour. With English summary.) *Jahr. Nationalökon. Statist.*, May 1973, *187* (4), pp. 301–29.

Laughhunn, D. J. and Forsyth, John D. Capital Rationing in the Face of Multiple Organizational Objectives. In *Cochrane, J. L. and Zeleny, M., eds.*, 1973, pp. 439–46.

Laumas, Prem S. and Mohabhat, Khan A. Money and Economic Development. *Indian Econ. J.*, April-June 1973, *20*(4–5), pp. 619–29.

Laumer, Helmut. Public Policy Toward Retailing: Uganda. In *Boddewyn, J. J. and Hollander, S. C., eds.*, 1972, pp. 327–36.

LaValle, Irving H. On Admissibility and Bayesness When Risk Attitude but Not the Preference Ranking Is Permitted to Vary. In *Cochrane, J. L. and Zeleny, M., eds.*, 1973, pp. 72–83.

Lave, Judith R.; Lave, Lester B. and Morton, Thomas E. Sources and Uses of Paramedical Personnel. In *Stein, B. and Miller, S. M., eds.*, 1973, pp. 37–68.

Lave, Lester B.; Morton, Thomas E. and Lave, Judith R. Sources and Uses of Paramedical Personnel. In *Stein, B. and Miller, S. M., eds.*, 1973, pp. 37–68.

_____ and **Seskin, Eugene P.** Air Pollution and Human Health. In *Enthoven, A. C. and Freeman, A. M., III, eds.*, 1973, pp. 88–99.

_____ and **Seskin, Eugene P.** An Analysis of the Association Between U.S. Mortality and Air Pollution. *J. Amer. Statist. Assoc.*, June 1973, *68*(342), pp. 284–90.

Lavely, Joe. Diversity of Interest Rates on Bank Savings Accounts. *Indiana Bus. Rev.*, September-October 1973, *48*, pp. 20–24.

Lavia, Alberto. Ricerche sui flussi distributivi. (Re-

search on the Distributive Fluctuations. With English summary.) *L'Impresa*, 1973, *15*(1), pp. 36–40.

Lawler, Edward E., III. Quality of Working Life and Social Accounts. In *Dierkes, M. and Bauer, R. A., eds.*, 1973, pp. 154–65.

Lawlor, Reed C. Copyright and Patent Protection for Computer Programs. In *The Diebold Group, Inc.*, 1973, pp. 204–12.

Lawson, H. B.; Newman, D. and Jones, H. J. M. Population Census: Some Recent British Developments in Methodology. *J. Roy. Statist. Soc.*, Part 4, 1973, *136*, pp. 505–20.

Layard, Richard. Denison and the Contribution of Education to National Income Growth: A Comment. *J. Polit. Econ.*, July-August 1973, *81*(4), pp. 1013–16.

_____ and **Jackman, Richard.** University Efficiency and University Finance. In *Parkin, M., ed.*, 1973, pp. 170–88.

Lazar, Fred and Donner, Arthur W. An Econometric Study of Segmented Labor Markets and the Structure of Unemployment: The Canadian Experience. *Int. Econ. Rev.*, June 1973, *14*(2), pp. 312–27.

_____ and **Donner, Arthur W.** Some Comments on the Canadian Phillips Curve. *Economica, N.S.*, May 1973, *40*(158), pp. 195–207.

Lazarcik, Gregor. Defense, Education and Health Expenditures and Their Relation to GNP in Eastern Europe, 1960-1970. *Amer. Econ.*, Spring 1973, *17*(1), pp. 29–34.

Lea, Richard B. Comments on Mock's Concepts of Information Value. *Accounting Rev.*, April 1973, *48*(2), pp. 389–93.

Leal de Araujo, Lucila. Extension of Social Security to Rural Workers in Mexico. *Int. Lab. Rev.*, October 1973, *108*(4), pp. 295–312.

Leamer, Edward E. Empirically Weighted Indexes for Import Demand Functions. *Rev. Econ. Statist.*, November 1973, *55*(4), pp. 441–50.

_____ Multicollinearity: A Bayesian Interpretation. *Rev. Econ. Statist.*, August 1973, *55*(3), pp. 371–80.

Leather, J. and Bennett, J. W. Investment Cut-off Rates for a Public Company. *Econ. Rec.*, June 1973, *49*(126), pp. 228–40.

Leathers, Charles G. and Evans, John S. Thorstein Veblen and the New Industrial State. *Hist. Polit. Econ.*, Fall 1973, *5*(2), pp. 420–37.

Lebédel, Claude. Public Policy Toward Retailing: East Germany. In *Boddewyn, J. J. and Hollander, S. C., eds.*, 1972, pp. 101–15.

Lebergott, Stanley. A New Technique for Time Series? Comment. *Rev. Econ. Statist.*, November 1973, *55*(4), pp. 525–27.

Lebowitz, Michael A. The Current Crisis of Economic Theory. *Sci. Soc.*, Winter 1973–1974, *37*(4), pp. 385–403.

Lécaillon, Jacques and Botalla-Gambetta, Brigitte. Inflation, répartition et chômage dans la France contemporaine. (Inflation, Distribution and Unemployment in Today's France. With English summary.) *Revue Écon.*, May 1973, *24*(3), pp. 373–400.

LeClerc, Guy and Marks, David H. Determination

of the Discharge Policy for Existing Reservoir Networks under Differing Objectives. *Water Resources Res.,* October 1973, *9*(5), pp. 1155–65.

Leclercq, M.; Hansen, P. and Brans, J. P. An Algorithm for Optimal Reloading of Pressurized Water Reactors. In *Ross, M., ed.,* 1973, pp. 417–28.

Leduc, Edgar and Baccanari, Samuel M. Interlocal Governmental Relations in Air Pollution Abatement. In *Gabriel, R. A. and Cohen, S. H., eds.,* 1973, pp. 113–28.

Lee, Alec M. Stochastic Processes: Discussant 1. In *Ross, M., ed.,* 1973, pp. 241–43.

Lee, Boyden E. The Euro-Dollar Multiplier. *J. Finance,* September 1973, *28*(4), pp. 867–74.

Lee, Douglass B., Jr. and Averous, Christian P. Land Allocation and Transportation Pricing in a Mixed Economy. *J. Reg. Sci.,* August 1973, *13*(2), pp. 173–85.

Lee, George E. and Nicholson, Raymond C. Managerial Information (Recording, Data, and Decision) Systems in Canada. *Amer. J. Agr. Econ.,* December 1973, *55*(5), pp. 921–29.

Lee, Jae Won and Kao, Charles H. C. An Empirical Analysis of China's Brain Drain into the United States. *Econ. Develop. Cult. Change,* April 1973, *21*(3), pp. 500–13.

Lee, Jong Ryool and Milstein, Jeffrey S. A Political Economy of the Vietnam War, 1965–1972. *Peace Sci. Soc.,* 1973, *21,* pp. 41–63.

Lee, Kok-Huat. Using Partially Balanced Designs for the Half Sample Replication Method of Variance Estimation. *J. Amer. Statist. Assoc.,* September 1973, *68*(343), pp. 612–14.

_____ Variance Estimation in Stratified Sampling. *J. Amer. Statist. Assoc.,* June 1973, *68*(342), pp. 336–42.

Lee, Maw Lin and Wallace, Richard L. Problems in Estimating Multiproduct Cost Functions: An Application to Hospitals. *Western Econ. J.,* September 1973, *11*(3), pp. 350–63.

Lee, Norman. Interactions between Economic and Eco-systems. In *Robinson, J., ed.,* 1973, pp. 125–33.

Lee, Ronald. Population in Preindustrial England: An Econometric Analysis. *Quart. J. Econ.,* November 1973, *87*(4), pp. 581–607.

Lee, Sang M. and Lerro, A. J. Optimizing the Portfolio Selection for Mutual Funds. *J. Finance,* December 1973, *28*(5), pp. 1087–1102.

Lee, S. Y. Some Basic Problems of Industrialization in Singapore. *J. Devel. Areas,* January 1973, *7*(2), pp. 185–216.

Lee, T.-C. and Seaver, S. K. A Positive Model of Spatial Equilibrium with Special Reference to the Broiler Markets. In *Judge, G. G. and Takayama, T., eds.,* 1973, pp. 443–63.

Lee, Wayne Y. and Krouse, Clement G. Optimal Equity Financing of the Corporation. *J. Financial Quant. Anal.,* September 1973, *8*(4), pp. 539–63.

Lees, Dennis and Doherty, Neil. Compensation for Personal Injury. *Lloyds Bank Rev.,* April 1973, (108), pp. 18–32.

Leet, Don R. and Shaw, John A. Research and Development and Productivity Change in the U.S.,

1948–1968. *J. Ind. Econ.,* December 1973, *22*(2), pp. 153–55.

de Leeuw, C. G. OR Aspects of a Management Information System. In *Ross, M., ed.,* 1973, pp. 465–74.

de Leeuw, Frank and Ekanem, Nkanta F. The Supply of Rental Housing: Reply. *Amer. Econ. Rev.,* June 1973, *63*(3), pp. 437–38.

_____ and Ekanem, Nkanta F. Time Lags in the Rental Housing Market. *Urban Stud.,* February 1973, *10*(1), pp. 39–68.

Lefeber, Louis. Income Distribution and Agricultural Development. In *[Rosenstein-Rodan, P.],* 1973, pp. 133–51.

_____ and Chakravarty, Sukhamoy. An Optimising Planning Model. In *Wadhva, C. D., ed.,* 1973, pp. 51–77.

Lefever, Harry G. The Involvement of the Men and Religion Forward Movement in the Cause of Labor Justice, Atlanta, Georgia, 1912–1916. *Labor Hist.,* Fall 1973, *14*(4), pp. 521–35.

Leff, Nathaniel H. Dependency Rates and Savings Rates: Reply. *Amer. Econ. Rev.,* March 1973, *63* (1), pp. 234.

_____ The Employment Problem in Development: Comment. In *Ayal, E. B., ed.,* 1973, pp. 275–77.

_____ Tropical Trade and Development in the Nineteenth Century: The Brazilian Experience. *J. Polit. Econ.,* May-June 1973, *81*(3), pp. 678–96.

Lefgren, John. Famine in Finland: 1867–1868. *Intermountain Econ. Rev.,* Fall 1973, *4*(2), pp. 17–31.

Lefter, Viorel and Sergent, Raisa. Utilizarea extensivă a capacităţilor de producţie şi influenţa ei asupra preţului de cost. (The Extensive Use of Production Capacities and its Influence on the Cost Price. With English summary.) *Stud. Cercet. Econ.,* 1973, (1), pp. 65–76.

Leftwich, Robert B. Foreign Direct Investments in the United States, 1962–71. *Surv. Curr. Bus.,* February 1973, *53*(2), pp. 29–40.

_____ and Boyke, Robert. Foreign Direct Investments in the United States in 1972. *Surv. Curr. Bus.,* August 1973, *53*(8), pp. 50–51.

Legey, L.; Ripper, M. and Varaiya, P. Effects of Congestion on the Shape of a City. *J. Econ. Theory,* April 1973, *6*(2), pp. 162–79.

Legler, John B. and Shapiro, Perry. Estimating Tax Revenue Changes in Response to Changes in Tax Rates. *Nat. Tax J.,* March 1973, *26*(1), pp. 111–13.

Lehman, Charles and Bogart, Leo. What Makes a Brand Name Familiar? *J. Marketing Res.,* February 1973, *10*(1), pp. 17–22.

Lehmann, David and Bell, Clive. The International Context of La Via Chilena. In *Zammit, J. A., ed.,* 1973, pp. 343–65.

Lehmann, Donald R. and Beckwith, Neil E. The Importance of Differential Weights in Multiple Attribute Models of Consumer Attitude. *J. Marketing Res.,* May 1973, *10*(2), pp. 141–45.

Lehtinen, Uolevi. On Some Possibilities of Taking Risk into Account in a Brand Choice Model. *Liiketaloudellinen Aikak.,* 1973, *22*(4), pp. 272–77.

Lehto, Sakari T. Nej till styrda kreditströmmar. ("No" to Directed Credit Flows. With English summary.) *Ekon. Samfundets Tidskr.,* 1973, *26* (2), pp. 101–03.

Leibenstein, Harvey. Competition and X-Efficiency: Reply. *J. Polit. Econ.*, May-June 1973, *81*(3), pp. 765–77.

_____ Notes on X-Efficiency and Technical Progress. In *Ayal, E. B., ed.*, 1973, pp. 18–38.

Leibowitz, Arleen. Intergenerational Determinants of Individual Incomes: Discussion. *Amer. Econ. Rev.*, May 1973, *63*(2), pp. 357–58.

Leigh, Arthur Hertel. von Thünen's Theory of Distribution and the Advent of Marginal Analysis. In *Rectenwald, H. C., ed.*, 1973, pp. 146–54.

Leigh, Duane E. and Rawlins, V. Lane. On the Stability of Relative Black-White Unemployment. *Mon. Lab. Rev.*, May 1973, *96*(5), pp. 30–32.

_____ and Ruffin, Roy J. Charity, Competition, and the Pricing of Doctors' Services. *J. Human Res.*, Spring 1973, *8*(2), pp. 212–22.

Leijonhufvud, Axel. Effective Demand Failures. *Swedish J. Econ.*, March 1973, *75*(1), pp. 27–48.

_____ Life Among the Econ. *Western Econ. J.*, September 1973, *11*(3), pp. 327–37.

_____ and Buchanan, James M. The Backbending Supply Curve of Labor: Comment on Buchanan, with His Reply. *Hist. Polit. Econ.*, Spring 1973, *5*(1), pp. 261–67.

_____ and Clower, Robert W. Say's Principle, What it Means and Doesn't Mean: Part I. *Intermountain Econ. Rev.*, Fall 1973, *4*(2), pp. 1–16.

Leinekugel-Le-Cocq, Armand R. and Tapiero, Charles S. Investissements, utilisation de capacité productive et amortissement: politiques optimales. (Investments, Capacity Utilization and Depreciation: Optimal Policies. With English summary.) *Revue Écon.*, May 1973, *24*(3), pp. 442–59.

Leininger, Wayne E. and Corcoran, A. Wayne. Stochastic Process Costing Models. *Accounting Rev.*, January 1973, *48*(1), pp. 105–14.

Leino, Unto. Lähdevero. (Source Tax. With English summary.) *Liiketaloudellinen Aikak.*, 1973, *22*(2), pp. 131–40.

Leitenberg, Milton. The Dynamics of Military Technology Today. *Int. Soc. Sci. J.*, 1973, *25*(3), pp. 336–57.

Leitmann, George and Stalford, Harold. Sufficiency Conditions for Nash Equilibria in N-Person Differential Games. In *Blaquière, A., ed.*, 1973, pp. 345–76.

Lekachman, Robert. Demand Theory and the Economist's Propensity to Assume: Comment. *J. Econ. Issues*, June 1973, *7*(2), pp. 241–43.

LeKashman, Raymond and Stolle, John F. The Total Cost Approach to Distribution. In *Britt, S. H. and Boyd, H. W., Jr., eds.*, 1973, pp. 441–58.

Lekvall, Per and Wahlbin, Clas. A Study of Some Assumptions Underlying Innovation Diffusion Functions. *Swedish J. Econ.*, December 1973, *75*(4), pp. 362–77.

Lell, Hans-Joachim. Integrated Regional Development. *Finance Develop.*, June 1973, *10*(2), pp. 23–25, 38.

Lemennicier, Bertrand. La contrainte budgétaire de l'Etat et l' "Optimal Policy Mix" en régime de change fixe et flexible. (The Optimal Policy Mix in a Fixed and Flexible Exchange Rate System Under the Constraint of Financing Monetary and Public Expenditure Policies. With English summary.) *Revue Écon.*, May 1973, *24*(3), pp. 473–504.

Lenehan, B.; O'Farrell, J. and Cantwell, J. Improving the Performance of a Local Authority Ambulance Service. In *Ross, M., ed.*, 1973, pp. 443–53.

Lent, George E. Taxation of Agricultural Income in Developing Countries. *Bull. Int. Fiscal Doc.*, August 1973, *27*(8), pp. 324–42.

_____; Casanegra, Milka and Guerard, Michèle. The Value-Added Tax in Developing Countries. *Int. Monet. Fund Staff Pap.*, July 1973, *20*(2), pp. 318–78.

Lenti, Libero. Business Cycles and Price Trend in Italy. *Rev. Econ. Cond. Italy*, May 1973, *27*(3), pp. 113–26.

Lentnek, Barry and Brown, Lawrence A. Innovation Diffusion in a Developing Economy: A Mesoscale View. *Econ. Develop. Cult. Change*, January 1973, *21*(2), pp. 274–92.

Lentz, Gary W.; Kendrick, James G. and Helmers, Glenn A. Specialization and Flexibility Considerations in a Polyperiod Firm Investment Model. *Can. J. Agr. Econ.*, February 1973, *21*(1), pp. 41–48.

Leonard, Walter J. The Development of the Black Bar. *Ann. Amer. Acad. Polit. Soc. Sci.*, May 1973, *407*, pp. 134–43.

Leonard, William N. Government in Political Economy. *Amer. Econ.*, Fall 1973, *17*(2), pp. 57–62.

_____ Research and Development in Industrial Growth: Reply. *J. Polit. Econ.*, September-October 1973, *81*(5), pp. 1249–52.

Leone, Fred C. and Moussa-Hamouda, Effat. Relative Efficiencies of 'O-BLUE' Estimators in Simple Linear Regression. *J. Amer. Statist. Assoc.*, December 1973, *68*(344), pp. 953–59.

Leontief, Wassily W. Explanatory Power of the Comparative Cost Theory of International Trade and Its Limits. In *[Tinbergen, J.]*, 1973, pp. 153–60.

_____ Input-Output Analysis in Business Planning. In *The Diebold Group, Inc.*, 1973, pp. 78–83.

_____ National Income, Economic Structure, and Environmental Externalities. In *Moss, M., ed.*, 1973, pp. 565–76.

Lermer, George. Evidence from Trade Data Regarding the Rationalizing of Canadian Industry. *Can. J. Econ.*, May 1973, *6*(2), pp. 248–56.

Lerner, Abba P. The Challenge of Full Employment with Price Stability: "Incomes Policies." In *Levy, M. E., ed.*, 1973, pp. 14–22.

_____ A Note on Socialist Economics. In *Farrell, M. J., ed.*, 1973, pp. 39–43.

Lerner, Eugene M. The Bank Holding Company—A Superior Device for Expanding Activities? Discussion. In *Federal Reserve Bank of Boston*, 1973, pp. 94–97.

_____ Simulating a Cash Budget. In *Thomas, W. E., Jr., ed.*, 1973, pp. 266–78.

_____ and Breen, William J. Corporate Financial Strategies and Market Measures of Risk and Return. *J. Finance*, May 1973, *28*(2), pp. 339–51.

LeRoy, Stephen F. Interest Rates and the Inflation Premium. *Fed. Res. Bank Kansas City Rev.*, May 1973, pp. 11–18.

―――― Property Tax Assessment: How Fair Is It? *Fed. Res. Bank Kansas City Rev.*, July-August 1973, pp. 7–16.

―――― Risk Aversion and the Martingale Property of Stock Prices. *Int. Econ. Rev.*, June 1973, *14*(2), pp. 436–46.

Lerro, A. J. and Lee, Sang M. Optimizing the Portfolio Selection for Mutual Funds. *J. Finance*, December 1973, *28*(5), pp. 1087–1102.

Lerviks, Alf-Erik. Synpunkter på ekonomiskt modellbyggande. (On Model Construction in Economic Sciences. With English summary.) *Ekon. Samfundets Tidskr.*, 1973, *26*(4), pp. 301–04.

Lesage, Richard and Sellekaerts, Willy. A Reformulation and Empirical Verification of the Administered Prices Inflation Hypothesis: The Canadian Case. *Southern Econ. J.*, January 1973, *39*(3), pp. 345–60.

Leslie, Dennis C.; Mazis, Michael B. and Settle, Robert B. Elimination of Phosphate Detergents and Psychological Reactance. *J. Marketing Res.*, November 1973, *10*(4), pp. 390–95.

Leslie, D. G. A Note on the Regional Distribution of Unemployment. *Oxford Bull. Econ. Statist.*, August 1973, *35*(3), pp. 233–37.

L'Esperance, Wilford L. Estimating Corporate Net Income in Ohio. *Ohio State U. Bull. Bus. Res.*, October 1973, *48*(10), pp. 4–5.

Lessard, Donald R. International Portfolio Diversification: A Multivariate Analysis for a Group of Latin American Countries. *J. Finance*, June 1973, *28*(3), pp. 619–33.

―――― and Bower, Richard S. An Operational Approach to Risk-Screening. *J. Finance*, May 1973, *28*(2), pp. 321–37.

Lester, Richard A. Manipulation of the Labor Market. In *Somers, G. G., ed.*, 1973, pp. 47–55.

Letwin, William. Four Fallacies about Economic Development. In *Reynolds, L. G.; Green, G. D. and Lewis, D. R., eds.*, 1973, pp. 502–17.

Leue, G. Transformation of Technical Forecasts into Market Predictions for the Computer Industry. In *Blohm, H. and Steinbuch, K., eds.*, 1973, pp. 73–78.

Leung, David T. W. The Concept of Effective Subsidy and its Application to the Canadian Flour Milling Industry. *Can. J. Agr. Econ.*, February 1973, *21*(1), pp. 1–9.

Leunis, J. V. and Vandenborre, R. J. An Interregional Analysis of the United States Soybean Industry. In *Judge, G. G. and Takayama, T., eds.*, 1973, pp. 274–97.

Leuschner, Dieter. Volkswirtschaftliche Kosten und Erträge der Beschäftigung ausländischer Arbeitnehmer. (With English summary.) *Z. ges. Staatswiss.*, October 1973, *129*(4), pp. 702–13.

Lev, Baruch. The RAS Method for Two-Dimensional Forecasts. *J. Marketing Res.*, May 1973, *10*(2), pp. 153–59.

―――― and Hirsch, Seev. Trade and Per Capita Income Differentials: A Test of the Burenstam-Linder Hypothesis. *World Devel.*, September 1973, *1*(9), pp. 11–17.

―――― and Orgler, Yair E. Analysis of the Lease-or-Buy Decision: Comment. *J. Finance*, September 1973, *28*(4), pp. 1022–23.

Levenbach, Hans. The Estimation of Heteroscedasticity from a Marginal Likelihood Function. *J. Amer. Statist. Assoc.*, June 1973, *68*(342), pp. 436–39.

Lever, William F. Cyclical Changes in Factors Affecting Industrial Location. *Land Econ.*, May 1973, *49*(2), pp. 218–21.

―――― A Markov Approach to the Optimal Size of Cities in England and Wales. *Urban Stud.*, October 1973, *10*(3), pp. 353–65.

Leveson, Irving. Cost-Benefit Analysis and Program Target Populations: The Narcotics Addiction Treatment Case. *Amer. J. Econ. Soc.*, April 1973, *32*(2), pp. 129–42.

―――― Strategies against Urban Poverty. In *Boulding, K. E.; Pfaff, M. and Pfaff, A., eds.*, 1973, pp. 130–59.

Levhari, David and Barkai, Haim. The Impact of Experience on Kibbutz Farming. *Rev. Econ. Statist.*, February 1973, *55*(1), pp. 56–63.

―――― and Peles, Yoram. Market Structure, Quality and Durability. *Bell J. Econ. Manage. Sci.*, Spring 1973, *4*(1), pp. 235–48.

―――― and Sheshinski, Eytan. Experience and Productivity in the Israel Diamond Industry. *Econometrica*, March 1973, *41*(2), pp. 239–53.

Levi, J. F. S. Migration from the Land and Urban Unemployment in Sierra Leone. *Oxford Bull. Econ. Statist.*, November 1973, *35*(4), pp. 309–26.

Levi, Maurice D. Errors in the Variables Bias in the Presence of Correctly Measured Variables. *Econometrica*, September 1973, *41*(5), pp. 985–86.

Levin, A. Problems in the Control of Consumer Demand. *Prob. Econ.*, December 1973, *16*(8), pp. 81–104.

Levin, Fred J. Examination of the Money-Stock Control Approach of Burger, Kalish, and Babb. *J. Money, Credit, Banking*, November 1973, *5*(4), pp. 924–38.

Levin, Harvey J. Television's Second Chance: A Retrospective Look at the Sloan Cable Commission. *Bell J. Econ. Manage. Sci.*, Spring 1973, *4*(1), pp. 343–65.

Levin, Jonathan. Government Finance and the Balance of Payments. In *[Halm, G. N.]*, 1973, pp. 199–210.

Levin, Samuel M. Economic Aspects of Modern Speed. In *Levin, S. M.*, 1973, pp. 65–77.

―――― The Economic Background of the National Labor Relations Act. In *Levin, S. M.*, 1973, pp. 89–98.

―――― The End of Ford Profit Sharing. In *Levin, S. M.*, 1973, pp. 51–64.

―――― Ford Profit Sharing, 1914–1920. In *Levin, S. M.*, 1973, pp. 33–50.

―――― The Ford Unemployment Policy. In *Levin, S. M.*, 1973, pp. 79–88.

―――― The Impact of War on Industrial Technology. In *Levin, S. M.*, 1973, pp. 99–114.

―――― John Dewey's Evaluation of Technology. In *Levin, S. M.*, 1973, pp. 157–74.

―――― Organized Labor and the Equality of Sacrifice Program. In *Levin, S. M.*, 1973, pp. 127–42.

―――― The Second Industrial Conference and Adjustment of Disputes. In *Levin, S. M.*, 1973, pp. 15–32.

—— Social Implications of Factory Labor. In *Levin, S. M.*, 1973, pp. 3–13.

—— Technology and Liberty. In *Levin, S. M.*, 1973, pp. 115–26.

—— Thoughts on Industrial Democracy. In *Levin, S. M.*, 1973, pp. 143–56.

Levin, Sharon G. and Shepherd, William G. Managerial Discrimination in Large Firms. *Rev. Econ. Statist.*, November 1973, *55*(4), pp. 412–22.

Levine, Daniel S. and Yett, Donald E. A Method for Constructing Proxy Measures of Health Status. In *Berg, R. L., ed.*, 1973, pp. 12–22.

Levine, Kenneth C. Corporate Modeling of a Life Insurance Company: A Developmental Game Plan. *J. Risk Ins.*, December 1973, *40*(4), pp. 555–64.

Levinson, F. James and Call, David L. A Systematic Approach to Nutrition Intervention Programs. In *Berg, A.; Scrimshaw, N. S. and Call, D. L., eds.*, 1973, pp. 165–97.

Levitan, Sar A. The Art of Giving Away Federal Dollars. In *Levitan, S. A., ed.*, 1973, pp. 1–20.

—— Manpower Programs for a Healthier Economy. In *Ulman, L., ed.*, 1973, pp. 102–16.

—— The Payoff of the Federal Social Dollar. In *Levitan, S. A., ed.*, 1973, pp. 259–72.

—— and Johnston, William B. Job Redesign, Reform, Enrichment: Exploring the Limitations. *Mon. Lab. Rev.*, July 1973, *96*(7), pp. 35–41.

—— and Marwick, David. Work and Training for Relief Recipients. *J. Human Res.*, Supplement 1973, *8*, pp. 5–18.

—— and Taggart R. Employment-Earnings Inadequacy: A Measure of Welfare. *Mon. Lab. Rev.*, October 1973, *96*(10), pp. 19–27.

Levy, Fred D., Jr. Economic Planning in Venezuela. In *Thurber, C. E. and Graham, L. S., eds.*, 1973, pp. 81–108.

Levy, Girard W. Urban Social Indicators and Corporate Social Accounts. In *Dierkes, M. and Bauer, R. A., eds.*, 1973, pp. 212–18.

Levy, Haim. The Demand for Assets Under Conditions of Risk. *J. Finance*, March 1973, *28*(1), pp. 79–96.

—— Stochastic Dominance Among Log-Normal Prospects. *Int. Econ. Rev.*, October 1973, *14*(3), pp. 601–14.

—— Stochastic Dominance, Efficiency Criteria, and Efficient Portfolios: The Multi-Period Case. *Amer. Econ. Rev.*, December 1973, *63*(5), pp. 986–94.

—— and Arditti, Fred D. Valuation, Leverage, and the Cost of Capital in the Case of Depreciable Assets. *J. Finance*, June 1973, *28*(3), pp. 687–93.

——; Arditti, Fred D. and Grinold, Richard C. The Investment-Consumption Decision under Capital Rationing: An Efficient Set Analysis. *Rev. Econ. Stud.*, July 1973, *40*(3), pp. 367–76.

Levy, Marion J., Jr. A Sociologist Who Knew Science. *Soc. Sci. Quart.*, December 1973, *54*(3), pp. 469–79.

Levy, Michael E. Major Economic Issues of the 1970's. In *Levy, M. E., ed.*, 1973, pp. 1–5.

—— and Torres, Juan. Grants and Revenue Shar-

ing Abroad: Canada, Australia, West Germany. In *Moskoff, W., ed.*, 1973, pp. 4–21.

Levy, Mildred B. and Wadycki, Walter J. The Influence of Family and Friends on Geographic Labor Mobility: An International Comparison. *Rev. Econ. Statist.*, May 1973, *55*(2), pp. 198–203.

Levy, Sidney J. Consumer Views of Bank Services. *J. Bank Res.*, Summer 1973, *4*(2), pp. 100–04.

Levy, Yvonne. Pollution Control: Two Industries. *Fed. Res. Bank San Francisco Rev.*, January-February 1973, pp. 12–20.

—— Recovery in Washington. *Fed. Res. Bank San Francisco Rev.*, September-October 1973, pp. 22–28.

——; Chen, Dean and Johnston, Verle. Boom in the West. *Fed. Res. Bank San Francisco Rev.*, May-June 1973, pp. 3–8.

Levy-Garboua, Louis. Rémunère-t-on les études? (Does Schooling Pay? With English summary.) *Consommation*, July-September 1973, *20*(3), pp. 57–81.

LeWarne, Charles P. On the Wobbly Train to Fresno. *Labor Hist.*, Spring 1973, *14*(2), pp. 264–89.

Lewellen, Wilbur G. and Edmister, Robert O. A General Model for Accounts-Receivable Analysis and Control. *J. Financial Quant. Anal.*, March 1973, *8*(2), pp. 195–206.

—— and Johnson, Robert W. Analysis of the Lease-or-Buy Decision: Reply. *J. Finance*, September 1973, *28*(4), pp. 1024–28.

—— and Lanser, Howard P. Executive Pay Preferences. *Harvard Bus. Rev.*, September-October 1973, *51*(5), pp. 115–22.

—— and Racette, George A. Convertible Debt Financing. *J. Financial Quant. Anal.*, December 1973, *8*(5), pp. 777–92.

Lewin, David. Public Employment Relations: Confronting the Issues. *Ind. Relat.*, October 1973, *12*(3), pp. 309–21.

—— Wage Parity and the Supply of Police and Firemen. *Ind. Relat.*, February 1973, *12*(1), pp. 77–85.

Lewin, Haskell and Morris, Jacob. The Skilled Labor Reduction Problem. *Sci. Soc.*, Winter 1973–1974, *37*(4), pp. 454–72.

Lewis, Darrell R.; Wentworth, Donald R. and Orvis, Charles C. Economics in the Junior Colleges: Terminal or Transfer? *J. Econ. Educ.*, Spring 1973, *4*(2), pp. 100–10.

Lewis, H. Gregg. Economic Analysis of Fertility in Israel: Point and Counterpoint: Comment. *J. Polit. Econ.*, Part II, March-April 1973, *81*(2), pp. S234–37.

—— and Becker, Gary S. On the Interaction between the Quantity and Quality of Children. *J. Polit. Econ.*, Part II, March-April 1973, *81*(2), pp. S279–88.

Lewis, John P. Grants, Loans, and Local-Cost Financing: Comment. In *Lewis, J. P. and Kapur, I., eds.*, 1973, pp. 77–81.

—— Wanted in India: A Relevant Radicalism. In *Wadhva, C. D., ed.*, 1973, pp. 216–32.

—— and Kapur, Ishan. The World Bank Group, Multilateral Aid, and the 1970s. In *Lewis, J. P. and Kapur, I., eds.*, 1973, pp. 1–11.

Lewis, M. K. and Hatch, J. H. Economies of Scale in Australian Banking: Reply. *Econ. Rec.*, September 1973, *49*(127), pp. 481–84.

Lewis, Morgan V. and Cohn, Elchanan. Recruiting and Retaining Participants in a Manpower Program. *Ind. Lab. Relat. Rev.*, January 1973, *26*(2), pp. 842–50.

Lewis, Stephen R., Jr. Agricultural Taxation and Intersectoral Resource Transfers. *Food Res. Inst. Stud.*, 1973, *12*(2), pp. 93–114.

Lewis, Wilfred, Jr. Economic Policy and Inflation in the 1960's—a Review Essay. *Mon. Lab. Rev.*, November 1973, *96*(11), pp. 49–52.

Lewis, William Cris. Public Investment Impacts and Regional Economic Growth. *Water Resources Res.*, August 1973, *9*(4), pp. 851–60.

Li, Wen L. Temporal and Spatial Analysis of Fertility Decline in Taiwan. *Population Stud.*, March 1973, *27*(1), pp. 97–104.

_____; Smith, Gerald W. and Udell, Jonathan. The Gambling Business in the U.S.A. *Ohio State U. Bull. Bus. Res.*, April 1973, *48*(4), pp. 1–3, 6–7.

Lianos, Theodore P. and Prodromidis, Kyprianos P. City Size and Patterns of Employment Structure. In *Mattila, J. M. and Thompson, W. R., eds.*, 1973, pp. 91–104.

Liao, Shu S. Responsibility Centers. *Manage. Account.*, July 1973, *55*(1), pp. 46–48.

Licari, J. A.; Neuberger, Egon and Brown, Alan A. A Dynamic CES Production Function Interpretation of Hungarian Growth. *Acta Oecon.*, 1973, *11*(4), pp. 305–24.

Lieber, Harvey and Rosinoff, Bruce. Evaluating the State's Role in Water Pollution Control. *Amer. Real Estate Urban Econ. Assoc. J.*, Fall 1973, *1*(2), pp. 73–87.

Lieberman, Sima. Economic Achievement in the German Democratic Republic 1949–1969. *Schweiz. Z. Volkswirtsch. Statist.*, December 1973, *109*(4), pp. 554–78.

Liebhafsky, H. H. "The Problem of Social Cost" —An Alternative Approach. *Natural Res. J.*, October 1973, *13*(4), pp. 615–76.

Lieftinck, Pieter. To Float or Not to Float. *Finance Develop.*, December 1973, *10*(4), pp. 27–29, 41–42.

Liepmann, Peter and Gerlach, Knut. Industrialisierung und Siedlungsstruktur—Bemerkungen zum regionalpolitischen Programm einer aktiven Sanierung der bayerischen Rückstandsgebiete. (Industrialization and Settlement Structure—Remarks on the Regional Program of the Promotion of Less Developed Regions in Bavaria. With English summary.) *Jahr. Nationalökon. Statist.*, August 1973, *187*(6), pp. 507–21.

Lierman, F.; Van Eeckhoudt, M. and Verheirstraeten, A. Het conjunctureel patroon van de termijnstructuur van de interestvoeten—met een grafische analyse voor België. *Tijdschr. Econ.*, 1973, *18*(4), pp. 545–89.

Liew, C. K. A Computer Program for Dynamic Multipliers. *Econometrica*, November 1973, *41*(6), pp. 1207.

Lifson, K. A. and Blackmarr, Brian R. Simulation and Optimization Models for Asset Deployment and Funds Sources Balancing Profit, Liquidity and

Growth. *J. Bank Res.*, Autumn 1973, *4*(3), pp. 239–55.

Lilley, William, III. The Homebuilders' Lobby. In *Pynoos, J.; Schafer, R. and Hartman, C. W., eds.*, 1973, pp. 30–48.

Lim, David. A Note on Supply Response of Tin Producers, 1949–1969. *Malayan Econ. Rev.*, October 1973, *18*(2), pp. 50–59.

Lin, Cheyeh. A Price Index for Life Insurance: Reply. *J. Risk Ins.*, December 1973, *40*(4), pp. 630.

Lin, Hui-Sheng; Speare, Alden, Jr. and Speare, Mary C. Urbanization, Non-Familial Work, Education, and Fertility in Taiwan. *Population Stud.*, July 1973, *27*(2), pp. 323–34.

Lin, Steven A. Y. Effects of Monetary Policy and Credit Conditions on the Housing Sector. *Amer. Real Estate Urban Econ. Assoc. J.*, June 1973, *1*(1), pp. 8–30.

Lind, Robert C. Spatial Equilibrium, the Theory of Rents, and the Measurement of Benefits from Public Programs. *Quart. J. Econ.*, May 1973, *87*(2), pp. 188–207.

Lindauer, John. Stabilization Inflation and the Inflation-Unemployment Trade-off. *Indian Econ. J.*, April-June 1973, *20*(4–5), pp. 541–47.

Lindbeck, Assar. Research on Internal Adjustment to External Disturbances: A European View. In *Bergsten, C. F., ed.*, 1973, pp. 61–74.

Lindberg, Leon N. and Scheingold, Stuart A. The Future of the European Community: Equilibrium and Beyond. In *Falk, R. A. and Mendlovitz, S. H., eds.*, 1973, pp. 435–54.

Lindblad, Sven and Hallencreutz, Ingrid. Public Policy Toward Retailing: Sweden. In *Boddewyn, J. J. and Hollander, S. C., eds.*, 1972, pp. 283–95.

Lindblom, Charles E. The Rediscovery of the Market. In *Reynolds, L. G.; Green, G. D. and Lewis, D. R., eds.*, 1973, pp. 532–43.

Lindholm, Richard W. State-Local School and Highway Expenditure Trends, 1965-1966 and 1969-1970. *Public Finance Quart.*, January 1973, *1*(1), pp. 29–34.

Lindley, Robert M. and Evans, Graham J. The Use of RAS and Related Models in Manpower Forecasting. *Econ. Planning*, 1973, *13*(1–2), pp. 53–73.

Lindsay, Cotton M. Real Returns to Medical Education. *J. Human Res.*, Summer 1973, *8*(3), pp. 331–48.

Lindström, Caj-Gunnar. Företagsekonomin som vetenskapsgren och undervisnings disciplin. (Business Economics as a Branch of Science and Educational Discipline. With English summary.) *Ekon. Samfundets Tidskr.*, 1973, *26*(3), pp. 201–10.

_____ Om beslutsplanering. (Decision Planning. With English summary.) *Ekon. Samfundets Tidskr.*, January 1973, *26*(1), pp. 32–38.

Ling, Robert F. A Probability Theory of Cluster Analysis. *J. Amer. Statist. Assoc.*, March 1973, *68*(341), pp. 159–64.

Link, Charles R. The Quantity and Quality of Education and Their Influence on Earnings: The Case of Chemical Engineers. *Rev. Econ. Statist.*, May 1973, *55*(2), pp. 241–47.

Liossatos, Panagis and Isard, Walter. Social Injustice

and Optimal Space-Time Development. *J. Peace Sci.*, Autumn 1973, *1*(1), pp. 69–93.

Lipsky, David B. Employer Role in Hard-Core Trainee Success. *Ind. Relat.*, May 1973, *12*(2), pp. 125–36.

———— **and Drotning, John E.** The Influence of Collective Bargaining on Teachers' Salaries in New York State. *Ind. Lab. Relat. Rev.*, October 1973, *27*(1), pp. 18–35.

Lisandru, N. Necesitatea verigii comerciale cu ridicata în organizarea circulaţiei mărfurilor. (The Necessity of a Wholesale Trade Link in Organizing the Circulation of Goods. With English summary.) *Stud. Cercet. Econ.*, 1973, (1), pp. 133–39.

Lissner, Will. Developing Agriculture in Low Income Countries. *Amer. J. Econ. Soc.*, October 1973, *32*(4), pp. 436–38.

Lister, R. J. Financing an Acquisition. In *Lister, R. J., ed.*, 1973, pp. 186–200.

van Lith, Jan A. Government Procurement in the Benelux Countries. In *Scaperlanda, A. E., ed.*, 1973, pp. 163–90.

Litschert, Robert L. and Nicholson, Edward A., Jr. Long-Range Planning in Banking: Ten Cases in the U.S. and Britain. *J. Bank Res.*, Spring 1973, *4*(1), pp. 31–40.

Little, Charles H. and Doeksen, Gerald A. Measurement of Leakage by the Use of an Input-Output Model: Reply. *Amer. J. Agr. Econ.*, Part I, November 1973, *55*(4), pp. 682.

Little, I. M. D. and Mirrlees, James A. Further Reflections on the OECD Manual of Project Analysis in Developing Countries. In *[Rosenstein-Rodan, P.]*, 1973, pp. 257–80.

Littlechild, S. C. Myopic Investment Rules and Toll Charges in a Transport Network. *J. Transp. Econ. Policy*, May 1973, *7*(2), pp. 194–204.

Littleton, A. C. and Paton, W. A. An Introduction to Corporate Accounting Standards. In *Thomas, W. E., Jr., ed.*, 1973, pp. 446–53.

Littrell, Earl K., III. A Note on Discounted Cash Flow Examples. *Accounting Rev.*, January 1973, *48*(1), pp. 132–34.

Litzenberger, Robert H. and Budd, A. P. Changes in the Supply of Money, the Firm's Market Value and Cost of Capital. *J. Finance*, March 1973, *28*(1), pp. 49–57.

———— **and Joy, O. Maurice.** Inter-Industry Profitability Under Uncertainty. *Western Econ. J.*, September 1973, *11*(3), pp. 338–49.

————; **Joy, O. Maurice and Jones, Charles P.** Leverage and the Valuation of Risk Assets: An Empirical Test. *J. Financial Quant. Anal.*, March 1973, *8*(2), pp. 227.

———— **and Kraus, Alan.** A State-Preference Model of Optimal Financial Leverage. *J. Finance*, September 1973, *28*(4), pp. 911–22.

Liu, Ta-Chung and Yeh, Kung-Chia. Chinese and Other Asian Economies: A Quantitative Evaluation. *Amer. Econ. Rev.*, May 1973, *63*(2), pp. 215–23.

Livesey, D. A. Optimum City Size: A Minimum Congestion Cost Approach. *J. Econ. Theory*, April 1973, *6*(2), pp. 144–61.

Liviatan, Nissan and Kemp, Murray C. Production

and Trade Patterns under Uncertainty. *Econ. Rec.*, June 1973, *49*(126), pp. 215–27.

Livingstone, I. and Bevin, J. H. Economic History and Economics Teaching. In *Livingstone, I., et al., eds.*, 1973, pp. 95–100.

————, **et al.** A Review of the Debate. In *Livingstone, I., et al., eds.*, 1973, pp. 17–39.

Lloyd, A. G. and Wills, Ian R. Economic Theory and Sheep-Cattle Combinations. *Australian J. Agr. Econ.*, April 1973, *17*(1), pp. 58–67.

Lloyd, P. J. Optimal Intervention in a Distortion-Ridden Open Economy. *Econ. Rec.*, September 1973, *49*(127), pp. 377–93.

Lluch, Constantino. The Extended Linear Expenditure System. *Europ. Econ. Rev.*, April 1973, *4*(1), pp. 21–32.

———— **and Morishima, M.** Demand for Commodities under Uncertain Expectation. In *Morishima, M., et al.*, 1973, pp. 169–83.

Loboda, I. On Certain Ways of Restructuring the Countryside. *Prob. Econ.*, January 1973, *15*(9), pp. 61–70.

Lockner, Allyn O. and Kim, Han J. Circuit-Breakers on Farm-Property-Tax Overload: A Case Study. *Nat. Tax J.*, June 1973, *26*(2), pp. 233–40.

Lockwood, Brian and Moulik, T. K. Seeds of Development in a Delhi Village. In *Epstein, T. S. and Penny, D. H., eds.*, 1973, pp. 157–72.

Loeb, Peter D. and Smith, V. Kerry. Misspecification and the Small Sample Properties of Econometric Estimators. *Appl. Econ.*, September 1973, *5*(3), pp. 167–79.

Loebner, Hugh and Driver, Edwin D. Differential Fertility in Central India: A Path Analysis. *Demography*, August 1973, *10*(3), pp. 329–50.

Loehman, Edna and Whinston, A. Reply to Forster and Logan. *Appl. Econ.*, March 1973, *5*(1), pp. 69–73.

Loevinger, Lee. The Closed Mind Strikes Again. *Antitrust Bull.*, Fall, 1973, *18*(3), pp. 581–87.

von Loewe, Karl. Commerce and Agriculture in Lithuania, 1400-1600. *Econ. Hist. Rev.*, 2nd Ser., February 1973, *26*(1), pp. 23–37.

Loewenstein, Louis K. and McGrath, Dorn C., Jr. The Planning Imperative in America's Future. *Ann. Amer. Acad. Polit. Soc. Sci.*, January 1973, *405*, pp. 15–24.

Löf, George O. G. Solar Energy: An Infinite Source of Clean Energy. *Ann. Amer. Acad. Polit. Soc. Sci.*, November 1973, *410*, pp. 52–64.

Lofthouse, Stephen. On Paradigms, Methodology and the Theory of the Firm. Part 2. *Rivista Int. Sci. Econ. Com.*, June 1973, *20*(6), pp. 566–607.

———— On Paradigms, Methodology and the Theory of the Firm. Part 1. *Rivista Int. Sci. Econ. Com.*, May 1973, *20*(5), pp. 406–48.

Logan, Charles H. Motives of Criminals: Comment. In *Rottenberg, S., ed.*, 1973, pp. 55–58.

Logan, John and Forster, Bruce A. The Welfare Economics of Water Resource Allocation Over Time: Comment. *Appl. Econ.*, March 1973, *5*(1), pp. 61–68.

Logue, Dennis E. On the Pricing of Unseasoned Equity Issues: 1965-1969. *J. Financial Quant. Anal.*, January 1973, *8*(1), pp. 91–103.

———— Premia on Unseasoned Equity Issues. *J. Econ.*

Bus., Spring-Summer 1973, *25*(3), pp. 133–41.

———— **and Barnea, Amir.** Stock-Market Based Measures of Corporate Diversification. *J. Ind. Econ.*, September 1973, *22*(1), pp. 51–60.

———— **and Merville, Larry J.** General Model of Imperfect Capital Markets. *Southern Econ. J.*, October 1973, *40*(2), pp. 224–33.

———— **and Simkowitz, Michael A.** The Interdependent Structure of Security Returns. *J. Financial Quant. Anal.*, March 1973, *8*(2), pp. 259–72.

Lomax, David F. Reserve Assets and Competition and Credit Control. *Nat. Westminster Bank Quart. Rev.*, August 1973, pp. 36–46.

Lombardini, Siro. Piano e mercato oggi in Italia. (Plan and Market in Italy Today. With English summary.) *L'industria, N. S.*, 1973, (1), pp. 27–34.

Lombardo, Enzo. La costruzione delle tavole ridotte di mortalità. (The Construction of Abridged Life Tables. With English summary.) *Statistica*, July-September 1973, *33*(3), pp. 437–54.

Lombra, Raymond E. and Torto, Raymond G. Federal Reserve "Defensive" Behavior and the Reverse Causation Argument. *Southern Econ. J.*, July 1973, *40*(1), pp. 47–55.

Long, Larry H. New Estimates of Migration Expectancy in the United States. *J. Amer. Statist. Assoc.*, March 1973, *68*(341), pp. 37–43.

Long, Norton E. The City as Reservation. In *Rasmussen, D. W. and Haworth, C. T., eds.*, 1973, pp. 229–44.

Long, Robert H. Planning for Tomorrow's Customer. *J. Bank Res.*, Summer 1973, *4*(2), pp. 93–99.

Long, Stanley G. Public Utility Regulation: Structure and Performance: Comment. In *Russell, M., ed.*, 1973, pp. 105–07.

Long, Virginia and Klein, Lawrence R. Capacity Utilization: Concept, Measurement, and Recent Estimates. *Brookings Pap. Econ. Act.*, 1973, (3), pp. 743–56.

Long, William F.; Schramm, Richard and Tollison, Robert D. The Economic Determinants of Antitrust Activity. *J. Law Econ.*, October 1973, *16*(2), pp. 351–64.

Longbrake, William A. Computers and the Cost of Producing Banking Services: Planning and Control Considerations. *J. Bank Res.*, Autumn 1973, *4*(3), pp. 194–202.

———— Murphy's Method for Determining the Weights Assigned to Demand Deposit Items: A Clarification and Extension. *J. Bank Res.*, Summer 1973, *4*(2), pp. 139–44.

———— **and Gilbert, Gary G.** The Effects of Branching by Financial Institutions on Competition, Productive Efficiency and Stability: An Examination of the Evidence. *J. Bank Res.*, Autumn 1973, *4*(3), pp. 154–67.

————; **Murphy, Neil B. and Daniel, Donnie L.** The Effect of Technology on Bank Economies of Scale for Demand Deposits. *J. Finance*, March 1973, *28*(1), pp. 131–46.

Lopreato, Joseph. Notes on the Work of Vilfredo Pareto. *Soc. Sci. Quart.*, December 1973, *54*(3), pp. 451–68.

Lorange, Peter and Norman, Victor D. Risk Prefer-

ence in Scandinavian Shipping. *Appl. Econ.*, March 1973, *5*(1), pp. 49–59.

Lord, William B. and Warner, Maurice L. Aggregates and Externalities: Information Needs for Public Natural Resource Decision-Making. *Natural Res. J.*, January 1973, *13*(1), pp. 106–17.

Lösche, Peter. Stages in the Evolution of the German Labor Movement. In *Sturmthal, A. and Scoville, J. G., eds.*, 1973, pp. 101–22.

Loschky, David J. Studies of the Navigation Acts: New Economic Non-History? *Econ. Hist. Rev., 2nd Ser.*, November 1973, *26*(4), pp. 689–91.

Lott, William F. and Miller, Stephen M. A Note on the Optimality Conditions for Excise Taxation. *Southern Econ. J.*, July 1973, *40*(1), pp. 122–23.

Lotti, Eraldo. L'eccedenza industriale. Analisi e calcola dell'incidenza delle anomalie del processo produttivo sull'eccedenza industriale. (Industrial Surplus. Analysis of Calculations of the Effect of Irregularities of the Productive Process of the Industrial Surplus. With English summary.) *L'Impresa*, 1973, *15*(3–4), pp. 245–51.

———— Nuove tecniche di organizzazione della produzione. Estensione di alcuni concetti di Ragnar Frisch. (New Techniques of Industrial Organization. An Extension of Some Ideas of Ragnar Frisch. With English summary.) *L'Impresa*, 1973, *15*(11–12), pp. 701–08.

Lotz, Jørgen R. Om refusioner eller generelle tilskud til kommunerne. (Grants-in-aid to Danish Local Governments—Matching or General? With English summary.) *Nationalokon. Tidsskr.*, 1973, *111*(2), pp. 205–20.

Lougheed, Alan L. and Glynn, Sean. A Comment on United States Economic Policy and the "Dollar Gap" of the 1920's. *Econ. Hist. Rev., 2nd Ser.*, November 1973, *26*(4), pp. 692–94.

Louis, R. Co-operative Development Centres. *Int. Lab. Rev.*, June 1973, *107*(6), pp. 539–51.

Louviere, Jordan; Reynolds, David R. and Horton, Frank E. Mass Transit Utilization: Individual Response Data Inputs. *Econ. Geogr.*, April 1973, *49* (2), pp. 122–33.

Love, Joseph. External Financing and Domestic Politics: The Case of São Paulo, Brazil, 1889–1937. In *Scott, R. E., ed.*, 1973, pp. 236–59.

Lovell, C. A. Knox. CES and VES Production Functions in a Cross-Section Context. *J. Polit. Econ.*, May-June 1973, *81*(3), pp. 705–20.

———— Estimation and Prediction with CES and VES Production Functions. *Int. Econ. Rev.*, October 1973, *14*(3), pp. 676–92.

———— Homotheticity and the Average Cost Function. *Western Econ. J.*, December 1973, *11*(4), pp. 506–13.

———— A Note on Aggregation Bias and Loss. *J. Econometrics*, October 1973, *1*(3), pp. 301–11.

———— Technology and Specification Error. *Southern Econ. J.*, July 1973, *40*(1), pp. 110–16.

———— **and Moroney, J. R.** Estimating the Elasticity of Substitution: A Correction and Some Further Results. *Southern Econ. J.*, January 1973, *39*(3), pp. 437–41.

Lovell, Malcolm R., Jr. The Politics of Manpower Planning. In *Aronson, R. L., ed.*, 1973, pp. 14–22.

Lovell, Michael C. The Minimum Wage Reconsidered. *Western Econ. J.,* December 1973, *11*(4), pp. 529–37.

——— The Production of Economic Literature: An Interpretation. *J. Econ. Lit.,* March 1973, *11*(1), pp. 27–55.

——— and Vogel, Robert C. A CPI–Futures Market. *J. Polit. Econ.,* July-August 1973, *81*(4), pp. 1009–12.

Lowell, Cym H. Collective Bargaining and the Professional Team Sport Industry. *Law Contemp. Probl.,* Winter-Spring 1973, *38*(1), pp. 3–41.

Lowry, S. Todd. Lord Mansfield and the Law Merchant: Law and Economics in the Eighteenth Century. *J. Econ. Issues,* December 1973, *7*(4), pp. 605–22.

Lowry, William R. and Aitken, Norman D. A Cross-Sectional Study of the Effects of LAFTA and CACM on Latin American Trade. *J. Common Market Stud.,* June 1973, *11*(4), pp. 326–36.

Loyns, R. M. A. and Lu, W. F. A Cross-Section and Time-Series Analysis of Canadian Egg Demand. *Can. J. Agr. Econ.,* July 1973, *21*(2), pp. 1–15.

Lu, W. F. and Loyns, R. M. A. A Cross-Section and Time-Series Analysis of Canadian Egg Demand. *Can. J. Agr. Econ.,* July 1973, *21*(2), pp. 1–15.

Lu, Yao-Chi and Tweeten, Luther G. The Impact of Busing on Student Achievement. *Growth Change,* October 1973, *4*(4), pp. 44–46.

Lübbers, P. J. M. and Haccou, J. F. Public Policy Toward Retailing: The Netherlands. In *Boddewyn, J. J. and Hollander, S. C., eds.,* 1972, pp. 245–70.

Lubell, Alfred M. and Mestre, Eloy R. Teaching Undergraduate Economics: An Experimental Program. *J. Econ. Educ.,* Spring 1973, *4*(2), pp. 138–40.

Lubell, Harold. Urban Development and Employment in Calcutta. *Int. Lab. Rev.,* July 1973, *108*(1), pp. 25–41.

Lubin, John Francis. Failures in the Procurement of Data Processing Equipment. In *The Diebold Group, Inc.,* 1973, pp. 199–203.

Lubitz, Raymond. Export-Led Growth in Industrial Economies. *Kyklos,* 1973, *26*(2), pp. 307–21.

Lucas, Robert E., Jr. Some International Evidence on Output-Inflation Tradeoffs. *Amer. Econ. Rev.,* June 1973, *63*(3), pp. 326–34.

——— Wage Inflation and the Structure of Regional Unemployment: Comment. *J. Money, Credit, Banking,* Part II, February 1973, *5*(1), pp. 382–84.

Lucero, Maryetta. New Mexico Travel Service Training Program. *N. Mex. Bus.,* March 1973, *26*(3), pp. 10–12.

Lucia, Joseph L. Money Market Strategy or Monetary Aggregates: An Analysis of Recent Federal Reserve Policy. *Econ. Soc. Rev.,* October 1973, *5*(1), pp. 31–45.

Lucier, Richard I. The Prediction of Public Choice Behavior in the Washington Tax Substitution Referendum. *Nat. Tax J.,* December 1973, *26*(4), pp. 625–30.

Ludlow, Nicholas. China Trade. In *Henley, D. S., ed.,* 1973, pp. 39–54.

Luey, Paul. Discrepancies in Trade Statistics: Rejoinder. *Malayan Econ. Rev.,* October 1973, *18*(2), pp. 79–81.

Lugovskaia, L. Current Problems of Urbanization. *Prob. Econ.,* May 1973, *16*(1), pp. 91–99.

Lumb, H. C. Economic Incentives to Control Pollution. In *Reynolds, L. G.; Green, G. D. and Lewis, D. R., eds.,* 1973, pp. 220–30.

Lumsden, Keith G. Summary of an Analysis of Student Evaluations of Faculty and Courses. *J. Econ. Educ.,* Fall 1973, *5*(1), pp. 54–56.

Lumsden, M. A.; Sturm, A. B. and Deane, R. S. Some Simulation Experiments with a New Zealand Model. In *Deane, R. S., ed.,* 1972, pp. 15–64.

Lundstedt, Sven. Using Information Theory in Administrative Systems. *Ohio State U. Bull. Bus. Res.,* February 1973, *48*(2), pp. 1–3, 6–7.

Luni, Paolo. La "società d'acquisti": premessa per una nuova e più rapida evoluzione del settore distributivo. (The "Purchasing Company": Ideas for New and Rapid Developments in the Distribution Sector. With English summary.) *L'Impresa,* 1973, *15*(9–10), pp. 631–33.

Luoma, Väinö. Yritys ja yhteiskunta. (The Enterprise and Society: The Social Responsibility of Management in Outline. With English summary.) *Liiketaloudellinen Aikak.,* 1973, *22*(1), pp. 18–28.

Lupo, Leonard A. Worldwide Sales by U.S. Multinational Companies. *Surv. Curr. Bus.,* January 1973, *53*(1), pp. 33–39.

Luscia, Fausta. Un risultato sull'indipendenza. (A Result on Independence. With English summary.) *Rivista Int. Sci. Econ. Com.,* October 1973, *20*(10), pp. 1025–28.

Lusztig, Peter. Analysis of the Lease-or-Buy Decision: Comment. *J. Finance,* September 1973, *28*(4), pp. 1017–18.

Luthans, Fred and Hodgetts, Richard M. Determining a Social-Responsibility Strategy. In *Klein, W. H. and Murphy, D. C., eds.,* 1973, pp. 292–95.

Lutins, Theodore and Piro, Paula A. Utilization and Reimbursements under Medicare for 1967 and 1968 Decedents. *Soc. Sec. Bull.,* May 1973, *36*(5), pp. 37–41, 58.

Lüttichau, Knud. Kvartalsresultater for pengelønsændringens determinanter for Danmark i mellem-og efter-krigstiden. (Quarterly Results Concerning the Determinants of Changes in Money Wage Rates in Denmark in the Interwar and Post–war Period. With English summary.) *Nationalokon. Tidsskr.,* 1973, *111*(1), pp. 92–111.

——— Pengelønsudviklingen for fire udvalgte fag for Danmark i mellemkrigstiden. (With English summary.) *Nationalokon. Tidsskr.,* 1973, *111*(3), pp. 382–96.

——— Pengelønsudviklingen for fire udvalgte fag for Danmark i efterkrigstiden. (The Changes in the Wage Rates for Four Trades in Denmark in the Post-War Period. With English summary.) *Nationalokon. Tidsskr.,* 1973, *111*(2), pp. 242–65.

Luttrell, Clifton B. Food and Agriculture in 1973. *Fed. Res. Bank St. Louis Rev.,* May 1973, *55*(5), pp. 1–16.

——— The Russian Wheat Deal—Hindsight vs. Foresight. *Fed. Res. Bank St. Louis Rev.,* October 1973, *55*(10), pp. 2–9.

Lybeck, Johan A. The Monetary Sector of RDX2: A Note on Some Puzzling Features. *Can. J. Econ.,* November 1973, *6*(4), pp. 595–98.

_____ The Monetary Sector of the Bank of Finland's Quarterly Model: A Critical Comment. *Ekon. Samfundets Tidskr.*, 1973, *26*(2), pp. 117–21.

Lybecker, Martin E. Regulation of Bank Trust Department Investment Activities. *Yale Law J.*, April 1973, *82*(5), pp. 977–1002.

Lyle, Jerolyn R. Factors Affecting the Job Status of Workers with Spanish Surnames. *Mon. Lab. Rev.*, April 1973, *96*(4), pp. 10–16.

_____ **and Zamoff, Richard.** Planning and Evaluation of Day Care at the Community Level. In *Young, D. R. and Nelson, R. R., eds.*, 1973, pp. 71–90.

Lynch, Edward. Propositions for Planning New Towns in Venezuela. *J. Devel. Areas*, July 1973, *7*(4), pp. 549–70.

Lynn, Mary and Kotz, Nick. You Are What You Eat: Feeding D.C.'s Hungry. In *Levitan, S. A., ed.*, 1973, pp. 143–74.

Lyon, George C. Fixed Characteristics of Variable Costs. *Manage. Account.*, October 1973, *55*(4), pp. 27–30.

Lyon, H. L. and Johnson, K. H. Experimental Evidence on Combining Cross-Section and Time Series Information. *Rev. Econ. Statist.*, November 1973, *55*(4), pp. 465–74.

Lytle, P. W. and Hill, Lowell D. Opportunities for New Investment in Country Elevator Facilities. *Ill. Agr. Econ.*, July 1973, *13*(2), pp. 6–11.

_____ **and Hill, Lowell, D.** The Optimum Combination of Resources Within and Among Country Elevators. *Amer. J. Agr. Econ.*, May 1973, *55*(2), pp. 202–08.

Lyttkens, Ejnar. The Fix-point Method for Estimating Interdependent Systems with the Underlying Model Specification. *J. Roy. Statist. Soc.*, Part 3 1973, *136*, pp. 353–75.

_____ Investigation of the Fix-Point (FP) and Iterative Instrumental Variables (IIV) and Related Estimation Methods: Various Theoretical Aspects. *Écon. Appl.*, 1973, *26*(2–3–4), pp. 423–70.

Lyutov, A. Economic Integration and the Socialist International Market. In *Kiss, T., ed.*, 1973, pp. 49–55.

Maass, Randal O. and Hutchins, Robert C. Measurement of Multicompany Diversification. *J. Econ. Bus.*, Fall 1973, *26*(1), pp. 74–77.

Mabogunje, Akin L. Manufacturing and the Geography of Development in Tropical Africa. *Econ. Geogr.*, January 1973, *49*(1), pp. 1–20.

Mabro, Robert and Knight, J. B. On the Determination of the General Wage Level: A Rejoinder. *Econ. J.*, June 1973, *83*(330), pp. 520–22.

Mabry, Bevars D. The Economics of Fringe Benefits. *Ind. Relat.*, February 1973, *12*(1), pp. 95–106.

Macario, Santiago P. The Role of World Trade Policy: A Latin American Viewpoint. In *Urquidi, V. L. and Thorp, R., eds.*, 1973, pp. 58–87.

MacAulay, T. G. and Huff, H. B. Summing Components of Real Capital Gains. *Amer. J. Agr. Econ.*, February 1973, *55*(1), pp. 69–72.

MacAvoy, Paul W. and Noll, Roger G. Relative Prices on Regulated Transactions of the Natural Gas Pipelines. *Bell J. Econ. Manage. Sci.*, Spring 1973, *4*(1), pp. 212–34.

_____ **and Pindyck, Robert S.** Alternative Regulatory Policies for Dealing with the Natural Gas Shortage. *Bell J. Econ. Manage. Sci.*, Autumn 1973, *4*(2), pp. 454–98.

MacBeth, James D. and Fama, Eugene F. Risk, Return, and Equilibrium: Empirical Tests. *J. Polit. Econ.*, May-June 1973, *81*(3), pp. 607–36.

Macbeth, Thomas G. and Downey, Gerald F. The Monetary Consequences of Demand Deposit Creation by Mutual Savings Banks—The Commonwealth of Massachusetts Case. *Marquette Bus. Rev.*, Spring 1973, *17*(1), pp. 1–8.

Maccarone, Salvatore. Aspetti e problemi della riforma del protesto. (Problems of the Italian Reform of the Protest. With English summary.) *Bancaria*, August 1973, *29*(8), pp. 951–62.

Maccini, Louis J. Delivery Lags and the Demand for Investment. *Rev. Econ. Stud.*, April 1973, *40*(2), pp. 269–81.

_____ On Optimal Delivery Lags. *J. Econ. Theory*, April 1973, *6*(2), pp. 107–25.

MacCluer, Jean W. and Dyke, Bennett. Estimation of Vital Rates by Means of Monte Carlo Simulation. *Demography*, August 1973, *10*(3), pp. 383–403.

MacCrimmon, Kenneth R. An Overview of Multiple Objective Decision Making. In *Cochrane, J. L. and Zeleny, M., eds.*, 1973, pp. 18–44.

MacDonald, A. S. Exchange Rates for National Expenditure on Research and Development. *Econ. J.*, June 1973, *83*(330), pp. 477–94.

MacDonald, B. A. Program Budgeting in the Government of Canada: Origin and Progress. In *Novick, D., ed.*, 1973, pp. 71–78.

MacDougall, Donald. Indian Balance of Payments. In *Wadhva, C. D., ed.*, 1973, pp. 430–38.

MacGregor, James. Skeptical Consumers, Tough Regulators Spur a New Candor in Ads. In *Murray, B. B., ed.*, 1973, pp. 310–15.

Mach, Milos. Planning Under Socialism. *Czech. Econ. Digest.*, August 1973, (5), pp. 64–88.

_____ **and Reizer, Jozef.** The Place of Commodity-Money Relations in the Socialist System and a Critical Review of the Theory of the So-Called Market Socialism. *Czech. Econ. Digest.*, December 1973, (8), pp. 71–101.

Machlis, Peter David. The Distributional Effects of Public Higher Education in New York City. *Public Finance Quart.*, January 1973, *1*(1), pp. 35–57.

Machlup, Fritz. Exchange Rate Flexibility: A Variety of Choices. In *Wiegand, G. C., ed.*, 1973, pp. 110–26.

_____ Exchange-Rate Flexibility. *Banca Naz. Lavoro Quart. Rev.*, September 1973, (106), pp. 183–205.

_____ Implications for International Reserves: Comment. In *Krause, L. B. and Salant, W. S., eds.*, 1973, pp. 247–49.

_____ Stateless Money. In *[Halm, G. N.]*, 1973, pp. 115–22.

Machol, Robert E. New Applications and Trends in OR in the US. In *Ross, M., ed.*, 1973, pp. 571–78.

MacKay, David B. Spatial Measurement of Retail Store Demand. *J. Marketing Res.*, November 1973, *10*(4), pp. 447–53.

_____ A Spectral Analysis of the Frequency of Supermarket Visits. *J. Marketing Res.*, February 1973, *10*(1), pp. 84–90.

Mackay, Robert J. Stein and Nagatani on Stabilization Policies in a Growing Economy. *Rev. Econ. Stud.*, October 1973, *40*(4), pp. 571–78.

MacKay, R. R. Employment Creation: A Resurrection. *Scot. J. Polit. Econ.*, June 1973, *20*(2), pp. 175–77.

Mackie, Arthur B. Patterns of World Agricultural Trade. In *Iowa State University Center for Agricultural and Rural Development*, 1973, pp. 69–86.

MacKinnon, James and Mills, Edwin S. Notes on the New Urban Economics. *Bell J. Econ. Manage. Sci.*, Autumn 1973, *4*(2), pp. 593–601.

MacLachlan, Colin M. The Indian Labor Structure in the Portuguese Amazon, 1700–1800. In *Alden, D., ed.*, 1973, pp. 199–230.

Macourt, M. P. A. An Exploratory Compartive Study of Catholic and Protestant Farmers in the Republic of Ireland. *Econ. Soc. Rev.*, July 1973, *4*(4), pp. 511–22.

MacPhee, Craig R. Insurance and Reciprocity: Comment. *J. Risk Ins.*, March 1973, *40*(1), pp. 139–41.

Macpherson, W. J. Economic Development in India under the British Crown, 1858–1947. In *Youngson, A. J., ed.*, 1973, pp. 126–91.

MacRae, Duncan, Jr. Normative Assumptions in the Study of Public Choice. *Public Choice*, Fall 1973, *16*, pp. 27–41.

Macura, Milos. World Population Prospects and Policies. *Econ. Bull. Ghana, Sec. Ser.*, 1973, *3*(2), pp. 22–30.

Madarász, A. Is Political Economy Timely? *Acta Oecon.*, 1973, *10*(2), pp. 177–200.

Maddala, G. S. and Grether, D. M. Errors in Variables and Serially Correlated Disturbances in Distributed Lag Models. *Econometrica*, March 1973, *41*(2), pp. 255–62.

⸺ **and Mount, T. D.** A Comparative Study of Alternative Estimators for Variance Components Models Used in Econometric Applications. *J. Amer. Statist. Assoc.*, June 1973, *68*(342), pp. 324–28.

⸺ **and Rao, A. S.** Tests for Serial Correlation in Regression Models with Lagged Dependent Variables and Serially Correlated Errors. *Econometrica*, July 1973, *41*(4), pp. 761–74.

Madden, Carl H. Construction Wages: The Great Consumer Robbery. In *Reynolds, L. G.; Green, G. D. and Lewis, D. R., eds.*, 1973, pp. 18–23.

⸺ Controls or Competition—What's at Issue? Reply. *Rev. Econ. Statist.*, November 1973, *55*(4), pp. 524–25.

⸺ Is Our Tax System Making Us Second-Rate? Tax Reform: Savings and Consumption. *Nat. Tax J.*, September 1973, *26*(3), pp. 403–07.

Maddock, Thomas, III. Management Model as a Tool for Studying the Worth of Data. *Water Resources Res.*, April 1973, *9*(2), pp. 270–80.

Madsen, Howard C. and Heady, Earl O. National and Interregional Models of Water Demand for Land Use and Agricultural Policies. In *Judge, G. G. and Takayama, T., eds.*, 1973, pp. 651–75.

Maekawa, Koichi. A Note on the Estimation of the Pareto Distribution. *Econ. Stud. Quart.*, December 1973, *24*(3), pp. 63–66.

Mafeje, Archie. Agrarian Revolution and the Land Question in Buganda. In *Institute for Development Research*, 1973, pp. 127–54.

⸺ The Fallacy of Dual Economies Revisited. In *Institute for Development Research*, 1973, pp. 25–52.

⸺ The Farmers—Economic and Social Differentiation. In *Richards, A. I.; Sturrock, F. and Fortt, J. M., eds.*, 1973, pp. 198–231.

⸺ **and Hougham, D. A.** Sampling and Fieldwork Methods. In *Richards, A. I.; Sturrock, F. and Fortt, J. M., eds.*, 1973, pp. 95–123.

⸺ **and Richards, A. I.** The Commercial Farmer and His Labour Supply. In *Richards, A. I.; Sturrock, F. and Fortt, J. M., eds.*, 1973, pp. 179–97.

Magaddino, Joseph P. Crime, Victim Compensation, and the Supply of Offenses. *Public Policy*, Summer 1973, *21*(3), pp. 437–40.

Magdoff, Harry and Sweezy, Paul M. The Merger Movement: A Study in Power. In *Andreano, R. L., ed.*, 1973, pp. R328–19.

Magee, Stephen P. Currency Contracts, Pass-through, and Devaluation. *Brookings Pap. Econ. Act.*, 1973, (1), pp. 303–23.

⸺ Factor Market Distortions, Production, and Trade: A Survey. *Oxford Econ. Pap.*, March 1973, *25*(1), pp. 1–43.

Magnani, Livio. Considerazioni sui flussi e sulle disponibilità. (Money Flows and Assets Formation. With English summary.) *Bancaria*, January 1973, *29*(1), pp. 83–103.

⸺ I recenti avvenimenti monetari internazionali. (The Recent International Monetary Events. With English summary.) *Bancaria*, February 1973, *29*(2), pp. 189–92.

Magnifico, Giovanni. The European and International Currency Problem. *Banca Naz. Lavoro Quart. Rev.*, December 1973, (107), pp. 375–95.

⸺ European Monetary Integration. In *Magnifico, G.*, 1973, pp. 199–222.

⸺ European Monetary Unification for Balanced Growth: A New Approach. In *Magnifico, G.*, 1973, pp. 1–42.

⸺ Further Considerations on the New Approach to European Monetary Unification. In *Magnifico, G.*, 1973, pp. 85–136.

⸺ The Theory of Optimum Currency Areas and European Monetary Unification. In *Magnifico, G.*, 1973, pp. 43–84.

⸺ Towards a European Money and Capital Market. In *Magnifico, G.*, 1973, pp. 137–98.

Magnusson, Leif. Cost-Benefit Analysis of Investment in Higher Education: Some Swedish Results. *Swedish J. Econ.*, June 1973, *75*(2), pp. 119–27.

Mahadevan, P. Nutrition and Agriculture. In *Berg, A.; Scrimshaw, N. S. and Call, D. L., eds.*, 1973, pp. 150–53.

Mahoney, D. M. and Jonson, P. D. Price Expectations in Australia. *Econ. Rec.*, March 1973, *49* (125), pp. 50–61.

Maier, Heribert. The International Free Trade Union Movement and International Corporations. In *Kujawa, D., ed.*, 1973, pp. 8–27.

Main, Jeremy. Industry Still Has Something to Learn About Congress. In *Murray, B. B., ed.*, 1973, pp. 192–99.

Main, T. R. N. and Fenske, G. A. Labour and the Gold Mines. *S. Afr. J. Econ.*, September 1973, *41* (3), pp. 298–304.

Maital, Shlomo. Public Goods and Income Distribution: Some Further Results. *Econometrica*, May 1973, *41*(3), pp. 561–68.

_____ Targets, Tradeoffs, and Economic Policy: A Generalized Phillips Curve. *Public Finance Quart.*, January 1973, *1*(1), pp. 67–83.

_____; **Prachowny, Martin F. J. and Boadway, Robin W.** Optimal Tariffs, Optimal Taxes and Public Goods. *J. Public Econ.*, November 1973, *2*(4), pp. 391–403.

Maiti, Pradip. Factor Price Equalization Theorem in Linear Programming. *J. Int. Econ.*, November 1973, *3*(4), pp. 367–78.

Maitra, Priyatosh. Relative Effects of Import Substitution in New Zealand. *Econ. Aff.*, May 1973, *18* (5), pp. 213–16, 234–40.

Maixner, Ladislav. Optimalizace kapacit zásobníků pružné automatické linky. (Optimalization of the Size of Magazines in an Elastic Production Line. With English summary.) *Ekon.-Mat. Obzor*, 1973, *9*(2), pp. 150–66.

Maizels, Alfred. Recent Trends in Latin America's Exports to the Industrialised Countries. In *Urquidi, V. L. and Thorp, R.*, eds., 1973, pp. 35–52.

Majumdar, Mukul and Bhattacharya, Rabindra Nath. Random Exchange Economies. *J. Econ. Theory*, February 1973, *6*(1), pp. 37–67.

Mak, James and Haites, Erik F. The Decline of Steamboating on the Ante-bellum Western Rivers: Some New Evidence and An Alternative Hypothesis. *Exploration Econ. Hist.*, Fall 1973, *11* (1), pp. 25–36.

_____ **and Walton, Gary M.** The Persistence of Old Technologies: The Case of Flatboats. *J. Econ. Hist.*, June 1973, *33*(2), pp. 444–51.

Makeenko, M. and Khalitov, R. Agroindustrial Associations and Their Effectiveness: Based on the Example of the Moldavian SSR. *Prob. Econ.*, January 1973, *15*(9), pp. 71–89.

Maki, Wilbur R. and Angus, James E. Development Planning. In *Judge, G. G. and Takayama, T.*, eds., 1973, pp. 43–64.

Makin, John H. Identifying a Reserve Base for the Euro-Dollar System. *J. Finance*, June 1973, *28*(3), pp. 609–17.

Makó, Csaba and Héthy, Lajos. Incentive Problems in the Centrally Planned Economy of Hungary. *Ind. Lab. Relat. Rev.*, January 1973, *26*(2), pp. 767–77.

Makower, H. The Pure Theory of International Trade: The Teaching of It. *Indian Econ. J.*, July–September 1973, *21*(1), pp. 1–18.

Malaker, C. R. Construction of Nuptiality Tables for the Single Population in India: 1901–1931. *Demography*, November 1973, *10*(4), pp. 525–35.

Malek, P.; Křikava, L. and Mašek, J. The Czech Experience in Nutrition Improvement. In *Berg, A.; Scrimshaw, N. S. and Call, D. L.*, eds., 1973, pp. 329–34.

Malenbaum, Wilfred. A Note on the Poor Nation Situation. In *Berg, A.; Scrimshaw, N. S. and Call, D. L.*, eds., 1973, pp. 81–86.

_____ World Resources for the Year 2000. *Ann.*

Amer. Acad. Polit. Soc. Sci., July 1973, *408*, pp. 30–46.

Mäler, Karl-Göran and Kneese, Allen V. Bribes and Charges in Pollution Control: An Aspect of the Coase Controversy. *Natural Res. J.*, October 1973, *13*(4), pp. 705–16.

Malgrange, Pierre; Deleau, Michel and Guesnerie, Roger. Planification, incertitude et politique économique. II—L'opération Optimix: Résultats numériques. (Planning, Uncertainty and Economic Policy. II—Optimix Operation: Numerical Results. With English summary.) *Revue Écon.*, November 1973, *24*(6), pp. 1072–1103.

_____; **Deleau, Michel and Guesnerie, Roger.** Planification, incertitude et politique économique. L'operation Optimix. Une procédure formalisée d'adaptation du Plan à l'aléa. (Planning Uncertainty and Economic Policy. A Formalized Procedure: "Optimix." With English summary.) *Revue Écon.*, September 1973, *24*(5), pp. 801–36.

Malinnikov, V. V. The Decompostiion Method in the Solution of Large-Scale Linear Programming Problems with Block Structure. *Matekon*, Spring 1973, *9*(3), pp. 41–46.

Malinvaud, E. Markets for an Exchange Economy with Individual Risks. *Econometrica*, May 1973, *41*(3), pp. 383–410.

Malisoff, Harry. Beyond the Limits of State Workmen's Compensation: Comment. *J. Risk Ins.*, June 1973, *40*(2), pp. 287–90.

Malizia, Emil. Imperialism Reconsidered. *Rev. Radical Polit. Econ.*, Summer 1973, *5*(2), pp. 87–92.

Malkiel, Burton G. and Malkiel, Judith A. Male-Female Pay Differentials in Professional Employment. *Amer. Econ. Rev.*, September 1973, *63*(4), pp. 693–705.

Malkiel, Judith A. and Malkiel, Burton G. Male-Female Pay Differentials in Professional Employment. *Amer. Econ. Rev.*, September 1973, *63*(4), pp. 693–705.

Malkovich, J. F. and Afifi, A. A. On Tests for Multivariate Normality. *J. Amer. Statist. Assoc.*, March 1973, *68*(341), pp. 176–79.

Mallinson, Eugenie and Pickering, Margaret H. New Series for Large Manufacturing Corporations. *Fed. Res. Bull.*, October 1973, *59*(10), pp. 731–33.

Malmgren, Harald B. The Impact of the Developed Countries. In *Streeten, P.*, ed., 1973, pp. 123–42.

Malysiak, James T. Toward a Substantive Private International Law of Trademarks: The Lessons of the *Carl Zeiss* Litigation. *Yale Law J.*, April 1973, *82*(5), pp. 1072–91.

Mammen, Thampy. Indian Money Market: An Econometric Study. *Int. Econ. Rev.*, February 1973, *14*(1), pp. 49–68.

Manca, G. Developments in the International Competitive Climate during the 1970s. In *Rybczynski, T. M.*, ed., 1973, pp. 18–36.

Manchester, Harland. Refuse is Reusable. In *Moskoff, W.*, ed., 1973, pp. 242–48.

Mandel, M. and Huszár, J. The Investment Decision-Making System in Hungary. *Eastern Europ. Econ.*, Spring 1973, *11*(3), pp. 27–49.

Mandelbrot, Benoit B. A Subordinated Stochastic Process Model with Finite Variance for Speculative Prices: Comment. *Econometrica,* January 1973, *41*(1), pp. 157–59.

Mandell, Lewis. The Changing Role of the American Consumer. In *Britt, S. H. and Boyd, H. W., Jr., eds.,* 1973, pp. 190–95.

Manderscheid, Lester V. Guidelines for Curriculum Changes in Agricultural Economics. *Amer. J. Agr. Econ.,* Part II, November 1973, *55*(4), pp. 740–47.

Mandich, Donald R. International Loans: Profit Center or Loss Leader. In *Henley, D. S., ed.,* 1973, pp. 420–32.

Mănescu, Gheorghe and Danciu, Constantin. Istoria contemporană a României şi reprezentarea viitorului. (The Contemporary History of Romania and the Representation of the Future. With English summary.) *Stud. Cercet. Econ.,* 1973, (3), pp. 5–18.

Manescu, Manea. The Planned Economic-Social Development of Romania. *Revue Roumaine Sci. Soc. Serie Sci. Econ.,* 1973, *17*(1), pp. 13–33.

Manfredini, Marialuisa. Il vantaggio comparato potenziale come principio-guida del processo di sviluppo. (On the Potential Comparative Advantage in International Trade: Theory and Evidence. With English summary.) *Rivista Int. Sci. Econ. Com.,* June 1973, *20*(6), pp. 546–65.

Mangahas, Mahar. A Note on "Income Inequality and Economic Growth: The Postwar Experience of Asian Countries." *Malayan Econ. Rev.,* April 1973, *18*(1), pp. 11–14.

Mangkusuwondo, Suhadi. Dilemmas in Indonesian Economic Development. *Bull. Indonesian Econ. Stud.,* July 1973, *9*(2), pp. 28–35.

Mangum, Garth L. Manpower Programs as Career Education. In *McClure, L. and Buan, C., eds.,* 1973, pp. 129–41.

———— **and Robson, R. Thayne.** Metropolitan Impact of Manpower Programs: A Four-City Comparison: Introduction. In *Mangum, G. L. and Robson, R. T., eds.,* 1973, pp. 1–5.

————; **Robson, R. Thayne and Bradley, Iver E.** Impact of Manpower Programs upon Employment and Earnings. In *Mangum, G. L. and Robson, R. T., eds.,* 1973, pp. 227–59.

————; **Robson, R. Thayne and Bradley, Iver E.** Total Impact of Manpower Programs. In *Mangum, G. L. and Robson, R. T., eds.,* 1973, pp. 260–93.

Manheim, Larry M. and Ginsburgh, Paul B. Insurance, Copayment, and Health Services Utilization: A Critical Review. *J. Econ. Bus.,* Spring-Summer 1973, *25*(3), pp. 142–53.

Manitzas, Nita R. The Setting of the Cuban Revolution. In *Barkin, D. P. and Manitzas, N. R., eds.,* 1973, pp. M260–18.

Mankoubi, Bawa Sandani. Savings Banks and Savings Facilities in African Countries: Togo. In *Alberici, A. and Baravelli, M., eds.,* 1973, pp. 111–13.

Mann, H. Michael. Concentration, Barriers to Entry, and Rates of Return Revisited: A Reply. *J. Ind. Econ.,* April 1973, *21*(2), pp. 203–04.

————; **Henning, John A. and Meehan, James W., Jr.** Advertising and Market Concentration: Comment. *Southern Econ. J.,* January 1973, *39*(3), pp. 448–51.

Mann, Jitendar S. A Dynamic Model of the U.S.

Tobacco Economy. *Agr. Econ. Res.,* July 1973, *25* (3), pp. 81–92.

Mannari, Hiroshi and Marsh, Robert M. Pay and Social Structure in a Japanese Firm. *Ind. Relat.,* February 1973, *12*(1), pp. 16–32.

Manne, Alan S. DINAMICO, A Dynamic Multi-Sector, Multi-Skill Model. In *Goreux, L. M. and Manne, A. S., eds.,* 1973, pp. 107–50.

———— Economic Alternatives for Mexico: A Quantitative Analysis. In *Goreux, L. M. and Manne, A. S., eds.,* 1973, pp. 151–72.

———— A Mixed Integer Algorithm for Project Evaluation. In *Goreux, L. M. and Manne, A. S., eds.,* 1973, pp. 477–97.

———— On Linking ENERGETICOS to DINAMICO. In *Goreux, L. M. and Manne, A. S., eds.,* 1973, pp. 277–89.

———— **and Fernández de la Garza, Guillermo.** ENERGETICOS, A Process Analysis of the Energy Sectors. In *Goreux, L. M. and Manne, A. S., eds.,* 1973, pp. 233–75.

————; **Franchet, Yves and Inman, Richard A.** Numerical Data for Multi-Sector Planning. In *Goreux, L. M. and Manne, A. S., eds.,* 1973, pp. 85–106.

———— **and Goreux, Louis M.** Multi-Level Planning: Case Studies in Mexico: Introduction. In *Goreux, L. M. and Manne, A. S., eds.,* 1973, pp. 1–14.

———— **and Keesing, Donald B.** Manpower Projections. In *Goreux, L. M. and Manne, A. S., eds.,* 1973, pp. 55–83.

————; **Valencia, José Alberto and Fernández de la Garza, Guillermo.** Multi-Level Planning for Electric Power Projects. In *Goreux, L. M. and Manne, A. S., eds.,* 1973, pp. 197–231.

Manning, Chris M. and Garnaut, Ross. An Economic Survey of West Irian, Part II. *Bull. Indonesian Econ. Stud.,* March 1973, *9*(1), pp. 30–64.

Manoff, Richard K. The Mass Media Contribution to Intervention Programs. In *Berg, A.; Scrimshaw, N. S. and Call, D. L., eds.,* 1973, pp. 217–22.

Manogaran, Chelvadurai. Economic Feasibility of Irrigating Southern Pipes. *Water Resources Res.,* December 1973, *9*(6), pp. 1485–96.

Manove, Michael. Non-Price Rationing of Intermediate Goods in Centrally Planned Economies. *Econometrica,* September 1973, *41*(5), pp. 829–52.

Mansfield, Edwin. Determinants of the Speed of Application of New Technology. In *Williams, B. R., ed.,* 1973, pp. 199–216.

———— The Production and Application of New Technology by American Business Firms. In *Edge, D. O. and Wolfe, J. N., eds.,* 1973, pp. 199–221.

Mansfield, N. and Watson, P. The Valuation of Time in Cost-benefit Studies. In *Wolfe, J. N., ed.,* 1973, pp. 222–32.

Mansinghka, Surendra K. and Weston, J. Fred. Performance of Conglomerate Firms: Reply. *J. Finance,* June 1973, *28*(3), pp. 759.

———— **and Weston, J. Fred.** Tests of the Efficiency Performance of Conglomerate Firms. In *Weston, J. F. and Ornstein, S. I., eds.,* 1973, pp. 203–24.

Manson, A. R.; Hader, R. J. and Cote, R. Minimum Bias Approximation of a General Regression

Model. *J. Amer. Statist. Assoc.*, September 1973, *68*(343), pp. 633–38.

Mantell, Edmund H. Labor Markets for Engineers of Differing Ability and Education. *Ind. Lab. Relat. Rev.*, October 1973, *27*(1), pp. 63–73.

_____ Suboptimal Land Use Induced by Transportation Planning for New Towns. *Land Econ.*, February 1973, *49*(1), pp. 89–92.

Mantoux, P. The Industrial Revolution in the Eighteenth Century, 1966. In *Tranter, N. L., ed.,* 1973, pp. 211–17.

Mantripragada, K. Capital Management and Capital Theory: Discussion. *J. Finance*, May 1973, *28*(2), pp. 369–72.

Manvel, Allen D. Tax Capacity Versus Tax Performance: Comment. *Nat. Tax J.*, June 1973, *26*(2), pp. 293–4.

Maragi, Mario. La problematica del prestito su pegno. (Pledge Loan Problems. With English summary.) *Bancaria,* July 1973, *29*(7), pp. 813–19.

Marangoni, Giandemetrio. Problemi d'ordinamento e decisioni aziendali. (Scheduling Problems and Firm Decisions. With English summary.) *Rivista Int. Sci. Econ. Com.*, November 1973, *20*(11), pp. 1116–26.

Marchand, James R. and Russell, Keith P. Externalities, Liability, Separability, and Resource Allocation. *Amer. Econ. Rev.*, September 1973, *63*(4), pp. 611–20.

Marchand, M. G. The Economic Principles of Telephone Rates Under a Budgetary Constraint. *Rev. Econ. Stud.*, October 1973, *40*(4), pp. 507–15.

Marchesini, Giambattista. Il ruolo del mercato del credito nel ciclo di produzione del reddito, I. (Role of the Credit Market in the Income Production Cycle, I. With English summary.) *Bancaria,* October 1973, *29*(10), pp. 1239–43.

_____ Il ruolo del mercato del credito nel ciclo di produzione del reddito, II. (Role of the Credit Market in the Income Production Cycle, II. With English summary.) *Bancaria,* November 1973, *29* (11), pp. 1346–57.

de Marchi, N. B. The Noxious Influence of Authority: A Correction of Jevons' Charge. *J. Law Econ.*, April 1973, *16*(1), pp. 179–89.

_____ and Sturges, R. P. Malthus and Ricardo's Inductivist Critics: Four Letters to William Whewell. *Economica, N.S.*, November 1973, *40* (160), pp. 379–93.

Marcis, Richard G. and Smith, V. Kerry. The Demand for Liquid Asset Balances by U.S. Manufacturing Corporations: 1959-1970. *J. Financial Quant. Anal.*, March 1973, *8*(2), pp. 207–18.

_____ and Smith, V. Kerry. Monetary Activity and Interest Rates: A Spectral Analysis. *Quart. Rev. Econ. Bus.*, Summer 1973, *13*(2), pp. 69–82.

Marckwardt, Albert M. Evaluation of an Experimental Short Interview Form Designed to Collect Fertility Data: The Case of Peru. *Demography,* November 1973, *10*(4), pp. 639–57.

Marcus, Irwin M. Labor Discontent in Tioga County, Pennsylvania, 1865-1905. *Labor Hist.*, Summer 1973, *14*(3), pp. 414–22.

Marcus, Morton J. The Indiana Housing Market: An Alternative View. *Indiana Bus. Rev.*, May-June 1973, *48*, pp. 13–14.

Marcus, Sumner. The Basic Issues: Societal Demands and the Viability of Social Accounting: Introduction. In *Dierkes, M. and Bauer, R. A., eds.,* 1973, pp. 43–49.

_____; Graham, Philip L., Jr. and Hermann, Donald H. G. Section 7 of the Clayton Act and Mergers Involving Foreign Interests. In *Henley, D. S., ed.,* 1973, pp. 155–84.

Marcuse, Peter. The Rise of Tenant Organizations. In *Pynoos, J.; Schafer, R. and Hartman, C. W., eds.,* 1973, pp. 49–54.

Marer, Paul and Brown, Alan A. Foreign Trade in the East European Reforms. In *Bornstein, M., ed.,* 1973, pp. 153–205.

Mares, Miroslav and Hrbek, Antonín. Prognostické ekonometrické modely strojírenstvi. (Prognostic Econometric Models of Machine Industry. With English summary.) *Ekon.-Mat. Obzor*, 1973, *9*(3), pp. 241–59.

Marfels, Christian. Relevant Market and Concentration: The Case of the U.S. Automobile Industry. *Jahr. Nationalökon. Statist.*, March 1973, *187*(3), pp. 209–17.

_____ Whither Industrial Organization? *Z. Nationalökon.*, 1973, *33*(3–4), pp. 435–45.

Mariano, Roberto S. Approximations to the Distribution Functions of Theil's *K*-Class Estimators. *Econometrica,* July 1973, *41*(4), pp. 715–21.

_____ Approximations to the Distribution Functions of the Ordinary Least-Squares and Two-Stage Least-Squares Estimators in the Case of Two Included Endogenous Variables. *Econometrica,* January 1973, *41*(1), pp. 67–77.

Marinacos, George N. Big Board: Does it Really Increase Market Price? *Marquette Bus. Rev.*, Winter 1973, *17*(4), pp. 197–200.

Markandya, Anil and Robinson, Sherman. Complexity and Adjustment in Input-Output Systems. *Oxford Bull. Econ. Statist.*, May 1973, *35*(2), pp. 119–34.

Markham, Jesse W. The Conglomerate Firm: A Factual Analysis. In *Weston, J. F. and Ornstein, S. I., eds.,* 1973, pp. 185–201.

Marks, David H. and Cohon, Jared L. Multiobjective Screening Models and Water Resource Investment. *Water Resources Res.*, August 1973, *9*(4), pp. 826–36.

_____ and LeClerc, Guy. Determination of the Discharge Policy for Existing Reservoir Networks under Differing Objectives. *Water Resources Res.*, October 1973, *9*(5), pp. 1155–65.

Marks, George P., III. The New Orleans Screwmen's Benevolent Association, 1850-1861. *Labor Hist.*, Spring 1973, *14*(2), pp. 259–63.

Marks, Leonard H. A Communications Satellite System for the United States. In *The Diebold Group, Inc.,* 1973, pp. 153–60.

Marks, Peter A. A Further Note on Tariff vs. Subsidy. *Kyklos,* 1973, *26*(4), pp. 870–71.

Marschak, Thomas A. Decentralizing the Command Economy: The Study of a Pragmatic Strategy for Reformers. In *Bornstein, M., ed.,* 1973, pp. 23–63.

Marsh, Arthur I. International Manual on Collective Bargaining for Public Employees: Great Britain. In *Kaye, S. P. and Marsh, A., eds.,* 1973, pp. 128–70.

Marsh, Robert M. and Mannari, Hiroshi. Pay and Social Structure in a Japanese Firm. *Ind. Relat.,* February 1973, *12*(1), pp. 16–32.

Marshall, Harold Emory. Cost Sharing and Multiobjectives in Water Resource Development. *Water Resources Res.,* February 1973, *9*(1), pp. 1–10.

Marshall, Harvey. Suburban Life Styles: A Contribution to the Debate. In *Masotti, L. H. and Hadden, J. K., eds.,* 1973, pp. 123–48.

Marsiglia, Alessandro. Considerazioni metodologiche. (Research on Distribution: Methodological Considerations. With English summary.) *L'Impresa,* 1973, *15*(1), pp. 53–58.

Marstrand, Pauline K. and Pavitt, K. L. R. The Agricultural Sub-system. In *Cole, H. S. D., et al., eds.,* 1973, pp. 56–65.

_____ **and Sinclair, T. C.** The Pollution Sub-system. In *Cole, H. S. D., et al., eds.,* 1973, pp. 80–89.

Martelli, Antonio. Transformazioni tecnologiche nell'industria tessile: implicazioni economiche e sociali. (Technological Changes in the Textile Industry: Economical and Social Implications. With English summary.) *L'Impresa,* 1973, *15*(7–8), pp. 434–38.

Martin, A. W. Australia and the Hartz 'Fragment' Thesis. *Australian Econ. Hist. Rev.,* September 1973, *13*(2), pp. 131–47.

Martin, David A. Beyond Positive Economics: Toward Moral Philosophy. *Amer. Econ.,* Spring 1973, *17*(1), pp. 60–69.

_____ Protecting the Fisc: Executive Impoundment and Congressional Power. *Yale Law J.,* July 1973, *82*(8), pp. 1636–58.

_____ 1853: The End of Bimetallism in the United States. *J. Econ. Hist.,* December 1973, *33*(4), pp. 825–44.

Martin, Donald L. Legal Constraints and the Choice of Organizational Form. *Amer. Econ. Rev.,* May 1973, *63*(2), pp. 326–34.

_____ Some Economics of Job Rights in the Longshore Industry. *J. Econ. Bus.,* Winter 1973, *25*(2), pp. 93–100.

Martin, M. J. Durable Goods as a Generalizer of Demand Theory. In *Morishima, M., et al.,* 1973, pp. 184–209.

Martin, Neil R., Jr. and Davison, Cecil W. Sensitivity of Beef Quantity and Prices—1980 Preview. *Ill. Agr. Econ.,* July 1973, *13*(2), pp. 33–37.

Martin, Randolph C. Spatial Distribution of Population: Cities and Suburbs. *J. Reg. Sci.,* August 1973, *13*(2), pp. 269–78.

Martin, Warren S. The Effects of Scaling on the Correlation Coefficient: A Test of Validity. *J. Marketing Res.,* August 1973, *10*(3), pp. 316–18.

_____; **Bruce, Grady D. and Witt, Robert E.** Interpersonal Orientation and Innovative Behavior. *Miss. Val. J. Bus. Econ.,* Winter 1973-74, *9*(2), pp. 35–42.

Martinoli, Gino. Formazione dei quadri e "stages" all'estero. (Cadres Training and "Stages" abroad. With English summary.) *L'Impresa,* 1973, *15*(2), pp. 147–56.

Martner, Gonzalo. The Popular Unity Government's Efforts in Planning. In *Zammit, J. A., ed.,* 1973, pp. 69–75.

Márton, J. The Vertical Integration of the Hungarian Food Economy. *Acta Oecon.,* 1973, *11*(1), pp. 81–96.

Martos, Béla and Kornai, János. Autonomous Control of the Economic System. *Econometrica,* May 1973, *41*(3), pp. 509–28.

Marty, Alvin L. Growth, Satiety, and the Tax Revenue from Money Creation. *J. Polit. Econ.,* September-October 1973, *81*(5), pp. 1136–52.

Martyn, Howe. Multinational Corporations in a Nationalistic World. In *Andreano, R. L., ed.,* 1973, pp. R332–06.

Marunová, Eva and Švábová, Milada. Zobecnění MODI-metody pro žiskání optimálního řesení jednoho typu trojrozmerného dopravního problému. (Generalization of Modi-Method for Getting the Optimal Solution of One Type of Three-Dimensional Transportation Problem. With English summary.) *Ekon.-Mat. Obzor,* 1973, *9*(2), pp. 201–11.

Marvulli, Roberto. Il messaggio pubblicitario sulla stampa quotidiana: un esame quantitativo. (An Analysis of the Quantitative Importance of the Advertising Message on the Daily Newspapers. With English summary.) *L'Impresa,* 1973, *15* (5–6), pp. 353–58.

Marwick, David and Levitan, Sar A. Work and Training for Relief Recipients. *J. Human Res.,* Supplement 1973, *8,* pp. 5–18.

Marz, Roger H.; Casstevens, Thomas W. and Casstevens, Harold T., II. The Hunting of the Paradox. *Public Choice,* Summer 1973, *15,* pp. 97–102.

Marzola, Pier L. Indicazioni verso l'aumento del prezzo ufficiale dell'oro per la ricostruzione del sistema monetario internazionale. (Towards a Rise of the Official Price of Gold as a Means to Rebuild the International Monetary System. With English summary.) *Rivista Int. Sci. Econ. Com.,* December 1973, *20*(12), pp. 1157–78.

Mascarenhas, R. C. A Conceptual Framework for Understanding Autonomy for Public Enterprises in India. In *Henley, D. S., ed.,* 1973, pp. 395–405.

Mas-Colell, Andreu and Razin, Assaf. A Model of Intersectoral Migration and Growth. *Oxford Econ. Pap.,* March 1973, *25*(1), pp. 72–79.

Mašek, J.; Malek, P. and Křikava, L. The Czech Experience in Nutrition Improvement. In *Berg, A.; Scrimshaw, N. S. and Call, D. L., eds.,* 1973, pp. 329–34.

Masera, Francesco. Autonomous Capital Movements: The Italian Experience in the Past Decade. *Aussenwirtschaft,* March-June 1973, *28* (1–2), pp. 83–106.

_____ European Fund for Monetary Cooperation: Objectives and Operating Guidelines. *Banca Naz. Lavoro Quart. Rev.,* September 1973, (106), pp. 269–86.

_____ I movimenti di capitali autonomi nell'esperienza italiana degli ultimi dieci anni. (Autonomous Movements of Capital Within the Range of Italian Experience During the Last Ten Years. With English summary.) *Bancaria,* June 1973, *29* (6), pp. 696–707.

Maslove, Allan and Mohring, Herbert. The Optimal Provision of Public Goods: Yet Another Comment. *J. Polit. Econ.,* May-June 1973, *81*(3), pp. 778–85.

Mason, Joseph Barry. Along the Interstate: Highway Interchange Land Use Development. *Growth Change*, October 1973, *4*(4), pp. 38–43.

———— **and Mayer, Morris L.** Insights into the Image Determinants of Fashion Specialty Outlets. *J. Bus. Res.*, Summer 1973, *1*(1), pp. 73–80.

Mason, R. Hal. The Multinational Firm and the Cost of Technology to Developing Countries. *Calif. Manage. Rev.*, Summer 1973, *15*(4), pp. 5–13.

———— Some Observations on the Choice of Technology by Multinational Firms in Developing Countries. *Rev. Econ. Statist.*, August 1973, *55*(3), pp. 349–55.

————; **Harris, Jerome and McLoughlin, John.** Corporate Strategy: A Point of View. In *Klein, W. H. and Murphy, D. C., eds.*, 1973, pp. 158–65.

Mason, William M. and Griliches, Zvi. Education, Income, and Ability. In *Goldberger, A. S. and Duncan, O. D., eds.*, 1973, pp. 285–316.

Masotti, Louis H. Epilogue: Suburbia in the Seventies . . . and Beyond. In *Masotti, L. H. and Hadden, J. K., eds.*, 1973, pp. 533–42.

———— Prologue: Suburbia Reconsidered—Myth and Counter-Myth. In *Masotti, L. H. and Hadden, J. K., eds.*, 1973, pp. 15–22.

Massel, M. S. Non-Tariff Barriers as an Obstacle to World Trade. In *Thorelli, H. B., ed.*, 1973, pp. 71–82.

Massetti, C. Les incertitudes quantitatives et qualitatives des prévisions du bilan et de l'approvisionnement énergétique européen: ses implications pour l'industrie pétrolière. (The Quantitative and Qualitative Uncertainties of Forecasting the European Energy Balance and Supply: Its Implications for the Mineral Oil Industry. With English summary.) *Schweiz. Z. Volkswirtsch. Statist.*, September 1973, *109*(3), pp. 411–20.

Masson, Robert Tempest. Costs of Search and Racial Price Discrimination. *Western Econ. J.*, June 1973, *11*(2), pp. 167–86.

Massy, William F. Issues in the Development of Information Systems. In *Britt, S. H. and Boyd, H. W., Jr., eds.*, 1973, pp. 647–55.

Masters, Gene C. and Miller, Bill R. A Short-Run Price Prediction Model for Eggs. *Amer. J. Agr. Econ.*, August 1973, *55*(3), pp. 484–89.

Masters, Stanley H. and Garfinkel, Irwin. Two Income Maintenance Plans, Work Incentives and the Closure of the Poverty Gap: Comment. *Ind. Lab. Relat. Rev.*, April 1973, *26*(3), pp. 1002–04.

Mastrapasqua, Frank and Bolten, Steven. A Note on Financial Analyst Evaluation. *J. Finance*, June 1973, *28*(3), pp. 707–12.

———— **and Moyer, R. Charles.** Socio-economic Accounting and External Diseconomies: A Comment. *Accounting Rev.*, January 1973, *48*(1), pp. 126–27.

Mate, Mavis. The Indebtedness of Canterbury Cathedral Priory, 1215–95. *Econ. Hist. Rev., 2nd Ser.*, May 1973, *26*(2), pp. 183–97.

Mathew, T. I. Social Security for the Rural Population: A Study of Some Social Services in Selected Rural Areas of India. *Int. Lab. Rev.*, October 1973, *108*(4), pp. 313–28.

Mathew, V. T. Restructuring of India's Banking System. In *Simha, S. L. N., ed.*, 1973, pp. 183–88.

Mathews, Russell. Budget Structure and Organisation in Developed and Developing Countries. In *[Hicks, U.]*, 1973, pp. 233–59.

———— Patterns of Educational Finance. *Australian Econ. Pap.*, December 1973, *12*(21), pp. 145–61.

Mathias, Peter. Debates in Economic History: Introduction. In *Perry, P. J., ed.*, 1973, pp. xi–xliv.

Mathias, Robert A. An Approach Toward Corporate Social Measures. In *Dierkes, M. and Bauer, R. A., eds.*, 1973, pp. 285–91.

Mathieson, Donald J. Traded Goods, Nontraded Goods, and the Balance of Payments. *Int. Econ. Rev.*, October 1973, *14*(3), pp. 615–24.

Mathur, A. B. L. India's Terms of Trade with U.S.A. 1951–52 to 1968–69. *Indian Econ. J.*, October–December 1973, *21*(2), pp. 73–90.

Mathur, Ashok. Consumption Lag, Harrod's Warranted Growth Path and Its Stability. *Indian Econ. Rev.*, October 1973, *8*(2), pp. 148–71.

Mathur, P. N. The Rate of Interest in a State of Economic Flux. In *Parkin, M., ed.*, 1973, pp. 330–42.

Mathur, Vijay K. Models of Air Pollution Damage Control in a Region. In *Mattila, J. M. and Thompson, W. R., eds.*, 1973, pp. 27–40.

Matiukha, I. The Rise in Living Standards of Working People in the USSR. *Prob. Econ.*, September 1973, *16*(5), pp. 60–71.

Matsuura, Tamotsu. L'evoluzione del pensiero economico moderno in Giappone. (The Evolution of Modern Economic Thought in Japan. With English summary.) *Rivista Int. Sci. Econ. Com.*, August-September 1973, *20*(8–9), pp. 839–52.

Mattfeldt, Harald. Zum Problem der wissenschaftlichen Politikberatung am Beispiel des Gesamtindikators des Sachverständigenrats. (With English summary.) *Z. ges. Staatswiss.*, October 1973, *129*(4), pp. 634–42.

———— Zum Verhältnis verschiedener finanzieller Aktiva im Portefeuille inländischer Nichtbanken der BRD. (On the Relationship Between Different Financial Assets of Non-bank Portfolio Composition in Western Germany. With English summary.) *Jahr. Nationalökon. Statist.*, March 1973, *187*(3), pp. 237–44.

Matthews, Jim; Womack, Abner and Heien, Dale. A Methods Note on the Gauss-Seidel Algorithm for Solving Econometric Models. *Agr. Econ. Res.*, July 1973, *25*(3), pp. 71–80.

Matthews, R. C. O. The Contribution of Science and Technology to Economic Development. In *Williams, B. R., ed.*, 1973, pp. 1–31.

———— Foreign Trade and British Economic Growth. *Scot. J. Polit. Econ.*, November 1973, *20*(3), pp. 195–209.

Matthiessen, Lars. Index-tied Income Taxes and Economic Policy. *Swedish J. Econ.*, March 1973, *75*(1), pp. 49–66.

———— Recent Experience with Fiscal Policy in Sweden. In *Giersch, H., ed.*, 1973, pp. 170–87.

Mattila, John M. A Metropolitan Income Determination Model and the Estimation of Metropolitan Income Multipliers. *J. Reg. Sci.*, April 1973, *13*(1), pp. 1–16.

Mattila, J. Peter. The Effects of Extending Minimum

Wages to Cover Household Maids. *J. Human Res.,* Summer 1973, *8*(3), pp. 365–82.

Mattox, Bruce W. and Stevens, Joe B. Augmentation of Salmon Stocks through Artificial Propagation: Methods and Implications. In *Sokoloski, A. A., ed.,* 1973, pp. 133–45.

Mattsson, Peter. Projektanalys. (Project Analysis. With English summary.) *Ekon. Samfundets Tidskr.,* 1973, *26*(2), pp. 95–100.

Matzner, Egon and Vak, Karl. Program Budgeting in Austria: An Essay in Persuasion. In *Novick, D., ed.,* 1973, pp. 61–64.

Mauer, Laurence Jay. Logical Consistency and Jacob Mosak's General Equilibrium in International Trade. *Indian Econ. J.,* July–September 1973, *21*(1), pp. 37–41.

_____ **and van de Gevel, A. J. W.** Non-Tariff Distortions in International Trade: A Methodological Review. In *Scaperlanda, A. E., ed.,* 1973, pp. 47–69.

_____ **and Scaperlanda, Anthony E.** The Impact of Controls on United States Direct Foreign Investment in the European Economic Community. *Southern Econ. J.,* January 1973, *39*(3), pp. 419–23.

Mauldon, R. G. Financial Control within Commercial Family Farms. *Australian J. Agr. Econ.,* April 1973, *17*(1), pp. 33–42.

Maurice, S. Charles and Ferguson, C. E. Factor Demand Elasticity under Monopoly and Monopsony. *Economica, N.S.,* May 1973, *40*(158), pp. 180–86.

Maurizi, Alex R. Minority Membership in Apprenticeship Programs in the Construction Trades: Reply. *Ind. Lab. Relat. Rev.,* October 1973, *27*(1), pp. 100–102.

_____ **and Isakson, Hans R.** The Consumer Economics of Unit Pricing. *J. Marketing Res.,* August 1973, *10*(3), pp. 277–85.

Maxwell, James A. Income Tax Discrimination Against the Renter. *Nat. Tax J.,* September 1973, *26*(3), pp. 491–97.

_____ The New 1971 Federal-Provincial Fiscal Arrangements Act in Canada. *Econ. Rec.,* June 1973, *49*(126), pp. 306–10.

May, Alfred N. An Index of Thirteenth-Century Peasant Impoverishment? Manor Court Fines. *Econ. Hist. Rev., 2nd Ser.,* August 1973, *26*(3), pp. 389–402.

May, Paul A. The Budgeting Process. *Manage. Account.,* January 1973, *54*(7), pp. 19–25.

May, Robert G. and Sundem, Gary L. Cost of Information and Security Prices: Market Association Tests for Accounting Policy Decisions. *Accounting Rev.,* January 1973, *48*(1), pp. 80–94.

Mayer, Harold M. Some Geographic Aspects of Technological Change in Maritime Transportation. *Econ. Geogr.,* April 1973, *49*(2), pp. 145–55.

Mayer, Kurt B. Die jüdische Bevölkerung der Schweiz. (The Jewish Population of Switzerland. With English summary.) *Schweiz. Z. Volkswirtsch. Statist.,* March 1973, *109*(1), pp. 91–100.

Mayer, Lawrence S. Estimating a Correlation Coefficient When One Variable Is Not Directly Observed. *J. Amer. Statist. Assoc.,* June 1973, *68* (342), pp. 420–21.

Mayer, Leo V. Regional Effects of Alternative Trade Policies. In *Iowa State University Center for Agricultural and Rural Development,* 1973, pp. 166–83.

Mayer, Morris L. and Mason, Joseph Barry. Insights into the Image Determinants of Fashion Specialty Outlets. *J. Bus. Res.,* Summer 1973, *1*(1), pp. 73–80.

Mayer, Wolfgang. A General Class of Production Functions with Nonlinear Isoclines. *Southern Econ. J.,* July 1973, *40*(1), pp. 1–8.

_____ **and Chang, Winston W.** Intermediate Goods in a General Equilibrium Trade Model. *Int. Econ. Rev.,* June 1973, *14*(2), pp. 447–59.

Mayers, David. Nonmarketable Assets and the Determination of Capital Asset Prices in the Absence of a Riskless Asset. *J. Bus.,* April 1973, *46*(2), pp. 258–67.

Maynard, Geoffrey. Special Drawing Rights and Development Aid. *J. Devel. Stud.,* July 1973, *9*(4), pp. 518–43.

Mayne, Lucille S. The Deposit Reserve Requirement Recommendations of the Commission on Financial Structure & Regulation: An Analysis and Critique. *J. Bank Res.,* Spring 1973, *4*(1), pp. 41–51.

Maynes, E. Scott. Consumerism: Origin and Research Implications. In *Sheldon, E. B., ed.,* 1973, pp. 270–94.

Mazis, Michael B. and Green, Robert. Implementing Social Responsibility. In *Klein, W. H. and Murphy, D. C., eds.,* 1973, pp. 296–304.

_____**; Settle, Robert B. and Leslie, Dennis C.** Elimination of Phosphate Detergents and Psychological Reactance. *J. Marketing Res.,* November 1973, *10*(4), pp. 390–95.

Mazumdar, D. Labour Supply in Early Industrialization: the Case of the Bombay Textile Industry. *Econ. Hist. Rev., 2nd Ser.,* August 1973, *26*(3), pp. 477–96.

Mazur, D. Peter. Fertility and Economic Dependency of Soviet Women. *Demography,* February 1973, *10*(1), pp. 37–51.

_____ Relation of Marriage and Education to Fertility in the U.S.S.R. *Population Stud.,* March 1973, *27*(1), pp. 105–15.

Mazza, Gertrude and Wentz, John. The Acquisitive Bank Holding Companies: A Bigger Role in Mortgage Banking. *Fed. Res. Bank Bus. Rev. Phila.,* October 1973, pp. 7–8.

M'Baye, M. Savings Banks and Savings Facilities in African Countries: Senegal. In *Alberici, A. and Baravelli, M., eds.,* 1973, pp. 83–86.

McAnaw, Richard. Bankers and Politicians: The Not So Strange Bedfellows. *Mich. Academician,* Spring 1973, *5*(4), pp. 505–13.

McCain, Roger A. Consumer Welfare and Product Differentiation: An Agnostic Comment. *Quart. Rev. Econ. Bus.,* Summer 1973, *13*(2), pp. 90–92.

_____ The Cost of Supervision and the Quality of Labor: A Determinant of X-Inefficiency. *Miss. Val. J. Bus. Econ.,* Spring 1973, *8*(3), pp. 1–16.

_____ Critical Note on Illyrian Economics. *Kyklos,* 1973, *26*(2), pp. 380–86.

McCalden, Gerald. Towards a Model for Prediction of Residential Water Use. In *Aislabie, C., ed.,* 1973, pp. 99–113.

McCall, Alan S. and Walker, David A. The Effects

of Control Status on Commercial Bank Profitability. *J. Financial Quant. Anal.*, September 1973, *8*(4), pp. 637–45.

McCall, David B. Profit: Spur for Solving Social Ills. *Harvard Bus. Rev.*, May-June 1973, *51*(3), pp. 46–54, 180–82.

McCalla, Alex F. Public Sector Research and Education and the Agribusiness Complex: Unholy Alliance or Socially Beneficial Partnership? Discussion. *Amer. J. Agr. Econ.*, December 1973, *55*(5), pp. 999–1002.

McCallum, B. T. Friedman's Missing Equation: Another Approach. *Manchester Sch. Econ. Soc. Stud.*, September 1973, *41*(3), pp. 311–28.

——— A Note Concerning Asymptotic Covariance Expressions. *Econometrica*, May 1973, *41*(3), pp. 581–83.

McCallum, John S. The Impact of the Capital Gains Tax on Bond Yields. *Nat. Tax J.*, December 1973, *26*(4), pp. 575–83.

McCann, James C. A More Accurate Short Method of Approximating Lotka's *r.*. *Demography*, November 1973, *10*(4), pp. 567–70.

McCarty, J. W. Australia as a Region of Recent Settlement in the Nineteenth Century. *Australian Econ. Hist. Rev.*, September 1973, *13*(2), pp. 148–67.

McCawley, Peter. Survey of Recent Developments. *Bull. Indonesian Econ. Stud.*, November 1973, *9* (3), pp. 1–27.

McClam, Warren D. The Control of Capital Movements: Comparative Policy Developments in the United States and Japan. *Aussenwirtschaft*, March-June 1973, *28*(1–2), pp. 107–29.

McClelland, Peter D. The New Economic History and the Burdens of the Navigation Acts: Comment. *Econ. Hist. Rev.*, 2nd Ser., November 1973, *26*(4), pp. 679–86.

McClelland, W. G. Public Policy Toward Retailing: The United Kingdom. In *Boddewyn, J. J. and Hollander, S. C., eds.*, 1972, pp. 351–66.

McCloskey, Donald N. New Perspectives on the Old Poor Law. *Exploration Econ. Hist.*, Summer 1973, *10*(4), pp. 419–36.

McClung, Nelson. Editing Census Microdata Files for Income and Wealth. *Ann. Econ. Soc. Measure*, April 1973, *2*(2), pp. 201–08.

McCollum, James F. Price-Expectations Effects on Interest Rates: Comment. *J. Finance*, June 1973, *28*(3), pp. 746–50.

McCord, William. The Japanese Model. In *Wilber, C. K., ed.*, 1973, pp. 278–83.

McCormick, B. J. Trade Unions and Wage Inflation in the UK: A Reappraisal: Discussion. In *Parkin, M., ed.*, 1973, pp. 328–29.

McCormick, James A. A Look at Poverty in New Mexico Through the 1970 Census. *N. Mex. Bus.*, June 1973, *26*(6), pp. 10–16.

McCracken, Paul W. Domestic Economic Policy and Convertibility. *Amer. Econ. Rev.*, May 1973, *63* (2), pp. 199–205.

——— Federal Budget Discipline and National Priorities of the 1970's. In *Levy, M. E., ed.*, 1973, pp. 8–13.

——— The Practice of Political Economy. *Amer. Econ. Rev.*, May 1973, *63*(2), pp. 168–71.

McCulloch, Rachel. When Are a Tariff and a Quota

Equivalent: *Can. J. Econ.*, November 1973, *6*(4), pp. 503–11.

——— and **Johnson, Harry G.** A Note on Proportionally Distributed Quotas. *Amer. Econ. Rev.*, September 1973, *63*(4), pp. 726–32.

McCumstie, R. F. The New South Wales Beef Cattle Industry: A Summary of BAE Survey Results, 1968–69 to 1970–71. *Quart. Rev. Agr. Econ.*, April 1973, *26*(2), pp. 117–39.

McDaniel, Paul R. Tax Shelters and Tax Policy. *Nat. Tax J.*, September 1973, *26*(3), pp. 353–88.

McDonald, Charles L. An Empirical Examination of the Reliability of Published Predictions of Future Earnings. *Accounting Rev.*, July 1973, *48*(3), pp. 502–10.

McDonald, James B. and Ebbeler, Donald H. An Analysis of the Properties of the Exact Finite Sample Distribution of a Nonconsistent GCL Structural Variance Estimator. *Econometrica*, January 1973, *41*(1), pp. 59–65.

McDonald, John G. French Mutual Fund Performance: Evaluation of Internationally-Diversified Portfolios. *J. Finance*, December 1973, *28*(5), pp. 1161–80.

——— and **Baron, Donald C.** Risk and Return on Short Positions in Common Stocks. *J. Finance*, March 1973, *28*(1), pp. 97–107.

McDonald, Richard J. and Barzel, Yoram. Assets, Subsistence, and The Supply Curve of Labor. *Amer. Econ. Rev.*, September 1973, *63*(4), pp. 621–33.

McDonnell, C. F. and Ozawa, Terutomo. On the Geometric Measurement of an Optimum Tariff. *Indian Econ. J.*, July–September 1973, *21*(1), pp. 33–36.

McDonough, Carol C. The Demand for Commuter Rail Transport. *J. Transp. Econ. Policy*, May 1973, *7*(2), pp. 134–43.

McDougall, Duncan M. The Domestic Availability of Manufactured Commodity Output, Canada, 1870–1915. *Can. J. Econ.*, May 1973, *6*(2), pp. 189–206.

McElroy, Jerome L. and Singell, Larry D. Some Structural Contours of the Recent Urban Crisis: An Empirical Analysis of the Social and Economic Conditions of Riot and Non-Riot Cities. In *Mattila, J. M. and Thompson, W. R., eds.*, 1973, pp. 177–91.

McElroy, Marjorie B. and Vernon, John M. Estimation of Structure-Profit Relationships: Comment. *Amer. Econ. Rev.*, September 1973, *63*(4), pp. 763–67.

McElyea, Steward D. Auditing Corporate Social Impact in a Period of Rising Social Concern. In *Dierkes, M. and Bauer, R. A., eds.*, 1973, pp. 308–14.

McEnally, Richard W. Some Portfolio-Relevant Risk Characteristics of Long-Term Marketable Securities. *J. Financial Quant. Anal.*, September 1973, *8*(4), pp. 565–85.

——— and **Tavis, Lee A.** Further Studies of Property-Liability Return Adequacy: Comment. *J. Risk Ins.*, September 1973, *40*(3), pp. 453–60.

McFadden, Daniel. On the Existence of Optimal Development Programmes in Infinite-Horizon Economies. In *Mirrlees, J. A. and Stern, N. H., eds.*, 1973, pp. 260–82.

McFarlane, Bruce. Price Rigidity and Excess Capacity in Socialist Economies. *Australian Econ. Pap.*, June 1973, *12*(20), pp. 36–41.

McFetridge, Donald G. The Determinants of Pricing Behaviour: A Study of the Canadian Cotton Textile Industry. *J. Ind. Econ.*, December 1973, *22*(2), pp. 141–52.

_____ Market Structure and Price-Cost Margins: An Analysis of the Canadian Manufacturing Sector. *Can. J. Econ.*, August 1973, *6*(3), pp. 344–55.

McGaughey, Stephen E. Project Selection and Macroeconomic Objectives: Reply. *Amer. J. Agr. Econ.*, February 1973, *55*(1), pp. 107–09.

McGee, Dean A. Assessing the "Energy Crisis"—Problems and Prospects. *Fed. Res. Bank Kansas City Rev.*, September-October 1973, pp. 14–20.

McGee, John S. Economies of Size in Auto Body Manufacture. *J. Law Econ.*, October 1973, *16*(2), pp. 239–73.

McGilvray, James and Simpson, David. The Commodity Structure of Anglo-Irish Trade. *Rev. Econ. Statist.*, November 1973, *55*(4), pp. 451–58.

McGowan, John J. The Supply of Equity Securities, 1952–68. In *Goldsmith, R. W., ed.,* 1973, pp. 165–203.

_____ and Hay, George A. External Diseconomies in Competitive Supply: Comment. *Amer. Econ. Rev.*, September 1973, *63*(4), pp. 738–40.

McGrail, George R. and Furlong, Daniel R. Absorption Break-Even. *Manage. Account.*, October 1973, *55*(4), pp. 31–35.

McGrath, Dorn C., Jr. and Loewenstein, Louis K. The Planning Imperative in America's Future. *Ann. Amer. Acad. Polit. Soc. Sci.*, January 1973, *405*, pp. 15–24.

McGregor, John R. Terre Haute, The "No Grow" Industrial Center. *Indiana Bus. Rev.*, March-April 1973, *48*, pp. 14–18.

McGregor, L. and Walters, A. A. Real Balances and Output: A Productivity Model of a Monetary Economy. In *Powell, A. A. and Williams, R. A., eds.,* 1973, pp. 233–59.

McGuigan, James R. and King, William R. Security Option Strategy under Risk Aversion: An Analysis. *J. Financial Quant. Anal.,* January 1973, *8*(1), pp. 1–15.

McGuire, Joseph W. The Social Responsibility of the Corporation. In *Klein, W. H. and Murphy, D. C., eds.,* 1973, pp. 284–91.

McGuire, Martin. Notes on Grants-in-Aid and Economic Interactions among Governments. *Can. J. Econ.*, May 1973, *6*(2), pp. 207–21.

McGuire, Thomas. A Note on Lindahl's Voluntary Exchange Theory. *Public Finance,* 1973, *28*(1), pp. 94–97.

McHale, John and McHale, Magda Cordell. Management: The Larger Perspective. In *The Conference Board,* 1973, pp. 298–370.

McHale, Magda Cordell and McHale, John. Management: The Larger Perspective. In *The Conference Board,* 1973, pp. 298–370.

McInerney, J. P. and Donaldson, G. F. Changing Machinery Technology and Agricultural Adjustment. *Amer. J. Agr. Econ.*, December 1973, *55*(5), pp. 829–39.

McIntyre, Edward V. Current-Cost Financial Statements and Common-Stock Investments Decisions. *Accounting Rev.*, July 1973, *48*(3), pp. 575–85.

McKay, L. E. Some Aspects of Diversification of Production in the Pastoral Zone of the Australian Sheep Industry. *Quart. Rev. Agr. Econ.*, April 1973, *26*(2), pp. 140–48.

McKay, Roberta V. Commuting Patterns of Inner-City Residents. *Mon. Lab. Rev.*, November 1973, *96*(11), pp. 43–48.

McKean, J. R. and Peterson, R. D. Demand Elasticity, Product Differentiation, and Market Structure. *J. Econ. Theory*, April 1973, *6*(2), pp. 205–09.

McKean, Roland N. An Outsider Looks at Urban Economics. *Urban Stud.*, February 1973, *10*(1), pp. 19–37.

_____ Government and the Consumer. *Southern Econ. J.*, April 1973, *39*(4), pp. 481–89.

_____ Growth vs. No Growth: An Evaluation. In *Olson, M. and Landsberg, H. H., eds.,* 1973, pp. 207–27.

_____ Spillovers from the Rising Value of Time. *Quart. J. Econ.*, November 1973, *87*(4), pp. 638–40.

McKee, David L. Regional Inequality and the Market Mechanism: Comment. *Kyklos,* 1973, *26*(3), pp. 624–26.

McKelvey, Edward F. and Joskow, Paul L. The Fogel-Engerman Iron Model: A Clarifying Note. *J. Polit. Econ.*, September-October 1973, *81*(5), pp. 1236–40.

McKenzie, Richard B. The Micro and Macro Economic Effects of Changes in the Statutory Tax Rates. *Rev. Soc. Econ.*, April 1973, *31*(1), pp. 20–30.

McKeown, James C. A Brief Exploration of the Goal Congruence of Net Realizable Value. *Accounting Rev.*, April 1973, *48*(2), pp. 386–88.

McKibben, Walt and Rosenberg, Barr. The Prediction of Systematic and Specific Risk in Common Stocks. *J. Financial Quant. Anal.*, March 1973, *8*(2), pp. 317–33.

McKie, James W. Public Utility Regulation: Structure and Performance. In *Russell, M., ed.,* 1973, pp. 85–105.

McKinnon, Ronald I. The Dual Currency System Revisited. In *Johnson, H. G. and Swoboda, A. K., eds.,* 1973, pp. 85–90.

_____ The Monetary Approach to Exchange-Rate Policy in Less Developed Countries. In *Grubel, H. G. and Morgan, T., eds.,* 1973, pp. 67–75.

_____ On Securing a Common Monetary Policy in Europe. *Banca Naz. Lavoro Quart. Rev.*, March 1973, (104), pp. 3–20.

_____ The Value-Added Tax and the Liberalization of Foreign Trade in Developing Economies: A Comment. *J. Econ. Lit.*, June 1973, *11*(2), pp. 520–24.

McKitterick, John B. Resource Allocation in the General Electric Company. In *Weston, J. F. and Ornstein, S. I., eds.,* 1973, pp. 123–27.

McLaren, J. Alec. An Income Tax Simulation Model for the State of Minnesota. *Nat. Tax J.*, March 1973, *26*(1), pp. 71–77.

McLaughlin, Donald H. The Triumph Not the Twilight of Gold. In *Wiegand, G. C., ed.,* 1973, pp. 30–32.

McLaughlin, Doris B. The Second Battle of Battle

Creek—The Open Shop Movement in the Early Twentieth Century. *Labor Hist.*, Summer 1973, *14*(3), pp. 323–39.

McLean, David. Commerce, Finance, and British Diplomatic Support in China, 1885–86. *Econ. Hist. Rev.*, 2nd Ser., August 1973, *26*(3), pp. 464–76.

McLean, I. W. The Adoption of Harvest Machinery in Victoria in the Late Nineteenth Century. *Australian Econ. Hist. Rev.*, March 1973, *13*(1), pp. 41–56.

—— Growth and Technological Change in Agriculture: Victoria 1870–1910. *Econ. Rec.*, December 1973, *49*(128), pp. 560–74.

McLean, John G. The United States Energy Outlook and Its Implications for National Policy. *Ann. Amer. Acad. Polit. Soc. Sci.*, November 1973, *410*, pp. 97–105.

McLennan, Marshall S. Land Tenure in the Philippines, An Heterogeneous Heritage. *Mich. Academician*, Summer 1973, *6*(1), pp. 17–27.

McLeod, Donald. Determinants of Jamaican Government Revenue Shares. *J. Devel. Stud.*, April 1973, *9*(3), pp. 427–37.

McLoughlin, John; Mason, R. Hal and Harris, Jerome. Corporate Strategy: A Point of View. In *Klein, W. H. and Murphy, D. C., eds.*, 1973, pp. 158–65.

McLure, Charles E., Jr. Economic Effects of Taxing Value Added. In *Musgrave, R. A., ed.*, 1973, pp. 155–204.

—— Gradualism and the New Economic Policy: Fiscal Economics in Transition. In *Cagan, P., et al.*, 1973, pp. 35–77.

—— Investment Life Insurance Versus Term Insurance and Separate Investment: A Determination of Expected-Return Equivalents: Comment. *J. Risk Ins.*, June 1973, *40*(2), pp. 291–93.

McMahon, P. C. and Harbury, C. D. Inheritance and the Characteristics of Top Wealth Leavers in Britain. *Econ. J.*, September 1973, *83*(331), pp. 810–33.

McNees, Stephen K. A Comparison of the GNP Forecasting Accuracy of the Fair and St. Louis Econometric Models. *New Eng. Econ. Rev.*, September-October 1973, pp. 29–34.

—— Deductibility of Charitable Bequests. *Nat. Tax J.*, March 1973, *26*(1), pp. 79–98.

—— The Predictive Accuracy of Econometric Forecasts. *New Eng. Econ. Rev.*, September-October 1973, pp. 3–27.

—— Tax Refunds and Consumer Spending. *New Eng. Econ. Rev.*, January-February 1973, pp. 3–11.

McNicol, David L. The Comparative Statics Properties of the Theory of the Regulated Firm. *Bell J. Econ. Manage. Sci.*, Autumn 1973, *4*(2), pp. 428–53.

McNulty, Paul J. Hoxie's Economics in Retrospect: The Making and Unmaking of a Veblenian. *Hist. Polit. Econ.*, Fall 1973, *5*(2), pp. 449–84.

McQuown, J. A. Technical and Fundamental Analysis and Capital Market Theory. *J. Bank Res.*, Spring 1973, *4*(1), pp. 8–17.

McShane, R. W. The Influence of Financial Factors on Household Meat Consumption. *Rev. Marketing Agr. Econ.*, March 1973, *41*(1), pp. 20–29.

McWilliams, James D. A Closer Look at Incentive Fees for Bank Managed Pension Funds. *J. Bank Res.*, Winter 1973, *3*(4), pp. 238–46.

Meacci, Ferdinando. Protezione dell'ambiente, aumento dei coefficienti tecnici e preferenze collettive. (Environmental Protection, Increase in Technical Coefficients and Collective Preferences. With English summary.) *Econ. Int.*, August-November 1973, *26*(3–4), pp. 393–412.

Mead, R. and Stern, R. D. The Use of a Computer in the Teaching of Statistics. *J. Roy. Statist. Soc.*, Part 2, 1973, *136*, pp. 191–205.

Meadows, Dennis L. Dynamic Systems Modelling. In *Hawkes, N., ed.*, 1973, pp. 60–77.

—— The Dynamics of Global Equilibrium. In *Hawkes, N., ed.*, 1973, pp. 78–95.

—— and Randers, Jørgen. System Simulation to Test Environmental Policy: A Sample Study of DDT Movement in the Environment. In *Hawkes, N., ed.*, 1973, pp. 96–143.

Meadows, Donella H., et al. The Limits to Growth. In *Enthoven, A. C. and Freeman, A. M., III, eds.*, 1973, pp. 212–29.

—— A Response to Sussex. In *Cole, H. S. D., et al., eds.*, 1973, pp. 216–40.

—— and Randers, Jørgen. The Carrying Capacity of Our Global Environment: A Look at the Ethical Alternatives. In *Daly, H. E., ed.*, 1973, pp. 283–306.

Meany, George. A Trade Policy for America. In *Reynolds, L. G.; Green, G. D. and Lewis, D. R., eds.*, 1973, pp. 443–51.

Meckler, Jack M. and Rossitch, Eugene. Foreign Currency Exposure Control. *Manage. Account.*, July 1973, *55*(1), pp. 29–37.

Medford, Derek. Il controllo dei processi technologici. (The Control of Technological Processes. With English summary.) *L'Impresa*, 1973, *15* (7–8), pp. 439–44.

Medler, Jerry F. and Tull, Donald S. Poll Positions and Win Probabilities: A Stochastic Model of the Electoral Process. *Public Choice*, Spring 1973, *14*, pp. 125–32.

Medoff, James; Brown, Charles and Fane, George. The Income Distribution as a Pure Public Good: Comment. *Quart. J. Econ.*, May 1973, *87*(2), pp. 296–303.

Medow, Paul. Towards a Reexamination of Ragnar Frisch's Proposal for a Multilateral Trade Clearing Agency in the Light of International Program Budgeting. *Amer. Econ.*, Fall 1973, *17*(2), pp. 51–55.

Mee, John F. Management Philosophy for Professional Executives. In *Klein, W. H. and Murphy, D. C., eds.*, 1973, pp. 43–49.

Meehan, James W., Jr. and Duchesneau, Thomas D. The Critical Level of Concentration: An Empirical Analysis. *J. Ind. Econ.*, September 1973, *22*(1), pp. 21–36.

—— ; Mann, H. Michael and Henning, John A. Advertising and Market Concentration: Comment. *Southern Econ. J.*, January 1973, *39*(3), pp. 448–51.

Meek, Ronald L. and Skinner, Andrew S. The Development of Adam Smith's Ideas on the Division of Labour. *Econ. J.*, December 1973, *83*(332), pp. 1094–1116.

Meeker, Edward. Allocation of Resources to Health Revisited. *J. Human Res.*, Spring 1973, *8*(2), pp. 257–59.

Meeker, L. D. and Burns, Tom. A Mathematical Model of Multi-Dimensional Evaluation, Decision-Making, and Social Interaction. In *Cochrane, J. L. and Zeleny, M., eds.*, 1973, pp. 141–63.

Megyeri, E. Optimal Utilization of Enterprise Funds and Some Problems of Measuring Effectiveness. *Acta Oecon.*, 1973, *11*(4), pp. 347–67.

Mehaffey, Bruce J.; Heeler, Roger M. and Kearney, Michael J. Modeling Supermarket Product Selection. *J. Marketing Res.*, February 1973, *10*(1), pp. 34–37.

Mehay, Stephen L. Police and Productivity: Can the Invisible Hand of Competition Extend the Long Arm of the Law? *Fed. Res. Bank Bus. Rev. Phila.*, May 1973, pp. 3–12.

Mehr, Robert I. Consumerism and Automobile Insurance: Discussion. *J. Risk Ins.*, June 1973, *40*(2), pp. 217–20.

———— **and Forbes, Stephen W.** The Risk Management Decision in the Total Business Setting. *J. Risk Ins.*, September 1973, *40*(3), pp. 389–401.

Mehran, Farhad. Variance of the MVUE for the Lognormal Mean. *J. Amer. Statist. Assoc.*, September 1973, *68*(343), pp. 726–27.

Mehren, George. Public Sector Research and Education and the Agribusiness Complex: Unholy Alliance or Socially Beneficial Partnership? Discussion. *Amer. J. Agr. Econ.*, December 1973, *55*(5), pp. 997–99.

Mehta, J. S. and Swamy, P. A. V. B. Bayesian Analysis of a Bivariate Normal Distribution with Incomplete Observations. *J. Amer. Statist. Assoc.*, December 1973, *68*(344), pp. 922–27.

———— Bayesian Analysis of Error Components Regression Models. *J. Amer. Statist. Assoc.*, September 1973, *68*(343), pp. 648–58.

Meidner, Rudolf and Andersson, Rolf. The Overall Impact of an Active Labor Market Policy in Sweden. In *Ulman, L., ed.*, 1973, pp. 117–58.

Meier, G. M. The Impact of the Developed Countries. In *Streeten, P., ed.*, 1973, pp. 105–22.

Meimaroglou, M. C. Break-Even Analysis with Stepwise Varying Marginal Costs and Revenues. In *Haynes, W. W.; Coyne, T. J. and Osborne, D. K., eds.*, 1973, pp. 250–63.

Meinander, Nils. The Finnmark Devaluation—Implications and Follow-Up Measures. In *Moskoff, W., ed.*, 1973, pp. 224–31.

Meinster, David R. and Johnson, Rodney D. An Analysis of Bank Holding Company Acquisitions: Some Methodological Issues. *J. Bank Res.*, Spring 1973, *4*(1), pp. 58–61.

Meisel, William S. Tradeoff Decisions in Multiple Criteria Decision Making. In *Cochrane, J. L. and Zeleny, M., eds.*, 1973, pp. 461–76.

Meiselman, David I. The Case Against the Case for Gold. In *Wiegand, G. C., ed.*, 1973, pp. 14–20.

———— Simulations of Stabilization Policies for 1966–1970 *and* A Comparison of Stabilization Policies: 1966–67 and 1969–70: Comment. *J. Money, Credit, Banking*, Part I, February 1973, *5*(1), pp. 43–46.

———— The 1973 Report of the President's Council of Economic Advisers: Whistling in the Dark. *Amer. Econ. Rev.*, September 1973, *63*(4), pp. 527–34.

Meissner, Werner. Econometric Models: Cognitive Aims and Aspiration Levels. *Écon. Appl.*, 1973, *26* (2–3–4), pp. 367–84.

Melamed, A.; Katzir, I. and Zusman, P. A Spatial Analysis of the EEC Trade Policies in the Market for Winter Oranges. In *Judge, G. G. and Takayama, T., eds.*, 1973, pp. 464–87.

Melichar, Emanuel. Financing Agriculture: Demand for and Supply of Farm Capital and Credit. *Amer. J. Agr. Econ.*, May 1973, *55*(2), pp. 313–25.

Melicher, Ronald W. and Nielsen, James F. A Financial Analysis of Acquisition and Merger Premiums. *J. Financial Quant. Anal.*, March 1973, *8*(2), pp. 139–48.

———— **and Rush, David F.** The Performance of Conglomerate Firms: Recent Risk and Return Experience. *J. Finance*, May 1973, *28*(2), pp. 381–88.

Melinte, T.; Horovicz, M. and Olteanu, I. World Market, Economic Cooperation and the Planning of the National Economy. In *Kiss, T., ed.*, 1973, pp. 127–33.

Mélitz, Jacques. Une tentative d'explication de l'offre de monnaie en France. (The French Money Supply: An Attempted Explanation. With English summary.) *Revue Écon.*, September 1973, *24*(5), pp. 761–800.

———— **and Pardue, Morris.** The Demand and Supply of Commercial Bank Loans. *J. Money, Credit, Banking*, May 1973, *5*(2), pp. 669–92.

Mellanby, Kenneth. The Biological Effects of Pollution—An Ecological Problem. In *Robinson, J., ed.*, 1973, pp. 189–99.

Mellon, W. Giles and Bernstein, Samuel J. Multi-Dimensional Considerations in the Evaluation of Urban Policy. In *Cochrane, J. L. and Zeleny, M., eds.*, 1973, pp. 530–43.

Mellor, Earl F. A Case Study: Costs and Benefits of Public Goods and Expenditures for a Ghetto. In *Boulding, K. E.; Pfaff, M. and Pfaff, A., eds.*, 1973, pp. 38–57.

———— **and Ryscavage, P. M.** The Economic Situation of Spanish Americans. *Mon. Lab. Rev.*, April 1973, *96*(4), pp. 3–9.

Mellor, John W. Accelerated Growth in Agricultural Production and the Intersectoral Transfer of Resources. *Econ. Develop. Cult. Change*, October 1973, *22*(1), pp. 1–16.

———— Nutrition and Economic Growth. In *Berg, A.; Scrimshaw, N. S. and Call, D. L., eds.*, 1973, pp. 70–73.

Melman, Seymour. Industrial Efficiency under Managerial vs. Cooperative Decision-Making: A Comparative Study of Manufacturing Enterprises in Israel. In *Wilber, C. K., ed.*, 1973, pp. 240–57.

———— The Pervasive Economic Impact of the Military. In *Haveman, R. H. and Hamrin, R. D., eds.*, 1973, pp. 127–34.

Melnik, A. and Pollatschek, M. A. Debt Capacity, Diversification and Conglomerate Mergers. *J. Finance*, December 1973, *28*(5), pp. 1163–73.

————; **Pollatschek, M. A. and Comay, Yochanan.** The Option Value of Education and the Optimal

Path for Investment in Human Capital. *Int. Econ. Rev.*, June 1973, *14*(2), pp. 421–35.

Melnyk, Z. Lew. Regional Contribution to Capital Formation in the USSR: The Case of the Ukrainian Republic. In *Bandera, V. N. and Melnyk, Z. L., eds.*, 1973, pp. 104–31.

_____ **and Bandera, V. N.** The Soviet Economy in Regional Perspective: Introduction. In *Bandera, V. N. and Melnyk, Z. L., eds.*, 1973, pp. xvii–xxi.

Melson, Robert. Political Dilemmas of Nigerian Labor. In *Damachi, U. G. and Seibel, H. D., eds.*, 1973, pp. 119–37.

Meltzer, Allan H. The Dollar as an International Money. *Banca Naz. Lavoro Quart. Rev.*, March 1973, (104), pp. 21–28.

_____ **and Arcelus, Francisco.** The Markets for Housing and Housing Services. *J. Money, Credit, Banking*, Part I, February 1973, *5*(1), pp. 78–99.

_____ **and Arcelus, Francisco.** The Markets for Housing and Housing Services: Reply. *J. Money, Credit, Banking*, November 1973, *5*(4), pp. 973–78.

_____ **and Brunner, Karl.** Mr. Hicks and the "Monetarists." *Economica, N.S.*, February 1973, *40*(157), pp. 44–59.

Melvin, James R. and Warne, Robert D. Monopoly and the Theory of International Trade. *J. Int. Econ.*, May 1973, *3*(2), pp. 117–34.

Mendelson, Morris. The *Martin Report* and its Aftermath. *Bell J. Econ. Manage. Sci.*, Spring 1973, *4*(1), pp. 250–69.

_____ The Eurobond Market: A Prospective Review. In *Henley, D. S., ed.*, 1973, pp. 223–39.

Menger, Karl. Austrian Marginalism and Mathematical Economics. In *Hicks, J. R. and Weber, W., eds.*, 1973, pp. 38–60.

Menges, Robert J.; Costin, Frank and Greenough, William T. Student Ratings of College Teaching: Reliability, Validity, and Usefulness. *J. Econ. Educ.*, Fall 1973, *5*(1), pp. 51–53.

Mentasti, Flaminio. Osservazioni cicliche attorno alla circolazione monetaria: filtrazione mediante processo di convoluzione. (Convolution Approach in Digital Filtering of Currency Circulation Time Series. With English summary.) *L'Industria*, January-June 1973, (1–2), pp. 176–87.

Menzies, Merril W. Grain Marketing Methods in Canada—The Theory, Assumptions, and Approach. *Amer. J. Agr. Econ.*, December 1973, *55*(5), pp. 791–99.

Mera, Koichi. On the Urban Agglomeration and Economic Efficiency. *Econ. Develop. Cult. Change*, January 1973, *21*(2), pp. 309–24.

Mercado, Abraham and Gisser, Micha. Economic Aspects of Ground Water Resources and Replacement Flows in Semiarid Agricultural Areas. *Amer. J. Agr. Econ.*, August 1973, *55*(3), pp. 461–66.

Mercer, Lloyd J. Corporate Farming in the United States: Discussion. *J. Econ. Hist.*, March 1973, *33*(1), pp. 291–95.

_____ Rates of Return and Government Subsidization of the Canadian Pacific Railway: An Alternate View. *Can. J. Econ.*, August 1973, *6*(3), pp. 428–37.

_____ **and Morgan, W. Douglas.** Housing Surplus in the 1920s? Another Evaluation. *Exploration Econ. Hist.*, Spring 1973, *10*(3), pp. 295–303.

Merchant, Stephen M. and Triplett, Jack E. The CPI and the PCE Deflator: An Econometric Analysis of Two Price Measures: Reply. *Ann. Econ. Soc. Measure*, July 1973, *2*(3), pp. 287–88.

_____ The CPI and the PCE Deflator: An Econometric Analysis of Two Price Measures. *Ann. Econ. Soc. Measure*, July 1973, *2*(3), pp. 263–82.

Merewitz, Leonard. Cost Overruns in Public Works. In *Niskanen, W. A., et al., eds.*, 1973, pp. 277–95.

Mergen, Bernard. Blacksmiths and Welders: Identity and Phenomenal Change: Reply. *Ind. Lab. Relat. Rev.*, January 1973, *26*(2), pp. 862–64.

Merican, Malik Ali. Exchange Rate Experience and Policy in Malaysia Since World War II. In *Grubel, H. G. and Morgan, T., eds.*, 1973, pp. 19–29.

Merk, Gerhard. Möglichkeiten einer vindikativen Devisenterminpolitik der Zentralbank. (The Possibilities of Vindicative Forward Exchange Policy of the Central Bank. With English summary.) *Z. Wirtschaft. Sozialwissen.*, 1973, *93*(3), pp. 323–40.

Merrett, A. J. and Sykes, Allen. Return on Equities and Fixed Interest Securities: 1919–66. In *Lister, R. J., ed.*, 1973, pp. 28–38.

Merriam, John H. Forecasting Business Cycle Downturns. *Quart. Rev. Econ. Bus.*, Winter 1973, *13*(4), pp. 71–78.

Merriam, Robert E. The Impact of Federal Tax Reform on State-Local Revenues. In *Tax Foundation, Inc.*, 1973, pp. 19–21.

Merriwether, Jacob D. Small Sample Properties of Distributed Lag Estimators with Misspecified Lag Structures. *J. Amer. Statist. Assoc.*, September 1973, *68*(343), pp. 568–74.

Merton, Robert C. An Intertemporal Capital Asset Pricing Model. *Econometrica*, September 1973, *41*(5), pp. 867–87.

_____ The Relationship Between Put and Call Option Prices: Comment. *J. Finance*, March 1973, *28*(1), pp. 183–84.

_____ Theory of Rational Option Pricing. *Bell J. Econ. Manage. Sci.*, Spring 1973, *4*(1), pp. 141–83.

Merville, Larry J. and Logue, Dennis E. General Model of Imperfect Capital Markets. *Southern Econ. J.*, October 1973, *40*(2), pp. 224–33.

_____ **and Tavis, Lee A.** A Generalized Model for Capital Investment. *J. Finance*, March 1973, *28*(1), pp. 109–18.

_____ **and Tavis, Lee A.** Optimal Working Capital Policies: A Chance-Constrained Programming Approach. *J. Financial Quant. Anal.*, January 1973, *8*(1), pp. 47–59.

van der Merwe, P. J. Manpower Policy in South Africa. *Finance Trade Rev.*, December 1972-June 1973, *10*(2–3), pp. 73–135.

Merz, C. M.; Gibson, T. A. and Seitz, C. Ward. Impact of the Space Shuttle Program on the National Economy. *Eng. Econ.*, January-February 1973, *18*(2), pp. 115–33.

Mesa-Lago, Carmelo. A Continuum Model to Compare Socialist Systems Globally. *Econ. Develop. Cult. Change*, Part I, July 1973, *21*(4), pp. 573–90.

Mestelman, Stuart. Highway User Fees and Vehicle

Transport Modes: An Old Rule Defended. *J. Polit. Econ.*, May-June 1973, *81*(3), pp. 786-95.

Mestmäcker, Ernst-Joachim. Power, Law and Economic Constitution. *Ger. Econ. Rev.*, 1973, *11*(3), pp. 177-92.

_____ Wettbewerbspolitik in der Industriegesellschaft. (Policy of Competition in the Industrial Society. With English summary.) *Z. ges. Staatswiss.*, February 1973, *129*(1), pp. 89-101.

Mestre, Eloy R. and Lubell, Alfred M. Teaching Undergraduate Economics: An Experimental Program. *J. Econ. Educ.*, Spring 1973, *4*(2), pp. 138-40.

Metcalf, Charles E. Making Inferences from Controlled Income Maintenance Experiments. *Amer. Econ. Rev.*, June 1973, *63*(3), pp. 478-83.

Metcalf, David. Pay Dispersion, Information, and Returns to Search in a Professional Labour Market. *Rev. Econ. Stud.*, October 1973, *40*(4), pp. 491-505.

_____ The Rate of Return to Investing in a Doctorate: A Case Study. *Scot. J. Polit. Econ.*, February 1973, *20*(1), pp. 43-51.

_____ Some Aspects of University Teachers' Labour Market in the UK. In *Parkin, M., ed.*, 1973, pp. 192-211.

Metcalf, Lee. The Vested Oracles: How Industry Regulates Government. In *Haveman, R. H. and Hamrin, R. D., eds.*, 1973, pp. 52-59.

Metcalfe, J. S. and Steedman, Ian. Heterogeneous Capital and the Heckscher-Ohlin-Samuelson Theory of Trade. In *Parkin, M., ed.*, 1973, pp. 50-60.

_____ **and Steedman, Ian.** The Non-Substitution Theorem and International Trade Theory. *Australian Econ. Pap.*, December 1973, *12*(21), pp. 267-69.

_____ **and Steedman, Ian.** On Foreign Trade. *Econ. Int.*, August-November 1973, *26*(3-4), pp. 516-28.

Metwally, Mohktar M. Australian Advertising Expenditure and its Relation to Demand. *Econ. Rec.*, June 1973, *49*(126), pp. 290-99.

_____ Economic Strategies of Firms Facing Asymptotic Demand: A Case Study. *Appl. Econ.*, December 1973, *5*(4), pp. 271-80.

_____ Entry Gap in New Zealand Markets for Manufactured Consumer Goods. *Econ. Rec.*, December 1973, *49*(128), pp. 575-87.

_____ **and Jensen, Rodney C.** A Note on the Measurement of Regional Income Dispersion. *Econ. Develop. Cult. Change*, October 1973, *22*(1), pp. 135-36.

_____ **and Timmaiah, G.** A Note on the Classical Utility Function for Purpose of the Theory of Taxation. *Finanzarchiv*, 1973, *31*(3), pp. 441-45.

Metwally, Mokhtar M. Economies of Size in Butter Production: The New Zealand Experience. *Econ. Anal. Pol.*, March 1973, *4*(1), pp. 33-44.

Metzler, Lloyd A. The Assumptions Implied in Least-Squares Demand Techniques. In *Metzler, L. A.*, 1973, pp. 575-98.

_____ Business Cycles and the Theory of Employment. In *Metzler, L. A.*, 1973, pp. 482-96.

_____ Exchange Rates and the International Monetary Fund. In *Metzler, L. A.*, 1973, pp. 112-58.

_____ Factors Governing the Length of Inventory Cycles. In *Metzler, L. A.*, 1973, pp. 440-64.

_____ Flexible Exchange Rates and the Theory of Employment. In *Metzler, L. A.*, 1973, pp. 275-307.

_____ Flexible Exchange Rates, the Transfer Problem, and the Balanced-Budget Theorem. In *Metzler, L. A.*, 1973, pp. 95-111.

_____ Graham's Theory of International Values. In *Metzler, L. A.*, 1973, pp. 234-57.

_____ Imported Raw Materials, the Transfer Problem, and the Concepts of Income. In *Metzler, L. A.*, 1973, pp. 70-94.

_____ A Multiple-Country Theory of Income Transfers. In *Metzler, L. A.*, 1973, pp. 545-67.

_____ A Multiple-Region Theory of Income and Trade. In *Metzler, L. A.*, 1973, pp. 516-44.

_____ The Nature and Stability of Inventory Cycles. In *Metzler, L. A.*, 1973, pp. 393-427.

_____ Partial Adjustment and the Stability of Inventory Cycles. In *Metzler, L. A.*, 1973, pp. 428-39.

_____ The Rate of Interest and the Marginal Product of Capital. In *Metzler, L. A.*, 1973, pp. 363-89.

_____ Stability of Multiple Markets: The Hicks Conditions. In *Metzler, L. A.*, 1973, pp. 499-515.

_____ The Structure of Taxes, Open-Market Operations, and the Rate of Interest. In *Metzler, L. A.*, 1973, pp. 345-62.

_____ Tariffs, International Demand, and Domestic Prices. In *Metzler, L. A.*, 1973, pp. 198-208.

_____ Tariffs, the Terms of Trade, and the Distribution of National Income. In *Metzler, L. A.*, 1973, pp. 159-97.

_____ Taxes and Subsidies in Leontief's Input-Output Model. In *Metzler, L. A.*, 1973, pp. 568-74.

_____ The Theory of International Trade. In *Metzler, L. A.*, 1973, pp. 1-49.

_____ Three Lags in the Circular Flow of Income. In *Metzler, L. A.*, 1973, pp. 465-81.

_____ The Transfer Problem Reconsidered. In *Metzler, L. A.*, 1973, pp. 50-69.

_____ Underemployment Equilibrium in International Trade. In *Metzler, L. A.*, 1973, pp. 258-74.

_____ Wealth, Saving, and the Rate of Interest. In *Metzler, L. A.*, 1973, pp. 311-44.

Meuller, Anders and Johnson, Björn. Interactions of Consumption and Metropolitan Growth. *Swedish J. Econ.*, September 1973, *75*(3), pp. 278-88.

Meyer, Eugene L. Urban Renewal and Housing: Rhetoric and Realtiy. In *Levitan, S. A., ed.*, 1973, pp. 226-58.

Meyer, John R. Is Growth Obsolete? Comment. In *Moss, M., ed.*, 1973, pp. 548-54.

_____ Knocking Down the Straw Men. In *Rasmussen, D. W. and Haworth, C. T., eds.*, 1973, pp. 190-98.

_____ Notes on Serfdom in Western and Eastern Europe: Discussion. *J. Econ. Hist.*, March 1973, *33*(1), pp. 100-105.

_____ **and Conrad, A. H.** The Economics of Slavery in the Antebellum South. In *Temin, P., ed.*, 1973, pp. 339-97.

_____ **and Kain, John F.** Transportation and Poverty. In *Grieson, R. E., ed.*, 1973, pp. 323-35.

_____; **Kain, John F. and Wohl, Martin.** Economic Change and the City: A Qualitative Evaluation and Some Hypotheses. In *Grieson, R. E., ed.*, 1973, pp. 55–72.

Meyer, Peter B. Differences in Taxation of Households: One Test of a Policy-Relevant Evaluative Technique. *Public Finance*, 1973, *28* (1), pp. 30–42.

Meyer, Richard L. and Power, Fred B. Total Insurance Costs and the Frequency of Premium Payments. *J. Risk Ins.*, December 1973, *40*(4), pp. 599–605.

Meyers, Frederic. Public Employee Unions: The French Experience. *Ind. Relat.*, February 1973, *12*(1), pp. 33–50.

Meyers, Stephen L. An Examination of the Relationship Between Interperiod Tax Allocation and Present-Value Depreciation. *Accounting Rev.*, January 1973, *48*(1), pp. 44–49.

––––––– A Re-Examination of Market and Industry Factors in Stock Price Behavior. *J. Finance*, June 1973, *28*(3), pp. 695–705.

––––––– The Stationarity Problem in the Use of the Market Model of Security Price Behavior. *Accounting Rev.*, April 1973, *48*(2), pp. 318–22.

Michael, Robert T. Education and the Derived Demand for Children. *J. Polit. Econ.*, Part II, March-April 1973, *81*(2), pp. S128–64.

––––––– Education in Nonmarket Production. *J. Polit. Econ.*, Part I, March-April 1973, *81*(2), pp. 306–27.

––––––– **and Becker, Gary S.** On the New Theory of Consumer Behavior. *Swedish J. Econ.*, December 1973, *75*(4), pp. 378–96.

Michal, Jan M. Size-Distribution of Earnings and Household Incomes in Small Socialist Countries. *Rev. Income Wealth*, December 1973, *19*(4), pp. 407–28.

Michelotti, Kopp. Young Workers: In School and Out. *Mon. Lab. Rev.*, September 1973, *96*(9), pp. 11–15.

Michetti, Ambrogio. The Mineral Water and Spa Industry in Italy. *Rev. Econ. Cond. Italy*, November 1973, *27*(6), pp. 410–20.

Miconi, Gastone. New Aspects of an Old Problem? Inflation. *Rev. Econ. Cond. Italy*, January-March 1973, *27*(1–2), pp. 53–64.

Mieszkowski, Peter and King, A. Thomas. Racial Discrimination, Segregation, and the Price of Housing. *J. Polit. Econ.*, May-June 1973, *81*(3), pp. 590–606.

Mighell, Ronald L. and Lane, Elizabeth. Writing and the Economic Researcher. *Agr. Econ. Res.*, January 1973, *25*(1), pp. 15–20.

Migliaro, Alfonso and Jain, Chaman L. Optimum Customer Investment Criteria in Mail Order Operation. *Rivista Int. Sci. Econ. Com.*, May 1973, *20*(5), pp. 470–78.

Mikesell, James J. Mobile Homes: An Important New Element in Rural Housing. *Agr. Finance Rev.*, July 1973, *34*, pp. 18–23.

Mikesell, John L. The Corporate Income Tax and Rate of Return in Privately Owned Utilities, 1948–1970. *Public Finance*, 1973, *28*(3–4), pp. 291–300.

––––––– **and Blair, John P.** A Note on the Empirical Nature of the Taxpayer Rebellion. *Public Choice*, Fall 1973, *16*, pp. 43–50.

––––––– **and Seifried, Edmond J.** Rates of Return in Public and Private Enterprise: Electric Utilities in the United States. *Miss. Val. J. Bus. Econ.*, Fall 1973, *9*(1), pp. 41–54.

Mikesell, Raymond F. and Zinser, James E. The Nature of the Savings Function in Developing Countries: A Survey of the Theoretical and Empirical Literature. *J. Econ. Lit.*, March 1973, *11* (1), pp. 1–26.

Mikitani, Ryoichi. Monetary Policy in Japan. In *Holbik, K., ed.*, 1973, pp. 246–81.

Miles, Barbara L. and Robinson, Thomas R. Residential Construction Boom, 1970–73. *Surv. Curr. Bus.*, May 1973, *53*(5), pp. 14–22.

Miles, Caroline. Employment in the Industrialized Countries. In *Hughes, H., ed.*, 1973, pp. 101–16.

Miles, Raymond E. and Vergin, Roger C. Behavioral Properties of Variance Controls. In *Thomas, W. E., Jr., ed.*, 1973, pp. 325–39.

Milgram, Grace. Estimates of the Value of Land in the United States Held by Various Sectors of the Economy, Annually, 1952 to 1968. In *Goldsmith, R. W., ed.*, 1973, pp. 343–77.

Militaru, St. Analiza statistică a corelaţiei dintre acumulare şi consum în R.S. România. (Statistical Analysis of the Correlation Between Accumulation and Consumption in the Socialist Republic of Romania. With English summary.) *Stud. Cercet. Econ.*, 1973, (3), pp. 105–20.

Miller, Bill R. and Masters, Gene C. A Short-Run Price Prediction Model for Eggs. *Amer. J. Agr. Econ.*, August 1973, *55*(3), pp. 484–89.

Miller, Edward. Farming of Manors and Direct Management: Rejoinder. *Econ. Hist. Rev., 2nd Ser.*, February 1973, *26*(1), pp. 138–40.

––––––– The Flight of the Native Born. *Growth Change*, October 1973, *4*(4), pp. 10–15.

––––––– Is Out-Migration Affected by Economic Conditions? *Southern Econ. J.*, January 1973, *39*(3), pp. 396–405.

––––––– Return and Nonreturn In-Migration. *Growth Change*, January 1973, *4*(1), pp. 3–9.

––––––– Some Implications of Land Ownership Patterns for Petroleum Policy. *Land Econ.*, November 1973, *49*(4), pp. 414–23.

Miller, Ervin. The Pains of Monetary Restraint. *Lloyds Bank Rev.*, July 1973, (109), pp. 36–51.

Miller, Etienne and Smith, Gordon P. International Travel, Passenger Fares, and Other Transportation in the U.S. Balance of Payments: 1972. *Surv. Curr. Bus.*, June 1973, *53*(6), pp. 12–16, 56.

Miller, Glenn H., Jr. and Cacy, J. A. Business and Financial Outlook—A Promising 1973. *Fed. Res. Bank Kansas City Rev.*, January 1973, pp. 11–20.

Miller, Herman P. Measuring Subemployment in Poverty Areas of Large U.S. Cities. *Mon. Lab. Rev.*, October 1973, *96*(10), pp. 10–18.

Miller, James C., III. The Optimal Pricing of Freight in Combination Aircraft. *J. Transp. Econ. Policy*, September 1973, *7*(3), pp. 258–68.

Miller, James E. Guidelines for Selecting a Health Status Index: Suggested Criteria. In *Berg, R. L., ed.*, 1973, pp. 243–46.

Miller, James J. and Gruebele, J. W. Effects of the Use of Spot Cases in the Sale of Selected Dairy Products in Retail Food Chains. *Ill. Agr. Econ.*,

July 1973, *13*(2), pp. 44–48.

Miller, Jerry D. Accounting for Warrants and Convertible Bonds. *Manage. Account.*, January 1973, *54*(7), pp. 26–28.

Miller, L. Charles, Jr. The Economics of Housing Code Enforcement. *Land Econ.*, February 1973, *49*(1), pp. 92–96.

Miller, Malcolm C. Goodwill—An Aggregation Issue. *Accounting Rev.*, April 1973, *48*(2), pp. 280–91.

Miller, Marcus H. "Competition and Credit Control" and the Open Economy. *Manchester Sch. Econ. Soc. Stud.*, March 1973, *41*(1), pp. 123–40.

Miller, Norman C. and Whitman, Marina v. N. Alternative Theories and Tests of U.S. Short-Term Foreign Investment. *J. Finance*, December 1973, *28* (5), pp. 1131–50.

Miller, Paul B. and Jones, David E. Regional Growth and Industrial Change in Ohio: A Shift-Share Analysis. *Ohio State U. Bull. Bus. Res.*, July 1973, *48*(7), pp. 1–4, 8.

Miller, Richard K. and Cohen, Jacob. A Flow-of-Funds Model of the Stock Market. *J. Econ. Bus.*, Winter 1973, *25*(2), pp. 71–82.

Miller, Robert B. and Cramer, Robert H. Development of a Deposit Forecasting Procedure for Use in Bank Financial Management. *J. Bank Res.*, Summer 1973, *4*(2), pp. 122–38.

Miller, Robert R. and Weigel, Dale R. Factors Affecting Resource Transfer Through Direct Investment. In *Alexandrides, C. G., ed.*, 1973, pp. 129–44.

Miller, Roger LeRoy. The Closed Enterprise System Opened Up. *Antitrust Bull.*, Fall, 1973, *18*(3), pp. 589–606.

_____ **and Williams, Raburn.** A Note on the Effects of Government Finance on Aggregate Demand for Goods and Services. *Public Finance*, 1973, *28* (3–4), pp. 393–96.

Miller, S. F. and Halter, A. N. Systems-Simulation in a Practical Policy-Making Setting: The Venezuelan Cattle Industry. *Amer. J. Agr. Econ.*, August 1973, *55*(3), pp. 420–32.

Miller, S. M. On Not Abusing Incentives. In *Stein, B. and Miller, S. M., eds.*, 1973, pp. 199–204.

_____ **and Corwin, R. D.** A qui profite l'impôt? Mythes et réalitiés. (Taxation and its Beneficiaries: The Manipulation of Symbols. With English summary.) *Consommation*, January-March 1973, *20*(1), pp. 17–35.

Miller, Stephen M. and Lott, William F. A Note on the Optimality Conditions for Excise Taxation. *Southern Econ. J.*, July 1973, *40*(1), pp. 122–23.

_____ **and Tabb, William K.** A New Look at a Pure Theory of Local Expenditures. *Nat. Tax J.*, June 1973, *26*(2), pp. 161–76.

Miller, Thomas A. Economic Adjustment Research for Policy Guidance: An Example from Agriculture. In *Judge, G. G. and Takayama, T., eds.*, 1973, pp. 65–88.

Miller, W. L. and Byers, D. M. Development and Display of Multiple-Objective Project Impacts. *Water Resources Res.*, February 1973, *9*(1), pp. 11–20.

Mills, Edwin S. and MacKinnon, James. Notes on the New Urban Economics. *Bell J. Econ. Manage.*

Sci., Autumn 1973, *4*(2), pp. 593–601.

Milne, Robin G. Family Planning in Malta. *Population Stud.*, July 1973, *27*(2), pp. 373–86.

Milstein, Jeffrey S. and Lee, Jong Ryool. A Political Economy of the Vietnam War, 1965–1972. *Peace Sci. Soc.*, 1973, *21*, pp. 41–63.

Minami, Ryoshin. Wage Adjustments in Postwar Japan: An Alternative Approach to the Phillips-Lipsey Curve. *Hitotsubashi J. Econ.*, June 1973, *14*(1), pp. 44–55.

Minc, Bronislaw. Il meccanismo di funzionamento dell'economia socialista. (The Functioning Mechanism of Socialist Economy. With English summary.) *Mondo Aperto*, October 1973, *27*(5), pp. 314–20.

Mincer, Jacob. Determining Who Are the "Hidden Unemployed." *Mon. Lab. Rev.*, March 1973, *96* (3), pp. 27–30.

Mingat, Alain. Cheminements aléatoires et modèles systématiques d'intervention. Bourse des valeures de Paris. (Random Walk Changes and Buying and Selling Models. With English summary). *Consommation*, January-March 1973, *20*(1), pp. 77–96.

Mingo, Kent A.; Caruthers, J. Kent and Pinches, George E. The Stability of Financial Patterns in Industrial Organizations. *J. Finance*, May 1973, *28* (2), pp. 389–96.

_____ **and Pinches, George E.** A Multivariate Analysis of Industrial Bond Ratings. *J. Finance*, March 1973, *28*(1), pp. 1–18.

Minnehan, Robert F. Multiple Objectives and Multigroup Decision Making in Physical Design Situations. In *Cochrane, J. L. and Zeleny, M., eds.*, 1973, pp. 506–16.

Minoguchi, Takeo. Reconsideration of the Theory of Rent. *Hitotsubashi J. Econ.*, February 1973, *13* (2), pp. 29–36.

Minsky, Hyman P. The Strategy of Economic Policy and Income Distribution. *Ann. Amer. Acad. Polit. Soc. Sci.*, September 1973, *409*, pp. 92–101.

Mintzberg, Henry. Strategy-Making in Three Modes. *Calif. Manage. Rev.*, Winter 1973, *16*(2), pp. 44–53.

Mirakhor, Abbas and Afzal, Mohammad. An Index of Export Performance as a Criterion of Export Policy for Developing Countries. *Pakistan Econ. Soc. Rev.*, Summer 1973, *11*(2), pp. 193–99.

Miranowski, John; Dixon, Orani and Dixon, Peter. Insecticide Requirements in an Efficient Agricultural Sector. *Rev. Econ. Statist.*, November 1973, *55*(4), pp. 423–32.

Mire, Joseph. European Workers' Participation in Management. *Mon. Lab. Rev.*, February 1973, *96* (2), pp. 9–15.

Mirer, Thad W. The Distributional Impact of the 1970 Recession. *Rev. Econ. Statist.*, May 1973, *55* (2), pp. 214–24.

_____ The Effects of Macroeconomic Fluctuations on the Distribution of Income. *Rev. Income Wealth*, December 1973, *19*(4), pp. 385–406.

Mirman, Leonard J. The Steady State Behavior of a Class of One Sector Growth Models with Uncertain Technology. *J. Econ. Theory*, June 1973, *6*(3), pp. 219–42.

_____ **and Brock, William A.** Optimal Economic

Growth and Uncertainty: The No Discounting Case. *Int. Econ. Rev.*, October 1973, *14*(3), pp. 560–73.

Miron, John R. On the Estimation of a Partial Adjustment Model with Autocorrelated Errors. *Int. Econ. Rev.*, October 1973, *14*(3), pp. 653–56.

Mirrlees, James A. A Comment on Some Uses of Mathematical Models in Urban Economics: Rejoinder—II. *Urban Stud.*, June 1973, *10*(2), pp. 267–69.

—— The Integration of Project and Sector Analysis: Discussion. In *Parkin, M., ed.*, 1973, pp. 167–69.

—— Models of Economic Growth: Introduction. In *Mirrlees, J. A. and Stern, N. H., eds.*, 1973, pp. xi–xxii.

—— National Income and Social Values: Rejoinder. *Bangladesh Econ. Rev.*, January 1973, *1*(1), pp. 101–02.

—— and **Diamond, Peter A.** Aggregate Production with Consumption Externalities. *Quart. J. Econ.*, February 1973, *87*(1), pp. 1–24.

—— and **Hammond, Peter J.** Agreeable Plans. In *Mirrlees, J. A. and Stern, N. H., eds.*, 1973, pp. 283–99.

—— and **Little, I. M. D.** Further Reflections on the OECD Manual of Project Analysis in Developing Countries. In *[Rosenstein-Rodan, P.]*, 1973, pp. 257–80.

Mirus, Rolf. Some Implications of Student Evaluation of Teachers. *J. Econ. Educ.*, Fall 1973, *5*(1), pp. 35–46.

Mishan, Ezra J. Growth and Antigrowth: What Are the Issues? In *Weintraub, A.; Schwartz, E. and Aronson, J. R., eds.*, 1973, pp. 3–38.

—— Ills, Bads, and Disamenities: The Wages of Growth. In *Olson, M. and Landsberg, H. H., eds.*, 1973, pp. 63–87.

—— The Nature of External Diseconomies. In *Grieson, R. E., ed.*, 1973, pp. 234–44.

—— Welfare Criteria: Resolution of a Paradox. *Econ. J.*, September 1973, *83*(331), pp. 747–67.

Mishra, G. P. Land Reform and Changing Structure of Indian Agriculture. *Econ. Aff.*, September-October 1973, *18*(9–10), pp. 455–65, 476.

—— Planning and Land Reform Policy in India. *Econ. Aff.*, May 1973, *18*(5), pp. 217–33.

——; **Tripathy, B. N. and Pandey, Ram Lala.** Role of Banking in Financing Rural Credit. *Econ. Aff.*, July 1973, *18*(7), pp. 313–25.

Mitchell, D. J. B. and Azevedo, R. A Pay Board Assessment of Wage Controls. *Mon. Lab. Rev.*, April 1973, *96*(4), pp. 21–23.

Mitchell, George W. Statement to Congress. *Fed. Res. Bull.*, October 1973, *59*(10), pp. 734–38.

—— Statements to Congress. *Fed. Res. Bull.*, December 1973, *59*(12), pp. 874–78.

—— Statements to Congress. *Fed. Res. Bull.*, April 1973, *59*(4), pp. 276–80.

Mitchell, Jeremy. The Consumer Movement and Technological Change. *Int. Soc. Sci. J.*, 1973, *25*(3), pp. 358–69.

Mitchell, William E. Equity Effects of Property Tax Relief for the Aged: The Circuit-Breaker Legislation. *Amer. J. Econ. Soc.*, October 1973, *32*(4), pp. 367–78.

Mitra, Asok. The Nutrition Movement in India. In *Berg, A.; Scrimshaw, N. S. and Call, D. L., eds.*, 1973, pp. 357–65.

Mitra, P. K. Rationale of Commercial Policy of Developing Countries. *Rivista Int. Sci. Econ. Com.*, February 1973, *20*(2), pp. 139–52.

Mitra, S. On the Efficiency of the Estimates of Life Table Functions. *Demography*, August 1973, *10*(3), pp. 421–26.

—— and **Romaniuk, A.** Pearsonian Type I Curve and Its Fertility Projection Potentials. *Demography*, August 1973, *10*(3), pp. 351–65.

Miura, Makoto. The Tax Appeals System in Japan. *Bull. Int. Fiscal Doc.*, January 1973, *27*(1), pp. 3–9.

Miyazaki, Yoshikazu. Rapid Economic Growth in Postwar Japan. In *Moskoff, W., ed.*, 1973, pp. 117–39.

Mizrahi, Andrée; Mizrahi, Arié and Rösch, Georges. Un indicateur de morbidité. (An Indicator of Morbidity. With English summary.) *Consommation*, July-September 1973, *20*(3), pp. 7–55.

Mizrahi, Arié; Rösch, Georges and Mizrahi, Andrée. Un indicateur de morbidité. (An Indicator of Morbidity. With English summary.) *Consommation*, July-September 1973, *20*(3), pp. 7–55.

Moag, Joseph M. Strategic Planning in Banks—A Behavioral Science Perspective. *J. Bank Res.*, Summer 1973, *4*(2), pp. 84–92.

Mochalov, B. On the Training of Economists. *Prob. Econ.*, July 1973, *16*(3), pp. 87–101.

Mock, Theodore J. Concepts of Information Value and Accounting: A Reply. *Accounting Rev.*, April 1973, *48*(2), pp. 394–97.

—— The Value of Budget Information. *Accounting Rev.*, July 1973, *48*(3), pp. 520–34.

Mockler, Robert J. The Systems Approach to Business Organization and Decision Making. In *Klein, W. H. and Murphy, D. C., eds.*, 1973, pp. 28–33.

Modigliani, Franco. International Capital Movements, Fixed Parities, and Monetary and Fiscal Policies. In *[Rosenstein-Rodan, P.]*, 1973, pp. 239–53.

—— and **Askari, Hossein.** The International Transfer of Capital and the Propagation of Domestic Disturbances Under Alternative Payment Systems. *Banca Naz. Lavoro Quart. Rev.*, December 1973, (107), pp. 295–310.

—— and **Shiller, Robert J.** Inflation, Rational Expectations and the Term Structure of Interest Rates. *Economica, N.S.*, February 1973, *40*(157), pp. 12–43.

—— and **Tarantelli, Ezio.** A Generalization of the Phillips Curve for a Developing Country. *Rev. Econ. Stud.*, April 1973, *40*(2), pp. 203–23.

Moeller, John F. Development of a Microsimulation Model for Evaluating Economic Implications of Income Transfer and Tax Policies. *Ann. Econ. Soc. Measure*, April 1973, *2*(2), pp. 183–87.

Moggridge, D. E. From the *Treatise* to *The General Theory*: An Exercise in Chronology. *Hist. Polit. Econ.*, Spring 1973, *5*(1), pp. 72–88.

Mogull, Robert G. Football Salaries and Race: Some Empirical Evidence. *Ind. Relat.*, February 1973, *12*(1), pp. 109–12.

Mohabhat, Khan A. and Laumas, Prem S. Money

and Economic Development. *Indian Econ. J.,* April-June 1973, *20*(4–5), pp. 619–29.

Mohammed, Azizali F. and Saccomanni, Fabrizio. Short-Term Banking and Euro-Currency Credits to Developing Countries. *Int. Monet. Fund Staff Pap.,* November 1973, *20*(3), pp. 612–38.

Mohindru, Rajesh K. The Structural Unemployment Controversy Revisited. *J. Econ. Bus.,* Winter 1973, *25*(2), pp. 122–26.

Mohr, Lawrence B. The Concept of Organizational Goal. *Amer. Polit. Sci. Rev.,* June 1973, *67*(2), pp. 470–81.

Mohring, Herbert and Maslove, Allan. The Optimal Provision of Public Goods: Yet Another Comment. *J. Polit. Econ.,* May-June 1973, *81*(3), pp. 778–85.

Moiola, David L. Regulation Q: A New Tool for Monetary Policy? *Intermountain Econ. Rev.,* Spring 1973, *4*(1), pp. 22–28.

Moirao, Sharon and Goldberg, Victor. Limit Pricing and Potential Competition. *J. Polit. Econ.,* November-December 1973, *81*(6), pp. 1460–66.

Moiseev, Nikita N. Principles of Simulation: Hierarchial Control Systems. In *Hawkes, N., ed.,* 1973, pp. 205–26.

——— Operations Research in the U.S.S.R.—Development and Perspectives. In *Ross, M., ed.,* 1973, pp. 41–55.

——— The Present State of Futures Research in the Soviet Union. In *Hawkes, N., ed.,* 1973, pp. 14–19.

Moldovan, Roman and Botez, Mihai C. Correlation Between Forecasting and Action—An Essential Feature in Planning. *Revue Roumaine Sci. Soc. Serie Sci. Econ.,* 1973, *17*(1), pp. 41–52.

Molitor, Bruno. Öffentliche Leistungen in verteilungspolitischer Sicht. (Social Goods and Income Redistribution. With English summary.) *Z. Wirtschaft. Sozialwissen.,* 1973, *93*(2), pp. 147–58.

Mollenkopf, John and Pynoos, Jon. Boardwalk and Park Place: Property Ownership, Political Structure, and Housing Policy at the Local Level. In *Pynoos, J.; Schafer, R. and Hartman, C. W., eds.,* 1973, pp. 55–74.

Monarchi, David E.; Kisiel, Chester C. and Duckstein, Lucien. Interactive Multiobjective Programming in Water Resources: A Case Study. *Water Resources Res.,* August 1973, *9*(4), pp. 837–50.

Monat, J. and Epstein, E. Labour Contracting and Its Regulation: I. *Int. Lab. Rev.,* May 1973, *107*(5), pp. 451–70.

——— Labour Contracting and Its Regulation: II. *Int. Lab. Rev.,* June 1973, *107*(6), pp. 513–28.

Moncarz, Raul. Monetary Aspects of the Central American Common Market. *J. Common Market Stud.,* December 1973, *12*(2), pp. 196–204.

Moncur, James E. T. Opportunity Costs of a Transbasin Diversion: 2. The Columbia River Basin. *Water Resources Res.,* February 1973, *9*(1), pp. 43–49.

Mondanga, Emony. Savings Banks and Savings Facilities in African Countries: Zaire. In *Alberici, A. and Baravelli, M., eds.,* 1973, pp. 129–31.

Mondani, Aristide. Alcune semplici rappresentazioni integrali di funzioni a gradino. (A Few Simple Integral Representations of Step Functions. With English summary.) *Rivista Int. Sci. Econ. Com.,* November 1973, *20*(11), pp. 1127–34.

Money, W. J. The Need to Sustain a Viable System of Local Democracy. *Urban Stud.,* October 1973, *10*(3), pp. 319–33.

Monissen, Hans G. Preise, Löhne und Beschäftigung in dynamischer Betrachtung: Eine einfache Exposition. (Prices, Wages and Employment in Dynamic Perspective: A Simple Exposition. With English summary.) *Kyklos,* 1973, *26*(3), pp. 545–58.

Monroe, Kent B. Buyers' Subjective Perceptions of Price. *J. Marketing Res.,* February 1973, *10*(1), pp. 70–80.

Monroe, Robert J. Financial Characteristics of Merged Firms: A Multivariate Analysis: Comment. *J. Financial Quant. Anal.,* March 1973, 8 (2), pp. 163–65.

Monroe, Wilbur F. The Contribution of Japanese Exports to Growth in Output. *Nebr. J. Econ. Bus.,* Winter 1973, *12*(1), pp. 11–21.

Monsen, R. Joseph. Is Social Accounting a Mirage? In *Dierkes, M. and Bauer, R. A., eds.,* 1973, pp. 107–10.

Montazer-Zohour, M. Generalization of Multiplier Theory. *Tahq. Eq.,* Winter & Spring 1973, *10*(29 & 30), pp. 106–45.

de Montbrial, Thierry. Intertemporal General Equilibrium and Interest Rates Theory. *Écon. Appl.,* 1973, *26*(2–3–4), pp. 877–917.

Montgomery, David B. and Morrison, Donald G. A Note on Adjusting R^2. *J. Finance,* September 1973, *28*(4), pp. 1009–13.

Montgomery, W. David and Krier, James E. Resource Allocation, Information Cost and the Form of Government Intervention. *Natural Res. J.,* January 1973, *13*(1), pp. 89–105.

Monti, Mario and Sdralevich, Alberto. I modelli macroeconomici per la politica monetaria in Italia: aggregazione e realismo. (Macroeconomic Models for Monetary Policy in Italy: Aggregation and Realism. With English summary.) *L'Industria,* January-June 1973, (1–2), pp. 36–58.

Montias, John Michael. A Framework for Theoretical Analysis of Economic Reforms in Soviet-type Economies. In *Bornstein, M., ed.,* 1973, pp. 65–122.

Montrie, Charles. The Organization and Functions of Foreign Aid. *Econ. Develop. Cult. Change,* Part I, July 1973, *21*(4), pp. 697–713.

Moor, R. Carl. The Economic Efficiency of Mixed Financing of Education in Economic Space. *Public Finance Quart.,* October 1973, *1*(4), pp. 399–408.

Moore, Arnold B.; Walgreen, John A. and Rastatter, E. H. The Economics of the United States Supersonic Transport. *J. Transp. Econ. Policy,* May 1973, *7*(2), pp. 186–93.

Moore, Barry and Rhodes, John. Evaluating the Effects of British Regional Economic Policy. *Econ. J.,* March 1973, *83*(329), pp. 87–110.

Moore, Basil J. Some Macroeconomic Consequences of Corporate Equities. *Can. J. Econ.,* November 1973, *6*(4), pp. 529–44.

Moore, Beverly C., Jr. Product Safety—Who Should

Absorb the Cost? In *Britt, S. H. and Boyd, H. W., Jr., eds.*, 1973, pp. 340–44.

_____ **and Green, Mark J.** The Nader Antitrust Report: A Tale of Two Critics. *Antitrust Bull.*, Fall, 1973, *18*(3), pp. 551–79.

_____ **and Green, Mark J.** Winter's Discontent: Market Failure and Consumer Welfare. *Yale Law J.*, April 1973, *82*(5), pp. 903–19.

Moore, Charles T. and Dawson, Lyndon E., Jr. Psychometric Measures of Inter-Media Advertising Effectiveness: A Case Study. *Marquette Bus. Rev.*, Summer 1973, *17*(2), pp. 73–83.

Moore, Dan H., II. Evaluation of Five Discrimination Procedures for Binary Variables. *J. Amer. Statist. Assoc.*, June 1973, *68*(342), pp. 399–404.

Moore, George S. The Monetary Crisis—From a Banker's Point of View. In *Wiegand, G. C., ed.*, 1973, pp. 35–38.

Moore, James C. and Chipman, John S. Aggregate Demand, Real National Income, and the Compensation Principle. *Int. Econ. Rev.*, February 1973, *14*(1), pp. 153–81.

Moore, John R., Jr. Planning an Efficient Regional Health System. In *Stein, B. and Miller, S. M., eds.*, 1973, pp. 13–35.

Moore, Mark H. Policies to Achieve Discrimination on the Effective Price of Heroin. *Amer. Econ. Rev.*, May 1973, *63*(2), pp. 270–77.

Moore, P. G. Relationship between Statisticians and Other Numerate Professions. *J. Roy. Statist. Soc.*, Part 1, 1973, *136*, pp. 89–94.

_____ **; Thomas, H. and Hampton, J. M.** Subjective Probability and Its Measurement. *J. Roy. Statist. Soc.*, Part 1, 1973, *136*, pp. 21–42.

_____ **; Thomas, H. and Hull, J.** Utility and its Measurement. *J. Roy. Statist. Soc.*, Part 2, 1973, *136*, pp. 226–47.

Moore, Philip W. Corporate Social Reform: An Activist's Viewpoint. *Calif. Manage. Rev.*, Summer 1973, *15*(4), pp. 90–96.

Moore, Robert L. Further Test of the Permanent Income Hypothesis Using Postwar Time-Series Data. *Southern Econ. J.*, October 1973, *40*(2), pp. 319–22.

Moore, Thomas Gale. Science, Technology, and Industry. In *Ott, D. J., et al.*, 1973, pp. 67–89.

Moore, William J. The Relative Quality of Graduate Programs in Economics, 1958-1972: Who Published and Who Perished. *Western Econ. J.*, March 1973, *11*(1), pp. 1–23.

Moorhouse, John C. Censorship, Revenue, and X-Rated Movie Taxes. *Quart. Rev. Econ. Bus.*, Summer 1973, *13*(2), pp. 83–89.

Moran, R. Allen. Cooperative Advertising: An Alternative Interpretation of Price Discrimination. *Calif. Manage. Rev.*, Summer 1973, *15*(4), pp. 61–63.

Morawetz, David. Harmonization of Economic Policies in a Free Trade Area: The Andean Group. *Weltwirtsch. Arch.*, 1973, *109*(4), pp. 579–600.

_____ Harmonization of Economic Policies in Customs Unions: The Andean Group. *J. Common Market Stud.*, June 1973, *11*(4), pp. 294–313.

_____ Personal Income Taxes and Consumer Spending in the United Kingdom, 1958–69. *Public Finance*, 1973, *28*(2), pp. 178–95.

Moreh, J. Human Capital: Deterioration and Net Investment. *Rev. Income Wealth*, September 1973, *19*(3), pp. 279–302.

Moretti, Giovanni. The Italian Plastic Materials Industry. *Rev. Econ. Cond. Italy*, May 1973, *27*(3), pp. 162–77.

Morgan, Daniel, Jr. and Gilmer, Robert W. The Equivalence of Flat Grants and Foundation Programs in State Education Aid Formulas. *Public Finance Quart.*, October 1973, *1*(4), pp. 437–47.

Morgan, E. Victor. Regional Problems and Common Currencies. *Lloyds Bank Rev.*, October 1973, (110), pp. 19–30.

_____ **and Harrington, R. L.** Reserve Assets and the Supply of Money. *Manchester Sch. Econ. Soc. Stud.*, March 1973, *41*(1), pp. 73–87.

Morgan, James N. and Baerwaldt, Nancy A. Trends in Inter-Family Transfers. In *Mandell, L., et al., eds.*, 1973, pp. 205–32.

Morgan, W. Douglas and Mercer, Lloyd J. Housing Surplus in the 1920s? Another Evaluation. *Exploration Econ. Hist.*, Spring 1973, *10*(3), pp. 295–303.

Morgenstern, Oskar. Ingolf Stahl: Bargaining Theory. *Swedish J. Econ.*, December 1973, *75*(4), pp. 410–13.

Morgenstern, Richard D. Direct and Indirect Effects on Earnings of Schooling and Socio-Economic Background. *Rev. Econ. Statist.*, May 1973, *55*(2), pp. 225–33.

Morgenthaler, George W. Guiding Technological Development. In *Ross, M., ed.*, 1973, pp. 617–40.

Mori, Kei and Klein, Lawrence R. The Impact of Disarmament on Aggregate Economic Activity: An Econometric Analysis. In *Udis, B., ed.*, 1973, pp. 59–77.

Moriguchi, C. Forecasting and Simulation Analysis of the World Economy. *Amer. Econ. Rev.*, May 1973, *63*(2), pp. 402–09.

_____ **and Tatemoto, M.** An Econometric Analysis of a Bilateral Model of International Economic Activity: Japan and U.S.A. In *Ball, R. J., ed.*, 1973, pp. 367–93.

Morin, Thomas L. Pathology of a Dynamic Programming Sequencing Algorithm. *Water Resources Res.*, October 1973, *9*(5), pp. 1178–85.

Morishima, M. Consumer Behaviour and Liquidity Preference. In *Morishima, M., et al.*, 1973, pp. 215–41.

_____ Demand for Durable Goods: A Note. In *Morishima, M., et al.*, 1973, pp. 210–11.

_____ Optimal Transactions Demand for Money. In *Morishima, M., et al.*, 1973, pp. 271–84.

_____ Separability and Intrinsic Complementarity. In *Morishima, M., et al.*, 1973, pp. 148–65.

_____ A Two-Parametric 'Revealed-Preference' Theory of Portfolio Selection. In *Morishima, M., et al.*, 1973, pp. 287–300.

_____ **and Allingham, M. G.** Qualitative Economics and Comparative Statics. In *Morishima, M., et al.*, 1973, pp. 3–69.

_____ **and Allingham, M. G.** Veblen Effects and Portfolio Selection. In *Morishima, M., et al.*, 1973, pp. 242–70.

_____ **and Geary, P. T.** Demand and Supply under

Separability. In *Morishima, M., et al.*, 1973, pp. 87–147.

———— and Lluch, Constantino. Demand for Commodities under Uncertain Expectation. In *Morishima, M., et al.*, 1973, pp. 169–83.

Morissey, M. J. and Burt, R. A Theory of Mineral Discovery: A Note. *Econ. Hist. Rev., 2nd Ser.*, August 1973, *26*(3), pp. 497–505.

Morley, Samuel A. Inflation and Stagnation in Brazil: Reply. *Econ. Develop. Cult. Change*, April 1973, *21*(3), pp. 530–33.

———— The Relationship Between Money, Income and Prices in the Short and Long Run. *J. Finance*, December 1973, *28*(5), pp. 1119–30.

———— and Smith, Gordon W. The Effect of Changes in the Distribution of Income on Labor, Foreign Investment, and Growth in Brazil. In *Stepan, A., ed.*, 1973, pp. 119–41.

Moroney, J. R. and Lovell, C. A. Knox. Estimating the Elasticity of Substitution: A Correction and Some Further Results. *Southern Econ. J.*, January 1973, *39*(3), pp. 437–41.

Morozov, F. Structural Problems in the Formation of an Agroindustrial Complex. *Prob. Econ.*, September 1973, *16*(5), pp. 72–93.

Morrall, John F., III and Vogel, Ronald J. The Impact of Medicaid on State and Local Health and Hospitals Expenditures, with Special Reference to Blacks. *J. Human Res.*, Spring 1973, *8*(2), pp. 202–11.

Morrill, Richard L. On the Size and Spacing of Growth Centers. *Growth Change*, April 1973, *4* (2), pp. 21–24.

———— Waves of Spatial Diffusion: Reply. *J. Reg. Sci.*, August 1973, *13*(2), pp. 297.

Morris, Carl and Efron, Bradley. Stein's Estimation Rule and Its Competitors—An Empirical Bayes Approach. *J. Amer. Statist. Assoc.*, March 1973, *68* (341), pp. 117–30.

Morris, Jacob and Lewin, Haskell. The Skilled Labor Reduction Problem. *Sci. Soc.*, Winter 1973–1974, *37*(4), pp. 454–72.

Morris, John P. In the Wake of the Flood. *Law Contemp. Probl.*, Winter-Spring 1973, *38*(1), pp. 85–98.

Morris, Stuart. Stalled Professionalism: The Recruitment of Railway Officials in the United States, 1885–1940. *Bus. Hist. Rev.*, Autumn 1973, *47*(3), pp. 317–34.

Morrison, Clarence C. and Higgins, Richard S. A Further Note on Distributional Equality. *Southern Econ. J.*, January 1973, *39*(3), pp. 442–43.

———— A Note on Comparative Statics Analysis in Equality Constrained Models. *Southern Econ. J.*, April 1973, *39*(4), pp. 638–41.

Morrison, Donald G. and Montgomery, David B. A Note on Adjusting R². *J. Finance*, September 1973, *28*(4), pp. 1009–13.

Morrison, Peter A. A Demographic Assessment of New Cities and Growth Centers as Population Redistribution Strategies. *Public Policy*, Summer 1973, *21*(3), pp. 367–82.

Morrisson, Christian and Cazenave, Philippe. Fonctions d'utilité interdépendantes et théorie de la redistribution en économie de production. (Interdependent Utility Functions and Redistribution Theory in a Production Economy. With English summary.) *Revue Écon.*, September 1973, *24*(5), pp. 725–60.

Morrock, Richard. Heritage of Strife: The Effects of Colonialist "Divide and Rule" Strategy Upon the Colonized Peoples. *Sci. Soc.*, Summer 1973, *37*(2), pp. 129–51.

Morse, Chandler. Natural Resources as a Constraint on Economic Growth: Discussion. *Amer. Econ. Rev.*, May 1973, *63*(2), pp. 126–28.

Morse, C. J. La crisi monetaria del 1971 e gli insegnamenti da trarne. Intervento. (The Monetary Crisis of 1971. The Lessons to be Learned. With English summary.) *Bancaria*, March 1973, *29*(3), pp. 314–18.

Morse, Edward L. The Political Context: Comment. In *Krause, L. B. and Salant, W. S., eds.*, 1973, pp. 55–62.

Morse, Wayne J. A Note on the Relationship Between Human Assets and Human Capital. *Accounting Rev.*, July 1973, *48*(3), pp. 589–93.

Morsell, John A. Ethnic Relations of the Future. *Ann. Amer. Acad. Polit. Soc. Sci.*, July 1973, *408*, pp. 83–93.

Morss, Elliott R. and Brannon, Gerard M. The Tax Allowance for Dependents: Deductions versus Credits. *Nat. Tax J.*, December 1973, *26*(4), pp. 599–609.

Mortensen, Dale T. Generalized Costs of Adjustment and Dynamic Factor Demand Theory. *Econometrica*, July 1973, *41*(4), pp. 657–65.

Morton, Henry W. Handbook of Soviet Social Science Data: Housing. In *Mickiewicz, E., ed.*, 1973, pp. 119–35.

Morton, Rogers C. B. The Nixon Administration Energy Policy. *Ann. Amer. Acad. Polit. Soc. Sci.*, November 1973, *410*, pp. 65–74.

Morton, Thomas E. and Aldrich, Carole A. A Note on Bayesian Modification of the Failure Rate Function. *J. Amer. Statist. Assoc.*, June 1973, *68* (342), pp. 483–84.

————; Lave, Judith R. and Lave, Lester B. Sources and Uses of Paramedical Personnel. In *Stein, B. and Miller, S. M., eds.*, 1973, pp. 37–68.

Moruzzi, Paolo. Situation and Prospects of the Furniture Industry in Italy. *Rev. Econ. Cond. Italy*, September 1973, *27*(5), pp. 326–35.

Moser, Claus A. Social Indicators—Systems, Methods and Problems. *Rev. Income Wealth*, June 1973, *19*(2), pp. 133–41.

———— Staffing in the Government Statistical Service. *J. Roy. Statist. Soc.*, Part 1, 1973, *136*, pp. 75–88.

———— and Beesley, I. B. United Kingdom Official Statistics and the European Communities. *J. Roy. Statist. Soc.*, Part 4, 1973, *136*, pp. 539–72.

Moses, Leon N. and Goldstein, Gerald S. A Survey of Urban Economics. *J. Econ. Lit.*, June 1973, *11* (2), pp. 471–515.

Mosher, A. T. Higher Education in the Rural Social Sciences. *Amer. J. Agr. Econ.*, Part II, November 1973, *55*(4), pp. 711–19.

Mosin, V. On the Creation of an Automated System of Planning. *Prob. Econ.*, April 1973, *15*(12), pp. 16–36.

Moskow, Michael H. Government in the Lead. In

Ginzberg, E. and Yohalem, A. M., eds., 1973, pp. 125–32.

Moss, Laurence S. Isaac Butt and the Early Development of the Marginal Utility Theory of Imputation. *Hist. Polit. Econ.*, Fall 1973, *5*(2), pp. 317–38.

Motley, Brian. Sales versus Income Taxes: A Pedagogic Note. *Oxford Econ. Pap.*, July 1973, *25*(2), pp. 204–12.

Mott, Charles H. Forecast Disclosure. *Manage. Account.*, July 1973, *55*(1), pp. 17–18, 28.

Mott, George Fox. Communicative Turbulence in Urban Dynamics—Media, Education, and Planning. *Ann. Amer. Acad. Polit. Soc. Sci.*, January 1973, *405*, pp. 114–30.

Moulik, T. K. and Lockwood, Brian. Seeds of Development in a Delhi Village. In *Epstein, T. S. and Penny, D. H., eds.*, 1973, pp. 157–72.

Mouly, Jean. Prices, Wages, Unemployment: Inflation in Contemporary Economic Theory. *Int. Lab. Rev.*, October 1973, *108*(4), pp. 329–43.

Mount, T. D. and Maddala, G. S. A Comparative Study of Alternative Estimators for Variance Components Models Used in Econometric Applications. *J. Amer. Statist. Assoc.*, June 1973, *68* (342), pp. 324–28.

Moussa-Hamouda, Effat and Leone, Fred C. Relative Efficiencies of 'O-BLUE' Estimators in Simple Linear Regression. *J. Amer. Statist. Assoc.*, December 1973, *68*(344), pp. 953–59.

Mowitz, Robert J. Pennsylvania's Planning, Programming, Budgeting System. In *Novick, D., ed.*, 1973, pp. 169–80.

Mowry, Glenn K. Steps Toward a Less-Check Society. In *The Diebold Group, Inc.*, 1973, pp. 169–79.

Moyer, R. International Market Analysis. In *Thorelli, H. B., ed.*, 1973, pp. 162–79.

Moyer, R. Charles and Mastrapasqua, Frank. Socioeconomic Accounting and External Diseconomies: A Comment. *Accounting Rev.*, January 1973, *48*(1), pp. 126–27.

_____ **and Sussna, Edward.** Registered Bank Holding Company Acquisition: A Cross-Section Analysis. *J. Financial Quant. Anal.*, September 1973, *8*(4), pp. 647–61.

Mueller, Dennis C. Constitutional Democracy and Social Welfare. *Quart. J. Econ.*, February 1973, *87* (1), pp. 60–80.

Mueller, Eva. Generating Micro Data in Less Developed Countries through Surveys: Some Experience in Asia. In *Ayal, E. B., ed.*, 1973, pp. 101–18.

Mueller, Marjorie Smith. Private Health Insurance in 1971: Health Care Services, Enrollment, and Finances. *Soc. Sec. Bull.*, February 1973, *36*(2), pp. 3–22.

Mueller, Willard F. Corporate Secrecy and the Need for Financial Disclosure. In *Haveman, R. H. and Hamrin, R. D., eds.*, 1973, pp. 283–91.

Muench, Thomas; Wallace, Neil and Kareken, John H. Optimal Open Market Strategy: The Use of Information Variables. *Amer. Econ. Rev.*, March 1973, *63*(1), pp. 156–72.

Mujahid, G. B. S. The Measurement of Disguised Unemployment: A Comment. *Can. J. Econ.*, February 1973, *6*(1), pp. 128–29.

_____ "Disguised" Unemployment Once Again:

East Pakistan, 1951–1961: Comment. *Amer. J. Agr. Econ.*, February 1973, *55*(1), pp. 118–19.

Mujica, Jorge G. and Behrman, Jere R. A Study of Quarterly Nominal Wage Change Determination in an Inflationary Developing Economy. In *Eckaus, R. S. and Rosenstein-Rodan, P. N., eds.*, 1973, pp. 399–416.

Mukherjee, M. and Rao, D. S. Prasada. On Consistent Intergroup Comparisons of Purchasing Power of Money. *Rev. Income Wealth*, March 1973, *19*(1), pp. 35–47.

Mukherjee, Ramkrishna. The Social Background of Bangladesh. In *Gough, K. and Sharma, H. P., eds.*, 1973, pp. 399–418.

Mukherji, Anjan. On the Sensitivity of Stability Results to the Choice of the Numeraire. *Rev. Econ. Stud.*, July 1973, *40*(3), pp. 427–33.

Mulaney, Charles W., Jr. Gasoline Marketing and the Robinson-Patman Act. *Yale Law J.*, July 1973, *82*(8), pp. 1706–18.

Mulholland, William D., Jr. Financial Simulation in Long-Range Project Planning. In *The Diebold Group, Inc.*, 1973, pp. 43–54.

Mullendore, Walter E. and Stanfield, J. Ronald. A Suggested Form of Benefit-Cost Analysis for an Evaluation of Urban Renewal Projects. *Land Econ.*, February 1973, *49*(1), pp. 81–86.

Müller, Jens. Appropriate Technology and Technological Dualism. In *Institute for Development Research*, 1973, pp. 161–76.

Müller, Paul. Protection of the Environment in Agriculture and Forestry. *Ger. Econ. Rev.*, 1973, *11*(1), pp. 77–88.

Muller, Peter O. Trend Surfaces of American Agricultural Patterns: A Macro-Thünian Analysis. *Econ. Geogr.*, July 1973, *49*(3), pp. 228–42.

Müller, Ronald. The Multinational Corporation and the Underdevelopment of the Third World. In *Wilber, C. K., ed.*, 1973, pp. 124–51.

Muller, Thomas. Income Redistribution Impact of State Grants to Public Schools: A Case Study of Delaware. In *Boulding, K. E.; Pfaff, M. and Pfaff, A., eds.*, 1973, pp. 226–45.

Müller, Udo and Rumm, Ulrich. Zur Gleichgewichtsproblematik im unvollkommenen Polypol. (The Problem of Equilibrium in the Polypol. With English summary.) *Z. ges. Staatswiss.*, May 1973, *129* (2), pp. 189–204.

Müller-Merbach, Heiner. Operational Research '72: Summing Up. In *Ross, M., ed.*, 1973, pp. 713–18.

Müller-Oehring, H. Determining the Coal Wagon Requirements in the Rhenish Lignite Mines. In *Ross, M., ed.*, 1973, pp. 391–404.

Mullet, Gary M. and Murray, Tracy. More on the Game of Maximizing R^2 *Australian Econ. Pap.*, December 1973, *12*(21), pp. 263–66.

Mullineaux, Donald J. Deposit-Rate Ceilings and Noncompetitive Bidding for U.S. Treasury Bills. *J. Money, Credit, Banking*, Part I, February 1973, *5*(1), pp. 201–12.

_____ Interest-Rate Ceilings and the Treasury-Bill Market: Disintermediation and the Small Saver. *New Eng. Econ. Rev.*, July-August 1973, pp. 19–26.

_____ Paying for Social Security: Is It Time To "Retire" the Payroll Tax? *Fed. Res. Bank Bus.*

Rev. Phila., April 1973, pp. 3–10.

Mulvey, C. and Trevithick, J. A. Trade Unions and Wage Inflation. *Econ. Soc. Rev.*, January 1973, *4* (2), pp. 209–29.

Mumphrey, Anthony J. and Seley, John. Simulation Approaches to Locational Conflicts. *Econ. Geogr.*, January 1973, *49*(1), pp. 21–36.

_____ **and Wolpert, Julian.** Equity Considerations and Concessions in the Siting of Public Facilities. *Econ. Geogr.*, April 1973, *49*(2), pp. 109–21.

Muncrief, George; Davis, Bob and Schreiner, Dean. Solid Waste Management for Rural Areas: Analysis of Costs and Service Requirements. *Amer. J. Agr. Econ.*, Part I, November 1973, *55*(4), pp. 567–76.

Mundell, Robert A. The Monetary Consequences of Jacques Rueff: Review Article. *J. Bus.*, July 1973, *46*(3), pp. 384–95.

_____ A Plan for a European Currency. In *Johnson, H. G. and Swoboda, A. K., eds.*, 1973, pp. 143–72.

_____ Uncommon Arguments for Common Currencies. In *Johnson, H. G. and Swoboda, A. K., eds.*, 1973, pp. 114–32.

Mundlak, Yair and Volcani, Zvi. The Correspondence of Efficiency Frontier as a Generalization of the Cost Function. *Int. Econ. Rev.*, February 1973, *14*(1), pp. 223–33.

Munro, Donald J. Man, State, and School. In *Oksenberg, M., ed.*, 1973, pp. 121–43.

Munsche, Richard C. International Competition and Tax Reform. In *Tax Foundation, Inc.*, 1973, pp. 59–64.

Munson, Fred C.; Griffith, John R. and Hancock, Walton M. Practical Ways to Contain Hospital Costs. *Harvard Bus. Rev.*, November-December 1973, *51*(6), pp. 131–39.

Murad, Howard; Belli, R. David and Allnutt, Smith W. Property, Plant, and Equipment Expenditures by Majority-Owned Foreign Affiliates of U.S. Companies: Revised Estimates for 1966–72 and Projections for 1973 and 1974. *Surv. Curr. Bus.*, December 1973, *53*(12), pp. 19–32.

Murdick, Robert G. The Long-Range Planning Matrix. In *Klein, W. H. and Murphy, D. C., eds.*, 1973, pp. 234–41.

_____ Nature of Planning and Plans. In *Klein, W. H. and Murphy, D. C., eds.*, 1973, pp. 224–33.

Murdock, E. Wayne and Brinker, Paul A. Children of the Severely Injured. *J. Human Res.*, Spring 1973, *8*(2), pp. 242–49.

Murie, A. S., et al. A Survey of Industrial Movement in Northern Ireland between 1965 and 1969. *Econ. Soc. Rev.*, January 1973, *4*(2), pp. 231–44.

Murphy, David C. and Klein, Walter H. Policy: Concepts in Organizational Guidance: Introduction. In *Klein, W. H. and Murphy, D. C., eds.*, 1973, pp. 1–12.

Murphy, J. Carter. The Adjustment Problem: Comment. In *Krause, L. B. and Salant, W. S., eds.*, 1973, pp. 191–97.

Murphy, Neil B. The Implications of Econometric Analysis of Bank Cost Functions for Bank Planning. *J. Bank Res.*, Autumn 1973, *4*(3), pp. 203–06.

_____; **Daniel, Donnie L. and Longbrake, William A.** The Effect of Technology on Bank Economies of Scale for Demand Deposits. *J. Finance*, March 1973, *28*(1), pp. 131–46.

Murray, Barbara B. Consumerism: The Eternal Triangle: Introduction. In *Murray, B. B., ed.*, 1973, pp. xi–xvii.

_____ Major Federal Consumer Protection Laws, 1906–1970. In *Murray, B. B., ed.*, 1973, pp. 78–85.

_____ A Pure Theory of Local Expenditures Revisited. In *Mattila, J. M. and Thompson, W. R., eds.*, 1973, pp. 129–39.

Murray, J. Alex; Fayerweather, John and Blake, David H. Perspectives for the Future. In *Fayerweather, J., ed.*, 1973, pp. 95–123.

Murray, Janet. Family Structure in the Preretirement Years. *Soc. Sec. Bull.*, October 1973, *36*(10), pp. 25–45.

Murray, Roger F. Pension Funds: Newest Among Major Financial Institutions. *J. Bank Res.*, Winter 1973, *3*(4), pp. 247–60.

Murray, Tracy. E.E.C. Enlargement and Preference for the Developing Countries. *Econ. J.*, September 1973, *83*(331), pp. 853–57.

_____ How Helpful is the Generalised System of Preferences to Developing Countries? *Econ. J.*, June 1973, *83*(330), pp. 449–55.

_____ Preferential Tariffs for the LDCs. *Southern Econ. J.*, July 1973, *40*(1), pp. 35–46.

_____ **and Edgmand, Michael R.** Full Employment, Trade Expansion, and Adjustment Assistance: Reply. *Southern Econ. J.*, July 1973, *40*(1), pp. 138–39.

_____ **and Ginman, Peter J.** Will Devaluation Improve the US Trade Deficit? *Kyklos*, 1973, *26*(4), pp. 844–48.

_____ **and Mullet, Gary M.** More on the Game of Maximizing R^2 *Australian Econ. Pap.*, December 1973, *12*(21), pp. 263–66.

Murry, Donald A. Practical Economics of Public Utility Regulation: An Application to Pipelines. In *Russell, M., ed.*, 1973, pp. 35–47.

Murthy, K. S. R. and Bodkin, Ronald G. The Orders-Shipments Mechanism in Canadian Producer Goods Industries. *J. Amer. Statist. Assoc.*, June 1973, *68*(342), pp. 297–305.

Musarra, Emanuele Parisi. Note sull'automazione elettronica per la gestione e la direzione aziendale bancaria. (Notes on the Electronic Automation for Bank Management. With English summary.) *Bancaria*, April 1973, *29*(4), pp. 447–52.

Muscat, Robert and Berg, Alan. Nutrition Program Planning: An Approach. In *Berg, A.; Scrimshaw, N. S. and Call, D. L., eds.*, 1973, pp. 247–74.

Musgrave, John C. Alternative Measures of Price Change for GNP, 1970–73. *Surv. Curr. Bus.*, August 1973, *53*(8), pp. 15–17.

Mustafa, Gholam. Measurement of Leakage by the Use of an Input-Output Model: Comment. *Amer. J. Agr. Econ.*, Part I, November 1973, *55*(4), pp. 680–82.

_____ **and Jones, Lonnie L.** RIMLOC: A Computer Algorithm for Regional Input-Output Analyses. *Ann. Econ. Soc. Measure*, July 1973, *2*(3), pp. 313–16.

Muth, Richard F. Capital and Current Expenditures in the Production of Housing. In *Harriss, C. L., ed.*, 1973, pp. 65–78.

_____ The Determinants of Dwelling-Unit Condition. In *Pynoos, J.; Schafer, R. and Hartman, C. W., eds.*, 1973, pp. 239–50.

Mutti, John H. and Baldwin, Robert. Policy Issues in Adjustment Assistance: The United States. In *Hughes, H., ed.*, 1973, pp. 149–77.

Mwanza, J. The Adaptation of Economics Teaching to the Needs of African Economic Development. In *Livingstone, I., et al., eds.*, 1973, pp. 41–45.

Myers, Charles A. Manpower Policies in the U.S. In *Somers, G. G., ed.*, 1973, pp. 72–82.

Myers, John G. Measuring and Monitoring the Impact of Advertising. In *Dierkes, M. and Bauer, R. A., eds.*, 1973, pp. 130–41.

Myers, Myron G.; Rogstad, Barry K. and Wehner, Harrison G. A Theoretical Evaluation of Alternative Subsidy Schemes for Regional Development. *Amer. J. Agr. Econ.*, May 1973, *55*(2), pp. 304–12.

Myers, Stewart C. A Simple Model of Firm Behavior Under Regulation and Uncertainty. *Bell J. Econ. Manage. Sci.*, Spring 1973, *4*(1), pp. 304–15.

Myhrman, Johan. An Analytical Treatment of Swedish Monetary Policy. *Swedish J. Econ.*, September 1973, *75*(3), pp. 221–37.

Myrdal, Gunnar. A Brief Note on Marx and "Marxism." In *Myrdal, G.*, 1973, pp. 308–16.

_____ Causes and Nature of Development. *Tahq. Eq.*, Winter & Spring 1973, *10*(29 & 30), pp. 3–16.

_____ Economics of an Improved Environment. *World Devel.*, February 1973, *1*(1-2), pp. 102–14.

_____ The Future of India. In *Myrdal, G.*, 1973, pp. 245–65.

_____ Growth and Social Justice. *World Devel.*, March-April 1973, *1*(3–4), pp. 119–20.

_____ How Scientific Are the Social Sciences? In *Myrdal, G.*, 1973, pp. 133–57.

_____ The Need for a Sociology and Psychology of Social Science and Scientists. *World Devel.*, May 1973, *1*(5), pp. 41–46.

_____ The Need for Radical Domestic Reforms. In *Myrdal, G.*, 1973, pp. 101–32.

_____ "Growth" and "Development." In *Myrdal, G.*, 1973, pp. 182–96.

_____ "Stagflation." In *Myrdal, G.*, 1973, pp. 17–32.

_____ The Place of Values in Social Policy. In *Myrdal, G.*, 1973, pp. 33–51.

_____ Politics and Economics in International Relations. In *Myrdal, G.*, 1973, pp. 167–81.

_____ Rôle des valeurs et politique sociale. (The Place of Values in Social Policy. With English summary.) *Consommation*, January-March 1973, *20*(1), pp. 5–16.

_____ The World Poverty Problem. In *Myrdal, G.*, 1973, pp. 65–100.

Mytelka, Lynn Krieger. Foreign Aid and Regional Integration: The UDEAC Case. *J. Common Market Stud.*, December 1973, *12*(2), pp. 138–58.

Nabseth, Lars. The Diffusion of Innovations in Swedish Industry. In *Williams, B. R., ed.*, 1973, pp. 256–80.

Nachtigal, Vladimír and Beck, Jiří. K problematice systému makroekonomických modelů v podmínkách ČSSR. (Problems of a System of Macroeconomic Models in the Conditions of Czechoslovakia. With English summary.) *Ekon.-Mat. Obzor*, 1973, *9*(1), pp. 13–29.

Nader, Ralph. A Case for More Consumer Protection. In *Reynolds, L. G.; Green, G. D. and Lewis, D. R., eds.*, 1973, pp. 181–89.

_____ A Citizen's Guide to the American Economy. In *Haveman, R. H. and Hamrin, R. D., eds.*, 1973, pp. 33–42.

_____ Efficiency and Regulatory Policy: Issues of Compliance, Disclosure, and Accountability. In *Haveman, R. H. and Hamrin, R. D., eds.*, 1973, pp. 267–72.

_____ The Great American Gyp. In *Murray, B. B., ed.*, 1973, pp. 39–51.

_____, et al. Government Secrecy and the People's Right to Know. In *Haveman, R. H. and Hamrin, R. D., eds.*, 1973, pp. 273–82.

_____ and Green, Mark J. Economic Regulation vs. Competition: Uncle Sam the Monopoly Man. *Yale Law J.*, April 1973, *82*(5), pp. 871–89.

Naert, Philippe A. Measuring Performance in a Decentralized Firm with Interrelated Divisions: Profit Center Versus Cost Center. *Eng. Econ.*, January-February 1973, *18*(2), pp. 99–114.

_____ and Bultez, Alain. Logically Consistent Market Share Models. *J. Marketing Res.*, August 1973, *10*(3), pp. 334–40.

Nag, Moni. Anthropology and Population: Problems and Perspectives. *Population Stud.*, March 1973, *27*(1), pp. 59–68.

Nagadevara, Vishnuprasad; Heady, Earl O. and Srivastava, Uma K. Resource Productivity, Returns to Scale and Farm Size in Indian Agriculture: Some Recent Evidence. *Australian J. Agr. Econ.*, April 1973, *17*(1), pp. 43–57.

Nagar, A. L. and Singh, Balvir. Determination of Consumer Unit Scales. *Econometrica*, March 1973, *41*(2), pp. 347–55.

_____ and Ullah, Aman. Note on Approximate Skewness and Kurtosis of the Two-Stage Least-Square Estimator. *Indian Econ. Rev.*, April 1973, *8*(1), pp. 69–80.

Nagata, Ernest A. The Cost Structure of Consumer Finance Small-Loan Operations. *J. Finance*, December 1973, *28*(5), pp. 1327–37.

Nagy, A. Industrial Projection Methods in Hungary. *Acta Oecon.*, 1973, *11*(4), pp. 381–402.

Naito, Takeshi. Japan's Changing Role. In *Wiegand, G. C., ed.*, 1973, pp. 139–42.

Nakamura, Satoru. The Historical Preconditions of the Formations of Capitalism in Japan. *Kyoto Univ. Econ. Rev.*, April–October 1973, *43*(1–2), pp. 30–44.

Nakanishi, Masao. Advertising and Promotion Effects on Consumer Response to New Products. *J. Marketing Res.*, August 1973, *10*(3), pp. 242–49.

Nakano, Isao. Homomorphism and Business Income Measurement. *Kobe Econ. Bus. Rev.*, 1973, *20*, pp. 61–77.

Nakao, Takeo. An Examination of Duesenberry's Hypothesis on the Growth of Demand for the New Product. (In Japanese.) *Econ. Stud. Quart.*, April 1973, *24*(1), pp. 18–32.

Nakayama, Toshiko. Price Increases Accelerate in First Quarter 1973. *Mon. Lab. Rev.*, June 1973, *96*(6), pp. 50–54.

_____ Second Quarter Price Pressures Bring Freeze, Phase 4. *Mon. Lab. Rev.*, September

1973, *96*(9), pp. 69–73.

———— and Bahr, Richard C. New CPI by Size of City Shows Larger Increases in Big Areas. *Mon. Lab. Rev.*, March 1973, *96*(3), pp. 55–57.

———— and Warsky, D. Measuring Regional Price Change in Urban Areas. *Mon. Lab. Rev.*, October 1973, *96*(10), pp. 34–38.

Namiki, Nobuyoshi. Future of the Economic Relations Between Japan and the European Community. *Rivista Int. Sci. Econ. Com.*, August-September 1973, *20*(8–9), pp. 758–85.

Nanus, Burt and Coffey, Robert E. Future-Oriented Business Education. *Calif. Manage. Rev.*, Summer 1973, *15*(4), pp. 28–34.

Naouri, Jean-Charles. Le financement des investissements publics. Les deux taux d'actualisation et la charge morte du transfert fiscal. (Financing Public Expenditure and the Deadweight Loss of Fiscal Transfers. With English summary.) *Revue Écon.*, July 1973, *24*(4), pp. 588–618.

Naqvi, Syed Nawab Haider. The Balance-of-Payments Problems in Developing Countries. *Pakistan Develop. Rev.*, Autumn 1973, *12*(3), pp. 259–72.

———— Pakistan's Export Possibilities. *Pakistan Develop. Rev.*, Spring 1973, *12*(1), pp. 1–30.

Naranjo, John and Porter, Richard C. The Impact of the Commonwealth Preference System on the Exports of Latin America to the United Kingdom. *J. Devel. Stud.*, July 1973, *9*(4), pp. 581–97.

Narayana, N. Changing Pattern of Indian Industries in the Plan Period 1950–70. *Econ. Aff.*, July 1973, *18*(7), pp. 338–46.

Narayanan, A. V. S. and Swanson, E. R. Evaluation of the Effect of Alternative Agricultural Systems on Water Quality: A Linear Programming Approach. In *Judge, G. G. and Takayama, T., eds.*, 1973, pp. 676–87.

Narayanaswamy, S. Banking Organisation: The Need for Service Orientation. In *Simha, S. L. N., ed.*, 1973, pp. 230–37.

Naseem, S. M. Import Substitution: A Survey of Concepts, Measures and Models. *Pakistan Develop. Rev.*, Spring 1973, *12*(1), pp. 31–47.

———— Mass Poverty in Pakistan: Some Preliminary Findings. *Pakistan Develop. Rev.*, Winter 1973, *12*(4), pp. 317–60.

———— and Berendsen, B. S. M. On Two Formulae for Calculating the Effective Rate of Protection. *Pakistan Develop. Rev.*, Summer 1973, *12*(2), pp. 189–93.

Nash, Christopher and Pearce, David. The Evaluation of Urban Motorway Schemes: A Case Study—Southampton. *Urban Stud.*, June 1973, *10*(2), pp. 129–43.

Näslund, Bertil. Labor Power and Income Distribution. *Swedish J. Econ.*, June 1973, *75*(2), pp. 128–42.

———— Pollution and the Value of Time. *Europ. Econ. Rev.*, June 1973, *4*(2), pp. 181–96.

Nasse, Ph. Un système complet de fonctions de demande: Les équations de Fourgeaud et Nataf. *Econometrica*, November 1973, *41*(6), pp. 1137–58.

Nasta, Eliza and Horja, Gavril. Conţinutul şi funcţiile contractelor economice în etapa actuală. (The Content and Functions of the Economic Contracts in the Present Stage. With English summary.) *Stud. Cercet. Econ.*, 1973, (4), pp. 47–53.

———— and Vasilescu, Floarea. Consideraţii asupra metodologiei de calcul a coeficientului elasticităţii. (Considerations of the Methodology of Calculating the Elasticity Coefficient. With English summary.) *Stud. Cercet. Econ.*, 1973, (1), pp. 99–109.

Natchez, Peter B. and Bupp, Irvin C. Policy and Priority in the Budgetary Process. *Amer. Polit. Sci. Rev.*, September 1973, *67*(3), pp. 951–63.

Nath, G. Baikunth. Correlation in a Truncated Bivariate Normal Distribution. *Statistica*, October-December 1973, *33*(4), pp. 563–87.

Nath, Shyam. Comparison of States' Tax Ratio, Marginal Tax Rate and Income Elasticity of Taxation. *Econ. Aff.*, April 1973, *18*(4), pp. 185–89, 196.

———— On Moping of the Agricultural Surplus. *Econ. Aff.*, January-February 1973, *18*(1-2), pp. 81–85.

Nath, Vishwa. Progress of New Agricultural Strategy in India. *Econ. Aff.*, September-October 1973, *18* (9–10), pp. 450–54.

Nathan, Robert R. Focusing Attention on Nutrition in Development Planning. In *Berg, A.; Scrimshaw, N. S. and Call, D. L., eds.*, 1973, pp. 282–84.

Nawas, Farid and Brown, William G. Impact of Aggregation on the Estimation of Outdoor Recreation Demand Functions. *Amer. J. Agr. Econ.*, May 1973, *55*(2), pp. 246–49.

Nawrocki, David N. and Philippatos, George C. The Behavior of Stock Market Aggregates: Evidence of Dependence on the American Stock Exchange. *J. Bus. Res.*, Fall 1973, *1*(2), pp. 102–14.

———— The Information Inaccuracy of Stock Market Forecasts: Some New Evidence of Dependence on the New York Stock Exchange. *J. Financial Quant. Anal.*, June 1973, *8*(3), pp. 445–58.

Naya, Seiji. Fluctuations in Export Earnings and Economic Patterns of Asian Countries. *Econ. Develop. Cult. Change*, Part I, July 1973, *21*(4), pp. 629–41.

Nayyar, Deepak. An Analysis of the Stagnation in India's Cotton Textile Exports During the Sixties. *Oxford Bull. Econ. Statist.*, February 1973, *35*(1), pp. 1–19.

Neal, Larry and Klotz, Benjamin P. Spectral and Cross-Spectral Analysis of the Long-Swing Hypothesis. *Rev. Econ. Statist.*, August 1973, *55*(3), pp. 291–98.

Neary, Peter. Relative Efficiency of Regression Using Original Data or First Differences: The Case of Autocorrelated Disturbances. *Econ. Soc. Rev.*, October 1973, *5*(1), pp. 47–58.

Neave, Edwin H. and Rorke, C. Harvey. Risk, Ruin, and Investment Analysis: Comment. *J. Financial Quant. Anal.*, June 1973, *8*(3), pp. 517–26.

Neece, Roger N. and Saini, Krishan G. Poverty versus Pollution: Is There a Choice? *Indian Econ. J.*, January-March 1973, *20*(3), pp. 452–68.

Needham, Douglas. Monetary and Fiscal Policy under Fixed Exchange Rates: Comment. *Swedish J. Econ.*, March 1973, *75*(1), pp. 112–18.

Neef, Arthur and Capdevielle, Patricia. Productivity and Unit Labor Costs in 12 Industrial Countries.

Mon. Lab. Rev., November 1973, *96*(11), pp. 14–21.

Neel, Gérard and Grandmont, Jean-Michel. Sur les taux d'intérêt en France. (About Interest Rates in France. With English summary.) *Revue Écon.*, May 1973, *24*(3), pp. 460–72.

Neenan, William B.; Akin, John S. and Fields, Gary S. A Socioeconomic Explanation of Demand for Public Goods. *Public Finance Quart.*, April 1973, *1*(2), pp. 169–89.

Negishi, Takashi. The Excess of Public Expenditures on Industries. *J. Public Econ.*, July 1973, *2*(3), pp. 231–40.

Nègre, Michel and Ousset, Jean. Des comptes nationaux aux comptes régionaux. L'exemple des comptes de l'Agriculture. (Regional and National Accounts: The Example of French Agricultural Accounts. With English summary.) *Revue Écon.*, July 1973, *24*(4), pp. 549–87.

Neild, P. G. The Construction and Estimation of a Coherent Labour-Market System. *Australian Econ. Pap.*, June 1973, *12*(20), pp. 106–23.

Neild, R. R. The Effect of Demand on Prices in British Manufacturing Industry: Comment. *Rev. Econ. Stud.*, January 1973, *40*(1), pp. 143–44.

Neiss, Hubert and Tyler, Geoffrey. Problems and Prospects in East-West Trade. *Finance Develop.*, September 1973, *10*(3), pp. 24–26.

Nekola, Jiří and Vrba, Josef. Optimalizace rozsahu výkumné a vývojové činnosti na základě produkčni funkce. (The Optimization of the Level of Research and Development Activity on the Basis of the Production Function. With English summary.) *Ekon.-Mat. Obzor*, 1973, *9*(1), pp. 51–67.

Nell, Edward J. Cyclical Accumulation: A Marxian Model of Development. *Amer. Econ. Rev.*, May 1973, *63*(2), pp. 152–59.

―――― The Fall of the House of Efficiency. *Ann. Amer. Acad. Polit. Soc. Sci.*, September 1973, *409*, pp. 102–11.

Nelles, H. V. and Armstrong, Christopher. Private Property in Peril: Ontario Businessmen and the Federal System, 1898–1911. *Bus. Hist. Rev.*, Summer 1973, *47*(2), pp. 158–76.

Nelson, Jane. Swiss Banks. In *Moskoff, W., ed.*, 1973, pp. 28–33.

Nelson, Jon P. An Interregional Recursive Programming Model of the U.S. Iron and Steel Industry. In *Judge, G. G. and Takayama, T., eds.*, 1973, pp. 368–93.

―――― and Day, Richard H. A Class of Dynamic Models for Describing and Projecting Industrial Development. *J. Econometrics*, June 1973, *1*(2), pp. 155–90.

Nelson, Paul E., Jr.; Hildreth, R. J. and Krause, Kenneth R. Organization and Control of the U.S. Food and Fiber Sector. *Amer. J. Agr. Econ.*, December 1973, *55*(5), pp. 851–59.

Nelson, Phillip. Economics of Information: Discussion. *Amer. Econ. Rev.*, May 1973, *63*(2), pp. 50–51.

―――― The Elasticity of Labor Supply to the Individual Firm. *Econometrica*, September 1973, *41*(5), pp. 853–66.

Nelson, Ralph L. Estimates of Balance Sheets and Income Statements of Foundations and Colleges and Universities. In *Goldsmith, R. W., ed.*, 1973, pp. 378–91.

Nelson, Richard R. Collective Bargaining Agreements in the Federal Service. *Mon. Lab. Rev.*, September 1973, *96*(9), pp. 76–78.

―――― Microeconomic Theory and Economic Development: Reflections on the Conference. In *Ayal, E. B., ed.*, 1973, pp. 278–85.

―――― Recent Exercises in Growth Accounting: New Understanding or Dead End? *Amer. Econ. Rev.*, June 1973, *63*(3), pp. 462–68.

―――― and Krashinsky, Michael. The Demand and Supply of Extra-Family Day Care. In *Young, D. R. and Nelson, R. R., eds.*, 1973, pp. 9–20.

―――― and Krashinsky, Michael. Two Major Issues of Public Policy: Public Subsidy and Organization of Supply. In *Young, D. R. and Nelson, R. R., eds.*, 1973, pp. 47–69.

―――― and Winter, Sidney G. Toward an Evolutionary Theory of Economic Capabilities. *Amer. Econ. Rev.*, May 1973, *63*(2), pp. 440–49.

―――― and Young, Dennis. National Day Care Policy. In *Young, D. R. and Nelson, R. R., eds.*, 1973, pp. 91–103.

Nelson, Robert H. Accessibility and Rent: Applying Becker's "Time Price" Concept to the Theory of Residential Location. *Urban Stud.*, February 1973, *10*(1), pp. 83–86.

Nemmers, Erwin E. Real as Opposed to Monetary Underconsumption or Hobson Revisited. *Nebr. J. Econ. Bus.*, Autumn 1973, *12*(4), pp. 69–76.

Nentjes, A. and Kuipers, S. K. Pollution in a Neo-Classical World: The Classics Rehabilitated? *De Economist*, January-February 1973, *121*(1), pp. 52–67.

Nentvichová, Božena and Vachel, Jan. 25 Years of Building Czechoslovakia's Socialist Economy. *Czech. Econ. Digest.*, February 1973, (1), pp. 3–93.

Nerlove, Marc and Schultz, T. Paul. Love and Life between the Censuses. In *Goldberger, A. S. and Duncan, O. D., eds.*, 1973, pp. 317–28.

Nesci, Vincenzo. Savings Banks and Savings Facilities in African Countries: Morocco. In *Alberici, A. and Baravelli, M., eds.*, 1973, pp. 69–76.

Nestel, Gilbert and Borus, Michael E. Response Bias in Reports of Father's Education and Socioeconomic Status. *J. Amer. Statist. Assoc.*, December 1973, *68*(344), pp. 816–20.

Neter, John and Yu, Seongjae. A Stochastic Model of the Internal Control System. *J. Acc. Res.*, Autumn 1973, *11*(2), pp. 273–95.

Netschert, Bruce C. and Stelzer, Irwin M. Energy and the Environment in New York State: A Balancing of Needs. *Amer. Econ.*, Fall 1973, *17*(2), pp. 143–47.

Netzer, Dick. Effects of the Property Tax in Urban Areas. In *Pynoos, J.; Schafer, R. and Hartman, C. W., eds.*, 1973, pp. 510–22.

―――― The Incidence of the Property Tax Revisited. *Nat. Tax J.*, December 1973, *26*(4), pp. 515–35.

Neu, Axel and Glismann, Hans H. Quantitative Aspects of Nontariff Distortions of Trade in the Federal Republic of Germany. In *Scaperlanda, A. E., ed.*, 1973, pp. 193–253.

Neuberger, Egon. The Plan and the Market: The Models of Oskar Lange. *Amer. Econ.*, Fall 1973, *17*(2), pp. 148–53.

———; **Brown, Alan A. and Licari, J. A.** A Dynamic CES Production Function Interpretation of Hungarian Growth. *Acta Oecon.*, 1973, *11*(4), pp. 305–24.

——— **and James, Estelle.** The Yugoslav Self-Managed Enterprise: A Systemic Approach. In *Bornstein, M., ed.*, 1973, pp. 245–84.

Neumann, Manfred J. M. On Public Expenditure and Taxation. *Public Finance*, 1973, *28*(3–4), pp. 377–83.

——— Special Drawing Rights and Inflation. *Weltwirtsch. Arch.*, 1973, *109*(2), pp. 232–52.

——— The 1972 Report of the German Council of Economic Experts: Inflation and Stabilization: Review Essay. *J. Money, Credit, Banking*, November 1973, *5*(4), pp. 950–59.

Neumann, Seev. Ownership and Performance: Stock and Mutual Life Insurance Companies: Comment. *J. Risk Ins.*, December 1973, *40*(4), pp. 631–35.

Newbold, P. and Granger, C. W. J. Some Comments on the Evaluation of Economic Forecasts. *Appl. Econ.*, March 1973, *5*(1), pp. 35–47.

Newell, William H. The Agricultural Revolution in Nineteenth-Century France. *J. Econ. Hist.*, December 1973, *33*(4), pp. 697–731.

Newhouse, Joseph P. The Economics of Group Practice. *J. Human Res.*, Winter 1973, *8*(1), pp. 37–56.

Newlon, Daniel H. and Greene, Kenneth V. Economic Factors Affecting the Likelihood of a Switch to a Volunteer Army. *Public Finance Quart.*, October 1973, *1*(4), pp. 388–98.

——— The Pareto Optimality of Eliminating a Lottery Draft. *Quart. Rev. Econ. Bus.*, Winter 1973, *13*(4), pp. 61–70.

Newlyn, Walter T. The Effect of Aid and Other Resource Transfers on Savings and Growth in Less-Developed Countries: A Comment. *Econ. J.*, September 1973, *83*(331), pp. 867–69.

Newman, D.; Jones, H. J. M. and Lawson, H. B. Population Census: Some Recent British Developments in Methodology. *J. Roy. Statist. Soc.*, Part 4, 1973, *136*, pp. 505–20.

Newman, Joseph W. and Werbel, Richard A. Multivariate Analysis of Brand Loyalty for Major Household Appliances. *J. Marketing Res.*, November 1973, *10*(4), pp. 404–09.

Newman, William H. Basic Objectives Which Shape the Character of a Company. In *Klein, W. H. and Murphy, D. C., eds.*, 1973, pp. 85–97.

——— Shaping the Master Strategy of Your Firm. In *Klein, W. H. and Murphy, D. C., eds.*, 1973, pp. 174–85.

Ng, Yew-Kwang. The Economic Theory of Clubs: Pareto Optimality Conditions. *Economica, N.S.*, August 1973, *40*(159), pp. 291–98.

——— Income Distribution as a Peculiar Public Good: The Paradox of Redistribution and the Paradox of Universal Externality. *Public Finance*, 1973, *28*(1), pp. 1–10.

——— Optimal Terms of Foreign Assistance: Comment. *J. Polit. Econ.*, Part I, March-April 1973, *81*(2), pp. 488–90.

Nguyen, D. T. Unwanted Amortisation Funds: A Comment. *Econ. J.*, March 1973, *83*(329), pp. 234–35.

Nibale, Gianfranco. Distribuzione automobilistica e dimensione d'impresa. (Automobile Distribution and Business Size. With English summary.) *Rivista Int. Sci. Econ. Com.*, October 1973, *20*(10), pp. 1013–24.

Niblack, William C. Operations of the Federal Reserve Bank of St. Louis—1972. *Fed. Res. Bank St. Louis Rev.*, February 1973, *55*(2), pp. 17–19, 22–24.

Nichols, Alan. External Diseconomies in Competitive Supply: Comment. *Amer. Econ. Rev.*, September 1973, *63*(4), pp. 741–42.

Nichols, Charles and Wittman, Donald A. Cheating and Control. *Public Choice*, Spring 1973, *14*, pp. 137–42.

Nichols, Donald R. and Fielitz, Bruce D. Awareness of Marginal Income Tax Rates Among Taxpayers. *Miss. Val. J. Bus. Econ.*, Spring 1973, *8*(3), pp. 39–46.

Nicholson, Edward A., Jr. and Litschert, Robert L. Long-Range Planning in Banking: Ten Cases in the U.S. and Britain. *J. Bank Res.*, Spring 1973, *4*(1), pp. 31–40.

——— **and Roderick, Roger D.** Correlates of Job Attitudes Among Young Women. *Nebr. J. Econ. Bus.*, Autumn 1973, *12*(4), pp. 77–89.

Nicholson, Raymond C. and Lee, George E. Managerial Information (Recording, Data, and Decision) Systems in Canada. *Amer. J. Agr. Econ.*, December 1973, *55*(5), pp. 921–29.

Nicholson, R. J. Econometrics: Measurement in Economics. *Bull. Econ. Res.*, May 1973, *25*(1), pp. 3–21.

——— Income and the Demand for Housing: Some Evidence for Great Britain: Discussion. In *Parkin, M., ed.*, 1973, pp. 85–88.

——— **and Topham, N.** Step-wise Regression and Principal Components Analysis in Estimating a Relationship in an Econometric Model. *Manchester Sch. Econ. Soc. Stud.*, June 1973, *41*(2), pp. 187–205.

Nicosia, Francesco M. Consumer Behavior: Can Economics and Behavioral Science Converge? *Calif. Manage. Rev.*, Winter 1973, *16*(2), pp. 71–78.

Niculescu, I. N. Folosirea metodei probelor curente în analiza procesului tehnologic. (Using the Method of Current Samples in Analysing the Technological Process. With English summary.) *Stud. Cercet. Econ.*, 1973, (4), pp. 73–87.

Niedercorn, John H. A Negative Exponential Model of Urban Land Use Densities and Its Implications for Metropolitan Development: Reply. *J. Reg. Sci.*, April 1973, *13*(1), pp. 139–40.

Niehans, Jürg. The Flexibility of the Gold-Exchange Standard. In *Johnson, H. G. and Swoboda, A. K., eds.*, 1973, pp. 46–64.

——— Veendorp on Optimal Payment Arrangements: Reply. *J. Money, Credit, Banking*, Part I, February 1973, *5*(1), pp. 213–14.

Nielsen, James F. and Joehnk, Michael D. Further Evidence on the Effects of Block Transactions on Stock Price Fluctuations. *Miss. Val. J. Bus. Econ.*,

Winter 1973-74, *9*(2), pp. 27–34.

_____ **and Melicher, Ronald W.** A Financial Analysis of Acquisition and Merger Premiums. *J. Financial Quant. Anal.*, March 1973, *8*(2), pp. 139–48.

Niemi, Albert W., Jr. Returns to Educated Blacks Resulting from Southern Outmigration. *Southern Econ. J.*, October 1973, *40*(2), pp. 330–32.

Niessen, A. M. Twelfth Valuation of the Railroad Retirement System: A Summary View. *Soc. Sec. Bull.*, December 1973, *36*(12), pp. 13–19.

Nieuwenhuysen, J. P. Macro-Economic Policy: South Africa. In *Perkins, J. O. N., ed.*, 1973, pp. 130–76.

_____ **and Perkins, J. O. N.** Macro-Economic Policies in the Four Countries. In *Perkins, J. O. N., ed.*, 1973, pp. 177–208.

_____ **and Perkins, J. O. N.** Macro-Economic Policy: Australia. In *Perkins, J. O. N., ed.*, 1973, pp. 17–56.

Nishimura, Osamu. Transaction Activity and Optimal Taxation. *Econ. Stud. Quart.*, August 1973, *24*(2), pp. 16–25.

Nishioka, Hisao and Krumme, Gunter. Location Conditions, Factors and Decisions: An Evaluation of Selected Location Surveys. *Land Econ.*, May 1973, *49*(2), pp. 195–205.

Niskanen, William and Berry, Robert. The 1973 Economic Report of the President. *J. Money, Credit, Banking*, May 1973, *5*(2), pp. 693–703.

Nissen, Anton. Revision of the Money Stock Measures and Member Bank Reserves and Deposits. *Fed. Res. Bull.*, February 1973, *59*(2), pp. 61–79.

Nixon, Richard M. Consumer Protection. In *Murray, B. B., ed.*, 1973, pp. 68–77.

Nizami, N. H.; Afzal, Mohammad and Hashmi, M. Iqbal. Marriage Patterns in a Rural Agglomeration. *Pakistan Develop. Rev.*, Autumn 1973, *12*(3), pp. 273–82.

Nlend, Emmanuel. Savings Banks and Savings Facilities in African Countries: Cameroon. In *Alberici, A. and Baravelli, M., eds.*, 1973, pp. 1–5.

Nobay, A. R. The Bank of England, Monetary Policy and Monetary Theory in the United Kingdom, 1951-1971. *Manchester Sch. Econ. Soc. Stud.*, March 1973, *41*(1), pp. 43–58.

_____ Manipulating Demand for Money: Discussion. In *Parkin, M., ed.*, 1973, pp. 386–88.

Nobukuni, Makoto and Fukuchi, Takao. The Economic Measurement of the Benefit of Public Transportation Investment. (In Japanese. With English summary.) *Econ. Stud. Quart.*, December 1973, *24*(3), pp. 43–53.

Nolan, Joseph T. The Social Audit: One Corporation's Experience. In *Dierkes, M. and Bauer, R. A., eds.*, 1973, pp. 292–96.

Nolan, Richard L. Computer Data Bases: The Future is Now. *Harvard Bus. Rev.*, September-October 1973, *51*(5), pp. 98–114.

Noll, Roger G. Selling Research to Regulatory Agencies. In *Park, R. E., ed.*, 1973, pp. 63–69.

_____ **and MacAvoy, Paul W.** Relative Prices on Regulated Transactions of the Natural Gas Pipelines. *Bell J. Econ. Manage. Sci.*, Spring 1973, *4*(1), pp. 212–34.

_____ **and Rivlin, Lewis A.** Regulating Prices in

Competitive Markets. *Yale Law J.*, June 1973, *82*(7), pp. 1426–34.

Nondasuta, Amorn. Suggested Components of Intervention Programs. In *Berg, A.; Scrimshaw, N. S. and Call, D. L., eds.*, 1973, pp. 223–28.

Nord, Walter. Adam Smith and Contemporary Social Exchange Theory. *Amer. J. Econ. Soc.*, October 1973, *32*(4), pp. 421–36.

Nordberg, Leif. Om möjligheterna att utnyttja data fran flera länder vid konstruktionen av ekonometriska modeller. (The Possibilities of Using Data from Several Countries in the Construction of Econometric Models. With English summary.) *Ekon. Samfundets Tidskr.*, 1973, *26*(2), pp. 105–16.

Nordbotten, Svein and Aukrust, Odd. Files of Individual Data and their Potentials for Social Research. *Rev. Income Wealth*, June 1973, *19*(2), pp. 189–201.

Nordhaus, William D. The Allocation of Energy Resources. *Brookings Pap. Econ. Act.*, 1973, (3), pp. 529–70.

_____ The Effects of Inflation on the Distribution of Economic Welfare. *J. Money, Credit, Banking*, Part II, February 1973, *5*(1), pp. 465–504.

_____ Some Skeptical Thoughts on the Theory of Induced Innovation. *Quart. J. Econ.*, May 1973, *87*(2), pp. 208–19.

_____ World Dynamics: Measurement Without Data. *Econ. J.*, December 1973, *83*(332), pp. 1156–83.

_____ **and Tobin, James.** Is Growth Obsolete? In *Moss, M., ed.*, 1973, pp. 509–32.

_____ **and Tobin, James.** Is Growth Obsolete? Reply to Denison and Usher. In *Moss, M., ed.*, 1973, pp. 554–63.

_____ **and Tobin, James.** Is Growth Obsolete? Reply to Meyer. In *Moss, M., ed.*, 1973, pp. 563–64.

Nordhauser, Norman. Origins of Federal Oil Regulation in the 1920's. *Bus. Hist. Rev.*, Spring 1973, *47*(1), pp. 53–71.

Norgaard, Richard B. and Hall, Darwin C. On the Timing and Application of Pesticides. *Amer. J. Agr. Econ.*, May 1973, *55*(2), pp. 198–201.

Norman, D. W. Crop Mixtures under Indigenous Conditions in the Northern Part of Nigeria. In *Ofori, I. M., ed.*, 1973, pp. 130–44.

_____ **and Simmons, E. B.** Determination of Relevant Research Priorities for Farm Development in West Africa. In *Ofori, I. M., ed.*, 1973, pp. 42–48.

Norman, Victor D. and Lorange, Peter. Risk Preference in Scandinavian Shipping. *Appl. Econ.*, March 1973, *5*(1), pp. 49–59.

North, Douglass C. and Thomas, Robert Paul. European Economic Growth: Comments on the North-Thomas Theory: Reply. *Econ. Hist. Rev.*, 2nd Ser., May 1973, *26*(2), pp. 293–94.

Norton, Arthur J. and Glick, Paul C. Perspectives on the Recent Upturn in Divorce and Remarriage. *Demography*, August 1973, *10*(3), pp. 301–14.

Norton, Hugh S. Reviewing Economics Textbooks: Some Comments on the Process. *J. Econ. Lit.*, September 1973, *11*(3), pp. 889–97.

Norton, Roger D. and Duloy, John H. CHAC Results: Economic Alternatives for Mexican Agriculture. In *Goreux, L. M. and Manne, A. S., eds.,* 1973, pp. 373–99.

———— and Duloy, John H. CHAC, A Programming Model of Mexican Agriculture. In *Goreux, L. M. and Manne, A. S., eds.,* 1973, pp. 291–337.

———— and Duloy, John H. Linking the Agricultural Model and the Economy-Wide Model. In *Goreux, L. M. and Manne, A. S., eds.,* 1973, pp. 435–61.

————; Duloy, John H. and Kutcher, Gary P. Investment and Employment Alternatives in the Agricultural District Model. In *Goreux, L. M. and Manne, A. S., eds.,* 1973, pp. 417–33.

Norton, W. E. and Henderson, J. F. The Structure of a Model of the Australian Economy. In *Powell, A. A. and Williams, R. A., eds.,* 1973, pp. 49–83.

Norwood, Bernard. The Next World Trade Negotiations. In *[Halm, G. N.],* 1973, pp. 125–48.

Nosari, Eldon J. and Anthony, William P. A Test of the Permanent Income Hypothesis. *J. Bus. Res.,* Summer 1973, *1*(1), pp. 43–48.

Nosse, Tetsuya. Patterns of Government Capital Formation in the Economic Development of Japan, 1878–1967. In *[Hicks, U.],* 1973, pp. 140–80.

Notkin, A. The Production Accumulation Norm. *Prob. Econ.,* February 1973, *15*(10), pp. 3–29.

Nour, Mohamed A. Planning Priorities in Nutrition and Development. In *Berg, A.; Scrimshaw, N. S. and Call, D. L., eds.,* 1973, pp. 87–90.

Nouri, Clement J. Comparative Job Attitudes—Iraqui and American Students. *Marquette Bus. Rev.,* Spring 1973, *17*(1), pp. 13–24.

Nourse, Robert E. M. and Vernon, John M. Profit Rates and Market Structure of Advertising Intensive Firms. *J. Ind. Econ.,* September 1973, *22*(1), pp. 1–20.

Novak, George J. Priorities for Statistical Development. *Finance Develop.,* September 1973, *10*(3), pp. 9–13.

Novara, Francesco. Job Enrichment in the Olivetti Company. *Int. Lab. Rev.,* October 1973, *108*(4), pp. 283–94.

Nove, Alec. Great Britain and Latin American Economic Development. In *Urquidi, V. L. and Thorp, R., eds.,* 1973, pp. 331–66.

———— Russia as an Emergent Country. In *Youngson, A. J., ed.,* 1973, pp. 79–97.

Novick, David. Brief History of Program Budgeting. In *Novick, D., ed.,* 1973, pp. 19–28.

———— Evaluating Program Budgeting in the 1960s. In *Novick, D., ed.,* 1973, pp. 49–53.

———— Program Budgeting, 1971. In *Novick, D., ed.,* 1973, pp. 29–47.

———— What Program Budgeting Is and Is Not. In *Novick, D., ed.,* 1973, pp. 5–17.

Nowacek, Charles G. Organizing Manpower Delivery Systems in Big Cities: Discussion. In *Aronson, R. L., ed.,* 1973, pp. 44–50.

Nowotny, Ewald. On the Incidence of Real Estate Taxation. *Z. Nationalökon.,* 1973, *33*(1–2), pp. 133–60.

Nowshirvani, Vahid F. A Note on the Elasticity of the Marketable Surplus of a Subsistence Crop—A Comment. In *Wadhva, C. D., ed.,* 1973, pp. 319–22.

Noyes, Guy E. The Multinational Firm: Bane or

Boon?: Discussion. *J. Finance,* May 1973, *28*(2), pp. 462–65.

Ntim, S. M. and Williams, T. David. Public Employment Centres as a Source of Data on Unemployment in Ghana. *Econ. Bull. Ghana, Sec. Ser.,* 1973, *3*(1), pp. 16–26.

Nugent, Jeffrey B. Exchange-Rate Movements and Economic Development in the Late Nineteenth Century. *J. Polit. Econ.,* September-October 1973, *81*(5), pp. 1110–35.

———— and Yotopoulos, Pan A. A Balanced-Growth Version of the Linkage Hypothesis: A Test. *Quart. J. Econ.,* May 1973, *87*(2), pp. 157–71.

Nukunya, G. K. Land Tenure and Agricultural Development in the Anloga Area of the Volta Region. In *Ofori, I. M., ed.,* 1973, pp. 101–06.

Nunnally, Nelson and Pollina, Ronald. Recent Trends in Industrial Park Location in the Chicago Metropolitan Area. *Land Econ.,* August 1973, *49*(3), pp. 356–61.

Nurnberg, Hugo. A Strange Animal. *J. Acc. Res.,* Autumn 1973, *11*(2), pp. 331–33.

Nussbaumer, Adolf. Financing the Generation of New Science and Technology. In *Williams, B. R., ed.,* 1973, pp. 169–89.

———— On the Compatibility of Subjective and Objective Theories of Economic Value. In *Hicks, J. R. and Weber, W., eds.,* 1973, pp. 75–91.

Nuti, Domenico M. On the Truncation of Production Flows. *Kyklos,* 1973, *26*(3), pp. 485–96.

Nuttall, T. The Industry Act and Regional Policy. *Nat. Westminster Bank Quart. Rev.,* November 1973, pp. 55–68.

Nwaneri, V. C. Income Distribution and Project Selection. *Finance Develop.,* September 1973, *10*(3), pp. 27–29, 33.

———— Income Distribution Criteria for the Analysis of Development Projects. *Finance Develop.,* March 1973, *10*(1), pp. 16–19, 37.

Nyanteng, V. K. and van Apeldoorn, G. J. Some Development Implications of Farmers' Problems in Marketing Their Foodcrops. In *Ofori, I. M., ed.,* 1973, pp. 263–77.

Nye, Joseph S. The Political Context. In *Krause, L. B. and Salant, W. S., eds.,* 1973, pp. 37–55.

———— Regional Institutions. In *Falk, R. A. and Mendlovitz, S. H., eds.,* 1973, pp. 78–93.

———— and Keohane, Robert O. World Politics and the International Economic System. In *Bergsten, C. F., ed.,* 1973, pp. 115–79.

Nye, Richard C. The Indiana Economic Forum. *Indiana Bus. Rev.,* May-June 1973, *48*, pp. 19–20.

Oakland, W. H.; Sparrow, Frederick T. and Stettler, H. Louis, III. More on Ghetto Multipliers. *J. Reg. Sci.,* April 1973, *13*(1), pp. 127–28.

Oates, Wallace E. The Effects of Property Taxes and Local Public Spending on Property Values: A Reply and Yet Further Results. *J. Polit. Econ.,* July-August 1973, *81*(4), pp. 1004–08.

Oaxaca, Ronald. Male-Female Wage Differentials in Urban Labor Markets. *Int. Econ. Rev.,* October 1973, *14*(3), pp. 693–709.

Obeng, F. A. and Rourke, B. E. Seasonality in the Employment of Casual Agricultural Labour in Ghana. *Econ. Bull. Ghana, Sec. Ser.,* 1973, *3*(3), pp. 3–13.

Oberhofer, W. and Kmenta, J. Estimation of Standard Errors of the Characteristic Roots of a Dynamic Econometric Model. *Econometrica,* January 1973, *41*(1), pp. 171–77.

O'Brien, James M. Inflation and Unemployment: The Great Debate. *Fed. Res. Bank Bus. Rev. Phila.,* January 1973, pp. 13–18.

O'Brien, Thomas and Ganz, Alexander. The City: Sandbox, Reservation, or Dynamo? *Public Policy,* Winter 1973, *21*(1), pp. 107–23.

O'Brien of Lothbury [Lord]. Le imprese multinazionali. (Multinational Enterprises. With English summary.) *Bancaria,* September 1973, *29*(9), pp. 1075–80.

O'Cofaigh, Thomas F. Programme Budgeting in Ireland. In *Novick, D., ed.,* 1973, pp. 119–24.

O'Connor, Melvin C. On the Usefulness of Financial Ratios to Investors in Common Stock. *Accounting Rev.,* April 1973, *48*(2), pp. 339–52.

Odewahn, Charles A. and Krislov, Joseph. Contract Rejections: Testing the Explanatory Hypotheses. *Ind. Relat.,* October 1973, *12*(3), pp. 289–96.

———— The Relationship Between Union Contract Rejections and the Business Cycle—A Theoretical Approach. *Nebr. J. Econ. Bus.,* Summer 1973, *12* (3), pp. 23–36.

Odland, J.; Casetti, Emilio and King, L. J. Testing Hypotheses of Polarized Growth Within a Central Place Hierarchy. *Econ. Geogr.,* January 1973, *49*(1), pp. 74–79.

Odling-Smee, J. C. Personal Saving Revisited: More Statistics, Fewer Facts. *Oxford Bull. Econ. Statist.,* February 1973, *35*(1), pp. 21–29.

O'Donnell, Cyril. Planning Objectives. In *Klein, W. H. and Murphy, D. C., eds.,* 1973, pp. 98–105.

O'Donnell, L. A. Rationalism, Capitalism and the Entrepreneur: The Views of Veblen and Schumpeter. *Hist. Polit. Econ.,* Spring 1973, *5*(1), pp. 199–214.

O'Donoghue, Patrick D. and Bish, Robert L. Public Goods, Increasing Cost, and Monopsony: Reply. *J. Polit. Econ.,* January-February 1973, *81*(1), pp. 231–36.

Ody, J. G. Economics of Change in Road Passenger Transport: Comment. *J. Transp. Econ. Policy,* September 1973, *7*(3), pp. 291–92.

Oehm, J. Kent. Controlling Professional Manpower Costs. *Manage. Account.,* March 1973, *54*(9), pp. 31–35.

O'Farrell, J.; Cantwell, J. and Lenehan, B. Improving the Performance of a Local Authority Ambulance Service. In *Ross, M., ed.,* 1973, pp. 443–53.

Ofer, Gur. Returns to Scale in Retail Trade. *Rev. Income Wealth,* December 1973, *19*(4), pp. 363–84.

Officer, R. R. The Variability of the Market Factor of the New York Stock Exchange. *J. Bus.,* July 1973, *46*(3), pp. 434–53.

Ofori, I. M. Land Tenure Interactions and Land Use Patterns in Ghanaian Agriculture: Some Basic Theoretical Considerations. In *Ofori, I. M., ed.,* 1973, pp. 91–100.

Ogawa, Kazuo and Watanabe, Tamao. Introduction to Japan-China Trade. *Chinese Econ. Stud.,* Fall 1973, *7*(1), pp. 3–137.

Ogram, Ernest W., Jr. The Multinational Corpora-

tion in the Future. In *Alexandrides, C. G., ed.,* 1973, pp. 273–83.

Ogren, Kenneth E. Exports of U.S. Capital and Technology and International Political Conflicts. In *Iowa State University Center for Agricultural and Rural Development,* 1973, pp. 210–24.

Ogur, Jonathan D. Higher Education and Housing: The Impact of Colleges and Universities on Local Rental Housing Markets. *Amer. J. Econ. Soc.,* October 1973, *32*(4), pp. 387–94.

Ogut, Soner; Baker, C. B. and Fettig, L. P. Effects of Financing and Employment Alternatives on a Modern Farm Village in Turkey. *Ill. Agr. Econ.,* July 1973, *13*(2), pp. 12–15.

Oh, Tai K. Estimating the Migration of U.S.-Educated Manpower from Asia to the United States. *Soc. Econ. Stud.,* September 1973, *22*(3), pp. 335–57.

O'Hagan, John and O'Higgins, Michael. Are Ireland's Social Security Payments too Small? Comment. *Econ. Soc. Rev.,* October 1973, *5*(1), pp. 113–21.

O'Higgins, Michael and O'Hagan, John. Are Ireland's Social Security Payments too Small? Comment. *Econ. Soc. Rev.,* October 1973, *5*(1), pp. 113–21.

Ohlin, Göran. Industrialization and Trade Trends: Some Issues for the 1970s: Comment. In *Hughes, H., ed.,* 1973, pp. 32–34.

Ohlsson, Ingvar and Blohm, Margareta. Experience in Measurement of Welfare Components and their Regional Implications. *Rev. Income Wealth,* June 1973, *19*(2), pp. 167–88.

Ohman, Carl I. An Integrated Radicalism: Comment. In *Lewis, J. P. and Kapur, I., eds.,* 1973, pp. 27–34.

Öhqvist, Henrik. Kapitalets produktivitet i industriföretag. (Capital Productivity in Industrial Enterprise. With English summary.) *Ekon. Samfundets Tidskr.,* 1973, *26*(3), pp. 159–66.

Ohta, H. and Greenhut, M. L. Spatial Configurations and Competitive Equilibrium. *Weltwirtsch. Arch.,* 1973, *109*(1), pp. 87–104.

Ohtsuki, Yoshitaka. Public Investment and Economic Growth—Fiscal Policy and Resource Allocation. (In Japanese. With English summary.) *Econ. Stud. Quart.,* December 1973, *24*(3), pp. 16–30.

Oi, Walter Y. The Economics of Product Safety. *Bell J. Econ. Manage. Sci.,* Spring 1973, *4*(1), pp. 3–28.

Oiso, Toshio. Nutrition in National Development: The Japanese Experience. In *Berg, A.; Scrimshaw, N. S. and Call, D. L., eds.,* 1973, pp. 366–69.

Okishio, Nobuo. On the Convergence of Marx's 'Transformation' Procedure. (In Japanese. With English summary.) *Econ. Stud. Quart.,* August 1973, *24*(2), pp. 40–45.

Okita, Saburo. Possible Modifications in Development Aid Policy. In *Berg, A.; Scrimshaw, N. S. and Call, D. L., eds.,* 1973, pp. 207–09.

Okner, Benjamin A. The Federal Revenue System: Discussion. *J. Finance,* May 1973, *28*(2), pp. 500–03.

Oksanen, Ernest H. and Denton, Frank T. Data Revisions and Forecasting Accuracy: An Econometric Analysis Based on Preliminary and Revised

National Accounting Estimates. *Rev. Income Wealth*, December 1973, *19*(4), pp. 437–52.

—— and George, P. J. Saturation in the Automobile Market in the Late Twenties: Some Further Results. *Exploration Econ. Hist.*, Fall 1973, *11*(1), pp. 73–85.

—— and Kliman, M. L. The Keynesian Demand-for-Money Function: Comment. *J. Money, Credit, Banking*, Part I, February 1973, *5*(1), pp. 215–20.

Okuguchi, Koji. Magnification Effect in a Two-Good Model with Intermediate Inputs. *Z. Nationalökon.*, 1973, *33*(3–4), pp. 413–18.

—— Quasi-Competitiveness and Cournot Oligopoly. *Rev. Econ. Stud.*, January 1973, *40*(1), pp. 145–48.

Okun, Arthur M. General Economic Conditions and National Elections: Comment. *Amer. Econ. Rev.*, May 1973, *63*(2), pp. 172–77.

—— Rules and Roles for Fiscal and Monetary Policy. In *Reynolds, L. G.; Green, G. D. and Lewis, D. R., eds.*, 1973, pp. 62–80.

—— Upward Mobility in a High-pressure Economy. *Brookings Pap. Econ. Act.*, 1973, (1), pp. 207–52.

Okuno, Nobuhiro. Consumption Externalities and Total Demand Curves. *Econ. Stud. Quart.*, August 1973, *24*(2), pp. 61–66.

Okwuosa, E. A. The Problem of Demand in Relation to Policy for Agricultural Development. In *Ofori, I. M., ed.*, 1973, pp. 20–25.

Olayide, S. Olajuwon. Some Aspects of Beef Production in Nigeria. In *Ofori, I. M., ed.*, 1973, pp. 240–50.

Oldham, C. H. G. Science and Technology Policies. In *Oksenberg, M., ed.*, 1973, pp. 80–94.

Oldham, James C. Organized Labor, the Environment, and the Taft-Hartley Act. *Mich. Law Rev.*, April 1973, *71*(5), pp. 935–1040.

Oleinik, I. and Iudina, E. Structural Changes in the Economies of Socialist Countries. *Prob. Econ.*, March 1973, *15*(11), pp. 21–43.

Ølgaard, Anders. Føres der pengepolitik i Danmark? (Danish Monetary Policy—Does it Exist? With English summary.) *Nationalokon. Tidsskr.*, 1973, *111*(1), pp. 9–24.

Olian, A. and Yaron, D. Application of Dynamic Programming in Markov Chains to the Evaluation of Water Quality in Irrigation. *Amer. J. Agr. Econ.*, August 1973, *55*(3), pp. 467–71.

Olienyk, John and Fan, Liang-Shing. Inflation in a Growing Economy: A Monetaristic Elucidation. *Intermountain Econ. Rev.*, Fall 1973, *4*(2), pp. 75–76.

Oliva, T. Extensions of Selected Graphical Techniques in International Economics: A Theoretical Approach. *Amer. Econ.*, Spring 1973, *17*(1), pp. 128–46.

Oliver, Henry. Study of Relationships Between Economic and Political Systems. *J. Econ. Issues*, December 1973, *7*(4), pp. 543–51.

Olivera, Julio H. G. On Bernoullian Production Sets. *Quart. J. Econ.*, February 1973, *87*(1), pp. 112–20.

Olivier, R. and Sabolo, Y. Simultaneous Planning of Employment, Production and Education. *Int. Lab. Rev.*, April 1973, *107*(4), pp. 359–72.

Olivieri, Dario. Tavole della dimensione minima di un campione necessaria per la stima di una probabilità. (Tables of a Sample Minimum Size Necessary for the Estimate of a Probability. With English summary.) *Rivista Int. Sci. Econ. Com.*, April 1973, *20*(4), pp. 371–98.

O'Loughlin, Carleen. What Is Agricultural Growth? In *Ofori, I. M., ed.*, 1973, pp. 7–13.

Olsen, Emilie S. and Ekelund, Robert B., Jr. Comte, Mill, and Cairnes: The Positivist-Empiricist Interlude in Late Classical Economics. *J. Econ. Issues*, September 1973, *7*(3), pp. 383–416.

Olsen, E. Odgers, Jr. Utility and Profit Maximization by an Owner-Manager. *Southern Econ. J.*, January 1973, *39*(3), pp. 389–95.

Olshavsky, Richard W. Customer-Salesman Interaction in Appliance Retailing. *J. Marketing Res.*, May 1973, *10*(2), pp. 208–12.

Olshen, Richard A. The Conditional Level of the F-Test. *J. Amer. Statist. Assoc.*, September 1973, *68*(343), pp. 692–98.

Olson, Edwin G. Determining Sample Size for State Tax Impact Studies. *Nat. Tax J.*, March 1973, *26*(1), pp. 99–102.

Olson, Mancur. Evaluating Performance in the Public Sector. In *Moss, M., ed.*, 1973, pp. 355–84.

—— Evaluating Performance in the Public Sector: Reply. In *Moss, M., ed.*, 1973, pp. 397–409.

—— The No-Growth Society: Introduction. In *Olson, M. and Landsberg, H. H., eds.*, 1973, pp. 1–13.

——; Landsberg, Hans H. and Fisher, Joseph L. The No-Growth Society: Epilogue. In *Olson, M. and Landsberg, H. H., eds.*, 1973, pp. 229–41.

Olteanu, I.; Melinte, T. and Horovicz, M. World Market, Economic Cooperation and the Planning of the National Economy. In *Kiss, T., ed.*, 1973, pp. 127–33.

Oluwasanmi, H. A. West African Agricultural Development in the '60's. In *Ofori, I. M., ed.*, 1973, pp. 1–6.

Onado, Marco and Porteri, Antonio. Savings Banks and Savings Facilities in African Countries: Lesotho. In *Alberici, A. and Baravelli, M., eds.*, 1973, pp. 45–46.

Onaka, Alvin T. and Yaukey, David. Reproductive Time Lost Due to Sexual Union Dissolution in San José, Costa Rica. *Population Stud.*, November 1973, *27*(3), pp. 457–65.

O'Neill, Dave M. Manpower. In *Ott, D. J., et al.*, 1973, pp. 153–70.

O'Neill, Helen. Regional Planning in Ireland—The Case for Concentration. *Irish Banking Rev.*, September 1973, pp. 9–20.

Oni, S. A. An Econometric Analysis of Western Nigerian Cocoa Output Response Relations. *Econ. Bull. Ghana, Sec. Ser.*, 1973, *3*(1), pp. 27–38.

Onibokun, Adepoju. Forces Shaping the Physical Environment of Cities in the Developing Countries: The Ibadan Case. *Land Econ.*, November 1973, *49*(4), pp. 424–31.

Onigkeit, Dietmar. Zur Berechnung von Einkommenselastizitäten für Prognosen. (The Computation of Income Elasticities for Forecasts. With English summary.) *Schweiz. Z. Volkswirtsch. Statist.*, December 1973, *109*(4), pp. 597–602.

Oniki, Hajime. Comparative Dynamics (Sensitivity Analysis) in Optimal Control Theory. *J. Econ. Theory,* June 1973, *6*(3), pp. 265–83.

Onitiri, H. M. A. The International Aspects of Economic Independence. In *Ghai, D., ed.,* 1973, pp. 35–44.

Onoe, Hisao. Problems of Japanese Economic Policy at the Turning-Point in Planning. *Rivista Int. Sci. Econ. Com.,* August-September 1973, *20*(8–9), pp. 794–803.

Onsi, Mohamed. Factor Analysis of Behavioral Variables Affecting Budgetary Slack. *Accounting Rev.,* July 1973, *48*(3), pp. 535–48.

Oohashi, Ryuken. Working Class in the Present World—Statistics and Their Meaning. *Kyoto Univ. Econ. Rev.,* April–October 1973, *43*(1–2), pp. 1–29.

Ooms, Van Doorn and Keohane, Robert O. The Multinational Enterprise and World Political Economy. In *Henley, D. S., ed.,* 1973, pp. 241–77.

Oosterveen, Karla and Laslett, Peter. Long-term Trends in Bastardy in England: A Study of the Illegitimacy Figures in the Parish Registers and in the Reports of the Registrar General, 1561–1960. *Population Stud.,* July 1973, *27*(2), pp. 255–86.

Ophek, Eli. On Samuelson's Analysis of Land Rent. *Amer. J. Econ. Soc.,* July 1973, *32*(3), pp. 306–10.

Ophir, Tsvi. Introducing Probabilities and Present Value Analysis into Taxation: A Comment. *Accounting Rev.,* July 1973, *48*(3), pp. 594.

_____ **and Falk, Haim.** The Effect of Risk on the Use of Financial Statements by Investment Decision-Makers: A Case Study. *Accounting Rev.,* April 1973, *48*(2), pp. 323–38.

_____ **and Falk, Haim.** The Influence of Differences in Accounting Policies on Investment Decisions. *J. Acc. Res.,* Spring 1973, *11*(1), pp. 108–16.

Ophuls, William. Leviathan or Oblivion? In *Daly, H. E., ed.,* 1973, pp. 215–30.

Opoku-Owusu, K. Problems in the Provision of Institutional Finance for Agricultural Development in Ghana. In *Ofori, I. M., ed.,* 1973, pp. 164–76.

Oppenheimer, Valerie K. A Sociologist's Skepticism. In *Ginzberg, E. and Yohalem, A. M., eds.,* 1973, pp. 30–38.

Orazem, Frank; Biere, Arlo and Sjo, John. Undergraduate Program Revision at Kansas State University. *Amer. J. Agr. Econ.,* Part I, November 1973, *55*(4), pp. 604–10.

Ord, H. W. The Employment of Economists in Africa. In *Livingstone, I., et al., eds.,* 1973, pp. 147–51.

Orgler, Yair E. and Lev, Baruch. Analysis of the Lease-or-Buy Decision: Comment. *J. Finance,* September 1973, *28*(4), pp. 1022–23.

O'Riordan, T. An Analysis of the Use and Management of Campgrounds in British Columbia Provincial Parks. *Econ. Geogr.,* October 1973, *49*(4), pp. 298–308.

O'Riordan, W. K. Elasticity of Demand for Petrol in Ireland: Reply. *Econ. Soc. Rev.,* October 1973, *5*(1), pp. 111–12.

Orita, Sadao. National Nutrition Survey in Japan. In *Berg, A.; Scrimshaw, N. S. and Call, D. L., eds.,* 1973, pp. 293–98.

Orleans, Leo A. and Suttmeier, Richard P. The Mao Ethic and Environmental Quality. In *Wilber, C. K., ed.,* 1973, pp. 258–65.

Ornstein, Stanley I. Concentration and Profits. In *Weston, J. F. and Ornstein, S. I., eds.,* 1973, pp. 87–102.

_____ Market Structure and Industry Growth: Comment. *Miss. Val. J. Bus. Econ.,* Fall 1973, *9*(1), pp. 83–86.

_____, **et al.** Determinants of Market Structure. *Southern Econ. J.,* April 1973, *39*(4), pp. 612–25.

_____ **and Weston, J. Fred.** Trends and Causes of Concentration—A Survey. In *Weston, J. F. and Ornstein, S. I., eds.,* 1973, pp. 3–21.

Oron, Yitzhak; Pines, David and Sheshinski, Eytan. Optimum vs. Equilibrium Land Use Pattern and Congestion Toll. *Bell J. Econ. Manage. Sci.,* Autumn 1973, *4*(2), pp. 619–36.

Orosel, Gerhard O. A Linear Growth Model Including Education. *Z. Nationalökon.,* 1973, *33*(3–4), pp. 251–79.

_____ A Note on the Factor–Price Frontier. *Z. Nationalökon.,* 1973, *33*(1–2), pp. 103–14.

O'Rourke, A. Desmond. Commonality, Fishery Resources, Potential and Policy: Reply. *Amer. J. Agr. Econ.,* August 1973, *55*(3), pp. 530–31.

Orr, John A. The Rise and Fall of Steel's Human Relations Committee. *Labor Hist.,* Winter 1973, *14*(1), pp. 69–81.

Orsi, Renzo; Adams, F. Gerard and Clavijo, Fernando. A Macroeconomic Model of Belgium: Anelise. *Rech. Écon. Louvain,* September 1973, *39*(3), pp. 303–26.

Orvis, Charles C.; Lewis, Darrell R. and Wentworth, Donald R. Economics in the Junior Colleges: Terminal or Transfer? *J. Econ. Educ.,* Spring 1973, *4*(2), pp. 100–10.

Osana, Hiroaki. Externalities and the Basic Theorems of Welfare Economics: A Supplementary Note. *J. Econ. Theory,* February 1973, *6*(1), pp. 91–93.

_____ On the Boundedness of an Economy with Externalities. *Rev. Econ. Stud.,* July 1973, *40*(3), pp. 321–31.

Osborn, Richards C. The Supply of Equity Capital by the SBICs. *Quart. Rev. Econ. Bus.,* Spring 1973, *13*(1), pp. 69–86.

Osborn, Richard Warren. The Fallacy of the Five Million Women: A Re-Estimate: Further Reactions. *Demography,* November 1973, *10*(4), pp. 673–77.

Osborne, D. K. On the Rationality of Limit Pricing. *J. Ind. Econ.,* September 1973, *22*(1), pp. 71–80.

Osgood, Russell K. Mutual-to-Stock Conversions and the Federal Home Loan Bank Board. *Yale Law J.,* January 1973, *82*(3), pp. 559–72.

Oshima, Keichi. Research and Development and Economic Growth in Japan. In *Williams, B. R., ed.,* 1973, pp. 310–23.

Oslizlok, J. S. Community Regional Policy. *Irish Banking Rev.,* December 1973, pp. 15–22.

Ossola, Rinaldo. Central Bank Interventions and Eurocurrency Markets. *Banca Naz. Lavoro Quart. Rev.,* March 1973, (104), pp. 29–45.

Osteryoung, Jerome S. Multiple Goals in the Capital Budgeting Decision. In *Cochrane, J. L. and Zel-*

eny, M., eds., 1973, pp. 447–57.

Ostlund, Lyman E. A Further Caution: It's Innovativeness Overlap. *J. Marketing Res.,* May 1973, *10* (2), pp. 225–26.

Ostrom, Elinor and Parks, Roger B. Suburban Police Departments: Too Many and Too Small? In *Masotti, L. H. and Hadden, J. K., eds.,* 1973, pp. 367–402.

Ostrom, Vincent. The Crisis of Confidence. In *Ostrom, V.,* 1973, pp. 1–22.

—— The Work of the Contemporary Political Economists. In *Ostrom, V.,* 1973, pp. 48–73.

Ostroy, Joseph M. The Informational Efficiency of Monetary Exchange. *Amer. Econ. Rev.,* September 1973, *63*(4), pp. 597–610.

Otani, Yoshihiko. Neo-Classical Technology Sets and Properties of Production Possibility Sets. *Econometrica,* July 1973, *41*(4), pp. 667–82.

Oţoiu, Alexandrina. Cu privire la metodele de evidenţă a cheltuielilor de producţie şi de calculaţie a preţului de cost. (On the Concept and Classification of the Accounts Keeping Methods of Production Expenses and of Cost Price Calculation. With English summary.) *Stud. Cercet. Econ.,* 1973, (1), pp. 141–49.

—— Probleme ale calculaţiei preţului de cost în industria de încălţăminte. (Problems of the Calculation of the Cost Price in the Footwear Industry. With English summary.) *Stud. Cercet. Econ.,* 1973, (3), pp. 121–39.

Ott, Attiat F. Education. In *Ott, D. J., et al.,* 1973, pp. 113–52.

—— and Ott, David J. The Effect of Nonneutral Taxation on the Use of Capital by Sector. *J. Polit. Econ.,* July-August 1973, *81*(4), pp. 972–81.

——; Penner, Rudolph G. and Ott, David J. Income Security. In *Ott, D. J., et al.,* 1973, pp. 193–214.

Ott, David J. The Budget Outlook: An Overview. In *Ott, D. J., et al.,* 1973, pp. 11–27.

—— The Federal Revenue System: Discussion. *J. Finance,* May 1973, *28*(2), pp. 499–500.

——, et al. Introduction and Summary of Findings. In *Ott, D. J., et al.,* 1973, pp. 1–9.

—— and Ott, Attiat F. The Effect of Nonneutral Taxation on the Use of Capital by Sector. *J. Polit. Econ.,* July-August 1973, *81*(4), pp. 972–81.

——; Ott, Attiat F. and Penner, Rudolph G. Income Security. In *Ott, D. J., et al.,* 1973, pp. 193–214.

—— and Vasquez, Thomas. Agriculture. In *Ott, D. J., et al.,* 1973, pp. 53–65.

Ouattara, Alassane D. Trade Effects of the Association of African Countries with the European Economic Community. *Int. Monet. Fund Staff Pap.,* July 1973, *20*(2), pp. 499–543.

Oudet, Bruno A. The Variation of the Return of Stocks in Periods of Inflation. *J. Financial Quant. Anal.,* March 1973, *8*(2), pp. 247–58.

—— and von Furstenberg, George M. The Valuation of Common Stocks During Periods of Inflation. *Z. Nationalökon.,* 1973, *33*(1–2), pp. 67–78.

Oulton, W. N. and Heath, J. B. A Cost-benefit Study of Alternative Runway Investments at Edinburgh (Turnhouse) Airport. In *Wolfe, J. N., ed.,* 1973, pp. 117–39.

Ousset, Jean and Nègre, Michel. Des comptes nationaux aux comptes régionaux. L'exemple des comptes de l'Agriculture. (Regional and National Accounts: The Example of French Agricultural Accounts. With English summary.) *Revue Écon.,* July 1973, *24*(4), pp. 549–87.

Over, Mead; Ahmad, Meekal A. and Flesher, John. An Econometric Test of a Zero Elasticity of Substitution Production Function for Pakistan. *Pakistan Econ. Soc. Rev.,* Winter 1973, *11*(4), pp. 443–53.

Overbeek, Johannes. Mercantilism, Physiocracy and Population Theory. *S. Afr. J. Econ.,* June 1973, *41* (2), pp. 167–74.

—— Wicksell on Population. *Econ. Develop. Cult. Change,* January 1973, *21*(2), pp. 205–11.

Ow, Chin Hock and Blitz, Rudolph C. A Cross-Sectional Analysis of Women's Participation in the Professions. *J. Polit. Econ.,* January-February 1973, *81*(1), pp. 131–44.

Owen, Bruce M. Newspaper and Television Station Joint Ownership. *Antitrust Bull.,* Winter 1973, *18* (4), pp. 787–807.

—— Pricing in Combined Gas and Electric Utilities: Reply. *Antitrust Bull.,* Spring 1973, *18*(1), pp. 99.

—— A View from the President's Office of Telecommunications Policy. In *Park, R. E., ed.,* 1973, pp. 3–14.

Owen, Carol and Witton, Ronald A. National Division and Mobilization: A Reinterpretation of Primacy. *Econ. Develop. Cult. Change,* January 1973, *21*(2), pp. 325–37.

—— A Note on Conditions Supporting the Covariation of External and Internal Conflict. *Econ. Develop. Cult. Change,* October 1973, *22* (1), pp. 114–23.

Owen, Joel and Brief, Richard P. Present Value Models and the Multi-Asset Problem. *Accounting Rev.,* October 1973, *48*(4), pp. 690–95.

—— A Reformulation of the Estimation Problem. *J. Acc. Res.,* Spring 1973, *11*(1), pp. 1–15.

Owen, John D. The Distribution of Educational Resources in Large American Cities: Reply. *J. Human Res.,* Fall 1973, *8*(4), pp. 518–19.

Owen, John E. The US Economy—Prosperity and Problems. *Rivista Int. Sci. Econ. Com.,* October 1973, *20*(10), pp. 973–84.

Oxenfeldt, Alfred R., et al. Attitudes and Pricing. In *Britt, S. H. and Boyd, H. W., Jr., eds.,* 1973, pp. 372–86.

Oyejide, T. Ademola. Tariff Protection and Industrialization via Import Substitution: An Empirical Analysis of the Nigerian Experience. *Econ. Bull. Ghana, Sec. Ser.,* 1973, *3*(3), pp. 20–27.

—— Tariff Protection and Industrialization via Import Substitution: An Empirical Analysis of the Nigerian Experience. *Bangladesh Econ. Rev.,* October 1973, *1*(4), pp. 331–40.

Oza, Ghanshyambhai. Inaugural Speech. *Artha-Vikas,* January-July 1973, *9*(1–2), pp. 5–10.

Ozawa, Terutomo and Hemley, David D. Intra-Racial and Minority Inter-Racial Discrimination. *J. Econ. Bus.,* Spring-Summer 1973, *25*(3), pp. 206–07.

—— and McDonnell, C. F. On the Geometric

Measurement of an Optimum Tariff. *Indian Econ. J.*, July–September 1973, *21*(1), pp. 33–36.

Özmucur, Süleyman and Krzyzaniak, Marian. The Distribution of Income and the Short-run Burden of Taxes in Turkey, 1968. *Finanzarchiv*, 1973, *32* (1), pp. 69–97.

de Pablo, Juan C. and Dagnino Pastore, José M. Sobre la restricción de ahorro-inversión en los modelos de dos brechas. (On the Savings Constraint in Two Gap Models. With English summary.) *Económica*, May-August 1973, *19*(2), pp. 157–64.

Pack, Janet Rothenberg. Determinants of Migration to Central Cities. *J. Reg. Sci.*, August 1973, *13*(2), pp. 249–60.

Packard, Philip C. On the Apparent Benefits of Higher Productivity: An Arithmetical Illustration: A Comment. *J. Devel. Stud.*, April 1973, *9*(3), pp. 451–52.

Packer, Arnold H. A Budget Structured to Reflect Economic Objectives. *J. Finance*, May 1973, *28* (2), pp. 467–80.

_____ **and Park, Seong H.** Distortions in Relative Wages and Shifts in the Phillips Curve. *Rev. Econ. Statist.*, February 1973, *55*(1), pp. 16–22.

Paelinck, J. and Van Rompuy, P. Regionaal en sectoraal subsidiebeleid: Economische theorie en modellen. (Regional and Sectoral Subsidies—Economic Theory and Models. With English summary.) *Tijdschr. Econ.*, 1973, *18*(1), pp. 39–55.

Paez-Franco, Jaime. The National Nutrition Program in Colombia. In *Berg, A.; Scrimshaw, N. S. and Call, D. L., eds.*, 1973, pp. 335–56.

Pagan, Adrian. Efficient Estimation of Models with Composite Disturbance Terms. *J. Econometrics*, December 1973, *1*(4), pp. 329–40.

Page, Benjamin I. and Brody, Richard A. Indifference, Alienation and Rational Decisions: The Effects of Candidate Evaluations on Turnout and the Vote. *Public Choice*, Summer 1973, *15*, pp. 1–17.

Pagé, Jean-Pierre and Bonnaud, Jean-Jacques. L'utilisation d'un modèle de simulation économique dans la procédure de préparation du VIe Plan (1970–1975). (The Utilisation of a Mathematical Economic Model in the Process of Elaboration of the French VIth Plan (1970–1975). With English summary.) *Revue Écon.*, November 1973, *24*(6), pp. 988–1025.

_____ **and Courbis, Raymond.** Techniques de projection macro-économique et choix du Plan français. (Macro-Economic Forecasting Techniques and Decision Making in the French Planning System. With English summary.) *Revue Écon.*, November 1973, *24*(6), pp. 951–87.

Page, Talbot. Failure of Bribes and Standards for Pollution Abatement. *Natural Res. J.*, October 1973, *13*(4), pp. 677–704.

_____ **and Ferejohn, John.** A Note on "Voting or a Price System in a Competitive Market Structure." *Amer. Polit. Sci. Rev.*, March 1973, *67*(1), pp. 157–60.

Page, William. The Non-renewable Resources Subsystem. In *Cole, H. S. D., et al., eds.*, 1973, pp. 33–42.

_____ Population Forecasting. In *Cole, H. S. D., et al., eds.*, 1973, pp. 159–74.

_____ The Population Sub-system. In *Cole, H. S. D., et al., eds.*, 1973, pp. 43–55.

Paglin, Morton and Fogarty, Michael. Equity and the Property Tax: A Reply. *Nat. Tax J.*, December 1973, *26*(4), pp. 651–52.

Pagoulatos, Emilio and Christian, James W. Domestic Financial Markets in Developing Economies: An Econometric Analysis. *Kyklos*, 1973, *26*(1), pp. 75–90.

Painter, William H. An Analysis of Recent Proposals for Reform of Federal Securities Legislation. *Mich. Law Rev.*, August 1973, *71*(8), pp. 1576–1638.

Paish, F. W. The Prospects for Increasing Output. *Lloyds Bank Rev.*, January 1973, (107), pp. 1–18.

Pajestka, Jøsef. Need for Greater World-Wide Rationality. In *[Tinbergen, J.]*, 1973, pp. 273–83.

_____ General Development Relationships and Social Factors for Progress. *Eastern Europ. Econ.*, Fall 1973, *12*(1), pp. 45–81.

_____ The Socio-Economic Factors of Progress. *Acta Oecon.*, 1973, *10*(1), pp. 3–20.

Pal, D. N. Agrarian Revolution. *Econ. Aff.*, September-October 1973, *18*(9–10), pp. 439–49.

Pal, Sasanka Shekhar. Productivity of Farm Labour in the Context of Rural Unemployment (A Case Study of 79 Farms in a Village) *Econ. Aff.*, May 1973, *18*(5), pp. 241–48.

Palánkai, T. and Veress, P. Effect of the United Kingdom's Entry Into the Common Market on Anglo-Hungarian Relations. *Acta Oecon.*, 1973, *10*(1), pp. 81–94.

Palda, Kristian S. Production Functions and Performance Evaluation. In *Palda, K. S., ed.*, 1973, pp. 34–42.

Paldam, Martin. An Empirical Analysis of the Relationship between Inflation and Economic Growth in 12 Countries, 1950 to 1969. *Swedish J. Econ.*, December 1973, *75*(4), pp. 420–27.

Palliser, David M. York under the Tudors: The Trading Life of the Northern Capital. In *Everitt, A., ed.*, 1973, pp. 39–59.

Palmer, John P. A Further Analysis of Provincial Trucking Regulation. *Bell J. Econ. Manage. Sci.*, Autumn 1973, *4*(2), pp. 655–64.

_____ The Profit Variability Effects of the Managerial Enterprise. *Western Econ. J.*, June 1973, *11*(2), pp. 228–31.

_____ The Profit-Performance Effects of the Separation of Ownership from Control in Large U.S. Industrial Corporations. *Bell J. Econ. Manage. Sci.*, Spring 1973, *4*(1), pp. 293–303.

_____ Public and Private Capital and the Capital Coefficient in Canada: Comment. *Quart. Rev. Econ. Bus.*, Spring 1973, *13*(1), pp. 97–100.

_____ **and Palomba, Neil A.** Skill Differentials and their Determinants. *Amer. Econ.*, Fall 1973, *17* (2), pp. 130–36.

Palmerio, Giovanni. Contributo alla teoria dello sviluppo dell'impresa. (A Contribution to the Theory of the Growth of the Firm. With English summary.) *L'Industria*, January-June 1973, (1–2), pp. 59–88.

Palomba, Neil A. and Palmer, John P. Skill Differentials and their Determinants. *Amer. Econ.*, Fall

1973, *17*(2), pp. 130–36.

Pandey, Ram Lala; Mishra, G. P. and Tripathy, B. N. Role of Banking in Financing Rural Credit. *Econ. Aff.*, July 1973, *18*(7), pp. 313–25.

Pandey, R. K. and Capel, R. E. Evaluating Demand for Deer Hunting: A Comparison of Methods. *Can. J. Agr. Econ.*, November 1973, *21*(3), pp. 6–14.

Pandey, V. K. and Takayama, T. Temporal Equilibrium Analysis of Rice and Wheat in India. In *Judge, G. G. and Takayama, T., eds.*, 1973, pp. 579–96.

Pandit, Shrikrishna A. IMF Resident Representatives. *Finance Develop.*, September 1973, *10*(3), pp. 30–33.

———— Nationalization of the Banks in India. *Finance Develop.*, March 1973, *10*(1), pp. 32–37.

Pang, Eng Fong. A Note on Labour Underutilization in Singapore. *Malayan Econ. Rev.*, April 1973, *18* (1), pp. 15–23.

Panić, M. and Close, R. E. Profitability of British Manufacturing Industry. *Lloyds Bank Rev.*, July 1973, (109), pp. 17–30.

Pant, S. P. and Takayama, T. An Investigation of Agricultural Planning Models: A Case Study of the Indian's Food Economy. In *Judge, G. G. and Takayama, T., eds.*, 1973, pp. 597–623.

Papadia, Francesco. Nota sugli indici di concentrazione. (Essays on the Indexes of Concentration. With English summary.) *L'Impresa*, 1973, *15* (3–4), pp. 265–72.

Papadopoulos, C. Factors Determining Australian Saleyard Prices for Beef Cattle. *Quart. Rev. Agr. Econ.*, July 1973, *26*(3), pp. 159–70.

Papageorgiou, G. J. The Impact of the Environment upon the Spatial Distribution of Population and Land Values. *Econ. Geogr.*, July 1973, *49*(3), pp. 251–56.

Papandreou, Andreas G. The Multinational Corporation. *Amer. Econ.*, Fall 1973, *17*(2), pp. 154–60.

———— The Multinational Firm: Bane or Boon?: Discussion. *J. Finance*, May 1973, *28*(2), pp. 455–57.

Papanek, Gustav F. Aid, Foreign Private Investment, Savings, and Growth in Less Developed Countries. *J. Polit. Econ.*, January-February 1973, *81*(1), pp. 120–30.

———— The Effect of Aid and Other Resource Transfers on Savings and Growth in Less-Developed Countries: A Reply. *Econ. J.*, September 1973, *83* (331), pp. 870–74.

Paraskevopoulos, Christos C. The Impact of Regional Wage Differentials. *Growth Change*, April 1973, *4*(2), pp. 40–42.

———— Shifts in Industry Employment, Population Size and the Wage Structure: An Analysis of Two National Industries. In *Mattila, J. M. and Thompson, W. R., eds.*, 1973, pp. 105–25.

Pardue, Morris and Melitz, Jacques. The Demand and Supply of Commercial Bank Loans. *J. Money, Credit, Banking*, May 1973, *5*(2), pp. 669–92.

Parguez, Alain. Sismondi et la théorie du déséquilibre macro-économique. (Sismondi and Macro-Disequilibrium Theory. With English summary.) *Revue Écon.*, September 1973, *24*(5), pp. 837–66.

Parikh, A. United States, European, and World Demand Functions for Coffee. *Amer. J. Agr. Econ.*,

August 1973, *55*(3), pp. 490–94.

Paris, Quirino and Rausser, Gordon C. Sufficient Conditions for Aggregation of Linear Programming Models. *Amer. J. Agr. Econ.*, Part I, November 1973, *55*(4), pp. 659–66.

Parish, E. M. A.; Sully, Floyd and Evans, R. G. Medical Productivity, Scale Effects, and Demand Generation. *Can. J. Econ.*, August 1973, *6*(3), pp. 376–93.

Parish, William L., Jr. Internal Migration and Modernization: The European Case. *Econ. Develop. Cult. Change*, Part I, July 1973, *21*(4), pp. 591–609.

Park, Rolla Edward. A Bayesian Framework for Thinking about the Role of Analysis. In *Park, R. E., ed.*, 1973, pp. 57–61.

———— The Role of Analysis in Regulatory Decision-making: The Case of Cable Television: Conclusion. In *Park, R. E., ed.*, 1973, pp. 71–78.

Park, Rosemary. Like Their Fathers Instead. In *Ginzberg, E. and Yohalem, A. M., eds.*, 1973, pp. 39–57.

Park, Se-Hark. On Input-Output Multipliers with Errors in Input-Output Coefficients. *J. Econ. Theory*, August 1973, *6*(4), pp. 399–403.

Park, Seong H. and Packer, Arnold H. Distortions in Relative Wages and Shifts in the Phillips Curve. *Rev. Econ. Statist.*, February 1973, *55*(1), pp. 16–22.

Park, Sung-Jo. Ökonomische und politische Zielkonflikte in der Gestaltung des kommunistischen Aussenhandels: Autarkie und Pragmatismus in der Aussenwirtschaftspolitik der Volksrepublik China. (Autarky and Pragmatism in the Foreign Trade Policy of the People's Republic of China. With English summary.) *Z. Wirtschaft. Sozialwissen.*, 1973, *93*(5), pp. 587–600.

———— and Kokulinsky, Detlef. Die Entwicklungshilfe als ein aussenpolitisches Instrument der Volksrepublik China. (Development Aid as Instrument of Foreign Policy of the People's Republic of China. With English summary.) *Z. ges. Staatswiss.*, August 1973, *129*(3), pp. 559–72.

Park, Yung C. The Role of Money in Stabilization Policy in Developing Countries. *Int. Monet. Fund Staff Pap.*, July 1973, *20*(2), pp. 379–418.

———— The Transmission Process and the Relative Effectiveness of Monetary and Fiscal Policy in a Two-Sector Neoclassical Model. *J. Money, Credit, Banking*, May 1973, *5*(2), pp. 595–622.

Parker, Edith H. New Directions in Agricultural Economics Curricula, University of California, Davis. *Amer. J. Agr. Econ.*, Part II, November 1973, *55*(4), pp. 748–49.

Parker, William N. Technology, Resources, and Economic Change in the West. In *Youngson, A. J., ed.*, 1973, pp. 62–78.

———— Through Growth and Beyond: Three Decades in Economic and Business History. In *[Williamson, H. F.]*, 1973, pp. 15–47.

Parkin, Michael. A Continuous Disequilibrium Econometric Model of the Domestic and International Portfolio Behaviour of the UK Banking System: Discussion. In *Parkin, M., ed.*, 1973, pp. 291–93.

———— The Discount Houses' Role in the Money Supply Control Process Under the "Competition and Credit Control" Regime. *Manchester Sch. Econ. Soc. Stud.*, March 1973, *41*(1), pp. 89–105.

_____ The Short-Run and Long-Run Trade-Offs Between Inflation and Unemployment in Australia. *Australian Econ. Pap.*, December 1973, *12*(21), pp. 127–44.

_____ The 1973 Report of the President's Council of Economic Advisers: A Critique. *Amer. Econ. Rev.*, September 1973, *63*(4), pp. 535–45.

_____ and Gray, M. R. Portfolio Diversification as Optimal Precautionary Behaviour. In *Morishima, M., et al.*, 1973, pp. 301–15.

Parks, Richard W. and Barten, Anton P. A Cross-Country Comparison of the Effects of Prices, Income and Population Composition on Consumption Patterns. *Econ. J.*, September 1973, *83*(331), pp. 834–52.

Parks, Roger B. and Ostrom, Elinor. Suburban Police Departments: Too Many and Too Small? In *Masotti, L. H. and Hadden, J. K., eds.*, 1973, pp. 367–402.

Parnes, Herbert S. The Role of Forecasting and Planning Manpower Programs: Discussion. In *Aronson, R. L., ed.*, 1973, pp. 62–64.

Paroush, Jacob. Efficient Purchasing Behavior and Order Relations in Consumption. *Kyklos*, 1973, *26*(1), pp. 91–112.

Parr, John B. Structure and Size in the Urban System of Lösch. *Econ. Geogr.*, July 1973, *49*(3), pp. 185–212.

_____ and Suzuki, Keisuke. Settlement Populations and the Lognormal Distribution. *Urban Stud.*, October 1973, *10*(3), pp. 335–52.

Parrinello, Sergio. Distribuzione, sviluppo e commercio internazionale. (Distribution, Growth and International Trade. With English summary.) *Econ. Int.*, May 1973, *26*(2), pp. 197–229.

Parrish, Charles J. Bureaucracy, Democracy, and Development: Some Considerations Based on the Chilean Case. In *Thurber, C. E. and Graham, L. S., eds.*, 1973, pp. 229–59.

Parrish, Evelyn M. U.S. Balance of Payments Developments: Fourth Quarter and Year 1972. *Surv. Curr. Bus.*, March 1973, *53*(3), pp. 22–30, 52.

Parrish, Thomas. The Foundation: "A Special American Institution." In *Heimann, F. F., ed.*, 1973, pp. 7–42.

Parry, Thomas G. The International Firm and National Economic Policy: A Survey of Some Issues. *Econ. J.*, December 1973, *83*(332), pp. 1201–21.

Parsons, Donald O. Quit Rates Over Time: A Search and Information Approach. *Amer. Econ. Rev.*, June 1973, *63*(3), pp. 390–401.

Parsons, S. A. and Girdlestone, J. N. The Regional Supply Pattern of Beef Cattle for Slaughter in Queensland. *Quart. Rev. Agr. Econ.*, January 1973, *26*(1), pp. 44–60.

Parthasarathy, L. S. Chit Funds: Commission's Report and Suggestions. In *Simha, S. L. N., ed.*, 1973, pp. 272–78.

Parvin, D. W., Jr. Estimation of Irrigation Response from Time-Series Data on Nonirrigated Crops. *Amer. J. Agr. Econ.*, February 1973, *55*(1), pp. 73–76.

Parzych, Kenneth M. The U.S. Balance-of-Payments:

A Restructuring of Commercial Policy. *Rivista Int. Sci. Econ. Com.*, December 1973, *20*(12), pp. 1179–89.

Pásara, Luís and Santistevan, Jorge. "Industrial Communities" and Trade Unions in Peru: A Preliminary Analysis. *Int. Lab. Rev.*, August-September 1973, *108*(2–3), pp. 127–42.

Pasour, E. C., Jr. Economic Growth and Agriculture: An Evaluation of the Compensation Principle. *Amer. J. Agr. Econ.*, Part I, November 1973, *55*(4), pp. 611–16.

_____ Real Property Taxes and Farm Real Estate Values: Incidence and Implications. *Amer. J. Agr. Econ.*, Part I, November 1973, *55*(4), pp. 549–56.

_____ and Hyman, David N. Real Property Taxes, Local Public Services, and Residential Property Values. *Southern Econ. J.*, April 1973, *39*(4), pp. 601–11.

_____ and Hyman, D. N. Note: Property Tax Differentials and Residential Rents in North Carolina. *Nat. Tax J.*, June 1973, *26*(2), pp. 303–07.

Passell, Peter. Corporate Farming in the United States: Discussion. *J. Econ. Hist.*, March 1973, *33* (1), pp. 296–98.

_____; Roberts, Marc J. and Ross, Leonard. The Limits to Growth: A Review. In *Enthoven, A. C. and Freeman, A. M., III, eds.*, 1973, pp. 230–34.

Passy, Ury and Pasternak, Hanoch. Bicriterion Functions in Annual Activity Planning. In *Ross, M., ed.*, 1973, pp. 325–41.

_____ Bicriterion Mathematical Programs with Boolean Variables. In *Cochrane, J. L. and Zeleny, M., eds.*, 1973, pp. 327–48.

Pasternak, Hanoch and Passy, Ury. Bicriterion Functions in Annual Activity Planning. In *Ross, M., ed.*, 1973, pp. 325–41.

_____ Bicriterion Mathematical Programs with Boolean Variables. In *Cochrane, J. L. and Zeleny, M., eds.*, 1973, pp. 327–48.

Patankar, H. R. Some Observations about Efficacy of Financial Incentives on Industrial Development in Backward Districts. *Artha-Vikas*, January-July 1973, *9*(1–2), pp. 220–29.

Patel, I. G. La crisi monetaria del 1971 e gli insegnamenti da trarne. Intervento. (The Monetary Crisis of 1971. The Lessons to be Learned. With English summary.) *Bancaria*, March 1973, *29*(3), pp. 319–25.

_____ Some Reflections on Trade and Development. In *Streeten, P., ed.*, 1973, pp. 35–48.

_____ The Strategy of Indian Planning. In *Wadhva, C. D., ed.*, 1973, pp. 108–15.

Patel, V. G. Promotion of Entrepreneurship and Regional Development. *Artha-Vikas*, January-July 1973, *9*(1–2), pp. 214–19.

_____ and Shah, Anil C. An Integrated Strategy for Backward Districts Industrial Development. *Artha-Vikas*, January-July 1973, *9*(1–2), pp. 203–13.

Pathak, H. N. Developing Entrepreneurship in Backward Regions. *Artha-Vikas*, January-July 1973, *9*(1–2), pp. 47–54.

Pathak, Mahesh T. Development of Backward Areas: Problems and Prospects. *Artha-Vikas*, January-July 1973, *9*(1–2), pp. 25–46.

_____; Desai, Mahendra D. and Charan, A. S. Development of Agriculture in Backward Regions of

Gujarat: Facts and Issues. *Artha-Vikas,* January-July 1973, *9*(1–2), pp. 100–38.

Pathak, Pravin G. and Alagh, Yoginder K. Industrial Development in Gujarat: Regional Structure and Policies. *Artha-Vikas,* January-July 1973, *9*(1–2), pp. 143–84.

Patinkin, Don. Frank Knight as Teacher. *Amer. Econ. Rev.,* December 1973, *63*(5), pp. 787–810.

—— In Search of the "Wheel of Wealth": On the Origins of Frank Knight's Circular-Flow Diagram. *Amer. Econ. Rev.,* December 1973, *63*(5), pp. 1037–46.

—— On the Monetary Economics of Chicagoans and Non-Chicagoans: Comment. *Southern Econ. J.,* January 1973, *39*(3), pp. 454–59.

Patman, Wright. Commercial Banks and Their Trust Activities. In *Andreano, R. L., ed.,* 1973, pp. R344–19.

Paton, W. A. and Littleton, A. C. An Introduction to Corporate Accounting Standards. In *Thomas, W. E., Jr., ed.,* 1973, pp. 446–53.

Patrick, D. L.; Bush, J. W. and Chen, M. M. Health Status Index in Cost Effectiveness: Analysis of PKU Program. In *Berg, R. L., ed.,* 1973, pp. 172–93.

Patrick, George F. and Kehrberg, Earl W. Costs and Returns of Education in Five Agricultural Areas of Eastern Brazil. *Amer. J. Agr. Econ.,* May 1973, *55*(2), pp. 145–53.

Patrick, Hugh T. and Wai, U Tun. Stock and Bond Issues and Capital Markets in Less Developed Countries. *Int. Monet. Fund Staff Pap.,* July 1973, *20*(2), pp. 253–317.

Patrick, John D. Establishing Convergent Decentralized Policy Assignment. *J. Int. Econ.,* February 1973, *3*(1), pp. 37–51.

Patrucco, Carlo. Dimensione sociale del fenomeno distributivo commerciale. (The Social Dimensions of the Distributive Phenomenon. With English summary.) *L'Impresa,* 1973, *15*(1), pp. 24–26.

—— Le imprese commerciali di fronte all'evoluzione strutturale del loro settore. (Trade Companies and the Developing Structures of their Sector. With English summary.) *L'Impresa,* 1973, *15*(9–10), pp. 619–22.

—— Ricerche geo-commerciali. (Geo-Commercial Research. With English summary.) *L'Impresa,* 1973, *15*(1), pp. 40–44.

Pattanaik, Prasanta K. On the Stability of Sincere Voting Situations. *J. Econ. Theory,* December 1973, *6*(6), pp. 558–74.

Patterson, D. Jeanne. Indiana's Regions: How Delimited? *Indiana Bus. Rev.,* January-February 1973, *48*, pp. 10–20.

Pattison, Allan. The Economics of Data Collection Systems. In *Aislabie, C., ed.,* 1973, pp. 119–44.

Pattison, John C. Some Aspects of Price Discrimination in the Airline Industry. *J. Econ. Issues,* March 1973, *7*(1), pp. 136–47.

Paukert, Felix. Income Distribution at Different Levels of Development: A Survey of Evidence. *Int. Lab. Rev.,* August-September 1973, *108*(2–3), pp. 97–125.

Paul, Robert J. Psychographics, Demographics and Affluence—Predictors of Individual Decision Pat-

terns? *Marquette Bus. Rev.,* Fall 1973, *17*(3), pp. 144–48.

Paulson, Albert S. and Garrison, Charles B. An Entropy Measure of the Geographic Concentration of Economic Activity. *Econ. Geogr.,* October 1973, *49*(4), pp. 319–24.

—— Entropy as a Measure of the Areal Concentration of Water-Oriented Industry. *Water Resources Res.,* April 1973, *9*(2), pp. 263–69.

Pauly, Mark V. Income Redistribution as a Local Public Good. *J. Public Econ.,* February 1973, *2*(1), pp. 35–58.

—— Public Utilities and the Theory of Power: Comment. In *Russell, M., ed.,* 1973, pp. 27–33.

—— **and Redisch, Michael.** The Not-For-Profit Hospital as a Physicians' Cooperative. *Amer. Econ. Rev.,* March 1973, *63*(1), pp. 87–99.

Pavitt, K. L. R. Malthus and Other Economists: Some Doomsdays Revisited. In *Cole, H. S. D., et al., eds.,* 1973, pp. 137–58.

—— **and Marstrand, Pauline K.** The Agricultural Sub-system. In *Cole, H. S. D., et al., eds.,* 1973, pp. 56–65.

Pavliuchenko, V. Some Problems in the Long-Term Planning of Purchases of Licenses. *Prob. Econ.,* March 1973, *15*(11), pp. 92–98.

Pavlov, N. V.; Belen'kii, V. Z. and Volkonskii, V. A. Dynamic Input-Output Models in Planning and Price Calculations and Economic Analysis. *Matekon,* Winter 1973-74, *10*(2), pp. 74–101.

Pawakaranond, Lamduan and Robinson, Warren C. Manpower Imbalances in Thailand: Comment. *Western Econ. J.,* September 1973, *11*(3), pp. 375–79.

Pazos, Felipe. Regional Integration of Trade Among Less Developed Countries. In *Streeten, P., ed.,* 1973, pp. 145–75.

Pchenitchny, Boris N. є-Strategies in Differential Games. In *Blaquière, A., ed.,* 1973, pp. 45–99.

Peabody, Gerald E. A Primer on the Critique of Marginal Distribution Theory. *Amer. Econ.,* Fall 1973, *17*(2), pp. 23–27.

Peacock, Alan T. Cost-benefit Analysis and the Political Control of Public Investment. In *Wolfe, J. N., ed.,* 1973, pp. 17–29.

—— Malthus in the Twentieth Century. In *Rectenwald, H. C., ed.,* 1973, pp. 91–98.

—— **and Rowley, Charles K.** Welfare Economics and the Public Regulation of Natural Monopoly: Reply. *J. Public Econ.,* February 1973, *2*(1), pp. 97–100.

—— **and Shaw, G. K.** Fiscal Measures to Create Employment: The Indonesian Case. *Bull. Int. Fiscal Doc.,* November 1973, *27*(11), pp. 443–54.

Peaker, A. Holiday Spending by the British at Home and Abroad. *Nat. Westminster Bank Quart. Rev.,* August 1973, pp. 47–55.

Pearce, David and Nash, Christopher. The Evaluation of Urban Motorway Schemes: A Case Study—Southampton. *Urban Stud.,* June 1973, *10*(2), pp. 129–43.

Pearce, David W. and Common, Michael S. Adaptive Mechanisms, Growth, and the Environment: The Case of Natural Resources. *Can. J. Econ.,* August 1973, *6*(3), pp. 289–300.

Pearce, I. F. and Wise, J. On the Uniqueness of

Competitive Equilibrium: Part I, Unbounded Demand. *Econometrica*, September 1973, *41*(5), pp. 817–28.

Pearse, R. A. and Dent, J. B. Operations Research, Agricultural Research and Agricultural Practice. In *Ross, M., ed.*, 1973, pp. 641–53.

Pechman, Joseph A. International Trends in the Distribution of Tax Burdens: Implications for Tax Policy. *Bull. Int. Fiscal Doc.*, December 1973, *27* (12), pp. 487–95.

_____ Responsiveness of the Federal Individual Income Tax to Changes in Income. *Brookings Pap. Econ. Act.*, 1973, (2), pp. 385–421.

_____ The Rich, the Poor, and the Taxes They Pay. In *Reynolds, L. G.; Green, G. D. and Lewis, D. R., eds.*, 1973, pp. 260–82.

Peck, Stephen C. and Zellner, Arnold. Simulation Experiments with a Quarterly Macroeconometric Model of the U.S. Economy. In *Powell, A. A. and Williams, R. A., eds.*, 1973, pp. 149–68.

Pécsi, K. Capital Movements and Joint Undertakings. In *Kiss, T., ed.*, 1973, pp. 227–34.

Pedersen, Peder J. Har finanspolitikken mistet sin effektivitet? (With English summary.) *Nationalokon. Tidsskr.*, 1973, *111*(3), pp. 327–41.

Peel, David A. The Non-uniqueness of the Dorfman-Steiner Condition: A Note. *Economica, N.S.*, May 1973, *40*(158), pp. 208–09.

_____ Some Implications of Utility Maximizing Firms: A Note. *Bull. Econ. Res.*, November 1973, *25*(2), pp. 148–51.

_____ **and Latham, R. W.** A Comment on Adjustments Costs and the Flexible Accelerator. *Rech. Écon. Louvain*, September 1973, *39*(3), pp. 371–76.

Peel, Evelyn and Scharff, Jack. Impact of Cost-Sharing on Use of Ambulatory Services Under Medicare, 1969. *Soc. Sec. Bull.*, October 1973, *36*(10), pp. 3–24.

Peeran, S. T. Control over Non-Banking Financial Intermediaries by the Reserve Bank. In *Simha, S. L. N., ed.*, 1973, pp. 252–64.

Peirson, C. G. and Bird, R. G. A Study of Convertible Notes Issued in Australia. *Australian Econ. Pap.*, June 1973, *12*(20), pp. 91–105.

Pejovich, Svetozar. The Banking System and the Investment Behavior of the Yugoslav Firm. In *Bornstein, M., ed.*, 1973, pp. 285–311.

_____ Good Old Economic History: Discussion. *J. Econ. Hist.*, March 1973, *33*(1), pp. 41–42.

_____ **and Furubotn, Eirik G.** Property Rights, Economic Decentralization, and the Evolution of the Yugoslav Firm, 1965–1972. *J. Law Econ.*, October 1973, *16*(2), pp. 275–302.

_____ **and Ghazalah, I. A.** The Economics of Vocational and Technical Education: A Report on Three Studies. *Rev. Soc. Econ.*, October 1973, *31* (2), pp. 191–98.

Peleg, Bezalel. A Weakly Maximal Golden-Rule Program for a Multi-Sector Economy. *Int. Econ. Rev.*, October 1973, *14*(3), pp. 574–79.

_____ **and Yaari, Menahem E.** On the Existence of a Consistent Course of Action when Tastes are Changing. *Rev. Econ. Stud.*, July 1973, *40*(3), pp. 391–401.

_____ **and Yaari, Menahem E.** Price Properties of

Optimal Consumption Programmes. In *Mirrlees, J. A. and Stern, N. H., eds.*, 1973, pp. 306–17.

Peles, Yoram and Levhari, David. Market Structure, Quality and Durability. *Bell J. Econ. Manage. Sci.*, Spring 1973, *4*(1), pp. 235–48.

Pelkmans, Jacques. Government Aid to Industry in the Benelux Countries. In *Scaperlanda, A. E., ed.*, 1973, pp. 107–62.

Pelleri, Paolo. Fatti e tendenze del mese in Borsa. (Facts and Tendencies in the Month. With English summary.) *Bancaria*, January 1973, *29*(1), pp. 104–08.

_____ Le borse estere nel 1972. (Foreign Stock Exchanges in 1972. With English summary.) *Bancaria*, February 1973, *29*(2), pp. 164–88.

_____ Le Borse italiane nel 1972. (Italian Stock Market in 1972. With English summary.) *Bancaria*, January 1973, *29*(1), pp. 40–75.

Pellicanò, Giuseppe. Research, Technological Innovation and Management in Italy. *Rev. Econ. Cond. Italy*, November 1973, *27*(6), pp. 381–96.

Peltzman, Sam. An Evaluation of Consumer Protection Legislation: The 1962 Drug Amendments. *J. Polit. Econ.*, September-October 1973, *81*(5), pp. 1049–91.

_____ The Effect of Government Subsidies-in-Kind on Private Expenditures: The Case of Higher Education. *J. Polit. Econ.*, January-February 1973, *81*(1), pp. 1–27.

Pen, Jan. Business Against the Consumer. In *Reynolds, L. G.; Green, G. D. and Lewis, D. R., eds.*, 1973, pp. 190–200.

_____ Trade Union Attitudes Toward Central Wage Policy: Remarks on the Dutch Experience. In *Sturmthal, A. and Scoville, J. G., eds.*, 1973, pp. 259–82.

Pendleton, William W. Blacks in Suburbs. In *Masotti, L. H. and Hadden, J. K., eds.*, 1973, pp. 171–84.

Pengilley, Warren. Australian Experience of Antitrust Regulation—A Vindication of the Per Se Approach. *Antitrust Bull.*, Summer 1973, *18*(2), pp. 355–74.

_____ The Register of Trade Practices Agreements —How Relevant Is It? *Econ. Anal. Pol.*, September 1973, *4*(2), pp. 18–42.

Penkava, Jaromír. Improvements of the Finance and Credit System in Czechoslovakia. *Czech. Econ. Digest.*, August 1973, (5), pp. 3–24.

Penn, J. B.; Candler, Wilfred V. and Cartwright, R. Wayne. The Substitution of Analytic for Simulation Algorithms: Comment. *Amer. J. Agr. Econ.*, May 1973, *55*(2), pp. 235–39.

Penner, Rudolph G. Health. In *Ott, D. J., et al.*, 1973, pp. 171–92.

_____ Housing and Community Development. In *Ott, D. J., et al.*, 1973, pp. 91–111.

_____; **Ott, David J. and Ott, Attiat F.** Income Security. In *Ott, D. J., et al.*, 1973, pp. 193–214.

_____ **and Silber, William L.** The Interaction Between Federal Credit Programs and the Impact on the Allocation of Credit. *Amer. Econ. Rev.*, December 1973, *63*(5), pp. 838–52.

Penny, David H. Development Studies: Some Reflections. In *Epstein, T. S. and Penny, D. H., eds.*, 1973, pp. 1–10.

———— and Singarimbun, Masri. Economic Activity among the Karo Batak of Indonesia: A Case Study in Economic Change. In *Epstein, T. S. and Penny, D. H., eds.*, 1973, pp. 86–113.

Penrose, Edith. International Patenting and the Less-Developed Countries. *Econ. J.,* September 1973, *83*(331), pp. 768–86.

Pepper, H. W. T. Taxing Pollution. *Bull. Int. Fiscal Doc.,* May 1973, *27*(5), pp. 189–93.

Peppers, Larry C. Full-Employment Surplus Analysis and Structural Change: The 1930s. *Exploration Econ. Hist.,* Winter 1973, *10*(2), pp. 197–210.

Pepson, Robert P. Job Vacancies, Hires, Quits, and Layoffs in Manufacturing, 1972. *Mon. Lab. Rev.,* April 1973, *96*(4), pp. 66–68.

Percy, M.; Jones, J. C. H. and Laudadio, Leonard. Market Structure and Profitability in Canadian Manufacturing Industry: Some Cross-Section Results. *Can. J. Econ.,* August 1973, *6*(3), pp. 356–68.

Perelman, Michael A. Mechanization and the Division of Labor in Agriculture. *Amer. J. Agr. Econ.,* August 1973, *55*(3), pp. 523–26.

———— Sacred Cows: Response. *Amer. J. Agr. Econ.,* May 1973, *55*(2), pp. 342–43.

Pérez, Louis A., Jr. Aspects of Underdevelopment: Tourism in the West Indies. *Sci. Soc.,* Winter 1973–1974, *37*(4), pp. 473–80.

Perkins, Brian B. Farm Income and Labour Mobility. *Amer. J. Agr. Econ.,* December 1973, *55*(5), pp. 913–20.

Perkins, Dwight H. Development of Agriculture. In *Oksenberg, M., ed.,* 1973, pp. 55–67.

———— Plans and Their Implementation in the People's Republic of China. *Amer. Econ. Rev.,* May 1973, *63*(2), pp. 224–31.

Perkins, J. O. N. Macro-Economic Policy: Introduction. In *Perkins, J. O. N., ed.,* 1973, pp. 11–16.

———— and Nieuwenhuysen, J. P. Macro-Economic Policies in the Four Countries. In *Perkins, J. O. N., ed.,* 1973, pp. 177–208.

———— and Nieuwenhuysen, J. P. Macro-Economic Policy: Australia. In *Perkins, J. O. N., ed.,* 1973, pp. 17–56.

Perl, Lewis J. Family Background, Secondary School Expenditure, and Student Ability. *J. Human Res.,* Spring 1973, *8*(2), pp. 156–80.

Perline, Martin M. and Presley, Ronald W. Mobility of Unemployed Engineers: A Case Study. *Mon. Lab. Rev.,* May 1973, *96*(5), pp. 41–43.

Perlman, Mark. Consumption Values of Trade Unions: Comment. *J. Econ. Issues,* June 1973, *7*(2), pp. 303–05.

———— The Editor's Comment. *J. Econ. Lit.,* March 1973, *11*(1), pp. 56–58.

———— On the Classification of Economics Material. *J. Econ. Lit.,* September 1973, *11*(3), pp. 898–99.

Perlman, Morris. The Roles of Money in an Economy and the Optimum Quantity of Money: Reply. *Economica, N.S.,* November 1973, *40*(160), pp. 432–41.

Perlmutter, Howard V. Super-Giant Firms in the Future. In *Andreano, R. L., ed.,* 1973, pp. R336–07.

Perloff, Harvey S. The Development of Urban Economics in the United States. *Urban Stud.,* October 1973, *10*(3), pp. 289–301.

———— and Clawson, Marion. Alternatives for Future Urban Land Policy. In *Clawson, M., ed.,* 1973, pp. 221–39.

Perlstein, William J. Revising the Private Placement Exemption. *Yale Law J.,* June 1973, *82*(7), pp. 1512–32.

Perrella, Vera C. Employment of Recent College Graduates. *Mon. Lab. Rev.,* February 1973, *96*(2), pp. 41–50.

Perren, R. The Landlord and Agricultural Transformation, 1870–1900. In *Perry, P. J., ed.,* 1973, pp. 109–28.

Perroux, François. The Economic Agent, Equilibrium, and the Choice of Formalisation. *Écon. Appl.,* 1973, *26*(2–3–4), pp. 250–85.

———— The Growth of the French Economy 1946–1970 a First Assessment. *Écon. Appl.,* 1973, *26*(2–3–4), pp. 641–46.

———— Multinational Investments and the Analysis of Development and Integration Poles. *Écon. Soc.,* May-June 1973, *7*(5–6), pp. 831–68.

Perry, Arnon. Heredity, Personality Traits, Product Attitude, and Product Consumption—An Exploratory Study. *J. Marketing Res.,* November 1973, *10*(4), pp. 376–79.

Perry, George L. Capacity in Manufacturing. *Brookings Pap. Econ. Act.,* 1973, (3), pp. 701–42.

———— The Success of Anti-Inflation Policies in the United States. *J. Money, Credit, Banking,* Part II, February 1973, *5*(1), pp. 569–93.

Perry, P. J. Where was the 'Great Agricultural Depression'? A Geography of Agricultural Bankruptcy in Late Victorian England and Wales. In *Perry, P. J., ed.,* 1973, pp. 129–48.

Persky, Joseph. The Dominance of the Rural-Industrial South, 1900–1930. *J. Reg. Sci.,* December 1973, *13*(3), pp. 409–19.

Personick, Martin E. Earnings Rise as Employment Dips in Petroleum and Gas. *Mon. Lab. Rev.,* August 1973, *96*(8), pp. 68–70.

———— Meat Department Workers Register Top Wage Rates in Grocery Stores. *Mon. Lab. Rev.,* May 1973, *96*(5), pp. 47–49.

———— Shorter Workweeks Dampen Earnings Gains in Contract Cleaning Services. *Mon. Lab. Rev.,* March 1973, *96*(3), pp. 53–55.

Pertot, Vladimir. Eastern European Trade and Financial Relations with Latin America. In *Urquidi, V. L. and Thorp, R., eds.,* 1973, pp. 400–419.

Pesando, James E. and Smith, Lawrence B. Monetary Policy in Canada. In *Holbik, K., ed.,* 1973, pp. 70–116.

Pesaran, M. Hashem. An Alternative Econometric Approach to the Permanent Income Hypothesis: An International Comparison: A Comment. *Rev. Econ. Statist.,* May 1973, *55*(2), pp. 259–61.

———— Exact Maximum Likelihood Estimation of a Regression Equation with a First-Order Moving-Average Error. *Rev. Econ. Stud.,* October 1973, *40*(4), pp. 529–35.

———— The Small Sample Problem of Truncation Remainders in the Estimation of Distributed Lag Models with Autocorrelated Errors. *Int. Econ. Rev.,* February 1973, *14*(1), pp. 120–31.

Peseau, Dennis E. and Boyes, William J. On Optimization in Models of Urban Land Use Densities:

Comment. *J. Reg. Sci.*, April 1973, *13*(1), pp. 129–33.

Pesek, Boris P. Equilibrium Level of Transaction Services of Money. *J. Finance,* June 1973, *28*(3), pp. 647–60.

Pessel', M. Credit and Its Development Under Current Conditions. *Prob. Econ.*, April 1973, *15*(12), pp. 86–99.

Pessemier, Edgar A. and Hustad, Thomas P. Will the Real Consumer Activist Please Stand Up: An Examination of Consumers' Opinions About Marketing Practices. *J. Marketing Res.*, August 1973, *10*(3), pp. 319–24.

_____ **and Wilkie, William L.** Issues in Marketing's Use of Multi-Attribute Attitude Models. *J. Marketing Res.*, November 1973, *10*(4), pp. 428–41.

Peston, Maurice. A Note on Tax Changes and Fluctuations in National Income. *J. Polit. Econ.*, November-December 1973, *81*(6), pp. 1467–70.

Peters, Hans-Rudolf. Hauptsächliche Determinanten von Wirtschaftsordnungen. (Main Determining Factors of Economic Orders. With English summary.) *Z. Wirtschaft. Sozialwissen.,* 1973, *93*(4), pp. 385–409.

Peters, Michael P. and Venkatesan, M. Exploration of Variables Inherent in Adopting an Industrial Product. *J. Marketing Res.*, August 1973, *10*(3), pp. 312–15.

Peters, William H. Income and Occupation as Explanatory Variables: Their Power Combined vs. Separate. *J. Bus. Res.*, Summer 1973, *1*(1), pp. 81–89.

Petersen, Gustav H. Latin America: Benign Neglect Is Not Enough. *Foreign Aff.*, April 1973, *51*(3), pp. 598–607.

Petersen, Russell J. Interindustry Estimation of General Price-level Impact on Financial Information. *Accounting Rev.*, January 1973, *48*(1), pp. 34–43.

_____ Price-Level Changes and Company Wealth. *Manage. Account.*, February 1973, *54*(8), pp. 17–20.

Peterson, David W. The Economic Significance of Auxiliary Functions in Optimal Control. *Int. Econ. Rev.*, February 1973, *14*(1), pp. 234–52.

Peterson, George E. Welfare, Workfare, and Pareto Optimality. *Public Finance Quart.*, July 1973, *1*(3), pp. 323–38.

_____ **and Galper, Harvey.** The Equity Effects of a Taxable Municipal Bond Subsidy. *Nat. Tax J.*, December 1973, *26*(4), pp. 611–24.

Peterson, Manferd O. Some Evidence on Intraregional Differences in Yields of Costs of Mortgage Lending. *Land Econ.*, February 1973, *49*(1), pp. 96–99.

_____ **and Boorman, John T.** Instability of Savings Flows and Mortgage Lending by Financial Intermediaries. *Southern Econ. J.*, October 1973, *40*(2), pp. 297–312.

Peterson, Peter G. The Art of Managing Change. In *The Diebold Group, Inc.*, 1973, pp. 3–10.

_____ The Russian Economy and Its Trade Potential. In *Henley, D. S., ed.*, 1973, pp. 25–38.

Peterson, R. D. and McKean, J. R. Demand Elasticity, Product Differentiation, and Market Structure. *J. Econ. Theory*, April 1973, *6*(2), pp. 205–09.

Peterson, Robert A. A Note on Optimal Adopter

Category Determination. *J. Marketing Res.*, August 1973, *10*(3), pp. 325–29.

_____ **and Cagley, James W.** The Effect of Shelf Space Upon Sales of Branded Products: An Appraisal. *J. Marketing Res.*, February 1973, *10*(1), pp. 103–04.

_____ **and Sharpe, Louis K.** Market Segmentation: Product Usage Patterns and Psychographic Configurations. *J. Bus. Res.*, Summer 1973, *1*(1), pp. 11–20.

Peterson, Willis and Hayami, Yujiro. Social Return to Public Information Services: Statistical Reporting of U.S. Farm Commodities: Reply. *Amer. Econ. Rev.*, December 1973, *63*(5), pp. 1020–21.

Petras, James F. Cuba: Fourteen Years of Revolutionary Government. In *Thurber, C. E. and Graham, L. S., eds.*, 1973, pp. 281–93.

Petrei, Amalio H. Rates of Return to Physical Capital in Manufacturing Industries in Argentina. *Oxford Econ. Pap.*, November 1973, *25*(3), pp. 378–404.

Petri, Enrico. Holding Gains and Losses as Cost Savings: A Comment on *Supplementary Statement No. 2* on Inventory Valuation. *Accounting Rev.*, July 1973, *48*(3), pp. 483–88.

Petridis, Anastasios. Alfred Marshall's Attitudes to the Economic Analysis of Trade Unions: A Case of Anomalies in a Competitive System. *Hist. Polit. Econ.*, Spring 1973, *5*(1), pp. 165–98.

Petrini, Bart F. and Grub, Phillip D. Product Management in High Technology Defense Industry Marketing. *Calif. Manage. Rev.*, Spring 1973, *15*(3), pp. 138–46.

Petrof, John V. Minority Representation in French Advertising. *Marquette Bus. Rev.*, Spring 1973, *17*(1), pp. 9–12.

Petrovsky, Boris. Progress in Public Health in the USSR, 1917–1967. In *Moskoff, W., ed.*, 1973, pp. 260–71.

Pettengill, Julian. The Financial Position of Private Community Hospitals, 1961–71. *Soc. Sec. Bull.*, November 1973, *36*(11), pp. 3–19.

Pettersen, Oystein. Stochastic Properties of Cumulative Feedback in a Simple Model. *Swedish J. Econ.*, September 1973, *75*(3), pp. 296–301.

Pettway, Richard H. Integer Programming in Capital Budgeting: A Note on Computational Experience. *J. Financial Quant. Anal.*, September 1973, *8*(4), pp. 665–72.

Petty, J. William and Klemkosky, Robert C. A Multivariate Analysis of Stock Price Variability. *J. Bus. Res.*, Summer 1973, *1*(1), pp. 1–10.

_____ **and Scott, David F., Jr.** An Analysis of Corporate Insider Trading Activity. *J. Econ. Bus.*, Fall 1973, *26*(1), pp. 19–24.

Pezzoli, Ettore and Gardini, Attilio. Relazioni statistiche di un semplice modello aggregativo dell'economia italiana (1951–1970). (Some Statistical Relationships in a Simple Aggregate Model of the Italian Economy (1951–1970).) With English summary.) *Statistica*, April-June 1973, *33*(2), pp. 241–73.

_____ Soluzione e qualche simulazione di un semplice modello statistico aggregato dell'economia italiana (1952–1970). (Solution and Some Simulations of a Simple Aggregate Model of the Italian Economy (1952–1970). With English summary.)

Statistica, July-September 1973, *33*(3), pp. 429–36.

Pfaff, Anita B. Transfer Payments to Large Metropolitan Poverty Areas: Their Distributive and Poverty-Reducing Effects. In *Boulding, K. E.; Pfaff, M. and Pfaff, A., eds.,* 1973, pp. 93–130.

Pfaff, Martin. Economic Life-Styles, Values, and Subjective Welfare—An Empirical Approach: Response. In *Sheldon, E. B., ed.,* 1973, pp. 126–38.

Pfeiffer, W. and Staudt, E. The Integration of Technological Prediction into Management Systems by Improvement of Forecasting Analysis. In *Blohm, H. and Steinbuch, K., eds.,* 1973, pp. 105–14.

Pfouts, Ralph W. Some Cost and Profit Relationships in the Multi-Product Firm. *Southern Econ. J.,* January 1973, *39*(3), pp. 361–65.

Pham, Chung. On Some Aspects of the Theory of Grants Economics. *Soc. Sci. Quart.,* December 1973, *54*(3), pp. 632–38.

Phan, Duc-Loï. Le modèle FIFI et la politique économique à moyen terme. (The Physico-Financial Model and the Medium Term Policy. With English summary.) *Revue Écon.,* November 1973, *24*(6), pp. 923–50.

Phares, Donald L. Impact of Spatial Tax Flows as Implicit Grants on State-Local Tax Incidence: With Reference to the Financing of Education. In *Boulding, K. E.; Pfaff, M. and Pfaff, A., eds.,* 1973, pp. 258–75.

Phelps, Edmund S. The Harried Leisure Class: A Demurrer. *Quart. J. Econ.,* November 1973, *87* (4), pp. 641–45.

———— Inflation in the Theory of Public Finance. *Swedish J. Econ.,* March 1973, *75*(1), pp. 67–82.

———— Optimal Stabilization Paths: Comment. *J. Money, Credit, Banking,* Part II, February 1973, *5*(1), pp. 563–65.

———— Taxation of Wage Income for Economic Justice. *Quart. J. Econ.,* August 1973, *87*(3), pp. 331–54.

Phelps Brown, E. H. How Phase II Worked in the United States. *Lloyds Bank Rev.,* July 1973, (109), pp. 1–16.

———— Levels and Movements of Industrial Productivity and Real Wages Internationally Compared, 1860-1970. *Econ. J.,* March 1973, *83*(329), pp. 58–71.

Philip, Kjeld. Nogle bemærkninger om kriterier for u-landsbistand. (With English summary.) *Nationalokon. Tidsskr.,* 1973, *111*(3), pp. 342–60.

Philippatos, George C. and Nawrocki, David N. The Behavior of Stock Market Aggregates: Evidence of Dependence on the American Stock Exchange. *J. Bus. Res.,* Fall 1973, *1*(2), pp. 102–14.

———— The Information Inaccuracy of Stock Market Forecasts: Some New Evidence of Dependence on the New York Stock Exchange. *J. Financial Quant. Anal.,* June 1973, *8*(3), pp. 445–58.

Phillips, Almarin. François Quesnay: The Tableau Économique as a Simple Leontief Model. In *Rectenwald, H. C., ed.,* 1973, pp. 16–21.

———— and Jacobs, Donald P. Overview of the Commission's Philosophy and Recommendations. In *Federal Reserve Bank of Boston,* 1973, pp. 9–20.

Phillips, Bruce D. The Spatial Distribution of Unemployment by Occupation: Reply. *J. Reg. Sci.,* December 1973, *13*(3), pp. 471.

Phillips, Llad. Crime Control: The Case for Deterrence. In *Rottenberg, S., ed.,* 1973, pp. 65–84.

———— and Pippenger, John E. Stabilization of the Canadian Dollar: 1952–1960. *Econometrica,* September 1973, *41*(5), pp. 797–815.

————; Votey, Harold L., Jr. and Hambor, John C. High School Inputs and Their Contribution to School Performance: A Comment. *J. Human Res.,* Spring 1973, *8*(2), pp. 260–63.

————; Votey, Harold L., Jr. and Hambor, John C. Optimal Community Educational Attainment: A Simultaneous Equation Approach. *Rev. Econ. Statist.,* February 1973, *55*(1), pp. 98–103.

Phillips, P. C. B. The Problem of Identification in Finite Parameter Continuous Time Models. *J. Econometrics,* December 1973, *1*(4), pp. 351–62.

Phlips, Louis. Illusions in Testing for Administered Prices: A Reply. *J. Ind. Econ.,* April 1973, *21*(2), pp. 196–99.

Piasentin, U. and Costa, P. A Dynamic Simulation Model of the Urban Development of Venice. In *Hawkes, N., ed.,* 1973, pp. 144–54.

Piché, Victor and George, M. V. Estimates of Vital Rates for the Canadian Indians, 1960–1970. *Demography,* August 1973, *10*(3), pp. 367–82.

Pickard, Jerome P. Growth of Urbanized Population in the United States: Past, Present, and Future. In *Rasmussen, D. W. and Haworth, C. T., eds.,* 1973, pp. 5–15.

Pickering, J. F., et al. Are Goods Goods? Some Empirical Evidence. *Appl. Econ.,* March 1973, *5*(1), pp. 1–18.

————; Harrison, J. A. and Cohen, C. D. Identification and Measurment of Consumer Confidence: Methodology and Some Preliminary Results. *J. Roy. Statist. Soc.,* Part 1, 1973, *136*, pp. 43–63.

Pickering, Margaret H. and Mallinson, Eugenie. New Series for Large Manufacturing Corporations. *Fed. Res. Bull.,* October 1973, *59*(10), pp. 731–33.

Pickett, Margaret S. and Bechter, Dan M. The Wholesale and Consumer Price Indexes: What's the Connection? *Fed. Res. Bank Kansas City Rev.,* June 1973, pp. 3–9.

Pickle, Hal B. and Rungeling, Brian S. Empirical Investigation of Entrepreneurial Goals and Customer Satisfaction. *J. Bus.,* April 1973, *46*(2), pp. 268–73.

Pidot, George B., Jr. and Gustman, Alan L. Interactions Between Educational Spending and Student Enrollment. *J. Human Res.,* Winter 1973, *8*(1), pp. 3–23.

Piehl, DeWayne and Ebert, Ronald J. Time Horizon: A Concept for Management. *Calif. Manage. Rev.,* Summer 1973, *15*(4), pp. 35–41.

Pierre, Joseph C. La gestion des ressources humaines: une approche intégrée et prévisionnelle. (The Management of Human Resources: An Integrated and Planned Approach. With English summary.) *Ann. Sci. Écon. Appl.,* 1973–1974, (1), pp. 17–45.

Pigram, John J. J. Urban-Rural Conflicts in Urban Water Supply. In *Aislabie, C., ed.,* 1973, pp. 145–54.

Pilgrim, John D. and Bloch, Ben W. A Reappraisal of Some Factors Associated with Fluctuations in the United States in the Interwar Period. *Southern Econ. J.,* January 1973, *39*(3), pp. 327–44.

Pinches, George E. and Mingo, Kent A. A Multivariate Analysis of Industrial Bond Ratings. *J. Finance,* March 1973, *28*(1), pp. 1–18.

_____; **Mingo, Kent A. and Caruthers, J. Kent.** The Stability of Financial Patterns in Industrial Organizations. *J. Finance,* May 1973, *28*(2), pp. 389–96.

_____ **and Sims, Edwin C., Jr.** Factors Related to the Performance of College Endowment Funds. *J. Econ. Bus.,* Spring-Summer 1973, *25*(3), pp. 198–205.

_____ **and Trieschmann, James S.** A Multivariate Model for Predicting Financially Distressed P-L Insurers. *J. Risk Ins.,* September 1973, *40*(3), pp. 327–38.

Pinder, John. The Community and the Developing Countries: Associates and Outsiders. *J. Common Market Stud.,* September 1973, *12*(1), pp. 53–77.

Pindling, Lynden O. Focus on the Bahamas: The Way to Independence. *World Devel.,* May 1973, *1*(5), pp. 47–48.

Pindyck, Robert S. Optimal Policies for Economic Stabilization. *Econometrica,* May 1973, *41*(3), pp. 529–60.

_____ **and Eisner, Mark.** A Generalized Approach to Estimation as Implemented in the TROLL/1 System. *Ann. Econ. Soc. Measure,* January 1973, *2*(1), pp. 29–51.

_____ **and MacAvoy, Paul W.** Alternative Regulatory Policies for Dealing with the Natural Gas Shortage. *Bell J. Econ. Manage. Sci.,* Autumn 1973, *4*(2), pp. 454–98.

Piñeiro, Martín and Hurtado, Hernán. Rentabilidad potencial de la investigación ganadera: Una estimación empírica. (Rateable of Livestock Research: An Empirical Estimation. With English summary.) *Económica,* May-August 1973, *19*(2), pp. 185–200.

Pines, David; Sheshinski, Eytan and Oron, Yitzhak. Optimum vs. Equilibrium Land Use Pattern and Congestion Toll. *Bell J. Econ. Manage. Sci.,* Autumn 1973, *4*(2), pp. 619–36.

Pinkerton, James R. The Changing Class Composition of Cities and Suburbs. *Land Econ.,* November 1973, *49*(4), pp. 462–69.

Pintilie, C. Concepte de bază ale ştiinţei conducerii societăţii socialiste, a ramurilor şi unităţilor lor componente. (Basic Concepts of the Science of Management of the Socialist Society, of their Component Branches and Units. With English summary.) *Stud. Cercet. Econ.,* 1973, (2), pp. 73–87.

Pinto, Aníbal and Kňakal, Jan. The Centre-Periphery System Twenty Years Later. *Soc. Econ. Stud.,* March 1973, *22*(1), pp. 34–89.

Piore, Michael J. Fragments of a "Sociological" Theory of Wages. *Amer. Econ. Rev.,* May 1973, *63*(2), pp. 377–84.

Pippenger, John E. Balance-of-Payments Deficits: Measurement and Interpretation. *Fed. Res. Bank St. Louis Rev.,* November 1973, *55*(11), pp. 6–14.

_____ The Case for Freely Fluctuating Exchange Rates: Some Evidence. *Western Econ. J.,* September 1973, *11*(3), pp. 314–26.

_____ The Determination of the Stock of Reserves and the Balance of Payments in a Neo-Keynesian Model: Comment. *J. Money, Credit, Banking,* May 1973, *5*(2), pp. 713–19.

_____ Speculation in the Flexible Exchange Re-Revisited. *Kyklos,* 1973, *26*(3), pp. 613–18.

_____ **and Phillips, Llad.** Stabilization of the Canadian Dollar: 1952–1960. *Econometrica,* September 1973, *41*(5), pp. 797–815.

Piro, Paula A. and Lutins, Theodore. Utilization and Reimbursements under Medicare for 1967 and 1968 Decedents. *Soc. Sec. Bull.,* May 1973, *36*(5), pp. 37–41, 58.

Pisano, Paolo G. International Manual on Collective Bargaining for Public Employees: Italy. In *Kaye, S. P. and Marsh, A., eds.,* 1973, pp. 210–63.

Pitchford, J. D. The Optimum Population and Growth: A Closer Look. *J. Econ. Theory,* February 1973, *6*(1), pp. 94–95.

Pittenger, Donald B. An Exponential Model of Female Sterility. *Demography,* February 1973, *10*(1), pp. 113–21.

Pittman, Clarence R. Organizational Behavior and the Management Accountant. *Manage. Account.,* July 1973, *55*(1), pp. 25–28.

Piven, Frances Fox and Cloward, Richard A. The Case Against Urban Desegregation. In *Pynoos, J.; Schafer, R. and Hartman, C. W., eds.,* 1973, pp. 97–107.

Pizzala, F. B. The Cost of Capital to the Private Sector: A Critique of Merrett and Sykes. In *Lister, R. J., ed.,* 1973, pp. 39–48.

Pizzorno, Alessandro. Vilfredo Pareto and the Crisis of Nineteenth Century Science. *Soc. Sci. Quart.,* December 1973, *54*(3), pp. 480–90.

Plant, Kenneth M. The Secondary Mortgage Market: Problems and Prospects. *Indiana Bus. Rev.,* January-February 1973, *48*, pp. 1–7.

Platt, D. C. M. Further Objections to an "Imperialism of Free Trade," 1830-60. *Econ. Hist. Rev., 2nd Ser.,* February 1973, *26*(1), pp. 77–91.

Plaunt, Darrel H. Agricultural Development Policies and Programs in Canada. *Amer. J. Agr. Econ.,* December 1973, *55*(5), pp. 903–12.

Plaxico, James S. and Ray, Daryll E. Implications for Agricultural Economists. *Amer. J. Agr. Econ.,* August 1973, *55*(3), pp. 399–403.

Plessas, Demetrius J. Airplane Noise: Some Analytic and Policy Perspectives. *Land Econ.,* February 1973, *49*(1), pp. 14–21.

Pliska, Stanley R. Supply of Storage Theory and Commodity Equilibrium Prices with Stochastic Production. *Amer. J. Agr. Econ., Part I,* November 1973, *55*(4), pp. 653–58.

Plott, Charles R. Path Independence, Rationality, and Social Choice. *Econometrica,* November 1973, *41*(6), pp. 1075–91.

Plowden, S. P. C. Indirect Taxation of Motorway and Alternative Consumption. *J. Transp. Econ. Policy,* September 1973, *7*(3), pp. 250–71.

Plowman, E. Grosvenor. The Logistics of Industrial Distribution. In *The Diebold Group, Inc.,* 1973, pp. 128–33.

Pochkin, P. The Effectiveness of Production in Bourgeois Literature. *Prob. Econ.,* June 1973, *16*(2), pp. 84–102.

Podder, N. and Kakwani, N. C. On the Estimation of Lorenz Curves from Grouped Observations. *Int. Econ. Rev.,* June 1973, *14*(2), pp. 278–92.

Podrebarac, Michael L.; Fernando, T. D. H. and Sengupta, S. Sankar. Probabilities of Optima in Multi-Objective Linear Programmes. In *Cochrane, J. L. and Zeleny, M., eds.,* 1973, pp. 217–35.

Pohlman, Jerry E. A Trade-off Analysis of Job Creation vs. Welfare. *J. Econ. Bus.,* Spring-Summer 1973, *25*(3), pp. 168–74.

Poindexter, J. Carl, Jr. and Benavie, Arthur. Deposit Ceilings and Monetary Policy. *Rev. Econ. Statist.,* November 1973, *55*(4), pp. 487–92.

—— **and Jones, C. P.** The Effect of Recent Tax Policy Changes on Manufacturing Investment. *Quart. Rev. Econ. Bus.,* Winter 1973, *13*(4), pp. 79–88.

Poirier, Dale J. Piecewise Regression Using Cubic Splines. *J. Amer. Statist. Assoc.,* September 1973, *68*(343), pp. 515–24.

Pol, Jorge E. F. A Note on the Generalized Production Function. *Rev. Econ. Stud.,* January 1973, *40* (1), pp. 139–40.

Polaczek, S. and Zdanowicz, J. Subsidy, Taxation and Foreign Trade. In *Kiss, T., ed.,* 1973, pp. 221–26.

Polanyi, George and Polanyi, Priscilla. Tax Credits: A Reverse Income Tax. *Nat. Westminster Bank Quart. Rev.,* February 1973, pp. 20–34.

Polanyi, Priscilla and Polanyi, George. Tax Credits: A Reverse Income Tax. *Nat. Westminster Bank Quart. Rev.,* February 1973, pp. 20–34.

Polasek, M. IMF Special Drawing Rights and Economic Aid to Less Developed Countries. *Econ. Rec.,* September 1973, *49*(127), pp. 358–76.

Polenske, Karen R. An Analysis of United States Commodity Freight Shipments. In *Judge, G. G. and Takayama, T., eds.,* 1973, pp. 163–79.

Poliak, R. A.; Primak, M. E. and Zukhovitskii, S. T. Concave Multiperson Games: Numerical Methods. *Matekon,* Summer 1973, *9*(4), pp. 10–30.

Polinsky, A. Mitchell. A Note on the Measurement of Incidence. *Public Finance Quart.,* April 1973, *1*(2), pp. 219–30.

Polk, Judd. American Labor and the U.S. Multinational Enterprise in an Emerging World Economy. In *Kujawa, D., ed.,* 1973, pp. 270–85.

—— The International Corporation. In *Andreano, R. L., ed.,* 1973, pp. R334–08.

—— International Perspectives on World Companies. In *Alexandrides, C. G., ed.,* 1973, pp. 261–71.

—— The New International Production. *World Devel.,* May 1973, *1*(5), pp. 15–20.

Polk, Lon. The Radical Paradigm and Urban Economics. In *Mattila, J. M. and Thompson, W. R., eds.,* 1973, pp. 206–23.

Pollak, Robert A. The Risk Independence Axiom. *Econometrica,* January 1973, *41*(1), pp. 35–39.

Pollakowski, Henry O. The Effects of Property Taxes and Local Public Spending on Property Values: A Comment and Further Results. *J. Polit. Econ.,* July-August 1973, *81*(4), pp. 994–1003.

Pollard, Sidney. Industrialization and the European Economy. *Econ. Hist. Rev., 2nd Ser.,* November 1973, *26*(4), pp. 636–48.

Pollatschek, M. A.; Comay, Yochanan and Melnik, A. The Option Value of Education and the Optimal Path for Investment in Human Capital. *Int. Econ. Rev.,* June 1973, *14*(2), pp. 421–35.

—— **and Melnik, A.** Debt Capacity, Diversification and Conglomerate Mergers. *J. Finance,* December 1973, *28*(5), pp. 1163–73.

Pollina, Ronald and Nunnally, Nelson. Recent Trends in Industrial Park Location in the Chicago Metropolitan Area. *Land Econ.,* August 1973, *49* (3), pp. 356–61.

Pollock, David H. Ideologies of Latin American Modernization. In *Pollock, D. H. and Ritter, A. R. M., eds.,* 1973, pp. 30–44.

—— The Pearson and Prebisch Reports: The Crucial Issue of Unemployment. In *Pollock, D. H. and Ritter, A. R. M., eds.,* 1973, pp. 70–85.

—— **and Ritter, Arch R. M.** Revolution in Latin America: An Overview. In *Pollock, D. H. and Ritter, A. R. M., eds.,* 1973, pp. 3–29.

Pollock, Richard. The Effect of Alternative Regulatory Treatment of Tax Depreciation on Utility Tax Payments. *Nat. Tax J.,* March 1973, *26*(1), pp. 43–57.

—— Supply of Residential Construction: A Cross-Section Examination of Recent Housing Market Behavior. *Land Econ.,* February 1973, *49*(1), pp. 57–66.

—— **and Hight, Joseph E.** Income Distribution Effects of Higher Education Expenditures in California, Florida and Hawaii. *J. Human Res.,* Summer 1973, *8*(3), pp. 318–30.

Polterovich, V. M. On the Formulation of Integer Linear Programming Problems. *Matekon,* Winter 1973-74, *10*(2), pp. 36–51.

Polzin, Paul E. Urban Employment Models: Estimation and Interpretation. *Land Econ.,* May 1973, *49*(2), pp. 226–32.

Pompermayer, Malori J. Dependency and Unemployment: Some Issues. In *Bonilla, F. and Girling, R., eds.,* 1973, pp. 63–82.

Pone, Maris. Recent Developments in Brazil: A Perspective. In *Pollock, D. H. and Ritter, A. R. M., eds.,* 1973, pp. 185–202.

Pontecorvo, Giulio. On the Utility of Bioeconomic Models for Fisheries Management. In *Sokoloski, A. A., ed.,* 1973, pp. 12–22.

Pool, A. Jonathan, et al. Handbook of Soviet Social Science Data: Education. In *Mickiewicz, E., ed.,* 1973, pp. 137–58.

Pool, D. I. Estimates of New Zealand Maori Vital Rates from the Mid-Nineteenth Century to World War I. *Population Stud.,* March 1973, *27*(1), pp. 117–25.

Poole, William. Wage-Price Controls: Where Do We Go from Here? *Brookings Pap. Econ. Act.,* 1973, (1), pp. 285–99.

—— **and Kornblith, Elinda B. F.** The Friedman-Meiselman CMC Paper: New Evidence on an Old Controversy. *Amer. Econ. Rev.,* December 1973, *63*(5), pp. 908–17.

Pope, David. Economic History and Scientific Inference. *Australian Econ. Hist. Rev.,* March 1973, *13* (1), pp. 1–15.

Popescu, C. and Sandu, C. Corelația între creșterea

In *Postan, M. M. (II)*, 1973, pp. 92–231.

――― Why Was Science Backward in the Middle Ages? In *Postan, M. M. (I)*, 1973, pp. 81–86.

Postgate, M. R. Field Systems of East Anglia. In *Baker, A. R. H. and Butlin, R. A., eds.*, 1973, pp. 281–324.

Poston, Dudley L., Jr. and Alvírez, David. On the Cost of Being a Mexican American Worker. *Soc. Sci. Quart.*, March 1973, *53*(4), pp. 697–709.

――――; **Schnirring, Paul and Haynes, Kingsley E.** Intermetropolitan Migration in High and Low Opportunity Areas: Indirect Tests of the Distance and Intervening Opportunities Hypotheses. *Econ. Geogr.*, January 1973, *49*(1), pp. 68–73.

Potáč, Svatopluk. The Role of Credit in the Plan-Based Management of the Czechoslovak Economy. *Czech. Econ. Digest.*, September 1973, (6), pp. 63–104.

Potgieter, J. F. The Poverty Datum Line. *S. Afr. J. Econ.*, June 1973, *41*(2), pp. 161–63.

Potter, Roger E. Characteristics of Two Groups of Investors. *Marquette Bus. Rev.*, Summer 1973, *17*(2), pp. 109–12.

Poullet, E. The PPBS Experiment in Belgium. In *Novick, D., ed.*, 1973, pp. 65–69.

Poulson, Barry W. and Dowling, J. Malcolm, Jr. The Climacteric in U.S. Economic Growth. *Oxford Econ. Pap.*, November 1973, *25*(3), pp. 420–34.

Pournarakis, E. Capital Accumulation and Industrialization in the Open Dual Economy—A Two Sector Model. *Econ. Int.*, August-November 1973, *26*(3–4), pp. 502–15.

Pousa, Aurora G.; Alemany, Ricardo and Fernandez, Pedro. Algorithm for Solving a Class of Linear Programing Problems Related to Reservoir Management and Design. *Water Resources Res.*, October 1973, *9*(5), pp. 1227–34.

Povey, George; Uyeno, Dean and Vertinsky, Ilan. Social Impact Index for Evaluation of Regional Resource Allocation. In *Berg, R. L., ed.*, 1973, pp. 104–14.

Powell, A. A. An ELES Consumption Function for the United States. *Econ. Rec.*, September 1973, *49*(127), pp. 337–57.

Powell, C. Randall. The Indiana MBA: Where Is He? *Indiana Bus. Rev.*, July-August 1973, *48*, pp. 8–11.

Powell, R. A. and Anderson, Jock R. Economics of Size in Australian Farming. *Australian J. Agr. Econ.*, April 1973, *17*(1), pp. 1–16.

Power, Fred B. and Meyer, Richard L. Total Insurance Costs and the Frequency of Premium Payments. *J. Risk Ins.*, December 1973, *40*(4), pp. 599–605.

Powers, John A. Symmetry of Production Stages and Uneconomic Production: Comment. *Southern Econ. J.*, October 1973, *40*(2), pp. 333–34.

Pozdniakova, N. On the Distribution of Incomes on Collective Farms. *Prob. Econ.*, January 1973, *15*(9), pp. 90–100.

Pozen, Robert. The Financing of Local Housing Authorities: A Contract Approach for Public Corporations. *Yale Law J.*, May 1973, *82*(6), pp. 1208–27.

van Praag, Bernard M. S. and Kapteyn, Arie. Further Evidence on the Individual Welfare Function of Income: An Empirical Investigation in The Netherlands. *Europ. Econ. Rev.*, April 1973, *4*(1), pp. 33–62.

Prachowny, Martin F. J. The Effectiveness of Stabilization Policy in a Small Open Economy. *Weltwirtsch. Arch.*, 1973, *109*(2), pp. 214–31.

――――; **Boadway, Robin W. and Maital, Shlomo.** Optimal Tariffs, Optimal Taxes and Public Goods. *J. Public Econ.*, November 1973, *2*(4), pp. 391–403.

Prachuabmoh, Visid and Knodel, John. Desired Family Size in Thailand: Are the Responses Meaningful? *Demography*, November 1973, *10*(4), pp. 619–37.

Praetz, P. D. A Spectral Analysis of Australian Share Prices. *Australian Econ. Pap.*, June 1973, *12*(20), pp. 70–78.

Prasad, K. N. The Value Approach in the Classical Theory of Distribution-II. *Econ. Aff.*, September-October 1973, *18*(9–10), pp. 475–76.

――― The Value Approach in the Classical Theory of Distribution—III. *Econ. Aff.*, November-December 1973, *18*(11–12), pp. 503–10.

――― The Value Approach in the Classical Theory of Distribution. *Econ. Aff.*, August 1973, *18*(8), pp. 372–80.

Prasad, S. Benjamin. Comparative Management Models: Structure and Research Potential. In *Alexandrides, C. G., ed.*, 1973, pp. 145–61.

Prato, Anthony A. Milk Demand, Supply, and Price Relationships, 1950–1968. *Amer. J. Agr. Econ.*, May 1973, *55*(2), pp. 217–22.

――― A Proposal for Reducing Nutrient Deficiencies with Economical Diets. *Can. J. Agr. Econ.*, November 1973, *21*(3), pp. 15–22.

――― **and Alcantara, Reinaldo.** Returns to Scale and Input Elasticities for Sugarcane: The Case of Sao Paulo, Brazil. *Amer. J. Agr. Econ.*, Part I, November 1973, *55*(4), pp. 577–83.

――― **and Ayob, Ahmad Mahzan.** United States Import Demand and Prices of Natural Rubber. *Malayan Econ. Rev.*, April 1973, *18*(1), pp. 24–35.

Pražák, Ivo and Zelinka, Jan. Systém programů pro ekonomicko-matematické úlohy. (System of Computer Programs for Economic-Mathematical Calculations. With English summary.) *Ekon.-Mat. Obzor*, 1973, *9*(4), pp. 393–403.

Prell, Michael J. How Well Do the Experts Forecast Interest Rates? *Fed. Res. Bank Kansas City Rev.*, September-October 1973, pp. 3–13.

――― The Long-Run Growth of Consumer Installment Credit—Some Observations. *Fed. Res. Bank Kansas City Rev.*, February 1973, pp. 3–13.

――― **and Hamblin, Mary.** Income of Men and Women: Why Do They Differ? *Fed. Res. Bank Kansas City Rev.*, April 1973, pp. 3–11.

Prescott, Edward C. Market Structure and Monopoly Profits: A Dynamic Theory. *J. Econ. Theory*, December 1973, *6*(6), pp. 546–57.

――― **and Cooley, Thomas F.** An Adaptive Regression Model. *Int. Econ. Rev.*, June 1973, *14*(2), pp. 364–71.

――― **and Cooley, Thomas F.** Systematic (Non-Random) Variation Models Varying Parameter Regression: A Theory and Some Applications. *Ann. Econ. Soc. Measure*, October 1973, *2*(4), pp. 463–73.

_____ and Cooley, Thomas F. Tests of an Adaptive Regression Model. *Rev. Econ. Statist.*, May 1973, *55*(2), pp. 248–56.

Presley, Ronald W. and Perline, Martin M. Mobility of Unemployed Engineers: A Case Study. *Mon. Lab. Rev.*, May 1973, *96*(5), pp. 41–43.

Presman, L. S. A Model of Industrial Location. *Matekon*, Spring 1973, *9*(3), pp. 6–21.

Pressman, Israel and Carol, Arthur. Behavior of the Firm Under Regulatory Constraint: Reply. *Amer. Econ. Rev.*, March 1973, *63*(1), pp. 238.

Prest, Alan R. On the Distinction between Direct and Indirect Taxation. In *[Hicks, U.]*, 1973, pp. 44–56.

_____ Public Finance: Backward Area or New Frontier? *Economica, N.S.*, May 1973, *40*(158), pp. 121–35.

Prič, Jozef and Fuchs, Tomáš. Meranie intenzity ekonomického rastu metódou úplne dynamizovanej substitučnej produkčnej funkcie Cobb-Douglasovho typu. (Measuring the Intensity of Economic Growth by the Method of Totally Dynamised Cobb-Douglas Type Production Function. With English summary.) *Ekon.-Mat. Obzor*, 1973, *9*(4), pp. 381–92.

Price, Daniel N. Cash Benefits for Short-Term Sickness, 1948-71. *Soc. Sec. Bull.*, January 1973, *36*(1), pp. 20–29.

Price, R. W. R. Some Aspects of the Progressive Income Tax Structure in the UK. *Nat. Inst. Econ. Rev.*, August 1973, (65), pp. 52–63.

Pricop, Mihai. Asigurarea ritmicității activității de servire a producției de bază. (Ensuring the Rhythmicity of the Activity of Serving Basic Production. With English summary.) *Stud. Cercet. Econ.*, 1973, (4), pp. 55–64.

Primak, M. E.; Zukhovitskii, S. T. and Poliak, R. A. Concave Multiperson Games: Numerical Methods. *Matekon*, Summer 1973, *9*(4), pp. 10–30.

Primeaux, Walter J. Price Variability and Price Discrimination: A Case Study. *Marquette Bus. Rev.*, Spring 1973, *17*(1), pp. 25–29.

Prince, Barry L. and Hansen, Thomas J. The Paradox of Voting: An Elementary Solution for the Case of Three Alternatives. *Public Choice*, Summer 1973, *15*, pp. 103–17.

Prindle, Allen and Sharples, Jerry. Income Characteristics of Farm Families in the Corn Belt. *Agr. Finance Rev.*, July 1973, *34*, pp. 12–17.

Pringle, John J. A Theory of the Banking Firm: Comment. *J. Money, Credit, Banking*, November 1973, *5*(4), pp. 990–96.

_____ and Cohn, Richard A. Imperfections in International Financial Markets: Implications for Risk Premia and the Cost of Capital to Firms. *J. Finance*, March 1973, *28*(1), pp. 59–66.

Pritchett, S. Travis. Operating Expenses of Life Insurers, 1961–70: Implications for Economies of Size. *J. Risk Ins.*, June 1973, *40*(2), pp. 157–65.

Prochaska, Fred J. and Schrimper, R. A. Opportunity Cost of Time and Other Socioeconomic Effects on Away-From-Home Food Consumption. *Amer. J. Agr. Econ.*, Part I, November 1973, *55*(4), pp. 595–603.

Prodromidis, Kyprianos P. Applied Economic Policy with a Quadratic Criterion Function: A Reply.

Appl. Econ., September 1973, *5*(3), pp. 229–31.

_____ and Lianos, Theodore P. City Size and Patterns of Employment Structure. In *Mattila, J. M. and Thompson, W. R., eds.*, 1973, pp. 91–104.

Prohaska, Charles R. and Taylor, Walton. Minimizing Losses in a Hostile Environment: The Costs of Defending One's Castle. *J. Risk Ins.*, September 1973, *40*(3), pp. 375–87.

Prosser, P. B. The Market for Beef in Japan. *Quart. Rev. Agr. Econ.*, April 1973, *26*(2), pp. 67–89.

Prothero, D. L. and Chatfield, C. Box-Jenkins Seasonal Forecasting: Problems in a Case-study. *J. Roy. Statist. Soc.*, Part 3 1973, *136*, pp. 295–315.

Proxmire, William. Qualifications for FTC Chairmanship: Competence, Concern, and Consumer Confidence. In *Murray, B. B., ed.*, 1973, pp. 92–97.

Prud'homme, Rémy. Costs and Financing of Urban Development in France. *Urban Stud.*, June 1973, *10*(2), pp. 189–98.

Pruitt, Eleanor M. State and Local Borrowing Anticipations and Realizations. *Fed. Res. Bull.*, April 1973, *59*(4), pp. 257–60.

Prybyla, Jan S. Soviet Economic Reforms in Agriculture. *Weltwirtsch. Arch.*, 1973, *109*(4), pp. 644–87.

Pryor, Frederic L. Simulation of the Impact of Social and Economic Institutions on the Size Distribution of Income and Wealth. *Amer. Econ. Rev.*, March 1973, *63*(1), pp. 50–72.

_____ Size of Establishments in Manufacturing: A Reply. *Econ. J.*, September 1973, *83*(331), pp. 900.

Psacharopoulos, George. Manpower Forecasting for all Occupations: France. In *Ahamad, B. and Blaug, M., eds.*, 1973, pp. 106–30.

_____ A Note on the Demand for Enrollment in Higher Education. *De Economist*, September-October 1973, *121*(5), pp. 521–25.

_____ Substitution Assumptions versus Empirical Evidence in Manpower Planning. *De Economist*, November-December 1973, *121*(6), pp. 609–25.

_____ and Williams, Gareth. Public Sector Earnings and Educational Planning. *Int. Lab. Rev.*, July 1973, *108*(1), pp. 43–57.

Psoinos, D. P. and Xirokostas, D. A. A Dynamic Programming Approach to Establishing Teaching Posts in a Centralized Educational System. In *Ross, M., ed.*, 1973, pp. 315–23.

Puckett, A. Marshall. Consumer Financial Management and Financial Institution Response—A Two-Decade Perspective: Response. In *Sheldon, E. B., ed.*, 1973, pp. 363–67.

Puckett, Richard H. Changes in Bank Lending Practices, 1972. *Fed. Res. Bull.*, July 1973, *59*(7), pp. 501–05.

_____ Monetary Policy Effectiveness: The Case of a Positively Sloped I-S Curve: Comment. *J. Finance*, December 1973, *28*(5), pp. 1362–64.

_____ and Vroman, Susan B. Rules Versus Discretion: A Simulation Study. *J. Finance*, September 1973, *28*(4), pp. 853–65.

Puig, Carlos M.; Aschoff, John and Simon, Julian L. A Duopoly Simulation and Richer Theory: An End to Cournot. *Rev. Econ. Stud.*, July 1973, *40*(3), pp. 353–66.

Pullinger, Barry F. A Method of Analysis of Residential Water Demand and Its Relation to Management. In *Aislabie, C., ed.,* 1973, pp. 155–70.

Purcărea, M. and Dumitru, Georgeta. Eficiența economică a diversificării producției industriale. (The Economic Efficiency of the Diversification of Industrial Production. With English summary.) *Stud. Cercet. Econ.,* 1973, (2), pp. 63–71.

Purcell, Wayne D. An Approach to Research on Vertical Coordination: The Beef System in Oklahoma. *Amer. J. Agr. Econ.,* February 1973, *55* (1), pp. 65–68.

Purdy, D. L. and Zis, G. Trade Unions and Wage Inflation in the UK: A Reappraisal. In *Parkin, M., ed.,* 1973, pp. 294–327.

Pursell, G. and Snape, R. H. Economies of Scale, Price Discrimination and Exporting. *J. Int. Econ.,* February 1973, *3*(1), pp. 85–91.

Purvis, Douglas D. Short-Run Dynamics in Models of Money and Growth. *Amer. Econ. Rev.,* March 1973, *63*(1), pp. 12–23.

Purvis, Malcolm J. The New Varieties Under Dryland Conditions: Mexican Wheats In Tunisia. *Amer. J. Agr. Econ.,* February 1973, *55*(1), pp. 54–57.

Puth, Robert C. From Enforced Segregation to Integration: Market Factors in the Development of a Negro Life Insurance. In *[Williamson, H. F.],* 1973, pp. 280–301.

Puu, Tönu and Vázquez, Andrés. Factor Demand Functions in the Long-Run Equilibrium. *Rivista Int. Sci. Econ. Com.,* December 1973, *20*(12), pp. 1209–29.

Pye, Gordon. Lifetime Portfolio Selection in Continuous Time for a Multiplicative Class of Utility Functions. *Amer. Econ. Rev.,* December 1973, *63* (5), pp. 1013–16.

Pyhrr, Stephen A. A Computer Simulation Model to Measure the Risk in Real Estate Investment. *Amer. Real Estate Urban Econ. Assoc. J.,* June 1973, *1*(1), pp. 48–78.

Pyle, Gerald F. Measles as an Urban Health Problem: The Akron Example. *Econ. Geogr.,* October 1973, *49*(4), pp. 344–56.

Pynoos, Jon and Mollenkopf, John. Boardwalk and Park Place: Property Ownership, Political Structure, and Housing Policy at the Local Level. In *Pynoos, J.; Schafer, R. and Hartman, C. W., eds.,* 1973, pp. 55–74.

———; **Schafer, Robert and Hartman, Chester W.** Housing Urban America: Introduction. In *Pynoos, J.; Schafer, R. and Hartman, C. W., eds.,* 1973, pp. 1–12.

Pyrke, Richard. The Growth of Efficiency. In *Tivey, L., ed.,* 1973, pp. 121–26.

Qayum, Abdul. Professor Tinbergen's Approach to Economic Planning. *Econ. Int.,* February 1973, *26*(1), pp. 95–115.

Quandt, Richard E. The Estimation of Constant Elasticities: Comment. *Southern Econ. J.,* January 1973, *39*(3), pp. 444–45.

——— **and Goldfeld, Stephen M.** The Estimation of Structural Shifts by Switching Regressions. *Ann. Econ. Soc. Measure,* October 1973, *2*(4), pp. 475–85.

——— **and Goldfeld, Stephen M.** A Markov Model for Switching Regressions. *J. Econometrics,* March 1973, *1*(1), pp. 3–15.

Quantius, Frances W. Commercial Banking and the Hunt Commission Report. *Ohio State U. Bull. Bus. Res.,* April 1973, *48*(4), pp. 4–5, 8.

Quddus, M. A. and Hossain, Mahabub. Some Economic Aspects of Jute Production in Bangladesh—An Inter-District Study. *Bangladesh Econ. Rev.,* July 1973, *1*(3), pp. 269–96.

Que, Agustin V. and Walter, James E. The Valuation of Convertible Bonds. *J. Finance,* June 1973, *28* (3), pp. 713–32.

Quinn, Robert P., et al. Evaluating Working Conditions in America. *Mon. Lab. Rev.,* November 1973, *96*(11), pp. 32–41.

Quintano, Claudio. Regressione e correlazione lineare di variabili multidimensionali. (Linear Regression and Linear Correlation of Multidimensional Variables. With English summary.) *Rivista Int. Sci. Econ. Com.,* January 1973, *20*(1), pp. 48–62.

Quirk, James. An Economic Analysis of Team Movements in Professional Sports. *Law Contemp. Probl.,* Winter-Spring 1973, *38*(1), pp. 42–66.

——— **and Habibagahi, Hamid.** Hicksian Stability and Walras' Law. *Rev. Econ. Stud.,* April 1973, *40* (2), pp. 249–58.

Qureshi, Sarfraz K. The Problem of Agricultural Taxation in West Pakistan and an Alternative Solution: A Comment. *Pakistan Develop. Rev.,* Winter 1973, *12*(4), pp. 433–37.

——— Reliability of Pakistani Agricultural Price Data. *Pakistan Develop. Rev.,* Summer 1973, *12* (2), pp. 168–80.

Qureshi, Usman A.; Cross, Edward M. and Sailors, Joel W. Empirical Verification of Linder's Trade Thesis. *Southern Econ. J.,* October 1973, *40*(2), pp. 262–68.

Rabe, B. Financiële modellen als beleidsinstrument in de onderneming. (Financial Models as Management Tools. With English summary.) *Econ. Soc. Tijdschr.,* April 1973, *27*(2), pp. 173–80.

Rabin, Yale. Highways as a Barrier to Equal Access. *Ann. Amer. Acad. Polit. Soc. Sci.,* May 1973, *407,* pp. 63–77.

Rabushka, Alvin and Roberts, Paul Craig. A Diagrammatic Exposition of an Economic Theory of Imperialism. *Public Choice,* Spring 1973, *14,* pp. 101–07.

Racette, George A. Earnings Retention, New Capital and the Growth of the Firm: A Comment. *Rev. Econ. Statist.,* February 1973, *55*(1), pp. 127–28.

——— **and Lewellen, Wilbur G.** Convertible Debt Financing. *J. Financial Quant. Anal.,* December 1973, *8*(5), pp. 777–92.

Racster, Ronald L. and Howard, Robert. Evaluation of Multiple Subsidy Programs in a Local Market. *Amer. Real Estate Urban Econ. Assoc. J.,* Fall 1973, *1*(2), pp. 104–18.

Rader, J. Trout. An Economic Approach to Social Choice. *Public Choice,* Summer 1973, *15,* pp. 49–75.

——— Nice Demand Functions. *Econometrica,* September 1973, *41*(5), pp. 913–35.

——— **and Van Moeseke, P.** Heckscher-Ohlin Hypothesis and Scarce-Factor Theorems. *Tijdschr.*

Econ., 1973, *18*(3), pp. 445–50.

Radhakrishnan, S. The Future Role of Some Non-Banking Financial Intermediaries. In *Simha, S. L. N., ed.*, 1973, pp. 265–71.

Radhu, Ghulam M. Some Aspects of Direct Foreign Private Investment in Pakistan. *Pakistan Develop. Rev.*, Spring 1973, *12*(1), pp. 68–80.

———— Trade Between East and West Pakistan at World Prices, 1960/61–1969/70. *Pakistan Develop. Rev.*, Summer 1973, *12*(2), pp. 148–55.

———— Transfer of Technical Know-How Through Multinational Corporations in Pakistan. *Pakistan Develop. Rev.*, Winter 1973, *12*(4), pp. 361–74.

Radner, Roy. Optimal Stationary Consumption with Stochastic Production and Resources. *J. Econ. Theory*, February 1973, *6*(1), pp. 68–90.

Rǎducanu, Constantin. Determinarea proporţiei dintre sectorul I şi sectorul II necesare realizǎrii echilibrului la nivel intersectorial între cerere şi ofertǎ. (Determining the Proportion Between Sector I and Sector II Necessary for Obtaining an Intersectorial Balance Between Supply and Demand. With English summary.) *Stud. Cercet. Econ.*, 1973, (1), pp. 43–52.

Raetsen, M. J. E. H. and Veldkamp, Gérard M. J. Temporary Work Agencies and Western European Social Legislation. *Int. Lab. Rev.*, February 1973, *107*(2), pp. 117–31.

Ragazzi, Giorgio. Theories of the Determinants of Direct Foreign Investment. *Int. Monet. Fund Staff Pap.*, July 1973, *20*(2), pp. 471–98.

Rahim, Sikander. Economic Development and Unequal Exchange. *Pakistan Econ. Soc. Rev.*, Winter 1973, *11*(4), pp. 463–72.

Rahman, Md. Anisur. National Income and Social Values. *Bangladesh Econ. Rev.*, January 1973, *1*(1), pp. 95–101.

Rahman El Sheikh, Ahmed Abdel. Savings Banks and Savings Facilities in African Countries: Sudan. In *Alberici, A. and Baravelli, M., eds.*, 1973, pp. 97–101.

Raiff, Donald L. and Young, Richard M. Budget Surpluses for State and Local Governments: Undercutting Uncle Sam's Fiscal Stance? *Fed. Res. Bank Bus. Rev. Phila.*, March 1973, pp. 19–28.

Rainoni, Antonio. Monetary Cooperation and the International Monetary System. In *Holbik, K., ed.*, 1973, pp. 525–71.

Raj, K. N. Direct Taxation of Agriculture. *Indian Econ. Rev.*, April 1973, *8*(1), pp. 1–15.

———— Presidential Address. *Indian Econ. J.*, January-March 1973, *20*(3), pp. 355–62.

Rakes, G. K. A Numerical Credit Evaluation Model for Residential Mortgages. *Quart. Rev. Econ. Bus.*, Autumn 1973, *13*(3), pp. 73–84.

Raman, A. Credit Planning—Role of the Reserve Bank of India. In *Simha, S. L. N., ed.*, 1973, pp. 331–39.

———— Expansion of Branches of Commercial Banks with Special Reference to 'Lead Bank' Scheme. In *Simha, S. L. N., ed.*, 1973, pp. 139–54.

Ramana, D. V. Towards an Appraisal and a Strategy of Development for the ECAFE Region Countries. *Malayan Econ. Rev.*, October 1973, *18*(2), pp. 16–36.

Ramanathan, R. Adjustment Time in the Two-Sector Growth Model with Fixed Coefficients. *Econ. J.*, December 1973, *83*(332), pp. 1236–44.

Ramanujam, M. S. Requirements of Technical Manpower in India: 1965–66 to 1980–81. *Indian Econ. Rev.*, October 1973, *8*(2), pp. 101–24.

Ramey, James T. The Promise of Nuclear Energy. *Ann. Amer. Acad. Polit. Soc. Sci.*, November 1973, *410*, pp. 11–23.

Ramsett, David E.; Johnson, Jerry D. and Adams, Curtis. Some Evidence on the Value of Instructors in Teaching Economic Principles. *J. Econ. Educ.*, Fall 1973, *5*(1), pp. 57–62.

Ramsey, J. A. East-West Business Cooperation: The Twain Meet. In *Thorelli, H. B., ed.*, 1973, pp. 58–63.

Randall, J. N. Shift-Share Analysis as a Guide to the Employment Performance of West Central Scotland. *Scot. J. Polit. Econ.*, February 1973, *20*(1), pp. 1–26.

Randall, Laura. Inflation and Economic Development in Latin America: Some New Evidence. *J. Devel. Stud.*, January 1973, *9*(2), pp. 317–22.

Randers, Jørgen and Meadows, Dennis L. System Simulation to Test Environmental Policy: A Sample Study of DDT Movement in the Environment. In *Hawkes, N., ed.*, 1973, pp. 96–143.

———— and **Meadows, Donella H.** The Carrying Capacity of Our Global Environment: A Look at the Ethical Alternatives. In *Daly, H. E., ed.*, 1973, pp. 283–306.

Rangi, P. S.; Sankhayan, P. L. and Singh, Balwinder. Relative Contributions of Area and Productivity in Increasing Production of Major Foodgrain Crops in Panjab (1960–61 to 1969–70) *Econ. Aff.*, March 1973, *18*(3), pp. 124–30.

Ranis, Gustav. The Exchange Constraint on Development—A Partial Solution to the Problem: A Comment. *Econ. J.*, March 1973, *83*(329), pp. 203–07.

———— Industrial Sector Labor Absorption. *Econ. Develop. Cult. Change*, April 1973, *21*(3), pp. 387–408.

Ransom, Roger and Sutch, Richard. The Ex-Slave in the Post-Bellum South: A Study of the Economic Impact of Racism in a Market Environment. *J. Econ. Hist.*, March 1973, *33*(1), pp. 131–48.

Ranuwihardjo, Sukadji. Exchange Rate Experience and Policy in Indonesia Since World War II. In *Grubel, H. G. and Morgan, T., eds.*, 1973, pp. 41–53.

Ranuzzi de Bianchi, Paolo. Le società multinazionali e la bilancia dei pagamenti americana. (Multinational Companies and the American Balance of Payments. With English summary.) *Bancaria*, September 1973, *29*(9), pp. 1090–93.

Rao, A. S. and Maddala, G. S. Tests for Serial Correlation in Regression Models with Lagged Dependent Variables and Serially Correlated Errors. *Econometrica*, July 1973, *41*(4), pp. 761–74.

Rao, B. Bhaskara. An Alternative Econometric Approach to the Permanent Income Hypothesis: An International Comparison: A Comment. *Rev. Econ. Statist.*, May 1973, *55*(2), pp. 261.

———— Price Behaviour in India: A Note on Professor Raj's Model. *Indian Econ. Rev.*, October 1973, *8*(2), pp. 186–92.

Rao, Cherukuri U. The Demand for Liquid Asset Balances by U.S. Manufacturing Corporations: 1959-1970: Comment. *J. Financial Quant. Anal.*, March 1973, *8*(2), pp. 223–25.

Rao, D. C. and Kaminow, Ira. Selective Credit Controls and the Real Investment Mix: A General Equilibrium Approach. *J. Finance*, December 1973, *28*(5), pp. 1103–18.

Rao, D. S. Prasada and Mukherjee, M. On Consistent Intergroup Comparisons of Purchasing Power of Money. *Rev. Income Wealth*, March 1973, *19*(1), pp. 35–47.

Rao, M. R. S. N. Proposed Role of GIIC in Industrialisation of Backward Districts. *Artha-Vikas*, January-July 1973, *9*(1–2), pp. 230–39.

Rao, Potluri. On Estimation of Demand and Supply Equations of a Commodity. *Indian Econ. Rev.*, April 1973, *8*(1), pp. 61–68.

Rao, S. L. N. On Long-Term Mortality Trends in the United States, 1850-1968. *Demography*, August 1973, *10*(3), pp. 405–19.

Rapp, William V. and Abegglen, James C. Japanese Managerial Behavior and "Excessive Competition." In *Henley, D. S., ed.,* 1973, pp. 65–82.

Rapping, Leonard A. U.S. Maritime Policy: Subsidizing Waste and Inefficiency. In *Haveman, R. H. and Hamrin, R. D., eds.,* 1973, pp. 215–19.

Rasaputram, Warnasena. Exchange Rate Experience and Policy in Sri Lanka (Ceylon) Since World War II. In *Grubel, H. G. and Morgan, T., eds.,* 1973, pp. 9–18.

Rasche, Robert H. A Comparative Static Analysis of Some Monetarist Propositions. *Fed. Res. Bank St. Louis Rev.*, December 1973, *55*(12), pp. 15–23.

———— Simulations of Stabilization Policies for 1966-1970. *J. Money, Credit, Banking*, Part I, February 1973, *5*(1), pp. 1–25.

Raskin, Barbara. The AFDC Numbers Game. In *Levitan, S. A., ed.,* 1973, pp. 119–42.

Rasminsky, Louis. Canadian Monetary Policy and the Problem of Inflation. In *Moskoff, W., ed.,* 1973, pp. 56–62.

Rasmussen, David W. Changes in the Relative Income of Nonwhite Males, 1948–1970. In *Rasmussen, D. W. and Haworth, C. T., eds.,* 1973, pp. 81–86.

———— **and Haworth, C. T.** Determinants of Metropolitan Cost of Living Variations. *Southern Econ. J.*, October 1973, *40*(2), pp. 183–92.

Rasmussen, Jon A. Applications of a Model of Endogenous Technical Change to US Industry Data. *Rev. Econ. Stud.*, April 1973, *40*(2), pp. 225–38.

Rasmussen, Jørgen. Dual Theories and the Classics. In *Institute for Development Research,* 1973, pp. 61–74.

Rasmussen, Nørregaard and Danø, Sven. Ragnar Frisch. *Nationalokon. Tidsskr.*, 1973, *111*(1), pp. 5–8.

Rastatter, E. H.; Moore, Arnold B. and Walgreen, John A. The Economics of the United States Supersonic Transport. *J. Transp. Econ. Policy*, May 1973, *7*(2), pp. 186–93.

Ratajczak, Donald and Williams, Robert M. Forecast. Another Year of Prosperity for 1973. *Calif. Manage. Rev.*, Spring 1973, *15*(3), pp. i–v.

Ratchford, B. U. Interest Rates and Inflation. *Nebr. J. Econ. Bus.*, Spring 1973, *12*(2), pp. 45–54.

Ratcliffe, Anne E. Labour in the South African Gold Mines. (Review article). *S. Afr. J. Econ.*, September 1973, *41*(3), pp. 257–67.

Ratford, Bruce E. A Note on Niedercorn's Negative Exponential Model of Urban Land Use. *J. Reg. Sci.*, April 1973, *13*(1), pp. 135–38.

Rath, Gustave J. and Thompson, Charles W. N. Planning Solutions Aided by Management and Systems Technology. *Ann. Amer. Acad. Polit. Soc. Sci.*, January 1973, *405*, pp. 151–62.

Raup, Phillip. Corporate Farming in the United States. *J. Econ. Hist.*, March 1973, *33*(1), pp. 274–90.

Rauscher, Walter J. The Implementation and Impact of SABRE: American Airlines. In *The Diebold Group, Inc.*, 1973, pp. 265–70.

Rausser, Gordon C. and Paris, Quirino. Sufficient Conditions for Aggregation of Linear Programming Models. *Amer. J. Agr. Econ.*, Part I, November 1973, *55*(4), pp. 659–66.

Ravazzi, Giancarlo. Evoluzione delle strutture commerciali: analisi funzionale e indicazioni prospettiche. (Development of Distribution Structures: A Functional Analysis and Prospects. With English summary.) *L'Impresa*, 1973, *15*(9–10), pp. 607–17.

———— La conoscenza come fattore di razionalizzazione del sistema distributivo-commerciale. (Knowledge As a Factor of Rationalization of the Distributive System. With English summary.) *L'Impresa*, 1973, *15*(1), pp. 12–19.

Raveed, Sion and Renforth, William C. Shifting World Wage Rates: What Do They Mean for Indiana? *Indiana Bus. Rev.*, September-October 1973, *48*, pp. 15–19.

Rawlins, V. Lane and Leigh, Duane E. On the Stability of Relative Black-White Unemployment. *Mon. Lab. Rev.*, May 1973, *96*(5), pp. 30–32.

Rawski, Thomas G. The Chinese Economy at the Present Juncture: Discussion. *Amer. Econ. Rev.*, May 1973, *63*(2), pp. 234–35.

———— Chinese Industrial Production, 1952-1971. *Rev. Econ. Statist.*, May 1973, *55*(2), pp. 169–81.

Ray, Alok. Non-Traded Inputs and Effective Protection: A General Equilibrium Analysis. *J. Int. Econ.*, August 1973, *3*(3), pp. 245–57.

Ray, Anandarup and Van der Tak, Herman G. The Economic Benefits of Road Transport Projects. In *Niskanen, W. A., et al., eds.,* 1973, pp. 132–73.

Ray, Daryll E. and Plaxico, James S. Implications for Agricultural Economists. *Amer. J. Agr. Econ.*, August 1973, *55*(3), pp. 399–403.

Ray, Edward J. The Sources of Finance in West Germany. *Z. ges. Staatswiss.*, October 1973, *129*(4), pp. 663–84.

———— **and Baack, Bennett D.** Tariff Policy and Comparative Advantage in the Iron and Steel Industry: 1870–1929. *Exploration Econ. Hist.*, Fall 1973, *11*(1), pp. 3–23.

Ray, Paramesh. Independence of Irrelevant Alternatives. *Econometrica*, September 1973, *41*(5), pp. 987–91.

Raymond, Richard. The Interregional Brain Drain and Public Education. *Growth Change,* July 1973, *4*(3), pp. 28–34.

Rayner, A. and Wolfson, M. Analytics of Choice in Fiscal Policy. In *Parkin, M., ed.,* 1973, pp. 345–68.

Rayner, P. J. and Hagger, A. J. The Excess Demand for Commodities in Australia, 1950-51 to 1968-69. *Econ. Rec.*, June 1973, *49*(126), pp. 161–93.

Razin, Assaf and Berglas, Eitan. Effective Protection and Decreasing Returns to Scale. *Amer. Econ. Rev.*, September 1973, *63*(4), pp. 733–37.

_____ and Berglas, E. Real Exchange Rate and Devaluation. *J. Int. Econ.*, May 1973, *3*(2), pp. 179–91.

_____ and Berglas, E. A Trade Model with Variable Returns to Scale. *Econ. Rec.*, March 1973, *49* (125), pp. 126–34.

_____; Hochman, Eitan and Hochman, Oded. Demand for Investment in Productive and Financial Capital. *Europ. Econ. Rev.*, April 1973, *4*(1), pp. 67–83.

_____ and Mas-Colell, Andreu. A Model of Intersectoral Migration and Growth. *Oxford Econ. Pap.*, March 1973, *25*(1), pp. 72–79.

Rea, John D. Trends and Cycles in Money and Bank Credit. *Fed. Res. Bank Kansas City Rev.*, March 1973, pp. 3–9.

Reading, Don C. New Deal Activity and the States, 1933 to 1939. *J. Econ. Hist.*, December 1973, *33* (4), pp. 792–810.

Reaume, David M. Cost-Benefit Techniques and Consumer Surplus: A Clarificatory Analysis. *Public Finance*, 1973, *28*(2), pp. 196–211.

Reay, J. S. S. Air Pollution. In *Robinson, J., ed.*, 1973, pp. 156–74.

Recktenwald, Horst Claus. From Public Finance to Public Economics. In *Rectenwald, H. C., ed.*, 1973, pp. 424–36.

_____ and Hicks, John R. [Sir]. Walras's Economic System. In *Rectenwald, H. C., ed.*, 1973, pp. 261–65.

Redclift, M. R. Squatter Settlements in Latin American Cities: The Response from Government. *J. Devel. Stud.*, October 1973, *10*(1), pp. 92–109.

Reddington, Donald A. Control Methods for Small Business. *Manage. Account.*, September 1973, *55* (3), pp. 15–17, 26.

Rédei, J. The System of Foreign Trade Agreements. In *Kiss, T., ed.*, 1973, pp. 167–75.

Redisch, Michael and Pauly, Mark V. The Not-For-Profit Hospital as a Physicians' Cooperative. *Amer. Econ. Rev.*, March 1973, *63*(1), pp. 87–99.

Redlich, Fritz. American Banking and Growth in the Nineteenth Century: Epistemological Reflections. *Exploration Econ. Hist.*, Spring 1973, *10*(3), pp. 305–14.

_____ and Carpenter, Kenneth E. Research Possibilities in the History of Political Economy Through a Bibliography of Translations. *Hist. Polit. Econ.*, Spring 1973, *5*(1), pp. 268–83.

Reed, Clyde G. Transactions Costs and Differential Growth in Seventeenth Century Western Europe. *J. Econ. Hist.*, March 1973, *33*(1), pp. 177–90.

_____ and Anderson, Terry L. An Economic Explanation of English Agricultural Organization in the Twelfth and Thirteenth Centuries: Comment. *Econ. Hist. Rev., 2nd Ser.*, February 1973, *26*(1), pp. 134–37.

Reed, Laurance. Policy Issues. In *Robinson, J., ed.*, 1973, pp. 175–88.

Reed, Merl E. The Augusta Textile Mills and the Strike of 1886. *Labor Hist.*, Spring 1973, *14*(2), pp. 228–46.

Rees, R. Public Sector Resource Allocation under Conditions of Risk. In *Parkin, M., ed.*, 1973, pp. 110–36.

Rees, R. D. Optimum Plant Size in United Kingdom Industries: Some Survivor Estimates. *Economica, N.S.*, November 1973, *40*(160), pp. 394–401.

Rees, Richard D. World Wheat Production and Trade. *Fed. Res. Bank Kansas City Rev.*, June 1973, pp. 10–16.

Reese, K. The Soviet Ruble and Comecon Countries. *S. Afr. J. Econ.*, June 1973, *41*(2), pp. 134–45.

Reeves, H. Clyde. System Value Determination in the Assessment of Railroads for Property Taxation. *Nat. Tax J.*, March 1973, *26*(1), pp. 133–35.

Regan, Opal G. Statistical Reforms Accelerated by Sixth Census Errors. *J. Amer. Statist. Assoc.*, September 1973, *68*(343), pp. 540–46.

Regev, Uri and Schwartz, Aba. Optimal Path of Interregional Investment and Allocation of Water. *Water Resources Res.*, April 1973, *9*(2), pp. 251–62.

Rehnberg, Bertil. Active Manpower Policy in Sweden. In *Moskoff, W., ed.*, 1973, pp. 85–91.

Reich, Michael and Finkelhor, David. The Military-Industrial Complex. In *Reynolds, L. G.; Green, G. D. and Lewis, D. R., eds.*, 1973, pp. 334–46.

_____; Gordon, David M. and Edwards, Richard C. A Theory of Labor Market Segmentation. *Amer. Econ. Rev.*, May 1973, *63*(2), pp. 359–65.

Reich, Utz-Peter. Die theoretischen Grundlagen des SPD-Langzeitprogramms. (Theoretical Frame-Work of the SPD-Long-Term-Program. With English summary.) *Z. Wirtschaft. Sozialwissen.*, 1973, *93*(5), pp. 513–35.

Reichenbach, H. and Scheper, W. Die Entwicklung der Anteile der Wirtschaftsbereiche am Bruttoinlandsprodukt—Eine Strukturprognose. (The Development of the Sectoral Shares of Production in Gross National Product. A Forecast of the Production Structure. With English summary) *Weltwirtsch. Arch.*, 1973, *109*(2), pp. 291–320.

Reid, Escott. McNamara's World Bank. *Foreign Aff.*, July 1973, *51*(4), pp. 794–810.

Reid, Frank J. Mundell on Growth and the Balance of Payments: A Note. *Can. J. Econ.*, November 1973, *6*(4), pp. 592–95.

Reid, G. K. R. and Thomas, D. A. Pastoral Production, Stocking Rate and Seasonal Conditions. *Quart. Rev. Agr. Econ.*, October 1973, *26*(4), pp. 217–27.

Reid, Joseph D. Sharecropping as an Understandable Market Response—The Post-Bellum South. *J. Econ. Hist.*, March 1973, *33*(1), pp. 106–30.

Reid, Margaret G. Education and the Derived Demand for Children: Comment. *J. Polit. Econ.*, Part II, March-April 1973, *81*(2), pp. S165–67.

Reid, Samuel Richardson. "The Bank Merger Act of 1960: A Decade After": Comment. *Antitrust Bull.*, Fall, 1973, *18*(3), pp. 449–62.

Reierson, Roy L. International Financial Markets: Problems and Prospects. In *Levy, M. E., ed.*, 1973, pp. 24–36.

Reilley, Ewing W. Planning the Strategy of the Business. In *Klein, W. H. and Murphy, D. C., eds.*, 1973, pp. 166–73.

Reilly, Frank K. Further Evidence on Short-Run Results for New Issue Investors. *J. Financial Quant. Anal.*, January 1973, *8*(1), pp. 83–90.

—— and **Drzycimski, Eugene F.** Tests of Stock Market Efficiency Following Major Events. *J. Bus. Res.*, Summer 1973, *1*(1), pp. 57–72.

—— and **Sherr, Lawrence A.** The Shift Method: A Technique for Measuring the Differential Performance of Stocks. *Miss. Val. J. Bus. Econ.*, Fall 1973, *9*(1), pp. 28–40.

—— and **Slaughter, William C.** The Effect of Dual Markets on Common Stock Market Making. *J. Financial Quant. Anal.*, March 1973, *8*(2), pp. 167–82.

Reilly, Raymond R. and **Wecker, William E.** On the Weighted Average Cost of Capital. *J. Financial Quant. Anal.*, January 1973, *8*(1), pp. 123–26.

Reimann, Guenter. Floating Rates and the Market Place. In *Wiegand, G. C., ed.*, 1973, pp. 160–68.

Rein, Martin. Recent British Experience with Negative Income Tax. *J. Human Res.*, Supplement 1973, *8*, pp. 69–89.

—— Work Incentives and Welfare Reform in Britain and the United States. In *Stein, B. and Miller, S. M., eds.*, 1973, pp. 151–95.

Reinhardt, Paul G. A Theory of Household Grocery Inventory Holdings. *Kyklos*, 1973, *26*(3), pp. 497–511.

Reinhardt, U. E. Break-Even Analysis for Lockheed's Tri Star: An Application of Financial Theory. *J. Finance*, September 1973, *28*(4), pp. 821–38.

Reinsel, Edward I. and **Browning, Thomas L.** Distribution of Farm Program Payments by Income of Sole Proprietors. *Agr. Econ. Res.*, April 1973, *25* (2), pp. 41–44.

—— and **Carlin, Thomas A.** Combining Income and Wealth: An Analysis of Farm Family "Well-Being." *Amer. J. Agr. Econ.*, February 1973, *55* (1), pp. 38–44.

Reints, William W. and **Vandenberg, Pieter A.** A Comment on the Risk Level Discriminatory Powers of the Wiesenberger Classifications. *J. Bus.*, April 1973, *46*(2), pp. 278–83.

Reisler, Mark. Mexican Unionization in California Agriculture, 1927–1936. *Labor Hist.*, Fall 1973, *14*(4), pp. 562–79.

Reiter, Stanley and **Hurwicz, Leonid.** On the Boundedness of the Feasible Set Without Convexity Assumptions. *Int. Econ. Rev.*, October 1973, *14*(3), pp. 580–86.

Reizer, Jozef and **Mach, Milos.** The Place of Commodity-Money Relations in the Socialist System and a Critical Review of the Theory of the So-Called Market Socialism. *Czech. Econ. Digest.*, December 1973, (8), pp. 71–101.

Rejda, George E. and **Shepler, Richard J.** The Impact of Zero Population Growth on the OASDHI Program. *J. Risk Ins.*, September 1973, *40*(3), pp. 313–25.

Remaley, William A. Suboptimization in Mean-Variance Efficient Set Analysis. *J. Finance*, May 1973, *28*(2), pp. 397–403.

Remes Lenicov, Jorge L. Algunos resultados de la política desarrollista (1958–64): el caso de la industria automotriz. (Some Results of the Development Policy 1958–64; the Case of the Automobile Industry. With English summary.) *Económica,* September-December 1973, *19*(3), pp. 293–329.

Renas, Steve. Short Run Marginal Cost and Marginal Productivity: A Note. *Pakistan Econ. Soc. Rev.,* Summer 1973, *11*(2), pp. 215–18.

—— Work Effort and the Progressive Income Tax: A Note. *Tijdschr. Econ.*, 1973, *18*(3), pp. 441–43.

Renaud, Bertrand M. Conflicts Between National Growth and Regional Income Equality in a Rapidly Growing Economy: The Case of Korea. *Econ. Develop. Cult. Change*, April 1973, *21*(3), pp. 429–45.

Renda, Benedetto. Credito, risparmio e banche nelle prospettive dell'integrazione europea. (Credit, Savings and Bank Systems in the Perspective of European Economic Integration. With English summary.) *Mondo Aperto*, February 1973, *27*(1), pp. 9–23.

Rendón, Teresa and **Bassoco, Luz María.** The Technology Set and Data Base for CHAC. In *Goreux, L. M. and Manne, A. S., eds.*, 1973, pp. 339–71.

Renforth, William C. and **Raveed, Sion.** Shifting World Wage Rates: What Do They Mean for Indiana? *Indiana Bus. Rev.*, September-October 1973, *48*, pp. 15–19.

Rennie, Henry G. Federal Tax Policy and Fixed Capital Expenditures by Ohio's Electric Utilities. *Ohio State U. Bull. Bus. Res.*, July 1973, *48*(7), pp. 5–7.

Reno, Virginia. Women Newly Entitled to Retired-Worker Benefits: Survey of New Beneficiaries. *Soc. Sec. Bull.*, April 1973, *36*(4), pp. 3–26.

Renshaw, Edward F. A Note on Mass Transit Subsidies. *Nat. Tax J.*, December 1973, *26*(4), pp. 638–44.

Reps, John W. Public Land, Urban Development Policy, and the American Planning Tradition. In *Clawson, M., ed.*, 1973, pp. 15–48.

Resnick, Stephen A. and **Birnberg, Thomas.** A Model of the Trade and Government Sectors in Colonial Economies. *Amer. Econ. Rev.*, September 1973, *63*(4), pp. 572–87.

—— and **Truman, Edwin M.** An Empirical Examination of Bilateral Trade in Western Europe. *J. Int. Econ.*, November 1973, *3*(4), pp. 305–35.

Retherford, Robert D. Cigarette Smoking and Widowhood in the United States. *Population Stud.*, July 1973, *27*(2), pp. 193–206.

Rettaroli, Riccardo. L'esperienza delle SICAV in Francia. (The SICAV Experience in France. With English summary.) *Bancaria*, April 1973, *29*(4), pp. 453–66.

Rettig, R. Bruce. Multiple Objectives for Marine Resource Management. In *Sokoloski, A. A., ed.*, 1973, pp. 23–27.

Reubens, Beatrice G. Manpower Training in Japan. *Mon. Lab. Rev.*, September 1973, *96*(9), pp. 16–24.

Reuss, Henry S. A Congressional View of the World's Monetary Problems. In *Wiegand, G. C., ed.*, 1973, pp. 145–50.

Revankar, Nagesh S. and **Hartley, Michael J.** An Independence Test and Conditional Unbiased Predictions in the Context of Simultaneous Equation Systems. *Int. Econ. Rev.*, October 1973, *14* (3), pp. 625–31.

ReVelle, Charles and **Eastman, John.** Linear Decision Rule in Reservoir Management and Design: 3. Direct Capacity Determination and Intraseasonal Constraints. *Water Resources Res.*, February 1973, *9*(1), pp. 29–42.

Reynaud, Paul and Zarca, Bernard. Les leçons d'une enquête sur les petits commerçants âgés (Action sociale et transformation du milieu sociologique). (The Lessons of a Survey of Old Small Shop-keepers. (Social Policy and Change of Social Settings.) With English summary.) *Consommation,* January-March 1973, *20*(1), pp. 59–76.

Reynaud, Pierre-Louis. The Work of Jean-Baptiste Say. In *Rectenwald, H. C., ed.,* 1973, pp. 110–18.

Reynolds, Clark W. Relations with Latin America: An American View. In *Urquidi, V. L. and Thorp, R., eds.,* 1973, pp. 235–82.

Reynolds, David R.; Horton, Frank E. and Louviere, Jordan. Mass Transit Utilization: Individual Response Data Inputs. *Econ. Geogr.,* April 1973, *49*(2), pp. 122–33.

Reynolds, Lloyd G. Labor in Less Developed Economies. In *Somers, G. G., ed.,* 1973, pp. 165–76.

Reynolds, Morgan O. and Brown, William W. Crime and "Punishment": Risk Implications. *J. Econ. Theory,* October 1973, *6*(5), pp. 508–14.

_____ Debt Peonage Re-examined. *J. Econ. Hist.,* December 1973, *33*(4), pp. 862–71.

Reyns, C. and De Coorde, F. Accountancy versus Management. (In Flemish. With English summary.) *Econ. Soc. Tijdschr.,* June 1973, *27*(3), pp. 277–86.

Rhoades, Stephen A. The Concentration-Profitability Relationship: Policy Implications and Some Empirical Evidence. *Antitrust Bull.,* Summer 1973, *18*(2), pp. 333–54.

_____ The Effect of Diversification on Industry Profit Performance in 241 Manufacturing Industries: 1963. *Rev. Econ. Statist.,* May 1973, *55*(2), pp. 146–55.

_____ and Cleaver, Joe M. The Nature of the Concentration—Price/Cost Margin Relationship for 352 Manufacturing Industries: 1967. *Southern Econ. J.,* July 1973, *40*(1), pp. 90–102.

Rhodes, John and Moore, Barry. Evaluating the Effects of British Regional Economic Policy. *Econ. J.,* March 1973, *83*(329), pp. 87–110.

Rhodes, R. A. W. The European Community and British Public Administration: The Case of Local Government. *J. Common Market Stud.,* June 1973, *11*(4), pp. 263–75.

Rhomberg, Rudolf R. Towards a General Trade Model. In *Ball, R. J., ed.,* 1973, pp. 9–20.

_____ and Artus, Jacques R. A Multilateral Exchange Rate Model. *Int. Monet. Fund Staff Pap.,* November 1973, *20*(3), pp. 591–611.

_____; Hickman, Bert G. and Klein, Lawrence R. Background, Organization and Preliminary Results of Project LINK. In *Alexandrides, C. G., ed.,* 1973, pp. 19–56.

_____ and Junz, Helen B. Price Competitiveness in Export Trade Among Industrial Countries. *Amer. Econ. Rev.,* May 1973, *63*(2), pp. 412–18.

Rhys, D. G. Economics of Change in Road Passenger Transport: Rejoinder. *J. Transp. Econ. Policy,* September 1973, *7*(3), pp. 292–93.

Ribich, Thomas I. Soft Sell for Soft Drinks: An Excise Tax Problem. *Nat. Tax J.,* March 1973, *26*(1), pp. 115–17.

Rica, Narciso A. Some Reflections on Permanent Tributary Reform. *Bull. Int. Fiscal Doc.,* May 1973, *27*(5), pp. 179–88.

Rice, E. B. and Dalrymple, Dana G. Review of Small Farmer Credit in Developing Nations. *Agr. Finance Rev.,* July 1973, *34*, pp. 35–37.

Rice, G. Randolph. Poverty and Industrial Growth Patterns: Some Cross-State Evidence. *J. Reg. Sci.,* December 1973, *13*(3), pp. 377–84.

Rich, Jack. Natural Resources and External Economies: Regulation of the Pacific Halibut Fishery. In *Sokoloski, A. A., ed.,* 1973, pp. 65–71.

Richard, Enrique P. Treatment of Royalties in Tax Conventions Between Developed and Developing Countries. *Bull. Int. Fiscal Doc.,* October 1973, *27*(10), pp. 407–14.

Richard, Jean F. and Zellner, Arnold. Use of Prior Information in the Analysis and Estimation of Cobb-Douglas Production Function Models. *Int. Econ. Rev.,* February 1973, *14*(1), pp. 107–19.

Richards, A. I. Characteristics of the Selected Farmers—A Summary. In *Richards, A. I.; Sturrock, F. and Fortt, J. M., eds.,* 1973, pp. 271–88.

_____ Government Policy and the Commercial Farmer. In *Richards, A. I.; Sturrock, F. and Fortt, J. M., eds.,* 1973, pp. 85–92.

_____ Some Conclusions. In *Richards, A. I.; Sturrock, F. and Fortt, J. M., eds.,* 1973, pp. 289–305.

_____ Subsistence to Commercial Farming in Present-Day Buganda: An Economic and Anthropological Survey: Introduction. In *Richards, A. I.; Sturrock, F. and Fortt, J. M., eds.,* 1973, pp. 1–13.

_____ The Traditional Administrative Structure and the Agricultural Development of Buganda. In *Richards, A. I.; Sturrock, F. and Fortt, J. M., eds.,* 1973, pp. 47–65.

_____ and Mafeje, Archie. The Commercial Farmer and His Labour Supply. In *Richards, A. I.; Sturrock, F. and Fortt, J. M., eds.,* 1973, pp. 179–97.

Richards, Douglas F.; Davis, Lawrence S. and Thompson, Emmett F. The South's Third Forest: A Critique. *Land Econ.,* February 1973, *49*(1), pp. 105–09.

Richards, E. S. Structural Change in a Regional Economy: Sutherland and the Industrial Revolution, 1780-1830. *Econ. Hist. Rev., 2nd Ser.,* February 1973, *26*(1), pp. 63–76.

Richards, J. H. and Halder, A. Structural Characteristics of India's Foreign Trade and its Effect on the Instability of Export Receipts. *Indian Econ. J.,* October-December 1973, *21*(2), pp. 132–46.

Richards, Louise G. Consumer Practices of the Poor. In *Murray, B. B., ed.,* 1973, pp. 426–41.

Richards, P. J. Job Mobility and Unemployment in the Ceylon Urban Labour Market. *Oxford Bull. Econ. Statist.,* February 1973, *35*(1), pp. 49–59.

Richards, Vincent A. E. Development Prospects in the Commonwealth Caribbean in the 1970s. In *Pollock, D. H. and Ritter, A. R. M., eds.,* 1973, pp. 269–86.

Richardson, Dennis W. The Emerging Era of Electronic Money: Some Implications for Monetary Policy. *J. Bank Res.,* Winter 1973, *3*(4), pp. 261–64.

Richardson, D. H. and Basmann, R. L. The Exact

Finite Sample Distribution of a Non-Consistent Structural Variance Estimator. *Econometrica*, January 1973, *41*(1), pp. 41–58.

Richardson, Harry W. A Comment on Some Uses of Mathematical Models in Urban Economics. *Urban Stud.*, June 1973, *10*(2), pp. 259–66.

——— A Comment on Some Uses of Mathematical Models in Urban Economics: Reply to Solow and Mirrlees. *Urban Stud.*, June 1973, *10*(2), pp. 269–70.

——— A Guide to Urban Economics Texts: A Review Article. *Urban Stud.*, October 1973, *10*(3), pp. 399–405.

——— A Markov Chain Model of Interregional Savings and Capital Growth. *J. Reg. Sci.*, April 1973, *13*(1), pp. 17–27.

——— The Spatial Distribution of Unemployment by Occupation: A Comment. *J. Reg. Sci.*, December 1973, *13*(3), pp. 467–69.

Richardson, J. David. Beyond (But Back To?) the Elasticity of Substitution in International Trade. *Europ. Econ. Rev.*, December 1973, *4*(4), pp. 381–92.

Richardson, Lee. Consumers in the Federal Decision-Making Process. *Calif. Manage. Rev.*, Winter 1973, *16*(2), pp. 79–84.

Richardson, Peter and Gardner, Bernard. The Fiscal Treatment of Shipping. *J. Ind. Econ.*, December 1973, *22*(2), pp. 95–117.

Richardson, Reed C. Delivery Systems for Manpower Services. In *Mangum, G. L. and Robson, R. T., eds.*, 1973, pp. 100–119.

——— The Economic, Social, and Political Environment. In *Mangum, G. L. and Robson, R. T., eds.*, 1973, pp. 95–99.

——— The Impact of Denver's Manpower Programs. In *Mangum, G. L. and Robson, R. T., eds.*, 1973, pp. 134–43.

——— Skills and Jobs for Denver's Disadvantaged. In *Mangum, G. L. and Robson, R. T., eds.*, 1973, pp. 120–33.

Richardson, Richard W. The Raising of Resources: Comment. In *Lewis, J. P. and Kapur, I., eds.*, 1973, pp. 57–63.

Richardson, Robert A. and Farris, Paul L. Farm Commodity Price Stabilization Through Futures Markets. *Amer. J. Agr. Econ.*, May 1973, *55*(2), pp. 225–30.

Riche, Martha F. and Robinowitz, Robert S. Productivity in the Ready-Mixed Concrete Industry. *Mon. Lab. Rev.*, May 1973, *96*(5), pp. 12–15.

Richelson, Jeffrey. A Note on Collective Goods and the Theory of Political Entrepreneurship. *Public Choice*, Fall 1973, *16*, pp. 73–75.

Richman, Barry. New Paths to Corporate Social Responsibility. *Calif. Manage. Rev.*, Spring 1973, *15*(3), pp. 20–36.

Richman, Raymond L. The Capitalization of Property Taxes and Subsidies. In *Harriss, C. L., ed.*, 1973, pp. 19–27.

Richmond, David and Kensicki, Peter R. Consumerism and Automobile Insurance. *J. Risk Ins.*, June 1973, *40*(2), pp. 209–17.

Richmond, Richard D. and Hagerman, Robert L. Random Walks, Martingales and the OTC. *J. Finance*, September 1973, *28*(4), pp. 897–909.

Richter, H. V. The Impact of Socialism on Economic Activity in Burma. In *Epstein, T. S. and Penny, D. H., eds.*, 1973, pp. 216–39.

Richter, Joseph J. Constitutional and Institutional Constraints in Agriculture and Agricultural Policy. *Can. J. Agr. Econ.*, February 1973, *21*(1), pp. 49–56.

——— Discussion: The Position of an Importer of Canadian Agricultural Products: Marketing Requirements for Pacific Rim Markets. In *Canadian Agricultural Economics Society*, 1973, pp. 38–42.

Richter, Rudolf. Full Employment and Stable Prices—Compatibility of Targets and Rules. *Ger. Econ. Rev.*, 1973, *11*(2), pp. 108–20.

Riddell, Tom. A Note on Radical Economics and the New Economists. *Rev. Radical Polit. Econ.*, Fall 1973, *5*(3), pp. 67–72.

de Ridder, P. B. and Verbaan, W. C. Uniforme modelstructuur voor meerdere landen. (A Uniform Model Structure for Several Countries. With English summary.) *De Economist*, September-October 1973, *121*(5), pp. 481–520.

Ridker, Ronald G. and Fisher, Joseph L. Population Growth, Resource Availability and Environmental Quality. *Amer. Econ. Rev.*, May 1973, *63*(2), pp. 79–87.

Ridzon, Donald S. Occupational Pay in Shirt Manufacturing. *Mon. Lab. Rev.*, January 1973, *96*(1), pp. 60–61.

——— Wages and Productivity Rise as Employment Falls in Cigar Plants. *Mon. Lab. Rev.*, June 1973, *96*(6), pp. 56–57.

Riedel, James and Glassburner, Bruce. Economic Development Lessons from Hong Kong: A Reply. *Econ. Rec.*, December 1973, *49*(128), pp. 637–43.

Rieder, George A. Performance Review—A Mixed Bag. *Harvard Bus. Rev.*, July-August 1973, *51*(4), pp. 61–67.

Riefler, Roger F. Interregional Input-Output: A State of the Arts Survey. In *Judge, G. G. and Takayama, T., eds.*, 1973, pp. 133–62.

Riesenfeld, Stefan A. Enforcement of Money Judgments in Early American History. *Mich. Law Rev.*, March 1973, *71*(4), pp. 691–728.

Riesz, M. The Main Issues of Credit Theory in the Past 25 Years. *Acta Oecon.*, 1973, *10*(2), pp. 233–46.

Riesz, Peter C. Size versus Price, or Another Vote for Tonypandy. *J. Bus.*, July 1973, *46*(3), pp. 396–403.

Riew, John. Migration and Public Policy. *J. Reg. Sci.*, April 1973, *13*(1), pp. 65–76.

Rifkin, Susan B. and Kaplinsky, Raphael. Health Strategy and Development Planning: Lessons from the People's Republic of China. *J. Devel. Stud.*, January 1973, *9*(2), pp. 213–32.

Riker, William H. Micropolitics and Macroeconomics: Discussion. *Amer. Econ. Rev.*, May 1973, *63*(2), pp. 178–80.

Riley, J. C. Dutch Investment in France, 1781–1787. *J. Econ. Hist.*, December 1973, *33*(4), pp. 732–60.

Riley, John G. "Gammaville": An Optimal Town. *J. Econ. Theory*, October 1973, *6*(5), pp. 471–82.

Riley, Kathleen M. An Estimate of the Age Distribution of the Dwelling Stock in Great Britain. *Urban Stud.*, October 1973, *10*(3), pp. 373–79.

Riley, Kevin. Productive Hours Analysis for a Small Shop. *Manage. Account.*, January 1973, *54*(7), pp. 17–18.

Ringrose, David R. European Economic Growth: Comments on the North-Thomas Theory. *Econ. Hist. Rev., 2nd Ser.*, May 1973, *26*(2), pp. 285–92.

_____ The Impact of a New Capital City: Madrid, Toledo, and New Castile, 1560–1660. *J. Econ. Hist.*, December 1973, *33*(4), pp. 761–91.

_____ War and the Birth of the Nation State: Discussion. *J. Econ. Hist.*, March 1973, *33*(1), pp. 222–27.

Ripley, Duncan M. Systematic Elements in the Linkage of National Stock Market Indices. *Rev. Econ. Statist.*, August 1973, *55*(3), pp. 356–61.

Ripley, Frank C. and Segal, Lydia. Price Determination in 395 Manufacturing Industries. *Rev. Econ. Statist.*, August 1973, *55*(3), pp. 263–71.

Ripman, Hugh B. Project Supervision. *Finance Develop.*, June 1973, *10*(2), pp. 14–18.

Ripper, M.; Varaiya, P. and Legey, L. Effects of Congestion on the Shape of a City. *J. Econ. Theory*, April 1973, *6*(2), pp. 162–79.

Ristea, Mihai. Conceptul de operativitate în sistemul informaţional contabil. (The Concept of Efficiency in the Book-keeping Information System. With English summary.) *Stud. Cercet. Econ.*, 1973, (4), pp. 99–109.

Ritchey, P. Neal. The Fertility of Negroes without Southern Rural Experience: A Re-examination of the 1960 GAF Study Findings with 1967 SEO Data. *Population Stud.*, March 1973, *27*(1), pp. 127–34.

Ritter, Arch R. M. Institutional Strategy and Economic Performance in Revolutionary Cuba. In *Pollock, D. H. and Ritter, A. R. M., eds.*, 1973, pp. 203–59.

_____ and Pollock, David H. Revolution in Latin America: An Overview. In *Pollock, D. H. and Ritter, A. R. M., eds.*, 1973, pp. 3–29.

Ritter, Lawrence S. Reordering National Priorities: A Day of Reckoning. In *Reynolds, L. G.; Green, G. D. and Lewis, D. R., eds.*, 1973, pp. 323–31.

Ritz, Philip M. and Roberts, Eugene P. Industry Inventory Requirements: An Input-Output Analysis. *Surv. Curr. Bus.*, November 1973, *53*(11), pp. 15–22.

Rivlin, Alice M. Measuring Performance in Education. In *Moss, M., ed.*, 1973, pp. 411–28.

Rivlin, Lewis A. and Noll, Roger G. Regulating Prices in Competitive Markets. *Yale Law J.*, June 1973, *82*(7), pp. 1426–34.

Rizek, R. L.; Judge, G. G. and Havlicek, J. A Spatial Analysis of the U.S. Livestock Economy. In *Judge, G. G. and Takayama, T., eds.*, 1973, pp. 261–73.

Rizvi, M. Haseeb and Solomon, Herbert. Selection of Largest Multiple Correlation Coefficients: Asymptotic Case. *J. Amer. Statist. Assoc.*, March 1973, *68*(341), pp. 184–88.

Robbins, Lionel [Lord]. Remarks upon Certain Aspects of the Theory of Costs. In *Buchanan, J. M. and Thirlby, G. F., eds.*, 1973, pp. 19–41.

_____ Summing Up: Mergers and the Legal Framework. In *Allen, G. C., et al.*, 1973, pp. 81–84.

Robbins, Sidney M. and Stobaugh, Robert B. The Bent Measuring Stick for Foreign Subsidiaries. *Harvard Bus. Rev.*, September-October 1973, *51*(5), pp. 80–88.

Roberts, B. K. Field Systems of the West Midlands. In *Baker, A. R. H. and Butlin, R. A., eds.*, 1973, pp. 188–231.

Roberts, Blaine. An Extension of Optimality Criteria: An Axiomatic Approach to Institutional Choice. *J. Polit. Econ.*, Part I, March-April 1973, *81*(2), pp. 386–400.

_____ Individual Decisions and Standardized Choice. *Z. Nationalökon.*, 1973, *33*(3–4), pp. 353–60.

_____ and Truett, Dale. Classical Production Functions, Technical Optimality, and Scale Adjustments of the Firms. *Amer. Econ. Rev.*, December 1973, *63*(5), pp. 975–82.

Roberts, C. A. Reorganization of the National Coal Board. In *Tivey, L., ed.*, 1973, pp. 242–48.

Roberts, Donald John. Existence of Lindahl Equilibrium with a Measure Space of Consumers. *J. Econ. Theory*, August 1973, *6*(4), pp. 355–81.

_____; Kamien, Morton I. and Schwartz, Nancy L. Exclusion, Externalities, and Public Goods. *J. Public Econ.*, July 1973, *2*(3), pp. 217–30.

Roberts, Eugene P. and Ritz, Philip M. Industry Inventory Requirements: An Input-Output Analysis. *Surv. Curr. Bus.*, November 1973, *53*(11), pp. 15–22.

Roberts, Karlene H. A Symposium: Cross-national Organizational Research: Overview. *Ind. Relat.*, May 1973, *12*(2), pp. 137–43.

Roberts, Marc J. On Reforming Economic Growth. In *Olson, M. and Landsberg, H. H., eds.*, 1973, pp. 119–37.

_____ On Time. *Quart. J. Econ.*, November 1973, *87*(4), pp. 646–50.

_____; Ross, Leonard and Passell, Peter. The Limits to Growth: A Review. In *Enthoven, A. C. and Freeman, A. M., III, eds.*, 1973, pp. 230–34.

Roberts, Paul Craig. The Theory of Socialist Planning: Reply. *J. Polit. Econ.*, Part I, March-April 1973, *81*(2), pp. 465–70.

_____ and Rabushka, Alvin. A Diagrammatic Exposition of an Economic Theory of Imperialism. *Public Choice*, Spring 1973, *14*, pp. 101–07.

Roberts, Robert E. Modernization and Infant Mortality in Mexico. *Econ. Develop. Cult. Change*, Part I, July 1973, *21*(4), pp. 655–69.

Roberts, R. W. and Schmitt, R. W. Program Budgeting R and D at General Electric. In *Novick, D., ed.*, 1973, pp. 139–50.

Robertson, A. F. Bugerere—A Country Case History: The Successful Commercial Farmer in an Immigrant Society. In *Richards, A. I.; Sturrock, F. and Fortt, J. M., eds.*, 1973, pp. 232–68.

Robertson, B. C.; Ellis, P. L. and Wilson, I. H. Rock Phosphate Mining in North West Queensland—A Cost-Benefit Analysis. *Econ. Anal. Pol.*, March 1973, *4*(1), pp. 23–32.

Robertson, David. Multilateral Trade Negotiations. *Nat. Westminster Bank Quart. Rev.*, February 1973, pp. 46–58.

Robertson, Ross M. Chartering, Branching, and the Concentration Problem: Discussion. In *Federal Reserve Bank of Boston*, 1973, pp. 40–45.

_____, et al. The Uncertain Outlook for 1974. *In-*

diana *Bus. Rev.*, November-December 1973, *48*, pp. 3–15.

Robichek, Alexander A.; Higgins, Robert C. and Kinsman, Michael. The Effect of Leverage on the Cost of Equity Capital of Electric Utility Firms. *J. Finance*, May 1973, *28*(2), pp. 353–67.

——— **and Jaedicke, Robert K.** Cost-Volume-Profit Analysis Under Conditions of Uncertainty. In *Thomas, W. E., Jr., ed.*, 1973, pp. 279–93.

Robie, Edward A. Challenge to Management. In *Ginzberg, E. and Yohalem, A. M., eds.*, 1973, pp. 9–29.

Robinowitz, Robert S. and Riche, Martha F. Productivity in the Ready-Mixed Concrete Industry. *Mon. Lab. Rev.*, May 1973, *96*(5), pp. 12–15.

Robinson, Albert J. A Planned New Town: The Canberra Experiment. *Land Econ.*, August 1973, *49* (3), pp. 362–65.

Robinson, Austin. John Maynard Keynes. In *Rectenwald, H. C., ed.*, 1973, pp. 395–405.

Robinson, Colin and Crook, Elizabeth M. Is There a World Energy Crisis? *Nat. Westminster Bank Quart. Rev.*, May 1973, pp. 46–60.

Robinson, Derek. Capital-Sharing Schemes. In *Robinson, D.*, 1973, pp. 137–57.

——— Forecasting Manpower Requirements: The Functioning of the Labour Market in Practice. In *Robinson, D.*, 1973, pp. 205–18.

——— Industrial Relations Aspects of Incomes Policies. In *Robinson, D.*, 1973, pp. 42–75.

——— Prices and Incomes Policies—Recent Developments in Some European Countries. In *Robinson, D.*, 1973, pp. 11–41.

——— Productivity Bargaining. In *Robinson, D.*, 1973, pp. 185–204.

——— Trade Union Views on Workers' Negotiated Savings Plans for Capital Formation. In *Robinson, D.*, 1973, pp. 76–104.

——— Trade Unions and Multinational Companies. In *Robinson, D.*, 1973, pp. 158–84.

——— Workers' Savings Plans for Capital Formation in Germany. In *Robinson, D.*, 1973, pp. 105–36.

Robinson, James W. and Turner, James T. An Empirical Investigation of the Theory Y Management—Theory X Union Hypothesis. *Miss. Val. J. Bus. Econ.*, Spring 1973, *8*(3), pp. 77–84.

Robinson, J. N. Applied Economic Policy with a Quadratic Criterion Function: A Comment. *Appl. Econ.*, September 1973, *5*(3), pp. 227–28.

Robinson, Joan. Chinese Agricultural Communes. In *Wilber, C. K., ed.*, 1973, pp. 209–15.

——— "Samuelson and Marx." *J. Econ. Lit.*, December 1973, *11*(4), pp. 1367.

——— What Has Become of the Keynesian Revolution? In *Robinson, J., ed.*, 1973, pp. 1–11.

Robinson, Randall S. BANKMOD: An Interactive Simulation Aid for Bank Financial Planning. *J. Bank Res.*, Autumn 1973, *4*(3), pp. 212–24.

Robinson, Richard D. Beyond the Multinational Corporation. In *Fayerweather, J., ed.*, 1973, pp. 17–26.

——— The Engagement of Host Government Interests upon the Entry of Foreign Business. In *Fayerweather, J., ed.*, 1973, pp. 39–48.

——— From Multinational Corporation to World Government? In *Alexandrides, C. G., ed.*, 1973, pp. 285–93.

Robinson, R. V. F. and Hebden, J. The Influence of Price and Trading Stamps on Retail Petrol Sales. *J. Ind. Econ.*, September 1973, *22*(1), pp. 37–50.

Robinson, Sherman and Markandya, Anil. Complexity and Adjustment in Input-Output Systems. *Oxford Bull. Econ. Statist.*, May 1973, *35*(2), pp. 119–34.

Robinson, Stephen M. Irreducibility in the von Neumann Model. *Econometrica*, May 1973, *41*(3), pp. 569–73.

——— **and Day, Richard H.** Economic Decisions with L** Utility. In *Cochrane, J. L. and Zeleny, M., eds.*, 1973, pp. 84–92.

Robinson, Thomas R. and Miles, Barbara L. Residential Construction Boom, 1970–73. *Surv. Curr. Bus.*, May 1973, *53*(5), pp. 14–22.

Robinson, Warren C. "Disguised" Unemployment Once Again: East Pakistan, 1951–1961: Reply. *Amer. J. Agr. Econ.*, February 1973, *55*(1), pp. 120.

——— **and Pawakaranond, Lamduan.** Manpower Imbalances in Thailand: Comment. *Western Econ. J.*, September 1973, *11*(3), pp. 375–79.

Robson, R. Thayne; Bradley, Iver E. and Mangum, Garth L. Impact of Manpower Programs upon Employment and Earnings. In *Mangum, G. L. and Robson, R. T., eds.*, 1973, pp. 227–59.

———; **Bradley, Iver E. and Mangum, Garth L.** Total Impact of Manpower Programs. In *Mangum, G. L. and Robson, R. T., eds.*, 1973, pp. 260–93.

——— **and Mangum, Garth L.** Metropolitan Impact of Manpower Programs: A Four-City Comparison: Introduction. In *Mangum, G. L. and Robson, R. T., eds.*, 1973, pp. 1–5.

di Roccaferrera, Giuseppe M. Ferrero. Behavioral Aspects of Decision Making Under Multiple Goals. In *Cochrane, J. L. and Zeleny, M., eds.*, 1973, pp. 635–56.

Roche, D. J. D., et al. Some Determinants of Labour Mobility in Northern Ireland. *Econ. Soc. Rev.*, October 1973, *5*(1), pp. 59–73.

Rochin, Refugio I. A Study of Bangladesh Farmers' Experiences with IR-20 Rice Variety and Complementary Production Inputs. *Bangladesh Econ. Rev.*, January 1973, *1*(1), pp. 71–94.

Rockoff, Hugh and Hinderliter, Roger H. The Management of Reserves by Ante-bellum Banks in Eastern Financial Centers. *Exploration Econ. Hist.*, Fall 1973, *11*(1), pp. 37–53.

Roden, D. Field Systems of the Chiltern Hills and Their Environs. In *Baker, A. R. H. and Butlin, R. A., eds.*, 1973, pp. 325–76.

Roderick, Roger D. and Nicholson, Edward A., Jr. Correlates of Job Attitudes Among Young Women. *Nebr. J. Econ. Bus.*, Autumn 1973, *12*(4), pp. 77–89.

Rodgers, James D. Distributional Externalities and the Optimal Form of Income Transfers. *Public Finance Quart.*, July 1973, *1*(3), pp. 266–99.

——— **and Hochman, Harold M.** Brennan and Walsh Reconsidered. (Mutt and Jeff Ride Again.) *Public Finance Quart.*, October 1973, *1*(4), pp. 359–71.

——— **and Hochman, Harold M.** Utility Interdependence and Income Transfers through Charity. In *Boulding, K. E.; Pfaff, M. and Pfaff, A., eds.*, 1973, pp. 63–77.

_____; Tullock, Gordon and Hochman, Harold M. The Income Distribution as a Pure Public Good: Comment. *Quart. J. Econ.*, May 1973, *87*(2), pp. 311–15.

Rodin, Burton and Rodin, Miriam. Student Evaluations of Teachers. *J. Econ. Educ.*, Fall 1973, *5*(1), pp. 5–21.

Rodin, Miriam and Rodin, Burton. Student Evaluations of Teachers. *J. Econ. Educ.*, Fall 1973, *5*(1), pp. 5–21.

Roe, Alan R. The Case for Flow of Funds and National Balance Sheet Accounts. *Econ. J.*, June 1973, *83*(330), pp. 399–420.

Roehl, Richard. War and the Birth of the Nation State: Discussion. *J. Econ. Hist.*, March 1973, *33*(1), pp. 228–31.

Roemer, Milton J. Development of Medical Services under Social Security in Latin America. *Int. Lab. Rev.*, July 1973, *108*(1), pp. 1–23.

Roenfeldt, Rodney L. and Tuttle, Donald L. An Examination of the Discounts and Premiums of Closed-End Investment Companies. *J. Bus. Res.*, Fall 1973, *1*(2), pp. 129–40.

Roethenmund, Otto. The Dollar Problem from the Point of View of a Swiss Banker. In *Wiegand, G. C., ed.*, 1973, pp. 127–30.

Rogers, Christopher D. Gli accordi internazionali per le materie prime. (The International Agreements on Raw Materials. With English summary.) *Mondo Aperto*, December 1973, *27*(6), pp. 415–28.

_____ International Commodity Agreements. *Lloyds Bank Rev.*, April 1973, (108), pp. 33–47.

Rogers, David. Organizing Manpower Delivery Systems in Big Cities. In *Aronson, R. L., ed.*, 1973, pp. 24–44.

Rogstad, Barry K.; Wehner, Harrison G. and Myers, Myron G. A Theoretical Evaluation of Alternative Subsidy Schemes for Regional Development. *Amer. J. Agr. Econ.*, May 1973, *55*(2), pp. 304–12.

Rohlíček, Rudolf. The Role of Finance in Plan-Based Management of the Development of the Czechoslovak Economy. *Czech. Econ. Digest.*, September 1973, (6), pp. 3–62.

Rohrlich, George F. The Potential of *Social* Ecology for Economic Science. *Rev. Soc. Econ.*, April 1973, *31*(1), pp. 31–39.

Rokoff, Gerald. Alternatives to the University Property Tax Exemption. *Yale Law J.*, November 1973, *83*(1), pp. 181–96.

Roll, Richard. Assets, Money, and Commodity Price Inflation Under Uncertainty: Demand Theory. *J. Money, Credit, Banking*, November 1973, *5*(4), pp. 903–23.

_____ Evidence on the "Growth-Optimum" Model. *J. Finance*, June 1973, *28*(3), pp. 551–66.

Rolph, Earl R. Discriminating Effects of the Income Tax Treatment of Owner-Occupants. *Nat. Tax J.*, September 1973, *26*(3), pp. 471–84.

_____ The Economics of the Nullification Movement. *Western Econ. J.*, December 1973, *11*(4), pp. 381–93.

Rolph, John E. and Carroll, Stephen J. A Stochastic Model of Discrimination in the Labor Market. *Econometrica*, January 1973, *41*(1), pp. 97–108.

Romacker, B. Problems of Product Planning. In *Blohm, H. and Steinbuch, K., eds.*, 1973, pp. 115–19.

Romaniuk, A. A Three Parameter Model for Birth Projections. *Population Stud.*, November 1973, *27*(3), pp. 467–78.

_____ and Mitra, S. Pearsonian Type I Curve and Its Fertility Projection Potentials. *Demography*, August 1973, *10*(3), pp. 351–65.

Ronen, J. and Dopuch, N. The Effects of Alternative Inventory Valuation Methods—An Experimental Study. *J. Acc. Res.*, Autumn 1973, *11*(2), pp. 191–211.

Roomkin, Myron. Economic Effects of Basic Education for Adults: The Milwaukee MDTA Experience. *Quart. Rev. Econ. Bus.*, Spring 1973, *13*(1), pp. 87–96.

Rooney, Robert F. Descartes' Rule and Multiple Internal Rates of Return. *Western Econ. J.*, June 1973, *11*(2), pp. 241.

Roop, Joseph M. Contingency Management in the Teaching of Economics: Some Results from an Intermediate Microeconomics Course. *Intermountain Econ. Rev.*, Spring 1973, *4*(1), pp. 53–71.

de Roos, F. Floating Exchange Rates. *S. Afr. J. Econ.*, June 1973, *41*(2), pp. 111–33.

_____ Zwevende wisselkoersen. (Fluctuating Exchange Rates. With English summary.) *De Economist*, January-February 1973, *121*(1), pp. 1–28.

Roper, Don E. Implications of the Gold-Exchange Standard for Balance of Payments Adjustment. *Econ. Int.*, August-November 1973, *26*(3–4), pp. 413–32.

Ropohl, G. Technological Forecasting: Between Speculation and Science. In *Blohm, H. and Steinbuch, K., eds.*, 1973, pp. 157–69.

_____ The Use of Systems Technology and Morphological Method in Technological Forecasting. In *Blohm, H. and Steinbuch, K., eds.*, 1973, pp. 29–38.

Rorke, C. Harvey and Neave, Edwin H. Risk, Ruin, and Investment Analysis: Comment. *J. Financial Quant. Anal.*, June 1973, *8*(3), pp. 517–26.

Rosa, Jean-Jacques. Keynes or Fisher? Monetary Channels and the 1967 Reform. *Econ. Int.*, August-November 1973, *26*(3–4), pp. 433–50.

Rösch, Georges; Mizrahi, Andrée and Mizrahi, Arié. Un indicateur de morbidité. (An Indicator of Morbidity. With English summary.) *Consommation*, July-September 1973, *20*(3), pp. 7–55.

Rose, Hugh. Effective Demand in the Long Run. In *Mirrlees, J. A. and Stern, N. H., eds.*, 1973, pp. 25–47.

_____ Optimal Stabilization Paths: Comment. *J. Money, Credit, Banking*, Part II, February 1973, *5*(1), pp. 566–67.

Rose, Klaus and Bender, Dieter. Flexible Wechselkurse und Inflationsimport. (Flexible Exchange Rates and Import of Inflation. With English summary.) *Jahr. Nationalökon. Statist.*, August 1973, *187*(6), pp. 481–506.

Rose, Louis A. The Development Value Tax. *Urban Stud.*, June 1973, *10*(2), pp. 271–75.

Rose, Manfred. Das fiskalische Ziel der Besteuerung. (The Fiscal Goal of Taxation. With English summary.) *Kyklos*, 1973, *26*(4), pp. 815–40.

Rose, Marshall. Market Problems in the Distribution

of Emission Rights. *Water Resources Res.,* October 1973, *9*(5), pp. 1132–44.

Rose, Peter S. The Impact of Policy Variables on Price-Level Movements. *Miss. Val. J. Bus. Econ.,* Fall 1973, *9*(1), pp. 1–11.

———— **and Fraser, Donald R.** Short-Run Bank Portfolio Behavior: An Examination of Selected Liquid Assets. *J. Finance,* May 1973, *28*(2), pp. 531–37.

———— **and Fraser, Donald R.** The Short-run Determinants of Loan Mix at Large Commercial Banks. *J. Econ. Bus.,* Fall 1973, *26*(1), pp. 1–9.

———— **and Hunt, Lacy H., II.** The Relative Importance of Monetary and Fiscal Variables in Determining Price Level Movements: Reply. *J. Finance,* March 1973, *28*(1), pp. 191–93.

Rose, Sanford. U.S. Foreign Trade: There's No Need to Panic. In *Reynolds, L. G.; Green, G. D. and Lewis, D. R., eds.,* 1973, pp. 452–62.

Rose-Ackerman, Susan. Effluent Charges: A Critique. *Can. J. Econ.,* November 1973, *6*(4), pp. 512–28.

———— Used Cars as a Depreciating Asset. *Western Econ. J.,* December 1973, *11*(4), pp. 463–74.

Rosen, Carol. Hidden Unemployment and Related Issues. *Mon. Lab. Rev.,* March 1973, *96*(3), pp. 31–37.

Rosenberg, Barr. The Analysis of a Cross Section of Time Series by Stochastically Convergent Parameter Regression. *Ann. Econ. Soc. Measure,* October 1973, *2*(4), pp. 399–428.

———— A Survey of Stochastic Parameter Regression. *Ann. Econ. Soc. Measure,* October 1973, *2*(4), pp. 381–97.

———— **and McKibben, Walt.** The Prediction of Systematic and Specific Risk in Common Stocks. *J. Financial Quant. Anal.,* March 1973, *8*(2), pp. 317–33.

Rosenberg, Nathan. The Direction of Technological Change: Reply. *Econ. Develop. Cult. Change,* January 1973, *21*(2), pp. 356–57.

———— Innovative Responses to Materials Shortages. *Amer. Econ. Rev.,* May 1973, *63*(2), pp. 111–18.

Rosenberg, W. Economic Development Lessons from Hong Kong: A Rejoinder. *Econ. Rec.,* December 1973, *49*(128), pp. 644–45.

———— Hong Kong Model for Development? *Econ. Rec.,* December 1973, *49*(128), pp. 629–36.

Rosenbloom, Richard S. The *Real* Productivity Crisis is in Government. *Harvard Bus. Rev.,* September-October 1973, *51*(5), pp. 156–64.

Rosenblum, Marc. The Great Labor Force Projection Debate: Implications for 1980. *Amer. Econ.,* Fall 1973, *17*(2), pp. 122–29.

Rosendale, Phyllis B. The Short-Run Pricing Policies of Some British Engineering Exporters. *Nat. Inst. Econ. Rev.,* August 1973, (65), pp. 44–51.

Rosenfeld, Barry D. The Displacement-Effect in the Growth of Canadian Government Expenditures. *Public Finance,* 1973, *28*(3–4), pp. 301–14.

Rosenstein-Rodan, Paul N. Planning for Full Employment in Latin America. In *Pollock, D. H. and Ritter, A. R. M., eds.,* 1973, pp. 86–96.

Rosenthal, Albert J. Employment Discrimination and the Law. *Ann. Amer. Acad. Polit. Soc. Sci.,* May 1973, *407,* pp. 91–101.

Rosenthal, Joel T. Medieval Longevity: And the Secular Peerage, 1350–1500. *Population Stud.,* July 1973, *27*(2), pp. 287–93.

Rosenthal, Neal H. Projected Changes in Occupations. *Mon. Lab. Rev.,* December 1973, *96*(12), pp. 18–26.

Rosenthal, Robert W. Taxation vs. Prohibition of an External Diseconomy by Direct Vote: A Game Theoretic Approach. *Int. Econ. Rev.,* June 1973, *14*(2), pp. 414–20.

Rosett, Richard N. and Huang, Lien-fu. The Effect of Health Insurance on the Demand for Medical Care. *J. Polit. Econ.,* Part I, March-April 1973, *81* (2), pp. 281–305.

Rosinoff, Bruce and Lieber, Harvey. Evaluating the State's Role in Water Pollution Control. *Amer. Real Estate Urban Econ. Assoc. J.,* Fall 1973, *1*(2), pp. 73–87.

Roskamp, Karl W. Pareto Optimal Redistribution, Utility Interdependence and Social Optimum. *Weltwirtsch. Arch.,* 1973, *109*(2), pp. 337–44.

Rosner, M., et al. Worker Participation and Influence in Five Countries. *Ind. Relat.,* May 1973, *12* (2), pp. 200–12.

Rosovsky, H. What are the 'Lessons' of Japanese Economic History. In *Youngson, A. J., ed.,* 1973, pp. 229–53.

Rosow, Jerome M. Work Requirements in Welfare and Unemployment Insurance. *Mon. Lab. Rev.,* April 1973, *96*(4), pp. 56–57.

Ross, Charles R. Electricity as a Social Force. *Ann. Amer. Acad. Polit. Soc. Sci.,* January 1973, *405,* pp. 47–54.

Ross, Howard N. Illusions in Testing for Administered Prices. *J. Ind. Econ.,* April 1973, *21*(2), pp. 187–95.

Ross, Kenneth H. Problems and Issues in Public Employee Retirement Systems: Discussion. *J. Risk Ins.,* March 1973, *40*(1), pp. 46–50.

Ross, Leonard; Passell, Peter and Roberts, Marc J. The Limits to Growth: A Review. In *Enthoven, A. C. and Freeman, A. M., III, eds.,* 1973, pp. 230–34.

Ross, Miceal. Procedures for Integrated Regional Planning. I: The Background to Decentralisation. *Econ. Soc. Rev.,* July 1973, *4*(4), pp. 523–42.

———— Systems and Management: A Review. *Econ. Soc. Rev.,* April 1973, *4*(3), pp. 365–94.

Ross, Myron H. Probability, Games, Regret and Investment Criteria. *Eng. Econ.,* April-May 1973, *18*(3), pp. 191–98.

————**; Collery, Arnold and Zelder, Raymond E.** Internal and External Balance in an "Almost Classical" World: Reply. *Western Econ. J.,* June 1973, *11*(2), pp. 238–40.

Ross, Russell and Tower, Edward. More on the Neutrality of Forward Market Intervention. *Weltwirtsch. Arch.,* 1973, *109*(4), pp. 701–03.

Ross, Stephen A. The Economic Theory of Agency: The Principal's Problem. *Amer. Econ. Rev.,* May 1973, *63*(2), pp. 134–39.

———— **and Wachter, Michael L.** Wage Determination, Inflation, and the Industrial Structure. *Amer. Econ. Rev.,* September 1973, *63*(4), pp. 675–92.

Ross, W. R. Pert/Cost Resource Allocation Procedure. In *Thomas, W. E., Jr., ed.,* 1973, pp. 249–63.

Rosser, Rachel and Watts, Vincent. Health and Welfare Systems. In *Ross, M., ed.*, 1973, pp. 655–69.

Rossi, Aldo. Pubblicità industriale per l' agricoltura. (Industrial Advertising for Agriculture. With English summary.) *L'Impresa*, 1973, *15*(5–6), pp. 359–64.

Rossitch, Eugene and Meckler, Jack M. Foreign Currency Exposure Control. *Manage. Account.*, July 1973, *55*(1), pp. 29–37.

Rostow, W. W. The Beginnings of Modern Growth in Europe: An Essay in Synthesis. *J. Econ. Hist.*, September 1973, *33*(3), pp. 547–80.

Roşu, V. Armonizarea intereselor în procesul de făurire a societăţii socialiste multilateral dezvoltate. (Harmonizing the Interests in Building the Many-sidedly Developed Socialist Society. With English summary.) *Stud. Cercet. Econ.*, 1973, (4), pp. 39–46.

Roth, Timothy P. Classical vs. Process Analysis and the Form of the Production Function. *Eng. Econ.*, October-November 1973, *19*(1), pp. 47–54.

Rothbard, Murray N. Value Implications of Economic Theory. *Amer. Econ.*, Spring 1973, *17*(1), pp. 35–39.

Rothenberg, Jerome. Spatial Economics: Discussion. *Amer. Econ. Rev.*, May 1973, *63*(2), pp. 67–70.

Rothman, Jack. The Ghetto Makers. In *Pynoos, J.; Schafer, R. and Hartman, C. W., eds.*, 1973, pp. 274–78.

Rothman, Mitchell P. and Scott, James H., Jr. Political Opinions and the TUCE. *J. Econ. Educ.*, Spring 1973, *4*(2), pp. 116–24.

Rothschild, Kurt W. Distributive Aspects of the Austrian Theory. In *Hicks, J. R. and Weber, W., eds.*, 1973, pp. 207–25.

_____ Military Expenditure, Exports and Growth. *Kyklos*, 1973, *26*(4), pp. 804–14.

Rothschild, Michael. Models of Market Organization with Imperfect Information: A Survey. *J. Polit. Econ.*, November-December 1973, *81*(6), pp. 1283–1308.

_____ and Hirschman, Albert O. The Changing Tolerance for Income Inequality in the Course of Economic Development; with a Mathematical Appendix. *Quart. J. Econ.*, November 1973, *87*(4), pp. 544–66.

_____ and Stiglitz, Joseph E. Some Further Results on the Measurement of Inequality. *J. Econ. Theory*, April 1973, *6*(2), pp. 188–204.

Rottenberg, Simon. The Economics of Crime and Punishment: Introduction. In *Rottenberg, S., ed.*, 1973, pp. 1–8.

Rotwein, Eugene. David Hume as an Economist. In *Rectenwald, H. C., ed.*, 1973, pp. 30–36.

_____ Empiricism and Economic Method: Several Views Considered. *J. Econ. Issues*, September 1973, *7*(3), pp. 361–82.

_____ The Ideology of Wealth and the Liberal Economic Heritage: The Neglected View. *Soc. Res.*, Summer 1973, *40*(2), pp. 269–92.

Rourke, B. E. and Obeng, F. A. Seasonality in the Employment of Casual Agricultural Labour in Ghana. *Econ. Bull. Ghana, Sec. Ser.*, 1973, *3*(3), pp. 3–13.

Rouse, Andrew M.; Harper, Edwin L. and Kramer, Fred A. Personnel Limitations of "Instant Analysis." In *Novick, D., ed.*, 1973, pp. 201–05.

Rousseas, Stephen. Paradigm Polishing versus Critical Thought in Economics. *Amer. Econ.*, Fall 1973, *17*(2), pp. 72–78.

Rousseau, Henri-Paul. Bargaining As Behavior Towards Risk. *Amer. Econ.*, Spring 1973, *17*(1), pp. 4–12.

Rousseaux, R. De liquiditeitenmassa in België en Nederland. (Currency in Belgium and the Netherlands. With English summary.) *Econ. Soc. Tijdschr.*, February 1973, *27*(1), pp. 73–89.

Routh, Guy. Methodology. In *Livingstone, I., et al., eds.*, 1973, pp. 51–58.

Rowan, D. C. The Monetary System in the Fifties and Sixties. *Manchester Sch. Econ. Soc. Stud.*, March 1973, *41*(1), pp. 19–42.

Rowe, A. J. and Bahr, F. R. A Heuristic Approach to Managerial Problem Solving. *J. Econ. Bus.*, Spring-Summer 1973, *25*(3), pp. 159–63.

Rowe, J. W. Macro-Economic Policy: New Zealand. In *Perkins, J. O. N., ed.*, 1973, pp. 94–129.

Rowley, Charles K. and Peacock, Alan T. Welfare Economics and the Public Regulation of Natural Monopoly: Reply. *J. Public Econ.*, February 1973, *2*(1), pp. 97–100.

Rowley, J. C. R. and Wilton, D. A. The Empirical Sensitivity of the Phillips Curve. *Amer. Econ.*, Fall 1973, *17*(2), pp. 90–112.

_____ Quarterly Models of Wage Determination Some New Efficient Estimates. *Amer. Econ. Rev.*, June 1973, *63*(3), pp. 380–89.

_____ Wage Determination: The Use of Instrumental Assumptions. *Int. Econ. Rev.*, June 1973, *14*(2), pp. 525–29.

Rowthorn, Bob. Neoclassical Economics and its Critics: A Marxist View. *Pakistan Econ. Soc. Rev.*, Autumn 1973, *11*(3), pp. 316–48.

Roxas, Sixto K. Exchange Rate Experience and Policy in the Philippines Since World War II. In *Grubel, H. G. and Morgan, T., eds.*, 1973, pp. 55–66.

Roy, Bernard. How Outranking Relation Helps Multiple Criteria Decision Making. In *Cochrane, J. L. and Zeleny, M., eds.*, 1973, pp. 179–201.

Roy, Patricia E. Direct Management from Abroad: The Formative Years of the British Columbia Electric Railway. *Bus. Hist. Rev.*, Summer 1973, *47*(2), pp. 239–59.

Roy, René. Cournot and Mathematical Economics. In *Rectenwald, H. C., ed.*, 1973, pp. 180–88.

_____ Demography and Economic Growth: Income Distribution and Way of Life. In *[Tinbergen, J.]*, 1973, pp. 257–71.

Roy, Sujit K. and Johnson, Phillip N. Econometric Models for Quarterly Shell Egg Prices. *Amer. J. Agr. Econ.*, May 1973, *55*(2), pp. 209–13.

Rubin, Leonard. Late Entitlement to Retirement Benefits: Findings from the Survey of New Beneficiaries. *Soc. Sec. Bull.*, July 1973, *36*(7), pp. 3–20.

Rubin, Lester and Burke, Donald R. Is Contract Rejection a Major Collective Bargaining Problem? *Ind. Lab. Relat. Rev.*, January 1973, *26*(2), pp. 820–33.

Rubin, Paul H. The Economic Theory of the Criminal Firm. In *Rottenberg, S., ed.*, 1973, pp. 155–66.

—— The Expansion of Firms. *J. Polit. Econ.*, July-August 1973, *81*(4), pp. 936–49.

—— A Paradox Regarding the Use of Time. *Indian Econ. J.*, January-March 1973, *20*(3), pp. 469–71.

Rubinfeld, Daniel. Credit Ratings and the Market for General Obligation Municipal Bonds. *Nat. Tax J.*, March 1973, *26*(1), pp. 17–27.

Rubinowitz, Leonard S. A Question of Choice: Access of the Poor and the Black to Suburban Housing. In *Masotti, L. H. and Hadden, J. K., eds.*, 1973, pp. 329–66.

Rubinshtein, M. Scientific and Technical Progress and Planned Price Formation. *Prob. Econ.*, July 1973, *16*(3), pp. 22–36.

Rubinstein, Mark E. A Comparative Statics Analysis of Risk Premiums. *J. Bus.*, October 1973, *46*(4), pp. 605–15.

—— Corporate Financial Policy in Segmented Securities Markets. *J. Financial Quant. Anal.*, December 1973, *8*(5), pp. 749–61.

—— The Fundamental Theorem of Parameter-Preference Security Valuation. *J. Financial Quant. Anal.*, January 1973, *8*(1), pp. 61–69.

—— A Mean-Variance Synthesis of Corporate Financial Theory. *J. Finance*, March 1973, *28*(1), pp. 167–81.

Ruckdeschel, Frederic Brill. The Determinants of a Direct Investment Outflow with Emphasis on the Supply of Funds. *Fed. Res. Bull.*, June 1973, *59*(6), pp. 403–04.

Rud, Jon. Freedom of Employment and Maintenance of Public Services: A Study of Obligatory Service for Dentists in Norway. In *Moskoff, W., ed.*, 1973, pp. 271–88.

Rudamoorthy, B. Financing Agriculture in Backward Regions. *Artha-Vikas,* January-July 1973, *9* (1–2), pp. 139–42.

Ruebling, Charlotte E. A Value Added Tax and Factors Affecting Its Economic Impact. *Fed. Res. Bank St. Louis Rev.*, September 1973, *55*(9), pp. 15–19.

Rueda-Williamson, Roberto. Top Priority Programs in National Development Plans. In *Berg, A.; Scrimshaw, N. S. and Call, D. L., eds.*, 1973, pp. 285–89.

Rueff, Jacques. The Lessons of Bretton Woods. In *Wiegand, G. C., ed.*, 1973, pp. 39–44.

—— Prolegomeni a qualsiasi riforma del sistema monetario internazionale. (Prolegomena to Any Reform Concerning the International Monetary System. With English summary.) *Bancaria,* June 1973, *29*(6), pp. 679–87.

—— and Carli, Guido. Dibattito sulla riforma del sistema monetario internazionale. (Debate on the Reform of the International Monetary System. With English summary.) *Bancaria,* August 1973, *29*(8), pp. 935–46.

Ruefli, Timothy W. Linked Multi-Criteria Decision Models. In *Cochrane, J. L. and Zeleny, M., eds.*, 1973, pp. 406–15.

Rueter, Frederick H. Externalities in Urban Property Markets: An Empirical Test of the Zoning Ordinance of Pittsburgh. *J. Law Econ.*, October 1973, *16*(2), pp. 313–49.

Ruff, Larry E. The Economic Common Sense of Pollution. In *Enthoven, A. C. and Freeman, A. M.,*

III, eds., 1973, pp. 37–53.

di Ruffia, Rodolfo B. Situation and Prospects of the Motor Industry in Italy. *Rev. Econ. Cond. Italy,* January-March 1973, *27*(1–2), pp. 43–52.

Ruffin, Roy J. and Leigh, Duane E. Charity, Competition, and the Pricing of Doctors' Services. *J. Human Res.,* Spring 1973, *8*(2), pp. 212–22.

Rugg, Donald. The Choice of Journey Destination: A Theoretical and Empirical Analysis. *Rev. Econ. Statist.,* February 1973, *55*(1), pp. 64–72.

Ruggeri, Giuseppe C. Automatic Stabilizers, Business Cycles, and Economic Growth. *Kyklos,* 1973, *26*(2), pp. 288–306.

Ruggles, Nancy and Ruggles, Richard. A Proposal for a System of Economic and Social Accounts. In *Moss, M., ed.,* 1973, pp. 111–46.

Ruggles, Richard and Ruggles, Nancy. A Proposal for a System of Economic and Social Accounts. In *Moss, M., ed.,* 1973, pp. 111–46.

Rugh, William. Emergence of a New Middle Class in Saudi Arabia. *Middle East J.,* Winter 1973, *27* (1), pp. 7–20.

Rugina, Anghel N. A Reorganization Plan of the International Monetary Fund as Oriented Toward Conditions of Stable Equilibrium. *Econ. Int.,* August-November 1973, *26*(3–4), pp. 451–67.

Ruh, Robert A.; Wallace, Roger L. and Frost, Carl F. Management Attitudes and the Scanlon Plan. *Ind. Relat.,* October 1973, *12*(3), pp. 282–88.

Rühl, G. Forecasting in Goods' Transport and Market Behaviour. In *Blohm, H. and Steinbuch, K., eds.,* 1973, pp. 91–102.

Ruiz-Palá, Ernesto and Avila Beloso, Carlos. Stochastic Processes: Discussant 2. In *Ross, M., ed.,* 1973, pp. 245–51.

Rumm, Ulrich and Müller, Udo. Zur Gleichgewichtsproblematik im unvollkommenen Polypol. (The Problem of Equilibrium in the Polypol. With English summary.) *Z. ges. Staatswiss.,* May 1973, *129* (2), pp. 189–204.

Rungeling, Brian S. and Pickle, Hal B. Empirical Investigation of Entrepreneurial Goals and Customer Satisfaction. *J. Bus.,* April 1973, *46*(2), pp. 268–73.

Ruozi, Roberto. Savings Banks and Savings Facilities in African Countries: Introduction. In *Alberici, A. and Baravelli, M., eds.,* 1973, pp. ix–xxiii.

Rupli, R. G. How to Improve Profits Through Simulation. *Manage. Account.,* November 1973, *55*(5), pp. 16–20.

Rürup, Bert. Handlungsverzögerungen diskretionärer Fiskalpolitik: Konstruktionsfehler oder Element rationaler Politik? (Decision Lags of Discretionary Fiscal Policy: Defects of Construction or Element of a Rational Policy. With English summary.) *Z. Wirtschaft. Sozialwissen.,* 1973, *93* (1), pp. 35–50.

Rush, David F. The Interdependent Structure of Security Returns: Comment. *J. Financial Quant. Anal.,* March 1973, *8*(2), pp. 289–91.

—— and Melicher, Ronald W. The Performance of Conglomerate Firms: Recent Risk and Return Experience. *J. Finance,* May 1973, *28*(2), pp. 381–88.

Rushing, Philip J. and Gillespie, Robert W. Expenditure Switching vs. Altering Absorption: An Empirical Approach. *Southern Econ. J.,* July 1973, *40* (1), pp. 26–34.

Russell, C. and Gregory, K. SIMPREP, A Computer Model for Coal Preparation. In *Ross, M., ed.,* 1973, pp. 379–89.

Russell, Clifford S. Application of Microeconomic Models to Regional Environmental Quality Management. *Amer. Econ. Rev.,* May 1973, *63*(2), pp. 236–43.

Russell, Keith P. and Marchand, James R. Externalities, Liability, Separability, and Resource Allocation. *Amer. Econ. Rev.,* September 1973, *63*(4), pp. 611–20.

Russell, Louise B. An Econometric Model of the Medicare System: Comment. *Quart. J. Econ.,* August 1973, *87*(3), pp. 482–89.

_____ The Impact of the Extended-Care Facility Benefit on Hospital Use and Reimbursements Under Medicare. *J. Human Res.,* Winter 1973, *8*(1), pp. 57–72.

Russell, Milton. Introduction: The Political Economy of Public Utilities. In *Russell, M., ed.,* 1973, pp. xix–xxviii.

Russell, Robert William. Political Distortions in Trade Negotiations among Industrialized Countries. In *Scaperlanda, A. E., ed.,* 1973, pp. 299–317.

Russett, Bruce M. International Regions and the International System. In *Falk, R. A. and Mendlovitz, S. H., eds.,* 1973, pp. 182–208.

Rutenberg, David P. Maneuvering Liquid Assets in a Multinational Company: Formulation and Deterministic Solution Procedures. In *Alexandrides, C. G., ed.,* 1973, pp. 109–28.

Rutgaizer, V. A Comprehensive Plan for the Development of the Service Sector. *Prob. Econ.,* September 1973, *16*(5), pp. 41–59.

Rutherford, Brent M.; Dunlap, Riley E. and Gale, Richard P. Concern for Environmental Rights Among College Students. *Amer. J. Econ. Soc.,* January 1973, *32*(1), pp. 45–60.

Rutman, Gilbert L. and Werner, David J. A Test of the 'Uneconomic Culture' Thesis: An Economic Rationale for the 'Sacred Cow'. *J. Devel. Stud.,* July 1973, *9*(4), pp. 566–80.

Ruttan, Vernon W. and Hayami, Yujiro. Induced Innovation in Agricultural Development. In *Ayal, E. B., ed.,* 1973, pp. 181–208.

_____ Professor Rosenberg and the Direction of Technological Change: Comment. *Econ. Develop. Cult. Change,* January 1973, *21*(2), pp. 352–55.

Ruttenberg, Stanley H. The Future of Manpower Planning. In *Aronson, R. L., ed.,* 1973, pp. 85–99.

Rutz, A. Die Kurse schweizerischer Aktien im letzten Jahrzehnt. Regressionstechnische Bestimmung möglicher Einflussgrössen. (The Swiss Stock Market During the Last Decade. With English summary.) *Schweiz. Z. Volkswirtsch. Statist.,* June 1973, *109*(2), pp. 147–69.

Ruzicka, L. T. Length of Working Life for Australian Males: 1933–66. *Econ. Rec.,* June 1973, *49*(126), pp. 280–89.

Rweyemamu, J. F. A Note on the Theories of Under-

development. In *Livingstone, I., et al., eds.,* 1973, pp. 79–81.

Ryan, Allan J. Medical Practices in Sports. *Law Contemp. Probl.,* Winter-Spring 1973, *38*(1), pp. 99–111.

Ryan, James G. Some Implications of Rice Price and Policy Changes for Irrigated Farms. *Rev. Marketing Agr. Econ.,* June and September 1973, *41* (2–3), pp. 39–52.

Ryan, Mary E. and Abel, Martin E. Oats and Barley Acreage Response to Government Programs. *Agr. Econ. Res.,* October 1973, *25*(4), pp. 105–14.

_____ Supply Response of U.S. Sorghum Acreage to Government Programs. *Agr. Econ. Res.,* April 1973, *25*(2), pp. 45–55.

Ryan, Terence M. C.E.S. Production Functions in British Manufacturing Industry: A Cross-section Study. *Oxford Econ. Pap.,* July 1973, *25*(2), pp. 241–50.

_____ The Demand for Financial Assets by the British Life Funds. *Oxford Bull. Econ. Statist.,* February 1973, *35*(1), pp. 61–67.

_____ Security Prices as Markov Processes. *J. Financial Quant. Anal.,* January 1973, *8*(1), pp. 17–36.

Ryan, Timothy J. An Empirical Investigation of the Harvest Operation Using Systems Simulation. *Australian J. Agr. Econ.,* August 1973, *17*(2), pp. 114–26.

Ryans, J. K., Jr. Is It Too Soon to Put a Tiger in Every Tank? In *Thorelli, H. B., ed.,* 1973, pp. 227–36.

Rybakov, O. Improvements in Planning Methods of Collaboration Among COMECON Countries. *Prob. Econ.,* March 1973, *15*(11), pp. 3–20.

_____ Some Organizational and Methodological Problems Relating to the Elaboration of Long-Range Plans for Collaboration Between the USSR and Socialist Countries. *Prob. Econ.,* October 1973, *16*(6), pp. 3–19.

Rybczynski, T. M. The Merchant Banks. *Manchester Sch. Econ. Soc. Stud.,* March 1973, *41*(1), pp. 107–21.

Rychlewski, Eugeniusz. The Investment System of a Socialist Economy. *Eastern Europ. Econ.,* Fall 1973, *12*(1), pp. 3–44.

Rydén, Rune; Vedder, Richard K. and Gallaway, Lowell E. Internal Labor Migration in Sweden, 1967. *Swedish J. Econ.,* September 1973, *75*(3), pp. 257–65.

Ryder, Harl E., Jr. and Heal, Geoffrey M. Optimum Growth with Intertemporally Dependent Preferences. *Rev. Econ. Stud.,* January 1973, *40*(1), pp. 1–33.

Ryder, Norman B. A Critique of the National Fertility Study. *Demography,* November 1973, *10*(4), pp. 495–506.

_____ A New Approach to the Economic Theory of Fertility Behavior: Comment. *J. Polit. Econ.,* Part II, March-April 1973, *81*(2), pp. S65–69.

_____ Two Cheers for ZPG. In *Olson, M. and Landsberg, H. H., eds.,* 1973, pp. 45–62.

Ryscavage, P. M. and Mellor, Earl F. The Economic Situation of Spanish Americans. *Mon. Lab. Rev.,* April 1973, *96*(4), pp. 3–9.

Ryvkin, A. A Conference on Problems of Long-Range Planning and Forecasting. *Prob. Econ.,* September 1973, *16*(5), pp. 31–40.

Rzhanitsina, L. Public Consumption Funds in the USSR. *Int. Lab. Rev.,* December 1973, *108*(6), pp. 516–35.

Sabā, Mohsen. The Economic Ideas of Khajeh Nasir ed-Din Tusi as Stated in the Nasirian Ethics. *Tahq. Eq.,* Summer & Autumn 1973, *10*(31&32), pp. 5–21.

Sabel, Hermann. On Pricing New Products. *Ger. Econ. Rev.,* 1973, *11*(4), pp. 292–311.

Sabella, Edward M. Equity and the Property Tax: A Comment and an Alternative Conceptual Framework. *Nat. Tax J.,* December 1973, *26*(4), pp. 645–50.

Sabolo, Y. and Olivier, R. Simultaneous Planning of Employment, Production and Education. *Int. Lab. Rev.,* April 1973, *107*(4), pp. 359–72.

Sacchetti, Ugo. Sharing the Burden of International Adjustment. *Banca Naz. Lavoro Quart. Rev.,* June 1973, (105), pp. 141–57.

Sacco, John F. Local Government and Air Quality Problems: A Study of Problem Solving Approaches. In *Gabriel, R. A. and Cohen, S. H., eds.,* 1973, pp. 32–60.

Saccomanni, Fabrizio and Mohammed, Azizali F. Short-Term Banking and Euro-Currency Credits to Developing Countries. *Int. Monet. Fund Staff Pap.,* November 1973, *20*(3), pp. 612–38.

Sacerdoti, Emilio. Economic Effects of the New Treasury Bill Market in Italy. *Rivista Int. Sci. Econ. Com.,* July 1973, *20*(7), pp. 651–68.

_____ A Note on Monetary Policy when Banks Have Managerial Objectives. *L'Industria,* January-June 1973, (1–2), pp. 89–108.

Sachs, Ignacy. Development, Environment and Technology Assessment. *Int. Soc. Sci. J.,* 1973, *25* (3), pp. 273–83.

_____ Outward-Looking Strategies: A Dangerous Illusion? In *Streeten, P., ed.,* 1973, pp. 51–61.

Sackett, David L.; Thomas, Warren H. and Torrance, George W. Utility Maximization Model for Program Evaluation: A Demonstration Application. In *Berg, R. L., ed.,* 1973, pp. 156–64.

Sadan, Ezra and Tropp, Zvi. Consumption Function Analysis in a Communal Household: Cross Section and Time Series. *Rev. Econ. Statist.,* November 1973, *55*(4), pp. 475–81.

Sadler, P. G. The Integration of Project and Sector Analysis. In *Parkin, M., ed.,* 1973, pp. 156–66.

Sadove, Robert. Urban Needs of Developing Countries. *Finance Develop.,* June 1973, *10*(2), pp. 26–31.

Sadowski, Dieter. Zur Berücksichtigung des Verteilungsaspektes in der Cost-Benefit-Analyse. (The Aspect of Distribution in Cost-Benefit-Analysis. With English summary.) *Z. ges. Staatswiss.,* May 1973, *129*(2), pp. 215–29.

Safarian, A. E. Perspectives on Foreign Direct Investment from the Viewpoint of a Capital Receiving Country. *J. Finance,* May 1973, *28*(2), pp. 419–38.

Sai, F. T. Problems in Nutrition and Diagnosis and Planning. In *Berg, A.; Scrimshaw, N. S. and Call, D. L., eds.,* 1973, pp. 154–58.

Sailors, Joel W.; Qureshi, Usman A. and Cross, Edward M. Empirical Verification of Linder's Trade Thesis. *Southern Econ. J.,* October 1973, *40*(2), pp. 262–68.

Saini, Krishan G. and Neece, Roger N. Poverty versus Pollution: Is There a Choice? *Indian Econ. J.,* January-March 1973, *20*(3), pp. 452–68.

Sakai, Yasuhiro. An Axiomatic Approach to Input Demand Theory. *Int. Econ. Rev.,* October 1973, *14*(3), pp. 735–52.

Sakashita, Noboru and Kamoike, Osamu. National Growth and Regional Income Inequality: A Consistent Model. *Int. Econ. Rev.,* June 1973, *14*(2), pp. 372–82.

Salaff, Janet W. Mortality Decline in the People's Republic of China and the United States. *Population Stud.,* November 1973, *27*(3), pp. 551–76.

Salamon, Gerald L. Models of the Relationship between the Accounting and Internal Rate of Return: An Examination of the Methodology. *J. Acc. Res.,* Autumn 1973, *11*(2), pp. 296–303.

Salant, Walter S. Implications for International Reserves. In *Krause, L. B. and Salant, W. S., eds.,* 1973, pp. 203–36.

_____ The Post-Devaluation Weakness of the Dollar. *Brookings Pap. Econ. Act.,* 1973, (2), pp. 481–97.

_____ Some Intellectual Contributions of the Truman Council of Economic Advisers to Policy-Making. *Hist. Polit. Econ.,* Spring 1973, *5*(1), pp. 36–49.

Salazar-Carrillo, Jorge. Price, Purchasing Power and Real Product Comparisons in Latin America. *Rev. Income Wealth,* March 1973, *19*(1), pp. 117–32.

_____ and **Ferber, Robert.** Experience in Generating Micro Data in Latin America. In *Ayal, E. B., ed.,* 1973, pp. 84–100.

Salgo, Harvey. The Obsolescence of Growth: Capitalism and the Environmental Crisis. *Rev. Radical Polit. Econ.,* Fall 1973, *5*(3), pp. 26–45.

Salin, Edgar. Die EWG im Koma. (EEC—A Fainting Patient. With English summary.) *Kyklos,* 1973, *26* (4), pp. 723–35.

_____ Johann Heinrich von Thünen in His Age. In *Rectenwald, H. C., ed.,* 1973, pp. 135–45.

Salkin, Jay S. The Optimal Level of Production in Generalized Production Functions an Application to South Vietnamese Rice Production. *Malayan Econ. Rev.,* October 1973, *18*(2), pp. 60–67.

Salmi, Timo. Monikansallinen yritys tarkasteltuna matemaattisen optimointimallin avulla. (Some Aspects of Production and Profit Adjustment in the Multinational Firm. With English summary.) *Liiketaloudellinen Aikak.,* 1973, *22*(2), pp. 114–26.

Salop, S. C. Systematic Job Search and Unemployment. *Rev. Econ. Stud.,* April 1973, *40*(2), pp. 191–201.

_____ Wage Differentials in a Dynamic Theory of the Firm. *J. Econ. Theory,* August 1973, *6*(4), pp. 321–44.

Salsbury, A. J. Medical Evidence: Blood Donation and the Australia Antigen. In *Alchian, A. A., et al.,* 1973, pp. 179–91.

Salvatore, Dominick. Regional Inequality and the Market Mechanism: Reply. *Kyklos,* 1973, *26*(3), pp. 627–33.

Samli, A. Coskun and Bellas, Carl J. Improving New Product Planning with GERT Simulation. *Calif. Manage. Rev.,* Summer 1973, *15*(4), pp. 14–21.

Samuels, Nathaniel. National Policies, the Balance of Payments and the Role of the Dollar. In *Levy, M. E., ed.,* 1973, pp. 37–44.

Samuels, Warren J. Adam Smith and the Economy as a System of Power. *Indian Econ. J.,* January-March 1973, *20*(3), pp. 363–81.

———— Adam Smith and the Economy as a System of Power. *Rev. Soc. Econ.,* October 1973, *31*(2), pp. 123–37.

———— Law and Economics: Introduction. *J. Econ. Issues,* December 1973, *7*(4), pp. 535–41.

———— Public Utilities and the Theory of Power. In *Russell, M., ed.,* 1973, pp. 1–27.

Samuelson, Paul A. Deadweight Loss in International Trade from the Profit Motive? In *[Halm, G. N.],* 1973, pp. 149–54.

———— Interrogativi un po' eretici sui meccanismi monetari internazionali. (Heretical Doubts about the International Monetary Mechanisms. With English summary.) *Bancaria,* April 1973, *29*(4), pp. 423–29.

———— Lord Keynes and the General Theory. In *Rectenwald, H. C., ed.,* 1973, pp. 407–13.

———— Monetarism Re-evaluated. In *Reynolds, L. G.; Green, G. D. and Lewis, D. R., eds.,* 1973, pp. 50–59.

———— "Samuelson and Marx": Reply. *J. Econ. Lit.,* December 1973, *11*(4), pp. 1367.

———— Proof that Properly Discounted Present Values of Assets Vibrate Randomly. *Bell J. Econ. Manage. Sci.,* Autumn 1973, *4*(2), pp. 369–74.

———— A Quantum-Theory Model of Economics: Is the Co-ordinating Entrepreneur Just Worth His Profit? In *[Rosenstein-Rodan, P.],* 1973, pp. 329–35.

———— Relative Shares and Elasticities Simplified: Comment. *Amer. Econ. Rev.,* September 1973, *63*(4), pp. 770–71.

———— Samuelson's "Reply on Marxian Matters." *J. Econ. Lit.,* March 1973, *11*(1), pp. 64–68.

Sanazaro, Paul J. Federal Health Services R&D Under the Auspices of the National Center for Health Services Research and Development. In *Flook, E. E. and Sanazaro, P. J., eds.,* 1973, pp. 150–83.

———— and **Flook, E. Evelyn.** Health Services Research: Origins and Milestones. In *Flook, E. E. and Sanazaro, P. J., eds.,* 1973, pp. 1–81.

Sánchez, Carlos E. and Arnaudo, Aldo A. The Economic Power of Argentine Manufacturing Labor Unions. In *Sturmthal, A. and Scoville, J. G., eds.,* 1973, pp. 178–98.

Sanchez, Nicolas and Sweeney, Richard J. The Allocation of Tariff Revenues and Optimum Trade Distortion. With Empirical Applications to United States Sugar Policy. *Weltwirtsch. Arch.,* 1973, *109*(3), pp. 382–401.

Sandberg, I. W. A Nonlinear Input-Output Model of a Multisectored Economy. *Econometrica,* November 1973, *41*(6), pp. 1167–82.

Sandee, J. A Linear Macro Production Function for Long-Term Use. In *[Tinbergen, J.],* 1973, pp. 99–110.

Sandford, C. T. Prospects for Wealth Taxes. *Nat. Westminster Bank Quart. Rev.,* November 1973, pp. 27–40.

Sandhu, H. S. and Gupta, J. R. Adoption and Performance of Recommended Practices—A Comparative Study of Two Villages in Ludhiana District. *Econ. Aff.,* August 1973, *18*(8), pp. 389–94.

Sandler, Todd M. Exchange Rate Systems, the Marginal Efficiency of Investment and Foreign Direct Capital Movements: A Comment. *Kyklos,* 1973, *26*(4), pp. 866–68.

———— The Rybczynski Theorem, the Gains from Trade and Non-Homogeneous Utility Functions. *Indian Econ. J.,* July–September 1973, *21*(1), pp. 19–32.

———— and **Hogan, Timothy D.** The Optimum Population and Growth: A Further Look. *J. Econ. Theory,* December 1973, *6*(6), pp. 582–84.

Sandmo, Agnar. Public Goods and the Technology of Consumption. *Rev. Econ. Stud.,* October 1973, *40*(4), pp. 517–28.

Sandor, Richard L. Innovation by an Exchange: A Case Study of the Development of the Plywood Futures Contract. *J. Law Econ.,* April 1973, *16*(1), pp. 119–36.

———— and **Arditti, Fred D.** A Note on Variable Patent Life. *J. Ind. Econ.,* April 1973, *21*(2), pp. 177–83.

Sands, Saul. Estimating Data Withheld in Grouped Size Distributions. *J. Amer. Statist. Assoc.,* June 1973, *68*(342), pp. 306–11.

Sandu, C. and Popescu, C. Corelaţia între creşterea productivităţii muncii şi salariul mediu şi influenţa ei asupra mărimii preţului de cost şi a rentabilităţii. (The Correlation Between the Increase of Labour Productivity and the Average Wage and Its Influence on the Proportion of the Cost Price and of Profitableness. With English summary.) *Stud. Cercet. Econ.,* 1973, (1), pp. 35–42.

Sanittanont, Sura. Exchange Rate Experience and Policy in Thailand Since World War II. In *Grubel, H. G. and Morgan, T., eds.,* 1973, pp. 31–40.

Sankar, U. Investment Behavior in the U.S. Telephone Industry—1949 to 1968. *Bell J. Econ. Manage. Sci.,* Autumn 1973, *4*(2), pp. 665–78.

———— A Utility Function for Wealth for a Risk-Averter. *J. Econ. Theory,* December 1973, *6*(6), pp. 614–17.

Sankaran, Sundaram. Population and the World Bank. *Finance Develop.,* December 1973, *10*(4), pp. 18–21, 41.

Sankhayan, P. L.; Singh, Balwinder and Rangi, P. S. Relative Contributions of Area and Productivity in Increasing Production of Major Foodgrain Crops in Panjab (1960–61 to 1969–70) *Econ. Aff.,* March 1973, *18*(3), pp. 124–30.

Santistevan, Jorge and Pásara, Luís. "Industrial Communities" and Trade Unions in Peru: A Preliminary Analysis. *Int. Lab. Rev.,* August-September 1973, *108*(2–3), pp. 127–42.

Santomero, Anthony M. A Note on Interest Rates and Prices in General Equilibrium. *J. Finance,* September 1973, *28*(4), pp. 997–1000.

Saraceno, Pasquale. The Process of Industrialization of an Overpopulated Agricultural Area—The Italian Experience. In *[Rosenstein-Rodan, P.],* 1973, pp. 185–98.

Saraiya, R. G. Banking Commission's Approach to Its Task. In *Simha, S. L. N., ed.,* 1973, pp. 62–68.

———— Reform of the Indian Banking System: Proceedings of a Seminar: Introductory Address.

In *Simha, S. L. N., ed.,* 1973, pp. 15–19.

Sargent, J. R. The Distribution of Scientific Manpower. In *Williams, B. R., ed.,* 1973, pp. 360–74.

Sargent, Thomas J. Interest Rates and Prices in the Long Run: A Study of the Gibson Paradox. *J. Money, Credit, Banking,* Part II, February 1973, *5*(1), pp. 385–449.

⸺ "Rational Expectations": A Correction. *Brookings Pap. Econ. Act.,* 1973, (3), pp. 799–800.

⸺ Rational Expectations, the Real Rate of Interest, and the Natural Rate of Unemployment. *Brookings Pap. Econ. Act.,* 1973, (2), pp. 429–72.

⸺ What Do Regressions of Interest on Inflation Show? *Ann. Econ. Soc. Measure,* July 1973, *2*(3), pp. 289–301.

⸺ and **Henderson, Dale W.** Monetary and Fiscal Policy in a Two-Sector Aggregative Model. *Amer. Econ. Rev.,* June 1973, *63*(3), pp. 345–65.

⸺ and **Wallace, Neil.** Rational Expectations and the Dynamics of Hyperinflation. *Int. Econ. Rev.,* June 1973, *14*(2), pp. 328–50.

⸺ and **Wallace, Neil.** The Stability of Models of Money and Growth with Perfect Foresight. *Econometrica,* November 1973, *41*(6), pp. 1043–48.

Särkisilta, Martti. Markkinoinnin informaatiojärjestelmän rakenne ja kehittämisen pääsuuntaviivat. (The Structure of a Marketing Information System and Main Lines for Development. With English summary.) *Liiketaloudellinen Aikak.,* 1973, *22*(1), pp. 3–17.

Sarnat, Marshall. Purchasing Power Risk, Portfolio Analysis, and the Case for Index-Linked Bonds: Comment. *J. Money, Credit, Banking,* August 1973, *5*(3), pp. 836–45.

Sarris, Alexander H. A Bayesian Approach to Estimation of Time-Varying Regression Coefficients. *Ann. Econ. Soc. Measure,* October 1973, *2*(4), pp. 501–23.

Sasaki, Kozo. Spatial Equilibrium Analysis of Livestock Products in Eastern Japan. In *Judge, G. G. and Takayama, T., eds.,* 1973, pp. 419–42.

Sassen, E. M. J. A. Ensuring Fair Competition in the European Community. In *Thorelli, H. B., ed.,* 1973, pp. 104–15.

Sastri, K. V. S. Federal Finance in Underdeveloped Countries. In *[Hicks, U.],* 1973, pp. 207–29.

Sato, Ryuzo. On the Stability Properties of Dynamic Economic Systems. *Int. Econ. Rev.,* October 1973, *14*(3), pp. 753–64.

⸺ and **Koizumi, Tetsunori.** On the Elasticities of Substitution and Complementarity. *Oxford Econ. Pap.,* March 1973, *25*(1), pp. 44–56.

⸺ and **Koizumi, Tetsunori.** The Production Function and the Theory of Distributive Shares. *Amer. Econ. Rev.,* June 1973, *63*(3), pp. 484–89.

⸺ and **Koizumi, Tetsunori.** Relative Shares and Elasticities Simplified: Reply. *Amer. Econ. Rev.,* September 1973, *63*(4), pp. 772.

Saul, John S. African Socialism in One Country: Tanzania. In *Arrighi, G. and Saul, J. S.,* 1973, pp. 237–335.

⸺ The Political Aspects of Economic Independence. In *Ghai, D., ed.,* 1973, pp. 123–50.

⸺ and **Arrighi, Giovanni.** Nationalism and Revolution in Sub-Saharan Africa. In *Arrighi, G. and*

Saul, J. S., 1973, pp. 44–102.

⸺ and **Arrighi, Giovanni.** Socialism and Economic Development in Tropical Africa. In *Arrighi, G. and Saul, J. S.,* 1973, pp. 11–43.

⸺ and **Woods, Roger.** Appendix: African Peasantries. In *Arrighi, G. and Saul, J. S.,* 1973, pp. 406–16.

Saul, S. B. The Nature and Diffusion of Technology. In *Youngson, A. J., ed.,* 1973, pp. 36–61.

Saulnier, Raymond J. Is a Tax Increase Inevitable? In *Tax Foundation, Inc.,* 1973, pp. 6–9.

Sauls, Eugene H. and Holstrum, Gary L. The Opportunity Cost Transfer Price. *Manage. Account.,* May 1973, *54*(11), pp. 29–33.

Saunders, N. C. and Eldridge, D. P. Employment and Exports, 1963–72. *Mon. Lab. Rev.,* August 1973, *96*(8), pp. 16–27.

Saunders, Robert J. and Coccari, Ronald L. Racial Earnings Differentials: Some Economic Factors. *Amer. J. Econ. Soc.,* July 1973, *32*(3), pp. 225–33.

Savage, Paul L. The Ecological Bind: The Political Imperative. In *Gabriel, R. A. and Cohen, S. H., eds.,* 1973, pp. 192–211.

Savin, N. E. Systems *k*-Class Estimators. *Econometrica,* November 1973, *41*(6), pp. 1125–36.

Saving, Thomas R. On the Neutrality of Money. *J. Polit. Econ.,* January-February 1973, *81*(1), pp. 98–119.

Savona, Paolo. Mercato internazionale delle valute e mercato italiano delle obbligazioni. (International Exchange Market and Italian Bond Market. With English summary.) *Bancaria,* December 1973, *29*(12), pp. 1467–73.

Savoré, Carlo. Nuovi problemi delle imprese di produzione di fronte all'evoluzione delle strutture commerciali. (New Problems of Manufacturing Companies and the Development of Distributive Structures. With English summary.) *L'Impresa,* 1973, *15*(9–10), pp. 623–26.

⸺ Ricerche aziendali. (Firm Research. With English summary.) *L'Impresa,* 1973, *15*(1), pp. 48–49.

Savost'ianov, V. V. Factors Determining the Effectiveness of Socialist Foreign Trade. *Prob. Econ.,* September 1973, *16*(5), pp. 94–105.

⸺ Quantitative Estimation of the Factors in Foreign Trade. *Matekon,* Winter 1973-74, *10*(2), pp. 26–35.

Sawa, Takamitsu. Almost Unbiased Estimator in Simultaneous Equations Systems. *Int. Econ. Rev.,* February 1973, *14*(1), pp. 97–106.

⸺ The Mean Square Error of a Combined Estimator and Numerical Comparison with the TSLS Estimator. *J. Econometrics,* June 1973, *1*(2), pp. 115–32.

⸺ and **Anderson, T. W.** Distributions of Estimates of Coefficients of a Single Equation in a Simultaneous System and Their Asymptotic Expansions. *Econometrica,* July 1973, *41*(4), pp. 683–714.

⸺ and **Hiromatsu, Takeshi.** Minimax Regret Significance Points for a Preliminary Test in Regression Analysis. *Econometrica,* November 1973, *41*(6), pp. 1093–1101.

Sawers, Larry and Wisman, Jon D. Wealth Taxation for the United States. *J. Econ. Issues,* September

1973, *7*(3), pp. 417–36.

Sawhill, Isabel V. The Economics of Discrimination Against Women: Some New Findings. *J. Human Res.*, Summer 1973, *8*(3), pp. 383–96.

Sawhney, Bansi L. and Sawhney, Pawan K. Capacity-Utilization, Concentration, and Price-Cost Margins: Results on Indian Industries. *J. Ind. Econ.*, April 1973, *21*(2), pp. 145–53.

Sawhney, Pawan K. and Sawhney, Bansi L. Capacity-Utilization, Concentration, and Price-Cost Margins: Results on Indian Industries. *J. Ind. Econ.*, April 1973, *21*(2), pp. 145–53.

Sawicki, David S. Studies of Aggregated Areal Data: Problems of Statistical Inference. *Land Econ.*, February 1973, *49*(1), pp. 109–14.

Sawyer, Alan G. The Effects of Repetition of Refutational and Supportive Advertising Appeals. *J. Marketing Res.*, February 1973, *10*(1), pp. 23–33.

Sawyer, J. A. The Invisible Components of the Current Account of the Balance of International Payments. In *Ball, R. J., ed.*, 1973, pp. 329–63.

Sawyer, M. C. The Earnings of Manual Workers: A Cross-Section Analysis. *Scot. J. Polit. Econ.*, June 1973, *20*(2), pp. 141–57.

Saxe, Jo. The Japanese Experience and Attitudes Toward Trade Adjustment: Comment. In *Hughes, H., ed.*, 1973, pp. 266–68.

Saxena, D. N. Commercial Banks in the Current Development Strategy in India. In *Simha, S. L. N., ed.*, 1973, pp. 125–38.

Saxena, P. S. and Dubey, R. M. Rural Unemployment: A Direct Approach. *Econ. Aff.*, June 1973, *18*(6), pp. 265–74, 304.

Sayeki, Yutaka and Vesper, Karl H. A Quantitative Approach for Policy Analysis. *Calif. Manage. Rev.*, Spring 1973, *15*(3), pp. 119–26.

Sazama, Geraldo W. and Davis, Harlan. Land Taxation and Land Reform. *Econ. Develop. Cult. Change*, Part I, July 1973, *21*(4), pp. 642–54.

Scadding, John L. The Sampling Distribution of the Liviatan Estimator of the Geometric Distributed Lag Parameter. *Econometrica*, May 1973, *41*(3), pp. 503–08.

Scanlon, Paul D. Anti-Competitive Advertising and the FTC: A Ban on Oligopoly-Creating-Ads? In *Murray, B. B., ed.*, 1973, pp. 363–69.

_____ Oligopoly and Deceptive Advertising: The Cereal Industry Affair. In *Murray, B. B., ed.*, 1973, pp. 125–34.

Scaperlanda, Anthony E. E.E.C. NTD's and Developing Economies. In *Scaperlanda, A. E., ed.*, 1973, pp. 255–80.

_____ Perspectives and Implications. In *Scaperlanda, A. E., ed.*, 1973, pp. 17–45.

_____ and Mauer, Laurence Jay. The Impact of Controls on United States Direct Foreign Investment in the European Economic Community. *Southern Econ. J.*, January 1973, *39*(3), pp. 419–23.

Scarfe, B. L. A Model of the Inflation Cycle in a Small Open Economy. *Oxford Econ. Pap.*, July 1973, *25* (2), pp. 192–203.

Scarth, William M. The Effects on Stabilization Policy of Several Monetary Reform Proposals. *J. Econ. Bus.*, Spring-Summer 1973, *25*(3), pp. 154–58.

_____ The Financing of Stabilization Policies: Evidence for the Canadian Economy. *Can. J. Econ.*, August 1973, *6*(3), pp. 301–18.

_____ and Warne, Robert D. The Elasticity of Substitution and the Shape of the Transformation Curve. *Economica, N.S.*, August 1973, *40*(159), pp. 299–304.

Schachter, Gustav. Some Developments in Economic Science Since 1965: Methods, Ideas, Approaches. *Amer. J. Econ. Soc.*, July 1973, *32*(3), pp. 331–35.

_____ and Cohen, Bruce. Influenze esterne sui mercati dei capitali degli Stati Uniti. (Foreign Influences on the U.S. Capital Markets. With English summary.) *Bancaria*, February 1973, *29*(2), pp. 156–63.

Schaeffer, Maurice. The European Economic Community and Latin American Development. In *Urquidi, V. L. and Thorp, R., eds.*, 1973, pp. 313–30.

Schafer, Robert and Field, Charles G. Section 235 of the National Housing Act: Homeownership for Low-income Families? In *Pynoos, J.; Schafer, R. and Hartman, C. W., eds.*, 1973, pp. 460–71.

_____; Hartman, Chester W. and Pynoos, Jon. Housing Urban America: Introduction. In *Pynoos, J.; Schafer, R. and Hartman, C. W., eds.*, 1973, pp. 1–12.

Schanz, John J., Jr. and Frank, Helmut J. The Future of American Oil and Natural Gas. *Ann. Amer. Acad. Polit. Soc. Sci.*, November 1973, *410*, pp. 24–34.

Scharff, Jack and Peel, Evelyn. Impact of Cost-Sharing on Use of Ambulatory Services Under Medicare, 1969. *Soc. Sec. Bull.*, October 1973, *36*(10), pp. 3–24.

Scharnau, Ralph. Elizabeth Morgan, Crusader for Labor Reform. *Labor Hist.*, Summer 1973, *14*(3), pp. 340–51.

Schatan, Jacobo and Barraclough, Solon. Technological Policy and Agricultural Development. *Land Econ.*, May 1973, *49*(2), pp. 175–94.

Schatz, Sayre P. Externalities, Divergences, and the Profitability Criterion. *Quart. Rev. Econ. Bus.*, Winter 1973, *13*(4), pp. 19–26.

Schechter, Henry B. Federally Subsidized Housing Program Benefits. In *Harriss, C. L., ed.*, 1973, pp. 31–63.

Schedvin, C. B. A Century of Money in Australia. *Econ. Rec.*, December 1973, *49*(128), pp. 588–605.

Scheel, William C. A Critique of the Interest-Adjusted Net Cost Index. *J. Risk Ins.*, June 1973, *40*(2), pp. 245–61.

Scheffman, D. T. Some Remarks on the Net Production Possibilities Set in Models with Intermediate Goods. *J. Int. Econ.*, August 1973, *3*(3), pp. 291–95.

Scheiber, Harry N. Property Law, Expropriation, and Resource Allocation by Government: The United States, 1789–1910. *J. Econ. Hist.*, March 1973, *33*(1), pp. 232–51.

Scheidell, John M. The Price Reducing Potential of Advertising. *Southern Econ. J.*, April 1973, *39*(4), pp. 535–43.

Scheinberg, Stephen. Invitation to Empire: Tariffs and American Economic Expansion in Canada.

Bus. Hist. Rev., Summer 1973, *47*(2), pp. 218–38.

Scheingold, Stuart A. Domestic and International Consequences of Regional Integration. In *Falk, R. A. and Mendlovitz, S. H., eds.,* 1973, pp. 133–51.

———— **and Lindberg, Leon N.** The Future of the European Community: Equilibrium and Beyond. In *Falk, R. A. and Mendlovitz, S. H., eds.,* 1973, pp. 435–54.

Schenker, Eric and Bunamo, Michael. A Study of the Corps of Engineers' Regional Pattern of Investments. *Southern Econ. J.,* April 1973, *39*(4), pp. 548–58.

Scheper, W. and Reichenbach, H. Die Entwicklung der Anteile der Wirtschaftsbereiche am Bruttoinlandsprodukt—Eine Strukturprognose. (The Development of the Sectoral Shares of Production in Gross National Product. A Forecast of the Production Structure. With English summary) *Weltwirtsch. Arch.,* 1973, *109*(2), pp. 291–320.

Schepsman, Martin and Stekler, H. O. Forecasting with an Index of Leading Series. *J. Amer. Statist. Assoc.,* June 1973, *68*(342), pp. 291–96.

Scherer, Frederic M. The Determinants of Industrial Plant Sizes in Six Nations. *Rev. Econ. Statist.,* May 1973, *55*(2), pp. 135–45.

———— Investment Variability, Seller Concentration, and Plant Scale Economies. *J. Ind. Econ.,* December 1973, *22*(2), pp. 157–60.

———— The Problem of Cost Overruns. In *Haveman, R. H. and Hamrin, R. D., eds.,* 1973, pp. 159–65.

Scherr, Bruce A. and Smith, Lawrence N. Social Return to Public Information Services: Statistical Reporting of U.S. Farm Commodities: Comment. *Amer. Econ. Rev.,* December 1973, *63*(5), pp. 1017–19.

Scheuren, Frederick J. Ransacking CPS Tabulations: Applications of the Log Linear Model to Poverty Statistics. *Ann. Econ. Soc. Measure,* April 1973, *2*(2), pp. 159–82.

Schiesser, W. E. The Club of Rome Model. In *Weintraub, A.; Schwartz, E. and Aronson, J. R., eds.,* 1973, pp. 219–29.

Schiff, Frank W. Alternative Tax and Spending Policies, 1971–1976. In *Giersch, H., ed.,* 1973, pp. 188–94.

Schilbred, Cornelius M. The Market Price of Risk. *Rev. Econ. Stud.,* April 1973, *40*(2), pp. 283–92.

Schiller, Bradley R. Empirical Studies of Welfare Dependency: A Survey. *J. Human Res.,* Supplement 1973, *8*, pp. 19–32.

———— Moving from Welfare to Workfare. *Public Policy,* Winter 1973, *21*(1), pp. 125–33.

Schiltknecht, Kurt and Zweifel, Peter. Voraussagen der Kommission für Konjunkturfragen und Modellprognosen 1967–1970. (Forecasts of the Federal Commission on Business Cycles and Model's Predictions 1967–1970. With English summary.) *Schweiz. Z. Volkswirtsch. Statist.,* December 1973, *109*(4), pp. 535–53.

Schimmler, Harry. On National Accounts at Constant Prices. *Rev. Income Wealth,* December 1973, *19*(4), pp. 457–61.

Schimmler, Jörg. Speculation, Profitability, and Price Stability—A Formal Approach. *Rev. Econ. Statist.,* February 1973, *55*(1), pp. 110–14.

Schink, George R. and Fromm, Gary. Aggregation and Econometric Models. *Int. Econ. Rev.,* February 1973, *14*(1), pp. 1–32.

Schips, B. and Stier, W. Einige Bemerkungen über die Rolle der Spektralanalyse in der empirischen Wirtschaftsforschung. (Some Remarks on the Role of Spectral Analysis for Empirical Economic Research. With English summary.) *Schweiz. Z. Volkswirtsch. Statist.,* June 1973, *109*(2), pp. 233–43.

Schirm, David; Havrilesky, Thomas M. and Yohe, William P. The Economic Affiliations of Directors of Federal Reserve District Banks. *Soc. Sci. Quart.,* December 1973, *54*(3), pp. 608–22.

Schleicher, Heinz. On European Social Rates of Discount: Survey. *Finanzarchiv,* 1973, *31*(3), pp. 434–40.

Schlenker, Jon A. and Bourgeois, Lawrence L. Family Assistance to Married University Students. *Southern Quart.,* January 1973, *11*(2), pp. 147–55.

Schlenker, Robert E. Optimal Mechanisms for Income Transfer: Note. *Amer. Econ. Rev.,* June 1973, *63*(3), pp. 454–57.

Schler, Michael L. and Kau, Randall K. C. Inflation and the Federal Income Tax. *Yale Law J.,* March 1973, *82*(4), pp. 716–44.

Schlesinger, Helmut and Bockelmann, Horst. Monetary Policy in the Federal Republic of Germany. In *Holbik, K., ed.,* 1973, pp. 161–213.

Schlichthaber, Roland. Verkehrsplanung in der Agglomeration aus der Sicht eines Ökonomen. (Traffic Planning in Agglomerations from the Economist's Point of View. With English summary.) *Schweiz. Z. Volkswirtsch. Statist.,* September 1973, *109*(3), pp. 375–84.

Schlissel, Martin R. Promotional Strategy in a High-Technology Industry. *J. Econ. Bus.,* Fall 1973, *26*(1), pp. 67–73.

Schloctern, F. J. M. Meyer Zu and Yajima, Akira. The OECD Trade Model 1970 Version. In *Alexandrides, C. G., ed.,* 1973, pp. 57–78.

Schloenbach, Knut. Studies on the Structure of the Armed Forces with the Aid of Simulation. On the Quantitative Methods of Analysis Employed by the Force Structure Commission. *Ger. Econ. Rev.,* 1973, *11*(4), pp. 361–68.

Schlossmacher, E. J. An Iterative Technique for Absolute Deviations Curve Fitting. *J. Amer. Statist. Assoc.,* December 1973, *68*(344), pp. 857–59.

Schlüter, Karl-Peter. Eignet sich die Wachstumstheorie zur wirtschaftspolitischen Anwendung? (With English summary.) *Z. ges. Staatswiss.,* October 1973, *129*(4), pp. 613–33.

Schmähl, Winfried. Zur Struktur von Rentenleistungen. (On the Structure of Pensions. With English summary.) *Z. ges. Staatswiss.,* February 1973, *129*(1), pp. 123–49.

Schmalen, Helmut. Rationale individuelle Berufswahl und die langfristige Entwicklung des Arbeitsmarktes. (Rational Individual Choice of Professions and the Long-Term Development of the Labor Market. With English summary.) *Z. ges. Staatswiss.,* May 1973, *129*(2), pp. 292–311.

Schmalensee, Richard. A Note on the Theory of Vertical Integration. *J. Polit. Econ.,* Part I, March-

April 1973, *81*(2), pp. 442–49.

Schmeidler, David; Zamir, Shmuel and Hildenbrand, Werner. Existence of Approximate Equilibria and Cores. *Econometrica*, November 1973, *41*(6), pp. 1159–66.

Schmenner, Roger W. The Determination of Municipal Employee Wages. *Rev. Econ. Statist.*, February 1973, *55*(1), pp. 83–90.

Schmid, A. Allan. The Role of Grants, Exchange, and Property Rights in Environmental Policy. **In** *Boulding, K. E.; Pfaff, M. and Pfaff, A., eds.*, 1973, pp. 340–49.

Schmidt, Ádám. Equilibrium of the Budget and of the National Economy. **In** *Földi, T., ed.*, 1973, pp. 89–115.

Schmidt, Benicio Viero. Dependency and the Multinational Corporation. **In** *Bonilla, F. and Girling, R., eds.*, 1973, pp. 17–33.

Schmidt, Herbert. Governmental Regulations and Quality of Work Environment. **In** *Dierkes, M. and Bauer, R. A., eds.*, 1973, pp. 191–211.

Schmidt, Peter. The Asymptotic Distribution of Dynamic Multipliers. *Econometrica*, January 1973, *41*(1), pp. 161–64.

———— Calculating the Power of the Minimum Standard Error Choice Criterion. *Int. Econ. Rev.*, February 1973, *14*(1), pp. 253–55.

———— On the Difference Between Conditional and Unconditional Asymptotic Distributions of Estimates in Distributed Lag Models with Integer-Valued Parameters. *Econometrica*, January 1973, *41*(1), pp. 165–69.

———— **and Guilkey, David K.** Estimation of Seemingly Unrelated Regressions with Vector Autoregressive Errors. *J. Amer. Statist. Assoc.*, September 1973, *68*(343), pp. 642–47.

———— **and Waud, Roger N.** The Almon Lag Technique and the Monetary Versus Fiscal Policy Debate. *J. Amer. Statist. Assoc.*, March 1973, *68*(341), pp. 11–19.

Schmidt, Richard A. and Henry, John P., Jr. Coal: Still Old Reliable? *Ann. Amer. Acad. Polit. Soc. Sci.*, November 1973, *410*, pp. 35–51.

Schmidt, Warren H. and Tannenbaum, Robert. How to Choose a Leadership Pattern. *Harvard Bus. Rev.*, May-June 1973, *51*(3), pp. 162–80.

Schmidt, William H.; Bramble, William J. and Wiley, David E. Studies of a Class of Covariance Structure Models. *J. Amer. Statist. Assoc.*, June 1973, *68*(342), pp. 317–23.

Schmidtchen, Dieter. Für eine konsequente Wettbewerbspolitik und über die Wege dorthin: Bemerkungen zum Wettbewerbsverständnis des Sachverständigenrates. (Consequent Competition Policy and the Ways Towards It: Remarks on the Understanding of Competition of the German Council of Economic Experts. With English summary.) *Z. ges. Staatswiss.*, February 1973, *129*(1), pp. 102–22.

Schmiedeskamp, Jay; Schwartz, M. Susan and Strumpel, Burkhard. The Function of Consumer Attitude Data Beyond Econometric Forecasts. **In** *Mandell, L., et al., eds.*, 1973, pp. 263–88.

Schmitt, Hans O. Development and Assistance: The View from Bretton Woods. *Public Policy*, Fall 1973, *21*(4), pp. 585–600.

Schmitt, R. W. and Roberts, R. W. Program Budgeting R and D at General Electric. **In** *Novick, D., ed.*, 1973, pp. 139–50.

Schmitter, Philippe C. The "Portugalization" of Brazil? **In** *Stepan, A., ed.*, 1973, pp. 179–232.

Schmitt-Rink, Gerhard. Marktform und Geldschöpfungsmultiplikator. (Market Structure and Multiple Money Expansion. With English summary.) *Jahr. Nationalökon. Statist.*, December 1973, *188*(1), pp. 1–9.

Schmitz, Andrew. Distortions and Product Specialization in International Trade. *Econ. Rec.*, June 1973, *49*(126), pp. 263–69.

———— **and Bawden, D. Lee.** A Spatial Price Analysis of the World Wheat Economy: Some Long-Run Predictions. **In** *Judge, G. G. and Takayama, T., eds.*, 1973, pp. 488–516.

———— **and Bieri, Jurg.** Export Instability, Monopoly Power, and Welfare. *J. Int. Econ.*, November 1973, *3*(4), pp. 389–96.

Schmulowitz, Jack. Recovery and Benefit Termination: Program Experience of Disabled-Worker Beneficiaries. *Soc. Sec. Bull.*, June 1973, *36*(6), pp. 3–15.

———— Spanish-Surnamed OASDI Beneficiaries in the Southwest. *Soc. Sec. Bull.*, April 1973, *36*(4), pp. 33–36.

Schnabel, Morton. A Model of Cigarette Advertising. *Antitrust Bull.*, Spring 1973, *18*(1), pp. 33–43.

Schnaiberg, Allan. The Concept and Measurement of Child Dependency: An Approach to Family Formation Analysis. *Population Stud.*, March 1973, *27*(1), pp. 69–84.

Schneider, Jan. New Perspectives on International Environmental Law. *Yale Law J.*, July 1973, *82*(8), pp. 1659–80.

Schneider, J. W. Intra-Benelux NTD's. **In** *Scaperlanda, A. E., ed.*, 1973, pp. 73–106.

Schnirring, Paul; Haynes, Kingsley E. and Poston, Dudley L., Jr. Intermetropolitan Migration in High and Low Opportunity Areas: Indirect Tests of the Distance and Intervening Opportunities Hypotheses. *Econ. Geogr.*, January 1973, *49*(1), pp. 68–73.

Schnittker, John A. Prospects for Freer Agricultural Trade. *Amer. J. Agr. Econ.*, May 1973, *55*(2), pp. 289–93.

———— The 1972–73 Food Price Spiral. *Brookings Pap. Econ. Act.*, 1973, (2), pp. 498–507.

Schofield, Roger. Dimensions of Illiteracy, 1750–1850. *Exploration Econ. Hist.*, Summer 1973, *10*(4), pp. 437–54.

Scholes, Myron S. Causes and Predictions of Rates of Return on Stocks and Bonds: Discussion. *J. Finance*, May 1973, *28*(2), pp. 315–18.

———— **and Black, Fischer.** The Pricing of Options and Corporate Liabilities. *J. Polit. Econ.*, May-June 1973, *81*(3), pp. 637–54.

Scholl, Robert. Managing the Scientific Mind. *Manage. Account.*, September 1973, *55*(3), pp. 48–50.

Scholl, Russell B. The International Investment Position of the United States: Developments in 1972. *Surv. Curr. Bus.*, August 1973, *53*(8), pp. 18–23.

Schollhammer, Hans. Organization Structures of Multinational Corporations. **In** *Henley, D. S., ed.*,

1973, pp. 445–65.

———— Le strutture organizzative delle aziende multinazionali. (Organizational Structures of Multinational Companies. With English summary.) *Mondo Aperto,* October 1973, *27*(5), pp. 321–40.

Schonberger, Richard J. Management Information Systems in Insurance: Comment. *J. Risk Ins.,* June 1973, *40*(2), pp. 294–96.

———— A Taxonomy of Systems Management. *Nebr. J. Econ. Bus.,* Spring 1973, *12*(2), pp. 35–44.

Schönfeld, Peter. A Note on the Measurability of the Pseudo-Inverse. *J. Econometrics,* October 1973, *1* (3), pp. 313–14.

Schott, Francis H. Consumer Financial Management and Financial Institution Response—A Two-Decade Perspective. In *Sheldon, E. B., ed.,* 1973, pp. 311–62.

Schotter, Andrew. Core Allocations and Competitive Equilibrium—A Survey. *Z. Nationalökon.,* 1973, *33*(3–4), pp. 281–313.

Schramm, Richard; Tollison, Robert D. and Long, William F. The Economic Determinants of Antitrust Activity. *J. Law Econ.,* October 1973, *16*(2), pp. 351–64.

Schreiner, Dean; Muncrief, George and Davis, Bob. Solid Waste Management for Rural Areas: Analysis of Costs and Service Requirements. *Amer. J. Agr. Econ.,* Part I, November 1973, *55*(4), pp. 567–76.

Schrimper, R. A. and Prochaska, Fred J. Opportunity Cost of Time and Other Socioeconomic Effects on Away-From-Home Food Consumption. *Amer. J. Agr. Econ.,* Part I, November 1973, *55*(4), pp. 595–603.

Schriver, William R. and Bowlby, Roger L. Academic Ability and Rates of Return to Vocational Training. *Ind. Lab. Relat. Rev.,* April 1973, *26*(3), pp. 980–90.

Schroeder, Gertrude E. Regional Differences in Incomes and Levels of Living in the USSR. In *Bandera, V. N. and Melnyk, Z. L., eds.,* 1973, pp. 167–95.

Schruben, Leonard W. Grain Marketing Methods in the U.S.A.—The Theory, Assumptions, and Approach. *Amer. J. Agr. Econ.,* December 1973, *55* (5), pp. 800–04.

Schubert, A. Eugene. Organizing to Supply Nuclear Energy. In *Weston, J. F. and Ornstein, S. I., eds.,* 1973, pp. 157–62.

Schuessler, Karl. Ratio Variables and Path Models. In *Goldberger, A. S. and Duncan, O. D., eds.,* 1973, pp. 201–28.

Schulenberg, T. W. Indiana's Regions: Emerging Policy and Management. *Indiana Bus. Rev.,* March-April 1973, *48,* pp. 19–24.

Schüler, Manfred. Fiscal Policy in Recession: The German Experience. In *Giersch, H., ed.,* 1973, pp. 195–202.

Schuler, Randall. Worker Background and Job Satisfaction: Comment. *Ind. Lab. Relat. Rev.,* January 1973, *26*(2), pp. 851–53.

Schultz, Theodore W. The Value of Children: An Economic Perspective. *J. Polit. Econ.,* Part II, March-April 1973, *81*(2), pp. S2–13.

Schultz, T. Paul. Explanation of Birth Rate Changes over Space and Time: A Study of Taiwan. *J. Polit.*

Econ., Part II, March-April 1973, *81*(2), pp. S238–74.

———— A Preliminary Survey of Economic Analyses of Fertility. *Amer. Econ. Rev.,* May 1973, *63*(2), pp. 71–78.

———— and Nerlove, Marc. Love and Life between the Censuses. In *Goldberger, A. S. and Duncan, O. D., eds.,* 1973, pp. 317–28.

Schultze, Charles L. The Economic Content of National Security Policy. *Foreign Aff.,* April 1973, *51* (3), pp. 522–40.

———— Evaluating Performance in the Public Sector: Comment. In *Moss, M., ed.,* 1973, pp. 384–94.

———— The Factors Behind Rising Military Expenditures. In *Haveman, R. H. and Hamrin, R. D., eds.,* 1973, pp. 117–26.

———— Perverse Incentives and the Inefficiency of Government. In *Haveman, R. H. and Hamrin, R. D., eds.,* 1973, pp. 15–22.

———— U.S. Farm Policy: Who Gets the Benefits. In *Haveman, R. H. and Hamrin, R. D., eds.,* 1973, pp. 182–90.

Schumacher, D. Technological Forecasting and Political Planning. In *Blohm, H. and Steinbuch, K., eds.,* 1973, pp. 145–49.

Schumacher, E. F. Buddhist Economics. In *Daly, H. E., ed.,* 1973, pp. 231–39.

———— Does Economics Help? An Exploration of Meta-economics. In *Robinson, J., ed.,* 1973, pp. 26–36.

Schumpeter, Joseph Alois. Capitalism, Socialism and Democracy: Marx the Economist. In *Rectenwald, H. C., ed.,* 1973, pp. 238–50.

Schürmann, Leo. Zur neueren Entwicklung der Kartell- und Wettbewerbspolitik aus schweizerischer Sicht. *Wirtsch. Recht,* 1973, *25* (2), pp. 77–109.

Schurr, Samuel. Minerals Trade and International Relations. In *Bergsten, C. F., ed.,* 1973, pp. 181–96.

Schuster, Helmut. Direktinvestitionen und Zahlungsbilanz in Entwicklungsländern. (Direct Investment and the Balance of Payments in Developing Countries. With English summary.) *Z. Wirtschaft. Sozialwissen.,* 1973, *93*(2), pp. 190–96.

———— Keynes' Disequilibrium Analysis. *Kyklos,* 1973, *26*(3), pp. 512–44.

———— On the Additivity of Consumers' Rents and the Assessment of External Rent Effects. *Ger. Econ. Rev.,* 1973, *11*(1), pp. 14–20.

Schwab, Bernhard and Brumelle, Shelby L. Capital Budgeting with Uncertain Future Opportunities: A Markovian Approach. *J. Financial Quant. Anal.,* January 1973, *8*(1), pp. 111–22.

Schwartz, Aba. Interpreting the Effect of Distance on Migration. *J. Polit. Econ.,* September-October 1973, *81*(5), pp. 1153–69.

———— and Regev, Uri. Optimal Path of Interregional Investment and Allocation of Water. *Water Resources Res.,* April 1973, *9*(2), pp. 251–62.

Schwartz, Anna J. Secular Price Change in Historical Perspective. *J. Money, Credit, Banking,* Part II, February 1973, *5*(1), pp. 243–69.

———— and Friedman, M. The Panic of 1907 and Banking Reform in Its Wake. In *Temin, P., ed.,*

1973, pp. 315–35.

Schwartz, Benjamin. China's Developmental Experience, 1949–72. In *Oksenberg, M., ed.*, 1973, pp. 17–26.

Schwartz, Eli and Aronson, J. Richard. Financing Public Goods and the Distribution of Population in a System of Local Governments. *Nat. Tax J.*, June 1973, *26*(2), pp. 137–60.

Schwartz, Ivo E. Creating a Common Market for Insurance: Harmonization of EEC Insurance Legislation. *Antitrust Bull.*, Spring 1973, *18*(1), pp. 103–16.

Schwartz, Lawrence E. Uncertainty Reduction Over Time in the Theory of Multiattributed Utility. In *Cochrane, J. L. and Zeleny, M., eds.*, 1973, pp. 108–23.

Schwartz, M. Susan; Strumpel, Burkhard and Schmiedeskamp, Jay. The Function of Consumer Attitude Data Beyond Econometric Forecasts. In *Mandell, L., et al., eds.*, 1973, pp. 263–88.

Schwartz, Nancy L. and Kamien, Morton I. Payment Plans and the Efficient Delivery of Health Care Services. *J. Risk Ins.*, September 1973, *40*(3), pp. 427–36.

———; **Roberts, Donald John and Kamien, Morton I.** Exclusion, Externalities, and Public Goods. *J. Public Econ.*, July 1973, *2*(3), pp. 217–30.

Schwartz, Robert A. and Altman, Edward I. Volatility Behavior of Industrial Stock Price Indices. *J. Finance*, September 1973, *28*(4), pp. 957–71.

Schwartz, Sandra L. Second-hand Machinery in Development, or How to Recognize a Bargain. *J. Devel. Stud.*, July 1973, *9*(4), pp. 544–55.

Schwartz, Stuart B. Free Labor in a Slave Economy: The *Lavrodores de Cana* of Colonial Bahia. In *Alden, D., ed.*, 1973, pp. 147–97.

Schwartzman, David. Competition and Efficiency: Comment. *J. Polit. Econ.*, May-June 1973, *81*(3), pp. 756–64.

——— The Cost-Elasticity of Demand and Industry Boundaries: Coal, Oil, Gas, and Uranium. *Antitrust Bull.*, Fall, 1973, *18*(3), pp. 483–507.

Schwarze, Jochen. Probleme der Fehlermessung bei quantitativen ökonomischen Prognosen. (Problems of Measuring of Errors in Quantitative Economic Forecasting. With English summary.) *Z. ges. Staatswiss.*, August 1973, *129*(3), pp. 535–58.

Schweiger, Irving. 1973 Forecast of Gross National Product, Consumer Spending, Saving, and Housing. *J. Bus.*, January 1973, *46*(1), pp. 6–10.

Schweikert, H. Zur Planung der Energieversorgung in städtischen Agglomerationen. (The Planning of Distribution of Energy in Urban Areas. With English summary.) *Schweiz. Z. Volkswirtsch. Statist.*, September 1973, *109*(3), pp. 421–39.

de Schweinitz, Karl, Jr. The Ethics of Economic Development. *Econ. Develop. Cult. Change*, Part I, July 1973, *21*(4), pp. 717–21.

Schweitzer, Stuart A. Economies of Scale and Holding Company Affiliation in Banking: Reply. *Southern Econ. J.*, July 1973, *40*(1), pp. 141–42.

Schwendiman, John S. Strategic and Long Range Planning in the International Firm. In *Alexandrides, C. G., ed.*, 1973, pp. 173–84.

Schwirian, Kent P. and Bleda, Sharon E. Ecological and Socio-Economic Factors in Neighborhood Housing Conditions: The Case of the Cleveland Metropolitan Area. *Ohio State U. Bull. Bus. Res.*, January 1973, *48*(1), pp. 1–3, 6–7.

Scioli, Frank P., Jr. and Cook, Thomas J. Experimental Design in Policy Impact Analysis. *Soc. Sci. Quart.*, September 1973, *54*(2), pp. 271–80.

Scitovsky, Tibor. Inequalities: Open and Hidden, Measured and Immeasurable. *Ann. Amer. Acad. Polit. Soc. Sci.*, September 1973, *409*, pp. 112–19.

——— A New Approach to the Theory of Consumer Behavior. *Amer. Econ.*, Fall 1973, *17*(2), pp. 29–32.

——— Notes on the Producer Society. *De Economist*, May-June 1973, *121*(3), pp. 225–50.

——— The Place of Economic Welfare in Human Welfare. *Quart. Rev. Econ. Bus.*, Autumn 1973, *13*(3), pp. 7–19.

——— A Reconsideration of the Theory of Tariffs. In *Farrell, M. J., ed.*, 1973, pp. 58–79.

Scott, Anthony. The Defense of Federalism, or, the Attack on Unitary Government. *Amer. Econ.*, Fall 1973, *17*(2), pp. 162–69.

Scott, David F., Jr. and Petty, J. William. An Analysis of Corporate Insider Trading Activity. *J. Econ. Bus.*, Fall 1973, *26*(1), pp. 19–24.

Scott, Donald E. Takings and the Public Interest in Railroad Reorganization. *Yale Law J.*, April 1973, *82*(5), pp. 1004–22.

Scott, James H., Jr. The Portfolio Balance Theory of the Expected Rate of Change of Prices: Comment. *Rev. Econ. Stud.*, October 1973, *40*(4), pp. 579–80.

——— The Test of Understanding in College Economics and Its Construct Validity: Comment. *J. Econ. Educ.*, Spring 1973, *4*(2), pp. 141–42.

——— **and Rothman, Mitchell P.** Political Opinions and the TUCE. *J. Econ. Educ.*, Spring 1973, *4*(2), pp. 116–24.

Scott, John T., Jr. and Chen, C. T. Expected Changes in Farm Organization When Industry Moves into a Rural Area. *Ill. Agr. Econ.*, January 1973, *13*(1), pp. 41–47.

Scott, Robert A. and Shore, Arnold R. Work Response and Family Composition Changes in a Negative Income Tax Experiment: Preliminary Mid-Experiment Results. In *Sheldon, E. B., ed.*, 1973, pp. 233–63.

Scott, Robert E. Latin America and Modernization. In *Scott, R. E., ed.*, 1973, pp. 1–21.

Scott, T. W. K. and Davies, S. W. Forecasting Industrial Production. *Nat. Inst. Econ. Rev.*, November 1973, (66), pp. 54–68.

Scott, Walter Giorgio. Proposta per una ricerca sui costi di distribuzione commerciale. (Proposal for Research on the Distribution Costs Met by Firms. With English summary.) *L'Impresa*, 1973, *15*(1), pp. 50–52.

Scott, William R. A Bayesian Approach to Asset Valuation and Audit Size. *J. Acc. Res.*, Autumn 1973, *11*(2), pp. 304–30.

Scotto di Carlo, Giovampietro. Effetto reddito ed effetto finanziario per la programmazione della politica di bilancio. (Income Effect and Financial Effect in the Planning of the Budget Policy. With English summary.) *L'Industria*, January-June

1973, (1–2), pp. 109–24.

———— Programmi quinquennali di spesa pubblica. Il sistema inglese e quello italiano. (Five-Year Public Expenditure Programmes. The British and Italian Systems. With English summary.) *Bancaria*, July 1973, *29*(7), pp. 832–38.

Scoville, James G.   Pre-Industrial Industrial Relations: The Case of Afghanistan. In *Sturmthal, A. and Scoville, J. G., eds.*, 1973, pp. 199–227.

———— The Role of Forecasting and Planning Manpower Programs. In *Aronson, R. L., ed.*, 1973, pp. 51–62.

———— Some Determinants of the Structure of Labor Movements. In *Sturmthal, A. and Scoville, J. G., eds.*, 1973, pp. 58–78.

Scoville, Orlin J.   The Agribusiness Sector—An Important Link in Economic Growth Models. *Amer. J. Agr. Econ.*, August 1973, *55*(3), pp. 520–23.

Scully, Gerald W.   Economic Discrimination in Professional Sports. *Law Contemp. Probl.*, Winter-Spring 1973, *38*(1), pp. 67–84.

———— Technical Progress, Factor Market Distortions, and the Pattern of Trade. *Econ. Int.*, February 1973, *26*(1), pp. 3–16.

———— and Gallaway, Lowell E.   A Spectral Analysis of the Demographic Structure of American Unemployment. *J. Bus.*, January 1973, *46*(1), pp. 87–102.

Sdralevich, Alberto and Monti, Mario.   I modelli macroeconomici per la politica monetaria in Italia: aggregazione e realismo. (Macroeconomic Models for Monetary Policy in Italy: Aggregation and Realism. With English summary.) *L'Industria*, January-June 1973, (1–2), pp. 36–58.

Seagraves, James A.   Economics of Heroin: Discussion. *Amer. Econ. Rev.*, May 1973, *63*(2), pp. 278–79.

———— On Appraising Environmental Institutions. *Amer. J. Agr. Econ.*, Part I, November 1973, *55*(4), pp. 617–21.

Seaver, S. K. and Lee, T.-C.   A Positive Model of Spatial Equilibrium with Special Reference to the Broiler Markets. In *Judge, G. G. and Takayama, T., eds.*, 1973, pp. 443–63.

Sebestyén, Joseph.   On Models of Planning Regional Development in Hungary. In *Judge, G. G. and Takayama, T., eds.*, 1973, pp. 26–42.

Sebold, Frederick D.; Harper, Richard D. and Venieris, Yiannis P.   The Impact of Economic, Technological and Demographic Factors on Aggregate Births. *Rev. Econ. Statist.*, November 1973, *55*(4), pp. 493–97.

Secchi, Carlo.   Il rinnovo della associazione tra la CEE e i SAMA e le tendenze della politica comunitaria verso i paesi sottosviluppati. (The Renewal of the Association Between the EEC and the AASM and the Prospects of the Community Policy Towards Underdeveloped Countries. With English summary.) *Rivista Int. Sci. Econ. Com.*, November 1973, *20*(11), pp. 1081–1108.

Seers, Dudley.   The Debate on the Teaching of Economics in Africa: Foreword. In *Livingstone, I., et al., eds.*, 1973, pp. 9–15.

Seetzen, J. and Ferrari, A.   La ricerca innovazionale in USA e in Europa. (Results of Innovation Research in USA and Europe. With English sum-

mary.) *L'Impresa*, 1973, *15*(7–8), pp. 425–32.

Seevers, G. L. and Keeton, W. R.   Interrelationships between the Levels of U.S. Exports and Imports. In *Iowa State University Center for Agricultural and Rural Development*, 1973, pp. 111–21.

Šefer, Berislav.   Income Distribution in Yugoslavia. In *Moskoff, W., ed.*, 1973, pp. 201–16.

Segal, David R. and Felson, Marcus.   Social Stratification and Family Economic Behavior. In *Sheldon, E. B., ed.*, 1973, pp. 143–64.

Segal, Lydia and Ripley, Frank C.   Price Determination in 395 Manufacturing Industries. *Rev. Econ. Statist.*, August 1973, *55*(3), pp. 263–71.

Segelhorst, Elbert W. and Kirkus, Larry D.   Parking Bias in Transit Choice. *J. Transp. Econ. Policy*, January 1973, *7*(1), pp. 58–70.

Segura, Edilberto L.   Optimal Fishing Effort in the Peruvian Anchoveta Fishery. In *Sokoloski, A. A., ed.*, 1973, pp. 57–64.

Seibel, H. Dieter.   The Process of Adaptation to Wage Labor. In *Damachi, U. G. and Seibel, H. D., eds.*, 1973, pp. 3–10.

Seiders, David.   Credit-Card and Check-Credit Plans at Commercial Banks. *Fed. Res. Bull.*, September 1973, *59*(9), pp. 646–53.

Seidman, Bert.   Welfare Reform Should Mean the Welfare of Children. *Mon. Lab. Rev.*, April 1973, *96*(4), pp. 57–59.

Seidman, Joel and Staudohar, Paul D.   The Hawaii Public Employment Relations Act: A Critical Analysis. *Ind. Lab. Relat. Rev.*, April 1973, *26*(3), pp. 919–37.

Seidman, Robert B.   Contract Law, the Free Market, and State Intervention: A Jurisprudential Perspective. *J. Econ. Issues*, December 1973, *7*(4), pp. 553–75.

Seifer, Daniel M.   Foreign Steel and U.S. Jobs, Trade, Environment, and Safety. *Ohio State U. Bull. Bus. Res.*, March 1973, *48*(3), pp. 4–7.

Seifert, Hans G. and Hauptmann, Harry.   Ein Oligopolspiel mit wirksamen Kapazitätsschranken. (An Oligopoly Game with Effective Capacity Bounds. With English summary.) *Jahr. Nationalökon. Statist.*, December 1973, *188*(1), pp. 51–64.

Seifried, Edmond J. and Mikesell, John L.   Rates of Return in Public and Private Enterprise: Electric Utilities in the United States. *Miss. Val. J. Bus. Econ.*, Fall 1973, *9*(1), pp. 41–54.

Seitz, C. Ward; Merz, C. M. and Gibson, T. A.   Impact of the Space Shuttle Program on the National Economy. *Eng. Econ.*, January-February 1973, *18*(2), pp. 115–33.

Seitz, Peter.   Mandatory Contract Arbitration: A Viable Process or Not, It Works (Sometimes). *Ind. Lab. Relat. Rev.*, April 1973, *26*(3), pp. 1009–12.

Sekine, Thomas T.   Classical Monetary Theory and the Non-Optimality Theorem. *Z. Nationalökon.*, 1973, *33*(1–2), pp. 1–24.

———— The Discovery of International Monetary Equilibrium by Vanderlint, Cantillon, Gervaise and Hume. *Econ. Int.*, May 1973, *26*(2), pp. 262–82.

Selander, Sharon L. and Korth, Christopher M.   The China Market: Boom or Bust? In *Henley, D. S., ed.*, 1973, pp. 55–64.

Selander, Stephen E.   Is Annual Style Change in the

Automobile Industry an Unfair Method of Competition? A Rebuttal. *Yale Law J.*, March 1973, *82* (4), pp. 691–710.

Seley, John and Mumphrey, Anthony J. Simulation Approaches to Locational Conflicts. *Econ. Geogr.*, January 1973, *49*(1), pp. 21–36.

Seligman, Ben Baruch. Max Weber and the Capitalist Spirit. In *Rectenwald, H. C., ed.*, 1973, pp. 348–56.

Seligson, Mitchell A. Transactions and Community Formation: Fifteen Years of Growth and Stagnation in Central America. *J. Common Market Stud.*, March 1973, *11*(3), pp. 173–90.

Sellekaerts, Brigette and Sellekaerts, Willy. Balance of Payments Deficits, the Adjustment Cost and the Optimum Level of International Reserves. *Weltwirtsch. Arch.*, 1973, *109*(1), pp. 1–18.

Sellekaerts, Willy. How Meaningful are Empirical Studies on Trade Creation and Diversion? *Weltwirtsch. Arch.*, 1973, *109*(4), pp. 519–53.

_____ The Soviet Managerial Evolution. *Marquette Bus. Rev.*, Summer 1973, *17*(2), pp. 84–97.

_____ and Lesage, Richard. A Reformulation and Empirical Verification of the Administered Prices Inflation Hypothesis: The Canadian Case. *Southern Econ. J.*, January 1973, *39*(3), pp. 345–60.

_____ and Sellekaerts, Brigette. Balance of Payments Deficits, the Adjustment Cost and the Optimum Level of International Reserves. *Weltwirtsch. Arch.*, 1973, *109*(1), pp. 1–18.

Sellier, François. The French Workers' Movement and Political Unionism. In *Sturmthal, A. and Scoville, J. G., eds.*, 1973, pp. 79–100.

Selowsky, Marcelo. An Attempt to Estimate Rates of Return to Investment in Infant Nutrition. In *Niskanen, W. A., et al., eds.*, 1973, pp. 410–28.

_____ Cost of Price Stabilization in a Strongly Inflationary Economy. *Quart. J. Econ.*, February 1973, *87*(1), pp. 44–59.

_____ and Dougherty, Christopher. Measuring the Effects of the Misallocation of Labour. *Rev. Econ. Statist.*, August 1973, *55*(3), pp. 386–90.

_____ and Taylor, Lance. The Economics of Malnourished Children: An Example of Disinvestment in Human Capital. *Econ. Develop. Cult. Change*, October 1973, *22*(1), pp. 17–30.

Semple, R. Keith. Recent Trends in the Spatial Concentration of Corporate Headquarters. *Econ. Geogr.*, October 1973, *49*(4), pp. 309–18.

Sen, Amartya K. Behaviour and the Concept of Preference. *Economica, N.S.*, August 1973, *40*(159), pp. 241–59.

_____ Brain Drain: Causes and Effects. In *Williams, B. R., ed.*, 1973, pp. 385–404.

_____ On Ignorance and Equal Distribution. *Amer. Econ. Rev.*, December 1973, *63*(5), pp. 1022–24.

_____; Starrett, David and Dasgupta, Partha. Notes on the Measurement of Inequality. *J. Econ. Theory*, April 1973, *6*(2), pp. 180–87.

Sen, Subrata K. and Blattberg, Robert C. An Evaluation of the Application of Minimum Chi-Square Procedures to Stochastic Models of Brand Choice. *J. Marketing Res.*, November 1973, *10*(4), pp. 421–27.

Senchagov, V. K. and Volkov, A. M. Problems of Depreciation and Its Reflection in the Input-Output Balance. *Matekon*, Spring 1973, *9*(3), pp. 55–66.

Seneca, Rosalind S. Inherent Advantage, Costs, and Resource Allocation in the Transportation Industry. *Amer. Econ. Rev.*, December 1973, *63*(5), pp. 945–56.

Senghore, Alhagi A. J. Savings Banks and Savings Facilities in African Countries: Gambia. In *Alberici, A. and Baravelli, M., eds.*, 1973, pp. 35–36.

Sengupta, J. K. Adaptive Control in Models of Optimum Economic Growth. *Z. ges. Staatswiss.*, October 1973, *129*(4), pp. 601–12.

Sengupta, S. Sankar; Podrebarac, Michael L. and Fernando, T. D. H. Probabilities of Optima in Multi-Objective Linear Programmes. In *Cochrane, J. L. and Zeleny, M., eds.*, 1973, pp. 217–35.

Senner, Eldon E.; Butterfield, D. Anthony and Farris, George F. Trust, Culture, and Organizational Behavior. *Ind. Relat.*, May 1973, *12*(2), pp. 144–57.

Sennholz, Hans F. Make Peace with Gold. In *Wiegand, G. C., ed.*, 1973, pp. 21–27.

Sergent, Raisa and Lefter, Viorel. Utilizarea extensivă a capacităților de producție și influența ei asupra prețului de cost. (The Extensive Use of Production Capacities and its Influence on the Cost Price. With English summary.) *Stud. Cercet. Econ.*, 1973, (1), pp. 65–76.

Seskin, Eugene P. Residential Choice and Air Pollution: A General Equilibrium Model. *Amer. Econ. Rev.*, December 1973, *63*(5), pp. 960–67.

_____ and Lave, Lester B. Air Pollution and Human Health. In *Enthoven, A. C. and Freeman, A. M., III, eds.*, 1973, pp. 88–99.

_____ and Lave, Lester B. An Analysis of the Association Between U.S. Mortality and Air Pollution. *J. Amer. Statist. Assoc.*, June 1973, *68*(342), pp. 284–90.

Sesnowitz, Michael. The Returns to Burglary: An Alternative to the Alternative. *Western Econ. J.*, September 1973, *11*(3), pp. 368–70.

Sethi, Narendra K. The Japanese Managerial Scene: An Introductory View. *Marquette Bus. Rev.*, Winter 1973, *17*(4), pp. 201–06.

Sethi, S. Prakash and Holton, Richard H. Country Typologies for the Multinational Corporation: A New Basic Approach. *Calif. Manage. Rev.*, Spring 1973, *15*(3), pp. 105–18.

_____ and Shocker, Allan D. An Approach to Incorporating Societal Preferences in Developing Corporate Action Strategies. *Calif. Manage. Rev.*, Summer 1973, *15*(4), pp. 97–105.

Sethi, Suresh P. A Note on Modeling Simple Dynamic Cash Balance Problems. *J. Financial Quant. Anal.*, September 1973, *8*(4), pp. 685–87.

Seton, Francis. Shadow Wages in Chile. In *Eckaus, R. S. and Rosenstein-Rodan, P. N., eds.*, 1973, pp. 49–119.

Settle, Robert B.; Leslie, Dennis C. and Mazis, Michael B. Elimination of Phosphate Detergents and Psychological Reactance. *J. Marketing Res.*, November 1973, *10*(4), pp. 390–95.

Sevaldson, Per. Price Differentiation and Computation of National Accounts Figures at Constant Prices. *Rev. Income Wealth*, December 1973, *19*(4), pp. 453–56.

de Seve, Charles W. Improved Pari-Mutual Taxation. *Nat. Tax J.*, December 1973, *26*(4), pp. 591–97.

Severn, Alan K. The Financing of the Multi-National Firm: Comment. *Kyklos*, 1973, *26*(4), pp. 852–56.

—— Further Evidence on the Formation of Price Expectations. *Quart. Rev. Econ. Bus.*, Winter 1973, *13*(4), pp. 27–35.

Sexton, R. N.; Jackson, R. and Bates, W. R. The Impact of Death Duties on the Rural Industries in Australia. *Quart. Rev. Agr. Econ.*, January 1973, *26*(1), pp. 25–43.

Seymour, Sally. Forging a Partnership with the States. *Mon. Lab. Rev.*, August 1973, *96*(8), pp. 28–34.

Shackle, G. L. S. Keynes and Today's Establishment in Economic Theory: A View. *J. Econ. Lit.*, June 1973, *11*(2), pp. 516–19.

Shafer, Ronald G. Consumers in Court. In *Murray, B. B., ed.*, 1973, pp. 373–77.

—— A Food Chain Recruits a Consumer Advocate to Shape Its Policies. In *Murray, B. B., ed.*, 1973, pp. 274–78.

Shaffer, James D. On the Concept of Subsector Studies. *Amer. J. Agr. Econ.*, May 1973, *55*(2), pp. 333–35.

Shaffer, Richard A. Consumers Gripe That Credit Reporting Law Doesn't Always Work. In *Murray, B. B., ed.*, 1973, pp. 138–42.

—— More Antitrust Suits Are Filed by States, Firms, Private Parties. In *Murray, B. B., ed.*, 1973, pp. 228–32.

Shafique, M.; Azhar, B. A. and Chaudhry, M. Ghaffar. A Model for Forecasting Wheat Production in the Punjab. *Pakistan Develop. Rev.*, Winter 1973, *12*(4), pp. 407–15.

Shah, Anil C. and Patel, V. G. An Integrated Strategy for Backward Districts Industrial Development. *Artha-Vikas*, January-July 1973, *9*(1–2), pp. 203–13.

Shamin, A.; Dubinkin, V. and Smirtiukov, V. Structural Analysis of the Network of Scientific Organizations. *Prob. Econ.*, December 1973, *16*(8), pp. 44–55.

Shanahan, James L. Mis-Match in the Supply of and Demand for Low Skill Jobs in the Inner City. In *Mattila, J. M. and Thompson, W. R., eds.*, 1973, pp. 192–205.

Shand, R. T. The Spectrum of Cash Crop Participation in New Guinea Villages. In *Epstein, T. S. and Penny, D. H., eds.*, 1973, pp. 69–85.

Shank, John K. Long Range Planning Systems: Achieving Both "Realism" and "Reach." *J. Bank Res.*, Autumn 1973, *4*(3), pp. 185–93.

Shannon, John. Residential Property Tax Relief—A Federal Responsibility? *Nat. Tax J.*, September 1973, *26*(3), pp. 499–513.

Shantakumar, G. A Note on the Recent Increase in Fertility in Singapore. *Malayan Econ. Rev.*, October 1973, *18*(2), pp. 43–49.

Shapiro, A. A. Inflation, Lags, and the Demand for Money. *Int. Econ. Rev.*, February 1973, *14*(1), pp. 81–96.

Shapiro, Alan C. Management Science Models for Multicurrency Cash Management. In *Alexandrides, C. G., ed.*, 1973, pp. 93–107.

—— Optimal Inventory and Credit-Granting

Strategies under Inflation and Devaluation. *J. Financial Quant. Anal.*, January 1973, *8*(1), pp. 37–46.

Shapiro, Benson P. Marketing for Nonprofit Organizations. *Harvard Bus. Rev.*, September-October 1973, *51*(5), pp. 123–32.

—— Price Reliance: Existence and Sources. *J. Marketing Res.*, August 1973, *10*(3), pp. 286–94.

Shapiro, David. Economy of Scale as a Cost Factor in the Operation of School Districts in Alberta. *Can. J. Econ.*, February 1973, *6*(1), pp. 114–21.

Shapiro, David L. Can Public Investment Have a Positive Rate of Return? *J. Polit. Econ.*, Part I, March-April 1973, *81*(2), pp. 401–13.

Shapiro, Eli. Proposals for Rechanneling Funds to Meet Social Priorities: Discussion. In *Federal Reserve Bank of Boston*, 1973, pp. 199–204.

Shapiro, Gary and Thompson, Marvin M. The Current Population Survey: An Overview. *Ann. Econ. Soc. Measure*, April 1973, *2*(2), pp. 105–29.

Shapiro, Harold T. Is Verification Possible? The Evaluation of Large Econometric Models. *Amer. J. Agr. Econ.*, May 1973, *55*(2), pp. 250–58.

—— Monetary and Fiscal Influences on U.S. Money Income, 1891–1970: Comment. *J. Money, Credit, Banking*, Part II, February 1973, *5*(1), pp. 304–10.

Shapiro, Jeremy F. Computer Research Center for Economics and Management Science: The Mathematical Programming Project (March 1973) *Ann. Econ. Soc. Measure*, April 1973, *2*(2), pp. 224–25.

Shapiro, Perry and Legler, John B. Estimating Tax Revenue Changes in Response to Changes in Tax Rates. *Nat. Tax J.*, March 1973, *26*(1), pp. 111–13.

Shapiro, S. H. On Computing Bayes Risks. *J. Amer. Statist. Assoc.*, June 1973, *68*(342), pp. 485–86.

Shapley, Lloyd S. Let's Block "Block." *Econometrica*, November 1973, *41*(6), pp. 1201–02.

Sharif, M. Raihan. Development Planning with Social Justice: Some Clarifications of Concepts and Applications. *Bangladesh Econ. Rev.*, July 1973, *1*(3), pp. 227–42.

Sharma, Hari P. The Green Revolution in India: Prelude to a Red One? In *Gough, K. and Sharma, H. P., eds.*, 1973, pp. 77–102.

Sharma, K. C. Indo-East European Trade—A Perspective. *Indian Econ. J.*, October–December 1973, *21*(2), pp. 91–106.

Sharma, M. L. Exports of Engineering Goods—Retrospect and Prospects. *Econ. Aff.*, January–February 1973, *18*(1-2), pp. 39–40, 73.

Sharma, P. L. and Dutta, M. Alternative Estimators and Predictive Power of Alternative Estimators: An Econometric Model of Puerto Rico. *Rev. Econ. Statist.*, August 1973, *55*(3), pp. 381–85.

Sharma, R. K. Grant Element in External Assistance to India. *Indian Econ. J.*, October–December 1973, *21*(2), pp. 124–31.

Sharman, Ben. Multinational Corporations and Trade Unions. *Mon. Lab. Rev.*, August 1973, *96*(8), pp. 56–58.

Sharman, F. A. A Network Analysis of Airport Accessibility in South Hampshire: A Comment. *J. Transp. Econ. Policy*, January 1973, *7*(1), pp. 102–03.

Sharot, T. Unemployment Dispersion as a Determinant of Wage Inflation in the U.K. 1925–66—A Note. *Manchester Sch. Econ. Soc. Stud.*, June 1973, *41*(2), pp. 225–28.

Sharpe, Ian G. A Mortgage Model: Some Theoretical and Empirical Results as Applied to Australian Savings Banks. *Australian Econ. Pap.*, December 1973, *12*(21), pp. 208–20.

———— A Quarterly Econometric Model of Portfolio Choice—Part I: Specification and Estimation Problems. *Econ. Rec.*, December 1973, *49*(128), pp. 518–33.

Sharpe, L. K. and Anderson, W. T., Jr. The New American Marketplace: Life-Style in Revolution. In *Thorelli, H. B., ed.*, 1973, pp. 146–53.

Sharpe, Louis K. and Peterson, Robert A. Market Segmentation: Product Usage Patterns and Psychographic Configurations. *J. Bus. Res.*, Summer 1973, *1*(1), pp. 11–20.

Sharpe, Ron. Models for Allocation of Water Resources. In *Aislabie, C., ed.*, 1973, pp. 171–76.

Sharples, Jerry and Prindle, Allen. Income Characteristics of Farm Families in the Corn Belt. *Agr. Finance Rev.*, July 1973, *34*, pp. 12–17.

Sharpston, C. H. Competition and the Developing Countries. In *Rybczynski, T. M., ed.*, 1973, pp. 46–54.

Shastiko, B. M. and Shiryaev, Y. S. Interrelations with Non-Socialist Markets. In *Kiss, T., ed.*, 1973, pp. 159–65.

Shauger, Donald and Cox, Steven R. Executive Compensation, Firm Sales, and Profitability. *Intermountain Econ. Rev.*, Spring 1973, *4*(1), pp. 29–39.

Shaw, Gaylord. Government as Promoter, Sustainer, and Subsidizer of "Private Enterprise." In *Haveman, R. H. and Hamrin, R. D., eds.*, 1973, pp. 47–51.

Shaw, G. K. and Peacock, Alan T. Fiscal Measures to Create Employment: The Indonesian Case. *Bull. Int. Fiscal Doc.*, November 1973, *27*(11), pp. 443–54.

Shaw, John A. Railroads, Irrigation, and Economic Growth: The San Joaquin Valley of California. *Exploration Econ. Hist.*, Winter 1973, *10*(2), pp. 211–27.

———— and Leet, Don R. Research and Development and Productivity Change in the U.S., 1948–1968. *J. Ind. Econ.*, December 1973, *22*(2), pp. 153–55.

Shaw, R. W. Investment and Competition from Boom to Recession: A Case Study in the Processes of Competition—The Dry Cleaning Industry. *J. Ind. Econ.*, July 1973, *21*(3), pp. 308–24.

Shaw, William H. Paradoxes, Problems and Progress. *J. Amer. Statist. Assoc.*, March 1973, *68*(341), pp. 7–10.

Shawcross, Hartley William [Lord]. The Structure of Public Company Boards. In *Allen, G. C., et al.*, 1973, pp. 45–54.

Shchori-Bachrach, Nira and Kislev, Yoav. The Process of an Innovation Cycle. *Amer. J. Agr. Econ.*, February 1973, *55*(1), pp. 28–37.

Shea, John R. Welfare Mothers: Barriers to Labor Force Entry. *J. Human Res.*, Supplement 1973, *8*, pp. 90–102.

Shearer, John C. High-Level Human Resources in Latin American Development. In *Thurber, C. E.*

and Graham, L. S., eds., 1973, pp. 133–47.

Shechter, Mordechai and Helman, Amir. Collective Decision-Making in a Kibbutz: A Case Study. *Public Finance*, 1973, *28*(2), pp. 139–50.

Sheehan, P. J. The Real Income Guarantee: A Fiscal Policy to Control Inflation. *Australian Econ. Rev.*, 4th Quarter 1973, pp. 9–14.

———— and Gregory, R. G. The Cyclical Sensitivity of Labour Force Participation Rates. *Australian Econ. Rev.*, 2nd Quarter 1973, pp. 9–20.

Sheehan, Robert. Proprietors in the World of Big Business. In *Andreano, R. L., ed.*, 1973, pp. R342–06.

Shefer, Daniel. Localization Economies in SMSA'S: A Production Function Analysis. *J. Reg. Sci.*, April 1973, *13*(1), pp. 55–64.

Sheifer, Victor J. Reconciling Labor Department and Stabilization Agency Wage Data. *Mon. Lab. Rev.*, April 1973, *96*(4), pp. 24–30.

Shell, Karl. Inventive Activity, Industrial Organisation and Economic Growth. In *Mirrlees, J. A. and Stern, N. H., eds.*, 1973, pp. 77–96.

Shell, Richard L. and Stelzer, David F. Systems Analysis: Aid to Decision Making. In *Klein, W. H. and Murphy, D. C., eds.*, 1973, pp. 34–39.

Shelton, John P. and Warren, James M. A Simultaneous Equation Approach to Financial Planning: Reply. *J. Finance*, September 1973, *28*(4), pp. 1039–42.

Shelton, Robert B. and Hogan, Timothy D. Interstate Tax Exportation and States' Fiscal Structures. *Nat. Tax J.*, December 1973, *26*(4), pp. 553–64.

———— A Note on Barlow's Local School Finance. *J. Polit. Econ.*, January-February 1973, *81*(1), pp. 192–98.

Shen, T. Y. Technology Diffusion, Substitution, and X-Efficiency. *Econometrica*, March 1973, *41*(2), pp. 263–84.

Shepard, Jon M. Specialization, Autonomy, and Job Satisfaction. *Ind. Relat.*, October 1973, *12*(3), pp. 274–81.

———— Worker Background and Job Satisfaction: Reply. *Ind. Lab. Relat. Rev.*, January 1973, *26*(2), pp. 856–59.

Shepherd, A. Ross. A Clarification of Rent Theory: Comment. *Southern Econ. J.*, July 1973, *40*(1), pp. 124–31.

———— External Diseconomies in Competitive Supply: Comment. *Amer. Econ. Rev.*, September 1973, *63*(4), pp. 743–44.

Shepherd, William G. Entry as a Substitute for Regulation. *Amer. Econ. Rev.*, May 1973, *63*(2), pp. 98–105.

———— and Levin, Sharon G. Managerial Discrimination in Large Firms. *Rev. Econ. Statist.*, November 1973, *55*(4), pp. 412–22.

Shepler, Richard J. and Rejda, George E. The Impact of Zero Population Growth on the OASDHI Program. *J. Risk Ins.*, September 1973, *40*(3), pp. 313–25.

Sheppard, Harold L. Asking the Right Questions on Job Satisfaction. *Mon. Lab. Rev.*, April 1973, *96* (4), pp. 51–52.

Sheppard, J. A. Field Systems of Yorkshire. In *Baker, A. R. H. and Butlin, R. A., eds.*, 1973, pp. 145–87.

Sher, William. An Alternative Proof of the B-M

Theorem on the Existence of the Firm's Optimal Capital Structure. *Quart. J. Econ.*, August 1973, *87*(3), pp. 474–81.

Sherman, Howard J. The Theory of Socialist Planning: Comment. *J. Polit. Econ.*, Part I, March-April 1973, *81*(2), pp. 450–58.

Sherman, Sally R. Assets on the Threshold of Retirement. *Soc. Sec. Bull.*, August 1973, *36*(8), pp. 3–17.

Sherr, Lawrence A. and Reilly, Frank K. The Shift Method: A Technique for Measuring the Differential Performance of Stocks. *Miss. Val. J. Bus. Econ.*, Fall 1973, *9*(1), pp. 28–40.

Sherwood, Frank P. Technical Assistance for Education in Public Administration: Lessons of Experience. In *Thurber, C. E. and Graham, L. S., eds.*, 1973, pp. 195–226.

Sheshinski, Eytan. Congestion and the Optimum City Size. *Amer. Econ. Rev.*, May 1973, *63*(2), pp. 61–66.

_____ **and Levhari, David.** Experience and Productivity in the Israel Diamond Industry. *Econometrica*, March 1973, *41*(2), pp. 239–53.

_____; **Oron, Yitzhak and Pines, David.** Optimum vs. Equilibrium Land Use Pattern and Congestion Toll. *Bell J. Econ. Manage. Sci.*, Autumn 1973, *4*(2), pp. 619–36.

Sheth, Jagdish N. A Review of Buyer Behavior. In *Britt, S. H. and Boyd, H. W., Jr., eds.*, 1973, pp. 126–68.

Sheth, V. K. Organizational Structure for Agricultural Credit. In *Simha, S. L. N., ed.*, 1973, pp. 106–14.

Shetler, Douglas. Monetary Aggregates Prior to the Civil War: A Closer Look: Comment. *J. Money, Credit, Banking*, November 1973, *5*(4), pp. 1000–06.

Shibata, Hirofumi. Public Goods, Increasing Cost, and Monopsony: Comment. *J. Polit. Econ.*, January-February 1973, *81*(1), pp. 223–30.

Shiller, Robert J. A Distributed Lag Estimator Derived from Smoothness Priors. *Econometrica*, July 1973, *41*(4), pp. 775–88.

_____ Rational Expectations and the Term Structure of Interest Rates: Comment. *J. Money, Credit, Banking*, August 1973, *5*(3), pp. 856–60.

_____ **and Modigliani, Franco.** Inflation, Rational Expectations and the Term Structure of Interest Rates. *Economica, N.S.*, February 1973, *40*(157), pp. 12–43.

Shimada, Toshiro. Industrial Dynamics Model of a Japanese University. In *Ross, M., ed.*, 1973, pp. 303–14.

Shin, Kilman. The Rate of Interest and Inflation: An International Comparison. *Econ. Int.*, August-November 1973, *26*(3–4), pp. 603–22.

Shinkai, Yoichi. The Accumulation of International Reserves under an Inflationary Pressure. *Z. Nationalökon.*, 1973, *33*(1–2), pp. 55–66.

_____ A Model of Imported Inflation. *J. Polit. Econ.*, July-August 1973, *81*(4), pp. 962–71.

_____ Problems in the Estimation of Price Elasticities of Exports and Imports: A Survey. (In Japanese. With English summary.) *Econ. Stud. Quart.*, August 1973, *24*(2), pp. 31–39.

Shipunov, V. Effectiveness of Vocational-Technical

Training of Workers. *Prob. Econ.*, August 1973, *16*(4), pp. 82–94.

Shiralkar, S. S. Non-Banking Financial Intermediaries. In *Simha, S. L. N., ed.*, 1973, pp. 241–51.

Shiratori, Masaki and Wittich, Günter. The Snake in the Tunnel. *Finance Develop.*, June 1973, *10*(2), pp. 9–13, 38.

Shiriaev, Iu. Developing Scientific Foundations for Joint Planning Activity of COMECON Countries. *Prob. Econ.*, October 1973, *16*(6), pp. 55–71.

Shiryaev, Y. S. and Shastiko, B. M. Interrelations with Non-Socialist Markets. In *Kiss, T., ed.*, 1973, pp. 159–65.

Shishankov, V. and Kazakevich, L. Economic Collaboration Between the USSR and the Socialist Countries. *Prob. Econ.*, October 1973, *16*(6), pp. 72–92.

Shiskin, Julius. Measuring Current Economic Fluctuations. *Ann. Econ. Soc. Measure*, January 1973, *2*(1), pp. 1–15.

Shitovitz, Benyamin. Oligopoly in Markets with a Continuum of Traders. *Econometrica*, May 1973, *41*(3), pp. 467–501.

Shivnan, Martin. The Bank Group Meeting. *Finance Develop.*, December 1973, *10*(4), pp. 34–37.

Shocker, Allan D. and Sethi, S. Prakash. An Approach to Incorporating Societal Preferences in Developing Corporate Action Strategies. *Calif. Manage. Rev.*, Summer 1973, *15*(4), pp. 97–105.

Shore, Arnold R. and Scott, Robert A. Work Response and Family Composition Changes in a Negative Income Tax Experiment: Preliminary Mid-Experiment Results. In *Sheldon, E. B., ed.*, 1973, pp. 233–63.

Short, Brock K. The Velocity of Money and *Per Capita* Income in Developing Economies: West Malaysia and Singapore. *J. Devel. Stud.*, January 1973, *9*(2), pp. 291–300.

Short, John H. Is Health Care an Economic Commodity? *Intermountain Econ. Rev.*, Spring 1973, *4*(1), pp. 14–21.

Shorter, Edward. Female Emancipation, Birth Control, and Fertility in European History. *Amer. Hist. Rev.*, June 1973, *78*(3), pp. 605–40.

Shoup, Carl S. Factors Bearing on an Assumed Choice between a Federal Retail-Sales Tax and a Federal Value-Added Tax. In *Musgrave, R. A., ed.*, 1973, pp. 215–26.

_____ Three Fiscal Reports on Colombia: A Review Article. *Nat. Tax J.*, March 1973, *26*(1), pp. 59–63.

_____ **and Head, John G.** Public, Private, and Ambiguous Goods Reconsidered. *Public Finance*, 1973, *28*(3–4), pp. 384–92.

Shoup, Donald C. Cost Effectiveness of Urban Traffic Law Enforcement. *J. Transp. Econ. Policy*, January 1973, *7*(1), pp. 32–57.

Shourie, Arun. Growth, Poverty and Inequalities. *Foreign Aff.*, January 1973, *51*(2), pp. 340–52.

Shoven, John B. and Whalley, John. General Equilibrium with Taxes: A Computational Procedure and an Existence Proof. *Rev. Econ. Stud.*, October 1973, *40*(4), pp. 475–89.

Shtern, Iu. Production Functions and the Possibility of Using Them in Economic Calculations. *Prob. Econ.*, November 1973, *16*(7), pp. 59–83.

Shubik, Martin. Commodity Money, Oligopoly,

Credit and Bankruptcy in a General Equilibrium Model. *Western Econ. J.*, March 1973, *11*(1), pp. 24–38.

———— Information, Duopoly and Competitive Markets: A Sensitivity Analysis. *Kyklos*, 1973, *26*(4), pp. 736–61.

———— Price Strategy Duopoly with Product Variation: Reply. *Kyklos*, 1973, *26*(3), pp. 612.

———— Some Aspects of Socio-Economic Modelling. In *Hawkes, N., ed.*, 1973, pp. 155–63.

———— **and Whitt, Ward.** Fiat Money in an Economy with One Nondurable Good and No Credit (A Noncooperative Sequential Game). In *Blaquière, A., ed.*, 1973, pp. 401–48.

Shulman, J. S. Transfer Pricing in the Multinational Firm. In *Thorelli, H. B., ed.*, 1973, pp. 312–22.

Shuman, Howard E. Federal Housing Policy and the HUD Bureaucracy. In *Haveman, R. H. and Hamrin, R. D., eds.*, 1973, pp. 243–49.

Shumway, C. Richard. Allocation of Scarce Resources to Agricultural Research: Review of Methodology. *Amer. J. Agr. Econ.*, Part I, November 1973, *55*(4), pp. 557–66.

Shuptrine, F. Kelly. Upper-Middle Class and Working Class Opinions of the Wage/Price Freeze. *Marquette Bus. Rev.*, Winter 1973, *17*(4), pp. 182–87.

Shwayder, Keith R. Two "Wrongs" Making a "Right." *J. Acc. Res.*, Autumn 1973, *11*(2), pp. 259–72.

Sichel, Werner. Vertical Integration as a Dynamic Industry Concept. *Antitrust Bull.*, Fall, 1973, *18* (3), pp. 463–82.

Sicherl, Pavle. Time-Distance as a Dynamic Measure of Disparities in Social and Economic Development. *Kyklos*, 1973, *26*(3), pp. 559–75.

Sidambaram, Mootoosamy. Savings Banks and Savings Facilities in African Countries: Mauritius. In *Alberici, A. and Baravelli, M., eds.*, 1973, pp. 65–67.

Siddiqui, M. M. and Gehan, Edmund A. Simple Regression Methods for Survival Time Studies. *J. Amer. Statist. Assoc.*, December 1973, *68*(344), pp. 848–56.

Sidel, Victor W. Medicine and Public Health. In *Oksenberg, M., ed.*, 1973, pp. 110–20.

Siebert, Horst. Environment and Regional Growth. *Z. Nationalökon.*, 1973, *33*(1–2), pp. 79–85.

Siebke, Jürgen and Krelle, Wilhelm. Vermögensverteilung und Vermögenspolitik in der Bundesrepublik Deutschland. Ein Überblick. (Distribution of Wealth and Policy of Wealth Distribution in the Federal Republic of Germany. A Survey. With English summary.) *Z. ges. Staatswiss.*, August 1973, *129*(3), pp. 478–503.

Siegel, Gilbert B. Brazil: Diffusion and Centralization of Power. In *Thurber, C. E. and Graham, L. S., eds.*, 1973, pp. 362–81.

Siegel, Philip H. The Location of Industry and Job Participation: An Econometric Study. *Econ. Aff.*, January–February 1973, *18*(1-2), pp. 54–58.

Siegfried, John J. A Reply to the Comment of Professors Battalio, Hulett, and Kagel on "The Publishing of Economic Papers and Its Impact on Graduate Faculty Ratings, 1960-1969." *J. Econ. Lit.*, March 1973, *11*(1), pp. 71–73.

———— **and White, Kenneth J.** Financial Rewards to Research and Teaching: A Case Study of Academic Economists. *Amer. Econ. Rev.*, May 1973, *63*(2), pp. 309–15.

———— **and White, Kenneth J.** Teaching and Publishing as Determinants of Academic Salaries. *J. Econ. Educ.*, Spring 1973, *4*(2), pp. 90–99.

Sielken, R. L., Jr. and Hartley, H. O. Two Linear Programming Algorithms for Unbiased Estimation of Linear Models. *J. Amer. Statist. Assoc.*, September 1973, *68*(343), pp. 639–41.

Sieper, E. and Swan, P. L. Monopoly and Competition in the Market for Durable Goods. *Rev. Econ. Stud.*, July 1973, *40*(3), pp. 333–51.

Sigurdson, Jon. Rural Economic Planning. In *Oksenberg, M., ed.*, 1973, pp. 68–79.

Silber, Sigmund. The Common Data-Base: Defining Its Role in the Information System. In *The Diebold Group, Inc.*, 1973, pp. 63–77.

Silber, William L. A Model of Federal Home Loan Bank System and Federal National Mortgage Association Behavior. *Rev. Econ. Statist.*, August 1973, *55*(3), pp. 308–20.

———— Monetary Policy Effectiveness: The Case of a Positively Sloped I-S Curve: Reply. *J. Finance*, December 1973, *28*(5), pp. 1365.

———— Selective Credit Policies: A Survey. *Banca Naz. Lavoro Quart. Rev.*, December 1973, (107), pp. 328–51.

———— **and Penner, Rudolph G.** The Interaction Between Federal Credit Programs and the Impact on the Allocation of Credit. *Amer. Econ. Rev.*, December 1973, *63*(5), pp. 838–52.

Silberberg, Eugene and Barzel, Yoram. Is the Act of Voting Rational? *Public Choice*, Fall 1973, *16*, pp. 51–58.

Silberman, Jonathan and Gwartney, James. Distribution of Costs and Benefits and the Significance of Collective Decision Rules. *Soc. Sci. Quart.*, December 1973, *54*(3), pp. 568–78.

Sileock, T. H. Rationality, Fluency and Impersonality in Rural Thailand. In *Epstein, T. S. and Penny, D. H., eds.*, 1973, pp. 203–15.

Silk, Alvin J. Testing the Inverse Ad Size-Selective Exposure Hypothesis: Clarifying Bogart. *J. Marketing Res.*, May 1973, *10*(2), pp. 221–23.

Silveira, Antonio M. The Demand for Money: The Evidence from the Brazilian Economy. *J. Money, Credit, Banking*, Part I, February 1973, *5*(1), pp. 113–40.

———— Interest Rate and Rapid Inflation: The Evidence from the Brazilian Economy. *J. Money, Credit, Banking*, August 1973, *5*(3), pp. 794–805.

Silver, Morris and Auster, Richard. Collective Goods and Collective Decision Mechanisms. *Public Choice*, Spring 1973, *14*, pp. 1–17.

Silverberg, Stanley C. Deposit Costs and Bank Portfolio Policy. *J. Finance*, September 1973, *28*(4), pp. 881–95.

Silverman, Bertram. Economic Organization and Social Conscience: Some Dilemmas of Cuban Socialism. In *Barkin, D. P. and Manitzas, N. R., eds.*, 1973, pp. R262–28.

———— Economic Organization and Social Conscience: Some Dilemmas of Cuban Socialism. In *Zammit, J. A., ed.*, 1973, pp. 391–418.

Silverman, Lester P. Credit Standards and Tight Money: Comment. *J. Money, Credit, Banking,* Part I, February 1973, *5*(1), pp. 221–23.

Silvers, J. B. An Alternative to the Yield Spread as a Measure of Risk. *J. Finance,* September 1973, *28* (4), pp. 933–55.

Silverstein, Leonard L. Federal Tax Policy for Tax Shelters. *Nat. Tax J.,* September 1973, *26*(3), pp. 347–51.

Simanis, Joseph G. Medical Care Expenditures in Seven Countries. *Soc. Sec. Bull.,* March 1973, *36* (3), pp. 39–42.

Simha, S. L. N. Evolution of Indian Banking. In *Simha, S. L. N., ed.,* 1973, pp. 20–43.

———— Future of the Subsidiaries of the State Bank of India. In *Simha, S. L. N., ed.,* 1973, pp. 189–202.

———— Reform of the Central Banking System in India. In *Simha, S. L. N., ed.,* 1973, pp. 309–21.

Simkowitz, Michael A. and Logue, Dennis E. The Interdependent Structure of Security Returns. *J. Financial Quant. Anal.,* March 1973, *8*(2), pp. 259–72.

Simmons, E. B. and Norman, D. W. Determination of Relevant Research Priorities for Farm Development in West Africa. In *Ofori, I. M., ed.,* 1973, pp. 42–48.

Simmons, G. H. An Evaluation of Use of Grab Samples in the Appraisal of Wool for Store Handling. *Quart. Rev. Agr. Econ.,* April 1973, *26*(2), pp. 89–99.

Simmons, Harvey. System Dynamics and Technocracy. In *Cole, H. S. D., et al., eds.,* 1973, pp. 192–208.

Simon, John G. Foundations and Public Controversy: An Affirmative View. In *Heimann, F. F., ed.,* 1973, pp. 58–100.

Simon, Julian L. Does Economic Growth Imply a Growth in Welfare? *J. Econ. Issues,* March 1973, *7*(1), pp. 130–36.

————; **Puig, Carlos M. and Aschoff, John.** A Duopoly Simulation and Richer Theory: An End to Cournot. *Rev. Econ. Stud.,* July 1973, *40*(3), pp. 353–66.

Simon, Larry G. The School Finance Decisions: Collective Bargaining and Future Finance Systems. *Yale Law J.,* January 1973, *82*(3), pp. 409–60.

Simon, Leonard S.; Alexis, Marcus and Haines, George H., Jr. An Analysis of Central City Neighborhood Food Trading Areas: A Reply. *J. Reg. Sci.,* August 1973, *13*(2), pp. 301.

Simon, William. Management and Man. In *The Conference Board,* 1973, pp. 275–97.

Simpson, David and McGilvray, James. The Commodity Structure of Anglo-Irish Trade. *Rev. Econ. Statist.,* November 1973, *55*(4), pp. 451–58.

Sims, Christopher A. Efficiency in the Construction Industry. In *Pynoos, J.; Schafer, R. and Hartman, C. W., eds.,* 1973, pp. 329–42.

Sims, Edwin C., Jr. and Pinches, George E. Factors Related to the Performance of College Endowment Funds. *J. Econ. Bus.,* Spring-Summer 1973, *25*(3), pp. 198–205.

Sinclair, T. C. Environmentalism: A la recherche du temps perdu—bien perdu? In *Cole, H. S. D., et al., eds.,* 1973, pp. 175–91.

———— **and Marstrand, Pauline K.** The Pollution Subsystem. In *Cole, H. S. D., et al., eds.,* 1973, pp. 80–89.

Singarimbun, Masri and Penny, David H. Economic Activity among the Karo Batak of Indonesia: A Case Study in Economic Change. In *Epstein, T. S. and Penny, D. H., eds.,* 1973, pp. 86–113.

Singell, Larry D. and McElroy, Jerome L. Some Structural Contours of the Recent Urban Crisis: An Empirical Analysis of the Social and Economic Conditions of Riot and Non-Riot Cities. In *Mattila, J. M. and Thompson, W. R., eds.,* 1973, pp. 177–91.

———— **and Yordon, Wesley J.** Incentives for More Efficient Education: The Development of a Model. In *Stein, B. and Miller, S. M., eds.,* 1973, pp. 71–91.

Singer, Dan and Walzer, Norman. The Distribution of Income in Large Urban Areas. *Nebr. J. Econ. Bus.,* Autumn 1973, *12*(4), pp. 91–101.

Singer, Hans and Jolly, Richard. Unemployment in an African Setting: Lessons of the Employment Strategy Mission to Kenya. *Int. Lab. Rev.,* February 1973, *107*(2), pp. 103–15.

Singer, Neil M. Federal Aid to Minority Business: Survey and Critique. *Soc. Sci. Quart.,* September 1973, *54*(2), pp. 292–305.

Singer, S. Fred. Is Growth Obsolete? Comment. In *Moss, M., ed.,* 1973, pp. 532–36.

———— Is There an Optimum Level of Population? In *Weintraub, A.; Schwartz, E. and Aronson, J. R., eds.,* 1973, pp. 154–64.

Singh, Anoop. An Enquiry into the Nature and Implications of a Foreign Exchange Constraint on Development. *Indian Econ. J.,* October–December 1973, *21*(2), pp. 147–57.

Singh, Balbir. Making Honesty the Best Policy. *J. Public Econ.,* July 1973, *2*(3), pp. 257–63.

Singh, Balvir and Nagar, A. L. Determination of Consumer Unit Scales. *Econometrica,* March 1973, *41*(2), pp. 347–55.

Singh, Balwinder; Rangi, P. S. and Sankhayan, P. L. Relative Contributions of Area and Productivity in Increasing Production of Major Foodgrain Crops in Panjab (1960–61 to 1969–70) *Econ. Aff.,* March 1973, *18*(3), pp. 124–30.

Singh, H. P. Export of Spices. *Econ. Aff.,* March 1973, *18*(3), pp. 131–42.

Singh, I. Recursive Programming Models of Agricultural Development. In *Judge, G. G. and Takayama, T., eds.,* 1973, pp. 394–416.

Singh, Manmohan. Export Strategy for the Take-off. In *Wadhva, C. D., ed.,* 1973, pp. 394–406.

Singh, Pritam. Land to the Landless. *Econ. Aff.,* July 1973, *18*(7), pp. 326–37.

Singh, Tarlok. Enlarging the Economic Base for Domestic Savings. In *[Hicks, U.],* 1973, pp. 181–88.

Singleton, Gregory H. The Genesis of Suburbia: A Complex of Historical Trends. In *Masotti, L. H. and Hadden, J. K., eds.,* 1973, pp. 29–50.

Sinha, J. N. Agrarian Reforms and Employment in Densely Populated Agrarian Economies: A Dissenting View. *Int. Lab. Rev.,* November 1973, *108* (5), pp. 395–421.

Sinha, R. K. A Note on Central Budget 1973–74.

Econ. Aff., April 1973, *18*(4), pp. 190–96.

_____ Report of the Committee on Taxation of Agricultural Wealth and Income—An Appraisal. *Econ. Aff.*, January–February 1973, *18*(1-2), pp. 17–28.

Sinkey, Joseph F., Jr. The Term Structure of Interest Rates: A Time-Series Test of the Kane Expected-Change Model of Interest-Rate Forecasting. *J. Money, Credit, Banking,* Part I, February 1973, *5*(1), pp. 192–200.

_____ **and Kurtz, Robert D.** Bank Disclosure Policy and Procedures, Adverse Publicity and Bank Deposit Flows. *J. Bank Res.*, Autumn 1973, *4*(3), pp. 177–84.

Sirenko, E. I. Methods for Solving Linear Programming Problems on Analogue Computers. *Matekon,* Winter 1973-74, *10*(2), pp. 56–63.

Sirken, Monroe G. Design of Household Sample Surveys to Test Death Registration Completeness. *Demography,* August 1973, *10*(3), pp. 469–78.

Sirmans, C. F. and Floyd, Charles F. Shift and Share Projections Revisited. *J. Reg. Sci.,* April 1973, *13*(1), pp. 115–20.

Sirota, David. The Multinational Corporation: Management Myths. In *Henley, D. S., ed.,* 1973, pp. 466–73.

Sisco, Anthony F., Jr. Overhead Variance Analysis and Corrective Action. *Manage. Account.,* October 1973, *55*(4), pp. 45–47, 51.

Sjaastad, Larry A. Notes on X-Efficiency and Technical Progress: Comment. In *Ayal, E. B., ed.,* 1973, pp. 38–40.

Sjo, John; Orazem, Frank and Biere, Arlo. Undergraduate Program Revision at Kansas State University. *Amer. J. Agr. Econ.,* Part I, November 1973, *55*(4), pp. 604–10.

Sjoquist, David Lawrence. Property Crime and Economic Behavior: Some Empirical Results. *Amer. Econ. Rev.,* June 1973, *63*(3), pp. 439–46.

Skarzhinskii, M. A Systems-Structural Approach to the Study of the Basic Economic Law of Socialism. *Prob. Econ.,* April 1973, *15*(12), pp. 3–15.

Skegg, J. L. and Atkinson, A. B. Anti-Smoking Publicity and the Demand for Tobacco in the U.K. *Manchester Sch. Econ. Soc. Stud.,* September 1973, *41*(3), pp. 265–82.

Skidmore, Thomas E. Politics and Economic Policy Making in Authoritarian Brazil, 1937–71. In *Stepan, A., ed.,* 1973, pp. 3–46.

Skinner, Andrew S. and Meek, Ronald L. The Development of Adam Smith's Ideas on the Division of Labour. *Econ. J.,* December 1973, *83*(332), pp. 1094–1116.

Skinner, Douglas E. and Yett, Donald E. Debility Index for Long-term-care Patients. In *Berg, R. L., ed.,* 1973, pp. 69–81.

Skogh, Göran. A Note on Gary Becker's "Crime and Punishment: An Economic Approach." *Swedish J. Econ.,* September 1973, *75*(3), pp. 305–11.

Skolnikoff, Eugene B. La tecnologia e la politica mondiale. (Technology and World Politics. With English summary.) *Mondo Aperto,* April 1973, *27*(2), pp. 101–11.

Skouras, Athanassios. On the Analysis of Property Tax Effects on Operating and Investment Decisions of Rental Property Owners. *Nat. Tax J.,* March 1973, *26*(1), pp. 123–25.

Skouras, Thanos; Krauss, Melvyn B. and Johnson, Harry G. On the Shape and Location of the Production Possibility Curve. *Economica, N.S.,* August 1973, *40*(159), pp. 305–10.

Skraly, Emile B. Manpower Planning and Economic Planning: The Two Perspectives: Discussion. In *Aronson, R. L., ed.,* 1973, pp. 80–84.

Slacik, Karl F. What Can You, the Financial Executive, Do About Customer Service? In *Thomas, W. E., Jr., ed.,* 1973, pp. 130–40.

Sláma, Jiří and Vogel, Heinrich. Zur Verbreitung neuer Technologien in der UdSSR—eine Fallstudie: das Oxygenblasstahlverfahren. (Diffusion of New Technologies in the USSR—the Case of Oxygene-Steel. With English summary.) *Jahr. Nationalökon. Statist.,* March 1973, *187*(3), pp. 245–61.

Slater, Paul B. Spatial and Temporal Effects in Residential Sales Prices. *J. Amer. Statist. Assoc.,* September 1973, *68*(343), pp. 554–61.

Slaughter, William C. and Reilly, Frank K. The Effect of Dual Markets on Common Stock Market Making. *J. Financial Quant. Anal.,* March 1973, *8*(2), pp. 167–82.

Slavin, Richard H. and Devine, Edward J. Multi-Discipline Design Teams for Transportation Facilities. *Land Econ.,* August 1973, *49*(3), pp. 241–50.

Slezak, Lester. Effects of Changes in Payment System on Productivity in Sweden. *Mon. Lab. Rev.,* March 1973, *96*(3), pp. 51–52.

van Slijpe, A. R. D. and de Wolff, P. The Relation Between Income, Intelligence, Education and Social Background. *Europ. Econ. Rev.,* October 1973, *4*(3), pp. 235–64.

Slitor, Richard E. Administrative Aspects of Expenditures Taxation. In *Musgrave, R. A., ed.,* 1973, pp. 227–63.

Sloan, John W. and Cochrane, James D. LAFTA and the CACM: A Comparative Analysis of Integration in Latin America. *J. Devel. Areas,* October 1973, *8*(1), pp. 13–37.

Sloane, P. J. and Chiplin, B. Real and Money Wages Revisited. *Appl. Econ.,* December 1973, *5*(4), pp. 289–304.

Sloss, Judith. Stable Outcomes in Majority Rule Voting Games. *Public Choice,* Summer 1973, *15*, pp. 19–48.

Smallhorn, P. J. Demand Elasticities for Raw Wool in Japan. *Quart. Rev. Agr. Econ.,* October 1973, *26*(4), pp. 253–62.

Smalls, Isaac S. Hospital Cost Controls. *Manage. Account.,* March 1973, *54*(9), pp. 17–20.

Smetherman, Bobbie B. and Smetherman, Robert M. Peruvian Fisheries: Conservation and Development. *Econ. Develop. Cult. Change,* January 1973, *21*(2), pp. 338–51.

Smetherman, Robert M. and Smetherman, Bobbie B. Peruvian Fisheries: Conservation and Development. *Econ. Develop. Cult. Change,* January 1973, *21*(2), pp. 338–51.

Smirtiukov, V.; Shamin, A. and Dubinkin, V. Structural Analysis of the Network of Scientific Organizations. *Prob. Econ.*, December 1973, *16*(8), pp. 44–55.

Smith, Allen G. and Carlin, Thomas A. A New Approach in Accounting for Our Nation's Farm Income. *Agr. Finance Rev.*, July 1973, *34*, pp. 1–6.

Smith, Blair J. Dynamic Programming of the Dairy Cow Replacement Program. *Amer. J. Agr. Econ.*, February 1973, *55*(1), pp. 100–04.

Smith, Bruce W. Analysis of the Location of Coal-Fired Power Plants in the Eastern United States. *Econ. Geogr.*, July 1973, *49*(3), pp. 243–50.

Smith, Curtis R. Despite Damage by Agnes...District Economy Forges Ahead in '72. *Fed. Res. Bank Bus. Rev. Phila.*, February 1973, pp. 12–18.

–––––– Will the Four-Day Week Work? *Fed. Res. Bank Bus. Rev. Phila.*, August 1973, pp. 14–21.

Smith, Dan Throop. Capital Gains and Losses in Income Taxation. In *Tax Foundation, Inc.*, 1973, pp. 43–47.

Smith, D. C. and Kaliski, S. F. Inflation, Unemployment and Incomes Policy. *Can. J. Econ.*, November 1973, *6*(4), pp. 574–91.

Smith, Douglas V. Opportunity for Village Development: The Tanks of Bangladesh. *Bangladesh Econ. Rev.*, July 1973, *1*(3), pp. 297–308.

Smith, Edward. An Economic Comparison of Urban Railways and Express Bus Services: Rejoinder. *J. Transp. Econ. Policy*, September 1973, *7*(3), pp. 297–99.

–––––– An Economic Comparison of Urban Railways and Express Bus Services. *J. Transp. Econ. Policy*, January 1973, *7*(1), pp. 20–31.

Smith, Gerald W.; Udell, Jonathan and Li, Wen L. The Gambling Business in the U.S.A. *Ohio State U. Bull. Bus. Res.*, April 1973, *48*(4), pp. 1–3, 6–7.

Smith, Glenn R. Has Social Science Research at the Experiment Stations Increased in Line with Society's Needs and Congressional Intent? *Amer. J. Agr. Econ.*, Part I, November 1973, *55*(4), pp. 667–69.

Smith, Gordon P. and Miller, Etienne. International Travel, Passenger Fares, and Other Transportation in the U.S. Balance of Payments: 1972. *Surv. Curr. Bus.*, June 1973, *53*(6), pp. 12–16, 56.

Smith, Gordon W. Marketing and Economic Development: A Brazilian Case Study, 1930–70. *Food Res. Inst. Stud.*, 1973, *12*(3), pp. 179–98.

–––––– and Morley, Samuel A. The Effect of Changes in the Distribution of Income on Labor, Foreign Investment, and Growth in Brazil. In *Stepan, A., ed.*, 1973, pp. 119–41.

Smith, Herbert L. The Natural Christmas Tree Industry. *Manage. Account.*, December 1973, *55*(6), pp. 9–11, 27.

Smith, James D. New Perspectives in Government Data Distribution: The Current Population Survey. *Ann. Econ. Soc. Measure*, April 1973, *2*(2), pp. 131–39.

Smith, Joel and Bromley, David G. The Historical Significance of Annexation as a Social Process. *Land Econ.*, August 1973, *49*(3), pp. 294–309.

Smith, John H. Aggregation of Preferences with Variable Electorate. *Econometrica*, November 1973, *41*(6), pp. 1027–41.

Smith, Keith V. A Financial Analysis of Acquisition and Merger Premiums: Comment. *J. Financial Quant. Anal.*, March 1973, *8*(2), pp. 159–62.

Smith, Lawrence B. Evaluating National Housing Criteria in Canada. *Amer. Real Estate Urban Econ. Assoc. J.*, Fall 1973, *1*(2), pp. 35–51.

–––––– and Pesando, James E. Monetary Policy in Canada. In *Holbik, K., ed.*, 1973, pp. 70–116.

–––––– and Winder, John W. L. Interest Rate Expectations and the Demand for Money in Canada: Reply. *J. Finance*, March 1973, *28*(1), pp. 213–14.

Smith, Lawrence N. and Scherr, Bruce A. Social Return to Public Information Services: Statistical Reporting of U.S. Farm Commodities: Comment. *Amer. Econ. Rev.*, December 1973, *63*(5), pp. 1017–19.

Smith, M. A. M. A Note on Fixed Factor Proportions and Net Saving Rates. *Rev. Econ. Stud.*, April 1973, *40*(2), pp. 297–98.

Smith, P. Seasonal Fluctuations in the Motor Vehicle Industry: A Comment. *J. Ind. Econ.*, April 1973, *21*(2), pp. 184–86.

Smith, Paul E. and Johnson, Stanley R. The Phillips Curve, Expectations, and Stability. *Quart. Rev. Econ. Bus.*, Autumn 1973, *13*(3), pp. 85–91.

–––––– and Kmenta, J. Autonomous Expenditures Versus Money Supply: An Application of Dynamic Multipliers. *Rev. Econ. Statist.*, August 1973, *55*(3), pp. 299–307.

Smith, Ralph E. Manpower Programs and Unemployment Statistics. *Mon. Lab. Rev.*, April 1973, *96*(4), pp. 63–65.

Smith, R. J. Medium-Term Forecasts Reassessed: IV. Domestic Appliances. *Nat. Inst. Econ. Rev.*, May 1973, (64), pp. 68–83.

Smith, Robert S. Labor Market Conditions and Employer Hiring Standards: Comment. *Ind. Relat.*, May 1973, *12*(2), pp. 248–49.

Smith, Theodore Reynolds. Community Development and Agrarian Reform in the East Asian Setting. *Amer. J. Econ. Soc.*, January 1973, *32*(1), pp. 73–86.

Smith, Vernon L. Depreciation, Market Valuations and Investment Theory. In *Haynes, W. W.; Coyne, T. J. and Osborne, D. K., eds.*, 1973, pp. 375–82.

Smith, Victor E. and Koo, Anthony Y. C. A General Consumption Technology in New Demand Theory. *Western Econ. J.*, September 1973, *11*(3), pp. 243–59.

Smith, V. Kerry. International Trade Theory Without Homogeneity: A Comment. *Quart. J. Econ.*, May 1973, *87*(2), pp. 288–89.

–––––– Least Squares Regression with Cauchy Errors. *Oxford Bull. Econ. Statist.*, August 1973, *35* (3), pp. 223–31.

–––––– and Cichetti, Charles J. Interdependent Consumer Decisions: A Production Function Approach. *Australian Econ. Pap.*, December 1973, *12*(21), pp. 239–52.

–––––– and Loeb, Peter D. Misspecification and the Small Sample Properties of Econometric Estimators. *Appl. Econ.*, September 1973, *5*(3), pp. 167–79.

–––––– and Marcis, Richard G. The Demand for Liquid Asset Balances by U.S. Manufacturing Corporations: 1959-1970. *J. Financial Quant. Anal.*, March 1973, *8*(2), pp. 207–18.

–––––– and Marcis, Richard G. Monetary Activity and Interest Rates: A Spectral Analysis. *Quart.*

Rev. Econ. Bus., Summer 1973, *13*(2), pp. 69–82.

Smithies, Richard M. The Changing Demand for Air Transport: The North Atlantic Case. *J. Transp. Econ. Policy,* September 1973, *7*(3), pp. 231–49.

Smolensky, Eugene. Poverty, Propinquity and Policy. *Ann. Amer. Acad. Polit. Soc. Sci.,* September 1973, *409,* pp. 120–24.

────── **and Behrens, Jean.** Alternative Definitions of Income Redistribution. *Public Finance,* 1973, *28* (3–4), pp. 315–32.

Smolinski, Leon. Karl Marx and Mathematical Economics. *J. Polit. Econ.,* September-October 1973, *81*(5), pp. 1189–1204.

Smyth, David J. Effect of Public Price Forecasts on Market Price Variation: A Stochastic Cobweb Example. *Amer. J. Agr. Econ.,* February 1973, *55*(1), pp. 83–88.

────── **and Cohen, Stanley.** Some Determinants of Price/Earnings Ratios of Industrial Common Stock. *Quart. Rev. Econ. Bus.,* Winter 1973, *13*(4), pp. 49–60.

──────; **Ireland, Norman J. and Briscoe, G.** Specification Bias and Short-run Returns to Labour: Some Evidence for the United Kingdom. *Rev. Econ. Statist.,* February 1973, *55*(1), pp. 23–27.

Snape, R. H. and Pursell, G. Economies of Scale, Price Discrimination and Exporting. *J. Int. Econ.,* February 1973, *3*(1), pp. 85–91.

Snell, Bradford C. Is Annual Style Change in the Automobile Industry an Unfair Method of Competition? A Reply. *Yale Law J.,* March 1973, *82*(4), pp. 711–14.

Snider, Thomas E. The Effect of Merger on the Lending Behavior of Rural Unit Banks in Virginia. *J. Bank Res.,* Spring 1973, *4*(1), pp. 52–57.

Snider, William D. Building an On-Line Financial Planning Model. *J. Bank Res.,* Autumn 1973, *4*(3), pp. 232–38.

Snooks, G. D. Depression and Recovery in Western Australia, 1928–29 to 1938–39: A Deviation from the Norm. *Econ. Rec.,* September 1973, *49*(127), pp. 420–39.

────── The Growth Process of the Firm: A Case Study. *Australian Econ. Pap.,* December 1973, *12* (21), pp. 162–74.

────── Innovation and the Growth of the Firm: Hume Enterprises 1910–40. *Australian Econ. Hist. Rev.,* March 1973, *13*(1), pp. 16–40.

Snow, John W. and Hexter, J. L. Entropy, Lorenz Curves, and Some Comments on Size Inequality Among the Largest U.S. Corporations. *Nebr. J. Econ. Bus.,* Winter 1973, *12*(1), pp. 43–50.

Snowbarger, Marvin and Kirk, John. A Cross-Sectional Model of Built-In Flexibility, 1954–1969. *Nat. Tax J.,* June 1973, *26*(2), pp. 241–49.

Snyder, Wayne W. Are the Budgets of State and Local Governments Destabilizing? A Six Country Comparison. *Europ. Econ. Rev.,* June 1973, *4*(2), pp. 197–213.

Sobbrio, Giuseppe and Genovese, Nicola M. Regional Inequality and the Market Mechanism: Comment. *Kyklos,* 1973, *26*(3), pp. 621–23.

Sobek, Robert S. A Manager's Primer on Forecasting. *Harvard Bus. Rev.,* May-June 1973, *51*(3), pp. 6–28, 181–83.

Sobol, Marion G. A Dynamic Analysis of Labor Force Participation of Married Women of Child-

bearing Age. *J. Human Res.,* Fall 1973, *8*(4), pp. 497–505.

Socher, Karl. Monetary Policy in Austria. In *Holbik, K., ed.,* 1973, pp. 1–38.

Soentoro, Gunawan Wiradi and Collier, William L. Recent Changes in Rice Harvesting Methods: Some Serious Social Implications. *Bull. Indonesian Econ. Stud.,* July 1973, *9*(2), pp. 36–45.

Sofranko, Andrew J. and Bealer, Robert C. Modernization Balance, Imbalance, and Domestic Instability. *Econ. Develop. Cult. Change,* October 1973, *22*(1), pp. 52–72.

Sokoloski, Adam A. The Status of Fisheries Management Research: An Overview. In *Sokoloski, A. A., ed.,* 1973, pp. 1–6.

Solar, Donald. Chile's Dilemma: An Interpretive Analysis. *Amer. Econ.,* Spring 1973, *17*(1), pp. 40–50.

Soldaczuk, J. Trade and Cooperation among CMEA Member Countries. In *Kiss, T., ed.,* 1973, pp. 137–42.

Soldi, Costantino. Ricerche economiche. (Economic Research. With English summary.) *L'Impresa,* 1973, *15*(1), pp. 32–36.

Soldner, Helmut. Public Policy Toward Retailing: West Germany. In *Boddewyn, J. J. and Hollander, S. C., eds.,* 1972, pp. 405–29.

Soldofsky, Robert M. and Jennings, Edward H. Risk-Premium Curves: Empirical Evidence on Their Changing Position, 1950 to 1970. *Quart. Rev. Econ. Bus.,* Spring 1973, *13*(1), pp. 49–68.

Soligo, Ronald and Besen, Stanley M. The Economics of the Network-Affiliate Relationship in the Television Broadcasting Industry. *Amer. Econ. Rev.,* June 1973, *63*(3), pp. 259–68.

Solís, Leopoldo and Barraza, Luciano. Agricultural Policies and the Role of the Sectoral Model. In *Goreux, L. M. and Manne, A. S., eds.,* 1973, pp. 463–75.

Sollenberger, Harold and Arens, Alvin A. Assessing Information Systems Projects. *Manage. Account.,* September 1973, *55*(3), pp. 37–42.

Solnik, Bruno H. Note on the Validity of the Random Walk for European Stock Prices. *J. Finance,* December 1973, *28*(5), pp. 1151–59.

Solomon, Arthur P. Housing and Public Policy Analysis. In *Pynoos, J.; Schafer, R. and Hartman, C. W., eds.,* 1973, pp. 558–77.

Solomon, Herbert and Rizvi, M. Haseeb. Selection of Largest Multiple Correlation Coefficients: Asymptotic Case. *J. Amer. Statist. Assoc.,* March 1973, *68*(341), pp. 184–88.

Solomon, Martin B., Jr. Uncertainty and Its Effect on Capital Investment Analysis. In *Haynes, W. W.; Coyne, T. J. and Osborne, D. K., eds.,* 1973, pp. 408–13.

Soloveytchik, George. Nordic Uncertainties and Realities. *Nat. Westminster Bank Quart. Rev.,* May 1973, pp. 31–45.

Solow, Robert M. A Comment on Some Uses of Mathematical Models in Urban Economics: Rejoinder—I. *Urban Stud.,* June 1973, *10*(2), pp. 267.

────── Congestion Cost and the Use of Land for Streets. *Bell J. Econ. Manage. Sci.,* Autumn 1973, *4*(2), pp. 602–18.

────── A Framework for the Measurement of Economic and Social Performance: Comment. In *Moss, M., ed.,* 1973, pp. 102–05.

_____ Is the End of the World at Hand? In *Weintraub, A.; Schwartz, E. and Aronson, J. R., eds.,* 1973, pp. 39–61.

_____ On Equilibrium Models of Urban Location. In *Parkin, M., ed.,* 1973, pp. 2–16.

_____ Some Evidence on the Short-Run Productivity Puzzle. In *[Rosenstein-Rodan, P.],* 1973, pp. 316–25.

_____ Technology and Unemployment. In *Reynolds, L. G.; Green, G. D. and Lewis, D. R., eds.,* 1973, pp. 89–99.

_____ What Happened to Full Employment? *Quart. Rev. Econ. Bus.,* Summer 1973, *13*(2), pp. 7–20.

_____ **and Blinder, Alan S.** Does Fiscal Policy Matter? *J. Public Econ.,* November 1973, *2*(4), pp. 319–37.

Soly, H. Grondspeculatie en kapitalisme te Antwerpen in de 16e eeuw. (Real Estate Speculation and Capitalism in Antwerp in the 16th Century. With English summary.) *Econ. Soc. Tijdschr.,* June 1973, *27*(3), pp. 291–302.

Somerhausen, Marc. International Manual on Collective Bargaining for Public Employees: Belgium. In *Kaye, S. P. and Marsh, A., eds.,* 1973, pp. 67–127.

Sommariva, A. Some Theoretical Implications of the Model of the Bank of Italy. *Tijdschr. Econ.,* 1973, *18*(2), pp. 207–34.

Sommers, Montrose S.; Kernan, Jerome B. and Greeno, Daniel W. Personality and Implicit Behavior Patterns. *J. Marketing Res.,* February 1973, *10*(1), pp. 63–69.

Sommers, Paul M. and Suits, Daniel B. Analysis of Net Interstate Migration. *Southern Econ. J.,* October 1973, *40*(2), pp. 193–201.

Somogyi, János and Amid-hozour, Esmail. East-West Trade. *Finance Develop.,* June 1973, *10*(2), pp. 32–37.

Sondermann, Dieter. Optimale Aggregation von grossen linearen Gleichungssystemen. (Optimal Aggregation of Great Systems of Linear Equations.) *Z. Nationalökon.,* 1973, *33*(3–4), pp. 235–50.

Songre, Ambroise. Mass Emigration from Upper Volta: The Facts and Implications. *Int. Lab. Rev.,* August-September 1973, *108*(2–3), pp. 209–25.

Sonne, A. Monopol-og priskontrol under en stabiliseringspolitik. (Monopoly and Price Control in a Stabilization Policy. With English summary.) *Nationalokon. Tidsskr.,* 1973, *111*(1), pp. 154–64.

Sonnenschein, Hugo. Do Walras' Identity and Continuity Characterize the Class of Community Excess Demand Functions? *J. Econ. Theory,* August 1973, *6*(4), pp. 345–54.

_____ The Utility Hypothesis and Market Demand Theory. *Western Econ. J.,* December 1973, *11*(4), pp. 404–10.

Sood, James H. The Computer Manufacturing Industry and the U.S. Balance of Payments. *Calif. Manage. Rev.,* Winter 1973, *16*(2), pp. 37–43.

Soper, John C. Programmed Instruction in Large-Lecture Courses. *J. Econ. Educ.,* Spring 1973, *4*(2), pp. 125–29.

_____ Soft Research on a Hard Subject: Student Evaluations Reconsidered. *J. Econ. Educ.,* Fall 1973, *5*(1), pp. 22–26.

Sorenson, L. Orlo. Rail-barge Competition in Transporting Winter Wheat. *Amer. J. Agr. Econ.,* December 1973, *55*(5), pp. 814–19.

Sorenson, Vernon L. Contradictions in U.S. Trade Policy. In *Iowa State University Center for Agricultural and Rural Development,* 1973, pp. 184–93.

Sorkin, Alan. Manpower Programs for American Indians. *J. Econ. Bus.,* Fall 1973, *26*(1), pp. 49–57.

Sorkin, Alan L. On The Occupational Status of Women, 1870–1970. *Amer. J. Econ. Soc.,* July 1973, *32*(3), pp. 235–43.

Sorter, G. H. and Horngren, Charles T. Asset Recognition and Economic Attributes—The Relevant Costing Approach. In *Thomas, W. E., Jr., ed.,* 1973, pp. 461–74.

Souders, Thomas L. and Killough, Larry N. A Goal Programming Model for Public Accounting Firms. *Accounting Rev.,* April 1973, *48*(2), pp. 268–79.

Soutar, Douglas. A Forward Look at Labor-Management Relations within the Framework of a Free Enterprise System. In *Somers, G. G., ed.,* 1973, pp. 157–63.

Southey, Clive. Peasants, Procreation, and Pensions: Note. *Amer. Econ. Rev.,* December 1973, *63*(5), pp. 983–85.

Southwick, Lawrence, Jr. The Higher Education Industry: Forecasts to 1990. *Rev. Soc. Econ.,* April 1973, *31*(1), pp. 1–19.

Şovei, George. Sistem informaţional bancar modern. (A Modern Banking Informational System. With English summary.) *Stud. Cercet. Econ.,* 1973, (4), pp. 127–40.

Sowey, Eric R. A Classified Bibliography of Monte Carlo Studies in Econometrics. *J. Econometrics,* December 1973, *1*(4), pp. 377–95.

_____ Stochastic Stimulation of Macroeconomic Models: Methodology and Interpretation. In *Powell, A. A. and Williams, R. A., eds.,* 1973, pp. 195–230.

Spandau, Arnt. Cross-Section Production Functions and Income-Shares in South African Industry. *S. Afr. J. Econ.,* September 1973, *41*(3), pp. 208–33.

_____ The Post-Keynesian Model of Income Distribution. *S. Afr. J. Econ.,* March 1973, *41*(1), pp. 1–16.

Sparks, Gordon; Frisch, Jack and Helliwell, John F. The Supply Price of Capital in Macroeconomic Models. In *Powell, A. A. and Williams, R. A., eds.,* 1973, pp. 261–83.

Sparrow, Frederick T.; Stettler, H. Louis, III and Oakland, W. H. More on Ghetto Multipliers. *J. Reg. Sci.,* April 1973, *13*(1), pp. 127–28.

Spaventa, Luigi. Notes on Problems of Transition between Techniques. In *Mirrlees, J. A. and Stern, N. H., eds.,* 1973, pp. 168–87.

Speare, Alden, Jr.; Speare, Mary C. and Lin, Hui-Sheng. Urbanization, Non-Familial Work, Education, and Fertility in Taiwan. *Population Stud.,* July 1973, *27*(2), pp. 323–34.

Speare, Mary C.; Lin, Hui-Sheng and Speare, Alden, Jr. Urbanization, Non-Familial Work, Education, and Fertility in Taiwan. *Population Stud.,* July

1973, _27_(2), pp. 323–34.

Spence, A. Michael. Job Market Signaling. _Quart. J. Econ.,_ August 1973, _87_(3), pp. 355–74.

―――― Time and Communication in Economic and Social Interaction. _Quart. J. Econ.,_ November 1973, _87_(4), pp. 651–60.

Spencer, Byron G. Determinants of the Labour Force Participation of Married Women: A Micro-Study of Toronto Households. _Can. J. Econ.,_ May 1973, _6_(2), pp. 222–38.

―――― **and Denton, Frank T.** A Simulation Analysis of the Effects of Population Change on a Neoclassical Economy. _J. Polit. Econ.,_ Part I, March-April 1973, _81_(2), pp. 356–75.

Spencer, Dustan S. C. Rice Production and Marketing in Sierra Leone. In _Ofori, I. M., ed.,_ 1973, pp. 217–30.

Spencer, Roger W. Business Recovery Continues. _Fed. Res. Bank St. Louis Rev.,_ February 1973, _55_ (2), pp. 2–7.

―――― The National Plans to Curb Unemployment and Inflation. _Fed. Res. Bank St. Louis Rev.,_ April 1973, _55_(4), pp. 2–13.

―――― Strong Credit Demands, But No "Crunch" in Early 1973. _Fed. Res. Bank St. Louis Rev.,_ June 1973, _55_(6), pp. 2–10.

Spengler, Joseph John. Quesnay: Philosopher, Empiricist, Economist. In _Rectenwald, H. C., ed.,_ 1973, pp. 11–16.

Spiller, Richard. Ownership and Performance: Stock and Mutual Life Insurance Companies: Reply. _J. Risk Ins.,_ December 1973, _40_(4), pp. 635–38.

Spiro, Alan and Arak, Marcelle. A Theoretical Explanation of the Interest Inelasticity of Money Demand. _Rev. Econ. Statist.,_ November 1973, _55_(4), pp. 520–23.

Spiro, Erwin. The 1973 Income Tax Changes in South Africa. _Bull. Int. Fiscal Doc.,_ September 1973, _27_(9), pp. 372–78.

Spiro, Michael H. and Adams, Earl W., Jr. Labor Force Adjustment in the Construction Trades. _J. Econ. Bus.,_ Fall 1973, _26_(1), pp. 78–80.

―――― **and Adams, Earl W., Jr.** Reducing the Lags in Government Spending: An Empirical Analysis of Highway Construction. _Public Finance,_ 1973, _28_(2), pp. 125–38.

―――― **and Byrne, Robert F.** On Taxation as a Pollution Control Policy. _Swedish J. Econ.,_ March 1973, _75_(1), pp. 105–09.

Spitäller, Erich. Incomes Policy in Austria. _Int. Monet. Fund Staff Pap.,_ March 1973, _20_(1), pp. 170–202.

Spornic, Aneta. Influenţa factorilor social-politici asupra creşterii productivităţii muncii. (The Influence of Social-Political Factors on the Increase of Labour Productivity. With English summary.) _Stud. Cercet. Econ.,_ 1973, (2), pp. 55–62.

Sprenger, Rolf-Ulrich. Zur Problematik der Treffsicherheit von langfristigen Verkehrsvorausschätzungen—Methodische Ansätze ter Treffsicherheitsanalyse und ihr Aussagewert für die prognostische Praxis. (Notes on Testing the Accuracy of Long-Term Traffic Forecasts. With English summary.) _Ifo-Studien,_ January 1973, _19_ (1/2), pp. 17–57.

Sprenkle, C. M. and Aigner, Dennis J. On Optimal Financing of Cyclical Cash Needs. _J. Finance,_

December 1973, _28_(5), pp. 1249–54.

Sprinkel, Beryl W. Continued Expansion in 1973 amid Growing Prosperity. _J. Bus.,_ January 1973, _46_(1), pp. 1–5.

Spulber, Nicolas and von Furstenberg, George M. Is There an Economic System Based on Sovereignty of Each Consumer? _Z. Nationalökon.,_ 1973, _33_ (3–4), pp. 361–74.

Squire, Lyn. Optimal Feeder Roads in Developing Countries: The Case of Thailand. _J. Devel. Stud.,_ January 1973, _9_(2), pp. 279–90.

―――― Some Aspects of Optimal Pricing for Telecommunications. _Bell J. Econ. Manage. Sci.,_ Autumn 1973, _4_(2), pp. 515–25.

Sreekantaradhya, B. S. Economic Integration Among Developing Countries with Special Reference to South-East Asia—I. _Econ. Aff.,_ November-December 1973, _18_(11–12), pp. 483–84, 511–16.

Sreenivas, M. A. Prices, Money Wages and Real Output: A Case Study of Indian Manufacturing Sector. _Indian Econ. J.,_ April-June 1973, _20_(4–5), pp. 604–18.

Srikantan, K. S. Regional and Rural-Urban Socio-Demographic Differences in Turkey. _Middle East J.,_ Summer 1973, _27_(3), pp. 275–300.

Srinivasan, M. Problems of Inputs (With Special Reference to Water and Fertilisers) in Indian Agriculture. _Econ. Aff.,_ September-October 1973, _18_(9–10), pp. 466–74.

Srinivasan, T. N. A Critique of the Optimising Planning Model. In _Wadhva, C. D., ed.,_ 1973, pp. 78–93.

―――― Tax Evasion: A Model. _J. Public Econ.,_ November 1973, _2_(4), pp. 339–46.

―――― **and Bhagwati, Jagdish N.** The General Equilibrium Theory of Effective Protection and Resource Allocation. _J. Int. Econ.,_ August 1973, _3_(3), pp. 259–81.

―――― **and Bhagwati, Jagdish N.** Smuggling and Trade Policy. _J. Public Econ.,_ November 1973, _2_ (4), pp. 377–89.

Srivastava, Uma K. and Heady, Earl O. Technological Change and Relative Factor Shares in Indian Agriculture: An Empirical Analysis. _Amer. J. Agr. Econ.,_ August 1973, _55_(3), pp. 509–14.

―――― ; **Nagadevara, Vishnuprasad and Heady, Earl O.** Resource Productivity, Returns to Scale and Farm Size in Indian Agriculture: Some Recent Evidence. _Australian J. Agr. Econ.,_ April 1973, _17_ (1), pp. 43–57.

Srivastava, V. K. The Efficiency of an Improved Method of Estimating Seemingly Unrelated Regression Equations. _J. Econometrics,_ December 1973, _1_(4), pp. 341–50.

Staaf, Robert J. and Freiden, Alan. Scholastic Choice: An Economic Model of Student Behavior. _J. Human Res.,_ Summer 1973, _8_(3), pp. 396–404.

―――― **and Tullock, Gordon.** Education and Equality. _Ann. Amer. Acad. Polit. Soc. Sci.,_ September 1973, _409,_ pp. 125–34.

Stabler, J. C. and Williams, P. R. The Changing Structure of the Central Place Hierarchy. _Land Econ.,_ November 1973, _49_(4), pp. 454–58.

Staelin, Charles. Indian Export Incentives: A Critical View. _Indian Econ. J.,_ October–December 1973,

21(2), pp. 107–23.

Staelin, Richard and Turner, Ronald E. Error in Judgmental Sales Forecasts: Theory and Results. *J. Marketing Res.*, February 1973, *10*(1), pp. 10–16.

Stafford, E. M. and Ellison, A. P. The Order Delivery Lag in the World's Civil Aircraft Industry. *Appl. Econ.*, March 1973, *5*(1), pp. 19–34.

Stafford, Frank P. and Johnson, George E. Social Returns to Quantity and Quality of Schooling. *J. Human Res.*, Spring 1973, *8*(2), pp. 139–55.

Stager, David A. A. and Cook, Gail C. A. Contingent Repayment Student Finance: The Problem of Non-Participants in the Labour Force. *Ann. Econ. Soc. Measure,* January 1973, *2*(1), pp. 65–67.

Stahl, Ingolf. Bargaining as a Decision Process: Comment. *Swedish J. Econ.*, December 1973, *75*(4), pp. 406–09.

Stahl, Sheldon W. and Cacy, J. A. For 1974—An Uncertain Outlook. *Fed. Res. Bank Kansas City Rev.*, December 1973, pp. 3–11.

_____ **and Harshbarger, C. Edward.** Free Enterprise Revisited—A Look at Economic Concentration. *Fed. Res. Bank Kansas City Rev.*, March 1973, pp. 10–16.

Staley, Charles E. A Note on Adam Smith's Version of the Vent for Surplus Model. *Hist. Polit. Econ.*, Fall 1973, *5*(2), pp. 438–48.

Stalford, Harold and Leitmann, George. Sufficiency Conditions for Nash Equilibria in N-Person Differential Games. In *Blaquière, A., ed.*, 1973, pp. 345–76.

Stamm, John H. and Jedel, Michael Jay. The Battle over Jobs: An Appraisal of Recent Publications on the Employment Effects of U.S. Multinational Corporations. In *Kujawa, D., ed.*, 1973, pp. 144–91.

Stammati, Gaetano. Il coordinamento delle politiche di bilancio nella C.E.E. (Coordination of Budget Policies in E.E.C. With English summary.) *Bancaria*, February 1973, *29*(2), pp. 151–55.

_____ Italian Experience with Fiscal Policy. In *Giersch, H., ed.*, 1973, pp. 203–09.

_____ Raffaele Mattioli. (Raffaele Mattioli. With English summary.) *Bancaria*, November 1973, *29* (11), pp. 1323–28.

Stan, Sorin and Dobrotă, Niță. Investiţiile şi creditele internaţionale—componente importante ale circuitului economic mondial. (International Investments and Credits—Important Components of the World Economic Circulation. With English summary.) *Stud. Cercet. Econ.*, 1973, (4), pp. 149–65.

Stanbridge, R. J. Sources and Uses of Funds in the New Zealand Farm Sector. *Australian J. Agr. Econ.*, April 1973, *17*(1), pp. 17–32.

Stanciu, Ion E. Eficienţa economică a diversificării produselor textile. (The Economic Efficiency of the Diversification of Textile Products. With English summary.) *Stud. Cercet. Econ.*, 1973, (4), pp. 141–48.

Standen, B. J. Where Are the Markets for Farm Poplar on the North Coast? *Rev. Marketing Agr. Econ.*, June and September 1973, *41*(2–3), pp. 91–92.

Standing, Guy and Taira, Koji. Labor Market Effects of Multinational Enterprises in Latin America. *Nebr. J. Econ. Bus.*, Autumn 1973, *12*(4), pp. 103–17.

Stanfield, J. Ronald and Mullendore, Walter E. A Suggested Form of Benefit-Cost Analysis for an Evaluation of Urban Renewal Projects. *Land Econ.*, February 1973, *49*(1), pp. 81–86.

Stanke, F.; Hennings, U. and Hüber, R. P. O. Delphi Interrogation Concerning Future Possibilities of the Employment of Robots. In *Blohm, H. and Steinbuch, K., eds.*, 1973, pp. 19–28.

Stanley, Kenneth B. International Telecommunications Industry: Interdependence of Market Structure and Performance Under Regulation. *Land Econ.*, November 1973, *49*(4), pp. 391–403.

Staples, Thomas G. Supplemental Security Income: The Aged Eligible. *Soc. Sec. Bull.*, July 1973, *36* (7), pp. 31–35.

Starler, Norman H. and Thomas, Robert W. Intergovernmental Education Grants and the Efficiency of Resource Allocation in School Districts. *Appl. Econ.*, September 1973, *5*(3), pp. 181–92.

Starostin, S. and Emdin, G. The Five-Year Plan and the Soviet Way of Life. *Prob. Econ.*, February 1973, *15*(10), pp. 81–103.

Starr, Martin K. Productivity is the USA's Problem. *Calif. Manage. Rev.*, Winter 1973, *16*(2), pp. 32–36.

Starr, Ross M. Optimal Production and Allocation under Uncertainty. *Quart. J. Econ.*, February 1973, *87*(1), pp. 81–95.

Starrett, David; Dasgupta, Partha and Sen, Amartya K. Notes on the Measurement of Inequality. *J. Econ. Theory*, April 1973, *6*(2), pp. 180–87.

Starrett, David A. Inefficiency and the Demand for "Money" in a Sequence Economy. *Rev. Econ. Stud.*, October 1973, *40*(4), pp. 437–48.

_____ A Note on Externalities and the Core. *Econometrica*, January 1973, *41*(1), pp. 179–83.

_____ **and Arrow, Kenneth J.** Cost- and Demand-theoretical Approaches to the Theory of Price Determination. In *Hicks, J. R. and Weber, W., eds.*, 1973, pp. 129–48.

Staudohar, Paul D. The Emergence of Hawaii's Public Employment Law. *Ind. Relat.*, October 1973, *12*(3), pp. 338–51.

_____ **and Seidman, Joel.** The Hawaii Public Employment Relations Act: A Critical Analysis. *Ind. Lab. Relat. Rev.*, April 1973, *26*(3), pp. 919–37.

Staudt, E. and Pfeiffer, W. The Integration of Technological Prediction into Management Systems by Improvement of Forecasting Analysis. In *Blohm, H. and Steinbuch, K., eds.*, 1973, pp. 105–14.

Staudte, Axel and Hansen, Gerd. Eine empirische Überprüfung der Permanent-Income-Hypothese: Eine Erwiderung auf H. Drost. (An Empirical Reexamination of the Permanent Income Hypothesis: A Comment. With English summary.) *Jahr. Nationalökon. Statist.*, March 1973, *187*(3), pp. 269–81.

Steckle, Jean. Changes in Food Use Patterns: Some Aspects of Household Enumeration in Measuring Levels of Living through Studies in Depth. In *Ofori, I. M., ed.*, 1973, pp. 49–56.

Steedman, Ian. Some Long-run Equilibrium Tax

Theory. *Public Finance*, 1973, *28*(1), pp. 43–51.

_____; Bell, D. J. and Brenneman, Ronald. A Control Theory Analysis of a Finite Optimum Savings Program in a Two-Sector Model. *Int. Econ. Rev.*, June 1973, *14*(2), pp. 520–24.

_____ and Metcalfe, J. S. Heterogeneous Capital and the Heckscher-Ohlin-Samuelson Theory of Trade. In *Parkin, M., ed.*, 1973, pp. 50–60.

_____ and Metcalfe, J. S. The Non-Substitution Theorem and International Trade Theory. *Australian Econ. Pap.*, December 1973, *12*(21), pp. 267–69.

_____ and Metcalfe, J. S. On Foreign Trade. *Econ. Int.*, August-November 1973, *26*(3–4), pp. 516–28.

Steeger, H. Cooperation in Planning. In *Kiss, T., ed.*, 1973, pp. 37–40.

Steel, William F. Complementarities and Conflicts Between Employment and Output Growth in Low-Income Countries. *Econ. Bull. Ghana, Sec. Ser.*, 1973, *3*(1), pp. 50–66.

Steenkamp, W. F. J. Labour and Management in Manufacturing Development. *S. Afr. J. Econ.*, December 1973, *41*(4), pp. 438–51.

Stefansky, Wilhelmine and Kaiser, Henry F. Note on Discrete Approximations. *J. Amer. Statist. Assoc.*, March 1973, *68*(341), pp. 232–34.

Steger, Wilbur A. Economic and Social Costs of Residential Segregation. In *Clawson, M., ed.*, 1973, pp. 83–113.

Stegman, Michael A. Private Participation in Low-income Housing. In *Pynoos, J.; Schafer, R. and Hartman, C. W., eds.*, 1973, pp. 532–35.

_____ Reducing the Cost of New Construction. In *Pynoos, J.; Schafer, R. and Hartman, C. W., eds.*, 1973, pp. 372–75.

Steib, Steve B. The Demand for Euro-Dollar Borrowings by U.S. Banks. *J. Finance*, September 1973, *28*(4), pp. 875–79.

Stein, Bruno. Incentives and Planning as Social Policy Tools. In *Stein, B. and Miller, S. M., eds.*, 1973, pp. 3–10.

Stein, Daniel D. and Denny, David L. Recent Developments in Trade between the U.S. and the P.-R.C.: A Legal and Economic Perspective. *Law Contemp. Probl.*, Summer-Autumn 1973, *38*(2), pp. 260–73.

Stein, Jerome L. and Infante, Ettore F. Optimal Growth with Robust Feedback Control. *Rev. Econ. Stud.*, January 1973, *40*(1), pp. 47–60.

_____ Optimal Stabilization Paths. *J. Money, Credit, Banking*, Part II, February 1973, *5*(1), pp. 525–62.

Stein, L. On the Third World's Narrowing Trade Gap: A Rejoinder. *Oxford Econ. Pap.*, March 1973, *25*(1), pp. 141–44.

Steinbruner, John D. and Jacoby, Henry D. Advanced Technology and the Problem of Implementation. In *Jacoby, H. D., et al.*, 1973, pp. 49–61.

_____ The Context of Current Policy Discussions. In *Jacoby, H. D., et al.*, 1973, pp. 9–26.

_____ Policy Analysis and the Public Sector. In *Jacoby, H. D., et al.*, 1973, pp. 1–8.

_____ Policy Options and Predicted Outcomes. In *Jacoby, H. D., et al.*, 1973, pp. 27–47.

_____ Salvaging the Federal Attempt to Control Auto Pollution. *Public Policy*, Winter 1973, *21*(1), pp. 1–48.

Steinbuch, K. Technological Forecasting in Practice: Conclusion. In *Blohm, H. and Steinbuch, K., eds.*, 1973, pp. 171–72.

Steindl, Frank G. The Appeal of Minimum Wage Laws and the Invisible Hand in Government. *Public Choice*, Spring 1973, *14*, pp. 133–36.

_____ Money and Bonds as Giffen Goods. *Manchester Sch. Econ. Soc. Stud.*, December 1973, *41*(4), pp. 418–24.

_____ Price Expectations and Interest Rates. *J. Money, Credit, Banking*, November 1973, *5*(4), pp. 939–49.

_____ A Structural Model of the Canadian Monetary Sector: Comment. *Southern Econ. J.*, April 1973, *39*(4), pp. 642.

Steiner, Gary A. The Creative Organization. In *Britt, S. H. and Boyd, H. W., Jr., eds.*, 1973, pp. 45–60.

Steiner, George A. Approaches to Long-Range Planning for Small Business. In *Klein, W. H. and Murphy, D. C., eds.*, 1973, pp. 250–63.

_____ Long-Range Planning: Concept and Implementation. In *Klein, W. H. and Murphy, D. C., eds.*, 1973, pp. 242–49.

Steiner, H. M. and Johnson, G. P. Evaluating Social Roads in Mexico. *J. Transp. Econ. Policy*, January 1973, *7*(1), pp. 98–101.

Steinherr, Alfred. Economic Policy in the Short Run under Fixed Exchange Rates. *Rech. Écon. Louvain*, December 1973, *39*(4), pp. 419–36.

Steinmann, Gunter. Informationsgewinnung und Preisentwicklung: Ein mikroökonomischer Erklärungsversuch für die verzögerte Preisanpassung im Konjunkturaufschwung mit Hilfe des Mills-Modells. (Information Problem and Price Development: A Mills-Model-Explanation for Lagged Adjustment of Prices in the Beginning Upswing. With English summary.) *Z. Wirtschaft. Sozialwissen.*, 1973, *93*(4), pp. 411–21.

_____ Lohnentwicklung und Beschäftigungsgrad: Die Neuauflage der Kontroverse zwischen der Keynesschen und der neoklassischen Theorie bei der Diskussion um die Phillips-Kurve. (Wages and the Rate of Employment. With English summary.) *Weltwirtsch. Arch.*, 1973, *109*(1), pp. 105–20.

Stekler, H. O. and Schepsman, Martin. Forecasting with an Index of Leading Series. *J. Amer. Statist. Assoc.*, June 1973, *68*(342), pp. 291–96.

Stelu, Şerban. Circuitul economic al ambalajelor. (The Economic Circuit of Packings. With English summary.) *Stud. Cercet. Econ.*, 1973, (2), pp. 157–69.

_____ Perfectarea contractelor economice. (The Conclusion of Economic Contracts. With English summary.) *Stud. Cercet. Econ.*, 1973, (3), pp. 141–52.

Stelzer, David F. and Shell, Richard L. Systems Analysis: Aid to Decision Making. In *Klein, W. H. and Murphy, D. C., eds.*, 1973, pp. 34–39.

Stelzer, Irwin M. and Netschert, Bruce C. Energy and the Environment in New York State: A Balancing of Needs. *Amer. Econ.*, Fall 1973, *17*(2), pp. 143–47.

Stephan, Paula and Haveman, Robert H. White Elephants, Waterways, and the Transportation Act of 1966. In *Haveman, R. H. and Hamrin, R. D., eds.,* 1973, pp. 220–25.

Stephens, J. Kirker. Input Quality, Obsolescence, and Unemployment. *Kyklos,* 1973, *26*(2), pp. 282–87.

————— Returns to Scale and the Average Cost Curve: Comment. *Swedish J. Econ.,* March 1973, *75*(1), pp. 110–11.

Stephenson, Charles M. Implications of PLLRC Tax Recommendations for Federal Hydro Projects and Power Facilities. *Land Econ.,* February 1973, *49*(1), pp. 67–75.

Stern, David. Effects of Alternative State Aid Formulas on the Distribution of Public School Expenditures in Massachusetts. *Rev. Econ. Statist.,* February 1973, *55*(1), pp. 91–97.

Stern, Ernest. Private Capital Markets for Development. In *[Halm, G. N.],* 1973, pp. 185–97.

Stern, James L. Bargaining and Arbitration in the British Civil Service. *Mon. Lab. Rev.,* August 1973, *96*(8), pp. 61–63.

Stern, Louis W.; Sternthal, Brian and Craig, C. Samuel. Managing Conflict in Distribution Channels: A Laboratory Study. *J. Marketing Res.,* May 1973, *10*(2), pp. 169–79.

Stern, Martin O. and Ayres, Robert U. Transportation Outlays: Who Pays and Who Benefits? In *Harriss, C. L., ed.,* 1973, pp. 117–54.

Stern, Nicholas. Homogeneous Utility Functions and Equality in "The Optimum Town." A Note. *Swedish J. Econ.,* June 1973, *75*(2), pp. 204–07.

Stern, Nicholas H. and Carr-Hill, R. A. An Econometric Model of the Supply and Control of Recorded Offences in England and Wales. *J. Public Econ.,* November 1973, *2*(4), pp. 289–318.

Stern, R. D. and Mead, R. The Use of a Computer in the Teaching of Statistics. *J. Roy. Statist. Soc.,* Part 2, 1973, *136,* pp. 191–205.

Stern, Robert M. Research on Internal Adjustment to External Economic Disturbances: An American View. In *Bergsten, C. F., ed.,* 1973, pp. 75–92.

————— Tariffs and Other Measures of Trade Control: A Survey of Recent Developments. *J. Econ. Lit.,* September 1973, *11*(3), pp. 857–88.

Stern, Robert N. and Becker, Theodore M. Professionalism, Professionalization, and Bias in the Commercial Human Relations Consulting Operation: A Survey Analysis. *J. Bus.,* April 1973, *46*(2), pp. 230–57.

Stern, Ronald J. and Ben-Israel, Adi. On Linear Optimal Control Problems with Multiple Quadratic Criteria. In *Cochrane, J. L. and Zeleny, M., eds.,* 1973, pp. 366–72.

Sternlieb, George. The City as Sandbox. In *Rasmussen, D. W. and Haworth, C. T., eds.,* 1973, pp. 125–32.

Sternthal, Brian; Craig, C. Samuel and Stern, Louis W. Managing Conflict in Distribution Channels: A Laboratory Study. *J. Marketing Res.,* May 1973, *10*(2), pp. 169–79.

Stettler, H. Louis, III; Oakland, W. H. and Sparrow, Frederick T. More on Ghetto Multipliers. *J. Reg. Sci.,* April 1973, *13*(1), pp. 127–28.

Steuer, M. D. and Gennard, John. The Industrial Relations of Foreign Owned Subsidiaries in the United Kingdom. In *Henley, D. S., ed.,* 1973, pp. 301–17.

Steuer, Ralph E. and Evans, John P. Generating Efficient Extreme Points in Linear Multiple Objective Programming: Two Algorithms and Computing Experience. In *Cochrane, J. L. and Zeleny, M., eds.,* 1973, pp. 349–65.

Stevens, Donald L. Financial Characteristics of Merged Firms: A Multivariate Analysis. *J. Financial Quant. Anal.,* March 1973, *8*(2), pp. 149–58.

Stevens, Guy V. G.; Kichline, James L. and Laub, P. Michael. Obtaining the Yield on a Standard Bond from a Sample of Bonds with Heterogeneous Characteristics. *Fed. Res. Bull.,* May 1973, *59*(5), pp. 327–28.

Stevens, Joe B. and Mattox, Bruce W. Augmentation of Salmon Stocks through Artificial Propagation: Methods and Implications. In *Sokoloski, A. A., ed.,* 1973, pp. 133–45.

Stevenson, Richard A. Brokerage Commissions and the Small Shareholder. *J. Bus. Res.,* Fall 1973, *1*(2), pp. 193–200.

————— Odd-Lot Trading in the Stock Market and its Market Impact: Comment. *J. Financial Quant. Anal.,* June 1973, *8*(3), pp. 527–33.

Stever, Guyford. Impact of Space on World Development. *World Devel.,* February 1973, *1*(1-2), pp. 116–21.

Stewart, Charles T. and Benson, Virginia. Job Migration Linkages Between Smaller SMSAs and Their Hinterlands. *Land Econ.,* November 1973, *49*(4), pp. 432–39.

Stewart, Frances. Trade and Technology. In *Streeten, P., ed.,* 1973, pp. 231–63.

————— **and Streeten, Paul.** Conflicts Between Output and Employment Objectives in Developing Countries. *Bangladesh Econ. Rev.,* January 1973, *1*(1), pp. 1–24.

Stewart, Max D. and Wyckham, Robert G. Public Policy Toward Retailing: Canada. In *Boddewyn, J. J. and Hollander, S. C., eds.,* 1972, pp. 81–99.

Stewart, Samuel S., Jr. A Behavioral Model for Predicting Stock Prices. *J. Bus. Res.,* Fall 1973, *1*(2), pp. 173–82.

————— Share Price Maximization: A Tool for Management Decision-Making. *Calif. Manage. Rev.,* Winter 1973, *16*(2), pp. 54–58.

————— Shifts in Equity Composition and Market Performance. *Miss. Val. J. Bus. Econ.,* Fall 1973, *9*(1), pp. 12–17.

Stier, W. and Schips, B. Einige Bemerkungen über die Rolle der Spektralanalyse in der empirischen Wirtschaftsforschung. (Some Remarks on the Role of Spectral Analysis for Empirical Economic Research. With English summary.) *Schweiz. Z. Volkswirtsch. Statist.,* June 1973, *109*(2), pp. 233–43.

Stigler, George J. The Economies of Scale. In *Haynes, W. W.; Coyne, T. J. and Osborne, D. K., eds.,* 1973, pp. 232–49.

————— General Economic Conditions and National Elections. *Amer. Econ. Rev.,* May 1973, *63*(2), pp. 160–67.

————— John Stuart Mill: The Nature and Role of Originality in Scientific Progress. In *Rectenwald,*

H. C., ed., 1973, pp. 207–10.

_____ The Kinky Oligopoly Demand Curve and Rigid Prices. In *Haynes, W. W.; Coyne, T. J. and Osborne, D. K., eds.*, 1973, pp. 281–99.

_____ The Ricardian Theory of Value and Distribution. In *Rectenwald, H. C., ed.*, 1973, pp. 131–34.

_____ A Sketch of the History of Truth in Teaching. *J. Polit. Econ.*, Part I, March-April 1973, *81*(2), pp. 491–95.

_____ and Kindahl, James K. Industrial Prices, as Administered by Dr. Means. *Amer. Econ. Rev.*, September 1973, *63*(4), pp. 717–21.

Stiglitz, Joseph E. Approaches to the Economics of Discrimination. *Amer. Econ. Rev.*, May 1973, *63* (2), pp. 287–95.

_____ The Badly Behaved Economy with the Well-Behaved Production Function. In *Mirrlees, J. A. and Stern, N. H., eds.*, 1973, pp. 117–37.

_____ Education and Inequality. *Ann. Amer. Acad. Polit. Soc. Sci.*, September 1973, *409*, pp. 135–45.

_____ Recurrence of Techniques in a Dynamic Economy. In *Mirrlees, J. A. and Stern, N. H., eds.*, 1973, pp. 138–61.

_____ Taxation, Corporate Financial Policy, and the Cost of Capital. *J. Public Econ.*, February 1973, *2*(1), pp. 1–34.

_____ and Rothschild, Michael. Some Further Results on the Measurement of Inequality. *J. Econ. Theory*, April 1973, *6*(2), pp. 188–204.

Stigum, Bernt P. Competitive Equilibria with Infinitely Many Commodities (II) *J. Econ. Theory*, October 1973, *6*(5), pp. 415–45.

_____ Revealed Preference—A Proof of Houthakker's Theorem. *Econometrica*, May 1973, *41*(3), pp. 411–23.

Stinson, John F. and Green, Gloria P. Changes in the Employment Situation in 1972. *Mon. Lab. Rev.*, February 1973, *96*(2), pp. 24–34.

Ştirbu, Cornelia and Condurache, Gheorghe. Determinarea timpului optim de înlocuire a unei linii tehnologice du sudură de la Uzina metalurgică—Iaşi. (Determining the Optimum Time for Replacing a Welding Technological Line at the Jassy Metallurgical Works. With English summary.) *Stud. Cercet. Econ.*, 1973, (4), pp. 89–98.

Stitelman, Leonard. The "Base Data-Cluster" Concept: A Regional Approach to a Governmental Information Network. *Mich. Academician*, Spring 1973, *5*(4), pp. 435–40.

Stobaugh, Robert B., et al. U.S. Multinational Enterprises and the U.S. Economy. In *Kujawa, D., ed.*, 1973, pp. 82–126.

_____ and Robbins, Sidney M. The Bent Measuring Stick for Foreign Subsidiaries. *Harvard Bus. Rev.*, September-October 1973, *51*(5), pp. 80–88.

_____; Telesio, Piero and de la Torre, Jose, Jr. U.S. Multinational Enterprises and Changes in the Skill Composition of U.S. Employment. In *Kujawa, D., ed.*, 1973, pp. 127–43.

Stöber, G. J. Technological Forecasting and Technology Policy. In *Blohm, H. and Steinbuch, K., eds.*, 1973, pp. 139–44.

Stockdale, Jerry D. Human Potential: A Perspective on Poverty and Quality of Life. *Growth Change*, October 1973, *4*(4), pp. 24–28.

Stoddard, Ellwyn R. The Adjustment of Mexican American Barrio Families to Forced Housing Relocation. *Soc. Sci. Quart.*, March 1973, *53*(4), pp. 749–59.

Stöhr, Walter and Friedmann, John. The Uses of Regional Science: Policy Planning in Chile. In *Friedmann, J.*, 1973, pp. 255–71.

Stoikov, Vladimir. Recurrent Education: Some Neglected Economic Issues. *Int. Lab. Rev.*, August-September 1973, *108*(2–3), pp. 187–208.

_____ Size of Firm, Worker Earnings, and Human Capital: The Case of Japan. *Ind. Lab. Relat. Rev.*, July 1973, *26*(4), pp. 1095–1106.

_____ The Structure of Earnings in Japanese Manufacturing Industries: A Human-Capital Approach. *J. Polit. Econ.*, Part I, March-April 1973, *81*(2), pp. 340–55.

Stokes, Charles J. How the General Accounting Office Evaluates Urban Housing Policies: An Analysis of Criteria and Procedures. *Amer. Real Estate Urban Econ. Assoc. J.*, Fall 1973, *1*(2), pp. 88–103.

Stokes, C. Shannon. Family Structure and Socio-economic Differentials in Fertility. *Population Stud.*, July 1973, *27*(2), pp. 295–304.

Stokes, Houston H. Spot Speculation, Forward Speculation, and Arbitrage: Comment. *Amer. Econ. Rev.*, December 1973, *63*(5), pp. 995–98.

Stolk, William C. Beyond Profitability: A Proposal for Managing the Corporation's Public Business. In *Klein, W. H. and Murphy, D. C., eds.*, 1973, pp. 305–07.

Stoll, Hans R. The Relationship Between Put and Call Option Prices: Reply. *J. Finance*, March 1973, *28*(1), pp. 185–87.

Stolle, John F. and LeKashman, Raymond. The Total Cost Approach to Distribution. In *Britt, S. H. and Boyd, H. W., Jr., eds.*, 1973, pp. 441–58.

Stolz, Peter. Flexibilitätsspielräume im Einsatz des Arbeitspotentials und bedarfsorientierte Modelle der Bildungsökonomie. (Manpower Forecasts and the Problem of Flexible Relationships between Educational Qualifications and Occupations. With English summary.) *Z. Wirtschaft. Sozialwissen.*, 1973, *93*(1), pp. 3–20.

Stone, Alan. The F.T.C. and Advertising Regulation: An Examination of Agency Failure. *Public Policy*, Spring 1973, *21*(2), pp. 203–34.

Stone, Bernell K. Cash Planning and Credit-Line Determination with a Financial Statement Simulator: A Case Report on Short-Term Financial Planning. *J. Financial Quant. Anal.*, December 1973, *8*(5), pp. 711–29.

_____ A General Class of Three-Parameter Risk Measures. *J. Finance*, June 1973, *28*(3), pp. 675–85.

_____ A Linear Programming Formulation of the General Portfolio Selection Problem. *J. Financial Quant. Anal.*, September 1973, *8*(4), pp. 621–36.

Stone, Courtenay C. and Gifford, Adam, Jr. Externalities, Liability and the Coase Theorem: A Mathematical Analysis. *Western Econ. J.*, September 1973, *11*(3), pp. 260–69.

Stone, Gary K. Life Insurance Sales Practices on the College Campus. *J. Risk Ins.*, June 1973, *40*(2), pp. 167–79.

Stone, James M. A Theory of Capacity and the Insurance of Catastrophe Risks (Part I) *J. Risk Ins.*, June

1973, *40*(2), pp. 231–43.

───── A Theory of Capacity and the Insurance of Catastrophe Risks (Part II) *J. Risk Ins.*, September 1973, *40*(3), pp. 339–55.

Stone, Michael E. Federal Housing Policy: A Political-Economic Analysis. In *Pynoos, J.; Schafer, R. and Hartman, C. W., eds.*, 1973, pp. 423–33.

Stone, P. The Massive Market for Simplicity. In *Thorelli, H. B., ed.*, 1973, pp. 204–08.

Stone, Richard. Economic and Demographic Accounts and the Distribution of Income. *Acta Oecon.*, 1973, *11*(2–3), pp. 165–76.

───── Personal Spending and Saving in Postwar Britain. In *[Tinbergen, J.]*, 1973, pp. 75–98.

───── Process, Capacity and Control in an Input-Output System. *L'Industria*, January-June 1973, (1–2), pp. 3–17.

───── A System of Social Matrices. *Rev. Income Wealth*, June 1973, *19*(2), pp. 143–66.

Stoner, James A. F. and Aram, John D. Effectiveness of Two Technical Assistance Efforts in Differing Environments. *J. Devel. Stud.*, July 1973, *9*(4), pp. 508–17.

Storey, David A. and Christensen, Robert L. Graduate Programs in Agricultural Economics: Results of a Survey. *Amer. J. Agr. Econ.*, February 1973, *55*(1), pp. 61–64.

Storgaard, Birgit. A Delayed Proletarianization of Peasants. In *Institute for Development Research*, 1973, pp. 103–25.

Stott, Alexander L. Capital Recovery in a World of Inflation. In *Tax Foundation, Inc.*, 1973, pp. 35–42.

Stoutjesdijk, A. LDC Regional Markets: Do They Work? In *Thorelli, H. B., ed.*, 1973, pp. 47–57.

Strangert, Per. Budget Simulation: A Tool for Adaptive Planning. In *Ross, M., ed.*, 1973, pp. 491–97.

Strangways, Raymond S. and Donaldson, Loraine. Can Ghetto Groceries Price Competitively and Make a Profit? *J. Bus.*, January 1973, *46*(1), pp. 61–65.

Strassl, Arthur. Equilibrium Growth of Capital and Labor. *Amer. Econ.*, Fall 1973, *17*(2), pp. 33–45.

Straszheim, Mahlon R. Estimation of the Demand for Urban Housing Services from Household Interview Data. *Rev. Econ. Statist.*, February 1973, *55*(1), pp. 1–8.

Straus, Alexis K. Role of Models in Corporate Decision Making: Discussant 2. In *Ross, M., ed.*, 1973, pp. 167–69.

Strauss, George. Minority Membership in Apprenticeship Programs in the Construction Trades: Comment. *Ind. Lab. Relat. Rev.*, October 1973, *27*(1), pp. 93–99.

Strayhorn, Martha. Changes in Time and Savings Deposits at Commercial Banks: April-July 1973. *Fed. Res. Bull.*, October 1973, *59*(10), pp. 724–30.

───── Changes in Time and Savings Deposits at Commercial Banks, July 1972–January 1973. *Fed. Res. Bull.*, April 1973, *59*(4), pp. 261–75.

───── Changes in Time and Savings Deposits, January-April 1973. *Fed. Res. Bull.*, July 1973, *59*(7), pp. 493–500.

Strazheim, Mahlon R. The Demand for Corporate Stock in the Postwar Period. In *Goldsmith, R. W., ed.*, 1973, pp. 204–65.

Streeten, Paul. An Institutional Critique of Development Concepts. In *Livingstone, I., et al., eds.*, 1973, pp. 82–94.

───── Industrialization and Trade Trends: Some Issues for the 1970s: Comment. In *Hughes, H., ed.*, 1973, pp. 35–39.

───── Some Comments on the Teaching of Economics. In *Livingstone, I., et al., eds.*, 1973, pp. 46–50.

───── Trade Strategies for Development: Some Themes for the Seventies. In *Streeten, P., ed.*, 1973, pp. 1–24.

───── **and Stewart, Frances.** Conflicts Between Output and Employment Objectives in Developing Countries. *Bangladesh Econ. Rev.*, January 1973, *1*(1), pp. 1–24.

Streissler, Erich W. Menger's Theories of Money and Uncertainty—A Modern Interpretation. In *Hicks, J. R. and Weber, W., eds.*, 1973, pp. 164–89.

───── **and Weber, Wilhelm.** The Menger Tradition. In *Hicks, J. R. and Weber, W., eds.*, 1973, pp. 226–32.

Strickland, Roger P., Jr. Alternative Analyses of Farm Growth. *Agr. Econ. Res.*, October 1973, *25* (4), pp. 99–104.

Stringer, John. Behavioral Science Models. In *Ross, M., ed.*, 1973, pp. 253–63.

Strober, Myra H. Economic Development and the Hierachy of Earnings. *Ind. Relat.*, February 1973, *12*(1), pp. 65–76.

Strøm, Steinar. Economic Growth and Biological Equilibrium. *Swedish J. Econ.*, June 1973, *75*(2), pp. 164–75.

Strong, Maurice F. One Year after Stockholm: An Ecological Approach to Management. *Foreign Aff.*, July 1973, *51*(4), pp. 690–707.

Stroobants-Vanden Bossche, G. Inflatie: een actueel probleem voor het bedrijfsleven? (Inflation: A Topical Business Problem? With English summary.) *Econ. Soc. Tijdschr.*, April 1973, *27*(2), pp. 115–28.

Strotz, Robert H. and Wright, Colin. Externalities, Welfare Economics, and Environmental Problems. In *Boulding, K. E.; Pfaff, M. and Pfaff, A., eds.*, 1973, pp. 359–73.

Stroup, Richard and Baden, John. Externality, Property Rights, and the Management of our National Forests. *J. Law Econ.*, October 1973, *16*(2), pp. 303–12.

───── **and Gwartney, James.** Measurement of Employment Discrimination According to Sex. *Southern Econ. J.*, April 1973, *39*(4), pp. 575–87.

Strout, Alan M. Foreign Capital and Indonesian Economic Growth. *Bull. Indonesian Econ. Stud.*, July 1973, *9*(2), pp. 77–90.

───── Foreign Capital and Indonesian Economic Growth: A Reply. *Bull. Indonesian Econ. Stud.*, July 1973, *9*(2), pp. 96–99.

Strumpel, Burkhard. Economic Life-Styles, Values, and Subjective Welfare—An Empirical Approach. In *Sheldon, E. B., ed.*, 1973, pp. 69–125.

─────; **Schmiedeskamp, Jay and Schwartz, M. Susan.** The Function of Consumer Attitude Data Beyond Econometric Forecasts. In *Mandell, L., et al., eds.*, 1973, pp. 263–88.

─────; **Zahn, E. and Katona, George.** The Sociocultural Environment. In *Thorelli, H. B., ed.,* 1973, pp. 135–45.

Struyk, Raymond J. Explaining Variations in the Hourly Wage Rates of Urban Minority Group Females. *J. Human Res.,* Summer 1973, *8*(3), pp. 349–64.

—— Price Determinants in the Republic of Vietnam, 1966–1970. *Malayan Econ. Rev.,* April 1973, *18*(1), pp. 74–80.

Strydom, P. D. F. Some Observations on Monetary Policy. *S. Afr. J. Econ.,* September 1973, *41*(3), pp. 234–56.

Studenmund, A. H. A Cross-Sectional Analysis of the Law of Declining International Trade. *Western Econ. J.,* December 1973, *11*(4), pp. 481–86.

Studer, Tobias. Untersuchungen über das Wachstum der Schweizer Städte. (Investigations Upon the Growth of Swiss Towns. With English summary.) *Schweiz. Z. Volkswirtsch. Statist.,* June 1973, *109*(2), pp. 187–99.

Stull, William J. A Note on Residential Bid Price Curves. *J. Reg. Sci.,* April 1973, *13*(1), pp. 107–13.

Sturdivant, Frederick D. Rationality and Racism in the Ghetto Marketplace. *Soc. Sci. Quart.,* September 1973, *54*(2), pp. 380–83.

—— and **Wilhelm, Walter T.** Poverty, Minorities, and Consumer Exploitation. In *Murray, B. B., ed.,* 1973, pp. 447–54.

Sturges, R. P. and de Marchi, N. B. Malthus and Ricardo's Inductivist Critics: Four Letters to William Whewell. *Economica, N.S.,* November 1973, *40*(160), pp. 379–93.

Sturgess, Ian. The Prospects of UK Cereal Surpluses. *Nat. Westminster Bank Quart. Rev.,* February 1973, pp. 35–45.

Sturgis, Richard B. and Clemente, Frank. Population Size and Industrial Diversification: A Rejoinder. *Urban Stud.,* October 1973, *10*(3), pp. 397.

Sturm, A. B.; Deane, R. S. and Lumsden, M. A. Some Simulation Experiments with a New Zealand Model. In *Deane, R. S., ed.,* 1972, pp. 15–64.

Sturmthal, Adolf. Industrial Relations Strategies. In *Sturmthal, A. and Scoville, J. G., eds.,* 1973, pp. 1–33.

Sturrock, Ford. The Comparative Viewpoint. In *Richards, A. I.; Sturrock, F. and Fortt, J. M., eds.,* 1973, pp. 306–19.

—— and **Hougham, D. A.** The Farms—Present-day Organisation. In *Richards, A. I.; Sturrock, F. and Fortt, J. M., eds.,* 1973, pp. 150–78.

Stutz, Frederick P. Distance and Network Effects on Urban Social Travel Fields. *Econ. Geogr.,* April 1973, *49*(2), pp. 134–44.

Su, Teddy T. Skill Obsolescence and Training: Comment. *Southern Econ. J.,* April 1973, *39*(4), pp. 645–48.

Subramaniam, V. Has the Indian Economy "Taken-Off" *Econ. Aff.,* August 1973, *18*(8), pp. 381–88.

Sudarsana Rao, J. and Krishnamoorthy, M. Some Characteristics of Project Duration for a Class of Stochastic Activity Networks. In *Ross, M., ed.,* 1973, pp. 509–18.

Sudit, Ephraim F. Additive Nonhomogeneous Production Functions in Telecommunications. *Bell J. Econ. Manage. Sci.,* Autumn 1973, *4*(2), pp. 499–514.

Sudman, Seymour and Bradburn, Norman M. Effects of Time and Memory Factors on Response in Surveys. *J. Amer. Statist. Assoc.,* December 1973, *68*(344), pp. 805–15.

Sufrin, Sidney C. and Henning, John A. Japan: Steady State or Explosion. *Rivista Int. Sci. Econ. Com.,* August-September 1973, *20*(8–9), pp. 786–93.

—— and **Wagner, Abraham.** U.S. Employment and Growth in the Immediate Future: A Guess. *Rivista Int. Sci. Econ. Com.,* January 1973, *20*(1), pp. 63–71.

Sugden, Robert and Williams, Alan. The Location Choices of Students in Lodgings and Flats. *Urban Stud.,* February 1973, *10*(1), pp. 87–90.

Suits, Daniel B. and Sommers, Paul M. Analysis of Net Interstate Migration. *Southern Econ. J.,* October 1973, *40*(2), pp. 193–201.

Šujan, Ivan and Tkáč, Miloslav. The Econometric Forecasting Model of Czechoslovakia. *Econ. Planning,* 1973, *13*(1–2), pp. 15–31.

Suliman, Ali A. Fiscal Incentives for Industrial Investment in the Sudan. *Bull. Int. Fiscal Doc.,* August 1973, *27*(8), pp. 315–23.

Sullivan, Jeremiah M. The Influence of Cause-Specific Mortality Conditions on the Age Pattern of Mortality with Special Reference to Taiwan. *Population Stud.,* March 1973, *27*(1), pp. 135–58.

Sully, Floyd; Evans, R. G. and Parish, E. M. A. Medical Productivity, Scale Effects, and Demand Generation. *Can. J. Econ.,* August 1973, *6*(3), pp. 376–93.

Sultan, Ralph. Product Line Pricing and Technological Change: The Case of Sophisticated Electrical Machinery. In *Weston, J. F. and Ornstein, S. I., eds.,* 1973, pp. 163–79.

Suman, H. N. P. S. Effect of Corporate Taxation on Saving and Capital Formation in Some Indian Industries. *Econ. Aff.,* November-December 1973, *18*(11–12), pp. 485–96.

Summers, Anita A. Equity in School Financing: The Courts Move In. *Fed. Res. Bank Bus. Rev. Phila.,* March 1973, pp. 3–13.

Summers, Gene F.; Beck, E. M. and Dotson, Louis. Effects of Industrial Development on Heads of Households. *Growth Change,* July 1973, *4*(3), pp. 16–19.

Summers, John O.; Kraft, Frederic B. and Granbois, Donald H. Brand Evaluation and Brand Choice: A Longitudinal Study. *J. Marketing Res.,* August 1973, *10*(3), pp. 235–41.

Summers, Robert. International Price Comparisons Based Upon Incomplete Data. *Rev. Income Wealth,* March 1973, *19*(1), pp. 1–16.

Sumner, M. T. Announcement Effects of Profits Taxation. In *Parkin, M., ed.,* 1973, pp. 17–32.

—— Investment and Corporate Taxation. *J. Polit. Econ.,* July-August 1973, *81*(4), pp. 982–93.

—— Recent Changes in Fiscal Investment Incentives: A Postscript. *Manchester Sch. Econ. Soc. Stud.,* June 1973, *41*(2), pp. 235–39.

Sun, Nai-Ching and Bunamo, Michael C. Competition for Handling U.S. Foreign Trade Cargoes: The Port of New York's Experience. *Econ. Geogr.,* April 1973, *49*(2), pp. 156–62.

Sundaram, K. Education and Class Structure: Further Evidence from India. *World Devel.*, May 1973, *1*(5), pp. 37–40.

Sundblom, Dan J. Investeringsbeslutets systematik. (Classification of Investment Decision. With English summary.) *Ekon. Samfundets Tidskr.*, 1973, *26*(3), pp. 177–200.

Sundem, Gary L. and May, Robert G. Cost of Information and Security Prices: Market Association Tests for Accounting Policy Decisions. *Accounting Rev.*, January 1973, *48*(1), pp. 80–94.

Sundquist, James L. Where Shall They Live? In *Rasmussen, D. W. and Haworth, C. T., eds.*, 1973, pp. 247–59.

Sundrum, R. M. Consumer Expenditure Patterns: An Analysis of the Socio-Economic Surveys. *Bull. Indonesian Econ. Stud.*, March 1973, *9*(1), pp. 86–106.

—— Money Supply and Prices: A Re-interpretation. *Bull. Indonesian Econ. Stud.*, November 1973, *9*(3), pp. 73–86.

—— **and Arndt, H. W.** Foreign Capital and Indonesian Economic Growth: A Comment. *Bull. Indonesian Econ. Stud.*, July 1973, *9*(2), pp. 90–95.

Sunkel, Osvaldo. The Pattern of Latin American Dependence. In *Urquidi, V. L. and Thorp, R., eds.*, 1973, pp. 3–25.

—— Transnational Capitalism and National Disintegration in Latin America. *Soc. Econ. Stud.*, March 1973, *22*(1), pp. 132–76.

Sunley, Emil M., Jr. Towards a More Neutral Investment Tax Credit. *Nat. Tax J.*, June 1973, *26*(2), pp. 209–20.

Supple, Barry. Thinking About Economic Development. In *Youngson, A. J., ed.*, 1973, pp. 19–35.

Suranyi-Unger, Theodore, Jr. Consumer Behavior and the Hypothesis of Standardized Choice. *Z. Nationalökon.*, 1973, *33*(3–4), pp. 325–51.

Surrey, A. J. and Bromley, A. J. Energy Resources. In *Cole, H. S. D., et al., eds.*, 1973, pp. 90–107.

Surrey, Stanley S. Tax Expenditures and Tax Reform. In *Haveman, R. H. and Hamrin, R. D., eds.*, 1973, pp. 82–91.

Suslov, I. Technical Progress and Effectiveness of Agriculture. *Prob. Econ.*, January 1973, *15*(9), pp. 47–60.

Susman, Gerald I. Job Enlargement: Effects of Culture on Worker Responses. *Ind. Relat.*, February 1973, *12*(1), pp. 1–15.

Sussman, Zvi. The Determination of Wages for Unskilled Labor in the Advanced Sector of the Dual Economy of Mandatory Palestine. *Econ. Develop. Cult. Change*, October 1973, *22*(1), pp. 95–113.

Sussna, Edward and Moyer, R. Charles. Registered Bank Holding Company Acquisition: A Cross-Section Analysis. *J. Financial Quant. Anal.*, September 1973, *8*(4), pp. 647–61.

Sussna, Stephen. Residential Densities or a Fool's Paradise. *Land Econ.*, February 1973, *49*(1), pp. 1–13.

Susuki, Shigemichi. A Method of Planning Yard Pass Trains on a General Network. In *Ross, M., ed.*, 1973, pp. 353–61.

Sutch, Richard and Ransom, Roger. The Ex-Slave in the Post-Bellum South: A Study of the Economic Impact of Racism in a Market Environment. *J.*

Econ. Hist., March 1973, *33*(1), pp. 131–48.

Suttmeier, Richard P. and Orleans, Leo A. The Mao Ethic and Environmental Quality. In *Wilber, C. K., ed.*, 1973, pp. 258–65.

Sutton, C. J. Management Behaviour and a Theory of Diversification. *Scot. J. Polit. Econ.*, February 1973, *20*(1), pp. 27–42.

Suzuki, Keisuke and Parr, John B. Settlement Populations and the Lognormal Distribution. *Urban Stud.*, October 1973, *10*(3), pp. 335–52.

Suzumura, Kotaro. Boundedness of the Closed Economy with Samuelson-Leontief Technology. *Hitotsubashi J. Econ.*, February 1973, *13*(2), pp. 43–46.

—— The Economic Theory of Organization and Planning: A Review Article. *Econ. Stud. Quart.*, April 1973, *24*(1), pp. 33–51.

—— Professor Uzawa's Equivalence Theorem: A Note. *Econ. Stud. Quart.*, August 1973, *24*(2), pp. 67–70.

Švábová, Milada and Marunová, Eva. Zobecnění MODI-metody pro žiskání optimálního řešení jednoho typu trojrozměrného dopravního problému. (Generalization of Modi-Method for Getting the Optimal Solution of One Type of Three-Dimensional Transportation Problem. With English summary.) *Ekon.-Mat. Obzor*, 1973, *9*(2), pp. 201–11.

Svendsen, K. E. Economic Theory and Public Policy. In *Livingstone, I., et al., eds.*, 1973, pp. 66–72.

Swamy, Dalip S. Optimum Interest Rates on Bank Deposits. *Indian Econ. J.*, April-June 1973, *20* (4–5), pp. 630–37.

Swamy, P. A. V. B. Criteria, Constraints and Multicollinearity in Random Coefficient Regression Models. *Ann. Econ. Soc. Measure*, October 1973, *2*(4), pp. 429–50.

—— **and Mehta, J. S.** Bayesian Analysis of a Bivariate Normal Distribution with Incomplete Observations. *J. Amer. Statist. Assoc.*, December 1973, *68*(344), pp. 922–27.

—— **and Mehta, J. S.** Bayesian Analysis of Error Components Regression Models. *J. Amer. Statist. Assoc.*, September 1973, *68*(343), pp. 648–58.

Swamy, Subramanian. Economic Growth in China and India, 1952–1970: A Comparative Appraisal. *Econ. Develop. Cult. Change*, Part II, July 1973, *21*(4), pp. 1–84.

Swan, Craig. Housing Subsidies and Housing Starts. *Amer. Real Estate Urban Econ. Assoc. J.*, Fall 1973, *1*(2), pp. 119–40.

—— The Markets for Housing and Housing Services: Comment. *J. Money, Credit, Banking*, November 1973, *5*(4), pp. 960–72.

Swan, Philip L. Decentralization and the Growth of Urban Manufacturing Employment. *Land Econ.*, May 1973, *49*(2), pp. 212–16.

—— The International Diffusion of an Innovation. *J. Ind. Econ.*, September 1973, *22*(1), pp. 61–69.

Swan, P. L. and Sieper, E. Monopoly and Competition in the Market for Durable Goods. *Rev. Econ. Stud.*, July 1973, *40*(3), pp. 333–51.

Swanson, Dorothy. Annual Bibliography of Periodical Articles on American Labor History, 1972. *Labor Hist.*, Fall 1973, *14*(4), pp. 580–98.

Swanson, E. R. and Finke, Jeffrey. Diversification in

Illinois Crop Production: 1938–1970. *Ill. Agr. Econ.*, January 1973, *13*(1), pp. 8–11.

_____ and Narayanan, A. V. S. Evaluation of the Effect of Alternative Agricultural Systems on Water Quality: A Linear Programming Approach. In *Judge, G. G. and Takayama, T., eds.*, 1973, pp. 676–87.

_____ and Taylor, C. R. Experimental Nitrogen Response Functions, Actual Farm Experience and Policy Analysis. *Ill. Agr. Econ.*, July 1973, *13* (2), pp. 26–32.

_____; Taylor, C. R. and Welch, L. F. Economically Optimal Levels of Nitrogen Fertilizer for Corn: An Analysis Based on Experimental Data, 1966–71. *Ill. Agr. Econ.*, July 1973, *13*(2), pp. 16–25.

Swanson, Gerald J.; Due, John F. and Friedlaender, Ann F. Estimating Sales Tax Revenue Changes in Response to Changes in Personal Income and Sales Tax Rates. *Nat. Tax J.*, March 1973, *26*(1), pp. 103–10.

Swanston, David. Poverty and Poor Health. In *Levitan, S. A., ed.*, 1973, pp. 175–97.

Swanston, Walterene. Community Organizations: The Voice of the Poor. In *Levitan, S. A., ed.*, 1973, pp. 198–225.

Sweeney, Richard J. and Sanchez, Nicolas. The Allocation of Tariff Revenues and Optimum Trade Distortion. With Empirical Applications to United States Sugar Policy. *Weltwirtsch. Arch.*, 1973, *109*(3), pp. 382–401.

Sweezy, Paul M. and Magdoff, Harry. The Merger Movement: A Study in Power. In *Andreano, R. L., ed.*, 1973, pp. R328–19.

Swidler, Joseph C. The Challenge to State Regulation Agencies: The Experience of New York State. *Ann. Amer. Acad. Polit. Soc. Sci.*, November 1973, *410*, pp. 106–19.

Swidrowski, Jozef. Export Controls and Export Promotion. *S. Afr. J. Econ.*, March 1973, *41*(1), pp. 49–59.

Swinth, Robert L.; Tollefson, John O. and Gaumnitz, Jack E. Simulation of Water Recreation Users' Decisions. *Land Econ.*, August 1973, *49*(3), pp. 269–77.

Swisher, Idella G. The Disabled and the Decline in Men's Labor Force Participation. *Mon. Lab. Rev.*, November 1973, *96*(11), pp. 53.

Swoboda, Alexander K. Monetary Policy under Fixed Exchange Rates: Effectiveness, the Speed of Adjustment and Proper Use. *Economica, N.S.*, May 1973, *40*(158), pp. 136–54.

_____ Policy Conflict, Inconsistent Goals, and the Coordination of Economic Policies. In *Johnson, H. G. and Swoboda, A. K., eds.*, 1973, pp. 133–42.

Sycheva, L. Economic Foundations of an Optimal Combination of Accumulation and Consumption on Collective Farms. *Prob. Econ.*, February 1973, *15*(10), pp. 46–61.

Syed, Hasan A. Demand for and Supply of Pulses in the Punjab. *Pakistan Econ. Soc. Rev.*, Winter 1973, *11*(4), pp. 363–77.

Sykes, Allen and Merrett, A. J. Return on Equities and Fixed Interest Securities: 1919–66. In *Lister, R. J., ed.*, 1973, pp. 28–38.

Sylla, Richard. Economic History "Von Unten Nach

Oben" and "Von Oben Nach Unten": A Reply to Fritz Redlich. *Exploration Econ. Hist.*, Spring 1973, *10*(3), pp. 315–18.

Symanski, Richard and Webber, M. J. Periodic Markets: An Economic Location Analysis. *Econ. Geogr.*, July 1973, *49*(3), pp. 213–27.

Syron, Richard F. Administered Prices and the Market Reaction: The Case of Urban Core Property Insurance. *J. Finance*, March 1973, *28*(1), pp. 147–56.

Syrquin, Moshe. Efficient Input Frontiers for the Manufacturing Sector in Mexico 1965–1980. *Int. Econ. Rev.*, October 1973, *14*(3), pp. 657–75.

Szabó, I. Economic Associations of Farming Cooperatives. *Acta Oecon.*, 1973, *11*(1), pp. 51–64.

Szabó, K. A Few Thoughts on the Evolution of a Uniform Marxist Theory of the Firm. *Acta Oecon.*, 1973, *11*(4), pp. 325–45.

Szakolczai, G. Capital Taxes, Self-Financing and Capital Transfer. *Acta Oecon.*, 1973, *10*(3–4), pp. 361–76.

Székely, B. and Szepesi, Gy. Some Features of the Economic Structure: An International Comparison. *Acta Oecon.*, 1973, *10*(2), pp. 129–46.

Szepesi, Gy. and Székely, B. Some Features of the Economic Structure: An International Comparison. *Acta Oecon.*, 1973, *10*(2), pp. 129–46.

Szeplaki, Leslie. Elements of Risk and Information in Business Decisions: Principles and Methodology. *Rivista Int. Sci. Econ. Com.*, April 1973, *20* (4), pp. 358–70.

_____ A Note on the Redistributive Effects of Socialist Wage and Price Policies. *Rivista Int. Sci. Econ. Com.*, November 1973, *20*(11), pp. 1109–15.

_____ Pricing and Taxation in a Marxian Two-Sector Model: A Brief Reflection. *J. Econ. Theory*, August 1973, *6*(4), pp. 404–08.

_____ Some Reflections on Marxian Equilibria and Socialist Economic Policy. *Indian Econ. J.*, January-March 1973, *20*(3), pp. 431–39.

Szilágyi, Gyorgy; Csernok, Attila and Ehrlich, Eva. Numerical Results of an International Comparison of Infrastructure Development Over the Last 100 Years. *Europ. Econ. Rev.*, April 1973, *4*(1), pp. 63–65.

Szpigel, Bernardo. Optimal Train Scheduling on a Single Track Railway. In *Ross, M., ed.*, 1973, pp. 343–52.

Szucs, Ferenc K. The Impact of Electoral Systems on Environmental Amelioration: A Comparative Study of London and Liege. In *Gabriel, R. A. and Cohen, S. H., eds.*, 1973, pp. 154–70.

Szybillo, George J. and Heslin, Richard. Resistance to Persuasion: Inoculation Theory in a Marketing Context. *J. Marketing Res.*, November 1973, *10* (4), pp. 396–403.

Szychowski, Mario L. Consideraciones analíticas respecto a un sistema alternativo del impuesto inmobiliario. (Analytical Considerations Regarding a System of Alternative Real Estate Tax. With English summary.) *Económica*, May-August 1973, *19*(2), pp. 201–16.

Tabb, William K. Black Power–Green Power. In *Reynolds, L. G.; Green, G. D. and Lewis, D. R., eds.*, 1973, pp. 284–99.

_____ and Miller, Stephen M. A New Look at a Pure

Theory of Local Expenditures. *Nat. Tax J.*, June 1973, *26*(2), pp. 161–76.

Taeuber, Richard C. Problems of Access: Some Comments. *Ann. Econ. Soc. Measure*, April 1973, *2*(2), pp. 215–20.

Taft, Philip. Internal Union Structure and Functions. In *Somers, G. G., ed.*, 1973, pp. 1–9.

Tagat, R. G. and Kaur, Surinderjit. India's Green Revolution: Socio-Economic and Political Implications. *Econ. Aff.*, September-October 1973, *18*(9–10), pp. 414–27, 433.

Taggart, R. and Levitan, S. A. Employment-Earnings Inadequacy: A Measure of Welfare. *Mon. Lab. Rev.*, October 1973, *96*(10), pp. 19–27.

Tagliacarne, Guglielmo. The Regions Twenty Years Later: Socio-Economic Dynamics of the Regions Between 1951 and 1971. *Rev. Econ. Cond. Italy*, May 1973, *27*(3), pp. 127–61.

Tahir, Pervez. Soviet Economic Reform: Progress and Problems. *Pakistan Develop. Rev.*, Spring 1973, *12*(1), pp. 62–67.

Tahmassebi, H. The General Equilibrium Analysis of Customs Union. *Tahq. Eq.*, Winter & Spring 1973, *10*(29 & 30), pp. 146–69.

Taira, Koji. Labor Markets, Unions, and Employers in Inter-war Japan. In *Sturmthal, A. and Scoville, J. G., eds.*, 1973, pp. 149–77.

—— **and Standing, Guy.** Labor Market Effects of Multinational Enterprises in Latin America. *Nebr. J. Econ. Bus.*, Autumn 1973, *12*(4), pp. 103–17.

Takagi, Tadao. Il problema salariale in Giappone. (Wage Problems in Japan. With English summary.) *Rivista Int. Sci. Econ. Com.*, August-September 1973, *20*(8–9), pp. 804–38.

Takayama, Akira and El-Hodiri, Mohamed. Behavior of the Firm Under Regulatory Constraint: Clarifications. *Amer. Econ. Rev.*, March 1973, *63*(1), pp. 235–37.

Takayama, T. and Pandey, V. K. Temporal Equilibrium Analysis of Rice and Wheat in India. In *Judge, G. G. and Takayama, T., eds.*, 1973, pp. 579–96.

—— **and Pant, S. P.** An Investigation of Agricultural Planning Models: A Case Study of the Indian's Food Economy. In *Judge, G. G. and Takayama, T., eds.*, 1973, pp. 597–623.

Takeuchi, Keiichi. Tendenze recenti degli studi di geografia economica in Giappone. (Recent Trends in the Studies of Economic Geography in Japan. With English summary.) *Rivista Int. Sci. Econ. Com.*, August-September 1973, *20*(8–9), pp. 918–26.

Talbot, Joseph E., Jr. Wage Changes and Bargaining Gains in 1972. *Mon. Lab. Rev.*, April 1973, *96*(4), pp. 17–20.

Talbot, Ross B. Effect of Domestic Political Groups and Forces on U.S. Trade Policy. In *Iowa State University Center for Agricultural and Rural Development*, 1973, pp. 141–54.

Talley, Ronald J. A "Real" Explanation of Interest Rate Movements. *Quart. Rev. Econ. Bus.*, Winter 1973, *13*(4), pp. 7–17.

Talonen, Pentti. Näkökohtia yrityksen kasvusta ja kannattavuudesta. Osa II. (Growth and Profitability of the Firm. Part II. With English summary.) *Liiketaloudellinen Aikak.*, 1973, *22*(4), pp. 248–62.

Tanago, A. G. and Hardaker, J. B. Assessment of the Output of a Stochastic Decision Model. *Australian J. Agr. Econ.*, December 1973, *17*(3), pp. 170–78.

Tan Boon Ann; Corsa, Leslie and Johnson, J. Timothy. Assessment of Family Planning Programme Effects on Births: Preliminary Results Obtained through Direct Matching of Birth and Programme Acceptor Records. *Population Stud.*, March 1973, *27*(1), pp. 85–96.

Tannenbaum, Robert and Schmidt, Warren H. How to Choose a Leadership Pattern. *Harvard Bus. Rev.*, May-June 1973, *51*(3), pp. 162–80.

Tanner, J. Ernest and Hodgins, Cyril D. Forecasting Non-residential Building Construction. *Can. J. Econ.*, February 1973, *6*(1), pp. 79–89.

Tantazzi, Angelo. Il controllo dei prezzi industriali. (The Control of Industrial Prices. With English summary.) *L'industria, N. S.*, 1973, (1), pp. 39–56.

Tapiero, Charles S. and Leinekugel-Le-Cocq, Armand R. Investissements, utilisation de capacité productive et amortissement: politiques optimales. (Investments, Capacity Utilization and Depreciation: Optimal Policies. With English summary.) *Revue Écon.*, May 1973, *24*(3), pp. 442–59.

Taplin, G. B. A Model of World Trade. In *Ball, R. J., ed.*, 1973, pp. 177–223.

Taqieddin, Nureddin and Gardner, B. Delworth. Net Migration and Population Distribution in the State of Utah. *Intermountain Econ. Rev.*, Fall 1973, *4*(2), pp. 32–44.

Tarantelli, Ezio and Modigliani, Franco. A Generalization of the Phillips Curve for a Developing Country. *Rev. Econ. Stud.*, April 1973, *40*(2), pp. 203–23.

Tarasanar, Hsiung. Recent Developments on the Gold Front. *Fed. Res. Bank Bus. Rev. Phila.*, November 1973, pp. 12–13.

Tarascio, Vincent J. The Pareto Law of Income Distribution. *Soc. Sci. Quart.*, December 1973, *54*(3), pp. 525–33.

—— Vilfredo Pareto: On the Occasion of the Translation of His Manuel. *Can. J. Econ.*, August 1973, *6*(3), pp. 394–408.

Tardos, M. Necessity of Direct Connections between Productive Enterprises and Difficulties of Their Development in the Foreign Trade between CMEA Countries. (In Russian. With English summary.) *Acta Oecon.*, 1973, *11*(4), pp. 369–80.

Tarnovsky, I. O. The Role of Market in the Socialist Economic Integration. In *Kiss, T., ed.*, 1973, pp. 41–48.

Tarpley, Fred A., Jr. and Kaatz, John R. Economies of Scale and Holding Company Affiliation in Banking: Comment. *Southern Econ. J.*, July 1973, *40*(1), pp. 140.

Tatalovich, Anne. John Stuart Mill: The Subjection of Women: An Analysis. *Southern Quart.*, October 1973, *12*(1), pp. 87–105.

Tate, Merle W. and Hyer, Leon A. Inaccuracy of the X^2 Test of Goodness of Fit when Expected Frequencies Are Small. *J. Amer. Statist. Assoc.*,

December 1973, *68*(344), pp. 836–41.

Tatemoto, M. and Moriguchi, C. An Econometric Analysis of a Bilateral Model of International Economic Activity: Japan and U.S.A. In *Ball, R. J., ed.,* 1973, pp. 367–93.

Tatham, Ronald L. and Dornoff, Ronald J. A Cautionary Note on Innovative Overlap. *J. Marketing Res.,* May 1973, *10*(2), pp. 224–25.

Taubman, Paul J. Occupational Coding. *Ann. Econ. Soc. Measure,* January 1973, *2*(1), pp. 71–87.

_____ **and Wales, Terence J.** Higher Education, Mental Ability, and Screening. *J. Polit. Econ.,* January-February 1973, *81*(1), pp. 28–55.

Tavela, John. If a Citation is Appealed. *Mon. Lab. Rev.,* August 1973, *96*(8), pp. 43–47.

Tavis, Lee A. and McEnally, Richard W. Further Studies of Property-Liability Return Adequacy: Comment. *J. Risk Ins.,* September 1973, *40*(3), pp. 453–60.

_____ **and Merville, Larry J.** A Generalized Model for Capital Investment. *J. Finance,* March 1973, *28*(1), pp. 109–18.

_____ **and Merville, Larry J.** Optimal Working Capital Policies: A Chance-Constrained Programming Approach. *J. Financial Quant. Anal.,* January 1973, *8*(1), pp. 47–59.

Taylor, Carl E. Nutrition and Population. In *Berg, A.; Scrimshaw, N. S. and Call, D. L., eds.,* 1973, pp. 74–80.

Taylor, C. R. An Analysis of Nitrate Concentrations in Illinois Streams. *Ill. Agr. Econ.,* January 1973, *13*(1), pp. 12–19.

_____ **and Swanson, E. R.** Experimental Nitrogen Response Functions, Actual Farm Experience and Policy Analysis. *Ill. Agr. Econ.,* July 1973, *13* (2), pp. 26–32.

_____; **Welch, L. F. and Swanson, E. R.** Economically Optimal Levels of Nitrogen Fertilizer for Corn: An Analysis Based on Experimental Data, 1966–71. *Ill. Agr. Econ.,* July 1973, *13*(2), pp. 16–25.

Taylor, Frank F. The Tourist Industry in Jamaica, 1919–1939. *Soc. Econ. Stud.,* June 1973, *22*(2), pp. 205–28.

Taylor, George W. Collective Bargaining in the Public Sector. In *Somers, G. G., ed.,* 1973, pp. 27–35.

Taylor, James R. Industrialization of the Mexican Border Region. *N. Mex. Bus.,* March 1973, *26*(3), pp. 3–9.

_____ **and Kinnear, Thomas C.** The Effect of Ecological Concern on Brand Perceptions. *J. Marketing Res.,* May 1973, *10*(2), pp. 191–97.

Taylor, Jim and Godfrey, Leslie G. Earnings Changes in the United Kingdom, 1954–70: Excess Labour Supply, Expected Inflation and Union Influence. *Oxford Bull. Econ. Statist.,* August 1973, *35*(3), pp. 197–216.

Taylor, Lance. Investment Project Analysis in Terms of a Model of Optical Growth: The Case of Chile. In *Eckaus, R. S. and Rosenstein-Rodan, P. N., eds.,* 1973, pp. 167–98.

_____ Neoclassical Projections of Foreign Exchange Needs in Chile. In *Eckaus, R. S. and Rosenstein-Rodan, P. N., eds.,* 1973, pp. 327–40.

_____ Two Generalizations of Discounting. In *Eck-*

aus, R. S. and Rosenstein-Rodan, P. N., eds., 1973, pp. 31–45.

_____ **and Bacha, Edmar.** Foreign Exchange Shadow Prices: A Critical Review of Current Theories. In *Eckaus, R. S. and Rosenstein-Rodan, P. N., eds.,* 1973, pp. 3–29.

_____ **and Bacha, Edmar.** Growth and Trade Distortions in Chile, and Their Implications in Calculating the Shadow Price of Foreign Exchange. In *Eckaus, R. S. and Rosenstein-Rodan, P. N., eds.,* 1973, pp. 121–46.

_____; **Bergendorff, Hans G. and Clark, Peter B.** Welfare Gains from Optimization in Dynamic Planning Models. *Econ. Planning,* 1973, *13*(1–2), pp. 75–90.

_____ **and Selowsky, Marcelo.** The Economics of Malnourished Children: An Example of Disinvestment in Human Capital. *Econ. Develop. Cult. Change,* October 1973, *22*(1), pp. 17–30.

Taylor, Ryland A. Resource Misallocation in Hospital Care: Comment. *Rev. Soc. Econ.,* October 1973, *31*(2), pp. 199–201.

Taylor, Vincent D. Incentives for Inefficiency in Medicare and Medicaid. In *Haveman, R. H. and Hamrin, R. D., eds.,* 1973, pp. 238–42.

Taylor, Walton and Prohaska, Charles R. Minimizing Losses in a Hostile Environment: The Costs of Defending One's Castle. *J. Risk Ins.,* September 1973, *40*(3), pp. 375–87.

Taymans, A. L. The Use of Productivity Gains in the Price Control Program of the United States. *Econ. Soc. Tijdschr.,* April 1973, *27*(2), pp. 181–90.

Teague, J. and Eilon, S. Productivity Measurement: A Brief Survey. *Appl. Econ.,* June 1973, *5*(2), pp. 133–45.

Tearle, D. and Gregory, R. G. Product Differentiation and International Trade Flows: An Application of the "Hedonic" Regression Technique. *Australian Econ. Pap.,* June 1973, *12*(20), pp. 79–90.

Tearney, Michael G. and Wolk, Harry I. Income Tax Allocation and Loss Carryforwards: Exploring Uncharted Ground. *Accounting Rev.,* April 1973, *48*(2), pp. 292–99.

Teeters, Nancy H. The Payroll Tax and Social-Security Finance. In *Musgrave, R. A., ed.,* 1973, pp. 87–112.

Tefertiller, K. R. Rural Development in an Urban Age. *Amer. J. Agr. Econ.,* December 1973, *55*(5), pp. 771–77.

Teigeiro, José D. and Elson, R. Anthony. Export Incentives in Colombia. *Finance Develop.,* December 1973, *10*(4), pp. 30–33.

_____ The Export Promotion System and the Growth of Minor Exports in Colombia. *Int. Monet. Fund Staff Pap.,* July 1973, *20*(2), pp. 419–70.

Telesio, Piero; de la Torre, Jose, Jr. and Stobaugh, Robert B. U.S. Multinational Enterprises and Changes in the Skill Composition of U.S. Employment. In *Kujawa, D., ed.,* 1973, pp. 127–43.

Telser, L. G. Searching for the Lowest Price. *Amer. Econ. Rev.,* May 1973, *63*(2), pp. 40–49.

Temin, Peter. Labor Scarcity in America. In *Temin, P., ed.,* 1973, pp. 165–80.

_____ **and Fisher, Franklin M.** Returns to Scale in Research and Development: What Does the

Schumpeterian Hypothesis Imply? *J. Polit. Econ.*, January-February 1973, *81*(1), pp. 56–70.

Teodorescu, N. Mathematical Modelling of Cybernetic Systems. In *Hawkes, N., ed.*, 1973, pp. 182–94.

Teplin, Mary F. U.S. International Transactions in Royalties and Fees: Their Relationship to the Transfer of Technology. *Surv. Curr. Bus.*, December 1973, *53*(12), pp. 14–18.

Tepper, Irwin. Revealed Preference Methods and the Pure Theory of the Cost of Capital. *J. Finance*, March 1973, *28*(1), pp. 35–48.

Terhune, Kenneth W. and Kaufman, Sol. The Family Size Utility Function. *Demography*, November 1973, *10*(4), pp. 599–618.

Teriba, O. The Demand for Money in Nigeria. *Econ. Bull. Ghana, Sec. Ser.*, 1973, *3*(4), pp. 14–22.

Terleckyj, Nestor E. Measuring Performance in Education: Comment. In *Moss, M., ed.*, 1973, pp. 435–37.

Ter-Minassian, Teresa and Borpujari, Jitendra G. The Weighted Budget Balance Approach to Fiscal Analysis: A Methodology and Some Case Studies. *Int. Monet. Fund Staff Pap.*, November 1973, *20*(3), pp. 801–31.

Terre, Norbert C.; Warnke, Dale W. and Ameiss, Albert P. Cost/Benefit Analysis of Public Projects. *Manage. Account.*, January 1973, *54*(7), pp. 34–37.

Terrell, R. D. and Hannan, E. J. Multiple Equation Systems with Stationary Errors. *Econometrica*, March 1973, *41*(2), pp. 299–320.

Teubal, Morris. Comparative Advantage and Technological Change: The Learning by Doing Case. *J. Int. Econ.*, May 1973, *3*(2), pp. 161–77.

_____ Heavy and Light Industry in Economic Development. *Amer. Econ. Rev.*, September 1973, *63*(4), pp. 588–96.

Thackray, John. International Banking: What's Behind Its Rage to Innovate? In *Henley, D. S., ed.*, 1973, pp. 433–41.

Thage, Bent. Udenrigshandelen i input-output analysen. (With English summary.) *Nationalokon. Tidsskr.*, 1973, *111*(3), pp. 361–81.

Tharakan, Mathew. India's Diamond Trade with Belgium. A Case-Study in "Cross-Hauling." *Econ. Soc. Tijdschr.*, February 1973, *27*(1), pp. 39–56.

_____ Indian Exports of Selected Primary Products and Semi-Manufactures to European Community. Problems and Prospects. *Tijdschr. Econ.*, 1973, *18*(2), pp. 235–61.

Thatcher, Lionel W. and Thompson, Howard E. Required Rate of Return for Equity Capital Under Conditions of Growth and Consideration of Regulatory Lag. *Land Econ.*, May 1973, *49*(2), pp. 148–62.

Theil, Henri. Measuring the Quality of the Consumer's Basket. *De Economist*, July-August 1973, *121*(4), pp. 333–46.

_____ A New Index Number Formula. *Rev. Econ. Statist.*, November 1973, *55*(4), pp. 498–502.

_____ A Simple Modification of the Two-Stage Least-Squares Procedure for Undersized Samples. In *Goldberger, A. S. and Duncan, O. D., eds.*, 1973, pp. 113–29.

_____ Some Recent Developments in Consumer

Demand Analysis. In *[Tinbergen, J.]*, 1973, pp. 41–73.

_____ and Friedman, Yoram. Regional Per Capita Incomes and Income Inequalities: Point Estimates and Their Standard Errors. *J. Amer. Statist. Assoc.*, September 1973, *68*(343), pp. 531–39.

Thimmaiah, G. The Changing Role of the Australian Commonwealth Grants Commission: A Reexamination. *Public Finance*, 1973, *28*(3–4), pp. 407–19.

Thirlby, G. F. The Economist's Description of Business Behaviour. In *Buchanan, J. M. and Thirlby, G. F., eds.*, 1973, pp. 201–24.

_____ The Ruler. In *Buchanan, J. M. and Thirlby, G. F., eds.*, 1973, pp. 163–98.

_____ The Subjective Theory of Value and Accounting 'Cost'. In *Buchanan, J. M. and Thirlby, G. F., eds.*, 1973, pp. 135–61.

Thirlwall, A. P. The Recent "Shift" in the U.S. Phillips Curve. *Ind. Relat.*, October 1973, *12*(3), pp. 297–306.

_____ and Kennedy, Charles. Technological Change and the Distribution of Income: A Belated Comment. *Int. Econ. Rev.*, October 1973, *14*(3), pp. 780–84.

Thirsk, J. Field Systems of the East Midlands. In *Baker, A. R. H. and Butlin, R. A., eds.*, 1973, pp. 232–80.

Thirunarayanan, R. Functional Efficiency of Rural Banks. In *Simha, S. L. N., ed.*, 1973, pp. 115–21.

Thoburn, J. T. Exports and Economic Growth in West Malaysia. *Oxford Econ. Pap.*, March 1973, *25*(1), pp. 88–111.

_____ Exports and the Malaysian Engineering Industry: A Case Study of Backward Linkage. *Oxford Bull. Econ. Statist.*, May 1973, *35*(2), pp. 91–117.

Thomann, Robert V. Effect of Longitudinal Dispersion on Dynamic Water Quality Response of Streams and Rivers. *Water Resources Res.*, April 1973, *9*(2), pp. 355–66.

Thomas, Brian. The Structure of Retailing and Economies of Scale. *Bull. Econ. Res.*, November 1973, *25*(2), pp. 122–28.

Thomas, D. A. and Reid, G. K. R. Pastoral Production, Stocking Rate and Seasonal Conditions. *Quart. Rev. Agr. Econ.*, October 1973, *26*(4), pp. 217–27.

Thomas, David B. How Reliable Are Those Price and Employment Measures? *Fed. Res. Bank Bus. Rev. Phila.*, April 1973, pp. 17–22.

Thomas, George. Regional Migration Patterns and Poverty Among the Aged in the South. *J. Human Res.*, Winter 1973, *8*(1), pp. 73–84.

Thomas, H. The Assessment of Project Worth with Applications to Research and Development. In *Wolfe, J. N., ed.*, 1973, pp. 88–114.

_____; Hampton, J. M. and Moore, P. G. Subjective Probability and Its Measurement. *J. Roy. Statist. Soc.*, Part 1, 1973, *136*, pp. 21–42.

_____; Hull, J. and Moore, P. G. Utility and its Measurement. *J. Roy. Statist. Soc.*, Part 2, 1973, *136*, pp. 226–47.

Thomas, L. Joseph and Bierman, Harold, Jr. Airline Overbooking Strategies and Bumping Procedures. *Public Policy*, Fall 1973, *21*(4), pp. 601–06.

Thomas, Lloyd B. Behavior of Flexible Exchange Rates: Additional Tests from the Post-World War I Episode. *Southern Econ. J.,* October 1973, *40*(2), pp. 167–82.

――――― Speculation in the Flexible Exchange Revisited—Another View. *Kyklos,* 1973, *26*(1), pp. 143–50.

Thomas, R. B. On the Definition of 'Shortages' in Administered Labour Markets. *Manchester Sch. Econ. Soc. Stud.,* June 1973, *41*(2), pp. 169–86.

Thomas, R. L. Unemployment Dispersion as a Determinant of Wage Inflation in the U.K. 1925–66—A Rejoinder. *Manchester Sch. Econ. Soc. Stud.,* June 1973, *41*(2), pp. 229–33.

Thomas, Robert Paul. Style Change and the Automobile Industry During the Roaring Twenties. In *[Williamson, H. F.],* 1973, pp. 118–38.

――――― and Anderson, Terry L. White Population, Labor Force and Extensive Growth of the New England Economy in the Seventeenth Century. *J. Econ. Hist.,* September 1973, *33*(3), pp. 634–67.

――――― and North, Douglass C. European Economic Growth: Comments on the North-Thomas Theory: Reply. *Econ. Hist. Rev., 2nd Ser.,* May 1973, *26*(2), pp. 293–94.

Thomas, Robert W. and Starler, Norman H. Intergovernmental Education Grants and the Efficiency of Resource Allocation in School Districts. *Appl. Econ.,* September 1973, *5*(3), pp. 181–92.

Thomas, Warren H.; Torrance, George W. and Sackett, David L. Utility Maximization Model for Program Evaluation: A Demonstration Application. In *Berg, R. L., ed.,* 1973, pp. 156–64.

Thomas, Wayne, et al. Separable Programming for Considering Risk in Farm Planning: Reply. *Amer. J. Agr. Econ.,* February 1973, *55*(1), pp. 117–18.

Thompson, Charles W. N. and Rath, Gustave J. Planning Solutions Aided by Management and Systems Technology. *Ann. Amer. Acad. Polit. Soc. Sci.,* January 1973, *405,* pp. 151–62.

Thompson, Duane E. and Borglum, Richard P. A Case Study of Employee Attitudes and Labor Unrest. *Ind. Lab. Relat. Rev.,* October 1973, *27*(1), pp. 74–83.

Thompson, Earl A. The Private Production of Public Goods: Comment. *J. Law Econ.,* October 1973, *16*(2), pp. 407–12.

Thompson, Edward. International Protection of Performers' Rights: Some Current Problems. *Int. Lab. Rev.,* April 1973, *107*(4), pp. 303–14.

Thompson, Emmett F.; Richards, Douglas F. and Davis, Lawrence S. The South's Third Forest: A Critique. *Land Econ.,* February 1973, *49*(1), pp. 105–09.

Thompson, Fred A. The Interaction of Cognition and Affect: The Issue of Free Trade. *J. Econ. Educ.,* Spring 1973, *4*(2), pp. 111–15.

Thompson, Howard E. A Note on the Value of Rights in Estimating the Investor Capitalization Rate. *J. Finance,* March 1973, *28*(1), pp. 157–60.

――――― and Thatcher, Lionel W. Required Rate of Return for Equity Capital Under Conditions of Growth and Consideration of Regulatory Lag. *Land Econ.,* May 1973, *49*(2), pp. 148–62.

Thompson, Mark and Cairnie, James. Compulsory Arbitration: The Case of British Columbia Teach-

ers. *Ind. Lab. Relat. Rev.,* October 1973, *27*(1), pp. 3–17.

Thompson, Marvin M. and Shapiro, Gary. The Current Population Survey: An Overview. *Ann. Econ. Soc. Measure,* April 1973, *2*(2), pp. 105–29.

Thompson, Richard G.; Callen, Richard W. and Wolken, Lawrence C. A Stochastic Investment Model for a Survival Conscious Fishing Firm. In *Sokoloski, A. A., ed.,* 1973, pp. 112–20.

Thompson, Russell G. Some Suggestions for the Development of a Bioeconomic Theory of the Fishery. In *Sokoloski, A. A., ed.,* 1973, pp. 92–95.

――――― , et al. A Stochastic Investment Model for a Survival Conscious Firm Applied to Shrimp Fishing. *Appl. Econ.,* June 1973, *5*(2), pp. 75–87.

――――― and Young, H. Peyton. Forecasting Water Use for Electric Power Generation. *Water Resources Res.,* August 1973, *9*(4), pp. 800–07.

――――― and Young, H. Peyton. Forecasting Water Use for Policy Making: A Review. *Water Resources Res.,* August 1973, *9*(4), pp. 792–99.

――――― and Young, H. Peyton. Least-Cost Allocation and Valuation Model for Water Resources. *Water Resources Res.,* October 1973, *9*(5), pp. 1186–95.

Thompson, S. C. The Substitution of Analytic for Simulation Algorithms: Response. *Amer. J. Agr. Econ.,* May 1973, *55*(2), pp. 240–41.

Thompson, Wilbur R. The City as a Distorted Price System. In *Grieson, R. E., ed.,* 1973, pp. 4–14.

――――― A Preface to Suburban Economics. In *Masotti, L. H. and Hadden, J. K., eds.,* 1973, pp. 409–30.

Thomson, Herbert F. Policy Alternatives for Ohio's Electric Power Industry. *Ohio State U. Bull. Bus. Res.,* December 1973, *48*(12), pp. 1–5.

Thomson, K. J. and Hazell, P. B. R. Reliability of Using the Mean Absolute Deviation to Derive Efficient *E, V* Farm Plans: Reply. *Amer. J. Agr. Econ.,* Part I, November 1973, *55*(4), pp. 677–78.

Thomson, Michael R. Forecasting for Financial Planning. *J. Bank Res.,* Autumn 1973, *4*(3), pp. 225–31.

Thomson, Roy Herbert [Lord]. Modernization of Newspaper Techniques. In *The Diebold Group, Inc.,* 1973, pp. 310–13.

Thomson, William; Kane, Julius and Vertinsky, Ilan. KSIM: A Methodology for Interactive Resource Policy Simulation. *Water Resources Res.,* February 1973, *9*(1), pp. 65–79.

Thorbecke, Erik. The Employment Problem: A Critical Evaluation of Four ILO Comprehensive Country Reports. *Int. Lab. Rev.,* May 1973, *107* (5), pp. 393–423.

――――― Sector Analysis and Models of Agriculture in Developing Countries. *Food Res. Inst. Stud.,* 1973, *12*(1), pp. 73–89.

Thore, Sten and Eriksen, Ib. Payment Clearing Networks. *Swedish J. Econ.,* June 1973, *75*(2), pp. 143–63.

Thorelli, Hans B. International Marketing Strategy: Introduction. In *Thorelli, H. B., ed.,* 1973, pp. 11–19.

――――― International Marketing: An Ecologic View. In *Thorelli, H. B., ed.,* 1973, pp. 23–40.

――――― Simulating International Business Operations. In *Alexandrides, C. G., ed.,* 1973, pp. 1–4.

Thornton, Richard M. and Kwon, Jene K. An Examination of the Financing of Federal Home Loan Bank Advances: A Reply. *Rev. Econ. Statist.*, May 1973, *55*(2), pp. 258.

_____ The Effect of FHLB Bond Operations on Savings Inflows at Savings and Loan Associations: Reply. *J. Finance*, March 1973, *28*(1), pp. 203–06.

Thorp, Edward O. and Bicksler, James L. The Capital Growth Model: An Empirical Investigation. *J. Financial Quant. Anal.*, March 1973, *8*(2), pp. 273–87.

Thrun, Walter J., Sr. A Systems Approach to Cash Flow Determination. *Manage. Account.*, February 1973, *54*(8), pp. 29–31.

Thurber, Clarence E. Islands of Development: A Political and Social Approach to Development Administration in Latin America. In *Thurber, C. E. and Graham, L. S., eds.*, 1973, pp. 15–46.

Thurow, Lester C. Discrimination. In *Grieson, R. E., ed.*, 1973, pp. 341–63.

_____ The Income Distribution as a Pure Public Good: Response. *Quart. J. Econ.*, May 1973, *87*(2), pp. 316–19.

_____ The Political Economy of Income Redistribution Policies. *Ann. Amer. Acad. Polit. Soc. Sci.*, September 1973, *409*, pp. 146–55.

_____ Proposals for Rechanneling Funds to Meet Social Priorities. In *Federal Reserve Bank of Boston*, 1973, pp. 179–89.

_____ Redistributional Aspects of Manpower Training Programs. In *Ulman, L., ed.*, 1973, pp. 83–101.

_____ Zero Economic Growth and the Distribution of Income. In *Weintraub, A.; Schwartz, E. and Aronson, J. R., eds.*, 1973, pp. 141–53.

Thygesen, Inge. Ranking of Interdependent Investment Projects. In *Ross, M., ed.*, 1973, pp. 531–40.

Thygesen, Niels. Monetary Policy, Capital Flows and Internal Stability: Some Experiences from Large Industrial Countries. *Swedish J. Econ.*, March 1973, *75*(1), pp. 83–99.

Tice, Helen Stone and Duff, Virginia A. Basic Statistical Data. In *Goldsmith, R. W., ed.*, 1973, pp. 269–342.

Tideman, T. Nicolaus. Defining Area Distress in Unemployment. *Public Policy*, Fall 1973, *21*(4), pp. 441–92.

Tiebout, Charles M. A Method of Determining Incomes and Their Variation in Small Regions. In *Grieson, R. E., ed.*, 1973, pp. 19–25.

Tietenberg, Thomas H. Controlling Pollution by Price and Standard Systems: A General Equilibrium Analysis. *Swedish J. Econ.*, June 1973, *75*(2), pp. 193–203.

_____ Specific Taxes and the Control of Pollution: A General Equilibrium Analysis. *Quart. J. Econ.*, November 1973, *87*(4), pp. 503–22.

Till, Thomas. The Extent of Industrialization in Southern Nonmetro Labor Markets in the 1960's. *J. Reg. Sci.*, December 1973, *13*(3), pp. 453–61.

Tillman, J. A. The Efficiency of Taking First Differences in Regression Analysis: A Note. *Econ. Soc. Rev.*, July 1973, *4*(4), pp. 543–49.

Tilly, Richard H. Zeitreihen zum Geldumlauf in Deutschland, 1870–1913. (Time Series Concerning the Aggregate Money Supply in Germany, 1870–1913. With English summary.) *Jahr. Na-*

tionalökon. Statist., May 1973, *187*(4), pp. 330–63.

Tilman, Rick. Thorstein Veblen: Incrementalist and Utopian. *Amer. J. Econ. Soc.*, April 1973, *32*(2), pp. 155–69.

Tilton, John E. Research and Development in Industrial Growth: Comment. *J. Polit. Econ.*, September-October 1973, *81*(5), pp. 1245–48.

Timár, M. Results of the New System of Economic Control and Management and its Further Development. *Acta Oecon.*, 1973, *10*(3–4), pp. 277–301.

Timberg, Thomas A. Revolution and Growth: Two Case Studies from India. *Polit. Sci. Quart.*, March 1973, *88*(1), pp. 86–93.

Timbrell, M. and Johnston, J. Empirical Tests of a Bargaining Theory of Wage Rate Determination. *Manchester Sch. Econ. Soc. Stud.*, June 1973, *41*(2), pp. 141–67.

Timmaiah, G. and Metwally, Mohktar M. A Note on the Classical Utility Function for Purpose of the Theory of Taxation. *Finanzarchiv*, 1973, *31*(3), pp. 441–45.

Timmer, C. Peter. Choice of Technique in Rice Milling in Java. *Bull. Indonesian Econ. Stud.*, July 1973, *9*(2), pp. 57–76.

Tinbergen, Jan. Naar de meetbaarheid van een rechtvaardige verdeling van de helft voor de helft. Naschrift. (An Approach to the Measurement of Just Distribution of One Half for One Half: Reply. With English summary.) *De Economist*, November-December 1973, *121*(6), pp. 628–29.

_____ Naar de meetbaarheid van een rechtvaardige verdeling. (An Approach to the Measurement of a Just Distribution of Income. With English summary.) *De Economist*, March-April 1973, *121*(2), pp. 106–21.

_____ Actual, Feasible and Optimal Income Inequality in a Three-Level Education Model. *Ann. Amer. Acad. Polit. Soc. Sci.*, September 1973, *409*, pp. 156–62.

_____ Exhaustion and Technological Development: A Macro-Dynamic Policy Model. *Z. Nationalökon.*, 1973, *33*(3–4), pp. 213–34.

_____ Labour with Different Types of Skills and Jobs as Production Factors. *De Economist*, May-June 1973, *121*(3), pp. 213–24.

_____ Some Thoughts on Mature Socialism. In *Judge, G. G. and Takayama, T., eds.*, 1973, pp. 9–25.

_____ Tendencies and Determinants of Income Distribution in Western Countries—A Note. In *[Rosenstein-Rodan, P.]*, 1973, pp. 178–84.

Tindale, L. V. D. New Era in Finance. In *Rybczynski, T. M., ed.*, 1973, pp. 96–105.

Tinic, Seha M. and West, Richard R. Portfolio Returns and the Random Walk Theory: Comment. *J. Finance*, June 1973, *28*(3), pp. 733–41.

Tintner, Gerhard and Ferghali, Salwa Ali S. A Note on Stochastic Programming in a Development Plan: Reply. *Kyklos*, 1973, *26*(2), pp. 399–401.

Tisdell, Clement A. The Australian Research Subsidy to Overseas Firms and Other Aspects of the Distribution of Research Grants. *Econ. Rec.*, June 1973, *49*(126), pp. 194–214.

_____ Certainty Equivalence and Bias in the Management of Production. *Rev. Marketing Agr.*

Econ., December 1973, *41*(4), pp. 166–78.

——— A Comment on Losses from Stabilization. *Australian J. Agr. Econ.*, August 1973, *17*(2), pp. 144–45.

——— Kangaroos: The Economic Management of a Common-Property Resource Involving Interdependence of Production. *Econ. Anal. Pol.*, September 1973, *4*(2), pp. 59–75.

——— and Walsh, Cliff. Non-marginal Externalities: As Relevant and As Not. *Econ. Rec.*, September 1973, *49*(127), pp. 447–55.

Titmuss, K. and Titmuss, R. Parents' Revolt, 1942. In *Tranter, N. L., ed.*, 1973, pp. 155–62.

Titmuss, R. and Titmuss, K. Parents' Revolt, 1942. In *Tranter, N. L., ed.*, 1973, pp. 155–62.

Tivey, Leonard. British Nationalization in the 1960s. In *Tivey, L., ed.*, 1973, pp. 11–17.

Tkáč, Miloslav and Šujan, Ivan. The Econometric Forecasting Model of Czechoslovakia. *Econ. Planning*, 1973, *13*(1–2), pp. 15–31.

Toan, Arthur B., Jr. Publicly Reporting on Corporate Social Impact. In *Dierkes, M. and Bauer, R. A., eds.*, 1973, pp. 327–44.

Tobin, James. Explanation of Birth Rate Changes over Space and Time: A Study of Taiwan: Comment. *J. Polit. Econ.*, Part II, March-April 1973, *81*(2), pp. S275–78.

——— More on Inflation: Reply. *J. Money, Credit, Banking*, November 1973, *5*(4), pp. 982–84.

——— Payments Imbalances and the Demand for International Reserves: A Theoretic and Empiric Inquiry. *Econ. Int.*, August-November 1973, *26* (3–4), pp. 529–39.

——— and Nordhaus, William D. Is Growth Obsolete? In *Moss, M., ed.*, 1973, pp. 509–32.

——— and Nordhaus, William D. Is Growth Obsolete? Reply to Denison and Usher. In *Moss, M., ed.*, 1973, pp. 554–63.

——— and Nordhaus, William D. Is Growth Obsolete? Reply to Meyer. In *Moss, M., ed.*, 1973, pp. 563–64.

Tobin, Norman. Planning under Uncertainty: Discussant 2. In *Ross, M., ed.*, 1973, pp. 127–29.

——— and Butfield, Terry. The Implementation of OR Models in Planning Procedures. In *Ross, M., ed.*, 1973, pp. 363–72.

Todaro, Michael P. and Edwards, Edgar O. Educational Demand and Supply in the Context of Growing Unemployment in Less Developed Countries. *World Devel.*, March-April 1973, *1* (3–4), pp. 107–117.

Todd, M. and Freestone, R. The Effect on Store Costs of a Trial Method for Rehandling Bulk-Class Wools: A Preliminary Analysis. *Quart. Rev. Agr. Econ.*, October 1973, *26*(4), pp. 263–76.

Todd, Ralph H. Evidence of Immediate Tax Shifting in U.S. Manufacturing, 1948–1967. *Nebr. J. Econ. Bus.*, Spring 1973, *12*(2), pp. 55–63.

Toffler, Alvin. "Soft Models", Hard Data, and Social Reality. In *Hawkes, N., ed.*, 1973, pp. 195–204.

Tokita, Tadahiko. Behavior of Oligopolistic Firm and Market Adjustment—A Short Run Macroeconomic Approach. (In Japanese.) *Econ. Stud. Quart.*, April 1973, *24*(1), pp. 9–17.

——— Determination of Income and Prices in the Short Run. (In Japanese. With English summary.)

Econ. Stud. Quart., December 1973, *24*(3), pp. 31–42.

Tolksdorf, Michael. Zur ökonomischen Begründung von Ausnahmebereichen. Bemerkungen zu E. Hoppmanns Erwiderung. (Economic Reasons for Exceptions to Competitive Policy Norms—A Comment to Hoppmanns Article. With English summary.) *Jahr. Nationalökon. Statist.*, August 1973, *187*(6), pp. 543–49.

Tollefson, John O.; Gaumnitz, Jack E. and Swinth, Robert L. Simulation of Water Recreation Users' Decisions. *Land Econ.*, August 1973, *49*(3), pp. 269–77.

Tollison, Robert D.; Long, William F. and Schramm, Richard. The Economic Determinants of Antitrust Activity. *J. Law Econ.*, October 1973, *16*(2), pp. 351–64.

——— and Willet, Thomas D. Some Simple Economics of Voting and Not Voting. *Public Choice*, Fall 1973, *16*, pp. 59–71.

——— and Willett, Thomas D. The University and the Price System. *J. Econ. Bus.*, Spring-Summer 1973, *25*(3), pp. 191–97.

———; Willett, Thomas D. and Amacher, Ryan C. Import Controls on Foreign Oil: Comment. *Amer. Econ. Rev.*, December 1973, *63*(5), pp. 1031–34.

Tomasini, Luigi M. Una nota sull'incertezza e la convenienza economica della lite giudiziaria. (A Note on Uncertainty and Economic Profitability of Legal Controversy. With English summary.) *L'Industria*, January-June 1973, (1–2), pp. 125–31.

Tomek, William G. R² in TSLS and GLS Estimation. *Amer. J. Agr. Econ.*, Part I, November 1973, *55*(4), pp. 670.

Tomescu, Gh. I. Tendinţe şi resorturi ale automatizării în capitalism. (Trends and Spheres of Automation in Capitalism. With English summary.) *Stud. Cercet. Econ.*, 1973, (4), pp. 167–76.

Tomic, Radomiro. One View of Chile's Present Political and Economic Situation. In *Zammit, J. A., ed.*, 1973, pp. 31–40.

Tommissen, Piet. La notion d'idéologie dans la pensée de Pareto. (The Meaning of Ideology in Pareto's Sociological Work. With English summary.) *Rivista Int. Sci. Econ. Com.*, March 1973, *20*(3), pp. 219–41.

Toms, Miroslav. The Labor Force and Relations Within the Production Process. *Eastern Europ. Econ.*, Summer 1973, *11*(4), pp. 3–59.

——— and Klacek, Jan. Prognostický model pro krátké období. (A Short-Run Forecasting Model. With English summary.) *Ekon.-Mat. Obzor*, 1973, *9*(1), pp. 68–83.

Tontz, Robert L. U.S. Trade Policy: Background and Historical Trends. In *Iowa State University Center for Agricultural and Rural Development*, 1973, pp. 17–48.

Topham, N. and Nicholson, R. J. Step-wise Regression and Principal Components Analysis in Estimating a Relationship in an Econometric Model. *Manchester Sch. Econ. Soc. Stud.*, June 1973, *41* (2), pp. 187–205.

Topham, Neville. Micro-Economic Risk and the Social Rate of Discount. In *Parkin, M., ed.*, 1973, pp. 139–55.

Torrance, George W. A Generalized Cost-Effectiveness Model for Health Planning. In *Ross, M., ed.*, 1973, pp. 455–64.

_____; **Sackett, David L. and Thomas, Warren H.** Utility Maximization Model for Program Evaluation: A Demonstration Application. In *Berg, R. L., ed.*, 1973, pp. 156–64.

de la Torre, Jose, Jr.; Stobaugh, Robert B. and Telesio, Piero. U.S. Multinational Enterprises and Changes in the Skill Composition of U.S. Employment. In *Kujawa, D., ed.*, 1973, pp. 127–43.

Torres, James F. Concentration of Political Power and Levels of Economic Development in Latin American Countries. *J. Devel. Areas*, April 1973, *7*(3), pp. 397–409.

Torres, Juan and Levy, Michael E. Grants and Revenue Sharing Abroad: Canada, Australia, West Germany. In *Moskoff, W., ed.*, 1973, pp. 4–21.

Torto, Raymond G. and Lombra, Raymond E. Federal Reserve "Defensive" Behavior and the Reverse Causation Argument. *Southern Econ. J.*, July 1973, *40*(1), pp. 47–55.

Tosterud, Robert J. and Tyrchniewicz, Edward W. A Model for Rationalizing the Canadian Grain Transportation and Handling System on a Regional Basis. *Amer. J. Agr. Econ.*, December 1973, *55*(5), pp. 805–13.

Tower, Edward. Commercial Policy Under Fixed and Flexible Exchange Rates. *Quart. J. Econ.*, August 1973, *87*(3), pp. 436–54.

_____ **and Dean, James W.** Internal and External Balance in an "Almost Classical" World: Rejoinder. *Western Econ. J.*, June 1973, *11*(2), pp. 240.

_____ **and Dean, James W.** More on Internal and External Balance in an "Almost Classical" World. *Western Econ. J.*, June 1973, *11*(2), pp. 232–37.

_____ **and Ross, Russell.** More on the Neutrality of Forward Market Intervention. *Weltwirtsch. Arch.*, 1973, *109*(4), pp. 701–03.

Townsend, Harry. Big Business and Competition. In *Rybczynski, T. M., ed.*, 1973, pp. 68–77.

Townsend, Robert C. America Inc.: A Review. In *Andreano, R. L., ed.*, 1973, pp. R326–05.

Toye, J. F. J. Structural Changes in the Government Sector of the Indian States, 1955-70. *J. Devel. Stud.*, January 1973, *9*(2), pp. 261–77.

Tracy, Martin B. Proposed Pension Reform in United Kingdom, 1972. *Soc. Sec. Bull.*, August 1973, *36*(8), pp. 45–49.

_____ Sweden: Cash Maternity Benefits for Fathers. *Soc. Sec. Bull.*, November 1973, *36*(11), pp. 37–39.

Trąmpczyński, Bolesław. Co-operatives of the Disabled in Poland. *Int. Lab. Rev.*, November 1973, *108*(5), pp. 423–37.

Trant, G. I. Adjustment Problems and Policies Within a Framework of Political Economy. *Amer. J. Agr. Econ.*, December 1973, *55*(5), pp. 888–91.

Trantner, N. L. Population and Industrialization: Introduction. In *Tranter, N. L., ed.*, 1973, pp. 9–32.

Trapeznikov, V. Scientific-Technical Progress and the Effectiveness of Science. *Prob. Econ.*, August 1973, *16*(4), pp. 23–46.

Trebilcock, Clive. British Armaments and European Industrialization, 1890–1914. *Econ. Hist. Rev.*, 2nd Ser., May 1973, *26*(2), pp. 254–72.

Treischmann, James S. Further Studies of Property-Liability Return Adequacy: Reply. *J. Risk Ins.*, September 1973, *40*(3), pp. 462–64.

Treitel, Ralph. Recovery of Disabled After Trust Fund Financing of Rehabilitation. *Soc. Sec. Bull.*, February 1973, *36*(2), pp. 23–31.

Trejo Reyes, Saúl. Comments on DINAMICO. In *Goreux, L. M. and Manne, A. S., eds.*, 1973, pp. 173–77.

_____ EXPORTA, A Multi-Sector Model for Optimal Growth and Export Policies. In *Goreux, L. M. and Manne, A. S., eds.*, 1973, pp. 179–95.

Treml, Vladimir G. and Gallik, Dimitri, M. Teaching the History of Economic Thought in the USSR. *Hist. Polit. Econ.*, Spring 1973, *5*(1), pp. 215–42.

Trenton, R. W. Successor to Bretton Woods. *Rivista Int. Sci. Econ. Com.*, December 1973, *20*(12), pp. 1140–56.

Trescott, Paul B. Secular Price Change in Historical Perspective: Comment. *J. Money, Credit, Banking*, Part II, February 1973, *5*(1), pp. 274–78.

Trevithick, J. A. and Mulvey, C. Trade Unions and Wage Inflation. *Econ. Soc. Rev.*, January 1973, *4* (2), pp. 209–29.

Treynor, Jack L. and Black, Fischer. How to Use Security Analysis to Improve Portfolio Selection. *J. Bus.*, January 1973, *46*(1), pp. 66–86.

Trezise, Philip H. Implications for U.S. Policy toward Europe. In *Krause, L. B. and Salant, W. S., eds.*, 1973, pp. 276–83.

Trezza, Bruno. La teoria del second best: una critica. (On the Theory of Second Best: a Critique. With English summary.) *L'Industria*, January-June 1973, (1–2), pp. 18–35.

Tribe, Laurence H. Policy Science: Analysis or Ideology? In *Niskanen, W. A., et al., eds.*, 1973, pp. 3–47.

Tribe, M. Economics Textbooks for Africa. In *Livingstone, I., et al., eds.*, 1973, pp. 181–89.

Trickōvić, Vidosav. Science Policy and Development Strategy in Developing Countries. In *Williams, B. R., ed.*, 1973, pp. 287–99.

Trieschmann, James S. and Pinches, George E. A Multivariate Model for Predicting Financially Distressed P-L Insurers. *J. Risk Ins.*, September 1973, *40*(3), pp. 327–38.

Triffin, Robert. The Collapse of the International Monetary System. In *Wiegand, G. C., ed.*, 1973, pp. 46–55.

_____ The Collapse of the International Monetary System: Structural Causes and Remedies. *De Economist*, July-August 1973, *121*(4), pp. 362–74.

_____ The International Monetary Chaos and the Way Out. *J. Common Market Stud.*, September 1973, *12*(1), pp. 104–17.

_____ La crisi del sistema monetario internazionale: cause strutturali e rimedi. (The Collapse of the International Monetary System: Structural Causes and Remedies. With English summary.) *Bancaria*, April 1973, *29*(4), pp. 430–36.

Tripathy, B. N.; Pandey, Ram Lala and Mishra, G. P. Role of Banking in Financing Rural Credit. *Econ. Aff.*, July 1973, *18*(7), pp. 313–25.

Triplett, Jack E. and Merchant, Stephen M. The CPI and the PCE Deflator: An Econometric Analysis of Two Price Measures. *Ann. Econ. Soc. Measure,* July 1973, *2*(3), pp. 263–82.

———— The CPI and the PCE Deflator: An Econometric Analysis of Two Price Measures: Reply. *Ann. Econ. Soc. Measure,* July 1973, *2*(3), pp. 287–88.

Trist, Eric. A Socio-Technical Critique of Scientific Management. In *Edge, D. O. and Wolfe, J. N., eds.,* 1973, pp. 95–116.

Trivedi, P. K. Retail Inventory Investment Behaviour. *J. Econometrics,* March 1973, *1*(1), pp. 61–80.

Trivelli, Hugo and Bitar, Sergio. The Cost of Capital in the Chilean Economy. In *Eckaus, R. S. and Rosenstein-Rodan, P. N., eds.,* 1973, pp. 147–65.

Trofimenko, Martha B. Legal Aspects of Economic Centralization. In *Bandera, V. N. and Melnyk, Z. L., eds.,* 1973, pp. 328–45.

Troie, L. Cu privire la eficienţa cheltuielilor cu reparaţiile şi întreţinerea utilajelor de producţie. (Considerations on the Efficiency of Expenses for the Repair and Maintenance of Production Equipment. With English summary.) *Stud. Cercet. Econ.,* 1973, (2), pp. 99–115.

Tropp, Zvi and Sadan, Ezra. Consumption Function Analysis in a Communal Household: Cross Section and Time Series. *Rev. Econ. Statist.,* November 1973, *55*(4), pp. 475–81.

Trubek, David M.; Branfman, Eric J. and Cohen, Benjamin I. Measuring the Invisible Wall: Land Use Controls and the Residential Patterns of the Poor. *Yale Law J.,* January 1973, *82*(3), pp. 483–508.

Trueger, Paul M. Contract Termination and Unabsorbed Overhead. *Manage. Account.,* February 1973, *54*(8), pp. 38–40.

Truett, Dale and Roberts, Blaine. Classical Production Functions, Technical Optimality, and Scale Adjustments of the Firms. *Amer. Econ. Rev.,* December 1973, *63*(5), pp. 975–82.

Truman, Edwin M. and Resnick, Stephen A. An Empirical Examination of Bilateral Trade in Western Europe. *J. Int. Econ.,* November 1973, *3*(4), pp. 305–35.

Truu, M. L. Some Effects of Regional Migration. *S. Afr. J. Econ.,* June 1973, *41*(2), pp. 98–110.

Tryfos, Peter. The Determinants of Prices and Employment in the Canadian Meat Industry. *Can. J. Agr. Econ.,* July 1973, *21*(2), pp. 25–42.

———— **and Tryphonopoulos, N.** Consumer Demand for Meat in Canada. *Amer. J. Agr. Econ.,* Part I, November 1973, *55*(4), pp. 647–52.

Tryphonopoulos, N. and Tryfos, Peter. Consumer Demand for Meat in Canada. *Amer. J. Agr. Econ.,* Part I, November 1973, *55*(4), pp. 647–52.

Tsaklanganos, Angelos A. Informal Organization: A Managerial Myth Revisited. *Marquette Bus. Rev.,* Winter 1973, *17*(4), pp. 167–73.

Tsang, Herbert H. Economic Hypotheses and the Derivation of Production Functions. *Econ. Rec.,* September 1973, *49*(127), pp. 456–63.

Tsiang, S. C. Interest Rate and Consumption: Comment. *Int. Econ. Rev.,* June 1973, *14*(2), pp. 493–96.

———— Risk, Return, and Portfolio Analysis: Com-

ment. *J. Polit. Econ.,* May-June 1973, *81*(3), pp. 748–52.

———— Spot Speculation, Forward Speculation, and Arbitrage: A Clarification and Reply. *Amer. Econ. Rev.,* December 1973, *63*(5), pp. 999–1002.

Tsuchiya, Masaya. Recent Developments in Sino-Japanese Trade. *Law Contemp. Probl.,* Summer-Autumn 1973, *38*(2), pp. 240–48.

Tsurumi, Hiroki. A Comparison of Alternative Optimal Models of Advertising Expenditures: Stock Adjustment vs. Control Theoretic Approaches. *Rev. Econ. Statist.,* May 1973, *55*(2), pp. 156–68.

———— A Comparison of Econometric Macro Models in Three Countries. *Amer. Econ. Rev.,* May 1973, *63*(2), pp. 394–401.

———— A Survey of Recent Canadian Macro-Econometric Models. *Can. J. Econ.,* August 1973, *6*(3), pp. 409–28.

———— **and Tsurumi, Yoshi.** An Econometric Model of a Japanese Pharmaceutical Company. In *Palda, K. S., ed.,* 1973, pp. 290–315.

Tsurumi, Yoshi and Tsurumi, Hiroki. An Econometric Model of a Japanese Pharmaceutical Company. In *Palda, K. S., ed.,* 1973, pp. 290–315.

Tuccillo, John A. and Billings, Brad. Determinants of the Money Multiplier: Comment. *Quart. Rev. Econ. Bus.,* Winter 1973, *13*(4), pp. 93–101.

———— **and Ford, William F.** Monetary Policy Implications of the Hunt Commission Report. *Quart. Rev. Econ. Bus.,* Autumn 1973, *13*(3), pp. 93–103.

Tucker, James F.; Weber, Warren E. and Goetz, Charles J. Student Incentive Payments and Academic Achievement: An Empirical Test. *Soc. Sci. Quart.,* June 1973, *54*(1), pp. 159–67.

Tucker, William H. Regulatory Constraint: The Need for a New Look. In *The Diebold Group, Inc.,* 1973, pp. 113–17.

Tuckman, Howard P. Local Colleges and the Demand for Higher Education: The Enrollment Inducing Effects of Location. *Amer. J. Econ. Soc.,* July 1973, *32*(3), pp. 257–68.

———— **and Canterbery, E. R.** The Income Distribution as a Pure Public Good: Comment. *Quart. J. Econ.,* May 1973, *87*(2), pp. 304–10.

Tuckwell, R. H. The Wage-Price Link. *Econ. Anal. Pol.,* September 1973, *4*(2), pp. 76–87.

Tull, Donald S. and Medler, Jerry F. Poll Positions and Win Probabilities: A Stochastic Model of the Electoral Process. *Public Choice,* Spring 1973, *14,* pp. 125–32.

Tuller, S. Mark. New Standards for Domination and Support under Section 8(a)(2). *Yale Law J.,* January 1973, *82*(3), pp. 510–32.

Tulloch, Peter. Developing Countries and the Enlargement of the EEC. In *Dinwiddy, B., ed.,* 1973, pp. 88–111.

Tullock, Gordon. The Charity of the Uncharitable. In *Alchian, A. A., et al.,* 1973, pp. 15–32.

———— Constitutional Choice and Simple Majority Rule: Reply. *J. Polit. Econ.,* Part I, March-April 1973, *81*(2), pp. 480–84.

———— Inflation and Unemployment: The Discussion Continued: Comment. *J. Money, Credit, Banking,* August 1973, *5*(3), pp. 826–35.

———— Inheritance Rejustified. *J. Law Econ.,* October

~~*73*~~, *16*(2), pp. 425–28.

—— Universities Should Discriminate Against Assistant Professors. *J. Polit. Econ.*, September-October 1973, *81*(5), pp. 1256–57.

——; Hochman, Harold M. and Rodgers, James D. The Income Distribution as a Pure Public Good: Comment. *Quart. J. Econ.*, May 1973, *87*(2), pp. 311–15.

—— and Staaf, Robert J. Education and Equality. *Ann. Amer. Acad. Polit. Soc. Sci.*, September 1973, *409*, pp. 125–34.

Tumlir, Jan. Trade Negotiations in the Field of Manufactures. In *Streeten, P., ed.*, 1973, pp. 279–99.

Turková, Dana and Glückaufová, Dagmar. Některá rozšíření metody zobecněných horních mezí. (Some Extensions of Generalized Upper Bounding Technique. With English summary.) *Ekon.-Mat. Obzor*, 1973, *9*(4), pp. 423–49.

Turner, H. A. and Jackson, D. A. S. A Riposte to Knight and Mabro. *Econ. J.*, June 1973, *83*(330), pp. 523–25.

—— and Jackson, Dudley. How to Provide More Employment in a Labour-Surplus Economy. *Int. Lab. Rev.*, April 1973, *107*(4), pp. 315–38.

Turner, James T. and Robinson, James W. An Empirical Investigation of the Theory Y Management—Theory X Union Hypothesis. *Miss. Val. J. Bus. Econ.*, Spring 1973, *8*(3), pp. 77–84.

Turner, John N. Canada: Bill C-222. *Bull. Int. Fiscal Doc.*, March 1973, *27*(3), pp. 87–94.

Turner, Ronald E. and Staelin, Richard. Error in Judgmental Sales Forecasts: Theory and Results. *J. Marketing Res.*, February 1973, *10*(1), pp. 10–16.

Turnovsky, Stephen J. Optimal Stabilization Policies for Deterministic and Stochastic Linear Economic Systems. *Rev. Econ. Stud.*, January 1973, *40*(1), pp. 79–95.

—— Optimal Stabilization Policies in a Market with Lagged Adjustment in Supply. *Econ. Rec.*, March 1973, *49*(125), pp. 31–49.

—— Production Flexibility, Price Uncertainty and the Behavior of the Competitive Firm. *Int. Econ. Rev.*, June 1973, *14*(2), pp. 395–413.

Tussing, A. Dale. Poverty Research and Policy Analysis in the United States: Implications for Ireland. *Econ. Soc. Rev.*, October 1973, *5*(1), pp. 75–98.

Tuttle, Donald L. and Roenfeldt, Rodney L. An Examination of the Discounts and Premiums of Closed-End Investment Companies. *J. Bus. Res.*, Fall 1973, *1*(2), pp. 129–40.

Tweeten, Luther G. Emerging Issues for Sparsely Populated Areas and Regions Under a National Growth Policy. *Amer. J. Agr. Econ.*, December 1973, *55*(5), pp. 840–50.

—— and Holland, David W. Human Capital Migration: Implications for Common School Finance. *Land Econ.*, August 1973, *49*(3), pp. 278–84.

—— and Lu, Yao-Chi. The Impact of Busing on Student Achievement. *Growth Change*, October 1973, *4*(4), pp. 44–46.

—— and White, Fred. Optimal School District Size Emphasizing Rural Areas. *Amer. J. Agr. Econ.*, February 1973, *55*(1), pp. 45–53.

Tybout, Richard A. Prices, Costs, and the Energy Crisis. *Ohio State U. Bull. Bus. Res.*, June 1973, *48*(6), pp. 4–8.

—— Pricing of Pollution: The Coase Theorem in the Long Run: Reply. *Bell J. Econ. Manage. Sci.*, Spring 1973, *4*(1), pp. 320–21.

Tyler, Geoffrey and Neiss, Hubert. Problems and Prospects in East-West Trade. *Finance Develop.*, September 1973, *10*(3), pp. 24–26.

Tyler, George R. and Hoffer, George E. Reform of the Non-Commercial Vehicle Liability Insurance Market. *J. Risk Ins.*, December 1973, *40*(4), pp. 565–74.

Tyler, William G. Exchange Rate Flexibility under Conditions of Endemic Inflation: A Case Study of the Recent Brazilian Experience. In *[Halm, G. N.]*, 1973, pp. 19–49.

—— Manufactured Export Promotion in a Semi-Industrialized Economy: The Brazilian Case. *J. Devel. Stud.*, October 1973, *10*(1), pp. 3–15.

—— A Model of Income Distribution and Economic Development. *Weltwirtsch. Arch.*, 1973, *109*(2), pp. 321–36.

Tyran, Michael R. A Financial Projection Plan. *Manage. Account.*, July 1973, *55*(1), pp. 19–23, 28.

Tyrchniewicz, Edward W. and Tosterud, Robert J. A Model for Rationalizing the Canadian Grain Transportation and Handling System on a Regional Basis. *Amer. J. Agr. Econ.*, December 1973, *55*(5), pp. 805–13.

Tyree, Andrea. Mobility Ratios and Association in Mobility Tables. *Population Stud.*, November 1973, *27*(3), pp. 577–88.

Udell, Jonathan; Li, Wen L. and Smith, Gerald W. The Gambling Business in the U.S.A. *Ohio State U. Bull. Bus. Res.*, April 1973, *48*(4), pp. 1–3, 6–7.

Udis, Bernard. The Economic Consequences of Reduced Military Spending: Overview and Summary. In *Udis, B., ed.*, 1973, pp. 1–15.

—— The End of Overrun: Prospects for the High Technology Defense Industry and Related Issues. *Ann. Amer. Acad. Polit. Soc. Sci.*, March 1973, *406*, pp. 59–72.

—— and Weidenbaum, Murray L. The Many Dimensions of the Military Effort. In *Udis, B., ed.*, 1973, pp. 17–57.

Udry, J. Richard and Bauman, Karl E. The Difference in Unwanted Births between Blacks and Whites. *Demography*, August 1973, *10*(3), pp. 315–28.

——; Bauman, Karl E. and Chase, Charles L. Population Growth Rates in Perfect Contraceptive Populations. *Population Stud.*, July 1973, *27*(2), pp. 365–71.

Uekawa, Yasuo; Kemp, Murray C. and Wegge, Leon L. P- and PN-Matrices, Minkowski- and Metzler-Matrices, and Generalizations of the Stolper-Samuelson and Samuelson-Rybczynski Theorems. *J. Int. Econ.*, February 1973, *3*(1), pp. 53–76.

—— and Khang, Chulsoon. The Production Possibility Set in a Model Allowing Interindustry Flows: The Necessary and Sufficient Conditions for its Strict Convexity. *J. Int. Econ.*, August 1973, *3*(3), pp. 283–90.

Uhr, Carl G. The Emergence of the "New Economics" in Sweden: A Review of a Study by Otto

Steiger. *Hist. Polit. Econ.*, Spring 1973, *5*(1), pp. 243–60.

Uitermark, P. J. The Theory of Socialist Planning: Comment. *J. Polit. Econ.*, Part I, March-April 1973, *81*(2), pp. 459–64.

Ujázy, Karol. An Analysis of the Situation in Capital Construction. *Czech. Econ. Digest.*, November 1973, (7), pp. 3–55.

Újhelyi, T. Foreign Trade in Agricultural and Food Products—The Hungarian National Economy and the World Market. *Acta Oecon.*, 1973, *11*(1), pp. 3–18.

Ullah, Aman and Nagar, A. L. Note on Approximate Skewness and Kurtosis of the Two-Stage Least-Square Estimator. *Indian Econ. Rev.*, April 1973, *8*(1), pp. 69–80.

Ullmo, Bernard. Trois problèmes posés par le modèle physico-financier. (Three Problems Set by the Physico-Financial Model. With English summary.) *Revue Écon.*, November 1973, *24*(6), pp. 1026–71.

Ullmo, Jean. Sur quelques concepts marxistes. (About Some Marxist Concepts. With English summary.) *Revue Écon.*, January 1973, *24*(1), pp. 109–38.

Ulman, Lloyd. Introduction: The Problems in Policy Context. In *Ulman, L., ed.*, 1973, pp. 1–13.

Ulmer, Melville J. The Non-Answer to Nixonomics. In *Reynolds, L. G.; Green, G. D. and Lewis, D. R., eds.*, 1973, pp. 81–86.

Umemoto, H. E. Marketing Requirements for the Pacific Rim: The Position of an Importer. In *Canadian Agricultural Economics Society*, 1973, pp. 27–37.

Underwood, Trevor G. Analysis of Proposals for Using Objective Indicators as a Guide to Exchange Rate Changes. *Int. Monet. Fund Staff Pap.*, March 1973, *20*(1), pp. 100–17.

Updegraff, David E. and Coates, Robert. The Relationship between Organizational Size and the Administrative Component of Banks. *J. Bus.*, October 1973, *46*(4), pp. 576–88.

Ureel, William L. Nuclear Fuel Accounting. *Manage. Account.*, July 1973, *55*(1), pp. 14–16, 24.

Uri, Pierre. The Role of the Multinational Corporation. In *Hughes, H., ed.*, 1973, pp. 69–90.

Urken, Arnold B. and Kushner, Harvey W. Measuring Power in Voting Bodies. *Public Choice*, Summer 1973, *15*, pp. 77–85.

Ursachi, I. Probleme ale planificării productivității muncii în întreprinderile industriei textile. (Problems of the Planning of Labour Productivity in the Enterprises of the Textile Industry. With English summary.) *Stud. Cercet. Econ.*, 1973, (3), pp. 41–50.

Usatov, I. The Elaboration of Plans and the System of Prices. *Prob. Econ.*, March 1973, *15*(11), pp. 44–62.

Uselding, Paul. An Early Chapter in the Evolution of American Industrial Management. In *[Williamson, H. F.]*, 1973, pp. 51–84.

———— **and Juba, Bruce.** Biased Technical Progress in American Manufacturing, 1839–1899. *Exploration Econ. Hist.*, Fall 1973, *11*(1), pp. 55–72.

Usher, Dan. An Imputation to the Measure of Economic Growth for Changes in Life Expectancy. In *Moss, M., ed.*, 1973, pp. 193–226.

———— Is Growth Obsolete? Comment. In *Moss, M., ed.*, 1973, pp. 540–45.

Utami, Widya and Ihalauw, John. Some Consequences of Small Farm Size. *Bull. Indonesian Econ. Stud.*, July 1973, *9*(2), pp. 46–56.

Uyeno, Dean and Vertinsky, Ilan. Demand for Health Services and the Theory of Time Allocation. *Appl. Econ.*, December 1973, *5*(4), pp. 249–60.

————; **Vertinsky, Ilan and Povey, George.** Social Impact Index for Evaluation of Regional Resource Allocation. In *Berg, R. L., ed.*, 1973, pp. 104–14.

Uzawa, Hirofumi. Towards a Keynesian Model of Monetary Growth. In *Mirrlees, J. A. and Stern, N. H., eds.*, 1973, pp. 53–70.

Vachel, Jan and Nentvichová, Božena. 25 Years of Building Czechoslovakia's Socialist Economy. *Czech. Econ. Digest.*, February 1973, (1), pp. 3–93.

Vachha, Homiar S. and Iyengar, Sampath S. Financial Institutions and Backward Regions: A Case Study of Gujarat. *Artha-Vikas*, January-July 1973, *9*(1–2), pp. 185–202.

Vaciago, Giacomo. Monetary Analysis and Policy: An Aggregated Model for the Italian Economy. *Banca Naz. Lavoro Quart. Rev.*, June 1973, (105), pp. 84–108.

Văduva, I. and Călin, O. Folosirea metodelor matematice în contabilitate. (Utilization of Mathematical Models in Book-keeping. With English summary.) *Stud. Cercet. Econ.*, 1973, (2), pp. 139–56.

Vági, F. The Basis and Main Features of the System of Wage-Mass Regulation. (In Russian.) *Acta Oecon.*, 1973, *11*(1), pp. 65–80.

Vais, T. The Topic of an International Symposium: Labor Resources in COMECON Nations. *Prob. Econ.*, July 1973, *16*(3), pp. 77–86.

Vaitsos, Constantine V. Strategic Choices in the Commercialization of Technology: The Point of View of Developing Countries. *Int. Soc. Sci. J.*, 1973, *25*(3), pp. 370–86.

Vaizey, John. Emergence of a British Economist. *Int. Soc. Sci. J.*, 1973, *25*(1–2), pp. 154–68.

Vak, Karl and Matzner, Egon. Program Budgeting in Austria: An Essay in Persuasion. In *Novick, D., ed.*, 1973, pp. 61–64.

Vakil, Firouz. Indian Saving Behavior: A Reconciliation of Time Series and Cross Section Evidence. *Rev. Income Wealth*, September 1973, *19*(3), pp. 307–23.

———— The Propensity to Consume Permanent Income in India. *Econ. Develop. Cult. Change*, April 1973, *21*(3), pp. 514–21.

Valdes, Nelson P. "Health and Revolution in Cuba": An Addendum. *Sci. Soc.*, Winter 1973–1974, *37* (4), pp. 481.

Valdés E., Alberto. Trade Policy and Its Effect on the External Agricultural Trade of Chile 1945–1965. *Amer. J. Agr. Econ.*, May 1973, *55*(2), pp. 154–64.

Valencia, José Alberto; Fernández de la Garza, Guillermo and Manne, Alan S. Multi-Level Planning for Electric Power Projects. In *Goreux, L. M. and*

~~nne, A. S., eds., 1973, pp. 197–231.

~~entine, T. J. The Demand for Very Liquid Assets in Australia. *Australian Econ. Pap.*, December 1973, *12*(21), pp. 196–207.

—— The Loan Supply Function of Australian Trading Banks: An Empirical Analysis. *Australian Econ. Pap.*, June 1973, *12*(20), pp. 57–69.

di Vallega, Adalberto. Aree industriali in Piemonte connesse con i porti liguri. (Industrial Areas in Pedemont Connected with Ligurian Harbors. With English summary.) *L'Impresa*, 1973, *15* (5–6), pp. 317–22.

Valticos, Nicolas. Temporary Work Agencies and International Labour Standards. *Int. Lab. Rev.*, January 1973, *107*(1), pp. 43–56.

Van Arkadie, Brian. Development of the State Sector and Economic Independence. In *Ghai, D., ed.*, 1973, pp. 88–122.

—— Problems of Socialism in Tanzania. In *Zammit, J. A., ed.*, 1973, pp. 421–39.

Van Belle, John J. A Neglected Aspect of the Modern Theory of Forward Exchange. *Southern Econ. J.*, July 1973, *40*(1), pp. 117–19.

—— Spot Rates, Forward Rates, and the Interest-Rate Differentials: Comment. *J. Money, Credit, Banking*, November 1973, *5*(4), pp. 997–99.

Vance, Jack O. The Anatomy of a Corporate Strategy. In *Klein, W. H. and Murphy, D. C., eds.*, 1973, pp. 150–57.

Van Cise, J. G. The Supreme Court and the Antitrust Laws: 1972–1973. *Antitrust Bull.*, Winter 1973, *18*(4), pp. 691–714.

Van Cleef, Eugene. The Economic Relation Between Cities and Their Immediate Environments. *Ohio State U. Bull. Bus. Res.*, November 1973, *48*(11), pp. 4, 6–7.

Vandenberg, Pieter A. A Further Note on the Analysis of Capital Investment Alternatives: Comment. *Miss. Val. J. Bus. Econ.*, Fall 1973, *9*(1), pp. 88–90.

—— and Reints, William W. A Comment on the Risk Level Discriminatory Powers of the Wiesenberger Classifications. *J. Bus.*, April 1973, *46*(2), pp. 278–83.

Vandenborre, R. J. and Leunis, J. V. An Interregional Analysis of the United States Soybean Industry. In *Judge, G. G. and Takayama, T., eds.*, 1973, pp. 274–97.

Vandendries, René. An Appraisal of the Reformist Development Strategy of Peru. In *Scott, R. E., ed.*, 1973, pp. 260–84.

—— Internal Migration and Economic Development in Peru. In *Scott, R. E., ed.*, 1973, pp. 193–207.

Vanderholm, Dale H. and Ward, Robert C. Cost-Effectiveness Methodologies for Data Acquisition in Water Quality Management. *Water Resources Res.*, June 1973, *9*(3), pp. 536–45.

Vandermeulen, Alice. Economics Journals: Policies, Trends, and a Warning: Comment. *Southern Econ. J.*, July 1973, *40*(1), pp. 146–48.

Van der Tak, Herman G. and Ray, Anandarup. The Economic Benefits of Road Transport Projects. In *Niskanen, W. A., et al., eds.*, 1973, pp. 132–73.

Van Der Tak, Jean and Gendell, Murray. The Size and Structure of Residential Families, Guatemala City, 1964. *Population Stud.*, July 1973, *27*(2), pp. 305–22.

Van Eeckhoudt, M. Least Squares Construction of Yield Curves for Belgian Government Bonds (1955–1972): A Note. *Tijdschr. Econ.*, 1973, *18*(4), pp. 591–96.

——; Verheirstraeten, A. and Lierman, F. Het conjunctureel patroon van de termijnstructuur van de interestvoeten—met een grafische analyse voor België. *Tijdschr. Econ.*, 1973, *18*(4), pp. 545–89.

Vanek, Jaroslav. A Contribution to the Problem of Economic Development of Bangladesh. *Bangladesh Econ. Rev.*, July 1973, *1*(3), pp. 324–27.

—— Some Fundamental Considerations on Financing and Form of Ownership under Labor Management. In *[Tinbergen, J.]*, 1973, pp. 139–52.

—— The Yugoslav Economy Viewed through the Theory of Labor Management. *World Devel.*, September 1973, *1*(9), pp. 39–56.

Van Geel, M. Alternatief-Economisch/2 Zero economische groei: betekenis en consequenties. (Zero Economic Growth: Significance and Consequences. With English summary.) *Econ. Soc. Tijdschr.*, August 1973, *27*(4), pp. 347–70.

Van Horne, James C. The Effect of FHLB Bond Operations on Savings Inflows at Savings and Loan Associations: Comment. *J. Finance*, March 1973, *28*(1), pp. 194–97.

—— Implied Fixed Costs of Long-Term Debt Issues. *J. Financial Quant. Anal.*, December 1973, *8*(5), pp. 821–33.

—— and Hendershott, Patric H. Expected Inflation Implied by Capital Market Rates. *J. Finance*, May 1973, *28*(2), pp. 301–14.

Vanik, Charles A. Corporate Federal Tax Payments and Federal Subsidies to Corporations. In *Andreano, R. L., ed.*, 1973, pp. R340–23.

Van Lam, Ngo. The Pursuit of Growth and Stability Through Taxation of Agricultural Exports: Thailand's Experience: A Comment. *Public Finance*, 1973, *28*(2), pp. 227–32.

Van Langendonck, Jozef. The European Experience in Social Health Insurance. *Soc. Sec. Bull.*, July 1973, *36*(7), pp. 21–30.

Van Long, Ngo. On a Paradox in the Theory of International Capital Movements. *Econ. Rec.*, September 1973, *49*(127), pp. 440–46.

Van Mechelen, C. and Heirman, W. Receptselective en receptcreatie in de vleeswarenindustrie met behulp van lineaire programmering. (Selection and Creation of Recipes. The Application of Linear Programming in the Meat Industry. With English summary.) *Econ. Soc. Tijdschr.*, August 1973, *27*(4), pp. 411–21.

Van Meir, Lawrence W. Problems in Implementing New Fishery Management Programs. In *Sokoloski, A. A., ed.*, 1973, pp. 9–11.

Van Moeseke, Paul and Fox, Karl A. Derivation and Implications of a Scalar Measure of Social Income. In *[Tinbergen, J.]*, 1973, pp. 21–40.

—— and Rader, J. Trout. Heckscher-Ohlin Hypothesis and Scarce-Factor Theorems. *Tijdschr. Econ.*, 1973, *18*(3), pp. 445–50.

Vanneman, Reeve D. Dominance and Achievement

in Entrepreneurial Personalities. In *Ayal, E. B.*, *ed.*, 1973, pp. 122–45.

Van Ness, John W. and Fisher, Lloyd. Admissible Discriminant Analysis. *J. Amer. Statist. Assoc.*, September 1973, *68*(343), pp. 603–07.

Vanni, Lido. Immagine aziendale e politica del personale. (Company Image and Personnel Policy. With English summary.) *L'Impresa*, 1973, *15* (9–10), pp. 549–60.

Vännman, Kerstin and Kulldorff, Gunnar. Estimation of the Location and Scale Parameters of a Pareto Distribution by Linear Functions of Order Statistics. *J. Amer. Statist. Assoc.*, March 1973, *68* (341), pp. 218–27.

Van Oenen, Richard. Exchange Rate Experience in Southeast Asia. In *Grubel, H. G. and Morgan, T.*, *eds.*, 1973, pp. 1–7.

Van Peeterssen, A. and Klein, Lawrence R. Forecasting World Trade within Project LINK. In *Ball, R. J.*, *ed.*, 1973, pp. 429–63.

Van Rompuy, E. De stop-go cyclus en de Europese monetaire integratie. (The Stop-go Cycle and the European Monetary Integration. With English summary.) *Tijdschr. Econ.*, 1973, *18*(3), pp. 457–79.

Van Rompuy, H. Het stagnatieprobleem. Verleden en heden. (The Stagnation-Thesis. With English summary.) *Tijdschr. Econ.*, 1973, *18*(1), pp. 65–86.

Van Rompuy, P. and Paelinck, J. Regionaal en sectoraal subsidiebeleid: Economische theorie en modellen. (Regional and Sectoral Subsidies—Economic Theory and Models. With English summary.) *Tijdschr. Econ.*, 1973, *18*(1), pp. 39–55.

Van Roy, Edward. Ngo Van Lam on the Rice Premium: A Rejoinder. *Public Finance*, 1973, *28* (2), pp. 233–36.

Vanthienen, L. Portfolio Theorie en Bedrijfsfinanciering. (With English summary.) *Tijdschr. Econ.*, 1973, *18*(4), pp. 597–627.

_____ **and Depre, F.** Methodologie voor empirish onderzoek op de kapitaalmarkt. (With English summary.) *Tijdschr. Econ.*, 1973, *18*(4), pp. 629–46.

Van Til, Jon and Van Til, Sally Bould. The Lower Class and the Future of Inequality. *Growth Change*, January 1973, *4*(1), pp. 10–16.

Van Til, Sally Bould and Van Til, Jon. The Lower Class and the Future of Inequality. *Growth Change*, January 1973, *4*(1), pp. 10–16.

Varaiya, P.; Legey, L. and Ripper, M. Effects of Congestion on the Shape of a City. *J. Econ. Theory*, April 1973, *6*(2), pp. 162–79.

Varga, Gy. On the System of Preferences. *Acta Oecon.*, 1973, *10*(1), pp. 52–66.

Vartholomeos, John. Corporate Taxes and the United States Balance of Trade: A Comment. *Nat. Tax J.*, December 1973, *26*(4), pp. 653–54.

Vartikar, V. S. On Optimizing the Rate of Investment. *Econ. Int.*, February 1973, *26*(1), pp. 17–31.

Vaselenak, Michael J. and Kariel, Herbert G. Waves of Spatial Diffusion Reconsidered: Comment. *J. Reg. Sci.*, August 1973, *13*(2), pp. 291–95.

Vasicek, Oldrich A. A Note on Using Cross-Sectional Information in Bayesian Estimation of Security

Betas. *J. Finance*, December 1973, *28*(5), pp. 1233–39.

Vasile, Radu. Premisele economice ale revoluției române de la 1848. (The Economic Conditions of the 1848 Romanian Revolution. With English summary.) *Stud. Cercet. Econ.*, 1973, (2), pp. 5–24.

Vasilescu, Floarea and Nasta, Eliza. Considerații asupra metodologiei de calcul a coeficientului elasticității. (Considerations of the Methodology of Calculating the Elasticity Coefficient. With English summary.) *Stud. Cercet. Econ.*, 1973, (1), pp. 99–109.

Vasil'ev, V. F. Some Properties of the Application of Mathematical Methods to Develop Labor Norms. *Matekon*, Winter 1973-74, *10*(2), pp. 64–73.

Vasquez, Thomas and Ott, David J. Agriculture. In *Ott, D. J., et al.*, 1973, pp. 53–65.

Vathana, C.; Hammonds, T. M. and Yadav, R. The Elasticity of Demand for Hired Farm Labor. *Amer. J. Agr. Econ.*, May 1973, *55*(2), pp. 242–45.

Vatter, William J. Capital Budget Formulae. In *Thomas, W. E., Jr., ed.*, 1973, pp. 176–200.

_____ Limitations of Overhead Allocation. In *Thomas, W. E., Jr., ed.*, 1973, pp. 484–503.

Vaughn, Karen I. Symmetry of Production Stages and Uneconomic Production: Reply. *Southern Econ. J.*, October 1973, *40*(2), pp. 334–35.

Väyrynen, Olavi. Priskontrollen i samhällspolitiken. (Price Control in Public Policy. With English summary.) *Ekon. Samfundets Tidskr.*, 1973, *26*(2), pp. 75–86.

Vázquez, Andrés and Puu, Tönu. Factor Demand Functions in the Long-Run Equilibrium. *Rivista Int. Sci. Econ. Com.*, December 1973, *20*(12), pp. 1209–29.

Vedder, James N. Multiattribute Decision Making under Uncertainty Using Bounded Intervals. In *Cochrane, J. L. and Zeleny, M., eds.*, 1973, pp. 93–107.

Vedder, Richard K. and Cebula, Richard J. A Note on Migration, Economic Opportunity, and the Quality of Life. *J. Reg. Sci.*, August 1973, *13*(2), pp. 205–11.

_____ **; Cebula, Richard J. and Kohn, Robert M.** Some Determinants of Interstate Migration of Blacks, 1965–1970. *Western Econ. J.*, December 1973, *11*(4), pp. 500–05.

_____ **; Gallaway, Lowell E. and Rydén, Rune.** Internal Labor Migration in Sweden, 1967. *Swedish J. Econ.*, September 1973, *75*(3), pp. 257–65.

Vedovato, Giuseppe. Situation and Prospects of the Italian Extractive Industry. *Rev. Econ. Cond. Italy*, July 1973, *27*(4), pp. 225–35.

Veendorp, E. C. H. Pure Competition in Disequilibrium Situations. *Weltwirtsch. Arch.*, 1973, *109*(3), pp. 476–94.

Veevers, J. E. Estimating the Incidence and Prevalence of Birth Orders: A Technique Using Census Data. *Demography*, August 1973, *10*(3), pp. 447–58.

Veldkamp, Gérard M. J. The Coherence of Social Security Policy. *Int. Lab. Rev.*, November 1973, *108*(5), pp. 357–69.

_____ **and Raetsen, M. J. E. H.** Temporary Work

Agencies and Western European Social Legislation. *Int. Lab. Rev.,* February 1973, *107*(2), pp. 117–31.

Velten, Terri and Jackson, Carolyn. Residence, Race, and Age of Poor Families in 1966. In *Rasmussen, D. W. and Haworth, C. T., eds.,* 1973, pp. 53–71.

Velupillai, K. A Note on the Origin of the 'Correspondence Principle'. *Swedish J. Econ.,* September 1973, *75*(3), pp. 302–04.

Vendig, Richard E. A Three-Part Transfer Price. *Manage. Account.,* September 1973, *55*(3), pp. 33–36.

Venieris, Yiannis P. Sales Expectations, Inventory Fluctuations, and Price Behavior. *Southern Econ. J.,* October 1973, *40*(2), pp. 246–61.

_____; Sebold, Frederick D. and Harper, Richard D. The Impact of Economic, Technological and Demographic Factors on Aggregate Births. *Rev. Econ. Statist.,* November 1973, *55*(4), pp. 493–97.

Venkatesan, M. and Peters, Michael P. Exploration of Variables Inherent in Adopting an Industrial Product. *J. Marketing Res.,* August 1973, *10*(3), pp. 312–15.

Ventriglia, Ferdinando. Results and Prospects of the Policy for Southern Italy. *Rev. Econ. Cond. Italy,* January-March 1973, *27*(1–2), pp. 5–28.

Verbaan, W. C. and de Ridder, P. B. Uniforme modelstructuur voor meerdere landen. (A Uniform Model Structure for Several Countries. With English summary.) *De Economist,* September-October 1973, *121*(5), pp. 481–520.

Verbist, Daniel. La gestion prévisionnelle des ressources humaines. (The Planning and Forecasting of Human Resources. With English summary.) *Ann. Sci. Écon. Appl.,* 1973–1974, (1), pp. 81–104.

Verbrugge, James A. The Effects of Pledging Regulations on Bank Asset Composition. *J. Bank Res.,* Autumn 1973, *4*(3), pp. 168–76.

_____ Idle Public Funds Policies: Some Additional Evidence. *Nebr. J. Econ. Bus.,* Spring 1973, *12*(2), pp. 9–19.

Vercruijsse, E. V. W. and Boyd, T. A. Evaluation of an Extension Programme in Agriculture. In *Ofori, I. M., ed.,* 1973, pp. 57–66.

Verdoorn, P. J. Some Long-Run Dynamic Elements of Factor Price Inflation. In *[Tinbergen, J.],* 1973, pp. 111–37.

Veress, P. and Palánkai, T. Effect of the United Kingdom's Entry Into the Common Market on Anglo-Hungarian Relations. *Acta Oecon.,* 1973, *10*(1), pp. 81–94.

Vergin, Roger C. and Miles, Raymond E. Behavioral Properties of Variance Controls. In *Thomas, W. E., Jr., ed.,* 1973, pp. 325–39.

Vergnano, Franco. Determinazione dello stanziamento pubblicitario. Una bibliografia e un commento introduttivo. (A Determination of the Advertising Budget. A Bibliography and Preliminary Notes. With English summary.) *L'Impresa,* 1973, *15*(5–6), pp. 365–72.

_____ La conoscenza di base: ricerche strutturali e funzionali. (The Basic Knowledge: Structural and Functional Research. With English summary.) *L'Impresa,* 1973, *15*(1), pp. 28–32.

de la Vergne, Pierre. Le società finanziarie in Fran-

cia—Attività e regime giuridico. (Finance Companies in France: Activities and Juridical Regime. With English summary.) *Bancaria,* January 1973, *29*(1), pp. 17–22.

Verheirstraeten, A. and Claessens, G. De technische analyse van het verloop van aandelenkoersen—met een toepassing op de beurs te Brussel. (With English summary.) *Tijdschr. Econ.,* 1973, *18*(4), pp. 647–81.

_____; Lierman, F. and Van Eeckhoudt, M. Het conjunctureel patroon van de termijnstructuur van de interestvoeten—met een grafische analyse voor België. *Tijdschr. Econ.,* 1973, *18*(4), pp. 545–89.

Verkhovskii, B. S. Optimal Redistribution of Water Resources. *Matekon,* Summer 1973, *9*(4), pp. 95–101.

Verma, Krishnanand. Price Rise in India (1949–72). *Econ. Aff.,* June 1973, *18*(6), pp. 281–90.

Verma, Pramod. Regional Wages and Economic Development: A Case Study of Manufacturing Wages in India, 1950–1960. *J. Devel. Stud.,* October 1973, *10*(1), pp. 16–32.

Vermishev, K. The Stimulation of Population Growth. *Prob. Econ.,* June 1973, *16*(2), pp. 3–13.

Vernon, Jack. Financial Disintermediation in a Macroeconomic Framework: Comment. *J. Finance,* September 1973, *28*(4), pp. 1029–32.

Vernon, John M. and McElroy, Marjorie B. Estimation of Structure-Profit Relationships: Comment. *Amer. Econ. Rev.,* September 1973, *63*(4), pp. 763–67.

_____ and Nourse, Robert E. M. Profit Rates and Market Structure of Advertising Intensive Firms. *J. Ind. Econ.,* September 1973, *22*(1), pp. 1–20.

Vernon, Raymond. A Program of Research on Foreign Direct Investment. In *Bergsten, C. F., ed.,* 1973, pp. 93–113.

_____ Rogue Elephant in the Forest: An Appraisal of Transatlantic Relations. *Foreign Aff.,* April 1973, *51*(3), pp. 573–87.

_____ U.S. Direct Investment in Canada: Consequences for the U.S. Economy. *J. Finance,* May 1973, *28*(2), pp. 407–17.

Verstraete, J. Effect of a Change in Scale in One of the Variables on the Coefficients in a Cobb-Douglas Production Function. A Note. *Tijdschr. Econ.,* 1973, *18*(1), pp. 87–91.

Vertinsky, Ilan; Povey, George and Uyeno, Dean. Social Impact Index for Evaluation of Regional Resource Allocation. In *Berg, R. L., ed.,* 1973, pp. 104–14.

_____; Thomson, William and Kane, Julius. KSIM: A Methodology for Interactive Resource Policy Simulation. *Water Resources Res.,* February 1973, *9*(1), pp. 65–79.

_____ and Uyeno, Dean. Demand for Health Services and the Theory of Time Allocation. *Appl. Econ.,* December 1973, *5*(4), pp. 249–60.

Vesely, Zdenek and Kostál, Miroslav. The Czechoslovak Socialist Republic and the Council for Mutual Economic Assistance. *Czech. Econ. Digest.,* August 1973, (5), pp. 25–43.

Vesper, Karl H. and Sayeki, Yutaka. A Quantitative Approach for Policy Analysis. *Calif. Manage. Rev.,* Spring 1973, *15*(3), pp. 119–26.

Veverka, Ján. Strukturní model pro vypocty zmen velkoobchodních cen. (Structure Models for Calculating Wholesale Prices Changes. With English summary.) *Ekon.-Mat. Obzor*, 1973, *9*(3), pp. 260–74.

Vianelli, Silvio. Problemi economici e programmazione ecologica per la difesa dell'uomo e del suo ambiente. (Economic Problems and Environmental Planning for the Defense of Mankind and its Habitat. With English summary.) *Mondo Aperto*, June-August 1973, *27*(3–4), pp. 185–223.

Vibe-Pedersen, J. and Gørtz, Erik. Livsindkomstberegninger og deres betydning. (Calculation and Significance of Lifetime Incomes. With English summary.) *Nationalokon. Tidsskr.*, 1973, *111*(1), pp. 25–59.

Vickrey, William. Measuring Social and Economic Change: Benefits and Costs of Environmental Pollution: Comment. In *Moss, M., ed.*, 1973, pp. 503–08.

Vieli, Klaus; Frick, Andreas and Kiener, Urs. Bodenpreise und Stadtentwicklung. Eine empirische Untersuchung. (Land Prices and Urban Development. With English summary.) *Schweiz. Z. Volkswirtsch. Statist.*, March 1973, *109*(1), pp. 101–15.

Vietorisz, Thomas and Harrison, Bennett. Labor Market Segmentation: Positive Feedback and Divergent Development. *Amer. Econ. Rev.*, May 1973, *63*(2), pp. 366–76.

Vikbladh, Inge. Monetary Policy in Sweden. In *Holbik, K., ed.*, 1973, pp. 375–422.

Vilas, Carlos M. Aspectos del desarrollo de las corporaciones multinacionales en Argentina. (Aspects of Multinational Corporations Development in Argentina. With English summary.) *Económica*, September-December 1973, *19*(3), pp. 331–68.

Villanueva, Delano P. A Neoclassical Monetary Growth Model: Reply. *J. Money, Credit, Banking*, May 1973, *5*(2), pp. 707–12.

Villard, Henry H. Some Reflections on Student Evaluation of Teaching. *J. Econ. Educ.*, Fall 1973, *5*(1), pp. 47–50.

Villasuso, Juan M. and Wilford, W. T. The Velocity of Money in Central America. *Bangladesh Econ. Rev.*, October 1973, *1*(4), pp. 375–86.

Villela, Annibal V. and Baer, Werner. Industrial Growth and Industrialization: Revisions in the Stages of Brazil's Economic Development. *J. Devel. Areas*, January 1973, *7*(2), pp. 217–34.

Viner, Jacob. Adam Smith and Laissez-Faire. In *Rectenwald, H. C., ed.*, 1973, pp. 54–62.

Vining, Daniel R., Jr. and Haran, E. G. P. A Modified Yule-Simon Model Allowing for Intercity Migration and Accounting for the Observed Form of the Size Distribution of Cities. *J. Reg. Sci.*, December 1973, *13*(3), pp. 421–37.

Vinney, Les C. Credit Creation in the Eurodollar Market: An Unresolved Issue. *Rivista Int. Sci. Econ. Com.*, January 1973, *20*(1), pp. 33–47.

Vinod, H. D. Interregional Comparison of Production Structures. *J. Reg. Sci.*, August 1973, *13*(2), pp. 261–67.

Vinson, Donald E. The Marketing Concept: an Examination. *Rivista Int. Sci. Econ. Com.*, March 1973, *20*(3), pp. 291–95.

Vişinoiu, N. Analiza factorială a unor indicatori sintetici ai economiei naţionale. (The Factorial Analysis of Some of the Synthetic Indicators of the National Economy. With English summary.) *Stud. Cercet. Econ.*, 1973, (2), pp. 127–38.

_____ Aspecte privind teoria tabelelor de indici. (Aspects on the Theory of Index Tables. With English summary.) *Stud. Cercet. Econ.*, 1973, (1), pp. 111–21.

_____ Utilizarea teoriei grafurilor în studiul relaţiilor dintre mărimile relative ale dinamicii produsului social. (The Utilization of the Theory of Graphs in Studying the Relations Between the Relative Sizes of the Dynamics of the Social Product. With English summary.) *Stud. Cercet. Econ.*, 1973, (3), pp. 85–98.

Visscher, Michael L. Welfare-Maximizing Price and Output with Stochastic Demand: Comment. *Amer. Econ. Rev.*, March 1973, *63*(1), pp. 224–29.

Vitaliano, Donald F. The Payment of Interest on the Federal Debt and the Distribution of Income. *J. Econ. Bus.*, Spring-Summer 1973, *25*(3), pp. 175–86.

_____ A Reconsideration of Some Aspects of the Utility Sacrifice Rules of Taxation. *Public Finance Quart.*, January 1973, *1*(1), pp. 59–65.

Vlček, Jaroslav. K teorii informačních systémů. (On a Theory of Information Systems. With English summary.) *Ekon.-Mat. Obzor*, 1973, *9*(4), pp. 361–80.

Vlerick, André. Unione Monetaria Europea. (The European Monetary Union. With English summary.) *Mondo Aperto*, June-August 1973, *27*(3–4), pp. 224–35.

Voet, James R. Current Economic Developments. *N. Mex. Bus.*, May 1973, *26*(5), pp. 11–20.

_____ Current Economic Developments in New Mexico: Business Conditions Monthly Summary and Economic Indicators. *N. Mex. Bus.*, June 1973, *26*(6), pp. 17, 26–27.

Vogel, Heinrich and Sláma, Jiří. Zur Verbreitung neuer Technologien in der UdSSR—eine Fallstudie: das Oxygenblasstahlverfahren. (Diffusion of New Technologies in the USSR—the Case of Oxygene-Steel. With English summary.) *Jahr. Nationalökon. Statist.*, March 1973, *187*(3), pp. 245–61.

Vogel, Robert C. and Hanson, James S. Inflation and Monetary Velocity in Latin America. *Rev. Econ. Statist.*, August 1973, *55*(3), pp. 365–70.

_____ and Lovell, Michael C. A CPI–Futures Market. *J. Polit. Econ.*, July-August 1973, *81*(4), pp. 1009–12.

Vogel, Ronald J. and Blair, Roger D. Heroin Addiction and Urban Crime. *Public Finance Quart.*, October 1973, *1*(4), pp. 457–66.

_____ and Morrall, John F., III. The Impact of Medicaid on State and Local Health and Hospitals Expenditures, with Special Reference to Blacks. *J. Human Res.*, Spring 1973, *8*(2), pp. 202–11.

Voivodas, Constantin S. Exports, Foreign Capital Inflow and Economic Growth. *J. Int. Econ.*, November 1973, *3*(4), pp. 337–49.

Volcani, Zvi and Mundlak, Yair. The Correspondence of Efficiency Frontier as a Generalization of the Cost Function. *Int. Econ. Rev.*, February

1973, *14*(1), pp. 223–33.

Volgenant, A. F.; Fase, M. M. G. and Koning, J. An Experimental Look at Seasonal Adjustment. *De Economist,* September-October 1973, *121*(5), pp. 441–80.

Völker, Gottfried E. Impact of Turkish Labour Migration on the Economy of the Federal Republic of Germany. *Ger. Econ. Rev.,* 1973, *11*(1), pp. 61–77.

Volkonskii, V. A.; Pavlov, N. V. and Belen'kii, V. Z. Dynamic Input-Output Models in Planning and Price Calculations and Economic Analysis. *Matekon,* Winter 1973-74, *10*(2), pp. 74–101.

Volkov, A. M. and Senchagov, V. K. Problems of Depreciation and Its Reflection in the Input-Output Balance. *Matekon,* Spring 1973, *9*(3), pp. 55–66.

Voronov, O. Paid Educational Leave in the USSR. *Int. Lab. Rev.,* June 1973, *107*(6), pp. 529–38.

Votaw, Dow. Corporate Social Reform: An Educator's Viewpoint. *Calif. Manage. Rev.,* Summer 1973, *15*(4), pp. 67–73.

—— Genius Becomes Rare: A Comment on the Doctrine of Social Responsibility Pt. II. *Calif. Manage. Rev.,* Spring 1973, *15*(3), pp. 5–19.

Votey, Harold L., Jr. The Choice of Technique and a Growing Real Wage. *Indian Econ. Rev.,* April 1973, *8*(1), pp. 81–84.

——; **Hambor, John C. and Phillips, Llad.** High School Inputs and Their Contribution to School Performance: A Comment. *J. Human Res.,* Spring 1973, *8*(2), pp. 260–63.

——; **Hambor, John C. and Phillips, Llad.** Optimal Community Educational Attainment: A Simultaneous Equation Approach. *Rev. Econ. Statist.,* February 1973, *55*(1), pp. 98–103.

Votiakov, A. A. Integer Programming: A Comparison of Cutoffs. *Matekon,* Summer 1973, *9*(4), pp. 80–94.

Vousden, Neil. Basic Theoretical Issues of Resource Depletion. *J. Econ. Theory,* April 1973, *6*(2), pp. 126–43.

Vrba, Josef and Nekola, Jiří. Optimalizace rozsahu výkumné a vývojové činnosti na základě produkčni funkce. (The Optimization of the Level of Research and Development Activity on the Basis of the Production Function. With English summary.) *Ekon.-Mat. Obzor,* 1973, *9*(1), pp. 51–67.

de Vries, Barend A. The Plight of Small Countries. *Finance Develop.,* September 1973, *10*(3), pp. 6–8, 34.

de Vries, Jan. On the Modernity of the Dutch Republic. *J. Econ. Hist.,* March 1973, *33*(1), pp. 191–202.

Vroman, Susan B. and Puckett, Richard H. Rules Versus Discretion: A Simulation Study. *J. Finance,* September 1973, *28*(4), pp. 853–65.

Vuchelen, Jozef. Het gezinsvermogen 1952–1971. (With English summary.) *Cah. Écon. Bruxelles,* 4th Quarter 1973, (60), pp. 573–605.

—— Gezinsbesparingen in inflatie: een mogelijke benadering voor de Belgische ervaring. (With English summary.) *Cah. Écon. Bruxelles,* 3rd Trimestre 1973, (59), pp. 413–42.

—— Likwiditeiten en de lange termijn rentevoet:
een empirische studie. (With English summary.) *Cah. Écon. Bruxelles,* First Trimestre 1973, (57), pp. 53–81.

Vuskovic, Pedro. The Economic Policy of the Popular Unity Government. In *Zammit, J. A., ed.,* 1973, pp. 49–56.

Wachtel, Howard M. Theses on Poverty and Inequality. *Amer. Econ.,* Fall 1973, *17*(2), pp. 17–22.

Wachter, Michael L. and Ross, Stephen A. Wage Determination, Inflation, and the Industrial Structure. *Amer. Econ. Rev.,* September 1973, *63* (4), pp. 675–92.

Wadhva, Charan D. Asian Regional Economic Cooperation in Indian Perspective. In *Wadhva, C. D., ed.,* 1973, pp. 478–96.

—— New Industrial Licensing Policy: An Appraisal. In *Wadhva, C. D., ed.,* 1973, pp. 199–215.

Wadsworth, J. E. The Banks and the Monetary System in the UK 1959–1971. In *Wadsworth, J. E., ed.,* 1973, pp. 1–16.

Wadycki, Walter J. and Greenwood, Michael J. Crime Rates and Public Expenditures for Police Protection: Their Interaction. *Rev. Soc. Econ.,* October 1973, *31*(2), pp. 138–51.

—— **and Levy, Mildred B.** The Influence of Family and Friends on Geographic Labor Mobility: An International Comparison. *Rev. Econ. Statist.,* May 1973, *55*(2), pp. 198–203.

Waelbroeck, J. The Methodology of Linkage. In *Ball, R. J., ed.,* 1973, pp. 45–61.

Wagenbuur, H. T. M. Labour and Development: An Analysis of the Time Budget of Lime Farmers in Southern Ghana. In *Ofori, I. M., ed.,* 1973, pp. 145–57.

Wagener, Hans-Jürgen. Rules of Location and the Concept of Rationality: The Case of the USSR. In *Bandera, V. N. and Melnyk, Z. L., eds.,* 1973, pp. 63–103.

Wagner, Abraham and Sufrin, Sidney C. U.S. Employment and Growth in the Immediate Future: A Guess. *Rivista Int. Sci. Econ. Com.,* January 1973, *20*(1), pp. 63–71.

Wagner, Antonin. Die Auswirkung der öffentlichen Haushalte auf den Konjunkturverlauf in der Schweiz, 1955–1970. (The Effects of Public Finance on Trade Cycles in Switzerland, 1955–1970. With English summary.) *Schweiz. Z. Volkswirtsch. Statist.,* March 1973, *109*(1), pp. 17–57.

Wagstaff, H. R. Employment Multipliers in Rural Scotland. *Scot. J. Polit. Econ.,* November 1973, *20* (3), pp. 239–61.

Wahlbin, Clas and Lekvall, Per. A Study of Some Assumptions Underlying Innovation Diffusion Functions. *Swedish J. Econ.,* December 1973, *75* (4), pp. 362–77.

Wai, U Tun and Patrick, Hugh T. Stock and Bond Issues and Capital Markets in Less Developed Countries. *Int. Monet. Fund Staff Pap.,* July 1973, *20*(2), pp. 253–317.

Waite, Charles A. and Wakefield, Joseph C. Federal Fiscal Programs. *Surv. Curr. Bus.,* February 1973, *53*(2), pp. 18–28, 40.

Waite, David. The Economic Significance of Small Firms. *J. Ind. Econ.,* April 1973, *21*(2), pp. 154–66.

Wakefield, Joseph C. and Waite, Charles A. Federal

Fiscal Programs. *Surv. Curr. Bus.*, February 1973, *53*(2), pp. 18–28, 40.

Wakoff, Gary I. On Shareholders' Indifference to the Proceeds Price in Preemptive Rights Offerings. *J. Financial Quant. Anal.*, December 1973, *8*(5), pp. 835–36.

Waldauer, Charles. External Effects of Education Grants on Tax Base-Sharing Municipal Governments. In *Boulding, K. E.; Pfaff, M. and Pfaff, A., eds.*, 1973, pp. 246–58.

_____ Grant Structures and Their Effects on Aided Government Expenditures: An Indifference Curve Analysis. *Public Finance*, 1973, *28*(2), pp. 212–26.

Walderhaug, Albert J. The Composition of Value Added in the 1963 Input-Output Study. *Surv. Curr. Bus.*, April 1973, *53*(4), pp. 34–44.

Waldorf, William H. Quality of Labor in Manufacturing. *Rev. Econ. Statist.*, August 1973, *55*(3), pp. 284–90.

Wales, Stephen H., Sr. and Cole, William A. The Investment Credit. *Manage. Account.*, March 1973, *54*(9), pp. 13–16, 35.

Wales, Terence J. The Effect of College Quality on Earnings: Results from the NBER-Thorndike Data. *J. Human Res.*, Summer 1973, *8*(3), pp. 306–17.

_____ The Effect of School and District Size on Education Costs in British Columbia. *Int. Econ. Rev.*, October 1973, *14*(3), pp. 710–20.

_____ Estimation of a Labor Supply Curve for Self-Employed Business Proprietors. *Int. Econ. Rev.*, February 1973, *14*(1), pp. 69–80.

_____ **and Taubman, Paul J.** Higher Education, Mental Ability, and Screening. *J. Polit. Econ.*, January-February 1973, *81*(1), pp. 28–55.

Walgreen, John A.; Rastatter, E. H. and Moore, Arnold B. The Economics of the United States Supersonic Transport. *J. Transp. Econ. Policy*, May 1973, *7*(2), pp. 186–93.

Walker, David A. and McCall, Alan S. The Effects of Control Status on Commercial Bank Profitability. *J. Financial Quant. Anal.*, September 1973, *8*(4), pp. 637–45.

Walker, Donald A. Edgeworth's Theory of Recontract. *Econ. J.*, March 1973, *83*(329), pp. 138–49.

Walker, Francis E. and Jacobson, Robert E. Efficiency Considerations in Butterfat Differential and Component Pricing of Milk. *Amer. J. Agr. Econ.*, May 1973, *55*(2), pp. 214–16.

Walker, Joseph. Labor-Management Relations at Hopewell Village. *Labor Hist.*, Winter 1973, *14* (1), pp. 3–18.

Walker, Michael C. and White, Daniel L. First Degree Price Discrimination and Profit Maximization. *Southern Econ. J.*, October 1973, *40*(2), pp. 313–18.

Walker, Odell; Boehlje, Michael and Eidman, Vernon. An Approach to Farm Management Education. *Amer. J. Agr. Econ.*, May 1973, *55*(2), pp. 192–97.

Wall, David. Fashionable Economics? Review Article. *Econ. Develop. Cult. Change*, April 1973, *21* (3), pp. 534–40.

_____ The Japanese Experience and Attitudes Toward Trade Adjustment: Comment. In *Hughes,*

H., ed., 1973, pp. 263–66.

Wallace, George J. The Logic of Consumer Credit Reform. *Yale Law J.*, January 1973, *82*(3), pp. 461–82.

Wallace, Helen and Wallace, William. The Impact of Community Membership on the British Machinery of Government. *J. Common Market Stud.*, June 1973, *11*(4), pp. 243–62.

Wallace, Neil; Kareken, John H. and Muench, Thomas. Optimal Open Market Strategy: The Use of Information Variables. *Amer. Econ. Rev.*, March 1973, *63*(1), pp. 156–72.

_____ **and Sargent, Thomas J.** Rational Expectations and the Dynamics of Hyperinflation. *Int. Econ. Rev.*, June 1973, *14*(2), pp. 328–50.

_____ **and Sargent, Thomas J.** The Stability of Models of Money and Growth with Perfect Foresight. *Econometrica*, November 1973, *41*(6), pp. 1043–48.

Wallace, Phyllis. Sex Discrimination: Some Societal Constraints on Upward Mobility for Women Executives. In *Ginzberg, E. and Yohalem, A. M., eds.*, 1973, pp. 69–84.

Wallace, Richard L. and Lee, Maw Lin. Problems in Estimating Multiproduct Cost Functions: An Application to Hospitals. *Western Econ. J.*, September 1973, *11*(3), pp. 350–63.

Wallace, Roger L.; Frost, Carl F. and Ruh, Robert A. Management Attitudes and the Scanlon Plan. *Ind. Relat.*, October 1973, *12*(3), pp. 282–88.

Wallace, T. D. and Brook, Richard. A Note on Extraneous Information in Regression. *J. Econometrics*, October 1973, *1*(3), pp. 315–16.

Wallace, William. British External Relations and the European Community: The Changing Context of Foreign Policy-Making. *J. Common Market Stud.*, September 1973, *12*(1), pp. 28–52.

_____ **and Wallace, Helen.** The Impact of Community Membership on the British Machinery of Government. *J. Common Market Stud.*, June 1973, *11*(4), pp. 243–62.

Wallich, Henry C. Could Galbraith be Wrong? In *Reynolds, L. G.; Green, G. D. and Lewis, D. R., eds.*, 1973, pp. 315–22.

_____ Discussion of the Implications of the Proposals of the Hunt Commission for the Mortgage and Housing Markets: An Empirical Study and Impact of the Proposed New Financial Structure on Mortgage Markets. In *Federal Reserve Bank of Boston*, 1973, pp. 173–78.

_____ The Economics of an Automated Payment System. In *The Diebold Group, Inc.*, 1973, pp. 161–68.

_____ La crisi monetaria del 1971 e gli insegnamenti da trarne. (The Monetary Crisis of 1971. The Lessons to be Learned. With English summary.) *Bancaria*, March 1973, *29*(3), pp. 295–313.

_____ Reconstructing Humpty Dumpty. In *Henley, D. S., ed.*, 1973, pp. 145–51.

_____ Why Fixed Rates? *Soc. Sci. Quart.*, June 1973, *54*(1), pp. 146–51.

Walsh, Cliff and Brennan, Geoffrey. Pareto-Optimal Redistribution Reconsidered. *Public Finance Quart.*, April 1973, *1*(2), pp. 147–68.

_____ **and Tisdell, Clem.** Non-marginal Externalities: As Relevant and As Not. *Econ. Rec.*, September 1973, *49*(127), pp. 447–55.

Walsh, Cornelius F. Does Listing Increase the Market Price of Common Stocks?: Comment. *J. Bus.*, October 1973, *46*(4), pp. 616–20.

Walter, Emil J. Technologische, wirtschaftliche und soziale Aspekte der wachsenden Bedeutung der Schichtarbeit. (Technological, Economic and Social Aspects of the Growing Importance of Shift Work. With English summary.) *Schweiz. Z. Volkswirtsch. Statist.*, March 1973, *109*(1), pp. 69–89.

Walter, Ingo. Commonwealth Preferences in Retrospect: Some Policy Implications for the Developing Countries. *Econ. Bull. Ghana, Sec. Ser.*, 1973, *3*(4), pp. 3–13.

———— Environmental Management and the International Economic Order. In *Bergsten, C. F., ed.,* 1973, pp. 293–346.

———— The Pollution Content of American Trade. *Western Econ. J.*, March 1973, *11*(1), pp. 61–70.

Walter, James E. and Que, Agustin V. The Valuation of Convertible Bonds. *J. Finance*, June 1973, *28* (3), pp. 713–32.

Walter, John P. The City as a Source of Regional Economic Disparity in Latin America. *Rev. Soc. Econ.*, April 1973, *31*(1), pp. 66–84.

Walters, A. A. Investments in Airports and the Economist's Role: John F. Kennedy International Airport: An Example and Some Comparisons. In *Wolfe, J. N., ed.,* 1973, pp. 140–54.

———— **and McGregor, L.** Real Balances and Output: A Productivity Model of a Monetary Economy. In *Powell, A. A. and Williams, R. A., eds.,* 1973, pp. 233–59.

Walters, J., Jr. Public Policy Toward Retailing: Poland. In *Boddewyn, J. J. and Hollander, S. C., eds.,* 1972, pp. 271–82.

Walters, Joan G. Finance and Banking: Refereed Papers II: Discussion. *J. Finance*, May 1973, *28*(2), pp. 538–39.

Walton, Alfred G. and Baumol, William J. Full Costing, Competition and Regulatory Practice. *Yale Law J.*, March 1973, *82*(4), pp. 639–55.

Walton, C. Lee, Jr. and Bower, Marvin. Gearing a Business to the Future. In *The Conference Board,* 1973, pp. 93–148.

Walton, Gary M. The Burdens of the Navigation Acts: Reply. *Econ. Hist. Rev., 2nd Ser.,* November 1973, *26*(4), pp. 687–88.

———— **and Mak, James.** The Persistence of Old Technologies: The Case of Flatboats. *J. Econ. Hist.*, June 1973, *33*(2), pp. 444–51.

Walzer, Norman and Singer, Dan. The Distribution of Income in Large Urban Areas. *Nebr. J. Econ. Bus.*, Autumn 1973, *12*(4), pp. 91–101.

Wang, Gisela C. Flexible Retirement Feature of German Pension Reform. *Soc. Sec. Bull.*, July 1973, *36*(7), pp. 36–39, 41.

Wang, Kenneth. Foreign Trade Policy and Apparatus of the People's Republic of China. *Law Contemp. Probl.*, Summer-Autumn 1973, *38*(2), pp. 182–200.

Wang, Tong-eng. Quantitative Analysis of the Progress of the Econometric Movement: An Exploration. *Hist. Polit. Econ.*, Spring 1973, *5*(1), pp. 151–64.

Ward, Benjamin. Appraising Yugoslav Socialism. In

Zammit, J. A., ed., 1973, pp. 441–55.

Ward, Richard J. The Widening Gaps: Are There Tolerance Levels? *Rev. Soc. Econ.*, April 1973, *31* (1), pp. 40–53.

Ward, Robert C. and Vanderholm, Dale H. Cost-Effectiveness Methodologies for Data Acquisition in Water Quality Management. *Water Resources Res.*, June 1973, *9*(3), pp. 536–45.

Ward, Terry and George, Kenneth D. Productivity Growth in the Retail Trade. *Oxford Bull. Econ. Statist.*, February 1973, *35*(1), pp. 31–47.

Ware, H. and Caldwell, J. C. The Evolution of Family Planning in Australia. *Population Stud.,* March 1973, *27*(1), pp. 7–31.

Warford, Jeremy J.; Bahl, Roy W. and Coelen, Stephen P. Land Value Increments as a Measure of the Net Benefits of Urban Water Supply Projects in Developing Countries: Theory and Measurement. In *Harriss, C. L., ed.,* 1973, pp. 171–88.

Waris, Klaus. Styrningen av kreditströmmarna. (Directing the Credit Flows. With English summary.) *Ekon. Samfundets Tidskr.*, 1973, *26*(2), pp. 87–94.

Warne, Clinton L. The Consumer Movement and the Labor Movement. *J. Econ. Issues,* June 1973, *7*(2), pp. 307–16.

Warne, Robert D. Factor Intensity and the Heckscher-Ohlin Theorem in a Three-Factor, Three-Good Model. *Can. J. Econ.,* August 1973, *6*(3), pp. 369–75.

———— The Heckscher-Ohlin Model with Three Factors and Two Goods. *Econ. Rec.,* June 1973, *49* (126), pp. 300–05.

———— **and Melvin, James R.** Monopoly and the Theory of International Trade. *J. Int. Econ.,* May 1973, *3*(2), pp. 117–34.

———— **and Scarth, William M.** The Elasticity of Substitution and the Shape of the Transformation Curve. *Economica, N.S.,* August 1973, *40*(159), pp. 299–304.

Warner, David C. and Porter, David O. How Effective Are Grantor Controls?: The Case of Federal Aid to Education. In *Boulding, K. E.; Pfaff, M. and Pfaff, A., eds.,* 1973, pp. 276–302.

Warner, Maurice L. and Lord, William B. Aggregates and Externalities: Information Needs for Public Natural Resource Decision-Making. *Natural Res. J.,* January 1973, *13*(1), pp. 106–17.

Warnke, Dale W.; Ameiss, Albert P. and Terre, Norbert C. Cost/Benefit Analysis of Public Projects. *Manage. Account.,* January 1973, *54*(7), pp. 34–37.

Warr, Peter G. Savings Propensities and the Shadow Wage. *Economica, N.S.,* November 1973, *40*(160), pp. 410–15.

Warren, James M. and Shelton, John P. A Simultaneous Equation Approach to Financial Planning: Reply. *J. Finance,* September 1973, *28*(4), pp. 1039–42.

Warriner, Doreen. Results of Land Reform in Asian and Latin American Countries. *Food Res. Inst. Stud.,* 1973, *12*(2), pp. 115–31.

Warsky, D. and Nakayama, Toshiko. Measuring Regional Price Change in Urban Areas. *Mon. Lab. Rev.,* October 1973, *96*(10), pp. 34–38.

Wart, James R.; Ferguson, Donald L. and Porter, R.

Burr. Efficient Algorithms for Conducting Stochastic Dominance Tests on Large Numbers of Portfolios. *J. Financial Quant. Anal.*, January 1973, *8*(1), pp. 71–81.

Wasserstein, Bruce. British Merger Policy from an American Perspective. *Yale Law J.*, March 1973, *82*(4), pp. 656–90.

Watanabe, Tamao and Ogawa, Kazuo. Introduction to Japan-China Trade. *Chinese Econ. Stud.*, Fall 1973, *7*(1), pp. 3–137.

Watanabe, Tsunehiko. The Process of Industrialization: A Dynamic Simulation. *Osaka Econ. Pap.*, March 1973, *21*(38), pp. 1–43.

Waters, Alan Rufus. Interregional Development and Urban Tribalism in Africa. *Growth Change,* April 1973, *4*(2), pp. 30–37.

_____ Migration, Remittances, and the Cash Constraint in African Smallholder Economic Development. *Oxford Econ. Pap.*, November 1973, *25* (3), pp. 435–54.

Waters, W. G., II and Hildebrand, D. G. Road Costs and Government Revenues from Heavy Vehicles in Canada. *Can. J. Econ.*, November 1973, *6*(4), pp. 608–12.

Watrin, Christian. On the Question of Measuring the Efficiency of Economic Systems. *Ger. Econ. Rev.*, 1973, *11*(2), pp. 89–107.

Watson, P. and Mansfield, N. The Valuation of Time in Cost-benefit Studies. **In** *Wolfe, J. N., ed.*, 1973, pp. 222–32.

Watson, Ronald D. Lotteries: Can the Public and State Both Win? *Fed. Res. Bank Bus. Rev. Phila.*, July 1973, pp. 3–11.

Watson, William D., Jr. Stochastic Operating Characteristics and Cost Functions of Electrostatic Precipitators. *Eng. Econ.*, January-February 1973, *18*(2), pp. 79–98.

Watters, Gil. A New Decision for Urban Investment and Pricing Decisions. **In** *Aislabie, C., ed.*, 1973, pp. 177–78.

Wattles, George M. The Rates and Costs of the United States Postal Service. *J. Law Econ.*, April 1973, *16*(1), pp. 89–117.

Watts, Ross. The Information Content of Dividends. *J. Bus.*, April 1973, *46*(2), pp. 191–211.

Watts, Vincent and Rosser, Rachel. Health and Welfare Systems. **In** *Ross, M., ed.*, 1973, pp. 655–69.

Waud, Roger N. Index Bonds and Economic Stability. *Public Finance,* 1973, *28*(1), pp. 52–68.

_____ Proximate Targets and Monetary Policy. *Econ. J.*, March 1973, *83*(329), pp. 1–20.

_____ A Reconsideration of Interest Rates, Money Growth Rates, Inflation and the 'Ease' or 'Tightness' of Money: Reply. *Kyklos,* 1973, *26*(1), pp. 156–58.

_____ and Gould, John P. The Neoclassical Model of Investment Behavior: Another View. *Int. Econ. Rev.*, February 1973, *14*(1), pp. 33–48.

_____ and Schmidt, Peter. The Almon Lag Technique and the Monetary Versus Fiscal Policy Debate. *J. Amer. Statist. Assoc.*, March 1973, *68*(341), pp. 11–19.

Waugh, Frederick V.; Bell, Frederick W. and Carlson, Ernest W. Production from the Sea. **In** *Sokoloski, A. A., ed.*, 1973, pp. 72–91.

Waverman, L. and Atkinson, A. B. Resource Alloca-

tion and the Regulated Firm: Comment. *Bell J. Econ. Manage. Sci.*, Spring 1973, *4*(1), pp. 283–87.

Weaver, James H. Economic Growth, Inequality, Hierarchy, Alienation: The Impact of Socialization Processes in Capitalist Society. *Amer. Econ.*, Fall 1973, *17*(2), pp. 9–16.

_____ Growth and Welfare. **In** *Wilber, C. K., ed.*, 1973, pp. 342–53.

Weaver, Jerry L. Bureaucracy during a Period of Social Change: The Case of Guatemala. **In** *Thurber, C. E. and Graham, L. S., eds.*, 1973, pp. 314–61.

_____ Health Care Costs as a Political Issue: Comparative Responses of Chicanos and Anglos. *Soc. Sci. Quart.*, March 1973, *53*(4), pp. 846–54.

_____ Mexican American Health Care Behavior: A Critical Review of the Literature. *Soc. Sci. Quart.*, June 1973, *54*(1), pp. 85–102.

Weaver, Robert C. Housing and Associated Problems of Minorities. **In** *Clawson, M., ed.*, 1973, pp. 49–81.

Webb, Don R. and Darling, John R. The Post-Use Problem—A Response from Management. *J. Bus. Res.*, Summer 1973, *1*(1), pp. 49–56.

Webb, Lee. The Swindling of the Average Taxpayer: The Story of Taxes in Vermont. *Rev. Radical Polit. Econ.*, Summer 1973, *5*(2), pp. 18–46.

Webber, M. J. and Daly, M. T. The Growth of the Firm Within the City. *Urban Stud.*, October 1973, *10*(3), pp. 303–17.

_____ and Symanski, Richard. Periodic Markets: An Economic Location Analysis. *Econ. Geogr.*, July 1973, *49*(3), pp. 213–27.

Webbink, Douglas W. Regulation, Profits and Entry in the Television Broadcasting Industry. *J. Ind. Econ.*, April 1973, *21*(2), pp. 167–76.

_____ A View from the Federal Communications Commission. **In** *Park, R. E., ed.*, 1973, pp. 35–41.

Weber, Harry. God as Portfolio Manager. *J. Finance,* December 1973, *28*(5), pp. 1353–55.

Weber, Jean E. and Hawkins, Clark A. The Estimation of Constant Elasticities: Reply. *Southern Econ. J.*, January 1973, *39*(3), pp. 445–47.

Weber, John A. Economics Journals: Policies, Trends, and a Warning: Reply. *Southern Econ. J.*, July 1973, *40*(1), pp. 148–49.

_____ A Note on Keeping Abreast of Developments in the Field of Finance. *J. Finance,* March 1973, *28*(1), pp. 161–65.

Weber, Warren E.; Goetz, Charles J. and Tucker, James F. Student Incentive Payments and Academic Achievement: An Empirical Test. *Soc. Sci. Quart.*, June 1973, *54*(1), pp. 159–67.

Weber, Wilhelm. Collective Goods and the Planning of Fiscal Programmes. **In** *Hicks, J. R. and Weber, W., eds.*, 1973, pp. 149–63.

_____ and Streissler, Erich W. The Menger Tradition. **In** *Hicks, J. R. and Weber, W., eds.*, 1973, pp. 226–32.

Webster, Frederick E., Jr. Does Business Misunderstand Consumerism? *Harvard Bus. Rev.*, September-October 1973, *51*(5), pp. 89–97.

Wecker, William E. and Reilly, Raymond R. On the Weighted Average Cost of Capital. *J. Financial Quant. Anal.*, January 1973, *8*(1), pp. 123–26.

Wedekind, H. Information Systems for Decision and

Control. In *Ross, M., ed.,* 1973, pp. 171–82.

Wedin, Dick. Externalities and Open Field Burning: A Case Study. *Amer. J. Agr. Econ.,* December 1973, *55*(5), pp. 1026–29.

Wegge, Leon L.; Uekawa, Yasuo and Kemp, Murray C. P- and PN-Matrices, Minkowski- and Metzler-Matrices, and Generalizations of the Stolper-Samuelson and Samuelson-Rybczynski Theorems. *J. Int. Econ.,* February 1973, *3*(1), pp. 53–76.

Wehner, Harrison G.; Myers, Myron G. and Rogstad, Barry K. A Theoretical Evaluation of Alternative Subsidy Schemes for Regional Development. *Amer. J. Agr. Econ.,* May 1973, *55*(2), pp. 304–12.

Weicher, John C. A Test of Jane Jacobs' Theory of Successful Neighborhoods. *J. Reg. Sci.,* April 1973, *13*(1), pp. 29–40.

—— **and Emerine, R. J., II.** Econometric Analysis of State and Local Aggregate Expenditure Functions. *Public Finance,* 1973, *28*(1), pp. 69–83.

—— **and Zerbst, Robert H.** The Externalities of Neighborhood Parks: An Empirical Investigation. *Land Econ.,* February 1973, *49*(1), pp. 99–105.

Weidenbaum, Murray L. Industrial Adjustments to Military Expenditure Shifts and Cutbacks. In *Udis, B., ed.,* 1973, pp. 253–87.

—— **and Udis, Bernard.** The Many Dimensions of the Military Effort. In *Udis, B., ed.,* 1973, pp. 17–57.

Weigand, Robert E. The Problems of Managing Reciprocity. *Calif. Manage. Rev.,* Fall 1973, *16*(1), pp. 40–48.

Weigel, Dale R. and Miller, Robert R. Factors Affecting Resource Transfer Through Direct Investment. In *Alexandrides, C. G., ed.,* 1973, pp. 129–44.

Weigner, Edward A. Tax Simplification. *Nat. Tax J.* September 1973, *26*(3), pp. 337–39.

Weil, Roman L. Annuitants Can Afford CREF's Projecting Earnings at a Rate Larger Than 4 Percent. *J. Risk Ins.,* September 1973, *40*(3), pp. 465–72.

—— Macaulay's Duration: An Appreciation. *J. Bus.,* October 1973, *46*(4), pp. 589–92.

Weiller, Augusto. Arbitrato e programmazione. (Arbitration and Planning. With English summary.) *Bancaria,* December 1973, *29*(12), pp. 1474–80.

Weinand, Herbert C. Some Spatial Aspects of Economic Development in Nigeria. *J. Devel. Areas,* January 1973, *7*(2), pp. 247–63.

Weinberger, Caspar W. Expenditure Priorities and Budget Reform. In *Tax Foundation, Inc.,* 1973, pp. 57–59.

Weingartner, H. Martin. Some New Views on the Payback Period and Capital Budgeting Decisions. In *Haynes, W. W.; Coyne, T. J. and Osborne, D. K., eds.,* 1973, pp. 393–407.

Weinrobe, Maurice D. Accounting for Pollution: Pollution Abatement and the National Product. *Land Econ.,* May 1973, *49*(2), pp. 115–21.

—— Corporate Taxes and the United States Balance of Trade: Reply. *Nat. Tax J.,* December 1973, *26*(4), pp. 655.

—— The Demand for Money by Six Non-Bank Financial Intermediaries. *Western Econ. J.,* June 1973, *11*(2), pp. 191–213.

Weinschenck, G.; Henrichsmeyer, W. and Hanf, C.

H. Experiences with Multi-Commodity Models in Regional Analysis. In *Judge, G. G. and Takayama, T., eds.,* 1973, pp. 307–26.

Weinschrott, David and Wolf, Charles, Jr. International Transactions and Regionalism: Distinguishing "Insiders" from "Outsiders." *Amer. Econ. Rev.,* May 1973, *63*(2), pp. 52–60.

Weinstein, James. Labor and Socialism in America. *Labor Hist.,* Summer 1973, *14*(3), pp. 429–34.

Weinstein, Milton C. and Clark, Ian D. Emissions Measurement and the Testing of New Vehicles. In *Jacoby, H. D., et al.,* 1973, pp. 63–111.

—— **and Zeckhauser, Richard J.** Critical Ratios and Efficient Allocation. *J. Public Econ.,* April 1973, *2*(2), pp. 147–57.

Weintraub, Andrew. The Economics of Lincoln's Proposal for Compensated Emancipation. *Amer. J. Econ. Soc.,* April 1973, *32*(2), pp. 171–77.

Weintraub, E. R.; Gusen, P. and Havrilesky, Thomas M. Potpourri: The Monetarist's Papers. *Intermountain Econ. Rev.,* Fall 1973, *4*(2), pp. 78–80.

Weintraub, Sidney. Introduction: Perspectives on Money Wages. In *Weintraub, S., et al.,* 1973, pp. 3–16.

—— Keynes and the Theory of Derived Demand. In *Weintraub, S., et al.,* 1973, pp. 51–70.

—— **and Davidson, Paul.** Money as Cause and Effect. *Econ. J.,* December 1973, *83*(332), pp. 1117–32.

Weisbord, Robert G. Birth Control and the Black American: A Matter of Genocide? *Demography,* November 1973, *10*(4), pp. 571–90.

Weisbrod, Burton A. Measuring Performance in Education: Comment. In *Moss, M., ed.,* 1973, pp. 428–33.

Weisgerber, P. The Impact of Wealth Benefits on Farm Returns in the Wheat Area. *Agr. Finance Rev.,* July 1973, *34,* pp. 31–34.

Weiss, E. B. The Corporate Deaf Ear. In *Murray, B. B., ed.,* 1973, pp. 260–70.

Weissbourd, Bernard. The Satellite Community as Suburb. In *Masotti, L. H. and Hadden, J. K., eds.,* 1973, pp. 495–532.

Weissbrodt, Sylvia R. Changes in State Labor Laws in 1972. *Mon. Lab. Rev.,* January 1973, *96*(1), pp. 27–36.

Weisskopf, Thomas E. An Econometric Test of Alternative Constraints on the Growth of Underdeveloped Countries: A Reply. *Rev. Econ. Statist.,* February 1973, *55*(1), pp. 133–34.

—— Capitalism and Underdevelopment in the Modern World. In *Reynolds, L. G.; Green, G. D. and Lewis, D. R., eds.,* 1973, pp. 518–29.

—— Dependence and Imperialism in India. *Rev. Radical Polit. Econ.,* Spring 1973, *5*(1), pp. 53–96.

Weisskopf, Walter A. The Dialetics of Equality. *Ann. Amer. Acad. Polit. Soc. Sci.,* September 1973, *409,* pp. 163–73.

—— Economic Growth versus Existential Balance. In *Daly, H. E., ed.,* 1973, pp. 240–51.

—— The Image of Man in Economics. *Soc. Res.,* Autumn 1973, *40*(3), pp. 547–63.

Weissler, Mark L. Snowmobiles and the Environment. *Yale Law J.,* March 1973, *82*(4), pp. 772–86.

von Weizsäcker, Carl Christian. Modern Capital Theory and the Concept of Exploitation. *Kyklos,*

1973, *26*(2), pp. 245–81.

———— Morishima on Marx. *Econ. J.*, December 1973, *83*(332), pp. 1245–54.

———— Notes on Endogenous Growth of Productivity. In *Mirrlees, J. A. and Stern, N. H.*, eds., 1973, pp. 101–10.

Welch, Finis. Black-White Differences in Returns to Schooling. *Amer. Econ. Rev.*, December 1973, *63* (5), pp. 893–907.

Welch, L. F.; Swanson, E. R. and Taylor, C. R. Economically Optimal Levels of Nitrogen Fertilizer for Corn: An Analysis Based on Experimental Data, 1966–71. *Ill. Agr. Econ.*, July 1973, *13*(2), pp. 16–25.

Welch, Wilford. The Business Outlook for Southeast Asia. *Harvard Bus. Rev.*, May-June 1973, *51*(3), pp. 72–84.

Weld, John. Coase, Social Cost and Stability: An Integrative Essay. *Natural Res. J.*, October 1973, *13*(4), pp. 595–613.

Welfeld, Irving H. Toward a New Federal Housing Policy. In *Grieson, R. E.*, ed., 1973, pp. 200–13.

———— Toward a New Federal Housing Policy. In *Pynoos, J.; Schafer, R. and Hartman, C. W.*, eds., 1973, pp. 543–47.

Wells, Donald A. and Frank, Helmut J. United States Oil Imports: Implications for the Balance of Payments. *Natural Res. J.*, July 1973, *13*(3), pp. 431–47.

Wells, Louis T., Jr. Economic Man and Engineering Man: Choice in a Low-Wage Country. *Public Policy*, Summer 1973, *21*(3), pp. 319–42.

———— Effects of Policies Encouraging Foreign Joint Ventures in Developing Countries. In *Ayal, E. B.*, ed., 1973, pp. 149–77.

———— Men and Machines in Indonesia's Light Manufacturing Industries. *Bull. Indonesian Econ. Stud.*, November 1973, *9*(3), pp. 62–72.

Wells, Paul. Keynes's Dynamic Disequilibrium Theory of Employment. *Quart. Rev. Econ. Bus.*, Winter 1973, *13*(4), pp. 89–93.

Wemelsfelder, J. Kapitaalvoorzieningsproblemen in een op arbeiderszelfbestuur gebaseerde industrie. Het voorbeeld van Joegoslavië. (Problems of Financing Labor-Managed Firms: The Case of Yugo-Slavia. With English summary.) *De Economist*, March-April 1973, *121*(2), pp. 122–56.

Wendel, Helmut F. and Galper, Harvey. Time Lags in the Federal Expenditure Process and their Stabilization Implications. *Public Finance Quart.*, April 1973, *1*(2), pp. 123–46.

Wenders, John T. Corrective Taxes and Pollution Abatement. *J. Law Econ.*, October 1973, *16*(2), pp. 365–68.

Wendt, Paul F. New Techniques in Financing Real Estate. *Amer. Real Estate Urban Econ. Assoc. J.*, June 1973, *1*(1), pp. 140–57.

Wentworth, Donald R.; Orvis, Charles C. and Lewis, Darrell R. Economics in the Junior Colleges: Terminal or Transfer? *J. Econ. Educ.*, Spring 1973, *4* (2), pp. 100–10.

Wentworth, Eric. Higher Education: The Reach Exceeds the Grasp. In *Levitan, S. A.*, ed., 1973, pp. 52–88.

Wentz, John and Mazza, Gertrude. The Acquisitive Bank Holding Companies: A Bigger Role in Mortgage Banking. *Fed. Res. Bank Bus. Rev. Phila.*, October 1973, pp. 7–8.

Weralski, Marian. The New Structure of Turnover and Income Taxes in Poland. *Bull. Int. Fiscal Doc.*, December 1973, *27*(12), pp. 497–506.

———— Problems of Budgetary Policy in Socialist Planned Economies. In *[Hicks, U.]*, 1973, pp. 260–69.

Werbel, Richard A. and Newman, Joseph W. Multivariate Analysis of Brand Loyalty for Major Household Appliances. *J. Marketing Res.*, November 1973, *10*(4), pp. 404–09.

van der Werf, D. Ein Beitrag zur Problematik der Konsumfunktion in der Bundesrepublik Deutschland. (A Contribution to the Problem of Consumption Function in the German Federal Republic. With English summary.) *Weltwirtsch. Arch.*, 1973, *109*(2), pp. 274–90.

Werlin, Herbert H. The Consequences of Corruption: The Ghanaian Experience. *Polit. Sci. Quart.*, March 1973, *88*(1), pp. 71–85.

Werner, David J. and Rutman, Gilbert L. A Test of the 'Uneconomic Culture' Thesis: An Economic Rationale for the 'Sacred Cow'. *J. Devel. Stud.*, July 1973, *9*(4), pp. 566–80.

Werner, Ray O. Buyer's Inducement of Discriminatory Prices Under the Robinson-Patman Act. *Nebr. J. Econ. Bus.*, Summer 1973, *12*(3), pp. 37–42.

Wert, James E. and Joehnk, Michael D. The Call-Risk Performance of the Discounted Seasoned Issue. *Miss. Val. J. Bus. Econ.*, Winter 1973-74, *9*(2), pp. 1–15.

Wery, René and Blandy, Richard. Population and Employment Growth: Bachue-1. *Int. Lab. Rev.*, May 1973, *107*(5), pp. 441–49.

Wesche, Rolf J. Montana Settlement as a Partial Solution to Peru's Economic and Demographic Problems. In *Pollock, D. H. and Ritter, A. R. M.*, eds., 1973, pp. 260–68.

Wesolowski, J. Monetary and Financial Relations. In *Kiss, T.*, ed., 0000, pp. 203–11.

West, E. G. The Bilateral Monopoly Theory of Public Goods: A Critique. *J. Polit. Econ.*, September-October 1973, *81*(5), pp. 1226–35.

West, P. A. Allocation and Equity in the Public Sector: The Hospital Revenue Allocation Formula. *Appl. Econ.*, September 1973, *5*(3), pp. 153–66.

West, Richard R. Bond Ratings, Bond Yields and Financial Regulation: Some Findings. *J. Law Econ.*, April 1973, *16*(1), pp. 159–68.

———— **and Largay, James A., III.** Margin Changes and Stock Price Behavior. *J. Polit. Econ.*, Part I, March-April 1973, *81*(2), pp. 328–39.

———— **and Tinic, Seha M.** Portfolio Returns and the Random Walk Theory: Comment. *J. Finance*, June 1973, *28*(3), pp. 733–41.

West, Robert LeRoy. Economic Dependence and Policy in Developing Countries. In *[Halm, G. N.]*, 1973, pp. 157–83.

Weston, J. Fred. Conglomerate Firm in Perspective. *Intermountain Econ. Rev.*, Spring 1973, *4*(1), pp. 1–13.

———— Large Firms and Economic Performance. In *Weston, J. F. and Ornstein, S. I.*, eds., 1973, pp. 225–46.

———— Pricing Behavior of Large Firms. In *Weston, J. F. and Ornstein, S. I., eds.,* 1973, pp. 143–55.

———— ROI Planning and Control as a Dynamic Management System. In *Weston, J. F. and Ornstein, S. I., eds.,* 1973, pp. 107–15.

———— and Hoskins, W. Lee. Geographic Aspects of Market Structure and Performance in Banking. *J. Bus. Res.,* Summer 1973, *1*(1), pp. 31–42.

———— and Mansinghka, Surendra K. Performance of Conglomerate Firms: Reply. *J. Finance,* June 1973, *28*(3), pp. 759.

———— and Mansinghka, Surendra K. Tests of the Efficiency Performance of Conglomerate Firms. In *Weston, J. F. and Ornstein, S. I., eds.,* 1973, pp. 203–24.

———— and Ornstein, Stanley I. Trends and Causes of Concentration—A Survey. In *Weston, J. F. and Ornstein, S. I., eds.,* 1973, pp. 3–21.

Wetherell, David. Nuovi orientamenti della "company image." (New Directions for the "Company Image." With English summary.) *L'Impresa,* 1973, *15*(9–10), pp. 562–67.

Wettstein, Jürg. Operations Research in the Swiss Telecommunication Services. In *Ross, M., ed.,* 1973, pp. 475–81.

Wever, F. Long-term Scientific Studies in NATO. In *Blohm, H. and Steinbuch, K., eds.,* 1973, pp. 79–81.

Whalley, John and Shoven, John B. General Equilibrium with Taxes: A Computational Procedure and an Existence Proof. *Rev. Econ. Stud.,* October 1973, *40*(4), pp. 475–89.

Whinston, A. and Loehman, Edna. Reply to Forster and Logan. *Appl. Econ.,* March 1973, *5*(1), pp. 69–73.

Whinston, Andrew B. and Davis, Otto A. The Economics of Urban Renewal. In *Grieson, R. E., ed.,* 1973, pp. 163–77.

Whipple, Daniel S. Employment Among the Poor of Six Central Cities. *Mon. Lab. Rev.,* October 1973, *96*(10), pp. 52–53.

Whipple, David. A Generalized Theory of Job Search. *J. Polit. Econ.,* September-October 1973, *81*(5), pp. 1170–88.

Whitbread, Michael and Kettle, Peter. An Ordinal Method of Evaluation: A Comment. *Urban Stud.,* February 1973, *10*(1), pp. 95–99.

White, Daniel L. and Walker, Michael C. First Degree Price Discrimination and Profit Maximization. *Southern Econ. J.,* October 1973, *40*(2), pp. 313–18.

White, Desmond A. Some Aspects of Recent In-Migration to the Albuquerque Area. *N. Mex. Bus.,* April 1973, *26*(4), pp. 9–14.

White, Fred and Tweeten, Luther G. Optimal School District Size Emphasizing Rural Areas. *Amer. J. Agr. Econ.,* February 1973, *55*(1), pp. 45–53.

White, Harold C. A Leadership Audit. *Manage. Account.,* August 1973, *55*(2), pp. 39–41.

White, Kenneth J. The Tax Structure and Discrimination Against Working Wives: A Comment. *Nat. Tax J.,* March 1973, *26*(1), pp. 119–22.

———— and Siegfried, John J. Financial Rewards to Research and Teaching: A Case Study of Academic Economists. *Amer. Econ. Rev.,* May 1973, *63*(2), pp. 309–15.

———— and Siegfried, John J. Teaching and Publishing as Determinants of Academic Salaries. *J. Econ. Educ.,* Spring 1973, *4*(2), pp. 90–99.

White, P. R. An Economic Comparison of Urban Railways and Express Bus Services: Comment. *J. Transp. Econ. Policy,* September 1973, *7*(3), pp. 294–95.

White, S. Douglass. Marketing in Bank: Philosophies and Actions. *J. Bank Res.,* Winter 1973, *3*(4), pp. 265–68.

Whitehead, Carlton J. and King, Albert S. Differences in Managers' Attitudes Toward Mexican and Non-Mexican Americans in Organizational Authority Relations. *Soc. Sci. Quart.,* March 1973, *53*(4), pp. 760–71.

Whitehead, C. M. E. Inflation and the New Housing Market. *Oxford Bull. Econ. Statist.,* November 1973, *35*(4), pp. 275–93.

———— and Foster, C. D. The Layfield Report on the Greater London Development Plan. *Economica, N.S.,* November 1973, *40*(160), pp. 442–54.

Whitehouse, F. Douglas. Demographic Aspects of Regional Economic Development in the USSR. In *Bandera, V. N. and Melnyk, Z. L., eds.,* 1973, pp. 154–66.

———— and Horwitz, Bertrand. Soviet Land Value and Enterprise Location. *Land Econ.,* May 1973, *49*(2), pp. 233–37.

Whitlam, E. G. Focus on Australia: Change Will Mean Opportunity. *World Devel.,* May 1973, *1* (5), pp. 65.

Whitman, Andrew F. and Williams, C. Arthur, Jr. Open Competition Rating Laws and Price Competition. *J. Risk Ins.,* December 1973, *40*(4), pp. 483–96.

Whitman, Marina v. N. and Miller, Norman C. Alternative Theories and Tests of U.S. Short-Term Foreign Investment. *J. Finance,* December 1973, *28* (5), pp. 1131–50.

Whitmore, G. A. Health State Preferences and the Social Choice. In *Berg, R. L., ed.,* 1973, pp. 135–45.

———— and Amey, Lloyd R. Capital Budgeting under Rationing: Comments on the Lusztig and Schwab Procedure. *J. Financial Quant. Anal.,* January 1973, *8*(1), pp. 127–35.

Whitney, J. B. R. Ecology and Environmental Control. In *Oksenberg, M., ed.,* 1973, pp. 95–109.

Whitt, Ward and Shubik, Martin. Fiat Money in an Economy with One Nondurable Good and No Credit (A Noncooperative Sequential Game). In *Blaquière, A., ed.,* 1973, pp. 401–48.

Whittington, G. Field Systems of Scotland. In *Baker, A. R. H. and Butlin, R. A., eds.,* 1973, pp. 530–79.

Whyman, John. A Hanoverian Watering-Place: Margate before the Railway. In *Everitt, A., ed.,* 1973, pp. 138–60.

Whyte, William F. Organizations for the Future. In *Somers, G. G., ed.,* 1973, pp. 129–40.

Wiar, Robert C. Economic Implications of Multiple Rates of Return in the Leveraged Lease Context. *J. Finance,* December 1973, *28*(5), pp. 1275–86.

Wible, Lyman and Fox, Irving K. Information Generation and Communication to Establish Environmental Quality Objectives. *Natural Res. J.,* January 1973, *13*(1), pp. 134–49.

Wichern, Dean W. and Haugen, Robert A. The Diametric Effects of the Capital Gains Tax on the Stability of Stock Prices. *J. Finance*, September 1973, *28*(4), pp. 987–96.

Wicke, Lutz. Zinserhöhungen bei festverzinslichen Wertpapieren während einer schleichdenden Inflation. (Are Increases in the Interest Rates of Fixed-Interest-Bearing Securities During a Creeping Inflation a Compensation for Losses of Real Value? With English summary.) *Z. Wirtschaft. Sozialwissen.*, 1973, *93*(5), pp. 567–85.

Wickens, M. R. and Greenfield, J. N. The Econometrics of Agricultural Supply: An Application to the World Coffee Market. *Rev. Econ. Statist.*, November 1973, *55*(4), pp. 433–40.

Widing, J. William, Jr. Reorganizing Your Worldwide Business. *Harvard Bus. Rev.*, May-June 1973, *51*(3), pp. 153–60.

Widner, Ralph R. Evaluating the Administration of the Appalachian Regional Development Program. *Growth Change*, January 1973, *4*(1), pp. 25–29.

Wieand, Kenneth F. Air Pollution and Property Values: A Study of the St. Louis Area. *J. Reg. Sci.*, April 1973, *13*(1), pp. 91–95.

Wiegand, G. C. America and the International Monetary Crisis. In *Wiegand, G. C., ed.*, 1973, pp. 56–62.

——— Whither the World? In *Wiegand, G. C., ed.*, 1973, pp. iii–vii.

Wiegner, Edward A. Tax Simplification. *Nat. Tax J.*, September 1973, *26*(3), pp. 337–39.

Wiener, Anthony J. The Future of Economic Activity. *Ann. Amer. Acad. Polit. Soc. Sci.*, July 1973, *408*, pp. 47–61.

Wiese, Karl E.; Blaquière, Austin and Juricek, Libuska. Geometry of Pareto Equilibria in N-Person Differential Games. In *Blaquière, A., ed.*, 1973, pp. 271–310.

Wilber, Charles K. Economic Development, Central Planning and Allocative Efficiency. In *Wilber, C. K., ed.*, 1973, pp. 221–39.

——— The Human Costs of Economic Development: The West, the Soviet Union, and Underdeveloped Countries Today. In *Wilber, C. K., ed.*, 1973, pp. 324–41.

Wilcsek, J. Interrelations between the National Economic Management Systems and the Socialist International Market Mechanism. In *Kiss, T., ed.*, 1973, pp. 99–107.

Wilder, Ronald P. Public Utility Advertising: Some Observations. *Land Econ.*, November 1973, *49*(4), pp. 458–62.

Wiles, Peter. Cost Inflation and the State of Economic Theory. *Econ. J.*, June 1973, *83*(330), pp. 377–98.

Wiley, David E. The Identification Problem for Structural Equation Models with Unmeasured Variables. In *Goldberger, A. S. and Duncan, O. D., eds.*, 1973, pp. 69–83.

———; Schmidt, William H. and Bramble, William J. Studies of a Class of Covariance Structure Models. *J. Amer. Statist. Assoc.*, June 1973, *68*(342), pp. 317–23.

Wilford, W. T. The Central American Common Market: Trade Patterns After a Decade of Union.

Nebr. J. Econ. Bus., Summer 1973, *12*(3), pp. 3–22.

——— Nutrition Levels and Economic Growth: Some Empirical Measures. *J. Econ. Issues*, September 1973, *7*(3), pp. 437–58.

——— and Christou, G. A Sectoral Analysis of Disaggregated Trade Flows in the Central American Common Market 1962–1970. *J. Common Market Stud.*, December 1973, *12*(2), pp. 159–75.

——— and Villasuso, Juan M. The Velocity of Money in Central America. *Bangladesh Econ. Rev.*, October 1973, *1*(4), pp. 375–86.

Wilhelm, Walter T. and Sturdivant, Frederick D. Poverty, Minorities, and Consumer Exploitation. In *Murray, B. B., ed.*, 1973, pp. 447–54.

Wilkie, William L. and Bass, Frank M. A Comparative Analysis of Attitudinal Predictions of Brand Preference. *J. Marketing Res.*, August 1973, *10*(3), pp. 262–69.

——— and Pessemier, Edgar A. Issues in Marketing's Use of Multi-Attribute Attitude Models. *J. Marketing Res.*, November 1973, *10*(4), pp. 428–41.

Wilkinson, Maurice. An Econometric Analysis of Fertility in Sweden, 1870–1965. *Econometrica*, July 1973, *41*(4), pp. 633–42.

Wilkinson, R. K. House Prices and the Measurement of Externalities. *Econ. J.*, March 1973, *83*(329), pp. 72–86.

——— The Income Elasticity of Demand for Housing. *Oxford Econ. Pap.*, November 1973, *25*(3), pp. 361–77.

——— and Burkitt, B. Wage Determination and Trade Unions. *Scot. J. Polit. Econ.*, June 1973, *20*(2), pp. 107–22.

Willard, Norman, Jr. Relating the Concept and Content to the Consumers. In *McClure, L. and Buan, C., eds.*, 1973, pp. 193–203.

Willassen, Yngve. Three Econometric Applications of Split-variable and NIPALS Modelling. *Écon. Appl.*, 1973, *26*(2–3–4), pp. 471–504.

Wille, Frank. Expanded Powers for Depositary Financial Institutions. In *Federal Reserve Bank of Boston*, 1973, pp. 55–63.

de Willebois, J. L. J. M. van Der Does. A Workshop for Married Women in Part-Time Employment: Implications of an Experiment in the Netherlands. In *Moskoff, W., ed.*, 1973, pp. 302–22.

Willet, Thomas D. and Tollison, Robert D. Some Simple Economics of Voting and Not Voting. *Public Choice*, Fall 1973, *16*, pp. 59–71.

Willett, Thomas D. Secular Inflation and the International Monetary System: Comment. *J. Money, Credit, Banking*, Part II, February 1973, *5*(1), pp. 520–23.

———; Amacher, Ryan C. and Tollison, Robert D. Import Controls on Foreign Oil: Comment. *Amer. Econ. Rev.*, December 1973, *63*(5), pp. 1031–34.

——— and Herring, Richard. The Relationship Between U.S. Direct Investment at Home and Abroad. *Rivista Int. Sci. Econ. Com.*, January 1973, *20*(1), pp. 72–82.

——— and Tollison, Robert D. The University and the Price System. *J. Econ. Bus.*, Spring-Summer 1973, *25*(3), pp. 191–97.

Williams, Alan. Cost-Benefit Analysis: Bastard

Science? And/Or Insidious Poison in the Body Politick? In *Niskanen, W. A., et al., eds.,* 1973, pp. 48–74.

———— Cost-benefit Analysis: Bastard Science? And/Or Insidious Poison in the Body Politick? In *Wolfe, J. N., ed.,* 1973, pp. 30–60.

———— and Sugden, Robert. The Location Choices of Students in Lodgings and Flats. *Urban Stud.,* February 1973, *10*(1), pp. 87–90.

Williams, Anne D. and Zellner, Arnold. Bayesian Analysis of the Federal Reserve–MIT–Penn Model's Almon Lag Consumption Function. *J. Econometrics,* October 1973, *1*(3), pp. 267–99.

Williams, B. R. The Basis of Science Policy in Market Economies. In *Williams, B. R., ed.,* 1973, pp. 416–31.

———— Science and Technology in Economic Growth: Introduction. In *Williams, B. R., ed.,* 1973, pp. xi–xvii.

Williams, C. Arthur, Jr. and Whitman, Andrew F. Open Competition Rating Laws and Price Competition. *J. Risk Ins.,* December 1973, *40*(4), pp. 483–96.

Williams, David O., Jr. Simplification of the Federal Tax Laws for Corporations. *Nat. Tax J.,* September 1973, *26*(3), pp. 331–36.

Williams, Fred E. The Effect of Market Organization on Competitive Equilibrium: The Multi-Unit Case. *Rev. Econ. Stud.,* January 1973, *40*(1), pp. 97–113.

———— On the Evaluation of Intertemporal Outcomes. In *Cochrane, J. L. and Zeleny, M., eds.,* 1973, pp. 429–38.

Williams, Gareth and Psacharopoulos, George. Public Sector Earnings and Educational Planning. *Int. Lab. Rev.,* July 1973, *108*(1), pp. 43–57.

Williams, Harold M. The Future of ARIA. *J. Risk Ins.,* March 1973, *40*(1), pp. 103–09.

Williams, Harold R. Exchange Rate Systems, the Marginal Efficiency of Investment, and Foreign Direct Capital Movements. *Kyklos,* 1973, *26*(1), pp. 58–74.

———— Exchange Rate Systems, the Marginal Efficiency of Investment and Foreign Direct Capital Movements: Reply. *Kyklos,* 1973, *26*(4), pp. 869.

———— Resource Allocation under Alternative Exchange Rate Systems: Reply. *Southern Econ. J.,* April 1973, *39*(4), pp. 651.

Williams, J. Allen, Jr.; Beeson, Peter G. and Johnson, David R. Some Factors Associated with Income Among Mexican Americans. *Soc. Sci. Quart.,* March 1973, *53*(4), pp. 710–15.

Williams, John D. Security Exchange Packages Utilized in Mergers. *J. Econ. Bus.,* Spring-Summer 1973, *25*(3), pp. 187–90.

Williams, Maurice J. A Bilateral Viewpoint: Comment. In *Lewis, J. P. and Kapur, I., eds.,* 1973, pp. 103–08.

Williams, P. R. and Stabler, J. C. The Changing Structure of the Central Place Hierarchy. *Land Econ.,* November 1973, *49*(4), pp. 454–58.

Williams, Raburn and Miller, Roger LeRoy. A Note on the Effects of Government Finance on Aggregate Demand for Goods and Services. *Public Finance,* 1973, *28*(3–4), pp. 393–96.

Williams, R. L. A Note on the Specification and Esti-

mation of a Bias in the Measurement of the Size and Growth of Real GDP in Jamaica. *Soc. Econ. Stud.,* September 1973, *22*(3), pp. 384–94.

Williams, Robert M. and Ratajczak, Donald. Forecast. Another Year of Prosperity for 1973. *Calif. Manage. Rev.,* Spring 1973, *15*(3), pp. i–v.

Williams, S. W. Potential of Soybeans as Food in India. *Ill. Agr. Econ.,* January 1973, *13*(1), pp. 1–7.

Williams, T. David and Ntim, S. M. Public Employment Centres as a Source of Data on Unemployment in Ghana. *Econ. Bull. Ghana, Sec. Ser.,* 1973, *3*(1), pp. 16–26.

Williams, Walter E. Why the Poor Pay More: An Alternative Explanation. *Soc. Sci. Quart.,* September 1973, *54*(2), pp. 375–79.

Williams, W. H.; Davis, E. G. and Dunn, D. M. Ambiguities in the Cross-Section Analysis of Per Share Financial Data. *J. Finance,* December 1973, *28*(5), pp. 1241–48.

Williams, Willard F. Another Look at Economies of Size of Cattle Feeding. *Can. J. Agr. Econ.,* February 1973, *21*(1), pp. 65.

Williams, William V., et al. The Stability, Growth and Stabilizing Influence of State Taxes. *Nat. Tax J.,* June 1973, *26*(2), pp. 267–74.

Williamson, Jeffrey G. Comparative Consumption Patterns, the Extent of the Market, and Alternative Development Strategies: Comment. In *Ayal, E. B., ed.,* 1973, pp. 80–83.

———— Late Nineteenth-Century American Retardation: A Neoclassical Analysis. *J. Econ. Hist.,* September 1973, *33*(3), pp. 581–607.

———— and Brito, Dagobert L. Skilled Labor and Nineteenth Century Anglo-American Managerial Behavior. *Exploration Econ. Hist.,* Spring 1973, *10*(3), pp. 235–51.

———— and Kelley, Allen C. Modeling Economic Development and General Equilibrium Histories. *Amer. Econ. Rev.,* May 1973, *63*(2), pp. 450–58.

———— and Kelley, Allen C. Sources of Growth Methodology in Low-Income Countries: A Critique. *Quart. J. Econ.,* February 1973, *87*(1), pp. 138–47.

Williamson, John. Another Case of Profitable Destabilising Speculation. *J. Int. Econ.,* February 1973, *3*(1), pp. 77–83.

———— Payments Objectives and Economic Welfare. *Int. Monet. Fund Staff Pap.,* November 1973, *20*(3), pp. 573–90.

———— Stability, Resource Transfers and Income Distribution. In *Wiegand, G. C., ed.,* 1973, pp. 73–76.

———— Surveys in Applied Economics: International Liquidity. *Econ. J.,* September 1973, *83*(331), pp. 685–746.

Williamson, John W. and Berdit, Martin. Function Limitation Scale for Measuring Health Outcomes. In *Berg, R. L., ed.,* 1973, pp. 59–65.

Williamson, Oliver E. Markets and Hierarchies: Some Elementary Considerations. *Amer. Econ. Rev.,* May 1973, *63*(2), pp. 316–25.

Willis, Robert J. An Imputation to the Measure of Economic Growth for Changes in Life Expectancy: Comment. In *Moss, M., ed.,* 1973, pp. 226–32.

———— A New Approach to the Economic Theory of

Fertility Behavior. *J. Polit. Econ.*, Part II, March-April 1973, *81*(2), pp. S14–64.

Willmore, L. N. Direct Foreign Investment and Industrial Entrepreneurship in Central America. In *Pollock, D. H. and Ritter, A. R. M., eds.*, 1973, pp. 287–300.

Wills, Ian R. and Lloyd, A. G. Economic Theory and Sheep-Cattle Combinations. *Australian J. Agr. Econ.*, April 1973, *17*(1), pp. 58–67.

Wills, Walter J. SIU's Curriculum in Agricultural Economics. *Amer. J. Agr. Econ.*, Part II, November 1973, *55*(4), pp. 750–51.

Wilson, A. G. Examination of Alternative Methods, Approaches, and Programs for Production and Market Stabilization with Particular Reference to the Pacific Rim Market. In *Canadian Agricultural Economics Society*, 1973, pp. 98–140.

———— **and Kulshreshtha, S. N.** A Harmonic Analysis of Cattle and Hog Cycles in Canada. *Can. J. Agr. Econ.*, November 1973, *21*(3), pp. 34–45.

Wilson, Alan. Maritime Business History: A Reconnaissance of Records, Sources, and Prospects. *Bus. Hist. Rev.*, Summer 1973, *47*(2), pp. 260–76.

Wilson, Carroll L. A Plan for Energy Independence. *Foreign Aff.*, July 1973, *51*(4), pp. 657–75.

Wilson, Charles J. The Operating Lease and the Risk of Obsolescence. *Manage. Account.*, December 1973, *55*(6), pp. 41–44.

Wilson, David A. A Note on "Environmental Complexity and Financial Reports" *Accounting Rev.*, July 1973, *48*(3), pp. 586–88.

Wilson, Douglas. The Economic Analysis of Malnutrition. In *Berg, A.; Scrimshaw, N. S. and Call, D. L., eds.*, 1973, pp. 129–44.

Wilson, Ewen M. The Gold Standard and Monetary Reform. *S. Afr. J. Econ.*, March 1973, *41*(1), pp. 17–25.

———— The Rhodesian Constitution and Predictions for Political Stability. *Public Choice*, Fall 1973, *16*, pp. 77–80.

Wilson, Franklin D. and Bumpass, Larry. The Prediction of Fertility among Catholics: A Longitudinal Analysis. *Demography*, November 1973, *10* (4), pp. 591–97.

Wilson, I. H.; Robertson, B. C. and Ellis, P. L. Rock Phosphate Mining in North West Queensland—A Cost-Benefit Analysis. *Econ. Anal. Pol.*, March 1973, *4*(1), pp. 23–32.

Wilson, James Q. The War on Cities. In *Rasmussen, D. W. and Haworth, C. T., eds.*, 1973, pp. 16–27.

Wilson, J. Harold. Statistics and Decision-making in Government— Bradshaw Revisited: The Address of the President (with Proceedings). *J. Roy. Statist. Soc.*, Part 1, 1973, *136*, pp. 1–20.

Wilson, J. S. G. The Australian Money Market. *Banca Naz. Lavoro Quart. Rev.*, March 1973, (104), pp. 46–69.

Wilson, Ruth. Banking the Boom. *Fed. Res. Bank San Francisco Rev.*, May-June 1973, pp. 9–13.

———— Where the Money Came From. *Fed. Res. Bank San Francisco Rev.*, January-February 1973, pp. 9–11.

Wilson, Thomas. Pensions, Inflation and Growth. *Lloyds Bank Rev.*, April 1973, (108), pp. 1–17.

———— Pensions, Inflation and Growth. In *Robinson, J., ed.*, 1973, pp. 88–114.

Wilson, William J. Consumer Reality and Corporate Image. *Calif. Manage. Rev.*, Winter 1973, *16*(2), pp. 85–90.

Wilton, D. A. and Rowley, J. C. R. The Empirical Sensitivity of the Phillips Curve. *Amer. Econ.*, Fall 1973, *17*(2), pp. 90–112.

———— Quarterly Models of Wage Determination Some New Efficient Estimates. *Amer. Econ. Rev.*, June 1973, *63*(3), pp. 380–89.

———— Wage Determination: The Use of Instrumental Assumptions. *Int. Econ. Rev.*, June 1973, *14*(2), pp. 525–29.

Winch, David M. The Pure Theory of Non-Pure Goods. *Can. J. Econ.*, May 1973, *6*(2), pp. 149–63.

Wind, Yoram; Jain, Arun K. and Green, Paul E. Analyzing Free-Response Data in Marketing Research. *J. Marketing Res.*, February 1973, *10*(1), pp. 45–52.

Winder, John W. L. and Smith, Lawrence B. Interest Rate Expectations and the Demand for Money in Canada: Reply. *J. Finance*, March 1973, *28*(1), pp. 213–14.

Windham, Douglas M. The Economics of Education: A Survey. In *Chamberlain, N. W., ed.*, 1973, pp. 159–217.

Windsor, James S. Optimization Model for the Operation of Flood Control Systems. *Water Resources Res.*, October 1973, *9*(5), pp. 1219–26.

Winegarden, C. R. Welfare 'Explosion': Determinants of the Size and Recent Growth of the AFDC Population. *Amer. J. Econ. Soc.*, July 1973, *32*(3), pp. 245–56.

Winer, Leon. The Effect of Product Sales Quotas on Sales Force Productivity. *J. Marketing Res.*, May 1973, *10*(2), pp. 180–83.

Winfield, Gerald F. The Impact of Urbanization on Agricultural Processes. *Ann. Amer. Acad. Polit. Soc. Sci.*, January 1973, *405*, pp. 65–74.

Wing, Paul. Operating Expenditures and Sponsored Research at U.S. Medical Schools: Reply. *J. Human Res.*, Fall 1973, *8*(4), pp. 522–24.

Wingate, Livingston L. The Politics of Manpower Planning: Discussion. In *Aronson, R. L., ed.*, 1973, pp. 22–23.

Winger, Alan R. Some Internal Determinants of Upkeep Spending by Urban Home-Owners. *Land Econ.*, November 1973, *49*(4), pp. 474–79.

Wingo, Lowdon. The Quality of Life: Toward a Microeconomic Definition. *Urban Stud.*, February 1973, *10*(1), pp. 3–18.

Winkle, Gary M. Perspectives on Life Insurance Financial Reporting: Discussion. *J. Risk Ins.*, March 1973, *40*(1), pp. 25–30.

Winkler, Robert L. Bayesian Models for Forecasting Future Security Prices. *J. Financial Quant. Anal.*, June 1973, *8*(3), pp. 387–405.

Winklevoss, Howard E. An Explanatory Analysis of the Insurable Value Concept. *J. Risk Ins.*, September 1973, *40*(3), pp. 437–42.

———— **and Zelten, Robert A.** An Empirical Analysis of Mutual Life Insurance Company Surplus. *J. Risk Ins.*, September 1973, *40*(3), pp. 403–25.

Winpisinger, William W. Job Enrichment: A Union View. *Mon. Lab. Rev.*, April 1973, *96*(4), pp. 54–56.

Winston, Gordon C. A Note on the Political Economy of Development Theory. *Bangladesh Econ. Rev.*, January 1973, *1*(1), pp. 115–17.

Winter, E. Radical Egalitarianism: The Chinese Experience. *Amer. Econ.*, Spring 1973, *17*(1), pp. 174–77.

Winter, Frederick W. A Laboratory Experiment of Individual Attitude Response to Advertising Exposure. *J. Marketing Res.*, May 1973, *10*(2), pp. 130–40.

Winter, Ralph K., Jr. Economic Regulation vs. Competition: Ralph Nader and Creeping Capitalism. *Yale Law J.*, April 1973, *82*(5), pp. 890–902.

Winter, Sidney G. and Nelson, Richard R. Toward an Evolutionary Theory of Economic Capabilities. *Amer. Econ. Rev.*, May 1973, *63*(2), pp. 440–49.

Wirt, Frederick M. Financial and Desegregation Reform in Suburbia. In *Masotti, L. H. and Hadden, J. K., eds.*, 1973, pp. 457–88.

Wise, Gordon L. The Business of Major League Baseball as a Spectator Sport. *Ohio State U. Bull. Bus. Res.*, October 1973, *48*(10), pp. 1–3, 6–7.

Wise, J. and Pearce, I. F. On the Uniqueness of Competitive Equilibrium: Part I, Unbounded Demand. *Econometrica*, September 1973, *41*(5), pp. 817–28.

Wiseman, Jack. Uncertainty, Costs, and Collectivist Economic Planning. In *Buchanan, J. M. and Thirlby, G. F., eds.*, 1973, pp. 227–43.

Wisman, Jon D. and Sawers, Larry. Wealth Taxation for the United States. *J. Econ. Issues*, September 1973, *7*(3), pp. 417–36.

de Wit, Y. B. The *Kabupaten* Program. *Bull. Indonesian Econ. Stud.*, March 1973, *9*(1), pp. 65–85.

Witney, Fred. Final-Offer Arbitration: The Indianapolis Experience. *Mon. Lab. Rev.*, May 1973, *96*(5), pp. 20–25.

Witt, Robert Charles. Pricing and Underwriting Risk in Automobile Insurance: A Probabilistic View. *J. Risk Ins.*, December 1973, *40*(4), pp. 509–31.

——— Pricing Problems in Automobile Insurance: An Economic Analysis. *J. Risk Ins.*, March 1973, *40*(1), pp. 75–93.

Witt, Robert E.; Martin, Warren S. and Bruce, Grady D. Interpersonal Orientation and Innovative Behavior. *Miss. Val. J. Bus. Econ.*, Winter 1973-74, *9*(2), pp. 35–42.

Witte, Ann Dryden. Employment in the Manufacturing Sector of Developing Economies: A Study of Mexico and Peru. *J. Devel. Stud.*, October 1973, *10*(1), pp. 33–49.

Wittenberg, J. I. The Effective Rate of Inflation. *Rev. Marketing Agr. Econ.*, June and September 1973, *41*(2–3), pp. 93–94.

Witthans, Fred. Estimates of Effective Rates of Protection for United States Industries in 1967. *Rev. Econ. Statist.*, August 1973, *55*(3), pp. 362–64.

Wittich, Günter and Shiratori, Masaki. The Snake in the Tunnel. *Finance Develop.*, June 1973, *10*(2), pp. 9–13, 38.

Wittkopf, Eugene R. Foreign Aid and United Nations Votes: A Comparative Study. *Amer. Polit. Sci. Rev.*, September 1973, *67*(3), pp. 868–88.

Wittman, Donald A. Parties as Utility Maximizers. *Amer. Polit. Sci. Rev.*, June 1973, *67*(2), pp. 490–98.

——— **and Nichols, Charles.** Cheating and Control. *Public Choice*, Spring 1973, *14*, pp. 137–42.

Witton, Ronald A. and Owen, Carol. National Division and Mobilization: A Reinterpretation of Primacy. *Econ. Develop. Cult. Change*, January 1973, *21*(2), pp. 325–37.

——— A Note on Conditions Supporting the Covariation of External and Internal Conflict. *Econ. Develop. Cult. Change*, October 1973, *22*(1), pp. 114–23.

van de Woestijne, W. J. Toepassing van de Wet van Pareto op de lage inkomens. (Application of Pareto's Law to Low Incomes. With English summary.) *De Economist*, January-February 1973, *121*(1), pp. 29–51.

Wogart, Jan P. Inflation and Stagnation in Brazil: Comment. *Econ. Develop. Cult. Change*, April 1973, *21*(3), pp. 526–29.

Wohl, Martin; Meyer, John R. and Kain, John F. Economic Change and the City: A Qualitative Evaluation and Some Hypotheses. In *Grieson, R. E., ed.*, 1973, pp. 55–72.

Wolf, Charles, Jr. Heresies About Time: Wasted Time, Double-Duty Time, and Past Time. *Quart. J. Econ.*, November 1973, *87*(4), pp. 661–67.

——— Military-Industrial Complexities. In *Andreano, R. L., ed.*, 1973, pp. R339–04.

——— **and Weinschrott, David.** International Transactions and Regionalism: Distinguishing "Insiders" from "Outsiders." *Amer. Econ. Rev.*, May 1973, *63*(2), pp. 52–60.

Wolf, Thomas A. A Note on the Restrictive Effect of Unilateral United States Export Controls. *J. Polit. Econ.*, January-February 1973, *81*(1), pp. 219–22.

Wolfe, Alan. Waiting for Righty: A Critique of the "Fascism" Hypothesis. *Rev. Radical Polit. Econ.*, Fall 1973, *5*(3), pp. 46–66.

Wolfe, J. N. Cost Benefit and Cost Effectiveness: Studies and Analysis: Introduction. In *Wolfe, J. N., ed.*, 1973, pp. 9–14.

——— Cost Escalation in Research and Development Activities. In *Edge, D. O. and Wolfe, J. N., eds.*, 1973, pp. 225–30.

Wolff, Edward. IOPE: Input/Output Program for Economists. *Ann. Econ. Soc. Measure*, July 1973, *2*(3), pp. 309–12.

de Wolff, P. and van Slijpe, A. R. D. The Relation Between Income, Intelligence, Education and Social Background. *Europ. Econ. Rev.*, October 1973, *4*(3), pp. 235–64.

Wolfson, M. and Rayner, A. Analytics of Choice in Fiscal Policy. In *Parkin, M., ed.*, 1973, pp. 345–68.

Wolfstetter, E. Surplus Labour, Synchronised Labor Costs and Marx's Labour Theory of Value. *Econ. J.*, September 1973, *83*(331), pp. 787–809.

Wolk, Harry I. and Tearney, Michael G. Income Tax Allocation and Loss Carryforwards: Exploring Uncharted Ground. *Accounting Rev.*, April 1973, *48*(2), pp. 292–99.

Wolken, Lawrence C.; Thompson, Richard G. and Callen, Richard W. A Stochastic Investment Model for a Survival Conscious Fishing Firm. In *Sokoloski, A. A., ed.*, 1973, pp. 112–20.

Wolkowitz, Benjamin. Estimation of a Set of Homothetic Production Functions: A Time Series Analysis of American Postwar Manufacturing. *Southern Econ. J.*, April 1973, *39*(4), pp. 626–37.

Wollheim, Richard. John Stuart Mill and the Limits of State Action. *Soc. Res.*, Spring 1973, *40*(1), pp. 1–30.

Wolpert, Julian and Mumphrey, Anthony J. Equity Considerations and Concessions in the Siting of Public Facilities. *Econ. Geogr.*, April 1973, *49*(2), pp. 109–21.

Womack, Abner; Heien, Dale and Matthews, Jim. A Methods Note on the Gauss-Seidel Algorithm for Solving Econometric Models. *Agr. Econ. Res.*, July 1973, *25*(3), pp. 71–80.

Womer, Norman K. Lancaster's Version of the Walras-Wald Model. *J. Econ. Theory*, October 1973, *6*(5), pp. 515–19.

Wong, John. Agricultural Production and Socialist Transformation in China: Two Decades After. *Malayan Econ. Rev.*, October 1973, *18*(2), pp. 1–15.

Wong, Stanley. The "F-Twist" and the Methodology of Paul Samuelson. *Amer. Econ. Rev.*, June 1973, *63*(3), pp. 312–25.

Woo, H. Nam and Barckley, Robert. Sources of Cost Differentials in Higher Education: The Case of California State Colleges. *Malayan Econ. Rev.*, October 1973, *18*(2), pp. 68–78.

Wood, G. Donald, Jr. Problems of Comparisons in Africa with Special Regard to Kenya. *Rev. Income Wealth*, March 1973, *19*(1), pp. 105–16.

Wood, Geoffrey E. Resource Allocation under Alternative Exchange Rate Systems: A Comment. *Southern Econ. J.*, April 1973, *39*(4), pp. 650–51.

Wood, Harold A. Obstacles to Development in Latin America: An Evaluation of the Planning Process. In *Pollock, D. H. and Ritter, A. R. M., eds.*, 1973, pp. 47–57.

Wood, William F. J. The Effect of Dual Markets on Common Stock Market Making: Comment. *J. Financial Quant. Anal.*, March 1973, *8*(2), pp. 191–92.

Woodfield, Alan. Biased Efficiency Growth and the Declining Relative Share of Labor in New Zealand Manufacturing. *Southern Econ. J.*, January 1973, *39*(3), pp. 373–80.

Woodhall, Maureen. Manpower Forecasting for Single Occupations: Engineers in India. In *Ahamad, B. and Blaug, M., eds.*, 1973, pp. 157–200.

Woods, Roger. Interdisciplinary Courses and Professional Training in East African Universities. In *Livingstone, I., et al., eds.*, 1973, pp. 105–17.

———— **and Saul, John S.** Appendix: African Peasantries. In *Arrighi, G. and Saul, J. S.*, 1973, pp. 406–16.

Woods, W. Fred. Impact of Estate and Inheritance Taxes on U.S. Farms. *Agr. Finance Rev.*, July 1973, *34*, pp. 7–11.

———— Tax-Loss Farming. *Agr. Finance Rev.*, July 1973, *34*, pp. 24–30.

Woodward, John T. Capital Spending Expected to Rise Through First Half of 1974. *Surv. Curr. Bus.*, December 1973, *53*(12), pp. 9–13.

———— Investment Programs and Sales Expectations for 1973. *Surv. Curr. Bus.*, March 1973, *53*(3), pp. 16–21.

———— 1973 Plant and Equipment Expenditure Pro-

grams. *Surv. Curr. Bus.*, June 1973, *53*(6), pp. 8–11.

Woodward, Robert S. The Iso-Outlay Function and Variable Transport Costs. *J. Reg. Sci.*, December 1973, *13*(3), pp. 349–55.

Woodworth, Laurence N. Tax Reform—Past and Present. In *Tax Foundation, Inc.*, 1973, pp. 10–13.

Wool, Harold. What's Wrong with Work in America?—A Review Essay. *Mon. Lab. Rev.*, March 1973, *96*(3), pp. 38–44.

Woolley, P. K. A Cost-Benefit Analysis of the Concorde Project: Rejoinder. *J. Transp. Econ. Policy*, September 1973, *7*(3), pp. 301–02.

Worcester, Dean A., Jr. New Estimates of the Welfare Loss to Monopoly, United States: 1956–1969. *Southern Econ. J.*, October 1973, *40*(2), pp. 234–45.

Worcester, Robert M. Il valore della "corporate image." (The Value of Corporate Image. With English summary.) *L'Impresa*, 1973, *15*(9–10), pp. 522–26.

Working, E. J. What Do Statistical "Demand Curves" Show? In *Haynes, W. W.; Coyne, T. J. and Osborne, D. K., eds.*, 1973, pp. 61–73.

Workman, Randy L. Ohio's Women Workers. *Ohio State U. Bull. Bus. Res.*, August 1973, *48*(8), pp. 4–6.

Worland, Stephen T. The Economic Significance of John Rawls' A Theory of Justice. *Nebr. J. Econ. Bus.*, Autumn 1973, *12*(4), pp. 119–26.

Woroniak, Alexander. Regional Aspects of Soviet Planning and Industrial Organization. In *Bandera, V. N. and Melnyk, Z. L., eds.*, 1973, pp. 261–304.

Worrell, DeLisle. Comment on Three Econometric Models of the Jamaican Economy. *Soc. Econ. Stud.*, June 1973, *22*(2), pp. 272–86.

Worthington, Nancy L. and Cooper, Barbara S. Age Differences in Medical Care Spending, Fiscal Year 1972. *Soc. Sec. Bull.*, May 1973, *36*(5), pp. 3–15.

———— National Health Expenditures, 1929–72. *Soc. Sec. Bull.*, January 1973, *36*(1), pp. 3–19, 40.

Wotruba, Thomas R. and Breeden, Joseph S. The Ideal Company Image and Self-Image Congruence. *J. Bus. Res.*, Fall 1973, *1*(2), pp. 165–72.

Wright, Chester. Recruiting and Developing PPB Staff. In *Novick, D., ed.*, 1973, pp. 193–200.

Wright, Colin and Strotz, Robert H. Externalities, Welfare Economics, and Environmental Problems. In *Boulding, K. E.; Pfaff, M. and Pfaff, A., eds.*, 1973, pp. 359–73.

Wright, Gavin. New and Old Views on the Economics of Slavery. *J. Econ. Hist.*, June 1973, *33*(2), pp. 452–66.

———— Race, Tenure, and Resource Allocation in Southern Agriculture, 1910: Discussion. *J. Econ. Hist.*, March 1973, *33*(1), pp. 170–76.

Wright, Peter L. The Cognitive Processes Mediating Acceptance of Advertising. *J. Marketing Res.*, February 1973, *10*(1), pp. 53–62.

———— **and Bither, Stewart W.** The Self-Confidence-Advertising Response Relationship: A Function of Situational Distraction. *J. Marketing Res.*, May 1973, *10*(2), pp. 146–52.

Wrighton, Fred M. and Brobst, Robert W. The Income Elasticity of Housing: A Cross-Sectional Analysis of New Orleans. *Miss. Val. J. Bus. Econ.,* Winter 1973-74, *9*(2), pp. 43–58.

Wrightsman, Dwayne. On the Rationality of Compensating Balance Requirements. *Southern Econ. J.,* January 1973, *39*(3), pp. 427–30.

Wrigley, Robert L., Jr. Small Cities Can Help to Revitalize Rural Areas. *Ann. Amer. Acad. Polit. Soc. Sci.,* January 1973, *405,* pp. 55–64.

Wu, De-Min. Alternative Tests of Independence Between Stochastic Regressors and Disturbances. *Econometrica,* July 1973, *41*(4), pp. 733–50.

Wu, Hsiu-Kwang. Odd-Lot Trading in the Stock Market and its Market Impact: Reply. *J. Financial Quant. Anal.,* June 1973, *8*(3), pp. 535.

Wu, Joseph S. K. and Herbst, Anthony F. Some Evidence of Subsidization: The U.S. Trucking Industry, 1900–1920. *J. Econ. Hist.,* June 1973, *33* (2), pp. 417–33.

Wu, Roland Y. On Some Aspects of Linearly Aggregated Macro Models. *Int. Econ. Rev.,* October 1973, *14*(3), pp. 785–88.

Wyckham, Robert G. and Stewart, Max D. Public Policy Toward Retailing: Canada. In *Boddewyn, J. J. and Hollander, S. C., eds.,* 1972, pp. 81–99.

Wyer, Rolfe. Learning Curve Techniques for Direct Labor Management. In *Thomas, W. E., Jr., ed.,* 1973, pp. 370–78.

Wykoff, Frank C. A User Cost Approach to New Automobile Purchases. *Rev. Econ. Stud.,* July 1973, *40*(3), pp. 377–90.

Wyman, Harold E. Financial Lease Evaluation Under Conditions of Uncertainty. *Accounting Rev.,* July 1973, *48*(3), pp. 489–93.

Wymer, C. R. A Continuous Disequilibrium Model of United Kingdom Financial Markets. In *Powell, A. A. and Williams, R. A., eds.,* 1973, pp. 301–34.

Xirokostas, D. A. and Psoinos, D. P. A Dynamic Programming Approach to Establishing Teaching Posts in a Centralized Educational System. In *Ross, M., ed.,* 1973, pp. 315–23.

Yaari, Menahem E. and Peleg, Bezalel. On the Existence of a Consistent Course of Action when Tastes are Changing. *Rev. Econ. Stud.,* July 1973, *40*(3), pp. 391–401.

———— Price Properties of Optimal Consumption Programmes. In *Mirrlees, J. A. and Stern, N. H., eds.,* 1973, pp. 306–17.

Yadav, R.; Vathana, C. and Hammonds, T. M. The Elasticity of Demand for Hired Farm Labor. *Amer. J. Agr. Econ.,* May 1973, *55*(2), pp. 242–45.

Yajima, Akira and Schloctern, F. J. M. Meyer Zu. The OECD Trade Model 1970 Version. In *Alexandrides, C. G., ed.,* 1973, pp. 57–78.

Yalem, Ronald. Theories of Regionalism. In *Falk, R. A. and Mendlovitz, S. H., eds.,* 1973, pp. 218–31.

Yamamoto, Hiromasa. Available Jobs and Employment in Japanese Foreign-Going Shipping. *Kobe Econ. Bus. Rev.,* 1973, *20*(20), pp. 51–59.

Yamamura, Kozo. The Development of Za in Medieval Japan. *Bus. Hist. Rev.,* Winter 1973, *47*(4), pp. 438–65.

———— Economic Responsiveness in Japanese Industrialization. In *[Williamson, H. F.],* 1973, pp. 173–97.

———— Toward a Reexamination of the Economic History of Tokugawa Japan, 1600–1867. *J. Econ. Hist.,* September 1973, *33*(3), pp. 509–46.

Yancey, T. A.; Bock, M. E. and Judge, G. G. Properties of Estimators After Preliminary Tests of Significance When Stochastic Restrictions Are Used in Regression. *J. Econometrics,* March 1973, *1*(1), pp. 29–47.

————; **Bock, M. E. and Judge, G. G.** Some Comments on Estimation in Regression After Preliminary Tests of Significance. *J. Econometrics,* June 1973, *1*(2), pp. 191–200.

————; **Judge, G. G. and Bock, M. E.** The Statistical Consequences of Preliminary Test Estimators in Regression. *J. Amer. Statist. Assoc.,* March 1973, *68*(341), pp. 109–16.

————; **Judge, G. G. and Bock, M. E.** Wallace's Weak Mean Square Error Criterion for Testing Linear Restrictions in Regression: A Tighter Bound. *Econometrica,* Nov. 1973, *41*(6), pp. 1203–06.

Yandle, Bruce, Jr. and Barnett, Andy H. Allocating Environmental Resources. *Public Finance,* 1973, *28*(1), pp. 11–19.

Yaron, D. and Olian, A. Application of Dynamic Programming in Markov Chains to the Evaluation of Water Quality in Irrigation. *Amer. J. Agr. Econ.,* August 1973, *55*(3), pp. 467–71.

Yarrow, G. K. Managerial Utility Maximization under Uncertainty. *Economica, N.S.,* May 1973, *40* (158), pp. 155–73.

Yaukey, David and Onaka, Alvin T. Reproductive Time Lost Due to Sexual Union Dissolution in San José, Costa Rica. *Population Stud.,* November 1973, *27*(3), pp. 457–65.

Yeager, Leland B. The Keynesian Diversion. *Western Econ. J.,* June 1973, *11*(2), pp. 150–63.

Yeats, Alexander J. An Analysis of the Effect of Mergers on Banking Market Structures. *J. Money, Credit, Banking,* May 1973, *5*(2), pp. 623–36.

———— An Evaluation of the Predictive Ability of the FRB Sensitive Price Index. *J. Amer. Statist. Assoc.,* December 1973, *68*(344), pp. 782–87.

Yeh, Kung-Chia and Liu, Ta-Chung. Chinese and Other Asian Economies: A Quantitative Evaluation. *Amer. Econ. Rev.,* May 1973, *63*(2), pp. 215–23.

Yeo, Edwin H., III. A Management View of Financial Planning or The Best Laid Schemes. *J. Bank Res.,* Autumn 1973, *4*(3), pp. 207–11.

Yeomans, K. A. and Davis, E. W. Competition and Credit Control: The Rubicon and Beyond. *Lloyds Bank Rev.,* January 1973, (107), pp. 44–55.

Yett, Donald E. and Levine, Daniel S. A Method for Constructing Proxy Measures of Health Status. In *Berg, R. L., ed.,* 1973, pp. 12–22.

———— **and Skinner, Douglas E.** Debility Index for Long-term-care Patients. In *Berg, R. L., ed.,* 1973, pp. 69–81.

Yeung, Patrick. Induced Innovation in Agricultural Development: Comment. In *Ayal, E. B., ed.,* 1973, pp. 208–11.

Ylä-Anttila, Pekka. Infrastruktuuri ja teollisuuden kehitys. (Overhead Capital and Industrial Development. With English summary.) *Liiketaloudellinen Aikak.,* 1973, *22*(4), pp. 278–87.

Yoder, Dale. Personnel Administration. In *Somers,*

G. G., ed., 1973, pp. 141–56.

Yohe, William P.; Schirm, David and Havrilesky, Thomas M. The Economic Affiliations of Directors of Federal Reserve District Banks. *Soc. Sci. Quart.*, December 1973, *54*(3), pp. 608–22.

Yona, Daniel A. N. Savings Banks and Savings Facilities in African Countries: Tanzania. In *Alberici, A. and Baravelli, M., eds.*, 1973, pp. 103–09.

Yordon, Wesley J. and Singell, Larry D. Incentives for More Efficient Education: The Development of a Model. In *Stein, B. and Miller, S. M., eds.*, 1973, pp. 71–91.

Yoshino, Michael Y. Japan: Rationalizing the Retail Structure. In *Boddewyn, J. J. and Hollander, S. C., eds.*, 1972, pp. 213–27.

Yotopoulos, Pan A. Agricultural and Factory Processes: Implications for Empirical Research. *Food Res. Inst. Stud.*, 1973, *12*(2), pp. 159–67.

_____ **and Lau, Lawrence J.** Micro Functions in a Macro Model: An Application to Agricultural Employment and Development Strategies. In *Ayal, E. B., ed.*, 1973, pp. 212–40.

_____ **and Lau, Lawrence J.** A Test for Relative Economic Efficiency: Some Further Results. *Amer. Econ. Rev.*, March 1973, *63*(1), pp. 214–23.

_____ **and Nugent, Jeffrey B.** A Balanced-Growth Version of the Linkage Hypothesis: A Test. *Quart. J. Econ.*, May 1973, *87*(2), pp. 157–71.

Youde, James G. and Carman, Hoy F. Alternative Tax Treatment of Orchard Development Costs: Impacts on Producers, Middlemen, and Consumers. *Amer. J. Agr. Econ.*, May 1973, *55*(2), pp. 184–91.

Younes, Yves and Grandmont, Jean-Michel. On the Efficiency of a Monetary Equilibrium. *Rev. Econ. Stud.*, April 1973, *40*(2), pp. 149–65.

Young, A. Behavioral Science Models: Discussant 2. In *Ross, M., ed.*, 1973, pp. 269–72.

Young, Allan H. The CPI and the PCE Deflator: An Econometric Analysis of Two Price Measures: Comment. *Ann. Econ. Soc. Measure*, July 1973, *2*(3), pp. 283–86.

Young, Anne M. Children of Working Mothers. *Mon. Lab. Rev.*, April 1973, *96*(4), pp. 37–40.

_____ Going Back to School at 35. *Mon. Lab. Rev.*, October 1973, *96*(10), pp. 39–42.

_____ The High School Class of 1972: More at Work, Fewer in College. *Mon. Lab. Rev.*, June 1973, *96*(6), pp. 26–32.

Young, Dennis and Jackson, Emma. Public Policy for Day Care of Young Children: Introduction. In *Young, D. R. and Nelson, R. R., eds.*, 1973, pp. 1–8.

_____ **and Nelson, Richard R.** National Day Care Policy. In *Young, D. R. and Nelson, R. R., eds.*, 1973, pp. 91–103.

Young, Edwin. Personnel Relations in Non-Profit Institutions. In *Somers, G. G., ed.*, 1973, pp. 198–204.

Young, Elmer, Jr. Corporate Social Responsibility to the Minority Community. In *Dierkes, M. and Bauer, R. A., eds.*, 1973, pp. 297–300.

Young, H. Peyton and Thompson, Russell G. Forecasting Water Use for Electric Power Generation. *Water Resources Res.*, August 1973, *9*(4), pp. 800–07.

_____ Forecasting Water Use for Policy Making: A Review. *Water Resources Res.*, August 1973, *9*(4), pp. 792–99.

_____ Least-Cost Allocation and Valuation Model for Water Resources. *Water Resources Res.*, October 1973, *9*(5), pp. 1186–95.

Young, Ralph. An Exploratory Analysis of Demand for the Public Library Lending Service. *Appl. Econ.*, June 1973, *5*(2), pp. 119–32.

_____ Institutional Credit in the Rural Sector: An Exploratory Analysis of Demand and Supply. *Quart. Rev. Agr. Econ.*, October 1973, *26*(4), pp. 228–38.

_____ **and Crestani, I.** Productivity Change and Farm Income. *Quart. Rev. Agr. Econ.*, July 1973, *26*(3), pp. 198–214.

Young, Richard M. Inflation and the Distribution of Income and Wealth: Are the Poor Really Hurt? *Fed. Res. Bank Bus. Rev. Phila.*, September 1973, pp. 16–25.

_____ **and Raiff, Donald L.** Budget Surpluses for State and Local Governments: Undercutting Uncle Sam's Fiscal Stance? *Fed. Res. Bank Bus. Rev. Phila.*, March 1973, pp. 19–28.

Young, Stanley. Organization as a Total System. In *Klein, W. H. and Murphy, D. C., eds.*, 1973, pp. 16–27.

Young, Warren L. Compulsory Loans and Consumption-Savings Behaviour: Some Micro- and Macro-Economic Aspects. *Public Finance*, 1973, *28*(3–4), pp. 333–53.

_____ Compulsory Loans, Disposable Income, and Quarterly Consumption Behaviour in Israel: 1964–1969. *Finanzarchiv*, 1973, *32*(1), pp. 98–115.

Youngson, A. J. Economic Development in the Long Run: Introduction. In *Youngson, A. J., ed.*, 1973, pp. 9–17.

Yu, P. L. Introduction to Domination Structures in Multicriteria Decision Problems. In *Cochrane, J. L. and Zeleny, M., eds.*, 1973, pp. 249–61.

Yu, Seongjae and Neter, John. A Stochastic Model of the Internal Control System. *J. Acc. Res.*, Autumn 1973, *11*(2), pp. 273–95.

Yuchtman, Ephraim. Reward Structure, the Quality of Work Environment, and Social Accounting. In *Dierkes, M. and Bauer, R. A., eds.*, 1973, pp. 183–90.

Yung-kuei, Ch'en. On Scientific Farming. *Chinese Econ. Stud.*, Summer 1973, *6*(4), pp. 56–74.

Yunker, James A. An Appraisal of Langian Socialism. *Indian Econ. J.*, January-March 1973, *20*(3), pp. 382–413.

_____ A Dynamic Optimization Model of the Soviet Enterprise. *Econ. Planning*, 1973, *13*(1–2), pp. 33–51.

_____ A Statistical Estimate of Optimum Population in the United States. *Nebr. J. Econ. Bus.*, Winter 1973, *12*(1), pp. 3–10.

Zabel, Edward. The Competitive Firm, Uncertainty, and Capital Accumulation. *Int. Econ. Rev.*, October 1973, *14*(3), pp. 765–79.

_____ Consumer Choice, Portfolio Decisions, and Transaction Costs. *Econometrica*, March 1973, *41*(2), pp. 321–35.

Zabler, Jeffrey F. More on Wage Rates in the Iron

Industry: Reply. *Exploration Econ. Hist.*, Fall 1973, *11*(1), pp. 95–99.

Zachariah, K. C. and Gholl, Joseph E. Toward the Year 2000. *Finance Develop.*, December 1973, *10* (4), pp. 22–26.

Zack, Arnold M. Meeting the Rising Cost of Public Sector Settlements. *Mon. Lab. Rev.*, May 1973, *96* (5), pp. 38–40.

Zadeh, Lotfi, A. Outline of a New Approach to the Analysis of Complex Systems and Decision Processes. In *Cochrane, J. L. and Zeleny, M., eds.*, 1973, pp. 686–725.

Zagoria, Sam. Resolving Impasses by Public Referendum. *Mon. Lab. Rev.*, May 1973, *96*(5), pp. 36–38.

Zahn, E.; Katona, George and Strumpel, Burkhard. The Sociocultural Environment. In *Thorelli, H. B., ed.*, 1973, pp. 135–45.

Zahn, Frank. A Test of the Escape from the Persistence of Backwardness. *J. Devel. Stud.*, April 1973, *9*(3), pp. 403–11.

―――― **and Hosek, William R.** Impact of Trade Credit on the Velocity of Money and the Market Rate of Interest. *Southern Econ. J.*, October 1973, *40*(2), pp. 202–09.

Zakheim, Dov S. Britain and the EEC-Opinion Poll Data 1970–72. *J. Common Market Stud.*, March 1973, *11*(3), pp. 191–233.

Zalba, Serapio R. Motives of Criminals: Comment. In *Rottenberg, S., ed.*, 1973, pp. 58–62.

Zaloom, Victor A. On the Proper Use of Compound Interest Factors—A Technical Note. *Eng. Econ.*, July-August 1973, *18*(4), pp. 257–64.

Zaman, M. Raquibuz. Sharecropping and Economic Efficiency in Bangladesh. *Bangladesh Econ. Rev.*, April 1973, *1*(2), pp. 149–72.

Zamir, Shmuel; Hildenbrand, Werner and Schmeidler, David. Existence of Approximate Equilibria and Cores. *Econometrica*, November 1973, *41*(6), pp. 1159–66.

Zammit, J. Ann. Introduction: The Context of the Round Table and Subsequent Events. In *Zammit, J. A., ed.*, 1973, pp. 5–13.

Zamoff, Richard and Lyle, Jerolyn R. Planning and Evaluation of Day Care at the Community Level. In *Young, D. R. and Nelson, R. R., eds.*, 1973, pp. 71–90.

Zanella, Angelo. Sulle procedure di classificazione simultanea. (Some Aspects of Simultaneous Test Procedures. With English summary.) *Statistica*, January-March 1973, *33*(1), pp. 63–120.

Zanetti, Giovanni. Elementi per un'analisi economica dell'impresa. (Elements for an Economic Analysis of the Firm. With English summary.) *L'Impresa*, 1973, *15*(3–4), pp. 191–207.

Zannetos, Zenon S. Some Thoughts on Internal Control Systems of the Firm. In *Thomas, W. E., Jr., ed.*, 1973, pp. 2–15.

Zarca, Bernard and Reynaud, Paul. Les leçons d'une enquête sur les petits commerçants âgés (Action sociale et transformation du milieu sociologique). (The Lessons of a Survey of Old Small Shop-keepers. (Social Policy and Change of Social Settings.) With English summary.) *Consommation*, January-March 1973, *20*(1), pp. 59–76.

Zdanowicz, J. and Polaczek, S. Subsidy, Taxation and Foreign Trade. In *Kiss, T., ed.*, 1973, pp. 221–26.

Zech, Charles E. and Brown, Kenneth M. Welfare Effects of Announcing Election Forecasts. *Public Choice*, Spring 1973, *14*, pp. 117–23.

Zecher, Richard. Short-run Monetary Adjustments in the Australian Economy, 1952–70. In *Powell, A. A. and Williams, R. A., eds.*, 1973, pp. 335–48.

Zeckhauser, Richard J. Coverage for Catastrophic Illness. *Public Policy*, Spring 1973, *21*(2), pp. 149–72.

―――― Determining the Qualities of a Public Good—A Paradigm on Town Park Location. *Western Econ. J.*, March 1973, *11*(1), pp. 39–60.

―――― The Risks of Growth. In *Olson, M. and Landsberg, H. H., eds.*, 1973, pp. 103–18.

―――― Time as the Ultimate Source of Utility. *Quart. J. Econ.*, November 1973, *87*(4), pp. 668–75.

―――― Voting Systems, Honest Preferences and Pareto Optimality. *Amer. Polit. Sci. Rev.*, September 1973, *67*(3), pp. 934–46.

―――― **and Weinstein, Milton C.** Critical Ratios and Efficient Allocation. *J. Public Econ.*, April 1973, *2*(2), pp. 147–57.

Zeisel, Rose N. Modernization and Manpower in Textile Mills. *Mon. Lab. Rev.*, June 1973, *96*(6), pp. 18–25.

Zelder, Raymond E.; Ross, Myron H. and Collery, Arnold. Internal and External Balance in an "Almost Classical" World: Reply. *Western Econ. J.*, June 1973, *11*(2), pp. 238–40.

Zeleny, Milan. Compromise Programming. In *Cochrane, J. L. and Zeleny, M., eds.*, 1973, pp. 262–301.

―――― **and Cochrane, James L.** A Priori and A Posteriori Goals in Macroeconomic Policy Making. In *Cochrane, J. L. and Zeleny, M., eds.*, 1973, pp. 373–91.

Zelinka, Jan and Pražák, Ivo. Systém programů pro ekonomicko-matematické úlohy. (System of Computer Programs for Economic-Mathematical Calculations. With English summary.) *Ekon.-Mat. Obzor*, 1973, *9*(4), pp. 393–403.

Zellner, Arnold; Huang, David S. and Chau, L. C. Real Balances and the Demand for Money: Comment. *J. Polit. Econ.*, Part I, March-April 1973, *81* (2), pp. 485–87.

―――― **and Peck, Stephen C.** Simulation Experiments with a Quarterly Macroeconometric Model of the U.S. Economy. In *Powell, A. A. and Williams, R. A., eds.*, 1973, pp. 149–68.

―――― **and Richard, Jean F.** Use of Prior Information in the Analysis and Estimation of Cobb-Douglas Production Function Models. *Int. Econ. Rev.*, February 1973, *14*(1), pp. 107–19.

―――― **and Williams, Anne D.** Bayesian Analysis of the Federal Reserve–MIT–Penn Model's Almon Lag Consumption Function. *J. Econometrics*, October 1973, *1*(3), pp. 267–99.

Zelten, Robert A. and Winklevoss, Howard E. An Empirical Analysis of Mutual Life Insurance Company Surplus. *J. Risk Ins.*, September 1973, *40*(3), pp. 403–25.

Zerbst, Robert H. and Weicher, John C. The Externalities of Neighborhood Parks: An Empirical Investigation. *Land Econ.*, February 1973, *49*(1), pp. 99–105.

Zhamin, V. Economic Progress and the Development of Higher Education. *Prob. Econ.*, August 1973, *16*(4), pp. 47–62.

―――― Forecasting the Level of Education. *Prob. Econ.*, March 1973, *15*(11), pp. 73–91.

Zhuravlev, Y. I. Algorithms for Assessing the Quality of Expert Data. In *Hawkes, N., ed.,* 1973, pp. 238–42.

Ziderman, Adrian. Does it Pay to Take a Degree? *Oxford Econ. Pap.*, July 1973, *25*(2), pp. 262–74.

―――― Estimating U.S. Human Capital Loss in Southeast Asia: Comment. *J. Human Res.*, Fall 1973, *8* (4), pp. 524–26.

―――― On the Ranking of Social Investments in Education: A Comment. *Public Finance*, 1973, *28* (3–4), pp. 424–30.

―――― Rates of Return on Investment in Education: Recent Results for Britain. *J. Human Res.*, Winter 1973, *8*(1), pp. 85–97.

―――― **and Driver, C.** A Markov Chain Model of the Benefits of Participating in Government Training Schemes. *Manchester Sch. Econ. Soc. Stud.*, December 1973, *41*(4), pp. 401–17.

Zimmer, Basil G. Residential Mobility and Housing. *Land Econ.*, August 1973, *49*(3), pp. 344–50.

Zimmerman, Dennis. Expenditure-Tax Incidence Studies, Public Higher Education, and Equity. *Nat. Tax J.*, March 1973, *26*(1), pp. 65–70.

Zimmermann, Karel. Solution of Some Optimization Problems in Extremal Vector Space. (In Russian. With English summary.) *Ekon.-Mat. Obzor*, 1973, *9*(3), pp. 336–50.

Zinam, Oleg. The Dilemma of Specialization versus Autarky in the USSR: Issues and Solutions. In *Bandera, V. N. and Melnyk, Z. L., eds.,* 1973, pp. 196–213.

―――― Impact of Modernization on USSR: Two Revolutions in Conflict. *Econ. Int.*, May 1973, *26*(2), pp. 283–302.

―――― Soviet Dilemma: Modernization Versus Non-Marxist Convergence. *Rivista Int. Sci. Econ. Com.*, June 1973, *20*(6), pp. 526–41.

Zink, Lee B. The New Mexico Economy in 1972 and 1973. *N. Mex. Bus.*, January-February 1973, *26* (1-2), pp. 3–7.

Zinser, James E. and Mikesell, Raymond F. The Nature of the Savings Function in Developing Countries: A Survey of the Theoretical and Empirical Literature. *J. Econ. Lit.*, March 1973, *11* (1), pp. 1–26.

Ziock, Richard W. A Realistic Profit Model for Individual Non-Participating Life Insurance. *J. Risk Ins.*, September 1973, *40*(3), pp. 357–73.

Zis, G. and Purdy, D. L. Trade Unions and Wage Inflation in the UK: A Reappraisal. In *Parkin, M., ed.,* 1973, pp. 294–327.

Zito, George V. A Note on the Population of Seventeenth Century London: Reply. *Demography*, November 1973, *10*(4), pp. 661–62.

Zlocha, Nikolaj. Further Progress in the Work Connected with the System of Plan-Based Management. *Czech. Econ. Digest.*, December 1973, (8), pp. 47–70.

―――― The Role of Economic Production Units/

VHJs/ and Enterprises. *Czech. Econ. Digest.*, May 1973, (3), pp. 52–77.

Zoutendijk, G. Nonlinear Programming. In *Ross, M., ed.,* 1973, pp. 555–57.

Zucker, Albert. Minimum Wages and the Long-run Elasticity of Demand for Low-Wage Labor. *Quart. J. Econ.*, May 1973, *87*(2), pp. 267–77.

Zucker, Jiří. Užití metody Monte Carlo k určení charakteristik souboru investic. (The Use of Monte Carlo Method for Determining the Characteristics of a Collection of Investment Assets. With English summary.) *Ekon.-Mat. Obzor*, 1973, *9*(2), pp. 134–49.

Zukhovitskii, S. T.; Poliak, R. A. and Primak, M. E. Concave Multiperson Games: Numerical Methods. *Matekon*, Summer 1973, *9*(4), pp. 10–30.

Županov, Josip. Two Patterns of Conflict Management in Industry. *Ind. Relat.*, May 1973, *12*(2), pp. 213–23.

Zusman, P.; Melamed, A. and Katzir, I. A Spatial Analysis of the EEC Trade Policies in the Market for Winter Oranges. In *Judge, G. G. and Takayama, T., eds.,* 1973, pp. 464–87.

Zuvekas, Clarence, Jr. and Blankstein, Charles S. Agrarian Reform in Ecuador: An Evaluation of Past Efforts and the Development of a New Approach. *Econ. Develop. Cult. Change*, October 1973, *22*(1), pp. 73–94.

Zvára, Karel. Odvození trístupnové metody nejmensích ctvercu prímym vyuzitím identifikacních omezení. (Derivation of the Three-Stage Least-Squares Method by Means of Direct Use of Identification Restrictions. With English summary.) *Ekon.-Mat. Obzor*, 1973, *9*(3), pp. 292–304.

Zweifel, Peter and Schiltknecht, Kurt. Voraussagen der Kommission für Konjunkturfragen und Modellprognosen 1967–1970. (Forecasts of the Federal Commission on Business Cycles and Model's Predictions 1967-1970. With English summary.) *Schweiz. Z. Volkswirtsch. Statist.*, December 1973, *109*(4), pp. 535–53.

Zweig, Martin E. An Investor Expectations Stock Price Predictive Model Using Closed-End Fund Premiums. *J. Finance*, March 1973, *28*(1), pp. 67–78.

Zweig, Michael. Foreign Investment and the Aggregate Balance of Payments for Underdeveloped Countries. *Rev. Radical Polit. Econ.*, Spring 1973, *5*(1), pp. 13–18.

Zwick, Charles J. Strategic Planning and its Role in the Banking Environment of the Seventies. *J. Bank Res.*, Summer 1973, *4*(2), pp. 74–78.

Zwick, David R. A Criticism of the Effluent Charge. In *Enthoven, A. C. and Freeman, A. M., III, eds.,* 1973, pp. 138–40.

―――― **and Benstock, Marcy.** Water Wasteland: Conclusions and Recommendations. In *Enthoven, A. C. and Freeman, A. M., III, eds.,* 1973, pp. 141–44.

Zwintz, Richard. Der Abwasserkoeffizient der Industrie und ihrer Gruppen. (The Waste Water Coefficient of the Industrial Activities. With English summary.) *Z. ges. Staatswiss.*, October 1973, *129*(4), pp. 714–37.

Topical Guide
To Classification Schedule

TOPICAL GUIDE TO CLASSIFICATION SCHEDULE

This index refers to the subject index *group, category,* or *subcategory* in which the listed topic may be found. The subject index classifications include, in most cases, related topics as well. The term *category* generally indicates that the topic may be found in all of the *subcategories* of the 3-digit code; the term *group,* indicates that the topics may be found in all of the *subcategories* in the 2-digit code. The classification schedule (pp. xxiv) serves to refer the user to cross references.

ABSENTEEISM: 8240

ACCELERATOR: 0233

ACCOUNTING: firm, 5410; national income, 2210, 2212; social, 2250

ADMINISTERED PRICES: theory, 0226; empirical studies, 6110; industry, 6354

ADMINISTRATION: 5130; planning, programming, and budgeting: national, 5130, 3226, state and local, 3241

ADVERTISING: industry, 6354; and marketing, 5310

AFFLUENT SOCIETY: 0510, 0110

AGING POPULATION: as a demographic component, 8410; in the labor force, 8260

AGGREGATION: 2118; in input-output analysis, 2220; from micro to macro, 0220, 0230

AGREEMENTS: collective, 832 category; commodity, 4220, 7130; international trade, 4220

AGRIBUSINESS: 7151

AGRICULTURAL: commodity exchanges, 3132, 7150; cooperatives, 7150; credit, 7140; research and innovation, 621 category; employment, 8131; marketing, 7150; outlook, 7120; productivity, 7110, 7160; situation, 7120; supply and demand analysis, 7110; surpluses, 7130

AGRICULTURE: 710 group; government programs and policy, 7130; and development, 7100, 1120

AIR TRANSPORTATION: 6150

AIRPORT: 6150, 9410

AIRCRAFT MANUFACTURING: 6314

ALLOCATION: welfare aspects, 0242; and general equilibrium, 0210

ALUMINUM INDUSTRY: 6312

ANCIENT ECONOMIC HISTORY: 043 category

ANCIENT ECONOMIC THOUGHT: 0311; individuals, 0322

ANTITRUST POLICY: 6120

APPLIANCE INDUSTRY: 6313

APPRENTICESHIP: 8110

ARBITRATION: labor, 832 category, 833 category

ASSISTANCE: foreign, 4430

ATOMIC ENERGY: conservation and pollution, 7220; industries, 6352, 7230

AUSTRIAN SCHOOL: 0315; individuals, 0322

AUTOMATION: employment: empirical studies, 8243, theory, 8210

AUTOMOBILE MANUFACTURING: 6314

BALANCE OF PAYMENTS: 431 category; accounting, 4310; empirical studies, 4313; theory, 4312

BANK FOR INTERNATIONAL SETTLEMENTS: 4320

BANKS: central, 3116; commercial, 3120; investment, 3140; other, 3140; portfolios, 3120; savings and loan, 3140; savings, 3140; supervision and regulation of, 3120, 3140, 3116

BARGAINING: collective, 832 category

BAYESIAN ANALYSIS: 2115

BENEFIT-COST ANALYSIS: theory 0242; applied, see individual fields

BEVERAGE INDUSTRIES: 6318

BIBLIOGRAPHY: 0110; see also the GENERAL heading under each subject

BIOGRAPHY: businessmen, 040 group; history of thought, 0322

BOND MARKET: 3132

BOOK PUBLISHING: 6352

BOYCOTTS, LABOR: 833 category; 832 category

BRAIN DRAIN: 8230, 8410

BRAND PREFERENCE: 5310; and consumers, 9212

BREAK-EVEN ANALYSIS: 5120

BRETTON WOODS AGREEMENT: 4320

BUDGETS: consumers, 9211; governments: theory, 3212, national studies, 3226, state and local studies, 3241